W9-AQU-603

HANDBOOK OF QUALITATIVE RESEARCH

SECOND EDITION

HANDBOOK OF QUALITATIVE RESEARCH

SECOND EDITION

NORMAN K. DENZIN
YVONNA S. LINCOLN
EDITORS

Sage Publications, Inc.
International Educational and Professional Publisher
Thousand Oaks ▪ London ▪ New Delhi

For information:

Sage Publications, Inc.
2455 Teller Road
Thousand Oaks, California 91320
E-mail: order@sagepub.com

Sage Publications Ltd.
6 Bonhill Street
London EC2A 4PU
United Kingdom

Sage Publications India Pvt. Ltd.
M-32 Market
Greater Kailash I
New Delhi 110 048 India

Printed in the United States of America

Library of Congress Cataloging-in-Publication Data

Main entry under title:

The handbook of qualitative research / edited by Norman K. Denzin
    and Yvonna S. Lincoln. — 2nd ed.
        p.   cm.
    Includes bibliographical references and index.
    ISBN 0-7619-1512-5 (cloth: acid free paper)
    1. Social sciences—Research. I. Denzin, Norman K. II. Lincoln, Yvonna S.
III. Title.
H62 .H2455 2000
300'.7'2—dc21

00-008104

02   03   04   05   06   7   6   5   4

Acquiring Editor:	Peter Labella
Editorial Assistant:	Amy Dunham
Production Editor:	Astrid Virding
Editorial Assistant:	Nevair Kabakian
Copy Editor:	Judy Selhorst
Typesetter/Designer:	Marion Warren/Janelle LeMaster
Indexer:	Cristina Haley
Cover Designer:	Ravi Balasuriya

CONTENTS

PREFACE

This second edition of the *Handbook of Qualitative Research* is virtually a new volume. More than half of the chapters from the first edition have been replaced by new contributions. Indeed, this edition includes 33 new chapter authors or coauthors. There are six totally new chapter topics, contributions on queer theory, performance ethnography, *testimonio*, focus groups in feminist research, applied ethnography, and anthropological poetics. All returning authors have substantially revised their original contributions, in many cases producing totally new chapters.

This second edition continues where the first edition ended. In the preface to the first edition, we observed that over the past two decades, a quiet methodological revolution had been occurring in the social sciences; a blurring of disciplinary boundaries was taking place. The social sciences and humanities were drawing closer together in a mutual focus on an interpretive, qualitative approach to research and theory. We suggested that although these trends were not new ones, the extent to which the "qualitative revolution" was taking over the social sciences and related professional fields was nothing short of amazing. The overwhelmingly positive reaction to the first edition of the *Handbook* affirmed these observations. We were astonished at the reception the first edition received. Researchers and teachers alike found useful materials in that volume from which to teach and launch new inquiries.

There were, and continue to be, three social science and humanities audiences for the *Handbook*: graduate students who want to learn how to do qualitative research, interested faculty hoping to become better informed about the field, and faculty who are experts in one or more of the areas discussed in the *Handbook* but who want to be informed about the latest developments in the field. We never imagined this audience would be so large. Nor did we imagine that the *Handbook* would become a text to be used in undergraduate and graduate research methods courses, but it did. In 1998, we created three paperback volumes based on the first edition of the *Handbook* for classroom use: *The Landscape of Qualitative Research*, *Strategies of Qualitative Inquiry*, and *Collecting and Interpreting Qualitative Materials*.

With Thomas Schwandt (Chapter 7, this volume), we may observe that qualitative inquiry, among other things, is the name for a "reformist movement that began in the early 1970s in the academy." The interpretive and critical paradigms, in their multiple forms, are central to this movement. Indeed, Schwandt argues that this movement encompasses multiple paradigmatic formulations. It also includes complex epistemological and ethical criticisms of traditional social science research. The movement now has its own journals, scientific associations, conferences, and faculty positions.

The transformations in the field of qualitative research that were taking place in the early 1990s continued to gain momentum as the decade unfolded. By century's end, few looked back with skepticism on the narrative turn. The turn had been taken, and that was all there was to say about it. Many have now told their tales from the field. Further, today we know that men and women write culture differently, and that writing itself is not an innocent practice.

Experimental ways of writing first-person ethnographic texts are now commonplace. Sociologists and anthropologists continue to explore new ways of composing ethnography, and many are writing fiction, drama, performance texts, and ethnographic poetry. Social science journals are holding fiction contests. Civic journalism is shaping calls for a civic, or public, ethnography.

There is a pressing need to show how the practices of qualitative research can help change the world in positive ways. So, at the beginning of the 21st century, it is necessary to reengage the promise of qualitative research as a generative form of inquiry (Peshkin, 1993) and as a form of radical democratic practice. This is the agenda of this second edition of the *Handbook,* to show how the discourses of qualitative research can be used to help create and imagine a free democratic society. Each of the chapters that follows takes up this project in one way or another.

A handbook, we were told by our publisher, should ideally represent the distillation of knowledge of a field; it should be a benchmark volume that synthesizes an existing literature, helping to define and shape the present and future of that discipline. This mandate organized the first edition. In metaphoric terms, if you were to take one book on qualitative research with you to a desert island (or to prepare for a comprehensive graduate examination), a handbook would be that book. In the spring and summer of 1996 we returned to this mandate, asking ourselves how best to map what had happened in the field since 1994.

◆ *The "Field" of*
Qualitative Research

The photograph of the Brooklyn Bridge on our cover is deliberate. Like that complex construction, this volume bridges the new and the old. It joins multiple interpretive communities; it stretches across different landscapes. It offers a pathway back and forth between the public and the private, between science and the sacred, between disciplined inquiry and artistic expression.

It did not take us long to discover that the "field" of qualitative research had undergone quantum leaps since the spring of 1991, when we began to plan the first edition. We once again learned that the field of qualitative research is defined primarily by a series of essential tensions, contradictions, and hesitations. These tensions—many of them emerging after 1991—work back and forth between competing definitions and conceptions of the field.

These tensions do not exist in a unified arena. We discovered that the issues and concerns of qualitative researchers in nursing and communications are decidedly different from those of researchers in cultural anthropology. Symbolic interactionist sociologists deal with different questions from those of interest to critical theorists in educational research. Nor do the disciplinary networks of qualitative researchers necessarily cross each other, speak to each other, read each other.

Our attempt, once again, then, is to solidify, interpret, and organize a field of qualitative research in the face of essential paradigmatic differences, inherent contradictions among styles and types of research, and over the barriers of disciplinary, national, racial, cultural, and gender differences. We present our definition of how these tensions resolve themselves in our introductory and concluding chapters. It is also evident in the implicit dialogue we carry on with various authors, many of whom view the field quite differently than we. For you, the reader, to understand why we resolved these dilemmas as we did, we must first locate ourselves in these tensions and contradictions.

Norman Denzin is committed to a cultural studies, performance-based, postmodern, poststructural position that stresses the importance of the social text and its construction. Yvonna Lincoln is an avowed constructionist who places great value on theory and paradigm formation. We share a belief in the limitations of positivism and its successor, postpositivism. Lincoln brings to the project the disciplines of education, psychology, and history, whereas Denzin's grounding is in sociology, communications, anthropology, and the humanities. These biases shaped the construction of this volume and entered directly into our dialogues with each other. Although we did not always agree—for example, on the question of whether paradigms could be crossed or integrated—our two voices are heard often in the following pages. Other editors, working from different perspectives, would define the field and construct this book in different ways, choose different spokespersons for each topic, focus on other concerns, emphasize different methods, or otherwise organize the contents differently.

◆ *Organization of This Volume*

The organization of the *Handbook* moves from the general to the specific, the past to the present. Part I locates the field, starting with history, then moving to applied qualitative research traditions, studying the other, and the politics and ethics of field research. Part II isolates what we regard as the major historical and contemporary paradigms now structuring and influencing qualitative research in the human disciplines. The chapters move from competing paradigms (positivist, postpositivist, constructivist, critical theory) to specific interpretive perspectives.

Part III isolates the major strategies of inquiry—historically the research methods—that researchers can utilize in concrete studies. The question of methods begins with the design of the qualitative research project. This always begins with a socially situated researcher who moves from a research question to a paradigm or perspective, to the empirical world. So located, the researcher then addresses the range of methods that can be employed in any study. The history and uses of these strategies are extensively explored in the 11 chapters in Part III.

Part IV examines methods of collecting and analyzing empirical materials. It moves from interviewing to observation; to the use of artifacts, documents, and records from the past; to visual, personal experience; to data management, computerized, narrative, content, and semiotic methods of analysis. Part V takes up the art of interpretation, including criteria for judging the adequacy of qualitative materials, the interpretive process, the written text, and qualitative policy research and evaluation. Part VI speculates on the future and promise of qualitative research.

◆ Preparation of the Revised Handbook

The idea of a revised *Handbook* was taken up seriously in an all-day meeting in Toronto in the summer of 1996. There the two of us met with our editors at Sage and AltaMira, Peter Labella and Mitch Allen. Once again it became clear in our lengthy discussions that we needed input from perspectives other than our own. To accomplish this, we assembled a highly prestigious international and interdisciplinary editorial board (the names of our board members are listed at the front of this volume) that assisted us in the selection of equally prestigious authors, the preparation of the table of contents, and the reading of (often multiple drafts of) each chapter. We used editorial board members as windows into their respective disciplines. We sought information on key topics, perspectives, and controversies that needed to be addressed. We also, with Peter Labella's help, reviewed survey responses from those who had used the first edition as a teaching text. We sought to discover what they found most useful about the work. In our selection of editorial board members and chapter authors, we attempted to crosscut disciplinary, gender, race, paradigm, and national boundaries. Our hope was to use their views to minimize our own disciplinary blinders.

We received extensive feedback from the editorial board, including suggestions for new chapters and different slants to take on each of the chapters, as well as suggestions regarding authors for different chapters. Each *Handbook* author—internationally recognized in his or her subject matter—was asked to treat such issues as history, epistemology, ontology, exemplary texts, key controversies, competing paradigms, and predictions about the future.

Responding to Critics

We were gratified by the tremendous responses from the field to the first *Handbook*, especially by those of the hundreds of professors from around the world who chose the *Handbook* (in one form or another) to be part of their assigned readings for their students.[1] We were also gratified by the critical responses to the work. The *Handbook* has helped open a space for dialogue that was long overdue. Many readers found problems with our approach to the field, and these problems indicate places where more conversations need to take place.

Among the criticisms of the first edition were the following: Our framework was unwieldy; we did not give enough attention to the Chicago school; there was too much emphasis on the postmodern period; we had an arbitrary historical model; we were too eclectic; we overemphasized the fifth moment and the crisis of representation; we gave too much attention to political correctness and not enough to knowledge for its own sake; there was not enough on how to do it. Some felt that a revolution had not occurred and wondered, too, how we proposed to evaluate qualitative research now that the narrative turn has been taken.

We cannot speak for the more than 80 authors who have contributed chapters to the first and second editions. Each person has taken a stance on these issues. As editors, we have attempted to represent a number of competing or at least contesting ideologies and frames of reference. This *Handbook* is not, nor is it intended to be, the view from the bridge of Denzin or Lincoln. We are not saying that there is only one way to do research, or that our way is best, or that the so-called old ways are bad. We are just saying this is one way to conceptualize this field, and it is a way that we find useful.

Of course, the *Handbook* is not a single thing. It transcends the sum of its parts, and there is enormous diversity within and between every chapter. It is our hope that readers find spaces within these spaces that work for them. It is our desire that new dialogue take place within these spaces. This will be a gentle, probing, neighborly, and critical conversation, a conversation that bridges the many diverse interpretive communities that today make up this field called qualitative research.

◆ Defining the Field

These communities consist of groups of globally dispersed persons who are attempting to implement a qualitative, interpretive approach that will help them (and others) make sense of the terrifying conditions that define daily life at the dawn of a new century.[2] These individuals employ constructivist, critical theory, feminist theory, queer theory, critical race theory, and cultural studies models of interpretation. They locate themselves on the borders between postpositivism and poststructuralism. They use any and all of the research strategies (case study, ethnography, phenomenology, grounded theory, biographical, historical, participatory, and clinical) discussed in Part III of this *Handbook*. As interpretive *bricoleurs,* the members of this group are adept at using all of the methods of collecting and analyzing empirical materials discussed by the authors of the chapters in Part IV. And, as writers and interpreters, these individuals wrestle with positivist, postpositivist, poststructural, and postmodern criteria for evaluating their written work.[3]

These scholars constitute a loosely defined international interpretive community. They are slowly coming to agreement on what constitutes "good," "bad," banal, and emancipatory, troubling analysis and interpretation. They are constantly challenging the distinction between the "real" and that which is constructed, understanding that all events and understandings are mediated and made real through interactional and material practices, through discourse, conversation, writing, narrative, scientific articles, realist, postrealist, and performance tales from the field.

This group works at both the centers and the margins of those emerging interdisciplinary formations that crisscross the borders separating communication, race, ethnic, religious, and women's studies, sociology, history, anthropology, literary criticism, political science, economics, social work, health care, and education. This work is characterized by a quiet change in outlook, a transnational, transdisciplinary conversation, a pragmatic change in practices and habits.

It is at this juncture—the uneasy crossroads between pragmatism and postmodernism—that a quiet revolution is occurring. This is so because pragmatism is itself a theoretical and philosophical concern, firmly rooted in the realist tradition. As such, it is a theoretical position that privileges *practice and method* over reflection and deliberative action. Indeed, postmodernism itself has no predisposition to privilege discourse over observation. Instead, postmodernism (and poststructuralism) would simply have us attend to discourse as seriously as we attend to observation (or any other fieldwork methods) and to recognize that our discourses are the vehicles for sharing our observations with those who were not in the field with us.

It is precisely the angst attending our recognition of the hidden powers of discourses that leaves us now at the threshold of postmodernism and that signals the advent of questions that will leave none of us untouched. It is true that contemporary qualitative, interpretive research exists within competing fields of discourse. Our present history of the field locates six moments plus a seventh—the future. These moments all circulate in the present, competing with and defining one another. This discourse is moving in several directions at the same time. This has the effect of simultaneously creating new spaces, new possibilities, and new formations for qualitative research methods while closing down others.

There are those who would marginalize and politicize the postmodern, poststructural versions of qualitative research, equating them with radical relativism, narratives of the self, and armchair commentary. Some would chastise this *Handbook* for not paying adequate homage to the hands-on, nuts-and-bolts approach to fieldwork, to texts that tell us how to study the "real" world. Still others would seek a preferred, canonical, but flexible version of this project, returning to the Chicago school or more recent formal, analytic, realist versions. Some would criticize the formation from within, contending that the privileging of discourse over observation does not yield adequate criteria for evaluating interpretive work, wondering what to do when left with only voice and interpretation. Many ask for a normative framework for evaluating their own work. None of these desires is likely to be satisfied anytime soon, however. Contestation, contradiction, and philosophical tensions make the achievement of consensus on any of these issues less than imminent.

We are not collating history here, although every chapter describes the history in a subfield. Our intention, which our contributors share, is to point to the future, to where the field of qualitative research methods will be 10 years from now. Of course, much of the field still works within frameworks defined by earlier historical moments. This is as it should be. There is no one way to do interpretive, qualitative inquiry. We are all interpretive *bricoleurs* stuck in the present working against the past as we move into the future.

◆ *Competing Definitions of Qualitative Research Methods*

The open-ended nature of the qualitative research project leads to a perpetual resistance against attempts to impose a single, umbrellalike paradigm over the entire project. There are multiple interpretive projects, including performance ethnographies; standpoint epistemologies; critical race theory; materialist, feminist ethnographies; projects connected to the British cultural studies and Frankfurt schools; grounded theories of several varieties; multiple strands of ethnomethodology; African American, prophetic, postmodern, and neopragmatic Marxism; an American-based critical cultural studies model; and transnational cultural studies projects.

The generic focus of each of these versions of qualitative research moves in four directions at the same time: (a) the "detour through interpretive theory" linked (b) to the analysis of the politics of representation and the textual analyses of literary and cultural forms, including their production, distribution, and consumption; (c) the ethnographic, qualitative study of these forms in everyday life; and (d) the investigation of new pedagogical and interpretive practices that interactively engage critical cultural analysis in the classroom and the local community.

◆ *Whose Revolution?*

To summarize: A single, several-part thesis organizes our reading of where the field of qualitative research methodology is today. First, this project has changed because the world that qualitative research confronts has changed. It has also changed because of the increasing sophistication—both theoretical and methodological—of interpretivist researchers everywhere. Disjuncture and difference define the global cultural economy. This is a postcolonial world. It is necessary to think beyond the nation, or the local group, as the focus of inquiry.

Second, this is a world where ethnographic texts circulate like other commodities in the electronic world economy. It may be that ethnography is one of the major discourses of the postmodern world, but if this is so, we can no longer take for granted what anyone means by *ethnography*, even in traditional, realist qualitative research (see Snow, 1999, p. 97).[4] Global and local legal processes have erased the personal and institutional distance between the ethnographer and those he or she writes about. We do not "own" the field notes we make about those we study. We do not have an undisputed warrant to study anyone or anything. Subjects now challenge how they have been written about, and more than one ethnographer has been taken to court.

Third, this is a gendered project. Feminist, postcolonial, and queer theorists question the traditional logic of the heterosexual, narrative ethnographic text that reflexively positions the ethnographer's gender-neutral (or masculine) self within a realist story. Today there is no solidified ethnographic identity. The ethnographer works within a "hybrid" reality. Experience, discourse, and self-understandings collide against larger cultural assumptions concerning race, ethnicity, nationality, gender, class, and age. A certain identity is never possible; the ethnographer must always ask, "Not *who* am I?" but "*When, where, how* am I?" (Trinh, 1992, p. 157).

Fourth, qualitative research is an inquiry project, but it is also a moral, allegorical, and therapeutic project. Ethnography is more than the record of human experience. The ethnographer writes tiny moral tales, tales that do more than celebrate cultural difference or bring another culture alive. The researcher's story is written as a prop, a pillar that, to paraphrase William Faulkner (1967, p. 724), will help men and women endure and prevail in the dawning years of the 21st century.

Fifth, although the field of qualitative research is defined by constant breaks and ruptures, there is a shifting center to the project: the avowed humanistic commitment to study the social world from the perspective of the interacting individual. From this principle flow the liberal and radical politics of action that are held by feminist, clinical, ethnic, critical, queer theory, critical race theory, and cultural studies researchers. Although multiple interpretive communities now circulate within the field of qualitative research, they are all united on this single point.

Finally, qualitative research's seventh moment will be defined by the work that ethnographers do as they implement the above assumptions. These situations set the stage for qualitative research's transformations in the 21st century.[5]

◆ Tales of the Handbook

Many of the difficulties in developing a volume such as this are common to any project of this magnitude. Others arose from the essential tensions and contradictions that operate in this field. As with the first edition, the "right" chapter authors were unavailable, too busy, overcommitted, or going overseas to do fieldwork. Consequently, we sought out others, who turned out to be more "right" than we imagined possible. Few overlapping networks cut across the many disciplines we were attempting to cover. Although we knew the territory somewhat better this time around, there were still spaces we entered with little knowledge about who should be asked to do what. We confronted disciplinary blinders—including our own—and discovered there were separate traditions surrounding each of our topics within distinct interpretive communities. It was often difficult to know how to bridge these differences, and our bridges were often makeshift constructions. We also had to cope with vastly different styles of thinking about a variety of different topics based on disciplinary, epistemological, gender, racial, ethnic, cultural, and national beliefs, boundaries, and ideologies.

In many instances we unwittingly entered into political battles over who should write a chapter or over how a chapter should be written. These disputes clearly pointed to the political nature of this project and to the fact that each chapter is a potential, if not real, site for multiple interpretations. Many times the politics of meaning came into play, as we attempted to negotiate and navigate our way through areas fraught with high emotion. On more than one occasion we disagreed with both an author and an editorial board member. We often found ourselves adjudicating between competing editorial reviews, working the hyphens between meaning making and diplomacy. Regrettably, in some cases we hurt feelings and perhaps even damaged long-standing friendships. With the clarity of hindsight there are many things we would do differently today, and we apologize for any damage we have done.

We, as well as our authors and advisers, struggled with the meanings we wanted to bring to such terms as *theory, paradigm, epistemology, interpretive framework, empirical materials* versus *data,* and *research strategies.* We discovered that the very term *qualitative research* means different things to many different people.

We abandoned the goal of comprehensiveness, even with more than 2,000 manuscript pages. We fought with authors over deadlines and the number of pages we would give them. We also fought with authors over how to conceptualize their chapters and found that what was clear to us was not necessarily clear to anyone else. We fought too over when a chapter was done, and constantly sought the forbearance of our authors as we requested yet more revisions.

◆ Reading the *Handbook*

Were we to write our own critique of this book, we would point to the shortcomings we see in it, and in many senses these are the same as those we saw in 1994—an overreliance on the perspectives of our respective disciplines (sociology, communications, and education), an absence of work on the self and its place in the fieldwork situation, and too little on the new social and cultural history—although we worked hard to avoid all of these problems. On the other hand, we have addressed some of the problems present in the first edition. We have made a greater effort to cover more areas of applied qualitative work. We have helped initiate dialogue between different chapter authors. We have created spaces for more voices from other disciplines, especially anthropology, but we still have a shortfall of voices representing people of color and of the Third World. You, the reader, will certainly have your own responses to this book that may highlight other issues that we do not see.

This is all in the nature of the *Handbook,* and in the nature of doing qualitative research. This volume is a social construction, a socially enacted, cocreated entity, and although it exists in a material form, it will no doubt be re-created in subsequent iterations as generations of scholars and graduate students use it, adapt it, and launch from it additional methodological paradigmatic, theoretical, and practical work. It is not a final statement. It is a starting point, a springboard for new thought and new work, work that is fresh and sensitive, and that blurs the boundaries of our disciplines, but always sharpens our understandings of the larger human project.

It is our hope that this project, with all its strengths and all its flaws, will contribute to the growing maturity and influence of qualitative research in the human disciplines. And, as we were originally mandated, we hope this convinces you, the reader, that qualitative research now constitutes a field of study in its own right, allowing you to better anchor and locate your own work in the qualitative research tradition. If this happens, we will have succeeded in building a bridge that serves us all well.

◆ Acknowledgments

This *Handbook* would not exist without its authors and the editorial board members who gave freely, often on very short notice, of their time, advice, and ever-courteous suggestions. We acknowledge en masse the support of the authors and the editorial board members, whose names are listed facing the title page. These individuals were able to offer both long-term, sustained commitments to the project and short-term emergency assistance.

There are other debts, intensely personal and closer to home. The *Handbook* would never have been possible without the ever-present help, support, wisdom, and encouragement of our editor, Peter Labella, and his predecessor, Mitch Allen. Their grasp of this field, its history, and diversity is extraordinary. Their conceptions of what this project should look like were extremely valuable. Their energy kept us moving forward. Furthermore, whenever we confronted a problem, Peter was there with his assistance and good-natured humor. And back home, at the Sage mother ship, Thomas Gay, Rolf Janke, and on more than one occasion Sara Miller McCune kept the ship called the *Handbook* moving in the right direction.

We would also like to thank the following individuals and institutions for their assistance, support, insights, and patience: our respective universities and departments, especially Yvonna's dean, Jane Conoley, Associate Dean Ernest Goetz, and Department Head Bryan R. Cole, each of whom facilitated this work in some important way. In Urbana, Jack Bratich was the sine qua non. His good humor and grace kept our ever-growing files in order and everyone on the same timetable. Without Jack this project would never have been completed. Elizabeth Wilson, Gina Manning, and Delores Jean Hill at the University of Illinois kept faxes moving among Urbana, Walnut Creek, Boston, College Station, and other far-flung worldly places.

Norman also gratefully acknowledges the moral, intellectual, and financial support given this project by Dean Kim Rotzoll of the College of Communication and Clifford Christians, director of the Institute of Communication Research. He also thanks Diane Tipps and Tom Galer-Unti, who kept the financial accounts straight, and John Lie, head of the Department of Sociology, for his generous support of the project as well. At Sage Publications, Astrid Virding helped move this project through production; we are extremely grateful to her, as well as to the copy editor, Judy Selhorst, and to those, including Eileen

Peronneau, Kris Bergstad, Cristina Haley, and Uma Pimplaskar, whose excellent proofreading and indexing skills have helped to polish this volume. Janelle LeMaster created the page design, Ravi Balasuriya designed the cover, and Marion Warren did the typesetting and layout. Our spouses, Katherine Ryan and Egon Guba, helped keep us on track, listened to our complaints, and generally displayed extraordinary patience, forbearance, and support.

Finally, there is another group of individuals who gave unstintingly of their time and energy to provide us with their expertise and thoughtful reviews when we needed additional guidance. Without the help of these individuals we would often have found ourselves with less than complete understandings of the various traditions, perspectives, and methods represented in this volume. We would like to acknowledge the important contributions of the following individuals to this project: Michael Agar, Anthropology, University of Maryland; David Fetterman, Education, Stanford University; Egon G. Guba, Education, Indiana University; Jeffrey M. Johnson, Institute for Marine Affairs, East Carolina University; Stephen Kemmis, Stephen Kemmis Research & Consulting Pty. Ltd.; J. Gary Knowles, Education, University of Michigan; Raymond Lee, Social Policy, University of London; Markku Lonkila, Sociology, University of Helsinki; Matthew B. Miles, Center for Policy Research, New York; John Ogbu, Anthropology, University of California, Berkeley; Dennis Palumbo, Justice Studies, Arizona State University; Jon H. Rieger, Sociology, University of Louisville; Renato Rosaldo, Anthropology, Stanford University; Tom Schwandt, Education, University of Illinois; John Seidel, Qualis Research Associates, Amherst, Massachusetts; Renata Tesch, Qualitative Research Management, Desert Springs, California; and Henry T. Trueba, Education, University of Wisconsin–Madison.

Norman K. Denzin
University of Illinois at Urbana-Champaign

Yvonna S. Lincoln
Texas A&M University

■ Notes

1. We thank Professor Isamu Ito for suggesting this section, and Peter Labella for his comments on it.
2. This section extends Denzin and Lincoln (1995).
3. These criteria range from those endorsed by postpositivists (variations on validity and reliability, including credibility and trustworthiness) to poststructural, feminist standpoint concerns emphasizing collaborative, evocative performance texts that create ethically responsible relations between researchers and those they study.
4. The realist text, Jameson (1990) argues, constructed its version of the world by "programming . . . readers; by training them in new habits and practices. . . . Such narratives must ultimately produce that very category of Reality . . . of the real, of the 'objective' or 'external' world, which itself historical, may undergo decisive modification in other modes of production, if not in later stages of this one" (p. 166). The new ethnographic text is producing its versions of reality and teaching readers how to engage this view of the social world.

5. Finally, we anticipate a continued performance turn in qualitative inquiry, with writers performing their texts for others.

■ *References*

Denzin, N. K., & Lincoln, Y. S. (1995). Transforming qualitative research methods: Is it a revolution? *Journal of Contemporary Ethnography, 24,* 349-358.

Faulkner, W. (1967). Address upon receiving the Nobel Prize for Literature. In *The portable Faulkner* (Rev. ed.; M. Cowley, Ed.; pp. 723-724). New York: Viking.

Jameson, F. (1990). *Signatures of the visible.* New York: Routledge.

Peshkin, A. (1993). The goodness of qualitative research. *Educational Researcher, 22*(2), 24-30.

Snow, D. (1999). Assessing the ways in which qualitative/ethnographic research contributes to social psychology: Introduction to special issue. *Social Psychology Quarterly, 62,* 97-100.

Trinh T. M. (1992). *Framer framed.* New York: Routledge.

1

INTRODUCTION

The Discipline and Practice of Qualitative Research

◆ Norman K. Denzin and Yvonna S. Lincoln

Qualitative research has a long, distinguished, and sometimes anguished history in the human disciplines. In sociology, the work of the "Chicago school" in the 1920s and 1930s established the importance of qualitative inquiry for the study of human group life. In anthropology, during the same time period, the discipline-defining studies of Boas, Mead, Benedict, Bateson, Evans-Pritchard, Radcliffe-Brown, and Malinowski charted the outlines of the fieldwork method (see Gupta & Ferguson, 1997; Stocking, 1986, 1989). The agenda was clear-cut: The observer went to a foreign setting to study the customs and habits of another society and culture (see in this volume Vidich & Lyman, Chapter 2; Tedlock, Chapter 17; see also Rosaldo, 1989, pp. 25-45, for criticisms of this tradition). Soon, qualitative research would be employed in other social and behavioral science disciplines, including education (especially the work of Dewey), history, political science, business, medicine, nursing, social work, and communications.

In the opening chapter in Part I of this volume, Vidich and Lyman chart many key features of this history. In this now classic analysis, they

AUTHORS' NOTE: We are grateful to many who have helped with this chapter, including Egon Guba, Mitch Allen, Peter Labella, Jack Bratich, and Katherine E. Ryan. We take our subtitle for this chapter from Gupta and Ferguson (1997).

note, with some irony, that qualitative research in sociology and anthropology was "born out of concern to understand the 'other.' " Furthermore, this other was the exotic other, a primitive, nonwhite person from a foreign culture judged to be less civilized than that of the researcher. Of course, there were colonialists long before there were anthropologists. Nonetheless, there would be no colonial, and now no postcolonial, history were it not for this investigative mentality that turned the dark-skinned other into the object of the ethnographer's gaze.

Thus does bell hooks (1990, pp. 126-128) read the famous photo that appears on the cover of *Writing Culture* (Clifford & Marcus, 1986) as an instance of this mentality (see also Behar, 1995, p. 8; Gordon, 1988). The photo depicts Stephen Tyler doing fieldwork in India. Tyler is seated some distance from three dark-skinned persons. A child is poking his or her head out of a basket. A woman is hidden in the shadows of a hut. A man, a checkered white-and-black shawl across his shoulder, elbow propped on his knee, hand resting along the side of his face, is staring at Tyler. Tyler is writing in a field journal. A piece of white cloth is attached to his glasses, perhaps shielding him from the sun. This patch of whiteness marks Tyler as the white male writer studying these passive brown and black persons. Indeed, the brown male's gaze signals some desire, or some attachment to Tyler. In contrast, the female's gaze is completely hidden by the shadows and by the words of the book's title, which cross her face (hooks, 1990, p. 127). And so this cover photo of perhaps the most influential book on ethnography in the last half of the 20th century reproduces "two ideas that are quite fresh in the racist imagination: the notion of the white male as writer/authority . . . and the idea of the passive brown/black man [and woman and child] who is doing nothing, merely looking on" (hooks, 1990, p. 127).

In this introductory chapter, we will define the field of qualitative research and then navigate, chart, and review the history of qualitative research in the human disciplines. This will allow us to locate this volume and its contents within their historical moments. (These historical moments are somewhat artificial; they are socially constructed, quasi-historical, and overlapping conventions. Nevertheless, they permit a "performance" of developing ideas. They also facilitate an increasing sensitivity to and sophistication about the pitfalls and promises of ethnography and qualitative research.) We will present a conceptual framework for reading the qualitative research act as a multicultural, gendered process, and then provide a brief introduction to the chapters that follow. Returning to the observations of Vidich and Lyman as well as those of hooks, we will conclude with a brief discussion of qualitative research and critical race theory (see also in this volume Ladson-Billings, Chapter 9; Denzin, Chapter 35). As we indicate in our preface, we use the metaphor of the bridge to structure what follows. We see this volume as a bridge connecting historical moments, research methods, paradigms, and communities of interpretive scholars.

◆ Definitional Issues

Qualitative research is a field of inquiry in its own right. It crosscuts disciplines, fields, and subject matters.[1] A complex, interconnected family of terms, concepts, and assumptions surround the term *qualitative research*. These include the traditions associated with foundationalism, positivism, postfoundationalism, postpositivism, poststructuralism, and the many qualitative research perspectives, and/or methods, connected to cultural and interpretive studies (the chapters in Part II take up these paradigms).[2] There are separate and detailed literatures on the many methods and approaches that fall under the category of qualitative research, such as case study, politics and ethics, participatory inquiry, interviewing, participant observation, visual methods, and interpretive analysis.

In North America, qualitative research operates in a complex historical field that crosscuts seven historical moments (we discuss these moments in detail below). These seven moments overlap and simultaneously operate in the present.[3] We define them as the traditional (1900-1950); the modernist or golden age (1950-1970); blurred genres (1970-1986); the crisis of representation (1986-1990); the postmodern, a period of experimental and new ethnographies (1990-1995); postexperimental inquiry (1995-2000); and the future, which is now (2000-). The future, the seventh moment, is concerned with moral discourse, with the development of sacred textualities. The seventh moment asks that the social sciences and the humanities become sites for critical conversations about democracy, race, gender, class, nation-states, globalization, freedom, and community.

The postmodern moment was defined in part by a concern for literary and rhetorical tropes and the narrative turn, a concern for storytelling, for composing ethnographies in new ways (Ellis & Bochner, 1996). Laurel Richardson (1997) observes that this moment was shaped by a new sensibility, by doubt, by a refusal to privilege any method or theory (p. 173). But now, at the beginning of the 21st century, the narrative turn has been taken. Many have learned how to write differently, including how to locate themselves in their texts. We now struggle to connect qualitative research to the hopes, needs, goals, and promises of a free democratic society.

Successive waves of epistemological theorizing move across these seven moments. The traditional period is associated with the positivist, foundational paradigm. The modernist or golden age and blurred genres moments are connected to the appearance of postpositivist arguments. At the same time, a variety of new interpretive, qualitative perspectives were taken up, including hermeneutics, structuralism, semiotics, phenomenology, cultural studies, and feminism.[4] In the blurred genres phase, the humanities became central resources for critical, interpretive theory, and for the qualitative research project broadly conceived. The researcher became a *bricoleur* (see below), learning how to borrow from many different disciplines.

The blurred genres phase produced the next stage, the crisis of representation. Here researchers struggled with how to locate themselves and their subjects in reflexive texts. A kind of methodological diaspora took place, a two-way exodus. Humanists migrated to the social sciences, searching for new social theory, new ways to study popular culture and its local, ethnographic contexts. Social scientists turned to the humanities, hoping to learn how to do complex structural and poststructural readings of social texts. From the humanities, social scientists also learned how to produce texts that refused to be read in simplistic, linear, incontrovertible terms. The line between text and context blurred. In the postmodern experimental moment researchers continued to move away from foundational and quasi-foundational criteria (see in this volume Smith & Deemer, Chapter 34; Richardson, Chapter 36; Gergen & Gergen, Chapter 40). Alternative evaluative criteria were sought, criteria that might prove evocative, moral, critical, and rooted in local understandings.

Any definition of qualitative research must work within this complex historical field. *Qualitative research* means different things in each of these moments. Nonetheless, an initial, generic definition can be offered: Qualitative research is a situated activity that locates the observer in the world. It consists of a set of interpretive, material practices that make the world visible. These practices transform the world. They turn the world into a series of representations, including field notes, interviews, conversations, photographs, recordings, and memos to the self. At this level, qualitative research involves an interpretive, naturalistic approach to the world. This means that qualitative researchers study things in their natural settings, attempting to make sense of, or to interpret, phenomena in terms of the meanings people bring to them.[5]

Qualitative research involves the studied use and collection of a variety of empirical materials—case study; personal experience; introspection; life story; interview; artifacts; cultural texts and productions; observational, historical, interactional, and visual texts—that describe routine and problematic moments and meanings in individuals' lives. Accordingly, qualitative researchers deploy a wide range of interconnected interpretive practices, hoping always to get a better understanding of the subject matter at hand. It is understood, however, that each practice makes the world visible in a different way. Hence there is frequently a commitment to using more than one interpretive practice in any study.

The Qualitative Researcher as Bricoleur and Quilt Maker

The qualitative researcher may take on multiple and gendered images: scientist, naturalist, field-worker, journalist, social critic, artist, performer, jazz musician, filmmaker, quilt maker, essayist. The many methodological practices of qualitative research may be viewed as soft science, journalism, ethnography, bricolage, quilt making, or montage. The researcher, in turn, may be seen as a *bricoleur,* as a maker of quilts, or, as in filmmaking, a person who assembles images into montages. (On montage, see the discussion below as well as Cook, 1981, pp. 171-177; Monaco, 1981, pp. 322-328. On quilting, see hooks, 1990, pp. 115-122; Wolcott, 1995, pp. 31-33.)

Nelson, Treichler, and Grossberg (1992), Lévi-Strauss (1966), and Weinstein and Weinstein (1991) clarify the meanings of *bricolage* and *bricoleur.*[6] A *bricoleur* is a "Jack of all trades or a kind of professional do-it-yourself person" (Lévi-Strauss, 1966, p. 17). There are many kinds of *bricoleurs*—interpretive, narrative, theoretical, political (see below). The interpretive *bricoleur* produces a bricolage—that is, a pieced-together set of representations that are fitted to the specifics of a complex situation. "The solution [bricolage] which is the result of the *bricoleur's* method is an [emergent] construction" (Weinstein & Weinstein, 1991, p. 161) that changes and takes new forms as different tools, methods, and techniques of representation and interpretation are added to the puzzle. Nelson et al. (1992) describe the methodology of cultural studies "as a bricolage. Its choice of practice, that is, is pragmatic, strategic and self-reflexive" (p. 2). This understanding can be applied, with qualifications, to qualitative research.

The qualitative researcher as *bricoleur* or maker of quilts uses the aesthetic and material tools of his or her craft, deploying whatever strategies, methods, or empirical materials are at hand (Becker, 1998, p. 2). If new tools or techniques have to be invented, or pieced together, then the researcher will do this. The choices as to which interpretive practices to employ are not necessarily set in advance. The "choice of research practices depends upon the questions that are asked, and the questions depend on their context" (Nelson et al., 1992, p. 2), what is available in the context, and what the researcher can do in that setting.

These interpretive practices involve aesthetic issues, an aesthetics of representation that goes beyond the pragmatic, or the practical. Here the concept of *montage* is useful (see Cook, 1981, p. 323; Monaco, 1981, pp. 171-172). Montage is a method of editing cinematic images. In the history of cinematography, montage is associated with the work of Sergei Eisenstein, especially his film *The Battleship Potemkin* (1925). In montage, several different images are superimposed onto one another to create a picture. In a sense, montage is like *pentimento,* in which something that has been painted out of a picture (an image the painter "repented," or denied) becomes visible again, creating something new. What is new is what had been obscured by a previous image.

Montage and pentimento, like jazz, which is improvisation, create the sense that images, sounds, and understandings are blending together, overlapping, forming a composite, a new creation. The images seem to shape and define one another, and an emotional, gestalt effect is produced. Often these images are combined in a swiftly run filmic sequence that produces a dizzily revolving collection of several images around a central or focused picture or sequence; such effects are often used to signify the passage of time.

Perhaps the most famous instance of montage is the Odessa Steps sequence in *The Battleship Potemkin.*[7] In the climax of the film, the citizens of Odessa are being massacred by czarist troops on the stone steps leading down to the harbor. Eisenstein cuts to a young mother as she pushes her baby in a carriage across the landing in front of the firing troops. Citizens rush past her, jolting the carriage, which she is afraid to push down to the next flight of stairs. The troops are above her firing at the citizens. She is trapped between the troops and the steps. She screams. A line of rifles pointing to the sky erupt in smoke. The mother's head sways back. The wheels of the carriage teeter on the edge of the steps. The mother's hand clutches the silver buckle of her belt. Below her people are being beaten by soldiers. Blood drips over the mother's white gloves. The baby's hand reaches out of the carriage. The mother sways back and forth. The troops advance. The mother falls back against the carriage. A woman watches in horror as the rear wheels of the carriage roll off the edge of the landing. With accelerating speed the carriage bounces down the steps, past the dead citizens. The baby is jostled from side to side inside the carriage. The soldiers fire their rifles into a group of wounded citizens. A student screams as the carriage leaps across the steps, tilts, and overturns (Cook, 1981, p. 167).[8]

Montage uses brief images to create a clearly defined sense of urgency and complexity. Montage invites viewers to construct interpretations that build on one another as the scene unfolds. These interpretations are built on associations based on the contrasting images that blend into one another. The underlying assumption of montage is that viewers perceive and interpret the shots in a "montage sequence not *sequentially*, or one at a time, but rather *simultaneously*" (Cook, 1981, p. 172). The viewer puts the sequences together into a meaningful emotional whole, as if in a glance, all at once.

The qualitative researcher who uses montage is like a quilt maker or a jazz improviser. The quilter stitches, edits, and puts slices of reality together. This process creates and brings psychological and emotional unity to an interpretive experience. There are many examples of montage in current qualitative research (see Diversi, 1998; Jones, 1999; Lather & Smithies, 1997; Ronai, 1998). Using multiple voices, different textual formats, and various typefaces, Lather and Smithies (1997) weave a complex text about women who are HIV positive and women with AIDS. Jones (1999) creates a performance text using lyrics from the blues songs sung by Billie Holiday.

In texts based on the metaphors of montage, quilt making, and jazz improvisation, many different things are going on at the same time—different voices, different perspectives, points of views, angles of vision. Like performance texts, works that use montage simultaneously create and enact moral meaning. They move from the personal to the political, the local to the historical and the cultural. These are dialogical texts. They presume an active audience. They create spaces for give-and-take between reader and writer. They do more than turn the other into the object of the social science gaze (see McCall, Chapter 15, this volume)

Qualitative research is inherently multimethod in focus (Flick, 1998, p. 229). However, the use of multiple methods, or triangulation, reflects an attempt to secure an in-depth understanding of the phenomenon in question. Objective reality can never be captured. We can know a thing only through its representations. Triangulation is not a tool or a strategy of validation, but an alternative to validation (Flick, 1998, p. 230). The combination of multiple methodological practices, empirical materials, perspectives, and observers in a single study is best understood, then, as a strategy that adds rigor, breadth, complexity, richness, and depth to any inquiry (see Flick, 1998, p. 231).

In Chapter 36 of this volume, Richardson disputes the concept of triangulation, asserting that the central image for qualitative inquiry is the crystal, not the triangle. Mixed-genre texts in the postexperimental moment have more than three sides. Like crystals, Eisenstein's montage, the jazz solo, or the pieces that make up a quilt, the mixed-genre text, as Richardson notes, "combines symmetry and substance with an infinite variety of shapes, substances, transmutations. . . . Crystals grow, change, alter. . . . Crystals are prisms that reflect externalities *and* refract within themselves, creating different colors, patterns, and arrays, casting off in different directions."

In the crystallization process, the writer tells the same tale from different points of view. For example, in *A Thrice-Told Tale* (1992), Margery Wolf uses fiction, field notes, and a scientific article to give an accounting of the same set of experiences in a native village. Similarly, in her play *Fires in the Mirror* (1993), Anna Deavere Smith presents a series of performance pieces based on interviews with people involved in a racial conflict in Crown Heights, Brooklyn, on August, 19, 1991 (see Denzin, Chapter 35, this volume). The play has multiple speaking parts, including conversations with gang members, police officers, and anonymous young girls and boys. There is no "correct" telling of this event. Each telling, like light hitting a crystal, reflects a different perspective on this incident.

Viewed as a crystalline form, as a montage, or as a creative performance around a central theme, triangulation as a form of, or alternative to, validity thus can be extended. Triangulation is the display of multiple, refracted realities simultaneously. Each of the metaphors "works" to create simultaneity rather than the sequential or linear. Readers and audiences are then invited to explore competing visions of the context, to become immersed in and merge with new realities to comprehend.

The methodological *bricoleur* is adept at performing a large number of diverse tasks, ranging from interviewing to intensive self-reflection and introspection. The theoretical *bricoleur* reads widely and is knowledgeable about the many interpretive paradigms (feminism, Marxism, cultural studies, constructivism, queer theory) that can be brought to any particular problem. He or she may not, however, feel that paradigms can be mingled or synthesized. That is, one cannot easily move between paradigms as overarching philosophical systems denoting particular ontologies, epistemologies, and methodologies. They represent belief systems that attach users to particular worldviews. Perspectives, in contrast, are less well developed systems, and one can more easily move between them. The researcher-as-*bricoleur*-theorist works between and within competing and overlapping perspectives and paradigms.

The interpretive *bricoleur* understands that research is an interactive process shaped by his or her personal history, biography, gender, social class, race, and ethnicity, and by those of the people in the setting. The political *bricoleur* knows that science is power, for all research findings have political implications. There is no value-free science. A civic social science based on a politics of hope is sought (Lincoln, 1999).

The gendered, narrative *bricoleur* also knows that researchers all tell stories about the worlds they have studied. Thus the narratives, or stories, scientists tell are accounts couched and framed within specific storytelling traditions, often defined as paradigms (e.g., positivism, postpositivism, constructivism).

The product of the interpretive *bricoleur*'s labor is a complex, quiltlike bricolage, a reflexive collage or montage—a set of fluid, interconnected images and representations. This interpretive structure is like a quilt, a performance text, a sequence of representations connecting the parts to the whole.

Qualitative Research as a Site of Multiple Interpretive Practices

Qualitative research, as a set of interpretive activities, privileges no single methodological practice over another. As a site of discussion, or discourse, qualitative research is difficult to define clearly. It has no theory or paradigm that is distinctly its own. As the contributions to Part II of this volume reveal, multiple theoretical paradigms claim use of qualitative research methods and strategies, from constructivist to cultural studies, feminism, Marxism, and ethnic models of study. Qualitative research is used in many separate disciplines, as we will discuss below. It does not belong to a single discipline.

Nor does qualitative research have a distinct set of methods or practices that are entirely its own. Qualitative researchers use semiotics, narrative, content, discourse, archival and phonemic analysis, even statistics, tables, graphs, and numbers. They also draw upon and utilize the approaches, methods, and techniques of ethnomethodology, phenomenology, hermeneutics, feminism, rhizomatics, deconstructionism, ethnography, interviews, psychoanalysis, cultural studies, survey research, and participant observation, among others.[9] All of these research practices "can provide important insights and knowledge" (Nelson et al., 1992, p. 2). No specific method or practice can be privileged over any other.

Many of these methods, or research practices, are used in other contexts in the human disciplines. Each bears the traces of its own disciplinary history. Thus there is an extensive history of the uses and meanings of ethnography and ethnology in education (see Fine, Weis, Weseen, & Wong, Chapter 4); of participant observation and ethnography in anthropology (see Tedlock, Chapter 17; Ryan & Bernard, Chapter 29; Brady, Chapter 37), sociology (see Gubrium & Holstein, Chapter 18; Harper, Chapter 27; Fontana & Frey, Chapter 24; Silverman, Chapter 31), communication (see Ellis & Bochner, Chapter 28), and cultural studies (see Frow & Morris, Chapter 11); of textual, hermeneutic, feminist, psychoanalytic, semiotic, and narrative analysis in cinema and literary studies (see Olesen, Chapter 8; Brady, Chapter 37); of archival, material culture, historical, and document analysis in history, biography, and archaeology (see Hodder, Chapter 26; Tierney, Chapter 20); and of discourse and conversational analysis in medicine, communications, and education (see Miller & Crabtree, Chapter 23; Silverman, Chapter 31).

The many histories that surround each method or research strategy reveal how multiple uses and meanings are brought to each practice. Textual analyses in literary studies, for example, often treat texts as self-contained systems. On the other hand, a researcher taking a cultural studies or feminist perspective will read a text in terms of its location within a historical moment marked by a particular gender, race, or class ideology. A cultural studies use of ethnography would bring a set of understandings from feminism, postmodernism, and poststructuralism to the project. These understandings would not be shared by mainstream postpositivist sociologists. Similarly, postpositivist and poststructuralist historians bring different understandings and uses to the methods and findings of historical research (see Tierney, Chapter 20). These tensions and contradictions are all evident in the chapters in this volume.

These separate and multiple uses and meanings of the methods of qualitative research make it difficult for researchers to agree on any essential definition of the field, for it is never just one thing.[10] Still, we must establish a definition for our purposes here. We borrow from, and paraphrase, Nelson et al.'s (1992, p. 4) attempt to define cultural studies:

> Qualitative research is an interdisciplinary, transdisciplinary, and sometimes counterdisciplinary field. It crosscuts the humanities and the social and physical sciences. Qualitative research is many things at the same time. It is multiparadigmatic in focus. Its practitioners are sensitive to the value of the multimethod approach. They are committed to the naturalistic perspective and to the interpretive understanding of human experience. At the same time, the field is inherently political and shaped by multiple ethical and political positions.
>
> Qualitative research embraces two tensions at the same time. On the one hand, it is drawn to a broad, interpretive, postexperimental, postmodern, feminist, and critical sensibility. On the other hand, it is drawn to more narrowly defined positivist, postpositivist, humanistic, and naturalistic conceptions of human experience and its analysis. Further, these tensions can be combined in the same project, bringing both postmodern and naturalistic or both critical and humanistic perspectives to bear.

This rather complex statement means that qualitative research, as a set of practices, embraces within its own multiple disciplinary histories constant tensions and contradictions over the project itself, including its methods and the forms its findings and interpretations take. The field sprawls between and crosscuts all of the human disciplines, even including, in some cases, the physical sciences. Its practitioners are variously committed to modern, postmodern, and postexperimental sensibilities and the approaches to social research that these sensibilities imply.

Resistances to Qualitative Studies

The academic and disciplinary resistances to qualitative research illustrate the politics embedded in this field of discourse. The challenges to qualitative research are many. Qualitative researchers are called journalists, or soft scientists. Their work is termed unscientific, or only exploratory, or subjective. It is called criticism and not theory, or it is interpreted politically, as a disguised version of Marxism or secular humanism (see Huber, 1995; see also Denzin, 1997, pp. 258-261).

These resistances reflect an uneasy awareness that the traditions of qualitative research commit the researcher to a critique of the positivist or postpositivist project. But the positivist resistance to qualitative research goes beyond the "ever-present desire to maintain a distinction between hard science and soft scholarship" (Carey, 1989, p. 99; see also in this volume Schwandt, Chapter 7; Smith & Deemer, Chapter 34). The experimental (positivist) sciences (physics, chemistry, economics, and psychology, for example) are often seen as the crowning achievements of Western civilization, and in their practices it is assumed that "truth" can transcend opinion and personal bias (Carey, 1989, p. 99; Schwandt, 1997b, p. 309). Qualitative research is seen as an assault on this tradition, whose adherents often retreat into a "value-free objectivist science" (Carey, 1989, p. 104) model to defend their position. They seldom attempt to make explicit, or to critique, the "moral and political commitments in their own contingent work" (Carey, 1989, p. 104; see also Lincoln & Guba, Chapter 6, this volume).

Positivists further allege that the so-called new experimental qualitative researchers write fiction, not science, and that these researchers have no way of verifying their truth statements. Ethnographic poetry and fiction signal the death of empirical science, and there is little to be gained by attempting to engage in moral criticism. These critics presume a stable, unchanging reality that can be studied using the empirical methods of objective social science (see Huber, 1995). The province of qualitative research, accordingly, is the world of lived experience, for this is where individual belief and action intersect with culture. Under this model there is no preoccupation with discourse and method as material interpretive practices that constitute representation and description. Thus is the textual, narrative turn rejected by the positivists.

The opposition to positive science by the postpositivists (see below) and the poststructuralists is seen, then, as an attack on reason and truth. At the same time, the positivist science attack on qualitative research is regarded as an attempt to legislate one version of truth over another.

This complex political terrain defines the many traditions and strands of qualitative research: the British tradition and its presence in other national contexts; the American pragmatic, naturalistic, and interpretive traditions in sociology, anthropology, communication, and education; the German and French phenomenological, hermeneutic, semiotic, Marxist, structural, and poststructural perspectives; feminist studies, African American studies, Latino studies, queer studies, studies of indigenous and aboriginal cultures. The politics of qualitative research create a tension that informs each of the above traditions. This tension itself is constantly being reexamined and interrogated, as qualitative research confronts a changing historical world, new intellectual positions, and its own institutional and academic conditions.

To summarize: Qualitative research is many things to many people. Its essence is twofold: a commitment to some version of the naturalistic, interpretive approach to its subject matter and an ongoing critique of the politics and methods of postpositivism. We turn now to a brief discussion of the major differences between qualitative and quantitative approaches to research. We then discuss ongoing differences and tensions within qualitative inquiry.

Qualitative Versus Quantitative Research

The word *qualitative* implies an emphasis on the qualities of entities and on processes and meanings that are not experimentally examined or measured (if measured at all) in terms of quantity, amount, intensity, or frequency. Qualitative researchers stress the socially constructed nature of reality, the intimate relationship between the researcher and what is studied, and the situational constraints that shape inquiry. Such researchers emphasize the value-laden nature of inquiry. They seek answers to questions that stress *how* social experience is created and given meaning. In contrast, quantitative studies emphasize the measurement and analysis of causal relationships between variables, not processes. Proponents of such studies claim that their work is done from within a value-free framework.

Research Styles: Doing the Same Things Differently?

Of course, both qualitative and quantitative researchers "think they know something about society worth telling to others, and they use a variety of forms, media and means to communicate their ideas and findings" (Becker, 1986, p. 122). Qualitative research differs from quantitative research in five significant ways (Becker, 1996). These points of difference turn on different ways of addressing the same set of issues. They return always to the politics of research, and to who has the power to legislate correct solutions to these problems.

Uses of positivism and postpositivism. First, both perspectives are shaped by the positivist and postpositivist traditions in the physical and social sciences (see the discussion below). These two positivist science traditions hold to naïve and critical realist positions concerning reality and its perception. In the positivist version it is contended that there is a reality out there to be studied, captured, and understood, whereas the postpositivists argue that reality can never be fully apprehended, only approximated (Guba, 1990, p. 22). Postpositivism relies on multiple methods as a way of capturing as much of reality as possible. At the same time, emphasis is placed on the discovery and verification of theories. Traditional evaluation criteria, such as internal and external validity, are stressed, as is the use of qualitative procedures that lend themselves to structured (sometimes statistical) analysis. Computer-assisted methods of analysis that permit frequency counts, tabulations, and low-level statistical analyses may also be employed.

The positivist and postpositivist traditions linger like long shadows over the qualitative research project. Historically, qualitative research was defined within the positivist paradigm, where qualitative researchers attempted to do good positivist research with less rigorous methods and procedures. Some mid-20th-century qualitative researchers (e.g., Becker, Geer, Hughes, & Strauss, 1961) reported participant observation findings in terms of quasi-statistics. As recently as 1998, Strauss and Corbin, two leaders of the grounded theory approach to qualitative research, attempted to modify the usual canons of good (positivist) science to fit their own postpositivist conception of rigorous research (but see Charmaz, Chapter 19, this volume; see also Glaser, 1992). Some applied researchers, while claiming to be atheoretical, often fit within the positivist or postpositivist framework by default.

Flick (1998, pp. 2-3) usefully summarizes the differences between these two approaches to inquiry. He observes that the quantitative approach has been used for purposes of isolating "causes and effects . . . operationalizing theoretical relations . . . [and] measuring and . . . quantifying phenomena . . . allowing the generalization of findings" (p. 3). But today doubt is cast on such projects, because "Rapid social change and the resulting diversification of life worlds are increasingly confronting social researchers with new social contexts and perspectives. . . . traditional deductive methodologies . . . are failing. . . . thus research is increasingly forced to make use of inductive strategies instead of starting from theories and testing them. . . . knowledge and practice are studied as local knowledge and practice" (p. 2).

Spindler and Spindler (1992) summarize their qualitative approach to quantitative materials: "Instrumentation and quantification are simply procedures employed to extend and reinforce certain kinds of data, interpretations and test hypotheses across samples. Both must be kept in their place. One must avoid their premature or overly extensive use as a security mechanism" (p. 69).

Although many qualitative researchers in the postpositivist tradition will use statistical measures, methods, and documents as a way of locating groups of subjects within larger populations, they will seldom report their findings in terms of the kinds of complex statistical measures or methods to which quantitative researchers are drawn (i.e., path, regression, or log-linear analyses).

Acceptance of postmodern sensibilities. The use of quantitative, positivist methods and assumptions has been rejected by a new generation of qualitative researchers who are attached to poststructural and/or postmodern sensibilities (see below; see also in this volume Vidich & Lyman, Chapter 2; Richardson, Chapter 36). These researchers argue that positivist methods are but one way of telling stories about society or the social world. These methods may be no better or no worse than any other methods; they just tell different kinds of stories.

This tolerant view is not shared by everyone (Huber, 1995). Many members of the critical theory, constructivist, poststructural, and postmodern schools of thought reject positivist and postpositivist criteria when evaluating their own work. They see these criteria as irrelevant to their work and contend that such criteria reproduce only a certain kind of science, a science that silences too many voices. These researchers seek alternative methods for evaluating their work, including verisimilitude, emotionality, personal responsibility, an ethic of caring, political praxis, multivoiced texts, and dialogues with subjects. In response, positivists and postpositivists argue that what they do is good science, free of individual bias and subjectivity. As noted above, they see postmodernism and poststructuralism as attacks on reason and truth.

Capturing the individual's point of view. Both qualitative and quantitative researchers are concerned with the individual's point of view. However, qualitative investigators think they can get closer to the actor's perspective through detailed interviewing and observation. They argue that quantitative researchers are seldom able to capture their subjects' perspectives because they have to rely on more remote, inferential empirical methods and materials. The empirical materials produced by interpretive methods are regarded by many quantitative researchers as unreliable, impressionistic, and not objective.

Examining the constraints of everyday life. Qualitative researchers are more likely to confront and come up against the constraints of the everyday social world. They see this world in action and embed their findings in it. Quantitative researchers abstract from this world and seldom study it directly. They seek a nomothetic or etic science based on probabilities derived from the study of large numbers of randomly selected cases. These kinds of statements stand above and outside the constraints of everyday life. Qualitative researchers, on the other hand, are committed to an emic, idiographic, case-based position, which directs their attention to the specifics of particular cases.

Securing rich descriptions. Qualitative researchers believe that rich descriptions of the social world are valuable, whereas quantitative researchers, with their etic, nomothetic commitments, are less concerned with such detail. Quantitative researchers are deliberately unconcerned with rich descriptions because such detail interrupts the process of developing generalizations.

The five points of difference described above (uses of positivism and postpositivism, postmodernism, capturing the individual's point of view, examining the constraints of everyday life, securing thick descriptions) reflect commitments to different styles of research, different epistemologies, and different forms of representation. Each work tradition is governed by its own set of genres; each has its own classics, its own preferred forms of representation, interpretation, trustworthiness, and textual evaluation (see Becker, 1986, pp. 134-135). Qualitative researchers use ethnographic prose, historical narratives, first-person accounts, still photographs, life histories, fictionalized "facts," and biographical and autobiographical materials, among others. Quantitative researchers use mathematical models, statistical tables, and graphs, and usually write about their research in impersonal, third-person prose.

Tensions Within Qualitative Research

It is erroneous to presume that all qualitative researchers share the same assumptions about the five points of difference described above. As the discussion below will reveal, positivist, postpositivist, and poststructural differences define and shape the discourses of qualitative research. Realists and postpositivists within the interpretive qualitative research tradition criticize poststructuralists for taking the textual, narrative turn. These critics contend that such work is navel gazing. It produces conditions "for a dialogue of the deaf between itself and the community" (Silverman, 1997, p. 240). Those who attempt to capture the point of view of the interacting subject in the world are accused of naive humanism, of reproducing "a Romantic impulse which elevates the experiential to the level of the authentic" (Silverman, 1997, p. 248).

Still others argue that lived experience is ignored by those who take the textual, performance turn. Snow and Morrill (1995) argue that "this performance turn, like the preoccupation with discourse and storytelling, will take us further from the field of social action and the real dramas of everyday life and thus signal the death knell of ethnography as an empirically grounded enterprise" (p. 361). Of course, we disagree.

With these differences within and between the two traditions now in hand, we must now briefly discuss the history of qualitative research. We break this history into seven historical moments, mindful that any history is always somewhat arbitrary and always at least partially a social construction.

◆ The History of Qualitative Research

The history of qualitative research reveals, as Vidich and Lyman remind us in Chapter 2 of this volume, that the modern social science disciplines have taken as their mission "the analysis and understanding of the patterned conduct and social processes of society." The notion that this task could be carried out presupposed that social scientists had the ability to observe this world objectively. Qualitative methods were a major tool of such observations.[11]

Throughout the history of qualitative research, investigators have always defined their work in terms of hopes and values, "religious faiths, occupational and professional ideologies" (Vidich & Lyman, Chapter 2). Qualitative research (like all research) has always been judged on the "standard of whether the work communicates or 'says' something to us" (Vidich & Lyman, Chapter 2), based on how we conceptualize our reality and our images of the world. *Epistemology* is the word that has historically defined these standards of evaluation. In the contemporary period, as we have argued above, many received discourses on epistemology are now being reevaluated.

Vidich and Lyman's history covers the following (somewhat) overlapping stages: early ethnography (to the 17th century); colonial ethnography (17th-, 18th-, and 19th-century explorers); the ethnography of the American Indian as "other" (late-19th- and early-20th-century anthropology); the ethnography of the "civic other," or community studies, and ethnographies of American immigrants (early 20th century through the 1960s); studies of ethnicity and assimilation (midcentury through the 1980s); and the present, which we call the *seventh moment*.

In each of these eras, researchers were and have been influenced by their political hopes and ideologies, discovering findings in their research that confirmed prior theories or beliefs. Early ethnographers confirmed the racial and cultural diversity of peoples throughout the globe and attempted to fit this diversity into a theory about the origins of history, the races, and civilizations. Colonial ethnographers, before the professionalization of ethnography in the 20th century, fostered a colonial pluralism that left natives on their own as long as their leaders could be co-opted by the colonial administration.

European ethnographers studied Africans, Asians, and other Third World peoples of color. Early American ethnographers studied the American Indian from the perspective of the conqueror, who saw the life world of the primitive as a window to the prehistoric past. The Calvinist mission to save the Indian was soon transferred to the mission of saving the "hordes" of immigrants who entered the United States with the beginnings of industrialization. Qualitative community studies of the ethnic other proliferated from the early 1900s to the 1960s and included the work of E. Franklin Frazier, Robert Park, and Robert Redfield and their students, as well as William Foote Whyte, the Lynds, August Hollingshead, Herbert Gans, Stanford Lyman, Arthur Vidich, and Joseph Bensman. The post-1960 ethnicity studies challenged the "melting pot" hypothesis of Park and his followers and corresponded to the emergence of ethnic studies programs that saw Native Americans, Latinos, Asian Americans, and African Americans attempting to take control over the study of their own peoples.

The postmodern and poststructural challenge emerged in the mid-1980s. It questioned the assumptions that had organized this earlier history in each of its colonializing moments. Qualitative research that crosses the "postmodern divide" requires one, Vidich and Lyman argue in Chapter 2, to "abandon all established and preconceived values, theories, perspectives . . . and prejudices as resources for ethnographic study." In this new era, the qualitative researcher does more than observe history; he or she plays a part in it. New tales from the field will now be written, and they will reflect the researcher's direct and personal engagement with this historical period.

Vidich and Lyman's analysis covers the full sweep of ethnographic history. Ours is confined to the 20th century and complements many of their divisions. We begin with the early foundational work of the British and French as well the Chicago, Columbia, Harvard, Berkeley, and British schools of sociology and anthropology. This early foundational period established the norms of classical qualitative and ethnographic research (see Gupta & Ferguson, 1997; Rosaldo, 1989; Stocking, 1989).

◆ The Seven Moments of Qualitative Research

As suggested above, our history of qualitative research in North America in this century divides into seven phases, each of which we describe in turn below.

The Traditional Period

We call the first moment the traditional period (this covers Vidich and Lyman's second and third phases). It begins in the early 1900s and continues until World War II. In this period, qualitative researchers wrote "objective," colonializing accounts of field experiences that were reflective of the positivist scientist paradigm. They were concerned with offering valid, reliable, and objective interpretations in their writings. The "other" who was studied was alien, foreign, and strange.

Here is Malinowski (1967) discussing his field experiences in New Guinea and the Trobriand Islands in the years 1914-1915 and 1917-1918. He is bartering his way into field data:

> Nothing whatever draws me to ethnographic studies. . . . On the whole the village struck me rather unfavorably. There is a certain disorganization . . . the rowdiness and persistence of the people who laugh and stare and lie discouraged me somewhat. . . . Went to the village hoping to photograph a few stages of the *bara* dance. I handed out half-sticks of tobacco, then watched a few dances; then took pictures—but results were poor. . . . they would not pose long enough for time exposures. At moments I was furious at them, particularly because after I gave them their portions of tobacco they all went away. (quoted in Geertz, 1988, pp. 73-74)

In another work, this lonely, frustrated, isolated field-worker describes his methods in the following words:

> In the field one has to face a chaos of facts. . . . in this crude form they are not scientific facts at all; they are absolutely elusive, and can only be fixed by interpretation. . . . *Only laws and generalizations are scientific facts,* and field work consists only and exclusively in the interpretation of the chaotic social reality, in subordinating it to general rules. (Malinowski, 1916/1948, p. 328; quoted in Geertz, 1988, p. 81)

Malinowski's remarks are provocative. On the one hand they disparage fieldwork, but on the other they speak of it within the glorified language of science, with laws and generalizations fashioned out of this selfsame experience.

The field-worker during this period was lionized, made into a larger-than-life figure who went into and then returned from the field with stories about strange people. Rosaldo (1989, p. 30) describes this as the period of the Lone Ethnographer, the story of the man-scientist who went off in search of his native in a distant land. There this figure "encountered the object of his quest . . . [and] underwent his rite of passage by enduring the ultimate ordeal of 'fieldwork' " (p. 30). Returning home with his data, the Lone Ethnographer wrote up an objective account of the culture studied. These accounts were structured by the norms of classical ethnography. This sacred bundle of terms (Rosaldo, 1989, p. 31) organized ethnographic texts in terms of four beliefs and commitments: a commitment to objectivism, a complicity with imperialism, a belief in monumentalism (the ethnography would create a museumlike picture of the culture studied), and a belief in timelessness (what was studied would never change). The other was an "object" to be archived. This model of the researcher, who could also write complex, dense theories about what was studied, holds to the present day.

The myth of the Lone Ethnographer depicts the birth of classic ethnography. The texts of Malinowski, Radcliffe-Brown, Margaret Mead, and Gregory Bateson are still carefully studied for what they can tell the novice about conducting fieldwork, taking field notes, and writing theory. Today this image has been shattered. The works of the classic ethnographers are seen by many as relics from the colonial past (Rosaldo, 1989, p. 44). Although many feel nostalgia for this past, others celebrate its passing. Rosaldo (1989) quotes Cora Du Bois, a retired Harvard anthropology professor, who lamented this passing at a conference in 1980, reflecting on the crisis in anthropology: "[I feel a distance] from the complexity and disarray of what I once found a justifiable and challenging discipline. . . . It has been like moving from a distinguished art museum into a garage sale" (p. 44).

Du Bois regards the classic ethnographies as pieces of timeless artwork contained in a museum. She feels uncomfortable in the chaos of the garage sale. In contrast, Rosaldo (1989) is drawn to this metaphor: "[The garage sale] provides a precise image of the postcolonial situation where cultural artifacts flow between unlikely places, and nothing is sacred, permanent, or sealed off. The image of anthropology as a garage sale depicts our present global situation" (p. 44). Indeed, many valuable treasures may be found if one is willing to look long and hard, in unexpected places. Old standards no longer hold. Ethnographies do not produce timeless truths. The commitment to objectivism is now in doubt. The complicity with imperialism is openly challenged today, and the belief in monumentalism is a thing of the past.

The legacies of this first period begin at the end of the 19th century, when the novel and the social sciences had become distinguished as separate systems of discourse (Clough, 1992, pp. 21-22; see also Clough, 1998). However, the Chicago school, with its emphasis on the life story and the "slice-of-life" approach to ethnographic materials, sought to develop an interpretive methodology that maintained the centrality of the narrated life history approach. This led to the production of texts that gave the researcher-as-author the power to represent the subject's story. Written under the mantle of straightforward, sentiment-free social realism, these texts used the language of ordinary people. They articulated a social science version of literary naturalism, which often produced the sympathetic illusion that a solution to a social problem had been found. Like the Depression-era juvenile delinquent and other "social problems" films (Roffman & Purdy, 1981), these accounts romanticized the subject. They turned the deviant into a sociological version of a screen hero. These sociological stories, like their film counterparts, usually had happy endings, as they followed individuals through the three stages of the classic morality tale: being in a state of grace, being seduced by evil and falling, and finally achieving redemption through suffering.

Modernist Phase

The modernist phase, or second moment, builds on the canonical works from the traditional period. Social realism, naturalism, and slice-of-life ethnographies are still valued. This phase extended through the postwar years to the 1970s and is still present in the work of many (for reviews, see Wolcott, 1990, 1992, 1995; see also Tedlock, Chapter 17, this volume). In this period many texts sought to formalize qualitative methods (see, for example, Bogdan & Taylor, 1975; Cicourel, 1964; Filstead, 1970; Glaser & Strauss, 1967; Lofland, 1971, 1995; Lofland & Lofland, 1984, 1995; Taylor & Bogdan, 1998).[12] The modernist ethnographer and sociological participant observer attempted rigorous qualitative studies of important social processes, including deviance and social control in the classroom and society. This was a moment of creative ferment.

A new generation of graduate students across the human disciplines encountered new interpretive theories (ethnomethodology, phenomenology, critical theory, feminism). They were drawn to qualitative research practices that would let them give a voice to society's underclass. Postpositivism functioned as a powerful epistemological paradigm. Researchers attempted to fit Campbell and Stanley's (1963) model of internal and external validity to constructionist and interactionist conceptions of the research act. They returned to the texts of the Chicago school as sources of inspiration (see Denzin, 1970, 1978).

A canonical text from this moment remains Boys in White (Becker et al., 1961; see also Becker, 1998). Firmly entrenched in mid-20th-century methodological discourse, this work attempted to make qualitative research as rigorous as its quantitative counterpart. Causal narratives were central to this project. This multimethod work combined open-ended and quasi-structured interviewing with participant observation and the careful analysis of such materials in standardized, statistical form. In a classic article, "Problems of Inference and Proof in Participant Observation," Howard S. Becker (1958/1970) describes the use of quasi-statistics:

> Participant observations have occasionally been gathered in standardized form capable of being transformed into legitimate statistical data. But the exigencies of the field usually prevent the collection of data in such a form to meet the assumptions of statistical tests, so that the observer deals in what have been called "quasi-statistics." His conclusions, while implicitly numerical, do not require precise quantification. (p. 31)

In the analysis of data, Becker notes, the qualitative researcher takes a cue from statistical colleagues. The researcher looks for probabilities or support for arguments concerning the likelihood that, or frequency with which, a conclusion in fact applies in a specific situation (see also Becker, 1998, pp. 166-170). Thus did work in the modernist period clothe itself in the language and rhetoric of positivist and postpositivist discourse.

This was the golden age of rigorous qualitative analysis, bracketed in sociology by Boys in White (Becker et al., 1961) at one end and The Discovery of Grounded Theory (Glaser & Strauss, 1967) at the other. In education, qualitative research in this period was defined by George and Louise Spindler, Jules Henry, Harry Wolcott, and John Singleton. This form of qualitative research is still present in the work of such persons as Strauss and Corbin (1998) and Ryan and Bernard (see Chapter 29, this volume).

The "golden age" reinforced the picture of qualitative researchers as cultural romantics. Imbued with Promethean human powers, they valorized villains and outsiders as heroes to mainstream society. They embodied a belief in the contingency of self and society, and held to emancipatory ideals for "which one lives and dies." They put in place a tragic and often ironic view of society and self, and joined a long line of leftist cultural romantics that included Emerson, Marx, James, Dewey, Gramsci, and Martin Luther King, Jr. (West, 1989, chap. 6).

As this moment came to an end, the Vietnam War was everywhere present in American society. In 1969, alongside these political currents, Herbert Blumer and Everett Hughes met with a group of young sociologists called the "Chicago Irregulars" at the American Sociological Association meetings held in San Francisco and shared their memories of the "Chicago years." Lyn Lofland (1980) describes the 1969 meetings as a

> moment of creative ferment—scholarly and political. The San Francisco meetings witnessed not simply the Blumer-Hughes event but a "counter-revolution." . . . a group first came to . . . talk about the problems of being a sociologist and a female. . . . the discipline seemed literally to be bursting with new . . . ideas: labelling theory, ethnomethodology, conflict theory, phenomenology, dramaturgical analysis. (p. 253)

Thus did the modernist phase come to an end.

Blurred Genres

By the beginning of the third stage (1970-1986), which we call the moment of blurred genres, qualitative researchers had a full complement of paradigms, methods, and strategies to employ in their research. Theories ranged from symbolic interactionism to constructivism, naturalistic inquiry, positivism and postpositivism, phenomenology, ethnomethodology, critical theory, neo-Marxist theory, semiotics, structuralism, feminism, and various racial/ethnic paradigms. Applied qualitative research was gaining in stature, and the politics and ethics of qualitative research—implicated as they were in various applications of this work—were topics of considerable concern. Research strategies and formats for reporting research ranged from grounded theory to the case study, to methods of historical, biographical, ethnographic, action, and clinical research. Diverse ways of collecting and analyzing empirical materials were also available, including qualitative interviewing (open-ended and quasi-structured) and observational, visual, personal experience, and documentary methods. Computers were entering the situation, to be fully developed as aids in the analysis of qualitative data in the next decade, along with narrative, content, and semiotic methods of reading interviews and cultural texts.

Two books by Geertz, *The Interpretation of Culture* (1973) and *Local Knowledge* (1983), defined the beginning and end of this moment. In these two works, Geertz argued that the old functional, positivist, behavioral, totalizing approaches to the human disciplines were giving way to a more pluralistic, interpretive, open-ended perspective. This new perspective took cultural representations and their meanings as its point of departure. Calling for "thick descriptions" of particular events, rituals, and customs, Geertz suggested that all anthropological writings are interpretations of interpretations.[13] The observer has no privileged voice in the interpretations that are written. The central task of theory is to make sense out of a local situation.

Geertz went on to propose that the boundaries between the social sciences and the humanities had become blurred. Social scientists were now turning to the humanities for models, theories, and methods of analysis (semiotics, hermeneutics). A form of genre diaspora was occurring: documentaries that read like fiction (Mailer), parables posing as ethnographies (Castañeda), theoretical treatises that look like travelogues (Lévi-Strauss). At the same time, other new approaches were emerging: poststructuralism (Barthes), neopositivism (Philips), neo-Marxism (Althusser), micro-macro descriptivism (Geertz), ritual theories of drama and culture (V. Turner), deconstructionism (Derrida), ethnomethodology (Garfinkel). The golden age of the social sciences was over, and a new age of blurred, interpretive genres was upon us. The essay as an art form was replacing the scientific article. At issue now is the author's presence in the interpretive text (Geertz, 1988). How can the researcher speak with authority in an age when there are no longer any firm rules concerning the text, including the author's place in it, its standards of evaluation, and its subject matter?

The naturalistic, postpositivist, and constructionist paradigms gained power in this period, especially in education, in the works of Harry Wolcott, Frederick Erickson, Egon Guba, Yvonna Lincoln, Robert Stake, and Elliot Eisner. By the end of the 1970s, several qualitative journals were in place, including *Urban Life and Culture* (now *Journal of Contemporary Ethnography*), *Cultural Anthropology, Anthropology and Education Quarterly, Qualitative Sociology,* and *Symbolic Interaction,* as well as the book series *Studies in Symbolic Interaction.*

Crisis of Representation

A profound rupture occurred in the mid-1980s. What we call the fourth moment, or the crisis of representation, appeared with *Anthropology as Cultural Critique* (Marcus & Fischer, 1986), *The Anthropology of Experience* (Turner & Bruner, 1986), *Writing Culture* (Clifford & Marcus, 1986), *Works and Lives* (Geertz, 1988), and *The Predicament of Culture* (Clifford, 1988). These works made research and writing more reflexive and called into question the issues of gender, class, and race. They articulated the consequences of Geertz's "blurred genres" interpretation of the field in the early 1980s.[14]

New models of truth, method, and representation were sought (Rosaldo, 1989). The erosion of classic norms in anthropology (objectivism, complicity with colonialism, social life structured by fixed rituals and customs, ethnographies as monuments to a culture) was complete (Rosaldo, 1989, pp. 44-45; see also Jackson, 1998, pp. 7-8). Critical, feminist, and epistemologies of color now competed for attention in this arena. Issues such as validity, reliability, and objectivity, previously believed settled, were once more problematic. Pattern and interpretive theories, as opposed to causal, linear theories, were now more common, as writers continued to challenge older models of truth and meaning (Rosaldo, 1989).

Stoller and Olkes (1987, pp. 227-229) describe how the crisis of representation was felt in their fieldwork among the Songhay of Niger. Stoller observes: "When I began to write anthropological texts, I followed the conventions of my training. I 'gathered data,' and once the 'data' were arranged in neat piles, I 'wrote them up.' In one case I reduced Songhay insults to a series of neat logical formulas" (p. 227). Stoller became dissatisfied with this form of writing, in part because he learned that "everyone had lied to me and . . . the data I had so painstakingly collected were worthless. I learned a lesson: Informants routinely lie to their anthropologists" (Stoller & Olkes, 1987, p. 9). This discovery led to a second—that he had, in following the conventions of ethnographic realism, edited himself out of his text. This led Stoller to produce a different type of text, a memoir, in which he became a central character in the story he told. This story, an account of his experiences in the Songhay world, became an analysis of the clash between his world and the world of Songhay sorcery. Thus Stoller's journey represents an attempt to confront the crisis of representation in the fourth moment.

Clough (1992) elaborates this crisis and criticizes those who would argue that new forms of writing represent a way out of the crisis. She argues:

> While many sociologists now commenting on the criticism of ethnography view writing as "downright central to the ethnographic enterprise" [Van Maanen, 1988, p. xi], the problems of writing are still viewed as different from the problems of method or fieldwork itself. Thus the solution usually offered is experiments in writing, that is a self-consciousness about writing. (p. 136)

It is this insistence on the difference between writing and fieldwork that must be analyzed. (Richardson is quite articulate about this issue in Chapter 36 of this volume.)

In writing, the field-worker makes a claim to moral and scientific authority. This claim allows the realist and experimental ethnographic texts to function as sources of validation for an empirical science. They show that the world of real lived experience can still be captured, if only in the writer's memoirs, or fictional experimentations, or dramatic readings. But these works have the danger of directing attention away from the ways in which the text constructs sexually situated individuals in a field of social difference. They also perpetuate "empirical science's hegemony" (Clough, 1992, p. 8), for these new writing technologies of the subject become the site "for the production of knowledge/power . . . [aligned] with . . . the capital/state axis" (Aronowitz, 1988, p. 300; quoted in Clough, 1992, p. 8). Such experiments come up against, and then back away from, the difference between empirical science and social criticism. Too often they fail to engage fully a new politics of textuality that would "refuse the identity of empirical science" (Clough, 1992, p. 135). This new social criticism "would intervene in the relationship of information economics, nation-state politics, and technologies of mass communication, especially in terms of the empirical sciences" (Clough, 1992, p. 16). This, of course, is the terrain occupied by cultural studies.

In this volume, Richardson (Chapter 36), Tedlock (Chapter 17), Brady (Chapter 37), Ellis and Bochner (Chapter 28) develop the above arguments, viewing writing as a method of inquiry that moves through successive stages of self-reflection. As a series of written representations, the field-worker's texts flow from the field experience, through intermediate works, to later work, and finally to the research text, which is the public presentation of the ethnographic and narrative experience. Thus fieldwork and writing blur into one another. There is, in the final analysis, no difference between writing and fieldwork. These two perspectives inform one another throughout every chapter in this volume. In these ways the crisis of representation moves qualitative research in new and critical directions.

A Triple Crisis

The ethnographer's authority remains under assault today (Behar, 1995, p. 3; Gupta & Ferguson, 1997, p. 16; Jackson, 1998; Ortner, 1997, p. 2). A triple crisis of representation, legitimation, and praxis confronts qualitative researchers in the human disciplines. Embedded in the discourses of poststructuralism and postmodernism (see Vidich & Lyman, Chapter 2; and Richardson, Chapter 36, this volume), these three crises are coded in multiple terms, variously called and associated with the *critical, interpretive, linguistic, feminist,* and *rhetorical* turns in social theory. These new turns make problematic two key assumptions of qualitative research. The first is that qualitative researchers can no longer directly capture lived experience. Such experience, it is argued, is created in the social text written by the researcher. This is the representational crisis. It confronts the inescapable problem of representation, but does so

within a framework that makes the direct link between experience and text problematic.

The second assumption makes problematic the traditional criteria for evaluating and interpreting qualitative research. This is the legitimation crisis. It involves a serious rethinking of such terms as *validity, generalizability,* and *reliability,* terms already retheorized in postpositivist (Hammersley, 1992), constructionist-naturalistic (Guba & Lincoln, 1989, pp. 163-183), feminist (Olesen, Chapter 8, this volume), interpretive (Denzin, 1997), poststructural (Lather, 1993; Lather & Smithies, 1997), and critical (Kincheloe & McLaren, Chapter 10, this volume) discourses. This crisis asks, How are qualitative studies to be evaluated in the contemporary, poststructural moment? The first two crises shape the third, which asks, Is it possible to effect change in the world if society is only and always a text? Clearly these crises intersect and blur, as do the answers to the questions they generate (see in this volume Schwandt, Chapter 7; Ladson-Billings, Chapter 9; Smith & Deemer, Chapter 34).

The fifth moment, the postmodern period of experimental ethnographic writing, struggled to make sense of these crises. New ways of composing ethnography were explored (Ellis & Bochner, 1996). Theories were read as tales from the field. Writers struggled with different ways to represent the "other," although they were now joined by new representational concerns (see Fine et al., Chapter 4, this volume). Epistemologies from previously silenced groups emerged to offer solutions to these problems. The concept of the aloof observer has been abandoned. More action, participatory, and activist-oriented research is on the horizon. The search for grand narratives is being replaced by more local, small-scale theories fitted to specific problems and particular situations.

The sixth (postexperimental) and seventh (the future) moments are upon us. Fictional ethnographies, ethnographic poetry, and multimedia texts are today taken for granted. Postexperimental writers seek to connect their writings to the needs of a free democratic society. The demands of a moral and sacred qualitative social science are actively being explored by a host of new writers from many different disciplines (see

Jackson, 1998; Lincoln & Denzin, Chapter 6, this volume).

Reading History

We draw four conclusions from this brief history, noting that it is, like all histories, somewhat arbitrary. First, each of the earlier historical moments is still operating in the present, either as legacy or as a set of practices that researchers continue to follow or argue against. The multiple and fractured histories of qualitative research now make it possible for any given researcher to attach a project to a canonical text from any of the above-described historical moments. Multiple criteria of evaluation compete for attention in this field (Lincoln, in press). Second, an embarrassment of choices now characterizes the field of qualitative research. There have never been so many paradigms, strategies of inquiry, or methods of analysis for researchers to draw upon and utilize. Third, we are in a moment of discovery and rediscovery, as new ways of looking, interpreting, arguing, and writing are debated and discussed. Fourth, the qualitative research act can no longer be viewed from within a neutral or objective positivist perspective. Class, race, gender, and ethnicity shape the process of inquiry, making research a multicultural process. It is to this topic that we now turn.

◆ Qualitative Research as Process

Three interconnected, generic activities define the qualitative research process. They go by a variety of different labels, including *theory, method, analysis, ontology, epistemology,* and *methodology.* Behind these terms stands the personal biography of the researcher, who speaks from a particular class, gender, racial, cultural, and ethnic community perspective. The gendered, multiculturally situated researcher approaches the world with a set of ideas, a framework (theory, ontology) that specifies a set of questions (epistemology) that he or she then examines in specific ways (methodology, analy-

sis). That is, the researcher collects empirical materials bearing on the question and then analyzes and writes about them. Every researcher speaks from within a distinct interpretive community that configures, in its special way, the multicultural, gendered components of the research act.

In this volume we treat these generic activities under five headings, or phases: the researcher and the researched as multicultural subjects, major paradigms and interpretive perspectives, research strategies, methods of collecting and analyzing empirical materials, and the art, practices, and politics of interpretation. Behind and within each of these phases stands the biographically situated researcher. This individual enters the research process from inside an interpretive community. This community has its own historical research traditions, which constitute a distinct point of view. This perspective leads the researcher to adopt particular views of the "other" who is studied. At the same time, the politics and the ethics of research must also be considered, for these concerns permeate every phase of the research process.

◆ The Other as Research Subject

Since its early-20th-century birth in modern, interpretive form, qualitative research has been haunted by a double-faced ghost. On the one hand, qualitative researchers have assumed that qualified, competent observers can, with objectivity, clarity, and precision, report on their own observations of the social world, including the experiences of others. Second, researchers have held to the belief in a real subject, or real individual, who is present in the world and able, in some form, to report on his or her experiences. So armed, researchers could blend their own observations with the self-reports provided by subjects through interviews and life story, personal experience, case study, and other documents.

These two beliefs have led qualitative researchers across disciplines to seek a method that would allow them to record accurately their own observations while also uncovering the meanings their subjects bring to their life experiences. This method would rely upon the subjective verbal and written expressions of meaning given by the individuals studied as windows into the inner lives of these persons. Since Dilthey (1900/1976), this search for a method has led to a perennial focus in the human disciplines on qualitative, interpretive methods.

Recently, as noted above, this position and its beliefs have come under assault. Poststructuralists and postmodernists have contributed to the understanding that there is no clear window into the inner life of an individual. Any gaze is always filtered through the lenses of language, gender, social class, race, and ethnicity. There are no objective observations, only observations socially situated in the worlds of—and between—the observer and the observed. Subjects, or individuals, are seldom able to give full explanations of their actions or intentions; all they can offer are accounts, or stories, about what they did and why. No single method can grasp all of the subtle variations in ongoing human experience. Consequently, qualitative researchers deploy a wide range of interconnected interpretive methods, always seeking better ways to make more understandable the worlds of experience they have studied.

Table 1.1 depicts the relationships we see among the five phases that define the research process. Behind all but one of these phases stands the biographically situated researcher. These five levels of activity, or practice, work their way through the biography of the researcher. We take them up briefly in order here; we discuss these phases more fully in the introductions to the individual parts of this volume.

Phase 1: The Researcher

Our remarks above indicate the depth and complexity of the traditional and applied qualitative research perspectives into which a socially situated researcher enters. These traditions locate the researcher in history, simultaneously guiding and constraining work that will be done in any specific study. This field has been characterized constantly by diversity and conflict, and these are its most enduring traditions (see Greenwood & Levin, Chapter 3, this volume). As a carrier of this complex and contradictory history, the researcher must also confront the ethics and politics of research (see Christians, Chapter 5, this volume). The age of value-free inquiry for the human disciplines is over (see Vidich & Lyman, Chapter 2; Fine et al., Chapter 4, this volume). Today researchers struggle to develop situational and transsituational ethics that apply to all forms of the research act and its human-to-human relationships.

Phase 2: Interpretive Paradigms

All qualitative researchers are philosophers in that "universal sense in which all human beings . . . are guided by highly abstract principles" (Bateson, 1972, p. 320). These principles combine beliefs about ontology (What kind of being is the human being? What is the nature of reality?), epistemology (What is the relationship between the inquirer and the known?), and methodology (How do we know the world, or gain knowledge of it?) (see Guba, 1990, p. 18; Lincoln & Guba, 1985, pp. 14-15; see also Lincoln & Guba, Chapter 7, this volume). These beliefs shape how the qualitative researcher sees the world and acts in it. The researcher is "bound within a net of epistemological and ontological premises which—regardless of ultimate truth or falsity—become partially self-validating" (Bateson, 1972, p. 314).

The net that contains the researcher's epistemological, ontological, and methodological premises may be termed a *paradigm,* or an interpretive framework, a "basic set of beliefs that guides action" (Guba, 1990, p. 17). All research is interpretive; it is guided by a set of beliefs and feelings about the world and how it should be understood and studied. Some beliefs may be taken for granted, invisible, only assumed, whereas others are highly problematic and controversial. Each interpretive paradigm makes particular demands on the researcher, including the questions he or she asks and the interpretations the researcher brings to them.

At the most general level, four major interpretive paradigms structure qualitative re-

TABLE 1.1   The Research Process

Phase 1: The Researcher as a Multicultural Subject
   history and research traditions
   conceptions of self and the other
   ethics and politics of research

Phase 2: Theoretical Paradigms and Perspectives
   positivism, postpositivism
   interpretivism, constructivism, hermeneutics
   feminism(s)
   racialized discourses
   critical theory and Marxist models
   cultural studies models
   queer theory

Phase 3: Research Strategies
   study design
   case study
   ethnography, participant observation, performance ethnography
   phenomenology, ethnomethodology
   grounded theory
   life history, *testimonio*
   historical method
   action and applied research
   clinical research

Phase 4: Methods of Collection and Analysis
   interviewing
   observing
   artifacts, documents, and records
   visual methods
   autoethnography
   data management methods
   computer-assisted analysis
   textual analysis
   focus groups
   applied ethnography

Phase 5: The Art, Practices, and Politics of Interpretation and Presentation
   criteria for judging adequacy
   practices and politics of interpretation
   writing as interpretation
   policy analysis
   evaluation traditions
   applied research

search: positivist and postpositivist, constructivist-interpretive, critical (Marxist, emancipatory), and feminist-poststructural. These four abstract paradigms become more complicated at the level of concrete specific interpretive communities. At this level it is possible to identify not only the constructivist, but also multiple versions of feminism (Afrocentric and poststructural)[15] as well as specific ethnic, Marxist, and cultural studies paradigms. These perspectives, or paradigms, are examined in Part II of this volume.

The paradigms examined in Part II work against and alongside (and some within) the positivist and postpositivist models. They all work within relativist ontologies (multiple constructed realities), interpretive epistemologies (the knower and known interact and shape one another), and interpretive, naturalistic methods.

Table 1.2 presents these paradigms and their assumptions, including their criteria for evaluating research, and the typical form that an interpretive or theoretical statement assumes in each paradigm.[16] These paradigms are explored in considerable detail in Part II by Lincoln and Guba (Chapter 6), Schwandt (Chapter 7), Olesen (Chapter 8), Ladson-Billings (Chapter 9), Kincheloe and McLaren (Chapter 10), Frow and Morris (Chapter 11), and Gamson (Chapter 12). We have discussed the positivist and postpositivist paradigms above. They work from within a realist and critical realist ontology and objective epistemologies, and rely upon experimental, quasi-experimental, survey, and rigorously defined qualitative methodologies. Ryan and Bernard (Chapter 29) develop elements of this paradigm.

The constructivist paradigm assumes a relativist ontology (there are multiple realities), a subjectivist epistemology (knower and respondent cocreate understandings), and a naturalistic (in the natural world) set of methodological procedures. Findings are usually presented in terms of the criteria of grounded theory or pattern theories (see in this volume Lincoln & Guba, Chapter 6; Charmaz, Chapter 19; Ryan & Bernard, Chapter 29). Terms such as *credibility, transferability, dependability,* and *confirmability* replace the usual positivist criteria of internal and external validity, reliability, and objectivity.

Feminist, ethnic, Marxist, and cultural studies and queer theory models privilege a materialist-realist ontology; that is, the real world makes a material difference in terms of race, class, and gender. Subjectivist epistemologies and naturalistic methodologies (usually ethnographies) are also employed. Empirical materials and theoretical arguments are evaluated in terms of their emancipatory implications. Criteria from gender and racial communities (e.g., African American) may be applied (emotionality and feeling, caring, personal accountability, dialogue).

Poststructural feminist theories emphasize problems with the social text, its logic, and its inability ever to represent the world of lived experience fully. Positivist and postpositivist criteria of evaluation are replaced by other terms, including the reflexive, multivoiced text that is grounded in the experiences of oppressed people.

The cultural studies and queer theory paradigms are multifocused, with many different strands drawing from Marxism, feminism, and the postmodern sensibility (see in this volume Frow & Morris, Chapter 11; Gamson, Chapter 12; Richardson, Chapter 36). There is a tension between a humanistic cultural studies, which stresses lived experiences (meaning), and a more structural cultural studies project, which stresses the structural and material determinants (race, class, gender) and effects of experience. Of course, there are two sides to every coin, and both sides are needed and are indeed critical. The cultural studies and queer theory paradigms use methods strategically—that is, as resources for understanding and for producing resistances to local structures of domination. Scholars may do close textual readings and discourse analyses of cultural texts (see Olesen, Chapter 8; Frow & Morris, Chapter 11; Silverman, Chapter 31) as well as conducting local ethnographies, openended interviewing, and participant observation. The focus is on how race, class, and gender are produced and enacted in historically specific situations.

Paradigm and personal history in hand, focused on a concrete empirical problem to examine, the researcher now moves to the next stage of the research process—namely, working with a specific strategy of inquiry.

Phase 3: Strategies of Inquiry and Interpretive Paradigms

Table 1.1 presents some of the major strategies of inquiry a researcher may use. Phase 3 begins with research design, which, broadly conceived, involves a clear focus on the research question, the purposes of the study, "what information most appropriately will answer specific research questions, and which strategies are most

TABLE 1.2   Interpretive Paradigms

Paradigm/Theory	Criteria	Form of Theory	Type of Narration
Positivist/ postpositivist	internal, external validity	logical-deductive, grounded	scientific report
Constructivist	trustworthiness, credibility, transferability, confirmability	substantive-formal	interpretive case studies, ethnographic fiction
Feminist	Afrocentric, lived experience, dialogue, caring, accountability, race, class, gender, reflexivity, praxis, emotion, concrete grounding	critical, standpoint	essays, stories, experimental writing
Ethnic	Afrocentric, lived experience, dialogue, caring, accountability, race, class, gender	standpoint, critical, historical	essays, fables, dramas
Marxist	emancipatory theory, falsifiable, dialogical, race, class, gender	critical, historical, economic	historical, economic, sociocultural analyses
Cultural studies	cultural practices, praxis, social texts, subjectivities	social criticism	cultural theory as criticism
Queer theory	reflexivity, deconstruction	social criticism, historical analysis	theory as criticism, autobiography

effective for obtaining it" (LeCompte & Preissle, 1993, p. 30; see also in this volume Janesick, Chapter 13; Cheek, Chapter 14). A research design describes a flexible set of guidelines that connect theoretical paradigms first to strategies of inquiry and second to methods for collecting empirical material. A research design situates researchers in the empirical world and connects them to specific sites, persons, groups, institutions, and bodies of relevant interpretive material, including documents and archives. A research design also specifies how the investigator will address the two critical issues of representation and legitimation.

A strategy of inquiry comprises a bundle of skills, assumptions, and practices that the researcher employs as he or she moves from paradigm to the empirical world. Strategies of inquiry put paradigms of interpretation into motion. At the same time, strategies of inquiry also connect the researcher to specific methods of collecting and analyzing empirical materials. For example, the case study relies on interviewing, observing, and document analysis. Research strategies implement and anchor paradigms in specific empirical sites, or in specific methodological practices, such as making a case an object of study. These strategies include the case study, phenomenological and ethnomethodological techniques, and the use of grounded theory, as well as biographical, autoethnographic, historical, action, and clinical methods. Each of these strategies is connected to a complex literature, and each has a separate history, exemplary works, and preferred ways for putting the strategy into motion.

Phase 4: Methods of Collecting and Analyzing Empirical Materials

The researcher has several methods for collecting empirical materials.[17] These methods are taken up in Part IV. They range from the interview to direct observation, the analysis of artifacts, documents, and cultural records, and the use of visual materials or personal experience. The researcher may also use a variety of different methods of reading and analyzing interviews or cultural texts, including content, narrative, and semiotic strategies. Faced with large amounts of qualitative materials, the investigator seeks ways of managing and interpreting these documents, and here data management methods and computer-assisted models of analysis may be of use. Ryan and Bernard (Chapter 29) and Weitzman (Chapter 30) discuss these techniques.

Phase 5: The Art and Politics of Interpretation and Evaluation

Qualitative research is endlessly creative and interpretive. The researcher does not just leave the field with mountains of empirical materials and then easily write up his or her findings. Qualitative interpretations are constructed. The researcher first creates a field text consisting of field notes and documents from the field, what Roger Sanjek (1990, p. 386) calls "indexing" and David Plath (1990, p. 374) calls "filework." The writer-as-interpreter moves from this text to a research text: notes and interpretations based on the field text. This text is then re-created as a working interpretive document that contains the writer's initial attempts to make sense of what he or she has learned. Finally the writer produces the public text that comes to the reader. This final tale from the field may assume several forms: confessional, realist, impressionistic, critical, formal, literary,

analytic, grounded theory, and so on (see Van Maanen, 1988).

The interpretive practice of making sense of one's findings is both artistic and political. Multiple criteria for evaluating qualitative research now exist, and those that we emphasize stress the situated, relational, and textual structures of the ethnographic experience. There is no single interpretive truth. As we argued earlier, there are multiple interpretive communities, each with its own criteria for evaluating an interpretation.

Program evaluation is a major site of qualitative research, and qualitative researchers can influence social policy in important ways. The contributions to this volume by Greenwood and Levin (Chapter 3), Kemmis and McTaggart (Chapter 22), Miller and Crabtree (Chapter 23), Chambers (Chapter 33), Greene (Chapter 38), and Rist (Chapter 39) trace and discuss the rich history of applied qualitative research in the social sciences. This is the critical site where theory, method, praxis, action, and policy all come together. Qualitative researchers can isolate target populations, show the immediate effects of certain programs on such groups, and isolate the constraints that operate against policy changes in such settings. Action-oriented and clinically oriented qualitative researchers can also create spaces for those who are studied (the other) to speak. The evaluator becomes the conduit through which such voices can be heard. Chambers, Greene, and Rist explicitly develop these topics in their chapters.

◆ Bridging the Historical Moments: What Comes Next?

Ellis and Bochner (Chapter 28), Gergen and Gergen (Chapter 40), and Richardson (Chapter 36) argue that we are already in the post "post" period—post-poststructuralist, post-postmodernist, post-postexperimental. What this means for interpretive ethnographic practices is still not clear, but it is certain that things will never again be the same. We are in a new age where messy, uncertain, multivoiced texts, cultural criticism, and new experimental works will become more common, as will more reflexive forms of fieldwork, analysis, and intertextual representation. We take as the subject of our final essay in this volume these fifth, sixth, and seventh moments. It is true that, as the poet said, the center no longer holds. We can reflect on what should be at the new center.

Thus we come full circle. Returning to our bridge metaphor, the chapters that follow take the researcher back and forth through every phase of the research act. Like a good bridge, the chapters provide for two-way traffic, coming and going between moments, formations, and interpretive communities. Each chapter examines the relevant histories, controversies, and current practices that are associated with each paradigm, strategy, and method. Each chapter also offers projections for the future, where a specific paradigm, strategy, or method will be 10 years from now, deep into the formative years of the 21st century.

In reading the chapters that follow, it is important to remember that the field of qualitative research is defined by a series of tensions, contradictions, and hesitations. This tension works back and forth between the broad, doubting postmodern sensibility and the more certain, more traditional positivist, postpositivist, and naturalistic conceptions of this project. All of the chapters that follow are caught in and articulate this tension.

■ Notes

1. Qualitative research has separate and distinguished histories in education, social work, communications, psychology, history, organizational studies, medical science, anthropology, and sociology.

2. Some definitions are in order here. *Positivism* asserts that objective accounts of the real world can be given. *Postpositivism* holds that only partially objective accounts of the world can be produced, because all methods for examining them are flawed. According to *foundationalism*, we can have an ultimate grounding for our knowledge claims about the world, and this involves the use of empiricist and positivist epistemologies (Schwandt, 1997a, p. 103). *Nonfoundationalism* holds that we can make statements about the world without "recourse to ultimate proof or foundations for that knowing" (p. 102). *Quasi-foundationalism* holds that certain knowledge claims can be made about the world based on neorealist criteria, including the correspondence concept of truth; there is an independent reality that can be mapped (see Smith & Deemer, Chapter 34, this volume).

3. Jameson (1991, pp. 3-4) reminds us that any periodization hypothesis is always suspect, even one that rejects linear, stagelike models. It is never clear to what reality a stage refers, and what divides one stage from another is always debatable. Our seven moments are meant to mark discernible shifts in style, genre, epistemology, ethics, politics, and aesthetics.

4. Some further definitions are in order. *Structuralism* holds that any system is made up of a set of oppositional categories embedded in language. *Semiotics* is the science of signs or sign systems—a structuralist project. According to *poststructuralism,* language is an unstable system of referents, thus it is impossible ever to capture completely the meaning of an action, text, or intention. *Postmodernism* is a contemporary sensibility, developing since World War II, that privileges no single authority, method, or paradigm. *Hermeneutics* is an approach to the analysis of texts that stresses how prior understandings and prejudices shape the interpretive process. *Phenomenology* is a complex system of ideas associated with the works of Husserl, Heidegger, Sartre, Merleau-Ponty, and Alfred Schutz. *Cultural studies* is a complex, interdisciplinary field that merges critical theory, feminism, and poststructuralism.

5. Of course, all settings are natural—that is, places where everyday experiences take place. Qualitative researchers study people doing things together in the places where these things are done (Becker, 1986). There is no field site or natural place where one goes to do this kind of work (see also Gupta & Ferguson, 1997, p. 8). The site is constituted through the researcher's interpretive practices. Historically, analysts have distinguished between experimental (laboratory) and field (natural) research settings, hence the argument that qualitative research is natural-

istic. Activity theory erases this distinction (Keller & Keller, 1996, p. 20; Vygotsky, 1978).

6. According to Weinstein and Weinstein (1991), "The meaning of *bricoleur* in French popular speech is 'someone who works with his (or her) hands and uses devious means compared to those of the craftsman.' . . . the *bricoleur* is practical and gets the job done" (p. 161). These authors provide a history of the term, connecting it to the works of the German sociologist and social theorist Georg Simmel and, by implication, Baudelaire. Hammersley (in press) disputes our use of this term. Following Lévi-Strauss, he reads the *bricoleur* as a mythmaker. He suggests the term be replaced with the notion of the boatbuilder. Hammersley also quarrels with our "moments" model of qualitative research, contending that it implies some sense of progress.

7. Brian De Palma reproduced this baby carriage scene in his 1987 film *The Untouchables.*

8. In the harbor, the muzzles of the *Potemkin's* two huge guns swing slowly toward the camera. Words onscreen inform us, "The brutal military power answered by guns of the battleship." A final famous three-shot montage sequence shows first a sculptured sleeping lion, then a lion rising from his sleep, and finally the lion roaring, symbolizing the rage of the Russian people (Cook, 1981, p. 167). In this sequence Eisenstein uses montage to expand time, creating a psychological duration for this horrible event. By drawing out this sequence, by showing the baby in the carriage, the soldiers firing on the citizens, the blood on the mother's glove, the descending carriage on the steps, he suggests a level of destruction of great magnitude.

9. Here it is relevant to make a distinction between techniques that are used across disciplines and methods that are used within disciplines. Ethnomethodologists, for example, employ their approach as a method, whereas others selectively borrow that method as a technique for their own applications. Harry Wolcott (personal communication, 1993) suggests this distinction. It is also relevant to make distinctions among topic, method, and resource. Methods can be studied as topics of inquiry; that is how a case study gets done. In this ironic, ethnomethodological sense, method is both a resource and a topic of inquiry.

10. Indeed, any attempt to give an essential definition of qualitative research requires a qualitative analysis of the circumstances that produce such a definition.

11. In this sense all research is qualitative, because "the observer is at the center of the research process" (Vidich & Lyman, Chapter 2, this volume).

12. See Lincoln and Guba (1985) for an extension and elaboration of this tradition in the mid-1980s, and for more recent extensions see Taylor and Bogdan (1998) and Creswell (1997).

13. Greenblatt (1997, pp. 15-18) offers a useful deconstructive reading of the many meanings and practices Geertz brings to the term *thick description.*

14. These works marginalized and minimized the contributions of standpoint feminist theory and research to this discourse (see Behar, 1995, p. 3; Gordon, 1995, p. 432).

15. Olesen (Chapter 8, this volume) identifies three strands of feminist research: mainstream empirical, standpoint and cultural studies, and poststructural, postmodern. She places Afrocentric and other models of color under the cultural studies and postmodern categories.

16. These, of course, are our interpretations of these paradigms and interpretive styles.

17. *Empirical materials* is the preferred term for what are traditionally described as data.

■ *References*

Aronowitz, S. (1988). *Science as power: Discourse and ideology in modern society.* Minneapolis: University of Minnesota Press.

Bateson, G. (1972). *Steps to an ecology of mind.* New York: Ballantine.

Becker, H. S. (1970). Problems of inference and proof in participant observation. In H. S. Becker, *Sociological work: Method and substance.* Chicago: Aldine. (Reprinted from *American Sociological Review,* 1958, *23,* 652-660)

Becker, H. S. (1986). *Doing things together.* Evanston: Northwestern University Press.

Becker, H. S. (1996). The epistemology of qualitative research. In R. Jessor, A. Colby, & R. A. Shweder (Eds.), *Ethnography and human development: Context and meaning in social in-*

quiry (pp. 53-71). Chicago: University of Chicago Press.

Becker, H. S. (1998). *Tricks of the trade: How to think about your research while you're doing it.* Chicago: University of Chicago Press.

Becker, H. S., Geer, B., Hughes, E. C., & Strauss, A. L. (1961). *Boys in white: Student culture in medical school.* Chicago: University of Chicago Press.

Behar, R. (1995). Introduction: Out of exile. In R. Behar & D. A. Gordon (Eds.), *Women writing culture* (pp. 1-29). Berkeley: University of California Press.

Bogdan, R. C., & Taylor, S. J. (1975). *Introduction to qualitative research methods: A phenomenological approach to the social sciences.* New York: John Wiley.

Campbell, D. T., & Stanley, J. C. (1963). *Experimental and quasi-experimental designs for research.* Chicago: Rand McNally.

Carey, J. W. (1989). *Communication as culture: Essays on media and society.* Boston: Unwin Hyman.

Cicourel, A. V. (1964). *Method and measurement in sociology.* New York: Free Press.

Clifford, J. (1988). *The predicament of culture: Twentieth-century ethnography, literature, and art.* Cambridge, MA: Harvard University Press.

Clifford, J., & Marcus, G. E. (Eds.). (1986). *Writing culture: The poetics and politics of ethnography.* Berkeley: University of California Press.

Clough, P. T. (1992). *The end(s) of ethnography: From realism to social criticism.* Newbury Park, CA: Sage.

Clough, P. T. (1998). *The end(s) of ethnography: From realism to social criticism* (2nd ed.). New York: Peter Lang.

Cook, D. A. (1981). *A history of narrative film.* New York: W. W. Norton.

Creswell, J. W. (1997). *Qualitative inquiry and research design: Choosing among five traditions.* Thousand Oaks, CA: Sage.

Denzin, N. K. (1970). *The research act.* Chicago: Aldine.

Denzin, N. K. (1978). *The research act* (2nd ed.). New York: McGraw-Hill.

Denzin, N. K. (1997). *Interpretive ethnography.* Thousand Oaks, CA: Sage.

Dilthey, W. L. (1976). *Selected writings.* Cambridge: Cambridge University Press. (Original work published 1900)

Diversi, M. (1998). Glimpses of street life: Representing lived experience through short stories. *Qualitative Inquiry, 4,* 131-137.

Ellis, C., & Bochner, A. P. (Eds.). (1996). *Composing ethnography: Alternative forms of qualitative writing.* Walnut Creek, CA: AltaMira.

Filstead, W. J. (Ed.). (1970). *Qualitative methodology.* Chicago: Markham.

Flick, U. (1998). *An introduction to qualitative research: Theory, method and applications.* London: Sage.

Geertz, C. (1973). *The interpretation of cultures: Selected essays.* New York: Basic Books.

Geertz, C. (1983). *Local knowledge: Further essays in interpretive anthropology.* New York: Basic Books.

Geertz, C. (1988). *Works and lives: The anthropologist as author.* Stanford, CA: Stanford University Press.

Glaser, B. G. (1992). *Emergence vs. forcing: Basics of grounded theory.* Mill Valley, CA: Sociology Press.

Glaser, B. G., & Strauss, A. L. (1967). *The discovery of grounded theory: Strategies for qualitative research.* Chicago: Aldine.

Gordon, D. A. (1995). Culture writing women: Inscribing feminist anthropology. In R. Behar & D. A. Gordon (Eds.), *Women writing culture* (pp. 429-441). Berkeley: University of California Press.

Gordon, D. A. (1988). Writing culture, writing feminism: The poetics and politics of experimental ethnography. *Inscriptions, 3/4(8),* 21-31.

Greenblatt, S. (1997). The touch of the real. In S. B. Ortner (Ed.), The fate of "culture": Geertz and beyond [Special issue]. *Representations, 59,* 14-29.

Guba, E. G. (1990). The alternative paradigm dialog. In E. G. Guba (Ed.), *The paradigm dialog* (pp. 17-30). Newbury Park, CA: Sage.

Guba, E. G., & Lincoln, Y. S. (1989). *Fourth generation evaluation.* Newbury Park, CA: Sage.

Gupta, A., & Ferguson, J. (1997). Discipline and practice: "The field" as site, method, and location in anthropology. In A. Gupta & J. Ferguson (Eds.), *Anthropological locations:*

Boundaries and grounds of a field science (pp. 1-46). Berkeley: University of California Press.

Hammersley, M. (1992). *What's wrong with ethnography? Methodological explorations.* London: Routledge.

Hammersley, M. (in press). Not bricolage but boatbuilding. *Journal of Contemporary Ethnography.*

hooks, b. (1990). *Yearning: Race, gender, and cultural politics.* Boston: South End.

Huber, J. (1995). Centennial essay: Institutional perspectives on sociology. *American Journal of Sociology, 101,* 194-216.

Jackson, M. (1998). *Minima ethnographica: Intersubjectivity and the anthropological project.* Chicago: University of Chicago Press.

Jameson, F. (1991). *Postmodernism; or, The cultural logic of late capitalism.* Durham, NC: Duke University Press.

Jones, S. H. (1999). Torch. *Qualitative Inquiry, 5,* 235-250.

Keller, C. M., & Keller, J. D. (1996). *Cognition and tool use: The blacksmith at work.* New York: Cambridge University Press.

Lather, P. (1993). Fertile obsession: Validity after poststructuralism. *Sociological Quarterly, 35,* 673-694.

Lather, P., & Smithies, C. (1997). *Troubling the angels: Women living with HIV/AIDS.* Boulder, CO: Westview.

LeCompte, M. D., & Preissle, J. (with Tesch, R.). (1993). *Ethnography and qualitative design in educational research* (2nd ed.). New York: Academic Press.

Lévi-Strauss, C. (1966). *The savage mind* (2nd ed.). Chicago: University of Chicago Press.

Lincoln, Y. S. (1999, June). *Courage, vulnerability and truth.* Keynote address delivered at the conference "Reclaiming Voice II: Ethnographic Inquiry and Qualitative Research in a Postmodern Age," University of California, Irvine.

Lincoln, Y. S. (in press). Varieties of validity: Quality in qualitative research. In J. S. Smart & C. Ethington (Eds.), *Higher education: Handbook of theory and research.* New York: Agathon Press.

Lincoln, Y. S., & Guba, E. G. (1985). *Naturalistic inquiry.* Beverly Hills, CA: Sage.

Lofland, J. (1971). *Analyzing social settings.* Belmont, CA: Wadsworth.

Lofland, J. (1995). Analytic ethnography: Features, failings, and futures. *Journal of Contemporary Ethnography, 24,* 30-67.

Lofland, J., & Lofland, L. H. (1984). *Analyzing social settings: A guide to qualitative observation and analysis* (2nd ed.). Belmont, CA: Wadsworth.

Lofland, J., & Lofland, L. H. (1995). *Analyzing social settings: A guide to qualitative observation and analysis* (3rd ed.). Belmont, CA: Wadsworth.

Lofland, L. (1980). The 1969 Blumer-Hughes Talk. *Urban Life and Culture, 8,* 248-260.

Malinowski, B. (1948). *Magic, science and religion, and other essays.* New York: Natural History Press. (Original work published 1916)

Malinowski, B. (1967). *A diary in the strict sense of the term* (N. Guterman, Trans.). New York: Harcourt, Brace & World.

Marcus, G. E., & Fischer, M. M. J. (1986). *Anthropology as cultural critique: An experimental moment in the human sciences.* Chicago: University of Chicago Press.

Monaco, J. (1981). *How to read a film: The art, technology, language, history and theory of film* (Rev. ed.). New York: Oxford University Press.

Nelson, C., Treichler, P. A., & Grossberg, L. (1992). Cultural studies: An introduction. In L. Grossberg, C. Nelson, & P. A. Treichler (Eds.), *Cultural studies* (pp. 1-16). New York: Routledge.

Ortner, S. B. (1997). Introduction. In S. B. Ortner (Ed.), The fate of "culture": Geertz and beyond [Special issue]. *Representations, 59,* 1-13.

Plath, D. W. (1990). Fieldnotes, filed notes, and the conferring of note. In R. Sanjek (Ed.), *Fieldnotes: The makings of anthropology* (pp. 371-384). Ithaca, NY: Cornell University Press.

Richardson, L. (1997). *Fields of play: Constructing an academic life.* New Brunswick, NJ: Rutgers University Press.

Roffman, P., & Purdy, J. (1981). *The Hollywood social problem film.* Bloomington: Indiana University Press.

Ronai, C. R. (1998). Sketching with Derrida: An ethnography of a researcher/erotic dancer. *Qualitative Inquiry, 4,* 405-420.

Rosaldo, R. (1989). *Culture and truth: The re-making of social analysis.* Boston: Beacon.

Sanjek, R. (Ed.). (1990). *Fieldnotes: The makings of anthropology.* Ithaca, NY: Cornell University Press.

Schwandt, T. A. (1997a). *Qualitative inquiry: A dictionary of terms.* Thousand Oaks, CA: Sage.

Schwandt, T. A. (1997b). Textual gymnastics, ethics and angst. In W. G. Tierney & Y. S. Lincoln (Eds.), *Representation and the text: Re-framing the narrative voice* (pp. 305-311). Albany: State University of New York Press.

Silverman, D. (1997). Towards an aesthetics of research. In D. Silverman (Ed.), *Qualitative research: Theory, method and practice* (pp. 239-253). London: Sage.

Smith, A. D. (1993). *Fires in the mirror: Crown Heights, Brooklyn, and other identities.* Garden City, NY: Anchor.

Snow, D., & Morrill, C. (1995). Ironies, puzzles, and contradictions in Denzin and Lincoln's vision of qualitative research. *Journal of Contemporary Ethnography, 22,* 358-362.

Spindler, G., & Spindler, L. (1992). Cultural process and ethnography: An anthropological perspective. In M. D. LeCompte, W. L. Millroy, & J. Preissle (Eds.), *The handbook of qualitative research in education* (pp. 53-92). New York: Academic Press.

Stocking, G. W., Jr. (1986). Anthropology and the science of the irrational: Malinowski's encounter with Freudian psychoanalysis. In G. W. Stocking, Jr. (Ed.), *Malinowski, Rivers, Benedict and others: Essays on culture and personality* (pp. 13-49). Madison: University of Wisconsin Press.

Stocking, G. W., Jr. (1989). The ethnographic sensibility of the 1920s and the dualism of the anthropological tradition. In G. W. Stocking, Jr. (Ed.), *Romantic motives: Essays on anthropological sensibility* (pp. 208-276). Madison: University of Wisconsin Press.

Stoller, P., & Olkes, C. (1987). *In sorcery's shadow: A memoir of apprenticeship among the Songhay of Niger.* Chicago: University of Chicago Press.

Strauss, A. L., & Corbin, J. (1998). *Basics of qualitative research: Techniques and procedures for developing grounded theory* (2nd ed.). Thousand Oaks, CA: Sage.

Taylor, S. J., & Bogdan, R. (1998). *Introduction to qualitative research methods: A guidebook and resource* (3rd ed.). New York: John Wiley.

Turner, V., & Bruner, E. (Eds.). (1986). *The anthropology of experience.* Urbana: University of Illinois Press.

Van Maanen, J. (1988). *Tales of the field: On writing ethnography.* Chicago: University of Chicago Press.

Vygotsky, L. S. (1978). *Mind in society: The development of higher psychological processes* (M. Cole, V. John-Steiner, S. Scribner, & E. Souberman, Eds.). Cambridge, MA: Harvard University Press.

Weinstein, D., & Weinstein, M. A. (1991). Georg Simmel: Sociological flaneur bricoleur. *Theory, Culture & Society, 8,* 151-168.

West, C. (1989). *The American evasion of philosophy: A genealogy of pragmatism.* Madison: University of Wisconsin Press.

Wolcott, H. F. (1990). *Writing up qualitative research.* Newbury Park, CA: Sage.

Wolcott, H. F. (1992). Posturing in qualitative inquiry. In M. D. LeCompte, W. L. Millroy, & J. Preissle (Eds.), *The handbook of qualitative research in education* (pp. 3-52). New York: Academic Press.

Wolcott, H. F. (1995). *The art of fieldwork.* Walnut Creek, CA: AltaMira.

Wolf, M. A. (1992). *A thrice-told tale: Feminism, postmodernism, and ethnographic responsibility.* Stanford, CA: Stanford University Press.

Part I

LOCATING THE FIELD

T his part of the *Handbook* begins with the history and traditions of qualitative methods in the social and human sciences. It then turns to action research and the relationship between universities and society. It next takes up issues surrounding the social, political, and moral responsibilities of the researcher as well as the ethics and politics of qualitative inquiry.

◆ *History and Tradition*

Chapter 2, by Arthur Vidich and Stanford Lyman, and Chapter 3, by Davydd Greenwood and Morten Levin, reveal the depth and complexity of the traditional and applied qualitative research perspectives that are consciously and unconsciously inherited by the researcher-as-interpretive-*bricoleur*.[1] These traditions locate the investigator in a system of historical (and organizational) discourse. This system guides and constrains the interpretive work that is done in any specific study.

Vidich and Lyman show how the ethnographic tradition extends from the Greeks through the 15th- and 16th-century interests of Westerners in the origins of primitive cultures; to colonial ethnology connected to the empires of Spain, England, France, and Holland; to several 20th-century transformations in the United States and Europe. Throughout this history, the users of qualitative research have displayed commitments to a small set of beliefs, including objectivism, the desire to contextualize experience, and a willingness to interpret theoretically what they have observed.

These beliefs supplement the positivist tradition of complicity with colonialism, commitment to monumentalism, and the production of timeless texts discussed in Chapter 1. The colonial model located qualitative inquiry in racial and sexual discourses that privileged white patriarchy. Of course, as we have indicated in our introductory chapter, recently these beliefs have come under considerable attack. Vidich and Lyman, as well as Gloria Ladson-Billings (Chapter 9), document the extent to which early qualitative researchers were implicated in these systems of oppression.

Greenwood and Levin expand upon and extend this line of criticism. They are quite explicit that scholars have a responsibility to do work that is socially meaningful and socially responsible. The relationships among researchers, universities, and society in general must change. Politically informed action research, inquiry committed to praxis and social change, is the vehicle for accomplishing this transformation.

Action researchers are committed to a set of disciplined, material practices that produce radical, democratizing transformations in the civic sphere. These practices involve collaborative dialogue, participatory decision making, inclusive democratic deliberation, and the maximal participation and representation of all relevant parties (Ryan & Destefano, 2000, p. 1; see also Stringer, 1996, p. 38). Action researchers literally help transform inquiry into praxis, or action. Research subjects become co-participants and stakeholders in the process of inquiry. Research becomes praxis—practical, reflective, pragmatic action—directed toward solving problems in the world.

These problems originate in the lives of the research co-participants—they do not come down from on high, by way of grand theory. Together, stakeholders and action researchers create knowledge that is pragmatically useful. In the process, they jointly define research objectives and political goals, co-construct research questions, pool knowledge, hone shared research skills, and fashion interpretations and performance texts that implement specific strategies for social change (see Conquergood, 1998).

Academic science in the 20th century was often unable to accomplish goals such as these. According to Greenwood and Levin, there are several reasons for this failure, including the inability of a so-called positivistic, value-free social science to produce useful social research; the increasing tendency of outside corporations to define the needs and values of the university; the loss of research funds to entrepreneurial and private sector research organizations; and bloated, inefficient internal administrative infrastructures.

Greenwood and Levin do not renounce the practices of science; rather, they call for a reformulation of what science is all about. Their model of pragmatically grounded action research is not a retreat from disciplined scientific inquiry.[2] This form of inquiry reconceptualizes science as a collaborative, communicative, communitarian, context-centered, moral project. Greenwood and Levin's chapter is a call for a civic social science, a pragmatic science that will lead to the radical reconstruction of the university's relationships with society, state, and community in the 21st century.

◆ Reflexivity, Social Responsibility, and the Ethics of Inquiry

The contributions of Michelle Fine, Lois Weis, Susan Weseen, and Loonmun Wong (Chapter 4) and Clifford Christians (Chapter 5) extend this call for a committed, moral, civic social science. Fine and her colleagues argue that a great deal of qualitative research has reproduced a colonizing discourse of the "Other"; that is, the Other is interpreted through the eyes and cultural standards of the researcher. They review the traditions that have led researchers to speak on behalf of the Other, especially those connected to the belief systems identified by Vidich and Lyman. They then offer a series of "writing-stories" from their on-going study of 150 poor and working-class men and women, white, African American, Latino, and Asian American. These stories reveal a set of knotty, emergent ethical and rhetorical dilemmas that the researchers encountered as they attempted to write for, with, and about these poor and working-class stakeholders.

These are the problems of the sixth and seventh moments. They turn on the issues of voice, reflexivity, "race," informed consent, good and bad stories, coming clean at the hyphen. Voice and reflexivity are primary. Fine and her coauthors struggled with how to locate themselves and their stakeholders in the text, including whether or not to tell stories that would reflect negatively on the working poor, especially given that conservatives welcome stories about persons who cheat to receive welfare. They avoided such tales. They struggled, as well, with how to write about "race," a floating, unstable fiction that is also an inerasable aspect of the self and its personal history.

Fine and her colleagues paid their respondents $40 per interview. Who owns an interview once it has been transcribed? Whose story is it, and what does informed consent mean when you pay for the story? Who is consenting to what, and who is being protected? Informed consent can work against the formation of open, sharing, collaborative relationships. At the same time, how does the researcher move to the other side of the hyphen, become an advocate for the stakeholder? What is lost, and what is gained, when this is done? How can one write in a way that answers the needs of the urban poor in time when, to paraphrase Fine and her coauthors, many people of color no longer trust whites or academics to do them or their communities any good?

◆ *A Feminist, Communitarian Ethical Framework*

Clifford Christians locates the ethics and politics of qualitative inquiry within a broader historical and intellectual framework. He first examines the Enlightenment model of positivism, value-free inquiry, utilitarianism, and utilitarian ethics. In a value-free social science, codes of ethics for professional societies become the conventional format for moral principles. By the 1980s, each of the major social science associations in the United States (contemporaneous with passage of federal laws and promulgation of national guidelines) had developed its own ethical code, with an emphasis on several guidelines: informed consent, nondeception, the absence of psychological or physical harm, privacy and confidentiality, and a commitment to collecting and presenting reliable and valid empirical materials. Institutional review boards (IRBs) implemented these guidelines, including ensuring that informed consent is always obtained in human subject research. However, Christians notes, as do Fine and her colleagues, that in reality IRBs protect institutions and not individuals.

Several events challenged the Enlightenment model, including the Nazi medical experiments, the Tuskegee Syphilis Study, Project Camelot in the 1960s, Milgram's deception of subjects in his psychology experiments, Humphrey's deceptive study of homosexuals, and the complicity of social scientists with military initiatives in Vietnam. In addition, charges of fraud, plagiarism, data tampering, and misrepresentation continue to the present day. Christians details the poverty of this model. It creates the conditions for deception, for the invasion of private spaces, for the duping of subjects, and for challenges to subject's moral worth and dignity (see also Angrosino & Pérez, Chapter 25, this volume; Guba & Lincoln, 1989, pp. 120-141).

Christians calls for the replacement of this model with an ethics based on the values of a feminist communitarianism. This is an evolving, emerging ethical framework that serves as a powerful antidote to the deception-based, utilitarian IRB system. It presumes a community that is ontologically and axiologically prior to the person. This community has common moral values, and research is rooted in a concept of care, shared governance, neighborliness, love, kindness, and the moral good. Accounts of social life should display these values and should be based on interpretive sufficiency. They should have sufficient depth to allow the reader to form a critical understanding about the world studied. These texts should exhibit an absence of race, class, and gender stereotyping. They should generate social criticism and lead to resistance, empowerment, and social action; they should stimulate positive change in the social world.

In the feminist, communitarian model, as with the model of action research advocated by Greenwood and Levin (see also Kemmis & McTaggart, Chapter 22), participants have a co-equal say in how research should be conducted, what should be studied, which methods should be used, which findings are valid and acceptable, how the findings are to be implemented, and how the consequences of such action are to be assessed. Spaces for disagreement are recognized at the same time discourse aims for mutual understanding, for the honoring of moral commitments.

A sacred, existential epistemology places us in a noncompetitive, nonhierarchical relationship to the earth, to nature, and to the larger world (Bateson, 1972, p. 335). This sacred epistemology stresses the values of empowerment, shared governance, care, solidarity, love, community, covenant, morally involved observers, and civic transformation. As Christians observes, this ethical epistemology recovers the moral values that were excluded by the rational, Enlightenment science project. This sacred epistemology is based on a philosophical anthropology that declares "all humans are worthy of dignity and sacred status without exception for class or ethnicity" (Christians, 1995, p. 129). A universal human ethic stressing the sacredness of life, human dignity, truth telling, and nonviolence derives from this position (Christians, 1997, pp. 12-15). This ethic is based on locally experienced, culturally prescribed protonorms (Christians, 1995, p. 129). These primal norms provide a defensible "conception of good rooted in universal human solidarity" (Christians, 1995, p. 129; see also Christians, 1997, 1998). This sacred epistemology recognizes and interrogates the ways in which race, class, and gender operate as important systems of oppression in the world today.

Thus Christians outlines a radical ethical path for the future. In so doing, he transcends the usual middle-of-the-road ethical models that focus on the problems associated with betrayal, deception, and harm in qualitative research. Christians's call for a collaborative social science research model makes the researcher responsible not to a removed discipline (or institution), but to those studied. This implements critical, action, and feminist traditions that forcefully align the ethics of research with a politics of the oppressed. Christians's framework reorganizes existing discourses on ethics and the social sciences.[3]

With Christians, we endorse a feminist, communitarian ethic that calls for collaborative, trusting, nonoppressive relationships between researchers and those studied. Such an ethic presumes that investigators are committed to recognizing personal accountability, the value of individual expressiveness and caring, the capacity for empathy, and the sharing of emotionality (Collins, 1990, p. 216).

■ Notes

1. Any distinction between applied and nonapplied qualitative research traditions is somewhat arbitrary. Both traditions are scholarly. Each has a long tradition and a long history, and each carries basic implications for theory and social change. Good theoretical research should also have applied relevance and implications. On occasion it is argued that applied and action research are nontheoretical, but even this conclusion can be disputed, as Kemmis and McTaggart demonstrate in Chapter 22 of this volume.

2. We will develop a notion of a sacred science below and in Chapter 41.

3. Given Christians's framework, there are primarily two ethical models: utilitarian and nonutilitarian. However, historically, and most recently, researchers have taken one of five ethical stances: absolutist, consequentialist, feminist, relativist, or deception. Often these stances merge with one another. The absolutist position argues that any method that contributes to a society's self-understanding is acceptable, but only conduct in the public sphere should be studied. The deception model says that any method, including the use of lies and misrepresentation, is justified in the name of truth. The relativist stance says that researchers have absolute freedom to study what they want; ethical standards are a matter of individual conscience. Christians's feminist, communitarian framework elaborates a contextual-consequential framework that stresses mutual respect, noncoercion, nonmanipulation, and the support of democratic values (see Guba & Lincoln, 1989, pp. 120-141; House, 1990; Smith, 1990; see also Collins, 1990, p. 216; Mitchell, 1993).

■ References

Bateson, G. (1972). *Steps to an ecology of mind.* New York: Ballantine.

Christians, C. G. (1995). The naturalistic fallacy in contemporary interactionist-interpretive research. *Studies in Symbolic Interaction: A Research Annual, 19,* 125-130.

Christians, C. G. (1997). The ethics of being in a communications context. In C. G. Christians & M. Traber (Eds.), *Communication ethics and universal values* (pp. 3-23). Thousand Oaks, CA: Sage.

Christians, C. G. (1998). The sacredness of life. *Media Development, 45*(2), 3-7.

Collins, P. H. (1990). *Black feminist thought: Knowledge, consciousness, and the politics of empowerment.* New York: Routledge.

Conquergood, D. (1998). Health theatre in a Hmong refugee camp: Performance, communication and culture. In J. Cohen-Cruz (Ed.), *Radical street performance: An international anthology* (pp. 220-229). New York: Routledge.

Guba, E. G., & Lincoln, Y. S. (1989). *Fourth generation evaluation.* Newbury Park, CA: Sage.

House, E. R. (1990). An ethics of qualitative field studies. In E. G. Guba (Ed.), *The paradigm dialog* (pp. 158-164). Newbury Park, CA: Sage.

Mitchell, R. J., Jr. (1993). *Secrecy and fieldwork.* Newbury Park, CA: Sage.

Ryan, K., & Destefano, L. (2000). Introduction. In K. Ryan & L. Destefano (Eds.), *Evaluation in a democratic society: Deliberation, dialogue and inclusion* (pp. 1-20). San Francisco: Jossey-Bass.

Smith, L. M. (1990). Ethics, field studies, and the paradigm crisis. In E. G. Guba (Ed.), *The paradigm dialog* (pp. 139-157). Newbury Park, CA: Sage.

Stringer, E. T. (1996). *Action research: A handbook for practitioners.* Thousand Oaks, CA: Sage.

2

QUALITATIVE METHODS

Their History in Sociology and Anthropology

◆ Arthur J. Vidich and Stanford M. Lyman

Modern sociology has taken as its mission the analysis and understanding of the patterned conduct and social processes of society, and of the bases in values and attitudes on which individual and collective participation in social life rests. It is presupposed that, to carry out the tasks associated with this mission, the sociologist has the following:

1. The ability to perceive and contextualize the world of his or her own experience as well as the capacity to project a meta-empirical conceptualization onto those contexts of life and social institutions with which he or she has not had direct experience. The sociologist requires a sensitivity to and a curiosity about both what is visible and what is not visible to immediate perception—and sufficient self-understanding to make possible an empathy with the roles and values of others.

2. The ability to detach him- or herself from the particular values and special interests of organized groups in order that he or she may gain a level of understanding that does not rest on a priori commitments. For every individual and group, ideologies and faiths define the distinction between good and evil and lead to such nonsociological but conventional orientations as are involved in everyday judging and decision making. The sociologist's

task in ethnography is not only to be a part of such thoughts and actions but also to understand them at a higher level of conceptualization.

3. A sufficient degree of social and personal distance from prevailing norms and values to be able to analyze them objectively. Usually, the ability to engage in self-objectification is sufficient to produce the quality of orientation necessary for an individual to be an ethnographic sociologist or anthropologist.

Qualitative ethnographic social research, then, entails an attitude of detachment toward society that permits the sociologist to observe the conduct of self and others, to understand the mechanisms of social processes, and to comprehend and explain why both actors and processes are as they are. The existence of this sociological attitude is presupposed in any meaningful discussion of methods appropriate to ethnographic investigation (see Adler, Adler, & Fontana, 1991; Hammersley, 1992).

Sociology and anthropology are disciplines that, born out of concern to understand the "other," are nevertheless also committed to an understanding of the self. If, following the tenets of symbolic interactionism, we grant that the other can be understood only as part of a relationship with the self, we may suggest a different approach to ethnography and the use of qualitative methods, one that conceives the observer as possessing a self-identity that by definition is re-created in its relationship with the observed—the other, whether in another culture or that of the observer.

In its entirety, the research task requires both the act of observation and the act of communicating the analysis of these observations to others (for works describing how this is accomplished, see Johnson, 1975; Schatzman & Strauss, 1973; see also Pratt, 1986). The relationships that arise between these processes are not only the determinants of the character of the final research product, but also the arena of sociological methods least tractable to conventionalized understanding. The data gathering process can never be described in its totality because these "tales of the field" are themselves part of an ongoing social process that in its minute-by-minute and day-to-day experience defies recapitulation. To take as one's objective the making of a total description of the method of gathering data would shift the frame of ethnological reference, in effect substituting the means for the end. Such a substitution occurs when exactitude in reporting research methods takes priority over the solution to substantive sociological problems.

In fact, a description of a particular method of research usually takes place as a retrospective account, that is, a report written after the research has been completed. This all-too-often unacknowledged fact illustrates the part of the research process wherein the acts of observation are temporally separated from the description of how they were accomplished. Such essays in methodology are reconstructions of ethnographic reality; they take what was experienced originally and shrink it into a set of images that, although purporting to be a description of the actual method of research, exemplify a textbook ideal.

The point may be clarified through a comparison of the world of a supposedly "scientific" sociologist with that of such artists as painters, novelists, composers, poets, dancers, or chess masters. Viewing a painting, listening to music, reading a novel, reciting a poem, watching a chess game, or attending to the performance of a ballerina, one experiences a finished production, the "front region," as Goffman (1959, p. 107) puts it. The method seems to be inherent in the finished form (Goffman, 1949, pp. 48-77). More appropriately, we might say that the method—of composing, writing, painting, performing, or whatever—is an intrinsic part of the creator's craftsmanship, without which the creation could not be made. If the artist were to be asked, "How did you do it? Tell me your method," his or her answer would require an act of ex post facto reconstruction: the method of describing the method. However, the original production would still retain its primordial integrity; that cannot be changed, whatever conclusions are to be drawn from later discussions about how it was accomplished. Speaking of sociological methods, Robert Nisbet (1977) recalls:

> While I was engaged in exploration of some of the sources of modern sociology [it occurred to me] that none of the great themes which have provided continuing challenge and also theoretical foundation for sociologists during the last century was ever reached through anything resembling what we are to-day fond of identifying as "scientific method." I mean the kind of method, replete with appeals to statistical analysis, problem design, hypothesis, verification, replication, and theory construction, that we find described in textbooks and courses on methodology. (p. 3)

From Nisbet's pointed observation we may conclude that the method-in-use for the production of a finished sociological study is unique to that study and can be neither described nor replicated as it actually occurred. That societal investigators may choose to use different kinds of material as their data—documents for the historian, quantified reports for the demographer, or direct perception of a portion of society for the ethnographer—does not alter the fact that social scientists are observers. As observers of the world they also participate in it; therefore, they make their observations within a mediated framework, that is, a framework of symbols and cultural meanings given to them by those aspects of their life histories that they bring to the observational setting. Lurking behind each method of research is the personal equation supplied to the setting by the individual observer (Clifford, 1986). In this fundamental sense all research methods are at bottom qualitative and are, for that matter, equally objective; the use of quantitative data or mathematical procedures does not eliminate the intersubjective element that underlies social research. Objectivity resides not in a method, per se, but in the framing of the research problem and the willingness of the researchers to pursue that problem wherever the data and their hunches may lead (Vidich, 1955; see also Fontana, 1980; Goffman, 1974).[1] If, in this sense, all research is qualitative—because the observer is at the center of the research process—does this mean that the findings produced by the method are no more than the peculiar reality of each observer (Atkinson, 1990)?

One simple answer is that we judge for ourselves on the standard of whether the work communicates or "says" something to us—that is, does it connect with our reality?[2] Does it provide us with insights that help to organize our own observations? Does it resonate with our image of the world? Or does it provide such a powerful incursion on the latter that we feel compelled to reexamine what we have long supposed to be true about our life world?

Or, put another way, if the method used is not the issue, by what standards are we able to judge the worth of sociological research (Gellner, 1979)? Each is free to judge the work of others and to accept it or reject it if it does not communicate something meaningful about the world; and what is meaningful for one person is not necessarily meaningful for another.

In the present and for the foreseeable future, the virtually worldwide disintegration of common values and a deconstruction of consensus-based societies evoke recognition of the fact that there exist many competing realities, and this fact poses problems not previously encountered by sociology. In effect, this situation sets up a condition wherein the number of possible theoretical perspectives from which the world, or any part of it, may be viewed sociologically is conditioned only by the number of extant scientific worldviews. As for the potential subjects of investigation, their outlooks are limited only by the many religious faiths, occupational and professional ideologies, and other *Weltanschauungen* that arise to guide or upset their lives. At the time of this writing, a new outlook on epistemology has come to the fore. It disprivileges all received discourses and makes discourse itself a topic of the sociology of knowledge.[3]

The history of qualitative research suggests that this has not always been the case (Douglas, 1974). In the past, the research problems for many investigators were given to them by their commitment to or against a religious faith or an ethnic creed, or by their identification with or opposition to specific national goals or socioeconomic programs. In the historical account of the use of qualitative methods that follows, we shall show that their use has been occasioned by more than the perspective of the individual observer, but also that the domain assumptions that once guided qualitative research have lost much of their force. However, the faiths, creeds, and hopes that had given focus to the work of our predecessors have not disappeared altogether from the sociologist's mental maps (Luhmann, 1986). Rather, they remain as a less-than-conscious background, the all-too-familiar furniture of the sociological mind. Milan Kundera (1988) has pointed to a central issue in our present dilemma in *The Art of the Novel*: "But if God is gone and man is no longer the master, then who is the master? The planet is moving through the void without any master. There it is, the unbearable lightness of being" (p. 41).

Throughout all of the eras during which social science made use of observational methods, researchers have entered into their studies with problems implicitly and, in some cases, explicitly defined by hopes and faiths. Focusing on the substance of these problems and their ideational adumbrations, we shall confine our discussion of this history to the qualitative methods used by anthropologists and sociologists in ethnographic research, that is, the direct observation of the social realities by the individual observer. Our history proceeds along a continuum that begins with the first encounters of early ethnographers with the New World and ends with the practical and theoretical problems facing the work of our contemporaries.

◆ Early Ethnography: The Discovery of the Other

Ethnos, a Greek term, denotes a people, a race or cultural group (A. D. Smith, 1989, pp. 13-18). When *ethno* as a prefix is combined with *graphic* to form the term *ethnographic,* the reference is to the subdiscipline known as descriptive anthropology—in its broadest sense, the science devoted to describing ways of life of humankind. *Ethnography,* then, refers to a social scientific description of a people and the cultural basis of

their peoplehood (Peacock, 1986). Both descriptive anthropology and ethnography are thought to be atheoretical, to be concerned solely with description. However, the observations of the ethnographer are always guided by world images that determine which data are salient and which are not: An act of attention to one rather than another object reveals one dimension of the observer's value commitment, as well as his or her value-laden interests.

Early ethnography grew out of the interests of Westerners in the origins of culture and civilization and in the assumption that contemporary "primitive" peoples, those thought by Westerners to be less civilized than themselves, were, in effect, living replicas of the "great chain of being" that linked the Occident to its prehistoric beginnings (Hodgen, 1964, pp. 386-432). Such a mode of ethnography arose in the 15th and 16th centuries as a result of fundamental problems that had grown out of Columbus's and later explorers' voyages to the Western hemisphere, the so-called New World, and to the island cultures of the South Seas.

The discovery of human beings living in non-Occidental environments evoked previously unimagined cosmological difficulties for European intellectuals, who felt it necessary to integrate the new fact into the canon of received knowledge and understanding.[4] Because the Bible, especially the book of Genesis, was taken to be the only valid source on which to rely for an understanding of the history of geography and processes of creation, and because it placed the origin of humankind in the Garden of Eden—located somewhere in what is today called the Middle East—all human beings were held to be descended from the first pair, and, later, in accordance with flood ethnography (Numbers, 1992), from the descendants of Noah and his family, the only survivors of a worldwide deluge. Linking Columbus's encounter with what we now know as the Taino, Arawak, and Carib (Keegan, 1992; Rouse, 1992) peoples in the New World to the biblical account proved to be difficult. Specifically, the existence of others outside the Christian brotherhood revealed by his "discovery" posed this question: How had the ancestors of these beings reached the Americas in pre-Columbian times? Any thesis that they had not migrated from Eurasia or Africa was held to be heresy and a claim that humankind might have arisen from more than one creative act by God.

In general, the racial and cultural diversity of peoples throughout the globe presented post-Renaissance Europeans with the problem of how to account for the origins, histories, and development of a multiplicity of races, cultures, and civilizations (see Baker, 1974; Barkan, 1992; Trinkhaus & Shipman, 1993). Not only was it necessary for the cosmologist to account for the disconcerting existence of the "other," [5] but such a scholar was obliged to explain how and why such differences in the moral values of Europeans and these "others" had arisen. In effect, such a profusion of values, cultures, and ways of life challenged the monopolistic claim on legitimacy and truth of the doctrines of Christianity. Such practices as infanticide, cannibalism, human sacrifice, and what at first appeared as promiscuity reopened the problem of contradictions among cultural values and the inquiry into how these contradictions might be both explained and resolved (Oakes, 1938).

These issues of value conflicts were conflated with practical questions about the recruitment, organization, and justification for the division of labor in the Spanish settlements in the Americas, and these confusions are to be found in the debates of Bartolome de Las Casas with Juan Gines de Sepulveda at the Council of Valladolid. Sepulveda, "who used Aristotle's doctrine of natural slavery in order to legitimize Spanish behavior against the Indians" (Hosle, 1992, p. 238), in effect won the day against Las Casas, who insisted that the peoples we now call Native Americans were "full fellow human beings, possessing valid traditions, dignity and rights" (Marty, 1992, p. xiii). Today, despite or perhaps because of the new recognition of cultural diversity, the tension between universalistic and relativistic values remains an unresolved conundrum for the Western ethnographer (Hosle, 1992).[6] In practice, it becomes this question: By which values are observations to be guided? The choices seem to be either the values of the ethnographer or the values of the observed—that is, in modern parlance, either the *etic* or the *emic* (Pike, 1967; for an excellent

discussion, see Harré, 1980, pp. 135-137). Herein lies a deeper and more fundamental problem: How is it possible to understand the other when the other's values are not one's own? This problem arises to plague ethnography at a time when Western Christian values are no longer a surety of truth and, hence, no longer the benchmark from which self-confidently valid observations can be made.

◆ Colonial Mentalities and the Persistence of the Other

Before the professionalization of ethnography, descriptions and evaluations of the races and cultures of the world were provided by Western missionaries, explorers, buccaneers, and colonial administrators. Their reports, found in church, national, and local archives throughout the world and, for the most part, not known to contemporary ethnologists, were written from the perspective of, or by the representatives of, a conquering civilization, confident in its mission to civilize the world (for pertinent discussion of this issue, see Ginsburg, 1991, 1993). Some of the 17th-, 18th-, and 19th-century explorers, missionaries, and administrators have provided thick descriptions of those practices of the "primitives" made salient to the observer by his Christian value perspective.[7] For societies studied by these observers (see, for example, Degerando, 1800/ 1969), the author's ethnographic report is a reversed mirror image of his own ethnocultural ideal. That these early ethnographies reveal as much about the West as about their objects of study may explain why they have not been recovered and reanalyzed by contemporary anthropologists: Present-day ethnographers hope to separate themselves from the history of Western conquest and reject the earlier ethnographies as hopelessly biased (see "Symposium on Qualitative Methods," 1993). Recently they have begun to take seriously the accounts the natives have given of their Western "discoverers" and to "decenter" or "disprivilege" the reports presented by the latter (Abeyesekere, 1992; Salmond, 1991; Todorov, 1984).

A rich resource, through which one can discern the effects that this early ethnographic literature had on the subjugation of these peoples, is to be found in the works of latter-day colonial administrators (e.g., Olivier, 1911/1970). Ethnology arose out of the reports written by administrators of the long-maintained seaborne empires of the Spanish, English, French, and Dutch (Maunier, 1949). These empires provided opportunities for amateur and, later, professional ethnologists not only to examine hosts of "native" cultures,[8] but also to administer the conditions of life affecting the "cultural advancement" of peoples over whom their metropole exercised domination (Gray, 1911/1970, pp. 79-85). In respect to the seaborne empires, European interest was often confined to exploiting the labor power of the natives, utilizing their territory for extractive industry and/or establishing it in terms of the strategic military advantage it provided them in their struggles against imperialist rivals (for some representative examples, see Aldrich, 1990; Boxer, 1965; Duffy, 1968; Gullick, 1956; Suret-Canale, 1988a, 1988b). Hence the anthropology that developed under colonial administrators tended toward disinterest in the acculturation of the natives and encouragement for the culturally preservative effects of indirect rule. Their approach came to be called pluralistic development (M. G. Smith, 1965). Colonial pluralism left the natives more or less under the authority of their own indigenous leaders so long as these leaders could be co-opted in support of the limited interests of the colonial administration (Lugard, 1922/1965). This tendency led to the creation of a market economy at the center of colonial society (Boeke, 1946; Furnivall, 1956) surrounded by a variety of local culture groups (Boeke, 1948), some of whose members were drawn willy-nilly into the market economy and suffered the effects of marginalized identity (Sachs, 1947).

Ethnographers who conducted their field studies in colonialized areas were divided with respect to their attitudes toward cultural and/or political nationalism and self-determination. A few became champions of ethnocultural liberation and anticolonial revolt. Some respected the autonomy of the traditional culture and opposed any tendency among natives in revolt against colonialism to seek further modernization of their lifestyles. The latter, some of whom were Marxists, admired the anticolonial movement but were concerned to see that the natives remained precapitalist. Some of these might have imagined that precapitalist natives would practice some form of primitive communism (see Diamond, 1963, 1972) as described by Friedrich Engels (1884) in *The Origins of the Family, Private Property and the State.* Engels, in fact, had derived his idea of primitive communism from Lewis Henry Morgan's (1877/1964) *Ancient Society,* an original study in the Comtean ethnohistorical tradition of American aborigines that conceived of the latter as "ancestors" to the ancient Greeks (for a critique, see Kuper, 1988). Others, no longer concerned to prove that "mother-right" preceded "father-right" by presenting ethnographic accounts of Melanesians, Tasmanians, Bantus, or Dayaks (for a fine example, see Hartland, 1921/1969), turned their attention to acculturation, and, unsure of how long the process might take and how well the formerly colonized subjects would take to Occidental norms, reinvoked "the doctrine of survivals" (Hodgen, 1936) to account for elements of the natives' culture that persisted (see, e.g., Herskovitz, 1958, 1966) or marveled at how well some native peoples had traded "new lives for old" (Mead, 1956/1975). These diverse value and ideological orientations are pervasive in the work of early professional ethnologists and provided anthropology the grounding for most of its theoretical debates.

◆ The "Evolution" of Culture and Society: Comte and the Comparative Method

Even before the professionalization of anthropology engulfed the discipline, the enlightened ethnographer had abandoned any attitude that might be associated with that of a merciless conqueror and replaced it with that of an avatar of beneficent evolutionary progress. Value conflicts arising within anthropology from the history of colonialism, and with the moral relativism associated with them were, in part, replaced by theories of social evolution. The application of Darwinian and Spencerian principles to the understanding of how societies and cultures of the world have developed over eons freed the ethnographer from the problems presented by moral relativism; it permitted the assertion that there existed a spatiotemporal hierarchy of values. These values were represented synchronically in the varieties of cultures to be found in the world, but might be classified diachronically according to the theory of developmental advance.

This new approach to comprehending how the lifeways of the Occident related to those of the others had first been formally proposed by Auguste Comte and was soon designated the "comparative method" (Bock, 1948, pp. 11-36). According to Comte and his followers (see Lenzer, 1975), the study of the evolution of culture and civilization would postulate three stages of culture and would hold fast to the idea that the peoples and cultures of the world are arrangeable diachronically, forming "a great chain of being" (Lovejoy, 1936/1960). Moreover, these stages are interpretable as orderly links in that chain, marking the epochs that occurred as human societies moved from conditions of primitive culture to those of modern civilization.[9] By using technological as well as social indicators, ethnographers could discover where a particular people belonged on the "chain" and thus give that people a definite place in the evolution of culture. (For a discussion and critique of Comte as a theorist of history and evolution, see R. Brown, 1984, pp. 187-212.) The seemingly inconvenient fact that all of these different cultures coexisted in time—that is, the time in which the ethnographer conducted his or her field study—was disposed of by applying the theory of "uneven evolution," that is, the assertion, in the guise of an epistemological assumption, that all cultures except that of Western Europe had suffered some form of arrested development (Sanderson, 1990; Sarana, 1975). In this way, and in the

absence of documentary historical materials, ethnographers could utilize their on-the-spot field studies to contribute to the construction of the prehistory of civilization and at the same time put forth a genealogy of morals. Following Comte, this diachrony of civilizational development was usually characterized as having three progressive and irreversible stages: savagery, barbarism, and civilization. The peoples assigned to each of these stages corresponded to a color-culture hierarchical diachrony and fitted the ethnocentric bias of the Occident (Nisbet, 1972).

In the 19th century, Comte had formalized this mode of thinking for both anthropologists and sociologists by designating as epochs of moral growth (Comte's terms) three stages that, he averred, occurred in the development of religion. The ethnologists' adaptation of Comte's comparative method to their own efforts provided them with a set of a priori assumptions on the cultures of "primitives"—assumptions that vitiated the need to grant respect to these cultures in their own terms—that is, from the perspective of those who are its participants (for a countervailing perspective, see Hill-Lubin, 1992). The imposition of a preconceived Eurocentric developmental framework made the work of the ethnographer much simpler;[10] the task became that of a classifier of cultural traits in transition, or in arrest. Ultimately, this approach was institutionalized in the Human Relations Area Files (HRAF) housed at Yale University, which became the depository for an anthropological database and the resource for a vast project dedicated to the classification and cross-classification of virtually all the extant ethnographic literature—in the drawers of the HRAF any and all items of culture found a secure classificatory niche (Murdock, 1949/1965). A Yale-produced handbook of categories provided the ethnographer with guidelines to direct his or her observations and provided the basis for the classification of these and other collections of cultural traits.[11] The trait data in the Yale cross-cultural files represent ethnography in a form disembodied from that of a lived social world in which actors still exist. They are a voluminous collection of disparate cultural items that represent the antithesis of the ethnographic method.

◆ 20th-Century Ethnography: Comteanism and the Cold War

Two 20th-century developments have undermined both the various "colonial" anthropological perspectives and evolutionary schemes. Within 30 years of the termination of World War II, the several decolonization movements in Africa and Asia succeeded in ending the direct forms of Western global colonialism. As part of the same movements, an anticolonial assault on Western ethnocentrism led to a critical attack on the idea of "the primitive" and on the entire train of ethnological thought that went with it (Montagu, 1968). In effect, by the 1960s anthropologists had begun not only to run out of "primitive" societies to study but also to abandon the evolutionary epistemology that had justified their very existence in the first place.

A new term, *underdeveloped,* tended to replace *primitive.* The colonial powers and their supporters became defendants in an academic prosecution of those who were responsible for the underdevelopment of the newly designated "Third World" and who had neglected to recognize the integrity of "black culture" and that of other peoples of color in the United States (see Willis, 1972).[12] Ethnologists discovered that their basic orientation was under attack. Insofar as that orientation had led them or their much-respected predecessors to cooperate with imperial governments in the suppression and exploitation of natives, or with the American military and its "pacification" programs in Vietnam, anthropologists began to suffer from the effects of a collective and intradisciplinary guilt complex (see Nader, 1972).[13]

Changes in what appeared to be the direction of world history led anthropologists to retool their approach to ethnography. Because, by definition, there were few, if any, primitives available for study, and because the spokespersons for the newly designated Third World of "underdeveloped" countries often held anthropologists to have contributed to the latter condition, access to tribal societies became more difficult

than it had been. As opportunities for fieldwork shrank, recourse was had to the study of linguistics, to the database of the Yale files, or to the discovery of the ethnographic possibilities for anthropological examinations of American society. Anthropology had come full circle, having moved back to a study of its own society, the point of departure—as well as the benchmark—for its investigation of more "primitive" cultures. Linguistics and databases lend themselves to the study of texts, as does the study of Western society, with its rich literary and historical archives. These tendencies opened ethnography to the modernist and, later, the postmodernist approaches to the study of exotic peoples and to the investigation of alien culture bearers residing within industrial societies of the Occident.

However, even as anthropology was convulsed by decolonization movements and constrained by restricted access to its traditional fieldwork sites, the Cold War gave to sociology an opportunity to revive Comte's and Spencer's variants of evolutionary doctrine in modernist form and to combine them with a secular theodicy harking back to America's Puritan beginnings.

Talcott Parsons's (1966, 1971) two-volume study of the development of society restored the Calvinist-Puritan imagery, applying the latter to those "others" not yet included in the Christian brotherhood of the Occident. Written during the decades of the U.S. global contest with the Soviet Union, it arranged selected nations and societies in a schema according to which the United States was said to have arrived at the highest stage of societal development; other peoples, cultures, and civilizations were presumed to be moving in the direction plotted by America, "the first new nation" (Lipset, 1979; for a critique, see Lyman, 1975), or to be suffering from an arrest of advancement that prevented them from doing so. That developmental scheme held to the idea that economic progress was inherent in industrialization and that nation building coincided with capitalism, the gradual extension of democratization, and the orderly provision of individual rights. Despite the pointed criticisms of the comparative method that would continue to be offered by the school of sociohistorical thought associated with Frederick J. Teggart (1941) and his followers (Bock, 1952, 1956, 1963, 1974; Hodgen, 1974; Nisbet, 1969, 1986; for a critical discussion of this school, see Lyman, 1978; see also Kuper, 1988), a Comtean outlook survived within sociology in the work of Talcott Parsons and his macrosociological epigoni.

Social scientific literature during the Cold War included such titles as Robert Heilbroner's *The Great Ascent,* A. F. K. Organski's *The Stages of Political Development,* and W. W. Rostow's *The Stages of Economic Growth.* The American political economy and a democratic social order replaced earlier images of the ultimate stage of cultural evolution. Changes in the rest of the nations of the world that seemed to herald movement toward adoption of an American social, political, and economic institutional structure became the standard by which social scientists could measure the "advance" of humankind. This standard provided the analyst-ethnographer with a new measure for evaluating the "progress" of the "other" (which, after 1947, included the peoples and cultures of the Soviet Union as well as those of the "underdeveloped" world). The matter reached epiphany in the early 1990s, when students and scholars of the cosmological, moral, economic, and military problems faced by claimants of the right to spread a benevolent variant of Christianized Western civilization throughout the world began to rejoice over the collapse of communism, the disintegration of the Soviet Union, and the decomposition of its allies and alliances in Eastern Europe (Gwertzman & Kaufman, 1992). But for some there arose a new apprehension: worry over whether these events signaled the very end of history itself (see Fukuyama, 1992).[14]

The end of the Cold War and the deconstruction of the Soviet Union revived nationalist and ethnic claims in almost every part of the world. In such a newly decentered world, cultural pluralism has become a new watchword, especially for all those who hope to distinguish themselves from ethnonational "others." The dilemmas once posed by cultural relativism have been replaced by the issues arising out of the supposed certainties of primordial descent. Ethnographers now find themselves caught in the cross fire of incommensurable but competing values.

◆ The Ethnography of the American Indian: An Indigenous "Other"

In the United States, the Calvinist variant of the Protestant errand into the wilderness began with the arrival of the Puritans in New England. Convinced of their own righteousness and of their this-worldly mission to bring to fruition God's kingdom on the "new continent," the Puritans initially set out to include the so-called Indians in their covenant of faith. But, having misjudged both the Indians' pliability and their resistance to an alien worldview, the Puritans did not succeed in their attempt (Calloway, 1991, pp. 57-90; A. T. Vaughan, 1965). Nevertheless, they continued their missionary endeavors throughout the 19th and 20th centuries (Coleman, 1985; Keller, 1983; Milner & O'Neil, 1985). American political and jurisprudential policy toward the Indian, as well as the ethnographic work on the cultures of Native Americans, derive from this failure and shape its results. As one consequence, the several tribes of North American aborigines would remain outside the ethnographic, moral, and cultural pale of both European immigrant enclaves and settled white American communities.

From the 17th through the 19th centuries—that is, during the period of westward expansion across the American continent—ethnographic reports on Indian cultures were written from the perspective of the Euro-American conqueror and his missionary allies (Bowden, 1981). Even more than the once-enslaved Africans and their American-born descendants, the Indians have remained in a special kind of "otherness." One salient social indicator of this fact is their confinement to reservations of the mind as well as the body. In the conventional academic curriculum, the study of Native Americans is a part of the cultural anthropology of "primitive" peoples, whereas that of European and Asian immigrants and American blacks is an institutionalized feature of sociology courses on "minorities" and "race and ethnic relations."

In the United States a shift in ethnographic perspective from that written by missionaries and military conquerors to that composed exclusively by anthropologists arose with the establishment of the ethnology section of the Smithsonian Institution (Hinsley, 1981). However, ethnographies of various Indian "tribes" had been written earlier by ethnologists in service to the Bureau of Indian Affairs (BIA) (Bieder, 1989; two representative examples of pre-Smithsonian Amerindian ethnography are found in McKenney & Hall, 1836/1972; Schoolcraft, 1851/1975). In addition to being "problem peoples" for those theorists who wished to explain Indian origins in America and to construct their ancestry in terms consistent with the creation and flood myths of the Bible, the presence of the Indians within the borders of the United States posed still another problem: their anomalous status in law (R. A. Williams, 1990). Politically, the Indian "tribes" regarded themselves as separate sovereign nations and, for a period, were dealt with as such by the colonial powers and the U.S. government. However, in 1831, their legal status was redesignated in a Supreme Court case, *Cherokee Nation v. Georgia* (1831). In his decision, Chief Justice Marshall declared the Indians to occupy a unique status in law. They form, he said, "a domestic dependent nation." As such, he went on, they fall into a special "ward" relationship to the federal government. The latter had already established the Bureau of Indian Affairs to deal with them. Within the confines and constraints of this decision, the BIA administered the affairs of the Indian. From the special brand of anthropology that it fostered, American ethnography developed its peculiar outlook on Native Americans.[15]

The BIA and later the Smithsonian Institution employed ethnographers to staff the various reservation agencies and to study the ways of the Indians. The focus of study for this contingent of observers was not the possible conversion of Indians, but rather the depiction of their cultures—ceremonies recorded, kinship systems mapped, technology described, artifacts collected—all carried out from a secular and administrative point of view.[16] The theoretical underpinning of the BIA's perspective was the civilized/primitive dichotomy that had already designated Indians as preliterates. In effect, the tribal lands and reservation habitats of these "domestic, dependent nationals" became a living anthropological museum from which ethnologists could glean descriptions of the early stages of primitive life. In those parts of the country where Indians lived in large numbers—especially the Southwest[17]—and where archaeological artifacts were numerous, the Comtean evolutionary perspective was used to trace the ancestry of existing tribes back to an origin that might be found by paleontological efforts. From the beginning, however, the Southwest would also be the setting where debates—over how ethnography was to be carried out, and what purpose it ought to serve—would break out and divide anthropologists not only from missionaries and from federal agents, but from one another (Dale, 1949/1984; Dockstader, 1985).

The life world of "the primitive" was thought to be a window through which the prehistoric past could be seen, described, and understood. At its most global representation, this attitude had been given the imprimatur of ethnological science at the St. Louis World's Fair in 1904, when a scientifically minded missionary, Samuel Phillips Verner, allowed Ota Benga, a pygmy from the Belgian Congo, to be put on display as a living specimen of primitivism. A year later, Ota Benga was exhibited at the Monkey House of the Bronx Zoo (Bradford & Blume, 1992). In 1911, the American anthropologist Alfred Kroeber took possession of Ishi, the last surviving member of the Yahi tribe, and placed him in the Museum of Anthropology at the University of California. In the two years before his death, Ishi dwelled in the museum and, like Ota Benga before him, became, in effect, a living artifact, a primitive on display, one to be viewed by the civilized in a manner comparable to their perspective on the presentation of Indians in American museum dioramas (see Kroeber, 1962, 1965; for contemporary accounts in newspapers and other media, see Heizer & Kroeber, 1979).

Although U.S. Indian policy established both the programs and the perspectives under which most ethnographers worked, its orthodoxy was not accepted by all of the early field-workers. Among these heterodoxical ethnologists, perhaps the most important was Frank Hamilton Cushing (1857-1900), who became a Zuni shaman and a war chief while working as an ethnologist for the Smithsonian Institution (see Cushing, 1920/1974, 1979, 1901/1988, 1990; see also Culin, 1922/1967).[18] Cushing's case stands out because, though he was an active participant in Zuni life, he continued to be a professional ethnographer who tried to describe both Zuni culture and the Zuni worldview from an indigenous perspective. Moreover, Cushing joined with R. S. Culin in proposing the heterodoxical thesis that America was the cradle of Asia, that is, that in pre-Columbian times the ancestors of the Zuni had migrated to Asia and contributed significantly to the development of Chinese, Japanese, Korean, and other Asiatic civilizations that in turn had been diffused over the centuries into Africa and Europe (Lyman, 1979, 1982a, 1982b).

Without attempting to become a native himself, Paul Radin (1883-1959) devoted a lifetime to the ethnographic study of the Winnebago Indians (see Radin, 1927, 1927/1957a, 1937/1957b, 1920/1963, 1933/1966, 1953/1971b, 1923/1973, 1956/1976).[19] Maintaining that an inner view of an alien culture could be accomplished only through a deep learning of its language and symbol system, Radin documented the myths, rituals, and poetry in Winnebago and, in his reports, provided English translations of these materials. Taking Cushing's and Radin's works as a standard for Amerindian ethnography, their perspective could be used to reinterpret the works of earlier ethnographers; they might enable future field investigators to comprehend the cultural boundedness of American Indian ethnography and at the same time provide the point of departure for a critical

sociology of ethnological knowledge (Vidich, 1966). But, in addition, their work recognizes both the historicity of preliterate cultures and the problems attendant upon understanding the world of the other from the other's point of view. In this, as in the work of Thucydides and in the Weberian conception of a sociology of understanding (*verstehende* sociology), Cushing and Radin transcended the problem of value incommensurability.

◆ *The Ethnography of the Civic Other: The Ghetto, the Natural Area, and the Small Town*

The Calvinist mission to save and/or include the Indian found its later counterpart in a mission to bring to the urban ghetto communities of blacks and Asian and European immigrants the moral and communitarian values of Protestantism. That these immigrants had carried their Catholic, Judaic, or Buddhist religious cultures to the United States and that the lifestyles of the recently emancipated blacks did not accord with those of the white citizens of the United States were causes for concern among representatives of the older settled groups, who feared for the future integrity of America's Protestant civilization (Contosta, 1980, pp. 121-144; Hartmann, 1948/1967; Jones, 1992, pp. 49-166). Initially, efforts to include these groups focused on Protestant efforts to preach and practice a "social gospel" that found its institutionalization in the settlement houses that came to dot the urban landscape of immigrant and ghetto enclaves (Holden, 1922/1970; Woods & Kennedy, 1922/1990).

About three decades after the Civil War, when it became clear that the sheer number and cultural variety of the new urban inhabitants had become too great to be treated by individual efforts, recourse was had to the statistical survey. It would provide a way to determine how many inhabitants from each denomination, nationality, and race there were in any one place, and to describe each group's respective problems of adjustment (C. A. Chambers, 1971; Cohen, 1981;

McClymer, 1980). In this manner, the "other" was transformed into a statistical aggregate and reported in a tabular census of exotic lifestyles. These quantified reports, sponsored in the first years by various churches in eastern cities of the United States, were the forerunners of the corporate-sponsored surveys of immigrants and Negroes and of the massive government-sponsored surveys of European, Asian, Mexican, and other immigrant laborers in 1911 (Immigration Commission, 1911/1970). The church surveys and their corporate and sociological successors were designed to facilitate the "moral reform" and social adjustment of newcomer and ghetto populations. What is now known as qualitative research in sociology had its origins in this Christian mission (see Greek, 1978, 1992).

It was out of such a movement to incorporate the alien elements within the consensual community that the first qualitative community study was carried out. W. E. B. Du Bois's (1899/1967) *The Philadelphia Negro,* a survey of that city's seventh ward, was supported by Susan B. Wharton, a leader of the University of Pennsylvania's college settlement. To Wharton, Du Bois, and their colleagues, the "collection and analysis of social facts were as much a religious as a scientific activity offered as a form of prayer for the redemption of dark-skinned people" (Vidich & Lyman, 1985, p. 128). This study, which included 5,000 interviews conducted by Du Bois, aimed not only at description, but also at the uplift of Philadelphia's Negro population by the Quaker community that surrounded it. The tone of noblesse oblige that inspires the final pages of Du Bois's book are a stark reminder of the paternalistic benevolence underlying this first ethnographic study of a community.

Church- and corporate-sponsored survey methods continued to dominate social research until the early 1920s (see Burgess, 1916), when Helen and Robert Lynd began their study of Middletown. Robert Lynd, a newly ordained Protestant minister, was selected by the Council of Churches, then concerned about the moral state of Christian communities in industrial America, to examine the lifeways of what was thought to be a typical American community. Rather suddenly catapulted into the position of a two-person research team, the Lynds con-

sulted the anthropologist Clark Wissler (1870-1947), then on the staff of the American Museum of Natural History,[20] for advice on how to conduct such a survey and how to report it once the data had been gathered. Wissler provided them with what was then known as the cultural inventory, a list of standard categories used by anthropologists to organize field data (see Wissler, 1923, chaps. 5, 7). Those categories—getting a living, making a home, training the young, using leisure, engaging in religious practices, engaging in community activities—became the organizing principle of Lynd and Lynd's (1929/1956) book and provided them with a set of cues for their investigation. Although the Middletown study was designed to provide its church sponsors with information that might be used to set church policy, the Lynds approached the Middletown community in the manner of social anthropologists. As Wissler (1929/1956) states in his foreword to the published volume of the study, "To most people anthropology is a mass of curious information about savages, and this is so far true, in that most of its observations are on the less civilized. . . . The authors of this volume have approached an American community as an anthropologist does a primitive tribe" (p. vi). In Middletown, the "other" of the anthropologist found its way into American sociological practice and purpose. Moreover, from the point of view of the policy makers in the central church bureaucracy, he who had once been assumed to be the civic "brother" had to all intents and purposes become the "other," an ordinary inhabitant of Muncie, Indiana.

Shortly after the publication of *Middletown* in 1929, the Great Depression set in. Soon, the Lynds were commissioned to do a restudy of Muncie. Published in 1937 as *Middletown in Transition: A Study in Cultural Conflicts,* this investigation reflected not only changes in the town, but also a transformation in the outlook of its two ethnographers. During the early years of the Depression, Robert Lynd, a church progressive, had begun to look to the Soviet Union for answers to the glaring contradictions of capitalism that seemed to have manifested themselves so alarmingly in Depression-ridden America. This new political orientation was reflected in both what the Lynds observed and how they reported it. Where the first volume had made no mention of the Ball family's domination of what was a virtual "company town," or of the family's philanthropic sponsorship of Ball State University and the local library and hospital, or its control over the banks, *Middletown in Transition* included a chapter titled "The X Family: A Pattern of Business-Class Control" and an appendix titled "Middletown's Banking Institutions in Boom and Depression." Responding to what they believed to be the utter failure of America's laissez-faire, free market economy, the Lynds abandoned the ethnographic categories they had used in *Middletown*. Choosing instead to employ categories and conceptualizations derived from their own recently acquired Marxist outlook, they shifted the sociological focus from religious to political values.

Middletown in Transition would become a standard and much-praised work of sociological ethnography for the next half century. At Columbia University, where Robert Lynd taught generations of students, explicit Christian values and rhetoric were replaced by those of an ethically inclined political radicalism. With the radicalization of many Columbia-trained youths (as well as of their fellow students at City College, many of whom would later become prominent sociologists), variants of Marxism would provide a counterperspective to that of the anthropologically oriented ethnographic observer of American communities. Ironically, however, Middletown's second restudy, conducted by a team of non-Marxist sociologists nearly 50 years after *Middletown in Transition* was published, returned the focus to the significance of kinship and family that had characterized the early anthropological perspective, combining it with the kind of concern for Protestant religiosity that had been the stock-in-trade of the earlier American sociological orientation (Caplow, Bahr, Chadwick, Hill, & Williamson, 1982, 1983).

Even before the Lynds' original study, ethnography as a method of research had become identified with the University of Chicago's Department of Sociology. The first generation of Chicago sociologists, led by Albion W. Small,

supposed that the discipline they professed had pledged itself to reassert America's destiny—the nation that would be "the city upon a hill." America would become a unified Christian brotherhood, committed to a covenant through which the right and proper values would be shared by all (Vidich & Lyman, 1985, p. 179). Small sought a sociological means to impress the values and morals of Protestantism upon the inhabitants of the newer ethnic, racial, and religious ghettos then forming in Chicago. However, this explicitly Christian attitude—in service to which the University of Chicago had been brought into existence by John D. Rockefeller in 1892—did not survive at Chicago. It was discarded after Robert E. Park, Ernest W. Burgess, W. I. Thomas, and Louis Wirth had become the guiding professoriat of Chicago's sociology, and after Park's son-in-law, Robert Redfield, had become an important figure in that university's anthropology program. Park's secular conceptualization of the "natural area" replaced the Christian locus of the unchurched in the city, while, at the same time, and in contradistinction to Park's point of view, Redfield's formulation of the morally uplifting "little community" introduced a counterimage to that of the metropolis then emerging in Chicago.

Park (1925/1967) conceived the city to be a social laboratory containing a diversity and heterogeneity of peoples, lifestyles, and competing and contrasting worldviews. To Park, for a city to be composed of others, ghettoized or otherwise, was intrinsic to its nature. Under his and Ernest W. Burgess's direction or inspiration, a set of ethnographic studies emerged focusing on singular descriptions of one or another aspect of human life that was to be found in the city. Frequently, these studies examined urban groups whose ways of life were below or outside the purview of the respectable middle classes. In addition to providing descriptions of the myriad and frequently incompatible values by which these groups lived, these ethnographies moved away from the missionary endeavor that had characterized earlier studies. Instead, Park and his colleagues occupied themselves with documenting the various forms of civil otherhood that they perceived to be emerging in the city (see Burgess & Bogue, 1967).

Central to Park's vision of the city was its architectonic as a municipal circumscription of a number of "natural areas," forming a mosaic of minor communities, each strikingly different from the other, but each more or less typical of its kind. Park (1952a) observed, "Every American city has its slums; its ghettos; its immigrant colonies, regions which maintain more or less alien and exotic cultures. Nearly every large city has its bohemias and hobohemias, where life is freer, more adventurous and lonely than it is elsewhere. These are called natural areas of the city" (p. 196). For more than three decades, urban ethnography in Chicago's sociology department focused on describing such "natural areas" as the Jewish ghetto (Wirth, 1928/1956), Little Italy (Nelli, 1970), Polonia (Lopata, 1967; Thomas & Znaniecki, 1958, pp. 1511-1646), Little Germany (Park, 1922/1971), Chinatown (Lee, 1978; Siu, 1987; Wu, 1926), Bronzeville and Harlem (Drake & Cayton, 1962; Frazier, 1931, 1937a, 1937b), the gold coast and the slum (Zorbaugh, 1929), hobo jungles (N. Anderson, 1923/1961), single-room occupants of furnished rooms (Zorbaugh, 1968), enclaves of cultural and social dissidents (Ware, 1935/1965),[21] the urban ecology of gangdom (Thrasher, 1927/1963), and the urban areas that housed the suicidal (Cavan, 1928/1965), the drug addicted (Dai, 1937/1970), and the mentally disturbed (Faris & Dunham, 1939/1965), and on the social and economic dynamics of real estate transactions and the human and metropolitical effects arising out of the occupational interests of realtors as they interfaced with the state of the economy (Hughes, 1928; McCluer, 1928; Schietinger, 1967). Park's (1952b, 1952c) orientation was that of Montesquieu; he emphasized the freedom that the city afforded to those who would partake of the "romance" and "magic" of its sociocultural multiverse.

Some of Park's students, on the other hand, following up an idea developed by Louis Wirth (1938), all too often took to contrasting its forms of liberty in thought and action—that is, its encouragement of "segmented" personalities and role-specific conduct and its fostering of impersonality, secondary relationships, and a

blasé attitude (see Roper, 1935, abstracted in Burgess & Bogue, 1967, pp. 231-244)—with what they alleged was the sense of personal security—that is, the gratification that came from conformity to custom, the comfort that arose out of familiar face-to-face contacts, the wholesomeness of whole personalities, and the companionability of primary relationships—to be found among the people who dwelt in rural, ethnoracially homogeneous small towns (see Bender, 1978, pp. 3-27; Redfield & Singer, 1973; see also M. P. Smith, 1979). For those who idealized the "folk society," and who conflated it with concomitant idealizations of the "little community," "primitive" primordialism, pastoral peace, and the small town, the impending urbanization of the countryside—heralded by the building of highways (Dansereau, 1961; McKenzie, 1968), the well-documented trend of young people departing to the city (for early documentation of this phenomenon, see Weber, 1899/1967), and the intrusion of the automobile (Bailey, 1988; Rae, 1965), the telephone (Ball, 1968; Pool, 1981), and the radio (Gist & Halbert, 1947, pp. 128, 505-507) on rural folkways—was a portent not merely of change but of irredeemable tragedy (see Blake, 1990; Gusfield, 1975; Lingeman, 1980; Tinder, 1980). On the other hand, for those ethnographers who concluded on the basis of their own field experiences that the processes as well as the anomalies of America's inequitable class structure had already found their way into and become deeply embedded within the language and customs of the nation's small towns, there was an equally portentous observation: America's Jeffersonian ideals were professed but not practiced in the very communities that had been alleged to be their secure repository. As August B. Hollingshead (1949/1961) would point out on the basis of his ethnographic study of "Elmtown's youth": "The . . . American class system is extra-legal . . . [but] society has other dimensions than those recognized in law. . . . It is the culture which makes men face toward the facts of the class system and away from the ideals of the American creed" (pp. 448, 453).

Ethnographic studies that followed in this tradition were guided by a nostalgia for 19th-century small-town values, an American past that no longer existed, but during the heyday of which—so it was supposed—there had existed a society in which all had been brothers and sisters.

However, neither the civil otherhood conceived by Park nor the classless brotherhood sought by Hollingshead could account for American society's resistance to the incorporation of blacks. It was to address this point that E. Franklin Frazier (1894-1962) would stress the "otherhood" of the American Negro. Building on the teachings of both Park and Du Bois, Frazier began his sociological studies in Chicago with an analysis of the various lifeways within the black ghetto. In the process, he discovered both the ghetto's separateness and its isolation from the larger social and political economy. In his later evaluation of the rise of the "black bourgeoisie" (1957a) he saw it as a tragic, although perhaps inevitable, outcome of the limited economic and social mobility available to the black middle classes. Based on his observations of largely university-based black middle classes, Frazier presented their lifestyle as an emulation of the lifestyle of the white middle classes: as such, his monograph on the subject should be regarded as much as a study of the white bourgeoisie as of the black. Frazier's ethnographic studies were based on almost a lifetime of observation, not only of this specific class, but also of African American ghetto dwellers in Harlem and Chicago, of black families in the rural South and the urban North, and of Negro youths caught up in the problems of their socioeconomic situation (see Frazier, 1925, 1957b, 1963, 1939/1966, 1940/1967, 1968). Frazier's work stands apart, not only because it points to the exclusion of blacks from both the American ideal of brotherhood and the then-emerging civic otherhood, but also because its research orientation drew on the life histories of Frazier's subjects and on his own experience.

The importance of personal experience in ethnographic description and interpretation is implicit in all of Frazier's work. His methodology and chosen research sites are comparable to those employed by a very different kind of ethnographer—Thorstein Veblen. In such studies of American university ghettos as *The Higher Learning in America: A Memorandum on the Conduct of Universities by Businessmen,* Veblen (1918/1965) drew on his own experiences at the University of Chicago, Stanford University, and the University of Missouri, three sites that provided the raw materials for his highly organized and prescient examination of the bureaucratic transformations then occurring in American universities.[22] Frazier's and Veblen's oeuvres are, in effect, examples of qualitative research based on data acquired over the course of rich and varied life experiences. In these studies it is impossible to disentangle the method of study from either the theory employed or the person employing it. Such a method would appear to be the ultimate desideratum of ethnographic research.

The ethnographic orientation at the University of Chicago was given a new twist by William Foote Whyte. Whyte made what was designed to be formal research into part of his life experience and called it "participant observation." The Chicago sociology department provided Whyte with an opportunity to report, in *Street Corner Society* (1943a, 1955, 1981), his findings about Italian Americans residing in the North End of Boston. That work, initially motivated by a sense of moral responsibility to uplift the slum-dwelling masses, has become the exemplar of the techniques appropriate to participant observation research: Whyte lived in the Italian neighborhood and in many but not all ways became one of the "Cornerville" boys.[23] Although he presents his findings about Cornerville descriptively, Whyte's theoretical stance remains implicit. The book has an enigmatic quality, because Whyte presents his data from the perspective of his relationships with his subjects. That is, Whyte is as much a researcher as he is a subject in his own book; the other had become the brother of Italian ghetto dwellers.

Anthropology at the University of Chicago was also informed by a qualitative orientation. Until 1929, anthropology and ethnology at that university had been subsumed under "historical sociology" in a department called the Department of Social Science and Anthropology. Anthropological and ethnological studies were at first directed by Frederick A. Starr, formerly head of ethnology at the American Museum of Natural History (Diner, 1975). Starr became a Japanophile after his first trip to Japan, while he was on assignment to bring a few of the Ainu people to be displayed, like Ota Benga, at the St. Louis World's Fair in 1904 (Statler, 1983, pp. 237-255). A separate Department of Anthropology was established in 1929, but, unlike Starr's, it reflected the orientation developed by the sociologists W. I. Thomas and Ellsworth Faris (see Faris, 1970, p. 16). One year before the advent of the new department, Robert Redfield presented his dissertation, *A Plan for the Study of Tepoztlan, Mexico* (1928). Borrowing from Tönnies's (1887/1957) dichotomous paradigm, gemeinschaft-gesellschaft, and drawing upon Von Wiese's and Becker's (1950/1962, 1932/1974) sacred-secular continuum, Redfield asserted the virtues of "the folk culture" and what he would later call "the little community" (Redfield, 1962, pp. 143-144; see also Redfield, 1930, 1941, 1960, 1950/1962b; Redfield & Rojas, 1934/1962a).

Regarding the metropolis as a congeries of unhappy and unfulfilled others, Redfield stood opposed to the values associated with urban life and industrial civilization. He extolled the lifestyles of those nonindustrial peoples and small communities that had resisted incorporation into the globally emerging metropolitan world. In his final essay, written in 1958, the year of his death, describing an imaginary conversation with a man from outer space, Redfield (1963) abjured the condition of mutually assured destruction that characterized the Cold War, despaired of halting the march of technocentric progress, conflated the pastoral with the premodern, and concluded by lamenting the rise of noncommunal life in the metropolitan city. Redfield's orientation, Rousseauean in its ethos, would provide a generation of anthropologists with a rustic outlook—a postmissionary attitude that sought to preserve and protect the lifeways of the primitive. His was the antiurban variant of Puritanism, a point of view that held small-scale, face-to-face communities to be superior to all others. To those ethnologists who followed in the ideological footsteps of Redfield, these com-

munal values seemed representative of primordial humanity.[24]

A counterimage to that of ethnography's romance with small-town, communitarian and primordial values of primitivism was offered in 1958 when Arthur J. Vidich and Joseph Bensman published their ethnographic account of "Springdale," a rural community in Upstate New York.[25] As their title forewarned, this was a "small town in mass society." [26] Its situation, moreover, was typical of other American towns. Springdale's much-vaunted localism, its claims to societal, economic, and political autonomy, were illusions of a bygone era. Their "central concern," the authors observed in their introduction to a revised edition released 10 years after the original publication of their monograph, "was with the processes by which the small town (and indirectly all segments of American society) are continuously and increasingly drawn into the central machinery, processes and dynamics of the total society" (Vidich & Bensman, 1968, p. xi).

In so presenting their findings, Vidich and Bensman reversed the direction and exploded what was left of the mythology attendant upon the gemeinschaft-gesellschaft (Parsons, 1937/1949, 1973) and folk-urban continua in American sociological thought (Duncan, 1957; Firey, Loomis, & Beegle, 1950; Miner, 1952). Although the theoretical significance of their study was often neglected in the wake of the controversy that arose over its publication and the charge that they had not done enough to conceal the identities of the town's leading citizens (Vidich & Bensman, 1968, pp. 397-476), their concluding observations—namely, that there had occurred a middle-class revolution in America, that the rise and predominance of the new middle classes had altered the character and culture of both the cities and towns of America, and that "governmental, business, religious and educational super-bureaucracies far distant from the rural town formulate policies to which the rural world can respond only with resentment" (p. 323; see also Bensman & Vidich, 1987)—challenged the older paradigms guiding field research on community life.

By 1963, Roland L. Warren would take note of what he called "the 'great change' in American communities" and point out how a developing division of labor, the increasing differentiation of interests and associations, the growing systemic relations to the larger society, a transfer of local functions to profit enterprises and to state and federal governments, urbanization and suburbanization, and the shifts in values that were both cause and consequences of these changes had been accompanied by a "corresponding decline in community cohesion and autonomy" (see Warren, 1972, pp. 53-94). In effect, community ethnography would not only have to adjust to the encroachment of the city and the suburb on the town, but also enlarge its outlook to embrace the effects of the state and the national political economy on the towns and villages of the Third World as well as of the United States (see, e.g., the ethnographies collected in Toland, 1993; see also Marcus, 1986). ("The point is," Maurice Stein [1964] observed in his reflection on nearly six decades of American community studies, "that both the student of the slum and of the suburb [and, he might have added, the small town] require some sort of total picture of the evolution of American communities and of emerging constellations and converging problems"; p. 230. Had the practitioners of American community studies taken their point of departure from Otto von Gierke's [1868/1990] or Friedrich Ratzel's [1876/1988] orientations, they might have been more critical of the "Rousseauean" variant of Tönnies's outlook from the beginning of their research [see McKinney, 1957].)[27]

◆ *The Ethnography of
Assimilation: The Other
Remains an Other*

A breakdown in another fundamental paradigm affected the ethnographic study of ethnic and racial minorities. Until the 1960s, much of the sociological outlook on race and ethnic relations had focused on the processes and progress of assimilation, acculturation, and amalgamation among America's multiverse of peoples.

Guided by the cluster of ideas and notions surrounding the ideology of the "melting pot," as well as by the prediction of the eventual assimilation of everyone that accompanied the widely held understanding of Robert E. Park's theory of the racial cycle, ethnographers of America's many minority groups at first sought to chart each people's location on a continuum that began with "contact," passed consecutively through stages of "competition and conflict" and "accommodation," and eventually culminated in "assimilation" (for critical evaluations of Park's cycle, see Lyman, 1972, 1990b, 1992b). Although by 1937 Park had come to despair of his earlier assertion that the cycle was progressive and irreversible (see Park, 1937/1969b), his students and followers would not give up their quest for a pattern and process that promised to bring an ultimate and beneficent end to interracial relations and their attendant problems.

When the ethnic histories of particular peoples in the United States seemed to defy the unidirectional movement entailed in Park's projected sequence—for example, when Etzioni's (1959) restudy of the Jewish ghetto showed little evidence that either religion or custom would be obliterated, even after many years of settlement in America; when Lee's (1960) discovery that Chinatowns and their old world-centered institutions persisted despite a decline in Sinophobic prejudices; when Woods's (1972) careful depiction of how 10 generations of settlement in America had failed to erode either the traditions or the ethnoracial identity of a marginalized people, the Letoyant Creoles of Louisiana (see also Woods, 1956); and, more generally, when Kramer (1970) had documented the many variations in minority community adaptation in America—there arose a cacophony of voices lamenting the failure of assimilation and calling for a resurgence of WASP hegemony (Brookhiser, 1991, 1993) or expressing grave apprehension about America's ethnocultural future (Christopher, 1989; Schlesinger, 1991; Schrag, 1973).

Even before popularizers and publicists announced the coming of an era in which there would be a "decline of the WASP" (Schrag, 1970) and a rise of the "unmeltable ethnics" (Novak, 1972), some sociologists had begun to reexamine their assumptions about ethnicity in America and to rethink their own and their predecessors' findings on the matter. In 1952, Nathan Glazer caused Marcus Lee Hansen's (1938/1952) hitherto overlooked work on the "law of third generation return" to be republished,[28] sparking a renewed interest in documenting whether, how, and to what extent the grandchildren of immigrants retained, reintroduced, rediscovered, or invented the customs of their old-world forebears in modern America (Kivisto & Blanck, 1990). Stanford M. Lyman (1974, 1986) combined participant observation with documentary and historical analyses to show that the solidarity and persistence over time of territorially based Chinatowns was related in great measure to persistent intracommunity conflict and to the web of traditional group affiliations that engendered both loyalty and altercation. Kramer and Leventman (1961) provided a picture of conflict resolution among three generations of American Jews who had retained many but not all aspects of their ethnoreligious traditions despite, or perhaps because of, the fact that the third generation had become "children of the gilded ghetto." Richard Alba (1985, 1989, 1990) reopened the questions of whether and how European ethnic survival had occurred in the United States, pointing to the several dimensions of its presentation, representation, and disintegration, and carrying out, once more, a study of Italian Americans, a group often chosen by sociologists for ethnographic studies seeking to support, oppose, modify, or reformulate the original assimilation thesis (see, e.g., Covello, 1967; Gans, 1962; Garbaccia, 1984; Landesco, 1968; Lopreato, 1970; Tricarico, 1984; Whyte, 1943a, 1943b).

The reconsideration of assimilation theory in general and Park's race relations cycle in particular produced a methodological critique so telling that it cast doubt on the substance of that hypothesis. In 1950, Seymour Martin Lipset observed that "by their very nature, hypotheses about the inevitability of cycles, whether they be cycles of race relations or the rise and fall of civilization, are not testable at all" (p. 479). Earlier, some ethnographers of racial minority groups in America had attempted to construct lengthier or alternative cycles that would be able to accommodate the findings of their field investigations. Bogardus's (1930, 1940; Ross & Bogardus, 1940) three distinctive cycles for California's diversified Japanese communities and Masuoka's (1946) warning that three generations would be required for the acculturation of Japanese in America and that the third generation would still be victims of "a genuine race problem" evidence the growing disappointment with assimilation's promise. Others, including W. O. Brown (1934), Clarence E. Glick (1955), Stanley Lieberson (1961), and Graham C. Kinloch (1974, pp. 205-209), came to conclusions similar to that of Park's 1937 reformulation—namely, that assimilation was but one possible outcome of sustained interracial contact, and that isolation, subordination, nationalist or nativist movements, and secession ought also to be considered.

Those seeking to rescue the discredited determinism of Park's original cycle from its empirically minded critics turned to policy proposals or hortatory appeals in its behalf. Wirth (1945) urged the adoption of programs that would alleviate the frustration experienced by members of minority groups who had been repeatedly rebuffed in their attempts to be incorporated within a democratic America; Lee (1960, pp. 429-430) converted her uncritical adherence to Park's prophecy into a plaintive plea that Chinese ghetto dwellers live up to it—that is, that they assimilate themselves as rapidly as possible (see also Lyman, 1961-1962, 1963). Still others resolved the ontological and epistemological problems in Park's cycle by treating it as a "logical" rather than "empirical" perspective. Frazier (1953) suggested that, rather than occurring chronologically, the stages in the theory might be spatiotemporally coexistent: "They represent logical steps in a systematic sociological analysis of the subject." Shibutani and Kwan (1965), after examining the many studies of integrative and disintegrative social processes in racial and ethnic communities, concurred, holding that although there were many exceptions to its validity as a descriptive theory, Park's stages provided a "useful way of ordering data on the manner in which immigrants become incorporated into an already-established society" (see pp. 116-135). And Geschwender (1978) went further, holding that Park's race relations cycle was "an abstract model of an 'ideal type' sequence which might develop" (p. 25).

In 1918, Edward Byron Reuter had defined America's race issue as "the problem of arriving at and maintaining mutually satisfactory working relations between members of two nonassimilable groups which occupy the same territory" (Reuter, 1918/1969, p. 18). After a half century of sociological studies had seemed to demonstrate that virtually none of the racial or ethnic groups had traversed the cyclical pathway to complete assimilation, America's race problem seemed not only to be immense, but also to have defied as well as defined the basic problematic of sociological theory. Such, at any rate, was the position taken by the ethnological anthropologist Brewton Berry (1963), whose field investigations would eventually include studies of various peoples in Latin America as well as several communities of previously unabsorbed racial hybrids in the United States (see also Lyman, 1964). Having shown that none of the proposed cycles of race relations could claim universal validity on the basis of available evidence, Berry and Tischler (1978) observed, "Some scholars . . . question the existence of any universal pattern, and incline rather to the belief that so numerous and so various are the components that enter into race relations that each situation is unique, and [that] the making of generalizations is a hazardous procedure" (p. 156). Berry's thesis, although not necessarily intended in this direction, set the tone for the subsequent plethora of ethnographies that offered little in the way of theoretical advancements but much more of the detail of everyday life among minorities and other human groups.

During the two decades after 1970, ethnological studies of African American, Amerindian, Mexican American, and Asian peoples also cast considerable doubt on whether, when, and to whose benefit the much-vaunted process of ethnocultural meltdown in America would occur. Ethnographies and linguistic studies of black enclaves, North and South, slave and free,

suggested that the tools employed in earlier community analyses had not been honed sufficiently for sociologists to be able to discern the cultural styles and social practices that set African American life apart from that of other segments of the society (see, e.g., Abrahams, 1964, 1970, 1992; E. Anderson, 1978; Bigham, 1987; Blassingame, 1979; Duneier, 1992; Evans & Lee, 1990; Joyner, 1984; Liebow, 1967; for an overview, see Blackwell, 1991). Other critics observed that sociological studies of the "American dilemma" had paid insufficient attention to politics, civil rights, and history (Boxhill, 1992; Button, 1989; Jackson, 1991; Lyman, 1972; V. J. Williams, 1989). Anthropological studies of the culture-preserving and supposedly isolated Native American nations and tribes had to give way in the face of a rising ethnoracial consciousness (Cornell, 1988; Martin, 1987; Sando, 1992), selective demands for the return of Amerindian museum holdings (Berlo, 1992; Clifford, 1990; Messenger, 1991; Milson, 1991-1992; "A Museum Is Set," 1993), Indian recourse to American courts in quest of redress and treaty rights (see T. L. Anderson, 1992; Jaimes, 1992), and political alliances and the tracing of ethnohistorical descent that would connect Amerindians with Hispanics, African Americans, and Jews (Forbes, 1973, 1988; Gutierrez, 1991; Tobias, 1990; Vigil, 1980). Mexican American studies moved from early historical institutional studies through ethnographies of farmworkers, and in the 1980s became part of the new postmodernist revolution.[29] To the Amerasian peoples conventionally treated by ethnographic sociologists—namely, the Chinese and Japanese—were added more recent arrivals, including Koreans, Thais, Vietnamese, Cambodians, Laotians, and the Hmong (see, e.g., Chan, 1991; Hune et al., 1991; Knoll, 1982; Nomura et al., 1989; Okihiro et al., 1988; Takaki, 1989). And, as in the instance of Mexican American ethnographers, a shift in issues and methods is beginning to emerge—moving away from debates about whether and how to measure assimilation and acculturation and toward such postmodern topics as the character, content, and implications of racial discourse about Asians in America (e.g., K. J. Anderson, 1991; Okihiro, 1988). As East Indians, Burmese, Oceanians, Malaysians, and other peoples of what used to be called "the Orient" began to claim common cause with the earlier-established Asian groups (Espiritu, 1992; Ignacio, 1976; Mangiafico, 1988), but insisted on each people's sociocultural and historical integrity, as well as the right of each to choose its own path within U.S. society, it became clear that the trend toward ethnographic postmodernism would continue (see, e.g., Hune et al., 1991; Leonard, 1992).

In 1980, Harvard University Press issued its mammoth *Harvard Encyclopedia of American Ethnic Groups* (Thernstrom, 1980), a work that includes not only separate entries for "Africans" and "Afro-Americans" but also individual essays devoted to each of 173 different tribes of American Indians and reports on each of the Asian peoples coming to the United States from virtually all the lands east of Suez. Harold J. Abrahamson's entry, "Assimilation and Pluralism," in effect announces American sociology's awakening not only from its dream of the eventual assimilation of every people in the country, but also from its conflation of assimilation with Americanization: "American society . . . is revealed as a composite not only of many ethnic backgrounds but also of many different ethnic responses. . . . There is no one single response or adaptation. The variety of styles in pluralism and assimilation suggest that ethnicity is as complex as life itself" (p. 160; see also Gleason, 1980; Novak, 1980; Walzer, 1980).

For the moment, pluralism had won its way onto paradigmatic center stage.[30] But even that orientation did not exhaust the possibilities or dispose of the problems arising out of the presence of diverse races and peoples in America. In 1993, together with Rita Jalali, Seymour Martin Lipset, who had criticized Park's formulation of an inevitable cycle leading to assimilation four decades earlier, observed that "race and ethnicity provide the most striking example of a general failure among experts to anticipate social developments in varying types of societies" (Jalali & Lipset, 1992-1993, p. 585). Moreover, the celebration of pluralism that now prevails in social thought obscures recognition of a fundamental problem: the self-restraint to be placed upon the competitive claims put forward by each ethnic and racial group.

◆ Ethnography Now: The Postmodern Challenge

Historically, the ethnographic method has been used by both anthropologists and sociologists. The guiding frameworks for those who have used this method in the past have all but been abandoned by contemporary ethnographers. The social-historical transformations of society and consciousness in the modern world have undermined the theoretical and value foundations of the older ethnography.

With the present abandonment of virtually every facet of what might now be recognized as the interlocked, secular, eschatological legacies of Comte, Tönnies, Wissler, Redfield, Park, and Parsons—that is, the recognition that the "comparative method" and the anthropology of primitivism is inherently flawed by both its Eurocentric bias and its methodological inadequacies; the determination that the gemeinschaft of the little community has been subverted by the overwhelming force of the national political economy of the gesellschaft; the discovery that assimilation is not inevitable; and the realization that ethnic sodalities and the ghettos persist over long periods of time (sometimes combining deeply embedded internal disharmonies with an outward display of sociocultural solidarity, other times existing as "ghost nations," or as hollow shells of claimed ethnocultural distinctiveness masking an acculturation that has already eroded whatever elementary forms of existence gave primordial validity to that claim, or, finally, as semiarticulated assertions of a peoplehood that has moved through and "beyond the melting pot" without having been fully dissolved in its fiery cauldron)—ethnography and ethnology could emerge on their own terms.[31]

No longer would ethnography have to serve the interests of a theory of progress that pointed toward the breakup of every ethnos. No longer would ethnology have to describe the pastoral peacefulness, proclaim the moral superiority, or document the psychic security supposed to be found in the villages of the nonliterate, the folk societies of non-Western peoples, the little communities of the woods and forests, the small towns of America, or the urban ethnic enclaves of U.S. or world metropolises. No longer would ethnography have to chart the exact position of each traditional and ascriptively based status group as it moved down the socioculturally determined pathway that would eventually take it into a mass, class, or civil society, and recompose it in the process.

Liberated from these conceptual and theoretical constraints, ethnography and ethnology are, for the first time as it were, in a position to act out their own versions of the revolution of "life" against "the forms of life"—a cultural revolution of the 20th century that Simmel (1968) foresaw as both imminent and tragic. Just as Simmel predicted that the cultural revolutionaries that he saw emerging in pre-World War I Europe would oppose both marriage and prostitution on the grounds that each was a form of the erotic and that they wished to emancipate the erotic from all forms of itself, so the new ethnographers proclaim themselves to be self-liberated from the weight of historical consciousness, relieved of the anxiety of influence (see Bloom, 1979),[32] and, in effect, content to become witnesses to and reporters of the myriad scenes in the quixotic world that has emerged out of the ruins of both religion and secular social theory (see Kundera, 1988).

The proclamation of ethnography as a self-defining orientation and practice in sociology and anthropology and the importation of the postmodernist outlook into it took place recently, irregularly, and in somewhat disorderly moves. Aleksandr Solzhenitsyn (1993) once pointed out that "no new work of art comes into existence (whether consciously or unconsciously) without an organic link to what was created earlier" (p. 3). Such also remains the case in social science, as will be shown with the new developments in sociological and anthropological ethnography.

One beginning of the emancipatory movement in ethnographic methodology is to be found in Peter Manning's seminal essay "Analytic Induction" (1982/1991). Seeking to set ethnography on an even firmer foundation of the symbolic interactionist perspective and

hoping to reinforce its connections to the classical period of the "Chicago school," Manning sought first to warn any practitioners of the sociological enterprise against employing any "concepts and theories developed to deal with the problems of such other disciplines as behavioristic psychology, economics, medicine, or the natural or physical sciences." He identified analytic induction as a procedure derivable from George Herbert Mead's and Florian Znaniecki's writings on scientific method, and he observed that it had been employed with greater or lesser precision by such classical Chicago ethnographers as Thomas and Znaniecki, and, later, by Robert Cooley Angell, Alfred Lindesmith, and Donald Cressey. Distinguishable from deductive, historical-documentary, and statistical approaches, analytic induction was "a nonexperimental qualitative sociological method that employs an exhaustive examination of cases in order to prove universal, causal generalizations." The case method was to be the critical foundation of a revitalized qualitative sociology.

The claim to universality of the causal generalizations is—in the example offered by Manning as exemplary of the method[33]—the weakest, for it is derived from the examination of a single case studied in light of a preformulated hypothesis that might be reformulated if the hypothesis does not fit the facts. And "practical certainty" of the (reformulated) hypothesis is obtained "after a small number of cases has been examined." Discovery of a single negative case is held to disprove the hypothesis and to require its reformulation. After "certainty" has been attained, "for purposes of proof, cases outside the area circumscribed by the definition are examined to determine whether or not the final hypothesis applies to them." If it does, it is implied, there is something wrong with the hypothesis, for "scientific generalizations consist of descriptions of conditions which are always present when the phenomenon is present but which are never present when the phenomenon is absent." The two keys to the entire procedure, Manning points out, are the definition of the phenomenon under investigation and the formulation of the tentative hypothesis. Ultimately, however, as Manning concedes, despite its aim, analytic induction does not live up to the scientific demand that its theories "understand, predict, and control events." After a careful and thoroughgoing critique of the procedure he has chosen over its methodological competitors, Manning asserts, "Analytic induction is not a means of prediction; it does not clearly establish causality; and it probably cannot endure a principled examination of its claims to [be] making universal statements." Indeed, Manning goes further, pointing out that, "according to the most demanding ideal standards of the discipline, analytic induction as a distinctive, philosophical, methodological perspective is less powerful than either enumerative induction or axiomatic-modelling methods." Manning's essay seems about to eject a method intrinsic to ethnography from the scientific community.

Manning's frank appraisal of the weaknesses of analytic induction is "drawn from a positivistic, deductive model of the scientific endeavor, a model seizing on a selected group of concerns." The proponents of that model seek to set the terms and limits of the social sciences according to its criteria. In fact, although few American scholars seem to know much about either the long history or the irresolution of debates over epistemological matters in the social sciences, the very issues of those debates are central to the questions the positivists are raising (see, in this regard, Rorty, 1982, pp. 191-210).

In his defense of analytic induction, Manning invokes an unacknowledged earlier critique by Sorokin (1965), namely, "that what is taken to be [appropriate] methodology at a given time is subject to fads, fashions, and foibles." Manning goes on to credit analytic induction with being a "viable source of data and concepts" and with helping investigators to sort out "the particulars of a given event [and to distinguish them from] those things that are general and theoretical." Erving Goffman, surely a sociological practitioner whose methodological orientation is akin to but not the same as analytic induction, goes even further, however. Opposing, in a defense of his own brand of ethnographic sociology, both system building and enumerative induction, in 1961 he wrote, "At present, if sociological con-

cepts are to be treated with affection, each must be traced back to where it best applies, followed from there wherever it seems to lead, and pressed to disclose the rest of its family. Better, perhaps, different coats to clothe the children well than a single splendid tent in which they all shiver" (p. xiv). A decade later, Goffman (1971) dismissed the scientific claims of positivistic sociologists altogether: "A sort of sympathetic magic seems to be involved, the assumption being that if you go through the motions attributable to science then science will result. But it hasn't" (p. xvi).

With the waning of interest in, support for, or faith in the older purposes for doing ethnology, by the 1970s there had also arisen a concomitant discontent with the epistemological claims as well as the latent or secretive political usages (see Diamond, 1992; Horowitz, 1967) of the mainstream perspectives of both sociology (see Vidich, Lyman, & Goldfarb, 1981) and anthropology (e.g., Clifford & Marcus, 1986; Fox, 1991; Manganaro, 1990). An outlook that could be used to carry out research projects and at the same time to treat the very resources of each discipline as a topic to be investigated critically was needed. Postmodernism appeared and seemed to fill that need.

Toward the end of his essay, Manning hints at the issue that would explode on the pages of almost every effort to come to terms with postwar and post-Cold War America: "In an age of existentialism, self-construction is as much a part of sociological method as theory construction." What he would later perceive as a reason for developing a formalistic and semiotic approach to doing fieldwork (Manning, 1987, pp. 7-24, 66-72) was that each construction would come to be seen as inextricably bound up with the other and that each would be said to provide a distorted mirror image of both the body (Cornwell, 1992; Featherstone, Hepworth, & Turner, 1991; Feher, 1989; Sheets-Johnstone, 1990, pp. 112-133; 1992) and the self (Kotarba & Fontana, 1987; Krieger, 1991; Zaner, 1981), of both one's *Umwelt* and the world of the other (the concept of *Umwelt* is developed by Gurwitsch, 1966). But for those who accepted the critique but rejected neoformalism as a technique for ethnography, there opened up a new field of investigation—representation. Hence some of the best postmodern ethnography has focused on the media that give imagery to real life (Bhabha, 1990b; Early, 1993; Gilman, 1991; Trinh, 1991). Justification for turning from the fields of lived experience to what is represented as such is the assumption that the former is itself perceived holographically, calling for the thematization of representation as a problem in the construction of "persuasive fictions" (Baudrillard, 1988a, pp. 27-106; Norris, 1990).

The postmodern ethnographer takes Simmel's tragedy of culture to be a fait accompli: It is not possible at the present time to emancipate free-floating life from all of its constraining forms (Strathern, 1990). The postmodern sociologist-ethnographer and his or her subjects are situated in a world suspended between illusory memories of a lost innocence and millennial dreams of a utopia unlikely to be realized. From such a position, not only is the standpoint of the investigator problematic (Lemert, 1992; Weinstein & Weinstein, 1991), but also that of the people to be investigated. Each person has in effect been "touched by the mass media, by alienation, by the economy, by the new family and child-care systems, by the unceasing technologizing of the social world, and by the threat of nuclear annihilation" (Denzin, 1989, p. 139). And, if the anthropologist-ethnographer is to proceed in accordance with the postmodern perspective, he or she must, on the one hand, become less fearful about "going primitive" (Torgovnick, 1990) and, on the other, contend with the claim that Eurocentric imagery has attended virtually all previous reports from the "primitive" world (Beverly, 1992; Bhabha, 1990a; Dirlik, 1987; Turner, 1992; West, 1992). For these ethnographers, Helmut Kuzmics (1988) observes, "The claim that the 'evolutionary gradualism' of the theory of civilization renders it incapable of explaining the simultaneous appearance of civilization (in a narrower sense than is presupposed by the highest values of the Enlighten-

ment) and 'barbarism' still needs to be confronted more thoroughly" (p. 161).

As analytic induction advocates propose, let us begin with a definition of the new outlook—the postmodern. Charlene Spretnak (1991), a critic of much of the postmodernism she surveys, provides one that is comprehensive and useful:

> A sense of detachment, displacement, and shallow engagement dominates deconstructive-postmodern aesthetics because groundlessness is the only constant recognized by this sensibility. The world is considered to be a repressive labyrinth of "social production," a construction of pseudoselves who are pushed and pulled by cultural dynamics and subtly diffused "regimes of power." Values and ethics are deemed arbitrary, as is "history," which is viewed by deconstructive postmodernists as one group or another's self-serving selection of facts. Rejecting all "metanarratives," or supposedly universal representations of reality, deconstructive postmodernists insist that the making of every aspect of human existence is culturally created and determined in particular, localized circumstances about which no generalizations can be made. Even particularized meaning, however, is regarded as relative and temporary. (pp. 13-14)

Spretnak's definition permits us to see how the postmodern ethnographer proceeds. The post-modernist ethnographer enters into a world from which he or she is methodologically required to have become detached and displaced. Such an ethnographer is in effect reconstituted as Simmel's (1950) "stranger" (see also Frisby, 1992) and Park's (1929/1969a) and Stonequist's (1937/1961) "marginalized" person (see also Wood, 1934/1969, pp. 245-284). Like those ideal-typical ethnographers-in-spite-of-themselves, this social scientist begins work as a self-defined newcomer to the habitat and life world of his or her subjects (see Agar, 1980; Georges & Jones, 1980; D. Rose, 1989). He or she is a citizen-scholar (Saxton, 1993) as well as a participant observer (Vidich, 1955). Older traditions and aims of ethnography, including especially the quest for valid generalizations and substantive conclusions, are temporarily set aside in behalf of securing "thick descriptions" (Geertz, 1973) that will in turn make possible "thick interpretations"—joining ethnography to both biography and lived experience (Denzin, 1989, pp. 32-34). History is banished from the ethnographic enterprise except when and to the effect that local folk histories enter into the vocabularies of motive and conduct employed by the subjects.[34] Because crossing the postmodern divide (Borgmann, 1992; I. Chambers, 1990) requires one to abandon all established and preconceived values, theories, perspectives, preferences, and prejudices as resources for ethnographic study, the ethnographer must bracket these, treating them as if they are arbitrary and contingent rather then hegemonic and guiding (Rosenau, 1992, pp. 25-76). Hence the postmodernist ethnographer takes seriously the aim of such deconstructionists as Derrida (e.g., 1976, 1981), Lyotard (e.g., 1989), and Baudrillard (e.g., 1981, 1983, 1988b), namely, to disprivilege all received texts and established discourses in behalf of an all-encompassing critical skepticism about knowledge. In so doing, the ethnographer displaces and deconstructs his or her own place on the hierarchy of statuses that all too often disguise their invidious character as dichotomies (see Bendix & Berger, 1959; for a postmodern analysis of a dichotomy, see Lyman, 1992a). To all of these, instead, is given contingency—the contingencies of language, of selfhood, and of community (Rorty, 1989; C. Taylor, 1989).

For anthropologists, the new forms for ethnography begin with a recognition of their irreducible limitation: the very presentation of ethnographic information in a monograph is a "text" and therefore subject to the entire critical apparatus that the postmodern perspective brings to bear on any text.[35] The ethnographic enterprise is to be conceived as a task undertaken all too often by an unacculturated stranger who is guided by whatever the uneasy mix of poetry and politics gives to his or her efforts to comprehend an alien culture. Above all, an ethnography is now to be regarded as a piece of writing—as such, it cannot be said either to present or to represent what the older and newly discredited ideology of former ethnography claimed for itself: an unmodified and unfiltered record of immediate experience and an accurate portrait of the culture of the "other."

The postmodern critique has engendered something of a crisis among present-day anthropologists. As in the responses to other crises, a new self-and-other consciousness has come to the fore, and the imperatives of reflexivity have shifted attention onto the literary, political, and historical features of ethnography as well as onto career imperatives, all of which have hitherto been overlooked. Engaging themselves with these issues, such disciplinary leaders as Clifford Geertz, Mary Douglas, Claude Lévi-Strauss, and the late Victor Turner have blurred the old distinction between art and science and challenged the very basis of the claim to exacting rigor, unblinking truth telling, and unbiased reporting that marked the boundary separating one from the other.

Rereading the works in the classical ethnographic canon has now become a critical task of the highest importance. A new form of structuralist method must be devised if we are to dig beneath the works and uncover both their hidden truths and their limiting blinders. That canon is now to be seen as a product of the age of Occidental colonialism and to have been methodologically constrained by the metropole ideologies and literary conventions that gave voice and quality to them. Yet these ethnographies are not to be relegated to the historical dustbin of a rejectable epoch of disciplinary childhood by today's and tomorrow's anthropologists. Rather, in consideration of the fact that few of the latter will follow career trajectories like those of Malinowski or Powdermaker—that is, either spending decades of their lives in residence with a nonliterate Oceanic people or moving from the ethnographic task of observing at close range a group of South Africans to another, living among blacks in a segregated Mississippi town, and then to still another, closely examining how the Hollywood film industry became a "dream factory,"—the ethnologist of the present age and the immediate future is likely to do but one ethnography—a dissertation that stakes his or her claim to the title of ethnologist and to the perquisites of an academic life spent largely away from the field. Moreover, career considerations are not the only element affecting ethnology. The "field" itself has become constricted by the march of decolonization and the modernization that has overtaken once "primitive" peoples. For these reasons, rereading old ethnographies becomes a vicarious way to experience the original ways of the discipline, whereas criticizing them provides the ethnologist with a way to distance him- or herself from modernist foibles. Except for the dissertation ethnography and for those anthropologists who choose to move in on the turf of the equally postmodern sociological ethnographers of urban and industrial settings, the ethnographic task of anthropology may become one devoted to reading texts and writing critiques. The "field" may be located in one's library or one's study.

Given the postmodern ethnographers' epistemological stance and disprivileged social status, two fundamental problems for the sociological version of the new ethnography are its relationship to social change and social action, and the applicable scope of its representations of reality.

The first problem has been posed as well as answered by Michael Burawoy et al. (1992) in their conception of "ethnography unbound" and the role of the "extended case method." They direct the ethnographer toward the macropolitical, economic, and historical contexts in which directly observed events occur, and perceive in the latter fundamental issues of domination and resistance (see also Feagin, Orum, & Sjoberg, 1991). Norman Denzin (1989), a leader of postmodern approaches to ethnography, approaches the generality issue in two distinct though related ways. His advice to ethnographers is that they first immerse themselves in the lives of their subjects and, after achieving a deep understanding of these through rigorous effort, produce a contextualized reproduction and interpretation of the stories told by the subjects. Ultimately, an ethnographic report will present an integrated synthesis of experience and theory. The "final interpretive theory is multivoiced and dialogical. It builds on native interpretations and in fact simply articulates what is implicit in those

interpretations" (p. 120). Denzin's strategic move out of the epistemological cul-de-sac presented by such daunting observations as Berry's specific skepticism about the possibility of making valid generalizations in an ethnoracially pluralist society, or by the growing skepticism about the kind and quality of results that sociologists' adherence to positivistic and natural science models will engender (T. R. Vaughan, 1993, p. 120), is to take the onset of the postmodern condition as the very occasion for presenting a new kind of ethnography. He encourages, in effect, an ethnographic attitude of engagement with a world that is ontologically absurd but always meaningful to those who live in it (see Lyman & Scott, 1989). Thus he concludes his methodological treatise by claiming that the world has now entered its Fourth Epoch (following Antiquity, the Middle Ages, and the Modern Age), and that this latest epoch is in fact the "postmodern period" (Denzin, 1989, p. 138). The ethnographic method appropriate to this period, Denzin goes on, is one that is dedicated "to understanding how this historical moment universalizes itself in the lives of interesting individuals" (p. 189). Method and substance are joined in the common recognition that everyone shares in the same world and responds to it somehow. The study of the common condition and the uncovering of the uncommon response become the warp and woof of the fragile but not threadbare sociological skein of the postmodern era.

The postmodern is a cultural form as well as an era of history. As the former, like all the forms noted by Simmel, it invites and evokes its counteracting and rebellious tendencies. It too, then, is likely to suffer the penultimate tragedy of culture—the inability to emancipate life from all of its forms (Weinstein & Weinstein, 1990). However, in this era, the sociologist-ethnographer will not merely observe that history; he or she will participate in its everlasting quest for freedom, and be a partner in and a reporter on "the pains, the agonies, the emotional experiences, the small and large victories, the traumas, the fears, the anxieties, the dreams, fantasies and the hopes" of the lives of the peoples. These constitute this era's ethnographies—true tales of the field (Van Maanen, 1988).

The methods of ethnography have become highly refined and diverse, and the reasons for doing ethnography have multiplied. No longer linked to the values that had guided and focused the work of earlier ethnographers, the new ethnography ranges over a vastly expanded subject matter, limited only by the varieties of experience in modern life; the points of view from which ethnographic observations may be made are as great as the choices of lifestyles available in modern society. It is our hope that the technological refinement of the ethnographic method will find its vindication in the discovery of new sets of problems that lead to a greater understanding of the modern world.

Although it is true that at some level all research is a uniquely individual enterprise—not part of a sacrosanct body of accumulating knowledge—it is also true that it is always guided by values that are not unique to the investigator: We are all creatures of our own social and cultural pasts. However, in order to be meaningful to others, the uniqueness of our own research experience gains significance when it is related to the theories of our predecessors and the research of our contemporaries. Ethnographers can find social and cultural understanding only if they are aware of the sources of the ideas that motivate them and are willing to confront them—with all that such a confrontation entails.

■ Notes

1. For a discussion of the fundamental similarities between so-called quantitative and qualitative methods, see Vidich and Bensman (1968, chap. 13).

2. Here we merely gloss a serious problem in the philosophy and epistemology of the social sciences and present one possible approach to it. Some of the issues are discussed and debated in such works as those by C. W. Smith (1979), Rabinow and Sullivan (1979), G. Morgan (1983), Fiske and Shweder (1986), Hare and Blumberg (1988), Ashmore (1989), Minnich (1990), Bohman (1991), Sadri (1992, pp. 3-32, 105-142), and Harré (1984).

3. Many of the issues raised by this new outlook are treated in the essays collected in A. Rose (1988).

4. The following draws on Lyman (1990a).

5. This orientation differs from that used by Thucydides (1972) in *History of the Peloponnesian War.* His observations were made from the perspective of a participant who detached himself from the norms of both warring sides while never making explicit his own values. His book has confounded legions of scholars who have attempted to find his underlying themes, not understanding that the work is replete with ambiguities that do not lend themselves to a single viewpoint. For various perspectives on Thucydides' work, see Kitto (1991, pp. 136-152), Kluckhohn (1961, pp. 4, 34-35, 55, 64-66), Humphreys (1978, pp. 94, 131, 143, 227-232, 300-307), and Grant (1992, pp. 5, 45, 148-149).

6. When discussing the crimes committed by the Spaniards against the Indians, Hosle (1992) states: "It is certainly not easy to answer the following question: Were the priests who accompanied the conquistadors also responsible, even if they condemned the violence committed, insofar as their presence in a certain sense legitimized the enterprise? It is impossible to deny that by their mere presence they contributed to Christianity appearing as an extremely hypocritical religion, which spoke of universal love and nevertheless was the religion of brutal criminals. Yet it is clear that without the missionaries' presence even more cruelties would have been committed. Hypocrisy at least acknowledges in theory certain norms, and by so doing gives the oppressed the possibility to claim certain rights. Open brutality may be more sincere, but sincerity is not the only value. Sincere brutality generates nothing positive; hypocrisy, on the other side, bears in itself the force which can overcome it" (p. 236). If it does anything, Hosle's defense of Christianity reveals the difficulty still remaining in debates over universalistic as opposed to relativistic values and leaves wide open any resolution of the problem. See also Lippy, Choquette, and Poole (1992). For further history and discussion of the de Las Casas-Sepulveda dispute and its implications for ethnohistory and ethnology of the Americas, see Hanke (1949/1965, 1959/1970, 1974).

7. A fine example is the ethnographic study by Bishop Robert Henry Codrington (1891) ti-

tled *The Melanesians.* Codrington's study provided the sole source for Yale University anthropologist Loomis Havemeyer's (1929) chapter on the Melanesians (pp. 141-160). See Codrington (1974) for an excerpt from *The Melanesians* titled "Mana." See also the critical discussion in Kuper (1988, pp. 152-170).

8. A good example that also illustrates the anthropologists' despair over the disastrous effects of missionary endeavor on native life and culture is to be found in the last published work of William Hale R. Rivers (1922/1974).

9. Thus if the reader wishes to peruse one well-known exposition of "primitive" culture, George Peter Murdock's (1934) *Our Primitive Contemporaries,* as an example of one aspect of the "comparative method," he or she will discover therein ethnographies of 18 peoples who occupy time and space coincident to that of the author, arranged in terms of geography, but—with the term *primitive* as the descriptive adjective in use throughout—making the title of the book historically (that is, diachronically) oxymoronic. For a thoughtful critique, see Bock (1966).

10. Two exceptions to this mode of ethnocentric expression are worthy of note: William Graham Sumner (1840-1910), who coined the term *ethnocentrism,* seemed also to suggest that the failure of either Congress or the courts to do anything to halt the lynching of Negroes in the South signaled something less than that nation's rise to perfected civilization that other ethnologists were willing to credit to America and to other republics of the Occident: "It is unseemly that anyone should be burned at the stake in a modern civilized state" (Sumner, 1906/1940, p. 471; see also Sumner, 1905/1969). Thorstein Veblen (1857-1929) used such categories as "savagery" and "barbarism" tongue-in-cheek, often treating the moral codes and pecuniary values of the peoples so labeled as superior to those of the peoples adhering to the Protestant ethic or the spirit of capitalism, and disputing the claims of Aryan superiority so much in vogue in his day (see Veblen, 1899/1959, 1914/1990, 1919/1961a, 1919/1961b; see also A. K. Davis, 1980; Diggins, 1978; Tilman, 1991).

11. The Human Relations Area Files were reproduced, marketed, and distributed to anthropology departments in other universities. This not only added an element of standardiza-

tion and uniformity to culture studies, but also made it possible for the analyst of ethnography to forgo a trip to the field. That this approach is still in vogue is illustrated by two researches by the Harvard sociologist Orlando Patterson (1982). Patterson relies on Murdock's "World Sample" of 61 slaveholding societies (out of a total of 186 societies), which are arranged geographically, but rearranges them temporally to make them serve a developmentalist thesis that seeks to uncover the variations in as well as the functional origins of slavery. On the basis of this method, it is not surprising to find that in the sequel to his study Patterson (1991) believes he can show that "the Tupinamba, the ancient Greeks and Romans, and the southerners of the United States, *so markedly different in time, place, and levels of sociocultural development,* nonetheless reveal the remarkable tenacity of this culture-character complex" (p. 15; emphasis added).

12. For the conceptualization of a sector of the world's peoples as belonging to the Third World, as well as for the conceptualization of "developed" and "undeveloped" or "underdeveloped" societies, see Worsley (1964, 1984).

13. That capitalism had contributed to underdevelopment in both the European overseas empires and America's homegrown "ghetto colonialism" became an assumption and even an article of faith that could shape the perspective of posttraditional ethnography (see Blauner, 1972; Marable, 1983; see also Hechter, 1975).

14. For a historical view on eschatological, millennial, sacred, and secular "end-times" theories, as well as other modes of chronologizing events, see Paolo Rossi (1987).

15. It should be noted that American ethnography up to the beginnings of World War II focused almost exclusively on American Indians and the aboriginal inhabitants of American colonies. Anthropologists' interests in the high cultures of Central and South America were archaeologically oriented and were designed both to fill in the "prehistoric record" and to fill museums. Some ethnographic work was carried out in the U.S.-controlled Pacific Islands (in association with the Bernice P. Bishop Museum in Hawaii). Margaret Mead worked on American Samoa and was one of the earliest of the nonmissionaries to ethnograph a Pacific Island. Her work, aimed in part at criticizing the Puritanical sexual mores of America, overstated the actual situation in Oceania and eventually led to a counterstate-

ment (see Freeman, 1983; Holmes, 1987; Mead, 1928/1960a, 1930/1960b, 1949/1960c, 1935/1960d).

16. This was the same perspective used by anthropologists who administered the Japanese relocation centers during World War II and who had had some of their training on the reservation. For accounts by those anthropologists who moved from Amerindian to Japanese American incarceration ethnography and administration, see Leighton (1945), Wax (1971), Spicer, Hansen, Luomala, and Opler (1969), and Myer (1971). For a spirited critique, see Drinnon (1987).

17. For some representative ethnographies of the southwestern Amerindian peoples, see Schwatka (1893/1977), Nordenskiold (1893/1979), McGee (1899/1971), Goddard (1913/1976), White (1933/1974), Spier (1933/1978), and Kluckhohn (1944). See also Eggan (1966, pp. 112-141).

18. A recent ethnography of the Zuni by Tedlock (1992) both reflects upon and critically appraises Cushing's work among that tribe.

19. Radin (1935/1970, 1936/1971a) also did fieldwork among the Italians and Chinese of San Francisco.

20. Clark Wissler (1940/1966a, 1938/1966b) established his credentials on the basis of a lifetime in service to ethnohistorical and ethnographic study of the United States.

21. Although not carried out at the University of Chicago, this study bears the stamp of that school's approach.

22. In that report, he was the first to see the new role of the university president as an administrative "Captain of Erudition," the beginnings of university public relations designed to protect the image of learning, and the business foundations in real estate and fund-raising (endowments) of the university system in the United States.

23. In 1992, when new questions were raised about the ethnocultural and ethical aspects of Whyte's study of "Cornerville," a symposium reviewed the matter extensively (see "Street Corner Society Revisited," 1992).

24. A social variant of Redfield's perspective found its way into some of the urban community, ethnic enclave, and small-town studies of America that were conducted or supervised by anthropologists or Chicago sociologists (see Hannerz, 1980; Lyon, 1987; Suttles, 1972, pp. 3-20). (A

revival of ecological studies rooted in the idea that the uses of space are socially constructed was begun with the publication of Lyman & Scott, 1967; see also Ericksen, 1980.) As early as 1914, M. C. Elmer, a promising graduate student at the University of Chicago, had written a Ph.D. dissertation on social surveys in urban communities that reflected the shift from the church to the "scientific" survey tradition in both the social gospel movement and the discipline of sociology; seven years later, Raleigh Webster Stone (1921) in effect signaled that the transition to a newer orientation was well under way when he offered *The Origin of the Survey Movement* as his Ph.D. dissertation at Chicago. In 1933, Albert Bailie Blumenthal submitted *A Sociological Study of a Small Town* as his doctoral dissertation at the same university (Faris, 1970, pp. 135-140). However, the central thrust of ethnological studies in Chicago's sociology department after Robert E. Park had joined its faculty concerned community and subcommunity organization within the city (see, e.g., N. Anderson, 1959), and, for some, how the gemeinschaft could be reconstituted in the metropolis (see Fishman, 1977; Quandt, 1970).

25. That ethnographies of small towns and large cities adopted an approach more or less consistent with the macropolitical-economic orientation emphasized by Vidich and Bensman is evidenced in works by P. Davis (1982), Wallace (1987), Arsenault (1988), Campbell (1992), Moorhouse (1988), and Reid (1992).

26. Earlier, Vidich (1952, 1980) had contributed to the reconsideration of anthropological approaches to so-called primitive societies, reconceiving such studies as requiring an orientation that focused on the effects of global colonialism and its rivalries on the structure and process of colonialized societies. For the connections between his anthropological study of Palau under various colonial administrations and the study of "Springdale," see Vidich (1986).

27. British approaches to the historical sociology of small towns did not adopt Tönnies's theoretical stance (see, e.g., Abrams & Wrigley, 1979).

28. See also Glazer (1954). "Hansen's law" was the basis for work by Kennedy (1944) and Herberg (1960).

29. For monographs illustrating the stages in the evolution of these studies, see Blackman (1891/1976), P. S. Taylor (1930/1970, 1983),

Gamio (1930/1969, 1931/1971), Bogardus (1934/1970), and Galarza (1964, 1970, 1977). For community studies in New Mexico, see Gonzalez (1967), Sanchez (1967), and Forrest (1989). For Arizona, see Sheridan (1986); for Texas, see Rubel (1971); for Indiana, see Lane and Escobar (1987); for Chicago, see Padilla (1985). For general and historical studies, see Burma (1985), Officer (1987), and D. J. Weber (1992). For the shift from eth-class to postmodern analysis, see Barrera (1979, 1988).

30. Subsequent works (e.g., Fuchs, 1990; Keyes, 1982; Kivisto, 1984, 1989; Lieberson, 1980; Lieberson & Waters, 1988; Royce, 1982; Steinberg, 1981; Waters, 1990) emphasized pluralism, contingency, and the voluntary and social constructionist aspects of race and ethnicity.

31. In anthropology, the shift toward a new outlook included a critical reevaluation and commentary on virtually every aspect of ethnology and ethnography in what has thus far produced seven volumes of essays edited by George W. Stocking, Jr. (1983, 1984, 1985, 1986, 1988, 1989, 1991). A turn toward the classics of antiquity and their relation to modern and postmodern anthropology was appraised by Redfield's son (see J. Redfield, 1991).

32. One element of intellectual and moral influence has given rise to anxiety, recriminations, and rhetorical attempts to excuse, justify, or escape from the burden it lays on those who believe that postmodernism is a countercultural orientation of the Left, namely, the accusation that its preeminent philosophical founders—Heidegger and de Man—were sympathetic to and supporters of the Hitler regime and Nazism. For debates on this far-from-resolved issue, see Habermas (1983), Farias (1989), Neske and Kettering (1990), Ferry and Renaut (1990), Lyotard (1990), Rockmore (1992), Derrida (1992), Hamacher, Hertz, and Keenan (1989), and Lehman (1992). Another important contributor to postmodernism, Michel Foucault, has aroused apprehension over the extent to which his sexual preferences and promiscuous lifestyle affected his philosophical perspective. For various opinions on the matter, see Poster (1987-1988), Foucault (1992), Eribon (1991), Miller (1993); and Nikolinakos (1990). See also Paglia (1991).

33. The procedural example used by Manning is from Cressey (1953, p. 16).

34. For a discussion of the several issues involved in the relationship of history to ethnography, see Comaroff and Comaroff (1992); compare Natanson (1962).

35. The following draws on the essays and commentaries in Clifford and Marcus (1986).

■ *References*

Abeyesekere, G. (1992). *The apotheosis of Captain Cook: European mythmaking in the Pacific.* Princeton, NJ: Princeton University Press.

Abrahams, R. D. (1964). *Deep down in the jungle: Negro narrative folklore from the streets of Philadelphia.* Hatboro, PA: Folklore Associates.

Abrahams, R. D. (1970). *Positively black.* Englewood Cliffs, NJ: Prentice Hall.

Abrahams, R. D. (1992). *Singing the master: The emergence of African American culture in the plantation South.* New York: Pantheon.

Abrahamson, H. J. (1980). Assimilation and pluralism. In S. Thernstrom (Ed.), *Harvard encyclopedia of American ethnic groups.* Cambridge, MA: Harvard University Press.

Abrams, P., & Wrigley, E. A. (Eds.). (1979). *Towns and societies: Essays in economic history and historical sociology.* Cambridge: Cambridge University Press.

Adler, P. A., Adler, P., & Fontana, A. (1987). Everyday life sociology. In K. Plummer (Ed.), *Symbolic interactionism: Vol. 1. Foundations and history* (pp. 436-454). Brookfield, VT: Edward Elgar.

Agar, M. H. (1980). *The professional stranger: An informal introduction to ethnography.* New York: Academic Press.

Alba, R. (1985). *Italian Americans: Into the twilight of ethnicity.* Englewood Cliffs, NJ: Prentice Hall.

Alba, R. (Ed.). (1989). *Ethnicity and race in the U.S.A.: Toward the twenty-first century.* New York: Routledge, Chapman Hall.

Alba, R. (1990). *Ethnic identity: The transformation of white America.* New Haven, CT: Yale University Press.

Aldrich, R. (1990). *The French presence in the South Pacific, 1842-1940.* Honolulu: University of Hawaii Press.

Anderson, E. (1978). *A place on the corner.* Chicago: University of Chicago Press.

Anderson, K. J. (1991). *Vancouver's Chinatown: Racial discourse in Canada, 1875-1980.* Montreal: McGill-Queen's University Press.

Anderson, N. (1959). *The urban community: A world perspective.* New York: Henry Holt.

Anderson, N. (1961). *The hobo: The sociology of the homeless man.* Chicago: University of Chicago Press. (Original work published 1923)

Anderson, T. L. (Ed.). (1992). *Property rights and Indian economics.* Lanham, MD: Rowman & Littlefield.

Arsenault, R. (1988). *St. Petersburg and the Florida dream, 1888-1950.* Norfolk, VA: Donning.

Ashmore, M. (1989). *The reflexive thesis: Writing sociology of scientific knowledge.* Chicago: University of Chicago Press.

Atkinson, P. (1990). *The ethnographic imagination: Textual constructions of reality.* London: Routledge.

Bailey, B. L. (1988). *From front porch to back seat: Courtship in twentieth century America.* Baltimore: Johns Hopkins University Press.

Baker, J. R. (1974). *Race.* New York: Oxford University Press.

Ball, D. W. (1968). Toward a sociology of telephones and telephoners. In M. Truzzi (Ed.), *Sociology and everyday life* (pp. 59-75). Englewood Cliffs, NJ: Prentice Hall.

Barkan, E. (1992). *The retreat of scientific racism: Changing concepts of race in Britain and the United States.* Cambridge: Cambridge University Press.

Barrera, M. (1979). *Race and class in the Southwest: A theory of racial inequality.* Notre Dame, IN: University of Notre Dame Press.

Barrera, M. (1988). *Beyond Aztlan: Ethnic autonomy in comparative perspective.* Notre Dame, IN: University of Notre Dame Press.

Baudrillard, J. (1981). *For a critique of the political economy of the sign* (C. Levin, Trans.). St. Louis, MO: Telos.

Baudrillard, J. (1983). *In the shadow of the silent majorities; Or, the end of the social and other essays* (P. Foss, J. Johnston, & P. Patton, Trans.). New York: Semiotext(e).

Baudrillard, J. (1988a). *America* (C. Turner, Trans.). London: Verso.

Baudrillard, J. (1988b). *The ecstasy of communication* (S. Lotringer, Ed.; B. Schutze & C. Schutze, Trans.). New York: Semiotext(e).

Becker, H. (1962). *Through values to social interpretation: Essays on social contexts, actions, types, and prospects.* New York: Greenwood. (Original work published 1950)

Becker, H. (1974). *Systematic sociology: On the basis of the* Beziehungslehre *and* Begildlehre *of Leopold von Wiese.* New York: Arno. (Original work published 1932)

Bender, T. (1978). *Community and social change in America.* New Brunswick, NJ: Rutgers University Press.

Bendix, R., & Berger, B. (1959). Images of society and problems of concept formation in sociology. In L. Gross (Ed.), *Symposium on sociological theory* (pp. 92-118). Evanston, IL: Row, Peterson.

Bensman, J., & Vidich, A. J. (1987). *American society: The welfare state and beyond* (2nd ed.). Amherst, MA: Bergin & Garvey.

Berlo, J. C. (Ed.). (1992). *The early years of Native American art history: The politics of scholarship and collecting.* Seattle: University of Washington Press.

Berry, B. (1963). *Almost white.* New York: Macmillan.

Berry, B., & Tischler, H. (1978). *Race and ethnic relations* (4th ed.). Boston: Houghton Mifflin.

Beverly, J. (1992). The margin at the center: On *testimonio* (testimonial narrative). In S. Smith & J. Watson (Eds.), *De/colonizing the subject: The politics of gender in women's autobiography.* Minneapolis: University of Minnesota Press.

Bhabha, H. K. (Ed.). (1990a). *Nation and narration.* London: Routledge.

Bhabha, H. K. (1990b). The other question: Differences, discrimination and the discourse of colonialism. In R. Ferguson, M. Gever, Trinh T. M., & C. West (Eds.), *Out there: Marginalization and contemporary cultures* (pp. 71-88). Cambridge: MIT Press.

Bieder, R. E. (1989). *Science encounters the Indian, 1820-1880: The early years of American ethnology.* Norman: University of Oklahoma Press.

Bigham, D. E. (1987). *We ask only a fair trial: A history of the black community of Evansville, Indiana.* Bloomington: Indiana University Press/University of Southern Indiana.

Blackman, F. M. (1976). *Spanish institutions of the Southwest*. Glorieta, NM: Rio Grande. (Original work published 1891)

Blackwell, J. E. (1991). *The black community: Diversity and unity* (3rd ed.). New York: HarperCollins.

Blake, C. N. (1990). *Beloved community: The cultural criticism of Randolph Bourne, Van Wyck Brooks, Waldo Frank, and Lewis Mumford*. Chapel Hill: University of North Carolina Press.

Blassingame, J. W. (1979). *The slave community: Plantation life in the antebellum South* (Rev. ed.). New York: Oxford University Press.

Blauner, R. (1972). *Racial oppression in America*. New York: Harper & Row.

Bloom, H. (1979). *The anxiety of influence: A theory of poetry*. London: Oxford University Press.

Blumenthal, A. B. (1933). *A sociological study of a small town*. Unpublished doctoral dissertation, University of Chicago.

Bock, K. E. (1948). *The comparative method*. Unpublished doctoral dissertation, University of California, Berkeley.

Bock, K. E. (1952). Evolution and historical process. *American Anthropologist, 54,* 486-496.

Bock, K. E. (1956). *The acceptance of histories: Toward a perspective for social science*. Berkeley: University of California Press.

Bock, K. E. (1963). Evolution, function and change. *American Sociological Review, 27,* 229-237.

Bock, K. E. (1966). The comparative method of anthropology. *Comparative Studies in Society and History, 8,* 269-280.

Bock, K. E. (1974). Comparison of histories: The contribution of Henry Maine. *Comparative Studies in Society and History, 16,* 232-262.

Boeke, J. H. (1946). *The evolution of the Netherlands Indies economy*. New York: Institute of Pacific Relations.

Boeke, J. H. (1948). *The interests of the voiceless Far East: Introduction to Oriental economics*. Leiden, Netherlands: Universitaire Pers Leiden.

Bogardus, E. S. (1930). A race relations cycle. *American Journal of Sociology, 35,* 612-617.

Bogardus, E. S. (1940). Current problems of Japanese Americans. *Sociology and Social Research, 25,* 63-66.

Bogardus, E. S. (1970). *The Mexican in the United States*. New York: Arno/New York Times. (Original work published 1934)

Bohman, J. (1991). *New philosophy of social science*. Cambridge: MIT Press.

Borgmann, A. (1992). *Crossing the postmodern divide*. Chicago: University of Chicago Press.

Bowden, H. W. (1981). *American Indians and Christian missions: Studies in cultural conflict*. Chicago: University of Chicago Press.

Boxer, C. R. (1965). *Portuguese society in the tropics: The municipal councils of Goa, Macao, Bahia, and Luanda*. Madison: University of Wisconsin Press.

Boxhill, B. R. (1992). *Blacks and social justice* (Rev. ed.). Lanham, MD: Rowman & Littlefield.

Bradford, P. V., & Blume, H. (1992). *Ota Benga: The Pygmy in the zoo*. New York: St. Martin's.

Brookhiser, R. (1991). *The way of the WASP: How it made America, and how it can save it, so to speak*. New York: Free Press.

Brookhiser, R. (1993, March 1). The melting pot is still simmering. *Time,* p. 72.

Brown, R. (1984). *The nature of social laws: Machiavelli to Mill*. Cambridge: Cambridge University Press.

Brown, W. O. (1934). Culture contact and race conflict. In E. B. Reuter (Ed.), *Race and culture contacts* (pp. 34-47). New York: McGraw-Hill.

Burawoy, M., Burton, A., Ferguson, A. A., Fox, K. J., Gamson, J., Gartrell, N., Hurst, L., Kurzman, C., Salzinger, L., Schiffman, J., & Ui, S. (Eds). (1992). *Ethnography unbound: Power and resistance in the modern metropolis*. Berkeley: University of California Press.

Burgess, E. W. (1916). The social survey: A field for constructive service by departments of sociology. *American Journal of Sociology, 21,* 492-500.

Burgess, E. W., & Bogue, D. J. (Eds.). (1967). *Contributions to urban sociology*. Chicago: University of Chicago Press.

Burma, J. H. (Ed.). (1985). *Mexican-Americans in comparative perspective*. Washington, DC: Urban Institute.

Button, J. W. (1989). *Blacks and social change: Impact of the civil rights movement in south-*

ern communities. Princeton, NJ: Princeton University Press.

Calloway, C. G. (Ed.). (1991). *Dawnland encounters: Indians and Europeans in northern New England.* Hanover, NH: University Press of New England.

Campbell, W. D. (1992). *Providence.* Atlanta: Longstreet.

Caplow, T., Bahr, H. M., Chadwick, B. A., Hill, R., & Williamson, M. H. (1982). *Middletown families: Fifty years of change and continuity.* Minneapolis: University of Minnesota Press.

Caplow, T., Bahr, H. M., Chadwick, B. A., Hill, R., & Williamson, M. H. (1983). *All faithful people: Change and continuity in Middletown's religion.* Minneapolis: University of Minnesota Press.

Cavan, R. S. (1965). *Suicide.* New York: Russell & Russell. (Original work published 1928)

Chambers, C. A. (1971). *Paul U. Kellogg and the survey: Voices for social welfare and social justice.* Minneapolis: University of Minnesota Press.

Chambers, I. (1990). *Border dialogues: Journeys into postmodernity.* London: Routledge.

Chan, S. (1991). *Asian Americans: An interpretive history.* Boston: Twayne.

Cherokee Nation v. Georgia, 30 U.S. (5 Pet.) 1 (1831).

Christopher, R. C. (1989). *Crashing the gates: The de-WASPing of America's power elite.* New York: Simon & Schuster.

Clifford, J. (1986). On ethnographic self-fashioning: Conrad and Malinowski. In T. C. Heller, M. Sosna, & D. E. Wellbery (Eds.), *Reconstructing individualism: Autonomy, individuality, and the self in Western thought* (pp. 140-162). Stanford, CA: Stanford University Press.

Clifford, J. (1990). On collecting art and culture. In R. Ferguson, M. Gever, Trinh T. M., & C. West (Eds.). *Out there: Marginalization and contemporary cultures* (pp. 1-169). Cambridge: MIT Press.

Clifford, J., & Marcus, G. E. (Eds.). (1986). *Writing culture: The poetics and politics of ethnography.* Berkeley: University of California Press.

Codrington, R. H. (1891). *The Melanesians.* Oxford: Clarendon.

Codrington, R. H. (1974). Mana. In A. Montagu (Ed.), *Frontiers of anthropology* (pp. 255-259). New York: G. P. Putnam's Sons. (Reprinted from *The Melanesians*, Oxford: Clarendon, 1891)

Cohen, S. R. (1981). *Reconciling industrial conflict and democracy: The Pittsburgh survey and the growth of social research in the United States.* Unpublished doctoral dissertation, Columbia University.

Coleman, M. C. (1985). *Presbyterian missionary attitudes toward American Indians, 1837-1893.* Jackson: University Press of Mississippi.

Comaroff, J., & Comaroff, J. (1992). *Ethnography and the historical imagination.* Boulder, CO: Westview.

Contosta, D. R. (1980). *Henry Adams and the American experiment.* Boston: Little, Brown.

Cornell, S. (1988). The transformation of tribe: Organization and self-concept in Native American ethnicities. *Ethnic and Racial Studies, 11,* 27-47.

Cornwell, R. (1992). Interactive art: Touching the "body in the mind." *Discourse: Journal for Theoretical Studies in Media and Culture, 14,* 203-221.

Covello, L. (1967). *The social background of the Italo-American school child: A study of the southern Italian family mores and their effect on the school situation in Italy and America* (F. Cordesco, Ed.). Leiden, Netherlands: E. J. Brill.

Cressey, D. R. (1953). *Other people's money: A study in the social psychology of embezzlement.* Glencoe, IL: Free Press.

Culin, S. (1967). Zuni pictures. In E. C. Parsons (Ed.), *American Indian life* (pp. 175-178). Lincoln: University of Nebraska Press. (Original work published 1922)

Cushing, F. H. (1974). *Zuni breadstuff.* New York: Museum of the American Indian, Keye Foundation. (Original work published 1920)

Cushing, F. H. (1979). *Zuni: Selected writings of Frank Hamilton Cushing* (J. Green, Ed.). Lincoln: University of Nebraska Press.

Cushing, F. H. (1988). *Zuni folk tales.* Tucson: University of Arizona Press. (Original work published 1901)

Cushing, F. H. (1990). *Cushing at Zuni: The correspondence and journals of Frank Hamilton*

Cushing, 1878-1884 (J. Green, Ed.). Albuquerque: University of New Mexico Press.

Dai, B. (1970). *Opium addiction in Chicago*. Montclair, NJ: Patterson Smith. (Original work published 1937)

Dale, E. E. (1984). *The Indians of the Southwest: A century of development under the United States*. Norman: University of Oklahoma Press. (Original work published 1949)

Dansereau, H. K. (1961). Some implications of modern highways for community ecology. In G. A. Theodorsen (Ed.), *Studies in human ecology* (pp. 175-187). Evanston, IL: Row, Peterson.

Davis, A. K. (1980). *Thorstein Veblen's social theory*. New York: Arno.

Davis, P. (1982). *Hometown: A contemporary American chronicle*. New York: Simon & Schuster.

Degerando, J.-M. (1969). *The observation of savage peoples* (F. C. T. Moore, Trans.). London: Routledge & Kegan Paul. (Original work published 1800)

Denzin, N. K. (1989). *Interpretive interactionism*. Newbury Park, CA: Sage.

Derrida, J. (1976). *Of grammatology* (G. C. Spivak, Trans.). Baltimore: Johns Hopkins University Press.

Derrida, J. (1981). *Positions* (A. Bass, Trans.). Chicago: University of Chicago Press.

Derrida, J. (1992). *The other heading: Reflections on today's Europe* (P.-A. Brault & M. B. Naas, Trans.). Bloomington: Indiana University Press.

Diamond, S. (1963). The search for the primitive. In I. Goldston (Ed.), *Man's image in medicine and anthropology* (pp. 62-115). New York: International University Press.

Diamond, S. (1972). Anthropology in question. In D. Hymes (Ed.), *Reinventing anthropology* (pp. 401-429). New York: Pantheon.

Diamond, S. (1992). *Compromised campus: The collaboration of universities with the intelligence community, 1945-1955*. New York: Oxford University Press.

Diggins, J. P. (1978). *The bard of savagery: Thorstein Veblen and modern social theory*. New York: Seabury.

Diner, S. J. (1975). Department and discipline: The Department of Sociology at the University of Chicago, 1892-1920. *Minerva, 13,* 518-519, 538.

Dirlik, A. (1987). Culturalism as hegemonic ideology and liberating practice. *Cultural Critique, 6,* 13-50.

Dockstader, F. J. (1985). *The Kachina and the white man: The influences of white culture on the Hopi Kachina religion* (Rev. ed.). Albuquerque: University of New Mexico Press.

Douglas, J. (1974). A brief history of sociologists of everyday life. In J. Douglas et al. (Eds.), *Introduction to the sociologies of everyday life* (pp. 182-210). Boston: Allyn & Bacon.

Drake, S. C., & Cayton, H. R. (1962). *Black metropolis: A study of Negro life in a northern city* (Rev. ed., Vols. 1-2). New York: Harper Torchbooks.

Drinnon, R. (1987). *Keeper of concentration camps: Dillon S. Myer and American racism*. Berkeley: University of California Press.

Du Bois, W. E. B. (1967). *The Philadelphia Negro: A social study*. New York: Benjamin Blom. (Original work published 1899)

Duffy, J. (1959). *Portuguese Africa*. Cambridge, MA: Harvard University Press.

Duncan, O. D. (1957). Community size and the rural-urban continuum. In P. K. Hatt & A. J. Reiss, Jr. (Eds.), *Cities and society: The revised reader in urban sociology* (pp. 35-45). Glencoe, IL: Free Press.

Duneier, M. (1992). *Slim's table: Race, respectability, and masculinity*. Chicago: University of Chicago Press.

Early, G. (Ed.). (1993). *Lure and loathing: Essays on race, identity, and the ambivalence of assimilation*. New York: Allen Lane/Penguin.

Eggan, F. (1966). *The American Indian: Perspectives for the study of social change* (The Lewis Henry Morgan Lectures). Cambridge: Cambridge University Press.

Elmer, M. C. (1914). *Social surveys of urban communities*. Unpublished doctoral dissertation, University of Chicago.

Engels, F. (1884). *The origins of the family, private property and the state*. Moscow: Foreign Languages.

Eribon, D. (1991). *Michel Foucault* (B. Wing. Trans.). Cambridge, MA: Harvard University Press.

Ericksen, E. G. (1980). *The territorial experience: Human ecology as symbolic interaction*. Austin: University of Texas Press.

Espiritu, Y. L. (1992). *Asian American panethnicity: Bridging institutions and identities.* Philadelphia: Temple University Press.

Etzioni, A. (1959). The ghetto: A re-evaluation. *Social Forces, 37,* 255-262.

Evans, A. S., & Lee, D. (1990). *Pearl City, Florida: A black community remembers.* Boca Raton: Florida Atlantic University Press.

Farias, V. (1989). *Heidegger and Nazism* (J. Margolis & T. Rickmore, Eds.; P. Burrell & G. Ricci, Trans.). Philadelphia: Temple University Press.

Faris, R. E. L. (1970). *Chicago sociology, 1920-1932.* Chicago: University of Chicago Press.

Faris, R. E. L., & Dunham, H. W. (1965). *Mental disorders in urban areas: An ecological study of schizophrenia and other psychoses.* Chicago: University of Chicago Press. (Original work published 1939)

Feagin, J. R., Orum, A., & Sjoberg, G. (1991). The present crisis in U.S. sociology. In J. R. Feagin, A. M. Orum, & G. Sjoberg, *A case for the case study* (pp. 269-278). Chapel Hill: University of North Carolina Press.

Featherstone, M., Hepworth, M., & Turner, B. S. (Eds.). (1991). *The body: Social process and cultural theory.* London: Sage.

Feher, M. (Ed.). (1989). *Fragments for a history of the human body* (Vols. 1-3). Cambridge: MIT Press/Zone.

Ferry, L., & Renaut, A. (1990). *Heidegger and modernity* (F. Philip, Trans.). Chicago: University of Chicago Press.

Firey, W., Loomis, C. P., & Beegle, J. A. (1950). The fusion of urban and rural. In J. Labatut & W. J. Lane (Eds.), *Highways in our national life: A symposium* (pp. 154-163). Princeton, NJ: Princeton University Press.

Fishman, R. (1977). *Urban utopias in the twentieth century: Ebenezer Howard, Frank Lloyd Wright, and Le Corbusier.* New York: Basic Books.

Fiske, D. W., & Shweder, R. A. (Eds.). (1986). *Metatheory in social science: Pluralisms and subjectivities.* Chicago: University of Chicago Press.

Fontana, A. (1974). Toward a complex universe: Existential sociology. In J. Douglas et al. (Eds.), *Introduction to the sociologies of everyday life* (pp. 155-181). Boston: Allyn & Bacon.

Forbes, J. D. (1973). *Aztecs del norte: The Chicanos of Aztlan.* Greenwich, CT: Fawcett.

Forbes, J. D. (1988). *Black Africans and Native Americans: Color, race and caste in the evolution of red-black peoples.* New York: Blackwell.

Forrest, S. (1989). *The preservation of the village: New Mexico's Hispanics and the New Deal.* Albuquerque: University of New Mexico Press.

Foucault, M. (1992). *Michel Foucault, philosopher* (T. J. Armstrong, Ed. & Trans.). New York: Routledge, Chapman & Hall.

Fox, R. G. (Ed.). (1991). *Recapturing anthropology: Working in the present.* Santa Fe, NM: School of American Research Press.

Frazier, E. F. (1925). Durham: Capital of the black middle class. In A. Locke (Ed.), *The new Negro* (pp. 333-340). New York: Albert & Charles Boni.

Frazier, E. F. (1931). *The Negro family in Chicago.* Unpublished doctoral dissertation, University of Chicago.

Frazier, E. F. (1937a). The impact of urban civilization upon Negro family life. *American Sociological Review, 2,* 609-618.

Frazier, E. F. (1937b). Negro Harlem: An ecological study. *American Journal of Sociology, 43,* 72-88.

Frazier, E. F. (1953). The theoretical structure of sociology and sociological research. *British Journal of Sociology, 4,* 292-311.

Frazier, E. F. (1957a). *Black bourgeoisie: The rise of a new middle class in the United States.* Glencoe, IL: Free Press/Falcon's Wing.

Frazier, E. F. (1957b). *The Negro in the United States* (Rev. ed.). New York: Macmillan.

Frazier, E. F. (1963). *The Negro church in America.* New York: Schocken.

Frazier, E. F. (1966). *The Negro family in the United States* (Rev. ed.). Chicago: University of Chicago Press/Phoenix. (Original work published 1939)

Frazier, E. F. (1967). *Negro youth at the crossways: Their personality development in the middle states.* New York: Schocken. (Original work published 1940)

Frazier, E. F. (1968). *E. Franklin Frazier on race relations: Selected papers* (G. F. Edwards, Ed.). Chicago: University of Chicago Press.

Freeman, D. (1983). *Margaret Mead and Samoa: The making and unmaking of an anthropolog-*

ical myth. Cambridge, MA: Harvard University Press.

Frisby, D. (1992). *Simmel and since: Essays on Georg Simmel's social theory.* London: Routledge.

Fuchs, L. H. (1990). *The American kaleidoscope: Race, ethnicity, and the civic culture.* Hanover, NH: University Press of New England.

Fukuyama, F. (1992). *The end of history and the last man.* New York: Free Press.

Furnivall, J. S. (1948). *Colonial policy and practice: A comparative study of Burma and Netherlands India.* New York: New York University Press.

Galarza, E. (1964). *Merchants of labor: The Mexican bracero story—an account of the managed migration of Mexican farm workers in California, 1942-1960.* San Jose, CA: Rosicrucian.

Galarza, E. (1970). *Spiders in the house and workers in the field.* Notre Dame, IN: University of Notre Dame Press.

Galarza, E. (1977). *Farm workers and agri-business in California, 1947-1960.* Notre Dame, IN: University of Notre Dame Press.

Gamio, M. (1969). *Mexican immigration to the United States: A study of human migration and adjustment.* New York: Arno/New York Times. (Original work published 1930)

Gamio, M. (1971). *The life story of the Mexican immigrant: Autobiographic documents.* New York: Dover. (Original work published 1931)

Gans, H. J. (1962). *The urban villagers: Group and class in the life of Italian-Americans.* New York: Free Press.

Garbaccia, D. R. (1984). *From Sicily to Elizabeth Street: Housing and social change among Italian immigrants, 1880-1930.* Albany: State University of New York Press.

Geertz, C. (1973). Thick description: Toward an interpretive theory of culture. In C. Geertz, *The interpretation of cultures: Selected essays* (pp. 3-32). New York: Basic Books.

Gellner, E. (1979). Beyond truth and falsehood, or no method in my madness. In E. Gellner, *Spectacles and predicaments: Essays in social theory* (pp. 182-198). Cambridge: Cambridge University Press.

Georges, R. A., & Jones, M. O. (1980). *People studying people: The human element in fieldwork.* Berkeley: University of California Press.

Geschwender, J. A. (1978). *Racial stratification in America.* Dubuque, IA: William C. Brown.

Gilman, S. L. (1991). *Inscribing the other.* Lincoln: University of Nebraska Press.

Ginsburg, C. (1991). *Ecstasies: Deciphering the witches' sabbath* (R. Rosenthal, Trans.). New York: Pantheon.

Ginsburg, C. (1993). The European (re)discovery of the shamans. *London Review of Books, 15,* 2.

Gist, N. P., & Halbert, L. A. (1947). *Urban society* (2nd ed.). New York: Thomas Y. Crowell.

Glazer, N. (1954). Ethnic groups in America: From national culture to ideology. In M. Berger, T. Able, & C. H. Page (Eds.), *Freedom and control in modern society* (pp. 158-173). New York: D. Van Nostrand.

Gleason, P. (1980). American identity and Americanization. In S. Thernstrom (Ed.), *Harvard encyclopedia of American ethnic groups* (pp. 31-58). Cambridge, MA: Harvard University Press.

Glick, C. E. (1955). Social roles and social types in race relations. In W. A. Lind (Ed.), *Race relations in world perspective* (pp. 239-262). Honolulu: University of Hawaii Press.

Goddard, P. E. (1976). *Indians of the Southwest.* Glorieta, NM: Rio Grande. (Original work published 1913)

Goffman, E. (1949). *Some characteristics of response to depicted experience.* Unpublished master's thesis, University of Chicago.

Goffman, E. (1959). *The presentation of self in everyday life.* Garden City, NY: Doubleday.

Goffman, E. (1961). *Asylums: Essays on the social situation of mental patients and other inmates.* Garden City, NY: Doubleday.

Goffman, E. (1971). *Relations in public: Microstudies of the public order.* New York: Basic Books.

Goffman, E. (1974). *Frame analysis: An essay on the organization of experience.* New York: Harper Colophon.

Gonzalez, N. L. (1967). *The Spanish Americans of New Mexico: A heritage of pride.* Albuquerque: University of New Mexico Press.

Grant, M. (1992). *A social history of Greece and Rome.* New York: Charles Scribner's Sons.

Gray, J. (1970). The intellectual standing of different races and their respective opportunities for culture. In G. Spiller (Ed.), *Papers on* inter-racial problems communicated to the First Universal Race Congress, University of London, July 26-29, 1911 (pp. 79-85). New York: Citadel. (Original work published 1911)

Greek, C. E. (1978). The social gospel movement and early American sociology, 1870-1915. Graduate Faculty Journal of Sociology, 3(1), 30-42.

Greek, C. E. (1992). The religious roots of American sociology. New York: Garland.

Gullick, J. M. (1956). The story of early Kuala Lumpur. Singapore: Donald Moore.

Gurwitsch, A. (1966). The last work of Edmund Husserl. In A. Gurwitsch, Studies in phenomenology and psychology. Evanston, IL: Northwestern University Press.

Gusfield, J. R. (1975). Community: A critical response. New York: Harper Colophon.

Gutierrez, R. A. (1991). When Jesus came the corn mothers went away: Marriage, sexuality and power in New Mexico, 1500-1846. Stanford, CA: Stanford University Press.

Gwertzman, B., & Kaufman, M. T. (Eds.). (1992). The decline and fall of the Soviet empire. New York: New York Times.

Habermas, J. (1983). Martin Heidegger: The great influence (1959). In J. Habermas, Philosophical-political profiles (F. G. Lawrence, Trans.; pp. 53-60). Cambridge: MIT Press.

Hamacher, W., Hertz, N., & Keenan, T. (Eds.). (1989). On Paul de Man's wartime journalism. Lincoln: University of Nebraska Press.

Hammersley, M. (1992). What's wrong with ethnography? Methodological explorations. London: Routledge.

Hanke, L. (1965). The Spanish struggle for justice in the conquest of America. Boston: Little, Brown. (Original work published 1949)

Hanke, L. (1970). Aristotle and the American Indians: A study in race prejudice in the modern world. Bloomington: Indiana University Press. (Original work published 1959)

Hanke, L. (1974). All mankind is one: A study of the disputation between Bartolome de Las Casas and Juan Gines de Sepulveda on the religious and intellectual capacity of the American Indians. De Kalb: Northern Illinois University Press.

Hannerz, U. (1980). Exploring the city: Inquiries toward an urban anthropology. New York: Columbia University Press.

Hansen, M. L. (1952). The problem of the third generation immigrant. Commentary, 14, 492-500. (Original work published 1938)

Hare, A. P., & Blumberg, H. H. (1988). Dramaturgical analysis of social interaction. New York: Praeger.

Harré, R. (1980). Social being: A theory for social psychology. Totowa, NJ: Rowman & Littlefield.

Harré, R. (1984). Personal being: A theory for individual psychology. Cambridge, MA: Harvard University Press.

Hartland, E. S. (1969). Primitive society: The beginnings of the family and the reckoning of descent. New York: Harper & Row. (Original work published 1921)

Hartmann, E. G. (1967). The movement to Americanize the immigrant. New York: AMS. (Original work published 1948)

Havemeyer, L. (1929). Ethnography. Boston: Ginn.

Hechter, M. (1975). Internal colonialism: The Celtic fringe in British national development, 1536-1966. London: Routledge & Kegan Paul.

Heizer, R. F., & Kroeber, T. (Eds.). (1979). Ishi the last Yahi: A documentary history. Berkeley: University of California Press.

Herberg, W. (1960). Protestant-Catholic-Jew: An essay in American religious sociology. Garden City, NY: Doubleday.

Herskovitz, M. (1958). The myth of the Negro past. Boston: Beacon. (Original work published 1941)

Herskovitz, M. (1966). The new world Negro: Selected papers in Afroamerican studies (F. S. Herskovitz, Ed.). Bloomington: Indiana University Press.

Hill-Lubin, M. A. (1992). "Presence Africaine": A voice in the wilderness, a record of black kinship. In V. Y. Mudimbe (Ed.), The surreptitious speech: Presence Africaine and the politics of otherness, 1947-1987 (pp. 157-173). Chicago: University of Chicago Press.

Hinsley, C. M., Jr. (1981). Savages and scientists: The Smithsonian Institution and the development of American anthropology, 1846-1910. Washington, DC: Smithsonian Institution Press.

Hodgen, M. T. (1936). The doctrine of survivals: A chapter in the history of scientific method in the study of man. London: Allenson.

Hodgen, M. T. (1964). *Early anthropology in the sixteenth and seventeenth centuries.* Philadelphia: University of Pennsylvania.

Hodgen, M. T. (1974). *Anthropology, history and cultural change.* Tucson: University of Arizona Press/Wenner-Gren Foundation for Anthropological Research.

Holden, A. C. (1970). *The settlement idea: A vision of social justice.* New York: Arno/New York Times. (Original work published 1922)

Hollingshead, A. B. (1961). *Elmtown's youth: The impact of social classes on adolescents.* New York: Science Editions. (Original work published 1949)

Holmes, L. D. (1987). *Quest for the real Samoa: The Mead/Freeman controversy and beyond.* South Hadley, MA: Bergin & Garvey.

Horowitz, I. L. (Ed.). (1967). *The rise and fall of Project Camelot: Studies in the relationship between social science and practical politics.* Cambridge: MIT Press.

Hosle, V. (1992). The Third World as a philosophical problem. *Social Research, 59,* 230-262.

Hughes, E. C. (1928). *A study of a secular institution: The Chicago Real Estate Board.* Unpublished doctoral dissertation, University of Chicago.

Humphreys, S. C. (1978). *Anthropology and the Greeks.* London: Routledge & Kegan Paul.

Hune, S., et al. (Eds.). (1991). *Asian Americans: Comparative and global perspectives.* Pullman: Washington State University Press.

Ignacio, L. F. (1976). *Asian Americans and Pacific Islanders (Is there such an ethnic group?).* San Jose, CA: Pilipino Development Associates.

Immigration Commission (W. P. Dillingham, Chair). (1970). *Immigrants in industry (25 parts).* New York: Arno/New York Times. (Original work published 1911)

Jackson, J. S. (Ed.). (1991). *Life in black America.* Newbury Park, CA: Sage.

Jaimes, M. E. (Ed.). (1992). *The state of Native America: Genocide, colonization and resistance.* Boston: South End.

Jalali, R., & Lipset, S. M. (1992-1993). Racial and ethnic conflicts: A global perspective. *Political Science Quarterly, 107*(4), 585-606.

Johnson, J. M. (1975). *Doing field research.* New York: Free Press.

Jones, J. (1992). *Soldiers of light and love: Northern teachers and Georgia blacks, 1865-1873.* Athens: University of Georgia Press.

Joyner, C. (1984). *Down by the riverside: A South Carolina slave community.* Urbana: University of Illinois Press.

Keegan, W. F. (1992). *The people who discovered Columbus: The prehistory of the Bahamas.* Gainesville: University Press of Florida.

Keller, R. W., Jr. (1983). *American Protestantism and United States Indian policy, 1869-1882.* Lincoln: University of Nebraska Press.

Kennedy, R. J. R. (1944). Single or triple melting pot: Intermarriage trends in New Haven, 1870-1940. *American Journal of Sociology, 44,* 331-339.

Keyes, C. F. (Ed.). (1982). *Ethnic change.* Seattle: University of Washington Press.

Kinloch, G. C. (1974). *The dynamics of race relations.* New York: McGraw-Hill.

Kitto, H. D. F. (1951). *The Greeks.* London: Penguin.

Kivisto, P. (1984). *Immigrant socialists in the United States: The case of Finns and the Left.* Cranbury, NJ: Associates University Presses.

Kivisto, P. (Ed.). (1989). *The ethnic enigma: The salience of ethnicity for European-origin groups.* Philadelphia: Balch Institute Press.

Kivisto, P., & Blanck, D. (Eds.). (1990). *American immigrants and their generations: Studies and commentaries on the Hansen thesis after fifty years.* Urbana: University of Illinois Press.

Kluckhohn, C. (1944). *Navajo witchcraft.* Boston: Beacon.

Kluckhohn, C. (1961). *Anthropology and the classics: The Colver Lectures in Brown University, 1960.* Providence, RI: Brown University Press.

Knoll, T. (1982). *Becoming Americans: Asian sojourners, immigrants and refugees in the western United States.* Portland, OR: Coast to Coast.

Kotarba, J. A., & Fontana, A. (Eds.). (1987). *The existential self in society.* Chicago: University of Chicago Press.

Kramer, J. R. (1970). *The American minority community.* New York: Thomas Y. Crowell.

Kramer, J. R., & Leventman, S. (1961). *Children of the gilded ghetto: Conflict resolutions of three generations of American Jews.* New Haven, CT: Yale University Press.

Krieger, S. (1991). *Social science and the self: Personal essays on an art form.* New Brunswick, NJ: Rutgers University Press.

Kroeber, T. (1962). *Ishi in two worlds: A biography of the last wild Indian in North America.* Berkeley: University of California Press.

Kroeber, T. (1965). *Ishi: Last of his tribe.* New York: Bantam.

Kundera, M. (1988). *The art of the novel* (L. Ascher, Trans.). New York: Grove.

Kuper, A. (1988). *The invention of primitive society: Transformations of an illusion.* London: Routledge.

Kuzmics, H. (1988). The civilizing process (H. G. Zilian, Trans.). In J. Keane (Ed.), *Civil society and the state: New European perspectives.* London: Verso.

Landesco, J. (1968). *Organized crime in Chicago* (Part 3 of the Illinois Crime Survey, 1929). Chicago: University of Chicago Press.

Lane, J. B., & Escobar, E. J. (Eds.). (1987). *Forging a community: The Latino experience in Northwest Indiana, 1919-1975.* Chicago: Cattails.

Lee, R. H. (1960). *The Chinese in the United States of America.* Hong Kong: Hong Kong University Press.

Lee, R. H. (1978). *The growth and decline of Chinese communities in the Rocky Mountain region.* New York: Arno.

Lehman, D. (1992). Signs of the times: Deconstruction and the fall of Paul de Man. *Contention: Debates in Society, Culture and Science, 1*(2), 23-38.

Leighton, A. H. (1945). *The governing of men: General principles and recommendations based on experience at a Japanese relocation camp.* Princeton, NJ: Princeton University Press.

Lemert, C. (1992). Subjectivity's limit: The unsolved riddle of the standpoint. *Sociological Theory, 10,* 63-72.

Lenzer, G. (Ed.). (1975). *Auguste Comte and positivism: The essential writings.* New York: Harper Torchbooks.

Leonard, K. I. (1992). *Making ethnic choices: California's Punjabi Mexican Americans.* Philadelphia: Temple University Press.

Lieberson, S. (1961). A societal theory of race and ethnic relations. *American Sociological Review, 26,* 902-910.

Lieberson, S. (1980). *A piece of the pie: Blacks and white immigrants since 1880.* Berkeley: University of California Press.

Lieberson, S., & Waters, M. C. (1988). *From many strands: Ethnic and racial groups in contemporary America.* New York: Russell Sage Foundation.

Liebow, E. (1967). *Tally's corner: A study of Negro street corner men.* Boston: Little, Brown.

Lingeman, R. (1980). *Small town America: A narrative history, 1620-the present.* New York: G. P. Putnam's Sons.

Lippy, C. H., Choquette, R., & Poole, S. (1992). *Christianity comes to the Americas, 1492-1776.* New York: Paragon.

Lipset, S. M. (1950, May). Changing social status and prejudice: The race theories of a pioneering American sociologist. *Commentary, 9,* 475-479.

Lipset, S. M. (1963). *The first new nation: The United States in historical and comparative perspective.* New York: Basic Books.

Lipset, S. M. (1979). *The first new nation: The United States in historical and comparative perspective* (Rev. ed.). New York: W. W. Norton.

Lopata, H. Z. (1967). The function of voluntary associations in an ethnic community: "Polonia." In E. W. Burgess & D. J. Bogue (Eds.), *Contributions to urban sociology* (pp. 203-223). Chicago: University of Chicago Press.

Lopreato, J. (1970). *Italian Americans.* New York: Random House.

Lovejoy, A. O. (1960). *The great chain of being: A study of the history of an idea.* New York: Harper Torchbooks.

Lugard, L. (1965). *The dual mandate in British tropical Africa.* Hamden, CT: Archon/Shoe String. (Original work published 1922)

Luhmann, N. (1986). The individuality of the individual: Historical meanings and contemporary problems. In T. C. Heller, M. Sosna, & D. E. Wellbery (Eds.), *Reconstructing individualism: Autonomy, individuality, and the self in Western thought* (pp. 313-328). Stanford, CA: Stanford University Press.

Lyman, S. M. (1961-1962). Overseas Chinese in America and Indonesia: A review article. *Pacific Affairs, 34,* 380-389.

Lyman, S. M. (1963). Up from the "hatchet man." *Pacific Affairs, 36,* 160-171.

Lyman, S. M. (1964). The spectrum of color. *Social Research, 31,* 364-373.

Lyman, S. M. (1972). *The black American in sociological thought: A failure of perspective.* New York: G. P. Putnam's Sons.

Lyman, S. M. (1974). Conflict and the web of group affiliation in San Francisco's Chinatown, 1850-1910. *Pacific Historical Review, 43*, 473-499.

Lyman, S. M. (1975). Legitimacy and consensus in Lipset's America: From Washington to Watergate. *Social Research, 42*, 729-759.

Lyman, S. M. (1978). The acceptance, rejection, and reconstruction of histories. In R. H. Brown & S. M. Lyman (Eds.), *Structure, consciousness and history* (pp. 53-105). New York: Cambridge University Press.

Lyman, S. M. (1979). Stuart Culin and the debate over trans-Pacific migration. *Journal for the Theory of Social Behaviour, 9*, 91-115.

Lyman, S. M. (1982a). Stewart Culin: The earliest American Chinatown studies and a hypothesis about pre-Columbian migration. *Annual Bulletin of the Research Institute for Social Science* (Ryukoku University, Kyoto, Japan), *12*, 142-162.

Lyman, S. M. (1982b). Two neglected pioneers of civilizational analysis: The cultural perspectives of R. Stewart Culin and Frank Hamilton Cushing. *Social Research, 44*, 690-729.

Lyman, S. M. (1986). *Chinatown and Little Tokyo: Power, conflict and community among Chinese and Japanese immigrants in America.* Millwood, NJ: Associated Faculty.

Lyman, S. M. (1990a). Asian American contacts before Columbus: Alternative understandings for civilization, acculturation, and ethnic minority status in America. In S. M. Lyman, *Civilization: Contents, discontents, malcontents and other essays in social theory.* Fayetteville: University of Arkansas Press.

Lyman, S. M. (1990b). *Civilization: Contents, discontents, malcontents and other essays in social theory.* Fayetteville: University of Arkansas Press.

Lyman, S. M. (1992a). The assimilation-pluralism debate: Toward a postmodern resolution of the American ethnoracial dilemma. *International Journal of Politics, Culture and Society, 6*, 181-210.

Lyman, S. M. (1992b). *Militarism, imperialism and racial accommodation: An analysis and interpretation of the early writings of Robert E. Park.* Fayetteville: University of Arkansas Press.

Lyman, S. M., & Scott, M. B. (1967). Territoriality: A neglected sociological dimension. *Social Problems, 15*, 236-248.

Lyman, S. M., & Scott, M. B. (1989). *A sociology of the absurd* (2nd ed.). Dix Hills, NY: General Hall.

Lynd, R. S., & Lynd, H. M. (1937). *Middletown in transition: A study in cultural conflicts.* New York: Harcourt, Brace.

Lynd, R. S., & Lynd, H. M. (1956). *Middletown: A study in modern American culture.* New York: Harcourt, Brace. (Original work published 1929)

Lyon, L. (1987). *The community in urban society.* Chicago: Dorsey.

Lyotard, J.-F. (1989). The sign of history. In A. Benjamin (Ed.), *The Lyotard reader* (pp. 393-411). Cambridge, MA: Blackwell.

Lyotard, J.-F. (1990). *Heidegger and "the Jews"* (A. Michel & M. Roberts, Trans.). Minneapolis: University of Minnesota Press.

Manganaro, M. (1990). Textual play, power, and cultural critique: An orientation to modernist anthropology. In M. Manganaro (Ed.), *Modern anthropology: From fieldwork to text* (pp. 3-47). Princeton, NJ: Princeton University Press.

Mangiafico, L. (1988). *Contemporary American immigrants: Patterns of Filipino, Korean, and Chinese settlement in the United States.* New York: Praeger.

Manning, P. K. (1987). *Semiotics and fieldwork.* Newbury Park, CA: Sage.

Manning, P. K. (1991). Analytic induction. In K. Plummer (Ed.), *Symbolic interactionism: Vol. 2. Contemporary issues* (pp. 401-430). Brookfield, VT: Edward Elgar. (Reprinted from *Qualitative methods,* by R. Smith & P. K. Manning, Eds., 1982, Cambridge, MA: Ballinger)

Marable, M. (1983). *How capitalism underdeveloped black America: Problems in race, political economy, and society.* Boston: South End.

Marcus, G. E. (1986). Contemporary problems of ethnography in the modern world system. In J. Clifford & G. E. Marcus (Eds.), *Writing culture: The poetics and politics of ethnography* (pp. 165-193). Berkeley: University of California Press.

Martin, C. (Ed.). (1987). *The American Indian and the problem of history.* New York: Oxford University Press.

Marty, M. E. (1992). Foreword. In Bartolome de Las Casas, *In defense of the Indians: The defense of the most reverend Lord, Don Fray Bartolome de Las Casas, of the Order of Preachers, late Bishop of Chiapa, against the persecutors and slanderers of the peoples of the New World discovered across the seas* (C. M. S. Poole, Ed. & Trans.). De Kalb: Northern Illinois University Press. (Original work published 1552)

Masuoka, J. (1946). Race relations and Nisei problems. *Sociology and Social Research, 30,* 452-459.

Maunier, R. (1949). *The sociology of colonies: An introduction to the study of race contact* (E. O. Lorimer, Ed. & Trans.; Vols. 1-2). London: Routledge & Kegan Paul.

McCluer, F. L. (1928). *Living conditions among wage-earning families in forty-one blocks in Chicago.* Unpublished doctoral dissertation, University of Chicago.

McClymer, J. F. (1980). *War and welfare: Social engineering in America, 1890-1925.* Westport, CT: Greenwood.

McGee, W. J. (1971). *The Seri Indians of Bahia Kino and Sonora, Mexico* (Seventeenth Annual Report of the Bureau of American Ethnology to the Secretary of the Smithsonian Institution, 1895-1896, part 1). Glorieta, NM: Rio Grande. (Original work published 1899)

McKenney, T. L., & Hall, J. (1972). *The Indian Tribes of North America—with biographical sketches and anecdotes of the principal chiefs* (Vols. 1-3). Totowa, NJ: Rowman & Littlefield. (Original work published 1836)

McKenzie, R. D. (1968). *On human ecology: Selected writings* (A. H. Hawley, Ed.). Chicago: University of Chicago Press.

McKinney, J. C., in collaboration with Loomis, C. P. (1957). The application of *Gemeinschaft* and *Gesellschaft* as related to other typologies. In F. Tönnies, *Community and society (Gemeinschaft und Gesellschaft)* (C. P. Loomis, Ed. & Trans.; pp. 12-29). East Lansing: Michigan State University Press.

Mead, M. (1960a). *Coming of age in Samoa: A psychological study of primitive youth for Western civilization.* New York: Mentor. (Original work published 1928)

Mead, M. (1960b). *Growing up in New Guinea: A comparative study of primitive education.* New York: Mentor. (Original work published 1930)

Mead, M. (1960c). *Male and female: A study of the sexes in a changing world.* New York: Mentor. (Original work published 1949)

Mead, M. (1960d). *Sex and temperament in three primitive societies.* New York: Mentor. (Original work published 1935)

Mead, M. (1975). *New lives for old: Cultural transformation—Manau, 1928-1953.* New York: William Morrow. (Original work published 1956)

Messenger, P. M. (Ed.). (1991). *The ethics of collecting cultural property: Whose culture? Whose property?* Albuquerque: University of New Mexico Press.

Miller, J. (1993). *The passion of Michel Foucault.* New York: Simon & Schuster.

Milner, C. A., II, & O'Neil, F. A. (Eds.). (1985). *Churchmen and the Western Indians, 1820-1920.* Norman: University of Oklahoma Press.

Milson, K. (1991-1992). (En)countering imperialist nostalgia: The Indian reburial issue. *Discourse: Journal for Theoretical Studies in Media and Culture, 14,* 58-74.

Miner, H. (1952). The folk-urban continuum. *American Sociological Review, 17,* 529-537.

Minnich, E. K. (1990). *Transforming knowledge.* Philadelphia: Temple University Press.

Montagu, A. (Ed.). (1968). The concept of the primitive. New York: Free Press.

Morgan, G. (Ed.). (1983). *Beyond method: Strategies for social research.* Beverly Hills, CA: Sage.

Morgan, L. H. (1964). *Ancient society* (L. White, Ed.). Cambridge, MA: Belknap.

Moorhouse, G. (1988). *Imperial city: New York.* New York: Henry Holt.

Murdock, G. P. (1965). *Social structure.* New York: Free Press. (Original work published 1949)

Murdock, G. P. (1934). *Our primitive contemporaries.* New York: Macmillan.

A museum is set to part with its Indian treasures. (1993, February 19). *New York Times,* p. A12.

Myer, D. S. (1971). *Uprooted Americans: The Japanese Americans and the War Relocation Authority during World War II.* Tucson: University of Arizona Press.

Nader, L. (1972). Up the anthropologist: Perspectives gained from studying up. In D.

Hymes (Ed.), *Reinventing anthropology* (pp. 284-311). New York: Pantheon.

Natanson, M. (1962). History as a finite province of meaning. In H. Natanson, *Literature, philosophy and the social sciences: Essays in existentialism and phenomenology* (pp. 172-178). The Hague: Martinus Nijhoff.

Nelli, H. S. (1970). *The Italians in Chicago, 1880-1930*. New York: Oxford University Press.

Neske, G., & Kettering, E. (1990). *Martin Heidegger and National Socialism: Questions and answers* (L. Harries & J. Neugroschel, Trans.). New York: Paragon House.

Nikolinakos, D. D. (1990). Foucault's ethical quandary. *Telos, 23*, 123-140.

Nisbet, R. A. (1969). *Social change and history: Aspects of the Western theory of development*. New York: Oxford University Press.

Nisbet, R. A. (1972). Ethnocentrism and the comparative method. In A. R. Desai (Ed.), *Essays on modernization of underdeveloped societies* (Vol. 1, pp. 95-114). New York: Humanities Press.

Nisbet, R. A. (1977). *Sociology as an art form*. New York: Oxford University Press.

Nisbet, R. A. (1986). Developmentalism: A critical analysis. In R. A. Nisbet, *The making of modern society* (pp. 33-69). New York: New York University Press.

Nomura, G. M., et al. (Eds.). (1989). *Frontiers of Asian American studies: Writing, research and commentary*. Pullman: Washington State University Press.

Nordenskiold, G. (1979). *The cliff dwellers of the Mesa Verde* (O. L. Morgan, Trans.). Glorieta, NM: Rio Grande. (Original work published 1893)

Norris, C. (1990). Lost in the funhouse: Baudrillard and the politics of postmodernism. In R. Boyne & A. Rattansi (Eds.), *Postmodernism and society* (pp. 119-153). New York: St. Martin's.

Novak, M. (1972). *The rise of the unmeltable ethnics: Politics and culture in the seventies*. New York: Macmillan.

Novak, M. (1980). Pluralism: A humanistic perspective. In S. Thernstrom (Ed.), *Harvard encyclopedia of American ethnic groups* (pp. 772-781). Cambridge, MA: Harvard University Press.

Numbers, R. (1992). *The creationists: The evolution of scientific creationism*. New York: Alfred A. Knopf.

Oakes, K. B. (1938). *Social theory in the early literature of voyage and exploration in Africa*. Unpublished doctoral dissertation, University of California, Berkeley.

Officer, J. E. (1987). *Hispanic Arizona, 1536-1856*. Tucson: University of Arizona Press.

Okihiro, G. Y. (1988). The idea of community and a "particular type of history." In G. Y. Okihiro et al. (Eds.), *Reflections on shattered windows: Promises and prospects for Asian American studies* (pp. 175-183). Pullman: Washington State University Press.

Okihiro, G. Y., et al. (Eds.). (1988). *Reflections on shattered windows: Promises and prospects for Asian American studies*. Pullman: Washington State University Press.

Olivier, S. (1970). The government of colonies and dependencies. In G. Spiller (Ed.), *Papers on inter-racial problems communicated to the First Universal Race Congress, University of London, July 26-29, 1911* (pp. 293-312). New York: Citadel. (Original work published 1911)

Padilla, F. M. (1985). *Latino ethnic consciousness: The case of Mexican Americans and Puerto Ricans in Chicago*. Notre Dame, IN: University of Notre Dame Press.

Paglia, C. (1991). Junk bonds and corporate raiders: Academe in the hour of the wolf. *Arion: A Journal of Humanities and the Classics* (third series), *1*(2), 139-212.

Park, R. E. (1952a). *The collected papers of Robert Ezra Park: Vol. 2. Human communities: The city and human ecology* (E. C. Hughes et al., Eds.). Glencoe, IL: Free Press.

Park, R. E. (1952b). Community organization and the romantic temper. In R. E. Park, *The collected papers of Robert Ezra Park: Vol. 2. Human communities: The city and human ecology* (E. C. Hughes et al., Eds.; pp. 64-72). Glencoe, IL: Free Press.

Park, R. E. (1952c). Magic, mentality and city life. In R. E. Park, *The collected papers of Robert Ezra Park: Vol. 2. Human communities: The city and human ecology* (E. C. Hughes et al., Eds.; pp. 102-117). Glencoe, IL: Free Press.

Park, R. E. (1967). The city: Suggestions for the investigation of human behavior in the urban environment. In R. E. Park, E. W. Burgess, & R. D. McKenzie (Eds.), *The city* (pp. 1-46). Chicago: University of Chicago Press. (Original work published 1925)

Park, R. E. (1969a). Human migration and the marginal man. In E. W. Burgess (Ed.), *Personality and the social group* (pp. 64-77). Freeport, NY: Books for Libraries Press. (Original work published 1929)

Park, R. E. (1969b). Introduction. In R. Adams, *Interracial marriage in Hawaii: A study of mutually conditioned responses to acculturation and amalgamation* (pp. xiii-xiv). Montclair, NJ: Patterson Smith. (Original work published 1937)

Park, R. E. (1971). *The immigrant press and its control: The acculturation of immigrant groups into American society.* Montclair, NJ: Patterson Smith. (Original work published 1922)

Parsons, T. (1949). *The structure of social action: A study on social theory with special reference to a group of recent European writers.* Glencoe, IL: Free Press. (Original work published 1937)

Parsons, T. (1966). *Societies: Evolutionary and comparative perspectives.* Englewood Cliffs, NJ: Prentice Hall.

Parsons, T. (1971). *The system of modern societies.* Englewood Cliffs, NJ: Prentice Hall.

Parsons, T. (1973). Some afterthoughts on *Gemeinschaft* and *Gesellschaft.* In W. J. Cahnman (Ed.), *Ferdinand Tönnies: A new evaluation* (pp. 140-150). Leiden, Netherlands: E. J. Brill.

Patterson, O. (1982). *Slavery and social death: A comparative study.* Cambridge, MA: Harvard University Press.

Patterson, O. (1991). *Freedom: Vol. 1. Freedom in the making of Western culture.* New York: Basic Books.

Peacock, J. L. (1986). *The anthropological lens: Harsh lights, soft focus.* Cambridge: Cambridge University Press.

Pike, K. (1967). *Language in relation to a unified theory of the structure of human behaviour.* The Hague: Mouton.

Pool, I. de S. (Ed.). (1981). *The social impact of the telephone.* Cambridge: MIT Press.

Poster, M. (1987-1988). Foucault, the present and history. *Cultural Critique, 8,* 105-121.

Pratt, M. L. (1986). Fieldwork in common places. In J. Clifford & G. E. Marcus (Eds.), *Writing culture: The poetics and politics of ethnography.* Berkeley: University of California Press.

Quandt, J. B. (1970). *From the small town to the great community: The social thought of the progressive intellectuals.* New Brunswick, NJ: Rutgers University Press.

Rabinow, P., & Sullivan, W. M. (Eds.). (1979). *Interpretive social science: A reader.* Berkeley: University of California Press.

Radin, P. (1927). *The story of the American Indian.* New York: Boni & Liveright.

Radin, P. (1957a). *Primitive man as philosopher.* New York: Dover. (Original work published 1927)

Radin, P. (1957b). *Primitive religion: Its nature and origin.* New York: Dover. (Original work published 1937)

Radin, P. (1963). *The autobiography of a Winnebago Indian: Life, ways, acculturation, and the peyote cult.* New York: Dover. (Original work published 1920)

Radin, P. (1966). *The method and theory of ethnology: An essay in criticism.* New York: Basic Books. (Original work published 1933)

Radin, P. (1970). *The Italians of San Francisco: Their adjustment and acculturation.* San Francisco: R&E Research Associates. (Original work published 1935)

Radin, P. (Ed.). (1971a). *The golden mountain: Chinese tales told in California, collected by Jon Lee.* Taipei: Caves. (Original work published 1936)

Radin, P. (1971b). *The world of primitive man.* New York: Dutton. (Original work published 1953)

Radin, P. (1973). *The Winnebago tribe.* Lincoln: University of Nebraska Press. (Original work published 1923)

Radin, P. (1976). *The trickster: A study in American Indian mythology.* New York: Schocken. (Original work published 1956)

Rae, J. B. (1965). *The American automobile: A brief history.* Chicago: University of Chicago Press.

Ratzel, F. (1988). *Sketches of urban and cultural life in North America* (S. A. Stehlin, Ed. & Trans.). New Brunswick, NJ: Rutgers University Press. (Original work published 1876)

Redfield, J. (1991). Classics and anthropology. *Arion: A Journal of Humanities and the Classics* (third series), *1*(2), 5-23.

Redfield, R. (1928). *A plan for the study of Tepoztlan, Mexico.* Unpublished doctoral dissertation, University of Chicago.

Redfield, R. (1930). *Tepoztlan—A Mexican village: A study of folk life.* Chicago: University of Chicago Press.

Redfield, R. (1941). *The folk culture of Yucatan.* Chicago: University of Chicago Press.

Redfield, R. (1960). *The little community and peasant society and culture.* Chicago: University of Chicago Press.

Redfield, R. (1962a). The folk society and civilization. In M. P. Redfield (Ed.), *The papers of Robert Redfield: Vol. 1. Human nature and the study of society.* Chicago: University of Chicago Press.

Redfield, R. (1962b). *A village that chose progress: Chan Kom revisited.* Chicago: University of Chicago Press. (Original work published 1950)

Redfield, R. (1963). Talk with a stranger. In M. P. Redfield (Ed.), *The papers of Robert Redfield: Vol. 2. The social uses of social science* (pp. 270-284). Chicago: University of Chicago Press.

Redfield, R., & Rojas, A. V. (1962). *Chan Kom: A Maya village.* Chicago: University of Chicago Press. (Original work published 1934)

Redfield, R., & Singer, M. B. (1973). The cultural role of the cities: Orthogenetic and heterogenetic change. In G. Germani (Ed.), *Modernization, urbanization, and the urban crisis* (pp. 61-71). Boston: Little, Brown.

Reid, D. (Ed.). (1992). *Sex, death and God in L.A.* New York: Pantheon.

Reuter, E. B. (1969). *The mulatto in the United States: Including a study of the role of mixed-blood races throughout the world.* New York: Negro Universities Press. (Original work published 1918)

Rivers, W. H. R. (1974). The psychological factor. In A. Montagu (Ed.), *Frontiers of anthropology* (pp. 391-409). New York: G. P. Putnam's Sons. (Reprinted from *Essays on the depopulation of Melanesia,* by W. H. R. Rivers, Ed., 1922, Cambridge: Cambridge University Press)

Rockmore, T. (1992). *On Heidegger's Nazism and philosophy.* Berkeley: University of California Press.

Roper, M. W. (1935). *The city and the primary group.* Unpublished doctoral dissertation, University of Chicago.

Rorty, R. (1982). *Consequences of pragmatism: Essays, 1972-1980.* Minneapolis: University of Minnesota Press.

Rorty, R. (1989). *Contingency, irony and solidarity.* Cambridge: Cambridge University Press.

Rose, A. (Ed.). (1988). *Universal abandon? The politics of postmodernism.* Minneapolis: University of Minnesota Press.

Rose, D. (1989). *Patterns of American culture: Ethnography and estrangement.* Philadelphia: University of Pennsylvania Press.

Rosenau, P. M. (1992). *Post-modernism and the social sciences: Insights, inroads, and intrusions.* Princeton, NJ: Princeton University Press.

Ross, R. H., & Bogardus, E. S. (1940). The third generation race relations cycle: A study in Issei-Nisei relationships. *Sociology and Social Research, 24,* 357-363.

Rossi, P. (1987). *The dark abyss of time: The history of the earth and the history of nations from Hooke to Vico* (L. G. Cochrane, Trans.). Chicago: University of Chicago Press.

Rouse, I. (1992). *The Tainos: Rise and decline of the people who greeted Columbus.* New Haven, CT: Yale University Press.

Royce, P. (1982). *Ethnic identity: Strategies of diversity.* Bloomington: Indiana University Press.

Rubel, A. J. (1971). *Across the tracks: Mexican Americans in a Texas city.* Austin: University of Texas Press.

Sachs, W. (1947). *Black anger.* New York: Grove.

Sadri, A. (1992). *Max Weber's sociology of intellectuals.* New York: Oxford University Press.

Salmond, A. (1991). *Two worlds: First meetings between Maori and Europeans, 1642-1772.* Honolulu: University of Hawaii Press.

Sanchez, G. S. (1967). *Forgotten people: A study of New Mexicans.* Albuquerque: Calvin Horn.

Sanderson, S. K. (1990). *Social evolutionism: A critical history.* Cambridge, MA: Blackwell.

Sando, J. S. (1992). *Pueblo nations: Eight centuries of Pueblo Indian history.* Santa Fe, NM: Clear Light.

Sarana, G. (1975). *The methodology of anthropological comparison: An analysis of comparative methods in social and cultural anthropology.* Tucson: University of Arizona Press.

Saxton, S. L. (1993). Sociologist as citizen-scholar: A symbolic interactionist alternative to normal sociology. In T. R. Vaughan, G. Sjoberg, & L. J. Reynolds (Eds.). *A critique of contemporary American sociology* (pp. 232-251). Dix Hills, NY: General Hall.

Schatzman, L., & Strauss, A. L. (1973). *Field research: Strategies for a natural sociology.* Englewood Cliffs, NJ: Prentice Hall.

Schietinger, E. F. (1967). Racial succession and changing property values in residential Chicago. In E. W. Burgess & D. J. Bogue (Eds.), *Contributions to urban sociology* (pp. 86-99). Chicago: University of Chicago Press.

Schlesinger, A. M., Jr. (1991). *The disuniting of America: Reflections on a multicultural society.* Knoxville, TN: Whittle.

Schoolcraft, H. R. (1975). *Personal memoirs of a residence of thirty years with the Indian tribes of the American frontiers, with brief notices of passing events, facts and opinions, A.D. 1812 to A.D. 1842.* New York: Arno. (Original work published 1851)

Schrag, P. (1970). *The decline of the WASP.* New York: Simon & Schuster.

Schrag, P. (1973). *The end of the American future.* New York: Simon & Schuster.

Schwatka, F. (1977). *In the land of cave and cliff dwellers.* Glorieta, NM: Rio Grande. (Original work published 1893)

Sheets-Johnstone, M. (1990). *The roots of thinking.* Philadelphia: Temple University Press.

Sheets-Johnstone, M. (Ed.). (1992). *Giving the body its due.* Albany: State University of New York Press.

Sheridan, T. E. (1986). *Los Tucsonenses: The Mexican community in Tucson, 1854-1941.* Tucson: University of Arizona Press.

Shibutani, T., & Kwan, K. M.(1965). *Ethnic stratification: A comparative approach.* New York: Macmillan.

Simmel, G. (1950). The stranger. In G. Simmel, *The sociology of Georg Simmel* (K. H. Wolff, Ed. & Trans.; pp. 402-408). Glencoe, IL: Free Press.

Simmel, G. (1968). *The conflict in modern culture and other essays* (K. P. Etzkorn, Ed. & Trans.). New York: Teachers College Press.

Siu, P. C. P. (1987). *The Chinese laundrymen: A study of social isolation* (J. K. W. Tchen, Ed.). New York: New York University Press.

Smith, A. D. (1989). *The ethnic origin of nations.* New York: Blackwell.

Smith, C. W. (1979). *A critique of sociological reasoning: An essay in philosophical sociology.* Oxford: Blackwell.

Smith, M. G. (1965). *The plural society in the British West Indies.* Berkeley: University of California.

Smith, M. P. (1979). *The city and social theory.* New York: St. Martin's.

Solzhenitsyn, A. (1993, February 7). The relentless cult of novelty and how it wrecked the century. *New York Times Book Review,* p. 3.

Sorokin, P. (1965). *Fads and foibles in modern sociology and related sciences.* Chicago: Henry Regnery-Gateway.

Spicer, E. A., Hansen, A. T., Luomala, K., & Opler, M. K. (1969). *Impounded people: Japanese-Americans in the relocation centers.* Tucson: University of Arizona Press.

Spier, L. (1978). *Yuman tribes of the Gila River.* New York: Dover. (Original work published 1933)

Spretnak, C. (1991). *States of grace: The recovery of meaning in the postmodern age.* New York: HarperCollins.

Statler, O. (1983). *Japanese pilgrimage.* New York: William Morrow.

Stein, M. (1964). The eclipse of community: Some glances at the education of a sociologist. In A. J. Vidich, J. Bensman, & M. Stein (Eds.), *Reflections on community studies.* New York: John Wiley.

Steinberg, S. (1981). *The ethnic myth: Race, ethnicity, and class in America.* New York: Atheneum.

Stocking, G. W., Jr. (Ed.). (1983). *Observers observed: Essays on ethnographic field work.* Madison: University of Wisconsin Press.

Stocking, G. W., Jr. (Ed.). (1984). *Functionalism historicized: Essays on British social anthropology.* Madison: University of Wisconsin Press.

Stocking, G. W., Jr. (Ed.). (1985). *Objects and others: Essays on museums and material culture.* Madison: University of Wisconsin Press.

Stocking, G. W., Jr. (Ed.). (1986). *Malinowski, Rivers, Benedict and others: Essays on culture and personality.* Madison: University of Wisconsin Press.

Stocking, G. W., Jr. (Ed.). (1988). *Bones, bodies, behavior: Essays on biological anthropology.* Madison: University of Wisconsin Press.

Stocking, G. W., Jr. (Ed.). (1989). *Romantic motives: Essays on anthropological sensibility*. Madison: University of Wisconsin Press.

Stocking, G. W., Jr. (Ed.). (1991). *Colonial situations: Essays on the contextualization of ethnographic knowledge*. Madison: University of Wisconsin Press.

Stone, R. W. (1921). *The origin of the survey movement*. Unpublished doctoral dissertation, University of Chicago.

Stonequist, E. V. (1961). *The marginal man: A study in personality and culture conflict*. New York: Russell & Russell. (Original work published 1937)

Strathern, M. (1990). Out of context: The persuasive fictions of anthropology, with comments by I. C. Jarvie, Stephen A. Tyler and George E. Marcus. In M. Manganaro (Ed.), *Modern anthropology: From fieldwork to text* (pp. 80-130). Princeton, NJ: Princeton University Press.

Street corner society revisited [Special issue]. (1992). *Journal of Contemporary Ethnography, 21*(1), 3-132.

Sumner, W. G. (1940). *Folkways: A study of the sociological importance of usages, manners, customs, mores, and morals*. Boston: Ginn. (Original work published 1906)

Sumner, W. G. (1969). Foreword. In J. E. Cutler, *Lynch-law: An investigation into the history of lynching in the United States* (p. v). Montclair, NJ: Patterson Smith. (Original work published 1905)

Suret-Canale, J. (1988a). The end of chieftancy in Guinea. In J. Suret-Canale, *Essays on African history: From the slave trade to neocolonialism* (C. Hurst, Trans.). Trenton, NJ: Africa World.

Suret-Canale, J. (1988b). Guinea in the colonial system. In J. Suret-Canale, *Essays on African history: From the slave trade to neocolonialism* (C. Hurst, Trans.). Trenton, NJ: Africa World.

Suttles, G. D. (1972). *The social construction of communities*. Chicago: University of Chicago Press.

Symposium on qualitative methods. (1993). *Contemporary Sociology, 22,* 1-15.

Takaki, R. (1989). *Strangers from a different shore: A history of Asian Americans*. New York: Penguin.

Taylor, C. (1989). *Sources of the self: The making of modern identity*. Cambridge, MA: Harvard University Press.

Taylor, P. S. (1970). *Mexican labor in the United States* (Vols. 1-2). New York: Arno/New York Times. (Original work published 1930)

Taylor, P. S. (1983). *On the ground in the thirties*. Salt Lake City: Peregrine Smith.

Tedlock, B. (1992). *The beautiful and the dangerous: Encounters with the Zuni Indians*. New York: Viking.

Teggart, F. J. (1941). *The theory and processes of history*. Berkeley: University of California Press.

Thernstrom, S. (Ed.). (1980). *Harvard encyclopedia of American ethnic groups*. Cambridge, MA: Harvard University Press.

Thomas, W. I., & Znaniecki, F. (1958). *The Polish peasant in Europe and America*. New York: Dover.

Thrasher, F. M. (1963). *The gang: A study of 1,313 gangs in Chicago*. Chicago: University of Chicago Press. (Original work published 1927)

Thucydides. (1972). *History of the Peloponnesian War* (R. Warner, Trans.). Harmondsworth: Penguin.

Tilman, R. (1991). *Thorstein Veblen and his critics, 1891-1963*. Princeton, NJ: Princeton University Press.

Tinder, G. (1980). *Community: Reflections on a tragic ideal*. Baton Rouge: Louisiana State University Press.

Tobias, H. J. (1990). *A history of the Jews in New Mexico*. Albuquerque: University of New Mexico Press.

Todorov, T. (1984). *The conquest of America* (R. Howard, Trans.). New York: Harper & Row.

Toland, J. D. (Ed.). (1993). *Ethnicity and the state*. New Brunswick, NJ: Transaction.

Tönnies, F. (1957). *Community and society (Gemeinschaft und Gesellschaft)* (C. P. Loomis, Ed. & Trans.). East Lansing: Michigan State University Press. (Original work published 1887)

Torgovnick, M. (1990). *Gone primitive: Savage intellects, modern lives*. Chicago: University of Chicago Press.

Tricarico, D. (1984). *The Italians of Greenwich Village: The social structure and transformation of an ethnic community*. Staten Island, NY: Center for Migration Studies of New York.

Trinh T. M. (1991). *When the moon waxes red: Representation, gender and cultural politics*. New York: Routledge.

Trinkhouse, E., & Shipman, P. (1993). *The Neanderthals: Changing the image of mankind*. New York: Alfred A. Knopf.

Turner, V. (1992). African ritual and Western literature: Is a comparative symbology possible? In V. Turner, *Blazing the trail: Way marks in the exploration of symbols* (E. Turner, Ed.; pp. 66-88). Tucson: University of Arizona Press.

Van Maanen, J. (1988). *Tales of the field: On writing ethnography*. Chicago: University of Chicago Press.

Vaughan, A. T. (1965). *New England frontier: Puritans and Indians, 1620-1675*. Boston: Little, Brown.

Vaughan, T. R. (1993). The crisis in contemporary American sociology: A critique of the discipline's dominant paradigm. In T. R. Vaughan, G. Sjoberg, & L. J. Reynolds (Eds.), *A critique of contemporary American sociology*. Dix Hills, NY: General Hall.

Veblen, T. (1959). *The theory of the leisure class*. New York: Mentor. (Original work published 1899)

Veblen, T. (1961a). The blond race and the Aryan culture. In T. Veblen, *The place of science in modern civilization and other essays*. New York: Russell & Russell. (Original work published 1919)

Veblen, T. (1961b). The mutation theory and the blond race. In T. Veblen, *The place of science in modern civilization and other essays*. New York: Russell & Russell. (Original work published 1919)

Veblen, T. (1965). *The higher learning in America: A memorandum on the conduct of universities by businessmen*. New York: Augustus M. Kelley. (Original work published 1918)

Veblen, T. (1990). *The instinct of workmanship and the state of the industrial arts*. New Brunswick, NJ: Transaction. (Original work published 1914)

Vidich, A. J. (1952). *The political impact of colonial administration*. Unpublished doctoral dissertation, Harvard University, Boston.

Vidich, A. J. (1955). Participant observation and the collection and interpretation of data. *American Journal of Sociology, 60*, 335-360.

Vidich, A. J. (1966). Introduction. In P. Radin, *The method and theory of ethnology: An essay in criticism* (pp. vii-cxv). New York: Basic Books.

Vidich, A. J. (1980). *The political impact of colonial administration*. New York: Arno.

Vidich, A. J. (1986). *Anthropology and truth: Some old problems*. Paper presented at the annual meeting of the American Anthropological Society, Philadelphia.

Vidich, A. J., & Bensman, J. (1968). *Small town in mass society: Class, power and religion in a rural community* (2nd ed.). Princeton, NJ: Princeton University Press.

Vidich, A. J., & Lyman, S. M. (1985). *American sociology: Worldly rejections of religion and their directions*. New Haven, CT: Yale University Press.

Vidich, A. J., Lyman, S. M., & Goldfarb, J. C. (1981). Sociology and society: Disciplinary tensions and professional compromises. *Social Research, 48*, 322-361.

Vigil, J. D. (1980). *From Indians to Chicanos: The dynamics of Mexican American culture*. Prospect Heights, IL: Waveland.

von Gierke, O. (1990). *Community in historical perspective: A translation of selections from Das Deutsche Genossenschaftsrecht (the German law of fellowship)* (A. Black, Ed.; M. Fischer, Trans.). Cambridge: Cambridge University Press. (Original work published 1868)

Wallace, A. F. C. (1987). *St. Clair: A nineteenth-century coal town's experience with a disaster-prone industry*. New York: Alfred A. Knopf.

Walzer, M. (1980). Pluralism: A political perspective. In S. Thernstrom (Ed.), *Harvard encyclopedia of American ethnic groups* (pp. 781-787). Cambridge, MA: Harvard University Press.

Ware, C. (1965). *Greenwich Village, 1920-1930: A comment on American civilization in the post-war years*. New York: Harper Colophon. (Original work published 1935)

Warren, R. L. (1963). *The community in America*. Chicago: Rand McNally.

Warren, R. L. (1972). *The community in America* (2nd ed.). Chicago: Rand McNally.

Waters, M. C. (1990). *Ethnic options: Choosing identities in America*. Berkeley: University of California Press.

Wax, R. H. (1971). *Doing fieldwork: Warnings and advice*. Chicago: University of Chicago Press.

Weber, A. F. (1967). *The growth of cities in the nineteenth century: A study in statistics*. Ithaca, NY: Cornell University Press. (Original work published 1899)

Weber, D. J. (1992). *The Spanish frontier in North America*. New Haven, CT: Yale University Press.

Weinstein, D., & Weinstein, M. A. (1990). Dimensions of conflict: Georg Simmel on modern life. In M. Kaern, B. H. Phillips, & R. S. Cohen (Eds.), *Georg Simmel and contemporary sociology* (pp. 341-356). Dordrecht, Netherlands: Kluwer.

Weinstein, D., & Weinstein, M. A. (1991). Simmel and the theory of postmodern society. In B. S. Turner (Ed.), *Theories of modernity and postmodernity* (pp. 75-87). London: Sage.

West, C. (1992). Diverse new world. In P. Berman (Ed.), *Debating P.C.: The controversy over political correctness on college campuses* (pp. 326-332). New York: Dell.

White, L. A. (1974). *The A'Coma Indians: People of the sky city* (Forty-Seventh Annual Report of the Bureau of American Ethnology to the secretary of the Smithsonian Institution, 1929-1930). Glorieta, NM: Rio Grande. (Original work published 1933)

Williams, R. A., Jr. (1990). *The American Indian in Western legal thought: The discourses of conquest*. New York: Oxford University Press.

Williams, V. J., Jr. (1989). *From a caste to a minority: Changing attitudes of American sociologists toward Afro-Americans, 1896-1945*. Westport, CT: Greenwood.

Willis, W. S., Jr. (1972). Skeletons in the anthropological closet. In D. Hymes (Ed.), *Reinventing anthropology* (pp. 121-152). New York: Pantheon.

Wirth, L. (1938). Urbanism as a way of life. *American Journal of Sociology, 44*, 1-24.

Wirth, L. (1945). The problem of minority groups. In R. Linton (Ed.), *The science of man in the world crisis* (pp. 347-372). New York: Columbia University Press.

Wirth, L. (1956). *The ghetto*. Chicago: University of Chicago Press. (Original work published 1928)

Wissler, C. (1923). *Man and culture*. New York: Thomas Y. Crowell.

Wissler, C. (1956). Foreword. In R. S. Lynd & H. M. Lynd, *Middletown: A study in modern American culture*. New York: Harcourt, Brace. (Original work published 1929)

Wissler, C. (1966a). *Indians of the United States* (Rev. ed.). Garden City, NY: Doubleday. (Original work published 1940)

Wissler, C. (1966b). *Red man reservations*. New York: Collier. (Original work published 1938)

Wood, M. M. (1969). *The stranger: A study in social relationships*. New York: AMS. (Original work published 1934)

Woods, F. J. (1956). *Cultural values of American ethnic groups*. New York: Harper & Brothers.

Woods, F. J. (1972). *Marginality and identity: A colored Creole family through ten generations*. Baton Rouge: Louisiana State University Press.

Woods, R. A., & Kennedy, A. J. (1990). *The settlement horizon*. New Brunswick, NJ: Transaction. (Original work published 1922)

Wu, C. C. (1926). *Chinese immigration in the Pacific area*. Unpublished doctoral dissertation, University of Chicago.

Whyte, W. F. (1943a). *Street corner society: The social structure of an Italian slum*. Chicago: University of Chicago Press.

Whyte, W. F. (1943b). A slum sex code. *American Journal of Sociology, 49*, 24-31.

Whyte, W. F. (1955). *Street corner society: The social structure of an Italian slum* (2nd ed.). Chicago: University of Chicago Press.

Whyte, W. F. (1981). *Street corner society: The social structure of an Italian slum* (3rd ed.). Chicago: University of Chicago Press.

Zaner, R. M. (1981). *The context of self: A phenomenological inquiry using medicine as a clue*. Athens: Ohio University Press.

Zorbaugh, H. W. (1929). *The Gold Coast and the slum*. Chicago: University of Chicago Press.

Zorbaugh, H. W. (1968). The dweller in furnished rooms: An urban type. In E. W. Burgess (Ed.), *The urban community: Selected papers from the Proceedings of the American Sociological Society, 1925* (pp. 98-105). Westport, CT: Greenwood.

■ *Suggested Further Readings*

Appiah, K. A., & Gutman, A. (1996). *Color conscious: The political morality of race*. Princeton, NJ: Princeton University Press.

Bensman, J., & Lilienfeld, R. (1991). *Craft and consciousness: Occupational technique and the development of world images* (2nd ed.). New York: Aldine de Gruyter.

Denzin, N. K. (1997). *Interpretive ethnography: Ethnographic practices for the 21st century.* Thousand Oaks, CA: Sage.

Fine, M., Powell, L. C., Weis, L., & Wong, L. M. (Eds.). (1997). *Off white: Readings on race, power and society.* New York: Routledge.

Goldberg, D. T. (1997). *Racial subjects: Writing on race in America.* New York: Routledge.

Habermas, J. (1996). *Between facts and norms: Contributions to a discourse theory of law and democracy* (W. Rehg, Trans.). Cambridge: MIT Press.

Haraway, D. J. (1991). *Simians, cyborgs, and women: The reinvention of nature.* New York: Routledge.

Hutchinson, J., & Smith, A. D. (Eds.). (1996). *Ethnicity.* New York: Oxford University Press.

Lopez, I. F. H. (1996). *White by law: The legal construction of race.* New York: New York University Press.

Lyman, S. M. (1997). *Postmodernism and a sociology of the absurd and other essays on the "nouvelle vague" in American social science.* Fayetteville: University of Arkansas Press.

Min, P. G. (1996). *Caught in the middle: Korean communities in New York and Los Angeles.* Berkeley: University of California Press.

Oakes, G., & Vidich, A. J. (1999). *Collaboration, reputation, and ethics in American academic life: Hans H. Genth and C. Wright Mills.* Urbana: University of Illinois Press.

Radin, P. (1987). *The method and theory of ethnology.* South Hadley, MA: Bergin & Garvey. (Original work published 1933)

Salomon, A. (1963). Symbols and images in the constitution of society. In A. Salomon, *In praise of enlightenment* (pp. 237-260). Cleveland, OH: World.

Schutz, A. (1967). On multiple realities. In A. Schutz, *Collected papers* (M. Natanson, Ed. & Trans.; pp. 207-259). The Hague: Martinus Nijhoff.

Soja, E. W. (1990). *Postmodern geographies: The reassertion of space in critical social theory.* London: Verso.

Vidich, A. J., Bensman, J., & Stein, M. R. (Eds.). (1964). *Reflections on community studies.* New York: John Wiley.

Waldinger, R. (1996). *Still the promised city? African-Americans and new immigrants in postindustrial New York.* Cambridge, MA: Harvard University Press.

Weber, M. (1949). *The methodology of the social sciences* (E. Shils & H. Finch, Ed. & Trans.). Glencoe, IL: Free Press. (See especially "The Meaning of Ethical Neutrality in Sociology and Economics," pp. 1-49; and "Objectivity in Social Science and Social Policy," pp. 50-112.)

3

RECONSTRUCTING THE RELATIONSHIPS BETWEEN UNIVERSITIES AND SOCIETY THROUGH ACTION RESEARCH

◆ Davydd J. Greenwood and Morten Levin

Two sets of relationships form the core of this essay: those between theory and praxis in the social sciences and those between the university and society, particularly as they affect the academic social sciences.[1] To get at these, we argue in favor of action research as a critique of the premises of conventional academic social science, as a vehicle for changing some of the internal structures of universities, and as a way to enhance the relationships between academic social researchers and their broader constituencies beyond the university.

In making these arguments, we dispute a number of standard premises of academic discourse, among them the clarity of the widely used distinctions between applied and pure research and between quantitative and qualitative research in the social sciences. We argue that these dichotomies do not line up with each other and that, despite the value of these conceptual distinctions, they are insufficient as guiding concepts for the practice of social research.[2]

Our critique of academia is blunt and uncompromising. We make it so in the interest of clar-

AUTHORS' NOTE: This chapter is a synthesis and expansion of arguments developed in three other pieces of our writing: "Action Research, Science, and the Co-optation of Social Research" (Greenwood & Levin, 1998a), "The Reconstruction of Universities: Seeking a Different Integration Into Knowledge Development Processes" (Greenwood & Levin, 1998c), and *Introduction to Action Research: Social Research for Social Change* (Greenwood & Levin, 1998b).

ity, but we realize that the world is not as simple as the picture of it presented here. Some social scientists do integrate practice and theory effectively, some social scientists link up to extra-university constituencies effectively, some multidisciplinary projects and teams have succeeded in academia, and some social researchers envision a complex combination of quantitative and qualitative research as central to reform in the social sciences. Nevertheless, the bulk of university-based social research has a decidedly antipraxis orientation built deeply into the current structure of the academic social sciences, and this influences the mind-sets of university administrators. We believe that, despite the efforts of a growing group of praxis-oriented social researchers, there is little sense of urgency about changing existing arrangements in fundamental ways in most parts of the university system.[3]

Even if a reader agrees with our highly critical portrait of academic institutions and the social sciences, there is still plenty of room for disagreement about the action implications deriving from it. We know there are many good and committed people at work in other institutions who are making a difference with their publications, their teaching, and their pressures for university reform. However, we personally do not believe that this kind of necessary but modestly incremental reform effort alone is going to be sufficient to achieve the necessary transformations. In our view, the current situation is overdetermined by a powerful constellation of forces and will require a more systematic, confrontational, and transnational reform effort. For this reason, we seek to move to a more direct confrontation through our writing and work, even though we also keep working incrementally at our own institutions and through networks with many colleagues around the world. Our uncompromising critique makes ethical and political sense only if we believe that the situation can indeed be changed. We do, and thus we see the following as a contribution to a constructive social process and not a mere jeremiad.

We believe that different, vibrant universities could be built out of existing institutions and that they would have important social functions to play. It is not evident that any new institution could now take the place of universities in educating new cadres of critical, reflected, literate, and socially engaged youth, even if we think they are doing a poor job of it now. We are deeply concerned that critical and socially engaged research efforts are being undermined by autopoetic and self-referential academic activities in universities dominated by career opportunism and by students who are treated as imitators of their teachers rather than as original thinkers in the making. The current educational system privileges imitative students, not creative, critical, and analytic professionals with a broad and independent understanding of society at large. The core challenge for universities is to turn away from conventional lecturing to learning situations based on the search for solutions to real-life, open-ended problems.

Why is it proper for us to hold academic social researchers accountable to higher standards of social responsibility? For generations, academic social scientists have argued for public and private support of their disciplines and activities with the claim that their work is valuable to society at large. We need only look at the mission statements of most of the professional social science societies to see such justifications. In spite of this, the behavior of many academic social scientists reveals the center of their lives to be dialogues with their own disciplinary colleagues. This is how they are socialized professionally from the beginning of their university training in most institutions. As a result, they either show a lack of concern with the application of the results of their work or reject such application outright, arguing either that connections to the world beyond the university invade their intellectual autonomy or, if they are positivists, that such linkages threaten their "objectivity." In criticizing this behavior, we draw attention to the inconsistencies between the justificatory statements for the academic social sciences and the daily practices of members of these disciplines.

While we advocate action research as a promising way of moving the academic social sciences to socially meaningful missions, we do not base our claims for action research only on its putative moral superiority. Central to our argument is the claim that action research creates the valid knowledge, theoretical development, and social improvements that the conventional social sciences have promised. Action research does better what academic social science claims to do. Thus we advocate action research as a fruitful replacement for conventional social science practice in academia. The only alternative seems to be for the academic social sciences to continue on their current path while openly acknowledging that they have no obligation to play a useful social role, either because they simply do not wish to or because they are unable to imagine how their work could be applied. Obviously, such an admission would have both institutional and financial consequences, but at least it would clear up any remaining confusion.

◆ *The History of Universities*

To understand how the dilemmas of the social sciences in contemporary universities arose, we need to develop some common ground about the history of universities. The following discussion is brief and superficial, but it contains an essential component of our argument.

Our universities have a monastic origin, and they have specialized in being centers of higher learning, functions originally given by the Church to monasteries. Although, initially, universities were Church institutions that provided advanced training to the clergy, over time they became both Church- and state-supported institutions for training doctors, lawyers, notaries, engineers, and other secular professionals. The earliest European universities date from the 13th century (e.g., Bologna, Salamanca).

The form of the university most familiar to us today is mainly a Prussian invention whose architect and champion was Wilhelm von Humboldt (1767-1835). Although not a lonely culture hero, Humboldt articulated the design and logic of the university in an especially clear way. One important operating principle in Humboldt's restructuring of the university was the union of research and teaching. University faculties and students were to be able to both study and conduct research because university teaching was to be based on research rather than on untested doctrines. Humboldt's university curriculum included history, philosophy, classical languages, and political economy, crossing boundaries that were generally not bridgeable in the earlier universities.

In Humboldt's system, freedom of thought and inquiry were the central imperatives in university life, a point that is central to our argument. Free inquiry meant that research was not to be limited by theological and political constraints. To protect this, the Humboldtian university gave the collegial system the final say about what could be or could not be taught or written, rather than leaving those determinations to Church or political authorities. Colleagues, presumed to be well-informed and driven by the quest for knowledge (rather than by Church authorities or political leaders), were empowered to regulate each other's intellectual activities.

This kind of university was enormously successful, and these institutions quickly became Western society's most "advanced" knowledge centers. In a short time, the Humboldtian university model took nearly unlimited control over setting the curriculum, conducting research, and teaching society's elites. These social elites then became supporters of the university, and the university-elite relationship became strongly self-reinforcing (see, e.g., Bourdieu, 1988). The university became a key instrument for the creation of "citizens" (Readings, 1996) to manage and celebrate the nation-state.

The collegial system and its related peer review structures centered on an effort to gain intellectual freedom from the constraints of theological doctrine and political manipulation. Although addressing this problem was obviously important, the solution adopted has subsequently done much to weaken the social articulation of the university to all groups other than powerful elites.

One of the main goals of the collegiate system was to create an environment for free and self-directed research based on the preferences and abilities of individual or groups of researchers. This made the university research process somewhat independent of the Church and state but at the cost of making the construction of research agendas highly self-referential and autopoetic within academia.[4] With the topics of research and the decisions about the appropriate frameworks for research being made within the research community, research was encouraged but the connection between the research agenda and the needs or interests of many parts of society beyond the university was diminished.

Although this division occurred as a by-product of the effort to secure freedom of thought and research, this dynamic created an ongoing tension between universities and the larger society supporting them. Many universities use significant public resources to finance their teaching and research operations, either through direct support or through tax benefits. Not surprisingly, society at large occasionally thinks it should be getting a more useful return for its investment and the freedom it gives to the professoriate. This situation is predictable because the autopoetic research process provides important supports for intellectual freedom but simultaneously opens the door to useless research and academic careerism divorced from attention to important public social issues.

Of course, we know that the university is not nearly as independent from society as the ideal Humboldtian model suggests. The professoriate is drawn from society at large and lives in a specific social context, taking on issues and agendas that emerge from general social life, even if indirectly. And the students who come from beyond the university's boundaries have to be made interested in the subjects being taught within it and must emerge from it able to function in the larger society after graduation. Despite the often feigned indifference of much university research to the extra-academic world, the history of research issues and intellectual topics in universities tracks major social forces closely: wars, immigration, racism, changing gender roles, ethnic conflict, the arms race, information systems, and the like (see Chomsky et al., 1997).

Another influence arises from the sizable investment in universities made by governments and large corporations. These entities have long treated universities as socially valuable research sites and have allocated financial resources to sustain them. It is hardly surprising, then, that they also channel university research activities by using their control of funds to emphasize projects of interest to them. Governments and industry also control the regulatory environment in which universities operate, including auditing university accounts, setting the legal frameworks within which universities operate, and requiring evaluations of both the institutions themselves and the work they do. Various kinds of science foundations and other national funding agencies, as well as large public and private sector corporations and foundations, have the ability to focus research in universities by setting terms of reference for funding research.

None of this is surprising. What is interesting, however, is that one of the features of Western universities that most contemporary academics take for granted is really a peculiar compromise between public and private sector control of universities and the peer review system. In most Western countries, as Richard Lewontin (1997) points out, the powerful funders utilize the very peer review system created to guarantee the independence of university research as a mechanism to evaluate proposals and to allocate funds on a competitive basis among investigators and universities. Thus governments and industry set the research agenda and yet use academic researchers and their universities to compete with and to police each other in the process of acquiring and expending those funds, an odd situation that deserves to be understood better.

The peer review system, important as it is, certainly is not a source of unambiguous liberation. Within each discipline there are dominating paradigms and methods, key actors, and powerful schools (Freidson, 1985; Kuhn, 1962). Research proposals that do not match these paradigms will not receive funding, and so, under current conditions, the peer review system mainly guarantees that research will be kept fully under the control of the elite (and older) members of the academic professions.

This is a fascinating blend of two apparently contradictory organizational principles: external control and internal autonomy. The complexity of the proposal and review processes is one of the labyrinths that all successful academic researchers and university administrators know how to navigate well. A good deal of postgraduate training in universities centers on learning how to operate in this complicated system.

The role of defense-related money in science and engineering research at universities is well-known, but a good deal of non-defense-related money also flows to universities. All told, in the United States, universities now garner "about 60 percent of federal expenditures for basic research . . . 30 percent of applied research and . . . about 7 percent of development [funding]" (Lewontin, 1997, pp. 20-21). These monies are not distributed equally over the entire set of universities. For example, in the United States, the top 10 universities currently control 95% of federal research and development monies (Lewontin, 1997, p. 25).

In addition, most colleges and universities depend on the government and the private sector in other ways. Universities are either directly supported by national and state taxes or receive important tax benefits. In the United States, private sector foundations (also tax advantaged in the way they are created) and private donors receive tax benefits for contributing money to universities. Thus the relationships among universities, governments, and the private sector are close. The autopoetic role of the faculty in setting much of the research agenda is largely a fantasy. Where some freedom of action is created is through the internal redistributions made by university administrations of the overhead funding received by faculty members with large, externally supported research projects. Administrations can support particular disciplines that do not support themselves through the internal reallocation of monies earned by such research operations. However, such reallocation creates all kinds of internal tensions and animosities among highly entrepreneurial researchers and departments.

This obviously is a complex and contradictory situation. On the one hand, universities gain both legitimacy and money by conducting research on subjects emphasized by governments and other extra-university agencies. On the other, the peer review process imposes a competitive dynamic on this process in which researchers from other (often competing) universities and institutes evaluate the research proposals. Rivalries, issues of privacy of information, and the like are constantly in play in these processes. Successful academic research entrepreneurs have to be very savvy politically; they definitely are not the "babes in the woods" that public stereotypes of professors often evoke, nor are their deans, provosts, vice presidents, presidents, rectors, or chancellors.

Despite its complexity, the system generally functions smoothly, but there is evidence that this autopoetic form of academic capitalism is less and less able to satisfy the needs of major social groups. Expressions of dissatisfaction and hostility toward universities from students, their parents, the general public, the private sector, and the government are commonplace, and not just from political conservatives who are offended by the supposed "liberal" ideologies promoted at many universities. In addition to the sheer complexity of the combined entrepreneurial-autopoetic research university, we think that the disconnection of a number of constituencies from universities is a key element in this growing dissatisfaction. Especially disaffected are the less powerful members of society, as well as some of the private sector actors who have been a main source of support for universities in the past.

Community, Small-Scale, Minority, and Other Disempowered Problem Owners

Many groups do not have significant impacts on the focus of university research. Community members, small-scale organizations, minorities, and other powerless or poor people who want assistance with broad social change issues are looking for solutions to everyday problems in particular contexts: poverty, addiction, racism, environmental degradation, and so on. It does not matter to them whether one university has more government grants than another or ranks above another in the annual *Business Week* university ratings; their concern is whether they can get help in producing research that will assist in solving their problems. Significance tests, fat research résumés, and prestige in the eyes of other academics are not central to their interests—results are.

These social groups, belonging to the middle and low end of society's power spectrum, are poorly connected to universities and rarely influence university research agendas. Given the presence of other pressures on the direction of university research from the government and big private sector players, it is no surprise that socially relevant research is marginalized within universities. This means that the majority of people cannot look to universities for assistance with solutions to their most pressing problems. If they are lucky, they can send their children to a university and hope that they will be able to join the elite in this way, but they have learned that they generally cannot expect direct assistance from most academic researchers in solving their own problems.

In the United States, it has occurred to many such people that the protected tax status of universities and the allocation of tax monies to support these institutions is a public investment that does not benefit them enough, and they are increasingly conveying these feelings to their elected representatives in the form of a "value for the dollar" approach to the cost of their children's education. Of course, this kind of change is slow because these voters are not very high on elected legislators' lists of constituents to satisfy. Still, they do vote and they do pay tuition, and what they say is heard to some degree.

Large Businesses

Oddly enough, one of the most powerful supporters and beneficiaries of university work is also now moving into a more contradictory relationship with universities. The troubled link between universities and the corporate world might appear puzzling, given what we have said above. After all, the big funders set the main research agendas, and professional academic associations and publications support those agendas quite unreflectively. The private sector players discussed above further focus the agendas of university researchers, including hiring them as private consultants so that they earn nice salaries in addition to their academic pay.

Despite their still-powerful role in supporting scientific and engineering research in universities, there is evidence that major corporate actors, important national stakeholders in any capitalist society, are becoming disconnected from universities in key ways. Although money still flows into university research from these sources, many corporations are showing dissatisfaction with the kinds of training universities are providing to the people the corporations need to employ. Because gainful employment of graduates is a sine qua non of university success, this is an important issue.

We know that corporations invest great amounts of money in employee training programs. Some of this investment is a consequence of a highly competitive business climate, which demands ongoing learning within corporations as a condition for survival. For a period of time, universities controlled a significant part of the market for corporate training, either through campus programs or through paid consulting in corporate settings. Now larger corporations appear increasingly to seek sources of training on their own, rather than relying on universities to provide it. They either create their own training institutions or use consulting companies that specialize in corporate training.

These training efforts seem to have two quite different components. One involves the training of recent university graduates who have just been hired. Most corporate executives we know do not find the training of recent university graduates to be adequate. Whereas some corporate training is actually socialization into the "corporate cultures" of particular firms, some of it is used to make up for the lack of practical work experience in university curricula. Although the picture is mixed and some in-house corporate training is always likely, it is clear that corporations are also showing dissatisfaction with the training that current graduates have.

The other training component centers on in-service training for corporate personnel. Here it seems that universities are losing out to in-house corporate training centers (Eurich, 1985), consulting companies, and, in the United States, to community colleges. Thus the same major corporations that exercise important influence in the setting of national political priorities—which ultimately include government funding priorities for university research—now increasingly look to their own mechanisms and other organizations to provide the kinds of training that universities once monopolized.

Although none of these conditions by itself is fatal, the combination of forces suggests to us that there is trouble on the horizon for the university-business-government research connection. We must not forget that for businesses and the government, funding university research is mainly a practical proposition, not an act of charity or commitment to the life of the mind. Universities have received research funds primarily because of their infrastructures and cohorts of graduate students who can serve as low-cost researchers. These made universities cheap and efficient sites for research compared with private sector research institutions and government research units. Such research units are a very expensive proposition to create and maintain when they have to provide full-time employment and support to researchers. By contrast, universities have tuition, tax benefits, state and federal allocations, and endowment revenues to keep the doors open and have been able to afford to do private sector and government research at competitive prices as a result.

But in recent years, the increasingly complex administrative apparatus universities have developed to manage research processes and revenues has decreased the responsiveness of the university research system to immediate private sector and government interests. Many universities have created remarkably costly and inefficient administrative infrastructures to manage research. These employ many people and bloat research costs to the point that we think the movement of much private sector and government research money to cheaper and more entrepreneurial extra-university locations is likely, if not already well under way. Not surprisingly, entrepreneurial academic researchers are fully aware of this, and many of the private research organizations that are taking these research monies away from universities are also staffed by current or former university faculty members, who serve them as either paid consultants or full-time employees.[5]

This movement of research away from the core research structures of universities has been occurring for a while in the sciences and engineering. Now it is expanding rapidly into areas of organizational development, leadership training, group dynamics, program evaluation, and so on, subjects that are increasingly in the hands of private, market-driven companies that hire university professors on lucrative private contracts, further diminishing the on-campus research capacity of the universities.

If this sketch is accurate, contemporary universities now satisfy a very specialized set of social interests and do not fully meet the needs of their key supporters. Because universities depend heavily on the goodwill of governments, communities, and parents and students, and on tax advantages for their funding, we doubt this situation is sustainable. It is not clear why major segments of society should continue to support universities. Big business and government may get their research done more cheaply elsewhere. Communities and social change actors whose interests are not heeded and needs are not being met also have a decreasing stake in the future of universities.

Although inertia may keep the current situation going for a while, we do not think it will last much longer. If universities choose not to redirect themselves to be more pluralistic in responding effectively to a wider array of stakeholder groups in society, then we think a significant amount of public and private funding for them not only will but *should* dry up.

As experienced academic researchers ourselves, we know that the complacency and arrogance of many university administrators and faculty members does not enable them to foresee this risky future. We expect universities to begin to feel these competitive pressures very soon, and we do not believe that most currently have the organizational capacity or institutional leadership to respond effectively.[6]

◆ Theory and Praxis in the Social Sciences

Now that we have set the broader historical and political economic context around universities, we can move into a discussion of the overall effect of this complex environment on the social sciences, our central interest here.[7] Our purpose is to describe a role for action research in connecting university social research to some of its primary social constituencies, thereby contributing to a positive restructuring of university-society relationships. How the scientists, engineers, and humanists will address these challenges is a matter for them to consider, although we think that our arguments at least provide them with some useful points upon which to reflect.

What was known at the inception of the social sciences around 1800 and by most social thinkers between Aristotle and the beginning of the 17th century (see Toulmin, 1990) is now more obvious than ever. Social research aimed at social improvement is not an inferior counterpart of "pure" social research. Social change-oriented research, specifically action research, is the form social research must take if it is to achieve valid results, bring about useful social change, and reconnect universities to the larger society.

By contrast, current university-based social research is an armchair activity that claims to embody the scientific study of the structure of society through the argument that being as socially disengaged as possible somehow makes social research more "scientific." It builds explanations of the causes of social processes while disavowing any need to test its speculations in practice.

University social science is the activity of paid groups of full-time academics whose principal social impact is on each other and on the generations of young people in their classrooms. These academics and their disciples show little interest in social change and do not often venture outside the university, except on expeditions to "collect" data. They select their problems according to the intellectual and professional agendas of the most prestigious members of their disciplinary organizations, not in response to needs defined by people outside of academia. As they pursue their studies and refine their methods, there is little chance that their actions will affect most nonuniversity people or that their work will upset the holders of power outside of academia.

Everyone knows that there are wide variances in the kinds of social science practiced in universities: quantitative, qualitative, mixed method, positivist, constructivist, postmodernist, poststructuralist, and so on. One oddity of universities is that, despite the withering critique of positivism over the years, anyone looking at the kind of social research mainly supported by the principal agencies and foundations and privileged by academic administrators will see that it is overwhelmingly positivist (see Scheurich, 1997). That this is the case, and that positivism rests on social disengagement, does not seem to us accidental. It is a product of the systematic removal of academic social research from social change efforts.

Positivism

Positivistically-based quantitative researchers employ the language of objectivity, distance, and control because they believe these are the keys to the conduct of real social science. While we firmly believe in the value of quantitative research that is well carried out under proper conditions for a useful purpose, we also note that the positivist version of quantitative research is socially convenient for those in power who do not want to be the "subjects" of social research and who do not want criticism of their social actions to be brought forward by social researchers. Invoking impartiality and objectivity, positivistic social science absents itself from the controverted social arenas in which the ills produced by bureaucracy, authoritarianism, and inequality are played out, or it washes out this profile through the deployment of numbers rather than words.

The constructivist and postmodernist critiques of recent academic generations have devastated the conceptual and methodological underpinnings of positivism but have had very little effect on displacing the positivist practices and the comfortable "arrangement" among the conventional social sciences, university administrations, and external funders. We are constantly surprised by conventional social scientists' ability to articulate strong criticisms of positivism and yet continue to accept and enact many elements of the positivist approach.[8] And on the other side, there are many (although not all) postmodernists and poststructuralists who argue that all knowledge is so epistemologically compromised that it is impossible to know or do anything about anything, an equally nihilistic self-removal from the field of social engagement.

Qualitative Research

Despite the obvious value of qualitative research, we believe this criticism also applies here. Although it seems that qualitative research could be used very effectively for social change and that some qualitative research includes social criticism, most qualitative work becomes mired in intraprofessional rivalries and ends up chasing the latest trends in the literature, trends that rarely coincide with the felt needs of any particular social group for analysis and support. Although antipositivist in attitude, qualitative research has not as yet succeeded in reconstructing the relationship between the social sciences and society in any fundamental way. And the hostility of many of its adherents

to quantification also weakens its credibility, even with the poor and oppressed who know that one must do battle with the powerful by arming oneself with all possible arguments, methods, and data.

While we acknowledge the importance of the qualitative/quantitative distinction and the flourishing productivity of current qualitative research, we are not inclined to give the qualitative/quantitative distinction a major role here because we do not see that this distinction alters our core assertion about the disconnection between social research and social praxis. Without the test of application, no research endeavor can ascertain the utility and validity of its theories, whether its center of gravity be quantitative or qualitative. In addition, action research is inherently multimethod research, including scientific experiments, quantitative social research, and qualitative research methods from as many disciplines as necessary to address the problem at hand. Effective action research cannot accept an a priori limitation to one or another research modality.

Applied Versus Pure Research

A widely used and misleading distinction separates applied and pure research, a distinction that has long been very problematic in the physical and biological sciences. In the United States, the Congress recently has tried to restrict national research funding to "applied" scientific research (which the Congress believes to be more "valuable," for its own confusing reasons). As a result, scientists have had to struggle to figure out how to couch what they do in applied language. Generally, most physical and biological scientists believe this distinction to be unworkable in practice, and they have mostly sought to evade it. Renaming basic research as applied research has not done much to change their patterns of behavior.

If this dichotomy is problematic in the basic sciences, it is much more so in the social sciences, where positivist claims to be "scientific" are made on the basis that positivist social research is not "applied" but "pure." [9] Positivist social scientists are imitating what they imagine to be the model of "real" science, whereas that model does not fit the behavior of "real" scientists in most respects. Given all this, we find the applied/pure distinction useless and misleading in general and devastating to the social sciences.

Social Research Redefined as Action Research

In our view, the answer to the dilemmas we have laid out above is action research. We define action research as research in which the validity and value of research results are tested through collaborative insider-professional researcher knowledge generation and application processes in projects of social change that aim to increase fairness, wellness, and self-determination. For us, action research is the only form of social research that enacts this agenda adequately. In action research, community or organizational stakeholders collaborate with professional researchers in defining the objectives, constructing the research questions, learning research skills, pooling knowledge and efforts, conducting the research, interpreting the results, and applying what is learned to produce positive social change. Action research ignores the boundaries between disciplines when they restrict effective understanding and action and advocates crossing the boundary between academia and society as a basic principle of operation.[10]

Despite defensive reactions to action research from positivist social researchers and disengaged interpretivists, we are hopeful that a fundamental change in the future of social research is on the way. We are realistic enough to know that such changes will not be easy to bring about and that change will not produce an even and smooth outcome in academia or beyond. The academic social sciences have developed strong professional structures with powerful peer review systems, and their current forms are built into the organizational metabolisms of most academic institutions. Shifting the balance of university social research to action research would challenge the hegemony of the professional organizations and the academic division of labor, both notoriously difficult to change. And, of course, social change-oriented social research would be quite upsetting to many power

holders in society. They can be counted on to defend themselves against it, especially in this era that Ira Shor (1996) calls the "conservative restoration." So we will press on, but we are not blindly optimistic.

To make our case for action research in the remainder of this chapter, we will do four things in a very short space:

1. Underpin our argument for action research philosophically;
2. Portray the ways the university and its academic research establishment are inimical to the promotion of action research;
3. Examine the larger social forces that make the continued analytic and political passivity of social research the most likely outcome under current conditions; and
4. Give brief examples of university-based action research.

Doing this briefly means that the structure of the argument can be clear, but the demonstration cannot be based on the presentation of much evidence.

◆ Why Action Research?

As we have pointed out above, action researchers reject arguments for separating praxis and theory in social research. Either social research is applied or it is not research. The terms *pure research* and *applied research* imply that a division of labor can exist between the pure and the applied, a division we believe makes social research impossible. For action researchers, social inquiry aims to generate knowledge and action in support of liberating social change. The "test" of social research is whether it provides effective support for the stakeholders' actions, organizations, and/or communities in their processes of self-determining social change. For us, the world divides into action research, which we support and practice, and conventional social research (subdivided into pure and applied social research and organized into professional subgroupings), which we reject on combined epistemological, methodological, and political grounds.

Action Research Is Not a Retreat From Science

Because of the dominance of the positivistic framework in the organization of the conventional social sciences, our view will automatically be heard as a retreat from the scientific method into activism. And for hard-line interpretivists, we will be seen as so naïve as not to understand that it is impossible to commit ourselves to any course of action on the basis of any kind of social research. The operating assumption in the conventional social sciences is that greater relevance and engagement automatically involve a loss of scientific validity or a loss of courage in the face of the yawning abyss of endless subjectivity.

Pragmatist Underpinnings

These arguments are spurious. A different grounding for social research can be found in pragmatic philosophy. Dewey, James, Peirce, and others offer an interesting and fruitful foundation for ontological and epistemological questions inherent in social research that is action relevant (see Diggins, 1994). Pragmatism seeks first of all to link theory and praxis. The core reflection process is connected to action outcomes that involve manipulating material and social factors in a given context. Experience emerges in a continual interaction between people and their environment and, accordingly, this process constitutes both the subjects and the objects of inquiry. The actions taken are purposeful and aim at creating desired outcomes. Hence the knowledge-creation process is based on the inquirer's norms, values, and interests.

Validity claims are identified as "warranted" assertions resulting from an inquiry process in which an indeterminate situation is made determinate through concrete actions in an actual context. The research logic is constituted in the inquiry process itself, and it guides the knowledge-generation process.

As action researchers, we strongly advocate the use of scientific methods and emphasize the importance and possibility of the creation of valid knowledge in social research (see Greenwood & Levin, 1998b). This kind of inquiry is a foundational element in democratic processes in society. John Dewey (1927/1954) especially focused his intellectual energy on issues of participative democracy. In his view, the ethics of participation are a core element in meaningful knowledge-creation processes.

These general characteristics of the pragmatist position ground the action research approach. Two central parameters stand out clearly: knowledge generation through action and experimentation in context and participative democracy as both a method and a goal. Neither of these is met in current university structures. The Cartesian ethos has separated mind from body, praxis from reflection, science from social action. Research questions are formulated according to professional standards and ignore the holistic nature of real-life problem situations.

An Action Research Theory of Science

Everyone is supposed to know by now that social research is different from the study of atoms, molecules, rocks, tigers, and so on. Yet we are amazed by the emphasis so many conventional social scientists still place on the claim that being "scientific" requires researchers to sever all relations with the observed. It is still largely unchallenged, particularly in the fields gaining the bulk of social science research money and dominating in social science publications (economics, sociology, and political science). This positivistic credo is obviously wrong and leads away from the production of reliable information, meaningful interpretations, and social actions in social research. It has been subjected to generations of critique, even from within the conventional social sciences.[11] Yet the credo persists, suggesting that its social embeddedness itself deserves attention.

We believe that broad action research interventions in the organization of universities and the academic professions will be required to root it out. Put more simply, the epistemological ideas underlying action research are not new ideas; they simply have been widely ignored as conventional social researchers on the right and left (and the social interests they serve—consciously or unconsciously) have rejected university engagement in social reform.

How Action Research Integrates Theory and Praxis

Action research aims to solve pertinent problems in given contexts through democratic inquiry in which professional researchers collaborate with local stakeholders to seek and enact solutions to problems of major importance to the stakeholders. We refer to this as *cogenerative inquiry* because it is built on professional researcher-stakeholder collaboration. Action research can be described as follows:

1. Action research is inquiry in which participants and researchers cogenerate knowledge through collaborative communicative processes in which all participants' contributions are taken seriously. The meanings constructed in the inquiry process lead to social action, or these reflections on action lead to the construction of new meanings.
2. Action research treats the diversity of experience and capacities within the local group as an opportunity for the enrichment of the research/action process.
3. Action research produces valid research results.
4. Action research is context centered; it aims to solve real-life problems in context.

We explain each of these elements briefly below.

Cogenerative inquiry. Central to action research are cogenerative inquiry processes in which trained professional researchers and knowledgeable local stakeholders work together to define the problems to be addressed, gather and organize relevant knowledge and data, analyze the resulting information, and design social change interventions. The relationship between the professional researcher and the local stake-

holders is based on bringing the diverse bases of all participants' knowledge and their distinctive social locations to bear on a problem collaboratively. The professional researcher often brings knowledge of other relevant cases and of relevant research methods and has experience in organizing research processes. The insiders have extensive and long-term knowledge of the problems at hand and the contexts in which they occur, as well as knowledge about how and from whom to get additional information. They also contribute urgency and focus to the process, because it centers on problems they are anxious to solve. Together these partners create a powerful research team.

Local knowledge/professional knowledge. Action research is built on an interaction between local knowledge and professional knowledge. Whereas conventional social research and consulting privilege professional knowledge over local knowledge, action research does not. Action research is based on the premise that professional knowledge is important and can be valuable, but local knowledge is a necessary ingredient in any research. Only local stakeholders, with their years of experience in a particular situation, have sufficient information and knowledge about the situation to design effective social change processes. Action research does not romanticize local knowledge and denigrate professional knowledge. It is a cogenerative research process precisely because both types of knowledge are essential to it.

Validity/credibility/reliability. Action researchers do not make claims to context-free knowledge, nor are they interested in achieving such knowledge. Credibility, validity, and reliability in action research are measured by the willingness of local stakeholders to act on the results of the action research, thereby risking their welfare on the "validity" of their ideas and the degree to which the outcomes meet their expectations. Thus contextual knowledge, holism, and validity demonstrated in warrants for action are central to action research. The core validity claim centers on the workability of the actual social change activity engaged in, and the test is whether or not the actual solution to a problem arrived at solves the problem.

With Stephen Toulmin, we advocate restarting Western intellectual history just before the wrong turn begun in the 17th century with the emergence of the Cartesian model, in which knowing how (*phronesis*) was separated from the world of reason, abstraction, and distance—the world of *techne*. Action research returns social research to *phronesis,* to "knowing how" by acting on the phenomena, and away from *techne*'s worlds of inaction and putative distance from the subject (Toulmin, 1990; Toulmin & Gustavsen, 1996).

Context-centered knowledge. How can context-centered knowledge be communicated effectively to academics and to other potential recipients? Action research focuses on solving real problems, and so the central inquiry processes of action research are linked to solving practical problems in specific locations. Whether the "problem" is a social/organizational or material one, the results of action research must be tangible in the sense that the participants can figure out whether or not the solution they have developed actually resolves the problem they set themselves. The action research inquiry process is therefore intimately linked to action. By linking inquiry to actions in a given context, action research emphasizes the role of human inquirers as acting subjects in a holistic situation.

The challenges of action research are much more difficult in the realm of communicating and abstracting results of action research in a way that others who did not participate in a particular project (including other stakeholder groups facing comparable but not identical situations) will understand and believe, and that will enable them to generate their own effective courses of action. Precisely because the knowledge is cogenerated, includes local knowledge and analyses, and is built deeply into the local context, it is a challenge to compare results across cases and to create generalizations.[12]

We do not think this is sufficient reason to hand over the territory of comparative generalization and abstract theorization to conventional social researchers. The approach of positivistic research to generalization has been to abstract from context, average out cases, lose sight of the world as lived in by human beings, and generally make the knowledge impossible to apply. Despite the vast sums of money and huge numbers of person-hours put into this kind of research, we find the theoretical harvest pretty slim. And the rejection of the possibility of learning and generalizing at all, typical of much interpretivism, constructivism, and vulgar postmodernism, strikes us as an open invitation to vapid intellectual posturing.

The action research view of generalization means that any single case that runs counter to a generalization invalidates it (Lewin, 1948) and requires the generalization to be reformulated. In contrast, positivist research often approaches exceptional cases by attempting to disqualify them in order to preserve the existing generalization. Rather than welcoming the opportunity to revise their generalization, researchers often react by finding a way to ignore it.

Greenwood became particularly well aware of this during his period of action research in the labor-managed cooperatives of Mondragón, the most successful labor-managed industrial cooperatives anywhere (see Greenwood & González Santos, 1992). Because the "official story" is that cooperatives cannot succeed, that Spaniards are not good at working or making money, and so on, the bulk of the literature on Mondragón published in the 1960s and 1970s attempted to explain the case away. Basque cultural predispositions, charismatic leadership, and so on were all tried as ways of making this exception one that could be ignored while the celebration of the supposedly greater competitiveness of the standard capitalist firm went on unaffected by this glaring exception. Positivist theorists did not want to learn from the case, in direct contravention of the requirements of scientific thinking, which views important exceptions as the most potentially valuable sources of new knowledge.

William Foote Whyte (1991) captures the idea of the productivity of exceptions in his concept of "social inventions." He proposes that all forms of business organizations could learn from this Basque case by trying to figure out how the unique social inventions the Basques had made helped explain their success. Having identified these, researchers could then begin the process of figuring out which of these could be generalized and diffused to other contexts where their utility could be tested, again in collaborative action. Of course, the key to this approach is that the validity of the comparison is also tested in action and not treated as a thought experiment.

If we readdress generalizations in light of what we have argued above, we reframe generalizations as including a process of reflection rather than seeing them as a structure of rule-based interpretations. Given our position that knowledge is context-bound, the key to utilizing this knowledge in a different setting is to follow a two-step model. First, it is important to understand the contextual conditions under which the knowledge has been created. This contextualizes the knowledge itself. Second, the transfer of this knowledge to a new setting implies understanding the contextual conditions of the new setting, how these differ from the setting in which the knowledge was produced, and involves reflection on what consequences this has for applying the actual knowledge in the new context. Hence generalization becomes an active process of reflection in which involved actors must make up their minds about whether or not the previous knowledge makes sense in the new context.

It would take much more space to make the full case (see Greenwood & Levin, 1998b), but we believe we have said enough to make it clear that action research is not some kind of a social science dead end. It is a disciplined way of developing valid knowledge and theory while promoting positive social change.

◆ Can Universities Promote the Kind of Knowledge Production Involved in Action Research?

We believe that the proper response to the epistemological, methodological, political economic, and ethical issues we have been raising is to reconstruct the relationships between the universities and the multiple stakeholders in society. We believe that part of the answer is to make ac-

tion research the central social research strategy. This is because action research, as we have explained above, involves research efforts in which the users (governments, social service agencies, corporations large and small, communities, nongovernmental organizations, and so on) have a definite stake in the problems under study and the research process integrates collaborative teaching/learning with the nonuniversity partners. We know that this kind of university-based action research is possible because there are a number of successful examples. We provide below accounts of two such successes, drawn from a much larger set.

Case 1: Social Science Engineering Research Relationships and University-Industry Cooperation: The Offshore Yard

This project began when the Norwegian Research Council awarded a major research and development contract to SINTEF, a Norwegian research organization located in Trondheim and closely linked to the Norwegian University of Science and Technology. This contract focused on what is called *enterprise modeling,* an information systems-centered technique for developing models of complex organizational processes both to improve efficiency and to restructure organizational behavior. SINTEF received the contract for this work as part of a major national initiative to support applied research and organizational development in manufacturing industries.

A key National Research Council requirement for this program was that engineering research on enterprise modeling had to be linked to social science research on organization and leadership. This required the collaboration of engineers and social scientists within SINTEF of a more intensive sort than usual. The National Research Council argued that enterprise modeling could not be reduced to a technical effort; rather, the enterprise models themselves had to deal with organizational issues as well, because their deployment would depend on the employees' ability to use the models as a "tool" in everyday work.

The research focus of this activity was not very clear at the outset. The instrumental goal for the national research organization was to create a useful enterprise model rather than one that would only be a nice puzzle for information technologists to solve. The research focus emerged in the form of an engineering focus on enterprise models as learning opportunities for all employees and a social science focus on participatory change processes.

The Offshore Yard agreed to be a partner in this effort, and the project was launched in early 1996.[13] The Yard employs approximately 1,000 persons and is located on the Trondheim fjord, about a 90-minute drive north of Trondheim. The Yard has a long history of specializing in the design and construction of the large and complex offshore installations used in North Sea oil exploration.

The project was to be co-managed by a joint group of engineers and social scientists. The key researchers were Ivar Blikø, Terje Skarlo, Johan Elvemo, and Ida Munkeby (two engineers and two social scientists) all employed at SINTEF. The expectation was that cooperation across professional boundaries would somehow arise as an automatic feature of their being engaged in the same project.

The process was by no means so simple. Throughout the initial phase of the project, the only cooperation seen was merely that team members were present at the company site at the same time. In part, this was because the two engineers on the team had a long history with the company. They had many years of contact with the company as consulting researchers and, before that, had worked as engineers on the staff of the Offshore Yard. As a result, the engineers took the lead in the early project activity.[14] They were running the project, and the social scientists seemed fairly passive. The engineers were working concretely on computer-based mock-ups of enterprise models, and, because this was a strong focus of planning interest in the company, they accordingly received a great deal of attention from the senior management of the Yard.

While this was going on, the social scientists were devoting their attention to a general survey of the company and making an ethno-graphic effort to learn about the organization and social realities of the company. This was considered important to give the social scientists a grasp of what the company was like. This research-based knowledge generation meant little to company people, as the work was neither understood nor valued by the company or by the engineering members of the team.

The first opening for social science knowledge came when the social researchers organized a search conference to address the problems of the organization of work at the shop-floor level.[15] This search conference produced results that captured the attention of both the local union and management and made it clear locally that the social scientists had skills that offered significant opportunities for learning and collaborative planning in the company. This was also the first time the researchers managed to include a fairly large number of employees from different layers of the organization in the same knowledge-production process.

As a consequence of this experience, university-Offshore Yard cooperation began to deepen. At that time, the company was developing a leadership training program. Through the social scientists, company leaders learned about other experiences in running such programs, and this helped them plan locally. They were better able to match their overall organizational development activity in their own training program because knowing about other programs helped them with their design. In addition, they felt it would be an advantage to them if company participants in the training also could get official university credits for their involvement. Thus the resulting program was designed through a university-company dialogue and, in the end, one of the social scientists on the team ran it. The program also gave official university-based credits to those participants who decided to take a formal exam. The leadership program became an effort that enhanced the formal skill levels of the participants, and the university diploma gave them recognition outside the context of the Yard.

The program was very successful, making evident how close collaboration between the company and the university could be mutually rewarding. The university people could experiment professionally and pedagogically in real-life contexts, and the company got access to cutting-edge knowledge from the university and from other companies through the university's contacts. As an interesting side effect, the Yard leadership decided to invite managers from neighboring plants to participate. They recognized that the Yard's own future depended on its having good relations with neighbors and suppliers. They decided that one way to improve this cooperation would be to share their program, as a gesture symbolizing their interdependent relationships and their mutual stake in each other's success.

Over the course of the project, the cooperation between engineers and social scientists began to grow and create new insights. A key first move in this direction was a redesign of the tube manufacturing facility at the Yard. The reorganization of work processes, which was cogeneratively developed through workers' participation, meant that shop-floor workers gained direct access to the computer-based production planning and scheduling used by the company engineers. Instead of having information from the system filtered down to them through the foreman, workers at the shop-floor level could utilize the information system and decide for themselves how to manage the production process. This form of organizational leveling would probably not have come about had it not been for the increased mutual understanding between the SINTEF engineers and social scientists and their company partners that emerged through their working together on the same concrete problems as a team.

Gradually, based on these experiences, a reconceptualization of the whole way to develop enterprise models emerged. The conventional engineering take on enterprise models was that the experts (e.g., the engineers) collected information, made an analysis, and then made expert decisions regarding what the model should look like. A new approach to enterprise modeling in the Offshore Yard was developed in which the involved employees actually have a direct say. Although this is a modest step in the direction of participation, it is potentially a very important one. It is fair to say that this changed focus toward participation would not have occurred if

the social scientists had not presented substantive knowledge on issues of organization and leadership that were testable through participatory processes.

As more mutual trust developed between company people and researchers, the marginalized position of the social scientists gradually changed and the company came to count on the social researchers as well. For example, one of the major challenges for the company in the future will be how to manage with a significant reduction in the number of employees humanely and without destroying company morale. These changes originated both from a restructuring of the corporation of which the Yard is a part and new engineering and production processes that are leading to a reduced need for laborers. The Yard has invited the researchers to take part seriously in this process by asking them to draw knowledge and diverse perspectives on this difficult subject from all over the world. In this process, the researchers have been able to support new and often critical knowledge that has changed or extended the company's understanding of its downsizing challenge.

The research team has now also been asked to assist in working on the learning atmosphere in the Yard. This has involved extensive interviewing of a broad spectrum of employees to build a view about how to improve the Yard's capacity for ongoing learning. The results of these interviews were fed back to the involved employees, and the researchers shaped dialogues with them that aimed at both presenting the results and examining the inferences made by the researchers through comparison with the local knowledge of the workers. Again we can see how models of learning with origins in social science circles can be applied to the local learning process, and the results are important factors in the researchers' assessments of the strength and value of their academic findings.

Perhaps the most interesting overall development in this project is how the company-university relationship has developed. The senior executive officer of the Offshore Yard is now a strong supporter of the fruitfulness of the company's relationship with the university. In public presentations, he credits the researchers with bringing relevant and important knowledge to the company and explains that he can see how this relationship can become increasingly important. It took him several years of cooperation to see these possibilities, but now he does and the university is glad to respond. While there is no reason to romanticize the relationship, given that differences of opinion and interest emerge, the relationship seems so robust that further developments are likely.

In the end, only through multidisciplinary action research over a sustained period of time were these results possible. The research values and the action values in the process have both been respected, and all the partners in the process have benefited.

Case 2: Collaborative Research for Organizational Transformation Within the Walls of the University

Here we report on an example of an action research initiative that occurred at Cornell University, resulting in reform of a major required university course: introductory physics. The protagonist of this effort was Michael Reynolds, who wrote this work up as a doctoral dissertation in science education at Cornell (Reynolds, 1994).[16] Universities are, among other things, redoubts of hierarchical and territorial behavior, and thus changes initiated by students or by graduate assistants and lecturers are quite infrequent.

At the time the project began, Reynolds was employed as a teaching assistant in an introductory physics course that is one of the requirements for students wishing to go on to medical school. This makes the course a key gatekeeping mechanism in the very competitive process of access to the medical profession and makes the stake the students have in doing well high and the power of the faculty and university over their lives considerable. It also means that the course has a guaranteed clientele, almost no matter how badly it is taught.

Although there is more than one physics course offered, this particular one is crucial for students' completion of premed requirements.

Because of a comprehensive reform undertaken in the late 1960s, this course was and is delivered in an "autotutorial" format. This means that students work through the course materials at their own pace (within limits), doing experiments and studying in a learning center, asking for advice there, and taking examinations on each unit (often many times) until they have achieved mastery of the material and the grades they seek. Despite the inviting and apparently flexible format, the course had become notoriously unpopular among the students. Performance on standardized national exams was poor, morale among the students and staff was relatively low, and the Physics Department was concerned.

The staff structure included a professor in charge, a senior lecturer who was the de facto principal course manager, and some graduate assistants. Among these, Reynolds was working as a teaching assistant in the course to support himself while he worked on his Ph.D. in education. Having heard about action research and finding it consistent with his view of the world, he proposed to the professor and lecturer in charge that they attempt an action research evaluation and reform of the course. With Greenwood's help, they got funding from the office of the vice president for academic programs to support the reform effort.

There followed a long and complex process, which Reynolds guided skillfully. It involved the undergraduate students, teaching assistants, lecturers, professor, and members of Reynolds's Ph.D. committee in a long-term process. It began with an evaluation of the main difficulties students had with the course and then involved the selection of a new text and pilot testing of the revised course. Reynolds guided this process patiently and consistently. Ultimately, the professor, the lecturer, instructors, teaching assistants, and students collaborated in redesigning the course through intensive meetings and debates.

One of the things they discovered was that the course had become unworkable in part because of its very nature. As new concepts and theories were developed in physics, they were added to the course, but there was no overall system for examining what materials should be eliminated or consolidated to make room for the new ones.

The result was an increasingly overstuffed course that the students found harder and harder to deal with. In bringing the whole course before all the stakeholders and in examining the choice of a possible new textbook, the group was able to confront these issues.

There were many conflicts on issues of substance and authority during the process, and it was stressful for all involved. Yet they stayed together and kept at the process until they had completely redesigned the course. It was then piloted and the results were a dramatic improvement in student performance on national tests and a considerable increase in student satisfaction with the course.

Reynolds then wrote the process up from his detailed field notes and journals and drafted his dissertation. He submitted the draft to his collaborators for comment and revision and then explained to them the revisions he would make. He also offered them the options of adding their own written comments in a late chapter of the dissertation and of using either their real names or pseudonyms.

This iteration of the process produced some significant changes in the dissertation and solidified the group's own learning process. Eventually, many of the collaborators attended Reynolds's dissertation defense and were engaged in the discussion, the first time we know of that such a "collaborative" defense occurred at Cornell. Subsequently, this kind of defense with collaborators present has been repeated with another Ph.D. candidate (Grudens-Schuck, 1998).

Interestingly, although the process was extremely stressful for the participants, the results were phenomenally good for the students. A proposal was made to extend this approach to curriculum reform to other courses at Cornell, but the university administration was unprepared to underwrite the process, despite its obvious great success in this case.

Perhaps the reform of a single course does not seem like much of a social change, but we think this case has portentous implications. It demonstrates that action research-based reform initiated from a position of little power within a profoundly bureaucratic and hierarchical organization, the university, is possible. The value of the knowledge of each category of

stakeholder was patent throughout, and the shared interests of all in a good outcome for the students helped hold the process together. That such reform is possible and successful means that those who write off the possibility of significant university reforms are simply wrong. Of course, it also shows that an isolated success does not add up to ongoing institutional change without a broader strategy to back it up. So it was a success, but an isolated one.

We are aware that the above two accounts constitute a very modest amount of case material to present in support of our contentions, but we believe that these cases at least give the reader a general sense of the direction of our thinking.

◆ Conclusion: How the Role of the University and Academic Intellectuals Would Change If Action Research Became the Centerpiece of University Social Research

Autopoesis Versus Participatory Evaluation

If action research were to become the central research strategy of universities, then universities would be connected to society in very different ways from those currently found. They would become social partners in a wide range of activities, and internal academic autopoesis would not cease, but its play would be drastically curtailed. Performance reviews of both faculty and administrators would necessarily involve evaluation by external stakeholders as well as by professional peers and students. We know from the history of the extension divisions of U.S. universities that stakeholder evaluations of the performance of university personnel are possible. However, we also know that these evaluations are rarely carried out in an action research framework. Developing strategies for the participatory evaluation of university performance would be an essential ingredient in this process.

The counterforces to university autopoesis would be experienced differently in different parts of the university. For many in engineering, the applied sciences, management, social services, and so on, the change would not be very noticeable, because they deal with external stakeholders all the time. For conventional social scientists, the change would be profound. After generations of claiming social relevance, they would be required to demonstrate the value of their work in practice to the satisfaction of extra-university stakeholders. For the extreme interpretivist and postmodernist humanists, this new situation would be a true shock. After claiming intellectual privilege and having taken an overwhelmingly critical posture toward society for decades while taking almost no positive social action, humanists would find the value of their work questioned in fundamental ways.[17] Many important elements of the humanities would be quite important to these changes (e.g., critical theory, discourse analysis, ethics). What would be different is that the value of these perspectives would have to be demonstrated effectively to extra-university stakeholders rather than to a small circle of professional colleagues. Of course, some humanists have already taken on this role effectively, which shows that it is possible (for example, Jürgen Habermas, Hans-Georg Gadamer, Charles Taylor, Richard Rorty).

Democratizing Research

At the center of these changes would be the overall challenge to democratize research, making the external stakeholders an integral part of the knowledge-generation and evaluation processes. Rather than trying to continue the strategy of claiming that the university is the only social location where competent research is possible, academics would take their skills outside the university to collaborate in broader knowledge-generation and evaluation processes as professional researchers and supporters of collaborative research processes. This is not an entirely new role for universities or academics, but, in our ideal scenario, this role would become the principal one, with autopoetic academic activities reserved for a targeted set of internal university initiatives. With the social support universities might gain by reaching out to a broad array of stakeholders, it could be possible for university-based researchers to isolate a few areas in which research without clear social relevance and intellectual capacity building would be seen as essential for the university to support society more effectively. And we can imagine the determination of the areas for this kind of work arising from consistent problems emerging from action research collaborations in which action is inhibited by a lack of key basic knowledge or techniques. Devoting some of the social subsidy to universities to resolving these recurrent problems and then deploying the results through further action research work would be defensible, especially if determined in democratic dialogue both within the universities and with the external stakeholders. For a wonderful recent example of this kind of work, see Patti Lather and Chris Smithies's *Troubling the Angels* (1997).

Co-optation

We imagine that some readers of these last paragraphs will immediately see the specter of "co-optation" here. One of the core ideas behind the autopoetic university supposedly was to free intellectual work from censorship and direct control by powerful social interests. Yet we seem to be recommending that universities co-opt themselves. There is no doubt that the danger of co-optation of universities to the projects of power is ever present. However, in our view, part of the point of making action research central to university-society relationships is to break the current patterns of co-optation in the social sciences. As we have pointed out, universities are now in the employ of government research agencies and big private sector actors. Although they may do work of value to these stakeholders, universities characteristically ignore the interests of a much more diverse and larger group of stakeholders who do not have the power and money of governments and large corporations. Conventional social scientists and humanists do little to break out of this pattern. Thus the university is co-opted now, and the socially passive quality of the conventional social sciences and humanities is a clear indicator of this status. From our perspective, making a commitment to a broad array of action research efforts in support of a purposely diverse set of social stakeholders who are brought into the projects as partners and colearners can break this pattern of co-optation by the few in favor of service to the many.

Will this automatically avoid co-optation? Certainly not, but it will make the negotiation of subjects of research and the debate about projects to support and to avoid more public. In the end, our experience of action research suggests to us that collaboration does not lead so much to co-optation as it does to radical challenges to the ability of universities to generate and communicate relevant knowledge. In our years of practice, we have found the most difficult theoretical, methodological, and empirical challenges as social researchers in the process of conducting action research. Our collaborators constantly demand more and better knowledge from us to help them achieve their goals. So we have found action research more intellectually challenging than autopoetic university research. Retaining the integrity of our research as good-quality research has been less a problem than has been creating the new knowledge required by our projects.

■ Notes

1. Preparing this chapter has been an extraordinarily fruitful intellectual experience because of the unique commitment to us made by the editors, Yvonna Lincoln and Norman Denzin, and the very helpful and challenging critiques provided by our readers: Orlando Fals Borda and Linda Smircich. All the comments were useful, but the final stages of this process were particularly rewarding. Yvonna Lincoln would not let the issues go because she deems them so important, and she proceeded to press us with a wonderful combination of critique and encouragement. At her urging, we rethought and clarified parts of our arguments in a three-way e-mail dialogue that embodied an "ideal speech situation" in a powerful way. These debates both clarified our arguments and enhanced our sense that collegial critique is truly a gratifying experience, and we think the readers will be the beneficiaries of this process.

2. This point may strike some readers as too obvious to mention. However, we are constantly surprised by the conflation of applied research with qualitative methods by both academic colleagues and consumers of social research. We think this conflation is an irrational corollary of the assumption that, because applied research supposedly cannot be scientific, it must somehow be qualitative.

3. Readers will note that we argue that social research must be open to change, to diversity of viewpoints, and to complexity of response. Yet, in an apparently authoritarian posture, we view action research as the most valuable kind of social research. Thus it seems that we are not really advocating pluralism because we do not take a "live and let live" posture toward our academic colleagues. Despite the apparent logic of this criticism, we reject it because we are advocating a view of the mission of the social sciences that is completely consistent with the general justifications that social scientists have given for their work since the inception of these disciplines. Our colleagues have consistently argued that the social science should exist and be funded because of the contributions they make to understanding and thereby improving society. We simply point out that the practices of conventional academic social scientists violate these announced principles, whereas action research lives up to them.

4. The term *autopoetic* refers to the self-referential and self-generating character of a social situation in which a narrow group of socially interdependent individuals generate standards for each other and judge each other's performance without regard to their contextualization within the interests of society at large.

5. We were quite surprised to discover how little literature there is on the size, growth, and costs of university administrative structures over the past 20 years. It is as if the academic community has purposely turned a blind eye to the study of its own immediate environment. Because of this, these assertions arise mainly from anecdotal information. We do acknowledge that some administrative increases are the logical consequence of changed societal conditions, such as the explosion of information technology and the desire to provide more comprehensive student services, but we also strongly believe that a significant portion of the increase in administrative structure has to do with the hierarchization of

power within universities and the centralization of university research as a "business." And we believe that, in many cases, this research management operation is both inept and directed at short-term profits at the expense of the creation of an enduring and mutually productive relationship between university research and society's needs.

6. Readers aware of the differences between the public universities in Europe and those in the United States will wonder how this argument applies to the European scene. It is different in important ways, but not as different as might be imagined. European public universities, to the extent that they lose social relevance, lose faculty members and money to private sector and government research institutes. Further, they increasingly lose their students to universities that are managing these relationships better. Although public universities face a different kind of competitive situation, it remains a competitive situation, and their dependence on public funds makes them vulnerable to criticism from a wide variety of political groups. Thus, in the end, universities everywhere have a major stake in satisfying the needs of a broad spectrum of social groups.

7. The arguments we are about to launch are by no means new. The field of adult education, through the work of Paolo Freire (1970) and Budd Hall (1975), and the fields of participatory research through the pathbreaking work of Orlando Fals Borda (see Fals Borda & Rahman, 1991), Rajesh Tandon (1997), and many others, launched this critique long ago. Orlando Fals Borda also recently organized a monumental meeting of action researchers in Cartagena, Colombia *(Convergencia),* attended by more than 1,800 people. A great percentage of the participants came from university environments, and the problematic relationship between universities and liberating social research was explored from many angles. Some of the results of this meeting have been published already in Fals Borda (1998) and more appear in a special issue of *Studies in Cultures, Organizations and Societies* edited by Timothy Pyrch (1998).

8. See Scheurich (1997, chap. 3) for an excellent discussion of this in his critique of Elliot Mishler's work on postpositivist interviewing.

9. Oddly, interpretivist claims to excellence seem to be made on the basis of being so pure as to be "inapplicable"; they thus support the applied/pure distinction from the other side.

10. For an excellent and succinct discussion of action research, see Brown and Tandon (1983).

11. A critique of this kind of blind positivism was central to the ideas of the major social thinkers who gave rise to the social sciences in the first place (Adam Smith, Karl Marx, Max Weber, Emile Durkheim, John Dewey, and so on). A good source of current critiques is Scheurich (1997).

12. For a full discussion of these issues, see Stake (1995).

13. The name "Offshore Yard" is a pseudonym.

14. Levin observed much of this process because he served as a member of the local steering committee for the project. He recollects how little linkage there was across engineering and the social sciences at the outset.

15. A search conference is a democratically organized action research method for bringing a group of problem owners together for an intensive process of reflection, analysis, and action planning. For a more detailed description, see Greenwood and Levin (1998b).

16. Greenwood served as a member of Reynolds's Ph.D. committee and worked with him throughout this research. However, the ideas, processes, and interpretations offered here are those generated by Reynolds, not Greenwood. As Reynolds is now hard at work on secondary school reform, he has not made a further write-up of his work, so we encourage the interested reader to consult his dissertation directly (Reynolds, 1994).

17. Interestingly, the language and writing teachers within the university might well prosper under these conditions. Their work is mainly a service to the students. They have generally suffered from a lack of prestige in comparison to the literary critics and philosophers. Possibly this prestige hierarchy would be reversed or at least undermined by the changes we suggest.

■ *References*

Bourdieu, P. (1988). *Homo academicus* (P. Collier, Trans.). Stanford, CA: Stanford University Press.

Brown, L. D., & Tandon, R. (1983). Ideology and political economy in inquiry: Action research and participatory research. *Journal of Applied Behavioral Sciences, 19,* 277-294.

Chomsky, N., Zinn, H., Lewontin, R. C., Montgomery, D., Wallerstein, I., Katznelson, I., Nader, L., Ohmann, R., & Siever, R. (1997). *The Cold War and the university: Toward an intellectual history of the postwar years.* New York: New Press.

Dewey, J. (1954). *The public and its problems.* Athens: Ohio University Press. (Original work published 1927)

Diggins, J. P. (1994). *The promise of pragmatism.* Chicago: University of Chicago Press.

Eurich, N. (1985). *Corporate classrooms: The learning business.* Princeton, NJ: Carnegie Foundation for the Advancement of Teaching/Princeton University Press.

Fals Borda, O. (Ed.). (1998). *People's participation: Challenges ahead.* New York: Apex.

Fals Borda, O., & Rahman, M. A. (Eds.). (1991). *Action and knowledge: Breaking the monopoly with participatory action-research.* New York: Apex.

Freidson, E. (1985). *Professional powers: A study of the institutionalization of formal knowledge.* Chicago: University of Chicago Press.

Freire, P. (1970). *Pedagogy of the oppressed* (M. B. Ramos, Trans.). New York: Herder & Herder.

Greenwood, D. J., & González Santos, J. L. (with Alonso, J. C., Markaide, I. G., Arruza, A. G., Nuin, I. L., & Amesti, K. S.). (1992). *Industrial democracy as process: Participatory action research in the Fagor Cooperative Group of Mondragón.* Assen-Maastricht, Netherlands: Van Gorcum.

Greenwood, D. J., & Levin, M. (1998a). Action research, science, and the co-optation of social research. In T. Pyrch (Ed.), Convergence [Special issue]. *Studies in Cultures, Organizations and Societies, 5*(1).

Greenwood, D. J., & Levin, M. (1998b). *Introduction to action research: Social research for social change.* Thousand Oaks, CA: Sage.

Greenwood, D. J., & Levin, M. (1998c). The reconstruction of universities: Seeking a different integration into knowledge development processes. *Concepts and Transformation, 2*(2), 145-163.

Grudens-Schuck, N. (1998). *When farmers design curricula: Participatory education for sustainable agriculture in Ontario, Canada.*

Unpublished doctoral dissertation, Cornell University.

Hall, B. (1975). Participatory research: An approach for change. *Convergence, 8* (2), 24-32.

Kuhn, T. S. (1962). *The structure of scientific revolutions.* Chicago: University of Chicago Press.

Lather, P., & Smithies, C. (1997). *Troubling the angels: Women living with HIV/AIDS.* Boulder, CO: Westview.

Lewin, K. (1948). *Resolving social conflicts.* New York: Harper & Row.

Lewontin, R. C. (1997). The Cold War and the transformation of the academy. In N. Chomsky, H. Zinn, R. C. Lewontin, D. Montgomery, I. Wallerstein, I. Katznelson, L. Nader, R. Ohmann, & R. Siever, *The Cold War and the university: Toward an intellectual history of the postwar years.* New York: New Press.

Pyrch, T. (Ed.). (1998). Convergence [Special issue]. *Studies in Cultures, Organizations and Societies, 5*(1).

Readings, B. (1996). *The university in ruins.* Cambridge, MA: Harvard University Press.

Reynolds, M. A. (1994). *Democracy in higher education: Participatory action research in the Physics 101-102 Curriculum Revision Project at Cornell University.* Unpublished doctoral dissertation, Cornell University.

Scheurich, J. J. (1997). *Research method in the postmodern.* London: Falmer.

Shor, I. (1996). *When students have power: Negotiating authority in a critical pedagogy.* Chicago: University of Chicago Press.

Stake, R. E. (1995). *The art of case study research.* Thousand Oaks, CA: Sage.

Tandon, R. (1997). *Struggle for knowledge: A personal journey.* Paper presented at the Convergence World Congress, Cartagena, Colombia. Available Internet: http://www.parnet.org

Toulmin, S. (1990). *Cosmopolis: The hidden agenda of modernity.* Chicago, University of Chicago Press.

Toulmin, S., & Gustavsen, B. (Eds.). (1996). *Beyond theory: Changing organizations through participation.* Philadelphia: John Benjamins.

Whyte, W. F. (1991). *Social theory social action: How individuals and organizations learn to change.* Newbury Park, CA: Sage.

4

FOR WHOM?

Qualitative Research, Representations, and Social Responsibilities

◆ **Michelle Fine, Lois Weis, Susan Weseen, and Loonmun Wong**

I grew up in a world in which talking about somebody's mama was a way of life, an everyday occurrence. For all of us, boys and girls, it was a kind of game or performance. Whether we called it "capping," "snapping," "ranking," "busting," or simply "the dozens," most of it was ridiculous, surreal humor bearing very little resemblance to reality: "Your mom's so fat she broke the food chain"; "Your mama's skin's so ashy she was a stand-in for Casper the Friendly Ghost"; "Your mama's so dumb she thought ring-around-the-collar was a children's game." More than anything, it was an effort to master the absurd metaphor, an art form intended to entertain rather than to damage. . . .

You would think that as a kid growing up in this world I could handle any insult, or at least be prepared for any slander tossed in the direction of my mom—or, for that matter, my whole family, my friends, or my friends' families. But when I entered college and began reading the newspaper, monographs, and textbooks on a regular basis, I realized that many academics, journalists, policymakers, and politicians had taken the "dozens" to another level. In all my years of playing the dozens, I have rarely heard vitriol as vicious as the words spouted by Riverside (California) county welfare director Lawrence Townsend: "Every time I see a bag lady on the street, I wonder, 'Was that an A.F.D.C. mother

AUTHORS' NOTE: This chapter expands on an earlier article by the first two authors titled "Writing the 'Wrongs' of Field Work" (Fine & Weis, 1996). The data reported here were collected with the generous support of both the Spencer Foundation and the Carnegie Foundation.

◆ 107

who hit the menopause wall—who can no longer reproduce and get money to support herself?' " I have had kids tell me that my hair was so nappy it looked like a thousand Africans giving the Black Power salute, but never has anyone said to my face that my whole family—especially my mama—was a "tangle of pathology." Senator Daniel Patrick Moynihan has been saying it since 1965 and, like the one about your mama tying a mattress to her back and offering "roadside service," Moynihan's "snap" has been repeated by legions of analysts and politicians, including Dinesh D'Souza, the boy wonder of the far Right. (Kelly, 1997, pp. 1-2)

In this essay, we work through the decisions we made about how to represent the consequences of poverty on the lives of poor and working-class men and women in times of punishing surveillance and scrutiny by the state. We have discussed some of these issues—alternately called *ethics, dilemmas,* and simply *research*—with friends and colleagues. Some think we make "much ado about nothing." Others are relieved that we are "saying aloud" this next generation of troubles. Many wish we would continue to hide under the somewhat transparent robe of qualitative research. And yet we are compelled to try to move a public conversation about researchers and responsibilities toward a sense of research for social justice.

Because we write between poor communities and social policy at a time of Right-wing triumph, and because we seek to be taken seriously by both audiences, we know it is essential to think through the power, obligations, and responsibilities of social research. Entering the contemporary montage of perverse representations of poor and working-class men and women, especially people of color, we write with and for community organizers, policy makers, local activists, the public, and graduate students.

This chapter represents a concrete analysis—an update, perhaps—of what Michelle Fine (1994) has called "working the hyphen":

Much of qualitative research has reproduced, if contradiction-filled, a colonizing discourse of the "Other." This essay is an attempt to review how qualitative research projects have *Othered* and to examine an emergent set of activist and/or postmodern texts that interrupt *Othering*. First, I examine the hyphen at which Self-Other join in the politics of everyday life, that is, the hyphen that both separates and merges personal identities with our inventions of Others. I then take up how qualitative researchers work this hyphen . . . [through] a messy series of questions about methods, ethics, and epistemologies as we rethink how researchers have spoken "of" and "for" Others while occluding ourselves and our own investments, burying the contradictions that percolate at the Self-Other hyphen. (p. 70)

We seek not necessarily to engage in simple reflexivity about how our many selves (Jewish, Asian, Canadian, woman, man, straight, gay) coproduce the empirical materials on which we report, although clearly that is an important piece of work (see Weis & Fine, in press). Instead, we gather here a set of self-reflective points of critical consciousness around the questions of how to represent responsibility, that is, transform public consciousness and "common sense" about the poor and working classes, write in ways that attach lives to racial structures and economies, and construct stories and analyses that interrupt and reframe the victim-blaming mantras of the 1990s.

Writing against the grain, we thought it would be useful to speak aloud about the politics and scholarship of decisions we have made.

◆ Flexing Our Reflexivities

In the social sciences, both historically and currently, the relationship between researcher and subject has been "obscured in social science texts, protecting privilege, securing distance, and laminating the contradictions" (Fine, 1994, p. 72). There has long been a tendency to view the self of the social science observer as a potential contaminant, something to be separated out, neutralized, minimized, standardized, and controlled. This bracketing of the researcher's world is evident in social science's historically dominant literary style (Madigan, Johnson, & Linton, 1995), which is predicated on a "clarion renunciation" of the subjective or personal aspects of experience (Morawski & Bayer, 1995), particularly those of researchers. As Ruth Behar (1993) explains, "We ask for revelations from others, but we reveal little or nothing of ourselves; we make others vulnerable, but we ourselves remain invulnerable" (p. 273). Our informants are then left carrying the burden of representations as we hide behind the cloak of alleged neutrality.

Although it may be true that researchers are never absent from our texts, the problem of just how to "write the self [and, we would add, our political reflexivities] into the text" (Billig, 1994, p. 326) remains. Simply briefly inserting autobiographical or personal information often serves to establish and assert the researcher's authority, and ultimately produces texts "from which the self has been sanitised" (Okely, 1992, p. 5). But flooding the text with ruminations on the researcher's subjectivities also has the potential to silence participants/"subjects" (Lal, 1996).

It should also be pointed out that a call for the inclusion of subjective experience of the researcher into what has traditionally been conceived of as subject matter bears different implications for differently situated researchers. In the hands of relatively privileged researchers studying those whose experiences have been marginalized, the reflexive mode's potential to silence subjects is of particular concern. It is easy for reflexivity to slip into what Patricia Clough (1992) has called a "compulsive extroversion of interiority" (p. 63). In the words of Renato Rosaldo (1989), "If classic ethnography's vice was the slippage from the ideal of detachment to actual indifference, that of present-day reflexivity is the tendency for the self-absorbed Self to lose sight altogether of the culturally different Other" (p. 7). Yet from an entirely different and overlapping perspective, some critical race theorists (e.g., Ladner, 1971; Lawrence, 1995; Matsuda, 1995) have suggested that for people of color whose stories have not been told, "the assertion of our subjective presence as creators and interpreters of text [is a] political act" (Lawrence, 1995, p. 349). According to Donna Haraway (1991), "Vision is always a question of the power to see—

and perhaps of the violence implicit in our visualizing practices" (p. 192); who is afforded—or appropriates—this power to see and speak about what is seen as well as what is hidden from scrutiny is a question that is at the heart of our examinations of our social responsibilities to write and re-present in a time of ideological assault on the poor. Thus we seek to narrate a form of reflexivity in our concerns with representation and responsibilities in these very mean times.

◆ The Textual Subject

In the remainder of this chapter, we reflect on the materials drawn for a book written by Michelle Fine and Lois Weis about poor and working-class city dwellers at the end of the 20th century, *The Unknown City* (1998). In this work, Michelle and Lois center the voices, politics, disappointments, and hopes of young urban adults. These men and women—African American, white, and Latino/Latina, poor and working-class—render oral histories of their struggles, victories, and passions, detailing lives filled with work (and its absence), schooling, family life, spirituality, sexuality, violence on the streets and in their homes, and social movements that seem no longer vibrant. Our analyses suggest that these young adults, men and women, constitute an unknown, unheard-from, and negatively represented constituency of the American democracy. Between the ages of 23 and 35, with neither the resources nor the sense of entitlement typically narrated by members of Generation X, they have been displayed and dissected in the media as the cause of national problems. Depicted as being the reason for the rise in urban crime, they are cast as if they embody the necessity for welfare reform, as if they sit at the heart of moral decay. Although much of contemporary social policy is designed to "fix" them, our investigation reveals that they have much to say back to policy makers and the rest of America.

The late 1990s witnessed a flood of books written about and sometimes despite those who have been grouped together as the poor and working class. But the members of this group, particularly the young, are fundamentally unknown, at once quite visible as "moral spectacle" (Roman, 1997) and yet fundamentally invisible (A. J. Franklin, personal communication, October 14, 1997). As our nation walks away from their needs, desires, strengths, and yearnings, we abandon a generation. Millions of poor and working-class children continue to grow up amid the wreckage of global corporate restructuring, in the shadows of once-bustling urban factories, reinvigorated U.S. nationalism and racism, and a wholesale depletion of the public safety net, at the same time witnessing increasing violence in their communities and often in their homes. And mostly, they blame themselves and each other. The state retreat from the social good and corporate flight from urban centers, the North, and the United States are shockingly absent as blame is doled out. As calls to reverse civil rights, affirmative action, welfare, and immigration policies gain momentum, it is noteworthy that the voices of the men and women in the poor and working classes are never heard.

The Unknown City reveals not only common pains among members of the poor and the working class, but a deeply fractured urban America in the late 20th century. In spite of legislation and social politics designed to lessen inequality and promote social cohesion in the 1960s, we stand as a nation in the late 1990s deeply divided along racial, ethnic, social class, and gender lines. Our goals in conducting the research for *The Unknown City*, then, were to examine the commonalities among Americans and the fractured nature of U.S. society, focusing on what we call "communities of difference," as low-income people settle for crumbs in one of the richest nations in the world. We sought, further, to place these voices at the center of national debates about social policy rather than at the margin, where they currently stand. This chapter consciously reflects back on the work of writing that book—the headaches and struggles we experienced as we entered the battle of representations happening on, about, and despite but rarely with poor and working-class urban dwellers at the end of the 20th century. Amid economic dislocation and a contracted public sphere, we seek to re-present men and women navigating lives of joy and disappointment, anger and laughter, despair and prayer.

Much as we sought to escape the narrow confines of demographic, essentialist categories, what we heard from both Jersey City and Buffalo tended to bring us back to these categories. That is, much as we all know, read, teach, and write about race, class, and gender as social constructions (see Fine, Powell, Weis, & Wong, 1997), loaded with power and complexity, always in quotation marks, when we listened to the taped interviews with African American men living in Jersey City or Buffalo, they were strikingly different from those of white men, or Latinas, or African American women. Indeed, both the very distinct material bases and cumulative historical circumstances of each of these groups and the enormous variety "within" categories demanded intellectual and political respect. So we tell the "big story" of people living in poverty as well as the particular stories narrated through gender, race, and ethnicity. Thus we write with and through poststructural understandings of identity and possibility, ever returning to "common" material bases (the economy, state, and the body) as we move through the nuances of "differences."

◆ On Framing the Work

On Community

Perhaps our most vexing theoretical dilemma swirled around the question, So, what constitutes a community? How do we write about real estate, land-bounded communities like Buffalo or Jersey City, geographically valid, zip-code-varied, "real" spaces in which we nevertheless found so little in the way of psychologically or socially shared biographies or visions?

We recognized from our theoretical interests, confirmed by the narratives we collected, that profound fractures, and variation, cut through lives within these communities. Simple demographic nuances, by race/ethnicity, gender, class, generation, and sexuality marked dramatic distinctions in experience. Within local neighbor-hoods or racial/ethnic groups, gender, sexuality, and generational divisions boldly sever what may appear to be, at first glance, internal continuities (see West, 1993). For instance, within the presumably "same" part of Jersey City, African Americans refer to local police practices with stories of harassment and fear, whereas whites are far more likely to complain about a rise in crime and to brag about a brother-in-law who's a cop. Whereas Jersey City whites described the "good old days" of economic security and pined for the day when they'd be moving to Bayonne, African Americans from the same block harbored few wistful memories of "good old days" and routinely avoided "getting stopped at red lights" in Bayonne, lest their stay be extended beyond what they expected.

At historic moments of job insecurity and economic hard times, the presumed harmony of working-class/poor communities is ravaged by further interior splits, finger-pointing, blame, and suspicion. Coalitions are few, even if moments of interdependence-for-survival are frequent. Within homes, differences and conflicts explode across genders and across generations. A full sense of community is fictional and fragile, ever vulnerable to external threats and internal fissures. Although there is a class-based story to be told, a sense of class-based coherence prevails only if our methods fail to interrogate differences by race/ethnicity, gender, and sexuality. And yet, at the same time, commonalities across cities—by demography and biography—are all the more striking.

We could, therefore, write about life within these two urban communities, Jersey City and Buffalo, as though the notion of community were unproblematic, a geographic space of shared experience. Or we could, with equal ease and discomfort, present a book about African American men and women, white men and women, and Latinos and Latinas as though each group experiences a social world totally insulated from those of the others. Although some of our data press toward the latter, our theoretical and political inclinations make us look toward the former, searching for common ground, shared languages, and parallel experiences. Our text tries to speak, at once, in these

two dialects, to issues of the common and the specific, without diluting either. We decided that *The Unknown City* would offer two chapter forms: one that privileges the unique experiences of groups (for example, African American men) and another that explores the ways in which poor and working-class people travel over similar terrain (schooling, motherhood, crime) in their lives. Scripting a story in which we float a semifictional portrait of each community, we layered over an analytic matrix of differences "within." For our analysis—within and between cities—we delicately move between coherence and difference, fixed boundaries and porous borders, neighborhoods of shared values and homes of contentious interpretations.

On "Race"

Robin Kelly (1997) describes his latest book as "a defense of black people's humanity and a condemnation of scholars and policymakers for their inability to see complexity" (p. 4). Some academics have addressed this complexity: Henry Louis Gates (1985) has written beautifully about "race," always using quotes on the word; Michael Dyson (1993) argues against narrow nationalistic or essentialist definitions for either skin color or language; Kimberlé Crenshaw (1995) forces us to theorize at the intersections of race and gender; and Stuart Hall (1981) narrates the contextual instability of racial identities, as do Michael Omi and Howard Winant (1986). Like these theorists, our informants use/employ/conceive of race as both a floating unstable fiction and a fundamental, unerasable aspect of biography and social experience. Indeed, some of our informants, like the one quoted below, suggest that "race" constitutes inherently indefinable territory, offering narratives not so much of denial as complexity.

Mun: Your dad?
Luisa: Yes, my dad was the craziest Puerto Rican you had ever seen in the 70s. Oh my Lord.
Mun: What is your mom's background?
Luisa: Mom, Mom was raised Catholic, but in my mother's days, when an Irish and German woman went with a Chinese guy, in those days that was like, oh no, no that cannot happen.

My grandfather had to drop his whole family for my grandmother, so they could be together. Everybody disowned him in his family.

Mun: Because he married a—

Luisa: Yeah, he married my grandmother.

Mun: What about your mom's side?

Luisa: That is my mom's side.

Mun: What about your grandfather's side?

Luisa: My grandfather, he was in Vietnam, World War II, oh, I forgot the name. It was a very big war, that I know.

Mun: Korean War?

Luisa: Yeah, something like that, I just can't remember what it was. Yeah, he had honors and everything my mother told me.

Mun: So you looked very different?

Luisa: Yeah, I'm a mixture.

Mun: You have Chinese blood?

Luisa: Right. I got Irish and German, I got Puerto Rican and Italian, I have a lot. I'm a mixed breed.

Mun: I was wondering. The first time I saw you I thought you were from the Middle East.

Luisa: From the Middle East?

Mun: Yeah.

Luisa: Oh, golly gee, no. I'm, like, really mixed. I'm like everything. I got all these different personalities that just come out all the time. I swear to God. No lie. No lie.

When we began our interviews in Jersey City and Buffalo, we too were taken by poststructural thinking on questions of "race." With Stuart Hall (1997) particularly in mind, willing to acknowledge the artificiality, the performances, and, indeed, the racist "roots" of the notion of race (1/32nd drop of blood and the like), we constructed an interview protocol that generously invited our informants to "play" with "race" as we had. So we asked, in many clever ways, for them to describe time- and context-specific racial identifications—when they fill out census forms, when they walk through supermarkets, when alone or among friends. Informants of color tried to be polite and follow us in our "play," but by hour three they grew exasperated with these questions. White interviewees were either sure we were calling them racist or avoided identifying as white—instead speaking about being Irish, Italian, or human. Needless to say, the "playfulness" of the questions didn't work.

Many argued that race *shouldn't* make much of a difference.[1] And we wanted, too, to write that book, not out of liberal foolishness but out of profound political commitments to class, race, and gender analyses and to "what should be." And yet, as we listened to our data, the life stories as narrated were so thoroughly drenched in racializing discourse that readers couldn't *not* know even an "anonymous" informant's racial group once they read the transcript. Personal stories of violence and family structure, narrative style, people's histories with money, willingness to trash (publicly) violent men and marriages, access to material resources, relations with kin and the state, descriptions of interactions with the police—all were talked through "race."

"Race" is a place in which poststructuralism and lived realities need to talk. "Race" is a social construction, indeed. But "race" in a racist society bears profound consequences for daily life, identity, and social movements and for the ways in which most groups "other." But how we write about "race" to a deeply race-bound audience worries us. Do we take the category for granted, as if it is unproblematic? By so doing, we (re)inscribe its fixed and essentialist positionality. Do we instead problematize it theoretically, knowing full well its full-bodied impact on daily life? Yes, "race" *is* a social construction, but it is so deeply confounded with racism that it bears enormous power in lives and communities. To the informants with whom we spoke, "race" does exist—it saturates every pore of their lives. How can we destabilize the notion theoretically at one and the same time as we recognize the lived presence of "race"?

To give a trivial, but telling, example: Here's a problem that may appear, at face value, to be a "sampling problem" related to "race." We struggled in both cities to find "equally poor" and "equally working-class" African American, Latino/Latina, and white young adults so that comparisons by race/ethnicity would not be confounded by class. Guess what? The world is lousy with confounds. Although we did find poor and working-class whites, the spread and depth of their poverty was nowhere near as severe as in the African American sample. Our ambitious search for sampling comparability, in spite of our meticulous combing of raced neighborhoods, lost hands down to the profound "lived realities" of multigenerational poverty disproportionately affecting poor and working-class families of color. What may appear to be a methodological problem has been revealed as constitutive of the very fabric of society. Neither problematizing nor (re)inscribing "race" in our writing will help us, as a society, to confront the very real costs and privileges of racial categorization.

◆ Inform(ing) and Consent: Who's Informed and Who's Consenting?

With frame more or less clear, we move to the interviews. At this point, we struggle through the ethics of constructing narratives with poor men and women, each paid $40 for an interview. So, we ask, what is consent? And for whom? Mun Wong confronted this dilemma often. The informed consent form for our interviews states:

> We are conducting interviews with young adults on their perceptions of high school experiences and since. We are particularly interested in discussing concerns, attitudes, and aspirations (then and now) developed during your years in high school. . . . I, [respondent's name], agree to participate in this study on the urban experiences of young adults growing up in Jersey City during the 1980s and 1990s. The interviews will be audiotaped, transcribed and written up in a book. No names will be attached to the interviews.

The consent form sits at the contradictory base of the institutionalization of research. Although the aim of informed consent is presumably to protect respondents, informing them of the possibility of harm in advance and inviting them to withdraw if they so desire, it also effec-

tively releases the institution or funding agency from any liability and gives control of the research process to the researcher. Commenting on this standard formulaic piece of the research process, M. Brinton Lykes (1989) writes, "Reflecting on my experiences with the [informed consent] form revealed the complexity of both my role as researcher/activist and the constraints on developing collaboration between subjects in a context of real power imbalances" (p. 177). She continues:

> The informed consent form which I introduced as a mechanism for "protecting the subjects" of the research project, was instead a barrier and forced me to confront the chasm between the needs and demands of research conducted within the boundaries of the university and the systems of trust and mistrust and of sharing and withholding that were already a part of this collaboration. (p. 178)

In our work, we have come to understand how the introduction of an informed consent form requires analysis as much as what are routinely and easily considered as "data"—such as the narratives of our participants. The (apparent) rapport that Mun had with respondents seemed to unravel whenever he presented the consent form. Many of them asked him, "What is this for?" He was always embarrassed when an explanation was required, in many cases simply mumbling an explanation. In some cases, contrary to official research protocol, he presented the consent form in the second part of the interview. Even so, many women simply signed the form as just another procedural matter, without reading the entire document. Their (apparent) nonchalance probably reflected their general attitude toward procedural matters. These respondents—women on welfare—are constantly required to read bureaucratic forms that are convoluted and technical, and are told to sign off on others' responsibilities while signing on to their own.

The informed consent form forced us to confront and contend with the explicitly differential relationships between the respondents and ourselves; it became a crude tool—a conscience—to remind us of our accountability and position. Stripping us of our illusions of friendship and reciprocity, it made "working the hyphen" even more difficult. No matter how hard Mun tried to downplay "differences" and find a common ground from which to proceed, our participants' responses to the informed consent form reminded us to dispel any artificial attempts at displacing differences (Borland, 1991).

Judith Stacey (1991) has argued that (feminist) ethnography depends upon human relationships, engagement, and attachment, with the research process potentially placing research subjects at grave risk of manipulation and betrayal. She writes:

> Situations of inauthenticity, dissimilitude, and potential, perhaps inevitable, betrayal situations are inherent in fieldwork research. For no matter how welcome, even enjoyable, the field worker's presence may appear to locals, social work often represents an intrusion and intervention into a system of relationships, a system of relationships that the researcher is far freer than the researched to leave. The inequality and potential treacherousness of this relationship is inescapable. (p. 113)

Dorcy came up to Mun after he finished his interview with Regina. She told him that she also wanted to be part of the study, and he told her that he would get to her when he completed the interviews with Melissa and Diane. So for the next 3 weeks or so, whenever Mun ran into Dorcy, she would ask, "When is my turn?" Mun would always give his typical reply to women who kept requesting interviews: "You are next, next week, okay?" "You better make sure," Dorcy laughed. Her repeated but friendly gestures, along with her gigglish laughs and timid smiles, were constant reminders: "I thought you said it was my turn."

At the beginning of their first interview, Dorcy and Mun sat facing each other in Room 216. Mun started off with his script: "Thanks for doing this. As you know, I am interviewing women about their experiences on welfare but also try to get a picture of their lives. This is a consent form and you may want to read it first. If you agree to abide by whatever is written there, please sign it. And I am going to tape-record this. Also, if you do not feel comfortable with what-

ever, just say you are going to skip it, okay?" She signed the form and the taped interview began.

Mun: How was your family . . . when you were growing up?

Dorcy: Oh, I had . . . I had a good growing . . . growing . . . I had it good. My mother, my father. My father died when I was 12. So, he was . . . he was always there for us, ya know. My mother, she's good. She's a strong woman. She love us and she take care of us . . . things we need. . . . and she help us out a lot . . . yeah.

Mun: How many brothers and sisters do you have?

Dorcy: Excuse me?

Mun: Brothers and sisters?

Dorcy: Oh . . . um . . . three sisters, I make three sisters, and five brothers. I have . . . one of my brother died of AIDS, in '91 . . . of November . . . he died of AIDS.

Mun: What number are you?

Dorcy: I'm 25.

Mun: I mean, number in the family.

Dorcy: Oh, I'm . . . I'm in the middle.

Mun: [laughs]

Dorcy: [laughs] . . . I'm the middle . . . middle child.

Mun: Is it good?

Dorcy: It's good.

Mun: I mean . . . what . . .

Dorcy: It has its ups and downs, but it's good.

Mun: What do you mean?

Dorcy: Huh?

Mun: Ups and downs?

Dorcy: Because like, the oldest get things first and the baby get . . . more . . . the most things before the middle child will get. [And the interview continued.]

At first glance, this extract does not seem different from interviews with the other women. But if one looks more closely—and especially if one listens to the tape—Dorcy's hesitations, monosyllabic answers, and reluctance to speak up become noticeable. This is in sharp contrast to her speech outside of the interview process, as well as that of most of the other women interviewed. At the end of the day, Mun recorded this short memo in his field notes:

> Interviewed Dorcy today. She has been urging me for the past two weeks to interview her. And when I was talking to her today, she was giving me monosyllabic answers and speaking in such a soft tone that I could hardly make out a word she was speaking. She was driving me nuts with her inarticulations and "I don't know" . . . she refuses to elaborate her stories and discuss about her life. I don't know why I chose her. . . . I should have stuck to my initial choice of either Mary or Annie.

Thinking that their bantering and gestures were a process in developing a friendship, Mun felt a sense of betrayal and wondered whether Dorcy's friendliness had been a kind of staged performance designed to win his confidence.

Judith Stacey (1991) contends that in our fieldwork, the lives, loves, and tragedies that informants share with researchers are ultimately data—"grist for the ethnographic mill, a mill that has a truly grinding power" (p. 113). When the women are informed and they consent, does this mean that their stories (and aspects of their lives they choose—or feel compelled—to share) no longer belong to them? Does, for example, Mun inform the welfare agency of their problems with particular staff members? Does he interrupt or simply collect narration of the women's racial antagonisms, between and among groups? What about the time Rosita told him in the corridor that she saw her batterer ex-boyfriend walking with the program administrator, Deborah, the person who generously opened the program for his research? How best to respond to the information presented in one of the focus groups that Rosita had been sexually harassed by one of the instructors? Mun found himself working between an organization that was generous enough to allow us "access" and the allegiance and hard-earned trust of respondents. In many of these cases, he was the opportunistic "fly on the wall," recording observations without seeming to become entangled in these ethical conundrums (Roman, 1993). But, as Stacey has noted, ethnographic method is more likely to leave subjects exposed

to exploitation: The greater the intimacy, according to Stacey, the greater the danger. And yet, contrary to this view, many of the women and men we interviewed both recognized and delightfully exploited the power inequalities in the interview process. They recognized that we could take their stories, their concerns, and their worries to audiences, policy makers, and the public in ways that they themselves could not, because they would not be listened to. They (and we) knew that we traded on class and race privilege to get a counternarrative out. And so they "consented." They were both informed and informing.

◆ Then, the Stories

Moving from worries of consent to worries about "bad stories" we collected:

Mun: Do you feel that your word is not trusted, that you need someone else to say, you need a lawyer or psychiatrist to say everything is okay now?

Tara: Because of DYFS [Division for Youth and Family Services], yes.

Mun: But you can't have . . .

Tara: They won't, yeah. They won't just take you for your word, no. You need to have—

Mun: You need to have somebody else say that for you?

Tara: Yes. DYFS, yes.

Mun: How would DYFS treat your kids, though?

Tara: Because when you get child, they say I put their life in danger, because I did, but I was . . . I was in jail, I was in the psychiatric ward. They had to do the best interest for the children, I couldn't take care of them at the time.

Mun: Oh, so DYFS took your kids?

Tara: Yeah, so DYFS gave them to their father. I'm in court now.

Mun: At least it's not foster care, though.

Tara: That's what I said. They're with family. They might hate it there, they can't stand it. My kids say that they're treated worse.

Mun: They hate their father?

Tara: No, they don't hate their father, they hate their grandmother, they hate the mother-in-law, they hate their grandmother. They don't like their grandmother.

Mun: His mother?

Tara: Yeah, they don't like their aunts, their uncles.

Mun: They are a lot of Puerto Ricans?

Tara: They're all Puerto Ricans, but my kids were always like the outcasts because they didn't like me so my kids, my kids, I mean, George was 7 years old, 7 years of George's life, George had to have seen his grandmother six times. Nicole, in the 3 years of her life, never seen them. You know, my kids got dumped into a family that they know nothing about.

What does it mean to uncover some of what we have uncovered? How do we handle "hot" information, especially in times when poor and working-class women and men are being demonized by the Right and by Congress? How do we connect theoretically, empirically, and politically troubling social/familial patterns with macrostructural shifts when our informants expressly do not make, or even refuse to make, the connections?

The hegemony of autonomous individualism forces a self-conscious, imposed theorizing (by us) of especially "bad stories," well beyond the perspectives expressed by most of our informants. So, for instance, what do we do with information about the ways in which women on welfare virtually have to become welfare cheats—"Sure he comes once a month and gives me some money. I may have to take a beating, but the kids need the money"—in order to survive (Edin & Lein, 1997)? A few use more drugs than we wished to know about; most are wonderful parents, but some underattend to their children well beyond neglect. These are the dramatic consequences, and perhaps also the "facilitators," of hard economic times. To ignore the information is to deny the effects of poverty, racism, and abuse. To report these stories is to risk their more than likely misuse, all the while *not* studying the tax evasion, use of drugs, and neglect of children perpetrated by elites.

In a moment in history when there are few audiences willing to reflect on the complex social roots of community and domestic violence, the economic impossibilities of sole reliance on welfare, or even the willingness to appreciate the complexity of love, hope, and pain that fills the poor and working class, how do we put out for display the voyeuristic dirty laundry that litters our transcripts? Historian Daryl Michael Scott (1997), in his provocative book *Contempt and Pity,* places in historical perspective the perverse historic use of the "damaged black psyche" by both the Left and the Right today. To what extent do we contribute to this perverse legacy? Is it better if white poor and working-class people are also portrayed as "damaged"? At the same time, isn't it unethical to romanticize, and thereby deny, the devastating impact of the current and historic assault on poor and working-class families launched through the state, the economy, neighbors, and sometimes kin? We are left, then, with two questions: First, must we (i.e., social scientists) document damage in order to justify claims about oppression and injustice? Second, what is the role of the public intellectual in rewriting—that is, interrupting—the "commonsense" script of "their" damage (and, of course, our wholeness) and offering up, instead, a discourse of national damage, outrage, and demands for justice?

With interviews over, we continue to struggle with how best to represent the stories that may do more damage than good, depending on who consumes/exploits them—stories that reveal the adult consequences of physical and sexual abuse in childhood; stories that suggest it is almost impossible to live exclusively on welfare payments, which encourages many to "lie" about their incomes so that they self-define as "welfare cheats"; stories in which white respondents, in particular, portray people of color in gross and dehumanizing ways; data on the depth of violence in women's lives, across race/ethnicity. To what extent are we responsible to add, "Warning! Misuse of data can be hazardous to our collective national health"?

There are some academics writing about such concerns (Cross, 1991; hooks, 1990; Lather, 1991), but few who write about and work with activists to reimagine social research for social justice (for wonderful such work, see Austin, 1992; Lykes, 1989; Saegert, 1997). It is up to all of us to figure out how to say what needs to be said without jeopardizing individuals and feeding perverse social representations (McCarthy et al., 1997).

As with bad stories, we worried about our voyeuristic search for "good stories." While engaged in interviewing, the research assistants would gather informally and share stories. We talked about respondents not showing up for their interviews, the lives of interviewees, "funny things that happened along the way," our pain, and our early understanding of the material. The words and phrases thrown around included "interesting," "boring," "nothing out of the ordinary," "you should have heard this," and "this one has great stories." But just what did we mean by "great stories"?

Great stories can be read as allegories that shed light on both the level of content and the implications of that content. Allegory, as James Clifford (1986) reminds us,

> denotes a practice in which a narrative fiction continuously refers to another pattern of ideas or events. It is a representation that "interprets" itself. . . . [It is] a story [that] has a propensity to generate another story in the mind of its reader (or hearer), to repeat and displace some prior story. . . . A recognition of allegory emphasizes the fact that realistic portraits, to the extent that they are "convincing" or "rich," are extended metaphors, patterns of associations that point to coherent (theoretical, esthetic, moral) additional meanings. . . . Allegory draws special attention to the narrative character of cultural representations, to the stories built into the representational process itself. (pp. 99-100)

We worry that what appear to be great stories might, however, feed our collective misunderstandings and renderings of the poor. Like experimenters who are inevitably inflicted with and inflicting "experimenter's bias," qualitative researchers carry misconceptions and "alluring fictions" (Clifford, 1986) of the subject. We enter the scene looking for stories and may, at times, "unintentionally behav[e] in such a way

as to make the prophesied event more likely to occur" (Suls & Rosnow, 1988, p. 168). By looking for great stories, we potentially walk into the field with constructions of the "other," however seemingly benevolent or benign, feeding the politics of representation and becoming part of the negative figuration of poor women and men.

For us, the fundamental "good story" is not simply one laced with "social problems" such as homelessness, welfare, and/or sexual harassment—a victim who is harassed, battered, and overwhelmed by problems. In retrospect, we admit that we also searched for agents who "resisted," enacting the role of the critic of the state and/or economic relations. As Mun's interviews with women on welfare proceeded, he always hoped that they would be perfect critics, able to pierce the veil of structured and state hypocrisy. It is interesting to note how so many hegemonic and victim-blaming positions were narrated by these profoundly oppressed men and women; judgments about "others" often resonated with a broad cultural discourse of holding victims of poverty, racism, and sexual violence accountable for their woes. In many of our interviews, poor women on welfare blamed other women, labeling them "welfare queens," "neglectful mothers," and "insensitive bureaucrats." Our own romanticized images of the resistor—one who desires to speak out against injustice and to act with a collective—turned on us.

Once we collect "great (and not so great) stories" from our respondents, the next difficult stage is the interpretation, representation, and analysis of data. We have, at times, consciously and deliberately left out some of these "great stories" that have the potential to become "bad data" to buttress stereotypes, reaffirm the ideology and rhetoric of the Right, and reinscribe dominant representations. As Hurtado and Stewart (1997) have written, the repetition of certain hurtful and vicious opinions and attitudes will inflict pain on those who are the "victims." In such cases, what is required is "minimal documentation, when views are all-too-familiar and oppressive, while holding ourselves and others to a very high standard of analytic depth when work carries such a high risk of causing suffering in those already the objects of daily racism" (p. 308)—and a close focus, as well, on the mundane.

What happens to the dull details of negotiating daily life in poverty that do not capture our attention in the way that "great stories" do?

> Well, I take . . . I get $424 a month, okay? And I get $270 in food stamps, so I take . . . there's four weeks to a month, so I take . . . I take the $270 and I divide it by four. And that's what I spend on food. It's just me and my daughters. And my oldest don't eat that much and I don't eat. . . . I only eat once a day. I only eat dinner. I'm not hungry in the morning and I don't have breakfast. I have a cup of coffee or hot chocolate. My little one is the one that eats a lot. And whatever I don't . . . like I spend $65 a week in food. I go and I buy meat every day and I buy their breakfast, their lunch, her snacks for school. And whenever I can . . . I work at night . . . I work . . . if I get a call I go and clean somebody's house. I do that. Their father gives me money, you know. So I do whatever I . . . you know, whatever it takes, you know? Shovel your snow . . . [laughs] I don't care. You know, to me money's money, as long as your kids got what they need. But basically their father helps me the most. You know, he'll come in . . . oh, my dad does this, too, and I get really pissed off at him. He'll come in and he'll start looking through my cabinets and in my refrigerator, and my closet. "Well, what do you have here?" And it's like, "I'm fine. Johnny's coming over later." "No! Blah, blah, blah." And he'll go out and he'll come back with food, and their father's always coming in looking through the refrigerator, and things like that, you know? I always . . . my kids have food, so that's good, you know? They never go hungry. You know, I . . . I hate to say this, but if I had . . . I mean, if it came to where my kids were gonna go hungry, I'd sell my body. To hell with that! My kids ain't gonna starve, you know? I'd do what it takes. I would give two shits. People could . . . my friends could tell me whatever they wanted. I have a . . . I have two friends that sell their bodies for money for their kids. And thank God, I have to knock on wood, I never had to take a loan, if I had to, I would. If that's what it took to feed my kids. . . . I mean, if their father . . . a lot of people that are on welfare have husbands worth shit. They don't care. If they had a father, but I guess that's, if that's what it took. . . . I would try every aspect before doing that. But if that's what it really took to feed my kids, that's what I would do. I would do whatever it takes to feed and clothe my kids, you know, and put a roof over their head. I wouldn't

> care what the hell it was. I guess that's what I would do, you know?

When we listen to and read narratives, researchers (we) tend to be drawn to—in fact, to *code for*—the exotic, the bizarre, the violent. As we reflect on narratives of poverty we nevertheless feel obligated to explore meticulously the very tedious and mundane sections of the transcripts, those huge sections that are not very exciting: the mundane spots, where "they" (the informants) do what "we" (the researchers) admit that "we" do—walk their kids to school, read the newspaper, turn on the television for a break, look for a doctor they can trust, hope their children are safe on the way home from school. These mundane rituals of daily living—obviously made much more difficult in the presence of poverty and discrimination, but mundane nonetheless—are typically left out of ethnographic descriptions of life in poverty. They don't make very good reading, and yet they are the stuff of daily life. We recognize how careful we need to be so that we do not construct life narratives spiked only with the hot spots.

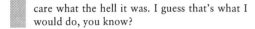

◆ Different Methods, Different Stories

Once the interviews are complete, triangulation surfaces as a critical element in the practice of social science: "adding" one layer of data to another to build a confirmatory edifice. In quantitative data analysis, triangulation occurs when multiple items within the same scale measure the same construct, or when two different scales join to measure the same construct. In psychological research in particular, and sociological research at times, the tendency is to use qualitative methods to supplement quantitative data.

However, in our work, conducted primarily through narratives but also through surveys on political engagement, we were not looking for a simple, coherent synthesis of data or methods. With a firm reliance on multiple methods, we sought to cross over, converse with, and tap into the different kinds of data; we searched for the very contradictions between methods that would most powerfully inform policy. We learned, as Fine and Weis (1996) have written elsewhere:

> Methods are not passive strategies. They differently produce, reveal, and enable the display of different kinds of identities. To be more specific, if individual interviews produce the most despairing stories, evince the most minimal sense of possibility, present identities of victimization, and voice stances of hopelessness, in focus groups with the same people the despair begins to evaporate, a sense of possibility sneaks through, and identities multiply as informants move from worker to mother, to friend, to lover, to sister, to spiritual healer, to son, to fireman, to once-employed, to welfare recipient. In the context of relative safety, trust, comfort, and counterhegemonic creativity offered by the few free spaces into which we have been invited, a far more textured and less judgmental sense of self is displayed. In these like-minded communities that come together to trade despair and build hope, we see and hear a cacophony of voices filled with spirit, possibility, and a sense of vitality absent in the individual data. (pp. 267-268)

We recognize that different methodologies are likely to illuminate different versions of men's and women's understandings of welfare, jobs, education, and violence. Convergence is unlikely and, perhaps, undesirable. Following a poststructuralist emphasis on contradiction, heterogeneity, and multiplicity, we produced a quilt of stories and a cacophony of voices speaking to each other in dispute, dissonance, support, dialogue, contention, and/or contradiction. Once women's and men's subjectivities are considered and sought after *as if* multiple, varied, conflicting, and contradictory, then the "data elicited" are self-consciously dependent upon the social locations of participants and the epistemological assumptions of the methods. We join Kum Kum Bhavnani (1993), who demands that multiple methods and a deep commitment to engaging with differences (particularly between researcher and researched) form the core of provocative, politically engaged so-

cial science, so that we "cannot be complicit with dominant representations which reinscribe inequality. It follows from a concern with power and positioning that the researcher must address the micropolitics of the conduct of research and . . . given the partiality of all knowledges, questions of differences must not be suppressed but built into research" (p. 98). Denzin and Lincoln (1994) suggest:

> Qualitative research is inherently multimethod in focus (Brewer & Hunter, 1989). However, the use of multiple methods, or triangulation, reflects an attempt to secure an in-depth understanding of the phenomenon in question. Objective reality can never be captured. Triangulation is not a tool or a strategy of validation, but an alternative to validation (Denzin, 1989a, 1989b, p. 244; Fielding & Fielding, 1986, p. 33; Flick, 1992, p. 194). The combination of multiple methods, empirical materials, perspectives and observers in a single study is best understood, then, as a strategy that adds rigor, breadth, and depth to any investigation (see Flick, 1992, p. 194). (p. 2)

◆ In Whose Voice?

Mark, a white working-class informant tells us:

> It goes into another subject where blacks, um, I have nothing against blacks. Um, whether you're black, white, you know, yellow, whatever color, whatever race. But I don't like the black movement where, I have black friends. I talk to them and they agree. You know, they consider themselves, you know, there's white trash and there's white, and there's black trash and there's blacks. And the same in any, you know, race. But as soon as they don't get a job, they right away call, you know, they yell discrimination.

In whose voice do we write? Well, of course, our own. But we also present long narratives, colorful and edited, drawn with/from informants. Some of these narratives, particularly from the sample of working-class and poor white men, contain hostile, sometimes grotesque references to "others"—people of color, women, black men on the corner. As theorists we refrain from the naïve belief that these voices should stand on their own or that voices should (or do) survive without theorizing. However, we also find ourselves differentially theorizing and contextualizing voices. That is, those voices that historically have been smothered—such as the voices of working-class white women, and men and women of color—we typically present on their own terms, perhaps reluctant to surround them with much of "our" theory (Weis, Marusza, & Fine, 1998). And yet when we present the voices of white men who seem eminently expert at fingering African American men for all the white men's pain and plight, we theorize boldly, contextualize wildly, rudely interrupting "them" to reframe "them" (Weis & Fine, 1996; Weis, Proweller, & Centrie, 1997).

Is this an epistemological double standard in need of reform, or is it a form of narrative affirmative action, creating discursive spaces where few have been in the past? Aida Hurtado and Abigail Stewart (1997), in a fascinating essay titled "Through the Looking Glass: Implications of Studying Whiteness for Feminist Methods," argue that feminist scholars should self-consciously underplay (e.g., not quote extensively) hegemonic voices in our essays and as relentlessly create textual room for counter-hegemonic narratives. Although we agree, we also think it is vitally important for us to analyze, critically, what it is that white men are saying about us, about "them," about economic and social relations. To do this, we interpret their words, their stories, and their assertions about "others."

This raises what we have come to think of as the "triple representational problem." We ponder how we present (a) ourselves as researchers choreographing the narratives we have collected; (b) the narrators, many of whom are wonderful social critics, whereas some, from our perspective, are talented ventriloquists for a hateful status quo; and (c) the "others" who are graphically bad-mouthed by these narrators, such as caseworkers blamed for stinginess and disrespect by women on welfare, African American men held responsible for all social evils by white men, and police officers held in contempt by communities of color, which have endured much abuse at the hands of the police. Do we have a responsibility to theorize the agency/innocence/collusion of these groups, too? When white men make disparaging comments about women of color, do we need to re-present women of color and denounce and re-place these representations? If not, are we not merely contributing to the archival representations of disdain that the social science literature has already so horrifically chronicled?

Given that all of these participants deserve to be placed within historical and social contexts, and yet power differences and abuses proliferate, how do theorists respect the integrity of informants' consciousness and narratives, place them within social and historical context, and yet not collude in the social scientific gaze, fixation, moral spectacularizing (Roman, 1997) of the poor and working-class? There are no easy answers to these dilemmas. In *The Unknown City* we try to contextualize the narratives as spoken within economic, social, and racial contexts so that no one narrator is left holding the bag for his or her demographic group, but indeed there are moments when, within the narratives, "others"—people of color, caseworkers, men, women, the neighbor next door—are portrayed in very disparaging ways. Then we wage the battle of *representation*. We work hard to figure out how to represent and contextualize our narrators, ourselves, and the people about whom they are ranting. We try, with the tutelage of historians Joan Scott (1992), Michael Katz (1995), Robin Kelly (1997), and Daryl Scott (1997), sociologist Joyce Ladner (1971), literary critic Eve Sedgwick (1990), and psychologist William Cross (1991), to understand how and why these binaries, these categories of analysis, these "others," these splittings, and these accusations are being cast at this moment in history, and who is being protected by this social science focus on blame (Opotow, 1990). Nevertheless, at times audiences have been alarmed at the language in our texts, at the vivid descriptions and the portraits, for instance, of seemingly cold and heartless social workers. We are working on these issues, and we welcome help from others who are also struggling with both theory and empirical data.

◆ What's Safe to Say Aloud— and by Whom?

> How hard it is for us to *think* we can choose to become writers, much less *feel* and *believe* that we can. What have we to contribute, to give? Our own expectations condition us. Does not our class, our culture as well as the white man tell us writing is not for women such as us?
>
> The white man speaks: *Perhaps if you scrape the dark off your face. Maybe if you bleach your bones. Stop speaking in tongues, stop writing left-handed. Don't cultivate your colored skins nor tongues of fire if you want to make it in a right-handed world.* (Anzaldúa, 1981, p. 166)

We have collected stories for the past 6 years on communities, economic and racial relationships, and individual lives deeply affected by public policies and institutions that had been rotten and rotting for many years before that. And yet these very same public policies and institutions, the ones about which we have deeply incriminating data, are today being excised, yanked away from communities as we speak—public schools, welfare, social services, public housing. Positioning a critique of the public sphere as it evaporates, or, more aptly, as it is targeted for downsizing and for demise, seems an academic waste of time. At its worst, it anticipates collusion with the Right. Nevertheless, the criticisms are stinging:

Tamara: I didn't want to be with the father of my children anymore. And at that time he really gave me a lot of headaches. "If you don't stay with me, then I'm not gonna help you with the kids." Which he really didn't do, which I'm thankful. But I just figured, "Well, the hell with it. Then I'll work . . . get the welfare." Because I pay $640 for this apartment. That's a lot of money for a two-bedroom apartment, you know? And the welfare only gives me $424, so I have to make up the difference. And plus I have a telephone, you know. I have cable for my daughters, you know. And it's just a lot of money. And I figure, you know, I figured, well, I couldn't make it on my own. I wasn't making enough

to make it on my own back then, so I had to go on welfare. So I did it, and it was . . . I didn't like it. I didn't like sitting there. I didn't like the waiting. I didn't like the questions they asked me, you know?

Mun: What kind of questions did—

Tamara: Well, they asked me if I was sexually active, how many times I went to bed with him, you know? And I told the guy, "I'm sorry, but that is none of your business," and I refuse to answer the questions. Because to me, well what, they ask you if you, he asked me if I slept with black men or white men, Puerto Rican men. What was my preference. And to me that was the questions—

Mun: Was this on a form, or he—

Tamara: No, he was just asking questions, you know? And I refused to answer them, you know. And he kind of like got upset. "We have to ask you this." I was like, "Bullshit." You know, they just wanted to, they asked, he asked me how many times I had sex in a day, and just really, you know, if I douched, if I was clean, if I took a shower. I don't think these are any of your business, you know? I take a shower every night and every day, you know? I think those are stupid questions he asked. I was, he asked me how many men I had in my life that I had, you know, if I have more than one man. And I turned around and told him, "I'm not your mother." I never heard of questions like—[laughs]

Mun: Neither have I. [laughs]

Tamara: They asked the weird questions.

Mun: So, how, what was the procedure like?

Tamara: It was embarrassing. Like, with Medicaid, for kids it's good. For kids, you know, you can go anywhere you want with the Medicaid. You can go to the doctors for kids. You know, they pay for braces. When it comes to an adult, I was going to, I was hemorrhaging. I was going to a doctor. I'd been bleeding since December, okay, and they're telling me, I've been going to a gynecologist through the welfare. "It's normal, it's normal. Don't worry about it. It's normal." So last week I was getting ready, for the past week I was feeling really dizzy and really weak, and I said the hell with it. Let me go see a gynecologist. And I paid her. Thank God, you know, the Medicaid took care of the hospital. But I had to pay her $700 for the procedure that I had to have done. [laughs] I had to do it. It was either that or bleed to death, you know. [laughs] But a lot of doctors, I asked her, because she used to take Medicaid. And I asked her, "Why don't you, you know, take Medicaid anymore?" And a lot of doctors that don't, doctors tell you because they don't pay them. She said she's been waiting for people that were on Medicaid to get paid for 2 years, 3 years, bills—that's how old the bills are and she's still waiting to get paid.

Our responsibility in this work, as we see it, is not to feed the dismantling of the state by posing a critique of the public sector as it has been, but instead to insist on a state that serves its citizenry well and responsibly. That is, social researchers must create vision and imagination for "what could be" and demand the resurrection of an accountable public sphere that has a full and participatory citizenship at its heart. Then we can layer on the critiques of "what has been." That said, it is important to note that it is not so easy when many are just waiting to use our narrative words to do away with welfare; when Brett Schundler, mayor of Jersey City, is desirous of getting voucher legislation passed in a city in which public schools enjoy little to no positive reputation; when Charles Murray (1984) will abduct our phrases as he paints poor women as lazy and irresponsible. Creating a safe space for intellectual, critical, and complicated discussion when the Right has been so able and willing to extract arguments that sustain the assault may be a naïve wish, but it is a worthwhile one.

◆ On "Safe Spaces"

In conducting our research for *The Unknown City,* we heard from young women and men who grew up within the working-class and poor segments of our society how they view economic opportunities; how they spin images of personal

and collective futures, especially as related to the power of schooling; how they conceptualize the shrinking public sector, the economy, labor, and the military; and how they reflect upon progressive social movements that have historically and dramatically affected their ancestors' and their own life chances. We heard about a disappearing public sphere but we tripped upon, as well, those urban pockets of counterhegemonic possibility, sites of critique, engagement, and outrage, excavated by these young men and women. Amid their despair lies hope. And hope appears to be cultivated in these "safe" spaces. So how to write on and through these spaces without romanticizing the tiny corners of sanctuary and possibility available to and created by the poor and working-class in the late 1990s? If people are surviving with hope and optimism, is devastation justified or managed?

The spaces into which we have been invited provide recuperation, resistance, and the makings of "home." They are not just a set of geographic/spatial arrangements, they are theoretical, analytic, and spatial displacements—a crack, a fissure in an organization or a community. Individual dreams, collective work, and critical thoughts are smuggled in and then reimagined. Not rigidly bounded by walls/fences, the spaces often are corralled by a series of (imaginary) borders where community intrusion and state surveillance are not permitted. These are spaces where trite social stereotypes are fiercely contested. That is, these young women and men, in their constant confrontation with harsh public representations of their races, ethnicities, classes, genders, and sexualities, use these spaces to break down these public images for scrutiny, and to invent new ones.

These spaces include the corners of the African American church where young men ponder how to "take back the streets" to "save the young boys"; the lesbian and gay center carved out quietly by working-class late adolescents and young adults seeking identities and networks when their geographic and cultural contexts deny them sexual expression; the Head Start and EPIC (Every Person Influences Children) programs in which poor mothers, and sometimes fathers, come together to talk about the delights and the minefields of raising children in a culture showered in racism and decimated by poverty; the cultural arts programs where men and women join self-consciously across racial and ethnic borders to create what is "not yet," a space, a set of images, a series of aesthetic products that speak of a world that could be (Weis & Fine, in press).

Spaces such as these spring from the passions and concerns of community members; they are rarely structured from "above." They may be one-time fictions, transitory, or quite stable. They can be designed to restore identities devastated by the larger culture, or they may be opportunities to try on identities and communities rejected by both mainstream culture and local ethnic groups. These spaces hold rich and revealing data about the resilience of young adults without denying the oppression that threatens the borders and interiors of community life amid urban poverty.

Legitimately, one may ask (and some have) whether we have any business floating through or writing about these sequestered quarters. Does our presence affect or interrupt the music of life within "free spaces"? Does our social scientific voyeurism shatter the sanctity of that which is presumably (although recognizably not) "free"?

We come down on these questions, for the moment at least, by presenting two different incidents. One occurred in a basement office in which New Jersey community activists met to discuss local politics. We were welcomed for the initial interview, but the notion of our continued presence clearly provoked discomfort. Not asked to return, we left—in good stead and with enormous respect. In contrast, for instance, we have been invited into some spaces (e.g., an EPIC parenting group, a black church, a community center, a lesbian and gay club) in which members, directors, and others indicate they are eager for documentation—anxious for others to know who they "really" are, what functions their programs serve, how deeply spiritual and religious "those teenage mothers" can be, how organized and supportive "those gays and lesbians" are. They have welcomed us into their

spaces to "exploit" our capacity—our class and professional positions and networks—and our willingness to write and to testify to those aspects of community life that the media ignore, that stereotypes deny, that mainstream culture rarely gets to see. And yet we seek not to romanticize resilience—for these spaces represent severe critique as well as warm comfort.

◆ On Responsibilities

We have certainly read much, and even written a fair amount, about researchers' subjectivities (Fine, 1994). Our obligation is to come clean "at the hyphen," meaning that we interrogate in our writings who we are as we coproduce the narratives we presume to "collect," and we anticipate how the public and policy makers will receive, distort, and misread our data. It is now acknowledged that critical ethnographers have a responsibility to talk about our identities, why we interrogate what we do, what we choose not to report, how we frame our data, on whom we shed our scholarly gaze, who is protected and not protected as we do our work. What is our participatory responsibility to research with and for a more progressive community life? As part of this discussion, we want to try to explain how we, as researchers, have worked with communities to capture and build upon exciting community and social movements. In other words, we will put forward parts of our ever-evolving political agenda, sharing the kinds of scholarship/action that we are focusing upon and how our work has been reshaped by the activism in the communities studied.

Thus far, in Jersey City and Buffalo we have been able to document how state policies and local economic/social shifts have affected young women's and men's belief systems, worldviews, social consciousness. Through individual interviews we have gathered much of this information. Through focus groups (e.g., in the lesbian and gay club, in the African American and white churches, in the EPIC parenting group, in the Latina homeless shelter, in the Pre-Cap college program for young adolescents), we have been able to create settings in which our interviewees have begun to weave together analyses about their commitments, for instance, to the "next generation of African American boys" or to "practicing the ways of my grandmother" around Latina spiritual rituals. An activist nun and a local director of Head Start have both invited us to work more closely with groups of women and men in their programs, running focus groups that would raise questions, press issues, and help the participants reshape programs. A college preparation program for "at-risk" youths (labels!) asked us for an evaluation to assist with further funding. In the EPIC group, we were told that the engagement of several members was raised due to the kind of individual and group work in which we were involved. For these women the group interviews offered them a way of piecing together the strengths of their lives, encouraging forward movement as they were raising their families in the midst of poverty. Indeed, Lois Weis was asked to facilitate an EPIC group on a long-term basis.

Further, throughout the course of our 5 years of research, we have moved across the researcher-researched hyphen and into a community of activists to apply our work to support local policy and community efforts. Michelle Fine testified at state hearings in Trenton and in Jersey City on the state takeover of the local schools, advocating with community groups that the state remain in control until authentic local participation can be encouraged and sustained; Mun Wong coordinated a project among women on welfare who were eager to document the differential supermarket prices of similar items at different points in the month and in different markets in the community; Lois Weis supplied testimony in support of continual funding for EPIC; and in Jersey City, we have provided census and qualitative data to city council members from the Latino community. Our graduate students have been deeply involved in various communities as they engage in dissertation work in an Irish community center, an African American church, a neighborhood center that serves white working-class youth, a neighborhood arts center, and numerous others. In all such spaces,

graduate students are "giving back" to the communities in which they are working. Across communities, numerous conversations have taken place with key policy makers on a number of issues arising from our data.

We take for granted that the purpose of social inquiry in the 1990s is not only to generate new knowledge but to reform "common sense" and inform critically public policies, existent social movements, and daily community life. A commitment to such "application," however, should not be taken for granted. This is a(nother) critical moment in the life of the social sciences, one in which individual scholars are today making decisions about the extent to which our work should aim to be "useful."

We have colleagues who embrace the commitment to "application," as we do, even if some think it is naïve for us to imagine our being able to infiltrate current policy talk on life within poor and working-class communities; other colleagues have long seen their own scholarship as explicitly aimed toward political and social change (see the work of Gittell, 1990, 1994; Lykes, 1994; Mullings, 1984; Piven & Cloward, 1971; Powell, 1994). And yet we hear a growing chorus of colleagues (on the Right and the Left) who presume that if one is interested in, engaged by, or drawn to policy, one's scholarship is less trustworthy, tainted by advocacy, commitments, passion, or responsibilities. This latter position was perhaps in retreat for a moment in time, but it seems to be returning to the academy in well-orchestrated volume. We do, of course, reject this latter position, but would ask again that academics who see y/our work as deeply nested in community life (recognizing that the notion of "community" is up for grabs) come together to argue cogently our responses to the litany: Is this science? Is this advocacy? Is only progressive work biased? Is this politics or policy?

We must probe to find the sites of intellectual leverage, responsibility, and obligation through which our work can begin to fissure public and political discourse, shifting the ideological and material grounds on which poor and working-class men and women are now being tortured. That said, we take our responsibilities to these communities seriously, and Lois and

Michelle are educating their graduate students to work with—not on or despite—local community efforts.

It is important to note another "underground debate" within community studies, which concerns the tension between representing historically oppressed groups as "victimized" and "damaged" or as "resilient" and "strong." This may seem an artificial and dangerous dichotomy—we think it is. But we have encountered colleagues within feminism, critical race theory, poverty work, disability studies, and, most recently, queer theory who argue across these intellectual stances, with these two "choices" carved out as the (presumably only) appropriate alternatives. We share the worries, but worry more about the fixed "choices" that are being offered. Simple stories of victimization, with no evidence of resistance, resilience, or agency, are seriously flawed and deceptively partial; they deny the rich subjectivities of persons surviving amid devastating social circumstances. Equally dreary, however, are the increasingly popular stories of individual heroes who thrive despite their difficulties, denying the burdens of surviving amid such circumstances.

We stretch toward writing that spirals around social injustice and resilience, that recognizes the endurance of structures of injustice and the powerful acts of agency, that appreciates the courage and the limits of individual acts of resistance but refuses to perpetuate the fantasy that "victims" are simply powerless. That these women and men are strong is not evidence that they have suffered no oppression. Individual and collective strength cannot be used against poor and working-class people as evidence—"See? It's not been so bad!" We need to invent an intellectual stance in which structural oppression, passion, social movements, and evidence of strength, health, and "damage" can all be recognized and theorized without erasing essential features of the complex story of injustice that constitutes urban life in poverty.

We take solace in the words of many of our African American male informants—drawn from churches and spiritual communities— who testify, as one said, that "only belief and hope

will save our communities. We have come a long, long way . . . and we have much further to go. Only belief will get us through." Amid the pain, the despair, survives hope. This, too, is a big part of community life, rarely seen in the light of day.

◆ Conclusion

We end this essay with a set of what might be called ethical invitations or, put more boldly, ethical injunctions. We offer these in the spirit of wedging open and contributing to a conversation about researcher responsibility, recognizing, of course, that questions of responsibility-for-whom will, and should, forever be paramount—because the "whom" is not a coherent whole, no single constituency, no unified community, group, or set of "others," and because the context in which we write today will change tomorrow, and so too will the readings of this text.

We write on the ethics of responsibility because we don't want to write only for and with friends; we hope to write in ways that contribute to a reshaping of the "common sense" about poverty, the economy, and social and human relations. We consider, then, the ethics of writing research in the interest of social justice and the ethics of publishing what Richardson (1995) has called "writing-stories." We offer the ideas below as lenses through which social analyses might be continually reassessed and (re)imagined.

On Reframing What Seems Like Good and Bad News

Our first injunction is that social researchers dare to speak hard truths with theoretical rigor and political savvy. By that, we mean that "bad stories," like "good stories," are always partial but/and deserve a hearing. They reveal as much as they conceal, whether informants seem too close or too far. Having witnessed the Right-wing assault on education, health care, welfare, and immigration in this country, we have become more convinced, not less, that progressive activists and researchers need to interrogate with deliberation—not camouflage with romance—some of the rough spots in our work. To obscure the bad news is to fool no one. Indeed, the suffocation of "bad stories" only tempers the very real stories of oppression we seek to tell. That there are (unevenly distributed) damaging consequences to all living under advanced capitalism, racist social relations, violent gendered relations, and homophobic community life is no great secret. That individuals engage in activities or behaviors deemed illegal, unethical, or immoral in contexts in which justice and fairness have no role is evidence of social injustice—not a reason to blame victims. That many thrive despite the odds is equally well-known. How survival, damage, and oppressive social/economic relations meld together is the task of explanation that lies before us. How to inform and encourage social movements for "what could be" is the task at hand. Thus, indeed, we err on the side of telling many kinds of stories, attached always to history, larger structures, and social forces, offered neither to glamorize nor to pathologize, but to re-view what has been, to re-imagine what could be in communities of poverty and the working class, and to re-visit, with critical speculation, lives, relations, and communities of privilege.

Upon Reflections

We ask, second, that beginning and veteran researchers, and all those in between, pose a set of questions to themselves as they move through the recursive "stages" of social analysis. These question are listed in no particular order, and have few right answers. But, we insist, they should be asked, as we all write what we write in a world not (necessarily) prepared to hear.

1. *Have I connected the "voices" and "stories" of individuals back to the set of historic, structural, and economic relations in which they are situated?* We mean this in no linear fashion, in no simple determinative progression, but only to recognize that what people say has a relation to the structures and ideologies around them in ways that will almost certainly not be narrated by interviewees themselves. The work of theory is to articulate these relations, excavating how qualitative narratives or even quantitative responses on a 5-point Likert scale are nested within a system of historic and material conditions.

2. *Have I deployed multiple methods so that very different kinds of analyses can be constructed?* In our work on *The Unknown City*, we found that individual and focus group interviews generated very different kinds of narrations—neither more true than the other, but different, particularly when it came to individuals expressing optimism or pessimism about the future and their place in it. We came to understand that it was important to theorize why and how responses took different forms, not seeking simple confirmation, or concluding too easily that there is contradiction, or one narration is more "true" than the other. Instead, we struggled to cultivate a theoretical relation between possibly very different responses, understanding that the issue of "triangulation" is not simple. Different people do, in fact, seem the same but different at times. The same person can do the same. We cannot see this as "contradictory," or worse, useless data, as this can cause us to miss important facets of individual and community life.

3. *Have I described the mundane?* As we have noted, we found it hard to resist the temptation to surf through our transcripts with a coding eye toward the exotic or the violent. Coding tends to lend itself to that. And yet most of our transcriptions reveal the boring details of life on the ground, day-to-day interactions with friends, kin, neighbors, children, and television. These portraits, although rarely stunning, constitute much of life in poverty and should not be relegated to the edited-out files.

4. *Have some informants/constituencies/participants reviewed the material with me and interpreted, dissented, challenged*

my interpretations? And then how do I report these departures/agreements in perspective? This is not a call for handing over veto power, but only a call for conversation, negotiated interpretations, texts in which multiple interpretations flourish, in which challenges are integrated into the manuscript. Much of this work can take place in follow-up focus groups to either participant observation work or individual interviews.

5. *How far do I want to go with respect to theorizing the words of informants?* That is, with respect to what Fine and Weis (1996) have called the triple representation problem, have you worked to understand your contribution to the materials/narrations provided and those silenced? Have you worked to explain to readers the position from which informants speak? Have you worked to recast the person(s) whom the informant chooses to "blame" or credit for social justice or injustice (be it a social worker, the informant's mother, black men)? Again, we do not hold out that all researchers must answer yes to these questions—only that researchers (faculty and graduate students) must ask themselves these questions and understand why it is that some answers must be no.

6. *Have I considered how these data could be used for progressive, conservative, repressive social policies?* How might the data be heard? Misread? Misappropriated? Do you need to add a "warning" about potential misuse?

7. *Where have I backed into the passive voice and decoupled my responsibility for my interpretations?* That is, where have you hidden your own authority behind "their" narrations or "their" participatory interpretations?

8. *Who am I afraid will see these analyses? Who is rendered vulnerable/responsible or exposed by these analyses? Am I willing to show him/her/them the text before publication? If not, why not? Could I*

publish his/her/their comments as an epilogue? What's the fear?

9. *What dreams am I having about the material presented?* What issues are pulling at/out of your own biography? Have you over- or underplayed them?

10. *To what extent has my analysis offered an alternative to the "commonsense" or dominant discourse? What challenges might very different audiences pose to the analysis presented?*

None of the above questions is intended to stifle scholarly license or to insist that there is one "right way" to answer them. Rather, these questions are intended to expand our work by helping us to recognize the potential influence of our writings: the pulls, fantasies, projections, and likely responses of very different kinds of audiences and the responsibility we have, therefore, to anticipate the relation between the texts we produce and the "common sense" that awaits/confronts them. By asking ourselves these questions, we push the issues, forcing ourselves to deal with what are serious dilemmas in our research. We repeat: not all of us will answer in the same ways. But we will clarify why we answer in the ways we do.

On Cautions

After reflections, we suggest that particularly those of us who write on questions of structural relations to the micropolitics of life in poverty should draft and publish a "Legend of Cautions: Ways to Misread, Misappropriate, and Misuse Presented Analyses." That is, we imagine such a legend that warns readers how *not* to read our work—for example, how not to use evidence of welfare fraud to cut payments or resurrect a welfare surveillance system, how not to exploit the real fears inside poor communities to generate support for the building of more prisons, how not to appropriate the anger of poor communities at their public schools as a rallying cry for vouchers likely to serve few but the relatively privileged. We recommend many, many drafts of these warnings, but anticipate that without such warnings the likelihood of our analyses being misappropriated is much higher than the likelihood of our analyses being deployed for ends of which we would approve.

On Educating Students in Multiple Genres

We exit this chapter with our fiercest injunction: that we have an ethical responsibility to retreat from the stance of dispassion all too prevalent in the academy and to educate our students toward analyzing, writing, and publishing in multiple genres at one and the same time—in policy talk, in the voices of empiricism, through the murky swamps of self-reflective "writing-stories," and in the more accessible languages of pamphlets, fliers, and community booklets. That is, if we are serious about enabling our students to be fluent across methods, to be engaged with community struggles, and to theorize conditions of social (in)justice, we must recognize that flickers and movements for social change happen in varied sites—courtrooms, legislative offices, the media, community-based organizations, and church groups, as well as the academy—and therefore through varied texts.

We recognize full well that there may be consequences for nontenured faculty who attempt to write across audiences in the way we are suggesting. Tenure review committees and external reviewers associated with these committees may not "count" writing other than traditional research (including qualitative analyses) as evidence that an individual is deserving of tenure or later promotion to full professor. It is important for junior faculty to establish credibility within a traditional research community. As one writes for a scholarly audience, however, it is possible to exercise simultaneously the option for writing in multiple tongues. We are not urging graduate students and junior faculty to write for broad-based audiences at the expense of writing for scholarly journals, authoring monographs, and so forth. Although the academy is changing, we recognize that the moves are slow, and resistance is always high.

With this caveat in mind, reflections on our responsibilities as social researchers must punctuate all texts we produce. Without such reflection, in the name of neutrality or researcher dispassion, we collude in a retreat from social responsibility, and the academy remains yet another institution without a soul in a world increasingly bankrupt of moral authority.

■ Note

1. Legal scholar Patricia Williams (1997) tells a story of her preschool-age son, who was seemingly unable to identify the colors of objects. Asked what color the grass was, for example, he would respond, "I don't know" or "It makes no difference." Eventually, Williams discovered that "the well-meaning teachers at his predominantly white school had valiantly and repeatedly assured their charges that color makes no difference. . . . Yet upon further investigation, the very reason that the teachers had felt it necessary to impart this lesson in the first place was that it did matter, and in predictably cruel ways: some of the children had been fighting about whether black people could play 'good guys' " (p. 3).

■ References

Anzaldúa, G. (1981). Speaking in tongues: A letter to Third World women writers. In C. Moraga & G. Anzaldúa (Eds.), *This bridge called my back: Writings by radical women of color* (pp. 165-173). New York: Kitchen Table/Women of Color Press.

Austin, R. (1992). "The black community," its lawbreakers, and a politics of identification. *Southern California Law Review, 65,* 1769-1817.

Behar, R. (1993). *Translated woman: Crossing the border with Esperanza's story.* Boston: Beacon.

Bhavnani, K. K. (1993). Tracing the contours: Feminist research and feminist objectivity. *Women's Studies International Forum, 16,* 95-104.

Billig, M. (1994). Repopulating the depopulated pages of social psychology. *Theory and Psychology, 4,* 307-335.

Borland, K. (1991). That's not what I said: Interpretive conflict in moral narrative research. In S. B. Gluck & D. Patai (Eds.), *Women's words: The feminist practice of oral history* (pp. 63-76). New York: Routledge.

Brewer, J., & Hunter, A. (1989). *Multimethod research: A synthesis of styles.* Newbury Park, CA: Sage.

Clifford, J. (1986). On ethnographic allegory. In J. Clifford & G. E. Marcus (Eds.), *Writing culture: The poetics and politics of ethnography* (pp. 98-121). Berkeley: University of California Press.

Clough, P. T. (1992). *The end(s) of ethnography: From realism to social criticism.* Newbury Park, CA: Sage.

Crenshaw, K. (1995). Mapping the margins: Intersectionality, identity politics, and violence against women of color. In K. Crenshaw, N. Gotanda, G. Peller, & K. Thomas (Eds.), *Critical race theory: The key writings that formed the movement* (pp. 357-383). New York: New Press.

Cross, W. E., Jr. (1991). *Shades of black: Diversity in African-American identity.* Philadelphia: Temple University Press.

Denzin, N. K. (1989a). *Interpretive interactionism.* Newbury Park, CA: Sage.

Denzin, N. K. (1989b). *The research act: A theoretical introduction to sociological methods* (3rd ed.). Englewood Cliffs, NJ: Prentice Hall.

Denzin, N. K., & Lincoln, Y. S. (1994). Introduction: Entering the field of qualitative research. In N. K. Denzin & Y. S. Lincoln (Eds.), *Handbook of qualitative research* (pp. 1-17). Thousand Oaks, CA: Sage.

Dyson, M. E. (1993). *Reflecting black: African-American cultural criticism.* Minneapolis: University of Minnesota Press.

Edin, K., & Lein, L. (1997). *Making ends meet: How single mothers survive welfare and low-wage work.* New York: Russell Sage Foundation.

Fielding, N. G., & Fielding, J. L. (1986). *Linking data.* Beverly Hills, CA: Sage.

Fine, M. (1994). Working the hyphens: Reinventing self and other in qualitative research. In N. R. Denzin & Y. S. Lincoln (Eds.), *Handbook of qualitative research* (pp. 70-82). Thousand Oaks, CA: Sage.

Fine, M., Powell, L. C., Weis, L., & Wong, L. M. (Eds.). (1997). *Off white: Readings on race, power, and society.* New York: Routledge.

Fine, M., & Weis, L. (1996). Writing the "wrongs" of fieldwork: Confronting our own research/writing dilemmas in urban ethnographies. *Qualitative Inquiry, 2,* 251-274.

Fine, M., & Weis, L. (1998). *The unknown city: The lives of poor and working-class young adults.* Boston: Beacon.

Flick, U. (1992). Triangulation revisited: Strategy of validation or alternative? *Journal for the Theory of Social Behaviour, 22,* 175-198.

Gates, H. L., Jr. (Ed.). (1985). *"Race," writing, and difference.* Chicago: University of Chicago Press.

Gittell, M. J. (1990). Women on foundation boards: The illusion of change. *Women and Foundations/Corporate Philanthropy, 1,* 1-2.

Gittell, M. J. (1994). School reform in New York and Chicago: Revisiting the ecology of local games. *Urban Affairs Quarterly, 30,* 136-151.

Hall, S. (1981). Moving right. *Socialist Review, 55,* 113-137.

Hall, S. (1997). Subjects in history: Making diasporic identities. In W. Lubiano (Ed.), *The house that race built: Black Americans, U.S. terrain* (pp. 289-299). New York: Pantheon.

Haraway, D. J. (1991). *Simians, cyborgs, and women: The reinvention of nature.* New York: Routledge.

hooks, b. (1990). *Yearning: Race, gender, and cultural politics.* Boston: South End Press.

Hurtado, A., & Stewart, A. J. (1997). Through the looking glass: Implications of studying whiteness for feminist methods. In M. Fine, L. C. Powell, L. Weis, & L. M. Wong (Eds.), *Off white: Readings on race, power and society* (pp. 297-311). New York: Routledge.

Katz, M. (1995). *Improving poor people.* Princeton, NJ: Princeton University Press.

Kelly, R. D. G. (1997). *Yo' mama's disfunktional! Fighting the culture wars in urban black America.* Boston: Beacon.

Ladner, J. A. (1971). *Tomorrow's tomorrow: The black woman.* Garden City, NY: Doubleday.

Lal, J. (1996). Situating locations. In D. L. Wolf (Ed.), *Feminist dilemmas in fieldwork* (pp. 185-214). Boulder, CO: Westview.

Lather, P. (1991). *Getting smart: Feminist research and pedagogy with/in the postmodern.* New York: Routledge.

Lawrence, C. R., III. (1995). The word and the river: Pedagogy as scholarship as struggle. In K. Crenshaw, N. Gotanda, G. Peller, & K. Thomas (Eds.), *Critical race theory: The key writings that formed the movement* (pp. 336-351). New York: New Press.

Lykes, M. B. (1989). Dialogue with Guatemalan Indian women: Critical perspectives on constructing collaborative research. In R. K. Unger (Ed.), *Representations: Social constructions of gender* (pp. 167-184). Amityville, NY: Baywood.

Lykes, M. B. (1994). Speaking against the silence: One Maya woman's exile and return. In C. E. Franz & A. J. Stewart (Eds.), *Women creating lives: Identities, resilience, and resistance* (pp. 97-114). Boulder, CO: Westview.

Madigan, R., Johnson, S., & Linton, P. (1995). The language of psychology: APA style as epistemology. *American Psychologist, 50,* 428-436.

Matsuda, M. (1995). Looking to the bottom: Critical legal studies and reparations. In K. Crenshaw, N. Gotanda, G. Peller, & K. Thomas (Eds.), *Critical race theory: The key writings that formed the movement* (pp. 63-79). New York: New Press.

McCarthy, C., Rodriguez, A., Meecham, S., David, S., Wilson-Brown, C., Godina, H., Supryia, K. E., & Buendia, E. (1997). Race, suburban resentment, and the representation of the inner city in contemporary film and television. In M. Fine, L. C. Powell, L. Weis, & L. M. Wong (Eds.), *Off white: Readings on race, power, and society* (pp. 229-241). New York: Routledge.

Morawski, J. G., & Bayer, B. M. (1995). Stirring trouble and making theory. In H. Landrine (Ed.), *Bringing cultural diversity to feminist psychology: Theory, research, and practice* (pp. 113-137). Washington, DC: American Psychological Association.

Mullings, L. (1984). Minority women, work and health. In W. Chavkin (Ed.), *Double exposure: Women's health hazards on the job and at home* (pp. 84-106). New York: Monthly Review Press.

Murray, C. (1984). *Losing ground: American social policy 1950-1980.* New York: Basic Books.

Okely, J. (1992). Anthropology and autobiography: Participatory experience and embodied knowledge. In J. Okely & H. Callaway (Eds.), *Anthropology and autobiography* (pp. 1-49). London: Routledge.

Omi, M. & Winant, H. (1986). *Racial formations in the United States: From the 1960s to the 1980s.* New York: Routledge.

Opotow, S. (1990). Moral exclusion and injustice: An introduction. *Journal of Social Issues, 46,* 1-20.

Piven, F. F., & Cloward, R. A. (1971). *Regulating the poor: The functions of public welfare.* New York: Pantheon.

Powell, L. (1994). Interpreting social defenses: Family group in an urban setting. In M. Fine (Ed.), *Chartering urban school reform: Reflections on public high schools in the midst of change* (pp. 112-121). New York: Teacher's College Press.

Richardson, L. (1995). Writing-stories: Co-authoring "The sea monster," a writing-story. *Qualitative Inquiry, 1,* 189-203.

Roman, L. (1993). Double exposure: The politics of feminist materialist ethnography. *Educational Theory, 43,* 279-308.

Roman, L. (1997). Denying (white) racial privilege: Redemption discourses and the uses of fantasy. In M. Fine, L. C. Powell, L. Weis, & L. M. Wong (Eds.), *Off white: Readings on race, power and society* (pp. 270-282). New York: Routledge.

Rosaldo, R. (1989). *Culture and truth: The remaking of social analysis.* Boston: Beacon.

Saegert, S. (1997, May). *Schools and the ecology of gender.* Paper presented at the Schools and the Urban Environment Conference, National Taiwan University, Taipei.

Scott, D. M. (1997). *Contempt and pity: Social policy and the image of the damaged black psyche 1880-1996.* Chapel Hill: University of North Carolina Press.

Scott, J. W. (1992). Experience. In J. Butler & J. W. Scott (Eds.), *Feminists theorize the political* (pp. 22-40). New York: Routledge.

Sedgwick, E. K. (1990). *Epistemology of the closet.* Berkeley: University of California Press.

Stacey, J. (1991). Can there be a feminist eth-nography? In S. B. Gluck & D. Patai (Eds.), *Women's words: The feminist practice of oral history* (pp. 111-119). New York: Routledge.

Suls, J. M., & Rosnow, R. L. (1988). Concerns about artifacts in psychological experi-ments. In J. G. Morawski (Ed.), *The rise of experimentation in American psychology* (pp. 163-187). New Haven, CT: Yale Uni-versity Press.

Weis, L., & Fine, M. (1996). Narrating the 1980s and 1990s: Voices of poor and work-ing class white and African American men. *Anthropology and Education, 27,* 1-24.

Weis, L., & Fine, M. (Eds.). (in press). *Speedbumps: A student-friendly guide to qualitative work.* New York: Teachers College Press.

Weis, L., Marusza, J., & Fine, M. (1998). Out of the cupboard: Kids, domestic violence and schools. *British Journal of Sociology of Educa-tion, 19,* 53-73.

Weis, L., Proweller, A., & Centrie, C. (1997). Re-examining "A moment in history": Loss of privilege inside white working-class masculin-ity in the 1990's. In M. Fine, L. C. Powell, L. Weis, & L. M. Wong (Eds.), *Off white: Read-ings on race, power and society* (pp. 210-226). New York: Routledge.

West, C. (1993). *Race matters.* Boston: Beacon.

Williams, P. J. (1997). *Seeing a color-blind future: The paradox of race.* New York: Farrar, Straus & Giroux.

5

ETHICS AND POLITICS IN QUALITATIVE RESEARCH

◆ Clifford G. Christians

The Enlightenment mind clustered around an extraordinary dichotomy. Intellectual historians usually summarize this split in terms of subject/object, fact/value, or material/spiritual dualisms. And all three of these are legitimate interpretations of the cosmology inherited from Galileo, Descartes, and Newton. None of them puts the Enlightenment into its sharpest focus, however. Its deepest root was a pervasive autonomy. The cult of human personality prevailed in all its freedom. Human beings were declared a law unto themselves, set loose from every faith that claimed their allegiance. Proudly self-conscious of human autonomy, the 18th-century mind saw nature as an arena of limitless possibilities in which the sovereignty of human personality was demonstrated by its mastery over the natural order. Release from nature spawned autonomous individuals who considered themselves independent of any authority. The freedom motif was the deepest driving force, first released by the Renaissance and achieving maturity during the Enlightenment.[1]

Obviously, one can reach autonomy by starting with the subject/object dualism. In constructing the Enlightenment worldview, the prestige of natural science played a key role in setting people free. Achievements in mathematics, physics, and astronomy allowed humans to dominate nature, which formerly had dominated them. Science provided unmistakable evidence that by applying reason to nature and human beings in fairly obvious ways, people could live progressively happier lives. Crime and insanity, for example, no longer needed repressive theological explanations, but were deemed capable of mundane empirical solutions.

Likewise, one can get to the autonomous self by casting the question in terms of a radical discontinuity between hard facts and subjective values. The Enlightenment did push values to the fringe through its disjunction between knowledge of what is and what ought to be. And Enlightenment materialism in all its forms isolated reason from faith, knowledge from belief. As Robert Hooke insisted three centuries ago, when he helped found London's Royal Society: "This Society will eschew any discussion of religion, rhetoric, morals, and politics." With factuality gaining a stranglehold on the Enlightenment mind, those regions of human interest that implied oughts, constraints, and imperatives simply ceased to appear. Certainly those who see the Enlightenment as separating facts and values have identified a cardinal difficulty. Likewise, the realm of the spirit can easily dissolve into mystery and intuition. If the spiritual world contains no binding force, it is surrendered to speculation by the divines, many of whom accepted the Enlightenment belief that their pursuit was ephemeral.

But the Enlightenment's autonomy doctrine created the greatest mischief. Individual self-determination stands as the centerpiece, bequeathing to us the universal problem of integrating human freedom with moral order. And in struggling with the complexities and conundrums of this relationship, the Enlightenment, in effect, refused to sacrifice personal freedom. Even though the problem had a particular urgency in the 18th century, its response was not resolution but a categorical insistence on autonomy. Given the despotic political regimes and oppressive ecclesiastical systems of the period, such an uncompromising stance for freedom at this juncture is understandable. The Enlightenment began and ended with the assumption that human liberty ought to be cut away from the moral order, never integrated meaningfully with it.

Jean-Jacques Rousseau was the most outspoken advocate of this radical freedom. He gave intellectual substance to free self-determination of the human personality as the highest good. Rousseau is a complicated figure. He refused to be co-opted by Descartes's rationalism, Newton's mechanistic cosmology, or Locke's egoistic

selves. And he was not merely content to isolate and sacralize freedom, either, at least not in his *Discourse on Inequality* or in the *Social Contract,* where he answers Hobbes.

Rousseau represented the romantic wing of the Enlightenment, revolting against its rationalism. He won a wide following well into the 19th century for advocating immanent and emergent values rather than transcendent and given ones. While admitting that humans were finite and limited, he nonetheless promoted a freedom of breathtaking scope—not just disengagement from God or the Church, but freedom from culture and from any authority. Autonomy became the core of the human being and the center of the universe. Rousseau's understanding of equality, social systems, axiology, and language were anchored in it. He recognized the consequences more astutely than those comfortable with a shrunken negative freedom. But the only solution that he found tolerable was a noble human nature that enjoyed freedom beneficently and, therefore, one could presume, lived compatibly in some vague sense with a moral order.

◆ Value-Free Experimentalism

Typically, debates over the character of the social sciences revolve around the theory and methodology of the natural sciences. However, the argument here is not how they resemble natural science, but their inscription into the dominant Enlightenment worldview. In political theory, the liberal state as it emerged in 17th- and 18th-century Europe left citizens free to lead their own lives without obeisance to the Church or the feudal order. Psychology, sociology, and economics—known as the human or moral sciences in the 18th and 19th centuries—were conceived as "liberal arts" that opened minds and freed the imagination. As the social sciences and liberal state emerged and overlapped historically, Enlightenment thinkers in Europe advocated the "facts, skills, and techniques" of experimental reasoning to support the state and citizenry (Root, 1993, pp. 14-15).

Consistent with the presumed priority of individual liberty over the moral order, the basic institutions of society were designed to ensure "neutrality between different conceptions of the good" (Root, 1993, p. 12). The state was prohibited "from requiring or even encouraging citizens to subscribe to one religious tradition, form of family life, or manner of personal or artistic expression over another" (Root, 1993, p. 12). Given the historical circumstances in which shared conceptions of the good were no longer broad and deeply entrenched, taking sides on moral issues and insisting on social ideals were considered counterproductive. Value neutrality appeared to be the logical alternative "for a society whose members practiced many religions, pursued many different occupations, and identified with many different customs and traditions" (Root, 1993, p. 11). The theory and practice of mainstream social science reflect liberal Enlightenment philosophy, as do education, science, and politics. Only a reintegration of autonomy and the moral order provides an alternative paradigm for the social sciences today.[2]

Mill's Philosophy of Social Science

For John Stuart Mill, "neutrality is necessary in order to promote autonomy. . . . A person cannot be forced to be good, and the state should not dictate the kind of life a citizen should lead; it would be better for citizens to choose badly than for them to be forced by the state to choose well" (Root, 1993, pp. 12-13). Planning our lives according to our own ideas and purposes is sine qua non for autonomous beings in Mill's *On Liberty* (1859/1978): "The free development of individuality is one of the principal ingredients of human happiness, and quite the chief ingredient of individual and social progress" (p. 50; see also Copleston, 1966, p. 303, n. 32). This neutrality, based on the supremacy of individual autonomy, is the foundational principle in his *Utilitarianism* (1861/

1957) and in *A System of Logic* (1843/ 1893) as well. For Mill, "the principle of utility demands that the individual should enjoy full liberty, except the liberty to harm others" (Copleston, 1966, p. 54). In addition to bringing classical utilitarianism to its maximum development and establishing with Locke the liberal state, Mill delineated the foundations of inductive inquiry as social scientific method. In terms of the principles of empiricism, he perfected the inductive techniques of Francis Bacon as a problem-solving methodology to replace Aristotelian deductive logic.

According to Mill, syllogisms contribute nothing new to human knowledge. If we conclude that because "all men are mortal" the Duke of Wellington is mortal by virtue of his manhood, then the conclusion does not advance the premise (see Mill, 1843/1893, II, 3, 2, p. 140). The crucial issue is not reordering the conceptual world but discriminating genuine knowledge from superstition. In the pursuit of truth, generalizing and synthesizing are necessary to advance inductively from the known to the unknown. Mill seeks to establish this function of logic as inference from the known, rather than certifying the rules for formal consistency in reasoning (Mill, 1843/1893, bk. 3). Scientific certitude can be approximated when induction is followed rigorously, with propositions empirically derived and the material of all our knowledge provided by experience.[3] For the physical sciences he establishes four modes of experimental inquiry: agreement, disagreement, residues, and the principle of concomitant variations (Mill, 1843/1893, III, 8, pp. 278-288). He considers them the only possible methods of proof for experimentation, as long as one presumes the realist position that nature is structured by uniformities.[4]

In Book 6 of *A System of Logic,* "On the Logic of the Moral Sciences," Mill (1843/1893) develops an inductive experimentalism as the scientific method for studying "the various phenomena which constitute social life" (VI, 6, 1, p. 606). Although he conceived of social science as explaining human behavior in terms of causal laws, he warned against the fatalism of full predictability. "Social laws are hypothetical, and statistically-based generalizations by their very nature admit of exceptions" (Copleston, 1966, p. 101; see also Mill, 1843/1893, VI, 5, 1, p. 596). Empirically confirmed instrumental knowledge about human behavior has greater predictive power when it deals with collective masses than when we are dealing with individual agents.

Mill's positivism is obvious throughout his work on experimental inquiry.[5] Based on the work of Auguste Comte, he defined matter as the "permanent possibility of sensation" (Mill, 1865b, p. 198) and believed that nothing else can be said about metaphysical substances.[6] With Hume and Comte, Mill insisted that metaphysical substances are not real and only the facts of sense phenomena exist. There are no essences or ultimate reality behind sensations; therefore Mill (1865a, 1865b) and Comte (1848/1910) argued that social scientists should limit themselves to particular data as a factual source out of which experimentally valid laws can be derived. For both, this is the only kind of knowledge that yields practical benefits (Mill, 1865b, p. 242); in fact, society's salvation is contingent upon such scientific knowledge (p. 241).[7]

As with his consequentialist ethics, Mill's philosophy of social science is built on a dualism of means and ends. Citizens and politicians are responsible for articulating ends in a free society, and science for the know-how for achieving them. Science is amoral, speaking to questions of means but with no wherewithal or authority to dictate ends. Methods in the social sciences must be disinterested regarding substance and content, and rigorously limited to the risks and benefits of possible courses of action. Protocols for practicing liberal science "should be prescriptive, but not morally or politically prescriptive and should direct against bad science but not bad conduct" (Root, 1993, p. 129). Research cannot be judged right or wrong, only true or false. "Science is political only in its applications" (Root, 1993, p. 213). Given his democratic liberalism, Mill advocates neutrality "out of concern for the autonomy of the individuals or groups" social science seeks to serve. It should "treat them as thinking, willing, active beings who bear respon-sibility for their choices and are free to choose" their own conception of the good life by majority rule (Root, 1993, p. 19).

Value Neutrality in Max Weber

When 20th-century mainstream social scientists contend that ethics is not their business, they typically invoke Weber's essays written between 1904 and 1917. Given Weber's importance methodologically and theoretically for sociology and economics, his distinction between political judgments and scientific neutrality is given canonical status.

Weber distinguishes between value freedom and value relevance. He recognizes that in the discovery phase, "personal, cultural, moral, or political values cannot be eliminated; . . . what social scientists choose to investigate . . . they choose on the basis of the values" they expect their research to advance (Root, 1993, p. 33). But he insists that social science be value-free in the presentation phase. Findings ought not to express any judgments of a moral or political character. Professors should hang up their values along with their coats as they enter their lecture halls.

"An attitude of moral indifference," Weber (1904/1949b) writes, "has no connection with scientific objectivity" (p. 60). His meaning is clear from the value-freedom/value-relevance distinction. For the social sciences to be purposeful and rational, they must serve the "values of relevance."

> The problems of the social sciences are selected by the value relevance of the phenomena treated. . . . The expression "relevance to values" refers simply to the philosophical interpretation of that specifically scientific "interest" which determines the selection of a given subject matter and problems of empirical analysis. (Weber, 1917/1949a, pp. 21-22)

> In the social sciences the stimulus to the posing of scientific problems is in actuality always given by practical "questions." Hence, the very recognition of the existence of a scientific problem coincides personally with the possession of specifically oriented motives and values. . . .

Without the investigator's evaluative ideas, there would be no principle of selection of subject matter and no meaningful knowledge of the concrete reality. Without the investigator's conviction regarding the significance of particular cultural facts, every attempt to analyze concrete reality is absolutely meaningless. (Weber, 1904/1949b, pp. 61, 82)

Whereas the natural sciences, in Weber's (1904/1949b, p. 72) view, seek general laws that govern all empirical phenomena, the social sciences study those realities that our values consider significant. Whereas the natural world itself indicates what reality to investigate, the infinite possibilities of the social world are ordered in terms of "the cultural values with which we approach reality" (1904/1949b, p. 78).[8] However, even though value relevance directs the social sciences, as with the natural sciences, Weber considers the former value-free. The subject matter in natural science makes value judgments unnecessary, and social scientists by a conscious decision can exclude judgments of "desirability or undesirability" from their publicationss and lectures (1904/1949b, p. 52). "What is really at issue is the intrinsically simple demand that the investigator and teacher should keep unconditionally separate the establishment of empirical facts . . . and his own political evaluations" (Weber, 1917/1949a, p. 11).

Weber's opposition to value judgments in the social sciences was driven by practical circumstances. Academic freedom for the universities of Prussia was more likely if professors limited their professional work to scientific know-how. With university hiring controlled by political officials, only if the faculty refrained from policy commitments and criticism would officials relinquish their control.

Few of the offices in government or industry in Germany were held by people who were well trained to solve questions of means. Weber thought that the best way to increase the power and economic prosperity of Germany was to train a new managerial class learned about means and silent about ends. The mission of the university, on Weber's view, should be to offer

such training. (Root, 1993, p. 41; see also Weber, 1973, pp. 4-8)[9]

Weber's practical argument for value freedom and his apparent limitation of it to the reporting phase have made his version of value neutrality attractive to 20th-century social science. He is not a positivist such as Comte or a thoroughgoing empiricist in the tradition of Mill. He disavowed the positivist's overwrought disjunction between discovery and justification, and developed no systematic epistemology comparable to Mill's. His nationalism was partisan compared to Mill's liberal political philosophy. Nevertheless, Weber's value neutrality reflects Enlightenment autonomy in a fundamentally similar fashion. In the process of maintaining his distinction between value relevance and value freedom, he separates facts from values and means from ends. He appeals to empirical evidence and logical reasoning rooted in human rationality. "The validity of a practical imperative as a norm," he writes, "and the truth-value of an empirical proposition are absolutely heterogeneous in character" (Weber, 1904/1949b, p. 52). "A systematically correct scientific proof in the social sciences" may not be completely attainable, but that is most likely "due to faulty data" not because it is conceptually impossible (1904/1949b, p. 58).[10] For Weber, as with Mill, empirical science deals with questions of means, and his warning against inculcating political and moral values presumes a means-ends dichotomy (see Weber, 1917/1949a, pp. 18-19; 1904/ 1949b, p. 52).

As Michael Root (1993) concludes, "John Stuart Mill's call for neutrality in the social sciences is based on his belief" that the language of science "takes cognizance of a phenomenon and endeavors to discover its laws." Max Weber likewise "takes it for granted that there can be a language of science—a collection of truths—that excludes all value-judgments, rules, or directions for conduct" (p. 205). In both cases, scientific knowledge exists for its own sake as morally neutral. For both, neutrality is desirable "because questions of value are not rationally resolvable" and neutrality in the social sciences is presumed to contribute "to political and personal autonomy"

(p. 229). In Weber's argument for value relevance in social science, he did not contradict the larger Enlightenment ideal of scientific neutrality between competing conceptions of the good.

Utilitarian Ethics

In addition to its this-worldly humanism, utilitarian ethics was attractive for its compatibility with scientific thought. It fit the canons of rational calculation as they were nourished by the Enlightenment's intellectual culture.

> In the utilitarian perspective, one validated an ethical position by hard evidence. You count the consequences for human happiness of one or another course, and you go with the one with the highest favorable total. What counts as human happiness was thought to be something conceptually unproblematic, a scientifically establishable domain of facts. One could abandon all the metaphysical or theological factors which made ethical questions scientifically undecidable. (Taylor, 1982, p. 129)

Utilitarian ethics replaces metaphysical distinctions with the calculation of empirical quantities. It follows the procedural demand that if "the happiness of each agent counts for one . . . the right course of action should be what satisfies all, or the largest number possible" (Taylor, 1982, p. 131). Autonomous reason is the arbiter of moral disputes.

With moral reasoning equivalent to calculating consequences for human happiness, utilitarianism presumes there is "a single consistent domain of the moral, that there is one set of considerations which determines what we ought morally to do." This "epistemologically-motivated reduction and homogenization of the moral" marginalizes the qualitative languages of admiration and contempt—integrity, healing, liberation, conviction, dishonesty, and self-indulgence, for example (Taylor, 1982, pp. 132-133). In utilitarian terms, these languages designate subjective factors that "correspond to nothing in reality. . . . They express the way we feel, not the way things are" (Taylor, 1982, p. 141). This single-consideration theory not only demands that we maximize general happiness, but

considers irrelevant other moral imperatives that conflict with it, such as equal distribution. One-factor models appeal to the "epistemological squeamishness" of value-neutral social science, which "dislikes contrastive languages." Moreover, utilitarianism appealingly offers "the prospect of exact calculation of policy through . . . rational choice theory" (Taylor, 1982, p. 143). "It portrays all moral issues as discrete problems amenable to largely technical solutions" (Euben, 1981, p. 117). However, to its critics, this kind of exactness represents "a semblance of validity" by leaving out whatever cannot be calculated (Taylor, 1982, p. 143).[11]

Given its dualism of means and ends, the domain of the good in utilitarian theory is extrinsic. All that is worth valuing is a function of their consequences. Prima facie duties are literally inconceivable. "The degree to which my actions and statements" truly express what is important to someone does not count. Ethical and political thinking in consequentialist terms legislate intrinsic valuing out of existence (Taylor, 1982, p. 144). The exteriority of ethics is seen to guarantee the value neutrality of experimental procedures.[12]

Codes of Ethics

In value-free social science, codes of ethics for professional and academic associations are the conventional format for moral principles. By the 1980s, each of the major scholarly associations had adopted its own code, with an overlapping emphasis on four guidelines for directing an inductive science of means toward majoritarian ends.

1. Informed consent. Consistent with its commitment to individual autonomy, social science in the Mill and Weber tradition insists that research subjects have the right to be informed about the nature and consequences of experiments in which they are involved. Proper respect for human freedom generally includes two necessary conditions. Subjects must agree voluntarily to participate—that is, without physical or psychological coercion. In addition, their agreement must be based on full and open information. "The Articles of the Nuremberg Tribunal and the Declaration of Helsinki both state that subjects must be told the duration, methods, possible risks, and the purpose or aim of the experiment" (Soble, 1978, p. 40; see also Veatch, 1996).

The self-evident character of this principle is not disputed in rationalist ethics. Meaningful application, however, generates ongoing disputes. As Punch (1994) observes, "In much fieldwork there seems to be no way around the predicament that informed consent—divulging one's identity and research purpose to all and sundry—will kill many a project stone dead" (p. 90). True to the privileging of means in a means-ends model, Punch reflects the general conclusion that codes of ethics should serve as a guideline prior to fieldwork, but not intrude on full participation. "A strict application of codes" may "restrain and restrict" a great deal of "innocuous" and "unproblematic" research (p. 90).

2. Deception. In emphasizing informed consent, social science codes of ethics uniformly oppose deception. Even paternalistic arguments for possible deception of criminals, children in elementary schools, or the mentally incapacitated are no longer credible. The ongoing exposé of deceptive practices since Stanley Milgram's experiments have given this moral principle special status—deliberate misrepresentation is forbidden. Bulmer (1982) is typical of hard-liners who conclude with the codes that deception is "neither ethically justified nor practically necessary, nor in the best interest of sociology as an academic pursuit" (p. 217; see also Punch, 1994, p. 92).

The straightforward application of this principle suggests that researchers design different experiments free of active deception. But with ethical constructions exterior to the scientific enterprise, no unambiguous application is possible. Given that the search for knowledge is obligatory and deception is codified as morally unacceptable, in some situations both criteria cannot be satisfied. Within both psychology and medicine some information cannot be ob-

tained without at least deception by omission. The standard resolution for this dilemma is to permit a modicum of deception when there are explicit utilitarian reasons for doing so. Opposition to deception in the codes is de facto redefined in these terms: If "the knowledge to be gained from deceptive experiments" is clearly valuable to society, it is "only a minor defect that persons must be deceived in the process" (Soble, 1978, p. 40).

3. Privacy and confidentiality. Codes of ethics insist on safeguards to protect people's identities and those of the research locations. Confidentiality must be assured as the primary safeguard against unwanted exposure. All personal data ought to be secured or concealed and made public only behind a shield of anonymity. Professional etiquette uniformly concurs that no one deserves harm or embarrassment as a result of insensitive research practices. "The single most likely source of harm in social science inquiry is" the disclosure of private knowledge considered damaging by experimental subjects (Reiss, 1979, p. 73; see also Punch, 1994, p. 93).

As Enlightenment autonomy was developed in philosophical anthropology, a sacred innermost self became essential to the construction of unique personhood. Already in John Locke, this private domain received nonnegotiable status. Democratic life was articulated outside these atomistic units, a secondary domain of negotiated contracts and problematic communication. In the logic of social science inquiry revolving around the same autonomy inscribed in being, invading persons' fragile but distinctive privacy is intolerable.

Despite the signature status of privacy protection, watertight confidentiality has proved to be impossible. Pseudonyms and disguised locations are often recognized by insiders. What researchers consider innocent is perceived by participants as misleading or even betrayal. What appears neutral on paper is often conflictual in practice. When government agencies or educational institutions or health organizations are studied, what private parts ought not be exposed? And who is blameworthy if aggressive media carry the research further? Encoding privacy protection is meaningless when "there is no consensus or unanimity on what is public and private" (Punch, 1994, p. 94).

4. *Accuracy.* Ensuring that data are accurate is a cardinal principle in social science codes as well. Fabrications, fraudulent materials, omissions, and contrivances are both nonscientific and unethical. Data that are internally and externally valid are the coin of the realm, experimentally and morally. In an instrumentalist, value-neutral social science, the definitions entailed by the procedures themselves establish the ends by which they are evaluated as moral.

Institutional Review Boards

As a condition of funding, government agencies in various countries have insisted that review and monitoring bodies be established by institutions engaged in research involving human subjects. Institutional review boards (IRBs) embody the utilitarian agenda in terms of scope, assumptions, and procedural guidelines.

In 1978, the U.S. National Commission for the Protection of Human Subjects in Biomedical and Behavioral Research was established. It developed broad ethical principles to serve as the basis upon which specific rules could be established. Three principles, published in what became known as the Belmont Report, were said to constitute the moral standards for research involving human subjects: respect for persons, beneficence, and justice.

1. The section on respect for persons reiterates the codes' demands that subjects enter the research voluntarily and with adequate information about the experiment's procedures and possible consequences. On a deeper level, respect for persons incorporates two basic ethical tenets: "First, that individuals should be treated as autonomous agents, and second, that persons with diminished autonomy [the immature and incapacitated] are entitled to protection" (University of Illinois, 1995).

2. Under the principle of beneficence, researchers are enjoined to secure the well-being of their subjects. Beneficent actions are understood in a double sense as avoiding harm altogether, and if risks are involved for achieving substantial benefits, minimizing as much harm as possible: "In the case of particular projects, investigators and members of their institutions are obliged to give forethought to the maximization of benefits and the reduction of risks that might occur from the research investigation. In the case of scientific research in general, members of the larger society are obliged to recognize the longer term benefits and risks that may result from the improvement of knowledge and from the development of novel medical, psychotherapeutic, and social procedures" (University of Illinois, 1995).

3. The principle of justice insists on fair distribution of both the benefits and burdens of research. An injustice occurs when some groups (e.g., welfare recipients, the institutionalized, or particular ethnic minorities) are overused as research subjects because of easy manipulation or their availability. And when research supported by public funds leads to "therapeutic devices and procedures, justice demands that these not provide advantages only to those who can afford them" (University of Illinois, 1995).

These principles reiterate the basic themes of value-neutral experimentalism—individual autonomy, maximum benefits and minimal risks, and ethical ends exterior to scientific means. The policy procedures based on them reflect the same guidelines as dominate the codes of ethics: informed consent, protection of privacy, and nondeception. The authority of IRBs was enhanced in 1989 when Congress passed the NIH Revitalization Act and formed the Commission on Research Integrity. The emphasis at that point was on the invention, fudging, and distortion of data. Falsification, fabrication, and plagiarism continue as federal categories of misconduct, with a new report in 1996 adding warnings against unauthorized use of confidential information, omission of important data, and interference (that is, physical damage to the materials of others).

With IRBs the legacy of Mill, Comte, and Weber comes into its own. Value-neutral science is accountable to ethical standards through rational procedures controlled by value-neutral academic institutions in the service of an impartial government. In its conceptual structure, IRB policy is designed to produce the best ratio of benefits to costs. IRBs ostensibly protect the subjects who fall under the protocols they approve. However, given the interlocking utilitarian functions of social science, the academy, and the state that Mill identified and promoted, IRBs in reality protect their own institutions rather than subject populations in society at large (see Vanderpool, 1996, chaps. 2-6).

Current Crisis

Mill and Comte, each in his own way, presumed that experimental social science benefited society by uncovering facts about the human condition. Durkheim and Weber believed that a scientific study of society could help people come to grips with "the development of capitalism and the industrial revolution" (Jennings & Callahan, 1983, p. 3). The American Social Science Association was created in 1865 to link "real elements of the truth" with "the great social problems of the day" (Lazarsfeld & Reitz, 1975, p. 1). This myth of beneficence was destroyed with "the revelations at the Nuremberg trials (recounting the Nazis' 'medical experiments' on concentration camp inmates) and with the role of leading scientists in the Manhattan Project" (Punch, 1994, p. 88).

The crisis of confidence multiplied with the exposure of actual physical harm in the Tuskegee Syphilis Study and the Willowbrook Hepatitis Experiment. In the 1960s, Project Camelot, a U.S. Army attempt to use social science to measure and forecast revolutions and insurgency, was bitterly opposed around the world and had to be canceled. Stanley Milgram's (1974) deception of unwitting sub-

jects and Laud Humphreys's (1970, 1972) deceptive research on homosexuals in a public toilet, and later in their homes, were considered scandalous for psychologically abusing research subjects. Noam Chomsky exposed the complicity of social scientists with military initiatives in Vietnam.

Vigorous concern for research ethics during the 1980s and 1990s, support from foundations, and the development of ethics codes and the IRB apparatus are credited by their advocates with curbing outrageous abuses. However, the charges of fraud, plagiarism, and misrepresentation continue on a lesser scale, with dilemmas, conundrums, and controversies unabated over the meaning and application of ethical guidelines. Entrepreneurial faculty competing for scarce research dollars are generally compliant with institutional control, but the vastness of social science activity in universities and research entities makes full supervision impossible.

Underneath the pros and cons of administering a responsible social science, the structural deficiencies in its epistemology have become transparent (Jennings, 1983, pp. 4-7). A positivistic philosophy of social inquiry insists on neutrality regarding definitions of the good, and this worldview has been discredited. The Enlightenment model setting human freedom at odds with the moral order is bankrupt. Even Weber's weaker version of contrastive languages rather than oppositional entities is not up to the task. Reworking the ethics codes so that they are more explicit and less hortatory will make no fundamental difference. Requiring ethics workshops for graduate students, redefining the mission of IRBs, and strengthening government policy are desirable but of marginal significance.

In utilitarianism, moral thinking and experimental procedures are homogenized into a unidimensional model of rational validation. Autonomous human beings are clairvoyant about aligning means and goals, presuming that they can objectify the mechanisms for understanding themselves and the social world surrounding them (see Taylor, 1982, p. 133). This restrictive definition of ethics accounts for some of the goods we seek, such as minimal harm, but those outside a utility calculus are excluded. "Emotionality and intuition" are relegated "to a secondary position" in the decision-making process, for example, and no attention is paid to an "ethics of caring" grounded in "concrete particularities" (Denzin, 1997, p. 273; see also Ryan, 1995, p. 147). The way power and ideology influence social and political institutions is largely ignored. Under a rhetorical patina of deliberate choice and the illusion of autonomous creativity, a means-ends system operates in fundamentally its own terms.

This constricted environment no longer addresses adequately the complicated issues we face in studying the social world. Celebrity social scientists generate status and prestige—McGeorge Bundy in the Kennedy years, political scientist Henry Kissinger, Daniel Moynihan in the Senate. But failure in the War on Poverty, contradictions over welfare, and ill-fated studies of urban housing have dramatized the limitations of a utility calculus that occupies the entire moral domain.[13]

Certainly, levels of success and failure are open to dispute even within the social science disciplines themselves. More unsettling and threatening to the empirical mainstream than disappointing performance is the recognition that neutrality is not pluralistic but imperialistic. Reflecting on past experience, disinterested research under presumed conditions of value freedom is increasingly seen as de facto reinscribing the agenda in its own terms. Empiricism is procedurally committed to equal reckoning, regardless of how research subjects may constitute the substantive ends of life. But experimentalism is not a neutral meeting ground for all ideas; rather, it is a "fighting creed" that imposes its own ideas on others while uncritically assuming the very "superiority that powers this imposition."[14] In Foucault's (1979, pp. 170-195) more decisive terms, social science is a regime of power that helps maintain social order by normalizing subjects into categories designed by political authorities (see Root, 1993, chap. 7). A liberalism of equality is not neutral but represents only one range of ideals, and is itself incompatible with other goods.

This noncontextual, nonsituational model that assumes "a morally neutral, objective ob-

server will get the facts right" ignores "the situatedness of power relations associated with gender, sexual orientation, class, ethnicity, race, and nationality." It is hierarchical (scientist-subject) and biased toward patriarchy. "It glosses the ways in which the observer-ethnographer is implicated and embedded in the 'ruling apparatus' of the society and the culture." Scientists "carry the mantle" of university-based authority as they venture out into "local community to do research" (Denzin, 1997, p. 272; see also Ryan, 1995, pp. 144-145).[15] There is no sustained questioning of expertise itself in democratic societies that belong in principle to citizens who do not share this specialized knowledge (see Euben, 1981, p. 120).

◆ Feminist Communitarianism

Social Ethics

Over the past decade, social and feminist ethics have made a radical break with the individual autonomy and rationalist presumption of canonical ethics (see Koehn, 1998). The social ethics of Agnes Heller (1988, 1990, 1996), Charles Taylor (1989, 1991; Taylor et al., 1994), Carole Pateman (1985, 1988, 1989), Edith Wyschogrod (1974, 1985, 1990, 1998), and Cornel West (1989, 1991) and the feminist ethics of Carol Gilligan (1982, 1983; Gilligan, Ward, & Taylor, 1988), Nel Noddings (1984, 1989, 1990), Virginia Held (1993), and Seyla Benhabib (1992) are fundamentally reconstructing ethical theory (see Code, 1991). Rather than searching for neutral principles to which all parties can appeal, social ethics rests on a complex view of moral judgments as integrating into an organic whole, everyday experience, beliefs about the good, and feelings of approval and shame, in terms of human relations and social structures. This is a philosophical approach that situates the moral domain within the general purposes of human life that people share contextually and across cultural, racial, and historical boundaries. Ideally, it engenders a new occupational role and normative core for social science research (White, 1995).

Carol Gilligan (1982, 1983; Gilligan et al., 1988) characterizes the female moral voice as an ethic of care. This dimension of moral development is rooted in the primacy of human relationships. Compassion and nurturance resolve conflicting responsibilities among people, standards totally opposite of merely avoiding harm.[16] In *Caring,* Nel Noddings (1984) rejects outright the "ethics of principle as ambiguous and unstable" (p. 5), insisting that human care should play the central role in moral decision making. For Julia Wood (1994), "an interdependent sense of self" undergirds the ethic of care, wherein we are comfortable acting independently while "acting cooperatively . . . in relationship with others" (pp. 108, 110). Feminism in Linda Steiner's work critiques the conventions of impartiality and formality in ethics while giving precision to affection, intimacy, nurturing, egalitarian and collaborative processes, and empathy. Feminists' ethical self-consciousness also identifies subtle forms of oppression and imbalance, and teaches us to "address questions about whose interests are regarded as worthy of debate" (Steiner, 1991, p. 158; see also Steiner, 1997).

While sharing in the turn away from an abstract ethics of calculation, Charlene Seigfried (1996) argues against the Gilligan-Noddings tradition. Linking feminism to pragmatism, in which gender is socially constructed, she contradicts "the simplistic equation of women with care and nurturance and men with justice and autonomy" (p. 206). Gender-based moralities de facto make one gender subservient to another. In her social ethics, gender is replaced with engendering: "To be female or male is not to instantiate an unchangeable nature but to participate in an ongoing process of negotiating cultural expectations of femininity and masculinity" (p. 206). Seigfried challenges us to a social morality in which caring values are central but contextualized in webs of relationships and constructed toward communities with "more autonomy for women and more connectedness for men" (p. 219). Agnes Heller and Edith Wyschogrod are two promising examples of

proponents of social ethics that meet Seigfried's challenge while confronting forthrightly today's contingency, mass murder, conceptual upheavals in ethics, and hyperreality.

Heller, a former student of Georg Lukács and a dissident in Hungary, is the Hannah Arendt Professor of Philosophy at the New School for Social Research. Her trilogy developing a contemporary theory of social ethics (Heller, 1988, 1990, 1996) revolves around what she calls the one decisive question: "Good persons exist— how are they possible?" (1988, p. 7). She disavows an ethics of norms, rules, and ideals external to human beings. Only exceptional acts of responsibility under duress and predicaments, each in their own way, are "worthy of theoretical interest" (1996, p. 3). Accumulated wisdom, moral meaning from our own choices of decency, and the ongoing summons of the Other together reintroduce love, happiness, sympathy, and beauty into a modern, nonabsolutist, but principled theory of morals.

In *Saints and Postmodernism,* Edith Wyschogrod (1990) asserts that antiauthority struggles are possible without assuming that our choices are voluntary. She represents a social ethics of self and Other in the tradition of Emmanuel Levinas (see Wyschogrod, 1974).[17] "The other person opens the venue of ethics, the place where ethical existence occurs." The Other, "the touchstone of moral existence, is not a conceptual anchorage but a living force." Others function "as a critical solvent." Their existence carries "compelling moral weight" (Wyschogrod, 1990, p. xxi). As a professor of philosophy and religious thought at Rice University, with a commitment to moral narrative, Wyschogrod believes that one venue for Otherness is the saintly life, defined as one in "which compassion for the Other, irrespective of cost to the saint, is the primary trait." Saints put their own "bodies and material goods at the disposal of the Other. . . . Not only do saints contest the practices and beliefs of institutions, but in a more subtle way they contest the order of narrativity itself" (1990, pp. xxii-xxiii).

In addition to the Other-directed across a broad spectrum of belief systems who have "lived, suffered, and worked in actuality," Wyschogrod (1990, p. 7) examines historical narratives for illustrations of how the Other's self-manifestation is depicted. Her primary concern is the way communities shape shared experience in the face of cataclysms and calamities, arguing for historians who situate themselves "in dynamic relationship to them" (1998, p. 218). The overriding challenge for ethics, in Wyschogrod's view, is how historians enter into communities that create and sustain hope in terms of immediacy—"a presence here and now" but "a presence that must be deferred" to the future (1998, p. 248). Unless it is tangible and actionable, hope serves those in control. Hope that merely projects a future redemption obscures abuses of power and human need in the present.

Martin Buber (1958) calls the human relation a primal notion in his famous lines, "in the beginning is the relation" and "the relation is the cradle of life" (pp. 69, 60, 3). Social relationships are preeminent. "The one primary word is the combination I-Thou." This irreducible phenomenon—the relational reality, the in-between, the reciprocal bond, the interpersonal—cannot be decomposed into simpler elements without destroying it. Given the primacy of relationships, unless we use our freedom to help others flourish, we deny our own well-being.

Rather than privileging an abstract rationalism, the moral order is positioned close to the bone, in the creaturely and corporeal rather than the conceptual. "In this way, ethics . . . is as old as creation. Being ethical is a primordial movement in the beckoning force of life itself" (Olthuis, 1997, p. 141). The ethics of Levinas is one example:

> The human face is the epiphany of the nakedness of the Other, a visitation, a meeting, a saying which comes in the passivity of the face, not threatening, but obligating. My world is ruptured, my contentment interrupted. I am already obligated. Here is an appeal from which there is no escape, a responsibility, a state of being hostage. It is looking into the face of the Other that reveals the call to a responsibility that is before any beginning, decision or initiative on my part. (Olthuis, 1997, p. 139)

Humans are defined as communicative beings within the fabric of everyday life. Through dialogic encounter, subjects create life together and nurture one another's moral obligation to it. Levinas's ethics presumes and articulates a radical ontology of social beings in relation (see, e.g., Levinas, 1981).

Moreover, in Levinasian terms, when I turn to the face of the Other, I not only see flesh and blood, but a third party arrives—the whole of humanity. In responding to the Other's need, a baseline is established across the human race. For Benhabib (1992), this is interactive universalism.[18] Our universal solidarity is rooted in the principle that "we have inescapable claims on one another which cannot be renounced except at the cost of our humanity" (Peukert, 1981, p. 11). Our obligation to sustain one another defines our existence. The primal sacredness for all without exception is the heart of the moral order (Christians, 1997a, 1998).

A Feminist Communitarian Model

Feminist communitarianism is Denzin's (1997, pp. 274-287) label for the ethical theory to lead us forward at this juncture.[19] This is a normative model that serves as an antidote to individualist utilitarianism. It presumes that the community is ontologically and axiologically prior to persons. Human identity is constituted through the social realm. We are born into a sociocultural universe where values, moral commitments, and existential meanings are negotiated dialogically. Fulfillment is never achieved in isolation, but only through human bonding at the epicenter of social formation.

For communitarians, the liberalism of Locke and Mill confuses an aggregate of individual pursuits with the common good. Moral agents need a context of social commitments and community ties for assessing what is valuable. What is worth preserving as a good cannot be self-determined in isolation, but can be ascertained only within specific social situations where human identity is nurtured. The public sphere is conceived as a mosaic of particular communities, a pluralism of ethnic identities and worldviews intersecting to form a social bond but each seriously held and competitive as well. Rather than pay lip service to the social nature of the self while presuming a dualism of two orders, communitarianism interlocks personal autonomy with communal well-being. Morally appropriate action intends community. Common moral values are intrinsic to a community's ongoing existence and identity.

Therefore, the mission of social science research is enabling community life to prosper—enabling people to come to mutually held conclusions. The aim is not fulsome data per se, but community transformation. The received view assumes that research advances society's interests by feeding our individual capacity to reason and make calculated decisions. Research is intended to be collaborative in its design and participatory in its execution. Rather than ethics codes in the files of academic offices and research reports prepared for clients, the participants themselves are given a forum to activate the polis mutually. In contrast to utilitarian experimentalism, the substantive conceptions of the good that drive the problems reflect the conceptions of the community rather than the expertise of researchers or funding agencies.

In the feminist communitarian model, participants have a say in how the research should be conducted and a hand in actually conducting it, "including a voice or hand in deciding which problems should be studied, what methods should be used to study them, whether the findings are valid or acceptable, and how the findings are to be used or implemented" (Root, 1993, p. 245). This research is rooted in "community, shared governance . . . and neighborliness." Given its cooperative mutuality, it serves "the community in which it is carried out, rather than the community of knowledge producers and policymakers" (Lincoln, 1995, pp. 280, 287; see also Denzin, 1997, p. 275). It finds its genius in the maxim that "persons are arbitrators of their own presence in the world" (Denzin, 1989, p. 81).

For feminist communitarians, humans have the discursive power "to articulate situated moral rules that are grounded in local community and group understanding." Moral reasoning goes forward because people are "able to share one another's point of view in the social situation." Reciprocal care and understanding, rooted in emotional experience and not in formal consensus, are the basis on which moral discourse is possible (Denzin, 1997, p. 277; see also Denzin, 1984, p. 145; Reinharz, 1993).

Multiple moral and social spaces exist within the local community, and "every moral act is a contingent accomplishment" measured against the ideals of a universal respect for the dignity of every human being regardless of gender, age, race, or religion (Denzin, 1997, p. 274; see also Benhabib, 1992, p. 6). Through a moral order we resist those social values that are divisive and exclusivist.

◆ Interpretive Sufficiency

Within a feminist communitarian model, the mission of social science research is interpretive sufficiency. In contrast to an experimentalism of instrumental efficiency, this paradigm seeks to open up the social world in all its dynamic dimensions. The thick notion of sufficiency supplants the thinness of the technical, exterior, and statistically precise received view. Rather than reducing social issues to financial and administrative problems for politicians, social science research enables people to come to terms with their everyday experience themselves.

Interpretive sufficiency means taking seriously lives that are loaded with multiple interpretations and grounded in cultural complexity (Denzin, 1989, pp. 81, 77). Ethnographic accounts "should possess that amount of depth, detail, emotionality, nuance, and coherence that will permit a critical consciousness to be formed by the reader. Such texts should also exhibit representational adequacy, including the absence of racial, class, and gender stereotyping" (Denzin, 1997, p. 283; see also Christians, Ferre, & Fackler, 1993, pp. 120-122).

From the perspective of a feminist communitarian ethics, interpretive discourse is authentically sufficient when it fulfills three conditions: represents multiple voices, enhances moral discernment, and promotes social transformation. Consistent with the community-based norms advocated here, the focus is not on professional ethics per se but on the general morality.

Multivocal and Cross-Cultural Representation

Within social and political entities are multiple spaces that exist as ongoing constructions of everyday life. The dialogical self is situated and articulated within these decisive contexts of gender, race, class, and religion. In contrast to contractarianism, where tacit consent or obligation is given to the state, promises are made and sustained to one another. Research narratives reflect a community's multiple voices through which promise keeping takes place.

In Carole Pateman's communitarian philosophy, sociopolitical entities are not to be understood first of all in terms of contracts. Making promises is one of the basic ways in which consenting human beings "freely create their own social relationships" (Pateman, 1989, p. 61; see also Pateman, 1985, pp. 26-29). We assume an obligation by making a promise. When individuals promise, they are obliged to act accordingly. But promises are made not primarily to authorities through political contracts, but to fellow citizens. If obligations are rooted in promises, obligations are owed to other colleagues in institutions and to participants in community practices. Therefore, only under conditions of participatory democracy can there be self-assumed moral obligation.

Pateman understands the nature of moral agency. We know ourselves primarily in relation, and derivatively as thinkers withdrawn from action. Only by overcoming the traditional dualisms between thinker and agent, mind and body, reason and will, can we conceive of being as "the mutuality of personal relationships" (MacMurray, 1961a, p. 38). Moral commitments arise out of action and return to action for their incarnation and verification. From a dialogical perspective, promise keeping through action and everyday language is not a supercilious pursuit, because our way of being is not inwardly generated but socially derived.

> We become full human agents, capable of understanding ourselves, and hence of defining our identity, through . . . rich modes of expression we learn through exchange with others. . . .

> My discovering my own identity doesn't mean that I work it out in isolation, but that I negotiate it through dialogue, partly overt, partly internal, with others. My own identity crucially depends on my dialogical relations with others. . . .
>
> In the culture of authenticity, relationships are seen as the key loci of self discovery and self-affirmation. (Taylor et al., 1994, pp. 32, 34, 36)

If moral bondedness flows horizontally and obligation is reciprocal in character, the affirming and sustaining of promises occur cross-culturally. But the contemporary challenge of cultural diversity has raised the stakes and made easy solutions impossible. One of the most urgent and vexing issues on the democratic agenda at present is how to recognize explicit cultural groups politically. "Nonrecognition or misrecognition can inflict harm, can be a form of oppression, imprisoning someone in a false, distorted and reduced mode of being" (Taylor et al., 1994, p. 26).

However, liberal proceduralism cannot meet this vital human need. Emphasizing equal rights with no particular substantive view of the good life "gives only a very restricted acknowledgement of distinct cultural identities" (Taylor et al., 1994, p. 52). Insisting on neutrality, and without collective goals, produces at best personal freedom, safety, and economic security understood homogeneously. As Bunge (1996) puts it: "Contractualism is a code of behavior for the powerful and the hard—those who write contracts, not those who sign on the dotted line" (p. 230). However, in promise-based communal formation the flourishing of particular cultures, religions, and citizen groups is the substantive goal to which we are morally committed as human beings. With the starting hypothesis that all human cultures have something important to say, social science research recognizes particular cultural values consistent with universal human dignity (Christians, 1997b, pp. 197-202).

Moral Discernment

Societies are embodiments of institutions, practices, and structures recognized internally as legitimate. Without allegiance to a web of ordering relations, society becomes, as a matter of fact, inconceivable. Communities are not only linguistic entities, but require at least a minimal moral commitment to the common good. Because social entities are moral orders and not merely functional arrangements, moral commitment constitutes the self-in-relation. Our identity is defined by what we consider good or worth opposing. According to Taylor, only through the moral dimension can we make sense of human agency. As Mulhall and Swift (1996) write:

> Developing, maintaining and articulating [our moral intuitions and reactions] is not something humans could easily or even conceivably dispense with. . . . We can no more imagine a human life that fails to address the matter of its bearings in moral space than we can imagine one in which developing a sense of up and down, right and left is regarded as an optional human task. . . .
> . . . A moral orientation is inescapable because the questions to which the framework provides answers are themselves inescapable. (pp. 106-108; see also Taylor, 1989, pp. 27-29)

A self exists only within "webs of interlocution," and all self-interpretation implicitly or explicitly "acknowledges the necessarily social origin of any and all their conceptions of the good and so of themselves." Moral frameworks are as fundamental for orienting us in social space as the need to "establish our bearings in physical space" (Mulhall & Swift, 1996, pp. 112-113; see also Taylor, 1989, pp. 27-29).

Moral duty is nurtured by the demands of social linkage and not produced by abstract theory. The core of a society's common morality is pretheoretical agreement. However, "what counts as common morality is not only imprecise but variable . . . and a difficult practical problem" (Bok, 1995, p. 99). Moral obligation must be articulated within the fallible and irresolute voices of everyday life. Among disagreements and uncertainty, we look for criteria and wisdom in settling disputes and clarifying confusions, and normative theories of an interactive sort can invigorate our common moral discourse. But generally accepted theories are not necessary for the common good to prosper. The common good is not "the complete morality of every participant . . . but a set of agreements among people who typically hold other, less widely shared ethical beliefs" (Bok, 1995, p. 99). Instead of expecting more theoretical coherence than history warrants, Reinhold Niebuhr inspires us to work through inevitable social conflicts while maintaining "an untheoretical jumble of agreements" called here the common good (Barry, 1967, pp. 190-191). Through a common morality we can approximate consensus on issues and settle disputes interactively. In Jürgen Habermas's (1993) terms, discourse in the public sphere must be oriented "toward mutual understanding" while allowing participants "the communicative freedom to take positions" on claims to final validity (p. 66; see also Habermas, 1990).

Communitarians challenge researchers to participate in a community's ongoing process of moral articulation. In fact, culture's continued existence depends on the identification and defense of its normative base. Therefore, ethnographic texts must enable us "to discover moral truths about ourselves"; narratives ought to "bring a moral compass into readers' lives" by accounting for things that matter to them (Denzin, 1997, p. 284). Feminist communitarianism seeks to engender moral reasoning (Benhabib, 1992, p. 10). Communities are woven together by narratives that invigorate their common understanding of good and evil, happiness and reward, the meaning of life and death. Recovering and refashioning religious word forms help to amplify our deepest humanness.

As a result, for social science research the moral task cannot be reduced to professional ethics. How the moral order works itself out in community formation is the issue, not first of all what practitioners consider virtuous. The challenge for those writing culture is not to limit their moral perspectives to their own codes of ethics, but to understand ethics and values in terms of everyday life.

Resistance and Empowerment

Ethics in the feminist communitarian mode generates social criticism, leads to resistance, and empowers the interactive self and others to action (see Habermas, 1971, pp. 301-317). Thus a basic norm for interpretive research is enabling the humane transformation of the multiple spheres of community life—religion, politics, ethnicity, gender, and so forth.

From his own dialogic perspective, Paulo Freire speaks of the need to reinvent the meaning of power:

> For me the principal, real transformation, the radical transformation of society in this part of the century demands not getting power from those who have it today, or merely to make some reforms, some changes in it. . . . The question, from my point of view, is not just to take power but to reinvent it. That is, to create a different kind of power, to deny the need power has as if it were metaphysics, bureaucratized, anti-democratic. (quoted in Evans, Evans, & Kennedy, 1987, p. 229)

Certainly oppressive power blocs and monopolies—economic, technological, and political—need the scrutiny of researchers. Given Freire's political-institutional bearing, power for him is a central notion in social analysis. But, in concert with him, feminist communitarian research refuses to deal with power in cognitive terms only. The issue is how we can empower people instead.

The dominant understanding of power is grounded in nonmutuality; it is interventionist power, exercised competitively and seeking control. In the communitarian alternative, power is relational, characterized by mutuality rather than sovereignty. Power from this perspective is reciprocity between two subjects, a relationship not of domination, but of intimacy and vulnerability—power akin to that of Alcoholics Anonymous, in which surrender to the community enables the individual to gain mastery. Dialogue is the key element in an emancipatory strategy that liberates rather than imprisons us in manipulation or antagonistic relationships. Although the control version of power considers mutuality weakness, the empowerment mode maximizes our humanity and thereby banishes powerlessness. In the research process, power is unmasked and engaged through solidarity. Rather than play semantic games with power, researchers themselves are willing to march against the barricades. As Freire insists, only with everyone filling his or her own political space, to the point of civil disobedience as necessary, will empowerment mean anything revolutionary (see, e.g., Freire, 1970b, p. 129).

What is nonnegotiable in Freire's theory of power is participation of the oppressed in directing cultural formation. If an important social issue needs resolution, the most vulnerable will have to lead the way: "Revolutionary praxis cannot tolerate an absurd dichotomy in which the praxis of the people is merely that of following the [dominant elite's] decisions" (Freire, 1970a, p. 120; see also Freire, 1978, pp. 17ff.).[20] Arrogant politicians—supported by a bevy of accountants, lawyers, economists, and social science researchers—trivialize the nonexpert's voice as irrelevant to the problem or its solution. On the contrary, transformative action from the inside out is impossible unless the oppressed are active participants rather than a leader's object. "Only power that springs from the weakness of the oppressed will be sufficiently strong to free both" (Freire, 1970b, p. 28).

In Freire's (1973) terms, the goal is conscientization, that is, a critical consciousness that directs the ongoing flow of praxis and reflection in everyday life. In a culture of silence, the oppressor's language and way of being are fatalistically accepted without contradiction. But a critical consciousness enables us to exercise the uniquely human capacity of "speaking a true word" (Freire, 1970b, p. 75). Under conditions of sociopolitical control, "the vanquished are dispossessed of their word, their expressiveness, their culture" (1970b, p. 134). Through conscientization the oppressed gain their own voice and collaborate in transforming their culture (1970a, pp. 212-213). Therefore, research is not the transmission of specialized data but, in style and content, a catalyst for critical consciousness. Without what Freire (1970b, p. 47) calls "a critical comprehension of reality" (that is, the oppressed "grasping with their minds the truth of their reality"), there is only acquiescence in the status quo.

Fulfilling the mission of interpretive sufficiency through the three moral principles described above creates for social science research a new set of ethical demands. It still lives with IRBs as a necessity of life and is relentlessly accurate. However, because the research-subject relation is reciprocal, invasion of privacy, informed consent, and deception are nonissues. In communitarianism, conceptions of the good are shared by the research subjects, and researchers collaborate in bringing these definitions into their own.

◆ Conclusion

As Guba and Lincoln (1994) argue, the issues in social science ultimately must be engaged at the worldview level. "Questions of method are secondary to questions of paradigm, which we define as the basic belief system or worldview that guides the investigator, not only in choices of method but in ontologically and epistemologically fundamental ways" (p. 105). The conventional view, with its extrinsic ethics, gives us a truncated and unsophisticated paradigm that needs to be ontologically transformed. This historical overview of theory and practice points to the need for an entirely new model of research ethics in which human action and conceptions of the good are interactive.

"Since the relation of persons constitutes their existence as persons, . . . morally right action is [one] which intends community" (MacMurray, 1961b, p. 119). In feminist communitarianism, personal being is cut into the very heart of the social universe. The common good is accessible to us only in personal form; it has its ground and inspiration in a social ontology of the human.[21] "Ontology must be rescued from submersion in things by being thought out entirely from the viewpoint of person and thus of Being" (Lotz, 1963, p. 294). "Ontology is truly itself only when it is personal and persons are truly themselves only as ontological" (Lotz, 1963, p. 297).

When rooted in a positivist worldview, explanations of social life are considered incompatible with the renderings offered by the participants themselves. In problematics, lingual

form, and content, research production presumes greater mastery and clearer illumination than the nonexperts who are the targeted beneficiaries. Protecting and promoting individual autonomy have been the philosophical rationale for value neutrality since its origins in Mill. But the incoherence in that view of social science is now transparent. By limiting the active involvement of rational beings or judging their self-understanding to be false, empiricist models contradict the ideal of rational beings who "choose between competing conceptions of the good" and make choices "deserving of respect." The verification standards of an instrumentalist system "take away what neutrality aims to protect: a community of free and equal rational beings legislating their own principles of conduct" (Root, 1993, p. 198). The social ontology of feminist communitarianism escapes this contradiction by reintegrating human life with the moral order.

■ Notes

1. For greater detail regarding this argument than I can provide in the summary below, see Christians et al. (1993, pp. 18-32, 41-44).

2. Michael Root (1993) is unique among philosophers of the social sciences in linking social science to the ideals and practices of the liberal state on the grounds that both institutions "attempt to be neutral between competing conceptions of the good" (p. xv). As he elaborates: "Though liberalism is primarily a theory of the state, its principles can be applied to any of the basic institutions of a society; for one can argue that the role of the clinic, the corporation, the scholarly associations, or professions is not to dictate or even recommend the kind of life a person should aim at. Neutrality can serve as an ideal for the operations of these institutions as much as it can for the state. Their role, one can argue, should be to facilitate whatever kind of life a student, patient, client, customer, or member is aiming at and not promote one kind of life over another" (p. 13). Root's interpretations of Mill and Weber are crucial to my own formulation.

3. Although committed to what he called "the logic of the moral sciences" in delineating the canons or methods for induction, Mill shared with natural science a belief in the uniformity of

nature and the presumption that all phenomena are subject to cause-and-effect relationships. His five principles of induction reflect a Newtonian cosmology.

4. Utilitarianism in John Stuart Mill was essentially an amalgamation of Bentham's greatest happiness principle, David Hume's empirical philosophy and concept of utility as a moral good, and Comte's positivist tenets that things-in-themselves cannot be known and knowledge is restricted to sensations. In his influential *A System of Logic,* Mill (1843/1893) is typically characterized as combining the principles of French positivism (as developed by August Comte) and British empiricism into a single system.

5. For an elaboration of the complexities in positivism—including reference to its Millian connections—see Lincoln and Guba (1985, pp. 19-28).

6. Mill's realism is most explicitly developed in his *Examination of Sir William Hamilton's Philosophy* (1865b). Our belief in a common external world, in his view, is rooted in the fact that our sensations of physical reality "belong as much to other human or sentient beings as to ourselves" (p. 196; see also Copleston, 1966, p. 306, n. 97).

7. Mill (1969) specifically credits to Comte his use of the inverse deductive or historical method: "This was an idea entirely new to me when I found it in Comte; and but for him I might not soon (if ever) have arrived at it" (p. 126). Mill explicitly follows Comte in distinguishing social statics and social dynamics. He published two essays on Comte's influence in the *Westminster Review,* which were reprinted as *Auguste Comte and Positivism* (Mill, 1865a; see also Mill, 1969, p. 165).

8. Emile Durkheim is more explicit and direct about causality in both the natural and the social worlds. While he argues for sociological over psychological causes of behavior and did not believe intention could cause action, he unequivocally sees the task of social science as discovering the causal links between social facts and personal behavior (see, e.g., Durkheim, 1966, pp. 44, 297-306).

9. As one example of the abuse Weber resisted, Root (1993, pp. 41-42) refers to the appointment of Ludwig Bernhard to a professorship of economics at the University of Berlin.

Though he had no academic credentials, the Ministry of Education gave Bernhard this position without a faculty vote (see Weber, 1973, pp. 4-30). In Shils's (1949) terms, "A mass of particular, concrete concerns underlies [his 1917] essay—his recurrent effort to penetrate to the postulates of economic theory, his ethical passion for academic freedom, his fervent nationalist political convictions and his own perpetual demand for intellectual integrity" (p. v).

10. The rationale for the Social Science Research Council in 1923 is multilayered, but in its attempt to link academic expertise with policy research, and in its preference for rigorous social scientific methodology, the SSRC reflects and implements Weber.

11. Often in professional ethics at present, we isolate consequentialism from a full-scale utilitarianism. We give up on the idea of maximizing happiness, but "still try to evaluate different courses of action purely in terms of their consequences, hoping to state everything worth considering in our consequence-descriptions." However, even this broad version of utilitarianism, in Taylor's terms, "still legislates certain goods out of existence." It is likewise a restrictive definition of the good that favors the mode of reasoned calculation and prevents us from taking seriously all facets of moral and normative political thinking (Taylor, 1982, p. 144). As Yvonna Lincoln observes, utilitarianism's inescapable problem is that "in advocating the greatest good for the greatest number, small groups of people (all minority groups, for example) experience the political regime of the 'tyranny of the majority.' " She refers correctly to "liberalism's tendency to reinscribe oppression by virtue of the utilitarian principle" (personal communication, February 16, 1999).

12. Given the nature of positivist inquiry, Jennings and Callahan (1983) conclude that only a short list of ethical questions are considered and they "tend to merge with the canons of professional scientific methodology. . . . Intellectual honesty, the suppression of personal bias, careful collection and accurate reporting of data, and candid admission of the limits of the scientific reliability of empirical studies—these were essentially the only questions that could arise. And, since these ethical responsibilities are not particularly controversial (at least in principle), it is not surprising that during this period [the 1960s]

neither those concerned with ethics nor social scientists devoted much time to analyzing or discussing them" (p. 6).

13. As Taylor (1982) puts it, "The modern dispute about utilitarianism is not about whether it occupies some of the space of moral reason, but whether it fills the whole space." "Comfort the dying" is a moral imperative in contemporary Calcutta, even though "the dying are in an extremity that makes [utilitarian] calculation irrelevant" (p. 134).

14. This restates the well-known objection to a democratic liberalism of individual rights: "Liberalism is not a possible meeting ground for all cultures, but is the political expression of one range of cultures, and quite incompatible with other ranges. Liberalism can't and shouldn't claim complete cultural neutrality. Liberalism is also a fighting creed. Multiculturalism as it is often debated today has a lot to do with the imposition of some cultures on others, and with the assumed superiority that powers this imposition. Western liberal societies are thought to be supremely guilty in this regard, partly because of their colonial past, and partly because of their marginalization of segments of their populations that stem from other cultures" (Taylor et al., 1994, pp. 62-63).

15. Denzin in this passage credits Smith (1987, p. 107) with the concept of a "ruling apparatus."

16. Gilligan's research methods and conclusions have been debated by a diverse range of scholars. For this debate and related issues, see Brabeck (1990), Card (1991), Tong (1989, pp. 161-168; 1993, pp. 80-157), Wood (1994), and Seigfried (1996).

17. Levinas (b. 1905) was a professor of philosophy at the University of Paris (Nanterre) and head of the Israelite Normal School in Paris. In Wyschogrod's (1974) terms, "He continues the tradition of Martin Buber and Franz Rosenweig" and was "the first to introduce Husserl's work into . . . the French phenomenological school" (pp. vii-viii). Although Wyschogrod is a student of Heidegger, Hegel, and Husserl (see, e.g., Wyschogrod, 1985)—and engaged with Derrida, Lyotard, Foucault, and Deleuze—her work on ethics appeals not to traditional philosophical discourse but to concrete expressions of self-Other transactions in

the visual arts, literary narrative, historiography, and the normalization of death in the news.

18. Martha Nussbaum (1993) argues for a version of virtue ethics in these terms, contending for a model rooted in Aristotle that has cross-cultural application without being detached from particular forms of social life. In her model, various spheres of human experience that are found in all cultures represent questions to answer and choices to make—attitudes toward the ill or good fortune of others, how to treat strangers, management of property, control over bodily appetites, and so forth. Our experiences in these areas "fix a subject for further inquiry" (p. 247). And our reflection on each sphere will give us a "thin or nominal definition" of a virtue relevant to this sphere. On this basis we can talk across cultures about behavior appropriate in each sphere (see Nussbaum, 1999).

19. Root (1993, chap. 10) also chooses a communitarian alternative to the dominant paradigm. In his version, critical theory, participatory research, and feminist social science are three examples of the communitarian approach. This chapter offers a more complex view of communitarianism developed in political philosophy and intellectual history, rather than limiting it to social theory and practical politics. Among the philosophical communitarians (Sandel, 1982; Taylor, 1989; Walzer, 1983, 1987), Carole Pateman (1985, 1989) is explicitly feminist, and her promise motif forms the axis for the principle of multivocal representation outlined below. In this chapter's feminist communitarian model, critical theory is integrated into the third ethical imperative—empowerment and resistance. In spite of that difference in emphasis, I agree with Root's (1993) conclusion: "Critical theories are always critical for a particular community, and the values they seek to advance are the values of that community. In that respect, critical theories are communitarian. . . . For critical theorists, the standard for choosing or accepting a social theory is the reflective acceptability of the theory by members of the community for whom the theory is critical" (pp. 233-234).

20. Mutuality is a cardinal feature of the feminist communitarian model generally, and therefore crucial to the principle of empowerment. For this reason, critical theory is inscribed into the third principle here, rather than following Root (see note 18, above), allowing it to stand by itself

as an illustration of communitarianism. Root (1993, p. 238) himself observes that critical theorists often fail to transfer the "ideals of expertise" to their research subjects or give them little say in the research design and interpretation. Without a fundamental shift to communitarian interactivity, research in all modes is prone to the distributive fallacy.

21. Michael Theunissen (1984) argues that Buber's relational self (and therefore its legacy in Levinas, Freire, Heller, Wyschogrod, and Taylor) is distinct from the subjectivity of Continental existentialism. The subjective sphere of Husserl and Sartre, for example, "stands in no relation to a Thou and is not a member of a We" (p. 20; see also p. 276). "According to Heidegger the self can only come to itself in a voluntary separation from other selves; according to Buber, it has its being solely in the relation" (p. 284).

■ References

Barry, B. (1967). Justice and the common good. In A. Quinton (Ed.), *Political philosophy* (pp. 190-191). Oxford: Oxford University Press.

Benhabib, S. (1992). *Situating the self: Gender, community and postmodernism in contemporary ethics.* Cambridge: Polity.

Bok, S. (1995). *Common values.* Columbia: University of Missouri Press.

Brabeck, M. M. (Ed.). (1990). *Who cares? Theory, research, and educational implications of the ethic of care.* New York: Praeger.

Buber, M. (1958). *I and thou* (2nd ed.; R. G. Smith, Trans.). New York: Scribner's.

Bulmer, M. (1982). The merits and demerits of covert participant observation. In M. Bulmer (Ed.), *Social research ethics* (pp. 217-251). London: Macmillan.

Bunge, M. (1996). *Finding philosophy in social science.* New Haven, CT: Yale University Press.

Card, C. (Ed.). (1991). *Feminist ethics.* Lawrence: University of Kansas Press.

Christians, C. G. (1997a). Social ethics and mass media practice. In J. M. Makau & R. C. Arnett (Eds.), *Communication ethics in an age of diversity* (pp. 187-205). Urbana: University of Illinois Press.

Christians, C. G. (1997b). The ethics of being. In C. G. Christians & M. Traber (Eds.), *Communication ethics and universal values* (pp. 3-23). Thousand Oaks, CA: Sage.

Christians, C. G. (1998). The sacredness of life. *Media Development, 45*(2), 3-7.

Christians, C. G., Ferre, J. P., & Fackler, P. M. (1993). *Good news: Social ethics and the press.* New York: Oxford University Press.

Code, L. (1991). *What can she know? Feminist theory and the construction of knowledge.* Ithaca, NY: Cornell University Press.

Comte, A. (1910). *A general view of positivism* (J. H. Bridges, Trans.). London: Routledge. (Original work published 1848; subsequently published as the first volume of *Positive philosophy,* 2 vols., H. Martineau, Trans., London: Trübner, 1853)

Copleston, F. (1966). *A history of philosophy: Vol. 8. Modern philosophy: Bentham to Russell.* Garden City, NY: Doubleday.

Denzin, N. K. (1984). *On understanding emotion.* San Francisco: Jossey-Bass.

Denzin, N. K. (1989). *Interpretive biography.* Newbury Park, CA: Sage.

Denzin, N. K. (1997). *Interpretive ethnography: Ethnographic practices for the 21st century.* Thousand Oaks, CA: Sage.

Durkheim, E. (1966). *Suicide: A study of sociology.* New York: Free Press.

Euben, J. P. (1981). Philosophy and the professions. *Democracy, 1*(2), 112-127.

Evans, A. F., Evans, R. A., & Kennedy, W. B. (1987). *Pedagogies for the non-poor.* Maryknoll, NY: Orbis.

Foucault, M. (1979). *Discipline and punish: The birth of the prison* (A. Sheridan, Trans.). New York: Random House.

Freire, P. (1970a). *Education as the practice of freedom: Cultural action for freedom.* Cambridge, MA: Harvard Educational Review/Center for the Study of Development.

Freire, P. (1970b). *Pedagogy of the oppressed.* New York: Seabury.

Freire, P. (1973). *Education for critical consciousness.* New York: Seabury.

Freire, P. (1978). *Pedagogy in process: The letters of Guinea-Bissau.* New York: Seabury.

Gilligan, C. (1982). *In a different voice: Psychological theory and women's development.* Cambridge, MA: Harvard University Press.

Gilligan, C. (1983). Do the social sciences have an adequate theory of moral development?

In N. Haan, R. N. Bellah, P. Rabinow, & W. M. Sullivan (Eds.), *Social science as moral inquiry* (pp. 33-51). New York: Columbia University Press.

Gilligan, C., Ward, J. V., & Taylor, J. M. (1988). *Mapping the moral domain*. Cambridge, MA: Harvard University, Graduate School of Education.

Guba, E. G., & Lincoln, Y. S. (1994). Competing paradigms in qualitative research. In N. K. Denzin & Y. S. Lincoln (Eds.), *Handbook of qualitative research* (pp. 105-117). Thousand Oaks, CA: Sage.

Habermas, J. (1971). *Knowledge and human interests* (J. J. Shapiro, Trans.). Boston: Beacon.

Habermas, J. (1990). *Moral consciousness and communicative action* (C. Lenhardt & S. W. Nicholson, Trans.). Cambridge: MIT Press.

Habermas, J. (1993). *Justification and application: Remarks on discourse ethics* (C. Cronin, Trans.). Cambridge: MIT Press.

Held, V. (1993). *Feminist morality: Transforming culture, society, and politics*. Chicago: University of Chicago Press.

Heller, A. (1988). *General ethics*. Oxford: Blackwell.

Heller, A. (1990). *A philosophy of morals*. Oxford: Blackwell.

Heller, A. (1996). *An ethics of personality*. Oxford: Blackwell.

Humphreys, L. (1970). *Tearoom trade: Impersonal sex in public places*. Chicago: Aldine.

Humphreys, L. (1972). *Out of the closet*. Englewood Cliffs, NJ: Prentice Hall.

Jennings, B. (1983). Interpretive social science and policy analysis. In D. Callahan & B. Jennings (Eds.), *Ethics, the social sciences, and policy analysis* (pp. 3-35). New York: Plenum.

Jennings, B., & Callahan, D. (1983, February). Social sciences and the policy-making process. *Hastings Center Report*, pp. 3-8.

Koehn, D. (1998). *Rethinking feminist ethics: Care, trust and empathy*. New York: Routledge.

Lazarsfeld, P., & Reitz, J. G. (1975). *An introduction to applied sociology*. New York: Elsevier.

Levinas, E. (1981). *Otherwise than being or essence*. The Hague: Martinus Nijhoff.

Lincoln, Y. S. (1995). Emerging criteria for quality in qualitative and interpretive inquiry. *Qualitative Inquiry, 1,* 275-289.

Lincoln, Y. S., & Guba, E. G. (1985). *Naturalistic inquiry*. Beverly Hills, CA: Sage.

Lotz, J. B. (1963). Person and ontology. *Philosophy Today, 7,* 294-297.

MacMurray, J. (1961a). *The form of the personal: Vol. 1. The self as agent*. London: Faber & Faber.

MacMurray, J. (1961b). *The form of the personal: Vol. 2. Persons in relation*. London: Faber & Faber.

Milgram, S. (1974). *Obedience to authority*. New York: Harper & Row.

Mill, J. S. (1865a). *Auguste Comte and positivism*. London.

Mill, J. S. (1865b). *Examination of Sir William Hamilton's philosophy and of the principal philosophical questions discussed in his writings*. London: Longman, Green, Roberts & Green.

Mill, J. S. (1893). *A system of logic, ratiocinative and inductive: Being a connected view of the principles of evidence and the methods of scientific investigation* (8th ed.). New York: Harper & Brothers. (Original work published 1843)

Mill, J. S. (1957). *Utilitarianism*. Indianapolis: Bobbs-Merrill. (Original work published 1861)

Mill, J. S. (1969). *Autobiography*. Boston: Houghton Mifflin. (Original work published posthumously 1873)

Mill, J. S. (1978). *On liberty*. Indianapolis: Hackett. (Original work published 1859)

Mulhall, S., & Swift, A. (1996). *Liberals and communitarians* (2nd ed.). Oxford: Blackwell.

Noddings, N. (1984). *Caring: A feminine approach to ethics and moral education*. Berkeley: University of California Press.

Noddings, N. (1989). *Women and evil*. Berkeley: University of California Press.

Noddings, N. (1990). Ethics from the standpoint of women. In D. L. Rhode (Ed.), *Theoretical perspectives on sexual difference* (pp. 160-173). New Haven, CT: Yale University Press.

Nussbaum, M. (1993). Non-relative virtues: An Aristotelian approach. In M. Nussbaum & A. Sen, *The quality of life* (pp. 242-269). Oxford: Clarendon.

Nussbaum, M. (1999). *Sex and social justice.* New York: Oxford University Press.

Olthuis, J. (1997). Face-to-face: Ethical asymmetry or the symmetry of mutuality? In J. Olthuis (Ed.), *Knowing other-wise* (pp. 134-164). New York: Fordham University Press.

Pateman, C. (1985). *The problem of political obligation: A critique of liberal theory.* Cambridge: Polity.

Pateman, C. (1988). *The sexual contract.* Stanford, CA: Stanford University Press.

Pateman, C. (1989). *The disorder of women: Democracy, feminism and political theory.* Stanford, CA: Stanford University Press.

Peukert, H. (1981). Universal solidarity as the goal of ethics. *Media Development, 28*(4), 10-12.

Punch, M. (1994). Politics and ethics in qualitative research. In N. K. Denzin & Y. S. Lincoln (Eds.), *Handbook of qualitative research* (pp. 83-97). Thousand Oaks, CA: Sage.

Reinharz, S. (1993). *Social research methods: Feminist perspectives.* New York: Elsevier.

Reiss, A. J., Jr. (1979). Governmental regulation of scientific inquiry: Some paradoxical consequences. In C. B. Klockars & F. W. O'Connor (Eds.), *Deviance and decency: The ethics of research with human subjects* (pp. 61-95). Beverly Hills, CA: Sage.

Root, M. (1993). *Philosophy of social science: The methods, ideals, and politics of social inquiry.* Oxford: Blackwell.

Ryan, K. E. (1995). Evaluation ethics and issues of social justice: Contributions from female moral thinking. In N. K. Denzin (Ed.), *Studies in symbolic interaction: A research annual* (Vol. 19, pp. 143-151). Greenwich, CT: JAI.

Sandel, M. J. (1982). *Liberalism and the limits of justice.* Cambridge: Cambridge University Press.

Seigfried, C. H. (1996). *Pragmatism and feminism: Reweaving the social fabric.* Chicago: University of Chicago Press.

Shils, E. A. (1949). Foreword. In M. Weber, *The methodology of the social sciences* (pp. iii-x). New York: Free Press.

Smith, D. E. (1987). *The everyday world as problematic: A feminist sociology.* Boston: Northeastern University Press.

Soble, A. (1978, October). Deception in social science research: Is informed consent possible? *Hastings Center Report,* pp. 40-46.

Steiner, L. (1991). Feminist theorizing and communication ethics. *Communication, 12*(3), 157-174.

Steiner, L. (1997). A feminist schema for analysis of ethical dilemmas. In F. L. Casmir (Ed.), *Ethics in intercultural and international communication* (pp. 59-88). Mahwah, NJ: Lawrence Erlbaum.

Taylor, C. (1982). The diversity of goods. In A. Sen & B. Williams (Eds.), *Utilitarianism and beyond* (pp. 129-144). Cambridge: Cambridge University Press.

Taylor, C. (1989). *Sources of the self: The making of the modern identity.* Cambridge, MA: Harvard University Press.

Taylor, C. (1991). *The ethics of authenticity.* Cambridge, MA: Harvard University Press.

Taylor, C., Appiah, K. A., Habermas, J., Rockefeller, S. C., Walzer, M., & Wolf, S. (1994). *Multiculturalism: Examining the politics of recognition* (A. Gutmann, Ed.). Princeton, NJ: Princeton University Press.

Theunissen, M. (1984). *The other: Studies in the social ontology of Husserl, Heidegger, Sartre, and Buber* (C. Macann, Trans.). Cambridge: MIT Press.

Tong, R. (1989). *Feminist thought.* Boulder, CO: Westview.

Tong, R. (1993). *Feminine and feminist ethics.* Belmont, CA: Wadsworth.

University of Illinois at Urbana-Champaign, Institutional Review Board. (1995, May). Part I: Fundamental principles for the use of human subjects in research. In *Handbook for investigators: For the protection of human subjects in research.* Urbana: Author. Available Internet: http://www.uiuc.edu/unit/vcres/irb/handbook/ sec1)

Vanderpool, H. Y. (Ed.). (1996). *The ethics of research involving human subjects: Facing the 21st century.* Frederick, MD: University Publishing Group.

Veatch, R. M. (1996). From Nuremberg through the 1990s: The priority of autonomy. In H. Y. Vanderpool (Ed.), *The ethics of research involving human subjects: Facing the 21st century* (pp. 45-58). Frederick, MD: University Publishing Group.

Walzer, M. (1983). *Spheres of justice: A defense of pluralism and equality.* New York: Basic Books.

Walzer, M. (1987). *Interpretation and social criticism.* Cambridge, MA: Harvard University Press.

Weber, M. (1949a). The meaning of ethical neutrality in sociology and economics. In M. Weber, *The methodology of the social sciences* (E. A. Shils & H. A. Finch, Eds. & Trans.). New York: Free Press. (Original work published 1917)

Weber, M. (1949b). Objectivity in social science and social policy. In M. Weber, *The methodology of the social sciences* (E. A. Shils & H. A. Finch, Eds. & Trans.). New York: Free Press. (Original work published 1904)

Weber, M. (1973). *Max Weber on universities* (E. A. Shils, Ed. & Trans.). Chicago: University of Chicago Press.

West, C. (1989). *The American evasion of philosophy: A genealogy of pragmatism.* Madison: University of Wisconsin Press.

West, C. (1991). *The ethical dimensions of Marxist thought.* New York: Monthly Review Books.

White, R. (1995). From codes of ethics to public cultural truth. *European Journal of Communication, 10,* 441-460.

Wood, J. (1994). *Who cares? Women, care, and culture.* Carbondale: Southern Illinois University Press.

Wyschogrod, E. (1974). *Emmanuel Levinas: The problem of ethical metaphysics.* The Hague: Martinus Nijhoff.

Wyschogrod, E. (1985). *Spirit in ashes: Hegel, Heidegger, and man-made death.* Chicago: University of Chicago Press.

Wyschogrod, E. (1990). *Saints and postmodernism: Revisioning moral philosophy.* Chicago: University of Chicago Press.

Wyschogrod, E. (1998). *An ethics of remembering: History, heterology, and the nameless others.* Chicago: University of Chicago Press.

Part II

PARADIGMS AND PERSPECTIVES IN TRANSITION

I n our introductory chapter, following Guba (1990, p. 17), we defined a paradigm as a basic set of beliefs that guide action. Paradigms deal with first principles, or ultimates. They are human constructions. They define the worldview of the researcher-as-interpretive *bricoleur.* These beliefs can never be established in terms of their ultimate truthfulness. Perspectives, in contrast, are not as solidified, or as well unified, as paradigms, although a perspective may share many elements with a paradigm, such as a common set of methodological assumptions or a particular epistemology.

A paradigm encompasses four concepts: ethics (axiology), epistemology, ontology, and methodology. *Ethics* asks, How will I be as a moral person in the world? *Epistemology* asks, How do I know the world? What is the relationship between the inquirer and the known? Every epistemology, as Christians indicates in Chapter 5 of this volume, implies an ethical-moral stance toward the world and the self of the researcher. *Ontology* raises basic questions about the nature of reality and the nature of the human being in the world. *Methodology* focuses on the best means for gaining knowledge about the world.

Part II of this volume examines the major paradigms and perspectives that now structure and organize qualitative research: positivism, postpositivism, constructivism, and participatory action frameworks. Alongside these paradigms are the perspectives of feminism (in its multiple forms), critical race theory, queer theory, and cultural studies. Each of these perspectives has developed its own criteria, assumptions, and methodological practices, which are then applied to disciplined inquiry within that framework. (Tables 6.1 and 6.2 in Chapter 6, by Lincoln and Guba, outline the major differences among the positivist, postpositivist, critical theory, constructivist, and participatory paradigms.)

We have provided a brief discussion of each paradigm and perspective in Chapter 1; here we elaborate them in somewhat more detail. However, before turning to this discussion, it is important to note that within the past decade, the borders and boundary lines separating these paradigms and perspectives have begun to blur. As Yvonna Lincoln and Egon Guba observe in Chapter 6, the various paradigms are beginning to "interbreed." Hence the title of this section, "Paradigms and Perspectives in Transition."

◆ Major Issues Confronting All Paradigms

Lincoln and Guba suggest in Chapter 6 that in the present moment all paradigms must confront seven basic, critical issues: axiology (ethics and values), accommodation and commensurability (can paradigms be fitted into one another?), action (what the researcher does in the world), control (who initiates inquiry, who asks questions), foundations of truth (foundationalism versus anti- and nonfoundationalism), validity (traditional positivist models versus poststructuralist-constructionist criteria), and voice, reflexivity, and postmodern representation (single-voice versus multivoiced representation).

Each paradigm takes a different stance on these topics. Of course the positivist and postpositivist paradigms provide the backdrop against which these other paradigms and perspectives operate. Lincoln and Guba analyze these two traditions in considerable detail, including their reliance on naïve realism, their dualistic epistemologies, their verificational approach to inquiry, and their emphasis on reliability, validity, prediction, control, and a building-block approach to knowledge. Lincoln and Guba discuss the inability of these paradigms to address adequately issues surrounding voice, empowerment, and praxis. They also allude to the failure of these paradigms to address satisfactorily the theory- and value-laden nature of facts, the interactive nature of inquiry, and the fact that the same sets of "facts" can support more than one theory.

◆ Constructivism, Interpretivism, and Hermeneutics

According to Lincoln and Guba, *constructivism* adopts a relativist ontology (relativism), a transactional epistemology, and a hermeneutic, dialectical methodology. Users of this paradigm are oriented to the production of reconstructed understandings of the social world. The traditional positivist criteria of internal and external validity are replaced by such terms as *trustworthiness* and *authenticity*. Constructivists value transactional knowledge. Their work overlaps with the several different participatory action approaches discussed by Kemmis and McTaggart in Chapter 22 of this volume. Constructivism connects action to praxis and builds on antifoundational arguments while encouraging experimental and multivoiced texts.

In Chapter 7, Thomas Schwandt offers a carefully nuanced, complex, and subtle analysis of the interpretivist, hermeneutic, and constructionist perspectives. He identifies major differences and strands of thought within each approach while indicating how they are unified by their opposition to positivism and their commitment to study the world from the point of view of the interacting individual. Yet these perspectives, as Schwandt argues, are distinguished more by their commitment to questions of knowing and being than by their specific methodologies, which basically enact an emic, idiographic approach to inquiry. Schwandt traces the theoretical and philosophical foundations of the constructivist and interpretivist traditions, connecting them back to the works of Schutz, Weber, Mead, Blumer, Winch, Heidegger, Gadamer, Geertz, Ricoeur, Gergen, Goodman, Guba, and Lincoln. The constructivist tradition, as Schwandt notes, is rich, deep, and complex. This complexity is evidenced in the ethical and political implications of these perspectives. The interpreter must always ask, How shall I be toward these people I am studying?

◆ *The Feminisms*

In Chapter 8, Virginia Olesen observes that feminist qualitative research is a highly diversified and contested site. Competing models blur together, but beneath the fray and the debate there is agreement that feminist inquiry is always dialectical and always committed to action in the world. Olesen's is an impassioned feminism. She contends that "rage is not enough"; we need "incisive scholarship to frame, direct, and harness passion in the interests of redressing grievous problems in many areas of women's health."

In her contribution to the first edition of this *Handbook,* Olesen (1994) identified three major strands of feminist inquiry: standpoint epistemology, empiricism, and postmodernism-cultural studies. Six years later, these strands have multiplied (see her Table 8.1) as the field has become much more complex and theoretically diverse. There are today separate feminisms associated with the writings of women of color, women problematizing whiteness, postcolonial discourse, lesbian research and queer theory, disabled women, standpoint theory, and postmodern and deconstructive theory. This complexity has problematized the researcher-participant relationship. It has destabilized the insider-outsider model of inquiry. It has produced a deconstruction of such traditional terms as *experience, difference,* and *gender* while simultaneously seeking a feminist solidarity in the service of the overthrow of oppression. Five newly framed issues have emerged from this discourse, focusing on the concepts of bias and objectivity, validity and trustworthiness, voice, and feminist ethics. On this last point, Olesen's masterful chapter elaborates the framework presented by Clifford Christians in Chapter 5.

◆ *Racialized Discourses and Ethnic Epistemologies*

In Chapter 9, Gloria Ladson-Billings moves critical race theory directly into the field of qualitative inquiry. Critical race theory "seeks to decloak the seemingly race-neutral, and color-blind ways . . . of constructing and administering race-based appraisals . . . of the law, administrative policy, electoral politics . . . political discourse [and education] in the USA" (Parker, Deyhle, Villenas, & Nebeker, 1998, p. 5). Critical race theory enacts an ethnic epistemology, arguing that ways of knowing and being are shaped by the individual's standpoint, or position in the world. This standpoint undoes the cultural, ethical, and epistemological logic (and racism) of the Eurocentric, Enlightenment paradigm.

Drawing on recent work by African American, Asian Pacific Islander, Asian American, Latino, and Native American scholars, Ladson-Billings introduces the concepts of multiple or double consciousness, *mestiza* consciousness, and tribal secrets. The analysis of these ideas allows her to show how the dominant cultural paradigms have produced fractured, racialized identities and experiences of exclusion for minority scholars. Critical race theorists experiment with multiple interpretive strategies, ranging from storytelling to auto-ethnography, case studies, textual and narrative analyses, traditional fieldwork, and, most important, collaborative, action-based inquiries and studies of race, gender, law, education, and ethnic oppression in daily life.

◆ Critical Theory

Multiple critical theories and Marxist and neo-Marxist models now circulate within the discourses of qualitative research. In Lincoln and Guba's framework this paradigm, in its many formulations, articulates an ontology based on historical realism, an epistemology that is transactional and a methodology that is both dialogic and dialectical. In Chapter 10, Joe Kincheloe and Peter McLaren trace the history of critical research (and Marxist theory) from the Frankfurt school through more recent transformations in poststructural, postmodern, feminist, critical pedagogy, and cultural studies theory. They outline a critical theory for the new millennium, beginning with the assumption that the societies of the West are not unproblematically democratic and free. Their version of critical theory rejects economic determinism and focuses on the media, culture, language, power, desire, critical enlightenment, and critical emancipation. Their framework (like Schwandt's) embraces a critical hermeneutics. Building on Dewey and Gramsci, Kincheloe and McLaren present a critical, pragmatic approach to texts and their relationships to lived experience. This leads to a "resistance" version of critical theory, a version connected to critical ethnography, and partisan, critical inquiry committed to social criticism and the empowerment of individuals. Critical theorists seek to produce practical, pragmatic knowledge that is cultural and structural, judged by its degree of historical situatedness and its ability to produce praxis, or action.

◆ Cultural Studies

Cultural studies cannot be contained within a single framework. There are multiple cultural studies projects, including those connected to the Birmingham school and the work of Stuart Hall and his associates (see Hall, 1996). Cultural studies research is historically self-reflective, critical, interdisciplinary, conversant with high theory, and focused on the global and the local, taking into account historical, political, economic, cultural, and everyday discourses. It focuses on "questions of community, identity, agency and change" (Grossberg & Pollock, 1998).

In its generic form, cultural studies involves an examination of how the history people live is produced by structures that have been handed down from the past. Each version of cultural studies is joined by a threefold concern with cultural texts, lived experience, and the articulated relationship between texts and everyday life. Within the cultural text tradition, some scholars examine the mass media and popular culture as sites where history, ideology, and subjective experiences come together. These scholars produce critical ethnographies of the audience in relation to particular historical moments. Other scholars read texts as sites where hegemonic meanings are produced, distributed, and consumed. Within the ethnographic tradition, there is a postmodern concern for the social text and its production.

The open-ended nature of the cultural studies project leads to a perpetual resistance against attempts to impose a single definition over the entire project. There are critical-Marxist, constructionist, and postpositivist paradigmatic strands within the formation, as well as emergent feminist and ethnic models. Scholars within the cultural studies project are drawn to historical realism and relativism as their ontology, to transactional epistemologies, and to dialogic methodologies, while remaining committed to a historical and structural framework that is action oriented.

In Chapter 11, John Frow and Meaghan Morris outline a critical materialist cultural studies project, noting that contemporary versions of cultural studies have been shaped by encounters among diverse feminisms; ethnic and critical race studies; gay, lesbian, and queer studies; postcolonial and diasporic research; and indigenous peoples' scholarship. These interactions have produced a sensitivity to culture in its multiple forms, including the aesthetic, the political, the anthropological, the performative, the historical, and the spatial. Thus there are collections and essays in Australian-Asian cultural studies; Asian Pacific cultural studies; Latin American, Mexican, and Chicana/o cultural studies; black British cultural studies; and Irish, British, Spanish, Italian, Nordic, and African cultural studies.

At the same time, students of cultural studies wrestle with the multiple meanings of such key terms as *identity, place, globalization, the local, nationhood,* and *difference.* These terms are constantly debated in the media and are played out in arenas defined and shaped by the new information and communication technologies. Cultural studies scholars examine how meanings move between and within various media formations. This has yielded studies of Madonna, Elvis, the Gulf War, and Anita Hill, as well as studies of the "memory-work" of museums, tourism, and shopping malls. In such work it becomes clear that culture is a contested, conflictual set of practices bound up with the meanings of identity and community.

The disciplinary boundaries that define cultural studies keep shifting, and there is no agreed-upon standard genealogy of the field's emergence as a serious academic discipline. Nonetheless, there are certain prevailing tendencies, including feminist understandings of the politics of the everyday and the personal; disputes among proponents of textualism, ethnography, and autoethnography; and continued debates surrounding the dreams of modern citizenship.

◆ Sexualities and Queer Theory

Critical race theory brought race and the concept of a complex racial subject squarely into qualitative inquiry. Next it remained for queer theory to do the same—namely, to question and deconstruct the concept of an unreflexive, unified sexual (and racialized) subject. In Chapter 12, Joshua Gamson documents the story of how mainstream social science was forced to confront the politics of sexuality along with the politics of race. He shows how the study of sexualities has long been intertwined with qualitative research (life stories, ethnographies). By troubling the place of the homo/heterosexual binary in everyday life, queer theory has created spaces for multiple discourses on gay, bisexual, transgendered, and lesbian subjects. This means that researchers must examine how any social arena is structured, in part, by this homo/hetero dichotomy. They must ask how the epistemology of the closet is central to the sexual and material practices of everyday life. Queer theory challenges this epistemology, just as it deconstructs the notion of unified subjects. Queerness becomes a topic and a resource for investigating the way group boundaries are created, negotiated, and changed. Institutional and historical analyses are central to this project, for they shed light on how the self and its identities are embedded in institutional and cultural practices.

◆ *In Conclusion*

The researcher-as-interpretive *bricoleur* cannot afford to be a stranger to any of the paradigms and perspectives discussed in Part II of this *Handbook*. The researcher must understand the basic ethical, ontological, epistemological, and methodological assumptions of each and be able to engage them in dialogue. The differences among paradigms and perspectives have significant and important implications at the practical, material, everyday level. The blurring of paradigm differences is likely to continue as long as proponents continue to come together to discuss their differences while seeking to build on those areas where they are in agreement.

It is also clear that there is no single "truth." All truths are partial and incomplete. As Lincoln and Guba argue in Chapter 6, there will be no single conventional paradigm to which all social scientists might ascribe. We occupy a historical moment marked by multivocality, contested meanings, paradigmatic controversies, and new textual forms. This is an age of emancipation; we have been freed from the confines of a single regime of truth and from the habit of seeing the world in one color.

■ *References*

Grossberg, L., & Pollock, D. (1998). Editorial statement. *Cultural Studies, 12*(2), 114.

Guba, E. G. (1990). The alternative paradigm dialog. In E. G. Guba (Ed.), *The paradigm dialog* (pp. 17-30). Newbury Park, CA: Sage.

Hall, S. (1996). Gramsci's relevance for the study of race and ethnicity. In D. Morley & K.-H. Chen (Eds.), *Stuart Hall: Critical dialogues in cultural studies* (pp. 411-444). London: Routledge.

Olesen, V. (1994). Feminisms and models of qualitative research. In N. K. Denzin & Y. S. Lincoln (Eds.), *Handbook of qualitative research* (pp. 158-174). Thousand Oaks, CA: Sage.

Parker, L., Deyhle, D., Villenas, S., & Nebeker, K. C. (1998). Guest editors' introduction: Critical race theory and qualitative studies in education. *International Journal of Qualitative Studies in Education, 11,* 5-6.

6

PARADIGMATIC CONTROVERSIES, CONTRADICTIONS, AND EMERGING CONFLUENCES

◆ Yvonna S. Lincoln and Egon G. Guba

n our chapter for the first edition of the *Handbook of Qualitative Research,* we focused on the contention among various research paradigms for legitimacy and intellectual and paradigmatic hegemony (Guba & Lincoln, 1994). The postmodern paradigms that we discussed (postmodernist critical theory and constructivism)[1] were in contention with the received positivist and postpositivist paradigms for legitimacy, and with one another for intellectual legitimacy. In the half dozen years that have elapsed since that chapter was published, substantial change has occurred in the landscape of social scientific inquiry.

On the matter of legitimacy, we observe that readers familiar with the literature on methods and paradigms reflect a high interest in ontologies and epistemologies that differ sharply from those undergirding conventional social science. Second, even those established professionals trained in quantitative social science (including the two of us) want to learn more about qualitative approaches, because new young professionals being mentored in graduate schools are asking serious questions about and looking for guidance in qualitatively oriented studies and dissertations. Third, the number of qualitative texts, research papers, workshops, and training materials has exploded. Indeed, it would be difficult to miss the distinct turn of the social sciences toward more interpretive, postmodern, and criticalist practices and theorizing (Bloland, 1989, 1995). This nonpositivist orientation has created a context (surround) in which virtually no study can go unchallenged by proponents of contending paradigms. Further, it is obvious that the number of practitioners of new-paradigm inquiry is growing daily. There can be no question that the legitimacy of postmodern paradigms is well established and at least equal to the legitimacy of received and conventional paradigms (Denzin & Lincoln, 1994).

On the matter of hegemony, or supremacy, among postmodern paradigms, it is clear that Geertz's (1988, 1993) prophecy about the "blurring of genres" is rapidly being fulfilled. Inquiry methodology can no longer be treated as a set of universally applicable rules or abstractions. Methodology is inevitably interwoven with and emerges from the nature of particular disciplines (such as sociology and psychology) and particular perspectives (such as Marxism, feminist theory, and queer theory). So, for instance, we can read feminist critical theorists such as Olesen (Chapter 8, this volume) or queer theorists such as Gamson (Chapter 12, this volume), or we can follow arguments about teachers as researchers (Kincheloe, 1991) while we understand the secondary text to be teacher empowerment and democratization of schooling practices. Indeed, the various paradigms are beginning to "interbreed" such that two theorists previously thought to be in irreconcilable conflict may now appear, under a different theoretical rubric, to be informing one another's arguments. A personal example is our own work, which has been heavily influenced by action research practitioners and postmodern critical theorists. Consequently, to argue that it is paradigms that are in contention is probably less useful than to probe where and how paradigms exhibit confluence and where and how they exhibit differences, controversies, and contradictions.

◆ *Major Issues Confronting All Paradigms*

In our chapter in the first edition of this *Handbook,* we presented two tables that summarized our positions, first, on the axiomatic nature of paradigms (the paradigms we considered at that time were positivism, postpositivism, critical theory, and constructivism; Guba & Lincoln, 1994, p. 109, Table 6.1); and second, on the issues we believed were most fundamental to differentiating the four paradigms (p. 112, Table 6.2). These tables are reproduced here as a way of reminding our readers of our previous statement. The axioms defined the ontological, epistemological, and methodological bases for both established and emergent paradigms; these are shown in Table 6.1. The issues most often in contention that we examined were inquiry aim, nature of knowledge, the way knowledge is accumulated, goodness (rigor and validity) or quality criteria, values, ethics, voice, training, accommodation, and hegemony; these are shown in Table 6.2. An examination of these two tables will reacquaint the reader with our original *Handbook* treatment; more detailed information is, of course, available in our original chapter.

Since publication of that chapter, at least one set of authors, John Heron and Peter Reason, have elaborated upon our tables to include the *participatory/cooperative* paradigm (Heron, 1996; Heron & Reason, 1997, pp. 289-290). Thus, in addition to the paradigms of positivism, postpositivism, critical theory, and constructivism, we add the participatory paradigm in the present chapter (this is an excellent example, we might add, of the hermeneutic elaboration so embedded in our own view, constructivism).

Our aim here is to extend the analysis further by building on Heron and Reason's additions and by rearranging the issues to reflect current thought. The issues we have chosen include our original formulations and the additions, revisions, and amplifications made by Heron and Reason (1997), and we have also chosen what we believe to be the issues most important today. We should note that *important* means several things to us. An important topic may be one that is widely debated (or even hotly contested)—validity is one such issue. An important issue may be one that bespeaks a new awareness (an issue such as recognition of the role of values). An important issue may be one that illustrates the influence of one paradigm upon another (such as the influence of feminist, action research, critical theory, and participatory models on researcher conceptions of action within and for the community in which research is carried out).

TABLE 6.1 Basic Belief (Metaphysics) of Alternative Inquiry Paradigms

Item	Positivism	Postpositivism	Critical Theory et al.	Constructivism
Ontology	Naïve realism—"real" reality but apprehendable	Critical realism—"real" reality but only imperfectly and probabilistically apprehendable	Historical realism—virtual reality shaped by social, political, cultural, economic, ethnic, and gender values; crystallized over time	Relativism—local and specific constructed realities
Epistemology	Dualist/objectivist; findings true	Modified dualist/objectivist; critical tradition/community; findings probably true	Transactional/subjectivist; value-mediated findings	Transactional/ subjectivist/ created findings
Methodology	Experimental/ manipulative; verification of hypotheses; chiefly quantitative methods	Modified experimental/ manipulative; critical multiplism; falsification of hypotheses; may include qualitative methods	Dialogic/dialectical	Hermeneutical/ dialectical

TABLE 6.2 Paradigm Positions on Selected Practical Issues

Item	Positivism	Postpositivism	Critical Theory et al.	Constructivism
Inquiry aim	explanation: prediction and control		critique and transformation; restitution and emancipation	understanding; reconstruction
Nature of knowledge	verified hypotheses established as facts or laws	nonfalsified hypotheses that are probable facts or laws	structural/historical insights	individual reconstructions coalescing around consensus
Knowledge accumulation	accretion—"building blocks" adding to "edifice of knowledge"; generalizations and cause-effect linkages		historical revisionism; generalization by similarity	more informed and sophisticated reconstructions; vicarious experience
Goodness or quality criteria	conventional benchmarks of "rigor": internal and external validity, reliability, and objectivity		historical situatedness; erosion of ignorance and misapprehension; action stimulus	trustworthiness and authenticity
Values	excluded—influence denied		included—formative	
Ethics	extrinsic: tilt toward deception		intrinsic: moral tilt toward revelation	intrinsic: process tilt toward revelation; special problems
Voice	"disinterested scientist" as informer of decision makers, policy makers, and change agents		"transformative intellectual" as advocate and activist	"passionate participant" as facilitator of multivoice reconstruction
Training	technical and quantitative; substantive theories	technical; quantitative and qualitative; substantive theories	resocialization; qualitative and quantitative; history; values of altruism and empowerment	
Accommodation	commensurable		incommensurable	
Hegemony	in control of publication, funding, promotion, and tenure		seeking recognition and input	

Or issues may be important because new or extended theoretical and/or field-oriented treatments for them are newly available—voice and reflexivity are two such issues.

Table 6.3 reprises the original Table 6.1 but adds the axioms of the participatory paradigm proposed by Heron and Reason (1997). Table 6.4 deals with seven issues and represents an update of selected issues first presented in the old Table 6.2. "Voice" in the 1994 version of Table 6.2 has been renamed "inquirer posture," and a redefined "voice" has been inserted in the current Table 6.5. In all cases except "inquirer posture," the entries for the participatory paradigm are those proposed by Heron and Reason; in the one case not covered by them, we have added a notation that we believe captures their intention.

We make no attempt here to reprise the material well discussed in our earlier *Handbook* chapter. Instead, we focus solely on the issues in Table 6.5: axiology; accommodation and commensurability; action; control; foundations of truth and knowledge; validity; and voice, reflexivity, and postmodern textual representation. We believe these seven issues to be the most important at this time.

While we believe these issues to be the most contentious, we also believe they create the intellectual, theoretical, and practical space for dialogue, consensus, and confluence to occur. There is great potential for interweaving of viewpoints, for the incorporation of multiple perspectives, and for borrowing or *bricolage,* where borrowing seems useful, richness enhancing, or theoretically heuristic. For instance, even though we are ourselves social constructivists/contructionists, our call to action embedded in the authenticity criteria we elaborated in *Fourth Generation Evaluation* (Guba & Lincoln, 1989) reflects strongly the bent to action embodied in critical theorists' perspectives. And although Heron and Reason have elaborated a model they call the *cooperative paradigm,* careful reading of their proposal reveals a form of inquiry that is post-postpositive, postmodern, and criticalist in orientation. As a result, the reader familiar with several theoretical and paradigmatic strands of research will find that echoes of many streams of thought come together in the extended table. What this means is that the categories, as Laurel Richardson (personal communication, September 12, 1998) has pointed out, "are fluid, indeed what should be a category keeps altering, enlarging." She notes that "even as [we] write, the boundaries between the paradigms are shifting." This is the paradigmatic equivalent of the Geertzian "blurring of genres" to which we referred earlier.

Our own position is that of the constructionist camp, loosely defined. We do not believe that criteria for judging either "reality" or validity are absolutist (Bradley & Schaefer, 1998), but rather are derived from community consensus regarding what is "real," what is useful, and what has meaning (especially meaning for action and further steps). We believe that a goodly portion of social phenomena consists of the meaning-making activities of groups and individuals around those phenomena. The meaning-making activities themselves are of central interest to social constructionists/constructivists, simply because it is the meaning-making/sense-making/attributional activities that shape action (or inaction). The meaning-making activities themselves can be changed when they are found to be incomplete, faulty (e.g., discriminatory, oppressive, or nonliberatory), or malformed (created from data that can be shown to be false).

We have tried, however, to incorporate perspectives from other major nonpositivist paradigms. This is not a complete summation; space constraints prevent that. What we hope to do in this chapter is to acquaint readers with the larger currents, arguments, dialogues, and provocative writings and theorizing, the better to see perhaps what we ourselves do not even yet see: where and when confluence is possible, where constructive rapprochement might be negotiated, where voices are beginning to achieve some harmony.

◆ Axiology

Earlier, we placed values on the table as an "issue" on which positivists or phenomenologists

TABLE 6.3 Basic Beliefs of Alternative Inquiry Paradigms—Updated

Issue	Positivism	Postpositivism	Critical Theory et al.	Constructivism	Participatory[a]
Ontology	naïve realism—"real" reality but apprehendable	critical realism—"real" reality but only imperfectly and probabilistically apprehendable	historical realism—virtual reality shaped by social, political, cultural, economic, ethnic, and gender values crystallized over time	relativism—local and specific constructed realities	participative reality—subjective-objective reality, cocreated by mind and given cosmos
Epistemology	dualist/objectivist; findings true	modified dualist/objectivist; critical tradition/community; findings probably true	Transactional/subjectivist; value-mediated findings	Transactional/subjectivist; created findings	critical subjectivity in participatory transaction with cosmos; extended epistemology of experiential, propositional, and practical knowing; cocreated findings
Methodology	experimental/manipulative; verification of hypotheses; chiefly quantitative methods	modified experimental/manipulative; critical multiplism; falsification of hypotheses; may include qualitative methods	dialogic/dialectic	hermeneutic/dialectic	political participation in collaborative action inquiry; primacy of the practical; use of language grounded in shared experiential context

a. Entries in this column are based on Heron and Reason (1997).

might have a "posture" (Guba & Lincoln, 1989, 1994; Lincoln & Guba, 1985). Fortunately, we reserved for ourselves the right to either get smarter or just change our minds. We did both. Now, we suspect (although Table 6.3 does not yet reflect it) that "axiology" should be grouped with "basic beliefs." In *Naturalistic Inquiry* (Lincoln & Guba, 1985), we covered some of the ways in which values feed into the inquiry process: choice of the problem, choice of paradigm to guide the problem, choice of theoretical framework, choice of major data-gathering and data-analytic methods, choice of context, treatment of values already resident within the context, and choice of format(s) for presenting findings. We believed those were strong enough reasons to argue for the inclusion of values as a major point of departure between positivist, conventional modes of inquiry and interpretive forms of inquiry.

A second "reading" of the burgeoning literature and subsequent rethinking of our own rationale have led us to conclude that the issue is much larger than we first conceived. If we had it to do all over again, we would make values or, more correctly, axiology (the branch of philosophy dealing with ethics, aesthetics, and religion) a part of the basic foundational philosophical dimensions of paradigm proposal. Doing so would, in our opinion, begin to help us see the embeddedness of ethics within, not external to, paradigms (see, for instance, Christians, Chapter 5, this volume) and would contribute to the consideration of and dialogue about the role of spirituality in human inquiry. Arguably, axiology has been "defined out of" scientific inquiry for no larger a reason than that it also concerns "religion." But defining "religion" broadly to encompass spirituality would move constructivists closer to participative inquirers and would move critical theorists closer to both (owing to their concern with liberation from oppression and freeing of the human spirit, both profoundly spiritual concerns). The expansion of basic issues to include axiology, then, is one way to achieving greater confluence among the various interpretivist inquiry models. This is the place, for example, where Peter Reason's profound concerns with

"sacred science" and human functioning find legitimacy; it is a place where Laurel Richardson's "sacred spaces" become authoritative sites for human inquiry; it is a place—or *the* place—where the spiritual meets social inquiry, as Reason (1993), and later Lincoln and Denzin (1994), proposed some years earlier.

◆ Accommodation and Commensurability

Positivists and postpositivists alike still occasionally argue that paradigms are, in some ways, commensurable; that is, they can be retrofitted to each other in ways that make the simultaneous practice of both possible. We have argued that at the paradigmatic, or philosophical, level, commensurability between positivist and postpositivist worldviews is not possible, but that within each paradigm, mixed methodologies (strategies) may make perfectly good sense (Guba & Lincoln, 1981, 1982, 1989, 1994; Lincoln & Guba, 1985). So, for instance, in *Effective Evaluation* we argued:

> The guiding inquiry paradigm most appropriate to responsive evaluation is . . . the naturalistic, phenomenological, or ethnographic paradigm. It will be seen that qualitative techniques are typically most appropriate to support this approach. There are times, however, when the issues and concerns voiced by audiences require information that is best generated by more conventional methods, especially quantitative methods. . . . In such cases, the responsive conventional evaluator will not shrink from the appropriate application. (Guba & Lincoln, 1981, p. 36)

As we tried to make clear, the "argument" arising in the social sciences was *not about method*, although many critics of the new naturalistic, ethnographic, phenomenological, and/or case study approaches assumed it was.[2] As late as 1998, Weiss could be found to claim that "Some evaluation theorists, notably Guba and Lincoln (1989), hold that it is impossible to combine qualitative and quantitative approaches responsibly

(Continued on p.174)

TABLE 6.4 Paradigm Positions on Selected Issues—Updated

Issue	Positivism	Postpositivism	Critical Theory et al.	Constructivism	Participatory[a]
Nature of knowledge	verified hypotheses established as facts or laws	nonfalsified hypotheses that are probable facts or laws	structural/historical insights	individual reconstructions coalescing around consensus	extended epistemology: primacy of practical knowing; critical subjectivity; living knowledge
Knowledge accumulation	accretion—"building blocks" adding to "edifice of knowledge"; generalizations and cause-effect linkages		historical revisionism; generalization by similarity	more informed and sophisticated reconstructions; vicarious experience	in communities of inquiry embedded in communities of practice
Goodness or quality criteria	conventional benchmarks of "rigor": internal and external validity, reliability, and objectivity		historical situatedness; erosion of ignorance and misapprehensions; action stimulus	trustworthiness and authenticity	congruence of experiential, presentational, propositional, and practical knowing; leads to action to transform the world in the service of human flourishing
Values	excluded—influence denied ⟶			included—formative ⟵	
Ethics	Extrinsic—tilt toward deception		intrinsic—moral tilt toward revelation	intrinsic—process tilt toward revelation	

Inquirer posture	"disinterested scientist" as informer of decision makers, policy makers, and change agents	"transformative intellectual" as advocate and activist	"passionate participant" as facilitator of multivoice reconstruction	primary voice manifest through aware self-reflective action; secondary voices in illuminating theory, narrative, movement, song, dance, and other presentational forms
Training	technical and quantitative; substantive theories	technical, quantitative, and qualitative; substantive theories	resocialization; qualitative and quantitative; history; values of altruism and empowerment	coresearchers are initiated into the inquiry process by facilitator/researcher and learn through active engagement in the process; facilitator/researcher requires emotional competence, democratic personality and skills

a. Entries in this column are based on Heron and Reason (1997), except for "ethics" and "values."

TABLE 6.5 Critical Issues of the Time

Issue	Positivism	Postpositivism	Critical Theory et al.	Constructivism	Participatory
Axiology	Propositional knowing about the world is an end in itself, is intrinsically valuable.		Propositional, transactional knowing is instrumentally valuable as a means to social emancipation, which as an end in itself, is intrinsically valuable.		Practical knowing about how to flourish with a balance of autonomy, cooperation, and hierarchy in a culture is an end in itself, is intrinsically valuable.
Accommodation and commensurability	commensurable for all positivist forms		incommensurable with positivist forms; some commensurability with constructivist, criticalist, and participatory approaches, especially as they merge in liberationist approaches outside the West		
Action	not the responsibility of the researcher; viewed as "advocacy" or subjectivity, and therefore a threat to validity and objectivity		found especially in the form of empowerment; emancipation anticipated and hoped for; social transformation, particularly toward more equity and justice, is end goal	intertwined with validity; inquiry often incomplete without action on the part of participants; constructivist formulation mandates training in political action if participants do not understand political systems	
Control	resides solely in researcher		often resides in "transformative intellectual"; in new constructions, control returns to community	shared between inquirer and participants	shared to varying degrees

Relationship to foundations of truth and knowledge	foundational	foundational	foundational within social critique	antifoundational	nonfoundational
Extended considerations of validity (goodness criteria)	traditional positivist constructions of validity; rigor, internal validity, external validity, reliability, objectivity		action stimulus (see above); social transformation, equity, social justice	extended constructions of validity: (a) crystalline validity (Richardson); (b) authenticity criteria (Guba & Lincoln); (c) catalytic, rhizomatic, voluptuous validities (Lather); (d) relational and ethics-centered criteria (Lincoln); (e) community-centered determinations of validity	see "action" above
Voice, reflexivity, postmodern textual representations	voice of the researcher, principally; reflexivity may be considered a problem in objectivity; textual representation unproblematic and somewhat formulaic		voices mixed between researcher and participants	voices mixed, with participants' voices sometimes dominant; reflexivity serious and problematic; textual representation an extended issue	voices mixed; textual representation rarely discussed, but problematic; reflexivity relies on critical subjectivity and self-awareness

Textual representation practices may be problematic—i.e., "fiction formulas," or unexamined "regimes of truth" within an evaluation" (p. 268), even though we stated early on in *Fourth Generation Evaluation* (1989) that

> those claims, concerns and issues that have *not* been resolved become the advance organizers for information collection by the evaluator. . . . *The information may be quantitative or qualitative.* Responsive evaluation does not rule out quantitative modes, as is mistakenly believed by many, but deals with whatever information is responsive to the unresolved claim, concern, or issue. (p. 43)

We had also strongly asserted earlier, in *Naturalistic Inquiry* (1985), that

> qualitative methods are stressed within the naturalistic paradigm not because the paradigm is antiquantitative but because qualitative methods come more easily to the human-as-instrument. *The reader should particularly note the absence of an antiquantitative stance,* precisely because the naturalistic and conventional paradigms are so often—mistakenly—equated with the qualitative and quantitative paradigms, respectively. Indeed, *there are many opportunities for the naturalistic investigator to utilize quantitative data—probably more than are appreciated.* (pp. 198-199; emphasis added)

Having demonstrated that we were not then (and are not now) talking about an antiquantitative posture or the exclusivity of *methods,* but rather the philosophies of which paradigms are constructed, we can ask the question again regarding commensurability: Are paradigms commensurable? Is it possible to blend elements of one paradigm into another, so that one is engaging in research that represents the best of both worldviews? The answer, from our perspective, has to be a cautious *yes.* This is especially so if the models (paradigms) share axiomatic elements that are similar, or that resonate strongly between them. So, for instance, positivism and postpositivism are clearly commensurable. In the same vein, elements of *interpretivist/postmodern* critical theory, constructivist and participative inquiry fit comfortably together. Commensurability is an issue only when researchers want to "pick and choose" among the axioms of positivist and interpretivist mod-

els, because the axioms are contradictory and mutually exclusive.

◆ The Call to Action

One of the clearest ways in which the paradigmatic controversies can be demonstrated is to compare the positivist and postpositivist adherents, who view action as a form of contamination of research results and processes, and the interpretivists, who see action on research results as a meaningful and important outcome of inquiry processes. Positivist adherents believe action to be either a form of advocacy or a form of subjectivity, either or both of which undermine the aim of objectivity. Critical theorists, on the other hand, have always advocated varying degrees of social action, from the overturning of specific unjust practices to radical transformation of entire societies. The call for action—whether in terms of internal transformation, such as ridding oneself of false consciousness, or of external social transformation—differentiates between positivist and postmodern criticalist theorists (including feminist and queer theorists).

The sharpest shift, however, has been in the constructivist and participatory phenomenological models, where a step beyond interpretation and *Verstehen,* or understanding, toward social action is probably one of the most conceptually interesting of the shifts (Lincoln, 1997, 1998a, 1998b). For some theorists, the shift toward action came in response to widespread nonutilization of evaluation findings and the desire to create forms of evaluation that would attract champions who might follow through on recommendations with meaningful action plans (Guba & Lincoln, 1981, 1989). For others, embracing action came as both a political and an ethical commitment (see, for instance, in this volume, Greenwood & Levin, Chapter 3; Christians, Chapter 5; Tierney, Chapter 20; see also Carr & Kemmis, 1986; Schratz & Walker, 1995).

Whatever the source of the problem to which inquirers were responding, the shift toward connecting research, policy analysis, evaluation, and/or social deconstruction (e.g., deconstruction of the patriarchal forms of oppression in social structures, which is the project informing much feminist theorizing, or deconstruction of the homophobia embedded in public policies) with action has come to characterize much new-paradigm inquiry work, both at the theoretical and at the practice and *praxis*-oriented levels. Action has become a major controversy that limns the ongoing debates among practitioners of the various paradigms. The mandate for social action, especially action designed and created by and for research participants with the aid and cooperation of researchers, can be most sharply delineated between positivist/postpositivist and new-paradigm inquirers. Many positivist and postpositivist inquirers still consider "action" the domain of communities other than researchers and research participants: those of policy personnel, legislators, and civic and political officials. Hard-line foundationalists presume that the taint of action will interfere with, or even negate, the objectivity that is a (presumed) characteristic of rigorous scientific method inquiry.

◆ *Control*

Another controversy that has tended to become problematic centers on *control* of the study: Who initiates? Who determines salient questions? Who determines what constitutes findings? Who determines how data will be collected? Who determines in what forms the findings will be made public, if at all? Who determines what representations will be made of participants in the research? Let us be very clear: The issue of control is deeply embedded in the questions of voice, reflexivity, and issues of postmodern textual representation, which we shall take up later, *but only for new-paradigm inquirers*. For more conventional inquirers, the issue of control is effectively walled off

from voice, reflexivity, and issues of textual representation, because each of those issues in some way threatens claims to rigor (particularly objectivity and validity). For new-paradigm inquirers who have seen the preeminent paradigm issues of ontology and epistemology effectively folded into one another, and who have watched as methodology and axiology logically folded into one another (Lincoln, 1995, 1997), control of an inquiry seems far less problematic, except insofar as inquirers seek to obtain participants' genuine participation (see, for instance, Guba & Lincoln, 1981, on contracting and attempts to get some stakeholding groups to do more than stand by while an evaluation is in progress).

Critical theorists, especially those who work in community organizing programs, are painfully aware of the necessity for members of the community, or research participants, to take control of their futures. Constructivists desire participants to take an increasingly active role in nominating questions of interest for any inquiry and in designing outlets for findings to be shared more widely within and outside the community. Participatory inquirers understand action controlled by the local context members to be the aim of inquiry within a community. For none of these paradigmatic adherents is control an issue of advocacy, a somewhat deceptive term usually used as a code within a larger metanarrative to attack an inquiry's rigor, objectivity, or fairness. Rather, for new-paradigm researchers control is a means of fostering emancipation, democracy, and community empowerment, and of redressing power imbalances such that those who were previously marginalized now achieve voice (Mertens, 1998) or "human flourishing" (Heron & Reason, 1997).

Control as a controversy is an excellent place to observe the phenomenon that we have always termed "Catholic questions directed to a Methodist audience." We use this description—given to us by a workshop participant in the early 1980s—to refer to the ongoing problem of illegitimate questions: questions that have no meaning because the frames of reference are those for which they were never intended. (We could as well call these "Hindu questions to a Muslim," to give another sense of how paradigms, or overarching philosophies—or theologies—are incommensurable, and how questions in one framework make little, if any, sense in another.) Paradigmatic formulations interact such that control becomes inextricably intertwined with mandates for objectivity. Objectivity derives from the Enlightenment prescription for knowledge of the physical world, which is postulated to be separate and distinct from those who would know (Polkinghorne, 1989). But if knowledge of the social (as opposed to the physical) world resides in meaning-making mechanisms of the social, mental, and linguistic worlds that individuals inhabit, then knowledge cannot be separate from the knower, but rather is rooted in his or her mental or linguistic designations of that world (Polkinghorne, 1989; Salner, 1989).

◆ Foundations of Truth and Knowledge in Paradigms

Whether or not the world has a "real" existence outside of human experience of that world is an open question. For modernist (i.e., Enlightenment, scientific method, conventional, positivist) researchers, most assuredly there is a "real" reality "out there," apart from the flawed human apprehension of it. Further, that reality can be approached (approximated) only through the utilization of methods that prevent human contamination of its apprehension or comprehension. For foundationalists in the empiricist tradition, the foundations of scientific truth and knowledge about reality reside in rigorous application of testing phenomena against a template as much devoid of human bias, misperception, and other "idols" (Francis Bacon, cited in Polkinghorne, 1989) as instrumentally possible. As Polkinghorne (1989) makes clear:

> The idea that the objective realm is independent of the knower's subjective experiences of it can be found in Descartes's dual substance theory, with its distinction between the objective and subjective realms. . . . In the splitting of reality into subject and object realms, what can be

> known "objectively" is only the objective realm. True knowledge is limited to the objects and the relationships between them that exist in the realm of time and space. Human consciousness, which is subjective, is not accessible to science, and thus not truly knowable. (p. 23)

Now, templates of truth and knowledge can be defined in a variety of ways—as the end product of rational processes, as the result of experiential sensing, as the result of empirical observation, and others. In all cases, however, the referent is the physical or empirical world: rational engagement with it, experience of it, empirical observation of it. Realists, who work on the assumption that there is a "real" world "out there," may in individual cases also be foundationalists, taking the view that all of these ways of defining are rooted in phenomena existing outside the human mind. Although we can think about them, experience them, or observe them, they are nevertheless transcendent, referred to but beyond direct apprehension. Realism is an ontological question, whereas foundationalism is a criterial question. Some foundationalists argue that real phenomena necessarily imply certain final, ultimate criteria for testing them as truthful (although we may have great difficulty in determining what those criteria are); nonfoundationalists tend to argue that there are no such ultimate criteria, only those that we can agree upon at a certain time and under certain conditions. Foundational criteria are discovered; nonfoundational criteria are negotiated. It is the case, however, that most realists are also foundationalists, and many nonfoundationalists or antifoundationalists are relativists.

An ontological formulation that connects realism and foundationalism within the same "collapse" of categories that characterizes the ontological-epistemological collapse is one that exhibits good fit with the other assumptions of constructivism. That state of affairs suits new-paradigm inquirers well. Critical theorists, constructivists, and participatory/cooperative inquirers take their primary field of interest to be precisely that subjective and intersubjective social knowledge and the active construction and cocreation of such knowledge by human agents that is produced by human consciousness. Further, new-paradigm inquirers take to the social knowledge field with zest, informed by a variety of social, intellectual, and theoretical explorations. These theoretical excursions include Saussurian linguistic theory, which views all relationships between words and what those words signify as the function of an internal relationship within some linguistic system; literary theory's deconstructive contributions, which seek to disconnect texts from any *essentialist* or transcendental meaning and resituate them within both author and reader historical and social contexts (Hutcheon, 1989; Leitch, 1996); feminist (Addelson, 1993; Alpern, Antler, Perry, & Scobie, 1992; Babbitt, 1993; Harding, 1993), race and ethnic (Kondo, 1990, 1997; Trinh, 1991), and queer theorizing (Gamson, Chapter 12, this volume), which seek to uncover and explore varieties of oppression and historical colonizing between dominant and subaltern genders, identities, races, and social worlds; the postmodern historical moment (Michael, 1996), which problematizes truth as partial, identity as fluid, language as an unclear referent system, and method and criteria as potentially coercive (Ellis & Bochner, 1996); and criticalist theories of social change (Carspecken, 1996; Schratz & Walker, 1995). The realization of the richness of the mental, social, psychological, and linguistic worlds that individuals and social groups create and constantly re-create and cocreate gives rise, in the minds of new-paradigm postmodern and poststructural inquirers, to endlessly fertile fields of inquiry rigidly walled off from conventional inquirers. Unfettered from the pursuit of transcendental scientific truth, inquirers are now free to resituate themselves within texts, to reconstruct their relationships with research participants in less constricted fashions, and to create re-presentations (Tierney & Lincoln, 1997) that grapple openly with problems of inscription, reinscription, metanarratives, and other rhetorical devices that obscure the extent to which human action is locally and temporally shaped. The processes of uncovering forms of inscription and the rhetoric of metanarratives is *genea-*logical—"expos[ing] the origins of the view that have become *sedimented and accepted as truths*" (Polkinghorne, 1989, p. 42; emphasis added)—or *archaeological* (Foucault, 1971; Scheurich, 1997).

New-paradigm inquirers engage the foundational controversy in quite different ways. Critical theorists, particularly critical theorists more positivist in orientation, who lean toward Marxian interpretations, tend toward foundational perspectives, with an important difference. Rather than locating foundational truth and knowledge in some external reality "out there," such critical theorists tend to locate the foundations of truth in specific historical, economic, racial, and social infrastructures of oppression, injustice, and marginalization. Knowers are not portrayed as *separate from* some objective reality, but may be cast as unaware actors in such historical realities ("false consciousness") or aware of historical forms of oppression, but unable or unwilling, because of conflicts, to act on those historical forms to alter specific conditions in this historical moment ("divided consciousness"). Thus the "foundation" for critical theorists is a duality: social critique tied in turn to raised consciousness of the possibility of positive and liberating social change. Social critique may exist apart from social change, but both are necessary for criticalist perspectives.

Constructivists, on the other hand, tend toward the antifoundational (Lincoln, 1995, 1998b; Schwandt, 1996). *Antifoundational* is the term used to denote a refusal to adopt any permanent, unvarying (or "foundational") standards by which truth can be universally known. As one of us has argued, truth—and any agreement regarding what is valid knowledge—arises from the relationship between members of some stakeholding community (Lincoln, 1995). Agreements about truth may be the subject of community *negotiations* regarding what will be accepted as truth (although there are difficulties with that formulation as well; Guba & Lincoln, 1989). Or agreements may eventuate as the result of a *dialogue* that moves arguments about truth claims or validity past the warring camps of objectivity and relativity toward "a communal test of validity through the argumentation of the participants in a discourse" (Bernstein, 1983; Polkinghorne, 1989; Schwandt, 1996). This "communicative and pragmatic concept" of validity (Rorty, 1979) is never fixed or unvarying. Rather, it is created by means of a community narrative, itself subject to the temporal and historical conditions that gave rise to the community. Schwandt (1989) has also argued that these discourses, or community narratives, can and should be bounded by moral considerations, a premise grounded in the emancipatory narratives of the critical theorists, the philosophical pragmatism of Rorty, the democratic focus of constructivist inquiry, and the "human flourishing" goals of participatory and cooperative inquiry.

The controversies around foundationalism (and, to a lesser extent, essentialism) are not likely to be resolved through dialogue between paradigm adherents. The likelier event is that the "postmodern turn" (Best & Kellner, 1997), with its emphasis on the social construction of social reality, fluid as opposed to fixed identities of the self, and the partiality of all truths, will simply overtake modernist assumptions of an objective reality, as indeed, to some extent, it has already done in the physical sciences. We might predict that, if not in our lifetimes, at some later time the dualist idea of an objective reality suborned by limited human subjective realities will seem as quaint as flat-earth theories do to us today.

◆ *Validity: An Extended Agenda*

Nowhere can the conversation about paradigm differences be more fertile than in the extended controversy about validity (Howe & Eisenhart, 1990; Kvale, 1989, 1994; Ryan, Greene, Lincoln, Mathison, & Mertens, 1998; Scheurich, 1994, 1996). Validity is not like objectivity. There are fairly strong theoretical, philosophical, and pragmatic rationales for examining the concept of objectivity and finding it wanting. Even within positivist frameworks it is viewed as conceptually flawed. But validity is a more irri-

tating construct, one neither easily dismissed nor readily configured by new-paradigm practitioners (Enerstvedt, 1989; Tschudi, 1989). Validity cannot be dismissed simply because it points to a question that has to be answered in one way or another: Are these findings sufficiently authentic (isomorphic to some reality, trustworthy, related to the way others construct their social worlds) that I may trust myself in acting on their implications? More to the point, would I feel sufficiently secure about these findings to construct social policy or legislation based on them? At the same time, radical reconfigurations of validity leave researchers with multiple, sometimes conflicting, mandates for what constitutes rigorous research.

One of the issues around validity is the conflation between method and interpretation. The postmodern turn suggests that no method can deliver on ultimate truth, and in fact "suspects all methods," the more so the larger their claims to delivering on truth (Richardson, 1994). Thus, although one might argue that some methods are more suited than others for conducting research on human construction of social realities (Lincoln & Guba, 1985), no one would argue that a single method—or collection of methods—is the royal road to ultimate knowledge. In new-paradigm inquiry, however, it is not merely method that promises to deliver on some set of local or context-grounded truths, it is also the processes of interpretation. Thus we have two arguments proceeding simultaneously. The first, borrowed from positivism, argues for a kind of rigor in the application of method, whereas the second argues for both a community consent and a form of rigor—defensible reasoning, plausible alongside some other reality that is known to author and reader—in ascribing salience to one interpretation over another and for framing and bounding an interpretive study itself. Prior to our understanding that there were, indeed, two forms of rigor, we assembled a set of methodological criteria, largely borrowed from an earlier generation of thoughtful anthropological and sociological methodological theorists. Those methodological criteria are still useful for a variety of reasons, not the least of which is that they ensure that such issues as prolonged engagement and persistent observation are attended to with some seriousness.

It is the second kind of rigor, however, that has received the most attention in recent writings: Are we *interpretively* rigorous? Can our cocreated constructions be trusted to provide some purchase on some important human phenomenon?

Human phenomena are themselves the subject of controversy. Classical social scientists would like to see "human phenomena" limited to those social experiences from which (scientific) generalizations may be drawn. New-paradigm inquirers, however, are increasingly concerned with the single experience, the individual crisis, the epiphany or moment of discovery, with that most powerful of all threats to conventional objectivity, feeling and emotion. Social scientists concerned with the expansion of what count as social data rely increasingly on the experiential, the embodied, the emotive qualities of human experience that contribute the narrative quality to a life. Sociologists such as Ellis and Bochner (see Chapter 28, this volume) and Richardson (see Chapter 36, this volume) and psychologists such as Michelle Fine (see Fine, Weis, Weseen, & Wong, Chapter 4, this volume) concern themselves with various forms of autoethnography and personal experience methods, both to overcome the abstractions of a social science far gone with quantitative descriptions of human life and to capture those elements that make life conflictual, moving, problematic.

For purposes of this discussion, we believe the adoption of the most radical definitions of social science are appropriate, because the paradigmatic controversies are often taking place at the edges of those conversations. Those edges are where the border work is occurring, and, accordingly, they are the places that show the most promise for projecting where qualitative methods will be in the near and far future.

Whither and Whether Criteria

At those edges, several conversations are occurring around validity. The first—and most radical—is a conversation opened by Schwandt (1996), who suggests that we say "farewell to criteriology," or the "regulative norms for removing doubt and settling disputes about what is correct or incorrect, true or false" (p. 59), which have created a virtual cult around criteria. Schwandt does not, however, himself say farewell to criteria forever; rather, he resituates social inquiry, with other contemporary philosophical pragmatists, within a framework that transforms professional social inquiry into a form of practical philosophy, characterized by "aesthetic, prudential and moral considerations as well as more conventionally scientific ones" (p. 68). When social inquiry becomes the practice of a form of practical philosophy—a deep questioning about how we shall get on in the world, and what we conceive to be the potentials and limits of human knowledge and functioning—then we have some preliminary understanding of what entirely different criteria might be for judging social inquiry.

Schwandt (1996) proposes three such criteria. First, he argues, we should search for a social inquiry that "generate[s] knowledge that complements or supplements rather than displac[ing] lay probing of social problems," a form of knowledge for which we do not yet have the *content,* but from which we might seek to understand the aims of practice from a variety of perspectives, or with different lenses. Second, he proposes a "social inquiry as practical philosophy" that has as its aim "enhancing or cultivating *critical* intelligence in parties to the research encounter," critical intelligence being defined as "the capacity to engage in moral critique." And finally, he proposes a third way in which we might judge social inquiry as practical philosophy: We might make judgments about the social inquirer-as-practical-philosopher. He or she might be "evaluated on the success to which his or her reports of the inquiry enable the training or calibration of human judgment" (p. 69) or "the capacity for practical wisdom" (p. 70).

Schwandt is not alone, however, in wishing to say "farewell to criteriology," at least as it has been previously conceived. Scheurich (1997) makes a similar plea, and in the same vein, Smith (1993) also argues that validity, if it is to survive at all, must be radically reformulated if it is ever to serve phenomenological research well (see also Smith & Deemer, Chapter 34, this volume).

At issue here is not whether we shall have criteria, or whose criteria we as a scientific community might adopt, but rather what the nature of social inquiry ought to be, whether it ought to undergo a transformation, and what might be the basis for criteria within a projected transformation. Schwandt (1989; also personal communication, August 21, 1998) is quite clear that both the transformation and the criteria are rooted in dialogic efforts. These dialogic efforts are quite clearly themselves forms of "moral discourse." Through the specific connections of the dialogic, the idea of practical wisdom, and moral discourses, much of Schwandt's work can be seen to be related to, and reflective of, critical theorist and participatory paradigms, as well as constructivism, although he specifically denies the relativity of truth. (For a more sophisticated explication and critique of forms of constructivism, hermeneutics, and interpretivism, see Schwandt, Chapter 7, this volume. In that chapter, Schwandt spells out distinctions between realists and nonrealists, and between foundationalists and nonfoundationalists, far more clearly than it is possible for us to do in this chapter.)

To return to the central question embedded in validity: How do we know when we have specific social inquiries that are faithful enough to some human construction that we may feel safe in acting on them, or, more important, that members of the community in which the research is conducted may act on them? To that question, there is no final answer. There are, however, several discussions of what we might use to make both professional and lay judgments regarding any piece of work. It is to those versions of validity that we now turn.

Validity as Authenticity

Perhaps the first nonfoundational criteria were those we developed in response to a challenge by John K. Smith (see Smith & Deemer, Chapter 34, this volume). In those criteria, we attempted to locate criteria for judging the *processes* and *outcomes* of naturalistic or constructivist inquiries (rather than the application of methods; see Guba & Lincoln, 1989). We described five potential outcomes of a social constructionist inquiry (evaluation is one form of disciplined inquiry; see Guba & Lincoln, 1981), each grounded in concerns specific to the paradigm we had tried to describe and construct, and apart from any concerns carried over from the positivist legacy. The criteria were instead rooted in the axioms and assumptions of the constructivist paradigm, insofar as we could extrapolate and infer them.

Those authenticity criteria—so called because we believed them to be hallmarks of authentic, trustworthy, rigorous, or "valid" constructivist or phenomenological inquiry—were fairness, ontological authenticity, educative authenticity, catalytic authenticity, and tactical authenticity (Guba & Lincoln, 1989, pp. 245-251). *Fairness* was thought to be a quality of balance; that is, all stakeholder views, perspectives, claims, concerns, and voices should be apparent in the text. Omission of stakeholder or participant voices reflects, we believe, a form of bias. This bias, however, was and is not related directly to the concerns of objectivity that flow from positivist inquiry and that are reflective of inquirer blindness or subjectivity. Rather, this fairness was defined by deliberate attempts to prevent marginalization, to act affirmatively with respect to inclusion, and to act with energy to ensure that all voices in the inquiry effort had a chance to be represented in any texts and to have their stories treated fairly and with balance.

Ontological and educative authenticity were designated as criteria for determining a raised level of awareness, in the first instance, by individual research participants and, in the second, by individuals about those who surround them or with whom they come into contact for some social or organizational purpose. Although we failed to see it at that particular historical moment (1989), there is no reason these criteria cannot be—at this point in time, with many miles under our theoretic and practice feet—reflective also of Schwandt's (1996) "critical intelligence," or capacity to engage in moral critique. In fact, the authenticity criteria we originally proposed had strong moral and ethical overtones, a point to which we later returned (see, for instance, Lincoln, 1995, 1998a, 1998b). It was a point to which our critics strongly objected before we were sufficiently self-aware to realize the implications of what we had proposed (see, for instance, Sechrest, 1993).

Catalytic and tactical authenticities refer to the ability of a given inquiry to prompt, first, action on the part of research participants, and second, the involvement of the researcher/evaluator in training participants in specific forms of social and political action if participants desire such training. It is here that constructivist inquiry practice begins to resemble forms of critical theorist action, action research, or participative or cooperative inquiry, each of which is predicated on creating the capacity in research participants for positive social change and forms of emancipatory community action. It is also at this specific point that practitioners of positivist and postpositivist social inquiry are the most critical, because any action on the part of the inquirer is thought to destabilize objectivity and introduce subjectivity, resulting in bias.

The problem of subjectivity and bias has a long theoretical history, and this chapter is simply too brief for us to enter into the various formulations that either take account of subjectivity or posit it as a positive learning experience, practical, embodied, gendered, and emotive. For purposes of this discussion, it is enough to say that we are persuaded that objectivity is a chimera: a mythological creature that never existed, save in the imaginations of those who believe that knowing can be separated from the knower.

Validity as Resistance, Validity as Poststructural Transgression

Laurel Richardson (1994, 1997) has proposed another form of validity, a deliberately "transgressive" form, the *crystalline*. In writing experimental (i.e., nonauthoritative, nonpositivist) texts, particularly poems and plays, Richardson (1997) has sought to "problematize reli-

ability, validity and truth" (p. 165), in an effort to create new relationships: to her research participants, to her work, to other women, to herself. She says that transgressive forms permit a social scientist to "conjure a different kind of social science . . . [which] means changing one's relationship to one's work, *how* one knows and tells about the sociological" (p. 166). In order to see "how transgression looks and how it feels," it is necessary to "find and deploy methods that allow us to uncover the hidden assumptions and life-denying repressions of sociology; resee/refeel sociology. Reseeing and retelling are inseparable" (p. 167).

The way to achieve such validity is by examining the properties of a crystal in a metaphoric sense. Here we present an extended quotation to give some flavor of how such validity might be described and deployed:

> I propose that the central imaginary for "validity" for postmodernist texts is not the triangle—a rigid, fixed, two-dimensional object. Rather the central imaginary is the crystal, which combines symmetry and substance with an infinite variety of shapes, substances, transmutations, multidimensionalities, and angles of approach. Crystals grow, change, alter, but are not amorphous. Crystals are prisms that reflect externalities *and* refract within themselves, creating different colors, patterns, arrays, casting off in different directions. What we see depends upon our angle of repose. Not triangulation, crystallization. In postmodernist mixed-genre texts, we have moved from plane geometry to light theory, where light can be *both* waves *and* particles. Crystallization, without losing structure, deconstructs the traditional idea of "validity" (we feel how there is no single truth, we see how texts validate themselves); and crystallization provides us with a deepened, complex, thoroughly partial understanding of the topic. Paradoxically, we know more and doubt what we know. (Richardson, 1997, p. 92)

The metaphoric "solid object" (crystal/text), which can be turned many ways, which reflects and refracts light (light/multiple layers of meaning), through which we can see both "wave" (light wave/human currents) and "particle" (light as "chunks" of energy/elements of truth, feeling, connection, processes of the research that "flow" together) is an attractive metaphor for validity. The properties of the crystal-as-metaphor help writers and readers alike see the interweaving of processes in the research: discovery, seeing, telling, storying, re-presentation.

Other "Transgressive" Validities

Laurel Richardson is not alone in calling for forms of validity that are "transgressive" and disruptive of the status quo. Patti Lather (1993) seeks "an incitement to discourse," the purpose of which is "to rupture validity as a regime of truth, to displace its historical inscription . . . via a dispersion, circulation and proliferation of counter-practices of authority that take the crisis of representation into account" (p. 674). In addition to catalytic validity (Lather, 1986), Lather (1993) poses *validity as simulacra/ironic validity; Lyotardian paralogy/neopragmatic validity*, a form of validity that "foster[s] heterogeneity, refusing disclosure" (p. 679); *Derridean rigor/rhizomatic validity*, a form of behaving "via relay, circuit, multiple openings" (p. 680); and *voluptuous/situated validity*, which "embodies a situated, partial tentativeness" and "brings ethics and epistemology together . . . via practices of engagement and self-reflexivity" (p. 686). Together, these form a way of interrupting, disrupting, and transforming "pure" presence into a disturbing, fluid, partial, and problematic presence—a poststructural and decidedly postmodern form of discourse theory, hence textual revelation.

Validity as an Ethical Relationship

As Lather (1993) points out, poststructural forms for validities "bring ethics and epistemology together" (p. 686); indeed, as Parker Palmer (1987) also notes, "every way of knowing contains its own moral trajectory" (p. 24). Peshkin reflects on Noddings's (1984) observation that "the search for justification often carries us farther and farther from the heart of morality" (p. 105; quoted in Peshkin, 1993, p. 24). The *way* in which we know is most assuredly tied up with

both *what* we know and our *relationships with our research participants*. Accordingly, one of us (Lincoln, 1995) worked on trying to understand the ways in which the ethical intersected both the interpersonal and the epistemological (as a form of authentic or valid knowing). The result was the first set of understandings about emerging criteria for quality that were also rooted in the epistemology/ethics nexus. Seven new standards were derived from that search: positionality, or standpoint, judgments; specific discourse communities and research sites as arbiters of quality; voice, or the extent to which a text has the quality of polyvocality; critical subjectivity (or what might be termed intense self-reflexivity); reciprocity, or the extent to which the research relationship becomes reciprocal rather than hierarchical; sacredness, or the profound regard for how science can (and does) contribute to human flourishing; and sharing the perquisites of privilege that accrue to our positions as academics with university positions. Each of these standards was extracted from a body of research, often from disciplines as disparate as management, philosophy, and women's studies (Lincoln, 1995).

◆ Voice, Reflexivity, and Postmodern Textual Representation

Texts have to do a lot more work these days than they used to. Even as they are charged by poststructuralists and postmodernists to reflect upon their representational practices, representational practices themselves become more problematic. Three of the most engaging, but painful, issues are the problem of voice, the status of reflexivity, and the problematics of postmodern/ poststructural textual representation, especially as those problematics are displayed in the shift toward narrative and literary forms that directly and openly deal with human emotion.

Voice

Voice is a multilayered problem, simply because it has come to mean many things to different researchers. In former eras, the only appropriate "voice" was the "voice from nowhere"—the "pure presence" of representation, as Lather terms it. As researchers became more conscious of the abstracted realities their texts created, they became simultaneously more conscious of having readers "hear" their informants—permitting readers to hear the exact words (and, occasionally, the paralinguistic cues, the lapses, pauses, stops, starts, reformulations) of the informants. Today voice can mean, especially in more participatory forms of research, not only having a real researcher—and a researcher's voice—in the text, but also letting research participants speak for themselves, either in text form or through plays, forums, "town meetings," or other oral and performance-oriented media or communication forms designed by research participants themselves. Performance texts, in particular, give an emotional immediacy to the voices of researchers and research participants far beyond their own sites and locales (see McCall, Chapter 15, this volume).

Rosanna Hertz (1997) describes voice as

> a struggle to figure out how to present the author's self while simultaneously writing the respondents' accounts and representing their selves. Voice has multiple dimensions: First, there is the voice of the author. Second, there is the presentation of the voices of one's respondents within the text. A third dimension appears when the self is the subject of the inquiry. . . . Voice is how authors express themselves within an ethnography. (pp. xi-xii)

But knowing how to express ourselves goes far beyond the commonsense understanding of "expressing ourselves." Generations of ethnographers trained in the "cooled-out, stripped-down rhetoric" of positivist inquiry (Firestone, 1987) find it difficult, if not nearly impossible, to "locate" themselves deliberately and squarely within their texts (even though, as Geertz [1988] has demonstrated finally and

without doubt, the authorial voice is rarely genuinely absent, or even hidden).[3] Specific textual experimentation can help; that is, composing ethnographic work into various literary forms—the poetry or plays of Laurel Richardson are good examples—can help a researcher to overcome the tendency to write in the distanced and abstracted voice of the disembodied "I." But such writing exercises are hard work. This is also work that is embedded in the practices of reflexivity and narrativity, without which achieving a voice of (partial) truth is impossible.

Reflexivity

Reflexivity is the process of reflecting critically on the self as researcher, the "human as instrument" (Guba & Lincoln, 1981). It is, we would assert, the critical subjectivity discussed early on in Reason and Rowan's edited volume *Human Inquiry* (1981). It is a conscious experiencing of the self as both inquirer and respondent, as teacher and learner, as the one coming to know the self within the processes of research itself.

Reflexivity forces us to come to terms not only with our choice of research problem and with those with whom we engage in the research process, but with our selves and with the multiple identities that represent the fluid self in the research setting (Alcoff & Potter, 1993). Shulamit Reinharz (1997), for example, argues that we not only "*bring* the self to the field . . . [we also] *create* the self in the field" (p. 3). She suggests that although we all have many selves we bring with us, those selves fall into three categories: research-based selves, brought selves (the selves that historically, socially, and personally create our standpoints), and situationally created selves (p. 5). Each of those selves comes into play in the research setting and consequently has a distinctive voice. Reflexivity—as well as the poststructural and postmodern sensibilities concerning quality in qualitative research—demands that we interrogate each of our selves regarding the ways in which research efforts are shaped and staged around the binaries, contradictions, and paradoxes that form our own lives. We must question our selves, too, regarding how those binaries and paradoxes shape not only the identities called forth in the field and later in the discovery processes of writing, but also our interactions with respondents, in who we become to them in the process of *becoming* to ourselves.

Someone once characterized qualitative research as the twin processes of "writing up" (field notes) and "writing down" (the narrative). But Clandinin and Connelly (1994) have made clear that this bitextual reading of the processes of qualitative research is far too simplistic. In fact, many texts are created in the process of engaging in fieldwork. As Richardson (1994, 1997; see also Chapter 36, this volume) makes clear, writing is not merely the transcribing of some reality. Rather, writing—of all the texts, notes, presentations, and possibilities—is also a process of discovery: discovery of the subject (and sometimes of the problem itself) and discovery of the self.

There is good news and bad news with the most contemporary of formulations. The good news is that the multiple selves—ourselves and our respondents—of postmodern inquiries may give rise to more dynamic, problematic, open-ended, and complex forms of writing and representation. The bad news is that the multiple selves we create and encounter give rise to more dynamic, problematic, open-ended, and complex forms of writing and representation.

Postmodern Textual Representations

There are two dangers inherent in the conventional texts of scientific method: that they may lead us to believe the world is rather simpler than it is, and that they may reinscribe enduring forms of historical oppression. Put another way, we are confronted with a crisis of authority (which tells us the world is "this way" when perhaps it is some other way, or many other ways) and a crisis of representation (which serves to silence those whose lives we appropriate for our social sciences, and which may also serve subtly to re-create *this* world, rather than some other,

perhaps more complex, but just one). Catherine Stimpson (1988) has observed:

> Like every great word, "representation/s" is a stew. A scrambled menu, it serves up several meanings at once. For a representation can be an image—visual, verbal, or aural. . . . A representation can also be a narrative, a sequence of images and ideas. . . . Or, a representation can be the product of ideology, that vast scheme for showing forth the world and justifying its dealings. (p. 223)

One way to confront the dangerous illusions (and their underlying ideologies) that texts may foster is through the creation of new texts that break boundaries; that move from the center to the margins to comment upon and decenter the center; that forgo closed, bounded worlds for those more open-ended and less conveniently encompassed; that transgress the boundaries of conventional social science; and that seek to create a social science about human life rather than *on* subjects.

Experiments with how to do this have produced "messy texts" (Marcus & Fischer, 1986). Messy texts are not typographic nightmares (although they may be typographically nonlinear); rather, they are texts that seek to break the binary between science and literature, to portray the contradiction and truth of human experience, to break the rules in the service of showing, even partially, how real human beings cope with both the eternal verities of human existence and the daily irritations and tragedies of living that existence. Postmodern representations search out and experiment with narratives that expand the range of understanding, voice, and the storied variations in human experience. As much as they are social scientists, inquirers also become storytellers, poets, and playwrights, experimenting with personal narratives, first-person accounts, reflexive interrogations, and deconstruction of the forms of tyranny embedded in representational practices (see Richardson, Chapter 36, this volume; Tierney & Lincoln, 1997).

Representation may be arguably the most open-ended of the controversies surrounding phenomenological research today, for no other reasons than that the ideas of what constitutes legitimate inquiry are expanding and, at the same time, the forms of narrative, dramatic, and rhetorical structure are far from being either explored or exploited fully. Because, too, each inquiry, each inquirer, brings a unique perspective to our understanding, the possibilities for variation and exploration are limited only by the number of those engaged in inquiry and the realms of social and intrapersonal life that become interesting to researchers.

The only thing that can be said for certain about postmodern representational practices is that they will proliferate as forms and they will seek, and demand much of, audiences, many of whom may be outside the scholarly and academic world. In fact, some forms of inquiry may never show up in the academic world, because their purpose will be use in the immediate context, for the consumption, reflection, and use of indigenous audiences. Those that are produced for scholarly audiences will, however, continue to be untidy, experimental, and driven by the need to communicate social worlds that have remained private and "nonscientific" until now.

◆ A Glimpse of the Future

The issues raised in this chapter are by no means the only ones under discussion for the near and far future. But they are some of the critical ones, and discussion, dialogue, and even controversies are bound to continue as practitioners of the various new and emergent paradigms continue either to look for common ground or to find ways in which to distinguish their forms of inquiry from others.

Some time ago, we expressed our hope that practitioners of both positivist and new-paradigm forms of inquiry might find some way of resolving their differences, such that all social scientists could work within a common discourse—and perhaps even several traditions—

once again. In retrospect, such a resolution appears highly unlikely and would probably even be less than useful. This is not, however, because neither positivists nor phenomenologists will budge an inch (although that, too, is unlikely). Rather, it is because, in the postmodern moment, and in the wake of poststructuralism, the assumption that there is no single "truth"—that all truths are but partial truths; that the slippage between signifier and signified in linguistic and textual terms creates re-presentations that are only and always shadows of the actual people, events, and places; that identities are fluid rather than fixed—leads us ineluctably toward the insight that there will be no single "conventional" paradigm to which all social scientists might ascribe in some common terms and with mutual understanding. Rather, we stand at the threshold of a history marked by multivocality, contested meanings, paradigmatic controversies, and new textual forms. At some distance down this conjectural path, when its history is written, we will find that this has been the era of emancipation: emancipation from what Hannah Arendt calls "the coerciveness of Truth," emancipation from hearing only the voices of Western Europe, emancipation from generations of silence, and emancipation from seeing the world in one color.

We may also be entering an age of greater spirituality within research efforts. The emphasis on inquiry that reflects ecological values, on inquiry that respects communal forms of living that are not Western, on inquiry involving intense reflexivity regarding how our inquiries are shaped by our own historical and gendered locations, and on inquiry into "human flourishing," as Heron and Reason (1997) call it, may yet reintegrate the sacred with the secular in ways that promote freedom and self-determination. Egon Brunswik, the organizational theorist, wrote of "tied" and "untied" variables—variables that were linked, or clearly not linked, with other variables—when studying human forms of organization. We may be in a period of exploring the ways in which our inquiries are both tied and untied, as a means of finding where our interests cross and where we can both be and promote others' being, as whole human beings.

■ Notes

1. There are several versions of critical theory, including classical critical theory, which is most closely related to neo-Marxist theory; postpositivist formulations, which divorce themselves from Marxist theory but are positivist in their insistence on conventional rigor criteria; and postmodernist, poststructuralist, or constructivist-oriented varieties. See, for instance, Fay (1987), Carr and Kemmis (1986), and Lather (1991). See also in this volume Kemmis and McTaggart (Chapter 22) and Kincheloe and McLaren (Chapter 10).

2. For a clearer understanding of how methods came to stand in for paradigms, or how our initial (and, we thought, quite clear) positions came to be misconstrued, see Lancy (1993) or, even more currently, Weiss (1998, esp. p. 268).

3. For example, compare this chapter with, say, Richardson's (Chapter 36) and Ellis and Bochner's (Chapter 28), where the authorial voices are clear, personal, vocal, and interior, interacting subjectivities. Although some colleagues have surprised us by correctly identifying which chapters each of us has written in given books, nevertheless, the style of this chapter more closely approximates the more distanced forms of "realist" writing than it does the intimate, personal "feeling tone" (to borrow a phrase from Studs Terkel) of other chapters. Voices also arise as a function of the material being covered. The material we chose as most important for this chapter seemed to demand a less personal tone, probably because there appears to be much more "contention" than calm dialogue concerning these issues. The "cool" tone likely stems from our psychological response to trying to create a quieter space for discussion around controversial issues. What can we say?

■ References

Addelson, K. P. (1993). Knowers/doers and their moral problems. In L. Alcoff & E. Potter (Eds.), *Feminist epistemologies* (pp. 265-294). New York: Routledge.

Alcoff, L., & Potter, E. (Eds.). (1993). *Feminist epistemologies*. New York: Routledge.

Alpern, S., Antler, J., Perry, E. I., & Scobie, I. W. (Eds.). (1992). *The challenge of feminist biography: Writing the lives of modern American women*. Urbana: University of Illinois Press.

Babbitt, S. (1993). Feminism and objective interests: The role of transformation experiences in rational deliberation. In L. Alcoff & E. Potter (Eds.), *Feminist epistemologies* (pp. 245-264). New York: Routledge.

Bernstein, R. J. (1983). *Beyond objectivism and relativism: Science, hermeneutics, and praxis*. Oxford: Blackwell.

Best, S., & Kellner, D. (1997). *The postmodern turn*. New York: Guilford.

Bloland, H. (1989). Higher education and high anxiety: Objectivism, relativism, and irony. *Journal of Higher Education, 60,* 519-543.

Bloland, H. (1995). Postmodernism and higher education. *Journal of Higher Education, 66,* 521-559.

Bradley, J., & Schaefer, K. (1998). *The uses and misuses of data and models*. Thousand Oaks, CA: Sage.

Carr, W. L., & Kemmis, S. (1986). *Becoming critical: Education, knowledge and action research*. London: Falmer.

Carspecken, P. F. (1996). *Critical ethnography in educational research: A theoretical and practical guide*. New York: Routledge.

Clandinin, D. J., & Connelly, F. M. (1994). Personal experience methods. In N. K. Denzin & Y. S. Lincoln (Eds.), *Handbook of qualitative research* (pp. 413-427). Thousand Oaks, CA: Sage.

Denzin, N. K., & Lincoln, Y. S. (Eds.). (1994). *Handbook of qualitative research*. Thousand Oaks, CA: Sage.

Ellis, C., & Bochner, A. P. (Eds.). (1996). *Composing ethnography: Alternative forms of qualitative writing*. Walnut Creek, CA: AltaMira.

Enerstvedt, R. (1989). The problem of validity in social science. In S. Kvale (Ed.), *Issues of validity in qualitative research* (pp. 135-173). Lund, Sweden: Studentlitteratur.

Fay, B. (1987). *Critical social science*. Ithaca, NY: Cornell University Press.

Firestone, W. (1987). Meaning in method: The rhetoric of quantitative and qualitative research. *Educational Researcher,* 16(7), 16-21.

Foucault, M. (1971). *The order of things: An archeology of the human sciences.* New York: Pantheon.

Geertz, C. (1988). *Works and lives: The anthropologist as author.* Cambridge: Polity.

Geertz, C. (1993). *Local knowledge: Further essays in interpretive anthropology.* London: Fontana.

Guba, E. G., & Lincoln, Y. S. (1981). *Effective evaluation: Improving the usefulness of evaluation results through responsive and naturalistic approaches.* San Francisco: Jossey-Bass.

Guba, E. G., & Lincoln, Y. S. (1982). Epistemological and methodological bases for naturalistic inquiry. *Educational Communications and Technology Journal, 31,* 233-252.

Guba, E. G., & Lincoln, Y. S. (1989). *Fourth generation evaluation.* Newbury Park, CA: Sage.

Guba, E. G., & Lincoln, Y. S. (1994). Competing paradigms in qualitative research. In N. K. Denzin & Y. S. Lincoln (Eds.), *Handbook of qualitative research* (pp. 105-117). Thousand Oaks, CA: Sage.

Harding, S. (1993). Rethinking standpoint epistemology: What is "strong objectivity"? In L. Alcoff & E. Potter (Eds.), *Feminist epistemologies* (pp. 49-82). New York: Routledge.

Heron, J. (1996). *Cooperative inquiry: Research into the human condition.* London: Sage.

Heron, J., & Reason, P. (1997). A participatory inquiry paradigm. *Qualitative Inquiry, 3,* 274-294.

Hertz, R. (1997). Introduction: Reflexivity and voice. In R. Hertz (Ed.), *Reflexivity and voice.* Thousand Oaks, CA: Sage.

Howe, K., & Eisenhart, M. (1990). Standards for qualitative (and quantitative) research: A prolegomenon. *Educational Researcher,* 19(4), 2-9.

Hutcheon, L. (1989). *The politics of postmodernism.* New York: Routledge.

Kincheloe, J. L. (1991). *Teachers as researchers: Qualitative inquiry as a path to empowerment.* London: Falmer.

Kondo, D. K. (1990). *Crafting selves: Power, gender, and discourses of identity in a Japanese workplace.* Chicago: University of Chicago Press.

Kondo, D. K. (1997). *About face: Performing race in fashion and theater.* New York: Routledge.

Kvale, S. (Ed.). (1989). *Issues of validity in qualitative research.* Lund, Sweden: Studentlitteratur.

Kvale, S. (1994, April). *Validation as communication and action.* Paper presented at the annual meeting of the American Educational Research Association, New Orleans.

Lancy, D. F. (1993). *Qualitative research in education: An introduction to the major traditions.* New York: Longman.

Lather, P. (1986). Issues of validity in openly ideological research: Between a rock and a soft place. *Interchange, 17*(4), 63-84.

Lather, P. (1991). *Getting smart: Feminist research and pedagogy with/in the postmodern.* New York: Routledge.

Lather, P. (1993). Fertile obsession: Validity after poststructuralism. *Sociological Quarterly, 34,* 673-693.

Leitch, V. B. (1996). *Postmodern: Local effects, global flows.* Albany: State University of New York Press.

Lincoln, Y. S. (1995). Emerging criteria for quality in qualitative and interpretive research. *Qualitative Inquiry, 1,* 275-289.

Lincoln, Y. S. (1997). What constitutes quality in interpretive research? In C. K. Kinzer, K. A. Hinchman, & D. J. Leu (Eds.), *Inquiries in literacy: Theory and practice* (pp. 54-68). Chicago: National Reading Conference.

Lincoln, Y. S. (1998a). *The ethics of teaching qualitative research.* Manuscript submitted for publication.

Lincoln, Y. S. (1998b). From understanding to action: New imperatives, new criteria, new methods for interpretive researchers. *Theory and Research in Social Education, 26*(1), 12-29.

Lincoln, Y. S., & Denzin, N. K. (1994). The fifth moment. In N. K. Denzin & Y. S. Lincoln (Eds.), *Handbook of qualitative research* (pp. 575-586). Thousand Oaks, CA: Sage.

Lincoln, Y. S., & Guba, E. G. (1985). *Naturalistic inquiry.* Beverly Hills, CA: Sage.

Marcus, G. E., & Fischer, M. M. J. (1986). *Anthropology as cultural critique: An experimen-*

tal moment in the human sciences. Chicago: University of Chicago Press.

Mertens, D. (1998). *Research methods in education and psychology: Integrating diversity with quantitative and qualitative methods.* Thousand Oaks, CA: Sage.

Michael, M. C. (1996). *Feminism and the post-modern impulse: Post-World War II fiction.* Albany: State University of New York Press.

Noddings, N. (1984). *Caring: A feminine approach to ethics and moral education.* Berkeley: University of California Press.

Palmer, P. J. (1987, September-October). Community, conflict, and ways of knowing. *Change, 19,* 20-25.

Peshkin, A. (1993). The goodness of qualitative research. *Educational Researcher, 22*(2), 24-30.

Polkinghorne, D. E. (1989). Changing conversations about human science. In S. Kvale (Ed.), *Issues of validity in qualitative research* (pp. 13-46). Lund, Sweden: Studentlitteratur.

Reason, P. (1993). Sacred experience and sacred science. *Journal of Management Inquiry, 2,* 10-27.

Reason, P., & Rowan, J. (Eds.). (1981). *Human inquiry.* London: John Wiley.

Reinharz, S. (1997). Who am I? The need for a variety of selves in the field. In R. Hertz (Ed.), *Reflexivity and voice* (pp. 3-20). Thousand Oaks, CA: Sage.

Richardson, Laurel (1994). Writing: A method of inquiry. In N. K. Denzin & Y. S. Lincoln (Eds.), *Handbook of qualitative research* (pp. 516-529). Thousand Oaks, CA: Sage.

Richardson, L. (1997). *Fields of play: Constructing an academic life.* New Brunswick, NJ: Rutgers University Press.

Rorty, R. (1979). *Philosophy and the mirror of nature.* Princeton, NJ: Princeton University Press.

Ryan, K. E., Greene, J. C., Lincoln, Y. S., Mathison, S., & Mertens, D. (1998). Advantages and challenges of using inclusive evaluation approaches in evaluation practice. *American Journal of Evaluation, 19,* 101-122.

Salner, M. (1989). Validity in human science research. In S. Kvale (Ed.), *Issues of validity in qualitative research* (pp. 47-72). Lund, Sweden: Studentlitteratur.

Scheurich, J. J. (1994). Policy archaeology. *Journal of Educational Policy, 9,* 297-316.

Scheurich, J. J. (1996). Validity. *International Journal of Qualitative Studies in Education, 9,* 49-60.

Scheurich, J. J. (1997). *Research method in the postmodern.* London: Falmer.

Schratz, M., & Walker, R. (1995). *Research as social change: New opportunities for qualitative research.* New York: Routledge.

Schwandt, T. A. (1989). Recapturing moral discourse in evaluation. *Educational Researcher, 18*(8), 11-16, 34.

Schwandt, T. A. (1996). Farewell to criteriology. *Qualitative Inquiry, 2,* 58-72.

Sechrest, L. (1993). *Program evaluation: A pluralistic enterprise.* San Francisco: Jossey-Bass.

Smith, J. K. (1993). *After the demise of empiricism: The problem of judging social and educational inquiry.* Norwood, NJ: Ablex.

Stimpson, C. R. (1988). Nancy Reagan wears a hat: Feminism and its cultural consensus. *Critical Inquiry, 14,* 223-243.

Tierney, W. G., & Lincoln, Y. S. (Eds.). (1997). *Representation and the text: Re-framing the narrative voice.* Albany: State University of New York Press.

Trinh, T. M. (1991). *When the moon waxes red: Representation, gender and cultural politics.* New York: Routledge.

Tschudi, F. (1989). Do qualitative and quantitative methods require different approaches to validity? In S. Kvale (Ed.), *Issues of validity in qualitative research* (pp. 109-134). Lund, Sweden: Studentlitteratur.

Weiss, C. H. (1998). *Evaluation* (2nd ed.). Upper Saddle River, NJ: Prentice Hall.

7

THREE EPISTEMOLOGICAL STANCES FOR QUALITATIVE INQUIRY

Interpretivism, Hermeneutics, and Social Constructionism

◆ Thomas A. Schwandt

Labels in philosophy and cultural discourse have the character that Derrida ascribes to Plato's pharmakon: they can poison and kill, and they can remedy and cure. We need them to help identify a style, a temperament, a set of common concerns and emphases, or a vision that has determinate shape. But we must also be wary of the ways in which they can blind us or can reify what is fluid and changing.

Richard J. Bernstein, "What Is the Difference That Makes a Difference?" 1986

Qualitative inquiry is the name for a reformist movement that began in the early 1970s in the academy.[1] The movement encompassed multiple epistemological, methodological, political, and ethical criticisms of social scientific research in fields and disciplines that favored experimental, quasi-experimental, correlational, and survey research strategies. Immanent criticism of these methodologies within these disciplines and fields as well as insights from external debates in philosophy of science and social science fueled the opposition.[2] Over the years, the movement has acquired a political as well as an intellectual place in the academy. It has its own journals, academic associations, conferences, and university positions, as well as the support of publishers, all of which have both sustained and, to some extent, created the movement. Moreover, it is not unreasonable to claim, given the influence that

AUTHOR'S NOTE: Special thanks to Barry Bull, Jeffrey Davis, Norman Denzin, Davydd Greenwood, Peter Labella, Yvonna Lincoln, and David Silverman for their suggestions on previous drafts of this chapter. Errors and confusions that remain here are probably the result of my not taking all of their good advice.

publishers exercise through the promotion and sales of ever more allegedly new and improved accounts of what qualitative inquiry is, that the movement at times looks more like an "industry."

Not surprisingly, considerable academic and professional politics are also entailed in the movement, particularly as it has drawn on intellectual developments in feminism, postmodernism, and poststructuralism. Current struggles over departmental organization, interdisciplinary alliances, what constitutes "legitimate" research, who controls the editorship of key journals, and so forth (compare, for example, Denzin, 1997, and Prus, 1996; see also Shea, 1998), in part, reflect the turmoil over what constitute the appropriate goals and means of human inquiry. Quarrels in university departments over the meaning and value of qualitative inquiry often reflect broader controversies in the disciplines of psychology, sociology, anthropology, feminist studies, history, and literature about the purpose, values, and ethics of intellectual labor.

Thus qualitative inquiry is more comprehensible as a site or arena for social scientific criticism than as any particular kind of social theory, methodology, or philosophy. That site is a "home" for a wide variety of scholars who often are seriously at odds with one another but who share a general rejection of the blend of scientism, foundationalist epistemology, instrumental reasoning, and the philosophical anthropology of disengagement that has marked "mainstream" social science. Yet how one further characterizes the site depends, in part, on what one finds of interest there.[3] For some researchers, the site is a place where a particular set of laudable virtues for social research are championed, such as fidelity to phenomena, respect for the life world, and attention to the fine-grained details of daily life. They are thus attracted to the fact that long-standing traditions of fieldwork research in sociology and anthropology have been revitalized and appropriated under the banner of "qualitative inquiry" while at the same time immanent criticism of those traditions has inspired new ways of thinking about the field-worker's interests, motivations, aims, obli-

gations, and texts. Others are attracted to the site as a place where debates about aims of the human sciences unfold and where issues of what it means to know the social world are explored. Still others may find social theory of greatest interest and hence look to the site for knowledge of the debate over the merits of symbolic interactionism, social systems theory, critical theory of society, feminist theory, and so forth. Finally, many current researchers seem to view the site as a place for experimentation with empirical methodologies and textual strategies inspired by postmodernist and poststructuralist thinking.

In this chapter, I focus on the site as an arena in which different epistemologies vie for attention as potential justifications for doing qualitative inquiry. I examine three of the philosophies that in various forms are assumed in the many books that explain the aims and methods of qualitative inquiry. Interpretivism, hermeneutics, and social constructionism embrace different perspectives on the aim and practice of understanding human action, different ethical commitments, and different stances on methodological and epistemological issues of representation, validity, objectivity, and so forth.[4] The chapter begins with an overview of each philosophy, and I indicate ways in which they are related to and at odds with one another. I then discuss several epistemological and ethical-political issues that arise from these philosophies and that characterize contemporary concerns about the purpose and justification of qualitative inquiry.

There is no denying that what follows is a Cook's tour of complicated philosophies that demand more detailed attention in their own right as well as in interaction. I apologize in advance for leaving the philosophically minded aghast at the incompleteness of the treatment and for encouraging the methodologically inclined to scurry to later chapters on tools. But I would be remiss were I not to add that the practice of social inquiry cannot be adequately defined as an atheoretical making that requires only methodological prowess. Social inquiry is a distinctive praxis, a kind of activity (like teaching) that in the doing transforms the very theory and aims that guide it. In other words, as one engages in the "practical" activities of generating and interpreting data to answer questions about the meaning of what others are doing and saying and then transforming that understanding into public knowledge, one inevitably takes up "theoretical" concerns about what constitutes knowledge and how it is to be justified, about the nature and aim of social theorizing, and so forth. In sum, acting and thinking, practice and theory, are linked in a continuous process of critical reflection and transformation.

◆ Background: Part 1

Interpretivism and hermeneutics, generally characterized as the *Geisteswissenschaftlichte* or *Verstehen* tradition in the human sciences, arose in the reactions of neo-Kantian German historians and sociologists (i.e., Dilthey, Rickert, Windleband, Simmel, Weber) in the late 19th and early 20th centuries to the then-dominant philosophy of positivism (and later, logical positivism). At the heart of the dispute was the claim that the human sciences (*Geisteswissenchaften*) were fundamentally different in nature and purpose from the natural sciences (*Naturwissenschaften*). Defenders of interpretivism argued that the human sciences aim to understand human action. Defenders of positivism and proponents of the unity of the sciences held the view that the purpose of any science (if it is indeed to be called a science) is to offer causal explanations of social, behavioral, and physical phenomena.

There was, of course, considerable debate among the neo-Kantians about the precise nature of the difference between the sciences. And to the present day, the issue of whether there is a critical distinction to be drawn between the natural and the human sciences on the basis of different aims—explanation (*Erklären*) versus understanding (*Verstehen*)—remains more or less unsettled.[5] Although it is important to understand how apologists for the uniqueness of the human sciences link their respective philosophies to this issue, in the interest of space, I will forgo that examination here and focus directly on key features of the philosophies themselves.

I begin with a sketch of the interpretivist theory of human action and meaning and then show how philosophical hermeneutics offers a critique of this view and a different understanding of human inquiry.

◆ Interpretivist Philosophies

From an interpretivist point of view, what distinguishes human (social) action from the movement of physical objects is that the former is inherently meaningful. Thus, to understand a particular social action (e.g., friendship, voting, marrying, teaching), the inquirer must grasp the meanings that constitute that action. To say that human action is meaningful is to claim either that it has a certain intentional content that indicates the kind of action it is and/or that what an action means can be grasped only in terms of the system of meanings to which it belongs (Fay, 1996; Outhwaite, 1975). Because human action is understood in this way, one can determine that a wink is not a wink (to use Ryle's example popularized by Geertz), or that a smile can be interpreted as wry or loving, or that very different physical movements can all be interpreted as acts of supplication, or that the same physical movement of raising one's arm can be variously interpreted as voting, hailing a taxi, or asking for permission to speak, depending on the context and intentions of the actor.

To find meaning in an action, or to say one understands what a particular action means, requires that one interpret in a particular way what the actors are doing. This process of interpreting or understanding (of achieving *Verstehen*) is differentially represented, and therein lie some important differences in philosophies of interpretivism and between interpretivism and philosophical hermeneutics. These differences can perhaps be most easily grasped through a consideration of four ways of defining (theorizing) the notion of interpretive understanding (*Verstehen*), three that constitute the interpretive tradition and a fourth that marks the distinction of philosophical hermeneutics from that tradition.

Empathic Identification

One way of defining the notion first appears in the earlier work of Wilhelm Dilthey and the *Lebensphilosophers.* Dilthey argued that to understand the meaning of human action requires grasping the subjective consciousness or intent of the actor from the inside.[6] *Verstehen* thus entails a kind of empathic identification with the actor. It is an act of psychological reenactment—getting inside the head of an actor to understand what he or she is up to in terms of motives, beliefs, desires, thoughts, and so on. This interpretivist stance (also called intentionalism) is explained in Collingwood's (1946/1961) account of what constitutes historical knowledge, and it lies at the heart of what is known as objectivist or conservative hermeneutics (e.g., Hirsch, 1976). Both approaches share the general idea that it is possible for the interpreter to transcend or break out of her or his historical circumstances in order to reproduce the meaning or intention of the actor. (I realize that introducing the term *hermeneutics* here is a bit confusing, given that I stated above that I wish to draw a distinction *between* interpretivist and hermeneutic philosophies. But *objectivist* hermeneutics shares the same epistemology as interpretivism, whereas *philosophical* hermeneutics, as I explain below, rejects this epistemology.)[7]

Whether it is possible to achieve interpretive understanding through a process of grasping an actors' intent is widely debated. Geertz (1976/1979), for example, argues that understanding comes more from the act of looking over the shoulders of actors and trying to figure out (both by observing and by conversing) what the actors think they are up to. Nonetheless, the idea of acquiring an "inside" understanding—the actors' definitions of the situation—is a powerful central concept for understanding the purpose of qualitative inquiry.

Phenomenological Sociology

A second way of making sense of the notion of interpretive understanding is found in the work of phenomenological sociologists and ethnomethodologists, including Cicourel and Garfinkel (I will address more recent developments in conversation analysis later). Influenced by the work of Alfred Schutz (1962, 1932/1967), phenomenological analysis is principally concerned with understanding how the everyday, intersubjective world (the life world, or *Lebenswelt*) is constituted. The aim is to grasp how we come to interpret our own and others' action as meaningful and to "reconstruct the genesis of the objective meanings of action in the intersubjective communication of individuals in the social life-world" (Outhwaite, 1975, p. 91). Two conceptual tools often used in that reconstruction are indexicality and reflexivity (Potter, 1996). The former signifies that the meaning of a word or utterance is dependent on its context of use. The latter directs our attention to the fact that utterances are not just about something but are also doing something; an utterance is in part constitutive of a speech act. These two notions are part of the means whereby phenomenological sociologists and ethnomethodologists come to understand how social reality, everyday life, is constituted in conversation and interaction. (For a fuller discussion of this perspective, see Gubrium & Holstein, Chapter 18, this volume.)

Language Games

A third definition of interpretive understanding is represented in analysis of language approaches that take their inspiration from Wittgenstein's *Philosophical Investigations,* especially the work of Peter Winch (1958). From Wittgenstein, Winch borrowed the notion that there are many games played with language (testing hypotheses, giving orders, greeting, and so on), and he extended this idea to language games as constituted in different cultures. Each of these games has its own rules or criteria that make the game meaningful to its participants. Reasoning by analogy, we can say that human action, like speech, is an element in communication governed by rules. More simply, human action is meaningful by virtue of the system of meanings (in Wittgenstein's terms, the "language game") to which it belongs. Understanding those systems of meanings (institutional and cultural norms, action-constituting rules, and so on) is the goal of *Verstehen* (Giddens, 1993; Habermas, 1967/1988; Outhwaite, 1975).

Shared Features

These first three ways of conceiving of the notion of interpretive understanding constitute the tradition of interpretivism. All three share the following features: (a) They view human action as meaningful; (b) they evince an ethical commitment in the form of respect for and fidelity to the life world; and (c) from an epistemological point of view, they share the neo-Kantian desire to emphasize the contribution of human subjectivity (i.e., intention) to knowledge without thereby sacrificing the objectivity of knowledge. In other words, interpretivists argue that it is possible to understand the subjective meaning of action (grasping the actor's beliefs, desires, and so on) yet do so in an objective manner. The meaning that the interpreter reproduces or reconstructs is considered the original meaning of the action. So as not to misinterpret the original meaning, interpreters must employ some kind of method that allows them to step outside their historical frames of reference. Method, correctly employed, is a means that enables interpreters to claim a purely theoretical attitude as observers (Outhwaite, 1975). The theoretical attitude or the act of scientific contemplation at a distance requires the cognitive style of the disinterested observer (Schutz, 1962). This, of course, does not necessarily deny the fact that in order to understand the intersubjective meanings of human action, the inquirer may have to, as a methodological requirement, "participate" in the life worlds of others.

Interpretivism generally embraces two dimensions of *Verstehen* as explicated by Schutz (1962, 1932/1967). *Verstehen* is, on a primary level, "the name of a complex process by which all of us in our everyday life interpret the meaning of our own actions and those of others with whom we interact" (Bernstein, 1976, p. 139). Yet *Verstehen* is also "a method peculiar to the

social sciences" (Schutz, 1962, p. 57), a process by which the social scientist seeks to understand the primary process. Hence interpretivists aim to reconstruct the self-understandings of actors engaged in particular actions. And in so doing, they assume that the inquirer cannot claim that the ways actors make sense of their experience are irrelevant to social scientific understanding because actors' ways of making sense of their actions are constitutive of that action (Giddens, 1993; Outhwaite, 1975).

Interpretivist epistemologies can in one sense be characterized as hermeneutic because they emphasize that one must grasp the situation in which human actions make (or acquire) meaning in order to say one has an understanding of the particular action (Outhwaite, 1975). This view draws upon the familiar notion of the hermeneutic circle as a method or procedure unique to the human sciences: In order to understand the part (the specific sentence, utterance, or act), the inquirer must grasp the whole (the complex of intentions, beliefs, and desires or the text, institutional context, practice, form of life, language game, and so on), and vice versa. Geertz's (1976/1979) oft-cited description of the process of ethnographic understanding portrays this conception of the hermeneutic circle as

> a continuous dialectical tacking between the most local of local detail and the most global of global structure in such a way as to bring both into view simultaneously. . . . Hopping back and forth between the whole conceived through the parts that actualize it and the parts conceived through the whole which motivates them, we seek to turn them, by a sort of intellectual perpetual motion, into explications of one another. (p. 239)

Garfinkel's (1967) claim about understanding how people make sense of their worlds is similar: "Not only is the underlying pattern derived from its individual documentary evidences, but the individual documentary evidences, in their turn, are interpreted on the basis of 'what is known' about the underlying pattern. Each is used to elaborate the other" (p. 78).

Finally, interpretivism assumes an epistemological understanding of understanding (*Verstehen*). That is, it considers understanding to be an intellectual process whereby a knower (the inquirer as subject) gains knowledge about an object (the meaning of human action). Accordingly, the notion of a hermeneutic circle of understanding is, as Bernstein (1983) explains,

> "object" oriented, in the sense that it directs us to the texts, institutions, practices, or forms of life that we are seeking to understand. . . . No essential reference is made to the interpreter, to the individual who is engaged in the process of understanding and questioning, except insofar as he or she must have the insight, imagination, openness, and patience to acquire this art—an art achieved through practice. (p. 135)[8]

Thus, in interpretive traditions, the interpreter objectifies (i.e., stands over and against) that which is to be interpreted. And, in that sense, the interpreter remains unaffected by and external to the interpretive process.

◆ Philosophical Hermeneutics

A fourth, and radically different, way of representing the notion of interpretive understanding is found in the philosophical hermeneutics of Gadamer (1975, 1977, 1981, 1996) and Taylor (1985a, 1985b, 1995) inspired by the work of Heidegger.[9] Let us begin with the premise that interpretivist philosophies, in general, define the role of the interpreter on the model of the exegete, that is, one who is engaged in a critical analysis or explanation of a text (or some human action) using the method of the hermeneutic circle.[10] Echoing the point made by Bernstein, Kerdeman (1998) explains that

> exegetical methodology plays the strange parts of a narrative [or some social action] off against the integrity of the narrative as whole until its strange passages are worked out or accounted for. An interpreter's self-understanding neither affects nor is affected by the negotiation of understanding. Indeed, insofar as interpreters and linguistic objects are presumed to be distinct, self-understanding is believed to bias and distort successful interpretation. (p. 251; see also Gadamer, 1981, pp. 98-101)

Both the phenomenological observer and the linguistic analyst generally claim this role of uninvolved observer.[11] The understanding that they acquire of some particular social action (or text) is exclusively reproductive and ought to be judged on the grounds of whether or not it is an accurate, correct, valid representation of that action and its meaning.

In several ways, philosophical hermeneutics challenges this classic epistemological (or, more generally, Cartesian) picture of the interpreter's task and the kind of understanding that he or she "produces." First, broadly conceived as a philosophical program, the hermeneutics of Gadamer and Taylor rejects the interpretivist view "that hermeneutics is an art or technique of understanding, the purpose of which is to construct a methodological foundation for the human sciences" (Grondin, 1994, p. 109). Philosophical hermeneutics argues that understanding is not, in the first instance, a procedure- or rule-governed undertaking; rather, it is a very condition of being human. Understanding *is* interpretation. As Gadamer (1970) explains, understanding is not "an isolated activity of human beings but a basic structure of our experience of life. We are always taking something *as* something. That is the primordial givenness of our world orientation, and we cannot reduce it to anything simpler or more immediate" (p. 87).

Second, in the act of interpreting (of "taking something *as* something"), sociohistorically inherited bias or prejudice is not regarded as a characteristic or attribute that an interpreter must strive to get rid of or manage in order to come to a "clear" understanding. To believe this is possible is to assume that the traditions and associated prejudgments that shape our efforts to understand are easily under our control and can be set aside at will. But philosophical hermeneutics argues that tradition is not something that is external, objective, and past—something from which we can free and distance ourselves (Gadamer, 1975). Rather, as Gallagher (1992) explains, tradition is "a living force that enters into all understanding" (p. 87), and, "despite the fact that traditions operate for the most part 'behind our backs,' they are already there, ahead of us, conditioning our interpretations" (p. 91).

Furthermore, because traditions "shape what we are and how we understand the world, the attempt to step outside of the process of tradition would be like trying to step outside of our own skins" (p. 87).

Thus reaching an understanding is not a matter of setting aside, escaping, managing, or tracking one's own standpoint, prejudgments, biases, or prejudices. On the contrary, understanding requires the *engagement* of one's biases.[12] As Garrison (1996) explains, prejudices are the very kinds of prejudgments "necessary to make our way, however tentatively, in everyday thought, conversation, and action. . . . The point is not to free ourselves of all prejudice, but to examine our historically inherited and unreflectively held prejudices and alter those that disable our efforts to understand others, and ourselves" (p. 434). The fact that we "belong" to tradition and that tradition in some sense governs interpretation does not mean that we merely reenact the biases of tradition in our interpretation. Although preconceptions, prejudices, or prejudices suggest the initial conceptions that an interpreter brings to the interpretation of an object or another person, the interpreter risks those prejudices in the encounter with what is to be interpreted.

Third, only in a dialogical encounter with what is not understood, with what is alien, with what makes a claim upon us, can we open ourselves to risking and testing our preconceptions and prejudices (Bernstein, 1983). Understanding is participative, conversational, and dialogic. It is always bound up with language and is achieved only through a logic of question and answer (Bernstein, 1983; Grondin, 1994; Taylor, 1991).[13] Moreover, understanding is something that is *produced* in that dialogue, not something *reproduced* by an interpreter through an analysis of that which he or she seeks to understand. The meaning one seeks in "making sense" of a social action or text is temporal and processive and always coming into being in the specific occasion of understanding (Aylesworth, 1991; Bernstein, 1983; Gadamer, 1975, p. 419).

This different conception of meaning signifies a radical departure from the interpretivist

idea that human action *has* meaning and that that meaning is in principle determinable or decidable by the interpreter. Philosophical hermeneutics has a nonobjectivist view of meaning: "The text [or human action] is not an 'object out there' independent of its interpretations and capable of serving as an arbiter of their correctness" (Connolly & Keutner, 1998, p. 17). Grondin (1994) notes that "in terms of its form, understanding is less like grasping a content, a noetic meaning, than like engaging in a dialogue" (p. 117).[14] In other words, meaning is negotiated mutually in the act of interpretation; it is not simply discovered.

In this sense, philosophical hermeneutics opposes a naïve realism or objectivism with respect to meaning and can be said to endorse the conclusion that there is never a finally correct interpretation. This is a view held by some constructivists as well, yet philosophical hermeneutics sees meaning not necessarily as constructed (i.e., created, assembled) but as negotiated (i.e., a matter of coming to terms). Bernstein (1983) summarizes Gadamer's notion of the processive, open, anticipatory character of the coming into being of meaning:

> We are always understanding and interpreting in light of our anticipatory prejudgments and prejudices, which are themselves changing in the course of history. That is why Gadamer tells us that to understand is always to understand differently. But this does not mean that our interpretations are arbitrary and distortive. We should always aim at a correct understanding of what the "things themselves" [the objects of our interpretation] say. But what the "things themselves" say will be different in light of our changing horizons and the different questions we learn to ask. Such analysis of the ongoing and open character of all understanding and interpretation can be construed as distortive only if we assume that a text possesses some meaning in itself that can be isolated from our prejudgments. (p. 139)

Finally, as is suggested in what has been said above, the kind of understanding that results from the encounter is always at once a kind of "application." In other words, in the act of understanding there are not two separate steps—first, acquiring understanding; second, applying that understanding. Rather, understanding is itself a kind of practical experience in and of the world that, in part, constitutes the kinds of persons that we are in the world. Understanding is "lived" or existential. Gadamer (1981) explains this in the following way:

> Understanding, like action, always remains a risk and never leaves room for the simple application of a general knowledge of rules to the statements or texts to be understood. Furthermore where it is successful, understanding means a growth in inner awareness, which as a new experience enters into the texture of our own mental experience. Understanding is an adventure and, like any other adventure is dangerous. . . . But . . . [i]t is capable of contributing in a special way to the broadening of our human experiences, our self-knowledge, and our horizon, for everything understanding mediates is mediated along with ourselves. (pp. 109-110)

A focus on understanding as a kind of moral-political knowledge that is at once embodied, engaged (and hence "interested"), and concerned with practical choice is a central element in the hermeneutic philosophies that draw, at least in part, on Gadamer and Heidegger (e.g., Dunne, Gallagher, Smith, and Taylor).[15]

Philosophical hermeneutics is not a methodology for "solving problems" of misunderstanding or problems concerned with the correct meaning of human action. Gadamer (1975) has repeatedly emphasized that the work of hermeneutics "is not to develop a procedure of understanding but to clarify the conditions in which understanding takes place. But these conditions are not of the nature of a 'procedure' or a method which the interpreter must of himself bring to bear on the text" (p. 263). The goal of philosophical hermeneutics is philosophical—that is, to understand what is involved in the process of understanding itself (Madison, 1991).

◆ Background: Part 2

Philosophical hermeneutics and social constructionist philosophies (like deconstructionist, crit-

ical theory, some feminist, and neopragmatic approaches) have their antecedents in the broad movement away from an empiricist, logical atomistic, designative, representational account of meaning and knowledge.[16] The philosophies of logical positivism and logical empiricism were principally concerned with the rational reconstruction of scientific knowledge by means of the semantic and syntactic analysis of two kinds of scientific statements (statements that explain, i.e., theories and hypotheses, and statements that describe, i.e., observations). In this analysis, social, cultural, and historical dimensions of understanding were regarded as extrascientific and hence irrelevant to any valid epistemological account of what constitutes genuine scientific knowledge and its justification. Logical empiricism worked from a conception of knowledge as correct representation of an independent reality and was (is) almost exclusively interested in the issue of establishing the validity of scientific knowledge claims.

In his essay "Overcoming Epistemology," Taylor (1987) argues that logical empiricism (or, more generally, any foundationalist epistemology) draws its strength from an interlocking set of assumptions about meaning, knowledge, language, and self. It embraces a philosophy of language that can be characterized broadly as empiricist and atomistic in that it assumes (a) that the meanings of words or sentences are explained by their relations to things or states of affairs in the world (in short, a designative view of language), (b) that language must exhibit a logical structure (syntax) that prescribes permissible relations among terms and sentences, and (c) that we ought not conflate or confuse the descriptive and evaluative functions of language, lest we "allow language that is really just the expression of a particular cultural or moral code to gain the appearance of objectively describing the world" (Smith, 1997, pp. 11-12).

The epistemology supported by this philosophy of language is that of pictorial description or conceptual representation of an external reality. Language and reason are understood as instruments of control in discovering and ordering the reality of the world (Taylor, 1985a). Further, the locus of representation is the autonomous, disengaged, cognizing agent, or what Bernstein (1983) characterizes as the Cartesian knower.[17] To be sure, there is considerable variation in the ways theories of inquiry and theories of knowledge draw on this concatenation of an empiricist theory of language, an atomistic theory of self, and a representational epistemology. Yet much contemporary social science practice, at least implicitly, continues to be informed by the idea that meaning and knowledge are best explicated by means of some kind of epistemology of representation (Shapiro, 1981; Taylor, 1995), although few social scientists are wedded to a crude correspondence theory of representation or naïvely accept that representation is mimesis.

◆ *Social Constructionism*

Social constructionist epistemologies aim to "overcome" representationalist epistemologies in a variety of ways.[18] They typically begin by drawing on an everyday, uncontroversial, garden-variety constructivism that might be described in the following way: In a fairly unremarkable sense, we are all constructivists if we believe that the mind is active in the construction of knowledge. Most of us would agree that knowing is not passive—a simple imprinting of sense data on the mind—but active; that is, mind does something with these impressions, at the very least forming abstractions or concepts. In this sense, constructivism means that human beings do not find or discover knowledge so much as we construct or make it. We invent concepts, models, and schemes to make sense of experience, and we continually test and modify these constructions in the light of new experience. Furthermore, there is an inevitable historical and sociocultural dimension to this construction. We do not construct our interpretations in isolation but against a backdrop of shared understandings, practices, language, and so forth.

This ordinary sense of constructionism is also called *perspectivism* in contemporary epistemology (e.g., Fay, 1996). It is the view that all knowledge claims and their evaluation take place within a conceptual framework through which the world is described and explained. Perspectivism opposes a naïve realist and empiricist epistemology that holds that there can be some kind of unmediated, direct grasp of the empirical world and that knowledge (i.e., the mind) simply reflects or mirrors what is "out there."

Philosophies of social constructionism also reject this naïve realist view of representation. But they often go much further in denying any interest whatsoever in an ontology of the real. Consider, for example, Potter's (1996) recent work explicating constructionism in the tradition of ethnomethodology and conversation analysis. He grounds his view in a critique of a representational theory of language and knowledge. He argues that "the world . . . is constituted in one way or another as people talk it, write it and argue it" (p. 98), yet he holds that social constructionism is not an ontological doctrine at all and thus takes no position on what sorts of things exist and what their status is. His primary concern is with how it is that a descriptive utterance is socially (i.e., interactionally) made to appear stable, factual, neutral, independent of the speaker, and merely mirroring some aspect of the world. For example, Potter states that "like money on the international markets, truth can be treated as a commodity which is worked up, can fluctuate, and can be strengthened or weakened by various procedures of representation" (p. 5). For Potter, social construction is interested in how utterances "work," and how they work is neither a matter of the cognitive analysis of how mental versions of the world are built nor a matter of the empirical analysis of semantic content and logical analysis of syntactical relations of words and sentences. Rather, how utterances work is a matter of understanding social practices and analyzing the rhetorical strategies in play in particular kinds of discourse.[19]

Like Potter, Denzin (1997) argues that discourse is the material practice that constitutes representation and description. He cites approvingly Stuart Hall's claim that "there is no way of experiencing the 'real relations' of a particular society outside of its cultural and ideological categories" (p. 245). Gergen (1985, 1994a, 1994b, 1995) is equally skeptical of the "real." He claims that social constructionism is mute or agnostic on matters of ontology: Social constructionism neither affirms nor denies the "world out there." For Gergen (1994a), constructionism is nothing more or less than a "form of intelligibility—an array of propositions, arguments, metaphors, narratives, and the like—that welcome inhabitation" (p. 78). Gergen subscribes to a relational theory of social meaning—"It is human interchange that gives language its capacity to mean, and it must stand as the critical locus of concern" (1994a, pp. 263-264)—and claims that social constructionism simply invites one to play with the possibilities and practices that are made coherent by various forms of relations.

All of these views take issue with what might be called *meaning realism*—the view that meanings are fixed entities that can be discovered and that exist independent of the interpreter. In this respect, these social constructionist views share with philosophical hermeneutics the broad critique of meaning as an object, and they display an affinity with the notion of the coming into being of meaning. Both philosophies endorse an expressivist-constructivist theory of language, in which, broadly conceived, language is understood as a range of activities in which we express and realize a certain way of being in the world. Language is seen neither as primarily a tool for gaining knowledge of the world as an objective process nor "as an instrument whereby we order the things in our world, but as what allows us to have the world we have. Language makes possible the disclosure of the human world" (Taylor, 1995, p. ix). Hence advocates for social constructionism and philosophical hermeneutics might agree on the claim that we are self-interpreting beings and that language constitutes this being (or that we dwell in language, as Gadamer and Heidegger have explained).

However, the similarity ends there. Although "constructionist" in its disavowal of an objectivist theory of meaning, philosophical hermeneutics trusts in the potential of language

(conversation, dialogue) to disclose meaning and truth (Gallagher, 1992; Smith, 1997). For both Gadamer and Taylor, there is a "truth to the matter" of interpretation, but it is conceived in terms of disclosure that transpires in actual interpretive practices "rather than as a relation of correspondence between an object and some external means of representation" as conceived in traditional epistemology (Smith, 1997, p. 22). In sharp contrast to the views of Gadamer and Taylor, many (but not all) constructionist accounts hold that there is no truth to the matter of interpretation.

"Weak" and "Strong" Constructionism

A general assumption of social constructionism is that knowledge is not disinterested, apolitical, and exclusive of affective and embodied aspects of human experience, but is in some sense ideological, political, and permeated with values (Rouse, 1996). This assumption is amenable to both weak and strong interpretations. A weak or moderate interpretation of the role that social factors play in what constitutes legitimate, warranted, or true interpretation may well reject definitions of such notions as knowledge, justification, objectivity, and evidence as developed within the representationalist-empiricist-foundationalist nexus. But the perspective will attempt to recast these notions in a different epistemological framework and thereby preserve some way of distinguishing better or worse interpretations. A strong or radical interpretation of the role that social factors play in what constitutes legitimate knowledge results in a more radically skeptical and even nihilistic stance.

"Weak" Constructionism: An Illustration

A moderate version of social constructionism, developed in the context of feminist philosophy of science, is provided by Longino (1990, 1993a, 1993b, 1996). Her aim is to develop "a theory of inquiry that reveals the ideological dimension of knowledge construction while at the same time offering criteria for the comparative evaluation of scientific theories and research programs" (1993a, p. 257). Longino argues that many feminist critiques of science, including both standpoint epistemologies and psychodynamic perspectives, rightly criticize traditional epistemology for focusing exclusively on the logic of justification of scientific claims while ignoring methods of discovery or heuristic biases. She provides examples of how heuristics (e.g., androcentrism, sexism, and gender ideology) "limit the hypotheses in play in specific areas of inquiry" and how different heuristics put different hypotheses into play (1993b, p. 102). Although they are successful critiques of empiricism to the extent that they help "redescribe the process of knowledge acquisition" (by introducing different heuristics), these feminist epistemologies stop short of offering an adequate account of how we are to decide or to justify decisions between what seem to be conflicting knowledge claims. In sum, Longino claims that many feminist epistemologies are descriptively adequate but normatively (or prescriptively) inadequate.

Longino's (1993a) solution to the problem of uniting the descriptive and the normative is something she calls "contextual empiricism." She defends a modest empiricism—one in which the real world constrains our knowledge construction—by claiming that experiential or observational data are the least easily dismissed bases of hypothesis and theory validation. At the same time, she argues that the methods employed to generate, analyze, and organize data and to link evidence to hypotheses are not under the control of an autonomous, disengaged, disembodied subject, knower, or ideal epistemic agent. Rather, such matters are "contextual" in that they are constituted by a context of intersubjectively determined background assumptions that are "the vehicles by which social values and ideology are expressed in inquiry and become subtly inscribed in theories, hypotheses, and models defining research programs" (1993a, p. 263).

Consequently, these background assumptions must be submitted to conceptual and evidential criticism that is not possible as long as we cling to the view that knowledge is a production of an individual cognitive process. But, according to Longino (1993b), if we conceive of the practices of inquiry and knowledge production as *social* and accept the thesis that objectivity is a function of social interactions, then we can begin to explore how to criticize background assumptions effectively. Longino goes on to explain that "effective criticism of background assumptions requires the presence and expression of alternative points of view . . . [which] allows us to see how social values and interests can become enshrined in otherwise acceptable research programs" (p. 112). She offers a set of criteria necessary for a given scientific community to "achieve the transformative dimension of critical discourse" that include recognized avenues/forums for criticism; community response to criticism, not merely tolerance of it; shared standards of evaluation; and equality of intellectual authority (p. 112).

Longino argues for a social epistemology in which ideological and value issues tied to sociocultural practices are interwoven with empirical ones in scientific inquiry.[20] She appears to steer a middle ground by acknowledging that scientific knowledge is in part the product of processes of social negotiation without claiming that such knowledge is *only* a matter of social negotiation. And, in endorsing objectivity and strongly defending the normative aspects of a theory of inquiry, she clearly avoids the relativist view that any interpretation is as good as another. Finally, as is characteristic of many feminist epistemologists, Longino both assumes and builds on an ontology of knowing that is concretely situated and more interactive, relational, and dialogic than representational (Rouse, 1996).

"Strong" Constructionism

One way in which this stance develops is as follows: Taking their cue from Wittgenstein's notion of language games (as elaborated by Winch, 1958), some radical social constructionists begin with the premise that language is embedded in social practices or forms of life.[21] Moreover, the rules that govern a form of life circumscribe and close that form of life off to others. Hence it is only within and with reference to a particular form of life that the meaning of an action can be described and deciphered (Giddens, 1993). Standards for rationally evaluating beliefs are completely dependent on the language games or forms of life in which those beliefs arise. Thus the meanings of different language games or different forms of life are incommensurable. When this view is coupled with an insistence on radical conceptual difference, as it often is in many standpoint epistemologies, it readily leads to epistemological relativism. As Fay (1996) explains, in epistemological relativism, "no cross-framework judgments are permissible [for] the content, meaning, truth, rightness, and reasonableness of cognitive, ethical, or aesthetic beliefs, claims, experiences or actions can only be determined from within a particular conceptual scheme" (p. 77).[22]

Curiously, radical social constructionists such as Gergen and Denzin apparently endorse this idea of the incommensurability of language games or forms of life yet simultaneously claim that social constructionist philosophy somehow leads to an improvement of the human condition. Gergen (1994a) argues that knowledge is the product of social processes and that all statements of the true, the rational, and the good are the products of various particular communities of interpreters and thus to be regarded with suspicion. Yet he links his social constructionist philosophy to an agenda of democratization, possibility, and reconstruction. Above all else, Gergen looks to social constructionism as a means of broadening and democratizing the conversation about human practices and of submitting these practices to a continuous process of reflection.

Likewise, in his defense of a postmodernist interpretive ethnography, Denzin (1997) adamantly rejects what he calls a realist epistemology, one that "asserts that accurate representations of the world can be produced, and [that] these representations truthfully map the worlds of real experience" (p. 265). He defends standpoint epistemologies that study the world of experience from the point of view of the historically and culturally situated individual. But he

simultaneously endorses an ethnographic practice given to writing moral and allegorical tales that are not mere records of human experience intended simply to celebrate cultural differences or bring other cultures to our awareness. In Denzin's view, these moral tales are a method of empowerment for readers and a means for readers to discover moral truths about themselves.

A similar paradox is evident in each of these two strong constructionist views. Of Gergen we might ask, Absent any criteria for deciding across various frameworks which is the better (the more just, more democratic, and so on) practice and if there is no epistemic gain or loss resulting from this comparison, why would we bother to engage in the conversation? [23] And of Denzin we might inquire, Does not the creation of moral tales assume that there is a (moral) truth to the matter of interpretation that arises from the comparison of historically and culturally situated experience? Does not such a move speak to the need for some criteria whereby we clarify and justify genuine moral truths, thereby distinguishing them from mere illusion or belief?

◆ Summary: Enduring Issues

The qualitative inquiry movement is built on a profound concern with understanding what other human beings are doing or saying. The philosophies of interpretivism, philosophical hermeneutics, and social constructionism provide different ways of addressing this concern. Yet cutting across these three philosophies are several perdurable issues that every qualitative inquirer must come to terms with using the resources of these (and other) philosophies. Three of the most salient issues are (a) how to define what "understanding" actually means and how to justify claims "to understand"; (b) how to frame the interpretive project, broadly conceived; and (c) how to envision and occupy the ethical space where researchers and researched (subjects, informants, respondents, participants, coresearchers) relate to one another on the sociotemporal occasion or event that is "research," and, consequently, how to determine the role, status, responsibility, and obligations the researcher has in and to the society he or she researches. These cognitive, social, and moral issues are obviously intertwined, but I distinguish them here for analytic purposes.

Understanding and Justifying Understanding[24]

All qualitative inquirers who have made the interpretive turn (Hiley et al., 1991; Rabinow & Sullivan, 1979) share a set of commitments.[25] They are highly critical of scientism and reject an anthropology of a disengaged, controlling, instrumental self (Smith, 1997; Taylor, 1995). They hold that the cognitive requirements involved in understanding others cannot be met through the use of foundationalist epistemological assumptions characteristic of logical empiricism (e.g., neutrality of observation, primordial "givenness" of experience, independence of empirical data from theoretical frameworks). Interpretivism, all varieties of social constructionism (including Nietzschean perspectivism, neopragmatism, and deconstructionism), and Gadamerian philosophical hermeneutics all "insist on rejecting the very idea of any foundational, mind-independent, and permanently fixed reality that could be grasped or even sensibly thought of without the mediation of human structuring" (Shusterman, 1991, p. 103), at least in the realm of human studies. Stated somewhat differently, knowledge of what others are doing and saying always depends upon some background or context of other meanings, beliefs, values, practices, and so forth. Hence, for virtually all postempiricist philosophies of the human sciences, understanding is interpretation all the way down.

But the cognitive requirements of understanding in qualitative methodologies are not exhausted by this claim of the inevitability of interpretation. It is necessary to spell out the consequences of this interpretive turn for our efforts to understand.[26] Broadly speaking, two different sets of consequences characterize the contemporary debate.

Strong Holism

On the one hand, there are strong holists who argue that from the fact that we always *see* (make sense of, know) everything through interpretation, we must conclude that everything in fact *is* constituted by interpretation. From the fact that knowledge is perspectival and contextual, they draw the strong skeptical conclusion that it is impossible to distinguish any particular interpretation as more correct, or better or worse, than any other.

In this scenario, the question of justifying an interpretation of what others are doing or saying is irrelevant. How or why justification is irrelevant depends on the particular kind of strong holism in question. Justification may be irrelevant because interpretations are always regarded as "our" interpretations and hence ethnocentric (Hoy, 1991). Justification may not matter because interpretations are thought to be always nothing more than an expression of personal or political subjectivity. Or justification may be a nonissue because it is assumed that an interpretation never goes beyond itself; it is not about justification, disclosure, or clarification of meaning, but "textualistic," caught up in the larger game called the play of signifiers.[27] A good deal of contemporary writing about qualitative inquiry (e.g., Clough, 1998; Denzin, 1994, 1997; Lather, 1993; Richardson, 1997), influenced by postmodern ethnography and other related intellectual currents, appears to be committed to some version of strong holism. Likewise, the radical social constructionists engaged in the social studies of science—Latour, Woolgar, Knorr-Cetina, Barnes, and Bloor—develop strong holistic theses about scientific knowledge.

The issue of evaluating and choosing among competing (different, contradictory, and so on) interpretations raises the question of what constitutes rational behavior. What does it mean to make a reasonable choice from among alternative interpretations? Often a common assumption in strong or skeptical holism is that "if we cannot come up with universal fixed criteria to measure the plausibility of competing interpretations, then this means that we have no *rational* basis for distinguishing better and worse, more plausible or less plausible interpretations, whether these be interpretations of texts, actions, or historical epochs" (Bernstein, 1986, p. 358). Given the impossibility of *foundational* criteria, strong holists, typically, reach one of several conclusions: (a) They hold that the very idea of being rational requires deconstruction; (b) they endorse a noncritical pluralism of views (i.e., "multiple realities," many equally acceptable interpretations, and so on) that requires no comparative evaluation; or (c) they claim that rhetorical criteria—whether an interpretation invites, persuades, compels, entertains, evokes, or delights—are the only proper ones for judging whether one interpretation is better than another.[28]

Weak Holism

Weak or nonskeptical holism argues that it is neither necessary nor desirable to draw such relativistic, suspicious (or, worse, nihilistic) conclusions from the fact that knowledge of others is always dependent on a background of understanding. Weak holists claim that the background (the "mediation" of all understanding) is "not strong enough to act as a fixed limit or to make it impossible to decide normatively between interpretations on the basis of evidence. Indeed such evaluation will always be comparative, fallibilistic, and revisable, in that yet a better interpretation could come along, encompassing the strengths and overcoming the weaknesses of previous interpretations" (Bohman, 1991a, p. 146).

Weak holism seeks to explicate a rational basis for deciding whether an interpretation is "valid" or justified. But there are a variety of ways in which justification is attempted. For example, Bohman (1991b), Fay (1996), and to some extent Longino, as explained above, appear committed to the view that justification of an interpretation is subject to epistemic norms of internal coherence as well as correctness based on empirical constraints. Other weak holists look to redefine rationality on the basis of practical reasoning, that is, how "we can and do make comparative judgments and seek to support them with arguments and the appeal to

good reasons" (Bernstein, 1986, p. 358). For example, Bernstein's (1983, 1986, 1991) "nonfoundational pragmatic humanism" (which he also finds as a common theme in Rorty, Habermas, and Gadamer) illustrates a case for weak holism built on themes of praxis, practice, discourse, and practical truth. Gadamer (1975) argues that although the act of understanding cannot be modeled as a determinate analysis of an object yielding a final, complete, or definitive interpretation, nonetheless understanding has a normative dimension manifest in the fact that understanding is a kind of practical-moral knowledge. In his explanation of choosing between competing interpretations, Taylor (1985a, 1989) denies that there can be any appeal to empirical evidence or any fixed criterion that would *decisively* determine the correctness of an interpretation. Yet he develops an argument for the comparative superiority of interpretations grounded in a narrative form of practical reason and linked to his particular explication of how it is that we are human beings for whom things matter. For Taylor, what counts as better interpretation is understood as the justified movement from one interpretation to another.[29]

Locating the Interpretive Project

There is little agreement among qualitative inquirers on the social and scientific goals or purposes of their shared interpretive project. Many qualitative inquirers locate the project squarely within an emancipatory and transformative agenda. Some neopragmatists, critical theorists, and feminists are committed to the task of interpretation for purposes of criticizing and dismantling unjust and undemocratic educational and social practices and transforming them (Howe, 1998).

Other neopragmatists and some defenders of philosophical hermeneutics share this general Enlightenment belief in the power of critical reflection to improve our lot, but connect the interpretive project less directly to political transformation and more closely to dialogue, conversation, and education understood as an interpretational interchange that is self-

transformative. They see understanding that results from interpretation less as something that
is at our disposal for us subsequently to do
something with by "applying" it and more as
participation in meaning, in a tradition, and ultimately in a dialogue (Grondin, 1994). In their
view, critical emancipation—release (or escape)
from reproductive, hegemonic, authoritarian
structures—never quite fully happens. Critical
reflection is always characterized by both autonomy and authority. As Gallagher (1992) explains, this way of conceiving of the interpretive
project does not deny the possibility of emancipation and subsequent transformation, but only
the possibility of absolute emancipation:
"Emancipation is an ongoing process within educational experience, rather than the end result
of critical reflection" (p. 272).

Many postmodernists are deeply suspicious
of either the emancipatory or the conversational framing of the interpretive project. They
opt instead for interpretation as a kind of spontaneous play or an incessant deciphering that
unravels the multiple meanings of such notions
as self, identity, objectivity, subjectivity, presence, truth, and being.

These different ways of framing the interpretive project reveal that, internally at least,
qualitative inquiry is a broadly contentious
movement. It is a loose coalition of inquirers
seemingly united only in their general opposition to what was earlier called the foundationalist-empiricist-representationalist nexus
of beliefs.

Ethical and Political
Considerations

Social inquiry is a practice, not simply a way
of knowing. Understanding what others are
doing or saying and transforming that knowledge into public form involves moral-political
commitments. Moral issues arise from the fact
that a theory of knowledge is supported by a
particular view of human agency. For example,
Taylor, Dunne, and others argue that the
foundationalist-empiricist-representationalist
nexus is built upon a stance of disengagement

and objectification: The subject (knower) stands
over and against the object of understanding.
Moreover, the political dimension of the practice
of social inquiry is wedded to the growth of what
Bauman (1992) describes as the politics of legislative reason central to the rise of the modern state.
Hence the practice of social research (including,
but not limited to, qualitative inquiry) is not immune to effects of the central forces of the culture
of modernity—technologization, institutionalization, bureaucratization, and professionalization.[30]

A good deal of current criticism of ethnographic realism, or what is more generally called
the crisis of representation in ethnography, is directed at the moral and political requirements of
social research practices, not just (or even) their
cognitive demands. At issue is how to answer the
fundamental question, How should I *be* toward
these people I am studying? There are at least two
sharply different answers to this question. Firmly
in line with the interpretivist tradition of disengagement, Prus (1996) defends what some qualitative researchers would perhaps criticize as a
conventional, modernist, and dangerous view of
the inquirer as one who "attempts to minimize
the obtrusiveness of the researcher in the field
and in the text eventually produced . . . an image
of a researcher who is more chameleon-like . . .
who fits into the situation with a minimum of disruption, and whose work allows the life-worlds
of the other to surface in as complete and unen-
cumbered a manner as possible" (p. 196). In
sharp contrast, Denzin (1994) aims

> to create a form of gazing and understanding fit-
> ted to the contemporary, mass-mediated, cine-
> matic societies called postmodern. Such a gaze
> would undermine from within the cold, analytic,
> abstract, voyeuristic, disciplinary gaze of Fou-
> cault's panopticon. This will be a newer, gentler,
> compassionate gaze which looks, and desires, not
> technical instrumental knowledge, but in-depth
> existential understandings. (p. 64)

How one understands the differences in the
ethical-political stances of the researcher illustrated by Prus and Denzin, and how one decides
what to do about one's own ethical-political
commitments as a researcher depend in part on

the ethical framework one draws on to make sense of these kinds of situations.[31] This observation takes us into the realm of ethics and moral philosophy, a topic beyond the scope of this chapter. For present purposes, it will have to suffice simply to point out that at present there is a rather lively ongoing dialogue and debate surrounding the standard framework for moral epistemology.

Very briefly, the standard framework embraces a common core of ideas: (a) that morality is deontological (primarily concerned with moral obligations and commitments), (b) that the moral point of view is marked by its impartiality and universalizability, and (c) that conflicts of rights and obligations are open to argumentative resolution. Taken collectively, these ideas constitute a largely formalistic understanding of morality. *Formalistic* here does not mean the well-known quarrel over which is the superior formal theory of ethics. Rather, it means that within the standard framework the moral point of view is defined in terms of formal criteria. Form is privileged over content, as Vetlesen (1997) explains:

> Universalizability, impartiality, and impersonality—the formal criteria instrumental in defining the "moral point of view"—now function as the features a given item must possess in order to qualify as actually having moral content. In other words, only issues, questions, problems, and dilemmas lending themselves to adjudication and consensual resolution by means of [these] formal criteria . . . are allowed to qualify as "moral" in content. (p. 4)

Although they display considerable differences in their views, thinkers such as Kierkegaard, Sartre, Buber, Gabriel Marcel, Levinas, Løgstrup, Nussbaum, Bauman, and Noddings oppose the way morality is defined in the standard framework. They all argue for an ethic of closeness, of care, of proximity, or of relatedness, and hold that morality must be theorized from an *experiential* basis, specifically in the experience of the I-thou relationship. Benhabib contrasts this orientation with the orientation of the standard way of theorizing morality in the following way: "The moral issues which preoccupy us most and which touch us

most deeply derive not from problems of justice in the economy and the polity, but precisely from the quality of our relations with others in the 'spheres of kinship, love, friendship, and sex' " (quoted in Vetlesen, 1997, p. 4). These relations demand what Nussbaum (1990) characterizes as attentiveness—"an openness to being moved by the plight of others," the willingness "to be touched by another's life" (p. 162). Normative attention, in turn, requires a way of knowing that is contextual and narrative rather than formal and abstract. *Context* refers both to each individual's specific history, identity, and affective-emotional constitution and to the relationship between parties in the encounter with *its* history, identity, and affective definition. These two elements are linked by narrative.

Moreover, because these relations are highly contingent and contextual, the moral act itself, as Bauman (1993) observes, "is endemically ambivalent, forever threading precariously the thin lines dividing care from domination and tolerance from indifference" (p. 181). The inherent fragility, precariousness, and incurable ambivalence of morality means that the moral life is not about decision making, calculation, or procedures. Rather, it is "that unfounded, non-rational, unarguable, no excuses given and non-calculable urge to stretch towards the other, to caress, to be for, to live for, happen what may" (p. 247). Bauman (1995) adds that what the moral life amounts to in this view is a "never-ending string of settlements between mildly attractive or unattractive eventualities" (p. 66). Here, the notion of settlement differs from a calculating decision; it is not a conclusion one reaches based on applying principles; it has no fixed procedure.

Completely absent in this way of thinking of the moral life is the notion that morality is about argumentative resolution of competing moral claims. The moral encounter does not mean rule following but expression and communication. Furthermore, in this framework, there is no teleological, liberalist idea of moral progress driven by a vision, albeit imperfect, of social utopia, or a belief that our values and our moral abilities are evolving to some better form.

In this alternative framework, ethical relationship is grounded in the notion of being-for the Other. The relationship of being-for is prior to intentionality, prior to choice. Morality in this alternative framework is not voluntary. Moral orientation comes prior to any calculating action on the part of the moral agent; it is prior to purposefulness, reciprocity, and contractuality. Morality, in the first instance, is not about a kind of moral decision making that precedes moral action. Morality is not optional. Noddings refers to this notion of morality as caring. But caring is not a method for doing ethics or a particular principle on which to form a professional service ethic. It is an ethical orientation, a particular ground of meaning and value with its own internal logic of relational work (Thompson, 1997).

Caring or being-for is a kind of responsibility that is prevoluntary, unremovable, noncontractual, nonreciprocal, and asymmetrical. As Vetlesen (1997) explains, "The core of being-for is neither right nor rights, neither the happiness nor the good of those concerned. Its core is responsibility. Responsibility not as freely assumed, not as socially or politically or legally sanctioned; and yet as coming from outside rather than inside, as originating from what is exterior not interior to the agent" (p. 9). He adds that matters of justice, goodness, happiness all matter, but come later, and they do not "taken together or singly, define morality the phenomenon, responsibility the task" (p. 9).

It would be both incorrect and naïve to argue that a formalistic theory of ethics and morality as sketched above maps directly onto some set of "quantitative" methodologies, whereas the alternative maps onto some set of "qualitative" methodologies. Linking this work in moral phenomenology and moral epistemology to thinking about the ethics and politics of qualitative (and, more generally, all social) research is a complex matter. Yet this work does suggest that how a researcher ought to relate to and consequently represent others can be framed in at least two ways. On the one hand, ethical-moral relations can be defined as a kind of "problem" that must be solved by adopting the right kind of research ethics for "gazing," or by using the right kind of textual form, or by employing the right kind of methodology. The

problem-solving approach assumes that we can draw on some resources for criticism and direction of our choices that somehow lie outside the particular occasion that demands a practical choice. It reduces the dilemmas of human existence to objective problems in need of solutions. On the other hand, the question of relations and representation can also be understood as a mystery about the union of knowing and being to be faced anew in each situation in which the researcher finds her- or himself. This approach understands the situation of "How shall I be toward these people I am studying?" as one that demands a particular kind of understanding noted above as practical-moral knowledge.

◆ Final Note

In outlining these philosophies it has not been my intention to offer a template or typology with which to sort current expressions of qualitative inquiry. (Moreover, the topics discussed here go well beyond any conception of qualitative studies to a concern with all current social inquiry.) It seems to be a uniquely American tendency to categorize and label complicated theoretical perspectives as either this or that.[32] Such labeling is dangerous, for it blinds us to enduring issues, shared concerns, and points of tension that cut across the landscape of the movement, issues that each inquirer must come to terms with in developing an identity as a social inquirer. In wrestling with the ways in which these philosophies forestructure our efforts to understand what it means to "do" qualitative inquiry, what we face is not a choice of which label—interpretivist, constructivist, hermeneuticist, or something else—best suits us. Rather, we are confronted with choices about how each of us wants to live the life of a social inquirer.

■ Notes

1. Of course, anthropologists and fieldwork sociologists had been doing "qualitative inquiry" for decades earlier. But methods for generating

and interpreting qualitative data acquired a particular currency in a variety of other human science fields in the 1970s. This is not the place to develop this historical account, but it seems reasonable to say that several developments in the disciplines converged in the 1970s, thereby providing fertile ground for the recovery of interest in fieldwork methodologies. These developments included the critique of statistical hypothesis testing and experimentation and the growing interest in "naturalistic" methods that was unfolding in psychology, the emergence of humanistic psychology, the renewed attention paid by some sociologists to explaining fieldwork methods, the critique of structural-functionalism and the concomitant development of interpretivist anthropology, and the widening awareness outside the community of philosophers of science of criticisms of the received view.

2. It is not coincidental that the movement in the United States began to flourish as more and more of the European philosophers' broad attack on scientism (Cooper, 1996) became available in English. For example, the first book-length treatment of *Verstehen* appeared in English in 1975 (Outhwaite, 1975); Schutz's *Der sinn hafte Aufbau der sozialen Welt* (*The Phenomenology of the Social World*), first published in German in 1932, appeared in an English translation in 1967; Habermas's monograph *Zur logik der Sozialwissenschaften* (*On the Logic of the Social Sciences*), first published in German in 1967, did not appear in English until 1988; and so on.

3. Sadly, some researchers seem drawn to qualitative inquiry for the simple fact that they do not wish to "deal with numbers." This is doubly tragic. First, it is based on faulty reasoning—there is nothing inherent in the epistemologies of qualitative inquiry that prohibits the use of numbers as data. Second, such a stance can be based in the illusion that so-called qualitative inquiry is somehow "easier" to do than so-called quantitative inquiry. But it is hard to imagine what criteria might be employed to determine that the level of effort and thought required for writing field notes, conducting and transcribing interviews, interpreting different kinds of qualitative data, and so on is somehow lower (or higher, for that matter) than that required for designing and executing a careful and meaningful test of a statistical hypothesis. These

inquiry tasks simply require different kinds of awareness, knowledge, and skills.

4. These are by no means the only philosophies that attract the attention of qualitative inquirers. For example, much contemporary "qualitative" work is firmly built on a post-empiricist philosophy of science. That is, its methodology takes seriously the implications of the underdetermination of theory by data, the theory-ladenness of observation, the fallibility of all claims to know, and so on, without being drawn into the Continental philosophers' critique of instrumental reason and scientism, Heideggerian concerns about "being," deconstructionism (whether that of Gadamer or Derrida), feminist critiques of objectivity, and so forth. Feminist, neopragmatic, ethnic, and critical theory philosophies are discussed elsewhere in this handbook. Some claim phenomenology as a founding epistemology for qualitative inquiry, but it is virtually impossible to discuss the relevance for qualitative inquiry of this complex, multifaceted philosophy in general terms without reducing the notion of phenomenology to a caricature. Phenomenology means something far more complicated than a romanticized notion of seeing the world of actors "as it really is." Moreover, simple formulations in introductory methods books (e.g., "Researchers in the phenomenological mode attempt to understand the meaning of events and interactions to ordinary people in particular situations"; Bogdan & Biklen, 1992, p. 34) are misleading because such definitions gloss the crucial difference for epistemologies of qualitative inquiry, namely, defining what *meaning* is. The complexity of the influence of phenomenology on qualitative inquiry is evident when we consider that the phenomenology of Heidegger, for example, figures prominently but in very different ways in both philosophical hermeneutics and deconstructionist approaches; Husserl's phenomenology considerably influenced the work of Alfred Schutz, who, in turn, served as a source of ideas for ethnomethodologists and other sociologists. Gubrium and Holstein take up issues in the tradition of phenomenological sociology in Chapter 18 of this volume.

5. However, this issue appears to be more of a concern among defenders of interpretivist/hermeneutic approaches to social science than it is between this group and the logical empiricists (Hiley, Bohman, & Shusterman,

1991). See, for example, the exchange between Geertz and Taylor on this issue in Tully (1994); see also Rouse (1991).

6. Dilthey (1958) emphasized the importance of the psychological reenactment (*Nacherleben*) of the experience of the other. Weber (1949) endorsed a similar notion of *Verstehen* as a "rational understanding of motivation" (p. 95). In his later writings, Dilthey de-emphasized the notion of empathic identification and spoke more of hermeneutic interpretation of cultural products.

7. See Bleicher (1980) and Gallagher (1992) for overviews of these distinctions in types of hermeneutics.

8. Bernstein (1983) adds that "there is no determinate method for acquiring or pursuing this art [of understanding], in the sense of explicit rules that are to be followed" (p. 135). Yet, within the interpretivist tradition, the epistemic status of rules, procedures, or methods is controversial. The work of Geertz, Wolcott, and Stake, I would argue, exemplifies a more artistic interpretation of how one achieves understanding. On the other hand, the work of Hammersley, Goffman, Lofland and Lofland, Miles and Huberman, Prus, Silverman, and Strauss and Corbin illustrates a more social scientific approach to the method of understanding. These scholars emphasize ways of generating and interpreting "understanding" that place a premium on the validity, relevance, and importance of both question and findings. Their methodologies are concerned with asking questions about the type, frequency, magnitude, structure, processes, causes, consequences, and meanings of sociopolitical phenomena and developing defensible answers to those questions. Answers typically take the form of substantive or middle-range theory that explains or accounts for the phenomena. Yet a "third way" of understanding the significance of method in achieving understanding is offered by Garfinkel and other ethnomethodologists who claim that both actors and observers (i.e., social scientists) are to be treated as "members" who produce and manage (i.e., accomplish) the social activity of organized everyday life. Thus sociological methods, for example, are nothing more or less than evidence of the practical sociological reasoning of sociologists.

9. I focus almost exclusively on philosophical or ontological hermeneutics here because the contours of both critical hermeneutics and radical hermeneutics are discussed elsewhere in this volume.

10. I use text and human action interchangeably here, following Ricoeur's (1981) argument for their analogous relationship in hermeneutic interpretation.

11. Again, it must be emphasized that *uninvolved observer* here does not mean that the interpretivist observes literally at a distance or from behind some kind of one-way mirror. What the term signifies is an epistemological relationship between subject (interpreter) and object of interpretation (text, human action) in which the interpreter is unaffected by (and, in this sense, external to) the act of interpretation. At issue here is the theoretical attitude noted above: the idea that the knower is not (or must not be) somehow bound up with the domain of the object he or she seeks to understand. Concerns for managing and tracking bias, inventorying subjectivities, keeping a reflexive journal, peer debriefing, and so forth (familiar procedures in the qualitative methodological literature) are all related to this bid to maintain the theoretical attitude.

12. Not to put too fine a point on it, but this notion of engagement entails more than a confession of positionality or simply inventorying "where one stands" relative to that which is being interpreted. Engagement means risking one's stance and acknowledging the ongoing liminal experience of living between familiarity and strangeness (see Kerdeman, 1998).

13. Grondin (1994) defends Gadamer's hermeneutics against the charge that it is a kind of linguistic idealism. According to Grondin, Gadamer maintains that understanding is *in principle* linguistic "because language embodies the sole means for carrying out the conversation that we are and that we hope to convey to each other. It is for this reason that hermeneutics permits itself an aphorism such as 'Being that can be understood is language.' The emphasis should be on the 'can.' Understanding, itself always linguistically formed and dealing with things verbal, must be capable of engaging the whole content of language in order to arrive at the being that language helps to bring to expression. The essential linguisticality of understanding expresses itself less in our statements than in our search for the language to say what we have on our minds and hearts. For hermeneutics, it is less constitutive that understanding is expressed in lan-

guage—which is true but trivial—than that it lives in the unending process of 'summoning the word' and the search for a sharable language. Indeed, understanding is to be conceived *as* this process" (p. 120). See also the exchange between Davey (1991) and Smith (1991) on whether Gadamer's critique of the statement, propositional language, and logic is justified.

14. See also Hekman's (1986, pp. 145ff.) argument that a fixed meaning of human action is the fundamental unit of social scientific analysis in Wittgensteinian social science (e.g., Winch, 1958), Schutz's phenomenology, and ethnomethodology.

15. In the philosophical hermeneutics of Gadamer and Taylor, understanding is linked both to the Aristotelian notion of *praxis* and to its distinct form of personal, experiential knowledge and reasoning called *phronesis* or practical wisdom. The latter (*allo eidos gnoseos,* that "other form of cognition") requires "responsiveness, flexibility, and perceptiveness in discerning what is needed" and sharply contrasts to the form of practical knowledge called *techne* (Dunne, 1993, p. 56). Gadamer connects understanding, interpretation, and application by modeling the activity of understanding on the notion of *phronesis* and by modeling the theory of understanding (hermeneutics) on practical philosophy (Bernstein, 1983, pp. 114-150; Dunne, 1993, pp. 154ff.; Gadamer, 1981).

16. This "movement" takes up an incredible variety of related developments in pragmatism (e.g., Mead's theory of the social self and the sociality of language, Dewey's epistemological behaviorism), theory of science (e.g., the Quine-Duhem thesis, Hanson, Kuhn), philosophy of language (e.g., Wittgenstein's *Philosophical Investigations,* the work of Austin and Louch in ordinary language philosophy), philosophy of social science (e.g., Winch), sociology of knowledge (e.g., Berger and Luckmann), phenomenology (e.g., Heidegger's ideas about language in *Being and Time*), ethnomethodology's concern for situated actions as publicly interpreted linguistic forms (e.g., Garfinkel), and so on. Bernstein (1991, pp. 326ff.) identifies a set of substantive pragmatic themes that characterize in a very general way many different postempiricist philosophies: antifoundationalism, thoroughgoing fallibilism, primary emphasis on the social character of the self, the need to culti-

vate a community of inquirers, awareness and sensitivity to radical contingency, and recognition that there is no escape from the plurality of traditions.

17. Taylor (1995) refers to this as the "first-person-singular self"; "the human agent as primarily a subject of representations, first, about the world outside; [and] second, about depictions of ends desired or feared. This subject is a monological one. We are in contact with an 'outside' world, including other agents, the objects we and they deal with, our own and others' bodies, but this contact is through representations we have 'within.' The subject is first of all an inner space, a 'mind' to use the old terminology, or a mechanism capable of processing representations, if we follow the more fashionable computer-inspired models of today" (p. 169).

18. Given limited space, I have chosen to focus on social versus psychological forms of constructionism. My primary concern here is with those philosophies that wrestle with joining social-political factors with epistemic concerns in their account of what constitutes a public body of knowledge. Of course, psychological constructionists also wrestle with the significance of social factors in knowledge construction, but their primary interest is in understanding how these play a role in individual acts of cognition. There is considerable within-group as well as between-group difference in psychological constructivist and social constructivist perspectives in social science, psychology, and education (Gergen, 1994a, 1994b; Phillips, 1995, 1997a, 1997b; Potter, 1996) that simply cannot be surveyed here. Moreover, there is a difference in terminology that can get rather confusing. Phillips, for example, divides social constructivists from psychological constructivists; Gergen calls the former group social constructionists and the latter constructivists. I use the terms *constructionist* and *constructionism* here in discussing the "social" end of the continuum.

19. In this emphasis on how language is used to accomplish something, we can find some parallels to issues taken up in informal logic, such as describing and evaluating reasoning and argumentation not in terms of deductive logic but in terms of criteria appropriate to different argument schemes or types of dialogue (Van Eemeren, Grootendorst, Blair, & Willard, 1987; Walton, 1989). Of course, for social construc-

tionists persuaded of radical perspectivalism or the infinite play of signifiers, there would not be much point to studying argumentation.

20. Dorothy Smith (1996) offers another example of this effort to interweave the social and the empirical that preserves the notion that our knowledge claims refer or are "about" something and not merely the infinite play of signifiers.

21. My concern here is with strong interpretations that continue to accord primacy to the role of social factors in knowledge construction, not with views that see the social as something to be undone. For example, references to Nietzsche's radical perspectivalism and Derrida's deconstructionism often appear in texts championing a radical social constructionist view. Yet they offer little support for *social constructionism*. Nietzsche (1979) holds that meaning (truth, knowledge) is nothing more than the product of processes of social negotiation: "What therefore is true? A mobile army of metaphors, metonymies, anthropomorphisms, . . . which after long use seem firm, canonical, and obligatory to a people; truths are illusions of which one has forgotten that they are illusions" (p. 174). But for him, the *social* construction of value has to be acknowledged and carefully criticized in order to make way for and justify the *individual* construction of value. These so-called social truths are, as Smith (1997) explains, "antagonistic to life, where 'life' connotes a vital force of creative energy, a flux of sensuous particularity which resists the conceptual categorization conditioning claims to truth" (p. 17). *Self*-creation and *self*-transformation are Nietzsche's goals. Derrida (1976, 1978) appears to hold a similar view, although of this I am not completely certain. On the one hand, Derrida is highly critical (and suspicious) of any interpretation that appeals to or seeks to reproduce some larger, more encompassing framework. He argues that the *individual* reader has a responsibility to open up or activate the textuality of the text, but this means the reader must open him- or herself to the text because any new reading of the text is not simply the reader's own doing. Meaning is constructed in the play of signifiers within the field of textuality that encompasses text and interpreter. Yet Derrida claims that there is no subjective and reflective control over this interpreta-

tion process. Hence he seems to endorse individual construction of meaning, but simultaneously holds that there is no subjective locus of meaning or interpretation (Derrida, 1976, 1978). To be sure, there is an affinity in the view I describe here with Nietzsche's and Derrida's views. All three assume more or less that everything we encounter is an interpretation in terms of our own subjective values and perspectives (or the values and perspectives of our group, community, culture, and the like). Hence the epistemological stance for all three views can be summarized as follows: "All knowledge is interpretation; interpretations are always value-laden; values are ultimately expressions of some heterogeneous non-cognitive faculty, process or event (such as the mechanics of desire, history, or the will to power); therefore truth claims are ultimately expressions of that non-cognitive faculty, process or event" (Smith, 1997, p. 16).

22. It is but a short step from epistemological relativism to ontological relativism: If all we can know about reality depends on our particular conceptual scheme, is it not the case that reality itself can only be how it seems in our conceptual scheme (Fay, 1996; Smith, 1997)?

23. In an exchange with Taylor (1988), Gergen (1988) disputes the idea of strong evaluation or the possibility of sorting out whether some interpretations are better than others. Moreover, Gergen (1994a) (wrongly) interprets the philosophical hermeneutics of Gadamer as endorsing some kind of "essence" of meaning. In my view, Gergen does not adequately come to terms with either Gadamer's or Taylor's view that interpretation as practical reason (*phronesis*) is not exhausted by tradition.

24. See Smith and Deemer (Chapter 34, this volume) for more extensive discussion of criteria and cognitive requirements for judging whether understanding has been accomplished.

25. Admittedly, what constitutes having made the "turn," so to speak, is not particularly easy to discern. In general, it means rejecting an epistemology of representation. But that can be wrongly interpreted as abandoning all interest in "traditional" social scientific concerns about validity, objectivity, and generalizability.

26. The argument developed here draws heavily on Bohman (1991a, 1991b), who develops this distinction between strong and weak holism and defends the latter. I do not necessarily

agree with the way in which he labels the various positions of Gadamer, Rorty, Derrida, Habermas, and so on in terms of these two kinds of holism, but that sorting and classifying is largely irrelevant to the point I am making here.

27. Gallagher (1992) explains Derrida's view as follows: "Interpretation occurs only within the diacritical system of signifiers and without recourse to a metaphysical reality of the referent. . . . Derrida's radical principle of play is an attempt (from the inside) to unravel the metaphysical belief in the reality and the identity of the referent—objectivity, subjectivity, presence, being, truth, or any other metaphysical concept operative in the Western tradition" (p. 283).

28. Deconstructionism or radical social constructionism (and Rortyian pragmatism) does not regard the absence of foundational criteria as a problem in need of correction. Smith (1997) explains: "On the contrary, the demand for foundations drives the ambition of the philosophical tradition weak hermeneutics [deconstructionism] aspires to overcome. The foundationalism of previous philosophy, it is alleged, encourages an intolerance of 'otherness' and the 'incommensurable.' Weak hermeneutics can take the form of strategies for circumventing or subverting that demand for answerability to reason through which, it is believed, power and control are exercised. The goal of these postmodern strategies is to make space in thought for that which is allegedly non-assimilable to reason: diversity, heterogeneity and difference" (p. 18).

29. Smith (1997) summarizes Taylor's notion of evaluation: "The correctness of a particular practical deliberation is determined by the comparative superiority of the interpretive positions on either side of a move. To be favored by reason is therefore not to be judged positively according to some fixed *criterion,* one that is applicable to *any* practical deliberation independent of context or horizon of self-interpretation. . . . practical reasoning works well when it perspicuously displays epistemic gains or loses in particular concrete cases. Typical ways of achieving this goal are through identifying and resolving a contradiction in the original interpretation, pointing to a confusion that interpretation relied on, or by acknowledging the importance of some factor which it screened out" (p. 61). Note that these *ways* in which perspicuous articulation can occur are not *criteria* for judging whether the interpretation per se is a good or bad one. What

counts as an "epistemic gain" cannot be determined independently or in advance of the actual occasion of interpretation. I have drawn on this idea of a criterionless weak holism to elaborate evaluative judgment (see Schwandt, 1996, 1997).

30. See Carr's (1997) discussion of how the 20th-century transformation of education into schooling was accompanied by a modern "methodical" approach to educational inquiry.

31. Understanding how to face the situation of knowing others also has a great deal to do with how researcher role and responsibility are shaped by discourses that dominate universities (Derrida, 1983). That topic is taken up by Greenwood and Levin in Chapter 3 of this volume.

32. The very idea of qualitative inquiry as a category distinct from quantitative inquiry is, of course, part of the origin of the movement portrayed in various ways in this *Handbook.* In the view of many, myself and many of my students included, it is highly questionable whether such a distinction is any longer meaningful for helping us understand the purpose and means of human inquiry. One of my students recently commented that we think we become researchers by learning methodologies, by developing some kind of allegiance to qualitative or quantitative approaches to inquiry. But, she continued, *all* research is interpretive, and we face a multiplicity of methods that are suitable for different kinds of understandings. So the traditional means of coming to grips with one's identity as a researcher by aligning oneself with a particular set of methods (or by being defined in one's department as a student of "qualitative" or "quantitative" methods) is no longer very useful. If we are to go forward, we need to get rid of that distinction.

■ *References*

Aylesworth, G. E. (1991). Dialogue, text, narrative: Confronting Gadamer and Ricoeur. In H. Silverman (Ed.), *Gadamer and hermeneutics* (pp. 63-81). New York: Routledge.

Bauman, Z. (1992). *Intimations of postmodernity.* London: Routledge.

Bauman, Z. (1993). *Postmodern ethics.* Oxford: Blackwell.

Bauman, Z. (1995). *Life in fragments: Essays in postmodern morality.* Oxford: Blackwell.

Bernstein, R. J. (1976). *The restructuring of social and political theory.* Philadelphia: University of Pennsylvania Press.

Bernstein, R. J. (1983). *Beyond objectivism and relativism: Science, hermeneutics, and praxis.* Philadelphia: University of Pennsylvania Press.

Bernstein, R. J. (1986). What is the difference that makes a difference? Gadamer, Habermas, and Rorty. In B. R. Wachterhauser (Ed.), *Hermeneutics and modern philosophy* (pp. 343-376). Albany: State University of New York Press.

Bernstein, R. J. (1991). *The new constellation: The ethical-political horizons of modernity/postmodernity.* Cambridge: MIT Press.

Bleicher, J. (1980). *Contemporary hermeneutics: Hermeneutics as method, philosophy, and critique.* London: Routledge & Kegan Paul.

Bogdan, R. C., & Biklen, S. K. (1992). *Qualitative research for education: An introduction to theory and methods* (2nd ed.). Boston: Allyn & Bacon.

Bohman, J. F. (1991a). Holism without skepticism: Contextualism and the limits of interpretation. In D. R. Hiley, J. F. Bohman, & R. Shusterman (Eds.), *The interpretive turn* (pp. 129-154). Ithaca, NY: Cornell University Press.

Bohman, J. F. (1991b). *New philosophy of social science: Problems of indeterminacy.* Cambridge: MIT Press.

Carr, W. (1997). Philosophy and method in educational research. *Cambridge Journal of Education, 27,* 203-209.

Clough, P. (1998). The end(s) of ethnography: Now and then. *Qualitative Inquiry, 4,* 3-14.

Collingwood, R. G. (1961). *The idea of history.* Oxford: Clarendon. (Original work published 1946)

Connolly, J. M., & Keutner, T. (1988). Introduction: Interpretation, decidability, and meaning. In J. M. Connolly & T. Keutner (Eds.), *Hermeneutics and science: Three German views* (pp. 1-66). Notre Dame, IN: University of Notre Dame Press.

Cooper, D. E. (1996). Modern European philosophy. In N. Bunnin & E. P. Tsui-James (Eds.)., *The Blackwell companion to philosophy* (pp. 702-721). Oxford: Blackwell.

Davey, R. N. (1991). A response to Christopher Smith. In H. Silverman (Ed.), *Gadamer and hermeneutics* (pp. 42-59). New York: Routledge.

Denzin, N. K. (1994). *Chan is missing*: The Asian eye examines cultural studies. *Symbolic Interaction, 17,* 63-89.

Denzin, N. K. (1997). *Interpretive ethnography: Ethnographic practices for the 21st century.* Thousand Oaks, CA: Sage.

Derrida, J. (1976). *Of grammatology* (G. C. Spivak, Trans.). Baltimore: Johns Hopkins University Press.

Derrida, J. (1978). *Writing and difference* (A. Bass, Trans.). Chicago: University of Chicago Press.

Derrida, J. (1983). The principle of reason: The university in the eyes of its pupils. *Diacritics, 13,* 3-20.

Dilthey, W. (1958). *Gesammelte Schriften.* Leipzig: B. G. Teubner.

Dunne, J. (1993). *Back to the rough ground: "Phronesis" and "techne" in modern philosophy and Aristotle.* Notre Dame, IN: University of Notre Dame Press.

Fay, B. (1996). *Contemporary philosophy of social science.* Oxford: Blackwell.

Gadamer, H.-G. (1970). On the scope and function of hermeneutical reflection (G. B. Hess & R. E. Palmer, Trans.). *Continuum, 8,* 77-95.

Gadamer, H.-G. (1975). *Truth and method* (2nd rev. ed.; J. Weinsheimer & D. G. Marshall, Eds. & Trans.). New York: Crossroad.

Gadamer, H.-G. (1977). Theory, technology, practice: The task of the science of man. *Social Research, 44,* 529-561.

Gadamer, H.-G. (1981). *Reason in the age of science* (F. G. Lawrence, Trans.). Cambridge: MIT Press.

Gadamer, H.-G. (1996). *The enigma of health.* Stanford, CA; Stanford University Press.

Gallagher, S. (1992). *Hermeneutics and education.* Albany: State University of New York Press.

Garfinkel, H. (1967). *Studies in ethnomethodology.* Englewood Cliffs, NJ: Prentice Hall.

Garrison, J. (1996). A Deweyan theory of democratic listening. *Educational Theory, 46,* 429-451.

Geertz, C. (1979). From the native's point of view: On the nature of anthropological understanding. In P. Rabinow & W. M. Sullivan (Eds.), *Interpretive social science: A reader* (pp. 225-241). Berkeley: University of California Press. (Reprinted from *Meaning in anthropology*, pp. 221-237, by K. H. Basso & H. A. Selby, Eds., 1976, Albuquerque: University of New Mexico Press)

Gergen, K. J. (1985). The social constructionist movement in modern psychology. *American Psychologist, 40,* 266-275.

Gergen, K. J. (1988). If person are texts. In S. Messer, L. A. Sass, & R. L. Woolfolk (Eds.), *Hermeneutics and psychological theory* (pp. 28-51). New Brunswick, NJ: Rutgers University Press.

Gergen, K. J. (1994a). *Realities and relationships: Soundings in social construction.* Cambridge, MA: Harvard University Press.

Gergen, K. J. (1994b). *Toward transformation in social knowledge* (2nd ed.). Thousand Oaks, CA: Sage.

Gergen, K. J. (1995). Social construction and the educational process. In L. P. Steffe & J. Gale (Eds.), *Constructionism in education* (pp. 17-39). Mahwah, NJ: Lawrence Erlbaum.

Giddens, A. (1993). *New rules of sociological method* (2nd ed.). Stanford, CA: Stanford University Press.

Grondin, J. (1994). *Introduction to philosophical hermeneutics* (J. Weinsheimer, Trans.). New Haven, CT: Yale University Press.

Habermas, J. (1988). *On the logic of the social sciences* (S. W. Nicholsen & J. A. Strak, Trans.). Cambridge: MIT Press.

Hekman, S. J. (1986). *Hermeneutics and the sociology of knowledge.* Notre Dame, IN: University of Notre Dame Press.

Hiley, D. R., Bohman, J. F., & Shusterman, R. (Eds.). (1991). *The interpretive turn.* Ithaca, NY: Cornell University Press.

Hirsch, E. D. (1976). *The aims of interpretation.* Chicago: University of Chicago Press.

Howe, K. (1998). The interpretive turn and the new debate in education. *Educational Researcher, 27*(8), 13-20.

Hoy, D. C. (1991). Is hermeneutics ethnocentric? In D. R. Hiley, J. F. Bohman, & R. Shusterman (Eds.), *The interpretive turn* (pp. 155-178). Ithaca, NY: Cornell University Press.

Kerdeman, D. (1998). Hermeneutics and education: Understanding, control, and agency. *Educational Theory, 48,* 241-266.

Lather, P. (1993). Fertile obsession: Validity after poststructuralism. *Sociological Quarterly, 34,* 673-693.

Longino, H. (1990). *Science as social knowledge.* Princeton, NJ: Princeton University Press.

Longino, H. (1993a). Essential tensions—phase two: Feminist, philosophical, and social studies of science. In L. M. Antony & C. Witt (Eds.), *A mind of one's own: Feminist essays on reason and objectivity* (pp. 257-272). Boulder, CO: Westview.

Longino, H. (1993b). Subjects, power, and knowledge: Description and prescription in feminist philosophies of science. In L. Alcoff & E. Potter (Eds.), *Feminist epistemologies* (pp. 101-120). New York: Routledge.

Longino, H. (1996). Cognitive and non-cognitive values in science: Rethinking the dichotomy. In L. H. Nelson & J. Nelson (Eds.), *Feminism, science, and the philosophy of science* (pp. 39-58). Dordrecht, Netherlands: Kluwer.

Madison, G. B. (1991). Beyond seriousness and frivolity: A Gadamerian response to deconstruction. In H. Silverman (Ed.), *Gadamer and hermeneutics* (pp. 119-134). New York: Routledge.

Nietzsche, F. (1979). *The complete works of Friedrich Nietzsche* (O. Levy, Ed.). New York: Russell & Russell.

Nussbaum, M. C. (1990). *Love's knowledge: Essays on philosophy and literature.* New York: Oxford University Press.

Outhwaite, W. (1975). *Understanding social life: The method called Verstehen.* London: George Allen & Unwin.

Phillips, D. C. (1995). The good, the bad, and the ugly: The many faces of constructivism. *Educational Researcher, 24*(7), 5-12.

Phillips, D. C. (1997a). Coming to grips with radical social constructivism. *Science and Education, 6,* 85-104.

Phillips, D. C. (1997b). How, why, what, when, and where: Perspectives on constructivism in psychology and education. *Issues in Education, 3*(2), 151-194.

Potter, J. (1996). *Representing reality: Discourse, rhetoric and social construction.* London: Sage.

Prus, R. (1996). *Symbolic interaction and ethnographic research.* Albany: State University of New York Press.

Rabinow, P., & Sullivan, W. M. (Eds.). (1979). *Interpretive social science: A reader.* Berkeley: University of California Press.

Richardson, L. (1997). *Fields of play: Constructing an academic life.* New Brunswick, NJ: Rutgers University Press.

Ricoeur, P. (1981). The model of the text: Meaningful action considered as text. In P. Ricoeur, *Hermeneutics and the human sciences* (J. B. Thompson, Ed. & Trans.). Cambridge: Cambridge University Press.

Rouse, J. (1991). Interpretation in natural and human science. In D. R. Hiley, J. F. Bohman, & R. Shusterman (Eds.), *The interpretive turn* (pp. 42-57). Ithaca, NY: Cornell University Press.

Rouse, J. (1996). Feminism and the social construction of scientific knowledge. In L. H. Nelson & J. Nelson (Eds.), *Feminism, science, and the philosophy of science* (pp. 195-215). Dordrecht, Netherlands: Kluwer.

Schutz, A. (1962). *Collected papers* (Vol. 1; M. Natanson, Ed.). The Hague: Martinus Nijhoff.

Schutz, A. (1967). *The phenomenology of the social world* (G. Walsh & F. Lehnert, Trans.). Evanston, IL: Northwestern University Press.

Schwandt, T. A. (1996). Farewell to criteriology. *Qualitative Inquiry, 2,* 58-72.

Schwandt, T. A. (1997). Evaluation as practical hermeneutics. *Evaluation, 3,* 69-83.

Shapiro, M. J. (1981). *Language and political understanding.* New Haven, CT: Yale University Press.

Shea, C. (1998, September 11). Tribal skirmishes in anthropology. *Chronicle of Higher Education,* pp. A17, A20.

Shusterman, R. (1991). Beneath interpretation. In D. R. Hiley, J. F. Bohman, & R. Shusterman (Eds.), *The interpretive turn* (pp. 102-128). Ithaca, NY: Cornell University Press.

Smith, D. (1996). Telling the truth after postmodernism. *Symbolic Interaction, 19,* 171-202.

Smith, N. H. (1997). *Strong hermeneutics: Contingency and moral identity.* New York: Routledge.

Smith, P. C. (1991). Plato as an impulse and obstacle in Gadamer's development of a hermeneutical theory. In H. Silverman (Ed.),

Gadamer and hermeneutics (pp. 23-41). New York: Routledge.

Taylor, C. (1985a). *Philosophical papers: Vol. 1. Human agency and language.* Cambridge: Cambridge University Press.

Taylor, C. (1985b). *Philosophical papers: Vol. 2. Philosophy and the human sciences.* Cambridge: Cambridge University Press.

Taylor, C. (1987). Overcoming epistemology. In K. Baynes, J. Bohman, & T. McCarthy (Eds.), *After philosophy: End or transformation?* (pp. 464-488). Cambridge: MIT Press.

Taylor, C. (1988). Wittgenstein, empiricism, and the question of the "inner": Commentary on Kenneth Gergen. In S. Messer, L. A. Sass, & R. L. Woolfolk (Eds.), *Hermeneutics and psychological theory* (pp. 52-58). New Brunswick, NJ: Rutgers University Press.

Taylor, C. (1989). *Sources of the self: The making of the modern identity.* Cambridge: Cambridge University Press.

Taylor, C. (1991). The dialogical self. In D. R. Hiley, J. F. Bohman, & R. Shusterman (Eds.), *The interpretive turn* (pp. 304-314). Ithaca, NY: Cornell University Press.

Taylor, C. (1995). *Philosophical arguments.* Cambridge, MA: Harvard University Press.

Thompson, A. (1997). Surrogate family values: The refeminization of teaching. *Educational Theory, 47,* 315-339.

Tully, J. (Ed.). (1994). *Philosophy in an age of pluralism.* Cambridge: Cambridge University Press.

Van Eemeren, F. H., Grootendorst, R., Blair, J. A., & Willard, C. A. (Eds.). (1987). *Argumentation: Across the lines of discipline* (Proceedings of the 1986 Conference on Argumentation). Dordrecht, Netherlands: Foris.

Vetlesen, A. J. (1997). Introducing an ethics of proximity. In H. Jodalen & A. J. Vetlesen (Eds.), *Closeness: An ethics* (pp. 1-19). Oslo: Scandinavian University Press.

Walton, D. (1989). *Informal logic: A handbook for critical argumentation.* Cambridge: Cambridge University Press.

Weber, M. (1949). *The methodology of the social sciences* (E. A. Shils & H. A. Finch, Trans.). Glencoe, IL: Free Press.

Winch, P. (1958). *The idea of a social science.* London: Routledge & Kegan Paul.

8

FEMINISMS AND QUALITATIVE RESEARCH AT AND INTO THE MILLENNIUM

♦ Virginia L. Olesen

At the approach of the new millennium, feminist qualitative research is highly diversified, enormously dynamic, and thoroughly challenging to its practitioners, its followers, and its critics. Competing models of thought jostle, divergent methodological and analytic approaches compete, once-clear theoretical differences (Fee, 1983) blur. Debates over the efficacy of such work abound. Feminist qualitative research is variegated and emergent, characteristics that I will explore in this chapter.

This chapter has its origins in an early feminist declaration I wrote for a 1975 conference on women's health, in which I argued that "rage is not enough" and called for incisive scholarship to frame, direct, and harness passion in the interests of redressing grievous problems in

many areas of women's health (Olesen, 1975, pp. 1-2). As a symbolic interactionist working primarily within the interactionist-social constructionist tradition (Denzin, 1992, pp. 1-21), I am sympathetic with deconstructive currents in interactionism and feminism that encourage provocative and productive unpacking of taken-for-granted ideas about women in specific material, historical, and cultural contexts. This avoids a "fatal unclutteredness" (Mukherjee, 1994, p. 6). I believe that research for rather than merely about women is possible through theoretical essays and a variety of qualitative modes using combinations of both experimental and text-oriented styles. Feminist work sets the stage for other research, other actions, and policy that transcend and transform (Olesen,

AUTHOR'S NOTE: Incisive criticisms from Norman Denzin, Yvonna Lincoln, Patricia Clough, Michelle Fine, and Meaghan Morris and continuing intellectual dialogue with Adele Clarke added to the quality of this chapter. I'm grateful to them all.

1993). For me, feminist inquiry is dialectical, with different views fusing to produce new syntheses that in turn become the grounds for further research, praxis, and policy (Nielsen, 1990b, p. 29; Westkott, 1979, p. 430).[1]

I will locate this exploration in changing currents of feminist thought (Benhabib, Butler, Cornell, & Fraser, 1995; Tong, 1989) and altering and sometimes controversial themes within qualitative research (Denzin, 1997; Gubrium & Holstein, 1997; Gupta & Ferguson, 1997; Miller & Dingwall, 1997; Scheurich, 1997). To position feminist qualitative research thus does not say it is merely a passive recipient of transitory intellectual themes and controversies. To the contrary, it has had influence, even if sometimes irksome in some people's views, on many aspects of qualitative research (Charmaz & Olesen, 1997; DeVault, 1996; Smith, 1996; Stacey & Thorne, 1996; Taylor, 1998).

Feminisms partake of different theoretical and pragmatic orientations and reflect national contexts among which feminist agendas differ widely. (For an analysis of this in psychology, see Morawski, 1997.) Nevertheless, without in any way positing a global, homogeneous, unified feminism, qualitative feminist research in its many variants, whether or not self-consciously defined as feminist, centers and makes problematic women's diverse situations as well as the institutions that frame those situations. It can refer the examination of that problematic to theoretical, policy, or action frameworks to realize social justice for women in specific contexts (Eichler, 1986, p. 68; 1997, pp. 12-13), or it can present new ideas generated in the research for destabilizing knowledges about oppressive situations for women, or for action or further research (Olesen & Clarke, 1999).[2] Many issues to be reviewed here have also been foregrounded in critical race studies and critical legal studies—for instance, Patricia Williams's (1991) application of literary theory to analysis of legal discourse to reveal the intersubjectivity of legal constructions and Mari Matsuda's (1996) interrogation of race, gender, and the law.

To provide some background, I will briefly outline the scope and types of feminist qualitative research, recognizing that this is only a partial glimpse of a substantial literature in many disciplines. This will lay the groundwork for a discussion of emergent complexities in feminist qualitative work and set the stage for a review of issues that feminist scholars currently debate. These include the obdurate worries (for some) of bias and believability, objectivity and subjectivity, and the demands (for others) posed by new experimental approaches in the realm of representation, voice, text, and ethical issues. I close the chapter with some questions about accomplishments of, shortfalls in, and the future of feminist qualitative research at the outset of the millennium.

It is well to remember that feminist research is highly diverse—experimental work with new complexities engages numerous investigators at the same time that many others remain oriented to views of gendered universals and more traditional approaches. Moreover, even within the same wings of feminist research (experimental or traditional) there are disagreements on issues ranging from treatment of voices to how to prepare research for policy use.

◆ Scope and Topics of Feminist Qualitative Research

Some (including feminists in an early period) may have assumed that qualitative research is most useful for and therefore limited to inquiries into subjective or interpersonal realms wherever found. This reflects early feminist interests in women's subjectivity as well as the erroneous assumption that qualitative research cannot handle large-scale issues. Feminist work has gone far beyond these limited views using a wide range of methods (see Reinharz, 1992, for descriptions of these) and for reasons found in new intellectual themes to be discussed shortly. Extensive feminist work in many disciplines ranges from assessments of women's lives and experiences that foreground the subjective to analyses of relationships through investigation of social movements and large-scale issues of policy and organization. (On qualitative feminist research on social movements, see Taylor, 1998; Taylor & Whittier, 1998, 1999.)

It is well-nigh impossible to cite even part of this work in these brief pages, but feminist qualitative research in two fields, education and health, merits mention. Within the educational realm, studies range widely, from Sandra Acker's (1994) acute observations of classroom experiences to Deborah Britzman's (1991) poststructuralist analysis of the "socialization" of student teachers, Diane Reay's (1998) research on social class in mothers' involvement in their children's schooling, Susan Chase's (1995) narrative analysis of women school superintendents struggling with inhibiting structures, and a study of how women "become gentlemen" in law school (Guinier, Fine, & Balin, 1997).

In the field of health and healing, Lora Bex Lempert's (1994) research links accounts of battered women's experiences to constructions of battering and structural issues. Lempert's clearly subjective approach contrasts with Dorothy Broom's (1991) account of how the emergence of state-sponsored women's health clinics in Australia created contradictions with feminist principles that feminists had to handle as they worked within the health care system.[3]

The arena of policy analysis, being largely quantitative and male dominated, has not been a receptive locus for feminist qualitative research whatever the field, and much remains to be done in two general areas: (a) the substance, construction, and emergence of specific policy issues; and (b) processes through which policy is accomplished.[4] However, there has been some noteworthy qualitative research on construction of policy issues for women: Through content analysis of scientific and lay publications, Patricia Kaufert and Sonja McKinlay (1985) have shown different concerns of clinicians, medical researchers, and feminists about estrogen replacement therapy. Accomplishing policy is a complex topic that feminists have scrutinized at a number of levels. In her theoretical critique of Barbara Ehrenreich and Frances Fox Piven's (1983) positive view of the state for women, Wendy Brown (1992) argues that they do not recognize issues of control. Rosalind

Petchesky's (1985) analysis reveals how women's health is framed in the abortion debate. Nancy Fraser's (1989) discourse analysis of women's needs and the state raises questions of emancipatory or controlling definitions. Theresa Montini's (1997) research on the breast cancer informed consent movement found that physicians deflected activists away from the policy goals the activists wanted.

Adele Clarke (1998) has called these latter studies "meso analysis," which refers to how societal and institutional forces mesh with human activity (Maines, 1982). Clarke's own feminist sociohistorical analysis shows how these processes play out around such issues as production of contraceptives. Such studies elevate the question of research for women to an important critique of contemporary and historically male-dominated science and policy making and control, not just of women but also of the policy processes. Linda Gordon's (1994) sociohistorical analysis of welfare mothers, which shows how outmoded ideas about women's place carry into new eras and misplaced policies, is a prime example of work in this category.

◆ Emergent Complexities

If any attribute could be said to characterize qualitative feminist research since the 1960s and the start of the so-called second phase (at least in the United States) of the women's movement, it would be increasing complexity in the feminist research enterprise: the nature of research, the definition of and relationship with those with whom research is done, the characteristics and location of the researcher, and the very creation and presentation of knowledges created in the research. And, indeed, if there is a dominant theme in this growing complexity, it is the question of knowledges. Whose knowledges? Where and how obtained and by whom, from whom, and for what purposes? As Liz Stanley and Sue Wise (1990) reflect, "Succinctly, feminist theorists have moved away from 'the reactive' stance of the feminist critiques of social science and into

TABLE 8.1   The Growing Complexity of Feminist Qualitative Research and Representative Texts

Strands in emergent complexities

Writings by women of color	Anzaldúa (1990), Collins (1986), Davis (1981), Dill (1979), Garcia (1989), Green (1990), hooks (1990), Hurtado (1989), Zavella (1987)
Problematizing unremitting whiteness	Frankenberg (1993), Hurtado and Stewart (1997)
Postcolonial feminist thought	Alexander and Mohanty (1997), Heng (1997), Mohanty (1988), Spivak (1988), Trinh (1989, 1992)
Lesbian research and queer theory	Anzaldúa (1990), Butler (1993), Kennedy and Davis (1993), Krieger (1983), Lewin (1993), Stevens and Hall (1991), Terry (1994), Weston (1991)
Disabled women	Asch and Fine (1992)
Standpoint theory	Collins (1990), Haraway (1991), Harding (1987), Hartsock (1983), Smith (1987)
Postmodern and deconstructive theory	Clough (1998), Collins (1998b), Flax (1987), Haraway (1991, 1997), Hekman (1990b), Nicholson (1990)

Consequences of complexity

Problematizing research and participant	Behar (1993), Ellis (1995), Frankenberg and Mani (1993), Lather and Smithies (1997), Lincoln (1993, 1997), Reay (1996a)
Destabilizing insider-outsider	Kondo (1990), Lewin (1993), Naples (1996), Narayan (1997a), Ong (1995), Weston (1996), Zavella (1996)
Deconstructing traditional concepts	
Experience	O'Leary (1997), Scott (1991)
Difference	Felski (1997), hooks (1990)
Gender	Butler (1990, 1993), Lorber (1994), West and Zimmerman (1987)

Newly framed issues

"Bias" and objectivity	Fine (1992a), Haraway (1997), Harding (1996, 1998), Holland and Ramazanoglu (1994), Phoenix (1994), Scheper-Hughes (1992)
"Validity" and trustworthiness	Lather (1993), Manning (1997), Richardson (1993)
Participants' voices	Fine (1992a), Kincheloe (1997), Lincoln (1993, 1997), Mascia-Lees et al. (1989), Opie (1992), Reay (1996), Ribbens and Edwards (1998)

TABLE 8.1	Continued
Presenting the account	Behar and Gordon (1995), Ellis (1995), Kondo (1995), Lather and Smithies (1997), McWilliam (1997), Richardson (1997)
Research ethics	Finch (1984), Fine and Weis (1996), Lincoln (1995), Reay (1996), Ribbens and Edwards (1998), Stacey (1988), D. L. Wolf (1996a)

the realms of exploring what 'feminist knowledge' could look like" (p. 37). This undergirds influential feminist writing such as Lorraine Code's (1991) question, "Who can know?" (p. ix), Donna Haraway's (1991) conceptualization of situated knowledges, Dorothy Smith's (1987) articulation of the everyday world as problematic, and a host of texts on feminist qualitative methods and methodology (Behar, 1996; Behar & Gordon, 1995; Butler, 1986; DeVault, 1999a; Fine, 1992a; Fonow & Cook, 1991; Hekman, 1990b; Lather, 1991; Lewin & Leap, 1996; Maynard & Purvis, 1994; Morawski, 1994; Nielsen, 1990a; Ribbens & Edwards, 1998; Roberts, 1981; Stanley, 1990; Stanley & Wise, 1983; Tom, 1989; Visweswaran, 1994; D. L. Wolf, 1996a). (For an exchange on the politics of feminist knowledge, see Hawkesworth, 1989, 1990a, 1990b; Hekman, 1990a; Shogan, 1990.)

This growing emphasis departed from two important themes of the early years of feminist research. First, Catharine MacKinnon's (1982, p. 353; 1983) assertion that "consciousness-raising" is the basis of feminist methodology gave way as more structural stances were foregrounded. Recognition that there are multiple knowledges grew, a point dramatically made by Patricia Hill Collins (1990) in her explication of black feminist thought, an influential work that— with the writings of Angela Davis (1981), Bonnie Thornton Dill (1979), Effie Chow (1987), bell hooks (1990), Rayna Green (1990), and Gloria Anzaldúa (1987,

1990)—began to dissolve an unremitting whiteness in feminist research. Further, awareness emerged that women are located structurally and in changing organizational and personal contexts that intertwine with subjective assessment to produce knowledge, as Sheryl Ruzek (1978) had earlier demonstrated in her analysis of the women's health movement. Second, important observations about women missing and invisible in certain arenas of social life, such as Judith Lorber's (1975) research on women and medicine and Cynthia Epstein's (1981) work on women in law, led to more complex analyses, such as Darlene Clark Hine's (1989) exploration of the structural, interactional, and knowledge-producing elements in the exclusion of and treatment of African American women in American nursing.

Parallel to these developments were research projects that initially conceptualized women as ubiquitous and invisible workers in the domestic sphere (Abel & Nelson, 1990; Finch & Groves, 1983; Graham, 1984, 1985; Nelson, 1990). Later, through Evelyn Nakano Glenn's (1990) work on Japanese domestic workers, Judith Rollins's (1985) participant observation study of doing housecleaning, and Mary Romero's (1992) interview study of Latina domestic workers, the race, class, and gender issues in domestic service and household work and concomitant contexts of knowledge, seemingly banal but ultimately critical to everyday life, were laid bare. Other work, such as Marjorie DeVault's (1991) research on domestic food preparation, Anne Murcott's (1993) analysis of conceptions of food, and Arlie Hochschild's (1989) findings that household labor is embedded in the political economy of household emotions, further demonstrated the dynamics of knowledge production within gendered relationships in the domestic sphere.

Thus the emergent complexities moved feminist research from justly deserved criticisms of academic disciplines (Stacey & Thorne, 1985, 1996) and social institutions, and of the lack of or flawed attention to women's lives and experiences, to debate and discussion of critical epistemological issues.[5] Paramount among these has been a growing recognition of the differentiation of persons with whom the research is done, the concomitant fading of the concept of a universalized "woman" or "women," and concerns about the researchers' own characteristics. Major strands within contemporary feminist research have fueled these growing and now mostly accepted awarenesses.

◆ Strands Contributing to Growing Complexities

Writing by Women of Color

Beyond the eye-opening work cited earlier in these pages, other work by women of color significantly shaped the new understandings that displaced taken-for-granted views of women of color and revealed the extent to which whiteness can be a factor in creating "otherness"—Asianness in Britain, for example (Puar, 1996). Aside from the critical task of differentiation, writings by Patricia Hill Collins (1986) and Aida Hurtado (1989) moved feminist research to greater recognition of the interplay of race, class, and gender in shaping women's oppression, as did empirical investigations by researchers such as Patricia Zavella (1987) on Mexican American cannery workers and Elaine Bell Kaplan (1997) in her myth-breaking study of black teenage mothers. At the same time these research projects, done in traditional qualitative style, were taking understanding of the lives of

women of color in the United States to new levels, Gloria Anzaldúa's (1987) experimental writing and work injected the conceptualization of borders and crossing borders and fluidities in women's lives—familial, national, sexual, international—adding further dimensions and complexities. Recognition of the importance of borders and fluidities, albeit in a very different form, has emerged in the work of feminist researchers concerned with women and immigration (Espin, 1995; Hondagneu-Sotelo, 1992). In spite of this work, feminist scholars Vanessa Bing and P. T. Reid (1996) warn against misapplication of white feminist knowledge, a warning echoed by legal scholar Kimberly Crenshaw (1992) in her discussion of white feminists' appropriation of the 1991 Clarence Thomas hearings.

Parallel to these developments have been critical investigations that problematize not only the construction of women of color in relationship to whiteness but whiteness itself. Ruth Frankenberg's (1993) interview study shifts that category from a privileged, unnamed taken-for-grantedness in research to a questionable issue that must be raised in thinking about all participants in the research process. Noting that "whiteness" is the "natural" state of affairs, Aida Hurtado and Abigail J. Stewart (1997, pp. 309-310) call for studies of whiteness from the standpoint of people of color to find what they call a critical, counterhegemonic presence in the research (see also Wyche & Crosby, 1996). These writings are not simple reminders of diversity among women. They emphasize that multiple identities (and subjectivities) are tentatively constructed in particular historical epochs and social contexts (Ferguson, 1993).

Postcolonial Feminist Thought

If the criticisms of an unremitting whiteness in feminist research in Western industrialized societies began to unsettle feminist research frames, powerful and sophisticated research and feminist thought from postcolonial theorists further shifted the very grounds of feminist research with regard to "woman" and "women" and, indeed, the very definitions of feminism itself. Feminism, they argued, takes many different forms depending on the context of contemporary nationalism (Alexander & Mohanty, 1997; Heng, 1997). Concerned about the invidious effects of "othering" (applying oppressive definitions to the persons with whom research is done), they argued that Western feminist models were inappropriate for thinking of research with women in postcolonial sites (Kirby, 1991, p. 398; see also Mascia-Lees, Sharpe, & Cohen, 1991). Questions such as Gayatri Chakravorti Spivak's (1988) cutting query as to whether subordinates can speak or are forever silenced by virtue of representation within elite thought, a question also raised by Chandra Mohanty (1988), arose. But beyond these issues, they raised questions about whether Third World women or indeed all women could be conceptualized as unified subjectivities easily located in the category of woman. Drawing on her expertise as a filmmaker, Trinh T. Minh-ha (1989, 1992) articulated a fluid framing of woman as other (and not other) and undermined the very doing of ethnographic research by undercutting the concept of woman, the assumptions of subjectivity and objectivity, and the utility of the interview. This literature also pointed to issues in globalization, such as unsafe and exploitative working conditions in offshore manufacturing and the international sex trade, as topics for feminist research.

Lesbian Research

In research that quickly laid to rest Stanley and Wise's (1990, pp. 29-34) criticism that little attention had been paid to lesbians, feminist scholars upended theoretical and research frames saturated with stigma that had essentially rendered lesbians invisible or, where visible, despicable. The new scholarship, such as Susan Krieger's (1983) ethnography of a lesbian community, Patricia Stevens and Joanne Hall's (1991) historical analysis of how medicine has invidiously defined lesbianism, Kath Weston's (1991) study of lesbian familial relationships, Ellen Lewin's (1993) research on lesbian mothers (which shows the surpassing im-

portance of the maternal rather the sexual identity), and Jennifer Terry's (1994) writing on theorizing "deviant" historiography, dissolved a homogeneous view of lesbians. Historical research such as Elizabeth Kennedy and Madeleine Davis's (1993) account of the Buffalo, New York, lesbian community, Gloria Anzaldúa's work noted earlier, and Ellen Lewin's (1996b) edited collection of cultural analyses of lesbian communities further differentiated these views by revealing race and class issues within lesbian circles and the multiple bases of lesbian identity.

The very meaning of gender also came in for incisive critical review by Judith Butler (1990, 1993), whose philosophical analysis for some feminists evoked themes in an earlier sociological statement by Candace West and Don Zimmerman (1987). In both cases, but for different theoretical reasons, these scholars pointed to sexual identity as performative rather than given or socially ascribed and thus undercut a dualistic conception of gender that had informed feminist thought for decades.

The emergence of the term *queer theory,* referring to those gay men and women who refuse assimilation into either gay culture or oppressive heterosexual culture, has been loosely used as a cover term for gay and lesbian studies, but it also refers to a more precise political stance (Lewin, 1996a, pp. 6-9). Ellen Lewin's (1998) research on gay and lesbian marriages shows how those ceremonies simultaneously reflect accommodation and subversion. This stance of resistance carries conceptual implications that bear directly on feminist research and that requires recognition of the complex contributions of race and class (Butler, 1994) to diverse expressions of identity(ies), always in formation and always labile.

Disabled Women

Recognition of differences among women also emerged with the disability rights movement and publication by feminist women who were themselves disabled. "Socially devalued, excluded from the playing field as women and invisible" (Gill, 1997, p. 96), disabled women were essentially depersonalized and degendered, sometimes even, regrettably, within feminist circles

(Lubelska & Mathews, 1997, p. 135). Carol Gill (1997) recalled that a prominent Canadian feminist, Bonnie Klein, was treated as an outsider at feminist gatherings after she suffered a disabling stroke (p. 97). She also noted that disabled women are regarded as not capable of or interested in having children, and hence are not part of reproductive health agendas (p. 102). Asch and Fine (1992), reviewing the emergence of disabled women as a problematic issue for feminists, pointed out that even sympathetic research on women with disabilities tended to view them solely in terms of their disabilities and to overlook disabled women as workers, lovers, mothers, friends, sportswomen, and activists.

Standpoint Research

Building on a loosely related set of theoretical positions by feminist scholars from several disciplines, standpoint research (and much of that noted earlier can be so categorized) took up the feminist criticism of the absence of women from or marginalized women in research accounts and foregrounded women's knowledge as emergent from women's situated experiences (Harding, 1987, p. 184). Aptly summarized by Donna Haraway (1997), whose influential work in history of science has been foundational and influential for standpoint thinking, "standpoints are cognitive-emotional-political achievements, crafted out of located social-historical-bodily experience—itself always constituted through fraught, noninnocent, discursive, material, collective practices" (p. 304, n. 32).[6] In the work of sociologist Dorothy Smith, sociologist Patricia Hill Collins, political scientist Nancy Hartsock, and philosopher Sandra Harding, the concept of essentialized, universalized woman disappeared in the lens of standpoint thinking to reappear as a situated woman with experiences and knowledge specific to her in the material division of labor and the racial stratification system. This carries with it the view that all knowledge claims are socially located and that some social locations, especially those at the bottom of social and economic hierarchies, are better than others as starting points for seeking knowledge not only about those particular women but others as well.

(This does *not* assume that the researcher's own life or group is the best starting point, nor does it assert the relativist position that all social locations are equally valuable for knowledge projects.)

Although they have been grouped under the rubric of *standpoint,* standpoint theorists are by no means identical, and in their differing versions they offer divergent approaches for qualitative researchers (Harding, 1997, p. 389). It is worthwhile, therefore, to discuss these theorists here, while recognizing the inevitable violence done to subtle thought in such a necessarily brief review.

Dorothy Smith focuses on women's standpoint and conceptualizes the everyday world as a problematic, that is, continually created, shaped, and known by women within it and its organization, which is shaped by external material factors or textually mediated relations (see Smith, 1987, p. 91). Thus the "everyday everynight activities" of women's lives are at the center. To understand that world, the researcher must not objectify the woman as would traditionally be done in sociology, which divides subject and object, researcher and participant. The researcher must be able to "work very differently than she is able to do with established sociological strategies of thinking and inquiry" (Smith, 1992, p. 96) that are not outside the relations of ruling. This requires a high degree of reflexivity from the researcher and a recognition of how feminist sociologists "participate as subjects in the relations of ruling" (p. 96). Smith's own work with Alison Griffith on mothers' work with children's schooling discloses how she and her colleague found in their own discussions the effects of the North American discourse on mothering of the 1920s and 1930s (Griffith & Smith, 1987; see also Smith, 1992, p. 97). A number of researchers have begun self-consciously and with awareness of one another's work to develop and use Smith's ideas of institutional ethnography (Campbell & Manicom, 1995) to discover how textually mediated relationships occur and are sustained in institutional settings, thus knitting an important link between the classic problem of micro and macro issues (Smith, 1990b, p. 10). (For criticisms of Smith, see Collins, 1992; Connell, 1992.)

Patricia Hill Collins's (1990) articulation of black women's standpoint is grounded in black women's material circumstances and political situation. Methodologically, this requires "an alternative epistemology whose 'criteria for substantiated knowledge' and 'methodological adequacy' will be compatible with the experiences and consciousness of Black women" (O'Leary, 1997, p. 62). Collins's writings and those of bell hooks (1984, 1990) shifted feminist thinking and research in the direction of more particularized knowledge and away from any sense of the universal. Collins (1998a) refuses to abandon situated standpoints and articulates a framework for black feminist thought in which she links the standpoint of black women with intersectionality, "the ability of social phenomena, race, class, and gender to mutually construct one another" (p. 205), but *always* within keen consideration for power and structural relations (pp. 201-228). This substantially amplifies standpoint theory. Thinking through this complexity is, as Collins recognizes, a "daunting task" (p. 225), and doing qualitative research within such a frame is equally daunting. Nevertheless, embracing new understandings of social complexity—and the locales of power relationships—is vital to the task of developing black feminist thought as critical social theory and new forms of visionary pragmatism (p. 228).

Sandra Harding, a philosopher, early recognized three types of feminist inquiry, which she termed "transitional epistemologies" (see Harding, 1987, p. 186). In keeping with Harding's concerns about modernity and science in general and science questions in feminism, these types are predicated on how those modes of inquiry relate to traditional science and the problem of objectivity:

1. *Feminist empiricism*, which is of two types: (a) "spontaneous feminist empiricism" (rigorous adherence to existing research norms and standards) and (b) following Helen Longino (1990), "contextual empiricism" (recognition of the influence of social values and interests in science; Harding, 1993, p. 53)

2. *Standpoint theory*, which "claims that all knowledge attempts are socially situated and that some of these objective social locations are better than others for knowledge projects" (Harding, 1993, p. 56; 1998, p. 163).

3. *Postmodern theories*, which void the possibility of a feminist science in favor of the many and multiple stories women tell about the knowledge they have (Harding, 1987, p. 188)

These are still useful ways to look at different styles of feminist qualitative work, but many projects display elements of several or all three as feminist researchers creatively borrow and innovate from multiple styles in their search "to escape damaging limitations of the dominant social relations and their schemes" (Harding, 1990, p. 101).

At issue here is the very form of science and whether "all possible science and epistemology . . . must be containable within modern, androcentric, Western, bourgeois forms" (Harding, 1990, p. 99). Harding argues that other forms of science are quite possible and likely. Her concerns with feminist research as a scientific activity and the attempt to generate "less false stories" prompted her to reject reliance on processes strictly governed by methodological rules and to argue that researchers should examine critically their own personal and historical commitments with which they construct their work (Harding, 1993, pp. 70-71). She points to the critical difference between sociological, cultural, and historical relativism (listening carefully to others' views) and judgmental relativism (abandoning any claims for adjudicating between different systems of beliefs and their social origins). Her solution is a posture of "strong objectivity" (Harding, 1991).[7] Strong objectivity contrasts sharply with value-free objectivity and posits the interplay of the researcher and participant. I discuss her contribution on "strong objectivity" in greater detail later in this chapter.

Nancy Hartsock's Marxist formulation of standpoint theory holds that women's circumstances in the material order provide them with experiences that generate particular and privileged knowledge that reflects both oppression and women's resistance (see Hartsock, 1983, 1985, 1998). Like the lives of the proletariat in Marxist theory, their knowledges provide an opening for a criticism of domination and for political action (Hartsock, 1997b, p. 98). This does not assume that such knowledge is innately essential, or that all women have the same experiences or indeed the same knowledge. Rather, in her recent formulations, Hartsock (1990) articulates the possibility of a "concrete multiplicity" of perspectives (p. 171). Each of these constitutes a different world, and each represents differential influence of power, a consideration that distinguishes standpoint theory from feminist empiricism (Hundleby, 1997, p. 41). Such knowledge is not merely individual, but derives from "interaction of people and groups with each other" and is always transitional (Hundleby, 1997, p. 36). As Hartsock (1997a) has observed, "The subjects who matter are not individual subjects, but collective subjects, or groups" (p. 371).

Standpoint theories and their implications for feminist qualitative research have not gone uncriticized. Some have fretted that standpoint theories contain risks of relativism (Harding, 1987, p. 187), are overly simplistic (Hawkesworth, 1989, p. 347), and raise issues around validity (Ramazanoglu, 1989). Criticisms have arisen about the potential for essentialism (Campbell, 1994; Lemert, 1992, p. 69), neglect of traditions of knowledge among women of color (Collins, 1992, p. 77), problems of evaluating accounts from different perspectives (Hekman, 1997b, p. 355; Longino, 1993, p. 104; Maynard, 1994b; Welton, 1997, p. 21), questions about understanding fragmented identities (Lemert, 1992, p. 68), and the potentially untenable use of experience as a basis for investigation if it is continually mediated and constructed from unconscious desire (Clough, 1993a). Others have argued that queer theory, with its destabilizing elements, undercuts the possibility for standpoint thinking, which, in this view, presumes the replication of heterosexual categories (Clough, 1994, p. 144).

For their part, standpoint theorists have not been silent. Dorothy Smith's (1993) robust ex-

change with Patricia Clough (1993a, p. 169; 1993b) highlights the centrality of experience, the place of desire, and the primacy of text. In this exchange, Clough argues that Smith has not gone far enough in deconstructing sociology as a dominant discourse of experience, a point Smith rejects, claiming that Clough's view is overly oriented to text and neglects experience. Susan Hekman's (1997a, 1997b) critical review of standpoint theory addresses questions of whether women's knowledge is privileged and how truth claims can be settled. Responses from Smith (1997), Patricia Hill Collins (1997), Nancy Hartsock (1997a), and Sandra Harding (1997) show clearly that standpoint theories have been and are continually being revised (see Harding, 1997, p. 389). Feminist qualitative researchers thinking of using standpoint theories in their work must read these theorists carefully and in their latest versions if they are to avoid misinterpretation and if they are to explore new connections between standpoint theories and postmodernism (Hirschmann, 1997). Indeed, Sandra Harding (1996) has observed that "poststructural approaches have been especially helpful in enabling standpoint theories systematically to examine critically pluralities of power relations, of the sort indicated in the earlier discussion of gender as shaped by class, race and other historical cultural forces and how these are disseminated through 'discourses' that are both structural and symbolic" (p. 451). Patricia Hill Collins (1998b), while warning about the corrosive effects of postmodern and deconstructive thought for black women's group authority and hence social action, also points to postmodernism's powerful analytic tools as useful in challenging not only dominant discourses, but the very rules of the game (pp. 143, 154).[8]

Postmodern and Deconstructive Thought

Complexities would probably have emerged in feminist qualitative research thanks to any of the themes discussed here, but the multiple and seductive intellectual sources of postmodern and deconstructive thought sharpened and enhanced the emerging complexities.[9] Indeed, in varying degrees postmodernism and deconstructionism are present in many of the themes noted above, sometimes constituting the central stance (as in Judith Butler or Trinh T. Minh-ha's analyses), sometimes anticipating future complexities (as in Frankenberg's deconstruction of whiteness), and sometimes reflecting trends and themes firmly set out by feminists not oriented to these modes of thought (as in Collins's analysis of black feminist thought or Lewin's research on lesbian cultures).

Concerned with the difficulties of ever producing more than a partial story of women's lives in oppressive contexts, postmodern feminists regard "truth" as a destructive illusion. Their view of the world is of a series of stories or texts that sustain the integration of power and oppression and actually "constitute us as subjects in a determinant order" (Hawkesworth, 1989, p. 349). These themes have emerged among feminist researchers working in anthropology, sociology, history, political science, cultural studies, and social studies of science as well as experimental wings in educational and nursing research (see the Australian journal *Nursing Inquiry*).

Carrying the imprint of feminist forebears from deconstruction and postmodernism (French feminists such as Irigaray and Cixous, and Foucault, Deleuze, Lyotard, and Baudrillard), feminist research in cultural studies stresses representation and text. This area is particularly complex for feminist researchers because some scholars also utilize Marxist theory from Althusser, French feminist theory, literary criticism (Abel, Christian, & Moglen, 1997), historical analysis, and psychoanalytic views (Lacan—though by no means do all feminists agree on Lacan's utility for feminist research; see Ferguson, 1993, p. 212, n. 3). In contrast to classical Marxist feminist studies of women, work, and social class, such as Karen Sacks's (1988) investigation of hospital workers and Nona Glazer's (1991) analysis of race and class issues in the profession of nursing, materialist feminist research in an Althusserian mode looks at ideology and its place in the shaping of subjectivity, desire, and authority (Clough, 1994, p. 75). Here enters the elusive question of how desire is expressed in or inferred from cultural products ranging from ethnographic accounts through films to confront the feminist qualitative researcher with difficult questions that go far beyond the easy recognition of intersubjectivity and invoke deeper cultural forms and questions.[10] (For a feminist materialist analysis of narrative, see Roman, 1992.)

These inquiries typically take the form of the analysis of cultural objects (such as films) and their meanings (Balsamo, 1993; Clough, in press; de Lauretis, 1987; Denzin, 1992, p. 80; Morris, 1988) or the analysis of places and contexts (Morris, 1998). This includes textual analysis of these objects and the discourses surrounding them, and the "study of lived cultures and experiences which are shaped by the cultural meanings that circulate in everyday life" (Denzin, 1992, p. 81). This anticipates Valerie Walkerdine's (1995) important call for the analysis of understanding the media as the site of production of subjectivity.

Here will be found the voluminous and growing feminist work in gender and science, wherein science, the sacred cow of the Enlightenment, modernity, and the contemporary moment, is dismembered as a culture to reveal its practices, discourses, and implications for control of women's lives (Haraway, 1991, 1997; Martin, 1987, 1999), including their health (Clarke & Olesen, 1999b), and to provide avenues for resistance and or intervention. Research about women's reproductive status, an issue central to feminist qualitative research from the very start and long productive of influential work (Ginsburg, 1998; Gordon, 1976; Joffe, 1995; Luker, 1984, 1996), is moving into the gender and science area (Balsamo, 1993, 1999; Casper, 1998; Hartouni, 1997). Because this work utilizes interdisciplinary borrowing, it is not easily classified. Studies often appear as hybrids and radical in terms of form, substance, and content, as, for instance, in Donna Haraway's (1997) deft interweaving of fiction, biology, history, humor, religion, and visual imagery in her feminist unpacking of technosciences. These productions for some may be at the least uncomfortable or threatening and subversive, not only for male-dominated institutions such as science, but for feminism itself.

These styles of thought sharpened and enhanced the emerging complexities: the sites (gender, race, and class) of where and how "women" are controlled, how the multiple, shifting identities and selves that supplant earlier notions of a stable identity (self) are produced (Clough, 1992, 1998; Ferguson, 1993; Flax, 1990; Fraser, 1997, p. 381). They emphasized the shift away from binary frameworks to fluid conceptualizations of women's experiences, places, and spaces (Anzaldúa, 1987; Trinh, 1989, 1992). This shift accompanied an emphasis on discourse, narrative, and text, a move to experimental writing away from standard forms of presenting the research account, an issue I will discuss more fully in a moment. Postmodernism and deconstructionism also called into question, as had standpoint theorists, feminist qualitative researchers' unexamined embrace of and adherence to traditional positivist qualitative approaches (known as feminist empiricism) that were thought to forward the feminist agenda, but that, the critics averred, merely repeated structures of oppression. The postmodern position produced an uneasy and sometimes anxious concern that the shifting sands of meaning, text, locale, and the continual proliferation of identities left no grounds for reform-oriented research, reinforced the status quo, erased structural power as well as failed to address problems or to represent a cultural system (Benhabib, 1995; Collins, 1998b; Hawkesworth, 1989; Johannsen, 1992; Mascia-Lees, Sharpe, & Cohen, 1989; Maynard, 1994b; Ramazanoglu, 1989). I will discuss some specific issues raised by this impact more fully below, in the section on issues in feminist qualitative research.

◆ Consequences of Growing Complexities

Thus writings from women of color, gay/lesbian/queer theorists, postcolonial researchers, disabled women, standpoint theorists, and analysts persuaded to a postmodern stance opened and up-ended taken-for-granted conceptualizations of the very grounds and process of doing feminist research as well as critical key concepts

such as experience, difference, and gender. Nowhere has this been more and incisively pursued than in the rethinking of the topic of woman as research participant, a point discussed above, and in the destabilization of the conception of the feminist researcher as an all-knowing, unified, distanced, and context-free seeker of objectified knowledge whose very gender guarantees access to women's lives and knowledges. Dissolution of this assumption pushed feminist research to greater awareness of researcher attributes and the impact of the research on the researcher.

Researcher Attributes

The researcher, too, has attributes, characteristics, a history, and gender, class, race, and social attributes that enter the research interaction. Yvonna Lincoln (1997) captures this in her comment, "If we are not just a single person, but rather a multitude of possibilities . . as ethnographers we could be about utilizing these multiple selves to create multiple texts" (p. 42). However, these possibilities are not static elements; they are, rather, reflections of the intersections of structures and practices. In this vein, borrowing from cultural studies, Ruth Frankenberg and Lata Mani (1993) articulate a conjecturalist approach that "firmly centers the analysis of subject formation and cultural practice within matrices of domination and subordination" and that "asserts that there is an effective but not determining relationship between subjects and their histories, a relationship that is complex, shifting and not 'free' " (p. 306). Although they are writing in a postcolonial, deconstructionist vein, their conceptualization of a conjecturalist approach still has applicability to the dynamics of feminist research wherever found, because it recognizes that both researcher and participant are positioned and are being positioned by virtue of history and context.

A number of feminist researchers have described the dynamics of conjecturalism in their work. Foregrounding her own trajectory from the working class to middle-class researcher, Diane Reay (1998) reflects on class in her analysis of mothers' involvement in their children's primary schooling; Ann Phoenix's (1994) work on young people's social identities demonstrates that the assumption that matching race and gender of interviewers is too simplistic; Catherine Kohler Riessman (1987) points out how ethnic and class differences override gender in achieving understandings in interviews; D. Millen (1997) examines potential problems when feminist researchers work with women who are not sympathetic to feminism.

Impact of the Research on the Feminist Researcher

In light of the multiple positions, selves, and identities at play in the research process, the subjectivity of the researcher, as much as that of the researched, became foregrounded, an indication of the blurring phenomenological and epistemological boundaries between the researcher and the researched. This development did not go unmarked among more traditional researchers, who worried that the emphasis on subjectivity comes "too close . . . to a total elimination of intersubjective validation of description and explanation" (Komarovsky, 1988, p. 592; see also Komarovsky, 1991). This issue led directly into the questions about objectivity, "validity and reliability," and the nature of the text and the voices in it, which will be discussed shortly. In spite of these misgivings, feminists began to publish provocative and even influential work that reflected the blurring of these boundaries: Ruth Behar's (1993) analysis of her Mexican respondent's life and her own crosses multiple national, disciplinary, and personal borders, as do Carolyn Ellis's (1995) poignant account of a terminal illness and Patti Lather and Chris Smithies's (1997) work with HIV-positive women.

These newer views of the researcher's part in the research also bred a host of influential research reflections that rethought the important issue of whether being an "insider" gave feminist researchers access to inside knowledge, a view that partook of Patricia Hill Collins's (1986) important conceptualization of "in-sider/outsider": Patricia Zavella (1996) discovered that her Mexican background did not suffice in her study of Mexican women doing factory work; Ellen Lewin's (1993) analysis of lesbian mothers showed the surpassing importance of motherhood over sexual orientation; Kirin Narayan (1997) asked, "How native is a 'native' anthropologist?"; Dorinne Kondo (1990) reported unexpected and sometimes unsettling experiences during her fieldwork in Japan around her Japanese identity. These works and others, such as Aihwa Ong's (1995) account of work with immigrant Chinese women and Nancy Naples's (1996) research with women in Iowa, problematized the idea that a feminist researcher who shares some attributes of a cultural background would, by virtue of that background, have full access to women's knowledge in that culture. They also troubled the hidden assumption that insider knowledge is unified, stable, and unchanging. Kath Weston's (1996) report of her struggles with these issues summarizes the problems: "A single body cannot bridge that mythical divide between insider and outsider, researcher and researched. I am neither, in any simple way, and yet I am both" (p. 275).

If the play of increasing complexities has destabilized once-secure views of the researcher and those with whom research is done, it has equally led to a critical examination of once taken-for-granted concepts with which feminist researchers have worked: experience and difference.

Experience

Although feminist qualitative researchers working in the empiricist and standpoint frames still foreground women's experience as key, there has been a growing recognition that merely focusing on experience does not take into account how that experience emerged (Morawski, 1990; Scott, 1991) and what the characteristics of the material, historical, and social circumstances were. One of the problems with taking experience in an unproblematic way is that the research, even standpoint research, although less prone to this problem, replicates rather than criticizes the oppressive system. Personal experience is not a self-authenticating claim to knowledge (O'Leary, 1997, p. 47), a point postmodernists raise in directing attention to the risk of essentialism in unthinking reliance on experience. Historian Joan Scott (1991) comments, "Experience is at once already an interpretation and in need of interpretation" (p. 779).

Feminist research in sociology and anthropology analyzes women's experience and the material, social, economic, and gendered conditions that articulate the experience: Arlie Hochschild's (1983) research on how flight attendants manage emotions, Nona Glazer's (1991) examination of racism and classism in professional nursing, Nancy Scheper-Hughes's (1992) exploration of motherhood and poverty in northeastern Brazil, Jennifer Pierce's (1995) ethnographic study of how legal assistants play a part in the production of their oppression in law firms. Historian Linda Kerber's (1998) analysis of women's legal obligations as well as their rights also falls into this category.

Difference

The recognition of difference, a conceptual move that pulled feminist thinkers and researchers away from the view of a shared gynocentric identity, surfaced in the dynamics of the trends just discussed, but very quickly gave way to concerns about the almost unassailable nature of the concept and whether its use would lead to an androcentric or imperialistic "othering" (Felski, 1997; hooks, 1990, p. 22). Arguing for the use of such concepts as hybridity, creolization, and metissage, Rita Felski (1997) claimed that these metaphors "not only recognize differences within the subject, fracturing and complicating holistic notions of identity, but also address connections between subjects by recognizing affiliations, cross-pollinations, echoes, and repetitions, thereby unseating difference from a position of absolute privilege" (p. 12).

Theorist Nancy Tuana (1993) enunciated a balance of possible common interests and observable differences in a way that would allow feminist qualitative researchers to grapple with these issues in their work:

> It is more realistic to expect pluralities of experiences that are related through various intersections or resemblances of some of the experiences of various women to some of the experiences of others. In other words, we are less likely to find a common core of shared experiences that are immune to economic conditions, cultural imperatives, etc., than a family of resemblances with a continuum of similarities, which allows for significant differences between the experience of, for example, an upper-class white American woman and an Indian woman from the lowest caste. (p. 283)

While echoing much of this thinking, bell hooks (1990) and Patricia Hill Collins (1990) nevertheless remind feminist researchers that identity cannot be dropped entirely. Rather, they see differences as autonomous, not fragmented, producing knowledge that accepts "the existence of and possible solidarity with, knowledges from other standpoints" (O'Leary, 1997, p. 63). These views reflect Gadamer's little-recognized concept of the "fusion of horizons," "which carries double or dual vision and dialectical notions a step further than do standpoint epistemologies because it indicates a transcendent third and new view or synthesis" (Nielsen, 1990b, p. 29).

Gender

Like the concepts of experience and difference, gender, the workhorse concept of feminist theory and research, has undergone sea changes that make contemporary use of this concept much more complex and differentiated than at the outset of the "second wave." Theoretical insights going as far back as Suzanne Kessler and Wendy McKenna's (1978) classic ethnomethodological framing of gender, including Judith Butler's (1990) philosophical outline of gender as performative and Judith Lorber's (1994, p. 5) argument that gender is wholly constructed, have shifted research possibilities. Whereas in an earlier time work on gender differences looked for explanations or characteristic of autonomous individuals (Gilligan, 1982), now production and realization of gender in a complex matrix of material, racial, and historical circumstances become the research foci, and differences among women as well as similarities between men and women are acknowledged

(Brabeck, 1996; Lykes, 1994). (Gender as causal explanation and as analytic category and the implications for research are examined by Hawkesworth, 1997a, and in responses to Hawkesworth by Connell, 1997; McKenna & Kessler, 1997; Scott, 1997; Smith, 1997. See also the reply to those responses from Hawkesworth, 1997b.)

◆ Issues and Tensions

The shifting currents depicted in the foregoing sections have emphasized and altered tensions within feminist qualitative research and produced new issues relevant to the conduct of the research itself. Whereas in an earlier era, concerns about the research enterprise tended to reflect traditional worries about the qualitative research enterprise (how to manage "bias," what about validity, and so on), the newer worries take the form of uneasiness about voice, the text, and ethical conduct, which I will discuss shortly. Feminist empiricists and those working within one of the standpoint frameworks are apt to share all of these concerns, whereas those who pursue a deconstructionist path are less likely to worry about bias and validity and more likely to be concerned with voice and text, key issues in representation, although there are important exceptions here (e.g., Lather & Smithies, 1997). Because there is a good deal of borrowing across these lines, many feminist researchers grapple simultaneously with these issues, sometimes muting, sometimes emphasizing, because much remains to be articulated, particularly in work that experiments with writing, narrative, voice, and form.

Bias

The dissolving of the distance between the researcher and those with whom the research is done and the recognition that both are labile, nonunitary subjects (Britzman, 1998, p. ix) steps beyond traditional criticisms about researcher bias (Denzin, 1992, pp. 49-52; Huber, 1973) and leads to strong arguments for "strongly reflexive" accounts about the researcher's own part in the research (Fine, 1992b; Holland & Ramazanoglu, 1994; Phoenix, 1994; Warren, 1988) and even reflections from the participants (Appleby, 1997). What Nancy Scheper-Hughes (1992) calls "the cultural self" that every researcher takes into her or his work is no longer a troublesome element to be eradicated or controlled, but rather a set of resources. Indeed, Susan Krieger (1991) early argued that utilization of the self is fundamental to qualitative work. If researchers are sufficiently reflexive about their projects, they can evoke these resources to guide the gathering, creation, and interpretation of data as well as their own behavior (Casper, 1997; Daniels, 1983; Stacey, 1998). Leslie Rebecca Bloom (1998, p. 41) goes further, urging that feminist researchers and their participants work out how they will communicate and that this be part of the research account. Nevertheless, researcher reflexivity needs to be tempered with an acuity as to what elements in the researchers' backgrounds, hidden or those of which they are unaware, contribute. Sherry Gorelick (1991) identifies potential problems when inductivist feminist researchers who espouse a Marxist framework "fail to take account of the hidden structure of oppression (the research participant is not omniscient) and the hidden relations of oppression (the participant may be ignorant of her relative privilege over and difference from other women)" (p. 461). Nancy Scheper-Hughes (1983) has also warned about feminists' unwitting replication of androcentric perspectives in their work.

Objectivity

Bias is related to the issue of subjectivity in feminist research and raises the problem of objectivity, which lurks in even the most liberated accounts (Cannon, Higginbotham, & Leung, 1991). Forgoing traditional and rigid ideas about objectivity, feminist researchers and scholars have opened new spaces in consideration of this enduring question. Arguing that observers' experiences can be useful, Sandra Harding (1993, p. 71) suggests a strategy of "strong objectivity" that takes the researchers as well as those researched as the focus of critical, causal, scientific explanations (Hirsh & Olson, 1995) and calls for critical examination of the researcher's social location (see Harding, 1996, 1998). Harding (1991) notes, "Strong objectivity requires that we investigate the relation between subject and object rather than deny the existence of, or seek unilateral control over this relation" (p. 152). She asks that feminist researchers see the participants in the inquiry as "gazing back" and that the researchers take the participants' view in looking at their own socially situated projects.[11] This goes beyond mere reflection on the conduct of the research and demands a steady, uncomfortable assessment of the interpersonal and interstitial knowledge-producing dynamics of qualitative research. As Janet Holland and Caroline Ramazanoglu (1994) illustrate in their research on young women's sexuality, there is no way to neutralize the social nature of interpretation. They argue:

> Feminist researchers can only try to explain the grounds on which selective interpretation has been made by making explicit the processes of decision making which produces the interpretation and the logic of the method on which these decisions are based. This entails acknowledging complexity and contradiction which may be beyond the researchers' experience, and recognizing the possibility of silences and absences in their data. (p. 133)[12]

Donna Haraway (1997, p. 16) urges researchers to go beyond even strong objectivity to the exercise of diffracting, which turns the lenses with which researchers view phenomena to show multiple fresh combinations and possibilities.

Rescuing feminist objectivity from being in thrall to classical positivist definitions and from being lost in an inchoate relativism (all views are equal), Haraway (1988) recognizes the merging of researcher and participant to foreground a position of situated knowledges, accountability (the necessity to avoid reproducing oppressive views of women), and partial truths. In Haraway's apt and oft-quoted phrase, "the view from nowhere" becomes "the view from somewhere," that of connected embodied, situated participants. (For an example of Haraway's conceptualization of objectivity in use, see the re-

search on young, working-class people in Britain conducted by Kum Kum Bhavnani, 1994.)

"Validity" and Trustworthiness

Related to the question of objectivity is the old question of the degree to which the account reflects or depicts what the researcher is looking at. Feminist qualitative researchers address or worry about validity, also known in more recent incarnations as "trustworthiness," in different ways depending on how they frame their approaches (Denzin, 1997, pp. 1-14). For those who work in a traditional vein reflecting the positivist origins of social science (reality is there to be discovered), the search for validity will involve well-established techniques. Those who disdain the positivistic origins of such techniques but nevertheless believe that there are ways of achieving validity that reflect the nature of qualitative work will seek out ways to establish credibility through such strategies as audit trails and member "validation," techniques that reflect their postpositivist views but that do not involve hard-and-fast criteria for according "authenticity" (Lincoln & Guba, 1985; Manning, 1997). Feminist qualitative researchers who worry about whether their research will respect or appreciate those with whom they work and whether, indeed, it may transform those others into another version of themselves, reach for something new, as in Laurel Richardson's (1993) manifesto:

> I challenge different kinds of validity and call for different kinds of science practices. The science practice I model is a feminist-postmodernist one. It blurs genres, probes lived experiences, enacts science, creates a female imagery, breaks down dualisms, inscribes female labor and emotional response as valid, deconstructs the myth of an emotion-free social science, and makes a space for partiality, self-reflexivity, tension and difference. (p. 695)

Among new ways of imagining validity (Denzin, 1997, pp. 9-14; Scheurich, 1997, pp. 88-92), Patti Lather's (1993) transgressive validity is the most completely worked-out feminist model, one that calls for a subversive move ("retaining the term to circulate and break with the signs that code it"; p. 674) in a feminist deconstructionist mode. To assure capturing differences but within a transformative space that can lead to a critical political agenda, Lather rests transgressive validity on four sub-types, here highly condensed: (a) ironic validity, which attends to the problems in representation; (b) paralogical validity, which seeks out differences, oppositions, uncertainties; (c) rhizomatic validity, which counters authority with multiple sites; and (d) voluptuous validity, which deliberately seeks excess and authority through self-engagement and reflexivity (pp. 685-686). Whether even in these bold steps Lather has gone far enough to overcome what some see as the almost obdurate problem in legitimation (the inevitable replication of researcher within the analyzed views of the researched; Scheurich, 1997, p. 90), this formulation nevertheless retains a feminist emancipatory stance while providing leads for feminist qualitative researchers to work out and work on the inherent problems in validity. Lather's own research with Chris Smithies on women with AIDS illustrates these strategies for achieving validity and challenges feminist qualitative researchers (Lather & Smithies, 1997).

◆ Problems of Voice, Reflexivity, and Text

A continuing and worrisome problem for all feminist qualitative researchers, irrespective of which approach they take, is the question of voice and, by implication, the nature of the account, which, as William Tierney and Yvonna Lincoln argue in their introduction to *Representation and the Text* (1997), now "comes under renewed scrutiny" (p. viii), a position echoed by the contributors to Rosanna Hertz's edited volume *Reflexivity and Voice* (1997). This issue goes back to the earliest beginnings of feminist research and the attempts, noted earlier in this chapter, to find and express women's voices.

When women of color and postcolonial critics raised concerns about how participants' voices are to be heard, with what authority and in what form, they sharpened and extended this issue. Within this question lie anxiety-provoking matters of whether the account will only replicate hierarchical conditions found in parent disciplines, such as sociology (Smith, 1989, p. 43), and the difficult problems of translating private matters from women's lives into the potentially oppressive and distorting frames of social science (Ribbens & Edwards, 1998). Addressing this latter concern, some feminist researchers have articulated strategies involving voice-centered relational methods (Mauthner & Doucet, 1998), reconstructing research narratives (Birch, 1998), and writing the voices of the less powerful (Standing, 1998).

Voices

How to make women's voices heard without exploiting or distorting those voices is an equally vexatious question. There may be hidden problems of control when literary devices are borrowed to express voice (Mascia-Lees et al., 1989, p. 30). Even though researchers and participants may both shape the flow of silences and comments in the interview situation, the researcher who writes up the account remains in the more powerful position (Phoenix, 1994; Stacey, 1998). Merely letting the tape recorder run and presenting the respondent's voice does not overcome the problem of representation, because the respondent's comments are already mediated when they are made in the interview (Lewin, 1991) and the researcher usually has the final responsibility for the text (Lincoln, 1997). Even taking the account back for comment or as simple courtesy or shaping the account with respondents may not work, as Joan Acker, Kate Barry, and Johanna Esseveld (1991) found in their participatory project; the women wanted them to do the interpreting. Moreover, the choice of audience shapes how voice is found and fashioned (Kincheloe, 1997; Lincoln, 1993, 1997).[13] Michelle Fine (1992b) explores worrisome issues about use of voices (use of pieces of narrative, taking individual voices to reflect group ideas, assuming that voices are free of power relations, researchers' failure to make clear their own positions in relationship to the voices or becoming "ventriloquists") and forcefully urges feminist researchers to "articulate how, how not, and within what limits" voices are framed and used (pp. 217-219).[14] Fine (personal communication, March 2, 1998) has also pointed to the critical tension between treating voices in the raw (as if they were untouched by ideology, hegemony, or interpretation) and critically analyzing those voices by understanding the contexts in which they arise and the hegemonic pressures out of which they are squeezed. J. Miller's (1997) respondents' resistance to her interpretations led her to question whose knowledge and whose interpretations prevail.

Nature of the Account

The issue of voice leads into questions of the form, nature, and content of the account, as well as theoretical issues in the production of ethnographic narratives (Britzman, 1995). There is by now a growing and substantial body of experimental writing, some of which is based on research work and some of which reflects highly reflexive and insightful interpretations of feminist researchers doing their work. Some writers manipulate or work within the printed text, whereas others opt for performances of the account.

Experimentation has bloomed in a number of fields.[15] Margery Wolf (1992) presents three versions of voices from an event in her anthropological field work in Taiwan: a piece of fiction, her anthropological field notes, and a social science article. Ruth Behar (1993) explodes the traditional anthropological form of life history to intertwine her own voice with that of her cocreator in an extended double-voiced text. Patti Lather and Chris Smithies (1997) use a split-page textual format to present the account of their research, their respondents' views, and their own reflections on themselves and the course and outcomes of their research. Richardson (1992, 1997) has pioneered writing and presenting sociological poetry and tales. (For greater detail on textual practice, see Richardson, Chapter 36, this volume.) Carolyn Ellis's (1995) accounts, both presented and written, deal with emotionally difficult topics, such as abortion, death in the family, an experience with black-white relations, and the death of her partner; this work has helped to give research in the sociology of emotions a decidedly experimental and feminist tone. *Autoethnography,* Ellis's term for this form, locates the deeply personal and emotional experiences of the researcher as subject in a context that relates to larger social issues (Ellis & Bochner, 1992, 1996). Here, the personal, biographical, political, and social are interwoven with the autoethnography, which in turn illuminates them (Denzin, 1997, p. 200), as Laura Ellingson (1998) does in her reflexive account of communications within a medical setting. These stances link the personal and political and undercut criticisms of personal reflections as mere solipsism (Patai, 1994).

At the same time, some feminists have created performance pieces—dramatic readings and plays. Michal McCall and Howard Becker's (1990) work on the art world and the late Marianne Paget's (1990) poignant play about a woman with an incorrect cancer diagnosis (based on her own research) are early examples. More recently, anthropologist Dorinne Kondo's play *Dis(Graceful)l Conduct,* about sexual and racial harassment in the academy, embraces a paradigm that shifts "away from the purely textural to the performative, the evanescent, the nondiscursive, the collaborative" and attempts to intervene in another register in what Kondo (1995) calls "powerfully engaging modes quite different from conventional academic prose" (p. 51). For more than a decade, some sessions featuring performance pieces have found a place on the programs of feminist and social science meetings, drawing appreciative, if not always comprehending, audiences. The critical question of how to evaluate such work has only begun to be examined by thoughtful practitioners of performance and dramatic work (McWilliam, 1997) and in questions raised by sympathetic reviewers of experimental writing (Brown, 1998).

◆ Ethics in Feminist Qualitative Research

Feminist qualitative research shares the many ethical concerns regarding privacy, consent, confidentiality, deceit, and deception that trouble the larger field, concerns that call for decent and fair conduct of the research to avoid harm of whatever sort (undue stress, unwanted publicity, loss of reputation) either in the course of data gathering and analysis or in the subsequent text. In research accounts such as Michelle Fine and Lois Weis's (1996) worries about their research with poor working-class respondents, Monica Casper's (1997) anxieties in her ethnographic work on fetal surgery, and Judith Stacey's (1998) candid revelations about relationships with her respondents and writings on research ethics (Ribbens & Edwards, 1998; M. A. Wolf, 1996), feminists have examined and foregrounded ethical issues. As is true with qualitative research in general, concerns for ethical issues in feminist work have become more complex and differentiated. Few researchers face the threat of having their data subpoenaed (Scarce, 1994), but in the face of federal regulations offering anyone access to data gathered in funded studies, for many there are renewed worries about assurances of privacy and confidentiality. Feminist researchers who work in the areas of women's reproductive health (especially abortion), sexual orientation, and homeless women are particularly sensitive to these issues.

These newer worries exist uneasily with older concerns about avoiding deceit and deception and fully informing participants of research goals, strategies, and styles. Contributors to the older qualitative or feminist literature tended to treat informed consent as somewhat problematic, but nevertheless mostly stable and durable during the full course of the research, including publication of findings. Rather rarely has it been noted that informed consent, freely given at one time, may fade or alter so that participants express curiosity or even skepticism about and resistance to the research at a later stage (May, 1980). Although little feminist research has been conducted covertly, there remains a gray area in which personal information about the researcher's life or experiences may be deliberately withheld or blurred (D. L. Wolf, 1996b, pp. 11-12) or other personal information, including views on sex, politics, money, social class, and race, is lost in the complexities of interactions characterized by mobile subjectivities and multiple realities of both participants and researcher. The former case is a research strategy; the latter is characteristic of everyday social life. In both cases the lack of information may influence the mutual construction of data by researcher and participants.

Thoughtful researchers now grapple with older issues and with newly problematic questions such as the intellectual and social processes discussed earlier in these pages that have shifted taken-for-granted feminist assumptions. As Yvonna Lincoln (1995, p. 287) has insightfully noted, standards for quality are now seen to be intertwined with issues of ethics—for example, the demand that the researcher conduct and make explicitly open and honest negotiations around data gathering, analysis, and presentation. These are closely tied to issues of how and where knowledge is created.

Although at the outset in feminist research, some believed that friendly relationships could grow out of research with women (Oakley, 1981), this quickly gave way to a somewhat more distanced view. Feminist qualitative researchers became sensitive to ethical issues arising from the theme that characterizes feminist qualitative work, namely, concern for and even involvement with participating individuals. Janet Finch's (1984) early concern about researchers' unwitting manipulation of participants hungry for social contact anticipated Judith Stacey's (1988) widely cited paper and one by Lila Abu-Lughod (1990) on contradictions in feminist qualitative methodology. Stacey called attention to the uncomfortable question of getting data from respondents as a means to an end and the difficult compromises that may be involved in promising respondents control over the report. These issues, however, as Elizabeth Wheatley (1994) later noted, are characteristic of qualitative work, which can never resolve all ethical dilemmas that arise.

Other ethical dilemmas lie in the potential for "stealing women's words" (Opie, 1992; Reay, 1996b). In a study that involved respondents in the meaning-making process, Sandra Jones (1997) encountered ethical dilemmas. The difficult question of validating or challenging women's taken-for-granted views when they do not accord with feminist perspectives presents another ethical quandary (Kitzinger & Wilson, 1997). Feminist nurse researchers have also pointed out that additional ethical dilemmas may arise when doing research in one's own professional field, where the professional and research roles may conflict (Field, 1991).

The view, long held in feminist research, that researchers occupy a more powerful position than research participants because the researchers are the writers of the accounts has occasioned ethical worries. However, as feminist qualitative researchers have looked more closely at the relations between researchers and participants, the image of the powerless respondent has altered with the recognition that researchers' "power" is often only partial (Ong, 1995), illusory (Visweswaran, 1997; M. A. Wolf, 1996), tenuous (D. L. Wolf, 1996b, p. 36), and confused with researcher responsibility (Bloom, 1998, p. 35), even though the researchers may be more powerfully positioned when out of the field, because they will write the accounts.

Ethics in Participatory Research

These ethical issues and those of voice and account emerge even more vividly in activist studies, where researchers and participants collaborate to enable women to do research for themselves and on topics of concern in their lives and worlds. Participatory research (fully discussed by Kemmis & McTaggart, Chapter 22, this volume) confronts both researchers and participants-who-are-also-researchers with challenges about women's knowledge; representations of women; modes of data gathering, analysis, interpretation, and writing of the account; and relationships between and among the collaborating parties. Although this kind of research is not done as widely as might be hoped, nevertheless there is a growing body of literature on such projects and thoughtful discussion of such issues as othering and dissemination (Lykes, 1997). Linda Light and Nancy Kleiber's (1981) early study of a Vancouver women's health collective describes their conversion from traditional field-workers to coresearchers with the members of the women's health collective and the difficulties of closing the distance between researchers and participants both fully engaged in the research. Questions of the ownership of the data also arise (Renzetti, 1997). Issues of power remain, as collaborative research does not dissolve competing interests (Lykes, 1989, p. 179). Alice McIntyre and M. Brinton Lykes (1998) urge that feminist participatory action researchers exercise reflexivity to interrogate power, privilege, and multiple hierarchies.

In a certain sense, participants are always "doing" research, for they, along with researchers, construct the meanings that become "data" for interpretation. Whereas in customary research the researcher frames interpretations, in participatory action research researchers and participants undertake this task (Cancian, 1992, 1996; Craddock & Reid, 1993). This raises issues of evaluation (Lykes, 1997) and management of distortion. Based on her collaborative work, Maria Mies's (1993) conceptualization of "conscious partiality," achieved through partial identification with research participants (p. 68), creates a critical conceptual distance between the researcher and participants to facilitate dialectically correction of distortions on both sides (see also Skeggs, 1994).

Feminist Research on Ethics

Feminist research on ethics has been done in two areas: (a) questions referential to larger issues of moral beingness and (b) practices and situations in health care. Research on moral beingness has a long history reaching back to Carol Gilligan's (1982) well-known and controversial study of young girls' moral development (Benhabib, 1987; Brabeck, 1996; Koehn, 1998; Larrabee, 1993). This history overlaps complex arguments around the question of care (Larrabee, 1993; Manning, 1992; Tronto, 1993) and the substantial conceptual and empirical feminist literature on caregiving (Olesen, 1997, p. 398). Recently, theorists and researchers have shifted away from the view that ethical or moral behavior is inherent in gender (the essentialist view that women are "natural" carers) to one sensitive to the social construction of gender, which recognizes that a trait such as caring emerges from an interaction between the individual and the milieu (Seigfried, 1996, p. 205). These newer positions on an ethic of care also go beyond a focus on personal relationships in the private sphere to concerns with the just community (Seigfried, 1996, p. 210) and the potential for transforming society in the public sphere (Tronto, 1993, pp. 96-97; see also Christians, Chapter 5, this volume).

Feminist researchers' long-standing concerns about and work on ethical (or nonethical) treatment of women in health care systems have carried into inquiries on aspects of new technologies, such as assisted reproduction, genetic screening, and the regrettably enduring problems of equitable care for elderly, poor women of all ethnic groups (Holmes & Purdy, 1992; Sherwin, 1992; Tong, 1997).

◆ Unrealized Agendas

Feminist qualitative research, as glimpsed in these pages, would appear to be at the beginning of the millennium a complex, diverse, and highly energized enterprise of which it can be said there is no single voice and no single voice can claim dominance or a privileged position. Given the substantive range, theoretical complexity, and empirical difficulties represented in the many topics on which feminist qualitative researchers are working, the multiplicity of voices is apt. This is not to argue that these approaches are beyond criticism that could sharpen and improve them for future work on these selfsame difficult topics; rather, the diversity and multiplicity of feminist qualitative re-

search are causes for celebration, not approbation. Having abandoned the strained binary that posed rigid adherence to traditional methods against the view that all competing knowledge claims are valid, feminist researchers in general have moved, as theorist Joan Alway (1995) has argued, "to try to produce less false, less partial and less perverse representations without making any claims about what is absolutely and always true" (p. 225). This posture rests on the important assumptions that women in specific contexts are best suited to help develop presentations of their lives and that contexts are located in specific structures and historical and material moments. The latter point is particularly critical as feminists work to understand—through texts, discourses, and encounters with women—how women's lives are contextualized and framed.

Yet there remain a number of unrealized agendas within the feminist qualitative research realm. Foremost among these is the deeper exploration of how meanings of race, class, and gender emerge and interlock, as well as their various effects, as Patricia Hill Collins (1999) has done in her analysis of "real mothers" and as Sheila Allen (1994) has proposed in her discussion of race, ethnicity, and nationality. Complicating this agenda is the still-unfinished job of problematizing whiteness, discussed earlier, and the realization of different agendas, contexts, and dynamics for women of color and varying social status. In this regard, Dorothy Smith's (1996) proposal to utilize the metaphor of the map to discover the ongoing ways in which people coordinate their activities, particularly "those forms of social organization and relations that connect up multiple and various sites of experience" (p. 194). offers a promising start. Olivia Espin's (1995) analysis of racism and sexuality in immigrant women's narratives does so as well.

Much remains to be done to open traditional feminist research approaches of data gathering, analysis, and representation to experimental moves, but some feminist researchers are appreciative of, if not sympathetic to, the new moves.[16] However, this poses two issues for all feminist qualitative researchers, irrespective of where they locate themselves in various research streams. First is the obdurate necessity to attend to representation, voice, and text in ways that avoid replication of the researcher and instead display representation of the participants. This is an issue that is not resolved through the simple presentation of research materials or findings in new or shocking ways. Rather, it speaks to the ethical and analytic difficulties inherent in the intertwining of researcher and participant and the mutual creation of data, which are brought to the fore usually by the researcher. There can be no dodging the researcher's responsibility for the account, the text, and the voices, as the research texts cited earlier make clear.

Further complicating this issue is the fact that, as Patricia Clough (1993a) notes, "the textuality never refers to a text, but to the processes of desire elicited and repressed, projected and interjected in the activity of reading and writing" (p. 175). Apt though this observation is, resolving this issue is a much more elusive prospect than choosing and positioning voices, texts, and so on. However, like the more traditional questions to be considered next, it merits much more work than has been done thus far.

A second and parallel task that would take different forms depending on the nature of the research is the question of the overarching issues of credibility and believability, or, put another way, how to indicate that the claims produced are less false, less perverse, and less partial without falling back into positivist standards that measure acceptability of knowledge in terms of some ideal, unchanging body of knowledge. The way forward on this problem, in the views of the authors reviewed here, involves scrupulous and open interrogation of the feminist researchers' own postures, views, and practices, turning back on themselves the very lenses with which they scrutinize the lives of the women with whom they work and always looking for tensions, contradictions, and complicities (Humphries, 1997, p. 7). Uncomfortable as this gaze may be, it is as much a strategy for feminist qualitative researchers reaching for new and experimental approaches as it is for those who take more familiar paths. Such unremitting reflexivity is not without difficulties: Rahel Wasserfall (1997) describes deep and tension-laden differences between herself and her participants; Rebecca

Lawthom (1997) reveals problems in her work as a feminist researcher in nonfeminist research; Kathy Davis and Ine Gremmen (1998) found that feminist ideals can sometimes stand in the way of doing feminist research.

◆ Contexts and Consequences

In this chapter I have emphasized recognition and awareness of the critical importance of context in women's lives, the situated knowledges that partake of local frames and overarching historical and material trends. It is therefore appropriate to try to locate feminist qualitative research in the many contexts that shape this enterprise and that it in turn shapes.

Academic Life

The traditional structure of academic life—at least in the United States—has influenced feminist qualitative research. Whereas much of the early impetus to reform and transformation emerged outside the academy, in recent decades the major intellectual energies in feminist qualitative research have been found in traditional departments, most usually anthropology, sociology, psychology, political science, philosophy, and history; in interdisciplinary women's studies and cultural studies programs; and in such professional programs as education, nursing, and social work, where it is not surprising to find published research essays focused on problems of quality, the utility of standpoint theory, and so on. Dispersal of feminist qualitative research as well as the feminisms that support it means highly variegated approaches and levels of maturity. It also points to differential reception of qualitative feminist work, which can range from dismissal or hostility to admiration if well, truly, and brilliantly done (depending on evaluators' predilection for traditional or experimental approaches). How these responses translate into job recruitment, tenure review, and acceptance of publications is a crucial question.

A parallel and intriguing issue is the extent to which strategies in qualitative feminist research, some borrowed from traditional approaches and then modified, are then reborrowed in other disciplines, creating a problem of differentiating feminist work from projects in these other realms. Many feminist qualitative researchers would argue that the criteria for feminist work noted early in these pages will continue to differentiate methodologically similar qualitative projects from feminist research.

The question of whether feminist qualitative research can transform traditional disciplines thus is lodged in the complexities of types of feminist research and the structural nature of the site. Sectors of sociology and psychology tenaciously hold positivistic outlooks, and there are diverse theoretical views within these disciplines that blunt or facilitate feminist transformation (Stacey & Thorne, 1985). Nevertheless, it remains to be seen whether such transformative research stances as Dorothy Smith's (1974, 1987, 1989, 1990a, 1990b) radical critique of sociology and Patricia Hill Collins's (1986, 1990) concerns about the impact of dualistic thought in sociology and the tendency to perpetuate racism will reshape sociology. Or will more deconstructive approaches of abandoning ethnography and focusing on "re-readings of representations in every form of information processing," which Patricia Clough (1992, p. 137) urges, or Ann Game's (1991, p. 47) embrace of discourses rather than a focus on "the social," reconfigure sociology? Within anthropology, Ruth Behar (1993) and Lila Abu-Lughod (1990) argue that many of the influential themes discussed earlier in this chapter (dissolution of self/other, subject/object boundaries) that are fundamental to traditional ethnographic approaches may liberate the discipline from its colonial and colonizing past (Behar, 1993, p. 302; for a different view, see Strathern, 1987). In psychology, Michelle Fine and Susan Merle Gordon (1992, p. 23) urge that feminist psychologists work in the space between the personal and the political to reconstitute psychology, and they urge activist research,[17] whereas Mary Gergen (in press) formulates a constructionist, postmodern agenda for revisioning psychology. Noting that feminists in psychology have made local and partial alterations to established methods rather than a programmatic metatheory, Jill Morawski (1994) foresees an emergent groundwork for radically new forms of psychological inquiry even though feminist psychology remains in transition.

The transformative potential of feminist cultural studies and the vital multidisciplined social studies of science remains to be seen. Here, as in other disciplinary sites, the plight of the fiscally strained academic department will shape feminist qualitative research. Downsized departments or programs relying on part-time faculty are not fertile arenas for experimental or even traditional transformative work. Counterbalancing this is the strong presence of established feminist researchers who take mentoring seriously and who connect politically to other scholars, feminist or not.

Parochialism and Publishing Practices

For at least the past decade and with no apparent end in sight, publishers have brought out hundreds of titles of feminist work—some theoretical, some empirical, some experimental, some methodological. Scholarly essays and books abound, an abundance that has had a beneficial effect on the emergence and growing complexity of qualitative feminist research. Much as this is a cause for rejoicing, given the relatively limited number of offerings three decades ago, it nevertheless presents a worrisome side concerning the quality and future of feminist research and, indeed, even the evaluation of that of the recent past. More specifically, much of this abundant and often very sophisticated literature, which includes some work by feminist scholars from non-English-speaking countries, has been published in English by publishing firms in the United States and Great Britain. Marketing pressures apparently make English-language publication necessary.[18] This means that feminist research that achieves publication is produced primarily in the United States or the United Kingdom. It is not surprising that this has resulted in undifferentiated views and limited or nonexistent understandings of feminist research done beyond Westernized, bureaucratized societies.

Fortunately, different perspectives such as those of postcolonial, Marxist feminists come through these publications to undercut Westernizing and homogenizing assumptions about "women" anywhere and everywhere. The leading English-language feminist journals publish essays by researchers from Asia, Africa, Latin America, the Arab Middle East, and Eastern Europe, although these publications are in the minority. Leading university and trade presses that feature feminist books frequently have publications by non-U.S. feminists on their lists.[19] Yet, as Meaghan Morris (personal communication, April 15, 1999) has pointed out, there is only a small flow of research publications from non-Western feminists because of translation and marketing problems, a criticism also made by Mary Maynard (1996) and Andre Schiffrin (1998). Even when published in English outside the United States or Great Britain, a feminist research-oriented monograph such as Cynthia Nelson and Soraya Altorki's *Arab Regional Women's Studies Workshop* (1997) may not easily reach interested Western feminists. International feminist conferences, such as that sponsored by Zentrum für Interdisziplinäre Frauenforschung at Humboldt Universität zu Berlin, have begun to discuss these issues.

Some, but not enough, of that work is heard at international conferences such as the International Congresses on Women's Health Issues, which meet biannually in such venues as New Zealand, Denmark, Botswana, Thailand, Egypt, and South Korea and draw substantial numbers of international participants from these regions.[20] In sum, there are some trickles of feminist research from international researchers that provide countervailing themes to dilute the weight of English-language publications and the dominance of English-language feminism. Given the economics of publishing, that probably will continue. However, given the increasing complexity in feminist qualitative research, some of which, as noted earlier, derives from postcolonial feminist thinking, new approaches

and tactics from international scholars will attract attention not only among open-minded English-language feminist researchers, but among publishers with an eye to profitable publication.

◆ Conclusion

Feminist qualitative research enters the new millennium in a stronger position than it began the "second wave" because both theorists and researchers have critically examined the foundations even as they have tried new research approaches, experimental and traditional. Above all, it appears that feminist qualitative researchers are much more self-conscious and much more aware of and sensitive to issues in the formulation and conduct of the research than was the case earlier. However, there is room for yet further sensitivity, as many of the essays cited in this chapter make clear. Happily, there are more sophisticated approaches and more incisive understandings with which to grapple with the innumerable problems in women's lives, contexts, and situations in the hope of, if not emancipation, at least some modest intervention and transformation. Given the diversity and complexity of feminist qualitative research, it is not likely that any orthodoxy—experimental or traditional—will prevail, nor in my opinion should it. All feminist qualitative researchers, in making women's lives and contexts problematic, should openly render their own practices problematic, as many researchers cited in this chapter urge.

Elsewhere, I have commented:

> It is important to recognize that knowledge production is continually dynamic—new frames open which give way to others which in turn open again and again. Moreover, knowledges are only partial. Some may find these views discomfiting and see in them a slippery slope of ceaseless constructions with no sure footing for action of whatever sort. It is not that there is no platform for action, reform, transformation or emancipation, but that the platforms are transitory. If one's work is overturned or altered by another researcher with a different, more effective approach, then one should rejoice and move on.... What is important for concerned feminists is that

new topics, issues of concerns and matters for feminist inquiry are continually produced and given attention to yield more nuanced understandings of action on critical issues. (Olesen & Clarke, 1999, p. 356)[21]

The range of problems is too great, and the issues are too urgent, for feminist researchers to do otherwise.

■ Notes

1. For a feminist view of public health that takes a similar position, see Lupton (1995).

2. Even though feminist qualitative research may not directly relieve women's suffering in certain contexts, the research can nevertheless contribute to legislation, policy, or agencies' actions (Maynard, 1994a). Beyond the relevance of the findings, the very conduct of the research provides grounds for evaluating the degree to which it is feminist: Does it depict the researched as abnormal, powerless, or without agency? Does it include details of the micropolitics of the research? How is difference handled in the study? Does it avoid replicating oppression (Bhavnani, 1994, p. 30)? Francesca Cancian (1992) enunciates a similar list of criteria for regarding research as feminist.

3. A classic interview study of women's health experiences that undercut medical taken-for-grantedness about female patients was conducted by Linda Hunt, Brigitte Jordan, Susan Irwin, and Carole Browner (1989); these researchers found that women did not comply with medical regimes for reasons that made sense in their own lives, and that the women were not "cranks," a finding similar to Anne Kasper's (1994) in her study of women with breast cancer. Alexandra Dundas Todd (1989) documented cultural conflicts between patients and female patients. At a different level, Sue Fisher's (1995) analysis showed that nurse practitioners provide more attentive care than do physicians, but still exert considerable control over patients. Addressing large-scale issues, Susan Yadlon's (1997) analysis of discourses around causes for breast cancer revealed that women are blamed for being poor mothers or for being too skinny and that environmental and other extracorporal causes are overlooked. Sarah Nettleton's (1991) deconstructive analy-

sis of discursive practices in dentistry showed how ideal mothers are created, and Kathy Davis's (1995) research on cosmetic surgery highlighted women's dilemmas. Building on her pioneering work on women's preparation of food (1991), Marjorie DeVault (1999b) questioned the "ownership of food and health."

4. Policy research raises the issue of "studying up" and invokes the oft-repeated comment that feminist researchers, like many other qualitative (and quantitative) investigators, find it easy to access respondents in social groups open to them rather than high-status lawmakers or elected officials, an important exception being Margaret Stacey's (1992) analysis of the British Medical Council. A second reason, however, may lie in a failure to explore policy made at local levels, where access may be easier (city governments, school boards, community activist organizations). In this regard the work developing Dorothy Smith's theories of institutional ethnography (Campbell & Manicom, 1995) and particularly Marie Campbell's (1998) analysis of how texts are enacted as policy in a Canadian nursing home offer new and promising leads in the area of feminist policy analysis. Carroll Estes and Beverly Edmonds's (1981) symbolic interactionist model on how emergent policy issues become framed remains a valuable approach for feminists interested in policy analysis. In the area of policy analysis qualitative feminist researchers, like feminist researchers in general, have more to contribute than they have been able to in the past. As Janet Finch (1986) has argued, qualitative research can make an important contribution to our understanding of the framing and making of policy.

5. This shift has evoked worried comments that feminist researchers have moved away from the political agendas of an earlier time concerned with understanding and alleviating women's oppression to descriptions of women's lives or arcane epistemological questions (Glucksman, 1994; Kelly, Burton, & Regan, 1994, p. 29). Clearly, widespread interest in epistemological issues flourishes among those seeking to understand, improve, or destabilize feminist approaches, but there is abundant work oriented toward intervention and change on numerous fronts. Patti Lather and Chris Smithies's (1997) participatory study with HIV-positive women combines poststructural approaches with a clear reform agenda, Rachel Pfeffer's (1997) ethnographic inquiry into lives of young homeless

women points to programmatic possibilities, and Diana Taylor and Katherine Dower's (1995) policy-oriented focus group research with community women in San Francisco details women's concerns. Olesen, Taylor, Ruzek, and Clarke (1997) extensively review feminist research oriented toward ameliorating women's health, and qualitative feminist researchers discuss difficult issues in researching sexual violence against women, such as sexual harassment of the researcher (Huff, 1997), cross-race research (Huisman, 1997), managing one's own and others' emotions (Mattley, 1997), and negotiating the territory between being an activist and being a researcher (Hippensteele, 1997). Adele Clarke and I argue that "discursive constructions and signifying practices can be handled as constitutive rather than determinative" (Clarke & Olesen, 1999a, p. 13). Sally Kenney and Helen Kinsella's (1997) edited volume details the political and reform implications of standpoint theory. Moreover, a number of journals (*Qualitative Research in Health Care, International Journal of Qualitative Studies in Education, Feminism and Psychology, Western Journal of Nursing Research, Journal of Social Issues, Sociology of Health and Illness, Qualitative Inquiry, Qualitative Sociology, Journal of Contemporary Ethnography, Feminist Studies, Feminist Review, Gender & Society,* and *Social Problems*) publish feminist qualitative reform-oriented research. However, there, as elsewhere, space limits on the size of essays (usually 25 pages double-spaced) make constructing both an argument and a reform stance difficult, given the necessity for detail in qualitative reporting. (On academy-community connections, see also *Feminist Collections: A Quarterly of Women's Studies Resources,* Vol. 20, No. 3, 1999, which includes a section titled "The Energizing Tension Between Scholars and Activists.")

6. Work by feminist legal scholars also falls within this genre (e.g., Ashe, 1988; Bartlett, 1990; Fry, 1992; MacKinnon, 1983; Matsuda, 1992, 1996; Williams, 1991).

7. Yvonna Lincoln (personal communication, March 4, 1999) has reminded me that relativism "spreads over a continuum" ranging from radical relativists who believe that "anything goes" to those who disavow absolute standards for evaluating accounts but hold that standards should be developed in specific contexts that incorporate participants' ideas of which account represents useful knowledge. This latter view does not jettison any notion of quality, but rather serves as a way to avoid utilizing "scientific standards" in contexts where "they act in oppressing, disabling or power-freighted ways."

8. Beyond the original texts of standpoint theorists cited here, useful interpretive reviews can be found in Denzin (1997), Clough (1998), and Kenney and Kinsella (1997). Harding's (1997, p. 387) summary of standpoint theories' chronology is also instructive.

9. The extensive literature on deconstructionism, postmodernism, and feminism is not always as accessible as it should be for those who are starting to explore or wish to deepen their understanding. Some useful works are the spring 1988 issue of *Feminist Studies,* Nicholson (1990, 1997), Hekman (1990b), Flax (1987, 1990), Rosenau (1992), Lemert (1997), Charmaz's (1995) insightful and evenly balanced analysis of positivism and postmodernism in qualitative research, and Collins's (1998b) incisive discussion of what postmodernism means for black feminists.

10. Feminist researchers who look to deconstruction or psychoanalytic feminist semiotics disavow attention to experience (Clough, 1993a, p. 179). They argue that, irrespective of how close the researcher, experience is always created in discourse and textuality. Text is central to incisive analysis as a fundamental mode of social criticism. In this work the emphasis on desire seems to refer to (a) passion, (b) the mysterious and mischievous contributions of the unconscious, (c) libidinal resources not squeezed out of us by childhood and adult socialization, and (d) the sexuality and politics of cultural life and its representations.

11. Kamela Visweswaran (1994) makes a useful differentiation between reflexive ethnography, which questions its own authority, confronts the researcher's processes of interpretation, and emphasizes how the researcher thinks she knows, and deconstructive ethnography, which abandons authority, confronts power in the interpretive process, and emphasizes how we think we know what we know is not innocent.

12. Other feminist accounts that have explicated how decisions were made include Janet Finch and Jennifer Mason's (1990) detailed report on how they sought "negative cases" and Catherine Kohler Riessman's (1990) worries about her analysis of divorced persons' reports and the sociologist's interpretive voice. Jennifer Ring (1987, p. 771), following Hegel, avers that

dialectical thought prevents stabilizing the border between objectivity and subjectivity.

13. Considerations of voice and preparation of text or alternative presentation raise the question of type of publication. Presenting research materials in popular magazines may reach audiences who would be unlikely to have access to or see more traditional or even experimental accounts in academic sources. At present few of the academic review processes leading to tenure, promotion, or even merit pay increases acknowledge these lay publications as important. Patti Lather and Chris Smithies (1997), in their research with HIV-positive women, in which they consulted with women throughout, initially took their manuscript directly to publication for the mass audience reachable through supermarkets and the like.

14. Earlier feminist accounts developed innovative ways to reflect and present voice, although not all would be free of the problems Fine (1992b) discusses. (For an extensive list of such accounts, see Mascia-Lees et al., 1989, pp. 7-8, n. 1.) Two contrasting examples: Marjorie Shostak (1981) gave a verbatim dialogic account of her voice and that of her !Kung respondent, Nisa, whereas Susan Krieger (1983) used the device of a polyphonic chorus to represent voices of women in a Midwest lesbian community. Krieger's voice is absent, although she clearly selected the materials for the account.

15. Under the editorship of Barbara and Dennis Tedlock, the flagship journal *American Anthropologist* adopted a policy of publishing experimental texts, as have several sociological journals long sympathetic to the new modes (*Qualitative Inquiry, Journal of Contemporary Ethnography, Midwest Sociological Quarterly, Qualitative Sociology*).

16. In a review essay discussing Laurel Richardson's *Fields of Play* (1997) cowritten by a group of women at the University of Michigan's Institute for Research on Women and Gender, Lora Bex Lempert argues that scholars who have moved into the experimental spaces have created intellectual and representation spaces for others in the work of social transformation, an agenda shared with the traditionalists (Dutton, Groat, Hassinger, Lempert, & Ruehl, 1998).

17. Activist-oriented research agendas in women's health are outlined by Narrigan, Zones, Worcester, and Grad (1997) and by Ruzek, Olesen, and Clarke (1997).

18. I am indebted here to a lively exchange on these issues with Meaghan Morris, Norman Denzin, Patricia Clough, and Yvonna Lincoln. In a helpful critical reading of this section, Annie George of the Department of Social and Behavioral Sciences Graduate Program in Sociology, University of California, San Francisco, raised an additional problem: Many English-language publications in non-Western countries are not listed or cited in major databases such as SocAbstracts and ERIC.

19. Notable recent issues of English-language feminist journals with space devoted to international feminist research include a special issue of *Feminist Review* (Mohammed, 1998) and a special section in *Signs* ("Gender, Politics and Islam," 1998). Research by Chinese and Japanese feminists on women office workers (Ogasawara, 1998) and on women factory workers in Hong Kong and south China (Lee, 1998) exemplify international work published by university and trade presses, as do writings by international scholars on their relationship to feminism and scholarship in their home and adopted societies (John, 1996; Narayan, 1997).

20. For those feminist qualitative researchers with computer resources and access to the Internet, a growing number of talk lists and Web sites among feminist organizations publicize international congresses held outside the United States. Computer and Internet resources, however, may not be readily available to less well supported feminist qualitative researchers, wherever they are located.

21. As Deborah Lupton (1995) has noted, "The point is not to seek a certain 'truth,' but to uncover varieties of truth that operate, to highlight the nature of truth as transitory and political and the position of subjects as fragmentary and contradictory" (pp. 160-161).

■ *References*

Abel, E., Christian, B., & Moglen, H. (Eds.). (1997). *Female subjects in black and white: Race, psychoanalysis, feminism.* Berkeley: University of California Press.

Abel, E. K., & Nelson, M. K. (Eds.). (1990). *Circles of care: Work and identity in women's lives.* Albany: State University of New York.

Abu-Lughod, L. (1990). Can there be a feminist ethnography? *Women and Performance,* 5(1), 7-27.

Acker, J., Barry, K., & Esseveld, J. (1991). Objectivity and truth: Problems in doing feminist research. In M. M. Fonow & J. A. Cook (Eds.), *Beyond methodology: Feminist scholarship as lived research* (pp. 133-153). Bloomington: Indiana University Press.

Acker, S. (1994). *Gendered education: Sociological reflections on women, teaching and feminism.* Milton Keynes, England: Open University Press.

Alexander, M. J., & Mohanty, C. T. (Eds.). (1997). *Feminist genealogies, colonial legacies, democratic futures.* New York: Routledge.

Allen, S. (1994). Race, ethnicity and nationality: Some questions of identity. In H. Afshar & M. Maynard (Eds.), *The dynamics of "race" and gender: Some feminist interventions* (pp. 85-105). London: Taylor & Francis.

Alway, J. (1995). The trouble with gender: Tales of the still missing feminist revolution in sociological theory. *Sociological Theory, 13,* 209-228.

Anzaldúa, G. (1987). *Borderlands/la frontera: The new mestiza.* San Francisco: Aunt Lute.

Anzaldúa, G. (Ed.). (1990). *Making face, making soul/haciendo caras: Creative and critical perspectives by feminists of color.* San Francisco: Aunt Lute.

Appleby, Y. (1997). How was it for you? Intimate exchanges in feminist research. In M. Ang-Lyngate, C. Corrin, & H. S. Millson (Eds.), *Desperately seeking sisterhood: Still challenging and building* (pp. 127-147). London: Taylor & Francis.

Asch, A., & Fine, M. (1992). Beyond the pedestals: Revisiting the lives of women with disabilities. In M. Fine (Ed.), *Disruptive voices: The possibilities of feminist research* (pp. 139-174). Ann Arbor: University of Michigan Press.

Ashe, M. (1988). Law-language of maternity: Discourse holding nature in contempt. *New England Law Review, 521,* 44-70.

Balsamo, A. (1993). On the cutting edge: Cosmetic surgery and the technological production of the gendered body. *Camera Obscura, 28,* 207-237.

Balsamo, A. (1999). Technologies of surveillance: Constructing cases of maternal neglect. In A. E. Clarke & V. L. Olesen (Eds.), *Revisioning women, health and healing: Feminist, cultural and technoscience perspectives* (pp. 231-253). New York: Routledge.

Bartlett, K. (1990). Feminist legal methods. *Harvard Law Review, 103,* 45-50.

Behar, R. (1993). *Translated woman: Crossing the border with Esperanza's story.* Boston: Beacon.

Behar, R. (1996). *The vulnerable observer: Anthropology that breaks your heart.* Boston: Beacon.

Behar, R., & Gordon, D. A. (Eds.). (1995). *Women writing culture.* Berkeley: University of California Press.

Benhabib, S. (1987). The generalized and the concrete other: The Kohlberg-Gilligan controversy and feminist theory. In S. Benhabib & D. Cornell (Eds.), *Feminism as critique* (pp. 77-95). Minneapolis: University of Minnesota Press.

Benhabib. S. (1995). Feminism and postmodernism: An uneasy alliance. In S. Benhabib, J. Butler, D. Cornell, & N. Fraser, *Feminist contentions: A philosophical exchange* (pp. 17-34). New York: Routledge.

Benhabib, S., Butler, J., Cornell, D., & Fraser, N. (1995). *Feminist contentions: A philosophical exchange.* London: Routledge.

Bhavnani, K.-K. (1994). Tracing the contours: Feminist research and feminist objectivity. In H. Afshar & M. Maynard (Eds.), *The dynamics of "race" and gender: Some feminist interventions* (pp. 26-40). London: Taylor & Francis.

Bing, V. M., & Reid, P. T. (1996). Unknown women and unknowing research: Consequences of color and class in feminist psychology. In N. Goldberger, J. Tarule, B. Clinchy, & M. Belenky (Eds.), *Knowledge, difference, and power: Essays inspired by Women's ways of knowing* (pp. 175-205). New York: Basic Books.

Birch, M. (1998). Reconstructing research narratives: Self and sociological identity in alternative settings. In J. Ribbens & R. Edwards (Eds.), *Feminist dilemmas in qualitative research: Public knowledge and private lives* (pp. 171-185). Thousand Oaks, CA: Sage.

Bloom, L. R. (1998). *Under the sign of hope: Feminist methodology and narrative interpretation.* Albany: State University of New York Press.

Brabeck, M. M. (1996). The moral self, values and circles of belonging. In K. F. Wyche & F. J. Crosby (Eds.), *Women's ethnicities: Journeys through psychology* (pp. 145-165). Boulder, CO: Westview.

Britzman, D. P. (1991). *Practice makes practice: A critical study of learning to teach.* Albany: State University of New York Press.

Britzman, D. P. (1995). The question of belief: Writing poststructural anthropology. *Qualitative Studies in Education, 8,* 229-238.

Britzman, D. P. (1998). Foreword. In L. R. Bloom, *Under the sign of hope, Feminist methodology and narrative interpretation* (pp. ix-xi). Albany: State University of New York Press.

Broom, D. (1991). *Damned if we do: Contradictions in women's health care.* Sydney: Allen & Unwin.

Brown, R. H. (1998). Review of *Fields of play: Constructing an academic life* by Laurel Richardson. *Contemporary Sociology, 27,* 380-383.

Brown, W. (1992). Finding the man in the state. *Feminist Studies, 18,* 7-34.

Butler, J. (1990). *Gender trouble: Feminism and the subversion of identity.* London: Routledge.

Butler, J. (1993). *Bodies that matter: On the discursive limits of "sex."* New York: Routledge.

Butler, J. (1994). Against proper objects. *Differences, 6,* 1-16.

Butler, O. (1986). *Feminist experiences in feminist research.* Manchester: University of Manchester Press.

Campbell, M. (1998). Institutional ethnography and experience as data. *Qualitative Sociology, 21,* 55-74.

Campbell, M., & Manicom, A. (Eds.). (1995). *Knowledge, experience and ruling relations.* Toronto: University of Toronto Press.

Campbell, R. (1984). The virtues of feminist empiricism. *Hypatia, 9,* 90-115.

Cancian, F. M. (1992). Feminist science: Methodologies that challenge inequality. *Gender & Society, 6,* 623-642.

Cancian, F. M. (1996). Participatory research and alternative strategies for activist sociology. In H. Gottfried (Ed.), *Feminism and social change* (pp. 187-205). Urbana: University of Illinois Press.

Cannon, L. W., Higginbotham, E., & Leung, M. L. A. (1991). Race and class bias in qualitative research on women. In M. M. Fonow & J. A. Cook (Eds.), *Beyond methodology: Feminist scholarship as lived research* (pp. 107-118). Bloomington: Indiana University Press.

Casper, M. J. (1997). Feminist politics and fetal surgery: Adventures of a research cowgirl on the reproductive frontier. *Feminist Studies, 23,* 233-262.

Casper, M. J. (1998). *The making of the unborn patient: Medical work and the politics of reproduction in experimental fetal surgery.* New Brunswick, NJ: Rutgers University Press.

Charmaz, K. (1995). Between positivism and postmodernism: Implications for methods. In N. K. Denzin (Ed.), *Studies in symbolic interaction* (Vol. 17, pp. 43-72). Greenwich, CT: JAI.

Charmaz, K., & Olesen, V. L. (1997). Ethnographic research in medical sociology: Its foci and distinctive contributions. *Sociological Methods & Research, 25,* 452-494.

Chase, S. E. (1995). *Ambiguous empowerment: The work narratives of women school superintendents.* Amherst: University of Massachusetts Press.

Chow, E. N. (1987). The development of feminist consciousness among Asian American women. *Gender & Society, 1,* 284-299.

Clarke, A. E. (1998). *Disciplining reproduction: Modernity, American life sciences, and the problems of sex.* Berkeley: University of California Press.

Clarke, A. E., & Olesen, V. L. (1999a). Revising, diffracting, acting. In A. E. Clarke & V. L. Olesen (Eds.), *Revisioning women, health and healing: Feminist, cultural and technoscience perspectives* (pp. 3-38). New York: Routledge.

Clarke, A. E., & Olesen, V. L. (Eds.). (1999b). *Revisioning women, health and healing: Feminist, cultural and technoscience perspectives.* New York: Routledge.

Clough, P. T. (1992). *The end(s) of ethnography: From realism to social criticism.* Newbury Park, CA: Sage.

Clough, P. T. (1993a). On the brink of deconstructing sociology: A critical reading of Dorothy Smith's standpoint epistemology. *Sociological Quarterly, 34,* 169-182.

Clough, P. T. (1993b). Response to Smith. *Sociological Quarterly, 34,* 193-194.

Clough, P. T. (1994). *Feminist thought: Desire, power and academic discourse.* Cambridge, MA: Blackwell.

Clough, P. T. (1998). *The end(s) of ethnography: From realism to social criticism* (2nd ed.). New York: Peter Lang.

Clough, P. T. (in press). *Autoaffection: The unconscious in the age of teletechnology.* Minneapolis: University of Minnesota Press.

Code, L. (1991). *What can she know? Feminist theory and the construction of knowledge.* Ithaca, NY: Cornell University Press.

Collins, P. H. (1986). Learning from the outsider within: The sociological significance of black feminist thought. *Social Problems, 33,* 14-32.

Collins, P. H. (1990). *Black feminist thought: Knowledge, consciousness, and the politics of empowerment.* New York: Routledge, Chapman & Hall.

Collins, P. H. (1992). Transforming the inner circle: Dorothy Smith's challenge to sociological theory. *Sociological Theory, 10,* 73-80.

Collins, P. H. (1997). Comment on Hekman's "Truth and method: Feminist standpoint theory revisited." *Signs, 22,* 375-381.

Collins, P. H. (1998a). *Fighting words: Black women and the search for justice.* Minneapolis: University of Minnesota Press.

Collins, P. H. (1998b). What's going on? Black feminist thought and the politics of postmodernism. In P. H. Collins, *Fighting words: Black women and the search for justice* (pp. 124-154). Minneapolis: University of Minnesota Press.

Collins, P. H. (1999). Will the "real" mother please stand up? The logic of eugenics and American national family planning. In A. E. Clarke & V. L. Olesen (Eds.), *Revisioning women, health and healing: Feminist, cultural and technoscience perspectives* (pp. 266-282). New York: Routledge.

Connell, R. W. (1992). A sober anarchism. *Sociological Theory, 10,* 81-87.

Connell, R. W. (1997). Comment on Hawkesworth's "Confounding gender." *Signs, 22,* 702-706.

Craddock, E., & Reid, M. (1993). Structure and struggle: Implementing a social model of a well woman clinic in Glasgow. *Social Science and Medicine, 19,* 35-45.

Crenshaw, K. (1992). Whose story is it, anyway? Feminist and antiracist appropriations of Anita Hill. In T. Morrison (Ed.), *Race-ing justice, en-gendering power: Essays on Anita Hill, Clarence Thomas, and the construction of social reality* (pp. 402-436). New York: Pantheon.

Daniels, A. K. (1983). Self-deception and self-discovery in field work. *Qualitative Sociology, 6,* 295-214.

Davis, A. Y. (1981). *Women, race and class.* London: Women's Press.

Davis, K. (1995). *Reshaping the female body: The dilemma of cosmetic surgery.* New York: Routledge.

Davis, K., & Gremmen, I. (1998). In search of heroines: Some reflections on normativity in feminist research. *Feminism and Psychology, 8,* 133-153.

de Lauretis, T. (1987). *Technologies of gender: Essays on theory, film, and fiction.* Bloomington: Indiana University Press.

Denzin, N. K. (1992). *Symbolic interactionism and cultural studies.* Newbury Park, CA: Sage.

Denzin, N. K. (1997). *Interpretive ethnography: Ethnographic practices for the 21st century.* Thousand Oaks, CA: Sage.

DeVault, M. L. (1991). *Feeding the family: The social organization of caring as gendered work.* Chicago: University of Chicago Press.

DeVault, M. L. (1996). Talking back to sociology: Distinctive contributions of feminist methodology. *Annual Review of Sociology, 22,* 29-50.

DeVault, M. L. (1999a). *Liberating method: Feminism and social research.* Philadelphia: Temple University Press.

DeVault, M. L. (1999b). Whose science of food and health? Narratives of profession and activism from public health nutrition. In A. E. Clarke & V. L. Olesen (Eds.), *Revisioning women, health and healing: Feminist, cultural and technoscience perspectives* (pp. 166-186). New York: Routledge.

Dill, B. T. (1979). The dialectics of black womanhood. *Signs, 4,* 543-555.

Dutton, J., Groat, L., Hassinger, J., Lempert, L. B., & Ruehl, C. (1998). [Review of the book *Fields of play: Constructing an academic life,* by Laurel Richardson]. *Qualitative Sociology, 21,* 195-204.

Ehrenreich, B., & Piven, F. F. (1983). Women and the welfare state. In I. Howe (Ed.), *Alter-*

natives: Proposals for America from the democratic left (pp. 30-45). New York: Pantheon.

Eichler, M. (1986). The relationship between sexist, non-sexist, woman-centered and feminist research. *Studies in Communication, 3,* 37-74.

Eichler, M. (1997). Feminist methodology. *Current Sociology, 45,* 9-36.

Ellingson, L. L. (1998). "Then you know how I feel": Empathy, identity, and reflexivity in fieldwork. *Qualitative Inquiry, 4,* 492-514.

Ellis, C. (1995). *Final negotiations: A story of love, loss, and chronic illness.* Philadelphia: Temple University Press.

Ellis, C., & Bochner, A. P. (1992). Telling and performing personal stories. In C. Ellis & M. G. Flaherty (Eds.), *Investigating subjectivity: Research on lived experience* (pp. 79-101). Newbury Park, CA: Sage.

Ellis, C., & Bochner, A. P. (Eds.). (1996). *Composing ethnography: Alternative forms of qualitative writing.* Walnut Creek, CA: AltaMira.

Epstein, C. F. (1981). *Women in law.* New York: Basic Books.

Espin, O. M. (1995). "Race," racism and sexuality in the life narratives of immigrant women. *Feminism and Psychology, 5,* 223-228.

Estes, C. L., & Edmonds, B. C. (1981). Symbolic interaction and social policy analysis. *Symbolic Interaction, 4,* 75-86.

Fee, E. (1983). Women and health care: A comparison of theories. In E. Fee (Ed.), *Women and health: The politics of sex in medicine* (pp. 10-25). Englewood Cliffs, NJ: Baywood.

Felski, R. (1997). The doxa of difference. *Signs, 23,* 1-22.

Ferguson, K. (1993). *The man question: Visions of subjectivity in feminist theory.* Berkeley: University of California Press.

Field, P. A. (1991). Doing fieldwork in your own culture. In J. M. Morse (Ed.), *Qualitative nursing research: A contemporary dialogue* (pp. 91-104). Newbury Park, CA: Sage.

Finch, J. (1984). "It's great to have someone to talk to": The ethics and politics of interviewing women. In C. Bell & H. Roberts (Eds.), *Social researching: Politics, problems, practice* (pp. 70-87). London: Routledge & Kegan Paul.

Finch, J. (1986). *Research and policy: The uses of qualitative research in social and educational research.* London: Falmer.

Finch, J., & Groves, D. (1983). *A labour of love: Women, work and caring.* London: Routledge & Kegan Paul.

Finch, J., & Mason, J. (1990). Decision taking in the fieldwork process: Theoretical sampling and collaborative working. In R. G. Burgess (Ed.), *Studies in qualitative methodology: Vol. 2. Reflections on field experience* (pp. 25-50). Greenwich, CT: JAI.

Fine, M. (Ed.). (1992a). *Disruptive voices: The possibilities of feminist research.* Ann Arbor: University of Michigan Press.

Fine, M. (1992b). Passions, politics and power: Feminist research possibilities. In M. Fine (Ed.), *Disruptive voices: The possibilities of feminist research* (pp. 205-232). Ann Arbor: University of Michigan Press.

Fine, M., & Gordon, S. M. (1992). Feminist transformations of/despite psychology. In M. Fine (Ed.), *Disruptive voices: The possibilities of feminist research* (pp. 1-25). Ann Arbor: University of Michigan Press.

Fine, M., & Weis, L. (1996). Writing the "wrongs" of fieldwork: Confronting our own research/writing dilemma in urban ethnographies. *Qualitative Inquiry, 2,* 151-174.

Fisher, S. (1995). *Nursing wounds: Nurse practitioners, doctors, women patients, and the negotiation of meaning.* New Brunswick, NJ: Rutgers University Press.

Flax, J. (1987). Postmodernism and gender relations in feminist theory. *Signs, 14,* 621-643.

Flax, J. (1990). *Thinking fragments: Psychoanalysis, feminism, and postmodernism in the contemporary West.* Berkeley: University of California Press.

Fonow, M. M., & Cook, J. A. (Eds.). (1991). *Beyond methodology: Feminist scholarship as lived research.* Bloomington: Indiana University Press.

Frankenberg, R. (1993). *White women, race matters: The social construction of whiteness.* Minneapolis: University of Minnesota Press.

Frankenberg, R., & Mani, L. (1993). Cross currents, cross talk: Race, postcoloniality and the politics of location. *Cultural Studies, 7,* 292-310.

Fraser, N. (1989). Struggle over needs: Outline of a socialist-feminist critical theory of late capitalist political culture. In N. Fraser, *Unruly practices: Power, discourse, and gender in contemporary social theory* (pp. 161-187). Minneapolis: University of Minnesota Press.

Fraser, N. (1997). *Justice interruptus: Critical reflections on the post-socialist condition.* New York: Routledge.

Fry, M. J. (1992). *Postmodern legal feminism.* London: Routledge.

Game, A. (1991). *Undoing the social: Towards a deconstructive sociology.* Milton Keynes, UK: Open University Press.

Garcia, A. M. (1989). The development of Chicana feminist discourse, 1970-1980. *Gender & Society, 3,* 217-238.

Gender, politics and Islam [Special section]. (1998, Winter). *Signs.*

Gergen, M. M. (in press). *Psychology and gender.* Thousand Oaks, CA: Sage.

Gill, C. J. (1997). The last sisters: Health issues of women with disabilities. In S. B. Ruzek, V. L. Olesen, & A. E. Clarke (Eds.), *Women's health: Complexities and differences* (pp. 96-112). Columbus: Ohio State University Press.

Gilligan, C. (1982). *In a different voice: Psychological theory and women's development.* Cambridge, MA: Harvard University Press.

Ginsburg, F. D. (1998). *Contested lives: The abortion debate in an American community* (Rev. ed.). Berkeley: University of California Press.

Glazer, N. Y. (1991). "Between a rock and a hard place": Women's professional organizations in nursing and class, racial, and ethnic inequalities. *Gender & Society, 5,* 351-372.

Glenn, E. N. (1990). The dialectics of wage work: Japanese-American women and domestic service, 1905-1940. In E. C. DuBois & V. L. Ruiz (Eds.), *Unequal sisters: A multi-cultural reader in U.S. women's history* (pp. 345-372). London: Routledge.

Glucksman, M. (1994). The work of knowledge and the knowledge of women's work. In M. Maynard & J. Purvis (Eds.), *Researching women's lives from a feminist perspective* (pp. 149-165). London: Taylor & Francis.

Gordon, L. (1976). *Women's body, women's right.* New York: Grossman.

Gordon, L. (1994). *Pitied but not entitled: Single mothers and the history of welfare.* New York: Free Press.

Gorelick, S. (1991). Contradictions of feminist methodology. *Gender & Society, 5,* 459-477.

Graham, H. (1984). *Women, health and the family.* Brighton: Wheatsheaf Harvester.

Graham, H. (1985). Providers, negotiators and mediators: Women as the hidden carers. In E. Lewin & V. L. Olesen (Eds.), *Women, health and healing: Toward a new perspective* (pp. 25-52). London: Tavistock.

Green, R. (1990). The Pocahontas perplex: The image of Indian women in American culture. In E. C. DuBois & V. L. Ruiz (Eds.), *Unequal sisters: A multi-cultural reader in U.S. women's history* (pp. 15-21). London: Routledge.

Griffith, A., & Smith, D. E. (1987). Constructing knowledge: Mothering as discourse. In J. Gaskell & A. McLaren (Eds.), *Women and education* (pp. 87-103). Calgary: Detselig.

Gubrium, J. F., & Holstein, J. A. (1997). *The new language of qualitative method.* New York: Oxford University Press.

Guinier, L., Fine, M., & Balin, J. (1997). *Becoming gentlemen: Women, law school and institutional change.* Boston: Beacon.

Gupta, A., & Ferguson, J. (Eds.). (1997). *Anthropological locations: Boundaries and grounds of a field science.* Berkeley: University of California Press.

Haraway, D. J. (1988). Situated knowledges: The science question in feminism and the privilege of partial perspective. *Feminist Studies, 14,* 575-599.

Haraway, D. J. (1991). *Simians, cyborgs, and women: The reinvention of nature.* New York: Routledge.

Haraway, D. J. (1997). *Modest_witness@second_millennium: Femaleman meets Oncomouse.* New York: Routledge.

Harding, S. (1987). Conclusion: Epistemological questions. In S. Harding (Ed.), *Feminism and methodology: Social science issues* (pp. 181-190). Bloomington: Indiana University Press.

Harding, S. (1990). Feminism, science and the anti-Enlightenment critiques. In L. J. Nicholson (Ed.), *Feminism/postmodernism* (pp. 83-105). New York: Routledge.

Harding, S. (1991). "Strong objectivity" and socially situated knowledge. In S. Harding, *Whose science? Whose knowledge? Thinking from women's lives* (pp. 138-163). Ithaca, NY: Cornell University Press.

Harding, S. (1993). Rethinking standpoint epistemology: What is "strong objectivity"? In L. Alcoff & E. Potter (Eds.), *Feminist epistemologies* (pp. 49-82). New York: Routledge.

Harding, S. (1996). Gendered ways of knowing and the "epistemological crisis" of the West. In N. Goldberger, J. Tarule, B. Clinchy, & M. Belenky (Eds.), *Knowledge, difference, and power: Essays inspired by* Women's ways of knowing (pp. 431-454). New York: Basic Books.

Harding, S. (1997). Comment on Hekman's "Truth and method: Feminist standpoint theory revisited." *Signs, 22,* 382-391.

Harding, S. (1998). *Is science multicultural? Postcolonialisms, feminisms, and epistemologies.* Bloomington: Indiana University Press.

Hartouni, V. (1997). *Cultural conceptions: On reproductive technologies and the remaking of life.* Minneapolis: University of Minnesota Press.

Hartsock, N. C. M. (1983). The feminist standpoint: Developing the ground for a specifically feminist historical materialism. In S. Harding & M. B. Hintikka (Eds.), *Discovering reality* (pp. 283-310). Amsterdam: D. Reidel.

Hartsock, N. C. M. (1985). *Money, sex and power: Towards a feminist historical materialism.* Boston: Northeastern University Press.

Hartsock, N. C. M. (1990). Foucault on power: A theory for women? In L. J. Nicholson (Ed.), *Feminism/postmodernism* (pp. 157-175). New York: Routledge.

Hartsock, N. C. M. (1997a). Comment on Hekman's "Truth and method: Feminist standpoint theory revisited": Truth or justice? *Signs, 22,* 367-374.

Hartsock, N. C. M. (1997b). Standpoint theories for the next century. In S. J. Kenney & H. Kinsella (Eds.), *Politics and feminist standpoint theories* (pp. 93-101). New York: Haworth.

Hartsock, N. C. M. (1998). *The feminist standpoint revisited and other essays.* Boulder, CO: Westview.

Hawkesworth, M. E. (1989). Knowers, knowing, known: Feminist theory and claims of truth. In M. R. Malson, J. F. O'Barr, S. Westphal Wihl, & M. Wyer (Eds.), *Feminist theory in practice and process* (pp. 327-351).

Chicago: University of Chicago Press. (Reprinted from *Signs,* 1989, *14,* 533-557)

Hawkesworth, M. E. (1990a). Reply to Hekman. *Signs, 15,* 420-423.

Hawkesworth, M. E. (1990b). Reply to Shogan. *Signs, 15,* 426-428.

Hawkesworth, M. E. (1997a). Confounding gender. *Signs, 22,* 649-686.

Hawkesworth, M. E. (1997b). Reply to McKenna and Kessler, Smith, Scott and Connell: Interrogating gender. *Signs, 22,* 707-713.

Hekman, S. (1990a). Comment on Hawkesworth's "Knowers, knowing, known: Feminist theory and claims of truth." *Signs, 15,* 417-419.

Hekman, S. (1990b). *Gender and knowledge: Elements of a post-modern feminism.* Boston: Northeastern University Press.

Hekman, S. (1997a). Reply to Hartsock, Collins, Harding and Smith. *Signs, 22,* 399-402.

Hekman, S. (1997b). Truth and method: Feminist standpoint theory revisited. *Signs, 22,* 341-365.

Heng, G. (1997). "A great way to fly": Nationalism, the state and varieties of Third World feminism. In M. J. Alexander & C. T. Mohanty (Eds.), *Feminist genealogies, colonial legacies, democratic futures* (pp. 30-45). New York: Routledge.

Hertz, R. (Ed.). (1997). *Reflexivity and voice.* Thousand Oaks, CA: Sage.

Hine, D. C. (1989). *Black women in white: Racial conflict and cooperation in the nursing profession, 1890-1950.* Bloomington: Indiana University Press.

Hippensteele, S. K. (1997). Activist research and social narratives: Dialectics of power, privilege, and institutional change. In M. D. Schwartz (Ed.), *Researching sexual violence against women: Methodological and personal perspectives* (pp. 74-85). Thousand Oaks, CA: Sage.

Hirschmann, N. J. (1997). Feminist standpoint as postmodern strategy. In S. J. Kenney & H. Kinsella (Eds.), *Politics and feminist standpoint theories* (pp. 73-92). New York: Haworth.

Hirsh, E., & Olson, G. A. (1995). Starting from marginalized lives: A conversation with Sandra Harding. In G. A. Olson & E. Hirsh (Eds.), *Women writing culture* (pp. 3-42). Albany: State University of New York Press.

Hochschild, A. R. (1983). *The managed heart: Commercialization of human feeling.* Berkeley: University of California Press.

Hochschild, A. R. (with MacHung, A.). (1989). *The second shift: Working parents and the revolution at home.* New York: Viking.

Holland, J., & Ramazanoglu, C. (1994). Coming to conclusions: Power and interpretation in researching young women's sexuality. In M. Maynard & J. Purvis (Eds.), *Researching women's lives from a feminist perspective* (pp. 125-148). London: Taylor & Francis.

Holmes, H. B., & Purdy, L. M. (Eds.). (1992). *Feminist perspectives in medical ethics.* Bloomington: Indiana University Press.

Hondagneu-Sotelo, P. (1992). Overcoming patriarchal constraints: The reconstruction of gender relations among Mexican immigrant women and men. *Gender & Society, 6,* 393-415.

hooks, b. (1984). *Feminist theory: From margin to center.* Boston: South End.

hooks, b. (1990). The politics of radical black subjectivity. In b. hooks, *Yearning: Race, gender, and cultural politics* (pp. 15-22). Boston: South End.

Huber, J. (1973). Symbolic interaction as a pragmatic perspective: The bias of emergent theory. *American Sociological Review, 38,* 274-284.

Huff, J. K. (1997). The sexual harassment of researchers by research subjects: Lessons from the field. In M. D. Schwartz (Ed.), *Researching sexual violence against women: Methodological and personal perspectives* (pp. 115-128). Thousand Oaks, CA: Sage.

Huisman, K. A. (1997). Studying violence against women of color: Problems faced by white women. In M. D. Schwartz (Ed.), *Researching sexual violence against women: Methodological and personal perspectives* (pp. 179-192). Thousand Oaks, CA: Sage.

Humphries, B. (1997). From critical thought to emancipatory action: Contradictory research goals. *Sociological Research Online, 2,* 1-9.

Hundleby, C. (1997). Where standpoint stands now. In S. J. Kenney & H. Kinsella (Eds.), *Politics and feminist standpoint theories* (pp. 25-44). New York: Haworth.

Hunt, L. M., Jordan, B., Irwin, S., & Browner, C. H. (1989). Compliance and the patient's perspective: Controlling symptoms in every-day life. *Culture, Medicine and Psychiatry, 13,* 315-334.

Hurtado, A. (1989). Relating to privilege: Seduction and rejection in the subordination of white women and women of color. *Signs, 14,* 833-855.

Hurtado, A., & Stewart, A. J. (1997). Through the looking glass: Implications of studying whiteness for feminist methods. In M. Fine, L. C. Powell, L. Weis, & L. M. Wong (Eds.), *Off white: Readings on race, power and society* (pp. 297-311). New York: Routledge.

Joffe, C. (1995). *Doctors of conscience: The struggle to provide abortion before and after Roe v. Wade.* Boston: Beacon.

Johannsen, A. M. (1992). Applied anthropology and post-modernist ethnography. *Human Organization, 51,* 71-81.

John, M. E. (1996). *Discrepant dislocations: Feminism, theory, and postcolonial histories.* Berkeley: University of California Press.

Jones, S. J. (1997). Reflexivity and feminist practice: Ethical dilemmas in negotiating meaning. *Feminism and Psychology, 7,* 348-353.

Kaplan, E. B. (1997). *Not our kind of girl: Unraveling the myths of black teenage motherhood.* Berkeley: University of California Press.

Kasper, A. (1994). A feminist qualitative methodology: A study of women with breast cancer. *Qualitative Sociology, 17,* 263-281.

Kaufert, P. A., & McKinlay, S. M. (1985). Estrogen-replacement therapy: The production of medical knowledge and the emergence of policy. In E. Lewin & V. L. Olesen (Eds.), *Women, health and healing: Toward a new perspective* (pp. 113-138). London: Tavistock.

Kelly, L., Burton, S., & Regan, L. (1994). Researching women's lives or studying women's oppression? Reflections on what constitutes feminist research. In M. Maynard & J. Purvis (Eds.), *Researching women's lives from a feminist perspective* (pp. 27-48). London: Taylor & Francis.

Kennedy, E. L., & Davis, M. D. (1993). *Boots of leather, slippers of gold: The history of a lesbian community.* New York: Routledge.

Kenney, S. J., & Kinsella, H. (Eds.). (1997). *Politics and feminist standpoint theories.* New York: Haworth.

Kerber, L. (1998). *No constitutional right to be ladies: Women and the obligation of citizenship.* New York: Hill & Wang.

Kessler, S., & McKenna, W. (1978). *Gender: An ethnomethodological approach.* New York: John Wiley.

Kincheloe, J. L. (1997). Fiction formulas: Critical constructivism and the representation of reality. In W. G. Tierney & Y. S. Lincoln (Eds.), *Representation and the text: Re-framing the narrative voice* (pp. 57-80). Albany: State University of New York Press.

Kirby, V. (1991). Comment on Mascia-Lees, Sharpe, and Cohen's "The postmodernist turn in anthropology: Cautions from a feminist perspective." *Signs, 16,* 394-400.

Kitzinger, C., & Wilkinson, S. (1997). Validating women's experiences? Dilemmas in feminist research. *Feminism and Psychology, 7,* 566-574.

Koehn, D. (1998). *Rethinking feminist ethics: Care, trust and empathy.* New York: Routledge.

Komarovsky, M. (1988). The new feminist scholarship: Some precursors and polemics. *Journal of Marriage and the Family, 50,* 585-593.

Komarovsky, M. (1991). Some reflections on the feminist scholarship in sociology. *Annual Review of Sociology, 17,* 1-25.

Kondo, D. K. (1990). *Crafting selves: Power, gender, and discourses of identity in a Japanese workplace.* Chicago: University of Chicago Press.

Kondo, D. K. (1995). Bad girls: Theater, women of color, and the politics of representation. In R. Behar & D. A. Gordon (Eds.), *Women writing culture* (pp. 49-64). Berkeley: University of California Press.

Krieger, S. (1983). *The mirror dance: Identity in a women's community.* Philadelphia: Temple University Press.

Krieger, S. (1991). *Social science and the self: Personal essays on an art form.* New Brunswick, NJ: Rutgers University Press.

Larrabee, M. J. (Ed.). (1993). *An ethic of care: Feminist and interdisciplinary perspectives.* New York: Routledge.

Lather, P. (1991). *Getting smart: Feminist research and pedagogy with/in the postmodern.* New York: Routledge.

Lather, P. (1993). Fertile obsession: Validity after poststructuralism. *Sociological Quarterly, 34,* 673-693.

Lather, P., & Smithies, C. (1997). *Troubling the angels: Women living with HIV/AIDS.* Boulder, CO: Westview.

Lawthom, R. (1997). What can I do? A feminist researcher in non-feminist research. *Feminism and Psychology, 7,* 533-538.

Lee, C. K. (1998). *Gender and the south China miracle: Two worlds of factory women.* Berkeley: University of California Press.

Lemert, C. (1992). Subjectivity's limit: The unsolved riddle of the standpoint. *Sociological Theory, 10,* 63-72.

Lemert, C. (1997). *Postmodernism is not what you think.* Malden, MA: Blackwell.

Lempert, L. B. (1994). Narrative analysis of abuse: Connecting the personal, the rhetorical, and the structural. *Journal of Contemporary Ethnography, 22,* 411-441.

Lewin, E. (1991). Writing gay and lesbian culture: What the natives have to say for themselves. *American Ethnologist, 18,* 786-792.

Lewin, E. (1993). *Lesbian mothers: Accounts of gender in American culture.* Ithaca, NY: Cornell University Press.

Lewin, E. (1996a). Introduction. In E. Lewin (Ed.), *Inventing lesbian cultures in America* (pp. 1-11). Boston: Beacon.

Lewin, E. (Ed.). (1996b). *Inventing lesbian cultures in America.* Boston: Beacon.

Lewin, E. (1998). *Recognizing ourselves: Ceremonies of lesbian and gay commitment.* New York: Columbia University Press.

Lewin, E., & Leap, W. L. (Eds.). (1996). *Out in the field: Reflections of lesbian and gay anthropologists.* Urbana: University of Illinois Press.

Light, L., & Kleiber, N. (1981). Interactive research in a feminist setting. In D. A. Messerschmidt (Ed.), *Anthropologists at home in North America: Methods and issues in the study of one's own society* (pp. 167-184). Cambridge: Cambridge University Press.

Lincoln, Y. S. (1993). I and thou: Method, voice, and roles in research with the silenced. In D. McLaughlin & W. G. Tierney (Eds.), *Naming silenced lives: Personal narratives and processes of educational change* (pp. 20-27). New York: Routledge.

Lincoln, Y. S. (1995). Emerging criteria for quality in qualitative and interpretive inquiry. *Qualitative Inquiry, 1,* 275-289.

Lincoln, Y. S. (1997). Self, subject, audience, text: Living at the edge, writing in the margins. In W. G. Tierney & Y. S. Lincoln (Eds.), *Rep-

resentation and the text: Re-framing the narrative voice (pp. 37-56). Albany: State University of New York Press.

Lincoln, Y. S., & Guba, E. G. (1985). *Naturalistic inquiry.* Beverly Hills, CA: Sage.

Longino, H. (1990). *Science as social knowledge.* Princeton, NJ: Princeton University Press.

Longino, H. (1993). Subjects, power, and knowledge: Description and prescription in feminist philosophies of science. In L. Alcoff & E. Potter (Eds.), *Feminist epistemologies* (pp. 101-120). New York: Routledge.

Lorber, J. (1975). Women and medical sociology: Invisible professionals and ubiquitous patients. In M. M. Millman & R. M. Kanter (Eds.), *Another voice: Feminist perspectives on social life and social science* (pp. 75-105). Garden City, NY: Anchor.

Lorber, J. (1994). *Paradoxes of gender.* New Haven, CT: Yale University Press.

Lubelska, C., & Mathews, J. (1997). Disability issues in the politics and processes of feminist studies. In M. Ang-Lygate, C. Corrin, & M. S. Henry (Eds.), *Desperately seeking sisterhood: Still challenging and building* (pp. 117-137). London: Taylor & Francis.

Luker, K. (1984). *Abortion and the politics of motherhood.* Berkeley: University of California Press.

Luker, K. (1996). *Dubious conceptions: The politics of teenage pregnancy.* Cambridge: Harvard University Press.

Lupton, D. (1995). *The imperative of health: Public health and the regulated body.* Thousand Oaks, CA: Sage.

Lykes, M. B. (1989). Dialogue with Guatemalan Indian women: Critical perspectives on constructing collaborative research. In R. K. Unger (Ed.), *Representations: Social constructions of gender* (pp. 167-184). Amityville, NY: Baywood.

Lykes, M. B. (1994). Whose meeting at which crossroads? A response to Brown and Gilligan. *Feminism and Psychology, 4,* 345-349.

Lykes, M. B. (1997). Activist participatory research among the Maya of Guatemala: Constructing meanings from situated knowledge. *Journal of Social Issues, 53,* 725-746.

MacKinnon, C. (1982). Feminism, Marxism, method and the state: An agenda for theory. *Signs, 7,* 515-544.

MacKinnon, C. (1983). Feminism, Marxism and the state: Toward feminist jurisprudence. *Signs, 8,* 635-658.

Maines, D. (1982). In search of the mesostructure: Studies in the negotiated order. *Urban Life, 11,* 267-279.

Manning, K. (1997). Authenticity in constructivist inquiry: Methodological considerations without prescription. *Qualitative Inquiry, 3,* 93-116.

Manning, R. C. (1992). *Speaking from the heart: A feminist perspective on ethics.* Boston: Rowan & Littlefield.

Martin, E. (1987). *The woman in the body: A cultural analysis of reproduction.* Boston: Beacon.

Martin, E. (1999). The woman in the flexible body. In A. E. Clarke & V. L. Olesen (Eds.), *Revisioning women, health and healing: Feminist, cultural and technoscience perspectives* (pp. 97-118). New York: Routledge.

Mascia-Lees, F. E., Sharpe, P., & Cohen, C. B. (1989). The postmodernist turn in anthropology: Cautions from a feminist perspective. *Signs, 15,* 7-33.

Mascia-Lees, F. E., Sharpe, P., & Cohen, C. B. (1991). Reply to Kirby. *Signs, 16,* 401-408.

Matsuda, M. (1992). *Called from within: Early women lawyers of Hawaii.* Honolulu: University of Hawaii Press.

Matsuda, M. (1996). *Where is your body? And other essays on race, gender and the law.* Boston: Beacon.

Mattley, C. (1997). Field research with phone sex workers: Managing the researcher's emotions. In M. D. Schwartz (Ed.), *Researching sexual violence against women: Methodological and personal perspectives* (pp. 101-114). Thousand Oaks, CA: Sage.

Mauthner, N., & Doucet, A. (1998). Reflections on a voice-centered relational method: Analyzing maternal and domestic voices. In J. Ribbens & R. Edwards (Eds.), *Feminist dilemmas in qualitative research: Public knowledge and private lives* (pp. 119-146). Thousand Oaks, CA: Sage.

May, K. A. (1980). Informed consent and role conflict. In A. J. Davis & J. C. Krueger (Eds.), *Patients, nurses, ethics* (pp. 109-118). New York: American Journal of Nursing.

Maynard, M. (1994a). Race, gender and the concept of "difference" in feminist thought. In H. Afshar & M. Maynard (Eds.), *The dy-*

namics of "race" and gender: Some feminist interventions (pp. 9-25). London: Taylor & Francis.

Maynard, M. (1994b). Methods, practice and epistemology: The debate about feminism and research. In M. Maynard & J. Purvis (Eds.), *Researching women's lives from a feminist perspective* (pp. 10-26). London: Taylor & Francis.

Maynard, M. (1996). Challenging the boundaries: Towards an anti-racist women's studies. In M. Maynard & J. Purvis (Eds.), *New frontiers in women's studies: Knowledge, identity and nationalism* (pp. 11-29). London: Taylor & Francis.

Maynard, M., & Purvis, J. (Eds.). (1994). *Researching women's lives from a feminist perspective.* London: Taylor & Francis.

McCall, M. M., & Becker, H. S. (1990). Performance science. *Social Problems, 37,* 116-132.

McIntyre, A., & Lykes, M. B. (1998). Who's the boss? Confronting whiteness and power differences within a feminist mentoring relationship in participatory action research. *Feminism and Psychology, 8,* 427-444.

McKenna, W., & Kessler, S. (1997). Comment on Hawkesworth's "Confounding gender": Who needs gender theory? *Signs, 22,* 687-691.

McWilliam, E. (1997). Performing between the posts: Authority, posture and contemporary feminist scholarship. In W. G. Tierney & Y. S. Lincoln (Eds.), *Representation and the text: Re-framing the narrative voice* (pp. 219-232). Albany: State University of New York Press.

Mies, M. (1993). Towards a methodology for feminist research. In M. Hammersley (Ed.), *Social research: Philosophy, politics and practice* (pp. 64-82). London: Sage.

Millen, D. (1997). Some methodological and epistemological issues raised by doing feminist research on non-feminist women. *Sociological Research Online, 2,* 2-18.

Miller, G., & Dingwall, R. (Eds.). (1997). *Context and method in qualitative research.* Thousand Oaks, CA: Sage.

Miller, J. (1997). Researching violence against street prostitutes: Issues of epistemology, methodology, and ethics. In M. D. Schwartz (Ed.), *Researching sexual violence against women: Methodological and personal per-*

spectives (pp. 144-156). Thousand Oaks, CA: Sage.

Mohammed, P. (1998, Summer). Rethinking Caribbean difference [Special issue]. *Feminist Review.*

Mohanty, C. T. (1988). Under Western eyes: Feminist scholarship and colonial discourses. *Feminist Review, 30,* 60-88.

Montini, T. (1997). Resist and redirect: Physicians respond to breast cancer informed consent legislation. *Women and Health, 12,* 85-105.

Morawski, J. (1990). Toward the unimagined: Feminism and epistemology in psychology. In R. Hare-Mustin & J. Marecek (Eds.), *Making a difference: Psychology and the construction of gender* (pp. 159-183). New Haven, CT: Yale University Press.

Morawski, J. (1994). *Practicing feminisms, reconstructing psychology: Notes on a liminal science.* Ann Arbor: University of Michigan Press.

Morawski, J. (1997). The science behind feminist research methods. *Journal of Social Issues, 53,* 667-681.

Morris, M. (1988). *The pirate's fiancée: Feminism, reading, postmodernism.* London: Verso.

Morris, M. (1998). *Too soon, too late: History in popular culture.* Bloomington: Indiana University Press.

Mukherjee, B. (1994). *The holder of the world.* London: Virago.

Murcott, A. (1993). On conceptions of good food; Or, anthropology between the laity and professionals. *Anthropology in Action, 14,* 11-13.

Naples, N. (1996). A feminist revisiting of the insider/outsider debate: The "outsider phenomenon" in rural Iowa. *Qualitative Sociology, 19,* 83-106.

Narayan, K. (1997). How native is a "native" anthropologist? In L. Lamphere, H. Ragone, & P. Zavella (Eds.), *Situated lives: Gender and culture in everyday life* (pp. 23-41). New York: Routledge.

Narayan, U. (1997). *Dislocating cultures: Identities, traditions, and Third World feminism.* New York: Routledge.

Narrigan, D., Zones, J. S., Worcester, N., & Grad, M. J. (1997). Research to improve women's health: An agenda for equity. In S. B. Ruzek, V. L. Olesen, & A. E. Clarke (Eds.), *Women's health: Complexities and differences* (pp. 551-579). Columbus: Ohio State University Press.

Nelson, C., & Altorki, S. (Eds.). (1997). Arab Regional Women's Studies Workshop [Special issue]. *Cairo Papers in Social Science, 20*(3).

Nelson, M. K. (1990). *Negotiated care: The experience of family day care givers.* Philadelphia: Temple University Press.

Nettleton, S. (1991). Wisdom, diligence and teeth: Discursive practices and the creation of mothers. *Sociology of Health and Illness, 13,* 98-111.

Nicholson, L. J. (Ed.). (1990). *Feminism/postmodernism.* New York: Routledge.

Nicholson, L. J. (Ed.). (1997). *The second wave: A reader in feminist theory.* New York: Routledge.

Nielsen, J. M. (Ed.). (1990a). *Feminist research methods: Exemplary readings in the social sciences.* Boulder, CO: Westview.

Nielsen, J. M. (1990b). Introduction. In J. M. Nielsen (Ed.), *Feminist research methods: Exemplary readings in the social sciences* (pp. 1-37). Boulder, CO: Westview.

Oakley, A. (1981). Interviewing women: A contradiction in terms. In H. Roberts (Ed.), *Doing feminist research* (pp. 30-61). London: Routledge.

Ogasawara, Y. (1998). *Office ladies and salaried men: Power, gender, and work in Japanese companies.* Berkeley: University of California Press.

O'Leary, C. M. (1997). Counteridentification or counterhegemony? Transforming feminist standpoint theory. In S. J. Kenney & H. Kinsella (Eds.), *Politics and feminist standpoint theories* (pp. 45-72). New York: Haworth.

Olesen, V. L. (1975). Rage is not enough: Scholarly feminism and research in women's health. In V. L. Olesen (Ed.), *Women and their health: Research implications for a new era* (DHEW Publication No. HRA-3138; pp. 1-2). Washington, DC: National Center for Health Services Research.

Olesen, V. L. (1993). Unfinished business: The problematics of women, health and healing. *Science of Caring, 5,* 27-32.

Olesen, V. L. (1997). Who cares? Women as informal and formal caregivers. In S. B. Ruzek, V. L. Olesen, & A. E. Clarke (Eds.), *Women's health: Complexities and differences* (pp.

397-424). Columbus: Ohio State University Press.

Olesen, V. L., Taylor, D., Ruzek, S. B., & Clarke, A. E. (1997). Strengths and strongholds in women's health research. In S. B. Ruzek, V. L. Olesen, & A. E. Clarke (Eds.), *Women's health: Complexities and differences* (pp. 580-606). Columbus: Ohio State University Press.

Olesen, V. L., & Clarke, A. E. (1999). Resisting closure, embracing uncertainties, creating agendas. In A. E. Clarke & V. L. Olesen (Eds.), *Revisioning women, health and healing: Feminist, cultural and technoscience perspectives* (pp. 355-357). New York: Routledge.

Ong, A. (1995). Women out of China: Traveling tales and traveling theories in postcolonial feminism. In R. Behar & D. A. Gordon (Eds.), *Women writing culture* (pp. 350-372). Berkeley: University of California Press.

Opie, A. (1992). Qualitative research, appropriation of the "other" and empowerment. *Feminist Review, 40,* 52-69.

Paget, M. (1990). Performing the text. *Journal of Contemporary Ethnography, 19,* 136-155.

Patai, D. (1994, February 23). Sick and tired of nouveau solipsism. *Chronicle of Higher Education,* p. A52.

Petchesky, R. P. (1985). Abortion in the 1980's: Feminist morality and women's health. In E. Lewin & V. L. Olesen (Eds.), *Women, health and healing: Toward a new perspective* (pp. 139-173). London: Tavistock.

Pfeffer, R. (1997). *Children of poverty: Studies on the effect of single parenthood, the feminization of poverty and homelessness.* New York: Garland.

Phoenix, A. (1994). Practicing feminist research: The intersection of gender and "race" in the research process. In M. Maynard & J. Purvis (Eds.), *Researching women's lives from a feminist perspective* (pp. 35-45). London: Taylor & Francis.

Pierce, J. L. (1995). *Gender trials: Emotional lives in contemporary law firms.* Berkeley: University of California Press.

Puar, J. K. (1996). Resituating discourses of "whiteness" and "Asianness" in northern England: Second-generation Sikh women and constructions of identity. In M. Maynard & J. Purvis (Eds.), *New frontiers in women's studies: Knowledge, identity and nationalism* (pp. 125-150). London: Taylor & Francis.

Ramazanoglu, C. (1989). Improving on sociology: The problems of taking a feminist standpoint. *Sociology, 23,* 427-442.

Reay, D. (1996a). Dealing with difficult differences. *Feminism and Psychology, 6,* 443-456.

Reay, D. (1996b). Insider perspectives or stealing the words out of women's mouths: Interpretation in the research process. *Feminist Review, 53,* 57-73.

Reay, D. (1998). Classifying feminist research: Exploring the psychological impact of social class on mothers' involvement in children's schooling. *Feminism and Psychology, 8,* 155-171.

Reinharz, S. (1992). *Feminist methods in social research.* Oxford: Oxford University Press.

Renzetti, C. M. (1997). Confessions of a reformed positivist: Feminist participatory research as good social science. In M. D. Schwartz (Ed.), *Researching sexual violence against women: Methodological and personal perspectives* (pp. 131-143). Thousand Oaks, CA: Sage.

Ribbens, J., & Edwards, R. (Eds.). (1998). *Feminist dilemmas in qualitative research: Public knowledge and private lives.* Thousand Oaks, CA: Sage.

Richardson, L. (1992). The consequences of poetic representation: Writing the other, rewriting the self. In C. Ellis & M. G. Flaherty (Eds.), *Investigating subjectivity: Research on lived experience* (pp. 125-140). Newbury Park, CA: Sage.

Richardson, L. (1993). The case of the skipped line: Poetics, dramatics and transgressive validity. *Sociological Quarterly, 34,* 695-710.

Richardson, L. (1997). *Fields of play: Constructing an academic life.* New Brunswick, NJ: Rutgers University Press.

Riessman, C. K. (1987). When gender is not enough: Women interviewing women. *Gender & Society, 2,* 172-207.

Riessman, C. K. (1990). *Divorce talk: Women and men make sense of personal relationships.* New Brunswick, NJ: Rutgers University Press.

Ring, J. (1987). Toward a feminist epistemology. *American Journal of Political Science, 31,* 753-772.

Roberts, H. (Ed.). (1981). *Doing feminist research.* London: Routledge.

Rollins, J. (1985). *Between women: Domestics and their employers.* Philadelphia: Temple University Press.

Roman, L. G. (1992). The political significance of other ways of narrating ethnography: A feminist materialist approach. In M. D. LeCompte, W. L. Millroy, & J. Preissle (Eds.), *The handbook of qualitative research in education* (pp. 555-594). New York: Academic Press.

Romero, M. (1992). *Maid in the U.S.A.* London: Routledge.

Rosenau, P. M. (1992). *Post-modernism and the social sciences: Insights, inroads, and intrusions.* Princeton, NJ: Princeton University Press.

Ruzek, S. B. (1978). *The women's health movement: Feminist alternatives to medical care.* New York: Praeger.

Ruzek, S. B., Olesen, V. L., & Clarke, A. E. (Eds.). (1997). *Women's health: Complexities and differences.* Columbus: Ohio State University Press.

Sacks, K. B. (1988). *Caring by the hour: Women, work and organizing at Duke University Medical Center.* Urbana: University of Illinois Press.

Scarce, R. (1994). (No) trial (but) tribulations: When courts and ethnography conflict. *Journal of Contemporary Ethnography, 34,* 123-149.

Scheper-Hughes, N. (1983). Introduction: The problem of bias in androcentric and feminist anthropology. *Women's Studies, 19,* 109-116.

Scheper-Hughes, N. (1992). *Death without weeping: The violence of everyday life in Brazil.* Berkeley: University of California Press.

Scheurich, J. J. (1997). The masks of validity: A deconstructive investigation. In J. J. Scheurich, *Research method in the postmodern* (pp. 80-93). London: Falmer.

Schiffrin, A. (1998, November 20). Transnational publishing in microcosm: The Frankfurt Book Fair. *Chronicle of Higher Education,* pp. B6-B7.

Scott, J. (1991). The evidence of experience. *Critical Inquiry, 17,* 773-779.

Scott, J. (1997). Comment on Hawkesworth's "Confounding gender." *Signs, 22,* 697-702.

Seigfried, C. H. (1996). *Pragmatism and feminism: Reweaving the social fabric.* Chicago: University of Chicago Press.

Sherwin, S. (1992). *No longer patient: Feminist ethics and health care.* Philadelphia: Temple University Press.

Shogan, D. (1990). Comment on Hawkesworth's "Knowers, knowing, known: Feminist theory and claims of truth." *Signs, 15,* 424-425.

Shostak, M. (1981). *Nisa: The life and words of a !Kung woman.* Cambridge, MA: Harvard University Press.

Skeggs, B. (1994). Situating the production of feminist ethnography. In M. Maynard & J. Purvis (Eds.), *Researching women's lives from a feminist perspective* (pp. 72-92). London: Taylor & Francis.

Smith, D. E. (1974). Women's perspective as a radical critique of sociology. *Sociological Inquiry, 4,* 1-13.

Smith, D. E. (1987). *The everyday world as problematic.* Boston: Northeastern University Press.

Smith, D. E. (1989). Sociological theory: Methods of writing patriarchy. In R. A. Wallace (Ed.), *Feminism and sociological theory* (pp. 34-64). Newbury Park, CA: Sage.

Smith, D. E. (1990a). *The conceptual practices of power: A feminist sociology of knowledge.* Boston: Northeastern University Press.

Smith, D. E. (1990b). *Texts, facts and femininity: Exploring the relations of ruling.* London: Routledge.

Smith, D. E. (1992). Sociology from women's experience: A reaffirmation. *Sociological Theory, 10,* 88-98.

Smith, D. E. (1993). High noon in Textland: A critique of Clough. *Sociological Quarterly, 34,* 183-192.

Smith, D. E. (1996). Telling the truth after postmodernism. *Symbolic Interaction, 19,* 171-202.

Smith, S. G. (1997). Comment on Hawkesworth's "Confounding gender." *Signs, 22,* 691-697.

Spivak, G. C. (1988). Subaltern studies: Deconstructing historiography. In G. C. Spivak, *In other worlds: Essays in cultural politics* (pp. 201-221). London: Routledge.

Stacey, J. (1988). Can there be a feminist ethnography? *Women's Studies International Forum, 11,* 21-27.

Stacey, J. (1998). *Brave new families: Stories of domestic upheaval in late-twentieth-century America.* Berkeley: University of California Press.

Stacey, J., & Thorne, B. (1985). The missing feminist revolution in sociology. *Social Problems, 32,* 301-316.

Stacey, J., & Thorne, B. (1996). Is sociology still missing its feminist revolution? *Perspectives: The ASA Theory Section Newsletter, 18,* 1-3.

Stacey, M. (1992). *Regulating British medicine: The General Medical Council.* New York: John Wiley.

Standing, K. (1998). Writing the voices of the less powerful. In J. Ribbens & R. Edwards (Eds.), *Feminist dilemmas in qualitative research: Public knowledge and private lives* (pp. 186-202). Thousand Oaks, CA: Sage.

Stanley, L., & Wise, S. (1983). *Breaking out: Feminist consciousness and feminist research.* London: Routledge & Kegan Paul.

Stanley, L., & Wise, S. (1990). Method, methodology and epistemology in feminist research processes. In L. Stanley (Ed.), *Feminist praxis: Research, theory and epistemology in feminist sociology* (pp. 20-60). London: Routledge.

Stanley, L. (Ed.). (1990). *Feminist praxis: Research, theory and epistemology in feminist sociology.* London: Routledge.

Stevens, P. E., & Hall, J. H. (1991). A critical historical analysis of the medical construction of lesbianism. *International Journal of Health Services, 21,* 271-307.

Strathern, M. (1987). An awkward relationship: The case of feminism and anthropology. *Signs, 12,* 684-790.

Taylor, D., & Dower, K. (1995). Toward a women centered health care system: Women's experiences, women's voices, women's needs. *Health Care for Women International, 18,* 407-422.

Taylor, V. (1998). Feminist methodology in social movements research. *Qualitative Sociology, 21,* 357-379.

Taylor, V., & Whittier, N. (Eds.). (1998). Gender and social movements: Part 1 [Special issue]. *Gender & Society, 12*(6).

Taylor, V., & Whittier, N. (Eds.). (1999). Gender and social movements: Part 2 [Special issue]. *Gender & Society, 13*(1).

Terry, J. (1994). Theorizing deviant historiography. In A. L. Shapiro (Ed.), *Feminists revision history* (pp 20-30). New Brunswick, NJ: Rutgers University Press.

Tierney, W. G., & Lincoln, Y. S. (1997). Introduction: Explorations and discoveries. In W. G. Tierney & Y. S. Lincoln (Eds.), *Representation and the text: Re-framing the narrative voice*. Albany: State University of New York Press.

Todd, A. D. (1989). *Intimate adversaries: Cultural conflict between doctors and women patients*. Philadelphia: University of Pennsylvania Press.

Tom, W. (1989). *Effects of feminist research on research methods*. Toronto: Wilfred Laurier.

Tong, R. (1989). *Feminist thought: A comprehensive introduction*. Boulder, CO: Westview.

Tong, R. (1997). *Feminist approaches to bioethics: Theoretical reflections and practical applications*. Boulder, CO: Westview.

Trinh T. M. (1989). *Woman, native, other: Writing postcoloniality and feminism*. Bloomington: Indiana University Press.

Trinh T. M. (1992). *Framer framed*. New York: Routledge.

Tronto, J. C. (1993). *Moral boundaries: A political argument for an ethic of care*. New York: Routledge.

Tuana, N. (1993). With many voices: Feminism and theoretical pluralism. In P. England (Ed.), *Theory on gender/feminism on theory* (pp. 281-289). New York: Aldine de Gruyter.

Visweswaran, K. (1994). *Fictions of feminist ethnography*. Minneapolis: University of Minnesota Press.

Walkerdine, V. (1995). Postmodernity, subjectivity and the media. In T. Ibanez & L. Iniguez (Eds.), *Critical social psychology* (pp. 169-177). London: Sage.

Warren, C. A. B. (1988). *Gender issues in field research*. Newbury Park, CA: Sage.

Wasserfall, R. R. (1997). Reflexivity, feminism, and difference. In R. Hertz (Ed.), *Reflexivity and voice* (pp. 150-168). Thousand Oaks, CA: Sage.

Welton, K. (1997). Nancy Hartsock's standpoint theory: From content to "concrete multiplicity." In S. J. Kenney & H. Kinsella (Eds.), *Politics and feminist standpoint theories* (pp. 7-24). New York: Haworth.

West, C., & Zimmerman, D. (1987). Doing gender. *Gender & Society, 1,* 125-151.

Westkott, M. (1979). Feminist criticism of the social sciences. *Harvard Educational Review, 4,* 422-430.

Weston, K. (1991). *Families we chose: Lesbians, gays, kinship*. New York: Columbia University Press.

Weston, K. (1996). Requiem for a street fighter. In E. Lewin & W. L. Leap (Eds.), *Out in the field: Reflections of lesbian and gay anthropologists* (pp. 274-286). Urbana: University of Illinois Press.

Wheatley, E. (1994). How can we engender ethnography with a feminist imagination? A rejoinder to Judith Stacey. *Women's Studies International Forum, 17,* 403-416.

Williams, P. J. (1991). *The alchemy of race and rights*. Cambridge, MA: Harvard University Press.

Wolf, D. L. (Ed.). (1996a). *Feminist dilemmas in fieldwork*. Boulder, CO: Westview.

Wolf, D. L. (1996b). Situating feminist dilemmas in fieldwork. In D. L. Wolf (Ed.), *Feminist dilemmas in fieldwork* (pp. 1-55). Boulder, CO: Westview.

Wolf, M. A. (1992). *A thrice-told tale: Feminism, postmodernism, and ethnographic responsibility*. Stanford, CA: Stanford University Press.

Wolf, M. A. (1996). Afterword: Musings from an old gray wolf. In D. L. Wolf (Ed.), *Feminist dilemmas in fieldwork* (pp. 215-222). Boulder, CO: Westview.

Wyche, K. F., & Crosby, F. J. (Eds.). (1996). *Women's ethnicities: Journeys through psychology*. Boulder, CO: Westview.

Yadlon, S. (1997). Skinny women and good mothers: The rhetoric of risk, control and culpability in the production of knowledge about breast cancer. *Feminist Studies, 23,* 645-677.

Zavella, P. (1987). *Women's work and Chicano families: Cannery workers of the Santa Clara Valley*. Ithaca, NY: Cornell University Press.

Zavella, P. (1996). Feminist insider dilemmas: Constructing ethnic identity with Chicana informants. In D. L. Wolf (Ed.), *Feminist dilemmas in fieldwork* (pp. 138-159). Boulder, CO: Westview.

9

RACIALIZED DISCOURSES
AND ETHNIC EPISTEMOLOGIES

◆ Gloria Ladson-Billings

> *I think, therefore I am.*
>
> René Descartes, *Le Discours de la Méthode,* 1637
>
> *Ubuntu [I am because we are].*
>
> African saying

When René Descartes proclaimed that he thought himself into being, he articulated a central premise upon which European (and Euro-American) worldviews and epistemology rest—that the individual mind is the source of knowledge and existence. In contrast, the African saying "*Ubuntu,*" translated "I am because we are," asserts that the individual's existence (and knowledge) is contingent upon relationships with others. These two divergent perspectives represent two distinct and often conflicting epistemological stances with which the academy has grappled since the mid- to late 1960s. The two traditions are not merely matters of "alternatives" or "preferences," but rather represent a deliberate choice between hegemony (Gramsci, 1971) and liberation. This strongly worded statement is not meant to be polemical; it is meant to be ur-

gent. I have chosen to explore this dichotomy to demonstrate the "effectively aggressive manner" (Ani, 1994) of the Euro-American epistemological tradition. And I will trace how different discourses and epistemologies serve as both counterknowledge and liberating tools for people who have suffered (and continue to suffer) from the Euro-American "regime of truth" (Foucault, 1973).

It is important to reinforce that the concept of epistemology is more than a "way of knowing." An epistemology is a "system of knowing" that has both an internal logic and external validity. This distinction between an epistemology and "ways of knowing" is not a trivial one. For example, literary scholars have created distinctions between literary genres such that some works are called *literature* whereas other works are termed *folklore.* Not surprisingly, the literature of peoples of color is more likely to fall into the folklore category. As a consequence, folklore is seen as less rigorous, less scholarly, and, perhaps, less culturally valuable than literature. The claim of an epistemological ground is a crucial legitimating force.

Epistemology is linked intimately to worldview. Shujaa (1997) argues that worldviews and systems of knowledge are symbiotic—that is, how one views the world is influenced by what knowledge one possesses, and what knowledge one is capable of possessing is influenced deeply by one's worldview. Thus the conditions under which people live and learn shape both their knowledge and their worldviews. The process of developing a worldview that differs from the dominant worldview requires active intellectual work on the part of the knower, because schools, society, and the structure and production of knowledge are designed to create individuals who internalize the dominant worldview and knowledge production and acquisition processes. The hegemony of the dominant paradigm makes it more than just another way to view the world—it claims to be the only legitimate way to view the world. In this chapter I argue that there are well-developed systems of knowledge, or epistemologies, that stand in contrast to the dominant Euro-American epistemology.

I look briefly at the ideological underpinnings of the Euro-American epistemological tradition through its construction of race, and then describe how the Euro-American tradition conflicts with those traditions established by people who have been subordinated in U.S. society and the world. Next, I investigate the notions of double consciousness (Du Bois, 1903/1953), *mestiza* consciousness (Anzaldúa, 1987), and "tribal secrets" (Warrior, 1995) discovered and uncovered by scholars of color to explicate the ways that discursive, social, and institutional structures have created a sense of "otherness" for those who are outside of the dominant culture paradigm. Then I explore two theoretical notions, "alterity" (Wynter, 1992) and "critical race theory" (Delgado, 1995a), as rubrics for considering the scholarship of racial and ethnic "others." Finally, I conclude the chapter with an examination of what these alternate paradigms mean for qualitative research methods.

◆ The Cultural Logic of the Eurocentric Paradigm

Traditional scientific method can't tell you where you ought to go, unless where you ought to go is a continuation of where you were going in the past.

Robert M. Pirsig,
*Zen and the Art of
Motorcycle Maintenance,* 1972

Ani (1994) says, "Rob the universe of its richness, deny the significance of the symbolic, simplify phenomena until it becomes mere object, and you have a knowable quantity. Here begins and ends the European epistemological mode" (p. 29). One such example of this epistemological stance is the way the construct of race has been formulated in the West (Omi & Winant, 1994). New languages and a new regime of truth (Foucault, 1973) were constituted around race. These new languages became "public" languages that are systems of knowledge whose object of inquiry is the social order in which the knower and inquirer are always already subjects.

Wynter (1992) argues that "such systems of knowledge, as 'acts of communication' which influence the behaviors of those being studied, are always generated from the 'paradigm of value and authority' on whose basis the order is instituted" (p. 21). The idea that "there exist three races, and that these races are 'Caucasoid,' 'Negroid,' and 'Mongoloid' is rooted in the European imagination of the Middle Ages, which encompassed only Europe, Africa, and the Near East" (Haney López, 1995, p. 194). The codification of this three-races theory occurred in the treatise of Count Arthur de Gobineau's *Essays on the Inequality of Races,* published in France in 1853-1855. That Gobineau excluded the peoples of the Americas, the Indian subcontinent, East and Southeast Asia, and Oceania (those living outside of the European imagination) reflects social and political decisions, not scientific ones.

Appleby, Hunt, and Jacob (1994) argue that by the 18th century, a small group of reformers established science as the "new foundation for truth" (p. 15). This new truth was much like the older truth established by the Christian church in that it transferred "a habit of mind associated with religiosity—the conviction that transcendent and absolute truth could be known—to the new mechanical understanding of the natural world" (p. 15). Eventually, this mode of thought and conviction was taken up by other forms of inquiry.

This new mode of thought, coming out of a period termed the Enlightenment, suggested that scientific knowledge was pure, elegant, and simple. Natural science could be summarized by its laws and employed an experimental method to seek truth. This mode of thought reasoned that everything from human biology to the art of governing could and should imitate science. Appleby et al. (1994) call this model of science heroic, "because it made scientific geniuses into cultural heroes" (p. 15). They note:

> Until quite recently, heroic science reigned supreme. The heroic model equated science with reason: disinterested, impartial, and, if followed closely, a guarantee of progress in this world. Science took its character from nature itself, which was presumed to be composed solely of matter in motion and hence to be "neutral." . . . The neutral, value-free, objective image of science inherited from the Enlightenment had wide influence in every discipline until well into the postwar era. (pp. 15-16)

This Enlightenment thinking permeated the thinking of the leaders of the American Revolution. However, these men—Washington, Jefferson, Madison, and others—had to rationalize their commitment to liberty, justice, and equality with the fact that they endorsed slavery (Zinn, 1980). Rather than being bound by a religious code that insisted on the dignity and worth of all people (however, a case for master-servant relationships was often made about Christianity), these leaders of the revolution relied on science to justify the injustice of slavery.

Jefferson, in his *Notes on the State of Virginia* (1784/1954), insisted that Blacks and Whites could never live together because there were "real distinctions" that "nature" had made between the two races. But we know that there is no biological basis to this concept of race. There are no genetic characteristics possessed by all the members of any group (Lewontin, Rose, & Kamin, 1984). Indeed, even the Enlightenment science demonstrates that there are more intragroup differences than intergroup ones. Current thinking about race argues that it is a social construction, and the process by which racial meanings arise is termed *racial formation* (Haney López, 1995).

Consider how this racial formation operates. According to Haney López (1995), "In the early 1800s, people in the United States ascribed to Latin American nationalities and, separate from these, races. Thus, a Mexican might also be White, Indian, Black, or Asian" (pp. 196-197). However, by the mid-1800s, when animosity developed in the U.S. Southwest between Anglos and Mexicans, social prejudices developed. These social prejudices soon became legal ones, with laws designed to reflect and reify racial prejudices. Enlightenment notions of science (and later, law) did not work independent of prevailing discourses of racial and class superiority. This discourse of Enlightenment science allowed the dominant culture to define, distance, and objectify the other.

Scheurich and Young (1997) identify epistemological racism that exists in the research paradigms that dominate academic and scholarly products. The epistemological challenge that is being mounted by some scholars of color is not solely about racism, however; it is also about the nature of truth and reality. Rosaldo (1993) argues that, in what he terms the classic period (from about 1921 to 1971), "norms of distanced normalizing description gained a monopoly on objectivity. Their authority appeared so self-evident that they became the one and only legitimate form for telling the literal truth about other cultures. . . . All other modes of composition were marginalized or suppressed altogether" (p. 106). As classic norms gain exclusive rights to objective truth, ethnography (as well as other social science methods) becomes "as likely to reveal where objectivity lies as where it tells the truth" (p. 115).

◆ Multiple Consciousness, Multiple Jeopardy

The Idea of a single civilization for everyone, implicit in the cult of progress and technique, impoverishes and mutilates us.
Octavio Paz,
The Labyrinth of Solitude, 1961

Although some scholars of color have attempted to find legitimacy in the dominant paradigm (see, e.g., Williams, 1882-1883) other scholars have looked to a different epistemological frame to describe the experiences and knowledge systems of peoples outside of the dominant paradigm.[1] In 1903, W. E. B. Du Bois wrote in *The Souls of Black Folk* that the African American "ever feels his two-ness . . . two souls, two thoughts, two unreconciled strivings" (1903/1953, p. 5). Historian David Levering Lewis (1993) lauds this conception, stating:

> It was a revolutionary concept. It was not just revolutionary; the concept of the divided self was profoundly mystical, for Du Bois invested this double consciousness with a capacity to see incomparably farther and deeper. The African American . . . possessed the gift of "second sight in this American world," an intuitive faculty enabling him/her to see and say things about American society that possessed heightened moral validity. (p. 281)

Du Bois's notion of double consciousness is being read here not as a pathetic state of marginalization and exclusion, but rather as a transcendent position allowing one to see and understand positions of inclusion and exclusion—margins and mainstreams.

An important synchronic aspect of Du Bois's work is that both he and African American scholar Carter G. Woodson (1933) mounted challenges to the dominant Euro-American scholarly paradigm at about the same time as the

formation of the Frankfurt school, out of which critical theories emerged. Max Horkheimer, Theodor Adorno, and Herbert Marcuse were the three primary scholars known for their engagement with the theoretical perspectives of Marx, Hegel, Kant, and Weber and their challenge to the "taken-for-granted empirical practices of American social science researchers" (Kincheloe & McLaren, 1998, p. 261). However, Du Bois and Woodson remain invisible in the scholarly canon except as "Negro" intellectuals concerned with the "Negro" problem. Their forthright and insightful critique of Euro-American scholarship was every bit as "critical" as that of the members of the Frankfurt school, but they would never be mentioned in the same breath as Horkheimer, Weber, Adorno, and Marcuse.

Du Bois's notion of double consciousness applies not only to African Americans but to any people who are constructed outside of the dominant paradigm. It is important to read this entire discussion of multiple consciousness as a description of complex phenomena. It is not an attempt to impose essentialized concepts of "Blackness," "Latina/oness," "Asian Americanness" or "Native Americanness" onto specific individuals or groups.[2] Rather, this discussion is about the multiple ways in which epistemological perspectives are developed. Indeed, the authors cited are not placed here to operate as proxies for what it means to be of a particular race, ethnicity, or cultural group. They are a few examples of the ways *particular* scholars have developed *specific* epistemological stances informed by their own cultural and identity positions.

Anzaldúa describes identities fractured not only by her gender, class, race, religion, and sexuality, but also by the reality of life along the U.S.-Mexico border. In one chapter of *Borderlands/La Frontera*, Anzaldúa (1987) explains the complexity of her life as a Mexican American living along the border:

> My "home" tongues are the languages I speak with my sister and brothers, with my friends. They are [*Pachuco* (called *calo*), Tex-Mex, Chicano Spanish, North Mexican Spanish dialect,

and Standard Mexican Spanish, with Chicano Spanish] being closest to my heart. From school, the media and job situations, I've picked up standard and working class English. From Mamagrande Locha and from reading Spanish and Mexican literature, I've picked up Standard Spanish and Standard Mexican Spanish. From *los recien llegados,* Mexican immigrants and *braceros,* I learned Northern Mexican dialect. (pp. 55-56)

Anzaldúa's work, which reflects a long intellectual history of Chicanas/os (see Acuña, 1972; Almaguer, 1974; Balderrama, 1982; Gomez-Quinones, 1977; Mirande & Enriquez, 1979; Padilla, 1987; Paz, 1961), has become a part of what Delgado Bernal (1998) calls a Chicana feminist epistemology. Chicana writers such as Alarcón (1990), Castillo (1995), and the contributors to de la Torre and Pesquera's (1993) edited collection exemplify these intersections of race, class, and gender.

But it is important not to assume a unified Latino/a (or even Chicano/a) subject. Oboler (1995) challenges the amalgamation of Spanish speakers in the Western Hemisphere under the rubric *Hispanic:* The Hispanic label belies the problematic inherent in attempts to create a unitary consciousness from one that is much more complex and multiple than imagined or constructed. According to Oboler:

Insofar as the ethnic label Hispanic homogenizes the varied social and political experiences of 23 million people of different races, classes, languages, and national origins, genders, and religions, it is perhaps not so surprising that the meanings and uses of the term have become the subject of debate in the social sciences, government agencies, and much of the society at large. (p. 3)

Similarly, American Indians have had to grapple with what it means to be Indian. Despite a movement toward "Pan-Indianism" (Hertzberg, 1971), the cultures of American Indians are very diverse. Broad generalizations about American Indians can be essentializing. However, the U.S. federal government movement to "civilize" and detribalize Indian children through boarding schools helped various groups

of Indians realize that the experiences of their tribes were not unique and that American Indians share any number of common problems and experiences (Snipp, 1995). Lomawaima (1995) argues that "since the federal government turned its attention to the 'problem' of civilizing Indians, its overt goal has been to educate Indians to be non-Indians" (p. 332). Much of the "double consciousness" Indians face revolves around issues of tribal sovereignty. A loss of sovereignty is amplified by four methods of disenfranchisement experienced by many American Indians (Lomawaima, 1995): relocation by colonial authorities (e.g., mission, reservations), systematic eradication of the native language, religious conversion (to Christianity), and restructured economies toward sedentary agriculture, small-scale craft industry, and gendered labor.

Warrior (1995) asks whether or not an investigation of early American Indian writers can have a significant impact on the way contemporary Native American intellectuals develop critical studies. He urges caution in understanding the scholarship of Fourth World formulations such as that of Ward Churchill and M. Annette Jaimes because it tends to be essentializing in its call for understanding American Indian culture as part of a global consciousness shared by all indigenous peoples in all periods of history. Warrior's work is a call for "intellectual sovereignty" (p. 87)—a position free from the tyranny and oppression of the dominant discourse.

Among Asian Pacific Islanders there are notions of multiple consciousness. Lowe (1996) expresses this in terms of "heterogeneity, hybridity, and multiplicity" (p. 60). She points out:

The articulation of an "Asian American identity" as an organizing tool has provided unity that enables diverse Asian groups to understand unequal circumstances and histories as being related. The building of "Asian American culture" is crucial to this effort, for it articulates and empowers the diverse Asian-origin community vis-à-vis the institutions and apparatuses that exclude and marginalize it. Yet to the extent that Asian American culture fixes Asian American identity and suppresses differences—of national origin, generation, gender, sexuality, class—it risks particular dangers: not only does it underestimate the differences and hybridities among Asians, but it may inadvertently support the racist discourse that constructs Asians as a homogeneous group. (pp. 70-71)

Espiritu (1992) also reminds us that "Asian American" as an identity category came into being within the past 30 years. Prior to that time, most members of the Asian-descent immigrant population "considered themselves culturally and politically distinct" from other Asian-descent groups (p. 19). Indeed, the historical enmity that existed between and among various Asian groups made it difficult for them to transcend their national allegiances to see themselves as one unified group. And the growing anti-Asian sentiments with which the various Asian immigrant groups were faced in the United States caused specific groups to "disassociate themselves from the targeted group so as not to be mistaken for members of it and suffer any possible negative consequences" (p. 20).

Trinh (1989) and Mohanty (1991) offer postmodern analyses of Asian Americanness that challenge any unitary definitions of *Asian American*. Rather than construct a mythical solidarity, these authors examine the ways that Asianness is represented in the dominant imagination. One of the most vivid examples of the distorted, imagined Asian shows up in the work of David Henry Hwang, whose play *M. Butterfly* demonstrates how a constellation of characteristics—size, temperament, submissiveness—allowed a French armed services officer to mistake a man for a woman even in intimate situations.

Lowe (1996) reminds us that "the grouping 'Asian American' is not a natural or static category; it is a socially constructed unity, a situationally specific position assumed for political reasons" (p. 82), but it coexists with the "dynamic fluctuation and heterogeneity of Asian American culture" (p. 68).

What all of these groups (i.e., African Americans, Native Americans, Latino/as, and Asian Americans) have in common is the experience of a racialized identity. Each group is constituted of myriad national and ancestral origins, but the dominant ideology of the Euro-American episte-

mology has forced each into an essentialized and totalized unit that is perceived to have little or no internal variation. However, at the same moment, members of these groups have used these unitary racialized labels for political and cultural purposes. Identification with the racialized labels means acknowledgment of some of the common experiences group members have had as outsiders and others.

◆ Life on the Margins

Anthropologist Jacob Pandian (1985) points out that in the Judeo-Christian local culture of the West (Geertz, 1983), the *True Christian* was the medieval metaphor of the *Self*. Alterity refers to the alter ego category of otherness that is specific to each culture's "metaphor of the self." Wynter (1992) argues that those constructed as other have a perspective advantage. This advantage does not speak to the economic, social, and political disadvantage that subordinated groups may experience, but rather to the way that not being positioned in the center allows for "wide-angle" vision. This advantage is not due to an inherent racial/cultural difference but is the result of the dialectical nature of constructed otherness that prescribes the liminal status of people of color as beyond the normative boundary of the conception of Self/Other (King, 1995).

King (1995) further argues that this epistemic project is more than simply adding on multiple perspectives or "pivoting" the center. Rather, this liminal position or point of alterity attempts to transcend an "either/or" epistemology. Alterity is not a dualistic position that there are multiple and equally partial standpoints that are either valid or inexorably ranked hierarchically. Recognizing the alterity perspective does not essentialize other perspectives, such as Blackness, Indianness, Asianness, Latino/aness, as homogenizing reverse epistemics (West, 1990).

Those occupying the liminal position do not seek to move from the margins to the mainstream because they understand the corrupting influences of the mainstream—its pull to maintain status quo relations of power and inequities. This liminal view is not unlike the view from the bottom that poor and working-class people have on the middle class. The poor and working classes have a perspective on their own experiences while simultaneously grasping the fundamentals of the workings of the dominant class. Because most poor and working-class people rely on the dominant class for food, clothing, shelter, and work, they are forced to learn dominant practices, at least minimally. The undocumented child-care workers or African American domestics find themselves inside the homes of dominant group members. There they have intimate access to sanctioned beliefs and patterns of behavior.[3]

Legesse (1973) suggests that the liminal group is that which is forcibly constrained to play the role of alter ego to the ideal self prescribed by the dominant cultural model. This dominant cultural model sets up prescriptive rules and canons for regulating thought and action in the society. Thus the "issue is about the 'nature of human knowing' of the social reality in a model of which the knower is already a socialized subject" (Wynter, 1992, p. 26).

> The system-conserving mainstream perspectives of each order (or well-established scholarship) therefore clash with the challenges made from the perspectives of alterity. . . . For it is the task of established scholarship to rigorously maintain those prescriptions which are critical to the order's existence. (Wynter, 1992, p. 27)

Thus the work of the liminal perspective is to reveal the ways that dominant perspectives distort the realities of the other in an effort to maintain power relations that continue to disadvantage those who are locked out of the mainstream. This liminal perspective is the condition of the dominant order's self-definition that "can empower us to free ourselves from the 'categories and prescriptions' of our specific or-

der and from its 'generalized horizon of understanding' " (Wynter, 1992, p. 27).

◆ Critical Race Theory: Challenging Mainstream Orthodoxy

One research paradigm in which racialized discourses and ethnic epistemologies or the liminal perspective may be deployed is critical race theory (CRT).[4] According to Delgado (1995b):

> Critical Race Theory sprang up in the mid-1970s with the early work of Derrick Bell and Alan Freeman, both of whom were deeply concerned over the slow pace of racial reform in the U.S. They argued that traditional approaches of filing *amicus* briefs, conducting protests and marches, and appealing to moral sensibilities of decent citizens produced smaller and fewer gains than in previous times. Before long, Bell and Freeman were joined by other legal scholars who shared their frustration with traditional civil rights strategies. (p. xiii)

Critical race theory is both an outgrowth of and a separate entity from an earlier legal movement called critical legal studies (CLS). Critical legal studies is a leftist legal movement that challenges the traditional legal scholarship that focuses on doctrinal and policy analysis (Gordon, 1990) in favor of a form of law that speaks to the specificity of individuals and groups in social and cultural contexts. CLS scholars also challenge the notion that "the civil rights struggle represents a long, steady march toward social transformation" (Crenshaw, 1988, p. 1334).

According to Crenshaw (1988), "Critical [legal] scholars have attempted to analyze legal ideology and discourse as a social artifact which operates to recreate and legitimate American society" (p. 1350). Scholars in the CLS movement decipher legal doctrine to expose both its internal and external inconsistencies and reveal the ways that "legal ideology has helped create, support, and legitimate America's present class structure" (p. 1350). The contribution of CLS to legal discourse is in its analysis of legitimating structures in society. Much of the CLS ideology emanates from the work of Gramsci (1971) and depends on the Gramscian notion of "hegemony" to describe the continued legitimacy of oppressive structures in American society (Unger, 1983). However, CLS fails to provide pragmatic strategies for material and social transformation. Cornel West (1993) asserts:

> Critical legal theorists fundamentally question the dominant liberal paradigms prevalent and pervasive in American culture and society. This thorough questioning is not primarily a constructive attempt to put forward a conception of a new legal and social order. Rather, it is a pronounced disclosure of inconsistencies, incoherences, silences, and blindness of legal formalists, legal positivists, and legal realists in the liberal tradition. Critical legal studies is more a concerted attack and assault on the legitimacy and authority of pedagogical strategies in law school than a comprehensive announcement of what a credible and realizable new society and legal system would look like. (p. 196)

CLS scholars have critiqued mainstream legal ideology for its portrayal of the United States as a meritocracy, but they have failed to include racism in their critique. Thus CRT became a logical outgrowth of the discontent of legal scholars of color.

CRT begins with the notion that racism is "normal, not aberrant, in American society" (Delgado, 1995b, p. xiv), and because it is so enmeshed in the fabric of the U.S. social order, it appears both normal and natural to people in this society. Indeed, Derrick Bell's major premise in *Faces at the Bottom of the Well* (1992) is that racism is a permanent fixture of American life. Therefore, the strategy of those who fight for racial social justice is to unmask and expose racism in all of its various permutations.

Second, CRT departs from mainstream legal scholarship by sometimes employing storytelling to "analyze the myths, presuppositions, and received wisdoms that make up the common culture about race and that invariably render blacks and other minorities one-down" (Delgado, 1995b, p. xiv). According to Barnes (1990), "Critical race theorists . . . integrate their

experiential knowledge, drawn from a shared history as 'other,' with their ongoing struggles to transform a world deteriorating under the albatross of racial hegemony" (pp. 1864-1865; emphasis added). Thus the experience of oppressions such as racism and sexism has important components for the development of a CRT perspective.

A third feature of CRT is its insistence on a critique of liberalism. Crenshaw (1988) argues that the liberal perspective of the "civil rights crusade as a long, slow, but always upward pull" (p. 1334) is flawed because it fails to understand the limits of the current legal paradigm to serve as a catalyst for social change because of its emphasis on incrementalism. CRT argues that racism requires sweeping changes, but liberalism has no mechanism for such change. Instead, liberal legal practices support the painstakingly slow process of arguing legal precedents to gain citizen rights for people of color.

Fourth, CRT argues that Whites have been the primary beneficiaries of civil rights legislation. For example, although the policy of affirmative action is under attack throughout the nation, it is a policy that also has benefited Whites. A close look at the numbers reveals that the major beneficiaries of affirmative action hiring policies have been White women (Guy-Sheftall, 1993). The logic of this argument is that many of these women earn incomes that support households in which other Whites live—men, women, and children. Thus White women's ability to secure employment ultimately benefits Whites in general.

In a recent compilation of key writings in critical race theory, the editors point out that there is no "canonical set of doctrines or methodologies to which [CRT scholars] all subscribe" (Crenshaw, Gotanda, Peller, & Thomas, 1995, p. xiii). But these scholars are unified by two common interests—understanding how a "regime of white supremacy and its subordination of people of color have been created and maintained in America" (p. xiii) and changing the bond that exists between law and racial power.

In the pursuit of these interests, legal scholars such as Patricia Williams (1991) and Derrick Bell

(1980, 1992) were among the early critical race theorists whose ideas reached the general public. Some might argue that their wide appeal was the result of their abilities to tell compelling stories into which they embedded legal issues. This use of story is of particular interest to social science scholars because of the growing popularity of narrative inquiry (Connelly & Clandinin, 1990). But merely because the research community is more receptive to story as a part of scholarly inquiry does not mean that all stories are judged as legitimate in knowledge construction and the advancement of a discipline.

Lawrence (1995) asserts that there is a tradition of storytelling in law and that litigation is highly formalized storytelling, although the stories of ordinary people, in general, have not been told or recorded in the literature of law (or any other discipline). But this failure to make it into the canons of literature or research does not make stories of ordinary people less important. The ahistorical and acontextual nature of much law and other "science" renders the voices of the dispossessed and marginalized group members mute. In response, much of the scholarship of CRT focuses on the role of "voice" in bringing additional power to the legal discourses of racial justice. Critical race theorists attempt to inject the cultural viewpoints of people of color, derived from a common history of oppression, into their efforts to reconstruct a society crumbling under the burden of racial hegemony (Barnes, 1990).

Until recently, little of CRT found its way into the literature outside of law. In my own work with Tate, we broached the subject as a challenge to traditional multicultural education paradigms (Ladson-Billings & Tate, 1995). We argued that race continues to be salient in U.S. society; that the nation was premised on property rights, not human rights; and that the intersection of race and property could serve as a powerful analytic tool for explaining social and educational inequities. Later, Tate (1997) provided a comprehensive description of critical race theory and its antecedents as a way to inform the educational research community more fully of CRT's meanings and possible uses in ed-

ucation. In his discussion he cites Calmore (1992), who identified CRT as

> a form of opposition scholarship . . . that challenges the universality of white experience/judgement as the authoritative standard that binds people of color and normatively measures, directs, controls, and regulates the terms of proper thought, expression, presentation, and behavior. As represented by legal scholars, critical race theory challenges the dominant discourses on race and racism as they relate to law. The task is to identify values and norms that have been disguised and subordinated in the law. . . . critical race scholars . . . seek to demonstrate that [their] experiences as people of color are legitimate, appropriate, and effective bases for analyzing the legal system and racial subordination. This process is vital to . . . transformative vision. This theory-practice approach, a praxis, if you will, finds a variety of emphases among those who follow it. . . . From this vantage, consider for a moment how law, society, and culture are texts—not so much like a literary work, but rather like a traditional black minister's citation of a text as a verse or scripture that would lend authoritative support to the sermon he is about to deliver. Here, texts are not merely random stories; like scripture, they are expressions of authority, preemption, and sanction. People of color increasingly claim that these large texts of law, society, and culture must be subjected to fundamental criticisms and reinterpretation. (pp. 2161-2162)

Although CRT has been used as an analytic tool for understanding the law (particularly civil rights law), as previously noted, it has not been deployed successfully in the practical world of courts and legal cases or schools. In fact, the first public exposure CRT received proved disastrous for presidential civil rights commission nominee Lani Guinier. CRT's radical theoretical arguments were seen as a challenge to "the American way." Guinier's (1994) writings about proportional representation were seen as antithetical to the U.S. constitutional notion of one "man," one vote. She had argued that in a postapartheid South Africa it would be necessary to ensure that the White minority had a political voice despite the fact that they were grossly outnumbered within the electorate. Similarly, she argued, people of color in the United States might have to seek new ways to be represented beyond that of majority rule through one person, one vote.

Guinier's ideas meant that she could not be confirmed, and the president did nothing to support her nomination.

◆ *CRT, the Knower, and the Known*

The power and pull of a paradigm is more than simply a methodological orientation. It is a means by which to grasp reality and give it meaning and predictability.
    Ray Rist, "On the Relations Among Educational Research Paradigms," 1990

What are the relationships among liminality, alterity, CRT, and new forms of qualitative research that incorporate racialized discourses and ethnic epistemologies? To answer this question we need to examine the relationship between the knower (the researcher) and the known (the subject, participant, informant, collaborator). Lorraine Code (1991) poses the question, Does the gender of the knower matter in the construction of knowledge? She contends that it does. I assert that along with the gender of the knower, the race, ethnicity, language, class, sexuality, and other forms of difference work to inform his or her relationship to knowledge and its production. However, Narayan (1993) argues that it is dangerous to presume that because the researcher (in her case as an anthropologist) is a member of a particular racial or ethnic group, she or he has emic knowledge of that particular group or community:

"Native" anthropologists, then, are perceived as insiders regardless of their complex backgrounds. The differences between kinds of "native" anthropologists are also obviously passed over. Can a person from an impoverished American minority background who, despite all prejudices, manages to get an education and study her own community be equated with a member of a Third World elite group who, backed by excellent schooling and parental funds, studies anthropology abroad yet returns home for fieldwork among the less privileged? Is it not insensitive to suppress the issue of location, acknowledging that a scholar who chooses an insti-

tutional base in the Third World might have a different engagement with Western-based theories, books, political stances, and technologies of written production? Is a middle-class white professional researching aspects of his own society also a "native" anthropologist? (p. 677)

Narayan's points are well-taken if we accept an essentialized view of what group membership means. We know that the categories we use to describe also delimit. Who and what constitutes group membership is always at play. However, the search for an approach to research that better represents indigenous and community knowledge remains a worthwhile one.

Asante (1987) builds upon the work of Woodson and Du Bois to craft an Afrocentric or "African-centered" approach to education. Although some other Black scholars have challenged his approach as essentialist and a form of ethnic "cheerleading" (e.g., Appiah, 1992), Asante's (1991) own words suggest that his search for an alternate paradigm is more directed at getting out from under the oppression of dominant perspectives:

Afrocentricity is *not* a black version of Eurocentricity. Eurocentricity is based on white-supremacist notions whose purposes are to protect white privilege and advantage in education, economics, politics, and so forth. Unlike Eurocentricity, Afrocentricity does not condone ethnocentric valorization at the expense of degrading other groups' perspectives. Moreover, Eurocentricity presents the particular historical reality of Europeans as the sum total of the human experience. It imposes Eurocentric realities as universal; i.e., that which is white is presented as applying to the human condition in general, while that which is nonwhite is viewed as group-specific and therefore not human. (p. 172)

Asante's (1987) major argument, as I see it, is that scholars of color have been searching for a "place to stand . . . in relation to Western standards, imposed as interpretative measures on other cultures" (p. 11). He argues for a "flexible frame of reference" (p. 11) that will allow a more dynamic and transformational interaction between the knower and the known.

Similarly, Anzaldúa (1987) reminds us that dominant culture is defined by the powerful and often operates as a kind of tyranny against those defined as other. Her response against the inequitable relationship between the knower and the known is to press toward a new *mestiza* consciousness that is a consciousness of the borderlands. Her work represents the complexity of identity, representation, and scholarship in the more dynamic way proposed by Asante. Her work moves in a fluid yet exciting way between exposition and art, prose and poetry, Spanish and English, displaying the borders in multiple ways. For instance, she writes in *"Una Lucha de Fronteras/*A Struggle of Borders" (p. 77):

> Because I, a *mestiza,*
>
> continually walk out of one culture,
>
> and into another,
>
> because I am in all cultures at the same time,
>
> *alma entre dos mundos, tres, cuatro,*
>
> *me zumba la cabeza con lo contradictorio.*
>
> *Estoy norteada por todas las voces que me hablan*
>
> *simultaneamente.*

She writes in an unapologetic, multivocal style to reinforce the multiple epistemological positions in which all human beings find themselves, even those who have assumed unitary voices.

Highwater (1981) raises similar issues when he argues that "the greatest distance between people is not space, but culture" (p. 3). He further asserts the importance of representation as a "complex and infinitely varied relationship between reality and the symbols used to depict it" (p. 70). The concept of representation can (and should) be extended to scholarship. Scholars must be challenged to ask not only *about* whom is the research, but also *for* whom is the research. The question of *for whom* is not merely about advocacy, but rather about who is capable to act and demonstrate agency. This

agency is enacted through both epistemological and discursive forms.

Fanon (1968) argues that although the oppressed resort to the language of the oppressor for their liberation, ultimately liberation will come from a new person with a new discourse. This new discourse represents the primary argument of Black feminist Audre Lorde (1984), who notes in her oft-quoted essay that "the master's tools will never dismantle the master's house." However, other scholars suggest that "the master's house will only be dismantled with the master's tools." [5] This epistemological limbo— between the old discourse and the new—is the place where many scholars of color find themselves. The mechanisms for scholarly recognition, promotion, tenure, and publication are controlled primarily by the dominant ideology. Scholars of color find themselves simultaneously having been trained in this dominant tradition and needing to break free of it.

This ambivalence about the research that scholars of color are trained to do and the research they ultimately do creates the condition that Delgado-Gaitan (1993) describes as "insider/outsider status." One initially begins as an outsider and gradually gains enough trust to be granted insider status. But the move from "outside" to "inside" can be a form of oppression and colonization. As Villenas (1966) notes, "By objectifying the subjectivities of the researched, by assuming authority, and by not questioning their own privileged positions, ethnographers have participated as colonizers of the researched" (p. 713). Rosaldo (1989) has also warned of the dangers the dominant discourse may have for ethnographers by describing the "Lone Ethnographer," who "rode off into the sunset in search of his 'natives' " (p. 30). After spending time among these "natives," this same Lone Ethnographer returned to the comfort and convenience of his (or her) office to write a "true" account of the culture. But scholars born of "new studies" have begun to ask different questions of themselves and their research.[6] Siddle-Walker (1996) raises the question of data versus "real" data. The insider status that scholars of color may have can alert them to the way oppressed peoples both protect themselves and subvert the dominant paradigm by withholding and "distorting" data. These actions may reflect the suspicions of the researched community rather than malice.

In my own research I have attempted to tell a story about myself as well as about my work (Ladson-Billings, 1997). This discursive turn is not merely a new narcissism; rather, it is a concern for situating myself as a researcher—who I am, what I believe, what experiences I have had—because it affects what, how, and why I research. My decision to research the exemplary practices of teachers who are successful with African American children was a decidedly political (not partisan) decision (Ladson-Billings, 1994). It also was a decision to demystify the research process in communities of color, the members of which are often the objects but rarely the beneficiaries of research.[7]

In my work I broke several canons of traditional research. I relied on low-income African American parents to help me locate excellent teachers. I allowed the teachers to assume responsibility for the theoretical leadership of the project, and I created a research collaborative in which I served as one of nine members along with the teachers, not as the expert/researcher. This changed relationship between researcher and researched forced me to participate in a more self-revealing, vulnerable way. Throughout the process, I sent the other members of the study copies of everything I wrote. They scolded me when I misrepresented their thoughts and ideas, and they affirmed me when I got it right. Over the course of 3 years we became a group of friends with a common concern about the education of African American children. This long-term, intensive form of research made it difficult for members to lie or hide their feelings. It also meant that the end of the funding could not mean the end of the relationship. So, 7 years later, we continue to consult each other and send each other greeting cards. I know who has suffered bereavement, who has coped with illness, whose children have entered college, who has become a grandparent. My research is a part of my life and my life is a part of my research.

The needs to know and to be known are powerful aspects of the human condition. Unfortu-

nately, knowledge of and by people of color has been repressed, distorted, and denied by a Euro-American cultural logic that represents an "aggressive seizure of intellectual space [that,] like the seizure of land, amounts to the aggressor occupying someone else's territory while claiming it as his own" (Asante, 1987, p. 9).

Critical race theory offers the researcher an opportunity to stand in a different relationship to the research (and researched). Some of the key features of CRT are storytelling, counter-storytelling, and "naming one's own reality" (see Delgado, 1995a). The value of storytelling in qualitative research is that it can be used to demonstrate how the same phenomenon can be told in different and multiple ways depending on the storytellers. For instance, where an anthropologist might describe the ritual scarification of a male infant's genitalia, Bertha Rosenfeld may tell of the wonderful bris performed on her new nephew as a part of her family's Jewish religious tradition (Ladson-Billings, 1993). Which story is true? Whose story is deemed legitimate? Who has the power to shape the public perception about the logic and worth of the event? One might argue that the example presented here is an exaggeration, much like that of Horace Miner's classic, "Body Ritual Among the Nacirema" (*Nacirema* is *American* spelled backward), but it is representative of the power of different storytellers. As Robert Williams (1995) notes:

> To be a Storyteller . . . is to assume the awesome burden of remembrance for a people, and to perform this paramount role with laughter and tears, joy and sadness, melancholy and passion, as the occasion demands. The Storyteller never wholly belongs to himself or herself. The Storyteller is the one who sacrifices everything in the tellings and retellings of the stories belonging to the tribe.
>
> . . . Whether the story gets the "facts" right is really not all that important. An Indian Storyteller is much more interested in the "truth" contained in a story. And a great Storyteller always makes that "truth" in the story fit the needs of the moment. (pp. xi-xii)[8]

No story was so widely disputed as that told at the murder trial of O.J. Simpson. The prosecutors told a story of a crazed and controlling man who after years of battering his ex-wife snapped when he learned of her romantic interests. They presented it as an open-and-shut case. They asserted that Simpson had motive and they had evidence of opportunity. But the defense attorneys told a different story. They talked about the implausibility of the prosecution's scenario and the deep-seated racism that is a part of the Los Angeles Police Department. They changed the focus of the case from one murder case to the general experiences of men of color (particularly Black and Latino men) with police departments in the United States. Although the telling of vastly differing stories is part of most legal cases, criminal or civil, the response of the jury to these two stories stunned White and/or middle-class Americans.

The posttrial analysis suggested that a "Black" jury failed to convict a Black celebrity defendant, even though the jury had at least one White and one Latino juror. Other analyses asserted that the jury was not intelligent enough to make the "right" decision. The O.J. Simpson murder trial came on the heels of the trials of four Los Angeles police officers for the beating of Rodney King. A predominantly White jury in the suburb of Simi Valley had acquitted the officers of a beating that the entire nation (including the jurors) had witnessed via videotape. In that trial, the defense attorneys told a story of how frame-by-frame analysis of the videotape could lead to an interpretation different from that evoked by real-time viewing. In the context of King's background and driving record, the defense's story was credible to the jurors.

Similarly, "stories" told in the research literature are received differently by different people. In the educational and social science research literature of the 1960s, the stories about children of color were stories of "cultural deprivation" and "cultural disadvantage" (see, e.g., Bettelheim, 1965; Bloom, Davis, & Hess, 1965; Ornstein & Vairo, 1968; Riessman, 1962). These were stories of the substandard, abnormal child of color and poverty, and they positioned White middle-class cultural expression as the normative and correct way of being

in school and society. Policy at federal and local levels flowed out of these stories in an attempt to "compensate" for the perceived inadequacies of children of color and their families.

Siddle-Walker's (1996) counterstory of the "good" segregated school presents a decidedly different picture of a working-class community of color. Indeed, throughout the southern United States there are counterstories of poor people working together to secure a better education for their children despite the neglect and antipathy of the dominant culture. The Historically Black Colleges and Universities, tribal colleges, and early ethnic studies programs are examples of some of the ways in which people of color have attempted to create educational structures and discourses that challenge the notion of exclusivity as the only route to excellence.

In 1969, the Asian American Studies Program at San Francisco State College (now San Francisco State University) operated an independent program of study that was conceived on democratic and inclusive principles (Hirabayashi & Alquizola, 1994). The program (in concert with the college's Ethnic Studies Program) grew out of the demands from a student strike staged by the Third World Liberation Front. The program goals were open admissions and the immediate admission of all "non-White" applicants, community control of the curriculum and hiring practices, and self-governance. This model of education represented a radical departure from the top-down, hierarchical, and bureaucratic forms that characterize much of higher education. The Asian American Studies Program dared to tell a counterstory, and it proved to be disruptive and destabilizing to the dominant paradigm.

◆ The Children of Field Hands Return to Do Fieldwork

My master used to read prayers in public to the ship's crew every Sabbath day; and when I first saw him read, I was never so surprised in my life, as when I saw the book talk to my master, for I thought it did, as I observed him to look

*upon it, and move his lips. I wished it would
do so with me. As soon as my master had
done reading, I followed him to the place
where he put the book . . . and when nobody
saw me, I opened it, and put my ear down
close upon it, in great hope that it would say
something to me.*

James Gronniosaw,
*A Narrative of the Most Remarkable
Particulars in the Life of James Albert
Ukawsaw Gronniosaw,* 1770

When I was a young child growing up in Philadelphia, there were groups of African American men (some from my family) who waited on street corners during the summer months for the farm labor bus. This broken-down yellow school bus arrived in the Black community looking for willing workers to go to the fields to do the harsh stoop labor of picking tomatoes, strawberries, or any other fruit or vegetable that was in season. Anyone who did not have a steady job could hope to be among those selected to go to the fields. This backbreaking labor did not yield much financial reward, but it was an honest day's work available to people who rarely could find work.

When I moved to California, I saw people with brown faces standing on street corners. This time, instead of a school bus, open-bed trucks would pull up to the curb and the men inside would select a few of those waiting on the corner to do a day's labor at a construction site. Not far from one of the nation's most prestigious universities was a strawberry ranch owned by the university, where a group of itinerant farmworkers lived and worked in inhumane and squalid conditions. Within a few years I began to see people with yellow faces scrubbing dishes and mopping floors in the kitchens of a growing number of restaurants in a community that boasted of a median home price of almost $300,000. The "real" fieldwork being done by people of color and poor people is rarely represented fully in the literature of the academy.

Today, as I attempt to do my own work I am struck by the growing number of scholars of color who have chosen to go back into those fields, construction sites, and kitchens to give voices to their own people—their perspectives, worldviews, and epistemologies. These scholars, like James Gronniosaw (quoted above), are attempting to have the lives of subordinated people "talk to them." Tired of bending their ears to hear the master's book talk, scholars of color are writing new texts from the lives and experiences of people much like themselves. The work of scholars such as Gwaltney (1980), Torres-Guzman (1992), Nieto (1992), Takaki (1989, 1993), Ellison (1986), Churchill (1992, 1993), Silko (1977, 1981), Spivak (1988), hooks (1984, 1989, 1992), and countless others has begun to reshape the contours of scholarly research about communities of color. Perhaps even more important is the work of scholars of color who have taken on the task of turning a critical gaze on the dominant paradigms. Scholars such as Said (1979), Ani (1994), Morrison (1992), and Hwang (1994) use deciphering knowledge to change "consciousness and [develop] cognitive autonomy . . . [in an] 'archaeology of knowledge' (Foucault, 1972) to expose the belief structures of race . . . and other discursive practices" (King, 1995, p. 276).

For example, although Collins (1990) has developed a theoretical rubric for explicating a Black feminist standpoint, this rubric also represents a framework for critique of Euro-American paradigms. Collins argues for concrete experiences as a criterion of meaning, the use of dialogue in the assessment of knowledge claims, an ethic of caring, and an ethic of personal accountability. In the vernacular, Collins asks, What have you been through? What are you talkin' about? How do I know you care and, by the way, who *are* you? Scrutiny about subjectivities generally is absent in positivist paradigms that rely on a notion of objectivity, even when it cannot be attained.

The return of researchers of color to communities of color and the casting of a critical eye on the Euro-American paradigm are not calls to a romantic, "noble savage" notion of otherness. Rather, this work is about uncovering the complexities of difference—race, class, and gender.

Work such as Gilroy's (1993) makes a compelling case for complex and multiple readings of race, ethnicity, and gender:

> The themes of nationality, exile, and cultural affiliation accentuate the inescapable fragmentation and differentiation of the [racialized] subject. This fragmentation has recently been compounded further by the questions of gender, sexuality, and male domination which have been made unavoidable by the struggles of [racial and ethnic minority] women. . . . As indices of differentiation, they are especially important because of the intracommunal antagonisms which appear between the local and immediate levels of our struggles and their hemispheric and global dynamics can only grow. (p. 35)

The point of working in racialized discourses and ethnic epistemologies is not merely to "color" the scholarship. It is to challenge the hegemonic structures (and symbols) that keep injustice and inequity in place. The work also is not about dismissing the work of European and Euro-American scholars. Rather, it is about defining the limits of such scholarship. The push from scholars of color is to raise the bar or up the ante of qualitative inquiry.

Perhaps a crude but relevant analogue for what racialized discourses and ethnic epistemologies can do for scholarship can be found in the world of sports. Prior to 1947, "America's favorite pastime"—professional baseball—was a game for White men. No players of color were considered "qualified" to play in the big leagues. Once a Black player was selected to play in the league, there was talk of "lowered standards." However, no such downward slide happened in professional baseball. Inclusion of players of color—African Americans, Latinos, Asians—has made for a more competitive game and a game more widely played throughout the world.

Similarly, scholars of color remain woefully underrepresented in the academy. Too often, concern is voiced that scholars of color will not be able to meet certain standards and that hiring such scholars will lower the prestige and status of the institution. But how can the full range of scholarship be explored if whole groups of people are systematically excluded from participating in the process of knowledge production? Some might argue that scholars of color who subscribe to these racialized discourses and ethnic epistemologies are "biased" in their approach to scholarly inquiry. But the point of the multiple-consciousness perspective and the view from the liminal is that scholars of color who have experienced racism and ethnic discrimination (yet survived the rigors of the degree credentialing process) have a perspective advantage. As Delgado (1995c) argues: "Many members of minority groups speak two languages, grow up in two cultures. . . . And so, . . . who has the advantage in mastering and applying critical social thought? Who tends to think of everything in two or more ways at the same time? Who is a postmodernist virtually as a condition of his or her being?" (p. 8).

The paradigm shifts that are occurring in qualitative research are both about representation and beyond representation. They are about developing a "tolerance for ambiguity" (Anzaldúa, 1987). Indeed, Anzaldúa (1987) has uttered prophetically:

> [*La mestiza*] has discovered that she can't hold concepts or ideas in rigid boundaries. The borders and walls that are supposed to keep the undesirable ideas out are entrenched habits and patterns of behavior; these habits and patterns are the enemy within. Rigidity means death. Only by remaining flexible is she able to stretch the psyche horizontally and vertically. *La mestiza* constantly has to shift out of habitual formations; from convergent thinking, analytical reasoning that tends to use rationality to move toward a single goal, to divergent thinking, characterized by movement away from set patterns and goals and toward a more whole perspective, one that includes rather than excludes. The new *mestiza* copes by developing a tolerance for contradictions, a tolerance for ambiguity. (p. 79)

The "gift" of the new *mestiza* is a new vision of scholarship. To be able to accept that gift, scholars must shed the bonds of rigid paradigms and stand in new relationship to knowledge, the knower, and the known. The position of alterity—the liminal—is not a privileged position, but it is an advantaged one. It offers an opportunity to create a "public scholarship" (J. E. King, personal communication, April 1998) that prompts social action and transformation.

◆ What Difference Can CRT Make for the Critical Qualitative Researcher?

Collins (1998) points out that rather than allow her language to "masquerade as seeming objectivity and apolitical authority," she chooses language through "both an intellectual and a political decision" (p. xxi). She cites legal scholar Patricia Williams, who asks, "What is 'impersonal' writing but denial of self?" (p. xxi). Thus CRT asks the critical qualitative researcher to operate in a self-revelatory mode, to acknowledge the double (or multiple) consciousness in which she or he is operating. My *decision* to deploy a critical race theoretical framework in my scholarship is intimately linked to my understanding of the political and personal stake I have in the education of Black children. All of my "selves" are invested in this work—the self that is a researcher, the self that is a parent, the self that is a community member, the self that is a Black woman. No technical-rational approach to this work would yield the deeply textured, multifaceted work I attempt to do. Nor would a technical-rational approach allow for the "archaeology of knowledge" (Foucault, 1972) that is necessary to challenge the inequitable social, economic, and political positions that exist between the mainstream and the margins.

The "gift" of CRT is that it unapologetically challenges the scholarship that would dehumanize and depersonalize us. The question we confront is not merely one of the difference between "quantitative" and "qualitative" scholarship. More than two decades ago, Cronbach (1975) tried to put to rest the false dichotomy of quantity versus quality. The significant issues with which we grapple are paradigmatic and epistemological. Out of those paradigms grow particular methodologies. Frankenstein (1990),

Nettles and Perna (1997), and Wilson (1987) have all used quantitative methods to turn a critical gaze on social inequity. The sheer volume and disparity of the numbers they present underscore the ways in which people are systematically subordinated and excluded from the society. Thus there is no magic in employing participant observation, narrative inquiry, or interviews. Indeed, the qualitative researcher must guard against the connotation that qualitative work represents some more "authentic" form of research. As we consider various examples of qualitative research we must be mindful of the ways "the research" may render the researcher invisible. The ethnographer stands as a kind of *deus ex machina* who tells a tightly organized and neatly contrived story. Unlike the television journalist who conducts an interview in plain sight of a huge audience, no critique of the questions, the format, or the tone of voice is offered to the researcher.[9]

In CRT the researcher makes a deliberate appearance in his or her work or, like Bell (1987, 1992, 1998) and Delgado (1992, 1993), may create an alter ego who can speak directly to power. For Bell, Geneva Crenshaw, a Black woman, served this purpose. Delgado created Rodrigo, Crenshaw's half brother, to argue against mainstream legal scholarship. The deeply personal rendering of social science that CRT scholars bring to their work helps break open the mythical hold that traditional work has on knowledge. When Williams (1991) presented the bill of sale of her enslaved great-great-grandmother in her law school contracts course, she destabilized the students' notions of contracts as documents devoid of human emotion and personal consequences.

CRT helps to raise some important questions about the control and production of knowledge—particularly knowledge about people and communities of color. Where is "race" in the discourse of critical qualitative researchers? To what degree have critical qualitative researchers reinscribed liberalism in their work? How has the quest to embrace the postmodern perspectives on human agency obscured the need for collective effort? In what ways will critical qualitative research be forced to "work the hyphens" or "probe how we are in relation with the contexts we study and with our informants, understanding that we are all multiple in those relations" (Fine, 1988, p. 135)?

◆ *Epilogue*

As I reflect back on what I have written in this chapter, I am reminded that the nagging questions about the "mixing" of race and ethnicity with "scholarship" persist. The claims of lack of objectivity and politicized inquiry nip at my heels. For me, Lucius Outlaw (1995) offers a fitting last word:

> Why race and ethnicity in relation to philosophy? In short because I am convinced that we are living through a period in which race and ethnicity are so challenging to the prospect of our enjoying a future in which we can and will flourish that we are compelled to undertake a fundamental revision of some of our basic convictions regarding who we are, what our lives should be about, and how we will achieve our goals, both individually and collectively. Since such concerns have provided the motivating core for much of Western philosophy (and its sibling fields of inquiry) for more than two thousand years. . . . Finally, there is the deeply personal dimension to . . . focusing on these issues, for they come together in a poignant way to constitute my very being and to inform my daily life, and thereby to condition the lives of all who interact with me: I am a philosopher; I teach portions of the history of the discipline; but I do so as a person of a racial/ethnic group whose existence in America . . . is marked by the holocaust of enslavement and other forms of oppression which have been rationalized by some of the "best" minds in the pantheon of Western philosophers. Thus, not only in practical living must I contend with constricting factors having to do with the politics of race and ethnicity, I must do battle as well, inside the very citadel of reason where enlightenment leading to enhanced living is supposed to have its wellspring. . . . I have committed myself to confronting this seedy aspect of its underside and to the clearing of intellectual and social spaces in which we might come together to work and dwell in peace and harmony with justice. (pp. 305-306)

■ *Notes*

1. The heading on this section is a reversal of Deborah King's (1988) "Multiple Jeopardy, Multiple Consciousness."

2. Although I refer to African Americans, Latinas/os, Asian Americans, Native Americans, and Whites throughout this essay, it is important not to reify what Hollinger (1995) terms the "ethnic pentagon." The boundaries separating various racial, ethnic, and cultural groups have become much more permeable and have created more complex and multifaceted identities in the late years of the 20th century.

3. Members of my own family made their livings by working as domestics in the homes of wealthy White people. From their jobs they learned about middle-class notions of etiquette, fashion, and financial sense.

4. Portions of this section are adapted from Ladson-Billings (1998).

5. This statement was made by Henry Louis Gates, Jr., in 1997 at a conference presenting the *Norton Anthology of African American Literature* at the University of Wisconsin–Madison.

6. Sylvia Wynter (1992) has referred to the ethnic studies of the 1960s—African American, American Indian, Asian American, Chicano, Puerto Rican, and Latino studies—as "New Studies" to represent their break from old paradigms and orthodoxy.

7. At a professional meeting, one of my colleagues, an African American woman, suggested that African American communities had become "data plantations" where researchers reap benefits without contributing much of substance.

8. This stance is particularly interesting in light of current controversies over the life story of Rigoberta Menchú (1984), titled *I, Rigoberta Menchú*. A Dartmouth researcher who visited Menchú's Guatemalan village discovered "inconsistencies" and "fabrications" in her autobiography (Stoll, 1999).

9. I am completing this chapter just after the airing of television journalist Barbara Walters's interview with the infamous Monica Lewinsky. I am struck by how many people commented after

the interview on the types of questions Walters asked, the way she asked them, and the kinds of questions she omitted.

■ References

Acuña, R. (1972). *Occupied America: The Chicano struggle toward liberation.* New York: Canfield.

Alarcón, N. (1990). Chicana feminism: In the tracks of "the" native woman. *Cultural Studies, 4,* 248-256.

Almaguer, T. (1974). Historical notes on Chicano oppression: The dialectics of racial and class domination in North America. *Aztlan, 5*(1-2), 27-56.

Ani, M. (1994). *Yurugu: An African-centered critique of European cultural thought and behavior.* Trenton, NJ: Africa World Press.

Anzaldúa, G. (1987). *Borderlands/la frontera: The new mestiza.* San Francisco: Aunt Lute.

Appiah, K. A. (1992). *In my father's house: Africa in the philosophy of culture.* New York: Oxford University Press.

Appleby, J., Hunt, L., & Jacob, M. (1994). *Telling the truth about history.* New York: W. W. Norton.

Asante, M. K. (1987). *The Afrocentric idea.* Philadelphia: Temple University Press.

Asante, M. K. (1991). The Afrocentric idea in education. *Journal of Negro Education, 60,* 170-180.

Balderrama, F. E. (1982). *In defense of la raza: The Los Angeles Mexican consulate and the Mexican community, 1929-1936.* Tucson: University of Arizona Press.

Barnes, R. (1990). Race consciousness: The thematic content of racial distinctiveness in critical race legal scholarship. *Harvard Law Review, 103,* 1864-1871.

Bell, D. (1980). *Brown v. Board of Education* and the interest convergence dilemma. *Harvard Law Review, 93,* 518-533.

Bell, D. (1987). *And we are not saved: The elusive quest for racial justice.* New York: Basic Books.

Bell, D. (1992). *Faces at the bottom of the well.* New York: Basic Books.

Bell, D. (1998). *Afrolantic legacies.* Chicago: Third World Press.

Bettelheim, B. (1965). Teaching the disadvantaged. *National Education Association Journal, 54,* 8-12.

Bloom, B., Davis, A., & Hess, R. (1965). *Comprehensive education for cultural deprivations.* Troy, MO: Holt, Rinehart & Winston.

Calmore, J. O. (1992). Critical race theory, Archie Shepp and fire music: Securing an authentic intellectual life in a multicultural world. *Southern California Law Review, 65,* 2129-2230.

Castillo, A. (1995). *Massacre of the dreamers: Essays on Xicanisma.* New York: Plume.

Churchill, W. (1992). *Fantasies of the master race: Literature, cinema, and the colonization of American Indians.* Monroe, ME: Common Courage.

Churchill, W. (1993). I am indigenist. In W. Churchill, *Struggle for the land: A land rights reader.* Monroe, ME: Common Courage.

Code, L. (1991). *What can she know? Feminist theory and the construction of knowledge.* Ithaca, NY: Cornell University Press.

Collins, P. H. (1990). *Black feminist thought: Knowledge, consciousness, and the politics of empowerment.* New York: Routledge, Chapman & Hall.

Collins, P. H. (1998). *Fighting words: Black women and the search for justice.* Minneapolis: University of Minnesota Press.

Connelly, F. M., & Clandinin, D. J. (1990). Stories of experience and narrative inquiry. *Educational Researcher, 19*(5), 2-14.

Crenshaw, K. (1988). Race, reform and retrenchment: Transformation and legitimation in anti-discrimination law. *Harvard Law Review, 101,* 1331-1387.

Crenshaw, K., Gotanda, N., Peller, G., & Thomas, K. (1995). Introduction. In K. Crenshaw, N. Gotanda, G. Peller, & K. Thomas (Eds.), *Critical race theory: The key writings that formed the movement.* New York: Free Press.

Cronbach, L. (1975). Beyond the two disciplines of scientific psychology. *American Psychologist, 30,* 116-127.

de la Torre, A., & Pesquera, B. (Eds.). (1993). *Building with our hands: New directions in Chicano studies.* Berkeley: University of California Press.

Delgado, R. (1992). Rodrigo's chronicle. *Yale Law Journal, 101,* 1357-1383.

Delgado, R. (1993). Rodrigo's sixth chronicle: Intersections, essences, and the dilemma of social reform. *New York University Law Review, 68*, 639-674.

Delgado, R. (Ed.). (1995a). *Critical race theory: The cutting edge.* Philadelphia: Temple University Press.

Delgado, R. (1995b). Introduction. In R. Delgado (Ed.), *Critical race theory: The cutting edge.* Philadelphia: Temple University Press.

Delgado, R. (1995c). Racial realism—after we're gone: Prudent speculations on America in a post-racial epoch. In R. Delgado (Ed.), *Critical race theory: The cutting edge.* Philadelphia: Temple University Press.

Delgado Bernal, D. (1998). Using a Chicana feminist epistemology in educational research. *Harvard Educational Review, 68,* 555-582.

Delgado-Gaitan, C. (1993). Researching change and changing the researcher. *Harvard Educational Review, 63*, 389-411.

Du Bois, W. E. B. (1953). *The souls of Black folk.* New York: Fawcett. (Original work published 1903)

Ellison, R. (1986). What America would be like without Blacks. In R. Ellison, *Going to the territory* (pp. 104-112). New York: Random House.

Espiritu, Y. L. (1992). *Asian American panethnicity: Bridging institutions and identities.* Philadelphia: Temple University Press.

Fanon, F. (1968). *The wretched of the earth.* New York: Grove.

Fine, M. (1998). Working the hyphens: Reinventing self and other in qualitative research. In N. K. Denzin & Y. S. Lincoln (Eds.), *The landscape of qualitative research: Theories and issues* (pp. 130-155). Thousand Oaks, CA: Sage.

Foucault, M. (1972). *The archaeology of knowledge* (A. M. Sheridan Smith, Trans.). New York: Harper & Row.

Foucault, M. (1973). *The order of things: An archaeology of the human sciences.* New York: Random House.

Frankenstein, M. (1990). Incorporating race, gender, and class issues into a critical mathematics literacy curriculum. *Journal of Negro Education, 59,* 336-351.

Geertz, C. (1983). *Local knowledge: Further essays in interpretive anthropology.* New York: Basic Books.

Gilroy, P. (1993). *Black Atlantic: Modernity and double consciousness.* Cambridge, MA: Harvard University Press.

Gomez-Quinones, J. (1977). On culture. *Revista Chicano-Riqueña, 5*(2), 35-53.

Gordon, R. (1990). New developments in legal theory. In D. Kairys (Ed.), *The politics of law: A progressive critique* (pp. 413-325). New York: Pantheon.

Gramsci, A. (1971). *Selections from the prison notebooks* (Q. Hoare & G. N. Smith, Eds. & Trans.). New York: International.

Guinier, L. (1994). *The tyranny of the majority: Fundamental fairness in representative democracy.* New York: Free Press.

Guy-Sheftall, B. (1993, April). *Black feminist perspectives on the academy.* Paper presented at the annual meeting of the American Educational Research Association, Atlanta.

Gwaltney, J. L. (1980). *Drylongso: A self-portrait of Black America.* New York: Random House.

Haney López, I. F. (1995). The social construction of race. In R. Delgado (Ed.), *Critical race theory: The cutting edge* (pp. 191-203). Philadelphia: Temple University Press.

Hertzberg, H. W. (1971). *The search for an American Indian identity.* Syracuse, NY: Syracuse University Press.

Highwater, J. (1981). *The primal mind: Vision and reality in Indian America.* New York: Meridian.

Hirabayashi, L. R., & Alquizola, M. C. (1994). Asian American studies: Re-evaluating for the 1990s. In K. Aguilar-San Juan (Ed.), *The state of Asian America: Activism and resistance in the 1990s* (pp. 351-364). Boston: South End.

Hollinger, P. (1995). *Postethnic America: Beyond multiculturalism.* New York: Basic Books.

hooks, b. (1984). *Feminist theory: From margin to center.* Boston: South End.

hooks, b. (1989). *Talking back: Thinking feminist, thinking Black.* Boston: South End.

hooks, b. (1992). *Black looks: Race and representation.* Boston: South End.

Hwang, D. H. (1994). Foreword: Facing the mirror. In K. Aguilar-San Juan (Ed.), *The state of Asian America: Activism and resistance in the 1990s* (pp. ix-xii). Boston: South End.

Jefferson, T. (1954). *Notes on the state of Virginia.* New York: W. W. Norton. (Original work published 1784)

Kincheloe, J. L., & McLaren, P. L. (1998). Rethinking critical theory and qualitative research. In N. K. Denzin & Y. S. Lincoln (Eds.), *The landscape of qualitative research: Theories and issues* (pp. 260-299). Thousand Oaks, CA: Sage.

King, D. K. (1988). Multiple jeopardy, multiple consciousness: The context of a Black feminist ideology. *Signs, 14,* 42-72.

King, J. E. (1995). Culture centered knowledge: Black studies, curriculum transformation, and social action. In J. A. Banks & C. M. Banks (Eds.), *Handbook of research on multicultural education* (pp. 265-290). New York: Macmillan.

Ladson-Billings, G. (1993). Through a looking glass: Politics and the history curriculum. *Theory and Research in Social Education, 21,* 84-92.

Ladson-Billings, G. (1994). *The dreamkeepers: Successful teachers of African American children.* San Francisco: Jossey-Bass.

Ladson-Billings, G. (1997). For colored girls who have considered suicide when the academy isn't enough: Reflections of an African American woman scholar. In A. Neumann & P. Peterson (Eds.), *Learning from our lives: Women, research and autobiography in education* (pp. 52-70). New York: Teachers College Press.

Ladson-Billings, G. (1998). Just what is critical race theory and what is it doing in a "nice" field like education? *International Journal of Qualitative Studies in Education, 11,* 7-24.

Ladson-Billings, G., & Tate, W. F. (1995). Toward a critical race theory of education. *Teachers College Record, 97,* 47-68.

Lawrence, C. (1995). The word and the river: Pedagogy as scholarship and struggle. In K. Crenshaw, N. Gotanda, G. Peller, & K. Thomas (Eds.), *Critical race theory: The writings that formed the movement* (pp. 336-351). New York: Free Press.

Legesse, A. (1973). *Three approaches to the study of an African society.* New York: Free Press.

Lewis, D. L. (1993). *W. E. B. Du Bois: Biography of a race 1868-1919.* New York: Henry Holt.

Lewontin, R. C., Rose, S., & Kamin, L. (1984). *Not in our genes: Biology, ideology and human nature.* New York: Pantheon.

Lomawaima, K. T. (1995). Educating Native Americans. In J. A. Banks & C. M. Banks (Eds.), *Handbook of research on multicultural education* (pp. 331-347). New York: Macmillan.

Lorde, A. (1984). *Sister outsider: Essays and speeches.* New York: Crossing.

Lowe, L. (1996). *Immigrant acts: On Asian American cultural politics.* Durham, NC: Duke University Press.

Menchú, R. (1984). *I, Rigoberta Menchú: An Indian woman in Guatemala* (E. Burgos-Debray, Ed.; A. Wright, Trans.). London: Verso.

Mirande, A., & Enriquez, E. (1979). *La Chicana: The Mexican American woman.* Chicago: University of Chicago Press.

Mohanty, C. T. (1991). Under Western eyes: Feminist scholarship and colonial discourses. In C. T. Mohanty, A. Russo, & L. Torres (Eds.), *Third World women and the politics of feminism* (pp. 50-80). Bloomington: Indiana University Press.

Morrison, T. (1992). *Playing in the dark: Whiteness and the literary imagination.* Cambridge, MA: Harvard University Press.

Narayan, K. (1993). How native is a "native" anthropologist? *American Anthropologist, 95,* 671-686.

Nettles, M., & Perna, L. (1997). *The African American education data book.* Fairfax, VA: Frederick D. Patterson Research Institute.

Nieto, S. (1992). We have stories to tell: A case study of Puerto Ricans in children's books. In V. A. Harris (Ed.), *Teaching multicultural literature in grades K-8* (pp. 171-201). Northwood, MA: Christopher-Gordon.

Oboler, S. (1995). *Ethnic labels, Latino lives: Identity and the politics of (re)presentation in the United States.* Minneapolis: University of Minnesota Press.

Omi, M., & Winant, H. (1994). *Racial formation in the United States: 1960-1990* (2nd ed.). New York: Routledge.

Ornstein, A., & Vairo, P. (1968). *How to teach disadvantaged youth.* New York: McKay.

Outlaw, L. (1995). Philosophy, ethnicity, and race. In F. L. Hord & J. S. Lee (Eds.), *I am because we are: Readings in Black philosophy* (pp. 304-328). Amherst: University of Massachusetts Press.

Padilla, F. (1987). *Latino ethnic consciousness.* Notre Dame, IN: Notre Dame University Press.

Pandian, J. (1985). *Anthropology and the Western tradition: Towards an authentic anthropology.* Prospects Heights, IL: Waveland.

Paz, O. (1961). *The labyrinth of solitude: Life and thought in Mexico.* New York: Random House.

Pirsig, R. M. (1972). *Zen and the art of motorcycle maintenance.* New York: Bantam.

Riessman, F. (1962). *The culturally deprived child.* New York: Harper & Row.

Rist, R. (1990). On the relations among educational research paradigms: From disdain to detentes. In K. Dougherty & F. Hammack (Eds.), *Education and society: A reader* (pp. 81-95). New York: Harcourt Brace Jovanovich.

Rosaldo, R. (1989). *Culture and truth: The remaking of social analysis.* Boston: Beacon.

Rosaldo, R. (1993). After objectivism. In S. During (Ed.), *The cultural studies reader* (pp. 104-117). New York: Routledge.

Said, E. W. (1979). *Orientalism.* New York: Vintage.

Scheurich, J. J., & Young, M. (1997). Coloring epistemologies: Are our research epistemologies racially biased? *Educational Researcher, 26*(4), 4-16.

Shujaa, M. (1997, April). *Transformation of the researcher working toward liberation.* Paper presented at the annual meeting of the American Educational Research Association, San Diego, CA.

Siddle-Walker, V. (1996). *Their highest potential: An African American school community in the segregated South.* Chapel Hill: University of North Carolina Press.

Silko, L. M. (1977). *Ceremony.* New York: Viking.

Silko, L. M. (1981). *Storyteller.* New York: Seaver.

Snipp, C. M. (1995). American Indian studies. In J. A. Banks & C. M. Banks (Eds.). *Handbook of research on multicultural education* (pp. 245-258). New York: Macmillan.

Spivak, G. C. (1988). *In other worlds: Essays in cultural politics.* New York: Routledge.

Stoll, D. (1999). *Rigoberta Menchú and the story of all poor Guatemalans.* Boulder, CO: Westview.

Takaki, R. (1989). *Strangers from a different shore: A history of Asian Americans.* Boston: Little, Brown.

Takaki, R. (1993). *A different mirror: A multicultural history of America.* Boston: Little, Brown.

Tate, W. F. (1997). Critical race theory and education: History, theory, and implications. In M. W. Apple (Ed.), *Review of research in education* (Vol. 22, pp. 191-243). Washington, DC: American Educational Research Association.

Torres-Guzman, M. E. (1992). Stories of hope in the midst of despair: Culturally responsive education for Latino students in an alternative high school in New York City. In M. Saravia-Shore & S. F. Arvizu (Eds.), *Cross cultural literacy: Ethnographies of communication in multiethnic classrooms* (pp. 477-490). New York: Garland.

Trinh T. M. (1909). *Woman, native, other: Writing postcoloniality and feminism.* Bloomington: Indiana University Press.

Unger, R. M. (1983). The critical legal studies movement. *Harvard Law Review, 96,* 561-675.

Villenas, S. (1966). The colonizer/colonized Chicana ethnographer: Identity, marginalization, and co-optation in the field. *Harvard Educational Review, 66,* 711-731.

Warrior, R. A. (1995). *Tribal secrets: Recovering American Indian intellectual traditions.* Minneapolis: University of Minnesota Press.

West, C. (1990). The new cultural politics of difference. In R. Ferguson, M. Gever, T. M. Trinh, & C. West (Eds.), *Out there: Marginalization and contemporary cultures* (pp. 19-36). Cambridge: MIT Press.

West, C. (1993). *Keeping faith: Philosophy and race in America.* New York: Routledge.

Williams, G. W. (1882-1883). *History of the Negro race in America from 1619 to 1880: Negroes as slaves, as soldiers, as citizens* (2 vols.). New York: G. P. Putnam's Sons.

Williams, P. (1991). *The alchemy of race and rights: Diary of a law professor.* Cambridge, MA: Harvard University Press.

Williams, R. (1995). Foreword. In R. Delgado, *The Rodrigo chronicles: Conversations about America and race* (pp. xi-xv). New York: New York University Press.

Wilson, W. J. (1987). *The truly disadvantaged: The inner city, the underclass, and public policy.* Chicago: University of Chicago Press.

Woodson, C. G. (1933). *The miseducation of the Negro.* Washington, DC: Association Press.

Wynter, S. (1992). *Do not call us "Negroes": How "multicultural" textbooks perpetuate racism.* San Francisco: Aspire.

Zinn, H. (1980). *A people's history of the United States.* New York: HarperCollins.

10

RETHINKING CRITICAL THEORY AND QUALITATIVE RESEARCH

◆ Joe L. Kincheloe and Peter McLaren

◆ The Roots of Critical Research

Some 70 years after its development in Frankfurt, Germany, critical theory retains its ability to disrupt and challenge the status quo. In the process, it elicits highly charged emotions of all types—fierce loyalty from its proponents, vehement hostility from its detractors. Such vibrantly polar reactions indicate at the very least that critical theory still matters. We can be against critical theory or for it, but, especially at the present historical juncture, we cannot be without it. Indeed, qualitative research that frames its purpose in the context of critical theoretical concerns still produces, in our view, undeniably dangerous knowledge, the kind of information and insight that upsets institutions and threatens to overturn sovereign regimes of truth.

Critical theory is a term that is often evoked and frequently misunderstood. It usually refers to the theoretical tradition developed by the Frankfurt school, a group of writers connected to the Institute of Social Research at the University of Frankfurt. However, none of the Frankfurt school theorists ever claimed to have developed a unified approach to cultural criticism. In its beginnings, Max Horkheimer, Theodor Adorno, and Herbert Marcuse initiated a conversation with the German tradition of philosophical and social thought, especially that of Marx, Kant, Hegel, and Weber. From the vantage point of these critical theorists, whose political sensibilities were influenced by the devastations of World War I, postwar Germany with its economic depression marked by inflation and unemployment, and the failed strikes and protests in Germany and Central Europe in this same period, the world was in urgent need of reinterpretation. From this perspective, they defied Marxist orthodoxy while deepening their belief that injustice and subjugation shape the lived world (Bottomore, 1984; Gibson, 1986; Held, 1980; Jay, 1973). Focusing their attention on the changing nature of capitalism, the early critical theorists analyzed the mutating forms of domination that accompanied this change (Agger, 1998; Gall, Gall, & Borg, 1999; Giroux, 1983, 1997; Kellner, 1989; Kincheloe & Pinar, 1991; McLaren, 1997).

Only a decade after the Frankfurt school was established, the Nazis controlled Germany. The danger posed by the exclusive Jewish membership of the Frankfurt school, and its association with Marxism, convinced Horkheimer, Adorno, and Marcuse to leave Germany. Eventually locating themselves in California, these critical theorists were shocked by American culture. Offended by the taken-for-granted empirical practices of American social science researchers, Horkheimer, Adorno, and Marcuse were challenged to respond to the social science establishment's belief that their research could describe and accurately measure any dimension of human behavior. Piqued by the contradictions between progressive American rhetoric of egalitarianism and the reality of racial and class discrimination, these theorists produced their major work while residing in the United States. In 1953, Horkheimer and Adorno returned to Germany and reestablished the Institute of Social Research. Significantly, Herbert Marcuse stayed in the United States, where he would find a new audience for his work in social theory. Much to his own surprise, Marcuse skyrocketed to fâme as the philosopher of the student movements of the 1960s. Critical theory, especially the emotionally and sexually liberating work of Marcuse, provided the philosophical voice of the New Left. Concerned with the politics of psychological and cultural revolution, the New Left preached a Marcusian sermon of political emancipation (Gibson, 1986; Hinchey, 1998; Kincheloe & Steinberg, 1997; Surber, 1998; Wexler, 1991, 1996b).

Many academicians who had come of age in the politically charged atmosphere of the 1960s focused their scholarly attention on critical theory. Frustrated by forms of domination emerging from a post-Enlightenment culture nurtured

by capitalism, these scholars saw in critical theory a method of temporarily freeing academic work from these forms of power. Impressed by critical theory's dialectical concern with the social construction of experience, they came to view their disciplines as manifestations of the discourses and power relations of the social and historical contexts that produced them. The "discourse of possibility" implicit within the constructed nature of social experience suggested to these scholars that a reconstruction of the social sciences could eventually lead to a more egalitarian and democratic social order. New poststructuralist conceptualizations of human agency and their promise that men and women can at least partly determine their own existence offered new hope for emancipatory forms of social research when compared with orthodox Marxism's assertion of the iron laws of history, the irrevocable evil of capitalism, and the proletariat as the privileged subject and anticipated agent of social transformation. For example, when Henry Giroux and other critical educators criticized the argument made by Marxist scholars Samuel Bowles and Herbert Gintis—that schools are capitalist agencies of social, economic, cultural, and bureaucratic reproduction—they contrasted the deterministic perspectives of Bowles and Gintis with the idea that schools, as venues of hope, could become sites of resistance and democratic possibility through concerted efforts among teachers and students to work within a liberatory pedagogical framework. Giroux (1988), in particular, maintained that schools can become institutions where forms of knowledge, values, and social relations are taught for the purpose of educating young people for critical empowerment rather than subjugation.

◆ Critical Humility: Our Idiosyncratic Interpretation of Critical Theory and Critical Research

Over the past 20 years of our involvement in critical theory and critical research, we have been asked by hundreds of people to explain more precisely what critical theory is. We find that question difficult to answer because (a) there are many critical theories, not just one; (b) the critical tradition is always changing and evolving; and (c) critical theory attempts to avoid too much specificity, as there is room for disagreement among critical theorists. To lay out a set of fixed characteristics of the position is contrary to the desire of such theorists to avoid the production of blueprints of socio-political and epistemological beliefs. Given these disclaimers, we will now attempt to provide one idiosyncratic "take" on the nature of critical theory and critical research at the beginning of the millennium. Please note that this is merely our subjective analysis and there are many brilliant critical theorists who will find many problems with our pronouncements.

In this humble spirit we tender a description of a reconceptualized, end-of-century critical theory that has been critiqued and overhauled by the "post-discourses" of the last quarter of the 20th century (Bauman, 1995; Carlson & Apple, 1998; Collins, 1995; Giroux, 1997; Kellner, 1995; Roman & Eyre, 1997: Steinberg & Kincheloe, 1998). In this context a reconceptualized critical theory questions the assumption that societies such as the United States, Canada, Australia, New Zealand, and the nations in the European Union, for example, are unproblematically democratic and free. Over the 20th century, especially since the early 1960s, individuals in these societies have been acculturated to feel comfortable in relations of domination and subordination rather than equality and independence. Given the social and technological changes of the last half of the century that led to new forms of information production and access, critical theorists argued that questions of self-direction and democratic egalitarianism should be reassessed. In this context critical researchers informed by the "post-discourses" (e.g., postmodern, critical feminism, poststructuralism) understand that individual's view of themselves and the world even more influenced by social and historical forces than previously believed. Given the changing social and informational conditions of late-20th-century media-saturated

Western culture, critical theorists needed new ways of researching and analyzing the construction of individuals (Agger, 1992; Flossner & Otto, 1998; Hinchey, 1998; Leistyna, Woodrum, & Sherblom, 1996; Quail, Razzano, & Skalli, 2000; Smith & Wexler, 1995; Sünker, 1998). The following points briefly delineate our interpretation of a critical theory for the new millennium.

◆ A Reconceptualized Critical Theory

In this context it is important to note that we understand a social theory as a map or a guide to the social sphere. In a research context it does not determine how we see the world but helps us devise questions and strategies for exploring it. A critical social theory is concerned in particular with issues of power and justice and the ways that the economy, matters of race, class, and gender, ideologies, discourses, education, religion and other social institutions, and cultural dynamics interact to construct a social system.

Critical enlightenment. In this context critical theory analyzes competing power interests between groups and individuals within a society—identifying who gains and who loses in specific situations. Privileged groups, criticalists argue, often have an interest in supporting the status quo to protect their advantages; the dynamics of such efforts often become a central focus of critical research. Such studies of privilege often revolve around issues of race, class, gender, and sexuality (Carter, 1998; Howell, 1998; Kincheloe & Steinberg, 1997; Kincheloe, Steinberg, Rodriguez, & Chennault, 1998; McLaren, 1997; Rodriguez & Villaverde, 1999; Sleeter & McLaren, 1995). In this context to seek critical enlightenment is to uncover the winners and losers in particular social arrangements and the processes by which such power plays operate (Cary, 1996; Fehr, 1993; King, 1996; Pruyn, 1994; Wexler, 1996a).

Critical emancipation. Those who seek emancipation attempt to gain the power to control their own lives in solidarity with a justice-oriented community. Here critical research attempts to expose the forces that prevent individuals and groups from shaping the decisions that crucially affect their lives. In this way greater degrees of autonomy and human agency can be achieved. At the beginning of the new millennium we are cautious in our use of the term *emancipation* because, as many critics have pointed out, no one is ever completely emancipated from the sociopolitical context that has produced him or her. Also, many have questioned the arrogance that may accompany efforts to emancipate "others." These are important criticisms and must be carefully taken into account by critical researchers. Thus, as critical inquirers who search for those forces that insidiously shape who we are, we respect those who reach different conclusions in their personal journeys (Butler, 1998; Cannella, 1997; Kellogg, 1998; Knobel, 1999; Steinberg & Kincheloe, 1998; Weil, 1998).

The rejection of economic determinism. A caveat of a reconceptualized critical theory involves the insistence that the tradition does not accept the orthodox Marxist notion that "base" determines "superstructure"—meaning that economic factors dictate the nature of all other aspects of human existence. Critical theorists understand at the beginning of the 21st century that there are multiple forms of power, including the aforementioned racial, gender, sexual axes of domination. In issuing this caveat, however, a reconceptualized critical theory in no way attempts to argue that economic factors are unimportant in the shaping of everyday life. Economic factors can never be separated from other axes of oppression (Aronowitz & DiFazio, 1994; Carlson, 1997; Gabbard, 1995; Gee, Hull, & Lankshear, 1996; Gibson, 1986; Haymes, 1995; Kincheloe, 1995, 1999; Kincheloe & Steinberg, 1999; Martin & Schumann, 1996; Rifkin, 1995).

The critique of instrumental or technical rationality. A reconceptualized critical theory sees instrumental/technology rationality as one of the most oppressive features of contemporary society. Such a form of "hyperreason" involves an obsession with means in preference to ends. Critical theorists claim that instrumental/technical rationality is more interested in method and efficiency than in purpose. It delimits its questions to "how to" instead of "why should." In a research context, critical theorists claim that many rationalistic scholars become so obsessed with issues of technique, procedure, and correct method that they forget the humanistic purpose of the research act. Instrumental/technical rationality often separates fact from value in its obsession with "proper" method, losing in the process an understanding of the value choices always involved in the production of so-called facts (Alfino, Caputo, & Wynyard, 1998; Giroux, 1997; Hinchey, 1998; Kincheloe, 1993; McLaren, 1998; Ritzer, 1993; Stallabrass, 1996; Weinstein, 1998).

The impact of desire. A reconceptualized critical theory appreciates poststructuralist psychoanalysis as an important resource in pursuing an emancipatory research project. In this context critical researchers are empowered to dig more deeply into the complexity of the construction of the human psyche. Such a psychoanalysis helps critical researchers discern the unconscious processes that create resistance to progressive change and induce self-destructive behavior. A poststructural psychoanalysis, in its rejection of traditional psychoanalysis's tendency to view individuals as rational and autonomous beings, allows critical researchers new tools to rethink the interplay among the various axes of power, identity, libido, rationality, and emotion. In this configuration the psychic is no longer separated from the sociopolitical realm; indeed, desire can be socially constructed and used by power wielders for destructive and oppressive outcomes. On the other hand, critical theorists can help mobilize desire for progressive and emancipatory projects. Taking their lead from feminist theory, critical researchers are aware of the patriarchal inscriptions within traditional psychoanalysis and work to avoid its bourgeois, ethnocentric, and misogynist practices. Freed from these blinders, poststructural psychoanalysis helps researchers gain a new sensitivity to the role of fantasy and imagination and the structures of sociocultural and psychological meaning they reference (Alford, 1993; Atwell-Vasey, 1998; Barrows, 1995; Block, 1995; Britzman & Pitt, 1996; Elliot, 1994; Gresson, 2000; Kincheloe, Steinberg, & Villaverde, 1999; Pinar, 1998; Pinar, Reynolds, Slattery, & Taubman, 1995; Samuels, 1993).

A reconceptualized critical theory of power: hegemony. Our conception of a reconceptualized critical theory is intensely concerned with the need to understand the various and complex ways that power operates to dominate and shape consciousness. Power, critical theorists have learned, is an extremely ambiguous topic that demands detailed study and analysis. A consensus seems to be emerging among criticalists that power is a basic constituent of human existence that works to shape the oppressive and productive nature of the human tradition. Indeed, we are all empowered and we are all unempowered, in that we all possess abilities and we are all limited in the attempt to use our abilities. Because of limited space, we will focus here on critical theory's traditional concern with the oppressive aspects of power, although we understand that an important aspect of critical research focuses on the productive aspects of power—its ability to empower, to establish a critical democracy, to engage marginalized people in the rethinking of their sociopolitical role (Apple, 1996b; Fiske, 1993; Freire, 2000; Giroux, 1997; Macedo, 1994; Nicholson & Seidman, 1995).

In the context of oppressive power and its ability to produce inequalities and human suffering, Antonio Gramsci's notion of hegemony is central to critical research. Gramsci understood that dominant power in the 20th century is not always exercised simply by physical force but also through social psychological attempts to win people's consent to domination through cultural institutions such as the media, the schools, the family, and the church. Gramscian hegemony recognizes that the winning of popular consent is a very complex process and must be researched carefully on a case-by-case basis. Students and researchers of power, educators, sociologists, all of us are hegemonized as our field of knowledge and understanding is structured by a limited exposure to competing definitions of the sociopolitical world. The hegemonic field, with its bounded sociopsychological horizons, garners consent to an inequitable power matrix—a set of social relations that are legitimated by their depiction as natural and inevitable. In this context critical researchers note that hegemonic consent is never completely established, as it is always contested by various groups with different agendas (Grossberg, 1997; Lull, 1995; McLaren, 1995a, 1995b; McLaren, Hammer, Reilly, & Sholle, 1995; West, 1993).

A reconceptualized critical theory of power: ideology. Critical theorists understand that the formation of hegemony cannot be separated from the production of ideology. If hegemony is the larger effort of the powerful to win the consent of their "subordinates," then ideological hegemony involves the cultural forms, the meanings, the rituals, and the representations that produce consent to the status quo and individuals' particular places within it. Ideology vis-à-vis hegemony moves critical inquirers beyond simplistic explanations of domination that have used terms such as *propaganda* to describe the way media, political, educational, and other sociocultural productions coercively manipulate citizens to adopt oppressive meanings. A reconceptualized critical research endorses a much more subtle, ambiguous, and situationally specific form of domination that refuses the propaganda model's assumption that people are passive, easily manipulated victims. Researchers operating with an awareness of this hegemonic ideology understand that dominant ideological practices and discourses shape our vision of reality (Lemke, 1995, 1998). Thus our notion of hegemonic ideology is a critical form of epistemological constructivism buoyed by a nuanced understanding of power's complicity in the constructions people make of the world and their role in it (Kincheloe, 1998). Such an awareness corrects earlier delineations of ideology as a monolithic, unidirectional entity that was imposed on individuals by a secret cohort of ruling-class czars. Understanding domination in the context of concurrent struggles among different classes, racial and gender groups, and sectors of capital, critical researchers of ideology explore the ways such competition engages different visions, interests, and agendas in a variety of social locales—venues previously thought to be outside the domain of ideological struggle (Brosio, 1994; Steinberg, 2000).

A reconceptualized critical theory of power: linguistic/discursive power. Critical researchers have come to understand that language is not a mirror of society. It is an unstable social practice whose meaning shifts, depending upon the context in which it is used. Contrary to previous understandings, critical researchers appreciate the fact that language is not a neutral and objective conduit of description of the "real world." Rather, from a critical perspective, linguistic descriptions are not simply about the world but serve to construct it. With these linguistic notions in mind, criticalists begin to study the way language in the form of discourses serves as a form of regulation and domination. Discursive practices are defined as a set of tacit rules that regulate what can and cannot be said, who can speak with the blessings of authority and who must listen, whose social constructions are valid and whose are erroneous and unimportant. In an educational context, for example, legitimated discourses of power insidiously tell educators what books may be read by students, what instructional methods may be utilized, and what belief systems and views of success may be taught. In all forms of research discursive power validates particular research strategies, narrative formats, and modes of representation. In this context power discourses undermine the multiple meanings of language, establishing one correct reading that implants a particular hegemonic/ideological message into the consciousness of the reader. This is a process often referred to as the attempt to impose discursive closure. Critical researchers interested in the construction of consciousness are very attentive to these power dynamics (Blades, 1997; Gee,

1996; Lemke, 1993; Morgan, 1996; McWilliam & Taylor, 1996; Steinberg, 1998).

Focusing on the relationships among culture, power, and domination. In the last decades of the 20th century, culture has taken on a new importance in the effort to understand power and domination. Critical researchers have argued that culture has to be viewed as a domain of struggle where the production and transmission of knowledge is always a contested process (Giroux, 1997; Kincheloe & Steinberg, 1997; McLaren, 1997; Steinberg & Kincheloe, 1997; Steinberg, 1998). Dominant and subordinate cultures deploy differing systems of meaning based on the forms of knowledge produced in their cultural domain. Popular culture, with its TV, movies, video games, computers, music, dance, and other productions, plays an increasingly important role in critical research on power and domination. Cultural studies, of course, occupies an ever-expanding role in this context, as it examines not only popular culture but the tacit rules that guide cultural production. Arguing that the development of mass media has changed the way the culture operates, cultural studies researchers maintain that cultural epistemologies at the beginning of the new millennium are different from those of only a few decades ago. New forms of culture and cultural domination are produced as the distinction between the real and the simulated is blurred. This blurring effect of hyperreality constructs a social vertigo characterized by a loss of touch with traditional notions of time, community, self, and history. New structures of cultural space and time generated by bombarding electronic images from local, national, and international spaces shake our personal sense of place. This proliferation of signs and images functions as a mechanism of control in contemporary Western societies. The key to successful counterhegemonic cultural research involves (a) the ability to link the production of representations, images, and signs of hyperreality to power in the political economy; and (b) the capacity, once this linkage is exposed and described, to delineate the highly complex effects of the reception of these images and signs on individuals located at various race, class, gender, and sexual coordinates in the web of reality (Ferguson & Golding, 1997; Garnham, 1997; Grossberg, 1995; Joyrich, 1996; Thomas, 1997).

The role of cultural pedagogy in critical theory. Cultural production can often be thought of as a form of education, as it generates knowledge, shapes values, and constructs identity. From our perspective, such a framing can help critical researchers make sense of the world of domination and oppression as they work to bring about a more just, democratic, and egalitarian society. In recent years this educational dynamic has been referred to as cultural pedagogy (Berry, 1998; Giroux, 1997; Kincheloe, 1995; McLaren, 1997; Pailliotet, 1998; Semali, 1998; Soto, 1998). *Pedagogy* is a useful term that has traditionally been used to refer only to teaching and schooling. By using the term *cultural pedagogy,* we are specifically referring to the ways particular cultural agents produce particular hegemonic ways of seeing. In our critical interpretive context, our notion of cultural pedagogy asserts that the new "educators" in the electronically wired contemporary era are those who possess the financial resources to use mass media. This corporate-dominated pedagogical process has worked so well that few complain about it at the beginning of the new millennium—such informational politics doesn't make the evening news. Can we imagine another institution in contemporary society gaining the pedagogical power that corporations now assert over information and signification systems? What if the Church of Christ was sufficiently powerful to run pedagogical "commercials" every few minutes on TV and radio touting the necessity for everyone to accept that denomination's faith? Replayed scenes of Jews, Muslims, Hindus, Catholics, and Methodists being condemned to hell if they rejected the official pedagogy (the true doctrine) would greet North Americans and their children 7 days a week. There is little doubt that many people would be outraged and would organize for political action. Western societies have to some degree capitulated to this corporate pedagogical threat to democracy,

passively watching an elite gain greater control over the political system and political consciousness via a sophisticated cultural pedagogy. Critical researchers are intent on exposing the specifics of this process (Deetz, 1993; Drummond, 1996; Molnar, 1996; Pfeil, 1995; Steinberg & Kincheloe, 1997).

◆ **Critical Research and the Centrality of Interpretation: Critical Hermeneutics**

One of the most important aspects of a critical theory-informed qualitative research involves the often-neglected domain of the interpretation of information. As we have taught and written about critical research in the 1990s, this interpretive or hermeneutical aspect has become increasingly important. Many students of qualitative research approach us in classes and presentations with little theoretical background involving the complex and multidimensional nature of data interpretation in their work. Although there are many moments within the process of researching when the *critical* dynamic of critical theory-informed research appears, there is none more important than the moment(s) of interpretation. In this context we begin our discussion of critical qualitative research, linking it as we go to questions of the relationship between critical hermeneutics and knowledge production (Madison, 1988; Slattery, 1995).

The critical hermeneutic tradition (Grondin, 1994; Gross & Keith, 1997; Rosen, 1987; Vattimo, 1994) holds that in qualitative research there is only interpretation, no matter how vociferously many researchers may argue that the facts speak for themselves. The hermeneutic act of interpretation involves in its most elemental articulation making sense of what has been observed in a way that communicates understanding. Not only is all research merely an act of interpretation, but, hermeneutics contends, perception itself is an act of interpretation. Thus the quest for understanding is a fundamental feature of human existence, as encounter with the unfamiliar always demands the attempt to make meaning, to make sense. The same, however, is also the case with the familiar. Indeed, as in the study of commonly known texts, we come to find that sometimes the familiar may be seen as the most strange. Thus it should not be surprising that even the so-called objective writings of qualitative research are interpretations, not value-free descriptions (Denzin, 1994; Gallagher, 1992; Jardine, 1998; Smith, 1999).

Learning from the hermeneutic tradition and the postmodern critique, critical researchers have begun to reexamine textual claims to authority. No pristine interpretation exists—indeed, no methodology, social or educational theory, or discursive form can claim a privileged position that enables the production of authoritative knowledge. Researchers must always speak/write about the world in terms of something else in the world, "in relation to . . . ." As creatures of the world, we are oriented to it in a way that prevents us from grounding our theories and perspectives outside of it. Thus, whether we like it or not, we are all destined as interpreters to analyze from within its boundaries and blinders. Within these limitations, however, the interpretations emerging from the hermeneutic process can still move us to new levels of understanding, appreciations that allow us to "live our way" into an experience described to us. Despite the impediments of context, hermeneutical researchers can transcend the inadequacies of thin descriptions of decontextualized facts and produce thick descriptions of social texts characterized by the contexts of their production, the intentions of their producers, and the meanings mobilized in the processes of their construction. The production of such thick descriptions/interpretations follows no step-by-step blueprint or mechanical formula. As with any art form, hermeneutical analysis can be learned only in the Deweyan sense—by doing it. Researchers in the context practice the art by grappling with the text to be understood, telling its story in relation to its contextual dynamics and other texts first to themselves and then to a public audience (Car-

son & Sumara, 1997; Denzin, 1994; Gallagher, 1992; Jardine, 1998; Madison, 1988).

Critical Hermeneutical Methods of Interpretation

These concerns with the nature of hermeneutical interpretation come under the category of philosophical hermeneutics. Working this domain, hermeneutical scholars attempt to think through and clarify the conditions under which interpretation and understanding take place. The critical hermeneutics that grounds critical qualitative research moves more in the direction of normative hermeneutics in that it raises questions about the purposes and procedures of interpretation. In its critical theory-driven context, the purpose of hermeneutical analysis is to develop a form of cultural criticism revealing power dynamics within social and cultural texts. Qualitative researchers familiar with critical hermeneutics build bridges between reader and text, text and its producer, historical context and present, and one particular social circumstance and another. Accomplishing such interpretive tasks is difficult, and researchers situated in normative hermeneutics push ethnographers, historians, semioticians, literary critics, and content analysts to trace the bridge-building processes employed by successful interpretations of knowledge production and culture (Gallagher, 1992; Kellner, 1995; Kogler, 1996; Rapko, 1998).

Grounded by the hermeneutical bridge building, critical researchers in a hermeneutical circle (a process of analysis in which interpreters seek the historical and social dynamics that shape textual interpretation) engage in the back-and-forth of studying parts in relation to the whole and the whole in relation to parts. No final interpretation is sought in this context, as the activity of the circle proceeds with no need for closure (Gallagher, 1992; Peters & Lankshear, 1994; Pinar et al., 1995). This movement of whole to parts is combined with an analytic flow between abstract and concrete. Such dynamics often tie interpretation to the interplay of larger social forces (the general) to the everyday lives of individuals (the particular). A critical hermeneutics brings the concrete, the parts, the particular into focus, but in a manner that grounds them contextually in a larger understanding of the social forces, the whole, the abstract (the general). Focus on the parts is the dynamic that brings the particular into focus, sharpening our understanding of the individual in light of the social and psychological forces that shape him or her. The parts and the unique places they occupy ground hermeneutical ways of seeing by providing the contextualization of the particular—a perspective often erased in traditional inquiry's search for abstract generalizations (Gallagher, 1992; Kellner, 1995; Miller & Hodge, 1998; Peters & Lankshear, 1994).

The give-and-take of the hermeneutical circle provokes analysts to review existing conceptual matrices in light of new understandings. Here the analysts reconsider and reconceptualize preconceptions so as to provide a new way of exploring a particular text. Making use of an author's insights hermeneutically does not mean replicating his or her response to his or her original question. In the hermeneutical process the author's answer is valuable only if it catalyzes the production of a new question for our consideration in the effort to make sense of a particular textual phenomenon (Gallagher, 1992). In this context participants in the hermeneutical circle must be wary of techniques of textual defamiliarization that have become clichéd. For example, feminist criticisms of Barbie's figure and its construction of the image of ideal woman became such conventions in popular cultural analysis that other readings of Barbie were suppressed (Steinberg, 1997). Critical hermeneutical analysts in this and many other cases have to introduce new forms of analysis to the hermeneutical circle— to defamiliarize conventional defamiliarizations—in order to achieve deeper levels of understanding (Berger, 1995; Steinberg, 1998).

Within the hermeneutical circle we may develop new metaphors to shape our analysis in ways that break us out of familiar modes. For example, thinking of movies as mass-mediated dreams may help critical researchers of popular culture to reconceptualize the interpretive act as a psychoanalytic form of dream study. In this way, critical researchers could examine psychoanalytic work in the analysis of dream symbolization for insights into their cultural studies of the popular culture and the meanings it helps individuals make through its visual images and narratives. As researchers apply these new metaphors in the hermeneutical circle, they must be aware of the implicit metaphors researchers continuously bring to the interpretive process (Berger, 1995; Clough, 1998). Such metaphors are shaped by the sociohistorical era, the culture, and the linguistic context in which the interpreter operates. Such awarenesses are important features that must be introduced into the give-and-take of the critical hermeneutical circle. As John Dewey (1916) observed decades ago, individuals adopt the values and perspectives of their social groups in a manner that such factors come to shape their views of the world. Indeed, the values and perspectives of the group help determine what is deemed important and what is not, what is granted attention and what is ignored. Hermeneutical analysts are aware of such interpretational dynamics and make sure they are included in the search for understanding (Madison, 1988; Mullen, 1999).

Critical researchers with a hermeneutical insight take Dewey's insight to heart as they pursue their inquiry. They are aware that the consciousness, and the interpretive frames, they bring to their research are historically situated, ever changing, ever evolving in relationship to the cultural and ideological climate (Hinchey, 1998; Kincheloe, Steinberg, & Hinchey, 1999). Thus there is nothing simple about the social construction of interpretive lenses—consciousness construction is contradictory and the result of the collision of a variety of ideologically oppositional forces. Critical qualitative researchers who understand the relationship between identity formation and interpretive lenses are better equipped to understand the etymology of their own assertions—especially the way power operates to shape them. Linguistic, discursive, and many other factors typically hidden from awareness insidiously shape the meanings researchers garner from their work (Goodson, 1997). It was this dynamic that Antonio Gramsci had in mind when he argued that a critical philosophy should be viewed as a form of self-criticism. The starting point, he concluded, for any higher understanding of self involves consciousness of oneself as a product of power-driven sociohistorical forces. A critical perspective, he once wrote, involves the ability of its adherents to criticize the ideological frames that they use to make sense of the world (see Coben, 1998).

Analyzing Dewey's and Gramsci's notions of self-production in light of the aims of critical hermeneutics vis-à-vis critical qualitative research, we begin to gain insight into how the ambiguous and closeted interpretive process operates. This moves us in a critical direction, as we understand that the "facts" do not simply demand particular interpretations.

Hermeneutical Horizons: Situating Critical Research

Researchers who fail to take these points into account operate at the mercy of unexamined assumptions. Because all interpretation is historically and culturally situated, it is the lot of critical researchers to study the ways both interpreters (often the analysts themselves) and the objects of interpretation are constructed by their time and place. In this context the importance of social theory emerges. Operating in this manner, researchers inject critical social theory into the hermeneutical circle to facilitate an understanding of the hidden structures and tacit cultural dynamics that insidiously inscribe social meanings and values (Cary, 1996; Gallagher, 1992; Kellner, 1995). This social and historical situating of interpreter and text is an extremely complex enterprise that demands a nuanced analysis of the impact of hegemonic and ideological forces that connect the microdynamics of everyday life with the macrodynamics of structures such as white supremacy, patriarchy, and class elitism. The central hermeneutic of many critical qualitative works involves the interactions among research, subject(s), and these situating sociohistorical structures.

When these aspects of the interpretation process are taken into account, analysts begin to understand Hans-Georg Gadamer's (1989) contention that social frames of reference influence researchers' questions, which, in turn, shape the nature of interpretation itself. In light of this situating process, the modernist notion that a social text has one valid interpretation evaporates into thin air. Researchers, whether they admit it or not, always have points of view, disciplinary orientations, social or political groups with which they identify (Kincheloe, 1991; Lugg, 1996). Thus the point, critical hermeneuts argue, is not that researchers should shed all worldly affiliations but that they should identify those affiliations and understand their impacts on the ways the researchers approach social and educational phenomena. Gadamer labels these world affiliations of researchers their "horizons" and deems the hermeneutic act of interpretation the "fusion of horizons." When critical researchers participate in the fusion of horizons, they enter into the tradition of the text. Here they study the conditions of its production and the circle of previous interpretations. In this manner they begin to uncover the ways the text has attempted to over determine meaning (Berger, 1995; Ellis, 1998; Jardine, 1998; Miller & Hodge, 1998; Slattery, 1995).

The hermeneutical tradition puts the politics of interpretation at center stage. Like ordinary human beings, critical researchers make history and live their lives within structures of meaning they have not necessarily chosen for themselves. Understanding this, critical hermeneuts realize that a central aspect of their sociocultural analysis involves dissecting the ways people connect their everyday experiences to the cultural representations of such experiences. Such work involves the unraveling of the ideological codings embedded in these cultural representations. This unraveling is complicated by the taken-for-grantedness of the meanings promoted in these representations and the typically undetected ways these meanings are circulated into everyday life (Denzin, 1992; Kogler, 1996). The better the analyst, the better he or she can expose these meanings in the domain of the "what-goes-without-saying," that activity previously deemed noise unworthy of comment.

At this historical juncture, electronic modes of communication become extremely important to the production of meanings and representations that culturally situate human beings in general and textual interpretations in particular (Goldman & Papson, 1994; Hall, 1997). In many ways it can be argued that the postmodern condition produces a secondhand culture, filtered and preformed in the marketplace and constantly communicated via popular and mass media. Critical analysts understand that the pedagogical effects of such a mediated culture can range from the political/ideological to the cognitive/epistemological. For example, the situating effects of print media tend to promote a form of linearity that encourages certain forms of rationality, continuity, and uniformity; on the other hand, electronic media promote a nonlinear immediacy that may encourage more emotional responses that lead individuals in very different directions (du Gay, Hall, Janes, MacKay, & Negus, 1997; Shelton & Kincheloe, 1999). Thus the situating influence and pedagogical impact of electronic media of the postmodern condition must be assessed by those who study cultural and political processes and, most important at the turn of the millennium, the research processes itself (Bell & Valentine, 1997; Berger, 1995; Bertman, 1998; Denzin, 1992; Kellner, 1995).

Critical Hermeneutics: Laying the Groundwork of Critical Research

Critical hermeneutics is suspicious of any model of interpretation that claims to reveal the final truth, the essence of a text or any form of experience (Goodson & Mangan, 1996). Critical hermeneutics is more comfortable with interpretive approaches that assume that the meaning of human experience can never be fully disclosed—neither to the researcher nor even to the human who experienced it. Because language is always slippery, with its meanings ever "in process," critical hermeneutics understands that interpretations will never be linguistically unproblematic, will never be direct representations. Critical hermeneutics seeks to understand how textual practices such as scientific research and classical theory work to maintain existing power relations and to support extant power structures (Denzin, 1992). As critical researchers we draw, of course, on the latter model of interpretation, with its treatment of the personal as political. Critical hermeneutics grounds a critical research that attempts to connect the everyday troubles individuals face to public issues of power, justice, and democracy. Typically, within the realm of cultural studies and cultural analysis in general critical hermeneutics has deconstructed sociocultural texts that promote demeaning stereotypes of the disempowered (Denzin, 1992; Gross & Keith, 1997; Rapko, 1998). In this context critical hermeneutics is also being deployed in relation to cultural texts that reinforce an ideology of privilege and entitlement for empowered members of the society (Allison, 1998; Fine, Weis, Powell, & Wong, 1997; Frankenberg, 1993; Kincheloe et al., 1998; Rains, 1998; Rodriguez & Villaverde, 1999).

In its ability to render the personal political, critical hermeneutics provides a methodology for arousing a critical consciousness through the analysis of the generative themes of the present era. Such generative themes can often be used to examine the meaning-making power of the contemporary cultural realm (Peters & Lankshear, 1994). Within the qualitative research community there is still resistance to the idea that movies, television, and popular music are intricately involved in the most important political, economic, and cultural battles of the contemporary epoch. Critical hermeneutics recognizes this centrality of popular culture in the postmodern condition and seeks to uncover the ways it impedes and advances the struggle for a democratic society (Kellner, 1995). Appreciating the material effects of media culture, critical hermeneutics traces the ways cultural dynamics position audiences politically in ways that not only shape their political beliefs but formulate their identities (Steinberg & Kincheloe, 1997). In this context, Paulo Freire's (1985) contribution to the development of a critical hermeneutics is especially valuable. Understanding that the generative themes of a culture are central features in a critical social analysis, Freire assumes that the interpretive process is both an ontological (pertaining to being) and an epistemological (pertaining to knowledge) act. It is ontological on the level that our vocation as humans, the foundation of our being, is grounded on the hermeneutical task of interpreting the world so we can become more fully human. It is epistemological in the sense that critical hermeneutics offers us a method for investigating the conditions of our existence and the generative themes that shape it. In this context we gain the prowess to both live with a purpose and operate with the ability to perform evaluative acts in naming the culture around us. This ability takes on an even greater importance in the contemporary electronic society, where the sociopolitical effects of the cultural domain have often been left unnamed, allowing our exploration of the shaping of our own humanness to go unexplored in this strange new social context. Critical hermeneutics addresses this vacuum (Kincheloe & Steinberg, 1997; McLaren, 1997; Peters & Lankshear, 1994).

Critical hermeneutics names the world as a part of a larger effort to evaluate it and make it better. Knowing this, it is easy to understand why critical hermeneutics focuses on domination and its negation, emancipation. Domination limits self-direction and democratic community building, whereas emancipation enables them. Domination, legitimated as it is by ideology, is decoded by critical hermeneuts who help critical researchers discover the ways they and their subjects have been entangled in the ideological process. The exposé and critique of ideology is one of the main objectives of critical hermeneutics in its effort to make the world better. As long as our vision is obstructed by the various purveyors of ideology, our effort to live in democratic communities will be thwarted (Gallagher, 1992). Power wielders with race, class, and gender privilege (Kincheloe & Steinberg, 1997) have access to the resources that allow them to promote ideologies and representations in ways individuals without such privilege cannot (Bartolomé, 1998; Carlson &

Apple, 1998; Denzin, 1992; Gresson, 1995; Hinchey, 1998; Jipson & Paley, 1997; Leistyna et al., 1996; Peters & Lankshear, 1994; Pinar, 1998).

◆ Partisan Research in a "Neutral" Academic Culture

In the space available here it is impossible to do justice to all of the critical traditions that have drawn inspiration from Marx, Kant, Hegel, Weber, the Frankfurt school theorists, Continental social theorists such as Foucault, Habermas, and Derrida, Latin American thinkers such as Paulo Freire, French feminists such as Irigaray, Kristeva, and Cixous, or Russian sociolinguists such as Bakhtin and Vygotsky—most of whom regularly find their way into the reference lists of contemporary critical researchers. Today there are criticalist schools in many fields, and even a superficial discussion of the most prominent of these schools would demand much more space than we have available.

The fact that numerous books have been written about the often-virulent disagreements among members of the Frankfurt school only heightens our concern with the "packaging" of the different criticalist schools. Critical theory should not be treated as a universal grammar of revolutionary thought objectified and reduced to discrete formulaic pronouncements or strategies. Obviously, in presenting our idiosyncratic version of a reconceptualized critical theory, we have defined the critical tradition very broadly for the purpose of generating understanding; as we asserted earlier, this will trouble many critical researchers. In this move we decided to focus on the underlying commonality among critical schools of thought, at the cost of focusing on differences. This, of course, is always risky business in terms of suggesting a false unity or consensus where none exists, but such concerns are unavoidable in a survey chapter such as this. We are defining a criticalist as a researcher or theorist who attempts to use her or his work as a form of social or cultural criticism and who accepts certain basic assumptions: that all thought is fundamentally mediated by power relations that are social and historically constituted; that facts can never be isolated from the domain of values or removed from some form of ideological inscription; that the relationship between concept and object and between signifier and signified is never stable or fixed and is often mediated by the social relations of capitalist production and consumption; that language is central to the formation of subjectivity (conscious and unconscious awareness); that certain groups in any society are privileged over others and, although the reasons for this privileging may vary widely, the oppression that characterizes contemporary societies is most forcefully reproduced when subordinates accept their social status as natural, necessary, or inevitable; that oppression has many faces and that focusing on only one at the expense of others (e.g., class oppression versus racism) often elides the interconnections among them; and, finally, that mainstream research practices are generally, although most often unwittingly, implicated in the reproduction of systems of class, race, and gender oppression (Kincheloe & Steinberg, 1997).

In today's climate of blurred disciplinary genres, it is not uncommon to find literary theorists doing anthropology and anthropologists writing about literary theory, or political scientists trying their hand at ethnomethodological analysis, or philosophers doing Lacanian film criticism. We offer this observation not as an excuse to be wantonly eclectic in our treatment of the critical tradition but to make the point that any attempts to delineate critical theory as discrete schools of analysis will fail to capture the hybridity endemic to contemporary critical analysis.

Readers familiar with the criticalist traditions will recognize essentially four different "emergent" schools of social inquiry in this chapter: the neo-Marxist tradition of critical theory associated most closely with the work of Horkheimer, Adorno, and Marcuse; the genealogical writings of Michel Foucault; the practices of poststructuralist deconstruction associated with Derrida; and postmodernist currents

associated with Derrida, Foucault, Lyotard, Ebert, and others. In our view, critical ethnography has been influenced by all of these perspectives in different ways and to different degrees. From critical theory, researchers inherit a forceful criticism of the positivist conception of science and instrumental rationality, especially in Adorno's idea of negative dialectics, which posits an unstable relationship of contradiction between concepts and objects; from Derrida, researchers are given a means for deconstructing objective truth, or what is referred to as "the metaphysics of presence." For Derrida, the meaning of a word is constantly deferred because the word can have meaning only in relation to its difference from other words within a given system of language; Foucault invites researchers to explore the ways in which discourses are implicated in relations of power and how power and knowledge serve as dialectically reinitiating practices that regulate what is considered reasonable and true. We have characterized much of the work influenced by these writers as the "ludic" and "resistance" postmodernist theoretical perspectives.

Critical research can be best understood in the context of the empowerment of individuals. Inquiry that aspires to the name *critical* must be connected to an attempt to confront the injustice of a particular society or public sphere within the society. Research thus becomes a transformative endeavor unembarrassed by the label *political* and unafraid to consummate a relationship with emancipatory consciousness. Whereas traditional researchers cling to the guard rail of neutrality, critical researchers frequently announce their partisanship in the struggle for a better world. Traditional researchers see their task as the description, interpretation, or reanimation of a slice of reality, whereas critical researchers often regard their work as a first step toward forms of political action that can redress the injustices found in the field site or constructed in the very act of research itself. Horkheimer (1972) puts it succinctly when he argues that critical theory and research are never satisfied with merely increasing knowledge (see also Agger, 1998; Andersen, 1989; Britzman, 1991; Giroux, 1983, 1988, 1997; Kincheloe, 1991; Kincheloe

& Steinberg, 1993; Quantz, 1992; Shor, 1996; Villaverde & Kincheloe, 1998).

Research in the critical tradition takes the form of self-conscious criticism—self-conscious in the sense that researchers try to become aware of the ideological imperatives and epistemological presuppositions that inform their research as well as their own subjective, intersubjective, and normative reference claims. Thus critical researchers enter into an investigation with their assumptions on the table, so no one is confused concerning the epistemological and political baggage they bring with them to the research site. Upon detailed analysis, these assumptions may change. Stimulus for change may come from the critical researchers' recognition that such assumptions are not leading to emancipatory actions. The source of this emancipatory action involves the researchers' ability to expose the contradictions of the world of appearances accepted by the dominant culture as natural and inviolable (Giroux, 1983, 1988, 1997; McLaren, 1992a, 1997; San Juan, 1992; Zizek, 1990). Such appearances may, critical researchers contend, conceal social relationships of inequality, injustice, and exploitation. For instance, if we view the violence we find in classrooms not as random or isolated incidents created by aberrant individuals willfully stepping out of line in accordance with a particular form of social pathology, but as narratives of transgression and resistance, then this could indicate that the "political unconscious" lurking beneath the surface of everyday classroom life is not unrelated to practices of race, class, and gender oppression but rather intimately connected to them.

◆ *Babes in Toyland: Critical Theory in Hyperreality*

Postmodern Culture

Over the last quarter of the 20th century, traditional notions of critical theory have had to come to terms with the rise of postmodernism.

Our reconceptualized notion of critical theory is our way of denoting the conversation between traditional criticalism and postmodernism (Kincheloe, Steinberg, & Tippins, 1999). We will first analyze postmodernism and then address the relationship between it and our notion of critical theory.

In a contemporary era marked by the delegitimation of the grand narratives of Western civilization, a loss of faith in the power of reason, and a shattering of traditional religious orthodoxies, scholars continue to debate what the term *postmodernism* means, generally positing it as a periodizing concept following modernism. Indeed, scholars have not agreed if this epochal break with the "modern" era even constitutes a discrete period. In the midst of such confusion it seems somehow appropriate that scholars are fighting over the application of the term *postmodernism* to the contemporary condition. Accepting postmodernism as an apt moniker for the end of the 20th century, a major feature of critical academic work has involved the exploration of what happens when critical theory encounters the postmodern condition, or hyperreality. *Hyperreality* is a term used to describe an information society socially saturated with ever-increasing forms of representation: filmic, photographic, electronic, and so on. These have had profound effects on the construction of the cultural narratives that shape our identities. The drama of living has been portrayed so often on television that individuals, for the most part, are increasingly able to predict the outcomes and consider such outcomes to be the "natural" and "normal" course of social life (Fraser, 1995; Gergen, 1991; Heshusius & Ballard, 1996; Kellner, 1994; Morley & Chen, 1996; Nicholson & Seidman, 1995).

As many postmodern analysts have put it, we become pastiches, imitative conglomerations of one another. In such a condition we approach life with low affect, with a sense of postmodern ennui and irremissible anxiety. Our emotional bonds are diffused as television, computers, VCRs, and stereo headphones assault us with representations that have shaped our cognitive and affective facilities in ways that still remain insufficiently understood. In the political arena, traditionalists circle their cultural wagons and fight off imagined bogeymen such as secular humanists, "extreme liberals," and utopianists, not realizing the impact that postmodern hyperreality exerts on their hallowed institutions. The nuclear family, for example, has declined in importance not because of the assault of "radical feminists" but because the home has been redefined through the familiar presence of electronic communication systems. Particular modes of information put individual family members in constant contact with specific subcultures. While they are physically in the home, they exist emotionally outside of it through the mediating effects of various forms of communication (Gergen, 1991; McGuigan, 1996; McLaren, 1997; Poster, 1989; Steinberg & Kincheloe, 1997). We increasingly make sense of the social world and judge other cultures through conventional and culture-bound television genres. Hyperreality has presented us with new forms of literacy that do not simply refer to discrete skills but rather constitute social skills and relations of symbolic power. These new technologies cannot be seen apart from the social and institutional contexts in which they are used and the roles they play in the family, the community, and the workplace. They also need to be seen in terms of how "viewing competencies" are socially distributed and the diverse social and discursive practices in which these new media literacies are produced (Buckingham, 1989; Hall, 1997; Taylor & Saarinen, 1994).

Electronic transmissions generate new formations of cultural space and restructure experiences of time. We often are motivated to trade community membership for a sense of pseudo-belonging to the mediascape. Residents of hyperreality are temporarily comforted by proclamations of community offered by "media personalities" on the 6 o'clock *Eyewitness News*. "Bringing news of your neighbors in the Tri-State community home to you," media marketers attempt to soften the edges of hyperreality, to soften the emotional effects of the social vertigo. The world is not brought into our homes by television as much as television brings its viewers to a quasi-fictional place—hyperreality (Luke, 1991).

Postmodern Social Theory

We believe that it is misleading to identify postmodernism with poststructuralism. Although there are certainly similarities involved, they cannot be considered discrete homologies. We also believe that it is a mistake to equate postmodernism with postmodernity or to assert that these terms can be contrasted in some simple equivalent way with modernism and modernity. As Michael Peters (1993) notes, "To do so is to frame up the debate in strictly (and naïvely) modernist terminology which employs exhaustive binary oppositions privileging one set of terms against the other" (p. 14). We are using the term *postmodernity* to refer to the postmodern condition that we have described as *hyperreality* and the term *postmodern theory* as an umbrella term that includes antifoundationalist writing in philosophy and the social sciences. Again, we are using this term in a very general sense that includes poststructuralist currents.

Postmodern theoretical trajectories take as their entry point a rejection of the deeply ingrained assumptions of Enlightenment rationality, traditional Western epistemology, or any supposedly "secure" representation of reality that exists outside of discourse itself. Doubt is cast on the myth of the autonomous, transcendental subject, and the concept of praxis is marginalized in favor of rhetorical undecidability and textual analysis of social practices. As a species of criticism, intended, in part, as a central requestioning of the humanism and anthropologism of the early 1970s, postmodernist social theory rejects Hegel's ahistorical state of absolute knowledge and resigns itself to the impossibility of an ahistorical, transcendental, or self-authenticating version of truth. The reigning conviction that knowledge is knowledge only if it reflects the world as it "really" exists has been annihilated in favor of a view in which reality is socially constructed or semiotically posited. Furthermore, normative agreement on what should constitute and guide scientific practice and argumentative consistency has become an intellectual target for epistemological uncertainty (Pinar et al., 1995; Shelton, 1996).

Postmodern criticism takes as its starting point the notion that meaning is constituted by the continual playfulness of the signifier, and the thrust of its critique is aimed at deconstructing Western metanarratives of truth and the ethnocentrism implicit in the European view of history as the unilinear progress of universal reason. Postmodern theory is a site of both hope and fear, where there exists a strange convergence between critical theorists and political conservatives, a cynical complicity with status quo social and institutional relations and a fierce criticism of ideological manipulation and the reigning practices of subjectivity in which knowledge takes place.

◆ Ludic and Resistance Postmodernism

Postmodernist criticism is not monolithic, and for the purposes of this essay we would like to distinguish between two theoretical strands. The first has been astutely described by Teresa Ebert (1991) as "ludic postmodernism" (p. 115)—an approach to social theory that is decidedly limited in its ability to transform oppressive social and political regimes of power. Ludic postmodernism generally occupies itself with a reality that is constituted by the continual playfulness of the signifier and the heterogeneity of differences. As such, ludic postmodernism (see, e.g., Lyotard, Derrida, Baudrillard) constitutes a moment of self-reflexivity in the deconstruction of Western metanarratives, asserting that "meaning itself is self-divided and undecidable."

We want to argue that critical researchers should assume a cautionary stance toward ludic postmodernism critique because, as Ebert (1991) notes, it tends to reinscribe the status quo and reduce history to the supplementarity of signification or the free-floating trace of textuality. As a mode of critique, it rests its case on interrogating specific and local enunciations

of oppression, but often fails to analyze such enunciations in relation to larger dominating structures of oppression (Aronowitz & Giroux, 1991; McLaren, 1995a; Sünker, 1998).

The kind of postmodern social theory we want to pose as a counterweight to skeptical and spectral postmodernism has been referred to as "oppositional postmodernism" (Foster, 1983), "radical critique-al theory" (Zavarzadeh & Morton, 1991), "postmodern education" (Aronowitz & Giroux, 1991), "resistance postmodernism" (Ebert, 1991), "affirmative postmodernism" (Slattery, 1995), "critical postmodernism" (Giroux, 1992; McLaren, 1992b, 1997; McLaren & Hammer, 1989), and "postformalism" (Kincheloe, 1993, 1995; Kincheloe & Steinberg, 1993; Kincheloe, Steinberg, & Hinchey, 1999; Kincheloe, Steinberg, & Villaverde, 1999). These forms of critique are not alternatives to ludic postmodernism but appropriations and extensions of this critique. Resistance postmodernism brings to ludic critique a form of materialist intervention because it is not based solely on a textual theory of difference but rather on one that is also social and historical. In this way, postmodern critique can serve as an interventionist and transformative critique of Western culture. Following Ebert (1991), resistance postmodernism attempts to show that "textualities (significations) are material practices, forms of conflicting social relations" (p. 115). The sign is always an arena of material conflict and competing social relations as well as ideas. From this perspective we can rethink a signifier as an ideological dynamic ever related to a contextually possible set of signifieds. In other words, difference is politicized by being situated in real social and historical conflicts.

The synergism of the conversation between resistance postmodernism and critical theory involves an interplay between the praxis of the critical and the radical uncertainty of the postmodern. As it invokes its strategies for the emancipation of meaning, critical theory provides the postmodern critique with a normative foundation (i.e., a basis for distinguishing between oppressive and liberatory social relations). Without such a foundation the postmodern critique is ever vulnerable to nihilism and inaction. Indeed, the normatively ungrounded postmodern critique is incapable of providing an ethically challenging and politically transformative program of action. Aronowitz, Giroux, Kincheloe, and McLaren argue that if the postmodern critique is to make a valuable contribution to the notion of schooling as an emancipatory form of cultural politics, it must make connections to those egalitarian impulses of modernism that contribute to an emancipatory democracy. In doing this, the postmodern critique can extend the project of an emancipatory democracy and the schooling that supports it by promoting new understandings of how power operates and by incorporating groups who had been excluded because of race, gender, or class (Aronowitz & Giroux, 1991; Codd, 1984; Godzich, 1992; Kincheloe, 1995, 1999; Lash, 1990; McLaren, 1997, 1999; Morrow, 1991; Pinar, 1994, 1998; Rosenau, 1992; Steinberg & Kincheloe, 1998; Surber, 1998; Welch, 1991; Wexler, 1996a, 1997; Yates, 1990).

◆ Critical Research and Cultural Studies

Cultural studies is an interdisciplinary, transdisciplinary, and sometimes counterdisciplinary field that functions within the dynamics of competing definitions of culture. Unlike traditional humanistic studies, cultural studies questions the equation of culture with high culture; instead, cultural studies asserts that myriad expressions of cultural production should be analyzed in relation to other cultural dynamics and social and historical structures. Such a position commits cultural studies to a potpourri of artistic, religious, political, economic, and communicative activities. In this context, it is important to note that although cultural studies is associated with the study of popular culture, it is not primarily about popular culture. The interests of cultural studies are much broader and generally tend to involve the production and

nature of the rules of inclusivity and exclusivity that guide academic evaluation—in particular, the way these rules shape and are shaped by relations of power. The rules that guide academic evaluation are inseparable from the rules of knowledge production and research. Thus cultural studies provides a disciplinary critique that holds many implications (Abercrombie, 1994; Ferguson & Golding, 1997; Grossberg, 1995; Hall & du Gay, 1996; McLaren, 1995a; Woodward, 1997).

One of the most important sites of theoretical production in the history of critical research has been the Centre for Contemporary Cultural Studies (CCCS) at the University of Birmingham. Attempting to connect critical theory with the particularity of everyday experience, the CCCS researchers have argued that all experience is vulnerable to ideological inscription. At the same time, they have maintained that theorizing outside of everyday experience results in formal and deterministic theory. An excellent representative of the CCCS's perspectives is Paul Willis, whose *Learning to Labour: How Working Class Kids Get Working Class Jobs* was published in 1977, seven years after Colin Lacey's *Hightown Grammar* (1970). Redefining the nature of ethnographic research in a critical manner, *Learning to Labour* inspired a spate of critical studies: David Robins and Philip Cohen's *Knuckle Sandwich: Growing Up in the Working-Class City* in 1978, Paul Corrigan's *Schooling the Smash Street Kids* in 1979, and Dick Hebdige's *Subculture: The Meaning of Style* in 1979.

Also following Willis's work were critical feminist studies, including an anthology titled *Women Take Issue* (Women's Studies Group, 1978). In 1985, Christine Griffin published *Typical Girls?* the first extended feminist study produced by the CCCS. Conceived as a response to Willis's *Learning to Labour, Typical Girls?* analyzes adolescent female consciousness as it is constructed in a world of patriarchy. Through their recognition of patriarchy as a major disciplinary technology in the production of subjectivity, Griffin and the members of the CCCS gender study group move critical research in a multicultural direction. In addition to the examination of class, gender and racial analyses are beginning to gain in importance (Quantz, 1992). Poststructuralism frames power not simply as one aspect of a society, but as the basis of society. Thus patriarchy is not simply one isolated force among many with which women must contend; patriarchy informs all aspects of the social and effectively shapes women's lives (see also Douglas, 1994; Finders, 1997; Fine et al., 1997; Frankenberg, 1993; Franz & Stewart, 1994; Shohat & Stam, 1994).

Cornel West (1993) pushes critical research even further into the multicultural domain as he focuses critical attention on women, the Third World, and race. Adopting theoretical advances in neo-Marxist postcolonialist criticism and cultural studies, he is able to shed greater light on the workings of power in everyday life. In this context, Ladislaus Semali and Joe Kincheloe, in *What Is Indigenous Knowledge? Voices from the Academy* (1999), explore the power of indigenous knowledge as a resource for critical attempts to bring about social change. Critical researchers, they argue, should analyze such knowledges in order to understand emotions, sensitivities, and epistemologies that move in ways unimagined by many Western knowledge producers. In this postcolonially informed context, Semali and Kincheloe employ concerns raised by indigenous knowledge to challenge the academy, its "normal science," and its accepted notions of certified information. Moving the conversation about critical research in new directions, these authors understand the conceptual inseparability of valuing indigenous knowledge, developing postcolonial forms of resistance, academic reform, the reconceptualization of research and interpretation, and the struggle for social justice.

In *Schooling as a Ritual Performance,* Peter McLaren (1999) integrates poststructuralist, postcolonialist, and Marxist theory with the projects of cultural studies, critical pedagogy, and critical ethnography. He grounds his theoretical analysis in the poststructuralist claim that the connection of signifier and signified is arbitrary yet shaped by historical, cultural, and economic forces. The primary cultural narrative that defines school life is the resistance by students to the school's attempts to marginalize

their street culture and street knowledge. McLaren analyzes the school as a cultural site where symbolic capital is struggled over in the form of ritual dramas. *Schooling as a Ritual Performance* adopts the position that researchers are unable to grasp themselves or others introspectively without social mediation through their positionalities with respect to race, class, gender, and other configurations. The visceral, bodily forms of knowledge, and the rhythms and gestures of the street culture of the students, are distinguished from the formal abstract knowledge of classroom instruction. The teachers regard knowledge as it is constructed informally outside of the culture of school instruction as threatening to the universalist and decidedly Eurocentric ideal of high culture that forms the basis of the school curriculum.

As critical researchers pursue the reconceptualization of critical theory pushed by its synergistic relationship with cultural studies, postmodernism, and poststructuralism, they are confronted with the post-discourses' redefinition of critical notions of democracy in terms of multiplicity and difference. Traditional notions of community often privilege unity over diversity in the name of Enlightenment values. Poststructuralists in general and poststructuralist feminists in particular see this communitarian dream as politically disabling because of the suppression of race, class, and gender differences and the exclusion of subaltern voices and marginalized groups whom community members are loath to engage. What begins to emerge in this instance is the movement of feminist theoretical concerns to the center of critical theory. Indeed, after the feminist critique, critical theory can never return to a paradigm of inquiry in which the concept of social class is antiseptically privileged and exalted as the master concept in the Holy Trinity of race, class, and gender. A critical theory reconceptualized by poststructuralism and feminism promotes a politics of difference that refuses to pathologize or exoticize the Other. In this context, communities are more prone to revitalization and revivification (Wexler, 1996b, 1997); peripheralized groups in the thrall of a condescending Eurocentric gaze are able to edge closer to the borders of respect, and "classified" objects of research potentially acquire the characteristics of subjecthood. Kathleen Weiler's *Women Teaching for Change: Gender, Class, and Power* (1988) serves as a good example of critical research framed by feminist theory. Weiler shows not only how feminist theory can extend critical research, but how the concept of emancipation can be reconceptualized in light of a feminist epistemology (Aronowitz & Giroux, 1991; Behar & Gordon, 1995; Bersani, 1995; Brents & Monson, 1998; Britzman, 1995; Christian-Smith & Keelor, 1999; Clatterbaugh, 1997; Clough, 1994; Cooper, 1994; Hammer, 1999; Hedley, 1994; Johnson, 1996; Kelly, 1996; King & Mitchell, 1995; Lugones, 1987; Maher & Tetreault, 1994; Morrow, 1991; Rand, 1995; Scott, 1992; Sedgwick, 1995; Steinberg, 1997; Young, 1990).

◆ Focusing on Critical Ethnography

As critical researchers attempt to get behind the curtain, to move beyond assimilated experience, to expose the way ideology constrains the desire for self-direction, and to confront the way power reproduces itself in the construction of human consciousness, they employ a plethora of research methodologies. In this context Patti Lather (1991, 1993) extends our position with her notion of catalytic validity. Catalytic validity points to the degree to which research moves those it studies to understand the world and the way it is shaped in order for them to transform it. Noncritical researchers who operate within an empiricist framework will perhaps find catalytic validity to be a strange concept. Research that possesses catalytic validity will not only display the reality-altering impact of the inquiry process, it will direct this impact so that those under study will gain self-understanding and self-direction.

Theory that falls under the rubric of *postcolonialism* (see McLaren, 1999; Semali & Kincheloe, 1999) involves important debates

over the knowing subject and object of analysis. Such works have initiated important new modes of analysis, especially in relation to questions of imperialism, colonialism, and neocolonialism. Recent attempts by critical researchers to move beyond the objectifying and imperialist gaze associated with the Western anthropological tradition (which fixes the image of the so-called informant from the colonizing perspective of the knowing subject), although laudatory and well-intentioned, are not without their shortcomings (Bourdieu & Wacquaat, 1992). As Fuchs (1993) has so presciently observed, serious limitations plague recent efforts to develop a more reflective approach to ethnographic writing. The challenge here can be summarized in the following questions: How does the knowing subject come to know the Other? How can researchers respect the perspective of the Other and invite the Other to speak (Abdullah & Stringer, 1999; Ashcroft, Griffiths, & Tiffin, 1995; Brock-Utne, 1996; Goldie, 1995; Macedo, 1994; Myrsiades & Myrsiades, 1998; Pieterse & Parekh, 1995; Prakash & Esteva, 1998; Rains, 1998; Scheurich & Young, 1997; Semali & Kincheloe, 1999; Viergever, 1999)?

Although recent confessional modes of ethnographic writing attempt to treat so-called informants as "participants" in an attempt to avoid the objectification of the Other (usually referring to the relationship between Western anthropologists and non-Western culture), there is a risk that uncovering colonial and postcolonial structures of domination may, in fact, unintentionally validate and consolidate such structures as well as reassert liberal values through a type of covert ethnocentrism. Fuchs (1993) warns that the attempt to subject researchers to the same approach to which other societies are subjected could lead to an " 'othering' of one's own world" (p. 108). Such an attempt often fails to question existing ethnographic methodologies and therefore unwittingly extends their validity and applicability while further objectifying the world of the researcher.

Michel Foucault's approach to this dilemma is to "detach" social theory from the epistemology of his own culture by criticizing the traditional philosophy of reflection. However, Foucault falls into the trap of ontologizing his own method-ological argumentation and erasing the notion of prior understanding that is linked to the idea of an "inside" view (Fuchs, 1993). Louis Dumont fares somewhat better by arguing that cultural texts need to be viewed simultaneously from the inside and from the outside. However, in trying to affirm a "reciprocal interpretation of various societies among themselves" (Fuchs, 1993, p. 113) through identifying both transin-dividual structures of consciousness and trans-subjective social structures, Dumont aspires to a universal framework for the comparative analy-sis of societies. Whereas Foucault and Dumont attempt to "transcend the categorical founda-tions of their own world" (Fuchs, 1993, p. 118) by refusing to include themselves in the process of objectification, Pierre Bourdieu integrates himself as a social actor into the social field un-der analysis. Bourdieu achieves such integration by "epistemologizing the ethnological content of his own presuppositions" (Fuchs, 1993, p. 121). But the self-objectification of the ob-server (anthropologist) is not unproblematic. Fuchs (1993) notes, after Bourdieu, that the chief difficulty is "forgetting the difference be-tween the theoretical and the practical relation-ship with the world and of imposing on the ob-ject the theoretical relationship one maintains with it" (p. 120). Bourdieu's approach to re-search does not fully escape becoming, to a cer-tain extent, a "confirmation of objectivism," but at least there is an earnest attempt by the re-searcher to reflect on the preconditions of his own self-understanding—an attempt to engage in an "ethnography of ethnographers" (p. 122).

Postmodern ethnography often inter-sects—to varying degrees—with the concerns of postcolonialist researchers, but the degree to which it fully addresses issues of exploitation and the social relations of capitalist exploitation remains questionable. Postmodern ethnogra-phy—and we are thinking here of works such as Paul Rabinow's *Reflections on Fieldwork in Morocco* (1977), James Boon's *Other Tribes, Other Scribes* (1982), and Michael Taussig's *Shamanism, Colonialism, and the Wild Man* (1987)—shares the conviction articulated by Marc Manganaro (1990) that "no anthropology

is apolitical, removed from ideology and hence from the capacity to be affected by or, as cru-cially, to effect social formations. The question ought not to be if an anthropological text is po-litical, but rather, what kind of sociopolitical af-filiations are tied to particular anthropological texts" (p. 35).

Judith Newton and Judith Stacey (1992-1993) note that the current postmodern textual experimentation of ethnography credits the "postcolonial predicament of culture as the op-portunity for anthropology to reinvent itself" (p. 56). Modernist ethnography, according to these authors, "constructed authoritative cul-tural accounts that served, however inadver-tently, not only to establish the authority of the Western ethnographer over native others but also to sustain Western authority over colonial cultures" (p. 56). They argue (following James Clifford) that ethnographers can and should try to escape the recurrent allegorical genre of colo-nial ethnography—the pastoral, a nostalgic, re-demptive text that preserves a primitive culture on the brink of extinction for the historical re-cord of its Western conquerors. The narrative structure of this "salvage text" portrays the na-tive culture as a coherent, authentic, and lamen-tably "evading past," whereas its complex, inauthentic, Western successors represent the future (p. 56).

Postmodern ethnographic writing faces the challenge of moving beyond simply the reani-mation of local experience, an uncritical cele-bration of cultural difference (including figural differentiations within the ethnographer's own culture), and the employment of a framework that espouses universal values and a global role for interpretivist anthropology (Silverman, 1990). What we have described as resistance postmodernism can help qualitative researchers challenge dominant Western research prac-tices that are underwritten by a foundational epistemology and a claim to universally valid knowledge at the expense of local, subju-gated knowledges (Peters, 1993). The choice is not one between modernism and postmodern-ism, but one of whether or not to challenge the presuppositions that inform the normalizing judgments one makes as a researcher. Vincent

Crapanzano (1990) warns that "the anthropologist can assume neither the Orphic lyre nor the crown of thorns, although I confess to hear salvationist echoes in his desire to protect his people" (p. 301).

Connor (1992) describes the work of James Clifford, which shares an affinity with ethnographic work associated with Georges Bataille, Michel Lerris, and the College de Sociologie, as not simply the "writing of culture" but rather "the interior disruption of categories of art and culture correspond[ing] to a radically dialogic form of ethnographic writing, which takes place across and between cultures" (p. 251). Clifford (1992) describes his own work as an attempt "to multiply the hands and discourses involved in 'writing culture' . . . not to assert a naïve democracy of plural authorship, but to loosen at least somewhat the monological control of the executive writer/anthropologist and to open for discussion ethnography's hierarchy and negotiation of discourses in power-charged, unequal situations" (p. 100). Citing the work of Marcus and Fischer (1986), Clifford warns against modernist ethnographic practices of "representational essentializing" and "metonymic freezing" in which one aspect of a group's life is taken to represent the group as a whole; instead, Clifford urges forms of multilocale ethnography to reflect the "transnational political, economic and cultural forces that traverse and constitute local or regional worlds" (p. 102). Rather than fixing culture into reified textual portraits, culture needs to be better understood as displacement, transplantation, disruption, positionality, and difference.

Although critical ethnography allows, in a way conventional ethnography does not, for the relationship of liberation and history, and although its hermeneutical task is to call into question the social and cultural conditioning of human activity and the prevailing sociopolitical structures, we do not claim that this is enough to restructure the social system. But it is certainly, in our view, a necessary beginning. We follow Patricia Ticineto Clough (1992) in arguing that "realist narrativity has allowed empirical social science to be the platform and horizon of social criticism" (p. 135). Ethnography needs to be analyzed critically not only in terms of its field methods but also as reading and writing practices. Data collection must give way to "rereadings of representations in every form" (p. 137). In the narrative construction of its authority as empirical science, ethnography needs to face the unconscious processes upon which it justifies its canonical formulations, processes that often involve the disavowal of oedipal or authorial desire and the reduction of differences to binary oppositions. Within these processes of binary reduction, the male ethnographer is most often privileged as the guardian of "the factual representation of empirical positivities" (p. 9).

◆ New Questions Concerning Validity in Critical Ethnography

Critical research traditions have arrived at the point where they recognize that claims to truth are always discursively situated and implicated in relations of power. Yet, unlike some claims made within "ludic" strands of postmodernist research, we do not suggest that because we cannot know truth absolutely that truth can simply be equated with an effect of power. We say this because truth involves regulative rules that must be met for some statements to be more meaningful than others. Otherwise, truth becomes meaningless and, if that is the case, liberatory praxis has no purpose other than to win for the sake of winning. As Phil Carspecken (1993, 1999) remarks, every time we act, in every instance of our behavior, we presuppose some normative or universal relation to truth. Truth is internally related to meaning in a pragmatic way through normative referenced claims, intersubjective referenced claims, subjective referenced claims, and the way we deictically ground or anchor meaning in our daily lives.

Carspecken explains that researchers are able to articulate the normative evaluative claims of others when they begin to see them in the same way as their participants by living inside the cultural and discursive positionalities that inform such claims. Claims to universality must be recognized in each particular normative claim, and questions must be raised about whether such norms represent the entire group. When the limited claim of universality is seen to be contradictory to the practices under observation, power relations become visible. What is crucial here, according to Carspecken, is that researchers recognize where they are ideologically located in the normative and identity claims of others and at the same time be honest about their own subjective referenced claims and not let normative evaluative claims interfere with what they observe. Critical research continues to problematize normative and universal claims in a way that does not permit them to be analyzed outside of a politics of representation, divorced from the material conditions in which they are produced, or outside of a concern with the constitution of the subject in the very acts of reading and writing.

In his book, *Critical Ethnography in Educational Research* (1996), Carspecken addresses the issue of critical epistemology, an understanding of the relationship between power and thought, and power and truth claims. In a short exposition of what is "critical" to critical epistemology, he debunks facile forms of social constructivism and offers a deft criticism of mainstream epistemologies by way of Continental phenomenology, poststructuralism, and postmodernist social theory, mainly the work of Edmund Husserl and Jacques Derrida. Carspecken makes short work of facile forms of constructivist thought purporting that what we see is strongly influenced by what we already value and that criticalist research simply indulges itself in the "correct" political values. For instance, some constructivists argue that all that criticalists need to do is to "bias" their work in the direction of social justice. This form of constructivist thought is not viable, according to Carspecken, because it is plainly ocularcentric; that is, it depends upon visual perception to form the basis of its theory. Rather than rely on perceptual metaphors found in mainstream ethnographic accounts, critical ethnography, in contrast, should emphasize communi-

cative experiences and structures as well as cultural typifications.

Carspecken argues that critical ethnography needs to differentiate among ontological categories (i.e., subjective, objective, normative-evaluative) rather than adopt the position of "multiple realities" defended by many constructivists. He adopts a principled position that research value orientations should not determine research findings, as much as this is possible. Rather, critical ethnographers should employ a critical epistemology; that is, they should uphold epistemological principles that apply to all researchers. In fecundating this claim, Carspecken rehabilitates critical ethnography from many of the misperceptions of its critics who believe that it ignores questions of validity.

To construct a socially critical epistemology, critical ethnographers need to understand holistic modes of human experience and their relationship to communicative structures. Preliminary stages of this process that Carspecken articulates include examining researcher bias and discovering researcher value orientations. Following stages include compiling the primary record through the collection of monological data, preliminary reconstructive analysis, dialogical data generation, discovering social systems relations, and using systems relations to explain findings. Anthony Giddens's work forms the basis of Carspecken's approach to systems analysis. Accompanying discussions of each of the complex stages Carspecken develops are brilliantly articulated approaches to horizontal and vertical validity reconstructions and pragmatic horizons of analysis. In order to help link theory to practice, Carspecken uses data from his study of an inner-city Houston elementary school program that is charged with helping students learn conflict management skills.

Another impressive feature is Carspecken's exposition and analysis of communicative acts, especially his discussion of meaning as embodiment and understanding as intersubjective, not objective or subjective. Carspecken works from a view of intersubjectivity that combines Hegel, Mead, Habermas, and Taylor. He recommends that critical ethnographers record body language carefully because the meaning of an action is not in the language, it is rather in the action and the actor's bodily states. In Carspecken's view, subjectivity is derivative from intersubjectivity (as is objectivity), and intersubjectivity involves the dialogical constitution of the "feeling body." Finally, Carspecken stresses the importance of macro-level social theories, environmental conditions, socially structured ways of meeting needs and desires, effects of cultural commodities on students, economic exploitation, and political and cultural conditions of action.

Much of Carspecken's inspiration for his approach to validity claims is taken from Habermas's theory of communicative action. Carspecken reads Habermas as grasping the prelinguistic foundations of language and intersubjectivity, making language secondary to the concept of intersubjectivity. Yet Carspecken departs from a strict Habermasian view of action by bringing in an expressive/praxis model roughly consistent with Charles Taylor's work. Although Habermas and Taylor frequently argue against each other's positions, Carspecken puts them together in a convincing manner. Taylor's emphasis on holistic modes of understanding and the act constitution that Carspecken employs make it possible to link the theory of communicative rationality to work on embodied meaning and the metaphoric basis of meaningful action. It also provides a means for synthesizing Giddens's ideas on part/whole relations, virtual structure, and act constitution with communicative rationality. This is another way in which Carspecken's work differs from Habermas and yet remains consistent with his theory and the internal link between meaning and validity.

◆ Recent Innovations in Critical Ethnography

In addition to Carspecken's brilliant insights into critically grounded ethnography, the late 1990s have witnessed a proliferation of deconstructive approaches as well as reflexive ap-

proaches (this discussion is based on Trueba & McLaren, in press). In her important book *Fictions of Feminist Ethnography* (1994), Kamala Visweswaran maintains that reflexive ethnography, like normative ethnography, rests on the "declarative mode" of imparting knowledge to a reader whose identity is anchored in a shared discourse. Deconstructive ethnography, in contrast, enacts the "interrogative mode" through a constant deferral or a refusal to explain or interpret. Within deconstructive ethnography, the identity of the reader with a unified subject of enunciation is discouraged. Whereas reflexive ethnography maintains that the ethnographer is not separate from the object of investigation, the ethnographer is still viewed as a unified subject of knowledge that can make hermeneutic efforts to establish identification between the observer and the observed (as in modernist interpretive traditions). Deconstructive ethnography, in contrast, often disrupts such identification in favor of articulating a fractured, destabilized, multiply positioned subjectivity (as in postmodernist interpretive traditions). Whereas reflexive ethnography questions its own authority, deconstructive ethnography forfeits its authority. Both approaches to critical ethnography can be used to uncover the clinging Eurocentric authority employed by ethnographers in the study of Latino/a populations. The goal of both these approaches is criticalist in nature: that is, to free the object of analysis from the tyranny of fixed, unassailable categories and to rethink subjectivity itself as a permanently unclosed, always partial, narrative engagement with text and context. Such an approach can help the ethnographer to caution against the damaging depictions propagated by Anglo observers about Mexican immigrants. As Ruth Behar (1993) notes, in classical sociological and ethnographic accounts of the Mexican and Mexican American family,

> stereotypes similar to those surrounding the black family perpetuated images of the authoritarian, oversexed, and macho husband and the meek and submissive wife surrounded by children who adore their good and suffering mother. These stereotypes have come under strong critique in the last few years, particularly by Chicana critics, who have sought to go beyond the vari-

ous "deficiency theories" that continue to mark the discussion of African-American and Latina/Latino family life. (p. 276)

The conception of culture advanced by critical ethnographers generally unpacks culture as a complex circuit of production that includes myriad dialectically reinitiating and mutually informing sets of activities such as routines, rituals, action conditions, systems of intelligibility and meaning making, conventions of interpretation, systems relations, and conditions both external and internal to the social actor (Carspecken, 1996). In her recent ethnographic study *A Space on the Side of the Road* (1996), Kathleen Stewart cogently illustrates the ambivalent character of culture, as well as its fluidity and ungraspable multilayeredness, when she remarks:

> Culture, as it is seen through its productive forms and means of mediation, is not, then, reducible to a fixed body of social value and belief or a direct precipitant of lived experience in the world but grows into a space on the side of the road where stories weighted with sociality take on a life of their own. We "see" it . . . only by building up multilayered narratives of the poetic in the everyday life of things. We represent it only by roaming from one texted genre to another—romantic, realist, historical, fantastic, sociological, surreal. There is no final textual solution, no way of resolving the dialogic of the interpreter/interpreted or subject/object through efforts to "place" ourselves in the text, or to represent "the fieldwork experience," or to gather up the voices of the other as if they could speak for themselves. (p. 210)

According to E. San Juan (1996), a renewed understanding of culture—as both discursive and material—becomes the linchpin for any emancipatory politics. San Juan writes that the idea of culture as social processes and practices that are thoroughly grounded in material social relations—in the systems of maintenance (economics), decision (politics), learning and communication (culture), and generation and nurture (the domain of social reproduction)—must be the grounding principle, or paradigm if you like, of any progressive and emancipatory approach (p. 177; Gresson, 1995).

Rejecting the characterization of anthropologists as either "adaptationalists" (e.g., Marvin Harris) or "ideationalists" (e.g., cognitivists, Lévi-Straussian structuralists, Schneiderian symbolists, Geertzian interpretivists), E. Valentine Daniel remarks in his recent ethnography *Charred Lullabies: Chapters in an Anthropology of Violence* (1996) that culture is "no longer something out there to be discovered, described, and explained, but rather something into which the ethnographer, as interpreter, enter[s]" (p. 198). Culture, in other words, is cocreated by the anthropologist and informant through conversation. Yet even this semeiosic conceptualization of culture is not without its problems. As Daniel himself notes, even if one considers oneself to be a "culture-comaking processualist," in contrast to a "culture-finding essentialist," one still has to recognize that one is working within a logocentric tradition that, to a greater or lesser extent, privileges words over actions.

Critical ethnography has benefited from this new understanding of culture and from the new hybridic possibilities for cultural critique that have been opened up by the current blurring and mixing of disciplinary genres—those that emphasize experience, subjectivity, reflexivity, and dialogical understanding. The advantage that follows such perspectives is that social life is not viewed as preontologically available for the researcher to study. It also follows that there is no perspective unspoiled by ideology from which to study social life in an antiseptically objective way. What is important to note here is the stress placed on the ideological situatedness of any descriptive or socioanalytic account of social life. Critical ethnographers such as John and Jean Comaroff (1992) have made significant contributions to our understanding of the ways in which power is entailed in culture, leading to practices of domination and exploitation that have become naturalized in everyday social life. According to Comaroff and Comaroff, hegemony refers to "that order of signs and practices, relations and distinctions, images and epistemologies—drawn from a historically situated cultural field—that come to be taken-for-granted as the natural and received shape of the world and everything that inhabits it" (p. 23). These axiomatic and yet ineffable discourses and practices that are presumptively shared become "ideological" precisely when their internal contradictions are revealed, uncovered, and viewed as arbitrary and negotiable. Ideology, then, refers to a highly articulated worldview, master narrative, discursive regime, or organizing scheme for collective symbolic production. The dominant ideology is the expression of the dominant social group.

Following this line of argument, hegemony "is nonnegotiable and therefore beyond direct argument," whereas ideology "is more susceptible to being perceived as a matter of inimical opinion and interest and therefore is open to contestation" (Comaroff & Comaroff, 1992, p. 24). Ideologies become the expressions of specific groups, whereas hegemony refers to conventions and constructs that are shared and naturalized throughout a political community. Hegemony works both through silences and repetition in naturalizing the dominant worldview. There also may exist oppositional ideologies among subordinate or subaltern groups— whether well formed or loosely articulated— that break free of hegemony. In this way hegemony is never total or complete; it is always porous.

◆ Conclusion: Critical Research in a Globalized, Privatized World

A critical postmodern research requires researchers to construct their perception of the world anew, not just in random ways but in a manner that undermines what appears natural, that opens to question what appears obvious (Slaughter, 1989). Oppositional and insurgent researchers as maieutic agents must not confuse their research efforts with the textual suavities of an avant-garde academic posturing in which they are awarded the sinecure of representation for the oppressed without actually having to return to those working-class communities where their studies took place.

Rather, they need to locate their work in a transformative praxis that leads to the alleviation of suffering and the overcoming of oppression. Rejecting the arrogant reading of metropolitan critics and their imperial mandates governing research, insurgent researchers ask questions about how what is has come to be, whose interests are served by particular institutional arrangements, and where our own frames of reference come from. Facts are no longer simply "what is"; the truth of beliefs is not simply testable by their correspondence to these facts. To engage in critical postmodern research is to take part in a process of critical world making, guided by the shadowed outline of a dream of a world less conditioned by misery, suffering, and the politics of deceit. It is, in short, a pragmatics of hope in an age of cynical reason. The obstacles that critical postmodern research has yet to overcome in terms of a frontal assault against the ravages of global capitalism and its devastation of the global working class has led McLaren to a more sustained and sympathetic engagement with Marx and the Marxist tradition.

The educational left in the United States has not been able to provide a counterforce to resist the ferocious orbit of capital and what we believe is the creation of a transnational global society in which the nation-state as the principal form of social organization has been superseded. We see as already under way an integration of all national markets into a single international market and division of labor and the erosion of national affiliations of capital (Robinson, 1998). The transnationalism of labor and capital has brought about material shifts in cultural practices and the proliferation of new contradictions between capitalism and labor. The deepening instability following in the wake of global capitalism has been driven by overaccumulation, overinvestment, overcapacity, overproduction, and new developments in the theater of global finance. The bottom line is the production of goods must return a profit by selling at market prices. Despite efforts of working classes throughout the globe to resist capital's drive to exploit their labor, capitalism is able dynamically and continuously to reorganize and reengineer itself such that its drive to accumulate is unhampered. Efforts at regulating markets are not effective at overcoming capital's reign of global terror. What is called for is the overturning of the basic laws of capitalism and the defeat of the dominion of capital itself. Capitalism's concentration, centralization, and transnationalism have reterritorialized the laws of motion of capital. We need to view the phenomena of globalized capitalism not merely in terms of market competition but rather from the perspective of production. Given that the logic of privatization and free trade—where social labor is the means and measure of value, and surplus social labor lies at the heart of profit—now odiously shapes archetypes of citizenship, manages our perceptions of what should constitute the "good society," and creates ideological formations that produce necessary functions for capital in relation to labor, it stands to reason that new ethnographic research approaches must take global capitalism not as an end point of analysis, but as a starting point. As schools are financed more by corporations that function as service industries for transnational capitalism, and as neoliberalism continues to guide educational policy and practice, the U.S. population faces a challenging educational reality (Kincheloe, 1999). It is a reality that is witnessing the progressive merging of cultural pedagogy and the productive processes within advanced capitalism (Giroux & Searles, 1996; McLaren, 1997). Although, as researchers, we may not be interested in global capitalism, we can be sure that it is interested in us.

Critical ethnography faces a daunting challenge in the years to come, especially because capitalism has been naturalized as commonsense reality—even as a part of nature itself—and the term *social class* has been replaced by the less antagonistic term *socioeconomic status*. The focus of much recent postmodern ethnography is on asymmetrical gender and ethnic relations, and although this focus is important, class struggle has become an outdated issue (Kincheloe & Steinberg, 1999). When social class is discussed, it is usually viewed as relational, not as oppositional. In the context of discussions of "social status" rather than "class struggle," postmodern ethnography has secured

a privileged position that is functionally advantageous to the socially reproductive logic of entrepreneurial capitalism, private ownership, and the personal appropriation of social production (McLaren, 1995b). More than ever before, critical research needs to address the objective, material conditions of the workplace and labor relations in order to prevent the further resecuring of the ideological hegemony of the neoliberal corporatist state.

In many ways the globalization process, and the strengthening of the free market capitalism that accompanies it, takes us back to the roots of critical research. As we have gained profound insights into the impact of the inscriptions of patriarchy, white supremacy, and class elitism on the consciousness of researchers operating under the banner of humanistic values, we also appreciate—mainly because it has profound implications for defeating the exploitation of human labor and the consolidation of a global ruling elite—critical insights into the domination of capital. In this context we envision important new developments of Marxist ethnographic practices that both complement and extend many of the exciting new approaches that we are witnessing within the precincts of postmodern and postcolonial ethnography. Future practitioners of critical research must take all of these crucial dynamics into account if their work is to help create a more just, democratic, and egalitarian world. The realm of the critical has yet to reach the potential it envisions. We hope that this essay challenges its readers to engage in the hard work and research necessary to move critical praxis closer to its realization.

■ References

Abdullah, J., & Stringer, E. (1999). Indigenous knowledge, indigenous learning, indigenous research. In L. Semali & J. L. Kincheloe (Eds.), *What is indigenous knowledge? Voices from the academy.* Bristol, PA: Falmer.

Abercrombie, N. (1994). Authority and consumer society. In R. Keat, N. Whiteley, &

N. Abercrombie (Eds.), *The authority of the consumer.* New York: Routledge.

Agger, B. (1992). *The discourse of domination: From the Frankfurt school to postmodernism.* Evanston, IL: Northwestern University Press.

Agger, B. (1998). *Critical social theories: An introduction.* Boulder, CO: Westview.

Alfino, M., Caputo, J., & Wynyard, R. (Eds.). (1998). *McDonaldization revisited: Critical essays on consumer and culture.* Westport, CT: Praeger.

Alford, C. (1993). Introduction to the special issue on political psychology and political theory. *Political Psychology, 14,* 199-208.

Allison, C. (1998). Okie narratives: Agency and whiteness. In J. L. Kincheloe, S. R. Steinberg, N. M. Rodriguez, & R. E. Chennault (Eds.), *White reign: Deploying whiteness in America.* New York: St. Martin's.

Anderson, G. (1989). Critical ethnography in education: Origins, current status, and new directions. *Review of Educational Research, 59,* 249-270.

Apple, M. (1996a). Dominance and dependency: Situating *The bell curve* within the conservative restoration. In J. L. Kincheloe, S. R. Steinberg, & A. D. Gresson III (Eds.), *Measured lies: The bell curve examined.* New York: St. Martin's.

Apple, M. (1966b). *Cultural politics and education.* New York: Teachers College Press.

Aronowitz, S., & DiFazio, W. (1994). *The jobless future.* Minneapolis: University of Minnesota Press.

Aronowitz, S., & Giroux, H. (1991). *Postmodern education: Politics, culture, and social criticism.* Minneapolis: University of Minnesota Press.

Ashcroft, B., Griffiths, G., & Tiffin, H. (Eds.). (1995). *The post-colonial studies reader.* New York: Routledge.

Atwell-Vasey, W. (1998). Psychoanalytic feminism and the powerful teacher. In W. F. Pinar (Ed.), *Curriculum: Toward new identities.* New York: Garland.

Barrows, A. (1995). The ecopsychology of child development. In T. Roszak, M. Gomes, & A. Kanner (Eds.), *Ecopsychology: Restoring the earth, healing the mind.* San Francisco: Sierra Club Books.

Bartolomé, L. I. (1998). *The misteaching of academic discourses: The politics of language in the classroom.* Boulder, CO: Westview.

Bauman, Z. (1995). *Life in fragments: Essays in postmodern morality.* Cambridge, MA: Blackwell.

Behar, R. (1993). *Translated woman: Crossing the border with Esperanza's story.* Boston: Beacon.

Behar, R., & Gordon, D. A. (Eds.). (1995). *Women writing culture.* Berkeley: University of California Press.

Bell, D., & Valentine, G. (1997). *Consuming geographies: We are where we eat.* New York: Routledge.

Berger, A. A. (1995). *Cultural criticism: A primer of key concepts.* Thousand Oaks, CA: Sage.

Berry, K. (1998). Nurturing the imagination of resistance: Young adults as creators of knowledge. In J. L. Kincheloe & S. R. Steinberg (Eds.), *Unauthorized methods: Strategies for critical teaching.* New York: Routledge.

Bersani, L. (1995). Loving men. In M. Berger, B. Wallis, & S. Watson (Eds.), *Constructing masculinity.* New York: Routledge.

Bertman, S. (1998). *Hyperculture: The human cost of speed.* Westport, CT: Praeger.

Blades, D. (1997). *Procedures of power and curriculum change: Foucault and the quest for possibilities in science education.* New York: Peter Lang.

Block, A. (1995). *Occupied reading: Critical foundations for an ecological theory.* New York: Garland.

Boon, J. A. (1982). *Other tribes, other scribes: Symbolic anthropology in the comparative study of cultures, histories, religions, and texts.* Cambridge: Cambridge University Press.

Bottomore, T. (1984). *The Frankfurt school.* London: Tavistock.

Bourdieu, P., & Wacquaat, L. (1992). *An invitation to reflexive sociology.* Chicago: University of Chicago Press.

Brents, B., & Monson, M. (1998). Whitewashing the strip: The construction of whiteness in Las Vegas. In J. L. Kincheloe, S. R. Steinberg, N. M. Rodriguez, & R. E. Chennault (Eds.), *White reign: Deploying whiteness in America.* New York: St. Martin's.

Britzman, D. (1991). *Practice makes practice: A critical study of learning to teach.* Albany: State University of New York Press.

Britzman, D. (1995). What is this thing called love? *Taboo: The Journal of Culture and Education, 1*, 65-93.

Britzman, D., & Pitt, A. (1996). On refusing one's place: The ditchdigger's dream. In J. L. Kincheloe, S. R. Steinberg, & A. D. Gresson III (Eds.), *Measured lies: The bell curve examined.* New York: St. Martin's.

Brock-Utne, B. (1996). Reliability and validity in qualitative research within Africa. *International Review of Education, 42*, 605-621.

Brosio, R. (1994). *The radical democratic critique of capitalist education.* New York: Peter Lang.

Buckingham, D. (1989). Television literacy: A critique. *Radical Philosophy, 51*, 12-25.

Butler, M. (1998). Negotiating place: The importance of children's realities. In S. R. Steinberg & J. L. Kincheloe (Eds.), *Students as researchers: Creating classrooms that matter* (pp. 94-112). London: Taylor & Francis.

Cannella, G. (1997). *Deconstructing early childhood education: Social justice and revolution.* New York: Peter Lang.

Carlson, D. (1997). *Teachers in crisis.* New York: Routledge.

Carlson, D., & Apple, M. (Eds.). (1998). *Power/knowledge/pedagogy: The meaning of democratic education in unsettling times.* Boulder, CO: Westview.

Carson, T. R., & Sumara, D. (Eds.). (1997). *Action research as a living practice.* New York: Peter Lang.

Carspecken, P. F. (1993). *Power, truth, and method: Outline for a critical methodology.* Unpublished manuscript.

Carspecken, P. F. (1996). *Critical ethnography in educational research: A theoretical and practical guide.* New York: Routledge.

Carspecken, P. F. (1999). *Four scenes for posing the question of meaning and other essays in critical philosophy and critical methodology.* New York: Peter Lang.

Carter, V. (1998). Computer-assisted racism: Toward an understanding of cyber-whiteness. In J. L. Kincheloe, S. R. Steinberg, N. M. Rodriguez, & R. E. Chennault (Eds.), *White reign: Deploying whiteness in America.* New York: St. Martin's.

Cary, R. (1996). I.Q. as commodity: The "new" economics of intelligence. In J. L. Kincheloe, S. R. Steinberg, & A. D. Gresson III (Eds.), *Measured lies: The bell curve examined.* New York: St. Martin's.

Christian-Smith, L., & Keelor, K. S. (1999). *Everyday knowledge and women of the academy: Uncommon Truths.* Boulder, CO: Westview.

Clatterbaugh, K. (1997). *Contemporary perspectives on masculinity: Men, women, and politics in modern society.* Boulder, CO: Westview.

Clifford, J. (1992). Traveling cultures. In L. Grossberg, C. Nelson, & P. A. Treichler (Eds.). *Cultural studies* (pp. 96-116). New York: Routledge.

Clough, P. T. (1994). *Feminist thought: Desire, power and academic discourse.* Cambridge, MA: Blackwell.

Clough, P. T. (1992). *The end(s) of ethnography: From realism to social criticism.* Newbury Park, CA: Sage.

Clough, P. T. (1998). *The end(s) of ethnography: From realism to social criticism* (2nd ed.). New York: Peter Lang.

Coben, D. (1998). *Radical heroes: Gramsci, Freire and the politics of adult education.* New York: Garland.

Codd, J. (1984). Introduction. In J. Codd (Ed.), *Philosophy, common sense, and action in educational administration* (pp. 8-28). Geelong, Victoria, Australia: Deakin University Press.

Collins, J. (1995). *Architectures of excess: Cultural life in the information age.* New York: Routledge.

Comaroff, J., & Comaroff, J. (1992). *Ethnography and the historical imagination.* Boulder, CO: Westview.

Connor, S. (1992). *Theory and cultural value.* Cambridge, MA: Blackwell.

Cooper, D. (1994). Productive, relational, and everywhere? Conceptualizing power and resistance within Foucauldian feminism. *Sociology, 28*, 435-454.

Corrigan, P. (1979). *Schooling the Smash Street kids.* London: Macmillan.

Crapanzano, V. (1990). Afterword. In M. Manganaro (Ed.). *Modernist anthropology: From fieldwork to text* (pp. 300-308). Princeton, NJ: Princeton University Press.

Daniel, E. V. (1996). *Charred lullabies: Chapters in an anthropology of violence.* Princeton, NJ: Princeton University Press.

Deetz, S. A. (1993, May). *Corporations, the media, industry, and society: Ethical imperatives and responsibilities.* Paper presented at the annual meeting of the International Communication Association, Washington, DC.

Denzin, N. K. (1992). *Symbolic interactionism and cultural studies.* Newbury Park, CA: Sage.

Denzin, N. K. (1994). The art and politics of interpretation. In N. K. Denzin & Y. S. Lincoln (Eds.), *Handbook of qualitative research* (pp. 500-515). Thousand Oaks, CA: Sage.

Dewey, J. (1916). *Democracy and education.* New York: Free Press.

Douglas, S. (1994). *Where the girls are: Growing up female in the mass media.* New York: Times Books.

Drummond, L. (1996). *American dreamtime: A cultural analysis of popular movies, and their implications for a science of humanity.* Lanham, MD: Littlefield Adams.

du Gay, P., Hall, S., Janes, L., MacKay, H., & Negus, K. (1997). *Doing cultural studies: The story of the Sony Walkman.* London: Sage.

Ebert, T. (1991). Political semiosis in/or American cultural studies. *American Journal of Semiotics, 8,* 113-135.

Elliot, A. (1994). *Psychoanalytic theory: An introduction.* Cambridge, MA: Blackwell.

Ellis, J. (1998). Interpretive inquiry as student research. In S. R. Steinberg & J. L. Kincheloe (Eds.), *Students as researchers: Creating classrooms that matter* (pp. 49-63). London: Taylor & Francis.

Fehr, D. (1993). *Dogs playing cards: Power-brokers of prejudice in education, art, and culture.* New York: Peter Lang.

Ferguson, M., & Golding, P. (Eds.). (1997). *Cultural studies in question.* London: Sage.

Finders, M. (1997). *Just girls: Hidden literacies and life in junior high.* New York: Teachers College Press.

Fine, M., Powell, L. C., Weis, L., & Wong, L. M. (Eds.). (1997). *Off white: Readings on race, power and society.* New York: Routledge.

Fiske, J. (1993). *Power works, power plays.* New York: Verso.

Flossner, G., & Otto, H. (Eds.). (1998). *Towards more democracy in social services: Models of culture and welfare.* New York: de Gruyter.

Foster, H. (Ed.). (1983). *The anti-aesthetic: Essays on postmodern culture.* Port Townsend, WA: Bay.

Frankenberg, R. (1993). *White women, race matters: The social construction of whiteness.* Minneapolis: University of Minnesota Press.

Franz, C., & Stewart, A. (Eds.). (1994). *Women creating lives.* Boulder, CO: Westview.

Fraser, N. (1995). Politics, culture, and the public sphere: Toward a postmodern conception. In L. J. Nicholson & S. Seidman (Eds.), *Social postmodernism: Beyond identity politics.* New York: Cambridge University Press.

Freire, A. M. A. (2000). Foreword by Ana Maria Araujo Freire. In P. McLaren, *Che Guevara, Paulo Freire, and the Pedagogy of Revolution.* Boulder, CO: Rowman and Littlefield.

Freire, P. (1985). *The politics of education: Culture, power, and liberation.* South Hadley, MA: Bergin & Garvey.

Fuchs, M. (1993). The reversal of the ethnological perspective: Attempts at objectifying one's own cultural horizon. Dumont, Foucault, Bourdieu? *Thesis Eleven, 34,* 104-125.

Gabbard, D. (1995). NAFTA, GATT, and Goals 2000: Reading the political culture of post-industrial America. *Taboo: The Journal of Culture and Education, 2,* 184-199.

Gadamer, H.-G. (1989). *Truth and method* (2nd rev. ed.; J. Weinsheimer & D. G. Marshall, Eds. & Trans.). New York: Crossroad.

Gall, J., Gall, M., & Borg, W. (1999). *Applying educational research: A practical guide.* New York: Longman.

Gallagher, S. (1992). *Hermeneutics and education.* Albany: State University of New York Press.

Garnham, N. (1997). Political economy and the practice of cultural studies. In M. Ferguson & P. Golding (Eds.), *Cultural studies in question.* London: Sage.

Gee, J. (1996). *Social linguistics and literacies: Ideology in discourses* (2nd ed.). London: Taylor & Francis.

Gee, J., Hull, G., & Lankshear, C. (1996). *The new work order: Behind the language of the new capitalism.* Boulder, CO: Westview.

Gergen, K. J. (1991). *The saturated self: Dilemmas of identity in contemporary life.* New York: Basic Books.

Gibson, R. (1986). *Critical theory and education*. London: Hodder & Stroughton.

Giroux, H. (1983). *Theory and resistance in education: A pedagogy for the opposition*. South Hadley, MA: Bergin & Garvey.

Giroux, H. (1988). Critical theory and the politics of culture and voice: Rethinking the discourse of educational research. In R. Sherman & R. Webb (Eds.), *Qualitative research in education: Focus and methods* (pp. 190-210). New York: Falmer.

Giroux, H. (1992). *Border crossings: Cultural workers and the politics of education*. New York: Routledge.

Giroux, H. (1997). *Pedagogy and the politics of hope: Theory, culture, and schooling*. Boulder, CO: Westview.

Giroux, H., & Searles, S. (1996). The bell curve debate and the crisis of public intellectuals. In J. L. Kincheloe, S. R. Steinberg, & A. D. Gresson III (Eds.), *Measured lies: The bell curve examined*. New York: St. Martin's.

Godzich, W. (1992). Afterword: Reading against literacy. In J.-F. Lyotard, *The postmodern explained*. Minneapolis: University of Minnesota Press.

Goldie, T. (1995). The representation of the indigene. In B. Ashcroft, G. Griffiths, & H. Tiffin (Eds.), *The post-colonial studies reader*. New York: Routledge.

Goldman, R., & Papson, S. (1994). The postmodernism that failed. In D. Dickens & A. Fontana (Eds.), *Postmodernism and social inquiry*. New York: Guilford Press.

Goodson, I. (1997). *The changing curriculum: Studies in social construction*. New York: Peter Lang.

Goodson, I., & Mangan, J. (1996). Exploring alternative perspectives in educational research. *Interchange, 27*(1), 41-59.

Gresson, A. (1995). *The recovery of race in America*. Minneapolis: University of Minnesota Press.

Gresson, A. (2000). *America's atonement: Racial pain, recovery discourse and the psychology of healing*. New York: Peter Lang.

Griffin, C. (1985). *Typical girls? Young women from school to the job market*. London: Routledge & Kegan Paul.

Grondin, J. (1994). *Introduction to philosophical hermeneutics* (J. Weinsheimer, Trans.). New Haven, CT: Yale University Press.

Gross, A., & Keith, W. (Eds.). (1997). *Rhetorical hermeneutics: Invention and interpretation in the age of science*. Albany: State University of New York Press.

Grossberg, L. (1995). What's in a name (one more time)? *Taboo: The Journal of Culture and Education, 1*, 1-37.

Grossberg, L. (1997). *Bringing it all back home: Essays on cultural studies*. Durham, NC: Duke University Press.

Hall, S. (Ed.). (1997). *Representation: Cultural representations and signifying practices*. London: Sage.

Hall, S., & du Gay, P. (Eds.). (1996). *Questions of cultural identity*. London: Sage.

Hebdige, D. (1979). *Subculture: The meaning of style*. London: Methuen.

Hedley, M. (1994). The presentation of gendered conflict in popular movies: Affective stereotypes, cultural sentiments, and men's motivation. *Sex Roles, 31*, 721-740.

Held, D. (1980). *Introduction to critical theory: Horkheimer to Habermas*. Berkeley: University of California Press.

Heshusius, L., & Ballard, K. (Eds.). (1996). *From positivism to interpretivism and beyond: Tales of transformation in educational and social research*. New York: Teachers College Press.

Hicks, D. E. (1999). *Ninety-five languages and seven forms of intelligence*. New York: Peter Lang.

Hinchey, P. (1998). *Finding freedom in the classroom: A practical introduction to critical theory*. New York: Peter Lang.

Horkheimer, M. (1972). *Critical theory*. New York: Seabury.

Howell, S. (1998). The learning organization: Reproduction of whiteness. In J. L. Kincheloe, S. R. Steinberg, N. M. Rodriguez, & R. E. Chennault (Eds.), *White reign: Deploying whiteness in America*. New York: St. Martin's.

Jardine, D. (1998). *To dwell with a boundless heart: Essays in curriculum theory, hermeneutics, and the ecological imagination*. New York: Peter Lang.

Jay, M. (1973). *The dialectical imagination: A history of the Frankfurt school and the Institute of Social Research 1923-1950*. Boston: Little, Brown.

Jipson, J., & Paley, N. (1997). *Daredevil research: Recreating analytic practice*. New York: Peter Lang.

Johnson, C. (1996). Does capitalism really need patriarchy? Some old issues reconsidered.

Women's Studies International Forum, 19, 193-202.

Joyrich, L. (1996). *Reviewing reception: Television, gender, and postmodern culture.* Bloomington: Indiana University Press.

Kellner, D. (1989). *Critical theory, Marxism, and modernity.* Baltimore: Johns Hopkins University Press.

Kellner, D. (Ed.). (1994). *Baudrillard: A critical reader.* Cambridge, MA: Blackwell.

Kellner, D. (1995). *Media culture: Cultural studies, identity and politics between the modern and the postmodern.* New York: Routledge.

Kellogg, D. (1998). Exploring critical distance in science education: Students researching the implications of technological embeddedness. In S. R. Steinberg & J. L. Kincheloe (Eds.), *Students as researchers: Creating classrooms that matter* (pp. 212-227). London: Falmer.

Kelly, L. (1996). When does the speaking profit us? Reflection on the challenges of developing feminist perspectives on abuse and violence by women. In M. Hester, L. Kelly, & J. Radford (Eds.), *Women, violence, and male power.* Bristol, PA: Open University Press.

Kincheloe, J. L. (1991). *Teachers as researchers: Qualitative paths to empowerment.* London: Falmer.

Kincheloe, J. L. (1993). *Toward a critical politics of teacher thinking: Mapping the postmodern.* Granby, MA: Bergin & Garvey.

Kincheloe, J. L. (1995). *Toil and trouble: Good work, smart workers, and the integration of academic and vocational education.* New York: Peter Lang.

Kincheloe, J. L. (1998). Critical research in science education. In B. Fraser & K. Tobin (Eds.), *International handbook of science education* (Pt. 2). Boston: Kluwer.

Kincheloe, J. L. (1999). *How do we tell the workers? The socioeconomic foundations of work and vocational education.* Boulder, CO: Westview.

Kincheloe, J. L., & Pinar, W. F. (1991). Introduction. In J. L. Kincheloe & W. F. Pinar, *Curriculum as social psychoanalysis: Essays on the significance of place* (pp. 1-23). Albany: State University of New York Press.

Kincheloe, J. L., & Steinberg, S. R. (1993). A tentative description of post-formal thinking: The critical confrontation with cogni-tive theory. *Harvard Educational Review, 63,* 296-320.

Kincheloe, J. L., & Steinberg, S. R. (1997). *Changing multiculturalism: New times, new curriculum.* London: Open University Press.

Kincheloe, J. L., Steinberg, S. R., & Hinchey, P. (Eds.). (1999). *The post-formal reader: Cognition and education.* New York: Falmer.

Kincheloe, J. L., Steinberg, S. R., Rodriguez, N. M., & Chennault, R. E. (Eds.). (1998). *White reign: Deploying whiteness in America.* New York: St. Martin's.

Kincheloe, J. L., Steinberg, S. R., & Tippins, D. (1999). *The stigma of genius: Einstein, consciousness and Education.* New York: Peter Lang.

Kincheloe, J. L., Steinberg, S. R., & Villaverde, L. (Eds.). (1999). *Rethinking intelligence: Confronting psychological assumptions about teaching and learning.* New York: Routledge.

King, J. (1996). Bad luck, bad blood, bad faith: Ideological hegemony and the oppressive language of hoodoo social science. In J. L. Kincheloe, S. R. Steinberg, & A. D. Gresson III (Eds.), *Measured lies: The bell curve examined.* New York: St. Martin's.

King, J., & Mitchell, C. (1995). *Black mothers to sons.* New York: Peter Lang.

Knobel, M. *Everyday literacies: Students, discourse, and social practice.* New York: Peter Lang.

Kogler, H. (1996). *The power of dialogue: Critical hermeneutics after Gadamer and Foucault.* Cambridge: MIT Press.

Lacey, C. (1970). *Hightown Grammar: The school as a social system.* London: Routledge & Kegan Paul.

Lash, S. (1990). Learning from Leipzig . . . or politics in the semiotic society. *Theory, Culture & Society, 7*(4), 145-158.

Lather, P. (1991). *Getting smart: Feminist research and pedagogy with/in the postmodern.* New York: Routledge.

Lather, P. (1993). Fertile obsession: Validity after poststructuralism. *Sociological Quarterly, 34,* 673-693.

Leistyna, P., Woodrum, A., & Sherblom, S. (1996). *Breaking free: The transformative power of critical pedagogy.* Cambridge, MA: Harvard Educational Review.

Lemke, J. (1993). Discourse, dynamics, and social change. *Cultural Dynamics, 6,* 243-275.

Lemke, J. (1995). *Textual politics: Discourse and social dynamics.* London: Taylor & Francis.

Lemke, J. (1998). Analyzing verbal data: Principles, methods, and problems. In B. Fraser & K. Tobin (Eds.), *International handbook of science education* (Pt. 2). Boston: Kluwer.

Lugg, C. (1996). Attacking affirmative action: Social Darwinism as public policy. In J. L. Kincheloe, S. R. Steinberg, & A. D. Gresson III (Eds.), *Measured lies: The bell curve examined.* New York: St. Martin's.

Lugones, M. (1987). Playfulness, "world"-traveling, and loving perception. *Hypatia, 2*(2), 3-19.

Luke, T. (1991). Touring hyperreality: Critical theory confronts informational society. In P. Wexler (Ed.), *Critical theory now* (pp. 1-26). New York: Falmer.

Lull, J. (1995). *Media, communication, culture: A global approach.* New York: Columbia University Press.

Macedo, D. (1994). *Literacies of power: What Americans are not allowed to know.* Boulder, CO: Westview.

Madison, G. B. (1988). *The hermeneutics of postmodernity: Figures and themes.* Bloomington: Indiana University Press.

Maher, F., & Tetreault, M. (1994). *The feminist classroom: An inside look at how professors and students are transforming higher education for a diverse society.* New York: Basic Books.

Manganaro, M. (1990). Textual play, power, and cultural critique: An orientation to modernist anthropology. In M. Manganaro (Ed.), *Modernist anthropology: From fieldwork to text* (pp. 3-47). Princeton, NJ: Princeton University Press.

Marcus, G. E., & Fischer, M. M. J. (1986). *Anthropology as cultural critique: An experimental moment in the human sciences.* Chicago: University of Chicago Press.

Martin, H., & Schuman, H. (1996). *The global trap: Globalization and the assault on democracy and prosperity.* New York: Zed Books.

McGuigan, J. (1996). *Culture and the public sphere.* New York: Routledge.

McLaren, P. (1992a). Collisions with otherness: "Traveling" theory, post-colonial criticism, and the politics of ethnographic practice—the mission of the wounded ethnographer. *International Journal of Qualitative Studies in Education, 5,* 77-92.

McLaren, P. (1992b). Literacy research and the postmodern turn: Cautions from the margins. In R. Beach, J. Green, M. Kamil, & T. Shanahan (Eds.), *Multidisciplinary perspectives on research.* Urbana, IL: National Council of Teachers of English.

McLaren, P. (1995a). *Critical pedagogy and predatory culture: Oppositional politics in a postmodern era.* New York: Routledge.

McLaren, P. (1995b). *Life in schools* (3rd ed.). New York: Longman.

McLaren, P. (1997). *Revolutionary multiculturalism: Pedagogies of dissent for the new millennium.* New York: Routledge.

McLaren, P. (1998). Revolutionary pedagogy in post-revolutionary times: Rethinking the political economy of critical education. *Educational Theory, 48,* 431-462.

McLaren, P. (1999). *Schooling as a ritual performance: Toward a political economy of educational symbols and gestures* (3rd ed.). Boulder, CO: Rowman & Littlefield.

McLaren, P. (2000). *Che Guevara, Paulo Freire, and the pedagogy of revolution.* Boulder, CO: Rowman & Littlefield.

McLaren, P., & Hammer, R. (1989). Critical pedagogy and the postmodern challenge. *Educational Foundations, 3*(3), 29-69.

McLaren, P., Hammer, R., Reilly, S., & Sholle, D. (1995). *Rethinking media literacy: A critical pedagogy of representation.* New York: Peter Lang.

McWilliam, E., & Taylor, P. (Eds.). (1996). *Pedagogy, technology, and the body.* New York: Peter Lang.

Miller, S., & Hodge, J. (1998). *Phenomenology, hermeneutics, and narrative analysis: Some unfinished methodological business.* Unpublished manuscript.

Molnar, A. (1996). *Giving kids the business: The commercialization of America's schools.* Boulder, CO: Westview.

Morgan, W. (1996). Personal training: Discourses of (self) fashioning. In E. McWilliam & P. Taylor (Eds.), *Pedagogy, technology, and the body.* New York: Peter Lang.

Morley, D., & Chen, K.-H. (Eds.). (1996). *Stuart Hall: Critical dialogues in cultural studies.* New York: Routledge.

Morrow, R. (1991). Critical theory, Gramsci and cultural studies: From structuralism to post-structuralism. In P. Wexler (Ed.), *Criti-*

cal theory now (pp. 27-69). New York: Falmer.

Mullen, C. (1999). Whiteness, cracks and ink-stains: Making cultural identity with Euro-american preservice teachers. In P. Diamond & C. Mullen (Eds.), *The postmodern educator: Arts-based inquiries and teacher development.* New York: Peter Lang.

Myrsiades, K., & Myrsiades, L. (Eds.). (1998). *Race-ing representation: Voice, history, and sexuality.* Lanham, MD: Rowman & Little-field.

Newton, J., & Stacey, J. (1992-1993). Learning not to curse, or, feminist predicaments in cultural criticism by men: Our movie date with James Clifford and Stephen Green-blatt. *Cultural Critique, 23,* 51-82.

Nicholson, L. J., & Seidman, S. (Eds.). (1995). *Social postmodernism: Beyond identity politics.* New York: Cambridge University Press.

Pailliotet, A. (1998). Deep viewing: A critical look at visual texts. In J. L. Kincheloe & S. R. Steinberg (Eds.), *Unauthorized methods: Strategies for critical teaching.* New York: Routledge.

Peters, M. (1993). *Against Finkielkraut's la defaite de la pensee: Culture, postmodernism and education.* Unpublished manuscript.

Peters, M., & Lankshear, C. (1994). Education and hermeneutics: A Freirean interpretation. In P. McLaren & C. Lankshear (Eds.), *Politics of liberation: Paths from Freire.* New York: Routledge.

Pfeil, F. (1995). *White guys: Studies in postmodern domination and difference.* New York: Verso.

Pieterse, J., & Parekh, B. (1995). Shifting imaginaries: Decolonization, internal decolonization, and postcoloniality. In J. Pieterse & B. Parekh (Eds.), *The decolonialization of imagination: Culture, knowledge, and power.* Atlantic Highlands, NJ: Zed.

Pinar, W. F. (1994). *Autobiography, politics, and sexuality: Essays in curriculum theory, 1972-1992.* New York: Peter Lang.

Pinar, W. F. (Ed.). (1998). *Curriculum: Toward new identities.* New York: Garland.

Pinar, W. F., Reynolds, W., Slattery, P., & Taubman, P. (1995). *Understanding curriculum.* New York: Peter Lang.

Poster, M. (1989). *Critical theory and post-structuralism: In search of a context.* Ithaca, NY: Cornell University Press.

Prakash, M., & Esteva, G. (1998). *Escaping education: Living as learning within grassroots cultures.* New York: Peter Lang.

Pruyn, M. (1994). Becoming subjects through critical practice: How students in an elementary classroom critically read and wrote their world. *International Journal of Educational Reform, 3*(1), 37-50.

Pruyn, M. (1999). *Discourse wars in Gotham-West: A Latino immigrant urban tale of resistance and agency.* Boulder, CO: Westview.

Quantz, R. A. (1992). On critical ethnography (with some postmodern considerations). In M. D. LeCompte, W. L. Millroy, & J. Preissle (Eds.), *The handbook of qualitative research in education* (pp. 447-505). New York: Academic Press.

Quail, C. B., Razzano, K. A., & Skalli, L. H. (2000). *Tell me more: Rethinking daytime talk shows.* New York: Peter Lang.

Rabinow, P. (1977). *Reflections on fieldwork in Morocco.* Berkeley: University of California Press.

Rains, F. (1998). Is the benign really harmless? Deconstructing some "benign" manifestations of operationalized white privilege. In J. L. Kincheloe, S. R. Steinberg, N. M. Rodriguez, & R. E. Chennault (Eds.), *White reign: Deploying whiteness in America.* New York: St. Martin's.

Rand, E. (1995). *Barbie's queer accessories.* Durham, NC: Duke University Press.

Rapko, J. (1998). Review of *The power of dialogue*: Critical hermeneutics after Gadamer and Foucault. *Criticism, 40*(1), 133-138.

Ritzer, G. (1993). *The McDonaldization of society.* Thousand Oaks, CA: Pine Forge.

Robins, D., & Cohen, P. (1978). *Knuckle sandwich: Growing up in the working-class city.* Harmondsworth: Penguin.

Robinson, W. (1998). Beyond nation-state paradigms: Globalization, sociology, and the challenge of transnational studies. *Sociological Forum, 13,* 561-594.

Rodriguez, N. M., & Villaverde, L. (2000). *Dismantling whiteness.* New York: Peter Lang.

Roman, L., & Eyre, L. (Eds.). (1997). *Dangerous territories: Struggles for difference and equality in education.* New York: Routledge.

Rosen, S. (1987). *Hermeneutics as politics.* New York: Oxford University Press.

Rosenau, P. M. (1992). *Post-modernism and the social sciences: Insights, inroads, and intrusion.* Princeton, NJ: Princeton University Press.

Samuels, A. (1993). *The political psyche.* New York: Routledge.

San Juan, E., Jr. (1992). *Articulations of power in ethnic and racial studies in the United States.* Atlantic Highlands, NJ: Humanities Press.

San Juan, E., Jr. (1996). *Mediations: From a Filipino perspective.* Pasig City, Philippines: Anvil.

Scheurich, J. J., & Young, M. (1997). Coloring epistemologies: Are our research epistemologies racially biased? *Educational Researcher, 26*(4), 4-16.

Scott, J. W. (1992). Experience. In J. Butler & J. W. Scott (Eds.), *Feminists theorize the political* (pp. 22-40). New York: Routledge.

Sedgwick, E. (1995). Gosh, Boy George, you must be awfully secure in your masculinity? In M. Berger, B. Wallis, & S. Watson (Eds.), *Constructing masculinity.* New York: Routledge.

Semali, L. (1998). Still crazy after all these years: Teaching critical media literacy. In J. L. Kincheloe & S. R. Steinberg (Eds.), *Unauthorized methods: Strategies for critical teaching.* New York: Routledge.

Semali, L., & Kincheloe, J. L. (1999). *What is indigenous knowledge? Voices from the academy.* New York: Falmer.

Shelton, A. (1996). The ape's I.Q. In J. L. Kincheloe, S. R. Steinberg, & A. D. Gresson III (Eds.), *Measured lies: The bell curve examined.* New York: St. Martin's.

Shohat, E., & Stam, R. (1994). *Unthinking Eurocentrism: Multiculturalism and the media.* New York: Routledge.

Shor, I. (1996). *When students have power: Negotiating authority in a critical pedagogy.* Chicago: University of Chicago Press.

Silverman, E. K. (1990). Clifford Geertz: Towards a more "thick" understanding? In C. Tilley (Ed.), *Reading material culture* (pp. 121-159). Cambridge, MA: Blackwell.

Slattery, P. (1995). *Curriculum development in the postmodern era.* New York: Garland.

Slaughter, R. (1989). Cultural reconstruction in the post-modern world. *Journal of Curriculum Studies, 3,* 255-270.

Sleeter, C., & McLaren, P. (Eds.). (1995). *Multicultural education, critical pedagogy, and the politics of difference.* Albany: State University of New York Press.

Smith, D. G. (1999). *Interdisciplinary essays in the Pedagon: Human sciences, pedagogy and culture.* New York: Peter Lang.

Smith, R., & Wexler, P. (Eds.). (1995). *After post-modernism: Education, politics, and identity.* London: Falmer.

Smyth, J. (1989). A critical pedagogy of classroom practice. *Journal of Curriculum Studies, 21*(6), 483-401.

Soto, L. (1998). Bilingual education in America: In search of equity and justice. In J. L. Kincheloe & S. R. Steinberg (Eds.), *Unauthorized methods: Strategies for critical teaching.* New York: Routledge.

Stallabrass, J. (1996). *Gargantua: Manufactured mass culture.* London: Verso.

Steinberg, S. (1997). Kinderculture: The cultural studies of childhood. In N. Denzin (Ed.), *Cultural studies: A research volume* (Vol. 2, pp. 17-44). Greenwich, CN: JAI.

Steinberg, S. (Ed.). (2000). *Multi/intercultural conversations.* New York: Peter Lang.

Steinberg, S. R. (1997). The bitch who has everything. In S. R. Steinberg & J. L. Kincheloe (Eds.), *Kinderculture: The corporate construction of childhood.* Boulder, CO: Westview.

Steinberg, S. R., & Kincheloe, J. L. (Eds.). (1997). *Kinderculture: Corporate constructions of childhood.* Boulder, CO: Westview.

Steinberg, S. R., & Kincheloe, J. L. (Eds.). (1998). *Students as researchers: Creating classrooms that matter.* London: Taylor & Francis.

Stewart, K. (1996). *A space on the side of the road: Cultural poetics in an "other" America.* Princeton, NJ: Princeton University Press.

Sünker, H. (1998). Welfare, democracy, and social work. In G. Flosser & H. Otto (Eds.), *Towards more democracy in social services: Models of culture and welfare.* New York: de Gruyter.

Surber, J. (1998). *Culture and critique: An introduction to the critical discourses of cultural studies.* Boulder, CO: Westview.

Taussig, M. (1987). *Shamanism, colonialism, and the wild man: A study in terror and healing.* Chicago: University of Chicago Press.

Taylor, M., & Saarinen, E. (1994). *Imagologies: Media philosophy.* New York: Routledge.

Thomas, S. (1997). Dominance and ideology in cultural studies. In M. Ferguson & P. Golding (Eds.), *Cultural studies in question.* London: Sage.

Trueba, E. T., & McLaren, P. (in press). Critical ethnography for the study of immigrants. In E. T. Trueba & L. I. Bartolomé (Eds.), *Immigrant voices: In search of educational equity.* Boulder, CO: Rowman & Littlefield.

Vattimo, G. (1994). *Beyond interpretation: The meaning of hermeneutics for philosophy.* Stanford, CA: Stanford University Press.

Viergever, M. (1999). Indigenous knowledge: An interpretation of views from indigenous peoples. In L. Semali & J. L. Kincheloe (Eds.), *What is indigenous knowledge? Voices from the academy.* Bristol, PA: Falmer.

Villaverde, L., & Kincheloe, J. L. (1998). Engaging students as researchers: Researching and teaching Thanksgiving in the elementary classroom. In S. R. Steinberg & J. L. Kincheloe (Eds.), *Students as researchers: Creating classrooms that matter* (pp. 149-166). London: Falmer.

Visweswaran, K. (1994). *Fictions of feminist ethnography.* Minneapolis: University of Minnesota Press.

Weil, D. (1998). *Towards a critical multi-cultural literacy: Theory and practice for education for liberation.* New York: Peter Lang.

Weiler, K. (1988). *Women teaching for change: Gender, class, and power.* South Hadley, MA: Bergin & Garvey.

Weinstein, M. (1998). *Robot world: Education, popular culture, and science.* New York: Peter Lang

Welch, S. (1991). An ethic of solidarity and difference. In H. Giroux (Ed.), *Postmodernism, feminism, and cultural politics: Redrawing educational boundaries* (pp. 83-99). Albany: State University of New York Press.

West, C. (1993). *Race matters.* Boston: Beacon.

Wexler, P. (1991). Preface. In P. Wexler (Ed.), *Critical theory now.* New York: Falmer.

Wexler, P. (1996a). *Critical social psychology.* New York: Peter Lang.

Wexler, P. (1996b). *Holy sparks: Social theory, education, and religion.* New York: St. Martin's.

Wexler, P. (1997). *Social research in education: Ethnography of being.* Paper presented at the International Conference on the Culture of Schooling, Halle, Germany.

Willis, P. E. (1977). *Learning to labour: How working class kids get working class jobs.* Farnborough, UK: Saxon House.

Women's Studies Group, Centre for Contemporary Cultural Studies. (1978). *Women take issue: Aspects of women's subordination.* London: Hutchinson, with Centre for Contemporary Cultural Studies, University of Birmingham.

Woodward, K. (Ed.). (1997). *Identity and difference.* London: Sage.

Yates, T. (1990). Jacques Derrida: "There is nothing outside of the text." In C. Tilley (Ed.), *Reading material culture* (pp. 206-280). Cambridge, MA: Blackwell.

Young, I. (1990). The ideal of community and the politics of difference. In L. J. Nicholson (Ed.), *Feminism/postmodernism* (pp. 300-323). New York: Routledge.

Zavarzadeh, M., & Morton, D. (1991). *Theory, (post)modernity, opposition.* Washington, DC: Maison-neuve.

Zizek, S. (1990). *The sublime object of ideology.* London: Verso.

11

CULTURAL STUDIES

◆ John Frow and Meaghan Morris

During the 1980s, as academics debated "postmodernism" and policy battles began to be waged about "globalization," the word *culture* came to be used by the media in a sense that seemed far removed from anything to do with artistic and literary texts. When an Australian politician declared that "resetting industrial policy is really a matter of reshaping cultural attitudes" (quoted in Loosley, 1991), he was not defining culture as a domain of aesthetic pleasure, as a set of masterpieces, or as an expression of national identity. Nor was he speaking in economic terms of culture as a major export industry, although he might have done so ("Culture Fills," 1990). Rather, he was referring to a complex of social customs, values, and expectations that affect our ways of working. So, too, was the media magnate Rupert Murdoch in a television interview aired in Australia in 1990. Just as the worst company crashes in Australian history ended an era of financial mismanagement and entrepreneurial

crime, the Melbourne host of ABC-TV's *The 7.30 Report* asked Murdoch what "we" should do to save our economy. Murdoch replied perfunctorily, "Oh, you know: Change the culture."

Murdoch expected us to "know" that he was quoting a formula of the neoliberal rhetoric now broadly shared in Australia, as elsewhere, by bureaucrats, politicians, economists, journalists, and financiers as well as union and corporate leaders: Economic problems need "cultural" solutions. Culture in this sense is not just a topic for specialized debate by an esoteric caste of interpreters ("critics"). On the contrary, "changing the culture" is a way of challenging the conduct of other people's everyday working lives, whether within the framework of a single company ("Changing the culture is not a quick process in something as old and as large as ARC," says a chief executive of Australia's main producer of concrete reinforcing steel), of an industry (a marketing expert offers a paper titled

AUTHORS' NOTE: For their assistance with the reference list, we would like to thank Chua Beng-Huat, Larry Grossberg, Gay Hawkins, Vivien Johnson, Allan Luke, Brian Massumi, Tony Mitchell, Elspeth Probyn, David Rowe, Darren Tofts, Keyan Tomaselli, Graeme Turner, and Rob Wilson.

◆ 315

"Changing Culture for Service: How to Effect a Change to the Service Culture in Shopping Centres"), or an entire national economy ("Professor Hughes said Australians 'have got to cultivate an export culture' ").[1]

In other words, culture itself is imagined as a plastic medium that politically powerful social elites may rework and remold at will. For these economic critics of everyday life, changing the culture primarily means that "fewer workers must produce more for less"; globalization is widely invoked as the inexorable force that makes this imperative rational. But this program has social implications, and these may vary from place to place. It means changing the minutiae of behavior ("work practices") at the workplace, and thus the texture and organization of home and family life. It can mean inducing workers to invest more actively in the corporate ethos. In some contexts, it can also mean improving race and gender relations in the interests of achieving an "international outlook." It can sharpen class consciousness by making "inequality of outcomes" and, therefore poverty more acceptable to people—at lest to those who have work. *Aesthetic* implications follow. In an Australian context, where the "ideology of the collective" (Knight, 1990, p. 5) has been strong, accepting these changes has meant questioning the value of canonical myths of our modern history—egalitarianism, "mateship" (solidarity), upward mobility, and a "fair go" for all—along with the associated ethical images of pleasure, personal development, and social worth that still circulate in our society (Morris, 1998a; Turner, 1994).

Despite appearances, then, the neoliberal critique of culture cannot be neatly disentangled from "artistic and literary" concerns. By the end of the 1980s it had prompted a media debate about the *worth* of various aspects of Australia's traditional national identity (hedonism and "welfarism" were popular topics for criticism; see Robinson, 1989), and over the next 10 years the economic and social arrangements that for a century had sustained social democracy in Australia were dismantled or undermined. However, this debate was only a fraction of the coverage devoted to the "cultural" dimensions of

East Asia's economic boom (Garnaut, 1989). Commentators promoted "Confucian capitalism" as a new model of development with cultural lessons to teach the West, and civilizational theories of history came back into mainstream fashion after decades in disrepute (Huntington, 1996; see also Chen, 1998a). After the Asian financial meltdown of 1997-1998, "crony capitalism" became for the very same commentators an object lesson in the need for "cultural reform" as prescribed by the International Monetary Fund (immiserating millions of people; see Arndt & Hill, 1999).

Shorn of its subordination of all other goals to that of economic productivity, and without the *moralism* (and determinism) of neoliberal rhetoric, this usage turns out to be strikingly close to one dimension of the way the word *culture* is used in contemporary cultural studies. In this context, too, culture is thought of as directly bound up with work and its organization; with relations of power and gender in the workplace, the home, the neighborhood, and the street; with the pleasures and the pressures of consumption; with the complex relations of class and kith and kin through which a sense of self and belonging is formed; and with the fantasies and desires through which social relations are carried and actively shaped. In short, *culture* is a term that can designate, in Raymond Williams's (1958/1961) phrase, the "whole way of life" (p. 16) of a social group as it is structured by representation and by power. It is not a detached domain for playing games of social distinction (Bourdieu, 1984) and "good" taste. It is a network of embedded practices and representations (texts, images, talk, codes of behavior, and the narrative structures organizing these) that shapes every aspect of social life.

◆ Identity and Community

The notion that culture is all-pervasive is often called anthropological, and, as Renato Rosaldo (1997) points out, one way of understanding cultural studies is as the product of a "rapid diffusion" of this notion "from anthropology to literary studies, law, social history, communication, business, media studies, and more" (p. 29). But to say that the concept of culture refers to the existence of social groups—their formation, their maintenance, their definition against other groups, the constant process of their re-formation—is to raise difficult questions about the kinds of unity that groups lay claim to. If for anthropologists "it no longer seems possible to study culture as an objectified thing or as a self-enclosed, coherent, patterned field of meaning" (Rosaldo, 1997, p. 29), we have all the more reason to ask at what level the concept of culture operates for cultural studies—that of the nation-state and/or of a "national" culture? That of class, gender, race, sexuality, age, ethnicity, community? The answer is that it may operate at any of these levels, and that they do not slot neatly into each other.

Much the same answer is given today right across the humanities and social sciences. With their colleagues in many other fields of qualitative research, practitioners of cultural studies have shared in decades of debate about cultural identity and difference, social location and movement, historical experience and change; any comprehensive cultural studies bibliography would overlap with many chapters in this *Handbook*. However, it is fair to say that for cultural studies these debates have not transformed an existing disciplinary formation but rather have directly constituted the field. As the most cursory survey of key publications will suggest, the very substance of cultural studies has been shaped in *encounters between* diverse feminisms (Butler, 1990; de Lauretis, 1986; Grewal & Kaplan, 1994; hooks, 1981; Hull, Scott, & Smith, 1982; Mohanty, Russo, & Torres, 1991; Probyn, 1993; Sheridan, 1988; Shiach, 1999; Wallace, 1978) interacting with class-conscious ethnic and critical race studies (Anzaldúa, 1987; Frankenberg, 1993; hooks, 1990; Jordan & Weedon, 1995; Matsuda, 1996; Moraga & Anzaldúa, 1981; Roediger, 1991; Ware, 1992), with gay, lesbian, and queer studies (Butler, 1993; Chang, 1998; Crimp, 1987; de Lauretis, 1991; Fuss, 1991; Sedgwick, 1993; Warner, 1993; Watney,

1987), with postcolonial and diasporic research (Ang, 1999; Bhabha, 1994; Chambers & Curti, 1996; Chow, 1991, 1993; Clifford, 1997; Gilroy, 1993; Hargreaves & McKinney, 1997; Morley & Chen, 1996; Prakash, 1995; Spivak, 1988, 1990), and with indigenous peoples' scholarship (Bennett & Blundell, 1995; Bennett, Turner, & Volkerling, 1994; Langton, 1993; Valaskakis, 1988, in press).

Given this history of interaction and often heated debate, most work in cultural studies has been acutely aware of the danger of positing imaginary social unities as the *explanatory* basis for its accounts of cultural texts. Its constant impetus is to think of cultures as being processes that divide as much as they bring together (see, e.g., Carby, 1982/1996; Chambers & Curti, 1996; Gilroy, 1987, 1996; hooks, 1992b; McRobbie, 1981; Steedman, 1986; Williams, 1985; Women's Studies Group, 1978), to stress the diversity and the contestation always involved in "defining" social groups (Frankenberg, 1997; Hall, 1996; Hall & du Gay, 1996; Lowe, 1996; Sedgwick, 1990), and to question those totalizing notions of culture that assume that at the end of cultural processes there lies the achievement of a whole and coherent "society" or "community" (Hunter, 1988b). At the same time, this very impetus pushes cultural studies to ask how groups "get to know themselves *as groups* (as a particular organization of individual and social interests, of sameness and difference) through cultural activity" (Frith, 1996a, p. 111); to investigate "the deep ambivalence of identification and desire" (Hall, 1996, p. 444) that can reach across and complicate the most rigid, historically deep-seated divisions and inequalities structuring *relationships* between groups (hooks, 1992a; Mercer, Ugwu, & Bailey, 1996; Muecke, 1997); and to seek a politics of connection and translation across prevailing boundaries rather than one of "unity" within or between radically separate groups (Benterrak, Muecke, & Roe, 1996; Clifford, 1997; Grossberg, 1992; Haraway, 1991; Hayward, 1998; McRobbie, 1994).

This double movement of critique and affirmation tends to put cultural studies at odds not only with an "evasive cosmopolitanism" (Willemen,

1994, p. 210) that denies the efficacy and the *burden* of actual boundaries between groups, treating difference as a consumable good and identity purely as fiction, but also with those militant cultural nationalisms, essentialisms, and particularisms that some critics fear will always arise with "the fateful question of culture" (Hartman, 1997). For example, Paul Gilroy (1992, 1993) rejects both a "notional pluralist" and an "exceptionalist" approach to black popular culture and outlines a third perspective, an "anti-antiessentialism" for which black identity is neither a freely disposable category nor an immutable racial essence but "the outcome of practical activity: language, gesture, bodily significations, desires," including the activities and impacts of racism. "Racialized subjectivity," Gilroy (1993) writes, is "the product of the social practices that supposedly derive from it" (p. 102). In a different context, Naoki Sakai (1997) makes a comparable argument about "the subject of 'Japan.'" Analyzing the complicity binding "universalism" to "particularism" in modern imperial nationalism, both in the West and in Japan, he shows that a rivalrous capacity to affirm the unity of a single language, *ethnos,* and nation is the outcome of a specific regime of translation installed in the 18th century (see Sakai, 1991), and not a precondition *for* translation.

Addressing debates in distinct academic areas, these arguments share with Willemen's work in cinema studies a disposition to see "the kinds of unity that groups lay claim to" not only as mobile and provisional (as the postmodern truism has it) but *also* as the real and consequential products of definite practices that it is the analyst's task to specify. Cultural studies has generally been less concerned with debating the pros and cons of essentialism as a philosophical stance (Fuss, 1989; see also Grossberg, 1997a, pp. 18-19; McRobbie, 1997b) than with examining the *political* conflicts at stake, in concrete contexts and for particular groups of people, between differing stories of community or nation (Baker, Diawara, & Lindeborg, 1996; D. Bennett, 1998; Chen, 1998b; Parker, Russo, Sommer, & Yaeger, 1992; Teer-Tomaselli & Roome, 1997) and with articulating the *histori-*

cal struggles occurring in the gaps between competing narrative programs (of "identity," for example) and the complex social experiences that these aspire to organize (Abbas, 1997; Berlant, 1997; Bhabha, 1990; Chakrabarty, in press; Chow, 1998a; Lilley, 1998; Morris, 1998a). Thus when Greg Noble, Scott Poynting, and Ken Tabar (1999) borrow from Gayatri Spivak (1990) the idea of a "strategic" essentialism, extending it to the study of cultural hybridity, they do so to investigate how young Arabic-speaking men in southwestern Sydney handle different contexts of everyday living by variably fashioning selves as migrants, as "Lebanese" (some are in fact from Syrian backgrounds), and as Australians inhabiting a socially particular place; for these young men, "the interplay of identity and context produces curiously practical amalgams" (Noble et al., 1999, p. 39).

Given this emphasis on material *contexts* (see Grossberg, 1993, 1998a)[2] of constraint and empowerment in everyday life, research in cultural studies in fact draws as deeply on geographic and historical ways of understanding culture as it does on anthropology in its recurring struggle with aesthetic concepts of culture (Clifford, 1988). Spatial and temporal framings of experience are equally important to contextual analysis, which seeks to grasp the complexity of the mundane processes, events, and *occasions* in which "identities" are formed and transformed; as Martin Allor (1997) puts it in an essay on "the Main" (Boulevard Saint-Laurent) in Montreal, a cultural studies aiming to render visible the politics of location "must focus precisely on [the] *coming into being* of forms of life" (p. 52).

◆ *Situating Cultural Studies*

One reason for this broadly skeptical approach to "culture" as the field's own unifying category lies in the complex international context in which cultural studies has developed since the 1970s. A smooth professional consensus about the limits and potentials of culture does not easily emerge when new struggles, conversations, and alliances are forming across once-formidable geopolitical and even linguistic boundaries while old colonial hierarchies, spacings, and "structures of feeling" (Williams, 1961b, p. 64; 1979) continue to shape the social meanings of events in landscapes newly produced or remade by economic globalization (Appadurai, 1996; Jacobs, 1996; Jameson & Miyoshi, 1998; Said, 1993; Wilson & Dissanayake, 1996; Wood, in press). For many scholars now, questions of identity and community are framed not only by issues of race, class, and gender but by a deeply political concern with place, cultural memory, and the variable terms of these scholars' access to an "international" space of debate dominated not only by Western preoccupations (Chen, 1992; Tomaselli, 1998b) but by the English language (Cho, 1996). In these conditions, as Jody Berland (1997a) observes, "culture and place demand our attention not because our concepts of them are definite or authoritative, but because they are fragile and fraught with dispute" (p. 9).

In cultural studies, as in other disciplines, globalization is contested both as *fact* and as *problematic,* to adapt a useful distinction from Allen Chun (1994; see also Chua, 1998; Grossberg, 1997b, 1999; King, 1991; Massey, 1997). Whatever value we accord this term, it is at least clear that large-scale economic, geopolitical, and technological changes have helped to transform both higher education and academic publishing over the past 30 years (Cohen, 1993; Morris, 1998b; Readings, 1996) and that these changes have not only shaped topics for work *in* cultural studies but have provided the conditions *for* its emergence as a transnational movement in scholarship. Those conditions include new opportunities and incentives for scholars to travel, talk, and publish, compare, and translate their work far more widely and diversely than before. However, they also include the corporatization of university life and its rationalization across national borders toward an increasing similarity at the level of institutional values and procedures. In some countries, conditions further include higher enrollments combined with a decline in state funding for public universities, thus making cultural studies attractive as a "cheap" form of pedagogy (Steedman, 1992b), and the reduction of formerly distinct faculties of "humanities" and "social sciences" into a single uneasy compound. It is not surprising, then, that an ambivalence about the "success" of cultural studies is one of its recurring themes (Ferguson & Golding, 1997; Grossberg, 1993; Kraniauskas, 1998; Morris, 1997a).

However, like English as a global language, cultural studies differs greatly according to the contexts in which it is practiced. The well-known difficulty of providing a "map" or an "overview" of the field is not simply a matter of epistemological squeamishness (disavowing the claim "to know"), but results from a practical limitation: There is always more going on than one is aware of from a particular situation *in* the field. For example, when James Carey (1997) regrets the passing of the "parochialism" of early British cultural studies, complaining as an American that cultural studies today is "pretty much a nowhere college," he reads the new internationalism of the field as just "a pattern of cross-reference and mutual citation spanning a couple of continents but hardly intellectually dominating on any campus" (p. 2; see also Carey, 1995). From our own situation on a third continent, Australia—where it is difficult to ignore work going on across parts of a fourth (East and Southeast Asia), and where cultural studies paradigms effectively dominate faculties at several "somewhere" colleges—Carey's account of the present seems not only parochial but wrong.

Yet it also has a certain plausibility. A general impression of cultural studies as a U.K./U.S. affair (give or take a few imported authors) is created by major anthologies (During, 1999; Grossberg, Nelson, & Treichler, 1992; Storey, 1996) as well as by some histories and thematic collections in wide distribution (Brantlinger, 1990; Ferguson & Golding, 1997; Hall & du Gay, 1996; Harris, 1992; McGuigan, 1997; McRobbie, 1997a; Nelson & Gaonkar, 1996). Read from elsewhere, however, these books do not appear from "nowhere"; on the contrary, they come from a strongly self-centralizing somewhere that is sometimes mistaken for everywhere. The problem, then, is how to situate, say, Carey's geography of "cultural studies" in relation to other ways of mapping the field, such as Kuan-Hsing Chen's (1998a) organization of an "inter-Asia cultural studies" around "the decolonization question," Peter Gibian's (1997) genealogy of a "North American" cultural studies based on the lively critiques of "mass culture" published by the journal *Tabloid,* or Keyan Tomaselli's (1998b) insistence that diverse African cultural studies will "derive from 'historicisation'; the recovery of African scholarship from all periods and societies within the frames of reference provided by various approaches within the field as a whole" (p. 395).

A bigger map won't do, although it's a start. What is striking about the geographically situated work easily available in our own vicinity is the flexibility of the categories in use; scanning the field, one can see nations begin to form regions, regions break up into areas, and areas form around communities within nations as well as between them. Thus there are collections of Australian cultural studies (Frow & Morris, 1993; Turner, 1993), of Australian-Asian "transactions" (Dever, 1997), and of "Asian and Pacific inscriptions" crossing Australia (Perera, 1995); others connect Australia with South Africa (Darien-Smith, Gunner, & Nuttall, 1996) and several countries historically linked by British colonialism (D. Bennett, 1998). There are collections of, and essays in, Asia-Pacific cultural studies (Birch, 1994; Wilson & Dirlik, 1995), Pacific cultural studies (Hereniko & Wilson, in press; Wilson, in press), Latin American cultural studies (García Canclini, 1995; Moreiras, 1999; Yudice, Franco, & Flores, 1992), Mexican cultural studies (García Canclini, 1993), and "Chicana/o" cultural studies (Chabram-Dernersesian, 1999; Fregoso & Chabram, 1990). Along with British cultural studies (Turner, 1996), we find Irish cultural studies (Gibbons, 1996; Sharkey, 1997; Waters, 1996) and "nationally" organized collections on French (Forbes & Kelly, 1996), German (Burns, 1995), Russian (Kelly & Shepherd, 1998), Spanish (Graham & Labanyi, 1996), and

Italian cultural studies (Forgacs & Lumley, 1996). We find "Nordic" cultural studies (Vainikkala & Eskola, 1994) and the continental frame of African cultural studies (Diawara, 1998; Tomaselli, 1998a; Wright, 1998). The diverse "inscriptions" situating projects in black cultural studies exemplify best the geopolitical fluidity of the field as well as the importance within it of precise contextualizations: Alongside transnational work on black popular culture (Dent, 1992) and black cultural studies (Mercer, 1994), there is an internationally edited collection of black British cultural studies (Baker et al., 1996); other essays consider black experience as regionalized within Britain (Owusu, 1999) and the United States (Lubiana, 1997), as well as diasporic between them (Gilroy, 1993).

Far from being produced in a nowhere college, then, these projects are actively developing a sense of the *situated* nature of intellectual work in its historical as well as social and geopolitical commitments—a point made in passing by Anthony Appiah (1992) when he describes as a "legacy" his father's capacity to make use of his many identities "as Asante, as a Ghanian, as an African, and as a Christian and a Methodist" (p. ix). If this sense of situatedness distances cultural studies from the context-free disciplinarity espoused by many social scientists, the understanding it entails of "situation" as an open, multiply directed, and relational *process* also contests the traditional claim of "language and literature" studies to read culture as expressive of a bounded nation or a civilization. National formations, after all, include the disciplines that define their ideal forms of unity. Aesthetics (sometimes conflated with "textualism" by scholars trained in the social sciences) has powerfully shaped modern Western thinking about culture not only through "self-shaping" pedagogies of reading (Hunter, 1988a, 1992) and writing (Clifford & Marcus, 1986; Steedman, 1997) but through the "national language" programs that linked it to history in the arts and humanities curriculum. Cultural studies refuses to privilege "the literary" and rejects any equation between "a language" and "a culture"; with its suspicion of homogenizing narratives, its affinity with "studies" areas generated by social movements, and its remapping of European universals as imperially powered provincialisms (Chakrabarty, 2000), cultural studies has been welcomed as a "challenge" by scholars "coming out of English" (Bennett, 1993), Chinese studies (Chow, 1991, 1998b), French (Chambers, 1996), and German (Bathrick, 1992), to mention only a few examples.

At a methodological level, whatever the geographies and histories at stake, cultural studies sets great store on "situating" particular objects for analysis (Hebdige, 1988). However, the notion of particularity is prized away from the values of opacity and untranslatability associated with it by modernist social theory (Harvey, 1989; Morris, 1992); it is not conceptualized in opposition to another register deemed "general" or "universal." Thus Alec McHoul (1997) argues that a *general* model for "finding the local specifics of cultural objects" becomes possible precisely when we shift our attention toward "the determination of particular cultural objects by their pragmatic and empirical (that is, their accidental) situatedness" (p. 15). Recently, cultural theorists drawing on the work of Michel de Certeau (1984), Gilles Deleuze and Félix Guattari (1987), and Giorgio Agamben (1993) have used the term *singularity* to designate a "mode of existence which is neither universal (i.e. conceptual) nor particular (i.e. individual)" (Grossberg, 1996, p. 103; see also Shaviro, 1997); as Brian Massumi (1992) explains, its singularity is precisely what "prevents a body from coinciding entirely with its identity category" (pp. 123-124), where identity is understood as a common property that differentiates a group.[3]

Taken up in cultural studies, these rather difficult arguments have practical implications for any work concerned with cultural identity and difference. Most immediately, they challenge the terms in which much debate about these issues is conducted, whether in social or geopolitical frames. For Grossberg (1996), they suggest a "concept of a belonging without identity," enabling new ways of thinking about

collective agency and *political* identities and alliances. Citing the U.S. civil rights movement as a successful example from the past, a "politics of singularity," he writes, "would need to define places people can belong to or, even more fundamentally, places people can find their way to" (pp. 103-104). In her aptly titled *Outside Belongings* (1996), Elspeth Probyn calls for a greater attention to the *movement* carried by the "wish to belong"; her descriptively rich, empirically alert studies of "interstitial moments" in the everyday politics of national, feminist, and queer belonging in the city of Montreal use the concept of singularity to "capture some of the ways in which we continually move in between categories of specificity" (p. 9).

◆ Culture, Cultural Studies, and the Media

The importance of the media in debates about identity, place, and community highlights the second contextual feature of cultural studies that we want to emphasize. If the widespread idea that the field is interested only in popular media culture is mistaken, cultural studies has nevertheless been shaped as a response to the *social uptake* of communications technologies in the second half of the 20th century (see Meyrowitz, 1985), and it is deeply concerned with the transformations wrought by this uptake in "whole ways of life" around the world.

Most work on modern popular culture discusses the media to varying degrees (see Dent, 1992; Grossberg, 1997c; McRobbie, 1994; Storey, 1994), and the sheer size of the literature on the interface between "popular" and "media" cultural studies makes any effort to sustain a hard distinction a matter of local convenience; cultural studies broadly thrives on the connection and overlap between them. However, this does not mean that studies of media are "typical" of cultural studies or interchangeable with it; a redefinition of the relations between the latter and the various branches of media studies has been a feature or even the focus in recent years of work on cinema (Diawara, 1993; Friedberg, 1993; Naficy & Gabriel, 1993; O'Regan & Miller, 1994; Willemen, 1994), journalism (Hartley, 1992a, 1996), music (Frith, 1996b; Keil & Feld, 1994; Lipsitz, 1994; Mitchell, 1996; Rose, 1994), music video (Frith, Goodwin, & Grossberg, 1993), radio (Johnson, 1988; Miller, 1992), and, perhaps most significant, television (Allen, 1987; Ang, 1996; Geraghty & Lusted, 1998; Hartley, 1992b; Mellencamp, 1990; Morley, 1992; Silverstone, 1994).

Television has been important to the development of cultural studies in part because of the obstacles it presents to any effort to divide the study of aesthetic forms from the study of their economics and their social uptake. As a primarily "domestic" object amenable to a multiplicity of public, communal, familial, and personal uses, television can be defined with equal plausibility as an art, as an industry, as a social force, as a pedagogical regime, as a sales medium, as a space-shaping feature of home and interior design, as a site of negotiation between markets and government, as a relay point in a "lifestyle" circuit or network of consumption (Kowinski, 1985), and, more recently, as potentially a terminal for home-based work as well as entertainment and education. John Hartley (1998) explains the implications for critical method: "TV is one of those many arts where form follows function, and thus 'textual analysis' is required of the semiotic environment surrounding the medium, not simply of individual shows or segments" (p. 42). Because the "semiotic" environment here includes practical political and economic activities as well as social relations (see Tomaselli, 1996), a rigorous reading of televisual textuality involves an analytic move to the "outside" of whatever boundaries may operate as given at the outset of a study (see Probyn, 1999b).

If this understanding of form as open-ended and "in process" distinguishes most work in cultural studies from the "close reading" techniques sometimes applied to films or TV shows but modeled on the kind of literary criticism that treats a poem as a self-contained artifact, it has also opened up new areas of study in which the media are positioned in wider net-

works of social and cultural activity that they create, transform, or enable but do not subsume. Alongside a continuing tradition of "subcultures" research (Gelder & Thornton, 1997; Hall & Jefferson, 1976; Hebdige, 1979; McRobbie, 1981, 1994), sports studies is rapidly developing as an interdisciplinary field in its own right (Martin & Miller, 1999; Morse, 1983; Rowe, 1995; Whannel, 1992), as is the study of scientific culture (Haraway, 1989, 1991; Ross, 1996) and of cyberspace and "technoculture" (Aronowitz, Martinsons, Menser, & Rich, 1996; Benedikt, 1991; Penley & Ross, 1991; Turkle, 1984); a growing literature on political culture is forming yet another area of study (Berlant, 1997; Chua, 1995; Clarke, 1991; Feuer, 1995; Grossberg, 1992; Hall, 1988; Massumi, 1996; Morris, 1998a; Street, 1997).

At the same time, the "close" (i.e., detailed and careful) study of aesthetic form is not abandoned; rather, it is extended and enriched by the inclusion of the semiotic "environment" in the object of study. For example, Patricia Mellencamp (1992) stretches fine-grained readings of films, media events, and TV situation comedies to grasp the nexus of "catastrophe, scandal, age, and comedy" that is organized *socioeconomically* around women in U.S. media culture; Barbara Browning (1995) uses her dancer's knowledge of bodily forms of eloquence to write a social history of Brazilian dance cultures as well as their political and religious stakes; and Jim Collins (1995) spills his case studies across several visual and performance media to show how the very stuff of art and cultural history is transformed in the richly localized uses of information technology that proliferate rather than vanish in an economy of media "excess."

In short, instead of isolating for study a single text, "author," industry, technology, or program format, cultural studies tends to emphasize questions or problems in circulation *between* various media and other spaces and times of social life. The fact that some studies do this by examining from multiple perspectives a widely distributed media event (Dayan & Katz, 1992; Wark, 1994) or a well-known media icon has prompted a caricature of the field as "Madonna studies" (see Benson & Metz, 1999). Well, there are also Barbie studies (Rand, 1995), Diana studies (Re:Public, 1997) and Elvis studies (Rodman, 1996), not to mention "Gulf War" studies (Kellner, 1992) and "mad cow disease" studies (McCalman, 1998). However, as Toni Morrison's (1992) collection of "Anita Hill" studies amply demonstrates, most of this work is not a coy celebration of this or that pop item but a critical investigation of media as a *force* that not only acts upon existing social conflicts, desires, and power relations, but continuously helps to produce them and sometimes to change them. This concern links the serious study of so-called pop ephemera to the significant work produced in recent years on the politics of the HIV/AIDS pandemic (Crimp, 1987, 1990; Erni, 1994; Patton, 1992, 1994) and indeed to "cultural studies" of ecological crisis and struggle (Berland, 1994; Jagtenberg & McKie, 1997; Langton, 1998; Ross, 1991, 1994; Slack & White, 1992).

Cultural studies itself has sometimes occasioned media events, creating controversy that travels well beyond the academy and across national borders. Following a fuss about "political correctness" in the U.S. academy in the early 1990s, the scandal over a "science wars" issue of the journal *Social Text* (Ross, 1996; see Michael, 1996; Nakayama, 1997; Slack & Semati, 1997) is the best-known recent example. These occasions usefully prompt academics to clarify their work for nonacademic audiences (see Berube, 1994; Gates, 1992; Lumby, 1997; Morris, 1997b; Wark, 1999). However, beyond inspiring self-defense, the media circulation of contending "images of cultural studies" is of interest because of the wider context of "representation wars" (Perera, 1993) in which it occurs. In her analysis of a major diplomatic wrangle between Australia and Malaysia in 1991 over an Australian TV drama series called *Embassy* (set in a fictitious "Asian" country apparently resembling Malaysia), Suvendrini Perera (1993) suggests that the show itself functioned "at once as agent and object" of dispute; relating this incident to others in which the media played an active role, she points out

that such crises raise "questions about cultural status and authority that need to be rearticulated within a number of global discursive fields" (in this instance, the Gulf War, the Rushdie affair, and postmodernism) but must also be understood in *"worldly,* historical frames" of conflict (pp. 19-21).

"Representation wars" are occurring with increasing frequency between and across societies, in part because new communications technologies are enabling more people to receive and compare differing local, regional, national, and "global" representations of their own and others' lives—and sometimes to take issue with what they see. However, this does not entail a more or less even progression toward a universal plenitude of "global culture." On the contrary, the impact of technological change (and the distributions of its costs and benefits) varies greatly according to the context in which it occurs. In some countries, for example, having access to a *national* space or network of representation may be more novel and consequential than saturation by "international" (i.e., American) media product; Tom O'Regan (1993) argues that in Australia it was not until satellite networking was introduced in the 1980s, together with changes in federal broadcasting regulations as well as in media markets, that a "space-binding," nationalizing emphasis could fully emerge in our once strongly regionalized media system. Paradoxically, he suggests, this emphasis has actually favored "decontextualized" ways of thinking about self, politics, and identity while simultaneously fostering a more national *and* international mind-set; it confirms as well as disconfirms state boundaries and regional autonomies while encouraging the further development of "corridors of information" (on these concepts see also Berland, 1992; Carey, 1989).

The pressure of these contradictory movements helps to explain the intensification of public debates about power, propriety, and representation; who has, and who should have, the power to represent whom, how, and under which conditions? If new national frames of reference are, in fact, emerging just as local, regional, and global flows of information are redrawing cultural and political boundaries, then the complex issue of *control* over image production, circulation, and consumption becomes enmeshed in a whole range of political, economic, legal, and diplomatic concerns in ways that vary between societies and from polity to polity (see Birch, 1994; Chua, 1995; Gaines, 1992; Im, 1998; Kang, 1999; Ma, 1999; Wark, 1994). At the same time, the technological and geoeconomic conditions forcing the question of "what is involved in the representation of another culture, especially when that representation is seen by members of that culture" (Chow, 1991, p. 19) to circulate among government, academic, and media agendas are precisely those that make it impossible for control to be fully assured from any point in a given system. Historically dense anxieties about "modern youth" and "the child" as victims and carriers of media uncontrollability are acquiring a new intensity in this context (see Davis, 1997; Grossberg, 1992; Jenkins, 1998; Johnson, 1993; Kim, 1998; Stratton, 1992).

Two major strands of cultural studies have been shaped by these developments. One of these is primarily historical, researching "representation wars" in the past as these have variously worked to install, legitimate, complicate, and sometimes challenge colonial regimes, nation-building programs, and/or the "domestic," everyday race, class, and gender divisions of particular social formations (Chun, 1994; Dyer, 1997; Lott, 1993; McClintock, 1995; Spigel, 1992; Stam, 1997; Tomaselli & Mpofu, 1997); a closely related body of work examines what Healy (1997) calls the "memory-work" of the museum as a powerful form of modern public cultural pedagogy (Bennett, 1995; Crimp, 1995; Dibley, 1997; Marrie, 1989). The second major strand focuses on the pluralized and networked "public cultures" of the media present and future, exploring the new practices of subjectivity, citizenship, democracy, and community that are emerging across and between them (Gilbert, Glover, Kapal, Taylor, & Wheeler, 1999; Hartley, 1996; Hawkins, 1999; Lumby, 1999; McGuigan, 1996; Miller, 1998; Moon & Davidson, 1995; Morris & McCalman, 1999; Robbins, 1993a; Wallace, 1990). In practice, these two strands are more closely entangled

than a sharp distinction between "cultural history" and "media studies" might lead us to expect: John Hartley's (1996) study of journalism in modernity is a scholarly history of "popular reality" as well as a vivid manifesto for a "postmodern public sphere"; Darren Tofts writes a prehistory of cyberculture that explores its continuity with older forms of "memory trade" (Tofts & McKeitch, 1998); and Emily Apter (1999) analyzes historically the implications of "virtual" citizenship for people living across the territories formed as "nations" by French colonialism.

Studies of tourism perhaps best illustrate the complex intertwining of ethical and "image" concerns with political and economic struggles that interests practitioners of cultural studies. As tourism has vastly expanded in scale and in importance to many local and regional economies, so conflict has intensified about its social costs and environmental effects (Craik, 1991; Lanfant, Allcock, & Bruner, 1995). An important influence in this context has come from indigenous peoples directly *confronting* those costs and effects on an international scale (Chiu, 1995; Palmer, 1998; Teaiwa, 1999). Historically used in Australia as targets for the technological practices, "nationing" experiments, and ethnocidal image campaigns of settler society (Mickler, 1998), Aboriginal groups have used the media to wage a representation "war" of their own to protect their languages and ways of life (Michaels, 1986, 1994), to increase their economic independence by developing their own artistic and tourist ventures (Healy, 1999; Johnson, 1994), to bring pressure to bear on governments sensitive to embarrassment and reactive to "credibility," to educate the public and demand more control over Aboriginal images (Johnson, 1996), and, by these means, to further their political struggle for self-determination in international as well as local and national contexts (see Bennett & Blundell, 1995; Fourmile, 1989; Langton, 1993; Meadows, 1996).

Although there is always controversy about the practical results of this kind of "symbolic" politics, Aboriginal media practices have, at the very least, challenged (and, we would argue, altered) the terms on which issues of race, colonialism, cultural value, national identity and history, landownership, and environmental ethics are publicly discussed in Australia—which is to say, they have powerfully affected our political and intellectual life (Muecke, 1992). So have feminist campaigns around images of women, and so, too, have the efforts of migrant groups to change the representational "norm" of an Anglo/Celtic Australia. In this context, it is not simply a conceit of cultural studies to claim that people can contest and transform the meanings circulated by the culture industries of a media society, perhaps the most famous claim associated with the field (Ang, 1985; Chambers, 1986; Hall & Jefferson, 1976; Hebdige, 1979; Fiske, 1989a, 1989b; Jenkins, 1992). On the contrary—the fact that people actually *do* this is a given of contemporary politics, and one determinant of the social context in which cultural studies is practiced.

◆ Concepts and Methods

At the beginning of his essay on the gift, Marcel Mauss (1970) writes:

> In these "early" societies, social phenomena are not discrete; each phenomenon contains all the threads of which the social fabric is composed. In these total social phenomena, as we propose to call them, all kinds of institutions find simultaneous expression: religious, legal, moral, and economic. In addition, the phenomena have their aesthetic aspect and they reveal morphological types. (p. 1)

For cultural studies, we suggest, a similar concentration of social relations is thought to occur in the pressure points of complex modern societies, but without the microcosmic expressiveness that Mauss finds in "archaic" social structures; rather, social relations are dispersed through these points, composing their complexity but permitting no read-off of a social totality. Instead of the "total social phenomenon," the corresponding concept for cultural studies

is perhaps that of the "site" (the point of intersection and of negotiation of radically different kinds of determination and semiosis), whereas "expression" is displaced by the concept of "event" (a moment of practice that crystallizes diverse temporal and social trajectories).

Thus a shopping mall—to take a banal but central example—offers no quintessential insight into the organization of an epoch or a culture (it is not an emblem or an essence of the postmodern condition or of consumer capitalism); it is a place where many different things happen and where many different kinds of social relations are played out. It is, of course, the end point of numerous chains of production and transportation of goods, as well as of the marketing systems that channel them to consumers (and of the financial structures that underlie all this); these chains belong to regional and national as well as to global circuits (the "gourmet" aisle in the supermarket or the shelves of a delicatessen make visible the global nature of the capitalist marketplace, and may evoke something of the history of its formation, whereas the produce section may or may not be quite local in its reach; in each case the forms of packaging and presentation—"exotic" or "fresh," for example—will carry particular ideologies and particular aesthetic strategies). In another of its dimensions, the mall is an architectural construct, designed in accordance with an international format (anchored strategically by one or two large stores, with a particular disposition of parking and pedestrian traffic, a particular mix of boutiques, of services, of facilities, and so on); it constructs (or perhaps fails to construct) a particular existence and image of community and works in calculated ways to display the rewards and pleasures that follow upon work (or, again, that fail to). It sets up a normative distinction between men's and women's interactions with this space, as well as distinctions among the uses of the space by adults, children, and teenagers; it distinguishes sharply, of course, between its affluent clientele (the proper subjects of its community) and those who are less welcome (some of them, such as schoolkids, it may tolerate; others, such as vagrants and drunks, it will not). The aesthetic organization of the mall has to do with the gratification of desire and the organization of bodies in space; it is a sensual, subtly coercive kind of space.

But it is also a space that is put to use, that is diverted to ends other than those foreseen by its architects and its managers and its guards. This is perhaps the most familiar lesson of cultural studies: that structures are always structures-in-use, and that uses cannot be contained in advance. The semiotic space of the shopping mall is a conflictual space, where meanings are negotiated and projected through quite different formations of fantasy and need. This is to suggest a certain freedom, a function perhaps merely of the complexity of these interactions; but, knowing how readily the appearance of freedom can itself be a ruse of power, a cultural studies critic is likely to be wary of positing any transcendental value for this ability to use public space.

In order to get at these disparate structures that meet in and flow through a complex site like a shopping mall, the theorist (because this is never simply a *descriptive* activity) will, of necessity, have to draw upon, and to cross, the discourses of a number of different disciplines— and again, this cross-disciplinary or "multiperspectival" (Kellner, 1997) approach is characteristic of the working methods of cultural studies. These might include the following:

- Several rather different forms of economic discourse; some relatively technical ways of discussing mall management, commodity supply and demand, and regional patterns of employment; and a more theoretical discourse about commodity production and circulation;
- An aesthetic discourse, relating particularly to architecture, but also to advertising and display; a discourse of musicology, or sociomusicology, to talk about the workings of Muzak or of live performance; and a higher-level discourse to deal with the interrelation between aesthetics and economics;
- A discourse of politics, both of the "mundane" kind that refers to zoning permits and struggles over property values and a

micrological discourse concerned with the politics of bodies in space; the first of these might draw in turn upon the discourses of the law and of town planning, and the latter upon a Foucauldian account of corporeal discipline, or upon symbolic interactionism or ethnomethodology, or upon urban geography;

- A discourse about gender (itself necessarily a mixed discourse) to analyze the organization of gender relations by a mythologized spatial structure, by the gender-specific targeting of consumer desire, by the structure of employment, by child-care provision or its absence, and so on;
- An ethnographic discourse, to get at the particularity of responses to and uses of the mall, to understand it as lived experience;
- A discourse of history, capable of talking about changes in the organization of consumption, perhaps in terms of the "postmodern" or "post-Fordist" centrality of consumption to a reorganized capitalist system, and of theorizing the changing modes of organization of community and of the public sphere;
- A discourse, one perhaps more specific to cultural studies, that would understand the mall as an intricate textual construct and understand shopping as a form of popular culture directly interrelated with other cultural forms and with an economy of representations and practices that make up a "way of life".

Governing the use of some of the discourses listed above might be a policy discourse, serving either the managers of and investors in shopping malls or local government, or perhaps community groups with an interest in reshaping the forms of community structured by the mall. And finally, one might draw upon some mix of sociology, semiotics, and philosophy to talk about the position(s) from which such an analysis can be enunciated—to come to terms with the odd duality that splits the critic into participant and observer, practitioner and reflexive intellectual, on the basis of the privilege given by the possession of cultural capital and a relation of some kind to the institutions of knowledge that make such reflexivity possible.

It is perhaps this "self-situating" and *limiting* moment of analysis that most clearly distinguishes work in cultural studies from some other modes of analysis on which its practitioners may draw. Unlike much positivist work in social science, cultural studies tends to incorporate in its object of study a critical account of its own motivating questions—and thus of the institutional frameworks and the disciplinary rules by which its research imperatives are formed. At the same time, cultural studies is not a form of that "multidisciplinarity" that dreams of producing an exhaustive knowledge map, and it does not posit (unlike some totalizing forms of Marxism) a transcendental space from which knowledges could be synthesized and a "general" theory achieved (see Deutsche, 1996; Morris, 1992).

On the contrary, work in cultural studies accepts its partiality (in both senses of the term); it is openly incomplete, and it is partisan in its insistence on the political dimensions of knowledge. For this reason, the "splitting" of critical practice among diverse and often conflicting social functions does not give rise, in cultural studies, to a discourse of intellectual *alienation*. Although there is no consensus about the politics of intellectual work shared by cultural studies imagined "as a whole," the intellectual project of cultural studies is always at some level marked, we would argue, by a discourse of social *involvement* (T. Bennett, 1998b; Frow, 1995; hooks, 1990; Robbins, 1993b; Ross, 1989).

The point of this discussion of an imaginary object (the shopping mall) is to give a sense not only of the working methods of cultural studies but of their rationale. Cultural studies often tends to operate in what looks like an eccentric way, starting with the particular, the detail, the scrap of ordinary or banal existence, and then working to unpack the density of relations and of intersecting social domains that inform it. To say that the shopping mall is organized by a range of diverse and overlapping systems (economic, aesthetic, demographic, regulatory,

spatial, and so on) and can be the object of very different discourses, none of which has a privileged relation to its object, is to say that it is subject to very different kinds of *readings,* and that there is no principle of totality that can bring these readings into a coherent complementarity. To cast it in terms of readings is then to suggest a relation between the specialized readings of the various disciplines of knowledge and the "folk" readings performed by the users of the site (readings that are bound up with the "things to do" in shopping centers rather than being detached analytic exercises—but that are also themselves, however, pleasurable and interesting "things to do"). This, too, is a characteristic move in cultural studies: a relativizing and democratizing move that seeks to ensure that talk about an object is not closed off on the assumption that we know everything there is to know about it and to ensure that the relationality of any discourse to the full range of others is kept constantly in view.

Another way of talking about all this might be to say that it has to do with the way we understand the concept of *genre.* The mixing of discourses and genres in much work in cultural studies has to do with methodological impurity, perhaps with a certain fruitful insecurity about the legitimacy of cultural studies as a discipline, but perhaps too with the way cultural studies conceives its object as being relational (a network of connections) rather than substantial. Anne Freadman (1992) puts it this way:

> With the professionalisation of the social sciences and of the humanities, we put ourselves at risk of writing and reading with carefully administered "methods" that can only be called monogeneric. . . . if I am right, that the conditions of sociality are best described as the occupation of, and enablement by, heterogeneous ranges of generic practices, then mono-generic strategies of interpretation will always miss the mark. (p. 280)

The concept of "sociality" here carries that active, processual sense that cultural studies gives to the concept of culture, and the two are directly related: Both have to do with the *practice* (rather than the implementation) of structures of meaning—genres or codes, for example—and with the construction of social space out of the weaving together, the crisscrossing, of such practices (there are clear analogies here with the way ethnomethodology understands the construction and maintenance of the social).

There is a precise sense in which cultural studies uses the concept of *text* as a fundamental model. However, the concept of text undergoes a mutation so that, rather than designating a place where meanings are constructed in a single level of inscription (writing, speech, film, dress, and so on), still less a single artifact ("a" text), it works as an interleaving of levels. If a shopping mall is conceived on the model of textuality, then this "text" involves practices, institutional structures and the complex forms of agency they entail, legal, political, and financial conditions of existence, and particular flows of power and knowledge, as well as a particular multilayered semantic organization. At the same time, this "text" exists only within a network of *intertextual* relations (the textual networks of commodity culture, let's say, of architecture, of formations of community, of postmodern spatiality); it is an ontologically mixed entity, and one for which there can be no privileged or "correct" form of reading. It is this, more than anything else, that forces the attention of cultural studies to the diversity of audiences or users of the structures of textuality it analyzes—that is, to the open-ended social life of texts—and that forces it, thereby, to question the authority or finality of its own readings (Ang, 1991, 1996; Hay, Grossberg, & Wartella, 1996; hooks, 1992a; Morley, 1992; Morris, 1990; Stacey, 1994).

◆ Cultural Studies and Disciplinarity

The conception of culture that, we argue, informs the discipline of cultural studies—that is, culture as a contested and conflictual set of practices of representation bound up with the processes of formation and re-formation of social groups—depends upon a theoretical paradox, because it presupposes an opposition (between culture and society, between representations and reality) that is the condition of its existence but that it must constantly work to undo. Both the undoing of these oppositions and the failure ever to resolve completely the tension between them are constitutive of work in cultural studies. If representations are dissolved into the real (if they are thought only to reflect or to re-present, in a secondary way and either more or less accurately, a reality that has an autonomous existence and against which the representation can thus be measured), then the sense of the ways in which the real is textually constructed (as story, as desire, as repetition) gets lost. Conversely, if the real is nothing more than the sum of its representations ("nothing but texts," as the caricature goes), then the sense of *urgency* to the cultural studies project gets lost.

The concerns of this project are not, however, primarily epistemological; rather, they have to do with the social processes by which the categories of the real and of group existence are formed. The word *social* here means at once semiotic and political, in the sense of involving relations of power. Foucault's concept of power/knowledge has provided one influential way of thinking this intertwining of meaning and social relationality (Burchell, Gordon, & Miller, 1991; Foucault, 1980; Frow, 1988; Morris & Patton, 1979). Another develops the Gramscian notion of "articulation" (Grossberg, 1992; Hanczor, 1997; Laclau, 1977; Morley & Chen, 1996; Tomaselli & Mpofu, 1997), and another derives from the linguistic concept of enunciation (Chambers, 1998, 1999; Morse, 1998; O'Regan, 1992; Probyn, 1993).

The concept of culture is an important one for many other disciplines, most notably perhaps for cultural anthropology and the sociology of culture. What, we might ask, is special or different about its use in cultural studies? One answer may be nothing; and it may be, too, that cultural studies should not be described as a "discipline." It is perhaps too young and unformed to have the strong sense of boundaries required of a discipline; it is also shaped—although this is a different issue—by its rebellion against disciplinarity itself (see T. Bennett, 1998a, 1998b; Nelson & Gaonkar, 1996; Striphas, 1998). Nevertheless, those who work in cultural studies tend to have strong opinions about what distinguishes their work from other fields of inquiry—"It does matter whether cultural studies is this or that" (S. Hall, 1992, p. 278)—and it might be useful to explore briefly both the differences and the overlap with these other fields.

The most obvious difference is in the object of study. Whereas anthropology is defined by its relation to an "allochronic" other (Fabian, 1983)—an other defined as such by its sociocultural difference within a quite different structure of time, and especially by what is understood as a qualitative difference in social organization—cultural studies takes as its object the ordinary culture (two very loaded words, but let them stand for the moment) of its own society. Certainly there are movements toward such an orientation in contemporary anthropology (see Augé, 1995), but often—for example, in ethnographic studies of rural or working-class communities or of the homeless—this continues to reproduce the same structure of otherness, an exoticism now caught within the home society. Cultural studies is sometimes caught in this trap, too, treating subcultures, for example, as an exotic or subversive other within the dominant culture, but its *impulse* is toward studying the diverse forms of cultural organization without recourse to such exoticization.

There are also, however, differences in methodological orientation. Although cultural studies has adopted many of the techniques of fieldwork observation and description developed by ethnography (Ang, 1985; Brunsdon & Morley, 1978; Radway, 1991; Skeggs, 1997; Thomas, 1999; Willis, 1977), its focus on complex industrialized societies means that other methodologies may also be appropriate. Information about cultural codes and practices can be obtained in many ways other than through discussion with informants and participant ob-

servation (vast archives of written and electronic texts are available in many instances), and sometimes the writer is a member of the culture that is being studied. Cultural studies tends, as a consequence, to make greater use of techniques of textual analysis, to make use of a greater diversity of sources, to make more eclectic use of methodologies, and, once again, to work with a perhaps more complex problematic of the relation between the writer and the culture being studied—that is, with an *intensification* of the anthropological problem of the tension between personal and political distance and personal and political involvement (Byrne, 1995; Field, 1991; Jackson, 1998; M. Z. Rosaldo, 1984; R. Rosaldo, 1989; Stewart, 1996; Taussig, 1997).

In relation to the sociology of culture, cultural studies has certainly learned from its use of statistical survey techniques (Bennett, Emmison, & Frow, 1999). The interest of cultural studies, however, tends to lie much more in the lived effects and formations of culture, and questions of the distribution of competence, preference, and access are usually made secondary to this concern. But the difference between the two disciplines is perhaps increasingly one of focus rather than of kind (see Alasuutari, 1995; Chaney, 1994; Denzin, 1992, 1997; Long, 1997), and the same holds true of the overlapping relationships between cultural studies and social as well as cultural history (Davis, 1983; Denning, 1996; C. Hall, 1992; Johnson, 1993; Pickering, 1997; Steedman, 1986, 1992a, 1992b; Steinberg, 1996) and between cultural studies and critical geography (Duncan & Ley, 1993; Fincher & Jacobs, 1998; Jacobs, 1996; Keith & Pile, 1993; Massey, 1994). One can observe, finally, an overlap with literary studies to the extent that the latter has retheorized its object in recent years to cover the analysis and history of social relations of textuality rather than texts or textual systems in themselves (Armstrong, 1987; Barrell, 1991; Brown, 1996; Chambers, 1999; Grewal, 1996; Guillory, 1993; Mignolo, 1995; Radway, 1997; Suleri, 1992; Viswanathan, 1989). It is worth noting that cultural studies is not restricted to the study of popular culture, and certainly has little in common with folkloric studies, including the "folkloric" orientation to mass-media studies. Rather, as Nelson, Treichler, and Grossberg (1992) write:

> Cultural studies does not require us to repudiate elite cultural forms—or simply to acknowledge, with Bourdieu, that distinctions between elite and popular cultural forms are themselves the products of relations of power. Rather, cultural studies requires us to identify the operation of specific practices, of how they continuously reinscribe the line between legitimate and popular culture, and of what they accomplish in specific contexts. (p. 13)

The concern of cultural studies is with the constitution and working of systems of relations rather than with the domains formed by these processes. Hence a further characteristic concern of cultural studies (one it shares with much poststructuralist thought): a concern with boundaries and limits, and especially with the fuzziness of such edges and the consequent impurity of genres and disciplines. For example, John Hartley (1992b) suggests that it is possible "to see in impurities not a problem but a fundamental criterion for cultural studies" (p. 102), and he defends an international television criticism on the grounds that neither television nor nations can be understood except in relational terms. Tom O'Regan (1992) reformulates the vexed question of the relationship between cultural criticism and cultural policy by considering both as "porous systems," and Helen Grace (1993) examines the increasingly fluid relations between value and utility, art and commerce, aesthetics and logic, "play" and "war" now being produced in the "serious business" of management culture.

The effect of this concern is not to dissolve analysis into an all-encompassing description ("cultural studies" as "studying culture"), but rather to foreground the question of the relation *between* the description of textual/cultural networks and the position of enunciation from which that description is possible (Hartley, 1999). This question is, again, at once *semiotic* (it has to do with the organization and enablement of textuality by structures of genre) and *political* (it has to do with the social relations of

textuality—that is, with the relative positioning of speakers and their discursive construction as the carriers of a certain social identity and authority). It follows that an interest in the concrete conditions and particular instances in which conflicts of authority and problems of authorship are negotiated (or not negotiated) and settled (or unsettled) is not confined to studies that are explicitly concerned with cross-cultural conflict and postcolonial struggle: McKenzie Wark's (1993) essay on the band Midnight Oil, for example, considers the politics of authority in popular media culture, and Ross Chambers (1998) reads three AIDS diaries (written in France, the United States, and Australia) to come to terms with "the problematics of survivorhood" shared among authors whose subject is their own dying and death and readers for whom the act of reading becomes a form of mourning. The self-situating impulse of cultural studies also foregrounds issues of *intellectual* authority and authorship as they arise in the course of particular projects; much work in cultural studies shares with other forms of qualitative inquiry a strong interest in the use of dialogic, collaborative, and composite modes of writing and research to foster more open and responsive relations between academics and the communities with whom they work (see, e.g., Frankenberg, 1993; Johnson, 1990; Langton, 1993; McRobbie, 1999; Muecke, 1997; Owusu, 1999; Ross, 1997).

◆ Genealogies and Potentials

In recent years a number of critical accounts have begun to take stock of the achievements and difficulties of cultural studies, many of them offering a "genealogy" of the emergence of cultural studies as a serious academic field (T. Bennett, 1998b; Brantlinger, 1990; Clarke, 1991; Crimp, 1999; Ferguson & Golding, 1997; Gilroy, 1987; Grossberg, 1997a; S. Hall, 1992; Harris, 1992; Rodman, 1997; Williams, 1989). In one sense, genealogies are as misleading for intellectual work as they are for studying personal behavior: They can tell us nothing about where we are going, or should go, or might want to go. However, if the best-known genealogy for cultural studies is British, this is so not least because it continues to provide a useful model against which other projects can define their own precedents and concerns (McNeil, 1998; Tomaselli, 1998b; Wright, 1998). The influential enterprise of "British cultural studies" took shape in the 1950s as a challenge to hierarchical distinctions between the public and the private, the major and the minor, the "great" and the "everyday," as these regulated the field of culture (and the discipline of English; Bennett, 1993) in Britain at the time.[4] Emerging as a program with the work of the Birmingham Centre for Contemporary Cultural Studies, founded in 1964 (where the study of subcultures and the politics of race and gender came to the foreground in the 1970s and early 1980s), British cultural studies developed an insistence on notions of agency in cultural theory. This means studying not how people *are* in a passively inherited culture but what we *do* with the cultural commodities that we encounter and use in daily life ("practice") and thus what we *make* as "culture." Inflected by poststructuralist theories of reading as well as by empirical audience research, this shift enabled a redefinition of popular culture not as a stratum (the "low" one) of aesthetic practice but as a social "zone of contestation," in Stuart Hall's (1981) famous phrase—the ground in and over which different interests struggle for hegemony (Hall, Critcher, Jefferson, Clarke, & Roberts, 1979).

This emphasis on agency and contestation is shared by cultural studies in most parts of the world today. However, other genealogies and other kinds of intellectual practice, we suggest, have been at least as important to the field's development. The pioneering work of the Canadian thinker Harold Innis on technology, imperialism, and space (Berland, 1997a, 1997b; Kroker, 1984) and of James Carey (1989) in the United States on space and communication (see also Munson & Warren, 1997) has been influential in linking the study of place and cultural history to work on media and cultural

policy (Bennett, 1992, 1998b; Meadows, 1996; O'Regan, 1993). Two texts by Foucault have been particularly influential: *The Archaeology of Knowledge* (1972) opened the way to a more extended and institutionally anchored model of discursivity than was available in other, language- and text-centered, notions of discourse; and the first volume of *The History of Sexuality* (1978) offered a complex microsociological mapping of social power as well as new ways of conceptualizing sexuality. The writings of Henri Lefebvre (1971/1984) and Michel de Certeau (1984) have also fed into the way cultural studies theorizes the structure and practice of everyday life; and Bourdieu's sociology of culture provides a strong countertradition to the culture-and-society line that descends from Raymond Williams.

The list of inputs into this emerging discipline could be extended almost indefinitely; it is perhaps the mark of the newness of a discipline that, lacking an established methodology and even a well-defined object, cultural studies draws eclectically and energetically upon a variety of theoretical sources as it seeks to define its own specificity. The influence of phenomenology and ethnomethodology can certainly be traced in its refusal to privilege the interpretations of "expert" readers and its concern with the experiential dimension of everyday life. The Gramscian understanding of culture as a site of contestation has been more recently inflected by postcolonial theory, as it variously draws on the works of, for example, Franz Fanon (Alessandrini, 1999), Ashish Nandy (1983; Chen, 1998a), C. L. R. James (Buhle, 1986; Grimshaw, 1992), and Ranajit Guha (1997) to give a more ambivalent and complex account of both the flow of power and the projective identifications and identities of actors in situations of cultural struggle.

As fundamental and lasting as any single intellectual influence, however, has been the feminist understanding of the politics of the everyday and of "personal" life. A critique of culture (and of theories of culture) was crucial to the "second wave" of the women's liberation movement in the early 1970s, and although it would be difficult to characterize the "effects" on cultural studies of such a complex and diverse social movement, we can point to two of the consequences that have followed from the influence of particular currents in feminism. One is a tendency to think of "the self" as a site of *social* creativity, rather than simply as a medium of individual expression. Many feminists, for example, have always taken the slogan "The personal is political" to mean that the resources of the state must be captured and used in the interests of transforming women's lives by increasing their access to social equity and power; work on cultural policy is able to refer for a precedent (although it does not always do so) to a record of significant feminist achievement. The other consequence is a tendency to assume that a politics of the everyday involves confronting not only the workings of class, racism, and colonialism as well as sex and gender, but their impact in intellectual life and in education. Ann Curthoys (1988) argued in 1970 that we "must analyse why public life has been considered to be the focus of history, and why public life has been so thoroughly occupied by men" (p. 4); cultural studies continues this line of questioning in an expanded framework today, as it develops both as a critique of education and as a pedagogical experiment (Giroux & Shannon, 1997; Luke, 1996; McCarthy & Crichlow, 1993; Striphas, 1998).

The point here is that cultural studies has not only been a response to the political and social movements of the past three decades but has also derived many of its themes, its research priorities, its polemics, and, in some ways, its theoretical emphases and privileged working methods from an *engagement* with those movements. For this reason, the most innovative work, in our view, continues to be more interested in developing the implications of particular forms of symbolic action and the consequences of particular moments of cultural practice—implications and consequences that experimental "genealogies" of the field may sometimes help us to see—than in proving the case for doing so against older theories of culture. It is not that cultural studies (as we see it) is in any way hostile to "theory"; theoretical work can also be considered a form of cultural practice. It is merely that the doctrinal disputes that have

marked the emergence of the field—disputes between humanism and formalism, formalism and Marxism, Marxism and poststructuralism, deconstruction and new historicism—are often resolved in practice by a kind of rigorous *mixing* (see Deutsche, 1996; Grace, 1993; Nightingale, 1996; O'Regan, 1996).

A similar tendency is at work, we would argue, in the "disciplinary" disputes that have intensified in recent years between proponents of "textualism" and ethnography (Ang, 1996; Hartley, 1992a, 1998; Morley, 1998; Murdock, 1995, 1997) and between political economy and "interpretive" cultural studies (Garnham, 1995a, 1995b; Gibson-Graham, 1996; Grossberg, 1995). However useful and necessary these debates continue to be for consolidating the field, its future directions are perhaps being shaped more directly by the experimental empiricism of, for example, Elspeth Probyn's (1998, 1999a) work on food, fashion, and agricultural economics; Kuan-Hsing Chen's (in press) political-historical mapping of the emergence of "KTV" (karaoke-TV) across the city of Taipei; or Julia Emberley's (1998) study of the cultural politics of the fur trade. Such empirical projects, far from being "antitheoretical," have to reflect on complex issues of disciplinary difference and convergence in order to articulate their aims.

In this they share a commitment to learning and thinking *from* practice with recent "theoretical" critiques of the pervasive concept of culture (Grossberg, 1998b; Massumi 1996, 1997; Readings, 1996; Spivak, 1993). Addressing the effects in academic as well as broader social and economic life of the neoliberalism we discussed at the beginning of this chapter, these critiques have begun to challenge, once again, the founding categories and the institutional formation of cultural studies itself—a necessary condition, perhaps, of its practice. Whatever the future of "culture," it is clear that both a commitment to empirical research and a constant questioning of the social and political frames in which that "research" is formulated and practiced will continue to be indispensable to a field so vitally concerned with the uncertain boundaries of "art" and "everyday life" in mediated societies; with the multiple ways in which "popular culture" informs the practices, and shapes the dreams, of modern citizenship; with the impact of institutional knowledges, and desires, on their objects of study; and the intricate, charged relations between stories and spaces, events and sites, "making history" and "taking place" in contemporary cultural economies.

■ Notes

1. These citations are taken from, respectively, the following newspaper items: "Swan Steels" (1989); an advertisement for a Shopping Centres Conference, published in *Australian Financial Review* (August 13, 1992); and "Poor Performance" (1989).

2. The concept of "context" does a lot of work in cultural studies, where it never refers (as it can in some sociologies of culture) to a background of influences and determinants detachable from a "text" or other object of study. In a number of essays on the problem of distinguishing cultural studies from other ways of "studying culture" (see Rodman, 1997), Lawrence Grossberg (1997a) argues that its "radical contextualism" is a feature "unique to cultural studies" (p. 253; see also Grossberg, 1997b, 1998a). In this usage, a "context" is not an environment but, on the contrary, a "specific bit of everyday life" positioned *between* culture, understood as "a specific body of practices," and "particular social forces, institutions and relations of power" (Grossberg, 1993, p. 9). The analyst's task is to specify this positioning, case by case: "The context of a particular research is not empirically given beforehand; it has to be defined by the project, by the political question that is at stake. The context can be as narrow as a neighbourhood at a particular moment, or an urban region, or perhaps even some local high school that is having race problems, or it can be as broad as global capitalism after the cold war. To put it succinctly, for cultural studies context is everything and everything is contextual" (Grossberg, 1997a, p. 255). In this view, cultural studies is primarily the study of contexts rather than "culture," insofar as contexts (including those of research, theorization, and conceptual definition) are produced *in* social practice. From this it follows that although anything can become an object of investigation in cultural studies, cultural studies does not, in fact, claim that *culture* is "everything" or that everything is cultural; construed as a specific body of practices, culture does not subsume the social and economic forces, institutions, and relations of power that both enable and *limit* those practices.

3. De Certeau (1984), for example, projected in his influential study of the practice of everyday life a "*science of singularity*; that is to say, a science of the relationship that links everyday pursuits to particular circumstances" (p. ix), whereas Agamben (1993) describes his philosophy as seeking a way past "the false dilemma that obliges knowledge to choose between the ineffability of the individual and the intelligibility of the universal" (p. 1).

4. According to the usual narrative, this challenge emerged from the "scholarship" generation of scholars formed, as Turner (1996) explains, by "the expansion of educational opportunities within Britain after the war, and the spread of adult education as a means of postwar reconstruction as well as an arm of the welfare state" (p. 44; see also Steele, 1997). Children of the working class, such as Richard Hoggart (1957) and Raymond Williams, saw their task as one of validating the culture of the common people over and against the canonical values of British high-cultural elitism; where the latter fostered a nostalgia for preindustrial English *folk* culture, the new intellectuals examined and affirmed the *popular* culture of the industrial working class. But, as Turner points out, this phase of educational modernization also corresponded to the postwar expansion of "industrial" *mass* culture—often American in source or inspiration. Early critical responses to this "inauthentic" development were ambiguous or negative; wedged between the "folk" and the "mass," the "popular" became an unstable and contested object of study (see Frow, 1995; Grossberg, 1997c; Hall, 1981; Miller & McHoul, 1999).

■ References

Abbas, A. (1997). *Hong Kong: Culture and the politics of disappearance*. Minneapolis: University of Minnesota Press.

Agamben, G. (1993). *The coming community* (M. Hardt, Trans.). Minneapolis: University of Minnesota Press.

Alasuutari, P. (1995). *Researching culture: Qualitative method and cultural studies.* London: Sage.

Alessandrini, A. C. (Ed.). (1999). *Frantz Fanon: Critical perspectives.* New York: Routledge.

Allen, R. C. (Ed.). (1987). *Channels of discourse: Television and contemporary criticism.* Chapel Hill: University of North Carolina Press.

Allor, M. (1997). Locating cultural activity: The "Main" as chronotope and heterotopia. *Topia, 1,* 42-54.

Ang, I. (1985). *Watching* Dallas: *Soap opera and the melodramatic imagination.* London: Methuen.

Ang, I. (1991). *Desperately seeking the audience.* London: Routledge.

Ang, I. (1996). *Living room wars: Rethinking media audiences for a postmodern world.* London: Routledge.

Ang, I. (1999). On not speaking Chinese: Postmodern ethnicity and the politics of diaspora. In M. Shiach (Ed.), *Feminism and cultural studies* (pp. 540-564). Oxford: Oxford University Press.

Anzaldúa, G. (1987). *Borderlands/la frontera: The new mestiza.* San Francisco: Aunt Lute.

Appadurai, A. (1996). *Modernity at large: Cultural dimensions of globalization.* Minneapolis: University of Minnesota Press.

Appiah, K. A. (1992). *In my father's house: Africa in the philosophy of culture.* Oxford: Oxford University Press.

Apter, E. (1999). *Continental drift: From national characters to virtual subjects.* Chicago: University of Chicago Press.

Armstrong, N. (1987). *Desire and domestic fiction: A political history of the novel.* New York: Oxford University Press.

Arndt, H. W., & Hill, H. (Eds.). (1999). *Southeast Asia's economic crisis: Origins, lessons and the way forward.* Sydney: Allen & Unwin.

Aronowitz, S., Martinsons, B., Menser, M., & Rich, J. (Eds.). (1996). *Technoscience and cyberculture.* London: Routledge.

Augé, M. (1995). *Non-places: Introduction to an anthropology of supermodernity* (J. Howe, Trans.). London: Verso.

Baker, H. A., Jr., Diawara, M., & Lindeborg, R. H. (Eds.). (1996). *Black British cultural studies: A reader.* Chicago: University of Chicago Press.

Barrell, J. (1991). *The infection of Thomas de Quincey: A psychopathology of imperialism.* New Haven, CT: Yale University Press.

Bathrick, D. (1992). Cultural studies. In J. Gibaldi (Ed.), *Introduction to scholarship in modern languages and literatures* (pp. 320-340). New York: Modern Language Association of America.

Benedikt, M. (Ed.). (1991). *Cyberspace: First steps.* Cambridge: MIT Press.

Bennett, D. (Ed.). (1998). *Multicultural states: Rethinking difference and identity.* London: Routledge.

Bennett, T. (1992). Putting policy into cultural studies. In L. Grossberg, C. Nelson, & P. A. Treichler (Eds.), *Cultural studies* (pp. 23-37). New York: Routledge.

Bennett, T. (1993). Coming out of English: A policy calculus for cultural studies. In K. K. Ruthven (Ed.), *Beyond the disciplines: The new humanities* (pp. 33-44). Canberra: Australian Academy of the Humanities.

Bennett, T. (1995). *The birth of the museum: History, theory, politics.* London: Routledge.

Bennett, T. (1998a). Cultural studies: A reluctant discipline. *Cultural Studies, 12,* 528-545.

Bennett, T. (1998b). *Culture: A reformer's science.* London/Sydney: Sage/Allen & Unwin.

Bennett, T., & Blundell, V. (Eds.). (1995). First peoples: Cultures, policies, politics [Special issue]. *Cultural Studies, 9*(1).

Bennett, T., Emmison, M., & Frow, J. (1999). *Accounting for tastes: Australian everyday cultures.* Cambridge: Cambridge University Press.

Bennett, T., Turner, G., & Volkerling, M. (Eds.). (1994). Post-colonial formations [Special issue]. *Culture and Policy, 6*(1).

Benson, C., & Metz, A. (Eds.). (1999). *The Madonna companion: Two decades of commentary.* New York: Schirmer.

Benterrak, K., Muecke, S., & Roe, P. (1996). *Reading the country* (Rev. ed.). Fremantle, Western Australia: Fremantle Arts Centre Press.

Berland, J. (1992). Angels dancing: Cultural technologies and the production of space. In L. Grossberg, C. Nelson, & P. A. Treichler

(Eds.), *Cultural studies* (pp. 38-55). New York: Routledge.

Berland, J. (1994). On reading "the weather." *Cultural Studies, 8,* 99-114.

Berland, J. (1997a). Nationalism and the modernist legacy: Dialogues with Innis. *Culture and Policy, 8*(3), 9-39.

Berland, J. (1997b). Space at the margins: Colonial spatiality and critical theory after Innis. *Topia, 1,* 55-82.

Berlant, L. (1997). *The queen of America goes to Washington City: Essays on sex and citizenship.* Durham, NC: Duke University Press.

Berube, M. (1994). *Public access: Literary theory and American cultural politics.* London: Verso.

Bhabha, H. K. (Ed.). (1990). *Nation and narration.* London: Routledge.

Bhabha, H. K. (1994). *The location of culture.* London: Routledge.

Birch, D. (Ed.). (1994). Cultural studies in the Asia Pacific [Special issue]. *Southeast Asian Journal of Social Science, 22*(1-2).

Bourdieu, P. (1984). *Distinction: A social critique of the judgement of taste* (R. Nice, Trans.). Cambridge. MA: Harvard University Press.

Brantlinger, P. (1990). *Crusoe's footprints: Cultural studies in Britain and America.* New York: Routledge.

Brown, B. (1996). *The material unconscious: American amusement, Stephen Crane, and the economics of play.* Cambridge, MA: Harvard University Press.

Browning, B. (1995). *Samba: Resistance in motion.* Bloomington: Indiana University Press.

Brunsdon, C., & Morley, D. (1978). *Everyday television: "Nationwide."* London: British Film Institute.

Buhle, P. (Ed.). (1986). *C. L. R. James: His life and work.* London: Allison & Busby.

Burchell, G., Gordon, C., & Miller, P. (1991). *The Foucault effect: Studies in governmentality.* London: Harvester Wheatsheaf.

Burns, R. (Ed.). (1995). *German cultural studies: An introduction.* Oxford: Oxford University Press.

Butler, J. (1990). *Gender trouble: Feminism and the subversion of identity.* New York: Routledge.

Butler, J. (1993). *Bodies that matter: On the discursive limits of "sex."* New York: Routledge.

Byrne, D. (1995). Intramuros' return. *UTS Review, 1*(2), 2-29.

Carby, H. (1996). White woman listen! In H. A. Baker, Jr., M. Diawara, & R. H. Lindeborg (Eds.), *Black British cultural studies: A reader* (pp. 223-239). Chicago: University of Chicago Press. (Reprinted from *The empire strikes back: Race and racism in seventies Britain,* pp. 212-235, by Centre for Contemporary Cultural Studies, Ed., 1982, London: Hutchinson)

Carey, J. W. (1989). *Communication as culture: Essays on media and society.* Boston: Unwin Hyman.

Carey, J. W. (1995). Abolishing the old spirit world. *Critical Studies in Mass Communication, 12*(1), 82-88.

Carey, J. W. (1997). Reflections on the project of (American) cultural studies. In M. Ferguson & P. Golding (Eds.), *Cultural studies in question* (pp. 1-24). London: Sage.

Chabram-Dernersesian, A. (Ed.). (1999). Chicana/o Latina/o cultural studies: Transnational and transdisciplinary movements [Special issue]. *Cultural Studies, 13*(2).

Chakrabarty, D. (in press). *Provincializing Europe: Postcolonial thought and historical difference.* Princeton, NJ: Princeton University Press.

Chambers, I. (1986). *Popular culture: The metropolitan experience.* London: Methuen.

Chambers, I., & Curti, L. (Eds.). (1996). *The post-colonial question: Common skies, divided horizons.* London: Routledge.

Chambers, R. (1996). Cultural studies as a challenge to French studies. *Australian Journal of French Studies, 33*(2), 137-156.

Chambers, R. (1998). *Facing it: AIDS diaries and the death of the author.* Ann Arbor: University of Michigan Press.

Chambers, R. (1999). *Loiterature.* Lincoln: University of Nebraska Press.

Chaney, D. (1994). *The cultural turn: Scene-setting essays on contemporary cultural history.* London: Routledge.

Chang, H.-H. (1998). Taiwan queer valentines. In K.-H. Chen (Ed.), *Trajectories: Inter-Asia cultural studies* (pp. 283-298). London: Routledge.

Chen, K.-H. (1992). Voices from the outside: Towards a new internationalist localism. *Cultural Studies, 6,* 476-484.

Chen, K.-H. (1998a). Introduction: The decolonization question. In K.-H. Chen (Ed.), *Trajectories: Inter-Asia cultural studies* (pp. 1-53). London: Routledge.

Chen, K.-H. (Ed.). (1998b). *Trajectories: Inter-Asia cultural studies.* London: Routledge.

Chen, K.-H. (in press). The formation and consumption of KTV in Taiwan. In B.-H. Chua (Ed.), *Consumption in Asia: Lifestyle and identity.* London: Routledge.

Chiu, Y.-L. (1995). From the politics of identity to an alternative cultural politics: On Taiwan primordial inhabitants' a-systemic movement. In R. Wilson & A. Dirlik (Eds.), *Asia/Pacific as space of cultural production* (pp. 120-144). Durham, NC: Duke University Press.

Cho, H. (1996). Feminist intervention in the rise of "Asian" discourse. In Asian Centre for Women's Studies, *The rise of feminist consciousness against the patriarchy* (pp. 144-170). Seoul: Ewha Woman's University.

Chow, R. (1991). *Woman and Chinese modernity: The politics of reading between West and East.* Minneapolis: University of Minnesota Press.

Chow, R. (1993). *Writing diaspora: Tactics of intervention in contemporary cultural studies.* Bloomington: Indiana University Press.

Chow, R. (1998a). *Ethics after idealism: Theory-culture-ethnicity-reading.* Bloomington: Indiana University Press.

Chow, R. (Ed.). (1998b). Modern Chinese literary and cultural studies in the age of theory: Reimagining a field [Special issue]. *Boundary 2, 25*(3).

Chua, B.-H. (1995). *Communitarian ideology and democracy in Singapore.* London: Routledge.

Chua, B.-H. (1998). Globalisation: Finding the appropriate words and levels. *Communal Plural, 6*(1), 117-124.

Chun, A. (1994). The culture industry as national enterprise: The politics of heritage in contemporary Taiwan. *Culture and Policy, 6*(1), 69-89.

Clarke, J. (1991). *New times and old enemies: Essays on cultural studies and America.* London: HarperCollins.

Clifford, J. (1988). *The predicament of culture: Twentieth-century ethnography, literature, and art.* Cambridge, MA: Harvard University Press.

Clifford, J. (1997). *Routes: Travel and translation in the late twentieth century.* Cambridge, MA: Harvard University Press.

Clifford, J., & Marcus, G. E. (Eds.). (1986). *Writing culture: The poetics and politics of ethnography.* Berkeley: University of California Press.

Cohen, S. (1993). *Academia and the luster of capital.* Minneapolis: University of Minnesota Press.

Collins, J. (1995). *Architectures of excess: Cultural life in the information age.* New York: Routledge.

Craik, J. (1991). *Resorting to tourism: Cultural policies for tourist development in Australia.* Sydney: Allen & Unwin.

Crimp, D. (Ed.). (1987). AIDS: Cultural analysis, cultural activism [Special issue]. *October, 43.*

Crimp, D. (with Rolston, A.). (1990). *AIDS demo graphics.* Seattle: Bay.

Crimp, D. (1995). *On the museum's ruins* (L. Lawler, Photog.). Cambridge: MIT Press.

Crimp, D. (1999). Getting the Warhol we deserve. *Social Text, 59,* 49-66.

Culture fills Aussie tills. (1990, October 11). *Daily Telegraph Mirror.*

Curthoys, A. (1988). *For and against feminism.* Sydney: Allen & Unwin.

Darien-Smith, K., Gunner, L., & Nuttall, S. (Eds.). (1996). *Text, theory, space: Land, literature and history in South Africa and Australia.* London: Routledge.

Davis, M. (1997). *Gangland: Cultural elites and the new generationalism.* Sydney: Allen & Unwin.

Davis, N. Z. (1983). *The return of Martin Guerre.* Cambridge, MA: Harvard University Press.

Dayan, D., & Katz, E. (1992). *Media events: The live broadcasting of history.* Cambridge, MA: Harvard University Press.

de Certeau, M. (1984). *The practice of everyday life* (S. F. Rendall, Trans.). Berkeley: University of California Press.

de Lauretis, T. (Ed.). (1986). *Feminist studies/critical studies.* Bloomington: Indiana University Press.

de Lauretis, T. (Ed.). (1991). Queer theory: Lesbian and gay sexualities [Special issue]. *Differences, 3*(1).

Deleuze, G., & Guattari, F. (1987). *A thousand plateaus: Capitalism and schizophrenia* (B. Massumi, Trans.). Minneapolis: University of Minnesota Press.

Denning, M. (1996). *The cultural front: The laboring of American culture in the twentieth century.* London: Verso.

Dent, G. (Ed.). (1992). *Black popular culture.* Seattle: Bay.

Denzin, N. K. (1992). *Symbolic interactionism and cultural studies.* Newbury Park, CA: Sage.

Denzin, N. K. (1997). *Interpretive ethnography: Ethnographic practices for the 21st century.* Thousand Oaks, CA: Sage.

Deutsche, R. (1996). *Evictions: Art and spatial politics.* Cambridge: MIT Press.

Dever, M. (Ed.). (1997). *Australia and Asia: Cultural transactions.* Richmond, UK: Curzon.

Diawara, M. (Ed.). (1993). *Black American cinema.* New York: Routledge.

Diawara, M. (1998). *In search of Africa.* Cambridge, MA: Harvard University Press.

Dibley, B. (1997). Museum, nation, narration: The Museum of New Zealand—Te Papa Tongarewa "telling New Zealand's story." *Culture and Policy, 8*(3), 97-118.

Duncan, J., & Ley, D. (Eds.). (1993). *Place/culture/representation.* London: Routledge.

During, S. (Ed.). (1999). *The cultural studies reader* (2nd ed.). London: Routledge.

Dyer, R. (1997). *White.* London: Routledge.

Emberley, J. V. (1998). *The cultural politics of fur.* Ithaca, NY: Cornell University Press.

Erni, J. N. (1994). *Unstable frontiers: Techno-medicine and the cultural politics of "curing" AIDS.* Minneapolis: University of Minnesota Press.

Fabian, J. (1983). *Time and the other: How anthropology makes its object.* New York: Columbia University Press.

Ferguson, M., & Golding, P. (Eds.). (1997). *Cultural studies in question.* London: Sage.

Feuer, J. (1995). *Seeing through the eighties: Television and Reaganism.* Durham, NC: Duke University Press.

Field, N. (1991). *In the realm of a dying emperor.* New York: Pantheon.

Fincher, R., & Jacobs, J. M. (Eds.). (1998). *Cities of difference.* New York: Guilford.

Fiske, J. (1989a). *Reading the popular.* Boston: Unwin Hyman.

Fiske, J. (1989b). *Understanding popular culture.* Boston: Unwin Hyman.

Forbes, J., & Kelly, M. (Eds.). (1996). *French cultural studies: An introduction.* Oxford: Oxford University Press.

Forgacs, D., & Lumley, R. (Eds.). (1996). *Italian cultural studies: An introduction.* Oxford: Oxford University Press.

Foucault, M. (1972). *The archaeology of knowledge* (A. M. Sheridan Smith, Trans.). London: Tavistock.

Foucault, M. (1978). *The history of sexuality: Vol. 1. An introduction* (R. Hurley, Trans.). New York: Random House.

Foucault, M. (1980). *Power/knowledge: Selected interviews and other writings, 1972-1977* (C. Gordon, Ed.; L. Marshall, J. Mepham, & K. Soper, Trans.). New York: Pantheon.

Fourmile, H. (1989). Aboriginal heritage legislation and self-determination. *Australian-Canadian Studies, 7*(1-2), 45-61.

Frankenberg, R. (1993). *White women, race matters: The social construction of whiteness.* Minneapolis: University of Minnesota Press.

Frankenberg, R. (Ed.). (1997). *Displacing whiteness: Essays in social and cultural criticism.* Durham, NC: Duke University Press.

Freadman, A. (1992). The vagabond arts. In *In the place of French: Essays in and around French studies in honour of Michael Spencer* (pp. 257-291). Mt. Nebo: University of Queensland/Boombana.

Fregoso, R. L., & Chabram, A. (Eds.). (1990). Chicana/o cultural representations [Special issue]. *Cultural Studies, 4*(3).

Friedberg, A. (1993). *Window shopping: Cinema and the postmodern.* Berkeley: University of California Press.

Frith, S. (1996a). Music and identity. In S. Hall & P. du Gay (Eds.), *Questions of cultural identity* (pp. 108-127). London: Sage.

Frith, S. (1996b). *Performing rites: The value of popular music.* Oxford: Oxford University Press.

Frith, S., Goodwin, A., & Grossberg, L. (Eds.). (1993). *Sound and vision: The music video reader.* London: Routledge.

Frow, J. (1988). Some versions of Foucault. *Meanjin, 47*(1-2), 144-156, 353-365.

Frow, J. (1995). *Cultural studies and cultural value.* Oxford: Oxford University Press.

Frow, J., & Morris, M. (Eds.). (1993). *Australian cultural studies: A reader*. Sydney/Chicago: Allen & Unwin/University of Illinois Press.

Fuss, D. (1989). *Essentially speaking: Feminism, nature, and difference*. New York: Routledge.

Fuss, D. (Ed.). (1991). *Inside/out: Lesbian theories, gay theories*. New York: Routledge.

Gaines, J. (1992). *Contested culture: The image, the voice and the law*. London: British Film Institute.

García Canclini, N. (1993). *Transforming modernity: Popular culture in Mexico*. Austin: University of Texas Press.

García Canclini, N. (1995). *Hybrid cultures: Strategies for entering and leaving modernity*. Minneapolis: University of Minnesota Press.

Garnaut, R. (1989). *Australia and the Northeast Asian ascendancy*. Canberra: Australian Government Publishing Service.

Garnham, N. (1995a). Political economy and cultural studies: Reconciliation or divorce? *Critical Studies in Mass Communication, 12*(1), 62-71.

Garnham, N. (1995b). Reply to Grossberg & Carey. *Critical Studies in Mass Communication, 12*(1), 95-100.

Gates, H. L., Jr. (1992). *Loose canons: Notes on the culture wars*. New York: Oxford University Press.

Gelder, K., & Thornton, S. (Eds.). (1997). *The subcultures reader*. London: Routledge.

Geraghty, C., & Lusted, D. (Eds.). (1998). *The television studies book*. London: Edward Arnold.

Gibbons, L. (1996). *Transformations in Irish culture*. Cork: Cork University Press.

Gibian, P. (Ed.). (1997). *Mass culture and everyday life*. New York: Routledge.

Gibson-Graham, J.-K. (1996). *The end of capitalism (as we knew it): A feminist critique of political economy*. Cambridge, MA: Blackwell.

Gilbert, J., Glover, D., Kapal, C., Taylor, J. B., & Wheeler, W. (Eds.). (1999). Diana and democracy [Special issue]. *New Formations, 36.*

Gilroy, P. (1987). *There ain't no black in the Union Jack: The cultural politics of race and nation*. London: Hutchinson.

Gilroy, P. (1992). Cultural studies and ethnic absolutism. In L. Grossberg, C. Nelson, & P. A. Treichler (Eds.), *Cultural studies* (pp. 187-198). New York: Routledge.

Gilroy, P. (1993). *The Black Atlantic: Modernity and double consciousness*. Cambridge, MA: Harvard University Press.

Gilroy, P. (1996). British cultural studies and the pitfalls of identity. In H. A. Baker, Jr., M. Diawara, & R. H. Lindeborg (Eds.), *Black British cultural studies: A reader* (pp. 223-239). Chicago: University of Chicago Press.

Giroux, H., & Shannon, P. (Eds.). (1997). *Education and cultural studies: Toward a performative practice*. London: Routledge.

Grace, H. (1993). A house of games: Serious business and the aesthetics of logic. In J. Frow & M. Morris (Eds.), *Australian cultural studies: A reader* (pp. 69-85). Sydney/Chicago: Allen & Unwin/University of Illinois Press.

Graham, H., & Labanyi, J. (Eds.). (1996). *Spanish cultural studies: An introduction*. Oxford: Oxford University Press.

Grewal, I. (1996). *Home and harem: Nation, gender, empire, and the cultures of travel*. Durham, NC: Duke University Press.

Grewal, I., & Kaplan, C. (Eds.). (1994). *Scattered hegemonies: Postmodernity and transnational feminist practices*. Minneapolis: University of Minnesota Press.

Grimshaw, A. (Ed.). (1992). *The C. L. R. James reader*. Oxford: Blackwell.

Grossberg, L. (1992). *We gotta get out of this place: Popular conservatism and postmodern culture*. New York: Routledge.

Grossberg, L. (1993). *Cultural studies: What's in a name?* [B. Aubrey Fisher Memorial Lecture]. Salt Lake City: University of Utah, Department of Communication.

Grossberg, L. (1995). Cultural studies vs. political economy: Is anyone else bored with this debate? *Critical Studies in Mass Communication, 12*(1), 72-81.

Grossberg, L. (1996). Identity and cultural studies: Is that all there is? In S. Hall & P. du Gay (Eds.), *Questions of cultural identity* (pp. 87-107). London: Sage.

Grossberg, L. (1997a). *Bringing it all back home: Essays on cultural studies*. Durham, NC: Duke University Press.

Grossberg, L. (1997b). Cultural studies, modern logics, and theories of globalisation. In A. McRobbie (Ed.), *Back to reality? Social experience and cultural studies* (pp. 7-35). Manchester: Manchester University Press.

Grossberg, L. (1997c). *Dancing in spite of myself: Essays on popular culture*. Durham, NC: Duke University Press.

Grossberg, L. (1998a). The cultural studies' crossroads blues. *European Journal of Cultural Studies, 1,* 64-82.

Grossberg, L. (1998b). The victory of culture: Part 1. Against the logic of mediation. *Angelaki, 3*(3), 3-29.

Grossberg, L. (1999). Speculations and articulations of globalization. *Polygraph, 11,* 11-48.

Grossberg, L., Nelson, C., & Treichler, P. A. (Eds.). (1992).*Cultural studies*. New York: Routledge.

Guha, R. (1997). *Dominance without hegemony: History and power in colonial India*. Cambridge, MA: Harvard University Press.

Guillory, J. (1993). *Cultural capital: The problem of literary canon formation*. Chicago: University of Chicago Press.

Hall, C. (1992). *White, male and middle-class: Explorations in feminism and history*. New York: Routledge.

Hall, S. (1981). Notes on deconstructing "the popular." In R. Samuel (Ed.), *People's history and socialist theory* (pp. 227-240). London: Routledge & Kegan Paul.

Hall, S. (1988). *The hard road to renewal: Thatcherism and the crisis of the left*. London: Verso.

Hall, S. (1992). Cultural studies and its theoretical legacies. In L. Grossberg, C. Nelson, & P. A. Treichler (Eds.), *Cultural studies* (pp. 277-294). New York: Routledge.

Hall, S. (1996). New ethnicities. In D. Morley & K.-H. Chen (Eds.), *Stuart Hall: Critical dialogues in cultural studies* (pp. 441-449). New York: Routledge.

Hall, S., Critcher, C., Jefferson, T., Clarke, J., & Roberts, B. (1979). *Policing the crisis: Mugging, the state, and law and order*. London: Macmillan.

Hall, S., & du Gay, P. (Eds.). (1996). *Questions of cultural identity*. London: Sage.

Hall, S., & Jefferson, T. (1976). *Resistance through rituals: Youth subcultures in post-war Britain*. London: Hutchinson.

Hanczor, R. S. (1997). Articulation theory and public controversy: Taking sides over *NYPD blue. Critical Studies in Mass Communication, 14*(1), 1-30.

Haraway, D. J. (1989). *Primate visions: Gender, race, and nature in the world of modern science*. New York: Routledge.

Haraway, D. J. (1991). *Simians, cyborgs, and women: The reinvention of nature*. New York: Routledge.

Hargreaves, A. G., & McKinney, M. (Eds.). (1997). *Post-colonial cultures in France*. London: Routledge.

Harris, D. (1992). *From class struggle to the politics of pleasure: The effects of Gramscianism on cultural studies*. London: Routledge.

Hartley, J. (1992a). *The politics of pictures: The creation of the public in the age of popular media*. London: Routledge.

Hartley, J. (1992b). *Tele-ology: Studies in television*. London: Routledge.

Hartley, J. (1996). *Popular reality: Journalism, modernity, popular culture*. London: Edward Arnold.

Hartley, J. (1998). Housing television: Textual traditions in TV and cultural studies. In C. Geraghty & D. Lusted (Eds.), *The television studies book* (pp. 33-50). London: Edward Arnold.

Hartley, J. (1999). "Text" and "audience": One and the same? Methodological tensions in media research. *Textual Practice, 13,* 491-512.

Hartman, G. H. (1997). *The fateful question of culture*. New York: Columbia University Press.

Harvey, D. (1989). *The condition of postmodernity: An enquiry into the origins of cultural change*. Oxford: Blackwell.

Hawkins, G. (1999). Public service broadcasting in Australia: Value and difference. In A. Calabrese & J. Burgelman (Eds.), *Communication, citizenship and social policy: Rethinking the welfare state* (pp. 173-187). Boulder, CO: Rowman & Littlefield.

Hay, J., Grossberg, L., & Wartella, E. (Eds.). (1996). *The audience and its landscape*. Boulder, CO: Westview.

Hayward, P. (Ed.). (1998). *Sound alliances: Indigenous peoples, cultural politics and popular music in the Pacific*. London: Cassell.

Healy, C. (1997). *From the ruins of colonialism: History as social memory*. Cambridge: Cambridge University Press.

Healy, C. (1999). White feet and black trails: Travelling cultures at the Lurujarri Trail. *Postcolonial Studies, 2*(1), 55-73.

Hebdige, D. (1979). *Subculture: The meaning of style*. London: Methuen.

Hebdige, D. (1988). *Hiding in the light: On images and things*. London: Routledge.

Hereniko, V., & Wilson, R. (Eds.). (in press). *Inside out: Literature, cultural politics, and identity in the new Pacific*. Boulder, CO: Rowman & Littlefield.

Hoggart, R. (1957). *The uses of literacy*. London: Chatto & Windus.

hooks, b. (1981). *Ain't I a woman: Black women and feminism*. Boston: South End.

hooks, b. (1990). *Yearning: Race, gender, and cultural politics*. Boston: South End.

hooks, b. (1992a). *Black looks: Race and representation*. Boston: South End.

hooks, b. (1992b). Representing whiteness in the black imagination. In L. Grossberg, C. Nelson, & P. A. Treichler (Eds.), *Cultural studies* (pp. 338-346). New York: Routledge.

Hull, G. T., Scott, P. B., & Smith, B. (Eds.). (1982). *All the women are white, all the blacks are men, but some of us are brave: Black women's studies*. Old Westbury, NY: Feminist Press.

Hunter, I. (1988a). *Culture and government: The emergence of literary education*. London: Macmillan.

Hunter, I. (1988b). Setting limits to culture. *New Formations, 4,* 103-124.

Hunter, I. (1992). Aesthetics and cultural studies. In L. Grossberg, C. Nelson, & P. A. Treichler (Eds.), *Cultural studies* (pp. 347-372). New York: Routledge.

Huntington, S. P. (1996). *The clash of civilizations and the remaking of world order*. New York: Simon & Schuster.

Im, Y.-H. (1998). The media, civil society and new social movements in Korea, 1985-93. In K.-H. Chen (Ed.), *Trajectories: Inter-Asia cultural studies* (pp. 330-345). London: Routledge.

Jackson, M. (1998). *Minima ethnographica: Intersubjectivity and the anthropological project*. Chicago: University of Chicago Press.

Jacobs, J. M. (1996). *Edge of empire: Postcolonialism and the city*. London: Routledge.

Jagtenberg, T., & McKie, D. (1997). *Eco-impacts and the greening of post-modernity*. London: Sage.

Jameson, F., & Miyoshi, M. (Eds.). (1998). *The cultures of globalization*. Durham, NC: Duke University Press.

Jenkins, H. (1992). *Textual poachers: Television fans and participatory cultures*. New York: Routledge.

Jenkins, H. (Ed.). (1998). *The children's culture reader*. New York: New York University Press.

Johnson, L. (1988). *The unseen voice: A cultural study of early Australian radio*. London: Routledge.

Johnson, L. (1993). *The modern girl: Childhood and growing up*. Sydney/Milton Keynes, UK: Allen & Unwin/Open University Press.

Johnson, V. (1990). *Radio birdman*. Sydney: Sheldon Booth.

Johnson, V. (1994). *Western desert artists: A biographical dictionary*. Sydney: Craftsman House.

Johnson, V. (1996). *"Copyrites": Aboriginal art in the age of reproductive technologies*. Sydney: Macquarie University/National Indigenous Arts Advocacy Association.

Jordan, G., & Weedon, C. (1995). *Cultural politics: Class, gender, race and the postmodern world*. Oxford: Blackwell.

Kang, M. K. (1999). Postmodern consumer culture without postmodernity: Copying the crisis of signification. *Cultural Studies, 13,* 18-33.

Keil, C., & Feld, S. (1994). *Music grooves*. Chicago: University of Chicago Press.

Keith, M., & Pile, S. (Eds.). (1993). *Place and the politics of identity*. London: Routledge.

Kellner, D. (1992). *The Persian Gulf TV war*. Boulder, CO: Westview.

Kellner, D. (1997). Critical theory and cultural studies: The missed articulation. In J. McGuigan (Ed.), *Cultural methodologies* (pp. 12-41). London: Sage.

Kelly, C., & Shepherd, D. (Eds.). (1998). *Russian cultural studies: An introduction*. Oxford: Oxford University Press.

Kim, S. (1998). "Cine-mania" or cinephilia: Film festivals and the identity question. *UTS Review, 4*(2), 174-187.

King, A. D. (Ed.). (1991). *Culture, globalization and the world system*. London: Macmillan.

Knight, S. (1990). *The selling of the Australian mind: From first fleet to third Mercedes*. Port Melbourne: Heinemann Australia.

Kowinski, W. S. (1985). *The malling of America: An inside look at the great consumer paradise*. New York: William Morrow.

Kraniauskas, J. (1998). Globalization is ordinary: The transnationalization of cultural studies. *Radical Philosophy, 90,* 9-19.

Kroker, A. (1984). *Technology and the Canadian mind: Innis, McLuhan, Grant*. Montreal: New World Perspectives.

Laclau, E. (1977). *Politics and ideology in Marxist theory*. London: Verso.

Lanfant, M.-F., Allcock, J. B., & Bruner, E. M. (Eds.). (1995). *International tourism: Identity and change*. London: Sage.

Langton, M. (1993). *"Well, I heard it on the radio and I saw it on the television . . . : An essay for the Australian Film Commission on the politics and aesthetics of filmmaking by and about Aboriginal people and things*. North Sydney: Australian Film Commission.

Langton, M. (1998). *Burning questions: Emerging environmental issues for indigenous peoples in Northern Australia*. Darwin: Northern Territory University, Centre for Indigenous Natural and Cultural Resource Management.

Lefebvre, H. (1984). *Everyday life in the modern world* (S. Rabinovitch, Trans.). New Brunswick, NJ: Transaction. (Original work published 1971)

Lilley, R. (1998). *Staging Hong Kong: Gender and performance in transition*. Richmond, UK: Curzon.

Lipsitz, G. (1994). *Dangerous crossroads*. London: Verso.

Long, E. (Ed.). (1997). *From sociology to cultural studies*. Oxford: Blackwell.

Loosley, S. (1991, March 17). Step towards real changes. *Sunday Telegraph*.

Lott, E. (1993). *Love and theft: Blackface minstrelsy and the American working class*. New York: Oxford University Press.

Lowe, L. (1996). *Immigrant acts: On Asian American cultural politics*. Durham, NC: Duke University Press.

Lubiana, W. (Ed.). (1997). *The house that race built*. New York: Pantheon.

Luke, C. (Ed.). (1996). *Feminisms and pedagogies of everyday life*. Albany: State University of New York Press.

Lumby, C. (1997). *Bad girls: The media, sex and feminism in the 90s*. Sydney: Allen & Unwin.

Lumby, C. (1999). *Gotcha: Life in a tabloid world*. Sydney: Allen & Unwin.

Ma, E. K.-W. (1999). *Culture, politics and television in Hong Kong*. London: Routledge.

Marrie, A. (1989). Museums and Aborigines: A case study in internal colonialism. *Australian-Canadian Studies, 7*(1-2), 63-80.

Martin, R., & Miller, T. (Eds.). (1999). *SportCult*. Minneapolis: University of Minnesota Press.

Massey, D. (1994). *Space, place and gender*. Cambridge: Polity.

Massey, D. (1997). Problems with globalisation. *Soundings, 7*, 7-12.

Massumi, B. (1992). *A user's guide to capitalism and schizophrenia: Deviations from Deleuze and Guattari*. Cambridge: MIT Press.

Massumi, B. (1996). The autonomy of affect. In P. Patton (Ed.), *Deleuze: A critical reader* (pp. 217-239). Oxford: Blackwell.

Massumi, B. (1997). The political economy of belonging and the logic of relation. In C. Davidson (Ed.), *Anybody* (pp. 174-189). Cambridge: MIT Press.

Matsuda, M. (1996). *Where is your body? And other essays on race, gender, and the law*. Boston: Beacon.

Mauss, M. (1970). *The gift: Forms and functions of exchange in archaic societies* (I. Cunnison, Trans.). London: Cohen & West.

McCalman, I. (Ed.). (1998). *Mad cows and modernity: Cross-disciplinary reflections on the crisis of Creutzfeldt-Jakob disease*. Canberra: Humanities Research Centre/National Academies Forum.

McCarthy, C., & Crichlow, W. (Eds.). (1993). *Race, identity and representation in education*. New York: Routledge.

McClintock, A. (1995). *Imperial leather: Race, gender and sexuality in the colonial contest*. New York: Routledge.

McGuigan, J. (1996). *Culture and the public sphere*. London: Routledge.

McGuigan, J. (Ed.). (1997). *Cultural methodologies*. London: Sage.

McHoul, A. (1997). Ordinary heterodoxies: Towards a theory of cultural objects. *UTS Review, 3*(2), 7-22.

McNeil, M. (1998). De-centring or re-focusing cultural studies: A response to Handel K. Wright. *European Journal of Cultural Studies, 1*, 57-64.

McRobbie, A. (1981). Settling accounts with subcultures: A feminist critique. In T. Bennett, G. Martin, C. Mercer, & J. Woollacott (Eds.), *Culture, ideology and social process: A reader* (pp. 113-123). London: Batsford Academic & Education.

McRobbie, A. (1994). *Postmodernism and popular culture*. London: Routledge.

McRobbie, A. (Ed.). (1997a). *Back to reality? Social experience and cultural studies*. Manchester: Manchester University Press.

McRobbie, A. (1997b). The Es and the anti-Es: New questions for feminism and cultural studies. In M. Ferguson & P. Golding (Eds.), *Cultural studies in question* (pp. 170-186). London: Sage.

McRobbie, A. (1999). *British fashion design: Rag trade or image industry?* London: Routledge.

Meadows, M. (1996). Indigenous cultural diversity: Television northern Canada. *Culture and Policy, 7*(1), 25-44.

Mellencamp, P. (Ed.). (1990). *Logics of television*. Bloomington: Indiana University Press.

Mellencamp, P. (1992). *High anxiety: Catastrophe, scandal, age, and comedy*. Bloomington: Indiana University Press.

Mercer, K. (1994). *Welcome to the jungle: New positions in black cultural studies*. London: Routledge.

Mercer, K., Ugwu, C., & Bailey, D. A. (Eds.). (1996). *Mirage: Enigmas of race, difference and desire*. London: ICA Editions.

Meyrowitz, J. (1985). *No sense of place: The impact of electronic media on social behavior*. New York: Oxford University Press.

Michael, J. (1996). Science friction and cultural studies: Intellectuals, interdisciplinarity, and the profession of truth. *Camera Obscura, 37*, 125-154.

Michaels, E. (1986). *The Aboriginal invention of television in central Australia 1982-1986*. Canberra: Australian Institute of Aboriginal Studies.

Michaels, E. (1994). *Bad Aboriginal art: Tradition, media, and technological horizons*. Minneapolis: University of Minnesota Press.

Mickler, S. (1998). *The myth of privilege: Aboriginal status, media visions, public ideas*. Fremantle, Western Australia: Fremantle Arts Centre Press.

Mignolo, W. D. (1995). *The darker side of the Renaissance: Literacy, territoriality and colonization*. Ann Arbor: University of Michigan Press.

Miller, T. (Ed.). (1992). Radio-sound [Special issue]. *Continuum, 6*(1).

Miller, T. (1998). *Technologies of truth: Cultural citizenship and the popular media*. Minneapolis: University of Minnesota Press.

Miller, T., & McHoul, A. (1999). *Popular culture and everyday life*. London: Sage.

Mitchell, T. (1996). *Popular music and local identity: Rock, pop and rap in Europe and Oceania*. Leicester: University of Leicester Press.

Mohanty, C. T., Russo, A., & Torres, L. (Eds.). (1991). *Third World women and the politics of feminism*. Bloomington: Indiana University Press.

Moon, M., & Davidson, C. N. (Eds.). (1995). *Subjects and citizens: Nation, race and gender from Oroonoko to Anita Hill*. Durham, NC: Duke University Press.

Moraga, C., & Anzaldúa, G. (Eds.). (1981). *This bridge called my back: Writings by radical women of color*. New York: Kitchen Table/Women of Color Press.

Moreiras, A. (1999). The order of order: On the reluctant culturalism of anti-subalternist critiques. *Journal of Latin American Cultural Studies, 8*(1), 125-145.

Morley, D. (1992). *Television, audiences and cultural studies*. London: Routledge.

Morley, D. (1998). So-called cultural studies: Dead ends and reinvented wheels. *Cultural Studies, 12,* 476-497.

Morley, D., & Chen, K.-H. (Eds.). (1996). *Stuart Hall: Critical dialogues in cultural studies*. New York: Routledge.

Morris, M. (1990). Banality in cultural studies. In P. Mellencamp (Ed.), *Logics of television* (pp. 14-43). Bloomington: Indiana University Press.

Morris, M. (1992). The man in the mirror: David Harvey's "condition" of postmodernity. In M. Featherstone (Ed.), *Cultural theory and cultural change* (pp. 253-279). London: Sage.

Morris, M. (1997a). A question of cultural studies. In A. McRobbie (Ed.), *Back to reality? Social experience and cultural studies* (pp. 36-57). Manchester: Manchester University Press.

Morris, M. (1997b). The truth is out there. *Cultural Studies, 11,* 367-375.

Morris, M. (1998a). *Too soon, too late: History in popular culture*. Bloomington: Indiana University Press.

Morris, M. (1998b). Truth and beauty in our times. In J. Bigelow (Ed.), *Our cultural heritage* (pp. 75-87). Canberra: Australian Academy of the Humanities.

Morris, M., & McCalman, I. (1999). "Public culture" and humanities research in Australia: A report. *Public Culture, 11*(2), 319-345.

Morris, M., & Patton, P. (Eds.). (1979). *Michel Foucault: Power, truth, strategy.* Sydney: Feral.

Morrison, T. (Ed.). (1992). *Race-ing justice, en-gendering power: Essays on Anita Hill, Clarence Thomas, and the construction of social reality.* New York: Pantheon.

Morse, M. (1983). Sport on television: Replay and display. In E. A. Kaplan (Ed.), *Regarding television* (pp. 44-66). Los Angeles: American Film Institute.

Morse, M. (1998). *Virtualities: Television, media art, and cyberculture.* Bloomington: Indiana University Press.

Muecke, S. (1992). *Textual spaces: Aboriginality and cultural studies.* Kensington: New South Wales University Press.

Muecke, S. (1997). *No road (bitumen all the way).* Fremantle, Western Australia: Fremantle Arts Centre Press.

Munson, E. S., & Warren, C. A. (Eds.). (1997). *James Carey: A critical reader.* Minneapolis: University of Minnesota Press.

Murdock, G. (1995). Across the great divide: Cultural analysis and the condition of democracy. *Critical Studies in Mass Communication, 12*(1), 89-95.

Murdock, G. (1997). Cultural studies at the crossroads. In A. McRobbie (Ed.), *Back to reality? Social experience and cultural studies* (pp. 58-73). Manchester: Manchester University Press.

Naficy, H., & Gabriel, T. H. (Eds.). (1993). *Otherness and the media: The ethnography of the imagined and the imaged.* Newark, NJ: Harwood.

Nakayama, T. K. (1997). The empire strikes back: The Sokal controversy and the vilification of cultural studies. *Journal of Communication Inquiry, 21*(2), 45-55.

Nandy, A. (1983). *The intimate enemy: Loss and recovery of self under colonialism.* Bombay: Oxford University Press.

Nelson, C., & Gaonkar, D. P. (Eds.). (1996). *Disciplinarity and dissent in cultural studies.* New York: Routledge.

Nelson, C., Treichler, P. A., & Grossberg, L. (1992). Cultural studies: An introduction. In L. Grossberg, C. Nelson, & P. A. Treichler (Eds.), *Cultural studies* (pp. 1-16). New York: Routledge.

Nightingale, V. (1996). *Studying audiences: The shock of the real.* London: Routledge.

Noble, G., Poynting, S., & Tabar, P. (1999). Youth, ethnicity and the mapping of identities: Strategic essentialism and strategic hybridity among male Arabic-speaking youth in south-western Sydney. *Communal Plural, 7*(1), 29-45.

O'Regan, T. (1992). Some reflections on the "policy moment." *Meanjin, 51,* 517-532.

O'Regan, T. (1993). *Australian television culture.* Sydney: Allen & Unwin.

O'Regan, T. (1996). *Australian national cinema.* London: Routledge.

O'Regan, T., & Miller, T. (Eds.). (1994). Screening cultural studies [Special issue]. *Continuum, 7*(2).

Owusu, K. (Ed.). (1999). *Black British culture and society.* London: Routledge.

Palmer, L. (1998). On or off the beaten track? Tourist trails in Thailand. *UTS Review, 4*(1), 67-91.

Parker, A., Russo, M., Sommer, D., & Yaeger, P. (Eds.). (1992). *Nationalisms and sexualities.* New York: Routledge.

Patton, C. (1992). From nation to family: Containing African AIDS. In A. Parker, M. Russo, D. Sommer, & P. Yaeger (Eds.), *Nationalisms and sexualities* (pp. 218-234). New York: Routledge.

Patton, C. (1994). *Last served? Gendering the HIV pandemic.* London: Falmer.

Penley, C., & Ross, A. (Eds.). (1991). *Technoculture.* Minneapolis: University of Minnesota Press.

Perera, S. (1993). Representation wars: Malaysia, *Embassy,* and Australia's *Corps Diplomatique.* In J. Frow & M. Morris (Eds.), *Australian cultural studies: A reader* (pp. 15-29). Sydney/Chicago: Allen & Unwin/University of Illinois Press.

Perera, S. (Ed.). (1995). *Asian and Pacific inscriptions: Identities, ethnicities, nationalities.* Bundoora, Victoria, Australia: Meridian.

Pickering, M. (1997). *History, experience and cultural studies.* London: Macmillan.

Poor performance "shooting Aust in the head." (1989, October 26). *Australian Financial Review.*

Prakash, G. (Ed.). (1995). *After colonialism: Imperial histories and postcolonial displacements.* Princeton, NJ: Princeton University Press.

Probyn, E. (1993). *Sexing the self: Gendered positions in cultural studies.* London: Routledge.

Probyn, E. (1996). *Outside belongings*. New York: Routledge.

Probyn, E. (1998). McIdentities: Food and the familial citizen. *Theory, Culture & Society, 15*(2), 155-173.

Probyn, E. (1999a). Beyond food/sex: Eating and an ethics of existence. *Theory, Culture & Society, 16*(2), 215-228.

Probyn, E. (1999b). Disciplinary desires: The outside of queer feminist cultural studies. In M. Shiach (Ed.), *Feminism and cultural studies* (pp. 431-458). Oxford: Oxford University Press.

Radway, J. A. (1991). *Reading the romance: Women, patriarchy and popular literature* (2nd ed.). Chapel Hill: University of North Carolina Press.

Radway, J. A. (1997). *Feeling for books: The Book-of-the-Month Club, literary taste, and middle-class desire*. Chapel Hill: University of North Carolina Press.

Rand, E. (1995). *Barbie's queer accessories*. Durham, NC: Duke University Press.

Readings, B. (1996). *The university in ruins*. Cambridge, MA: Harvard University Press.

Re:Public. (Ed.). (1997). *Planet Diana: Cultural studies and global mourning*. Nepean: University of Western Sydney, Research Centre in Intercommunal Studies.

Robbins, B. (Ed.). (1993a). *The phantom public sphere*. Minneapolis: University of Minnesota Press.

Robbins, B. (1993b). *Secular vocations: Intellectuals, professionalism, culture*. London: Verso.

Robinson, P. (1989, June 18). Fair go, we're all bludgers. *Sun Herald*.

Rodman, G. (1996). *Elvis after Elvis: The posthumous career of a living legend*. New York: Routledge.

Rodman, G. (1997). Subject to debate: (Mis)reading cultural studies. *Journal of Communication Inquiry, 21*(2), 56-69.

Roediger, D. R. (1991). *The wages of whiteness: Race and the making of the American working class*. London: Verso.

Rosaldo, M. Z. (1984). Toward an anthropology of self and feeling. In R. A. Shweder & R. A. Levine (Eds.), *Culture theory: Essays on mind, self and emotion* (pp. 137-157). Cambridge: Cambridge University Press.

Rosaldo, R. (1989). *Culture and truth: The remaking of social analysis*. Boston: Beacon.

Rosaldo, R. (1997). Whose cultural studies? Cultural studies and the disciplines. In P. Gibian (Ed.), *Mass culture and everyday life* (pp. 26-33). New York: Routledge.

Rose, T. (1994). *Black noise: Rap music and black culture in contemporary America*. Boston: Wesleyan University Press.

Ross, A. (1989). *No respect: Intellectuals and popular culture*. New York: Routledge.

Ross, A. (1991). *Strange weather: Culture, science and technology in the age of limits*. London: Verso.

Ross, A. (1994). *The Chicago gangster theory of life: Nature's debt to society*. London: Verso.

Ross, A. (Ed.). (1996). *Science wars*. London: Duke University Press.

Ross, A. (Ed.). (1997). *No sweat: Fashion, free trade and the rights of garment workers*. London: Verso.

Rowe, D. (1995). *Popular cultures: Rock music, sport and the politics of pleasure*. London: Sage.

Said, E. W. (1993). *Culture and imperialism*. London: Chatto & Windus.

Sakai, N. (1991). *Voices of the past: The status of language in eighteenth-century Japanese discourse*. Ithaca, NY: Cornell University Press.

Sakai, N. (1997). *Translation and subjectivity: On "Japan" and cultural nationalism*. Minneapolis: University of Minnesota Press.

Sedgwick, E. K. (1990). *Epistemology of the closet*. Berkeley: University of California Press.

Sedgwick, E. K. (1993). *Tendencies*. Durham, NC: Duke University Press.

Sharkey, S. (1997). Irish cultural studies and the politics of Irish studies. In J. McGuigan (Ed.), *Cultural methodologies* (pp. 155-177). London: Sage.

Shaviro, S. (1997). Beauty lies in the eye. *Canadian Review of Comparative Literature, 25*, 461-471.

Sheridan, S. (Ed.). (1988). *Grafts: Feminist cultural criticism*. London: Verso.

Shiach, M. (Ed.). (1999). *Feminism and cultural studies*. Oxford: Oxford University Press.

Silverstone, R. (1994). *Television and everyday life*. London: Routledge.

Skeggs, B. (1997). *Formations of class and gender*. London: Sage.

Slack, J. D., & Semati, M. M. (1997). Intellectual and political hygiene: The "Sokal affair." *Critical Studies in Mass Communication, 14*(3), 201-227.

Slack, J. D., & White, L. A. (1992). Ethics and cultural studies. In L. Grossberg, C. Nelson, & P. A. Treichler (Eds.), *Cultural studies* (pp. 571-592). New York: Routledge.

Spigel, L. (1992). *Make room for TV: Television and the family ideal in postwar America.* Chicago: University of Chicago Press.

Spivak, G. C. (1988). *In other worlds: Essays in cultural politics.* London: Routledge.

Spivak, G. C. (1990). *The post-colonial critic: Interviews, strategies, dialogues.* New York: Routledge.

Spivak, G. C. (1993). *Outside in the teaching machine.* New York: Routledge.

Stacey, J. (1994). *Star gazing: Hollywood cinema and female spectatorship.* London: Routledge.

Stam, R. (1997). *Tropical multiculturalism: A comparative history of race in Brazilian cinema and culture.* Durham, NC: Duke University Press.

Steedman, C. (1986). *Landscape for a good woman: A story of two lives.* London: Virago.

Steedman, C. (1992a). Culture, cultural studies, and the historians. In L. Grossberg, C. Nelson, & P. A. Treichler (Eds.), *Cultural studies* (pp. 613-622). New York: Routledge.

Steedman, C. (1992b). *Past tenses: Essays on writing, autobiography and history.* London: Rivers Oram.

Steedman, C. (1997). Writing the self: The end of the scholarship girl. In J. McGuigan (Ed.), *Cultural methodologies* (pp. 106-125). London: Sage.

Steele, T. (1997). *The emergence of cultural studies 1945-65: Cultural politics, adult education and the English question.* London: Lawrence & Wishart.

Steinberg, M. P. (1996). Cultural history and cultural studies. In C. Nelson & D. P. Gaonkar (Eds.), *Disciplinarity and dissent in cultural studies* (pp. 103-129). New York: Routledge.

Stewart, K. (1996). *A space on the side of the road: Cultural poetics in an "other" America.* Princeton, NJ: Princeton University Press.

Storey, J. (Ed.). (1994). *Cultural theory and popular culture.* Hertfordshire: Harvester Wheatsheaf.

Storey, J. (Ed.). (1996). *What is cultural studies? A reader.* London: Edward Arnold.

Stratton, J. (1992). *The young ones: Working-class culture, consumption and the category of youth.* Perth, Western Australia: Black Swan.

Street, J. (1997). *Politics and popular culture.* Cambridge: Polity.

Striphas, T. (Ed.). (1998). The institutionalization of cultural studies [Special issue]. *Cultural Studies, 12*(4).

Suleri, S. (1992). *The rhetoric of English India.* Chicago: University of Chicago Press.

Swan steels ARC for competition. (1989, November 26). *Sunday Telegraph.*

Taussig, M. (1997). *The magic of the state.* New York: Routledge.

Teaiwa, T. (1999). Reading Gauguin's *Noa Noa* with Hau'ofa's Nederends: "Militourism," feminism and the "Polynesian" body. *UTS Review, 5*(1), 53-69.

Teer-Tomaselli, R. E., & Roome, D. (Eds.). (1997). Popular culture and identity [Special issue]. *Critical Arts, 11*(1-2).

Thomas, M. (1999). *Dreams in the shadows: Australian-Vietnamese lives in transition.* Sydney: Allen & Unwin.

Tofts, D., & McKeitch, M. (1998). *Memory trade: A prehistory of cyberculture.* Sydney: 21C/Interface.

Tomaselli, K. G. (1996). *Appropriating images: The semiotics of visual representation.* Durban/Hojbjerg: Smyrna/Intervention.

Tomaselli, K. G. (1998a). African cultural studies: Excavating for the future. *International Journal of Cultural Studies, 1*(1), 143-153.

Tomaselli, K. G. (1998b). Recovering praxis: Cultural studies in Africa. *European Journal of Cultural Studies, 1,* 387-402.

Tomaselli, K. G., & Mpofu, A. (1997). The rearticulation of meaning of national monuments: Beyond apartheid. *Culture and Policy, 8*(3), 57-76.

Turkle, S. (1984). *The second self: Computers and the human spirit.* New York: Simon & Schuster.

Turner, G. (Ed.). (1993). *Nation, culture, text: Australian cultural and media studies.* London: Routledge.

Turner, G. (1994). *Making it national: Nationalism and Australian popular culture.* Sydney: Allen & Unwin.

Turner, G. (1996). *British cultural studies: An introduction* (Rev. ed.). Boston: Unwin Hyman.

Vainikkala, E., & Eskola, K. (Eds.). (1994). Nordic cultural studies [Special issue]. *Cultural Studies, 8*(2).

Valaskakis, G. (1988). The Chippewa and the other: Living the heritage of Lac du Flambeau. *Cultural Studies, 2,* 267-293.

Valaskakis, G. (in press). *Being native in North America.* Boulder, CO: Westview.

Viswanathan, G. (1989). *Masks of conquest: Literary study and British rule in India.* New York: Columbia University Press.

Wallace, M. (1978). *Black macho and the myth of the superwoman.* New York: Dial.

Wallace, M. (1990). *Invisibility blues: From pop to theory.* London: Verso.

Ware, V. (1992). *Beyond the pale: White women, racism and history.* London: Verso.

Wark, M. (1993). Homage to catatonia: Culture, politics and Midnight Oil. In J. Frow & M. Morris (Eds.), *Australian cultural studies: A reader* (pp. 105-116). Sydney/Chicago: Allen & Unwin/University of Illinois Press.

Wark, M. (1994). *Virtual geography: Living with global media events.* Bloomington: Indiana University Press.

Wark, M. (1999). *Celebrities, culture and cyberspace.* St. Leonards: Allen & Unwin.

Warner, M. (Ed.). (1993). *Fear of a queer planet: Queer politics and social theory.* Minneapolis: University of Minnesota Press.

Waters, J. P. (1996). Ireland and Irish cultural studies [Special issue]. *South Atlantic Quarterly, 95*(1).

Watney, S. (1987). *Policing desire: Pornography, AIDS, and the media.* Minneapolis: University of Minnesota Press.

Whannel, G. (1992). *Fields in vision: Television sport and cultural transformation.* London: Routledge.

Willemen, P. (1994). *Looks and frictions: Essays in cultural studies and film theory.* London/Bloomington: British Film Institute/Indiana University Press.

Williams, R. (1961a). *Culture and society 1780-1950.* Harmondsworth: Penguin. (Original work published 1958)

Williams, R. (1961b). *The long revolution.* London: Chatto & Windus.

Williams, R. (1979). *Politics and letters.* London: New Left.

Williams, R. (1985). *The country and the city.* London: Hogarth.

Williams, R. (1989). The future of cultural studies. In R. Williams, *The politics of modernism* (pp. 151-162). London: Verso.

Willis, P. E. (1977). *Learning to labour: How working class kids get working class jobs.* Farnborough, UK: Saxon House.

Wilson, R. (in press). *Reimagining the American Pacific: From "South Pacific" to Bamboo Ridge and beyond.* London: Duke University Press.

Wilson, R., & Dissanayake, W. (Eds.). (1996). *Global/local: Cultural production and the transnational imaginary.* Durham, NC: Duke University Press.

Wilson, R., & Dirlik, A. (Eds.). (1995). *Asia/Pacific as space of cultural production.* Durham, NC: Duke University Press.

Women's Studies Group, Centre for Contemporary Cultural Studies. (1978). *Women take issue: Aspects of women's subordination.* London: Hutchinson, with Centre for Contemporary Cultural Studies, University of Birmingham.

Wood, H. (in press). *Displacing native: The rhetorical production of Hawai'i.* Boulder, CO: Rowman & Littlefield.

Wright, H. K. (1998). Dare we de-centre Birmingham? Troubling the "origin" and trajectories of cultural studies. *European Journal of Cultural Studies, 1,* 33-56.

Yudice, G., Franco, J., & Flores, J. (Eds.). (1992). *On edge: The crisis of contemporary Latin American culture.* Minneapolis: University of Minnesota Press.

12

SEXUALITIES, QUEER THEORY, AND QUALITATIVE RESEARCH

♦ Joshua Gamson

W hen social researchers began discovering and investigating homosexual lives in the early part of this
century, they faced obvious pragmatic obstacles
to finding research participants. At a time when
homosexuality was subject to severe social stigmatization and onerous penalties, when people
with same-sex desires and practices were the
keepers of great secrets and the livers of fragile
"double lives," finding homosexuals to study
was not an easy task. Some half a century later,
when movements for lesbian and gay rights and
liberation have altered the terrain considerably,
one would think that willing subjects would be
easy enough to track down.

Indeed, on one level, this is the case. Despite
the ongoing strength of stigma, penalty, and secrecy, lesbians and gay men living lesbian and
gay lives openly and unapologetically, often as
members of organized communities, are no longer tough to find and study. The history of social
research on sexualities has elements familiar
from the histories of women's studies, ethnic
studies, and the like: It is a history intertwined
with the politics of social movements, wary of
the ways "science" has been used against the
marginalized, and particularly comfortable
with the strategies of qualitative research—
which at least appear to be less objectifying of
their subjects, to be more concerned with cultural and political meaning creation, and to
make more room for voices and experiences
that have been suppressed. Thus, on the one
hand, the coming-of-age of the field is a com-

AUTHOR'S NOTE: This chapter benefited enormously from the insightful comments of Patricia Clough, Norman
Denzin, Rosanna Hertz, Yvonna Lincoln, and William Tierney.

ing-to-voice of new sexual subjects on the terrains of both politics and academia. It is about invisible people becoming visible.

Yet as soon as the subject began to appear, she began to disappear. Over the past decade, in particular, the research subject has become problematic and elusive in striking new ways. With the growth of "queer theory," which took social constructionist insights and forcefully added a poststructuralist critique of the unified, autonomous self, the lesbian and gay subject has become, in a different way, increasingly hard to recognize, let alone research. Like many other recent intellectual developments, queer studies is largely a deconstructive enterprise, taking apart the view of a self defined by something at its core, be it sexual desire, race, gender, nation, or class. This is the central piece of the story I want to tell: of how we have gone from unreflective confidence in the existence of sexual subjects—who only needed to be found and documented—to a boom in lesbian and gay studies filled with subjects speaking and writing about their own lives, to a suspicion that sexual subjects do not exactly exist to be studied, an ongoing deconstruction of sexual subjectivity. This is a story, moreover, that runs parallel to, meets up with, and contributes to a similar history in the nature and meaning of qualitative research; as Norman Denzin and Yvonna Lincoln (1994) argue, the early traditional enterprise of "objective" study of stable subjects has, over time, in large part given way to a postmodern questioning of objectivity and embrace of "an always shifting center" (Lincoln & Denzin, 1994, p. 575).

As I trace these linked histories, I want to point to several key tensions built into the field that are ultimately productive for qualitative research on sexualities: over what it really means for researchers to include in their study people calling themselves lesbian, gay, bisexual, or transgender; over what it means to do qualitative research that is at most skeptical about the stability and literal reality of the social categories gay, bisexual, transgender, and lesbian; over the place of "lived experience" in such research and representation; and over what it means to research the discursive and the institutional si-

multaneously, especially in a field where research and politics are so closely tied.

◆ The Politics of Sexuality Studies: The Qualitative Push

The study of sexualities in general, and homosexualities in particular, has long been closely intertwined with qualitative research—by which, as a general starting point that I will quickly complicate, I mean a loose set of research practices (ethnography and participant observation, in-depth interviewing, textual analysis, historical research, and the like) distinct from quantitative methods and often suspicious of the epistemological assumptions of positivism, and a correspondingly loose but distinct set of research foci (cultural meaning creation and interpretive processes, collective and personal identities, social interaction, the practices of everyday life, and so on).

The qualitative push has come largely from the political context in which sexualities research has taken shape. Although there has been a long-standing stream of social science research on sexuality, there has been an even stronger, well-founded suspicion that positivist sciences, and some scientific professions, have been at odds with the interests of self-defining homosexuals—pathologizing, stigmatizing, seeking the "cause" of deviant sexualities and, by implication, their cure. This suspicion has given qualitative research an inside track. Further, qualitative methods, with their focus on meaning creation and the experiences of everyday life, fit especially well with movement goals of visibility, cultural challenge, and self-determination. Finally, as lesbian and gay studies gave rise to its own new theoretical developments—in particular, a critical focus on the social construction of sexual categories and identities, and then a "queer" focus on the broad role of the homo/heterosexual binary in contemporary life—it put the spotlight on interpretive issues especially suited to qualitative research.

At the same time, qualitative research, in part pushed by the entry of previously silent voices into its activities, has undergone a series of twists and turns that have affected, and been affected by, sexualities study. Denzin and Lincoln (1994) have identified five key "moments" in the history of qualitative research, and sexualities study has taken its place within this complex chronology: from traditional "colonializing accounts of field experiences," concerned with "valid, reliable, and objective interpretations" (1900-1950); to modernist attempts at formalized qualitative research presenting causal narratives (1950-1970); to a period in which boundaries between social sciences and humanities became blurred, and in which the observer came to have "no privileged voice in the interpretations that were written" (1970-1986); to a subsequent "crisis of representation," in which research and writing became more reflexive and the assumption that "qualitative researchers can directly capture lived experience" was undercut (1986-1990); to the current "postmodern moment," in which both "grand theories" and the "concept of the aloof researcher" have been abandoned (pp. 7, 9, 11).

Qualitative research, clearly, has meant and been different things in its different moments. In fact, none of the terms in the story I'm telling stays still for long—which is actually the central story line. I use the broad term *sexualities* here to underline the point that, although the fields to which I refer are largely focused on nonheterosexual, nonconforming sexual statuses, identities, and practices, how those objects of analysis are conceived has changed in important ways: Studying homosexuality or homosexualities is not necessarily the same as studying gays and lesbians or gayness, which is not necessarily the same as studying queers or queerness, which is not necessarily the same as studying society from a queer perspective. *Gay and lesbian studies* and even the more recent *queer studies* have changed meaning, largely through the various political struggles to which these terms have been attached. *Lesbian, bisexual, gay, homosexual,* and *transgender* have all been typically used to capture sexual and gen-

der identities, senses of self that are either inherently stable or stabilized through various social processes; the term *lesbian and gay studies* (and, more recently, *lesbian, gay, bisexual, and transgender studies*) has typically been used to capture the study of these populations. *Queer* has been a more vexed, conflict-ridden and confusing term, both as identity and disciplinary marker (Gamson, 1995). Although it has sometimes been used as a "people of color"-like shorthand for *gay, lesbian, bisexual, and transgender,* a politically volatile expansion of the identity category to include all sorts of sex and gender outsiders, I use it here in its more distinctive sense, as a marker of the instability of identity. *Queer* marks an identity that, defined as it is by a deviation from sex and gender norms either by the self inside or by specific behaviors, is always in flux; *queer theory* and *queer studies* propose a focus not so much on specific populations as on sexual categorization processes and their deconstruction. Each term, that is, comes with its own set of politics.

The Ambivalent Relationship to Positivism

Especially after the growth of the feminist and lesbian and gay movements in the 1960s and 1970s, sexuality studies have been, to begin with, closely allied with a political project of redressing the pathologized and stigmatized status of homosexuals (Adam, 1995). Because, historically, positivist natural and social sciences had been heavily involved in bolstering the notion of homosexuality as illness or deviance or both, much post-Stonewall sexuality study has tended to be ambivalent about, if not openly hostile to, "scientific" approaches to sexuality. The relationship to positivist social research has therefore often been an adversarial one.

The earliest approaches to homosexuality, for instance, conducted primarily by sex researchers trained in medicine and natural sciences, worked from a positivist model, searching for the objective truths of nature that moralizing about sexuality had apparently obscured. Although they often began with a liberalizing intent—to rescue sexuality from the clutches of religion—these studies often began and ended with the assumption that homosexuality is a deviation from the normal; their aim was more often than not to decipher the roots of the pathology (Weeks, 1985). To put it simply, researchers, however liberal, tended to share the taken-for-granted picture of homosexuals as sick, dangerous, or criminal.[1] That homosexuality officially remained a psychiatric disorder until 1973, when it was removed from the American Psychiatric Association's *Diagnostic and Statistical Manual of Mental Disorders* after much struggle, captures the political link between "scientific" study of homosexuality and the stigmatized, pathologized social status of homosexuals (Bayer, 1981).[2] It is no wonder, then, that qualitative approaches—especially those that search for and interpret meaning rather than "facts"—have often seemed more attractive to scholars politically aligned with lesbian and gay movements, because they put some distance between the researcher and the "master's tools."

There has, of course, been a long, effective, and significant tradition of quantitatively oriented scientific research on sexual practices and opinions, much of it focused on same-sex practices, much of which has gone far toward demonstrating the normality and respectability of nonnormative sexualities: from Kinsey in the 1940s and 1950s (Kinsey, Pomeroy, & Martin, 1948; Kinsey, Pomeroy, Martin, & Gebhard, 1953) to Masters and Johnson (1966) in the 1960s and 1970s to the 1990s' massive survey-based *Social Organization of Sexuality* (Laumann, Gagnon, Michael, & Michaels, 1994). The strategy of the Kinsey reports, according to one biographer, for example, "was to shout 'Science!' through an exhaustive accumulation of technical jargon and massed statistics" (Jones, 1997, p. 107). Kinsey's contributions—the notion of a sexual continuum, the revelation of how widespread and typical so-called deviant practices are—revolutionized popular discourse on sexuality by offering "scientific evidence conducive to a reevaluation of conventional moral attitudes" (D'Emilio, 1983, p. 33), with the result that "the extent of premarital sex, adultery, and homosexuality became ac-

ceptable topics of polite conversation" (Jones, 1997, p. 100). Similarly, Evelyn Hooker's (1958) studies comparing the psychological profiles of a sample of homosexual men to their nonhomosexual counterparts helped to "demonstrate empirically the 'normality' of the homosexual" (Nardi & Schneider, 1998, p. 3).

Such myth-bashing studies continue to this day—although now typically conducted by those identifying personally, or aligning politically, with the sexually marginalized. Indeed, especially in the discipline of psychology, and to a lesser degree in political science and economics, social researchers have often attempted to beat heterosexist science at its own game, using the tools and logic of science to bash myths about gay people: studies demonstrating that the children of lesbians and gay men differ very little from those of heterosexuals (e.g., Patterson, 1992, 1995), documenting the extent of antigay or homophobic public opinion in various populations and the prevalence and nature of hate crimes (e.g., Herek, 1989, 1997), or analyzing the economic circumstances of lesbians and gay men (e.g., Badgett, 1995). Tellingly, this is often essentially defensive social research, testing and disconfirming the hypotheses of a homophobic society with "facts." [3] As the mission statement of the Institute for Gay and Lesbian Strategic Studies, an organization "designed to conduct impartial and independent academic research and analysis on public policy issues of critical concern to the gay, lesbian, bisexual and transgender communities," puts it, "It is vital that we produce the unbiased, independent research which will counter [right-wing] lies" (Institute for Gay and Lesbian Strategic Studies, 1998). Even when the natural science model has been taken up by sexuality researchers, that is, it has been informed by the historically problematic relationship between science and lesbian and gay lives.

Another early response to the problematic relationship between sexuality and science was to investigate the "deviants" themselves, in their own space and time, in methodological (and sometimes political) departures. Research on sexualities partook of the tendencies of the "traditional" and "modernist" periods' qualitative work: "Reflective of the positivist scientist paradigm," fieldwork studied "alien, foreign, and strange" others, in "a social science version of literary naturalism" that often "romanticized the subject" (Denzin & Lincoln, 1994, pp. 7, 8). Although moving the researcher much closer to the subjective experience of the participants, such research did not of course suddenly jump from its political environment. Qualitative sociological work on male homosexuality through the early 1970s, for instance, focused largely on stigma management (e.g., Humphreys, 1970; Leznoff & Westley, 1956; Reiss, 1961), studying the homosexual as "part of a deviant sexual underworld of hustlers, prostitutes, prisons, tearooms, baths, and bars" (Seidman, 1996, p. 7). Yet, as Steven Seidman (1996) points out, although "much of this sociology aimed to figure the homosexual as a victim of unjust discrimination," such work "contributed to the public perception of the homosexual as a strange, exotic human type in contrast to the normal, respectable heterosexual" (p. 7). As gay and lesbian movements grew in strength, however, the strange, exotic humans started doing their own research, researching and reporting on themselves, triggering along the way new complications for both sexualities study and qualitative research.

Movements, Minority Research, and Narratives of the Self

In the 1970s and 1980s, taking their cues from feminist-inspired women's studies and civil rights-inspired African American and ethnic studies, scholars developing the new field of lesbian and gay studies (themselves mostly identifying as gay and lesbian) began the still-ongoing task of "uncovering" the "hidden" history of gay and lesbian people, both "reclaiming the gay and lesbian past" (Duberman, Vicinus, & Chauncey, 1989; see also Faderman, 1981; Katz, 1976) and recording the experiential present (e.g., Krieger, 1983; Levine, 1979; Newton, 1972). Much of this took place through conventional historical and ethnographic study, but it was also joined

by, and shared assumptions with, a sort of qualitative reporting that emerged outside of the academy, in which personal narratives and experiential truths were used to reclaim a gay or lesbian subjectivity that had been historically denied (Jay & Young, 1972). The further one went from the white, heterosexual male center, the more one found, in fact, autobiographical work written from the personal standpoint of the marginalized, in classic collections such as *This Bridge Called My Back: Writings by Radical Women of Color* (Moraga & Anzaldúa, 1981).[4]

This politically charged enterprise of "telling our own stories" not only gave qualitative research an extra edge, it came with an implicit epistemological critique of objective scientific research. Like feminist and Afrocentric standpoint theories, which makes the everyday experiences of marginality a ground for theory building (Collins, 1990; Harding, 1987; Smith, 1974), built into the strategies of personal narratives, and the reclaiming of gay and lesbian lives both past and present, was an implication that the experience of the outsider provides a unique outlook on social and political life, that what have been presented as the objective facts of sexuality are instead the subjective view from a heterosexual male standpoint—indeed, ultimately, that all knowledge is socially situated. The drama of such a change cannot be overstated: Lesbians studying lesbians was not only a great political challenge in an environment that had stigmatized lesbians as invisible or ill, but also a more general challenge to qualitative research in which the objectivity of an "outsider" was thought to lend validity, and in which the nonnative researcher retained "the power to represent the subject's story" (Denzin & Lincoln, 1994, p. 8). The lesbian or gay self, given voice through interviews, ethnographies, autobiography, and historical re-creation, while plainly resting on claims of authenticity, gave the lie to objectivity.

These various strands of research and representation also tended to share "essentialist" assumptions about the self, and the collections of selves gathering strength in neighborhoods and institutions after Stonewall, with the relatively new "sexual minority" movement to which they were tied: that whatever their roots, sexual differences are natural variations; that sexual categories are congruent with those natural variations; and that homosexuals therefore constitute a minority much like racial and ethnic minorities. When scholars in the early 1980s, for instance, began uncovering and describing the ins and outs of lesbian and gay life both past and present, *gay* and *lesbian* were typically assumed to describe similar types of individuals and a stable chunk of a population across time and space. As Steven Epstein (1987) has argued, and as John D'Emilio (1983) has documented, models of sexuality as "essence" and of sexual communities as "minorities" were critical political mobilization tools. The ethnic self-characterization running through both the politics and the research of the 1970s and 1980s, Epstein (1987) suggests, "has a clear political utility, for it has permitted a form of group organizing that is particularly suited to the American experience, with its history of civil-rights struggles and ethnic-based, interest-group competition" (p. 20). Research in sexualities developed, that is, not only in the midst of an ambivalent stance toward positivist science, but also in response to the American political tradition of minority group organizing; qualitative research would bring the shared, lived experience of sexual minorities into the spotlight. With an emphasis on the shared characteristics of the authentic lesbian or gay self, this was minority group research.

The Constructionist Turn

Effective and legitimating as these various approaches have been—especially in a political environment filled with myths and stereotypes about nonnormative sexuality and sensitive to the claims of minorities—they have also set pathways for profound challenges to their own assumptions, challenges that have given qualitative research a further significance and centrality. "Assuming the specificity of gay identity and gay experience," as Patricia Clough (1994) puts it, "only opened both to further specification and to the elaboration of their specific historical and cultural constructions, eventually undermining any sense of a uniform gay experience or

a unified gay identity" (p. 143). As the scattershot, multidisciplinary field of sexualities study began to congeal and consolidate, its major "essentialist" premises came quickly under fire. The notion that sexual subjects share a sexual core (an orientation or a preference), that underneath the skin they have the same kind of self, was questioned; shaken along with it was the claim that, being the same sorts of beings, they therefore share a minority status. The related, more general view that there is a "truth" of sexuality provided by nature, and therefore to be investigated along the lines of other natural subjects, a truth beyond the meanings attached socially to sex, bodies, and desire, also began to break apart (on critiques of sexual "essentialism," see Stein, 1992).

Indeed, over time the positivist tradition of sexuality studies has been very much overshadowed by a strategy that rejects the notion that the tools and assumptions of natural science are appropriate for the study of sexuality. Like feminism, from which many activists and some researchers took their cues—and which, in lesbian feminism, was directly tied to lesbian (and gay) politics (Phelan, 1989; Whittier, 1995)—lesbian and gay scholars criticized positivist approaches for mistaking the social order of sexuality for a natural one. These objections had early roots in the work of social researchers within distinctly qualitative fields (symbolic interactionists, phenomenologists, and labeling theorists) who argued for the need to distinguish the social and interactional processes by which bodies and desires are given meaning, are transformed into social categories with political significance and into bases for the sorts of collective action taking strong shape at the time.

Tied to a more general rebellion against positivist social research, the loose field of sexuality studies began to fix itself, from the 1970s onward, in "denaturalizing" gear: Sexuality was not a stable phenomenon of nature to be studied like plants or cells, but a set of meanings attached to bodies and desires by individuals, groups, and societies (Gagnon & Simon, 1973). "Against naturalized conceptions of sexuality as a biological given, against Freudian models of the sexual drive, and against the Kinseyan obsession with the tabulation of behavior," as Steven Epstein (1996) summarizes it, "sociologists asserted that sexual meanings, identities, and categories were intersubjectively negotiated social and historical products—that sexuality was, in a word, constructed" (p. 145). Historians and anthropologists documented the variability of cultural and historical systems of sexual meaning (e.g., Greenberg, 1988; Ortner & Whitehead, 1981) as focus shifted from research about "the homosexual" as a universal entity and oddity to "homosexual" (and later "heterosexual") as a social category and identity that "should itself be analyzed and its relative historical, economic, and political base be scrutinized" (Nardi & Schneider, 1998, p. 4; see also McIntosh, 1968; Plummer, 1981, 1992).

Although often theoretical in orientation, the constructionist approach focused attention on questions particularly suited to qualitative research, with its attempts "to make sense of, or interpret, phenomena in terms of the meanings people bring to them" (Denzin & Lincoln, 1994, p. 2): How do sexual categories get created and challenged, and with what effects? How do same-sex practices relate to identities that are built, or not built, around them? Whereas positivist approaches took sexual categories for granted and investigated those assumed to belong to them (how homosexuals live, the etiology of homosexuality, and so on), students of sexualities began to investigate the politics, history, and sociology of the *categories and identities* themselves; the various "sex/gender systems" (Rubin, 1975) giving meaning to bodies and pleasures became a focal point. In one early study, Barbara Ponse (1978), for instance, used ethnographic methods to explicate "the social construction of identity and its meanings within the lesbian subculture," and many subsequent studies used similar methods for similar purposes. Given the profoundly interpretive nature of the questions asked by a constructionist framework, moreover, qualitative research methods—ethnographic, sociohistorical, and so on—began to establish themselves as the cutting edge.[5] And given the growing antipathy to the "essen-tialist" assumptions about sexuality rooted largely in sexual science, the gap between quantitative and qualitative studies of sexuality widened even more.[6]

At the same time, within the political movements to which many scholars were tied, related category challenges were being raised by those who found themselves defined *out* of the collective identity (working-class people, people of color, sex radicals, and so on). These critiques added to the focus on the problematic construction of sexual identities, to the ongoing critical deconstruction of the homosexual "minority," and to the relationships among race, gender, and sexual identity (e.g., Clarke, 1981; Hemphill, 1991; Seidman, 1993). Who "we" are, these conflicts suggested, is never a given, and is much more complex and multiple than gay minority studies was assuming. In an important precursor to the queer critique, those marginalized *within* the gay scene argued that asserting the primacy of sexuality forced false choices (between an identity as lesbian and as black, for instance) and obscured the important connections among race, gender, ethnicity, sexuality, physical ability, and class.

These movement-driven concerns with exclusion and diversity made their way, gradually, into qualitative research: Tomás Almaguer, for instance, reviewed ethnographic and autobiographical writings to map the ways Chicano male homosexuals negotiated their ways through two distinct sexual systems, a European American one emphasizing the gay-straight axis, and a Mexican/Latin American one organized along the passive-active axis (Almaguer, 1991). Coinciding with a period in which the "boundaries between the social sciences and the humanities had become blurred" (Denzin & Lincoln, 1994, p. 9), moreover, much of the retheorizing of sexual-identities-as-multiple came through the interpretive voices of gay men and lesbians of color working in fields such as film and literary studies, or from outside of the academy (e.g., Harper, 1991; Hemphill, 1991; Trujillo, 1991).

The sociological roots of constructionism and the political roots of multiple-identity arguments met up, of course, with the highly influential work of Michel Foucault (1978), and those influenced by him, from historical studies (e.g., Greenberg, 1988). The forceful entry of Foucault's work both solidified the tie between qualitative research and the study of sexualities and began a new phase in the theorizing of sexual identities. The homosexual was distinguished as a contemporary historical and cultural "invention" made possible by a conflation of acts with identities: In Foucault's (1978) famous statement, whereas sodomy had been a "category of forbidden acts" and temporary aberration, over the course of the "discursive explosion" of the 19th century the homosexual became "a species," "a personage, a past, a case history, a life form" (p. 43).

Foucault's *History of Sexuality* (1978) focused attention more than ever on the social construction of sexual "discourse," reinforced a skepticism about scientific knowledge as progress, and encouraged a renewed questioning of the categories of sexuality still taken for granted by many working within the field. While institutional analyses became somewhat sidelined, the *discourses* through which sexuality became, and continues to be, the "truth of our being"—including the "counterdiscourses" such as minority identity, and especially scientific sex research—now became subject to analysis and deconstruction. With category construction, discourse, meaning creation, and identity work becoming firmly entrenched subjects for investigation, qualitative approaches to sexualities study moved even more to the center of the stage.

Yet that stage was also beginning to be guided by a sort of methodological and epistemological turmoil. The crises of authority and legitimation for qualitative researchers that came to fruition in the late 1980s (see, e.g., Clifford & Marcus, 1986) were also given, in the field of sexualities and elsewhere, a firm push by Foucault, whose critique of methodological practices such as the psychoanalytic case study forcefully suggested that all methods take their place in particular "regimes of truth," and that no knowledge creation is divorced from political relations. Queer theory and queer studies emerged out of this methodologically critical, epistemologically skeptical mix.

◆ "Queer Theory" and the Critique of Identity

As quantitative study of sexuality continued on its own path, albeit increasingly divorced from and eclipsed by qualitative approaches in lesbian and gay studies,[7] research on sexuality entered a new phase in the early 1990s with the emergence of "queer theory." Heavily influenced by poststructuralist theory, emerging primarily from humanities-based cultural studies, and tied somewhat loosely to a confrontational, antinormative "queer" politics, queer theory first began to take shape in a series of late 1980s academic conferences (Epstein, 1996; Gamson, 1995; Stein & Plummer, 1996). Queer theory built on the insights of constructionism and Foucault, but moved poststructuralist and postmodernist concerns to the forefront—critiques of identity and identity politics, an emphasis on discourse and its deconstruction, a suspicion of "grand narratives" (Kellner, 1988; Seidman & Wagner, 1991). With queer theory, the postmodern moment in qualitative inquiry—with its elusive center that "shifts and moves as new, previously oppressed or silenced voices enter the discourse" (Lincoln & Denzin, 1994, p. 575)—arrived full force in sexualities study. Not only the foci of inquiry but also what *counts* as qualitative research were, through a process that continues to be contested, starting to shape-shift.

Queer theory put forth several core changes and challenges, dramatically altering the terrain of qualitative research for those taking the challenges to heart. For one thing, the substantive territory of analysis was broadened: It was not so much the lives or identities of gays and lesbians, or the construction of homosexual identities or minority status, that required attention, but the ways the very homo/hetero distinction underpinned all aspects of contemporary life. "An understanding of virtually any aspect of modern Western culture," wrote Eve Kosovsky Sedgwick, for example, in *Epistemology of the Closet* (1990), generally considered the founding text of queer theory, "must be, not merely incomplete, but damaged in its central substance to the degree that it does not incorporate a critical analysis of modern homo/heterosexual definition" (p. 1).

This was quite a departure from the theory and research that preceded queer theory and made it possible, moving the aim from "explaining the modern homosexual to questions of the operation of the hetero/homosexual binary, from an exclusive preoccupation with homosexuality to a focus on heterosexuality as a social and political organizing principle, and from a politics of minority interest to a politics of knowledge and difference" (Seidman, 1996, p. 9). The deconstruction and criticism of "heteronormativity" in its various forms and guises, of the notion that "humanity and heterosexuality are synonymous" (Warner, 1993, p. xxiii), became a key goal and rallying cry of queer studies.

Queer theory, moreover, often called for theoretical interventions that paralleled the antiassimilationist, in-your-face, antinormative, deconstructive spirit of queer politics (Berlant & Freeman, 1993; Cohen, 1997; Duggan, 1992). As Alexander Doty (1993) puts it, "Queerness should challenge and confuse our understanding and uses of sexual and gender categories" (p. xvii). Just as bisexual and transgender people were being included in the "queer" political category, sharing the status of sex and gender dissidents (Gamson, 1995), for instance, bisexuality and transgenderism became much more central subjects for theory and research, celebrated in queer studies for their capacity to confound sex and gender categories (e.g., Epstein & Straub, 1991; Garber, 1995; Stryker, 1998a). Built into these substantive shifts were epistemological and methodological perspectives that have shaken the ground for qualitative research on sexualities.

Discourse, Language, and Identity

One dynamic set in motion by these changes, not surprisingly, has been a methodological one: Field study of lesbians, gay men,

transsexuals, bisexuals, and so on has consistently been edged out in queer studies by discourse analysis, with literary criticism at the head. Like much qualitative inquiry of the early 1990s more generally, queer theory questions the assumption that lived experience can be captured and directly represented by researchers, and looks instead at the textual and linguistic practices (including the discourse of "social research") through which sexual subjectivity takes shape. As Steven Seidman (1996) explains:

> Queer theorists view heterosexuality and homosexuality not simply as identities or social statuses but as categories of knowledge, a language that frames what we know as bodies, desires, sexualities, identities. This is a normative language as it shapes moral boundaries and political hierarchies. . . . Queer theory is suggesting that the study of homosexuality should not be a study of a minority—the making of the lesbian/gay/bisexual subject—but a study of those knowledges and social practices that organize "society" as a whole by sexualizing—heterosexualizing or homosexualizing—bodies, desires, acts, identities, social relations, knowledges, culture, and social institutions. (pp. 12-13)

It is this study of knowledges, language, and discourse that makes the tools of literary analysis so key for queer theorists. Indeed, as Patricia Clough (1994) points out, for queer theorists, "gender [or sexuality] is not a literal reality, not even a socially constructed reality, but rather a literary reality," and thus theorists such as Judith Butler propose "a new mode of reading the social that collapses the distinction between fantasy and reality, fiction and history, polemic and academic discourse, social science and literary criticism—all figured in the opposition of homosexuality and heterosexuality" (p. 155).

Seen through a "queer" lens, qualitative researchers investigating the "reality" of, say, lesbian and gay experiences of the closet, or of major heterosexist institutions such as the military or schools, tend to appear naïve in their assumptions about "social reality" and their methods for getting at it. Indeed, the poststructuralist collapsing of the social into the literary, and the practice of "reading" the social as text, has often meant an edging out of field research on social behavior, be it individual, collective, or institutional. "To the extent that poststructuralists reduce cultural codes to textual practice," Seidman (1993) argues effectively, "and to the extent that these practices are abstracted from institutional contexts, we come up against the limits of poststructuralism as social critique" (p. 135). Queer theoretical perspectives have begun to redefine what "counts" as qualitative research, with literary techniques taking up territory—although not without strenuous objections (e.g., Plummer, 1998)—previously claimed by empirical social researchers.

Yet if the focus with queer theory moves from the lived experiences of sexuality to "the grammar of culture," the "relationship of language and discourse to power and the production, organization, and circulation of diverse texts and institutions" (Tierney, 1997, pp. 9-10), this is only partially due to the intellectual imperialism of cultural studies. Central to the poststructuralist turn in sexuality studies is a profound and well-articulated skepticism about the existence of social subjects who preexist their discursive constitution, whose "experience" can simply be studied and represented. Underlying the focus on knowledge, language, sexualizing, and so on is a core objection by queer theory to "the dominant foundational concept of both homophobic and affirmative homosexual theory: the assumption of a unified homosexual identity" (Seidman, 1996, p. 11).

The critique of identity runs throughout queer theoretical writings: Identities are multiple, contradictory, fragmented, incoherent, disciplinary, disunified, unstable, fluid—hardly the stuff that allows a researcher to confidently run out and study sexual subjects as if they are coherent and available social types. "I'm permanently troubled by identity categories," says Judith Butler (1991), for instance, "consider them to be invariable stumbling-blocks, and understand them, even promote them, as sites of necessary trouble" (p. 14). Identity is, she argues, a "necessary error" (Butler, 1993, p. 21). Queer theorists, Shane Phelan (1993) suggests, "while retaining *lesbian* as a meaningful category," have "worked against reification of lesbians, toward views of lesbianism as a *critical site of gen-*

der deconstruction rather than as a unitary experience with a singular political meaning" (p. 766). Michael Warner (1993) notes:

> A lesbian and gay population is defined by multiple boundaries that make the question of who is and is not "one of them" not merely ambiguous but rather a perpetually and necessarily contested issue. Identity as a lesbian or gay is ambiguously given and chosen, in some ways the product of the performative act of coming out. . . . "Queer" therefore also suggests the difficulty in defining the population whose interests are at stake in queer politics. (pp. xxv-xxvi)

Identity, that is, cannot be taken as a starting point for social research, can never be assumed by a researcher to be standing still, ready for its close-up.

In fact, according to the poststructuralist queer critique, the subject does not precede his or her recognition as a subject, but is created through discursive processes—such as social research—and the continual bodily repetition, or "performance," of gender and sexuality. Butler (1993) writes:

> The discursive condition of social recognition *precedes and conditions* the formation of the subject: recognition is not conferred on a subject, but forms that subject. Further, the impossibility of a full recognition, that is, of ever fully inhabiting the name by which one's social identity is inaugurated and mobilized, implies the instability and incompleteness of subject-formation. (p. 18)

Thus, as Ken Plummer (1992) puts it a bit more simply, "there is no essential object of study . . . gay and lesbian studies 'construct' an object for analysis that is itself much more diffuse, fragmented, overlapping, and multiple: it forces a unity that does not exist" (p. 11).[8] The forms of agency and subjectivity that had been assumed by earlier sexualities research, then, are shot full of holes by the queer theoretical "refusal to name a subject" (Seidman, 1993, p. 132). This is not, of course, unique to the study of sexuality—feminist scholars and activists, for instance, have been working through such issues for years (Nicholson, 1990; Spelman, 1989)—but it is acutely present in queer studies.

The rise of queer studies has been, not surprisingly, filled with conflict, much of it focused on what Ken Plummer (1998) has called "the overtextualization of lesbian and gay experiences," in which "analyses of discourse overtake the analysis of real world events." As he writes:

> There are important studies to be done in the empirical world, and an obsession with texts is dangerous indeed. It is time to move beyond the text—and rapidly. Whilst lesbian and gay studies "plays" more and more fancifully with a wide array of poems, novels, and films, relatively little research actually exists on what is going on in lesbian and gay worlds right now. (p. 611)

Plummer may overstate the case. In fact, plenty of research continues on gay and lesbian lives that is not "queer" in the sense I have been using the term, work that is untouched by or simply rejects the poststructuralist identity critique: studies on the experiences of gay men in corporations (Woods & Lucas, 1994), on sexual diversity in Native American cultures (Williams, 1992), on media coverage of lesbians and gays (Alwood, 1996), on the experiences of lesbian and gay youth (Herdt & Boxer, 1993), to name just a few. That such work continues testifies not simply to disciplinary division, but to an important and ongoing struggle over what qualitative inquiry into sexualities can and should look like, especially given the undeniable experience of political and social marginalization, institutionalized heterosexism, and antigay mobilizations to which lesbian and gay people are subject. Whatever the complexities of identity this work points up, the societies and institutions in which gay, lesbian, bisexual, and transgender subjects live their lives seem to have no difficulty recognizing and targeting them.

Yet while the direction of the qualitative sexualities study is far from settled, the issues raised by queer approaches, and the turmoil they provoke over the study of "lived experience," have become increasingly difficult to shake. Just as sexuality studies was establishing itself, it began to take itself apart. The qualitative focus especially, given its own twist by queer theory, has wound up twisting and turning on the wrenches thrown into it. The queer theoretical challenge to the unified subject creates epistemological difficulties that translate into methodological ones. If lived experiences of "the social" are always constituted by systems of discourse, then to study such experiences as *experiences* rather than narratives, or to report on them autobiographically as though reporting were a direct translation of reality, is hopelessly distorted. If the idea of an autonomous, gendered self is a "literary reality" produced by "heteronormativity," a fiction of sorts that exists only in a series of ongoing bodily performances, taking such a self as a basis for research naïvely reproduces rather than interrupts the workings of heteronormativity. If "gay" and "lesbian" are provisional, discursively produced, unstable, performative, and decidedly partial identities—if they are forever in quotation marks— how does one go about studying sexuality and sexually identified populations? Even taking normative discourse as the object of analysis, how does one study its operation when one is, by definition, not "outside" of it? On what grounds does a researcher or author, herself a discursively created subject, himself available for textual deconstruction, wage a critique of normatively constructed sexuality? What's a researcher to do?

◆ Shared Challenges for Qualitative Inquiry

The strands of research and theory I have recounted—lesbian and gay minority studies, constructionist sexualities research, queer theory—coexist in considerable tension within sexualities study, with their differently constituted objects of study, their different disciplinary roots, their different rules of evidence, and their different assumptions about the intellectual and political utility of identity categories. Although they often share a profoundly qualitative focus on meaning construction and a concern for the relationship between research and the politics of sexuality, each has had somewhat different implications for the sort of research that can and should be done. Taken together, however, they both intentionally and inadvertently pose significant theoretical and substantive challenges to researchers.

The Substantive Challenge of Queer Inclusion in Qualitative Research

Like other fields with origins in identity-based movements, lesbian and gay studies, and especially queer theory, have waged systematic challenges to the research agendas of more traditional fields of scholarship. If "the closet" is indeed a central organizing feature of Western thought and practices, all investigations, as Sedgwick has suggested, must arguably consider it. Thus a primary substantive challenge currently issuing to and from the field of sexuality studies is not simply to "include" gay and lesbian subjects in research areas that have rendered them invisible, but even more fundamentally to uncover the ways *any* social arena (including, of course, the production of social scientific knowledge) is structured in part by the homo/hetero dichotomy. There is great productive promise for new topics of qualitative research as this charge is asserted and absorbed.

Thus far, the action has rarely taken place through empirical work; it is happening instead through a tracing out of the reconceptualizations that queer thinking implies, but such rethinking has also begun to trigger new research directions. Lisa Duggan (1998), for instance, has argued for "queering the state" through strategies that "work to destabilize heteronormativity rather than to naturalize gay identities" (p. 570), and legal scholars, political scientists, and sociologists have begun to investigate the ways the state in fact depends on intersecting racial, sexual, and gender codes (Alexander, 1991; Eaton, 1994), revealing the state's heteronormativity through detailed deconstruction of its legal discourse (e.g., Duggan & Hunter, 1995, pt. II). Similar substantive direc-

tions can be expected as other social processes and institutions are subjected to an analysis that asks not just how gay men, lesbians, bisexuals, and transgendered people fit into this picture but how particular institution's work to heterosexualize and gender, and with what material effects.[9] This remains a question for which qualitative research and analysis are particularly suited.

The Deconstruction of Unified Subjects

Queer theory undercuts earlier notions of an autonomous, coherent self (and collection of selves) defined by gender and desire, raising, as we have seen, epistemological and methodological questions that make trouble for research and writing on sexualities. Although many of these questions will remain, perhaps healthfully, in the air for a good long time, researchers have begun to take these complexities of identity into account as they go about their work. One strategy is to build on the long-standing tradition of making identity itself the focus of research while integrating the instability, multiplicity, and partiality of identities into the research program and analysis. Sociologist Arlene Stein, for instance, based her *Sex and Sensibility* (1997) on "self stories"—that is, interviews in which women told stories "of and about the self in relation to an experience, in this case the development of a lesbian identity, that positions the self of the teller centrally in the narrative" (p. 7). The queer influence is embedded in this formulation of the research project: Stein's is not a study of the ways a "true self" gets revealed, but of the ever-changing stories that get told as people conduct "identity work." It takes into account "the permanently unsettled nature of identities and group boundaries," as Stein puts it, "a decentered model of identity [that] mirrors the decentering of lesbian culture and communities" (p. 201). Indeed, the booming interest in bisexual and transgender lives and identities is driven by a similar agenda, the analysis of confounding identities—in the words of Susan Stryker (1998b), their promise of "a profound destabilization of naturalized heteronormative configurations of gender, embodiment, and identity" (p. 145).

In another related vein, researchers on sexuality-based social movements have been among those at the forefront of making "collective identity" the subject of empirical and theoretical revision. Rather than assuming a group "we-ness" that preexists social movement action, researchers have investigated the ways group boundaries, interests, and consciousness are established and negotiated (Phelan, 1989; Taylor & Whittier, 1992). Queerness here becomes both a topic and a resource for investigating logics of collective action. In an article on debates over "queerness," for instance, I myself have argued:

> Queerness spotlights a dilemma shared by other identity movements (racial, ethnic, and gender movements, for example): Fixed identity categories are both the basis for oppression and the basis for political power. . . . If identities are indeed much more unstable, fluid, and constructed than movements have tended to assume—if one takes the queer challenge seriously, that is—what happens to identity-based social movements such as gay and lesbian rights? . . . The case of queerness . . . calls for a more developed theory of collective identity formation and its relationship to both institutions and meanings, an understanding that *includes the impulse to take apart the identity from within.* (Gamson, 1995, p. 391)

Taking queer critiques of identity seriously pushed forward for me a different set of investigations—necessarily qualitative ones, because they involve everyday identity work: how, when and why collective identity gets deconstructed as well as solidified, how collective identity is shaped by specific organizational exigencies and communication environments (Gamson, 1996, 1997).

Although these studies remain relatively conventional in their data collection and representational strategies, social researchers have begun to take queer problematizing of representation to heart as well. Although the older tradition of autobiographical writing as both political act and representation of an authentic sexual self continues, in queer qualitative texts the researcher's authoritative voice is increasingly positioned as one among many competing, partial voices—none and all of them "authentic." The notion that a gay ethnography is "one in which the identity of the ethnographer as a lesbian or as a gay man is an explicit and integral part of the text" (Wafer, 1996, p. 261) does not sit easily with poststructuralist notions that such an identity is neither unitary nor stable; in its place, increasingly, is "a growing focus in lesbian [and gay] ethnography on the permeability of both communities and identities and on our Hexpanding awareness of the instability of identity, particularly in complex cultural settings" (Lewin, 1995, p. 327). Ethnographic research, rather than being a site for the revelation of identity, is redefined as "yet another context for defining identity" with and against the various others (however they are defining themselves) in the field (Lewin, 1995, p. 332).

Kath Weston's *Render Me, Gender Me* (1996), for instance, uses a mix of personal narratives to represent what could be called a queer take on the gendering process. "Anything and anybody can be gendered in a variety of ways," Weston writes; the point of placing same-sex relationships at the center is not to make lesbians more visible, as it was in earlier studies, but to make "the modes of gendering more obvious" (pp. 2-3). Importantly, doing so also involves a more experimental strategy of representation, in which the author's voice and the author's version of lesbian identity are not privileged. Thus Weston brings together long passages from interviews with a variety of lesbian-identified women—teachers, writers, factory workers, nurses, artists, strippers, women from all sorts of racial, class, and religious backgrounds—with her own analytic observations. This is a textual strategy informed by queer thinking. "Representations," Weston asserts, "do not do a very good job of depicting the specific people assigned to cultural categories" (p. 4). Her book is designed to make that explicit, and accordingly to invite a different reading strategy:

> I have deliberately edited and organized [the] interviews to call into question the concept of identity. Lesbians who consistently named themselves "androgynous" or "butch" or "femme" appear alongside lesbians who used these terms sparingly or not at all. This strategic juxtaposition shifts oral history away from chronology toward montage in order to disrupt cultural assumptions about what makes women women, lesbians women, and gay women gay. The back-and-forth movement between interview and commentary . . . opens a space for you, the reader, to gender yourself alternately as storyteller, anthropologist, traveling companion, theorist, voyeur . . . [and] to walk the fine line that weaves difference together with desire. (p. 5)

Although such a representational strategy remains rare, it makes very plain the potential impact on qualitative research reporting that serious considerations of queer identity critiques can provoke.

Researching and Theorizing the Institutions-Discourse Relationship

The final and perhaps most productive challenge comes not from queer theory and gay and lesbian studies themselves, but from the differences between them and the growing attempts to reconcile them. "In both defenders of identity politics and its poststructural critics," Steven Seidman (1993) has argued, "there is a preoccupation with the self and the politics of representation. Institutional and historical analysis and an integrative political vision seems to have dropped out." He urges "a shift away from the preoccupation with self and representations characteristic of identity politics and poststructuralism to an analysis that embeds the self in institutional and cultural practices" (pp. 136-137). Or, put somewhat differently: Whereas lesbian and gay studies, including its more sophisticated constructionist versions rooted in sociology, has underplayed the *discursive,* queer

theory, with its heavy, humanities-driven analysis on social-life-as-text, has underplayed the *institutional.* The *relationship* between the institutional and the discursive (a strong tension within political activism as well; see Gamson, 1995) is therefore itself undertheorized and underresearched. This predicament has been exacerbated by a disciplinary divide between social researchers (often more attuned to institutional forces) and humanities scholars (often more attuned to the dynamics of discourse), and between empirical work and theoretical work—divisions that are only beginning to be bridged in the field.

The complex tension between institutionally oriented qualitative analysis of lesbian and gay studies and the discursively oriented queer theory, however, can and should itself be a resource for important new directions in qualitative research. There is much at stake here, not just for research and theory but for everyday politics: Collective action, be it organizing for protection against discrimination (or for benefits) on the base of existing social categories of "gay" and "lesbian" and "bisexual" and "transsexual" or challenging the boundaries and utility of those categories through cultural interventions, requires sophisticated inquiry into the simultaneous, and linked, processes by which the experiences of sexual desire are given institutional, textual, and experiential shape. In the coming years, qualitative social researchers have a critical role to play in closing the angst-ridden, politically volatile gaps between different qualitative pursuits, not by choosing between text and experience, or between discourse and institution, not by settling the necessary competition between queer fluidity and gay solidity, but by transforming the tensions on which sexuality studies has been built into new sources of productivity.

■ Notes

1. This is actually an important way in which the terms of oppression for homosexuals dif-

fered from those of other marginalized groups: Although women, for instance, were stereotyped in various ways (for example, as having a propensity for hysteria), the status of female was not itself seen as an illness or as abnormal; although racist research treated African Americans as inferior in a variety of ways (including a propensity for criminality), the status of black was not itself seen as criminal or in need of a cure.

2. This association, Jeffrey Weeks (1985) argues, has been a constant in sexual science: "In the rush to protect themselves, many sexologists have become little more than propagandists of the sexual norm, whatever it is at any particular time. The call upon science then becomes little more than a gesture to legitimize interventions governed largely by specific relations of power. The production of a body of knowledge that is apparently scientifically neutral (about women, about sexual variants, delinquents or offenders) can become a resource for utilization in the production of normative definitions that limit and demarcate erotic behavior" (p. 79).

3. These studies have been especially good at directing attention toward institutionalized heterosexism and homophobia, providing an institutional focus that, as we will see, has gotten somewhat lost as qualitative research has become more prominent.

4. It is interesting to note that as the budding bisexual movement took shape in the 1980s, much of the writing by bisexuals and about bisexuality used the same strategy of personal narrative. See, for example, Hutchins and Ka'ahumanu (1990).

5. Constructionist thought and work, despite its challenges to the assumptions of "essentialism," also partook of the minority building of the 1980s; while historicizing the process by which "the homosexual" was created, for instance, and rejecting the notion of a universal homosexual subject, the study of "the social factors that produced a homosexual identity which functioned as the foundation for homosexuals as a new ethnic minority" also "legitimated a model of lesbian and gay subcultures as ethnic-like minorities" (Seidman, 1996, p. 9).

6. Much has been written on the "essentialist-constructionist" debate (Stein, 1992),

and I will not belabor it here. It is worth noting, however, that although essentialism and constructionism do not line up neatly with quantitative and qualitative methods, constructionist conceptualizations of sexuality do tend to favor qualitative approaches, and essentialist conceptualizations are often more closely aligned with positivist science, as in the search for the biological roots of homosexuality (Burr, 1996).

7. The divorce is at times quite extreme, so much so that a 1995 Social Science Research Council report on sexuality research in the social and behavioral sciences could call for a "much-needed framework" of "sexual behaviors in the context of society and culture" and for recognizing that "sexuality is not a series of individual, episodic behaviors linked to specific acts and the physical body, but represents a range of sexual activities and norms, whose meaning and significance for both the individual and society change over time" (di Mauro, 1995, pp. 4-5)—that is, could treat as novel the very assumptions of most qualitative research on sexuality of the past two decades.

8. As Plummer (1992) notes, the elusiveness of the object of analysis is embedded in the constructionist arguments that preceded and fed into queer theory; also, queer theory makes explicit and problematizes the role of lesbian and gay studies itself, among other practices, in the construction of a false unity of "lesbian and gay" subjects.

9. For an example of this approach applied to entertainment media, see *Freaks Talk Back: Tabloid Talk Shows and Sexual Nonconformity* (Gamson, 1998).

■ References

Adam, B. (1995). *The growth of a gay and lesbian movement* (2nd ed.). Boston: Twayne.

Alexander, J. (1991). Redrafting morality: The postcolonial state and the Sexual Offences Bill of Trinidad and Tobago. In C. T. Mohanty, A. Russo, & L. Torres (Eds.), *Third World women and the politics of feminism* (pp. 133-152). Bloomington: Indiana University Press.

Almaguer, T. (1991). Chicano men: A cartography of homosexual identity and behavior. *differences, 3,* 75-100.

Alwood, E. (1996). *Straight news: Gays, lesbians, and the news media.* New York: Columbia University Press.

Badgett, M. V. L. (1995). The wage effects of sexual orientation discrimination. *Industrial and Labor Relations Review, 48*(4).

Bayer, R. (1981). *Homosexuality and American psychiatry.* New York: Basic Books.

Berlant, L., & Freeman, E. (1993). Queer nationality. In M. Warner (Ed.), *Fear of a queer planet: Queer politics and social theory* (pp. 193-229). Minneapolis: University of Minnesota Press.

Burr, C. (1996). *A separate creation: The search for the biological origins of sexual orientation.* New York: Hyperion.

Butler, J. (1991). Imitation and gender insubordination. In D. Fuss (Ed.), *Inside/out: Lesbian theories, gay theories* (pp. 13-31). New York: Routledge.

Butler, J. (1993). Critically queer. *GLQ, 1,* 17-32.

Clarke, C. (1981). Lesbianism: An act of resistance. In C. Moraga & G. Anzaldúa (Eds.), *This bridge called my back: Writings by radical women of color* (pp. 128-137). New York: Kitchen Table/Women of Color Press.

Clifford, J., & Marcus, G. E. (Eds.). (1986). *Writing culture: The poetics and politics of ethnography.* Berkeley: University of California Press.

Clough, P. T. (1994). *Feminist thought: Desire, power and academic discourse.* Cambridge, MA: Blackwell.

Cohen, C. (1997). Punks, bulldaggers, and welfare queens: The radical potential of queer politics? *GLQ, 3,* 437-465.

Collins, P. H. (1990). *Black feminist thought: Knowledge, consciousness, and the politics of empowerment.* New York: Routledge, Chapman & Hall.

D'Emilio, J. (1983). *Sexual politics, sexual communities.* Chicago: University of Chicago Press.

Denzin, N. K., & Lincoln, Y. S. (1994). Introduction: Entering the field of qualitative research. In N. K. Denzin & Y. S. Lincoln (Eds.), *Handbook of qualitative research* (pp. 1-22). Thousand Oaks, CA: Sage.

di Mauro, D. (1995). *Sexuality research in the United States: An assessment of the social and behavioral sciences* (Executive summary). New York: Social Science Research Council.

Doty, A. (1993). *Making things perfectly queer: Interpreting mass culture.* Minneapolis: University of Minnesota Press.

Duberman, M., Vicinus, M., & Chauncey, G. (Eds.). (1989). *Hidden from history: Reclaiming the gay and lesbian past.* New York: Penguin.

Duggan, L. (1992). Making it perfectly queer. *Socialist Review, 22,* 11-32.

Duggan, L. (1998). Queering the state. In P. M. Nardi & B. E. Schneider (Eds.), *Social perspectives in lesbian and gay studies* (pp. 564-572). London: Routledge.

Duggan, L., & Hunter, N. D. (1995). *Sex wars: Sexual dissent and political culture.* New York: Routledge.

Eaton, M. (1994). Homosexual unmodified: Speculations on law's discourse, race, and the construction of sexual identity. In D. Herman & C. Stychin (Eds.), *Legal inversions: Lesbians, gay men, and the politics of law* (pp. 46-73). Philadelphia: Temple University Press.

Epstein, J., & Straub, K. (Eds.). (1991). *Body guards: The cultural politics of gender ambiguity.* New York: Routledge.

Epstein, S. (1987). Gay politics, ethnic identity: The limits of social constructionism. *Socialist Review, 93/94,* 9-54.

Epstein, S. (1996). A queer encounter: Sociology and the study of sexuality. In S. Seidman (Ed.), *Queer theory/sociology* (pp. 145-167). Cambridge, MA: Blackwell.

Faderman, L. (1981). *Surpassing the love of men: Romantic friendship and love between women from the Renaissance to the present.* New York: William Morrow.

Foucault, M. (1978). *The history of sexuality: Vol. 1. An introduction* (R. Hurley, Trans.). New York: Vintage.

Gagnon, J., & Simon, W. (1973). *Sexual conduct.* Chicago: University of Chicago Press.

Gamson, J. (1995). Must identity movements self-destruct? A queer dilemma. *Social Problems, 42,* 390-407.

Gamson, J. (1996). The organizational shaping of collective identity: The case of lesbian and gay film festivals in New York. *Sociological Forum, 11,* 231-262.

Gamson, J. (1997). Messages of exclusion: Gender, movements, and symbolic boundaries. *Gender & Society, 11,* 178-199.

Gamson, J. (1998). *Freaks talk back: Tabloid talk shows and sexual nonconformity.* Chicago: University of Chicago Press.

Garber, M. (1995). *Vice versa: Bisexuality and the eroticism of everyday life.* New York: Simon & Schuster.

Greenberg, D. (1988). *The construction of homosexuality.* Chicago: University of Chicago Press.

Harding, S. (1987). Conclusion: Epistemological questions. In S. Harding (Ed.), *Feminism and methodology: Social science issues* (pp. 181-190). Bloomington: Indiana University Press.

Harper, P. B. (1991). Eloquence and epitaph: Black nationalism and the homophobic impulse in responses to the death of Max Robinson. *Social Text, 28*(9), 68-86.

Hemphill, E. (Ed.). (1991). *Brother to brother: New writings by black gay men.* Boston: Alyson.

Herdt, G. H., & Boxer, A. M. (1993). *Children of Horizons: How gay and lesbian teens are leading a new way out of the closet.* Boston: Beacon.

Herek, G. M. (1989). Hate crimes against lesbians and gay men. *American Psychologist, 44,* 948-955.

Herek, G. M. (1997). Heterosexuals' attitudes towards lesbians and gay men. In M. Duberman (Ed.), *A queer world: The Center for Lesbian and Gay Studies reader* (pp. 331-344). New York: New York University Press.

Hooker, E. (1958). Male homosexuality in the Rorschach. *Journal of Projective Techniques, 22,* 33-54.

Humphreys, L. (1970). *Tearoom trade: Impersonal sex in public places.* Chicago: Aldine.

Hutchins, L., & Ka'ahumanu, L. (Eds.). (1990). *Bi any other name: Bisexual people speak out.* Boston: Alyson.

Institute for Gay and Lesbian Strategic Studies. (1998). Mission statement [On-line]. Available Internet: http://www.iglss.org

Jay, K., & Young, A. (Eds.). (1972). *Out of the closets: Voices of gay liberation.* New York: Harcourt Brace Jovanovich.

Jones, J. H. (1997, August 25-September 1). Dr. Yes. *New Yorker,* pp. 98-113.

Katz, J. N. (1976). *Gay American history.* New York: Thomas Y. Crowell.

Kellner, D. (1988). Postmodernism as social theory: Some challenges and problems. *Theory, Culture & Society, 5,* 239-269.

Kinsey, A. C., Pomeroy, W. B., & Martin, C. E. (1948). *Sexual behavior in the human male.* Philadelphia: W. B. Saunders.

Kinsey, A. C., Pomeroy, W. B., Martin, C. E., & Gebhard, P. (1953). *Sexual behavior in the human female.* Philadelphia: W. B. Saunders.

Krieger, S. (1983). *The mirror dance: Identity in a women's community.* Philadelphia: Temple University Press.

Laumann, E. O., Gagnon, J. H., Michael, R. T., & Michaels, S. (1994). *The social organization of sexuality: Sexual practices in the United States.* Chicago: University of Chicago Press.

Levine, M. (1979). Gay ghetto. *Journal of Homosexuality, 4,* 363-377.

Lewin, E. (1995). Writing lesbian ethnography. In R. Behar & D. A. Gordon (Eds.), *Women writing culture* (pp. 322-335). Berkeley: University of California Press.

Leznoff, M., & Westley, W. A. (1956). The homosexual community. *Social Problems, 3,* 257-263.

Lincoln, Y. S., & Denzin, N. K. (1994). The fifth moment. In N. K. Denzin & Y. S. Lincoln (Eds.), *Handbook of qualitative research* (pp. 575-586). Thousand Oaks, CA: Sage.

Masters, W., & Johnson, V. (1966). *Human sexual response.* Boston: Little, Brown.

McIntosh, M. (1968). The homosexual role. *Social Problems, 16,* 182-192.

Moraga, C., & Anzaldúa, G. (Eds.). (1981). *This bridge called my back: Writings by radical women of color.* New York: Kitchen Table/ Women of Color Press.

Nardi, P. M., & Schneider, B. E. (1998). Looking: The sociological baselines [Part introduction]. In P. M. Nardi & B. E. Schneider (Eds.), *Social perspectives in lesbian and gay studies* (pp. 3-4). London: Routledge.

Newton, E. (1972). *Mother camp*. Chicago: University of Chicago Press.

Nicholson, L. (Ed.). (1990). *Feminism/postmodernism*. New York: Routledge.

Ortner, S., & Whitehead, H. (Eds.). (1981). *Sexual meanings: The cultural construction of gender and sexuality*. Cambridge: Cambridge University Press.

Patterson, C. (1992). Children of lesbian and gay parents. *Child Development, 63*, 1025-1043.

Patterson, C. (1995). Families of the lesbian baby boom: Parents' division of labor and children's adjustment. *Developmental Psychology, 31*, 115-124.

Phelan, S. (1989). *Identity politics: Lesbian feminism and the limits of community*. Philadelphia: Temple University Press.

Phelan, S. (1993). (Be)coming out: Lesbian identity and politics. *Signs, 18*, 765-790.

Plummer, K. (1981). Homosexual categories: Some research problems in the labelling perspective of homosexuality. In K. Plummer (Ed.), *The making of the modern homosexual* (pp. 53-75). London: Hutchinson.

Plummer, K. (1992). Speaking its name: Inventing a lesbian and gay studies. In K. Plummer (Ed.), *Modern homosexualities: Fragments of a lesbian and gay experience* (pp. 3-25). London: Routledge.

Plummer, K. (1998). Afterword: The past, present, and futures of the sociology of same-sex relations. In P. M. Nardi & B. E. Schneider (Eds.), *Social perspectives in lesbian and gay studies* (pp. 605-614). London: Routledge.

Ponse, B. (1978). *Identities in the lesbian world: The social construction of self*. Westport, CT: Greenwood.

Reiss, A. J. (1961). The social integration of queers and peers. *Social Problems, 9*, 102-120.

Rubin, G. (1975). The traffic in women. In R. Reiter (Ed.), *Toward an anthropology of women* (pp. 157-210). New York: Monthly Review Press.

Sedgwick, E. K. (1990). *Epistemology of the closet*. Berkeley: University of California Press.

Seidman, S. (1993). Identity and politics in a "postmodern" gay culture: Some historical and conceptual notes. In M. Warner (Ed.), *Fear of a queer planet: Queer politics and social theory* (pp. 105-142). Minneapolis: University of Minnesota Press.

Seidman, S. (1996). Introduction. In S. Seidman (Ed.), *Queer theory/sociology* (pp. 1-29). Cambridge, MA: Blackwell.

Seidman, S., & Wagner, D. (Eds.). (1991). *Postmodernism and social theory*. New York: Blackwell.

Smith, D. E. (1974). Women's perspective as a radical critique of sociology. *Sociological Inquiry, 4*, 1-13.

Spelman, E. V. (1989). *Inessential woman: Problems of exclusion in feminist thought*. Boston: Beacon.

Stein, A. (1997). *Sex and sensibility: Stories of a lesbian generation*. Berkeley: University of California Press.

Stein, A., & Plummer, K. (1996). "I can't even think straight": "Queer" theory and the missing sexual revolution in sociology. In S. Seidman (Ed.), *Queer theory/sociology* (pp. 129-144). Cambridge, MA: Blackwell.

Stein, E. (Ed.). (1992). *Forms of desire: Sexual orientation and the social constructionist controversy*. New York: Routledge.

Stryker, S. (Ed.). (1998a). The transgender issue [Special issue]. *GLQ, 4*(2).

Stryker, S. (1998b). The transgender issue: An introduction. *GLQ, 4*, 145-158.

Taylor, V., & Whittier, N. (1992). Collective identity in social movement communities: Lesbian feminist mobilization. In A. Morris & C. Mueller (Eds.), *Frontiers in social movement theory* (pp. 104-129). New Haven, CT: Yale University Press.

Tierney, W. G. (1997). *Academic outlaws: Queer theory and cultural studies in the academy*. Thousand Oaks, CA: Sage.

Trujillo, C. (Ed.). (1991). *Chicana lesbians: The girls our mothers warned us about*. Berkeley, CA: Third Woman.

Wafer, J. (1996). Out of the closet and into print: Sexual identity in the textual field. In E. Lewin & W. L. Leap (Eds.), *Out in the field: Reflections of lesbian and gay anthropologists* (pp. 261-273). Urbana: University of Illinois Press.

Warner, M. (1993). Introduction. In M. Warner (Ed.), *Fear of a queer planet: Queer politics and social theory* (pp. vii-xxxi). Minneapolis: University of Minnesota Press.

Weeks, J. (1985). *Sexuality and its discontents.* New York: Routledge.

Weston, K. (1996). *Render me, gender me: Lesbians talk sex, class, color, nation, studmuffins . . . .* New York: Columbia University Press.

Whittier, N. (1995). *Feminist generations: The persistence of the radical women's movement.* Philadelphia: Temple University Press.

Williams, W. (1992). *The spirit and the flesh: Sexual diversity in American Indian culture.* Boston: Beacon.

Woods, J. D., & Lucas, J. H. (1994). *The corporate closet: The professional lives of gay men in America.* New York: Free Press.

Part III

STRATEGIES
OF INQUIRY

C ivic-minded qualitative researchers think historically, interactionally, and structurally. They attempt to identify the many persuasions, prejudices, and cultural motifs, and the varieties of men and women who prevail, in a given historical period (Mills, 1959, p. 7). Such scholars seek to examine the major public and private issues and personal troubles that define a particular historical moment. In so doing, qualitative researchers self-consciously draw upon their own experience as a resource in such inquiries. They always think reflectively and historically as well as biographically. They seek strategies of empirical inquiry that will allow them to make connections among lived experience, larger social and cultural structures, and the here and now. These connections are forged out of the interpretations and empirical materials generated in any given inquiry.

Empirical inquiry, of course, is shaped by paradigm commitments and by the recurring questions that any given paradigm or interpretive perspective asks about human experience, social structure, and culture. More deeply, however, qualitative researchers always ask how the practices of qualitative inquiry can be used to help create a free democratic society. Critical theorists, for example, examine the material conditions and systems of ideologies that reproduce class and economic structures. Queer, constructivist, cultural studies, critical race, and feminist researchers examine the stereotypes, prejudices, and injustices connected to race, ethnicity, and gender. There is no such thing as value-free inquiry, and in qualitative research this premise is presented with clarity. Such clarity permits the value commitments of researchers to be transparent.

The researcher-as-interpretive-*bricoleur* is always already in the material world of values and empirical experience. This world is confronted and constituted through the lens that the scholar's paradigm or interpretive perspective provides. The world so conceived ratifies the individual's commitment to the paradigm or perspective in question. This paradigm is connected at a higher ethical level to the values and politics of an emancipatory, civic social science.

As researchers plan and carry out specific investigations, they must immediately confront two issues: research design and choice of strategy of inquiry.[1] We take these up in order below. Each devolves into a variety of related questions and issues that must also be addressed.

◆ *Research Design*

The research design, as we discuss in our introduction to this *Handbook,* and as Janesick and Cheek note in their contributions to Part III, situates the investigator in the world of experience.[2] Five basic questions structure the issue of design: (a) How will the design connect to the paradigm or perspective being used? That is, how will empirical materials be informed by and interact with the paradigm in question? (b) How will these materials allow the researcher to speak to the problems of praxis and change? (c) Who or what will be studied? (d) What strategies of inquiry will be used? (e) What methods or research tools will be used for collecting and analyzing empirical materials? (These questions are examined in detail in Part IV.)

Paradigm, Perspective, and Metaphor

The positivist, postpositivist, constructionist, and critical paradigms dictate, with varying degrees of freedom, the design of a qualitative research investigation. This can be viewed as a continuum moving from rigorous design principles on one end to emergent, less well-structured directives on the other. Positivist research designs place a premium on the early identification and development of a research question, a set of hypotheses, a research site, and a statement concerning sampling strategies as well as a specification of the research strategies and methods of analysis that will be employed. A research proposal may be written, laying out the stages and phases of the study. In interpretive research, a priori design commitments may block the introduction of new understandings. Consequently, although qualitative researchers may design procedures beforehand, designs should always have built-in flexibility to allow for discoveries of new and unexpected empirical materials and growing sophistication.

The stages of research design can be conceptualized as involving reflection, planning, entry, data collection, withdrawal from the field, analysis, and write-up. As Julianne Cheek observes in Chapter 14, the degree of detail involved in the research proposal will vary depending on the funding agency. Funding agencies fall into at least six categories: local community funding units, special-purpose agencies, family-sponsored agencies, corporate foundations, national foundations, and federal government agencies. The proposal may include a budget, a review of the relevant literature, a statement concerning human subjects protection, a copy of consent forms, interview schedules, and a timeline. Positivist designs attempt to anticipate all of the problems that may arise in a qualitative study (whereas interpretivist designs do not). Such designs provide rather well defined road maps for the researcher. The scholar working in this tradition hopes to produce a work that will find its place in the literature on the topic being studied.

In contrast, much greater ambiguity and flexibility are associated with postpositivist and nonpositivist designs—those based, for example, on the constructivist or critical theory paradigms, or the critical race, feminist, queer, or cultural studies perspectives. In studies shaped by these paradigms and perspectives there is less emphasis on formal grant proposals, well-formulated hypotheses, tightly defined sampling frames, structured interview schedules, and predetermined research strategies and methods and forms of analysis. The researcher may follow a path of discovery, using as a model qualitative works that have achieved the status of classics in the field. Enchanted, perhaps, by the myth of the Lone Ethnographer, the scholar hopes to produce a work that has the characteristics of a study done by one of the giants from the past (Malinowski, Mead, Bateson, Goffman, Becker, Strauss, Wolcott). Conversely, qualitative researchers often at least begin by undertaking studies that can be completed by one individual after prolonged engagement.

In Chapter 14, Cheek complicates and deconstructs the relationships among money, ethics, and research markets. She shows how qualitative research is a commodity that circulates and is exchanged in this political economy. She discusses the problems associated with institutional review boards and ethics committees. She notes that many times qualitative researchers are unable to answer in advance all of the questions that are raised by such committees. Issues of control over the research are also central. As Cheek observes, "Taking funding from someone in order to conduct research is not a neutral act." This issue shades into another, namely: What happens when the researcher's findings do not please the funder?

Choreographing the Dance of Design

In Chapter 13, Valerie Janesick presents a fluid view of the design process. She observes that the essence of good qualitative research design requires the use of a set of procedures that are at once open-ended and rigorous. Influenced by Martha Graham, Merce Cunningham, Alvin Ailey, Elliot Eisner, and John Dewey, she approaches the problem of research design from an aesthetic, artistic, and metaphoric perspective. With Dewey and Eisner, she sees research design as a work of improvisational, rather than composed, art—as an event, a process, with phases connected to different forms of problematic experience and their interpretation and representation. Art molds and fashions experience. In its dance form, art is a choreographed, emergent production, with distinct phases: warming up, stretching exercises and design decisions, cooling down, interpretation, and writing the narrative.

Qualitative research design decisions parallel the warm-up, exercise, and cool-down periods of dance. Just as dance mirrors and creates life, so research designs adapt, change, and mold the very phenomena they are intended to examine. Janesick fits traditional design questions, the research question, the research site, the timeline, and the research strategy into this framework. She then addresses the problems involved in pilot studies, interdisciplinary triangulation, and alternative views of triangulation (crystallization), validity, reliability, and generalizability. She offers a compelling criticism of the methodolatry (preoccupation with method) of many traditional, positivist approaches to these topics. Her suggestions for journal writing represent a way to implement a more reflective, critical approach to inquiry.

Who and What Will Be Studied?

The who and what of qualitative studies involve cases, or instances of phenomena, or social processes. Three generic approaches may be taken to the question of who or what will be studied. First, a single case, or single process, may be studied, what Robert Stake in Chapter 16 calls the intrinsic case study. Here the researcher examines in detail a single case or instance of the phenomenon in question, such as a classroom, an arts program, or a death in the family.

Second, the researcher may focus on a number of cases. Stake calls this the collective case approach. These cases are then analyzed in terms of specific and generic properties. Third, the researcher can examine multiple instances of a process, as that process is displayed in a variety of different cases. In his study of relapse in the careers of recovering alcoholics, for example, Denzin (1993) examined types of relapses across several different types of recovering careers. This process approach is then grounded or anchored in specific cases.

Research designs vary, of course, depending on the needs of multifocus or single-focus case and process inquiries. Different sampling issues arise in each situation. These needs and issues also vary according to the paradigm that is being employed. Every instance of a case or process bears the stamp of the general class of phenomena to which it belongs. However, any given instance is likely to be particular and unique. Thus, for example, any given classroom is like all classrooms, but no two classrooms are the same.

For these reasons, many postpositivist, constructionist, and critical theory qualitative researchers employ theoretical or purposive, and not random, sampling models. They seek out groups, settings, and individuals where and for whom the processes being studied are most likely to occur. At the same time, a process of constant comparison (see Charmaz, Chapter 19, this volume)—of groups, concepts, and observations—is necessary, as the researcher seeks to develop an understanding that encompasses all instances of the process or case under investigation. A focus on negative cases is a key feature of this process.

These sampling and selection issues would be addressed differently by a postmodern ethnographer in the cultural studies tradition. This investigator would be likely to place greater stress on the intensive analysis of a small body of empirical materials (cases and processes), arguing, after Sartre (1981, p. ix), that no individual or case is ever just an individual or a case. He or she must be studied as a single instance of more universal social experiences and social processes. The person, Sartre states, is "summed up and for this reason universalized by his epoch, he in turn resumes it by reproducing himself in it as a singularity" (p. ix). Thus to study the particular is to study the general. For this reason, any case will necessarily bear the traces of the universal; consequently, there is less interest in the traditional positivist and postpositivist concerns with negative cases, generalizations, and case selection. The researcher assumes that the readers will be able, as Stake argues, to generalize subjectively from the case in question to their own personal experiences.

An expansion on this strategy appears in the "method of instances" (see Denzin, 1999; Psathas, 1995). Following Psathas (1995, p. 50), the method of instances takes each instance of a phenomenon as an occurrence that evidences the operation of a set of cultural understandings currently available for use by cultural members. An analogy may be useful. In discourse analysis, "no utterance is representative of other utterances, though of course it shares structural features with them; a discourse analyst studies utterances in order to understand how the potential of the linguistic system can be activated when it intersects at its moment of use with a social system" (Fiske, 1994, p. 195). This is the argument for the method of instances. The analyst examines those moments when an utterance intersects with another utterance, giving rise to an instance of the system in action.

Psathas (1995) clarifies the meaning of an instance: "An instance of something is an occurrence . . . an event whose features and structures can be examined to discover how it is organized" (p. 50). An occurrence is evidence that "the machinery for its production is culturally available . . . [for example] the machinery of turn-taking in conversation" (pp. 50-51).

The analyst's task is to understand how this instance and its intersections work, to show what rules of interpretation are operating, to map and illuminate the structure of the interpretive event itself. The analyst inspects the actual course of the interaction "by observing what happens first, second, next, etc., by noticing what preceded it; and by examining what is actually done and said by the participants" (Psathas, 1995, p. 51). Questions of meaning are referred back to the actual course of interaction, where it can be shown how a given utterance is acted upon and hence given meaning. The pragmatic maxim obtains here (Peirce, 1905). The meaning of an action is given in the consequences that are produced by it, including the ability to explain past experience and predict future consequences.

Whether the particular utterance occurs again is irrelevant. The question of sampling from a population is also not an issue, for it is never possible to say in advance what an instance is a sample of (Psathas, 1995, p. 50). Indeed, collections of instances "cannot be assembled in advance of an analysis of at least one, because it cannot be known in advance what features delineate each case as a 'next one like the last' " (Psathas, 1995, p. 50). This means there is little concern for empirical generalization. Psathas is clear on this point. The goal is not an abstract or empirical generalization; rather, the aim is "concerned with providing analyses that meet the criteria of unique adequacy" (p. 50). Each analysis must be fitted to the case at hand, each "must be studied to provide an analysis *uniquely adequate* for that particular phenomenon (p. 51).

◆ *Strategies of Inquiry*

The strategy of inquiry comprises the skills, assumptions, enactments, and material practices that the researcher-as-methodological-*bricoleur* uses in moving from a paradigm and a research design to the collection of empirical materials. Strategies of inquiry connect researchers to specific approaches and methods for collecting and analyzing empirical materials. The case study, for example, relies on interviewing, observation, and document analysis. Research strategies locate researchers and paradigms in specific empirical, material sites and in specific methodological practices—for example, making a case an object of study (Stake, Chapter 16).

We turn now to a brief review of the strategies discussed in this volume. Each is connected to a complex literature with its own history, its own exemplary works, and its own set of preferred ways for putting the strategy into motion. Each strategy also has its own set of problems involving the positivist, postpositivist, and postmodern legacies.

Performance Ethnography

In Chapter 15, Michal McCall offers a detailed history of the performance text, performance art, and performance ethnography movements in the arts, humanities, and social sciences. She distinguishes early social science uses of this form, noting her place in this history and contrasting the performance science work she, Morris, and Becker have done with the parodic ethnography of performance artists. With Linda Gammell and Sandra Taylor, McCall has produced a series of recent performance ethnographies based on work with midwestern women who practice sustainable agriculture. These texts extend the work of Anna Deavere Smith, Della Pollock, and Marianne Paget. Like Pollock and Smith, McCall wanted to return the stories to the communities out of which they emerged. She arranged for workshops where women who had participated in earlier workshops took roles in a play. McCall offers many useful guidelines for creating, staging, and casting performance texts. In this way her work complements the ethnodrama performance movement inspired by Jim Mienczakowski (2000).

The Case Study

Robert Stake argues in Chapter 16 that not all case studies are qualitative, although many are. Focusing on those that are attached to the naturalistic, holistic, cultural, and phenomenological paradigms, he contends that the case study is not a methodological choice, but a choice of object to be studied, such as a child or a classroom. Ultimately the researcher is interested in a process or a population of cases, not an individual case. Stake identifies several types of case studies (intrinsic, instrumental, collective). Each case is a complex historical and contextual entity. Case studies have unique conceptual structures, uses, and problems (bias, theory, triangulation, telling the story, case selection, ethics). Researchers routinely provide information on such topics as the nature of the case, its historical background, and its relation to its contexts and other cases as well as to the informants who have provided information. In order to avoid ethical problems, the case study researcher needs constant input "from conscience, from stakeholders, and from the research community."

Ethnography and Participant Observation

In Chapter 17, Barbara Tedlock reminds us that "ethnography involves an ongoing attempt to place specific encounters, events, and understandings into a fuller, more meaningful content." Ethnography combines research design, fieldwork, and various methods of inquiry to produce representations of human group life. Ethnographic works draw on personal experience and autobiography. Ethnography is perhaps the most hotly contested site in qualitative research today. Traditionalists (positivists), postpositivists, and postmodernists compete over the definitions of this field, the criteria that are applied to its texts, and the place of the reflexive researcher in the interpretive process. Tedlock shows how participant observation has become the observation of participation. As a consequence, the doing, framing, representation, and reading of ethnography have been dramatically changed in the past decade. In the process, the genre of narrative ethnography has moved to claim the center of attention in contemporary discourse. Many now understand that the ethnographic text is fashioned out of the researcher's engagement with the world studied. Such a text is best evaluated in terms of its ability to create a sense of verisimilitude for the reader. Others set forth rigorous criteria for the production and evaluation of ethnographic texts (see also in this volume, Angrosino & Pérez, Chapter 25; Ryan & Bernard, Chapter 29; Smith & Deemer, Chapter 34).

Analyzing Interpretive Practice

In Chapter 18, Jaber Gubrium and James Holstein extend the arguments made in their recent book, *The New Language of Qualitative Method* (1997), in which they examine various contemporary idioms of qualitative inquiry, from naturalism to ethnomethodology, emotional sociology, postmodernism, and poststructuralism. They then offer a new language of qualitative research that builds on ethnomethodology, conversation analysis, institutional studies of local culture, and Foucault's critical approach to history and discourse analysis (see also Kendall & Wickham, 1999). Gubrium and Holstein capture a developing consensus in the interpretive community. This consensus seeks to show how social constructionist approaches can be profitably combined with poststructuralist discourse analysis and the situated study of meaning and order as local, social accomplishments. (This chapter is profitably read alongside Schwandt's contribution in Part II.)

Gubrium and Holstein draw attention to the interpretive procedures and practices that give structure and meaning to everyday life. These reflexive practices are both the topic of and the resources for qualitative inquiry. Knowledge is always local, situated in a local culture, and embedded in organizational and interactional sites. Everyday stereotypes and ideologies, including understandings about race, class, and gender, are enacted in these sites. The systems of power, what Dorothy Smith (1993) calls the ruling apparatuses, and relations of ruling in society are played out in these sites. Gubrium and Holstein build on Smith's project, elaborating a critical theory of discourse and social structure. They then show how reflexive discourse and discursive practices transform the processes of analytic and critical bracketing. Such practices make the foundations of local social order visible. This emphasis on interpretive resources and local resources enlivens and dramatically extends the reflexive turn in qualitative research.

Grounded Theory

Kathy Charmaz is a leading proponent of the constructivist approach to grounded theory. She suggests that grounded theory, in its essential form, consists of systematic inductive guidelines for collecting and analyzing empirical materials to build middle-range theoretical frameworks that explain collected empirical materials. In Chapter 19, she outlines the history of this approach, from the early work of Glaser and Strauss to its transformations in more recent statements by Glaser, Strauss, and Corbin. She contrasts the positivist-objectivist positions of these authors with her own more interpretive constructivist approach, which stakes out a middle ground between postmodernism and positivism. Grounded theory may be the most widely employed interpretive strategy in the social sciences today. It gives the researcher a specific set of steps to follow that are closely aligned with the canons of "good science." But on this point Charmaz is clear: It is possible to use grounded theory without embracing earlier proponents' positivist leanings (a position long adopted by Lincoln & Guba, 1985; see also Chapter 6, this volume).

Charmaz reviews the basic strategies used by grounded theorists. She grounds her discussion in materials from her own research, showing how she has used theoretical sampling, the constant comparison method, systematic coding, and memo writing while seeking conceptual density. She also takes up computer-assisted analysis, briefly discussing those programs that are explicitly designed to assist in grounded theory analysis (NUD•IST and Ethnograph; see also Weitzman, Chapter 30, this volume), and reviews critical challenges to grounded theory. In Charmaz's hands, constructivist grounded theory becomes a very powerful analytic framework for implementing multiple interpretive approaches to social life. In these ways she disarms the many criticisms that have been directed at earlier versions of this framework (see also Strauss & Corbin, 1998, pp. 275-295).

The Life History Method

In Chapter 20, William Tierney reminds us that every life history text is gendered. Queer theory extends this argument. Gamson (Chapter 12) and Tierney suggest that all autobiographical and biographical texts are shaped by cultural apparatuses that regulate sexuality, sexual identity, and sexual desire. Thus does Tierney startle the reader when he opens his chapter with two assertions. He first argues that Meriwether Lewis was a gay man in love with his fellow explorer William Clark. He then suggests that Stephen Ambrose could not write this fact in his account of the Lewis and Clark expedition because the discourses for writing about gay explorers did not exist in the 19th century, when Lewis and Clark began their journey. Hence Lewis's life history and his relationship to Clark receive a different telling from Ambrose and other historians.

Framing his opening in this way allows Tierney to bring queer theory and postmodernism into his analysis of the life history method, in particular the *testimonio,* which is an important new form of the life history (see also Beverley, Chapter 21; Madriz, Chapter 32). A *testimonio* is a first-person political text told by a narrator who is the protagonist in, or witness to, the events that are reported upon. These tellings report on torture, imprisonment, social upheaval, and other struggles for survival. These works are intended to produce (and record) social change. Their truth is contained in the telling of the events that are recorded by the narrator. The author is not a researcher, but rather a person who testifies on behalf of history and personal experience.

Understood this way, a life history document is an entry into a life, a portal into a culture different from that of the reader. Such texts become vehicles for self-understanding. They connect memory and history to reflexive political action. They create spaces for the voices of previously silenced persons to be heard. In this way the postmodern historian-ethnographer helps create liberating texts.

The New Histories and the Historical Method

Texts such as Tierney's simultaneously build upon and advance the projects of the contemporary cultural historian (see Jenkins, 1997), including the new cultural Marxism; the new social histories of everyday life; interpretive anthropology (Geertz); critical psychoanalytic and Marxist studies of women, gender, and sexuality; the discursive, linguistic turn in history since Foucault (see also in this volume Vidich & Lyman, Chapter 2; Lincoln & Guba, Chapter 6; Schwandt, Chapter 7; Olesen, Chapter 8; Kincheloe & McLaren, Chapter 10).

All social phenomena need to be studied in their historical contexts. This involves the use of historical documents and written records of the past, including diaries, letters, newspapers, census tract data, novels and other popular literature, and popular culture documents. To understand historical documents, one must have an interpretive point of view. This point of view shapes how one gathers, reads, and analyzes historical materials. A historian's account of the past is a social text that constructs and reconstructs the realities of the past.

History is always the story of somebody's lived experience. The stories that tell history are always biased; none can ever document the "truth." Together, these stories present a revealing montage that should speak to us today. But how history speaks reveals the politics of power, for history is not purely referential—it is constructed by the historian. Written history both reflects and creates relations of power. Today's struggles are, then, about how we shall know the past and how the past will be constituted in the present. Every historical method implies a different way of telling these stories.

Testimonio as Narrative, Method, and Discourse

John Beverley's seminal discussion of *testimonio* in Chapter 21 extends the treatment Tierney gives this method in Chapter 20. Beverley traces the contemporary history of this method back to Oscar Lewis's life history analysis in *Children of Sánchez*. Beverley suggests that a predominant formal aspect of the *testimonio* is the voice that speaks to the reader in the form of an "I"—a real, rather than fictional, person. This is a voice that refuses to be silenced, and the person speaks on behalf of others. Yet, unlike autobiography, *testimonio* involves an erasure of the concept of author. The *testimonio* uses a voice that stands for a larger whole. This creates a democratic, egalitarian form of discourse.

The *testimonio* is an open-ended, interpretive work. It may contain passages and reflections that are social constructions, fabrications, or arrangements of selected events from the actual world. These constructions may deal with events that did not happen. In this sense, the *testimonio* is an object of interpretation. It is not a mirror of the world; rather, it stands in critical relationship to the world of actual events. The *testimonio I, Rigoberta Menchú* (1984) does this. It asks that the reader identify with the text, and believe in the truth of the text, as the text asserts its interpretations of the world. In this context, Beverley takes up the controversy surrounding *I, Rigoberta Menchú* (see also our discussion of this text in Chapter 41). Beverley concludes with a very valuable bibliographic note on the preparation of testimonios. It is certain that in the 21st century the testimonio will continue to be an important form of critical interpretive writing.

Participatory Action Research

According to Stephen Kemmis and Robin McTaggart (Chapter 22), participatory action research (PAR) is an alternative philosophy of research (and social life) associated with liberation theology, neo-Marxist approaches to community development, and human rights activism. There are several different strands of PAR, from critical action research to classroom action research, action learning, action science, and industrial action research. Participatory action researchers believe in the shared ownership of research projects as well as the value of community-based analyses of social problems. They have a commitment to local community action, but take care to protect the welfare and interests of those with whom they work. Participatory action scholars reject the concept of value neutrality while also rejecting the criticisms of those who claim that PAR scholarship lacks scientific rigor and is too political.

Kemmis and McTaggart identify three different forms of PAR: the third-person instrumental, second-person practical, and first-person critical approaches. They value those forms of PAR that involve first-person relationships. The material practices of PAR transform practitioners' theories and the theories that operate at the community level. Such transformations help to shape the conditions of life, connecting the local and the global, the personal and the political. Work in this tradition attempts to make qualitative research more humanistic, holistic, and relevant to the lives of human beings. In this worldview, human beings cocreate their reality through participation, experience, and action. Participatory action researchers help make this happen.

Clinical Models

Participatory action research has a natural affinity with clinical methods. Both traditions reflect commitment to change, although clinical research displays greater concern for diagnosis and treatment than for large-scale social change per se. Historically, the biomedical, positivist, and postpositivist paradigms have dominated clinical, medical research. In Chapter 23, William Miller and Benjamin Crabtree present a qualitative alternative approach that locates clinical research in the nexus of applied anthropology and the practice of primary health care—family practice in particular. They outline an experience-based, interpretive view of clinical practice, a view that makes the clinical practitioner and the patient coparticipants in the realities of medical treatment. They ask how questions emerging from the racialized, gendered clinical experience can frame the conversations that occur between doctors and patients.

Miller and Crabtree offer a compelling critical analysis of the biomedical paradigm as it is rooted in a patriarchal positivism. Their perspective blends experience-based medicine with a participatory, action-based, multimethod approach. Methodologically, this model draws on experimental, survey, documentary, and field methods. It also uses the analytic framework of grounded theory, personal experience methods, clinical interviews, and participant observation. This model treats the medical and social body as a contested (and gendered) site for multiple personal and medical narratives. The multimethod approach that Miller and Crabtree advocate represents an attempt to change biomedical culture radically. Their chapter speaks to the politics of qualitative research. In the clinical model, as in other areas of qualitative research, the multimethod approach is often the only avenue to a more interpretive conception of the research process.

Like Kemmis and McTaggart, Miller and Crabtree show how qualitative research can be used as a tool to create social change. Miller and Crabtree want to change consciousness in the medical setting by changing the language and the paradigm that physicians and patients now use. The tools that these four authors advocate are powerful agents for social change.

At the same time, Miller and Crabtree want to change how medical texts are written. They want to create new forms of textuality, forms that will hold a place for those who have not yet been heard. Once the previously silenced are heard, they can then speak for themselves as agents of social change. In these kinds of texts, research is connected to political action, systems of language and meaning are changed, and paradigms are challenged. How to interpret these voices is the topic of Part IV of this *Handbook*. In the meantime, listen to the voices in Part III; these are calls to action.

■ Notes

1. In keeping with our commitment to the applied and civic implications of qualitative research, we have once again included two chapters on research design. Julianne Cheek presents an incisive treatment of this topic that is directly fitted to the needs of those researchers who increasingly find themselves in situations where they must secure external support for their projects. Valerie Janesick presents another version of the design process that is less geared to such concerns.

2. Mitch Allen's comments have significantly shaped our treatment of the relationship between paradigms and research designs.

■ References

Denzin, N. K. (1993). *The alcoholic society: Addiction and recovery of self.* New Brunswick, NJ: Transaction.

Denzin, N. K. (1999). Cybertalk and the method of instances. In S. Jones (Ed.), *Doing Internet research: Critical issues and methods for examining the Net* (pp. 107-126). Thousand Oaks, CA: Sage.

Fiske, J. (1994). Audiencing: Cultural practice and cultural studies. In N. K. Denzin & Y. S. Lincoln (Eds.), *Handbook of qualitative research* (pp. 189-198). Thousand Oaks, CA: Sage.

Gubrium, J. F., & Holstein, J. A. (1997). *The new language of qualitative method.* New York: Oxford University Press.

Jenkins, K. (Ed.). (1997). *The postmodern history reader.* New York: Routledge.

Kendall, G., & Wickham, G. (1999). *Using Foucault's methods.* London: Sage.

Lincoln, Y. S., & Guba, E. G. (1985). *Naturalistic inquiry.* Beverly Hills, CA: Sage.

Menchú, R. (1984). *I, Rigoberta Menchú: An Indian woman in Guatemala* (E. Burgos-Debray, Ed.; A. Wright, Trans.). London: Verso.

Mienczakowski, J. (2000). Ethnodrama: Performed research—limitations and potential. In P. Atkinson, S. Delamont, & A. Coffey (Eds.), *Handbook of ethnography.* London: Sage.

Mills, C. W. (1959). *The sociological imagination.* New York: Oxford University Press.

Peirce, C. S. (1905, April). What pragmatism is. *Monist, 15,* 161-181.

Psathas, G. (1995). *Conversation analysis.* Thousand Oaks, CA: Sage.

Sartre, J.-P. (1981). *The family idiot: Gustave Flaubert, 1821-1857* (Vol. 1). Chicago: University of Chicago Press.

Smith, D. E. (1993). High noon in Textland: A critique of Clough. *Sociological Quarterly, 34,* 183-192.

Strauss, A. L., & Corbin, J. (1998). *Basics of qualitative research: Techniques and procedures for developing grounded theory* (2nd ed.). Thousand Oaks, CA: Sage.

13

THE CHOREOGRAPHY OF QUALITATIVE RESEARCH DESIGN

Minuets, Improvisations, and Crystallization

◆ Valerie J. Janesick

> *Movement never lies. It is a barometer telling the state of the soul—to all who can read it.*
>
> Martha Graham

Qualitative research design is very much like choreography. As Flick (1998) reminds us, the essence of good qualitative research design turns on the use of a set of procedures that are simultaneously open-ended and rigorous and that do justice to the complexity of the social setting under study. A good choreographer captures the complexity of the dance/story by using rigorous and tested procedures and in fact refuses to be limited to one approach to choreography. In this chapter, I wish to develop this metaphor through the use of two kinds of dances: a precisely set piece, a minuet, and a piece that has

structure and form yet is totally free, the approach known as improvisation. Finally, I will discuss my views on crystallization as an alternative to triangulation in qualitative research design.

I have selected the metaphor of choreography to extend my earlier writing (Janesick, 1994a, 1998a) using the dance metaphor for two reasons. First, dance is the art form to which I am most devoted, having been a dancer, dance teacher, and choreographer for more than 25 years. I became a choreographer as a matter of natural evolution, following in the footsteps of many of my dear and influential teachers, and as a matter of survival. I have choreographed dances for various groups and my own dance company in three states, and I continued to study dance long after giving up my work as a choreographer. I have spent summers in New York City studying technique at the schools of Martha Graham, Merce Cunningham, Alvin Ailey, and Erick Hawkins.[1] While studying at Michigan State University at the Institute for Research on Teaching, I taught all levels of modern dance, choreography, dance history, and anatomy for the dancers at Lansing Community College in addition to my research internship. In fact, it was this simultaneous experience in dance and research studies that prepared me for my academic career as an ethnographic researcher, teacher of qualitative research methods, and designer of qualitative research projects.

Second, the metaphor of choreography is simply a tool to make the reader think about metaphor. Metaphor in general creeps up on you, surprises you. It defies the one-size-fits-all approach to a topic. I can only wholeheartedly agree with Eisner (1991) when he discusses metaphor:

> What is ironic is that in the professional socialization of educational researchers, the use of metaphor is regarded as a sign of imprecision; yet, for making public the ineffable, nothing is more precise than the artistic use of language. Metaphoric precision is the central vehicle for revealing the qualitative aspects of life. (p. 227)

Consequently, I invite the reader to embrace this metaphor of choreography, to stretch your imagination and broaden your view of qualitative research design. Choreography is about the art of making dances. Because dance and choreography are about lived experience, choreography seems to me the perfect metaphor for discussing qualitative research design. Because the qualitative researcher is the research instrument, the metaphor is even more apropos for this discussion, as the body is the instrument of dance.

The qualitative researcher is remarkably like a choreographer at various stages in the design process, in terms of situating and recontextualizing the research project within the shared experience of the researcher and the participants in the study. When choreographers are asked what they do, they typically speak of each individual piece, case by case, within the social context of the given choreographic study. This similarity with the work of qualitative researchers is striking. For example, as a choreographer, Doris Humphrey (1959/1987) was one of the first to write about choreography as a field of study. She viewed choreographic theory and the study of it as a craft. She did not eschew talent or genius, but she believed that it is not possible to teach someone to "create" a dance, for example. This is like the architect who still must know about glass and steel no matter what level of giftedness he or she possesses. For Humphrey, the craft of making dances was about learning the principles, then expanding and embroidering. Similarly, as newcomers to the field of qualitative research begin the task of designing research projects, the first stage for them is to learn the principles, so that they can then expand and embroider. This ancient concept was captured centuries ago in the writings of the Chinese master painters:

> Some set great value on method, while others pride themselves on dispensing with method. To be without method is deplorable, but to depend on method entirely is worse. You must first learn to observe the rules faithfully; afterwards, modify them according to your intelligence and capacity. The end of all method is to have no method. (Lu Ch'ai)

The qualitative researcher and the choreographer are similar in yet another way: Both refuse to separate art from ordinary experience. Choreographers and qualitative researchers can routinely benefit from the view, expressed more than 65 years ago by John Dewey (1934/1958), that art is about communication and experience. Although Dewey was roundly criticized in his time for this idea, over time many have come to see the value of his thinking. Dewey wrote about art as providing a sense of the whole of something, much like the qualitative researcher and the choreographer, who do this very thing in their work. As Dewey (1934/1958) noted, "The artist should restore continuity between the refined and intensified forms of experience that are works of art and the everyday events, doings, and sufferings that are universally recognized to constitute experience" (p. 3). This thoughtful and critical approach to everyday experience and to art as experience is very much like the approaches taken by the qualitative researcher and the choreographer.

◆ Of Minuets and Improvisations

A good choreographer refuses to be limited to just one approach or one technique from dance history. Likewise, the qualitative researcher refuses to be limited; as Flick (1998) has recently observed, the qualitative researcher uses various techniques and rigorous and tested procedures in working to capture the nuance and complexity of the social situation under study. From the amazing range of types of dances that have been described thus far in dance history, I have chosen two seemingly unrelated forms, the minuet and improvisation, to illustrate my discussion of the design process in qualitative research studies. The minuet represents the most confined approach, with a prescribed set of steps in a given dance piece. It is a dance with definite steps, definite turns, and prescribed patterns of foot and arm movements. On the other end of the spectrum is improvisational dance. Imagine yourself as a choreographer and consider how you might approach the challenge of choreographing both kinds of dances.

First, let us look at the minuet. At the risk of sounding like Forrest Gump, I must point out that dance history writers have noted that life is like a minuet: The dancer makes a few turns in order to curtsy or bow and end up in the same place where the dance began. However, the minuet is not as simple as it seems. Imagine yourself in France in the year 1650. It is a period of luxury and calm for those who are able to enjoy music and dance. Strict rules apply to manners, customs, art, music, ceremonies, life as a whole, and certainly daily dress. Millions are spent on the production of the minuet at parties and court gatherings. Costumers, choreographers, set designers, musicians, jesters, and poets are called upon to see that the perfect minuet is danced. In fact, dancing teachers and choreographers of the period are revered as angels, architects of god; all would-be dancers of the minuet bow to these teachers as they look for instruction in this dance.

Now imagine yourself in the present day, about to choreograph an improvisation. Improvisation is probably the approach to dance most unlike the minuet. It first appeared in the 1960s as part of postmodern dance in general. Improvisation is spontaneous and reflective of the social condition; it is up to the individual dancer to interpret an idea, given a set problem or context in which to work. Improvisation in dance is like any creative endeavor. It relies on (a) preparation, (b) exploration, and (c) illumination and formulation. For example, I recall one of my dance teachers saying, in an improvisation session, "Think of a favorite poem. Now listen to this music I am playing. Now *move*." This is an example of a choreographic study of an improvisation. As with any dance, one must be keenly aware of the body and kinesiology, phrasing, core imagery, and the idea to be expressed to an audience. Likewise, the choreographer is balancing all this as he or she prompts an improvisation. The point is that all dance, all choreography, begins with an idea, whether the dance is defined in an exact form or spontaneous. I see a connection to the qualitative researcher's work in Blom and Chaplin's (1988) description of improvisational dance components:

> Certainly and easily we can say that spontaneity is one of its constituent parts. At the same time it is not without direction. It is at once intentional and reactive. . . . An organic plan emerges to take us forward in time, yet it only becomes articulated as we move. Because improv is a phenomenological process, we cannot examine any product per se. But it does exist and is perceivable. What we can do is examine the route it takes and our consciousness of it, a route which is on the way to creating itself while being itself. (p. 7)

Thus the qualitative researcher may learn from the choreographic forms of both minuet and improvisation. The design of the study begins with some fixed movements: precise interviews are planned, observations are scheduled, documents are reviewed and analyzed. In this way the researcher is like the choreographer/dancer of the minuet. At the same time, within the parameters of the interviews, information is disclosed that allows the researcher to improvise, to find out more about some critical event or moment in the lives of the participants. So the researcher begins to use the techniques of the improvisational choreographer/dancer. Even the act of charting observations and interviews is sometimes improvisational. One interview may lead the researcher to find out that another individual may become part of the study for one reason or another. One document may lead to many more, and so on. Likewise, the researcher charts the progress and examines the route of the study as it proceeds by keeping track of his or her own role in the research process. A good way for the researcher to do this is to keep a reflective journal of the research process (Janesick, 1999). Like choreographers who document their thinking and work in their notes and on videotape, the researcher may do the same to contribute to the historical record.

◆ *Qualitative Research Design as Choreography*

All choreographers make a statement and begin, explicitly or implicitly, with the question, What do I want to say in this dance? In much the same way, the qualitative researcher begins with a similar question: What do I want to know in this study? This is a critical beginning point. Regardless of the researcher's point of view, and quite often because of that point of view, the researcher constructs and frames a question for inquiry. After this question is clear, the researcher selects the most appropriate methodology to proceed with the research project. For the qualitative researcher, the question cannot be entirely separated from the method, in the same way the dancer cannot be separated from

the dance or the choreographer from what is danced. Qualitative research design, like choreography, begins with a question, or at least an intellectual curiosity if not a passion for a particular topic. Of course, a qualitative researcher designs a study with real individuals in mind, and with the intent of living in that social setting over time. The qualitative researcher studies a social setting to understand the meaning of participants' lives in the participants' own terms. This contrasts with the work of the quantitative researcher, who is perfectly comfortable with aggregating large numbers of people without communicating with them face-to-face. So the questions the qualitative researcher asks will be quite different from those asked by the quantitative researcher. In general, questions that are suited to qualitative inquiry have long been the questions of many educational researchers and theorists, sociologists, anthropologists, students of organizations, and historians. For example:

1. Questions concerning the quality of a given innovation or program;
2. Questions regarding the meaning or interpretation of some component of the context under study;
3. Questions that relate to organizations and society in terms of their sociolinguistic aspects;
4. Questions related to the whole system, as in a classroom, school, school district, city, country, organization, hospital, or prison;
5. Questions regarding the political, economic, or sociopsychological aspects of organizations and society;
6. Questions regarding the hidden curriculum or hidden agendas in an organization;
7. Questions pertaining to the social context of an organization;
8. Questions pertaining to participants' implicit theories about their work;
9. Questions about the meaning of an individual's life;
10. Questions that afflict the comfortable and comfort the afflicted.

This list is not meant to be exhaustive; it serves only to illustrate the basic areas where research has been completed and has employed qualitative techniques because of, among other things, the suitability of the technique and the question.

Just as the choreographer begins with stages of completion of a choreographic piece, I like to think of qualitative design as made up of three stages of design. First is the warm-up, preparation, or prechoreographic stage of design decisions at the beginning of the study; second is the exploration or tryout and total workout stage, when design decisions are made throughout the study; and third is the illumination and formulation or completion stage, when design decisions are made at the end or near the end of the study. At the same time, the qualitative researcher, like the choreographer, follows set routines (such as those found in the minuet) as well as improvisational moments. Likewise, just as the choreographer relies on the spine of the dancer for the power and coherence of the dance, the qualitative researcher relies on the design of the study. Both are elastic. Like the dancer who finds her center from the base of the spine and the connection between the spine and the body, the qualitative researcher is centered by a series of design decisions. A dancer who is centered may tilt forward and backward and from side to side, yet always return to the center, the core of the dancer's strength. If one thinks of the design of the study as the spine, and the base of the spine as the beginning of the warm-up in dance, one can see that the beginning decisions in a study are very much like the warm-up for the dancer and the predesign decisions made by the choreographer.

◆ *Warming Up and Preparation: Design Decisions at the Beginning of the Study and Elements for Choreography*

The first set of design decisions have to do with what is studied, under what circum-

stances, for what duration of time, and with whom. For the choreographer, motivation for movement, themes for the dance, dynamics, rhythm, and phrasing are first considerations. As a researcher, I always start any given research project with a question. For example, when I was studying deaf culture in Washington, D.C., over a 4-year period, my basic question was, How do some deaf adults manage to succeed academically and in the workplace given the stigma of deafness in our society (Janesick, 1994b)? This basic question informed all my observations and interviews and led me to use focus groups and oral history techniques later in the study. Both the focus groups and oral histories evolved after I came to know the perspectives on deafness of the twelve individuals in my study. I then used theoretical sampling techniques to select three individuals to participate in an oral history component of the study.[2] I use this example to illustrate the elasticity of qualitative design. Focus groups allowed me to moderate and observe interactions among three of my participants on their perspectives on deafness, something I could not have planned in the first days in the field. Nor could I have realized at the beginning of the study the value of incorporating these techniques, which allowed me to capture a richer interpretation of participants' perspectives on deafness as well as to experience the use of various techniques and disciplines. Choreographers must also make adjustments as they create choreographic studies. For example, questions about the use of space, the types of dancers, types of soloists, and use of movement are preperformance decisions. During rehearsals, the choreographer may reorganize and adjust many of these elements as the work proceeds.

Further examples to illustrate this point come from the qualitative research projects conducted by Judith Gouwens, Patricia Williams-Boyd, and Byron DeFreese. Gouwens (1995) studied the principals of two Chicago schools to determine their personal realities regarding their professional roles. After deciding to describe and explain how the principals do what they do, she was able to determine that interviews, observations, and document reviews were appropriate techniques for her research project. Similarly,

Boyd (1996) studied a full-service school and its effects on the community in which it is located. By living in the setting, interviewing, observing, and taking photographs, Boyd documented the everyday lives of the actors involved and extracted meaning from their lived experience so as to guide prospective practitioners in this area. DeFreese (1996) studied an assistant school superintendent to find out how he made decisions and how he viewed his role. Through careful interviews over time and by reviewing documents related to this person's life, DeFreese found a way to do justice to a life of service to the community. Thus qualitative researchers have open minds, but not empty minds. They formulate questions to guide their studies, but those questions are under constant revision and are continually taking new shapes. On a regular basis, I am confronted by colleagues who state that qualitative researchers just hang around aimlessly until something pops up; or worse, they claim that there are no questions in qualitative projects. Nothing could be further from the truth.

Simultaneous with formulating the question that guides the study, the qualitative researcher needs to select a site and develop a rationale for the choice of that site. Access and entry are sensitive components in qualitative research, and the researcher must establish trust, rapport, and authentic communication patterns with participants. By establishing trust and rapport at the beginning of the study, the researcher is better able to capture the nuances and meanings of each participant's life from the participant's point of view. This also ensures that participants will be more willing to share everything, warts and all, with the researcher. Maintaining trust and rapport continues through the length of the study and long after in fact. Yet it must begin at the beginning. It would be difficult to imagine establishing trust, say, 6 months into a study. All of us who have done fieldwork know how critical the initial interactions in the field are, as a precursor to establishing trust and rapport. This holds true in dance as well. There must be trust between choreographer and dancers if they are to create a dance.

Once the researcher has a question, a site, a participant or a number of participants, and a reasonable period of time in which to undertake the study, he or she needs to decide what data collection strategies are most suited to the study. The selection of these strategies is intimately connected to how the researcher views the purpose of the work—that is, how to understand the social setting under study. Most often, qualitative researchers use some combination of participant observation, interviews, and document analysis. The use of such approaches and strategies in qualitative studies is well documented in the literature (Bogdan & Biklen, 1992; Creswell, 1997; Denzin, 1989; Goetz & LeCompte, 1984; Guba & Lincoln, 1994; Janesick, 1998a; LeCompte, Millroy, & Priessle, 1992; Lincoln & Guba, 1985; Marshall & Rossman, 1995; Maxwell, 1996; Spradley, 1979, 1980; Strauss & Corbin, 1990; Wolcott, 1990b, 1994). For example, in education and human services over the past three decades, case study, oral history (including narrative and life history approaches), grounded theory, literary criticism, and ethnographic approaches to research have been discovered and used because of their fit with research questions. Education has, at long last, embraced the techniques of the anthropologist, the sociologist, and the historian. This makes sense, given that these are the very approaches that allow researchers to deal with individuals. Choreographers must make similar design decisions before they create their dances. First, there is usually some inspiration for the dance in the first place. In Alvin Ailey's work, for example, there is no getting away from the major idea that prompts the dance. Ailey's ability to combine music for effect, costumes, lighting, and selection of the perfect soloist can be compared with the researcher's ability to make design decisions that he or she can rely upon throughout the study.

Summary

In summary, the warm-up period, or the period of making decisions at the beginning of the study, includes decisions regarding the following:

1. The questions that guide the study;
2. Selection of a site and participants;

3. Access and entry to the site and agreements with participants;
4. Timeline for the study;
5. Selection of appropriate research strategies, which may include some of the following (this list is not meant to be inclusive of all possibilities):
   a. ethnography
   b. life history
   c. oral history
   d. ethnomethodology
   e. case study
   f. participant observation
   g. field research or field study
   h. naturalistic study
   i. phenomenological study
   j. ecological descriptive study
   k. descriptive study
   l. symbolic interactionist study
   m. microethnography
   n. interpretive research
   o. action research
   p. narrative research
   q. historiography
   r. literary criticism
6. The place of theory in the study;
7. Identification of the researcher's own beliefs and ideology;
8. Identification of appropriate informed consent procedures and willingness to deal with ethical issues as they present themselves.

Regarding the last two categories listed above, I would like to point out that qualitative researchers accept the fact that research is ideologically driven. There is no value-free or bias-free design. Early on, the qualitative researcher identifies his or her own biases and articulates the ideology or conceptual frame for the study. By identifying one's biases, one can see easily where the questions that guide the study are crafted. The researcher owns up to his or her perspective on the study and may even track its evolution by keeping a critical reflective journal on the entire research process and the particular role of the researcher. This is a big difference between paradigms. I have yet to see a study in the quantitative arena in which

the researcher discusses the ideology that guided and shaped the study. The myth that research is objective in some way can no longer be taken seriously. At this point in time, all researchers should be free to challenge prevailing myths, such as this myth of objectivity. As we try to make sense of our social world and give meaning to what we do as researchers, we continually raise awareness of our own beliefs. There is no attempt to pretend that research is value-free. Likewise, qualitative researchers, because they deal with individuals face-to-face on a daily basis, are attuned to making decisions regarding ethical concerns, because this is part of life in the field. From the beginning moments of informed consent decisions, to other ethical decisions in the field, to the completion of the study, qualitative researchers need to allow for the possibility of recurring ethical dilemmas and problems in the field. Ethical issues arise regularly in the field. For example, questions regarding how much to disclose in the final report and how much to keep out of the final report are ever present. The researcher and participants in the project—or coresearchers, if you will—decide how to present the information that best captures the social setting yet will not compromise or harm any members in the study.

In addition to the decisions made at the beginning of the study, it is helpful for researchers to consider some characteristics of qualitative design (again, the following list is not meant to be exhaustive; it is meant to be used merely as a heuristic tool):

1. Qualitative design is holistic. It looks at the larger picture, the whole picture, and begins with a search for understanding of the whole. Qualitative research is not constructed to prove something or to control people.
2. Qualitative design looks at relationships within systems or cultures.
3. Qualitative design is concerned with the personal, face-to-face, and immediate.
4. Qualitative design is focused on understanding given social settings, not necessarily making predictions about those settings.

5. Qualitative design demands that the researcher stay in the setting over time.

6. Qualitative design demands time in analysis equal to the time in the field.

7. Qualitative design sometimes requires that the researcher develop a model of what occurred in the social setting. (I like to encourage this because developing a model comes close to choreographic work or artistic work and serves as a heuristic tool. I am sure there are many qualitative researchers who do not need or value model development; however, like the scene designer or architect who builds a model, the choreographer or dancer who captures the dance on film, or the artist who creates a drawing or series of drawings, the researcher can use the model as a tool for further work or it can serve as a simple historical record.)

8. Qualitative design requires the researcher to become the research instrument. This means the researcher must have the ability to observe behavior and must sharpen the skills necessary for observation and face-to-face interview. (Like the dancer and the choreographer, the qualitative researcher must be in tune with the body: The eyes must be taught to see, the ears must be taught to hear, and so on.)

9. Qualitative design incorporates informed consent decisions and is responsive to ethical concerns.

10. Qualitative design incorporates room for description of the role of the researcher as well as description of the researcher's own biases and ideological preference.

11. Qualitative design requires the construction of an authentic and compelling narrative of what occurred in the study and the various stories of the participants.

12. Qualitative design requires ongoing analysis of the data.

Other chapters in this volume discuss many of these characteristics in depth, and the reader will benefit from those discussions. Once the researcher begins the study and is in the field, another set of decision points emerges.

◆ *Stage 2: Exploration and Exercises—Design Decisions Throughout the Course of the Study and Choreography as a Work in Progress*

Stretching Exercises and Background Work

Before researchers devote themselves to the arduous and significant time commitments of qualitative studies, it is a good idea for them to do some background work, or what I have called "stretching exercises." (I have in the past used the term *pilot study,* but I now reject that term as far too limiting for qualitative researchers.) Stretching exercises allow prospective qualitative researchers to practice interview, observation, writing, reflection, and artistic skills to refine their research instruments, which are the researchers themselves. In dance, as I have written earlier, the dancer stretches to move beyond the current starting point (Janesick, 1998c). Likewise, qualitative researchers in training need to stretch their imaginations as well as their bodies—their eyes for observation, their ears for listening, their hands for writing, and so on. During this short period, preinterviews with selected key participants and a period of observations and document review can be helpful to researchers in a number of ways.

Also at this point, the researcher should take a trip to the library or go on-line to investigate what has been done before, historically, in his or her field. Just as the choreographer makes a dance from a historical posture, so the qualitative researcher designs a research project from some set of historical antecedents. It is a good idea for the researcher to identify those historical antecedents in the background work for the study. This background work will allow the researcher to focus on particular areas that previously may have been unclear. In addition, the researcher may use preinterviews to test certain questions.

This initial part of the process allows the researcher to begin to develop and solidify rapport with participants as well as to establish effective communication patterns. By including some time for reviewing records and documents, the researcher may uncover some insight into the shape of the study that previously was not apparent. To use another example from my study on deaf culture: Prior to my interviews with participants, I spent time in the Gallaudet University archives, reading journals, looking at newspaper clippings, and viewing videotapes, all of which helped me to understand the historical influences that led to the "Deaf President Now" movement.[3] I saw, in retrospect, common themes and categories in the subsequent interview transcripts that made perfect sense given a series of historical situations in a 125-year period prior to the selection of Gallaudet University's first deaf president. Thus the time invested in background work can be valuable and enriching for later phases of the study. In addition, graduate students who are getting ready to write the proposals for their dissertations should first and foremost check the past 10 years of *Dissertation Abstracts* to see what research projects have preceded them in their fields.

Other decisions made during the study usually concern effective use of time, participants' issues, or researcher issues. Because working in the field is unpredictable a good deal of the time, the qualitative researcher must be ready to readjust schedules and interview times, add or subtract observations or interviews, replace participants in the event of trauma or tragedy, and even rearrange terms of the original agreement. My own experiences in conducting long-term ethnographic studies have led me to refine and readjust study design constantly as I proceed, especially at this phase. While totally immersed in the immediate and local actions and statements of belief of participants, the researcher must be ready to deal with the substantive focus of the study and with his or her

own presuppositions. Simply observing and interviewing do not ensure that the research is qualitative; the qualitative researcher must also interpret the beliefs and behaviors of participants. To offer an example: I was recently asked to review some proposals for research projects funded in-house. One of the proposals was for a study that the proposal author claimed would be both qualitative and quantitative. The proposal described a lengthy survey (quantitative) and journal writing (qualitative). However, the author forgot to say what was to be done with the journals. How would they be integrated into the project? How would they be protected, ethically speaking? How would they connect to the survey? So you see, this was hardly a qualitative component. It was like an extra lump of clay in the hands of an indecisive sculptor: Should he throw it on the existing piece or not? If it can be integrated into the sculpture and will make sense, of course he should consider using it. If it will not make sense and will add nothing to the integrity of the final work of art, why would he use it?

Merely employing a qualitative technique here and there does not make a study qualitative. There seems to be a prevailing misunderstanding of qualitative work, and only those of us in the field can work to rectify this through careful documentation of our work on qualitative research projects. Painstaking, detailed descriptions and explanations of the design and conduct of studies are required not only for our own use but for future generations of qualitative researchers.

In a sense, while in the field the researcher is constantly immersed in a combination of deliberate decisions about hypotheses generated and tested on the one hand and intuitive reactions on the other. The researcher can find in the vast literature of sociology, anthropology, and education some common rules of thumb on which most researchers agree:

1. Look for meaning, the perspectives of the participants in the study.
2. Look for relationships regarding the structure, occurrence, and distribution of events over time.

3. Look for points of tension: What does not fit? What are the conflicting points of evidence in the case?

It is much the same in the dance world. Although the Graham technique represented a paradigm shift from ballet into modern dance, elements of ballet are still used within the idiom of modern dance. Furthermore, modern dance has embraced multiple competing and rival techniques, such as those developed by Cunningham and Tharp. As a choreographer presents an idea for an audience, you can be sure that many adjustments were made in the tryouts and rehearsals prior to the actual performance. Even dancing the minuet, with its set style in form and steps, every body is different, and one footstep from a 4-foot body is very different from that same step made by a 6-foot body. Similarly, improvisational dance is constantly changing depending on design decisions within each case, moment by moment. Basically, the qualitative researcher as designer of the research project will be making decisions at all stages of the project. Warm-up decisions and preparations made before entering the field constitute the first set of decisions. Exercises and exploration, the second stage of decisions, occur within the period of data collection in the field. The third stage of design decisions encompasses those that are made at the end of the study, what I call cooling down, illumination and formulation, or the decisions the researcher makes after leaving the field.

◆ Cooling Down: Illumination and Formulation—Design Decisions Made at the End of the Study

Design decisions at the end of the study are similar to the cooling-down portion of the dance movement or the choreographer's decision to come to completion of the choreographic study. The researcher must decide when to actually leave the field setting, often an emotional and traumatic event because of the close rapport developed during the course of the study. I usually

ease out of the setting, much as a dancer will cool down gradually. For example, in my study of a teacher's classroom perspective, after observing on a daily basis for 6 months, I started staggering my observations and interviews in the seventh month of fieldwork from the 5 days per week, to 3 days, to once a week, and then to meetings with the teacher to go over interview transcripts at his convenience (Janesick, 1982).

Following the process of leaving the field, final data analysis can begin. Of course, the qualitative researcher has been developing categories from the data, through constant comparative analysis,[4] over the entire time frame of the study. The process of reduction of data into a compelling, authentic, and meaningful statement constitutes an end goal of qualitative research design. As Richardson (1994) suggests, narrative writing is in itself a type of inquiry. Every qualitative researcher must inevitably be a good writer in order to do justice to the complexity and substance of the life stories of participants in any study. The researcher must continually reassess and refine concepts while conducting the fieldwork. As the analysis proceeds, the researcher may develop working models or theories in action that explain the behavior under study. As the analysis continues, the researcher may identify relationships that connect portions of the description with the explanations offered in the working models. The researcher can attempt to determine the significance of the various elements in the working models and then try to verify these by checking through field notes, interview transcripts, and documents. Not all qualitative researchers agree about the use of working models. I am suggesting this from the standpoint of choreography, which employs this kind of approach. The choreographer develops working models as the work proceeds in order to work toward the final artistic statement. The work is always open to discussion and critique from the dancers, the audience, and so on. Similarly, I am suggesting that in qualitative research design, researchers develop working models, because they are more like artists than they may think.

Following the fieldwork, the researcher needs to present the data in a narrative form supported by evidence from the statements and behaviors recorded in field notes, critical reflection journals, and interviews. In other words, the researcher must make empirical assertions supported by direct quotations from notes and interviews. The researcher also needs to provide some interpretive commentary framing the key findings in the study. The theoretical discussion should be traceable in the data. In addition, the researcher should describe his or her own role thoroughly, so that readers will understand the relationship between the researcher and the participants. This allows the researcher to confront the major assertions in the study with credibility while surveying the full range of evidence. Because qualitative work recognizes early on the perspective of the researcher as it evolves through the study, the description of the role of the researcher is a critical component of the written report of the study. The researcher must describe and explain his or her social, philosophical, and physical location in the study. The qualitative researcher must honestly probe his or her own biases at the onset of the study, during the study, and at the end of the study by clearly describing and explaining the precise role of the researcher in the study.

Recently, a colleague called me to ask, "Are there any textbooks or journals on qualitative methods?" As an educator I felt I had to try to explain the current rich store of superb books and journals and in fact sent him information that I thought would be helpful, such as an annotated bibliography, my course syllabus for "Qualitative Methods," and a packet of information including on-line list servers and resources. I mention this only to illustrate that the qualitative researcher, in addition to the responsibility of designing his or her own study, may have to take on the added responsibility of explaining the most basic information to individuals who are not researchers or who are unaware of the substantial discussion on qualitative research methods in written texts, professional journals, on-line dialogues and other resources, and even such progress in their own fields. In fact, every one of my students who has done a qualitative dissertation has had

to start early in the proposal writing stage to educate members of their committees, who may have forgotten about reading the books and journals available in this field. Inevitably, this becomes a responsibility for the qualitative researcher, and I see this as part of the social location of the researcher.

◆ Major Considerations in Writing the Narrative and Other Points

The qualitative researcher uses inductive analysis, which means that categories, themes, and patterns come from the data. The categories that emerge from field notes, documents, and interviews are not imposed prior to data collection. Early on, the researcher must develop a system for coding and categorizing the data. There is no one best system for analysis. The researcher may follow rigorous guidelines described in the literature (see Eisner, 1991; Fetterman, 1989; Goetz & LeCompte, 1984; Lincoln & Guba, 1985; Miles & Huberman, 1994; Patton, 1990), but the ultimate decisions about the narrative reside with the researcher. Like the choreographer, the researcher must find the most effective way to tell the story and to convince the audience of the meaning of the study. Staying close to the data is the most powerful means of telling the story, just as in dance the story is told through the body itself. As in the quantitative arena, the purpose of conducting a qualitative study is to produce findings. The methods and strategies used are not ends in themselves. There is a danger in becoming so taken up with methods that the substantive findings are obscured.

In fact, a problem that concerns me in doctoral programs is obsession with method. For example, many doctoral students take a number of statistics classes and, for whatever reason, hire others to do the statistics for their studies and in fact the analysis and interpretation. Qualitative researchers do not fall into this trap. The role of the qualitative researcher, like that of the dancer or the choreographer, demands a presence, an attention to detail, and a powerful use of the researcher's own mind and body in analysis and interpretation of the data. No one can dance your dance, so to speak. No one can choreograph your dance but you. No one can interpret your data but you. Qualitative researchers do not hire people to analyze and interpret their data. This is a critical difference between the two paradigms, and it illustrates the usefulness once again of the dance metaphor. It also prompts us as researchers to begin a dialogue on methodolatry, and whether or not we are actually contributing to methodolatry by either allowing others to analyze and interpret data for our studies, as in the case of many quantitative researchers, or standing by and not questioning this practice as professors of qualitative research. After all, the entire point of doing a dissertation is to pass through the rites of passage of designing a study, implementing the study, and disseminating the findings of the study. If someone else does two-thirds of that work, what rite of passage has the student completed?

◆ Methodolatry

I use the term *methodolatry,* a combination of *method* and *idolatry,* to describe a preoccupation with selecting and defending methods to the exclusion of the actual substance of the story being told. Methodolatry is the idolatry of method, or a slavish attachment and devotion to method, that so often overtakes the discourse in the education and human services fields. Methodolatry manifests itself in many ways. A good example of methodolatry at its worst is found in the cases of survey researchers who throw out survey responses that don't match the answers they are looking for in order that they might do the only statistical techniques they were taught (and this is aside from the ethical issues raised by such practices). Another great example is the dissertation that contains 30 *t* tests or more about no particular issue, always in good faith, of course, but with very little reflection. In my lifetime, I have witnessed an almost constant obsession with the trinity of validity,

reliability, and generalizability. It is always tempting to become obsessed with methods, but when this happens, experience is separated from knowing. Methodolatry is another way to move away from understanding the actual experience of participants in the research project. In the final stage of writing up the project, it is probably wise for the qualitative researcher to avoid being overly preoccupied with method. In other words, the researcher should immediately focus on the substance of the findings. Qualitative research depends on the presentation of solid descriptive data, so that the researcher leads the reader to an understanding of the meaning of the experience under study.

In classic terms, sociologists and anthropologists have shown us that finding categories and the relationship and patterns between and among categories leads to completeness in the narrative. Spradley (1980) suggests searching for cultural themes or domains. Denzin (1989) follows Husserl's earlier conception of bracketing, which is to hold the phenomenon up for serious inspection, and suggests the following steps:

1. Locate within the personal experience, or self-story, key phrases and statements that speak directly to the phenomenon in question.
2. Interpret the meanings of these phrases as an informed reader.
3. Obtain the participants' interpretation of these findings, if possible.
4. Inspect these meanings for what they reveal about the essential, recurring features of the phenomenon being studied.
5. Offer a tentative statement or definition of the phenomenon in terms of the essential recurring features identified in Step 4.

In the process of bracketing, the researcher has the opportunity to treat the data in all its forms equally. Then the researcher may categorize, group, and cluster the data in order to interpret the data. The researcher uses constant comparative analysis to look for statements and indices of behavior that occur over time and in a variety of periods during the study. In addition, bracketing allows the researcher to find points of tension and conflict and what doesn't fit. After total immersion in the setting, the researcher needs time for analysis and contemplation of the data. By allowing sufficient time to go over the data carefully, the researcher opens up possibilities for uncovering the meaning in participants' lives. I have found Moustakis (1990) helpful in providing a heuristic approach here. He offers room to use inductive analysis through five phases. First, immersion in the setting starts the inductive process. Second, the incubation process allows for thinking, becoming aware of nuance and meaning in the setting, and capturing intuitive insights, to achieve understanding. Third, there is a phase of illumination that allows for expanding awareness. Fourth, and most understandably, is a phase of explication that includes description and explanation to capture the experience of individuals in the study. Finally, creative synthesis enables the researcher to synthesize and bring together as a whole the individual's story, including the meaning of the lived experience. These phases are similar to what the choreographer registers through the stages of preparation, exploration, and illumination.

The purposes of these disciplined approaches to analysis are, of course, to describe and to explain the essence of experience and meaning in participants' lives. Essentially this is what dancers do in interpreting a dance, and most assuredly what choreographers do in designing choreographic studies. Patton (1990) suggests a balance between description and interpretation. Denzin (1989) elaborates further by suggesting that thick description makes thick interpretation possible. Endless description is not useful if the researcher is to present a powerful narrative. Analysis and interpretation effectively balance description. There is no one way to accomplish this balance. Many beginning students ask me, "How many interviews must I do?" or "How long should I observe?" or "How many documents should I look at?" All of these are legitimate questions, of course, and all flow out of the psychometric—How long? How many? and so on. What the qualitative researcher needs to do is begin to reframe

these questions in a language of interpretation and meaning, much as dancers and choreographers do—indeed, as any artist does. Rather than ask, for example, "How many interviews should I do?" the researcher can pose the question as a choreographer might: "What type of interview and with which actors would be most sensible given the purpose of my study and the exploratory questions that guide my study?" Such a question will yield answers that are far more textured and demanding. I am always amazed at the resistance to qualitative research by fellow professors who manage only to ask the child's question, "How many?" or, even more transparent, "Where's the control group?" rather than really think as qualitative researchers and ask solid, meaningful, textured questions. I am convinced that what separates good researchers from mediocre or bad ones is the same as what separates good choreographers from mediocre ones—the basic ability to formulate a meaningful textured question or statement.

◆ Crystallization Instead of Triangulation in Research Projects

If one reviews the literature in the area of qualitative research methods and design, one sees that historically there have been periodic discussions of triangulation as an important part of the design process. In the 1970s, Denzin (1978) identified four basic types of triangulation:

1. *Data triangulation:* the use of a variety of data sources in a study;
2. *Investigator triangulation:* the use of several different researchers or evaluators;
3. *Theory triangulation:* the use of multiple perspectives to interpret a single set of data;
4. *Methodological triangulation:* the use of multiple methods to study a single problem.

In the 1990s, I initially wrote of interdisciplinary triangulation (Janesick, 1994a). Now, as we move toward the new millennium, I am in agreement with Richardson (1994), who offers the idea of crystallization as a better lens through which to view qualitative research designs and their components. Richardson elegantly explains the concept of crystallization as part of the postmodern project. Crystallization recognizes the many facets of any given approach to the social world as a fact of life. The image of the crystal replaces that of the land surveyor and the triangle. We move on from plane geometry to the new physics. The crystal "combines symmetry and substance with an infinite variety of shapes, substances, transmutations, multidimensionalities, and angles of approach. Crystals grow, change, and alter, but are not amorphous" (Richardson, 1994, p. 522). What we see when we view a crystal, for example, depends on how we view it, how we hold it up to the light or not. Richardson continues, "Crystallization provides us with a deepened, complex, thoroughly partial, understanding of the topic. Paradoxically, we know more and doubt what we know" (p. 522).

I like to think that crystallization incorporates the use of other disciplines, such as art, sociology, history, dance, architecture, and anthropology, to inform our research processes and broaden our understanding of method and substance. For example, in the discipline of history, historians rely on documents and interviews almost entirely. There is constant discussion of method, but this is connected to content. We might learn a great deal from historians on this point alone. Returning to the arts and choreography, just the awareness of the choreographer's concerns with rhythm, tempo, the use of negative space, and action, for example, may broaden our own views on our respective research projects. Too often we become comfortable in our worlds and, to paraphrase Goethe, sometimes the most obvious things are hardest to see because they are right in front of our eyes. Thus I propose that we use the notion of crystallization to include incorporation of various disciplines as part of multifaceted qualitative research design.

To illustrate, I require all my students to incorporate journal writing, in which they reflect on the research process, into their preparatory work before they go out into the field for their dissertation work. The act of journal writing is a rigorous documentary tool (Janesick, 1998b, 1999). The students keep journals as do the researcher and the participants in the study in their roles as coresearchers on the project. Often, if students elect to do so, interactive journals between researcher and participants as coresearchers are also used. These techniques, borrowed from the arts and the humanities, are extremely helpful for focusing individuals on the project at hand; they also serve as a useful tool for describing the role of the researcher. If keeping journals is not a viable option, letter writing between members of the study, actual short essays, and other written work can provide a useful data set for further understanding in the research project. I like to think of these activities as multidisciplinary. I also use other artistic techniques, such as collages, mounted constructions, and haiku and other poetry, during class activities to get prospective researchers thinking in an artistic frame and stretching that part of their brains. I ask students to dig deep into their souls to create haiku, a traditional Japanese poetry form containing only 17 syllables, about their work in their research projects. Here are two haiku examples that appear in my book *Stretching Exercises for Qualitative Researchers* (1998c); the first is my own, and the second was written by Judith Gouwens:

Willingness to fail,
Easing into Silence,
Stumbling upon secrets.

Seeing past happening,
Hearing between words,
Touching heart stories.

This is what I mean by *stretching exercises;* for me, at least, such activities fit with the idea of crystallization.

The Issue of Credibility

The qualitative research literature contains many valuable and useful treatments of the issue of credibility (see, e.g., Eisner, 1991; Lincoln & Guba, 1985; Patton, 1990). Basically, qualitative researchers have been patiently responding to questions usually formulated from a psychometric perspective. Most often, questions addressed to qualitative researchers are constructed from the psychometric paradigm and revolve around the trinity of validity, reliability, and generalizability, as if there were no other linguistic representations for questions.

Replacing Validity, Generalizability, and Reliability With Qualitative Referents

Many qualitative researchers have struggled to identify more appropriately how we do what we do. So, rather than take terms from the quantitative paradigm, qualitative researchers have correctly offered alternative ways to think about descriptive validity and the unique qualities of case study work. In order to explain this, I rely on experience and the literature. The description of persons, places, and events has been the cornerstone of qualitative research. I believe it will remain the cornerstone, because this is the qualitative researcher's reason for being. What has happened recently, as Wolcott (1990a, 1995) reminds us, is that the term *validity,* for example, which is overspecified in one domain, has become confusing because it is reassigned to another. Validity in the quantitative arena has a set of technical microdefinitions, and the reader is most likely well aware of those. Validity in qualitative research has to do with description and explanation and whether or not the explanation fits the description. In other words, is the explanation credible? In addition, qualitative researchers do not claim that there is only one way of interpreting an event. There is no one "correct" interpretation.

By applying the suggestions of Lincoln and Guba (1985) and others, we may cross-check our work through member checks and audit trails. As a rule, in writing up the narrative, the qualitative researcher must decide what form the member check will take. For example, quite often, participants in a study move, leave the area, or request that they omit being part of the member check. The researcher needs to find a way to allow for the participants to review the material one way or another. For years, anthropologists and sociologists have incorporated a kind of member check by having an outsider read their field notes and interview transcripts (see Janesick, 1998b). This current variation is a good one, for educational research is always public, open to the public, and in many cases funded under federal mandates. Implicit in the member check directive, however, is the psychometric assumption that the trinity of validity, generalizability, and reliability, all terms from the quantitative paradigm, are to be adhered to in research. I think it is time to question that trinity and the use of psychometric language, and in fact to replace that language with language that more accurately captures the complexity and texture of qualitative research. The excellent suggestions of Flick (1998), Lincoln and Guba (1985), Janesick (1994a), and Wolcott (1995), to name a few, offer us heuristic tools to reconceptualize this space. There is no need for us to go over again and again those terms that more correctly apply to another paradigm.

Wolcott (1990a, 1995) presents provocative discussions about seeking and rejecting validity. He argues for understanding the absurdity of validity by developing a case for no single "correct" interpretation. Dancers and choreographers know this as well. Even, for example, if we consider the minuet, with its set movements and prescribed gestures, one dancer's arm movements may be very different from another's, even as both are dancing the same dance. Similarly, Donmoyer (1990) makes an even stronger case for rejecting traditional notions of generalizability for those researchers in education and human services who are concerned with individuals and the meaning in their lives. Donmoyer argues that traditional ways of thinking about generalizability are inadequate. He does not eschew generalizability altogether; for example, bureaucrats and policy makers seem to prefer aggregated numbers about certain social conditions, but only because no one has taken the time to offer them sensible or viable alternatives. In fact, the research community is often silent on such points. Is it time for the research community to assert itself and offer bureaucrats and policy makers some range of options for understanding the social settings under study? For the needs of the bureaucrats, the old notions of generalizability seem to make sense, if only for expediency. On the other hand, for those of us who are interested in questions of meaning and interpretation in individual cases—the kind of research done in education and human services and in the arts and humanities—traditional thinking about generalizability falls short, and in fact may do serious damage to individual persons. The traditional view of generalizability limits the ability to reconceptualize the role of social science in education and human services. In addition, the whole history of case study research in anthropology, education, sociology, and history stands solidly on its merits. In fact, the value of the case study is its uniqueness; consequently, reliability in the traditional sense of replicability is pointless here. I hope that we can move beyond discussions of this trinity of psychometrics and get on with the discussion of powerful statements from carefully done, rigorous long-term studies that uncover the meanings of events in individuals' lives.

Somehow we have lost the human and passionate element of research. Becoming immersed in a study requires passion: passion for people, passion for communication, and passion for understanding people. This is the contribution of qualitative research, and it can only enhance educational and human services practice. In the other paradigm, people are taken out of the formula and, worse, are often lumped together in some undefinable aggregate as if they were not individual persons. In the qualitative arena the individual is not only inserted into the study, the individual is the backbone of the study. We can take a lesson about this from dance and choreography. It would be difficult indeed to find a dancer or choreographer who lacks passion for his or her work, or who looks away from the individual person who is part of the dance. For too long we have allowed psychometrics to rule our research and subsequently have decontextualized individual persons. By depersonalizing the most personal of social events, education and human services, we have lost our way. Now it is time to return to a discourse on the personal, on what it means to

be alive. We need to capture the lived experience of individuals and their stories, much like the choreographer who crafts a dance.

◆ Meaning and Choreography: Revisiting Minuets and Improvisations

We had the experience but missed the meaning. And approach to the meaning restores the experience

In a different form

T. S. Eliot

Isn't it remarkable that the entire history of dance has been characterized by a deep division, the division between classical ballet and modern and postmodern forms? What might we learn from this? All arts and sciences draw upon tradition, and a first step in understanding them is to understand their past. Dance and choreography are tied to the past in a peculiar way. Dance and choreography originated from one element of society, the courts of kings and queens. However, as society developed and organized, dividing into tribes, nations, and classes, the function of dance became much more complicated. Its language, steps, and movements no longer only represented kings and queens, but included the dances of ordinary people in the form of folk dances. Dance became divided.

One form of this division survives as folk dance from the ancient primitive thread of communal dances. The other thread emerged from society's ruling class, the court, center of social power. It was not long before ballet became an official lexicon of the court and the court dances a definite class and status symbol. It was not until the 20th century that the ruling influence in dance, ballet, was challenged by a determined, frail woman from Vermont, Martha Graham. The field today in dance is well into a postmodern era, mostly due to choreographers such as Merce Cunningham. Essentially, Cunningham made the following claims (Banes, 1980, p. 6):

1. Any movement can be material for dance.
2. Any procedure can be valid.
3. Any part or parts of the body can be used, subject to nature's limitation.
4. Music, costume, lighting, and dancing have their own separate logics and identities.
5. Any dancer in a company may be a soloist.
6. Any space may be danced in.
7. Dancing can be about anything, but it is fundamentally and primarily about the human body and its movements, beginning with walking.

Cunningham's dances decentralize space and stretch out time. They do away with what is familiar and easy. They are unpredictable. They sometimes do not even turn out as planned. He may use chance methods, such as tossing coins. (Banes, 1980, points out that although this was to be random, the dancers' movements were determined by this chance event.) Chance subverts habits and allows for new combinations and interpretations. Cunningham truly makes the word *radical*, returning to the root, come alive. He preserves continuity and a physical logic to his search for meaning in movement and the desire to tell a story. In thinking about dance as a metaphor for qualitative research design, I find that the meaning for me lies in the fact that the substance of dance is the familiar; walking, running, and any movement of the body. The qualitative researcher is like the dancer or the choreographer, then, in seeking to describe, explain, and make understandable the familiar in a contextual, personal, and passionate way.

◆ *Summary, Afterthoughts, and Future Directions*

The qualitative researcher's design decisions can be thought of as similar to the dancer's three stages of warm-up, exercises, and cool-down, or, as the choreographer might say, preparation, exploration, and illumination/ formulation. The qualitative researcher makes a series of decisions at the beginning, middle, and end of the study. Qualitative research design has an elastic quality, much like the elasticity of the dancer's spine. Just as dance mirrors and adapts to life, qualitative design is adapted, changed, and redesigned as the study proceeds, due to the social realities of doing research among and with the living. The qualitative researcher focuses on description and explanation, and all design decisions ultimately relate to these acts. Built into qualitative research design is a system of checks and balances that include staying in a setting over time and capturing and interpreting the meaning in individual persons' lives. By staying in a setting over time, the researcher has the opportunity to use crystallization, whereby he or she may view the approaching work in the study through various facets to deepen understanding of what is going on in the study. This allows for multiple ways of framing the problem, selecting research strategies, and extending discourse across several fields of study. This is exactly the opposite of the quantitative approach, which relies on one mind-set, the psychometric, and which prefers to aggregate numbers that are one or more steps removed from social reality. The qualitative researcher is uncomfortable with methodolatry and prefers to capture the lived experience of participants in order to understand their meaning perspectives, case by case. Finally, the qualitative researcher is like the choreographer who creates a dance to make a statement. For the researcher, the story told is like the dance, in all its complexity, context, originality, and passion. In addition, the researcher is, like the dancer, always a part of the research project and, like the choreographer, an intellectual critic throughout the study. Whether or not the dancer is performing a minuet or an improvisation, like the qualitative researcher, she is involved in interpretation. Qualitative research design is an act of interpretation from beginning to end.

Future Directions

I am optimistic concerning the future directions in our field in general and in qualitative research design in particular. In looking over the

current writings in the arts, humanities, and social sciences, one can only be optimistic. Here
are my reasons for this statement.

1. We live in a postmodern world where the
old boundaries, voices, and power structures
are constantly being questioned. In fact, the locus of psychometric control is eroding, simply
because when psychometric practices are called
into question, the same old tired arguments are
used—they didn't work in the first place. Look
at the critics of education, for example: Many of
these writers have pointed out that the past half
century of educational research has yielded little in the way of results. The public, members of
Congress, business executives, and leaders in
the field often point out that indeed schools are
no better places today than they were, say, 50
years ago, all other factors aside. In fact, the
kinds of questions educational researchers have
pursued are often termed trivial because they
have little to do with teachers, students, and the
underlying work of schools. Postmodernists and
post-postmodernists (or whatever we end up
calling the next wave of critics) have forced us to
return to the heart of the matter: individual lives
and how they are exploited in organizations on
a daily basis. We should all be thankful for the
postmodern questions.

2. With the hostile political context in Congress, and the consistent cutting of funds for education and educational research since the Rea-
gan-Bush-Quayle years, researchers are finding
fewer dollars for their research projects. Thus
they will have to turn to research that relies on
historical techniques and archival expertise;
they will have to go to libraries and other reposi-
tories of information. In general, I see a return
to those techniques used by artists and humani-
tarians. Researchers will be forced to confront
historical contexts and, instead of working in
big, grant-funded shops, may have to work individually in archives, libraries, and other reposi-
tories of written texts.

3. With corporate sponsors stepping in to finance artworks such as public murals, dance
concerts, and symphonies, there may be an opportunity for researchers to argue persuasively
for corporate sponsorship of oral history, life
history, and other narrative projects to docu-

ment the lived experience of community members. For example, the Disney Corporation
funded Julie Taymor's creation and direction of
the highly original, imaginative, and successful
Broadway hit *The Lion King*. At no time did Disney interfere with the project because of its utter
faith in this remarkable artist. I see such developments as expanding our notion of how corporations might work with qualitative researchers
at some point in the future.

4. Foundations may also be interested in
partnerships with qualitative researchers. Indeed, foundations may continue their support
of careful long-term case studies, as the Ford
Foundation did with the case studies on immigration captured by Louise Lamphere's (1992)
edited volume. The Ford Foundation also
funded the research described in later work by
Lamphere, Stepick, and Grenier (1994) on restructuring the U.S. economy. This is a positive
and important sign that shows how foundations
might work with qualitative researchers over
extended periods of time to document the narratives of newcomers in the workplace.

5. With the renewed emphasis on communitarianism and the call to re-vision particular
communities, individual qualitative researchers
may find a growing demand for documentation
of the lived experience of key members of given
communities through long-term, carefully done
studies. A bit of ingenuity and library time can
uncover many funding sources, such as civic organizations and foundations, for research in any
given community. Each semester, I am called
upon to talk to community workers who would
like to do oral history projects in the community
and are looking for information on finding exemplars in that area.

6. Cultivation of the art of writing, and thus
a return to communication, will be central to
our future work: writing journals, writing letters, writing sensible e-mail messages. In fact, I
teach my students to include in their final research reports written testimony from participants in their projects, in as many forms as possible. Most often, these appear as letters, short
essays, and journal entries. After all, in the end,
the written narrative is indeed a type of permanent insurrection. Choreographers, other art-

ists, and qualitative researchers are also part of this permanent insurrection.

7. I think there will be a need for researchers to develop their imaginations and to use those imaginations when it comes to designing qualitative research projects. For far too long, research has been for the few, and, in the field of education at least, research is often forgotten as soon as it is reported (with a few exceptions). One of the reasons for this is that research traditionally has been reported without passion or imagination, and in many cases without wisdom. It is time to rekindle the researcher's imagination. I foresee that those who can use imagination in their work will be a significant force in shaping future research projects.

■ Notes

1. I went to New York because it is the center of the dance world. From Erick Hawkins I learned that creativity and the body/mind are one, and I was introduced to Eastern thought. Hawkins and all his teachers were inspiring and brilliant persons. From Merce Cunningham and the teachers at Westbeth, I learned to trust the body and to draw upon lived experience in my work as a choreographer. For Cunningham, dance is a *chance* encounter between movement, sound, and light through space. The viewer makes of it what the viewer will. Cunningham pursues the process of dance in a Zen-like manner. He has also been called the anarchist of modern dance as well as the beginning point of the postmodern movement in dance. All dances are grounded in some experience, and all stories that are told about that experience rely on the body, which is the research instrument. The body is the instrument through which life is lived. In dance, the body cannot deny the impulse to express the lived experience. It is virtually impossible for the body to tell a lie or to cover up the truth in the dance. As the painter Salvador Dalí remarked, "Drawing is the honesty of art. There is no possibility of cheating."

2. I first learned of theoretical sampling in my training as an ethnographer of the symbolic interactionist school, by reading Glaser and Strauss (1967). Theoretical sampling is the heart of grounded theory approaches to research. It allows for the use of the constant comparative method in data collection and analysis. Theoretical sampling allows for direction in the study and allows the researcher to have confidence in his or her categories, because they emerge from the data and are constantly and selectively reformulated along the way. The data in any study do not speak for themselves. The researcher must make sense of the data in a meaningful way, and any technique that allows the researcher to find an active way of searching the data is welcome. This is only one of many approaches to qualitative analysis. However, it is most helpful to students who have studied only psychometric approaches to research. This seems to be a transition tool for many who have approached research as a boilerplate activity.

3. Gallaudet University is the only liberal arts university dedicated to educating deaf individuals.

4. Constant comparative analysis allows the researcher to develop grounded theory. A grounded theory is one inductively derived from the study. Data collection, analysis, and theory are related reciprocally. The researcher grounds the theory in the data from statements of belief and behavior of participants in the study. See Glaser and Strauss (1967) and Strauss and Corbin (1990) for more detailed descriptions of grounded theory. It is basically opposite to the use of theory in the quantitative paradigm. Instead of proving a theory, the qualitative researcher studies a setting over time and develops theory grounded in the data. This is only one of many approaches to analysis, but it is a solid one and is especially useful for beginners. To move further, I suggest we look to the arts and humanities, particularly choreography and writing, to expand our notions of how to make sense of, analyze, and interpret qualitative data.

■ References

Banes, S. (1980). *Terpsichore in sneakers: Post-modern dance.* Boston: Houghton Mifflin.

Blom, L. A., & Chaplin, L. (1988). *The moment of movement: Dance improvisation.* Pittsburgh, PA: University of Pittsburgh Press.

Bogdan, R. C., & Biklen, S. K. (1992). *Qualitative research for education: An introduction to theory and methods* (2nd ed.). Boston: Allyn & Bacon.

Creswell, J. W. (1997). *Qualitative inquiry and research design: Choosing among five traditions.* Thousand Oaks, CA: Sage.

DeFreese, B. (1996). *A case study of an assistant superintendent.* Unpublished doctoral dissertation, University of Kansas.

Denzin, N. K. (1978). *The research act: A theoretical introduction to sociological methods* (2nd ed.). New York: McGraw-Hill.

Denzin, N. K. (1989). *Interpretive interactionism.* Newbury Park, CA: Sage.

Dewey, J. (1958). *Art as experience.* New York: Capricorn. (Original work published 1934)

Donmoyer, R. (1990). Generalizability and the single-case study. In E. W. Eisner & A. Peshkin (Eds.), *Qualitative inquiry in education: The continuing debate* (pp. 175-200). New York: Teachers College Press.

Eisner, E. (1991). *The enlightened eye: Qualitative inquiry and the enhancement of educational practices.* New York: Macmillan.

Fetterman, D. M. (1989). *Ethnography: Step by step.* Newbury Park, CA: Sage.

Flick, U. (1998). *An introduction to qualitative research: Theory, method and applications.* London: Sage.

Glaser, B. G., & Strauss, A. L. (1967). *The discovery of grounded theory: Strategies for qualitative research.* Chicago: Aldine.

Goetz, J. P., & LeCompte, M. D. (1984). *Ethnography and qualitative design in educational research.* New York: Academic Press.

Gouwens, J. A. (1995). *Leadership for school change: An interview observation study of two Chicago elementary principals.* Unpublished doctoral dissertation, University of Kansas.

Guba, E. G., & Lincoln, Y. S. (1994). Competing paradigms in qualitative research. In N. K. Denzin & Y. S. Lincoln (Eds.), *Handbook of qualitative research* (pp. 105-117). Thousand Oaks, CA: Sage.

Humphrey, D. (1987). *The art of making dances.* Penington, NJ: Princeton Book. (Original work published 1959)

Janesick, V. J. (1982). Of snakes and circles: Making sense of classroom group processes through a case study. *Curriculum Inquiry, 12,* 161-185.

Janesick, V. J. (1994a). The dance of qualitative research design: Metaphor, methodolatry, and meaning. In N. K. Denzin & Y. S. Lincoln (Eds.), *Handbook of qualitative research* (pp. 209-219). Thousand Oaks, CA: Sage.

Janesick, V. J. (1994b). *Of heart windows and utopias: A case study of deaf culture.* Paper presented at the Ethnography in Education Forum, University of Pennsylvania, Philadelphia.

Janesick, V. J. (1998a). The dance of qualitative research design: Metaphor, methodolatry, and meaning. In N. K. Denzin & Y. S. Lincoln (Eds.), *Strategies of qualitative inquiry.* Thousand Oaks, CA: Sage.

Janesick, V. J. (1998b). *Journal writing as a qualitative research technique: History, issues, and reflections.* Paper presented at the annual meeting of the American Educational Research Association, San Diego, CA.

Janesick, V. J. (1998c). *Stretching exercises for qualitative researchers.* Thousand Oaks, CA: Sage.

Janesick, V. J. (1999). A journal about journal writing as a qualitative research technique. *Qualitative Inquiry, 5*(4).

Lamphere, L. (Ed.). (1992). *Structuring diversity: Ethnographic perspectives on the new immigration.* Chicago: University of Chicago Press.

Lamphere, L., Stepick, A., & Grenier, G. (1994). *Newcomers in the workplace: Immigrants and the restructuring of the U.S. economy.* Philadelphia: Temple University Press.

LeCompte, M. D., Millroy, W. L., & Preissle, J. (Eds.). (1992). *The handbook of qualitative research in education.* New York: Academic Press.

Lincoln, Y. S., & Guba, E. G. (1985). *Naturalistic inquiry.* Beverly Hills, CA: Sage.

Marshall, C., & Rossman, G. (1995). *Designing qualitative research* (2nd ed.). Thousand Oaks, CA: Sage.

Maxwell, J. A. (1996). *Qualitative research design: An interactive approach.* Thousand Oaks, CA: Sage.

Miles, M. B., & Huberman, A. M. (1994). *Qualitative data analysis: An expanded sourcebook* (2nd ed.). Thousand Oaks, CA: Sage.

Moustakis, C. (1990). *Heuristic research design, methodology, and applications.* Newbury Park, CA: Sage.

Patton, M. Q. (1990). *Qualitative evaluation and research methods* (2nd ed.). Newbury Park, CA: Sage.

Richardson, L. (1994). Writing: A method of inquiry. In N. K. Denzin & Y. S. Lincoln (Eds.), *Handbook of qualitative research* (pp. 516-529). Thousand Oaks, CA: Sage.

Spradley, J. P. (1979). *The ethnographic interview.* New York: Holt, Rinehart & Winston.

Spradley, J. P. (1980). *Participant observation.* New York: Holt, Rinehart & Winston.

Strauss, A. L., & Corbin, J. (1990). *Basics of qualitative research: Grounded theory procedures and techniques.* Newbury Park, CA: Sage.

Williams-Boyd, P. (1996). *A case study of a full service school: A transformational dialectic of empowerment, collaboration, and commu-nitarianism.* Unpublished doctoral dissertation, University of Kansas.

Wolcott, H. F. (1990a). On seeking and rejecting validity in qualitative research. In E. W. Eisner & A. Peshkin (Eds.), *Qualitative inquiry in education: The continuing debate* (pp. 121-152). New York: Teachers College Press.

Wolcott, H. F. (1990b). *Writing up qualitative research.* Newbury Park, CA: Sage.

Wolcott, H. F. (1994). *Transforming qualitative data: Description, analysis, and interpretation.* Thousand Oaks, CA: Sage.

Wolcott, H. F. (1995). *The art of fieldwork.* Walnut Creek, CA: AltaMira.

14

AN UNTOLD STORY?

Doing Funded Qualitative Research

♦ Julianne Cheek

♦ The Untold Story

Ever-increasing numbers of articles, book chapters, and even books are available on how to "do" funded research. Although not many of these are written with qualitative research specifically in mind, much of what is stated can be applied to research using qualitative approaches. However, too often the discussion begins at what I see as the middle stage in the process of doing research rather than at the start. For example, working out who to approach for funding, and how this should be done, is as important as knowing how to prepare research proposals or fill in application guidelines. Yet often it is taken for granted that researchers in-stinctively know how to go about identifying and approaching potential funders. Similarly, most discussions about applying for funding come to an end at the point where the proposal has been prepared and submitted, giving the impression that somehow the research process from there on is smooth sailing—which in my experience it certainly is not. Insights into the process of allocating funding, and ways in which researchers can interact with that process and learn from it, remain very much outside the major focus of conventional literature about doing funded research. Questions that need to be addressed, although more often than not they are ignored, include the following: What are some of the things researchers need to consider before accepting funds? Does accepting funding

AUTHOR'S NOTE: I would like to acknowledge the critical but constructive feedback on various drafts of this chapter provided by Yvonna Lincoln, Norman Denzin, Ann Austin, and William Tierney. Their comments have helped me to tighten and focus the discussion. In particular, I would like to thank Yvonna Lincoln for helping me to overcome a dilemma I faced in wanting to create a text that focuses on the practicalities of doing funded qualitative research while at the same time troubling what I perceive as the subtle (and not so subtle) commodification of research. Her suggestion of using Patti Lather's notion of writing in a different register for each perspective helped me to go some way toward meeting the competing demands of reviewers and thus, I hope, to reach the readers of this chapter.

affect in any way the qualitative research process? What are the ethical issues bound up in both the search and selection process for funding and the actual research itself? What other issues might researchers face while actually conducting funded qualitative research?

Thus, for many would-be researchers, doing funded qualitative research remains shrouded in mystique. In short, it is largely "an unknown story" ("The Leading Edge," 1996). In response to this, what follows is my attempt to make known certain aspects of the story of "doing" funded qualitative research that are seldom told. Consequently, I offer no detailed information as to how to write the various sections of a research proposal. Nor do I address specific research approaches and methods. Rather, I present detailed discussion of those aspects of "doing" funded qualitative research that otherwise may not get attention yet are vitally important to the smooth conduct of a research project. At all times, I try to concentrate on points that I believe have particular relevance to *qualitative* research that is funded.

My aim in writing this chapter is thus to begin to tell a story that for whatever reason tends to remain untold. I do not claim to tell the full story or the only story possible—rather, it is my story, drawn from my experiences and the experiences and writings of others. It is also a story with no end. I hope that readers will be able to add to the story from their own experiences and from understandings they gain from either considering or "doing" funded qualitative research.

◆ *Setting the Parameters for the Chapter: The Notion of Funded Qualitative Research*

Funded research, particularly funded *qualitative* research, forms the focus of the discussion to follow. Funded research is research carried out with financial support, which can take various forms. The researcher could receive a certain amount of money to be used directly for salaries, equipment, travel, or other expenses

identified as having been incurred in carrying out the research. In some cases, support for projects is offered "in-kind": Rather than supplying cash, the funder may choose to provide the researcher with access to specialist staff or equipment as a means of supporting the research. This type of support can be very useful, as it may give the researcher access to resources that otherwise may not be available and without which he or she could not undertake the research. Thus when we talk about *funded* qualitative research, it is not always money that we are talking about.

Each form of support for qualitative research places its own unique demands on both the researcher and the research project. In particular, the amount of freedom the researcher has in terms of the project design and the form the "products" of the research take will vary depending on what type of support is received. For example, when a researcher initiates a project, he or she is free to develop the aims and objectives as well as the general direction of the research. However, in projects that are funded as components of larger studies, such as some evaluation projects, the researcher in all probability cannot assume the freedom to develop the aims and direction of the research to be undertaken.

It is apparent from this introductory discussion that there are a range of ways in which qualitative research might be funded and a number of different purposes that such funded research might serve. Funded qualitative research is not a homogeneous category that can be reduced to a single understanding. In the same way that qualitative approaches to research are varied in focus and purpose, so are funded qualitative projects. Thus it is not possible to provide a single "recipe" to follow for researchers who wish to undertake funded qualitative research. In the remainder of this chapter, I explore some of the issues and questions that may arise for researchers either when they are "doing" funded qualitative research or when they are thinking about the notion of funded qualitative research. Of course, some of what follows is not necessarily unique to qualitative approaches but applies across the board to all research, whether qualitative or not.

Following this section, in which I set the parameters for the chapter and examine the notion of funded qualitative research, the next section explores the craft of attracting funds for qualitative research. In this very practical discussion, I address how researchers can go about identifying and building relationships with funding bodies, approaching potential funders, crafting proposals to request funding, and navigating the application process, including building on initial failure, to attract funds. I then explore issues the researcher may encounter when undertaking funded qualitative research. Most of what I discuss arises from issues that I have had to confront and grapple with while either doing, or contemplating doing, funded qualitative research. Thus the discussion is grounded in the reality of doing such research. Issues to be explored include how funding can affect considerations around the ethics of the research, matters pertaining to the control of the research, and the effect funding might have on the relationships among the various parties involved in the research.

Following that discussion, I make a shift in register (Lather, 1996) to explore the notion of the research "market" and whether or not there is the potential for funded qualitative research to be privileged over unfunded research. In this exploration I aim to trouble the concept of qualitative funded research—not to set up a polemic between unfunded and funded research, but rather to encourage readers to think about their own assumptions about funded research and how such assumptions have embedded within them many taken-for-granteds about the nature of research and research "products." In the concluding section, the various threads that have been woven throughout the chapter are drawn together. I end the chapter where I began—urging readers to think deeply about all aspects of funded qualitative research, not just the "how-to," but issues such as the "use" to which research products will be put.

Finally, in terms of setting the parameters for what is to follow, I wish to state up front the positions (for they are plural) from which I am writing this chapter. To a large extent these positions provide the "con-text," that is, the "text

that is 'with' " (Halliday & Hasan, 1989, p. 11) the discussion that occurs. Any analysis of what I have written in this chapter must consider, among other things, the wider processes in its development. Such an analysis must situate the text that is this chapter in terms of the texts that inform and are "with" the main text. In other words, it is important to ask what texts are framing the discussion that occurs in this chapter. On reflecting upon this question, I have identified some of the con-texts that I am aware have affected the text that you are reading now. First, I write from the position of an individual committed to qualitative approaches to research. Second, I write as someone who recognizes that funded qualitative research is not only possible, but actually opens up opportunities that otherwise may not be available to researchers in terms of types of projects, scope of projects, and simply the ability to undertake research that is as person- and time-intensive as many qualitative studies are.

However, equally I write as someone who has discovered many pitfalls when doing funded qualitative studies. Most of these pitfalls could not be predicted, and they forced me to confront some very fundamental questions about what research is for and how much, as a researcher, I am prepared to give up in order to conform to funding requirements. From another position altogether, I write as an academic who has grappled with the requirement to produce performance outcomes measured by, for instance, the amount of funding received for research. I write also as one who has faced the dilemma of whether the funding or the project should assume primary importance. Finally, I write with the aim of consciously trying to avoid setting up any form of polemic in the discussion that is to follow.

Thus I am not arguing for or against doing funded qualitative research—rather, I am exploring what "doing" funded qualitative research might mean for both the researcher and the research. In so doing, I aim to provide practical details for researchers but also to encourage readers to think carefully about the con-texts that are in operation at any point in time, including while they are doing funded qualitative research. Any text has embedded within it assumptions about the reality in question and a certain view that is being conveyed to the reader of the text. This is the subtext or "the hidden script" (Sachs, 1996, p. 633). Put another way, the subtext is "the assumptions that every text makes in presuming it will be understood" (Agger, 1991, p. 112). This chapter has embedded within it a critical subtext that aims to challenge aspects of doing funded qualitative research that can otherwise come to be taken for granted. The chapter should not be read as either for or against funded or any other type of research. Rather, it should be read as a text that takes a particular view of doing funded qualitative research. It is up to the readers how they position themselves with respect to that view.

◆ Getting Started: Turning a Research Idea Into a Submission for Funding

One of the first things that researchers do when trying to attract funding for a research proposal, or to be in a position to know about contracts/tenders that are offered for various research projects, is to identify potential funding sources. Zagury (1997) has identified six categories of potential funding sources: local community funds, special-purpose foundations, family-sponsored foundations, national foundations, government grants, and corporate foundations and/or corporate funding. It is important to be aware that there are distinct national differences in types and patterns of funding. Hence it may well be that in certain countries some of the above categories of funders are of less significance than in others. However, regardless of the actual mix of funding sources in any particular country or part of a country (for there are regional variations in many nations), it is imperative that researchers "do their homework" with respect to uncovering potential funding sources.

One place for researchers to start is by obtaining publications that list the names of potential funders for research. For example, in Aus-

tralia one such publication is *The Australian Grants Register,* whose author states that it has been compiled "to give everyone ready access to information concerning grants in Australia, and to enable forward planning so that applications are well prepared" (Summers, 1998, p. vii). It is useful for those beginning to investigate funding sources to investigate what types of grant registers exist in their local contexts. Watching advertisements in newspapers, particularly in the contract/tender section, is another way of identifying potential funding sources, as is getting on the mailing list of the university research office, for those who work in university settings. Another very useful way researchers can get to know about potential funding sources that may not be advertised or appear in any grants register or list is by talking to people who have received funding in areas similar to the proposed research. I have found that, on the whole, people are only too willing to share their experiences. Often they can provide the names of contacts who might be interested in the type of research being considered.

Once potential funding sources have been identified, the real work begins. It is important for the researcher to get as much information as possible about those funding agencies identified as potential sources of support. One way of doing this is to obtain copies of the agencies' funding guidelines and/or annual reports. These documents, among other things, give a good overview of what types of projects the agencies appear to fund and the amount of funding available for projects. From this, the researcher can assess whether the proposed research seems to fit the priorities and interests of the funders concerned.

If, after the researcher has absorbed the documentation from an agency, it remains a potential funder for the research in question, then the researcher will need to approach the agency directly to discuss the research idea. How this is done will vary, depending on the type of sponsor. For example, if the funder calls for proposals on an annual basis, the researcher may initiate contact with the office that deals with those applications, so as to gain information about the process and to introduce both the research and the researcher(s) to the people who are likely to be administratively dealing with the application. Speaking with representatives of the agency can give the researcher insight into the processes and practices of the agency with respect to the way that funding is allocated. Further, it should be possible for the researcher to ascertain more information about what has been funded in the past. The agency may even supply reports of completed research and/or copies of proposals for projects that have been funded. Such documents are invaluable; from them, the researcher can ascertain the format and scope expected of a proposal, and they can help the researcher to formulate ideas in language appropriate to the funder in question. Furthermore, they can enable the researcher to locate the proposed study better in terms of work already done in the area. Situating the research in terms of what has preceded it is crucial; this enables the researcher to better address questions from the funder such as: Can this research be done? Is there a need? Will the research deliver? What is the researcher's expertise? What do others think? (See Zagury, 1997.) It is thus critical that the researcher have personal communication with potential funding bodies, as this can provide insights and advice not readily available elsewhere.

Further, depending on the agency's policy, representatives of the agency may put the researcher in contact with members of the agency's funding decision-making committee. Such contact is invaluable, particularly if members of the committee are not used to proposals oriented toward a qualitative approach to research. As Lidz and Ricci (1990) point out, reviewers and funders, like all of us, have "culturally prescribed ideas about 'real' research" (p. 114). If a particular granting committee seems to have an aversion to funding qualitative research, then it may be necessary for the researcher to look elsewhere for potential funders. At the same time, this does not mean that the researcher should not agitate for change; it is possible to get the composition of panels changed, the better to reflect an appreciation of all types of research. I recently had the experience of being invited onto a granting

panel for just this purpose. I found that the other members of the panel, although not opposed to qualitative research as such, simply did not have the expertise to judge the merits of qualitative proposals, given their backgrounds. My task as a member is to provide this input.

Much of what I have discussed above also applies when a researcher approaches a funding agency that does not call for proposals, but that tends to fund research on a more ad hoc basis. One difference is that it may not be immediately obvious to the researcher which person he or she should contact in the sponsor's organization. It is important that the researcher find the right person, in the right section of the organization, to talk to about the intended research and the possibility of funding for it. In this way, the researcher becomes familiar with the organization and the members of the organization get to know the researcher. This is important, as a crucial question for any funding agency is whether it can trust a particular researcher to complete a worthwhile project successfully once the agency has committed money to it.

When speaking to the agency representative, the researcher should present a clear, simple idea that is both researchable and likely to produce valuable benefits and outcomes from the funder's perspective. The researcher might consider submitting a concept paper first, either by mail or in person, before making contact with the individual representative of the organization. The concept paper could include any preliminary work done or data already collected. This would allow the researcher to address the points identified by Bogdan and Biklen (1998) as important in the initiation of contact with funders: "1. What have you done already? 2. What themes, concerns, or topics have emerged in your preliminary work? What analytic questions are you pursuing?" (p. 70).

Accompanying the concept paper should be a statement of the researcher's track record. It is important that the researcher demonstrate that there is every likelihood, based on past experience, of his or her being able to complete the project on time and within budget. Not only is it important to sell the research idea, it is also important to sell the researcher. For instance, the advantages of being associated with a researcher situated in a particular organization may be attractive to the funder. Zagury (1997) provides a useful set of self-reflective questions for the researcher to ask in this situation: "What qualities make my organization the best at what it does? Do we offer our clients/patients/customers something that they cannot get elsewhere, what is this special offering? What strengths does my organization have over our competitors? Are there specific, identifiable and unique capabilities that the funding source can only get from my organization?" (p. 26).

One of the problems facing many researchers is the catch-22 situation of needing a track record to attract funding while not being able to get the funding needed to build up a track record. One way a researcher can get around this is to join a research team that has already established a track record in the same or a closely related area of research, and to work as part of that team. This has the advantage of allowing the researcher to establish contact with the research expertise that is collectively present. It is an ideal way for an individual to learn about the research process in a safe way and can lead to the formation of enduring research relationships between colleagues. Another strategy for building a track record is for the researcher to gain some form of seed funding from their employing organization, which may be less competitive than larger funding bodies and directed to more novice researchers. Such seed funding, although invariably modest in amount, can be enough for a researcher to begin a small research project that can lead to publications and thus provide a foundation on which other research can be built.

What should be evident by now is that gaining funding is not a quick or easy process. Much lead time is often needed for planning and for establishing research credentials and rapport with funding sources. It all takes time, a lot of energy, and, above all, courage. There will be the inevitable failures, and it is very difficult not to take these personally. However, in my experience, persistence does pay off.

Other researchers can provide valuable advice and support throughout this process. As I pointed out previously, many research textbooks begin their discussions of how to gain funding by talking about proposal writing. This, I believe, is nowhere near the beginning. The strategies I have just discussed—those the researcher must employ to get to the point where he or she can write a proposal for a specific funding agency—represent, in my opinion, the actual start of "doing" funded qualitative research.

The Next Step: Crafting a Proposal for Funding

Having identified a potential funder, the researcher must take the next step—crafting a proposal to seek funding for the research. I use the word *crafting* deliberately here, because proposal writing is a craft requiring a unique set of skills, most of which are learned as a result of practice. Writing a proposal involves shaping and tailoring the research idea to fit the guidelines or application process imposed by the intended funding agency. Different applications, even for the same proposal, will vary depending on the characteristics and requirements of the funders being approached. When a proposal is written for a potential sponsor's consideration, it is written for a particular audience that has assumptions and expectations of the form a proposal should take and the language it should use. Thus, as I have emphasized before, it is important for the researcher to know that audience and its expectations.

Writing a proposal is to some extent a political process. The researcher will need to consider whether the approach proposed and the likely outcomes of the research "fit" the agenda of the funding body. It is quite reasonable for those who provide funding for research to ask whether or not the proposed project represents an appropriate use of the funds for which they have responsibility. The majority of funders take the allocation of monies very seriously indeed. They have to weigh up the relative merits, from their point of view, of proposals competing for limited resources. Thus it is essential that the researcher submit a proposal that is clear in terms of its purpose and rationale. Are the outcomes of the project stated? Are they important and useful—able to make a difference in people's lives? Some funding bodies may be a little self-serving in their reasons for funding specific proposals, but, on the whole, funders do make a genuine effort to fund worthy research proposals, and most treat the selection process very seriously.

In the following discussion, I draw on my own experience in preparing proposals to share some insights into the *process* of formulating the application. I place particular emphasis on issues and problems that qualitative approaches may pose for the researcher attempting to craft a proposal. Hence what follows is not about proposal writing, per se, as much has been written about this in many research textbooks (see the appendix to this chapter for information on three such books). Rather, the emphasis is on continuing to expose aspects of what otherwise may remain the untold story of the funding process.

All application forms or guidelines that are put out by research funding agencies contain often unwritten and unspoken assumptions and rules—the subtext of the guidelines. It is important that the researcher excavate these assumptions and understandings so as to work out how best to fit the research proposal to the rules. Hence the researcher must read the guidelines and application form carefully, not only for what they say but also for what they *do not* say. Further, it should go without saying that the researcher must follow these instructions carefully. I have reviewed many research funding applications, and although it may seem somewhat strange, even patronizing, for me to write this, it is all too evident that some researchers do not follow instructions when applying for support. For example, when asked to confine an application to a certain page limit or word limit, the researcher should do so. Similarly, if asked to explain something in lay terms, the researcher should do so. No one is impressed by impenetrable language.

Perhaps most crucial is that the researcher follow instructions meticulously with respect to the detail required about the research budget

and the way the funds will be used. Many ambitious claims appear in proposals for amounts that are obviously well beyond, or outside, the funding parameters of the grants program in question. Put simply, the researcher must tailor the proposal to the guides, not the guides to the proposal. Asking colleagues to read their draft proposals and provide critical comment is one strategy employed by many successful researchers to ensure that their proposals closely approximate the guidelines.

One issue that faces many researchers writing applications for funding for qualitative research is that their research approaches may not fit the guidelines in terms of the language used. For instance, I have been confronted with application forms asking me to write sections on, for example, the hypotheses to be tested. My response has been to write in terms related to the qualitative approaches that I am using and to discuss why it is not appropriate to state hypotheses in this particular study. I make the point that there are issues or problems driving the research, rather than hypotheses, which assume a certain research orientation. However, I have noticed that many application guides and forms have begun to develop language that is more inclusive of different research approaches. For example, guidelines may ask that a proposal include a discussion of considerations to do with "sample size/participant selection," where once the requirement would simply have been "sample size."

Where guidelines remain inflexible in terms of the language used, this may well be a good indication that the funding body is not suitable after all to support qualitative approaches. This is another reason why it is useful for the researcher to find out as much as possible about the funding body that will be the "audience" for the proposal and to consider what that audience's expectations are likely to be. Apart from the organization itself, this also applies to the specific assessors of the proposal (who may act in a consulting role from elsewhere). What might reviewers of the proposal be looking for? If they are not particularly familiar with qualitative techniques, will they still be able to work out clearly what is actually going to happen in the proposed study, how, and why? It is vital that the researcher address any concerns they may have, especially questions pertaining to what they might term *validity* and *reliability*. The researcher must stand, as it were, on the other side of the process, looking in, to consider how assessors are likely to view the proposal. This is an important principle for the researcher to consider when he or she is asked to provide names of assessors whom the funding agency might approach. The researcher needs to put as much thought into this as he or she puts into the actual development of the proposal.

A key point for the researcher to bear in mind is that any research proposal, qualitative or not, must formulate a clear issue or question—the initial idea that provided the impetus for the research must have been transformed into a researchable focus. Schutt (1996) provides certain criteria that he believes can be used, regardless of the research approach employed, to distinguish what he terms "good research questions from mediocre ones. A good research question will be *feasible* within the time and resources available, it will be *socially important*, and it will be *scientifically relevant*" (p. 35). The rest of the proposal must unpack that research question and demonstrate how the approach to be taken will enable it to be answered. The proposed research must be contextualized in terms of what has preceded it. The study must be situated in terms of what others are doing, and how this research links to that. It must be justified in terms of approach and design, having a clear direction and focus with clearly achievable outcomes in line with the funder's priorities and stated goals. The credentials of the researcher or research team will also need to be established.

The amount of information the researcher needs to give about the research design, analysis, and data collection will be in part determined by the format of the guides or application form. However, it will also be determined by whether the reader of the proposal can clearly understand from the document what is intended for the study and why. More information does not necessarily mean a better proposal. As stated previously, one of the best ways for the researcher to get a sense of the level of detail required is by obtaining copies of proposals that have already been successful with certain funding bodies. If that is not possible, then the researcher could ask those who have gained funding to provide copies of their proposals, or at least to engage in discussion about the development process.

Once the researcher has written and submitted the proposal, it is important that he or she ascertain the timelines involved and the procedures followed by the decision-making person/committee. In other words, it is important that the researcher gain insight into the agency's process of allocating funds. Such insight will prepare the researcher to expect a response in a certain format within a set time and will inform any necessary follow-up.

When the decision about funding is finally made, there are usually three possible outcomes. The request may be successful; in this case the researcher receives funding and the research commences as soon as all appropriate permissions, such as ethics clearance, are obtained. Another possible outcome is that the researcher may be asked to add or change something—for instance, to supply more information about one or more aspects of the proposal. This should be interpreted as a positive sign; more often than not it means that the funder is considering the request seriously and feels it has some merit, but requires clarification about certain aspects of it. As another example, the decision-making committee may ask the researcher to consider linking up with another researcher or group of researchers who have applied for funding on a similar project. It is important that the researcher think carefully about such a request, for, although collaboration has many benefits, it requires much goodwill and give-and-take to work successfully.

In another version of this outcome, the researcher may be asked if the study could be conducted with a reduced budget and, if so, how. This is not unusual. Sometimes funders have set amounts to allocate; if a proposed study is toward the end of the list of projects an agency wishes to fund, it may be able to offer only a proportion of the funds requested. It is important that the researcher think carefully about whether to accept such funding. I believe that funded research should not be attempted without adequate support for the activities necessary to the research. It is very tempting to accept any funding offered, but inadequate funding can lead to all sorts of problems in actually doing the research. Clearly, the process of securing research funding poses moral issues, not only about the wise use of funds, but also about the wisdom of whether or not to accept funds in the first place.

The third possible outcome is one that is becoming all too common, given the increasing competition for grants—namely, the request for funding is rejected. If this happens, it is important that the researcher get as much feedback as possible. He or she should make an appointment to speak to the Chair of the committee or a representative of the trust/foundation making the decision and use that meeting to find out as much as possible. Copies of the reviewers' reports may be made available; these often contain very useful critiques that can help the researcher in preparing the proposal for resubmission. If it is not possible for the researcher to see these reports, then he or she may be able to request a list of the projects that *were* successful; this may shed some light on whether the researcher's idea did in fact match the funding priorities of the funder. If all this fails and no feedback at all is available, then the researcher should ask those researchers who *have* been funded to review the unsuccessful proposal and help in debriefing the process just undergone. Talking it through may help the researcher to see things he or she can do differently the next time.

In many grants programs in Australia, the success rate is below 20%. Such low success rates are increasingly the case in most countries, as the competition for shrinking funding sources grows relentlessly. This means that it is much more likely for researchers *not* to gain funding than to be successful. Researchers should not take rejection personally, but should build on it. It may simply be the case that there is not enough money; this does not necessarily reflect on the personal worthiness of the researcher. Nevertheless, research proposals do

take much time and effort to complete, and it is hard to cope with constant rejection. Remember that no researcher is alone. By keeping contact with others and setting in place the strategies outlined so far in this chapter, they can maximize their chances of success.

◆ Issues That May Arise in the "Doing" of Funded Qualitative Research

I turn now to a consideration of some of the issues that may arise when the researcher is "doing" funded qualitative research. The issues discussed in this section are not the only issues that may confront the researcher; I have chosen these because they seem to me to have particular relevance to funded qualitative research. Put another way, I believe that a funded qualitative study puts a particular "spin" on the issues. The discussion to follow is structured around three interrelated sets of issues. The first group of issues have to do with the ethics of research, including some fundamental questions for the researcher to consider when thinking about accepting funding. The next group of issues pertain to the question of who controls the research and how this can pose unique dilemmas for the funded qualitative researcher. The issues in the third group focus on the effects that doing funded qualitative research can have on relationships among the various players in the research enterprise.

Ethical Considerations for Researchers "Doing" Funded Qualitative Research

The first, and central, ethical consideration for a researcher thinking about doing funded qualitative research is whether or not to apply to a particular funding agency. The researcher must consider the potentially conflicting agendas of funders, participants, and researchers. For example, at the university in which I work, we have just had a major debate over whether to accept funds from the tobacco industry. The arguments revolve around the ethics of taking money from an industry that is associated with health risks as well as questionable targeting of young people in product promotion. A question was also raised as to what would happen if funds were accepted for research whose findings did not support the tobacco industry in some way. The outcome of the debate was that the university decided, as a general principle, neither to seek nor to accept funding from the tobacco industry. This is just one example; no doubt, there are many more instances of question marks over the ethics of accepting funding from certain industries, agencies, or even governments. Considerations may include whether a particular industry is involved in questionable environmental activities or health practices, or whether it is a multinational company involved in possible exploitation of Third World workforces. Taking money from a sponsor is not a neutral activity. It links the researcher and the research inexorably with the values of that funder.

Another important issue for the researcher to consider early on is whether or not the proposed research should, in fact, be done. Do the potential benefits of the research outweigh the potential harm caused by the research? The notion of harm as interpreted by ethics committees has, at times, in my opinion, become somewhat narrow. These committees tend to place emphasis on more obvious (and still important) ethical issues to do with, for example, anonymity for participants and confidentiality of data, rather than the broader picture of the potential effects on participants of the research findings and actions arising therefrom. Guba and Lincoln (1989) identify, as part of this broader picture of potential harm, "the loss of dignity, the loss of individual agency and autonomy, and the loss of self-esteem that occur upon discovering that one has been duped and objectified" (p. 121). I would argue that this is particularly the case for qualitative research, with its much closer relationship between researcher and researched. I concur with Guba and Lincoln's assertion that harm "has been construed entirely too narrowly. . . . 'harm' is a concept that needs much more consideration, and that could possibly benefit from expanded definition" (p. 121).

Elsewhere, Lincoln (1995) has explored what she terms "emerging criteria" for quality in qualitative and interpretive research, and has argued that "nearly all of the emerging criteria are relational, that is they recognize and validate relationships between the inquirer and those who participate in the inquiry" (p. 278). This does not simply mean that the researcher communicated well with the participants once the research got under way, or that the participants were involved in decision making once the researcher had defined the issues and the approach to be taken. It is far more than that. Quality involves the *ethics* of the research, and one of the most fundamental questions to be asked is whether or not this research should be done in relation to the broader conception of harm discussed above. Indeed, Lincoln (1995) argues that "standards for quality in interpretive social science are also standards for ethics" (p. 287).

When they think about the ethics involved in research, many researchers immediately think of the process of getting the research approved by the appropriate ethics committees or institutional review boards. Most funding bodies require that evidence of ethics approval be submitted with the application as part of their approval process; or they may make funding conditional upon the receipt of such approval. It is important that the researcher identify the committees he or she needs to approach for approval; there may be several. If the research involves particularly vulnerable and historically exploited groups, such as indigenous peoples, then there is a further requirement for approval from ethics committees that deal specifically with research involving these groups. Not all ethics committees will recognize the approval of other committees, so several ethics applications may be necessary if, for example, a research study spans several sites, such as a group of hospitals. More often than not, these committees require that the research application be made according to their particular guidelines.

The same principles outlined earlier in this chapter about approaching funding bodies apply to working with, and approaching, ethics boards. The researcher must find out as much as possible about the processes used by each review board, and should ask to see examples of proposals that have been accepted. These will help the researcher to get an idea of both the level of detail and the format that the committee requires. The researcher should speak to others who have applied for ethics approval to the committee in question. Ethics boards and committees usually require clear statements about informed consent, guarding from harm and deception, and ensuring the privacy of participants; their focus is usually on the confidentiality of data collected and the anonymity of participants (see Guba & Lincoln, 1989). As Guba and Lincoln (1989) note, such issues often pertain to reasonably conventional safeguards and fairly standard ways of dealing with both data and participants in research.

It is clearly important for researchers undertaking funded qualitative research to remember that they will need to secure ethics approvals. However, gaining clearances can take a great deal of time. Ethics committees may meet only monthly and may require researchers to submit modified proposals to be taken up at future meetings before they grant approval. Researchers should take into consideration the potential for delays in obtaining ethics approval when they are developing the timelines for funded projects.

One problem that is somewhat unique to qualitative research (but not necessarily to funded qualitative research) is that ethics committees often take detailed interest in exactly who participants will be, how they will be approached, and what they will be asked if, for example, interviews are being used. In some qualitative studies, it may not be possible for the researchers to be specific about such information. I have found it useful to write to ethics committees and explain how I have filled in their forms and why I have done so, especially with respect to not being able to conceptualize certain details of the research fully until the study is actually under way. It is possible to state how the initial approach will be made to participants, and to outline the general principles that will be employed regarding confidentiality, and so forth. I have also stated that, if the

committee members would find it useful, I would be happy to talk about the research and discuss any concerns they might have. I have found most committees willing to listen and quite reasonable. However, sometimes compromises have been necessary. There have been instances where interim approval was given and I had to submit details progressively as they became available. Although this was tedious, I do not believe it compromised the research in any way.

Another time, a student of mine and I were dealing with an extremely traditional hospital's medical ethics committee, for which the proposal in question was the committee members' first experience of a certain approach, and thus something of a culture shock. We agreed to change the word *participant* to *patient* on the consent forms and information sheets that would be given to participants in the research. We had to think deeply about this, but in the end considered that it was more important for the research to go forward than to take a stand on this issue. However, this does raise an important point. At times, researchers may find themselves asked to modify proposals in ways that appear to compromise the approaches they wish to take. In instances like this, they must make what I would argue is a fundamentally ethical decision: Can the research proceed under these conditions? Grappling with such decisions is often another part of the untold story of doing funded qualitative research.

Who Controls the Research?

A related set of issues emerges from a consideration of who controls the qualitative research that is funded. It is a fact that, once the researcher has accepted funding for research, he or she is not an entirely free agent with respect to the direction and outcome of that research. However, depending on the policies and attitudes of the funder, the degree of freedom allowed the researcher in carrying out the research (such as changing its direction if the need arises as a result of findings, and talking and writing about the research) may vary considerably. The researcher needs to engage in careful negotiation about the issue of control in the very early stages of the research, as it is often too late once the project is well under way. Yet too often researchers either ignore or are simply unaware of the problems that can arise. Taking funding from someone in order to conduct research is not a neutral act. It implies a relationship with that funder that has certain obligations for both parties. It is important that the researcher discuss with the funder all the expectations and assumptions, spoken and unspoken, that both of them may have about the research.

As an example, one such expectation relates to what can be said about the research, and by whom. Put another way, this is an issue about who actually owns the data or findings that result from the study, and how those data can be used both during and after the study. Some researchers have found themselves in the situation of not being able to write about the research in the way they want to, if at all. For example, I carried out a funded piece of research, using qualitative approaches, that produced four main findings, each of which was accompanied by a series of recommendations. When I submitted the report, I found that the funding body was willing to act on two of the findings, as the agency believed these were within their statutory remit, but not on the others. Although this seems reasonable at one level, I was concerned that the remaining two findings were in danger of being lost. The recommendations associated with those findings were important and needed to be acted on. I was even more concerned when the funder wanted to alter the report to include only the two findings the funding body believed were relevant to it. Fortunately, a solution was found whereby the report was framed to highlight the findings considered relevant by the funder while making reference to the other findings as well. In some ways, this may seem like an uneasy compromise, but at least the whole picture was given with respect to the findings. In retrospect, I realize that I was somewhat naïve in not anticipating the issue arising as to what data and findings should or could be included in a study, or what data, conversely, might be excluded. I am now much more careful to negotiate how the findings of a study will be reported, the use of the data, and my rights to publish the study findings in full, myself, in scholarly literature.

A related issue can arise when the findings of a study do not please the funder. What happens if the findings are, or have the potential to be, beneficial to the participants but may displease the sponsor? Who has the say as to whether or not these findings will be published? As Parahoo (1991) points out, "Too often those who control the purse tend to act in their own interests when they veto the publication of research. To others this is an abuse of power and office, and a waste of public money" (p. 39). This is a particularly important question if the research involves working with groups that are relatively powerless or disenfranchised. A real dilemma is posed for qualitative researchers, in that much of their research is built on developing relationships of trust with participants. Researchers have found themselves in the position of not being able to publish or even disseminate results in any way because of contractual arrangements they have entered into when accepting funds. When a contract is finalized, the researcher should check it carefully to be sure that he or she is comfortable and can live with the conditions set down.

Issues such as these make it clear that the researcher must invest careful thought in deciding whether or not to accept money from a particular funder. Funders, just like researchers, have motives for wanting research to be done. Some bodies may be entirely altruistic, others less so. Some funders, particularly in the evaluation area, may overtly be funding research to "vindicate policies and practices" (Parahoo, 1991, p. 37). As Guba and Lincoln (1989) note in writing about evaluation studies, "Often evaluation contracts are issued as requests for proposals just as research contracts are; in this way, winning evaluators are often those whose definitions of problems, strategies, and methods exhibit 'fit' with the clients' or funders' values" (p. 124). This is why Bogdan and Biklen (1998) assert, "You can only afford to do evaluation or policy research [or, I would add, any funded form of qualitative research] if you can afford not to do so" (p. 209).

None of this is to suggest that qualitative researchers should not seek funding. Rather, what it does suggest is the need for close self-scrutiny on the part of any researcher considering taking funding for a project. It is important for the researcher to consider whether it is possible for him or her to retain integrity and independence as a researcher when paid by someone else or provided with the support to do research. Key questions for the researcher to ask are, How much freedom will I lose if someone else is paying? How do I feel about this? Funding for projects is a means to an end; it must not become an end in itself.

The final issue I want to consider concerning the control of research pertains to the need for clarity about exactly what will be "delivered" to the funder in return for the funding received. What is it that the researcher is contracting with the funder to provide? This is a very important area, as many potential problems arise if both parties involved do not understand this in the same way. It is very easy and tempting for researchers, particularly if they are inexperienced, to underestimate the amount of time and energy needed to conduct research projects. Consequently, they may "over commit" in terms of what they promise to deliver to funders. The researcher must consider carefully what it is reasonable to provide for the funding received and make this explicit to the funder. Time frames should be placed against each deliverable so that both parties are aware of what will be produced and when it can be expected.

Some funders may approach researchers to produce summaries of their research, or to present the findings for them in forums, once the final report has been submitted. It is important for the researcher to distinguish such requests from the core deliverables that form part of the research contract. When faced with such requests, which are really over and above the requirements for the research, I have negotiated with the funders concerned. If the request is to present the findings at a local meeting, then I will usually agree. If, however, I am asked to present the findings at some location further away or if the work otherwise involves expense

to myself, I will then claim costs, because they are not covered by the funding received for the project. If I am asked to produce a shortened version of a research report, suitable for a particular audience for whom I had not written the original report, then I will usually agree to do so, but only if the funder provides the necessary editorial support. I make it clear that I do so as a gesture of goodwill, and that I have neither the time nor the resources to physically produce the additional report. I believe it is important to take this position, as otherwise the potential exists for researchers to be exploited, whether intentionally or not. The key to all of this is the researcher's establishment of open and clear communication with the funder from the outset. I have found working with funding bodies, on the whole, to be an enjoyable and mutually satisfying experience.

The Effect of Funding on Relationships in the Research

Qualitative approaches to research are premised on an honest and open working relationship between the researcher and the participants in the research. Inevitably in such studies the researcher spends a great deal of time with participants, getting to know aspects of their world and learning about the way they live in that world. At the center of a good working relationship in qualitative research is the development of trust. Further, as qualitative researchers, we have all dealt with issues such as participants' feeling threatened by the research and therefore concealing information, or participants' being anxious to please us and giving us the information they think we want to hear or that they think we need to know. These issues can become even more complicated for researchers who are doing funded qualitative research.

When doing funded research it is important for researchers to tell participants who is providing the funding and what that funding is being given for. Successful researchers report the importance of making their own relationship to the funder clear—for example, are they acting as paid employees of the funder or are they independent? Equally crucial to a successful relationship between researchers and participants is that the researchers ensure, and give assurances, that the participants will remain anonymous and that the confidentiality of their individual information will be safeguarded. This is a major concern for some participants, who may believe they will be identified and "punished" in some way by the funder if, for example, the funder is their employer and the participants are critical of the organization. When conducting research in specific settings among specified groups of people, it may be very difficult for researchers to ensure the anonymity of participants. It is crucial that researchers be clear about this issue and that they discuss it with participants, who need to know what will happen to specific information in the project, who will have access to that information, and how their rights to confidentiality are being assured. Individuals may choose not to participate if they have concerns about a particular funder having access to information they have given, or if they question the motives for that funding being given in the first place.

Further, if there are any restrictions on what can or cannot be said about the findings of the research and the research undertaking itself, then it is important for the researchers to make potential participants aware of this as well. Part of the constant process of giving feedback to participants must include feedback about any issues that arise about ownership of the research and the way it will be disseminated. All of this is to empower participants to make informed decisions about whether or not to participate and to give them some idea about the use to which the research is likely to be put. This enables them to be better positioned to follow up the research findings and to have a say in what happens as a result of them. It is a part of valuing all perspectives in the research, and of treating participants as more than simply research objects who are subject to the findings of a research agenda that has been imposed on them.

It is important in a research team that all team members share similar approaches to the issues that have been raised. This needs to be discussed from the outset of the formation of the team, and is just as important to the smooth functioning of the team as the particular expertise each team member brings to the project. There must be trust among team members that decisions made will be adhered to. Further, it is important for team members to talk about how team decisions will be made. Who will control the budget? What happens if there is disagreement about the way the research is proceeding? The involvement of a third party—namely, the funder—makes the need to be clear about these issues all the more imperative. Furthermore, the team needs to have clear guidelines about which member(s) will communicate with the funder and how. Working as part of a research team offers the individual researcher the advantages of a team approach that is multiskilled and often multidisciplinary in focus. However, funding increases the need for good communication in the team and clear understandings of each member's role, both in terms of the research itself and in terms of dealing with the funder. Strategies that research teams can employ to assist in the smooth functioning of funded projects include outlining all members' responsibilities, including their contributions to the final report; drawing up timelines for all members to adhere to; upholding all members' access to support and funds; and holding regular meetings for team members to discuss issues.

Obtaining funding creates another research relationship that needs to be developed during the conduct of the research—namely, that between funder and researcher. All funding bodies require reports about the progress of research projects. When communicating with and reporting to the funder, which often involves reporting to an individual nominated by the funder as a point of contact, it is important that the researcher be honest and up-front. This applies particularly if something has gone "wrong" or if for some reason the research plan has had to be changed. In my experience, funders would much rather find out about these things as they arise than be faced at the end with a project that has not met expectations.

The extent of funding bodies' involvement in research can vary considerably, ranging from researchers' submission of one or two reports a year to a very hands-on approach where a representative of the agency seeks to play an active role in the research undertaken. Whatever approach is adopted, it is important that there be clear communication as to the role each party will play in the research. It is also important for the researcher to clarify that, if research is being carried out in which participants will be known to the representative of the agency, then there may have to be restrictions on access to information put in place, so as to protect the participants' rights to confidentiality. Similarly, if a funder requires that an advisory board be established to provide guidance on the progress and direction of the research, it is important that both researcher and funder understand the parameters within which the board will operate. Often such boards can be invaluable in assisting researchers with broad issues pertaining to the substantive focus of the research. Indeed, many experienced researchers, recognizing the value of advisory boards for helping them to think through aspects of doing their projects, interpreting the findings, and considering the routes for dissemination, may constitute such boards regardless of funder requirements. However, clear understandings must be put in place as to what access, if any, the board can have to specific sets of information collected in the study, especially if board members are connected in any way to the study site and/or to participants.

Thus the funding of research can affect the nature of relationships between the research participants and the researcher. Funded research can also result in the development of a new set of relationships, especially between the researcher/research team and the funding agency, and between the researcher and any other structures the funder may wish to put in place, such as advisory boards. When there is clear communication, these relationships can enhance the research effort and assist its smooth functioning. However, such relationships cannot be taken for granted; all parties involved need to work on them actively. The development of these relationships is another part of the too often untold story of doing funded qualitative research.

◆ "The Research Market": The Potential for Privileging Funded Research

Up to this point, the discussion has focused on the everyday issues and realities confronting the funded qualitative researcher. This chapter, so far, has been unashamedly practical in orientation, but in a way that explores, not just prescribes, strategies with which to approach funded qualitative research. I wish now to change register (Lather, 1996) overtly. In so doing, I shift the focus of the discussion from the practicalities of doing funded qualitative research to a much more macro level—a kind of supercontext where the focus is on larger social issues and forces that impact on the funded qualitative researcher. The shift in register is reflected by my use of a more critical voice, one that probes, challenges, and tests assumptions about what I have termed the research market and the concomitant commodification of research. As Lather (1996) puts it, "Here the text turns back on itself, putting the authority of its own affirmations in doubt" (p. 533). It is to this task that I now turn.

The late 1990s have seen the emergence of a climate of economic restraint and funding cuts by governments in most Western countries. These cuts have had severe impacts on the availability of funding for research in that many funding agencies, particularly government departments, no longer have the resources to support research to the extent that they once did. At the same time, educational institutions such as universities have also experienced cuts to their funding. One of the consequences of such cuts to university operating budgets has been the imperative for staff to be able to generate income for the institution. In some cases such income has become part of academics' salaries; in others this income has been factored into the operating budget of the institution to pay for the basic resources needed to continue teaching and research programs. One way in which academics are able to generate income is by winning research grants. This, in some instances, has created a whole new imperative for gaining funding—the funding itself, rather than the research, has become highly prized. Put another way, it is possible that what is becoming important to some university administrations is the amount of funding gained rather than the contribution of the research and its associated scholarship to new knowledge and problem solving. In such a climate there is the potential to privilege funded research over unfunded research.

Historically there has always been a place for both funded and unfunded research in universities and elsewhere. Some types of research simply have not required funding, yet have been able to produce significant contributions to knowledge for which they have been valued. Further, research serves a variety of purposes. On one hand, it can be carried out to investigate a well-defined issue or problem arising in a specific area or field; on the other, it can be conducted to probe or explore what the issues might be in the first place. Research can also be carried out simply for the pleasure of investigating new and different ways of thinking about aspects of our reality. Some research projects might incorporate all of the above. In other words, just as there are a variety of research approaches and associated techniques, so there are a range of purposes for which research might be carried out. Each research project has its own intended audience who will relate to the assumptions framing the problem to be investigated, as embedded within that piece of research.

However, with the imperative for academics to generate income, there has been a subtle, and at times not so subtle, shift in thinking toward valuing research that is funded more highly than research that is not, simply on the basis of funding alone. As Keat (1991) notes about the United Kingdom, "Academics complain that . . . the value of their research is now being judged by intellectually facile considerations of 'marketability' " (p. 216). Given this, the question can be asked as to whether we are seeing the emergence of what Derrida (1976) terms a binary opposition with respect to funded/unfunded research.

Derrida holds that any positive representation of a concept in language, such as "funded research," rests on the negative representation of its "opposite"—in this case, unfunded research. In a binary opposition there is always a dominant or prior term, and, conversely, there is always a subordinate or secondary term. For example, consider such common binary oppositions as masculine/feminine and reason/emotion. In each case the first-named term is given priority over the second, which is often defined in terms of "not" the dominant. However, as I have noted elsewhere, "the definitional dynamic extends to the primary term as well in that it can only sustain its definition by reference to the secondary term. Thus the definition and status of the primary term is in fact maintained by the negation and opposition of the secondary partner" (Cheek, Shoebridge, Willis, & Zadoroznyj, 1996, p. 189). Derrida points out that binary oppositions are constructions of certain worldviews. They are not natural givens that can be taken for granted. In the instance of funded/unfunded research, it is important to recognize that there is a binary opposition in operation and to explore both how it has come to be and how it is maintained. An interesting way to commence such an exploration is to reverse the binary pairing and note the effect. What is the effect on the way research is viewed and understood if unfunded research assumes primacy and funded research becomes the secondary or derivative term?

In a climate where funded research is assuming ever-increasing importance, the power of funding agencies to set research agendas has increased markedly. As Parahoo (1991) notes: "A successful researcher is sometimes defined by the ability to attract funds, and most researchers know that in order to do so one must submit proposals on subjects which sponsors are prepared to spend money on. This can mean that the real issues that concern practitioners are sometimes ignored" (p. 37). Although it is not unreasonable that sponsors should be able to fund research that is relevant to them, a problem arises if funds are not available for researcher-initiated research in order to address questions that have arisen from the field. If funding alone drives research agendas, then this may infringe on the academic freedom of researchers to pursue topics of importance and interest. As Porter (1997) notes, "Pressure is therefore exerted on academics to tailor their work in order to meet the requirements of funders" (p. 655). Creativity may be sacrificed for expediency in that some research topics will have more currency than others in terms of their likeliness to attract funding. Drawing on Mills (1959), Stoesz (1989) observes that "to the extent that this happens, an enormous problem emerges—social science [read research] becomes a commodity, the nature of which is defined by the bureaucracies of the corporate and governmental sectors" (p. 122).

Further, a trend that is emerging in times of fiscal restraint is for some funding bodies to decline to fund chief investigators' salaries, arguing that the salaries of these researchers are already paid by the institutions at which they work (such as universities) and therefore the funders should not have to pay second, supplementary salaries. This is the case in Canada and in Australia, to give but two instances, with respect to many major grants programs. In my experience, one interesting effect of the reluctance of many funding bodies to pay investigators' salaries has been the emergence of a trend in universities, in many parts of the world, to insist that researchers put in their research budgets an amount (for example, in Australia usually somewhere between 10% and 30% of the grant total) to be paid to the university for indirect costs, such as infrastructure charges for the project. The argument is that universities should not be asked to supplement funding bodies by providing "free" research infrastructure. This has led to problems for researchers in some grants programs as funders have refused to fund such levies, agreeing to award funding only for the amount requested minus the levy. This, of course, leaves the researchers in a dilemma—should they take the reduced funds, knowing that the levy will still be taken from them, and thereby effectively ensure that the research remains underfunded?

The emerging emphasis on funded research, in terms of its ability to produce income for institutions, has, in my opinion, led to an increasing view of research as a commodity to be bought and sold on the research market. Information and data from research projects are seen as "products" to be traded on this market and sold to the highest bidders. Researchers increasingly find themselves struggling with the often competing demands of research as the generation of new knowledge and research as a commodity to be traded on the marketplace. Turpin and Hill (1995) describe this as a boundary struggle between the different domains of research activity:

> On the one hand researchers are concerned with the generation and transfer of new knowledge through research and teaching, on the other hand they are encouraged through various policy mechanisms, to be concerned with securing and maintaining market niches for selling that knowledge. The two domains of work are dominated by different sets of reward criteria, different sets of objectives, different ways of measuring success, different modes of communication. . . . in short they are culturally distinct. (p. 185)

This struggle is exacerbated by a trend in which the act of winning funding for research is itself viewed as currency to be traded in the academic marketplace. For example, promotion and tenure committees in many universities see the amount of funding individuals have received as a measure of research success. This has the effect of maintaining the binary opposition of funded/unfunded research in that performance in terms of funded research is valued whereas the absence of funding—that is, unfunded research—is not. Further, large quantitative studies usually require more funds than do most qualitative projects, which are often on a smaller scale and do not require expensive equipment. There is a very real danger that using amount of funding to measure things for which it was never intended, such as academic performance, will have the effect of making the pursuit of funds an end in itself rather than the means to an end, as it was always intended to be.

The idea of research being perceived as a commodity, along with the trend to privilege funded research over unfunded research, poses some particular dilemmas for qualitative researchers. For instance, it is still true that, despite progress, most funding in some disciplinary fields, such as medicine, is attracted by research projects using traditional scientific methods. As Gilbert (1995) points out, "The present forms of truth and rationality determine the issues acceptable for research monies and for publication" (p. 869). This means that it is harder in these fields to gain funding for qualitative research. If success in gaining funding is used, rightly or wrongly, to measure performance and to put a value on research, then there is a real danger that qualitative research could be marginalized, because it is not as easy to attract funds for research using qualitative approaches.

All of this is to bring into sharp focus some very fundamental questions that qualitative researchers need to grapple with. These questions relate to the background assumptions about research and research performance that are driving many research agendas and researchers. Assumptions about how research performance should be measured and valued need to be exposed. They can then be considered and explored in terms of the effects they have on the two notions of what research is for and what the nature of a research product should be. Funding is important in that it enables research to be carried out that would otherwise not happen because of resource constraints. It is not funding itself that is the issue here; rather, it is the uses to which the act of gaining funding is being put, apart from enabling specific pieces of research to proceed. I am not arguing against funded qualitative research—far from it. What I am suggesting is that researchers need to think about their own assumptions about funded research and how such assumptions have embedded within them many taken-for-granteds about the nature of research and research products. Research is not, and must not be reduced to, a commodity to be sold to the highest bidder in a market driven by expediency. Resisting such reductionism poses one of the biggest challenges facing qualitative researchers—indeed, all researchers—as we enter the new millennium.

◆ Conclusion: Thinking Deeply About Doing Funded Qualitative Research

Doing funded qualitative research is more than developing a proposal or carrying out a piece of research. It is a process that a researcher undertakes, involving various stages. The process begins with the researcher's identification of potential funding sources for the project, initiation of contact with the potential funder, and development of a proposal for funding; only then does it move to the stages in which the research is carried out and the findings are disseminated. Each of these stages involves a number of issues that qualitative researchers must face in order to maintain their own integrity and that of the research. Facing these issues is as much a part of "doing" funded qualitative research as the actual fieldwork itself.

At the same time, it is imperative that researchers think deeply about all aspects of doing qualitative research, from developing the idea right through to the "use" to which the final product is put. In order to think deeply, researchers must consider the con-texts that accompany research as text and the effects that these can have on the way the research is viewed. This is particularly crucial in a climate where, increasingly, funded research is enjoying a privileged status because of the income it provides for cash-strapped institutions. Doing funded qualitative research is not a neutral and value-free activity. Researchers must constantly examine their motives for doing the research and the motives of funding bodies in funding the research.

However, given this, as I have emphasized throughout this chapter, in no way should my writing be viewed as arguing against "doing" funded qualitative research. Quite to the contrary—used well, funding can enhance and enable projects to proceed that otherwise could not do so. Satisfying relationships can be developed between funders and researchers. Participants can benefit from research that has been funded. Rather, what I have been arguing for is the ability to do funded qualitative research in a way that retains the integrity of the researcher, the participants, the research project, *and* the funding body.

At the outset of this chapter, I stated that my aim in writing about "doing" funded research was to tell a story that has largely remained untold. An accompanying aim has been my attempt to create, at least in part, a "multivoiced text that moves through different registers and that speaks to multiple audiences" (Lather, 1996, p. 525). I hope that readers of this chapter will be able to take up their own position(s) with respect to the position(s) I have taken. I have told my part of the story, it is now up to readers to add their stories to it.

◆ Appendix: Annotated Bibliography of Works on Proposal Writing

Locke, L. F., Spirduso, W. W., & Silverman, S. J. (1993). *Proposals that work: A guide for planning dissertations and grant proposals* (3rd ed.). Newbury Park, CA: Sage.

This book has two major parts: Part I focuses on writing the proposal, and Part II contains four specimen proposals—for an experimental design, a qualitative study, a quasi-experimental design, and a funded grant. The book appears to be aimed at postgraduate students or beginning researchers. The first part covers a range of topics, including the basic elements of a proposal, ethical issues, developing a thesis/dissertation, content and form of the proposal, asking for money, and preparing a grant proposal. One chapter, subtitled "Different Assumptions," is dedicated to the preparation of proposals for qualitative research. The authors state that it is written with an emphasis on experimental and quasi-experimental studies, mainly because this was the "most economical method for assisting readers who have a wide variety of research interests" (p. xii).

Ogden, T. E., & Goldberg, I. A. (1995). *Research proposals: A guide to success* (2nd ed.). New York: Raven.

This book is a how-to guide to preparing grant proposals for the National Institutes of Health (NIH). As the title suggests, it concentrates on how to obtain funding for grants, especially for experimental, scientific research proposals. It discusses topics such as the review process, enhancing proposal effectiveness, and NIH programs and procedures. It is divided into three sections: "Basic Grantsmanship," "Advanced Grantsmanship," and "Advice for New Scientists."

Reif-Lehrer, L. (1995). *Grant application writer's handbook.* Boston: Jones & Bartlett.

This volume is a comprehensive guide to preparing successful NIH and National Science Foundation grants in the United States. The author goes beyond simply detailing how to write a research grant proposal. Sections are "Getting Started," which includes where to get information about available grants; "Understanding the Review Process"; "Parts of the Grant Application"; "Planning the Research Plan"; "Writing the Research Plan"; "Submitting and Tracking the Grant Application"; "Summary Statements, Rebuttals, and Revisions"; and "Some Final Words." Finally, the book includes extensive appendices with details of specific grant awards to apply for and examples of various proposal sections.

■ References

Agger, B. (1991). Critical theory, poststructuralism, postmodernism: Their sociological relevance. *Annual Review of Sociology, 17,* 105-131.

Bogdan, R. C., & Biklen, S. K. (1998). *Qualitative research for education: An introduction to theory and methods* (3rd ed.). Boston: Allyn & Bacon.

Cheek, J., Shoebridge, J., Willis, E., & Zadoroznyj, M. (1996). *Society and health: Social theory for health workers.* Melbourne: Longman Australia.

Derrida, J. (1976). *Of grammatology* (G. C. Spivak, Trans.). Baltimore: Johns Hopkins University Press.

Gilbert, T. (1995). Nursing: Empowerment and the problem of power. *Journal of Advanced Nursing, 21,* 865-871.

Guba, E. G., & Lincoln, Y. S. (1989). Ethics and politics: The twin failures of positivist science. In E. G. Guba & Y. S. Lincoln, *Fourth generation evaluation* (pp. 117-141). Newbury Park, CA: Sage.

Halliday, M. A. K., & Hasan, R. (1989). Context of situation. In M. A. K. Halliday & R. Hasan (Eds.), *Language, context, and text: Aspects of language in a social-semiotic perspective* (pp. 3-14). Geelong, Victoria, Australia: Deakin University Press.

Keat, R. (1991). Consumer sovereignty and the integrity of practices. In R. Keat & N. Abercrombie (Eds.), *Enterprise culture* (pp. 216-230). London: Routledge.

Lather, P. (1996). Troubling clarity: The politics of accessible language. *Harvard Educational Review, 66,* 525-545.

The leading edge. (1996). *A Closer Look, 25*(6), 4.

Lidz, C. W., & Ricci, E. (1990). Funding large scale qualitative sociology. *Qualitative Sociology, 13*(2), 113-126.

Lincoln, Y. S. (1995). Emerging criteria for quality in qualitative and interpretive inquiry. *Qualitative Inquiry, 1,* 275-289.

Mills, C. W. (1959). *The sociological imagination.* New York: Oxford University Press.

Parahoo, K. (1991). Politics and ethics in nursing research. *Nursing Standard, 6*(1), 35-39.

Porter, S. (1997). The degradation of the academic dogma. *Journal of Advanced Nursing, 25,* 655-656.

Sachs, L. (1996). Casualty, responsibility and blame: Core issues in the cultural construction and subtext of prevention. *Sociology of Health and Illness, 18,* 632-652.

Schutt, R. (1996). *Investigating the social world: The process and practice of research.* Thousand Oaks, CA: Pine Forge.

Stoesz, D. (1989). Provocation on the politics of government funded research: Part 1. *Social Epistemology, 4*(1), 121-123.

Summers, J. (1998). *The Australian grants register.* Melbourne: Australian Scholarly Publishing.

Turpin, T., & Hill, S. (1995). Researchers, cultural boundaries, and organizational change. *Research in the Sociology of Work, 5,* 179-204.

Zagury, C. S. (1997). Grant writing: The uncertain road to funding: Part V. From the other side: How reviewers look at proposals. *Alternative Health Practitioner, 3*(1), 25-29.

15

PERFORMANCE ETHNOGRAPHY

A Brief History and Some Advice

◆ Michal M. McCall

The term *performance* entered art critical and academic discourses in the 1970s, to name a new visual art form and to distinguish dramatic scripts from particular productions of them—that is, from performances on-stage.[1] Similar terms were *events* and *happenings* in the 1950s and 1960s and *body art* and *experimental theater* in the 1970s and 1980s. Conventional histories locate the roots of performances, events, happenings, body art, and experimental theater in the futurist, dadaist, and surrealist movements of the early 20th century. Here, in excerpts from two such histories, are an overview and brief descriptions of those movements.

Overview

Members of the historic avant-garde movement throughout Europe (ca. 1900-1935) wanted to propose an "other" theatre, different in every way from what had gone before: a theatre freed from the chains of literature, constituted as an autonomous art form; a theatre which did not imitate a reality which actually existed, but which created its own reality; a theatre which nullified the radical split between stage and spectator and which developed new forms of communication between them, so that the chasm between art (theatre) and life, so typical and characteristic of bourgeois society, might be bridged. (Fischer-Lichte, 1997, p. 115)

Futurism

The launching of futurism in 1909 was a typical example, with a manifesto by Filippo Marinetti in . . . *Le Figaro*. Futurism is in fact rather better known for its manifestos than for its actual artistic achievements, but both contributed importantly to the performance tradition of this century. The interest of the futurists in movement and change drew them away from the static work of art and provided an important impetus for the general shift in modern artistic interest from product to process, turning even painters and sculptors into performance artists. (Carlson, 1996, p. 89)

Dadaism

[From the] founding of the Cabaret Voltaire in 1916 in Zurich . . . [all] dadaist activities were directed at the spectator. While at first they only aimed to "épater le bourgeois," these ventures occurred increasingly in the form of an organized assault on the audience, a "strategy of revolt" . . . aimed at challenging and reexamining the purely passive attitude of expectation and customary practices of spectator reception. In this way, they attempted to dissolve the discrepancies between art and society for the duration of the performance. (Fischer-Lichte, 1997, pp. 267-268)

Surrealism

Perhaps the most important contribution of the surrealist movement to subsequent experimental theater and performance was the theoretical writing of Antonin Artaud, which exerted an enormous influence in the 1960s and 1970s. In his visionary *The Theater and Its Double,* Artaud advanced his own powerful version of the argument found throughout the early twentieth-century avant-garde that the traditional theatre had lost contact with the deeper and more significant realms of human life by its emphasis on plot, language, and intellectual and psychological concerns. The subjugation of the theatre to the written text must be ended, to be replaced by a spectacle of "direct" and "objective" action: "cries, groans, apparitions, surprises, theatricalities of all kinds, magic beauty of costumes taken from certain ritual models; resplendent lighting, incantational beauty of voices, the charms of harmony, rare notes of music, colors of objects, physical rhythm of movements . . . masks, effigies yards high, sudden changes of light." (Carlson, 1996, pp. 91-92)

◆ Events

An *Untitled Event* produced in 1952 at Black Mountain College in North Carolina by composer John Cage, dancer Merce Cunningham, painter Robert Rauschenberg, and others "has

often been cited as the model for the wave of happenings and related performance events that swept the art world in the late 1950s and early 1960s. In many respects, this event recapitulated many of the motifs and practices of earlier avant-gardes," according to one historian (Carlson, 1996, p. 95). In *Untitled Event,* performances, "each timed to the second, took place in and around an arena audience" (Carlson, 1996, p. 95):

Each performer was given a "score" which consisted purely of "time brackets" to indicate moments of action, inaction, and silence that each individual performer was expected to fill. . . . Cage, in a black suit and tie, stood on a stepladder and read a text on "the relation of music to Zen Buddhism" and excerpts from Meister Eckhart. Later he performed a "composition with a radio." At the same time, Rauschenberg played old records on a wind-up gramophone with a trumpet while a dog sat beside it listening, and David Tudor played a "prepared piano." A little later, Tudor started to pour water from one bucket to another. . . . Cunningham and others danced through the aisles chased by the dog. . . . Rauschenberg projected abstract slides (created by colored gelatin sandwiched between the glass) and clips of film onto [his "white paintings"] on the ceiling; the film clips showed first the school cook and then, as they gradually moved from the ceiling down the walls, the setting sun. (Fischer-Lichte, 1997, pp. 233-234)

◆ Happenings

In the late 1950s, Allan Kaprow invented "happenings," and this label was applied to all sorts of experimental performances in the 1960s.

A key event in the history of modern performance was the presentation in 1959 of Allan Kaprow's *18 Happenings in 6 Parts* at the Reuben Gallery [in New York City]. This first public demonstration established the "happening" for public and press as a major new avant-garde activity, so much so that a wide range of performance work during the following years was characterized as "happenings," even when many creators of such events specifically denied the term. Audiences at Kaprow's happening were seated in three different rooms where they witnessed six fragmented events, performed simultaneously in all three spaces. The events included slides, playing of musical instruments, posed scenes, the reading of fragmentary notes from placards, and artists painting canvas walls. (Carlson, 1996, pp. 95-96)

◆ *Body Art and Experimental Theater*

In the 1970s and 1980s, visual and theater artists developed two different forms of "performance art": the "body art" of Vito Acconci, Chris Burden, Carolee Schneemann, Hannah Wilke, and other visual artists; and the "elaborate spectacles not based on the body or the psyche of the individual artist but devoted to the display of nonliterary aural and visual images, often involving spectacle, technology, and mixed media" (Carlson, 1996, pp. 104-105; see also Sayre, 1995) of Laurie Anderson, Lee Bruer, Richard Foreman, Robert Wilson, and, later, Spalding Gray, Bill Irwin, and other theatrical storytellers, jugglers, and clowns.

According to Amelia Jones (1998), the "body art" of the 1960s and 1970s was a "set of performative practices" that used "passionate and convulsive relationships (often explicitly sexual)" with audiences (whether physically present or viewing documentary photographs, films, videos and other texts), to "instantiate the dislocation or decentering of the Cartesian subject of modernism" (p. 1). Furthermore, and not incidentally, because it was "dramatically intersubjective," body art undercut the "masculinist and racist ideology of individualism shoring up modernist formalism" in art criticism (p. 3). For example:

> *Interior Scroll* [was] originally performed in 1975. . . . Her face and body covered in strokes of paint, [Carolee] Schneemann pulled a long, thin coil of paper from her vagina ("like a ticker tape . . . plumb line . . . the umbilicus and tongue"), unrolling it to read a narrative text to the audience. Part of this text read as follows: "I met a happy man,/a structuralist filmmaker . . . he said we are fond of you/ you are charming/ but don't ask us/to look at your films/. . . we cannot look at/*the personal clutter/the persis-*

> *tence of feelings/the hand-touch sensibility."* (Jones, 1998, p. 3)

> In *Transference Zone* (1972), [Vito] Acconci locked himself in a room with a group of photographs and objects owned by seven significant people in his life. One at a time, he let in visitors who knocked on the door, transferring his feelings about these "prime" people onto the unsuspecting recipient. . . . Playing out Freudian notions of transference—a dynamic involving the projection of one's subconscious conflicts and desires onto another—Acconci's piece opens out the contingency and performativity of identity and subjectivity itself. (Jones, 1998, pp. 139-140)

Experimental theater performances, on the other hand, "developed the aesthetic of a new theatre through productions which picked up the program of the historical avant-garde movement . . . and seemed to fulfill it: the 'retheatricalization' of theatre which was to be a radical move away from the literary theatre predominant in Western culture since the eighteenth century" (Fischer-Lichte, 1997, p. 200). An example is Robert Wilson's visual opera of the 1970s:

> His manipulation of space and time, his fusion of visual, aural, and performing arts, his utilization of chance and collage techniques in construction, his use of language for sound and evocation rather than discursive meaning, all show his close relationship to earlier experimental work in theatre, music, the visual arts, and dance. Speaking of *Einstein on the Beach* [1976], Wilson advised: "You don't have to think about the story, because there isn't any. You don't have to listen to words, because the words don't mean anything. You just enjoy the scenery, the architectural arrangements in time and space, the music, the feelings they all evoke. Listen to the pictures." (Carlson, 1996, p. 110)

◆ *Performance Ethnography*

In the late 1980s and early 1990s, sociologists began to turn their ethnographic field notes into performances, and theater artists and academics in performance studies began to produce or adapt ethnographies in order to perform them (see Becker, McCall, & Morris, 1989; Conquergood, 1985; Denzin, 1997; McCall, 1993; Mienczakowski, 2000; Paget, 1990; Pollock, 1990; Richardson, 1997; Siegel & Conquergood, 1985, 1990; Smith, 1993, 1994). The performance ethnographies of theater artists and people in performance studies were surely informed by the history of "performance art" and "experimental theater" in the 20th century. Ours certainly were not—despite the veiled reference to performance art in "performance science," the name Becker, Morris, and I gave our early pieces (see McCall & Becker, 1990). Our work was very much text based: There was a story, the words did mean something, and there were very few images to "listen to."

We based three performance pieces—*Local Theatrical Communities*; *Theatres and Communities: Three Scenes*; and *Performance Science*—on "formal interviews with seventy actors, directors and other theater workers (playwrights, critics, administrators, and technical people)" in "three metropolitan areas: Chicago, San Francisco, and Minneapolis/St. Paul" (Becker et al., 1989, p. 93). In performances we carried and read from scripts, did not wear costumes or use props, sat in chairs or stood behind podiums, and moved only to exchange seats or to get from chairs to podiums and back. We played multiple characters: ourselves, as sociologists, and various people one of us had interviewed. In *Theatres and Communities: Three Scenes*, for example, we played a total of 25 characters. We shifted body positions and visual focus, and occasionally stood, to mark character and scene changes and to guide audience attention.

> For example, we addressed the audience directly when we were making analytic statements, but turned and looked at one another when we were conversing, as "sociologists" and other characters. In the body of [published] script[s], italicized stage directions indicate[d] who was being addressed in each speech; a longer stage direction at the beginning of the first scene explain[ed] where we sat and looked and how we held our scripts to focus attention on the voices of the people we interviewed. (Becker et al., 1989, p. 96)

Likewise, the parodic ethnography of performance artists Coco Fusco and Guillermo Gómez-Peña was explicitly not based in the history of "avant-garde" movements, although, like other performance art, Fusco and Gómez-Peña's work depended less on text than on visual images. As Fusco (1995) notes: "Performance Art in the West did not begin with Dadaist 'events.' Since the early days of European 'conquest,' 'aboriginal samples' of people from Africa, Asia, and the Americas were brought to Europe for aesthetic contemplation, scientific analysis, and entertainment" (p. 41). Fusco states, "My collaborator, Guillermo Gómez Peña, and I were intrigued by this legacy of performing the identity of an Other for a white audience, sensing its implications for us as performance artists dealing with cultural identity in the present" (p. 37).

> Our plan was to live in a golden cage for three days, presenting ourselves as undiscovered Amerindians from an island in the Gulf of Mexico that had somehow been overlooked by Europeans for five centuries. We called our homeland Guatinau, and ourselves Guatinauis. We performed our "traditional tasks," which ranged from sewing voodoo dolls and lifting weights to watching television and working on a laptop computer. A donation box in front of the cage indicated that, for a small fee, I would dance (to rap music), Guillermo would tell authentic Amerindian stories (in a nonsensical language), and we would pose for Polaroids with visitors. Two "zoo guards" would be on hand to speak to visitors (since we could not understand them), take us to the bathroom on leashes, and feed us sandwiches and fruit. At the Whitney Museum in New York we added sex to our spectacle, offering a peek at authentic Guatinaui male genitals for $5. A chronology with highlights from the history of exhibiting non-Western peoples was on one didactic panel and a simulated Encyclopedia Britannica entry with a fake map of the Gulf of Mexico showing our island was on another. . .
>
> . . . We did not anticipate that our self-conscious commentary . . . could be believable. We underestimated the public faith in museums as bastions of truth, and institutional investment in that role. Furthermore, we did not anticipate that literalism would dominate the interpretation of our work. Consistently from city to city, more than half of our visitors believed our fic-

tion and thought we were "real." . . . As we moved our performance from public site to natural history museum, pressure mounted from institutional representatives . . . to correct audience misinterpretation. . . . we were perceived as either noble savages or evil tricksters, dissimulators who discredit museums and betray public trust. (Fusco, 1995, pp. 39, 50)

The ethnographic performances of theater artists and academics in performance studies are more theatrical than those of sociologists and more like performance art. They combine texts and visual elements such as movement, settings, costumes, and props. Emilie Beck's adaptation of a sociological text and Della Pollock's adaptation of an oral history are good examples.

Emilie Beck adapted an article that Marianne Paget (1990) wrote "about the erroneous construction of a medical diagnosis of a woman who was a cancer patient" (p. 136) and directed a performance of it titled *The Work of Talk: Studies in Misunderstandings*. There were seven characters, played by performance studies and theater students: the narrator, the doctor, the patient, and a panel of four experts "(two women, two men)," each of whom "was a rather singular and one-dimensional type. One was rather prim, like our stereotype of the librarian. Another was young and precocious. He was constantly unmasking the doctor and enjoyed it. The third was all business and matter of fact, and the fourth was rather lewd, a guy 'on the make' " (Paget, 1990, p. 144). The narrator was Cancer.

"The doctor and patient enacted dialogue" based on a series of transcripts Paget analyzed in the article. "Sometimes they commented on what they had said or would soon say, just as I had done in the original article. Sometimes they reacted to the panel" (Paget, 1990, p. 138). They also "danced together. They tangoed. . . . Sometimes, as she sat on a small table, he examined or asked her questions. . . . The experts reported the science" of Paget's analysis. "Sometimes they also 'gossiped' about what was going on between the doctor and patient. Sometimes they mimicked their dialogue or

acted like a chorus." Once the "cast acted as a machine, a many levered instrument producing work along a line. Everyone bleated or bayed a mechanical sound and moved synchronously. The machine (cast) surrounded the patient," miming "the physician's oddly mechanical talk" (pp. 139-140).

Cancer wore a long white dress, carried an evening bag and was barefooted.

She was both lovely and flirtatious. . . . Throughout the performance, she pays close attention to the patient. She dresses her up, coming at one point to apply makeup and at another to give her a chocolate. The patient belongs to Cancer. Occasionally panel members also try to help the patient. At one point panel member #1 drops glitter on her back; at another time she massages her back. These attentions to her back foreshadow the final moments when the patient reports that she has gone to another clinic and has been told that she has cancer of the spine. (Paget, 1990, pp. 139-141)

Della Pollock directed performances of *Like a Family: The Making of a Southern Cotton Mill World* (Hall et al., 1987), an oral history based on 300 interviews with former cotton mill workers in the Carolina Piedmont region. Eleven undergraduates "were selected by application" for "an independent study project that would give [them] credit for learning mill history through performance" (Pollock, 1990, p. 4). Pollock and her students developed the script and the performances together. The students played multiple roles, including themselves, and were costumed in "the long skirts and wool pants of the early twentieth century mill worker." Sets "consisted of chairs borrowed from the audience's seating area and prop pieces (a washboard, a tin kettle) borrowed from a distinctly 'other' era" (Pollock, 1990, p. 18).

[Performances] began with actors in costume ushering audience members to their seats while other actors set up the stage area, tuned guitars, etc. The lights remained bright. A selection of traditional songs buoyed both the actors and audience members. A general hubbub ensued until all of the actors—in both the stage and audience areas—joined in a round of "I Saw the Light." At the song's conclusion, the usher/actors took seats in the audience and one of the actors on stage came forward to introduce the performance and herself. She was followed by four others, each telling a brief story about his or her relation to the mill world. . . . As part of their introduction, the actors then recalled questions the *Like a Family* interviewers had asked former mill workers. . . In a spirit of genuine curiosity, the actors asked, How much free time did you have? Did you go to church? What happened when the union organizers came in?

We then gently, playfully blurred the performance frame. Actors stood in the audience to respond to the stage actors' questions. Rather than convincing shills, these were clearly actors: they were the ushers in costume who greeted audience members at the door and then sat next to them or their neighbor. When the actor stood to declare that she was Icy Norman or that he was Hoyle McCorkle, he or she was quite explicitly acting—representing someone else, expressing a point of view not his or her own. This kind of self-conscious theatricality helped us to confuse conventional distinctions between actor and audience and yet to maintain unconventional distinctions between actor and character. In this way we invited audience members to participate. (Pollock, 1990, p. 21)

At the end of the performance,

one of the *Like a Family* authors was invited to join the performers, to tell his or her own story and to invite, in turn, the audiences' stories and comments. Closing applause was thus postponed until after audience members had also assumed the role of performer. . . . When applause did occur, it was mutual: performers clapped for audience members and audience members for performers. Their roles were blurred in the expression of general pleasure. (p. 23)

The performance ethnographies I wrote, performed, and/or cast in the mid-1990s were influenced by Pollock's work. From 1992 through 1998, I worked with a photographer, Linda Gammell, and a sculptor, Sandra M. Taylor, on a study of midwestern women who practiced and/or advocated sustainable agriculture.[2] During that period we held seven daylong "workshops"—group interviews, really—with 52 women farmers.

We began the workshops by asking the women to answer the question "Who are you and what is your connection to the land?" After the introductions, Gammell and Taylor presented a slide lecture on stereotypes of rural women in art and advertising. Next, each woman described the object or objects she had brought to "represent farm life and/or farm women" and added it or them to a "centerpiece" on the table we sat around. Gammell photographed the centerpiece and, later, made portraits of the objects in the women's hands (see Taylor, Gammell, & McCall, 1994). We closed the workshops with open-ended questions such as, "If you were to have a very public opportunity to communicate something about women and rural life and the changes that are happening in rural culture, what would you say?" As the participants left, we gave each a roll of film and asked her to photograph her own landscape and mail the used film back to us; we had the film developed and sent the women copies of their prints. Gammell also made slides from their negatives.

A grant from the Blandin Foundation, which funded our work in the summer of 1993 and allowed us to hire three student research assistants, required that we and the students collaboratively report our findings to foundation officials and other grant recipients at an October conference. I wrote *Not "Just" a Farmer and Not Just a "Farm Wife"* (McCall, 1993) for that purpose. Only five of us could attend the conference, so I based the script on a workshop with four farm women, played by the students and me, and added the role of "questioner" and slide projector operator for Taylor. The performance began and ended with a tape recording of Patty Kakac, a workshop participant, singing "I'm Just a Farmer," a song she wrote. Throughout the performance, Taylor showed slides of the landscape photographs taken by women in four workshops. Although we read from scripts, sitting on stools, and were not costumed, the addition of music and visual images made this performance a bit less "text-bound" and more like Pollock's adaptation of *Like a Family* than my previous work with Becker and Morris.

Like Pollock, I wanted to "return the stories to the communities out of which they emerged." I understood that "telling personal, traditional and historical tales at work, on a front porch, or during an interview was itself performative action," and I "hoped we could realize their performative nature" by "re-performing these tales" (Pollock, 1990, p. 4). So I arranged three more performances in which women who participated in the workshops played the parts of Michal and Sandra; Sara, Michelle, and Liza (the students); and Patty, Alice, Gloria, and Donna (the farm women) for Minnesota Food Association Board members (our other sponsors) and workshop participants.

◆ *Some Tips*

Performance ethnography requires at least the following from the ethnographer or adapter: He or she must write a script and then cast and/or perform and/or stage it (adding movement, sets, costumes, props). Writing a script is the easiest task for a sociologist/ethnographer, I think, because we always turn our field notes and interview transcripts into written texts— even if these are normally meant for readers and not for performers and audiences. Emerson, Fretz, and Shaw (1995) call the texts ethnographers usually write "thematic narratives" and explain them as follows:

> In coding and memo-writing, the ethnographer has started to create and elaborate analytic themes. In writing an ethnographic text, the writer organizes some of these themes into a coherent "story" about life and events in the setting studied. Such a narrative requires selecting only some small portion of the total set of fieldnotes and then linking them into a coherent text representing some aspect or slice of the world studied. (p. 170)

Emerson et al. explain to student ethnographers how to "jot" notes in the field, how to "write them up" to create "scenes on the page," how to "discover" members' meanings in field notes, and how to "process" field notes through "open coding, focused coding and integrative memos" (pp. v-vii). In a chapter titled "Writing an Ethnography," they explain how to "build up piece by piece a coherent,

fieldnote-centered story" (p. 179). They advise students to write "excerpt-commentary units" using field notes and initial memos; an "excerpt-commentary unit" includes an analytic point, orienting information (e.g., the social statuses of speakers), an excerpt from the field notes, and analytic commentary (pp. 182-183). Next, Emerson et al. tell students to order these units within a section and to order sections within the text and, finally, to write an introduction, a "literature review," and a conclusion to the ethnography.

Writing an ethnographic performance script is very similar, except that "orienting information" and "analytic points and commentary" are unnecessary: The first is embodied, and the second can be done by the "characters." And, of course, dialogue replaces description and narration. Still, ethnographic scriptwriters must read and reread their field notes or transcripts to "create and elaborate analytic themes" and "organize some of these into a coherent story."

To write *Not "Just" a Farmer,* I read and reread the transcript of a workshop we held in St. Cloud, Minnesota, on August 21, 1993. It was approximately 120 pages long, representing 6 hours of audiotaped conversation. I needed to produce a script that would take 30 minutes to perform (the time allotted to us at the Blandin conference); as it turned out, this meant the script was 10½ pages long—only a "small portion of the total set of fieldnotes."

The St. Cloud workshop was organized by Barb Thomes, who had participated in a 1992 workshop. Barb lived on a farm and worked for Lutheran Social Services, providing crisis counseling and other services to farm families. She invited four women to participate in the 1993 workshop. Donna Johnson and her husband lost their farming operation, but not his maternal grandparents' farm, in the 1980s "farm crisis." Patty Kakac and her husband lived on a 160-acre farm, kept bees and sold honey, and grew their own food, but she earned her living as a folksinger. She and Alice Tripp were political activists; Alice was a retired dairy farmer and former candidate for governor of Minnesota. Gloria Schneider owned a 200-acre dairy farm, which she had farmed alone since 1989, when her husband died suddenly; she was hoping her son would move back and farm with her. It is not surprising, then, that the dominant themes in the workshop were the difficulties family farmers have earning a living; the vast wealth and power, by comparison, of corporate food processors, retailers, and transportation, seed, and chemical companies; the loss of farmland to urban migration, suburban sprawl, and the depressed rural economy; and our responsibilities, as urban eaters, to learn where our food comes from and, where possible, to buy it from local family farmers who grow it without chemical herbicides, pesticides, or fertilizers. Secondary themes were the importance of women's work on traditional farms, the diversity of rural women's work lives in the present, and the opportunities for women in sustainable agriculture. I organized the script around these themes.

It began with the question, "What is your connection to the land?" directed to the audience and asked in unison by four of us, seated on tall stools, onstage. Next, Sara and I, Michelle and Liza, and Sandra, who was seated in the audience near the slide projector, introduced ourselves by answering that question. Then, Sara, Michelle, Liza, and I changed places and introduced "ourselves" as Donna (Sara), Gloria (me), Patty (Michelle), and Alice (Liza). As we became the other characters, Sandra began to project the slides. She also asked questions and made comments; I used quotes from the transcript, mostly her own words, but I rearranged them to provide transitions from topic to topic and to motivate or explain comments and answers from the other participants. An example is the first segment of the script after the introductions:

Sandra: [We've] noticed that there isn't a very true picture of women and land in the media. Or the fine arts. So that's what we're going to talk about today and ask you for your help: to give us better information. About what it means to be a woman associated with the land in the 1990s and beyond. So thank you for coming to help us. . . . And now, if you could, take whatever you brought and put it in the middle [of the table].

Sandra: Linda [Gammell] brought some good stuff. [She said] she brought this little cow because she was "interested in the idea of how people depict animals. And how animals then become dolls and toys."

Patty: Somehow the cow became really popular in the, you know, cutesy art stuff. Just as farmers [were losing their farms]. . . . And it just kind of made me sick. I go to Craft Fairs, selling for my friend. And people who sold cows—you know, you can make lots of money selling cows! God this is not right! There's something screwy about this. That you can make money selling little cows but you can't make money selling food from it. . . . I've noticed, throughout the country, no matter what product you make if it's for food you can't make a living on it. But if you can entertain people . . . And that's how a lot of farmers are going. Having people come out and they have vacations on the farm.

Donna: Uh-huh. Bed and Breakfasts.

Patty: To make money.

Sandra: Really?

Patty: Yeh, that's one alternative to making money [farming].

Donna: It's like supplemental income.

Patty: Yeh, people raising vegetables go to raising dried flowers. To make money. They can make money on dried flowers but not on vegetables.

Sandra: Is it that people don't see a difference between supermarket food and food that's grown on a farm?

Donna: I don't think there's any connection left.

Patty: There also is, there was a policy in this country, you know, established. That food would be cheap. Which allowed some people to make money on it, but not others.

Sandra: Which ones? Who gets to make money?

Patty: Those who

Alice: process. General Mills.

Patty: The supermarkets, the handlers.

Alice: Food processors.

[Sara]: Fertilizer people.

Patty: Yeh.

Donna: Banks, anybody. I'm not much of a TV person—much at all. But there was just an ad not too long ago, about the price of corn being, let's say, two dollars in nineteen—pick a number—twenty. And at this point it's two dollars again. And all the costs [have gone up]. Say the newspaper cost a nickel at that time, or whatever it was. Did anybody see that ad?

Patty: I didn't see that ad but I've seen similar things. Yeh.

Alice: There used to be a Department of Agriculture bulletin that said it cost three dollars a bushel to *raise* corn. So how are you going to make money? Yeh.

Donna: Yeh, but the public doesn't see that.

Alice: Yeh, right.

Patty: Umhuh.

Donna: The public will see this commercial and nice colors and . . .

Patty: Sure.

This script was less artificial than the scripts I wrote with Becker and Morris because it was based on a group interview. Those early scripts were based on individual interviews that were not tape-recorded; we used the information in them as much as we used the interviewers' and interviewees' actual words when we "made up" the dialogue. We also let the "sociologists" make the analytic points and do the commentary. In *Theatres and Communities: Three Scenes,* for example, the "sociologists" made 61% of all 165 speeches and all but 8 of 67 "analytic" speeches. I didn't have to "make up" the dialogue in *Not "Just" a Farmer*—it was already there, recorded in the transcript. The "analytic commentary" was also in the transcript, provided by the women farmers themselves. The "questioner" needed only to introduce the performance and provide context and transitions.

◆ Casting

I learned what I know about casting as a "participant observer" in the community theater world. My husband directed 23 plays, with amateur actors, in 3 years at two community theaters and, as the "director's wife," I observed

auditions, rehearsals, and performances; participated in backstage activities; and listened to endless discussions about the artistic choices and decisions a director makes. I learned there is a discrepancy between actors' casting expectations and directors' casting purposes. Amateur actors think the "best" actor (sometimes simply the highest-status person in the community) should get the "biggest" part. The director, on the other hand, wants to cast a strong, balanced ensemble of actors. As my husband's teacher has explained:

> Actors at the point of auditioning should be aware that the director wants to arrive at a comfortable solution of the casting problem. The director wants to do as little work or readjustment as possible, and tries to develop an almost extrasensory awareness as to whether or not the chosen actor will be sympathetic with the character which is to be played. . . .
>
> Certainly it is helpful to have a sprinkling of previously successful experience in the cast, mainly to help create rapport and sympathetic relationships. . . . When I know the pluses and minuses of the actors and the script, it becomes my job to meld them together and put the strong people where they will lend strength—not necessarily in the strongest plot roles. Often the strongest part is so well-written that a person who is adequate will develop the necessary strength while rehearsing and playing. But in the weaker sections of the play, where it could fall apart, the stronger actors may be needed more sorely. (Spayde, 1993, pp. 43-45)

For the original performance of *Not "Just" a Farmer and Not Just a "Farm Wife,"* I had to cast the five of us who conducted the research and could attend the Blandin conference. Indeed, I chose to work with the St. Cloud transcript because it had the right number of characters, including the generic "questioner." However, as I cast the five of us I did try make sure each "actor" would be "sympathetic with the character" she played. Like Donna and her husband, Sara's parents lost their farming operation but still lived on a farm. Both Patty and Michelle were singers. (Michelle's "object" was a tape recording of Minnesota musicians, and she talked about singing when she introduced herself: "My mother and my sister and I always sang. And in California it was something that just *we* did. And when we moved to Fergus Falls [Minnesota], one of the most interesting things was that singing was something that *everyone* did, together. There were so many songs that everyone knew, that we didn't know.") I cast Liza as Alice because Alice was about the same age as Liza's great-grandmother, of whom she said: "I feel like my strongest connection to the land is my great-grandma who lives in a small town in Illinois and we're pretty close. She's eighty-four and she runs greenhouses so she can sell for the Lord." I cast myself as Gloria because I thought she was the least sympathetic character—less politicized than the others and more traditional in her farming and her gender practices, she was boisterous and talked too much, before she left early. Because she was the "outsider" in the workshop the other "actors" participated in, I was afraid they might not give her a sympathetic reading. I thought perhaps I could, because I was aware of the problem.

◆ Directing and Performing

I won't presume to give the reader acting advice. Instead I will quote from one of hundreds of books of advice to actors, written by experts. According to playwright David Mamet (1997), "To act means to perform an action, to do something" (p. 72). He asserts:

> To you, to the actor, it is not the words which carry the meaning—it is the actions. Moment to moment and night to night the play will change, as you and your adversaries onstage change, as your conflicting actions butt up against each other. That play, that interchange, is drama. But the words are set and unchanging. Any worth in them was put there by the author. His or her job is done, and the best service you can do them is accept the words as is, and speak them simply and clearly in an attempt to get what you want from another actor. (pp. 62-63)

Mamet also states:

> The plane is designed to fly; the pilot is trained to direct it. Likewise, the play is designed, if cor-

rectly designed, as a series of incidents in which and through which the protagonist struggles toward his or her goal. It is the job of the actor to show up, and use the lines and his or her will and common sense, to attempt to achieve a goal similar to that of the protagonist. And that is the end of the actor's job. (p. 12)

Of course *we* were not acting; we were simply reading aloud the traces of a conversation among ourselves and four women farmers. Instead of "directing" the "actors," I tried to make the words in my script easy to speak "simply and clearly," requiring little interpretive work, by transcribing the *sounds* of words and pauses in our conversations, the music of our speech, and transferring these to the script. This way of working is consistent with Anna Deavere Smith's (1993) idea that you "find a character's psychological reality by 'inhabiting' that character's words" (p. xxvii).

Since the mid-1980s, Smith has created a series of performances "based on actual events" (Smith, 1994, p. xvii) that she calls *On the Road: A Search for American Character*. The best-known performances in the series are *Fires in the Mirror*, about 3 days of riots, marches, and demonstrations that broke out in Crown Heights, Brooklyn, after "one of the cars in a three-car procession carrying the Lubavitcher Hasidic rebbe (spiritual leader) ran a red light, hit another car, and swerved onto a sidewalk," where it "struck and killed Gavin Cato, a seven-year-old Black boy from Guyana, and seriously injured his cousin Angela" and after "a group of young Black men fatally stabbed Yankel Rosenbaum, a 29-year-old Hasidic scholar from Australia" in retaliation (Smith, 1933, p. xliii); and *Twilight: Los Angeles, 1992*, about the civil disturbances in Los Angeles in April 1992.

> Each *On the Road* performance evolves from interviews I conduct with individuals directly or indirectly involved in the event I intend to explore. Basing my scripts entirely on this interview material, I perform the interviewees on stage using their own words. *Twilight: Los Angeles, 1992* is the product of my search for the character of Los Angeles in the wake of the initial Rodney King verdict. (Smith, 1994, p. xvii)

As an acting student, Smith learned "the importance of thinking on the word, rather than between the words in order to discover the character" (Smith, 1993, p. xxiv). Following her Shakespeare teacher's instructions, she said a 14-line speech from *Richard III* "over and over well into the wee hours of the morning." Because she did not try to "control the words," Smith learned "about the power of rhythm and imagery to evoke the spirit of a character, of a play, of a time" (p. xxiv). Later she realized she could "create the illusion of being another person by reenacting something they had said *as they had said it*" (p. xxvi).

> Actors . . . are trained to develop aspects of our memories that are more emotional and sensory than intellectual. The general public often wonders how actors remember their lines. What's more remarkable to me, is how actors remember, recall, and reiterate feelings and sensations. The body has a memory just as the mind does. The heart has a memory, just as the mind does. The act of speech is a physical act. It is powerful enough that it can create, with the rest of the body, a kind of cooperative dance. That dance is a sketch of something that is inside a person, and not fully revealed by the words alone. I came to realize that if I were able to record part of the dance—that is, the spoken part—and re-enact it, the rest of the body would follow. (Smith, 1993, pp. xxv-xxvi)

At first, Smith used published interviews to "engage" her "students in putting themselves in other people's shoes" (p. xxvi). Later, she began to conduct her own interviews and, later still, to perform them herself.

> I wanted to develop an alternative to the self-based [acting] technique, a technique that would begin with the other and come to the self, a technique that would empower the other to find the actor rather than the other way around. I needed very graphic evidence that the manner of speech could be a mark of individuality. If we were to inhabit the speech pattern of another, and walk in the speech of another, we could find the individuality of the other and experience that individuality viscerally. I became increasingly convinced that the activity of reenactment could tell us as much, if not more, about another individual than the process of learning about the other by using the self as a

> frame of reference. The frame of reference for the other would *be* the other. (Smith, 1993, p. xxvii)

◆ Staging

Besides casting and coaching actors, the director of a performance or play also "*stages the event*" by "controlling the mise-en-scène": sets, lighting, costumes, props, and movement (Bordwell & Thompson, 1993, p. 145). As I have said, the staging has been minimal in the performances I have done, so I cannot tell the reader "how to" do it. Nor are other published descriptions of performance ethnography very helpful. Staging requires interpretive choices. Anna Deavere Smith works with professional directors, dramaturges, and set, sound, lighting, and costume designers in making these choices. And although they explain their interpretive purposes, neither Pollock nor Paget/Beck tells us how these interpretive choices were made. Pollock (1990) says that she hoped "re-performing" the oral histories of cotton mill workers would "invigorate their claim to self-representation" (p. 4) and "help to recover their historical life" (p. 5). She wanted to avoid "the illusion that the past was present" because she thought this would turn "drama's advantage of immediacy towards the end of time-warp titillation" (p. 6). The interpretive choices she made to achieve her goals included keeping costumes, sets, and props simple (to avoid "the illusion that the past was present") and casting performers in multiple roles, so that "the audience member is liberated from any particular historical position (including his or her own) but constrained within a dialectic of history-making" because the "audience member identifies . . . above all [with] the actor's power to transform him or herself and, in the process, the world" (p. 18).

Because Marianne Paget (1990) has published the description of "On the Work of Talk," we do not know how Emilie Beck, the director, made her interpretive choices. However, in discussing the alternative choices she imagined Beck might have made, Paget does provide one small clue:

I thought of the performed text as Emilie Beck's version. Making Cancer the narrator was a stunning interpretive act which had many implications for the production of the performance's meaning. . . . Excluding the author and investigator was another interpretive act. Including me as the investigator, Emilie Beck argued, interfered with the production of a necessary atmosphere that would engage the audience. Here is one of the conundrums of the performance. [It] made fantastic some of the facts in order to state them. (pp. 144-145)

Performance ethnography is a relatively new form. Perhaps, with time, people who are trained in theater and performance techniques will write books of advice for directors of such ethnographies. In the meantime, I can recommend a book of advice for theater directors. Titled *Backwards and Forwards: A Technical Manual for Reading Plays* and written by David Ball (1983), an experienced playwright and director, it "reveals a script not only as literature, but as raw material for theatrical performance," as director Michael Langham (1983, p. vii) says in his foreword to the book.

There is all the difference in the world between literature and drama. A play's sound, music, movement, looks, dynamics—and much more—are to be discovered deep in the script, yet cannot be detected through strictly literary methods of reading and analysis. [In] this little book . . . there is guidance and illumination about the nature of scripts [even for directors with] a lot of experience. (Langham, 1983, pp. vii-viii)

■ Notes

1. The distinction was new to theater critics, but not to theater artists (see Mamet, 1997, pp. 62-63).

2. An agriculture more sustainable than the current agribusiness system would rely less on petrochemicals (which, in some cases, "cost" more calories than the food they produce and can cause water, soil, and air pollution and a host of health problems), less on long-distance transportation (buying and selling food locally are basic tenets of sustainable agriculture), and less on "middlemen" (buying directly from farmers at farmers' markets or through memberships in Community Supported Agriculture is also a basic tenet).

■ References

Ball, D. (1983). *Backwards and forwards: A technical manual for reading plays*. Carbondale: Southern Illinois University Press.

Becker, H. S., McCall, M. M., & Morris, L. V. (1989). Theatres and communities: Three scenes. *Social Problems, 36*, 93-116.

Bordwell, D., & Thompson, K. (1993). *Film art: An introduction*. New York: McGraw-Hill.

Carlson, M. (1996). *Performance: A critical introduction*. New York: Routledge.

Conquergood, D. (1985). Performing as a moral act: Ethical dimensions of the ethnography of performance. *Literature in Performance, 5*, 1-13.

Denzin, N. K. (1997). *Interpretive ethnography: Ethnographic practices for the 21st century*. Thousand Oaks, CA: Sage.

Emerson, R. M., Fretz, R. I., & Shaw, L. L. (1995). *Writing ethnographic fieldnotes*. Chicago: University of Chicago Press.

Fischer-Lichte, E. (1997). *The show and the gaze of theatre: A European perspective*. Iowa City: University of Iowa Press.

Fusco, C. (1995). *English is broken here: Notes on cultural fusion in the Americas*. New York: New Press.

Hall, J. D., Leloudis, J., Korstad, R., Murphy, M., Jones, L. A., & Daly, C. B. (1987). *Like a family: The making of a southern cotton mill world*. Chapel Hill: University of North Carolina Press.

Jones, A. (1998). *Body art/performing the subject*. Minneapolis: University of Minnesota Press.

Langham, M. (1983). Foreword. In D. Ball, *Backwards and forwards: A technical manual for reading plays* (pp. vii-viii). Carbondale: Southern Illinois University Press.

Mamet, D. (1997). *True and false: Heresy and common sense for the actor*. New York: Pantheon.

McCall, M. M., & Becker, H. S. (1990). Performance science. *Social Problems, 37*, 116-132.

McCall, M. M. (1993). *Not "just" a farmer and not just a "farm wife."* Unpublished performance script.

Mienczakowski, J. (2000). Ethnodrama: Performed research—limitations and potential. In P. Atkinson, S. Delamont, & A. Coffey (Eds.), *Handbook of ethnography.* London: Sage.

Paget, M. A. (1990). Performing the text. *Journal of Contemporary Ethnography, 19,* 136-155.

Pollock, D. (1990). Telling the told: Performing like a family. *Oral History Review, 18,* 1-36.

Richardson, L. (1997). *Fields of play: Constructing an academic life.* New Brunswick, NJ: Rutgers University Press.

Sayre, H. (1995). Performance. In F. Lentricchia & T. McLaughlin (Eds.), *Critical terms for literary study* (pp. 91-104). Chicago: University of Chicago Press.

Siegel, T., & Conquergood, D. (Producers & Directors). (1985). *Between two worlds: The Hmong shaman in America* [Video documentary].

Siegel, T., & Conquergood, D. (Producers & Directors). (1990). *The heart broken in half* [Video documentary].

Smith, A. D. (1993). *Fires in the mirror: Crown Heights, Brooklyn, and other identities.* Garden City, NY: Anchor.

Smith, A. D. (1994). *Twilight: Los Angeles, 1992.* Garden City, NY: Anchor.

Spayde, S. H. (with Mackey, D. A.). (1993). *Doors into the play: A few practical keys for theatricians.* San Bernardino, CA: Borgo.

Taylor, S. M., Gammell, L., & McCall, M. M. (1994). *The one about the farmer's daughter: Stereotypes and self-images.* St. Paul: Minnesota Food Association.

16

CASE STUDIES

◆ Robert E. Stake

Case studies have become one of the most common ways to do qualitative inquiry, but they are neither new nor essentially qualitative. Case study is not a methodological choice but a choice of what is to be studied. By whatever methods, we choose to study the case. We could study it analytically or holistically, entirely by repeated measures or hermeneutically, organically or culturally, and by mixed methods—but we concentrate, at least for the time being, on the case.

The physician studies the child because the child is ill. The child's symptoms are both qualitative and quantitative. The physician's record is more quantitative than qualitative. The social worker studies the child because the child is neglected. The symptoms of neglect are both qual- itative and quantitative. The formal record the social worker keeps is more qualitative than quantitative.[1] In many professional and practical fields, cases are studied and recorded. As a form of research, case study is defined by interest in individual cases, not by the methods of inquiry used.

Perhaps a majority of researchers doing case-work call their studies by some other name. Howard Becker (personal communication, 1980), for example, when asked what he called his own studies, reluctantly said, "Fieldwork," adding that such labels contribute little to the understanding of what researchers do. Some of us emphasize the name *case study* because it draws attention to the question of what specially can be learned from the single case. That

AUTHOR'S NOTE: This revision of my chapter of the same title in the first edition of the *Handbook of Qualitative Research* has been enhanced by the fine contributions to *What Is a Case?* edited by Charles Ragin and Howard Becker (1992), as well as by the critical readings of Norman Denzin, Yvonna Lincoln, Orlando Fals Borda, Morten Levin, Linda Mabry, and Rita Davis.

◆ 435

epistemological question is the driving question of this chapter: What can be learned from the single case? I will emphasize designing the study to optimize understanding of the case rather than generalization beyond.

◆ Identification of the Case

A case may be simple or complex. It may be a child, or a classroom of children, or an incident such as a mobilization of professionals to study a childhood condition. It is one among others. In any given study, we will concentrate on the one. The time we may spend concentrating our inquiry on the one may be long or short, but, while we so concentrate, we are engaged in case study.

Custom has it that not everything is a case. A child may be a case. A doctor may be a case—but *his doctoring* probably lacks the specificity, boundedness, to be called a case.[2] An agency may be a case. But the *reasons* for child neglect or the *policies* of dealing with neglectful parents will seldom be considered a case. We think of those topics as generalities rather than specificities. The case is a specific One.

If we are moved to study it, the case is almost certainly going to be a functioning specific. The case is a "bounded system" (Flood, as reported in Fals Borda, 1998). In the social sciences and human services, the case has working parts; it is purposive; it often has a self. It is an integrated system. However immature, the child is a working combination of physiological, psychological, cultural, aesthetic, and other forces. Similarly, the hospital as case, the agency as case. Functional or dysfunctional, rational or irrational, the case is a system.

Its behavior is patterned. Coherence and sequence are prominent. It is common to recognize that certain features are within the system, within the boundaries of the case, and other features outside. Some are significant as context. William Goode and Paul Hatt (1952) observe

that it is not always easy for the case researcher to say where the child ends and the environment begins. But boundedness and behavior patterns are useful concepts for specifying the case (Stake, 1988).

Ultimately, we may be interested in a general phenomenon or a population of cases more than in the individual case. And we cannot understand this case without knowing about other cases. But while we are studying it, our meager resources are concentrated on trying to understand *its* complexities. For the while, we probably will not study comparison cases. We may simultaneously carry on more than one case study, but each case study is a concentrated inquiry into a single case.

Charles Ragin (1992) gives emphasis to the question of "What is it a case of?" as if "membership in" or "representation of" something else were the main consideration in case study. He makes detailed reference to the casework of Michel Wieviorka (1988) on terrorism. Ragin was writing for the social scientist seeking theoretical generalization, justifying the study of the particular only if it serves an understanding of grand issues or explanations. He recognized that even in formal experimentation and statistical survey work there is interest in the illustrative or deviant case. But historians, program evaluators, institutional researchers, practitioners in all professions are interested in the individual case without necessarily caring what it is a case of.

Even if my definition of case study were agreed upon,[3] and it is not, the terms *case* and *study* defy full specification (Kemmis, 1980). A case study is both a process of inquiry about the case and the product of that inquiry. Lawrence Stenhouse (1984) advocates calling the latter, the product, a *case record,* and occasionally we do, but the practice of calling the final report a *case study* is widely established. Here and there, researchers call a great variety of things case studies.[4] But the more the object of study is a specific, unique, bounded system, the greater the usefulness of the epistemological rationales described in this chapter.

◆ *Intrinsic and Instrumental*
   Interest in Cases

I find it useful to identify three types of case study. I call a study an *intrinsic case study* if it is undertaken because, first and last, the researcher wants better understanding of this particular case. Here, it is not undertaken primarily because the case represents other cases or because it illustrates a particular trait or problem, but because, in all its particularity *and* ordinariness, this case itself is of interest. The researcher at least temporarily subordinates other curiosities so that the stories of those "living the case" will be teased out. The purpose is not to come to understand some abstract construct or generic phenomenon, such as literacy or teenage drug use or what a school principal does. The purpose is not theory building—although at other times the researcher may do just that. Study is undertaken because of an intrinsic interest in, for example, this particular child, clinic, conference, or curriculum. Writings illustrating intrinsic case study include the following:

- *The Education of Henry Adams: An Autobiography* (Adams, 1918)
- *God's Choice* (Peshkin, 1986)
- *Bread and Dreams: A Case Study of Bilingual Schooling in the U.S.A.* (MacDonald, Adelman, Kushner, & Walker, 1982) (and most program evaluation studies; see Mabry, 1998)
- *An Aberdeenshire Village Propaganda: Forty Years Ago* (Smith, 1889)
- *The Swedish School System* (Stenholm, 1984)

I call it *instrumental case study* if a particular case is examined mainly to provide insight into an issue or to redraw a generalization. The case is of secondary interest, it plays a supportive role, and it facilitates our understanding of something else. The case still is looked at in depth, its contexts scrutinized, its ordinary activities detailed, but all because this helps the researcher to pursue the external interest. The case may be seen as typical of other cases or not. (In a later section, I will discuss when typicality is important.) Here the choice of case is made to advance understanding of that other interest. Because the researcher simultaneously has several interests, particular and general, there is no line distinguishing intrinsic case study from instrumental; rather, a zone of combined purpose separates them. Writings illustrating instrumental case study include these:

- "Campus Response to a Student Gunman" (Asmussen & Creswell, 1995/1997)
- *Boys in White: Student Culture in Medical School* (Becker, Geer, Hughes, & Strauss, 1961)
- "Thrown Overboard: The Human Costs of Health Care Rationing" (Kolker, 1996)
- *On the Border of Opportunity: Education, Community, and Language at the U.S.-Mexico Line* (Pugach, 1998)
- "A Nonreader Becomes a Reader: A Case Study of Literacy Acquisition by a Severely Disabled Reader" (McCormick, 1994)

With even less intrinsic interest in one particular case, a researcher may jointly study a number of cases in order to investigate a phenomenon, population, or general condition. I call this *collective case study*.[5] It is instrumental study extended to several cases. Individual cases in the collection may or may not be known in advance to manifest some common characteristic. They may be similar or dissimilar, redundancy and variety each important. They are chosen because it is believed that understanding them will lead to better understanding, perhaps better theorizing, about a still larger collection of cases. Works illustrating collective case study include the following:

- *Teachers' Work* (Connell, 1985)
- "Researching Practice Settings: A Case Study Approach" (concerning medical clinics; Crabtree & Miller, 1999)

- *Savage Inequalities* (Kozol, 1991)
- *Bold Ventures: Patterns Among U.S. Innovations in Science and Mathematics Education* (Raisin & Britton, 1997)
- "The Dark Side of Organizations: Mistake, Misconduct and Disaster" (Vaughan, 1999)

Reports (and authors) often do not fit neatly into such categories. I see these three as heuristic more than determinative. Alan Peshkin (personal communication, October 1992) responded to my classification of *God's Choice* (1986) as an intrinsic case study by saying: "I mean to present my case so that it can be read with interest in the case itself, but I always have another agenda—to learn from the case about some class of things. Some of what that will be remains an emergent matter for a long time." In this work, for 3 years Peshkin studied a single school, Bethany Baptist Academy. Until the final chapter, he does not tell the reader about the emergent matters of great importance to him and to the school people and citizens broadly. The first order of business was to understand the case, and a harsh understanding it turned out to be. But the immediate, if not ultimate, interest was intrinsic. The methods Peshkin used centered on the case, only latently taking up his abiding concern for community, freedom, and survival. Yes, this work could also have been called an instrumental study.

Other types of case study have been acknowledged. Harrison White (1992) categorizes social science casework according to three purposes: case studies for identity, explanation, or control. Similarly, Yvonna Lincoln and Egon Guba (1985) discuss five functions. Ragin (1992) sorts the studies two by two, conceptualizing cases as empirical units or theoretical constructs, general or specific. Historians and political scientists regularly examine singular episodes or movements or eras, such as Norman Gottwald's (1979) study of the emergence of Jewish identity. But I choose not to call such investigations case studies when the episodes or relationships—however complex, impacting, and bounded—are not easily thought of as organic and systemic, laced with purpose and self.

Elsewhere there is a common form of cases used in teaching to illustrate a point, a condition, a category, something important for instruction (Kennedy, 1979). For decades, law school and school of business professors have gallaried these cases.[6] For staff development and management training, such reports constitute the articles of the *Journal of Case Research,* key publication of the North American Case Research Association. Used for instruction and consultation, they result from instrumental case study.

One could also make a separate category for biography. Bill Tierney's contribution to this volume (Chapter 20) is case centered, noting that biography calls for special attention to chronological structures and to procedures for the protection of human subjects. Similarly, television documentaries, many of them easily classifiable as case studies, require their own methods. The work of ethnographers, critical theorists, institutional demographers, and many others follows conceptual and stylistic patterns that not only amplify the taxonomy but also extend the foundation for case study research in the social sciences and social services. My purpose here in categorization is not taxonomic; rather, I want to emphasize variation in concern for and methodological orientation to *the case.* Thus I focus on three types: intrinsic, instrumental, and collective.

◆ Study of the Particular

Case researchers seek both what is common and what is particular about the case, but the end result regularly portrays something of the uncommon (Stouffer, 1941), drawing from all of the following:

1. The nature of the case;
2. The case's historical background;
3. The physical setting;
4. Other contexts (e.g., economic, political, legal, and aesthetic);

5. Other cases through which this case is recognized;
6. Those informants through whom the case can be known.

To study the case, to show particularity, many researchers gather data on all of the above.

The search for particularity competes with the search for generalizability. What all should be said about a single case is quite different from what should be said about all cases. Each case has important atypical features, happenings, relationships, and situations. Pursuit of understanding of those atypicalities not only robs time from the study of the generalizable but also diminishes the value, to some extent, that we place on demographic and policy issues.

Most academic researchers are supportive of the study of cases only if there is clear expectation of generalizability to other cases. Case-by-case uniqueness is seldom an ingredient of scientific theory. Case study research has been constrained even by qualitative methodologists who grant less than full regard to study of the particular (Denzin, 1989; Glaser & Strauss, 1967; Herriott & Firestone, 1983; Yin, 1989). These and other social scientists have written about case study as if intrinsic study of a particular case is not as important as studies to obtain generalizations pertaining to a population of cases.[7] Some have emphasized case study as typification of other cases, as exploration leading up to generalization-producing studies, or as an occasional early step in theory building. At least as I see it, case study method has been too little honored as the intrinsic study of a valued particular, as it is in biography, institutional self-study, program evaluation, therapeutic practice, and many lines of work. Generalization should not be emphasized in all research (Feagin, Orum, & Sjoberg, 1991; Simons, 1980).

Reflecting upon the pertinent literature, I find case study methodology written largely by people who presume that the research should contribute to scientific generalization. The bulk of case study work, however, is done by individuals who have *intrinsic* interest in the case

and little interest in the advance of science. Their designs aim the inquiry toward understanding of what is important about that case within its own world, which is seldom the same as the worlds of researchers and theorists. Those designs develop what is perceived to be the case's own issues, contexts, and interpretations, its *thick description*. In contrast, the methods of instrumental case study draw the researcher toward illustrating how the concerns of researchers and theorists are manifest in the case. Because the critical issues are more likely to be known in advance and following disciplinary expectations, such a design can take greater advantage of already developed instruments and preconceived coding schemes.

In intrinsic case study, researchers do not avoid generalization—they cannot. Certainly they generalize to happenings of their cases at times yet to come and in other situations. They expect readers to comprehend the reported interpretations but to modify their (the readers') own. Thus researchers use the methods for casework that they actually use to learn enough about their cases to encapsulate complex meanings into finite reports—and thus to describe the cases in sufficient descriptive narrative so that readers can vicariously experience these happenings and draw conclusions (which may differ from those of the researchers).

Even intrinsic case study can be seen as a small step toward grand generalization (Campbell, 1975; Vaughan, 1992), especially in the case that runs counter to the existing rule. Damage occurs when the commitment to generalize or to theorize runs so strong that the researcher's attention is drawn away from features important for understanding the case itself.[8] The case study researcher faces a strategic decision in regard to how much and how long the complexities of the case should be studied. Not everything about the case can be understood—how much needs to be? Each researcher has choices to make.

Contexts and Situations

With its own unique history, the case is a complex entity operating within a number of contexts—physical, economic, ethical, aesthetic, and so on. The case is singular, but it has subsections (e.g., production, marketing, sales departments), groups (e.g., students, teachers, parents), occasions (e.g., workdays, holidays, days near holidays), a concatenation of domains—many so complex that at best they can only be sampled.

Holistic case study calls for the examination of these complexities. As Yvonna Lincoln and Egon Guba point out in Chapter 6 of this volume, much qualitative research is based on a holistic view that social phenomena, human dilemmas, and the nature of cases are situational and influenced by happenings of many kinds. Qualitative researchers are sometimes disposed toward causal determination of events (Becker, 1992) but more often tend to perceive, as does Tolstoy in *War and Peace*, events not simply and singly caused. Many find the search for cause of little value, and dramatize instead the coincidence of events, seeing some events as purposive, some as situational, many of them interrelated. They favor inquiry designs that seek data describing diverse operations of the case. To do case studies does not require examination of diverse issues and contexts, but that is the way that most qualitative researchers do them.

Organizing Around Issues

A case study, like research of all kinds, has conceptual structure. It is usually organized around a small number of research questions. These are not just information questions, such as "Who influenced her career choice?" or "What was the impact of his teaching?" They are issues or thematic lines, such as "In what ways did the change in hiring policy require a change in performance standards?" or "Did the addiction therapy, originally developed for male clients, need reconceptualization for women?"

Issues are complex, situated, problematic relationships. They invite attention to ordinary experience but also to the language and understanding of the common disciplines of knowledge, such as sociology, economics, ethics, and literary criticism. Seeking a different purview

from that of most crafters of experiments and testers of hypotheses, qualitative case researchers orient to complexities connecting ordinary practice in natural habitats to the abstractions and concerns of diverse academic disciplines. This broader purview is applied to the single case, but does not replace it as focus. Generalization and proof (Becker, 1992) linger in the mind of the researcher, so a tension exists.[9]

The issues mentioned two paragraphs back were aimed at a particular case, but their statement can be more general: "Does change in hiring policy away from affirmative action require change in performance standards?" or "Does addiction therapy originally developed for male clients need reconceptualization for women?" But even when stated for generalization, the issues, as organizers for case study, serve to deepen understanding of the specific case.

Starting with a topical concern, researchers may pose "foreshadowed problems,"[10] concentrate on issue-related observations, interpret patterns of data that reform the issues as assertions. The transformation I have experienced in my work in program evaluation is illustrated by the sequence displayed in Table 16.1, issues for a hypothetical case study of a music education program.

In choosing issues to organize their studies, researchers reflect their orientations to intrinsic or instrumental study. To treat the case as an exemplar, they ask, Which issues bring out our initial concerns, the dominant theme? To maximize understanding of the case, they ask, Which issues seek out compelling uniquenesses? For an evaluation study, they ask, Which issues help reveal merit and shortcoming? But in general, they ask, Which issues facilitate the planning and activities of inquiry, including inspiring and rehabilitating the researcher? Issues are chosen partly in terms of what can be learned within the opportunities for study. They will be chosen differently depending on the purpose of the study, and differently by different researchers. One might say a contract is drawn between researcher and phenomenon. For all the devotion to science or to a client, What can be learned *here* that a researcher needs to know?

TABLE 16.1   An Example of Issue Evolution in a Study

---

1. *Topical issue:* The goals of the music education program.

2. *Foreshadowed problem:* The majority of the community supports the present emphasis on band, chorus, and performances, but a few teachers and community leaders want a more intellectual emphasis, including history, literature, and critical review of music.

3. *Issue under development:* What are the pros and cons of having this teaching staff teach music theory and music as a discipline in courses required of everyone?

4. *Assertion:* This community was found (by the researcher) to be not supportive of the extra funding necessary to provide intellectual learning of music for all secondary school students.

The issues used to organize the study may or may not be the ones used to report the case to others. Observing is different work from presenting the case report. At the end, it may be the anticipated issues of readers that will structure the report.

Storytelling

Some call for letting the case "tell its own story" (Carter, 1993; Coles, 1989). We cannot be sure that a case, telling its own story, will tell all or tell well—but the ethos of *interpretive* study, seeking out emic meanings held by the people within the case, is strong. The choices of presentation styles are many. John Van Maanen (1988) identifies these: realistic, impressionistic, confessional, critical, formal, literary, and jointly told. One cannot know at the outset what the issues, the perceptions, the theory will be. Case researchers enter the scene expecting, even knowing, that certain events, problems, and relationships will be important, yet they discover that some of them this time will be of little consequence (Parlett & Hamilton, 1976; Smith, 1994). Case content evolves even in the last phases of writing.

Storytelling as cultural representation and as sociological text emerges from many traditions, but nowhere more strongly than oral history and folklore, and is becoming more disciplined in a line of work called *narrative inquiry* (Clandinin & Connelly, 1999; Ellis & Bochner, 1996; Lockridge, 1988; Richardson, 1997; see also the *Journal of Narrative and Life History*).

Even when empathic and respectful of each person's realities, the researcher decides what the case's *own story* is, or at least what will be included in the report. More will be pursued than was volunteered. Less will be reported than was learned. Even though the competent researcher will be guided by what the case somehow indicates is most important, even though patrons, other researchers, and those researched will advise, what is necessary for an understanding of the case will be decided by the researcher.[11] What results may be the case's own story, but the report will be the researcher's dressing of the case's own story. This is not to dismiss the aim of finding the story that best represents the case but to remind the reader that, usually, the researcher ultimately decides criteria of representation.[12]

Many a researcher would like to tell the whole story but of course cannot; the whole story exceeds anyone's knowing, anyone's telling. Even those inclined to tell all find strong the obligation to winnow and consolidate. A continuum runs from telling lots to telling nothing. The holistic researcher, like the single-issue researcher, must choose. Criteria for selecting content are many (Van Maanen, 1988). Some are set by funding agencies, prospective readers, rhetorical convention, the researcher's career pattern, and the prospect of publication. Some criteria are set by a notion of what represents the case most fully, most appreciably for the hospitality received, most comprehensibly. These are subjective choices not unlike those all researchers make in choosing what to study. Some are made while the case study is being designed, but some continue to be made through the final hours.

◆ Learning From the
   Particular Case

The researcher is a teacher using at least two pedagogical methods (Eisner, 1985). Teaching *didactically*, the researcher teaches what he or she has learned. Arranging for what educationists call *discovery learning*, the researcher provides material for readers to learn, on their own, things the teacher does not know as well as those he or she does know. What can one learn from a single case? Donald Campbell (1975), David Hamilton (1980), Stephen Kemmis (1980), and Robert Yin (1989) are among those who have advanced the epistemology of the particular.[13] How we learn from the singular case is related to how the case is like and unlike other cases (i.e., comparisons). Yet, in the words of Charles Ragin, "variable oriented comparative work (e.g., quantitative cross-national research) as compared with case oriented comparative work disembodies and obscures cases" (Ragin & Becker, 1992, p. 5).

From case reports we increase both propositional and experiential knowledge (Geertz, 1983; Polanyi, 1962; Rumelhart & Ortony, 1977; von Wright, 1971). Readers assimilate certain descriptions and assertions into memory. When the researcher's narrative provides opportunity for vicarious experience, readers extend their memories of happenings. Naturalistic, ethnographic case materials, to some extent, parallel actual experience, feeding into the most fundamental processes of awareness and understanding. Deborah Trumbull and I have called these processes *naturalistic generaliza-*

tion (Stake & Trumbull, 1982). The reader comes to know some things told, as if he or she had experienced it. Enduring meanings come from encounter, and are modified and reinforced by repeated encounter.

In life itself, this occurs seldom to the individual alone but in the presence of others. In a social process, together they bend, spin, consolidate, and enrich their understandings. We come to know what has happened partly in terms of what others reveal as their experience. The case researcher emerges from one social experience, the observation, to choreograph another, the report. Knowledge is socially constructed, so we constructivists believe (see Schwandt, Chapter 7, this volume), and, in their experiential and contextual accounts, case study researchers assist readers in the construction of knowledge.

Knowledge Transfer From Researcher to Reader

Both researcher and reader bring their conceptual structures, for example, advanced organizers (Ausubel & Fitzgerald, 1961), schemata (Anderson, 1977), and an unfolding of realization (Bohm, 1985). Some such frameworks for thought are unconscious. Communication is facilitated by carefully crafted structures. Thought itself, conversation surely, and writing especially draw phrases into paragraphs, append labels onto constructs. Meanings aggregate or attenuate. Associations become relationships; relationships become theory (Robinson, 1951). Generalization can be an unconscious process for both researcher and reader.

In private and personal ways, ideas are structured, highlighted, subordinated, connected, embedded *in* contexts, embedded *with* illustration, laced with favor and doubt. However moved to share ideas, however clever and elaborated their writings, case researchers, like others, pass along to readers some of their personal meanings of events and relationship—and fail to pass along others. They know that the reader, too, will add and subtract, invent and shape—reconstructing the knowledge in ways that leave it differently connected and more likely to be personally useful.

A researcher's knowledge of the case faces hazardous passage from writing to reading. The writer seeks ways of safeguarding the trip. Even as reading begins, often much earlier, the case assumes a place in the company of previously known cases. Conceptually for the reader, the new case cannot be but some combination of cases already known. A new case without commonality cannot be understood. Yet a new case without distinction will not be noticed. Researchers cannot know well the already known cases, the peculiarities of mind, of their readers. They seek ways to protect and substantiate the transfer of knowledge.

The researcher recognizes a need to accommodate the readers' preexisting knowledge. Although everyone deals with this need every day and draws upon a lifetime of experience, we know precious little about how new experience merges with old. According to Spiro, Vispoel, Schmitz, Samarapungavan, and Boerger (1987), most personal experience is *ill-structured,* neither pedagogically nor epistemologically neat. It follows that a well-structured, propositional presentation will often not be the better way to *transfer* experiential knowledge. The reader has a certain *cognitive flexibility,* the readiness to assemble a situation-relative schema from the knowledge fragments of a new encounter. Spiro et al. contend that

> the best way to learn and instruct in order to attain the goal of cognitive flexibility in knowledge representation for future application is by a method of case-based presentations which treats a content domain as a landscape that is explored by "criss-crossing" it in many directions, by reexamining each case "site" in the varying contexts of different neighboring cases, and by using a variety of abstract dimensions for comparing cases. (p. 178)

Transfer remains difficult to understand. And even less understood is how a small aspect of the case may be found by many readers to modify an existing understanding about cases in general, even when the case is not typical.[14]

In a ghetto school, I observed a teacher with one set of rules for classroom decorum—except that for Adam, a nearly expelled, indomitable youngster, a more liberal set had to be continuously invented (Stake, 1995). Reading my account, teachers from very different schools agreed with both. "Yes, you have to be strict with the rules." "Yes, sometimes you have to bend the rules." They recognized in the report an unusual but generalizable circumstance. People find in case reports certain insights into the human condition, even while being well aware of the atypicality of the case. They may be *too* quick to accept the insight. The case researcher needs to provide grounds for validating both the observation and generalization.

Triangulation

With reporting and reading both "ill-structured" (and within an atmosphere of constructivism), it is not surprising to find here a tolerance of ambiguity and the championing of multiple perspectives. Still, I have yet to meet any case researchers who are unconcerned about the clarity and validity of their own communications. Even if meanings do not transfer intact but squeeze into the conceptual space of the reader, there is no less urgency for researchers to assure that their senses of situation, observation, reporting, and reading stay within some limits of correspondence. However accuracy is construed, researchers don't want to be inaccurate, caught without confirmation. Joseph Maxwell (1992) has written of the need for thinking of validity separately for descriptions, interpretations, theories, generalizations, and evaluative judgments.

To reduce the likelihood of misinterpretation, researchers employ various procedures, two of the most common being redundancy of data gathering and procedural challenges to explanations (Denzin, 1989; Goetz & LeCompte, 1984). For qualitative casework, these procedures generally are called *triangulation.* Triangulation has been generally considered a process of using multiple perceptions to clarify meaning, verifying the repeatability of an observation or interpretation.[15] But, acknowledging that no observations or interpretations are perfectly repeatable, triangulation serves also to clarify meaning by identifying different ways the phenomenon is being seen (Flick, 1998; Silverman, 1993; see also Smith, Chapter 34, this volume).

Comparisons

Researchers report their cases as cases, knowing they will be compared to others. They differ as to how much they will take responsibility for making comparisons, setting up comparative cases for the reader or acknowledging reference cases different for each reader. Most naturalistic, ethnographic, phenomenological researchers will concentrate on describing the present case in sufficient detail so that the reader can make good comparisons. Sometimes the researcher will point out comparisons that might be made. Many quantitative and evaluation case researchers will try to provide some comparisons, sometimes by presenting one or more reference cases, sometimes by providing statistical norms for reference groups from which a hypothetical reference case can be imagined. Both the quantitative and qualitative approaches provide narrow grounds for strict comparison of cases, even though a tradition of grand comparison exists within comparative anthropology and related disciplines (Ragin, 1987; Sjoberg, Williams, Vaughan, & Sjoberg, 1991; Tobin, 1989).

I see comparison as actually competing with learning about and from the particular case. Comparison is a grand epistemological strategy, a powerful conceptual mechanism, fixing attention upon one or a few attributes. And it obscures case knowledge that fails to facilitate comparison. Comparative description is the opposite of what Clifford Geertz (1973) calls "thick description." Thick description of a music program, for example, would include conflicting perceptions of the staffing, recent program changes, the charisma of the choral director, the working relationship with a church organist, diverse interest in a critical vote of the school board, and the lack of student interest in

taking up the clarinet. In these particularities lie the vitality, trauma, and uniqueness of the case. Comparison might be made on any of these characteristics, but it tends to be made on more general variables traditionally noted in the organization of music programs, such as staffing, budget, and tour policy. With concentration on the bases for comparison, uniquenesses and complexities will be glossed over. A research design featuring comparison substitutes (a) *the comparison* for (b) *the case* as the focus of the study.

Regardless of the type of case study—intrinsic, instrumental, or collective—readers often learn little from control or reference cases chosen only for comparison. When there are multiple cases of intrinsic interest, then, of course, it can be useful to compare them.[16] But more often than not, there is but one case of intrinsic interest, if any at all. Readers with intrinsic interest in the case learn more of it directly from the description, not ignoring comparisons with other cases but not concentrating on comparisons. Readers examining instrumental case studies are shown how the phenomenon exists within particular cases. As to accuracy, differences are fundamentally more inaccurate than simple measurements. Similarly, conclusions about the differences between any two cases are less to be trusted than conclusions about one. Still, illustration as to how a phenomenon occurs in the circumstances of several exemplars can provide valuable and trustworthy knowledge (Vaughan, in press).

Many are the ways of conceptualizing cases to maximize learning from the case. The case is expected to be something that functions, that operates; the study is the observation of operations. There is something to be described and interpreted. The conceptions of most naturalistic, holistic, ethnographic, phenomenological case studies need accurate description and subjective, yet disciplined, interpretation; a respect and curiosity for culturally different perceptions of phenomena; and empathic representation of local settings—all blending (perhaps clumped) within a constructivist epistemology.

◆ Arrangements for the Study

Perhaps the simplest rule for method in qualitative casework is this: Place your best intellect into the thick of what is going on. The brain work ostensibly is observational, but, more basically, it is *reflective*.[17] In being ever reflective, the researcher is committed to pondering the impressions, deliberating recollections and records—but not necessarily following the conceptualizations of theorists, actors, or audiences (Carr & Kemmis, 1986). Local meanings are important; foreshadowed meanings are important; and readers' consequential meanings are important. The case researcher teases out meanings of these three kinds and, for whatever reason, works on one kind more than the other two. In each case, the work is reflective.[18]

If we typify qualitative casework, we see data sometimes precoded but continuously interpreted, on first sighting and again and again. Records and tabulations are perused not only for classification and pattern recognition but also for "crisscrossed" reflection (Spiro et al., 1987). An observation is interpreted against one issue, perspective, or utility, then interpreted against others. Qualitative case study is characterized by researchers spending extended time, on site, personally in contact with activities and operations of the case, reflecting, revising meanings of what is going on.

Teaming

Naturalistic, ethnographic, phenomenological caseworkers seek to see what is *ordinary* in happenings, in settings, in expressions of value. Blumer (1969, p. 149) calls for us to accept, develop, and use the distinctive expression (of the particular case) in order to detect and study the common. What detail of life the researchers are unable to see for themselves they obtain by interviewing people who did see it or by finding documents recording it. Part IV of this *Handbook* deals extensively with the methods of qualitative research, particularly observation, interview, coding, data management, and interpretation. These pertain, of course, to qualitative case study.

Documenting the ordinary takes a lot of time for data gathering, and more for arrangements, analysis, and write-up. In many studies, there are no clear stages: Issue development continues to the end of the study; write-up begins with preliminary observations. A speculative, page-allocating outline for the report helps anticipate how issues will be handled and how the case will become visible. For most researchers, to set out upon an unstructured, open-ended study is a calamity in the making. Still, the caseworker needs to anticipate the need to recognize and develop late-emerging issues. Many qualitative fieldworkers invest little in instrument construction, partly because even the familiar case is too little known. And the budget is too quickly consumed by devising and field testing instruments to pursue what turn out to be too many foreshadowing questions, with some of them maturing, some dying, some moving to new levels of complexity. The ordinary is too complicated to be mastered in the time available.

When the case is too large for one researcher to know well or for a collective case study, teaming is an important option. The method requires integrated, holistic comprehension of the case, but in the larger studies, no one individual can handle the complexity. Coding can be a great help if the team is experienced in the process and with each other. But learning a detailed analytic coding system within the study period often is too great a burden (Smith & Dwyer, 1979), reducing observations to simple categories, eating up the on-site time. As much as possible, sites, key groups or actors, and issues should be assigned to single team members, including junior members. The case's parts to be studied and the research issues need to be pared down to what can be comprehended by the collection of team members. It is better to negotiate the parts to be studied and the parts not, and then do an in-depth study pursuing a few key issues. Each team member writes up his or her parts; other team members need to read and critique them.

Usually the team leader needs to write the synthesis, getting critiques from the team, data sources, and selected skeptical friends.

Case Selection

Perhaps the most unique aspect of case study in the social sciences and human services is the selection of cases to study. Intrinsic casework regularly begins with cases already identified. The doctor, the social worker, the program evaluator receive their cases; they do not choose them. The cases are of prominent interest before formal study begins. Instrumental and collective casework regularly requires researchers to choose their cases. Understanding the critical phenomena depends on choosing the case well (Patton, 1990; Vaughan, 1992; Yin, 1989). Suppose we are trying to understand the behavior of people who take hostages and decide to probe the phenomenon using a case study. Hostage taking does not happen often—in the whole world there are few cases to choose. Current options, let us imagine, boil down to a bank robber, an airline hijacker, an estranged father who kidnapped his own child, and a Shi'ite Muslim group. We want to generalize about hostage-taking behavior, yet realize that each of these cases, each sample of one, weakly *represents* the larger group of interest.

When one designs a study in the manner advocated by Michael Huberman and Matthew Miles (1994) and by Gery Ryan and Russell Bernard in Chapter 29 of this volume, nothing is more important than making a proper selection of cases. For this design, formal sampling is needed. The cases are expected to represent some population of cases. The phenomenon of interest observable in the case represents the phenomenon writ large. For Huberman and Miles, Yin, and Malinowski, the main work is science, an enterprise to gain the best possible explanations of phenomena (von Wright, 1971). In the beginning, phenomena are given; the cases are opportunities to study the phenomena. But even in the larger collective case studies, the sample sizes are usually much too small to warrant random selection. For qualitative fieldwork, we draw a purposive sample, building in variety and acknowledging opportunities for intensive study.

The phenomenon on the table is hostage taking. We want to improve our understanding of hostage taking, to fit it into what we know about criminology, conflict resolution, human relations—that is, various *abstract dimensions*.[19] We recognize a large population of hypothetical cases, a small subpopulation of accessible cases. We want to generalize about hostage taking without special interest in any of those cases available for study. On representational grounds, the epistemological opportunity seems small, but we are optimistic that we can learn some important things from almost any case. We choose one or a small number of exemplars. Hostages usually are strangers to their captors who happen to be available. We might rule out studying a father who takes his own child as hostage. Such kidnappings may actually be more common, but we rule out the father. We are more interested in hostage taking accompanying a criminal act, hostage taking in order to gain refuge. The researcher examines various interests in the phenomenon, selecting a case of some typicality, but leaning toward those cases that seem to offer *opportunity to learn*. My choice would be to examine that case from which we feel we can learn the most.[20] That may mean taking the one most accessible, the one we can spend the most time with. Potential for learning is a different and sometimes superior criterion to representativeness. Isn't it better to learn a lot from an atypical case than a little from a seemingly typical case?

Another illustration: Suppose we are interested in the attractiveness of interactive displays (which the visitor manipulates and gets feedback from) in children's museums. We have resources to study four museums, to do a collective study of four cases. It is likely that we would set up a typology, perhaps of (a) museum types (namely, art, science, and history), (b) city types (namely, large and very large), and (c) program types (namely, exhibitory and participative), making a 12-cell matrix. Examples probably cannot be found for all 12 cells, but resources do not allow us to study 12 anyway. With four to be studied, we are likely to start out thinking we should have one art, one history, and two science museums (because interactive displays are more common in science museums), two located in large cities and two in very large cities, and two each of the program types. But when we actually look at existing cases, the logistics, the potential reception, the resources, and additional characteristics of relevance, we move toward choosing four museums to study that offer variety (falling short of structured representation) across the attributes, the four that give us the best opportunities to learn about interactive displays.[21] Any best possible selection of four museums from a balanced design would not give us compelling representation of museums as a whole, and certainly not a statistical basis for generalizing about interactions between interactivity and site characteristics. Several desirable types usually have to be omitted. Even for collective case studies, selection by sampling of attributes should not be the highest priority. Balance and variety are important; opportunity to learn is of primary importance.

Cases Within the Case

The same process of selection will occur as part of intrinsic case study. Even though the case is decided in advance (usually), there are subsequent choices to make about persons, places, and events to observe. Here again, training and intuition tell us to seek a good sample. Suppose that we are studying a program for placing computers in the homes of fourth graders for scholastic purposes.[22] The cases—that is, the school sites—have already been selected. Although there is a certain coordination of activity, each participating researcher has one case study to develop. A principal issue has to do with impact on the family, because certain expectations of computer use accompany placement in the home. (The computer should be available for word processing, record keeping, and games by family members, but certain time should be set aside for fourth-grade homework.) At one site, 50 homes now have computers. The researcher can get certain information from every home, but observation in the home can occur only in a

small number. Which homes should be selected? Just as in the collective case study, the researcher notes attributes of interest: gender of the fourth grader, siblings, family structure, home discipline, previous use of computers and other technology in the home, and so on. The researcher discusses these characteristics with informants, gets recommendations, visits several homes, and gets attribute data. The choices are made, assuring variety but not necessarily representativeness, without strong argument for typicality, again weighted by considerations of access and even by hospitality, for the time is short and perhaps too little can be learned from inhospitable parents.[23] Here, too, the primary criterion is opportunity to learn.

Ethics

Ethical considerations for qualitative research are reviewed by Clifford Christians in Chapter 5 of this volume (and elsewhere by such as Coles, 1997; Graue & Walsh, 1998). Case studies often deal with matters of public interest but for which there is neither public nor scholarly "right to know." Funding, scholarly intent, or a passed preliminary oral does not constitute license to invade the privacy of others. The value of the best research is not likely to outweigh injury to a person exposed. Qualitative researchers are guests in the private spaces of the world. Their manners should be good and their code of ethics strict.

Along with much qualitative work, case study research shares an intense interest in personal views and circumstances. Those whose lives and expressions are portrayed risk exposure and embarrassment, as well as loss of standing, employment, and self-esteem. Something of a contract exists between researcher and the researched, a disclosing and protective covenant, usually informal, but best not silent—a moral obligation (Schwandt, 1993).[24] Risks to well-being cannot be inventoried but should be exemplified. Issues of observation and reportage should be discussed in advance. Limits to access should be suggested and agreements heeded. It is important (but never sufficient) for targeted persons to receive drafts revealing how they are presented, quoted, and interpreted and for the researcher to listen well for signs of concern. It is important that researchers exercise great caution to minimize the risks. Even with good information, the researched cannot be expected to protect themselves against the risks inherent in participation. Researchers must follow rules for protection of human subjects (yet should protest those rules when they serve only to protect the institution from litigation). Researchers should go beyond those rules, avoiding low-priority probing of sensitive issues and drawing in advisers and reviewers to help extend the protective system.

Ethical problems arise (inside and outside the research topics) with nondisclosure of malfeasance and immorality. When rules of study are set that prevent the researcher from "whistle-blowing" or that limit the exercise of compassion, a problem exists. Where an expectation has been raised that propriety is being examined and no mention is made of serious impropriety observed, the report is deceptive. Breach of ethics is seldom a simple matter; often it occurs when two contradictory standards apply, such as withholding full disclosure (as per the contract) in order to protect a good but vulnerable agency (Mabry, 1999). Ongoing and summative review procedures are needed, with impetus from conscience, from stakeholders, and from the research community.

◆ Summary

The major conceptual responsibilities of the qualitative case researcher are as follows:

1. Bounding the case, conceptualizing the object of study;
2. Selecting phenomena, themes, or issues— that is, the research questions—to emphasize;
3. Seeking patterns of data to develop the issues;
4. Triangulating key observations and bases for interpretation;
5. Selecting alternative interpretations to pursue;

6. Developing assertions or generalizations about the case.

Except for the first of these, the steps are similar to those taken by other qualitative researchers. The more the researcher has intrinsic interest in the case, the more the focus of study will be on the case's uniqueness, particular context, issues, and story.

Some major stylistic options for case researchers include the following:

1. How much to make the report a story;
2. How much to compare with other cases;
3. How much to formalize generalizations or leave that to readers;
4. How much to include description in the report of the researcher interacting;
5. Whether or not and how much to anonymize.

Case study is a part of scientific methodology, but its purpose is not limited to the advance of science. Single or a few cases are poor representation of a population of cases and questionable grounds for advancing grand generalization. Yet, "because more than one theoretical notion may be guiding an analysis, confirmation, fuller specification, and contradiction all may result from one case study" (Vaughan, 1992, p. 175). For example, we lose confidence in the generalization that a child of separated parents is better off placed with the mother when we find a single instance of resulting injury. Case studies are of value for refining theory and suggesting complexities for further investigation, as well as helping to establish the limits of generalizability.

Case study can also be a disciplined force in public policy setting and reflection on human experience. Vicarious experience is an important basis for refining action options and expectation. Formal epistemology needs further development, but somehow people draw, from the description of an individual case, implications for other cases—not always correctly, but with a confidence shared by people of dissimilar views.

The purpose of a case report is not to represent the world, but to represent the case. Criteria for conducting the kind of research that leads to valid generalization need modification to fit the search for effective particularization. The utility of case research to practitioners and policy makers is in its extension of experience. The methods of qualitative case study are largely the methods of disciplining personal and particularized experience.

■ Notes

1. Many case studies are both qualitative and quantitative. In search of fundamental pursuits common to both qualitative and quantitative research, Robert Yin (1992) analyzed three well-crafted research efforts: (a) a quantitative investigation to resolve disputed authorship of the *Federalist Papers,* (b) a qualitative study of Soviet intent at the time of the Cuban missile crisis, and (c) his own studies of the recognizability of human faces. He found four common commitments: to bring expert knowledge to bear upon the phenomena studied, to round up all the relevant data, to examine rival interpretations, and to ponder and probe the degree to which the findings have implication elsewhere. These commitments are as important in case research as in any other kind of research.

2. Ethnomethodologists study *methods* as topics of inquiry, examining how certain things, such as work or play, get done (Garfinkel, 1967). Coming to understand a case usually requires extensive examination of how things get done, but the prime referent in case study is the case, not the methods by which cases operate.

3. Definition of the case is not independent of interpretive paradigm or methods of inquiry. Seen from different worldviews and in different situations, the "same" case *is* different. And however we originally define the case, the working definition changes as we study. And the definition of the case changes in different ways under different methods of study. The case of Theodore Roosevelt was not just differently portrayed but differently defined as biographer Edmund Morris (1979) presented him as "the Dude from New York," "the Dear Old Beloved Brother," "the Snake in the Grass," "the Rough Rider," and "the Most Famous Man in America."

4. The history of case study, like the history of curiosity and common sense, is found throughout the library. Peeps at that history can be found in the work of Bogdan and Biklen (1982), Delamont (1992), Feagin, Orum, and Sjoberg (1991), Stake (1978), White (1992), and Wieviorka (1992), as well as throughout this volume.

5. Collective case study is essentially what Herriott and Firestone (1983) call "multisite qualitative research." Multisite program evaluation is another common example. A number of German sociologists, such as Martin Kohli and Fritz Schütze, have used collective case studies with Strauss's grounded theory approach.

6. In law, the *case* has a special definition; the practice of law itself could be called case study.

7. In a thoughtful review of a draft of this chapter, Orlando Fals Borda urged me to abandon the effort to promote intrinsic casework and the study of particularity. In persisting here, I think it important to support disciplined and scholarly study that takes up important questions but has no scientific aspiration.

8. In 1922, Bronislaw Malinowski said, "One of the first conditions of acceptable Ethnographic work certainly is that it should deal with the totality of all social, cultural and psychological aspects of the community" (1922/1984, p. xvi). Good spirit there, although totalities defy the acuity of the eye and the longevity of the watch.

9. Generalization from collective case study has been discussed by Herriott and Firestone (1983), Miles and Huberman (1994), and Vaughan (1992).

10. Malinowski (1922/1984) claims that we can distinguish between arriving with closed minds and arriving with an idea of what to look for. He notes: "Good training in theory, and acquaintance with its latest results, is not identical with being burdened with 'preconceived ideas.' If a man sets out on an expedition, determined to prove certain hypotheses, if he is incapable of changing his views constantly and casting them off ungrudgingly under the pressure of evidence, needless to say his work will be worthless. But the more problems he brings with him into the field, the more he is in the habit of moulding his theories according to facts, and of seeing facts in their bearing upon theory, the better he is equipped for the work. Preconceived ideas are pernicious in any scientific work, but *foreshadowed problems* are the main endowment of a scientific thinker, and these problems are first revealed to the observer by his theoretical studies" (p. 9).

11. It appears I claim here there is no such thing as participatory evaluation (Cousins & Earl, 1992; Greene, Chapter 38, this volume) or participatory action research (Fals Borda, 1998; Heron, 1996; Whyte, 1991). There is. Shared responsibility for design, data gathering, and interpretation are to be found, and can be what is needed. Most researchers make some effort to negotiate interpretations, but ultimately decide themselves what array of interpretations to present. However interactive the researcher is, there is an abiding professional responsibility for him or her to decide what will be included under his or her byline. In those situations where the values of the study have been collaboratively set, it is important for the reader to know it.

12. The case report is a representation of the case or, more considerately, a collection of representations. The presumptuousness of representations has been a "hot topic" in postmodern discussions (Clifford, 1983). Researchers need to locate themselves somewhere between extruding description from the template of their personal experience and saying nothing.

13. Among the earlier philosophers of science providing groundwork for qualitative contributions to theory elaboration were Herbert Blumer, Barney Glaser, Bronislaw Malinowski, and Robert Merton.

14. Sociologists have used the term *micro/macro* to refer to the leap from understanding individual cases or parts to understanding the system as a whole. Even without an adequate epistemological map, sociologists do leap, and so do our readers (Collins, 1981).

15. Creative use of "member checking," submitting drafts for review by data sources, is one of the most needed forms of validation of qualitative research (Glesne & Peshkin, 1992; Lincoln & Guba, 1985).

16. Evaluation studies comparing the innovative program to a control case regularly fail to make the comparison credible. No matter how well studied, the control case too weakly represents cases currently known by the reader. By comprehensively describing the program case, the researcher should help the reader draw naturalistic generalizations.

17. I would prefer to call it *interpretive* to emphasize the production of meanings, but ethnographers have used that term to mean "learn the special views of actors, the local meanings" (see Erickson, 1986; Schwandt, Chapter 7, this volume).

18. Ethnographic use of the term *reflective* sometimes limits attention to the need for self-challenging the researcher's etic issues, frame of reference, cultural bias (see Tedlock, Chapter 17, this volume). That challenge is important, but, following Donald Schön (1983), I refer to a general frame of mind when I call qualitative casework *reflective*.

19. As indicated in a previous section, I call them issues or issue areas. Mary Kennedy (1979) calls them "relevant attributes." Spiro et al. (1987) call them "abstract dimensions." Malinowski (1922/1984) calls them "theories." In our research, these will be our "working theories" more than the "grand theories" of the disciplines.

20. My emphasis is on learning the most about both the individual case and the phenomenon, especially the latter if the special circumstances may yield unusual insight into an issue.

21. Firestone (1993) advises maximizing diversity and being "as like the population of interest as possible."

22. This in fact happened with the Buddy Project, a component of the Indiana public school reform effort of 1990-1993 (see Quinn & Quinn, 1992).

23. Patton (1990), Strauss and Corbin (1990), and Firestone (1993) have discussed successive selection of cases over time.

24. A special obligation exists to protect those with limited resources. Those who comply with the researcher's requests, who contribute in some way to the making of the case, should not thus be hurt—usually. When continuing breaches of ethics or morality are discovered, or are the reason for the study, the researcher must take some ameliorative action. Exposé and critique are legitimate within case study, but luring self-indictment out of a respondent is no more legitimate in research than in the law.

■ References

Adams, H. (1918). *The education of Henry Adams: An autobiography*. Boston: Houghton Mifflin.

Anderson, R. C. (1977). The notion of schema and the educational enterprise. In R. C. Anderson, R. J. Spiro, & W. E. Montague (Eds.), *Schooling and the acquisition of knowledge* (pp. 415-431). Hillsdale, NJ: Lawrence Erlbaum.

Asmussen, K. J., & Creswell, J. W. (1997). Campus response to a student gunman. In J. W. Creswell, *Qualitative inquiry and research design: Choosing among five traditions* (pp. 357-373). Thousand Oaks, CA: Sage. (Reprinted from *Journal of Higher Education*, 1995, 66, 575-591)

Ausubel, D. P., & Fitzgerald, D. (1961). Meaningful learning and retention: Interpersonal cognitive variables. *Review of Educational Research, 31*, 500-510.

Becker, H. S. (1992). Cases, causes, conjunctures, stories, and imagery. In C. C. Ragin & H. S. Becker (Eds.), *What is a case? Exploring the foundations of social inquiry* (pp. 205-216). Cambridge: Cambridge University Press.

Becker, H. S., Geer, B., Hughes, E. C., & Strauss, A. L. (1961). *Boys in white: Student culture in medical school*. Chicago: University of Chicago Press.

Blumer, H. (1969). *Symbolic interactionism: Perspective and method*. Englewood Cliffs, NJ: Prentice Hall.

Bogdan, R. C., & Biklen, S. K. (1982). *Qualitative research for education: An introduction to theory and methods*. Boston: Allyn & Bacon.

Bohm, D. (1985). *Unfolding meaning: A weekend of dialogue with David Bohm*. New York: Routledge.

Campbell, D. T. (1975). Degrees of freedom and case study. *Comparative Political Studies, 8*, 178-193.

Carr, W. L., & Kemmis, S. (1986). *Becoming critical: Education, knowledge and action research*. London: Falmer.

Carter, K. (1993). The place of story in the study of teaching and teacher education. *Educational Researcher, 22*(1), 5-12.

Clandinin, D. J., & Connelly, F. M. (1999). *Narrative inquiry: Experience and story in qualitative research*. San Francisco: Jossey-Bass.

Clifford, J. (1983). On anthropological authority. *Representations, 1*, 118-146.

Coles, R. (1989). *The call of stories: Teaching and the moral imagination*. Boston: Houghton Mifflin.

Coles, R. (1997). *Doing documentary work*. Oxford: Oxford University Press.

Collins, R. (1981). On the microfoundations of macrosociology. *American Journal of Sociology, 86*, 984-1014.

Connell, R. W. (1985). *Teachers' work*. Sydney: George Allen & Unwin.

Cousins, J. B., & Earl, L. M. (1992). The case for participatory evaluation. *Educational Evaluation and Policy Analysis, 14*, 397-418.

Crabtree, B. F., & Miller, W. L. (1999). Researching practice settings: A case study approach. In B. F. Crabtree & W. L. Miller (Eds.), *Doing qualitative research* (2nd ed.). Thousand Oaks, CA: Sage.

Delamont, S. (1992). *Fieldwork in educational settings: Methods, pitfalls and perspectives*. London: Falmer.

Denzin, N. K. (1989). *The research act: A theoretical introduction to sociological methods* (3rd ed.). Englewood Cliffs, NJ: Prentice Hall.

Eisner, E. W. (Ed.). (1985). *Learning and teaching the ways of knowing* (84th yearbook of the National Society for the Study of Education). Chicago: University of Chicago Press.

Erickson, F. (1986). Qualitative methods in research on teaching. In M. C. Wittrock (Ed.), *Handbook of research on teaching* (3rd ed., pp. 119-161). New York: Macmillan.

Fals Borda, O. (Ed.). (1998). *People's participation: Challenges ahead*. New York: Apex.

Feagin, J. R., Orum, A. M., & Sjoberg, G. (1991). *A case for the case study*. Chapel Hill: University of North Carolina Press.

Ellis, C., & Bochner, A. P. (Eds.). (1996). *Composing ethnography: Alternative forms of qualitative writing*. Walnut Creek, CA: AltaMira.

Firestone, W. A. (1993). Alternative arguments for generalizing from data as applied to qualitative research. *Educational Researcher, 22*(4), 16-23.

Flick, U. (1998). *An introduction to qualitative research: Theory, method and applications*. London: Sage.

Garfinkel, H. (1967). *Studies in ethnomethodology*. Englewood Cliffs, NJ: Prentice Hall.

Geertz, C. (1973). Thick description: Toward an interpretive theory of culture. In C. Geertz, *The interpretation of cultures: Selected essays* (pp. 3-30). New York: Basic Books.

Geertz, C. (1983). *Local knowledge: Further essays in interpretive anthropology.* New York: Basic Books.

Glaser, B. G., & Strauss, A. L. (1967). *The discovery of grounded theory: Strategies for qualitative research.* Chicago: Aldine.

Glesne, C., & Peshkin, A. (1992). *Becoming qualitative researchers: An introduction.* White Plains, NY: Longman.

Goetz, J. P., & LeCompte, M. D. (1984). *Ethnography and qualitative design in educational research.* New York: Academic Press.

Goode, W. J., & Hatt, P. K. (1952). The case study. In W. J. Goode & P. K. Hatt, *Methods of social research* (pp. 330-340). New York: McGraw-Hill.

Gottwald, N. K. (1979). *The tribes of Jahweh: A sociology of the religion of liberated Israel, 1250-1050 B.C.E.* Maryknoll, NY: Orbis.

Graue, M. E., & Walsh, D. J. (1998). *Studying children in context: Theories, methods, ethics.* Thousand Oaks, CA: Sage.

Hamilton, D. (1980). Some contrasting assumptions about case study research and survey analysis. In H. Simons (Ed.), *Towards a science of the singular* (pp. 76-92). Norwich, England: University of East Anglia, Centre for Applied Research in Education.

Heron, J. (1996). *Co-operative inquiry: Research into the human condition.* London: Sage.

Herriott, R. E., & Firestone, W. A. (1983). Multisite qualitative policy research: Optimizing description and generalizability. *Educational Researcher, 12*(2), 14-19.

Huberman, A. M., & Miles, M. B. (1994). Data management and analysis methods. In N. K. Denzin & Y. S. Lincoln (Eds.), *Handbook of qualitative research* (pp. 428-444). Thousand Oaks, CA: Sage.

Kemmis, S. (1980). The imagination of the case and the invention of the study. In H. Simons (Ed.), *Towards a science of the singular* (pp. 93-142). Norwich, England: University of East Anglia, Centre for Applied Research in Education.

Kennedy, M. M. (1979). Generalizing from single case studies. *Evaluation Quarterly, 3,* 661-678.

Kolker, A. (1996). Thrown overboard: The human costs of health care rationing. In C. Ellis & A. P. Bochner (Eds.), *Composing ethnography: Alternative forms of qualitative writing* (pp. 132-159). Walnut Creek, CA: AltaMira.

Kozol, J. (1991). *Savage inequalities.* New York: Harper.

Lincoln, Y. S., & Guba, E. G. (1985). *Naturalistic inquiry.* Beverly Hills, CA: Sage.

Lockridge, E. (1988). Faithful in her fashion: Catherine Barkley, the invisible Hemingway heroine. *Journal of Narrative Technique, 18,* 170-178.

Mabry, L. (1998). Case study methods. In H. J. Walberg & A. J. Reynolds (Eds.), *Advances in educational productivity: Vol. 7. Evaluation research for educational productivity* (pp. 155-170). Greenwich, CT: JAI.

Mabry, L. (1999). Circumstantial ethics. *American Journal of Evaluation, 20,* 199-212.

MacDonald, B., Adelman, C., Kushner, S., & Walker, R. (1982). *Bread and dreams: A case study in bilingual schooling in the U.S.A.* Norwich, England: University of East Anglia, Centre for Applied Research in Education.

Malinowski, B. (1984). *Argonauts of the western Pacific.* Prospect Heights, IL: Waveland. (Original work published 1922)

Maxwell, J. A. (1992). Understanding and validity in qualitative research. *Harvard Educational Review, 63,* 279-300.

McCormick, S. (1994). A nonreader becomes a reader: A case study of literacy acquisition by a severely disabled reader. *Reading Research Quarterly, 29*(2), 157-176.

Miles, M. B., & Huberman, A. M. (1994). *Qualitative data analysis: An expanded sourcebook* (2nd ed.). Thousand Oaks, CA: Sage.

Morris, E. (1979). *The rise of Theodore Roosevelt.* New York: Coward, McCann & Geognegan.

Parlett, M., & Hamilton, D. (1976). Evaluation as illumination: A new approach to the study of innovative programmes. In G. V Glass (Ed.), *Evaluation studies review annual* (Vol. 1, pp. 141-157). Beverly Hills, CA: Sage.

Patton, M. Q. (1990). *Qualitative evaluation and research methods* (2nd ed.). Newbury Park, CA: Sage.

Peshkin, A. (1986). *God's choice.* Chicago: University of Chicago Press.

Polanyi, M. (1962). *Personal knowledge: Towards a post-critical philosophy.* Chicago: University of Chicago Press.

Pugach, M. C. (1998). *On the border of opportunity: Education, community, and language at the U.S.-Mexico line.* Mahwah, NJ: Lawrence Erlbaum.

Quinn, W., & Quinn, N. (1992). *Buddy evaluation.* Oakbrook, IL: North Central Regional Educational Laboratory.

Ragin, C. C. (1987). *The comparative method.* Berkeley: University of California Press.

Ragin, C. C. (1992). Cases of "What is a case?" In C. C. Ragin & H. S. Becker (Eds.), *What is a case? Exploring the foundations of social inquiry* (pp. 1-18). Cambridge: Cambridge University Press.

Ragin, C. C., & Becker, H. S. (Eds.). (1992). *What is a case? Exploring the foundations of social inquiry.* Cambridge: Cambridge University Press.

Raisin, S., & Britton, E. D. (Eds.). (1997). *Bold ventures: Patterns among U.S. innovations in science and mathematics education.* Dordrecht, Netherlands: Kluwer Academic.

Richardson, L. (1997). *Fields of play: Constructing an academic life.* New Brunswick, NJ: Rutgers University Press.

Robinson, W. S. (1951). The logical structure of analytic induction. *American Sociological Review, 16,* 812-818.

Rumelhart, D. E., & Ortony, A. (1977). The representation of knowledge in memory. In R. C. Anderson, R. J. Spiro, & W. E. Montague (Eds.), *Schooling and the acquisition of knowledge* (pp. 99-135). Hillsdale, NJ: Lawrence Erlbaum.

Schön, D. (1983). *The reflective practitioner: How professionals think in action.* New York: Basic Books.

Schwandt, T. A. (1993). Theory for the moral sciences: Crisis of identity and purpose. In G. Mills & D. J. Flinders (Eds.), *Theory and concepts in qualitative research* (pp. 5-23). New York: Teachers College Press.

Silverman, D. (1993). *Interpreting qualitative data.* London: Sage.

Simons, H. (Ed.), (1980). *Towards a science of the singular.* Norwich, England: University of East Anglia, Centre for Applied Research in Education.

Sjoberg, G., Williams, N., Vaughan, T. R., & Sjoberg, A. (1991). The case approach in social research: Basic methodological issues. In J. R. Feagin, A. M. Orum, & G. Sjoberg, *A case for the case study* (pp. 27-79). Chapel Hill: University of North Carolina Press.

Smith, L. M. (1994). Biographical method. In N. K. Denzin & Y. S. Lincoln (Eds.), *Handbook of qualitative research* (pp. 286-305). Thousand Oaks, CA: Sage.

Smith, L. M., & Dwyer, D. (1979). *Federal policy in action: A case study of an urban education project.* Washington, DC: National Institute of Education.

Smith, R. (1889). *An Aberdeenshire village propaganda: Forty years ago.* Edinburgh: David Douglas.

Spiro, R. J., Vispoel, W. P., Schmitz, J. G., Samarapungavan, A., & Boerger, A. E. (1987). Knowledge acquisition for application: Cognitive flexibility and transfer in complex content domains. In B. C. Britton (Ed.), *Executive control processes* (pp. 177-199). Hillsdale, NJ: Lawrence Erlbaum.

Stake, R. E. (1978). The case study method of social inquiry. *Educational Researcher, 7*(2), 5-8.

Stake, R. E. (1988). Case study methods in educational research: Seeking sweet water. In R. M. Jaeger (Ed.), *Complementary methods for research in education* (pp. 253-278). Washington, DC: American Educational Research Association.

Stake, R. E. (1995). *The art of case study research.* Thousand Oaks, CA: Sage.

Stake, R. E., & Trumbull, D. J. (1982). Naturalistic generalizations. *Review Journal of Philosophy and Social Science, 7,* 1-12.

Stenholm, B. (1984). *The Swedish school system.* Stockholm: Swedish Institute.

Stenhouse, L. (1984). Library access, library use and user education in academic sixth forms: An autobiographical account. In R. G. Burgess (Ed.), *The research process in educational settings: Ten case studies* (pp. 211-234). London: Falmer.

Stouffer, S. A. (1941). Notes on the case-study and the unique case. *Sociometry, 4,* 349-357.

Strauss, A. L., & Corbin, J. (1990). *Basics of qualitative research: Grounded theory procedures and techniques*. Newbury Park, CA: Sage.

Tobin, J. (1989). *Preschool in three cultures*. New Haven, CT: Yale University Press.

Van Maanen, J. (1988). *Tales of the field: On writing ethnography*. Chicago: University of Chicago Press.

Vaughan, D. (1992). Theory elaboration: The heuristics of case analysis. In C. C. Ragin & H. S. Becker (Eds.), *What is a case? Exploring the foundations of social inquiry* (pp. 173-292). Cambridge: Cambridge University Press.

Vaughan, D. (1999). The dark side of organizations: Mistake, misconduct and disaster. *Annual Review of Sociology, 25*, 271-305.

Vaughan, D. (in press). *Theorizing: Analogy, cases, and comparative social organization*. Chicago: University of Chicago Press.

von Wright, G. H. (1971). *Explanation and understanding*. London: Routledge & Kegan Paul.

White, H. C. (1992). Cases are for identity, for explanation, or for control. In C. C. Ragin & H. S. Becker (Eds.), *What is a case? Exploring the foundations of social inquiry* (pp. 83-104). Cambridge: Cambridge University Press.

Whyte, W. F. (Ed.). (1991). *Participatory action research*. London: Sage.

Wieviorka, M. (1988). *Sociétés et terrorisme*. Paris: Fayard.

Wieviorka, M. (1992). Case studies: History or sociology? In C. C. Ragin & H. S. Becker (Eds.), *What is a case? Exploring the foundations of social inquiry* (pp. 159-172). Cambridge: Cambridge University Press.

Yin, R. K. (1989). *Case study research: Design and methods* (2nd ed.). Newbury Park, CA: Sage.

Yin, R. K. (1992, November). *Evaluation: A singular craft*. Paper presented at the annual meeting of the American Evaluation Association, Seattle, WA.

17

ETHNOGRAPHY AND ETHNOGRAPHIC REPRESENTATION

◆ Barbara Tedlock

E thnography involves an ongoing attempt to place specific encounters, events, and understandings into a fuller, more meaningful context. It is not simply the production of new information or research data, but rather the way in which such information or data are transformed into a written or visual form. As a result, it combines research design, fieldwork, and various methods of inquiry to produce historically, politically, and personally situated accounts, descriptions, interpretations, and representations of human lives. As an inscription practice, ethnography is a continuation of fieldwork rather than a transparent record of past experiences in the field. The ongoing nature of fieldwork connects important personal experiences with an area of knowledge; as a result, it is located between the interiority of autobiography and the exteriority of cultural analysis.

Because ethnography is both a process and a product, ethnographers' lives are embedded within their field experiences in such a way that all of their interactions involve moral choices. Experience is meaningful, and human behavior is generated from and informed by this meaningfulness. Because ethnographers traverse both territorial and semantic boundaries, fashioning cultures and cultural understandings through an intertwining of voices, they appear heroic to some and ludicrous to others. They are cross-dressers, outsiders wearing insiders' clothes while gradually acquiring the language and behaviors that go along with them.

Long enshrined as a method, a theoretical orientation, and even a philosophical paradigm within anthropology, ethnography has recently been extended (primarily as a useful methodology) to cultural studies, literary theory, folklore,

◆ 455

women's studies, sociology, cultural geography, and social psychology. It has also proved useful in a number of applied areas, including education, counseling, organization studies, planning, clinical psychology, nursing, psychiatry, law, criminology, management, and industrial engineering. Wherever it has been adopted, a key assumption has been that by entering into close and relatively prolonged interaction with people (one's own or other) in their everyday lives, ethnographers can better understand the beliefs, motivations, and behaviors of their subjects than they can by using any other approach (Hammersley, 1992).

◆ A Brief Historical Sketch of Ethnography

Over the past two centuries, anthropologists have used a number of ethnographic methods to collect, analyze, and represent information. In the late 19th century the British Association for the Advancement of Science published *Notes and Queries on Anthropology* (1874). The purpose of this circular was to help theorists obtain "accurate anthropological observation on the part of travelers, and to enable those who are not anthropologists themselves to supply the information which is wanted for the scientific study of anthropology at home" (p. iv). This document, filled with ethnocentric ideas and leading questions, was distributed widely to travelers, merchants, missionaries, and government officials. Edward Tylor, keeper of the university museum and reader in anthropology at Oxford University, helped to revise the earlier questionnaire, but soon decided that some of the more promising results should be subject to "a personal survey" by a trained scientist (Stocking, 1983, p. 73). To that end, he established a committee "for the purpose of investigating and publishing reports on the physical characters, languages, and industrial and social condition of the North-western Tribes of the Dominion of Canada" (Tylor, 1884). A similar circular was created by James Frazer, *Questions*

on the Manners, Customs, Religion, Superstitions, etc. of Uncivilized or Semi-Civilized Peoples (1887). Because his pamphlet was produced with the express aim of facilitating his own comparative research for *The Golden Bough* (1890/1981), it was designed to gather exactly the sort of information that would fit into his own theories (Richards, 1994, pp. 150-153). This early unsuccessful use of questionnaires as a method of inquiry resulted in a desire on the part of scholars to undertake their own fieldwork in order to gather their own, perhaps more reliable, information.

The new concept of firsthand scholarly "fieldwork" was derived from the discourse of field naturalists by Alfred Cort Haddon. In his 1903 presidential address to the Anthropological Institute in London, he spoke of the pressing need for "fresh investigations in the field." He warned against the "rapid collector" and emphasized the necessity for the researcher not simply "to gather specimens" but to take the time "to coax out of the native by patient sympathy" the deeper connections and meanings of the materials collected (quoted in Stocking, 1983, pp. 80-81). His idea of using a sympathetic method was already standard practice in North America. By the end of the 19th century, thanks to the fieldwork carried out among Native Americans by Matilda Cox Stevenson, Alice Fletcher, Franz Boas, and Frank Hamilton Cushing, the model of experientially gained knowledge of other cultures had displaced armchair methods (Visweswaran, 1998). Cushing, at Zuni Pueblo, New Mexico (1879-1884), wrote to his employer, Spencer Baird of the Smithsonian Institution: "My *method* must succeed. I live among the Indians, I eat their food, and sleep in their houses. . . . On account of this, thank God, my notes will contain much which those of all other explorers have failed to communicate" (Cushing, 1979, pp. 136-137).

Although Cushing was among the earliest ethnographers to realize that his own direct participation in the ongoing lives of his subjects was the basis of his method, it is Bronislaw Malinowski who has been credited with formulating fieldwork as a paradigm or theory (Firth, 1985). The practice of fieldwork, however, was clearly not invented by Malinowski; what he actually accomplished was the enshrinement of fieldwork as a central element of "ethnography" as a new genre (Rabinow, 1985, p. 4). Ever since Malinowski (1922) suggested that an ethnographer's goal should be to grasp the "native's point of view" (p. 25), there has been an expectation that "participant observation" would lead to human understanding through a field-worker's learning to see, think, feel, and sometimes even behave as an insider or "native." Because of the emphasis on an experiential approach, in which the researcher acquires entrance into and at least partial socialization by the society he or she studies, it has become commonplace to suggest that a field-worker adopt the stance of a "marginal native" (Freilich, 1970) or "professional stranger" (Agar, 1980). As "self-denying emissaries" (Boon, 1982), field-workers bring forward an ethnography about the social settings they study. In these roles ethnographers are expected to maintain a polite distance from those studied and to cultivate rapport, not friendship; compassion, not sympathy; respect, not belief; understanding, not identification; admiration, not love. If the researcher were to cultivate friendship, sympathy, belief, identification, and love, then, so we are told, he or she would run the risk of taking up "complete membership" (Adler & Adler, 1987) or "going native."

The negative portrayal of "going native" appeared in late-19th-century colonial fiction, in which the colonizers were created and then embraced within a deeply racialized discourse that also represented the colonial other. Although the colonizers were shown as being at the top of the evolutionary cultural and racial hierarchies, they were also imagined as capable of falling from this pinnacle. Degeneration, "going native," or, in its most excessive form, "going troppo" became a common theme in narratives of white travel and residence in tropical lands (Eves, 1999; Pick, 1989; Young, 1995). Two classic narratives of this sort are Joseph Conrad's *Heart of Darkness* and Jack London's *The Call of the Wild*. In Conrad's depiction of Kurtz's descent into savagery, he produces a narrative of degeneration that re-

veals the vulnerability of colonists in foreign lands. London's characters, like many ethnographers, do not live as the locals do, and they maintain the marks of colonial prestige, power, and authority vested in material objects such as clothing, watches, and radios. Their way of "going native" is through moral degeneration rather than the adoption of the surface trappings and cultural inscriptions of the native other, such as tattoos.

Early ethnographic examples of "gone-native field-workers" include Alexandra David-Neel, Curt Unkel, and Verrier Elwin. These European ethnographers (French, German, and English, respectively) went into the field early in the 20th century in order to study the cultures of indigenous peoples. They stayed for most, or all, of the rest of their lives, fluently speaking the languages of their hosts and becoming deeply identified with their cultures. David-Neel, during her more than 14 years of living in Sri Lanka, India, Nepal, Sikkim, Japan, China, and Tibet, learned to speak a number of non-European languages, including all of the Tibetan dialects. She meditated in lonely caves and on snowy mountaintops with yogi hermits and studied philosophical Buddhism as well as Tibetan Tantra (David-Neel, 1936, 1959). After her initiation, she traveled in disguise to meet the Dalai Lama in Lhasa, which was closed to all foreigners at the time (David-Neel, 1927). Although she became a devout Buddhist, proficient in creating disembodied thought forms, visions, and control of her own body heat, she retained the philosophic skepticism of René Descartes. She wrote that "psychic training, rationally and scientifically conducted, can lead to desirable results. That is why the information gained about such training . . . constitutes useful documentary evidence worthy of our attention" (David-Neel, 1932, p. vi).

Curt Unkel was formally adopted by the Guaraní Indians in Brazil and took the name Nimuendajú, but he maintained a European-style home in the city of Belém, where he wrote detailed ethnographic monographs (Nimuendajú, 1914/1978, 1939, 1942, 1946, 1952). Although he had little formal training prior to his fieldwork, he collaborated with the well-known ethnographer Robert H. Lowie in such a way that his mode of writing might be called "dialogic" (Damatta, 1994, p. 123). Verrier Elwin, an Englishman who went to India during the 1930s, married into a tribe, was naturalized an Indian citizen, and became recognized as an important pioneer Indian anthropologist (Misra, 1973). He published extraordinarily detailed ethnographies and collections of folklore much admired in both India and England (Elwin, 1932, 1942, 1946, 1947, 1954, 1961).

For these pioneer ethnographers, fieldwork was not merely a rite of passage. Rather, the lived reality of their ethnographic experience was the center of their intellectual and emotional lives. As Elwin (1964) expresses it in his autobiography: "For me anthropology did not mean 'field-work': it meant my whole life. My method was to settle down among the people, live with them, share their life as far as an outsider could and generally do several books together. . . . This meant that I did not depend merely on asking questions, but knowledge of the people gradually sank in until it was part of me" (p. 142). These individuals were so fully incorporated into their host communities that they might be described as "complete members" (Lee, 1995, p. 61). This role can be further divided into "converts," who enter the setting as outsiders but become members, and "double agents," who, although they also may be inducted into full group membership, do so with the sole intention of describing the setting and then departing. Cushing was in fact a double agent. During his fieldwork at Zuni he was adopted into a clan and initiated into the war priesthood (Cushing 1882, 1883). Because of these activities, he has been described repeatedly, and erroneously, as having "gone native" (Gronewold, 1972). However, according to his own field notes and letters, his sole purpose in seeking membership within these organizations was to gain entrance into secret meetings in order to observe, write field notes, and make sketches (Brandes, 1965, p. 48; Cushing, 1979, p. 135; Cushing, 1990, pp. 237-246, 353, 401). When he was recalled to Washington, D.C., by the Bureau of American Ethnology, he switched his research interests from ethnography to ar-

chaeological exploration and museum work, never to return to Zuni (Cushing, 1990, p. 26).

Because these early ethnographers retained key European values and philosophies while becoming (to an impressive degree) members of non-Western cultures, it might be better to bracket the question of intentionality and describe them as having become "bicultural" (Tedlock, 1991). Just as one can become "bilingual," given enough time and effort, so one can learn to behave appropriately within a different cultural setting and even acquire a second worldview. The main way this is accomplished is through direct participation in the practices of the new culture. That undertaking this experiential method is not the same thing as simply going native is made clear by the fact that many ethnographers have been able to combine the talents of scholar with those of apprentice.[1] Undergoing an apprenticeship has long been considered a way to equalize power differentials between ethnographers and their consultants. By dismantling and reorganizing the social interaction from that of an inquiring outsider to a relationship between teacher and student, apprenticeship becomes a negotiated ethnographic endeavor. It empowers consultants by allowing them to choose the topics of inquiry, the way of learning, and even the manner of writing essays or a book about the knowledge and experience shared. Apprentices and other participatory ethnographers have given their consultants the power to vet entire manuscripts, or sections of manuscripts, before publication (Simonelli & Winters, 1997). Afterward, they may invite these ethnographic subjects to become coauthors of the ethnography. These sorts of relationships have usually occurred between First World anthropologists and Third or Fourth World consultants (Bahr, Gregorio, Lopez, & Alvarez, 1974; Fischer & Abedi, 1990; Gudeman & Rivera, 1990; Humphrey, 1996; Lambek, 1997; Tehindrazanarivelo, 1997) or between middle-class social scientists and members of a lower class or a criminal subculture (Prus & Irini, 1980; Prus & Sharper, 1977).

When ethnographers began to undertake intensive long-term participant observation fieldwork in European, American, and Middle Eastern urban centers, their work involved "studying up" (concentrating on elite institutions) or "across" (working with people in a similar class or power location) rather than "down" (studying subcultures and marginal peoples).[2] In these new sorts of collaborations, with individuals who participated in highly elaborated and well-established local traditions, texts often became important sources of data and strategic sites of negotiation (Archetti, 1994, pp. 11-13; Rogers, 1997; Shryock, 1996, 1997; Terrio, 1998, pp. 27-28). In working with their cultural contemporaries, the researchers became increasingly aware not only of the dialogical understandings of the emergence of data and knowledge, but also of the political and literary issues involved in the processes of writing, publishing, and reading ethnographies.

◆ Genres of Ethnography

Although there has been some discussion concerning the different styles of ethnography—classical, modernist, postmodernist, poststructuralist—that discussion has, for the most part, been rather general and superficial.[3] What has been ignored in these debates is the fact that thousands of works written in many languages and genres have been encoded as "ethnographic." Researchers can and do inscribe the same material in many different ways, using different formats, styles, and genres. Because audiences have expectations—including overall form and organization, metaphors, and images—regarding texts they may want to read, it is important for ethnographers, like other authors, to know these parameters (Gerhart, 1992; L. Richardson, 1990). Thus, although genre is often thought of in relation to the work of authoring, it also plays an important role in the work of reading. Because the meanings readers derive from a text are shaped by the discourse communities to which they belong, an author needs a clear idea of which readers he or

she wishes to address. Over the course of a career, an ethnographer typically utilizes a number of genres to create and communicate findings to and for different groups of readers.

An ethnographer may begin with an extended monograph based on either a master's thesis or a doctoral dissertation. Each chapter unfolds spatially and logically, treating a standard topic—environment, social relations, identity, or worldview—constructed by means of a repetitive accumulation of equivalent episodes and data. The chapter headings are designed to suggest exhaustive coverage, such as that found in an encyclopedia or a catalog (Thornton, 1988). Later the ethnographer may take up writing more clearly narrative genres that, because they depend on lived experience and have a strongly linear arrangement, are more accessible to the general educated public (MacClancy, 1996). These include personal documents such as biographies and life stories of consultants, memoirs and autobiographies of both consultants and ethnographers, and field diaries and chronicles. Alternative forms of documentation, such as travelogues and autoethnographies, are also popular. More self-consciously literary genres, such as novels, novellas, short stories, poems, and plays, have also been used as vehicles of ethnographic documentation and representation.

One of the earliest and most popular narrative genres to be developed by ethnographers is the biography, or "life history." Although biographies can be produced on the basis of interview materials alone, the most frequent way they emerge is from the fieldwork context itself. The use of life histories as an alternative form of ethnographic documentation goes back at least as far as Thomas and Znaniecki's publication of *The Polish Peasant in Europe and America* (1918-1920) and Paul Radin's *Crashing Thunder* (1920). At that time, ethnographers' aim in collecting life histories was to illuminate cultural, historical, and social facts rather than individual lives or aspects of personality (Shaw, 1930; Underhill, 1936). Life histories depend upon the use of the rhetorical figure of synecdoche, in which a "representative" individual is selected and made to stand for an entire culture. Thus, according to Ricardo Pozas, his biography *Juan the Chamula* (1962) "should be considered a small monograph on the culture of the Chamulas" (p. 1). It was only later that an interest in personality was added to the life history (Langness & Frank, 1981, pp. 21-23). Oscar Lewis energetically promoted the life history as primarily a cultural document. He began his family biography approach to ethnography and developed his idea of a "culture of poverty" with his now-classic book, *Five Families* (1959). In the introduction, he describes the family portraits he constructs as neither "fiction nor conventional ethnography. For want of a better term I would call them ethnographic realism, in contrast to literary realism" (p. 5). His writing technique depends upon the layering of synecdoches in which a single family stands for a common type of family and a single day stands for any day, or every day. He sets before his readers five perfectly ordinary days—days not marked by any unusual events, such as births, baptisms, or funerals—in the lives of five ordinary, representative Mexican families. This book was soon followed by more truly biographical and emotionally moving accounts: *The Children of Sánchez* (1961), *Pedro Martínez* (1964), and *La Vida* (1965).

The second type of personal document is the "memoir," in which an author takes the reader back to a corner of the author's own life in the field that was unusually vivid, full of affect, or framed by unique events. By narrowing the lens, the author provides a window into a segment of his or her life in the field. Although most ethnographers who have published memoirs have done so under their own names, some have used pseudonyms. Margaret Field published her memoir of doing ethnography among the Gâ of West Africa, *Stormy Dawn* (1947), under the name Mark Freshfield. Laura Bohannan novelized her experiences as a neophyte ethnographer in West Africa, *Return to Laughter* (1954), under the name Elenore Smith Bowen. Philip Drucker published his Mexican ethnographic memoir, *Tropical Frontier* (1969), under the name Paul Record. Karla Poewe published her memoir of African fieldwork, *Reflections of a Woman Anthropologist* (1982), under the name

Manda Cesara. One reason some authors might distance themselves from their memoirs by using pseudonyms is that this enables them to publish their fieldwork experiences for a general readership and keep this activity totally separate, even secret, from their professional peers. This distancing move may indicate that these authors feel that publishing personal materials could damage their credibility as scientists. Later in life, however, as in the cases of Laura Bohannan and Karla Poewe, they might choose to reveal their pseudonyms to their profession and take credit for their books.

A third ethnographic genre, the "narrative ethnography," evolved from the overlapping of the first two genres, life history and memoir. This hybrid form was created when individuals attempted to portray accurately the subjects of biographies but also to include their own experiences in their texts. For example, Vincent Crapanzano in *Tuhami* (1980) documents the life of his Moroccan subject and his own emotional and intellectual responses in working with him. He dwells at length on the psychological and cultural tensions and yearnings present in his extended face-to-face interactions with Tuhami, showing how each of them became engrossed in the encounter as a consequence of becoming the "object of transference" to the other. Thus, although Tuhami was initially the primary focus of the biography, Crapanzano became a secondary focus, produced during the writing process. The result is a psychodynamically rich double portrait in the form of a narrative ethnography. A similar intertwining of a biography with the story of the ethnographic encounter, both in the field and in retrospect, structures Laurel Kendall's book *The Life and Hard Times of a Korean Shaman* (1988). Here, in a series of shamanic autobiographical exchanges, reproduced from memory and captured on tape, Kendall represents herself and her field assistant as sympathetic students of a woman shaman. With the addition of Kendall's personal and theoretical interludes, which occur in typographically marked sections throughout the book, we witness the multiple narrative event of a female shaman actively engaging with a female ethnographer, her female field assistant, and her readers.

An overlap between biography and personal memoir also structures Ruth Behar's *Translated Woman* (1993). Here Behar confesses how worried, yet relieved, she was when she realized that after nearly 3 years of studying what colonial women had said to their inquisitors and developing relationships with a number of townswomen, she had let one of her subjects take over her research. Throughout the text, she portrays her inner feelings by using an italic font: "*I am remembering the hurt I had felt several days before. While I was sitting in the half-open doorway reading, a boy had run past, gotten a peek at me, and yelled out with what to me sounded like venom in his voice, 'Gringa!'*" (p. 250). Because Behar is a Cuban American, she found this verbal insult from another Hispanic quite unexpected and painful.

What these psychologically rich documents contributed was an unsettling of the boundaries that had been central to the notion of a self studying an other. This form of border-zone cultural production became the new direction of ethnographic interchange and cultural inscription. At its inception, this sea change in ethnographic representation of both the self and other within a single text was lumped together with other writing strategies and labeled as part of a mythic "experimental moment in the human sciences" (Marcus & Fischer, 1986, p. 165). However, as Renato Rosaldo (1989, p. 231) indicates, this analysis embodied a facile application of Thomas Kuhn's notion of experimentalism as occurring only during scientific paradigm shifts. The ongoing historical refiguration of social thought and practice should not be described as part of a unique and radically ahistorical "experimental moment," but should be recognized for what it was: a major change in ethnographic epistemology and methodology embodying key historical, political, ethical, analytic, and authorial issues.

Just as in feminist critical theory, which denies the split between epistemology and politics, ethnographic critical theory became simultaneously reflexive and political.[4] There

emerged a passionate interest in coproducing ethnographic knowledge, creating and representing it in the only way it could be, within a critical interactive self-other conversation or dialogue.[5] An extreme yearning for such a dialogic embrace is poignantly portrayed by the French ethnographer Pierre Clastres in his chronicle of fieldwork. In South America during the mid-1960s, he encountered the Atchei people in Paraguay, who had only recently been contacted by outsiders. When he met them they refused to accept his gifts or to speak with him, even though he spoke a neighboring dialect of their language. As he describes the scene, "they were still green," "hardly touched, hardly contaminated by the breezes of our civilization," a society "so healthy that it could not enter into a dialogue with me, with another world" (Clastres, 1998, p. 97). Clastres's translator, the novelist Paul Auster (1998), notes that the chronicle is "the true story of a man's experiences," that "the result is not just a portrait of the people he is studying, but a portrait of himself," and that "he writes with the cunning of a good novelist" (p. 8). In other words, his chronicle takes the form of a narrative ethnography.

That a fiction writer might recognize Clastres's novelistic cunning should not be surprising given that the most popular literary genre read or written by social scientists is the novel—especially the kind that is based on a combination of the author's personal history and background, scholarly training, and field experiences.[6] Although some of these fictive works can be categorized as science fiction, mysteries, or historical novels, most are also what have come to be called "ethnographic novels" (Buelow, 1973; Langness & Frank, 1978; Schmidt, 1981, 1984). This genre is different from other novelistic categories in that it conforms not only to the principles set up within the text itself, but also to those within the external culture the novel describes. Thus ethnographic novels combine internal textual accuracy with external cultural accuracy. For this type of novel to be considered ethnographically complete, it must contain accurate information on how the ethnic group portrayed is organized and how it relates, or refuses to relate, to the wider world.

The Swiss archaeologist Adolf F. Bandelier was the originator of this genre. His novel *The Delight Makers* (1890/1971) is set in the American Southwest among the Pueblo Indians. Bandelier noted that although the plot was his own, he was true to the geographic nature of the country as well as the indigenous architecture, traditions, manners, and customs that he and other ethnologists had observed. He actually witnessed the scenes the novel describes, and the people portrayed are complicated human beings living in a structured and regulated society. Although the novel was immediately recognized by both archaeologists and anthropologists as a classic, it failed to attract the general public for whom it was written. As Stefan Jovanovich (1971) points out, this was due to the fact that Bandelier "had taken the adventure out of the Old West; he had written about the enemy, the Indians, as if they were real (that is, white) people struggling in a muddled social world rather than mythical creatures grazing in a long-extinct forest" (p. xvii). Indeed, it would be nearly 40 years before the general public was ready to appreciate ethnographic fiction about Indians as real people. In 1929, Oliver La Farge won the Pulitzer Prize in Literature for his ethnographic novel *Laughing Boy* (1929). The main characters in the novel are Laughing Boy, a model of everything good in traditional Navajo culture, and Slim Girl, an acculturated Navajo raised in a mission school. They fall in love, and through the various social interactions that arise from their marriage we learn that the Navajo are matrilineal, matrilocal, semisedentary, horticulturists, and herders and that they consider reconciliation to be the most important positive result of legal proceedings. Inherent in Laughing Boy's actions is the importance placed by Navajo culture upon a unity of mind, body, and spirit. Because his wife lacks this integrative faculty, Laughing Boy is threatened and almost destroyed.[7]

In Latin America, at about the same time, the Peruvian ethnologist José María Arguedas became the major Indianist novelist of his time. He invented a language for his ethnographic novels using native Quechua syntax with Spanish vocabulary. In what is widely considered his best novel, *Yawar Fiesta* (1941/1985), he dramatically portrays the clash between Indian and Hispanic cultures in Puquio, the highland village where he lived during his early childhood and adolescence. A more recent literary ethnographer is John Stewart, who has taught English literature as well as anthropology. The Royal Society of Literature awarded him its Winifred Holthy Memorial Prize for his novel *Last Cool Days* (1971). Because this novel, as well as his other ethnographic fiction, is based on a combination of his West Indian birth and upbringing together with his more recent black American experience, it is as much an exercise in self-exploration as it is cultural portraiture. He shares this dual identity, resulting from a field situation in which the ethnographer is among his or her own chief informants, with Arguedas. This work is also closely associated with W. E. B. Du Bois's (1903/1969, p. 45) notion of a "double consciousness" within African American life.

Chad Oliver was 22 years old when he sold his first short story, "The Boy Next Door" (1951), to Anthony Boucher, the editor of the magazine *Fantasy and Science Fiction*. Martha Foley listed it that season on her prestigious register of "Distinctive Short Stories in American Magazines" (Nolan, 1968, p. 110). A year later, Oliver finished his master's thesis in anthropology at the University of Texas, titled *They Built a Tower: The Story of Science Fiction* (1952), and began teaching there. He soon became a prime contender for the Heinlein-Clarke front rank of what Boucher called "genuine science fiction, in which the science is as accurately absorbing as the fiction is richly human" (Oliver, 1957, cover blurb). Oliver's science fiction novel *Shadows in the Sun* (1954), which explores the theme of humanlike aliens on earth, was cited by the *New York Times* as "tops in its field" for that year. Throughout his academic career, Oliver (1962, 1981) published ethnography and introduced anthropological themes into science fiction. His novella *Guardian Spirit,* first published in 1958, examines the ultimate definition of civilization by exploring the relation between technological man and primitive man. A later novel, *The Shores of Another Sea* (1971), is set in Kenya, where Oliver undertook his doctoral fieldwork. In this story, a scientist who runs a baboonery suddenly finds that his animals have changed. The detached look in their eyes reveals to him that they have been taken over by an alien intelligence. They are now studying him. He realizes that he is no longer the hunter, but the hunted. Oliver's combination of traditional science fiction themes—early man, lost races, and future wars—and ethnographic reflexivity resulted in classic works of ethnographic fiction.[8]

A number of social scientists have chosen other fictive genres—such as the short story, novella, and play—for representing ethnographic materials.[9] Hilda Kuper (1947, 1960), a well-known South African ethnographer, published several literary works based on her ethnographic fieldwork, including a novel, a play, and short stories (1965, 1970, 1943/ 1984). In a panel at the Africanists' meetings in 1981, she declared that her best ethnographic writing was her play, *A Witch in My Heart*. Several other plays centering on ethnographers and ethnographic field experiences have been performed and published.[10] Dennis Tedlock (1986, 1998) and Dorinne Kondo (1995, 1997, p. 22) have written ethnographic plays and worked with professional theater groups as producers and dramaturges. The ethnographer Catherine Allen and the playwright Nathan Garner collaborated in teaching a course, then wrote and co-produced an ethnographic play, *Condor Qatay* (1993). They later wrote both an essay and a book about the process, suggesting that playwriting provides an appropriate vehicle not only for ethnographic description but also for interpretation and analysis (Allen & Garner, 1995, p. 69; 1997). Robert Laughlin served as an ethnographic consultant, dramaturge, and impresario for a play written and performed by Mayans about the sociopoli-

tical conditions behind the Zapatista uprising in Chiapas, Mexico (Laughlin, 1994; Skomal, 1995).

Another way of communicating ethnographic experiences intertwined with emotional response has been to weave them together; these works may take the form of travelogues, chronicles, or diaries.[11] Ethnographic travelogues often take on the easygoing, chatty tone of travel brochures, whereas chronicles and diaries tend to reveal the inner thoughts, bittersweet emotions, and prejudices of their authors. In *Tristes Tropiques*, Claude Lévi-Strauss (1973) writes lyrically, "The bay at Rio eats right into the heart of the city: you land in the centre, as if the other half, like the fabled town of Ys, had already been engulfed by waves" (p. 76). Zora Neale Hurston, in *Tell My Horse* (1938), uses a chatty tone: "If you go to Jamaica you are going to want to visit the Maroons of Accompong. They are under the present rule of Colonel Rowe, who is an intelligent, cheerful man. But I warn you in advance not to ride his wall-eyed, pot-bellied mule" (p. 21). Brian Moeran's *Okubo Diary: Portrait of a Japanese Valley* (1985) is a refashioning of the contents of three journals Moeran kept during his 4 years of fieldwork in rural Japan. In part because his son was seriously injured while in primary school and Moeran ended up having to sue the local school board, the diary is filled with estrangement and melancholy self-reflection: "These mountain silhouettes that I know so well, these sounds of birds calling, of the wind in the pear trees, of the bamboo swaying. They will never be mine. Perhaps they never, after all, were mine. I who am caught in this bridge of dreams" (p. 204).

There have also been tell-all ethnographic diaries. The French poet and ethnographer Michel Leiris published his rather shocking field diary *L'Afrique fantôme* (*Phantom Africa*, 1934), documenting the activities of the Dakar-Djibouti expedition to the Dogon of Sanga and the Ethiopians of Gondar, together with the activities of various African subjects (Beaujour, 1987). He revealed the strained relationships between the European members of the research team and the unethical museum collecting procedures of the expedition. These revelations were to be the cause of Leiris's permanent break with his friend and colleague Marcel Griaule. In a later work, *L'Age d'homme* (1939), translated as *Manhood* (1983), which combines novelistic fiction with an intimate journal, Leiris goes beyond the merely chronological collection of anecdotes and snapshots to construct a story on the model of photomontage. This anthology of the self cultivates a photographic viewpoint with no attempt to speak from the heart. It is a fable of disenchantment, combining an acute sense of the futility of existence with a strong desire to salvage its meaningful details in the form of perception, quotation, and memory. By interrupting the smooth ethnographic story of an access to Africa, Leiris undermines the assumption that self and other can ever be gathered in a stable narrative coherence. He ends abruptly with words quoted from a dream: "I explain to my mistress how necessary it is to construct a wall around oneself by means of clothing" (1983, p. 146).

Perhaps the most scandalous ethnographic field diary of all time is Bronislaw Malinowski's posthumously published *A Diary in the Strict Sense of the Term* (1967). It reveals the self-proclaimed inventor of participant observation and the hidden authorial voice of *Argonauts of the Western Pacific* (1922) as a person who not only participated very little in Kiriwinian culture, but was racially prejudiced (Willis, 1969, p. 140). As a response to the controversy caused by the revelation of this secret diary, ethnographers became self-conscious about their own political, ethnic, and racial backgrounds and prejudices, as well as about the nature of their participation, or lack of participation, in the cultures they lived in and wrote about (Caulfield, 1979; Nash & Wintrob, 1972). They were shaken also by Malinowski's imperialist ideas and embarrassed by the colonialist practices within social science (Asad, 1973; Banaji, 1970; Gough, 1968; Lewis, 1973; Stavenhagen, 1971). A small group of anthropologists dared publicly to ask themselves the painful question, "If the discipline did not exist, would it have to be invented?" To which Dell Hymes and the other contributors to his

edited volume *Reinventing Anthropology* (1969) answered no. To a second question, "If anthropology were reinvented, would it be the anthropology we have now?" the answer was also no. Instead, as Bob Scholte (1969) suggested, a reinvented anthropology ought to become "a critical and emancipatory discipline."

This new critical self-awareness was further enhanced by a second major controversy within social science. This time, debate surrounded the publication, in the journal *Science,* of an essay titled "On Being Sane in Insane Places" (Rosenhan, 1973). The essay describes a novel research design in which eight social scientists invented symptoms and then presented themselves to psychiatric outpatient clinics with the aim of being admitted to inpatient psychiatric wards. Upon admission to the wards, they never again referred to their symptoms and were never spotted as researchers. When the research was published, the clinicians were outraged and accused the social scientists of manufacturing the data, which they had not. Although some undercover ethnographic work continued (Rose, 1987), covert observation was deemed unethical and became unfashionable (Brink, 1993).

These controversies contributed to an exploration of both ethical and authorial issues involved in the process of generating ethnographic information and in the writing and publishing of ethnographic accounts. Some researchers began to advocate a more humanly involved and politically savvy role for ethnographers, together with the blending in single texts of epistemological and personal understandings (Dwyer, 1979, 1982; Scholte, 1969; Thomas, 1983). And it was just this combination of a new vantage point and critical practice that resulted in the shift from participant observation to "the observation of participation" (Tedlock, 1991), in which ethnographers both experience and observe their own and others' coparticipation within the ethnographic scene of encounter. The shift entailed a major representational transformation in which, instead of having to choose between writing a memoir or autobiography centering on the self or a life history or standard monograph centering on the other, the ethnographer can present both self and other together within a single narrative frame that focuses on the process and character of the ethnographic dialogue.

◆ From Participant Observation to the Observation of Participation

Participant observation was originally forged as a method in the study of small, relatively homogeneous societies. An ethnographer lived in a society for an extended period of time, learned the local language, participated in daily life, and steadily observed. The oxymoron *participant observation* implies simultaneous emotional involvement and objective detachment. Ethnographers attempted to be both engaged participants and coolly dispassionate observers of the lives of others. This strangely empathic yet impassive methodology was widely believed to produce documentary data that somehow reflected the natives' own points of view. It has even been argued that because we cannot study the social world without being a part of it, all social research is a form of participant observation (Hammersley & Atkinson, 1983).

The privileging of the trope of participant observation as a scientific method encouraged ethnographers to demonstrate both their observational skills and their social participation by producing radically different forms of writing: scholarly monographs and personal documents, such as life histories and memoirs. This dualistic approach split public from private and objective from subjective realms of experience. John Beattie (1960), for example, first published a scholarly monograph based on his doctoral thesis, which he felt was an "objective" ethnographic account. Five years later, at the suggestion of his publisher, he wrote a second version of his field research, which he described as a "subjective" first-person account (Beattie, 1965). Even though this second book emphasizes overt methodologies—the use of assistants, informants, questionnaires, house-

to-house surveys, note taking, photography, keeping a diary, and writing up the research— he is nonetheless apologetic about being "autobiographical" or subjective, remarking in his preface on his "somewhat immodest undertaking."[12]

Discomfort with the act of revealing the self within a serious ethnography can also be detected in Paul Rabinow's (1977) memoir, in which he refers to his 1975 monograph as a "more traditionally anthropological treatment of the same data" (p. 7). Jean-Paul Dumont, like Rabinow, published his standard ethnographic monograph (1976) before his first-person fieldwork account (1978). However, he revealed a different attitude toward including himself in his ethnography. For him the work of self-representation was no less "traditional" than the standard representation of the ethnographic other. In fact, as Peter Rivière (1980) has pointed out, we learn rather more about the Panaré in Dumont's first-person account than we do in Dumont's monograph. Part of the reason for this is that Dumont self-consciously centered his field account around the question of who he was for the Panaré rather than who the Panaré were for him, this latter being the implicit question most ethnographies explore.

Unlike these authors, Nigel Barley released his ethnographic monograph and fieldwork account simultaneously. The monograph, *Symbolic Structures: An Exploration of the Culture of the Dowayos* (1983b), is a Lévi-Straussian structuralist study. The first-person ethnographic field account, *Adventures in a Mud Hut* (1983a), is a funny, warts-and-all, first-person narrative of Barley's West African fieldwork. The remarkable difference in tone, tenor, and material presented in these two books reveals Barley's extreme discomfort with representing himself in an ethnographic account. In his experiential ethnography he comes off as a silly, sad, incompetent slapstick character who marched, limped, and finally was carried through his initiatory field research. The natives also come off as clowns; foolish old men stare at photographs of lions and leopards, turning them in all directions and saying things like, "I do not know this man" (Barley, 1983a, p. 96). Here, what purports to be a personal document ends up as a lampoon of the entire ethnographic enterprise.

Instead of focusing on the embarrassing or funny edges of the ethnographic encounter (De Vita, 1990), some ethnographers have chosen to explore the complex personal and political dimensions involved in crossing cultural boundaries. Kurt Wolff (1964) describes how, during his field research in a northern New Mexico village, he opened himself to the risk of being hurt by becoming so totally involved and identified with the community that everything he saw or experienced became relevant to him: "It was years before I understood what had happened to me: I had fallen through the web of culture patterns and assorted conceptual meshes into the chaos of love; I was looking everywhere, famished, with a ruthless glance" (p. 235). It is precisely these risks that Ruth Behar, in *The Vulnerable Observer* (1996), portrays as the central ethnographic project. No matter how much care the ethnographer devotes to the project, its success depends upon more than individual effort. It is tied to outside social forces, including local, national, and sometimes even international relationships that make the research possible as well as to a readership that accepts the endeavor as meaningful. The issues are not so much objectivity, neutrality, and distance as they are risk, the possibility of failure, and the hope of success. More recently, such intimate topics as fear of physical violence, rape, friendship, love, sexuality, and erotic fieldwork encounters—both homosexual and heterosexual—have begun to be inscribed as social science.[13]

◆ Autoethnography and Feminist Ethnography

Another key factor in ethnographers' changing choices and development of alternative topics and styles of research and representation is found in the changes in the population of individuals electing to become ethnographers. In terms of class, more ethnographers are now from middle- and lower-class backgrounds. Concerning gender and sexuality, more are now women as well as open gays and lesbians. In terms of ethnicity, more are minority, hybrid (Eurasians, *mestizos,* and so on), as well as Third and Fourth World scholars. Such transformations have spurred not only a democratization of knowledge but a new critical awareness, resulting in the suggestion that the class, race, culture, and gender beliefs and behaviors of the inquirer be placed within the same historical moment, or critical plane, as those of the subjects of inquiry.[14]

These changes have been stimulated by the emergence of an articulate population of "native" and "feminist" ethnographers, including various bicultural inside/outsiders. Although it is undoubtedly true that insiders may have easier access to certain types of information, especially in the area of daily routines (Jones, 1970; Ohnuki-Tierney, 1984), native ethnography can be distinguished from indigenous ethnography in that native ethnographers are those who have their origins in non-European or non-Western cultures and who share a history of colonialism, or an economic relationship based upon subordination. Just as being born female does not automatically result in "feminist" consciousness, being born an ethnic minority does not automatically result in "native" consciousness. Nonetheless, it has been suggested that women's binary view or "dual consciousness"— similar to the double consciousness attributed to blacks and other racial minorities—gives women a certain advantage in understanding oppressed peoples worldwide.[15]

Native ethnographers have critiqued Western ethnocentric practices in social science (Harrison, 1991; Hsu & Textor, 1978). They have pointed out the strange preoccupation with issues such as caste in South Asia (Appadurai, 1986; Daniel, 1984) and the lack of systematic portrayal of sentiments in studies of kinship, exchange, and reciprocity. Tongan anthropologist Epeli Hau'ofa (1982) notes that the scarcity of attention to emotions within these highly charged areas of human relations "has rendered most such studies in Oceania (and probably elsewhere) incomplete and therefore half-meaningful" (p. 222). He illustrates the serious moral consequences of this form of misrepresentation, noting that when Melanesian leaders were reduced to a "caricature of the quintessential Western capitalist" (Hau'ofa, 1975, p. 285), this resulted in Polynesian racist feelings against Melanesians. Native ethnographers have also objected to the application of the term *matriarchal* only to a hypothetical society completely ruled by women. The Igbo anthropologist Ifi Amadiume (1987, p. 189) has called for the recognition of such factors as matrifocality, matricentrism, and female orientation in West Africa as aspects of matriarchal cultures.

These scholars have worked to bridge the gulf between self and other by revealing both parties as vulnerable experiencing subjects working to coproduce knowledge (Abu-Lughod, 1993). The observer and the observed are not entirely separate categories, they argue. For them, theory is not a transparent, culture-free zone, not a duty-free intellectual marketplace hovering between cultures, lacking all connection to embodied, lived experience. Knowledge and experience from outside fieldwork should be brought into ethnographic narratives; ethnographers should demonstrate how ideas matter to them, bridging the gap between their narrow academic world and wide cultural experiences. As Vietnamese ethnographer and cinematographer Trinh T. Minh-ha (1989) states, "In writing close to the other of the other, I can only choose to maintain a self-reflexively critical relationship toward the material, a relationship that defines both the subject written and the writing subject, undoing the I while asking 'what do I want wanting to know you or me?' " (p. 76). Or, as Jean-Paul Dumont (1978) says at the close of his narrative ethnography, "Who was I for them?" (p. 200).

Writing for and about the community in which one has grown up and lived, or at least achieved some degree of insider status, should produce engaged writing centering on the ongoing dialectical political-personal relationship between self and other. This is not a new idea. In 1972, Martin Yang published an important essay discussing the role of both his gradu-

ate education and what he called his "firsthand fieldwork" in the production of his highly acclaimed ethnography *A Chinese Village* (1945). His field research was conducted in the village in which he lived until he went away to college. As Yang (1972) notes, "My fieldwork was my own life and the lives of others in which I had an active part" (p. 63). This type of ethnographic experience has been called variously *ethnosociology, ethnoethnography, autoanthropology,* and *autoethnography* (Deck, 1990; Fogelson, 1984; Hayano, 1979; Reed-Danahay, 1997; Strathern, 1987a). Yang was by no means the first indigenous anthropologist to publish an ethnography about his own group. Jomo Kenyatta (1938), Fei Hsiao Tung (1939), and Chie Nakane (1970), among others, had already done so. But Yang, unlike the others, wrote a self-reflexive essay about the experience of doing an auto-ethnography.

What has received far too little attention to date are the political exchanges and verbal encounters between ethnographers and natives who have different interests and goals (Chilungu, 1976). Roger Keesing (1985) has provided an important example of the cross-gender micropolitics of talk. In his fieldwork among the Kwaio, a traditional group living in the Solomon Islands of the South Pacific, he found that men told their life stories eagerly and artfully, even though Kwaio lack the genre we call autobiography. At the same time, he found that he was not able to elicit autobiographical narratives from women. They spoke to him in a fragmented, inarticulate, and joking way, this in front of the elder men who had urged them to cooperate. Eight years later, during a subsequent joint field trip with a woman ethnographer, he found that in sessions in which they were both present Kwaio women took control of the encounters and even brought female friends along as audience members for their recording sessions. Unlike the men, who provided personal life stories and societal rules, the women created moral texts about the virtues of womanhood, inserting only enough personal experience to illustrate a woman's possible path through life. Clearly, the women's initial inarticulateness and subsequent "voice," as much as the men's systematization of their culture, were responses to wider fields of force that assure that some genres are more powerful than others.

Feminist scholars might have predicted the changes produced by the presence of women anthropologists. They would have understood that the genre of autobiography is problematic, not only because it is culturally specific to the West, but because it has been shaped by a gender ideology that assumes a male subject. Kwaio women's refusal to recite the personal narratives and societal rules characteristic of men's responses and their insistence on moral justifications of womanhood evoke a parallel strategy in other women's autobiographies. In these, a recurring figure of "divided consciousness" can be detected, revealing the authors' awareness that they are being read as women and thus judged differently from men in their self-constructions (Gal, 1991; Tedlock, 1995).

Women's ethnographic and autobiographical intentions are often powered by the motive to convince readers of the authors' self-worth, to clarify and authenticate their self-images. Many of these self-images are projected by understatement, the very means individuals use to distance or detach themselves from intimacy. Women ethnographers often either tend toward straightforward and objective representation of their experiences or write obliquely and elliptically, using a free-indirect or stream-of-consciousness style (DeVault, 1990; Stanley & Wise, 1983). Sometimes they poke fun at themselves as field-workers in order to camouflage their professional desires and will to power. Over and over again, women ethnographers, be they novices or experienced researchers, reveal their uncertainty about fieldwork and about ethnographic writing. Kirin Narayan, in *Storytellers, Saints and Scoundrels* (1989), undermines her own ethnographic authority by not offering a romantic insider's view of an alien culture. Instead, she subtly portrays the irony of an inside/outside woman who, while sitting among the South Asian people with whom she grew up and with whom she felt a comfortable sense of solidarity, was partly rejected as an academic outsider listening to religious teachings for material, rather than spiritual, reasons. She

reports that her guru said to her: "You're taking this on tape. You'll take this and do a business. . . . In your university you'll say, I saw this, I saw that. This is what Bhagavan is. That's why you learn this: not to understand it" (p. 59).

Masculine ethnographic and autobiographical intentions, on the other hand, are often powered by the desire to unify a work by concentrating on one period of a life or a single characteristic of a personality. It is not surprising that with men socially conditioned to pursue successful careers, we find harmony and orderliness in their autobiographies. The unidirectionality of men's lives seems somehow appropriately cast into self-assured progressive narratives. Thus anthropologist Kenneth Read's (1986) self-portrayal of fieldwork is beatific: "Looking back now, I believe I was permanently elated most of the time I was there. At least this is the only name I can give to a state of mind in which certainty in my own abilities and discovery of myself joined with a compassion for others and a gratitude for the lessons in acceptance that they taught me" (p. 6).

Narratives of women's lives, by contrast, are often neither chronological nor progressive but disjointed, fragmentary, or organized into self-sustained units rather than connecting chapters (Krieger, 1983). Feminist authors and critics have been weaving autobiography into history and criticism, journals into analysis, and the spirit of poetry into interdisciplinary prose. A number of women ethnographers have used the female mode, constructing their texts of fragments: letters from the field, diary extracts, musings, poems, dreams, drawings, and stories. One of the most radical and truly successful examples of this type of experimentation is Karen McCarthy Brown's *Mama Lola* (1991), an ethnographic study of Vodou in New York City. In this beautifully crafted book, Brown employs four separate vocal registers: the voice of Alourdes, the Vodou priestess who is the main character; the scholarly voice of Karen Brown, the ethnographer; the personal intimate voice of Brown, as narrator and character in the tale she herself is constructing; and the mythic voice of Gede, the teller of ancestral fictional tales. The feminine narrative is also often marked by conflicts between the personal and the professional. There may be a tension between the conventional role of wife, mother, sister, or daughter and another, unconventional role that includes ambition or a vocation. In her memoir, *Nest in the Wind* (1989), Martha Ward undermines her own authority by noting, "I have probably imparted more wisdom to myself in recounting these events than I deserve. The written accounts, letters, field notes, and reports from this period have provided a framework, but memory and shifts in my own consciousness alter my perspectives." This admittedly unreliable narrator also notes that "this book was not written for my peers or professional colleagues. It is only what John Van Maanen [1988] calls 'an impressionist tale' " (p. 3).

Women ethnographers have revealed not only lack of rapport and even bad faith during fieldwork, but also their accidental, informal, or personal rather than professional reasons for undertaking field research. Barbara Bode's stated motive for doing research in Peru was to fill the void in herself created by the loss of her baby. She explains, in the introduction to *No Bells to Toll* (1989), that she went to Peru primarily in order to catapult herself out of her own personal tragedy. Marjorie Shostak, in her biography *Nisa: The Life and Words of a !Kung Woman* (1981), admits that the impetus for her collection of personal information from Nisa arose because she herself felt lonely and hoped that more structured interactions might allow her to share in other people's lives. Judith Stacey (1995) notes that she undertook her "accidental ethnography" of the families of white working-class people in California's Silicon Valley because of the demands and delights of "delayed mothering," which confined her field research options to locations close to her San Francisco Bay Area home. She structured her trade book *Brave New Families* (1990) as two first-person documentary novellas within an overall third-person expository account of the historical changes in family life within the United States.

These gendered textual practices are learned partly through reading. In the not-too-distant past, wherever a husband and wife worked in the same region, it was the man who wrote about what were considered more centrally important topics and adopted the expository mode. The woman wrote on what were considered more peripheral topics and adopted the narrative mode.[16] An early example of this segmentation is the joint ethnographic career of Charles and Brenda Seligman. Upon marriage, Brenda Salaman gave up her premedical training to become an ethnographic field partner with her husband among the Veddahs of Ceylon and the Nuba in the Sudan (Stocking, 1995, p. 117). While she became a specialist in kinship and social organization, her husband collected data on what were considered more important topics at the time: physical types and material culture. They published their research jointly (Seligman & Seligman, 1911, 1932).

Another couple who researched and wrote jointly were the South Africans Eileen Jensen Krige and Jack Krige. In this case, Eileen was the trained ethnographer and included her lawyer husband in her research among the Lovedu of the northern Transvaal, but the result was similar. The book they published was based on fieldwork they conducted together during the 1930s. When they constructed their joint ethnography *The Realm of a Rain-Queen* (1943), she took primary responsibility for what they describe as the "more feminine" topics, including health, fertility, the family, children, drum and rain cults, and the Rain-Queen. Her husband handled what they describe as the "more masculine" topics, including subsistence, economic exchange, social groups, tribal history, politics, and law. This split reflects the gendered typification of feminine domestic versus masculine public spheres. The book is united with evocative descriptions of everyday life written by Eileen Krige (Hammond-Tooke, 1997, pp. 85-89).

A similar segmentation of writing tasks along gender lines appeared more recently in Elizabeth and Robert Fernea's coauthored ethnographies *The Arab World* (1985) and *Nubian Ethnographies* (1991). Here the wife narrates the couple's encounters in a breezy travel-diary style while the husband contributes abstractions and commentaries that are typifying and authoritative.

While Elizabeth represents herself as experiencing various locations and cultures, Robert takes up a strategic location within the authoritative "heart" of Arab culture as it was known and described by earlier scholars. These textual strategies, representing alternative modes of reading and claiming very different audiences, coexist within both books. The effect of these strongly gendered accounts is to highlight the points of difference rather than the Ferneas' shared observations and interpretations.

Just as men have sometimes cast their lives into heroic molds in order to project their universal import, women can also exaggerate, mythologize, or monumentalize their own lives or those of their consultants. Judith Okely (1992) reports that her stories about fieldwork with Gypsies "naturally" became heroically embellished through numerous tellings and retellings to her male colleagues. This masculinization of an ethnographic narrative is not at all surprising, given that professional identity, like sexual identity, is acquired through a process of language learning that constitutes the social person. During the early days of anthropology, women like Audrey Richards may even have succeeded, to a certain degree, in achieving disciplinary equality by becoming "honorary males." Professional masculinization is also revealed when they claim that honorary-male status has been bestowed upon them during their fieldwork. However, most women trying to be men have actually found themselves perceived as "pseudomales," occupying neither a male nor a female role. Jean Jackson (1986), an ethnographer in South America, wrote home to her family and friends, "I am like a man from Mars here; I suppose I should say woman except that I am so foreign to the Bará they probably don't see much difference" (p. 263).

Ifi Amadiume (1987) has suggested that the ideas and practices leading to this honorary-male or pseudomale role during fieldwork ought to be examined, modified, and perhaps rejected. She points out that assuming such a role may in fact be neopatriarchal as well as neocolonialist. During ethnographic research in her own matrilineal Igbo community, when she found that an important women's council was excluded from the constitution by local male leaders, she chose not to identify with the men but rather spoke up about the unfairness of a situation that seriously diminished the status of local women. After becoming directly involved in raising the women's consciousness about this situation, however, she decided on a self-imposed exile in England, where she has reported that she plans to do research and use her pen to contribute to the political struggle back home.

Women can, and often do, enter into women's worlds during their field research, writing from a politically involved, woman-centered perspective. This movement from honorary-male ethnographer to woman-centered ethnographer is revealed in the plotting, rhetoric, and texture of writing produced through a strongly participatory feminist consciousness (Maguire, 1996). Feminist ethnographers today, although they exist within what has been described as a patriarchal discipline, are practicing an antilogocentric or antiphallocentric approach to writing by speaking "otherwise"—against, even outside, paternal truth, reason, and phallic desire.

◆ *Conclusions*

Long enshrined as a theoretical orientation and philosophical paradigm within anthropology, ethnography has been adopted more recently as a useful methodology in cultural studies, literary theory, folklore, women's studies, nursing, law, planning, and even industrial engineering. Wherever this has happened, a key assumption has been that by entering into firsthand interaction with people in their everyday lives, ethnographers can reach a better understanding of the beliefs, motivations, and behaviors of their subjects than they can by using any other method.

In the past, the human sciences modeled themselves on the physical sciences, which emphasize the structures of reality outside the area of meaning. However, because human beings exist within the realm of meaning as well as in the material and organic realms, ethnographers now pay careful attention to this dimension. One of the most important forms for creating meaning is a narrative that attends to the temporal dimension of human existence and shapes events into a unity. Ethnographers who have recently provided models for the investigation of narrative have realized that the human sciences, instead of striving toward natural science, need to conceive of themselves as multiple sciences. The human being, the object and subject of their inquiry, exists in multiple strata of reality, which are organized in different ways. The realm of meaning is emergent from the material and organic strata rather than a product of them.

Following the controversies caused by the posthumous publication of Malinowski's diary and the repudiation of undercover observation, there was a movement away from participant observation toward the observation of participation. The shift from an objectifying methodology to an intersubjective methodology entails a representational transformation. The exploration of ethical issues involved in the process of generating ethnographic information and publishing ethnographic accounts encouraged ethnographers to combine the political, philosophical, and personal within single accounts. Instead of choosing between writing an ethnographic memoir centering on the self or a life history or standard monograph centering on the other, an ethnographer can allow both self and other to appear together within a single narrative that carries a multiplicity of dialoguing voices.

Experience is intersubjective and embodied, not individual and fixed, but social and processual. Intersubjectivity and dialogue involve situations where bodies marked by the social—that is, by difference (gender, ethnicity, race)—may be presented as partial identities. The experience of being a woman, or being black, or being Muslim, can never be singular. It will always be dependent on a multiplicity of locations and positions that are socially constructed. These positionings are different for each individual, as well as for each culture that ethnographers come into contact with as

field-workers, observant participants, and collectors of life stories.

In part, the shifts in the practice and construction of ethnography reflect an important change in the population of ethnographers and readers of ethnographies. With more middle- and lower-class individuals, more minority as well as Third and Fourth World scholars, and more women reading and practicing ethnography, the class, race, culture, and gender beliefs and behaviors of the inquirers have been placed within the same historical moment, or critical plane, as those of the subjects of inquiry. As a result, the doing, framing, representation, and reading of ethnography have been changed in both ethical and encoding practices. Participant observation has become the observation of participation, and the genre of narrative ethnography has emerged from the margins and moved to claim the center.

■ Notes

1. Individuals who have taken on a strongly participatory role, and in some cases even undergone apprenticeships, include Reichard (1934), Hurston (1938), Dunham (1969), Jules-Rosette (1975), Maquet (1975), Riesman (1977), Chernoff (1980), Cooper (1980), Harner (1980), Peters (1981), Hayano (1982), Schipper (1982), Tedlock (1982), Dalby (1983), Johnson (1984), Turner (1985, 1993), Rose (1987), Coy (1989), Dilley (1989), Stoller (1989a), Wafer (1991), Seremetakis (1993), Knab (1995), Friedson (1996), Emad (1997), Tarn (1997), and Prechtel (1998).

2. Ever since Laura Nader (1969) advocated "studying up," there have been a growing number of studies of power elites, especially those involved in the most prestigious areas within Western science and biomedicine; see Latour (1987), Martin (1987), Traweek (1988), and Cassell (1991, 1998). There has also been attention to "studying horizontally" (Cassell, 1988, p. 89), in which there are only small power differences between the researcher and the research partners. For an instructive comparison of the benefits and problems involved in studying up, down, and sideways, see Schrijvers (1991).

3. For useful discussions of ethnography as a modernist, postmodernist, or nonmodern en-

deavor, see Ardener (1985), Strathern (1987b), Ashley (1991), Crapanzano (1990), Manganaro (1990), Wolf (1992), Denzin (1993), Visweswaran (1994, pp. 85-94), Hastrup (1995, pp. 49-51), Pool (1995), and Dawson (1996).

4. Both critical feminism and critical ethnography have close ties to the critical theory of society explored by members of the Frankfurt school; see Wellmer (1971) and Geuss (1981).

5. More about the role of reflexivity in feminist and ethnographic critical theory can be found in Scholte (1969), Babcock (1980), Ruby (1982), Caplan (1988), and Stacey (1988). For examples of dialogical anthropology, discussions about dialogical approaches to ethnography, and critical dialogue, see Stavenhagen (1971), Dwyer (1977, 1979, 1982), D. Tedlock (1979, 1987), Webster (1982), Crapanzano (1985), Buckley (1987), Feld (1987), Tyler (1987a, 1987b), Page (1988), Fischer and Abedi (1990), Harrison (1991), Jordan (1991), B. Tedlock (1991), and Tedlock and Mannheim (1995). In sociology these same issues, but focusing on naturally occurring conversation rather than the trope of dialogue, are covered within symbolic interactionism, ethnomethodology, and the sociology of knowledge (Rapport, 1997).

6. Some of the novels written by ethnographers—both members of the cultures described and outsiders—are those of Bandelier (1890), Haggard and Lang (1890), Driberg (1930), Coon (1933, 1940), Griaule (1934), McNickle (1936, 1978), Hurston (1937), Elwin (1937, 1938), Underhill (1940), Arguedas (1941/1985, 1958/1978), Osgood (1953), Ekvall (1954, 1981), Miller (1959), Matthiessen (1965, 1975), Leighton (1971), Stewart (1971), Buelow (1973), Wendt (1973, 1979), Wilson (1974), Bista (1980), Salerno and Vanderburgh (1980), Jaffe (1983), Bennett (1986), Ghosh (1986, 1993, 1996), M. Jackson (1986), Thomas (1987), Deloria (1988), Courlander (1990), Gear and Gear (1990), Narayan (1995b), and Price (1998).

7. La Farge went on to write other novels that depended upon ethnographic knowledge of the indigenous peoples of the American Southwest and Guatemala (1931, 1937, 1945, 1951). He also wrote two collections of short stories based on ethnography and ethnographers (1957, 1965).

8. *The Wolf Is My Brother* (1967), which won the Golden Spur Award as best western his-

torical novel, is set in the American Southwest, where Oliver lived. His last novel, *Broken Eagle* (1989), is an epic of the Old West with a Cheyenne warrior whose wife and child were killed at the Sand Creek Massacre as the hero. More recently, Kathy Reichs, of the University of North Carolina at Charlotte, has used her knowledge of and experiences in forensic anthropology to become a best-selling mystery writer. Her ethnographic novel *Déjà Dead* (1997) is built upon a composite of cases she actually worked on, and the novel's heroine, Temperance Brennan, is based on her own professional background. Her protagonist's personal problems with alcoholism and marital troubles, however, are "purely fictional" (Montell, 1997).

9. Ethnographic short stories and novellas include those of Stewart (1975, 1989, 1995), Nelson (1980), Frank (1981), Jaffe (1982, 1995), M. Richardson (1984, 1990), Applebaum (1985), Skafte (1986), B. Tedlock (1986), Waldorf (1986), Stacey (1990), McNickle (1992), Wolf (1992), Altork (1994), Nimmo (1994), Zedeño (1994), Goldschmidt (1995), Narayan (1995a), Reck (1995), Ruiz (1995), Springwater (1996), and Flynn (1997).

10. Some of the ethnographic plays that have been written and/or produced include those of Kuper (1970), Brook (1976), Higgins and Canan (1984), D. Tedlock (1986, 1998), Grindal and Shephard (1987), Richardson and Lockridge (1991), and Kondo (1995, 1997). The lives of ethnographers have also been at the center of theatrical productions. Kirsten Hastrup (1992) discusses her experience of being an object of dramatic representation. A play about the relationship between the feminist ethnographer Marjorie Shostak and her !Kung subject, Nisa, written by Brenda Bynum (1995) based on the ethnographer's field notes, journals, and letters home, was performed at the American Anthropological Association meeting in Atlanta, Georgia, in December 1995. The following year, at the AAA annual meeting in San Francisco, a staged reading was presented of a play, *Myth of the Docile Woman*, centering on Louise Lamphere's ethnographic research among sweatshop seamstresses and her own successful sex-discrimination lawsuit against Brown University (Schevill & Gordon, 1996).

11. Ethnographic diaries, letters, and travelogues include those of Leiris (1934), Elwin (1936), Lévi-Strauss (1955), Condominas (1957),

Matthiessen (1962), Bista (1979), Ribeiro (1979), Chaffetz (1981), Brandão (1982), Moeran (1985), Good (1991), Behar (1995), Price and Price (1992), Goodale (1996), Turner (1996), Kirk (1997), Yu (1997), and Clastres (1998).

12. Colin Turnbull reversed this process by publishing an accessible first-person account of his fieldwork among the Congo pygmies (1961) and then releasing a coolly distanced, more authoritative monograph on the same topic (1965). Paul Stoller first published a jointly written memoir centering on his African fieldwork cowritten with his first wife, Cheryl Olkes (1987). Two years later, he released two solely authored books: a formal ethnography and a theoretical text (Stoller, 1989a, 1989b).

13. For examples of works touching on such topics, see Weston (1991, 1993), Scheper-Hughes (1992), Kleinman and Copp (1993), Newton (1993), Wade (1993), Blackwood (1995), Bolton (1995), Dubisch (1995), Grindal and Salomone (1995), Kulick (1995), Kulick and Willson (1995), Lewin (1995), Nordstrom and Robben (1995), Behar (1996), Daniel (1996), Kennedy and Davis (1996), Lewin and Leap (1996), Wafer (1996), and Willson (1997).

14. Important attempts to grapple with the intersections of class, gender, "race" and racism, ethnicity, nationalism, and sexuality are found in the work of Brah (1996) and Lewis (1996). Examples of feminist and native ethnographers (who often form an overlapping category) include Visweswaran (1988, 1994), Abu-Lughod (1990), Bell (1993), Narayan (1993), Hong (1994), Kanaaneh (1997), and Rang (1997). Discussion of these important changes can be found in Harding (1987, p. 9), Rose (1990, p. 10), D'Amico-Samuels (1991), Harrison (1991), Panini (1991), and Strathern (1987a).

15. For background reading in this contested area of "native" versus "indigenous" ethnographic practice, including the concept of "dual consciousness" that theoretically gives women and other subalterns a special ethnographic advantage, see Fahim (1977, 1987), Huizer (1979), Nash (1980), Fei (1981), Madan (1987), McClaurin-Allen (1989), Deck (1990), Kim (1990), Harrison (1991), Limón (1991), Driessen (1993), Jones (1995), and Motzafi-Haller (1997).

16. Compare the gendered discourse strategies used by women field-workers and their husbands: D. A. Talbot (1915) with P. A. Talbot (1923, 1969), E. W. Fernea (1965, 1975) with R. A. Fernea (1970, 1973), D. Dwyer (1978) with K. Dwyer (1982), E. Turner (1987, 1996) with V. Turner (1967, 1969), and Meyerson (1990) with Urton (1981). Family or "accompanied" fieldwork has only recently been described and theorized; see Cassell (1987), Gottlieb and Graham (1993), and Flinn, Marshall, and Armstrong (1998).

■ References

Abu-Lughod, L. (1990). Can there be a feminist ethnography? *Women and Performance, 5*(1), 7-27.

Abu-Lughod, L. (1993). *Writing women's worlds: Bedouin stories.* Berkeley: University of California Press.

Adler, P. A., & Adler, P. (1987). *Membership roles in field research.* Newbury Park, CA: Sage.

Agar, M. H. (1980). *The professional stranger: An informal introduction to ethnography.* New York: Academic Press.

Allen, C. J., & Garner, N. (1993). *Condor Qatay* [Play]. (Produced and performed at George Washington University, Dorothy Betts Marvin Theater, March 31, 1994)

Allen, C. J., & Garner, N. (1995). *Condor Qatay*: Anthropology in performance. *American Anthropologist, 97*(1), 69-82.

Allen, C. J., & Garner, N. (1997). *Condor Qatay: Anthropology in performance.* Prospect Heights, IL: Waveland.

Altork, K. (1994). Working Norman's birthday. *Anthropology and Humanism, 19*(2), 159-162.

Amadiume, I. (1987). *Male daughters, female husbands: Gender and sex in an African society.* New York: Zed.

Appadurai, A. (1986). Theory in anthropology: Center and periphery. *Comparative Studies in Society and History, 28,* 356-361.

Applebaum, H. A. (1985). *Blue chips.* Lawrenceville, VA: Brunswick.

Archetti, E. P. (1994). Introduction. In E. P. Archetti (Ed.), *Exploring the written: Anthropology and the multiplicity of writing* (pp. 11-28). Oslo: Scandinavian University Press.

Ardener, E. W. (1985). Social anthropology and the decline of modernism. In J. Overing (Ed.), *Reason and morality*. London: Tavistock.

Arguedas, J. M. (1985). *Yawar Fiesta* (F. H. Barraclough, Trans.). Austin: University of Texas Press. (Original work published 1941)

Arguedas, J. M. (1978). *Deep rivers* (F. H. Barraclough, Trans.). Austin: University of Texas Press. (Original work published 1958)

Asad, T. (Ed.). (1973). *Anthropology and the colonial encounter*. Atlantic Highlands, NJ: Humanities Press.

Ashley, D. (1991). Critical theory, poststructuralism, postmodernism: Their sociological relevance. *Annual Review of Sociology, 17*, 105-131.

Auster, P. (1998). Translator's note. In P. Clastres, *Chronicle of the Guayaki Indians* (pp. 7-13). New York: Zone.

Babcock, B. (1980). Reflexivity: Definitions and discriminations. *Semiotica, 30*(1-2), 1-14.

Bahr, D., Gregorio, J., Lopez, D., & Alvarez, A. (1974). *Piman shamanism and staying sickness*. Tucson: University of Arizona Press.

Banaji, J. (1970). The crisis of British anthropology. *New Left Review, 64*.

Bandelier, A. F. (1971). *The delight makers: A novel of prehistoric Pueblo Indians*. New York: Harcourt Brace Jovanovich. (Original work published 1890)

Barley, N. (1983a). *Adventures in a mud hut: An innocent anthropologist abroad*. New York: Vanguard.

Barley, N. (1983b). *Symbolic structures: An exploration of the culture of the Dowayos*. Cambridge: Cambridge University Press.

Beattie, J. (1960). *Bunyoro: An African kingdom*. New York: Holt, Rinehart & Winston.

Beattie, J. (1965). *Understanding an African kingdom*. New York: Holt, Rinehart & Winston.

Beaujour, M. (1987). Michel Leiris: Ethnography or self-portrayal? *Cultural Anthropology, 2*, 470-480.

Behar, R. (1993). *Translated woman: Crossing the border with Esperanza's story*. Boston: Beacon.

Behar, R. (1995). Writing in my father's name: A diary of *Translated woman*'s first year. In R. Behar & D. A. Gordon (Eds.), *Women writing*

culture (pp. 65-82). Berkeley: University of California Press.

Behar, R. (1996). *The vulnerable observer: Anthropology that breaks your heart*. Boston: Beacon.

Bell, D. (1993). Yes Virginia, there is a feminist ethnography: Reflections from three Australian fields. In D. Bell, P. Caplan, & W. J. Karim (Eds.), *Gendered fields: Women, men and ethnography* (pp. 28-43). London: Routledge.

Bennett, J. A. W. (1986). *Downfall people*. Toronto: McClelland & Stewart.

Bista, D. B. (1979). *Report from Lhasa*. Kathmandu: Sajha Prakashan.

Bista, D. B. (1980). *Shotala*. Kathmandu, Nepal: Sajha Prakashan.

Blackwood, E. (1995). Falling in love with an-Other lesbian: Reflections on identity in fieldwork. In D. Kulick & M. Willson (Eds.), *Taboo: Sex, identity and erotic subjectivity in anthropological fieldwork* (pp. 51-75). New York: Routledge.

Bode, B. (1989). *No bells to toll: Destruction and creation in the Andes*. New York: Scribner's Sons.

Bolton, R. (1995). Tricks, friends, and lovers: Erotic encounters in the field. In D. Kulick & M. Willson (Eds.), *Taboo: Sex, identity and erotic subjectivity in anthropological fieldwork* (pp. 140-167). New York: Routledge.

Boon, J. A. (1982). *Other tribes, other scribes: Symbolic anthropology in the comparative study of cultures, histories, religions, and texts*. Cambridge: Cambridge University Press.

Bowen, E. S. (pseudonym of L. Bohannan). (1954). *Return to laughter: An anthropological novel*. New York: Harper & Row.

Brah, A. (1996). *Cartographies of diaspora: Contesting identities*. London: Routledge.

Brandão, C. R. (1982). *Diário de campo: A antropologia com alegoria*. São Paulo: Brasiliense.

Brandes, R. S. (1965). *Frank Hamilton Cushing: Pioneer Americanist*. Ann Arbor, MI: University Microfilms International.

Brink, P. J. (1993). Studying African women's secret societies. In C. M. Renzetti & R. M. Lee (Eds.), *Researching sensitive topics* (pp. 235-248). Newbury Park, CA: Sage.

British Association for the Advancement of Science. (1874). *Notes and queries on anthro-*

pology, for the use of travellers and residents in uncivilized lands. London: CRAA.

Brook, J. P. (1976). *The Ik* [Play]. (Directed and produced by Peter Brook, Round House Theatre, London)

Brown, K. M. (1991). *Mama Lola: A Vodou priestess in Brooklyn.* Berkeley: University of California Press.

Buckley, T. (1987). Dialogue and shared authority: Informants as critics. *Central Issues in Anthropology, 7*(1), 13-23.

Buelow, G. D. (1973). *The ethnographic novel in Africa.* Unpublished doctoral dissertation, University of Oregon.

Bynum, B. (1995, December). *My heart is still shaking.* Play performed at the annual meeting of the American Anthropological Association, Atlanta, GA.

Caplan, P. (1988). Engendering knowledge: The politics of ethnography. *Anthropology Today, 4*(5), 8-12.

Cassell, J. (1987). *Children in the field: Anthropological experiences.* Philadelphia: Temple University Press.

Cassell, J. (1988). The relationship of observer to observed when studying up. In R. Burgess (Ed.), *Studies in qualitative methodology* (Vol. 1, pp. 89-108). London: JAI.

Cassell, J. (1991). *Expected miracles: Surgeons at work.* Philadelphia: Temple University Press.

Cassell, J. (1998). *The woman in the surgeon's body.* Cambridge, MA: Harvard University Press.

Caulfield, M. D. (1979). Participant observation or partisan participation? In G. Huizer & B. Mannheim (Eds.), *The politics of anthropology: From colonialism and sexism toward a view from below* (pp. 309-318). The Hague: Mouton.

Cesara, M. (pseudonym of K. Poewe). (1982). *Reflections of a woman anthropologist: No hiding place.* London: Academic Press.

Chaffetz, D. (1981). *A journey through Afghanistan: A memorial.* Chicago: University of Chicago Press.

Chernoff, J. M. (1980). *African rhythm and African sensibility.* Chicago: University of Chicago Press.

Chilungu, S. W. (1976). Issues in the ethics of research method: An interpretation of the Anglo-American perspective. *Current Anthropology, 17,* 457-481.

Clastres, P. (1998). *Chronicle of the Guayaki Indians* (P. Auster, Trans.). New York: Zone.

Condominas, G. (1957). *Nous avons mangé la forêt de la Pierre-Génie Gôo.* Paris: Mercure de France.

Coon, C. S. (1933). *The ruffian.* Boston: Little, Brown.

Coon, C. S. (1940). *Flesh of the wild ox.* New York: Morrow.

Cooper, E. (1980). *The woodcarvers of Hong Kong: Craft production in the world capitalist periphery.* New York: Cambridge University Press.

Courlander, H. (1990). *The Bordeaux narrative.* Albuquerque: University of New Mexico Press.

Coy, M. W. (1989). Being what we pretend to be: The usefulness of apprenticeship as a field method. In M. W. Coy (Ed.), *Apprenticeship: From theory to method and back again* (pp. 115-135). Albany: State University of New York Press.

Crapanzano, V. (1980). *Tuhami: Portrait of a Moroccan.* Chicago: University of Chicago Press.

Crapanzano, V. (1985). *Waiting: The whites of South Africa.* New York: Random House.

Crapanzano, V. (1990). Afterword. In M. Manganaro (Ed.), *Modernist anthropology: From fieldwork to text* (pp. 300-308). Princeton, NJ: Princeton University Press.

Cushing, F. H. (1882). My adventures in Zuñi. *Century Illustrated Monthly Magazine, 25,* 191-207, 500-511.

Cushing, F. H. (1883). My adventures in Zuñi. *Century Illustrated Monthly Magazine, 26,* 28-47.

Cushing, F. H. (1979). *Zuñi: Selected writings of Frank Hamilton Cushing* (J. Green, Ed.). Lincoln: University of Nebraska Press.

Cushing, F. H. (1990). *Cushing at Zuni: The correspondence and journals of Frank Hamilton Cushing 1879-1884* (J. Green, Ed.). Albuquerque: University of New Mexico Press.

Dalby, L. C. (1983). *Geisha.* Berkeley: University of California Press.

Damatta, R. (1994). Some biased remarks on interpretivism: A view from Brazil. In R. Borofsky (Ed.), *Assessing cultural anthropology* (pp. 119-132). New York: McGraw-Hill.

D'Amico-Samuels, D. (1991). Undoing fieldwork: Personal, political, theoretical and methodological implications. In F. V. Harrison (Ed.), *Decolonizing anthropology: Moving further toward an anthropology for liberation* (pp. 68-87). Washington, DC: Association of Black Anthropologists/American Anthropological Association.

Daniel, E. V. (1984). *Fluid signs: Being a person the Tamil way.* Berkeley: University of California Press.

Daniel, E. V. (1996). *Charred lullabies: Chapters in an anthropology of violence.* Princeton, NJ: Princeton University Press.

David-Neel, A. A. (1927). *My journey to Lhasa: The personal story of the only white woman who succeeded in entering the Forbidden City.* London: William Heinemann.

David-Neel, A. A. (1932). *Magic and mystery in Tibet.* New York: Claude Kendall.

David-Neel, A. A. (1936). *Le bouddhisme, ses doctrines et ses methodes.* Paris: Plon.

David-Neel, A. A. (1959). *Initiations and initiates in Tibet.* New York: University.

Dawson, L. L. (1996). Postmodern ethnography and the sociology of religion. *Research in the Social Scientific Study of Religion, 7,* 3-41.

Deck, A. A. (1990). Autoethnography: Zora Neale Hurston, Noni Jabavu, and cross-disciplinary discourse. *Black American Literature Forum, 24,* 237-256.

Deloria, E. C. (1988). *Waterlily.* Lincoln: University of Nebraska Press.

Denzin, N. K. (1993). The postmodern sensibility. In N. K. Denzin (Ed.), *Studies in symbolic interaction* (pp. 179-188). Greenwich, CT: JAI.

DeVault, M. L. (1990). Women write sociology: Rhetorical strategies. In A. Hunter (Ed.), *The rhetoric of social research: Understood and believed* (pp. 97-110). New Brunswick, NJ: Rutgers University Press.

De Vita, P. R. (Ed.). (1990). *The humbled anthropologist: Tales from the Pacific.* Belmont, CA: Wadsworth.

Dilley, R. M. (1989). Secrets and skills: Apprenticeship among Tukolor weavers. In M. W. Coy (Ed.), *Apprenticeship: From theory to method and back again* (pp. 181-198). Albany: State University of New York Press.

Driberg, J. H. (1930). *People of the small arrow.* New York: Payson & Clarke.

Driessen, H. (1993). *The politics of ethnographic reading and writing: Confrontations of Western and indigenous views.* Saarbrücken, Germany: Verlag.

Dubisch, J. (1995). Lovers in the field: Sex, dominance, and the female anthropologist. In D. Kulick & M. Willson (Eds.), *Taboo: Sex, identity and erotic subjectivity in anthropological fieldwork* (pp. 29-50). New York: Routledge.

Du Bois, W. E. B. (1969). *The souls of black folk: Essays and sketches.* New York: Fawcett. (Original work published 1903)

Dumont, J.-P. (1976). *Under the rainbow: Nature and supernature among the Panaré Indians.* Austin: University of Texas Press.

Dumont, J.-P. (1978). *The headman and I: Ambiguity and ambivalence in the fieldworking experience.* Austin: University of Texas Press.

Dunham, K. (1969). *Island possessed.* Chicago: University of Chicago Press.

Dwyer, D. (1978). *Images and self-images: Male and female in Morocco.* New York: Columbia University Press.

Dwyer, K. (1977). On the dialogic of fieldwork. *Dialectical Anthropology, 2,* 143-151.

Dwyer, K. (1979). The dialogic of ethnology. *Dialectical Anthropology, 4,* 205-224.

Dwyer, K. (1982). *Moroccan dialogues: Anthropology in question.* Baltimore: Johns Hopkins University Press.

Ekvall, R. B. (1954). *Tents against the sky.* London: Victor Gollancz.

Ekvall, R. B. (1981). *The lama knows.* Novato, CA: Chandler & Sharp.

Elwin, V. (1932). *Truth and India: Can we get it?* London: George Allen & Unwin.

Elwin, V. (1936). *Leaves from the jungle: Life in a Gond village.* London: Oxford University Press.

Elwin, V. (1937). *Phulmat of the hills.* London.

Elwin, V. (1938). *A cloud that is dragonish.* London.

Elwin, V. (1942). *The Agaria.* London: Oxford University Press.

Elwin, V. (1946). *Folk-songs of Chhattisgarh.* London: Oxford University Press.

Elwin, V. (1947). *The Muria and their ghotul.* Bombay: Oxford University Press.

Elwin, V. (1954). *Tribal myths of Orissa.* Bombay: Oxford University Press.

Elwin, V. (1961). *Nagaland.* Shillong: Adviser's Secretariat.

Elwin, V. (1964). *The tribal world of Verrier Elwin.* Bombay: Oxford University Press.

Emad, M. (1997). Twirling the needle: Pinning down anthropologists' emergent bodies in the disclosive field of American acupuncture. *Anthropology of Consciousness, 8*(2-3), 88-96.

Eves, R. (1999). Going troppo: Images of white savagery, degeneration and race in turn-of-the-century colonial fictions of the Pacific. *History and Anthropology, 11,* 351-385.

Fahim, H. (1977). Foreign and indigenous anthropology: The perspectives of an Egyptian anthropologist. *Human Organization, 36,* 80-86.

Fahim, H. (Ed.). (1987). *Indigenous anthropology in non-Western countries.* Durham, NC: Carolina Academic Press.

Fei H. T. (1939). *Peasant life in China.* London: Kegan Paul, Trench & Trubner.

Fei H. T. (1981). *Toward a people's anthropology.* Beijing: New World.

Feld, S. (1987). Dialogic editing: Interpreting how Kaluli read *Sound and sentiment. Cultural Anthropology, 2,* 190-210.

Fernea, E. W. (1965). *Guests of the sheik: An ethnography of an Iraqi village.* Garden City, NY: Doubleday.

Fernea, E. W. (1975). *A street in Marrakech.* Garden City, NY: Doubleday.

Fernea, E. W., & Fernea, R. A. (1985). *The Arab world: Personal encounters.* Garden City, NY: Doubleday.

Fernea, E. W., & Fernea, R. A. (1991). *Nubian ethnographies.* Prospect Heights, IL: Waveland.

Fernea, R. A. (1970). *Shaykh and effendi: Changing patterns of authority among the El Shaban of southern Iraq.* Cambridge, MA: Harvard University Press.

Fernea, R. A. (1973). *Nubians in Egypt.* Austin: University of Texas Press.

Firth, R. (1985). Degrees of intelligibility. In J. Overing (Ed.), *Reason and morality.* London: Tavistock.

Fischer, M. M., & Abedi, M. (1990). *Debating Muslims: Cultural dialogues in postmodernity and tradition.* Madison: University of Wisconsin Press.

Flinn, J., Marshall, L., & Armstrong, J. (Eds.). (1998). *Fieldwork and families: Constructing new models for ethnographic research.* Honolulu: University of Hawaii Press.

Flynn, S. I. (1997). A feast of mangoes. *Anthropology and Humanism, 22*(1), 119-124.

Fogelson, R. D. (1984). Who were the Ani-Kutani? An excursion into Cherokee historical thought. *Ethnohistory, 31,* 255-263.

Frank, G. (1981). Mercy's children. *Anthropology and Humanism Quarterly, 6*(4), 8-12.

Frazer, J. G. (1887). *Questions on the manners, customs, religion, superstitions, etc. of uncivilized or semi-civilized peoples* [Pamphlet]. London: Author.

Frazer, J. G. (1981). *The golden bough: The roots of religion and folklore.* New York: Avenel. (Original work published 1890)

Freilich, M. (1970). *Marginal natives: Anthropologists at work.* New York: Harper & Row.

Freshfield, M. (pseudonym of M. Field). (1947). *Stormy dawn.* London: Faber.

Friedson, S. M. (1996). *Dancing prophets: Musical experience in Tumbuka healing.* Chicago: University of Chicago Press.

Gal, S. (1991). Between speech and silence: The problematics of research on language and gender. In M. di Leonardo (Ed.), *Gender at the crossroads of knowledge* (pp. 175-203). Berkeley: University of California Press.

Gear, W. M., & Gear, K. O. (1990). *People of the wolf.* New York: Tor.

Gerhart, M. (1992). *Genre choices, gender questions.* Norman: University of Oklahoma Press.

Geuss, R. (1981). *The idea of a critical theory: Habermas and the Frankfurt school.* Cambridge: Cambridge University Press.

Ghosh, A. (1986). *The circle of reason.* New York: Viking.

Ghosh, A. (1993). *In an antique land.* New York: Alfred A. Knopf.

Ghosh, A. (1996). *Calcutta chromosome: A novel of fevers, delirium, and discovery.* London: Picador.

Goldschmidt, W. (1995). Pietro's house. *Anthropology and Humanism, 20*(1), 47-51.

Good, K. (with Chanoff, D.). (1991). *Into the heart: One man's pursuit of love and knowledge among the Yanomama.* New York: Simon & Schuster.

Goodale, J. C. (with Chowning, A.). (1996). *The two-party line: Conversations in the field.* Lanham, MD: Rowman & Littlefield.

Gottlieb, A., & Graham, P. (1993). *Parallel worlds: An anthropologist and a writer encounter Africa.* New York: Crown.

Gough, K. (1968). Anthropology: Child of imperialism. *Monthly Review, 19*(11).

Griaule, M. (1934). *Les flambeurs d'hommes.* Paris: Calmann-Lévy.

Grindal, B., & Salomone, F. (Eds.). (1995). *Bridges to humanity: Narratives on anthropology and friendship.* Prospect Heights, IL: Waveland.

Grindal, B., & Shephard, W. H. (1987). Redneck girl: From experience to performance. *Journal of the Steward Anthropological Society, 17*(1-2), 193-218.

Gronewold, S. (1972). Did Frank Hamilton Cushing go native? In S. T. Kimball & J. B. Watson (Eds.), *Crossing cultural boundaries: The anthropological experience* (pp. 33-50). San Francisco: Chandler.

Gudeman, S., & Rivera, A. (1990). *Conversations in Colombia: The domestic economy in life and text.* Cambridge: Cambridge University Press.

Haggard, H. R., & Lang, A. (1890). *The world's desire.* London: Longman, Green.

Hammersley, M. (1992). *What's wrong with ethnography? Methodological explorations.* London: Routledge.

Hammersley, M., & Atkinson, P. (1983). *Ethnography: Principles in practice.* London: Tavistock.

Hammond-Tooke, W. D. (1997). *Imperfect interpreters: South Africa's anthropologists 1920-1990.* Johannesburg: Witwatersrand University Press.

Harding, S. (Ed.). (1987). *Feminism and methodology: Social science issues.* Bloomington: Indiana University Press.

Harner, M. (1980). *The way of the shaman.* New York: Harper & Row.

Harrison, F. V. (1991). Ethnography as politics. In F. V. Harrison (Ed.), *Decolonizing anthropology: Moving further toward an anthropology for liberation* (pp. 88-109). Washington, DC: Association of Black Anthropologists/American Anthropological Association.

Hastrup, K. (1992). Out of anthropology: The anthropologist as an object of dramatic representation. *Cultural Anthropology, 7,* 327-345.

Hastrup, K. (1995). *A passage to anthropology: Between experience and theory.* London: Routledge.

Hau'ofa, E. (1975). Anthropology and Pacific islanders. *Oceania, 45,* 283-289.

Hau'ofa, E. (1982). Anthropology at home: A South Pacific islands experience. In H. Fahim (Ed.), *Indigenous anthropology in non-Western countries* (pp. 213-222). Durham, NC: Carolina Academic Press.

Hayano, D. M. (1979). Auto-ethnography: Paradigms, problems, and prospects. *Human Organization, 38,* 113-120.

Hayano, D. M. (1982). *Poker faces.* Berkeley: University of California Press.

Higgins, C., & Canan, D. (1984). *The Ik* [Play].

Hong, K. (1994). Experiences of being a "native": Observing anthropology. *Anthropology Today, 10*(3), 6-9.

Hsu, F. L., & Textor, R. (1978). Third World anthropologists and the reprisal of anthropological paradigms. *Anthropology Newsletter, 19*(1), 5.

Huizer, G. (1979). Anthropology and politics: From naïveté toward liberation? In G. Huizer & B. Mannheim (Eds.), *The politics of anthropology: From colonialism and sexism toward a view from below* (pp. 3-141). The Hague: Mouton.

Humphrey, C. (with Onon, U.). (1996). *Shamans and elders: Experience, knowledge, and power among the Daur Mongols.* Oxford: Clarendon.

Hurston, Z. N. (1937). *Their eyes were watching God.* New York: Collier.

Hurston, Z. N. (1938). *Tell my horse.* Philadelphia: J. B. Lippincott.

Hymes, D. (Ed.). (1969). *Reinventing anthropology.* New York: Random House.

Jackson, J. (1986). On trying to be an Amazon. In T. L. Whitehead & M. E. Conaway (Eds.), *Self, sex, and gender in cross-cultural fieldwork* (pp. 263-274). Urbana: University of Illinois Press.

Jackson, M. (1986). *Barawa and the ways birds fly in the sky.* Washington, DC: Smithsonian Institution Press.

Jaffe, H. (1982). *Mourning crazy horses: Stories.* New York: Fiction Collective.

Jaffe, H. (1983). *Dos indios.* New York: Thunder's Mouth.

Jaffe, H. (1995). *Straight razor: Stories.* Normal, IL: Black Ice.

Johnson, N. B. (1984). Sex, color, and rites of passage in ethnographic research. *Human Organization, 43,* 108-120.

Jones, D. J. (1970). Towards a native anthropology. *Human Organization, 29*(4), 1-59.

Jones, D. J. (1995). Anthropology and the oppressed: A reflection on "native" anthropology. In E. L. Cerroni-Long (Ed.), *Insider anthropology* (pp. 58-70). Washington, DC: American Anthropological Association.

Jordan, G. H. (1991). On ethnography in an intertextual situation: Reading narratives or deconstructing discourse? In F. V. Harrison (Ed.), *Decolonizing anthropology: Moving further toward an anthropology for liberation* (pp. 42-67). Washington, DC: Association of Black Anthropologists/American Anthropological Association.

Jovanovich, S. (1971). Adolf Bandelier: An introduction. In A. F. Bandelier, *The delight makers: A novel of prehistoric Pueblo Indians* (pp. v-xix). New York: Harcourt Brace Jovanovich.

Jules-Rosette, B. (1975). *African apostles: Ritual and conversion in the church of John Maranke*. Ithaca, NY: Cornell University Press.

Kanaaneh, M. (1997). The "anthropologicality" of indigenous anthropology. *Dialectical Anthropology, 22*, 23-49.

Keesing, R. (1985). "Kwaio women speak": The micropolitics of autobiography in a Solomon Island society. *American Anthropologist, 87*(12), 27-39.

Kendall, L. (1988). *The life and hard times of a Korean shaman: Of tales and the telling of tales*. Honolulu: University of Hawaii Press.

Kennedy, E. L., & Davis, M. D. (1996). *Boots of leather, slippers of gold: The history of a lesbian community*. New York: Routledge.

Kenyatta, J. (1938). *Facing Mount Kenya: The tribal life of the Gikuyu*. London: Secker & Warburg.

Kim, C. S. (1990). The role of the non-Western anthropologist reconsidered: Illusion versus reality. *Current Anthropology, 31*, 191-201.

Kirk, R. (1997). *The monkey's paw: New chronicles from Peru*. Amherst: University of Massachusetts Press.

Kleinman, S., & Copp, M. A. (1993). *Emotions and fieldwork*. Newbury Park, CA: Sage.

Knab, T. J. (1995). *A war of witches: A journey into the underworld of the contemporary Aztecs*. San Francisco: Harper.

Kondo, D. K. (1995). Bad girls: Theater, women of color, and the politics of representation. In R. Behar & D. A. Gordon (Eds.), *Women writing culture* (pp. 49-64). Berkeley: University of California Press.

Kondo, D. K. (1997). *About face: Performing race in fashion and theater*. New York: Routledge.

Krieger, S. (1983). *The mirror dance: Identity in a women's community*. Philadelphia: Temple University Press.

Krige, E. J., & Krige, J. D. (1943). *The realm of a rain-queen: A study of the pattern of Lovedu society*. London: Oxford University Press.

Kulick, D. (1995). The sexual life of anthropologists: Erotic subjectivity and ethnographic work. In D. Kulick & M. Willson (Eds.), *Taboo: Sex, identity and erotic subjectivity in anthropological fieldwork* (pp. 1-28). New York: Routledge.

Kulick, D., & Willson, M. (Eds.). (1995). *Taboo: Sex, identity and erotic subjectivity in anthropological fieldwork*. New York: Routledge.

Kuper, H. (1947). *An African aristocracy: Rank among the Swazi*. London: Oxford University Press.

Kuper, H. (1960). *Indian people in Natal*. Natal, Brazil: Natal University Press.

Kuper, H. (1965). *Bite of hunger: A novel of Africa*. New York: Harcourt, Brace & World.

Kuper, H. (1970). *A witch in my heart: A play set in Swaziland in the 1930s*. London: Oxford University Press.

Kuper, H. (1984). Work, misses? *Anthropology and Humanism Quarterly, 9*, 15-17. (Original work published 1943)

La Farge, O. (1929). *Laughing boy*. New York: Literary Guild of America.

La Farge, O. (1931). *Sparks fly upward*. Boston: Houghton Mifflin.

La Farge, O. (1937). *The enemy gods*. Boston: Houghton Mifflin.

La Farge, O. (1945). *Raw material*. Boston: Houghton Mifflin.

La Farge, O. (1951). *Behind the mountain*. Boston: Houghton Mifflin.

La Farge, O. (1957). *A pause in the desert*. Boston: Houghton Mifflin.

La Farge, O. (1965). *The door in the wall*. Boston: Houghton Mifflin.

Lambek, M. (1997). Pinching the crocodile's tongue: Affinity and the anxieties of influence in fieldwork. *Anthropology and Humanism, 22*(1), 31-53.

Langness, L. L., & Frank, G. (1978). Fact, fiction, and the ethnographic novel. *Anthropology and Humanism Quarterly, 3*(1-2), 18-22.

Langness, L. L., & Frank, G. (1981). *Lives: An anthropological approach to biography.* Novato, CA: Chandler & Sharp.

Latour, B. (1987). *Science in action.* Cambridge, MA: Harvard University Press.

Laughlin, R. (1994, March 24). *From all for all.* Play performed at the conference "La Sabiduria Maya ah Idzatil: The Wisdom of the Maya," University of Florida.

Lee, R. M. (1995). *Dangerous fieldwork.* Thousand Oaks, CA: Sage.

Leighton, A. H. (1971). *Come near.* New York: W. W. Norton.

Leiris, M. (1934). *L'Afrique fantôme.* Paris: Plon (Terre Humaine).

Leiris, M. (1939). *L'age d'homme.* Paris: Editions Gallimard.

Leiris, M. (1983). *Manhood: A journey from childhood into the fierce order of virility* (R. Howard, Trans.). Chicago: University of Chicago Press.

Lévi-Strauss, C. (1955). *Tristes tropiques.* Paris: Plon (Terre Humaine).

Lévi-Strauss, C. (1973). *Tristes tropiques.* New York: Washington Square Press.

Lewin, E. (1995). Writing lesbian ethnography. In R. Behar & D. A. Gordon (Eds.), *Women writing culture* (pp. 322-335). Berkeley: University of California Press.

Lewin, E., & Leap, W. L. (Eds.). (1996). *Out in the field: Reflections of lesbian and gay anthropologists.* Urbana: University of Illinois Press.

Lewis, D. K. (1973). Anthropology and colonialism. *Current Anthropology, 14,* 581-597.

Lewis, O. (1959). *Five families: Mexican case studies in the culture of poverty.* New York: Basic Books.

Lewis, O. (1961). *The children of Sánchez: Autobiography of a Mexican family.* New York: Random House.

Lewis, O. (1964). *Pedro Martínez: A Mexican peasant and his family.* New York: Random House.

Lewis, O. (1965). *La vida: A Puerto Rican family in the culture of poverty—San Juan and New York.* New York: Vintage.

Lewis, R. (1996). *Gendering Orientalism: Race, femininity and representation.* London: Routledge.

Limón, J. (1991). Representation, ethnicity, and the precursory ethnography: Notes of a native anthropologist. In R. G. Fox (Ed.), *Recapturing anthropology: Working in the present* (pp. 115-135). Santa Fe, NM: School of American Research Press.

MacClancy, J. (1996). Popularizing anthropology. In J. MacClancy & C. McDonaugh (Eds.), *Popularizing anthropology* (pp. 1-57). London: Routledge.

Madan, T. N. (1987). Indigenous anthropology in non-Western counties: An overview. In H. Fahim (Ed.), *Indigenous anthropology in non-Western countries* (pp. 263-268). Durham, NC: Carolina Academic Press.

Maguire, P. (1996). Considering more feminist participatory research: What's congruency got to do with it? *Qualitative Inquiry, 2,* 106-118.

Malinowski, B. (1922). *Argonauts of the western Pacific: An account of native enterprise and adventure in the archipelagoes of Melanesian New Guinea.* New York: E. P. Dutton.

Malinowski, B. (1967). *A diary in the strict sense of the term* (N. Guterman, Trans.). New York: Harcourt, Brace & World.

Manganaro, M. (1990). Textual play, power, and cultural critique: An orientation to modernist anthropology. In M. Manganaro (Ed.), *Modernist anthropology: From fieldwork to text* (pp. 3-47). Princeton, NJ: Princeton University Press.

Maquet, J. (1975). Meditation in contemporary Sri Lanka: Idea and practice. *Journal of Transpersonal Psychology, 7*(2), 182-195.

Marcus, G. E., & Fischer, M. M. J. (1986). *Anthropology as cultural critique: An experimental moment in the human sciences.* Chicago: University of Chicago Press.

Martin, E. (1987). *The woman in the body: A cultural analysis of reproduction.* Boston: Beacon.

Matthiessen, P. (1962). *Under the mountain wall: A chronicle of two seasons in Stone Age New Guinea.* London: Penguin.

Matthiessen, P. (1965). *At play in the fields of the Lord.* New York: Random House.

Matthiessen, P. (1975). *Far Tortuga.* New York: Random House.

McClaurin-Allen, I. (1989). *Theorizing "native" anthropology: Who, what, why and how.* Unpublished manuscript.

McNickle, D. (1936). *The surrounded.* New York: Dodd, Mead.

McNickle, D. (1978). *Wind from an enemy sky.* San Francisco: Harper & Row.

McNickle, D. (1992). *The hawk is hungry and other stories.* Tucson: University of Arizona Press.

Meyerson, J. (1990). *'Tambo: Life in an Andean village.* Austin: University of Texas Press.

Miller, W. (1959). *The cool world.* New York: Fawcett.

Misra, B. (1973). *Verrier Elwin: A pioneer Indian anthropologist.* New York: Asia.

Moeran, B. (1985). *Okubo diary: Portrait of a Japanese valley.* Stanford, CA: Stanford University Press.

Montell, G. (1997, October 24). An anthropologist's best-selling thriller. *Chronicle of Higher Education,* p. A8.

Motzafi-Haller, P. (1997). Writing birthright: On native anthropologists and the politics of representation. In D. E. Reed-Danahay (Ed.), *Auto/ethnography: Rewriting the self and the social* (pp. 195-222). New York: Berg.

Nader, L. (1969). Up the anthropologist: Perspectives gained from studying up. In D. Hymes (Ed.), *Reinventing anthropology* (pp. 284-311). New York: Random House.

Nakane, C. (1970). *Japanese society.* Berkeley: University of California Press.

Narayan, K. (1989). *Storytellers, saints and scoundrels: Folk narrative in Hindu religious teaching.* Philadelphia: University of Pennsylvania Press.

Narayan, K. (1993). How native is a "native" anthropologist? *American Anthropologist, 5,* 671-686.

Narayan, K. (1995a). Come out and serve. *Anthropology and Humanism, 20*(1), 51-59.

Narayan, K. (1995b). *Love stars and all that.* New York: Washington Square.

Nash, D., & Wintrob, R. (1972). The emergence of self-consciousness in ethnography. *Current Anthropology, 13,* 527-542.

Nash, J. (1980). A critique of social science roles in Latin America. In J. Nash & H. Safa (Eds.), *Sex and class in Latin America* (pp. 1-22). South Hadley, MA: Bergin & Garvey.

Nelson, R. K. (1980). *Shadow of the hunter: Stories of Eskimo life.* Chicago: University of Chicago Press.

Newton, E. (1993). My best informant's dress: The erotic equation in fieldwork. *Cultural Anthropology, 8,* 3-23.

Nimmo, H. A. (1994). *The songs of Salanda and other stories of Sulu.* Seattle: University of Washington Press.

Nimuendajú, C. (pseudonym of C. Unkel). (1939). *The Apinayé.* Washington, DC: Catholic University of America.

Nimuendajú, C. (pseudonym of C. Unkel). (1942). *The Serente.* Boston: Frederick Webb Hodge Anniversary Publication Fund.

Nimuendajú, C. (pseudonym of C. Unkel). (1946). *The eastern Timbira* (Publications in American Archaeology and Ethnology No. 14). Berkeley: University of California.

Nimuendajú, C. (pseudonym of C. Unkel). (1952). *The Tukuna.* Berkeley: University of California Press.

Nimuendajú, C. (pseudonym of C. Unkel). (1978). *Los mitos de creación y de destrucción del mundo como fundamentos de la religión de los Apapokuva-Guarani.* Lima: Centro Amazonico de Antropología y Aplicación Practica. (Original work published 1914)

Nolan, W. F. (1968). Chad Oliver. In W. F. Nolan (Ed.), *3 to the highest power: Bradbury, Oliver, Sturgeon* (pp. 109-160). New York: Avon.

Nordstrom, C., & Robben, A. C. G. M. (Eds.). (1995). *Fieldwork under fire: Contemporary studies of violence and survival.* Berkeley: University of California Press.

Ohnuki-Tierney, E. (1984). Native anthropologists. *American Ethnologist, 3,* 584-586.

Okely, J. (1992). Anthropology and autobiography: Participatory experience and embodied knowledge. In J. Okely & H. Callaway (Eds.), *Anthropology and autobiography* (pp. 1-28). London: Routledge.

Oliver, C. (1951, June). The boy next door. *Fantasy and Science Fiction.*

Oliver, (S.) C. (1952). *They builded a tower: The story of science fiction.* Unpublished master's thesis, University of Texas.

Oliver, C. (1954). *Shadows in the sun.* New York: Ballantine.

Oliver, C. (1957). *The winds of time.* New York: Doubleday.

Oliver, C. (1962). *Ecology and cultural continuity as contributing factors in the social organization of the Plains Indians.* Berkeley: University of California Press.

Oliver, C. (1967). *The wolf is my brother.* New York: Bantam.

Oliver, C. (1971). *The shores of another sea.* New York: Crown.

Oliver, C. (1981). *The discovery of humanity: An introduction to anthropology.* New York: Bantam.

Oliver, C. (1989). *Broken eagle.* New York: Bantam.

Osgood, C. (1953). *Winter.* New York: W. W. Norton.

Page, H. E. (1988). Dialogic principles of interactive learning in the ethnographic relationship. *Journal of Anthropological Research, 44,* 163-181.

Panini, M. N. (Ed.). (1991). *From the female eye: Accounts of women fieldworkers studying their own society.* Delhi: Hindustan.

Peters, L. (1981). *Ecstasy and healing in Nepal: An ethnopsychiatric study of Tamang shamanism.* Malibu, CA: Undena.

Pick, D. (1989). *Faces of degeneration: A European disorder, c. 1848-1918.* Cambridge: Cambridge University Press.

Pool, R. (1995). Breaking the conspiracy of silence: Some reflections on fieldwork and new modes of ethnographic writing. In K. Geuijen, D. Raven, & J. de Wolf (Eds.), *Post-modernism and anthropology: Theory and practice* (pp. 108-119). Assen-Maastricht, Netherlands: Van Gorcum.

Pozas, R. (1962). *Juan the Chamula: An ethnological re-creation of the life of a Mexican Indian.* Berkeley: University of California Press.

Prechtel, M. (1998). *Secrets of the talking jaguar: A Mayan shaman's journey to the heart of the indigenous soul.* New York: Jeremy P. Tarcher.

Price, R. (1998). *The convict and the colonel.* Boston: Beacon.

Price, R., & Price, S. (1992). *Equatoria.* New York: Routledge.

Prus, R., & Irini, S. (1980). *Hookers, rounders, and desk clerks: The social organization of the hotel community.* Salem, WI: Sheffield.

Prus, R., & Sharper, C. R. D. (1977). *Road hustler: Career contingencies of professional card and dice hustlers.* Lexington, MA: Lexington.

Rabinow, P. (1975). *Symbolic domination: Cultural form and historical change in Morocco.* Chicago: University of Chicago Press.

Rabinow, P. (1977). *Reflections on fieldwork in Morocco.* Berkeley: University of California Press.

Rabinow, P. (1985). Discourse and power: On the limits of ethnographic texts. *Dialectical Anthropology, 10,* 1-13.

Radin, P. (1920). Crashing Thunder: The autobiography of an American Indian. *University of California Publications in American Archaeology and Ethnology, 16,* 381-473.

Rang, S. (1997). Native anthropology and other problems. *Dialectical Anthropology, 22,* 23-49.

Rapport, N. (1997). Culture as conversation: Representation as conversation. In A. James, J. Hockey, & A. Dawson (Eds.), *After writing culture: Epistemology and praxis in contemporary anthropology* (pp. 177-193). New York: Routledge.

Read, K. E. (1986). *Return to the high valley.* Berkeley: University of California Press.

Reck, G. (1995). Resurrection. *Anthropology and Humanism, 20*(2), 160-164.

Record, P. (pseudonym of P. Drucker). (1969). *Tropical frontier.* New York: Alfred A. Knopf.

Reed-Danahay, D. E. (Ed.). (1997). *Auto/ethnography: Rewriting the self and the social.* New York: Berg.

Reichard, G. A. (1934). *Spider Woman: A story of Navajo weavers and chanters.* New York: Macmillan.

Reichs, K. J. (1997). *Déjà dead.* New York: Scribner.

Ribeiro, B. G. (1979). *Diário do Xingu.* São Paulo: Editora Paz e Terra.

Richards, D. (1994). *Masks of difference: Cultural representations in literature, anthropology and art.* Cambridge: Cambridge University Press.

Richardson, L. (1990). *Writing strategies: Reaching diverse audiences.* Newbury Park, CA: Sage.

Richardson, L., & Lockridge, E. (1991). *The sea monster*: An ethnographic drama. *Symbolic Interaction, 14,* 335-340.

Richardson, M. (1984). The museum. *Southern Review, 20,* 919-927.

Richardson, M. (1990). *Cry lonesome and other accounts of the anthropologist's project.* Albany: State University of New York Press.

Riesman, P. (1977). *Freedom in Fulani social life.* Chicago: University of Chicago Press.

Rivière, P. (1980). Review of *The headman and I: Ambiguity and ambivalence in the field-working experience. American Ethnologist, 7,* 213.

Rogers, S. C. (1997). Explorations in terra cognita. *American Anthropologist, 99,* 717-719.

Rosaldo, R. I. (1989). *Culture and truth: The remaking of social analysis.* Boston: Beacon.

Rose, D. (1987). *Black American street life.* Philadelphia: University of Pennsylvania Press.

Rose, D. (1990). *Living the ethnographic life.* Newbury Park, CA: Sage.

Rosenhan, D. L. (1973). On being sane in insane places. *Science, 179,* 250-258.

Ruby, J. (Ed.). (1982). *A crack in the mirror: Reflexive perspectives in anthropology.* Philadelphia: University of Pennsylvania Press.

Ruiz, O. (1995). Testimony. *Anthropology and Humanism, 20*(2), 164-166.

Salerno, N. F., & Vanderburgh, R. M. (1980). *Shaman's daughter.* New York: Dell.

Scheper-Hughes, N. (1992). *Death without weeping: The violence of everyday life in Brazil.* Berkeley: University of California Press.

Schevill, J., & Gordon, A. (1996). *The myth of the docile woman.* San Francisco: California OnStage.

Schipper, K. (1982). *Le corps taoïste.* Paris: Librairie Arthème Fayard.

Schmidt, N. J. (1981). The nature of ethnographic fiction: A further inquiry. *Anthropology and Humanism Quarterly, 6*(1), 8-18.

Schmidt, N. J. (1984). Ethnographic fiction: Anthropology's hidden literary style. *Anthropology and Humanism Quarterly, 9*(4), 11-14.

Scholte, B. (1969). Toward a reflexive and critical anthropology. In D. Hymes (Ed.), *Reinventing anthropology* (pp. 430-457). New York: Random House.

Schrijvers, J. (1991). Dialectics of a dialogical ideal: Studying down, studying sideways and studying up. In L. Nencel & P. Pels (Eds.), *Constructing knowledge: Authority and critique in social science* (pp. 162-179). London: Sage.

Seligman, C. G., & Seligman, B. Z. (1911). *The Veddas.* The Hague: Osterhout.

Seligman, C. G., & Seligman, B. Z. (1932). *Pagan tribes of the Nilotic Sudan.* London.

Seremetakis, C. N. (1993). *The last word: Women, death and divination in inner Mani.* Chicago: University of Chicago Press.

Shaw, C. (1930). *The jack-roller: A delinquent boy's own story.* Chicago: University of Chicago Press.

Shostak, M. (1981). *Nisa: The life and words of a !Kung woman.* Cambridge, MA: Harvard University Press.

Shryock, A. (1996). Tribes and the print trade: Notes from the margins of literate culture in Jordan. *American Anthropologist, 98,* 26-40.

Shryock, A. (1997). *Nationalism and the genealogical imagination: Oral history and textual authority in tribal Jordan.* Berkeley: University of California Press.

Simonelli, J. M., & Winters, C. D. (1997). *Crossing between worlds: The Navajos of Canyon de Chelly.* Santa Fe, NM: School of American Research Press.

Skafte, P. (1986). Narayan's road: The wheel of change in Nepal. *Anthropology and Humanism Quarterly, 11,* 102-104.

Skomal, S. (1995). Monkey business in Chiapas. *Anthropology Newsletter, 36*(7), 41.

Springwater, C. (1996). Stories of red clay: Man of the mesa. *Anthropology and Humanism, 21*(2), 192-199.

Stacey, J. (1988). Can there be a feminist ethnography? *Women's Studies International Forum, 11,* 21-27.

Stacey, J. (1990). *Brave new families: Stories of domestic upheaval in late-twentieth-century America.* New York: Basic Books.

Stacey, J. (1995). Disloyal to the disciplines: A feminist trajectory in the borderlands. In D. C. Stanton & A. J. Steward (Eds.), *Feminisms in the academy* (pp. 311-329). Ann Arbor: University of Michigan Press.

Stanley, L., & Wise, S. (1983). *Breaking out: Feminist consciousness and feminist research.* London: Routledge & Kegan Paul.

Stavenhagen, R. (1971). Decolonizing applied social sciences. *Human Organization, 39,* 333-357.

Stewart, J. O. (1971). *Last cool days.* London: Andre Deutsch.

Stewart, J. O. (1975). *Curving road.* Urbana: University of Illinois Press.

Stewart, J. O. (1989). *Drinkers, drummers, and decent folk: Ethnographic narratives of village Trinidad.* Albany: State University of New York Press.

Stewart, J. O. (1995). Carnival mourning. In B. Grindal & F. Salamone (Eds.), *Bridges to hu-*

manity (pp. 213-230). Prospect Heights, IL: Waveland.

Stocking, G. W., Jr. (1983). The ethnographer's magic: Fieldwork in British anthropology from Tylor to Malinowski. In G. W. Stocking, Jr. (Ed.), *Observers observed: Essays on ethnographic research* (pp. 70-120). Madison: University of Wisconsin Press.

Stocking, G. W., Jr. (1995). *After Tylor: British social anthropology 1888-1951*. Madison: University of Wisconsin Press.

Stoller, P. (1989a). *The taste of ethnographic things: The senses in anthropology*. Philadelphia: University of Pennsylvania Press.

Stoller, P. (1989b). *Fusion of the worlds: An ethnography of possession among the Songhay of Niger*. Chicago: University of Chicago Press.

Stoller, P., & Olkes, C. (1987). *In sorcery's shadow: A memoir of apprenticeship among the Songhay of Niger*. Chicago: University of Chicago Press.

Strathern, M. (1987a). The limits of auto-anthropology. In A. Jackson (Ed.), *Anthropology at home* (pp. 59-67). London: Tavistock.

Strathern, M. (1987b). Out of context: The persuasive fictions of anthropology. *Current Anthropology, 28*, 251-282.

Talbot, D. A. (1915). *Woman's mysteries of a primitive people: The Ibibios of southern Nigeria*. London: Frank Cass.

Talbot, P. A. (1923). *Life in Southern Nigeria: The magic, beliefs, and customs of the Ibibio tribe*. London: Frank Cass.

Talbot, P. A. (1969). *The peoples of southern Nigeria*. London: Frank Cass.

Tarn, N. (with Prechtel, M.). (1997). *Scandals in the house of birds: Shamans and priests on Lake Atitlan*. New York: Marsilio.

Tedlock, B. (1982). *Time and the highland Maya*. Albuquerque: University of New Mexico Press.

Tedlock, B. (1986). Keeping the breath nearby. *Anthropology and Humanism Quarterly, 11*, 92-94.

Tedlock, B. (1991). From participant observation to the observation of participation: The emergence of narrative ethnography. *Journal of Anthropological Research, 47*, 69-94.

Tedlock, B. (1995). Works and wives: On the sexual division of textual labor. In R. Behar & D. A. Gordon (Eds.), *Women writing cul-*

ture (pp. 267-286). Berkeley: University of California Press.

Tedlock, D. (1979). The analogical tradition and the emergence of a dialogical anthropology. *Journal of Anthropological Research, 35*, 387-400.

Tedlock, D. (1986). *The translator* or *Why the crocodile was not disillusioned*: A play in one act. *Translation Review, 20*, 6-8.

Tedlock, D. (1987). Questions concerning dialogical anthropology. *Journal of Anthropological Research, 43*, 325-344.

Tedlock, D. (1998, April 24-25). *Man of Rabinal: The Mayan dance of the trumpets of sacrifice*. Linguistic and cultural translation of a Mayan play produced and performed in the Katharine Cornell Theater, State University of New York at Buffalo.

Tedlock, D., & Mannheim, B. (Eds.). (1995). *The dialogic emergence of culture*. Urbana: University of Illinois Press.

Tehindrazanarivelo, E. D. (1997). Fieldwork: The dance of power. *Anthropology and Humanism, 22*(1), 54-60.

Terrio, S. J. (1998). Deconstructing fieldwork in contemporary urban France. *Anthropological Quarterly, 71*(1), 18-31.

Thomas, E. M. (1987). *Reindeer moon*. New York: Pocket Books.

Thomas, J. (1983). Toward a critical ethnography. *Urban Life, 11*, 477-490.

Thomas, W. I., & Znaniecki, G. (1918-1920). *The Polish peasant in Europe and America* (5 vols.). Boston: Richard G. Badger.

Thornton, R. J. (1988). The rhetoric of ethnographic holism. *Cultural Anthropology, 3*, 285-303.

Traweek, S. (1988). *Beamtimes and lifetimes: The world of high energy physicists*. Cambridge, MA: Harvard University Press.

Trinh T. M. (1989). *Woman, native, other: Writing postcoloniality and feminism*. Bloomington: Indiana University Press.

Turnbull, C. (1961). *The forest people: A study of the Pygmies of the Congo*. New York: Simon & Schuster.

Turnbull, C. (1965). *Wayward servants: The two worlds of the African Pygmies*. Garden City, NY: Natural History Press.

Turner, E. (1985). Prologue: From the Ndembu to Broadway. In E. Turner (Ed.), *On the edge of the bush: Anthropology as experience* (pp. 1-15). Tucson: University of Arizona Press.

Turner, E. (1987). *The Spirit and the drum: A memoir of Africa.* Tucson: University of Arizona Press.

Turner, E. (1993). The reality of spirits: A tabooed or permitted field of study? *Anthropology of Consciousness, 4*(1), 9-12.

Turner, E. (1996). *The hands feel it: Healing and spirit presence among a northern Alaskan people.* De Kalb: Northern Illinois University Press.

Turner, V. (1967). *The forest of symbols: Aspects of Ndembu ritual.* Ithaca, NY: Cornell University Press.

Turner, V. (1969). *The ritual process: Structure and anti-structure.* Ithaca, NY: Cornell University Press.

Tyler, S. A. (1987a). *The unspeakable: Discourse, dialogue, and rhetoric in the postmodern world.* Madison: University of Wisconsin Press.

Tyler, S. A. (1987b). On "writing-up/off" as "speaking-for." *Journal of Anthropological Research, 43,* 338-342.

Tylor, E. B. (1884). American aspects of anthropology. In *Report of the 54th meeting of the British Association for the Advancement of Science* (pp. 898-924). London: British Association for the Advancement of Science.

Underhill, R. (1936). *Chona, Papago woman.* Menasha, WI: American Anthropological Association.

Underhill, R. (1940). *Hawk over whirlpools.* New York: J. J. Augustin.

Urton, G. (1981). *At the crossroads of the earth and the sky: An Andean cosmology.* Austin: University of Texas Press.

Van Maanen, J. (1988). *Tales of the field: On writing ethnography.* Chicago: University of Chicago Press.

Visweswaran, K. (1988). Defining feminist ethnography. *Inscriptions, 3-4,* 7-44.

Visweswaran, K. (1994). *Fictions of feminist ethnography.* Minneapolis: University of Minnesota Press.

Visweswaran, K. (1998). "Wild West" anthropology and the disciplining of gender. In H. Silverberg (Ed.), *Gender and American social science: The formative years*

(pp. 86-123). Princeton, NJ: Princeton University Press.

Wade, P. (1993). Sexuality and masculinity among Colombian blacks. In D. Bell, P. Caplan, & W. J. Karim (Eds.), *Gendered fields: Women, men and ethnography* (pp. 199-214). London: Routledge.

Wafer, J. (1991). *The taste of blood: Spirit possession in Brazilian candomblé.* Philadelphia: University of Pennsylvania Press.

Wafer, J. (1996). Out of the closet and into print: Sexual identity in the textual field. In E. Lewin & W. L. Leap (Eds.), *Out in the field: Reflections of lesbian and gay anthropologists* (pp. 261-273). Urbana: University of Illinois Press.

Waldorf, S. (1986). The pig man. *Anthropology and Humanism Quarterly, 11,* 95-101.

Ward, M. C. (1989). *Nest in the wind: Adventures in anthropology on a tropical island.* Prospect Heights, IL: Waveland.

Webster, S. (1982). Dialogue and fiction in ethnography. *Dialectical Anthropology, 7,* 91-114.

Wellmer, A. (1971). *Critical theory of society.* New York: Herder & Herder.

Wendt, A. (1973). *Sons for the return home.* Auckland, New Zealand: Longman Paul.

Wendt, A. (1979). *Leaves of the banyan tree.* Harmondsworth: Penguin.

Weston, K. (1991). *Families we choose: Lesbians, gays, kinship.* New York: Columbia University Press.

Weston, K. (1993). Lesbian/gay studies in the house of anthropology. *Annual Review of Anthropology, 22,* 339-367.

Willis, W. S. (1969). Skeletons in the anthropological closet. In D. Hymes (Ed.), *Reinventing anthropology* (pp. 121-152). New York: Random House.

Willson, M. (1997). Playing the dance, dancing the game: Race, sex and stereotype in anthropological fieldwork. *Ethnos, 62*(3-4), 24-48.

Wilson, C. (1974). *Crazy February: Death and life in the Maya highlands of Mexico.* Berkeley: University of California Press.

Wolf, M. A. (1992). *A thrice-told tale: Feminism, postmodernism, and ethnographic responsibility.* Stanford, CA: Stanford University Press.

Wolff, K. H. (1964). Surrender and community study: The study of Loma. In A. J. Vidich, J.

Bensman, & M. R. Stein (Eds.), *Reflections on community studies* (pp. 233-263). New York: John Wiley.

Yang, M. M. C. (1945). *A Chinese village.* New York: Columbia University Press.

Yang, M. M. C. (1972). How *A Chinese village* was written. In S. T. Kimball & J. B. Watson (Eds.), *Crossing cultural boundaries: The anthropological experience* (pp. 63-73). San Francisco: Chandler.

Young, R. J. C. (1995). *Colonial desire: Hybridity in theory, culture and race.* London: Routledge.

Yu, P.-L. (1997). *Hungry lightning: Notes of a woman anthropologist in Venezuela.* Albuquerque: University of New Mexico Press.

Zedeño, M. N. (1994). Saint versus the hummingbird. *Anthropology and Humanism, 19*(2), 162-164.

18

ANALYZING INTERPRETIVE PRACTICE

◆ Jaber F. Gubrium and James A. Holstein

Qualitative inquiry's analytic pendulum is constantly in motion. There have been times when naturalism was on the upswing, when the richly detailed description of social worlds was the goal. At other times, analysis has shifted toward the processes by which these worlds and their experiences are socially constructed. The pendulum has even doubled back on itself as postmodern sensibilities have refocused the analytic project on itself, viewing it as a source of social reality in its own right (see Gubrium & Holstein, 1997). Although it can be unsettling, this oscillation invariably clears new space for growth.

This chapter capitalizes on a momentum that is currently building among qualitative researchers interested in the social accomplishment of meaning and order. As social constructionist analysis expands, diversifies, and claims an increasingly prominent place on the qualitative scene, analysts are drawing new inspiration from ingenious "misreadings" and innovative admixtures of canonical sources. Recently, ethnomethodological sensibilities have been appropriated to the constructionist move (see Gubrium & Holstein, 1997; Holstein & Gubrium, 1994, 2000), heightening and broadening its analytic acuity. At the same time, yet riding a different current in the discursive and linguistic flow of the social sciences, poststructuralist discourse analysis has suffused constructionism with cultural, institutional, and historical concerns as well. This chapter outlines one attempt to explore and extend the discursive and interactional terrain that is emerging at the intersection of ethnomethodology and Foucauldian discourse analysis.

For some time, qualitative researchers have been interested in documenting the processes by which social reality is constructed, managed, and sustained. Alfred Schutz's (1962, 1964, 1967, 1970) social phenomenology, Peter Berger and Thomas Luckmann's (1967) social constructionism, and process-oriented strains of symbolic interactionism (e.g., Blumer, 1969; Hewitt, 1997; Weigert, 1981) have all contributed to the constructionist project, but ethnomethodology arguably has been the most analytically radical and empirically productive in specifying the actual procedures through which social order is accomplished (see Garfinkel, 1967; Heritage, 1984; Holstein & Gubrium, 1994; Maynard & Clayman, 1991; Mehan & Wood, 1975; Pollner, 1987, 1991).[1] The analytic emphasis throughout has been on the question of *how* social reality is constructed, with ethnomethodology taking the lead in documenting the mechanisms by which this is accomplished in everyday life.

Recently, a new set of concerns has emerged in relation to ethnomethodology, reflecting a heretofore suspended interest in *what* is being accomplished, under *what* conditions, and out of *what* resources. Older naturalistic questions are being resurrected, but with a more analytically sophisticated, empirically sensitive mien. Analyses of reality construction are now reengaging questions concerning the broad cultural and institutional contexts of meaning making and social order. The emerging empirical horizons, although still centered on processes of social accomplishment, are increasingly viewed in terms of "interpretive practice"—the constellation of procedures, conditions, and resources through which reality is apprehended, understood, organized, and conveyed in everyday life (Gubrium & Holstein, 1997; Holstein, 1993; Holstein & Gubrium, 1994, 2000). Interpretive practice engages both the *hows* and the *whats* of social reality; it is centered both in how people methodically construct their experiences and their worlds and in the configurations of meaning and institutional life that inform and shape their reality-constituting activity. A growing attention to both the *hows* and the *whats* of the social construction process echoes Karl Marx's (1956) adage that people actively construct their worlds, but not completely on, or in, their own terms. An analytics of interpretive practice is emerging to address these dual concerns, complete with its own conceptual vocabulary. This chapter will sketch a version of this analytics, beginning from its conceptual foundations in several major sociological traditions.

◆ Foundational Matters

An analytics of interpretive practice has diverse conceptual bases. These range from Schutz's development of a social phenomenology to the related empirical concerns embodied in ethnomethodological programs of research developed in the wake of Harold Garfinkel's (1967) early studies, to studies of talk and interaction (see Sacks, 1992; Silverman, 1998), and to the contemporaneous studies of institutional and historical discourses presented by Michel Foucault (see Dreyfus & Rabinow, 1982). Let us consider these in turn as they point us toward more recent developments.

Phenomenological Background

Edmund Husserl's (1970) philosophical phenomenology provides the point of departure for Schutz and other social phenomenologists. Concerned with the experiential underpinnings of knowledge, Husserl argues that the relation between perception and its objects is not passive. Rather, human consciousness actively constitutes objects of experience. Consciousness, in other words, is always consciousness-of-something. It does not stand alone, over and above experience, more or less immaculately perceiving and conceiving objects and actions but, instead, exists always already—from the start—as a constitutive part of what it is conscious of. Although the term *construction* came into fashion much later, we might say that consciousness constructs as much as it perceives the world. Husserl's project is to investigate the structures of consciousness that make it possible to apprehend an empirical world.

Schutz (1962, 1964, 1967, 1970) turns Husserl's philosophical project toward the ways in which ordinary members of society attend to their everyday lives, introducing a set of tenets that also align with ethnomethodological studies. Schutz argues that the social sciences should focus on the ways that the life world—the world every individual takes for granted—is experienced by its members. He cautions that "the safeguarding of [this] subjective point of view is the only but sufficient guarantee that the world of social reality will not be replaced by a fictional non-existing world constructed by the scientific observer" (1964, p. 8). From this perspective, the scientific observer deals with how the social world is made meaningful. The observer's focus is on *how* members of the social world apprehend and act upon the objects of their experience as if they are things separate and distinct from themselves. Emile Durkheim's (1961, 1964) formulation of a sociology based on the emergence of categories sui generis, separate and distinct from individual thought and action, resonates with this aim.

This is a radical departure from the assumptions underlying what Schutz calls "the natural attitude," which is the stance that takes the world to be principally "out there," so to speak, categorically distinct from acts of perception or interpretation. In the natural attitude, it is assumed that the life world exists before members are present and it will be there after they depart. Schutz's recommendation for studying members' attention to this life world is to first "bracket" it for analytic purposes. That is, the analyst must temporarily set aside belief in its reality. This makes it possible to view the constitutive processes—the *hows*—by which a separate and distinct empirical world becomes an objective reality for members. Ontological judgments about the nature and essence of things and events are temporarily suspended so that the observer can focus on the ways that members of the life world subjectively constitute the objects and events they take to be real—that is, to exist independent of their attention to, and presence in, the world.

Schutz's orientation to the subjectivity of the life world pointed him to the commonsense knowledge that members use to "objectify" (make into objects) its social forms. He noted that individuals approach the life world with a stock of knowledge composed of ordinary constructs and categories that are social in origin. These images, folk theories, beliefs, values, and attitudes are applied to aspects of experience, thus making them meaningful and giving them a semblance of everyday familiarity. The stock of knowledge produces a world with which members already seem to be acquainted. In part this is because of the categorical manner by which knowledge of particular objects and events is articulated. The myriad phenomena of everyday life are subsumed under a delimited number of shared constructs (or types). These "typifications" make it possible for individuals to account rationally for experience, rendering various things and sundry occurrences recognizable as particular types of objects or events. Typification, in other words, organizes the flux of life into recognizable form, making it meaningful. In turn, as experience is given shape, the stock of knowledge is itself elaborated and altered in practice.

Ordinary language is the modus operandi. In the natural attitude, the meaning of a word is taken principally to be what it references or stands for in the real world, following a correspondence theory of meaning; in this framework, the leading task of language is to convey accurate information. Viewed as a process of typification, however, words and categories are the constitutive building blocks of the social world. Typification through ordinary language use creates the sense among users that the life world is familiarly organized and substantial, which simultaneously gives it shape and meaning. Individuals who interact with one another do so in an environment that is concurrently constructed and experienced in fundamentally the same terms by all parties, even while mistakes may be made in its particular apprehensions. Taking for granted that we intersubjectively share the same reality, we assume further that we can understand each other in its terms. Intersubjectivity is thus a social accomplishment, a set of understandings sustained in and through the shared assumptions of interaction and recurrently sustained in processes of typification.

Ethnomethodological Formulations

Although indebted to Schutz, ethnomethodology is not a mere extension of his social phenomenological program. Ethnomethodology addresses the problem of order by combining a "phenomenological sensibility" (Maynard & Clayman, 1991) with a paramount concern for everyday social practice (Garfinkel, 1967). From an ethnomethodological standpoint, the social world's facticity is accomplished by way of members' constitutive interactional work, the mechanics of which produces and maintains the accountable circumstances of their lives.[2] In a manner of speaking, ethnomethodologists focus on how members actually "do" social life, aiming in particular to document how they concretely construct and sustain social entities, such as gender, self, and family.

Although Garfinkel's studies were phenomenologically informed, his overall project also was a response to his teacher Talcott Parsons's theory of action (Heritage, 1984; Lynch, 1993). According to Parsons, social order is made possible through socially integrating systems of norms and values, a view that leaves little room for the everyday production of social order. Garfinkel sought an alternative to this approach, which in his judgment portrays actors as "cultural dopes" who automatically respond to external social forces and internalized moral imperatives. Garfinkel's (1952) response was a vision of social order built from the socially contingent, practical reasoning of ordinary members of society. He viewed members as possessing ordinary linguistic and interactional skills through which the accountable features of everyday life are produced. This approach deeply implicates members in the production of social order. Rather than more or less playing out moral directives, Garfinkel conceptualized members as actively using them, thus *working* to give their world a sense of orderliness. Ethnomethodology's research topic became members' integral "methods" for accomplishing everyday reality.

The empirical investigation of members' methods takes its point of departure from phenomenological bracketing. Adopting the parallel policy of "ethnomethodological indifference" (Garfinkel & Sacks, 1970), the investigator temporarily suspends all commitments to a priori or privileged versions of the social world, focusing instead on how members accomplish a sense of social order. Social realities such as crime or mental illness are not taken for granted; instead, belief in them is temporarily suspended in order to make visible how they become realities for those concerned. Analysis then centers on the ordinary constitutive work that produces the locally unchallenged appearance of stable realities. This policy vigorously resists judgmental characterizations of the correctness of members' activities. Contrary to the common sociological tendency to ironicize and criticize commonsense formulations from the standpoint of ostensibly correct sociological views, ethnomethodology takes members' practical reasoning for what it is—circumstantially adequate ways of interpersonally orienting to and interpreting the world at hand. The abiding guideline is succinctly conveyed by Melvin Pollner (personal communication, May 1983): "Don't argue with the members!"

Ethnomethodologists have examined many facets of social order. One aim has been to document how recognizable structures of behavior, systems of motivation, or causal ties between motivations and social structures are evidenced in members' practical reasoning (Zimmerman & Wieder, 1970). Whereas conventional sociology orients to rules, norms, and shared meanings as exogenous explanations for members' actions, ethnomethodology turns this around to consider how members themselves orient to and use rules, norms, and shared meanings to account for the regularity of their actions. Ethnomethodology sets aside the idea that actions are externally rule governed or internally motivated in order to observe how members themselves establish and sustain social regularities. The appearance of action as being the consequence of a rule is treated as just that—the *appearance* of action as compliant or non-compliant. In "accounting" for their actions by prospectively invoking rules or retrospectively offering rule-motivated explanations for action, members convey a sense of structure and order and, in the process, cast their actions as rational, coherent, precedented, and reproducible for all practical purposes (Zimmerman, 1970).

For example, a juror in the midst of deliberation may account for her opinion by saying that the judge's instructions on how to consider the case in question compel her to think as she does. She actively uses the judge's instructions to make sense of her opinion, thereby giving it the semblance of rationality, legality, and correctness because it was formed "according to the rule" invoked (Holstein, 1983). In contrast, another juror might account for his opinion by saying that it is serving the interests of justice, citing a value or moral principle in explanation (Maynard & Manzo, 1993). From an ethnomethodological standpoint, the rationality or correctness of these opinions and the reasoning involved are not at issue. Instead, the focus is on the individuals' use of instructions, values, moral principles, and other accounts to construct a sense of coherence in social action, in this case a shared understanding among jurors of what led them to form their opinions and reach a verdict.

The accountable display of social order forms ethnomethodology's analytic horizon. Rather than assuming a priori that members share meanings and definitions of situations, ethnomethodologists consider how members achieve them by applying a native capacity to account "artfully" for their actions, rendering them orderly. Social order is not externally imposed by proverbial social forces, nor is it the expression of more or less socialized members of society; instead, ethnomethodologists view it as locally produced by way of the practices of mundane reason (Pollner, 1987). If social order is accomplished in and through its practices, then social worlds and circumstances are self-generating. Members, as we noted earlier, are continually "doing" social life in the very actions they take to communicate and make sense of it. Their language games, to borrow

from Ludwig Wittgenstein (1958), virtually constitute their everyday realities; in this sense, the games are "forms of life."

This implicates two properties of ordinary social action. First, all actions and objects are "indexical"; they depend upon (or "index") context. Objects and events have equivocal or indeterminate meanings without a discernible context. It is through contextualization that practical meaning is derived. Second, the circumstances that provide meaningful contexts are themselves self-generating. Each reference to, or account for, an action—such as the juror's comment that she is expressly following the judge's directives—establishes a context (in this case, of procedural dutifulness) for evaluating the selfsame and related actions of the juror herself and the actions of others. The account simultaneously establishes a particular context, which in turn becomes a basis for the juror's making her own and others' actions accountable. Having established this context, the juror can then virtually turn around and account for her actions by saying, for example, "That's why I feel as I do," in effect parlaying the context she has constructed for her actions into something recognizable and reasonable (accountable), if not ultimately acceptable. Practical reasoning, in other words, is simultaneously in and about the settings to which it orients, and that it describes. Social order and its practical realities are thus "reflexive." Accounts or descriptions of a setting constitute that setting while they are simultaneously being shaped by the contexts they constitute.

Procedurally, ethnomethodological research is keenly attuned to naturally occurring talk and social interaction, orienting to them as constitutive elements of the settings studied (see Atkinson & Drew, 1979; Maynard, 1984, 1989; Mehan & Wood, 1975; Sacks, 1972). This has taken different empirical directions, in part depending upon whether the interactive meanings or the structure of talk is emphasized. Ethnographic studies tend to focus on locally crafted meanings and the settings within which social interaction constitutes the practical realities in question. Such studies consider the situated content of talk in relation to local meaning making (see Gubrium, 1992; Holstein, 1993; Lynch & Bogen, 1996; Miller, 1991; Pollner, 1987; Wieder, 1988). They combine attention to how social order is built up in everyday communication with detailed descriptions of place settings as those settings and their local understandings and perspectives mediate the meaning of what is said in the course of social interaction. The texts produced from such studies are highly descriptive of everyday life, with both conversational extracts from the settings and ethnographic accounts of interaction used to convey the methodical production of the subject matter in question. To the extent the analysis of talk in relation to social interaction and setting is in place, this tends to take the form of (non-Foucauldian) discourse analysis (DA), emphasizing how talk and conversation are used to make meaning (see Potter, 1996, 1997; Potter & Wetherell, 1987).

Studies that emphasize the structure of talk itself examine the conversational "machinery" through which meaning emerges. The focus here is on the sequential, utterance-by-utterance, socially structuring features of talk or "talk-in-interaction," the now familiar bailiwick of conversation analysis (CA; see Heritage, 1984; Sacks, Schegloff, & Jefferson, 1974; Silverman, 1998; Zimmerman, 1988; see also Silverman, Chapter 31, this volume). The analyses produced from such studies are detailed explications of the communicative processes by which speakers methodically and sequentially construct their concerns in conversational practice. Often bereft of ethnographic detail except for brief lead-ins that describe place settings, the analytic sense conveyed is that biographical and social particulars can be understood as artifacts of the unfolding conversational machinery, although the analysis of what is called "institutional talk" or "talk at work" has struck a greater balance in this regard (see, for example, Drew & Heritage, 1992). Whereas some contend that CA's connection to ethnomethodology is tenuous because of this lack of concern with ethnographic detail (Atkinson, 1988; Lynch, 1993; Lynch & Bogen, 1994; for counterarguments, see Maynard & Clayman, 1991; ten Have, 1990), CA clearly shares ethnomethodology's interest in the local and methodical construction of social action (Maynard & Clayman, 1991).

John Heritage (1984) summarizes the fundamentals of conversation analysis in three premises. First, interaction is sequentially organized, and this may be observed in the regularities of ordinary conversation. All aspects of interaction can be found to exhibit stable and identifiable features that are independent of speakers' individual characteristics. This sets the stage for the analysis of talk as structured in and through social interaction, not by internal sources such as motives or by external determinants such as social status. Second, social interaction is contextually oriented in that talk is simultaneously productive of, and reflects, the circumstances of its production. This premise highlights both the local conditioning and the local constructiveness of talk and interaction, exhibiting the dual properties of indexicality and reflexivity noted earlier. Third, these properties characterize all social interaction, so that no form of talk or interactive detail can be dismissed as irrelevant.

Conversation analysis has come under fire from ethnomethodologists who argue that the in situ details of everyday life are ignored at the risk of reducing social life to recorded talk and conversational sequencing. Michael Lynch, for example, has drawn a parallel between CA and molecular biology. On one hand, this serves to underscore Lynch's claims about CA's basic formalism and scientism. On the other, it projects the image of conversation as a relatively predictable set of socially structured techniques through which orderly social activities are assembled. Conversation analysts, according to Lynch (1993), attempt to describe "a simple order of structural elements and rules for combining them, and thus they undertake a reductionist program not unlike molecular biology" (p. 259), which attempts to deconstruct DNA for its molecular structures and rules of combination.

As a "molecular sociology" (Lynch, 1993), CA focuses on the normative, sequential "machinery" of conversation that constitutes social action. This machinery in many ways inverts conventional understandings of human agency, substituting the demands of a moral order of conversation for psychological and motivational imperatives. Although this does not strip participants of all agency, it does place them in the midst of a "liberal economy" of conversational rights and obligations (Lynch, 1993) that tests ethnomethodological tolerance for deterministic formulations.

In contrast to what Lynch and David Bogen (1994) have labeled the "enriched positivism" of CA, Garfinkel, Lynch, and others have elaborated what they refer to as a "postanalytic" ethnomethodology that is less inclined to universalistic generalizations regarding the enduring structures or machinery of social interaction (see Garfinkel, 1988; Lynch, 1993; Lynch & Bogen, 1996). This program of research centers on the highly localized competencies that constitute specific domains of everyday "work," especially the (bench)work of astronomers (Garfinkel, Lynch, & Livingston, 1981), biologists and neurologists (Lynch, 1985), and mathematicians (Livingston, 1986). The aim is to document the "haecceity"—the "just thisness"—of social practices within circumscribed domains of knowledge and activity (Lynch, 1993). The practical details of the real-time work of these activities are viewed as *incarnate* features of the knowledges they produce. It is impossible to separate the knowledges from the highly particularized occasions of their production. The approach is theoretically minimalist in that it resists a priori conceptualization or categorization, especially historical time, while advocating detailed descriptive studies of the specific, local practices that manifest order and render it accountable (Bogen & Lynch, 1993).

Despite their success at displaying a panoply of social accomplishment practices, CA and postanalytic ethnomethodology in their separate ways tend to disregard an important balance in the conceptualizations of talk, setting, and social interaction that was evident in Garfinkel's early work and Harvey Sacks's (1992) pioneering lectures on conversational practice (see Silverman, 1998, and Chapter 31, this volume). Neither Garfinkel nor Sacks envisioned the machinery of conversation as productive of recognizable social forms in its own right. Attention to the constitutive *hows* of social realities was balanced with attention to the meaningful *whats*. Settings, cultural understandings, and their everyday mediations were viewed as reflexively interwoven with talk and social interaction (see Silverman, Chapter 31, this volume). Sacks, in particular, understood culture to be a matter of practice, something that served as a resource for discerning the possible linkages of utterances and exchanges. Whether they wrote of (Garfinkel's) "good organizational reasons" or (Sacks's) "membership categorization devices," both initially avoided the reduction of social practice to highly localized or momentary haecceities of any kind.

As such, some of the original promise of ethnomethodology has been short-circuited as CA and postanalytic ethnomethodology have increasingly restricted their investigations to the relation between social practices and the immediate accounts of those practices. If the entire goal of postanalytic and CA projects is to describe the accounting practices by which descriptions are made intelligible in the immediate circumstances of their production, then constructionists may need to formulate a new project that retains ethnomethodology's interactional sensibilities while extending its scope to both the constitutive and constituted *whats* of everyday life. Michel Foucault, among others, is a valuable resource for such a project.

Foucauldian Discourse Analysis

Whereas ethnomethodology engages the accomplishment of everyday life at the interactional level, Foucault has undertaken a parallel project in a different empirical register. Appearing on the analytic stage during the early 1960s, at about the same time ethnomethodologists did, Foucault considers how historically and culturally located systems of power/knowledge construct subjects and their worlds. Foucauldians refer to these systems as "discourses," emphasizing that they are not merely bodies of ideas, ideologies, or other symbolic formulations, but are also working attitudes, modes of address, terms of reference, and courses of action suffused into social practices. Foucault (1972) himself explains that discourses are not "a mere intersection of things and words: an obscure web of things, and a manifest, visible, colored chain of words" (p. 48). Rather, they are "practices that systematically form the objects [and subjects] of which they speak" (p. 49). Even the design of buildings such as prisons reveals the social logic that specifies ways of interpreting persons and the physical and social landscapes they occupy (Foucault, 1979).

As in the ethnomethodological view of social interaction, Foucault views discourse as socially reflexive, both constitutive and meaningfully descriptive of the world and its subjects. But, for him, the analytic accent is as much on the constructive *whats* that discourse constitutes as it is on the *hows* of discursive technology. While this represents a swing of the analytic pendulum toward the culturally "natural," Foucault's treatment of discourse as social practice suggests, in particular, the importance of understanding the practices of subjectivity. If he offers a vision of subjects and objects constituted through discourse, he also allows for an unwittingly active subject who shapes discourse and puts it to work (Best & Kellner, 1991). As Foucault (1988) explains:

> If now I am interested . . . in the way in which the subject constitutes himself in an active fashion, by the practices of the self, these practices are nevertheless not something that the individual invents by himself. They are patterns that he finds in his culture and which are proposed, suggested and imposed on him by his culture, his society and his social group. (p. 11)

This complements ethnomethodology's interest in documenting the accomplishment of order in the everyday practice of talk and social interaction. Foucault is particularly concerned with social locations or institutional sites—the asylum, the hospital, and the prison, for example—that specify the practical operation of discourses, linking the discourse of particular subjectivities with the construction of lived experience. As in ethnomethodology, there is an interest in the constitutive quality of systems of discourse; it is an orientation to practice that views social worlds and their subjectivities as always already embedded and embodied in its discursive conventions.

Several commentators have pointed to the striking parallel between what Foucault (1980) refers to as systems of "power/knowledge" (or discourses) and ethnomethodology's formulation of the constitutive power of language use (Atkinson, 1995; Gubrium & Holstein, 1997; Heritage, 1997; Miller, 1997b; Potter, 1996; Prior, 1997; Silverman, 1993). The apparent correspondence suggests that what Foucault documents historically as "discourses-in-practice" in varied institutional or cultural sites may be likened to what ethnomethodology traces as "discursive practice" in varied forms of social interaction.[3] We will continue to apply these terms—*discourses-in-practice* and *discursive practice*—throughout this chapter to emphasize the parallel.

Although ethnomethodologists and Foucauldians draw from different intellectual traditions and work in distinct empirical registers, we want to emphasize their respective concerns with social practice; they both attend to the reflexivity of discourse. Neither discourse-in-practice nor discursive practice is viewed as being caused or explained by external social forces or internal motives; rather, both are taken to be the working mechanism of social life itself, as actually known or performed in time and place. For both, "power" lies in the articulation of distinctive forms of social life as such, not in the application of particular resources by some to affect the lives of others. Although discourses-in-practice are represented by "regimens/regimes" or lived patterns of action that broadly (historically and institutionally) "discipline" or encompass their adherents' lives and discursive practice is manifest in patterns of talk and interaction that constitute everyday life, the practices refer in common to the lived "doing," or ongoing accomplishment, of social worlds.

For Foucault, power operates in and through discourse as the other face of knowledge, thus the term *power/knowledge*. Discourse not only puts words to work, it gives them their meaning, constructs perceptions, and formulates understanding and ongoing courses of interaction. The "work" entailed simultaneously and reflexively constitutes the realities that words are taken otherwise merely to reference or specify. To deploy a particular discourse of subjectivity is not simply a matter of representing a subject; in practice, it simultaneously constitutes the kinds of subjects that are meaningfully embedded in the discourse itself. For example, to articulate the discourse of medicine in today's world automatically generates the roles of professional healer and patient, each of whose actions in turn articulate the application and reception of technologies of healing served by the social dominance of scientific knowledge. The taken-for-grantedness of this socially encompassing discourse makes challenges to this way of "thinking" (or speaking) seem oddly misplaced. Even the weak "powerfully" participate in the discourse that defines them as weak. This is a kind of knowledge-in-social-practice, and it is powerful because it not only represents but ineluctably puts into practice what is known and shared. Language is not just more or less correlated with what it represents, but is always already a "form of life," to again put it in Wittgenstein's (1958) terms. If ethnomethodologists attend to *how* members use everyday methods to account for their activities and their worlds, Foucault makes us aware of the related conditions of possibility for *what* the results are likely to be. For example, in a Western postindustrial world, to think seriously of medicine and voodoo as equally viable paradigms for understanding sickness and healing would seem idiosyncratic, if not amusing or preposterous, in most conventional situations. The power of the medical discourse partially lies in its ability to be "seen but unnoticed," in its ability to appear as *the* only possibility while other possibilities are outside the plausible realm.

Both ethnomethodology's and Foucault's approach to empirical material are "analytics," not theoretical frameworks in the traditional sense. Conventionally understood, theory purports to explain the state of the matters in question. It provides answers to *why* concerns, such as why the suicide rate is rising or why individuals are suffering depression. Ethnomethodology and the Foucauldian project, in contrast, aim to answer how it is that individual experience comes to be understood in particular terms such as these. They are pretheoretical in this sense, respectively seeking to arrive at an understanding of how the subject matter of theory comes into existence in the first place and of what the subject of theory might possibly become. The parallel lies in the common goal of documenting the social bases of such realities.

Still, this remains a parallel. Because Foucault's project (and most Foucauldian projects) operates in a historical register, real-time talk and social interaction are understandably missing from chosen bodies of empirical material. Although Foucault himself points to sharp turns in the discursive formations that both form and inform the shifting realities of varied institutional spheres, contrasting extant social forms with the "birth" of new ones, he provides little or no sense of the *everyday* technology by which this is achieved (see Atkinson, 1995; Holstein & Gubrium, 2000). Certainly, he elaborates the broad birth of new technologies, such as the emergence of new regimes of surveillance in medicine and modern criminal justice systems (Foucault, 1975, 1979), but he does not provide us with a view of how these operate in social interaction. Neither do latter-day Foucauldians—such as Nikolas Rose (1990), who informatively documents the birth and rise of the technical apparatus for "governing the soul" that forms a private self—offer much insight into the everyday processes through which such regimes are accomplished.

Conversely, ethnomethodology's commitment to documenting the real-time, interactive processes by which reality is built up into accountable structures precludes a broader perspective on constitutive resources, possibilities, and limitations. It is one thing to show in interactive detail that our everyday encounters with reality are an ongoing accomplishment; it is quite another matter to derive an understanding of what the general parameters of those everyday encounters might be. The machinery of talk-in-interaction tells us little about the massive work and resources that inform or guide the operation of conversation, or about the consequences of producing particular results and not others, each of which is an important ingredient of practice. Members speak their worlds and their subjectivities, but they also articulate particular forms of life as they do so. What Foucauldian considerations offer ethnomethodology in this regard is an analytic sensitivity to the discursive opportunities and possibilities at work in talk and social interaction, without making it necessary to take these up as external templates for the everyday production of social order.

◆ *Toward an Analytics of*
Interpretive Practice

If we are concerned with interpretive practice and reality construction, we clearly need to draw ethnomethodological and Foucauldian analytics together more explicitly. This is not simply another attempt to bridge the so-called macro/micro divide. That debate usually centers on the question of how to conceptualize the relationship between preexisting larger and smaller social forms, the assumption being that these are categorically distinct and separately discernible. Issues raised in the debate perpetuate the distinction between, say, social systems on the one hand and social interaction on the other. In contrast, those who consider ethnomethodology and Foucauldian analytics to be parallel operations focus their attention instead on the interactional, institutional, and cultural variabilities of socially constituting discursive practice and discourses-in-practice, as the case might be. They are concerned with how the social construction process is shaped across various domains of everyday life, not with how separate theories of macro and micro domains can be linked together for a fuller account of social organization. Doctrinaire accounts of Garfinkel, Sacks, Foucault, and others may continue to sustain a variety of distinct projects, but these pro-

jects are not likely to inform one another, nor will they lead to profitable "conversations" between dogmatic practitioners who insist on viewing themselves as speaking different analytic languages.[4] Instead, we need a new, hybridized analytics of reality construction at the crossroads of institutions, culture, and social interaction—an analytics that "misreads" and co-opts useful insights from established traditions in order to appreciate the possible complementarity of analytic idioms without losing sight of their distinctive utilities, limitations, and contributions.

Beyond Ethnomethodology

Some conversation analysts have edged in this direction by analyzing the sequential machinery of talk-in-interaction as it is patterned by institutional context. Their studies of "talk at work" aim to specify how the "simplest systematics" of ordinary conversation (Sacks et al., 1974) is shaped in various ways by the reflexively constructed speech environments of particular interactional regimes (see Boden & Zimmerman, 1991; Drew & Heritage, 1992). Ethnomethodologically oriented ethnographers approach the problem from another direction by asking how institutions and their respective representational cultures are brought into being, managed, and sustained in and through members' social interaction (or "reality work") (see Atkinson, 1995; Dingwall, Eekelaar, & Murray, 1983; Emerson, 1969; Emerson & Messinger, 1977; Gubrium, 1992; Holstein, 1993; Mehan, 1979; Miller, 1991, 1997a). Self-consciously Foucauldian ethnographers, too, have drawn links between everyday discursive practice and discourses-in-practice to document in local detail how the formulation of everyday texts, such as psychiatric case records or coroners' reports, reproduces institutional discourses (see Prior, 1997).

In their own fashions, these efforts consider both the *hows* and the *whats* of reality construction. But this is analytically risky business. Asking *how* questions without having an integral way of getting an analytic handle on *what* questions makes concern with the *whats* arbitrary. Although talk-in-interaction is locally "artful," as Garfinkel (1967) puts it, not just anything goes. On the other hand, if we swing too far analytically in the direction of contextual or cultural imperatives, we end up with the cultural, institutional, or judgmental "dopes" that Garfinkel (1967) decries.

The admonition that "not just anything goes" has been taken seriously, but cautiously, by both ethnomethodologists and conversation analysts as they have sought to document carefully the practical contours of interaction in the varied circumstances in which it unfolds. Systematic attention to everyday reasoning and to the sequential organization of conversations has made it clear that outcomes are constructed in the interactional apparatuses within which their antecedents are made topical. But this is a very delimited approach to the constitutive *whats* of social construction, one that lacks a broad view of the institutional and cultural discourses that serve as resources for what is likely to be constructed, when, and where in everyday life.

To broaden and enrich ethnomethodology's analytic scope and repertoire, we have extended its reach into the institutional and cultural *whats* that come into play in social interaction. This need not be a historical extension, as was Foucault's metier, although that certainly should not be ruled out. Rather, we appeal to a "cautious" (and self-conscious) naturalism that addresses the practical and sited production of everyday life (Gubrium, 1993). The analytics of interpretive practice is such an effort. It centers on the *interplay,* not the synthesis, of discursive practice and discourses-in-practice, the tandem projects of ethnomethodology and Foucauldian discourse analysis. This analytics assiduously avoids theorizing social forms, lest the discursive practices associated with the construction of these forms be taken for granted. By the same token, it concertedly keeps institutional or cultural discourses in view, lest they be dissolved into localized displays of practical reasoning or forms of sequential organization for talk-in-interaction. First and foremost, an analytics of interpretive practice takes us, in real time, to

the "going concerns" of everyday life, as Everett Hughes (1984) liked to call social institutions. There, we can focus on how members artfully put discourses to work as they constitute their subjectivities and related social worlds.

The emphasis on the interplay between the *hows* and *whats* of interpretive practice is paramount. Interplay connotes a dynamic relationship. We assiduously avoid analytically privileging either discursive practice or discourses-in-practice. Putting it in ethnomethodological terms, the aim of an analytics of interpretive practice is to document the interplay between the practical reasoning and conversational machinery entailed in constructing a sense of everyday reality on the one hand and the institutional conditions, resources, and related discourses that substantively nourish and interpretively mediate interaction on the other. Putting it in Foucauldian terms, the goal is to describe the interplay between institutional discourses and the "dividing practices" that constitute local subjectivities and their worlds of experience (Foucault, 1965). The symmetry of real-world practice requires that we give equal treatment to both its articulative and its substantive engagements.

Qualitative researchers are increasingly focusing on these two sides of interpretive practice, looking to both the artful processes and the substantive conditions of meaning making and social order. Douglas Maynard (1989), for example, notes that most ethnographers have traditionally asked, "How do participants see things?" whereas ethnomethodologically informed discourse studies have asked, "How do participants do things?" Although his own work typically begins with the latter question, Maynard cautions us not to ignore the former. He explains that, in the interest of studying how members *do* things, ethnomethodological studies have tended to de-emphasize factors that condition their actions. Recognizing that "external social structure is used as a resource for social interaction at the same time as it is constituted within it," Maynard suggests that ethnographic and discourse studies can be mutually informative, allowing researchers to document more fully the ways in which the "structure of interaction, while being a local production, simultaneously enacts matters whose origins are externally initiated" (p. 139). "In addition to knowing how people 'see' their workaday worlds," writes Maynard, researchers should try to understand how people "discover and exhibit features of these worlds so that they can be 'seen' " (p. 144).

Expressing similar interests and concerns, Hugh Mehan (1979) has developed a discourse-oriented program of "constitutive ethnography" that puts "structure and structuring activities on an equal footing by showing *how* the social facts of the world emerge from structuring work to become external and constraining" (p. 18). Mehan (1991) examines "contrastive" instances of interpretation in order to describe both the "distal" and "proximate" features of the reality-constituting work people do "within institutional, cultural, and historical contexts" (pp. 73, 81).

Beginning from similar ethnomethodological and discourse-analytic footings, David Silverman (1993) likewise attends to the institutional venues of talk and social construction (see also Silverman, 1985, 1997). Seeking a mode of qualitative inquiry that exhibits both constitutive and contextual sensibilities, he suggests that discourse studies that consider the varied institutional contexts of talk bring a new perspective to qualitative inquiry. Working in the same vein, Gale Miller (1994) has proposed "ethnographies of institutional discourse" that serve to document "the ways in which setting members use discursive resources in organizing their practical actions, and how members' actions are constrained by the resources available in the settings" (p. 280; see also Miller, 1997b). This approach makes explicit overtures to both conversation analysis and Foucauldian discourse analysis.

Miller's (1997a) ethnography of the discourses characterizing a therapy agency is instructive, especially as it sheds light on the discursive production of the client in therapy. His 12-year ethnographic study of Northland Clinic, an internationally prominent center of "brief therapy," describes a marked shift in client subjectivity that accompanied a conscious alteration of treatment philosophy. When Miller began his fieldwork, Northland employed "ecosystemic brief therapy," which emphasized the social contexts of clients' lives and problems. In this therapeutic environment, clients' subjectivity was linked with the systems of social relationships that were taken to form and fuel their problems. The approach required the staff to discern the state of these systems and to intervene so as to alter their dynamics and thereby effect change. Miller notes that this approach was informed by a "modern" discourse of the reality of the problems in question.

Several years into the fieldwork, Northland shifted to a more "postmodern" approach, articulating intervention in an everyday linguistic and constructivist discourse. Therapists began to apply what was called "solution-focused brief therapy," which meant viewing troubles as ways of talking about everyday life. This prompted the staff to orient to the therapy process as a set of language games, expressly appropriating Wittgenstein's sense of the term. The idea here was that troubles were as much constructions—ways of talking or forms of life—as they were real difficulties for the clients in question. This transformed clients' institutional subjectivity, from their being relatively passive agents of systems of personal troubles and negative stories to being active problem solvers with a potential to formulate positive stories about themselves and design helpful solutions. As an everyday language of solutions, not a discourse of problems, became the basis of intervention, the narrative identities of clients were transformed to reveal entirely different selves. As the therapy agency itself changed over time, so did both the discourse-in-practice and discursive practices. This resulted in the construction of distinctly different "clients" and "problems" that were institutionally formulated and addressed.

Dorothy Smith (1987, 1990) has been quite explicit in addressing a version of the interplay between the *whats* and *hows* of social life from a feminist point of view. Hers has been an analytics informed by ethnomethodological and, increasingly, Foucauldian sensibilities. Moving beyond ethnomethodology, Smith (1990) calls for what she refers to as a "dialectics of discourse and the everyday" (p. 202). Stressing the "play and interplay" of discourse, Smith articulates her view of women's "active" placement in their worlds:

> It is easy to misconstrue the discourse as having an overriding power to determine the values and interpretation of women's appearances in local settings, and see this power as essentially at the disposal of the fashion industry and media. But women are active, skilled, make choices, consider, are not fooled or foolish. Within discourse there is play and interplay. (p. 202)

Philosopher Calvin Schrag (1997) similarly emphasizes the advantage of the strategy of analytic interplay over theoretical integration. Schrag puts this in the context of the need to guard against, on the one hand, reducing what we refer to as discursive practice to mere speech acts or talk-in-interaction or, on the other, supplanting the local artfulness of social interaction with its institutional discourses. Considering the self after postmodernity, Schrag echoes our own aim to keep both the constructive *whats* and *hows* in balance at the forefront of an analytics, lest the study of lived experience neglect or overemphasize one or the other.

> We must stand guard to secure the space of discourse as temporalized event of speaking *between* the objectification of speech acts and language on the one hand and the abstractions and reifications in the structuralist designs of narratology on the other hand. The event of discourse as a saying of something by someone to someone is threatened from both "below" and "above"—from below in terms of a tendency toward an ontology of elementarism fixated on the isolable, constitutive elements of speech acts and linguistic units . . . and from above in the sense of a predilection toward an abstract holism of narratological structures that leave the event of discourse behind. Only by sticking to the terrain of the "between" will the subject as the who of discourse and the who of narrative remain visible. It is on this terrain, which we will later come to call the terrain of lived-experience, that we are able to observe the august event of a self understanding itself

through the twin moments of discourse and narration. (pp. 22-23)

Indeed, we echo Schrag's warning against integrating an analytics of discursive practice with an analytics of discourse-in-practice. To integrate one with the other is to reduce the empirical purview of a common enterprise. Reducing the analytics of discourse-in-practice into discursive practice risks losing the lessons of attending to institutional differences and cultural configurations as they mediate and are not "just talked into being" through social interaction. Conversely, figuring discursive practice as the mere residue of institutional discourse risks a totalized marginalization of local artfulness.

Analytic Bracketing

Rather than attempting synthesis or integration, we view an analytics of interpretive practice as more like a skilled juggling act, concentrating alternately on the myriad *hows* and *whats* of everyday life. This requires a new form of bracketing to capture the interplay between discursive practice and discourses-in-practice. We have called this technique of oscillating indifference to the realities of everyday life *analytic bracketing* (see Gubrium & Holstein, 1997).

Recall that ethnomethodology's interest in the *hows* by which realities are constructed requires a studied, temporary indifference to those realities. Like phenomenologists, ethnomethodologists begin their analysis by setting aside belief in the real in order to bring into view the everyday practices by which subjects, objects, and events come to have a sense of being observable, rational, and orderly for those concerned. The ethnomethodological project moves forward from there, documenting how discursive practice constitutes social structures. As Wittgenstein (1958, p. 19) might put it, language is "taken off holiday" in order to make visible how language works to construct the objects it is otherwise viewed as principally describing.

Analytic bracketing works somewhat differently. It is employed throughout analysis, not just at the start. As analysis proceeds, the observer intermittently orients to everyday realities as both the *products* of members' reality-constructing procedures and the *resources* from which realities are constituted. At one moment, the analyst may be indifferent to the structures of everyday life in order to document their production through discursive practice. In the next analytic move, he or she brackets discursive practice in order to assess the local availability, distribution, and/or regulation of resources for reality construction. In Wittgensteinian terms, this translates into attending to both language-at-work and language-on-holiday, alternating considerations of how languages games, in particular institutional discourses, operate in everyday life and what games are likely to come into play at particular times and places. In Foucauldian terms, it leads to alternating considerations of discourses-in-practice on the one hand and the locally fine-grained documentation of related discursive practices on the other.

Analytic bracketing amounts to an orienting procedure for alternately focusing on the *whats* and then the *hows* of interpretive practice (or vice versa) in order to assemble both a contextually scenic and a contextually constructive picture of everyday language-in-use. The objective is to move back and forth between discursive practice and discourses-in-practice, documenting each in turn and making informative references to the other in the process. Either discursive machinery or available discourses becomes the provisional phenomenon, while interest in the other is temporarily deferred, but not forgotten. The constant interplay between the analysis of these two sides of interpretive practice mirrors the lived interplay among social interaction, its immediate surroundings, and its going concerns.

Because discursive practice and discourses-in-practice are mutually constitutive, one cannot argue that analysis should begin or end with either one, although there are predilections in this regard. As those who are ethnographically oriented are wont to do, Smith (1987, 1990), for example, advocates beginning "where people are." We take her to mean where people are located in the institutional landscape of every-

day life. Conversely, conversation analysts insist on beginning with discursive practice, even though a variety of unanalyzed *whats* typically inform their efforts.[5]

Wherever one starts, neither the cultural and institutional details of discourse nor its interpolations in social interaction predetermine the other. If we set aside the need for an indisputable resolution to the question of which comes first, last, or has priority, we can designate a suitable point of departure and proceed from there, so long as we keep firmly in mind that the interplay within interpretive practice requires that we move back and forth analytically between its leading components. Of course, we don't want to reify the components; we continuously remind ourselves that the analytic task centers on the dialectics of two fields of play, not the reproduction of one by the other.

Although we advocate no rule for where to begin, there is no need to fret that the overall task is impossible or logically incoherent. Maynard (1998), for example, compares analytic bracketing to "wanting to ride trains that are going in different directions, initially hopping on one and then somehow jumping to the other." He asks, "How do you jump from one train to another when they are going in different directions?" (p. 344). The question is, in fact, merely an elaboration of the issue of how one brackets in the first place, which is, of course, the basis for Maynard's and other ethnomethodologists' and conversation analysts' own projects. The answer is simple: Knowledge of the *principle* of bracketing (and unbracketing) makes it possible. Those who bracket the life world or treat it indifferently, as the case might be, readily set reality aside every time they get to work on their respective corpuses of empirical material. It becomes as routine as rising in the morning, having breakfast, and going to the workplace.[6] On the other hand, the desire to operationalize bracketing of any kind, analytic bracketing included, into explicitly codified and sequenced procedural moves would turn bracketing into a set of recipelike, analytic directives, something surely to be avoided. We would assume that no one, except the most recalcitrant operationalist, would want to substitute a recipe book for an analytics.[7]

Analytic bracketing, however, is far from undisciplined; it has distinct procedural implications. As we have noted, the primary directive is to examine alternately both sides of interpretive practice. Researchers engaging in analytic bracketing must constantly turn their attention in more than one direction. This is increasingly resulting in new methodological hybrids. Some analysts undertake a more content-oriented form of discourse analysis (see Potter, 1996; Potter & Wetherell, 1987). Others develop methods of "constitutive ethnography" (Mehan, 1979), the "ethnography of practice" (Gubrium, 1988), or other discursively sensitive ethnographic approaches (see Holstein, 1993; Miller, 1991, 1997a). The distinguishing feature of such studies is their disciplined focus on both discourse-in-practice and discursive practice.

The dual focus should remind us that, in describing the constitutive role of discourses-in-practice, we must take care not to appropriate these naïvely into our analysis. We must sustain ethnomethodology's desire to distinguish between members' resources and our own. As a result, as we consider discourses-in-practice, we must attend to how they mediate, not determine, members' socially constructive activities. Analytic bracketing is always substantively temporary. It resists full-blown attention to discourses as systems of power/knowledge, separate from how they unfold in lived experience. It also is enduringly empirical in that it does not take the operation of discourses for granted as the operating truths of a setting *tout court*.[8]

Working Against Totalization

Centered at the crossroads of discursive practice and discourses-in-practice, an analytics of interpretive practice works against totalization. It restrains the propensity of a Foucauldian analytics to view all interpretations as artifacts of particular regimes of power/knowledge. Writing in relation to the broad sweep of his "histories of the present," Foucault was inclined to overemphasize the predominance of discourses in constructing the horizons of meaning at particular times or places, conveying the sense that discourses fully detail the nuances of everyday life. A more interactionally sensitive analytics of discourse— one tied to discursive practice—resists this tendency.

Because interpretive practice is mediated by discourse through institutional functioning, we discern the operation of power/knowledge in the separate going concerns of everyday life. Yet what one institutional site brings to bear is not necessarily what another puts into practice. Institutions constitute distinct, yet sometimes overlapping, realities. While one may deploy a gaze that confers agency or subjectivity upon individuals, for example, another may constitute subjectivity along different lines, such as the family systems that are called into question as subjects and agents of troubles in family therapy (see Gubrium, 1992; Miller, 1997a).

Still, if interpretive practice is complex and fluid, it is not socially arbitrary. In the practice of everyday life, discourse is articulated in myriad sites and is socially variegated; actors methodically build up their shared realities in diverse, locally nuanced, and biographically informed terms. Although this produces considerable slippage in how discourses do their work, it is far removed from the uniform hegemonic regimes of power/knowledge presented in some Foucauldian readings. Social organization nonetheless is evident in the going concerns referenced by participants, to which they hold their talk and interaction accountable.

An analytics of interpretive practice must deal with the perennial question of what realities and/or subjectivities are being constructed in the myriad sites of everyday life. In practice, diverse articulations of discourse intersect, collide, and work against the construction of common or uniform subjects, agents, and social realities. Interpretations shift in relation to the institutional and cultural markers they reference, which, in turn, fluctuate with respect to the varied settings in which social interaction unfolds. Discourses-in-practice refract one another as they are methodically adapted to practical exigencies, local discursive practice serving up variation and innovation in the process (see Abu-Lughod, 1991, 1993; Chase, 1995).

From How and What to Why

Traditionally, qualitative inquiry has concerned itself with *what* and *how* questions. *Why* questions have been the hallmark of quantitative sociology, which seeks to explain and ostensibly predict behavior. Qualitative researchers typically approach *why* questions cautiously. Explanation is tricky business, one that qualitative inquiry embraces discreetly in light of its appreciation for interpretive elasticity. It is one thing to describe what is going on and how things or events take shape, but the question of why things happen the way they do can lead to inferential leaps and empirical speculations that propel qualitative analysis far from its stock-in-trade. The challenge is to respond to *why* questions in ways that are empirically and conceptually consonant with qualitative inquiry's traditional concerns.

An analytics of interpretive practice provides a limited basis for raising particular kinds of *why* question in the context of qualitative inquiry. In order to pursue *why* questions, one needs to designate a domain of explanation for that which is to be explained. The familiar distinction in sociology between macrosociological and microsociological domains, for example, specifies two kinds of explanatory footing. Most commonly, macrosociological variables are used as footing for explaining microsociological phenomena, for example, using the rural/urban or the traditional/modern distinction to explain qualities of face-to-face relationships. Parsons's (1951) social system framework was once a leading model of this kind of explanation, using macro-level systemic variables to explain functioning and variation in individual lives and actions.

One way for qualitative inquiry to approach *why* questions without endangering its traditional analytic interests is to proceed from the *whats* and *hows* of social life. Provisional ex-

planatory footing can be found at the junction of concerns for what is going on in everyday life in relation to how that is constructed, centered in the space we have located as interpretive practice. Bracketing the *whats,* footing for explaining the constructive nuances of social patterns can be found in discursive practice. Bracketing the *hows,* footing for explaining the delimited patterns of meaning consequent to social construction processes can be found in discourses-in-practice.

The interplay between discourses-in-practice and discursive practice is a source of two kinds of answers for why things are organized as they are in everyday life. One kind stems from the explanatory footings of discursive practice, directing us to the artful talk and interaction that design and designate the local contours of our social worlds. From such footings, we learn why discourses are not templates for action. Their articulation is subject to the everyday contingencies of discursive practice. Discourses-in-practice are talked into action, so to speak; they do not dictate what is said and done from the outside or from the inside, as if they were separate and distinct sources of influence. To answer why social structures are as circumstantially nuanced as they are, one can bracket the constitutive *whats* of the matter in order to reveal how recognizable activities and systems of meaning are constituted in particular domains of everyday life. Discursive practice, in other words, provides the footing for answering why recognizable constellations of social order take on locally distinctive shapes.

We may also answer limited *why* questions that are related to discursive practice, questions such as why discursive actions unfold in specific directions or why they have particular consequences. Answers emerge when we bracket the constitutive work that shapes who and what we are and what it is that we do. By itself, the machinery of conversation gives us few clues as to when, where, or what particular patterns of meaning or action will be artfully produced and managed. The machinery is like a galloping horse, but we have little or no sense of when it began to run, where it is headed, what indeed it is up to, and what might happen when it gets there. Is it racing, fleeing, playing polo, delivering the mail, or what? Each of these possibilities requires a discourse to set its course and to tell us what messages it might be conveying. This can then inform us in delimited ways of why the machinery of speech environments is organized and propelled in the ways it is. Discourse-in-practice provides the footing for answering why discursive practice proceeds in the direction it does, toward what end, in pursuit of what goals, in relation to what meanings.

◆ Sustaining a Critical Consciousness

The interplay of discourse-in-practice and discursive practice sustains an integral critical consciousness for qualitative inquiry. Each component of interpretive practice serves as an *endogenous* basis for raising serious questions relating to the empirical assumptions of ongoing inquiry. Critical consciousness is built into the analytics; it is not external to it. Indeed, it is the other face of analytic bracketing. If, for purposes of broadening our knowledge of everyday life, analytic bracketing provides a means of combining attention to constitutive *hows* with substantive *whats*, it simultaneously enjoins us to pay attention continuously to what we may be shortchanging in the service of one of these questions or the other. The continuing enterprise of analytic bracketing does not keep us comfortably ensconced throughout the research process in a domain of indifference to the lived realities of experience, as a priori bracketing does. Nor does analytic bracketing keep us comfortably engaged in the unrepentant naturalism of documenting the world of everyday life the way it really is. Rather, it continuously jerks us out of the analytic lethargies of both endeavors.

When questions of discourse-in-practice take the stage, there are grounds for problematizing or politicizing the sum and substance of what otherwise can be too facilely viewed as arbitrarily or individualistically constructed,

managed, and sustained. The persistent urgency of *what* questions cautions us not to assume that interpersonal agency, artfulness, or the machinery of social interaction is the whole story. The urgency prompts us to inquire into the broader sources of matters that are built up across time and circumstance in discursive practice, the contemporaneous conditions that inform and shape the construction process, and the personal and interpersonal consequences for those involved of having constituted their world in the way they have. Although the analytics of interpretive practice does not orient naturalistically to the "real world," neither does it take everyday life as built from the ground up in talk-in-interaction on each and every conversational or narrative occasion. The political consequence of this is an analytics that turns to matters of social organization and control, implicating a reality that doesn't rest completely on the machinery of talk or the constructive quality of social interaction. It turns us to wider contexts in search of other sources of change or stability.

When discursive practice commands the spotlight, there is a basis for critically challenging the representational security of taken-for-granted realities. The continual urgency of *how* questions warns us not to assume that the world as it now is, is the world that must be. This warning prompts us to "unsettle" realities in search of their construction to reveal the constitutive processes that produce and sustain particular realities as the processes are engaged, not for time immemorial. In an analytics of interpretive practice, *how* concerns caution us to remember that the everyday realities of our lives—whether they are being normal, abnormal, law-abiding, criminal, male, female, young, or old—are realities we *do*. Having done them, we move on to do others, producing and reproducing, time and again, the worlds we inhabit. Politically, this presents the recognition that we could enact alternate possibilities or alternative directions, although the apparent organization of our lives might appear to make that impossible. If we make visible the constructive fluidity and malleability of social forms, we also reveal a potential for change (see Gubrium & Holstein, 1990, 1994, 1995, 1998; Holstein & Gubrium, 2000).

The critical consciousness of this analytics deploys the continuous imperative to take issue with discourse or discursive practice when either one is foregrounded, thus turning the analytics on itself as it pursues its goals. Reflexively framed, the interplay of discourse and discursive practice transforms analytic bracketing into critical bracketing, offering a basis not only for documenting interpretive practice, but also for commenting critically on its own constructions, putting the analytic pendulum in motion in relation to itself.

■ Notes

1. Some self-proclaimed ethnomethodologists, however, would reject the notion that ethnomethodology is in any sense a "constructionist" or "constructivist" enterprise (see Lynch, 1993). Some reviews of the ethnomethodological canon also clearly imply that constructionism is anathema to the ethnomethodological project (see Maynard, 1998; Maynard & Clayman, 1991).

2. While clearly reflecting Garfinkel's pioneering contributions, this characterization of the ethnomethodological project is perhaps closer to the version conveyed in the work of Melvin Pollner (1987, 1991) and D. Lawrence Wieder (1988) than some of the more recent "postanalytic" or conversation-analytic forms of ethnomethodology. Indeed, Garfinkel (1988), Lynch (1993), and others might object to how we ourselves portray ethnomethodology. We would contend, however, that there is much to be gained from a studied "misreading" of the ethnomethodological "classics," a practice that Garfinkel himself advocates for the sociological classics more generally (see Lynch, 1993). With the figurative "death of the author" (Barthes, 1977), those attached to doctrinaire readings of the canon should have little grounds for argument.

3. Other ethnomethodologists have drawn upon Foucault, but without necessarily endorsing these affinities or parallels. Lynch (1993), for example, writes that Foucault's studies can be relevant to ethnomethodological investigations in a "restricted and 'literal' way" (p. 131) and resists the generalization of discursive regimes across highly occasioned "language games." See McHoul (1986) and Lynch and Bogen (1996) for exemplary ethnomethodological appropriations of Foucauldian insights.

4. There is still considerable doctrinaire sentiment for maintaining "hard-headed, rigorous investigation in one idiom" while recognizing its possible "incommensurability" with others (Maynard, 1998, p. 345). The benefit, according to Maynard (1998), would be "strongly reliable understanding in a particular domain of social life, and it need not imply narrowness, fragmentation, limitation, or isolation" (p. 345). Our sense is that such conversations do produce fragmentation and isolation (see Hill & Crittenden, 1968, for a vivid example of nonproductive conversation deriving from incompatible analytic idioms), resulting in the stale reproduction of knowledge and, of course, the equally stale representation of the empirical world. In our view, reliability has never been a strong enough incentive for analysts to ignore the potential validities of new analytic horizons.

5. The CA argument for this point of departure is that ostensibly distinct patterns of talk and interaction are constitutive of particular settings, and therefore must be the point of departure. This is tricky, however. CA's practitioners routinely designate and describe particular institutional contexts *before* the analysis of the conversations that those conversations are said to reveal. CA would have us believe that setting, as a distinct context for talk and interaction, would be visibly (hearably) constituted *in the machinery of talk* itself (see Schegloff, 1991). This would mean that no scene setting would be necessary (or even need to be provided) for the production of the discursive context to be apparent. One wonders if what is demonstrated in these studies could have been produced in the unlikely event that no prior knowledge of the settings had been available, or if prior knowledge were rigorously bracketed.

CA studies always admit to being about conversation in *some* context. Even the myriad studies of telephone interaction make that discursive context available to readers *before* the analysis begins. Indeed, titles of research reports literally announce institutional context at the start. For example, one of Heritage's (1984) articles is titled "Analyzing News Interviews: Aspects of the Production of Talk for an Overhearing Audience." Immediately, the reader knows and, in a manner of speaking, is prepared to get the gist of what conversation is "doing" in what follows. In a word, the *productivity* of talk relies as much on this analytically under-recognized start as on what the analysis proper aims to show. In such studies, context inevitably sneaks in the front door, in titles and "incidental" stage setting. Apparently, analysts fail to recognize that some measure of discursive context is being imported to assist in the explanation of how context is indigenously constructed.

Strictly speaking, researchers cannot hope to attribute institutional patterns completely to the machinery of conversation. Nor can they completely disattend to discourse-in-practice and meaning while describing the sequential flow of conversation. Analytically, one must at some point reappropriate institutions and external cultural understandings in order to know what is artfully and methodically going on in that talk and interaction. Centered as analytic bracketing is on both sides of interpretive practice, there is concerted warrant for the continual return of the analytic gaze to discourse-in-practice.

6. There are other useful metaphors for describing how analytic bracketing changes the focus from discourse-in-practice to discursive practice. One can liken the operation to "shifting" gears while driving a motor vehicle equipped with a manual transmission. One mode of analysis may prove quite productive, but it will eventually strain against the resistance engendered by its own temporary analytic orientation. When the analyst notes that the analytic "engine" is laboring under, or being constrained by, the restraints of what it is currently "geared" to accomplish, he or she can decide to virtually "shift" analytic "gears" in order to gain further purchase on the aspects of interpretive interplay that were previously bracketed. Just as there can be no prescription for shifting gears while driving (i.e., one can never specify in advance at what speed one should shift up or down), changing analytic brackets always remains an artful enterprise, awaiting the empirical circumstances it encounters. Its timing cannot be prespecified. As in shifting gears while driving, changes are not arbitrary or undisciplined. Rather, they respond to the analytic challenges at hand in a principled, if not predetermined, fashion.

7. This may be the very thing Lynch (1993) decries with respect to conversation analysts who attempt to formalize and professionalize CA as a "scientific" discipline.

8. Some critics have worried that analytic bracketing represents a selective objectivism, a form of "ontological gerrymandering" (see Denzin, 1998). These, of course, have become fighting words among constructionists. But we should soberly recall that Steve Woolgar and Dorothy Pawluch (1985) have suggested that carving out some sort of analytic footing may be a pervasive and unavoidable feature of any sociological commentary. Our own constant attention to the *interplay* between discourse-in-practice and discursive practice—as they are understood and used by members—continually reminds us of their reflexive relationship. Gerrymanderers stand their separate ground and unreflexively deconstruct; analytic bracketing, in contrast, encourages a continual and methodical deconstruction of empirical groundings themselves. This may produce a less-than-tidy picture, but it also is designed to keep reification at bay and ungrounded signification under control.

■ *References*

Abu-Lughod, L. (1991). Writing against culture. In R. G. Fox (Ed.), *Recapturing anthropology: Working in the present* (pp. 137-162). Santa Fe, NM: School of American Research Press.

Abu-Lughod, L. (1993). *Writing women's worlds: Bedouin stories.* Berkeley: University of California Press.

Atkinson, J. M., & Drew, P. (1979). *Order in court.* Atlantic Highlands, NJ: Humanities Press.

Atkinson, P. A. (1988). Ethnomethodology: A critical review. *Annual Review of Sociology, 14,* 441-465.

Atkinson, P. A. (1995). *Medical talk and medical work.* London: Sage.

Barthes, R. (1977). *Image, music, text* (S. Heath, Trans.). New York: Hill & Wang.

Berger, P. L., & Luckmann, T. (1967). *The social construction of reality: A treatise in the sociology of knowledge.* Garden City, NY: Doubleday.

Best, S., & Kellner, D. (1991). *Postmodern theory: Critical interrogations.* New York: Guilford.

Blumer, H. (1969). *Symbolic interactionism: Perspective and method.* Englewood Cliffs, NJ: Prentice Hall.

Boden, D., & Zimmerman, D. (Eds.). (1991). *Talk and social structure: Studies in ethnomethodology and conversation analysis.* Cambridge: Polity.

Bogen, D., & Lynch, M. (1993). Do we need a general theory of social problems? In J. A. Holstein & G. Miller (Eds.), *Reconsidering social constructionism: Debates in social problems theory* (pp. 213-237). Hawthorne, NY: Aldine de Gruyter.

Chase, S. E. (1995). *Ambiguous empowerment: The work narratives of women school superintendents.* Amherst: University of Massachusetts Press.

Denzin, N. K. (1998). The new ethnography. *Journal of Contemporary Ethnography, 27,* 405-415.

Dingwall, R., Eekelaar, J., & Murray, T. (1983). *The protection of children: State intervention and family life.* Oxford: Blackwell.

Drew, P., & Heritage, J. C. (Eds.). (1992). *Talk at work.* Cambridge: Cambridge University Press.

Dreyfus, H. L., & Rabinow, P. (1982). *Michel Foucault: Beyond structuralism and hermeneutics.* Chicago: University of Chicago Press.

Durkheim, E. (1961). *The elementary forms of the religious life.* New York: Collier-Macmillan.

Durkheim, E. (1964). *The rules of the sociological method* (S. S. Solovay & J. H. Mueller, Trans.; G. E. G. Catlin, Ed.). New York: Free Press.

Emerson, R. M. (1969). *Judging delinquents.* Chicago: Aldine.

Emerson, R. M., & Messinger, S. (1977). The micro-politics of trouble. *Social Problems, 25,* 121-134.

Foucault, M. (1965). *Madness and civilization.* New York: Random House.

Foucault, M. (1972). *The archaeology of knowledge.* New York: Pantheon.

Foucault, M. (1975). *The birth of the clinic: An archaeology of medical perception.* New York: Vintage.

Foucault, M. (1979). *Discipline and punish: The birth of the prison* (A. Sheridan, Trans.). New York: Vintage.

Foucault, M. (1980). *Power/knowledge: Selected interviews and other writings, 1972-1977* (C. Gordon, Ed.; L. Marshall, J. Mepham, & K. Soper, Trans.). New York: Pantheon.

Foucault, M. (1988). The ethic of care for the self as a practice of freedom. In M. Foucault, *The final Foucault* (J. Bernauer & G. Rasmussen, Eds.; pp. 1-20). Cambridge: MIT Press.

Garfinkel, H. (1952). *The perception of the other: A study in social order.* Unpublished doctoral dissertation, Harvard University.

Garfinkel, H. (1967). *Studies in ethnomethodology.* Englewood Cliffs, NJ: Prentice Hall.

Garfinkel, H. (1988). Evidence for locally produced, naturally accountable phenomena of order, logic, reason, meaning, method, etc. in and as of the essential quiddity of immortal ordinary society (I of IV): An announcement of studies. *Sociological Theory, 6,* 103-109.

Garfinkel, H., Lynch, M., & Livingston, E. (1981). The work of a discovering science construed with materials from the optically discovered pulsar. *Philosophy of the Social Sciences, 11,* 131-158.

Garfinkel, H., & Sacks, H. (1970). On the formal structures of practical actions. In J. C. McKinney & E. A. Tiryakian (Eds.), *Theoretical sociology* (pp. 338-366). New York: Appleton-Century-Crofts.

Gubrium, J. F. (1988). *Analyzing field reality.* Newbury Park, CA: Sage.

Gubrium, J. F. (1992). *Out of control: Family therapy and domestic disorder.* Newbury Park, CA: Sage.

Gubrium, J. F. (1993). For a cautious naturalism. In J. A. Holstein & G. Miller (Eds.), *Reconsidering social constructionism: Debates in social problems theory* (pp. 89-101). Hawthorne, NY: Aldine de Gruyter.

Gubrium, J. F., & Holstein, J. A. (1990). *What is family?* Mountain View, CA: Mayfield.

Gubrium, J. F., & Holstein, J. A. (1994). *Constructing the life course.* Dix Hills, NY: General Hall.

Gubrium, J. F., & Holstein, J. A. (1995). Life course malleability: Biographical work and deprivatization. *Sociological Inquiry, 65,* 207-223.

Gubrium, J. F., & Holstein, J. A. (1997). *The new language of qualitative method.* New York: Oxford University Press.

Gubrium, J. F., & Holstein, J. A. (1998). Narrative practice and the coherence of personal stories. *Sociological Quarterly, 39,* 163-187.

Heritage, J. C. (1984). *Garfinkel and ethnomethodology.* Cambridge: Polity.

Heritage, J. C. (1987). Ethnomethodology. In A. Giddens & J. Turner (Eds.), *Sociological theory today* (pp. 224-271). Stanford, CA: Stanford University Press.

Heritage, J. C. (1997). Conversation analysis and institutional talk: Analysing data. In D. Silverman (Ed.), *Qualitative research: Theory, method and practice* (pp. 161-182). London: Sage.

Hewitt, J. P. (1997). *Self and society.* Boston: Allyn & Bacon.

Hill, R. J., & Crittenden, K. S. (Eds.). (1968). *Proceedings of the Purdue Symposium on Ethnomethodology.* West Lafayette, IN: Purdue Research Foundation.

Holstein, J. A. (1983). Jurors' use of judges' instructions. *Sociological Methods & Research, 11,* 501-518.

Holstein, J. A. (1993). *Court-ordered insanity: Interpretive practice and involuntary commitment.* Hawthorne, NY: Aldine de Gruyter.

Holstein, J. A., & Gubrium, J. F. (1994). Phenomenology, ethnomethodology, and interpretive practice. In N. K. Denzin & Y. S. Lincoln (Eds.), *Handbook of qualitative research* (pp. 262-272). Thousand Oaks, CA: Sage.

Holstein, J. A., & Gubrium, J. F. (2000). *The self we live by: Narrative identity in a postmodern world.* New York: Oxford University Press.

Hughes, E. C. (1984). Going concerns: The study of American institutions. In E. C. Hughes, *The sociological eye: Selected papers* (D. Riesman & H. S. Becker, Eds.; pp. 52-64). New Brunswick, NJ: Transaction.

Husserl, E. (1970). *Logical investigation.* Atlantic Highlands, NJ: Humanities Press.

Livingston, E. (1986). *The ethnomethodological foundations of mathematics.* London: Routledge & Kegan Paul.

Lynch, M. (1985). *Art and artifact in laboratory science.* London: Routledge & Kegan Paul.

Lynch, M. (1993). *Scientific practice and ordinary action.* Cambridge: Cambridge University Press.

Lynch, M., & Bogen, D. (1994). Harvey Sacks' primitive natural science. *Theory, Culture & Society, 11,* 65-104.

Lynch, M., & Bogen, D. (1996). *The spectacle of history: Speech, text, and memory at the Iran-Contra hearings.* Durham, NC: Duke University Press.

Marx, K. (1956). *Selected writings in sociology and social philosophy* (T. Bottomore, Ed.). New York: McGraw-Hill.

Maynard, D. W. (1984). *Inside plea bargaining: The language of negotiation.* New York: Plenum.

Maynard, D. W. (1989). On the ethnography and analysis of discourse in institutional settings. In J. A. Holstein & G. Miller (Eds.), *Perspectives on social problems* (Vol. 1, pp. 127-146). Greenwich, CT: JAI.

Maynard, D. W. (1998). On qualitative inquiry and extramodernity. *Contemporary Sociology, 27,* 343-345.

Maynard, D. W., & Clayman, S. E. (1991). The diversity of ethnomethodology. *Annual Review of Sociology, 17,* 385-418.

Maynard, D. W., & Manzo, J. (1993). On the sociology of justice. *Sociological Theory, 11,* 171-193.

McHoul, A. (1986). The getting of sexuality: Foucault, Garfinkel, and the analysis of sexual discourse. *Theory, Culture & Society, 3,* 65-79.

Mehan, H. (1979). *Learning lessons: Social organization in the classroom.* Cambridge, MA: Harvard University Press.

Mehan, H. (1991). The school's work of sorting students. In D. Boden & D. Zimmerman (Eds.), *Talk and social structure: Studies in ethnomethodology and conversation analysis* (pp. 71-90). Cambridge: Polity.

Mehan, H., & Wood, H. (1975). *The reality of ethnomethodology.* New York: John Wiley.

Miller, G. (1991). *Enforcing the work ethic.* Albany: State University of New York Press.

Miller, G. (1994). Toward ethnographies of institutional discourse. *Journal of Contemporary Ethnography, 23,* 280-306.

Miller, G. (1997a). *Becoming miracle workers: Language and meaning in brief therapy.* New York: Aldine de Gruyter.

Miller, G. (1997b). Building bridges: The possibility of analytic dialogue between ethnography, conversation analysis, and Foucault. In D. Silverman (Ed.), *Qualitative research: Theory, method and practice* (pp. 24-44). London: Sage.

Parsons, T. (1951). *The social system.* New York: Free Press.

Pollner, M. (1987). *Mundane reason.* Cambridge: Cambridge University Press.

Pollner, M. (1991). Left of ethnomethodology: The rise and decline of radical reflexivity. *American Sociological Review, 56,* 370-380.

Potter, J. (1996). *Representing reality: Discourse, rhetoric and social construction.* London: Sage.

Potter, J. (1997). Discourse analysis as a way of analysing naturally-occurring talk. In D. Silverman (Ed.), *Qualitative research: Theory, method and practice* (pp. 144-160). London: Sage.

Potter, J., & Wetherell, M. (1987). *Discourse and social psychology: Beyond attitudes and behaviour.* London: Sage.

Prior, L. (1997). Following in Foucault's footsteps: Text and context in qualitative research. In D. Silverman (Ed.), *Qualitative research: Theory, method and practice* (pp. 63-79). London: Sage.

Rose, N. (1990). *Governing the soul: The shaping of the private self.* New York: Routledge.

Sacks, H. (1972). An initial investigation of the usability of conversational data for doing sociology. In D. Sudnow (Ed.), *Studies in social interaction* (pp. 31-74). New York: Free Press.

Sacks, H. (1992). *Lectures on conversation* (Vols. 1-2). Oxford: Blackwell.

Sacks, H., Schegloff, E. A., & Jefferson, G. (1974). A simplest systematics for the organization of turn-taking for conversation. *Language, 50,* 696-735.

Schegloff, E. A. (1991). Reflections on talk and social structure. In D. Boden & D. Zimmerman (Eds.), *Talk and social structure: Studies in ethnomethodology and conversation analysis* (pp. 44-70). Cambridge: Polity.

Schrag, C. O. (1997). *The self after postmodernity.* New Haven, CT: Yale University Press.

Schutz, A. (1962). *The problem of social reality.* The Hague: Martinus Nijhoff.

Schutz, A. (1964). *Studies in social theory.* The Hague: Martinus Nijhoff.

Schutz, A. (1967). *The phenomenology of the social world.* Evanston, IL: Northwestern University Press.

Schutz, A. (1970). *On phenomenology and social relations.* Chicago: University of Chicago Press.

Silverman, D. (1985). *Qualitative methodology and sociology.* Aldershot, England: Gower.

Silverman, D. (1993). *Interpreting qualitative data: Strategies for analysing talk, text and interaction.* London: Sage.

Silverman, D. (Ed.). (1997). *Qualitative research: Theory, method and practice.* London: Sage.

Silverman, D. (1998). *Harvey Sacks: Social science and conversation analysis.* Cambridge: Polity.

Smith, D. E. (1987). *The everyday world as problematic.* Boston: Northeastern University Press.

Smith, D. E. (1990). *Texts, facts, and femininity.* London: Routledge.

ten Have, P. (1990). Methodological issues in conversation analysis. *Bulletin de Methodologie Sociologique, 27,* 23-51.

Weigert, A. J. (1981). *Sociology of everyday life.* New York: Longman.

Wieder, D. L. (1988). *Language and social reality.* Washington, DC: University Press of America.

Wittgenstein, L. (1958). *Philosophical investigations.* New York: Macmillan.

Woolgar, S., & Pawluch, D. (1985). Ontological gerrymandering. *Social Problems, 32,* 214-227.

Zimmerman, D. H. (1970). The practicalities of rule use. In J. D. Douglas (Ed.), *Understanding everyday life: Toward a reconstruction of social knowledge* (pp. 221-238). Chicago: Aldine.

Zimmerman, D. H. (1988). On conversation: The conversation analytic perspective. In J. A. Anderson (Ed.), *Communication yearbook 11* (pp. 406-432). Newbury Park, CA: Sage.

Zimmerman, D. H., & Wieder, D. L. (1970). Ethnomethodology and the problem of order. In J. D. Douglas (Ed.), *Understanding everyday life: Toward a reconstruction of social knowledge* (pp. 285-295). Chicago: Aldine.

19

GROUNDED THEORY

Objectivist and Constructivist Methods

◆ Kathy Charmaz

Grounded theory served at the front of the "qualitative revolution" (Denzin & Lincoln, 1994, p. ix). Barney G. Glaser and Anselm L. Strauss wrote *The Discovery of Grounded Theory* (1967) at a critical point in social science history. They defended qualitative research and countered the dominant view that quantitative studies provide the only form of systematic social scientific inquiry. Essentially, grounded theory methods consist of systematic inductive guidelines for collecting and analyzing data to build middle-range theoretical frameworks that explain the collected data. Throughout the research process, grounded theorists develop analytic interpretations of their data to focus further data collection, which they use in turn to inform and refine their developing theoretical analyses. Since Glaser and Strauss developed grounded theory methods, qualitative researchers have claimed the use of these methods to legitimate their research.

Now grounded theory methods have come under attack from both within and without.

AUTHOR'S NOTE: I made an earlier statement of my position on constructivism in a paper titled *Studying Lived Experience Through Grounded Theory: Objectivist and Constructivist Methods,* presented at the Qualitative Research Conference "Studying Human Lived Experience: Symbolic Interaction and Ethnographic Research '93," at the University of Waterloo, Ontario, Canada, May 19-22, 1993. I am grateful to Robert Prus, who invited me to present my ideas in the conference paper; to Lyn Lofland, who wrote a detailed review of it; and to members of my first Sonoma State University writing group, Julia Allen, Patrick Jackson, and Catherine Nelson, who encouraged me to pursue the topic. I thank Julianne Cheek, Norman K. Denzin, Udo Kelle, Kyrina Kent, and Yvonna Lincoln for their supportive and thoughtful comments on earlier drafts of this chapter.

Postmodernists and poststructuralists dispute obvious and subtle positivistic premises assumed by grounded theory's major proponents and within the logic of the method itself (see, e.g., Denzin, 1994, 1996, 1998; Richardson, 1993; Van Maanen, 1988). What grounded theory is and should be is contested. Barney G. Glaser and the late Anselm Strauss, with his more recent coauthor, Juliet Corbin, have moved the method in somewhat conflicting directions (Glaser, 1992; Strauss, 1987; Strauss & Corbin, 1990, 1994, 1998). Nonetheless, both their positions remain imbued with positivism, with its objectivist underpinnings (Guba & Lincoln, 1994). Glaser's (1978, 1992) position often comes close to traditional positivism, with its assumptions of an objective, external reality, a neutral observer who discovers data, reductionist inquiry of manageable research problems, and objectivist rendering of data. Strauss and Corbin's (1990, 1998) stance assumes an objective external reality, aims toward unbiased data collection, proposes a set of technical procedures, and espouses verification. Their position moves into postpositivism because they also propose giving voice to their respondents, representing them as accurately as possible, discovering and acknowledging how respondents' views of reality conflict with their own, and recognizing art as well as science in the analytic product and process (see Strauss & Corbin, 1998). By taking these points further, I add another position to the fray and another vision for future qualitative research: constructivist grounded theory.[1]

Constructivist grounded theory celebrates firsthand knowledge of empirical worlds, takes a middle ground between postmodernism and positivism, and offers accessible methods for taking qualitative research into the 21st century. Constructivism assumes the relativism of multiple social realities, recognizes the mutual creation of knowledge by the viewer and the viewed, and aims toward interpretive understanding of subjects' meanings (Guba & Lincoln, 1994; Schwandt, 1994). The power of grounded theory lies in its tools for understanding empirical worlds. We can reclaim these tools from their positivist underpinnings to form a re-

vised, more open-ended practice of grounded theory that stresses its emergent, constructivist elements. We can use grounded theory methods as flexible, heuristic strategies rather than as formulaic procedures.

A constructivist approach to grounded theory reaffirms studying people in their natural settings and redirects qualitative research away from positivism. My argument is threefold: (a) Grounded theory strategies need not be rigid or prescriptive; (b) a focus on meaning while using grounded theory *furthers*, rather than limits, interpretive understanding; and (c) we can adopt grounded theory strategies without embracing the positivist leanings of earlier proponents of grounded theory. Certainly, a continuum can be discerned between objectivist and constructivist grounded theory. In addition, individual grounded theorists have modified their approaches over time (see, e.g., Glaser, 1994; Strauss, 1995; Strauss & Corbin, 1990, 1994, 1998). For clarity, I juxtapose objectivist and constructivist approaches throughout the following discussion, but note shifts as proponents have developed their positions.

In this chapter, I provide an overview of grounded theory methods, discuss recent debates, and describe a constructivist approach, which I illustrate with examples from my earlier studies. Researchers can use grounded theory methods with either quantitative or qualitative data, although these methods are typically associated with qualitative research. And researchers can use these methods whether they are working from an objectivist or a constructivist perspective.

The rigor of grounded theory approaches offers qualitative researchers a set of clear guidelines from which to build explanatory frameworks that specify relationships among concepts. Grounded theory methods do not detail data collection techniques; they move each step of the analytic process toward the development, refinement, and interrelation of concepts. The strategies of grounded theory include (a) simultaneous collection and analysis of data, (b) a two-step data coding process, (c) comparative methods, (d) memo writing aimed at the construction of conceptual analyses, (e) sampling to refine the researcher's emerging theoretical ideas, and (f) integration of the theoretical framework.

Glaser (1978, 1992) establishes the following criteria for evaluating a grounded theory: fit, work, relevance, and modifiability. Theoretical categories must be developed from analysis of the collected data and must fit them; these categories must explain the data they subsume. Thus grounded theorists cannot shop their disciplinary stores for preconceived concepts and dress their data in them. Any existing concept must earn its way into the analysis (Glaser, 1978). A grounded theory must work; it must provide a useful conceptual rendering and ordering of the data that explains the studied phenomena. The relevance of a grounded theory derives from its offering analytic explanations of actual problems and basic processes in the research setting. A grounded theory is durable because it accounts for variation; it is flexible because researchers can modify their emerging or established analyses as conditions change or further data are gathered.

Many grounded theory studies reflect the objectivist approaches and perspectival proclivities of the founders of grounded theory (see, e.g., Biernacki, 1986; Johnson, 1991; Reif, 1975; Swanson & Chenitz, 1993; Wiener, 1975).[2] However, researchers starting from other vantage points—feminist, Marxist, phenomenologist— can use grounded theory strategies for their empirical studies. These strategies allow for varied fundamental assumptions, data gathering approaches, analytic emphases, and theoretical levels.

Thus diverse researchers can use grounded theory methods to develop constructivist studies derived from interpretive approaches. Grounded theorists need not subscribe to positivist or objectivist assumptions. Rather, they may still study empirical worlds without presupposing narrow objectivist methods and without assuming the truth of their subsequent analyses. Hence constructivist grounded theory studies of subjective experience can bridge Blumer's (1969) call for the empirical study of meanings with current postmodernist critiques.

◆ *Grounded Theory Then and Now*

The Development of Grounded Theory

In their pioneering book, *The Discovery of Grounded Theory* (1967), Barney G. Glaser and Anselm L. Strauss first articulated their research strategies for their collaborative studies of dying (Glaser & Strauss, 1965, 1968). They challenged the hegemony of the quantitative research paradigm in the social sciences. Chicago school sociology (see, e.g., Park & Burgess, 1925; Shaw, 1930; Thomas & Znaniecki, 1918-1920; Thrasher, 1927/1963; Zorbaugh, 1929) had long contributed a rich ethnographic tradition to the discipline. However, the ascendancy of quantitative methods undermined and marginalized that tradition. Scientistic assumptions of objectivity and truth furthered the quest for verification through precise, standardized instruments and parsimonious quantifiable variables. Field research waned. It became viewed as a preliminary exercise through which researchers could refine quantitative instruments before the real work began, rather than as a viable endeavor in its own right. The ascendancy of quantification also led to a growing division between theory and empirical research. Theorists and researchers lived in different worlds and pursued different problems. Presumably, quantitative research tested existing theory as prescribed by the logico-deductive model. However, much of this research remained atheoretical and emphasized controlling variables rather than theory testing.

Glaser and Strauss's (1967) work was revolutionary because it challenged (a) arbitrary divisions between theory and research, (b) views of qualitative research as primarily a precursor to more "rigorous" quantitative methods, (c) claims that the quest for rigor made qualitative research illegitimate, (d) beliefs that qualitative methods are impressionistic and unsystematic, (e) separation of data collection and analysis, and (f) assumptions that qualitative research could produce only descriptive case studies rather than theory development (Charmaz, 1995c). With the publication of *Discovery,* Glaser and Strauss called for qualitative research to move toward theory development.[3] They provided a persuasive intellectual rationale for conducting qualitative research that permitted and encouraged novices to pursue it. And they gave guidelines for its successful completion.

Prior to the publication of *Discovery,* most qualitative analysis had been taught through an oral tradition of mentoring, when taught at all. Glaser and Strauss led the way in providing written guidelines for systematic qualitative data analysis with explicit analytic procedures and research strategies. Glaser applied his rigorous positivistic methodological training in quantitative research from Columbia University to the development of qualitative analysis. Grounded theory methods were founded upon Glaser's epistemological assumptions, methodological terms, inductive logic, and systematic approach. Strauss's training at the University of Chicago with Herbert Blumer and Robert Park brought Chicago school field research and symbolic interactionism to grounded theory. Hence, Strauss brought the pragmatist philosophical study of process, action, and meaning into *empirical* inquiry through grounded theory.

Glaser's 1978 book *Theoretical Sensitivity* substantially advanced explication of grounded theory methods. However, the abstract terms and dense writing Glaser employed rendered the book inaccessible to many readers. Strauss's *Qualitative Analysis for Social Scientists* (1987) made grounded theory more accessible, although perhaps more theoretically diffuse than the earlier methods texts would suggest.

Reformulation and Repudiation

Grounded theory gained a wider audience, a new spokesperson, and more disciples with the appearance of Strauss's 1990 coauthored book with Juliet Corbin, *Basics of Qualitative Research: Grounded Theory Procedures and Techniques.*[4] This book aims to specify and to develop grounded theory methodology. It takes the reader through several familiar analytic steps, illustrates procedures with examples, and

stirs a new technical armamentarium into the mix. *Basics* gained readers but lost the sense of emergence and open-ended character of Strauss's earlier volume and much of his empirical work. The improved and more accessible second edition of *Basics* (Strauss & Corbin, 1998) reads as less prescriptive and aims to lead readers to a new way of thinking about their research and about the world. In both editions, the authors pose concerns (1990, p. 7; 1998, p. x) about valid and reliable data and interpretations and researcher bias consistent with "normal science" (Kuhn, 1970). Strauss and Corbin impart a behaviorist, rather than interpretive, cast to their analysis of key hypothetical examples (see 1990, pp. 63-65, 78-81, 88-90, 145-147).[5] Perhaps the scientific underpinnings of the 1990 book reflect both Corbin's earlier training and Strauss's growing insistence that grounded theory is verificational (A. L. Strauss, personal communication, February 1, 1993).[6] Whether *Basics* advances grounded theory methods or proposes different technical procedures depends on one's point of view.

Glaser (1978, 1992) emphasizes emergence of data and theory through the analysis of "basic social processes." Glaser's position (see also Melia, 1996) becomes clear in his 1992 repudiation of Strauss and Corbin (1990). He advocates gathering data without forcing either preconceived questions or frameworks upon it. In *Basics of Grounded Theory Analysis: Emergence vs. Forcing* (1992), Glaser answers Strauss and Corbin's work in *Basics.* Over and over, he finds Strauss and Corbin to be forcing data and analysis through their preconceptions, analytic questions, hypotheses, and methodological techniques (see, e.g., Glaser, 1992, pp. 33, 43, 46-47, 50-51, 58-59, 63, 78, 96-100). For Glaser, the use of systematic comparisons is enough. "Categories emerge upon comparison and properties emerge upon more comparison. And that is all there is to it" (Glaser, 1992, p. 43).

In addition to Glaser's trenchant critique, readers may find themselves caught in a maze of techniques that Strauss and Corbin propose as significant methodological advancements. Linda Robrecht (1995) asserts that the new procedures divert the researcher from the data and result in poorly integrated theoretical frameworks. Glaser declares that Strauss and Corbin invoke contrived comparisons rather than those that have emerged from analytic processes of comparing data to data, concept to concept, and category to category. He views their approach as "full conceptual description," not grounded theory. Glaser argues that the purpose of grounded theory methods is to generate theory, not to verify it. His point is consistent with quantitative research canons in which verification depends upon random sampling and standardized procedures. Strauss and Corbin do not answer Glaser directly, but, as Kath Melia (1996) notes, they do state their view of the essentials of grounded theory in their contribution to the first edition of this *Handbook,* while suggesting that the method will continue to evolve (Strauss & Corbin, 1994). Similarly, Strauss and Corbin do not respond to Glaser's charge that they abandoned grounded theory in favor of full conceptual description in their second edition of *Basics* (1998). However, they do offer an elegant statement of the significance of description and conceptual ordering for theory development (pp. 16-21).

Both Strauss and Corbin's *Basics* and Glaser's critique of it assert views of science untouched by either epistemological debates of the 1960s (Adler, Adler, & Johnson, 1992; Kleinman, 1993; Kuhn, 1970; Lofland, 1993; Snow & Morrill, 1993) or postmodern critiques (Clough, 1992; Denzin, 1991, 1992a, 1996; Marcus & Fischer, 1986). Both endorse a realist ontology and positivist epistemology, albeit with some sharp differences. Glaser remains in the positivist camp; Strauss and Corbin less so. They move between objectivist and constructivist assumptions in various works, although *Basics,* for which they are best known, stands in the objectivist terrain. For example, in their efforts to maintain objectivity, they advocate taking "appropriate measures" to minimize the intrusion of the subjectivity of the researcher into the research (Strauss & Corbin, 1998, p. 43). Both Glaser and Strauss and Corbin assume an external reality that re-

searchers can discover and record—Glaser through discovering data, coding it, and using comparative methods step by step; Strauss and Corbin through their analytic questions, hypotheses, and methodological applications. In their earlier writings, Glaser and Strauss (1967) imply that reality is independent of the observer and the methods used to produce it. Because both Glaser and Strauss and Corbin follow the canons of objective reportage, both engage in silent authorship and usually write about their data as distanced experts (Charmaz & Mitchell, 1996), thereby contributing to an objectivist stance.[7] Furthermore, the didactic, prescriptive approaches described in early statements about grounded theory coated these methods with a positivist, objectivist cast (see Charmaz, 1983; Glaser, 1992; Stern, 1994b; Strauss, 1987; Strauss & Corbin, 1990, 1994).

So who's got the real grounded theory? Glaser (1998) contends that he has the pure version of grounded theory. That's correct—if one agrees that early formulations should set the standard.[8] Different proponents assume that grounded theory essentials *ought* to include different things. Their "oughts" shape their notions of the real grounded theory. Must grounded theory be objectivist and positivist? No. Grounded theory offers a set of flexible strategies, not rigid prescriptions. Should grounded theorists adopt symbolic interactionism? Not always. Emphases on action and process and, from my constructivist view, meaning and emergence within symbolic interactionism complement grounded theory. Symbolic interactionism also offers a rich array of sensitizing concepts. However, grounded theory strategies can be used with sensitizing concepts from other perspectives. Pragmatism? Yes, because applicability and usefulness are part of the criteria for evaluating grounded theory analyses. Should we expect grounded theorists to remain committed to their written statements? Not completely. Published works become separated from the contexts of their creation. Neither their authors' original purpose nor intended audience may be apparent. Authors may write mechanistic prescriptions for beginners to get them started but compose more measured pieces for peers. New developments may influence them. But readers may reify these authors' earlier written words. Strauss and Corbin's (1994) chapter in the first edition of this *Handbook* has a considerably more flexible tone than is found in the first edition of *Basics* (1990), both in describing methods and in positioning grounded theory. For example, they note that future researchers may use grounded theory in conjunction with other approaches, which I argue here. A simplified, constructivist version of grounded theory such as outlined below can supply effective tools that can be adopted by researchers from diverse perspectives.[9]

◆ *Grounded Theory Strategies*

Regarding Data

Grounded theory methods specify analytic strategies, not data collection methods. These methods have become associated with limited interview studies, as if limiting grounded theory methods *to* interviews and limiting the number *of* interviews are both acceptable practices (see, e.g., Creswell, 1997). Researchers can use grounded theory techniques with varied forms of data collection (for historical analyses, see Clarke, 1998; Star, 1989). Qualitative researchers should gather extensive amounts of rich data with thick description (Charmaz, 1995c; Geertz, 1973). Grounded theorists have been accused, with some justification, of slighting data collection (Lofland & Lofland, 1984). Nonetheless, a number of grounded theorists have gathered thorough data, even those who have relied primarily on interviews (see, e.g., Baszanger, 1998; Biernacki, 1986; Charmaz, 1991, 1995b). Perhaps because grounded theory methods focus on the development of early analytic schemes, data gathering remains problematic and disputed.

Glaser (1992) raises sharp differences with Strauss and Corbin (1990) about forcing data

through preconceived questions, categories, and hypotheses. Perhaps both are right, although in different ways. Glaser's comparative approach and emphasis on process provide excellent strategies for making data analysis efficient, productive, and exciting—without formulaic techniques. Every qualitative researcher should take heed of his warnings about forcing data into preconceived categories through the imposition of artificial questions. However, data collecting may demand that researchers ask questions and follow hunches, if not in direct conversation with respondents, then in the observers' notes about what to look for. Researchers construct rich data by amassing pertinent details. Strauss and Corbin's many questions and techniques may help novices improve their data gathering. Glaser (1998) assumes that data become transparent, that we researchers will see the basic social process in the field through our respondents' telling us what is significant. However, what researchers see may be neither basic nor certain (Mitchell & Charmaz, 1996). What respondents assume or do not apprehend may be much more important than what they talk about. An acontextual reliance on respondents' overt concerns can lead to narrow research problems, limited data, and trivial analyses.

Most grounded theorists write as if their data have an objective status. Strauss and Corbin (1998) write of "the reality of the data" and tell us, "The data do not lie" (p. 85). Data are narrative constructions (Maines, 1993). They are reconstructions of experience; they are not the original experience itself (see also Bond, 1990). Whether our respondents ply us with data in interview accounts they recast for our consumption or we record ethnographic stories to reflect experience as best we can recall and narrate, data remain reconstructions.

As we gather rich data, we draw from multiple sources—observations, conversations, formal interviews, autobiographies, public records, organizational reports, respondents' diaries and journals, and our own tape-recorded reflections. Grounded theory analyses of such materials begin with our coding, take form with memos, and are fashioned into conference papers and articles. Yet our statement of the ideas seldom ends with publication. Rather, we revisit our ideas and, perhaps, our data and re-create them in new form in an evolving process (Connelly & Clandinin, 1990).[10]

Coding Data

How do we do grounded theory? Analysis begins early. We grounded theorists code our emerging data as we collect it. Through coding, we start to define and categorize our data. In grounded theory coding, we create codes as we study our data. We do not, or should not, paste catchy concepts on our data. We should interact with our data and pose questions to them while coding them. Coding helps us to gain a new perspective on our material and to focus further data collection, and may lead us in unforeseen directions. Unlike quantitative research that requires data to fit into *preconceived* standardized codes, the researcher's interpretations of data shape his or her emergent codes in grounded theory.

Coding starts the chain of theory development. Codes that account for our data take form together as nascent theory that, in turn, explains these data and directs further data gathering. Initial or open coding proceeds through our examining each line of data and then defining actions or events within it—line-by-line coding (see especially Glaser, 1978). This coding keeps us studying our data. In addition to starting to build ideas inductively, we are deterred by line-by-line coding from imposing extant theories or our own beliefs on the data. This form of coding helps us to remain attuned to our subjects' views of their realities, rather than assume that we share the same views and worlds. Line-by-line coding sharpens our use of sensitizing concepts—that is, those background ideas that inform the overall research problem. Sensitizing concepts offer ways of seeing, organizing, and understanding experience; they are embedded in our disciplinary emphases and perspectival proclivities. Although sensitizing concepts may

deepen perception, they provide starting points for building analysis, not ending points for evading it. We may use sensitizing concepts *only* as points of departure from which to study the data.

Line-by-line coding likely leads to our refining and specifying any borrowed extant concepts. Much of my work on the experience of illness has been informed by concepts of self and identity. The woman whose statement is quoted in Table 19.1 talked of having loved her job as an advocate for nursing-home residents. Through coding her statement line by line, I created the code "identity trade-offs" and later developed it into a category. Line-by-line coding keeps us thinking about what meanings we make of our data, asking ourselves questions of it, and pinpointing gaps and leads in it to focus on during subsequent data collection. Note that I kept the codes active. These action codes give us insight into what people are doing, what is happening in the setting.

Generating action codes facilitates making comparisons, a major technique in grounded theory. The constant comparative method of grounded theory means (a) comparing different people (such as their views, situations, actions, accounts, and experiences), (b) comparing data from the same individuals with themselves at different points in time, (c) comparing incident with incident, (d) comparing data with category, and (e) comparing a category with other categories (Charmaz, 1983, 1995c; Glaser, 1978, 1992).

Glaser (1978, 1992) stresses constant comparative methods. Strauss (1987) called for comparisons in his research and teaching—often hypothetical comparisons or, when he was teaching, comparisons from students' lives—at every level of analysis (see also Star, 1997).[11] Strauss and Corbin (1990) introduce new procedures: dimensionalizing, axial coding, and the conditional matrix. These procedures are intended to make researchers' emerging theories denser, more complex, and more precise. Dimensionalizing and axial coding can be done during initial coding; creating a conditional matrix comes later. Schatzman (1991) had earlier developed the concept of dimensionality to rec-

---

TABLE 19.1   Example of Line-by-Line Coding of an Interview Statement

Line-by-Line Coding	*Interview Statement*[a]
Deciding to relinquish Accounting for costs Weighing the balance Relinquishing identity Making identity trade-offs	And so I decided, this [pain, fatigue, and stress accruing during her workday] isn't a way to live. I don't have to work. . . . So it was with great regret, and not something I planned, I turned in my resignation. It was the best thing I ever did.

a. From Charmaz (1995b, p. 671).

---

ognize and account for complexity beyond one meaning of a property or phenomenon. Strauss and Corbin (1990) build on his notion by urging researchers to divide properties into dimensions that lie along a continuum. In turn, we can develop a "dimensional profile" of the properties of a category. Strauss and Corbin further propose techniques for reassembling data in new ways through what they call "axial coding." This type of coding is aimed at making connections between a category and its subcategories. These include conditions that give rise to the category, its context, the social interactions through which it is handled, and its consequences.

Selective or focused coding uses initial codes that reappear frequently to sort large amounts of data. Thus this coding is more directed and, typically, more conceptual than line-by-line coding (Charmaz, 1983, 1995c; Glaser, 1978). These codes account for the most data and categorize them most precisely. Making explicit decisions about selecting codes gives us a check on the fit between the emerging theoretical framework and the empirical reality it explains. Of the initial codes shown in Table 19.1, "identity trade-offs" was the only one I treated analytically in the published article. When comparing respondents' interviews, I found similar statements and concerns about identity.

Our categories for synthesizing and explaining data arise from our focused codes. In turn, our categories shape our developing analytic frameworks. Categories often subsume several codes. For example, my category of "significant events" included positive events and relived negative events (Charmaz, 1991). Categories turn description into conceptual analysis by specifying properties analytically, as in the following example:

> A significant event stands out in memory because it has boundaries, intensity, and emotional force. . . . The emotional reverberations of a single event echo through the present and future and therefore, however subtly, shade thoughts.

In their discussion of selective coding, Strauss and Corbin (1990) introduce the "conditional matrix," an analytic diagram that maps the range of conditions and consequences related to the phenomenon or category. They describe this matrix as a series of circles in which the outer rings represent those conditions most distant from actions and interactions and the inner rings represent those closest to actions and interactions. Strauss and Corbin propose that researchers create matrices to sensitize themselves to the range of conditions conceivably affecting the phenomena of interest and to the range of hypothetical consequences. Such matrices can sharpen researchers' explanations of and predictions about the studied phenomena.

Memo Writing

Memo writing is the intermediate step between coding and the first draft of the completed analysis. This step helps to spark our thinking and encourages us to look at our data and codes in new ways. It can help us to define leads for collecting data—both for further initial coding and later theoretical sampling. Through memo writing, we elaborate processes, assumptions, and actions that are subsumed under our codes. Memo writing leads us to explore our codes; we expand upon the processes they identify or suggest. Thus our codes take on substance as well as a structure for sorting data.

Action codes (e.g., as illustrated above) spur the writing of useful memos because they help us to see interrelated processes rather than static isolated topics. As we detail the properties of our action codes in memos, we connect categories and define how they fit into larger processes. By discussing these connections and defining processes in memos early in our research, we reduce the likelihood that we will get lost in mountains of data—memo writing keeps us focused on our analyses and involved in our research.

Memo writing aids us in linking analytic interpretation with empirical reality. We bring raw data right into our memos so that we maintain those connections and examine them directly. Raw data from different sources provide the grist for making precise comparisons, fleshing out ideas, analyzing properties of categories, and seeing patterns. The first excerpt below is the first section of an early memo. I wrote this memo quickly in 1983 after comparing data from a series of recent interviews.[12]

Developing a Dual Self

The dual self in this case is the *contrast* between the *sick self* and the *monitoring self* (actually *physical* self might be a better term [than *sick self*] since some of these people try to see themselves as "well" but still feel they must constantly monitor in order to maintain that status—they also rather easily sink into self-blame when the monitoring doesn't work).

With Sara S. we see definite conversations held between the physical and monitoring self. Through her learning time or body education, self-taught and self-validated she has not only developed a sense of what her body "*needs*" she has developed a finely honed *sense of timing* about how to handle those needs.

With the dual self, the monitoring self *externalizes* the internal messages from the physical self and makes them concrete. It is as if dialogue and negotiation with ultimate validation of the physical self take place between the two dimensions of the dual self. Consequently, the competent monitoring self must be able to attend to the messages given by the physical self. The learning time is the necessary amount of concentration, trial and error to become an effective monitoring self.

Mark R., for example, illustrates the kind of dialogue that takes place between the monitoring and physical selves when he talks about person to kidney talks and what is needed to sustain that new transplanted kidney in his body.

The dual self in many ways is analogous to the dialogue that Mead describes between the I and the me. The me monitors and attends to the I which is creating, experiencing, feeling. The monitoring me defines those feelings, impulses and sensations. It evaluates them and develops a line of action so that what is defined as needed is taken care of. The physical self here is then taken as an object held up to view which can be compared with past physical (or for that matter, psychological selves), with perceived statuses of others, with a defined level of health or well-being, with signals of potential crises etc.

A consequence of the monitoring self is that it may be encouraged by practitioners (after all, taking responsibility for one's body is the message these days, isn't it?) when it seems to "work," yet it may be condemned when the person's tactics for monitoring conflict with practitioners' notions of reasonable action or are unsuccessful.

The following passage shows how the memo appeared in the published version of the research (Charmaz, 1991). The combination of analytic clarity and empirical grounding makes the memo above remarkably congruent with the published excerpt. Memos record researchers' stages of analytic development. Memo writing helps researchers (a) to grapple with ideas about the data, (b) to set an analytic course, (c) to refine categories, (d) to define the relationships among various categories, and (e) to gain a sense of confidence and competence in their ability to analyze data.

Developing a Dialectical Self

The dialectical self is the contrast between the sick or physical self and the monitoring self. Keeping illness contained by impeding progression of illness, rather than merely hiding it, leads to developing a monitoring self. Developing a dialectical self means gaining a heightened awareness of one's body. People who do so believe that they perceive nuances of physical changes. By his second transplant, for example, Mark Reinertsen felt that he had learned to perceive the first signs of organ rejection.

When people no longer view themselves as "sick," they still monitor their physical selves to save themselves from further illness. To illustrate, Sara Shaw explained that she spent months of "learning time" to be able to discover what her body "needed" and how to handle those needs. She commented, "I got to know it [her ill body]; I got to understand it, and it was just me and mixed connective tissue disease [her diagnosis changed], you know, and I got to respect it and I got to know—to have a real good feeling for time elements and for what my body was doing, how my body was feeling." When I asked her what she meant by "time elements," she replied:

> There's times during the month, during the course of a month, when I'm much more susceptible, and I can feel it. I can wake up in the morning and I can feel it. . . . So I really learned what I was capable of and when I had to stop, when I had to slow down. And I learned to like—give and take with that. And I think that's all programmed in my mind now, and I don't even have to think about it now, you know; I'll know. I'll know when, no matter what's going on, I've gotta go sit down . . . and take it easy, . . . that's a requirement of that day. And so consequently, I really don't get sick.

In the dialectical self, the monitoring self externalizes the internal messages from the physical self and makes them concrete. It is as if dialogue and negotiation with ultimate validation of the physical self take place. For example, Mark Reinertsen engaged in "person to kidney" talks to encourage the new kidney to remain with him (see also McGuire and Kantor 1987). A competent monitoring self attends to messages from the physical self and over time, as Sara Shaw's comment suggests, monitoring becomes taken for granted.

In many ways, the dialectical self is analogous to the dialogue that Mead (1934) describes between the "I" and the "me." The "me" monitors and attends to the "I" that creates, experiences, and feels. The monitoring "me" defines the "I's" behaviors, feelings, impulses, and sensations. It evaluates them and plans action to meet defined needs. Here, an ill person takes his or her physical self as an object, appraises it and compares it with past physical selves, with perceived health statuses of others, with ideals of physical or mental well-being, with signals of potential crises and so forth (cf. Gadow 1982).

The dialectical self is one of ill people's multiple selves emerging in the face of uncertainty. Whether or not ill people give the dialectical self validity significantly affects their actions. For someone like Sara Shaw, the dialectical self provided guidelines for organizing time, for taking jobs, and for developing relationships with others. With jobs, she believed that she had to guard herself from the stress of too many demands. With friends, she felt she had to place her needs first. With physicians, she resisted their control since she trusted her knowledge about her condition more than theirs.

Practitioners may encourage a monitoring self when it seems to "work," yet condemn it when unsuccessful, or when monitoring tactics conflict with their advice (cf. Kleinman 1988). The development of the dialectical self illuminates the active stance that some people take toward their illnesses and their lives. In short, the dialectical self helps people to keep illness in the background of their lives. (Charmaz, 1991, pp. 70-72)

Note the change in the title of the category in the published version. This change reflects my attempt to choose terms that best portrayed the empirical descriptions that the category subsumed. I was trying to address the liminal relationship certain respondents described with their bodies in which they gained a heightened awareness of cues that other people disavow, disregard, or do not discern. The term *dialectical self* denotes a more dynamic process than does the term *dual self*.

Although many grounded theorists concentrate on overt actions and statements, I also look for subjects' unstated assumptions and implicit meanings.[13] Then I ask myself how these assumptions and meanings relate to conditions in which a category emerges. For example, some people with chronic illnesses assumed that their bodies had become alien and hostile battlegrounds where they warred with illness. Their assumptions about having alien bodies and being at war with illness affected if and how they adapted to their situations. When I developed the category "surrendering to the sick body," I asked what conditions fostered surrendering (Charmaz, 1995b). I identified three: (a) "relinquishing the quest for control over one's body," (b) "giving up notions of victory over illness," and (c) "affirming, however implicitly, that one's self is tied to the sick body" (p. 672).

Theoretical Sampling

As we grounded theorists refine our categories and develop them as theoretical constructs, we likely find gaps in our data and holes in our theories. Then we go back to the field and collect delimited data to fill those conceptual gaps and holes—we conduct theoretical sampling. At this point, we choose to sample specific issues only; we look for precise information to shed light on the emerging theory.

Theoretical sampling represents a defining property of grounded theory and relies on the comparative methods within grounded theory. We use theoretical sampling to develop our emerging categories and to make them more definitive and useful. Thus the aim of this sampling is to refine *ideas,* not to increase the size of the original sample. Theoretical sampling helps us to identify conceptual boundaries and pinpoint the fit and relevance of our categories.

Although we often sample people, we may sample scenes, events, or documents, depending on the study and where the theory leads us. We may return to the same settings or individuals to gain further information. I filled out my initial analysis of one category, "living one day at a time," by going back to respondents with whom I had conducted earlier interviews. I had already found that people with chronic illnesses took living one day at time as a strategy

to maintain some control over their uncertain lives. Only by going back to selected respondents did I learn that this strategy also had consequences for how they viewed the future when they later allowed themselves to think of it. The passage of time and the events that had filled it allowed them to give up earlier cherished plans and anticipated futures without being devastated by loss.

Theoretical sampling is a pivotal part of the development of formal theory. Here, the level of abstraction of the emerging theory has explanatory power across substantive areas because the processes and concepts within it are abstract and generic (Prus, 1987). Thus we would seek comparative data in substantive areas through theoretical sampling to help us tease out less visible properties of our concepts and the conditions and limits of their applicability. For example, I address identity loss in several analyses of the experience of illness. I could refine my concepts by looking at identity loss in other situations, such as bereavement and involuntary unemployment. Comparative analysis of people who experience unanticipated identity gains, such as unexpected job promotions, could also net conceptual refinements.

The necessity of engaging in theoretical sampling means that we researchers cannot produce a solid grounded theory through one-shot interviewing in a single data collection phase. Instead, theoretical sampling demands that we have completed the work of comparing data with data and have developed a provisional set of relevant categories for explaining our data. In turn, our categories take us back to the field to gain more insight about when, how, and to what extent they are pertinent and useful.

Theoretical sampling helps us to define the properties of our categories; to identify the contexts in which they are relevant; to specify the conditions under which they arise, are maintained, and vary; and to discover their consequences. Our emphasis on studying process combined with theoretical sampling to delineate the limits of our categories also helps us to define gaps between categories. Through using comparative methods, we specify the conditions under which they are linked to other categories. After we decide which categories best explain what is happening in our study, we treat them as concepts. In this sense, these concepts are useful for helping us to understand many incidents or issues in the data (Strauss & Corbin, 1990). Strauss (personal communication, February 1, 1993) advocates theoretical sampling early in the research. I recommend conducting it later in order that relevant data and analytic directions emerge without being forced. Otherwise, early theoretical sampling may bring premature closure to the analysis.

Grounded theory researchers take the usual criteria of "saturation" (i.e., new data fit into the categories already devised) of their categories for ending the research (Morse, 1995). But what does saturation mean? In practice, saturation seems elastic (see also Flick, 1998; Morse, 1995). Grounded theory approaches are seductive because they allow us to gain a handle on our material quickly. Is the handle we gain the best or most complete one? Does it encourage us to look deeply enough? The data in works claiming to be grounded theory pieces range from a handful of cases to sustained field research. The latter more likely fulfills the criterion of saturation and, moreover, has the resonance of intimate familiarity with the studied world.

As we define our categories as saturated (and some of us never do), we rewrite our memos in expanded, more analytic form. We put these memos to work for lectures, presentations, papers, and chapters. The analytic work continues as we sort and order memos, for we may discover gaps or new relationships.

Computer-Assisted Analysis

Computer-assisted techniques offer some shortcuts for coding, sorting, and integrating the data. Several programs, including NUD•IST and the Ethnograph, are explicitly aimed at assisting in grounded theory analyses. Hyper-Research, a program designed to retrieve and group data, serves qualitative sociologists across a broad range of analytic applications.[14] Such programs can prove enormously helpful with the problem of mountains of data—that is, data

management. Amanda Coffey, Beverly Holbrook, and Paul Atkinson (1996) point out that other advantages of computer coding include the ability to do multiple searches using more than one code word simultaneously and the fact that it enables researchers to place memos at points in the text. Data analysis programs are also effective for mapping relationships visually onscreen. They do not, however, think for the analyst—perhaps to chagrin of some students (see also Seidel, 1991). Nonetheless, Thomas J. Richards and Lyn Richards (1994) argue that the code-and-retrieve method supports the emergence of theory by searching the data for codes and assembling ideas. Further, Renata Tesch (1991) notes that conceptual operations follow or accompany mechanical data management.

Qualitative analysis software programs do not escape controversy. Coffey et al. (1996) and Lonkila (1995) express concern about qualitative programs based on conceptions of grounded theory methods and their uncritical adoption by users. They fear that these programs overemphasize coding and promote a superficial view of grounded theory; they also note that mechanical operations are no substitute for nuanced interpretive analysis. However, Nigel G. Fielding and Raymond M. Lee (1998) do not find substantial empirical evidence for such concerns in their systematic field study of users' experiences with computer-assisted qualitative data analysis programs.[15] I still have some reservations about these programs for four reasons: (a) Grounded theory methods are often poorly understood; (b) these methods have long been used to *legitimate,* rather than to conduct, studies; (c) these software packages appear more suited for objectivist grounded theory than constructivist approaches; and (d) the programs may unintentionally foster an illusion that interpretive work can be reduced to a set of procedures. Yvonna Lincoln (personal communication, August 21, 1998) asks her students, "Why would you want to engage in work that connects you to the deepest part of human existence and then turn it over to a machine to 'mediate'?" Part of interpretive work is gaining a sense of the whole—the whole interview, the whole story, the whole body of data. No matter how helpful computer programs may prove for managing the parts, we can see only their fragments on the screen.[16] And these fragments may seem to take on an existence of their own, as if objective and removed from their contextual origins and from our constructions and interpretations. Because objectivist grounded theory echoes positivism, computer-assisted programs based on it may promote widespread acceptance not just of the software, but of a one-dimensional view of qualitative research.

◆ Critical Challenges to Grounded Theory

As is evident from the discussion above, recent debates have resulted in reassessments of grounded theory. Objectivist grounded theory has shaped views of what the method is and where it can take qualitative research. Over the years, a perception of how leading proponents have used grounded theory has become melded with the methods themselves. Subsequently, critics make assumptions about the nature of the method and its limitations (see, e.g., Conrad, 1990; Riessman, 1990a, 1990b). Riessman (1990a) states that grounded theory methods were insufficient to respect her interviewees and to portray their stories. Richardson (1993) found prospects of completing a grounded theory analysis to be alienating and turned to literary forms. Richardson (1994) also has observed that qualitative research reports are not so straightforward as their authors represent them to be. Authors choose evidence selectively, clean up subjects' statements, unconsciously adopt value-laden metaphors, assume omniscience, and bore readers.

These criticisms challenge authors' representations of their subjects, their authority to interpret subjects' lives, and their writer's voice, criticisms ethnographers have answered (see, e.g., Best, 1995; Dawson & Prus, 1995; Kleinman, 1993; Sanders, 1995; Snow & Morrill, 1993). These criticisms imply that grounded theory methods gloss over meanings within respondents' stories.[17] Conrad (1990) and Riessman (1990b) suggest that "fracturing the data" in grounded theory research might limit understanding because grounded theorists aim for analysis rather than the portrayal of subjects' experience in its fullness. From a grounded theory perspective, fracturing the data means creating codes and categories as the researcher defines themes within the data. Glaser and Strauss (1967) propose this strategy for several reasons: (a) to help the researcher avoid remaining immersed in anecdotes and stories, and subsequently unconsciously adopting subjects' perspectives; (b) to prevent the researcher's becoming immobilized and overwhelmed by voluminous data; and (c) to create a way for the researcher to organize and interpret data. However, criticisms of fracturing the data imply that grounded theory methods lead to separating the experience from the experiencing subject, the meaning from the story, and the viewer from the viewed.[18] In short, the criticisms assume that the grounded theory method (a) limits entry into subjects' worlds, and thus reduces understanding of their experience; (b) curtails representation of both the social world and subjective experience; (c) relies upon the viewer's authority as expert observer; and (d) posits a set of objectivist procedures on which the analysis rests.[19]

Researchers can use grounded theory methods to further their knowledge of subjective experience and to expand its representation while neither remaining external from it nor accepting objectivist assumptions and procedures. A constructivist grounded theory assumes that people create and maintain meaningful worlds through dialectical processes of conferring meaning on their realities and acting within them (Bury, 1986; Mishler, 1981). Thus social reality does not exist independent of human action. Certainly, my approach contrasts with a number of grounded theory studies, methodological statements, and research texts (see, e.g., Chenitz & Swanson, 1986; Glaser, 1992; Martin & Turner, 1986; Strauss & Corbin, 1990; Turner, 1981). By adopting a constructivist grounded theory approach, the researcher can move grounded theory methods further into the realm of interpretive social science consistent with a Blumerian (1969) emphasis on meaning, without assuming the existence of a unidimensional external reality. A constructivist grounded theory recognizes the interactive nature of both data collection and analysis, resolves recent criticisms of the method, and reconciles positivist assumptions and postmodernist critiques. Moreover, a constructivist grounded theory fosters the development of qualitative traditions through the study of experience from the standpoint of those who live it.

The Place of Grounded Theory in Qualitative Research

Grounded theory research fits into the broader traditions of fieldwork and qualitative analysis. Most grounded theory studies rely on detailed qualitative materials collected through field, or ethnographic, research, but they are not ethnographies in the sense of total immersion into specific communities. Nor do grounded theorists attempt to study the social structures of whole communities. Instead, we tend to look at slices of social life. Like other forms of qualitative research, grounded theories can only portray moments in time. However, the grounded theory quest for the study of basic social processes fosters the identification of connections between events. The social world is always in process, and the lives of the research subjects shift and change as their circumstances and they themselves change. Hence a grounded theorist—or, more broadly, a qualitative researcher—constructs a picture that draws from, reassembles, and renders subjects' lives. The product is more like a painting than a photograph (Charmaz, 1995a). I come close to Atkinson's (1990, p. 2) depiction of ethnography as an "artful product" of objectivist description, careful organization, and interpretive commentary. The tendency to reify the findings and the picture of reality may result more from interpreters of the work than from its author.[20] Significantly, however, many researchers who adopt grounded theory strategies do so precisely to construct objectivist—that is, positivist—qualitative studies.

Grounded theory provides a systematic analytic approach to qualitative analysis of ethnographic materials because it consists of a set of explicit strategies. Any reasonably well-trained researcher can employ these strategies and develop an analysis. The strengths of grounded theory methods lie in (a) strategies that guide the researcher step by step through an analytic process, (b) the self-correcting nature of the data collection process, (c) the methods' inherent bent toward theory and the simultaneous turning away from acontextual description, and (d) the emphasis on comparative methods. Yet, like other qualitative approaches, grounded theory research is an emergent process rather than the product of a single research problem logically and deductively sequenced into a study—or even one logically and inductively sequenced. The initial research questions may be concrete and descriptive, but the researcher can develop deeper analytic questions by studying his or her data. Like wondrous gifts waiting to be opened, early grounded theory texts imply that categories and concepts inhere within the data, awaiting the researcher's discovery (Charmaz, 1990, 1995c). Not so. Glaser (1978, 1992) assumes that we can gather our data unfettered by bias or biography. Instead, a constructivist approach recognizes that the categories, concepts, and theoretical level of an analysis emerge from the researcher's interactions within the field and questions about the data. In short, the narrowing of research questions, the creation of concepts and categories, and the integration of the constructed theoretical framework reflect what and how the researcher thinks and does about shaping and collecting the data.

The grounded theorist's analysis tells a story about people, social processes, and situations. The researcher composes the story; it does not simply unfold before the eyes of an objective viewer. This story reflects the viewer as well as the viewed. Grounded theory studies typically lie between traditional research methodology and the recent postmodernist turn. Radical empiricists shudder at grounded theorists' contamination of the story because we shape the data collection and redirect our analyses as new issues emerge. Now postmodernists and post-structuralists castigate the story as well. They argue that we compose our stories unconsciously, deny the oedipal logic of authorial desire (Clough, 1992), and deconstruct the subject. In addition, Denzin (1992a) states that even the new interpretive approaches "privilege the researcher over the subject, method over subject matter, and maintain commitments to outmoded conceptions of validity, truth, and generalizability" (p. 20). These criticisms apply to much grounded theory research. Yet we can use them to make our empirical research more reflexive and our completed studies more contextually situated. We can claim only to have interpreted *a* reality, as we understood both our own experience and our subjects' portrayals of theirs.

A re-visioned grounded theory must take epistemological questions into account. Grounded theory can provide a path for researchers who want to continue to develop qualitative traditions without adopting the positivistic trappings of objectivism and universality. Hence the further development of a constructivist grounded theory can bridge past positivism and a revised future form of interpretive inquiry. A revised grounded theory preserves realism through gritty, empirical inquiry and sheds positivistic proclivities by becoming increasingly interpretive.

In contradistinction to Clough's (1992) critique, ethnographies can refer to a feminist vision to construct narratives that do not claim to be literal representations of the real. A feminist vision allows emotions to surface, doubts to be expressed, and relationships with subjects to grow. Data collection becomes less formal, more immediate, and subjects' concerns take precedence over researchers' questions.

A constructivist grounded theory distinguishes between the real and the true. The constructivist approach does not seek truth—single, universal, and lasting. Still, it remains realist because it addresses human *realities* and assumes the existence of real worlds. However, neither human realities nor real worlds are unidimensional. We act within and upon our realities and worlds and thus develop dialectical relations among what we do, think, and feel. The constructivist approach assumes that what we take as real, as objective knowledge and truth, is based upon our perspective (Schwandt, 1994). The pragmatist underpinnings in symbolic interactionism emerge here. W. I. Thomas and Dorothy Swaine Thomas (1928) proclaim, "If human beings define their situations as real, they are real in their consequences" (p. 572). Following their theorem, we must try to find what research participants define as real and where their definitions of reality take them. The constructivist approach also fosters our self-consciousness about what we attribute to our subjects and how, when, and why researchers portray these definitions as real. Thus the research products do not constitute the reality of the respondents' reality. Rather, each is a rendering, one interpretation among multiple interpretations, of a shared or individual reality. That interpretation is objectivist only to the extent that it seeks to construct analyses that show how respondents and the social scientists who study them construct those realities—*without viewing those realities as unidimensional, universal, and immutable.* Researchers' attention to detail in the constructivist approach sensitizes them to multiple realities and the multiple viewpoints within them; it does not represent a quest to capture a single reality.

Thus we can recast the obdurate character of social life that Blumer (1969) talks about. In doing so, we change our conception of it from a real world to be discovered, tracked, and categorized to a world *made real* in the minds and through the words and actions of its members. Thus the grounded theorist constructs an image of *a* reality, not *the* reality—that is, objective, true, and external.

◆ Objectivist Versus Constructivist Grounded Theory

A constructivist grounded theory recognizes that the viewer creates the data and ensuing analysis through interaction with the viewed. Data do not provide a window on reality. Rather, the "discovered" reality arises from the interactive process and its temporal, cultural, and structural contexts. Researcher and subjects frame that interaction and confer meaning upon it. The viewer then is part of what is viewed rather than separate from it. What a viewer sees shapes what he or she will define, measure, and analyze. Because objectivist (i.e., the majority of) grounded theorists depart from this position, this crucial difference reflects the positivist leanings in their studies.[21]

Causality is suggestive, incomplete, and indeterminate in a constructivist grounded theory. Therefore, a grounded theory remains open to refinement. It looks at how "variables" are grounded—given meaning and played out in subjects' lives (Dawson & Prus, 1995; Prus, 1996). Their meanings and actions take priority over researchers' analytic interests and methodological technology. A constructivist grounded theory seeks to define conditional statements that interpret how subjects construct their realities. Nonetheless, these conditional statements do not approach some level of generalizable truth. Rather, they constitute a set of hypotheses and concepts that other researchers can transport to similar research problems and to other substantive fields. As such, they answer Prus's (1987) call for the development and study of generic concepts. Thus the grounded theorist's hypotheses and concepts offer both explanation and understanding and fulfill the pragmatist criterion of usefulness.

In contrast, objectivist grounded theorists adhere more closely to positivistic canons of traditional science (see Glaser, 1978, 1992; Glaser & Strauss, 1967; Strauss & Corbin, 1990, 1994; Wilson & Hutchinson, 1991).[22] They assume that following a systematic set of methods leads them to discover reality and to construct a provisionally true, testable, and ultimately verifiable "theory" of it (Strauss, 1995; Strauss & Corbin, 1990, 1994).[23] This theory provides not only understanding but prediction. Three extensions of this position follow: (a) Systematic application of grounded theory strategies answers the positivist call for reliability and validity, because specifying procedures permits reproducibility;[24] (b) hypothesis testing in

grounded theory leads to confirmation or disconfirmation of the emerging theory; and (c) grounded theory methods allow for the exertion of controls, and therefore make changing the studied reality possible.

Objectivist grounded theory accepts the positivistic assumption of an external world that can be described, analyzed, explained, and predicted: truth, but with a small *t*. That is, objectivist grounded theory is modifiable as conditions change. It assumes that different observers will discover this world and describe it in similar ways. That's correct—to the extent that subjects have comparable experiences (e.g., people with different chronic illnesses may experience uncertainty, intrusive regimens, medical dominance) and viewers bring similar questions, perspectives, methods, and, subsequently, concepts to analyze those experiences. Objectivist grounded theorists often share assumptions with their research participants—particularly the professional participants. Perhaps more likely, they assume that respondents share their meanings. For example, Strauss and Corbin's (1990) discussion of independence and dependence assumes that these terms hold the same meanings for patients as for researchers.

Guidelines such as those offered by Strauss and Corbin (1990) structure objectivist grounded theorists' work. These guidelines are didactic and prescriptive rather than emergent and interactive. Clinton Sanders (1995) refers to grounded theory procedures as "more rigorous than thou instructions about how information should be pressed into a mold" (p. 92). Strauss and Corbin categorize steps in the process with scientific terms such as *axial coding* and *conditional matrix* (Strauss, 1987; Strauss & Corbin, 1990, 1993). As grounded theory methods become more articulated, categorized, and elaborated, they seem to take on a life of their own. Guidelines turn into procedures and are reified into immutable rules, unlike Glaser and Strauss's (1967) original flexible strategies. By taking grounded theory methods as prescriptive scientific rules, proponents further the positivist cast to objectivist grounded theory.

Given the positivist bent in objectivist grounded theory, where might a constructivist approach take us? How might it reconcile both positivist leanings and postmodernist critiques in grounded theory? A constructivist grounded theory lies between postmodernist (Denzin, 1991; Krieger, 1991; Marcus & Fischer, 1986; Tyler, 1986) and postpositivist approaches to qualitative research (Rennie, Phillips, & Quartaro, 1988; Turner, 1981). Researchers no longer provide a solitary voice rendering the dialogue only from their standpoints. Constructivists aim to include multiple voices, views, and visions in their rendering of lived experience. How does one accomplish this?

◆ *Constructing*
Constructivism

What helps researchers develop a constructivist grounded theory? How might they shape the data collection and analysis phases? Gaining depth and understanding in their work means that they can fulfill Blumer's (1969) call for "intimate familiarity" with respondents and their worlds (see also Lofland & Lofland, 1984, 1995). In short, constructing constructivism means seeking meanings— both respondents' meanings and researchers' meanings.

To seek respondents' meanings, we must go further than surface meanings or presumed meanings. We must look for views and values as well as for acts and facts. We need to look for beliefs and ideologies as well as situations and structures. By studying tacit meanings, we clarify, rather than challenge, respondents' views about reality.[25]

A constructivist approach necessitates a relationship with respondents in which they can cast their stories in their terms. It means listening to their stories with openness to feeling and experience. In my studies of chronic illness, several people mentioned that they saw me as someone to whom they could express their private thoughts and feelings. Sometimes, however, researchers frame their questions in ways that cloak raw experience and mute feelings. In studies that tap suffering, we may unwittingly give off cues that we do not welcome respondents' going too deep. Furthermore, one-shot interviewing lends itself to a partial, sanitized view of experience, cleaned up for public discourse. The very structure of an interview may preclude private thoughts and feelings from emerging. Such a structure reinforces whatever proclivities a respondent has to tell only the public version of the story. Researchers' sustained involvement with research participants lessens these problems.

The conceptual level of coding, writing memos, and developing categories likely differ in objectivist and constructivist grounded theory. For example, Strauss and Corbin (1990, 1998) stick close to their depiction of overt data. I aim to understand the assumptions underlying the data by piecing them together. For example, "living one day at a time" is a taken-for-granted explanation of how one manages troubles. Everyone knows what living one day at a time is. But what does it assume? Ill people report living one day at a time or having good days and bad days as self-evident facts. Not until they are asked what these terms mean experientially— that is, how they affect their relating to time, what feelings these experiences elicit, and so on—do they start to define a form and content for "living one day at a time" or "good" and "bad" days.

Objectivist grounded theory studies may offer rich description and make conditional statements, but they may remain outside of the experience. Furthermore, objectivist grounded theory methods foster externality by invoking procedures that increase complexity at the expense of experience. Axial coding can lead to awkward scientist terms and clumsy categories. Terms and categories take center stage and distance readers from the experience, rather than concentrate their attention upon it. Processual diagrams and conceptual maps can result in an overly complex architecture that obscures experience. Any form of grounded theory can generate jargon. Objectivist grounded theory especially risks cloaking analytic power in jargon.

Making our categories consistent with studied life helps to keep that life in the foreground. Active codes and subsequent categories preserve images of experience. For example, in my discussion of immersion in illness, my categories were "Recasting Life," "Facing Dependency," "Pulling In," "Slipping Into Illness Routines," and "Weathering a Serious Episode." [26]

Coding and categorizing processes sharpen the researcher's ability to ask questions about the data. Different questions can flow from objectivist and constructivist starting points. These questions can be concrete, as described by Strauss and Corbin (1990, 1998), or more abstract. Concrete questions are revealed in their discussion of two categories—pain experience and pain relief: "Who gives pain relief to people with arthritis?" "What gives relief?" "How is the pain experienced and handled?" "How much relief is needed?" "When does the pain occur and when does she institute relief?" "Why is pain relief important?" (1990, pp. 78-79). Here the categories take on an objective, external character—objective because these questions assume answers that reflect "facts"; objective because the answers assume that the researcher discovers what being in pain "really is all about"; objective because the topic of pain now takes on an external character that can be identified, addressed, and managed.

In contrast, I start by viewing the topic of pain subjectively as a feeling, an experience that may take a variety of forms. Then I ask these questions: What makes pain, pain? (That is, what is essential to the phenomenon as defined by those who experience it?) What defining properties or characteristics do ill people attribute to it? When do they do so? These questions lead into a question I share with Strauss and Corbin (1990, 1998): How does the person experience this pain, and what, if anything, does he or she do about it? My questions aim to get at meaning, not at truth. As a result, a constructivist grounded theory may remain at a more intuitive, impressionistic level than an objectivist approach.

My version of grounded theory fosters the researcher's viewing the data afresh, again and again, as he or she develops new ideas. Researchers can code and recode data numerous times (see also Glaser & Strauss, 1967). Posing new questions to the data results in new analytic points. I go back and forth between data and the drafts of chapters or papers many times. I take explicit findings in certain interviews and see if they remain implicit in other interviews. Then I go back to respondents and ask specific questions around the new category. For example, when I returned to a young woman with colitis to ask how the slow, monotonous time of convalescence might seem in memory, she understood my line of questioning immediately and cut in without skipping a beat: "It seems like a wink" (Charmaz, 1991, p. 92).

Every qualitative researcher makes multiple analytic decisions. Foremost among these is how much complexity to introduce. How much is necessary to convey the story with depth and clarity? How much seems like hairsplitting that will irritate or confuse the reader? At what point does collapsing categories result in conceptual muddiness and oversimplification? To achieve the right level of complexity, we must know the potential audience and sense the appropriate style and level at which to write for it.

◆ Rendering Through Writing

The analysis of qualitative data does not cease when the grounded theorist has developed a theoretical framework; it proceeds into the writing (Mitchell & Charmaz, 1996). A grounded theorist's proclivities toward objectivism or constructivism also come through in his or her writing about the research. The image of a scientific laboratory comes to mind with objectivist grounded theory, reflected in carefully organized and stated written reports of concepts, evidence, and procedures. Constructivist grounded theory spawns an image of a writer at a desk who tries to balance theoretical interpretation with an evocative aesthetic. To illustrate how analysis proceeds into writing constructivist grounded theory, I provide several writing strategies and examples from earlier work.

As Laurel Richardson (1990) declares, writing matters. Consistent with the postmodernist turn, I attempt to evoke experiential feeling through how I render it in writing. This means taking the reader into a story and imparting its mood through linguistic style and narrative exposition. This strategy removes the writing from typical scientific format without transforming the final product into fiction, drama, or poetry. I frame key definitions and distinctions in words that reproduce the tempo and mood of the experience:

> *Existing* from day to day occurs when a person plummets into continued crises that rip life apart. (Charmaz, 1991, p. 185)

> Others wait to map a future. And wait. They monitor their bodies and their lives. They look for signs to indicate what steps to take next. They map a future or move to the next point on the map only when they feel assured that the worst of their illness is over. These people map a future or move to the next point when they feel distant enough from illness to release their emotions from it. (p. 191)

Analogies and metaphors can explicate tacit meanings and feelings subsumed within a category (see also Charmaz & Mitchell, 1996; Richardson, 1994):

> Such men and women feel coerced into living one day at a time. They force it upon themselves, almost with clenched teeth. Here, living one day at a time resembles learning an unfamiliar, disagreeable lesson in grammar school; it is an unwelcome prerequisite to staying alive. (Charmaz, 1991, p. 179)

> Drifting time, in contrast [to dragging time], spreads out. Like a fan, drifting time unfolds and expands during a serious immersion in illness. (p. 91)

Simple language and straightforward ideas make theory readable. Theory remains embedded in the narrative, in its many stories. The theory becomes more accessible but less identifiable as theory. Several strategies foster making the writing accessible. Catching experien-tial rhythm and timing allows the researcher to reproduce it within the writing:

> From embarrassment to mortification. From discomfort to pain. Endless uncertainty. What follows? Regimentation. (Charmaz, 1991, p. 134)

> Days slip by. The same day keeps slipping by. Durations of time lengthen since few events break up the day, week, or month. Illness seems like one long uninterrupted duration of time. (p. 88)

Questions help tie main ideas together or redirect the reader. Sometimes I adopt the role of a chronically ill person and ask questions as she would.

> Is it cancer? Could it be angina? Pangs of uncertainty spring up when current, frequently undiagnosed, symptoms could mean a serious chronic illness. (Charmaz, 1991, p. 32)

Immediacy draws the reader into the story. A story occurring in the present as if now unfolding draws the reader in. I sacrificed immediacy for accuracy by writing about respondents in the past because the events described took place in the past.[27] Where authors place their stories and how they frame them can bring experience to life or wholly obscure it.

A mix of concrete detail with analytic categories connects the familiar with the unfamiliar or even esoteric. Thus I kept material in *Good Days, Bad Days* (Charmaz, 1991) that had been covered before, such as the chapter on living with chronic illness. I took the reader through messy houses, jumbled schedules, pressures to simplify life, fragile pacing, and enormous efforts to function to the relief when remission occurs. This detail gave readers imagery on which to build when I moved into a more elusive analysis of time.

Writers use a linear logic to organize their analyses and make experience understandable. Yet experience is not necessarily linear, nor is it always readily drawn with clear boundaries. For example, experiencing illness, much less all its spiraling consequences, does not fit neatly into one general process. The grounded theory method emphasizes the analysis of a basic process the researcher discovers in the data. Although I pondered over organizing the book around one process, I could not identify an overarching theme. Experiencing illness consists of many processes, not a single process that subsumes others. Further, illness ebbs and flows. Chronically ill people define periods of relative "health" as well as spells of sickness. Thus I chose to collapse time and experience to cover illness.

Written images portray the tone the writer takes toward the topic and reflect the writer's relationships with his or her respondents. I aim for curiosity without condescension, openness without voyeurism, and participation without domination. Maintaining balance is difficult, because I try to portray respondents' worlds and views. Throughout the research and writing of *Good Days, Bad Days,* I tried to go beyond respondents' public presentation of self in illness. Otherwise, the knotty problems, the fear and pain, the moral dilemmas and ambivalent decisions do not come through.

Writers makes moral choices about portraying respondents, designing how to tell their stories, and delineating ways to interpret them. These choices also lead to the researcher's assuming a role as the writer (Krieger, 1991). In my book, I remain in the background as a storyteller whose tales have believable characters, not as an omniscient social scientist. My tone, style, and imagery reduce omniscience. However, because I stayed with the conceptual categories and built the stories around them, my work remains consistent with grounded theory and much social scientific writing.

Revising a manuscript can result in changes in style, possibly even of genre. Carefully crafted grounded theory categories work well as signposts in professional journals. A book editor may delete all the subheadings in one quick read. As signposts go, the narrative style changes. A more straightforward scientific style recedes as a more literary style evolves. Of course, how one sees that style and whether one defines it as scientific or literary depends upon where one stands. The postmodernist may see this style as objectivist, realist, and scientific; the positivist may see it as disconcertingly literary. I agree with Atkinson (1990) that impressionist

tales are often embedded in realist accounts. I try to pull readers in so they might sense and situate the feeling of the speaker in the story. Here, what Van Maanen (1988) calls impressionist tales sounds exactly what Clough (1992) calls "emotional realism." Perhaps, however, portraying moods, feelings, and views evokes an aesthetic verisimilitude of them.

◆ *Summary and Conclusion*

Given the analysis above, what conclusions can we draw about grounded theory studies? What might be the future of grounded theory? First, grounded theory methods evolve in different ways depending upon the perspectives and proclivities of their adherents. I aim to move researchers toward an explicitly constructivist approach. If we examine our epistemological premises, we can acknowledge the limits of our studies and the ways we shape them. In this way, adopting and refining grounded theory methods furthers the study of empirical worlds.

Second, we can reduce or resolve tensions between postmodernism and constructivist grounded theory when we use the former to illuminate and extend the latter. In short, postmodernism can *inform* realist study of experience rather than simply serve as justification for abandoning it. The postmodernist turn has forced renewed awareness of our relationships with and representation of subjects that will long influence qualitative research, possibly longer than the term *postmodernism* itself holds sway. Similarly, the importance of situating qualitative research in historical and cultural context is underscored. We grounded theorists can profit from the current trend toward linguistic and rhetorical analysis by becoming more reflexive about how we frame and write our studies. This trend supports constructivist approaches in grounded theory because it explicitly treats authors' works *as* constructions instead of as objectified products.

Third, the future of grounded theory lies with both objectivist and constructivist visions.

Scientific institutions and conventions are unlikely to undergo rapid change. Granting agencies and tenure review committees may long favor objectivist work over constructivist craft. The qualitative revolution has opened up possibilities and potentials, but gatekeepers are likely to reward scholars whose work comes closest to their own. Thus, we can expect to see growing numbers of large studies with small qualitative components and more team projects in multiple sites. Does this mean that constructivist grounded theory will wither and wane? No. The trend toward interpretive study, the quest for understanding, and the challenge to the imagination impel us to take our inquiry into the world. Through sharing the worlds of our subjects, we come to conjure an image of their constructions and of our own.

■ Notes

1. For my comparisons of objectivist and constructivist grounded theory, see the section below headed "Objectivist Versus Constructivist Grounded Theory."

2. For example, in his definitive study of natural recovery from heroin addiction, Patrick Biernacki (1986) controlled his referral chains for obtaining interviews for sampling, theoretical, and verificational considerations (pp. 214-219). Some colleagues have placed Biernacki's work in the emerging postmodern ethnography. However, in our conversations before he died, it was clear that he saw his work as realist qualitative research in which the investigator tries to achieve accurate reporting of a world. We both agreed that my use of grounded theory is more phenomenological and constructivist than his own. Anselm Strauss made the same assessment of my work relative to his (Strauss's) as well.

3. Lindesmith (1947) and Cressey (1953) both attempted earlier to codify analytic methods for qualitative research through analytic induction. Their work has been preserved in the criminology and deviance literatures but has faded in general methodological discussions.

4. Juliet Corbin has a strong background and a doctorate in nursing science. She has long been a leader in the establishment of qualitative methods in nursing; since the publication of *Ba-sics,* she has attained prominence in the social sciences and other professions as well.

5. To illustrate, when discussing conceptualizing data as the first step in analysis, Strauss and Corbin (1990) provide the following hypothetical example from a restaurant: "While waiting for your dinner, you notice a lady in red. She appears to be just standing there in the kitchen, but your common sense tells you that a restaurant wouldn't pay a lady in red just to stand there, especially in a busy kitchen. Your curiosity is piqued, so you decide to do an inductive analysis to see if you can determine just what her job is. (Once a grounded theorist, always a grounded theorist).

"You notice that she is intently looking around the kitchen area, **a work site,** focusing here and then there, taking a mental note of what is going on. *You ask yourself, what is she doing here? Then you label it* watching. Watching what? **Kitchen work**" (pp. 63-64).

This example continues in the same vein. It relies on careful observation of the overt behavior of the woman in the restaurant, from the objective observer's viewpoint. It does not take into account what that reality is like from the perspective of the restaurant worker. Nor do the categories develop from comparative study of other restaurants.

6. Anselm Strauss critiqued the draft of my 1995 paper on grounded theory in which I then claimed that grounded theory is not verificational (Charmaz, 1995c). He said that I was wrong.

7. For example, when writing about "mutual pretense," Glaser and Strauss (1965) state: "This particular awareness context cannot exist, of course, unless both the patient and staff are aware that he is dying. Therefore all the structural conditions which contribute to the existence of open awareness (and which are absent in closed and suspicion awareness) contribute also to the existence of mutual pretense. In addition, at least one interactant must indicate a desire to pretend that the patient is not dying and the other must agree to the pretense, acting accordingly" (p. 67). Corbin and Strauss (1987) also adopt a distanced voice in the following passage: "The impact of body failure and consequent performance failure can be measured by the impact that it has on each dimension of the BBC (biographical body conceptions). Since each dimension (biographical time, body, self conceptions) exists in a tightly bound relationship with the other, the conse-

quences of body failure with regard to one aspect are further felt with the other two. It is the combined impact of the three aspects of the BBC that profoundly affects biographical continuity and meaning" (p. 260). Several of Corbin and Strauss's works on chronic illness, such as *Unending Work and Care* (1988), read as if much less distanced than other works. Two factors may contribute to the difference: Strauss's experience with chronic illness and Corbin's direct involvement in data gathering.

8. Stern (1994a) agrees. She sees recent developments in grounded theory methods as eroding the method and the power of the subsequent analyses.

9. For a more developed discussion of how to do constructivist grounded theory, see Charmaz (1995c).

10. Grounded theorists work up and out from data. Not every qualitative researcher does. Rena Lederman (1990) observes that some anthropologists avoid using their field notes when developing their finished work. She writes of how anthropological field notes fulfill different functions for the researcher while he or she is away in the field and later, when the researcher is home. Ethnographers write as both close to and distant from their respondents while in the field, but their loyalties shift to the professional community when they reach home. Then the same field notes that provided a concrete grasp of reality in the field impart a sense of doubt. Lederman argues that conceptions of field notes as fixed and stable data crumble at this point. Instead, field notes can assume multiple meanings and are open to reinterpretation and contradiction.

11. Strauss's remarkably facile mind could not stop making comparisons. He taught students to compare unlikely categories of people, actions, settings, and organizations to tease out the properties of a category (see also Star, 1997).

12. The original memo was considerably longer and contained snippets of data throughout. The more distanced tone of the 1983 memo reflects my earlier socialization in writing and in grounded theory. It also reflects tensions between the relativism I adopted during my first year of graduate school and the objectivism in my grounded theory training (see Charmaz, 1983). By 1990, when *Good Days, Bad Days* went to press, this material reads as less distanced and more constructivist although it is essentially the same as the 1983 memo. In the interim, I came closer to integrating my realist intention to study empirical problems with the relativism inherent in constructivism (see Charmaz, 1990). In addition, I worked on making abstract ideas accessible.

13. I use the term *subjects* not because I view them as subordinate, or subjected to inquiry, but because the term *research participants* is so cumbersome.

14. For guidelines in choosing a data analysis software program, see Weitzman and Miles (1995).

15. However, recent listserv discussions of qualitative computer analysis indicate that some users still view the programs as too mechanical. For example, Aksel Hn Tjorca (MedSoc Listserv, November 17, 1998) found NUD•IST to be useful in sorting data initially but feared that hierarchical categories embedded in the program might work against the relational nature of the data.

16. To gain a sense of the whole on which we are working, we may need to have entire documents, if not the complete data set, before us. Yvonna Lincoln (personal communication, August 21, 1998) tells me that she works with all her data spread out on a large table. That way, she can gain a sense of the whole and, simultaneously, plan how to assemble the parts.

17. There are tensions between the constructivist assumptions of varied and problematic meaning and objectivist assumptions of the world as real, obdurate, external, and predictable. A constructivist grounded theory acknowledges realities of enduring worlds and tries to show how they are socially created through action, intention, and routine.

18. For a detailed report on how diverse scholars have responded to such concerns, see the 1992 debate in the *Journal of Contemporary Ethnography* about reality and interpretation in William Foote Whyte's *Street Corner Society* (Adler et al., 1992). Mariane Boelen (1992) challenges the veracity of Whyte's study and, by doing so, challenges reifications made of it (but not the notion of reifying ethnography itself). The responses to her challenge, however, range from accepting objectivist premises to questioning them (see Denzin, 1992b; Orlandella, 1992; Richardson, 1992; Vidich, 1992; Whyte, 1992). Vidich (1992) points out that Boelen assumes only one possible view of reality and that Whyte missed it. Denzin (1992b) and Richardson

(1992), however, question the objectivist premises that both Whyte and Boelen share.

19. To my knowledge, those who raise these criticisms have not resolved them through using grounded theory. Their recommendations range from abandoning empirical study to moving toward narrative analysis. To the extent that narrative analysis focuses on or drifts into emphasizing the type and structure of the narrative rather than respondents' meanings, I fail to see it as a better alternative than grounded theory studies. Nor do I see recording respondents' statements in one-line stanzas as offering a better frame for meaning than interview excerpts.

20. An author may call attention to an issue, frame a manuscript on it, but assume that the one issue constitutes the entire empirical reality. For example, before my analyses of illness focused squarely on the self, I argued that loss of self is *a* fundamental form of suffering. Readers reified my argument and concluded that I erroneously saw loss of self as the only experience of illness (see Robinson, 1990).

21. Glaser and Strauss (1967; Glaser, 1992; Strauss, 1987) have long stated that the core issues become apparent in the research setting, as if any trained observer will discover them. Similarly, they write as if neither standpoint nor status affects what observers see and find.

22. For a good outline of positivist premises, see Denzin (1989).

23. Strauss and Corbin (1994) call for grounded theory advocates to abandon the quest for truth. However, they also make a strong case for aiming for verification, which assumes a quest for truth. In their 1994 chapter, they also affirm two points I raised earlier, that the researcher's analysis is an interactive product of the views of the researcher and the data, and that the early works are written as if the researcher discovers an external order in the data (see Charmaz, 1983, 1990).

24. Strauss and Corbin (1998) state that exact replication is not possible, but sufficient reproducibility is. They propose that other researchers with similar theoretical premises, data gathering procedures, and research conditions develop similar theoretical explanations.

25. By making our early drafts available to those subjects who wish to read them, we make it possible for them to challenge and correct our views.

26. It is important to distinguish when the actor has agency and when he or she is acted upon. A hazard of any inductive method such as the constructivist approach is overemphasis on the individual. The constructivist approach leads to a style that emphasizes the active, reflective actor. Yet larger social forces also act upon this actor. So the researcher needs to learn how these social forces affect the actor and what, if anything, the actor thinks, feels, and does about them.

27. See, in contrast, Catherine Riessman (1990a) for presenting stories in the present.

■ *References*

Adler, P. A., Adler, P., & Johnson, J. M. (1992). New questions about old issues. *Journal of Contemporary Ethnography, 21,* 3-10.

Atkinson, P. A. (1990). *The ethnographic imagination: Textual constructions of reality.* London: Routledge.

Baszanger, I. (1998). *Inventing pain medicine: From the laboratory to the clinic.* New Brunswick, NJ: Rutgers University Press.

Best, J. (1995). Lost in the ozone again: The postmodernist fad and interactionist foibles. In N. K. Denzin (Ed.), *Studies in symbolic interaction: A research annual* (Vol. 17, pp. 125-134). Greenwich, CT: JAI.

Biernacki, P. L. (1986). *Pathways from heroin addiction: Recovery without treatment.* Philadelphia: Temple University Press.

Blumer, H. (1969). *Symbolic interactionism: Perspective and method.* Englewood Cliffs, NJ: Prentice Hall.

Boelen, W. A. M. (1992). *Street corner society:* Cornerville revisited. *Journal of Contemporary Ethnography, 21,* 11-51.

Bond, G. C. (1990). Fieldnotes: Research in past occurrences. In R. Sanjek (Ed.), *Fieldnotes: The makings of anthropology* (pp. 273-289). Ithaca, NY: Cornell University Press.

Bury, M. R. (1986). Social constructionism and the development of medical sociology. *Sociology of Health and Illness, 8,* 137-169.

Charmaz, K. (1983). The grounded theory method: An explication and interpretation. In R. M. Emerson (Ed.), *Contemporary field research* (pp. 109-126). Boston: Little, Brown.

Charmaz, K. (1990). Discovering chronic illness: Using grounded theory. *Social Science and Medicine, 30,* 1161-1172.

Charmaz, K. (1991). *Good days, bad days: The self in chronic illness and time.* New Brunswick, NJ: Rutgers University Press.

Charmaz, K. (1995a). Between positivism and postmodernism: Implications for methods. In N. K. Denzin (Ed.), *Studies in symbolic interaction: A research annual* (Vol. 17, pp. 43-72). Greenwich, CT: JAI.

Charmaz, K. (1995b). Body, identity, and self: Adapting to impairment. *Sociological Quarterly, 36,* 657-680.

Charmaz, K. (1995c). Grounded theory. In J. A. Smith, R. Harré, & L. Van Langenhove (Eds.), *Rethinking methods in psychology* (pp. 27-49). London: Sage.

Charmaz, K., & Mitchell, R. G. (1996). The myth of silent authorship: Self, substance, and style in ethnographic writing. *Symbolic Interaction, 19,* 285-302.

Chenitz, W. C., & Swanson, J. M. (Eds.). (1986). *From practice to grounded theory: Qualitative research in nursing.* Reading, MA: Addison-Wesley.

Clarke, A. E. (1998). *Disciplining reproduction: Modernity, American life sciences, and the problems of sex.* Berkeley: University of California Press.

Clough, P. T. (1992). *The end(s) of ethnography: From realism to social criticism.* Newbury Park, CA: Sage.

Coffey, A., Holbrook, B., & Atkinson, P. (1996). Qualitative data analysis: Technologies and representations. *Sociological Research Online, 1*(1). Available Internet: http://www.socresonline.org.uk/socresonline/1/1/4.html

Connelly, F. M., & Clandinin, D. J. (1990). Stories of experience and narrative inquiry. *Educational Researcher, 19*(5), 2-14.

Conrad, P. (1990). Qualitative research on chronic illness: A commentary on method and conceptual development. *Social Science and Medicine, 30,* 1257-1263.

Corbin, J., & Strauss, A. L. (1987). Accompaniments of chronic illness: Changes in body, self, biography, and biographical time. In J. A. Roth & P. Conrad (Eds.), *Research in the sociology of health care: The experience and management of chronic illness* (Vol. 6, pp. 249-282). Greenwich, CT: JAI.

Corbin, J., & Strauss, A. L. (1988). *Unending work and care: Managing chronic illness at home.* San Francisco: Jossey-Bass.

Cressey, D. R. (1953). *Other people's money: A study in the social psychology of embezzlement.* Glencoe, IL: Free Press.

Creswell, J. W. (1997). *Qualitative inquiry and research design: Choosing among five traditions.* Thousand Oaks, CA: Sage.

Dawson, L. L., & Prus, R. C. (1995). Postmodernism and linguistic reality versus symbolic interactionism and obdurate reality. In N. K. Denzin (Ed.), *Studies in symbolic interaction: A research annual* (Vol. 17, pp. 105-124). Greenwich, CT: JAI.

Denzin, N. K. (1989). *Interpretive interactionism.* Newbury Park, CA: Sage.

Denzin, N. K. (1991). *Images of postmodern society.* Newbury Park, CA: Sage.

Denzin, N. K. (1992a). The many faces of emotionality: Reading *Persona.* In C. Ellis & M. G. Flaherty (Eds.), *Investigating subjectivity: Research on lived experience* (pp. 17-30). Newbury Park, CA: Sage.

Denzin, N. K. (1992b). Whose Cornerville is it anyway? *Journal of Contemporary Ethnography, 21,* 120-132.

Denzin, N. K. (1994). The art and politics of interpretation. In N. K. Denzin & Y. S. Lincoln (Eds.), *Handbook of qualitative research* (pp. 500-515). Thousand Oaks, CA: Sage.

Denzin, N. K. (1996). Prophetic pragmatism and the postmodern: A comment on Maines. *Symbolic Interaction, 19,* 341-356.

Denzin, N. K. (1998). Review of *Pragmatism and feminism: Reweaving the social fabric. Symbolic Interaction, 21,* 221-223.

Denzin, N. K., & Lincoln, Y. S. (1994). Preface. In N. K. Denzin & Y. S. Lincoln (Eds.), *Handbook of qualitative research* (pp. ix-xii). Thousand Oaks, CA: Sage.

Fielding, N. G., & Lee, R. M. (1998). *Computer analysis and qualitative research.* London: Sage.

Flick, U. (1998). *An introduction to qualitative research: Theory, method and applications.* London: Sage.

Gadow, S. (1982). Body and self: A dialectic. In V. Kestenbaum (Ed.), *The humanity of the ill.* Knoxville: University of Tennessee Press.

Geertz, C. (1973). *The interpretation of cultures: Selected essays.* New York: Basic Books.

Glaser, B. G. (1978). *Theoretical sensitivity*. Mill Valley, CA: Sociology Press.

Glaser, B. G. (1992). *Basics of grounded theory analysis: Emergence vs. forcing*. Mill Valley, CA: Sociology Press.

Glaser, B. G. (Ed.). (1994). *More grounded theory: A reader*. Mill Valley, CA: Sociology Press.

Glaser, B. G. (1998, February 19). [Contribution to workshop]. In B. G. Glaser & P. Stern (Leaders), *Advanced grounded theory, workshop II*. Workshop conducted at the Qualitative Health Research Conference, Vancouver.

Glaser, B. G., & Strauss, A. L. (1965). *Awareness of dying*. Chicago: Aldine.

Glaser, B. G., & Strauss, A. L. (1967). *The discovery of grounded theory: Strategies for qualitative research*. Chicago: Aldine.

Glaser, B. G., & Strauss, A. L. (1968). *Time for dying*. Chicago: Aldine.

Guba, E. G., & Lincoln, Y. S. (1994). Competing paradigms in qualitative research. In N. K. Denzin & Y. S. Lincoln (Eds.), *Handbook of qualitative research* (pp. 105-117). Thousand Oaks, CA: Sage.

Johnson, J. L. (1991). Learning to live again: The process of adjustment. In J. M. Morse & J. L. Johnson (Eds.), *The illness experience: Dimensions of suffering* (pp.13-88). Newbury Park, CA: Sage.

Kleinman, A. (1988). *The illness narratives: Suffering, healing and the human condition*. New York: Basic Books.

Kleinman, S. (1993). The textual turn. *Contemporary Sociology, 22*, 11-13.

Krieger, S. (1991). *Social science and the self: Personal essays on an art form*. New Brunswick, NJ: Rutgers University Press.

Kuhn, T. S. (1970). *The structure of scientific revolutions* (2nd ed.). Chicago: University of Chicago Press.

Lederman, R. (1990). Pretexts for ethnography: On reading fieldnotes. In R. Sanjek (Ed.), *Fieldnotes: The makings of anthropology* (pp. 71-91). Ithaca, NY: Cornell University Press.

Lindesmith, A. R. (1947). *Opiate addiction*. Bloomington, IN: Principia.

Lofland, J., & Lofland, L. H. (1984). *Analyzing social settings* (2nd ed.). Belmont, CA: Wadsworth.

Lofland, J., & Lofland, L. H. (1995). *Analyzing social settings* (3rd ed.). Belmont, CA: Wadsworth.

Lofland, L. H. (1993). Fighting the good fight—again. *Contemporary Sociology, 22*, 1-3.

Lonkila, M. (1995). Grounded theory as an emerging paradigm for computer-assisted qualitative data analysis. In U. Kelle (Ed.), *Computer-aided qualitative data analysis: Theory, methods and practice* (pp. 41-51). London: Sage.

Maines, D. R. (1993). Narrative's moment and sociology's phenomena: Toward a narrative sociology. *Sociological Quarterly, 34*, 17-38.

Marcus, G. E., & Fischer, M. M. J. (1986). *Anthropology as cultural critique: An experimental moment in the human sciences*. Chicago: University of Chicago Press.

Martin, P. Y., & Turner, B. A. (1986). Grounded theory and organizational research. *Journal of Applied Behavioral Science, 22*, 141-157.

McGuire, M. B., & Kantor, D. J. (1987). Belief systems and illness experience. In J. A. Roth & P. Conrad (Eds.), *Research in the sociology of health care: The experience and management of chronic illness* (Vol. 6, pp. 241-248). Greenwich, CT: JAI.

Mead, G. H. (1934). *Mind, self, and society: From the standpoint of a social behaviorist* (C. W. Morris, Ed.). Chicago: University of Chicago Press.

Melia, K. M. (1996). Rediscovering Glaser. *Qualitative Health Research, 6*, 368-378.

Mishler, E. G. (1981). The social construction of illness. In E. G. Mishler, L. R. Amara Singham, S. T. Hauser, R. Liem, S. D. Osherson, & N. Waxler (Eds.), *Social contexts of health, illness and patient care* (pp. 141-168). New York: Cambridge University Press.

Mitchell, R. G., Jr., & Charmaz, K. (1996). Telling tales, writing stories: Postmodernist visions and realist images in ethnographic writing. *Journal of Contemporary Ethnography, 25*, 144-166.

Morse, J. M. (1995). The significance of saturation. *Qualitative Health Research, 5*, 147-149.

Orlandella, A. R. (1992). Boelen may know Holland, Boelen may know Barzini, but Boelen "doesn't know diddle about the North End!" *Journal of Contemporary Ethnography, 21*, 69-79.

Park, R. E., & Burgess, E. W. (1925). *The city.* Chicago: University of Chicago Press.

Prus, R. C. (1987). Generic social processes: Maximizing conceptual development in ethnographic research. *Journal of Contemporary Ethnography, 16,* 250-293.

Prus, R. C. (1996). *Symbolic interaction and ethnographic research: Intersubjectivity and the study of human lived experience.* Albany: State University of New York Press.

Reif, L. (1975). Ulcerative colitis: Strategies for managing life. In A. L. Strauss (Ed.), *Chronic illness and the quality of life* (pp. 81-89). St. Louis, MO: C. V. Mosby.

Rennie, D. L., Phillips, J. R., & Quartaro, G. K. (1988). Grounded theory: A promising approach to conceptualization in psychology? *Canadian Psychology, 29,* 139-150.

Richards, T. J., & Richards, L. (1994). Using computers in qualitative research. In N. K. Denzin & Y. S. Lincoln (Eds.), *Handbook of qualitative research* (pp. 445-462). Thousand Oaks, CA: Sage.

Richardson, L. (1990). *Writing strategies: Reaching diverse audiences.* Newbury Park, CA: Sage.

Richardson, L. (1992). Trash on the corner: Ethics and technography. *Journal of Contemporary Ethnography, 21,* 103-119.

Richardson, L. (1993). Interrupting discursive spaces: Consequences for the sociological self. In N. K. Denzin (Ed.), *Studies in symbolic interaction: A research annual* (Vol. 14, pp. 77-84). Greenwich, CT: JAI.

Richardson, L. (1994). Writing: A method of inquiry. In N. K. Denzin & Y. S. Lincoln (Eds.), *Handbook of qualitative research* (pp. 516-529). Thousand Oaks, CA: Sage.

Riessman, C. K. (1990a). *Divorce talk: Women and men make sense of personal relationships.* New Brunswick, NJ: Rutgers University Press.

Riessman, C. K. (1990b). Strategic uses of narrative in the presentation of self and illness: A research note. *Social Science and Medicine, 30,* 1195-1200.

Robinson, I. (1990). Personal narratives, social careers and medical courses: Analysing life trajectories in autobiographies of people with multiple sclerosis. *Social Science and Medicine, 30,* 1173-1186.

Robrecht, L. C. (1995). Grounded theory: Evolving methods. *Qualitative Health Research, 5,* 169-177.

Sanders, C. R. (1995). Stranger than fiction: Insights and pitfalls in post-modern ethnography. In N. K. Denzin (Ed.), *Studies in symbolic interaction: A research annual* (Vol. 17, pp. 89-104). Greenwich, CT: JAI.

Schatzman, L. (1991). Dimensional analysis: Notes on an alternative approach to the grounding of theory in qualitative research. In D. R. Maines (Ed.), *Social organization and social processes: Essays in honor of Anselm Strauss* (pp. 303-314). New York: Aldine de Gruyter.

Schwandt, T. A. (1994). Constructivist, interpretivist approaches to human inquiry. In N. K. Denzin & Y. S. Lincoln (Eds.), *Handbook of qualitative research* (pp. 118-137). Thousand Oaks, CA: Sage.

Seidel, J. (1991). Method and madness in the application of computer technology to qualitative data analysis. In N. G. Fielding & R. M. Lee (Eds.), *Using computers in qualitative research* (pp. 107-116). London: Sage.

Shaw, C. (1930). *The jack-roller: A delinquent boy's own story.* Chicago: University of Chicago Press.

Snow, D., & Morrill, C. (1993). Reflections upon anthropology's crisis of faith. *Contemporary Sociology, 22,* 8-11.

Star, S. L. (1989). *Regions of the mind: Brain research and the quest for scientific certainty.* Stanford, CA: Stanford University Press.

Star, S. L. (1997). Another remembrance: Anselm Strauss: An appreciation. In N. K. Denzin (Ed.), *Studies in symbolic interaction: A research annual* (Vol. 21, pp. 39-48). Greenwich, CT: JAI.

Stern, P. N. (1994a). Eroding grounded theory. In J. M. Morse (Ed.), *Critical issues in qualitative research methods* (pp. 212-223). Thousand Oaks, CA: Sage.

Stern, P. N. (1994b). The grounded theory method: Its uses and processes. In B. G. Glaser (Ed.), *More grounded theory: A reader* (pp. 116-126). Mill Valley, CA: Sociology Press.

Strauss, A. L. (1987). *Qualitative analysis for social scientists.* New York: Cambridge University Press.

Strauss, A. L. (1995). Notes on the nature and development of general theories. *Qualitative Inquiry, 1,* 7-18.

Strauss, A. L., & Corbin, J. (1990). *Basics of qualitative research: Grounded theory procedures and techniques.* Newbury Park, CA: Sage.

Strauss, A. L., & Corbin, J. (1994). Grounded theory methodology: An overview. In N. K. Denzin & Y. S. Lincoln (Eds.), *Handbook of qualitative research* (pp. 273-285). Thousand Oaks, CA: Sage.

Strauss, A. L., & Corbin, J. (1998). *Basics of qualitative research: Techniques and procedures for developing grounded theory* (2nd ed.). Thousand Oaks, CA: Sage.

Swanson, J. M., & Chenitz, C. W. (1993). Regaining a valued self: The process of adaptation to living with genital herpes. *Qualitative Health Research, 3,* 270-297.

Tesch, R. (1991). Software for qualitative researchers: Analysis needs and program capacities. In N. G. Fielding & R. M. Lee (Eds.), *Using computers in qualitative research* (pp. 16-37). London: Sage.

Thomas, W. I., & Thomas, D. S. (1928). *The child in America.* New York: Alfred A. Knopf.

Thomas, W. I., & Znaniecki, F. (1918-1920). *The Polish peasant in Europe and America* (5 vols.). Boston: Richard G. Badger.

Thrasher, F. M. (1963). *The gang: A study of 1,313 gangs in Chicago.* Chicago: University of Chicago Press. (Original work published 1927)

Turner, B. A. (1981). Some practical aspects of qualitative data analysis: One way of organizing the cognitive processes associated with the generation of grounded theory. *Quality and Quantity, 15,* 225-247.

Tyler, S. A. (1986). Post-modern ethnography: From document of the occult to occult document. In J. Clifford & G. E. Marcus (Eds.), *Writing culture: The poetics and politics of ethnography* (pp. 122-140). Berkeley: University of California Press.

Van Maanen, J. (1988). *Tales of the field: On writing ethnography.* Chicago: University of Chicago Press.

Vidich, A. J. (1992). Boston's North End: An American epic. *Journal of Contemporary Ethnography, 21,* 80-102.

Weitzman, E. A., & Miles, M. B. (1995). *Computer programs for qualitative data analysis: A software sourcebook.* Thousand Oaks, CA: Sage.

Whyte, W. F. (1992). In defense of *Street corner society. Journal of Contemporary Ethnography, 21,* 52-68.

Wiener, C. (1975). The burden of rheumatoid arthritis. In A. L. Strauss (Ed.), *Chronic illness and the quality of life* (pp. 71-80). St. Louis, MO: C. V. Mosby.

Wilson, H. S., & Hutchinson, S. A. (1991). Triangulation of qualitative methods: Heideggerian hermeneutics and grounded theory. *Qualitative Health Research, 1,* 263-276.

Zorbaugh, H. (1929). *The Cold Coast and the slum.* Chicago: University of Chicago Press.

UNDAUNTED COURAGE

Life History and the Postmodern Challenge

◆ William G. Tierney

Who built Thebes of the seven gates?
In the books you will find the names of kings.
Did the kings haul up the lumps of rock? . . .

Philip of Spain wept when his armada
Went down. Was he the only one to weep?

Bertolt Brecht, "Questions From
a Worker Who Reads," 1934

Almost two centuries ago, Thomas Jefferson commissioned Meriwether Lewis to command an expedition to the Pacific. In *Undaunted Courage* (1996), Stephen Ambrose writes of this journey, its trials and tribulations. For his efforts, Ambrose won acclaim and his book ended up a best-seller. The result of Meriwether Lewis's work was somewhat less salutary; he committed suicide in the fall of 1809.

Although Ambrose's book includes in its subtitle *Thomas Jefferson and the Opening of the American West,* the text's major focus is on Captain Lewis. What kind of man would set off across a continent about which he knew little? Why would Lewis suggest that he share his post equally with his friend George Rogers Clark, when the military always has operated as a hierarchical chain of command? And, most tragically, why would Lewis kill himself after he had completed such a remarkable voyage and earned

AUTHOR'S NOTE: Michael Bamberg, Norm Denzin, Patrick Dilley, Yen Espiritu, Alexander Jun, Yvonna Lincoln, and Michael Olivas offered helpful comments on an earlier version of this chapter.

the praise of the country in general and of his friend Thomas Jefferson in particular?

Ambrose concludes his lyrical text by trying to guess what Lewis thought during his final moments at the hotel where he shot himself in a hamlet outside of Nashville, Tennessee. Perhaps he worried about his finances, or cursed himself for his drinking, suggests Ambrose. Or Lewis may have thought of his enemies, or he may have recalled his more heroic exploits. The reader is left really with only one conclusion—Lewis had a depressive personality and ultimately it got the better of him.

One might read *Undaunted Courage* on any number of levels. To some readers it is a rip-roaring adventure story that stretches the imagination about how anyone could possibly have navigated a crew across the North American continent—and then turned back and did it again. Jefferson's belief in Manifest Destiny and Americans' rapacious appetite for conquest provide another way to read it. Some might read the book as a map for understanding the roots of capitalism in the United States. The relationship that Lewis developed with Native Americans may be read one way by some and other ways by others. And then there is the case of Lewis himself and what the reader might make of him. Ambrose outlines a multitude of reasonable interpretations about why Lewis might have taken his life, absent one. Permit me to provide a different reading of his life.

Meriwether Lewis was a confirmed bachelor who was in love with Captain Clark. Lewis asked Clark to share his command. The book details how they were inseparable. On the trip out to the Pacific and upon the return home, every man in the party but one contracted syphilis—Lewis did not sleep with women. Lewis returned to Washington and Philadelphia but was always unsuccessful in his courtships. In fact, he more often than not wrote about the women he courted, yet his friends never met these women. Clark, on the other hand, returned home and soon married. One might plausibly conclude that Lewis killed himself a year or two later because of a broken heart.

Lewis of course may not have been gay and may not have died of heartbreak. I am neither a historian of early America nor a psychologist. I raise the issue about Lewis's suicide here because it goes to the heart of the issues with which authors and readers must contend as they develop and read life histories and life stories. For example, on one level, I find it remarkable that an author as skillful as Ambrose does not even raise a question about Lewis's sexual identity. On another, I wonder how many readers who are not gay would suggest the possibility that Lewis had fallen in love with another man.

On yet another level, what would it have meant to have been homosexual at the beginning of the 19th century? Surely a gay identity signifies more than that Meriwether was *shtupping* George, but it also ought not mean, cannot mean, what queer theorists contend a gay man is as the 20th century ends. As Joshua Gamson comments in Chapter 12 of this volume, queer theory, with its roots in postmodernism, points to an "ongoing deconstruction of sexual subjectivity" such that identities—authors, subjects, readers—are never unified, never stable.

Some might posit that a theoretical framework that raises questions about the past (postmodernism) and a method that deals in what has happened (life history) make strange bedfellows. I will argue, however, that the relationship between postmodernism and life history affords authors and readers critical insights into not so much the dead past as the developing future. As Stephen Best and Douglas Kellner (1991) note:

> Postmodern theory provides a critique of representation and the modern belief that theory mirrors reality, taking instead "perspectivist" and relativist positions that theories at best provide partial perspectives on their objects and that all cognitive representations of the world are historically and linguistically mediated. (p. 4)

To be sure, a concrete definition of postmodernism does not exist; indeed, such a definition would be ironic given postmodernism's basic tenets pertaining to indeterminacy and constant deconstruction/reconstruction. There is also a great deal of confusion between postmodernism and poststructuralism and various strands of postmodernism. As I will discuss later in this chapter, the framework I work from here is informed by critical theory; I oppose modernist notions of rational, autonomous subjects, totalizing discourses, and foundationalist epistemologies. Thus a singular view of why someone acted in a particular way—Meriwether Lewis's suicide, for example—is rejected in favor of the creation of alternative interpretations that take into account the fluid nature of identity and the role of the researcher/author in the development of a text.

This chapter, then, is in many ways a history of the present. I investigate the creation of the past as a comment on the present condition. I seek neither to outline yet again the basic tenets of postmodernism nor to offer a cookbook of methodological recipes for those who wish to do life stories. Instead, in what follows I first discuss one form of life history, the *testimonio,* and outline what the project of postmodern life histories might be. I then consider the interstices of memory and history as a way to highlight the inevitable tension between fact and myth. I conclude by considering how authors might decolonize subjects by way of the construction and presentation of the narrative. My purpose here is to trouble the method, to bring into question various facets of life history work that often have gone unquestioned. In doing so, I aim to move the genre toward new projects, new relationships between the researcher and the researched, and away from previously constructed colonizations of the "Other."

◆ *Life History and the* Testimonio: "*I, Meriwether Lewis . . .* "

Life history is a term that has meant many things to many people. Schwandt (1997) notes that it is also called "the biographical method" (p. 82). Watson and Watson-Franke (1985) state that a "life history is any retrospective account by the individual of his life in whole or part, in written or oral form, that has been elicited or prompted by another person" (p. 2).

Watson (1976) argues elsewhere that the only direct purpose of life history "is as a commentary of the individual's very personal view of his own experience as he understands it" (p. 97). Dollard (1935), in a classic text, has written that the life history is "an attempt to define the growth of a person in a cultural milieu and to make theoretical sense of it" (p. 3). In a helpful table summarizing the biographical method, Denzin (1989) succinctly observes that a life history is an "account of a life based on interviews and observations" (p. 48). Hatch and Wisniewski (1995) suggest that "an analysis of the social, historical, political and economic contexts of a life story by the researcher is what turns a life story into a life history" (p. 125).

Clearly, the definition of life history varies depending on the perspective one chooses. For example, if I were to engage in life histories of Asian Americans, I might use autobiography (e.g., Lee, 1990), or perhaps oral histories (e.g., Lee, 1991) or life stories (Chow, 1998; Espiritu, 1995).

To some, the life history falls within a taxonomic biographical structure, and its emphasis is on the interactions between the researcher and the researched and on the researched's relationships to others. Life history is a culturally produced artifact in one light and an interpretive document in another. It might be defined by way of method (interviews and observations), theoretical vantage point (hermeneutics, phenomenology), or disciplinary perspective (psychology, anthropology, sociology).

I obviously am not suggesting the development of a universal definition of life history on which everyone will agree; rather, I am underscoring the multiple definitions that have surrounded the idea of life history. Often, as with the definitions I have just listed, what one finds is not so much that authors disagree but that they speak past one another.

Certainly, as the authors cited above suggest, life history is related to biography, it is a retrospective account, and it involves some form of narrative statement. However, my goal in this chapter is not to regurgitate what has been said before, but to provoke commentary on what researchers, readers, and activists might do next. I suggest that (a) the purpose of the text, (b) the truth of the text, and (c) the author of the text come into question at the end of the 20th century in ways that did not concern life historians a century ago, much less in the time of Lewis and Clark.

Although there are different formats of the life history that I might highlight in this chapter, I have chosen to feature the *testimonio*. By no means do I intend to suggest that researchers should use only the *testimonio* when attempting life history work. However, I have chosen to discuss the *testimonio* because this form of life history has the least overtly intrusive hand of an author and is the most indigenously derived of the qualitative techniques discussed in this volume. Further, as John Beverley (1992) has observed, the *testimonio* "is by nature a protean and demotic form not yet subject to legislation by a normative literary establishment" (p. 93). It is my hope that, by highlighting a literary form that is not encased by normative frames, I might contribute to our ability to consider ways to change, alter, and reconfigure other forms that are.

Perhaps the most famous *testimonio* is *I, Rigoberta Menchú: An Indian Woman in Guatemala* (1984). The book begins:

> My name is Rigoberta Menchú. I am twenty three years old. This is my testimony. I didn't learn it from a book and I didn't learn it alone. I'd like to stress that it's not only *my* life, it's also the testimony of my people. . . . My story is the story of all poor Guatemalans. My personal experience is the reality of a whole people. (p. 1)

Because I have quoted from the first page, one might reasonably conclude that I have provided the opening of the book, but actually, in a preface the volume's editor, Elisabeth Burgos-Debray (1984), writes of how the project was developed:

> When we began to use the tape recorder, I initially gave her a schematic outline, a chronology: childhood, adolescence, family involvement in the struggle. . . . As we continued, Rigoberta made more and more digressions, introduced descriptions of cultural practices into her story

and generally upset my chronology. . . . I became what I really was: Rigoberta's listener. I allowed her to speak and then became her instrument, her double, by allowing her to make the transition from the spoken to the written word. (pp. xix-xx)

The *testimonio* has developed, in large part, not from Western Europe or the United States, but from Latin America. Unlike in oral history, the narrator bears witness to a social urgency; the text frequently falls within what Barbara Harlow (1987) defines as "resistance literature." The roots of *testimonio* go back to colonial *crónicas* and the war diaries of Simón Bolívar or José Martí. Over the past generation the focal points of the *testimonio* have been of those who have been silenced, excluded, and marginalized by their societies. Frequently, *testimonios* come from individuals who cannot write (e.g., Barnet, 1994; Dalton, 1982).

Some might argue (wrongly) that a *testimonio* actually erases the author function. In a traditionally defined life history or a biography, the hand of the researcher is ever present, whereas in the *testimonio* the researcher's role seems to fall to what Burgos-Debray defines as becoming the "instrument" of the individual who testifies. In this light the *testimonio* is a fundamentally different kind of document from other biographical undertakings. Whereas a life history is a written account elicited through interviews by an individual who seeks to understand a life in order to gain a greater understanding of cultural notions, the *testimonio* is developed by the one who testifies in the hope that his or her life's story will move the reader to action in concert with the group with which the testifier identifies. There is an urgency to the *testimonio* that is not always apparent in life histories or biographies and is most often absent in autoethnographies, which are more concerned with literary structures than with changing oppressive structures. In the *testimonio,* the testifier's life is directly linked to social movements and change.

Beverley (1992) defines the *testimonio* as "a novella-length narrative in book or pamphlet form, told in the first person by a narrator who is also the real protagonist or witness of the events he or she recounts, and whose unit of narration is usually a 'life' or a significant life experience" (p. 92). Thus a *testimonio* differs from an autobiography or autoethnography in that a moral or social imperative exists for the protagonist to tell his or her story. Although the *testimonio* might be circumscribed by everyday events that have happened to the individual, the centerpieces of the text pertain to issues such as torture, imprisonment, social upheaval, and the struggle for survival.

According to Beverley (1992), "Testimonio represents an affirmation of the individual subject, . . . but in connection with a group or class situation marked by marginality, oppression, and struggle. If it loses this connection, it ceases to be testimonio and becomes autobiography" (p. 103). The author of a *testimonio* is usually defined not as an author, but as an activist who is centrally tied to the struggle about which he or she writes. The individual has not risen "above" or "beyond" the struggle. Autobiography frequently looks back at a life, with the author speaking about life's challenges from a distance. The struggles may have been overcome or not, but the recollections are more reminiscence than call to action. Thus, if we return to my earlier concerns, we might initially summarize what a *testimonio* is by suggesting that (a) the *purpose* is social change, (b) the *truth* is created through the telling of an individual's events that have otherwise been occluded or ignored, and (c) the *author* is he or she who testifies, and not a researcher. Unfortunately, in a postmodern world, tidy summaries such as this are not so easy.

Textual Purpose

What is the purpose of the creation of a text? Clearly, the "disengaged" modernist who presumes him- or herself to be discovering knowledge has a very different purpose from the interlocutor of a *testimonio*. Indeed, the purpose of a text is dependent on any number of contextual issues.

Would it have been possible, for example, for Meriwether Lewis to pen a *testimonio* about his longings for Clark and bring into question the nature of sexual orientation in 1809? Presumably, even a white man of privilege who is able to write might develop a *testimonio* in the late 20th century about the oppression that gay and lesbian individuals face, or the marginalization someone who is disabled must deal with. But social constructs, Michel Foucault (1973) has taught us, are contextually and historically framed. As Jeffrey Weeks (1995, p. 5) and others have noted (e.g., Halperin, 1997; Sedgwick, 1990; see also Gamson, Chapter 12, this volume), it is deeply problematic to think of sexuality as a purely natural phenomenon, outside the boundaries of society and culture. If homosexuality was not "invented" in the manner that we have come to think of it today until the late 20th century, then Lewis could not have written a testimony to its oppression. He either would have been unable to understand his longings for George Clark or would not have had a name for them. As Montero (1997) has pointed out, gender definition is less a rigid identity than a series of repeated performances that intersect at various times with other identities—social, cultural, racial, ethnic, and so on.

Similarly, Ray McDermott and Herve Varenne (1995, p. 344) have observed that the idea of "disability" is not an individual condition but a cultural construct determined by the individual and group relations in which people function and develop meaning. I am suggesting that we cannot use the ways we define identity today to define identities of yesterday or of cultures different from those of us who do the defining.

The point, of course, is not to deny or downplay the horrific episodes that someone like Rigoberta Menchú relates, but instead to acknowledge that the individual is not an autonomous, essentialized agent capable of independently inventing him- or herself. Individual lives are constant constructs embedded in societal and cultural forces that seek to constrain some and enable others. However critical a *testimonio* is at a specific moment, and however much I urge our work to be more involved in social change, I am

542 ◆ STRATEGIES OF INQUIRY

arguing that authors run the risk of re-creating a modernist fallacy if they assume that individual identity is not constrained by specific power relations.

I surely am not suggesting that researchers must forgo the struggle to overcome inequities. Instead, as Popkewitz (1998) has pointed out, all such work is defined by "effects of power which, when they go unnoticed in contemporary research and policy, may inter and enclose the possibility of change by reinscribing the very rules of reason and practice that need to be struggled against" (p. 3). The challenge is not to dismiss the *testimonio,* but to engage the text in ways that enable authors to enact change by acknowledging the relations of speaker, writer, and reader to truth.

Textual Truth

Recently, there has been a brouhaha about Rigoberta Menchú's version of truth. David Stoll (1999), an anthropologist who has spent a great deal of time in Central America, charges that Menchú's text is mistaken on several counts. Menchú says she never went to school, but Stoll's research reveals that her neighbors say she was sent away to a Catholic school. The point is not merely a geographic disagreement about her whereabouts: She could not have been an eyewitness to the events she relates if she was attending boarding school. Further, Menchú paints her father as a victim of *ladino* landlords and the state; Stoll (1998) interviewed Menchú's family and argues that actually her father's in-laws, cousins, and uncles had beaten him up because they thought he was stealing their land (p. 9).

Such charges have created a maelstrom. Stoll's point is more than a simple demand for veracity; rather, he turns the *testimonio* (and, by implication, life history, biography, and other such methods) back on itself. The determiner of truth becomes not the text and the reader. Instead, "we would have to acknowledge that there is no substitute for our capacity to judge competing versions of events, to exercise our authority as scholars" (Stoll, 1998, p. 11). On the face of it, what Stoll suggests has merit. One

ought not believe that someone died at the hands of X when Y was actually responsible. One ought not say, "I saw a murder happen," if one did not. Certainly, analyses of contradictions between narrative and experience need to be explored and examined in any document.

However, one wonders if "truth" in a *testimonio* is to be defined in the manner that Stoll does, especially in a postmodern world where such terms are inevitably contested, argued over, and perspectival. Greg Grandin (1998) disagrees with Stoll: "I have no doubt that Menchú's testimony contains exaggerations, contradictions, if not outright fabrications. But can this come as a surprise to anyone who treats Mayans as political actors, capable of developing their own political agenda?" (p. 52). The concern here is that Stoll would have readers judge narratives as seamless and hermetically sealed, rather than through multiple filters. *Testimonio*—as well as life history, life story, autoethnography, and the like—is situated within a series of complex and ambiguous political and cultural relations. Texts are surely to be interrogated in the manner that Stoll has done, but for the interrogators the end result should not be the declamation of a scholarly "gotcha" when they find contradictions; rather, they should try to piece together how these multiple presentations account for contested versions of reality.

In her text about five women, Mary Catherine Bateson (1990) matter-of-factly states, "I have not tried to verify these narratives, beyond attending to issues of internal consistency and checking them against my knowledge of the individuals. . . . The accounts are shaped by each person's choice and selective memory. . . . These are stories I have used to think with" (p. 33). Such a statement stands in contradistinction to the empiricism of Stoll's fact checking. Again, the point here is not that facts of the kind Stoll has examined are wrong or irrelevant, but that how we use facts determines how we think about truth and how we read a text.

Lewis's omission of any discussion of his homosexuality in his journals, for example, does not necessarily mean that he was lying; at the same time, the lack of such information also ought not suggest that therefore he was a heterosexual. The heterosexual reader may not even have considered such "facts." Proponents of Stoll's position might rightfully argue that if we were able to transport ourselves back to the early 19th century and we then found evidence of Lewis's homosexuality, then it needs to be reported—and I concur. But what makes a fact a fact is not merely the act one sees or does, but the interconnections between who sees what when and how it gets reported by whom. "A fact is like a sack which won't stand up when it is empty," says Pirandello (1921/1952). "In order that it may stand up, one has to put into it the reason and sentiment which have caused it to exist" (p. 230).

The Author of the Text

From the earliest life histories to the most recent texts, such as those by Menchú, Domitila Barrios de Chungara (1978), Fernandez and Gutierrez (1996), and Elvira Alvarado (1987), the role of the author has been in question. As noted, individuals such as Burgos-Debray (1984) claim that they are their interviewees' "instruments," as if their role is little more than that of human tape recorder. However, we must disavow the notion that any text is singularly created, even in a genre that is perhaps the most responsive to the individual who provides his or her "testimony."

Listen, for example, to Alfred Kroeber's (1908) presentation of Black-Wolf's description of war: "When I was a boy, I heard about great deeds in war, and resolved to follow in the tracks of such men" (p. 197). Kroeber also had Watches-All comment on supernatural powers by observing, "Medicine-men cured the sick by sucking the body and by brushing it. As is customary among Indians, they were believed to suck through the skin without biting, cutting or puncturing it" (p. 222). Does anyone seriously believe that a native speaker—or anyone—talks in that way? Here we have an interviewer gathering a story in a language different from his own, and the reader discovers that Native Americans speak in a manner akin to the reader's.

Further, authors often interpret the spoken words of others in various ways, in large part because the speakers' language is different from theirs. Translation is always provisional; different translators translate the same texts in different ways. Conversely, authors increasingly are studying individuals and groups with whom they share much in common; that is, an African American author might study African Americans, or a lesbian might investigate a lesbian community. Once again, we cannot presume that because an author is similar to those he or she studies that the author function is irrelevant. From a postmodern perspective, all authors, all narrators, are situated; the challenge is to come to terms with the positions in which authors locate themselves.

A text is always created not simply by the speaker of the narrative and the individual who owns the tape recorder, but also by the multiple editorial decision makers who oversee the story's production. On the one hand are the questions of the interviewer. Susan Chase (1995) notes that the questions she asked framed how her interviewee thought about what to say: "Despite my repeated statements of interest in her experience, [the interviewee] heard that my primary interest lay in the connection between her experience and sociological ideas" (p. 7). One cannot escape that the individual who collects the data is doing more than merely collecting them. As Gelles (1998) asks, "What [would] Menchú's narrative have looked like if it had been solicited by a sympathetic and politically attuned Maya-speaking *ladino* or indigenous intellectual from Guatemala?" (p. 17). His observation is not that Burgos-Debray had sinister or mistaken motives, but that any text is coproduced. As researchers we are participants in the creation of the data.

And on the other hand, the editor or author also shapes the data on the written page. For example, Hones (1998) has suggested that "the rhythmic repetitions and formulaic language present in traditional oral cultures such as the Hmong should be represented in the form of poetry instead of prose" (p. 240; see also Tedlock,

1983; Tierney & Lincoln, 1997). The forms that have been employed throughout the 20th century in what constitutes academic scholarship exist in large part because of formulas derived from modernism and the Western mind. Themes, with beginnings and ends, populate texts—but not all people construct their lives in such a manner. Greg Sarris (1994) makes precisely such a point in his instructions to a medicine woman with whom he was doing a life history: "When you write a book there has to be a story, or idea, a theme." She replied, "Well, theme I don't know nothing about. That's somebody else's rule" (p. 5).

People speak expressively, with body and facial movements that help explain and extend the words they use, but usually such movements do not make it into texts dependent upon language. If we are to believe the vast majority of life histories that exist, those individuals whose lives have been reported are among the most grammatically correct and logical speakers we know; they speak in complete sentences and they develop ideas in chronological sequence. Academic rules help to shape life stories to such an extent that narrative texts cannot be seen as other than cocreated.

As Rinehart (1998) nicely summarizes: "How we choose to name other people and groups—how we categorize them—often tells more about us, about our stance on how things are, than it does about any truth of who they are. It tells more about that which is true to the namer" (p. 201). Even in a *testimonio*, then, we must accept that the document is mediated in any number of ways.

Such acceptance will raise concerns on the part of those who are wedded to a modernist framework. Indeed, much of what I have raised here should be of concern to the modernist. One might wrongly assume that in a world where facts are not facts and authors are always involved in the creation of data, I am suggesting anything goes. However, no one I know who subscribes to postmodernism suggests that the veracity of a statement should go unchecked, or that because all life histories are cocreated, one is as good as another. To be sure, one challenge that I leave for a later text is to delineate how

one might evaluate the kinds of texts I am discussing here.

For now, the challenge in a world that we view as constructed on multiple levels by multiple parties is to seek some sense of voice and agency that enables action. "The autobiographical occasion," write Smith and Watson (1992), "becomes a site on which cultural ideologies intersect and dissect one another, in contradiction, consonance, and adjacency" (p. xix). The narrative site is full of potential. Our struggle is to enact that potential—and to this challenge I now turn.

◆ Between Memory and History

"History is perpetually suspicious of memory," writes Pierre Nora (1989), "and its true mission is to suppress and destroy it" (p. 9). Those who utilize the life history, the *testimonio*, the life story, the autoethnography, all begin with the assumption that it is helpful to remember. The written text, a narrative archive, on a material level seeks to assert what has occurred—that, in fact, a past existed and humanity is not always in the present. Such a statement may seem matter-of-fact—Who could argue that a past does not exist?—except that in an age consumed by the present, individuals develop historical amnesia; they are unable to grasp histories of groups and individuals except as these are constructed (or not) by current ideological forces. History, in this sense, has been hidden from memory. The past is a foreign country where a different language is spoken; too often, historians have simply assumed that history is discovery of patterns, places, and people.

Relatedly, Marjorie Becker (1997) points out that "the linear approach to historical writing so frequently employed in the twentieth century gives the impression that human experience moves sequentially, act by act, with each experience slightly more significant than the last" (p. 344). The problem with such an approach is that no two individuals engage time in the same manner. No one temporal structure can express the multitude of experiences for all people, across all times.

Scholars traditionally have attached importance to the life history for any number of reasons—perhaps to create a sense of nostalgia ("the way we were"), to develop ideological images (the "noble savage"), to re-create symbolic virtue in a world that ostensibly has been deritualized. A society such as exists at the end of the 20th century, which has been so deeply absorbed in transformation and renewal, generally has used life history as fleeting memory. Those who suggest that history is little more than collective memory overlook how ideology frames, constructs, and defines what is seen and/or obscured. Memory is assuredly not outside of history; rather, the two are conjoined in mutual constructions.

In an earlier work, I observed that discussions about the purpose of life history revolve around the twin concepts of *portal* and *process* (Tierney, 1998). A life history might be done as a portal, an entryway, through which the author and reader might understand a culture different from their own. The assumption is that a life history's purpose is to enable the reader to come to terms with different social phenomena, perhaps, or to learn vicariously about a world quite different from his or her own.

The portal approach to life history generally assumes that the author and the reader are different from the person whose story is told. A *testimonio,* obviously, is in contradistinction to the portal approach with regard to the author. However mediated a testimonio might be, the individual whose story is heard is directly involved in its construction. The purpose of the text is not merely for a foreign reader to gain a sense of an alien culture, but for an individual to testify about a compelling social problem. The portal approach to life history exoticizes the Other and tries to enable the reader to understand the life fantastic. An undertaking of this kind inevitably privileges the researcher and reinforces social relations circumscribed by power insofar as a dynamic is created in which the author has control over the final production of a text about someone else's life story.

A life history also may represent a process whereby the researcher and reader come to understand the semiotic means by which someone else makes sense of the world. "Life story researchers," explains Gelya Frank (1995), "examine the cultural scripts and narrative devices speakers use to make sense of their own life experiences" (p. 255). Through this use of the life history, the researcher and reader hopefully are able to reflect on their own lives. They achieve some understanding of one another and of the multiple realities involved in the creation of meaning. I am suggesting that the text—a life history, a life story, a *testimonio*—be seen as a personal narrative whose ontological status as a spoken interaction between two (or more) individuals helps create, define, reinforce, or change reality. Thus the process approach to life history more easily fits within a postmodern framework and enables the development and encouragement of texts such as *testimonios.*

The life history text, then, exists somewhere between history and memory. Memory is not a spontaneous word association. Speakers and researchers build memory from the shared perspective of the present. Memories are recalled for reasons that are important to someone—the speaker, the interviewer—in large part because of present contextual definitions of what constitutes identity, society, and culture. The life history not only represents the memory of an individual, it also produces identity. The challenge to us as researchers is to ensure that individuals are not the object of our discourses, but rather the agents of complex, partial, and contradictory identities that help transform the worlds they and we inhabit.

A handful of years ago, the challenge might have been to "name silenced lives" (McLaughlin & Tierney, 1993) as a way to provide voice for those who had been left out of history's picture. If one were to read only formalized histories, one might mistakenly presume, for example, that African Americans, American Indians, gay and lesbian people, and other marginalized groups did not exist prior to a generation ago. Certainly the women's movement is significantly responsible for enabling us to realize that a history of a particular epoch that speaks only of men's work is partial and incomplete.

However, the simple "naming" of silenced lives is insufficient. Yes, histories in general, and life histories in particular, are helpful for enabling societies to come to terms with individuals and groups who have been omitted from official versions of the past. But we ought not fool ourselves into thinking that simply by adding a few voices here and there our work is done if we have proven that omitted characters from official histories have representational value. Life histories are helpful not merely because they add to the mix of what already exists, but because of their ability to refashion identities. Rather than a conservative goal based on nostalgia for a paradise lost, or a liberal one of enabling more people to take their places at humanity's table, a goal of life history work in a postmodern age is to break the stranglehold of metanarratives that establishes rules of truth, legitimacy, and identity. The work of life history becomes the investigation of the mediating aspects of culture, the interrogation of its grammar, and the decentering of its norms (Tierney, 1997). In doing such work, life histories are successful in a liberal fashion—groups previously excluded from official versions of history get included—but more important, those previously excluded groups as well as other individuals and groups become redefined and redescribed. Smith and Watson (1992) are worth quoting at length here:

> Western autobiography colludes in cultural mythmaking. . . . It functions as an exclusionary genre against which the utterances of other subjects are measured and misread. While inviting all subjects to participate in its practices, it provides the constraining template or the generic "law" against which those subjects and their diverse forms of self-narrative are judged and found wanting. In order to unstick both this Man and his meanings, we need to adjust, to reframe, our understanding of traditional and countertraditional autobiographical practices. (p. xviii)

In his analysis of Menchú's *testimonio,* Stoll (1998) argues that the text is more mythopoesis than history. He defines mythopoesis as "the act of mythmaking in which people tell certain stories to justify their preferred interpretation of the world" (p. 9). One senses, of course, Stoll's

very real concern that myth is not the stuff of history. Active mythmaking is intellectual fraud; myths that develop where the speaker is simply mistaken are one reason researchers must exercise their authority as scholars.

On the other hand, Beverley (1992) approvingly comments that Menchú's work "is a kind of testimonial expressionism, or magic realism" (p. 101). Lincoln and Denzin (1994) might define such a tactic as "deconstructive verisimilitude" (p. 580) insofar as Stoll accepts the idea of a singular reality that can be proved/not proved. What Beverley is trying to convey is the sense that a text is a site of political struggle over the "real" and its meanings. The challenge set forth, as Lincoln and Denzin (1994) note, is "to reproduce and deconstruct the reproductions and simulations that structure the real" (p. 580).

Susan Krieger (1996) and Carolyn Steedman (1986) offer texts that operate within the interstices of history and memory. Steedman (1986) writes, "This book is about interpretations, about the places where we rework what has already happened to give current events meaning" (p. 5); she continues, "Personal interpretations of past time . . . are often in deep and ambiguous conflict with the official interpretative devices of a culture" (p. 6). Steedman's word choice is purposive, specific. She is not simply saying that her work is about a reconfiguration of the past—a naming of a silenced life—she is saying that the text takes issue with the "interpretive devices" of that past. One of those key devices is history. The researcher's work, however, needs to be more than the stimulation of memory that reaches for easy reminiscence, for if all the researcher is doing is evoking a nostalgia for the past irrespective of ideology, then he or she has stripped the work of any possibility for change. Thus the site for a researcher's work is between memory and history, lost in the interstices.

◆ Decolonizing Meriwether

At the close of the 20th century, we have seen a variety of experiments with the writing of life histories. Autoethnography is one form that is being used in which the author is more explicitly involved within the text. The life story utilizes specific moments in a speaker's life that are conveyed through a story; less attention is paid to textual veracity than to what the implicit semiotic meanings of the text may be. Ruth Behar (1996) has written that "the genres of life history and life story are merging with the testimonio, which speaks to the role of witnessing in our time as a key form of approaching and transforming reality" (p. 27). Heretofore, scholars of the *testimonio* would have disagreed that an overtly mediated text such as a life history could approximate what a *testimonio* struggles to do. Obviously, there will be differences of tone, style, and urgency between the *testimonio* and some life histories and autoethnographies, but the recent past has brought forth a significant number of texts that utilize recent advances in postmodernism in a manner akin to the narrative structure of *testimonio* (Behar, 1993; Brown, 1991).

Rather than texts by distant observers who interview subjects to glean facts about their lives in order to make "objective" assertions, we have postmodern texts that work from different assumptions and frameworks. They have three different conditions from life histories of the past and follow from the overarching comments made earlier. The first is that the reality of the exchange, the data collected, is constructed. The second condition pertains to the nature of the voice and the vulnerability necessary for such a voice, what Soderqvist (1991) calls "embodied construction and reflexivity" (p. 145). The third condition involves why we write what we write. These three conditions, relating back to the discussion in the first section of this chapter, combine in a way that creates the possibility for researchers to decolonize subjects and to open up avenues for change. Researchers disavow any idea of "discovering" data as if it were waiting "out there" to be found; instead, data are created. A danger is that each condition is not well understood, and a certain authorial narcissism is capable of overpowering a text so that, rather than create a dynamic for democratic change, authors re-create a different version of the imperialist

author. Because writers are embarking on uncharted methodological terrain, they do not have a map of the research design; nevertheless, a sense of general direction becomes apparent from the postmodern conditions noted above.

Storytelling

Life histories that worked from a modernist framework assumed that an underlying goal was to present verifiable information about different phenomena. Given what I have argued for, the postmodern challenge is to accept the multiple mediations at work in the creation of the text and expose them, rather than try to hide them, wish them away, or assume that they can be resolved. In this light, how to categorize and frame a life becomes of central import. The naming of individuals and groups structures how we see them.

Barely over a generation ago, for example, a life history of a gay man might well have been framed as an exploration of deviance, or a life story of a homeless person might have left unexamined the structural conditions that enable the idea of homelessness to get enacted. Similarly, a life history of a Native American would have been attempted as a way to understand the exotic "Other," but a life history of a white male who was a corporate executive would have been overlooked insofar as he was not the "Other." Life histories informed by postmodernism will begin with the assumption that identity is partial, contested, and, at times, contradictory. Such a position enables the possibility for the decolonization of previously colonized peoples—be they Native Americans, the disabled, or gay men who commit suicide because of their sexual orientation.

Well-meaning modernists may shake their heads at the implications of what I am suggesting. On the one hand, I criticize the observer who seeks to record the lives of those individuals on the border—Native Americans, lesbian and gay individuals, and the like—as an ethnographic voyeur. On the other hand, I have criticized the absence from traditional texts of those of us on the border. Am I not, some might ask, placing life historians in an untenable double bind in which they are intellectually dammed if they do (life histories) and dammed if they don't?

The answer depends on the framework employed. The point is surely not that one must eschew life histories of colonized peoples, or that the attempt to understand the Other is a fruitless undertaking. Rather, the researcher must begin with an understanding of the fragmented nature of identity and build a text that enables readers to see how the author/narrator/speaker has created a particular identity that is fraught with contested meanings.

Toward the end of his elegiac memoir *Before Night Falls* (1993), Reinaldo Arenas writes, "Witches have played an important part in my life" (p. 294). The empiricist would try to prove whether witches actually exist or, more likely, examine Arenas's mental condition and explain why Arenas could believe such a magical idea. I am suggesting, as with the earlier comments about Menchú's testimony, that if such empiricism goes unquestioned, researchers miss a great deal by simply answering whether or not witches exist. The postmodern challenge is in part for the researcher to come to terms with alternative realities different from his or her own, not to exoticize them so that the researcher might put them on display, but instead to help create the conditions for decolonization whereby the researcher tries to understand the life of a gay Cuban man dying of AIDS in an empathic manner. Such a position resituates the research endeavor of the life historian. The researcher does not simply try to find or explain away witches, but reflects back on why such a question is important and others are not. The relationship of the researcher/author to the individual and to the text of necessity comes in for questioning and analysis.

Embodied Construction and Vulnerability

Over the past generation there has been a sea change concerning the use of the first person in texts. Although representation still exists within a quite narrow context, at least qualitative researchers have moved beyond the assumption that the only tenable way to present themselves in life histories is by authorial absence or through the third person. Indeed, a good deal of recent work in ethnographic research either advocates using or utilizes the first person (Denzin, 1994; Ellis & Bochner, 1996; Ellis & Flaherty, 1992; Richardson, 1998; Tierney & Lincoln, 1997). I welcome such a stance. Nevertheless, I also wish to suggest that writers need to extend the authorial role yet again. There needs to be greater vulnerability to the author's voice and work. Permit me to elaborate, and to do so on a personal level.

Western epistemology was shaped by the belief that emotion needed to be cut out of the process of knowledge production. The authorial response of the postmodernist has been to insert the first person into the text. And yet one need not be a postmodernist to recognize that there are multiple ways an author might utilize the voice of the first person. Indeed, as a gay man I am only too well aware of how I utilize my voice as an out gay academic. There is the "I" who can say, "I am gay—do you want to make something out of it?" as a defiant assertion in a peremptory manner, for I know that there are individuals—academics, readers—who hate me for no reason other than that I am gay. I have employed such a narrative strategy at times in my own work and in my life; I assume that anyone who has faced similar oppression and marginalization understands the defensive posture that brings forth such a voice.

Another way to use the voice of the "I" is in the manner in which I use it initially in this text. If the reader will return to the introduction to the chapter, he or she will find that I do not say there that I am gay; instead, I suggest it when I raise a question about Meriwether's sexual orientation. In this way, I employ the first person in a cool, stripped-down academic manner akin to what might be used by modernists who employ the omniscient narrator. The "I" is used presumably to move the text along, and the author is not overly intrusive. There are, of course, multiple additional possibilities for the use of the first person.

I suggest here that we also become able to make our work and ourselves vulnerable. Yes, there are times when I should be a defiant queer man; yes, there are moments when a return to the voice of the cerebral gay academic is sufficient—but there also ought to be a place where my voice is vulnerable and passionate. As we enter the new century, for example, I am only too aware of how many friends I have lost to AIDS; such loss has unalterably tinged my life—all of it, personal, political, academic. At times in our work such vulnerability also needs to be heard, for without it, we hold on to a unified voice that is power laden and dominant.

I agree with Ruth Behar (1996) when she writes: "Since I have put myself in the ethnographic picture, readers feel they have come to know me. They have poured their own feelings into their construction of me and in that way come to identify with me, or at least their fictional image of who I am" (p. 16). When we write vulnerably, we invite others to respond vulnerably. Surely not every qualitative text that is written needs to provoke a vulnerable response in the reader; just as surely, however, some texts should.

If we are to shed the role of the disengaged observer who records data from afar, then our voices must reflect our own vulnerabilities. At times I am troubled that the recent use of the first person is often akin to what I have pointed out about my own voice as a gay man. Sometimes I hear in a text the author symbolically saying, "There. I've used the first person. I've done it!" Perhaps the voice is first person, but it remains cool and disengaged. Again, I understand why as researchers and authors we have used such a voice, and I am in agreement that at times we are correct in its employment. After all, as Jane Tompkins (1993) has noted, "to break with the convention is to risk not being heard at all" (p. 26). We want to be listened to, and we have a good deal of justification about feeling defensive. However, the vulnerability of our work, our identities, and our voices also needs to be heard if we are to create the conditions for decolonization.

Praxis and the Other

We ought not lose sight of the fact that, however flawed the research endeavor, the possibility exists that in some of our work we might be able to bring about change with those with whom we work. While we employ the first person and make ourselves vulnerable, we have yet another task and obligation, and that concerns those individuals whose life histories, stories, and *testimonios* we help create.

When a text is done, one goal the writer ought to have is that the reader will have a sense of who the author is. Such a goal should not be, cannot be, the only goal. Again, if I mentioned earlier that I am troubled by the maintenance of a power-laden voice even if it is in the first person, I am equally troubled by a narcissistic voice that eschews a concern for those with whom the author works. The work of life history has to be more than the celebration of my authorial voice, for if nothing else has been accomplished, all that I have achieved is a narrative trick, a linguistic sleight of hand. I have employed the first person in a manner akin to what modernists have done with other voices. The researcher/author remains in control, and the individual with whom he or she has worked yet again takes a textual backseat to the academic narrator.

Not all research will have the social urgency of a Guatemalan peasant's *testimonio* about her people being murdered. Nevertheless, there is a strand of postmodernism that assumes change is impossible, or not a worthy goal. The focus of that form of postmodernism centers on irony and wordplay. The version of postmodernism I have worked from here, however, is informed by critical theory (Tierney, 1993, 1997). The challenge becomes the desire to change the more oppressive aspects of life that silence and marginalize some and privilege others. One certainly cannot wish away power. But the work of life history ought to try to understand the conditions in which people live and work and die, so that everyone engaged in the life history—researcher, storyteller, reader—has the possibility of reconfiguring his or her life.

◆ Conclusion

I began this chapter with a discussion of Meriwether Lewis and the possibility that he was gay. As I have suggested, some readers may well be unconvinced by the "evidence" that Lewis was gay. My point in using the example of Lewis, however, was to highlight the multiple interpretations that researchers and readers bring to events and people of the past. Lewis may have been gay, and certainly that thought will cross the minds of many gay readers as they work their way through Ambrose's text. The empiricist will demand proof, and I have suggested that such proof is a modernist fallacy.

I then turned to a discussion of life history in general and the *testimonio* in particular. Many readers may be unfamiliar with the *testimonio;* my choice of life history strategy is not simply to suggest yet another tool to add to our methodological kit. And I certainly have had no desire to convince all life historians that henceforth the *testimonio* is the only valid way to construct life's stories. Rather, in large part because it has not yet been subjected to normalizing frameworks, the *testimonio* enables a particularly compelling discussion about what I have termed three turning points in life history. As one undertakes a life history, one needs to consider (a) the purpose of the text (What is the author trying to do and why?), (b) the veracity of the text (How does one deal with the truth of what is presented?), and (c) the author of the text (Who pens a story?). Although I have not suggested that there are hard-and-fast rules that must be observed regardless of context or situation, I have argued that one needs to consider these issues as one interprets, constructs, and reads texts.

I have elaborated on these points by considering the relationship between history and memory. I have suggested that life history is something more than collective memory. Ideology and social and cultural frames help define how we see the past and construct its stories. Identity is not something fixed and predetermined; rather, it is constantly re-created. In this re-creation, the past's histories help construct the future. I have also suggested that, like the *testimonio* in particular, life histories in general cannot be simply the unearthing of untold stories. Rather, informed by the critical postmodern framework that I have employed, I have argued that texts fail if they are little more than literary experiments or the telling of untold tales.

Of consequence, life histories of the kind I have discussed here eschew the paternalism that has imbued so much social science research in the 20th century, and instead seek to create ways to decolonize those who have been silenced, forgotten, or mangled by life's forces. Such a task, I have argued, demands not only new ways of thinking about constructing texts but different relationships with those who are studied and a different stance with regard to the "Other." Instead of a disengaged empiricism, we need a greater sense of vulnerability on the part of the new life historian and an elaborated sense of social responsibility with regard to those with whom we work.

Some might argue that I have made fundamental errors in logic. I have titled this text "Undaunted Courage," which suggests that writing a life history is as difficult and daunting as crossing the continent was two centuries ago. I also have suggested that Meriwether Lewis was gay and that he be decolonized; thus a man who helped colonize America is now himself a candidate for decolonization. Those who subscribe to postmodernism also might criticize the use of the word *courage* in the title of this chapter insofar as I have borrowed it from Stephen Ambrose's book on Meriwether Lewis. Ambrose works from a modernist construction of a hero. The hero carries "courage" with him across the continent.

Courage, like voice, comes in different forms. The modernist definition of courage that explores unexplored external terrain is one viewpoint. The courage I have suggested here is of a form that allows the author to reach across boundaries and within him- or herself. The author forgoes romantic notions about truth or knowledge, but also accepts the task of trying to bridge differences. The modernist courage of

Meriwether Lewis is that he reached the Pacific Ocean and then turned around and returned home.

The postmodern life historian helps create texts that are voyages of creation—for the historian, the person who speaks, and the person who ultimately reads the final product. Texts have been used to colonize people by framing individuals and groups in one light and silencing them in another. The project of decolonization is not a simple task of authorial enlightenment, nor can it be divorced from the daily situations in which authors, speakers, and readers find themselves. Indeed, a next step in the project outlined here might be further development of the parameters of what makes for a good text.

The power the author has is the ability to develop a reflexive text. Such a text enables readers to understand the author a bit better, to come to grips with the individual whose life is retold, and to reflect back on their own lives. A reflexive work of the kind I have argued for leaves a writer and speaker and reader vulnerable. Vulnerability is not a position of weakness, but one from which to attempt change and social fellowship.

■ *References*

Alvarado, E. (1987). Foreword. In M. Benjamin (Ed.), *Don't be afraid, gringo: A Honduran woman speaks from the heart.* San Francisco: Institute for Food and Development Policy.

Ambrose, S. E. (1996). *Undaunted courage: Meriwether Lewis, Thomas Jefferson, and the opening of the American West.* New York: Simon & Schuster.

Arenas, R. (1993). *Before night falls: A memoir.* New York: Penguin.

Barnet, M. (1994). *Biography of a runaway slave* (W. N. Hill, Trans.). Willimantic, CT: Curbstone.

Barrios de Chungara, D. (1978). *Let me speak! Testimony of Domitila, a woman of the Bolivian mines.* New York: Monthly Review Press.

Bateson, M. C. (1990). *Composing a life: Life as a work in progress.* New York: Penguin.

Becker, M. (1997). When I was a child, I danced as a child, but now that I am old, I think about salvation. *Rethinking History, 1*, 343-355.

Behar, R. (1993). *Translated woman: Crossing the border with Esperanza's story.* Boston: Beacon.

Behar, R. (1996). *The vulnerable observer: Anthropology that breaks your heart.* Boston: Beacon.

Best, S., & Kellner, D. (1991). *Postmodern theory: Critical interrogations.* New York: Guilford.

Beverley, J. (1992). The margin at the center: On testimonio (testimonial narrative). In S. Smith & J. Watson (Eds.), *De/colonizing the subject: The politics of gender in women's autobiography* (pp. 91-114). Minneapolis: University of Minnesota Press.

Brown, K. M. (1991). *Mama Lola: A Vodou priestess in Brooklyn.* Berkeley: University of California Press.

Burgos-Debray, E. (1984). Preface. In R. Menchú, *I, Rigoberta Menchú: An Indian woman in Guatemala* (E. Burgos-Debray, Ed. & Trans.). New York: Verso.

Chase, S. E. (1995). Taking narrative seriously: Consequences for method and theory in interview studies. In R. Josselson & A. Liebech (Eds.), *Interpreting experience: The narrative study of lives* (pp.1-26). Thousand Oaks, CA: Sage.

Chow, C. S. (1998). *Leaving deep water: The lives of Asian American women at the crossroads of two cultures.* New York: E. P. Dutton.

Dalton, R. (1982). *Miguel Marmol* (M. Randall & M. Argueta, Trans.). Willimantic, CT: Curbstone.

Denzin, N. K. (1989). *Interpretive biography.* Newbury Park, CA: Sage.

Denzin, N. K. (1994). The art and politics of interpretation. In N. K. Denzin & Y. S. Lincoln (Eds.), *Handbook of qualitative research* (pp. 500-515). Thousand Oaks, CA: Sage.

Dollard, J. (1935). *Criteria for the life history: With analysis of six notable documents.* New Haven, CT: Yale University Press.

Ellis, C., & Bochner, A. P. (Eds.). (1996). *Composing ethnography: Alternative forms of qualitative writing.* Walnut Creek, CA: AltaMira.

Ellis, C., & Flaherty, M. G. (Eds.). (1992). *Investigating subjectivity: Research on lived experience.* Newbury Park, CA: Sage.

Espiritu, Y. L. (1995). *Filipino American lives.* Philadelphia: Temple University Press.

Fernandez, R. V., & Gutierrez, C. E. (Eds.). (1996). *Andean lives: Gregario Condori Mamani and Asunta Quispe Huamán* (P. H. Gelles & G. M. Escobar, Trans.). Austin: University of Texas Press.

Frank, G. (1995). Life histories in occupational therapy clinical practice. *American Journal of Occupational Therapy, 50,* 251-264.

Foucault, M. (1973). *The order of things: An archaeology of the human sciences* (E. Gallimard, Trans.). New York: Vintage.

Gelles, P. H. (1998, April). Testimonio, ethnography, and processes of authorship. *Anthropology Newsletter,* pp. 16-17.

Grandin, G. (1998, April). She said, he said. *Anthropology Newsletter,* p. 52.

Halperin, D. (1997). Questions of evidence. In M. Duberman (Ed.), *Queer representations: Reading lives, reading cultures* (pp. 39-55). New York: New York University Press.

Harlow, B. (1987). *Resistance literature.* New York: Methuen.

Hatch, J. A., & Wisniewski, R. (1995). Life history and narrative: Questions, issues, and exemplary works. In J. A. Hatch & R. Wisniewski (Eds.), *Life history and the narrative* (pp. 113-136). Philadelphia: Taylor & Francis.

Hones, D. F. (1998). Known in part: The transformational power of narrative inquiry. *Qualitative Inquiry, 4,* 225-248.

Krieger, S. (1996). *The family silver: Essays on relationships among women.* Berkeley: University of California Press.

Kroeber, A. (1908). Ethnology of the Gros Ventre. *Anthropological Papers of the American Museum of Natural History, 1*(4), 196-222.

Lee, J. F. (1991). *Asian American experiences in the United States: Oral histories of first to fourth generation Americans from China, the Philippines, Japan, India, the Pacific islands, Vietnam and Cambodia.* Jefferson, NC: McFarland.

Lee, M. P. (1990). *Quiet odyssey: A pioneer Korean woman in America* (S. Chan, Ed.). Seattle: University of Washington Press.

Lincoln, Y. S., & Denzin, N. K. (1994). The fifth moment. In N. K. Denzin & Y. S. Lincoln (Eds.), *Handbook of qualitative research* (pp. 575-586). Thousand Oaks, CA: Sage.

McDermott, R., & Varenne, H. (1995). Culture as disability. *Anthropology and Education Quarterly, 26,* 324-348.

McLaughlin, D., & Tierney, W. G. (1993). *Naming silenced lives: Personal narratives and the process of educational change.* New York: Routledge.

Menchú, R. (1984). *I, Rigoberta Menchú: An Indian woman in Guatemala* (E. Burgos-Debray, Ed.; A. Wright, Trans.). London: Verso.

Montero, O. (1997). Notes for a queer reading of Latin American Literature. In M. Duberman (Ed.), *Queer representations: Reading lives, reading cultures* (pp. 216-225). New York: New York University Press.

Nora, P. (1989). Between memory and history: Les lieux de memoire. *Representations, 26,* 7-25.

Pirandello, L. (1952). Six characters in search of an author. In E. Bentley (Ed.), *Naked masks: Five plays by Luigi Pirandello.* New York: Meridian. (Original work published 1921)

Popkewitz, T. S. (1998). The culture of redemption and the administration of freedom as research. *Review of Educational Research, 68,* 1-34.

Richardson, L. (1998). The politics of location: Where am I now? *Qualitative Inquiry, 4,* 41-48.

Rinehart, R. (1998). Fictional methods in ethnography: Believability, specks of glass, and Chekhov. *Qualitative Inquiry, 4,* 200-224.

Sarris, G. (1994). *Mabel McKay: Weaving the dream.* Berkeley: University of California Press.

Schwandt, T. A. (1997). *Qualitative inquiry: A dictionary of terms.* Thousand Oaks, CA: Sage.

Sedgwick, E. K. (1990). *Epistemology of the closet.* Berkeley: University of California Press.

Smith, S., & Watson, J. (1992). Introduction: De/colonization and the politics of discourse in women's autobiographical practices. In S. Smith & J. Watson (Eds.), *De/colonizing the subject: The politics of gender in women's autobiography.* Minneapolis: University of Minnesota Press.

Soderqvist, T. (1991). Biography or ethno-biography or both? Embodied reflexivity and the deconstruction of knowledge-power. In F. Steier (Ed.), *Method and reflexivity: Knowing as systemic social construction* (pp. 143-162). London: Sage.

Steedman, C. (1986). *Landscape for a good woman: A story of two lives.* London: Virago.

Stoll, D. (1998, April). Life history as mythopoesis. *Anthropology Newsletter,* pp. 9-11.

Stoll, D. (1999). *Rigoberta Menchú and the story of all poor Guatemalans.* Boulder, CO: Westview.

Tedlock, D. (1983). *The spoken word and the work of interpretation.* Philadelphia: University of Pennsylvania Press.

Tierney, W. G. (1993). *Building communities of difference: Higher education in the twenty-first century.* South Hadley, MA: Bergin & Garvey.

Tierney, W. G. (1997). *Academic outlaws: Queer theory and cultural studies in the academy.* Thousand Oaks, CA: Sage.

Tierney, W. G. (1998). Life history's history: Subjects foretold. *Qualitative Inquiry, 4,* 49-70.

Tierney, W. G., & Lincoln, Y. S. (Eds.). (1997). *Representation and the text: Re-framing the narrative voice.* Albany: State University of New York Press.

Tompkins, J. (1993). Me and my shadow. In D. P. Freedman, O. Frey, & F. M. Zauhar (Eds.), *The intimate critique: Autobiographical literary criticism.* Durham, NC: Duke University Press.

Watson, L. C. (1976). Understanding a life history as a subjective document: Hermeneutical and phenomenological perspectives. *Ethos, 4*(1), 95-131.

Watson, L. C., & Watson-Franke, M. (1985). *Interpreting life histories.* New Brunswick, NJ: Rutgers University Press.

Weeks, J. (1995). *Invented moralities: Sexual values in an age of uncertainty.* New York: Columbia University Press.

21

TESTIMONIO, SUBALTERNITY, AND NARRATIVE AUTHORITY

◆ John Beverley

In a justly famous essay, Richard Rorty (1985) distinguishes between what he calls the "desire for solidarity" and the "desire for objectivity" as cognitive modes:

> There are two principal ways in which reflective human beings try, by placing their lives in a larger context, to give sense to those lives. The first is by telling the story of their contribution to a community. This community may be the actual historical one in which they live, or another actual one, distant in time or place, or a quite imaginary one, consisting perhaps of a dozen heroes and heroines selected from history or fiction or both. The second way is to describe themselves as standing in an immediate relation to a nonhuman reality. This relation is immediate in the sense that it does not derive from a relation between such a reality and their tribe, or their nation, or their imagined band of comrades. I shall say that stories of the former kind exemplify the desire for solidarity, and that stories of the latter kind exemplify the desire for objectivity. (p. 3)[1]

The question of *testimonio*—testimonial narrative—has come prominently onto the agenda of the human and social sciences in recent years in part because *testimonio* intertwines the "desire for objectivity" and "the desire for solidarity" in its very situation of production, circulation, and reception.

Testimonio is by nature a demotic and heterogeneous form, so any formal definition of it is bound to be too limiting.[2] But the following might serve provisionally: A *testimonio* is a novel or novella-length narrative, produced in the form of a printed text, told in the first person by a narrator who is also the real protagonist or witness of the events she or he recounts. Its unit of narration is usually a "life" or a significant life experience. Because in many cases the direct narrator is someone who is either functionally illiterate or, if literate, not a professional writer, the production of a *testimonio* generally involves the tape-recording and then the transcription and editing of an oral account by an interlocutor who is a journalist, ethnographer, or literary author.

Although one of the antecedents of *testimonio* is undoubtedly the ethnographic life history of the *Children of Sánchez* sort, *testimonio* is not exactly commensurable with the category of life history (or oral history). In the life history it is the intention of the interlocutor-recorder (the ethnographer or journalist) that is paramount; in *testimonio*, by contrast, it is the intention of the direct narrator, who *uses* (in a pragmatic sense) the possibility the ethnographic interlocutor offers to bring his or her situation to the attention of an audience—the bourgeois public sphere—to which he or she would normally not have access because of the very conditions of subalternity to which the *testimonio* bears witness.[3] *Testimonio* is not intended, in other words, as a reenactment of the anthropological function of the native informant. In René Jara's (1986, p. 3) phrase, it is rather a "narración de urgencia"— an "emergency" narrative—involving a problem of repression, poverty, marginality, exploitation, or simply survival that is implicated in the act of narration itself. In general, *testimonio* could be said to coincide with the feminist slogan "The personal is the political." The contemporary appeal of *testimonio* for educated, middle-class, transnational publics is perhaps related to the importance given in various forms of 1960s counterculture to oral testimony as a form of personal and/or collective catharsis and liberation in (for example) the consciousness-raising sessions of the early women's movement, the practice of "speaking bitterness" in the Chinese Cultural Revolution, or psychotherapeutic encounter groups.

The predominant formal aspect of the *testimonio* is the voice that speaks to the reader through the text in the form of an I that demands to be recognized, that wants or needs to stake a claim on our attention. Eliana Rivero (1984-1985) notes that "the act of speaking faithfully recorded on the tape, transcribed and then 'written' remains in the *testimonio* punctuated by a repeated series of interlocutive and

conversational markers . . . which constantly put the reader on the alert, so to speak: True? Are you following me? OK? So?" (pp. 220-221). The result, she argues, is a "snail-like" discourse (*discurso encaracolado*) that keeps turning in on itself and that in the process invokes the complicity of the reader through the medium of his or her counterpart in the text, the direct interlocutor.

This presence of the voice, which the reader is meant to experience as the voice of a *real* rather than fictional person, is the mark of a desire not to be silenced or defeated, to impose oneself on an institution of power and privilege from the position of the excluded, the marginal, the subaltern. Hence the insistence on the importance of personal name or identity evident sometimes in titles of *testimonios*, such as *I, Rigoberta Menchú* (even more strongly in the Spanish: *Me llamo Rigoberta Menchú y así me nació la conciencia*), *I'm a Juvenile Delinquent* (*Soy un delincuente*), and *Let Me Speak* (*Si me permiten hablar*).

This insistence suggests an affinity between testimony and autobiography (and related forms, such as the autobiographical *bildungsroman*, the memoir, and the diary). Like autobiography, *testimonio* is an affirmation of the authority of personal experience, but, unlike autobiography, it cannot affirm a self-identity that is separate from the subaltern group or class situation that it narrates. *Testimonio* involves an erasure of the function and thus also of the textual presence of the "author" that is so powerfully present in all major forms of Western literary and academic writing.[4] By contrast, in autobiography or the autobiographical *bildungsroman*, the very possibility of "writing one's life" implies necessarily that the narrator is no longer in the situation of marginality and subalternity that his or her narrative describes, but has now attained precisely the cultural status of an author (and, generally speaking, middle- or upper-class economic status). Put another way, the transition from storyteller to author implies a parallel transition from *gemeinschaft* to *gesellschaft,* from a culture of primary and secondary orality to writing, from a traditional group identity to the privatized, modern identity that forms the subject of liberal political and economic theory.

The metonymic character of testimonial discourse—the sense that the voice that is addressing us is a part that stands for a larger whole—is a crucial aspect of what literary critics would call the convention of the form: the narrative contract with the reader it establishes. Because it does not require or establish a hierarchy of narrative authority, *testimonio* is a fundamentally democratic and egalitarian narrative form. It implies that *any* life so narrated can have a symbolic and cognitive value. Each individual *testimonio* evokes an absent polyphony of other voices, other possible lives and experiences (one common formal variation on the first-person singular *testimonio* is the polyphonic *testimonio* made up of accounts by different participants in the same event).

If the novel is a closed form, in the sense that both the story and the characters it involves end with the end of the text, in *testimonio*, by contrast, the distinctions between text and history, representation and real life, public and private spheres, objectivity and solidarity (to recall Rorty's alternatives) are transgressed. It is, to borrow Umberto Eco's expression, an "open work." The narrator in *testimonio* is an actual person who continues living and acting in an actual social space and time, which also continue. *Testimonio* can never create the illusion—fundamental to formalist methods of textual analysis—of the text as autonomous, set against and above the practical domain of everyday life and struggle. The emergence of *testimonios*, for the form to have become more and more popular in recent years, means that there are experiences in the world today (there always have been) that cannot be expressed adequately in the dominant forms of historical, ethnographic, or literary representation, that would be betrayed or misrepresented by these forms.

Because of its reliance on voice, *testimonio* implies in particular a challenge to the loss of the authority of orality in the context of processes of cultural modernization that privilege literacy and literature as a norm of expression. The inequalities and contradictions of gender, class, race, ethnicity, nationality, and cultural authority that determine the "urgent" situation of the testimonial narrator may also reproduce themselves in the relation of the narrator to the interlocutor, especially when (as is generally the case) that narrator requires to produce the *testimonio* a "lettered" interlocutor from a different ethnic and/or class background in order first to elicit and record the narrative, and then to transform it into a printed text and see to its publication and circulation as such. But it is equally important to understand that the testimonial narrator is not the subaltern as such either; rather, she or he functions as an organic intellectual (in Antonio Gramsci's sense of this term) of the subaltern, who speaks to the hegemony by means of a metonymy of self in the name and in the place of the subaltern.

By the same token, the presence of subaltern voice in the *testimonio* is in part a literary illusion—something akin to what the Russian formalists called *skaz*: the textual simulacrum of direct oral expression. We are dealing here, in other words, not with reality itself but with what semioticians call a "reality effect" that has been produced by both the testimonial narrator—using popular speech and the devices of oral storytelling—and the interlocutor-compiler, who, according to hegemonic norms of narrative form and expression, transcribes, edits, and makes a story out of the narrator's discourse. Elzbieta Sklodowska (1982) cautions in this regard that

> it would be naïve to assume a direct homology between text and history [in testimonio]. The discourse of a witness cannot be a reflection of his or her experience, but rather a refraction determined by the vicissitudes of memory, intention, ideology. The intention and the ideology of the author-editor further superimposes the original text, creating more ambiguities, silences, and absences in the process of selecting and editing the material in a way consonant with norms of literary form. Thus, although the testimonio uses a series of devices to gain a sense of veracity and authenticity—among them the point of view of the first-person witness-narrator—the play between

fiction and history reappears inexorably as a problem. (p. 379, my translation; see also Sklodowska, 1996)

The point is well-taken, but perhaps overstated. Like the identification of *testimonio* with life history (which Sklodowska shares), it concedes agency to the interlocutor-editor of the testimonial text rather than to its direct narrator. It would be better to say that what is at stake in *testimonio* is the *particular* nature of the reality effect it produces. Because of its character as a narrative told in the first person to an actual interlocutor, *testimonio* interpellates the reader in a way that literary fiction or third-person journalism or ethnographic writing does not. The word *testimonio* carries the connotation in Spanish of the act of testifying or bearing witness in a legal or religious sense. Conversely, the situation of the reader of *testimonio* is akin to that of a jury member in a courtroom. *Something* is asked of us by *testimonio*, in other words. In this sense, *testimonio* might be seen as a kind of speech act that sets up special ethical and epistemological demands. (When we are addressed directly by an actual person, in such a way as to make a demand on our attention and capacity for judgment, we are under an obligation to respond in some way or other; we can act or not on that obligation, but we cannot ignore it.)

What *testimonio* asks of its readers is in effect what Rorty means by solidarity—that is, the capacity to identify their own identities, expectations, and values with those of another. To understand how this happens is to understand how *testimonio works* ideologically as discourse, rather than what it *is*.

In one of the most powerful sections of her famous *testimonio I, Rigoberta Menchú* (1984), which has come to be something like a paradigm of the genre, Menchú describes the torture and execution of her brother Petrocinio by elements of the Guatemalan army in the plaza of a small highland town called Chajul, which is the site of an annual pilgrimage by worshipers of the local saint. Here is part of that account:

After he'd finished talking the officer ordered the squad to take away those who'd been "pun-

ished," naked and swollen as they were. They dragged them along, they could no longer walk. Dragged them to this place, where they lined them up all together within sight of everyone. The officer called to the worst of the criminals—the *Kaibiles,* who wear different clothes from other soldiers. They're the ones with the most training, the most power. Well, he called the *Kaibiles* and they poured petrol over each of the tortured. The captain said, "This isn't the last of their punishments, there's another one yet. This is what we've done with all the subversives we catch, because they have to die by violence. And if this doesn't teach you a lesson, this is what'll happen to you too. The problem is that the Indians let themselves be led by the communists. Since no-one's told the Indians anything, they go along with the communists." He was trying to convince the people but at the same time he was insulting them by what he said. Anyway, they [the soldiers] lined up the tortured and poured petrol on them; and then the soldiers set fire to each one of them. Many of them begged for mercy. Some of them screamed, many of them leapt but uttered no sound—of course, that was because their breathing was cut off. But—and to me this was incredible—many of the people had weapons with them, the ones who'd been on their way to work had machetes, others had nothing in their hands, but when they saw the army setting fire to the victims, everyone wanted to strike back, to risk their lives doing it, despite all the soldiers' arms. . . . Faced with its own cowardice, the army itself realized that the whole people were prepared to fight. You could see that even the children were enraged, but they didn't know how to express their rage. (pp. 178-179)

This passage is undoubtedly compelling and powerful. It invites the reader into the situation it describes through the medium of the eyewitness narrator, and it is the sharing of the experience through the medium of Menchú's account that constitutes the possibility of solidarity. But "what if much of Rigoberta's story is not true?" the anthropologist David Stoll (1999, p. viii) asks. On the basis of interviews in the area where the massacre was supposed to have occurred, Stoll concludes that the killing of Menchú's brother did not happen in exactly this way, that Menchú could not have been a direct witness to the event as her account suggests, and that therefore this account, along with other details of her *testimonio*, amounts to, in Stoll's words, a "mythic inflation" (pp. 63-70, 232).

It would be more accurate to say that what Stoll is able to show is that *some* rather than "much" of Menchú's story is not true. He does not contest the fact of the murder of Menchú's brother by the army, and he stipulates that "there is no doubt about the most important points [in her story]: that a dictatorship massacred thousands of indigenous peasants, that the victims included half of Rigoberta's immediate family, that she fled to Mexico to save her life, and that she joined a revolutionary movement to liberate her country" (p. viii). But he does argue that the inaccuracies or omissions in her narrative make her less than a reliable spokesperson for the interests and beliefs of the people for whom she claims to speak. In response to Stoll, Menchú herself has publicly conceded that she grafted elements of other people's experiences and stories onto her own account. In particular, she has admitted that she was not herself present at the massacre of her brother and his companions in Chajul, and that the account of the event quoted in part above came instead from her mother, who (Menchú claims) was there. She says that this and similar interpolations were a way of making her story a collective one, rather than a personal autobiography. But the point remains: If the epistemological and ethical authority of testimonial narratives depends on the assumption that they are based on personal experience and direct witness, then it might appear that, as Stoll puts it, "*I, Rigoberta Menchú* does not belong in the genre of which it is the most famous example, because it is not the eyewitness account it purports to be" (p. 242).

In a way, however, the argument between Menchú and Stoll is not so much about what really happened as it is about who has the authority to narrate. (Stoll's quarrel with Menchú and *testimonio* is a *political* quarrel that masquerades as an epistemological one.) And that question, rather than the question of "what really happened," is crucial to an understanding of how *testimonio* works. What seems to bother Stoll above all is that Menchú *has* an agenda.

He wants her to be in effect a native informant who will lend herself to *his* purposes (of ethnographic information gathering and evaluation), but she is instead functioning in her narrative as an organic intellectual, concerned with producing a text of local history—that is, with elaborating hegemony.

The basic idea of Gayatri Spivak's famous, but notoriously difficult, essay "Can the Subaltern Speak?" (1988) might be reformulated in this way: If the subaltern could speak—that is, speak in a way that really *matters* to us, that we would feel compelled to listen to, then it would not be subaltern. Spivak is trying to show that behind the gesture of the ethnographer or solidarity activist committed to the cause of the subaltern in allowing or enabling the subaltern to speak is the trace of the construction of an other who is available to speak to us (with whom we *can* speak or with whom we would feel comfortable speaking), neutralizing thus the force of the reality of difference and antagonism to which our own relatively privileged position in the global system might give rise. She is saying that one of the things being subaltern means is not mattering, not being worth listening to, or not being understood when one is "heard."

By contrast, Stoll's argument with Rigoberta Menchú is precisely with how her *testimonio* comes to matter. He is bothered by the way it was used by academics and solidarity activists to mobilize international support for the Guatemalan armed struggle in the 1980s, long after (in Stoll's view) that movement had lost whatever support it may have initially enjoyed among the indigenous peasants for whom Menchú claims to speak. That issue—"how outsiders were using Rigoberta's story to justify continuing a war at the expense of peasants who did not support it" (Stoll, 1999, p. 241)—is the main problem for Stoll, rather than the inaccuracies or omissions themselves. From Stoll's viewpoint, by making Menchú's story seem (in her own words) "the story of all poor Guatemalans"—that is, by its participating in the very metonymic logic of *testimonio*—*I, Rigoberta Menchú* misrepresents a more complex and ideologically contradictory situation among the indigenous peasants. It reflects back to the reader not the subaltern as such, but a narcissistic image of what the subaltern *should be:*

> Books like *I, Rigoberta Menchú* will be exalted because they tell academics what they want to hear. . . . What makes *I, Rigoberta Menchú* so attractive in universities is what makes it misleading about the struggle for survival in Guatemala. We think we are getting closer to understanding Guatemalan peasants when actually we are being borne away by the mystifications wrapped up in an iconic figure. (Stoll, 1999, p. 227)

In one sense, of course, there is a coincidence between Spivak's concern with the production in metropolitan ethnographic and literary discourse of what she calls a "domesticated Other" and Stoll's concern with the conversion of Menchú into an icon of academic political correctness. But Stoll's argument is also explicitly *with* Spivak, as a representative of the very kind of "postmodern scholarship" that would privilege a text like *I, Rigoberta Menchú,* even to the extent of wanting to deconstruct its metaphysics of presence. Thus, Stoll states, for example:

> Following the thinking of literary theorists such as Edward Said and Gayatri Spivak, anthropologists have become very interested in problems of narrative, voice, and representation, especially the problem of how we misrepresent voices other than our own. In reaction, some anthropologists argue that the resulting fascination with texts threatens the claim of anthropology to be a science, by replacing hypothesis, evidence, and generalization with stylish forms of introspection. (p. 247)

Or: "Under the influence of postmodernism (which has undermined confidence in a single set of facts) and identity politics (which demands acceptance of claims to victimhood), scholars are increasingly hesitant to challenge certain kinds of rhetoric" (p. 244). Or: "With postmodern critiques of representation and authority, many scholars are tempted to abandon the task of verification, especially when they construe the narrator as a victim worthy of their support" (p. 274).

Where Spivak is concerned with the way in which hegemonic literary or scientific representation effaces the effective presence and agency of the subaltern, Stoll's case against Menchú is precisely that: a way of, so to speak, *resubalternizing* a narrative that aspired to (and to some extent achieved) cultural authority. For in the process of constructing her narrative and articulating herself as a political icon around its circulation, Menchú is becoming not-subaltern, in the sense that she is functioning as what Spivak calls a subject of history. Her *testimonio* is a *performative* rather than simply descriptive or denotative discourse. Her narrative choices, and silences and evasions, entail that there are versions of "what really happened" that she does not or cannot represent without relativizing the authority of her own account.

It goes without saying that in any social situation, indeed even within a given class or group identity, it is always possible to find a variety of points of view or ways of telling that reflect contradictory, or simply differing, agendas and interests. "Obviously," Stoll (1999) observes, "Rigoberta is a legitimate Mayan voice. So are all the young Mayas who want to move to Los Angeles or Houston. So is the man with a large family who owns three worn-out acres and wants me to buy him a chain saw so he can cut down the last forest more quickly. Any of these people can be picked to make misleading generalizations about Mayas" (p. 247). The presence of these other voices makes Guatemalan indigenous communities—indeed even Menchú's own immediate family—seem irremediably driven by internal rivalries, contradictions, and disagreements.

But to insist on this is, in a way, to deny the possibility of subaltern agency as such, because a hegemonic project by definition points to a possibility of collective will and action that depends precisely on the transformation of the conditions of cultural and political disenfranchisement, alienation, and oppression that underlie these rivalries and contradictions. The appeal to diversity ("any of these people") leaves intact the authority of the outside observer (the ethnographer or social scientist) who is alone in the position of being able to both hear and sort through all the various conflicting testimonies.

The concern about the connection between *testimonio* and identity politics that Stoll evinces is predicated on the fact that multicultural rights claims carry with them what Canadian philosopher Charles Taylor (1994) has called a "presumption of equal worth" (and *I, Rigoberta Menchú* is, among other things, a strong argument for seeing the nature of American societies as irrevocably multicultural and ethnically heterogeneous). That presumption in turn implies an epistemological relativism that coincides with the postmodernist critique of the Enlightenment paradigm of scientific objectivity. If there is no one universal standard for truth, then claims about truth are contextual: They have to do with how people construct different understandings of the world and historical memory from the same sets of facts in situations of gender, ethnic, and class inequality, exploitation, and repression. The truth claims for a testimonial narrative like *I, Rigoberta Menchú* depend on conferring on the form a special kind of epistemological authority as embodying subaltern voice and experience. Against the authority of that voice— and, in particular, against the assumption that it can represent adequately a collective subject ("all poor Guatemalans")—Stoll wants to affirm the authority of the fact-gathering and -testing procedures of anthropology and journalism, in which accounts like Menchú's will be treated simply as ethnographic data that must be processed by more objective techniques of assessment, which, by definition, are not available to the direct narrator. But, in the final analysis, what Stoll is able to present as evidence against the validity of Menchú's account are, precisely, *other testimonios*: other voices, narratives, points of view, in which, it will come as no surprise, he can find something *he* wants to hear.

We know something about the nature of this problem. There is not, outside the realm of human discourse itself, a level of facticity that can guarantee the truth of this or that representation, given that society itself is not an essence prior to representation, but rather the consequence of struggles to represent and over representation. That is the deeper meaning of Walter Benjamin's aphorism "Even the dead are not safe": Even the historical memory of the past is conjunctural, relative, perishable. *Testimonio* is both an art and a strategy of subaltern memory.

We would create yet another version of the native informant of classical anthropology if we were to grant testimonial narrators like Rigoberta Menchú only the possibility of being witnesses, and not the power to create their own narrative authority and negotiate its conditions of truth and representativity. This would amount to saying that the subaltern can of course speak, but only through *us*, through our institutionally sanctioned authority and pretended objectivity as intellectuals, which give us the power to decide what counts in the narrator's raw material. But it is precisely that institutionally sanctioned authority and objectivity that, in a less benevolent form, but still claiming to speak from the place of truth, the subaltern must confront every day in the forms of war, economic exploitation, development schemes, obligatory acculturation, police and military repression, destruction of habitat, forced sterilization, and the like.[5]

There is a question of agency here. What *testimonio* obliges us to confront is not only the subaltern as a (self-) represented victim, but also as the agent—in that very act of representation—of a transformative project that aspires to become hegemonic in its own right. In terms of this project, which is not our own in any immediate sense and which may in fact imply structurally a contradiction with our own position of relative privilege and authority in the global system, the testimonial text is a *means* rather than an end in itself. Menchú and the persons who collaborated with her in the creation of *I, Rigoberta Menchú* were certainly aware that the text would be an important tool in human rights and solidarity work that might have a positive effect on the genocidal conditions the text itself describes. But *her* interest in the text is not to have it become an object for us, our means of getting the "whole truth"—"toda la realidad"—of her experience. It is rather to act tactically in a way she hopes and expects will advance the interests of the community and social groups and classes her *testimonio* represents: "poor" (in her own description) Guatemalans. That is as it should be, however, because it is not only *our* desires and purposes that count in relation to *testimonio*.

This seems obvious enough, but it is a hard lesson to absorb fully, because it forces us to, in Spivak's phrase, "unlearn privilege." And unlearning privilege means recognizing that it is not the intention of subaltern cultural practice simply to signify its subalternity to us. If that is what *testimonio* does, then critics like Sklodowska are right in seeing it as a form of the status quo, a kind of postmodernist *costumbrismo*.

The force of a *testimonio* such as *I, Rigoberta Menchú* is to displace the centrality of intellectuals and what they recognize as culture—including history, literature, journalism, and ethnographic writing. Like any testimonial narrator (like anybody), Menchú is of course also an intellectual, but in a sense she is clearly different from what Gramsci meant by a traditional intellectual—that is, someone who meets the standards and carries the authority of humanistic and/or scientific high culture. The concern with the question of subaltern agency and authority in *testimonio* depends, rather, on the suspicion that intellectuals and writing practices are themselves complicit in maintaining relations of domination and subalternity.

The question is relevant to the claim made by Dinesh D'Souza (1991) in the debate over the Stanford Western Culture undergraduate requirement (which centered on the adoption of *I, Rigoberta Menchú* as a text in one of the course sections) that *I, Rigoberta Menchú* is not good or great literature. D'Souza writes, "To celebrate the works of the oppressed, apart from the standard of merit by which other art and history and literature is judged, is to romanticize their suffering, to pretend that it is naturally creative, and to give it an aesthetic status that is not shared or appreciated by those who actually endure the oppression" (p. 87). It could be argued that *I, Rigoberta Menchú* is one of the most powerful works of *literature* produced in Latin America in the past several decades; but there is

also some point in seeing it as a provocation in the academy, as D'Souza feels it to be. The subaltern, by definition, is a social position that is not, and cannot be, adequately represented in the human sciences or the university, if only because the human sciences and the university are among the institutional constellations of power/knowledge that create and sustain subalternity.

This is not, however, to draw a line between the world of the academy and the subaltern, because the point of *testimonio* is, in the first place, to intervene in that world—that is, in a place where the subaltern is not. In its very situation of enunciation, which juxtaposes radically the subject positions of the narrator and interlocutor, *testimonio* is involved in and constructed out of the opposing terms of a master/slave dialectic: metropolis/periphery, nation/region, European/indigenous, creole/mestizo, elite/popular, urban/rural, intellectual/manual, male/female, "lettered"/illiterate or semiliterate. *Testimonio* is no more capable of transcending these oppositions than are more purely literary or scientific forms of writing or narrative; that would require something like a cultural revolution that would abolish or invert the conditions that produce relations of subordination, exploitation, and inequality in the first place. But *testimonio* does involve a new way of articulating these oppositions and a new, collaborative model for the relationship between the intelligentsia and the popular classes.

To return to Rorty's point about the "desire for solidarity," a good part of the appeal of *testimonio* must lie in the fact that it both represents symbolically and enacts in its production and reception a relation of solidarity between ourselves—as members of the professional middle class and practitioners of the human sciences—and subaltern social subjects like Menchú. *Testimonio* gives voice to a previously anonymous and voiceless popular-democratic subject, but in such a way that the intellectual or professional is interpellated, in his or her function as interlocutor/reader of the testimonial account, as being in alliance with (and to some extent dependent on) this subject, without at the same time losing his or her identity as an intellectual.

If first-generation *testimonio*s such as *I, Rigoberta Menchú* effaced textually in the manner of the ethnographic life story (except in their introductory presentations) the presence of the interlocutor, it is becoming increasingly common in what is sometimes called the "new ethnography" to put the interlocutor into the account, to make the dynamic of interaction and negotiation between interlocutor and narrator part of what *testimonio* testifies to. Ruth Behar's *Translated Woman: Crossing the Border with Esperanza's Story* (1993), for example, is often mentioned as a model for the sort of ethnographic text in which the authority (and identity) of the ethnographer is counterpointed against the voice and authority of the subject whose life history the ethnographer is concerned with eliciting. In a similar vein, Philippe Bourgois's innovative ethnography of Puerto Rican crack dealers in East Harlem, *In Search of Respect* (1995), often pits the values of the investigator—Bourgois—against those of the dealers he befriends and whose stories and conversations he transcribes and reproduces in his text. In *Event, Metaphor, Memory: Chauri Chaura, 1922-1992* (1995), the subaltern studies historian Shahid Amin is concerned with retrieving the "local memory" of an uprising in 1922 in a small town in northern India in the course of which peasants surrounded and burned down a police station, leading to the deaths of 23 policemen. But he is also concerned with finding ways to incorporate formally the narratives that embody that memory into his own history of the event, abandoning thus the usual stance of the historian as omniscient narrator and making the heterogeneous voices of the community itself the historian(s).

These ways of constructing testimonial material (obviously, the examples could be multiplied many times over) make visible that what happens in *testimonio* is not only the textual staging of a "domesticated Other," to recall Spivak's telling objection, but the confrontation through the text of one person (the reader and/or immediate interlocutor) with another (the direct narrator or narrators) at the level of a *possible* solidarity. In this sense, *testimonio* also embodies a new possibility of political agency (it is essentially that possibility to which Stoll objects). But that possibility—a postmodernist form of Popular Front-style alliance politics, if you will—is necessarily built on the recognition of and respect for the radical incommensurability of the situation of the parties involved. More than empathic liberal guilt or political correctness, what *testimonio* seeks to elicit is *coalition*. As Doris Sommer (1996) puts it succinctly, *testimonio* "is an invitation to a tête-à-tête, not to a heart to heart" (p. 143).

◆ Bibliographic Note

Margaret Randall, who has organized testimonial workshops in Cuba and Nicaragua (and who has herself edited a number of *testimonio*s on the roles of women in the Cuban and Nicaraguan revolutions), is the author of a very good, albeit hard to find, handbook on how to prepare a *testimonio* titled *Testimonios: A Guide to Oral History* (1985). The first significant academic discussion of *testimonio* that I am aware of was published in the 1986 collection *Testimonio y literatura*, edited by René Jara and Hernán Vidal at the University of Minnesota's Institute for the Study of Ideologies and Literature. The most comprehensive representation of the debate around *testimonio* in the literary humanities in the ensuing decade or so is the collection edited by Georg Gugelberger titled *The Real Thing: Testimonial Discourse and Latin America* (1996), which incorporates two earlier collections: one by Gugelberger and Michael Kearney for a special issue of *Latin American Perspectives* (vols. 18-19, 1991), and the other by myself and Hugo Achugar titled *La voz del otro: Testimonio, subalternidad, y verdad narrativa*, which appeared as a special issue of *Revista de Crítica Literaria Latinoamericana* (1992). The initial literary "manifesto" of *testimonio* was the essay by the Cuban novelist-ethnographer Miguel Barnet (*apropos* his own *Biography of a Runaway Slave*), "La novela-*testimonio*: Socioliteratura" (1986), originally published in the late 1960s in the Cuban journal *Unión*. On the academic incorporation of *testimonio* and its consequences for pedagogy, see Carey-Webb and Benz (1996).

Jara and Vidal's (1986) collection happened to coincide with the famous collection on ethnographic authority and writing practices edited by James Clifford and George Marcus, *Writing Culture* (1986), which exercised a wide influence in the fields of anthropology and history. One should note also in this respect the pertinence of the work of the South Asian Subaltern Studies Group (see, e.g., Guha, 1997; Guha & Spivak, 1988) and of the Latin American Subaltern Studies Group (see Rabasa, Sanjinés, & Carr, 1994/1996). For both social scientists and literary critics, a touchstone for conceptualizing *testimonio* should be Walter Benjamin's great essay from the 1930s, "The Storyteller" (see Benjamin, 1969).

■ Notes

1. Rorty's (1985) distinction may recall for some readers Marvin Harris's well-known distinction between *emic* and *etic* accounts (where the former are personal or collective "stories" and the latter are representations given by a supposedly objective observer based on empirical evidence).

2. Widely different sorts of narrative texts could in given circumstances function as *testimonios*: confession, court testimony, oral history, memoir, autobiography, autobiographical novel, chronicle, confession, life story, *novela-testimonio*, "nonfiction novel" (Truman Capote), or "literature of fact" (Roque Dalton).

3. Mary Louise Pratt (1986) describes the *testimonio* usefully in this respect as "autoethnography."

4. In Miguel Barnet's (1986) phrase, the author has been replaced in *testimonio* by the function of a "compiler" (*compilador*) or "activator" (*gestante*), somewhat on the model of the film producer.

5. "Any statement of authority has no other guarantee than its very enunciation, and it is pointless for it to seek another signifier, which could not appear outside this locus in any way. Which is what I mean when I say that no metalanguage can be spoken, or, more aphoristically, that there is no Other of the Other. And when

the Legislator (he who claims to lay down the Law) presents himself to fill the gap, he does so as an impostor" (Lacan, 1977, pp. 310-311).

■ References

Amin, S. (1995). *Event, metaphor, memory: Chauri Chaura 1922-1992.* Berkeley: University of California Press.

Barnet, M. (1986). La novela-*testimonio*: Socioliteratura. In R. Jara & H. Vidal (Eds.), *Testimonio y literatura.* Minneapolis: University of Minnesota, Institute for the Study of Ideologies and Literatures.

Behar, R. (1993). *Translated woman: Crossing the border with Esperanza's story.* Boston: Beacon.

Benjamin, W. (1969). *Illuminations* (H. Zohn, Trans.). New York: Schocken.

Beverley, J., & Achugar, H. (Eds.). (1992). *La voz del otro: Testimonio, subalternidad, y verdad narrativa* [Special issue]. *Revista de Crítica Literaria Latinoamericana, 36.*

Bourgois, P. (1995). *In search of respect.* Cambridge: Cambridge University Press.

Carey-Webb, A., & Benz, S. (Eds.). (1996). *Teaching and testimony.* Albany: State University of New York Press.

Clifford, J, & Marcus, G. E. (Eds.). (1986). *Writing culture: The poetics and politics of ethnography.* Berkeley: University of California Press.

D'Souza, D. (1991). *Illiberal education.* New York: Free Press.

Gugelberger, G. M. (Ed.). (1996). *The real thing: Testimonial discourse and Latin America.* Durham, NC: Duke University Press.

Gugelberger, G. M., & Kearney, M. (Eds.). (1991). [Special issue]. *Latin American Perspectives, 18-19.*

Guha, R. (Ed.). (1997). *A subaltern studies reader.* Minneapolis: University of Minnesota Press.

Guha, R., & Spivak, G. C. (Eds.). (1988). *Selected subaltern studies.,* New York: Oxford University Press.

Jara, R. (1986). Prólogo. In R. Jara & H. Vidal (Eds.), *Testimonio y literatura* (pp. 1-3). Minneapolis: University of Minnesota, Institute for the Study of Ideologies and Literatures.

Jara, R., & Vidal, H. (Eds.). (1986). *Testimonio y literatura*. Minneapolis: University of Minnesota, Institute for the Study of Ideologies and Literatures.

Lacan, J. A. (1977). *Écrits: A selection*. New York: W. W. Norton.

Menchú, R. (1984). *I, Rigoberta Menchú: An Indian woman in Guatemala* (E. Burgos-Debray, Ed.; A. Wright, Trans.). London: Verso.

Pratt, M. L. (1986). Fieldwork in common places. In J. Clifford & G. E. Marcus (Eds.), *Writing culture: The poetics and politics of ethnography*. Berkeley: University of California Press.

Rabasa, J., Sanjinés, J., & Carr, R. (Eds.). (1996). Subaltern studies in the Americas [Special issue]. *dispositio/n, 19*(46). (Contributions written in 1994)

Randall, M. (1985). *Testimonios: A guide to oral history*. Toronto: Participatory Research Group.

Rivero, E. (1984-1985). Testimonio y conversaciones como discurso literario: Cuba y Nicaragua. *Literature and Contemporary Revolutionary Culture, 1*.

Rorty, R. (1985). Solidarity or objectivity? In J. Rajchman & C. West (Eds.), *Post-analytic philosophy* (pp. 3-19). New York: Columbia University Press.

Sklodowska, E. (1982). La forma testimonial y la novelística de Miguel Barnet. *Revista/Review Interamericana, 12*, 368-380.

Sklodowska, E. (1996). Spanish American testimonial novel: Some afterthoughts. In G. M. Gugelberger (Ed.), *The real thing: Testimonial discourse and Latin America* (pp. 84-100). Durham, NC: Duke University Press.

Sommer, D. (1996). No secrets. In G. M. Gugelberger (Ed.), *The real thing: Testimonial discourse and Latin America* (pp. 130-160). Durham, NC: Duke University Press.

Spivak, G. C. (1988). Can the subaltern speak? In C. Nelson & L. Grossberg (Eds.), *Marxism and the interpretation of culture* (pp. 280-316). Urbana: University of Illinois Press.

Stoll, D. (1999). *Rigoberta Menchú and the story of all poor Guatemalans*. Boulder, CO: Westview.

Taylor, C. (1994). The politics of recognition. In C. Taylor, K. A. Appiah, J. Habermas, S. C. Rockefeller, M. Walzer, & S. Wolf, *Multiculturalism: Examining the politics of recognition* (A. Gutmann, Ed.). Princeton, NJ: Princeton University Press.

22

PARTICIPATORY ACTION RESEARCH

◆ Stephen Kemmis and Robin McTaggart

P articipatory action research is a contested concept applied to a variety of research approaches employed in a diversity of fields and settings. The nomenclature itself reflects the contestation, with the rubric *action research* perhaps best encompassing most of the approaches, with *participatory research* overlapping to include the rest. In our own work we initially used the term *collaborative action research* to emphasize the interdependence of the activities of university academics and educators in particular. More recently we have used the term *participatory action research,* in recognition of practical and theoretical convergences between our work and the activities of people engaged in "participatory research" in several different fields.

We begin by briefly describing some key approaches and some typical criticisms of them, but our aim in this chapter is to set out a particular view of participatory action research developed in our own theory and practice in recent years.

◆ The Field of "Participatory Action Research"

In this section, we outline several different approaches to inquiry for which the term *participatory action research* is sometimes used. Our synopsis includes only those kinds of inquiry that have attracted some support in relevant research literature.[1] Of course, there is considerable contestation between and within the approaches identified here, usually around questions such as the following: (a) Is this defensible as research? (b) How crucial is participation and how is it expressed here? (c) Is this research really about social improvement, or is it only about efficiency, with basic values unquestioned? (d) What are the appropriate roles for researchers, research, and other social agents in the enhancement of the human condition?

Despite the contestation, there is some convergence of interest among researchers in each of the approaches identified, and the vitality of the debates provides evidence of some shared views as well as differences. We present each approach beginning with a basic outline; we then indicate the sites and settings where the approach has been practiced most explicitly and identify what we see as some key criticisms of the approach. We present the criticisms somewhat naturalistically, expressed informally as we see them emerging in the field. In later sections we provide a more developed theoretical perspective that is useful for reflection on the nature of these criticisms.

Participatory Research

Participatory research (often called PR) is an alternative philosophy of social research (and social life, *vivencia*) often associated with social transformation in the Third World. It has roots in liberation theology and neo-Marxist approaches to community development (in Latin America, for example), but also has rather liberal origins in human rights activism (in Asia, for example). Three particular attributes are often used to distinguish PR from conventional research: shared ownership of research projects, community-based analysis of social problems, and an orientation toward community action. Given PR's commitment to social, economic, and political development responsive to the needs and opinions of ordinary people, proponents of this approach have highlighted the politics of conventional social research, arguing that orthodox social science, despite its claim to value neutrality, normally serves the ideological function of justifying the position and interests of the wealthy and powerful (Fals Borda & Rahman, 1991; Forester, Pitt, & Welsh, 1993; Freire, 1982/1988; Hall, Gillette, & Tandon, 1982; Horton, 1990; McTaggart, 1997a; Oliveira & Darcy, 1975; Park, Brydon-Miller, Hall, & Jackson, 1993).

Sites and settings. In developing countries, PR is typically undertaken by members of urban communities in *barrios* and *favellas,* remote and resource-poor rural areas, unregulated industries, and neighborhoods with high levels of unemployment, and by street dwellers. Its propo-

nents are often the poorest of the poor, deprived and exploited people working in collaboration with *animateurs* from universities, agricultural extension agencies, community development organizations, churches, and labor unions. In "developed countries," many of those who have adopted PR approaches have been academics committed to integrating university responsibilities with community work. PR has been conducted in a variety of settings and with a variety of groups in education, social work, health care, natural resource management, and urban planning.

Criticisms. Criticisms leveled against PR include that it lacks scientific rigor, confusing social activism and community development with research. Such practices may employ desirable means and serve desirable ends, but to confuse them with research—or, worse still, to disguise or dignify them as research—is a fundamental form of deception and manipulation, in this view. Proponents of PR are sometimes accused of such close identification with the communities they study that they see themselves as special and different and they alienate potential allies among alternative research proponents in the academy.

The association of the practice of PR with activists occasionally leads to accusations that it is politically motivated outsiders, not the poor, deprived, and exploited themselves, who take the initiative in identifying problems to be investigated. This in turn may lead to the charge that the welfare, livelihoods, and, in some cases, lives of disadvantaged people are put at risk as a consequence of their involvement in PR. Further, in extreme cases, proponents of PR may be dismissed as malcontents, subversives, and "communists."

Critical Action Research

Critical action research expresses a commitment to bring together broad social analyses: the self-reflective collective self-study of practice, the way language is used, organization and power in a local situation, and action to improve things. Critical action research is strongly represented in the literatures of educational action research, and emerges from dissatisfactions with classroom action research, which typically does not take a broad view of the role of the relationship between education and social change. Critical action research has a strong commitment to participation as well as to the social analyses in the critical social science tradition that reveal the disempowerment and injustice created in industrialized societies. In recent times it has attempted also to take account of disadvantage attributable to gender and ethnicity as well as to social class, its initial point of reference (Carr & Kemmis, 1986; Fay, 1987; Henry, 1991; Kemmis, 1991; Marika, Ngurruwutthun, & White, 1992; McTaggart, 1991a, 1991b, 1991c, 1997a, 1997b; Zuber-Skerritt, 1996).

Sites and settings. Critical action research projects typically include mixed groups of participants, for example, university researchers, teachers and principals, curriculum consultants, community members, and others with interests and expertise in the area of action and inquiry. Networking is important as participants are aware that change and innovation requires broad-based support. Groups may seek input from others to help inform, initiate, and sustain changes and improvements.

Criticisms. Criticisms of critical action research echo some of the criticisms of participatory research. Critical action research may be regarded as a "dangerous" vehicle for importing "radical" ideology into social settings. This view suggests that critical action research makes social participants dependent on "radical theorists" and denies that social participants' self-understandings can alone constitute a source of critical self-reflection and emancipation. In other words, critical action research may simply be yet another vehicle for the imperialism of academic (patriarchal) discourses over participants' own ways of describing and engaging their experience. In the same vein, but perhaps more generously, critical action research may be considered a "romantic" aspira-

tion, overemphasizing people's willingness and capacity to participate in programs of reform.

Classroom Action Research

Classroom action research typically involves the use of qualitative, interpretive modes of inquiry and data collection by teachers (often with help from academics) with a view to teachers' making judgments about how to improve their own practices. The practice of classroom action research has a long tradition but has swung in and out of favor, principally because the theoretical work that justified it lagged behind the progressive educational movements that breathed life into it at certain historical moments (McTaggart, 1991a; Noffke, 1990, 1997a, 1997b). Primacy is given to teachers' self-understandings and judgments. The emphasis is "practical"—that is, on the interpretations teachers and students are making and acting on in the situation. That is, classroom action research is practical not just idealistically, in a utopian way, or just about how interpretations might be different "in theory," but practical in Aristotle's sense of practical reasoning about how to act rightly and properly in a situation with which one is confronted. If university researchers are involved, their role is a service role to the teachers. Such university researchers are often advocates for "teachers' knowledge" and may disavow or seek to diminish the relevance of more theoretical discourses such as critical theory (Dadds, 1995; Elliott, 1976-1977/1988; Sagor, 1992; Stenhouse, 1975; Weiner, 1989).

Sites and settings. As the name implies, key participants in classroom action research are teachers, and sites are typically school settings (although action research is becoming more common in university classrooms). Other participants may be university researchers and occasionally curriculum consultants and students, but generally the professional ethics and substantive responsibilities of teachers take center stage.

Criticisms. Classroom action research is sometimes criticized for the prominence it gives to teachers' knowledge in comparison with other views of what is happening in schools. This privileging of teachers' knowledge masks the assumption that significant improvement in classrooms can be accomplished in the absence of broader patterns of community support and social change (thereby ignoring the literature on educational change; Fullan, 1982, 1991). Further, it implies that consciousness-raising among teachers is possible without the theoretical resources of traditions of feminism, racism, critical theory, postcolonialist, and other such discourses (movements that more often arose in universities and communities, not schools).

Action Learning

Action learning has its origins in the work of advocate Reg Revans, who saw traditional approaches to management inquiry as unhelpful in solving the problems of organizations. Revans's early work with colliery managers attempting to improve workplace safety marks a significant turning point for the role of professors—engaging them directly in management problems in organizations.

The fundamental idea of action learning is bringing people together to learn from each other's experience. There is emphasis on studying one's own situation, clarifying what the organization is trying to achieve, and working to remove obstacles. Key aspirations are organization efficacy and efficiency, although advocates of action learning affirm the moral purpose and content of their own work and of the managers they seek to engage in the process (Clark, 1972; Pedler, 1991; Revans, 1980, 1982).

Sites and settings. Action learning began as an approach to management (and manager) development and still has that focus. However, broader participation has been used with good effect in some settings. It is used most often in business settings (early work was with colliery managers), but has been employed in the public sector (hospitals and public housing estates), especially where organizations were seeking to emulate what were perceived to be (and are in many circumstances) successful collaborative business management practices.

Criticisms. The early work on action learning began with the practice of colliery management. Some argue that its emphasis on management and on the common practice of composing action learning "sets" (groups) primarily of managers restricts its capacity to bring about change and to respond to different workplace participants' concerns. Its tendency toward an emphasis on "efficiency" (or potential co-optability) ignores the broader questions of the values and social purposes of the organization and the different values and concerns of participants at different levels and in different parts of organizations. The emphasis on "workplace learning" and on individual organizational development is argued to deny a critical perspective—reducing "learning" to simply applying routines invented by others, believing reasons invented by others, servicing aspirations invented by others, realizing goals invented by others, and giving expression to values advocated by others. An emphasis on "problem solving" distracts attention from what is going on in the literature about similar workplaces and restricts the coherence aspired to in generating a theoretical rationale for the work of the organization or industry.

Action Science

Action science emphasizes the study of practice in organizational settings as a source of new understandings and improved practice. The field of action science systematically builds the relationship between academic organizational psychology and practical problems as they are experienced in organizations. It identifies two aspects to professional knowledge: the formal knowledge that all competent members of the profession are thought to share and into which professionals are inducted during their initial training, and the professional knowledge of interpretation and enactment. A distinction is also made between the professional's "espoused theory" and "theories in use," and "gaps" between these are used as points of reference for change. A key factor in analyzing these gaps between theory and practice is helping the professional to unmask the "cover-ups" that are put in place, especially when participants are feeling anxious or threatened. The approach aspires to the development of the "reflective practitioner" (Argyris, 1990; Argyris, Putnam, & Smith, 1985; Argyris & Schön, 1974, 1978; Reason, 1988; Schön, 1983, 1987, 1991).

Sites and settings. The action science approach has been used in a wide variety of professional occupations. Educators have often espoused it, perhaps most notably in advocacies for more symmetrical and reciprocal versions of "clinical supervision" and for "reflective practice."

Criticisms. Action science faces criticisms similar to those aimed at action learning, encompassed by the term *technicism.* Participants are exposed to the judgment that an "espoused theory" does not match a *researcher*-described "theory in use." Implicit is the assumption that an espoused theory could ever adequately specify action, basically a flaw in the cognitivist position on the relationship between theory and practice. The identified gap between theory and practice then automatically exposes the participant to the intervention of the outsider, especially his or her role in "unmasking" the defenses of participants. Further, the approach can be somewhat individualistic, making each participant subject to outsider intervention and vulnerable after the intervention. The criticism also suggests unclear specification of the role and composition of the "group" of participants and the relationship between the group and researchers and consultants.

Soft Systems Approaches

Soft systems approaches have their origins in organizations that use so-called hard systems of engineering especially for industrial production. Soft systems methodology is the human "systems" analogy for systems engineering that has developed as the science of product and information flow. It is defined as oppositional to positivistic science, with its emphasis on hypothesis testing. The researcher (typically an outside consultant) assumes a role as discussion partner or trainer in a real problem situation.

The researcher works with participants to generate some (systems) models of the situation and uses the models to question the situation and to suggest a revised course of action (Checkland, 1981; Checkland & Scholes, 1990; Davies & Ledington, 1991; Flood & Jackson, 1991; Jackson, 1991; Kolb, 1984).

Sites and settings. Soft systems methodologies have been used in a variety of industrial and public sector organizational settings. Participants usually include an external management consultant who assumes a key role in making meaning from the attempts to bring about improvement. The consultant explicitly defers to the values of the organization avowed by participants and presents as a "neutral" process management consultant.

Criticisms. Criticisms of soft systems methodology include the ambiguous notion of participation and the potentially influential role played by the consultant. The association (typically contractual) between the consultant and the management of the organization leads to concerns about the interests underlying the role played by the consultant. The consultant is often described as "facilitator" or "process manager," and the assumption that this is a value-free, neutral, or politically inert role is strongly contested. It is suggested that there is a weak relationship between the process of inquiry and the literature and critique of the organization from a theoretically informed position. There is deference to the view that organizational reform is a "process" (and a one-off process) that requires an emphasis on processual input and consultant diagnosis at the expense of substantive input or input from sources other than the consultant.

Industrial Action Research

Industrial action research has an extended history, dating back to the post-Lewinian influence in organizational psychology and organizational development at the Tavistock Institute of Human Relations in Britain and the Research Center for Group Dynamics in the United States. It is typically consultant driven, with very strong advocacies for collaboration between social scientists and members of different levels of the organization. The work is often couched in the language of workplace democratization, but more recent explorations have aspired more explicitly to the democratization of the research act itself, following the theory and practice of the participatory research movement. Especially in its more recent manifestations, industrial action research is differentiated from "action science" and its emphasis on cognition, taking a preferred focus on reflection and the need for broader organizational and social change. Some advocacies have used critical theory as a resource to express aspirations for more participatory forms of work and evaluation, but more usually the style is somewhat humanistic and individualistic rather than "critical." Emphases on social systems in organizations, such as improving organizational effectiveness and employee relations, are common, and the Lewinian aspiration to learn from trying to bring about change is a strong theme (Bravette, 1996; Elden, 1983; Emery & Thorsrud, 1976; Emery, Thorsrud, & Trist, 1969; Foster, 1972; Levin, 1985; Pasmore & Friedlander, 1982; Sandkull, 1980; Torbert, 1991; Warmington, 1980; Whyte, 1989, 1991).

Sites and settings. Participants in industrial action research are typically shop-floor employees, middle managers, and professional consultants from outside the organization working in collaboration. The approach has been documented in a wide variety of industrial (and service) settings, and persuasive evidence of the broad positive effect of workplace "democratization" using action research approaches is widespread.

Criticisms. It is suggested that industrial action research has not adequately engaged the problem of the hierarchies and goals of industrial settings. In this view, "participation" is too limited to the lower echelons of organizations, and thereby senior management, company directors, and shareholders are insulated from questions about basic organizational values and di-

rections. The work draws more thoughtfully on social theory than do other forms of action research in industrial settings, but criticisms from the participatory research movement indicate a profound wariness about the adoption of that movement's cherished ideas and hard-won practices in the very transnational corporations that have created serious dysfunction and poverty in Third World settings. Although industrial action research may constitute organizational development and an expression of democracy in some parts of the organization, it is feared that it may too easily drift back into technicist, co-optive, and control practices such as quality circles and quality assurance.

◆ Research and Social Practice

Much contemporary participatory action research has evolved as an extension of applied research into practical social settings, with participants taking on roles formerly occupied by social researchers from outside the settings (Adelman, 1997; Altrichter & Gstettner, 1997). By contrast, participatory research and collaborative action research emerged more or less deliberately as forms of resistance to conventional research practices that were perceived by particular kinds of participants as acts of colonization—that is, as a means of normalizing or domesticating people to research and policy agendas imposed on a local group or community from central agencies often far removed from local concerns and interests.

This switch of perspective is not just of "political" or historical interest. It challenges some fundamental presuppositions about the nature of research as a social practice, including (for example) presuppositions about the nature of social life and about who can be a researcher (we discuss some of these issues later in this chapter). Theorizing participatory action research requires articulating and—to an extent—formalizing what is implied when participants in a social setting decide to take the construction and reconstruction of their social reality into their own hands, knowing that they are not alone in constructing or reconstructing it, but nevertheless taking an active, agential role in changing the processes of construction of social realities.

One way to understand this shift in perspective is to see it historically. Some histories of this kind are available (Fals Borda, 1979, 1988; McTaggart, 1991a, 1997a; Noffke, 1990, 1997a, 1997b). It is also possible to understand it (auto-)biographically or phenomenologically, from the perspectives of some of the people who have advocated and undertaken participatory action research as part of their engagement in a politics of resistance nourished by research undertaken by and for groups experiencing one or another form of oppression. Works of this kind also exist (Horton, 1990; McTaggart, 1999), some related to the histories of participatory research. In this chapter, we would like to take a different approach, partly to draw out some of the logic of what is implied by participatory research and partly to build some bridges between the participant perspective and the conventional literature of social research methodology—as a contribution to going beyond the "paradigm wars" that have bedeviled social research over much of the past century.

As Anthony Giddens (1979, p. 71) pointed out some years ago, participants in social settings are not "cultural dopes"—they can give cogent reasons for their intentions and actions, and generally demonstrate a sophisticated (although not necessarily social scientific) understanding of the situations they inhabit. Moreover, unlike social theorists attempting theoretical constructions of a setting from within a particular tradition of social theory, they are not obliged to foreclose options about how to "see" their situation—that is, to "see" it theoretically, in a way that can be construed as a contribution to a particular tradition of theorizing. Indeed, participants frequently shift from one way of seeing something to another, not only to see it from their own points of view and from the points of view of relevant others, but also to see it both from the perspective of

individuals and from a "big-picture" perspective on the setting, which means seeing the local setting as connected to wider social and historical conditions.

There is also a sense in which, when participants are dissatisfied with the way things are, they do not just want things to be different; they understand that things have to be made different by themselves and others. To the extent that this is so, it indicates that participants are generally aware that social settings are constituted through social practices, and that making change is itself a practice.

Participatory action research (not always by that name) frequently emerges in situations where people want to make changes thoughtfully—that is, after critical reflection. It emerges when people want to think "realistically" about where they are now, how things came to be that way, and, from these starting points, how, in practice, things might be changed.

Taking a "realistic" perspective on changing social practices in a setting usually means that participants have to take a multifaceted view of practice—not seeing it in a narrow way. In this, participants are sometimes regarded as "naïve" or "primitive" from the point of view of social theory, but we cannot accept these descriptions. On the contrary, we want to assert that participants are far from naïve. The participant perspective poses a substantial challenge to social theory: to articulate "common" sense in a way that will be regarded as authentic and compelling by participants themselves, without converting participants to the imposed perspective of a specialist social theorist. This process of making the familiar unfamiliar (and making the unfamiliar familiar) involves treading a fine line between taking an attitude toward the situation that aims to "uncover" or "unmask" hidden forces at work in the situation (the attitude of the outsider who claims special insight into the setting) and illuminating and clarifying interconnections and tensions between elements of a setting in terms that participants themselves regard as authentic (which may include giving more weight to relationships participants had previously discounted or devalued in their deliberations). The criterion of authenticity involves a dialectic sometimes described in terms of "the melting of horizons" (Gadamer, 1975)—seeing things intersubjectively, from one's own point of view and from the point of view of others (from the inside and the outside).

In the following subsections we briefly examine the notion of "practice" as a way to build a bridge between a participant perspective on practice and different theoretical traditions in the study of practice, and then briefly examine the participant perspective as a distinctive standpoint in terms of the social relations of social research.

Different Traditions in the Study of Practice

Despite its ubiquity and familiarity, what the term *practice* means is by no means self-explanatory. In theory and research, it turns out to mean very different things to different people. Perhaps one reason for this is that researchers who examine practice from different intellectual traditions tend to focus on different aspects of practice when they investigate it. The result is confusion. On the basis of their different views about how practice itself should be understood, different theorists take different views on how it can and should be improved.

To make a start in clearing up some of these confusions, it may help if we distinguish five different aspects of practice emphasized in different investigations of practice:

1. The individual performances, events, and effects that constitute practice as it is viewed from the "objective," external perspective of an outsider (the way the practitioner's individual behavior appears to an outside observer);

2. The wider social and material conditions and interactions that constitute practice as it is viewed from the "objective," external perspective of an outsider (the way the patterns of social interaction among those involved in the practice appear to an outside observer);

3. The intentions, meanings, and values that constitute practice as it is viewed from the "subjective," internal perspective of individual practitioners themselves (the way individual practitioners' intentional actions appear to them as individual cognitive subjects);

4. The language, discourses, and traditions that constitute practice as it is viewed from the "subjective," internal social perspective of members of the participants' own discourse community who must represent (describe, interpret, evaluate) practices in order to talk about and develop them, as happens, for example, in the discourse communities of professions (the way the language of practice appears to communities of practitioners as they represent their practices to themselves and others);

5. The change and evolution of practice—taking into account all four of the aspects of practice just mentioned—that comes into view when it is understood as reflexively restructured and transformed over time, in its historical dimension.

Different approaches to the study of practice have tended to focus on one or another of these different aspects of practice, with the result that, over time, different traditions in the study of practice have emerged. Some regard these different traditions as mutually exclusive and competing, based on their view that just one is the "correct" way to view practice. Others regard these different traditions pluralistically, seeing them as different but not necessarily in competition with one another, based on their view that each will simply go its own way in the research literature. Still others regard these different traditions as talking past one another—as failing to engage with one another in reciprocal critique and debate that could permit the exploration of complementarities and points of connection between them. And still others take the view that the different traditions can be interrelated within broader, perhaps synthetic, frameworks of theory and practice. There is merit in exploring the possibilities of complementarity and connection among these different approaches, even if for the time being it seems premature to say how a broad and unifying synthesis of the different perspectives can be achieved.

Epistemological Perspectives

Although different schools of thought in theorizing and research about practice in different fields are very diverse in terms of the problems and phenomena they study and the methods they employ, it is possible to bring some of their presuppositions about problems, phenomena, and methods to the fore by making some distinctions around which these differences can be arrayed. Generally speaking, these are regarded as epistemological questions—questions about the nature of the "truth" in the human and social sciences—in the case we are considering here, the "truth" about practice. For the moment, we will focus on just two dichotomies that have divided approaches to the human and social sciences: first, the division between (a) those approaches that see human and social life largely in *individualistic* terms and (b) those that see human and social life largely in terms of the *social realm;* and second, the division between (a) those approaches that conceive of their problems, phenomena, and methods largely in *objective* terms (from an "external" perspective, as it were) and (b) those that conceive their problems, phenomena, and methods largely in *subjective* terms (from an "internal" perspective, as it were). In each case, we want to suggest that these are false dichotomies, and that we can escape from the partiality of each by seeing the two sides of the dichotomies not as opposites, only one of which can be true, but as dialectically related—that is, as mutually constitutive aspects of one another, both of which are necessary to achieve a more comprehensive perspective on practice.

The move from thinking in terms of dichotomies to thinking in dialectical terms might be characterized as a move from "either/or" thinking to "never either, always both" thinking. (The logic of what these figures of speech imply will become clearer in what follows.) For the time being, however, it suffices to say that we can transcend each of these two dichotomies—individual-social and objective-subjective—by seeing both in dialectical terms. We can use these two distinctions as a basis for a taxonomy of different approaches to the study of practice (see Figure 22.1).

1. Practice as individual behavior, to be studied objectively. The first perspective on practice sees it primarily "from the outside," as individual behavior. Those adopting this perspective frequently understand the science of behavior as "objective" and apply this view to their understanding of practice. A variety of traditions in psychology, including the behaviorist and the cognitivist, adopt this view of practice.

Research on practice from this perspective adopts correlational or quasi-experimental methods; it is likely to use descriptive and inferential statistics and to adopt an instrumental view of the relationship between the researcher and the researched, in which the field being studied is understood in the "third person" (as objects whose behavior is to be changed). This approach to the study of practice is likely to be adopted when the research question is one asked by people administering organizations who want to provoke change by changing the inputs, processes, and outputs of the organization as a system (in which people are seen as elements of the system).

2. Practice as group behavior or ritual, to be studied objectively. The second perspective also views practice "from the outside," but sees it in terms of the social group. Those adopting this perspective also understand the study of group behavior as "objective." A variety of social psychological perspectives, and structural-functionalist perspectives in sociology, adopt this view of practice, as do some forms of systems theory in the social sciences.

Research on practice from this perspective is also likely to adopt correlational or quasi-experimental methods; it is also likely to use descriptive and inferential statistics and to adopt an instrumental view of the relationship between the

Focus:	The individual	The social	Both: Reflexive-dialectical view of individual-social relations and connections
Perspective			
Objective	(1) Practice as individual behavior, seen in terms of performances, events & effects: behaviorist and most cognitivist approaches in psychology	(2) Practice as social interaction (e.g., ritual, system-structured: structure-fuctionalist and social systems approaches	
Subjective	(3) Practice as intentional action, shaped by meaning and values: psychological *verstehen* (empathetic understanding) and most contructivist approaches	(4) Practice as socially structured, shaped by discourses, tradition: interpretive, aesthetic-historical *verstehen* & post-structuralist approaches	
Both: *Reflexive-dialectical* view of subjective-objective relations and connections			(5) Practice as socially and historically constituted, and as reconstituted by human agency and social action: critical theory, critical social science

Figure 22.1. Relationships Among Different Traditions in the Study of Practice

researcher and the researched, in which the field being studied is understood in the "third person" (as objects whose behavior is to be changed). And, like the first perspective, this perspective would also be likely to be adopted when the research question is one asked by people administering systems who want to change them by changing system inputs, processes, and outputs.

3. *Practice as individual action, to be studied from the perspective of the subjective.* The third perspective attempts to understand practice

"from the inside"—from the perspective of the individual practitioner. In this view, human action (including practice) cannot be understood as "mere" behavior; it must be seen as shaped by the values, intentions, and judgments of the practitioner. Because this view takes into account these elements of practice, as far as possible, from the perspective of the practitioner, it is frequently said to be a "subjective" view of practice (although it should be recognized that describing it as "subjective" is not to say that it is any less capable of laying claim to being scientific in its approach to the study of practice—indeed, there is a very strong tradition in the human and social sciences based on just this view). A variety of approaches in psychology take this view of practice (among them some clinical, some "humanistic," and some "gestalt" approaches, to give just a few examples). A much older and stronger tradition in the study of people and their actions—one that can be traced directly back to Aristotle in the Western philosophical tradition—is also based on understanding motives, intentions, values, and notions of virtue, and it understands practice (in the sense of praxis) as the exercise of human judgment by people acting in (practical) situations in which they are obliged to act, knowing that action in real historical circumstances is always uncertain and never fully justified by appeal to technical rules or principles, but must always reflect the best judgment of the actor. As well as being found in certain kinds of humanistic philosophy, this view of practice is found in some theological writings on practice.

Research on practice from this perspective generally adopts qualitative methods (including autobiographical, idiographic, and phenomenological methods), is likely to make only limited use of statistics, and is likely to adopt a "practical" view of the relationship between the researcher and the researched, in which the field being studied is understood in the "second person" (that is, as knowing, responsible, and autonomous subjects—persons who, like the researcher her- or himself, must make their own decisions about how to act in the situations in which they find themselves). This perspective is likely to be adopted when the research question is one asked by people who understand themselves to be autonomous and responsible persons acting in life worlds of human relationships and interactions, who believe that changing these life worlds requires engaging, and perhaps re-forming, selves and relationships in shared life-world settings.

4. *Practice as social action or tradition, to be understood from the perspective of the subjective.* A fourth perspective on practice also attempts to view it "from the inside," but understands it not from the perspective of the individual acting alone, but as part of a social

structure that contributes to forming the way in which action (practice) is understood by people in the situation. It also takes a "subjective" view, but it takes into account that people and the way they act are also formed historically—that they always come to situations that have been preformed, and in which only certain kinds of action are now appropriate or possible. Moreover, this view is also conscious that it must take into account that people's own perspectives, and their very words, have all been formed historically and in the interactions of social life—they are historically, socially, and discursively constituted. Much social theory, much social and moral philosophy, and much theology is based on this view of practice.

Such a view is captured in Alasdair MacIntyre's (1983) careful definition of a practice as

> any coherent and complex form of socially-established cooperative human activity through which goods internal to that activity are realized, in the course of trying to achieve those standards of excellence which are appropriate to, and partially definitive of, that form of activity, with the result that human powers to achieve excellence, and human conceptions of the ends and goods involved, are systematically extended. (p. 175)

MacIntyre gives some examples of practices and distinguishes practices from institutions:

> Practices must not be confused with institutions. Chess, physics and medicine are practices; chess clubs, laboratories, universities and hospitals are institutions. Institutions are characteristically and necessarily concerned with . . . external goods. They are involved in acquiring money and other material goods; they are structured in terms of power and status, and they distribute money, power and status as rewards. Nor could they do otherwise if they are to sustain not only themselves, but also the practices of which they are bearers. For no practices can survive any length of time unsustained by institutions. . . . institutions and practices characteristically form a single causal order in which the ideals and the creativity of the practice are always vulnerable to the acquisitiveness of the institution, in which the co-operative care for common goods of the practice is always vulnerable to the competitiveness of the institution. (p. 181)

Research on practice from this perspective is similar to the third perspective in its likely research methods (although it may also adopt clinical or critical ethnography as a research method, or particular kinds of methods that are very explicit about the role of the researcher in the research—as in advocacies for some feminist approaches to research), its view about practical reasoning, and its view of the standpoint of the researcher in relation to others in the situation being studied. In this case, however, the researcher would understand her- or himself not only as another actor in a social situation, but also as a human agent who, with others, must act at any particular moment in a situation that is already socially, historically, and discursively formed, and in which he or she is also, to some extent, a representative of a tradition that contests the ground with other traditions (because different and competing traditions about different things typically are simultaneously at play in any particular situation). In this sense, research in this tradition is likely to understand itself as in some sense "political"—just as the situations it studies are "political."

5. Practice as reflexive, to be studied dialectically. The fifth view of practice understands that it is "political" in an even more self-conscious sense: It understands that to study practice is to change it, that the process of studying it is also "political," and that its own standpoint is liable to change through the process of action—that it is a process of enlightenment about the standpoint from which one studies practice as well as about the practice itself.

This view of practice challenges the dichotomies or dualisms that separate the first four views from one another: the dualisms of the individual versus the social and the objective versus the subjective. It attempts to see each of these dimensions not in terms of polar opposites, but in terms of the mutuality and relationship between these different aspects of things. Thus it sees the individual and the social, and the objective and the subjective, as related aspects of human life and practice, to be understood dialectically—that is, as mutually opposed (and often contradictory) but mutually

necessary aspects of human, social, and historical reality, in which each aspect helps to constitute the other.

In this view, it is necessary to understand practice as enacted by individuals who act in the context of history and in ways constituted by a vast historical web of social interactions among people. Similarly, it is necessary to understand practice as having both objective (externally given) and subjective (internally understood and interpreted) aspects, both of which are necessary to understand how any practice is really practiced, how it is constituted historically and socially, and how it can be transformed. This view of the relationship between the objective and the subjective is sometimes also described as "reflexive," because changing the objective conditions changes the way in which a situation is interpretively understood, which in turn changes how people act on the "external," "objective" world, which means that what they do is understood and interpreted differently, and that others also act differently, and so on. This dynamic process of reflection and self-reflection gives human action in history its dynamic, fluid, and reflexive character. In this view of practice, practitioners regard themselves explicitly as engaged in action that makes history, and they are likely to regard research as a process of learning from action and history—a process conducted within action and history, not standing outside it in the role of recorder or commentator, or above it in the role of conductor or controller.

The reflexive-dialectical perspective on practice thus attempts to find a place for the four previous perspectives in a broader framework of historical, social, and discursive construction and reconstruction, and does its best to recognize not only that people's actions are caused by their intentions and circumstances, but also that people cause intentions and circumstances—that is, that people are made by action in the world, and that they also make action and history. And it aims to see how these processes occur within the ambit of the research process itself.

Research on practice from this perspective is likely to adopt research methods that are reflexive—methods like those used in critical social science (Carr & Kemmis, 1986; Fay, 1987), collaborative action research (Kemmis & McTaggart, 1988), and "memory work" (Haug, 1987). They are reflexive in the sense that they engage participants in a collaborative process of social transformation in which they learn from, and change the way they engage in, the process of transformation. Research conducted from this perspective adopts an "emancipatory" view of the point and purpose of the research, in which coparticipants attempt to remake and improve their own practice to overcome distortions, incoherence, contradictions, and injustices. It adopts a "first-person" perspective in which people construct the research process as a way of collaborating in the process of transforming their practices, their understanding of their practices, and the situations in which they practice. Like the fourth perspective on practice, it understands that research is "political," but it aims to make the research process into a politics that will in some definite ways supersede and reconstruct the preexisting politics of the settings in which it is conducted—indeed, it aims to be a process in which various aspects of social life in the setting (cultural, economic, and political) can be transformed through collaborative action (although recognizing that the internal social processes of the setting and the research are connected to, and sometimes conflict with, wider social and historical processes that the coresearchers cannot suspend or change simply by changing themselves, so they work in relation to these wider forces rather than simply "for" or "against" them).

Although the other four traditions are all necessary in their own ways, and for particular kinds of purposes, this fifth tradition is of special interest to those who want to change practices through their own efforts, and especially by their efforts in participatory, collaborative research. It is a tradition in the study of practice that aims to make explicit connections across the dimensions of "objective" and "subjective," the focus on the individual and the focus on the social, the aspects of structure and agency, and the connections between the past and the future.

The significance of the word *connections* here deserves special notice. The study of a practice as complex as the practice of education, or nursing, or public administration (to give just a few examples) is a study of connections—of many different kinds of communicative, productive, and organizational relationships among people in socially, historically, and discursively constituted media of language (discourse), work, and power—all of which must be understood dynamically and relationally. And we should recognize that there are research approaches that aim to explore these connections and relationships by participating in them and, through changing the forms in which people participate in them, to change the practice, the way it is understood, and the situations in which the practice is conducted. At its best, such a research tradition aims to help people understand themselves both as "objective" forces impinging on others and as subjects who have intentions and commitments they share with others, and both as people who act in ways framed by discourses formed beyond any one of us individually and as people who make meaning for ourselves in communication with the others alongside whom we stand, and whose fates—one way or another—we share.

Traditions of Research Into Practice as Constructed Through Social and Material Practices

Research practices are constituted in social and material relationships. To take a tough materialist stance, we might even want to think of research practices in terms of Louis Althusser's (1971) definition of a practice: "By practice in general, I shall mean any process of transformation of a determinate given raw material into a determinate product, a transformation effected by determinate human labor, using determinate means of production" (quoted in Bennett, 1979, p. 111). This definition of a practice probably rests most comfortably in the second of the five traditions outlined earlier (with the particular partialities of that perspective). It nevertheless draws attention to the concreteness of the social and material relationships that constitute practice—concrete relationships between people and things (which may include symbolic kinds of relationships and relationships between people's interpretations of people and things). Althusser nominates processes of transformation involving "raw materials," "products," "human labor," and "means of production"—all of which are determinate in any given case. We might ask ourselves what elements of the social and material relationships of any particular piece of research on practice (in education, nursing, or public administration, for example) can be described using each of these terms, and about the nature of the relationships among them.

Methodological Perspectives

At one level, considering the means of production involved in different traditions of research into practice, we may examine the kinds of research techniques these traditions typically employ. Different researchers into practice emphasize different aspects of practice in their investigations and rely on different research methods and techniques that seem appropriate in the study of practice viewed from the particular perspectives they adopt. That is, different methodological perspectives in research on practice are related to different epistemological perspectives on the nature of practice; from this it follows that different research techniques "construct" the objects of their study (practices) as phenomena of rather different kinds. Figure 22.2 outlines some of the kinds of methods and techniques that have characteristically been employed in different traditions in the study of practice.

These remarks have implications for the contemporary debate between "quantitative" and "qualitative" approaches in social and educational science. They suggest that it would be a mistake to conclude that truth and certainty reside with quantitative methods, or that they reside with qualitative methods. It is an illusion to believe that research methods and techniques provide secure paths to truth and certainty. Sadly, however, there are some who still cling to these illusions. At another extreme, however, are those who believe that, because truth and certainty cannot be attained, there is no sense in science except aesthetic or poetic sense—in short, that social science is just words,

symbols, and images that can claim no power to represent the social world in any compelling way, except, perhaps, with the compulsion of narrative or myth (for example, Lyotard, 1984). These views share the mistaken assumption that truth is certain or it cannot be truth at all. There is a path between this Scylla and Charybdis, however: the view that what we call "truth" is always and only provisional, that it is always fallible, that it is always shaped by particular views and material-social-historical circumstances, and that it can be approached only intersubjectively—through exploration of the extent to which it seems accurate, morally right and appropriate, and authentic in the light of our lived experience. From this view, it is the task of a social or educational science to create the conditions under which provisional, fallible, intersubjectively based claims to truth can be explored. In our view, this is the rich and complex work required in theorizing practice.

There is a kind of self-fulfilling prophecy, then, in research methods and techniques that construct practices in different ways. They do produce "pictures" of practice, but, like all pictures, they construct the world from a particular observational standpoint or perspective, in the particular terms and observational categories of the media (or discourse) of the particular observational techniques employed. Thus, for example, one tradition sees practice in terms of behavior, another sees it in terms of participants' values and interests, and another sees it in terms of discursive formation. For some, these perspectives are simply incommensurable;[2] for others, they may be complementary. At the level of research methods and techniques, we must certainly concede that there is a plurality of perspectives. The question is whether this plurality can be understood as suggesting a higher-order perspective in which we can triangulate these different perspectives against one another to arrive at a more multifaceted perspective that, even if it does not promise completeness, wholeness, or a higher-level unification of the perspectives it gathers together, at least poses a problem of how the different perspectives can be interrelated.

Focus:	The individual	The social	Both: *Reflexive-dialectical view of individual-social relations and connections*
Perspective			
Objective	(1) Practice as individual behavior: Quantitative, correlational-experimental methods. Psychometric and observational techniques, tests, interaction schedules.	(2) Practice as social and systems behavior: Quantitative, correlational-experimental methods. Observational techniques, sociometrics, systems analysis, social ecology.	
Subjective	(3) Practice as intentional action: Qualitative, interpretive methods. Clinical analysis, interview, questionnaire, diaries, journals, self-report, introspection	(4) Practice as socially structured, shaped by discourses and tradition: Qualitative, interpretive, historical methods. Discourse analysis, document analysis.	
Both: *Reflexive-dialectical* view of subjective-objective relations and connections			(5) Practice as socially and historically constituted, and as reconstituted by human agency and social action: Critical methods. Dialectical analysis (multiple methods).

Figure 22.2. Methods and Techniques Characteristic of Different Approaches to the Study of Practice

◆ Participatory Action Research as Practice

Like other forms of social research, participatory action research is sometimes conducted principally from within one or another of the traditions outlined in this taxonomy. More generally, however, it takes a more encompassing view of practice, simply because partici-

pants in most settings cannot readily exclude one or another of these perspectives on the grounds that it is not relevant to the way participants—and others with whom they interact in the setting—see things. And, even more significant, participatory action research generally occurs very much in the dimension of historical time (Perspective 5): Participants make, and learn from, changes they make as they go.

Our own work in Aboriginal teacher education in the Northern Territory of Australia pro-

582 ◆ STRATEGIES OF INQUIRY

vides an example. Aboriginal teachers wanted to explore practices that made the schools in which they taught more expressive of Aboriginal culture. Western domination expressed itself in curriculum, pedagogy, and organization, and Aboriginal resistance to this domination is encapsulated in the words of Wesley Lanhupuy, Northern Territory parliamentarian representing the electorate of Arnhem and an Aboriginal elder from northeast Arnhemland, who described the problem Aboriginal teachers face in this way:

Schools have been part of the process of the colonisation of Australia and its original inhabitants. Schools were introduced and imposed on Aborigines following the fierce struggles for the land between Aborigines and the new white settlers. This occurred in a predictable pattern as each state and territory of Australia was progressively colonised over the past two hundred years.

This colonisation process has taken place within living memory in the Northern Territory and unfortunately continues in many of our schools today. These have been difficult times, in which schools have been used quite openly to capture the minds of Aboriginal children and to turn them towards the dominant balanda culture. So schools have been most significant in the attempt by non-Aboriginal Australians to assimilate Aborigines into the balanda society. . . .

The strong balanda cultural orientation of the [school] and the dominating position of balanda teachers and administrators inevitably work to influence the minds of children in ways that undervalue the Aboriginal heritage. Aboriginal people now understand that if schools are to serve the political social and economic purposes of their own people, the school, as an institution, needs to be accommodated within Aboriginal society itself. Only when the cultural orientation of the school becomes Yolngu [Aboriginal], will schools become integral to the movement of Aborigines toward self-determination. The decolonisation of schools in Aboriginal communities is the challenge for Aborigines now. (Lanhupuy, 1987, p. 31)[3]

In the teacher education program we developed with help from Aboriginal teachers upgrading qualifications and from colleagues at Batchelor College in the Northern Territory of Australia, several aspects of practice were engaged and transformed: curriculum practices, teaching practices, administrative practices,

practices of relating to communities, and the research practices we worked through with Aboriginal teachers to inform our work.

The curriculum, teaching, and organizational practices of both schools and Deakin University were changed as teachers and teacher educators began to understand the aspirations of Aboriginal communities. As teacher educators in this setting, we followed the lead of the Aboriginal teachers, who were changing their own teaching, curricular, and organizational practices to express more faithfully their emergent understandings of what they came to call "Aboriginal pedagogies," or, in four of their own languages, *Blekbala Wei, Deme Nayin, Yolngu Rom,* and *Ngini Nginingawula Ngawurranungurumagi* (Bunbury, Hastings, Henry, & McTaggart, 1991; Marika et al., 1992; Yirrkala Homeland Schools, 1996). Aboriginal teachers' reflections on their changing work was paralleled by documentation of the emergent rationale and critique of non-Aboriginal teacher educators' own practice (Kemmis, 1988; McTaggart, 1987, 1988, 1991b, 1991c). The enhancement of practice was informed by the principles of participatory action research expressed in various ways (Carr & Kemmis, 1986; Kemmis & McTaggart, 1988) and by an understanding of the ways the ideology, institutionalization, and practices of colonialism were insinuated into the lives of Aboriginal people and into our own lives. Only by understanding the historical location of our own work and by examining these understandings with Aboriginal people could we participate adequately in changing the work. It was an attempt to express what we now term Perspective 5: to articulate simultaneously a theory of educational practice and a theory of educational research practice that mutually support, inform, and challenge each other.

Social Relationships in the Study of Practice

A science of practice must itself be a practice. It will be describable in terms of the five kinds of aspects of practice mentioned earlier. Moreover, like other practices, a science of practice will be constructed in social relations and will involve elements of technical, practical, and critical reasoning about practice. How it understands itself in terms of the social relations of the research act is important for an understanding of what kind of a science of practice it will be.

The differences among research perspectives are not due to questions of the machinery of research (research techniques) alone; they are also differences of standpoint that reveal something of the location of the researcher in the research act—as Habermas's (1972, 1974) attempt to articulate the politics of knowledge production and distribution as well as his theory of knowledge-constitutive interests have shown. Different kinds of research serve different kinds of knowledge-constitutive interests (the reasons that frame and justify the search for knowledge through research), and they are based in different kinds of reasoning, sometimes described as "instrumental" or "technical" reason, "practical" reason, and "critical" or "emancipatory" reason (Carr & Kemmis, 1986; Grundy, 1987; Habermas, 1972, 1974).

Since Aristotle, technical reason has been understood as the kind of reason employed when we aim to improve the efficacy or efficiency of a means (for example, a strategy, a method, or a policy) in achieving pregiven and accepted goals. The ends are not in question, only the means to those ends. According to some views of educational and social science, this form of reason is at the heart of the scientific enterprise: improving the ways things are done in order to achieve established ends. Proponents of these forms of educational and social science frequently see their work as essentially continuous with the work of the natural and physical sciences, and thus adopt the attitude of those sciences toward their objects—as if these were physical phenomena rather than knowing subjects like the researchers themselves.

Practical reason, by contrast, treats both ends and means as problematic. In science, it frequently takes the view that the physical and social sciences are discontinuous, and thus require different methods. It recognizes that the objects of its studies are knowing subjects whose actions are not entirely determined by

physical laws, but shaped by actors' reasons and perspectives—reasons and perspectives that can change, reflexively changing what they do. More particularly, however, practical reason is to be understood as the form of reason we employ when we have to act in complex situations, knowing that our actions and their consequences will be judged in terms of complex and sometimes conflicting values. Practical reason is at its most evident in situations described as "tragic"—that is, in situations where actors are forced to choose between conflicting sets of values, knowing that to succeed in terms of one set is to fail in terms of another. Reid (1978) gives an excellent description of the kinds of situations that require practical reasoning—practical problems, or what he calls "uncertain practical questions":

> First of all, they are questions that have to be answered—even if the answer is to decide to do nothing. In this, they differ from academic, or theoretic, questions which do not demand an answer at any particular time, or indeed any answer at all. Second, the grounds on which decisions should be made are uncertain. Nothing can tell us infallibly whose interests should be consulted, what evidence should be taken into account, or what kinds of arguments should be given precedence. Third, in answering practical questions, we always have to take some existing state of affairs into account. We are never in a position to make a completely fresh start, free from the legacy of past history and present arrangements. Fourth, and following from this, each question is in some ways unique, belonging to a specific time and context, the particulars of which we can never exhaustively describe. Fifth, our question will certainly compel us to adjudicate between competing goals and values. We may choose a solution that maximises our satisfaction across a range of possible goals, but some will suffer at the expense of others. Sixth, we can never predict the outcome of the particular solution we choose, still less know what the outcome would have been had we made a different choice. Finally, the grounds on which we decide to answer a practical question in a particular way are not grounds that point to the desirability of the action chosen as an act in itself, but grounds that lead us to suppose that the action will result in some desirable state of affairs. (p. 42)

Practical reason is what we do many times every day when we are confronted with choices about what to do, knowing that our decisions and their consequences are open to evaluation in terms of our own and others' values.

A science—and forms of research—that aims to support and strengthen practical reason is necessarily addressed to actors as people who will confront practical questions and must make decisions about what to do. It addresses these actors as persons—knowing subjects—who could make wiser and more prudent decisions in the light of a richer understanding of the situations in which they find themselves. Unlike a science aiming to support and inform technical reason, it does not aim to achieve control (in the sense of improving the means to known ends) but to educate actors or practitioners in ways that will help those persons to understand the nature and consequences of their actions more fully, and to assist them in weighing what should be done as a guide to (but not a prescription for) action.

Critical reason in some ways extends both technical and practical reason. It recognizes the primacy of practical reason—the necessity of deciding what to do when confronted with uncertain practical questions—but it does not address the problem from the perspective of the individual actor deciding alone. It aims to comprehend how a situation has come about as a result of human choices (see the third of the characteristics of uncertain practical questions that Reid mentions) and to consider how things might be reconstructed so that they could be different in the future—so that actors may have different choices from the ones forced upon them by "the way things are" currently. In a sense, this is to say that critical reason also involves an element of technical reasoning about the means to given ends, but it involves considering the kinds of ends that have shaped the way things are, judging the suitability of those ends in the light of their consequences (for example, considering whether the way educational goals have been interpreted and the way the means to those goals have been realized are adequate in terms of their historical consequences). In particular, critical reason involves evaluating situations in the light of their consequences—in terms of the extent to which, in practice, their consequences are irrational, unjust, alienating,

or unsatisfying for those involved in and affected by what happens in the situation. On this basis, it aims to assist people involved in and affected by the situation in identifying, confronting, and collectively overcoming the conditions that produce these untoward consequences—even though, as in practical reasoning, it is impossible for them to describe the situation exhaustively or predict with certainty what the outcomes of their transformative action will be.

Technical, practical, and critical reasoning are realized in different patterns of social relationships between the person doing the reasoning and the people—or social systems or institutions—reasoned about. Although there is no smooth one-to-one correspondence about this, in contemporary contexts where people are interested in developing, reforming, transforming, or otherwise changing practices, instrumental (technical) approaches to practice presuppose what might be described as a "third-person" relationship between the person thinking about the practice and the practitioners of the practice (and other people inhabiting the systems or settings to be changed); practical approaches presuppose a "second-person" relationship, and critical (and especially emancipatory) approaches presuppose a "first-person" relationship.

In technical reasoning about practice, the researcher adopts an objectifying stance toward the others involved in the practice setting, perhaps treating them as elements of a "system." The researcher is therefore predisposed to regard these others, in a sense, as "them"—that is, in the third person. As in social research more generally, some kinds of action research (for example, some cases of action learning and action science) adopt this third-person perspective on practice. They treat practice as a form of strategic action—a means to an end. In this view, the point of conducting research into practice is to modify and improve it as a means to some given end—that is, it adopts a technical or instrumental view of the purpose of the research.

In practical reasoning about practice, the researcher adopts a more "subjective" stance to the practice setting, treating the practitioners and others involved as members of a shared life world—as persons who, like the researcher him- or herself, deserve the respect due to knowing subjects who are not only "others" but also autonomous and responsible agents. The researcher is therefore predisposed to regard these others as "you"—that is, in the second person. Also as in social research more generally, some kinds of action research adopt this second-person perspective (for example, some cases of classroom research). They treat practice as intentional action informed by the values and meanings of practitioners. In this view, the point of conducting research into practice is to educate practitioners and to inform practitioners' practical deliberation about the nature and conduct of their practice in particular cases. It adopts a practical view of the purpose of the research.

In critical reasoning about practice, the researcher adopts a more dialectical stance with respect to the "objective" and "subjective" and the individual and social aspects of the setting. From such a stance, the researcher treats the others involved in the setting as coparticipants who, through their participation in the practices that daily constitute and reconstitute the setting, can work together collaboratively to change the ways in which they constitute it. The researcher is therefore predisposed to regard such people as members of a group understood as "us"—that is, in the first person. As in social research more generally, some kinds of action research (for example, some cases of critical action research and participatory research) adopt this first-person (especially first-person plural) perspective. They treat practice as discursively, socially, and historically constructed, in addition to being realized in the behavior and intentional actions of practitioners. But they do not treat practice as produced only by participants—they also understand that, to a greater or lesser extent, participants enter practices that are partly preformed by discourses, social relationships, and the histories of the settings they inhabit. In this view, the purpose of research into practice is to change practice, practitioner, and practice setting (or, we might say, the work, the worker, and the workplace)—because changing prac-

tices requires changing not only behavior or intentional action (including the way the practitioner understands the practice and the practice setting) but also the situation in which the practice is conducted.

Insofar as they imply different moral and political stances toward the people in the social systems and life worlds involved, these forms of reasoning, loosely correlated with third-person, second-person, and first-person standpoints on the social relationships of the setting, manifest themselves in quite different attitudes toward the process of change. In general, instrumental (technical) reasoning manifests itself in attitudes of systematization, regulation, and control—focusing on the "system" aspects of the social settings involved (which are regarded in a rather abstract, generalized, and disembedded way). By contrast, practical reason manifests itself in attitudes that value wise and prudent judgment about what to do in shared social contexts (understood in a more localized, concrete, and historically specific way). And critical-emancipatory reasoning manifests itself in attitudes of collaborative reflection, theorizing, and political action directed toward emancipatory reconstruction of the setting (understood more dialectically as both constituting and constituted by the personal as well as the political, the local as well as the global).

Arguably, the first two approaches, the instrumental and the practical, were more intertwined and interrelated in social theory, policy, and practice in the West at the end of the 19th century, and they diverged in sharply opposed theories, policies, and practices in the 20th. The third, the critical approach, emerged early in the 20th century (in response to emerging problems of Marxist theory) as some researchers' self-conscious attempt to overcome the increasing polarization between instrumental and practical tendencies in social and political theory and practice. It would be wrong to conclude, however, that critical approaches have actually been successful, in any practical sense, in overcoming such polarizations—far from it. At the beginning of the 21st century, all three approaches have their advocates, many apparently implacably opposed to one another, so that contemporary debates over the nature and objectives of social reform are consistently confused and politicized (in the narrow sense) as advocates of the different approaches contest the ground in theory, policy, and practice.

We could extend the "map" of different research traditions in the study of practice by including their general affinities with different kinds knowledge-constitutive interests, as in Figure 22.3.

Reconciling Different Traditions in the Study of Practice

Different traditions of research on practice emphasize different aspects of practice. Earlier, we suggested that it might be possible to explore complementarities and connections among these traditions, although not necessarily by combining the research methods and techniques characteristically employed by these different traditions, because each has built-in limitations and blindnesses as well as particular ways of illuminating practice. Instead, we suggested that we would need to find more encompassing ways of theorizing practice. We want now to suggest one possible way of doing this theorizing.

In Figures 22.1 and 22.2, we have outlined some relationships among different traditions in the study of practice. In Figure 22.4, we represent these relationships in terms of dimensions of practice to be interrelated in a more encompassing perspective on practice. In the view of practice presented here, real practices can be understood more richly, and in more complex ways, if they are understood in terms of all of the five aspects of practice outlined earlier—or, to put it another way, by reference to all of the three dimensions in the space described in Figure 22.4. (As we shall see, it is in this space that we might be said to be "orienting ourselves in the process of changing practices" through action research.)

In volume 2 of his *Theory of Communicative Action,* titled *Lifeworld and System: A Critique of Functionalist Reason,* Habermas (1987b) makes a point about the lack of connections among different streams of social theory.

Habermas does not make the point in the form of a plea for tolerance across theoretical perspectives and paradigms, however, but in an argument for a new view in social theory that can bring together perspectives that are currently at odds with one another in addressing "the phenomenon of modern societies." [4] His argument leads him to propose a "two-level" social theory that can overcome the one-sidedness of existing positions:

> If we leave to one side the insufficiently complex approach of behaviorism, there are today three main lines of inquiry occupied with the phenomenon of modern societies. [Here he is referring to (a) theories of structural differentiation, which aim to give a more or less descriptive, rather than explanatory, account of the ways modern societies developed their characteristic elaborate divisions of labor, structure, and functioning; (b) the systems-theoretical approach, which sets out to explain the functioning of modern societies in terms of systems functions and their consequences; and (c) the action-theoretical approach, characteristic of interpretive sociology, which sets out to explain modern societies in terms of the way they are experienced by participants—at worst, from the viewpoint of the "victims" of modern society.] We cannot even say that they are in competition, for they scarcely have anything to say to one another.
>
> Efforts at theory comparison do not issue in reciprocal critique; fruitful critique that might foster a common understanding can hardly be developed across these differences, but at most within one or another camp. There is good reason for this mutual incomprehension: the object domains of the competing approaches do not come into contact, for they are the result of one-sided abstractions that unconsciously cut the ties between system and lifeworld constitutive for modern societies. (pp. 375-376)

Different approaches and traditions in the study of practice suffer from mutual incomprehension of the kind Habermas observes in social theory—an incomprehension is similarly founded in different views about the object domains of research into practice. The object domains constituted by different research paradigms and traditions in the study of practice are the expressions of different views about the problems and phenomena to be addressed by theory and research, characteristically employ-

Traditions in the study of practice			Knowledge-constitutive interests		
Perspective:	*Focus:*	*View of practice*			
Objective	*The individual*	(1) Practice as individual behavior	*Technical*		
	The social	(2) Practice as social behavior - e.g., ritual, system- structured		*Practical*	*Critical-emancipatory*
Subjective	*The individual*	(3) Practice as intentional action, shaped by values			
	The social	(4) Practice as socially-structured, shaped by discourses and tradition			
Reflexive/dialectical view of relationships between subjective-objective and individual-social		(5) Practice as socially-, historically- and discursively constituted by human agency and social action			

Figure 22.3. General Relationships Among Different Research Traditions and Different Knowledge-Constitutive Interests

ing different research methods that they regard as appropriate to the problems and phenomena with which they are concerned.

We have described this diversity in terms of a three-dimensional matrix within which different traditions in the study of practice may be located: (a) the dimension of the individual versus the social, versus a reflexive-dialectical perspective embracing both; (b) the dimension of the objective versus the subjective, versus a reflexive-dialectical perspective embracing both; and (c) the dimension of time and history (which could be elaborated in terms of the synchronic versus the diachronic, versus a reflexive-dialectical perspective embracing both). Although Habermas does not describe the different kinds of theories he discusses in terms of this three-dimensional space, his formulation of the relationship between system and life world offers a new way of conceptualizing social change and the process of changing social and educational practices.

For reasons he makes clear in *The Theory of Communicative Action* (especially 1987b, pp. 113-198, 374-403), Habermas believes that the three approaches he discusses (the theory of structural differentiation, the systems-theoreti-

cal approach, and the action-theoretical approach) are all partial, with the result that each is inadequate to the task of explaining the character and problems of modern society. Theories of structural differentiation, Habermas says, fail to distinguish dynamics of differentiation in two different arenas of modern society, both of which are crucial to understanding it: society seen from the perspective of system (loosely speaking, as we see it from the perspective of its institutions, structures, and functions—as when we consider our work in terms of roles and functions) and society seen from the perspective of life worlds (loosely speaking, as we see it from the perspective of the local settings in which we relate to others, making sense of ourselves, our coparticipants, and our relationships in the settings of family, workplace, neighborhood, and so on). Theories of structural differentiation confuse and confound these aspects in a general descriptive approach that attempts to make sense of the whole without adequately distinguishing and then interconnecting patterns or dynamics of differentiation seen from the interacting perspectives of system and life world.

The two other main approaches suffer from complementary partialities—one might even say

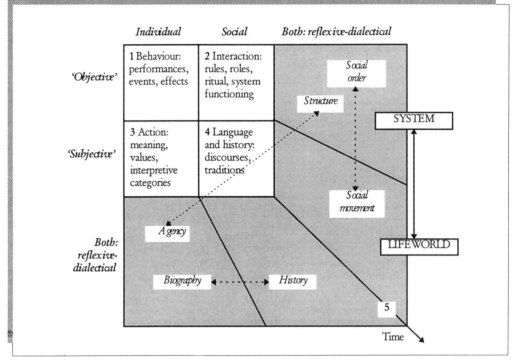

Figure 22.4. A More Encompassing View of Practice

"blindnesses." The systems-theoretical approach deals with the social life of modern societies very much from the perspective of systems integration (see also Giddens, 1979) and in terms of various kinds of functions of social systems of increasing complexity. In doing so, it neglects participants' perspectives on the social life it describes. Habermas believes that the protagonists of systems-theoretical approaches have developed their formulations in ways that have suppressed or abandoned some of the central problems that have traditionally occupied social theory, with the result that,

> once systems functionalism is cleansed of the dross of the sociological tradition, it becomes insensitive to social pathologies that can be discerned chiefly in the structural features of socially integrated domains of action. It hoists the vicissitudes of communicatively structured lifeworlds up to the level of media dynamics; by assimilating them, from the observer perspective, to disequilibria in intersystemic exchange relations, it robs them of the significance of

> identity-threatening deformations, which is how they are experienced from the participant perspective. (p. 377)

The action-theoretical approach, by contrast, sees social life very much from the perspective of social integration and in terms of the ways participants in social life interpret and experience their world, occasionally

> condens[ing] to fragments of history written from the point of view of its victims. Then modernization appears as the sufferings of those who had to pay for the establishment of the new mode of production and the new system of states in the coin of disintegrating traditions and forms of life. Research of this type sharpens our perception of historical asynchronicities; they provide a stimulus to critical recollection. . . . But it has as little place for the internal systemic dynamics of economic development, of nation and state building, as it does for the structural logics of rationalized lifeworlds. As a result, the subcultural mirrorings in which the sociopathologies of modernity are refracted and re-

flected retain the subjective and accidental character of uncomprehended events. (p. 377)

The task Habermas sets himself in *The Theory of Communicative Action* is to develop a "two-level" theory that can escape the limitations of formulations that either confuse system and life-world dynamics or give precedence to either the systems perspective or the life-world perspective (Habermas, 1984, 1987a, 1987b, 1990, 1992; for critical views, see also Bernstein, 1985, 1992; Fraser & Nicholson, 1988; Honneth & Joas, 1991; Honneth, McCarthy, Offe, & Wellmer, 1992; Rorty, 1985, 1989; Thompson & Held, 1982). This is a complex task, and Habermas undertakes it by reconstructing key conceptual choices made by precursor social theorists, including Marx, Weber, Durkheim, Parsons, and George Herbert Mead.

We find compelling Habermas's argument that the three major contemporary approaches to the study of "the phenomenon of modern society" are unable to offer one another the possibility of reciprocal critique—indeed, they could hardly be said even to be competitors—because they take such different views of the object domain of their inquiries. Earlier, we sought to show that different traditions in the study of practice take similarly different views of practice as an object domain of study. For Habermas, one way of overcoming the partiality of the major approaches in social theory is to concede that the relationship between system and life world is a crucial constituent of the phenomenon of modern society, and that the resources of each of the three principal approaches he mentions (theories of structural differentiation, systems theory, and action theory) can be reconstructed in the light of the distinction between system and life world, so that each may bring relevant resources to the overall problem of understanding and explaining modern society.

It is our view that educational theory and research can also learn from the system/life-world distinction, because it illuminates some of the burning issues of contemporary educa-

tional practice and policy—perhaps it even throws light on some of the characteristic differences in approach that separate the study of educational practice (which is frequently, although not invariably, conducted from an action-theoretical perspective) from the study of educational policy (which is frequently, although not invariably, conducted from a systems-theoretical perspective). It might also be true to say that some contemporary theories in education (such as those concerned with the history and social formation of education and those concerned with the conditioning of contemporary educational policies and practices by particular metadiscourses and power-knowledge configurations) offer parallels to the approach taken by theories of structural differentiation, and—following Habermas—it might be argued that they also fail to discriminate adequately between social dynamics rooted in system functioning and those rooted in life-world processes.

The social formation of education—in practice and in policy—seems to us to be an important arena in which the larger dynamics of system and life world are played out. The theory of communicative action seems to us to be a promising source for a more encompassing approach to problems of practice and policy in educational theory and research in the future.

In our view, the theory also provides a basis on which to understand the nature and work of participatory action research. Although few participants would put it in these terms, we contend that, on the one side, participants understand themselves and their practices as formed by system structures and functions that shape and constrain their actions, and that their efforts to change their practices necessarily involve encountering and reconstructing the system aspect of their social world. On the other side, we contend, participants also understand themselves and their practices as formed through the life-world processes of cultural reproduction, social integration, and socialization-individuation, and that their efforts to change their practices necessarily involve changing the substance of these processes. In addition, we contend, participants understand that there are tensions and interconnections between these two aspects of their social world, each shaping and constraining the other, and they recognize that changing their practices necessarily involves taking into account the nature and substance of these tensions and interconnections.

Participatory action research is a form of "insider research" in which participants move between two thought positions: on the one side, seeing themselves, their understandings, their practices, and the settings in which they practice from the perspective of insiders who see these things in an intimate, even "natural" way that may be subject to the partiality of view characteristic of the insider perspective; and, on the other side, seeing themselves, their understandings, their practices, and the setting from the perspective of an outsider (sometimes by adopting the perspective of an abstract, imagined outsider, and sometimes by trying to see things from the perspective of real individuals or role incumbents in and around the setting) who do not share the partiality of the inside view but who also do not have the benefit of "inside knowledge." Alternating between these perspectives gives the insider critical distance—the seed of the critical perspective that allows insiders to consider the possible as well as the actual in their social world.

For many research methodologists, this alternation of perspective is too fallible to be regarded as a secure methodological grounding for social research; for them, participatory action research will never be a method of choice. Our view is the contrary: Because only the insider has access to "inside knowledge" and can thus counterpose inside knowledge with the external view, the method of choice in social research will often be participatory action research—although it necessarily involves the development of processes of education and self-education among participants that make critical enlightenment possible. This is not to say that the aim of the process is to produce social researchers qualified in the usual academic terms; rather, it is to say that participants can develop skill and sophistication in shifting between the perspectives illustrated in Figure 22.1: seeing themselves, their understandings,

their practices, and their settings from the perspective of *individuals* in and around the setting, and then from the perspective of *the social* (in terms of both system integration and social integration, under the aspect of both system and life world); from the *"subjective"/insider* perspective, and from the *"objective"/outsider* perspective; and from the *synchronic* perspective of "how things are" and from the *diachronic* perspective of "how they came to be" or "can come to be." In short, in participatory action research, participants can and do develop the skills and sophistication necessary and sufficient to explore their social world in terms of the three dimensions represented schematically in Figure 22.4 as a more encompassing perspective on social life.

The participant perspective is not only a privileged perspective on a setting; it is also the perspective in terms of which much—but not all—of the social life of the setting is constituted. Although changes to external structures and functions may also be required if participants, their understandings, their practices, and the setting are to change, change cannot be secured if participants do not change themselves, their understandings, their practices, or their constitution of the setting. Participant change is the *sine qua non* of social change (social movement), and it is for this reason we conclude that participatory action research is the preferred approach to social and educational research aimed at social and educational change—although we concede that resources and circumstances are not always available to do it and do it well. On the other hand, it seems to us that research other than participatory action research that *does* contribute to social and educational change frequently approximates participatory action research in the way it engages participants in rethinking themselves, their understandings, their practices, and their settings. To the extent that it does so, social and educational research is likely to be regarded by participants as legitimate and thus to secure their consent and commitment. To the extent that social research ignores the participant view, or imposes itself (in process or findings) on participants, it is likely to be regarded as illegitimate, to foster alienation or hostility, and thus to provoke resistance.

Is Participatory Action Research "Good" Research?

In earlier sections, we outlined some epistemological perspectives (Figure 22.1) and methodological perspectives (Figure 22.2) characteristic of different traditions in the study of practice and related these to different research purposes (knowledge-constitutive interests; Figure 22.3). We indicated that different views of research on practice in the human and social sciences occupy different locations in these tables, and that different kinds of action research similarly take different views of the nature of practice and the purpose of research into practice. We proposed a more comprehensive view of the nature of practice (Figure 22.4) that could interconnect and interrelate different aspects of practice (dialectically interrelating objective and subjective, individual and social, and synchronic and diachronic aspects of practice).

Adopting this perspective is a tall order. In our view, it requires more of what might be called *symposium research*—interrelated studies by researchers specializing in different traditions in the study of social practice, working together to investigate the formation and transformation of practices, in particular historical circumstances and conditions.

In the case of participatory action research, the task appears even more difficult—is it possible for local participants in a particular setting to develop the specialist epistemological and methodological knowledge that seems necessary to conduct this kind of symposium research in a way that could satisfy the criteria of excellence appropriate in evaluating research in every one of the traditions of research we have described? We know of no cases where participatory action researchers have attempted this task *explicitly,* and of only a few where researchers have attempted anything like it—and then only *implicitly*—as in the case of the project conducted by Gloria Maria Braga

Blanco, Jose María Rozada Martínez, César Cascánte Fernández, and their colleagues (1995) in Asturias in Northern Spain. In this case, groups of teachers working in early childhood education, primary education, secondary education (one group in humanities and one group in science and mathematics), and university education have investigated their practice over many years, exploring the theme of democracy in and for education (see also Kemmis, 1998). The research group has used a variety of specialized research methods and techniques as part of an overall participatory action research project, although even in this case the researchers have not used all of the approaches to research on practice summarized in Figure 22.2.

In most action research, including participatory action research, the researchers make sacrifices in methodological and technical rigor in exchange for more immediate gains in face validity: whether the evidence they collect makes sense *to them, in their contexts.* For this reason, we sometimes characterize participatory action research as "low-tech" research: It sacrifices methodological sophistication in order to generate timely evidence that can be used and further developed in a real-time process of transformation (of practices, practitioners, and practice settings).

Some researchers wonder whether this tendency toward being low-tech makes participatory action research "bad" research—even if it may be "good" in terms of practical contributions to democratic processes of transformation in a setting. This concern presupposes that what makes research "good" can be determined on grounds of *methodology* rather than epistemology (what counts as good evidence in terms of what participants—using the evidence critically—think is accurate, relevant, appropriate, and pertinent to their purposes). It turns out that there may be a trade-off between methodological sophistication and "truth" in the sense of timely evidence capable of giving participants critical purchase on a real situation in which they find themselves. Of course, this is not to argue that validity is not an important issue for participatory action research, or to accept that the conventional canons of validity do not require revision (McTaggart, 1998).

It seems to us that some loss of methodological sophistication is a price worth paying in most practical contexts of transformative social action. Methodological sophistication is a primary concern most often when the research being conducted is of a third-person or second-person kind, where interpretation and analysis generally occur away from the setting under investigation, and where findings need to withstand scrutiny from people (generally other researchers) who have little interest in the particular case under investigation—people who are interested in more general or universalized phenomena. Frequently, too, such other audiences have no significant connection with the lived realities of participants, whereas *participants live with the consequences of the transformations they make.* The inevitability—for participants—of having to live with the consequences of transformation provides a very concrete "reality check" on the quality of their transformative work, in terms of whether their practices are more efficacious, their understandings are clearer, and the settings in which they practice are more rational, just, and productive of the kinds of consequences they are intended to achieve. For participants, the point of collecting compelling evidence is to achieve these goals, or, more precisely, to avoid subverting them intentionally or unintentionally by their action. Evidence sufficient for this kind of "reality checking" can often be low-tech (in terms of research methods and techniques) or impressionistic (from the perspective of an outsider who lacks the contextual knowledge that the insider draws on in interpreting the evidence). But it may still be "high-fidelity" evidence from the perspective of understanding the nature and consequences of particular interventions and transformations made by participants, in their own contexts—where they are privileged observers (not "cultural dopes," to use Giddens's phrase).

Most action research (and most participatory action research) is, in our view, correct to choose practical significance over methodological sophistication in the trade-off between epistemological and methodological gains—the choice between what evidence makes critical sense to participants and what evidence would satisfy the contextually nonspecific methodological criteria likely to satisfy external researchers. On the other hand, we suggest, most action research would be strengthened—for participants, not just outsiders—if more evidence were collected from across the range of different perspectives represented in Figures 22.2 and 22.3. That is, most action researchers would be well-advised to collect and consider evidence about practice as individual performance viewed as others see the practitioner (tradition 1 in Figures 22.2 and 22.3); evidence about practice as ritual and system, viewed from an external perspective (tradition 2); evidence about practice as meaningful and significant intentional action viewed from the perspectives of those involved (tradition 3); evidence about practice as discursively, socially, and historically constructed viewed from within the history and traditions of the practice (tradition 4); and evidence of all of these kinds seen as in a continuing process of historical formation and critical transformation shaped by participants themselves (tradition 5).

Orlando Fals Borda (1979) has written of action research as "investigating reality in order to transform it." We agree, but add that action research also transforms reality in order to investigate it. Here we are speaking not of some metaphysical "Reality" that stands above and beyond any particular local context, but about the day-to-day lived realities of participants in their ordinary work and lives. The aim of action research is to make a difference in these day-to-day lived realities—the ordinary settings in which people live and work, in which some thrive and some suffer. Action research aims to set in motion processes by which participants collectively make critical analyses of the nature of their practices, their understandings, and the settings in which they practice in order to confront and overcome irrationality, injustice, alienation, and suffering *in these practice settings* and *in relation to the consequences of their practices in these settings.* In our view, this—more than a metaphysical Truth or methodological sophistication—is the criterion against which the quality of action research is to be evaluated *as research*. Research cannot be regarded as self-justifying, or as justified solely by reference to internal criteria (for example, methodological criteria); research is also a social practice, to be evaluated against criteria of the kind we have listed as the aims of action research—that is, in terms of the extent to which it contributes to confronting and overcoming irrationality, injustice, alienation, and suffering, both in the research setting and more generally in terms of its broader consequences.

Participatory Action Research: The Future

As we suggested at the beginning of this chapter, action research takes a variety of forms. It is not a unitary approach. In our view, its evolution has owed more to the press of the contexts in which it has been practiced than to the working out of some set of problems immanent in action research understood as a research *method*.

On the other hand, what most distinguishes action from other approaches to research is a kind of shared resistance to some conventional views about research, including views of the researcher (for example, notions about who can be a researcher) and the relationship of research to social practice (for example, the notion that theory—especially "academic" theory—and research methodology stand in a mediating role between research and social practice, as if transforming practice can be warranted only by reference to grand claims to "Truth" or methodological purity). Much action research insists that the practitioner can be a researcher, with or without specialized training, and that research conducted within—not just on—practice can yield evidence and insights that can and do assist in the critical transformation of practice.

The press of the different contexts in which action research occurs will continue to shape its future. Some forms of action research will continue to develop as a species of field research by which practitioners aim to improve their practice principally in technical terms; some forms will continue to develop as an approach by which practitioners aim to improve their practice in practical terms (for example, through continuing development of the notion of the self-reflective practitioner, or the reflective professional; Schön, 1983, 1987); and some will continue to develop as a form of critical social science aimed at collective transformation of practices, practitioners, and practice settings.

Perhaps paradoxically, we believe that *participatory* action research will become both more practical and more theoretically sophisticated in the decade ahead. It will become more practical in the sense that it will be more widespread, more convivial as a form of social practice, and more congenial to practitioners in terms of the kinds of research techniques it employs. It will become more theoretically sophisticated in the sense that it will involve a more complex view of what social practice is, how particular social practices are shaped, and how they can be transformed by collective social action.

Already, participatory action researchers (along with some other kinds of action researchers) have successfully challenged the relative monopoly of "academic" researchers over the social practice of research. To some extent, they have been abetted by the modernist beliefs of a variety of state and other authorities who have insisted that practitioners must play an increasingly significant role in improving their practices (especially, but not only, in the technical terms favored by advocates of quality improvement). Research, as a social practice, has to some extent been "liberated" from the control of the academy and other highly specialized institutes and agencies. At the same time, there is a growing awareness among these practice-based practitioners of participatory action research that the social conditions that shape their practice cannot be swept away by purely local ideas and interventions. The obstacles to transformation are not just technical circumstances that participants can alter at will; they include social structures and media that may yield—and sometimes only gradually—to sustained collective effort. Social transformation is not just a technical matter, it is also political, cultural, social, and cognitive.

For this reason, we expect a continuing development of participatory action research as a form of involved and committed critique. In future, it may be less wedded to the specific modernist forms of critique characteristic of the forms of Marxian theory that informed some versions of participatory action research in the past; instead, it is likely to become more theoretically eclectic while still sustaining the hope that through collective action people can transform circumstances that oppress them. Similarly, it may be less bound to operating within established institutional frameworks (such as the school, the hospital, or the government agency) of the social order; instead, in a kind of "flanking" move, it is likely to become more explicit about its connections to social movements that challenge and test the taken-for-granted assumptions and presuppositions that shape practice in many of our key social institutions.

It follows from this that we expect participatory action research in the future to take a more complex view of practice of the kind represented schematically in Figure 22.4. The "paradigm wars" in social research were waged primarily on methodological grounds, based on competing views about the nature of truth in the human sciences. The competition between these positions has become fruitless; it is clear that they are incommensurable, and that "Truth" sides with no one view. What is now required is more extensive interchange between these rival positions, undertaken with the aim of exploring the extent to which together they can contribute to greater intersubjective understanding and agreement about the nature, dynamics, and consequences of specific practices under specific conditions and historical circumstances.

Participatory action research will provide especially fertile ground for this kind of cooperation and collaboration—the kind of cooperation and collaboration characteristic of what we have described as symposium research. It will do so for a reason given earlier—because what constitutes a "reality check" for its protagonists is making a difference in terms of practical actions and their consequences, not the esoteric demands of epistemology or methodology. Despite the conditions of late modernity, where participants increasingly feel that life and work

are risky, uncertain, and alienating, and where the legitimacy of social systems is increasingly in doubt, participatory action research offers practitioners a collective way of reconnecting with questions of meaning, value, and significance, and of exercising personal and collective agency for the common good. It revives practical and critical reason despite the ubiquity of the functional reason characteristic of the social systems that structure great tracts of our social realities. And it revives a kind of humanism that was displaced by the rationalism of Descartes and the scientism (the belief in science as a privileged way of knowing) of the past century (Toulmin, 1990).

Toulmin (1990) dates modernity from the end of the period of "Renaissance humanism" at the end of the 16th century. He argues that the early-modern shift from Renaissance humanism to Cartesian rationalism can best be understood in terms of four subsidiary shifts: (a) from an *oral* culture in which the theory and practice of rhetoric played a central role to a *written* culture in which formal logic played a central role in establishing the credentials of an argument; (b) from a practical concern with understanding and acting on *particular* cases to a more theoretical concern with the development of *universal* principles; (c) from a concern with the *local*, in all its concrete diversity, to the *general*, understood in terms of abstract axioms; and (d) from the *timely* (a concern with making wise and prudent decisions in the transitory situations of everyday life and society) to the *timeless* (a concern with understanding and explaining the enduring, perhaps eternal, nature of things). In the late-modern period, there is renewed interest in what has been occluded in these shifts— renewed interest in oral culture and the theory and practice of rhetoric, in understanding and acting on particular cases, in the local as against the general and abstract, and in the timely as against the timeless. Whether or not these interests signal a more general revival in the humanism of the Renaissance, they do seem to be characteristic of many groups conducting participatory action research in their local settings and circumstances. And this more humanistic approach fosters the kind of practicality and cooperative spirit likely to counter the dogmatism of the era of the paradigm wars and to encourage the kind of symposium research that we believe will be found in the participatory action research of the future.

If we are correct in thinking that participatory action research will continue to thrive because of its commitment to making a difference, it also seems to us likely that established authorities (including the state and in some entrenched areas of the academy) will make more strenuous efforts to co-opt and domesticate participatory action research. To the extent that these efforts are *not* successful, it is likely that participatory action research will be eschewed and rejected as "unscientific"—even treated as renegade. For this reason, we expect that the debate about whether participatory action research is or should be regarded as research (or "good research") will continue, and will continue to strengthen participatory action research in theory and in practice.

◆ *Key Features
of Participatory
Action Research*

Although the process of participatory action research is only poorly described in terms of a mechanical sequence of steps, it is generally thought to involve a spiral of self-reflective cycles of

planning a change,
acting and observing the process and consequences of the change,
reflecting on these processes and consequences, and then
replanning,
acting and observing,
reflecting, and so on . . .

In reality, the process may not be as neat as the spiral of self-contained cycles of planning, acting and observing, and reflecting suggests. The stages overlap, and initial plans quickly become obsolete in the light of learning from experience. In reality, the process is likely to be more fluid, open, and responsive. The criterion of success is not whether participants have followed the steps faithfully, but whether they have a strong and authentic sense of development and evolution in their practices, their understandings of their practices, and the situations in which they practice.

Each of the steps outlined in the spiral of self-reflection is best undertaken collaboratively by coparticipants in the participatory action research process. Not all theorists of participatory action research place this emphasis on participatory action research as a collaborative process; they argue that it is frequently a solitary process of systematic self-reflection. We concede that it is often so, but nevertheless hold that participatory action research is best conceptualized in collaborative terms. One reason we say this is that participatory action research is itself a social—and educational—process. A second and more compelling reason is that participatory action research is directed toward studying, reframing, and reconstructing practices that are, by their very nature, social. If practices are constituted in social interactions among people, then changing practices is a social process. To be sure, one person may change so that others are obliged to react or respond differently to that individual's changed behavior, but the willing and committed involvement of those whose interactions constitute the practice is necessary, in the end, to secure the change. Participatory action research offers an opportunity to create forums in which people can join one another as coparticipants in the struggle to remake the practices in which they interact—forums in which rationality and democracy can be pursued together, without an artificial separation ultimately hostile to both. In his 1996 book *Between Facts and Norms,* Habermas describes this process in terms of "opening communicative space." At its best, this is a collaborative social process of learning, realized by groups of people who join together in changing the practices through which they interact in a shared social world—a shared social world in which, for better or for worse, we live with the consequences of one another's actions.

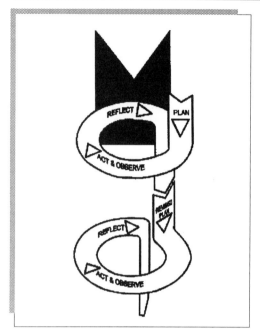

Figure 22.5. The Action Research Spiral

We should also stress that action research concerns actual, not abstract, practices. It involves learning about the real, material, concrete, particular practices of particular people in particular places. Although of course it is not possible to suspend the inevitable abstraction that occurs whenever we use language to name, describe, interpret, and evaluate things, action research differs from other forms of research in that it is more obstinate about changing particular practitioners' particular practices, rather than focusing on practices in general or in the abstract. In our view, action researchers need make no apology for seeing their work as mundane and mired in history; there are philosophical and practical dangers in the idealism that suggests that a more abstract view of practice might make it possible to transcend or rise above history, and delusions in the view that it is possible to find safe haven in abstract propositions that construe but do not themselves constitute practice. Action research is a learning process, the fruits of which are the real and material changes in (a) what people do, (b) how they interact with the world and with others, (c) what they mean and what they value, and (d) the dis-

courses in which they understand and interpret their world.

Through action research, people can come to understand their social and educational practices as located in particular material, social, and historical circumstances that produced (and reproduce) them—and in which it may be possible to transform them. Focusing on practices in a concrete and specific way makes those practices accessible for reflection, discussion, and reconstruction as products of past circumstances that are capable of being modified in and for present and future circumstances. While recognizing that every practice is transient and evanescent, and that it can be conceptualized only in the inevitably abstract (although comfortingly imprecise) terms that language provides, action researchers aim to understand their own particular practices as they emerge in their own particular circumstances, without reducing them to the ghostly status of the general, the abstract, or the ideal—or, perhaps one should say, the unreal.

If action research is understood in such terms, then, through their investigations, action researchers may want to become especially sensitive to the ways in which their particular practices involve

social practices of material, symbolic, and social
- production,
- communication, and
- social organization;
which shape and are shaped by social structures in
- the cultural,
- the economic, and
- the political realms;
which shape and are shaped by the social media of
- language/discourses,
- work, and
- power;
which largely shape, but can also be shaped by, participants' own knowledge, expressed in participants'
- understandings,

- skills, and
- values;

which, in turn, shape and are shaped by their acts of material, symbolic, and social

- production,
- communication, and
- social organization . . .

Action researchers might consider, for example, how their acts of communication, production, and social organization are intertwined and interrelated in the real and particular practices that connect them to others in the real situations in which they find themselves (such as communities, neighborhoods, families, schools, and other workplaces). They might consider how, by collaboratively changing the ways they participate with others in these practices, they can change the practices, their understandings of these practices, and the situations in which they live and work.

For many people, the image of the spiral of cycles of self-reflection (planning, acting and observing, reflecting, replanning, and so on) has become the dominant feature of action research as an approach. In our view, participatory action research has seven other key features that are at least as important as the self-reflective spiral. They are as follows:

1. *Participatory action research is a social process.* Participatory action research deliberately explores *the relationship between the realms of the individual and the social.* It recognizes that "no individuation is possible without socialization, and no socialization is possible without individuation" (Habermas, 1992, p. 26), and that the processes of individuation and socialization continue to shape individuals and social relationships in all the settings in which we find ourselves. Participatory action research is a process followed in research in settings, such as those of education and community development, where people, individually and collectively, try to understand how they are formed and re-formed as individuals and in relation to one another in a variety of settings—for example, when teachers work together or with students to improve processes of teaching and learning in the classroom.

2. *Participatory action research is participatory.* Participatory action research engages people in examining their *knowledge* (understandings, skills, and values) and interpretive categories (the ways they interpret themselves and their action in the social and material world). It is a process in which each individual in a group tries to get a handle on the ways his or her knowledge shapes his or her sense of identity and agency and reflects critically on how that present knowledge frames and constrains his or her action. It is also participatory in the sense that people can do action research only "on" themselves, individually or collectively. It is not research done "on" others.

3. *Participatory action research is practical and collaborative.* Participatory action research engages people in examining the *social practices* that link them with others in social interaction. It is a process in which people explore their practices of communication, production, and social organization and try to explore how to improve their interactions by changing the acts that constitute them—to reduce the extent to which participants experience these interactions (and their longer-term consequences) as irrational, unproductive (or inefficient), unjust, and/or unsatisfying (alienating). Participatory action researchers aim to work together in reconstructing their social interactions by reconstructing the acts that constitute them.

4. *Participatory action research is emancipatory.* Participatory action research aims to help people recover, and release themselves, from the constraints of irrational, unproductive, unjust, and unsatisfying *social structures* that limit their self-development and self-determination. It is a process in which people explore the ways in which their practices are shaped and constrained by wider social (cultural, economic, and political) structures and consider whether they can intervene to release themselves from these con-

straints—or, if they can't, how best to work within and around them to minimize the extent to which they contribute to irrationality, lack of productivity (inefficiency), injustice, and dissatisfactions (alienation) among people whose work and lives contribute to the structuring of a shared social life.

5. Participatory action research is critical. Participatory action research aims to help people recover, and release themselves, from the constraints embedded in the *social media* through which they interact: their language (discourses), their modes of work, and the social relationships of power (in which they experience affiliation and difference, inclusion and exclusion—relationships in which, grammatically speaking, they interact with others in the third, second, or first person). It is a process in which people deliberately set out to contest and to reconstitute irrational, unproductive (or inefficient), unjust, and/or unsatisfying (alienating) ways of interpreting and describing their world (language/discourses), ways of working (work), and ways of relating to others (power).

6. Participatory action research is recursive (reflexive, dialectical). Participatory action research aims to help people to investigate reality in order to change it (Fals Borda, 1979) and (we might add) to change reality in order to investigate it—in particular by changing their practices through a spiral of cycles of critical and self-critical action and reflection, as a deliberate social process designed to help them learn more about (and theorize) their practices, their knowledge of their practices, the social structures that shape and constrain their practices, and the social media in which their practices are expressed. In our view, this is what theorizing practice means. Participatory action research does not take an armchair view of theorizing, however; it is a process of learning, with others, by doing—changing the ways we interact in a shared social world in which, for better or for worse, we live with the consequences of our own and one another's actions. Figure 22.6 represents an attempt to sketch the recursive char-

acter of the relationships among knowledge, social practices, social structures, social media.

7. Participatory action research aims to transform both theory and practice. Participatory action research does not regard either theory or practice as preeminent in the relationship between theory and practice; it aims to articulate and develop each in relation to the other through critical reasoning about both theory and practice and their consequences. It does not aim to develop forms of theory that can stand above and beyond practice, as if practice could be controlled and determined without regard to the particulars of the practical situations that confront practitioners in their ordinary lives and work. Nor does it aim to develop forms of practice that might be regarded as self-justifying, as if practice could be judged in the absence of theoretical frameworks that give them their value and significance and that provide substantive criteria for exploring the extent to which practices and their consequences turn out to be irrational, unjust, alienating, or unsatisfying for the people involved in and affected by them. Participatory action research thus involves "reaching out" from the specifics of particular situations, as understood by the people within them, to explore the potential of different perspectives, theories, and discourses that might help to illuminate particular practices and practical settings as a basis for developing critical insights and ideas about how things might be transformed. Equally, it involves "reaching in" from the standpoints provided by different perspectives, theories, and discourses to explore the extent to which these provide practitioners themselves with a critical grasp of the problems and issues they actually confront in specific local situations. Participatory action research thus aims to transform *both* practitioners' theories and their practices *and* the theories and practices of others whose perspectives and practices may help to shape the conditions of life and work in particular local settings. In this way, participatory action research aims to connect the local and the global, and to live out the slogan, "The personal is the political."

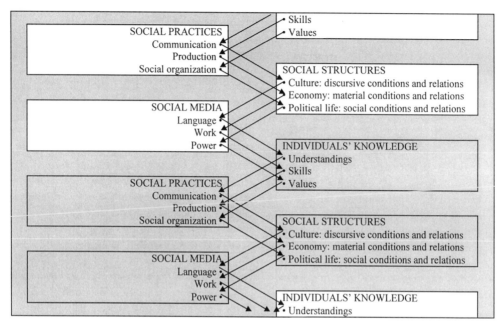

Figure 22.6. Recursive Relationships of Social Mediation That Action Research Aims to Transform

These seven are the principal features of participatory action research as we see it. We take a particular, and perhaps partisan, view. There are writers on action research who prefer to move immediately from a general description of the action research process (especially the self-reflective spiral) to questions of methodology and research technique—a discussion of the ways and means for collecting data in different social and educational settings. This is a somewhat methodologically driven view of action research; it suggests that research methods are what makes action research "research."

In terms of the five aspects of practice and the five traditions in the study of practice outlined earlier, however, it seems to us that a methodologically driven view of participatory action research finds itself mired in the assumptions about practice to which one or another of the different traditions of research on practice is committed. Depending on which of these sets of presuppositions it adopts, it may find itself unable to approach (the study of) practice in a sufficiently rich and multifaceted way—that is, in terms that recognize different aspects of practice and do justice to its social, historical, and discursive construction.

If participatory action research is to explore practice in terms of each of the five aspects outlined earlier, it will need to consider how different traditions in the study of practice, and different research methods and techniques, can provide multiple resources for the task. It must also avoid accepting the assumptions and limitations of particular methods and techniques. For example, the participatory action researcher may legitimately eschew the narrow empiricism of those approaches that attempt to construe practice entirely "objectively," as if it were possible to exclude consideration of participants' intentions, meanings, values, and interpretive categories from an understanding of practice, or as if it were possible to exclude consideration of the frameworks of language, discourse, and tradition by which people in different groups construe their practices. It does not follow from this that quantitative approaches are never relevant in participatory action research; on the contrary, they may be—but without the constraints many quantitative researchers put on these methods and techniques. Indeed, when quantitative researchers use questionnaires to convert participants' views into numerical data, they tacitly concede that they cannot understand practice without taking participants' views into account. Participatory researchers will differ from one-sidedly quantitative researchers in the ways they collect and use such data, because the participatory action researcher will regard the data as crude approximations to the ways participants understand themselves, not (as quantitative researchers may assert) as more rigorous (valid, reliable) because they are scaled.

On the other hand, participatory action research will differ from the one-sidedly qualitative approach that asserts that action can be understood only from a qualitative perspective—for example, through close clinical or phenomenological analysis of an individual's views or close analysis of the discourses and traditions that shape the way a particular practice is understood by participants. The participatory action researcher will also want to explore how changing "objective" circumstances (performances, events, effects; patterns of interaction, rules, roles, and system functioning) shape and are shaped by the "subjective" conditions of participants' perspectives.

In our view, questions of research methods should not be regarded as unimportant, but (by contrast with the methodologically driven view) we would want to assert that what makes participatory action research "research" is not the machinery of research techniques but an abiding concern with the relationships between social and educational theory and practice. In our view, before we can decide questions about what kinds of research methods are appropriate, we must decide what kinds of things "practice" and "theory" are—for only then can we decide what kinds of data or evidence might be relevant in describing practice and what kinds

of analyses are relevant in interpreting and evaluating people's real practices in the real situations in which they work. In this view of participatory action research, a central question is how practices are to be understood "in the field," as it were, so they become available for more systematic theorizing; once we have arrived at a general view of what it means to understand (theorize) practice in the field, we can work out what kinds of evidence, and hence what kinds of research methods and techniques, might be appropriate for advancing our understanding of practice at any particular time.

The theoretical scheme depicted in Figure 22.6 takes a view of what theorizing a practice might be like: locating practice within frameworks of participants' knowledge, in relation to social structures, and in terms of social media. By adopting a more encompassing view of practice such as the one outlined earlier (in Figure 22.4), we may be able to understand and theorize it more richly, and in more complex ways, so that powerful social dynamics (like the tensions and interconnections between system and life world) can be construed and reconstituted through a critical social practice like participatory action research.

■ *Notes*

1. Dr. Colin Henry of Deakin University assisted with the compilation of an earlier version of this synopsis.

2. Describing two of the great traditions in 20th-century philosophy of social science, positivism (which he relates to a Galilean worldview) and hermeneutics (which he relates to an Aristotelian worldview), Georg Henrik von Wright (1971) draws the conclusion that they are incommensurable—but with the reservation that there is a kind of dialogue between them that might suggest that some progress is possible: "I have tried to relate some developments in the philosophy of social science to two great traditions in the history of ideas. We have seen how in the last hundred years philosophy of science has successively clung to one or the other of two basically opposed positions. After Hegel came pos-

itivism; after the antipositivist and partly neohegelian reaction around the turn of the century came neopositivism; now the pendulum is again swinging toward the Aristotelian thematics that Hegel revived.

"It would surely be an illusion to think that truth itself unequivocally sided with one of the two opposed positions. In saying this I am not thinking of the triviality that both positions contain some truth and that a compromise can be achieved on some questions. This may be so. But there is also a basic opposition, removed from the possibility both of reconciliation and of refutation—even, in a sense, removed from truth. It is built into the choice of primitives, of basic concepts for the whole argumentation. This choice, one could say, is 'existential.' It is a choice of a point of view that cannot be further grounded.

"There is nevertheless dialogue between the positions, and a kind of progress. The temporary dominance of one of the two trends is usually the result of a breakthrough following a period of criticism of the other trend. What emerges after the breakthrough is never merely a restoration of something that was there before, but also bears the impress of the ideas through whose criticism it emerged. The process illustrates what Hegel described with the words *aufgehoben* and *aufbewart,* perhaps best rendered in English as 'superseded' and 'retained.' The position which is in a process of becoming superseded usually wastes its polemical energies on fighting already outmoded features in the opposed view, and tends to see what is retained in the emerging position as only a deformed shadow of its own self. This is what happens, for example, when positivist philosophers of science in our days object to Verstehen with arguments perhaps valid against Dilthey or Collingwood, or when they mistake Wittgenstein's philosophy of psychology for just another form of behaviorism" (pp. 32-33).

3. The term *balanda* is used by the Yolngu Matha language group of Aboriginal people in northeast Arnhemland—the northeast corner of the "top end" of Australia's Northern Territory—in speaking of Caucasians. The origin of the term in Yolngu-matha (the language of the Yolngu) has its roots in the word for "Hollanders" used by indigenous Indonesians (Malaccans) to refer to the Dutch colonial invaders of Indonesia. (In like manner, apparently, *Holland* was rendered by the Malaccans as *Beland.*) Indigenous Indonesians visited the coastal waters of northeast Arnhemland in search of trepang (bêche-de-mer) for hundreds of years before white settlement of Australia and, according to the Yolngu, gave the Yolngu this word for white people long before white people arrived in Arnhemland. The early cross-cultural contact between indigenous peoples of Indonesia and Australia was quite benign by comparison with the savagery of white invasion of the 18th and 19th centuries.

4. Note that Habermas speaks here of "the phenomenon," not "the phenomena" of modern societies, as he is interested in theories that make "modern society" comprehensible as a particular kind of social form—the product of particular processes of social formation and the framework that shapes particular patterns and dynamics of social life.

■ *References*

Adelman, C. (1997). Action research and the problem of participation. In R. McTaggart (Ed.), *Participatory action research: International contexts and consequences* (pp. 79-106). Albany: State University of New York Press.

Althusser, L. (1971). *Lenin and philosophy and other essays* (B. Brewster, Trans.). London: New Left.

Altrichter, H., & Gstettner, P. (1997). Action research: A closed chapter in the history of German social science? In R. McTaggart (Ed.), *Participatory action research: International contexts and consequences* (pp. 45-78). Albany: State University of New York Press.

Argyris, C. (1990). *Overcoming organizational defenses: Facilitating organizational learning.* Boston: Allyn & Bacon.

Argyris, C., Putnam, R., & Smith, D. M. (1985). *Action science: Concepts, methods, and skills for research and intervention.* San Francisco: Jossey-Bass.

Argyris, C., & Schön, D. A. (1974). *Theory in practice: Increasing professional effectiveness.* San Francisco: Jossey-Bass.

Argyris, C., & Schön, D. A. (1978). *Organizational learning: A theory of action perspective*. Reading, MA: Addison-Wesley.

Bennett, T. (1979). *Formalism and Marxism*. London: Methuen.

Bernstein, R. J. (Ed.). (1985). *Habermas and modernity*. Cambridge: MIT Press.

Bernstein, R. J. (1992). *The new constellation: The ethical-political horizons of modernity/postmodernity*. Cambridge: MIT Press.

Braga Blanco, G. M., Rozada Martínez, J. M., Cascánte Fernández, C., et al. (1995). Hacia un modelo dialectico-critico en la enseñanza: Grupos asociados para la investigación-acción. In Departamento de Didáctica y Organización Escolar (Ed.), *Teoría crítica e investigación acción* (pp. 162-172). Madrid: Departamento de Didáctica y Organización Escolar.

Bravette, G. (1996). Reflection on a black woman's management learning. *Women in Management Review, 11*(3), 3-11.

Bunbury, R., Hastings, W., Henry, J., & McTaggart, R. (Eds.). (1991). *Towards Aboriginal pedagogy: Aboriginal teachers speak out, Blekbala Wei, Deme Nayin, Yolngu Rom, and Ngini Nginingawula Ngawurranungurumagi*. Geelong, Victoria, Australia: Deakin University Press.

Carr, W., & Kemmis, S. (1986). *Becoming critical: Education, knowledge and action research*. London: Falmer.

Checkland, P. (1981). *Systems thinking, systems practice*. Chichester: John Wiley.

Checkland, P., & Scholes, J. (1990). *Soft systems methodology in action*. Chichester: John Wiley.

Clark, P. A. (1972). *Action research and organisational change*. London: Harper & Row.

Dadds, M. (1995). *Passionate enquiry and school development: A story about teacher action research*. London: Falmer.

Davies, L., & Ledington, P. (1991). *Information in action: Soft systems methodology*. Basingstoke, Hampshire, England: Macmillan.

Elden, M. (1983). Participatory research at work. *Journal of Occupational Behavior, 4*(1), 21-34.

Elliott, J. (1988). Developing hypotheses about classrooms from teachers' practical constructs: An account of the work of the Ford Teaching Project. In S. Kemmis & R. McTaggart (Eds.), *The action research reader* (3rd ed., pp. 195-213). Geelong, Victoria, Australia: Deakin University Press. (Reprinted from *Interchange, 7*[2], 1976-1977, 2-22)

Emery, F. E., & Thorsrud, E. (1976). *Democracy at work : The report of the Norwegian Industrial Democracy Program*. Leiden, Netherlands: Martinus Nijhoff.

Emery, F. E., Thorsrud, E., & Trist, E. (1969). *Form and content in industrial democracy: Some experiences from Norway and other European countries*. London: Tavistock.

Fals Borda, O. (1979). Investigating reality in order to transform it: The Colombian experience. *Dialectical Anthropology, 4,* 33-55.

Fals Borda, O. (1988). *Knowledge and people's power*. New Delhi: Indian Social Institute.

Fals Borda, O., & Rahman, M. A. (Eds.). (1991). *Action and knowledge: Breaking the monopoly with participatory action-research*. New York: Apex.

Fay, B. (1987). *Critical social science: Liberation and its limits*. Cambridge: Polity.

Flood, R. L., & Jackson, M. C. (1991). *Creative problem solving: Total systems intervention*. Chichester: John Wiley.

Forester, J., Pitt, J., & Welsh, J. (Eds.). (1993). *Profiles of participatory action researchers*. Ithaca, NY: Cornell University, Department of Urban and Regional Planning.

Foster, M. (1972). An introduction to the theory and practice of action research in work organizations. *Human Relations, 25,* 529-566.

Fraser, N., & Nicholson, L. J. (1988). Social criticism without philosophy: An encounter between feminism and postmodernism. *Theory, Culture & Society, 5,* 373-394.

Freire, P. (1988). Creating alternative research methods: Learning to do it by doing it. In S. Kemmis & R. McTaggart (Eds.), *The action research reader* (3rd ed., pp. 291-313). Geelong, Victoria, Australia: Deakin University Press. (Reprinted from *Creating knowledge: A monopoly?* pp. 29-37, by B. Hall, A. Gillette, & R. Tandon, Eds., 1982, New Delhi: Society for Participatory Research in Asia)

Fullan, M. (1982). *The meaning of educational change*. New York: Teachers College Press.

Fullan, M. (1991). The new meaning of educational change. London: Cassell.

Gadamer, H.-G. (1975). *Truth and method* (2nd rev. ed.; J. Weinsheimer & D. G. Marshall, Eds. & Trans.). New York: Crossroad.

Giddens, A. (1979). *Central problems in social theory: Action, structure, and contradiction in social analysis.* London: Macmillan.

Grundy, S. (1987). *Curriculum: Product or praxis?* London: Falmer.

Habermas, J. (1972). *Knowledge and human interests* (J. J. Shapiro, Trans.). London: Heinemann.

Habermas, J. (1974). *Theory and practice* (J. Viertel, Trans.). London: Heinemann.

Habermas, J. (1984). *Theory of communicative action: Vol. 1. Reason and the rationalization of society* (T. McCarthy, Trans.). Boston: Beacon.

Habermas, J. (1987a). *The philosophical discourse of modernity: Twelve lectures* (F. G. Lawrence, Trans.). Cambridge: MIT Press.

Habermas, J. (1987b). *Theory of communicative action: Vol. 2. Lifeworld and system: A critique of functionalist reason* (T. McCarthy, Trans.). Boston: Beacon.

Habermas, J. (1990). *Moral consciousness and communicative action* (C. Lenhardt & S. W. Nicholson, Trans.). Cambridge: MIT Press.

Habermas, J. (1992). *Postmetaphysical thinking: Philosophical essays* (W. M. Hohengarten, Trans.). Cambridge: MIT Press.

Habermas, J. (1996). *Between facts and norms: Contributions to a discourse theory of law and democracy* (W. Rehg, Trans.). Cambridge: MIT Press.

Hall, B., Gillette, A., & Tandon, R. (Eds.). (1982). *Creating knowledge: A monopoly?* New Delhi: Society for Participatory Research in Asia.

Haug, F. (1987). *Female sexualization: A collective work of memory.* London: Verso.

Henry, C. (1991). If action research were tennis. In O. Zuber-Skerritt (Ed.), *Action learning for improved performance* (pp. 102-114). Brisbane: AEBIS.

Honneth, A., & Joas, H. (Ed.). (1991). *Communicative action.* Cambridge: MIT Press.

Honneth, A., McCarthy, T., Offe, C., & Wellmer, A. (Eds.). (1992). *Philosophical interventions in the unfinished project of enlightenment.* Cambridge: MIT Press.

Horton, M. (with Kohl, J., & Kohl, H.). (1990). *The long haul: An autobiography.* Garden City, NY: Doubleday.

Jackson, M. C. (1991). *Systems methodology for the management sciences.* New York: Plenum.

Kemmis, S. (1988, May). *Critical educational research.* Paper prepared for the Critical Theory Preconference of the North American Adult Education Association Research Conference, University of Calgary, Alberta, Canada.

Kemmis, S. (1991). Action research and post-modernisms. *Curriculum Perspectives, 11*(4), 59-66.

Kemmis, S. (1998). Action research exemplary projects: The Asturias project. In J. Angwin (Ed.), *The essence of action research.* Geelong, Victoria, Australia: Deakin University, Centre for Education and Change.

Kemmis, S., & McTaggart, R. (1988). *The action research planner* (3rd ed.). Geelong, Victoria, Australia: Deakin University Press.

Kolb, D. (1984). *Experiential learning: Experience as the source of learning and development.* Englewood Cliffs, NJ: Prentice Hall.

Lanhupuy, W. (1987). Balanda education: A mixed blessing for Aborigines. *Aboriginal Child at School, 15*(3), 31-36.

Levin, M. (1985). *Participatory action research in Norway.* Trondheim: ORAL.

Lyotard, J.-F. (1984). *The postmodern condition: A report on knowledge* (G. Bennington & B. Massumi, Trans.). Minneapolis: University of Minnesota Press.

MacIntyre, A. (1983). *After virtue: A study in moral theory* (2nd ed.). London: Duckworth.

Marika, R., Ngurruwutthun, D., & White, L. (1992). Always together, Yaka gäna: Participatory research at Yirrkala as part of the development of Yolngu education. *Convergence, 25*(1), 23-39.

McTaggart, R. (1987). Pedagogical principles for Aboriginal teacher education. *Aboriginal Child at School, 15*(4), 21-33.

McTaggart, R. (1988). Aboriginal pedagogy versus colonisation of the mind. *Curriculum Perspectives, 8*(2), 83-92.

McTaggart, R. (1991a). *Action research: A short modern history.* Geelong, Victoria, Australia: Deakin University Press.

McTaggart, R. (1991b). Principles for participatory action research. *Adult Education Quarterly, 4*(3), 168-187.

McTaggart, R. (1991c). Western institutional impediments to Aboriginal education. *Journal of Curriculum Studies, 23,* 297-325.

McTaggart, R. (Ed.). (1997a). *Participatory action research: International contexts and consequences.* Albany: State University of New York Press.

McTaggart, R. (1997b). Revitalising management as a scientific activity. *Management Learning, 28*(2), 177-195.

McTaggart, R. (1998). Is validity really an issue for action research? *Studies in Cultures, Organizations and Societies, 4,* 211-236.

McTaggart, R. (1999). Reflection on the purposes of research, action and scholarship: A case of cross-cultural participatory action research. *Systemic Practice and Action Research, 12*(5).

Noffke, S. E. (1990). *Action research: A multidimensional analysis.* Unpublished doctoral dissertation, University of Wisconsin–Madison.

Noffke, S. E. (1997a). Professional, personal, and political dimensions of action research. In M. W. Apple (Ed.), *Review of research in education* (Vol. 22, pp. 305-343). Washington, DC: American Educational Research Association.

Noffke, S. E. (1997b). Themes and tensions in US action research: Towards historical analysis. In S. Hollinsworth (Ed.), *International action research: A casebook for educational reform* (pp. 2-16). London: Falmer.

Oliveira, R., & Darcy, M. (1975). *The militant observer: A sociological alternative.* Geneva: IDAC.

Park, P., Brydon-Miller, M., Hall, B., & Jackson, T. (Eds.). (1993). *Voices of change: Participatory research in the United States and Canada.* Toronto: OISE.

Pasmore, W., & Friedlander, F. (1982). An action-research program for increasing employee involvement in problem-solving. *Administrative Science Quarterly, 27,* 342-362.

Pedler, M. (Ed.). (1991). *Action learning in practice.* Aldershot, England: Gower.

Reason, P. (Ed.). (1988). *Human inquiry in action: Developments in new paradigm research.* London: Sage.

Reid, W. A. (1978). *Thinking about the curriculum: The nature and treatment of curriculum problems.* London: Routledge & Kegan Paul.

Revans, R. W. (1980). *Action learning: New techniques for management.* London: Blond & Briggs.

Revans, R. W. (1982). *The origins and growth of action learning.* Bromley, England: Chartwell-Bratt.

Rorty, R. (1985). Habermas and Lyotard on modernity. In R. J. Bernstein (Ed.), *Habermas and modernity.* Cambridge: MIT Press.

Rorty, R. (1989). *Contingency, irony and solidarity.* Cambridge: Cambridge University Press.

Sagor, R. (1992). *How to conduct collaborative action research.* Alexandria, VA: ASCD.

Sandkull, B. (1980). Practice of industry: Mismanagement of people. *Human Systems Management, 1,* 159-167.

Schön, D. A. (1983). *The reflective practitioner: How professionals think in action.* New York: Basic Books.

Schön, D. A. (1987). *Educating the reflective practitioner.* San Francisco: Jossey-Bass.

Schön, D. A. (Ed.). (1991). *The reflective turn: Case studies in and on educational practice.* New York: Teachers College Press.

Stenhouse, L. (1975). *An introduction to curriculum research and development.* London: Heinemann.

Thompson, J. B., & Held, D. (Eds.). (1982). *Habermas: Critical debates.* Cambridge: MIT Press.

Torbert, W. R. (1991). *The power of balance: Transforming self, society, and scientific inquiry.* Newbury Park, CA: Sage.

Toulmin, S. (1990). *Cosmopolis: The hidden agenda of modernity.* New York: Free Press.

von Wright, G. H. (1971). *Explanation and understanding.* London: Routledge & Kegan Paul.

Warmington, A. (1980). Action research: Its methods and its implications. *Journal of Applied Systems Analysis, 7,* 23-39.

Weiner, G. (1989). Professional self-knowledge versus social justice: A critical analysis of the teacher-researcher movement. *British Educational Research Journal, 15*(1), 41-51.

Whyte, W. F. (1989). Introduction to action research for the twenty-first century: Participation, reflection, and practice. *American Behavioral Scientist, 32,* 502-512.

Whyte, W. F. (Ed.). (1991). *Participatory action research.* London: Sage.

Yirrkala Homeland Schools. (1996, May). Linking business. *Big Link, 5,* 2-6.

Zuber-Skerritt, O. (Ed.). (1996). *New directions in action research.* London: Falmer.

23

CLINICAL RESEARCH

◆ William L. Miller and Benjamin F. Crabtree

◆ Conversing at the Wall

We are closer to Eden. The war against breast cancer advances and the local and national media stage another heroic celebration of the latest miracle. A drug prevents breast cancer. At multiple sites in the United States in 1992, 13,388 hopeful women with risk factors for breast cancer enrolled in an explanatory, double-blind, randomized controlled trial designed to demonstrate the efficacy of tamoxifen for preventing breast cancer. Several years later, the trial ended early because success appeared evident to the investigators (Fisher et al., 1998). Despite serious concerns about the drug's short-term side effects, two conflicting European studies (Powles et al., 1998; Veronesi et al., 1998), and no knowledge of the drug's social, emotional, or long-term consequences, a successful national marketing effort was launched to convince the Food and Drug Administration, physicians, and

women to consider seriously the large-scale use of tamoxifen.

These are the complex interactions of many well-intentioned individuals, an expectant and frightened public, and institutional dynamics. There are intense escalating pressures for academic health centers to get research grant money as a way of surviving, with the vast majority of those moneys being spent for basic biomolecular/genetic "bench" research and randomized clinical trials. The large pharmaceutical conglomerates are driven to identify new markets for drugs requiring enormous investment to develop and test. Career pathways and success are linked to these same pressures. Special interest groups, the media, and cultural forces continue to push, with intense urgency, for cures and fixes, for immortality inside the genome. The research imperative to find universal (i.e., generalizable) interventions or drugs that work in preplanned, standardized ways and that sell is overwhelming. "Just give me the evidence" means "Give me the numbers," which means "Demonstrate a good profit line," which means "Assure my endangered, privileged status." Welcome to the clinical research space.

Meanwhile, amid a Middle Atlantic landscape of small farms, crowded urban streets, and rigid walls of private property, Camille joins the clan of one-breasted women (Williams, 1991). She is confused and worried. Poor, frightened, and 50, she knows the breast cancer is spreading. Her life, composed of memories, children, career, lovers, and anticipated hopes, appears shredded; she fears no one is listening. She was in the Breast Cancer Prevention Trial (Fisher et al., 1998), took the drug and still got cancer. She feels punished and ignored. Her doctors hide their fears and lose their empathy behind liver enzyme tests and offers of experimental chemotherapy clinical trial protocols. They feel tired, overregulated, angry at the continued emphasis on cost cutting, and inadequate in the face of death, but they conceal their emotions behind a wall of professional "objectivity" and the afterglow of the tamoxifen breakthrough. Camille's friend Gloria was also in the study and did well, but is not sure the drug is worth it. She didn't like taking a pill every day; it made her feel like something was wrong with her body. She worries more about everything since she joined the study, and she's stopped taking the pill. Alice is outright angry about the study. She also got the tamoxifen and not the placebo, but she developed a large blood clot in her leg and now has chronic leg and back pain and can barely walk. Meanwhile, marketing researchers for Zeneca Pharmaceuticals are conducting focus groups to learn more effective ways to convince women and physicians of tamoxifen's value. But these are not the stories known by the "public." These stories are hidden, if known at all, by conscious concealment and by the forces of unconscious cultural preference. They are also hidden behind academic walls of qualitative jargon and disciplinary tradition. Thus potential openings in the walls that barricade us all are lost in obscurity.

This is a typical tale in medical research. The story of interest and of hope for qualitative clin-

ical researchers is in what is missing and how the story is framed. *Suffering is standardized.* The suffering related to breast cancer in "typical medical research" is framed as a universal need for some marketable product that prevents. The complexities and individualities of suffering are suppressed within this frame. Important voices and evidence are missing. Knowing the efficacy of the drug, its internal validity, is sufficient to approve using all means necessary to convince all women to "choose" the pill as a requirement for healthy life. Camille's experience of taking a daily pill that labels her formerly healthy self and body as endangered is missing. The voices of her husband and children and parents are missing. Relationships and moral discourse are missing. Feeling, spirituality, and ecology are missing. The "victory," the illusion of Eden, is possible only because depth and context have been reduced or eliminated and relationships have been isolated and alienated. But the victory is not total. As the drug enters the world of lived experience, its flaws will be exposed, its market value will fall, and disappointment will rise until the next "breakthrough." Fortunately, public discontent also continues to rise and manifests itself as growing interest in alternative and complementary healing approaches, spirituality and/or fundamentalisms, and anger with health care reform efforts and services.

This is the clinical research space we have witnessed—many conversations behind walls, but increased suffering, confusion, and searching in the clinical world despite technological "advances." The public discontent and the missing evidence are the hope upon which this chapter builds. We imagine a clinical research space where Camille, her doctors, the biomedical products industry, and the researchers meet and seek transformation. This chapter imagines a conversation at the walls (Brueggemann, 1991)—at the place where the walls meet clinical reality. At the walls separating clinician from patient, qualitative from quantitative, academy from practice, very different ways or cultures of knowing can meet and converse. This *Handbook* celebrates the qualitative research community's conversation behind the wall—the internal discourse about who we are and what we do, and about the faith and hope for our own transformation that are sustained there. The opportunity to translate this conversation outside the wall and into the clinical research space has never been better. Calls made a decade ago for a shift away from a strictly positivist position and for greater methodological diversity, including the use of qualitative research methods (e.g., Freymann, 1989; McWhinney, 1986, 1989; Waitzkin, 1991), are being answered, and qualitative approaches are finding their way into funding agency agendas, especially in primary health care, health services, and nursing. The use of qualitative methods and multiple paradigms is expanding, but such endeavors are still only a patchwork, found more in the tributaries of clinical research than in the mainstream. Patients and clinicians are increasingly being invited into the research conversations.[1] The methods are also evolving, beginning to separate from their parent traditions (such as ethnography, phenomenology, and grounded theory) and generating new hybrids in the clinical research space.

This chapter is about continuing and accelerating the flow, the exploration, the conversations at the walls. The understanding of clinical research that we present arises from the nexus of applied anthropology and the practice of primary health care, family practice in particular. Both of us have appointments in family medicine, and both are trained in anthropology; we are each on both sides of several walls. Our social science roots were fed by the development of clinically applied anthropology (Chrisman, 1977; Chrisman & Maretzki, 1982; Fabrega, 1976, 1979; Foster, 1974; Foster & Anderson, 1978; Polgar, 1962) in the 1970s, nurtured by the later work of Kleinman (1988, 1992, 1995; Kleinman, Eisenberg, & Good, 1978), Good and Good (1981; Good, 1994), Lock (1982, 1986, 1993), Pelto and Pelto (1978, 1990), and Young (1982a, 1982b), and currently challenged by the poststructuralist debate (Burawoy et al., 1991; Clifford & Marcus, 1986; Haraway, 1993; Jackson, 1989) and critical theory (Baer, 1993; Morsy,

1996; Singer, 1995). One of us (WLM) has a busy urban family practice, directs a residency program, and chairs a clinical department; the other (BFC) directs a family practice research division and is a national research consultant. We are both active participants in the politics and discourse of academic biomedicine and academic social science. The biomedical influence, with its perceived therapeutic imperative, steers toward pragmatic interventions and the desire for explicitness and coherence in information gathering and decision making and highlights the appeal of positivism and technology. The actual relationships that emerge within patient care reveal the uncertainty and particularity (McWhinney, 1989) of clinical praxis and turn one toward storytelling, relationship, and interpretation. Trying to get grants funded, to publish storied knowledge in biomedical journals, and to change dominant behaviors exposes the realities of power and hegemony.

Our guiding premise is that the questions emerging from clinical experience frame conversation and determine research design (Brewer & Hunter, 1989; Diers, 1979; Miller & Crabtree, 1999b). Clinical researchers have at least six discernible research styles available: experimental, survey, documentary-historical, field (qualitative), philosophical, and action/participatory (Lather, 1991, chap. 23). The clinical research space needs to be open to all of these possible sources and types of knowledge. Thus we structure this chapter around the following three goals: (a) *creating a space* for research that is open and celebrates qualitative and multi-paradigmatic approaches to the clinical world, (b) *providing the tools and translations* necessary for the discovery and interpretation of the clinical stories and knowledge within this space, and (c) identifying and describing the means for *telling the stories* and sharing the knowledge. Our emphasis is on the clinical text of Western biomedicine and the particular subtext of primary health care because of our own location in that place, but the discussion is easily transferred to other clinical contexts, such as nursing care, education, and organizational management (see also Berg & Smith, 1988; Bogdan & Biklen,

1992; Morse & Field, 1997; Sapsford & Abbott, 1992; Schein, 1987; Symon & Cassell, 1998).

◆ Creating a Space

The dominant biomedical world and the smaller qualitative research community both tend to maintain methodological and academic rigidity. Creating a clinical research space requires bringing both groups outside their walls and finding common ground and common language. *The clinical questions at the wall are the common ground* (Taylor, 1993). These questions call us to rediscover the missing evidence (the people, experiences, and contexts), the richness and depth of what "effectiveness" means; to explore the human implications of rationing and cost issues, biotechnology and genetic engineering; and to enter the conflicted landscape of alternative and conventional medicine, the world between the "garden" and the "machine" (Beinfield & Korngold, 1991). We describe two core strategies for creating and entering this common ground and transforming clinical research. The first of these consists of stepping directly into the biomedical world as it is now; the second involves joining the evidence-based medicine (EBM) space. We also mention four additional strategies: using theory more explicitly; expanding cross-disciplinary collaborations; thinking in more open, multimethod, and longitudinal ways; and doing more participatory research and advocacy. These strategies assume that change is more experience based than rational and that clinical participants must actively try methods if they are to adopt them. Thus there is an emphasis on clinical participants, including patients, answering their own questions using methods appropriate for those questions.

Entering Biomedicine

Walking and working inside the walls of technocratic biomedicine is daunting and fre-quently challenges intellectual and personal integrity. Thriving in this world requires understanding the biomedical cultural context while also clearly articulating a model that highlights the clinical implications of qualitative clinical research. This knowledge, if also joined by patients and other community participants, facilitates bargaining, mediation, and the formation of common language that makes possible the creation of a new research space just outside the walls. This is where, in languages the existing clinical world and patients understand, a space for more expansive imagination is created, tools for listening and seeing are shared, and transforming stories are enacted.

The dominant biomedical paradigm is rooted in a patriarchal positivism; *control through rationality and separation is the overriding theme.* The biomedical model is typified by the following nine basic premises:

1. Scientific *rationality;*
2. Emphasis on *individual autonomy,* rather than on family or community;
3. The *body as machine,* with emphasis on physiochemical data and objective, numerical measurement;
4. *Mind/body separation* and dualism;
5. *Diseases as entities;*
6. *Patient as object* and the resultant alienation of physician from patient;
7. Emphasis on the *visual;*
8. Diagnosis and treatment from the *outside;*
9. *Reductionism* and the seeking of *universals* (Davis-Floyd & St. John, 1998; Gordon, 1988).

The everyday characteristics of the clinical medical world that follow from this model include these:

1. Male-centeredness;
2. Physician-centeredness;
3. Specialist orientation;
4. Emphasis on credentials;
5. High value on memory;
6. A process orientation accentuating ritual, with supervaluation on "science" and technology;

7. Therapeutic activism with emphasis on short-term results;
8. Death seen as defeat;
9. Division of the clinical space into "front" (receptionists, billing clerks, and office managers) and "back" (doctors, nurses, and phlebotomists);
10. The definition, importance, and sanctity of "medical time";
11. Emphasis on patient satisfaction;
12. Profit-driven system;
13. Reverence for the privacy of the doctor-patient relationship;
14. Intolerance of other modalities (Davis-Floyd & St. John, 1998; Helman, 1994; Pfifferling, 1981; Stein, 1990).

These are the assumptions, values, and beliefs that characterize the dominant voice of the medical clinic and that currently define the preferred boundaries of clinical research. Biomedical culture is reinforced and sustained by its comfortable fit within the prevailing cultural norms of the United States. These "normalizing ideologies" include control over the environment, rational determinism, future orientation, life as an ordered and continuous whole, and individualism with emphasis on productivity, perseverance, self-determination, and self-reliance. They are manifested in daily discourses about family, self, gender identity, and aging. Both patients and physicians refer to these ideologies and their associated discourses to help them restore order and normalcy to the disruptions of sickness (Becker, 1997).

This reigning voice of biomedicine has now been successfully corporatized in the United States, and its apparent goal is the elimination of pain, suffering, and disease. The research tends to be atheoretical, hospital based, and disease oriented. In many ways, the present situation represents the triumph of commodification and universalism, with its emphasis on cost, customers, products, outcomes, effectiveness, standardization, and evidence. The reasons for focusing on outcomes are to inform choices (market approach), to provide accountability (regulatory approach), and to improve care (management approach). Fortu-

nately for qualitative researchers, the clinic has many additional, usually unheard, voices. If these voices are entered into the conversation as evidence, the clinical research space is expanded and potentially transformed.

Successfully entering the biomedical world as a qualitative clinical researcher requires a many-eyed *model of mediation.* The biomedical model views the world through its one eye of "objectivity." Qualitative clinical researchers need to learn the discipline of seeing with three eyes—the biomedical eye, the inward searching eye of reflexivity, and a third eye that looks for the multiple, nested contexts that hold and shape the research questions. Like the shamanistic tricksters of mythology (Hyde, 1998; Hynes & Doty, 1993; Radin, 1955), we enter the biomedical world as eye jugglers (Frey, 1994), skilled at mediating multiple perspectives. This qualitative clinical model of mediation features the following nine premises:

1. Center yourself in the *clinical world,* in the eye of the storm.
2. Focus on the *questions* that dawn there.
3. Assume *both/and;* acknowledge what is of value in biomedicine *and* highlight what is missing, what is silent, invisible, ignored; expand on the already existing tension between care and competence (Good & Good, 1993); hold quantitative objectivisms in one hand and qualitative revelations in the other.
4. Follow a *natural history* path that characterizes indigenous medical traditions and the early history of Western medicine and is still an important aspect of primary health care (Harris, 1989).
5. Be *participatory;* include patients and clinicians in your inquiry work.
6. Preserve and celebrate *anomalies,* the discoveries and data that do not fit; anomalies are the levers for transformation.
7. Allow "truth" to be *emergent* and not preconceived, defensive, or forceful.
8. Respect the plea for *clinical action* and the perceived need for coherence voiced by nearly all participants in the clinical world.

9. Practice *humility and patience;* these will enable everything else.

Qualitative clinical researchers can bring several powerful perspectives to the clinical encounter that can help surface the unseen and unheard and add depth to what is already present. These include an understanding of disease as a cultural construction (Berger & Luckmann, 1967); knowledge of additional medical models, such as the biopsychosocial or humanistic model (Engels, 1977; Smith, 1996), the holistic model (Gordon, 1996; Weil, 1988), and homeopathy (Swayne, 1998), and non-Western models such as traditional Chinese (Beinfield & Korngold, 1991), Ayurvedic (Sharma & Clark, 1998), and shamanism (Drury, 1996); and recognition of faith and the importance of spirituality in human life. Qualitative researchers also recognize that the therapeutic or healing process occurs not only in the clinical moment, but also in the everyday life between clinical events. Thus the study of everyday life offers additional perspectives, additional voices to the research space being created outside the walls. Carrying the staff of your many-eyed model of mediation, you are ready to enter the clinic.

The clinic is a public sanctuary for the voicing of trouble and dispensation of relief.[2] Each clinic participant crafts meaning out of the "facts" and "feelings" inherent in each clinical encounter and seeks to weave a comforting cloth of *support.* Camille and her family, Alice and her friend, and Gloria and her family all come and meet their clinician and her staff at the clinic. These participants bring into the clinic all of their past ghosts; the emotional, physical, conceptual, sociocultural, and spiritual contingencies and competing demands of their presents; and their hopes and fears for their futures. This is the real world of clinical practice involving material bodies, intentions, meanings, intersubjectivity, values, personal knowledge, physical ecology, and ethics. Yet most published clinical research consists of observational epidemiology (Feinstein, 1985; Kelsey, Thompson, & Evans, 1986; Kleinbaum, Kupper, & Morgenstern, 1982; Sackett, 1991) and clinical trial designs (Meinert, 1986; Pocock, 1983).

These studies involve separating variables of interest from their local, everyday milieu, entering them into a controlled research environment, and then trying to fit the results back into the original context. For example, Alice's clinician is aware of randomized controlled trials demonstrating clinical efficacy for short-term bed rest in patients with back pain (Deyo, Diehl, & Rosenthal, 1986; Wiesel et al., 1980). But the practitioner encounters difficulty in applying this information to the particular back pain and disability Alice is experiencing. The evidences needed to inform this encounter are many. Ideally, the clinical participants will study themselves and thus challenge their own situated knowledges and empower their own transformations. This requires that they bring qualitative methods to the clinical experience. Let's join the evidence-based medicine research space.

Joining Evidence-Based Medicine

Evidence-based medicine (EBM) is the new wonder child in clinical care and in clinical research. The premise is that individual clinical expertise must be integrated "with the best available external clinical evidence from systematic research" (Sackett, Richardson, Rosenberg, & Haynes, 1997, p. 2). Randomized clinical trials (RCTs) and meta-analyses (systematic reviews of multiple RCTs) are considered to produce the best external evidence for use in answering questions about therapeutic interventions. An international group of clinicians, methodologists, and consumers have formed the Cochrane Collaboration as a means of facilitating the collection, implementation, and dissemination of such systematic reviews (Fullerton-Smith, 1995). They have created the Cochrane Library, which is available on CD-ROM, on the Internet, and in secondary publications through the *British Medical Journal.* Major initiatives are under way to assure that all physicians, especially at the primary care level, use this evidence to guide their clinical decision making (Shaughnessy, Slawson, & Bennett, 1994; Slawson, Shaughnessy, & Bennett, 1994). The proliferation of clinical practice guidelines is one result of these initiatives. Another result is the relative reduced value of qualitative studies. But EBM actually offers qualitative clinical investigators multiple opportunities for creating a space outside the walls—there is so much *missing evidence*!

The double-blind (closed) RCT has high internal validity but often dubious external validity and almost no information about *context,* as noted in our introductory discussion of the Breast Cancer Prevention Trial. Read any RCT report, and the only voice you hear is the cold sound of the intervention and faint echoes of the investigator's biases. The cacophonous music of patients, clinicians, insurance companies, lawyers, government regulatory bodies, consumer interest groups, community agencies, office staff, corporate interests, and family turmoil is mute. Local politics and contradictory demands become the sound of thin hush. There has also been little research into the *individual clinical expertise* side of the EBM equation and the associated areas of relationship dynamics, communication, and patient preference; there is much to be learned about how patients and clinicians actually implement "best evidence." Additionally, there are many gray zones of clinical practice where the evidence about competing clinical options is incomplete or contradictory (Naylor, 1995). Breast cancer prevention is a good example. Should women at high risk of developing breast cancer undergo prophylactic mastectomy, take tamoxifen for life, have more frequent screening mammography with or without regular physician examination and rigorous breast self-examination, eat macrobiotic food and take antioxidant vitamins, and/or live life as it comes? Where is the helpful qualitative clinical research? Here are the openings for clinical researchers. We can join the EBM and RCT space and expand its vision.

The new gold standard, if there should be any at all, needs to include qualitative methods along with the RCT. In addition to those areas noted above, qualitative methods can help formalize the learning curve, test theory, inform hypothesis testing and future work, and enhance the transferability of the clinical trial into clinical practice. We propose conceptualizing the *multimethod RCT* as a double-stranded helix of DNA. On one strand are qualitative methods addressing issues of context, meaning, power, and complexity, and on the other are quantitative methods providing measurement and a focused anchor. The two strands are connected by the research questions. The qualitative and quantitative strands twist and spiral around the questions in an ongoing interaction, creating codes of understanding that get expressed in better clinical care. We hope that clinical researchers will seek out those doing clinical trials on symptom management, treatments, clinical processes, and community interventions and advocate for adding the qualitative strand. This work will also help to identify new outcomes that transpose the emphasis on individual cure and elimination of pain and disease toward care, growth, quality of life, healthier relationships, and more sustainable communities and ecosystems.

Examples showing the way already exist. Jolly, Bradley, Sharp, Smith, and Mant (1998), using RCT technology, tested a nurse-led intervention to help patients who had survived heart attacks maintain a rehabilitation program and improve health habits. The quantitative RCT strand yielded statistically insignificant results; fortunately, Wiles (1998) also conducted a qualitative depth interview study with 25 of the participants at 2 weeks and 5 months during the trial and uncovered several clinically valuable findings. At 2 weeks, most of the patients trusted the official accounts of what had happened to them and what they needed to do to prevent future problems. By 5 months, most of the patients had lost that trust because the official accounts had not adequately addressed the experienced random nature of their heart attacks, their severity, and the patients' levels of recovery. Many of the patients perceived their survival to mean that their heart attacks were mild, and, because the doctors had reassured them everything would be normal in 6 weeks, the patients assumed they could return to their original "normal" lifestyles in 6 weeks. Another example of the DNA model for RCTs concerns smoking cessation interventions and is found in the work of Willms and Wilson and their colleagues at McMaster University.

These researchers learned that the meanings patients attributed to their cigarettes had more influence on their stopping smoking than did the use of nicotine gum and counseling (Willms, 1991; Willms et al., 1990; Wilson et al., 1988). Let us join in opening the imagination inside the genome with qualitative questions and approaches.

What are the clinically grounded questions that serve as windows for opening imagination at the walls? Clinicians and patients seeking *support* in the health care setting confront four fundamental questions of clinical praxis:

1. What is going on with our *bodies*?
2. What is happening with our *lives*?
3. Who has what *power*?
4. What are the complex *relationships* among our bodies, our lives, and power?

Each of these questions has emotional, physical/behavioral, conceptual/attributional, cultural/social/historical, and spiritual/energetic ramifications. For example, from the stories of Camille, Gloria, and Alice, there are body questions about support. What are the emotions of living with a high risk for breast cancer? Is tamoxifen more effective than lifestyle change at preventing breast cancer? How will either affect my family and social bodies? What is the lived experience and meaning of breast cancer risk for patients and clinicians? What is happening in the practice or clinic as "organizational body" that helps or hinders Camille's, Gloria's, or Alice's care? There are questions concerning the support of one's life or biography. Do explanatory models of breast cancer relate to the experience and outcome of risk? How does one's self-concept relate to breast cancer risk and response to tamoxifen? What are patients' and clinicians' hopes, despairs, fears, and insecurities concerning breast cancer? How does past experience connect to the immediate experience of breast cancer risk or participation in a clinical trial? There are questions of power about how people are supported. What is happening when patients with high risk of breast cancer present to clinicians in different organi-

zational contexts of care? How is emotional distress surfaced or suppressed? What patterns exist in these different settings? Who influences whom? How is the patient or clinician's power undermined or enhanced (Fahy & Smith, 1999)? What are the local politics? There are questions about the support of relationships. What actions in the clinical encounter enhance family relationships? How do the individuals, the families, and the clinic function as complex adaptive systems? Many of these questions are addressed adequately only if qualitative methods enter into the clinical research space.

This is the evidence needed! We need to apply these four question categories to the critically important issues of the next decade, such as rationing and cost, biotechnology and genetic products, and the often conflicted landscape where alternative medicine and biomedicine meet. How does rationing of health care affect our bodies? What are the emotional, physical, conceptual, social, and spiritual consequences? The same questions can be asked of the many new (and old) products of biotechnology. What are their impacts on our lives? Where is the power and how is it used and resisted? What are the relationships and complex systems that are affected and through which the technologies are deployed? What are the unanticipated consequences? How do patients decide about therapies? How do they juggle seeing their bodies both as gardens and as machines? What other metaphors are used, and when and how do these change outcomes? The questions are infinite and challenging. Primary care, at its core, is a context-dependent craft. EBM lacks context in its present form; it cries out for qualitative methods. Let's get to work!

Using Theory

The multimethod RCT also creates an opportunity for clinical researchers to reintroduce theory into clinical research. Theory is frequently missing from standard quantitative clinical studies, and this often results in ungrounded a posteriori speculation. Qualitative data help to surface hidden theoretical assumptions and suggest new possibilities and connections. Theory can also help bridge the dominant biomedical and other cultural worlds. Recent theoretical discussions among medical anthropologists, phenomenologists, semioticians, and sociologists concerning the metaphor of the "body" challenge biomedical assumptions about the human body and its boundaries and highlight the culturally and socially constructed aspects of the "body" that extend far beyond its corporeality (Csordas, 1994; Gordon, 1990; Johnson, 1987; Kirmayer, 1992; Martin, 1994; Scheper-Hughes & Locke, 1987; Shildrick, 1997; Turner, 1992). There is an individual body, a social body, and a body politic. There are medical bodies, the earth as body, and communicative bodies. Bodies are imagined as flexible, leaky, or effervescent, as machines or gardens, and these imaginations both shape and are shaped by the social body, the body politic, and the world body. Arthur Frank (1995), for example, has described the use of storytelling as a means of restoring voice to the body. Bodily symptoms are understood as the infolding of cultural traumas into the body; as these bodies create history, the symptoms outfold into social space. Because of their complexity, social bodies such as practice organizations are often best characterized through the use of metaphors; they might be described as *brains, machines, organisms,* or *ugly faces* (Morgan, 1998). Qualitative methods become a primary source for hearing these stories and their associated metaphors, caring in relationships, and resisting the colonizing narrative of institutionalized medicine. The study of bodies and their place in the production and expression of sickness and health becomes a core strategy for clinical research that enables the bridging of paradigms and opens the clinical research space.

Collaborating Across Disciplines

This opened clinical research space requires collaboration that emphasizes multiple linkages and different types of cross-disciplinary relationships. Linkages can occur vertically, where one moves up and down through different levels or scales, such as the molecular, individual, local, and regional levels, or linkages can be horizontal, across different sectors at the same level of social organizations such as medical practices, schools, and local businesses. Linkages also occur over time or at different times. Finally, there are multiple academic linkages, including those with the "public," with practitioners, with policy makers, and with research participants (Miller, 1994).

Multimethod and Longitudinal Strategies

Orchestrating this type of multimethod, cross-disciplinary research requires the skills and mind-set of a generalist researcher using a framework of critical multiplism (Coward, 1990; Miller, 1994). The skills and perspectives of the generalist researcher consist of negotiation, translation, theoretical pluralism, methodological pluralism, a community orientation, and comfort with and rootedness in clinical practices. These skills and attitudes are successfully implemented through a critical multiplist framework. Critical multiplism assumes that multiple ways of knowing are necessary and that these options require critical thought and choice. *Multiplism* refers not only to multiple methods but also to multiple triangulation, multiple stakeholders, multiple studies, and multiple paradigms and perspectives. *Critical* refers to the critical selection of these options based on local history, the role of power and patterns of domination, and how the different methods complement each other. Six principles help to guide the complex work of the critical multiplist: (a) Know why you choose to do something, (b) preserve method and paradigm integrity, (c) pay attention to units of analysis, (d) remember the research questions, (e) select options whose strengths and weaknesses complement each other, and (f) continually evaluate methodology throughout the study. Critical multiplism is a particularly powerful framework for doing participatory clinical research.

Participatory and Advocacy Strategies

Participatory research (Macaulay et al., 1998, chap. 23; Thesen & Kuzel, 1999) provides another entry into transforming the research space and brings us around, full circle, to the research questions. We propose that clinical researchers investigate questions emerging from the clinical experience with the clinical participants, pay attention to and reveal any underlying values and assumptions, and direct the results toward clinical participants and policy makers. This refocuses the gaze of clinical research onto the clinical experience and redefines its boundaries so as to answer three questions: Whose question is it? Are hidden assumptions of the clinical world revealed? For whom are the research results intended? (That is, who is the stakeholder or audience?) Patients and clinicians are invited to explore their own and/or each other's questions and concerns with whatever methods are necessary. Clinical researchers share ownership of the research with clinical participants, thus undermining the patriarchal bias of the dominant paradigm and opening its assumptions to investigation. This is the situated knowledge, the "somewhere in particular" (Haraway, 1991, p. 196), where space is created to find a larger, more inclusive vision of clinical research.

Getting these many kinds of evidence will require the clinical researcher to join the evidence-based medicine space, to develop cross-disciplinary collaborations, to use multiple methods with a critical multiplist conceptualization, to use bridging metaphors and theories such as the "body," and, often, to emphasize participatory and advocacy approaches. With these strategies, the clinical research space opens for the tools of the generalist clinical researcher. Qualitative researchers have seen and heard the stories and sufferings of Camille, Gloria, and Alice, but they have been retold in a language that patients and clinicians don't understand (e.g., Fisher, 1986; Fisher & Todd, 1983; Lazarus, 1988; Mishler, 1984; West, 1984;

Williams, 1984). Neither clinicians nor patients know the languages of "ethnomethodology," "hermeneutics," "phenomenology," "semiotics," and "interpretive interactionism." Most qualitative clinical research is published in a language and in places that benefit researchers, not the patients and practitioners. Qualitative researchers have asked that clinicians join, listen to, and speak the "voice of the lifeworld" (Mishler, 1984). We ask clinical qualitative researchers to do the same.

◆ Providing the Tools and Translations

In this section we present the tools and translations necessary for bringing qualitative methods and traditions into the clinical research space. We begin by comparing the qualitative research process with the clinical process. The almost direct correspondence enables the clinical researcher to make qualitative methods transparent to clinicians and patients. This is followed by a brief overview of qualitative methods and how to create mixed-method research designs in the clinical setting. Finally, we put it all together with an example of clinical research that uses some of the strategies discussed.

Research Process

The clinical research space is created when the researcher focuses on the questions arising from the clinical experience, thus opening many possibilities for using the full range of qualitative data gathering and analysis methods. (Many of these qualitative approaches are presented elsewhere in this volume, and we discuss them in more detail in a text for primary care qualitative researchers; see Crabtree & Miller, 1999a.) The challenge for the researcher is to translate qualitative collection and analysis methods into clear, jargon-free language without sacrificing the methods' integrity rooted in the disciplinary conversations behind the wall.

A fundamental tenet of the proposed translation is that *the question and clinical context are primary; methods must adjust to the clinical setting and the clinical questions.* Interpretive social science has traditionally feared mixed methods because this has usually meant treating qualitative research as only a method subservient to the positivist paradigm or materialistic inquiry. We imagine a clinical research space where qualitative methods are empowered and constructivist and critical/ecological paradigms are included. The key is to recognize the similarity between the qualitative research process and the clinical process, particularly as it presents itself in primary health care.

Figure 23.1 is a diagram of the relationship-centered clinical method (RCCM), an emerging tool for teaching and doing the primary care clinical encounter (Stewart et al., 1995; Tresolini & Pew-Fetzer Task Force, 1994). Notice that the overall approach consists of four separate processes—exploring, understanding, finding common ground, and self-reflection. These four processes flow sequentially, but all iterate with each other during any particular encounter, and the whole process usually cycles multiple times for any given illness episode. Chronic illness care, for example, will occur over a lifetime of visits, whereas an episode of ear infection may require only one to three visits (i.e., one, two, or three iterations of the clinical method cycle).

For example, when Camille presents her embodied story of spreading breast cancer, she and her clinician begin their encounter by *exploring* specific disease issues, such as a newly discovered lump. But they also share Camille's fears and expectations and weave these into the fabric of her ongoing health story. Meanwhile, the clinician is seeking to *understand* how all of this relates to Camille's family, community, and ecological context. New information from the exploration and from *self-reflection* inform the emerging understanding, which, in turn, suggests new questions to ask. Shortly after the encounter begins, Camille and her clinician also start *finding common ground* about the issues of most concern, the goals of care, and their respective roles. This process also is informed by and informs the other three.

Doing this clinical method feels like doing qualitative research in fast-forward mode—and it is. The four clinical processes of the RCCM correspond directly to the four processes of qualitative research: gathering, analysis, interpretation, and reflexivity. These parallel processes are illustrated in Figure 23.2 (the clinical equivalents appear in parentheses above the research processes). If we use qualitative research language to describe the clinical process, the parallels and the translation of qualitative jargon become clearer. Clinicians begin their encounters by gathering data using purposeful or information-rich sampling. They focus their interviewing, participant observing, and touching on possible explanations related to the patient's presenting concern or opening story. The exploration seeks "disease" information, following the biomedical model, but the process also searches for understanding of the patient's health story and his or her illness experience, especially the patient's ideas, expectations, and feelings about the health concern and its effects on the patient's everyday living. The clinician almost immediately begins analyzing the data while continuing to gather additional information. This analysis seeks to understand the patient's concern within the context of his or her life world—the patient's personal, family, community, and ecological stories. This understanding is organized around sensitizing concepts, diagnostic categories, personal experience templates or scripts, and connections looked for and then corroborated against the known evidence. Using a participatory framework, the clinician periodically shares the emerging understanding with the patient (or others) and, together, they seek a common interpretation. Throughout this iterative process, the clinician is using self-reflection, personal feelings, and intuition to inform the gathering, analyzing, and interpreting. The visit ends when the practitioner and patient agree they have sufficient data (i.e., saturation) to implement an initial course of action. The outcomes are a course of action for the patient and a report describing the encounter written (or dictated) by the clini-

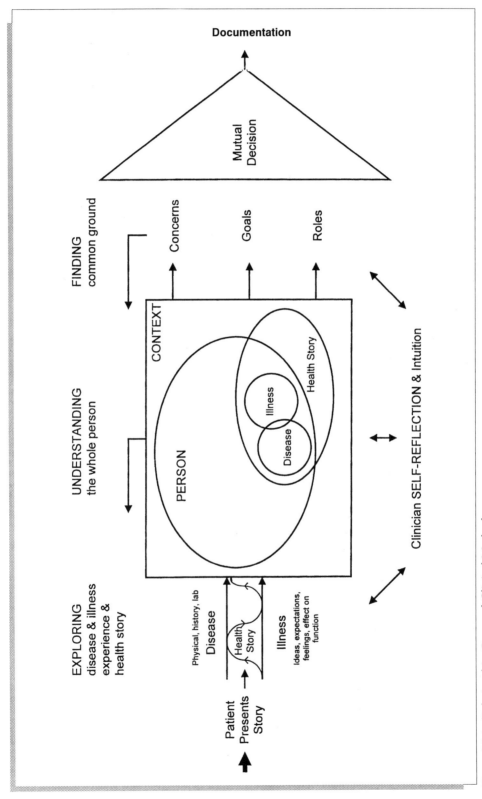

Figure 23.1. Relationship-Centered Clinical Method

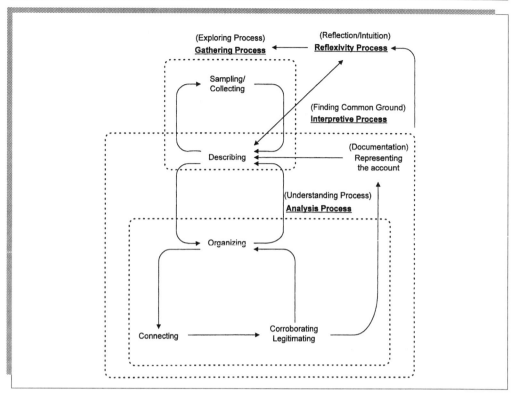

Figure 23.2. Qualitative Research Processes and Their Clinical Parallels

cian. The clinician's reports occasionally undergo peer review. This sounds like, looks like, and feels like qualitative research—only most clinicians don't know it. Researchers need to use clinical language to translate qualitative methods and standards.

It is helpful to notice how clinical care also mirrors the DNA-like, multimethod RCT described earlier. In both, simplified coherence for action ("disease") is in dynamic tension with personal/social/cultural complexity ("illness" and "health story"), and the tension is held through the quest for care, through the research questions. This is most possible when participatory and cognizant of the power imbalances inherent in the relationships and in the greater health care system (such as the system is). All of the many voices must be surfaced, and attention must be paid to them. Out of this tapestry of relational forces, within given biocultural boundaries, are woven senses. The methods must parallel the clinical process and

provide self-critique and correction. This is where doing science and reflexivity intersect.

Research Design

Research designs in clinical research inherently require multimethod thinking, or critical multiplism, with the particular combinations of data gathering, analysis, and interpretation approaches being driven by the research question and the clinical context. There are infinite possibilities for integrating qualitative and quantitative methods, with the design being created for each study and often evolving as a study progresses in response to the emerging questions. In clinical research, the design may be wholly qualitative or quantitative, including the use of a single method, but increasingly designs are employing combinations of these, in what have been referred to as mixed methods (Tashakkori & Teddlie, 1998). Clinical researchers must maintain multimethod thinking and remain free to mix and match methods as driven by particular clinically based questions.

There are many questions and contexts that require only a single method; however, these single-method designs should still be considered within a multimethod context. When the investigator starts with the question and considers all possible methods before deciding that a single method is appropriate for the question, he or she is maintaining multimethod thinking. Most clinical research questions are complex and require multiple approaches. Particular mixed-method combinations of qualitative and quantitative methods are generally presented in terms of typologies of multimethod designs (Stange, Miller, Crabtree, O'Connor, & Zyzanski, 1994). In actual practice, condensing these into typologies is too prescriptive and tends to oversimplify the complex dance of the research process. In conceptualizing a study, the clinical investigator creates a design from the full range of data collection and analysis tools, much as a child (or Will Miller) makes creations from the sticks and wheels of Tinkertoys or from Lego bricks. A child may make multiple airplanes, cars, windmills, and buildings, but rarely are any two exactly alike.

An important dimension of multimethod designs is the longitudinal nature of the research process. Most clinical research questions are complex and multifaceted and cannot be addressed in a single study. In constructing the design, the clinical researcher is constantly balancing the desire to address the question fully with the feasibility of being able to complete the study. Narrowing the focus potentially compromises the integrity of the question, whereas trying to accomplish too much can be overwhelming and possibly unfundable. Thus, in conceptualizing study designs, the researcher may decide to do a series of studies in a longitudinal process that fits the larger research agenda. How a design is finally put together depends on the questions and the setting. Snadden and Brown (1991) wondered about the impact of stigmatization on adults with asthma. Answering this question required them to take two

steps. First, they had to identify patients with asthma who felt they were stigmatized; then, they had to explore the perceived effects of that stigmatization in the patients' lives. The researchers solved these issues by initially using a questionnaire measuring attitudes concerning asthma to identify respondents reporting high levels of stigma. They then interviewed these individuals using qualitative interview and analysis methods.

Multiple methods can also be directly integrated within a single study in a number of ways. For example, sometimes it may be helpful if two independent studies are conducted concurrently on the same study population and the results then converged. This is the approach recommended for the multimethod RCT (see Wiles, 1998; Willms, 1991). Another widely used approach to designing multimethod research involves the more intimate integration of multiple methods within a single research study. For example, Borkan, Quirk, and Sullivan (1991) had noticed that breaking a hip was often a turning point toward death for many elderly patients. They puzzled about what distinguished those patients from others who recovered with minimal complications, as the research literature did not reveal any obvious traditional biomedical factors. The researchers wondered if patients' stories about their fractures had any connection with their outcomes. They used an epidemiological cross-sectional design with a sample of hospitalized elderly patients with hip fractures. Multiple biomedical indicators were measured as independent variables, along with rehabilitation outcome measures as the dependent variable. There is nothing unusual here—this design would assure acceptance by the intended clinical audience. What distinguished this study was that the researchers also conducted in-depth interviews with each patient concerning how the patient understood the hip fracture within his or her life story. Several distinguishable injury narratives emerged. The researchers organized the narratives according to type and then entered these as another independent variable in the statistical outcome modeling. They found narrative type to be the most powerful predictor of rehabilitation outcome.

When discussing qualitative research design with clinicians and patients, we simplify the jargon. We divide data gathering methods into interviewing, observing, and document review (which includes videotapes). We further subdivide interviews into depth, focus group, and ethnographic (or key informant; see Mitchell, 1998). We describe participant observation as either short-term or prolonged. We frame the many traditions, techniques, and "confusing" jargon of qualitative analysis as a "dance of interpretation" in which three idealized organizing styles—immersion/crystallization, editing, and template (for details, see Figure 23.3; see also Miller & Crabtree, 1999a)—promote the dynamic, creative, iterative, yet disciplined craft of qualitative interpretation. All three organizing styles may be used at some time during the different gathering/interpreting iterations of a particular research project.

Putting It Together

We will now review a case study focusing on family medicine practice patterns to further demonstrate the use of a multimethod framework (Crabtree, Miller, Aita, Flocke, & Stange, 1998; Stange et al., 1998). This study was funded by a large federal grant—a fact that provides evidence for the widening acceptance of the multimethod approach.

The Direct Observation of Primary Care (DOPC) study was designed to illuminate the "black box" of clinical practice by describing patient visits to family physicians in community practices with a special emphasis on the delivery of preventive health services. This largely quantitative cross-sectional descriptive study focused on the content and context of the outpatient visit through the direct observation of patient visits using a variation on the highly structured Davis Observation Code (Callahan & Bertakis, 1991) along with checklists of patient visits, patient exit questionnaires, medical record reviews, billing data abstractions, and physician questionnaires. To supplement and enhance these quantitative data, the research nurses dictated observational field notes immediately after each visit to provide richer descriptions of the variables under study. These ethnographic data were impressionistic and focused on describing the practices in terms of key features, such as the practice location, office relationships, and how the practice functioned. The data eventually totaled more than 2,000 pages of field notes from observations of 138 physicians in 84 different family practices. The quantitative descriptions provided valuable insights into the overall content of family medicine practice (Stange et al., 1998) as well as into many other facets of family practice (see the entire May 1998 issue of *Journal of Family Practice*). The qualitative field notes identified a long list of key features that appear to be important for understanding how practices operate on a day-to-day basis, particularly in the delivery of preventive services (Crabtree et al., 1998). The qualitative data were also used to formulate a new theoretical model of practice organization based on complexity theory. This model now provides the basis for two subsequent, federally funded studies (Miller, Crabtree, McDaniel, & Stange, 1998). These new studies include in-depth comparative case studies of family practices using ethnographic techniques (see Crabtree & Miller, 1999b) and a multimethod clinical trial using complexity theory as an intervention strategy for improving preventive health services delivery in family practices. In addition, these two studies are more participatory and directly involve the practices in analysis and feedback. These three large studies are providing data-based insights into family practice that extend well beyond their prevention focus. The progression from a multimethod observational study to an in-depth comparative case study to an intervention trial grounded in insights from the previous work shows the potential for multisite, multimethod, collaborative study.

An important aspect of all of these studies is their use of a collaborative research team. The team included physicians, epidemiologists, statisticians, a psychologist, anthropologists, an economist, and a sociologist. We designed the

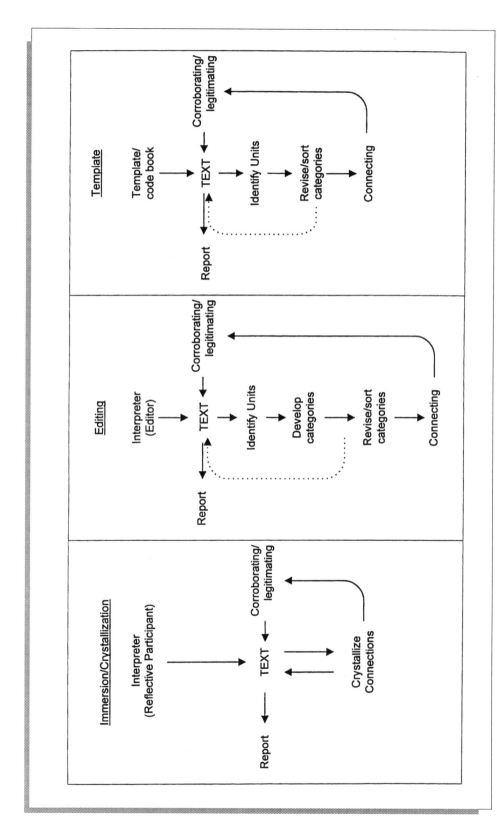

Figure 23.3. Three Organizing Styles of Analysis
SOURCE: Crabtree and Miller (1999a).

study together, met frequently during the study to review the qualitative data and make adjustments in the study, and did intensive reflexivity work (Barry, Britten, Barber, Bradley, & Stevenson, 1999). This long-term collaborative teamwork has enabled the group to expand its use of qualitative methods and its operating paradigms.

◆ Telling the Stories

Writing Strategies

Some specific writing strategies can be useful in facilitating communication of and receptivity to qualitative clinical research (Richardson, 1990; Wolcott, 1990). The most important of these is for the writer to *avoid jargon*; the language should be kept simple and concrete. Using typologies and continua as rhetorical frames is helpful because these initially appear rational and measurable, qualities valued by traditional clinical researchers. Researchers can maintain the interpretive aspects of their work by emphasizing their studies' cultural/historical and/or inductive construction and grounding in lived clinical experience. It is also useful for researchers to communicate either in the biomedically dominant visual mode (through the use of tables, charts, diagrams, and data matrices) or in the clinically familiar narrative mode of case reports. The latter often take the form of first-person voice pathographies (Hawkins, 1993) or first-person accounts by physicians of their patient encounters (Loxterkamp, 1997; Sacks, 1984).

The dominant audience for clinical research perceives the issues of "validity," "reliability," and "generalizability" as scientific fundamentalist dogma, resulting in heightened concerns about bias. In reporting on their collaborative multimethod study, Daly and McDonald (1992) describe the impact of echocardiography on patients' perceptions of self. Their story describes how difficult it can be to have a conversation at the wall: "The biggest problem

was that physicians saw qualitative research methods as . . . prone to bias. Highly structured methods of analyzing qualitative data were effectively used . . . and are probably necessary for 'covering one's back' in multidisciplinary teams" (p. 416). Daly and McDonald present strategies that qualitative researchers can use to translate their wisdom from behind the wall and engage in conversations at the wall. The methodological guidelines for quantitative methods are not relevant for qualitative clinical researchers. The rules of evidence for qualitative clinical research can be translated for clinical audiences as telling methodologically, rhetorically, and clinically convincing stories.

Telling Convincing Stories

A *methodologically convincing story* answers the question, How was the research designed and done? It is important that the researcher make explicit how and why the research design, sampling strategies, and data collection and analysis techniques fit the question and research context, as discussed earlier in this chapter. It is helpful for the researcher to mention when the research design is cross-sectional, prospective, case control, or similar to some other design from observational epidemiology (Ward, 1993). He or she should also address specific techniques, such as triangulation, member checking, and searching for disconfirming evidence (Guba & Lincoln, 1989; Kuzel & Like, 1991), when applicable.

Relationship is essential to the clinical experience. Kahn (1993) has proposed that a language of relationship be used to judge the methodological adequacy of clinical qualitative research. A methodologically convincing story addresses three different relationships: the investigator's *relationship with informants,* noting how each influenced the other during the research process; the investigator's *relationship with the data,* particularly the circularity or iterative aspects of the research experience; and the investigator's *relationship with the readers,* so that authorial intent is clear.

Methodological issues are especially important if the researcher is entering the EBM space.

One popular approach for helping primary care clinicians become "information masters," or EBM experts, involves teaching them to recognize POEMS, or "patient-oriented evidence that matters" (Slawson et al., 1994). In the first step, the clinician scans an article's abstract and determines if the results relate to outcomes that are common or important in everyday clinical practice and matter to patients, and if the results might potentially change what he or she currently does in practice. If the answers are yes, the clinician takes the second step: He or she reads the article and decides whether the conclusions are methodologically sound. There are simple one-page checklists for quantitative studies. The following checklist, which we have developed, is currently being used in the evaluation of qualitative articles:

1. Is the method appropriate for the question?
2. Is the sampling adequate and information rich?
3. Is the research process iterative?
4. Is the interpretive process thorough and clearly described?
5. Is reflexivity addressed?

A methodologically convincing story is not one that pleases a positivist; rather, it is one that pleases qualitative research peers, clinicians, and patients. Thus the use of explicit guidelines and checklists is helpful, but must be tempered with a large dose of flexibility so as not to put off the doing of qualitative research (Chapple & Rogers, 1998). The approach described above is consistent with Altheide and Johnson's (1998) idea of "validity-as-reflexive-accounting," where researcher or team, the sense-making processes, and the question or topic are in interaction, with a focus on how meanings are constructed. This is a good description of the validity process in clinical care.

A *rhetorically convincing story* answers the question, How believable is this text? Readers are drawn into the story and begin imagining that the story is about them. When this occurs, the conclusions make more sense for them. The language and style of writing need to be familiar to the audience. Some of the quotations and observations selected to illustrate interpretations also need to reflect the readers' experience and/or values. A rhetorically convincing story assures readers that the writer has walked in their shoes. Bunge (1961) reviews some of the features that characterize a believable story.

A *clinically convincing story* answers the question, Does this study make clinical sense? A story is clinically convincing if it successfully addresses three features important in the clinical research space. The *question* must matter to clinical participants and the results must specifically address that question. This usually means attention is directed to the pragmatic intervention and policy focus of the clinical world. The *audience* or stakeholder is also a clinical participant for whom the results matter, and this should be obvious in the text. Finally, the manuscript reveals *assumptions* about the physical/behavioral, social/emotional, cultural/historical, or spiritual aspects of clinical participants' bodies, lives, and/or power.

Qualitative clinical research is convincing if the methods are appropriate for the question and the investigator's relationships with informants, data, and audience are clearly addressed; if the audience recognizes itself in the findings; and if the question and results matter to clinical participants. All of these criteria are more easily satisfied if a collaborative team does the research. When this team includes clinical participants, a community of discourse is created where conversations at the walls can begin (see Denz-Penhey & Murdoch, 1993).

Where to Tell the Stories

Qualitative clinical research is widely presented and published in primary care internal medicine and family medicine, nursing, social work, and educational research books and journals. Much of this success over the past decade is owed to specific efforts to translate and introduce qualitative research in workshops within professional meetings, through newsletters, and through methods' publications emphasizing clinical usefulness. Qualitative clinical research is now appearing in clinical journals, especially in the field of primary care. *Qualitative Health Research, Qualitative Inquiry,* and *Culture, Medicine, and Psychiatry* serve as bridge-building publications with an almost exclusive emphasis on qualitative clinical research. All of the primary care journals have reviewers trained in qualitative research and readily publish qualitative studies. The *Journal of Family Practice* now provides space on its Web site to "publish" supplementary materials, thus making it possible for authors to condense articles into the space requirements of medical journals. The next steps are to expand presentations to the larger general medical journals, such as the *New England Journal of Medicine* and the *Journal of the American Medical Association,* and to improve ways for communicating results with the patient population. The use of the World Wide Web may become a valuable means of presenting findings to patients and the broader community.

◆ Summary

There are many clinical worlds. Each of them is a place where support is sought and power invoked. The clinical world and people's needs for support occur in nursing, primary health care, specialized medical care, administration and management, education, social work, family therapy, mental health care, public health, engineering, and law. In each of these worlds, there are questions emerging from practice. These are the questions, the settings, and the participants for doing qualitative clinical research. This is where the conversation starts. The research is judged by the clinical difference it makes.

People continue to meet in clinics, hoping to weave a comforting cloth of support, but the created relationships and patterns are now more varied, more confusing, and often too expensive. Concerns about access and cost do matter, but we cannot address them adequately without facing the abusive and dismembering experience of being a woman in the medical clinic, the pervasive delegitimation of patient experience, clinicians' increasing sense of helpless imprisonment, and the mounting problems, discontinuities, cultural conflicts, and ecological degradation within local communities. Knowing the probabilities is not enough and is often inappropriate. The stories, uniquenesses, and contexts are also essential threads in the fabric. Without them, care and moral discourse remain narrowly defined; our bodies and lives remain fragmented and power is imposed. Camille remains isolated within the clan of one-breasted women. She, and we, need the breath of qualitative research. She, and we, need *relationship* restored to the clinical world.

Ten years have passed. Camille, Gloria, and Alice are now members of a community health advisory group that provides counsel for several local primary care practices and a regional health network and hospital system. They are meeting with an interdisciplinary team of researchers, clinicians, local employers, pharmaceutical industry representatives, and a fellow from the National Institutes of Health. This group is designing a new regional research initiative jointly funded by the NIH and a local foundation that will test a promising new drug for the prevention of breast cancer using a multimethod RCT design that includes the extensive use of qualitative methods. The women's daughters will be in the locally controlled study. The analysis of the qualitative data will occur independent of the RCT analysis and will be ongoing throughout the trial. Camille, Gloria, and Alice are members of the qualitative analysis team. They have authority to end the study for any reason, at any time.

Qualitative methods are needed now more than ever, but with a participatory, collaborative, multimethod twist. Qualitative clinical researchers must move from behind their walls, engage the clinical experience and its questions, and practice humility and fidelity within a community of discourse at the walls. This is a dangerous, but exciting, conversation because it promises that no one can stay the same. Beware the idolatry of control, the idolatry of measurement. If measurement is required, insist on inviting the patients and the clinicians into the research process; insist on measuring suffering and love. Include the local ecology. Complicate the outcomes. Measure the dance of life's attachments and detachments, of mystery and grace, of breathing and the rhythms of life. Measure the process of healing. Our research needs to risk restoring relationship to the clinical world. Clinical research can heal by transforming into praxis. In time, all walls crumble, power shifts, and healing begins. We are not any closer to that dangerous and unconscious Eden. Thank heavens. It is much better than that—we are beginning to make sense of life together.

■ Notes

1. The word *patient* derives from the Latin word *patiens,* meaning "to suffer," and from the Latin *paene,* meaning "almost," and *penuria,* meaning "need." People seek clinicians because they have need and are suffering. They are no longer complete; they lack adequate support; they are merely "almost human." People go to clinicians because they do not perceive themselves as equal and/or whole. They are "patients" in need of movement toward wholeness.

2. The word *clinic* derives from the Greek words *klinikos,* meaning "of a bed," and *klinein,* " meaning "to lean" or "to recline." From this sense, a clinic is a physical and social place for those in need of support (this support can be medical, managerial, educational, legal, economic, religious, nursing, social, or psychological). This understanding defines clinic as a bounded text for research.

■ References

Altheide, D.L., & Johnson, J. M. (1998). Criteria for assessing interpretive validity in qualitative research. In N. K. Denzin & Y. S. Lincoln (Eds.), *Collecting and interpreting qualitative materials* (pp. 283-312). Thousand Oaks, CA: Sage.

Baer, H. A. (1993). How critical can clinical anthropology be? *Medical Anthropology, 15,* 299-317.

Barry, C. A., Britten, N., Barber, N., Bradley, C., & Stevenson, F. (1999). Using reflexivity to optimize teamwork in qualitative research. *Qualitative Health Research, 9,* 26-44.

Becker, G. (1997). *Disrupted lives: How people create meaning in a chaotic world.* Berkeley: University of California Press.

Beinfield, H., & Korngold, E. (1991). *Between heaven and earth: A guide to Chinese medicine.* New York: Ballantine.

Berg, D. N., & Smith, K. K. (Eds.). (1988). *The self in social inquiry: Researching methods.* Newbury Park, CA: Sage.

Berger, P. L., & Luckmann, T. (1967). *The social construction of reality: A treatise in the sociology of knowledge.* Garden City, NY: Anchor.

Bogdan, R. C., & Biklen, S. K. (1992). *Qualitative research for education: An introduction to theory and methods* (2nd ed.). Boston: Allyn & Bacon.

Borkan, J. M., Quirk, M., & Sullivan, M. (1991). Finding meaning after the fall: Injury narratives from elderly hip fracture patients. *Social Science and Medicine, 33,* 947-957.

Brewer, J., & Hunter, A. (1989). *Multimethod research: A synthesis of styles.* Newbury Park, CA: Sage.

Brueggemann, W. (1991). *Interpretation and obedience: From faithful reading to faithful living.* Minneapolis: Fortress.

Bunge, M. (1961). The weight of simplicity in the construction and assaying of scientific theories. *Philosophy of Science, 28,* 120-149.

Burawoy, M., Burton, A., Ferguson, A. A., Fox, K. J., Gamson, J., Gartrell, N., Hurst, L., Kurzman, C., Salzinger, L., Schiffman, J., & Ui, S. (1991). *Ethnography unbound: Power and resistance in the modern metropolis.* Berkeley: University of California Press.

Callahan, E. J., & Bertakis, K. D. (1991). Development and validation of the Davis observation code. *Family Medicine, 23,* 19-24.

Chapple, A., & Rogers, A. (1998). Explicit guidelines for qualitative research: A step in the right direction, a defense of the "soft" option, or a form of sociological imperialism? *Family Practice, 15,* 556-561.

Chrisman, N. J. (1977). The health seeking process: An approach to the natural history of illness. *Culture, Medicine, and Psychiatry, 1,* 351-377.

Chrisman, N. J., & Maretzki, T. W. (Eds.). (1982). *Clinically applied anthropology: Anthropologists in health science settings.* Boston: D. Reidel.

Clifford, J., & Marcus, G. E. (Eds.). (1986). *Writing culture: The poetics and politics of ethnography.* Berkeley: University of California Press.

Coward, D. D. (1990). Critical multiplism: A research strategy for nursing science. *Image: Journal of Nursing Scholarship, 22*(3), 163-167.

Crabtree, B. F., & Miller, W. L. (Eds.). (1999a). *Doing qualitative research* (2nd ed.). Thousand Oaks, CA: Sage.

Crabtree, B. F., & Miller, W. L. (1999b). Researching practice settings: The case study approach. In B. F. Crabtree & W. L. Miller (Eds.), *Doing qualitative research* (2nd ed.). Thousand Oaks, CA: Sage.

Crabtree, B. F., Miller, W. L., Aita, V., Flocke, S. A., & Stange, K. C. (1998). Primary care practice organization and preventive services delivery: A qualitative analysis. *Journal of Family Practice, 46,* 403-409.

Csordas, T. (Ed.). (1994). *Embodiment and experience: The existential ground of culture and self.* Cambridge: Cambridge University Press.

Daly, J., & McDonald, I. (1992). Covering your back: Strategies for qualitative research in clinical settings. *Qualitative Health Research, 2,* 416-438.

Davis-Floyd, R., & St. John, G. (1998). *From doctor to healer: The transformative journey.* New Brunswick, NJ: Rutgers University Press.

Denz-Penhey, H., & Murdoch, J. C. (1993). Service delivery for people with chronic fatigue syndrome: A pilot action research study. *Family Practice, 10,* 14-18.

Deyo, R. A., Diehl, A. K., & Rosenthal, M. (1986). How many days of bedrest for acute low back pain? A randomized clinical trial. *New England Journal of Medicine, 315,* 1064-1070.

Diers, D. (1979). *Research in nursing practice.* Philadelphia: J. B. Lippincott.

Drury, N. (1996). *Shamanism.* Shaftesbury, England: Element.

Engels, G. L. (1977). The need for a new medical model: A challenge for biomedicine. *Science, 196,* 129-136.

Fabrega, H., Jr. (1976). The function of medical care systems: A logical analysis. *Perspectives in Biology and Medicine, 20,* 108-119.

Fabrega, H., Jr. (1979). The ethnography of illness. *Social Science and Medicine, 13A,* 565-575.

Fahy, K., & Smith, P. (1999). From the sick role to subject positions: A new approach to the medical encounter. *Health, 3*(1), 71-93.

Feinstein, A. R. (1985). *Clinical epidemiology: The architecture of clinical research.* Philadelphia: W. B. Saunders.

Fisher, B., Costantino, J. P., Wickerham, D. L., Redmond, C. K., Kavanah, M., Cronin, W. M., Vogel, V., Robidoux, A., Dimitrov, N., Atkins, J., Daly, M., Wieand, S., Tan-Chiu, E., Ford, L., & Wolmark, N. (1998). Tamoxifen for prevention of breast cancer: Report of the National Surgical Adjuvant Breast and Bowel Project P-1 Study. *Journal of the National Cancer Institute, 90,* 1371-1388.

Fisher, S. (1986). *In the patient's best interest: Women and the politics of medical decisions.* New Brunswick, NJ: Rutgers University Press.

Fisher, S., & Todd, A. D. (Eds.). (1983). *The social organization of doctor-patient communication.* Washington, DC: Center for Applied Linguistics.

Foster, G. M. (1974). Medical anthropology: Some contrasts with medical sociology. *Medical Anthropology Newsletter, 6,* 1-6.

Foster, G. M., & Anderson, B. G. (1978). *Medical anthropology.* New York: John Wiley.

Frank, A. W. (1995). *The wounded storyteller: Body, illness, and ethics.* Chicago: University of Chicago Press.

Frey, R. (1994). *Eye juggling: Seeing the world through a looking glass and a glass pane.* Lanham, MD: University Press of America.

Freymann, J. G. (1989). The public's health care paradigm is shifting: Medicine must swing with it. *Journal of General Internal Medicine, 4,* 313-319.

Fullerton-Smith, I. (1995). How members of the Cochrane Collaboration prepare and maintain systematic reviews of the effects of health care. *Evidence-Based Medicine, 1,* 7-8.

Good, B. J. (1994). *Medicine, rationality, and experience.* Cambridge: Cambridge University Press.

Good, B. J., & Good, M. D. (1981). The meaning of symptoms: A cultural hermeneutic model for clinical practice. In L. Eisenberg & A. M. Kleinman (Eds.), *The relevance of social science for medicine* (pp. 165-196). Boston: D. Reidel.

Good, B. J., & Good, M. D. (1993). "Learning medicine": The constructing of medical knowledge at Harvard Medical School. In S. Lindenbaum & M. Lock (Eds.), *Knowledge, power, and practice: The anthropology of medicine and everyday life* (pp. 81-107). Berkeley: University of California Press.

Gordon, D. R. (1988). Tenacious assumptions in Western medicine. In M. Lock & D. R. Gordon (Eds.), *Biomedicine examined* (pp. 19-56). Boston: D. Reidel.

Gordon, D. R. (1990). Embodying illness, embodying cancer. *Culture, Medicine, and Psychiatry, 14,* 275-297.

Gordon, J. (1996). *Manifesto for a new medicine: Your guide to healing partnerships and the wise use of alternative therapies.* Reading, MA: Addison-Wesley.

Guba, E. G., & Lincoln, Y. S. (1989). *Fourth generation evaluation.* Newbury Park, CA: Sage.

Haraway, D. J. (1991). *Simians, cyborgs, and women: The reinvention of nature.* New York: Routledge.

Haraway, D. J. (1993). The biopolitics of postmodern bodies: Determinations of self in immune system discourse. In S. Lindenbaum & M. Lock (Eds.), *Knowledge, power, and practice: The anthropology of medicine and everyday life* (pp. 364-410). Berkeley: University of California Press.

Harris, C. M. (1989). Seeing sunflowers. *Journal of the Royal College of General Practitioners, 39,* 313-319.

Hawkins, A. H. (1993). *Reconstructing illness: Studies in pathography.* West Lafayette, IN: Purdue University Press.

Helman, C. G. (1994). *Culture, health and illness.* Oxford: Butterworth Heinemann.

Hyde, L. (1998). *Trickster makes this world: Mischief, myth, and art.* New York: Farrar, Straus & Giroux.

Hynes, W. J., & Doty, W. G. (Eds.). (1993). *Mythical trickster figures: Contours, contexts, and criticisms.* Tuscaloosa: University of Alabama Press.

Jackson, M. (1989). *Paths toward a clearing: Radical empiricism and ethnographic inquiry.* Bloomington: Indiana University Press.

Johnson, M. (1987). *The body in the mind.* Chicago: University of Chicago Press.

Jolly, K., Bradley, F., Sharp, S., Smith, H., & Mant, D. (1998). Follow-up care in general practice of patients with myocardial infarction or angina pectoris: Initial results of the SHIP trial. *Family practice, 15,* 548-555.

Kahn, D. L. (1993). Ways of discussing validity in qualitative nursing research. *Western Journal of Nursing Research, 15,* 122-126.

Kelsey, J. L., Thompson, W. D., & Evans, A. S. (1986). *Methods in observational epidemiology.* New York: Oxford University Press.

Kirmayer, L. J. (1992). The body's insistence on meaning: Metaphor as presentation and representation in illness experience. *Medical Anthropology Quarterly, 6,* 323-346.

Kleinbaum, D. G., Kupper, L. L., & Morgenstern, H. (1982). *Epidemiologic research: Principles and quantitative methods.* Belmont, CA: Lifetime Learning.

Kleinman, A. M. (1988). *The illness narratives: Suffering, healing, and the human condition.* New York: Basic Books.

Kleinman, A. M. (1992). Local worlds of suffering: An interpersonal focus for ethnographies of illness experience. *Qualitative Health Research, 2,* 127-134.

Kleinman, A. M. (1995). *Writing at the margin: Discourse between anthropology and medicine.* Berkeley: University of California Press.

Kleinman, A. M., Eisenberg, L., & Good, B. (1978). Culture, illness, and care: Clinical lessons from anthropologic and cross-cultural research. *Annals of Internal Medicine, 88,* 251-258.

Kuzel, A. J., & Like, R. C. (1991). Standards of trustworthiness for qualitative studies in primary care. In P. G. Norton, M. Stewart, F. Tudiver, M. J. Bass, & E. V. Dunn (Eds.), *Primary care research: Traditional and innovative approaches* (pp. 138-158). Newbury Park, CA: Sage.

Lather, P. (1991). *Getting smart: Feminist research and pedagogy with/in the postmodern.* New York: Routledge.

Lazarus, E. S. (1988). Theoretical considerations for the study of the doctor-patient relationship: Implications of a perinatal study. *Medical Anthropology Quarterly, 2,* 34-58.

Lock, M. (1982). On revealing the hidden curriculum. *Medical Anthropology Quarterly, 14,* 19-21.

Lock, M. (1986). The anthropological study of the American medical system: Center and periphery. *Social Science and Medicine, 22,* 931-932.

Lock, M. (1993). Cultivating the body: Anthropology and epistemologies of bodily practice and knowledge. *Annual Reviews of Anthropology, 22,* 133-156.

Loxterkamp, D. (1997). *A measure of my days: The journal of a country doctor.* Hanover, NH: University Press of New England.

Macaulay, A., Gibson, N., Commander, L., McCabe, M., Robbins, C., & Twohig, P. (1998). *Responsible research with communities: Participatory research in primary care* [On-line publication of the North American Primary Care Research Group]. Available Internet: http://views.vcu.edu/views/fap/napcrg.html

Martin, E. (1994). *Flexible bodies: The role of immunity in American culture from the days of polio to the age of AIDS.* Boston: Beacon.

McWhinney, I. R. (1986). Are we on the brink of a major transformation of clinical method? *Canadian Medical Association Journal, 135,* 873-878.

McWhinney, I. R. (1989). An acquaintance with particulars . . . . *Family Medicine, 21,* 296-298.

Meinert, C. L. (1986). *Clinical trials: Design, conduct, and analysis.* New York: Oxford University Press.

Miller, W. L. (1994). Common space: Creating a collaborative research conversation. In B. F. Crabtree, W. L. Miller, R. B. Addison, V. J. Gilchrist, & A. Kuzel (Eds.), *Exploring collaborative research in primary care* (pp. 265-288). Thousand Oaks, CA: Sage.

Miller, W. L., & Crabtree, B. F. (1999a). The dance of interpretation. In B. F. Crabtree & W. L. Miller (Eds.), *Doing qualitative research* (2nd ed.). Thousand Oaks, CA: Sage.

Miller, W. L., & Crabtree, B. F. (1999b). Primary care research: A multimethod typology and qualitative roadmap. In B. F. Crabtree & W. L. Miller (Eds.), *Doing qualitative research* (2nd ed.). Thousand Oaks, CA: Sage.

Miller, W. L., Crabtree, B. F., McDaniel, R., & Stange, K. C. (1998). Understanding change in primary care practice using complexity theory. *Journal of Family Practice, 46,* 369-376.

Mishler, E. G. (1984). *The discourse of medicine: Dialectics of medical interviews.* Norwood, NJ: Ablex.

Mitchell, M. L. (1998). *Employing qualitative methods in the private sector.* Thousand Oaks, CA: Sage.

Morgan, G. (1998). *Images of organization: The executive edition.* San Francisco: Berrett-Koehler.

Morse, J. M., & Field, P. A. (1997). *Principles of qualitative methods.* Thousand Oaks, CA: Sage.

Morsy, S. A. (1996). Political economy in medical anthropology. In C. F. Sargent & T. M. Johnson (Eds.), *Medical anthropology: Contemporary theory and method* (Rev. ed., pp. 21-40). Westport, CT: Praeger.

Naylor, C. D. (1995). Grey zones of clinical practice: Some limits to evidence-based medicine. *Lancet, 345,* 840-842.

Pelto, P. J., & Pelto, G. H. (1978). *Anthropological research: The structure of inquiry* (2nd ed.). New York: Cambridge University Press.

Pelto, P. J., & Pelto, G. H. (1990). Field methods in medical anthropology. In T. M. Johnson & C. F. Sargent (Eds.), *Medical anthropology: Contemporary theory and method* (pp. 269-297). New York: Praeger.

Pfifferling, J. H. (1981). A cultural prescription for medicocentrism. In L. Eisenberg & A. M. Kleinman (Eds.), *The relevance of social science for medicine* (pp. 197-222). Boston: D. Reidel.

Pocock, S. J. (1983). *Clinical trials: A practical approach.* New York: John Wiley.

Polgar, S. (1962). Health and human behavior: Areas of interest common to the social and medical sciences. *Current Anthropology, 3,* 159-205.

Powles, T., Eeles, R., Ashley, S., Easton, D., Chang, J., Dowsett, M., Tidy, A., Viggers, J., & Davey, J. (1998). Interim analysis of the incidence of breast cancer in the Royal Marsden Hospital tamoxifen randomised chemoprevention trial. *Lancet, 352,* 98-101.

Radin, P. (1955). *The trickster: A study in American Indian mythology.* New York: Schocken.

Richardson, L. (1990). *Writing strategies: Reaching diverse audiences.* Newbury Park, CA: Sage.

Sackett, D. L. (1991). *Clinical epidemiology: A basic science for clinical medicine* (2nd ed.). Boston: Little, Brown.

Sackett, D. L., Richardson, W. S., Rosenberg, W., & Haynes, R. B. (1997). *Evidence-based medicine: How to practice and teach EBM*. London: Churchill Livingstone.

Sacks, O. (1984). *A leg to stand on*. New York: Summit.

Sapsford, R., & Abbott, P. (1992). *Research methods for nurses and the caring professions*. Bristol, PA: Open University Press.

Schein, E. H. (1987). *The clinical perspective in fieldwork*. Newbury Park, CA: Sage.

Scheper-Hughes, N., & Locke, M. (1987). The mindful body: A prolegomenon to future work in medical anthropology. *Medical Anthropology Quarterly, 1*, 6-41.

Sharma, H., & Clark, C. (1998). *Contemporary ayurveda: Medicine and research in maharishi ayur-veda*. Philadelphia: Churchill Livingstone.

Shaughnessy, A. F., Slawson, D. C., & Bennett, J. H. (1994). Becoming an information master: A guidebook to the medical information jungle. *Journal of Family Practice, 39*, 489-499.

Shildrick, M. (1997). *Leaky bodies and boundaries: Feminism, postmodernism and (bio) ethics*. London: Routledge.

Singer, M. (1995). Beyond the ivory tower: Critical praxis in medical anthropology. *Medical Anthropology Quarterly, 9*, 80-106.

Slawson, D. C., Shaughnessy, A. F., & Bennett, J. H. (1994). Becoming a medical information master: Feeling good about not knowing everything. *Journal of Family Practice, 38*, 505-513.

Smith, R. C. (1996). *The patient's story: Integrated patient-doctor interviewing*. Boston: Little, Brown.

Snadden, D., & Brown, J. B. (1991). Asthma and stigma. *Family Practice, 8*, 329-335.

Stange, K. C., Miller, W. L., Crabtree, B. F., O'Connor, P. J., & Zyzanski, S. J. (1994). Multimethod research: Approaches for integrating qualitative and quantitative methods. *Journal of General Internal Medicine, 9*(5), 278-282.

Stange, K. C., Zyzanski, S. J., Jaen, C. R., Callahan, E. J., Kelly, R. B., Gillanders, W. R., Shank, J. C., Chao, J., Medalie, J. H., Miller, W. L., Crabtree, B. F., Flocke, S. A., Gilchrist, V. J., Langa, D. M., & Goodwin, M. A. (1998). Illuminating the "black box": A description of 4454 patient visits to 138 family physicians. *Journal of Family Practice, 46*, 377-389.

Stein, H. F. (1990). *American medicine as culture*. Boulder, CO: Westview.

Stewart, M., Brown, J. B., Weston, W. W., McWhinney, I. R., McWilliam, C. L., & Freeman, T. R. (1995). *Patient-centered medicine: Transforming the clinical method*. Thousand Oaks, CA: Sage.

Swayne, J. (1998). *Homeopathic method: Implications for clinical practice and medical science*. London: Churchill Livingstone.

Symon, G., & Cassell, C. (Eds.). (1998). *Qualitative methods and analysis in organizational research: A practical guide*. London: Sage.

Tashakkori, A., & Teddlie, C. (1998). *Mixed methodology: Combining qualitative and quantitative approaches*. Thousand Oaks, CA: Sage.

Taylor, B. (1993). Phenomenology: One way to understand nursing practice. *International Journal of Nursing Studies, 30*, 171-179.

Thesen, J., & Kuzel, A. (1999). Participatory inquiry. In B. F. Crabtree & W. L. Miller (Eds.), *Doing qualitative research* (2nd ed.). Thousand Oaks, CA: Sage.

Tresolini, C. P., & Pew-Fetzer Task Force. (1994). *Health professions education and relationship-centered care*. San Francisco: Pew Health Professions Commission.

Turner, B. (1992). *Regulating bodies: Essays in medical sociology*. New York: Routledge.

Veronesi, U., Maisonneuve, P., Costa, A., Sacchini, V., Maltoni, C., Robertson, C., Rotmensz, N., & Boyle, P. (on behalf of the Italian Tamoxifen Prevention Study). (1998). Prevention of breast cancer with tamoxifen: Preliminary findings from the Italian randomised trial among hysterectomised women. *Lancet, 352*, 93-97.

Waitzkin, H. (1991). *The politics of medical encounters: How patients and doctors deal with social problems*. New Haven, CT: Yale University Press.

Ward, M. M. (1993). Study design in qualitative research: A guide to assessing quality. *Journal of General Internal Medicine, 8*, 107-109.

Weil, A. (1988). *Health and healing*. Boston: Houghton Mifflin.

West, C. (1984). *Routine complications: Troubles with talk between doctors and patients*. Bloomington: Indiana University Press.

Wiesel, S. W., Cuckler, J. M., DeLuca, F., Jones, F., Zeide, M. S., & Rothman, R. H. (1980). Acute low back pain: An objective analysis of conservative therapy. *Spine, 5,* 324-330.

Wiles, R. (1998). Patients' perceptions of their heart attack and recovery: The influence of epidemiological "evidence" and personal experience. *Social Science and Medicine, 46,* 1477-1486.

Williams, G. (1984). The genesis of chronic illness: Narrative re-construction. *Sociology of Health and Illness, 6,* 175-200.

Williams, T. T. (1991). *Refuge: An unnatural history of family and place.* New York: Pantheon.

Willms, D. G. (1991). A new stage, a new life: Individual success in quitting smoking. *Social Science and Medicine, 33,* 1365-1371.

Willms, D. G., Best, J. A., Taylor, D. W., Gilbert, J. R., Wilson, D. M. C., Lindsay, E. A., & Singer, J. (1990). A systematic approach for using qualitative methods in primary prevention research. *Medical Anthropology Quarterly, 4,* 391-409.

Wilson, D. M. C., Taylor, D. W., Gilbert, J. R., Best, J. A., Lindsay, E. A., Willms, D. G., & Singer, J. (1988). A randomized trial of a family physician intervention for smoking cessation. *Journal of the American Medical Association, 260,* 1570-1574.

Wolcott, H. F. (1990). *Writing up qualitative research.* Newbury Park, CA: Sage.

Young, A. (1982a). The anthropologies of illness and sickness. In B. Siegel, A. Beals, & S. Tyler (Eds.), *Annual review of anthropology* (Vol. 11, pp. 257-285). Palo Alto, CA: Annual Reviews.

Young, A. (1982b). When rational men fall sick: An inquiry into some assumptions made by medical anthropologists. *Culture, Medicine, and Psychiatry, 5,* 317-335.

METHODS OF COLLECTING AND ANALYZING EMPIRICAL MATERIALS

The socially situated researcher creates through interaction the realities that constitute the places where empirical materials are collected and analyzed. In such sites, the interpretive practices of qualitative research are implemented. These methodological practices represent different ways of generating empirical materials grounded in the everyday world. The contributions to Part IV examine the multiple practices and methods of analysis that qualitative researchers-as-methodological-*bricoleurs* now employ.

◆ *The Interview*

We live in an interview society, in a society whose members seem to believe that interviews generate useful information about lived experience and its meanings. The interview has become a taken-for-granted feature of our mediated, mass culture. But the interview is a negotiated text, a site where power, gender, race, and class intersect. In Chapter 24, Andrea Fontana and James Frey review the history of the interview in the social sciences, noting its three major forms—structured, unstructured, and open-ended—and showing how the tool is modified and changed during use. They also discuss group (or focused) interviews (see also Madriz, Chapter 32), oral history interviews, creative interviewing, and gendered, feminist, and postmodern, or multivoiced, interviewing.

The interview is a conversation, the art of asking questions and listening. It is not a neutral tool, for at least two people create the reality of the interview situation. In this situation answers are given. Thus the interview produces situated understandings grounded in specific interactional episodes. This method is influenced by the personal characteristics of the interviewer, including race, class, ethnicity, and gender.

Fontana and Frey review the important work of feminist scholars on the interview, especially the arguments of Behar, Reinharz, Hertz, Richardson, Clough, Collins, Smith, and Oakley. British sociologist Oakley (1981) and other feminist scholars have identified a major contradiction between scientific, positivistic research, which requires objectivity and detachment, and feminist-based interviewing, which requires openness, emotional engagement, and the development of a potentially long-term, trusting relationship between the interviewer and the subject.

A feminist interviewing ethic, as Fontana and Frey suggest, redefines the interview situation. This ethic transforms interviewer and respondent into coequals who are carrying on a conversation about mutually relevant, often biographically critical, issues. This narrative, storytelling framework challenges the informed consent and deception models of inquiry discussed by Christians in Chapter 5. This ethic changes the interview into an important tool for both applied action research (see Kemmis & McTaggart, Chapter 22) and clinical research (see Miller & Crabtree, Chapter 23).

◆ *Observational Methods*

Going into a social situation and looking is another important way of gathering materials about the social world. In Chapter 25, Michael Angrosino and Kimberly Mays de Pérez fundamentally rewrite the methods and practices of naturalistic observation. All observation involves the observer's participation in the world being studied. There is no pure, objective, detached observation; the effects of the observer's presence can never be erased. Further, the colonial concept of the subject (the object of the observer's gaze) is no longer appropriate. Observers now function as collaborative participants in action inquiry settings. Angrosino and Pérez argue that observational interaction is a tentative, situational process. It is shaped by shifts in gendered identity as well as by existing structures of power. As relationships unfold, participants validate the cues generated by others in the setting. Finally, during the observational process people assume situational identities that may not be socially or culturally normative.

Like Christians in Chapter 5, Angrosino and Pérez offer compelling criticisms of institutional review boards (IRBs), noting that positivistic, experimental social scientists seldom recognize the needs of observational ethnographers. In many universities, the IRBs are tied to the experimental, hypothesis-testing, so-called scientific paradigm. This paradigm creates problems for postmodern observers, for scholars who become part of the worlds they study. In order to get approval for their research, scholars may have to engage in deception (in this instance of the IRB). This leads some ethnographers to claim that their research will not be intrusive and hence will not cause harm. Yet interactive observers are by definition intrusive. When collaborative inquiry is undertaken, subjects become stakeholders, persons who shape the inquiry itself. What this means for consent forms—and forms of participatory inquiry more broadly—is not clear. Alternative forms of ethnographic writing, including the use of fictionalized stories, represent one avenue for addressing this ethical quandary.

Angrosino and Pérez offer an ethic of "proportionate reason." This utilitarian ethic attempts to balance the benefits, costs, and consequences of actions in the field, asking if the means to an end are justified by the importance and value of the goals attained. These authors demystify the observation method. Observation is no longer the key to some grand analysis of culture or society. Instead, observational research is a method that focuses on differences, on the lives of particular people in concrete, but constantly changing, human relationships. The relevance and need for a feminist ethics of care and commitment become even more apparent.

◆ *Reading Material Culture and Its Records*

Mute evidence—that is, written texts and cultural artifacts—endures physically and leaves its traces on the material past. It is impossible to talk to and with these materials. Researchers must interpret them, for in them are found important meanings about the human shape of lived cultures. Archaeologists study material culture. In an essay that moves with ease across and within the postpositivist and postmodern sensibilities, Ian Hodder (Chapter 26) shows how this is done. Central to his position is the constructionist (and constructivist) argument that researchers create, through a set of interpretive practices, the materials and evidence they then theoretically analyze. Today it is understood that material culture, in all its forms, is a gendered, social, and political construction. Previous theories of culture, evolution, and the material past are being rewritten. How the past is reconstructed and interpreted very much determines how it will be constituted in the present and remembered in the future.

◆ *Reimagining Visual Methods*

Today, visual sociologists and anthropologists use photography, motion pictures, the World Wide Web, interactive CDs, CD-ROMs, and virtual reality as ways of forging connections between human existence and visual perception. These forms of visual representation constitute different ways of recording and documenting what passes as social life. Often called the mirror with a memory, photography takes the researcher into the everyday world, where the issues of observer identity, the subject's point of view, and what to photograph become problematic. In Chapter 27, Douglas Harper presents a history of this method and brings it up against postmodern developments in virtual and real ethnography.

Historically, visual sociology began within the postpositivist tradition; researchers provided visual information to support the realist tales of traditional ethnography. Photographs were a part of the unproblematic "facts" that constituted the "truth" of these tales. Now, visual sociology, like ethnography, is in a period of deep questioning and great change. Visual sociology, Harper contends, must find a place in this new ethnography. He engages this new turn through a close, storied reading of a series of photographs he made on the streets of Bologna. This bicycling sequence is a visual narrative. It tells many different stories at the same time as it mixes and combines multiple images, cultural meanings, points of view, geographic spaces, interactional sequences, and shifting, gendered forms of the gaze. Harper also analyzes the ideological aspects of representation, the social construction of images, the authority of visual knowledge, the mechanical capabilities of the camera, framing (point of view), printing techniques, editing, and image sequencing.

As Harper's bicycle shots indicate, sequences of photos can be connected through visual narratives, stories that connect images to first-person accounts, and cultural stories that unfold through time and space. Of course, every image tells a story, but visual narratives attempt to tell the stories of a culture, of individuals, and of institutions, and their interrelationships. Photo elicitation is one method used to elaborate these meanings.

We need to learn how to experiment with visual (and nonvisual) ways of thinking. We need to develop a critical, visual sensibility, a sensibility that will allow us to bring the gendered material world into play in critically different ways. We need to interrogate critically the hyperlogics of cyberspace and its virtual realities. We also need to understand more fully the rules and methods for establishing truth that hold these worlds together.

◆ *Autoethnography and the Researcher as Subject*

Personal experience reflects the flow of thoughts and meanings that persons have in their immediate situations. These experiences can be routine or problematic. They occur within the life of a person. When they are talked about, they assume the shape of a story, or a narrative. We cannot study lived experience directly, because language, speech, and systems of discourse mediate and define the very experience we attempt to describe. We study the representations of experience, not experience itself. We examine the stories people tell one another about the experiences they have had. These stories may be personal experience narratives or self-stories, interpretations made up as the person goes along.

Many now argue that we can study only our own experiences. The researcher becomes the research subject. This is the topic of autoethnography. In Chapter 28, Carolyn Ellis and Arthur Bochner reflexively present the arguments for writing reflexive, personal narratives. Indeed, their dialogic text is an example of such writing; it performs its own narrative reflexivity. Ellis and Bochner masterfully review the arguments for studying personal experience narratives, anchoring their text in the discourses of poststructuralism and postmodernism, especially the works of Rorty and Richardson.

They review the history of this writing form, starting with David Hayano's introduction of the term *autoethnography* in 1979. A variety of terms and methodological strategies are associated with the meanings and uses of autoethnographies, including personal narratives, narratives of the self, writing stories, self-stories, auto-observation, personal ethnography, literary tales, critical autobiography, radical empiricism, evocative narratives, reflexive ethnography, biographical method, co-constructed narrative, indigenous anthropology, anthropological poetics, and performance ethnography. Ellis and Bochner use the case of Sylvia Smith, Ph.D. candidate in psychology, to illustrate the value of this form of writing.

They then turn to their own intellectual biographies, showing how they came to their current understandings concerning the need to write about the researcher as subject. They show that the commitment to this style of writing does not come easily. It involves learning how to write differently, including how to use personal experience and the first-person voice as vehicles for authorizing claims to truth and knowledge. And there are many critics, including those who wonder about narrative truth, emotional recall, and layered texts, who question the point of a storied life and worry as well about such traditional issues as reliability and validity.

Of course, this autoethnography can be read as a variation on the *testimonio* and the first-person life history. Thus Ellis and Bochner's chapter complements Tierney's (Chapter 20) and Beverley's (Chapter 21) treatments of these narrative forms.

◆ Data Management and Analytic Techniques

The management, analysis, and interpretation of qualitative empirical materials is a complex process involving highly technical languages and systems of discourse. It also entails the mastery of a special set of interpretive practices and narrative techniques. In Chapter 29, Gery Ryan and H. Russell Bernard advance perhaps the most sophisticated and comprehensive model of this process and its discourses.

The management and analysis of empirical materials involves arguments concerning the differences between empiricism (there is a real world out there) and constructivism (the world is constructed). It also involves disputes between empiricists and nonempiricists—between those who would translate their observations into words and those who would translate their observations into numbers. Like others, Ryan and Bernard also distinguish two approaches to texts, the narrative or the linguistic and the sociological. The narrative approach to texts treats them as objects of narrative, conversation, performance, or formal analysis. The sociological approach treats texts as windows into experience and includes both texts generated by the analyst and free-flowing texts, or narratives.

Ryan and Bernard focus on methods used in the sociological tradition, that is, methods for collecting such materials (free lists, pile sorts, frame elicitations, and triad tests) and techniques for their analysis (taxonomies, mental maps, componential analysis). They also discuss methods for analyzing free-flowing texts, starting with texts that use raw text input (key-words-in-context, word counts, semantic network analysis, cognitive maps). They then take up methods that reduce texts to codes: grounded theory, schema analysis, classic content analysis, content dictionaries, analytic induction, and ethnographic decision models.

This is a far-reaching, encyclopedic, elegant, and systematic postpositivist approach to the issues surrounding the rigorous analysis of empirical materials. Ryan and Bernard's treatment of grounded theory, conversation analysis, and computer-assisted models of analysis should be read in conjunction with the treatment of these topics by, respectively, Charmaz (Chapter 19), Silverman (Chapter 31), and Weitzman (30).

◆ Computer-Assisted Qualitative Analysis

It is now becoming relatively commonplace for researchers to use computer software programs to assist them in their analysis of qualitative empirical materials. Lee and Fielding

(1998, p. 1) call such programs "computer-assisted qualitative data analysis software," or CAQDAS. In Chapter 30, Eben Weitzman presents a comprehensive and user-friendly survey of a wide array of CAQDAS currently available to support qualitative analysis. He reviews computer-based tools that can help researchers to record, store, index, cross-index, code, sort, and interconnect text-based materials. Of course, these tools are not ideologically neutral (Schwandt, 1997, p. 18). They structure the work of interpretation and presume a particular gendered stance toward the material world. They frequently impose a rational, hierarchical, linear or quasi-linear, and sequential framework on the world and its empirical materials. This can create the impression that meaningful patterns actually exist in the data, when in fact they are created by the software and analytic frameworks being used (in the case of analysis that is not assisted by computer, of course, it is the researcher who creates the seeming "order"). These tools can also distance researchers from their fieldwork and their empirical materials. These methods presume an objectivist, realist, foundational epistemology, and their use too often takes for granted the interpretive procedures and assumptions that transform field notes into text-based materials.

Weitzman divides the most frequently used programs into five main software families: textbase managers, code programs, retrieve programs, code-based theory builders, and conceptual network builders. These programs have multiple text management uses, such as helping researchers to locate and retrieve key materials based on phrases and words, build conceptual models, sort categories, attach key words and codes to text segments, isolate negative or deviant cases, and create indices. Multimedia software programs are just now appearing that allow researchers to use audio and video as well as text-based data. CD-ROMs are also functioning as sites where field notes and other versions of ethnographies are stored and made accessible for hypertextual analysis (see Coffey & Atkinson, 1996, p. 186).

Such powerful tools of graphic, visual, and audio representation allow researchers to consolidate and establish patterns of consistency in their materials. However, they can also create negative effects, including the false hope that such programs can actually write a theory (or a case) for researchers. They may even encourage quick-and-dirty, or "blitzkrieg," research. Coding and retrieval schemes can lead to an overemphasis on the discovery of categories and indicators, with a corresponding underemphasis on the multiple meanings of experience in concrete situations (see Fielding & Lee, 1998, pp. 120-121). The search for grounded theory can shift attention away from the theories of interpretation that operate in the social world.

Software programs for the qualitative researcher need to be interactive, allowing for many different interpretive spaces to emerge, spaces that connect patterns with meanings and experience. Nonetheless, it is important that the researcher avoid letting the computer (and the software) determine the form and content of interpretive activity. An emphasis on codes and categories can produce endless variable analyses that fail to take account of important situational and contextual factors.[1] There is frequently a tendency among researchers doing computer-assisted analysis to reduce field materials to only those data that are codable. There is also the danger that researchers will turn over the transcription of their field notes to persons who lack intimate familiarity with the field setting and the processes being studied (Lee & Fielding, 1991, p. 12).

Seidel (1991) speaks of a form of analytic madness that can accompany the use of these methods. This madness can lead researchers to an infatuation with the large volumes of data the computer allows them to deal with. In addition, researchers may develop understandings based on misunderstandings; that is, patterns identified in the data may be "artefacts of a relationship [they] have with the data" (Seidel, 1991, p. 114). Finally, researchers may focus only on those aspects of their research that can be helped by computer methods (Agar, 1991, p. 193). They then select and ready particular software for use in analyzing the materials they gather. Thus the problem arises: Frequently, researchers conduct research that fits the available software and then report that the software constituted their methodology. This is the methodological tail wagging the ethnographic dog.

Finally, ethical problems may arise from the use of such programs. Akeroyd (1991) isolates the crux of the matter: the potential loss of personal privacy that can occur when a personal, confidential database is developed on an individual or group. When such materials are entered into a computer, the problem of security is immediately created. In multiuser systems, privacy cannot be guaranteed (Akeroyd, 1991, p. 100). Nothing is any longer completely private or completely secure.

Fielding and Lee (1998, pp. 186-189) have speculated on the future of CAQDAS, and they suggest that the field is entering a period of "winnowing out," with some software packages becoming more sophisticated and others remaining undeveloped since their initial release. Some developers have left the field. The Windows operating system seems to have "caused a major shake-out of those willing to keep up with its programming and development requirements" (Fielding & Lee, 1998, p. 186). Software that permits the direct transcription of speech stored on CD-ROM continues to be developed. In some programs the speech is actually heard as it is being transcribed. This raises issues about the differences involved in interpreting heard versus written words (Fielding & Lee, 1998, p. 188).

The Internet has also produced changes in CAQDAS. Large-scale projects can now be located on Web sites. Such use of the Internet is not without problems, including the commodification of information, the control of encryption devices, electronic privacy, and the development of ethical protocols to produce subjects (Fielding & Lee, 1998, p. 188). Clearly, computer technology as a whole continues to transform and complicate qualitative research.

◆ *Analyzing Talk and Text*

Qualitative researchers study spoken and written records of human experience, including transcribed talk, films, novels, and photographs. Historically, there have been three major social science and literary approaches to textual-discourse analysis. Each is associated with a long theoretical and research tradition: content analysis with the quantitative approach to media studies; semiotics with the structural tradition in literary criticism; and narrative, discourse analysis with the recent poststructural development in interpretive theory (see Lieblich, Tuval-Mashiach, & Zilber, 1998, p. 18).

David Silverman contends that the world's business gets done in talk and in conversation. Hence field data are always linguistic, and in Chapter 31 he analyzes three kinds of linguistically mediated data: interviews, texts, and transcripts. With Fontana and Frey (Chapter 24), and Gubrium and Holstein (Chapter 18), Silverman treats interview materials as narrative accounts rather than as true pictures of reality. He poses five questions for interview researchers, including how they use their narrative data to make theoretical claims about the world.

Texts are based on transcriptions of interviews and other forms of talk. These texts are social facts; they are produced, shared, and used in socially organized ways. Silverman objects to those forms of text-based analyses that use the methods of content analysis. Content analyses reify the taken-for-granted understandings persons bring to words, terms, or experiences. Content analyses, he contends, obscure the interpretive processes that turn talk into text.

It is important that researchers not use text-based documentary materials as stand-ins for other kinds of evidence. These documents are social productions. They are not transparent representations of organizational routines, or of decision-making processes. They are situated constructions, particular kinds of representations shaped by certain conventions and understandings (Atkinson & Coffey, 1997, p. 47). Such documents are properly studied through the methods of semiotics, narrative, and discourse analysis. Membership categorization analysis (MCA) is a less familiar form of narrative analysis. Drawing on the work of Harvey Sacks, Silverman illustrates the logic of MCA (on Sacks, see Silverman, 1998). With this method, the researcher asks how persons use everyday terms and categories in their interactions with others. Silverman turns next to transcripts of talk. There are two main social science traditions that inform the analysis of transcripts; conversation analysis (CA) and discourse analysis (DA). Silverman reviews and offers examples of both traditions. He concludes his chapter with four arguments, contending that qualitative research (a) is not based on a set of freestanding techniques, (b) has special strengths for revealing how social interactions are routinely enacted, (c) shows us how people do things, and (d) has uses that extend far beyond exploratory purposes.

To summarize: Text-based documents of experience are complex. But if talk constitutes much of what we have, then the forms of analysis that Silverman outlines represent significant ways of making the world and its words more visible.

◆ Focus Groups in Feminist Research

In Chapter 24, Fontana and Frey note that the group, or focus group, interview relies upon the systematic questioning of several individuals simultaneously in a formal or informal setting. In Chapter 32, Esther Madriz significantly advances the discourse on this method by showing how focus groups are used in feminist research with women of color.[2] Using a feminist/postmodern approach, she offers a model of focus group interviewing that emphasizes a feminist ethic of empowerment, moral community, emotional engagement, and the development of long-term, trusting relationships. This method gives a voice to women of color who have long been silenced. Focus groups facilitate women writing culture together. As a Latina feminist, Madriz places focus groups within the context of collective testimonies and group resistance narratives (see Beverley, Chapter 21; Tierney, Chapter 20). Focus groups reduce the distance between the researcher and the researched. The multivocality of the participants limits the control of the researcher over the research process. The unstructured nature of focus group conversations also reduces the researcher's control over the interview process. Madriz illustrates these points with examples drawn from her study of lower-class women of color.

Drawing on recent developments in critical race theory and feminist theory (see, respectively, Ladson-Billings, Chapter 9; Olesen, Chapter 8), Madriz reminds us that women of color experience a triple subjugation based on class, race, and gender oppression. Focus groups create the conditions for the emergence of a critical race consciousness, a consciousness focused on social change. It seems that with focus groups, critical race theory has found its methodology.

◆ *Applied Ethnography*

The applied, action themes of Part IV are continued in Erve Chambers's comprehensive analysis of the history, forms, and uses of applied ethnography in Chapter 33. Applied research is inquiry intentionally developed within a context of decision making and directed toward the interests of one or more clients. So framed, applied (or action) ethnography is about research that advocates social change and increased cultural understandings between different social groups.

Chambers discusses three distinct traditions within applied ethnography: cognitive, semiotic, and semantic approaches; micro/macro analyses; and action and clinical models. Cognitive approaches attempt to map the native point of view in particular situations, to isolate the language, categories, and terms used in specific locales. Micro/macro analyses examine local contexts with an eye to generalizing to larger, more macro structures—for example, moving from the economy of a local community to the national economy. Action and clinical approaches follow an advocacy model. Researchers build collaborative relations with a variety of different types of persons in the local community, from indigenous experts to informed insiders, leaders in churches, schools, and local government, and representatives of state and federal bureaucracies.

Chambers notes that applied research places great ethical responsibility on the shoulders of the researcher (see also Trotter & Schensul, 1998, p. 692). It carries human, social, and ecological consequences that are immediate and sometimes critical to the life of a community. Its results are change oriented and can be very disruptive.

Chambers also takes up the issue of professional ethics. He indicates that the principle of informed consent has proven to be particularly difficult for applied ethnographers. Maintaining the confidentiality of research subjects can also be problematic. At the same time, applied ethnographers confront moral issues, such as questions of for whom they should advocate and whether or not their services should be available without discrimination.

◆ Conclusion

The researcher-as-methodological-*bricoleur* should have a working familiarity with all of the methods of collecting and analyzing empirical materials presented in this section of the *Handbook*. This familiarity should include an understanding of the history of each method and technique as well as hands-on experience with each. Only in this way can a researcher fully appreciate the limitations and strengths of the various methods and, at the same time, see clearly how each, as a set of practices, creates its own subject matter.

In addition, the researcher must understand that each paradigm and perspective, as presented in Part II, has a distinct history with each of these methods of research. Although methods-as-tools are somewhat universal in application, they are not uniformly used by researchers from all paradigms. And when they are used, they are fitted and adapted to the particularities of the paradigm in question.

Of the six specific methods and techniques addressed in Part IV (interviews, observation, cultural artifacts, visual methods, autoethnography, focus groups), positivists and postpositivists are most likely to make use of structured interviews and those cultural artifacts that lend themselves to formal analysis. Constructionists and critical theorists also have histories of using each of the methods, as do feminists, queer theorists, ethnic researchers, and cultural studies investigators. Similarly, researchers from all paradigms and perspectives can profitably make use of the data management and analysis methods, as well as the computer-assisted models discussed.

■ Notes

1. The continued shift toward variable analysis has moved computer-assisted methods firmly in the direction of postpositivist models of interpretation.
2. Also recall Fine, Weis, Weseen, and Wong's discussion of focus groups in Chapter 4.

■ References

Agar, M. (1991). The right brain strikes back. In N. G. Fielding & R. M. Lee (Eds.), *Using computers in qualitative research* (pp. 181-194). London: Sage.

Akeroyd, A. V. (1991). Personal information and qualitative research data: Some practical and ethical problems arising from data protection legislation. In N. G. Fielding & R. M. Lee (Eds.), *Using computers in qualitative research* (pp. 89-106). London: Sage.

Atkinson, P., & Coffey, A. (1997). Analysing documentary realities. In D. Silverman (Ed.), *Qualitative research: Theory, method and practice* (pp. 45-62). London: Sage.

Coffey, A., & Atkinson, P. (1996). *Making sense of qualitative data: Complementary research strategies.* Thousand Oaks, CA: Sage.

Fielding, N. G., & Lee, R. M. (1998). *Computer analysis and qualitative research.* London: Sage.

Hayano, D. M. (1979). Auto-ethnography: Paradigms, problems, and prospects. *Human Organization, 38,* 113-120.

Lee, R. M., & Fielding, N. G. (1991). Computing for qualitative research: Options, problems and potential. In N. G. Fielding & R. M. Lee (Eds.), *Using computers in qualitative research* (pp. 1-13). London: Sage.

Lieblich, A., Tuval-Mashiach, R., & Zilber, T. (1998). *Narrative research.* Thousand Oaks, CA: Sage.

Oakley, A. (1981). Interviewing women: A contradiction in terms. In H. Roberts (Ed.), *Doing feminist research* (pp. 30-61). London: Routledge & Kegan Paul.

Schwandt, T. A. (1997). *Qualitative inquiry: A dictionary of terms.* Thousand Oaks, CA: Sage.

Seidel, J. (1991). Method and madness in the application of computer technology to qualitative data analysis. In N. G. Fielding & R. M. Lee (Eds.), *Using computers in qualitative research* (pp. 107-116). London: Sage.

Silverman, D. (1998). *Harvey Sacks: Social science and conversation analysis.* Cambridge: Polity.

Trotter, R. T., & Schensul, J. J. (1998). Methods in applied anthropology. In H. R. Bernard (Ed.), *Handbook of cultural methods in cultural anthropology* (pp. 691-736). Walnut Creek, CA: AltaMira.

24

THE INTERVIEW

From Structured Questions to Negotiated Text

◆ **Andrea Fontana and James H. Frey**

Hamlet: Do you see yonder cloud that's almost in shape of a camel?
Polonius: By the mass, and 'tis like a camel, indeed.
Hamlet: Methink it is like a weasel.
Polonius: It is backed like a weasel.
Hamlet: Or like a whale?
Polonius: Very like a whale.

William Shakespeare, *Hamlet*, act 3, scene 2

Hamlet's interview . . . approximates the threefold ideal of being interpreted, validated and communicated. . . .
*   The interview appears as a display of the power relations at a royal court. . . .*
*   Hamlet's interview may . . . be seen as an illustration of a pervasive doubt about the appearance of the world. [Or, we would like to add, the interview can emerge as an example of a negotiated text.]*

Kvale, *InterViews*, 1996

Asking questions and getting answers is a much harder task than it may seem at first. The spoken or written word has always a residue of ambiguity, no matter how carefully we word the questions and how carefully we report or code the answers. Yet interviewing is one of the most common and powerful ways in which we try to understand our fellow human beings. Interviewing includes a wide variety of forms and a multiplicity of uses. The most common form of interviewing involves individual, face-to-face verbal interchange, but interviewing can also take the form of face-to-face group interchange, mailed or self-administered questionnaires, and telephone surveys. It can be structured, semistructured, or unstructured. Interviewing can be used for marketing research, political opinion polling, therapeutic reasons, or academic analysis. It can be used for the purpose of measurement or its scope can be the understanding of an individual or a group perspective. An interview can be a one-time, brief event—say, 5 minutes over the telephone—or it can take place over multiple, lengthy sessions, at times spanning days, as in life history interviewing.

The use of interviewing to acquire information is so extensive today that it has been said that we live in an "interview society" (Atkinson & Silverman, 1997; Silverman, 1993). Increasingly, qualitative researchers are realizing that interviews are not neutral tools of data gathering but active interactions between two (or more) people leading to negotiated, contextually based results. Thus the focus of interviews is moving to encompass the *hows* of people's lives (the constructive work involved in producing order in everyday life) as well as the traditional *whats* (the activities of everyday life) (Cicourel, 1964; Dingwall, 1997; Gubrium & Holstein, 1997, 1998; Holstein & Gubrium, 1995; Kvale, 1996; Sarup, 1996; Seidman, 1991; Silverman, 1993, 1997a).

In this chapter, after discussing the interview society, we examine interviews by beginning with structured methods of interviewing and gradually moving to more qualitative types, ending with interviews as negotiated texts. We begin by briefly outlining the history of interviewing, then we turn to a discussion of the academic uses of interviewing. Although the focus of this volume is qualitative research, in order to demonstrate the full import of interviewing, we need to discuss the major types of interviewing (structured, group, and unstructured) as well as other ways to conduct interviews. A caveat: In discussing the various interview methods, we use the language and rationales employed by practitioners of these methods; we note our differences with these practitioners and our criticisms later in the chapter, in our discussion of gendered and other new types of qualitative interviewing. Following our examination of structured interviewing, we address in detail the various elements of qualitative interviewing. We then discuss the

problems related to gendered interviewing as well as issues of interpretation and reporting, and we broach some considerations related to ethical issues. Finally, we note some of the new trends in qualitative interviewing.

◆ The Interview Society

Before embarking on our journey through interviewing per se, we want to comment briefly on the tremendous reliance on interviewing in U.S. society today, which has reached such a level that a number of scholars have referred to the United States as "the interview society" (Atkinson & Silverman, 1997; Silverman, 1993). Both qualitative and quantitative researchers tend to rely on the interview as the basic method of data gathering, whether the purpose is to obtain a rich, in-depth experiential account of an event or episode in the life of the respondent or to garner a simple point on a scale of 2 to 10 dimensions. There is inherent faith that the results are trustworthy and accurate and that the relation of the interviewer to respondent that evolves in the interview process has not unduly biased the account (Atkinson & Silverman, 1997; Silverman, 1993). The commitment to and reliance on the interview to produce narrative experience reflects and reinforces the view of the United States as an interview society.

It seems that everyone, not just social researchers, relies on the interview as a source of information, with the assumption that interviewing results in true and accurate pictures of respondents' selves and lives. One cannot escape being interviewed; interviews are everywhere, in the forms of political polls, questionnaires about doctor's visits, housing applications, forms regarding social service eligibility, college applications, talk shows, news programs—the list goes on and on. The interview as a means of data gathering is no longer limited to use by social science researchers or police detectives; it is a "universal mode of systematic inquiry" (Holstein & Gubrium, 1995, p. 1). It seems that almost any type of question—personal, sensitive, probing, upsetting, accusatory—is fair game and permissible in the interview setting. Almost all interviews, no matter their purposes (and these can be varied—to describe, to interrogate, to assist, to test, to evaluate), seek various forms of biographical description. As Gubrium and Holstein (1998) have noted, the interview has become a means of contemporary storytelling, where persons divulge life accounts in response to interview inquiries. The media have been especially adept at using this technique.

As a society we rely on the interview and by and large take it for granted. The interview and the norms surrounding the enactment of the respondent and researcher roles have evolved to the point where they are institutionalized and no longer require extensive training; rules and roles are known and shared. However, there is a growing group of individuals who increasingly question the traditional assumptions of the interview—we address their concerns in our later discussion of gendered interviewing and new trends in interview. Many practitioners continue to use and take for granted traditional interviewing techniques. It is as if interviewing is now part of the mass culture, so that it has actually become the most feasible mechanism for obtaining information about individuals, groups, and organizations in a society characterized by individuation, diversity, and specialized role relations. Thus, many feel that it is not necessary to reinvent the wheel for each interview situation, as "interviewing has become a routine technical practice and a pervasive, taken-for-granted activity in our culture" (Mishler, 1986, p. 23).

This is not to say, however, that the interview is so technical and the procedures so standardized that interviewers can ignore contextual, societal, and interpersonal elements. Each interview context is one of interaction and relation; the result is as much a product of this social dynamic as it is a product of accurate accounts and replies. The interview has become a routine, almost unnoticed, part of everyday life. Yet response rates continue to decline, indicating that fewer people are willing to disclose their "selves" or that they are so overburdened by requests for interviews that they are becoming more selective regarding which interviews to grant. Social scientists are more likely to recognize, however, that interviews are interactional encounters and that the nature of the social dynamic of the interview can shape the nature of the knowledge generated. Interviewers with less training and experience than social scientists may not recognize that interview participants are "actively" constructing knowledge around questions and responses (Holstein & Gubrium, 1995).

We turn now to a brief history of interviewing to frame its roots and development.

◆ The History of Interviewing

One form of interviewing or another has been with us for a very long time. Even ancient Egyptians conducted population censuses (Babbie, 1992). In more recent times, the tradition of interviewing evolved from two trends. First, interviewing found great popularity and widespread use in clinical diagnosis and counseling, where the concern was with the quality of responses. Second, during World War I interviewing came to be widely employed in psychological testing; here the emphasis was on measurement (Maccoby & Maccoby, 1954).

The individual generally credited with being the first to develop a social survey relying on interviewing was Charles Booth (Converse, 1987). In 1886, Booth embarked on a comprehensive survey of the economic and social conditions of the people of London, published as *Life and Labour of the People in London* (1902-1903). In his early study, Booth embodied what were to become separate interviewing methods, because he not only implemented survey research but triangulated his work by relying on unstructured interviews and ethnographic observations:

> The data were checked and supplemented by visits to many neighborhoods, streets and homes, and by conferences with various welfare and community leaders. From time to time Booth lived as a lodger in districts where he was not known, so that he could become more intimately acquainted

with the lives and habits of the poorer classes (Parten, 1950, pp. 6-7)

Many other surveys of London and other English cities followed, patterned after Booth's example. In the United States a similar pattern ensued. Among others, an 1895 study attempted to do in Chicago what Booth had done in London (see Converse, 1987), and in 1896, self-admittedly following Booth's lead, the American sociologist W. E. B. Du Bois studied the black population of Philadelphia (see Du Bois, 1899). Surveys of cities and small towns followed, most notable among them R. S. Lynd and H. M. Lynd's *Middletown* (1929) and *Middletown in Transition* (1937).

Opinion polling was another early form of interviewing. Some polling took place well before the start of the 20th century, but it really came into its own in 1935 with the formation of the American Institute of Public Opinion by George Gallup. Preceding Gallup, in both psychology and sociology in the 1920s there was a movement toward the study (and usually measurement) of attitudes. W. I. Thomas and Florian Znaniecki used the documentary method to introduce the study of attitudes in social psychology. Thomas's influence, along with that of Robert Park, a former reporter who believed sociology was to be found out in the field, sparked a number of community studies at the University of Chicago that came to be known collectively as the works of the Chicago school. Many other researchers were also greatly influential, such as Albion Small, George H. Mead, E. W. Burgess, Everett C. Hughes, Louis Wirth, W. Lloyd Warner, and Anselm Strauss (for a recent discussion of the relations and influence of various Chicagoans, see Becker, 1999).

Although the members of the Chicago school are reputed to have used the ethnographic method in their inquiries, some disagree, and have noted that many of the Chicago school studies lacked the analytic component of modern-day ethnography, and so were, at best, "firsthand descriptive studies" (Harvey, 1987, p. 50). Regardless of the correct label for the Chicagoans' fieldwork, they clearly relied on a combination of observation, personal documents, and informal interviews in their studies. Interviews

were especially in evidence in the work of Thrasher (1927/1963), who in his study of gang members relied primarily on about 130 qualitative interviews, and in that of Nels Anderson (1923), whose classic study of hoboes relied on informal, in-depth conversations.

It was left to Herbert Blumer and his former student Howard Becker to formalize and give impetus to sociological ethnography in the 1950s and 1960s, and interviewing began to lose both the eclectic flavor given to it by Charles Booth and the qualitative accent of the Chicagoans. Understanding gang members or hoboes through interviews lost importance; what became relevant was the use of interviewing in survey research as a tool to quantify data. This was not new, as opinion polls and market research had been doing it for years. But during World War II there was a tremendous increase in survey research as the U.S. armed forces hired great numbers of sociologists as survey researchers. More than half a million American soldiers were interviewed in one manner or another (Young, 1966), and their mental and emotional lives were reported in a four-volume survey titled *Studies in Social Psychology in World War II*, the first two volumes of which were directed by Samuel Stouffer and titled *The American Soldier*. This work had tremendous impact and led the way to widespread use of systematic survey research.

What was new, however, was that quantitative survey research moved into academia and came to dominate sociology as the method of choice for the next three decades. An Austrian immigrant, Paul Lazarsfeld, spearheaded this move. He welcomed *The American Soldier* with great enthusiasm. In fact, Robert Merton and Lazarsfeld (1950) edited a book of reflections on *The American Soldier*. Lazarsfeld moved to Columbia in 1940, taking with him his market research and other applied grants, and became instrumental in the directing of the Bureau of Applied Social Research. Two other "survey organizations" were also formed: one in 1941, by Harry Field, the National Opinion Research Center, first at Denver and then at Chicago; and one in 1946, by Likert and his group, the Survey Research Center at Michigan.

Academia at the time was dominated by theoretical concerns, and there was some resistance toward this applied, numbers-based kind of sociology. Sociologists and other humanists were critical of Lazarsfeld and the other survey researchers. Herbert Blumer, C. Wright Mills, Arthur Schlesinger, Jr., and Pitirin Sorokin, among others, voiced their displeasure. According to Converse (1987), Sorokin felt that "the new emphasis on quantitative work was obsessive, and he called the new practitioners 'quantophrenics'—with special reference to Stouffer and Lazarsfeld" (p. 253). And Converse quotes Mills: "Those in the grip of the methodological inhibition often refuse to say anything about modern society unless it has been through the fine little mill of the Statistical Ritual" (p. 252). Schlesinger, Converse notes, called the survey researchers "social relations hucksters" (p. 253).

But the survey researchers had powerful allies also, such as Merton, who joined the Survey Center at Columbia in 1943, and government moneys were becoming increasing available for survey research. The 1950s saw a growth of survey research in the universities and a proliferation of survey research texts. Gradually, survey research increased its domain over sociology, culminating in 1960 with the election of Lazarsfeld to the presidency of the American Sociological Association. The methodological dominance of survey research continued unabated through the 1970s, 1980s, and 1990s, although other methods began to erode the prominence of survey methods.

Qualitative interviewing continued to be practiced, hand in hand with participant observation methods, but it too assumed some of the quantifiable scientific rigor that so preoccupied survey research. This was especially visible in grounded theory (Glaser & Strauss, 1967), with its painstaking emphasis on coding data, and in ethnomethodology, with its quest for invariant properties of social action (Cicourel, 1970). Other qualitative researchers suggested variations. John Lofland (1971) criticized grounded theory for paying little attention to data gathering techniques, Jack Douglas (1985) suggested lengthy, existential one-on-one interviews lasting one or more days, and James Spradley (1980) tried to clarify the difference between ethnographic observation and ethnographic interviewing.

Recently, postmodernist ethnographers have concerned themselves with some of the assumptions present in interviewing and with the controlling role of the interviewer. These concerns have led to new directions in qualitative interviewing focusing on increased attention to the voices of the respondents (Marcus & Fischer, 1986), the interviewer-respondent relationship (Crapanzano, 1980), the importance of the researcher's gender in interviewing (Gluck & Patai, 1991), and the roles of other elements, such as race, social status, and age (Seidman, 1991).

◆ Structured Interviewing

In structured interviewing, the interviewer asks all respondents the same series of preestablished questions with a limited set of response categories. There is generally little room for variation in responses except where open-ended questions (which are infrequent) may be used. The interviewer records the responses according to a coding scheme that has already been established by the project director or research supervisor. The interviewer controls the pace of the interview by treating the questionnaire as if it were a theatrical script to be followed in a standardized and straightforward manner. Thus all respondents receive the same set of questions asked in the same order or sequence by an interviewer who has been trained to treat all interview situations in a like manner. There is very little flexibility in the way questions are asked or answered in the structured interview setting. Instructions to interviewers often include some of the following guidelines:

- Never get involved in long explanations of the study; use the standard explanation provided by the supervisor.
- Never deviate from the study introduction, sequence of questions, or question wording.

- Never let another person interrupt the interview; do not let another person answer for the respondent or offer his or her opinions on the question.
- Never suggest an answer or agree or disagree with an answer. Do not give the respondent any idea of your personal views on the topic of the question or the survey.
- Never interpret the meaning of a question; just repeat the question and give instructions or clarifications that are provided in training or by the supervisors.
- Never improvise, such as by adding answer categories or making wording changes.

Interviews by telephone, face-to-face interviews in respondents' households, intercept interviews in malls and parks, and interviews generally associated with survey research are most likely to be included in the structured interview category.

This interview context calls for the interviewer to play a neutral role, never interjecting his or her opinion of a respondent's answer. The interviewer must establish what has been called "balanced rapport"; he or she must be casual and friendly on the one hand, but directive and impersonal on the other. The interviewer must perfect a style of "interested listening" that rewards the respondent's participation but does not evaluate the responses (Converse & Schuman, 1974).

In a structured interview, hopefully, nothing is left to chance. However, response effects, or nonsampling errors, that can be attributed to the questionnaire administration process commonly evolve from three sources. The first of these is respondent behavior. The respondent may deliberately try to please the interviewer or to prevent the interviewer from learning something about the respondent. In order to do this, the respondent may embellish a response, give what is described as a "socially desirable" response, or omit certain relevant information (Bradburn, 1983, p. 291). The respondent may also err due to faulty memory. The second source of error is found in the nature of the task: the method of questionnaire administration (face-to-face or telephone) or the sequence or

wording of the questions. The third source of error is the interviewer, whose characteristics or questioning techniques can impede proper communication of the questions (Bradburn, 1983). It is the degree of error assigned to the interviewer that is of greatest concern.

Most structured interviews leave little room for the interviewer to improvise or exercise independent judgment, but even in the most structured interview situation not every contingency can be anticipated, and not every interviewer behaves according to the script (Bradburn, 1983; Frey, 1989). In fact, one study of interviewer effects found that interviewers changed the wording to as many as one-third of the questions (Bradburn, Sudman, & Associates, 1979).

In general, research on interviewer effects has shown interviewer characteristics such as age, gender, and interviewing experience to have relatively small impact on responses (Singer & Presser, 1989). However, there is some evidence that student interviewers produce larger response effects than do nonstudents, higher-status interviewers produce larger response effects than do lower-status interviewers, and the race of an interviewer makes a difference only on questions specifically related to race (Bradburn, 1983; Hyman, 1954; Singer, Frankel, & Glassman, 1983).

The relatively minor impact of the interviewer on response quality in structured interview settings is directly attributable to the inflexible, standardized, and predetermined nature of this type of interviewing. There is simply little room for error. However, those who are advocates of structured interviewing are not unaware that the interview takes place in a social interaction context and that it is influenced by that context. Good interviewers recognize this fact and are sensitive to how interaction can influence responses. Converse and Schuman (1974) observe, "There is no single interview style that fits every occasion or all respondents" (p. 53). This means that interviewers must be aware of respondent differences and must be able to make the proper adjustments called for by unanticipated developments. As Raymond Gorden (1992) states, "Interviewing skills are not simple motor skills like riding a bicycle: rather, they involve a high-order combination of observation, empathic sensitivity, and intellectual judgment" (p. 7).

It is not enough to understand the mechanics of interviewing, it is also important to understand the respondent's world and forces that might stimulate or retard response (Kahn & Cannel, 1957). Still, the structured interview proceeds under a stimulus-response format, assuming that the respondent will truthfully answer questions previously determined to reveal adequate indicators of the variable in question, as long as those questions are properly phrased. This kind of interview often elicits rational responses, but it overlooks or inadequately assesses the emotional dimension.

◆ Group Interviews

The group interview is essentially a qualitative data gathering technique (see Madriz, Chapter 32, this volume) that relies upon the systematic questioning of several individuals simultaneously in a formal or informal setting. Thus this technique straddles the line between formal and informal interviewing.

The use of the group interview has ordinarily been associated with marketing research under the label of *focus group,* where the purpose is to gather consumer opinion on product characteristics, advertising themes, or service delivery. This format has also been used to a considerable extent by political parties and candidates who are interested in voter reaction to issues and policies. The group interview has also been used in sociological research. Bogardus used it to test his social distance scale in 1926, Zuckerman (1972) interviewed Nobel laureates, Thompson and Demerath (1952) looked at management problems in the military, Morgan and Spanish (1984) studied health issues, we investigated older-worker labor force reentry (Fontana & Frey, 1990), and Merton and his associates studied the impact of propaganda using group interviews (see Frey & Fontana, 1991). In fact, Merton, Fiske, and

Kendall (1956) coined the term *focus group* to apply to a situation in which the researcher/interviewer asks very specific questions about a topic after having already completed considerable research. There is also some evidence that established anthropologists such as Malinowski used this technique, although they did not report it (Frey & Fontana, 1991). Today, all group interviews are often generically designated *focus group* interviews, even though there are considerable variations in the natures and types of group interviews.

In a group interview, the interviewer/moderator directs the inquiry and the interaction among respondents in a very structured fashion or in a very unstructured manner, depending on the interview's purpose. The purpose may be exploratory; for example, the researcher may bring several persons together to test a methodological technique, to try out a definition of a research problem, or to identify key informants. An extension of this exploratory intent is the use of the group interview for the purpose of pretesting questionnaire wording, measurement scales, or other elements of a survey design. This is now quite common in survey research (Desvousges & Frey, 1989). Group interviews can also be used successfully to aid respondents' recall of specific events or to stimulate embellished descriptions of events (e.g., a disaster or a celebration) or experiences shared by members of a group. Group interviews can also be used for triangulation purposes or can be used in conjunction with other data gathering techniques. For example, group interviews could be helpful in the process of "indefinite triangulation," by putting individual responses into a context (Cicourel, 1974). Finally, phenomenological purposes may be served whether group interviews are the sole basis for gathering data or they are used in association with other techniques.

Group interviews can take different forms depending on their purposes. They can be brainstorming sessions with little or no structure or direction from the interviewer, or they can be very structured, as in nominal, Delphi, and marketing focus groups. In the latter cases the role of the interviewer is very prominent and directive. Fieldwork settings provide both formal and informal occasions for group interviews. The field researcher can bring respondents into a formal setting in the field context and ask very directed questions, or a natural field setting, such as a street corner or a neighborhood tavern, can be a conducive setting for casual but purposive inquiries.

Group interviews can be compared on several dimensions. First, the interviewer can be very formal, taking a very directive and controlling posture, guiding discussion strictly, and not permitting digression or variation from topic or agenda. This is the mode of focus and nominal/Delphi groups. In the latter case participants are physically isolated but share views through a coordinator/interviewer. The nondirective approach is more likely to be implemented in naturally established field settings, such as a street corner, or in controlled settings (e.g., research labs) where the research purpose is phenomenological, to establish the widest range of meaning and interpretation for the topic. Groups can also be differentiated by question format and purpose, which in the case of group interviews usually means exploration, pretest, or phenomenological. Exploratory interviews are designed to establish familiarity with a topic or setting; the interviewer can be very directive (or the opposite), but the questions are usually unstructured or open-ended. The same format is used in interviews with phenomenological purposes, where the intent is to tap intersubjective meaning with depth and diversity. Pretest interviews are generally structured in question format and the interviewer is directive in style. Table 24.1 compares the types of group interviews on various dimensions.

The skills that are required to conduct the group interview are not significantly different from those needed for individual interviews. The interviewer must be flexible, objective, empathic, persuasive, a good listener, and so on. But the group format does present some problems not found in the individual interview. Merton et al. (1956) note three specific problems: First, the interviewer must keep one person or small coalition of persons from dominating the group; second, the interviewer must encourage recalcitrant respondents to participate; and

third, the interviewer must obtain responses from the entire group to ensure the fullest coverage of the topic. In addition, the interviewer must balance the directive, interviewer role with the role of moderator, which calls for the management of the dynamics of the group being interviewed; the group interviewer must simultaneously worry about the script of questions and be sensitive to the evolving patterns of group interaction.

Group interviews have some advantages over individual interviews: They are relatively inexpensive to conduct and often produce rich data that are cumulative and elaborative; they can be stimulating for respondents, aiding recall; and the format is flexible. Group interviews are not, however, without problems: The results cannot be generalized; the emerging group culture may interfere with individual expression, and the group may be dominated by one person; and "groupthink" is a possible outcome. The requirements for interviewer skills are greater than those for individual interviewing because of the group dynamics that are present. In addition, it is difficult to research sensitive topics using this technique. Nevertheless, the group interview is a viable option for both qualitative and quantitative research.

◆ Unstructured Interviewing

Unstructured interviewing can provide a greater breadth of data than the other types, given its qualitative nature. In this section we discuss the traditional type of unstructured interview: the open-ended, ethnographic (in-depth) interview. Many qualitative researchers differentiate between in-depth (or ethnographic) interviewing and participant observation. Yet, as Lofland (1971) points out, the two go hand in hand, and many of the data gathered in participant observation come from informal interviewing in the field. Consider the following report, from Malinowski's (1967/1989) diary:

TABLE 24.1	Types of Group Interviews and Dimensions			
Type	Setting	Role of Interviewer	Question Format	Purpose
Focus group	formal-preset	directive	structured	exploratory pretest
Brainstorming	formal or informal	nondirective	very structured	exploratory
Nominal/delphi	formal	directive	structured	pretest exploratory
Field, natural	informal spontaneous	moderately nondirective	very structured	exploratory phenomenological
Field, formal	preset, but in field	somewhat directive	semistructured	phenomenological

SOURCE: Frey and Fontana (1991, p. 184).

Saturday 8 [December 1917]. Got up late, felt rotten, took enema. At about 1 I went out; I heard cries; [people from] Kapwapu were bringing *uri* to Teyava. I sat with the natives, talked, took pictures. Went back. Billy corrected and supplemented my notes about *wasi*. At Teyava, an old man talked a great deal about fishes, but I did not understand him too well. Then we moved to his *bwayama*. Talked about *lili'u*. They kept questioning me about the war—In the evening I talked to the policeman about *bwaga'u, lili'u* and *yoyova*. I was irritated by their laughing. Billy again told me a number of interesting things. Took quinine and calomel. (p. 145)

Malinowski's "day in the field" shows how very important unstructured interviewing is in the conduct of fieldwork and clearly illustrates the difference between structured and unstructured interviewing. Malinowski has some general topics he wishes to know about, but he does not use closed-ended questions or a formal approach to interviewing. What's more, he commits (as most field-workers do) what structured interviewers would see as two "capital offenses": (a) He answers questions asked by the respondents, and (b) he lets his personal feelings influence him (as all field-workers do), thus he deviates from the "ideal" of a cool, distant, and rational interviewer.

Malinowski's example captures the differences between structured and unstructured interviewing: The former aims at capturing precise data of a codable nature in order to explain behavior within preestablished categories, whereas the latter attempts to understand the complex behavior of members of society without imposing any a priori categorization that may limit the field of inquiry.

In a way, Malinowski's interviewing is still structured to some degree—that is, there is a setting, there are identified informants, and the respondents are clearly discernible. In other types of interviewing there may be no setting; for instance, Rosanna Hertz (1995, 1997b, 1997c) focused on locating women in a historic moment rather than in a place. Additionally, in their study of single mothers, Hertz and Ferguson (1997) interviewed women who did not know each other, who were not part of a single group or village. At times, informants are not readily accessible or identifiable, but anyone the researcher meets may become a valuable source of information. Hertz and Ferguson relied on tradespeople and friends to identify single mothers for their study. Fontana and Smith (1989) found that respondents are not always readily identifiable. In studying Alzheimer's disease patients, they discovered it was often possible to confuse caregivers and patients in the early stages of the disease. Also, in Fontana's (1977) research on poor elderly, he had no fixed setting at all; he simply wandered from bench to bench in the park where the old folks were sitting, talking to any disheveled old person who would talk back.

Spradley (1979) aptly differentiates among various types of interviewing. He describes the following interviewer-respondent interaction, which would be unthinkable in traditional sociological circles yet is the very essence of unstructured interviewing—the establishment of a human-to-human relation with the respondent and the desire to *understand* rather than to *explain*:

> Presently she smiled, pressed her hand to her chest, and said: "Tsetchwe." It was her name. "Elizabeth," I said, pointing to myself. "Nisabe," she answered. . . . Then, having surely suspected that I was a woman, she put her hand on my breast gravely, and, finding out that I was, she touched her own breast. Many Bushmen do this; to them all Europeans look alike. "Tasu si" (women), she said. Then after a moment's pause Tsetchwe began to teach me. (pp. 3-4)

Spradley goes on to discuss all the things an interviewer learns from the natives about them, their culture, their language, their ways of life. Although each and every study is different, these are some of the basic elements of unstructured interviewing. These elements have been discussed in details already, and we need not elaborate upon them too much (for detailed accounts of unstructured interviewing, see, among others, Adams & Preiss, 1960; Denzin, 1989b; Lofland, 1971; Spradley, 1979). Here we provide brief synopses. Please remember that these are presented only as heuristic devices; every study uses slightly different elements and often in different combinations.

Later in this chapter, in discussing new trends, we will deconstruct these notions as we frame the interview as an active, emergent process. We contend that our interview society gives people instructions on how to comply with these heuristics (see Silverman, 1993, 1997a, 1997b). Similarly, James Scheurich (1997) is openly critical of both positivistic and interpretive interviewing, as they are both based on modernist assumptions. Rather than being a process "by the numbers," for Scheurich, interviewing (and its language) are "persistently slippery, unstable, and ambiguous from person to person, from situation to situation, from time to time" (p. 62).

Accessing the setting. How do we "get in"? That, of course, varies according to the group one is attempting to study. One may have to disrobe and casually stroll in the nude if doing a study of nude beaches (Douglas & Rasmussen, 1977), or one may have to buy a huge motorbike and frequent seedy bars in certain locations if attempting to befriend and study the Hell's Angels (Thompson, 1985). The different ways and attempts to "get in" vary tremendously, but they all share the common goal of gaining access to the setting. Sometimes there is no setting per se, as when Fontana (1977) attempted to study poor elderly on the streets and had to gain access anew with each and every interviewee.

Understanding the language and culture of the respondents. Rosalie Wax (1960) gives perhaps the most poignant description of learning the language and culture of the respondents in her study of "disloyal" Japanese in concentration camps in the United States between 1943 and 1945. Wax had to overcome a number of language and cultural problems in her study. Although respondents may be fluent in the language of the interviewer, there are different ways of saying things and, indeed, certain things that should not be said at all, linking language and cultural manifestations. Wax makes this point:

I remarked that I would like to see the letter. The silence that fell on the chatting group was almost palpable, and the embarrassment of the hosts was painful to see. The *faux pas* was not asking to see a letter, for letters were passed about rather freely. It rested on the fact that one did not give a Caucasian a letter in which the "disloyal" statement of a friend might be expressed. (p. 172)

Some researchers, especially in anthropological interviews, tend to rely on interpreters, and thus become vulnerable to added layers of meanings, biases, and interpretations, which may lead to disastrous misunderstandings (Freeman, 1983). At times, specific jargon, such as the medical metalanguage of physicians, may be a code that is hard for nonmembers to understand.

Deciding on how to present oneself. Do we present ourselves as representatives from academia studying medical students (Becker, 1956)? Do we approach the interview as a woman-to-woman discussion (Spradley, 1979)? Do we "dress down" to look like the respondents (Fontana, 1977; Thompson, 1985)? Do we represent the colonial culture (Malinowsky, 1922), or do we humbly present ourselves as "learners" (Wax, 1960)? This decision is very important, because once the interviewer's presentational self is "cast," it leaves a profound impression on the respondents and has great influence over the success (or lack of it) of the study. Sometimes, inadvertently, the researcher's presentational self may be misrepresented, as John Johnson (1976) discovered in studying a welfare office, when some of the employees assumed he was a "spy" for management despite his best efforts to the contrary.

Locating an informant. The researcher must find an insider, a member of the group studied, who is willing to be an informant and act as a guide and a translator of cultural mores and, at times, jargon or language. Although the researcher can conduct interviews without an informant, he or she can save much time and avoid mistakes if a good informant becomes available. The "classic" sociological informant is Doc in William Foote Whyte's *Street Corner Society* (1943). Without Doc's help and guidance, it is doubtful that Whyte would have been able to access his subjects at the level he did. Very instructive is Paul Rabinow's (1977) discussion of his relationship with his main informant, Abd al-Malik ben Lahcen. Malik acted as a translator but also provided Rabinow with access to the cultural ways of the subjects, and by his actions provided Rabinow with insights into the vast differences between a University of Chicago researcher and a native Moroccan.

Gaining trust. Survey researchers asking respondents whether they would or would not favor the establishment of a nuclear dump in their state (Frey, 1993) do not have too much work to do in the way of gaining trust; respondents have opinions about nuclear dumps and are very willing to express them, sometimes forcefully. But it is clearly a different story if one wants to ask about a person's frequency of sexual intercourse or preferred method of birth control. The interviewer needs to establish some trust with the respondents (Cicourel, 1974). Paul Rasmussen (1989) had to spend months as a "wallflower" in the waiting room of a massage parlor before any of the masseuses gained enough trust in him to divulge to him, in unstructured interviews, the nature of their "massage" relations with clients. Gaining trust is essential to the success of the interviews and, once gained, trust can still be very fragile. Any faux pas by the researcher may destroy days, weeks, or months of painfully gained trust.

Establishing rapport. Because the goal of unstructured interviewing is *understanding*, it is paramount that the researcher establish rapport with respondents; that is, the researcher must be able to take the role of the respondents and attempt to see the situation from their viewpoint, rather than superimpose his or her world of academia and preconceptions upon them. Although a close rapport with the respondents opens the doors to more informed research, it may create problems as the researcher may become a spokesperson for the group studied, losing his or her distance and objectivity, or may "go native" and become a member of the group and forgo his or her academic role. At times, what the researcher may feel is good rapport turns out not to be, as Thompson (1985) found out in a nightmarish way when he was subjected to a brutal beating by the Hell's Angels just as his study of them was coming to a close. At the other end of the spectrum, some researchers may never feel they have established rapport with their subjects. Malinowski (1967/1989), for example, always mistrusted the motives of the natives and at times was troubled by their brutish sensuality or angered by their outright lying or deceptions: "After lunch I [carried] yellow calico and spoke about the *baloma*. I made a small *sagali, Navavile*. I was *fed up* with the *niggers*" (p. 154).

Collecting empirical materials. Being out in the field does not afford researchers the luxury of video cameras, soundproof rooms, and high-quality recording equipment. Lofland (1971) provides detailed information on doing and writing up interviews and on the types of field notes researchers ought to take and how to organize them. Yet field-workers often must make do; their "tales" of their methods range from holding a miniature tape recorder as inconspicuously as possible to taking mental notes and then rushing to the privacy of a bathroom to jot notes down, on toilet papers at times. We agree with Lofland that regardless of the circumstances, researchers ought to (a) take notes regularly and promptly: (b) write everything down, no matter how unimportant it may seem at the time; (c) try to be as inconspicuous as possible in note taking; and (d) analyze their notes frequently.

◆ Other Types of Unstructured Interviewing

We consider the issues of interpreting and reporting empirical material later in this chapter. In this section, we briefly outline some different types of unstructured interviews.

Oral History

The oral history differs from other unstructured interviews in purpose, but not methodologically. The oral collection of historical materials goes back to ancient times, but its modern-day formal organization can be traced to 1948, when Allan Nevins began the Oral History Project at Columbia University (Starr, 1984, p. 4). Oral history captures a variety of forms of life, from common folks talking about their jobs in Studs Terkel's *Working* (1975) to the historical recollections of president Harry Truman in Merle Miller's *Plain Speaking* (1974; see Starr, 1984). Often, oral history transcripts are not published, but many may be found in libraries, silent memoirs waiting for someone to rummage through them and bring their testimony to life. Recently, oral history has found great popularity among feminists (Gluck & Patai, 1991), who see it as a way to understand and bring forth the history of women in a culture that has traditionally relied on masculine interpretation: "Refusing to be rendered historically voiceless any longer, women are creating a new history—using our own voices and experiences" (Gluck, 1984, p. 222).

Relevant to the study of oral history (and, in fact, to all interviewing) is the study of memory and its relation to recall. For instance, Barry Schwartz (1999) has examined the ages at which we recall critical episodes in our lives; he concludes that "biographical memory . . . is better understood as a social process" and that "as we look back, we find ourselves remembering our lives in terms of our experience with others" (p. 15; see also Schwartz, 1996). Carolyn Ellis (1991) has resorted to the use of "sociological introspection" to reconstruct biographical episodes of her past life. Notable among Ellis's works in this genre is her reconstruction of her 9-year relationship with her partner, Gene Weinstein, in which she describes the emotional negotiations the two of them went through as they coped with his downward-spiraling health, until the final negotiation with death (Ellis, 1995).

Creative Interviewing

Close to oral history, but used more conventionally as a sociological tool, is Jack Douglas's (1985) "creative interviewing." Douglas argues against "how-to" guides to conducting interviews because unstructured interviews take place in the largely situational everyday worlds of members of society. Thus interviewing and interviewers must necessarily be creative, forget how-to rules, and adapt themselves to the ever-changing situations they face. Similar to oral historians, Douglas sees interviewing as collecting oral reports from the members of society. In creative interviewing, these reports go well beyond the length of conventional unstructured interviews and may become "life histories," with interviewing taking place in multiple sessions over many days with the subject(s).

Postmodern Interviewing

Douglas's concern with the important role played by the interviewer qua human being, which is also shared by feminist oral historians, became a paramount element in the interviewing approaches of postmodern anthropologists and sociologists in the mid-1980s. Marcus and Fischer (1986) address ethnography at large, but their discussion is germane to unstructured interviewing because, as we have seen, such interviewing constitutes the major way of collecting data in fieldwork. Marcus and Fischer voice reflexive concerns about the ways in which the researcher influences the study, both in the methods of data collection and in the techniques of reporting findings; this concern leads to new ways to conduct interviews, in the hope of minimizing, if not eliminating, interviewer influence. One such way is *polyphonic* interviewing, in which the voices of the subjects are recorded with minimal influence from the researcher and are not collapsed together and reported as one, through the interpretation of the researcher. Instead, the multiple perspectives of the various subjects are reported and differences and problems encountered are discussed,

rather than glossed over (see Krieger, 1983). *Interpretive* interactionism follows in the footsteps of creative and polyphonic interviewing, but, borrowing from James Joyce, adds a new element, that of epiphanies, which Denzin (1989a) describes as "those interactional moments that leave marks on people's lives [and] have the potential for creating transformational experiences for the person" (p. 15). Thus the topic of inquiry becomes dramatized by the focus on existential moments in people's lives, hopefully producing richer and more meaningful data. Finally, as postmodernists seek new ways of understanding and reporting data, we wish to note the concept of *oralysis,* which refers "to the ways in which oral forms, derived from everyday life, are, with the recording powers of video, applied to the analytical tasks associated with literate forms" (Ulmer, 1989, p. xi). In oralysis, the traditional product of interviewing, talk, is coupled with the visual, providing, according to Ulmer (1989), a product consonant with a society that is dominated by the medium of television.

◆ Gendered Interviews

The housewife goes into a well-stocked store to look for a frying pan. Her thinking probably does not proceed exactly this way, but it is helpful to think of the many possible two-way choices she might make: Cast iron or aluminum? Thick or thin? Metal or wooden handle? Covered or not? Deep or shallow? Large or small? This brand or that? Reasonable or too high in price? To buy or not? Cash or charge? Have it delivered or carry it. . . . The two-way question is simplicity itself when it comes to recording answers and tabulating them. (Payne, 1951, pp. 55-56)

The above quote represents the prevalent paternalistic attitude toward women in interviewing (see Oakley, 1981, p. 39) as well as the paradigmatic concern with coding answers and therefore with presenting limited, dichotomous choices. Apart from a tendency to be condescending to women, the traditional interview paradigm does not account for gendered differ-

658 ◆ METHODS OF COLLECTING AND ANALYZING EMPIRICAL MATERIALS

ences. In fact, Babbie's classic text *The Practice of Social Research* (1992) briefly references gender only three times and says nothing about the influence of gender on interviews. As Ann Oakley (1981) cogently points out, both the interviewers and the respondents are considered faceless and invisible, and they must be if the paradigmatic assumption of gathering value-free data is to be maintained. Yet, as Denzin (1989a, p. 116) tells us, "gender filters knowledge"; that is, the sex of the interviewer and that of the respondent do make a difference, as the interview takes place within the cultural boundaries of a paternalistic social system in which masculine identities are differentiated from feminine ones.

In the typical interview there exists a hierarchical relation, with the respondent being in the subordinate position. The interviewer is instructed to be courteous, friendly, and pleasant:

> The interviewer's manner should be friendly, courteous, conversational and unbiased. He should be neither too grim nor too effusive; neither too talkative nor too timid. The idea should be to put the respondent at ease, *so that he will talk freely and fully.* (Selltiz, Jahoda, Deutsch, & Cook, 1965, p. 576; emphasis added)

Yet, as the last above-quoted line shows, this demeanor is a ruse to gain the trust and confidence of the respondent without reciprocating those feelings in any way. Interviewers are not to give their own opinions and are to evade direct questions. What seems to be a conversation is really a one-way pseudoconversation, raising the ethical dilemma (Fine, 1983-1984) inherent in the study of people for opportunistic reasons. When the respondent is female, the interview presents added problems, because the preestablished format directed at information relevant for the study tends both to ignore the respondent's own concerns and to curtail any attempts to digress and elaborate. This format also stymies any revelation of personal feelings and emotions.

Warren (1988) discusses problems of gender in both anthropological and sociological fieldwork, and many of these are found as well in the ethnographic interview. Some of these problems are the traditional ones of entrée and trust,

which may be heightened by the sex of the interviewer, especially in highly sex-segregated societies: "I never witnessed any ceremonies that were barred to women. Whenever I visited compounds I sat with the women while the men gathered in the parlors or in front of the compound. . . . I never entered any of the places where men sat around to drink beer or palm wine and to chat" (Sudarkasa, 1986; quoted in Warren, 1988, p. 16).

Solutions to the problem have been to view the female anthropologist as androgyne or to grant her honorary male status for the duration of her research. Warren (1988) also points to some advantages of a researcher's being female and therefore seen as harmless or invisible. Other problems are associated with the researcher's status and race and with the context of the interview; again, these problems are magnified for female researchers in a paternalistic world. Female interviewers at times face the added burden of sexual overtures or covert sexual hassle (Warren, 1988, p. 33).

Feminist researchers have suggested ways to circumvent the traditional interviewing paradigm. Oakley (1981) notes that interviewing is a masculine paradigm, embedded in a masculine culture and stressing masculine traits while at the same time excluding traits such as sensitivity, emotionality, and others that are culturally viewed as feminine traits. There is, however, a growing reluctance, especially among female researchers (Oakley, 1981; Reinharz, 1992; Smith, 1987), to continue interviewing women as "objects," with little or no regard for them as individuals. Although this reluctance stems from moral and ethical reasons, it is also relevant methodologically. As Oakley (1981) points out, in interviewing there is "no intimacy without reciprocity" (p. 49). Thus the emphasis is shifting to allow the development of a closer relation between interviewer and respondent; researchers are attempting to minimize status differences and are doing away with the traditional hierarchical situation in interviewing. Interviewers can show their human side and answer questions and express feelings. Methodologically, this new approach provides a greater spectrum of responses and greater insight into the lives of respondents—or "participants," to avoid the hierarchical pitfall (Reinharz, 1992, p.22)—because it encourages them to control the sequencing and the language of the interview and also allows them the freedom of open-ended responses (Oakley, 1981; Reinharz, 1992; Smith, 1987). To wit: "Women were always . . . encouraged to 'digress' into details of their personal histories and to recount anecdotes of their working lives. Much important information was gathered in this way" (Yeandle, 1984; quoted in Reinharz, 1992, p. 25).

Rosanna Hertz (1997a) makes the self of the researcher visible and suggests that it is only one of many selves the researcher takes to the field. She asserts that interviewers need to be reflexive; that is, they need "to have an ongoing conversation about experience while simultaneously living in the moment" (p. viii). By doing so, they will heighten the understanding of differences of ideologies, cultures, and politics between interviewers and interviewees.

Hertz also underscores the importance of "voices"—how we, as authors, express and write our stories, which data we include and which we exclude, whose voices we choose to represent and which we do not. The concern with voices is also found, very powerfully, in a volume edited by Kim Marie Vaz titled *Oral Narrative Research With Black Women* (1997). One of the contributors, Christine Obbo (1997), states:

> This chapter is a modest exercise in giving expression to women's voices and in rescuing their perceptions and experiences from being mere murmurs or backdrop to political, social and cultural happenings. Women's voices have been devalued by male chronicles of cultural history even when the men acknowledge female informants; they are overshadowed by the voice of male authority and ascendance in society. (pp. 42-43)

This commitment to maintaining the integrity of the phenomena and preserving the viewpoint of the subjects, as expressed in their everyday language, is akin to the stand taken by phenomenological and existential sociologies (Douglas & Johnson, 1977; Kotarba & Fontana, 1984) and also reflects the concerns of postmodern ethnographers (Marcus & Fischer, 1986). The differences are (a) the heightened moral concern for subjects/participants, (b) the attempt to redress the male/female hierarchy and existing paternalistic power structure, and (c) the paramount importance placed upon membership, because the effectiveness of male researchers in interviewing female subjects has been largely discredited.

Ruth Behar (1996) addresses the ambiguous nature of the enterprise of interviewing by asking: Where do we locate the researcher in the field? How much do we reveal about ourselves? How do we reconcile our different roles and positions? Behar makes us see that interviewer, writer, respondent, and interview are not clearly distinct entities; rather, they are intertwined in a deeply problematic way.

Some feminist sociologists have gone beyond concerns with interviewing or fieldwork in itself. Laurel Richardson (1992a) is striving for new forms of expression to report her findings and has presented some of her fieldwork in the form of poetry. Patricia Clough (1998) questions the whole enterprise of fieldwork under the current paradigm and calls for a reassessment of the whole sociological enterprise and for a rereading of existing sociological texts in a light that is not marred by a paternalistic bias. Their voices echo the concern of Dorothy Smith (1987), who eloquently states:

> The problem [of a research project] and its particular solution are analogous to those by which fresco painters solved the problems of representing the different temporal moments of a story in the singular space of the wall. The problem is to produce in a two-dimensional space framed as a wall a world of action and movement in time. (p. 281)

A growing number of researchers feel that we cannot isolate gender from other important elements that also "filter knowledge." Among others, Patricia Hill Collins (1990) has written eloquently about the filtering of knowledge through memberships—of being black and female in American culture, in her case. Kath Weston (1998) makes just as powerful a case for sexuality, which, she contends, should not be treated as a compartmentalized subspecialty, because it underlies and is integral to the whole of the social sciences. Clearly, gender, sexuality, and race cannot be considered in isolation; race, class, hierarchy, status, and age (Seidman, 1991) are all part of the complex, yet often ignored, elements that shape interviewing.

◆ Framing and Interpreting Interviews

Aside from the problem of framing real-life events in a two-dimensional space, we face the added problems of how the framing is being done and who is doing the framing. In sociological terms, this means that the type of interviewing selected, the techniques used, and the ways of recording information all come to bear on the results of the study. Additionally, data must be interpreted, and the researcher has a great deal of influence on what part of the data will be reported and how it will be reported.

Framing Interviews

Numerous volumes have been published on the techniques of structured interviewing (see, among others, Babbie, 1992; Bradburn et al., 1979; Gorden, 1980; Kahn & Cannel, 1957). There is also a voluminous literature on group interviewing, especially in marketing and survey research (for a comprehensive review of literature in this area, see Stewart & Shamdasani, 1990). The uses of group interviewing have also been linked to qualitative sociology (Morgan, 1988). Unstructured interviewing techniques have been covered thoroughly (Denzin, 1989b; Lofland, 1971; Lofland & Lofland, 1984; Spradley, 1979).

As we have noted, unstructured interviews vary widely, given their informal nature and depending on the nature of the setting, and some eschew the use of any preestablished set of techniques (Douglas, 1985). Yet there are techniques involved in interviewing whether the inter-

viewer is just being "a nice person" or is following a format. Techniques can be varied to meet various situations, and varying one's techniques is known as using tactics. Traditionally, the researcher is involved in an informal conversation with the respondent, thus he or she must maintain a tone of "friendly" chat while trying to remain close to the guidelines of the topic of inquiry he or she has in mind. The researcher begins by "breaking the ice" with general questions and gradually moves on to more specific ones, while also—as inconspicuously as possible—asking questions intended to check the veracity of the respondent's statements. The researcher should avoid getting involved in a "real" conversation in which he or she answers questions asked by the respondent or provides personal opinions on the matters discussed. A researcher can avoid "getting trapped" by shrugging off the relevance of his or her opinions ("It doesn't matter how I feel, it's your opinion that's important") or by feigning ignorance ("I really don't know enough about this to say anything; you're the expert"). Of course, as we have seen in the case of gendered interviewing, the researcher may reject these techniques and "come down" to the level of the respondent to engage in a "real" conversation, with give-and-take and shared empathic understanding.

The use of language, particularly the use of specific terms, is important in the creation of a "sharedness of meanings" in which both interviewer and respondent understand the contextual nature of specific referents. For instance, in studying nude beaches, Douglas and Rasmussen (1977) discovered that the term *nude beach virgin* had nothing to do with chastity; rather, it referred to the fact that a person's buttocks were white, thus indicating to others that he or she was a newcomer to the nude beach. Language is also important in delineating the type of question (broad, narrow, leading, instructive, and so on).

Nonverbal techniques are also important in interviewing. There are four basic modes of nonverbal communication:

Proxemic communication is the use of interpersonal space to communicate attitudes, *chronemics* communication is the use of pacing of speech and length of silence in conversation, *kinesic* communication includes any body movements or postures, and *paralinguistic* communication includes all the variations in volume, pitch and quality of voice. (Gorden, 1980, p. 335)

All four of these modes represent important techniques for the researcher; in addition, the researcher should carefully note and record respondents' uses of these modes, for interview data are more than verbal records and should include, as much as possible, nonverbal features of the interaction. Finally, techniques vary with the groups being interviewed; for instance, interviewing a group of children requires a different approach from the one an interviewer might use when interviewing a group of elderly widows (Lopata, 1980).

Interpreting Interviews

Many studies using unstructured interviews are not reflexive enough about the interpreting process; common platitudes proclaim that the data speak for themselves, that the researcher is neutral, unbiased, and "invisible." The data reported tend to flow nicely, there are no contradictory data and no mention of what data were excluded and/or why. Improprieties never happen and the main concern seems to be the proper, if unreflexive, filing, analyzing, and reporting of events. But anyone who has engaged in fieldwork knows better; no matter how organized the researcher may be, he or she slowly becomes buried under an increasing mountain of field notes, transcripts, newspaper clippings, and audiotapes. Traditionally, readers were presented with the researcher's interpretation of the data, cleaned and streamlined and collapsed in rational, noncontradictory accounts. More recently, sociologists have come to grips with the reflexive, problematic, and, at times, contradictory nature of data and with the tremendous, if unspoken, influence of the researcher as author. What Van Maanen (1988) calls "confessional style" began in earnest in the 1970s (see Johnson, 1976) and continues unabated to our day, in a soul cleansing by researchers of problematic feelings and sticky situations in the field. Although perhaps somewhat overdone at times, these "confessions" are very valuable, as they make the readers aware of the complex and cumbersome nature of interviewing people in their natural settings and lend a tone of realism and veracity to studies. For example: "Yesterday I slept very late. Got up around 10. The day before I had engaged Omaga, Koupa, and a few others. They didn't come. Again I fell into a rage" (Malinowski, 1967/1989, p. 67).

Showing the human side of the researcher and the problematics of unstructured interviewing has taken new forms in deconstructionism (Derrida, 1976). Here the influence of the author is brought under scrutiny. Thus the text created by the researcher's rendition of events is "deconstructed"; the author's biases and taken-for-granted notions are exposed, and, at times, alternative ways to look at the data are introduced (Clough, 1998).

Postmodern social researchers, as we have seen, attempt to expose and minimize the role of the researcher qua field-worker and qua author. Thus, for instance, Crapanzano (1980) reports Tuhami's accounts, whether they be sociohistorical renditions, dreams, or outright lies, because they all constitute a part of this Morrocan Arab subject's sense of self and personal history. In interviewing Tuhami, Crapanzano learns not only about his subject but about himself:

As Tuhami's interlocutor, I became an active participant in his life history, even though I rarely appear directly in his recitations. Not only did my presence, and my questions, prepare him for the text he was to produce, but they produced what I read as a change of consciousness in him. They produced a change of consciousness in me too. We were both jostled from our assumptions about the nature of the everyday world and ourselves and groped for common reference points within this limbo of interchange. (p. 11)

No longer pretending to be faceless subject and invisible researcher, Tuhami and Crapanzano are portrayed as individual human beings with their own personal histories and idiosyncrasies, and we, the readers, learn about two people and two cultures.

◆ Ethical Considerations

Because the objects of inquiry in interviewing are human beings, researchers must take extreme care to avoid any harm to them. Traditionally, ethical concerns have revolved around the topics of *informed consent* (receiving consent by the subject after having carefully and truthfully informed him or her about the research), *right to privacy* (protecting the identity of the subject), and *protection from harm* (physical, emotional, or any other kind).

No sociologist or other social scientist would dismiss these three ethical concerns. Yet, there are other concerns that are less unanimously upheld. The controversy concerning overt/covert fieldwork is more germane to participant observation, but could include the surreptitious use of tape-recording devices. Warwick (1973) and Douglas (1985) argue for the use of covert methods, because they mirror the deceitfulness of everyday-life reality, whereas others, including Kai Erikson (1967), are vehemently opposed to the study of uninformed subjects.

Another problematic issue stems from the researcher's degree of involvement with the group under study. Whyte (1943) was asked to vote more than once during the same local elections (i.e., to vote illegally) by members of the group he had gained access to, and befriended, gaining their trust. He used "situational ethics," judging the legal infraction to be minor in comparison to the loss of his fieldwork if he refused to vote. Thompson (1985) was faced with a more serious possible legal breach. He was terrified of having to witness one of the alleged rapes for which the Hell's Angels had become notorious, but, as he reports, none took place during his research. The most famous, and widely discussed, case of questionable ethics in qualitative sociology took place during Laud Humphreys's research for *Tearoom Trade* (1970). Humphreys studied homosexual encounters in public restrooms in parks ("tearooms") by acting as a lookout ("watchqueen"). Although this fact in itself may be seen as ethically incorrect, it is the following one that has raised many academic eyebrows.

Humphreys, unable to interview the men in the "tearoom," recorded their cars' license-plate numbers, which led him to find their residences with the help of police files. He then interviewed many of the men in their homes without being recognized as having been their "watchqueen."

Another ethical problem is raised by the veracity of the reports made by researchers. For example, Whyte's (1943) famous study of Italian street corner men in Boston has come under severe scrutiny (Boelen, 1992), as some have alleged that Whyte portrayed the men in demeaning ways that did not reflect their visions of themselves. Whyte's case is still unresolved, but it does illustrate the delicate issue of ethical decisions in the field and in reporting field notes, even more than 50 years later (Richardson, 1992b).

A growing number of scholars, as we have seen (Oakley, 1981), feel that most of traditional in-depth interviewing is unethical, whether wittingly or unwittingly. The techniques and tactics of interviewing, they say, are really ways of manipulating the respondents while treating them as objects or numbers rather than individual human beings. Should the quest for objectivity supersede the human side of those we study? Consider the following:

> One day while doing research at the convalescent center, I was talking to one of the aides while she was beginning to change the bedding of one of the patients who had urinated and soaked the bed. He was the old, blind, ex-wrestler confined in the emergency room. Suddenly, the wrestler decided he was not going to cooperate with the aide and began striking violently at the air about him, fortunately missing the aide. Since nobody else was around, I had no choice but to hold the patient pinned down to the bed while the aide proceeded to change the bedding. It was not pleasant: The patient was squirming and yelling horrible threats at the top of his voice; the acid smell of urine was nauseating; I was slowly loosing my grip on the much stronger patient, while all along feeling horribly like Chief Bromden when he suffocates the lobotomized Mac Murphy in Ken Kesey's novel. *But there was no choice, one just could not sit back and take notes while the patient tore apart the aide.* (Fontana, 1977, p. 187; emphasis added)

Clearly, as we move forward with sociology, we cannot, to paraphrase what Herbert Blumer said so many years ago, let the methods dictate our images of human beings. As Punch (1986) suggests, as field-workers we need to exercise common sense and responsibility, and, we would like to add, to our subjects first, to the study next, and to ourselves last.

◆ New Trends in Interviewing

The latest trends in interviewing have come some distance from structured questions; we have reached the point of interview as negotiated text. Ethnographers have realized for quite some time that researchers are not invisible, neutral entities; rather, they are part of the interactions they seek to study and influence those interactions. At last, interviewing is being brought in line with ethnography. There is a growing realization that interviewers are not the mythical, neutral tools envisioned by survey research. Interviewers are increasingly seen as active participants in interactions with respondents, and interviews are seen as negotiated accomplishments of both interviewers and respondents that are shaped by the contexts and situations in which they take place. As Schwandt (1997) notes, "It has become increasingly common in qualitative studies to view the interview as a form of discourse between two or more speakers or as a linguistic event in which the meanings of questions and responses are contextually grounded and jointly constructed by interviewer and respondent" (p. 79). We are beginning to realize that we cannot lift the results of interviews out of the contexts in which they were gathered and claim them as objective data with no strings attached.

Interview as Negotiated Accomplishment

Let us briefly recap the two traditional approaches to the interview, following Holstein and Gubrium (1995, 1997). These authors use

Jean Converse and Howard Schuman's *Conversations at Random* (1974) as an exemplar of the interview as used in survey research. In this context the interviewer is carefully instructed to remain as passive as possible, so as to reduce his or her influence—the scope of the interviewer's function is to access respondents' answers. This is a *rational* type of interviewing; it assumes that there is an objective knowledge out there and that if one is skilled enough one can access it, just as a skilled surgeon can remove a kidney from a donor and use it in a different context (e.g., for a patient awaiting transplant).

Holstein and Gubrium (1995, 1997) regard Jack Douglas's (1985) creative interviewing as a romanticist type of interviewing. Creative interviewing is based on *feelings*; it assumes that researchers, qua interviewers, need to "get to know" respondents beneath their rational facades, and that researchers can reach respondents' deep wells of emotion by engaging them, by sharing feelings and thoughts with them. Douglas's interviewer is certainly more active and far less neutral than Converse and Schuman's, but the assumptions are still the same: that it is the *skills* of interviewers that will provide access to knowledge and that there is a *core knowledge* that researchers can access.

Holstein and Gubrium finally consider the new type of interviewing—well, "new" isn't exactly accurate, given that their reference for this is the work of Ithiel de Sola Pool, published in 1957. To wit: "Every interview . . . is an interpersonal drama with a developing plot" (Pool, 1957, p. 193; quoted in Holstein & Gubrium, 1995, p. 14). Holstein and Gubrium (1995) go on to note that thus far we have focused on the *whats* of the interview, the substantive findings, and it is time that we pay attention to the *hows* of the interview—the contexts, particular situations, nuances, manners, people involved, and so on in which interview interactions take place. This concept harks back to ethnomethodology, according to Holstein and Gubrium (1995): "To say that the interview is an interpersonal drama with a developing plot is part of a broader claim that reality is an ongoing, interpretive accomplishment" (p. 16). Garfinkel, Sacks, and others clearly stated in the late 1960s that reality is an ever-changing, ongoing accomplishment based on the practical reasoning of the members of society. It is time to consider the interview as a practical production, the meaning of which is accomplished at the intersection of the interaction of interviewer and respondent.

In a later essay, Gubrium and Holstein (1998) continue their argument by looking at interviews as storytelling, which they see as a practical production used by members of society to accomplish coherence in their accounts. Once more they encourage us to examine the *hows* as well as the *whats* of storytelling. Similarly, Madan Sarup (1996) tells us:

> Each narrative has two parts; a story (*histoire*) and a discourse (*discourse*). The story is the content, or chain of events. The story is the "what" in a narrative, the discourse is the "how." The discourse is rather like a plot, how the reader becomes aware of what happened, the order of appearance of the events. (p. 17)

Gubrium and Holstein are not alone in advocating this reflexive approach to interviews. Both David Silverman (1993) and Robert Dingwall (1997) credit Cicourel's classic work *Method and Measurement in Sociology* (1964) with pointing to the interview as a social encounter. Dingwall (1997) notes:

> If the interview is a social encounter, then, logically, it must be analyzed in the same way as any other social encounter. The products of an interview are the outcome of a socially situated activity where the responses are passed through the role-playing and impression management of both the interviewer and the respondent. (p. 56)

I. E. Seidman (1991) discusses interviewing as a relationship by relying upon a principal intellectual antecedent of the ethnomethodologist Alfred Schutz (1967). Seidman analyzes the interviewer-respondent relation in terms of Schutz's "I-thou" relation, in which the two share a reciprocity of perspective and, by both being "thou" oriented, create a "we" relationship. Thus the respondent is no longer "an object or a type" (Seidman, 1991, p. 73) but becomes an equal participant in the interaction.

The Problematics of New Approaches

Some of the proponents of the ethnomethodologically informed interview are critical of interactionist as well as positivist interview methods. Dingwall (1997), as well as others, speaks of the romantic movement in ethnography (and interviewing)—the idea that the nearer we come to the respondent, the closer we are to apprehending the "real self." This assumption neglects the fact that the self is a process, ever negotiated and accomplished in the interaction. Dingwall also faults the "postmodern" turn; that is, if there is no real self, there is no real world and I can create one of my own. Finally, he is troubled by the "crusading" nature of the romantics and asks, "What is the value of a scholarly enterprise that is more concerned with being 'right on' than with being right?" (p. 64).

In a similar vein, Atkinson and Silverman (1997) reject the postmodern notion of "polyphonic voices," correctly noting that interviewer and respondent collaborate together to create an essentially monologic view of reality. This same rejection could be made using Schutz's (1967) argument—that is, "I" and "thou" create a unified "we," not two separate versions of it.

Ethnomethodologically informed interviewing is not, however, immune from criticism itself. Schutz assumes a reciprocity of perspective that may not exist. Granted, in our interview society we all know the commonsense routines and ground rules of interviewing, but in other societies this may not be the case. Isabel Bowler (1997) attempted to interview Pakistani women about their experience with maternity services and found a total lack of understanding of the value of social research and interviewing: "I had told them that I was writing a book on my findings. Yams, who spoke the better English, translated this with a look of disbelief on her face, and then they both dissolved into laughter. The hospitals were very good. There weren't any problems. All was well" (p. 72). Bowler was forced to conclude that interviewing may not work where there is no "shared notion of the process of research" (p. 66).

Silverman (1993) envisions a different problem. He seems to feel that some ethnomethodologists have suspended their interest in substantive concerns of everyday life, claiming that they cannot address them until they know more about the ways (methods) in which these realities are accomplished. He notes, "Put simply, according to one reading of Cicourel, we would focus on the conversational skills of the participants rather than on the content of what they are saying and its relation to the world outside the interview" (p. 98).

Cicourel (1970) states that sociologists need to outline a workable model of the actor before engaging in the study of self and society. Garfinkel held similar beliefs. For instance, in his famous study of a transsexual, Agnes, Garfinkel (1967) was examining the routines by which societal members pass as males or females; he had little or no interest in issues of transsexuality per se. Thus it would follow that, according to Silverman's reading of ethnomethodology, we should learn the conversational methods before attempting to learn substantive matters in interviewing.

Future Directions

To borrow from Gubrium and Holstein (1997): "Where do we go from here?" (p. 97). We share with these two authors a concern with appreciating the new horizons of postmodernism while simultaneously remaining conservatively committed to the empirical description of everyday life. Gubrium and Holstein (1998) introduce a technique they call "analytic bracketing" to deal with the multiple levels of interviewing (and ethnography):

> We may focus, for example, on *how* a story is being told, while temporarily deferring our concern for the various *whats* that are involved—for example, the substance, structure, or plot of the story, the context within which it is told, or the audience to which it is accountable. We can later return to these issues. (p. 165)

The use of this analytic bracketing allows the authors to analyze interviewing in its coherence

and diversity as an event collaboratively achieved, in which product and process are mutually constituted.

A pressing problem in interviewing concerns the kinds of standards we should apply to these new and different types of interviews. To assume absolute relativism is not the solution, for it would lead, in Silverman's (1997b) words, to the "sociology of navel-gazing" (p. 240). Silverman proposes an aesthetics for research; he rejects attempts to use literary forms in sociology: "If I want to read a good poem, why on earth should I turn to a social science journal?" (p. 240). Silverman's critique of interactionist sociology and proposal for aesthetic values seems to focus on the following three points: (a) He attacks the grandiose, political theorizing of British sociology and invokes a return to more modest, more minute goals; (b) he rejects the romanticist notion of equating experience (from the members' viewpoint) with authenticity; and (c) he notes that in sociology we mimic the mass media of the interview society, thus succumbing to the trivial, the kitschy, the gossipy, and the melodramatic and ignoring simplicity and profundity.

Silverman's notion that we should pay attention to minute details in sociological studies, rather than embarking on grandiose, abstract projects, in a way is not dissimilar to Lyotard's appeal for a return to local elements and away from metatheorizing. For Silverman, the "minute" are the small details that go on in front of our eyes in our everyday lives—very similar to Garfinkel's mundane routines, which allow us to sustain the world and interact with each other.

We are in agreement with Silverman that we need to stop deluding ourselves that in our particular method (whichever it may be) we have the key to the understanding of the self. We also agree that it is imperative that we look for new standards, as we are quickly digressing into a new form of the theater of the absurd (without the literary flair, we fear). But we cannot wait to find a model of the methods used by participants in interviews or in everyday life before we proceed; Cicourel's (1970) invariant properties of interaction turned out to be so general as to be of little use to sociological inquiry.

We need to proceed by looking at the substantive concerns of the members of society while simultaneously examining the constructive activities used to produce order in everyday life, and, all along, remaining reflexive about how interviews are accomplished (see Gubrium & Holstein, 1997, 1998). For instance, as Carolyn Baker (1997) points out, a researcher's telling a respondent "I am a mother of three" versus telling her "I am a university professor" accesses different categories and elicits different accounts. We need to move on with sociological inquiry, even though we realize conditions are less than perfect. To paraphrase Robert Solow, as cited by Geertz (1973): Just because complete asepsis is impossible it doesn't mean we may just as well perform surgery in a sewer.

A different kind of future direction for interviewing stems largely from the new feminist interviewing practices. Traditional interview has painstakingly attempted to maintain neutrality and achieve objectivity, and has kept the role of the interviewer as invisible as possible. Feminists, instead, are rebelling at the practice of *exploiting* respondents and wish to use interviewing for ameliorative purposes. To wit: "As researchers with a commitment to change, we must decenter ourselves from the 'ivory tower' and construct more participatory, democratic practices. *We must keep people and politics at the center of our research*" (Benmayor, 1991, pp. 172-173; emphasis added). Denzin (1989a) refers to this approach as the "feminist, communitarian ethical model" (see also Lincoln, 1995) and tells us:

> The feminist, communitarian researcher does not invade the privacy of others, use informed consent forms, select subjects randomly, or measure research designs in term of their validity. This framework presumes a researcher who builds collaborative, reciprocal, trusting, and friendly relations with those studied. . . . It is also understood that those studied have claims of ownership over any material that are produced in the research process, including field notes.

Combining the roles of the scholar and the feminist may be problematic and, at times, may lead to conflict if the researcher has a different political orientation than that of the people studied (Wasserfall, 1993), but this approach may also be very rewarding in allowing the researcher to see positive results stemming from the research (see Gluck, 1991).

Electronic Interviewing

Another direction currently being taken in interviewing is related to the changing technologies available. The reliance on the interview as a means of information gathering has most recently expanded to electronic outlets, with questionnaires being administered via fax, electronic mail, and Web site. Estimates suggest that nearly 50% of all households have computers, and nearly half of these utilize the Internet. Software is now available that allows researchers to schedule and archive interview data gathered via chat-room interviews. The limited population of potential respondents with access to computers makes general-population surveys infeasible, but electronic interviewing can reach 100% of some specialized populations (Schaefer & Dillman, 1998).

It is now possible to engage in "virtual interviewing," in which Internet connections are used synchronously or asynchronously to obtain information. The advantages include low cost, as the result of no telephone or interviewer charges, and speed of return. Of course, face-to-face interaction is eliminated, as is the possibility, for both interviewer and respondent, of reading nonverbal behavior or of cuing from gender, race, age, class, and other personal characteristics. Thus, establishing an interviewer-interviewee "relationship" and "living the moment" while gathering information (Hertz, 1997a) is difficult, if not impossible. Internet surveys make it easy for respondents to manufacture fictional social realities without anyone knowing the difference (Markham, 1998). Of course, interviewers can also deceive respondents by claiming experiences or characteristics they do not have in hopes of establishing better rapport. They can feign responses for the same purpose by claiming "false nonverbals," such as telling respondents that they "laughed" or "were pained" by particular comments.

Markham (1998), in her autoethnography of Internet interviewing, reports that electronic interviews take longer than their traditional counterparts and that responses are more cryptic and less in depth, but the interviewer has more time to phrase follow-up questions or probes properly.

It is also virtually impossible to preserve anonymity in Internet e-mail surveys, but chat rooms and similar sites do permit the use of pseudonyms. Although electronic interviews are currently used primarily for quantitative research and usually employ structured questionnaires, it is only a matter of time before researchers adapt these techniques to qualitative work, just as they have adapted electronic techniques of data analysis. For example, Markham immersed herself in the process of engaging with various electronic or Internet formats (i.e., chat rooms, listservs) to interview other participants and to document her journey in the virtual world, learning the experience of cyberspace and the meaning participants attached to their on-line lifestyles. She asks an intriguing question: "Can I have a self where my body does not exist?" (p. 8).

The future may see considerable ethnography by means of computer-mediated communication, where virtual space rather than a living room or a workplace is the setting of the interview. It remains to be seen whether electronic interviewing will allow researchers to obtain "thick descriptions" or accounts of subjective experiences, and whether such interviewing will provide the "process context" so important to qualitative interviews. In addition, researchers conducting such interviewing can never be sure they are receiving answers from desired or eligible respondents. Interviewing via the Internet is so prominent today that researchers are studying its effects on response quality. Schaefer and Dillman (1998), for example, found that e-mail surveys achieved similar response rates to mail surveys but yielded better-quality data in terms of item completion and more detailed responses to open-ended questions.

There are clearly many unanswered questions and problems related to the use of elec-

tronic interviewing. This mode of interviewing will obviously increase in the forthcoming millennium, as people rely increasingly on electronic modes of communication. But just how much Internet communication will displace face-to-face interviewing is a matter that only time will tell.

◆ Conclusion

In this chapter we have examined the interview, from structured types to interview as negotiated text. We have outlined the history of interviewing, with its qualitative and quantitative origins. We have looked at structured, group, and various types of unstructured interviewing. We have examined the importance of gender in interviewing and the ways in which framing and interpreting affect interviews. We have examined the importance of ethics in interviewing, and, finally we have discussed the latest trends in interviewing.

We have included discussion of the whole gamut of interviews, despite the fact that this book is concerned with qualitative research, because we believe that researchers must be cognizant of all the various types of interviews if they are to gain a clear understanding of interviewing. Clearly, certain types of interviewing are better suited to particular kinds of situations, and researchers *must be aware of the implications, pitfalls, and problems of the types of interviews they choose.* If we wish to find out how many people oppose the establishment of a nuclear repository in their area, a structured type of interview, such as that used in survey research, is the best tool; we can quantify and code the responses and use mathematical models to explain our findings. If we are interested in opinions about a given product, a focus group interview will provide us with the most efficient results, whereas if we wish to know about the lives of Palestinian women in the resistance (Gluck, 1991), we need to interview them at length and in depth in an unstructured way. In the first example used above, and perhaps in the second, we can speak in the formal language of scientific rigor and verifiability of findings; in the third example we can speak of understanding a negotiated way of life.

More scholars are realizing that to pit one type of interviewing against another is futile, a leftover from the paradigmatic quantitative/qualitative hostility of past generations. Thus an increasing number of researchers are using multimethod approaches to achieve broader and often better results. This multimethod approach, referred to as *triangulation* (Denzin, 1989b; Flick, 1998), allows researchers to use different methods in different combinations. For instance, group interviewing has long been used to complement survey research and is now being used to complement participant observation (Morgan, 1988). Human beings are complex, and their lives are ever changing; the more methods we use to study them, the better our chances to gain some understanding of how they construct their lives and the stories they tell us about them.

The brief journey we have taken through the world of interviewing should allow us to be better informed and perhaps more sensitized to the problematics of asking questions for sociological reasons. We must remember that each individual has his or her own social history and an individual perspective on the world. Thus we cannot take our task for granted. As Oakley (1981) notes, "Interviewing is rather like a marriage: everybody knows what it is, an awful lot of people do it, and yet behind each closed front door there is a world of secrets" (p. 41). She is quite correct—we all think we know how to ask questions and talk to people, from common, everyday folks to highly qualified quantophrenic experts. Yet to learn about people we must treat them as people, and they will work with us to help us create accounts of their lives. As long as many researchers continue to treat respondents as unimportant, faceless individuals whose only contribution is to fill one more boxed response, the answers we, as researchers, get will be commensurable with the questions we ask and the ways we ask them. We are no different from Gertrude Stein, who, on her deathbed, asked her lifelong companion, Alice B. Toklas, "What is the answer?" And when Alice could not bring

herself to speak, Gertrude asked, "In that case, what is the question?"

■ *References*

Adams, R. N., & Preiss, J. J. (Eds.). (1960). *Human organizational research: Field relations and techniques.* Homewood, IL: Dorsey.

Anderson, N. (1923). *The hobo: The sociology of the homeless man.* Chicago: University of Chicago Press.

Atkinson, P., & Silverman, D. (1997). Kundera's *Immortality*: The interview society and the invention of self. *Qualitative Inquiry, 3,* 304-325.

Babbie, E. (1992). *The practice of social research* (6th ed.). Belmont, CA: Wadsworth.

Baker, C. (1997). Membership categorization and interview accounts. In D. Silverman (Ed.), *Qualitative research: Theory, method and practice* (pp. 130-143). London: Sage.

Becker, H. S. (1956). Interviewing medical students. *American Journal of Sociology, 62,* 199-201.

Becker, H. S. (1999). The Chicago school, so-called. *Qualitative Sociology, 22,* 3-12.

Behar, R. (1996). *The vulnerable observer: Anthropology that breaks your heart.* Boston: Beacon.

Benmayor, R. (1991). Testimony, action research, and empowerment: Puerto Rican women and popular education. In S. B. Gluck & D. Patai (Eds.), *Women's words: The feminist practice of oral history* (pp. 159-174). New York: Routledge.

Boelen, W. A. M. (1992). *Street corner society*: Cornerville revisited. *Journal of Contemporary Ethnography, 21,* 11-51.

Bogardus, E. S. (1926). The group interview. *Journal of Applied Sociology, 10,* 372-382.

Booth, C. (1902-1903). *Life and labour of the people in London.* London: Macmillan.

Bowler, I. (1997). Problems with interviewing: Experiences with service providers and clients. In G. Miller & R. Dingwall (Eds.), *Context and method in qualitative research* (pp. 66-76). Thousand Oaks, CA: Sage.

Bradburn, N. M. (1983). Response effects. In P. H. Rossi, J. D. Wright, & A. B. Anderson

(Eds.), *Handbook of survey research* (pp. 289-328). New York: Academic Press.

Bradburn, N. M., Sudman, S., & Associates. (1979). *Improving interview method and questionnaire design*. San Francisco: Jossey-Bass.

Cicourel, A. (1964). *Method and measurement in sociology*. New York: Free Press.

Cicourel, A. (1970). The acquisition of social structure: Toward a developmental sociology of language and meaning. In J. D. Douglas (Ed.), *Understanding everyday life: Toward a reconstruction of social knowledge* (pp. 136-168). Chicago: Aldine.

Cicourel, A. (1974). *Theory and method in a study of Argentine fertility*. New York: John Wiley.

Clough, P. T. (1998). *The end(s) of ethnography: From realism to social criticism* (2nd ed.). New York: Peter Lang.

Collins, P. H. (1990). *Black feminist thought: Knowledge, consciousness, and the politics of empowerment*. New York: Routledge, Chapman & Hall.

Converse, J. M. (1987). *Survey research in the United States: Roots and emergence 1890-1960*. Berkeley: University of California Press.

Converse, J. M., & Schuman, H. (1974). *Conversations at random: Survey research as interviewers see it*. New York: John Wiley.

Crapanzano, V. (1980). *Tuhami: Portrait of a Moroccan*. Chicago: University of Chicago Press.

Denzin, N. K. (1989a). *Interpretive interactionism*. Newbury Park, CA: Sage.

Denzin, N. K. (1989b). *The research act: A theoretical introduction to sociological methods* (3rd ed.). Englewood Cliffs, NJ: Prentice Hall.

Derrida, J. (1976). *Of grammatology* (G. C. Spivak, Trans.). Baltimore: Johns Hopkins University Press.

Desvousges, W. H., & Frey, J. H. (1989). Integrating focus groups and surveys: Examples from environmental risk surveys. *Journal of Official Statistics, 5*, 349-363.

Dingwall, R. (1997). Accounts, interviews, and observations. In G. Miller & R. Dingwall (Eds.), *Context and method in qualitative research* (pp. 51-65). Thousand Oaks, CA: Sage.

Douglas, J. D. (1985). *Creative interviewing*. Beverly Hills, CA: Sage.

Douglas, J. D., & Johnson, J. M. (1977). *Existential sociology*. Cambridge: Cambridge University Press.

Douglas, J. D., & Rasmussen, P. (with Flanagan, C. A.). (1977). *The nude beach*. Beverly Hills, CA: Sage.

Du Bois, W. E. B. (1899). *The Philadelphia Negro: A social study*. Philadelphia: Ginn.

Ellis, C. (1991). Sociological introspection and emotional experience. *Symbolic Interaction, 14*, 23-50.

Ellis, C. (1995). *Final negotiations: A story of love, loss, and chronic illness*. Philadelphia: Temple University Press.

Erikson, K. T. (1967). A comment on disguised observation in sociology. *Social Problems, 14*, 366-373.

Fine, M. (1983-1984). Coping with rape: Critical perspectives on consciousness. *Imagination, Cognition and Personality, 3*, 249-267.

Flick, U. (1998). *An introduction to qualitative research: Theory, method and applications*. London: Sage.

Fontana, A. (1977). *The last frontier: The social meaning of growing old*. Beverly Hills, CA: Sage.

Fontana, A., & Frey, J. H. (1990). Postretirement workers in the labor force. *Work and Occupations, 17*, 355-361.

Fontana, A., & Smith, R. (1989). Alzheimer's disease victims: The "unbecoming" of self and the normalization of competence. *Sociological Perspectives, 32*, 35-46.

Freeman, D. (1983). *Margaret Mead and Samoa: The making and unmaking of an anthropological myth*. Cambridge, MA: Harvard University Press.

Frey, J. H. (1989). *Survey research by telephone* (2nd ed.). Newbury Park, CA: Sage.

Frey, J. H. (1993). Risk perception associated with a high-level nuclear waste repository. *Sociological Spectrum, 13*, 139-151.

Frey, J. H., & Fontana, A. (1991). The group interview in social research. *Social Science Journal, 28*, 175-187.

Garfinkel, H. (1967). *Studies in ethnomethodology*. Englewood Cliffs, NJ: Prentice Hall.

Geertz, C. (1973). Thick description: Toward an interpretive theory of culture. In C. Geertz,

The interpretation of cultures: Selected essays (pp. 3-30). New York: Basic Books.

Glaser, B. G., & Strauss, A. L. (1967). *The discovery of grounded theory: Strategies for qualitative research.* Chicago: Aldine.

Gluck, S. B. (1984). What's so special about women: Women's oral history. In D. Dunaway & W. K. Baum (Eds.), *Oral history: An interdisciplinary anthology* (pp. 221-237). Nashville, TN: American Association for State and Local History.

Gluck, S. B. (1991). Advocacy oral history: Palestinian women in resistance. In S. B. Gluck & D. Patai (Eds.), *Women's words: The feminist practice of oral history* (pp. 205-220). New York: Routledge.

Gluck, S. B., & Patai, D. (Eds.). (1991). *Women's words: The feminist practice of oral history.* New York: Routledge.

Gorden, R. L. (1980). *Interviewing: Strategy, techniques, and tactics.* Homewood, IL: Dorsey.

Gorden, R. L. (1992). *Basic interviewing skills.* Itasca, IL: F. E. Peacock.

Gubrium, J. F., & Holstein, J. A. (1997). *The new language of qualitative method.* New York: Oxford University Press.

Gubrium, J. F., & Holstein, J. A. (1998). Narrative practice and the coherence of personal stories. *Sociological Quarterly, 39,* 163-187.

Harvey, L. (1987). *Myths of the Chicago school of sociology.* Aldershot, England: Avebury.

Hertz, R. (1995). Separate but simultaneous interviewing of husbands and wives: Making sense of their stories. *Qualitative Inquiry, 1,* 429-451.

Hertz, R. (1997a). Introduction: Reflexivity and voice. In R. Hertz (Ed.), *Reflexivity and voice.* Thousand Oaks, CA: Sage.

Hertz, R. (Ed.). (1997b). *Reflexivity and voice.* Thousand Oaks, CA: Sage.

Hertz, R. (1997c). A typology of approaches to child care: The centerpiece of organizing family life for dual-earner couples. *Journal of Family Issues, 18,* 355-385.

Hertz, R., & Ferguson, F. (1997). Kinship strategies and self-sufficiency among single mothers by choice: Postmodern family ties. *Qualitative Sociology, 20*(2), 13-37.

Holstein, J. A., & Gubrium, J. F. (1995). *The active interview.* Thousand Oaks, CA: Sage.

Holstein, J. A., & Gubrium, J. F. (1997). Active interviewing. In D. Silverman (Ed.), *Qualita-*

tive research: Theory, method and practice (pp. 113-129). London: Sage.

Humphreys, L. (1970). *Tearoom trade: Impersonal sex in public places.* Chicago: Aldine.

Hyman, H. H. (1954). *Interviewing in social research.* Chicago: University of Chicago Press.

Johnson, J. (1976). *Doing field research.* New York: Free Press.

Kahn, R., & Cannell, C. F. (1957). *The dynamics of interviewing.* New York: John Wiley.

Kotarba, J. A., & Fontana, A. (Eds.). (1984). *The existential self in society.* Chicago: University of Chicago Press.

Krieger, S. (1983). *The mirror dance: Identity in a women's community.* Philadelphia: Temple University Press.

Kvale, S. (1996). *InterViews: An introduction to qualitative research interviewing.* Thousand Oaks, CA: Sage.

Lincoln, Y. S. (1995). The sixth moment: Emerging problems in qualitative research. In N. K. Denzin (Ed.), *Studies in symbolic interaction: A research annual* (Vol. 19, pp. 37-55). Greenwich, CT: JAI.

Lofland, J. (1971). *Analyzing social settings.* Belmont, CA: Wadsworth.

Lofland, J., & Lofland, L. H. (1984). *Analyzing social settings: A guide to qualitative observation and analysis* (2nd ed.). Belmont, CA: Wadsworth.

Lopata, H. Z. (1980). Interviewing American widows. In W. Shaffir, R. Stebbins, & A. Turowetz (Eds.), *Fieldwork experience: Qualitative approaches to social research* (pp. 68-81). New York: St. Martin's.

Lynd, R. S., & Lynd, H. M. (1929). *Middletown: A study in American culture.* New York: Harcourt, Brace.

Lynd, R. S., & Lynd, H. M. (1937). *Middletown in transition: A study in cultural conflicts.* New York: Harcourt, Brace.

Maccoby, E. E., & Maccoby, N. (1954). The interview: A tool of social science. In G. Lindzey (Ed.), *Handbook of social psychology: Vol. 1. Theory and method* (pp. 449-487). Reading, MA: Addison-Wesley.

Malinowski, B. (1922). *Argonauts of the western Pacific.* New York: E. P. Dutton.

Malinowski, B. (1989). *A diary in the strict sense of the term.* Stanford, CA: Stanford University Press. (Original work published 1967)

Marcus, G. E., & Fischer, M. M. J. (1986). *Anthropology as cultural critique: An experi-*

mental moment in the human sciences. Chicago: University of Chicago Press.

Markham, A. N. (1998). *Life online: Researching real experience in virtual space.* Walnut Creek, CA: AltaMira.

Merton, R. K., Fiske, M., & Kendall, P. L. (1956). *The focused interview.* Glencoe, IL: Free Press.

Merton, R. K., & Lazarsfeld, P. F. (Eds.). (1950). *Continuities in social research: Studies in the scope and method of "The American soldier."* Glencoe, IL: Free Press.

Miller, M. (1974). *Plain speaking: An oral biography of Harry S Truman.* New York: Putnam.

Mishler, E. G. (1986). *Research interviewing: Context and narrative.* Cambridge, MA: Harvard University Press.

Morgan, D. (1988). *Focus groups as qualitative research.* Newbury Park, CA: Sage.

Morgan, D., & Spanish, M. T. (1984). Focus groups: A new tool for qualitative research. *Qualitative Sociology, 7,* 253-270.

Oakley, A. (1981). Interviewing women: A contradiction in terms. In H. Roberts (Ed.), *Doing feminist research* (pp. 30-61). London: Routledge & Kegan Paul.

Obbo, C. (1997). What do women know? . . . As I was saying! In K. M. Vaz (Ed.), *Oral narrative research with black women* (pp. 41-63). Thousand Oaks, CA: Sage.

Parten, M. (1950). *Surveys, polls, and samples.* New York: Harper.

Payne, S. L. (1951). *The art of asking questions.* Princeton, NJ: Princeton University Press.

Pool, I. de S. (1957). A critique of the twentieth anniversary issue. *Public Opinion Quarterly, 21,* 190-198.

Punch, M. (1986). *The politics and ethics of fieldwork.* Newbury Park, CA: Sage.

Rabinow, P. (1977). *Reflections on fieldwork in Morocco.* Berkeley: University of California Press.

Rasmussen, P. (1989). *Massage parlor prostitution.* New York: Irvington.

Reinharz, S. (1992). *Feminist methods in social research.* New York: Oxford University Press.

Richardson, L. (1992a). The poetic representation of lives: Writing a postmodern sociology. In N. K. Denzin (Ed.), *Studies in symbolic interaction: A research annual* (Vol. 13, pp. 19-28). Greenwich, CT: JAI.

Richardson, L. (1992b). Trash on the corner: Ethics and technography. *Journal of Contemporary Ethnography, 21,* 103-119.

Sarup, M. (1996). *Identity, culture and the postmodern world.* Athens: University of Georgia Press.

Schaefer, D. R., & Dillman, D. A. (1998). Development of a standard e-mail methodology. *Public Opinion Quarterly, 62,* 378-397.

Scheurich, J. J. (1997). *Research method in the postmodern.* London: Falmer.

Schutz, A. (1967). *The phenomenology of the social world.* Evanston, IL: Northwestern University Press.

Schwandt, T. A. (1997). *Qualitative inquiry: A dictionary of terms.* Thousand Oaks, CA: Sage.

Schwartz, B. (Ed.). (1996). Collective memory [Special issue]. *Qualitative Sociology, 19*(3).

Schwartz, B. (1999). Memory and the practice of commitment. In B. Glassner & R. Hertz (Eds.), *Qualitative sociology as everyday life.* Thousand Oaks, CA: Sage.

Seidman, I. E. (1991). *Interviewing as qualitative research.* New York: Teachers College Press.

Selltiz, C., Jahoda, M., Deutsch, M., & Cook, S. W. (1965). *Research methods in social relations.* London: Methuen.

Silverman, D. (1993). *Interpreting qualitative data: Strategies for analysing talk, text and interaction.* London: Sage.

Silverman, D. (Ed.). (1997a). *Qualitative research: Theory, method and practice.* London: Sage.

Silverman, D. (1997b). Towards an aesthetics of research. In D. Silverman (Ed.), *Qualitative research: Theory, method and practice* (pp. 239-253). London: Sage.

Singer, E., Frankel, M., & Glassman, M. B. (1983). The effect of interviewer characteristics and expectations on response. *Public Opinion Quarterly, 47,* 68-83.

Singer, E., & Presser, S. (1989). *Survey research methods.* Chicago: University of Chicago Press.

Smith, D. E. (1987). *The everyday world as problematic: A feminist sociology.* Boston: Northeastern University Press.

Spradley, J. P. (1979). *The ethnographic interview.* New York: Holt, Rinehart & Winston.

Spradley, J. P. (1980). *Participant observation.* New York: Holt, Rinehart & Winston.

Starr, L. (1984). Oral history. In D. Dunaway & W. K. Baum (Eds.), *Oral history: An interdisciplinary anthology* (pp. 3-26). Nashville, TN: American Association for State and Local History.

Stewart, D., & Shamdasani, P. (1990). *Focus groups: Theory and practice*. Newbury Park, CA: Sage.

Sudarkasa, N. (1986). In a world of women: Field work in a Yoruba community. In P. Golde (Ed.), *Women in the field: Anthropological experiences* (pp. 167-191). Berkeley: University of California Press.

Terkel, S. (1975). *Working*. New York: Avon.

Thompson, H. (1985). *Hell's Angels*. New York: Ballantine.

Thompson, J., & Demerath, M. J. (1952). Some experiences with the group interview. *Social Forces, 31*, 148-154.

Thrasher, F. M. (1963). *The gang: A study of 1,313 gangs in Chicago*. Chicago: University of Chicago Press. (Original work published 1927)

Ulmer, G. (1989). *Teletheory: Grammatology in an age of video*. New York: Routledge.

Van Maanen, J. (1988). *Tales of the field: On writing ethnography*. Chicago: University of Chicago Press.

Vaz, K. M. (Ed.). (1997). *Oral narrative research with black women*. Thousand Oaks, CA: Sage.

Warren, C. A. B. (1988). *Gender issues in field research*. Newbury Park, CA: Sage.

Warwick, D. P. (1973). Tearoom trade: Means and ends in social research. *Hastings Center Studies, 1*, 27-38.

Wasserfall, R. (1993). Reflexivity, feminism and difference. *Qualitative Sociology, 16*, 23-41.

Wax, R. (1960). Twelve years later: An analysis of field experiences. In R. N. Adams & J. J. Preiss (Eds.), *Human organizational research: Field relations and techniques* (pp. 166-178). Homewood, IL: Dorsey.

Weston, K. (1998). *Long slow burn: Sexuality and social science*. New York: Routledge.

Whyte, W. F. (1943). *Street corner society: The social structure of an Italian slum*. Chicago: University of Chicago Press.

Yeandle, S. (1984). *Women's working lives: Patterns and strategies*. New York: Tavistock.

Young, P. (1966). *Scientific social surveys and research* (4th ed.). Englewood Cliffs, NJ: Prentice Hall.

Zuckerman, H. (1972). Interviewing an ultra-elite. *Public Opinion, 36*, 159-175.

25

RETHINKING OBSERVATION

From Method to Context

♦ Michael V. Angrosino and
Kimberly A. Mays de Pérez

♦ Observation: Basic Assumptions

Observation has been characterized as "the fundamental base of all research methods" in the social and behavioral sciences (Adler & Adler, 1994, p. 389) and as "the mainstay of the ethnographic enterprise" (Werner & Schoepfle, 1987, p. 257). Even studies based on direct interviews employ observational techniques to note body language and other gestural cues that lend meaning to the words of the persons being interviewed. Social scientists are observers both of human activities and of the physical settings in which such activities take place. Some such ob-

servation may take place in a lab or clinic, in which case the activity may be the result of a controlled experiment. On the other hand, it is also possible to conduct observations in settings that are the "natural" loci of those activities. Some scholars have criticized the very concept of the "natural" setting, particularly when fieldwork is conducted in Third World locations (or in domestic inner-city sites) that are the products of inherently "unnatural" colonial relationships (Gupta & Ferguson, 1996c, p. 6), but the designation is still prevalent throughout the literature. In that case, it is proper to speak of "naturalistic observation," or fieldwork, which is the focus of this chapter.

AUTHORS' NOTE: We thank Alvin W. Wolfe and Kathryn Borman for sharing their insights and experiences with us during the preparation of this chapter. We also gratefully acknowledge the advice and constructive criticism of Arthur Bochner, Norman Denzin, Yvonna Lincoln, and Barbara Tedlock.

♦ 673

Observations in natural settings can be rendered as descriptions either through open-ended narrative or through the use of published checklists or field guides (Rossman & Rallis, 1998, p. 137; see Stocking, 1983a, for a historical overview of this dichotomy). In either case, it has generally been assumed that naturalistic observation does not interfere with the people or activities under observation. Most social scientists have long recognized the possibility of the observer's affecting what he or she observes, but careful researchers are nonetheless supposed to adhere to rigorous standards of objective reporting designed to overcome that potential bias. Even cultural anthropologists, who have usually thought of themselves as "participant observers" and who have deliberately set out to achieve a degree of subjective immersion in the cultures they study (Cole, 1983, p. 50; Wolcott, 1995, p. 66), still claim to be able to maintain their scientific objectivity. Failure to do so would mean that they had "gone native," with their work consequently rendered suspect as scientific data (Pelto & Pelto, 1978, p. 69). The achievement of the delicate balance between participation and observation remains the ideal of anthropologists (Stocking, 1983b, p. 8), even though it is no longer "fetishized" (Gupta & Ferguson, 1996c, p. 37). Objectivity remains central to the self-images of most practitioners of the social and behavioral *sciences*. Objective rigor has most often been associated with quantitative research methods, and so important has been the harmonization of empathy and detachment that even those dedicated to qualitative methods have devoted considerable effort to organizing their observational data in the most nearly objective form (i.e., the form that looks most quantitative) for analysis (see, e.g., Altheide & Johnson, 1994; Bernard, 1988; Miles & Huberman, 1994; Silverman, 1993).

Adler and Adler (1994) have, in fact, suggested that in the future, observational research will be found as "part of a methodological spectrum," but that in that spectrum, it will serve as "the most powerful source of validation" (p. 389). Observation, they claim, rests on "something researchers can find constant," by which they mean "their own direct knowledge and their own judgment" (p. 389). In social science research, as in legal cases, eyewitness testimony from trustworthy observers has been seen as a particularly convincing form of verification (Pelto & Pelto, 1978, p. 69). In actuality, the production of a convincing narrative report of the research has most often served as de facto validation, even if the only thing it validates is the ethnographer's writing skill and not his or her observational capacities (Kuklick, 1996, p. 60).

Whatever else may be said about the postmodernist turn in contemporary studies of society and culture, its critique of assumptions about the objectivity of science and its presumed authoritative voice has raised issues that all qualitative researchers need to address.[1] Earlier criticism might have been directed at particular researchers, with the question being whether they had lived up to the expected standards of objective scholarship. In the postmodernist milieu, by contrast, the criticism is directed at the standards themselves. In effect, it is now possible to question whether observational objectivity is either desirable or feasible as a goal. James Clifford (1983a), who has written extensively and critically about the study of culture and society, has called into question even the work of the revered Bronislaw Malinowski, the archetype of the scientific participant observer, who, according to Stocking (1983a), is the scholar most directly responsible for the "shift in the conception of the ethnographer's role, from that of inquirer to that of participant 'in a way' in village life" (p. 93). Perhaps more surprisingly, Clifford has also questioned the research of the very influential contemporary interpretivist Clifford Geertz; he takes Geertz to task for suggesting that through empathy, the ethnographer can describe a culture in terms of the meanings specific to members of that culture. In other words, the ethnographer, as a distinct person, disappears—just as he or she was supposed to do in Malinowski's more openly positivistic world. This assessment is echoed by Sewell (1997), who points out that Geertz did not expect fieldworkers to "achieve some miracle of empathy with the people whose lives they briefly and incompletely share; they acquire no preternatural capacity to think, feel, and perceive like a native" (p. 40). The problem is not that Geertz failed to achieve some sort of idealized empathic state; rather, the question is whether such a state is even relevant to ethnographic research, and whether it is desirable to describe and/or interpret cultures as if those depictions could exist without the ethnographer's being part of the action.

The postmodernist critique, which emphasizes the importance of understanding the ethnographer's "situation" (e.g., his or her gender, class, ethnicity) as part of interpreting the ethnographic product, is particularly salient because the remote, traditional folk societies that were the anthropologists' stock-in-trade have virtually disappeared; most cultural anthropology is now carried out in literate societies that are part of global communication and transportation networks. Like sociologists, anthropologists now "study up" (i.e., conduct research among elites) almost as often as they study the poor and the marginalized. Doing so overcomes some of the problems associated with the lingering colonialist bias of traditional ethnography (D. L. Wolf, 1996, p. 37), but it raises new issues regarding the position and status of the observational researcher. For one thing, ethnographers can no longer claim to be the sole arbiters of knowledge about the societies and cultures they study, because they are in a position to have their analyses read and contested by those for whom they presume to speak (Bell & Jankowiak, 1992; Larcom, 1983, p. 191). In effect, objective truth about a society or a culture cannot be established, because there are inevitably going to be conflicting versions of what happened. Sociologists and other social scientists were working in such settings long before the anthropologists came on the scene, and were already beginning to be aware of the problems inherent in claiming the privilege of objective, authoritative knowledge when there are all too many "natives" ready and able to challenge them. As Margery Wolf (1992) wryly comments: "We can no longer assume that an isolated village will not within an amazingly short period of time move into the circuit of rapid social and economic change. A

barefoot village kid who used to trail along after you *will* one day show up on your doorstep with an Oxford degree and your book in hand" (p. 137). The validity of the traditional assumption, that the truth can be established through careful cross-checking of ethnographers' and insiders' reports, is no longer universally granted, as contemporary social and behavioral scientists are increasingly inclined to expect differences in testimony grounded in gender, class, ethnicity, and other factors that are not easy to mix into a consensus. Ethnographic truth has come to be seen as a thing of many parts, and no one perspective can claim exclusive privilege in the representation thereof. Indeed, the result of ethnographic research "is never reducible to a form of knowledge that can be packaged in the monologic voice of the ethnographer alone" (Marcus, 1997, p. 92).

Some ethnographers (of various disciplines) have responded to this new situation by revising the ways in which they conduct observation-based research and present their analyses. No longer can it be taken for granted that ethnographers operate at a distance from their subjects. Indeed, the very term *subject,* with its implicit colonialist connotations, is no longer appropriate. Rather, there is said to be a *dialogue* between researchers and those whose cultures/societies are to be described.[2] Discussions of ethnographers' own interactions, relationships, and emotional states while in the field have as a result been moved from their traditional discreet place in acknowledgments or forewords to the centers of the ethnographies themselves. Although this practice has certainly opened up new horizons in ethnographic reportage, it raises further issues of its own. For example, because it is likely to be the ethnographers who write up (or at least collate or edit) the results of the field studies, do they not continue to claim the implicit status of arbiters/mediators of social/cultural knowledge (Wolf, 1992, p. 120)? Ethnographers may assert that they represent the many voices involved in the research, but we still have only their assurance that such is the case.

Nonetheless, we now function in a context of "collaborative" research. *Collaboration* no longer refers only to the conduct of multidisciplinary teams of professional researchers; it often means the presumably equal participation of professional researchers and their erstwhile "subjects" (Kuhlmann, 1992; D. L. Wolf, 1996, p. 26). Matsumoto (1996), for example, sent a prepared list of questions to the people she was interested in interviewing for an oral history project. She assured them all that any questions to which they objected would be eliminated. The potential respondents reacted favorably to this invitation to participate in the formulation of the research design. As such situations become more common, it is important that we rethink our received notions about "observation"— what it is, how it is done, what role it plays in the generation of ethnographic knowledge. To that end, it might be useful to shift from a concentration on observation as a "method" per se to a perspective that emphasizes observation as a context for interaction among those involved in the research collaboration.

◆ Observation: The Classic Tradition

As a prelude to an exploration of observation-as-context, we will briefly review the traditions of observation-as-method that form the basis of our exercise in "rethinking." Conscientious ethnographers have, in fact, long been aware that in naturalistic settings, the interaction of researcher and subjects of study can change behaviors in ways that would not have occurred in the absence of such interaction. They have believed, however, that it is both possible and desirable to develop standardized procedures that can "maximize observational efficacy, minimize investigator bias, and allow for replication and/or verification to check out the degree to which these procedures have enabled the investigator to produce valid, reliable data that, when incorporated into his or her published report, will be regarded by peers as objective findings" (Gold, 1997, p. 397). True objectivity has been held to be the result of agreement between participants and observers as to what is

really going on in a given situation. Such agreement has been thought to be attained through the elicitation of feedback from those whose behaviors were being reported. Ethnography's "self-correcting investigative process" has typically included adequate and appropriate sampling procedures, systematic techniques for gathering and analyzing data, validation of data, avoidance of observer bias, and documentation of findings (Clifford, 1983b, p. 129; Gold, 1997, p. 399). The main difference between sociological and anthropological practitioners of ethnography seems to have been that the former have generally felt the need to validate their eyewitness accounts through other forms of documentation, whereas the latter have tended to use participant observation, "relatively unsystematized" though it may be, as the ultimate reality check on "all the other, more refined, research techniques" (Pelto & Pelto, 1978, p. 69).

The possibility of "observer bias" looms large in the thinking of both sociologists and anthropologists in the ethnographic tradition (Werner & Schoepfle, 1987, p. 259). Even setting aside the expected distortion of ethnocentrism (which can presumably be controlled for as long as the ethnographer is conscious of it), the plain fact is that each person who conducts observational research brings his or her distinctive talents and limitations to the enterprise; therefore, the quality of what is *recorded* becomes the measure of usable observational data (because it can be monitored and replicated) rather than the quality of the observation itself (which is, by definition, idiosyncratic and not subject to replication). Although theoretical or conceptual frames of analysis inevitably direct observers' observations, it was traditionally assumed that researchers could keep these in the background when recording basic observational data. For this reason, the emphasis was placed on observational *methods,* the basic theme of which was, as one important manual of field procedures puts it, "Primary reporting of concrete events and things in field work should proceed at as low a level of abstraction as possible" (Pelto & Pelto, 1978, p. 70). Theoretical analysis was therefore an epiphenomenon to the process of observation.

According to Gold (1958), the sociological ethnographers of the first half of the 20th century often made implicit reference to a typology of roles that might characterize naturalistic research: the complete participant (a highly subjective stance whose scientific validity was suspect), the participant-as-observer (only slightly less problematic), the observer-as-participant, and the complete observer. The complete observer was one who was to all intents and purposes removed from the setting, and who functioned without interacting in any way with those being observed. Because of the difficulty of maintaining the purity of such a stance (Werner & Schoepfle, 1987, p. 259), and because such research was sometimes conducted without the informed consent of the observed (an ethical lapse that is no longer tolerated by responsible social researchers), the observer-as-participant role was considered an acceptable compromise, allowing the researcher to interact "casually and nondirectively" with subjects; the researcher remained a researcher, however, and did not cross over the line into friendship (Adler & Adler, 1994, p. 380). Perhaps the most important contemporary use of this role is in classroom observational studies conducted by educational researchers (Rossman & Rallis, 1998, p. 137).

Ethnographers trained in sociology are nowadays more inclined than were their predecessors to accept participation as a legitimate base from which to conduct observation. Adler and Adler (1987) have therefore proposed a modification of Gold's familiar typology in recognition of the increasing emphasis in contemporary ethnographic research on "membership roles" as opposed to roles grounded in pure observation. In other words, the older assumption that "participation" (which bothered sociologists more than it did anthropologists) seriously compromises the validity of observational data has given way to the realities of contemporary research, which is often conducted with a greater degree of researcher immersion (deliberate or otherwise) in the culture under study than was once considered desirable. Adler and Adler describe, for example, "peripheral-member researchers" as those who believe that they can develop a desirable insider's perspective without participating in those activities constituting the core of group membership. By contrast, "active-member researchers" are those who become involved with the central activities of the group, sometimes even assuming responsibilities that advance the group; they do not, however, necessarily fully commit themselves to members' values and goals. A third category, that of "complete-member researchers," is composed of those who study settings in which they are already members or with which they become fully affiliated in the course of research. Even though practitioners in this category celebrate the "subjectively lived experience," they still strive to use their membership "so as not to alter the flow of interaction unnaturally" (Adler & Adler, 1994, p. 380).

Traditional anthropological ethnographers did not question the utility of participation or membership as a base for observation, but they often worried about the unsystematic nature of their observational methods. Werner and Schoepfle (1987, pp. 262-264) have addressed this concern by suggesting a typology of observation undertaken in naturalistic settings that focuses on process rather than on role. In this system, there are three types of observational process, representing increasingly deep understanding of the social group under study. First, there is "descriptive observation," which is, to all intents and purposes, the observation of everything. The ethnographer assumes a childlike attitude, assuming that he or she knows nothing about what is going on and taking nothing for granted. Such an approach quickly leads to a morass of "irrelevant minutiae," although it is only with increased exposure to the culture that the ethnographer begins to understand what is and is not irrelevant. At that point, he or she moves into "focused observation," in which certain things, defined as irrelevant, can be ignored. Focused observation necessarily entails interviewing, because the insights gleaned from the experience of "natives" guide the ethnographer in his or her decisions about what is more or less important in that culture. Focused observations usually concentrate on well-defined types of group activity (e.g., religious rituals, classroom instruction, political elections). Finally, and most systematically, there is "selective observation," in which the ethnographer concentrates on the attributes of different types of activities (e.g., apart from the obvious difference in content, what makes instructing a class in language arts different from instructing a class in social studies?)

◆ *Rethinking Observation as Context of Interaction*

Contemporary social research may be characterized by (a) the increasing willingness of ethnographers to affirm or develop a "membership" role in the communities they study, (b) the recognition of the possibility that it may be neither feasible nor possible to harmonize observer and "insider" perspectives so as to achieve a consensus about "ethnographic truth," and (c) the transformation of the erstwhile "subjects" of research into ethnographers' collaborative partners. The traditional concern with process and method has therefore been supplemented with (but by no means supplanted by) an interest in the ways in which ethnographic observers interact with or enter into a dialogic relationship with members of the group being studied. In this section, we discuss several selected works by contemporary ethnographers in order to illustrate these supplemental factors in the contemporary interactive context of observational research. We use five very general principles of social interaction to organize the following review of this otherwise quite disparate body of theoretical, methodological, and substantive literature.

The Conscious Adoption of a Situational Identity

The first principle is as follows: *The basis of social interaction is the decision (which may be spontaneous or part of a careful plan) to take part in a social setting rather than react passively to a position assigned by others.* In some of the older sociological literature, this process is referred to as "role making," as opposed to "role

taking." In the context of this discussion, this principle animates those ethnographers who actively seek out situational identities based on "membership" rather than on "observation" as traditionally understood.

For example, Angrosino has conducted a long-term study of adults with mental retardation and/or chronic mental illness who are served by community-based agencies in the United States. The question at the heart of this research project concerned how these adults, who had been socialized as youths in large-scale institutions, adapted to life in the community in the wake of the move to deinstitutionalize all but the most seriously disturbed individuals. Answering such a question required an immersion into the lives of these people, because they would not likely respond adequately to questionnaires or clinical survey instruments. Angrosino also expressed a desire to understand what it might feel like to be mentally "disabled" in a society that places high value on technical competence. To investigate this issues, it would not be reasonable to "observe" people served by the selected agencies in the older, neutralist, objective manner discussed above, because the ethnographer could not presume to be able to "read" the attitudes and responses of people whose behavioral cues were, by definition, not "normal." On the other hand, engaging in intensive interviewing in and of itself would not work very well, because the clients would not likely trust someone with whom they were not already familiar outside the interview setting.

Angrosino therefore actively sought out a membership role in the world in which the clients lived and worked. He did not want to adopt one of the recognized professional roles that would have been familiar to the clients (e.g., therapist, social worker, teacher, parole officer) because the very familiarity would have resulted in stereotypical responses. On the other hand, he could not just "hang out." Unlike other kinds of communities, where strangers do often show up and stay to become friends, no one just "shows up" in a sheltered workshop or at a group home. So Angrosino opted for a role as a "volunteer." He assisted the teacher as a tutor in the classroom, he occasionally drove clients to and from appointments, he clerked at the thrift shop run by one of the agencies as a fund-raising effort and that was staffed by the clients, and he helped out at special events (e.g., he helped to organize a charity softball game). By assuming these duties, he made it clear that he fit no preconceived model of what someone did in this community, and yet he was able to demonstrate that he did indeed have a meaningful function (other than simply "researcher," which would not have explained anything as far as the clients were concerned). He was thus able to spend a considerable amount of time making detailed observations of the settings in which the clients lived and worked, because his presence after a while ceased to be novel enough to be disruptive, and he was able to conduct interviews with the clients, who had already learned that he was someone who could be trusted. (For further details about this project, see Angrosino, 1992, 1994, 1995a, 1997b, 1998; Angrosino & Zagnoli, 1992.)

Behar's (1993) study of Esperanza illustrates the ways in which an ethnographer was led, by the force of her collaborator's personality, to adopt more of a membership role than she had originally expected. Indeed, that study could fairly be described as an account by a feminist ethnographer who realized only in the course of writing the book that she was a feminist. In relating the story of a poor Mexican Indian woman who has defined herself through her life's struggles, Behar comes to understand more about herself as a Cuban immigrant to the United States who had always felt outside the social and academic systems in which she sought membership. Behar first encountered Esperanza when the latter was selling flowers on a street corner. Behar asked the woman permission to photograph her, expecting some sort of deferential acquiescence. Instead, Esperanza asked her (in a "haughty" manner) why she needed the picture. Behar (1993) admits, "I jumped on her as an alluring image of Mexican womanhood, ready to create my own exotic portrait of her, but the image turned around and spoke back to me, questioning my project and daring me to carry it out" (p. 4). Behar responded to Esperanza's challenge by questioning her own assumptions about the power relationship in ethnographic research (see also D. L. Wolf, 1996, p. 2; M. A. Wolf, 1992, p. 5); in this case, Behar felt herself to be directed by the more assertive woman she wished to study. Esperanza could in no sense be described as a "subject" of research. If she wished to understand Esperanza and the world in which she lived, Behar would ultimately have to become part of Esperanza's family network; she did so, becoming *comadre* to Esperanza's daughter in the process.

The decision to insert oneself in a social setting other than one's own has emotional consequences, which Behar (1996) discusses at some length. She translates the old anthropological problem of establishing rapport without "going native" (a question of methodology, with strong *ethical* overtones) into a problem of allowing oneself to be vulnerable without being "too" vulnerable (a question of personal psychology, with strong *moral* overtones). She is wary of using the language of theory and analysis; it is her only tool for "making sense" of new experiences, but it is also a way of distancing herself from an emotionally affecting (and perhaps painful) encounter.

An even more emotionally affecting (and definitely more painful) encounter is reported by Eva Moreno (a pseudonym), who writes about being raped while conducting fieldwork in Ethiopia. Moreno (1995, p. 246) admits that it is neither feasible nor desirable to "maintain a fiction of a genderless self" while in the field, which means that when an ethnographer chooses how to express her own sexuality, she must always be aware of the degree to which she thereby makes herself the object of attention of others who may see her as a target of (unwanted) sexual advances. Moreno suspects that the sexual violence she suffered was directed as much against her "professional" identity as against her "private" self—there was, at the time of her research, a generalized hostility aimed at foreigners, particularly those who presented themselves as "experts" and who were blamed for the civil disorder that had overtaken the country. She had heard, for example, that at least one other foreign woman had been raped by the very police to whom she had gone to report an assault perpetrated by local men. Moreno (1995) concludes that "women must always, everywhere, deal with the spectre of sexual violence" (p. 248). It is difficult to believe that males are not also victimized in this way—although it is much less likely that they would discuss it openly—but Moreno is undoubtedly correct in her assumption that as a generalized pattern, sexual violence is most often, in most situations, directed against women. It would therefore be a painfully naïve female ethnographer who was not prepared to factor this possibility into her plan for her observations, as "reasonable precautions" should almost certainly affect what, where, how, and with whom one conducts research.

In sum, "making a role" may mean assuming a quasi-professional stance, becoming part of a family network, or becoming hyperconscious of one's sexuality—or some combination of them all. In no case is it advantageous for the ethnographer to be passive in the face of the assumptions of the community he or she is studying.

The Perception of Power

The second principle is as follows: *In most social interactions, people assess behavior not in terms of its conformity to social or cultural norms in the abstract, but in regard to its consistency, which is a perceived pattern that somehow makes sense to others in a given social situation.* This principle is related to the traditional anthropological distinction between "ideal" and "real" culture. An ethnographer who took the observer-as-participant role was largely concerned with the ideal culture and took steps not to transgress general norms of propriety. But an ethnographer who actively makes a membership role must be more familiar with behavior as it is lived. Members of a social group typically work their way through given situations in ways that do not necessarily conform to the principles enshrined in ideal tradition.

We often function in terms of an ideology that leads us to expect (and, therefore, possibly also to see) power working downward from white, Western institutions (and their representatives, such as ethnographers) to various subordinated or marginalized peoples. Yet the literature is increasingly filled with examples of "how

people in subordinate positions managed to oppose and evade the predations of higher powers" (Maddox, 1996, p. 277). We also have a lingering bias in favor of conceptualizing both culture and society as unified, cohesive wholes. Yet ethnographers increasingly find themselves studying "communities" that are defined as much by their conflicts, factions, and divisions as they are by their commonalities (Hubbard, 1997; McCall, Ngeva, & Mbebe, 1997).

For example, Angrosino (1991) compiled an oral history of a Benedictine monastery in Florida on the occasion of the centennial of its founding. He spent a month living at the monastery while conducting the interviews, during which time he adhered to the round of daily prayer, work, and reflective leisure that is prescribed by the Rule of St. Benedict. The research was approved by the abbot (to whom all the monks in the community have vowed obedience), and although Angrosino was not a vowed member of the community, the abbot made it clear that he expected the same deference from the ethnographer that he received from the monks. The abbot was always very cordial, but he demarcated his position very clearly in ways both subtle (sitting behind a desk when it came time for his interview) and blatant (reserving the final say as to which members of the community Angrosino could approach for interviews). The other members of the community claimed to be very supportive of the research, but Angrosino found that a fair number of them gave very truncated interviews, explaining that it is not seemly for a monk to speak too much about his own experiences—doing so smacks of vanity. In the course of living in and observing the community, Angrosino came to realize that this humble reticence, although sincere to a point, covered other motives. For one thing, it expressed a quiet rebellion against the authority of the abbot, who had mandated their cooperation. In the ordinary course of things, they would not have dared to be seen as less than eager to carry out the abbot's wishes, but because the ethnographer was, for all his temporary immersion in the life of the monastery, an outsider, he could be disobliged in a way that would have spelled trouble had it been directed against any insider, much less the abbot himself. Moreover, this tactic allowed some of the monks to make an oblique criticism of those who had been more fully cooperative; their own humility was a kind of symbolic indictment of their brothers, who could be seen as either toadying to the abbot or preening in their own vanity by "telling all" to the researcher. In any event, it was clear that the ideal arrangements of monastic life—with its formal, even codified system of hierarchy and deference—were not what happened in real life. Even in such a highly circumscribed culture, people could experiment with styles of interaction and involve the visitor in subtle, yet very revealingly subversive, power games, games that inevitably shaped both *what* the ethnographer observed and *how* he interpreted what he saw.

Behar (1993) discusses her inclination to fit Esperanza's story into the prevailing model of feminist studies of Latin American women. She realized, however, that Esperanza could not fit the part of the "exemplary feminist heroine." The reality of Esperanza was no less admirable and heroic, for her life was a kind of epic of female struggle, rage, and defiance of the patriarchal institutions of her culture; but she was a flesh-and-blood woman capable of "misbehavior," and not a stereotypical Third World feminist plaster saint. Behar concludes that an ethnographer's desire to produce stories that empower the people she studies must be grounded in an allowance for the way women in other cultures "misbehave." There must be respect for their "different ways of making sense," even if their sense does not conform to the European or North American expectations of the feminist ideal (p. 270). In a similar vein, Hirsh and Olson (1995, p. 23) cite Sandra Harding to the effect that feminist scholarship in general has sought to surmount the established categories of social knowledge, which have been developed from a male point of view (even when applied in the past by female scholars). Margery Wolf (1992), however, asks "whether by studying our subjects we are also exploiting them and whether by attempting to improve women's living situations we are imposing another (powerful) society's values" (p. 2). More-

over, it may be misleading to conceptualize the "power relationship" as that obtaining between researcher and "subject." In fact, Hsiung (1996) claims that this standard binary view overlooks the patriarchal context in which both the (female) ethnographer and her female informants are situated. It may be more useful to think in terms of a "multidimensional power relationship, of which the patriarchal/capitalist system, individual agents of the system, female informants, and female feminist researcher are the key constituents" (p. 123).

The injunction to pay attention to what makes sense in a given setting takes on particular importance when, as is now so often the case, ethnography is conducted "without the ethnos" (Gupta & Ferguson, 1996b, p. 2). In other words, few ethnographers function within the circumscribed communities that lent coherence to the cultures or societies that figured so prominently in the conceptual frameworks of earlier generations of observational researchers. It is no longer possible to assume that "the cultural object of study is fully accessible within a particular site" (Marcus, 1997, p. 96). Much of the contemporary ethnographic field consists of studies of those who inhabit the "borders between culture areas," of localities that demonstrate a diversity of behavioral and attitudinal patterns, of "postcolonial hybrid cultures," and of the social changes and cultural transformations that typically are found "within interconnected spaces" (Gupta & Ferguson, 1996a, p. 35). People, after all, "live in different overlapping but not always overdetermining spaces and times: domestic spaces; national spaces; broadcasting and narrowcasting spaces; biographical times; daily times; scheduled, spontaneous, but also socio-geological times" (Abu-Lughod, 1997, p. 112). Malkki (1996b), for example, describes working in "accidental communities of memory," which include "people who have experienced war together . . . ; people who were bombed in Hiroshima or Nagasaki; people who all fled a particular revolution; people who are stricken by a particular illness; or people who worked together on a particular humanitarian or development project" (p. 92). In all of these cases, "it is the communities that are accidental, not the happenings" (p. 92). The ethnographer therefore no longer enjoys the luxury of assuming that the local scene he or she is observing is somehow typical or representative of "a" culture of "a" society. It is a nexus of interactions defined by "interstitiality and hybridity" (Gupta & Ferguson, 1996a, p. 48), factors of "the globalizing discourses and images of the media" (Peters, 1996, p. 81), that the ethnographer, the classic neither-here-nor-there person, helps to define. In some cases, the ethnographer may even be said to *create* a community simply by virtue of studying certain people and by implying that the links he or she has perceived among them constitute a society. The "street corner society" studied by Whyte (1955), or Liebow (1967), or Hannerz (1969) became a "society" only because an ethnographer chose to treat that "nexus of interaction" as a site. Oral historians are often in the position of creating virtual communities by linking several personal experiences around a central theme of their own choosing (Hareven, 1996).

The principle is confounded when gender—that "enormous, extreme" question, in the words of Jean-François Lyotard (quoted in Olson, 1995a, p. 186)—and sexual orientation enter the picture, because "differing sexualized perspectives of 'the field' influence the kind of relationship that the ethnographer has with the field and this, in turn, affects interpretation" (Willson, 1995, p. 253). Gender and sexual orientation are extremely meaningful elements in defining an ethnographer's personal identity; they can also become filters through which the observation of communities is mediated. The problem is that the meanings shift from one community to another. The observer cannot assume a universal, let alone an ideal, symbolism of gender and/or sexual orientation. The cues of personal identity must always be interpreted in the context of the reality of a given social setting.

Dubisch (1995, p. 34), for example, notes that female anthropologists, simply by virtue of being female, have not been granted the indulgence to engage in casual sex, whether their sexual encounters occur at home or in the field. Male anthropologists, by contrast, have long been assumed to have had casual flings while in the field (Newton, 1993, p. 5). There was a tacit assumption that such male behavior did not matter because it was expected and approved by all parties, whereas analogous behavior by women was always disruptive because it was neither expected nor approved. This assumption must now be called into question, because the decision of *any* ethnographer to insert him- or herself into the social setting in a sexual manner must be seen to have repercussions with respect to what he or she is able to observe. Whether or not such behavior is approved is less important than the recognition that it will make a difference to the entire set of relationships initiated by the ethnographer, and hence to the type and quality of observations he or she is able to conduct. In recognition of this reality, Killick (1995) seems to counsel abstinence, noting that "while in the field, the fear of upsetting the delicate balance of relationships with informants is likely to be a significant curb on the libido" (p. 81). On the other hand, Killick advises those whose libidos are unrestrained by such methodological niceties to "keep quiet about it if their behavior is likely to be seen as either uninteresting (a possibility we should not discount) or reprehensible" (p. 81). Altork (1995), however, argues against both repression and concealment. She believes that "instead of blocking out [the] wealth of sensory (and sensual) input, or relegating it to private field journals, we might consider making room for our sensual responses in our work" (p. 116). In her view, whether or not one "did it" in the field is less important than whether or not one is able to be honest in acknowledging what did or did not happen and why, because such admissions leave the ethnographer "open to the fertile possibilities for dialogue about the ways in which 'it' changed, enhanced, or detracted from what we felt, witnessed, and interpreted in the field" (p. 121). In an ironic twist on this old (but only recently public) dilemma, Altork suggests that "perhaps by acknowledging our own feelings and desires, we might actually look at other people and places *more objectively,* by being able to ferret out our own biases and distortions as we do our work" (p. 132; emphasis added).

The process of open acknowledgment may be hindered in the case of lesbian or gay ethnographers, who may be habituated to a degree of concealment in both their personal and professional lives. Goodman (1996, p. 50) notes that lesbian and gay male ethnographers *expect* to engage in subterfuge while in the field, but Burkhart (1996) believes that his initial efforts at concealment (rationalized as an effort to achieve the "ideal of observer neutrality") led only to "spells of inertia and depression" (p. 34). Williams (1996, p. 74) suggests a compromise: being completely honest with people in the community although less so with granting agencies. He claims to have had positive experiences with people to whom he divulged his sexual orientation in the communities in which he conducted research, but he has found it prudent to apply for funding by stressing other research topics, and then studying homosexual behavior once in the field. Even AIDS research, now a reasonably well-funded area for social scientists, was initially not something funding agencies wanted to hear about, because it was assumed that AIDS was a purely homosexual concern (Bolton, 1996, p. 157).

Lesbians and gay men are used to "constant, and conscious, identity management" and have typically carried this mind-set from their personal lives into their research settings (Lewin & Leap, 1996, p. 13). A fair number of homosexual ethnographers have chosen to study homosexual behavior in the field (apparently on the assumption that they have a ready point of reference), but it is easy to be disappointed if one assumes that the understanding of and manifestation of homosexuality is the same in all communities, just as it is easy to be misled into assuming that female ethnographers are in an advantaged position when it comes to understanding women in all cultures (Lewin & Leap, 1996, p. 17). The point is that one's gender, as well as one's sexual orientation, are matters that must be taken into conscious account when one endeavors to conduct observational ethnography; but neither factor can be considered a source of privileged knowledge in and of itself. As Lang (1996) notes, "Quite obviously, there is no 'universal gay community' "

(p. 103). At the very least, homosexuality does not "override the social hierarchies of the contemporary world" (Kennedy & Davis, 1996, p. 193); it is still necessary to investigate the impact of "the hierarchies of class and race" even within a presumed "gay community."

In any case, it is clear that "no longer is it generally acceptable for [ethnographic researchers] to conceal or deny the significance of their gender identity, age, class, or ethnicity. (Sexual identity represents a sort of final frontier in this regard.) Instead, contemporary ethnographic writing tends to acknowledge these attributes as factors that shape an [ethnographer's] interpretations of what she or he observed in the field" (Weston, 1996, p. 276). For example, Edelman (1996) discusses the varying impacts his Jewish ethnicity had in three different field sites. Other factors, less well established as demographic categories, may also play a part in how an ethnographer relates to what is studied—for example, the ethnographer's personal struggle with bulimia (Tillman-Healy, 1996) or breast cancer (Kolker, 1996), or the ethnographer's having survived a nonmainstream childhood (Fox, 1996; Ronai, 1996) or having undergone detoxification therapy (Mienczakowski, 1996). In all of the cases just cited, the ethnographers' personal experiences were the main focus of both observation and interpretation. But it is clear that if these ethnographers should go on to study other people with those same characteristics, they would have to shift from a perspective that implicitly elevates the personal to the normative in order to observe what is going on in a natural setting.

Negotiating a Situational Identity

The third principle is as follows: *Interaction is always a tentative process that involves the continuous testing by all participants of the conceptions they have of the roles of others.* In other words, ethnographers and their collaborators do not step into fixed and fully defined positions; rather, their behaviors and expectations of each other are part of a dynamic process that continues to grow (one hopes in healthy ways, although the outcome is sometimes problematic) throughout the course of single research projects or as they move from one project to another (Wolcott, 1995, p. 77). Giroux (1995) speaks of the need for "intellectuals" in general (and ethnographers in particular) to "reinvent themselves in diverse sites" (p. 197). Denzin (1997a) discusses the "mobile consciousness" of an ethnographer who is aware of his or her "relationship to an ever-changing external world" (p. 46).

For example, Angrosino (1997a) conducted an oral history of the Southern Anthropological Society on the occasion of the 30th anniversary of its founding. He had been a member of the SAS almost since its establishment and had served over the years in both elective and appointive offices. As a professional anthropologist affiliated with a department at a university in the South, and whose research often dealt with aspects of life in the contemporary South, he was in terms of status a fully integrated member of the institutional culture of the organization. Moreover, he had long-term personal and professional ties with all of the people who were scheduled to be interviewed. The bulk of the interviews were conducted during the special anniversary meetings of the society, and Angrosino brought along three graduate students to work as his assistants—and, more important, to serve as "reality checks" to make sure that he did not act like too much of an "insider" and thereby miss important cues or take for granted too many items that outsiders would find in need of clarification. The interviews, however, began awkwardly, as many of the participants seemed annoyed at being questioned by someone they assumed already knew the answers. "Oh, you remember what happened in New Orleans in '70 . . ." someone would say. "Well, why don't you tell about it in your own words?" Angrosino would respond. They usually sighed in frustration at that suggestion. It was very difficult for professional anthropologists to act as informants, particularly when the interviewer was already assumed to be in the know. Some others decided to short-circuit an uncomfortable situation and, in effect, to hijack the interview, carrying on in lecture/monologue fashion without paying attention to the interviewer's questions. Still others demanded to be interviewed by one of the graduate assistants; "I can't talk to

you with a straight face," one of them told Angrosino.

After a while, the awkwardness wore off, presumably as members began to share with one another their reactions to having been interviewed. They reaffirmed all the reasons they had thought of collecting an oral history in the first place, primarily because doing so would be a good idea "for posterity." The later interviews went much more smoothly, as participants had clearly made a tacit decision to treat the overly familiar Angrosino as simply a naïve outsider to whom *everything* needed to be explained. The ethnographer came to think of himself as if he were one of his students, so that he would remember to ask all the questions that someone who had not been in on the action would want ask. Although most ethnographers seek to move from outsider status to a status of participant/member, Angrosino in this case (abetted by his collaborators) reinvented himself from complete insider to interested-but-ignorant bystander. Within the interactive context of observational research, roles mutate in response to changing circumstances and are never defined with finality.

Behar describes this process in terms of her own evolution from "feminist anthropologist" to "feminist ethnographer," by which she means a researcher who is attentive to the "reflexiveness about the politics of practicing feminism and experimental cultural writing." The focus of such reflexiveness must be "women's relationships to other women" (Behar, 1993, p. 301) rather than a scientific observer's relationship to a "subject" of research. For Behar (1996, p. 5), the very term *participant observation* is an "oxymoron." The ethnographer must, Behar suggests, be defined by the creative tension in the role of member/observer, not by some finite quantity of information gathered by one who plays that role. According to Ferguson (1996, p. 153), the exploration of how shifting connections frame experiences of place, community, and society among "the partially and provisionally dislocated" may well represent the most fertile ground for future ethnographic research.

Blackwood (1995, p. 53) therefore speaks of the *identities* assumed by the ethnographer in the field in terms of the many different ways he or she is perceived by "others." As a woman, she has "continually tacked back and forth between various assigned and constructed identities: researcher, friend, daughter, professional, American" (p. 58), and she concludes that "identities [in the field] are never stable, never simply defined" (p. 70). At this point in the psychosocial history of Western culture, it is probably clear that our "identities" in the existential sense are always in a process of evolution and never achieve a fixed, final point. The naïve assumption that ethnographers' identities in the field should be clearly defined and finite is, perhaps, the last vestige of the old belief that "wholeness" means personal autonomy and fixity of identity. Nevertheless, there is a very strong sense in which ethnographers continue to believe, as they have since the days of the ascendancy of the Freudian perspective in social analysis, that doing fieldwork is a way in which they can come to terms with themselves. "Sharing a different lifestyle," according to Barnett (1983), "has a mirror effect, providing glimpses of an observer's foibles as well as his dignity" (p. 169).

Walters (1996) expresses this view with an interesting figure of speech: In the matter of establishing one's identity, one must "constantly . . . pivot the center" (p. 63). She was led to this perspective when it became necessary for her to deal with the problem of bringing her partner to the field—the Yemen Arab Republic. She assumed that a conservative Islamic society would not be a friendly place for two openly homosexual women, and she considered various strategies of concealment (e.g., claiming to be relatives, going through a process of adoption); she finally decided to refer to the other woman as her "companion," which, while perfectly true, seemed vague enough to avoid the suspicion of the authorities. (It even had a whiff of Victorian propriety about it—a young woman traveling in the company of an older female companion has long been a well-known image in many parts of the world.)

Despite such occasionally successful strategies, it remains true that women researchers often feel pressured to conform to the gender behavior norms of the cultures they study, even if those norms are not the ones they would freely choose for themselves, and even if they have to resort to a certain amount of deception so as to appear to conform. According to Diane Wolf (1996), "Feminist fieldworkers have lied about their marital status, . . . about their national identity or ethnic/religious background . . . , about divorce and former marriages . . . , and about their class background" (p. 11). Even in those cases where the deception did no real harm to the people the researcher was observing, the ethnographers often felt guilty, in part because the very act of deception "directly contradicts attempts at a more feminist approach to fieldwork, which includes attempts to equalize a relationship and create more of a friendship" (Berik, 1996, p. 56; see also D. L. Wolf, 1996, p. 12). On the other hand, the refusal to deceive—in effect, to defy the norms of the community being studied in order to make a principled stand for what one actually believes—can sometimes have unintended negative consequences. Berik (1996, p. 65), for example, admits that her openly feminist stance while conducting research in a Turkish village unwittingly led to one of her female informants' being beaten by an outraged husband, who assumed she was being led astray by the insufficiently submissive ethnographer.

Lang (1996) conducted a research project focusing on Native American lesbians. Although she is openly gay herself, she found it unacceptable to locate potential informants in bars or other obvious meeting places. She was concerned lest the other women assume, because she was hanging out in a bar, that she was therefore interested in finding sexual, rather than research, partners. She decided that it would be unethical to pose as a potential sexual partner in order to elicit information (Lang, 1996, p. 94), and so she had to seek her "community" in less symbolically charged environments. In this case, Lang decided that her status as "ethnographer" would take precedence over her sexual orientation as a way of defining herself to the people she intended to study, despite the fact that sexual orientation was the thematic focus of her study. Her decision was a matter of strategy dictated by her reading of the nature of the particular community.

Much of the recent literature bearing on the creation, maintenance, and creative evolution of observers' identities (and on the pros and cons of deception and disclosure) has dealt with issues particular to women and lesbians/gay men, as shown above. It is worth mentioning, however, that there are other issues of identity that are of concern to researchers who study situations of political unrest and who come to be identified with politically proscribed groups (Hammond, 1996; Mahmood, 1996; Sluka, 1990), or who work with groups that are defined by their need for deceptive concealment, such as illegal migrants (Chavez, Flores, & Lopez-Garza, 1990; Stepick & Stepick, 1990) or those involved in criminal activities (Agar & Feldman, 1980; Brewer, 1992; Dembo, Hughes, Jackson, & Mieczkowski, 1993; Koester, 1994; van Gelder & Kaplan, 1992).

Criteria for Validation

The fourth principle is as follows: *Participants validate the cues generated by others in the setting by internal and/or external criteria.* Internal criteria are those by which members of a community check their behavior against the prevailing norms of their own group. External criteria are those by which members of a community check their behavior in terms of presumably universal standards. In other words, participants in the interaction ask, "Does it work?" or, perhaps less nobly, "Can I get away with it?" (that is, "Does my interpretation help me and my potential collaborator work out a viable relationship?") rather than, "Is it correct?" (That is, "Does 'the culture' somehow 'require' people to act in a certain manner?")

For example, Angrosino (1995b) led a team of graduate students in a study of local responses to the AIDS epidemic. The research centered on a particular agency that provided limited direct service (mostly testing) but was far more important as an information and referral network. The agency had been founded by partners and relatives of people who had contracted AIDS; these people believed that their personal involvement

in—indeed, their emotional commitment to—the cause was a primary reason for the success of their project. They were somewhat put out by the apparent transformation of the agency into a more professional outfit, with leadership positions being increasingly taken by human service managers and development specialists with no special concern for the particular characteristics of the AIDS crisis except for the recognition that it was a major public health concern. The professional managers were helpful to the researchers, but in a rather distant fashion; by contrast, the "old-line" founders were eager to draw the team members into a kind of social circle, the better for them to learn "what it's really all about."

This situation was one in which internal and external criteria seemed to work at cross-purposes. On the one hand, the two factions within the agency were reacting to very different criteria for validation. One side validated its activities and sense of mission with reference to the *quality* of interpersonal interactions (an internal criterion) and to general humanitarian concerns (an external criterion). The other group sought validation in the *efficiency* of interpersonal interactions (an internal criterion) and in "objective" standards of professional conduct (an external criterion). There was clearly no "correct" corporate culture in such an agency or in the client community it served; the question was, "What worked?" and the answer was, "It depends on what you want to accomplish." The founders vigorously sought to convince the ethnographers that the key to success in the crisis was to "work from the heart, not from the head." People with AIDS and their caretakers needed emotional support more than sound fiscal management from an agency like theirs. They did not deny that the clients appreciated good management, but believed that a coolly competent accountant was not the "face" potential clients wanted to see when they contacted the agency for help. They sought empathy, having already gotten quite enough unfeeling "competence" in clinical settings. The ethnographers, for their part, tended to agree, although they certainly appreciated the way in which the "competent" managers facilitated the research process for them.

It may be useful to characterize this aspect of the interactive context in terms of the ways in which personal experience serves as an organizing principle in the process of mediating internal and external criteria in social settings. For Denzin (1997a), "the starting point is experience" (p. 55), which leads to a discourse between the ethnographer and other members of the community, a discourse that "often begins from the painful autobiographical experiences of the writer" (p. 57). Indeed, there is increasing tolerance for a discourse that ends with those same experiences as well (Quinney, 1996). "Life in the field," Hinsley (1983) points out, "is an individual experience" (p. 55), and "ethnography" (despite the traditional connotation of the term as the study of "a people") is seen in certain quarters as a species of autobiography, the "personal ethnography" (Quinney, 1996). Olson (1995b) cites Donna Haraway to the effect that ethnographic observation must be translated into written representations that place "the writer's own situatedness in history" in the foreground (p. 46). Denzin's (1997a)—and, more obliquely, Olson's—remarks are directed mainly to the production of "standpoint texts" that flow from the particular experiences of those who have been excluded from "the dominant discourses in the human disciplines" (p. 55). Stocking (1983b) refers to the same trend in somewhat less favorable terms as the proliferation of "adjectival anthropologies" (p. 4).

It is nevertheless certainly possible to apply the same perspective to anyone engaging in ethnographic research. Even those who come from traditionally "dominant" social groups must engage in a process of consciousness-raising about the nature and effects of their interaction with others. For them, as for those previously marginalized, the starting point of observational research *is* experience, for their own existential immersion in the "cultural displacement" of people, things, and cultural products is a defining quality of the state of the world today (Malkki, 1996a, p. 53). According to Mary Belenky: "We all need to understand how writing the same material for different audiences changes the voice. This is very empowering knowledge to have" (quoted in Ashton-Jones & Thomas, 1995, p. 86). On the other hand, one cannot be "preoccupied" with one's audience, because such a focus can lead to "self-censorship," according to bell hooks (quoted in Olson & Hirsh, 1995, p. 110). In effect, the ethnographer who is a member/observer is an artifact of the very situation of cultural displacement that he or she intends to study. It may not, in fact, be possible to resolve the tension between what the ethnographer "is" and what he or she must "become" in the field; rather than fret about that tension, it may now be time to "find some practical use" for it in our analysis (M. A. Wolf, 1996, p. 217).

Bolton (1995) points out that when the topic of an ethnographic study is sexuality, the ethnographer is limited by his or her inability to "observe" the behavior in the strict, traditional sense of the term. Much of the social scientific discourse on sexual behavior has been recorded via hearsay rather than eyewitness testimony, although it has often been conducted within the compass of supposedly observational research designs. The best way for the ethnographer to overcome this limitation, Bolton suggests, is through participation, *if* the ethnographer feels comfortable doing so. He admits that "I learned more through participation than by simple observation or direct interviewing" (p. 148). This solution raises some additional issues of an interactional nature: Is the ethnographer who "participates" in this manner really learning about the norms of sexual practice in the community he or she is studying, or is the ethnographer importing attitudes and emotions from his or her own culture into the field setting? Is the ethnographer, in effect, confusing internal and external criteria? More provocatively, is he or she participating in the creation of a new set of norms or standards that are specific to this particular interaction, and not of either the host community or the home community? If the latter, is the ethnographer still doing social research, or has a new field for observation been introduced, requiring at minimum the much-discussed "blurring of genres" in reporting and at maximum a blurring of traditional academic/disciplinary boundaries in order to conceive of a new topic of discourse? As Murray (1996) notes: "Having sex with the natives is not a royal road to insight about alien sexuality. . . . In answering questions or inscribing life histories at a researcher's behest, as in having sex with them, the person whose sexuality is being studied is likely to be guessing what the researcher wants to hear rather than representing his or her most fundamental desires and identities" (p. 250).

A female variant of Bolton's point of view is provided by Gearing (1995), who fell in love with and married her "best informant" while conducting field research. Ethnographic research, she contends, is always a "joint endeavor" between the would-be observer and those he or she would observe; it is therefore dependent on the "quality of our personal relationships" (p. 207). Gearing advocates abandoning the "model of the dispassionate participant observer" and adopting instead the persona of "an emotionally aware inter-actor engaged with other actors" (p. 211).

The validation of the individual experience of the ethnographer has traditionally been bound up in the ethnography (usually written) produced as the result of observational research. The only audience that really matters has been the academic, although there have been recent attempts to write for an audience composed (at least in part) of the "subjects" of research. Nevertheless, there are now many formats in which a report can be generated (Polkinghorne, 1997), reflecting the variety of constituencies to which the ethnographer is now responsible. Thus the ethnographic observer must be concerned with the different "voices" in which he or she presents material. Traditional ethnographic reportage favored the supposedly objective third-person voice, emanating from the "omniscient narrator," as Tierney (1997, p. 27) notes. The move toward greater participation allowed the ethnographer to acknowledge his or her own presence, although this was often done via circumlocution, with the ethnographer referring to him- or herself, for example, as "the inter-

viewer" (Tierney, 1997, p. 26). The once-banned "I" is now much more common as subjective experience comes to the fore (Tierney, 1997, p. 25; see also Ellis, 1997; Lather, 1997; Tanaka, 1997). Wolcott (1995) declares his preference for "an approach that keeps humans always visibly present, researcher as well as the researched" (p. 15). Margery Wolf (1992, p. 52) suggests that it was women and others previously marginalized by the academic world who first dared challenge orthodoxy by writing in the first person, a trend that she believes has now entered the mainstream—now that male academics are also doing so. These shifts in reference are not irrelevant matters of style; they reflect evolving self-images of the ethnographic observer, changing relations between the observer and the observed, and new perceptions about the diverse (and possibly even contradictory) audiences to whom ethnographic research must now be addressed. Certain kinds of ethnographic texts can have professional, participatory, lay, and aesthetic audiences (Denzin, 1997b, p. 188). It is clear that validating what "I" say is a very different matter—philosophically as well as scientifically—from validating what "the interviewer" says.

Perhaps the most widely cited case study of the subtle interplay of internal and external criteria is the "thrice-told tale" of Margery Wolf (1992). In her book, Wolf embarks on a personal, reflexive journey by revisiting a fictional short story she had written some 30 years earlier, when she was the wife/assistant of an anthropologist conducting his first field research in Taiwan. Since that time, she had become an anthropologist in her own right, as well as a feminist. The original story (which was based on real events) is reprinted first, followed by the field notes and journal entries referring to the same events. The third part of the book is a formal ethnographic article that was originally published in *American Ethnologist*, a mainstream academic journal. Each section of the book is followed by commentary in which Wolf explains what she remembers about the events as represented in each of the three written accounts and what she now thinks about those same events from the perspective of three decades. In the process she sees changes in herself as both a woman and an ethnographer. For example, she notes, "Where once I was satisfied to describe what I thought I saw and heard as accurately as possible, to the point of trying to resolve differences of opinion among my informants, I have come to realize the importance of retaining these 'contested meanings' " (p. 4).

Wolf's point is that no ethnographic research, including supposedly objective naturalistic observation, can be considered complete and valid until it has undergone what Polkinghorne (1997) describes as the transformation of a "list or sequence of disconnected research events into a unified story with a thematic point" (p. 14). A good observer can develop the skill of catching cultural meanings as members of the community themselves understand them, but equally important is the skill of writing up the report in such a way as "to convey that meaning to an interested reader from another culture" (Wolf, 1992, p. 5).

Contextualizing Meaning

The fifth principle is as follows: *People come into interactions by assuming situational identities that enhance their own self-conceptions or serve their own needs, which may be context specific rather than socially or culturally normative.* Members of the community are reacting to *this particular ethnographer* and the cues he or she generates, not to "an outsider" in a generic sense. Some of those cues are matters over which the ethnographer can exercise some control if he or she is made aware of them (e.g., improving language facility, dressing in an "appropriate" way), although many others are simply part of the package (e.g., gender, race/ethnicity, relative age). In the latter case, the ethnographer may need to realize that what *he or she* observes is conditioned by who *he or she* is, and that different ethnographers—equally well trained and well versed in theory and method but of different gender, race, or age—might well stimulate a very different set of interactions, and hence a different set of observations leading to a different set of conclusions.

Angrosino, for example, has been involved with a long-term project documenting the patterns and impacts of inter-island labor migration in the Netherlands Antilles. One of his informants was an elderly woman now living on Saba, the smallest of the islands, and he published her life history in an anthology devoted to the Saba part of the project. Shortly thereafter, the same woman was interviewed by a Saba-born folklorist (and political leader) who was publishing a collection dedicated to "the island's treasures" (i.e., the accumulated wisdom of its senior citizens). The general outlines of the woman's life story were the same in both accounts, but there were clear differences as well. As might be expected, the story she told Angrosino had many more explanatory details than the one she told her fellow islander. Angrosino had obviously asked her many questions to clarify matters about which a nonnative would have no knowledge. But there were more subtle, yet telling differences. The woman had lived a life of great hardship, and yet she had survived to raise (virtually single-handedly) a large family; all of her children had gone on to become pillars of the community, and she herself was recognized as a person of the utmost integrity. When she told her story to the ethnographer, she allowed herself a bit of pride in recounting how she had surmounted all her travails; she comes across in that account as a humble, yet definitely heroic figure. In the story she told her fellow Sabian, she is considerably more self-deprecating; the island culture is not very cordial to those who "try to get above themselves." On the other hand, she included anecdotes in her discourse with the Sabian about her defiance of the white establishment, incidents she suppressed when talking with the (white) ethnographer. The point is that Angrosino, who is white, from another country, and of the same generation as this woman's grandsons, evoked a qualitatively different story from the one she told the black Sabian of her own generation. There is little evidence of conscious dissimulation; she merely responded to cues both obvious and covert in her two "audiences," and, like any good performer, she engaged her interlocutors in terms that resonated most clearly with them and their personal circumstances. (For a more detailed comparison of the two life stories, see Angrosino, 1989.) As Behar (1996) notes, citing George Devereux, the observer "*never* observes the behavioral event which 'would have taken place' in his absence, nor hears an account identical with that which the same narrator would give to another person" (p. 6).

Denzin (1997a) points out that it is now important to be aware of class, race, gender, and ethnicity, and of how these factors "shape the process of inquiry, thereby making research a multicultural process" (p. 19). This insight is not in and of itself new; what is new and important for the purposes of this discussion is the implication that the ethnographer must become aware of these factors not to minimize them or "hold them constant," as classic observers were taught to do, but to integrate them creatively into both the process of observation and the production of a written representation of the fruits of that observation. Diane Wolf (1996) echoes this position in a feminist context; she advises ethnographers to analyze their field research in terms that use, rather than deny, their "intuition, feelings, and viewpoint" (p. 5).

Morton (1995), for example, conducted research in Tonga, a "seductive," "exotic" culture. On her first visit, she "nearly" succumbed to the seduction; 10 years later, she was pregnant while conducting research, and she was able to wear her pregnancy as a "chastity belt" to avoid sexual pursuit (p. 168). The reader assumes that Morton had other motives for her pregnancy, but it certainly helped her out of an undesirable situation (that of being sexually active in the field); it probably also meant that she was able to hear a significantly different side of the story of Tongan culture from the one to which she was privy as a single, childless woman.

◆ The Ethical Dimension of Observational Research

Observation was once thought of as a data collection technique employed primarily by ethnographers who thought of themselves as ob-

jective researchers extrinsic to the social settings they studied. It has become a context in which researchers who define themselves as members of those social settings interact in dialogic fashion with other members of those settings. This transition has also effected a shift in the parameters of our ongoing reflections on the ethics of social research.

Institutional Structures

For good or ill, virtually all social research in our time is governed by the structure of institutional review boards (IRBs), which grew out of federal regulations beginning in the 1960s that mandated informed consent for all those participating in federally funded research. The perceived threat was from "intrusive" research (usually biomedical), participation in which was to be under the control of the "subjects," who had a right to know what was going to happen to them and to agree formally to all provisions of the research. The right of informed consent, and the review boards that were eventually created to enforce it at each institution receiving federal moneys (assuming a function originally carried out by the federal Office of Management and Budget), radically altered the power relationship between researcher and "subject," allowing both parties to have a say in the conduct and character of research. (For more detailed reviews of this history, see Fluehr-Lobban, 1994; Wax & Cassell, 1979.)

Ethnographic researchers, however, have always been uncomfortable with this situation—not, of course, because they wanted to conduct covert, harmful research, but because they did not believe that their research was "intrusive." Such a claim was of a piece with the assumptions typical of the "observer-as-participant" role, although it is certainly possible to interpret it as a relic of the "paternalism" that traditional researchers often adopted with regard to their "subjects" (Fluehr-Lobban, 1994, p. 8). Ethnographers were also concerned that the proposals sent to IRBs had to be fairly complete, so that all possibilities for doing harm might be adequately assessed. Their research, they argued, often grew and changed as it went along and could not always be set out with the kind of predetermined specificity that the legal experts seemed to expect. They further pointed out that the statements of professional ethics promulgated by the relevant disciplinary associations already provided for informed consent, such that IRBs were merely being redundant in their oversight.

In the 1980s, social scientists won from the federal Department of Health and Human Services an exemption from review for all social research except that dealing with children, people with disabilities, and others defined as members of "vulnerable" populations. Nevertheless, legal advisers at many universities (including the University of South Florida, where we are both based) have opted for caution and have been very reluctant to allow this near-blanket exemption to be applied. Indeed, at USF it is possible for a research proposal to undergo "expedited" (or "partial") review if it seems to meet the federal criteria for exemption, and even those that are judged worthy of full exemption must still be on file. USF now has two IRBs— one for biomedical research and one for "behavioral research." Because the latter is dominated by psychologists (by far the largest department in the social sciences division of the College of Arts and Sciences), this separate status rarely works to the satisfaction of ethnographic researchers. The psychologists, used to dealing with hypothesis-testing, experimental, or clinical or lab-based research, have been reluctant to recognize a subcategory of "observational" research design. As a result, the form currently required by the behavioral research IRB is couched in terms of the individual subject rather than in terms of populations or communities, and it mandates the statement of a hypothesis to be tested and a "protocol for the experiment." Concerned ethnographers at USF have discovered that some other institutions have developed forms more congenial to their particular needs, but as of this writing they have had no success in convincing the USF authorities to adopt any of them as an alternative to the current "behavioral research" form for review.

It is interesting to note that the only kind of "observational" research that is explicitly mentioned and routinely placed in the "exempt" category at USF is that defined as "public"—for example, studying patterns of where people sit in airport waiting rooms, one of the rare remaining classic "pure observer" types of ethnography. The exemption, however, disappears if the researcher intends to publish photos or otherwise identify the people who make up "the public."

Issues for Contemporary Observational Researchers

Ethical ethnographers who adopt more clearly "membership"-oriented identities—certainly a very strong trend, as this review has demonstrated—are therefore caught between two equally untenable models of research. On the one hand is the official IRB, which is tied to the experimental, hypothesis-testing, clinical model. On the other hand are those ethnographers who, in their zeal to win exemption from irrelevant and time-consuming strictures, appear to be claiming that their research is not, should not be, "intrusive" at all. Yet the interactive, membership-oriented researchers *are,* by definition, intrusive— not in the negative sense of the word, to be sure, but they are still deeply involved in the lives and activities of the communities they study, a stance fraught with all sorts of possibilities for "harm." There are ethnographers with an "applied" orientation (i.e., those who seek to use their research to effect social or institutional change), those interested in using their research as part of a project for social criticism, and those who advocate for "universalistic" values (e.g., women's rights, ecological justice) even when the local communities they happen to be studying act in ways inimical to those values. All of these researchers may do "harm" in the strict sense of the term, but it has not been satisfactorily determined whether such "harm" is necessarily and inevitably to be avoided by the ethical researcher. It is difficult to prepare an informed consent form when one cannot even begin to anticipate the possibilities that might flow from personalized interaction. In principle, at least, it might be possible to say that because research collaborators are no longer subjects, by definition they have as much power as do researchers in shaping the research agenda; they do not need to be warned or protected. But in reality, the researcher is still in a privileged position, at least insofar as actually *doing* the research and disseminating its results are concerned. The researcher probably does not want to retreat to the objective cold of the classic observer role, but neither does he or she want to shirk the responsibility for doing everything possible to avoid hurting or embarrassing people who have been trusting partners in the research endeavor. As Fluehr-Lobban (1994) concludes:

> Openness and disclosure; reference in social studies to participants instead of informants; models of collaborative research that incorporate informed consent; all are components of [ethnographic] research, whether academic or applied, federally or privately funded, that is fully current with developments taking place in the world we study and the professions that study it. Informed consent may only be a convenient summary term for what has taken place in biomedical and social science research, but when its spirit is implemented it results in better researchers and better research. (p. 8)

An Interim Solution

This ethical dilemma would seem to be the pivot on which further developments in observational research will turn, although there have been only provisional efforts to resolve it. One example of such an attempt is Angrosino's *Opportunity House* (1998), his summative report on the study, discussed above, of nearly two decades' duration of community-based agencies serving adult clients with mental disabilities. Informed consent was secured from those clients who were classified as "legally competent" and from the legal guardians of those who were not. Nevertheless, Angrosino never felt confident that the people with whom he worked fully understood the ramifications of their consent, particularly given that much of the ethnographic research was conducted in the form of extended life history interviews that often went off in directions that could not have been predicted at the time the original study was proposed and approved. Various interim publications about the

project were written in the standard authoritative voice of the objective scientist, with aggregated observations and limited excerpts from interview data (attributed to pseudonymous informants) as illustrations. When it came time to write an overall analysis of the entire project, Angrosino found that such a strategy seemed inadequate. It was necessary to draw the reader into both the experiences of people with mental disabilities (people who are so much like us, and yet with a critical difference somewhat beyond our capacities to imagine) and the experiences of a researcher trying to figure out the patterns of the communities in which those people interact. But doing so by means of an implicitly distancing language of expository scientific writing and a blurring of individual differences was not an attractive option.

Angrosino therefore decided to try a form of "alternative ethnographic writing" and to present his material in the form of fictionalized stories that preserved the truth of individual experience without making explicit identifications of particular people with specific situations. There are many valid reasons for experimenting with nonexpository presentations of ethnographic material, but it may also be useful to think of such alternative genres as one response to the ethical quandary of observational research in transition.

Steps Toward an Ethic of Proportionate Reason in Observational Research

Because observational research, as it has evolved in recent times, is essentially a matter of interpersonal interaction and not a matter of objective hypothesis testing, it would seem that a standard for the making of ethical judgments appropriate to the analysis of "the morality of human action" (Gula, 1989, p. 272) is in order. Human action must always be interpreted in situational context, and not in terms of objective "codes." As Gula (1989) has pointed out, "No one enjoys an ahistorical vantage point which will give absolute certitude on moral matters" (p. 275). The notion of "proportionate reason" is the key to such an interpretation (Cahill, 1981; Curran, 1979; Hoose, 1987; Walter, 1984). *Proportionalism* can sometimes refer to a strictly utilitarian cost-benefit analysis, but it is more properly thought of in this context as that which gives an action its moral meaning. In that sense, " 'proportionate' refers to the relation between the specific value at stake and the . . . limitations, the harm, or the inconvenience which will inevitably come about in trying to achieve that value" (Gula, 1989, p. 273). In other words, it is certainly important to "weigh the consequences" of an action, but consequences are only one part of the total meaning of the action. From this perspective, proportionate reason defines what a person is doing in an action (as an ethnographer engaged in an observational context) and not something merely added to the action already defined (i.e., the old notion of the ethnographic observer as extrinsic to the "action" he or she was recording).

There are three criteria that help us decide whether a proper relationship exists between the specific value and the other elements of the act (McCormick, 1973; McCormick & Ramsey, 1978). First, *the means used will not cause more harm than necessary to achieve the value.* In traditional moral terms, the ends cannot be said to justify the mans. If we take "the value" to refer to the production of some form of ethnography, then we must be careful to assure that "the means used" (e.g., inserting oneself into a social network, using photographs or other personal records) do not cause disproportionate harm. We might all agree that serving as *comadre* to an "informant's" child is sufficiently proportionate; we might well argue about whether becoming the lover of an "informant" (particularly if that sexual liaison is not intended to last beyond the time of the research) does more harm than an ethnographic book, paper, or presentation might be worth. Volunteering as a classroom tutor in a program serving adults with mental retardation whom one is interested in observing and interviewing is probably sufficiently proportionate; becoming a bill-paying benefactor to induce cooperation would, by contrast, be morally questionable.

The second criterion is that *no less harmful way exists at present to protect the value.* Some might argue that observational research always and inevitably compromises personal privacy, such that no form of research can ethically protect that cherished value. But most researchers (and others) would probably reject such an extreme view and take the position that there is real value in disseminating the fruits of ethnographic research so as to increase our knowledge and understanding of cultural diversity, or the nature of coping strategies, or any number of currently salient social justice issues. Granted that *all* methods have the potential to harm, we must be sure to choose those that do the *least* amount of harm, but that still enable us to come up with the sort of product that will be effective in communicating the valuable message. The strategy of writing ethnographic fiction, for example, is certainly not foolproof, as anyone with a knowledge of the population with which the ethnographer worked would be able to identify the "characters." But there is far less chance that an outside reader would be able to do so than would be the case with a report based on "objective" materials that are on the public record.

The third criterion is that *the means used to achieve the value will not undermine it.* If one sets out, for example, to use research in order to promote the dignity of people defined as mentally disabled, one must make sure that the research techniques do not subject such people to ridicule. Videotaping a group of people with mental retardation as they play a game of softball might conceivably result in viewers' concluding that such people are gallantly trying their best, but more likely it will result in confirming the popular stereotypes of such people as clumsy and inept, objects of pity (at best) or of scorn (at worst) rather than dignified individuals. Videotaping as an ethnographic method is ethically neutral; its appropriateness must be evaluated in this proportionate context.

McCormick (1973) suggests three modes of knowing whether there is a proportionate reason to carry out a suggested action. First, we know that a proper relation exists between a specific value and all other elements of an act through *experience*, which sometimes amounts to plain common sense. For example, although we may think that it is important to encourage individual expression, we know from experience that doing so in the context of a community (such as a monastery) in which the individual is, by tradition, subordinate to the group will do real violence to the precepts by which the people we are intent on studying have historically formed themselves into a community. Experience might suggest that we rethink a decision to collect personal life histories of people in such groups in favor of focusing on the collective reconstruction of remembered common activities or events.

Second, we may know that a proper relationship exists through our own *intuition* that some actions are inherently disproportionate, even if we do not have personal experience of their being so. Janssens (1979, p. 63) asserts that we can discover disproportion through "feelings of disunity" within the self. For example, we should intuitively know that publishing personal material collected from people living in an oppressive, totalitarian society might ultimately result in that material being used against them, even in the absence of a direct or explicit threat. Our righteous goal of exposing the tyrannical regime might well backfire on the very people we are trying to help. Our intuition might warn us that an otherwise praiseworthy research proposal (e.g., to collect life histories or genealogies, or to observe the daily activities at the local market) could have harmful consequences if the product of the research were to fall into the wrong hands. A perception of what *could* happen (the result of intuition) is, of course, different from a perception of what *will* happen (the result of experience), and we are clearly not well served by dreaming up every conceivable disaster. It serves no purpose to allow ourselves to be paralyzed beforehand by overactive guilty consciences. But there is certainly a commonsensical hierarchy of plausibility that obtains in such cases—some things that *could* happen are more likely to come about than others.

Third, we know through *trial and error.* This is a mode of knowing that would be completely impossible under current institutional ethical guidelines. But the fact is that we do not and cannot know all possible elements in any given human social interaction, and the idea that we can

predict—and thereby forestall—all harm is naïve in the extreme. An ethical research design would omit (or seek to modify) that which experience and intuition tell us is most likely to do harm; we can then proceed, but only on the understanding that the plan will be modified in the midst of the action when it becomes clear what is feasible and desirable in the real-life situation. For those uncomfortable with the indeterminacy of the term *trial and error,* Walter (1984) suggests "rational analysis and argument" (p. 38). By gathering evidence and formulating logical arguments, we try to give reasons to support our choices for certain actions over others. But the plain fact is that this way of knowing does, indeed, involve the possibility of committing an "error," perhaps one that may have unexpected harmful consequences. It is nonetheless disingenuous to hold that all possibility of harm can be anticipated and that any human action (including a research project based on interpersonal interaction) can be made risk-free. The moral advantage of the proportionate reasoning strategy is that it encourages the researcher to admit to an error once it has occurred, to correct it as far as possible, and to move on; the "objective" mode of research ethics, by contrast, encourages researchers to believe that they have eliminated all such problems, so that they are disinclined to own up to those problems that (perhaps inevitably) crop up and hence are less capable of repairing the damage. Those who work with people with developmental disabilities are familiar with the expression "the dignity of risk"; it is used to describe the "habilitation" of clients for full participation in the community. To deny the clients the possibility of making mistakes (by assuming that all risk can be eliminated beforehand and by failing to provide training in reasonable problem-solving techniques) is to deny them one of the fundamental characteristics of responsible adult living. One either lives in a shelter, protected from risk by objectified "codes," or one lives real life. The ethical paradigm suggested here does nothing more than allow the observational researcher the dignity of risk.

The logic of proportionate reason as a foundation for an ethical practice of social research might seem, at first glance, to slide into subjective relativism. Indeed, the conscience of the individual researcher plays a very large part in determining the morality of a given interaction. But proper proportionalism cannot be reduced to a proposition that an action can mean anything an individual wants it to mean, or that ethics is simply a matter of personal soul-searching. The strategy, rather, is based on a sense of community—the individual making the ethical decision must ultimately be guided by a kind of "communal discernment" (Gula, 1989, p. 278). When we speak of "experience," for example, we refer not just to personal experience, but to the "wisdom of the past" as it is embodied in the community's traditions. As such, it "demands broad consultation to seek the experience and reflection of others in order to prevent the influence of self interest from biasing perception and judgment. Using proportionalism requires more moral consultation with the community than would ever be required if the morality of actions were based on only one aspect . . . apart from its relation to all the . . . features of the action" (Gula, 1989, p. 278). That being the case, the ideal IRB would not be content with a utilitarian checklist of presumed consequences; it would constitute a circle of "wise" peers with whom the researcher could discuss and work out the sometimes conflicting demands of experience, intuition, and the potential for rational analysis and argument. The essential problem with current ethical codes, from the standpoint of qualitative observational researchers, is that they set up an arbitrary—and quite unnecessary—adversarial relationship between researchers and the rest of the scholarly community. The framework of proportionate reason implies that ethical research is the product of shared discourse, not of a species of prosecutorial inquisition.

◆ Prospects for Observational Research

As Adler and Adler (1994) remark in their chapter appearing in the first edition of this *Handbook,* "Forecasting the wax and wane of social

science research methods is always uncertain" (p. 389), although they were able to do so by extrapolating from existing trends. In that same cautious spirit, we suggest that the future of observational research will most likely be in the direction of what Barrett (1996) refers to as "qualitative investigation with a difference" (p. 237). Barrett refers to the "demystification" of methodology; whereas once ethnographers spoke in a vague way about "rapport" or "empathy," they now publish and lecture extensively in the soul-baring manner suggested by the preceding literature review. One important result of that demystification is that observation can no longer be said to be a key to those grand, but somewhat opaque, units of analysis, "culture" and "society." Abu-Lughod (1991) has, indeed, urged qualitative researchers to use their techniques to undermine those concepts, which, she feels, have become the contemporary equivalents of "race"—categories that separate people, arrange them into hierarchies, and freeze the system so that institutionalized inequality prevails. To speak in such terms reifies the treatment of difference and hierarchy as somehow "natural." Observational research, by contrast, has the potential to turn our attention to what Abu-Lughod (1991) calls "the ethnography of the particular" (p. 154). Rather than attempting to describe the composite culture of a group or analyze the full range of institutions that supposedly constitute the society, the observational ethnographer will be able to provide a rounded account of the lives of particular people, the focus being on individuals and their ever-changing relationships rather than on the supposedly homogeneous, coherent, patterned, and (particularly in the case of traditional anthropologists) timeless nature of the supposed "group."

Abu-Lughod's position was foreshadowed by Geertz (1973) more than two decades ago (an indication of how slowly it takes some predictions to come to pass). Geertz advocated setting aside the traditional social science concern for "complexes of concrete behavior patterns" in favor of a "concern with the particular" based on the interpretation of "significant symbols" (p. 44). The above literature review clearly indicates that this shift is already taking place, in the interest of feminists and postmodernists of all persuasions in life history and "meaning." At present, the type of social science represented by this approach to the observation of the particular coexists uneasily with more quantitative and positivistic schools of sociology, anthropology, and social psychology. There is, however, considerable doubt as to how long that link can survive, given the very different aims and approaches of the diverging branches of the once epistemologically unified social sciences. It seems not unlikely that observational techniques will find a home in a redefined genre of cultural studies (composed of the qualitative elements of the older disciplines), leaving their positivist colleagues to carry on in a redefined social science discipline.

Humanists though they may be, observational researchers are as dependent on the evolution of technology as their quantitative colleagues. *Observation* once implied a notebook and pencil, and perhaps a sketch pad; first still and then motion pictures were later added to the ethnographer's resources. Tape recorders have been supplemented (and, in some cases, even supplanted) by video recorders. Note taking has been enhanced by the advent of the laptop computer, and computer programs for the analysis of narrative data are being developed at a brisk pace. Observation-based ethnographers are, as a consequence, being pulled in two directions. On the one hand, they speak the theoretical language of "situatedness," indeterminacy, and relativism; but on the other hand, they rely more and more on technology that suggests the capturing of "reality" in ways that could be said to transcend the individual researcher's relatively limited capacity to interpret. The technology makes it possible for the ethnographer to record and analyze people and events with a degree of particularity that would have been impossible just a decade ago, but it also has the potential to privilege what is captured on the record at the expense of the lived experience as the ethnographer has personally known it. It would be foolish to suggest that for the sake of consistency, observation-based ethnographers should eschew further traffic with sophisticated recording and analyzing technology. But it would be equally foolish to assume that the current very strong trend in the direction of individualized

particularization can continue without significant modification in the face of technology that has the perceived power to objectify and turn into "data" everything it encounters. Perhaps it will become necessary for us to turn our observational powers on the very process of observation, to understand ourselves not only as psychosocial creatures (which is the current tendency) but as users of technology. As Postman (1993) has pointed out, technological change is never merely additive or subtractive, never simply an aid to doing what has always been done. It is, rather, "ecological" in the sense that a change in one aspect of behavior has ramifications throughout the entire system of which that behavior is a part. "Surrounding every technology are institutions whose organization . . . reflects the world-view promoted by that technology" (p. 18). Under those circumstances, perhaps the most effective use we can make of observational techniques in the near future will be to discern the ethos of the technology that we can no longer afford to think of as a neutral adjunct to our business-as-usual. It is a technology that itself has the capacity to define our business. We need to turn our observational powers to what happens not just when "we" encounter "them," but when "we" do so with a particular kind of totalizing technology.

Nevertheless, it seems quite clear that the ·once-unquestioned hegemony of positivistic epistemology that encompassed even so fundamentally humanistic a research technique as observation has now been shaken to its roots. One telling indication of the power of that transition—and a challenging indication of things to come—is a recent comment by Stephen Jay Gould (1998), the renowned paleontologist and historian of science, who has ruefully admitted:

> No faith can be more misleading than an unquestioned personal conviction that the apparent testimony of one's eyes must provide a purely objective account, scarcely requiring any validation beyond the claim itself. Utterly unbiased observation must rank as a primary myth and shibboleth of science, for we can only see what fits into our mental space, and all description includes interpretation as well as sensory reporting. (p. 72)

▪ Notes

1. The critique of objectivity was certainly not invented by the postmodernists. Indeed, a good case can be made that the prescient, discipline-spanning scholar Gregory Bateson (1972) was contributing rigorous and systematic analyses of the place of observers in the field long before it was considered possible to question the rationale of striving to eliminate "observer bias." His "cybernetic" theory suggested that the observer is inevitably tied to what is observed. Nevertheless, the debate that currently commands the attention of ethnographic researchers was jump-started by critics of the cultural studies persuasion, and the debate is most deeply informed by their vocabulary as well as by their specific epistemological concerns.

2. *Dialogue* need not be taken literally to mean a conversation between two parties; in practice, it often consists of multiple—even contradictory—voices.

▪ References

Abu-Lughod, L. (1991). Writing against culture. In R. G. Fox (Ed.), *Recapturing anthropology: Working in the present* (pp. 137-162). Santa Fe, NM: School of American Research Press.

Abu-Lughod, L. (1997). The interpretation of culture(s) after television. *Reflections, 59,* 109-134.

Adler, P. A., & Adler, P. (1987). *Membership roles in field research.* Newbury Park, CA: Sage.

Adler, P. A., & Adler, P. (1994). Observational techniques. In N. K. Denzin & Y. S. Lincoln (Eds.), *Handbook of qualitative research* (pp. 377-392). Thousand Oaks, CA: Sage.

Agar, M., & Feldman, H. (1980). A four-city study of PCP users: Methodology and findings. In C. Akins & G. Beschner (Eds.), *Ethnography: A research tool for policymakers in the drug and alcohol fields* (pp. 80-146). Rockville, MD: National Institute on Drug Abuse.

Altheide, D. L., & Johnson, J. M. (1994). Criteria for assessing interpretive validity in qualitative research. In N. K. Denzin & Y. S. Lincoln (Eds.), *Handbook of qualitative research* (pp. 485-499). Thousand Oaks, CA: Sage.

Altork, K. (1995). Walking the fire line: The erotic dimension of the fieldwork experience. In D. Kulick & M. Willson (Eds.), *Taboo: Sex, identity and erotic subjectivity in anthropological fieldwork* (pp. 107-139). London: Routledge.

Angrosino, M. V. (1989). The two lives of Rebecca Levenstone: Symbolic interaction in the generation of the life history. *Journal of Anthropological Research, 45,* 315-326.

Angrosino, M. V. (1991). Conversations in a monastery. *Oral History Review, 19,* 55-73.

Angrosino, M. V. (1992). Metaphors of stigma: How deinstitutionalized mentally retarded adults see themselves. *Journal of Contemporary Ethnography, 21,* 171-199.

Angrosino, M. V. (1994). On the bus with Vonnie Lee: Explorations in life history and metaphor. *Journal of Contemporary Ethnography, 23,* 14-28.

Angrosino, M. V. (1995a). Eutaw Jack: The man born blind. In B. Grindal & F. Salamone (Eds.), *Bridges to humanity: Narratives on anthropology and friendship* (pp. 7-22). Prospect Heights, IL: Waveland.

Angrosino, M. V. (1995b). *The Tampa AIDS Network: An oral history.* Tampa: University of South Florida, Center for Applied Anthropology.

Angrosino, M. V. (1997a). Among the savage Anthros: Reflections on the SAS oral history project. *Southern Anthropologist, 24,* 25-32.

Angrosino, M. V. (1997b). The ethnography of mental retardation: An applied perspective. *Journal of Contemporary Ethnography, 26,* 98-109.

Angrosino, M. V. (1998). *Opportunity House: Ethnographic stories of mental retardation.* Walnut Creek, CA: AltaMira.

Angrosino, M. V., & Zagnoli, L. J. (1992). Gender constructs and social identity: Implications for community-based care of retarded adults. In T. Whitehead & B. Reid (Eds.), *Gender constructs and social issues* (pp. 40-69). Urbana: University of Illinois Press.

Ashton-Jones, E., & Thomas, D. K. (1995). Composition, collaboration, and women's ways of knowing: A conversation with Mary Belenky. In G. A. Olson & E. Hirsh (Eds.),

Women writing culture (pp. 81-104). Albany: State University of New York Press.

Barnett, H. G. (1983). Learning about culture: Reconstruction, participation, administration, 1934-1954. In G. W. Stocking, Jr. (Ed.), *Observers observed: Essays on ethnographic fieldwork* (pp. 157-174). Madison: University of Wisconsin Press.

Barrett, S. R. (1996). *Anthropology: A student's guide to theory and method.* Toronto: University of Toronto Press.

Bateson, G. (1972). *Steps to an ecology of mind: Collected essays in anthropology, psychiatry, evolution, and epistemology.* San Francisco: Chandler.

Behar, R. (1993). *Translated woman: Crossing the border with Esperanza's story.* Boston: Beacon.

Behar, R. (1996). *The vulnerable observer: Anthropology that breaks your heart.* Boston: Beacon.

Bell, J., & Jankowiak, W. R. (1992). The ethnographer vs. the folk expert: Pitfalls of contract ethnography. *Human Organization, 51,* 412-417.

Berik, G. (1996). Understanding the gender system in rural Turkey: Fieldwork dilemmas of conformity and intervention. In D. L. Wolf (Ed.), *Feminist dilemmas in fieldwork* (pp. 56-71). Boulder, CO: Westview.

Bernard, H. R. (1988). *Research methods in cultural anthropology.* Newbury Park, CA: Sage.

Blackwood, E. (1995). Falling in love with an-Other lesbian: Reflections on identity in fieldwork. In D. Kulick & M. Willson (Eds.), *Taboo: Sex, identity and erotic subjectivity in anthropological fieldwork* (pp. 51-75). London: Routledge.

Bolton, R. (1995). Tricks, friends, and lovers: Erotic encounters in the field. In D. Kulick & M. Willson (Eds.), *Taboo: Sex, identity and erotic subjectivity in anthropological fieldwork* (pp. 140-167). London: Routledge.

Bolton, R. (1996). Coming home: The journey of a gay ethnographer in the years of the plague. In E. Lewin & W. L. Leap (Eds.), *Out in the field: Reflections of lesbian and gay anthropologists* (pp. 147-170). Urbana: University of Illinois Press.

Brewer, D. D. (1992). Hip hop graffiti writers' evaluations of strategies to control illegal graffiti. *Human Organization, 51,* 188-196.

Burkhart, G. (1996). Not given to personal disclosure. In E. Lewin & W. L. Leap (Eds.), *Out in the field: Reflections of lesbian and gay anthropologists* (pp. 31-48). Urbana: University of Illinois Press.

Cahill, L. S. (1981). Teleology, utilitarianism, and Christian ethics. *Theological Studies, 42,* 601-629.

Chavez, L. R., Flores, E. T., & Lopez-Garza, M. (1990). Here today, gone tomorrow? Undocumented settlers and immigration reform. *Human Organization, 49,* 193-205.

Clifford, J. (1983a). On ethnographic authority. *Representations, 1,* 118-146.

Clifford, J. (1983b). Power and dialogue in ethnography: Marcel Griaule's initiation. In G. W. Stocking, Jr. (Ed.), *Observers observed: Essays on ethnographic fieldwork* (pp. 121-156). Madison: University of Wisconsin Press.

Cole, D. (1983). "The value of a person lies in his *Herzenbildung*": Franz Boas' Baffin Island letter-diary, 1883-1884. In G. W. Stocking, Jr. (Ed.), *Observers observed: Essays on ethnographic fieldwork* (pp. 13-52). Madison: University of Wisconsin Press.

Curran, C. E. (1979). Utilitarianism and contemporary moral theology: Situating the debates. In C. E. Curran & R. A. McCormick (Eds.), *Readings in moral theology* (pp. 341-362). Ramsey, NJ: Paulist Press.

Dembo, R., Hughes, P., Jackson, L., & Mieczkowski, T. (1993). Crack cocaine dealing by adolescents in two public housing projects: A pilot study. *Human Organization, 52,* 89-96.

Denzin, N. K. (1997a). *Interpretive ethnography: Ethnographic practices for the 21st century.* Thousand Oaks, CA: Sage.

Denzin, N. K. (1997b). Performance texts. In W. G. Tierney & Y. S. Lincoln (Eds.), *Representation and the text: Re-framing the narrative voice* (pp. 179-218). Albany: State University of New York Press.

Dubisch, J. (1995). Lovers in the field: Sex, dominance, and the female anthropologist. In D. Kulick & M. Willson (Eds.), *Taboo: Sex, identity and erotic subjectivity in anthropological fieldwork* (pp. 29-50). London: Routledge.

Edelman, M. (1996). Devil, not-quite-white, rootless cosmopolitan: *Tsuris* in Latin America, the Bronx, and the USSR. In C. Ellis & A.

P. Bochner (Eds.), *Composing ethnography: Alternative forms of qualitative writing* (pp. 267-300). Walnut Creek, CA: AltaMira.

Ellis, C. (1997). Evocative autoethnography: Writing emotionally about our lives. In W. G. Tierney & Y. S. Lincoln (Eds.), *Representation and the text: Re-framing the narrative voice* (pp. 115-142). Albany: State University of New York Press.

Ferguson, J. (1996). The country and the city on the copperbelt. In A. Gupta & J. Ferguson (Eds.), *Culture, power, place: Explorations in critical anthropology* (pp. 137-154). Durham, NC: Duke University Press.

Fluehr-Lobban, C. (1994). Informed consent in anthropological research: We are not exempt. *Human Organization, 53,* 1-10.

Fox, K. V. (1996). Silent voices: A subversive reading of child sexual abuse. In C. Ellis & A. P. Bochner (Eds.), *Composing ethnography: Alternative forms of qualitative writing* (pp. 330-356). Walnut Creek, CA: AltaMira.

Gearing, J. (1995). Fear and loving in the West Indies: Research from the heart (as well as the head). In D. Kulick & M. Willson (Eds.), *Taboo: Sex, identity and erotic subjectivity in anthropological fieldwork* (pp. 186-218). London: Routledge.

Geertz, C. (1973). *The interpretation of cultures: Selected essays.* New York: Basic Books.

Giroux, H. A. (1995). Writing the space of the public intellectual. In G. A. Olson & E. Hirsh (Eds.), *Women writing culture* (pp. 195-198). Albany: State University of New York Press.

Gold, R. L. (1958). Roles in sociological field observation. *Social Forces, 36,* 217-223.

Gold, R. L. (1997). The ethnographic method in sociology. *Qualitative Inquiry, 3,* 388-402.

Goodman, L. (1996). Rites of passing. In E. Lewin & W. L. Leap (Eds.), *Out in the field: Reflections of lesbian and gay anthropologists* (pp. 49-57). Urbana: University of Illinois Press.

Gould, S. J. (1998). The sharp-eyed lynx, outfoxed by nature (part two). *Natural History, 107,* 23-27, 69-73.

Gula, R. M. (1989). *Reason informed by faith.* New York: Paulist Press.

Gupta, A., & Ferguson, J. (1996a). Beyond "culture": Space, identity, and the politics of difference. In A. Gupta & J. Ferguson (Eds.), *Culture, power, place: Explorations in critical anthropology* (pp. 33-52). Durham, NC: Duke University Press.

Gupta, A., & Ferguson, J. (1996b). Culture, power, place: Ethnography at the end of an era. In A. Gupta & J. Ferguson (Eds.), *Culture, power, place: Explorations in critical anthropology* (pp. 1-32). Durham, NC: Duke University Press.

Gupta, A., & Ferguson, J. (1996c). Discipline and practice: "The field" as site, method, and location in anthropology. In A. Gupta & J. Ferguson (Eds.), *Anthropological locations: Boundaries and grounds of a field science* (pp. 1-46). Berkeley: University of California Press.

Hammond, J. L. (1996). Popular education in the Salvadoran guerrilla army. *Human Organization, 55,* 436-445.

Hannerz, U. (1969). *Soulside.* New York: Columbia University Press.

Hareven, T. (1996). The search for generational memory. In D. K. Dunaway & W. K. Baum (Eds.), *Oral history: An interdisciplinary anthology* (2nd ed., pp. 241-256). Walnut Creek, CA: AltaMira.

Hinsley, C. (1983). Ethnographic charisma and scientific routine: Cushing and Fewkes in the American Southwest, 1879-1893. In G. W. Stocking, Jr. (Ed.), *Observers observed: Essays on ethnographic fieldwork* (pp. 53-69). Madison: University of Wisconsin Press.

Hirsh, E., & Olson, G. A. (1995). Starting from marginalized lives: A conversation with Sandra Harding. In G. A. Olson & E. Hirsh (Eds.), *Women writing culture* (pp. 3-44). Albany: State University of New York Press.

Hoose, B. (1987). *Proportionalism.* Washington: Georgetown University Press.

Hsiung, P.-C. (1996). Between bosses and workers: The dilemma of a keen observer and a vocal feminist. In D. L. Wolf (Ed.), *Feminist dilemmas in fieldwork* (pp. 122-137). Boulder, CO: Westview.

Hubbard, A. S. (1997). Face-to-face at arm's length: Conflict norms and extra-group relations in grassroots dialogue groups. *Human Organization, 56,* 265-274.

Janssens, L. (1979). Ontic evil and moral evil. In C. E. Curran & R. A. McCormick (Eds.), *Readings in moral theology* (pp. 49-72). Ramsey, NJ: Paulist Press.

Kennedy, E. L., & Davis, M. (1996). Constructing an ethnohistory of the Buffalo lesbian community: Reflexivity, dialogue, and politics. In E. Lewin & W. L. Leap (Eds.), *Out in the field: Reflections of gay and lesbian anthropologists* (pp. 171-199). Urbana: University of Illinois Press.

Killick, A. P. (1995). The penetrating intellect: On being white, straight, and male in Korea. In D. Kulick & M. Willson (Eds.), *Taboo: Sex, identity and erotic subjectivity in anthropological fieldwork* (pp. 76-106). London: Routledge.

Koester, S. K. (1994). Copping, running, and paraphernalia laws: Contextual variables and needle risk behavior among injection drug users in Denver. *Human Organization, 53,* 287-295.

Kolker, A. (1996). Thrown overboard: The human costs of health care rationing. In C. Ellis & A. P. Bochner (Eds.), *Composing ethnography: Alternative forms of qualitative writing* (pp. 132-159). Walnut Creek, CA: AltaMira.

Kuhlmann, A. (1992). Collaborative research among the Kickapoo tribe of Oklahoma. *Human Organization, 51,* 274-283.

Kuklick, H. (1996). After Ishmael: The fieldwork tradition and its future. In A. Gupta & J. Ferguson (Eds.), *Anthropological locations: Boundaries and grounds of a field science* (pp. 47-65). Berkeley: University of California Press.

Lang, S. (1996). Traveling woman: Conducting a fieldwork project on gender variance and homosexuality among North American Indians. In E. Lewin & W. L. Leap (Eds.), *Out in the field: Reflections of lesbian and gay anthropologists* (pp. 86-110). Urbana: University of Illinois Press.

Larcom, J. (1983). Following Deacon: The problem of ethnographic reanalysis, 1926-1981. In G. W. Stocking, Jr. (Ed.), *Observers observed: Essays on ethnographic fieldwork* (pp. 175-195). Madison: University of Wisconsin Press.

Lather, P. (1997). Creating a multilayered text: Women, AIDS, and angels. In W. G. Tierney & Y. S. Lincoln (Eds.), *Representation and the text: Re-framing the narrative voice* (pp. 233-258). Albany: State University of New York Press.

Lewin, E., & Leap, W. L. (1996). Introduction. In E. Lewin & W. L. Leap (Eds.), *Out in the field: Reflections of lesbian and gay anthropologists* (pp. 1-30). Urbana: University of Illinois Press.

Liebow, E. (1967). *Tally's corner: A study of Negro street corner men.* Boston: Little, Brown.

Maddox, R. (1996). Bombs, bikinis, and the popes of rock 'n' roll: Reflections on resistance, the play of subordinations, and liberalism in Andalusia and academia, 1983-1995. In A. Gupta & J. Ferguson (Eds.), *Culture, power, place: Explorations in critical anthropology* (pp. 277-290). Durham, NC: Duke University Press.

Mahmood, C. K. (1996). Why Sikhs fight. In A. Wolfe & H. Yang (Eds.), *Anthropological contributions to conflict resolution* (pp. 7-30). Athens: University of Georgia Press.

Malkki, L. H. (1996a). National geographic: The rooting of peoples and the territorialization of national identity among scholars and refugees. In A. Gupta & J. Ferguson (Eds.), *Culture, power, place: Explorations in critical anthropology* (pp. 53-74). Durham, NC: Duke University Press.

Malkki, L. H. (1996b). News and culture: Transitory phenomena and the fieldwork tradition. In A. Gupta & J. Ferguson (Eds.), *Anthropological locations: Boundaries and grounds of a field science* (pp. 86-101). Berkeley: University of California Press.

Marcus, G. E. (1997). The uses of complicity in the changing mise-en-scène of anthropological fieldwork. *Reflections, 59,* 85-108.

Matsumoto, V. (1996). Reflections on oral history: Research in a Japanese American community. In D. L. Wolf (Ed.), *Feminist dilemmas in fieldwork* (pp. 160-169). Boulder, CO: Westview.

McCall, G. J., Ngeva, J., & Mbebe, M. (1997). Mapping conflict cultures: Interpersonal disputing in a South African black township. *Human Organization, 56,* 71-78.

McCormick, R. A. (1973). *Ambiguity and moral choice.* Milwaukee, WI: Marquette University Press.

McCormick, R. A., & Ramsey, P. (1978). *Doing evil to achieve good.* Chicago: Loyola University Press.

Mienczakowski, J. (1996). An ethnographic act: The construction of consensual theater. In C. Ellis & A. P. Bochner (Eds.), *Composing ethnography: Alternative forms of qualitative writing* (pp. 244-266). Walnut Creek, CA: AltaMira.

Miles, M. B., & Huberman, A. M. (1994). *Qualitative data analysis: An expanded sourcebook* (2nd ed.). Thousand Oaks, CA: Sage.

Moreno, E. (1995). Rape in the field: Reflections from a survivor. In D. Kulick & M. Willson (Eds.), *Taboo: Sex, identity and erotic subjectivity in anthropological fieldwork* (pp. 219-250). London: Routledge.

Morton, H. (1995). My "chastity belt": Avoiding seduction in Tonga. In D. Kulick & M. Willson (Eds.), *Taboo: Sex, identity and erotic subjectivity in anthropological fieldwork* (pp. 168-185). London: Routledge.

Murray, S. P. (1996). Male homosexuality in Guatemala: Possible insights and certain confusions from sleeping with the natives. In E. Lewin & W. L. Leap (Eds.), *Out in the field: Reflections of lesbian and gay anthropologists* (pp. 236-260). Urbana: University of Illinois Press.

Newton, E. (1993). My best informant's dress: The erotic equation in fieldwork. *Cultural Anthropology, 8,* 3-23.

Olson, G. A. (1995a). Resisting a discourse of mastery: A conversation with Jean-François Lyotard. In G. A. Olson & E. Hirsh (Eds.), *Women writing culture* (pp. 169-194). Albany: State University of New York Press.

Olson, G. A. (1995b). Writing, literacy and technology: Toward a cyborg writing. In G. A. Olson & E. Hirsh (Eds.), *Women writing culture* (pp. 45-80). Albany: State University of New York Press.

Olson, G. A., & Hirsh, E. (1995). Feminist praxis and the politics of literacy: A conversation with bell hooks. In G. A. Olson & E. Hirsh (Eds.), *Women writing culture* (pp. 105-140). Albany: State University of New York Press.

Pelto, P. J., & Pelto, G. H. (1978). *Anthropological research: The structure of inquiry* (2nd ed.). New York: Cambridge University Press.

Peters, J. D. (1996). Seeing bifocally: Media, place, culture. In A. Gupta & J. Ferguson (Eds.), *Culture, power, place: Explorations in critical anthropology* (pp. 75-92). Durham, NC: Duke University Press.

Polkinghorne, D. E. (1997). Reporting qualitative research as practice. In W. G. Tierney & Y. S. Lincoln (Eds.), *Representation and the text: Re-framing the narrative voice* (pp. 3-22). Albany: State University of New York Press.

Postman, N. (1993). *Technopoly: The surrender of culture to technology.* New York: Vintage.

Quinney, R. (1996). Once my father traveled west to California. In C. Ellis & A. P. Bochner (Eds.), *Composing ethnography: Alternative forms of qualitative writing* (pp. 357-382). Walnut Creek, CA: AltaMira.

Ronai, C. R. (1996). My mother is mentally retarded. In C. Ellis & A. P. Bochner (Eds.), *Composing ethnography: Alternative forms of qualitative writing* (pp. 109-131). Walnut Creek, CA: AltaMira.

Rossman, G. B., & Rallis, S. F. (1998). *Learning in the field: An introduction to qualitative research.* Thousand Oaks, CA: Sage.

Sewell, W. H. (1997). Geertz and history: From synchrony to transformation. *Reflections, 59,* 35-55.

Silverman, D. (1993). *Interpreting qualitative data: Strategies for analysing talk, text and interaction.* London: Sage.

Sluka, J. A. (1990). Participant observation in violent social contexts. *Human Organization, 49,* 114-126.

Stepick, A., & Stepick, C. D. (1990). People in the shadows: Survey research among Haitians in Miami. *Human Organization, 49,* 64-77.

Stocking, G. W., Jr. (1983a). The ethnographer's magic: Fieldwork in British anthropology from Tylor to Malinowski. In G. W. Stocking, Jr. (Ed.), *Observers observed: Essays on ethnographic fieldwork* (pp. 70-120). Madison: University of Wisconsin Press.

Stocking, G. W., Jr. (1983b). History of anthropology: Whence/whither. In G. W. Stocking, Jr. (Ed.), *Observers observed: Essays on ethnographic fieldwork* (pp. 3-12). Madison: University of Wisconsin Press.

Tanaka, G. (1997). Pico College. In W. G. Tierney & Y. S. Lincoln (Eds.), *Representation and the text: Re-framing the narrative voice* (pp. 259-304). Albany: State University of New York Press.

Tierney, W. G. (1997). Lost in translation: Time and voice in qualitative research. In W. G. Tierney & Y. S. Lincoln (Eds.), *Representation and the text: Re-framing the narrative voice* (pp. 23-36). Albany: State University of New York Press.

Tillman-Healy, L. M. (1996). A secret life in a culture of thinness: Reflections on body, food, and bulimia. In C. Ellis & A. P. Bochner (Eds.), *Composing ethnography: Alternative forms of qualitative writing* (pp. 76-108). Walnut Creek, CA: AltaMira.

van Gelder, P. J., & Kaplan, C. D. (1992). The finishing moment: Temporal and spatial features of sexual interactions between streetwalkers and car clients. *Human Organization, 51*, 253-263.

Walter, J. (1984). Proportionate reason and its three levels of inquiry: Structuring the ongoing debate. *Louvain Studies, 10*, 30-40.

Walters, D. M. (1996). Cast among outcastes: Interpreting sexual orientation, racial, and gender identity in the Yemen Arab Republic. In E. Lewin & W. L. Leap (Eds.), *Out in the field: Reflections of lesbian and gay anthropologists* (pp. 58-69). Urbana: University of Illinois Press.

Wax, M. L., & Cassell, J. (1979). *Federal regulations: Ethical issues and social research.* Boulder, CO: Westview.

Werner, O., & Schoepfle, G. M. (1987). *Systematic fieldwork: Vol. 1. Foundations of ethnography and interviewing.* Newbury Park, CA: Sage.

Weston, K. (1996). Requiem for a street fighter. In E. Lewin & W. L. Leap (Eds.), *Out in the field: Reflections of lesbian and gay anthro-*

pologists (pp. 274-286). Urbana: University of Illinois Press.

Whyte, W. F. (1955). *Street corner society: The social structure of an Italian slum* (2nd ed.). Chicago: University of Chicago Press.

Williams, W. L. (1996). Being gay and doing fieldwork. In E. Lewin & W. L. Leap (Eds.), *Out in the field: Reflections of lesbian and gay anthropologists* (pp. 70-85). Urbana: University of Illinois Press.

Willson, M. (1995). Perspective and difference: Sexualization, the field, and the ethnographer. In D. Kulick & M. Willson (Eds.), *Taboo: Sex, identity and erotic subjectivity in anthropological fieldwork* (pp. 251-275). London: Routledge.

Wolcott, H. F. (1995). *The art of fieldwork.* Walnut Creek, CA: AltaMira.

Wolf, D. L. (1996). Situating feminist dilemmas in fieldwork. In D. L. Wolf (Ed.), *Feminist dilemmas in fieldwork* (pp. 1-55). Boulder, CO: Westview.

Wolf, M. A. (1992). *A thrice-told tale: Feminism, postmodernism, and ethnographic responsibility.* Stanford, CA: Stanford University Press.

Wolf, M. A. (1996). Afterword: Musings from an old gray wolf. In D. L. Wolf (Ed.), *Feminist dilemmas in fieldwork* (pp. 215-222). Boulder, CO: Westview.

26

THE INTERPRETATION OF DOCUMENTS AND MATERIAL CULTURE

◆ Ian Hodder

This chapter is concerned with the interpretation of mute evidence—that is, with written texts and artifacts. Such evidence, unlike the spoken word, endures physically and thus can be separated across space and time from its author, producer, or user. Material traces thus often have to be interpreted without the benefit of indigenous commentary. There is often no possibility of interaction with spoken emic "insider" as opposed to etic "outsider" perspectives. Even when such interaction is possible, actors often seem curiously inarticulate about the reasons they dress in particular ways, choose particular pottery designs, or discard dung in particular locations. Material traces and residues thus pose special problems for qualitative research. The main disciplines that have tried to develop appropriate theory and method are history, art history, archaeology, anthropology, sociology, cognitive psychology, technology, and modern material culture studies, and it is from this range of disciplines that my account is drawn.

◆ Written Documents and Records

Lincoln and Guba (1985, p. 277) distinguish documents and records on the basis of whether the text was prepared to attest to some formal transaction. Thus records include marriage certificates, driving licenses, building contracts, and banking statements. Documents, on the other hand, are prepared for personal rather than official reasons and include diaries, memos, letters, field notes, and so on. In fact, the two terms are often used interchangeably, although the distinction is an important one and has some parallels with the distinction between writing and speech, to be discussed below. Documents, closer to speech, require more contextualized interpretation. Records, on the other hand, may have local uses that become very distant from officially sanctioned meanings. Documents involve a personal technology, and records a full state technology of power. The distinction is also relevant for qualitative research, in that

◆ 703

researchers may often be able to get access to documents, whereas access to records may be restricted by laws regarding privacy, confidentiality, and anonymity.

Despite the utility of the distinction between documents and records, my concern here is more the problems of interpretation of written texts of all kinds. Such texts are of importance for qualitative research because, in general terms, access can be easy and low cost, because the information provided may differ from and may not be available in spoken form, and because texts endure and thus give historical insight.

It has often been assumed, for example, in the archaeology of historical periods, that written texts provide a "truer" indication of original meanings than do other types of evidence (to be considered below). Indeed, Western social science has long privileged the spoken over the written and the written over the nonverbal (Derrida, 1978). Somehow it is assumed that words get us closer to minds. But as Derrida has shown, meaning does not reside in a text but in the writing and reading of it. As the text is reread in different contexts it is given new meanings, often contradictory and always socially embedded. Thus there is no "original" or "true" meaning of a text outside specific historical contexts. Historical archaeologists have come to accept that historical documents and records give not a better but simply a different picture from that provided by artifacts and architecture. Texts can be used alongside other forms of evidence so that the particular biases of each can be understood and compared.

Equally, different types of texts have to be understood in the contexts of their conditions of production and reading. For example, the analyst will be concerned with whether a text was written as a result of firsthand experience or from secondary sources, whether it was solicited or unsolicited, edited or unedited, anonymous or signed, and so on (Webb, Campbell, Schwartz, & Sechrest, 1966). As Ricoeur (1971) demonstrates, concrete texts differ from the abstract structures of language in that they are written to do something. They can be understood only as what they are—a form of artifact produced under certain material conditions (not everyone can write, or write in a certain way, or have access to relevant technologies of reproduction) embedded within social and ideological systems.

Words are, of course, spoken to do things as well as to say things—they have practical and social impact as well as communication function. Once words are transformed into a written text, the gap between the "author" and the "reader" widens and the possibility of multiple reinterpretations increases. The text can "say" many different things in different contexts. But also the written text is an artifact, capable of transmission, manipulation, and alteration, of being used and discarded, reused and recycled—"doing" different things contextually through time. The writing down of words often allows language and meanings to be controlled more effectively, and to be linked to strategies of centralization and codification. The word, concretized or "made flesh" in the artifact, can transcend context and gather through time extended symbolic connotations. The word made enduring in artifacts has an important role to play in both secular and religious processes of the legitimation of power. Yet there is often a tension between the concrete nature of the written word, its enduring nature, and the continuous potential for rereading meanings in new contexts, undermining the authority of the word. Text and context are in a continual state of tension, each defining and redefining the other, saying and doing things differently through time.

In a related way, the written texts of anthropologists and archaeologists are increasingly coming under scrutiny as employing rhetorical strategies in order to establish positions of authority (e.g., Tilley, 1989). Archaeologists are used to the idea that their scientific activities leave traces and transform the worlds they study. Excavations cannot be repeated, and the residues of trenches, spoil tips, and old beer cans remain as specific expressions of a particular way of looking at the world. The past has been transformed into a present product, including the field notes and site reports. Ethnographic field notes (Sanjek, 1990) also transform the object of study into a historically situated product, "capturing" the "other" within a familiar routine. The field text has to be contextualized within specific historical moments.

I shall in this chapter treat written texts as special cases of artifacts, subject to similar interpretive procedures. In both texts and artifacts the problem is one of situating material culture within varying contexts while at the same time entering into a dialectic relationship between those contexts and the context of the analyst. This hermeneutical exercise, in which the lived experience surrounding the material culture is translated into a different context of interpretation, is common for both texts and other forms of material culture. I will note various differences between language and material culture in what follows, but the interpretive parallels have been widely discussed in the consideration of material culture as text (e.g., Hodder, 1991; Moore, 1986; Tilley, 1990).

◆ Artifact Analysis and Its Importance for the Interpretation of Social Experience

Ancient and modern buildings and artifacts, the intended and unintended residues of human activity, give alternative insights into the ways in which people perceived and fashioned their lives. Shortcuts across lawns indicate preferred traffic patterns, foreign-language signs indicate the degree of integration of a neighborhood, the number of cigarettes in an ashtray betrays a nervous tension, and the amount of paperwork in an "in" tray is a measure of workload or of work efficiency and priority (Lincoln & Guba, 1985, p. 280). Despite the inferential problems surrounding such evidence, I wish to establish at the outset that material traces of behavior give an important and different insight from that provided by any number of questionnaires.

"What people say" is often very different from "what people do." This point has perhaps been most successfully established over recent years by research stemming from the work of Bill Rathje (Rathje & Murphy, 1992; Rathje & Thompson, 1981). In studies in Tucson, Arizona, and elsewhere, Rathje and his colleagues collected domestic garbage bags and itemized the contents. It became clear that, for example, people's estimates about the amounts of garbage they produced were wildly incorrect, that discarded beer cans indicated a higher level of alcohol consumption than was admitted to, and that in times of meat shortage people threw away more meat than usual as a result of overhoarding. Thus a full sociological analysis cannot be restricted to interview data. It must also consider the material traces.

In another series of studies, the decoration of rooms as well as pots and other containers has been interpreted as a form of silent discourse conducted by women, whose voice has been silenced by dominant male interests. Decoration may be used to mark out, silently, and to draw attention to, tacitly, areas of female control, such as female areas of houses and the preparation and provision of food in containers. The decoration may at one level provide protection from female pollution, but at another level it expresses female power (Braithwaite, 1982; Donley, 1982; Hodder, 1991).

The study of material culture is thus of importance for qualitative researchers who wish to explore multiple and conflicting voices, differing and interacting interpretations. Many areas of experience are hidden from language, particularly subordinate experience. Ferguson (1991) has shown how study of the material traces of food and pots can provide insight into how slaves on plantations in the American South made sense of and reacted to their domination. The members of this normally silenced group expressed their own perspective in the mundane activities of everyday life.

Analysis of such traces is not a trivial pursuit, as the mundane and the everyday, because unimportant to dominant interests, may be of great importance for the expression of alternative perspectives. The material expression of power (parades, regalia, tombs, and art) can be set against the expression of resistance. The importance of such analysis is increased by the realization that material culture is not simply a passive by-product of other areas of life. Rather, material culture is active (Hodder, 1982). By this I mean that artifacts are produced so as to transform, materially, socially, and ideologically. It is the exchange of artifacts themselves that constructs social relationships; it is the style of spear that creates a feeling of common identity; it is the badge of authority that itself confers authority. Material culture is thus *necessary for* most social constructs. An adequate study of social interaction thus depends on the incorporation of mute material evidence.

◆ *Toward a Theory of Material Culture*

Having established that the study of material culture can be an important tool for sociological and anthropological analysis, we must attempt to build a theory on which the interpretation of material culture can be based. A difficulty here has been the diversity of the category "material culture," ranging from written texts to material symbols surrounding death, drama, and ritual to shopping behavior and to the construction of roads and airplanes. As a result, theoretical directions have often taken rather different paths, as one can see by comparing attempts to build a comprehensive theory for technological behavior (Lemonnier, 1986) and attempts to consider material culture as text (Tilley, 1990).

Ultimately, material culture always has to be interpreted in relation to a situated context of production, use, discard, and reuse. In working toward that contextual interpretation, it may be helpful to distinguish some general characteristics and analogies for the different types of material culture. In this attempt to build a general theory, recent research in a range of disciplines has begun to separate two areas of material meaning.

Some material culture is designed specifically to be communicative and representational. The clearest example is a written text, but this category extends, for example, to the badge and uniform of certain professions, to red and green stop and go traffic lights, to smoke signals, to the images of Christ on the cross. Because this category includes written texts, it is to be expected that meaning in this category might be organized in ways similar to language. Thus, as with words in a language, the material symbols are, outside a historical context, often arbitrary. For example, any design on a flag could be used as long as it differs from the designs on other flags and is recognizable with its own identity. Thus the system of meanings in the case of flags is constructed through similarities and differences in a semiotic code. Miller (1982) has shown how dress is organized both syntagmatically and paradigmatically. The choice of hat, tie, shirt, trousers, shoes, and so on for a particular occasion is informed by a syntax that allows a particular set of clothes to be put together. On the other hand, the distinctions among different types of hats (bowler, straw, cloth, baseball) or jackets constitute paradigmatic choices.

The three broad areas of theory that have been applied to this first type of material meaning derive from information technology, Marxism, and structuralism. In the first, the aim has been to account for the ways in which material symboling can provide adaptive advantage to social groups. Thus the development of complex symboling systems allows more information to be processed more efficiently (e.g., Wobst, 1977). This type of approach is of limited value to qualitative research because it is not concerned with the interpretation and experience of meaningful symbols. In the second, the ideological component of symbols is identified within relations of power and domination (Leone, 1984; Miller & Tilley, 1984) and increasingly power and systems of value and prestige are seen as multiple and dialectical (Miller, Rowlands, & Tilley, 1989; Shanks & Tilley, 1987). The aim of structuralist analysis has been to examine design (e.g., Washburn, 1983) or spatial relationships (e.g., Glassie, 1975; McGhee, 1977) in terms of underlying codes, although here too the tendency has been to emphasize multiple meanings contested within active social contexts as the various directions of poststructuralist thought have been debated (Tilley, 1990).

In much of this work the metaphor of language has been applied to material culture relatively unproblematically. The pot appears to "mean" in the same way as the word *pot*. Recent work has begun to draw attention to the limitations of this analogy between material culture and language, as will become clear in my consideration of the second type of material culture meaning. One can begin to explore the limitations of the analogy by considering that many examples of material culture are not produced to "mean" at all. In other words, they are not produced with symbolic functions as primary. Thus the madeleine cookie discussed in Proust's *A la recherche du temps perdu* (*Swann's Way*) was produced as an enticing food made in a shape representing a fluted scallop. But Proust describes its meaning as quite different from this symbolic representation. Rather, the meaning was the evocation of a whole series of childhood memories, sounds, tastes, smells surrounding Proust's having tea with his mother in winter.

Many if not most material symbols do not work through rules of representation, using a language-like syntax. Rather, they work through the evocation of sets of practices within individual experience. It would be relatively difficult to construct a grammar or dictionary of material symbols except in the case of deliberately representational or symbolic items, such as flags and road signs. This is because most material symbols do not mean in the same way as language. Rather, they come to have abstract meaning through association and practice. Insofar as members of society experience common practices, material symbols can come to have common evocations and common meanings. Thus, for example, the ways in which certain types of food, drink, music, and sport are experienced are embedded within social convention and thus come to have common meaning. A garlic crusher may not be used overtly in Britain to represent or symbolize class, but through a complex set of practices surrounding food and its preparation, the crusher has come to mean class through evocation.

Because objects endure, have their own traces, their own grain, individual objects with unique evocations can be recognized. The specific memory traces associated with any particular object (a particular garlic crusher) will vary from individual to individual. The particularity of material experience and meaning derives not only from the diversity of human life but also from the identifiability of material objects. The identifiable particularity of material experience always has the potential to work against and transform societywide conventions through practice. Because of this dialectic between structure and practice, and because of the multiple local meanings that can be given to things, it would be difficult to construct dictionaries and grammars for most material culture meanings.

Another reason for the inability to produce dictionaries of material culture returns us to the difficulty with which people give discursive accounts of material symbolism. The meanings often remain tacit and implicit. A smell or taste of a madeleine cookie may awake strong feelings, but it is notoriously difficult to describe a taste or a feel or to pin down the emotions evoked. We may know that in practice this or that item of clothing "looks good," "works well," or "is stylish," but we would be at a loss to say what it "means" because the item does not mean—rather, it is embedded in a set of practices that include class, status, goals, aesthetics. We may not know much about art, but we know what we like. On the basis of a set of practical associations, we build up an implicit knowledge about the associations and evocations of particular artifacts or styles. This type of embedded, practical experience seems to be different from the manipulation of rules of representation and from conscious analytic thought. Material symbolic meanings may get us close to lived experience, but they cannot easily be articulated.

The importance of practice for the social and symbolic meanings of artifacts has been emphasized in recent work on technology (Schlanger, 1990). Each technical operation is linked to others in operational chains (Leroi-Gourhan, 1964) involving materials, energy, and gestures. For example, some clays are better for throwing than others, so the type of clay constrains whether a manufacturer can make thrown pots or hand-built statuettes. Quality of clay is related to types of temper that should be used. All such operational chains are nondeterministic, and some degree of social choice is involved (Lemonnier, 1986; Miller, 1985). All operational chains involve aspects of production, exchange, and consumption, and so are part of a network of relations incorporating the material, the economic, the social, and the conceptual.

The practical operational chains often have implications that extend into not only social but also moral realms. For example, Latour (1988) discusses hydraulic door closers, devices that automatically close a door after someone has opened it. The material door closer thus takes the place of, or delegates, the role of a porter, someone who stands there and makes sure that the door stays shut after people have gone through. But use of this particular delegate has various implications, one of which is that very young or infirm people have difficulty getting through the door. A social distinction is unwittingly implied by this technology. In another example, Latour discusses a key used by some inhabitants of Berlin. This double-ended key forces the user to lock the door in order to get the key out. The key delegates for staff or signs that might order a person to "relock the door behind you." Staff or signs would be unreliable—they could be outwitted or ignored. The key enforces a morality. In the same way, "sleeping policemen" (speed bumps) force the driver of a car to be moral and to slow down in front of a school, but this morality is not socially encoded. That would be too unreliable. The morality is embedded within the practical consequences of breaking up one's car by driving too fast over the bumps. The social and moral meanings of the door closer, the Berlin key, or the speed bump are thoroughly embedded in the implications of material practices.

I have suggested that in developing a theory of material culture, the first task is to distinguish at least two different ways in which material culture has abstract meaning beyond primary utilitarian concerns. The first is through rules of representation. The second is through practice and evocation—through the networking, interconnection, and mutual implication of material and nonmaterial. Whereas it may be the case that written language is the prime example of the first category and tools the prime example of the second, language also has to be worked out in practices from which it derives much of its meaning. Equally, we have seen that material items can be placed within language-like codes. But there is some support from cognitive psychology for a general difference between the two types of knowledge. For example, Bechtel (1990, p. 264) argues that rule-based models of cognition are naturally good at quite different types of activity from connectionist models. Where the first is appropriate for problem solving, the second is best at tasks such as pattern recognition and motor control. It seems likely, then, that the skills involved in material practice and the social, symbolic, and moral meanings that are implicated in such practices might involve different cognitive systems from those involved in rules and representations.

Bloch (1991) argues that practical knowledge is fundamentally different from linguistic knowledge in the way it is organized in the mind. Practical knowledge is "chunked" into highly contextualized information about how to "get on" in specific domains of action. Much cultural knowledge is nonlinear and purpose dedicated, formed through the practice of closely related activities. I have argued here that even the practical world involves social and symbolic meanings that are not organized representational codes but that are chunked or contextually organized realms of activity in which emotions, desires, morals, and social relations are involved at the level of implicit taken-for-granted skill or know-how.

It should perhaps be emphasized that the two types of material symbolism—the representational and the evocative or implicative—often work in close relation to each other. Thus a set of practices may associate men and women with different parts of houses or times of day, but in certain social contexts these associations might be built upon to construct symbolic rules of separation and exclusion and to build an abstract representational scheme in which mythology and cosmology play a part (e.g., Yates, 1989). Such schemes also have ideological components that feed back to constrain the practices. Thus practice, evocation, and representation interpenetrate and feed off each other in many if not all areas of life. Structure and practice are recursively related in the "structuration" of material life (Giddens, 1979; see also Bourdieu, 1977).

◆ *Material Meanings in Time*

It appears that people both experience and "read" material culture meanings. There is much more that could be said about how material culture works in the social context. For instance, some examples work by direct and explicit metaphor, where similarities in form refer to historical antecedents, whereas others work by being ambiguous and abstract, by using spectacle or dramatic effect, by controlling the approach of the onlooker, by controlling perspective. Although there is not space here to explore the full range of material strategies, it is important to establish the temporal dimension of lived experience.

As already noted, material culture is durable and can be given new meanings as it is separated from its primary producer. This temporal variation in meaning is often related to changes in meaning across space and culture. Archaeological or ethnographic artifacts are continually being taken out of their contexts and reinterpreted within museums within different social and cultural contexts. The Elgin Marbles housed in the British Museum take on new meanings that are in turn reinterpreted antagonistically in some circles in Greece. American Indian human and artifact remains may have a scientific meaning for archaeologists and biological anthropologists, but they have important emotive and identity meanings for indigenous peoples.

Material items are continually being reinterpreted in new contexts. Also, material culture can be added to or removed from, leaving the traces of reuses and reinterpretations. In some cases, the sequence of use can give insight into the thought processes of an individual, as when flint flakes that have been struck off a core in early prehistory are refitted by archaeologists today (e.g., Pelegrin, 1990) in order to rebuild the flint core and to follow the decisions made by the original flint knapper in producing flakes and tools. In other cases, longer frames of time are involved, as when a monument such as Stonehenge is adapted, rebuilt, and reused for divergent purposes over millennia up to the present day (Chippindale, 1983). In such an example, the narrative held within traces on the artifact has an overall form that has been produced by multiple individuals and groups, often unaware of earlier intentions and meanings. Few people today, although knowledgeable about Christmas practices, are aware of the historical reasons behind the choice of Christmas tree, Santa Claus, red coats, and flying reindeer.

There are many trajectories that material items can take through shifting meanings. For example, many are made initially to refer to or evoke metaphorically, whereas through time the original meaning becomes lost or the item becomes a cliché, having lost its novelty. An artifact may start as a focus but become simply a frame, part of an appropriate background. In the skeuomorphic process a functional component becomes decorative, as when a gas fire depicts burning wood or coal. In other cases the load of meaning invested in an artifact increases through time, as in the case of a talisman or holy relic. Material items are often central in the backward-looking invention of tradition, as when the Italian fascist movement elevated the Roman symbol of authority—a bundle of rods—to provide authority for a new form of centralized power.

This brief discussion of the temporal dimension emphasizes the contextuality of material culture meaning. As is clear from some of the examples given, changing meanings through time are often involved in antagonistic relations between groups. Past and present meanings are continually being contested and reinterpreted as part of social and political strategies. Such conflict over material meanings is of particular interest to qualitative research in that it expresses and focuses alternative views and interests. The reburial of American Indian and Australian Aboriginal remains is an issue that has expressed, but perhaps also helped to construct, a new sense of indigenous rights in North America and Australia. As "ethnic cleansing" reappears in Europe, so too do attempts to reinterpret documents, monuments, and artifacts in ethnic terms. But past artifacts can also be used to help local communities in productive and practical ways. One example of the active use of the past in the present is provided by the work of Erickson (1988) in the area around Lake Titicaca in Peru. Information from the archaeological study of raised fields was used to reconstruct agricultural systems on the ancient model, with the participation and to the benefit of local farmers.

◆ Method

The interpretation of mute material evidence puts the interactionist view under pressure. How can an approach that gives considerable importance to interaction with speaking subjects (e.g., Denzin, 1989) deal with material traces for which informants are long dead or about which informants are not articulate?

I have already noted the importance of material evidence in providing insight into other components of lived experience. The methodological issues that are raised are not, however, unique. In all types of interactive research the analyst has to decide whether or not to take commentary at face value and how to evaluate spoken or unspoken responses. How does what is said fit into more general understanding? Analysts of material culture may not have much spoken commentary to work with, but they do have patterned evidence that has to be evaluated in relation to the full range of available information. They too have to fit different aspects of the evi-

dence into a hermeneutical whole (Hodder, 1992; Shanks & Tilley, 1987). They ask, How does what is done fit into more general understanding?

In general terms, the interpreter of material culture works between past and present or between different examples of material culture, making analogies between them. The material evidence always has the potential to be patterned in unexpected ways. Thus it provides an "other" against which the analyst's own experience of the world has to be evaluated and can be enlarged. Although the evidence cannot "speak back," it can confront the interpreter in ways that enforce self-reappraisal. At least when a researcher is dealing with prehistoric remains, there are no "member checks" because the artifacts are themselves mute. On the other hand, material culture is the product of and is embedded in "internal" experience. Indeed, it could be argued that some material culture, precisely because it is not overt, self-conscious speech, may give deeper insights into the internal meanings according to which people lived their lives. I noted above some examples of material culture being used to express covert meanings. Thus the lack of spoken member checks is counteracted by the checks provided by unspoken material patterning that remain able to confront and undermine interpretation.

An important initial assumption made by those interpreting material culture is that belief, idea, and intention are important to action and practice (see above). It follows that the conceptual has some impact on the patterning of material remains. The ideational component of material patterning is not opposed to but is integrated with its material functioning. It is possible therefore to infer both utilitarian and conceptual meaning from the patterning of material evidence.

The interpreter is faced with material data that are patterned along a number of different dimensions simultaneously. Minimally, archaeologists distinguish technology, function, and style, and they use such attributes to form typologies and to seek spatial and temporal patterning. In practice, however, as the discussion above has shown, it has become increasingly difficult to separate technology from style or to separate types from their spatial and temporal contexts. In other words, the analytic or pattern-recognition stage has itself been identified as interpretive.

Thus at all stages, from the identification of classes and attributes to the understanding of high-level social processes, the interpreter has to deal simultaneously with three areas of evaluation. First, the interpreter has to identify the contexts within which things had similar meaning. The boundaries of the context are never "given"; they have to be interpreted. Of course, physical traces and separations might assist the definition of contextual boundaries, such as the boundaries around a village or the separation in time between sets of events. Ritual contexts might be more formalized than or may invert mundane contexts. But despite such clues there is an infinity of possible contexts that might have been constructed by indigenous actors. The notion of context is always relevant when different sets of data are being compared and where a primary question is whether the different examples are comparable, whether the apparent similarities are real.

Second, in conjunction with and inseparable from the identification of context is the recognition of similarities and differences. The interpreter argues for a context by showing that things are done similarly, that people respond similarly to similar situations, within its boundaries. The assumption is made that within the context similar events or things had similar meaning. But this is true only if the boundaries of the context have been correctly identified. Many artifacts initially identified as ritual or cultic have later been shown to come from entirely utilitarian contexts. Equally, claimed cross-cultural similarities always have to be evaluated to see if their contexts are comparable. Thus the interpretations of context and of meaningful similarities and differences are mutually dependent.

The identification of contexts, similarities, and differences within patterned materials depends on the application of appropriate social and material culture theories. The third evaluation that has to be made by the interpreter is of the relevance of general or specific historical theories to the data at hand. Observation and interpretation are theory laden, although theories can be changed in confrontation with material evidence in a dialectical fashion. Some of the appropriate types of general theory for material culture have been identified above. The more specific theories include the intentions and social goals of participants, or the nature of ritual or cultic as opposed to secular or utilitarian behavior.

In terms of the two types of material meaning identified earlier, rules of representation are built up from patterns of association and exclusion. For example, if a pin type is exclusively associated with women in a wide variety of contexts, then it might be interpreted as representing women in all situations. The aspect of womanhood that is represented by this association with pins is derived from other associations of the pins—perhaps with foreign, nonlocal artifacts (Sorensen, 1987). The more richly networked the associations that can be followed by the interpreter, and the thicker the description (Denzin, 1989) that can be produced, the subtler the interpretations that can be made.

For the other type of material meaning, grounded in practice, the initial task of the interpreter is to understand all the social and material implications of particular practices. This is greatly enhanced by studies of modern material culture, including ethnoarchaeology (Orme, 1981). Experimental archaeologists (Coles, 1979) are now well experienced in reconstructing past practices, from storage of cereals in pits to flaking flint tools. Such reconstructions, always unavoidably artificial to some degree, allow some direct insight into another lived experience. On the basis of such knowledge the implications of material practices, extending into the social and the moral, can be theorized. But again it is detailed thick description of associations and contexts that allows the material practices to be set within specific historical situations and the particular evocations to be understood.

An example of the application of these methods is provided by Merriman's (1987) interpretation of the intentions behind the building of a wall around the elite settlement of Heuneberg,

Germany, in the sixth century B.C. (an example similar to that provided by Collingwood, 1956). In cultural terms, the Hallstatt context in central Europe, including Germany, can be separated from other cultural areas such as the Aegean at this time. And yet the walls are made of mud brick and they have bastions, both of which have parallels only in the Aegean. In practice, mud brick would not have been an effective long-term form of defense in the German climate. Thus some purpose other than defense is supposed. The walls are different from other contemporary walls in Germany and yet they are similar to walls found in the Aegean context. Other similarities and differences that seem relevant are the examples of prestige exchange—valuable objects such as wine flagons traded from the Aegean to Germany. This trade seems relevant because of a theory that elites in central Europe based their power on the control of prestige exchange with the Mediterranean. It seems likely, in the context of such prestige exchange, that the walls built in a Mediterranean form were also designed to confer prestige on the elites who organized their construction. In this example the intention of the wall building is interpreted as being for prestige rather than for defense. The interpretation is based on the simultaneous evaluation of similarities and differences, context and theory. Both representational symbolism (conferring prestige) and practical meanings (the building of walls by elites in a non-Mediterranean climate) are considered. For other examples of the method applied to modern material culture, see Hodder (1991) and Moore (1986).

◆ Confirmation

How is it possible to confirm such hypotheses about the meanings of mute material and written culture? Why are some interpretations more plausible than others? The answers to such questions are unlikely to differ radically from the procedures followed in other areas of interpretation, and so I will discuss them relatively

briefly here (see Denzin, 1989; Lincoln & Guba, 1985). However, there are some differences in confirming hypotheses regarding material objects. Perhaps the major difficulty is that material culture, by its very nature, straddles the divide between a universal, natural science approach to materials and a historical, interpretive approach to culture. There is thus a particularly marked lack of agreement in the scientific community about the appropriate basis for confirmation procedures. In my view, an interpretive position can and should accommodate scientific information about, for example, natural processes of transformation and decay of artifacts. It is thus an interpretive position that I describe here.

The twin struts of confirmation are coherence and correspondence. Coherence is produced if the parts of the argument do not contradict each other and if the conclusions follow from the premises. There is a partial autonomy of different types of theory, from the observational to the global, and a coherent interpretation is one in which these different levels do not produce contradictory results. The partial autonomy of different types of theory is especially clear in relation to material culture. Because material evidence endures, it can continually be reobserved, reanalyzed, and reinterpreted. The observations made in earlier excavations are continually being reconsidered within new interpretive frameworks. It is clear from these reconsiderations of earlier work that earlier observations can be used to allow different interpretations—the different levels of theory are partially autonomous. The internal coherence between different levels of theory is continually being renegotiated.

As well as internal coherence there is external coherence—the degree to which the interpretation fits theories accepted in and outside the discipline. Of course, the evaluation of a coherent argument itself depends on the application of theoretical criteria, and I have already noted the lack of agreement in studies of material culture about foundational issues such as the importance of a natural science or humanistic approach. But whatever their views on such issues, most of those working with material culture seem to accept implicitly the importance of simplicity and elegance. An argument in which too much special pleading is required in order to claim coherence is less likely to be adopted than is a simple or elegant theory. The notion of coherence could also be extended to social and political issues within and beyond disciplines, but I shall here treat these questions separately.

The notion of correspondence between theory and data does not imply absolute objectivity and independence, but rather embeds the fit of data and theory within coherence. The data are made to cohere by being linked within theoretical arguments. Similarly, the coherence of the arguments is supported by the fit to data. On the other hand, data can confront theory, as already noted. Correspondence with the data is thus an essential part of arguments of coherence. There are many aspects of correspondence arguments that might be used. One is the exactness of fit, perhaps measured in statistical terms, between theoretical expectation and data, and this is a particularly important aspect of arguments exploiting the mute aspects of material culture. Other arguments of correspondence include the number of cases that are accounted for, their range in space and time, and the variety of different classes of data that are explained. However, such numerical indications of correspondence always have to be evaluated against contextual relevance and thick description to determine whether the different examples of fit are relevant to each other. In ethnographic and historical contexts correspondence with indigenous accounts can be part of the argument that supports contextual relevance.

Other criteria that affect the success of theories about material culture meaning include fruitfulness—how many new directions, new lines of inquiry, new perspectives are opened up. Reproducibility concerns whether other people, perhaps with different perspectives, come to similar results. Perhaps different arguments, based on different starting points, produce similar results. I have already noted that one of the advantages of material evidence is that it can continually be returned to, unexcavated parts of sites excavated and old trenches dug out and reexamined. Inter-

subjective agreement is of considerable importance although of particular difficulty in an area that so completely bridges the science-humanity divide. The success of interpretations depends on peer review (either informal or formally in journals) and on the number of people who believe, cite, and build on them.

But much depends too on the trustworthiness, professional credentials, and status of the author and supporters of an interpretation. Issues here include how long the interpreter spent in the field and how well she or he knows the data: their biases, problems, and unusual examples. Has the author obtained appropriate degrees and been admitted into professional societies? Is the individual an established and consistent writer, or has he or she yet to prove her- or himself? Does the author keep changing her or his mind?

In fact, the audience does not respond directly to an interpretation but to an interpretation written or staged as an article or presentation. The audience thus responds to and reinterprets a material artifact or event. The persuasiveness of the argument is closely tied to the rhetoric within which it is couched (Gero, 1991; Hodder, 1989; Spector, 1991; Tilley, 1989). The rhetoric determines how the different components of the discipline talk about and define problems and their solutions.

◆ Conclusion

Material culture, including written texts, poses a challenge for interpretive approaches that often stress the importance of dialogue with and spoken critical comment from participants. Material culture evidence, on the other hand, may have no living participants who can respond to its interpretation. Even if such participants do exist, they may often be unable to be articulate about material culture meanings. In any case, material culture endures, and so the original makers and users may be able to give only a partial picture of the full history of meanings given to an object as it is used and reinterpreted through time.

The challenge posed by material culture is important for anthropological and sociological analysis because material culture is often a medium in which alternative and often muted voices can be expressed. But the "reader" of material culture must recognize that only some aspects of material culture meaning are language-like. The meaning of much material culture comes about through use, and material culture knowledge is often highly chunked and contextualized. Technical operations implicate a wide network of material, social, and symbolic resources and the abstract meanings that result are closely tied in with the material.

The methods of interpretation of material culture center on the simultaneous hermeneutical procedures of context definition, the construction of patterned similarities and differences, and the use of relevant social and material culture theory. The material culture may not be able directly to "speak back," but if appropriate procedures are followed, there is room for the data and for different levels of theory to confront interpretations. The interpreter learns from the experience of material remains—the data and the interpreter bring each other into existence in dialectical fashion. The interpretations can be confirmed or made more or less plausible than others using a fairly standard range of internal and external (social) criteria.

■ *References*

Bechtel, W. (1990). Connectionism and the philosophy of mind: An overview. In W. G. Lycan (Ed.), *Mind and cognition: A reader.* Oxford: Basil Blackwell.

Bloch, M. (1991). Language, anthropology and cognitive science. *Man, 26,* 183-198.

Bourdieu, P. (1977). *Outline of a theory of practice.* Cambridge: Cambridge University Press.

Braithwaite, M. (1982). Decoration as ritual symbol. In I. Hodder (Ed.), *Symbolic and structural archaeology* (pp. 80-88). Cambridge: Cambridge University Press.

Chippindale, C. (1983). *Stonehenge complete.* London: Thames & Hudson.

Coles, J. M. (1979). *Experimental archaeology.* London: Academic Press.

Collingwood, R. (1956). *The idea of history.* Oxford: Oxford University Press.

Denzin, N. K. (1989). *Interpretive interactionism.* Newbury Park, CA: Sage.

Derrida, J. (1978). *Writing and difference.* London: Routledge & Kegan Paul.

Donley, L. (1982). House power: Swahili space and symbolic markers. In I. Hodder (Ed.), *Symbolic and structural archaeology* (pp. 63--73). Cambridge: Cambridge University Press.

Erickson, C. L. (1988). Raised field agriculture in the Lake Titicaca Basin: Putting ancient agriculture back to work. *Expedition, 30*(3), 8-16.

Ferguson, L. (1991). Struggling with pots in colonial South Carolina. In R. McGuire & R. Paynter (Eds.), *The archaeology of inequality* (pp. 28-39). Oxford: Basil Blackwell.

Gero, J. (1991). Who experienced what in prehistory? A narrative explanation from Queyash, Peru. In R. Preucel (Ed.), *Processual and postprocessual archaeologies* (pp. 126-189). Carbondale: Southern Illinois University.

Giddens, A. (1979). *Central problems in social theory.* London: Macmillan.

Glassie, H. (1975). *Folk housing in middle Virginia.* Knoxville: University of Tennessee Press.

Hodder, I. (1982). *Symbols in action.* Cambridge: Cambridge University Press.

Hodder, I. (1989). Writing archaeology: Site reports in context. *Antiquity, 63,* 268-274.

Hodder, I. (1991). *Reading the past.* Cambridge: Cambridge University Press.

Hodder, I. (1992). *Theory and practice in archaeology.* London: Routledge.

Latour, B. (1988). Mixing humans and nonhumans together: The sociology of a door closer. *Social Problems, 35,* 298-310.

Lemonnier, P. (1986). The study of material culture today: Towards an anthropology of technical systems. *Journal of Anthropological Archaeology, 5,* 147-186.

Leone, M. (1984). Interpreting ideology in historical archaeology. In D. Miller & C. Tilley (Eds.), *Ideology, power and prehistory* (pp. 25-36). Cambridge: Cambridge University Press.

Leroi-Gourhan, A. (1964). *Le geste et la parole.* Paris: Michel.

Lincoln, Y. S., & Guba, E. G. (1985). *Naturalistic inquiry.* Beverly Hills, CA: Sage.

McGhee, R. (1977). Ivory for the sea woman. *Canadian Journal of Archaeology, 1,* 141-159.

Merriman, N. (1987). Value and motivation in prehistory: The evidence for "Celtic spirit." In I. Hodder (Ed.), *The archaeology of contextual meanings* (pp. 111-116). London: Unwin Hyman.

Miller, D. (1982). Artifacts as products of human categorisation processes. In I. Hodder (Ed.), *Symbolic and structural archaeology* (pp. 89-98). Cambridge: Cambridge University Press.

Miller, D. (1985). *Artifacts as categories.* Cambridge: Cambridge University Press.

Miller, D., Rowlands, M., & Tilley, C. (1989). *Domination and resistance.* London: Unwin Hyman.

Miller, D., & Tilley, C. (1984). *Ideology, power and prehistory.* Cambridge: Cambridge University Press.

Moore, H. (1986). *Space, text and gender.* Cambridge: Cambridge University Press.

Orme, B. (1981). *Anthropology for archaeologists.* London: Duckworth.

Pelegrin, J. (1990). Prehistoric lithic technology. *Archaeological Review From Cambridge, 9,* 116-125.

Rathje, W., & Murphy, C. (1992). *Rubbish! The archaeology of garbage.* New York: HarperCollins.

Rathje, W., & Thompson, B. (1981). *The Milwaukee Garbage Project.* Washington, DC: American Paper Institute, Solid Waste Council of the Paper Industry.

Ricoeur, P. (1971). The model of the text: Meaningful action considered as text. *Social Research, 38,* 529-562.

Sanjek, R. (Ed.). (1990). *Fieldnotes: The makings of anthropology.* Albany: State University of New York Press.

Schlanger, N. (1990). Techniques as human action: Two perspectives. *Archaeological Review From Cambridge, 9,* 18-26.

Shanks, M., & Tilley, C. (1987). *Reconstructing archaeology.* Cambridge: Cambridge University Press.

Sorensen, M.-L. (1987). Material order and cultural classification. In I. Hodder (Ed.), *The archaeology of contextual meanings* (pp. 90-101). Cambridge: Cambridge University Press.

Spector, J. (1991). What this awl means: Toward a feminist archaeology. In J. M. Gero & M. W. Conkey (Eds.), *Engendering archaeology* (pp. 388-406). Oxford: Basil Blackwell.

Tilley, C. (1989). Discourse and power: The genre of the Cambridge inaugural. In D. Miller, M. Rowlands, & C. Tilley (Eds.), *Domination and resistance* (pp. 41-62). London: Unwin Hyman.

Tilley, C. (Ed.). (1990). *Reading material culture.* Oxford: Basil Blackwell.

Washburn, D. (1983). *Structure and cognition in art.* Cambridge: Cambridge University Press.

Webb, E. J., Campbell, D. T., Schwartz, R. C., & Sechrest, L. (1966). *Unobtrusive measures: Nonreactive research in the social sciences.* Chicago: University of Chicago Press.

Wobst, M. (1977). Stylistic behavior and information exchange. *University of Michigan Museum of Anthropology, Anthropological Paper, 61,* 317-342.

Yates, T. (1989). Habitus and social space. In I. Hodder (Ed.), *The meanings of things* (pp. 248-262). London: Unwin Hyman.

■ *Suggested Further Readings*

Hodder, I. (1999). *The archaeological process.* Oxford: Basil Blackwell.

Hodder, I., & Shanks, M. (1995). *Interpreting archaeology.* London: Routledge.

Miller, D. (Ed.). (1997). *Material cultures.* London: University College Press.

Tilley, C. (1994). *The phenomenology of landscape.* London: Berg.

Tilley, C. (1999). *Metaphor and material culture.* Oxford: Basil Blackwell.

27

REIMAGINING VISUAL METHODS

Galileo to *Neuromancer*

◆ Douglas Harper

This chapter is based on my sense that the chapter I prepared for the first edition of this *Handbook* might help a researcher understand the relationship between visual and other methods, but it would not be very useful to a student or researcher trying to use visual methods, or to a researcher looking for a framework in which to understand visual methods.[1] In this chapter I take a different approach. First, I suggest a context in which to see photography and social research, this being the history of recorded perception. Next, I present visual sociology as fieldwork photography guided by several research traditions. Third, I describe the social influences around which "picture making" has taken place, noting how the social power involved in making images redefines institutions, groups, and individuals. Finally, I suggest that visual sociology is, above all, a process of seeing guided by theory. Because visual sociology is a grab bag of research approaches and perspec-

tives on understanding images in society, I aim to make several attenuated arguments and to weave them into a whole.

◆ Visual Methods and the History of Recorded Perception

Logical positivism assumed its modern form in the 16th century, when Roger Bacon suggested that observable data are the basis of knowledge. Bacon also argued that knowledge ought to be practically applied to solving social problems, anticipating Comte's mandate for sociology in the early 19th century. I note that Bacon's insights traced to the rationalist philosophers of 6th-century B.C. Greece to remind us that the roots of this perspective are nearly as old as recorded thought.

Bacon and logical positivism were contemporary to the invention of the telescope and the microscope, tools that showed that the world observed with human eyes was not complete or even correct. In the 16th century this was such a challenging idea that philosophers at the University of Padua, where Galileo was a professor, refused to look through the telescope. Galileo, censured and threatened with death, recanted the discoveries his telescope had revealed. But, of course, the scientific revolution was not stopped by the violence of the Church, and the revolution inspired by Galileo and Bacon flourished in the 17th century and became the basis of the modern scientific world.

In the 19th century, the camera became part of the revolution in seeing and understanding that was the scientific revolution, and several subsequent instruments and tools, which I will describe below, further redefined the relationship between seeing and knowing.

There are two important implications to the changes brought by Galileo's telescope. The first is that the new, instrument-based perception was treated as more real than was the world based on faith and belief. It became understood that to see through an instrument (such as the telescope or microscope, and, eventually, the camera) was to see a more profound reality than could be observed by the eye. The second implication of these changes is that the legitimacy of science came to be based in large part on its claim to describe a world in visual terms. In this way the eye became the privileged sense of science, and of modernism.

The hegemony of science and the image did not last, due a succession of tools and instruments that redefined both image making and the social role of images. The first and perhaps most important of these is the camera itself. The cameras used today are essentially similar to cameras designed 150 years ago, although they have the ability to see farther, closer, faster, and in lower light. In surprising ways, the public use of cameras has remained constant. The middle-class public enthusiastically adopted photography in the 19th century and continues to do so. Different social classes and groups, of course, use photography differently (Bourdieu, 1990), but the 19th-century family snapshooter would have no trouble interpreting the modern-day family album.

In the meantime, motion pictures, video, the World Wide Web, and virtual reality have offered new connections between human existence and visual perception. These new instruments influence the meanings of images, their relationship to spoken words and sounds, and the emergence and development of visual sociology.

By the end of the 19th century, it became possible to link individual frames of film together, giving a succession of images a verisimilitude the still image could never achieve. Suddenly it seemed that the process of life itself could be recorded. But at first this record was limited to images alone (synchronized sound could not be recorded with the images), and because cameras were bulky and heavy, filming the flow of natural life was nearly impossible. The earliest documentary films, such as *Nanook of the North* (filmed during the 1920s), were thus extraordinary technical achievements. Because there was no sound track (except for a piano score for a live musician), the film contained frames of typed words between sequences of images. These had to be brief statements, quickly readable by an audience impatient to rejoin the visual narrative of the film. These texts were what we now call "captions," and they performed the same function, which was to summarize the visual text.

By the 1930s it became possible to add sound to film, but it was nearly impossible to do so outside of a studio. Documentaries such as Pare Lorentz's *The River* and *The Plow That Broke the Plains* (see Snyder, 1968) introduced voice-over commentary. This commentary functioned as did the captions of the silent film, in that it defined and provided closure for the images. In this sense it can be thought of as the confident voice of (modernist) science.

The era of television brought documentaries in this form to the living rooms of America in the weekly *Omnibus* series shown during the 1950s. Again, the voice-over-image narrator supplied the logic that tied the film statements together. As a result, these films are linear and narrative in organization, and unambiguous in structure and message.

Portable cameras that could simultaneously record sound were developed in the early 1960s. These capabilities potentially eliminated the hegemony of image and scientific authority. Film could now explain itself; it leaped closer to reality, and the results resembled the messy flow of life. Interestingly enough, the movement was called cinema verité, or truth-cinema. Jean Rouch and Edgar Morin's (a French sociologist) *Chronique d'un Eté* (*Chronicle of a Summer*; 1960), one of the first cinema verité films, took cameras to the streets of Paris to measure the public reaction to the Algerian war and to comment on several cultural themes. In a departure from previous film structure, in *Chronique d'un Eté* the subjects of the film are shown watching their earlier filmed interviews, adding a layer of interpretation to the already ambiguous film statement.

In the United States, the early cinema verité movement (see Mamber, 1974) coincided with the emergence of experimental ethnography, although only a handful of sociological filmmakers and sociologists and anthropologists made the connection. Several films of this era offered bridges between ethnography and experimental filmmaking. These included the Maysles brothers' documentary *The Salesman* (1969), which follows the day-to-day routines of a Bible salesman; Robert Drew's *Primary* (1960), which shows the mundane events of a political primary; and Richard Leacock's *Happy Mother's Day* (1963), which explores how a small town experienced and marketed the birth of quintuplets. Frederick Wiseman's *Titicut Follies* (1967), which depicts the day-to-day routines of a prison for the criminally insane, was the first in a series of more than 20 cinema verité studies of mostly American institutions that offered an extraordinary resource for experimental sociology and anthropology. Cinema verité showed sociological dimensions to everyday life, and the movement embraced a technology that redefined what, in fact, could be filmed. Sadly for the social sciences, the potential of this technology has been little used or even recognized.

Although cinema verité redefined the relationship between film and reality, its adoption, for example, as a common research technique was limited by its expense. By the early 1980s a typical budget for a documentary film, not including salaries, was more than $1,000 per minute. The cameras could record only a few minutes of simultaneous sound and images, and generally there needed to be a sound recorder working in tandem with the filmmaker, which added to the intrusion of the recorders of reality on reality itself.

Advances in video technology, dating to the early 1980s, made it possible for videographers to record hours of synchronized visual and audio information at a fraction of the cost of film. Video cameras have become smaller and yet produce higher-quality images and sound (most recently in the Hi 8 format), and they have also become simpler to operate and cheap enough to be a routine home expense. Video wrested image making from the monopoly of well-heeled experts. It is reasonable to say that with this change, visual representations of the world lost their close connection with the authority of science. Yet the implications of this change are ambiguous. For the most part, the video revolution has not worked hand in hand with experimental ethnography to redefine the social science. Indeed, the social effects have been trivialized into "funniest home videos" television programs (now worldwide), in which the extraordinary power of the camera is used to present the lowest common denominator of public life.

Contemporary electronic technologies continue to redefine the image and its social meaning. Now that images can be created and/or changed digitally, the connection between image and "truth" has been forever severed. What was once disturbing (such as the addition of Hitler-like visual cues to a portrait of Saddam Hussein on the cover of a national newsmagazine) is now commonplace. Electronically altered images have become part of our entertainment (in *Zelig*, Woody Allen appears alongside Lenin; in *Forrest Gump*, Tom Hanks is shown in conversation with John Kennedy); advertising juxtaposes the images of people who have nothing to do with each other, who in fact do not even live in the same era, presenting them as enthusiastic product spokespersons.

But the electronic revolution is a great deal more than the ability to alter photographic or video images. Because of what is now called *hyperlogic,* there is an alternative to linear or narrative form of visual presentation. Hyperlogic, which began in the Hypercard program (packaged with early Macintosh computers) is the basis of the World Wide Web. As is common knowledge today, the Web is organized so that viewers can create their own paths through text, images, and even film or video clips. The most successful current example is Peter Biella, Napoleon Chagnon, and Gary Seaman's (1997) interactive CD-ROM of the anthropological film *The Ax Fight,* by Timothy Asch, and additional hyperlinked materials. The interactive CD allows a viewer to view the actual film in any of several possible ways (in real time, backward as well as forward, frame by frame, in slow motion, or keyed to significant moments as identified by the anthropologists). The viewer can also link to scene-by-scene descriptions of the film, or can link to any individual shown in the film to get information on that person's age, sex, spouses, children, birthplace, lineage, residence, year of death, place in the kin systems (presented in kin charts), and other anthropological details. The CD contains complete footage and edited versions of the film, hundreds of photographs, and several full-length essays. The viewer can access any part of the film and digress to any of several analyses.

The CD is a curious step in the evolution I have described. On one hand, it represents the scientific expert whose claims are reinforced visually; on the other, it deconstructs the authority of the scientist and makes the viewer the author of the viewing and learning experience.

The last step in the process that began with Galileo's telescope is the jumbling up of our senses through electronic manipulation, called *virtual reality.* Giovanni Artieri (1996) suggests that the "technological image is the real marker of the postmodern, able to trace out subjects' experience as border lines between natural and artificial" (p. 56). By wearing machines that transform nerve stimuli into visual and tactile

sensations, users alter the boundaries separating the body and society, and experience itself loses its link to authenticity. Now it is no longer what we see (or hear and feel) that is real, as in the case of a science based on unchallenged claims to represent the world. Rather, we choose to immerse ourselves in a fictional perceptional reality— that is, a perceptual world that is the result of our imagination and a machine. In the next step, still fictional (best represented in cyberpunk novels such as William Gibson's *Neuromancer,* 1985), computer chips implanted into the brain allow a person to jack directly into the Web, to experience viscerally what is a fictional, yet operative, space.

Because visual sociology comprises images and science, it is appropriate that we study the relationship between these elements. The images that visual sociologists make are also part of these issues; we should study our work as part of the study of visual society. As new technologies alter what and how we see (even changing the nature of sight, reality, and imagination), the issues will become both more complex and more important.

◆ A Visual Social Science Through Research Photography

The above comments offer a broad view. I now shift to the mundane operation of visual sociology, showing the operation of several paradigms of visual methodology in photos of a bike ride in Italy.[2]

I made the photographs that accompany this text while I was teaching visual sociology at the University of Bologna, experiencing a culture I was pretty much new to. My students and I explored the idea of seeing (and photographing) forms and levels of social control. In all cultures, the relationship between formal and informal social control is complex, and in Italy it seems extremely so. It would be only fair, I reasoned, for me to explore this assignment myself. Participating in traffic from the vantage point of a bicycle seemed sufficiently complex and visual to be a suitable photographic project. Thus, armed with my intrepid Leica, I photographed the same route, a main street that bisects the circle of the inner city of Bologna, on several occasions.

From a personal standpoint, I certainly found it intimidating to mount my beaten-up (pink) bike and take on Italian traffic, with or without a camera. I was a guest of my colleague Patrizia Faccioli, who told me to simply follow her through the moving maze of dangerous vehicles and vulnerable, darting pedestrians. Of course, this is the point: Things taken for granted by a cultural insider (which rules are followed, which norms guide behavior that is not regulated by rules, and what areas of social life lie primarily outside the perusal or rules) are not obvious to cultural outsiders. In the case of negotiating the street, not knowing is dangerous.

I had already photographed a different European city from a bicycle, and I'd become rather adept at the process. My camera is not automatic, so I steered with my left hand, holding the camera in my right. I focused and set apertures and shutter speeds before starting off. I framed the images as I biked, advancing the film with the thumb of my right hand. The resulting photos can be used to illustrate complementary paradigms of visual research, which is to say that their sociological meanings can be organized within the logics of at least four research strategies.

The first of these strategies can be referred to (cautiously!) as *empirical*. This orientation toward photography recognizes that a photographic image is created when light leaves its trace on an element that has a memory. For the image to exist, there had to be light reflected off a subject; thus the photograph is a record of the subject at a particular moment.

From this perspective, the photographs document several levels of social life. The simplest is a bicycle commute through Italian traffic. The photographs record such mundane information as how many vehicles of what types share the Italian streets at a certain time of day. The photographs suggest some of the jockeying that regulates a complex mix of human interac-

tion mediated by machines. If they are read carefully, with the help of a cultural insider, they begin to offer evidence of normative behavior. This is simple information, but it is precisely the daily occurrences of life that are often the basis of sociological analysis. Above all, the visual cataloging of life is efficient; it would take a lot of words to convey the information in the photographs.

Although these images produce what I consider to be empirical data, I do not claim that these images represent "objective truth." The very act of observing is interpretive, for to observe is to choose a point of view. To elaborate: As a photographer, I choose a point of view by aiming the camera and by choosing the focal length of the lens. Camera lenses do not see precisely what the human eye sees—some magnify a small visual area, like a telescope; some see wider than the normal vision but move the foreground of the subject farther away; others act as microscopes. For the bike photographs, I used a 35mm focal-length lens because it sees nearly what the eye sees (but cuts off the edges of normal vision); thus when I hold the camera in front of my face I need not look through the range finder to imagine the image I'll make. The person looking at the photograph sees the frame as familiar because it is rather close to how the eye records information. Thus the decisions of the image maker have profound effects on the kinds of sociological statements that result from their images.[3]

In this project I used 400 ASA (black-and-white) film, which is properly exposed with a small amount of light. Thus I could use a fast shutter speed (freezing the motion in the frame), and I could also use a small aperture, which created a deep depth of field (in lay terms, the images are in focus from the front nearly to the back). These are decisions that rendered the photographs a certain way. Different film, shutter speeds, apertures, and lenses would have created different visual statements. These statements would not be "better" or "worse," but they would be decidedly different. For example, Photo 5 freezes the action of about 10 individuals on different kinds of two-wheeled vehicles in an extremely dangerous confluence. The image, crisp and frozen, suggests order. Likewise, the el-

1

2

3

4

5

6

7

8

9

10

11

12

13

14

15   (route on right side of frame)

All photographs © by Douglas Harper

derly man in Photo 8 is not a passive spectator, as he appears, but a pedestrian about to make a decision as to whether or not to venture into my path. If I had used different shutter speeds and even different angles of the frame (point of view), the photographs would have communicated more of the chaos and uncertainties in the negotiation of the public space.

It is easy to see that empirical evidence is both constructed and real. Becoming a visual ethnographer means becoming conscious of the potential to make visual statements by knowing how the camera interprets social reality. This means learning how cameras work, making the technical decisions that, in fact, create the photograph self-consciously, and relegating the automatic camera to the wastebasket.

◆ Visual Narratives

To expand the idea of empirical data in single images to a sequence of photos is to introduce the concept of visual narrative. Sociologists use verbal narratives to tell sociological stories, both as first-person accounts and as cultural stories that unfold through time and space. On the level of microanalysis, the narrative view is consistent with symbolic interaction, which makes us sensitive to how we process interaction based on interpretations. Interaction, by definition, is narrative; it embodies the flow of human experience.

Visual materials are often narrative in form. The most common visual narrative is film or video, as described above: single images taken sequentially (often many per second) that, when viewed in rapid succession, seem to re-create the movement the eye sees. But still photographs can also create sociological narratives (Harper, 1982, 1987). For example, a succession of photographs of a tramp worker coming down from a drunk, boarding a freight train for a 1,500-mile trip, reassembling his identity as a worker, and taking on another job tells the story of a culture, a story that is repeated with subtle variations. The most respected photojournalists have used

this narrative form to great advantage. Eugene Smith and Ailene Smith's (1975) visual narrative of a social movement surrounding the lethal poisoning of a fishing village by a corporation describes the scenarios of several social groups. Kent Klich's visual narrative *The Book of Beth* (1989) traces events in the life of a Swedish heroin addict who is also a prostitute; here the sad narrative moves from the individual to several institutional connections.

My narrative study of the cultural phenomenon of bicycling down the same street at the same time of day over several days is constructed in several ways. It mixes images made at different times on the same route, which is indicated by the varying patterns of light and shadows that appear in different images. Even assembled in this way, the sequence is a sociological narrative, although the relationship of these images to the narrative flow of time is arbitrary.

The bicycle narrative is framed at either end by images that suggest the cultural definition of the bicycle and that locate the narrative in a larger geographic context. The advertising image that opens the sequence suggests that the bicycle represents both utility and fashion. The final image was taken from a tower (the same tower that appears in Photos 9-13), looking down at the street along which the bicyclist travels. The increasingly larger tower in the photos is a way to note the progress of the sequence. Seeing the context of the photographs from the bird's-eye view of the tower, one realizes that the path of the bicycle trip is through one of the main drags of the inner city of Bologna. The overview is a visual summary of the images that precede it.

The second image in the series frames the series from the perspective of a spectator rather than a participant. We gain the sense that cars, motor scooters, and bicycles are waiting for the signal to begin a race. In fact, that is exactly what the moment is like, as recorded in Photo 3. At the intersection where we wait, a small street suddenly becomes a much larger street, and oncoming traffic crosses immediately to the right. Photo 4 shows the moment just out of the "starting gate," with several different kinds of bikes and scooters roughly following the white lines marking a place for two-wheelers. Noteworthy is the presence of a "sportsman" on a touring bike, seemingly out of place in the urban stop-and-go traffic. The two buses pictured are going opposite directions, one leading traffic to the right and the other bearing toward the dispersing traffic. The remaining images show different points on the route, as recorded on different days (note the presence of shadows on some images, and disappearing buses and cars). Photo 5 shows the close reckoning between the scooters that are turning left immediately after the scooters moving ahead (a crash seems imminent, as is often the case). Photo 11 records a moment in a game of "chicken" where I did not faint at the onrush of a cab (and a woman on a scooter), causing the cabbie to slam on his brakes halfway through his turn into my path. Several images show how pedestrians and motorized traffic interact. The elderly man in Photo 8 appears alone halfway across the street; several groups in Photo 12 are crossing the street using different strategies. Finally, in Photo 7 I am observed photographing and the onlookers seem surprised, perhaps perturbed. This is such usual behavior it is by itself a norm violation. In any case, it is a record of the impact of the researcher on the reality he studies. By choosing images from several bike trips along the same path, I was able to include several events that occurred at different times.

Every visual narrative involves a decision concerning how much information to include per time unit. A film or video shows so much information it appears to reproduce reality. Thus it is not surprising that video and film are used in the analysis of face-to-face interaction. The example here stretches a small number of images over several minutes of social life. It may be in the sequence that questions of social norms can be approached, but it is clear that one would need more visual information to explore this subject in satisfying depth. Probably video, with simultaneous sound, would yield more meaningful data.

The visual narrative, like the individual frames from which it is made, is a result of choices and decisions. If the researcher is conscious of these choices, the visual narrative may

become a useful way to study certain kinds of social patterns. The methods used will, of course, influence the questions asked.

◆ Eliciting Cultural Explanation

Photo elicitation has become a familiar, if underutilized, qualitative method.[4] Simply described, in using this technique, rather than asking a subject, for example, "What is the role of the bicycle in Italian culture?" a researcher might present a set of images such as those in this chapter to an Italian or a group of Italians to elicit their explanations. Of course, responses to the images could well vary according to whether the respondents participate in the pictured reality as bicyclists, scooter or car drivers, or pedestrians. As such, the images function as a kind of "cultural Rorschach" test.

To demonstrate how photo elicitation works, I presented these images to my Italian colleague Patrizia Faccioli (PF), who appears in Photos 9 and 13 as lead driver in our convoy. Because she is a visual sociologist, the photo-elicitation interview provided a natural way for her to share her responses to the photographs. Her responses to these few images filled several pages; the edited excerpts presented below show the range of topics and the depth of the information produced but do not reflect the full range of her responses. As a demonstration, this is the tip of a larger cultural study iceberg.

The photos led PF to comment generally on the overall meanings of the bike in Italian culture:

> The bicycle stands for: rapidity, convenience, physical exercise, danger, risk, challenge, reduction of stress, increase of stress, cancer in the lungs, cold in the winter, hot in the summer . . . flexibility of the [traffic] rules, aggressiveness, attention, negotiation, social conscience, no pollution, autonomy.

> The bike increases your stress; you must have 1,000 eyes open (behind you, in front of you, at right, at left, above, under . . .) because every 10 seconds you risk your life. Nobody in the street cares about cyclists; they seem not to exist: pedes-

trians who suddenly cross the road, ignoring that you are coming; motorbikes which pass you on right and left and almost touch you; cars which don't give you the way even if you have the right of way. And the buses . . . It seems that among the bus drivers in Bologna, there is a sort of bet on who can pass the most closely to a bike without touching it.

So, using the bike means paying much attention, but also being aggressive and brutal. You have to stare at the car or motor scooter driver (the bus is too high) telling him, through the eyes, that you are going to pass first and that you will not stop.

In reference to Photos 5 and 6, PF comments:

The light has turned green and the scooters and the bikes went quickly in front of the cars, because the light is green also for those coming from the other side who want to turn left. The challenge is to pass first, before the others cross. You can see this in Photo 5; those going toward the two towers have the right of way, but if those arriving from the direction of the two towers can arrive first to turn left, they will turn and the others will have to stop. That is especially the case if you are on a bike (recall what I said about the use of the eyes to communicate you are going to pass anyway). This is one of the most dangerous moments in my everyday experience of going to work.

Understanding the experience of the bicyclist, PF tells us, leads us to understand what Italians call "minor deviance":

Using the bike means . . . not being obligated to follow rules. You are half machine and half pedestrian, and you are not very dangerous for the others, you can glance around and, if possible, pass when the light is red. When there is a traffic jam you can enter the portico [the covered sidewalks of Bologna, which weave 42 kilometers through the city, visible in Photos 8 and 11] and move among pedestrians. You can go the opposite direction in one-way streets, paying attention to the cars, of course. As an American you might say: "The rule is the rule, always and anyway!" But you are wrong! . . . Certain types of rules have to be evaluated in order to decide if it is right to follow them or not. This attitude is very diffused in Italy, especially regarding the rules of the road. Of course it's not the same for the penal code . . . but regarding certain types of rules we Italians think that we have the right to

judge the rule and behave accordingly. For example, Italian people decided (with their behavior) that the safety belts are important and useful on the freeways, but not in the town. The police have tried for a long time to have the rule followed, but nothing could bring this about. So now the police have accepted that behavior, as if there were an unwritten rule that tolerates the absence of belts when people drive in towns. . . . We can't accept any sort of rule just because someone decided that the rule is right. People who make rules can also make mistakes; people who live every day in the road can understand which is the best behavior.

A bicycle in a window display with female models is a difficult cultural symbol for an outsider to understand. Referring to Photo 1, PF explains the cultural meaning of several forms of transportation:

This perfume shop shows a bike that is the prize drawn by lot among those who buy a certain product, the perfume. The statement translates "The autographed bike could be yours." That's an indicator of how much the bike has become part of Italian culture and everyday life. Women who wear a famous perfume use bikes in everyday life: the woman in the poster is wearing elegant dresses, not sport ones. In the '60s those who used bikes were people belonging to the working class, who did not have money to buy (or to use every day) a car. A lot of people used the car only on Sunday, with their family. Nowadays, because of the increased standard of living . . . all people have one or more cars and the towns, mainly the old centers, are crowded. So the bike has become an alternative to the car, not linked to social class or money. It has become one of the most rapid ways to move across town. This is a similar consideration for the scooters: students, young people, but also employees, lawyers, doctors (teachers like me), etc., have scooters more and more fine and expensive, costing as much as $3,000. So the scooter means both rapidity and a status symbol. The motorcycles are different; used mainly for vacation or races on the road. In a town you can see scooters (for the rich people) or mopeds (for poor people) or bikes (for both the very poor people and the urban "ecologist"). These are ideal types, of course. The reality is more complex and mixed.

These interview excerpts show how images elicit cultural information that ranges from the micro (normative negotiation of social action) to cultural definition. The photo-elicitation interview is really a completion of the empirical and narrative efforts, the critical point being that the meaning supplied is from a cultural insider. This is in recognition that what constitutes a "fact" is culturally defined.

◆ *Experience and Image*

I next address a fourth way to look at these images, which I call the *phenomenological mode*. The vantage point from this view is the self, in this instance a self who happens to be driving a bicycle through crowded streets of an alien culture. From the phenomenological perspective, photographs express the artistic, emotional, or experiential intent of the photographer. Here sociology borrows from art; the phenomenological mode draws from early photographic art movements, as photographers sought to define themselves as more than technicians and to assert that photographic expression is equivalent to artistic expression in other media.[5]

Treating photographs phenomenologically is not common in sociology. Perhaps the best examples are found in the work of Richard Quinney (e.g., 1991, 1995), who uses images to interpret and render his own experiences, reflections, and memories. In the case of the Italian bicycle photography, my intent was to photograph what was new to me, but routine to natives.

There was a mix of euphoria and fear in the experience of biking to work. To photograph the experience was to look as I was doing—a harder thing than one might imagine. If you look at the photographs with this in mind, you see the photographer choosing points of view that illuminate different aspects of the unfolding social reality. The sentiments behind the image making must be understood through another mode of expression: a diary, a poem, or other expressive form. The photographs by themselves seem curiously detached, even quiet

and subdued, yet they emerged from an adrenaline-saturated experience. Here I question whether the same photographs serve both the empirical and the phenomenological mode equally well. The clinical distance in the crisp images of the empirical rendering does not communicate the experience of the moment.

Photography can produce data that enlarge our understanding of sociological processes, from the formation of one's own definition of the situation to the negotiation of actors with different machines. Photographs record details that may engage viewers to reflect upon larger cultural realities. Using photos as sequences allows us to see how social actions take place.

The example above shows how the most mundane of events, biking through a city street, may be thought about in several sociological ways. These four approaches do not begin to exhaust the possibilities for using photography in the research process.

◆ *The Social Construction of Photography and Visual Sociology*

It is not enough to describe visual research in the terms offered above. Like all research, visual research depends upon and redistributes social power. In the case of visual research, these issues are compounded by the power associated with photography. Thus we speak of the "social construction of the photograph" as part of the discussion of the politics of visual sociology itself.

The photograph is socially constructed in the sense that the social positions of the photographer and the subject come into play when a photograph is made. It takes social power to make photographs (Tagg, 1988), partly because making photographs defines identities (Spence, 1988), institutional relationships (Jackson, 1977), and histories (Copeland, 1969; Rieger, 1996). A father may photograph his children in ridiculous poses, but the children do not generally have the social power to photograph their parents arguing (or making love) and to present those images as the "official" family story (Chalfen, 1987). Sociologists and anthropologists have assumed that it is their right to photograph the people they study, and thus to present them as academic subjects (and in ways in which the ideological bases of their relationships are disguised). Edwards's (1992) collection of essays on early British anthropological photography demonstrates exactly this point: The images are not objective renderings of objects of scientific studies, as interpreted by early-20th-century anthropologists; rather, they are markers of colonial relationships. Anthropology was a science of the colonizer, and the images made in the service of anthropology defined the native in ways that reified the relationships of superiority and inferiority endemic to colonialism. There are no photographic records made by natives of colonialism (or colonials), but in recent decades prior "natives" have assumed the right to make their own images and tell their own visual stories. This has, of course, called the relationships of traditional anthropology into question.

The social construction of photography is also a matter of gender. For example, in my current research I am using about 110 documentary photographs made just after World War II in a study of the evolution of dairy farming in the northeastern United States. The photographs are part of a collection of nearly 70,000 images produced under the sponsorship of Standard Oil of New Jersey and directed by Roy Stryker. My farming collection includes about 40 images made by a female photographer, Charlotte Brooks, and about 70 by several male photographers. When I compared the photographs on the basis of the gender of the photographers, I was startled by what I found. For the men, the farm women's work was largely invisible. They did not photograph women as productive parts of the farm, nor did they photograph the work of maintaining and provisioning the house (and taking care of children). Brooks's photographs, however, cover many of these excluded topics. The difference is significant because it shows clearly that if we regard these photographs as a document of farm life during the World War II era, we accept an incomplete portrait as a full record. Indeed, the photos, in this case, are a result

of the social construction of "maleness" and "femaleness" typical of 1940s America. The role of gender in creating photographic meaning is yet another largely unexplored subject.[6]

Social scientists should be aware of the social construction of the image for several reasons. We need to acknowledge that photography embodies the unequal relationships that are part of most research activities. I can enter into the worlds of the poor by living temporarily on the street, and I can photograph the worlds I encounter there, but a homeless person cannot infiltrate and photograph the life of my university president. This realization has led many social scientists to abandon the use of photography. For others it is a cautioning awareness that should help us to overcome the inevitable power differentials of subject and researcher. Some sociologists have confronted the issue by giving up their own photography and instead teaching their subjects to use photography and writing to investigate their own cultures and, perhaps, to empower themselves. Wendy Ewald is a leader in this field, for she takes on the asymmetry of adult/child as well as First World/Third World power differences. Her first published project on Appalachian children is a good introduction to this approach. The photographs and writings of her students contradict the stereotypes long associated with the internal colony of Appalachia (Ewald, 1985). In this method, photographs (often accompanied by text that expands upon the images) represent inspired reflection—they are not social science in and of themselves, but data that sociologists and others should put to use.

◆ The Essence of Visual Sociology; and, Where Are We Going?

Assuming we are talking about research methods (given that this is a handbook of qualitative methods), and assuming we are speaking about the photographic end of the movement, the simplest way to do visual sociology is to photograph with sociological consciousness. Howard

Becker (1974) was the first to make this argument and the point has not been made more elegantly since then.

Becker suggests that we think theoretically when we do photography. What does this mean, exactly? For Becker, all photography is done from a theoretical perspective, but little of the theory is sociological. Our normal views of the world (which Becker calls "lay" theory) tell us where to point the camera and how to use the camera (speaking technically) to make images. Thus, when we photograph, we re-create our unexamined, taken-for-granted perceptions. We are interpreting sociological topics in our unexamined theorizing, and our photographs are our conclusions. If we are photojournalists (see Hagaman, 1996), we learn to present the theories of our newspaper editors and the recent conventions of photojournalism. We do this not only by choosing topics and specific images of those topics, but by using particular lenses (frames), apertures, and shutter speeds. If we are sociologists, we presumably have theoretical knowledge of our subject, the way Bateson and Mead (1942) knew the Balinese before they began photographing their still unequaled study of Bali culture. This prior knowledge will tell the researcher: "There is the enactment of a ritual my subjects have described. . . . It lasts 20 minutes and has four stages. . . . I will photograph it to highlight the transitions and interactions among actors." From this perspective, the work of visual sociology is straightforward: We bring it into the research process to extend our knowledge of the subject.

But not all field-workers have the kind of preexisting knowledge that Bateson and Mead had. There are at least two alternatives for visual sociologists. The first is to use the camera as an information-gathering instrument, to discover what Glaser and Strauss (1967) call "grounded theory." Photographs made during the research experience concretize the observations that field-workers use continually to redefine their theories. In this way photographs help build theory. In fact, the need to make photographs in the field requires that the field-worker look at something, and these beginning observations can be the starting point for making theory.

The second alternative is to use photographs to confirm and develop existing theory through photo elicitation, as described above. Researchers may use photos of events people experienced in the past to draw out memories of their history. Margolis (1998) studied the political consciousness of coal miners, using decades-old photos of mine work to interview elderly miners about events and their interpretations. In this case, one senses that the intervening years between when the photographs were taken and their interpretation led to deeper reflection than would normally be associated with the photo-elicitation process.

Other researchers have engaged subjects in the photography as well as the interviews in photo-elicitation research. Van der Dos, Gooskens, Liefting, and van Mierlo (1992) photographed a multiethnic Dutch neighborhood under the direction of five subjects. The researchers then interviewed their subjects using the images made on their earlier "photo tour." Finally, the researchers interviewed other informants using photos made by their neighbors, who were of a different age, gender, and ethnic background. The result is that as researchers we understand that a neighborhood is made up of people who share a material space but define it differently; but in this case, the five subjects also came to understand and appreciate the perspectives of their neighbors.

In all examples of photo-elicitation research, the photograph loses its claim to objectivity. Indeed, the power of the photo lies in its ability to unlock the subjectivity of those who see the image differently from the researcher.

A final thought: One can say that visual sociologists seek to find a way to integrate seeing into the research process. A sensitive field-worker is already nearly equipped to do visual sociology. It helps a great deal to understand how the camera records information, and it is important to understand the impact of photography on the research process. Finally, it is important to understand how various constructions (technical and social) influence how the photograph is made and interpreted.

We are living in a time of electronic revolution, which, as I have pointed out, has affected how images are made, distributed, experienced, and understood. Surely these changes should have an impact on visual sociology. Yet we are in a curious place. Sociology remains essentially uninterested in visual culture (Denzin, 1995, being an exception) or visual methods. Our textbooks contribute to the problem rather than solve it. The books most professors use for first courses in sociology are filled with colorful, uncomplicated images (chosen by art directors primarily to spiff up pages of text). The photographs restate the most obvious themes of the already watered-down text. Given that these images are the entirety of what most sociologists experience as "visual sociology," it is perhaps not surprising that the visual sociology movement remains tangential rather than in the mainstream of the discipline. In anthropology, with its long tradition of anthropological filmmaking and examples like Bateson and Mead's still-admired visual ethnography, the case is a bit better. Still, most articles published in the two journals of visual anthropology are primarily words-about-images rather than reports of experiments and demonstrations of visual thinking.

What is the future? One possibility has visual sensibility leading an energized social science that is experimentally ethnographic and theoretically interdisciplinary. The new technologies promise myriad ways to bring changing visual experience into the production of social science and the understanding of visual dimensions of society. Another possible future has social science largely unconnected with a rapidly changing technological world, only mildly interested in studying society as an observed phenomenon. In this scenario, those of us in the small movement of visually inspired thinkers continue to wave our banners from the sidelines. I suppose the actual future will be some mix of the two.

■ Notes

1. In my chapter for the first edition of this book, I suggest that the area in visual sociology

most relevant to qualitative methods is photographic fieldwork, or visual ethnography; I note that visual ethnography, however, is the focal point of several criticisms (Harper, 1994). These include a postmodern critique of scientific ethnography, a postmodern critique of documentary photography, and a criticism that the portrayal of subjects inevitable in much visual ethnography violates ethical principles of fieldwork. These critiques raise substantial and serious issues, but I argue that it is better to reform visual methods than to discard visual ethnography in a sweeping rejection of modernism, science, ethnography, and documentary photography. Because that paper was subsequently updated (Harper, 1998), I have sought new ground for this chapter.

2. I first suggested these "types" of visual sociology in a paper that was inspired by Nichols's (1981) discussion of film theory (Harper, 1988). For a broader view of visual sociology, see also John Grady's (1996) argument for an enlarged scope for visual sociology and Charles Suchar's (1997) plea for an "interrogatory principle" for visual sociology. A collection edited by Chris Jenks (1995b) explores several dimensions of the sociology of visual perception on this general theme. Jenks (1995a) notes that " 'idea' derives from the Greek verb meaning 'to see.' This lexical etymology reminds us that the way that we think about the way that we think in Western culture is guided by a visual paradigm" (p. 1). Jenks later anticipates some ideas I have offered in this chapter with the statement: "The modern world is very much a 'seen' phenomenon. Sociology, however, itself in many senses the emergent discourse of modernity, has been rather neglectful of addressing cultural ocular conventions and has subsequently become somewhat inarticulate in relation to the visual dimensions of social relations" (p. 2).

3. Steiger's (1995) analysis of the relationship between photographers' choices and sociological statements is the best place to become acquainted with this topic.

4. Collier (1967; Collier & Collier, 1986) first described photo elicitation, a process used in the 1950s in Cornell University research on rural assimilation to urban centers in Canada. The researchers came to the realization that without photographs to indicate common understandings, their interviews did not make a great deal of sense. Photographs made in the re-

search became a bridge between the subjects and the researchers.

5. A good place to start on this topic is with Dorothy Norman's (1960) study of Alfred Stieglitz, for whom photography was integral to the emergence of modern art.

6. After a thorough search (and on-line discussion), I found no references to the influence of gender in documentary expression. There have been many studies of the impact of gender on artistic photography. Thus although my example is limited because of the difficulty of comparing the work of a single female to the work of several men, it is an interesting first study.

■ *References*

Artieri, G. (1996). The virtual image: Technology, media, and construction of the visual reality. *Visual Sociology, 11*(2), 56-61.

Bateson, G., & Mead, M. (1942). *Balinese character: A photographic analysis.* New York: New York Academy of Sciences.

Becker, H. S. (1974). Photography and sociology. *Studies in the Anthropology of Visual Communication, 1*(1), 1-19.

Biella, P., Chagnon, N., & Seaman, G. (1997). *Yanomamo interactive: The ax fight* [CD-ROM and text]. New York: Harcourt Brace Jovanovich.

Bourdieu, P. (1990). *Photography: A middle-brow art.* Stanford, CA: Stanford University Press.

Chalfen, R. (1987). *Snapshot versions of life.* Bowling Green, OH: Bowling Green Popular Press.

Collier, J., Jr. (1967). *Visual anthropology: Photography as a research method.* New York: Holt, Rinehart & Winston.

Collier, J., Jr., & Collier, M. (1986). *Visual anthropology: Photography as a research method* (Rev. ed.). Albuquerque: University of New Mexico Press.

Copeland, A. (Ed.). (1969). *People's Park.* New York: Ballantine.

Denzin, N. K. (1995). *The cinematic society: The voyeur's gaze.* Thousand Oaks, CA: Sage.

Edwards, E. (Ed.). (1992). *Anthropology and photography 1860-1920.* New Haven, CT: Yale University Press.

Ewald, W. (1985). *Portraits and dreams: Photographs and stories by children of the Appalachians.* New York: Writers & Readers.

Gibson, W. (1985). *Neuromancer.* New York: Ace.

Glaser, B. G., & Strauss, A. L. (1967). *The discovery of grounded theory: Strategies for qualitative research.* Chicago: Aldine.

Grady, J. (1996). The scope of visual sociology. *Visual Sociology, 11*(2), 10-24.

Hagaman, D. (1996). *How I learned not to be a photojournalist.* Lexington: University Press of Kentucky.

Harper, D. (1982). *Good company.* Chicago: University of Chicago Press.

Harper, D. (1987). The visual ethnographic narrative. *Visual Anthropology, 1*(1), 1-19.

Harper, D. (1988). Visual sociology: Expanding sociological vision. *American Sociologist, 19*(1), 54-70.

Harper, D. (1994). On the authority of the image: Visual methods at the crossroads. In N. K. Denzin & Y. S. Yvonna Lincoln (Eds.), *Handbook of qualitative research* (pp. 403-412). Thousand Oaks, CA: Sage.

Harper, D. (1998). An argument for visual sociology. In J. Prosser (Ed.), *Image-based research: A sourcebook for qualitative researchers* (pp. 24-41). London: Falmer.

Jackson, B. (1977). *Killing time.* Ithaca, NY: Cornell University Press.

Jenks, C. (1995a). The centrality of the eye in Western culture: An introduction. In C. Jenks (Ed.), *Visual culture* (pp. 1-25). London: Routledge.

Jenks, C. (Ed.). (1995b). *Visual culture.* London: Routledge.

Klich, K. (1989). *The book of Beth.* Millertown, NY: Aperture.

Mamber, S. (1974). *Cinema vérité in America: Studies in uncontrolled documentary.* Cambridge: MIT Press.

Margolis, E. (1998). Picturing labor: A visual ethnography of the coal mine labor process. *Visual Sociology, 13*(2), 5-37.

Nichols, B. (1981). *Ideology and the image.* Bloomington: Indiana University Press.

Norman, D. (1960). *Alfred Stieglitz: An American seer.* New York: Random House.

Quinney, R. (1991). *Journey to a far place.* Philadelphia: Temple University Press.

Quinney, R. (1995). A sense sublime: Visual sociology as a fine art. *Visual Sociology, 10*(1-2), 61-84.

Rieger, J. (1996). Photographing social change. *Visual Sociology, 11*(1), 5-49.

Smith, W. E., & Smith, A. (1975). *Minamata.* New York: Holt, Rinehart & Winston.

Snyder, R. L. (1968). *Pare Lorentz and the documentary film.* Norman: Oklahoma University Press.

Spence, J. (1988). *Putting myself in the picture: A political, personal and photographic autobiography.* Seattle: Real Comet.

Steiger, R. (1995). First children and family dynamics. *Visual Sociology, 10*(1-2), 28-49.

Suchar, C. (1997). Grounding visual sociology research in shooting scripts. *Qualitative Sociology, 20*, 33-55.

Tagg, J. (1988). *The burden of representation: Essays on photographies and histories.* Basingstoke, Hampshire, England: Macmillan.

van der Dos, S. E., Gooskens, I., Liefting, M., & van Mierlo, M. (1992). Reading images: A study of a Dutch neighborhood. *Visual Sociology, 7*(1), 4-68.

AUTOETHNOGRAPHY, PERSONAL NARRATIVE, REFLEXIVITY

Researcher as Subject

◆ Carolyn Ellis and Arthur P. Bochner

◆ Overview: Extending the Handbook Genre

"Hi, glad it's you," I say, relieved to hear Art's voice on the other end of the line.

"You sound upset. What's the matter?" Art asks.

"Oh, it's been a zoo in the office today—long distance calls, forms to fill out, a barrage of e-mail, one student after another. I'm feeling that end-of-the-semester panic. I'd hoped to finish reading class papers and turn in semester grades, but I haven't gotten to them yet. How's everything at home? Are the dogs okay?"

"They're fine," Art replies quickly, "but I'm not. I started working on our chapter for the *Handbook of Qualitative Research*. The more I think about it, the more frustrated I become."

"I thought you really wanted to do this."

"Well, the first edition of the *Handbook* didn't sufficiently highlight autoethnography and personal narrative. So I initially thought it would be a good opportunity to show how important it is to make the researcher's own experience a topic of investigation in its own right."

"Well, the timing is right now to do that," I respond. "When the first edition was published a lot of academics were trying to figure out how to write their way out of the crisis of representation, but there weren't many examples of au-

AUTHORS' NOTE: Thanks to our graduate students at University of South Florida and to Mitch Allen, Norman Denzin, Rosanna Hertz, Yvonna Lincoln, Laurel Richardson, and William Tierney for commenting on the chapter manuscript. Carolyn Ellis gave a short portion of this article as a keynote address at The International Advances in Qualitative Methods Conference held in Edmonton, Alberta, Canada, February 1999, and published it in *Qualitative Health Research* (Vol. 9, no. 5, September 1999, pp. 653-667) as "Heartful Autoethnography."

thors who made themselves and their personal experience a central focus of their research. Over the past 5 years, however, that's changed significantly, what with the beginning of the Ethnographic Alternatives series, Denzin's emphasis on personal writing in *Interpretive Ethnography*, Behar's *The Vulnerable Observer. . .*"

"Granted, there's been a wave of interest in more personal, intimate, and embodied writing," Art assents.

"So what's the problem?"

"I think we've underestimated the constraints imposed by the genre of the handbook chapter as a form of writing," Art continues, apparently deep in thought.

"But you've written many handbook chapters before," I point out. "Why is this different?"

"Because those chapters conformed to the conventions of the handbook genre. They were essays, not stories. But in this piece we want to *show,* not just tell *about* autoethnography. Look at any handbook on your shelf and what you'll find is that most chapters are written in third-person, passive voice. It's as if they're written from nowhere by nobody. The conventions militate against personal and passionate writing. These books are filled with dry, distant, abstract, propositional essays."

"That's called academic writing, darling." When Art doesn't laugh, I continue in a more serious tone, "But some of the authors in the first edition of the *Handbook of Qualitative Research* wrote in first person."

"Yes, but the 'I' usually disappeared after the introduction and then reappeared abruptly in the conclusion," Art replies.

"And the 'I' usually was a 'we,' and an ambiguous 'we' at best, which sometimes referred to the authors as writers of the chapters and sometimes included all of us, whoever we might be," I add.

"And the authors almost never became characters in the stories they wrote . . ."

"They couldn't," I interrupt, now immersed in the conversation, "because their chapters weren't really stories. They included little in the way of dialogue, dramatic tension, or plotline, for that matter."

"But, look, handbooks do provide a service," I continue, fearing that Art will decide not to collaborate on the chapter. "They provide citations and sources, a sense of history, and arguments others can use as justifications for their own work."

"I don't question that they serve an important purpose. Hundreds of students have been inspired to do qualitative research by the first edition of the *Handbook of Qualitative Research,* for example."

"That's true, and we can't criticize handbook writers for failing to do what they're not asked to do."

"But we can ask why authors aren't encouraged to write academic articles in the first person, " Art retorts. "Why should we take it for granted that an author's personal feelings and thoughts should be omitted in a handbook chapter? After all, who is the person collecting the evidence, drawing the inferences, and reaching the conclusions? By not insisting on some sort of personal accountability, our academic publications reinforce the third-person, passive voice as the standard, which gives more weight to abstract and categorical knowledge than to the direct testimony of personal narrative and the first-person voice. It doesn't even occur to most authors that writing in the first person is an option. They've been shaped by the prevailing norms of scholarly discourse within which they operate. Once the anonymous essay became the norm, then the personal, autobiographical story became a delinquent form of expression."

Just as I'm beginning to doubt that we can do this project, Art says, "This morning I wrote out some of my concerns in conventional social science prose. Maybe this will give us a place to start. If you have a minute, I'd like to read it to you."

Relieved, I say, "Sure, go ahead." I glance toward the large stack of term papers. They'll have to wait.

Art reads:

Like most social scientists educated in the 1960s and 1970s, I was socialized into the legacy of empiricism. I developed an appetite for generalizable abstractions and unified knowl-

edge. The first social science handbooks were published when I was in graduate school, and they fed this hunger for received knowledge. My professors pressed the point that scientific knowledge is cumulative and linear, so every once in a while scholars have to step back and assess the state of the field. Ironically, these assessments sometimes were referred to as "state-of-the-art" essays (an art that was supposedly science). That's what a handbook did—it gave an objective, neutral read on the evidence. The authors were the experts, but they wrote as if they were anonymous. Because it wasn't important who gathered the evidence or who judged and weighed it, handbook writers followed the conventions of using a passive voice that erases subjectivity and personal accountability.

After I earned my Ph.D., I became increasingly circumspect about the possibilities and limitations of the human sciences. In the mid-1970s, one of my colleagues, who was teaching a graduate seminar on "the rhetoric of science," suggested that I study the growing literature on "the crisis of confidence" in social science. I began by reading Kuhn (1962), who showed that the building-block model of science lacked foundations; then Rorty (1982), Toulmin (1969), and other philosophers who illustrated how the "facts" scientists see are inextricably connected to the vocabulary they use to express or represent them; Lyotard (1984) debunked the belief in a unified totality of knowledge, questioning whether master narratives were either possible or desirable; poststructuralist and deconstructionist writers, such as Barthes (1977), Derrida (1978, 1981), and Foucault (1970), effectively obliterated the modernist conception of the author, altering how we understand the connections among author, text, and readers; under the influence of Bakhtin (1981), the interpretive space available to the reader was broadened, encouraging multiple perspectives, unsettled meanings, plural voices, and local and illegitimate knowledges that transgress against the claims of a unitary body of theory; feminist critical theorists such as Clough (1994), Harding (1991), Hartsock

(1983), and Smith (1990, 1992) promoted the unique and marginalized standpoints and particularities of women; and standpoint boundary-crossing textualists such as Trinh (1989, 1992), Anzaldúa (1987), and Behar (1993, 1996) opened our eyes and ears to the necessity of exposing how the complex contingencies of race, class, sexuality, disability, and ethnicity are woven into the fabric of concrete, personal lived experiences, championing the cause of reflexive, experimental, autobiographical, and vulnerable texts.

In the wake of these developments, I doubt whether a handbook chapter can help guide the work of those who have turned toward autoethnography and personal narrative if it holds to the voice and authority of a form of writing that this work seeks to transgress. How helpful would it be to list references, define terms, abstract from and critique exemplars, formulate criteria for evaluation, or theorize the perspective of the "I," so readers can make our knowledge theirs? No, we need a form that will allow readers to feel the moral dilemmas, think with our story instead of about it, join actively in the decision points that define an autoethnographic project, and consider how their own lives can be made a story worth telling.

When Art stops reading, I say, "Well, that's clever. Although you started with the 'I,' you quickly fell into using the handbook genre to argue against writing in the handbook genre." I can't stop laughing. "Reminds me of how so many of our texts argue in postmodern abstract jargon for greater accessibility and experimental forms."

"See how powerful the conventions are?" Art agrees, now chuckling as well. Then he adds more seriously, "Let's just write to Norman and Yvonna and bow out. Think of the time we could spend on the beach instead. Get some immediate gratification for a change."

"It's tempting, especially given how we've been feeling lately that our life is too dominated by our work—but no way. Not after I've already agonized over writing the section on 'what is autoethnography?' You know how I resist doing this kind of writing. At the same time, I know it's important," I reply, as I hear a knock at my door.

"I don't think I'll be satisfied, nor will you, unless we find a way to transgress the conventions. What if we were to create a story that would work within the handbook genre but also outside it, showing what we do as we tell about it? That could be fun," Art suggests playfully.

"How delightfully paradoxical," I add in a mischievous tone. "But we'd have to be careful not to give the impression that we're being oppositional and advocating that everyone should write the way we do," I warn, expressing something we hear often and try hard to dispel. Then I get back into the irony of Art's idea. "Won't our critics love it—you know, the ones who already accuse us of being irreverent, self-absorbed, sentimental, and romantic?"

Before Art can answer, I tell him I have to go. "Someone's at the door. Bye—Come in," I say in one breath, in response to the third knock.

◆ Introduction to Autoethnography

A woman in her mid-40s opens the door and hesitates in the entryway. A large-brimmed, floppy straw hat covered with purple bangles hides her face. A matching scarf hangs loosely around her neck. "Professor Ellis?" I nod. "My name is Sylvia Smith. I'm a Ph.D. student in the Psychology Department. I'm planning to do my dissertation on breast cancer, and your name was given to me as a social scientist interested in research on illness. I'd like you to be on my dissertation committee. Three members of my committee are from the Psychology Department and the fourth is a research oncologist."

"Hold it," I say, my hands extended in front of me to slow down her monologue. "Back up. Have a seat and let's talk about your project."

Sylvia removes her scarf and hat with a sweeping crisscross motion of both hands and continues speaking as rapidly as before. "I want to interview breast cancer survivors to understand how they're adjusting after cancer. I hope to combine qualitative and quantitative ap-proaches. Send out a survey and then interview . . . oh, maybe 30 women and include African Americans and lesbians, older and young women, professional and working-class women. That way I can generalize . . ."

"How'd you get interested in this topic?" I interrupt.

"Well, uh," she says, now slowing down and looking at me quizzically, "I've had breast cancer." Then, going back to her rapid-fire, assertive style, "But I won't let that bias my research. You can count on that."

"Of course you will," I say, and she immediately assumes a downcast, defeated posture, before I add, "as you should."

"What do you mean?" she asks, looking straight at me with penetrating eyes. "I thought I had to keep my personal experience out of my research. If I want my study to be valid, I can't mention to my participants that I've had cancer, can I?"

"Hold that question," I say again, and move my chair closer to hers. "Would you be willing to tell me a little about your breast cancer first? It'll help me understand more about your academic interest in the topic. Are you okay talking about your own experience?"

"Of course," she responds, "but I didn't think anybody at the university would be interested in my personal experience." She breathes deeply and slowly begins her story about the lump she discovered 7 years before, her mastectomy, and follow-up chemotherapy. Then, "And it's had a big impact on my family, especially my relationship with my daughter, and how I see myself . . . ," she says, her voice trailing off.

"How has it impacted your relationship with your daughter?" I ask quietly.

"She has to worry about getting cancer as well now. You know, the genetic link, and we seem to have trouble talking openly about the risks and about our feelings."

Sylvia continues to talk about her daughter, and after a while, I ask, "And your self-image?"

"I could write a book about that," she says, shaking her head back and forth. "You know, I'm a therapist. I thought I could deal with it all. But it's hard to feel like a whole person. I don't mean because I lost a breast. Good riddance, I say to that. They were always too big anyway. I had breast reduction on the other one when I had reconstruction. It's just . . . well . . . my life has changed so drastically, except the day-to-day, well actually that's not all that different . . ."

She becomes animated as she tells her story. Sensing that she is comfortable and desires to keep going, I continue asking questions. Her story inspires thoughts about myself. How would I feel if I had a breast removed? As she talks, I glance at her small breasts, then casually glide my hands across my own large ones. I can't imagine their not being there. Wouldn't I feel incomplete, desexualized? Did she really feel "good riddance" or is that a cover?

". . . And the hair," I hear her say through my thoughts. "Just look at my fuzz. It never really grew back like before. Shaving it was the most difficult yet exhilarating thing I've ever done." The thin, inch-long brown and gray strands don't move as she casually tosses her head from side to side. My fingers reach for my fine-textured, shoulder-length brown hair—I'd feel naked without it. I even resist pulling my hair back from my face. I wonder why she cuts hers so short now, as if she's drawing attention to having had cancer. But what about the hat and scarf? Does she use them in case she wants to "pass"? I wonder.

Sylvia and I are about the same age. This could happen to me. No, it couldn't. I get an annual mammogram.

". . . I'd had a mammogram just a few months before I found the lump," her voice intrudes into my thoughts.

But I do self-examinations every month, I argue back from inside my head.

"I found it during my monthly self-exam," she continues, shaking the false predictability of my world. I listen intently, understanding that Sylvia has a lot to teach me.

"Anyway, I'm interested in other women's experience," she says, adding hesitantly, "you know, how it compares to mine. That's not something I've admitted before, the personal part, I mean."

I nod. What do I do now? I don't want to wean another student off the science model and deal with a science-oriented committee. And

I'm wary of getting involved in another study that simplifies, categorizes, slices and dices the illness process. But Sylvia is a therapist and forthcoming about her feelings and what happened to her. Maybe her study could explore the feelings associated with breast cancer and be useful for other women. The pain on Sylvia's face, in spite of the casualness of her words, also makes me think that this study might be a useful exploration for her. And I know it could be a valuable experience for me as well. But what am I getting into?

"Do you have any idea what I do?" I ask.

"Just that you study illness and do qualitative work. Nobody does qualitative research in my department. But I've taken a qualitative course in education and I think I could get my committee to accept grounded theory for my dissertation research."

"I don't use grounded theory much anymore," I say. "Most of what I do is autoethnography."

"What's that?" she asks, writing the word *autoethnography* on her notepad as she looks at me.

"I start with my personal life. I pay attention to my physical feelings, thoughts, and emotions. I use what I call systematic sociological introspection and emotional recall to try to understand an experience I've lived through. Then I write my experience as a story. By exploring a particular life, I hope to understand a way of life, as Reed-Danahay says."

"Who?" she asks, pen poised in the air.

"Reed-Danahay, an anthropologist who wrote a book on autoethnography."

"How do I get a copy?"

"Don't worry about that yet. There's plenty of time to read *about* autoethnography. I want you to *experience* autoethnography first."

I ignore Sylvia's confused look, as I dig through my file cabinet. "So if I understand you correctly, the goal is to use your life experience to generalize to a larger group or culture," Sylvia speaks to my back.

"Yes, but that's not all. The goal is also to enter and document the moment-to-moment, concrete details of a life. That's an important way of knowing as well."

"So, you just write about your life? That doesn't sound too difficult," Sylvia says casually.

I turn around, stare at her for a moment, as though I'll get a sign as to whether I should promote autoethnography to Sylvia. When no sign is forthcoming, I say, "Oh, it's amazingly difficult. It's certainly not something that most people can do well. Most social scientists don't write well enough to carry it off. Or they're not sufficiently introspective about their feelings or motives, or the contradictions they experience. Ironically, many aren't observant enough of the world around them. The self-questioning autoethnography demands is extremely difficult. So is confronting things about yourself that are less than flattering. Believe me, honest autoethnographic exploration generates a lot of fears and doubts—and emotional pain. Just when you think you can't stand the pain anymore, well, that's when the real work has only begun. Then there's the vulnerability of revealing yourself, not being able to take back what you've written or having any control over how readers interpret it. It's hard not to feel your life is being critiqued as well as your work. It can be humiliating. And the ethical issues," I warn, "just wait until you're writing about family members and loved ones who are part of your story."

Sylvia holds on to her chair, her eyes wide. I smile and let out the breath I've been holding. "I'm sorry. I get really passionate about all this," I say more gently. "Of course, there are rewards too—for example, you come to understand yourself in deeper ways. And with understanding yourself comes understanding others. Autoethnography provides an avenue for doing something meaningful for yourself and the world . . ."

"Ah, here they are," I interrupt myself as I pull two stapled papers from my autoethnography file. "The one on top is 'Survivors,' a paper I wrote about my brother's death. The other one's a chapter from Butler and Rosenblum's book *Cancer in Two Voices,* a co-constructed narrative about a woman with breast cancer and her lesbian lover who takes care of her."

"Co-constructed?"

"We'll talk about that later. For now, just see how you respond to these stories. I think that af-

ter you've read them, what I've been saying will be clearer. If you're still interested then, leave me a note and I'll mail you some other materials."

"One more thing," I add, pointing to the syllabi on my desk. "I'll want to meet often and you'll have to read the assignments from my classes on 'illness narratives' and 'communicating emotion.' Also, I want you to meet with Art Bochner, my coauthor, who teaches courses on narrative and, by the way, also happens to be my husband." Her down-turned mouth changes to a smile for a brief moment, until I add, "These are minimum requirements if I'm going to be on your committee."

"Oh, my. I don't know if I'll have time, given my program," she says. "I still have to take 'Tests and Measurement' and 'Advanced Experimental Research Design.' I hope to finish my course work during this coming fall, and then take my prelims in early spring and finish my proposal by the beginning of next summer."

I shrug my shoulders as I stand and open the door. My exuberance, the warnings, all the requirements—any of these could scare her off. Oh, well, better if it happens now than later. Suspecting this will be the last I see of her, I'm glad I've given her an easy way out. Sylvia winds her scarf around her neck, throws her hat along with the papers I've given her into her large open bag, says good-bye, and quickly scurries from view.

Two days later, I arrive at school and find a faxed message from Sylvia.

> Dear Professor Ellis:
>   This is some of the most powerful writing I've ever read. I identified with your grief over losing your brother so suddenly. You reminded me of how I felt when I found out I had cancer. So did Butler and Rosenblum. I recall experiencing that kind of turmoil, confusion, and meaninglessness. This work violates everything I've been taught about social science research, but I'm fascinated and want to know more. Will you mail some materials to help clarify the origins and practices of autoethnography? Maybe some kind of a literature review would suffice. While you're at it, do you mind including a few more autoethnographies?

I smile and pull out articles from my autoethnography file. Jago, Kiesinger, Kolker,

Ronai, Tillmann-Healy—that ought to do it—and a section on defining autoethnography I have just written as part of a chapter for Denzin and Lincoln's second edition of the *Handbook of Qualitative Research*. I pause to read the draft, which is titled "What Is Autoethnography?"

◆ *What Is*
Autoethnography?

Autoethnography is an autobiographical genre of writing and research that displays multiple layers of consciousness, connecting the personal to the cultural. Back and forth autoethnographers gaze, first through an ethnographic wide-angle lens, focusing outward on social and cultural aspects of their personal experience; then, they look inward, exposing a vulnerable self that is moved by and may move through, refract, and resist cultural interpretations (see Deck, 1990; Neumann, 1996; Reed-Danahay, 1997). As they zoom backward and forward, inward and outward, distinctions between the personal and cultural become blurred, sometimes beyond distinct recognition. Usually written in first-person voice, autoethnographic texts appear in a variety of forms—short stories, poetry, fiction, novels, photographic essays, personal essays, journals, fragmented and layered writing, and social science prose. In these texts, concrete action, dialogue, emotion, embodiment, spirituality, and self-consciousness are featured, appearing as relational and institutional stories affected by history, social structure, and culture, which themselves are dialectically revealed through action, feeling, thought, and language.

The term *autoethnography* has been in circulation for at least two decades. Although anthropologist Karl Heider referred in 1975 to the Dani's own account of what people do as autoethnography, David Hayano (1979) usually is credited as the originator of the term. Hayano limited the term to cultural-level studies by anthropologists of their "own people," in which

the researcher is a full insider by virtue of being "native," acquiring an intimate familiarity with the group, or achieving full membership in the group being studied (p. 100).

Like many terms used by social scientists, the meanings and applications of autoethnography have evolved in a manner that makes precise definition and application difficult. It seems appropriate now to include under the broad rubric of autoethnography those studies that have been referred to by other similarly situated terms, such as personal narratives (Personal Narratives Group, 1989), narratives of the self (Richardson, 1994b), personal experience narratives (Denzin, 1989), self-stories (Denzin, 1989), first-person accounts (Ellis, 1998a), personal essays (Krieger, 1991), ethnographic short stories (Ellis, 1995d), writing-stories (Richardson, 1997); complete-member research (Adler & Adler, 1987), auto-observation (Adler & Adler, 1994), opportunistic research (Riemer, 1977), personal ethnography (Crawford, 1996), literary tales (Van Maanen, 1988), lived experience (Van Maanen, 1990), critical autobiography (Church, 1995), self-ethnography (Van Maanen, 1995), radical empiricism (Jackson, 1989), socioautobiography (Zola, 1982), autopathography (Hawkins, 1993), evocative narratives (Bochner, Ellis, & Tillmann-Healy, 1997), personal writing (DeVault, 1997), reflexive ethnography (Ellis & Bochner, 1996a), confessional tales (Van Maanen, 1988), ethnographic memoir (Tedlock, 1991), ethnobiography (Lejeune, 1989), autobiology (Payne, 1996), collaborative autobiography (Goldman, 1993), ethnographic autobiography (Brandes, 1982), emotionalism (Gubrium & Holstein, 1997), experiential texts (Denzin, 1997), narrative ethnography (Abu-Lughod, 1993), autobiographical ethnography (Reed-Danahay, 1997), ethnographic poetics (Marcus & Fischer, 1986), native ethnography (Ohnuki-Tierney, 1984), indigenous ethnography (Gonzalez & Krizek, 1994), and ethnic autobiography (Reed-Danahay, 1997). Nevertheless, social scientists often discuss autoethnography as a subtype of some other forms, such as impressionistic accounts (Van Maanen, 1988), narrative ethnography (Tedlock, 1991), interpretive biography (Denzin, 1989), new or experimental ethnography (Ellis & Bochner, 1996b), sociopoetics (Ellis

& Bochner, 1996a), or postmodern ethnography (Tyler, 1986).

Various methodological strategies have been developed in connection with autoethnographic projects, although they may be applied to other forms of qualitative research as well. These include systematic sociological introspection (Ellis, 1991b), biographical method (Denzin, 1989), personal experience methods (Clandinin & Connelly, 1994), feminist methods (Reinharz, 1992), experiential analysis (Reinharz, 1979), narrative inquiry (Bochner, 1994), consciousness-raising methods (Hollway, 1989), co-constructed narrative (Bochner & Ellis, 1992), and interactive interviewing (Ellis, Kiesinger, & Tillmann-Healy, 1997). In some disciplines, terms endemic to a particular field have evolved, such as in sociology, personal sociology (Higgins & Johnson, 1988), autobiographical sociology (Friedman, 1990), sociological autobiography (Merton, 1972/1988), private sociology (Shostak, 1996), and emotional sociology (Ellis, 1991a); in anthropology, anthropological autobiography (Brandes, 1982), native anthropology (Narayan, 1993), indigenous anthropology (Tedlock, 1991), autoanthropology (Strathern, 1987), self-conscious anthropology (Cohen, 1992), anthropology of the self (Kondo, 1990), anthropology at home (Jackson, 1987), anthropological poetics (Brady, 1991), and autoethnology (Lejeune, 1989); and in communication, rhetorical autoethnography (French, 1998), performance autobiography (Miller & Taylor, 1997), and autoethnographic performance (Park-Fuller, 1998). Increasingly, however, autoethnography has become the term of choice in describing studies and procedures that connect the personal to the cultural, frequently appearing in titles of books, theses, sections of books, articles, special issues of journals, and book series (for example, Clough, 1997; Deck, 1990; Ellis, 1997, 1998a; Ellis & Bochner, 1996a; Gravel, 1997; Herndon, 1993; Lionnet, 1989; Pratt, 1994; Reed-Danahay, 1997; Trotter, 1992).

Autoethnographers vary in their emphasis on the research process (graphy), on culture (ethnos), and on self (auto) (see Reed-Danahay, 1997, p. 2). Different exemplars of autoethnography fall at different places along the contin-

uum of each of these three axes. Researchers disagree on the boundaries of each category and on the precise definitions of the types of autoethnography. Indeed, many writers move back and forth among terms and meanings even in the same articles. Recognizing this limitation, I will mention, for heuristic purposes, a few widely used expressions that provide a sense of the range of approaches associated with autoethnography.

Although **reflexive ethnographies** primarily focus on a culture or subculture, authors use their own experiences in the culture reflexively to bend back on self and look more deeply at self-other interactions. In native ethnographies, researchers who are natives of cultures that have been marginalized or exoticized by others write about and interpret their own cultures for others. In texts by **"complete-member researchers,"** researchers explore groups of which they already are members or in which, during the research process, they have become full members with complete identification and acceptance. In **personal narratives,** social scientists take on the dual identities of academic and personal selves to tell autobiographical stories about some aspect of their experience in daily life. In **literary autoethnographies,** an author's primary identification is as an autobiographical writer rather than a social scientist, and the text focuses as much on examining a self autobiographically as on interpreting a culture for a nonnative audience (see Deck, 1990).

In **reflexive ethnographies,** the researcher's personal experience becomes important primarily in how it illuminates the culture under study. Reflexive ethnographies range along a continuum from starting research from one's own experience to ethnographies where the researcher's experience is actually studied along with other participants, to confessional tales where the researcher's experiences of doing the study become the focus of investigation.

Feminism has contributed significantly to legitimating the autobiographical voice associated with reflexive ethnography (for example, Behar, 1996; Behar & Gordon, 1995; Krieger, 1991, 1996; Personal Narratives Group, 1989; Richardson, 1997). Many feminist writers have advocated starting research from one's own experience (e.g., Smith, 1979). Thus, to a greater or lesser extent, researchers incorporate their personal experiences and standpoints in their research by starting with a story about themselves, explaining their personal connection to the project, or by using personal knowledge to help them in the research process (for examples, see Jones, 1998; Linden, 1992; for a summary of reflexive studies, see Reinharz, 1992, pp. 258-263).

Jackson (1989) uses the term **radical empiricism** to refer to a process that includes the ethnographer's experiences and interaction with other participants as vital parts of what is being studied. Reflexive ethnographers ideally use all their senses, their bodies, movement, feeling, and their whole being—they use the "self" to learn about the other (Cohen, 1992; Jackson, 1989; Okely, 1992; Turner & Bruner, 1986). Particularly controversial is the notion of the role of sexuality in learning about the other (Kulick & Willson, 1995; Lewin & Leap, 1996).

In summarizing reflexive ethnography and tracing its history thoroughly, Tedlock (1991) distinguishes between ethnographic memoir (also called confessional tales by Van Maanen, 1988), in which the ethnographer, who is the focus of the story, tells a personal tale of what went on in the backstage of doing research, and narrative ethnography, where the ethnographer's experiences are incorporated into the ethnographic description and analysis of others and the emphasis is on the "ethnographic dialogue or encounter" between the narrator and members of the group being studied (p. 78). The ethnographic memoir is rooted historically in the personal diaries and journals kept by Malinowski (1967). Standing on his shoulders, many ethnographers who followed wrote confessional tales about their research in volumes separate from their research documents (e.g., Dumont, 1976, 1978; Rabinow, 1975, 1977); some wrote under pen names in order to avoid losing academic credibility (e.g., Bowen, 1954). The development of this kind of reflexive writing is connected, according to Tedlock (1991), to a shift in the 1970s from an emphasis on participant observation to the "observation of participation" and to an emphasis on the process of writing. This shift was inspired by the epistemological doubt associated with the crisis of representation and the changing composition of those who become ethnographers, with more women, lower-class, ethnic and racial groups, and Third and Fourth World scholars now represented (Bochner & Ellis, 1999).

This changing composition also is associated with concerns about power and praxis and with more ethnographers writing about their own people. **Native ethnography**, for example, is written by researchers from the Third and Fourth Worlds who share a history of colonialism or economic subordination, including subjugation by ethnographers who have made them subjects of their work. Now as bicultural insiders/outsiders, native ethnographers construct their own cultural stories (often focusing on their own autobiographies; for example, see Kinkaid, 1988; Rodriguez, 1983), raise serious questions about the interpretations of others who write about them, and use their dual positionality to problematize the distinction between observer and observed, insider and outsider (see, for example, Motzafi-Haller, 1997; Trinh, 1989; for more detailed discussions, see Neumann, 1996; Reed-Danahay, 1997; Tedlock, 1991).

Complete-member researchers is a term coined by Adler and Adler (1987) to refer to researchers who are fully committed to and immersed in the groups they study. During the research process, the "convert" researcher identifies with the group and "becomes the phenomenon" (Mehan & Wood, 1975) being studied. For example, Jules-Rosette (1975) became a baptized true believer in the African Apostolic church she studied. The "opportunistic" researcher (Riemer, 1977; sometimes called an indigenous researcher in anthropology—see Tedlock, 1991) studies settings of which he or she is already a member (such as Hayano's 1982 study of poker or Krieger's 1983 study of a lesbian community).

In contrast to complete-member research, where the emphasis is on the research process and the group being studied, social scientists recently have begun to view themselves as the phenomenon and to write *evocative personal narratives* specifically focused on their academic as well as their personal lives. Their primary purpose is to understand a self or some aspect of a life lived in a cultural context. In personal narrative texts, authors become "I," readers become "you," subjects become "us." Participants are encouraged to participate in a personal relationship with the author/researcher, to be treated as coresearchers, to share authority, and to author their own lives in their own voices. Readers, too, take a more active role as they are invited into the author's world, evoked to a feeling level about the events being described, and stimulated to use what they learn there to reflect on, understand, and cope with their own lives. The goal is to write meaningfully and evocatively about topics that matter and may make a difference, to include sensory and emotional experience (Shelton, 1995), and to write from an ethic of care and concern (Denzin, 1997; Noddings, 1984; Richardson, 1997).

Literary and cultural critics often join social scientists in employing the term autoethnography in reference to autobiographies that self-consciously explore the interplay of the introspective, personally engaged self with cultural descriptions mediated through language, history, and ethnographic explanation (see Deck, 1990; Lionnet, 1989; Pratt, 1994). For example, Lionnet (1989) and Deck (1990) both label and explore Hurston's (1942/1991) memoirs as autoethnography, in which the traditional historical frame and specific dates and events associated with autobiography are minimized and the attempt to demonstrate the lived experience and humanity of authors and their peoples to outside audiences is maximized. As Hurston (1942/1991) explains about the folk songs she gathered in her own research, "The words do not count. . . . The tune is the unity of the thing" (p. 144). Deck compares literary autoethnographies to self-reflexive fieldwork accounts, such as Shostak's Nisa: The Life and Words of a !Kung Woman (1981) and Crapanzano's Tuhami: Portrait of a Moroccan (1980), in which the authors ground themselves in their field experiences, reference other social scientists who serve to validate the characters in their stories, keep the autobiographical components mainly in the introductions and

epilogues, and focus personal revelations directly on the fieldwork at hand rather than on their own personal development.

Social scientists also write literary and poetic ethnography. Dan Rose (1991), for example, distinguishes between his own personal poetry, which is not connected to his anthropology, and the poetry of other anthropologists such as Stanley Diamond (1982), which focuses on the ethnographic experience of anthropologists as observers. Many anthropologists, such as Edward Sapir and Ruth Benedict, have published realist ethnography in mainstream anthropology journals and personal poetry in literary outlets (Bruner, 1993). Now Anthropology and Humanism publishes fiction and poetry by anthropologists. In sociology, Laurel Richardson, for example, has published essays in literary (1995) and social science journals (1996) and poetry as ethnography (1994a).

Autoethnography, native ethnography, self-ethnography, memoir, autobiography, even fiction, have become blurred genres. In many cases, whether a social science work is called an autoethnography or an ethnography depends on the claims made by those who write and those who write about the work. Whether a work is called fiction or fact, autoethnography or memoir, is connected to writing practices—social science autoethnographies usually contain citations to other academics and use an academic, disciplinary vocabulary; publishing practices—who publishes the book, how it is promoted (for example, the field identified on the outside cover) and labeled (ISBN number), and who the targeted audience is; and reviewing practices—who endorses it, who reviews it, and who writes about it. Literary critics treat some autobiographies as autoethnographies and not others; Hurston, who sees herself as essayist, anthropologist, and fiction writer (Lionnet, 1989), provides a good example of the messiness and overlap. Mainstream social science tends to classify autoethnographies (for example, Ellis, 1995b) and life histories about academic careers (for example, Berger, 1990; Goetting & Fenstermaker, 1995; Riley, 1988) into the genre of memoir or autobiography (see Zussman, 1996). Perhaps the loose application of the term autoethnography only signifies a *greater tolerance now for the diverse goals of ethnography and a better understanding of the fallibility and indeterminacy of language and concepts.*

Smiling at the social science prose, I place the copy of the *Handbook* draft in the package with the stories I'm sending Sylvia. I try to imagine how she will take it in.

A week later, Sylvia again appears at my door. "Okay, I read everything you sent me. Wow, those personal narratives just blew me away. Your autoethnography piece was interesting, but hard to get through. It'll be more helpful later, I'm sure," she reassures, then continues quickly, "but now I'm very confused."

"Listen, I only have 5 minutes," I say. "I'm going to a department colloquium."

"Oh, I'm sorry. I'll come back another time," Sylvia responds, retreating through the doorway.

"No, wait. What confuses you?" I ask.

"Well, in my methods classes I was taught that I had to protect against my own biases interfering with my observations and that my research should produce general knowledge and theory. But the articles you gave me emphasize concrete expressions over abstractions. So, I'm confused about what my objectives would be if I do an autoethnography. Why would others be interested? How could I prove that what I have to say about my experience is true? Autoethnography isn't really social science, is it?"

"Your timing is perfect. Come with me," I say, grabbing my keys and walking down the hall. "I want you to hear somebody."

We enter a crowded room where a talk is about to begin. "That's Art, my partner, the good-looking guy sitting at the table," I whisper to Sylvia, as we take seats in the back.

"Welcome to another session of our Interdisciplinary Colloquium Series on Interpretive Research in the Social Sciences," says Jim Spiro, a departmental colleague who organizes the talks. "Today's speaker is Art Bochner, who teaches a Ph.D. seminar on 'narrative inquiry.' "

"We have these talks every week," I whisper to Sylvia. "They're pretty informal."

"Art will present his remarks for about 15 minutes and then turn to questions from the audience," Jim announces. "I've asked him to talk about what some writers have called 'the narrative turn in the human sciences' and to focus specifically on personal narratives. His talk is entitled 'Why Personal Narrative Matters.' Please welcome Art Bochner."

Art stands with his right foot hooked behind his left leg, runs his fingers through his hair, and begins.

◆ Why Personal Narrative Matters

It's my pleasure to be here today and to have this opportunity to speak on a topic about which I feel so passionately. As many of you know, I was educated as a traditional empiricist and spent most of the first decade of my academic life plying the trade I had learned as a graduate student. In the late 1970s I began to feel uneasy about the political, philosophical, ethical, and ideological foundations of social science research (Bochner, 1981). In my chosen field, communication research, empiricism rested largely on the premise that communication between humans could be described as an object. But human communication is not an object, or a discipline studying objects. Communication is a process consisting of sequences of interactions and the dynamic human activity of studying them. Moreover, as communicating humans studying humans communicating, we are inside what we are studying. The reflexive qualities of human communication should not be bracketed "in the name of science." They should be accommodated and integrated into research and its products.

Like many other social scientists who took these matters seriously, my confidence in orthodox, social science methodology was shaken by the critiques of poststructuralist, postmodernist, and feminist writers. I turned to narrative as a mode of inquiry because I was persuaded that social science texts needed to construct a different relationship between researchers and subjects and *between authors and readers. I wanted a more personal, collaborative, and interactive relationship, one that centered on the question of how human experience is endowed with meaning and on the moral and ethical choices we face as human beings who live in an uncertain and changing world. I also wanted to understand the conventions that constrain which stories we can tell and how we can tell them, and to show how people can and do resist the forms of social control that marginalize or silence counternarratives, stories that deviate from or transgress the canonical ones. The texts produced under the rubric of what I call **narrative inquiry** would be stories that create the effect of reality, showing characters embedded in the complexities of lived moments of struggle, resisting the intrusions of chaos, disconnection, fragmentation, marginalization, and incoherence, trying to preserve or restore the continuity and coherence of life's unity in the face of unexpected blows of fate that call one's meanings and values into question.*

I refer to these personal stories as evocative narratives *(Bochner, Ellis, & Tillmann-Healy, 1997, 1998). The word* evocative *contrasts the expressive and dialogic goals of this work with the more traditional orientations of mainstream, representational social science. Usually the author of an evocative narrative writes in the first person, making herself the object of research and thus breaching the conventional separation of researcher and subjects (Jackson, 1989); the story often focuses on a single case and thus breaches the traditional concerns of research from generalization across cases to generalization within a case (Geertz, 1973); the mode of storytelling is akin to the novel or biography and thus fractures the boundaries that normally separate social science from literature; the accessibility and readability of the text repositions the reader as a coparticipant in dialogue and thus rejects the orthodox view of the reader as a passive receiver of knowledge; the disclosure of hidden details of private life highlights emotional experience and thus challenges the rational actor model of social performance; the narrative text refuses the impulse to abstract and explain, stressing the journey over the destination, and thus eclipses the scientific illusion of control and mastery; and the*

episodic portrayal of the ebb and flow of relationship experience dramatizes the motion of connected lives across the curve of time, and thus resists the standard practice of portraying social life and relationships as a snapshot. Evocative stories activate subjectivity and compel emotional response. They long to be used rather than analyzed; to be told and retold rather than theorized and settled; to offer lessons for further conversation rather than undebatable conclusions; and to substitute the companionship of intimate detail for the loneliness of abstracted facts.

Personal writing akin to evocative narrative has recently proliferated in the mainstream press, in new journalism, in creative nonfiction, and in the genres of literary memoir, autobiography, and autopathography (Buford, 1996; Harrington, 1997; Hawkins, 1993; Parini, 1998; "True Confessions," 1996). All of the life writing genres (Tierney, 1998; see also Chapter 20, this volume) seem to have turned toward more intimate, personal, and self-conscious writing. I think the move in the social sciences toward less anonymous, more personal writing parallels the same trend in literature and journalism (Denzin, 1997; Neumann, 1996). Whatever the reasons, I see ample evidence of a burgeoning interest among diverse fields of social science in the genres of personal narrative and autoethnography. The examples I have in mind include the recent special issues of such journals as Journal of Contemporary Ethnography *(Ellis & Bochner, 1996b) and* Qualitative Sociology *(Glassner, 1997; Hertz, 1996); the book series* Ethnographic Alternatives, *published by AltaMira Press; the edited collections by anthropologists (Benson, 1993; Brady, 1991; Okely & Callaway, 1992), sociologists (Ellis & Flaherty, 1992; Hertz, 1997), and educators (Tierney & Lincoln, 1997); the many articles and monographs published in academic journals such as* American Anthropologist, Anthropology and Humanism Quarterly, Feminist Studies, Journal of Personal and Interpersonal Loss, Qualitative Inquiry, Sociological Quarterly, Symbolic Interaction, Text and Performance Quarterly, Western Journal of Communication, *and* Women's Studies International Forum.

By way of example, let me briefly mention three published evocative narratives. Each highlights the communicative practices through which the author's identity evolves, is displayed, and put to use (Bruner, 1990). In particular, these writers illustrate how certain metaphors and meanings are narrativized into their lives. Mukaia (1989) shows the lived experience of "anorexia from within," expressing the ways in which food and starvation are emplotted into her identity; Ronai (1992) presents a layered story in which she performs her situated, multiple selves, expressing her tortured ambivalence in assuming the dual identities of social science researcher and erotic dancer; and Ellis (1993) navigates the emotional maze of shock and grief as she copes with conflicting academic and family personas in the aftermath of her brother's sudden death in an airplane crash. Each is a first-person account, written as a story, that expresses vivid details about the author's own experience. The "research text" is the story, complete (but open) in itself, largely free of academic jargon and abstracted theory. The authors privilege stories over analysis, allowing and encouraging alternative readings and multiple interpretations. They ask their readers to feel the truth of their stories and to become coparticipants, engaging the story line morally, emotionally, aesthetically, and intellectually (Richardson, 1994b).

The question that I'm usually asked is, "To what kind of truth do these stories aspire?" Often this question is asked in a tone that expresses skepticism, doubt, and even hostility. Some critics (e.g., Mink, 1969-1970; Shotter, 1987) argue that stories give life a structure it does not have and, thus, stories fictionalize life. Since the experiences on which narratives are based may be vague and uncertain, the stories they arouse can never be determinate or complete (e.g. Shotter, 1987). Given the distortions of memory and the mediation of language, narrative is always a story about the past and not the past itself.

A second criticism is that personal narrative reflects or advances a "romantic construction of the self" (Atkinson, 1997) unworthy of being classified as part of social science. If you are "a storyteller rather than a story analyst," argues Atkinson (1997, p. 335), then your goal becomes therapeutic rather than analytic. Atkinson believes that a text that acts as an agent of self-discovery or self-creation—precisely the narrative challenge one faces when an expected life story is interrupted by illness, violence, or accident—cannot be an academic text. Presumably, if you don't subject narrative to sociological, cultural, or some other form of analysis, treating stories as "social facts," then you are not doing social science. While passionately protesting the ways in which some writers want "to privilege certain kinds and occasions of narrative performance," Atkinson (1997) aims to redeem (and privilege) the standard version of representational social science by trivializing or dismissing any work that does not, in his words, "use narrative to achieve serious social analysis" (pp. 338-339).

Let me briefly address the reservations expressed by these critics. First, there is the question of narrative truth. What is the point of a storied life? Narrative truth seeks to keep the past alive in the present. Stories show us that the meanings and significance of the past are incomplete, tentative, and revisable according to contingencies of our present life circumstances, the present from which we narrate. Doesn't this mean that the stories we tell always run the risk of distorting the past? Of course, it does. After all, stories rearrange, redescribe, invent, omit, and revise. They can be wrong in numerous ways—tone, detail, substance, etc. Does this attribute of storytelling threaten the project of personal narrative? Not at all, because a story is not a neutral attempt to mirror the facts of one's life; it does not seek to recover already constituted meanings. Only within the memoro-politics surrounding the accuracy of recovered memories, which emerged within the context of positivist psychology, would such a criticism be threatening (Hacking, 1995).

The truth of narrative is not akin to correspondence with prior meanings assumed to be located in some sort of prenarrative experience. One narrative interpretation of events can be judged against another, but there is no standard by which to measure any narrative against the meaning of events themselves, because the meaning of prenarrative experience is constituted in its narrative expression. Life and narrative are inextricably connected. Life both anticipates telling and draws meaning from it. Narrative is both about living and part of it.

I titled this little talk "Why Personal Narrative Matters" to emphasize that we live within the tensions constituted by our memories of the past and anticipations of the future. Personal narrative, the project of telling a life, is a response to the human problem of authorship, the desire to make sense and preserve coherence over the course of our lives. Our personal identities seem largely contingent on how well we bridge the remembered past with the anticipated future to provide what Stephen Crites (1971) calls "a continuity of experience over time." The narrative challenge that we face as narrators is the desire for continuity, to make sense of our lives as a whole. "The present of things past and the present of things future," says Crites (1971), "are the tension of every moment of experience, both united in that present and qualitatively differentiated by it" (p. 302). The work of self-narration is to produce this sense of continuity: to make a life that sometimes seems to be falling apart come together again, by retelling and restorying the events of one's life. Thus, narrative matters to us because, as David Carr (1986) observes, "coherence seems to be a need imposed upon us whether we seek it or not" (p. 97). At stake in our narrative attempts to achieve a coherent sense of ourselves are the very integrity and intelligibility of our selfhood, which rest so tenderly and fallibly on the story we use to link birth to life to death (MacIntyre, 1981). In the final analysis, the self is indistinguishable from the life story it constructs for itself out of what is inherited, what is experienced, and what is desired (Freeman, 1993, 1998; Kerby, 1991).

So the question is not, "Does my story reflect my past accurately?" as if I were holding a mirror to my past. Rather I must ask, "What are the consequences my story produces? What kind of a person does it shape me into? What new possibilities does it introduce for living my life?" The crucial issues are what narratives do, what consequences they have, to what uses they can be put. These consequences often precede rather than follow the story because they are enmeshed in the act of telling. "The story of our lives becomes our lives," writes Adrienne Rich (1978, p. 34). Thus personal narrative is part of the human, existential struggle to move life forward. Through the narrative activity of self-creation we seek to become identical to the story we tell. Anaïs Nin underscores this desire for self-created, narrative meaning when she announces, "I could not live in any of the worlds offered to me. . . . I believe one writes because one has to create a world in which to live" (quoted in Oakley, 1984).

I get impatient with writers who belittle or diminish the therapeutic consequences of stories. They tend to draw a hard-and-fast distinction between therapy and social research, implying that narratives are useful only insofar as they advance sociological, anthropological, or psychological theory. For these critics, narrative threatens the whole project of science. They reply angrily, shouting the canonically given, professional response: "If you can't pitch a theory, then you can't play in the big leagues." The most important thing is to be smart, clever, analytical; that's what it means to be academic. What they oppose is what they equate with the therapeutic: the sentimental, the mushy, the popular. Thus they engage surreptitiously in what feminist critic Jane Tompkins (1989) calls "the trashing of emotion," a war waged ceaselessly by academic intellectuals "against feeling, against women, against what is personal" (p. 138).

A text that functions as an agent of self-discovery or self-creation, for the author as well as for those who read and engage the text, is only threatening under a narrow definition of social inquiry, one that eschews a social science with a moral center and a heart. Why should caring and empathy be secondary to controlling and knowing? Why must academics be conditioned to believe that a text is important only to the extent it moves beyond the merely personal? We need to question our assumptions, the metarules that govern the institutional workings of social science—arguments over feelings, theories over stories, abstractions over concrete events, sophisticated jargon over accessible prose. Why should we be ashamed if our work has therapeutic or personal value? Besides, haven't our personal stories *always been embedded in our research mono-graphs? The question is whether we should ex-press our vulnerability and subjectivity openly in the text or hide them behind "social analysis."*

Sometimes I think: Art, if only you could do a better job communicating the important differ-ences between a representational and an evoca-tive social science. Why is it so hard to grasp that personal narrative is moral work and ethical practice? When the narrator is the investigator, to a certain extent she is always asking what it is right to do and good to be. At its most extreme, those who want "to put narrative in its place" (Atkinson, 1997, p. 343) seem to think there is only one right place to put it. They seek to pre-serve what already has been lost (Gergen, 1994; Schwandt, 1996). They think that if these per-sonal voices can be silenced, then perhaps they can return to business as usual in the social sci-ences, protected against the contingencies of hu-man experience, restored in their traditional be-lief in a transcendent position from which to speak (and interpret) with authority, freed of moral choices and emotional dilemmas, and in-spired to champion control over fate, facts over meanings, and rigor over peace of mind.

"Well, I guess this is a good place to stop and throw this session open for comments or ques-tions," Art invites. People in the audience shuf-fle in their seats anxiously, then several hands go up. "Yes, Billy," Art says, pointing toward a philosophy professor I recognize.

"Art, you mentioned that your turn toward narrative was provoked by postmodernism. Could you elaborate on that?"

"I had read Thomas Kuhn's *The Structure of Scientific Revolutions* and was impressed by his argument that there was no way to distinguish unequivocally what's in our minds from what's out there in the world. About the same time, I was introduced to the writings of Wittgenstein (1953), Heidegger (1971), Gadamer (1989), and Derrida (1978), and to speech act theory. In quite diverse ways, all of this work stood in opposition to the view—that now seems incred-ibly naïve—that language could be a neutral or transparent medium of communication.

Whether we apply language to ourselves or to the world there always is slippage, inexactness, inde-terminacy. Then along came Richard Rorty's *Phi-losophy and the Mirror of Nature* (1979), which provided a powerful synthesis of the challenges to our most venerable notions about truth and knowledge. It was hard to read Rorty without feeling totally shaken. I came away convinced that the foundations of traditional epistemology were fallible. No strong case could be made that human knowledge was independent of the hu-man mind. All truths were contingent on the de-scribing activities of human beings. No sharp dis-tinctions could be made between facts and values. If you couldn't eliminate the influence of the ob-server on the observed, then no theories or find-ings could ever be completely free of human val-ues. The investigator would always be implicated in the product. So why not observe the observer, focus on turning our observations back on our-selves? And why not write more directly, from the source of your own experience? Narratively. Po-etically. Evocatively. No longer was there any deep reason to believe that social science is closer to physics than to literature or poetry. Besides, I became a social scientist because I thought it was a way to address deep and troubling questions about how to live a meaningful, useful, and ethi-cal life. Somewhere along the way these ques-tions took a backseat to methodological rigor. Now I felt liberated to grapple with these ques-tions again, more dialogically, through personal narrative."

A woman I don't recognize stands and shouts from the back of the room, "I've always found the postmodernists depressing and cynical. They seem to be saying you can't know anything. It all seems so destructive." Laughter circulates through the audience and I notice a number of people nodding in agreement.

Art responds, "Well there's an affirming strain of postmodernism too. At least I read it that way. In the writings of certain postmodernists and par-ticularly within feminist and queer theory you see a renewed appreciation for emotion, intuition, personal experience, embodiment, and spiritual-ity. They've helped us cross some of the bound-aries separating the arts and the sciences and to focus attention on diversity and difference instead of unity and similarity. I don't regard these moves as negative or depressing. Perhaps, like you, I find them unsettling, even painful at times. But that's where the learning is. We lose our innocence and our lost innocence validates some good values. We gain tolerance and humility. Sometimes we're ashamed of how much we've excluded from our experience, tried not to see, hidden from. And we should be. We don't need to run from the fear or anxiety we feel. We need to learn from it. Racism, sexism, poverty, homophobia, disability—these issues touch all of us. We can't hide from them. We're all complicit in some way. No one's immune, invulnerable. So it's important to get exposed to local stories that bring us into worlds of experience that are unknown to us, show us the concrete daily details of people whose lives have been underrepresented or not represented at all, help us reduce their marginalization, show us how partial and situated our understanding of the world is. Maybe that's depressing to some of you, but I think it's enlightening and possibly transforming."

"I think you misunderstood her," a man in the front row interjects. I recognize the voice of a colleague wedded to mainstream social science methods. "The resistance and political dimensions are clear enough, but some of us still want to know how we can tell when we're right, when our representations are accurate and we can generalize."

Art sighs in frustration and continues, "We may have to agree to disagree. I take the crisis of representation more seriously than you do. For me, it necessitates a radical transformation in the goals of our work—from description to communication. That's the inspiration for the narrative turn. As I see it, the practices of human communication—the negotiation and performance of acts of meaning—should become our model for how we tell about the empirical world (Bochner & Waugh, 1995). Then, we would feel compelled to produce narrative, evocative, dialogic texts that show human beings, including ourselves, in the process of creating, negotiating, and performing meaning in a world of others,

making our way through a world that poses obstacles, interruptions, contingencies, turning points, epiphanies, and moral choices."

"So what are the goals? I don't quite follow," the same man continues. "Could you be more precise?"

"The goal is to encourage compassion and promote dialogue. Actually, I would be pleased if we understood our whole endeavor as a search for better conversation in the face of all the barriers and boundaries that make conversation difficult. The stories we write put us into conversation with ourselves as well as with our readers. In conversation with ourselves, we expose our vulnerabilities, conflicts, choices, and values. We take measure of our uncertainties, our mixed emotions, and the multiple layers of our experience. Our accounts seek to express the complexities and difficulties of coping and feeling resolved, showing how we changed over time as we struggled to make sense of our experience. Often our accounts of ourselves are unflattering and imperfect, but human and believable. The text is used, then, as an agent of self-understanding and ethical discussion.

"In conversation with our readers, we use storytelling as a method for inviting them to put themselves in our place. Our dialogue centers on moral choices, questions having more to do, as Michael Jackson (1995) observes, with how to live than with how to know. The usefulness of these stories is their capacity to inspire conversation from the point of view of the readers, who enter from the perspective of their own lives. The narrative rises or falls on its capacity to provoke readers to broaden their horizons, reflect critically on their own experience, enter empathically into worlds of experience different from their own, and actively engage in dialogue regarding the social and moral implications of the different perspectives and standpoints encountered. Invited to take the story in and use it for themselves, readers become coperformers, examining themselves through the evocative power of the narrative text."

Art pauses to take a sip of water. Jim, the colloquium organizer, turns toward him and says, "I liked your attempt to enter into dialogue with the critics of narrative inquiry, but you left out one of my main reservations. How do you react to critics who say that personal narratives simulate reality TV? Aren't these narratives reflective of the culture of confession and victimization and don't they end up as spectacles that sentimentalize, humiliate, and take pleasure in revealing anguish and pain? Personal narratives remind me of victim art. They play on your sympathies and manipulate your emotions."

"I've heard that one before, Jim. My first response is to consider the source. That's a particular reading, by a particular person. So it's always the case, in my view, that the criticism speaks the critic's life too. The text's meanings are never transparent. There is always a connection being made between the reader's consciousness and what is being read. So I want to know something about the reader—her interests, desires, values, premises, and what she resists and why.

"So, Jim, where are you in this picture?" Art teases. He pauses and smiles gently as the audience chuckles and Jim looks around quizzically, shrugging his shoulders.

"Seriously, Jim," Art continues. "I didn't mean to put you on the spot. Well, maybe I did. But, as a critic, I don't think it's your job to condemn something categorically. I think you have to look at the merits of each case. It's hard for me to respond in terms of some general principle. If you take a genre of stories that might be called 'illness narratives,' for example, the sorts of stories that Arthur Frank (1995) has analyzed, well, I think the goal is to reduce the stigma and marginalization of illness and disability. Most of these stories are written by people who don't want to surrender to the victimization and marginal identities promoted by the canonical narrative of medicine. Many of them try to write themselves as survivors, displaying their embodiment as a source of knowledge. It's hard to understand how anyone could read Anatole Broyard (1992) or Nancy Mairs (1986, 1990, 1998) or Audre Lorde (1980)—and I could name dozens more—as victim confessionals. They aren't seeking pity and they don't portray themselves as pathetic, helpless, down-

trodden characters. If anything, they use narrative as a source of empowerment and a form of resistance to counter the domination and authority of canonical discourses. I think that Couser (1997) thoroughly discredits the 'victim art' argument by showing that the vast majority of narratives focused on the 'recovering body' 'are much more likely to *de*victimize their subjects and others like them' (p. 291). Their main function is to confirm and humanize the experience of illness by bearing witness to what it means to live with bodily dysfunction and to gain agency through testimony. So, what are the choices, Jim? Erasure? Silence? Surrender? I think you have to understand some of the identity politics that are involved here too. Whose stories get told? By whom? And for what purpose? I know you're interested in cultural and political implications of narrative. Don't you think these stories help us understand how culture and politics are written on the body?"

"I see your point," Jim says, "but I still worry about voyeurism and the way these personal stories indulge our culture's perverse curiosity about the private, peeking in on damaged selves. How do we judge the merits of these stories? When do we know they're reliable and telling?"

"I think it's the same judgment we make about any author or any character. Is the work honest or dishonest? Does the author take the measure of herself, her limitations, her confusion, ambivalence, mixed feelings? Do you gain a sense of emotional reliability? Do you sense a passage through emotional epiphany to some communicated truth, not resolution per se, but some transformation from an old self to a new one (Rhett, 1997)? Does the story enable you to understand and feel the experience it seeks to convey? There is complexity, multiplicity, uncertainty, desire. Phillip Lopate (1994) refers to the personal essay as something akin to basic research on the self that ends up as 'a mode of being' (p. xliv). It's not science; it's not philosophy. The same can be said for the evocative, personal story. It's an existential struggle for honesty and expansion in an uncertain world."

I tap Sylvia's shoulder and whisper, "Notice how Art dodges questions that try to get him to stipulate categorical criteria. He always wants to balance rigor and imagination. He thinks if you're too bound up with rules, you probably won't do anything interesting. Anyway, I've got to meet another student in my office for a makeup exam. I'll meet you back here after the talk."

When I return, Sylvia is standing alone watching the students gathered around Art talking passionately about their writing projects. "The woman facing us is Lisa Tillmann-Healy," I tell Sylvia. "She's published a story about her own eating disorder, and she's recently finished her dissertation on straight couples' relationships with gay men, telling the story of her own friendships. The woman to her left is Deborah Austin, who writes lyrical poems and did her dissertation on African American marriages in the aftermath of the Million Man March. For her dissertation defense, she performed a script she wrote based on focus groups she studied. Christine Kiesinger, the woman talking to Art, has published several stories from her dissertation on women with eating disorders. You might be interested in looking at her dissertation to see how she weaves her story with the story of one of her participants. Over there, that's Laura Ellingson," I say, nodding just to the left of the group. "She published an article recently in *Qualitative Inquiry* on how her own illness affected her understanding of other cancer patients and the organizational environment at the cancer hospital she is studying, and how, in turn, this experience helped her reinterpret her own illness. I'll give you a reprint. Laura is talking with Leigh Berger, who published a story about her relationship with her hearing-impaired sister and another about her father who was institutionalized for mental illness. She's studying Messianic Judaism now, observing her own transformation as she participates in a religious group. Come, I'll introduce you to them."

"I read the articles by Lisa and Christine," Sylvia reminds me. "Interesting that they are all women," she says thoughtfully, and then exclaims, "Wow! This is exciting!" I smile, but before I can say anything, Sylvia blurts out, "I want to write my story. But I haven't been keeping notes or anything. How would I do it? Where would I start?"

◆ Doing Autoethnography: Considerations

"Answering your questions will take a while. Let's go get a cup of coffee. You can meet the other students later," I decide, waving to them over my shoulder. "There are a number of ways to go about writing autoethnography," I say as we walk. "It really depends on where along the continuum of art and science you want to locate yourself. What claims do you want to make? If you want to claim you're following traditional rules of ethnographic method, then it would be best if you had kept notes on the experience as it happened. The notes would serve as field notes and you'd write from those."

"If you didn't have notes, how would you remember what actually happened?" Sylvia asks.

"Do you think the notes would tell you what actually happened? Aren't they partial interpretations as well?"

"Well, yes, but then how would I make sure that what I said was truthful?"

"The truth is that we can never capture experience. As Art said, 'Narrative is always a story about the past,' and that's really all field notes are—one selective story about what happened written from a particular point of view for a particular purpose. But if representation is your goal, it's best to have as many sources and levels of story recorded at different times as possible. Even so, realize that every story is partial and situated."

I take four quarters from my pocket and insert them into the coffee machine. "I'm buying," I say. "Cream and sugar?"

"Oh, no. Let me pay," she insists, opening her purse.

"Next time. Okay?"

"Okay. Just black for me." We take our coffees outside and sit under a tree to enjoy the perfect Florida spring day. "Is there a way other than representation to think about personal narrative?" Sylvia asks.

"Well, yes, if you viewed your project as closer to art than science, then your goal would not be so much to portray the *facts* of what happened to you accurately, but instead to convey the *meanings* you attached to the experience. You'd want to tell a story that readers could enter and feel a part of. You'd write in a way to evoke readers to feel and think about your life, and their lives in relation to yours. You'd want them to experience the experience you're writing about—in your case, breast cancer."

"If these were your goals," I continue, "writing notes at the time the experience occurred would have been helpful, but not absolutely necessary. If you're writing about an epiphany, which you usually are in this kind of research, you may be too caught up in living it to write about it."

"But then how do you remember all the dialogue and details later?"

"When I wrote *Final Negotiations,* about the chronic illness and death of my first husband, I didn't actually remember everything I wrote about, certainly not the exact words we spoke, anyway. I had notes for much of what I described, but I still had to construct scenes and dialogue from the partial descriptions in my notes. And I hadn't kept immediate notes for everything I wrote about, though I constructed them later. But it's amazing what you can recall, and for how long, if the event was emotionally evocative. Another story I wrote, about race relations in a small town, was constructed without notes more than 25 years after the event occurred."

"But how can that be valid?"

"It depends on your definition of validity. I start from the position that language is not transparent and there's no single standard of truth. To me validity means that our work seeks verisimilitude; it evokes in readers a feeling that the experience described is lifelike, believable, and possible. You might also judge validity by whether it helps readers communicate with others different from themselves, or offers a way to improve the lives of participants and readers or

even your own. Take a look at Lather's discussion of validity and counterpractices of authority in the *Sociological Quarterly,* 1993, I believe it is."

Sylvia looks up from her note taking and grimaces, "What about reliability?"

"Since we always create our personal narrative from a situated location, trying to make our present, imagined future, and remembered past cohere, there's no such thing as orthodox reliability in autoethnographic research. However, we can do reliability checks. When other people are involved, you might take your work back to them and give them a chance to comment, add materials, change their minds, and offer their interpretations."

"Generalizability? Is that a concern?"

"Of course, though again not in the usual sense. Our lives are particular, but they also are typical and generalizable, since we all participate in a limited number of cultures and institutions. We want to convey both in our stories. A story's generalizability is constantly being tested by readers as they determine if it speaks to them about their experience or about the lives of others they know. Likewise, does it tell them about unfamiliar people or lives? Does a work have what Stake calls 'naturalistic generalization,' meaning that it brings 'felt' news from one world to another and provides opportunities for the reader to have vicarious experience of the things told?"

"That's sure different from what I've learned, but I think I understand. Still I don't know where to start my own project."

"Why don't you start by writing a draft of your story. Think of it as making retrospective field notes on your life. Include all the details you can recall. I find it helpful to organize my writing chronologically first, using the main events to structure the tale. I try to write daily, rereading what I wrote the day before, then filling in new memories. Remember, you are creating this story; it is not there waiting to be found. Your final story will be crafted from these notes."

"But how will I know when I'm writing from my perspective then and when my current perspective is clouding my memory of what happened?"

"Well, you won't really. Memory doesn't work in a linear way, nor does life, for that matter. As Denzin and also Ronai say in *Investigating Subjectivity,* the book I edited with Michael Flaherty, thoughts and feelings circle around us, flash back, then forward, the topical is interwoven with the chronological, thoughts and feelings merge, drop from our grasp, then reappear in another context. In real life, we don't always know when we know something. Remember Art's talk—events in the past are always interpreted from our current position. Yet that doesn't mean there's no value in trying to disentangle now from then, as long as you realize it's not a project you'll ever complete or get completely right; instead, you strive to get it 'differently contoured and nuanced' in a meaningful way, as Richardson says in her *Handbook* chapter."

"What do you mean? How do you do that?"

"I use a process of emotional recall in which I imagine being back in the scene emotionally and physically. If you can revisit the scene emotionally, then you remember other details. The advantage of writing close to the time of the event is that it doesn't take much effort to access lived emotions—they're often there whether you want them to be or not. The disadvantage is that being so involved in the scene emotionally means that it's difficult to get outside of it to analyze from a cultural perspective. Yet both of these processes, moving in and moving out, are necessary to produce an effective autoethnography. That's why it's good to write about an event while your feelings are still intense, and then to go back to it when you're emotionally distant. I've had students who were great at getting *inside* emotional experience, but they had tunnel vision. They couldn't move around in the experience. They were unable to see it as it might appear to others. They had trouble analyzing their thoughts and feelings as socially constructed processes. I'll give you my article on systematic sociological introspection, which talks more about introspection as a social process."

"I'd like that. But I'm not sure I'd want to feel all those emotions again. And some of the feelings I've had and still have about my cancer I wouldn't want to share. I'd feel so vulnerable."

"Well, that's your call. But if you're not willing to become a vulnerable observer, then maybe you ought to reconsider doing autoethnography. If you let yourself be vulnerable, then your readers are more likely to respond vulnerably, and that's what you want, vulnerable readers. I agree with Ruth Behar, who wrote in *The Vulnerable Observer* that social science 'that doesn't break your heart just isn't worth doing.' My goal is the same as Dorothy Allison's—'to take the reader by the throat, break her heart, and heal it again.' Vulnerability can be scary, but it also can be the source of growth and understanding."

"I've always assumed my task as a social scientist was to deliver knowledge and stay invulnerable," Sylvia responds. "I didn't know I had a choice.

"So, suppose I am willing to be vulnerable," she continues slowly. "How do I get from field notes to writing in a way that opens up myself and readers to being vulnerable?"

"Do you ever read fiction?" When she nods, I continue, "Well, think about how a good novel makes you feel. It does make you feel, right?" She nods again, waiting for what I will say next. "What provokes these feelings?"

"Sometimes I identify with the characters. I feel for them. Or I think about being in the situations they're in, doing what they're doing, or imagine what I'd do in the same situation. And sometimes I stop reading to think about how my life is different or similar."

"Exactly. Good fiction writers make you feel the feelings of the characters, smell the smells, see the sights, hear the sounds, as though you were there. They do this with devices of fictional writing such as internal monologue, dialogue among the characters, dramatic recall, strong imagery, things like scene setting, character development, flashbacks, suspense, and action. You enter the reality of the novel through a dramatic plotline, which is developed through the specific actions of specific characters with specific bodies doing specific things."

"Then how is what you do different from fiction writing?"

"A number of social scientists have addressed your question. Take a look at Denzin's discussion of the relationship of social science writers to the new journalists in *Interpretive Ethnography.* Susan Krieger's early piece on fiction and social science and Richardson and Lockridge's new work on fiction and ethnography also might be helpful."

"The two genres are more similar than different," I continue. "As Walt Harrington says about intimate journalism, in autoethnography you try to write from inside the heads of participants and evoke the tone of their felt lives."

"Of course, writing and publishing conventions are different," I add, now switching gears. "You're a social scientist, so that probably will affect what you look at and how you see. And, among social scientists, autoethnography often has more of an overt analytic purpose and an analytic frame. Remember how Carol Ronai in the piece I gave you layers analysis through her personal narrative? But in *Final Negotiations,* I emphasized that analysis can come through story and dialogue too. Arthur Frank says in *The Wounded Storyteller* that it is important to think *with* a story, not just about a story. Thinking with a story means allowing yourself to resonate with the story, reflect on it, become a part of it.

"I'd suggest you read some exemplars of this work and note the different ways authors intersect story and analytic frame. Look at some of the books in the AltaMira Ethnographic Alternatives series edited by Art and me. For example, Jones's *Kaleidoscope Notes* uses conversation, songs, poetry, stories, performance, and autoethnography to examine women's music, a folk music club, and ethnography; Angrosino's *Opportunity House* is made up of fictional stories of adults with mental illness that are based on his decade of participant observation work; and Markham's *Life Online* uses her own experiences to study life on the Internet. Our *Composing Ethnography* and *Fiction and Social Research* by Banks and Banks both showcase a multitude of creative forms of narrative writing."

"Aren't decisions social scientists make different from fiction writers?"

"Well, generally, autoethnographers limit themselves, unlike fiction writers, to what they remember actually happened. Or at least they don't tell something they know to be false. Well, even that's not so clear-cut. It depends . . ."

"On what?"

"Well, say you want to protect the privacy of a character in your story. Then you might use composites or change some identifying information. Or you might collapse events to write a more engaging story, which might be more truthful in a narrative sense though not in a historical one."

When Sylvia looks at me questioningly, I say, "You know—the story evokes in readers the feeling that the tale is true. The story is coherent. It connects readers to writers and provides continuity in their lives." When I see a look of recognition on Sylvia's face, I continue, "Even realist ethnographers, who claim to follow the rules for doing science, use devices such as composites or collapsing events to tell better stories and protect their participants. Yet they worship 'accuracy' in description. A friend of mine, Sherryl Kleinman, says, If it didn't happen, don't tell it. That's another version of 'Don't put words in participants' mouths if they didn't say them.' But, of course, ethnographers do put words in participants' mouths all the time."

"Really? How can they get away with that?"

"By relying on memory, editing, and selecting verbatim prose out of context and then surrounding it with their own constructed analytic contexts. When it comes to analysis, most traditional ethnographers have no problems reaching beyond description for all kinds of interpretation."

"Give me an example."

"Oh, from limited time and access in the field, they create the 'typical' person or day, the 'common' event. They use ambiguous and qualifying descriptors like *most, some, frequent,* and *few.* And, of course, they reify concepts such as social structure and organizational climate. I did this too in my first study of two fishing villages. Let me tell you, when community members read what I wrote—well, what I saw as typical was certainly not what they saw as typical. What I wrote told you more about how I organize my world than how they organized theirs."

"Don't believe the propaganda," Art says, suddenly walking toward us with a stack of books piled in his arms.

I laugh and ask, "Hi, where have you been?"

"In the library, retrieving some sources for our *Handbook* paper."

"They look pretty heavy to me," I say, smiling as I eye the titles on the spines of the books. "Art, this is my student Sylvia, the one who is studying breast cancer."

"Oh, yes, hi. I noticed you sitting next to Carolyn at my talk today."

"Yes, I found it very interesting," Sylvia replies.

"We were just talking about how autoethnography differs from fiction," I explain.

"Oh, was Carolyn giving you her rap on how you have to be systematic and stick to the facts?" Art asks, turning to Sylvia. "Just the facts, ma'am," he mimics.

"Ah . . . ," Sylvia stalls.

"Art, stop it," I say playfully. Then turning to Sylvia, I explain, "Art and I have this running commentary on writing autoethnography. I argue that you try to construct the story as close to the experience as you can remember it, especially in the initial version. That doing so helps you work through the meaning and purpose of the story. He likes to argue that what's important is the usefulness of the story. Of course, I agree that our stories should have therapeutic value . . ."

"Therapeutic value?" Sylvia stammers.

"Yes, I think of it as action research for the individual. Though therapy might not be the major objective in our research, it often is a useful result of good writing," I respond.

"That reminds me, Art . . . uh, may I call you Art?" Sylvia inquires. When Art nods, she continues, "What you said in your talk about the focus of stories, well, I thought therapy and research were separate entities. I mean, I'm a therapist, but I assumed I had to keep that role separate from my interviewer identity, because if I acted as a therapist it might bias the data. And wouldn't it be unethical?"

Art and I look at each other and try not to smile. Her questions and concerns help us realize how close together our positions are. I quickly interject, "But you told me you hoped your research would provide understanding of what happened to you and help others who face similar circumstances cope. So what will you do

if an interviewee breaks down or if you see a place where you could be of help?"

She looks at me, waiting for the answer, then murmurs, "I'm not sure."

"What would you want someone in a similar situation to do for you if you were a research participant?"

"Well, I'd want them to care about me and try to understand where I was coming from, " she responds softly. "Otherwise I wouldn't want to share my life stories with them."

"And wouldn't it be unethical for a researcher not to help or empathize with you if you were in need?"

"I've never thought of it that way before, but I would want my subjects to feel that I care about them. What good would my research be if it doesn't help others who are going through this experience, especially my subjects?"

"Participants," I say quietly.

"Participants," she repeats, her face turning red. "But isn't it true that not everybody can do good therapy? I mean most academics aren't trained therapists."

"Being able to do therapy and being a trained therapist are not synonymous," I respond, and Sylvia nods in agreement. "In fact, ethnographic training might be just as important for a therapist as therapeutic training."

"And therapeutic training probably should be a prerequisite to being an ethnographer," Art adds, laughing.

I smile and continue, "But you're right, not everybody is comfortable or capable of dealing with emotionality. Those who aren't probably shouldn't be doing this kind of research in the first place, or directing students who are."

"Perhaps you should give her citations to articles on some of these issues, like the ethic of caring and personal accountability, maybe Collins," Art suggests, as several of his books fall to the ground.

"I will," I say, helping to retrieve the books. "Other feminist writers would be helpful too. Let's see, Lieblich, Miller, Cook and Fonow, and Oakley. They'd be a good start," I say, marking them off as I return each book to Art's stack.

"And there are good summaries in Reinharz and also in Denzin's *Interpretive Ethnography*," Art adds. He then turns to Sylvia, "But enough literature, I want to know more about how you'd respond if you were an interviewee. What would make you comfortable enough to tell your story?"

"To know the other person was listening, really listening. I'd want someone I could cry in front of, actually who might cry with me. A person who might tell me some of her story if she had been through a similar experience."

"So are you going to share your story with your participants?" I ask.

"Ah . . . I think . . ."

"Go on."

"Well, I was going to say that my story would contaminate theirs, but I'm not so sure anymore."

Art and I smile. "This is probably enough for now," I say. "We've come a long way. Why don't you think about how this conversation provides clues for how you might want to do your own interviews and let's pick up this topic next time we meet."

We say our good-byes, and Art and I make our way to our car. "Are you sure this is the right move?" Art asks. "Is she ready to write her story?"

"Oh, I think she's ready. I sense she wants to tell her story."

"What if it opens up things for her that are just too painful?"

"I'll keep in close contact with her, just in case. But in my experience with personal narrative, people pretty quickly find their own comfort zone. They know when the time's right. But I'll make sure to provide opportunities for her to pull back or change gears in the project, if she needs to. She can always do that survey," I add, playfully tugging at his arm and then skipping ahead.

"I admire how much you're willing to risk with your students," Art says lovingly when I return to help him pick up the books that once again have toppled to the ground. "And how much you care about them."

"Same with you," I say.

"It's not easy being vulnerable, especially in the academy, where you're expected to be in control and keep your private life removed from your professional life. That's what I tried to say in 'It's About Time.' "

"It's scary, when you think about the professor at Colby who asked students to write personal narratives and ended up being charged with sexual harassment. Of course, we don't know what really happened there; we have only Ruth Shalit's report," I add. "Maybe his private and professional lives did become too entwined."

"That's certainly a possibility. But what about the article in the *Chronicle of Higher Education* that described how some of Jane Tompkins's colleagues attacked her for suggesting that the emotional and spiritual lives of university students are just as important as their intellects?"

"Maybe we should just write fiction," I offer.

"Now wait a minute," Art reprimands. "You know everything we write is fiction . . ."

◆ *Doing Autoethnography: Method and Form*

Two weeks later, Sylvia appears in my office. "Hi, I've written most of my story about my past now, and I waited until I was almost finished before I began reading other personal narratives of breast cancer. It's been very therapeutic," she says, "to write and to read. But I'm not sure I'm getting anywhere on my dissertation. I have so many questions."

"Like what?" I ask.

"Why would anybody want to read my story? How does my story differ from what's already published? And how will my story fit with the interviews I want to do of other women?"

"Slow down. Are you learning anything?"

"Oh, yes, at every turn."

"Tell me what you're learning."

"Well, that I have a lot in common with other women's breast cancer stories. For example, most women tell of their discovery of the lump—that's always a traumatic event—then the diagnosis and assessment of treatment options, then they describe waking up from the surgery, going through the follow-up treatment, and finally there's recovery and some kind of resolution at the end."

"Interesting, that's almost exactly how Couser summarized breast cancer narratives in his book on illness narratives," I respond, pleased with how much reading Sylvia has done.

"Most survivors describe making decisions about reconstructive surgery, shopping for a prosthesis—if they decide to wear one—their hair falling out, and seeking alternative treatment," she continues without skipping a beat. "I wrote about these things as well, and . . ."

"And have you learned anything new from writing *your* story? Sorry, I didn't mean to cut you off, but I'm curious."

"Yes, that cancer is more than a medical story, it's a feeling story. I learned how scared I am even though I've been a survivor now for 7 years. And that's the interesting thing—there's little about long-term survivors in stories or in social science research. Most survivors tell their stories soon after recovery from treatment and they're usually pretty optimistic about recovery and often claim to be better off at the end than the beginning.

"I felt that too, the optimism I mean, immediately after my treatment was over, that is," Sylvia continues passionately. "But I don't feel that way now. I try so hard to pretend that I'm an upbeat, optimistic person with no worries, a warrior who has learned from her experiences. But what I had to face as I wrote my story is that I'm scared all the time that the cancer will come back. I've had carpal tunnel syndrome and it's probably from the chemo. And now I have sweats at night, and I don't know if it's early menopause—another gift of chemo—or signs of the cancer returning. I'm sorry, but cancer has not improved my life and I can't make it into a gift. Holding in these feelings, all these years, has been difficult and I think it's had negative effects on my psychological and physical well-being and on my family."

Sylvia begins to cry. I touch her shoulder and hand her a Kleenex. We sit silently for a while, sadness connecting us. Needing to stay in the role of adviser, I hold back my tears. "Do you still want to continue this project?" I ask gently. "Or is it too painful?"

"Oh, no, I *have* to continue it," she responds forcefully, although her voice shakes. "What I'm experiencing is important to me. It was hard pretending; sometimes I thought I was going crazy. Now I realize I don't have to pretend. There are other stories to live and write. Maybe through writing and talking with other women about their experiences, I can figure out another story to live, one that might help me cope better and not take so much out of me. Maybe I can write myself as a survivor in a deeper, more meaningful way, like Art was talking about. You know, I can't help wondering how other women feel years after their treatment. That's what I want to know—how it feels to them, how they cope . . . or don't," she adds, the tears starting up again. "Does the experience continue to be as fresh and scary to them as it still is to me? Maybe I can both contribute to knowledge and help others—and myself—write a story we can live with. How I'm living now, denying my feelings—well, this is no way to live."

"Okay, we're getting somewhere now," I say softly. "I think you have your topic. I imagine that other women share your sense of vulnerability and loss of control over their lives. I think I would," I add, involuntarily shivering as I imagine how difficult it would be to have cancer hanging over me in such an intrusive way. "Now how do we find out how other long-term survivors experience cancer?"

"I'd like to do intensive interviews with survivors of more than 5 years," Sylvia responds energetically, "and include an African American woman—there's so little on their experience of breast cancer—and maybe even a lesbian woman, because I think their experiences might be different. How many participants would I need? Twenty-five?"

"Oh no," I laugh. "If you're going to do intensive interviews, you'd need only a few, maybe five or six including yourself. You'll want to interview each woman a number of times to build trust in the relationship, and also so they can read and respond to each transcript before you follow up with the next interview."

"How much will I participate?"

"Given that you share aspects of their experience, the interviews should be an interactive conversation, I would think. But you have to play that by ear. Rather than overlay method onto experience, you want to relate your approach to each woman's life and think about what would help her to tell her story. In some cases, participants will feel comfortable having a conversation, if you set it up that way. But as a society, we're so accustomed to the authoritative interview situation that some women still will expect you to be the authority and ask all the questions. Some might inquire about your story; others will be too glad for an opportunity to tell their own to pay attention to yours. They'll want you to be the researcher and therapist. Perhaps a few of the women will want to write their stories. Remind me next time to give you an article on interactive interviewing that I wrote with Christine Kiesinger and Lisa Tillmann-Healy, where we had conversations over dinner about eating disorders. It'll get you thinking about form and the problems of doing interactive interviews—the time involved and the emotional commitment and ethical issues of dealing in such a personal realm. I'll also give you a piece I wrote with Art on co-constructed narrative, which describes a two-part process of individually writing stories that are then shared and co-constructed by several participants."

"I guess there's no interview schedule then?" Sylvia asks, but since she's smiling, I don't respond. "How will the chapters look and where will my story be?" she asks, this time seriously.

"The form will evolve during the research process. You might start the dissertation with a short personal story, to position yourself for the reader, or tell your longer story as a chapter. Or you might integrate parts of your experience into each participant's story, each of which could form separate chapters. Or write your story in comparison to one of the participants who is similar to you, as Christine Kiesinger did in her study of eating disorders.

"Perhaps you will write each chapter in a unique form to reflect the different experiences you had in each interview," I continue, "or to reflect something about the character of each woman's story. For example, if a participant tells her story without much input or questioning from you, you might write in the thoughts you had as you listened to her and reflected on your life. If another interview is interactive, you might write dialogue to show the process of communication and interpretation that occurred between you. If you're successful, you should not only 'unmask' them and yourself for others, but, as Harold Rosen says, you should also discover the face under the mask.

"Or," I continue hesitantly, "you could write the dissertation, as Elliot Eisner suggests, in the form of a novel. The plot would consist of your research journey. You'd let readers experience with you your search for understanding, the questions you ask, how the women respond, what their answers open up for you, new questions that arise, and how you interpret their stories. In that case, you might end by showing how your stories compare and finally how your story changed as you took in and interacted with the other women's stories. You'd have to be careful, though, that your story didn't overshadow theirs."

"Yes, and it would probably be hard to get my committee to buy a novel."

I nod in agreement, and then remind her, "No matter how you tell the story, the writing has to be engaging and evocative. That's not how social scientists have been taught to write. You'll essentially have to learn how to write by reading novels, and by writing and rewriting and getting feedback. Of course, I'll provide response, but you might want to consider joining a writing group as well."

"That's a good idea," Sylvia responds, jotting down notes as she talks. "Won't I also have to do traditional writing? What about analysis, for example? Will I do grounded theory?"

"Well, your committee will demand an analytic chapter, you can bet on that. I also think you need one. The article I wrote on stigma convinced me of the benefits of moving between narrative and categorical knowledge, though I don't think that is necessary in every study."

I continue hesitantly, "You could do a straight grounded theory analysis. Then you'd divide chapters by concepts that emerge, or types, or some kind of category. Or each chapter might represent a stage in the illness process, like David Karp did in his study of depression. If you choose grounded theory, you'd need to pay a lot of attention to coding your materials and comparing and analyzing your data along the way, and you'd write in an authoritative voice about the patterns you saw. If you choose this strategy, I'd recommend you follow the procedures that Kathy Charmaz describes in the new *Handbook of Qualitative Research.*"

"What would happen then to the women's stories? And my story?"

"Well, you'd use snippets from all the stories where they applied in each chapter."

Sylvia pauses for a moment, jots down some notes, and then says thoughtfully, "I don't think so. It seems to me that would take away from the evocative nature of the stories as a whole, which is the value of my study. Besides, the women deserve to tell their own stories, though I know I'll influence how they get told . . ."

"I agree," I interrupt, relieved, "given the nature of your project and your goals. But just because we decide to do analysis doesn't mean we have to do it traditionally." Sylvia's eyes open wide. "What about inviting all your participants to read each other's stories and then meet together and tape-record the discussion? This could serve as the basis for your analysis—you'd 'ground' the analysis in your participants' understandings, as well as your own. You might provide your own interpretations for them to respond to."

"Okay," Sylvia says, leaning forward, speaking passionately. "I really like this idea. I'll invite my participants over for dinner one night. It'll be my way of doing something for them. Before they come, I'll send them the stories I wrote about each of the women. Then . . ."

"As long as you get permission," I caution.

"Oh, yes, I know that's important. Maybe I'll only send them their own stories." She pauses, then suddenly blurts, "What if somebody wants me to leave out something?"

"Then you might omit it, or ask your participant to help you rewrite it. Or you could fictionalize a detail in a way that camouflages the actual event but still conveys the meaning you want to get across. Or use pseudonyms or composite characters, if that helps."

"I'd also want them to listen and respond to my interpretations. But what if they disagree with my analysis?" she asks suddenly, frowning.

"That can happen, so you have to have some understanding up front about how you'll handle that. Perhaps you'll put alternative interpretations, yours and theirs, into the text. Or you could listen to their interpretations without giving them yours."

To provide an example, I say, "Susan Chase, a sociologist, chose not to give her analysis to participants to read before publication, though she asked for permission to use their words and gave them an opportunity to amend their narratives. She makes a distinction between what she wanted to communicate in her analysis—how culture shapes narrative process—and what her participants wanted to communicate in their narrations—their life experiences.

"In any case," I continue, "you'll need to explain in your dissertation the kinds of decisions you made and on what grounds you made them. You owe that to readers.

"It's a hard balance," I continue, suddenly reminded of readers, "giving readers the information they expect without betraying the trust of participants, I mean. As Ruth Josselson says, when we get to the writing stage, we tend to take ourselves out of relationship with our participants to form a relationship with readers. How can we help then but have feelings of betraying our participants?

"Oh, and it gets even more complicated," I say to Sylvia, whose hand covers her open mouth as she shakes her head in disbelief. "We haven't even talked about your family members yet. They may become central characters in your very personal story. Say your husband or daughter doesn't want you to reveal things about them or your relationship to them. What do you do then?"

"Oh, my, I hadn't thought of that," she says quietly. "But I'd *have* to talk about my family in order to penetrate the depths of my experience.

How could I ask my participants to do this, if I couldn't?"

"This is one of the most important ethical problems in this kind of research. Because now we're not just talking about faceless, nameless, unidentifiable subjects—if we ever were. Your intimates are identifiable individuals with names. Don't they deserve the same consideration as your participants who have given you permission to write about them?"

"Well, of course . . ."

"Are there any situations in which the 'greater good' outweighs individuals' rights to privacy, in which you have a right to tell your story even if other characters in it object?"

When I see the look of defeat on Sylvia's face, I realize that I am transferring too many of my own concerns to her too quickly. "Hey, these issues don't all have to be resolved today. I just wanted you to know that they will come up. We'll discuss each one as it arises and try to make good, ethical decisions."

Then, before Sylvia has a chance to be too relieved, I add, "But by the next time we talk, we do have to consider how to get your proposal past the IRB committee. You'll want to read Michael Angrosino and Kimberly Mays de Pérez's discussion of IRBs in the new *Handbook*. You'll have to be strategic in writing your proposal, because the first thing the committee will ask is about your independent and dependent variables. Then they'll want to see a copy of your interview schedule. All the talk of risk and ceding of responsibility by the university that they'll want you to put into your consent form, well, that will likely scare away some participants. But we have to go through the process to protect the university and ourselves, especially since you're dealing with an at-risk population. The board will be concerned with how you're protecting your participants—their identities and their well-being. At the least, you'll have to provide the name of a therapist your participants can see. I don't know how the board would respond to your telling them that you'll be the therapist," I laugh. Then I add more seriously, "But really protecting the participants

and your family members—well, in the end that's left up to you and me." I pick up the book I was reading when Sylvia arrived to indicate our time is up.

"I think I'm ready for those syllabi now. You know, from the courses you've taught." I smile and hand Sylvia the syllabi waiting on my desk. In turn, she hands me a folded piece of paper. "It's a poem I wrote about losing my breast. I know it isn't research, but . . ."

"Of course it's research. Think about including it as part of your story. Have you read any of Laurel Richardson's ethnographic poetry?"

I'm about to get started again, when Sylvia says with a twinkle in her eye, "So will you be on my committee?"

"Only if you're still planning to do that survey," I say, both of us chuckling as we wave good-bye.

◆ Defending and Expanding Autoethnography (One Year Later)

"Hi, Art, I just had to call."

"Why? What's the matter?"

"I just got out of Sylvia's proposal defense. Actually it wasn't as bad as I expected. I think she held her ground. Hey, would you quiet the dogs? I can hardly hear you."

"Oh, yeah. I guess that antibark contraption you bought for Christmas isn't working any better than all the other ones we've purchased. Likker, Traf, Ande, Sunya—quiet, your mom's on the phone," Art yells, and I'm amazed when they actually stop barking. "So what happened?"

"Well, I started the questioning and at first it went very well. Committee members seemed to understand what we were proposing. But then when it was their turn to ask questions, suddenly we moved from talking about the experience of breast cancer to talking about bias, validity, eligibility criteria, operationalization, control variables, confounding factors, building models, replicability, and objectivity. In response, I found myself giving long speeches peppered with words like *literature, literary license, evocative, vulnerable, narrative truth, verisimilitude, interactive,* and *therapeutic.*"

"Nothing like these forays out into the other world to make you realize how fortunate we are to have created what we have in the Communication Department, where we take the significance of this work for granted," Art responds.

"That's for sure. The experience gave me a lot of empathy for what students and young faculty members in other universities may have to go through to do this kind of work.

"But," I continue, "something very interesting happened near the end of the defense. I was listening to the oncologist talk about prediction and control when I began thinking about how important these goals must seem in his daily work life. So instead of giving yet another speech, I asked the oncologist what it is like to have to tell women the bad news, to deal with illness and death all the time. Before I knew it, we were having a conversation about feelings, how emotionally difficult his job is, and how he'd like to do it better. He told the story of how upset he was yesterday, when he had to tell a 34-year-old women, a mother of two young children, that she probably has less than 6 months to live and how bad he felt when she apologized for taking up too much of his time. He had tears in his eyes when he was telling the story. I mentioned Robert Cole's work and he told me he had read *The Call of Stories* and admired the writings of William Carlos Williams. I tried to show him how the goals of Sylvia's work relate to what Coles was saying about how we use stories to try to figure out how to live our lives meaningfully. I felt I had reached him where he lived, at the site of his subjectivity and deep feelings. Unlike the first part of the meeting, it seemed both of us had let down our guards and were communicating with each other as human beings."

"Wow, that must have been some moment."

"It was. You know, I think this is the future of what we do. To figure out how to introduce personal ethnography into the practical contexts of everyday life, to people whose work would be enhanced by it, like doctors, nurses, social workers, administrators, and teachers."

"I've been giving that issue a great deal of thought lately," Art responds. "I think there's a lot to gain from extending all of ethnography beyond the academy so that we stop thinking of it as exclusively an academic practice. Couldn't the work of many people in the service and helping professions be thought of as ethnography? To do their work effectively, service workers have to gain intersubjective understanding in contexts that cross the boundaries of age, ability, race, class, and ethnicity. I mean any time the success of your work depends on developing some degree of intercultural understanding, then you have to use the social skills we associate with ethnographic empathy. Wouldn't you say that psychotherapists do this? Aren't they ethnographers of the self?"

"Of course. And good teaching involves ethnography too," I add. "Over time you try to work your way through the barriers of unfamiliarity, distance, and difference toward a spirit of collaboration, understanding, and openness to experience and participation. When we learn how to open ourselves to ourselves and to each other, we find it easier to drop some of our resistance to different ideas. I like to think of this as working toward an ethnographic consciousness in the classroom that is personal, intimate, and empathic."

"That's very close to how I see the private geriatric care managers I've been studying for the past 2 years," Art responds. "As they work between long-distanced families and their elderly relatives, they become ethnographers of aging. They aren't academics. They don't do academic research and they don't write articles. Yet in every other respect they think and act as ethnographers. In each case they manage, they function as a channel through which pass the emotional, economic, medical, and social crises that must be negotiated by families coping with the contingencies of aging. They occupy a unique, dynamic, holistic, and engaged perspective. They are participants and observers and their private lives are deeply affected by their public and professional services. As storytellers and autoethnographers, they have as much, if not more, to teach us about the concrete, everyday details associated with aging as do scholars of aging."

"We like to think we have a lot to teach people in the public sector, but they have a lot to teach us as well, if we just listen," I add. "Yet I know, as Elliot Eisner discusses, that it will be difficult to wean scholars and the American public from a view that measuring, comparison, and outcomes are all that matter."

"But I think we're slowly knocking down some of the walls," Arts says encouragingly. "We've opened a space to write between traditional social science prose and literature and to stimulate more discussion of working the spaces between subjectivity and objectivity, passion and intellect, and autobiography and culture. Look at all the book manuscripts we've received to review for our series. I take that as strong evidence that more and more academics think it's possible to write from the heart, to bring the first-person voice into their work, and to merge art and science. I don't think there's any danger of going back to the way it used to be, not in our lifetimes anyway."

"Yes, we've encouraged writers to make ethnography readable, evocative, engaging, and personally meaningful. And it's working. Autoethnography is being read widely by graduate and undergraduate students. Now it's time to show its usefulness in the public realm. It's interesting that this is the same argument being made in some of the mainstream sociology journals. Have you seen the symposium in *Contemporary Sociology* on 'engaging publics in social dialogue'?" I ask.

"Yes, I read it yesterday. Perhaps our purposes are coming together for a change. After all, that's what we are trying to do in the Ethnographic Alternatives series, to publish books that say something meaningful and attract a wide audience."

"Like Mike Angrosino's stories of adult mental illness. Now we just need to get the book into the hands of those who work with and make policies about mental illness."

"I don't know if this *Handbook* piece will help with that," Art says. "But it may encourage more people to do autoethnography and help legitimate this approach for those students and young faculty members you're worried about. Those are important goals we've tried to achieve in our chapter. I'm glad we've written it."

"Me, too," I say, smiling as I think of Art's initial resistance to writing for the *Handbook*.

"So, then, we're finished with this piece?" Art asks.

"Looks like it," I reply. "Let's reward ourselves and go to the beach for the weekend. We need to get out of our offices and engage in some other life experiences, or else the only thing we're going to be able to write about is writing."

"But what about the chapter for the *Handbook of Loss and Trauma* and the one for the *Handbook of Interpersonal Communication* we just committed to do? We really should get started," Art says.

"Art!" I yell, as I hear simultaneously his laughter and a knock on my office door.

■ *References*

Abu-Lughod, L. (1993). *Writing women's worlds: Bedouin stories.* Berkeley: University of California Press.

Adler, P. A., & Adler, P. (1987). *Membership roles in field research.* Newbury Park, CA: Sage.

Adler, P. A., & Adler, P. (1994). Observational techniques. In N. K. Denzin & Y. S. Lincoln (Eds.), *Handbook of qualitative research* (pp. 377-392). Thousand Oaks, CA: Sage.

Allison, D. (1994). *Skin: Talking about sex, class, and literature.* Ithaca, NY: Firebrand.

Angrosino, M. (1998). *Opportunity House: Ethnographic stories of mental retardation.* Walnut Creek, CA: AltaMira.

Anzaldúa, G. (1987). *Borderlands/la frontera: The new mestiza.* San Francisco: Aunt Lute.

Atkinson, P. (1997). Narrative turn in a blind alley? *Qualitative Health Research, 7,* 325-344.

Austin, D. (1996). Kaleidoscope: The same and different. In C. Ellis & A. P. Bochner (Eds.), *Composing ethnography: Alternative forms of qualitative writing* (pp. 206-230). Walnut Creek, CA: AltaMira.

Austin, D. (1998). *Understanding close relationships among African Americans in the context of the Million Man March.* Unpublished doctoral dissertation, University of South Florida.

Bakhtin, M. M. (1981). *The dialogic imagination: Four essays* (M. Holquist, Ed.; M. Holquist & C. Emerson, Trans.). Austin: University of Texas Press.

Banks, A., & Banks, S. P. (Eds.). (1998). *Fiction and social research: By ice or fire.* Walnut Creek, CA: AltaMira.

Barthes, R. (1977). *Image, music, text* (S. Heath, Trans.). New York: Hill & Wang.

Behar, R. (1993). *Translated woman: Crossing the border with Esperanza's story.* Boston: Beacon.

Behar, R. (1996). *The vulnerable observer: Anthropology that breaks your heart.* Boston: Beacon.

Behar, R., & Gordon, D. A. (Eds.). (1995). *Women writing culture.* Berkeley: University of California Press.

Benson, P. (Ed.). (1993). *Anthropology and literature.* Urbana: University of Illinois Press.

Berger, B. (Ed.). (1990). *Authors of their own lives: Intellectual autobiographies by twenty American sociologists.* Berkeley: University of California Press.

Berger, L. (1997). Between the candy store and the mall: The spiritual loss of a father. *Journal of Personal and Interpersonal Loss, 2,* 397-409.

Berger, L. (1998). Silent movies: Scenes from a life. In A. Banks & S. P. Banks (Eds.), *Fiction and social research: By ice or fire* (pp. 137-146). Walnut Creek, CA: AltaMira.

Bochner, A. P. (1981). Forming warm ideas. In C. Wilder-Mott & J. H. Weakland (Eds.), *Rigor and imagination: Essays from the legacy of Gregory Bateson* (pp. 65-81). New York: Praeger.

Bochner, A. P. (1994). Perspectives on inquiry II: Theories and stories. In M. L. Knapp & G. R. Miller (Eds.), *Handbook of interpersonal communication* (2nd ed., pp. 21-41). Thousand Oaks, CA: Sage.

Bochner, A. P. (1997). It's about time: Narrative and the divided self. *Qualitative Inquiry, 3,* 418-438.

Bochner, A. P., & Ellis, C. (1992). Personal narrative as a social approach to interpersonal communication. *Communication Theory, 2,* 165-172.

Bochner, A. P., & Ellis, C. (1999). Which way to turn? *Journal of Contemporary Ethnography, 28,* 500-509.

Bochner, A. P., Ellis, C., & Tillmann-Healy, L. (1997). Relationships as stories. In S. Duck (Ed.), *Handbook of personal relationships: Theory, research and interventions* (2nd ed., pp. 307-324). New York: John Wiley.

Bochner, A. P., Ellis, C., & Tillmann-Healy, L. (1998). Mucking around looking for truth. In B. M. Montgomery & L. A. Baxter (Eds.). *Dialectical approaches to studying personal relationships* (pp. 41-62). Mahwah, NJ: Lawrence Erlbaum.

Bochner, A. P., & Waugh, J. B. (1995). Talking-with as a model for writing-about: Implications of Rortyean pragmatism. In L. Langsdorf & A. R. Smith (Eds.), *Recovering pragmatism's voice: The classical tradition, Rorty, and the philosophy of communication* (pp. 211-233). Albany: State University of New York Press.

Bowen, E. S. (1954). *Return to laughter: An anthropological novel.* New York: Harper & Row.

Brady, I. (Ed.). (1991). *Anthropological poetics.* Savage, MD: Rowman & Littlefield.

Brandes, S. (1982). Ethnographic autobiographies in American anthropology. In E. A. Hoebel, R. Currier, & S. Kaiser (Eds.), *Crisis in anthropology: View from Spring Hill, 1980* (pp. 187-202). New York: Garland.

Broyard, A. (1992). *Intoxicated by my illness and other writings on life and death.* New York: Fawcett-Columbine.

Bruner, J. (1990). *Acts of meaning.* Cambridge, MA: Harvard University Press.

Bruner, J. (1993). Introduction: The ethnographic self and the personal self. In P. Benson (Ed.), *Anthropology and literature* (pp. 2-26). Urbana: University of Illinois Press.

Buford, B. (1996, June 24). The seductions of storytelling. *New Yorker,* pp. 11-12.

Butler, S., & Rosenblum, B. (1991). *Cancer in two voices.* San Francisco: Spinster.

Carr, D. (1986). *Time, narrative, and history.* Bloomington: Indiana University Press.

Charmaz, K. (1991). *Good days, bad days: The self in chronic illness and time.* New Brunswick, NJ: Rutgers University Press.

Chase, S. (1996). Personal vulnerability and interpretive authority in narrative research. In R. Josselson (Ed.), *Ethics and process in the narrative study of lives* (pp. 45-59). Thousand Oaks, CA: Sage.

Church, K. (1995). *Forbidden narratives: Critical autobiography as social science.* Newark, NJ: Gordon & Breach.

Clandinin, D. J., & Connelly, F. M. (1994). Personal experience methods. In N. K. Denzin & Y. S. Lincoln (Eds.), *Handbook of qualitative research* (pp. 413-427). Thousand Oaks, CA: Sage.

Clough, P. T. (1994). *Feminist thought: Desire, power and academic discourse.* Cambridge, MA: Blackwell.

Clough, P. (1997). Autotelecommunication and autoethnography: A reading of Carolyn Ellis's *Final negotiations. Sociological Quarterly, 38,* 95-110.

Cohen, A. (1992). Self-conscious anthropology. In J. Okely & H. Callaway (Eds.), *Anthropology and autobiography* (pp. 221-241). London: Routledge.

Coles, R. (1989). *The call of stories: Teaching and the moral imagination.* Boston: Houghton Mifflin.

Collins, P. H. (1986). Learning from the outsider within: The sociological significance of black feminist thought. *Social Problems, 33,* 14-32.

Cook, J. A., & Fonow, M. M. (1986). Knowledge and women's interests: Issues of epistemology and methodology in feminist sociological research. *Sociological Inquiry, 56,* 2-27.

Couser, G. T. (1997). *Recovering bodies: Illness, disability, and life writing.* Madison: University of Wisconsin Press.

Crapanzano, V. (1980). *Tuhami: Portrait of a Moroccan.* Chicago: University of Chicago Press.

Crawford, L. (1996). Personal ethnography. *Communication Monographs, 63,* 158-170.

Crites, S. (1971). The narrative quality of experience. *Journal of the American Academy of Religion, 39,* 291-311.

Deck, A. (1990). Autoethnography: Zora Neale Hurston, Noni Jabavu, and cross-disciplinary discourse. *Black American Literature Forum, 24,* 237-256.

Denzin, N. K. (1989). *Interpretive biography.* Newbury Park, CA: Sage.

Denzin, N. K. (1997). *Interpretive ethnography: Ethnographic practices for the 21st century.* Thousand Oaks, CA: Sage.

Denzin, N. K., & Lincoln, Y. S. (Eds.). (1994). *Handbook of qualitative research.* Thousand Oaks, CA: Sage.

Derrida, J. (1978). *Writing and difference* (A. Bass, Trans.). Chicago: University of Chicago Press.

Derrida, J. (1981). *Positions* (A. Bass, Trans.). Chicago: University of Chicago Press.

DeVault, M. (1997). Personal writing in social science: Issues of production and interpretation. In R. Hertz (Ed.). *Reflexivity and voice* (pp. 216-228). Thousand Oaks, CA: Sage.

Diamond, S. (1982). *Totems.* Barrytown, NY: Open Book/Station Hill.

Dumont, J.-P. (1976). *Under the rainbow: Nature and supernatural among the Panare Indians.* Austin: University of Texas Press.

Dumont, J.-P. (1978). *The headman and I: Ambiguity and ambivalence in the fieldworking experience.* Austin: University of Texas Press.

Eisner, E. (1996). Should a novel count as a dissertation in education? *Research in the Teaching of English, 30,* 403-427.

Eisner, E. (1997). The new frontier in qualitative research methodology. *Qualitative Inquiry, 3,* 259-273.

Ellingson, L. (1998). "Then you know how I feel": Empathy, identification, and reflexivity in fieldwork. *Qualitative Inquiry, 4,* 492-514.

Ellis, C. (1986). *Fisher folk: Two communities on Chesapeake Bay.* Lexington: University Press of Kentucky.

Ellis, C. (1991a). Emotional sociology. In N. K. Denzin (Ed.), *Studies in symbolic interaction: A research annual* (Vol. 12, pp. 123-145). Greenwich, CT: JAI.

Ellis, C. (1991b). Sociological introspection and emotional experience. *Symbolic Interaction, 14,* 23-50.

Ellis, C. (1993). "There are survivors": Telling a story of sudden death. *Sociological Quarterly, 34,* 711-730.

Ellis, C. (1995a). Emotional and ethical quagmires in returning to the field. *Journal of Contemporary Ethnography, 24,* 711-713.

Ellis, C. (1995b). *Final negotiations: A story of love, loss, and chronic illness.* Philadelphia: Temple University Press.

Ellis, C. (1995c). The other side of the fence: Seeing black and white in a small, southern town. *Qualitative Inquiry, 1,* 147-167.

Ellis, C. (1995d). Speaking of dying: An ethnographic short story. *Symbolic Interaction, 18,* 73-81.

Ellis, C. (1997). Evocative autoethnography: Writing emotionally about our lives. In W. G. Tierney & Y. S. Lincoln (Eds.), *Representation and the text: Re-framing the narrative voice* (pp. 115-142). Albany: State University of New York Press.

Ellis, C. (1998a). Exploring loss through autoethnographic inquiry: Autoethnographic stories, co-constructed narratives, and interactive interviews. In J. H. Harvey (Ed.), *Perspectives on loss: A sourcebook* (pp. 49-62). Philadelphia: Taylor & Francis.

Ellis, C. (1998b). "I hate my voice": Coming to terms with minor bodily stigmas. *Sociological Quarterly, 39,* 517-537.

Ellis, C., & Bochner, A. P. (1992). Telling and performing personal stories: The constraints of choice in abortion. In C. Ellis & M. G. Flaherty (Eds.), *Investigating subjectivity: Research on lived experience* (pp. 79-101). Newbury Park, CA: Sage.

Ellis, C., & Bochner, A. P. (Eds.). (1996a). *Composing ethnography: Alternative forms of qualitative writing.* Walnut Creek, CA: AltaMira.

Ellis, C., & Bochner, A. P. (Eds.). (1996b). Taking ethnography into the twenty-first century [Special issue]. *Journal of Contemporary Ethnography, 25*(1).

Ellis, C., & Flaherty, M. G. (Eds.). (1992). *Investigating subjectivity: Research on lived experience.* Newbury Park, CA: Sage.

Ellis, C., Kiesinger, C., & Tillmann-Healy, L. (1997). Interactive interviewing: Talking about emotional experience. In R. Hertz (Ed.), *Reflexivity and voice* (pp. 119-149). Thousand Oaks, CA: Sage.

Engaging publics in sociological dialogue [Symposium]. (1998). *Contemporary Sociology, 27,* 435-462.

Foucault, M. (1970). *The order of things: An archaeology of the human sciences.* New York: Random House.

Frank, A. (1991). *At the will of the body: Reflections on illness.* Boston: Houghton Mifflin.

Frank, A. (1994). Reclaiming an orphan genre: The first-person narrative of illness. *Literature and Medicine, 13,* 1-21.

Frank, A. (1995). *The wounded storyteller: Body, illness, and ethics.* Chicago: University of Chicago Press.

Freeman, M. (1993). *Rewriting the self: History, memory, narrative.* London: Routledge.

Freeman, M. (1998). Mythical time, historical time, and the narrative fabric of self. *Narrative Inquiry, 8,* 27-50.

French, D. (1998). *Through the eyes of the comic mask: An ethnographic exploration of the identity of a stand-up comedian.* Unpublished doctoral dissertation, University of South Florida.

Friedman, N. (1990, Spring). Autobiographical sociology. *American Sociologist, 21,* 60-66.

Gadamer, H.-G. (1989). *Truth and method* (2nd rev. ed.; J. Weinsheimer & D. G. Marshall, Eds. & Trans.). New York: Crossroad.

Geertz, C. (1973). *The interpretation of cultures: Selected essays.* New York: Basic Books.

Gergen, K. J. (1994). *Realities and relationships: Soundings in social construction.* Cambridge, MA: Harvard University Press.

Glassner, B. (Ed.). (1997). Qualitative sociology as everyday life [Special issue]. *Qualitative Sociology, 20*(4).

Goetting, A., & Fenstermaker, S. (1995). *Individual voices, collective visions: Fifty years of women in sociology.* Philadelphia: Temple University Press.

Goldman, A. (1993, Fall). Is that what she said? The politics of collaborative autobiography. *Cultural Critique,* pp. 177-204.

Gonzalez, M. C., & Krizek, R. L (1994). *Indigenous ethnography.* Paper presented at the annual meeting of the Western States Communication Association, San Jose, CA.

Gravel, A. (1997). *The ideological functions of autoethnography.* Unpublished manuscript, University of Wisconsin–Whitewater.

Gubrium, J. F., & Holstein, J. A. (1997). *The new language of qualitative method.* New York: Oxford University Press.

Hacking, I. (1995). *Rewriting the soul: Multiple personality and the sciences of memory.* Princeton, NJ: Princeton University Press.

Harding, S. (1991). *Whose science? Whose knowledge? Thinking from women's lives.* Ithaca, NY: Cornell University Press.

Harrington, W. (1997). *Intimate journalism: The art and craft of reporting everyday life.* Thousand Oaks, CA: Sage.

Hartsock, N. C. M. (1983). The feminist standpoint: Developing the ground for a specifically feminist historical materialism. In S. Harding & M. B. Hintikka (Eds.), *Dis-*

covering reality (pp. 283-310). Amsterdam: D. Reidel.

Harvey, J. (Ed.). (in press). *Handbook of loss and trauma.* London: Taylor & Francis.

Hawkins, A. H. (1993). *Reconstructing illness: Studies in pathography.* West Lafayette, IN: Purdue University Press.

Hayano, D. M. (1979). Auto-ethnography: Paradigms, problems, and prospects. *Human Organization, 38,* 113-120.

Hayano, D. M. (1982). *Poker faces.* Berkeley: University of California Press.

Heidegger, M. (1971). *On the way to language* (P. D. Hertz & J. Stambaugh, Trans.). New York: Harper & Row.

Herndon, C. (1993). *Gendered fictions of self and community: Autobiography and autoethnography in Caribbean women's writing.* Unpublished doctoral dissertation, University of Texas at Austin.

Hertz, R. (Ed.). (1996). Ethics, reflexivity and voice [Special issue]. *Qualitative Sociology, 19*(1).

Hertz, R. (Ed.). (1997). *Reflexivity and voice.* Thousand Oaks, CA: Sage.

Higgins, P., & Johnson, J. (Eds.). (1988). *Personal sociology.* New York: Praeger.

Hollway, W. (1989). *Subjectivity and method in psychology: Gender, meaning and science.* London: Sage.

Hurston, Z. N. (1991). *Dust tracks on a road.* New York: HarperCollins. (Original work published 1942)

Jackson, A. (Ed.). (1987). *Anthropology at home.* London: Tavistock.

Jackson, M. (1989). *Paths toward a clearing: Radical empiricism and ethnographic inquiry.* Bloomington: Indiana University Press.

Jackson, M. (1995). *At home in the world.* Durham, NC: Duke University Press.

Jago, B. (1996). Postcards, ghosts, and fathers: Revising family stories. *Qualitative Inquiry, 2,* 495-516.

Jones, S. H. (1998). *Kaleidoscope notes: Writing women's music and organizational culture.* Walnut Creek, CA: AltaMira.

Josselson, R. (1996). On writing other people's lives: Self-analytic reflections of a narrative researcher. In R. Josselson (Ed.), *Ethics and process in the narrative study of lives* (pp. 60-71). Thousand Oaks, CA: Sage.

Jules-Rosette, B. (1975). *African apostles.* Ithaca, NY: Cornell University Press.

Karp, D. (1996). *Speaking of sadness.* New York: Oxford University Press.

Kerby, A. (1991). *Narrative and the self.* Bloomington: Indiana University Press.

Kiesinger, C. (1995). *Anorexic and bulimic lives: Making sense of food and eating.* Unpublished doctoral dissertation, University of South Florida.

Kiesinger, C. (1998a). From interviewing to story: Writing Abbie's life. *Qualitative Inquiry, 4,* 71-95.

Kiesinger, C. (1998b). Portrait of an anorexic life. In A. Banks & S. P. Banks (Eds.), *Fiction and social research: By ice or fire* (pp. 115-136). Walnut Creek, CA: AltaMira.

Kinkaid, J. (1988). *A small place.* New York: Penguin.

Kleinman, S. (1997). Essaying the personal: Making sociological stories stick. *Qualitative Sociology, 20,* 553-564.

Kolker, A. (1996). Thrown overboard: The human costs of health care rationing. In C. Ellis & A. P. Bochner (Eds.), *Composing ethnography: Alternative forms of qualitative writing* (pp. 132-159). Walnut Creek, CA: AltaMira.

Kondo, D. (1990). *Crafting selves: Power, gender, and discourses of identity in a Japanese workplace.* Chicago: University of Chicago Press.

Krieger, S. (1983). *The mirror dance: Identity in a women's community.* Philadelphia: Temple University Press.

Krieger, S. (1984). Fiction and social science. In N. K. Denzin (Ed.), *Studies in symbolic interaction: A research annual* (Vol. 5, pp. 269-286). Greenwich, CT: JAI.

Krieger, S. (1991). *Social science and the self: Personal essays on an art form.* New Brunswick, NJ: Rutgers University Press.

Krieger, S. (1996). *The family silver: Essays on relationships among women.* Berkeley: University of California Press.

Kuhn, T. (1962). *The structure of scientific revolutions.* Chicago: University of Chicago Press.

Kulick, D., & Willson, M. (Eds.). (1995). *Taboo: Sex, identity and erotic subjectivity in anthropological fieldwork.* London: Routledge.

Lather, P. (1986). Research as praxis. *Harvard Educational Review, 56,* 257-277.

Lather, P. (1993). Fertile obsession: Validity after poststructuralism. *Sociological Quarterly, 34,* 673-693.

Lejeune, P. (1989). *On autobiography* (K. Leary, Trans.). Minneapolis: University of Minnesota Press.

Lewin, E., & Leap, W. L. (Eds.). (1996). *Out in the field: Reflections of lesbian and gay anthropologists.* Urbana: University of Illinois Press.

Lieblich, A. (1996). Some unforeseen outcomes of conducting narrative research with people of one's own culture. In R. Josselson (Ed.). *Ethics and process in the narrative study of lives* (pp. 151-184). Thousand Oaks, CA: Sage.

Linden, R. R. (1992). *Making stories, making selves: Feminist reflections on the Holocaust.* Columbus: Ohio State University Press.

Lionnet, F. (1989). Autoethnography: The an-archic style of *Dust tracks on a road.* In F. Lionnet, *Autobiographical voices: Race, gender, self-portraiture* (pp. 97-129). Ithaca, NY: Cornell University Press.

Lopate, P. (1994). Introduction. In P. Lopate (Ed.), *The art of the personal essay: An anthology from the classical era to the present.* Garden City, NY: Anchor.

Lorde, A. (1980). *The cancer journals.* Argyle, NY: Spinsters.

Lyotard, J.-F. (1984). *The postmodern condition: A report on knowledge* (G. Bennington & B. Massumi, Trans.). Minneapolis: University of Minnesota Press.

MacIntyre, A. (1981). *After virtue: A study in moral theory.* Notre Dame, IN: University of Notre Dame Press.

Mairs, N. (1986). *Plain text.* Tucson: University of Arizona Press.

Mairs, N. (1990). *Carnal acts: Essays.* New York: Harper.

Mairs, N. (1998). *Waist-high in the world: A life among the nondisabled.* Boston: Beacon.

Malinowski, B. (1967). *A diary in the strict sense of the term.* (N. Guterman, Trans.). New York: Harcourt, Brace & World.

Marcus, G. E., & Fischer, M. M. J. (1986). *Anthropology as cultural critique: An experimental moment in the human sciences.* Chicago: University of Chicago Press.

Markham, A. (1998). *Life online: Researching real experience in virtual space.* Walnut Creek, CA: AltaMira.

Mehan, H., & Wood, H. (1975). *The reality of ethnomethodology.* New York: John Wiley.

Merton, R. (1988). Some thoughts on the concept of sociological autobiography. In M. Riley (Ed.), *Sociological lives* (pp. 17-21). Newbury Park, CA: Sage. (Original work published 1972)

Miller, L., & Taylor, J. (1997). Performing autobiography: Editors' introduction. *Text and Performance Quarterly, 4,* v-vi.

Miller, M. (1996). Ethics and understanding through interrelationship: I and thou in dialogue. In R. Josselson (Ed.), *Ethics and process in the narrative study of lives* (pp. 129-147). Thousand Oaks, CA: Sage.

Mink, L. (1969-1970). History and fiction as modes of comprehension. *New Literary History, 1,* 541-558.

Motzafi-Haller, P. (1997). Writing birthright: On native anthropologists and the politics of representation. In D. Reed-Danahay, *Auto/ethnography: Rewriting the self and the social* (pp. 195-222). Oxford: Berg.

Mukaia, T. (1989). A call for our language: Anorexia from within. *Women's Studies International Forum, 12,* 613-638.

Narayan, K. (1993). How native is a "native" anthropologist? *American Anthropologist, 95,* 671-686.

Neumann, M. (1996). Collecting ourselves at the end of the century. In C. Ellis & A. P. Bochner (Eds.), *Composing ethnography: Alternative forms of qualitative writing* (pp. 172-198). Walnut Creek, CA: AltaMira.

Noddings, N. (1984). *Caring: A feminine approach to ethics and moral education.* Berkeley: University of California Press.

Oakley, A. (1981). Interviewing women: A contradiction in terms. In H. Roberts (Ed.), *Doing feminist research* (pp. 30-61). London: Routledge & Kegan Paul.

Oakley, A. (1984). *Taking it like a woman.* New York: Random House.

Ohnuki-Tierney, E. (1984). Native anthropologists. *American Ethnologist, 2,* 584-586.

Okely, J. (1992). Participatory experience and embodied knowledge. In J. Okely & H. Callaway (Eds.), *Anthropology and autobiography* (pp. 1-28). London: Routledge.

Okely, J., & Callaway, H. (Eds.). (1992). *Anthropology and autobiography.* London: Routledge.

Parini, J. (1998, July 10). The memoir versus the novel in a time of transition. *Chronicle of Higher Education,* p. A40.

Park-Fuller, L. (1998). *Introduction to session on arguing the shifting shapes and speaking tongues of autoethnographic performance.* Paper presented at the annual meeting of the National Communication Association, New York.

Payne, D. (1996). Autobiology. In C. Ellis & A. P. Bochner (Eds.), *Composing ethnography: Alternative forms of qualitative writing* (pp. 49-75). Walnut Creek, CA: AltaMira.

Personal Narratives Group. (1989). *Interpreting women's lives: Feminist theory and personal narratives*. Bloomington: Indiana University Press.

Pratt, M. L. (1994). Transculturation and autoethnography: Peru 1615/1980. In F. Barker, P. Holme, & M. Iverson (Eds.), *Colonial discourse/postcolonial theory* (pp. 24-46). Manchester: Manchester University Press.

Quinney, R. (1991). *Journey to a far place: Autobiographical reflections*. Philadelphia: Temple University Press.

Rabinow, P. (1975). *Symbolic domination: Cultural form and historical change in Morocco*. Chicago: University of Chicago Press

Rabinow, P. (1977). *Reflections on fieldwork in Morocco*. Berkeley: University of California Press.

Reed-Danahay, D. (1997). *Auto/ethnography: Rewriting the self and the social*. Oxford: Berg.

Reinharz, S. (1979). *On becoming a social scientist: From survey research and participation to experiential analysis*. San Francisco: Jossey-Bass.

Reinharz, S. (1992). *Feminist methods in social research*. New York: Oxford University Press.

Rhett, K. (Ed.). (1997). *Survival stories: Memoirs of crisis*. Garden City, NY: Doubleday.

Rich, A. (1978). *On lies, secrets and silence: Selected prose 1966-1978*. New York: W. W. Norton.

Richardson, L. (1990a). Narrative and sociology. *Journal of Contemporary Ethnography, 19,* 116-135.

Richardson, L. (1990b). *Writing strategies: Reaching diverse audiences*. Newbury Park, CA: Sage.

Richardson, L. (1994a). Nine poems: Marriage and the family. *Journal of Contemporary Ethnography, 23,* 3-14.

Richardson, L. (1994b). Writing: A method of inquiry. In N. K. Denzin & Y. S. Lincoln (Eds.), *Handbook of qualitative research* (pp. 516-529). Thousand Oaks, CA: Sage.

Richardson, L. (1995). Vespers. *Chicago Review, 41,* 129-146.

Richardson, L. (1996). Speech lessons. In C. Ellis & A. P. Bochner (Eds.), *Composing ethnography: Alternative forms of qualitative writing* (pp. 231-239). Walnut Creek, CA: AltaMira.

Richardson, L. (1997). *Fields of play: Constructing an academic life*. New Brunswick, NJ: Rutgers University Press.

Richardson, L., & Lockridge, E. (1998). Fiction and ethnography: A conversation. *Qualitative Inquiry, 4,* 328-336.

Riemer, J. W. (1977). Varieties of opportunistic research. *Urban Life, 5,* 467-477.

Riley, M. W. (1988). *Sociological lives*. Newbury Park, CA: Sage.

Rodriguez, R. (1983). *Hunger of memory: The education of Richard Rodriguez*. New York: Bantam.

Ronai, C. R. (1992). The reflexive self through narrative: A night in the life of an erotic dancer/researcher. In C. Ellis & M. G. Flaherty (Eds.), *Investigating subjectivity: Research on lived experience* (pp. 102-124). Newbury Park, CA: Sage.

Ronai, C. R. (1995). Multiple reflections of child sex abuse: An argument for a layered account. *Journal of Contemporary Ethnography, 23,* 395-426.

Rorty, R. (1979). *Philosophy and the mirror of nature*. Princeton, NJ: Princeton University Press.

Rorty, R. (1982). *Consequences of pragmatism (essays 1972-1980)*. Minneapolis: University of Minnesota Press.

Rose, D. (1991). In search of experience: The anthropological poetics of Stanley Diamond. In I. Brady (Ed.), *Anthropological poetics* (pp. 219-233). Savage, MD: Rowman & Littlefield.

Rosen, H. (1988). The autobiographical impulse. In D. Tannen (Ed.), *Linguistics in context: Connecting observation and understanding* (pp. 69-88). Norwood, NJ: Ablex.

Schneider, A. (1998, July 10). Jane Tompkins's message to academe: Nurture the individual, not just the intellect. *Chronicle of Higher Education*, pp. A8-A10.

Schwandt, T. A. (1996). Farewell to criteriology. *Qualitative Inquiry, 2,* 58-72.

Shalit, R. (1998, February). The man who knew too much. *Lingua Franca*, pp. 32-40.

Shelton, A. (1995). Foucault's Madonna: The secret life of Carolyn Ellis. *Symbolic Interaction, 18,* 83-87.

Shostak, A. (Ed.). (1996). *Private sociology: Unsparing reflections, uncommon gains.* Dix Hills, NY: General Hall.

Shostak, M. (1981). *Nisa: The life and words of a !Kung woman.* Cambridge, MA: Harvard University Press.

Shotter, J. (1987). The social construction of an "us": Problems of accountability and narratology. In R. Burnett, P. McGee, & D. Clarke (Eds.), *Accounting for relationships: Explanation, representation, and knowledge* (pp. 225-247). London: Methuen.

Smith, D. (1979). A sociology for women. In J. Sherman & E. Beck (Eds.), *The prism of sex: Essays in the sociology of knowledge.* Madison: University of Wisconsin Press.

Smith, D. (1990). *The conceptual practices of power: A feminist sociology of knowledge.* Boston: Northeastern University Press.

Smith, D. (1992). Sociology from women's perspective: A reaffirmation. *Sociological Theory, 10,* 88-97.

Sontag, S. (1978). *Illness as a metaphor.* New York: Farrar, Straus & Giroux.

Stake, R. E. (1994). Case studies. In N. K. Denzin & Y. S. Lincoln (Eds.). *The handbook of qualitative research* (pp. 236-247). Thousand Oaks, CA: Sage.

Strathern, M. (1987). The limits of auto-anthropology. In A. Jackson (Ed.), *Anthropology at home* (pp. 59-67). London: Tavistock.

Tedlock, B. (1991). From participant observation to the observation of participation: The emergence of narrative ethnography. *Journal of Anthropological Research, 41,* 69-94.

Tierney, W. (1998). Life history's history: Subjects foretold. *Qualitative Inquiry, 4,* 49-70.

Tierney, W. G., & Lincoln, Y. S. (Eds.). (1997). *Representation and the text: Re-framing the narrative voice.* Albany: State University of New York Press.

Tillmann-Healy, L. (1996). A secret life in a culture of thinness: Reflections on body, food, and bulimia. In C. Ellis & A. P. Bochner (Eds.), *Composing ethnography: Alternative forms of qualitative writing* (pp. 76-108). Walnut Creek, CA: AltaMira.

Tillmann-Healy, L. (1999). *Life projects: A narrative ethnography of gay-straight friendship.* Unpublished doctoral dissertation, University of South Florida.

Tompkins, J. (1989). Me and my shadow. In L. Kauffman (Ed.), *Gender and theory: Dialogues on feminist criticism* (pp. 121-139). Cambridge, MA: Blackwell.

Toulmin, S. (1969). Concepts and the explanation of human behavior. In T. Mischel (Ed.), *Human action* (pp. 71-104). New York: Academic Press.

Trinh T. M. (1989). *Woman, native, other: Writing postcoloniality and feminism.* Bloomington: Indiana University Press.

Trinh T. M. (1992). *Framer framed.* New York: Routledge.

Trotter, M. (1992). *Life writing: Exploring the practice of autoethnography in anthropology.* Unpublished master's thesis, University of Illinois, Urbana-Champaign.

True confessions: The age of the literary memoir [Special issue]. (1996, May 12). *New York Times Magazine.*

Turner, V., & Bruner, E. (Eds.). (1986). *The anthropology of experience.* Urbana: University of Illinois Press.

Tyler, S. (1986). Post-modern ethnography: From document of the occult to occult document. In J. Clifford and G. E. Marcus (Eds.), *Writing culture: The poetics and politics of ethnography* (pp. 122-140). Berkeley: University of California Press.

Van Maanen, J. (1988). *Tales of the field: On writing ethnography.* Chicago: University of Chicago Press.

Van Maanen, J. (1995). An end to innocence: The ethnography of ethnography. In J. Van Maanen (Ed.), *Representation in ethnography* (pp. 1-35). Thousand Oaks, CA: Sage.

Van Maanen, M. (1990). *Researching lived experience: Human science for an action sensitive pedagogy.* Albany: State University of New York Press.

Wittgenstein, L. (1953). *Philosophical investigations* (G. Anscombe, Trans.). New York: Macmillan.

Zola, I. K. (1982). *Missing pieces: A chronicle of living with a disability.* Philadelphia: Temple University Press.

Zussman, R. (1996). Autobiographical occasions. *Contemporary Sociology, 25,* 143-148.

DATA MANAGEMENT
AND ANALYSIS METHODS

◆ Gery W. Ryan and H. Russell Bernard

◆ *Texts Are Us*

This chapter is about methods for managing and analyzing qualitative data. By *qualitative data* we mean text: newspapers, movies, sitcoms, e-mail traffic, folktales, life histories. We also mean narratives—narratives about getting divorced, about being sick, about surviving hand-to-hand combat, about selling sex, about trying to quit smoking. In fact, most of the archaeologically recoverable information about human thought and human behavior is text, the "good stuff" of social science.

Scholars in content analysis began using computers in the 1950s to do statistical analysis of texts (Pool, 1959), but recent advances in technology are changing the economics of the social sciences. Optical scanning today makes light work of converting written texts to machine-readable form. Within a few years, voice-recognition software will make light work of tran-

scribing open-ended interviews. These technologies are blind to epistemological differences. Interpretivists and positivists alike are using these technologies for the analysis of texts, and will do so more and more.

Like Tesch (1990), we distinguish between the *linguistic tradition,* which treats text as an object of analysis itself, and the *sociological tradition,* which treats text as a window into human experience (see Figure 29.1). The linguistic tradition includes narrative analysis, conversation (or discourse) analysis, performance analysis, and formal linguistic analysis. Methods for analyses in this tradition are covered elsewhere in this *Handbook.* We focus here on methods used in the sociological tradition, which we take to include work across the social sciences.

There are two kinds of written texts in the sociological tradition: (a) words or phrases generated by techniques for systematic elicitation and (b) free-flowing texts, such as narratives, discourse, and responses to open-ended interview

◆ 769

questions. In the next section, we describe some methods for collecting and analyzing words or phrases. Techniques for data collection include free lists, pile sorts, frame elicitations, and triad tests. Techniques for the analysis of these kinds of data include componential analysis, taxonomies, and mental maps.

We then turn to the analysis of free-flowing texts. We look first at methods that use raw text as their input—methods such as key-words-in-context, word counts, semantic network analysis, and cognitive maps. We then describe methods that require the reduction of text to codes. These include grounded theory, schema analysis, classical content analysis, content dictionaries, analytic induction, and ethnographic decision models. Each of these methods of analysis has advantages and disadvantages. Some are appropriate for exploring data, others for making comparisons, and others for building and testing models. Nothing does it all.

◆ Collecting and Analyzing Words or Phrases

Techniques for Systematic Elicitation

Researchers use techniques for systematic elicitation to identify lists of items that belong in a cultural domain and to assess the relationships among these items (for detailed reviews of these methods, see Bernard, 1994; Borgatti, 1998; Weller, 1998; Weller & Romney, 1988). Cultural domains comprise lists of words in a language that somehow "belong together." Some domains (such as animals, illnesses, things to eat) are very large and inclusive, whereas others (animals you can keep at home, illnesses that children get, brands of beer) are relatively small. Some lists (such as the list of terms for members of a family or the names of all the Major League Baseball teams) are agreed on by all native speakers of a language; others (such as the list of carpenters' tools) represent highly specialized knowledge, and still others (like the list of great left-handed baseball pitchers of the 20th cen-

tury) are matters of heated debate. Below we review some of the most common systematic elicitation techniques and discuss how researchers analyze the data they generate.

Free Lists

Free lists are particularly useful for identifying the items in a cultural domain. To elicit domains, researchers might ask, "What kinds of illnesses do you know?" Some short, open-ended questions on surveys can be considered free lists, as can some responses generated from in-depth ethnographic interviews and focus groups. Investigators interpret the frequency of mention and the order in which items are mentioned in the lists as indicators of items' salience (for measures of salience, see Robbins & Nolan, 1997; Smith, 1993; Smith & Borgatti, 1998). The co-occurrence of items across lists and the proximity with which items appear in lists may be used as measures of similarity among items (Borgatti, 1998; Henley, 1969; for a clear example, see Fleisher & Harrington, 1998).

Paired Comparisons, Pile Sorts, Triad Tests

Researchers use paired comparisons, pile sorts, and triads tests to explore the *relationships* among items. Here are two questions we might ask someone in a paired comparison test about a list of fruits: (a) "On a scale of 1 to 5, how similar are lemons and watermelons with regard to sweetness?" (b) "Which is sweeter, watermelons or lemons?" The first question produces a set of fruit-by-fruit matrices, one for each respondent, the entries of which are scale values on the similarity of sweetness among all pairs of fruits. The second question produces, for each respondent, a perfect rank ordering of the set of fruits.

In a pile sort, the researcher asks each respondent to sort a set of cards or objects into piles. Item similarity is the number of times each pair of items is placed in the same pile (for examples, see Boster, 1994; Roos, 1998). In a triad test, the researcher presents sets of three items and asks each respondent either to "choose the two most similar items" or to "pick the item that is the

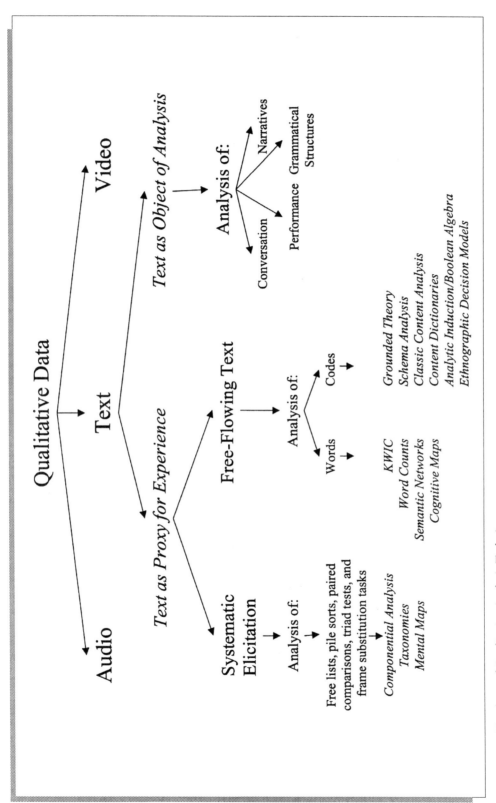

Figure 29.1. Typology of Qualitative Analysis Techniques

most different." The similarity among pairs of items is the number of times people choose to keep pairs of items together (for some good examples, see Albert, 1991; Harman, 1998).

Frame Substitution

In the frame substitution task (D'Andrade, 1995; D'Andrade, Quinn, Nerlove, & Romney, 1972; Frake, 1964; Metzger & Williams, 1966), the researcher asks the respondent to link each item in a list of items with a list of attributes. D'Andrade et al. (1972) gave people a list of 30 illness terms and asked them to fill in the blanks in frames such as "You can catch _____ from other people," "You can have _____ and never know it," and "Most people get _____ at one time or other" (p. 12; for other examples of frame substitution, see Furbee & Benfer, 1983; Young, 1978).

Techniques for Analyzing Data About Cultural Domains

Researchers use these kinds of data to build several kinds of models about how people think. *Componential analysis* produces formal models of the elements in a cultural domain, and *taxonomies* display hierarchical associations among the elements in a domain. *Mental maps* are best for displaying fuzzy constructs and dimensions. We treat these in turn.

Componential Analysis

As we have outlined elsewhere, componential analysis (or feature analysis) is a formal, qualitative technique for studying the content of meaning (Bernard, 1994; Bernard & Ryan, 1998). Developed by linguists to identify the features and rules that distinguish one sound from another (Jakobson & Halle, 1956), the technique was elaborated by anthropologists in the 1950s and 1960s (Conklin, 1955; D'Andrade, 1995; Frake, 1962; Goodenough, 1956; Rushforth, 1982; Wallace, 1962). (For a particularly good description of how to apply the method, see Spradley, 1979, pp. 173-184.)

Componential analysis is based on the principle of distinctive features. Any two items (sounds, kinship terms, names of plants, names of animals, and so on) can be distinguished by some minimal set ($2n$) of binary features—that is, features that either occur or do not occur. It takes two features to distinguish four items ($2^2 = 4$, in other words), three features to distinguish eight items ($2^3 = 8$), and so on. The trick is to identify the smallest set of features that best describes the domain of interest. Table 29.1 shows that just three features are needed to describe kinds of horses.

Componential analysis produces models based on logical relationships among features. The models do not account for variations in the meanings of terms across individuals. For example, when we tried to do a componential analysis on the terms for cattle (*bull, cow, heifer, calf, steer,* and *ox*), we found that native speakers of English in the United States (even farmers) disagreed about the differences between *cow* and *heifer,* and between *steer* and *ox.* When the relationships among items are less well defined, taxonomies or mental models may be useful. Nor is there any intimation that componential analyses reflect how "people really think."

Taxonomies

Folk taxonomies are meant to capture the hierarchical structure in sets of terms and are commonly displayed as branching tree diagrams. Figure 29.1 presents a taxonomy of our own understanding of qualitative analysis techniques. Figure 29.2 depicts a taxonomy we have adapted from Pamela Erickson's (1997) study of the perceptions among clinicians and adolescents of methods of contraception. Researchers can elicit folk taxonomies directly by using successive pile sorts (Boster, 1994; Perchonock & Werner, 1969). This involves asking people to continually subdivide the piles of a free pile sort until each item is in its own individual pile. Taxonomic models can also be created with cluster analysis on the similarity data from paired comparisons, pile sorts, and triad tests. *Hierarchical cluster analysis* (Johnson, 1967) builds a taxo-

TABLE 29.1	A Componential Analysis of Six Kinds of Horses		
Name	Female	Neuter	Adult
Mare	+	−	+
Stallion	−	−	+
Gelding	−	+	+
Foal	−	+	−
Filly	+	−	−
Colt	−	−	−

SOURCE: Adapted from D'Andrade (1995).

nomic tree where each item appears in only one group.

Interinformant variation is common in folk taxonomies. That is, different people may use different words to refer to the same category of things. Some of Erickson's (1997) clinician informants referred to the "highly effective" group of methods as "safe," "more reliable," and "sure bets." Category labels need not be simple words, but may be complex phrases; for example, see the category in Figure 29.2 comprising contraceptive methods in which you "have to pay attention to timing." Sometimes, people have no labels at all for particular categories—at least none that they can dredge up easily—and categories, even when named, may be fuzzy and may overlap with other categories. *Overlapping cluster analysis* (Hartigan, 1975) identifies groups of items where a single item may appear in multiple groups.

Mental Maps

Mental maps are visual displays of the similarities among items, whether or not those items are organized hierarchically. One popular method for making these maps is by collecting data about the cognitive similarity or dissimilarity among a set of objects and then applying multidimensional scaling, or MDS, to the similarities (Kruskal & Wish, 1978).

Cognitive maps are meant to be directly analogous to physical maps. Consider a table of distances between all pairs of cities on a map. Objects (cities) that are very dissimilar have high mileage between them and are placed far apart on the map; objects that are less dissimilar have low mileage between them and are placed closer together. Pile sorts, triad tests, and paired comparison tests are measures of cognitive distance. For example, Ryan (1995) asked 11 literate Kom speakers in Cameroon to perform successive pile sorts on Kom illness terms. Figure 29.3 presents an MDS plot of the collective mental map of these terms. The five major illness categories, circled, were identified by hierarchical cluster analysis of the same matrix used to produce the MDS plot.[1]

Data from frame substitution tasks can be displayed with correspondence analysis (Weller & Romney, 1990).[2] Correspondence analysis scales both the rows and the columns into the same space. For example, Kirchler (1992) analyzed 562 obituaries of managers who had died in 1974, 1980, and 1986. He identified 31 descriptive categories from adjectives used in the obituaries and then used correspondence analysis to display how these categories were associated with men and women managers over time. Figure 29.4 shows that male managers who died in 1974 and 1980 were seen by their surviving friends and family as *active, intelligent, outstanding, conscientious,* and *experienced experts.* Although the managers who died in 1986 were still respected, they were more likely to be described as *entrepreneurs, opinion leaders,* and *decision makers.* Perceptions of female managers also changed, but they did not become more like their male counterparts. In 1974 and 1980, female managers were remembered for being nice people. They were described as *kind, likable,* and *adorable.* By 1986, women were remembered for their *courage* and *commitment.* Kirchler interpreted these data to mean that gender stereotypes changed in

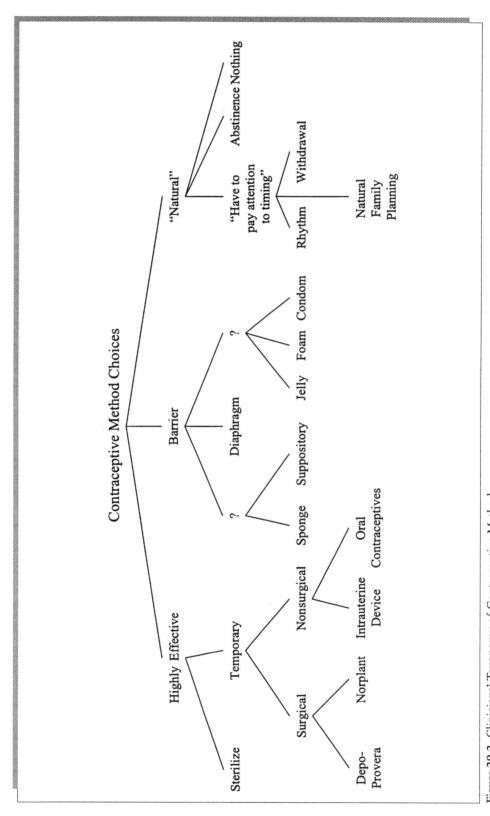

Figure 29.2. Clinicians' Taxonomy of Contraceptive Methods
SOURCE: Based on Erickson (1997).

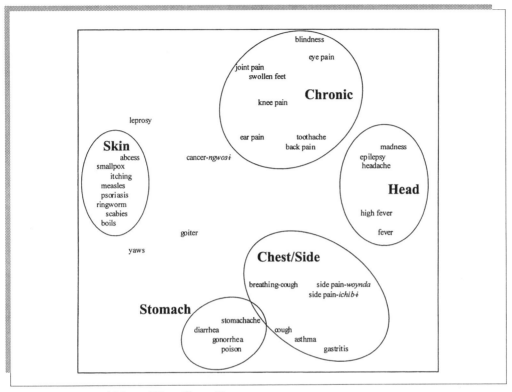

Figure 29.3. Mental Map of Kom Illness Terms

the early 1980s. By 1986, both male and female managers were perceived as working for success, but men impressed their colleagues through their knowledge and expertise, whereas women impressed their colleagues with motivation and engagement.

◆ Methods for Analyzing Free-Flowing Text

Although taxonomies, MDS maps, and the like are useful for analyzing short phrases or words, most qualitative data come in the form of free-flowing texts. There are two major types of analysis. In one, the text is segmented into its most basic meaningful components: words. In the other, meanings are found in large blocks of text.

Analyzing Words

Techniques for word analysis include key-words-in-context, word counts, structural analysis, and cognitive maps. We review each below.

Key-Words-in-Context

Researchers create key-words-in-context (KWIC) lists by finding all the places in a text where a particular word or phrase appears and printing it out in the context of some number of words (say, 30) before and after it. This produces a *concordance*. Well-known concordances have been done on sacred texts, such as the Old and New Testaments (Darton, 1976; Hatch & Redpath, 1954) and the Koran (Kassis, 1983), and on famous works of literature from Euripides (Allen & Italie, 1954) to Homer (Prendergast, 1971), to Beowulf (Bessinger, 1969), to Dylan Thomas (Farringdon & Farringdon, 1980). (On

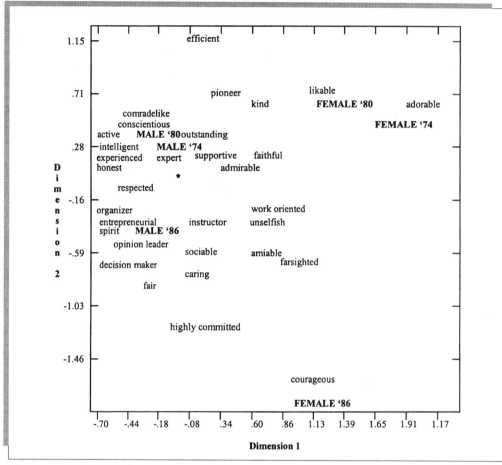

Figure 29.4. Correspondence Analysis of the Frequencies of 31 Disruptive Obituary Categories by Gender and Year of Publication
SOURCE: Erich Kirchler, "Adorable Woman, Expert Man: Changing Gender Images of Women and Men in Management," *European Journal of Social Psychology*, 22 (1992), p. 371. Copyright 1992 by John Wiley & Sons Limited. Reproduced by permission of John Wiley & Sons Limited.

the use of concordances in modern literary studies, see Burton, 1981a, 1981b, 1982; McKinnon, 1993.)

Word Counts

Word counts are useful for discovering patterns of ideas in any body of text, from field notes to responses to open-ended questions. Students of mass media have used use word counts to trace the ebb and flow of support for political figures over time (Danielson & Lasorsa, 1997; Pool, 1952). Differences in the use of words common to the writings of James Madi-

son and Alexander Hamilton led Mosteller and Wallace (1964) to conclude that Madison and not Hamilton had written 12 of the *Federalist Papers*. (For other examples of authorship studies, see Martindale & McKenzie, 1995; Yule 1944/1968.)

Word analysis (like constant comparison, memoing, and other techniques) can help researchers to discover themes in texts. Ryan and Weisner (1996) instructed fathers and mothers of adolescents in Los Angeles: "Describe your children. In your own words, just tell us about them." Ryan and Weisner identified all the unique words in the answers they got to that grand-tour question and noted the number of times each word was used by mothers and by fathers. Mothers, for example, were more likely to use words like *friends, creative, time,* and *honest;* fathers were more likely to use words like *school, good, lack, student, enjoys, independent,* and *extremely.* This suggests that mothers, on first mention, express concern over interpersonal issues, whereas fathers appear to prioritize achievement-oriented and individualistic issues. This kind of analysis considers neither the contexts in which the words occur nor whether the words are used negatively or positively, but distillations like these can help researchers to identify important constructs and can provide data for systematic comparisons across groups.

Structural Analysis and Semantic Networks

Network, or structural, analysis examines the properties that emerge from relations among things. As early as 1959, Charles Osgood created word co-occurrence matrices and applied factor analysis and dimensional plotting to describe the relations among words. Today, semantic network analysis is a growing field (Barnett & Danowski, 1992; Danowski, 1982, 1993). For example, Nolan and Ryan (1999) asked 59 undergraduates (30 women and 29 men) to describe their "most memorable horror film." The researchers identified the 45 most common adjectives, verbs, and nouns used across the descriptions of the films. They produced a 45(word)-by-59(person) matrix, the cells of which indicated whether each student had used each key word in his or her description. Finally, Nolan and Ryan created a 59(person)-by-59(person) similarity matrix of *people* based on the co-occurrence of the words in their descriptions.

Figure 29.5 shows the MDS of Nolan and Ryan's data. Although there is some overlap, it is pretty clear that the men and women in their study used different sets of words to describe horror films. Men were more likely to use words such as *teenager, disturbing, violence, rural, dark, country,* and *hillbilly,* whereas women were more likely to use words such as *boy, little, devil, young, horror, father,* and *evil.* Nolan and Ryan interpreted these results to mean that the men had a fear of rural people and places, whereas the women were more afraid of betrayed intimacy and spiritual possession. (For other examples of the use of word-by-word matrices, see Jang & Barnett, 1994; Schnegg & Bernard, 1996.) This example makes abundantly clear the value of turning qualitative data into quantitative data: Doing so can produce information that engenders deeper interpretations of the meanings in the original corpus of qualitative data. Just as in any mass of numbers, it is hard to see patterns in words unless one first does some kind of data reduction. More about this below.

As in word analysis, one appeal of semantic network analysis is that the data processing is done by computer. The only investigator bias introduced in the process is the decision to include words that occur at least 10 times or 5 times or whatever. (For discussion of computer programs that produce word-by-text and word-by-word co-occurrence matrices, see Borgatti, 1992; Doerfel & Barnett, 1996.) There is, however, no guarantee that the output of any word co-occurrence matrix will be meaningful, and it is notoriously easy to read patterns (and thus meanings) into any set of items.

Cognitive Maps

Cognitive map analysis combines the intuition of human coders with the quantitative methods of network analysis. Carley's work with this technique is instructive. Carley argues that if cognitive models or schemata exist, they are expressed in the texts of people's speech and can be represented as networks of concepts (see Carley & Palmquist, 1992, p. 602), an approach also suggested by D'Andrade (1991). To the extent that cognitive models are widely shared, Carley asserts, even a very small set of texts will contain the information required for describing the models, especially for narrowly defined arenas of life.

In one study, Carley (1993) asked students some questions about the work of scientists. Here are two examples she collected:

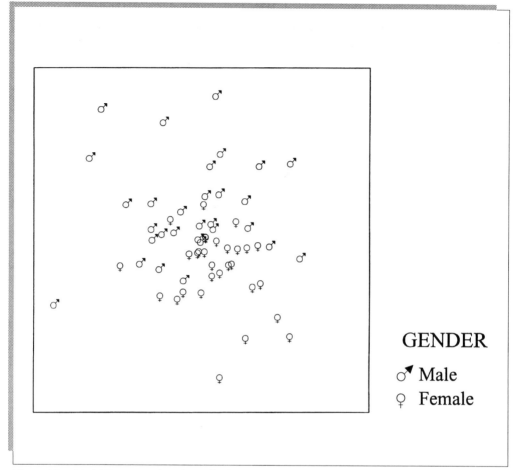

Figure 29.5. Multidimensional Scaling of Informants Based on Words Used in Descriptions of Horror Films
SOURCE: Based on data in Nolan and Ryan (in press).

Student A: I found that scientists engage in research in order to make discoveries and generate new ideas. Such research by scientists is hard work and often involves collaboration with other scientists which leads to discoveries which make the scientists famous. Such collaboration may be informal, such as when they share new ideas over lunch, or formal, such as when they are coauthors of a paper.

Student B: It was hard work to research famous scientists engaged in collaboration and I made many informal discoveries. My research showed that scientists engaged in collaboration with other scientists are coauthors of at least one paper containing their new ideas. Some scientists

make formal discoveries and have new ideas. (p. 89)

Carley compared the students' texts by analyzing 11 concepts: *I, scientists, research, hard work, collaboration, discoveries, new ideas, formal, informal, coauthors, paper.* She coded the concepts for their strength, sign (positive or negative), and direction (whether one concept is logically prior to others), not just for their existence. She found that although students used the same concepts in their texts, the concepts clearly had different meanings. To display the differences in understandings, Carley advocates the

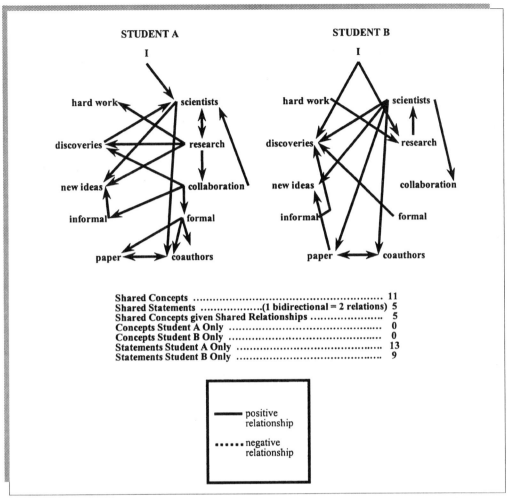

STUDENT A

STUDENT B

Shared Concepts 11
Shared Statements ....(1 bidirectional = 2 relations) 5
Shared Concepts given Shared Relationships 5
Concepts Student A Only 0
Concepts Student B Only 0
Statements Student A Only 13
Statements Student B Only 9

——— positive
relationship

••••• negative
relationship

Figure 29.6. Coded Maps of Two Students' Texts
SOURCE: Kathleen Carley, "Coding Choices for Textual Analysis: A Comparison of Content Analysis and Map Analysis," in P. Marsden (Ed.), *Sociological Methodology* (Oxford: Blackwell, 1993), p. 104. Copyright 1993 by the American Sociological Association. Reproduced by permission of the American Sociological Association.

use of maps that show the relations between and among concepts. Figure 29.6 shows Carley's maps of two of the texts.

Carley's approach is promising because it combines the automation of word counts with the sensitivity of human intuition and interpretation. As Carley recognizes, however, a lot depends on who does the coding. Different coders will produce different maps by making different coding choices. In the end, native-language competence is one of the fundamental methodological requirements for analysis (see also

Carley, 1997; Carley & Kaufer, 1993; Carley & Palmquist, 1992; Palmquist, Carley, & Dale, 1997).

Key-words-in-context, word counts, structural analysis, and cognitive maps all reduce text to the fundamental meanings of specific words. These reductions make it easy for researchers to identify general patterns and make comparisons across texts. With the exception of KWIC, however, these techniques remove words from the contexts in which they occur. Subtle nuances are likely to be lost—which brings us to the analysis of whole texts.

Analyzing Chunks of Text: Coding

Coding is the heart and soul of *whole-text analysis*. Coding forces the researcher to make judgments about the meanings of contiguous blocks of text. The fundamental tasks associated with coding are sampling, identifying themes, building codebooks, marking texts, constructing models (relationships among codes), and testing these models against empirical data. We outline each task below. We then describe some of the major coding traditions: grounded theory, schema analysis, classic content analysis, content dictionaries, analytic induction, and ethnographic decision trees. We want to emphasize that no particular tradition, whether humanistic or positivistic, has a monopoly on text analysis.

Sampling

Investigators must first identify a *corpus of texts,* and then select the *units of analysis within the texts.* Selection can be either random or purposive, but the choice is not a matter of cleaving to one epistemological tradition or another. Waitzkin and Britt (1993) did a thoroughgoing interpretive analysis of encounters between patients and doctors by selecting 50 texts at random from 336 audiotaped encounters. Trost (1986) used classical content analysis to test how the relationships between teenagers and their families might be affected by five different dichotomous variables. He intentionally selected five cases from each of the 32 possible combinations of the five variables and conducted $32 \times 5 = 160$ interviews.

Samples may also be based on extreme or deviant cases, cases that illustrate maximum variety on variables, cases that are somehow typical of a phenomenon, or cases that confirm or disconfirm a hypothesis. (For reviews of nonrandom sampling strategies, see Patton, 1990, pp. 169-186; Sandelowski, 1995b.) A single case may be sufficient to display something of substantive importance, but Morse (1994) suggests using at least six participants in studies where one is trying to understand the essence of

experience. Morse also suggests 30-50 interviews for ethnographies and grounded theory studies. Finding themes and building theory may require fewer cases than comparing across groups and testing hypotheses or models.

Once the researcher has established a sample of texts, the next step is to identify the basic units of analysis. The units may be entire texts (books, interviews, responses to an open-ended question on a survey), grammatical segments (words, word senses, sentences, themes, paragraphs), formatting units (rows, columns, or pages), or simply chunks of text that reflect a single theme—what Krippendorf (1980, p. 62) calls *thematic units.* In general, where the objective is to compare across texts (as in the case of classical content analysis), the units of analysis need to be nonoverlapping. (For discussion of additional kinds of units of analysis, see Krippendorf, 1980, pp. 57-64; Tesch, 1990.)

Finding Themes

Themes are abstract (and often fuzzy) constructs that investigators identify before, during, and after data collection. Literature reviews are rich sources for themes, as are investigators' own experiences with subject matter. More often than not, however, researchers induce themes from the text itself.

There is more than one way to induce themes. Grounded theorists suggest a careful, line-by-line reading of the text while looking for processes, actions, assumptions, and consequences. Schema analysts suggest looking for metaphors, for repetitions of words, and for shifts in content (Agar & Hobbs, 1985). Content analysts have used KWIC to identify different meanings. Spradley (1979, pp. 199-201) suggests looking for evidence of social conflict, cultural contradictions, informal methods of social control, things that people do in managing impersonal social relationships, methods by which people acquire and maintain achieved and ascribed status, and information about how people solve problems. Each of these arenas is likely to yield major themes in cultures. Barkin, Ryan, and Gelberg (1999) had multiple coders independently sort informants' statements into thematic piles. They then used multidimensional scaling and cluster analysis on the pile-sort data to identify subthemes shared across coders. (For another example, see Patterson, Bettini, & Nussbaum, 1993.)

Willms et al. (1990) and Miles and Huberman (1994) suggest that researchers start with some general themes derived from reading the literature and add more themes and subthemes as they go. Shelley (1992) followed this advice in her study of how social networks affect people with end-stage kidney disease. She used the *Outline of Cultural Materials* (Murdock, 1971) as the basis of her coding scheme and then added additional themes based on a close reading of the text. Bulmer (1979) lists 10 different sources of themes, including literature reviews, professional definitions, local commonsense constructs, and researchers' values and prior experiences. He also notes that investigators' general theoretical orientations, the richness of the existing literature, and the characteristics of the phenomena being studied influence the themes researchers are likely to find.

No matter how the researcher actually *does* inductive coding, by the time he or she has identified the themes and refined them to the point where they can be applied to an entire corpus of texts, a lot of interpretive analysis has already been done. Miles and Huberman (1994) say simply, "Coding is analysis" (p. 56).

Building Codebooks

Codebooks are simply organized lists of codes (often in hierarchies). How a researcher can develop a codebook is covered in detail by Dey (1993, pp. 95-151), Crabtree and Miller (1992), and Miles and Huberman (1994, pp. 55-72). MacQueen, McLellan, Kay, and Milstein (1998) suggest that a good codebook should include a detailed description of each code, inclusion and exclusion criteria, and exemplars of real text for each theme. If a theme is particularly abstract, we suggest that the researcher also provide examples of the theme's

boundaries and even some cases that are closely related but *not* included within the theme. Coding is supposed to be data *reduction,* not proliferation (Miles, 1979, pp. 593-594). The codes themselves are mnemonic devices used to identify or mark the specific themes in a text. They can be either words or numbers—whatever the researcher finds easiest to remember and to apply.

Qualitative researchers working as a team need to agree up front on what to include in their codebook. Morse (1994) suggests beginning the process with a group meeting. MacQueen et al. (1998) suggest that a single team member should be designated "Keeper of the Codebook"—we strongly agree.

Good codebooks are developed and refined as the research goes along. Kurasaki (1997) interviewed 20 *sansei*—third-generation Japanese Americans—and used a grounded theory approach to do her analysis of ethnic identity. She started with seven major themes. As the analysis progressed, she split the major themes into subthemes. Eventually, she combined two of the major themes and wound up with six major themes and a total of 18 subthemes. (Richards & Richards, 1991, discuss the theoretical principles related to hierarchical coding structures that emerge out of the data. Araujo, 1995, uses an example from his own research on the traditional British manufacturing industry to describe the process of designing and refining hierarchical codes.)

The development and refinement of coding categories have long been central tasks in classical content analysis (see Berelson, 1952, pp. 147-168; Holsti, 1969, pp. 95-126) and are particularly important in the construction of concept dictionaries (Deese, 1969; Stone, Dunphy, Smith, & Ogilvie, 1966, pp. 134-168). Krippendorf (1980, pp. 71-84) and Carey, Morgan, and Oxtoby (1996) note that much of codebook refinement comes during the training of coders to mark the text and in the act of checking for intercoder agreement. Disagreement among multiple coders shows when the codebook is ambiguous and confusing. The first run also allows the researcher to identify good examples to include in the codebook.

Marking Texts

The act of coding involves the assigning of codes to contiguous units of text. Coding serves two distinct purposes in qualitative analysis. First, codes act as *tags* to mark off text in a corpus for later retrieval or indexing. Tags are not associated with any fixed units of text; they can mark simple phrases or extend across multiple pages. Second, codes act as *values* assigned to fixed units (see Bernard, 1991, 1994; Seidel & Kelle, 1995). Here, codes are nominal, ordinal, or ratio scale values that are applied to fixed, nonoverlapping units of analysis. The non-overlapping units can be texts (such as paragraphs, pages, documents), episodes, cases, or persons. *Codes as tags* are associated with grounded theory and schema analysis (reviewed below). *Codes as values* are associated with classic content analysis and content dictionaries. The two types of codes are not mutually exclusive, but the use of one gloss—*code*—for both concepts can be misleading.

Analyzing Chunks of Texts: Building Conceptual Models

Once the researcher identifies a set of things (themes, concepts, beliefs, behaviors), the next step is to identify how these things are linked to each other in a theoretical model (Miles & Huberman, 1994, pp. 134-137). Models are sets of abstract constructs and the relationships among them (Bulmer, 1979). Grounded theory, schema analysis, ethnographic decision modeling, and analytic induction all include model-building phases.

Once a model starts to take shape, the researcher looks for negative cases—cases that don't fit the model. Negative cases either disconfirm parts of a model or suggest new connections that need to be made. In either instance, negative cases need to be accommodated. Negative case analysis is discussed in detail by Becker, Geer, Hughes, and Strauss (1961, pp. 37-45), Strauss and Corbin (1990, pp. 108-109), Lincoln and Guba (1985, pp. 309-313), Dey (1993, pp. 226-233), Miles and Huberman (1994, p. 271), and Becker (1998), and is used by

schema analysts (Quinn, 1997), ethnographic decision modelers (Gladwin, 1989), and scholars who use analytic induction (Bloor, 1976; Cressey, 1953/1971; Lindesmith, 1947/1968).

In ethnographic decision modeling and in classical content analysis, models are built on one set of data and tested on another. In their original formulation, Glaser and Strauss (1967) emphasized that building grounded theory models is a step in the research process and that models need to be validated. Grounded theorists and schema analysts today are more likely to validate their models by seeking confirmation from expert informants than by analyzing a second set of data. For example, Kearney, Murphy, and Rosenbaum (1994) checked the validity of their model of crack mothers' experiences by presenting it to knowledgeable respondents who were familiar with the research.

Regardless of the kind of reliability and validity checks, models are simplifications of reality. They can be made more or less complicated and may capture all or only a portion of the variance in a given set of data. It is up to the investigator and his or her peers to decide how much a particular model is supposed to describe.

Below we review some of the most common methods researchers use to analyze blocks of texts. These include grounded theory, schema analysis, classical content analysis, content dictionaries, analytic induction, and ethnographic decision tree analysis.

Grounded Theory

Grounded theorists want to understand people's experiences in as rigorous and detailed a manner as possible. They want to identify categories and concepts that emerge from text and link these concepts into substantive and formal theories. The original formulation of the method (Glaser & Strauss, 1967) is still useful, but later works are easier to read and more practical (Charmaz, 1990; Lincoln & Guba, 1985; Lonkila, 1995; Strauss, 1987). Strauss and Corbin (1990), Dey (1993), and Becker (1998) provide especially useful guidance. (For some recent examples of grounded theory research, see Hunt & Ropo, 1995; Irurita, 1996; Kearney et al., 1994; Kearney, Murphy, Irwin, & Rosenbaum, 1995; Sohier, 1993; Strauss & Corbin, 1997; Wilson & Hutchinson, 1996; Wright, 1997.)

Grounded theory is an iterative process by which the analyst becomes more and more "grounded" in the data and develops increasingly richer concepts and models of how the phenomenon being studied really works. To do this, the grounded theorist collects verbatim transcripts of interviews and reads through a small sample of text (usually line by line). Sandelowski (1995a) observes that analysis of texts begins with proofreading the material and simply underlining key phrases "because they make some as yet inchoate sense" (p. 373). In a process called "open coding," the investigator identifies potential themes by pulling together real examples from the text (Agar, 1996; Bernard, 1994; Bogdan & Biklen, 1992; Lincoln & Guba, 1985; Lofland & Lofland, 1995; Strauss & Corbin, 1990; Taylor & Bogdan, 1984). Identifying the categories and terms used by informants themselves is called "*in vivo* coding" (Strauss & Corbin, 1990). As grounded theorists develop their concepts and categories, they often decide they need to gather more data from informants.

As coding categories emerge, the investigator links them together in theoretical models. One technique is to compare and contrast themes and concepts. When, why, and under what conditions do these themes occur in the text? Glazer and Strauss (1967, pp. 101-116) refer to this as the "constant comparison method," and it is similar to the contrast questions Spradley (1979, pp. 160-172) suggests researchers ask informants. (For other good descriptions of the comparison method, see Glaser, 1978, pp. 56-72; Strauss & Corbin, 1990, pp. 84-95.)

Another useful tool for building theoretical models is the conditional matrix described by Strauss and Corbin (1990, pp. 158-175). The conditional matrix is a set of concentric circles, each level corresponding to a different unit of influence. At the center are actions and interactions; the outer rings represent international and national concerns, and the inner rings represent individual and small group influences on action. The matrix is designed to help investigators to be more sensitive to conditions, actions/interactions, and consequences of a phenomenon and to order these conditions and consequences into theories.

Memoing is one of the principal techniques for recording relationships among themes. Strauss and Corbin (1990, pp. 18, 73-74, 109-129, 197-219) discuss three kinds of memos: code notes, theory notes, and operational notes. Code notes describe the concepts that are being discovered in "the discovery of grounded theory." In theory notes, the researcher tries to summarize his or her ideas about what is going on in the text. Operational notes are about practical matters.

Once a model starts to take shape, the researcher uses negative case analysis to identify problems and make appropriate revisions. The end results of grounded theory are often displayed through the presentation of segments of text—verbatim quotes from informants—as exemplars of concepts and theories. These illustrations may be prototypical examples of central tendencies or they may represent exceptions to the norm. Grounded theory researchers also display their theoretical results in maps of the major categories and the relationships among them (Kearney et al., 1995; Miles & Huberman, 1994, pp. 134-137). These "concept maps" are similar to the personal semantic networks described by Leinhardt (1987, 1989), Strauss (1992), and D'Andrade (1991) (see below).

Schema Analysis

Schema analysis combines elements of the linguistic and sociological traditions. It is based on the idea that people must use cognitive simplifications to help make sense of the complex information to which they are constantly exposed (Casson, 1983, p. 430). Schank and Abelson (1977) postulate that schemata—or scripts, as they call them—enable culturally skilled people to fill in details of a story or event. It is, says Wodak (1992, p. 525), our schemata that lead us to interpret Mona Lisa's smile as evidence of her perplexity or her desperation.

From a methodological view, schema analysis is similar to grounded theory. Both begin with a careful reading of verbatim texts and seek to discover and link themes into theoretical models. In a series of articles, Quinn (1982, 1987, 1992, 1996, 1997) has analyzed hundreds of hours of interviews to discover concepts underlying American marriage and to show how these concepts are tied together. Quinn's (1997) method is to "exploit clues in ordinary discourse for what they tell us about shared cognition—to glean what people must have in mind in order to say the things they do" (p. 140). She begins by looking at patterns of speech and the repetition of key words and phrases, paying particular attention to informants' use of metaphors and the commonalities in their reasoning about marriage. Quinn found that the hundreds of metaphors in her corpus of texts fit into just eight linked classes, which she calls lastingness, sharedness, compatibility, mutual benefit, difficulty, effort, success (or failure), and risk of failure.

Metaphors and proverbs are not the only linguistic features used to infer meaning from text. D'Andrade (1991) notes that "perhaps the simplest and most direct indication of schematic organization in naturalistic discourse is the repetition of associative linkages" (p. 294). He observes that "indeed, anyone who has listened to long stretches of talk—whether generated by a friend, spouse, workmate, informant, or patient—knows how frequently people circle through the same network of ideas" (p. 287).

In a study of blue-collar workers in Rhode Island, Claudia Strauss (1992) refers to these ideas as "personal semantic networks." She describes such a network from one of her informants. On rereading her intensive interviews with one of the workers, Strauss found that her informant repeatedly referred to ideas associated with greed, money, businessmen, siblings, and "being different." She displays the relationships among these ideas by writing the concepts on a page of paper and connecting them with lines and explanations.

Price (1987) observes that when people tell stories, they assume that their listeners share with them many assumptions about how the world works, and so they leave out information

that "everyone knows." Thus she looks for what is *not* said in order to identify underlying cultural assumptions (p. 314).

For more examples of the search for cultural schemata in texts, see Holland's (1985) study of the reasoning that Americans apply to interpersonal problems, Kempton's (1987) study of ordinary Americans' theories of home heat control, Claudia Strauss's (1997) study of what chemical plant workers and their neighbors think about the free enterprise system, and Agar and Hobbs's (1985) analysis of how an informant became a burglar. We next turn to the two other methods used across the social sciences for analyzing text: classical content analysis and content dictionaries.

Displaying Concepts and Models

Visual displays are an important part of qualitative analysis. Selecting key quotes as exemplars, building matrices or forms, and laying theories out in the form of flowcharts or maps are all potent ways to communicate ideas visually to others. Models are typically displayed using boxes and arrows, with the boxes containing themes and the arrows representing the relationships among them. Lines can be unidirectional or bidirectional. For example, taxonomies are models in which the lines represent the super- and subordinate relationships among items. Relationships can include causality, association, choices, and time, to name a few.

A widely used method for describing themes is the presentation of direct quotes from respondents—quotes that lead the reader to understand quickly what it may have taken the researcher months or years to figure out. The researcher chooses segments of text—verbatim quotes from respondents—as exemplars of concepts, of theories, and of negative cases. Ryan (1999) has used multiple coders to identify typical quotes. He asks 10 coders to mark the same corpus of text for three themes. Ryan argues that the text marked by all the coders represents the central tendency or typical examples of the abstract constructs, whereas text marked by only some of the coders represents less typical examples and is more typical of the "edges" of the construct.

Tables can be used to organize and display raw text or can be used to summarize qualitative data along multiple dimensions (rows and columns). The cells can be filled with verbatim quotes (Bernard & Ashton-Voyoucalos, 1976; Leinhardt & Smith, 1985, p. 254; Miles & Huberman, 1994, p. 130), summary statements (Yoder, 1995), or symbols (Fjellman & Gladwin, 1985; Van Maanen, Miller, & Johnson, 1982). (For a range of presentation formats, see Bernard, 1994; Miles & Huberman, 1994; Werner & Schoepfle, 1987.)

Classical Content Analysis

Whereas grounded theory is concerned with the discovery of data-induced hypotheses, classical content analysis comprises techniques for reducing texts to a unit-by-variable matrix and analyzing that matrix quantitatively to test hypotheses. The researcher can produce a matrix by applying a set of codes to a set of qualitative data (including written texts as well as audio and video media). Unlike grounded theory or schema analysis, content analysis assumes that the codes of interest have already been discovered and described.

Once the researcher has selected a sample of texts, the next step in classical content analysis is to code each unit for each of the themes or variables in the codebook. This produces a unit-by-variable matrix that can be analyzed using a variety of statistical techniques. For example, Cowan and O'Brien (1990) tested whether males or females are more likely to be survivors in slasher films. Conventional wisdom about such films suggests that victims are mostly women and slashers are mostly men. Cowan and O'Brien selected a corpus of 56 slasher films and identified 474 victims. They coded each victim for gender and survival. They found that slashers are mostly men, but it turned out that victims are equally likely to be male or female. Women who survive are less likely to be shown engaging in sexual behavior and are less likely to be physically attractive than their nonsurviving counterparts. Male victims are cynical, egotistical, and dictatorial. Cowan and O'Brien conclude that, in slasher films, sexually

pure women survive and "unmitigated masculinity" leads to death (p. 195).

The coding of texts is usually assigned to multiple coders so that the researcher can see whether the constructs being investigated are shared and whether multiple coders can reliably apply the same codes. Typically, investigators first calculate the percentage of agreement among coders for each variable or theme. They then apply a correction formula to take account of the fact that some fraction of agreement will always occur by chance. The amount of that fraction depends on the number of coders and the precision of measurement for each code. If two people code a theme present or absent, they could agree, ceteris paribus, on any answer 25% of the time by chance. If a theme, such as wealth, is measured ordinally (low, medium, high), then the likelihood of chance agreement changes accordingly. Cohen's (1960) kappa, or K, is a popular measure for taking these chances into account. When K is zero, agreement is what might be expected by chance. When K is negative, the observed level of agreement is less than one would expect by chance. How much intercoder agreement is enough? The standards are still ad hoc, but Krippendorf (1980, pp. 147-148) advocates agreement of at least .70 and notes that some scholars (e.g., Brouwer, Clark, Gerbner, & Krippendorf, 1969) use a cutoff of .80. Fleiss (1971) and Light (1971) expand kappa to handle multiple coders. For other measures of intercoder agreement, see Krippendorf (1980, pp. 147-154) and Craig (1981).

Reliability "concerns the extent to which an experiment, test, or any measuring procedure yields the same results on repeated trials" (Carmines & Zeller, 1979, p. 11). A high level of intercoder agreement is evidence that a theme has some external validity and is not just a figment of the investigator's imagination (Mitchell, 1979). Not surprisingly, investigators have suggested many ways to assess validity (for reviews of key issues, see Campbell, 1957; Campbell & Stanley, 1963; Cook & Campbell, 1979; Denzin, 1997; Fielding & Fielding, 1986; Guba, 1981; Guba & Lincoln, 1982; Hammersley, 1992; Kirk & Miller, 1986; Lincoln & Guba, 1985). Bernard (1994) argues that, ultimately, the validity of a concept depends on the utility of the device that measures it and the collective judgment of the scientific community that a construct and its measure are valid. "In the end," he says, "we are left to deal with the effects of our judgments, which is just as it should be. Valid measurement makes valid data, but validity itself depends on the collective opinion of researchers" (p. 43). *Generalizability* refers to the degree to which the findings are applicable to other populations or samples. It draws on the degree to which the original data were representative of a larger population.

For reviews of work in content analysis, see Pool (1959); Gerbner, Holsti, Krippendorf, Paisley, and Stone (1969); Holsti (1969); Krippendorf (1980); Weber (1990); and Roberts (1997). Examples of classical content analysis can be found in media studies (Hirschman, 1987; Kolbe & Albanese, 1996; Spiggle, 1986), political rhetoric (Kaid, Tedesco, & McKinnon, 1996), folklore (Johnson & Price-Williams, 1997), business relations (Spears, Mowen, & Chakraborty, 1996), health care delivery (Potts, Runyan, Zerger, & Marchetti, 1996; Sleath, Svarstad, & Roter, 1997), and law (Imrich, Mullin, & Linz, 1995). Classical content analysis is also the fundamental means by which anthropologists test cross-cultural hypotheses (Bradley, Moore, Burton, & White, 1990; Ember & Ember, 1992; White & Burton, 1988). For early, but fundamental, criticisms of the approach, see Kracauer (1953) and George (1959).

Content Dictionaries

Computer-based, general-purpose content analysis dictionaries allow investigators to automate the coding of texts. To build such dictionaries, researchers assign words, by hand, to one or more categories (there are typically 50-60 categories in computerized content analysis dictionaries) according to a set of rules. The rules are part of a computer program that parses new texts, assigning words to categories.

Work on content dictionaries began in the 1960s with the General Inquirer and continues to this day (Kelly & Stone, 1975; Stone et al., 1966; Zuell, Weber, & Mohler, 1989). The General Inquirer is a computer program that uses a dictionary (the *Harvard Psychosocial Dictionary*) to parse and assign text to coded categories. Over time, the dictionary has been updated. The latest version (*Harvard IV*) contains more than 10,000 words and can distinguish among multiple meanings of words (Rosenberg, Schnurr, & Oxman, 1990, p. 303). Because such dictionaries do not contain all the words in the English language, investigators can assign unrecognized words to categories as they see fit, a process of further modifying the "codebook."

How effective are computer-based dictionaries? An early version of the General Inquirer was tested on 66 suicide notes—33 written by men who had actually taken their own lives and 33 written by men who were asked to produce simulated suicide notes. The program parsed the texts and picked the actual suicide notes 91% of the time (Ogilvie, Stone, & Schneidman, 1966). Content dictionaries do not need to be very big to be useful. Colby (1966) created a simple dictionary to distinguish between Navaho and Zuni responses to thematic apperception tests. For additional examples of special-purpose dictionaries in content analysis, see Fan and Shaffer (1990), Furbee (1996), Holsti (1966), Jehn and Werner (1993), Laffal (1990, 1995), McTavish and Pirro (1990), and Schnurr, Rosenberg, Oxman, and Tucker (1986).

Content dictionaries are attractive because they are entirely reliable and automated, but, as Shapiro (1997) argues, this may be offset by a decrease in validity. For the time being, only humans can parse certain subtleties of meaning reflected in context (Viney, 1983), but computer-based dictionaries are getting better all the time. For example, texts are now scored by computer for the Gottschalk-Gleser psychological scales (measuring various forms of anxiety and hostility) with greater than .80 reliability (Gottschalk & Bechtel, 1993).

Analytic Induction and Boolean Tests

Analytic induction is a formal, nonquantitative method for building up causal explanations of phenomena from a close examination of cases. It was proposed as an alternative to statistical analysis by Znaniecki (1934, pp. 249-331), modified by Lindesmith (1947/1968) and Cressey (1953/1971), and is discussed by Denzin (1978), Bulmer (1979), Manning (1982), and Becker (1998), among others. (For critiques of the approach, see Robinson, 1951.) The method is a formal kind of negative case analysis.

The technique can be described in a series of steps: First, define a phenomenon that requires explanation and propose an explanation. Next, examine a case to see if the explanation fits. If it does, then examine another case. An explanation is accepted until a new case falsifies it. When a case is found that doesn't fit, then, under the rules of analytic induction, the alternatives are to change the explanation (so that you can include the new case) or redefine the phenomenon (so that you exclude the nuisance case). Ideally, the process continues until a universal explanation for all known cases of a phenomenon is attained. Explaining cases by declaring them all unique is a tempting but illegitimate option. Classic examples of analytic induction include Lindesmith's (1947/1968) study of drug addicts, Cressey's (1953/1971) study of embezzlers, and McCleary's (1978) study of how parole officers decide when one of their charges is in violation of parole. For a particularly clear example of the technique, see Bloor's (1976, 1978) analysis of how doctors decide whether or not to remove children's tonsils.

Ragin (1987, 1994) formalized the logic of analytic induction, using a Boolean approach, and Romme (1995) applies the approach to textual data. Boolean algebra involves just two states (true and false, present and absent), but even with such simple inputs, things can get very complicated, very quickly. With just three dichotomous causal conditions (A and not A, B and not B, and C and not C) and one outcome variable (D and not D), there are 16 possible cases: A, B, C, D; A, not B, C, D; A, B, not C, D; and so on. Boolean analysis involves setting up what is known as a truth table, or a matrix of the actual versus the possible outcomes. (For more on truth tables and how they are related to negative case analysis, see Becker, 1998, pp. 146-214.)

Schweizer (1991, 1996) applied this method in his analysis of conflict and social status among residents of Chen Village, China. (For a discussion of Schweizer's data collection and analysis methods, see Bernard & Ryan, 1998.) All the data about the actors in this political drama were extracted from a historical narrative about Chen Village. Like classic content analysis and cognitive mapping, analytic induction requires that human coders read and code text and then produce an event-by-variable matrix. The object of the analysis, however, is not to show the relationships among all codes, but to find the minimal set of logical relationships among the concepts that accounts for a single dependent variable. With more than three variables, the analysis becomes much more difficult. Computer programs such as QCA (Drass, 1980) and ANTHROPAC (Borgatti, 1992) test all possible multivariate hypotheses and find the optimal solution. (QCA is reviewed in Weitzman & Miles, 1995.)

Ethnographic Decision Models

Ethnographic decision models (EDMs) are qualitative, causal analyses that predict behavioral choices under specific circumstances. An EDM, often referred to as a decision tree or flowchart, comprises a series of nested *if-then* statements that link criteria (and combinations of criteria) to the behavior of interest (Figure 29.7). EDMs have been used to explain how fishermen decide where to fish (Gatewood, 1983), what prices people decide to place on their products (Gladwin, 1971; Quinn, 1978), and which treatments people choose for an illness (Mathews & Hill, 1990; Ryan & Martínez, 1996; Young, 1980).

EDMs combine many of the techniques employed in grounded theory and classic content analysis. Gladwin (1989) lays out the fundamental steps for building an ethnographic decision tree model. (For other clear descriptions of the steps, see Hill, 1998; Ryan & Martínez, 1996.)

EDMs require exploratory data collection, preliminary model building, and model testing. First, researchers identify the decisions they want

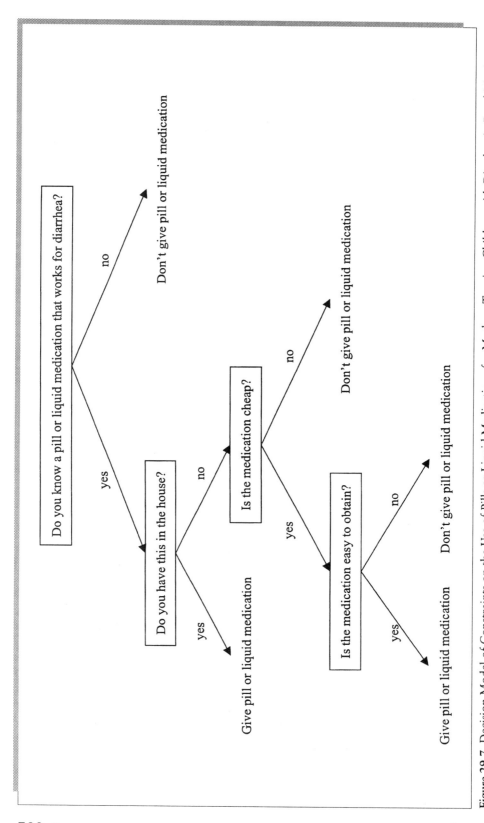

Figure 29.7. Decision Model of Constraints on the Use of Pills or Liquid Medications for Mothers Treating Children with Diarrhea in Rural Mexico
SOURCE: Based on data in Ryan and Martínez (1996).

to explore and the alternatives that are available. Typically, EDMs are done on simple yes/no types of behaviors. They can be used, however, to predict multiple behaviors (Mathews & Hill, 1990; Young, 1980) as well as the order of multiple behaviors (Ryan & Martínez, 1996).

Next, the researchers conduct open-ended interviews to discover the criteria people use to select among alternatives. The researchers first ask people to recall the most recent example of an actual—not a hypothetical—behavior and to recall *why* they did or did not do the behavior. Here is an example from a study we've done recently: "Think about the last time you had a can of something to drink in your hand—soda, juice, water, beer, whatever. Did you recycle the can? Why [Why not]?" This kind of question generates a list of *decision criteria*. To understand how these criteria might be linked, EDM researchers ask people to compare the latest decision with other similar decisions made in the past. Some researchers have used vignettes to elicit the relationships among criteria (e.g., Weller, Ruebush, & Klein, 1997; Young, 1980).

With a list of decision criteria in hand, the researchers' next step is to systematically collect data, preferably from a new group of people, about how each criterion applies or does not apply to a recent example of the behavior. "Was a recycling bin handy?" and "Do you normally recycle cans at home?" are 2 of the 30 questions we've asked people in our study of recycling behavior. The data from this stage are used to build a preliminary model of the decision process for the behavior under scrutiny. Cases that do not fit the model are examined closely and the model is modified. Researchers tweak, or tune, the model until they achieve a satisfactory level of postdictive accuracy—understood to be at least 80% among EDM researchers. Parsimonious models are favored over more complicated ones. (For automated ways of building and pruning decision trees, see Mingers, 1989a, 1989b.)

The process doesn't end there—the same data are used in building a preliminary model and in testing its postdictive accuracy. When EDM researchers feel confident in their model,

they test it on an independent sample to see if it predicts as well as it postdicts. Typically, EDMs predict more than 80% of whatever behavior is being modeled, far above what we expect by chance. (For more detailed arguments on how to calculate accuracy in EDMs, see Ryan & Martínez, 1996; Weller et al., 1997.)

Because of the intensive labor involved, EDMs have been necessarily restricted to relatively simple decisions in relatively small and homogeneous populations. Recently, however, we found we could effectively test, on a nationally representative sample, our ethnographically derived decision models for whether or not to recycle cans and whether or not to ask for paper or plastic bags at the grocery store (Bernard, Ryan, & Borgatti, 1999).

EDMs can be displayed as decision trees (e.g., Gladwin, 1989), as decision tables (Mathews & Hill, 1990; Young, 1980), or as sets of rules in the form of *if-then* statements (Ryan & Martínez, 1996). Like componential analysis, folk taxonomies, and schema analysis, EDMs represent an aggregate decision process and do not necessarily represent what is going on inside people's heads (Garro, 1998).

◆ Breaking Down the Boundaries

Text analysis as a research strategy permeates the social sciences, and the range of methods for conducting text analysis is inspiring. Investigators examine words, sentences, paragraphs, pages, documents, ideas, meanings, paralinguistic features, and even what is missing from the text. They interpret, mark, retrieve, and count. By turns, they apply interpretive analysis and numerical analysis. They use text analysis for exploratory and confirmatory purposes. Researchers identify themes, describe them, and compare them across cases and groups. Finally, they combine themes into conceptual models and theories to explain and predict social phenomena.

Figure 29.1 depicts a broad range of analysis techniques found across the social sciences. To conform our presentation with the literature on qualitative methods, we have organized these techniques according to the goals of the investigators and the kinds of texts to which the techniques are typically applied.

In this chapter, we focus on the sociological tradition that uses text as a "window into experience" rather than the linguistic tradition that describes how texts are developed and structured. Texts such as conversations, performances, and narratives are analyzed by investigators from both the sociological and linguistic traditions. Although the agendas of the investigators may differ, we see no reason why many of the sociological techniques we describe could not be useful in the linguistic tradition and vice versa.

We also distinguish between those analyses associated with systematically elicited data and those associated with free-flowing texts. We argue, however, that these data-analytic pairings are ones of convention rather than necessity. Investigators want to (a) identify the range and salience of key items and concepts, (b) discover the relationships among these items and concepts, and (c) build and test models linking these concepts together. They use free-listing tasks, KWIC, word counts, and the exploratory phases of grounded theory, schema analysis, and EDM to discover potentially useful themes and concepts.

Researchers use pile sorts, paired comparisons, triads tests, frame substitution tasks, semantic networks, cognitive maps, content analysis and content dictionaries, and the modeling phases of grounded theory, schema analysis, and EDM to discover how abstract concepts are related to each other. They display the relationships as models or frameworks. These frameworks include formal models that rely on Boolean logic (componential analysis and analytic induction), hierarchical models (taxonomies and ethnographic decision models), probabilistic models (classic content analysis and content dictionaries), and more abstract models such as those produced by grounded theory and schema analysis. Below we describe two important examples of studies in which researchers

combined methods to understand their data more fully.

Jehn and Doucet (1996, 1997) used word counts, classical content analysis, and mental mapping to examine conflicts among Chinese and U.S. business associates. They asked 76 U.S. managers who had worked in Sino-American joint ventures to describe recent interpersonal conflicts with business partners. Each person described a situation with a same-culture manager and a different-cultural manager. The researchers made sure that each manager interviewed included information about his or her relationship to the other person, who was involved, what the conflict was about, what caused the conflict, and how the conflict was resolved.

After collecting the narratives, Jehn and Doucet asked their informants to help identify the emic themes in the narratives. First, they generated separate lists of words from the intercultural and intracultural conflict narratives. They asked three expatriate managers to act as judges and to identify all the words that were related to conflict. They settled on a list of 542 conflict words from the intercultural list and 242 conflict words from the intracultural list. Jehn and Doucet then asked the three judges to sort the words into piles or categories. The experts identified 15 subcategories for the intercultural data (things like *conflict, expectations, rules, power,* and *volatile*) and 15 categories for the intracultural data (things like *conflict, needs, standards, power, contentious,* and *lose*). Taking into consideration the total number of words in each corpus, conflict words were used more in intracultural interviews and resolution terms were more likely to be used in intercultural interviews.

Jehn and Doucet also used traditional content analysis on their data. The had two coders read the 152 conflict scenarios (76 intracultural and 76 intercultural) and evaluate (on a 5-point scale) each on 27 different themes they had identified from the literature. This produced two 76 × 27 scenario-by-theme profile matrices— one for the intracultural conflicts and one for the intercultural conflicts. The first three factors from the intercultural matrix reflect (a) interpersonal animosity and hostility, (b) aggravation, and (c) the volatile nature of the conflict. The first two factors from the intracultural matrix reflect (a) hatred and animosity with a volatile nature and (b) conflicts conducted calmly with little verbal intensity.

Finally, Jehn and Doucet identified the 30 intracultural and the 30 intercultural scenarios that they felt were the clearest and pithiest. They recruited 50 *more* expatriate managers to assess the similarities (on a 5-point scale) of 60-120 randomly selected pairs of scenarios. When combined across informants, the managers' judgments produced two aggregate, scenario-by-scenario, similarity matrices—one for the intracultural conflicts and one for the intercultural conflicts. Multidimensional scaling of the intercultural similarity data identified four dimensions: (a) open versus resistant to change, (b) situational causes versus individual traits, (c) high- versus low-resolution potential based on trust, and (d) high- versus low-resolution potential based on patience. Scaling of the intracultural similarity data identified four different dimensions: (a) high versus low cooperation, (b) high versus low confrontation, (c) problem solving versus accepting, and (d) resolved versus ongoing.

The work of Jehn and Doucet is impressive because the analysis of the data from these tasks produced different sets of themes. All three emically induced theme sets have some intuitive appeal, and all three yield analytic results that are useful. The researchers could have also used the techniques of grounded theory or schema analysis to discover even more themes.

Jehn and Doucet are not the only researchers ever to combine different analytic techniques. In a series of articles on young adult "occasional" drug users, Agar (1979, 1980, 1983) used grounded theory methods to build models of behavior. He then used classical content analysis to test his hypotheses. Agar conducted and transcribed three interviews with each of his three informants. In his 1979 article, Agar describes his initial, intuitive analysis. He

pulled all the statements that pertained to informants' interactions or assessments of other people. He then looked at the statements and sorted them into piles based on their content. He named each pile as a theme and assessed how the themes interacted. He found that he had three piles. The first contained statements in which the informant was expressing negative feelings toward a person in a dominant social position. The second was made up of statements emphasizing the other's knowledge or awareness. The statements in the third small cluster emphasized the importance of change or openness to new experiences.

From this intuitive analysis, Agar felt that his informants were telling him that those in authority were only interested in displaying their authority unless they had knowledge or awareness; that knowledge or awareness comes through openness to new experience; and that most in authority are closed to new experience or change.

To test his intuitive understanding of the data, Agar (1983) used all the statements from a single informant and coded the statements for their role type (kin, friend/acquaintance, educational, occupational, or other), power (dominant, symmetrical, subordinate, or undetermined), and affect (positive, negative, ambivalent, or absent). Agar was particularly interested in whether negative sentiments were expressed toward those in dominant social roles. For one informant, Agar found that out of 40 statements coded as dominant, 32 were coded negative and 8 were coded positive. For the 36 statements coded as symmetrical, 20 were coded positive and 16 negative, lending support to his original theory.

Next, Agar looked closely at the deviant cases—the 8 statements where the informant expressed positive affect toward a person in a dominant role. These counterexamples suggested that the positive affect was expressed toward a dominant social other when the social other possessed, or was communicating to the informant, knowledge that the informant valued.

Finally, Agar (1980) developed a more systematic questionnaire to test his hypothesis further. He selected 12 statements, 4 from each of the control, knowledge, and change themes identified earlier. He matched these statements with eight roles from the informant's transcript (father, mother, employer, teacher, friend, wife, coworker, and teammate). Agar then returned to his informant and asked if the resulting statements were true, false, or irrelevant. (In no case did the informant report "irrelevant.") Agar then compared the informant's responses to his original hypotheses. He found that on balance his hypotheses were correct, but discrepancies between his expectations and his results suggested areas for further research.

These examples show that investigators can apply one technique to different kinds of data and they can apply multiple techniques to the same data set. Text analysis is used by avowed positivists and interpretivists alike. As we have argued elsewhere (Bernard, 1993; Bernard & Ryan, 1998), methods are simply tools that belong to everyone.

◆ What's Next?

We do not want to minimize the profound *intellectual* differences in the epistemological positions of positivists and interpretivists. We think, however, that when researchers can move easily and cheaply between qualitative and quantitative data collection and analysis, the distinctions between the two epistemological positions will become of less *practical* importance. That is, as researchers recognize the full array of tools at their disposal, and as these tools become easier to use, the pragmatics of research will lessen the distinction between qualitative and quantitative data and analysis.

The process is under way—and is moving fast—with the development of increasingly useful software tools for qualitative data analysis. Useful tools create markets, and market needs create increasingly useful tools. Qualitative data analysis packages (ATLAS/ti, NUD•IST, Code-A-Text, the Ethnograph, AnSWR, and others) have improved dramatically over the past few years (Fischer, 1994; Kelle, 1995; Weitzman & Miles, 1995). These products, and

others, make it easier and easier for researchers to identify themes, build codebooks, mark text, create memos, and develop theoretical models. Based loosely on a grounded theory type of approach to qualitative analysis, many program suites have recently folded in techniques from classical content analysis. Several programs, for example, allow researchers to export data to matrices that they can then analyze using other programs.

Investigators, however, remain constrained by program-defined units of analysis—usually marked blocks of text or informants. Researchers need the flexibility to create matrices on demand, whether they be word-by-theme or word-by-informant matrices for word analysis and sentence-by-code or paragraph-by-code matrices for content analysis. A series of word analysis functions would greatly enhance the automated coding features found in programs that are geared to the interests of scholars in the grounded theory school. Investigators should be able to code a section of text using grounded theory, then identify the key words associated with each theme. They should be able to use key words to search for additional occurrences of the theme in large corpuses of text.

When programs make it easy to use multiple coders and to identify intercoder agreements and disagreements systematically, researchers will be better able to describe themes and to train assistants. Adding a variety of measures for calculating intercoder agreement, which only some programs do, would also be helpful. Some programs offer researchers the option of recording the marking behavior of multiple coders, yet offer no direct way to measure intercoder agreement.

The evolution of text analysis software is just beginning. Some 15 years ago, spell checkers, thesauruses, and scalable fonts were all sold separately. Today, these functions are integrated into all full-featured word-processing packages. Just 10 years ago, graphics programs were sold separately from programs that do statistical analysis. Today, graphics functions are integrated into all full-featured packages for statistical analysis. As programmers of text analysis software compete for market share, packages will become more inclusive, incorporating methods from both sides of the epistemological divide. It can't happen too soon.

■ Notes

1. MDS displays are highly evocative. They beg to be interpreted. In fact, they *must* be interpreted. Why are some illnesses at the top of Figure 29.3 and some at the bottom? We think the illnesses at the top are more of the chronic variety, whereas those at the bottom are more acute. We also think that the illnesses on the left are less serious than those on the right. We can test ideas like these by asking key informants to help us understand the arrangement of the illnesses in the MDS plot. (For more examples of mental maps, see Albert, 1991; D'Andrade et al., 1972; Erickson, 1997.) (There is a formal method, called property fitting analysis, or PROFIT, for testing ideas about the distribution of items in an MDS map. This method is based on linear regression. See Kruskal & Wish, 1978.)

2. Alternatively, profile matrices (the usual thing-by-variable attribute matrix ubiquitous in the social sciences) can be converted to similarity matrices (thing-by-thing matrices in which the cells contain measures of similarity among pairs of things) and then analyzed with MDS (for step-by-step instructions, see Borgatti, 1999).

■ References

Agar, M. (1979). Themes revisited: Some problems in cognitive anthropology. *Discourse Processes, 2,* 11-31.

Agar, M. (1980). Getting better quality stuff: Methodological competition in an interdisciplinary niche. *Urban Life, 9,* 34-50.

Agar, M. (1983). Microcomputers as field tools. *Computers and the Humanities, 17,* 19-26.

Agar, M. (1996). *Speaking of ethnography* (2nd ed.). Thousand Oaks, CA: Sage.

Agar, M., & Hobbs, J. (1985). How to grow schemata out of interviews. In J. W. D.

Dougherty (Ed.), *Directions in cognitive anthropology* (pp. 413-431). Urbana: University of Illinois Press.

Albert, S. M. (1991). Cognition of caregiving tasks: Multidimensional scaling of the caregiver task domain. *The Gerontologist, 31,* 726-734.

Allen, J. T., & Italie, G. (1954). *A concordance to Euripides.* Berkeley: University of California Press.

Araujo, L. (1995). Designing and refining hierarchical coding frames. In U. Kelle (Ed.), *Computer-aided qualitative data analysis: Theory, methods and practice* (pp. 96-104). London: Sage.

Barkin, S., Ryan, G. W., & Gelberg, L. (1999). What clinicians can do to further youth violence primary prevention: A qualitative study. *Injury Prevention, 5,* 53-58.

Barnett, G. A., & Danowski, J. A. (1992). The structure of communication: A network analysis of the International Communication Association. *Human Communication Research, 19,* 164-285.

Becker, H. S. (1998). *Tricks of the trade: How to think about your research while you're doing it.* Chicago: University of Chicago Press.

Becker, H. S., Geer, B., Hughes, E. C., & Strauss, A. L. (1961). *Boys in white: Student culture in medical school.* Chicago: University of Chicago Press.

Berelson, B. (1952). *Content analysis in communication research.* Glencoe, IL: Free Press.

Bernard, H. R. (1991). About text management and computers. *CAM Newsletter, 3*(1), 1-4, 7, 12.

Bernard, H. R. (1993). Methods belong to all of us. In R. Borofsky (Ed.), *Assessing cultural anthropology* (pp. 168-178). New York: McGraw-Hill.

Bernard, H. R. (1994). *Research methods in anthropology: Qualitative and quantitative approaches* (2nd ed.). Walnut Creek, CA: AltaMira.

Bernard, H. R., & Ashton-Voyoucalos, S. (1976). Return migration to Greece. *Journal of the Steward Anthropological Society, 8*(1), 31-51.

Bernard, H. R., & Ryan, G. W. (1998). Qualitative and quantitative methods of text analysis. In H. R. Bernard (Ed.), *Handbook of methods in cultural anthropology* (pp. 595-646). Walnut Creek, CA: AltaMira.

Bernard, H. R., Ryan, G. W., & Borgatti, S. (1999). *Green cognition and behaviors.* Report submitted to Ford Research Laboratories, Dearborn, MI.

Bessinger, J. B. (1969). *A concordance to Beowulf.* Ithaca, NY: Cornell University Press.

Bloor, M. (1976). Bishop Berkeley and the adenotonsillectomy dilemma. *Sociology, 10,* 43-61.

Bloor, M. (1978). On the analysis of observational data: A discussion of the worth and uses of inductive techniques and respondent validation. *Sociology, 12,* 545-557.

Bogdan, R. C., & Biklen, S. K. (1992). *Qualitative research for education: An introduction to theory and methods* (2nd ed.). Boston: Allyn & Bacon.

Borgatti, S. P. (1992). *ANTHROPAC 4.0.* Columbia, SC: Analytic Technologies. Available Internet: http://www.analytictech.com

Borgatti, S. P. (1998). The methods. In V. C. De Munck & E. J. Sobo (Eds.), *Using methods in the field: A practical introduction and casebook* (pp. 249-252). Walnut Creek, CA: AltaMira.

Borgatti, S. P. (1999). Elicitation methods for cultural domain analysis. In J. Schensul, M. LeCompte, S. Borgatti, & B. Nastasi (Eds.), *The ethnographer's toolkit: Vol. 3. Enhanced ethnographic methods* (pp. 115-151). Walnut Creek, CA: AltaMira.

Boster, J. (1994). The successive pile sort. *Cultural Anthropology Methods Journal, 6*(2), 11-12.

Bradley, C., Moore, C. C., Burton, M. L., & White, D. R. (1990). A cross-cultural historical analysis of subsistence change. *American Anthropologist, 92,* 447-457.

Brouwer, M., Clark, C. C., Gerbner, G., & Krippendorf, K. (1969). The television world of violence. In R. K. Baker & S. J. Ball (Eds.), *Mass media and violence: A report to the National Commission on the Causes and Prevention of Violence* (pp. 311-339, 519-591). Washington, DC: Government Printing Office.

Bulmer, M. (1979). Concepts in the analysis of qualitative data. *Sociological Review, 27,* 651-677.

Burton, D. M. (1981a). Automated concordances and word indexes: The early sixties and the early centers. *Computers and the Humanities, 15,* 83-100.

Burton, D. M. (1981b). Automated concordances and word indexes: The process, the programs, and the products. *Computers and the Humanities, 15,* 139-154.

Burton, D. M. (1982). Automated concordances and word indexes: Machine decisions and editorial revisions. *Computers and the Humanities, 16,* 195-218.

Campbell, D. T. (1957). Factors relevant to the validity of experiments in social settings. *Psychological Bulletin, 54,* 297-312.

Campbell, D. T., & Stanley, J. C. (1963). *Experimental and quasi-experimental designs for research.* Chicago: Rand McNally.

Carey, J. W., Morgan, M., & Oxtoby, M. J. (1996). Intercoder agreement in analysis of responses to open-ended interview questions: Examples from tuberculosis research. *Cultural Anthropology Methods Journal, 8*(3), 1-5.

Carley, K. (1993). Coding choices for textual analysis: A comparison of content analysis and map analysis. In P. Marsden (Ed.), *Sociological methodology* (pp. 75-126). Oxford: Blackwell.

Carley, K. (1997). Network text analysis: The network position of concepts. In C. W. Roberts (Ed.), *Text analysis for the social sciences: Methods for drawing statistical inferences from texts and transcripts* (pp. 79-100). Mahwah, NJ: Lawrence Erlbaum.

Carley, K., & Kaufer, D. S. (1993). Semantic connectivity: An approach for analyzing semantic networks. *Communication Theory, 3,* 182-213.

Carley, K., & Palmquist, P. (1992). Extracting, representing, and analyzing mental models. *Social Forces, 70,* 601-636.

Carmines, E. G., & Zeller, R. A. (1979). *Reliability and validity assessment.* Beverly Hills, CA: Sage.

Casson, R. (1983). Schemata in cultural anthropology. *Annual Review of Anthropology, 12,* 429-462.

Charmaz, K. (1990). "Discovering" chronic illness: Using grounded theory. *Social Science and Medicine, 30,* 1161-1172.

Cohen, J. (1960). A coefficient of agreement for nominal scales. *Educational and Psychological Measurement, 20,* 37-48.

Colby, B. N. (1966). The analysis of culture content and the patterning of narrative concern in texts. *American Anthropologist, 68,* 374-388.

Conklin, H. (1955). Hanunóo color categories. *Southwest Journal of Anthropology, 11,* 339-344.

Cook, T. D., & Campbell, D. T. (1979). *Quasi-experimentation: Design and analysis issues for field settings.* Chicago: Rand McNally.

Cowan, G., & O'Brien, M. (1990). Gender and survival versus death in slasher films: A content analysis. *Sex Roles, 23*(3-4), 187-196.

Crabtree, B. F., & Miller, W. L. (1992). A template approach to text analysis: Developing and using codebooks. In B. F. Crabtree & W. L. Miller (Eds.), *Doing qualitative research* (pp. 93-109). Newbury Park, CA: Sage.

Craig, R. T. (1981). Generalization of Scott's index of intercoder agreement. *Public Opinion Quarterly, 45,* 260-264.

Cressey, D. R. (1971). *Other people's money: A study in the social psychology of embezzlement.* Montclair, NJ: Patterson Smith. (Original work published 1953)

D'Andrade, R. (1991). The identification of schemas in naturalistic data. In M. J. Horowitz (Ed.), *Person schemas and maladaptive interpersonal patterns* (pp. 279-301). Chicago: University of Chicago Press.

D'Andrade, R. (1995). *The development of cognitive anthropology.* Cambridge: Cambridge University Press.

D'Andrade, R., Quinn, N., Nerlove, S., & Romney, A. K. (1972). Categories of disease in American-English and Mexican-Spanish. In A. K. Romney et al. (Eds.), *Multidimensional scaling: Theory and applications in the behavioral sciences* (Vol. 2, pp. 9-54). New York: Seminar.

Danielson, W. A., & Lasorsa, D. L. (1997). Perceptions of social change: 100 years of front-page content in the *New York Times* and the *Los Angeles Times.* In C. W. Roberts (Ed.), *Text analysis for the social sciences: Methods for drawing statistical inferences from texts and transcripts* (pp. 103-116). Mahwah, NJ: Lawrence Erlbaum.

Danowski, J. A. (1982). A network-based content analysis methodology for computer-mediated communication: An illustration with a computer bulletin board. In M.

Burgoon (Ed.), *Communication yearbook 6* (pp. 904-925). Beverly Hills, CA: Sage.

Danowski, J. A. (1993). Network analysis of message content. In W. D. Richards & G. A. Barnett (Eds.), *Progress in communication science* (Vol. 12, pp. 197-221). Norwood, NJ: Ablex.

Darton, M. (1976). *Modern concordance to the New Testament.* Garden City, NY: Doubleday.

Deese, J. (1969). Conceptual categories in the study of content. In G. Gerbner, O. R. Holsti, K. Krippendorf, W. J. Paisley, & P. J. Stone (Eds.), *The analysis of communication content: Developments in scientific theories and computer techniques* (pp. 39-56). New York: John Wiley.

Denzin, N. K. (1978). *The research act: A theoretical introduction to sociological methods* (2nd ed.). New York: McGraw-Hill.

Denzin, N. K. (1997). *Interpretive ethnography: Ethnographic practices for the 21st century.* Thousand Oaks, CA: Sage.

Dey, I. (1993). *Qualitative data analysis: A user-friendly guide for social scientists.* London: Routledge & Kegan Paul.

Doerfel, M. L., & Barnett, G. A. (1996). The use of Catpac for text analysis. *Cultural Anthropology Methods Journal, 8*(2), 4-7.

Drass, K. (1980). The analysis of qualitative data: A computer program. *Urban Life, 9,* 332-353.

Ember, C. R., & Ember, M. (1992). Resource unpredictability, mistrust, and war: A cross-cultural study. *Journal of Conflict Resolution, 36,* 242-262.

Erickson, P. (1997). Contraceptive methods: Do Hispanic adolescents and their family planning care providers think about contraceptive methods the same way? *Medical Anthropology, 17,* 65-82.

Fan, D. P., & Shaffer, C. L. (1990). Use of open-ended essays and computer content analysis to survey college students' knowledge of AIDS. *College Health, 38,* 221-229.

Farringdon, J. M., & Farringdon, M. G. (1980). *A concordance and word-lists to the poems of Dylan Thomas.* Swansea, England: Ariel House.

Fielding, N. G., & Fielding, J. L. (1986). *Linking data.* Beverly Hills, CA: Sage.

Fischer, M. D. (1994). *Applications in computing for social anthropologists.* London: Routledge.

Fjellman, S. M., & Gladwin, H. (1985). Haitian family patterns of migration to South Florida. *Human Organization, 44,* 301-312.

Fleisher, M. S., & Harrington, J. A. (1998). Freelisting: Management at a women's federal prison camp. In V. C. De Munck & E. J. Sobo (Eds.), *Using methods in the field: A practical introduction and casebook* (pp. 69-84). Walnut Creek, CA: AltaMira.

Fleiss, J. L. (1971). Measuring nominal scale agreement among many raters. *Psychological Bulletin, 76,* 378-382.

Frake, C. O. (1962). The ethnographic study of cognitive systems. In T. Gladwin & W. C. Sturtevant (Eds.), *Anthropology and human behavior* (pp. 72-85). Washington, DC: Anthropology Association of Washington.

Frake, C. O. (1964). Notes on queries in ethnography. *American Anthropologist, 66,* 132-145.

Furbee, L. (1996). *The religion of politics in Chiapas: Founding a cult of communicating saints.* Paper presented at the 96th Annual Meeting of the American Anthropological Association, San Francisco.

Furbee, L., & Benfer, R. (1983). Cognitive and geographic maps: Study of individual variation among Tojolabal Mayans. *American Anthropologist, 85,* 305-333.

Garro, L. (1998). On the rationality of decision-making studies: Part 1. Decision models of treatment choice. *Medical Anthropology Quarterly, 12,* 319-340.

Gatewood, J. B. (1983). Deciding where to fish: The skipper's dilemma in Southeast Alaskan salmon seining. *Coastal Zone Management Journal, 10,* 347-367.

George, A. L. (1959). Quantitative and qualitative approaches to content analysis. In I. de S. Pool (Ed.), *Trends in content analysis* (pp. 7-32). Urbana: University of Illinois Press.

Gerbner, G., Holsti, O. R., Krippendorf, K., Paisley, W. J., & Stone, P. J. (Eds.). (1969). *The analysis of communication content: Developments in scientific theories and computer techniques* New York: John Wiley.

Gladwin, C. (1989). *Ethnographic decision tree modeling.* Newbury Park, CA: Sage.

Gladwin, H. (1971). *Decision making in the Cape Coast (Fante) fishing and fish marketing system.* Unpublished doctoral dissertation, Stanford University.

Glaser, B. G. (1978). *Theoretical sensitivity.* Mill Valley, CA: Sociology Press.

Glaser, B. G., & Strauss, A. L. (1967). *The discovery of grounded theory: Strategies for qualitative research.* Chicago: Aldine.

Goodenough, W. H. (1956). Componential analysis and the study of meaning. *Language, 32,* 195-216.

Gottschalk, L. A., & Bechtel, R. J. (1993). *Psychological and neuropsychiatric assessment applying the Gottschalk-Gleser content analysis method to verbal sample analysis using the Gottschalk-Bechtel computer scoring system.* Palo Alto, CA: Mind Garden.

Guba, E. G. (1981). Criteria for assessing the trustworthiness of naturalistic inquiries. *Educational Communications and Technology Journal, 29,* 75-92.

Guba, E. G., & Lincoln, Y. S. (1982). Epistemological and methodological bases for naturalistic inquiry. *Educational Communications and Technology Journal, 30,* 233-252.

Hammersley, M. (1992). *What's wrong with ethnography? Methodological explorations.* London: Routledge.

Harman, R. C. (1998). Triad questionnaires: Old age in Karen and Maya cultures. In V. C. De Munck & E. J. Sobo (Eds.), *Using methods in the field: A practical introduction and casebook* (pp. 121-138). Walnut Creek, CA: AltaMira.

Hartigan, J. A. (1975). *Clustering algorithms.* New York: John Wiley.

Hatch, E., & Redpath, H. (1954). *A concordance to the Septuagint and the other Greek versions of the Old Testament.* Graz, Austria: Akademische Druck-u. Verlagsanstalt.

Henley, N. M. (1969). A psychological study of the semantics of animal terms. *Journal of Verbal Learning and Verbal Behavior, 8,* 176-184.

Hill, C. E. (1998). Decision modeling: Its use in medical anthropology. In V. C. De Munck & E. J. Sobo (Eds.), *Using methods in the field: A practical introduction and casebook* (pp. 139-164). Walnut Creek, CA: AltaMira.

Hirschman, E. C. (1987). People as products: Analysis of a complex marketing exchange. *Journal of Marketing, 51,* 98-108.

Holland, D. (1985). From situation to impression: How Americans get to know themselves and one another. In J. W. D. Dougherty (Ed.), *Directions in cognitive anthropology* (pp. 389-412). Urbana: University of Illinois Press.

Holsti, O. R. (1966). External conflict and internal consensus: The Sino-Soviet case. In P. J. Stone, D. C. Dunphy, M. S. Smith, & D. M. Ogilvie (Eds.), *The General Inquirer: A computer approach to content analysis* (pp. 343-358). Cambridge: MIT Press.

Holsti, O. R. (1969). *Content analysis for the social sciences and humanities.* Reading, MA: Addison-Wesley.

Hunt, J. G., & Ropo, A. (1995). Multi-level leadership: Grounded theory and mainstream theory applied to the case of General Motors. *Leadership Quarterly, 6,* 379-412.

Imrich D. J., Mullin, C., & Linz, D. (1995). Measuring the extent of prejudicial pretrial publicity in major American newspapers: A content analysis. *Journal of Communication, 45*(3), 94-117.

Irurita, V. F. (1996). Hidden dimensions revealed: Progressive grounded theory study of quality care in the hospital. *Qualitative Health Research, 6,* 331-349.

Jakobson, R., & Halle, M. (1956). *Fundamentals of language.* The Hague: Mouton.

Jang, H.-Y., & Barnett, G. A. (1994, September). Cultural differences in organizational communication: A semantic network analysis. *Bulletin de Méthodologie Sociologique, 44,* 31-59.

Jehn, K. A., & Doucet, L. (1996). Developing categories from interview data: Part 1. Text analysis and multidimensional scaling. *Cultural Anthropology Methods Journal, 8*(2), 15-16.

Jehn, K. A., & Doucet, L. (1997). Developing categories for interview data: Part 2. Consequences of different coding and analysis strategies in understanding text. *Cultural Anthropology Methods Journal, 9*(1), 1-7.

Jehn, K. A., & Werner, O. (1993). Hapax Legomenon II: Theory, a thesaurus, and word frequency. *Cultural Anthropology Methods Journal, 5*(1), 8-10.

Johnson, A., & Price-Williams, D. R. (1997). *Oedipus ubiquitous: The family complex in world folk literature.* Stanford, CA: Stanford University Press.

Johnson, S. C. (1967). Hierarchical clustering schemes. *Psychometrika, 32,* 241-253.

Kaid, L. L., Tedesco, J. C., & McKinnon, L. M. (1996). Presidential ads as nightly news: A content analysis of 1988 and 1992 televised Adwatches. *Journal of Broadcasting Electronic Media, 40,* 297-308.

Kassis, H. (1983). *A concordance of the Qur'an.* Berkeley: University of California Press.

Kearney, M. H., Murphy, S., Irwin, K., & Rosenbaum, M. (1995). Salvaging self: A grounded theory of pregnancy on crack cocaine. *Nursing Research, 44,* 208-213.

Kearney, M. H., Murphy, S., & Rosenbaum, M. (1994). Mothering on crack cocaine: A grounded theory analysis. *Social Science and Medicine, 38,* 351-361.

Kelle, U. (1995). An overview of computer-aided methods in qualitative research. In U. Kelle (Ed.), *Computer-aided qualitative data analysis: Theory, methods and practice* (pp. 1-18). London: Sage.

Kelly, E. F., & Stone, P. J. (1975). *Computer recognition of English word senses.* Amsterdam: North-Holland.

Kempton, W. (1987). Two theories of home heat control. In D. Holland & N. Quinn (Eds.), *Cultural models in language and thought* (pp. 222-242). Cambridge: Cambridge University Press.

Kirchler, E. (1992). Adorable woman, expert man: Changing gender images of women and men in management. *European Journal of Social Psychology, 22,* 363-373.

Kirk, J., & Miller, M. L. (1986). *Reliability and validity in qualitative research.* Beverly Hills, CA: Sage.

Kolbe, R. H., & Albanese, J. P. (1996). Man to man: A content analysis of sole-male images in male-audience magazines. *Journal of Advertising, 25*(4), 1-20.

Kracauer, S. (1953. The challenge of qualitative content analysis. *Public Opinion Quarterly, 16,* 631-642.

Krippendorf, K. (1980). *Content analysis: An introduction to its methodology.* Beverly Hills, CA: Sage.

Kruskal, J. B., & Wish, M. (1978). *Multidimensional scaling.* Beverly Hills, CA: Sage.

Kurasaki, K. S. (1997). *Ethnic identity and its development among third-generation Japanese*

Americans. Unpublished doctoral dissertation, DePaul University.

Laffal, J. (1990). *A concept dictionary of English, with computer programs for content analysis.* Essex, CT: Gallery.

Laffal, J. (1995). A concept analysis of Jonathan Swift's *A tale of a tub* and *Gulliver's travels. Computers and the Humanities, 29,* 339-361.

Leinhardt, G. (1987). Development of an expert explanation: An analysis of a sequence of subtraction lessons. *Cognition and Instruction, 4,* 225-282.

Leinhardt, G. (1989). Math lessons: A contrast of novice and expert competence. *Journal for Research in Mathematics Education, 20*(1), 52-75.

Leinhardt, G., & Smith, D. A. (1985). Expertise in mathematics instruction: Subject matter knowledge. *Journal of Educational Psychology, 77,* 247-271.

Light, R. J. (1971). Measures of response agreement for qualitative data: Some generalizations and alternatives. *Psychological Bulletin, 76,* 365-377.

Lincoln, Y. S., & Guba, E. G. (1985). *Naturalistic inquiry.* Beverly Hills, CA: Sage.

Lindesmith, A. R. (1968). *Addiction and opiates.* Chicago: Aldine. (Original work published 1947)

Lofland, J., & Lofland, L. H. (1995). *Analyzing social settings* (3rd ed.). Belmont, CA: Wadsworth.

Lonkila, M. (1995). Grounded theory as an emerging paradigm for computer-assisted qualitative data analysis. In U. Kelle (Ed.), *Computer-aided qualitative data analysis: Theory, methods and practice* (pp. 41-51). London: Sage.

MacQueen, K. M., McLellan, E., Kay, K., & Milstein, B. (1998). Codebook development for team-based qualitative research. *Cultural Anthropology Methods Journal, 10*(2), 31-36.

Manning, P. K. (1982). Analytic induction. In R. Smith & P. K. Manning (Eds.), *Handbook of social science methods: Vol. 2. Qualitative methods* (pp. 273-302). New York: Harper.

Martindale, C., & McKenzie, D. (1995). On the utility of content analysis in author attribution: The Federalist. *Computers and the Humanities, 29,* 259-270.

Mathews, H. F., & Hill, C. (1990). Applying cognitive decision theory to the study of regional patterns of illness treatment choice. *American Anthropologist, 91,* 155-170.

McCleary, R. (1978). *Dangerous men: The sociology of parole.* Beverly Hills, CA: Sage.

McKinnon, A. (1993). The multi-dimensional concordance: A new tool for literary research. *Computers and the Humanities, 27,* 165-183.

McTavish, D. G., & Pirro, E. B. (1990). Contextual content analysis. *Quality and Quantity, 24,* 44-63.

Metzger, D., & Williams, G. (1966). Some procedures and results in the study of native categories: Tzeltal "firewood." *American Anthropologist, 68,* 389-407.

Miles, M. B. (1979). Qualitative data as an attractive nuisance: The problem of analysis. *Administrative Science Quarterly, 24,* 590-601.

Miles, M. B., & Huberman, A. M. (1994). *Qualitative data analysis: An expanded sourcebook* (2nd ed.). Thousand Oaks, CA: Sage.

Mingers, J. (1989a). An empirical comparison of pruning methods for decision tree induction. *Machine Learning, 4,* 227-243.

Mingers, J. (1989b). An empirical comparison of selection measures for decision-tree induction. *Machine Learning, 3,* 319-342.

Mitchell, S. K. (1979). Interobserver agreement, reliability, and generalizability of data collected in observational studies. *Psychological Bulletin, 86,* 376-390.

Morse, J. M. (1994). Designing funded qualitative research. In N. K. Denzin & Y. S. Lincoln (Eds.), *Handbook of qualitative research* (pp. 220-235). Thousand Oaks, CA: Sage.

Mosteller, F., & Wallace, D. L. (1964). *Inference and disputed authorship: The Federalist Papers.* Reading, MA: Addison-Wesley.

Murdock, G. P. (1971). *Outline of cultural materials* (4th rev. ed.). New Haven, CT: Human Relations Area Files.

Nolan, J., & Ryan, G. W. (in press). *Fear and loathing at the cinemaplex: Differences in gender perceptions and descriptions of slasher films.* Manuscript submitted for publication.

Ogilvie, D. M., Stone, P. J., & Schneidman, E. S. (1966). Some characteristics of genuine versus simulated suicide notes. In P. J. Stone, D. C. Dunphy, M. S. Smith, & D. M. Ogilvie

(Eds.), *The General Inquirer: A computer approach to content analysis* (pp. 527-535). Cambridge: MIT Press.

Osgood, C. (1959). The representational model and relevant research methods. In I. de S. Pool (Eds.), *Trends in content analysis* (pp. 33-88). Urbana: University of Illinois Press.

Palmquist, M., Carley, K., & Dale, T. (1997). Applications of computer-aided text analysis: Analyzing literary and nonliterary texts. In C. W. Roberts (Ed.), *Text analysis for the social sciences: Methods for drawing statistical inferences from texts and transcripts* (pp. 171-189). Mahwah, NJ: Lawrence Erlbaum.

Patterson, B. R., Bettini, L., & Nussbaum, J. F. (1993). The meaning of friendship across the life-span: Two studies. *Communication Quarterly, 41,* 145-160.

Patton, M. Q. (1990). *Qualitative evaluation and research methods* (2nd ed.). Newbury Park, CA: Sage.

Perchonock, N., & Werner, O. (1969). Navaho systems of classification. *Ethnology, 8,* 229-242.

Pool, I. de S. (1952). *Symbols of democracy.* Stanford, CA: Stanford University Press.

Pool, I. de S. (Ed.). (1959). *Trends in content analysis.* Urbana: University of Illinois Press.

Potts R., Runyan, D., Zerger, A., & Marchetti, K. (1996). A content analysis of safety behaviors of television characters: Implications for children's safety and injury. *Journal of Pediatric Psychology, 21,* 517-528.

Prendergast, G. L. (1971). *A complete concordance to the Iliad of Homer.* Hildesheim, Germany: G. Olms.

Price, L. (1987). Ecuadorian illness stories. In D. Holland & N. Quinn (Eds.), *Cultural models in language and thought* (pp. 313-342). Cambridge: Cambridge University Press.

Quinn, N. (1978). Do Mfantse fish sellers estimate probabilities in their heads? *American Ethnologist, 5,* 206-226.

Quinn, N. (1982). "Commitment" in American marriage: A cultural analysis. *American Ethnologist, 9,* 755-798.

Quinn, N. (1987). Convergent evidence for a cultural model of American marriage. In D. Holland & N. Quinn (Eds.), *Cultural models in language and thought* (pp. 173-192). Cambridge: Cambridge University Press.

Quinn, N. (1992). The motivational force of self-understanding: Evidence from wives' inner conflicts. In R. D'Andrade & C. Strauss (Eds.), *Human motives and cultural models* (pp. 90-126). New York: Cambridge University Press.

Quinn, N. (1996). Culture and contradiction: The case of Americans reasoning about marriage. *Ethos, 24,* 391-425.

Quinn, N. (1997). Research on shared task solutions. In C. Strauss & N. Quinn (Eds.), *A cognitive theory of cultural meaning* (pp. 137-188). Cambridge: Cambridge University Press.

Ragin, C. C. (1987). *The comparative method: Moving beyond qualitative and quantitative strategies.* Berkeley: University of California Press.

Ragin, C. C. (1994). Introduction to qualitative comparative analysis. In T. Janowski & A. M. Hicks (Eds.), *The comparative political economy of the welfare state* (pp. 299-317). Cambridge: Cambridge University Press.

Richards, T. J., & Richards, L. (1991). The NUD•IST qualitative data analysis system. *Qualitative Sociology, 14,* 307-325.

Robbins, M. C., & Nolan, J. M. (1997). A measure of dichotomous category bias in free listing tasks. *Cultural Anthropology Methods Journal, 9*(3), 8-12.

Roberts, C. W. (1997). A theoretical map for selecting among text analysis methods. In C. W. Roberts (Ed.), *Text analysis for the social sciences: Methods for drawing statistical inferences from texts and transcripts* (pp. 275-283). Mahwah, NJ: Lawrence Erlbaum.

Robinson, W. S. (1951). The logical structure of analytic induction. *American Sociological Review, 16,* 812-818.

Romme, A. G. L. (1995). Boolean comparative analysis of qualitative data: A methodological note. *Quality and Quantity, 29,* 317-329.

Roos, G. (1998). Pile sorting: "Kids like candy." In V. C. De Munck & E. J. Sobo (Eds.), *Using methods in the field: A practical introduction and casebook* (pp. 97-110). Walnut Creek, CA: AltaMira.

Rosenberg, S. D., Schnurr, P. P., & Oxman, T. E. (1990). Content analysis: A comparison of manual and computerized systems. *Journal of Personality Assessment, 54,* 298-310.

Rushforth, S. (1982). A structural semantic analysis of Bear Lake Athapaskan kinship classification. *American Ethnologist, 9, 559-577.*

Ryan, G. W. (1995). *Medical decision making among the Kom of Cameroon: Modeling how characteristics of illnesses, patients, caretakers, and compounds affect treatment choice in a rural community.* Unpublished doctoral dissertation, University of Florida, Gainesville.

Ryan, G. W. (1999). Measuring the typicality of text: Using multiple coders for more than just reliability and validity checks. *Human Organization, 58*(3), 313-322.

Ryan, G. W., & Martínez, H. (1996). Can we predict what mothers do? Modeling childhood diarrhea in rural Mexico. *Human Organization, 55,* 47-57.

Ryan, G. W., & Weisner, T. (1996). Analyzing words in brief descriptions: Fathers and mothers describe their children. *Cultural Anthropology Methods Journal, 8*(3), 13-16.

Sandelowski, M. (1995a). Qualitative analysis: What it is and how to begin. *Research in Nursing and Health, 18,* 371-375.

Sandelowski, M. (1995b). Sample size in qualitative research. *Research in Nursing and Health, 18,* 179-183.

Schank, R. C., & Abelson, R. P. (1977). *Scripts, plans, goals, and understanding: An enquiry into human knowledge structures.* Hillsdale, NJ: Lawrence Erlbaum.

Schnegg, M., & Bernard, H. R. (1996). Words as actors: A method for doing semantic network analysis. *Cultural Anthropology Methods Journal, 8*(2), 7-10.

Schnurr, P. P., Rosenberg, S. D., Oxman, T. E., & Tucker, G. (1986). A methodological note on content analysis: Estimates of reliability. *Journal of Personality Assessment, 50,* 601-609.

Schweizer, T. (1991). The power struggle in a Chinese community, 1950-1980: A social network analysis of the duality of actors and events. *Journal of Quantitative Anthropology, 3,* 19-44.

Schweizer, T. (1996). Actor and event orderings across time: Lattice representation and Boolean analysis of the political disputes in Chen Village, China. *Social Networks, 18,* 247-266.

Seidel, J., & Kelle, U. (1995). Different functions of coding in the analysis of textual data. In U. Kelle (Ed.), *Computer-aided qualitative data analysis: Theory, methods and practice* (pp. 52-61). London: Sage.

Shapiro, G. (1997). The future of coders: Human judgments in a world of sophisticated software. In C. W. Roberts (Ed.), *Text analysis for the social sciences: Methods for drawing statistical inferences from texts and transcripts* (pp. 225-238). Mahwah, NJ: Lawrence Erlbaum.

Shelley, G. A. (1992). *The social networks of people with end-stage renal disease: Comparing hemodialysis and peritoneal dialysis patients.* Unpublished doctoral dissertation, University of Florida.

Sleath, B., Svarstad, B., & Roter, D. (1997). Physician versus patient initiation of psychotropic prescribing in primary care settings: A content analysis of audiotapes. *Social Science and Medicine, 44,* 541-548.

Smith, J. J. (1993). Using ANTHROPAC 3.5 and a spreadsheet to compute a free-list salience index. *Cultural Anthropology Methods Journal, 5*(3), 1-3.

Smith, J. J., & Borgatti, S. P. (1998). Salience counts—and so does accuracy: Correcting and updating a measure for free-list-item salience. *Journal of Linguistic Anthropology, 7,* 208-209.

Sohier, R. (1993). Filial reconstruction: A theory on development through adversity. *Qualitative Health Research, 3,* 465-492.

Spears, N. E, Mowen, J. C., & Chakraborty, G. (1996). Symbolic role of animals in print advertising: Content analysis and conceptual development. *Journal of Business Research, 37*(2), 87-95.

Spiggle, S. (1986). Measuring social values: A content analysis of Sunday comics and underground comix. *Journal of Consumer Research, 13,* 100-113.

Spradley, J. P. (1979). *The ethnographic interview.* New York: Holt, Rinehart & Winston.

Stone, P. J., Dunphy, D. C., Smith, M. S., & Ogilvie, D. M. (Eds.). (1966). *The General Inquirer: A computer approach to content analysis.* Cambridge: MIT Press.

Strauss, A. L. (1987). *Qualitative analysis for social scientists.* New York: Cambridge University Press.

Strauss, A. L., & Corbin, J. (1990). *Basics of qualitative research: Grounded theory procedures and techniques.* Newbury Park, CA: Sage.

Strauss, A. L., & Corbin, J. (Eds.). (1997). *Grounded theory in practice.* Thousand Oaks, CA: Sage.

Strauss, C. (1992). What makes Tony run? Schemas as motive reconsidered. In R. D'Andrade & C. Strauss (Eds.), *Human motives and cultural models* (pp. 191-224). New York: Cambridge University Press.

Strauss, C. (1997). Research on cultural discontinuities. In C. Strauss & N. Quinn (Eds.), *A cognitive theory of cultural meaning* (pp. 210-251). Cambridge: Cambridge University Press.

Taylor, S. J., & Bogdan, R. C. (1984). *Introduction to qualitative research methods: The search for meanings* (2nd ed.). New York: John Wiley.

Tesch, R. (1990). *Qualitative research: Analysis types and software tools.* New York: Falmer.

Trost, J. E. (1986). Statistically nonrepresentative stratified sampling: A sampling technique for qualitative studies. *Qualitative Sociology, 9,* 54-57.

Van Maanen, J., Miller, M., & Johnson, J. (1982). An occupation in transition: Traditional and modern forms of commercial fishing. *Work and Occupations, 9,* 193-216.

Viney, L. L. (1983). The assessment of psychological states through content analysis of verbal communications. *Psychological Bulletin, 94,* 542-563.

Waitzkin, H., & Britt, T. (1993). Processing narratives of self-destructive behavior in routine medical encounters: Health promotion, disease prevention, and the discourse of health care. *Social Science and Medicine, 36,* 1121-1136.

Wallace, A. F. C. (1962). Culture and cognition. *Science, 135,* 352-357.

Weber, R. (1990). *Basic content analysis* (2nd ed.). Newbury Park, CA: Sage.

Weitzman, E. A., & Miles, M. B. (1995). *Computer programs for qualitative data analysis: A software sourcebook.* Thousand Oaks, CA: Sage.

Weller, S. C. (1998). Structured interviewing and questionnaire construction. In H. R. Bernard (Ed.), *Handbook of methods in cultural anthropology* (pp. 365-409). Walnut Creek, CA: AltaMira.

Weller, S. C., & Romney, A. K. (1988). *Systematic data collection.* Newbury Park, CA: Sage.

Weller, S. C., & Romney, A. K. (1990). *Metric scaling: Correspondence analysis.* Newbury Park, CA: Sage.

Weller, S. C., Ruebush, T. K., II, & Klein, R. E. (1997). Predicting treatment-seeking behavior in Guatemala: A comparison of the health services research and decision-theoretic approaches. *Medical Anthropology Quarterly, 11,* 224-245.

Werner, O., & Schoepfle, G. M. (1987). *Systematic fieldwork: Vol. 2. Ethnographic analysis and data management.* Newbury Park, CA: Sage.

White, D. R., & Burton, M. L. (1988). Causes of polygyny: Ecology, economy, kinship, and warfare. *American Anthropologist, 90,* 871-887.

Willms, D. G., Best, J. A., Taylor, D. W., Gilbert, J. R., Wilson, D. M. C., Lindsay, E. A., & Singer, J. (1990). A systematic approach for using qualitative methods in primary prevention research. *Medical Anthropology Quarterly, 4,* 391-409.

Wilson, H. S., & Hutchinson, S. A. (1996). Methodological mistakes in grounded theory. *Nursing Research, 45,* 122-124.

Wodak, R. (1992). Strategies in text production and text comprehension: A new perspective. In D. Stein (Ed.), *Cooperating with written texts* (pp. 493-528). New York: Mouton de Gruyter.

Wright, K. B. (1997). Shared ideology in Alcoholics Anonymous: A grounded theory approach. *Journal of Health Communication, 2*(2), 83-99.

Yoder, S. (1995). Examining ethnomedical diagnoses and treatment choices for diarrheal disorders in Lubumbashi Swahili. *Medical Anthropology, 16,* 211-248.

Young, J. C. (1978). Illness categories and action strategies in a Tarascan town. *American Ethnologist, 5,* 81-97.

Young, J. C. (1980). A model of illness treatment decisions in a Tarascan town. *American Ethnologist, 7,* 106-151.

Yule, G. U. (1968). *The statistical study of literary vocabulary.* Hamden, CT: Archon. (Original work published 1944)

Znaniecki, F. (1934). *The method of sociology.* New York: Farrar & Rinehart.

Zuell, C., Weber, R. P., & Mohler, P. (Eds.). (1989). *Computer-assisted text analysis for the social sciences: The General Inquirer III.* Mannheim, Germany: Center for Surveys, Methods, and Analysis (ZUMA).

30

SOFTWARE AND QUALITATIVE RESEARCH

◆ Eben A. Weitzman

The array of software available to support the work of qualitative researchers is maturing. A wide variety of useful tools are now available to support many different approaches to qualitative research. Most qualitative researchers can now find software that is appropriate to their analysis plans, the structure of their data, and their ease-of-use and cost preferences. However, making that appropriate match still requires systematic analysis of the needs of the project and the researcher(s), and careful comparison of the software options available at the time of purchase with an eye kept fixed firmly on those needs. There is still no one best program.

To help researchers understand what software can and cannot do to support their research efforts, understand both the potential benefits and pitfalls of using computers in qualitative research projects, and find software that is suited to their needs, I provide in this chapter (a)

an introduction to and overview of the role of software in qualitative research, (b) a discussion of the critical debates and concerns in the field about the impact and appropriateness of using qualitative data analysis (QDA) software, (c) guidelines for choosing software to match individual needs, and (d) an indication of future directions for both scholarship on the use of QDA software and development of such software.

◆ A Minihistory of the Use of Computers in Qualitative Research

Traditionally, qualitative researchers have carried out the mechanics of analysis by hand: typing up field notes and interviews, photocopying them, "coding" by marking them up with mark-

AUTHOR'S NOTE: My thanks to Norman Denzin, Nigel Fielding, Udo Kelle, Ray Lee, and Morten Levin for their comments on an earlier draft of this chapter.

ers or pencils, cutting and pasting the marked segments onto file cards, sorting and shuffling cards, and typing up their analyses. This picture has been slowly changing since the early to mid-1980s. At that point, some researchers were beginning to use word processors for the typing work, and just a few were beginning to experiment with database programs for storing and accessing their texts. Most qualitative methods textbooks at the time (e.g., Bogdan & Biklen, 1982; Goetz & LeCompte, 1984; Lofland & Lofland, 1984; Miles & Huberman, 1984) made little, if any, reference to the use of computers.

In the early 1980s, a couple of programs designed specifically for the analysis of qualitative data began to appear (Drass, 1980; Seidel & Clark, 1984; Shelly & Sibert, 1985). Early programs like QUALOG and the first versions of The Ethnograph and NUD•IST reflected the state of computing at that time. Researchers typically accomplished the coding of texts (tagging chunks of text with labels—codes—that indicate the conceptual categories the researcher wants to sort them into) by typing in line numbers and code names at a command prompt, and there was little or no facility for memoing or other annotation or markup of text. In comparison to marking up text with colored pencils, this felt awkward to many researchers. And computer support for the analysis of video or audio data was at best a fantasy.

But the landscape has changed dramatically, in terms of both software and the literature devoted to it. By the time the late Matt Miles and I wrote *Computer Programs for Qualitative Data Analysis* (Weitzman & Miles, 1995b), we reviewed no fewer than 24 different programs that were useful for analyzing qualitative data. Half of those programs had been developed specifically for qualitative data analysis, whereas the other half had been developed for more general-purpose applications, such as text search and storage. Since then, the field has continued to grow rapidly. Programs are being revised at a regular rate, new programs appear on the scene at the rate of one or two a year, and programs that don't find users disappear. There has been some convergence as good features in one program are imitated by the developers of others.

And there has also been divergence, as developers look for new and different ways to conceptualize support for analysis.

There are now tools available that can help researchers who are using a wide variety of research and analysis methodologies, from grounded theory to textual analysis to narrative analysis to interpretive interactionism. It is important to emphasize that software is not now, if it ever was, something that is relevant only to "positivist" or "quasi-positivist" approaches to qualitative research. If you see language in this chapter that does not match your approach, you may find it helpful to do some speculative translation. For example, if the discussion is about "verification" or "hypothesis testing" and your approach is postmodern, the discussion may seem irrelevant. But it may be that there is a way to understand the concept that makes sense from your perspective, such as "looking to see whether there is more material supporting, or contradicting, a certain assumption or interpretation." The same software tools that someone else might use for classical hypothesis testing might be very useful for *your* purposes.

Many programs now allow the researcher to specify relationships among codes and use these relationships in analysis, and to write memos and link them to text and codes. Some programs allow the researcher to create links between different points in the text (hypertext), and a small but growing handful allow the use of audio and video in place of, or in addition to, text. And there are a variety of approaches to linking categorical and quantitative data (e.g., demographics, test scores, quantitative ratings) to text and for exporting categorical and quantitative data (e.g., word frequencies or coding summaries) to quantitative analysis programs for statistical analysis. Finally, there are now some free programs available, notably two from the U.S. Centers for Disease Control: EZ-Text, which focuses on qualitative surveys, and AnSWR, intended for a more general range of qualitative data. The software continues to vary widely, and it remains very much the case that there is no one best program for all needs.

In parallel with the growth in software, literature reporting studies and commenting on the software has begun to appear regularly. There has been an outpouring of journal articles, a series of international conferences on computers and qualitative methodology, thoughtful books on the topic (Fielding & Lee, 1991, 1998; Kelle, 1995; Tesch, 1990; Weitzman & Miles, 1995b), and special journal issues (Mangabeira, 1996; Tesch, 1991).

Periodically, commentators have raised concerns about whether the range of available software is dominated by a particular approach, methodology, or epistemology (see, e.g., Coffey, Holbrook, & Atkinson, 1996; Lonkila, 1995). Although there is certainly room for further development to support certain specific analytic processes (I offer some suggestions later in this chapter, and the list appearing in the chapter titled "Reflections and Hopes" in Weitzman & Miles, 1995b, has only begun to be addressed), these concerns are clearly missing the mark. In this chapter, I suggest a wide variety of types of programs that are available to support a wide variety of research approaches. Qualitative researchers are not limited only to coding-oriented programs, or even to programs explicitly marketed to qualitative researchers. For example, as Fielding and Lee (1998) point out, there are a variety of options for those wishing to follow the suggestion of Coffey and Atkinson (1996) that text retrievers may be more helpful for discourse analysis than code-and-retrieve programs. Fielding and Lee go on to argue that

> developers of CAQDAS [computer-aided qualitative data analysis software] programs have increasingly included facilities for proximity searching, which might be useful for narrative analysis, and for "autocoding" which could be adapted to some kinds of semiotic analysis. The provision of new features in CAQDAS programs reflects the generally close relationship between users and developers characteristic of the field, and the general willingness of developers to incorporate features desired by users even if these do not always accord with the epistemological preferences of the developer. Since packages increasingly support procedures, routines and features which are new to qualitative analysis or make procedures possible that were not practicable without the power of the computer, it is less and less plausible either to argue that the software is merely an aid to code-and-retrieve or to argue that code-and-

 retrieve is the *sine qua non* of qualitative analysis. (p. 175)

I address these issues at more length through much of this chapter, particularly in the subsections below headed "False Hopes and Fears," "Real Hopes," and "Real Fears," and in the later section headed "Debates in the Field."

◆ What Software Can and Cannot Do

Simply put, software can provide tools to help you analyze qualitative data, but it cannot do the analysis for you, not in the same sense in which a statistical package like SPSS or SAS can do, say, multiple regression. Many researchers have had the hope—for others it is a fear—that the computer could somehow read the text and decide what it all means. That is, generally speaking, not the case.[1] Thus it is particularly important to emphasize that using software cannot be a substitute for learning data analysis methods: The researcher must know what needs to be done, and do it. The software provides tools to do it with.

The following are some of the things computers *can* be used for to facilitate the analysis process:

1. *Making notes* in the field;
2. *Writing up* or transcribing field notes;
3. *Editing:* correcting, extending, or revising field notes;
4. *Coding:* attaching key words or tags to segments of text, graphics, audio, or video to permit later retrieval;
5. *Storage:* keeping text in an organized database;
6. *Search and retrieval:* locating relevant segments of text and making them available for inspection;
7. *Data "linking":* connecting relevant data segments to each other, forming categories, clusters, or networks of information;
8. *Memoing:* writing reflective commentaries on some aspect of the data, theory, or method as a basis for deeper analysis;

9. *Content analysis:* counting frequencies, sequences, or locations of words and phrases;

10. *Data display:* placing selected or reduced data in a condensed, organized format, such as a matrix or network, for inspection;

11. *Conclusion drawing and verification:* aiding in the interpretation of displayed data and the testing or confirmation of findings;

12. *Theory building:* developing systematic, conceptually coherent explanations of findings; testing hypotheses;

13. *Graphic mapping:* creating diagrams that depict findings or theories;

14. *Report writing:* interim and final (adapted from Miles & Huberman, 1994, p. 44).

Obviously, many of these are things that researchers can do with a word processor. Other software, which is the focus of this chapter, helps with the other tasks. The developments seen in recent years have made it possible for researchers to do these things more and more easily, and more and more powerfully. In the section headed "Types and Functions of Software for QDA," below, you will find more specific details about what software can do. But first, consider some of the hopes and fears, both real and false, that people have concerning QDA software.

False Hopes and Fears

In Weitzman and Miles (1995b), we argue:

> As Pfaffenberger . . . points out, it's equally naïve to believe that a program is (a) a neutral technical tool or (b) an overdetermining monster. The issue is understanding a program's properties and presuppositions, and how they can support or constrain your thinking to produce unanticipated effects. (p. 330)

As already mentioned, many people apparently continue to believe that QDA software intends to *do* the data analysis. Skeptical researchers raise challenges to the notion of "dumping my text into a program and seeing what comes out."

Others express this more as a hope that if they buy the right program, they will not have to engage in the often very time-consuming process of analyzing all that text themselves. QDA software provides tools that help you do these things; it does not do them for you.

In an extension of this concern, many researchers have worried about the software going yet a step further and "building theory." But, as Miles and I also argued in 1995, "Software will never 'do' theory building for you . . . , but it can explicitly support your intellectual efforts, making it easier for you to think coherently about the meaning of your data" (Weitzman & Miles, 1995b, p. 330).

This situation may change in the coming years. There are some current efforts to use artificial intelligence (AI) approaches to get computers to interpret text. For example, the SPSS module TextSmart uses information about frequency of occurrence of words and proximity of words to each other to categorize text responses automatically. Microsoft Word97 has an "Auto Summarize" feature that aims to identify the most important "concepts" in a document according to word frequency. Other developers are thinking about using AI techniques to get software to participate in the theory-building process with researchers. These approaches rely on things like frequency to indicate importance and proximity in the text to indicate relatedness. For some qualitative researchers these are acceptable assumptions, but for many others they are not, and for such researchers the results of these approaches do not yield useful interpretations of text.

Real Hopes

What can we really expect to gain from the use of software? QDA software provides tools for searching, marking up, linking, and reorganizing the data, and representing and storing your own reflections, ideas, and theorizing. Some of it gives you tools for further exploration—which in some cases might amount to hypothesis testing or conclusion verification—based on your theorizing and interpretive work.

Consistency. Software can help with consistency. If I can search for *all* the places a given key word appears, or *all* the places where a given code or combination of codes was applied, or always see the relationship between two features of the data that I have recorded, it becomes possible for me to be more consistent in a couple of ways. I can be much more careful about not missing the data that contradict my brilliant, but wrong, new hypothesis. I can easily review all the data I assigned to a given conceptual category or theme and check to see if they (a) all belong together and (b) still seem to support the interpretation I started out with; if not, I can easily reorganize. (Note that the problem of my making bad interpretations has not been removed. But the kinds of facilities mentioned here can be tremendously helpful to competent researchers in checking their own work, as well as in allowing colleagues or research participants to check it and provide feedback.)

Speed. The speed of computers is a critical issue in making QDA software helpful. First, a caution: It can take time to learn to use a program, and once you have, it can take some time to prepare and set up the data for analysis. But once that is done, the speed of the computer quickly pays for that investment. Being able to search and re-search almost instantaneously encourages the researcher to conduct multiple searches to zero in on the data that really apply to a particular question. Being able to quickly re-sort a database, redefine codes, and reassign chunks of text enables and encourages the researcher to revise the analysis and the thinking about it whenever necessary. Being able to quickly pull together all the text for cells in a complex matrix display enables and encourages the researcher to run down provocative leads and new ideas—as well as worries that the current conclusions may be way off track—much more often and with much less cost.

An example from quantitative research may be instructive. In the days of slide rules, and even of handheld calculators, before statistical software was available, doing factor analysis was a months-long enterprise. Now a factor analysis can be run in minutes or seconds on a desktop computer. As a result, researchers can run factor analyses much more often, as part of other analyses rather than only as major undertakings of their own, and on multiple sets of scores in the same project. The speed of the computer alone can change what researchers even contemplate undertaking.

Representation. Software that allows dynamic, real-time representation of a researcher's thinking can be a substantial aid to theorizing. Software that provides a graphic map of relationships among codes, text segments, or cases can help researchers to visualize and extend their thinking about the data or theory at hand. Researchers often use drawings to depict these relationships, but software can keep maps tied to the underlying project, so that changes to the links in the drawing change the links among the objects in the database, and vice versa.

Consolidation. Finally, allowing the researcher to record field notes, interviews, codes, memos, annotations, reflective remarks, diagrams, audio and video recordings, demographic variables, and structural maps of the data and the theory all in one place can be a tremendously powerful support to the analysis process. If the design of the program is such that it allows the researcher to move from one intellectual activity to another with minimal effort, and carry over the results of one sort of thinking to others, it can both free up large amounts of energy for the critical tasks and help the researcher to see and keep track of connections that might otherwise easily fall through the cracks.

Real Fears

What do we really have to be worried about? Many of the advantages touted above have flip sides. The very ease, speed, and power of the software have the potential to encourage the kind of thinking I have referred to as "false hopes and fears" above. Although the software will not figure out what a complex account of a childhood trauma really means in the context of the current study, the ease of searching for key words and "autocoding" them may encourage the researcher to take shortcuts. We may fail to check to see what passages were actually coded in the autocoding process, and to use their own intelligence to analyze whether they fit. There is the real potential that we will get lazy. As Lee and Fielding (1991) have noted, "There is the possibility that the use of computers may tempt qualitative researchers into 'quick and dirty' research with its attendant danger of premature theoretical closure" (p. 8).

It is also possible that the availability of software may tempt researchers to skip over the process of learning properly about research. Again from Lee and Fielding (1991):

> Of course, the ultimate fear here is of Franken-stein's monster. It is susceptible to the same caveats, too. Like the monster, the programs are misunderstood. The programs are innocent of guile. It is their misapplication which poses the threat. It was exposure to human depravity which made a threat of Frankenstein's creation. Equally, the untutored use of analysis programs can certainly produce banal, unedifying and off-target analyses. But the fault would lie with the user. This is why teaching the use of the programs to novice researchers has to be embedded in a pedagogy which has a sense of the exemplars of qualitative analysis, rather than as skills and techniques to be mechanically applied. (p. 8)

The final fear that has some truth to it is that the conceptual assumptions behind the program—for example, that the relationships among codes are always strictly hierarchical—will shape the analysis. This fear both has truth to it and is often overstated. For example, if the program allows you to directly represent hierarchical relationships among codes, but not nonhierarchical relationships, such as circular loops or unstructured networks, it will probably encourage you to think primarily or only in terms of hierarchical relationships among your codes/concepts. If you are aware of the assumptions behind a program, you have a couple of options: You can choose another program or you can find a way to work around the assumptions in the program—for example, by keeping an ever-changing, nonhierarchical code map pinned to the wall. More on this in the section headed "Debates in the Field," below.

◆ Types and Functions of Software for QDA

In this section I offer a rough sorting of available software into types. There is naturally quite a bit of overlap among categories, with individual programs having functions that would seem to belong to more than one type. However, it is possible to focus on the "heart and soul" of a program: what it is mainly intended for. This categorization scheme was first presented in Weitzman and Miles (1995b).

Text Retrievers

Text retrievers specialize in finding all the instances of words and phrases in text, in one or several files. They typically also allow you to search for places where two or more words or phrases coincide within a specified distance (a number of words, sentences, pages, and so on) and allow you to sort the resulting passages into different output files and reports. They may do other things as well, such as content analysis functions like counting, displaying key words in context or creating concordances (organized lists of all words and phrases in their contexts), or they may allow you to attach annotations or even variable values (for things like demographics or source information) to points in the text. Examples of text retrievers are Sonar Professional, the Text Collector, and ZyINDEX; there are also a variety of free (but hard to use) GREP tools available on the World Wide Web.

Textbase Managers

Textbase managers are database programs specialized for storing text in more or less organized fashion. They are good at holding text, together with information about it, and allowing you to quickly organize and sort your data in a variety of ways and retrieve it according to different criteria. Some are better suited to highly structured data that can be organized into "records" (that is, specific cases) and "fields" (variables—information that appears for each case), whereas others easily manage "free-form" text.

They may allow you to define fields in the fixed manner of a traditional database such as Microsoft Access® or FileMaker Pro®, or they may allow significantly more flexibility, for example, allowing different records to have different field structures. Their search operations may be as good as, or sometimes even better than, those of some text retrievers. Examples of textbase managers are askSam, Folio Views, Idealist, InfoTree32 XT, and TEXTBASE AL-PHA.

Code-and-Retrieve Programs

Code-and-retrieve programs are often developed by qualitative researchers specifically for the purpose of qualitative data analysis. The programs in this category specialize in allowing you to apply category tags (codes) to passages of text and later retrieve and display the text according to your coding. These programs have at least some search capacity, allowing you to search either for codes or words and phrases in the text. They may have a capacity to store memos. Even the weakest of these programs represent a quantum leap forward from the old scissors-and-paper approach: they're more systematic, more thorough, less likely to miss things, more flexible, and much, much faster. Examples of code-and-retrieve programs are HyperQual2, Kwalitan, QUALPRO, Martin, and the Data Collector.

Code-Based Theory Builders

Most of the code-based theory-building programs are also based on a code-and-retrieve model, but they go beyond the functions of code-and-retrieve programs. They do not, nor would you want them to, build theory for you. Rather, they have special features or routines that go beyond those of code-and-retrieve programs in supporting *your* theory-building efforts. For example, they may allow you to represent relations among codes, build higher-order classifications and categories, or formulate and test theoretical propositions about the data. They may have more powerful memoing features (allowing you, for example, to categorize or code your memos) or more sophisticated search-and-retrieval functions than code-and-retrieve programs. They may have extended and sophisticated hyperlinking features, allowing you to link segments of text together or to create links among segments of text, graphics, photos, video, audio, Web sites, and more. They may also offer capabilities for "system closure," allowing you to feed results of your analyses (such as search results or memos) back into the system as data. Examples of code-based theory builders are AFTER, AnSWR, AQUAD, ATLAS/ti, Code-A-Text, HyperRESEARCH, NUD•IST, NVivo, QCA, the Ethnograph, and winMAX. Two of these programs, AQUAD and QCA, support cross-case configural analysis (Ragin, 1987), QCA being dedicated wholly to this method and not having any text-coding capabilities.

Conceptual Network Builders

Conceptual network builders are programs that emphasize the creation and analysis of network displays. Some of them are focused on allowing you to create network drawings: graphic representations of the relationships among concepts. Examples of these are Inspiration, Meta-Design, and Visio. Others are focused on the analysis of cognitive or semantic networks, for example, the program MECA. Still others offer some combination of the two approaches, for example, SemNet and Decision Explorer. Finally, ATLAS/ti, a program also mentioned above under code-based theory builders, also has a fine graphical network builder connected to the analytic work you do with your text and codes.

Summary

In concluding this discussion of the five main software family types, I want to emphasize that functions often cross type boundaries. For example, Folio VIEWS can code and retrieve, and has an excellent text search facility. ATLAS/ti, NUD•IST, NVivo, the Ethnograph, and winMAX graphically represent the relationships among codes, although among these, only ATLAS/ti allows you to work with and manipulate the drawing.[2] The Ethnograph and win-MAX both have systems for attaching variable values (text, date, numeric, and so on) to text files and/or cases. Sphinx Survey allows you to work with survey data consisting of a mix of qualitative and quantitative data. The implication: Do not decide too early which family you want to choose from. Instead, stay focused on the functions you need.

Multimedia. Multimedia capabilities are just beginning to emerge as a significant issue in software choice. There are now several programs in the code-based theory builder category that allow you to use audio and video, as well as text, as data: AFTER, ATLAS/ti, and Code-A-Text all allow you to code and annotate audio and video files, and search and retrieve from them, in ways quite similar to the ways they let you manipulate text, as does version 2 of HyperRESEARCH, which is under development at the time of this writing. In these programs, you can play a media file (audio or video), mark the beginning and ending points of segments, and then treat those segments much like segments of text. A program now in beta testing called InterClipper is designed primarily for audio files, with the assumption that you only bother to transcribe the segments that you find most important (it is targeted at focus group researchers in commercial environments who need to be able to generate analyses and reports quickly). This program will probably fall in the code-and-retrieve family when it is ready for release. There is also a growing field of software dedicated exclusively to managing video.

◆ *How to Make Intelligent, Individualized Software Choices*

I have emphasized from the beginning of this chapter that there is no one best software program for analyzing qualitative data. Furthermore, there is no one best program for a particular type of research or analytic method. Researchers will sometimes ask, What's the best program for a school ethnography? or, What's the best program for doing grounded theory? or, What's the best program for analyzing focus groups? None of these questions has a good answer. Instead, analysts need to approach choice based on the structure of the data, the specific things they will want to do as part of the analysis, and their needs around issues such as ease of use, cost, time available, and collaboration.

Researchers can ask themselves four broad questions, as well as consider two cut-across issues, to help guide their choices (Weitzman & Miles, 1995a, 1995b). These guidelines for choice have seen wide use in practice since their original formulation, and have proven to be effective for guiding researchers to appropriate choices. Because this approach to choice emphasizes matching functions, rather than specific programs, to particular needs, these guidelines can continue to be useful long after the programs referenced here as examples have evolved into new versions and new programs have arrived on the scene.[3]

Specifically, there are four key questions you need to ask and answer as you move toward choosing one or more software packages:

1. What kind of computer user am I?
2. Am I choosing for one project or for the next few years?
3. What kind of project(s) and database(s) will I be working on?
4. What kinds of analyses am I planning to do?

In addition to these four key questions, there are two cut-across issues to bear in mind:

- How important is it to you to maintain a sense of "closeness" to your data?
- What are your financial constraints when buying software and the hardware it needs to run on?

With these basic issues clear, you will be able to look at specific programs in a more active, deliberate way, seeing what does or does not meet your needs. (You may find it helpful to organize your answers to these questions on a worksheet, such as the one proposed in Weitzman & Miles, 1995b, which has rows for each of the questions below and columns for answers, implications/notes, and candidate programs.) Work your way from answering questions, to the implications of those answers for program choice, to candidate programs. For example, if you are working on a complex evaluation study, with a combination of structured interviews, focus groups, and case studies, you will need strong tools for tracking cases through different documents. You might find good support for this in a program's code structures, or through the use of speaker identifiers that track individuals throughout the database (see Question 3, below). Such suggestions are elaborated below.

Question 1: What Kind of Computer User Are You?

Your present level of computer use is an important factor in choice of a program. If you are new to computers, your best bet is probably to choose a word-processing program with advice from friends and begin using it, learning to use your computer's operating system (e.g., MS-DOS, Windows, or Mac) and getting comfortable with the idea of creating text, moving around in it, and revising it. That would bring you to what we'll call Level 1. Or you may have gotten acquainted with several different programs, use your operating system easily, and feel comfortable with the idea of exploring and learning new programs (Level 2). Or you may be a person with active interest in the ins and outs of how programs work (Level 3) and feel easy with customization, writing macros, and the like. (I will not deal here with the "hacker," a Level 4 person who lives and breathes computing.)

Being more of a novice does not mean you have to choose a "baby" program, or even that you shouldn't choose a very complex program. It does mean, however, allowing for extra learning time, perhaps placing more emphasis on user-friendliness, and finding sources of support for your learning, such as friends or colleagues, or on-line discussion groups on the Internet. People at different levels seem to have quite different reactions to the same programs. So, for example, a person at Level 2 or 3 might like a program that puts the maximum information on one screen because this allows her to find what she wants quickly, and she might learn the program very quickly. A person at Level 1 might find all that information overwhelming at first, and might take a little longer to learn that program because of it. But, once he has learned the program, our Level 1 person would probably benefit from the layout in the same way as the more advanced computer user.

Question 2: Are You Choosing for One Project or for the Next Few Years?

A word processor does not care what you are writing about, so most people pick one and stick with it until something better comes along and they feel motivated to learn it. But particular qualitative analysis programs tend to be good for certain types of analyses. Switching will cost you learning time and money. Think about whether you should choose the best program for this project or the program that best covers the kinds of projects you are considering over the next few years. For example, a particular code-and-retrieve program might look adequate for the current project and be cheaper or look easier to learn than some other program. But if you are likely to need a more fully featured code-based theory builder down the road, it might make more sense to get started with one of those now (assuming you choose one that includes good code-and-retrieve capabilities).

Question 3: What Kind of Database and Project Will You Be Working On?

Here the questions begin to get a bit more specific. As you look at detailed software features, you need to play them against a series of detailed issues. Because of the nature of computers, it becomes essential to give careful attention to the issue of understanding the nature and structure of qualitative data sets. The issues here have to do with the physical and logical form of the data:

how structured and how consistent it is, how data about a case are organized, and so on. In terms of the issues presented below, there may be great variation from project to project, even within a given analytic approach (say, grounded theory, ethnography, or narrative analysis). Epistemological issues, such as the interpretive nature of observational notes, coding, or memos, or the social construction of interview data, although very important for research methodology, do not come into play here; the question is whether the program you choose provides the organizational tools for the text, graphics, audio, or video you want to put into it.

Data sources per case: single versus multiple. You may be collecting data on a case from many different sources (say your case is defined as a student, and you talk with several teachers, the student's parents and friends, the principal, and the student herself). Some programs are specifically designed to handle data organized like this, others are not designed this way but can handle multiple sources pretty well, and some really do not have the flexibility you'll need. As mentioned above, you should look for strong tools for tracking cases through different documents. Some programs provide good support for this in code structures (particularly programs with highly structured code systems, like NUD•IST and NVivo, and to lesser degrees in programs with flexible code systems like ATLAS/ti) or through the use of speaker identifiers in programs like AFTER, the Ethnograph, or Code-A-Text. Also, look for programs that are good at making links, such as those with hypertext capability, and that attach "source tags" telling you where information is coming from.

Single versus multiple cases. If you have multiple cases, you usually will want to sort them out according to different patterns or configurations, and/or work with only some of the cases, and/or do cross-case comparisons. Multicase studies can get complicated. For example, your cases might be students (and you might have data from multiple sources for each student). Your students might all be "nested" in (grouped by) classrooms, which might be nested within

schools, which in turn might be nested in districts. Look for software that will easily select different portions of the database, and/or do configurational analysis (Ragin, 1987) across your cases; software that can help you create multiple-case matrix displays, usually by gathering together the data that correspond to the different cells of the matrix, is also useful.

Fixed records versus revised. Will you be working with data that are fixed (such as official documents or survey responses) or data that will be revised (with corrections, added codes, annotations, memos, and so on)? Some programs make database revision easy, whereas others are quite rigid, so that revising can use up a lot of time and energy. Some will let you revise annotations and coding easily, but not the underlying text, and some will let you revise both. Although this has been a constraining issue up to now, the trend in new programs and upcoming revisions of existing ones is toward programs that allow you to edit underlying text easily.

Structured versus open. Are your data strictly organized (for example, responses to a standard questionnaire or interview) or free-form (running field notes, participant observation, and so on)? Highly organized data can usually be more easily, quickly, and powerfully managed in programs set up to accommodate them—for example, those with well-defined "records" for each case and "fields" (or variables) with data for each record. Structured surveys may benefit from survey-oriented programs like Sphinx Survey or EZ-Text, which take advantage of predictable structure to provide good data-manipulation tools. Free-form text demands a more flexible program. There are programs that specialize in one or the other type of data, and some that work fairly well with either.

Uniform versus diverse entries. Your data may all come from interviews, or you may have information of many sorts: archival documents, field observations, questionnaires, pictures, audiotapes, videotapes (this issue overlaps with single versus multiple sources, above). Some programs handle diverse data types easily, and others are narrow and stern in their requirements. If you will have diverse entries, look for software designed to handle multiple sources and types of data, with good source tags and good linking features in a hypertext mode. The ability to handle "off-line" data—referring you to material not actually loaded into your program—is a plus. Many programs can be tricked into doing this if you are clever about it. If you want to be able to code, and then retrieve, audio or video, look for programs like AFTER, ATLAS/ti, Code-A-Text, and InterClipper, which let you treat these media much like text.

Size of database. A program's database capacity may be expressed in terms of numbers of cases, numbers of data documents (files), size of individual files, and/or total database size, often expressed in kilobytes (K) or megabytes (MB). (Roughly, consider that a *single*-spaced page of printed text is about 2 to 3K.) Estimate your total size in whatever terms the program's limits are expressed, and at least double it. Most programs today are generous in terms of total database size. A few are still stingy when it comes to the size of individual texts. For example, in some programs when a document goes beyond about 10 pages, the program will insist on breaking it into smaller chunks or will open it only in a "read-only mode" browser.[4]

Question 4: What Kind of Analyses Are You Planning to Do?

As mentioned above, identifying the name of your analysis methodology really won't do the trick here. Your choice of software depends on how you expect to go about analysis. This does not mean a detailed analysis plan, but a general sense of the style and approach you are expecting, which in turn will tell you the kinds of things you will need to be able to do with the data. For an excellent overview of a range of approaches to qualitative data analysis, and a discussion of some of the procedures associated with them, see Fielding and Lee (1998, chap. 2).

If you will be coding your data, you need a program that will let you code the way your

methodology requires. If you are doing narrative analysis you may need to track temporal or narrative structures in certain ways. Or you may be focusing on building a web of hypertext links as a way of understanding the phenomena in your data, and your needs may be better served by one or another way of creating and representing that hypertext web. Coding is probably the best-supported approach at the current writing, and many researchers who use other approaches may find that their best option is to use a "coding" system for their own purposes—for example, to mark up the narrative structure of a text. More on this in the section headed "The Future," below.

The subsections below, laying out the parts of Question 4, should help you move beyond just the name of your methodology. They should help you identify the specific analytic moves you will need to make; the specific operations you will need to perform; the kinds of insights, inferences, and interpretations you will need to record; and the manner in which you plan to record them. In other words, they should help you to get specific about the things you would do if working with paper and to translate these into the functions you will need from software.

Exploratory versus confirmatory. Are you mainly planning to poke around in your data to see what they are like, evolving your ideas inductively? Or do you have some specific hypotheses in mind linked to an existing theory to test deductively? If the former, it is especially important that you have features of fast and powerful search and retrieval, easy coding and revision, along with good text and/or graphic display.

If, on the other hand, you have a beginning theory and want to test some specific hypotheses, programs with strong theory-building and -testing features are better bets. Look for programs that test propositions, or those that help you develop and extend conceptual networks.

Coding scheme firm at start versus evolving. Does your study have a fairly well defined a priori scheme for codes (categories, key words), perhaps theoretically derived, that you will apply to your data? Or will such a scheme evolve as you go, in a grounded theory style, using the "constant comparative" method (Glaser, 1965; Glaser & Strauss, 1967; Strauss & Corbin, 1998)? If the latter, it is especially important that you have easy on-screen coding (rather than being required to code on hard copy, or having to deal with cumbersome on-screen coding procedures) and features supporting easy or automated revision of codes. Hypertext linking capabilities are helpful here too. "Automated" coding (in which the program applies a code according to a rule you set up, such as when a certain phrase or a combination of other codes exists) can be helpful in either case.

Multiple versus single coding. Some programs let you assign several different codes to the same segment of text, including higher-order codes, and may let you overlap or nest coded "chunks" (the ranges of text you apply codes to). Others are stern: one chunk, one code. Still other programs will let you apply more than one code to a chunk, but will not "know" that there are multiple codes on the chunk—they'll treat it like two chunks, one for each code.

Iterative versus one pass. Do you want—and do you have the time—to keep walking through your data several times, taking different and revised cuts? Or will you limit yourself to one pass? An iterative intent should point you toward programs that give you a good display of your previous coding, are flexible, invite repeated runs, make coding revision easy, have good search and autocoding features, allow you to track connections between different parts of the text with hypertext, and can make a log of your work as you go. (See also the question of whether your records are fixed or revisable during analysis.)

Fineness of analysis. Will your analysis focus on specific words? Or lines of text? Or sentences? Paragraphs? Pages? Whole files? Look to see what the program permits (or requires, or forbids) you to do. How flexible is it? Can you look at *varying* sizes of chunks in your data? Can you define free-form segments with ease? Some programs make you choose the size of your codable

segments when you first import the data, whereas others let you mix and match chunk sizes as you go.

Interest in context of data. When the program pulls out chunks of text in response to your search requests, how much surrounding information do you want to have? Do you need only the word, phrase, or line itself? Do you want the preceding and following lines/sentences/paragraphs? Do you want to see the entire file? Do you need to be able to jump right to that place in the file and do some work on it (e.g., code, edit, annotate)? Do you want the information to be marked with a "source tag" that tells you where it came from (e.g., Interview 3 with Janice Chang, page 22, line 6)? Or do you just want the source information without the text itself? Programs vary widely on this.

Intentions for displays. Analysis goes much better when you can see organized, compressed information in one place rather than in page after page of unreduced text. Some programs produce output in list form (lists of text segments, hits, codes, and so on). Some can help you produce matrix displays. They may list text segments or codes for each cell of a matrix, although you will have to actually arrange them in a matrix for display. Look for programs that let you edit, reduce, or summarize hits before you put them into a text-filled matrix with your word processor. Some programs can give you quantitative data (generally frequencies) in a matrix. Others can give you networks or hierarchical diagrams, the other major form of data display.

Qualitative only or numbers included. If your data, and/or your analyses, include the possibility of number crunching, look to see whether the program will count things and/or whether it can share information with quantitative analysis programs such as SPSS or SAS. Think carefully about what kind of quantitative analysis you'll be doing, and make sure the program you are thinking about can arrange the data appropriately. Consider, too, whether the program can link qualitative and quantitative data in a meaningful way (in terms of the analytic approach you are taking). For example, do you need to be able to select subsets of your qualitative data based on quantitative scores or demographics? Or do you need to use your qualitative coding to generate scaled variables for statistical analysis in SPSS? Or do you want to be able to generate word or code frequency tables for statistical analysis?

Collaboration. If you will be working with a team and more than one of you will be working on data analysis, look to see how the program supports collaboration. Some are fine if you just want to divide up the work with each of you coding different parts of the data and then combining the work. Others will support comparing multiple researchers' interpretations of the same data. Some programs will allow multiple users to access a shared database over a network; others will allow you to merge periodically separate copies of the database that different researchers have been working on. Programs differ in how much control they give you over the merge process. Some allow you to specify what the program will do if it finds, say, codes or memos with the same name in each of the copies being merged, whereas others follow a fixed rule. Some programs are good at letting you tell which copy a code, memo, or other object came from; others lose all identifying information so you have to use tricks like using different names in each copy (e.g., I might start the names of all codes I create with my initials, and you start yours with your initials). Some programs offer specific features for letting you compare the coding of two different researchers, for example, by showing you a table in which you can see the coding done by each.

Cut-Across Issues

The two main cut-across issues are closeness to the data and financial resources. Let's dispense quickly with the latter question first. Software varies dramatically in price. The range of prices for the programs we reviewed in Weitzman and Miles (1995b) was $0 to $1,644 per user. That is still the range. (Look for dis-

counts for educational users and multiple-user "site licenses.") In addition, programs vary a lot in the hardware they require to run efficiently. You obviously cannot use a program if it is too expensive for you, if it requires a machine you cannot afford, or if it runs on the wrong platform—say, PC instead of Mac. Happily, the U.S. Centers for Disease Control now distributes two programs free via the Web: EZ-Text for qualitative surveys and AnSWR for unstructured text. Also happily, reports from the field are that the Macintosh computers being sold today (the G3 is today's top Mac) run even the most powerful new PC programs satisfactorily with PC "emulation" software. This will, presumably, continue to be the case with future generations of Macs.

The remaining issue, closeness to the data, is more complex, and I also address it below in the section headed "Debates in the Field." For choice purposes, remember to think about what *kind* of closeness to the data is important to you. Many researchers fear that working with qualitative data on a computer will have the effect of "distancing" them from their data. This can in fact be the case. You may wind up looking at only small chunks of text at a time, or maybe even just line-number references to where the text is. This is a far cry from the feeling of deep immersion in the data that comes from reading and flipping through piles of paper.

But other programs minimize this effect. They typically keep your data files onscreen in front of you at all times; show you search results by scrolling to the hit, so that you see it in its full context; and allow you to execute most or all actions from the same data-viewing screen. Programs that allow you to build in hypertext links between different points in your data, provide good facilities for keeping track of where you are in the database, display your coding and memoing, and allow you to pull together related data quickly can in some ways help you get even *closer* to the data than you can with paper transcripts. If you choose with this consideration in mind, software can *help,* rather than hinder, your work at staying close to the data. It can, in fact, help keep you from drowning in those piles of paper.

However, having software that enhances the sense of closeness to the data may not be a crucial issue for everyone. Some researchers do not mind relying heavily on printed transcripts to get a feeling of closeness, whereas others think such heavy reliance defeats the purpose of QDA software. Furthermore, some projects simply do not require intense closeness to the data. You may be doing more abstract work, and in fact may *want* to move away from the raw data.

◆ Debates in the Field

A number of debates have taken place over the past two decades in the qualitative research community about whether the use of software is a good idea and, if so, what kinds of software are a good idea. I will address four of the debated issues here: closeness to the data, whether software drives methodology, whether new researchers should start off doing analysis by hand, and whether software really affects rigor, consistency, and thoroughness.[5]

Closeness to the Data

The issue of closeness to the data, which I have just discussed in terms of program choice, has been one of the big concerns raised by qualitative researchers over the years. Experienced researchers have often found that as difficult as it was, the process of spending endless hours sitting on the floor surrounded by piles and piles of paper led them, by necessity, to a very rich and thorough familiarity with their data. But as I have tried to argue above, software need not cut down on this familiarity. Software neither makes it better nor worse, it simply changes it. Although some programs still create the sense that you are staring at just a small window of text with no sense of what lies around it, there are now many programs available that provide rich contextual information (such as source information, graphical maps of hypertext links, navigable outlines, and linked lists of codes, documents, and text segments), and may in fact help you get to know your data better than ever before.

Does Software Drive Methodology?

Another concern has been that researchers might wind up adapting their research to the software they use, rather than the other way around (Coffey et al., 1996; Kelle, 1997; Lonkila, 1995)—that is, that the software will impose a methodological or conceptual approach. In fact, software developers bring assumptions, conceptual frameworks, and sometimes even methodological and theoretical ideologies to the development of their products. These have important implications for the impact that using a particular program will have on your analyses. However, as I have argued elsewhere, you need not, and in fact should not, be trapped by these assumptions and frameworks; there are often ways of bending a program to your own purposes (see Weitzman, in press). For example, a program may allow you to define only hierarchical relations among codes. You might work around this by creating redundant codes in different parts of the hierarchy, or by keeping track of the extra relationships *you* want to define with memos and network diagrams.

The fact that developers bring conceptual assumptions to their work is in fact one of the strengths of the field. Many of the developers, particularly of code-and-retrieve and code-based theory builder programs, are researchers themselves. They have invested enormous intellectual energy in finding the right tools for analyses of different types, and the user can benefit greatly from their investment.

It is also true that the design of the software can have an impact on analysis. For example, different programs work with different "metaphors"—that is, different ways of presenting the relationships among codes, and between codes and text. Kwalitan, NUD•IST, the Ethnograph, and winMAX all allow hierarchical relations among codes. For studies in which you are organizing your conceptual categories hierarchically, these programs offer significant strengths. If you want to represent nonhierarchical relationships, even if you choose to try to work around this metaphor, it may be less comfortable than using a program like ATLAS/ti that explicitly supports more flexible networks. HyperRESEARCH emphasizes the relationship between codes and cases, rather than codes and chunks of text. When you code a chunk of text, you create an entry on what looks like an index card for a particular case. This strongly supports and encourages thinking that stresses casewise and cross-case phenomena, but makes it harder to look for and think about relationships among codes *within* a text (although version 2, under development at the time of this writing, appears to be solving this problem). Finally, Code-A-Text offers a quite different set of coding metaphors: (a) codes arranged into "scales" (you can assign only one code from each scale to a segment of text, useful if you want to code your text chunks by making mutually exclusive judgments on a variety of factors), (b) codes automatically assigned according to words in the text, and (c) open-ended "interpretations" you write about each text chunk. Working with this collection of coding metaphors could be expected to lead you to consider your text in somewhat different ways than with one of the other metaphors described above.

Similar issues exist in the choice of other types of software, such as textbase managers. InfoTree32 XT allows you to arrange texts in a hierarchical tree and lets you drag texts around to rearrange them. Folio Views also allows you to create a hierarchical outline, but gives you the additional capability of creating multiple, nonsequential "groupings" of texts that you can activate any time you wish. Folio Views and askSam let you insert fields whenever and wherever you want in any given record, whereas InfoTree32 XT requires that you use a standard field set (of your own design) throughout the whole database. Idealist not only lets you customize the field set for each record, you can also create a variety of record types, each with its own set of fields, and mix them in the same database. Finally, whereas most of these programs show you just one record at a time, Folio Views shows you a word processor-like view in which records appear one right after the other as paragraphs. Clearly, each of these programs shows you a quite different view of your data, and so each may encourage different ways of thinking

about your data. The different programs all have different strengths and weaknesses. It is also true that a clever user will be able to bend each of these flexible packages to a wide variety of different tasks, overcoming many of the differences between them.

Each of these assumptions is both a benefit for some modes of analysis and a constraint. The key, then, is not to get trapped by the assumptions of the program. If you are aware of what they are, you can be clever and work around them. The program should serve *your* analytic needs, goals, and assumptions, not the other way around. Researchers interested in empirical work on the impacts of different programs on research are again encouraged to refer to Fielding and Lee (1998).

Should New Researchers Start Off Doing Analysis by Hand?

There is no clear-cut answer to this question. Certainly, it is important that new researchers begin by learning about how to do good analysis, rather than just how to use a program. Whether that means doing a first project by hand or learning about analysis and software to do it with in the same course is a question best left to teachers. I have taught both ways, and in my experience students benefit from having some experience with manual methods, if only a few coding exercises, so that they can get the feel of what is happening analytically before they start worrying about using the software.

Does Software Really Affect Rigor? Consistency? Thoroughness?

Some researchers are dedicated to the notion that software makes for more rigorous research. There are even rumors floating around of federal funding agencies requiring the use of software in grant proposals. Yet, as I have argued above, software will not pull good work out of a poor researcher. On the other hand, for all the reasons outlined above in the subsection headed "Real Hopes," software can in fact help competent researchers do more rigorous, consistent, and thorough analysis than they otherwise might. The issue should be conceptualized not as whether the software makes the work more rigorous, but whether the researcher uses the software to do more rigorous work than he or she could without it.

◆ The Future

It is my hope that the future will see a continuation of current trends, both in scholarship and in software development. Some of my specific hopes are outlined below.

Needs for Scholarship on the Topic

Ongoing review work. In addition to books like Weitzman and Miles (1995b) and its upcoming revision (which I am coauthoring with Nigel Fielding and Ray Lee), which offer comprehensive comparative reviews of the range of software available at a particular time, there is a need for regularly appearing reviews of new and revised programs as they appear. The journal *Field Methods* (formerly *Cultural Anthropology Methods*) offers regular software reviews (of quantitative as well as qualitative programs) in the same way that many journals feature regular book reviews. More journals that serve qualitative research audiences should follow this lead.

Debate on methodological questions. The kind of controversial issues addressed in this chapter need to be subjected to continued debate in the literature and among researchers. We need to be both wary of unintended influences of software and actively participating in shaping the future development of software by arguing (constructively) with developers about what we need and what we do not like.

More empirical work. The kind of empirical work on the impact of software on analysis that has been pioneered by Fielding and Lee (1998), Weaver and Atkinson (1995), Horney and Healey (1991), and Walker (1993) needs to be continued. Opinions about the impact of soft-

ware are nice, but we also need to continue to subject our hypotheses to empirical research.

Needs for Software Development

We can at this point identify some of the needs of researchers that are not yet met. For example, the field is still lagging in its support for case-oriented work. A few programs have features built in for explicitly tracking individual cases through multiple documents, but few programs are set up with a strong case-oriented structure.

Display building, especially of matrices, still needs much development. A product newly released at the time of this writing, NVivo (from the developers of NUD•IST), allows you to build an interactive matrix in which you can click on cells to call up the corresponding text. Matt Miles's dream of a program that would combine this sort of functionality with the ability to actually compose the summary text for the output matrix (rather than switching to a word processor) is still one step away.

Tools for narrative and discourse analysis are still lagging as well. Researchers using these approaches continue to call for features that let them flexibly describe the structure of text and discourse, and longitudinal researchers do not yet have much in the way of tools built explicitly for tracking cases over time, though NVivo has an "attributes" feature that allows you to attach date values to codes or documents.[6] In each of these cases, researchers can either adapt coding systems to their needs or look for yet other kinds of software (such as hypertext authoring programs, project schedulers, and so on) that they can adapt to their needs.

Finally, because no one program will ever do it all best, researchers need developers to create the possibility of importing and exporting marked-up, coded, annotated data from one program to another. At this writing, there is just a little of this beginning to happen. The developers of Code-A-Text, the Ethnograph, and winMAX have agreed to work on a common structure, partially realized at this point. And ATLAS/ti has become the first program to support export of fully developed projects in XML, a new markup language that may succeed HTML, the World Wide Web formatting standard. A common standard like this, if adopted by other developers, would allow researchers to move fully developed projects easily from one program to another, just as we can now move tabular data among multiple spreadsheet and database programs.

◆ Conclusion

Unlike the situation just a decade or so ago, qualitative researchers now have available to them an array of very good software tools to assist in their research, and the use of software—including, but not limited to, word processors—seems more and more to be a regular part of the qualitative research process. There is still no one "best" program, not even for a particular methodology, and that's good. It means that researchers have to think through their methods and choose programs that fit, which should keep them from becoming reliant on the software to lead them. As researchers continue to hunt around for programs that will do the things they want, and do them better, software developers will likely continue to respond by making their programs more and more useful.

What else can we hope will come out of this collaboration between users and developers in the near future? More and better tools for sharing analyses and raw data, perhaps by allowing posting of project databases, with analytic markups, links, and memos, to the World Wide Web, as ATLAS/ti allows, or on CDs; tools for building complex reports that include analyses and data right in the report itself; and more and better tools for supporting collaboration among research teams, and for involving informants in the research process without intensive computer training.

■ Notes

1. I discuss some exceptions in the subsection below headed "False Hopes and Fears."

2. The first release of NVivo lets you draw diagrams, but any connections you draw are represented only in the diagram, they are not representations of the defined relationships among codes and other objects, as in ATLAS/ti. You see the actual relationships among codes in a hierarchical "explorer" with expandable and collapsible branches, as in NUD•IST, the Ethnograph, and winMAX.

3. This section does not contain much in the way of references to specific software, both because the landscape changes every few years and because a single chapter does not allow for responsible comparisons among programs.

4. For any warning like this, check at the time you are choosing to see if the program under consideration presents this problem. This type of problem is worked at so regularly by developers that it would be unfair and unhelpful for me to name particular programs. Things change.

5. The reader interested in pursuing these questions further is referred to Fielding and Lee (1998) for reports of users' experiences of these and other issues when using different programs.

6. You can, in fact, attach not only date values, but text or numerical values as well.

■ References

Bogdan, R. C., & Biklen, S. K. (1982). *Qualitative research for education: An introduction to theory and methods.* Boston: Allyn & Bacon.

Coffey, A., & Atkinson, P. (1996). *Making sense of qualitative data: Complementary research strategies.* Thousand Oaks, CA: Sage.

Coffey, A., Holbrook, B., & Atkinson, P. (1996). Qualitative data analysis: Technologies and representations. *Sociological Research Online, 1*(1). Available Internet: http://www.socresonline.org.uk/socresonline/1/1/4.html

Drass, K. A. (1980). The analysis of qualitative data: A computer program. *Urban Life, 9,* 322-353.

Fielding, N. G., & Lee, R. M. (Eds.). (1991). *Using computers in qualitative research.* London: Sage.

Fielding, N. G., & Lee, R. M. (1998). *Computer analysis and qualitative research.* London: Sage.

Glaser, B. G. (1965). The constant comparative method of qualitative analysis. *Social Problems, 12,* 436-445.

Glaser, B. G., & Strauss, A. L. (1967). *The discovery of grounded theory: Strategies for qualitative research.* Chicago: Aldine.

Goetz, J. P., & LeCompte, M. D. (1984). *Ethnography and qualitative design in educational research.* New York: Academic Press.

Horney, M. A., & Healey, D. (1991, April). *Hypertext and database tools for qualitative research.* Paper presented at the annual meeting of the American Educational Research Association, Chicago.

Kelle, U. (Ed.). (1995). *Computer-aided qualitative data analysis: Theory, methods and practice.* London: Sage.

Kelle, U. (1997). Theory building in qualitative research and computer programs for the management of textual data. *Sociological Research Online, 2*(2). Available Internet: http://www.socresonline.org.uk/socresonline/2/2/1.html

Lee, R. M., & Fielding, N. G. (1991). Computing for qualitative research: Options, problems and potential. In N. G. Fielding & R. M. Lee (Eds.), *Using computers in qualitative research* (pp. 1-13). London: Sage.

Lofland, J., & Lofland, L. H. (1984). *Analyzing social settings: A guide to qualitative observation and analysis* (2nd ed.). Belmont, CA: Wadsworth.

Lonkila, M. (1995). Grounded theory as an emerging paradigm for computer-assisted qualitative data analysis. In U. Kelle (Ed.), *Computer-aided qualitative data analysis: Theory, methods and practice* (pp. 41-51). London: Sage.

Mangabeira, W. (Ed.). (1996). Qualitative sociology and computer programs: Advent and diffusion of CAQDAS [Special issue]. *Current Sociology, 44*(1).

Miles, M. B., & Huberman, A. M. (1984). *Qualitative data analysis: A sourcebook of new methods.* Beverly Hills, CA: Sage.

Miles, M. B., & Huberman, A. M. (1994). *Qualitative data analysis: An expanded sourcebook* (2nd ed.). Thousand Oaks, CA: Sage.

Ragin, C. C. (1987). *The comparative method: Moving beyond qualitative and quantitative strategies.* Berkeley: University of California Press.

Seidel, J. V., & Clark, J. A. (1984). The Ethnograph: A computer program for the analysis of qualitative data. *Qualitative Sociology, 7,* 110-125.

Shelly, A., & Sibert, E. (1985). *The QUALOG users' manual.* Syracuse, NY: Syracuse University, School of Computer and Information Science.

Strauss, A. L., & Corbin, J. (1998). *Basics of qualitative research: Techniques and procedures for developing grounded theory* (2nd ed.). Thousand Oaks, CA: Sage.

Tesch, R. (1990). *Qualitative research: Analysis types and software tools.* New York: Falmer.

Tesch, R. (1991). Computers and qualitative data II. *Qualitative Sociology, 14*(3).

Walker, B. L. (1993). Computer analysis of qualitative data: A comparison of three packages. *Qualitative Health Research, 3*(1), 91-111.

Weaver, A., & Atkinson, P. (1995). From coding to hypertext: Strategies for microcomputing and qualitative data analysis. In R. G. Burgess (Ed.), *Studies in qualitative methodology.* Greenwich, CT: JAI.

Weitzman, E. A. (1999). Analyzing qualitative data with computer software. *Health Services Research, 34*(5), 1241-1263.

Weitzman, E. A., & Miles, M. B. (1995a). Choosing software for qualitative data analysis: An overview. *Cultural Anthropology Methods, 7*(1), 1-5.

Weitzman, E. A., & Miles, M. B. (1995b). *Computer programs for qualitative data analysis: A software sourcebook.* Thousand Oaks, CA: Sage.

31

ANALYZING TALK AND TEXT

◆ David Silverman

The linguistic character of field data is most obvious in the case of texts and interviews. Even if our aim is to search for supposedly "external" realities (e.g., class, gender, power), our raw material is inevitably the words written in documents or spoken by interview respondents. Moreover, although observational data should properly include descriptions of contextual aspects of social interaction (what Stimson, 1986, calls "the sociology of space and place"), much of what we observe in formal and informal settings will inevitably consist of conversations.

Of course, if our data are transcripts of audiotapes, then we come face-to-face with how talk organizes the world. Although talk is sometimes seen as trivial ("mere" talk), it has increasingly become recognized as the primary medium through which social interaction takes place. In households and in more "public" settings, families and friends assemble their activi-

ties through talk. At work, we converse with one another and have accounts of our activities placed in dossiers and files. As Heritage (1984) argues, "The social world is a pervasively conversational one in which an overwhelming proportion of the world's business is conducted through the medium of spoken interaction" (p. 239). Indeed, what Heritage calls "the world's business" includes such basic features as telling news, deciding if one should commit suicide, and children's learning how to converse with their mothers (see Sacks, 1992a; Silverman, 1998b, chap. 1).

Yet a curiously prelinguistic sensibility pervades much social research. This is most obvious in quantitative researchers' preference for "operational definitions" that arbitrarily define the meaning of (linguistically mediated) phenomena. Less apparently, an inattention to participants' talk-in-interaction is shown by those qualitative researchers who claim to have direct

AUTHOR'S NOTE: I am most grateful for the comments of Norman Denzin, Jaber Gubrium, and Yvonna Lincoln on a first draft of this chapter.

access to the external "realities" mentioned earlier. These "realities" are often simply "read off" interview respondents' answers or transcripts of talk, with little or no reference to whether (and how) they are made reference to by the speakers. So, for instance, our "knowledge" that the speaker is a woman or that the setting is, say, a medical consultation is of no analytic relevance unless we can demonstrate the relevance of these features in the actions of the parties concerned (see Schegloff, 1991).

By contrast, 20th-century thought has resisted such researchers' assumptions that words are simply a transparent medium to "reality." From Saussure (1974), the Swiss linguist, we learn that signs derive meaning from their relation to other signs. From Wittgenstein (1968), the philosopher, we understand that the meaning of a word derives largely from its *use*. Consequently, as Wittgenstein puts it,

> when philosophers use a word—"knowledge," "being," "object" (etc.) . . . —and try to grasp the *essence* of the thing, one must first ask oneself: is the word ever actually used in this way in the language-game which is its original home?
>
> What *we* do is to bring words back from their metaphysical to their everyday use. (para. 116)

Wittgenstein's critique of some philosophers can, of course, be turned upon those quantitative researchers who arbitrarily construct "operational definitions" of phenomena without ever studying the "language-game" in which a phenomenon has its everyday home. However, what Wittgenstein is saying constitutes an equally relevant critique of qualitative research that claims to discover social "realities" unaddressed by participants.

As Garfinkel (1967) implies, both quantitative researchers' scientism and qualitative researchers' claims for "empathic understanding" are deeply commonsensical, because both trade off the capacity of societal members to "see through" appearances to an underlying reality. In this sense, there is a strong similarity between social researchers who claim to be able to access some social structure or emotion "behind" their data and, say, TV sports commentators who tell their audiences what sportspeople are "feeling." Both parties use (as a tacit resource) what

Garfinkel calls the "documentary method of interpretation" to produce their "findings" (see Gubrium & Holstein, Chapter 18, this volume).

This link between social research and society is hardly surprising. Such activities as observation and interviewing are not unique to social researchers. For instance, as Foucault (1977) has noted, the observation of the prisoner has been at the heart of modern prison reform, and the method of questioning used in the interview reproduces many of the features of the Catholic confessional or the psychoanalytic consultation. Its pervasiveness is reflected by the centrality of the interview study in so much contemporary social research. Think, for instance, of how much interviews are a central (and popular) feature of mass-media products, from "talk shows" to "celebrity interviews." Perhaps we all live in what might be called an "interview society," in which interviews seem central to making sense of our lives (see Atkinson & Silverman, 1997).

This broader societal context may explain qualitative researchers' temptation to gloss their methodology as "empathic understanding" and to use methods such as the interview. Of course, such a link between culture and method should be an opportunity to question ourselves about our methodological preferences. However, such self-questioning (sometimes—mistakenly, I think—referred to as reflexivity) does not itself provide a warrant for the choices we make.[1] As I argue below, such a warrant depends on our preparedness to describe societal members' actual methods for achieving whatever they do achieve.

These large-scale questions need, of course, to be embedded in our data analysis. I now turn to such issues, examining three kinds of linguistically mediated data: interviews, texts, and transcripts. It should be apparent that here, as elsewhere, I am concerned with data *analysis* rather than the mechanics of data gathering.

◆ Interviews

For the qualitative-minded researcher, the open-ended interview apparently offers the opportunity for an authentic gaze into the soul of another, or even for a politically correct dialogue in which researcher and researched offer mutual understanding and support. The rhetoric of interviewing "in depth" repeatedly hints at such a collection of assumptions. Here we see a stubbornly persistent romantic impulse in contemporary sociology: the elevation of the experiential as the authentic—the selfsame gambit that can make the TV talk-show or news interview so appealing.

Such qualitative researchers share survey researchers' assumption that interview responses index some external reality ("facts" or "events" for the latter group and "feelings" or "meanings" for the former). Both groups build into their research designs various devices to ensure the accuracy of their interpretations. So you can try to ensure that you have accurately depicted such realities and experiences by such measures as intercoder agreement and computer-assisted qualitative data programs. And you can check the accuracy of what your respondents tell you through other observations. Let us call this a *realist* approach to interview data.

An alternative approach treats interview data as accessing various stories or narratives through which people describe their worlds (see Holstein & Gubrium, 1995, 1997). This *narrative* approach claims that, by abandoning the attempt to treat respondents' accounts as potentially "true" pictures of "reality," we open up for analysis the culturally rich methods through which interviewers and interviewees, in concert, generate plausible accounts of the world (e.g., Gubrium, 1993; Voysey, 1975).

I am aware that many readers of this volume will favor the former approach. In this light, I want to give an example of how one realist interview study was eventually driven in a narrative direction. Jody Miller and Barry Glassner (1997) describe a study involving in-depth, open-ended interviews with young women (aged 13 to 18) who claim affiliation with youth gangs in their communities (Miller, 1996). These interviews followed the completion of survey interviews administered by Miller. Here is how Miller and Glassner (1997) describe the purposes of each form of data:

> While the survey interview gathers information about a wide range of topics, including the individual, her school, friends, family, neighborhood, delinquent involvement, arrest history, sexual history, and victimization, in addition to information about the gang, the in-depth interview is concerned exclusively with the roles and activities of young women in youth gangs, and the meanings they describe as emerging from their gang affiliation. (p. 105)

Let us focus on the data that Miller obtained in her in-depth interviews. This is one example:

> Describing why she joined her gang, one young women told Miller, "well, I didn't get any respect at home. I wanted to get some love and respect from somebody somewhere else." (p. 107)

Here is another respondent's explanation of why she joined a gang:

> I didn't have *no* family. . . . I had nothin' else. (p. 107)

Another young woman, when asked to speculate on why young people join gangs, suggested:

> Some of 'em are like me, don't have, don't really have a basic home or steady home to go to, you know, and they don't have as much love and respect in the home so they want to get it elsewhere. And, and, like we get, have family members in gangs or that were in gangs, stuff like that. (p. 107)

Let us assume that you have gathered these data and now want to begin analysis. Put at its starkest, what are you to do with them?

In line with the realist approach, using programs such as the Ethnograph or NUD•IST (see Weitzman, Chapter 30, this volume), you may start by coding respondents' answers into the different sets of reasons they give for participation in gangs. From these data, two reasons seem to predominate: "push" factors (unsupportive families) and "pull" factors (supportive gangs).

Moreover, given the availability of survey data on the same respondents, you are now in a position to correlate each factor with various background characteristics that they have. This seems to set up your research in good shape. Not only can you search for the "subjective" meanings of adolescent gangs, you can relate these meanings to "objective" social structures.

The realist approach thus has a high degree of plausibility to social scientists who theorize the world in terms of the impact of (objective) social structures upon (subjective) dispositions. Moreover, the kind of research outputs that this approach seeks to deliver are precisely those demanded by "users" in the community, who seek immediate practical payoffs from social science research.

Calling their approach a "methodology for listening," Miller and Glassner (1997) are thus centrally concerned with "seeing the world from the perspective of our subjects" (Glassner & Loughlin, 1987, p. 37). In this respect, they share the same assumptions about the "authenticity" of "experience" as other realists and, therefore, fail to detect culturally (and locally) specific elements in several "personal" tales (see Gubrium, 1993; Voysey, 1975).

However, say we are not entirely satisfied by the apparent plausibility of realism. How can the narrative approach kick-start data analysis? Miller and Glassner (1997, pp. 103-104) suggest that one way to begin is to think about how respondents are using culturally available resources in order to construct their stories. They refer to Richardson's (1990) suggestion that "participation in a culture includes participation in the narratives of that culture, a general understanding of the stock of meanings and their relationships to each other" (p. 24).

How, then, can the data above be read in these terms? The idea is to see respondents' answers as *cultural stories*. This means examining the rhetorical force of what interviewees say as "interviewees deploy these narratives to make their actions explainable and understandable to those who otherwise may not understand" (Miller & Glassner, 1997, p. 107).

In the data already presented, Miller and Glassner note that respondents make their actions understandable in two ways. First, they do not attempt to challenge public views of gangs as bad. But, second, they do challenge the notion that the interviewee herself is bad. However, Miller and Glassner (1997) note that not all their respondents glibly recycle conventional

cultural stories. As they put it, "Some of the young women go farther and describe their gang involvement in ways that directly challenge prevailing stereotypes about gangs as groups that are inherently bad or antisocial and about females' roles within gangs" (p. 108). Here are some of the respondents' accounts that they have in mind:

> It was really, it was just normal life, the only difference was, is, that we had meetings. (p. 109)

> [We] play cards, smoke bud, play dominoes, play video games. That's basically all we do is play. You would be surprised. This is a bunch of big kids. It's a bunch of big old kids in my set. (p. 109)

In accounts like these, Miller and Glassner argue that there is an explicit challenge to what the interviewees know to be popular beliefs about youth gangs. Instead of accepting the conventional definition of their behavior as "deviant," the girls attempt to convey the normalcy of their activities.

These narratives directly challenge stereotypical cultural stories of the gang. Following Richardson, Miller and Glassner (1997) refer to such accounts as "collective stories" that "resist the cultural narratives about groups of people and tell alternative stories" (Richardson, 1990, p. 25). Miller and Glassner's sensitive address of the narrative forms from which perspectives arise suggests an alternative path for interview analysis (for a more developed version of the narrative approach, see Gubrium & Holstein, 1997).

Summary

In light of the discussion above, I suggest below five questions that interview researchers might ask themselves.

What status do you attach to your data? Many interview studies are used to elicit respondents' perceptions. How far is it appropriate to think that people attach single meanings to their experiences? May there not be multiple meanings of a situation (e.g., living in a community home) or of an activity (e.g., being a male football fan) represented by what people say to the researcher, to each other, to caregivers, and so on (Gubrium, 1975/1997)?

This raises the important methodological issue of whether interview responses are to be treated as giving direct access to "experience" or as actively constructed "narratives" involving activities that themselves demand analysis (Holstein & Gubrium, 1995; Silverman, 1993). Both positions are entirely legitimate, but you need to justify and explain the position you take.

Is your analytic position appropriate to your practical concerns? Some ambitious analytic positions (e.g., hermeneutics, discourse analysis) may actually cloud the issue if your aim is simply to respond to a given social problem (e.g., living and coping in a community of elderly people, students' views of evaluation and feedback). If so, it might be simpler to acknowledge that there are more complex ways of addressing your data but to settle on presenting your research as a *descriptive* study based upon a clear social problem.

Do interview data really help in addressing your research topic? If you are interested in, say, what happens in school classrooms, should you be using interviews as your major source of data? Think about exactly why you have settled on an interview study. Certainly, it can be relatively quick to gather interview data, but not as quick as, say, gathering texts and documents. How far are you being influenced by the prominence of interviews in the media (see Atkinson & Silverman, 1997)?

In the case of the classroom, couldn't you observe what people do there instead of asking them what they think about it? Or gather documents that routinely arise in schools, such as pupils' reports, mission statements, and so on? Of course, you may still want to do an interview study. But, whatever your method, you will need to justify it and show you have thought through the practical and analytic issues involved in your choice.

Are you making too-large claims about your research? It always helps to make limited claims about your own research. Grandiose claims about originality, scope, or applicability to social problems are all hostages to fortune. Be careful in how you specify the claims of your approach. Show that you understand that it constitutes one way of "slicing the cake" and that other approaches, using other forms of data, may not be directly competitive.

Does your analysis go beyond a mere list? Identifying the main elements in your data according to some theoretical scheme should be only the first stage of your data analysis. By examining how these elements are linked together, you can bring out the active work of both interviewer and interviewee and, like them, say something lively and original.

◆ Texts

To introduce a separate section on "texts" now begins to look a little artificial. After all, to treat an interview as a narrative can mean looking for the same textual features as researchers working with printed material. Indeed, the mere act of transcription of an interview turns it into a written text. In this section, I use *text* as a heuristic device to identify data consisting of words and images that have become recorded without the intervention of a researcher (e.g., through an interview).

Of course, every way of seeing is also a way of not seeing. As Atkinson (1992, p. 459) points out, one of the disadvantages of the coding schemes used in both interview and text-based analysis is that, because they are based upon given sets of categories, they furnish "a powerful conceptual grid" from which it is difficult to escape. Although this grid is very helpful for organizing the data analysis, it also deflects attention away from uncategorized activities.

In part, Atkinson's critique vitiates the claims of many quantitative researchers in their attempts to produce reliable evidence about large samples of texts. Their favored method is "content analysis," in which the researchers establish a set of categories and then count the number of instances that fall into each category. The crucial requirement is that the categories are sufficiently precise to enable different coders to arrive at the same results when the same body of material (e.g., newspaper headlines) is examined (see Berelson, 1952).

The meat of the problem with content analysis (and its relatives) is not simply Atkinson's point about overlooked categories, but how analysts usually simply trade off their tacit members' knowledge in coining and applying whatever categories they do use. For instance, in a lecture given in the 1960s, Harvey Sacks compared the social psychologist Bales's (1950) tendency to produce immediate categories of "interaction process" with the relatively long time taken by experienced physicians to read the output of electroencephalographs. According to Sacks (1992b), one should not "categorize . . . as it comes out" (p. 28). Indeed, as we shall see shortly, our ability to categorize quickly is properly treated as a research topic rather than a research resource.

By contrast, in some qualitative research, small numbers of texts and documents may be analyzed for a very different purpose. The aim is to understand the participants' categories and to see how these are used in concrete activities such as telling stories (Propp, 1968; Sacks, 1974), assembling files (Cicourel, 1968; Gubrium & Buckholdt, 1982), and describing "family life" (Gubrium, 1992). The theoretical orientation of these qualitative researchers makes them more concerned with the processes through which texts depict "reality" than with whether such texts contain true or false statements. As Atkinson and Coffey (1997) put it:

> In paying due attention to such materials, however, one must be quite clear about what they can and cannot be used for. They are "social facts," in that they are produced, shared and used in socially organised ways. They are not, however, transparent representations of organizational routines, decision-making processes, or professional diagnoses. They construct particular kinds of representations with their own conventions. (p. 47)

The implications of this are clear:

> We should not use documentary sources as surrogates for other kinds of data. We cannot, for instance, learn through records alone how an organization actually operates day-by-day. Equally, we cannot treat records—however "official"—as firm evidence of what they report. . . . That strong reservation does not mean that we should ignore or downgrade documentary data. On the contrary, our recognition of their existence as social facts alerts us to the necessity to treat them very seriously indeed. We have to approach them for what they are and what they are used to accomplish. (p. 47)

What does it mean to approach texts "for what they are"? Potential examples are semiotics, ethnographically oriented narrative analysis, and discourse analysis. In crude terms, semiotics treats texts as systems of signs on the basis that no meaning every resides in a single term (see Silverman, 1993, pp. 71-80), narrative analysis focuses on how accounts artfully use local cultural resources (e.g., Atkinson & Coffey, 1997; Denzin, 1990; Holstein & Gubrium, 1997), and discourse analysis focuses on how different versions of the world are produced through the use of interpretive repertoires, claims to "stakes" in an account (see Potter, 1997), and constructions of knowing subjects (Prior, 1997).

Following my interest in ethnomethodology's focus on members' methods, I will sketch out a less familiar example—Sacks's account of membership categorization analysis (see also Silverman, 1998b; Watson, 1997).

Membership Categorization Analysis

Like some contemporary ethnographers concerned with narratives, Sacks (1992b) believes the issue is not to second-guess societal members, but to try to work out "how it is that people can produce sets of actions that provide that others can see such things . . . [as] persons doing intimacy . . . persons lying, etc." (p. 119). Given that many categories can be used to describe the same person or act, Sacks's task was "to find out how they [members] go about choosing among the available sets of categories for grasping some event" (p. 41). So Sacks does not mean to imply that "society" determines which category one chooses. Instead, he wants to show the active interpretive work involved in rendering any description and the local implications of choosing any particular category. Whether or not we choose to use Sacks's precise method, he offers an inspiring way to begin to analyze the productivities of any text.

As we have already seen, "coding" is not the preserve of research scientists. All of us "code" what we hear and see in the world around us. This is what Garfinkel (1967) and Sacks (1992a) mean when they say that societal members, like social scientists, make the world observable and reportable. Put at its simplest, this means that researchers must be very careful how they use categories. For instance, Sacks (1992b) quotes from two linguists who appear to have no problem characterizing particular (invented) utterances as "simple," "complex," "casual," or "ceremonial." For Sacks (1992a), such rapid characterizations of data assume "that we can know that [such categories are accurate] without an analysis of what it is [members] are doing" (p. 429).

At this point, the experienced researcher might respond that Sacks has characterized conventional research as overly naïve. In particular, most researchers are aware of the danger of assuming any one-to-one correspondence between their categories and the aspects of "reality" that they purport to describe. Instead, following Weber (1949), many researchers claim that they are simply using hypothetical constructs (or "ideal types") that are to be judged only in relation to whether they are *useful*, not whether they are "accurate" or "true." However, Sacks (1992a) was aware of this argument:

It is a very conventional way to proceed in the social sciences to propose that the machinery you use to analyze some data you have is acceptable if it is not intendedly the analysis of real phenomena. That is, you can have machinery which is a "valid hypothetical construct," and it can analyze something for you. (p. 315)

By contrast, the "machinery" in which Sacks is interested is not a set of "hypothetical constructs." Instead, Sacks's (1992a) ambitious claim throughout is "to be dealing with the real world" (p. 316). The "machinery" he sets out, then, is not to be seen as a set of more or less useful categories, but as the *actual* categories and mechanisms that members use.

Let us take a concrete example. In two of Harvey Sacks's lectures, he refers to a *New York Times* story about an interview with a U.S. Navy pilot about the pilot's missions in the Vietnam War (see Sacks, 1992b, pp. 205-222, 306-311). Sacks is especially interested in the story's report of the pilot's reported answer to a question:

How did he feel about knowing that even with all the care he took in aiming only at military targets someone was probably being killed by his bombs?

"I certainly don't like the idea that I might be killing anybody," he replied. "But I don't lose any sleep over it. You have to be impersonal in this business. Over North Vietnam I condition myself to think that I'm a military man being shot at by another military man like myself." (Sacks, 1992b, p. 205)

Sacks invites us to see how the pilot's immediate reply ("I certainly don't like the idea") shows his commitment to the evaluational scheme offered by the journalist's question. For instance, if the pilot had instead said, "Why do you ask?" he would have shown that he did not necessarily subscribe to the same moral universe as the reporter (and, by implication, the readers of the article) (Sacks, 1992b, p. 211).

Having accepted this moral schema, the pilot, as Sacks shows, now builds an answer that helps us to see him in a favorable light. The category "military man" works to defend his bombing as a category-bound activity that reminds us this is, after all, what military pilots do. The effect of this is magnified by the pilot's identification of his coparticipant as "another military man like myself." In this way, the pilot creates a pair (military man/military man) with recognizable mutual obligations (bombing/shooting at the other). In terms of this pair, the other party cannot properly complain, or, as Sacks (1992b) puts it, "there are no complaints to be offered on their part about the error of his ways, except if he happens to violate the norms that, given the device used, are operative" (p. 206).

Notice also that the pilot suggests, "You have to be impersonal in this business." Note how the category "this business" sets up the terrain on which the specific pair of military men will shortly be used. So this account could be offered by either pair-part. However, as Sacks (1992b) argues, the implication is that "this business" is one of many where impersonality is required, for "if it were the case that, that you had to be impersonal in this business held only for this business, then it might be that doing this business would be wrong in the first instance" (p. 206).

Moreover, the impersonality involved is of a special sort. Sacks points out that we hear the pilot as saying not that it is unfortunate that he cannot kill "personally," but rather that being involved in this "business" means that one must not consider that one is killing persons (p. 209). However, the pilot is only *proposing* a pair of military man/military man. In that sense, he is inviting the North Vietnamese to "play the game" in the same way a child might say to another, "I'll be third base." However, as Sacks (1992b) notes, in children's baseball, such proposals can be rejected: "If you say 'I'll be third base,' unless someone else says 'and I'll be . . .' another position, and the others say they'll be the other positions, then you're not that thing. You can't play" (p. 307).

Of course, the North Vietnamese indeed did reject the pilot's proposal. Instead, they proposed the identification of the pilot as a "criminal" and defined themselves as "doing police action." As Sacks notes, these competing definitions had implications that went beyond mere propaganda. For instance, if the navy pilot were shot down, then the Geneva Conventions about his subsequent treatment would be properly applied only if he indeed were a "military man" rather than a "criminal" (p. 307).

Unlike more formalistic accounts of action (Mead, 1934; Parsons, 1937), Sacks's analysis shows us the nitty-gritty mechanisms through which we construct moral universes "involving

appropriate kinds of action and particular actors with motives, desires, feelings, aspirations and sense of justice" (J. F. Gubrium, personal communication, January 1997). Like Garfinkel (1967), Sacks wants to avoid treating people as "cultural dopes," representing the world in ways that some culture demanded. Instead, Sacks approaches "culture" as an "inference-making machine": a descriptive apparatus, administered and used in specific contexts.

Summary

I will conclude my discussion of texts with a further summary statement. Here I will not use questions, but take the risk of offering three pieces of advice that emerge out of the preceding discussion (for a development of this argument, see Silverman, 2000).

Have a clear analytic approach. Successful textual studies recognize the value of working with a clearly defined approach. Having chosen your approach (e.g., Foucauldian discourse analysis, Saussurian semiotics, Sacks's analysis of membership categorizations), treat it as a "toolbox" providing a set of concepts and methods to select your data and to illuminate your analysis.

Recognize that successful analysis goes beyond a list. I make no apology for repeating a point that I made above in my discussion of interview studies. It seems to me that the distinctive contribution qualitative researchers can make is in utilizing their theoretical resources in the deep analysis of small bodies of publicly shareable data. This means that, unlike many quantitative researchers, we are not satisfied with a simple coding of data. Instead, we have to work to show how the (theoretically defined) elements we have identified are assembled or mutually laminated.

Limit your data. Like many other qualitative approaches, textual analysis depends upon very detailed data analysis. To make such analysis effective, it is imperative that you have a limited body of data with which to work. So, although it may be useful initially to explore different kinds of data (e.g., newspaper reports, scientific textbooks, magazine advice pages), you should usually do this only to establish the data set with which you can most effectively work. Having chosen your data set, you should limit your material further by taking only a few texts or parts of texts (e.g., headlines).

◆ Transcripts

The three types of qualitative data discussed here all end up in the form of some kind of text. In interviews, researchers usually work with written transcripts. Similarly, audiotapes of naturally occurring interaction are usually transcribed prior to (and as part of) the analysis.

The two main social science traditions that inform the analysis of transcripts of tapes are conversation analysis (CA) and discourse analysis (DA). For an introduction to CA, see ten Have (1998); on DA, see Potter and Wetherell (1987) and Potter (1997).[2] In the rest of this chapter, I will deal with two more practical issues: (a) the advantages of working with tapes and transcripts of naturally occurring talk and (b) the elements of how to do analysis of such tapes.

Why Work With Tapes?

> The kind of phenomena I deal with are always transcriptions of actual occurrences in their actual sequence. (Sacks, 1984, p. 25)

In contemporary philosophy, Sacks was attracted to speech-act theory, which, like him, treats talk as an activity. However, Austin (1962) and Searle (1969) did not study actual talk but worked with invented examples and their own intuitions about what it makes sense to say. Sacks (1992b), on the contrary, notes:

> One cannot invent new sequences of conversation and feel happy with them. You may be able to take "a question and answer," but if we have to extend it very far, then the issue of whether somebody would really say that, after, say, the fifth utterance, is one which we could not confidently argue. One doesn't have a strong intuition for sequencing in conversation. (p. 5)

The earlier ethnographers had generally relied on recording their observations through field notes. Why did Sacks prefer to use an audio recorder? Sacks's answer is that we cannot rely on our recollections of conversations. Certainly, depending on our memories, we can usually summarize what different people said. But it is simply impossible to remember (or even to note at the time) such matters as pauses, overlaps, and inbreaths.

Now, whether you think these kinds of things are important or not will depend upon what you can show with or without them. Indeed, you may not even be convinced that conversation itself is a particularly interesting topic. But, at least by studying tapes of conversations, you are able to focus on the "actual details" of one aspect of social life. As Sacks (1992b) puts it:

> My research is about conversation only in this incidental way, that we can get the actual happenings on tape and transcribe them more or less, and therefore have something to begin with. If you can't deal with the actual detail of actual events then you can't have a science of social life. (p. 26)

Tapes and transcripts also offer more than just "something to begin with." In the first place, they are a public record, available to the scientific community, in a way that field notes are not. Second, they can be replayed and transcriptions can be improved, and analyses can take off on different tacks unlimited by the original transcript. As Sacks (1992b) told his students:

> I started to play around with tape recorded conversations, for the single virtue that I could replay them; that I could type them out somewhat, and study them extendedly, who knew how long it might take. . . . It wasn't from any large interest in language, or from some theoretical formulation

of what should be studied, but simply by virtue of that; I could get my hands on it, and I could study it again and again. And also, consequentially, others could look at what I had studied, and make of it what they could, if they wanted to disagree with me. (p. 622)

A third advantage of detailed transcripts is that, if you want to, you can inspect sequences of utterances without being limited to the extracts chosen by the first researcher. For it is within these sequences, rather than in single turns of talk, that we make sense of conversation. As Sacks (1992b) points out:

Having available for any given utterance other utterances around it, is extremely important for determining what was said. If you have available only the snatch of talk that you're now transcribing, you're in tough shape for determining what it is. (p. 729)

There remains the potential charge that data based mainly on audio recordings is incomplete. We see Sacks's response to this issue when a student asks a question about "leaving out things like facial expressions" from his analysis (1992b, p. 26). Sacks at once concedes that "it would be great to study them [such things]. It's an absence." Nonetheless, he constructs a two-part defense of his data.

First, the idea of "completeness" may itself be an illusion. Surely, there cannot be totally "complete" data any more than there can be a "perfect" transcript? Second, Sacks (1992b, pp. 26-27) recognized some of the undoubted technical problems involved in camera positioning and the like if one were to use videos. These are the very issues that have been addressed, if not resolved, by more recent work based on video-recorded data (e.g., Heath, 1986, 1997; Heath & Luff, 1992). Rather, as always in science, everything will depend on what you are trying to do and where it seems that you may be able to make progress. As Sacks (1992b) puts it, "One gets started where you can maybe get somewhere" (p. 26).

It should not be assumed that the preparation of transcripts is simply a technical detail prior to the main business of the analysis. The

convenience of transcripts for presentational purposes is no more than an added bonus. As Atkinson and Heritage (1984) point out, the production and use of transcripts are essentially "research activities." They involve close, repeated listenings to recordings that often reveal previously unnoted recurring features of the organization of talk. Such listenings can most fruitfully be done in group data sessions. As described by Paul ten Have (1998), work in such groups usually begins with the members listening to an extract from a tape with a draft transcript and agreeing upon improvements to the transcript. Then

the participants are invited to proffer some observations on the data, to select an episode which they find "interesting" for whatever reason, and formulate their understanding or puzzlement, regarding that episode. Then anyone can come in to react to these remarks, offering alternatives, raising doubts, or whatever. (p. 124)

However, as ten Have makes clear, such group data sessions should be rather more than anarchic free-for-alls:

Participants are, on the one hand, *free* to bring in anything they like, but, on the other hand, *required* to ground their observations in the data at hand, although they may also support them with reference to their own data-based findings or those published in the literature. (p. 124)

Analyzing Tapes

As with any kind of data, the analysis of tapes and transcripts depends upon the generation of some research problem out of a particular theoretical orientation. Like the writing of field notes, the preparation of a transcript from an audio- or videotape is a theoretically saturated activity. Where there is more than one researcher, debate about what you are seeing and hearing is never just about collating data—it is data *analysis*.

But how do you push the analysis beyond an agreed transcript? The temptation is to start at line 1 of your transcript and work your way down the page, making observations as you go. However, the danger of proceeding in this way is that your observations are likely to be ad hoc and commonsensical. Moreover, if you are committed to an approach (like CA or DA) that looks at how the participants coproduce some meaning, then beginning with a single utterance gets you off on the wrong foot.

How else can you proceed? Jennifer Mason (1996) suggests that you can formulate a research topic in terms of different kinds of puzzles. Identifying a puzzle can also be a way to kick-start the analysis of a transcript. Once you have found your puzzle, the best method is often to *work back and forth* through your transcript to see how the puzzle arises and is resolved. This implies a strongly inductive bent to this kind of research. It follows that any research claims need to be identified in precise analyses of detailed transcripts. It is therefore necessary to avoid premature theory construction and the "idealization" of research materials that uses only general, nondetailed characterizations. Heritage (1984) sums up these assumptions as follows:

> Specifically, analysis is strongly "data-driven"—developed from phenomena which are in various ways evidenced in the data of interaction. Correspondingly, there is a strong bias against *a priori* speculation about the orientations and motives of speakers and in favour of detailed examination of conversationalists' actual actions. Thus the empirical conduct of speakers is treated as the central resource out of which analysis may develop. (p. 243)

In practice, Heritage adds, this means that it must be demonstrated that the regularities described can be shown to be produced by the participants and attended to by them as grounds for their own inferences and actions. Further, deviant cases, in which such regularities are absent, must be identified and analyzed.

However, the way in which CA obtains its results is rather different from how we might intuitively try to analyze talk. It may be helpful, therefore, if I conclude this section by offering a crude set of prescriptions about how to do CA (Table 31.1) and a list of things to avoid in

TABLE 31.1 How to Do Conversation Analysis

1. Always try to identify sequences of related talk.
2. Try to examine how speakers take on certain roles or identities through their talk (e.g., questioner/answerer or client-professional).
3. Look for particular outcomes in the talk (e.g., a request for clarification, a repair, laughter) and work backward to trace the trajectory through which a particular outcome was produced.

SOURCE: Silverman (1998a).

TABLE 31.2 Common Errors in Conversation Analysis

1. Explaining a turn at talk by reference to the speaker's intentions (except insofar as such intentions are topicalized in the conversation).
2. Explaining a turn at talk by reference to a speaker's role or status (e.g., as a doctor or as a man or woman).
3. Trying to make sense of a single line of transcript or utterance in isolation from the surrounding talk.

SOURCE: Silverman (1998a).

doing CA (Table 31.2). If we follow these rules, the analysis of conversations does not require exceptional skills. As Schegloff (1992) puts it in his introduction to Sacks's collected lectures, all we need to do is "begin with some observations, then find the problem for which these observations could serve as . . . the solution" (p. xlviii).

This means that doing the kind of systematic data analysis that CA demands is not an impossibly difficult activity. As Harvey Sacks (1992a) once pointed out, in doing CA we are only reminding ourselves about things we already know:

> I take it that lots of the results I offer, people can see for themselves. And they needn't be afraid to. And they needn't figure that the results are wrong because they can see them. . . . [It is] as if we found a new plant. It may have been a plant in your garden, but now you see it's different than something else. And you can look at it to see how it's different, and whether it's different in the way that somebody has said. (p. 488)

Wittgenstein (although mentioned only twice in Sacks's lectures), and his concern for assembling reminders of what we know already, is clearly relevant. Wittgenstein (1968) writes: "The aspects of things that are most important for us are hidden because of their simplicity and familiarity" (para. 129). Now Wittgenstein, of course, is referring to what is hidden from philosophers. But the same issue often arises for social scientists—to whom things can be "hidden because of their simplicity and familiarity."

◆ Conclusion

In a sense, nearly all qualitative research touches upon talk and text. In this chapter, however, I have resisted such inclusiveness in favor of a much more strictly defined version of appropriate ways of responding to the linguistically mediated character of qualitative data.

Although my own approach derives from Garfinkel's and Sacks's concern with members' methods, I have nonetheless tried to avoid adopting a "take it or leave it" approach. In particular, I have highlighted points of contact with a wide range of other approaches, including narrative-based ethnography, discourse analysis, and semiotics.

Above all, I have endeavored to offer practical advice to novice researchers who may be considering setting out in this direction. However, rather than offering a simple cookbook of techniques, this chapter, I hope, derives from a coherent set of principles. At the risk of restating what is already obvious, I conclude with a statement of four of those principles:

- Qualitative research is best viewed not as a set of freestanding techniques but as based on some analytically defined perspective.
- From my perspective, the particular strength of qualitative research, for both researchers and practitioners, is its ability to focus on actual practice in situ, looking at how social interactions are routinely *enacted*.
- The fashionable identification of qualitative method with an analysis of how people "see things" ignores the importance of how people "do things." This means that the apparent identification of non-quantitative social science with the open-ended interview needs to be reexamined. This does *not* mean that we should never interview, but that, as a minimum, we should first think through the alternatives.
- Qualitative researchers ought to question the conventional wisdom that their kind of research can only be "exploratory" or "anecdotal." Case study methods can be applied to large data sets and standard issues of "reliability" can, in part, be addressed by systematic transcription of data (see Peräkylä, 1997; Silverman, 1993, pp. 144-170).

■ Notes

1. In Garfinkel's (1967) sense, *reflexivity* refers not to self-questioning but to how context is constituted through interaction (see Gubrium & Holstein, Chapter 18, this volume).

2. The difference between DA and CA is a matter for debate. Some DA researchers find CA's refusal to engage directly with cultural and

political context disconcerting (see Wetherell, 1998). Equally, CA specialists question the validity of some DA researchers' appeals to their own sense of context (see Schegloff, 1998).

■ *References*

Atkinson, J. M., & Heritage, J. C. (Eds.). (1984). *Structures of social action.* Cambridge: Cambridge University Press.

Atkinson, P. A. (1992). The ethnography of a medical setting: Reading, writing and rhetoric. *Qualitative Health Research, 2,* 451-474.

Atkinson, P. A., & Coffey, A. (1997). Analysing documentary realities. In D. Silverman (Ed.), *Qualitative research: Theory, method and practice* (pp. 45-62). London: Sage.

Atkinson, P. A., & Silverman, D. (1997). Kundera's *Immortality*: The interview society and the invention of self. *Qualitative Inquiry, 3,* 304-325.

Austin, J. L. (1962). *How to do things with words.* Oxford: Clarendon.

Bales, R. F. (1950). *Interaction process analysis.* Cambridge, MA: Addison-Wesley.

Berelson, B. (1952). *Content analysis in communicative research.* New York: Free Press.

Cicourel, A. (1968). *The social organization of juvenile justice.* New York: John Wiley.

Denzin, N. K. (1990). Harold and Agnes: A feminist narrative's undoing. *Sociological Theory, 8,* 198-216.

Foucault, M. (1977). *Discipline and punish: The birth of the prison* (A. Sheridan, Trans.). New York: Pantheon.

Garfinkel, H. (1967). *Studies in ethnomethodology.* Englewood Cliffs, NJ: Prentice Hall.

Glassner, B., & Loughlin, J. (1987). *Drugs in adolescent worlds: Burnouts to straights.* New York: St. Martin's.

Gubrium, J. F. (1992). *Out of control: Family therapy and domestic disorder.* Newbury Park, CA: Sage.

Gubrium, J. F. (1993). *Speaking of life: Horizons of meaning for nursing home residents.* New York: Aldine de Gruyter.

Gubrium, J. F. (1997). *Living and dying at Murray Manor.* Charlottesville: University Press of Virginia. (Original work published 1975)

Gubrium, J. F., & Buckholdt, D. (1982). *Describing care: Image and practice in rehabilitation.* Cambridge, MA: Oelschlager, Gunn & Hain.

Gubrium, J. F., & Holstein, J. A. (1997). *The new language of qualitative method.* New York: Oxford University Press.

Heath, C. C. (1986). *Body movement and speech in medical interaction.* Cambridge: Cambridge University Press.

Heath, C. C. (1997). Using video: Analysing activities in face to face interaction. In D. Silverman (Ed.), *Qualitative research: Theory, method and practice* (pp. 183-200). London: Sage.

Heath, C. C., & Luff, P (1992). Collaboration and control: Crisis management and multimedia technology in London underground line control rooms. *Journal of Computer Supported Cooperative Work, 1*(1-2), 69-94.

Heritage, J. C. (1984). *Garfinkel and ethnomethodology.* Cambridge: Polity.

Holstein, J. A., & Gubrium, J. F. (1995). *The active interview.* Thousand Oaks, CA: Sage.

Holstein, J. A., & Gubrium, J. F. (1997). Active interviewing. In D. Silverman (Ed.), *Qualitative research: Theory, method and practice* (pp. 113-129). London: Sage.

Mason, J. (1996). *Qualitative researching.* London: Sage.

Mead, G. H. (1934). *Mind, self, and society: From the standpoint of a social behaviorist* (C. W. Morris, Ed.). Chicago: University of Chicago Press.

Miller, J. (1996). *Female gang involvement in the Midwest: A two-city comparison.* Unpublished doctoral dissertation, University of Southern California.

Miller, J., & Glassner, B. (1997). The "inside" and the "outside": Finding realities in interviews. In D. Silverman (Ed.), *Qualitative research: Theory, method and practice* (pp. 99-112). London: Sage.

Parsons, T. (1937). *The structure of social action.* New York: McGraw-Hill.

Peräkylä, A. (1997). Reliability and validity in research based upon transcripts. In D. Silverman (Ed.), *Qualitative research: Theory, method and practice* (pp. 201-220). London: Sage.

Potter, J. (1997). Discourse analysis as a way of analysing naturally-occurring talk. In D. Silverman (Ed.), *Qualitative research: Theory, method and practice* (pp. 144-160). London: Sage.

Potter, J., & Wetherell, M. (1987). *Discourse and social psychology: Beyond attitudes and behaviour.* London: Sage.

Prior, L. (1997). Following in Foucault's footsteps: Text and context in qualitative research. In D. Silverman (Ed.), *Qualitative research: Theory, method and practice* (pp. 63-79). London: Sage.

Propp, V. I. (1968). *The morphology of the folktale* (L. A. Wagner, Ed.; 2nd rev. ed.). Austin: University of Texas Press.

Richardson, L. (1990). *Writing strategies: Reaching diverse audiences.* Newbury Park, CA: Sage.

Sacks, H. (1974). On the analyzability of stories by children. In R. Turner (Ed.), *Ethnomethodology* (pp. 216-232). Harmondsworth: Penguin.

Sacks, H. (1984). Notes on methodology. In J. M. Atkinson & J. Heritage (Eds.), *Structures of social action: Studies in conversation analysis* (pp. 21-27). Cambridge: Cambridge University Press.

Sacks, H. (1992a). *Lectures on conversation* (G. Jefferson, Ed.; Vol. 1). Oxford: Blackwell.

Sacks, H. (1992b). *Lectures on conversation* (G. Jefferson, Ed.; Vol. 2). Oxford: Blackwell.

Saussure, F. de. (1974). *Course in general linguistics.* London: Fontana.

Schegloff, E. A. (1991). Reflections on talk and social structure. In D. Boden & D. Zimmerman (Eds.), *Talk and social structure: Studies in ethnomethodology and conversation analysis* (pp. 44-70). Cambridge: Polity.

Schegloff, E. A. (1992). Introduction. In H. Sacks, *Lectures on conversation* (G. Jefferson, Ed.; Vol. 1). Oxford: Blackwell.

Schegloff, E. A. (1998). Reply to Wetherell. *Discourse and Society, 9,* 413-416.

Searle, J. R. (1969). *Speech acts.* Cambridge: Cambridge University Press.

Silverman, D. (1993). *Interpreting qualitative data: Strategies for analysing talk, text and interaction.* London: Sage.

Silverman, D. (1998a). Analysing conversation. In C. Seale (Ed.), *Researching society and culture* (pp. 261-274). London: Sage.

Silverman, D. (1998b). *Harvey Sacks: Social science and conversation analysis.* Cambridge: Polity.

Silverman, D. (2000). *Doing qualitative research: A practical handbook.* London: Sage.

Stimson, G. (1986). Place and space in sociological fieldwork. *Sociological Review, 34,* 641-656.

ten Have, P. (1998). *Doing conversation analysis: A practical guide.* Thousand Oaks, CA: Sage.

Voysey, M. (1975). *A constant burden.* London: Routledge.

Watson, R. (1997). Ethnomethodology and textual analysis. In D. Silverman (Ed.), *Qualitative research: Theory, method and practice* (pp. 80-98). London: Sage.

Weber, M. (1949). *The methodology of the social sciences* (E. A. Shils & H. A. Finch, Eds. & Trans.). New York: Free Press.

Wetherell, M. (1998). Positioning and interpretative repertoires: Conversation analysis and post-structuralism in dialogue. *Discourse and Society, 9,* 387-412.

Wittgenstein, L. (1968). *Philosophical investigations.* Oxford: Basil Blackwell.

32

FOCUS GROUPS IN FEMINIST RESEARCH

◆ Esther Madriz

Me gusta mas conversar así, con un grupo de mujeres. . . . Cuando estoy sola con un entrevistador, me siento intimidada, asustada. Y, si ellos me llaman por el telefono, yo nunca les contesto sus preguntas. ¿Como puedo saber quienes son o que quieren?

[I'd rather talk this way, with a group of women. . . . When I am alone with an interviewer, I feel intimidated, scared. And if they call me over the telephone, I never answer their questions. How can I know what they really want or who they are?]

María Fernández, 25-year-old Dominican woman
(participant in a focus group I led in Washington
Heights, New York City, spring 1995)

The two major techniques used by researchers to collect qualitative data are participant observation and individual interviews. Focus groups, or group interviews, possess elements of both techniques while maintaining their own uniqueness as a distinctive research method (Morgan, 1988). Fundamentally, they are "a way of listening to people and learning from them" (Morgan, 1998, p. 9). As María Fernández's words suggest, focus groups allow access to research participants who may find one-on-one, face-to-face interaction "scary" or "intimidating." By creating multiple lines of communication, the group interview offers participants such as María a safe environment where they can share ideas, be-

liefs, and attitudes in the company of people from the same socioeconomic, ethnic, and gender backgrounds. Some of the studies that have been conducted on focus groups show that group participants find the experience more gratifying and stimulating than individual interviews (Morgan, 1988; Wilkinson, 1998).

This chapter deals specifically with the use of focus groups from a feminist/postmodernist framework. The major concerns of feminist/postmodernist ethnographers are the moral dilemmas present in the process of interviewing and the role of the interviewer in this process. These concerns have given particular significance to the voices and feelings of the participants (Fontana & Frey, 1994). Moreover, by acknowledging the absence and invisibility that have surrounded certain population groups in the social sciences, and more specifically women of color, feminist/postmodernist researchers have made the race and ethnicity of the researchers and the respondents focal points in their studies.

For years, the voices of women of color have been silenced in most research projects. Focus groups may facilitate women of color "writing culture together" by exposing not only the layers of oppression that have suppressed these women's expressions, but the forms of resistance that they use every day to deal with such oppressions. In this regard, I argue that focus groups can be an important element in the advancement of an agenda of social justice for women, because they can serve to expose and validate women's everyday experiences of subjugation and their individual and collective survival and resistance strategies.

The focus group is a collectivistic rather than an individualistic research method that focuses on the multivocality of participants' attitudes, experiences, and beliefs. In the social sciences, however, individualistic research methods have been prevalent for several reasons. First, the dominance of positivistic, quantitative studies, particularly in the United States, has led to a preference for the individual questionnaire as the favored and more accepted data gathering method. Second, even among qualitative researchers, the one-to-one, face-to-face interview is the most widely used research tool. It is only recently that collective testimonies and narratives have gained limited ascendancy among qualitative researchers. Even among feminist scholars, who—paradoxically—emphasize the communal and collectivist nature of women's lives, the most important research method is still the individual interview (Finch, 1984; Oakley, 1981; Wilkinson, 1998). As a Latina feminist, I place focus groups within the context of collective testimonies and group resistance narratives. They can be used by women in general and by women of color in particular to unveil specific and little-researched aspects of women's daily existences, their feelings, attitudes, hopes, and dreams.

The singularity of focus groups is that they allow social scientists to observe the most important sociological process—collective human interaction. Furthermore, they enable researchers to gather large amounts of information about such interactions in limited periods of time. Curiously, although focus groups have been used extensively in market research, it has taken some time for qualitative and ethnographic social researchers to accept them and to get acquainted with the method. Hence the existing information regarding focus groups is not only scarce but unsystematic. As Morgan and Krueger (1993) suggest, "Social science and evaluation research are still at a stage at which most of our knowledge about focus groups comes from personal experience rather than systematic investigation" (p. 3). During the past 5 years, however, group interviews have gained in popularity among a few feminist and postmodernist social researchers.

Compared with participant observation, focus groups have the disadvantage of—sometimes—taking place outside of the settings where social interaction typically occurs. Therefore, the range of behavioral information that can be gathered through group interviews is narrower and is—with some exceptions—limited to verbal communication, body language, and self-report data. In addition, given the necessary presence of a facilitator, it is difficult to discern how "authentic" the social interaction in a focus group really is. This last limitation, however, is also shared with participant observation, for it has been argued that the presence of the researcher may also alter the behavior of those he or she observes.

Compared with individual interviews, the clear advantage of focus groups is that they make it possible for researchers to observe the interactive processes occurring among participants. Often these processes include spontaneous responses from the members of the group that ease their involvement and participation in the discussion. Moreover, the interaction among group participants often decreases the amount of interaction between the facilitator and the individual members of the group. This gives more weight to the participants' opinions, decreasing the influence the researcher has over the interview process.

◆ *History of Focus Groups*

Morgan (1998) explains how focus groups developed in three phases: First, during the 1920s, social scientists used the technique for a variety of purposes, one of the most important being the development of survey questionnaires. Second, between World War II and the 1970s, focus groups were used mainly by market researchers to understand people's wants and needs. Finally, from the 1980s to the present, focus group interviews have been used by various professionals to do research on issues dealing with health, sexual behavior, and other social issues. Indeed, in recent years, social scientists have begun to consider the focus group to be an important qualitative research technique.

Although some early field researchers acknowledged using group interviews, few made explicit reference to them as a distinctive methodology. Bronislaw Malinowski, for example, one of the major figures in cultural anthropology, acknowledged in his diaries conversations among groups of native Trobriand Islanders. Nevertheless, he did not explicitly describe the particularities of these group interviews in his reports (Frey & Fontana, 1993). William Foote Whyte, author of *Street Corner Society* (1943), made use of group interviews with gang members in Boston, but he did not explicitly acknowledge the use of group interviews as a unique research technique.

During the early 1940s, Robert Merton and Paul Lazarsfeld introduced the method of group interviewing into the social sciences. In their pioneering work, they used focused group interviews to evaluate the reaction of a group of subjects to wartime radio programs at the Office of Radio Research at Columbia University (Merton, 1987; Stewart & Shamdasani, 1990). Since then, focus group interviews have been used consistently, especially by market researchers, among whom they are one of the favored qualitative research techniques (Morgan, 1988).

For about 40 years after Merton and Lazarsfeld's work, there was little acceptance of group interviews as a method of social science inquiry. Since the late 1980s, however, there has been a renewed interest in promoting the use of group interviews as a recognized social science research method. This interest is not limited to sociologists and anthropologists. Indeed, a diversity of social scientists and other professionals are finding this qualitative technique useful. Political scientists, for example, are using focus groups to assess the public perceptions of political candidates and their views on specific issues. Stewart and Shamdasani (1990) document how focus groups were used in the 1980s during President Ronald Reagan's administration to understand the perception of U.S. and Soviet citizens regarding relations between the two countries. Similarly, they illustrate their own use of this technique to learn about consumer practices in the purchase of new automobiles. In sum, focus groups have become a valuable tool for social researchers and other professionals, regardless of their particular fields of inquiry (Frey & Fontana, 1993; Morgan, 1998).

In the social sciences, group interviews developed as reservations concerning the effectiveness of individual information gathering techniques grew. Such reservations focused on the influence of the interviewer on research participants and on the limitations imposed by closed-ended questions. Traditional interview techniques, which used highly structured questionnaires, had a major disadvantage—the interviewer's framework, viewpoint, and beliefs, consciously or not, influenced the nature of the questions asked and the choices given to research participants (Krueger, 1994). Less directed methods were based on the premise that they were more appropriate to elicit responses that better reflected the social reality of the interviewee.

As Krueger (1994) argues, the acceptance of qualitative techniques, especially focus group interviews, has been slow due to the positivistic legacy of reliance on numbers as the most accepted way to measure social reality and due to the emphasis on quantitative methods, considered more "scientific" than qualitative methods. Although quantitative methods have dominated the social sciences, particularly in the United States, many contemporary social researchers are interested in learning more about research participants' opinions, attitudes, and everyday interactions. Feminist and postmodernist researchers, particularly, believe that traditional methods are alien to population groups who have been traditionally marginalized. These researchers also consider such methods inappropriate to recover the voices of members of marginalized groups because, among other reasons, those methods force upon participants an agenda that it is not their own but the researcher's (Maynard & Purvis, 1994). Even more important, feminist and postmodern researchers believe that traditional research methods do not result in high-quality data (Wilkinson, 1998).

◆ Focus Groups, Postmodernism, and Feminism

Influenced by feminist and postmodernist ethnographic studies, a few social researchers have "rediscovered" focus groups and are now increasingly utilizing them in their specific areas of research. This technique is particularly useful to postmodernist ethnographers, who attempt to remain as close as possible to accounts of everyday life while trying to minimize the distance between themselves and their research participants. It is believed that the group situation may reduce the influence of the interviewer on the research subjects by tilting the balance of power toward the group. Because focus groups emphasize the collective, rather than the individual, they foster free expression of ideas, encouraging the members of the group to speak up (Denzin, 1986; Frey & Fontana, 1993).

Feminist scholars, disenchanted with the disengagement and aloofness of positivistic research and with its inability to explore women's experiences and life situations, have also begun to advocate a more integrative, experiential approach to research. Such an approach regards women's everyday experiences as an important area of study that necessitates alternative methods of scrutiny. Among these methods, ethnography has been regarded as "particularly suited to feminist research" (Stacey, 1991, p. 112). Feminists have advanced many arguments to justify their preference for ethnographic research over traditional survey research methods. First, they have pointed to the potential for one-to-one interviewing to reproduce power relationships between the researcher and the participants (Finch, 1984; Oakley, 1981; Wilkinson, 1998). Their argument is that the researcher usually dominates the whole research process, from the selection of the topic to the choice of the method and the questions asked, to the imposition of her own framework on the research findings. Focus groups minimize the control the researcher has during the data gathering process by decreasing the power of the researcher over research participants. The collective nature of the group interview empowers the participants and validates their voices and experiences.

Second, feminist research attempts to lessen the dichotomy that traditional research imposes between thought and feeling, between the personal and the political, between the observed and the observer, between "dispassionate" or "objective" research and "passionate" or "subjective" knowledge. Giving voice to the subjective experiences of women becomes the focus of inquiry (Stacey, 1991). Rather than seeing research as a linear, one-way process, feminist researchers emphasize the contradictions and complexities encountered in their work.

It should be noted, however, that feminist researchers hold several and conflicting views; they do not take one unified approach. Olesen (1994) characterizes three types of feminist research. First is standpoint research, which emphasizes the need to focus on women's experiences in everyday life as it is familiar to them. Those experiences are constantly shaped, created, and re-created by women. Second is feminist empiricism, which adheres to "the standards of the current norms of qualitative inquiry" (p. 163). This also creates new and strict research practices to make research findings believable. Third is postmodernist feminism, which focuses on stories and narratives and on the construction and reproduction of knowledge. In spite of their differences, however, feminist researchers share the common need of centering and "problematizing" women's diversity of views and life experiences. Group interviews, I believe, offer a viable qualitative research method that satisfies the requirements of all three models of feminist research. Group interviews are particularly suited for uncovering women's daily experience through collective stories and resistance narratives that are filled with cultural symbols, words, signs, and ideological representations that reflect the different dimensions of power and domination that frame women's quotidian experiences.

However, in order to enhance the requirements and standards of qualitative inquiry (Olesen, 1994), as feminist empiricists demand, we must pay greater attention to the following questions: How can a social scientist conduct ethical research that uses subjects not only as providers of information but as human agents with potential to exert social change? What is the potential of group interviews and of qualitative research projects in general for fostering such change? Can the focus group be a data gathering technique as well as part of a consciousness-raising process through which human sharing and interaction take place? Is the focus group a valid research method that minimizes the voice and influence of the researcher?

Black feminists (e.g., Collins, 1986; hooks, 1990), Latina feminists (e.g., Benmayor, 1991; Garcia, 1989; Madriz, 1997), and Asian feminists (e.g., Chow, 1987; Espiritu, 1997) remind us that women of color experience a triple subjugation based on class, race, and gender oppression. Researchers should take such subjugation into account in their selection of methods for studying women's lives. Not all methods are suitable for interviewing women and much less women of color, who, under-

standably, may feel apprehensive about talking with an interviewer about their lives. As Collins (1998) argues, the contemporary debate about quantitative versus qualitative research reflects the polarization that exists between what is male, White, and scientific on one side and what is considered soft, subjective, female, and possibly Black, Latino, or Asian on the other.

Some researchers have documented the reluctance of some Latinas and African American women to participate in survey research and other studies that use positivistic methodologies. This reluctance is especially strong among undocumented women, women who do not speak or are not fluent in English, and women who engage in nontraditional activities or activities involving the informal or the underground economy (Madriz, 1998). As a response, a few qualitative feminist researchers are advocating the use of focus groups for interviewing women (Fine, 1994; Jarrett, 1993; Madriz, 1997, 1998; Wilkinson, 1998). Jarrett (1993) has emphasized the importance of the use of focus groups in research with women of lower socioeconomic status, particularly women of color (see also Madriz, 1998).

Focus groups not only encourage researchers to listen to the voices of those who have been subjugated, they also represent a methodology that is consistent with the particularities and everyday experiences of women of color. Women have historically used conversation with other women as a way to deal with their oppression. For African American, Latina, and Asian American women, for example, sharing with other women has been an important way to confront and endure their marginality. Historically, women have gathered to talk about issues important to them and to get involved in political activism. Referring to African American women, for example, Cheryl Townsend Gilkes (1994, p. 235) documents how, after slavery ended, churchwomen and teachers gathered to organize throughout the South. Women's clubs were also important places where women learned from each other how to challenge male domination in the existing male-controlled organizations. Similarly, Mexican women have been instrumental in keeping traditional practices through getting together to cook, to organize birthday and *quinceaños* parties, and to talk and keep alive their rich oral traditions (Dill, 1994). Finally, Yen Le Espiritu (1997, p. 39) explains how, in 1937, Chinese women employed in San Francisco's Chinatown organized themselves and struck against the garment factory owned by the National Dollar Store. All these examples illustrate how women's gathering and sharing with other women has the potential to result in actions and movements for social change.

◆ Shattering Otherization as a Way to Promote Social Change

Focus groups are similar to other research methods in that they enable researchers to have access to the opinions, viewpoints, attitudes, and experiences of individuals. They also provide social scientists access to individual and collective life stories. However, as a qualitative methodology, focus groups have a lot to offer social researchers interested in building new paradigms of social research and promoting social change. Obviously, no research method per se can facilitate such change. My point, however, is that some methodologies are more suitable than others for shattering a colonizing discourse in which images of research subjects as the Other are constantly reproduced (Fine, 1994; Madriz, 1998).

Several feminist researchers who have worked with focus groups have reported how participants begin to discuss issues of interest to them without even waiting for questions from the moderator. Griffin (1986), for example, found in her research dealing with young women's experiences that some of her participants' focus group conversations did not even fall within the areas she had anticipated asking about. Thus group interviews heighten the opportunities for participants to decide the direction and content of the discussion.

As Michel Fine (1994) remarks, qualitative researchers collaborate in the construction of the self-other hyphen. In fact, it has been as-

serted that the relationship between researcher and participants reproduces colonial and postcolonial structures. I argue that group interviews minimize some of the self-other distance in various ways. First, the multivocality of the participants limits the control of the moderator, who has less power over a group than over a single individual (Holstein & Gubrium, 1995; Wilkinson, 1998). Second, the unstructured character of the focus group interview guide (the instrument favored by feminist ethnographers) decreases the control of the researcher over the interview process. Structured questionnaires, which consist of closed- or open-ended questions, maximize the influence of the researcher over the direction of the conversation and introduce the researcher's preconceived notions and opinions and even words and concepts. Indeed, it is possible to have a focus group without an interview guide, entirely eliminating the researcher's prejudices from the interaction (Morgan, 1988; Wilkinson, 1998). Finally, focus groups involve not only "vertical interaction," or interaction between the moderator and the interviewees, but also "horizontal interaction" among the group participants. Although it can be argued that there is a potential for power relations to surface among the participants, these relations, if they arise, are the participants' *own* power relations, in their *own* constructed hierarchies. Indeed, observing and documenting the development of these hierarchies may provide the researcher with some very important data.

Rather than giving voice to the other, or knowing the other, focus groups open possibilities of listening to the plural voices of Others "as constructors and agents of knowledge" (Fine, 1994, p. 75) and as agents of social change. Jenny Kitzinger (1994) explains how the group situation ensures that precedence is given to the participants' hierarchies of importance, their own words and language, and the frameworks they use to describe their own experiences. Language is of particular importance because a sensitive understanding of people's lives requires shared symbols, meanings, and vocabularies. Therefore, the power that research participants hold at the data collection stage of focus groups is not only a matter of ethics. Many researchers have also reported how the interaction among participants leads to the gathering of high-quality data (Wilkinson, 1998). By asking questions, participants contribute to challenge each other's contradictions and responses. In my own use of focus groups while doing research on fear of crime, participants confronted each other in this manner:

Maria: No, I tell you, *de verdad,* I am not afraid of crime.
Juana: Well, you are saying now that you are not afraid of crime. So, then why did you say before that you don't like to go out alone at night?
Rosa: Yes, that's true. You did say that before.
Maria: Okay, I am talking more in general. I try not to be afraid.

In this and many similar instances, participants challenged each other on responses that seemed to reflect contradictions between what they said and the ways they behaved when confronted with particular situations.

Group interviews are especially significant in that they allow the researcher to witness one of the most important processes for the social sciences—social interaction (Berg, 1998). Unlike more traditional research techniques, such as face-to-face interviews, in group interviews researchers observe participants engaging in dialogue, sharing ideas, opinions, and experiences, and even debating with each other. Indeed, it is this sharing that creates the socially constructed interactional experiences necessary for what Denzin (1989) calls "interpretive interactionism." The plurality of actors involved in the focus groups makes the process of interviewing more active and dynamic, facilitating the social construction of meaning (Holstein & Gubrium, 1995). Therefore, the group interaction becomes a very important aspect of the research, contributing to "the development of shared stocks of knowledge" (Holstein & Gubrium, 1995, p. 71). This shared stock of knowledge is essential to the process of writing history and culture together. For women of color, whose experiences—as researchers as

well as subjects of research—have often been neglected in the social sciences, this writing is especially important because it contributes to tearing down the walls of silence that have hidden women of color's triple and overlapping marginality: being female, being of color, and, usually, being poor.

Obviously, focus groups are not a solution to the reproduction of the Other. However, at the data gathering stage, they facilitate researchers' hearing the *plural voices* of the participants (Fine, 1994, p. 75). The multivocality of the group situation validates the subjects' experiences with other subjects of similar socioeconomic, gender, and racial/ethnic backgrounds. This validation empowers participants, contributing to the construction of a research agenda embedded in the struggles for social justice (West, 1988). In a culture that highlights individualism and separation, shifting the research agenda in the direction of commonality and togetherness is, in itself, subversive.

When engaged in participant observation, the researcher is able to observe the unfolding of social processes in their actual social environment. It could be argued that this does not occur in the environment of the focus group, because the place where the group meets is decided by the researcher. As Frey and Fontana (1993) argue, qualitative research methods can be placed on a continuum; focus groups use more familiar settings than other research techniques and less familiar settings than field research or ethnographic studies. Evidently, there is a wide variation in how researchers use focus groups, with some even using special facilities, one-way mirrors, and videotaping in an attempt to create a more unfamiliar environment. Among feminist and postmodernist researchers, however, the tendency is to use the participants' own settings to carry out "in the field" group interviews. In my work, I have purposefully used participants' familiar settings, such as their living rooms and kitchens, a senior citizen's dining area, a church basement, a classroom, and even a teenager's bedroom. Using the participants' familiar spaces further diffuses the power of the researcher, decreasing the possibilities of "Otherization."

◆ *The Use of Focus Groups as Collective Testimony*

Feminist researchers have objected to the use of conventional, positivistic methodologies in the study of women and, more specifically, women of color and women of lower socioeconomic status (Etter-Lewis, 1991; Fonow & Cook, 1991; Reinharz, 1992). Some of the most compelling issues addressed by feminists deal with research into women's everyday lives and their particularities, and thus with gaining access into their lives. Hence feminists are attempting to use and develop research methods geared toward facilitating forms of communication with women and among women. Some the most common questions raised by feminist researchers include these: Doing research for whom and by whom? How is it conducted? Whose words are privileged (Benmayor, 1991)? One of the principles of feminist research has been expressed in the phrase "research by, about, and for women" (Acker, Barry, & Esseveld, 1983; Harding, 1987). This has resulted in a large amount of literature on women based on oral histories, in-depth interviews, and testimonies aimed at narrating the everyday reality of women's lives. Interestingly, very few books dealing with feminist research methods have included discussions on the use of focus groups (Wilkinson, 1998).

Since the 1960s, the entrance of African American, Latina, Asian American, and Native American women into the social sciences in small but unparalleled numbers has led to mounting criticism of the absence of women of color from many research projects and of the colonizing nature of many of those research projects. Third World feminists have joined these criticisms of the postcolonial nature of research practices.

As a Latina feminist researcher, I regard the use of focus groups as a form of collective testimony. "Multivocal conversations" have been used by women for generations in the form of exchanges with their mothers, sisters, and female neighbors and friends. In a male-centered culture, some of these conversations have been caricatured as "idle talk" or even "gossip." However, these dialogues have traditionally been a major way in which women have faced their social isolation and their oppression. Thus testimonies, individual or collective, become a vehicle for capturing the socioeconomic, political, and human challenges that women face (Randall, 1980).

The interaction occurring within the group accentuates empathy and commonality of experiences and fosters self-disclosure and self-validation. Communication among women can be an awakening experience and an important element in the consciousness-raising process. It asserts women's right to validate their own experience, and it allows them to build on each other's opinions and thoughts (Oakley, 1981). The awareness that other women experience similar problems or share analogous ideas is important in that it contributes to women's realization that their opinions are legitimate and valid. This awareness may contribute to raising consciousness among women that their problems are not just individual but structural and that these problems are shared by other women. This awareness is also consistent with a social research agenda inserted into movements for social change.

Latina women, for example, belong to a culture in which *mi familia y mi comunidad* (my family and my community) take precedence (Heyck, 1994; Marin & VanOss Marin, 1991; Moore, 1970). Because extended kinship groups are common, sharing is a customary practice, but sharing with other women is especially important for Latinas. In many Latina families, women sit around a kitchen table to plan the meals, drink coffee, and share stories and concerns. Hence communication exchange through the use of focus groups can be considered a practice with which many Latina women are accustomed. Similar claims can be made about African American women, who have faced centuries of oppression and the legacy of slavery. Sharing with other women has been an important way in which African American women have dealt with their oppression. Moreover, as Glenn (1986) notes, Asian American women "kept many customs alive by cooking ethnic foods, organizing traditional celebrations, practicing folk healing methods, and transmitting folklore" (p. 196). They performed most of these activities while engaging in dialogue and conversations with other women.

Rina Benmayor (1991), a Puerto Rican scholar, is one of the few to have pointed out the transformative experience of collective oral history. Benmayor asserts that group testimonies empower people, either individually or collectively: "Social empowerment enables people to speak and speaking empowers" (p. 159). Focus groups, as a form of collective testimony, can become an empowering experience for women in general, and for women of color in particular.

◆ Using Focus Groups to Study Lower-Socioeconomic-Class Women of Color

Patricia Hill Collins (1998) argues that "breaking silence enables individual African-American women to reclaim humanity in a system that gains part of its strength by objectifying Black women" (p. 47). Similar words can be applied to Latina, Native American, and Asian American women, especially those of lower socioeconomic status. By speaking collectively, women of color not only reclaim their humanity but, at the same time, empower themselves by making sense of their experience of vulnerability and subjugation.

I decided to use focus groups based on several theoretical and methodological considerations. First, because fear of crime has been related to social vulnerability, I believed it was particularly important for me to gain access to women who, by virtue of their race and class, occupy socially devalued positions. More specifically, for my research goals it was crucial that I interview Latina and African American women of lower socioeconomic background. Second, I was concerned that women of color,

who are usually more afraid of crime than members of other groups, would feel intimidated by face-to-face, one-on-one interviews. The fact that several women were present at the same time in a room definitely eased some of these concerns. Third, it was necessary to include undocumented women, who face unique situations of socioeconomic and political vulnerability. I believe that because the undocumented women involved in my project were interviewed in the company of other undocumented and documented women, rather than individually, they were more willing to participate in the study and were more open to entering into the discussion.

Collins (1990) has written about systems of inequality or matrices of domination. In the case of lower-socioeconomic-status women of color, the intersection of race, class, and gender puts them in an extremely vulnerable position, making it difficult in many cases for researchers to gain access into their lives. In the case of undocumented Latinas and Asian American women, who are considered "illegal" or "criminal" by virtue of their not having legal resident status in the United States, their situation places them in a particularly defenseless position. Indeed, the multiple and overlapping vulnerabilities of undocumented, lower-class Latinas and Asian American women make them one of the most extreme cases of "Otherization." Aura, a 16-year-old Puerto Rican who participated in one of the focus groups for my study and who lives in a Latino neighborhood in Brooklyn, New York, expressed her feelings of multiple subjugation in a vivid manner:

> Like my mother said, you are born with two strikes already: you are Puerto Rican and you are a woman. So, if something happens to you nobody is going to help. I think it is worse for us Latinas, because we are in the middle, between Black and white. . . . so, it's like, we get it from both ways, you know? (quoted in Madriz, 1997, p. 54)

In sum, I believed that traditional methodologies were not appropriate for my study. As a feminist, I wanted to minimize as much as possible the separation between myself and the participants, although my being a middle-class professor contributed to this separation. I believed that the focus group method would limit the imposition of my own ideas and beliefs onto the women and amplify the power of the participants while also diminishing my own influence on the conversations. It was also extremely important for me to observe the interaction among participants and to witness how they were building on each other's words, ideas, and feelings. The following is an example of a conversation on the subject of carrying some form of protection. The participants are all Latina teenagers:

Carmen: I usually carry something on me.
Isabel: Like a weapon or something
Gloria: I also carry a weapon with me . . . like keys or other sharp things to protect myself.
Carmen: Come on! Tell her the truth.
Gloria: Yes, I carry a knife.
Carmen: And she carries a small gun. (quoted in Madriz, 1997, p. 141)

One important consideration for my study was how I might gain access to lower-socioeconomic-status women of color. As a Latina researcher, I believe that impersonal recruiting strategies—often preferred by positivistic researchers—do not work with lower-socioeconomic-status women of color, and especially with undocumented women. Other social scientists who have done research with women of color have reported similar experiences (Cannon, Higginbotham, & Leung, 1988; Jarrett, 1993). Jarrett (1993) considers impersonal recruiting strategies inappropriate for research with low-income minority populations. In her study of low-income African American women, she visited Head Start programs in poor neighborhoods throughout Chicago and talked to women directly about her study in order to gain their participation.

My sources of recruitment were personal networks such as friends, students, community leaders, and friends of friends who worked in nonprofit, community organizations. The first contact with the recruiter was usually face-to-face; in a few instances, first contact took place over the telephone. In cases where I did

not know the recruiter personally, I asked my friends and students to initiate the contact. They would mention my name to the recruiter, indicating that I was a professor doing a study on fear of crime and informing him or her that I would call at a later date. They usually informed the person that I was a professor involved in social justice and social change. As one of my students said, "I told the director of the organization that you are okay." This personalistic approach was extremely useful given the reluctance many people of color, and particularly undocumented women, feel about participating in research (Zinn, 1979).

Although this personal approach works better than other methods for reaching populations of color, it is still a challenge to gain the participation of members of some lower socioeconomic groups, such as lower-class Latinas. Some feel apprehensive about participating in group discussions, especially if they are recent immigrants or undocumented women, live on welfare or engage in any nonnormative behavior (such as alternative family living arrangements), or work in the underground economy. I found that economic incentives definitely increased the likelihood of participation in the project, and I believe participants should be offered such incentives as a reward for giving their time.

Some social scientists claim that Latinos are more willing to participate in research projects (Marin, Perez-Stable, & VanOss Marin, 1989). However, my experience in doing focus groups with low-income Latinas shows otherwise. Several factors influence the participation of Latinas in research projects. First, many Latinas, especially those of lower socioeconomic status, fulfill traditional roles within the family. Indeed, most of them carry full responsibility for the care of the children and the house. Second, traditional Latino families are hierarchical institutions in which men are considered the *cabeza de familia* (head of the family). Often, Latinas exercise their power in the family *por debajo* (behind the scenes; see Heyck, 1994). Frequently, in traditional Latino families—even in two-wage-earner families—women still perform more of the household work (Pesquera,

1993). Latinas fulfill many functions as mothers, caretakers, cooks, and keepers of the house. They often feel that they should be fully available to their spouses and to their children, making it difficult for some low-socioeconomic-status Latinas to attend activities outside of the house. Third, often these women have more unforeseen demands on their time and less control over their schedules than do other women (Krinitzky, 1990; Stack, 1974). Hence it is my experience that often Latinas fail to arrive at interviews or come late. In my experience, in spite of overrecruiting, only a few women will show up out of 12 to 15 who had confirmed their participation. Providing transportation for participants, either by picking them up or by sending drivers to bring them to the meeting place, or just offering to reimburse them for transportation costs improves attendance. But it is even better to meet them at their most convenient place, such as the soup kitchen where they have dinner or the church or English-as-a-second-language school they attend.

One reason for the high rate of nonattendance among lower-socioeconomic-status women is that they may feel uncomfortable saying no and turning down an invitation. In the case of Latinas, Latina *simpatía* emphasizes cordial and affable relationships. However, it may interfere with recruitment because it makes it more socially acceptable to say yes and accept an invitation. Thus a commitment to participate in a group may be made, but later the promise may not be fulfilled (Marin & VanOss Marin, 1991, p. 13).

In addition, I have found that it is not unusual for these women participants to encounter emergencies at the last minute that prevent them from participating in the group—a child gets sick or gets into trouble at school, a relative needs help with child care or needs to be accompanied to some appointment, or a basic service breaks down at home, such as water or electricity.

It was especially important for my study to have homogeneous groups in terms of age, class, and race because it was evident that participants felt freer to express their ideas about images and cultural representations of crime, criminals, and victims when discussing them with other women from their own backgrounds. Explaining this need to the recruiter, however, became a very sensitive issue. On several occasions, I was asked questions such as "Why do you want a group of all Latinas?" Or "Why only Black girls?" "Why can't we mix them up with White girls?" In most cases, after I carefully explained the nature of the topic, the recruiter understood the need for homogeneous focus groups.

I held 18 focus groups involving between 5 and 12 White, Black, and Latina women. I avoided using larger groups because of the difficulties they would pose for handling the discussion and keeping the conversation around the topic of research. Moreover, larger groups make it more difficult for all the participants to have their opinions heard. I acted as the facilitator in all the focus groups, except for one that was led by a student acting as a research assistant. The discussions typically lasted from 90 minutes to 2 hours. With the permission of the participants, the discussions were taped and later transcribed (Madriz, 1997).

One of the major dilemmas in data gathering concerns the question of the race/ethnicity of the facilitator versus that of the participants. My experience with focus groups has been similar to that found in other studies: A facilitator of the same race/ethnicity as participants usually enhances rapport and increases the willingness of participants to respond (Jarrett, 1993). A facilitator of the same racial or ethnic background contributes to participants' feelings that the facilitator shares with them common experiences. Although I believe this to be true with many other methodologies, it is especially important in the case of focus groups, where establishing rapport with the participants is key to eliciting high-quality information. Although research on Latinas and the race of the interviewer is scarce, studies with African Americans show that the race of the interviewer has an effect on responses (Jarrett, 1993). For example, a study on race-related attitudes of African Americans showed that when they were interviewed by Whites, they were more likely to express closeness toward

Whites than when they were interviewed by African Americans (Anderson, Silver, & Abramson, 1988).

For my focus groups, I developed an unstructured interview guide with some introductory remarks. I first asked a very general question dealing with the participants' opinions about the incidence of crime in the place where they lived. Only after framing the topic did I begin to ask more specific questions about their fears and images of crime and the cultural representations associated with those fears. Because the topic of fear of crime was very relevant to the participants, they easily became willing participants in the discussion. On many occasions the participants moved away from the interview guide, tapping into areas of the topic that I had not previously considered. This process added a wealth of information to my research and gave me new insights into the topic of fear or crime.

One problem with the use of group interviews is that some lower-socioeconomic-status women have been socialized to reserve their opinions. Thus some may be less likely to participate in the discussion than others. Under these circumstances, it can be a challenge to elicit responses from particular women. They may feel uncomfortable in a group, especially when asked to express their opinions in front of strangers. Moreover, some women may feel uneasy disagreeing with others, and that may prevent them from expressing their opinions and feelings in the group. When there are a few timid or reticent participants in a group, the dynamic changes and interaction becomes less spontaneous and more directed by the facilitator. This problem may be minimized in groups that are homogeneous not only in terms of race, gender, and class, but in terms of ethnic cultures and languages. To include in the same group Latinas of different ethnic backgrounds—such as Caribbean and Mexican women—may be a mistake, because there are many differences among different Latina groups. For example, language differences may create problems of communication. Rules of interaction are also different among various Latina groups, with some being more comfortable when addressed with the formal pronoun *usted* and others being

more comfortable with the use of the informal pronoun *tu*.

I found it very useful to let the groups know that the opinions of all the participants were important for the research project and were valued. Also, I emphasized that there could be no "right" or "wrong" answers to my questions. Because one of the dangers of the group discussion is that people may feel pressured to agree with others, it is important to let participants know that it is acceptable—and in fact desirable—for them to disagree on issues. Disagreements allow the researcher to understand the range of opinions on a topic. This is especially important in the case of focus groups with low-socioeconomic-status women, some of whom have been socialized to agree outwardly with others' opinions and to reserve their own.

Finally, it is important to note that conducting focus groups with people who speak Spanish, or Chinese, or any other language different from English, can result in additional expenses for such things as hiring bilingual facilitators, research assistants, and transcribers. In addition, given the time constraints and multiple demands experienced by lower socioeconomic women, researchers studying this group may find that cancellations are common. Group cancellations that lead to the need for replacement focus groups mean that the researcher incurs additional costs. In most social research, where funds are scarce, any unexpected expense can put a strain on the study budget. Researchers must take such likely expenses into consideration when applying for research grants. Because many social researchers are, like me, also professors with limited time for their research, cancellations impose additional hardships on their tight schedules.

◆ Focus Groups and the Ethics of Empowerment for Women of Color

Some scholars have pointed out the role of social theories in the reproduction of social inequality (Collins, 1998; van Dijk, 1993). According to Patricia Hill Collins (1998), elite discourses "represent the interest of those privileged by hierarchical power relations of race, economic class, gender, sexuality, and nationality" (pp. 44-45). For centuries, "scientific" theories justifying racial and gender inferiority have been commonplace. For example, in my area of research, criminology, biological theories have related physical characteristics of Blacks and other non-White groups to a predisposition to engage in criminal behavior. Similarly, theories of female criminality usually present women offenders as inferior beings who emulate male criminality because of "penis envy," or else as social misfits who do not follow mainstream gender expectations. Therefore, female offenders are often regarded as "bad girls" (Klein, 1995).

In the same way that elitist social theories have served to perpetuate inequalities, traditional methodologies have played an important role in the reproduction of race, class, and gender inequalities. Aside from perpetuating fallacious and insubstantial information about certain groups, the knowledge generated by positivistic research tends to reproduce discrimination and prejudice against those groups whose members do not "perform" according to social expectations or do not conform to the stereotypical ideas of researchers.

The predominant use of quantitative techniques and one-to-one interviewing among social scientists in the United States has resulted in an array of individualistic research methods. This individualism has even permeated ethnographic studies and feminist research. However, as Sue Wilkinson (1998) points out, "research methods that isolate individuals from their social context should clearly be viewed as inappropriate" for feminist researchers (p. 111). This observation is even more valid in the case of research with women of color and women of lower socioeconomic status. In the case of many women of color who belong to communitarian cultures, individualistic research methods place them in artificial, unfamiliar, and even "unsafe" environments.

As Rina Benmayor (1991) has stated, collective testimonies have the potential for "impacting directly on individual and collective empowerment" (p. 159). This, I believe, is the potential of focus groups for research into women's lives and particularly the lives of women of color. The shared dialogues, stories, and knowledge generated by the group interview have the potential to help such women to develop a sense of identity, self-validation, bonding, and commonality of experiences. Focus groups tend to create environments in which participants feel open to telling their stories and to giving their testimonies in front of other women like themselves.

Although the use of focus groups has plenty of challenges, this method is particularly well suited to research concerning low-socioeconomic-status women of color. Focus groups have great potential for uncovering the complexity of layers that shape women's collective, and individual, life experiences. Therefore, the properties inherent in focus groups allow them to be a culturally sensitive data gathering method. The experience of women of color in the United States is shaped by the intersection of multiple and overlapping hierarchies—gender, race, and class together with culture, language, and legal status. Some women of color, such as Asian and Latina immigrants in the United States, are trying to adapt to an alien culture and occupy socially, economically, and politically vulnerable positions. They are often part of cultures in which women's opinions and concerns are systematically devalued. In this context, I regard focus group interviewing as an appropriate methodology for women in general, and particularly for low-socioeconomic-status women of color. Focus groups offer a way of listening to multivocal conversations on topics relevant to the understanding of these women's lives, feelings, and thoughts. The collective experience of the focus group empowers participants to take control of the discussion process, moving the conversation toward areas of the topic relevant to *them*, sometimes encouraging and even compelling the researcher to reconsider her views on a certain subject. Focus group methods can contribute to correcting the individualistic bias existing in social research by offering a unique opportunity to study individuals in their social contexts, by generating high-quality interactive data, by contributing to the social construction of meaning, and by accessing women's shared, and often ignored, stocks of knowledge.

◆ The Future of Focus Groups

Although focus groups represent a sound method of inquiry with much potential for the study of women of color, their use in the future depends on researchers' abilities to understand when and where it becomes appropriate to use them. Some researchers may be lured into using the technique for many of the reasons developed in this chapter: the fact that participants enjoy the opportunity to take part in the discussion, the quality and quantity of information gathered, the possibility of interviewing several people at once and to witness their interaction, the empowerment of participants, and the enthusiasm generated toward the subject matter. However, it is important for researchers to recognize that in some instances other research techniques, such as individual interviews, may be more appropriate for the goals of the research. For instance, in a situation where a researcher needs participants to share very intimate details about their lives, a focus group would not be the most appropriate technique. Furthermore, researchers should avoid the use of focus groups in cases where participants may not feel comfortable with each other. For example, in some work situations, individuals may not feel comfortable opening up and presenting their views in front of their supervisors or other superiors (Morgan, 1998). Researchers should also avoid bringing together in a group individuals who have strong disagreements or who are hostile toward each other. Finally, focus groups are not appropriate when the researcher needs to be able to generalize from the research results. When generalizability is a requirement, the researcher must employ quantitative research techniques and adequate sampling methods.

Focus groups have become an important technique because they offer a way for researchers to listen to the plural voices of others. They are especially important for making audible the voices of oppressed people who are demanding to be heard. Many people want politicians, policy makers, academics, and others in position of power to listen to them (Krueger, 1994). Focus groups, although not a solution to the silencing of the oppressed, may help to facilitate this listening. For those social scientists interested in social change, the hope embedded in the use of focus groups is that they may contribute to some individuals' recognition and awareness of their own subjugation. Using their own words and their own framework, this awareness may lead to the participants' involvement as change agents in the affairs that affect their neighborhoods and their communities.

■ References

Acker, J., Barry, K., & Esseveld, J. (1983). Objectivity and truth: Problems in doing feminist research. *Women's Studies International Forum, 6,* 423-435.

Anderson, B. A., Silver, B. D., & Abramson, P. R. (1988). The effects of the race of the interviewer on race-related attitudes of black respondents in SRC/CPS national election studies. *Public Opinion Quarterly, 52,* 289-324.

Benmayor, R. (1991). Testimony, action research, and empowerment: Puerto Rican women and popular education. In S. B. Gluck & D. Patai (Eds.), *Women's words: The feminist practice of oral history* (pp. 159-174). New York: Routledge.

Berg, B. L. (1998). *Qualitative research methods for the social sciences.* Boston: Allyn & Bacon.

Cannon, L. W., Higginbotham, E., & Leung, M. L. A. (1988). Race and class bias in qualitative research on women. *Gender & Society, 2,* 449-462.

Chow, E. N. (1987). The development of feminist consciousness among Asian American women. *Gender & Society, 1,* 284-299.

Collins, P. H. (1986). Learning from the outsider within: The sociological significance of black feminist thought. *Social Problems, 33,* 14-32.

Collins, P. H. (1990). *Black feminist thought: Knowledge, consciousness, and the politics of empowerment.* New York: Routledge, Chapman & Hall.

Collins, P. H. (1998). *Fighting words: Black women and the search for justice.* Minneapolis: University of Minnesota Press.

Denzin, N. K. (1986). A postmodern social theory. *Sociological Theory, 4,* 194-204.

Denzin, N. K. (1989). *Interpretive interactionism.* Newbury Park, CA: Sage.

Dill, B. T. (1994). Fictive kin, paper sons, and compadrazgo: Women of color and the struggle for family survival. In M. B. Zinn & B. T. Dill (Eds.), *Women of color in U.S. society* (pp. 149-169). Philadelphia: Temple University Press.

Espiritu, Y. L. (1997). *Asian American women and men: Labor, laws, and love.* Thousand Oaks, CA: Sage.

Etter-Lewis, G. (1991). Black women's life stories: Reclaiming self in narrative texts. In S. B. Gluck & D. Patai (Eds.), *Women's words: The feminist practice of oral history* (pp. 43-58). New York: Routledge.

Finch, J. (1984). "It's great to have someone to talk to": The ethics and politics of interviewing women. In C. Bell & H. Roberts (Eds.), *Social researching: Politics, problems, practice* (pp. 70-87). London: Routledge & Kegan Paul.

Fine, M. (1994). Working the hyphens: Reinventing self and other in qualitative research. In N. K. Denzin & Y. S. Lincoln (Eds.), *Handbook of qualitative research* (pp. 70-82). Thousands Oaks, CA: Sage.

Fonow, M. M., & Cook, J. A. (Eds.). (1991). *Beyond methodology: Feminist scholarship as lived research.* Bloomington: Indiana University Press.

Fontana, A., & Frey, J. H. (1994). Interviewing: The art of science. In N. K. Denzin & Y. S. Lincoln (Eds.), *Handbook of qualitative research* (pp. 361-376). Thousands Oaks, CA: Sage.

Frey, J. H., & Fontana, A. (1993). The group interview in social research. In D. L. Morgan (Ed.), *Successful focus groups: Advancing the state of the art* (pp. 20-34). Newbury Park, CA: Sage.

Garcia, A. M. (1989). The development of Chicana feminist discourse 1970-1980. *Gender & Society, 3,* 217-238.

Gilkes, C. T. (1994). "If it wasn't for the women . . . ": African American women, community work and social change. In M. B. Zinn & B. T. Dill (Eds.), *Women of color in U.S. society* (pp. 229-246). Philadelphia: Temple University Press.

Glenn, E. N. (1986). *Issei, nisei, war bride: Three generations of Japanese American women in domestic service.* Philadelphia: Temple University Press.

Griffin, C. (1986). Qualitative methods and female experience: Young women from school to the job market. In S. Wilkinson (Ed.), *Feminist social psychology: Developing theory and practice* (pp. 173-191). Milton Keynes, England: Open University Press.

Harding, S. (1987). Introduction: Is there a feminist method? In S. Harding (Ed.), *Feminism and methodology: Social science issues* (pp. 1-14). Bloomington: Indiana University Press.

Heyck, D. L. D. (1994). *Barrios and borderlands: Cultures of Latinos and Latinas in the United States.* New York: Routledge.

Holstein, J. A., & Gubrium, J. F. (1995). *The active interview.* Thousand Oaks, CA: Sage.

hooks, b. (1990). The politics of radical black subjectivity. In b. hooks, *Yearning: Race, gender, and cultural politics* (pp. 15-22). Boston: South End.

Jarrett, R. L. (1993). Focus group interviewing with low-income minority populations: A research experience. In D. L. Morgan (Ed.), *Successful focus groups: Advancing the state of the art* (pp. 184-201). Newbury Park, CA: Sage.

Kitzinger, J. (1994). The methodology of focus groups: The importance of interaction between research participants. *Sociology of Health and Illness, 16,* 103-121.

Klein, D. (1995). The etiology of female crime: A review of the literature. In B. R. Price & N. J. Sokoloff (Eds.), *The criminal justice system and women: Offenders, victims, and workers* (pp. 30-53). New York: McGraw-Hill.

Krinitzky, N. (1990). *Welfare dependence and psychological distress: A study of Puerto Rican women in New York City.* Unpublished doctoral dissertation, New York University.

Krueger, R. A. (1994). *Focus groups: A practical guide to applied research.* Thousand Oaks, CA: Sage.

Madriz, E. (1997). *Nothing bad happens to good girls: The impact of fear of crime on women's lives.* Berkeley: University of California Press.

Madriz, E. (1998). Using focus groups with lower socioeconomic status Latina women. *Qualitative Inquiry, 4,* 114-128.

Marin, G., Perez-Stable, E. J., & VanOss Marin, B. (1989). Cigarette smoking among San Francisco Hispanics: The role of acculturation and gender. *American Journal of Public Health, 79,* 196-198.

Marin, G., & VanOss Marin, B. (1991). *Research with Hispanic populations.* Newbury Park, CA: Sage.

Maynard, M., & Purvis, J. (1994). Doing feminist research. In M. Maynard & J. Purvis (Eds.), *Researching women's lives from a feminist perspective* (pp. 1-9). London: Taylor & Francis.

Merton, R. (1987). Focused interviews and focus groups: Continuities and discontinuities. *Public Opinion Quarterly, 51,* 550-566.

Moore, J. W. (1970). *Mexican-Americans.* Englewood Cliffs, NJ: Prentice Hall.

Morgan, D. L. (1988). *Focus groups as qualitative research.* Newbury Park, CA: Sage.

Morgan, D. L. (1998). *The focus group guidebook.* Thousand Oaks, CA: Sage.

Morgan, D. L., & Krueger, R. A. (1993). When to use focus groups and why. In D. L. Morgan (Ed.), *Successful focus groups: Advancing the state of the art* (pp. 3-19). Newbury Park, CA: Sage.

Oakley, A. (1981). Interviewing women: A contradictions in terms. In H. Roberts (Ed.), *Doing feminist research* (pp. 30-61). London: Routledge & Kegan Paul.

Olesen, V. (1994). Feminisms and models of qualitative research. In N. K. Denzin & Y. S. Lincoln (Eds.), *Handbook of qualitative research* (pp. 158-174). Thousand Oaks, CA: Sage.

Pesquera, B. M. (1993). In the beginning he wouldn't even lift a spoon: The division of household labor. In A. de la Torre & B. M. Pesquera (Eds.), *Building with our hands: New directions in Chicana studies* (pp. 181-195). Berkeley: University of California Press.

Randall, M. (1980). *Todas estamos despiertas.* Mexico City: Editorial Siglo XXI.

Reinharz, S. (1992). *Feminist methods in social research.* New York: Oxford University Press.

Stacey, J. (1991). Can there be a feminist ethnography? In S. B. Gluck & D. Patai (Eds.), *Women's words: The feminist practice of oral history* (pp. 111-119). New York: Routledge.

Stack, C. B. (1974). *All our kin: Strategies for survival in a black community.* New York: Harper & Row.

Stewart, D. W., & Shamdasani, P. N. (1990). *Focus groups: Theory and practice.* Newbury Park, CA: Sage.

van Dijk, T. A. (1993). *Elite discourse and racism.* Newbury Park, CA: Sage.

West, C. (1988). Marxist theory and the specificity of Afro-American oppression. In C. Nelson & L. Grossberg (Eds.), *Marxism and the interpretation of culture* (pp. 17-29). Urbana: University of Illinois Press.

Wilkinson, S. (1998). Focus groups in feminist research: Power, interaction, and the co-construction of meaning. *Women's Studies International Forum, 21,* 111-125.

Whyte, W. F. (1943). *Street corner society: The social structure of an Italian slum.* Chicago: University of Chicago Press.

Zinn, M. B. (1979). Field research in minority communities: Ethical, methodological and political observations by an insider. *Social Problems, 27,* 209-219.

33

APPLIED ETHNOGRAPHY

◆ Erve Chambers

There is no general agreement within the social sciences as to the definition or value of either of the words that make up the title of this chapter. Both words are imbued with assumptions of common meaning and yet subject to many conflicting and largely unexpressed distinctions. Accordingly, the subject of this chapter needs to be qualified in both of its terms. What is it that makes a piece of research or a kind of practice specifically *applied,* and what do we mean by the term *ethnography*?

The question of how social inquiry becomes applied is intriguing and can include considerations of intent as well as of research design and product. I opt here for a broad definition. Applied work helps people make decisions and is generally directed toward informing others of the possible consequences of policy options or of programs of directed change. These consequences may be anticipated (as in impact studies and forecasting), or they may be determined in retrospect (as in evaluation research). In this chapter I consider a variety of approaches to applied ethnography, focusing primarily on cognitive approaches, micro/macro analyses, and action or clinical models. A major difference between basic and applied research rests with the criteria used to judge their significance. For basic research, the ultimate measure of significance is a research product's contribution to theory and disciplinary knowledge. The most immediate measure of the significance of applied research is its contribution to decision making. This is not to say that a piece of research cannot be judged by both criteria, but only that it need not be. At any rate, the close association with decision making accounts for much of the variation in approaches to applied ethnography. It seems inevitable that the kinds of settings in which ethnographers work, ranging from federal bureaucracies to local activist organizations, should help determine the kinds of problems they are likely to address, as well as their methodological approaches to trying to understand those problems.

I reserve the term *applied research* for inquiry that is intentionally developed within a context of decision making and that is directed toward the interests of one or more clients. Basic research can certainly be usefully applied, but in order for the transition to occur between its potential for usefulness and its actual use, there must be a deliberate act of transfer from the one realm to the other. This can be accomplished through various kinds of *practice* in which individuals bring ethnographic knowledge to bear on particular human problems. Although this latter role might be realized in several ways (E. Chambers, 1985), I will discuss it here primarily in the context of what are sometimes referred to as clinical modes of practice.

In contrast to the above, my definition of *ethnography* will seem fairly narrow to some readers. This is because in many quarters the term has come to be regarded as virtually synonymous with qualitative research. Following Wolcott's (1995) clear but frequently unheeded counsel, I restrict my use of the term here to those varieties of inquiry that aim to describe or interpret the place of culture in human affairs. In other words, ethnography is principally defined by its subject matter, which is *ethnos,* or culture, and not by its methodology, which is often but not invariably qualitative.

The term *culture* is itself ambiguous and has been subject to a variety of interpretations, each implying somewhat different methodological approaches. In my view, culture is composed of those understandings and ways of understanding that are judged to be characteristic of a discernible group. As such, culture is an *abstraction* that has been applied, with various degrees of success, to small groups (i.e., the "culture" of the classroom) and to large groups (i.e., nation-states); an operational definition might be that culture is apparent when distinctly shared meanings are discovered to be present in any given group. Within most definitions of culture there is also an expectation that its features must have some lasting quality—durable enough, at

least, to be acquired by newcomers to a group. It is important to recognize that cultural understanding can be acquired from a variety of data. It might, for example, be extracted out of observable patterns of human behavior, drawn from "native" accounts of explicit standards of value and behavior, discovered through the discernment of rules or patterns of interpretation that are particular to a group, or realized through the study of the more tacit dimensions of cognitive or symbolic processes. In practice, ethnographers often combine these data in ways that they feel will be productive given particular research aims.

The problem with the concept of culture as an abstraction that is attributed to particular societies or groups is that it has not been helpful for the anticipation of actual behaviors, which seem almost invariably to result from interaction between cultural groups. It has taken most anthropologists some time to realize that the concept is more useful and representational when applied to actual processes of cultural negotiation. Accordingly, the attribution of culture to shared meanings within groups does not necessarily imply that ethnographers are solely interested in describing such groups in isolation; in fact, they are becoming less so interested. Neither does the expectation of some degree of lastingness suggest that a group's culture is not subject to change. Early ethnographers generally did emphasize the uniqueness of neatly bounded cultures, and often assumed that cultural patterns were deeply rooted in human consciousness and resistant to change. They were more interested in describing durable and distinct cultural units than they were in discerning the processes by which culture becomes meaningful. More recently, however, many ethnographers have shifted their attention to these issues of process, trying to understand how culture is constructed and negotiated, particularly as a result of interactions between groups (or, if you will, between cultures). It is not yet entirely clear what this shift might mean to the special interests apparent in an *applied* ethnography, which has built most of its relationships with clients and with the general public on the basis of advocating for the significance of cultural understanding in its earlier incarnation.

◆ *Early Applications of the Ethnographic Approach*

Although ethnography is no longer the sole province of anthropologists, it clearly developed with a close relationship to the discipline, and its first applications follow closely on anthropology's early commitment to the study of presumably traditional and predominantly non-Western societies. By the time anthropology became established as a discipline in its own right, most such peoples were in one way or another politically or economically subject to Western nations. It is not surprising that many of the earliest opportunities to apply ethnography were closely related to problems that representatives of colonial or quasi-colonial systems encountered in administering these subject peoples. Two early defenses of an applied "anthropology" (i.e., ethnography) that is directed to the problems of administering subject peoples stand out, both for the reasonableness of their arguments and for their contrasting views of the kinds of data applied ethnographers might collect.

The first of these is Bronislaw Malinowski's essay "Practical Anthropology" (1929), which offers his views of how ethnographic understanding might assist British colonial administrators in Africa. Malinowski's argument for the usefulness of ethnographic data in colonial administration rests principally on the anthropologist's presumed grasp of what is sometimes called "the native point of view." Because the anthropologist has (more or less) lived within native communities and often participated in as well as observed their practices, he or she is in a better position to interpret the meanings and possible consequences of their behaviors in a cultural context. The promise of a distinctly applied ethnography rests, however, upon ethnographers' being willing to direct their research interests to matters of particular con-

cern to administrators. Malinowski chided his colleagues for paying too little attention to understanding the subtleties of language use, and for ignoring such vital administrative issues as local practices related to land tenure, labor, and justice. He did not challenge the premises of colonial rule, but argued that a more practical ethnography would provide administrators with the kinds of information they needed to make more effective as well as more humane decisions regarding native peoples.

Malinowski's defense of applied ethnography rests primarily on the ethnographer's ability to observe behaviors and to explain their significance in relation to their functions in a larger institutional and cultural context. Another rationale for applied ethnography was offered by Clyde Kluckhohn in his article "Covert Culture and Administrative Problems" (1947). Writing on the basis of his experience with the U.S. Indian Service, Kluckhohn noted that the agency had made considerable strides in integrating cultural concepts and ethnographic data as part of their policy and program development. He argued that further progress might be made if ethnographers were to pay more attention to the covert dimensions of culture, or to those cultural configurations that lie somewhere beyond a people's conscious awareness of their own culture. This is a different justification for applied ethnography from one that relies solely on the discernment of the native point of view. Kluckhohn suggested that ethnography could uniquely serve to make explicit those cultural configurations that inform human behavior, even though they may not be explicitly recognized or easily verbalized by the "native." This kind of interpretation could be particularly useful in instances where there were striking differences between the configurations of particular Indian groups and those of the predominantly white administrators—two examples provided by Kluckhohn included Navajo configurations that relate sexual rights closely with property rights and the relative lack of "guilt" as a motivating or sanctioning factor in Navajo society. Kluckhohn was vague as to the kinds of ethnographic methods that might provide a better understanding of covert culture. He encouraged ethnographers not to limit themselves to those features of culture that could be "measured or quantitatively validated," and suggested that informed speculation based on long-term familiarity with another culture might well be appropriate.

A third distinct approach to applied ethnography was offered by Sol Tax (1958) as a result of his work with the Fox Indians in Iowa. Tax described his research team's efforts both as "action anthropology" and as "participant interference," playing on the familiarity of the term *participant observation* as a mainstay of ethnographic technique. Although action anthropology did not suggest any new methodological approaches, it did indicate a strikingly different way of applying ethnographic expertise. The Fox Project began in 1948, at a time when most of the ethnography devoted to American Indian communities was focused on documenting cultural traditions. Tax's team directed its interest instead to the problems that the Fox were then facing, most notably the effects of internal factionalism and difficulties in their relations with whites. The researchers committed themselves to a style of research and action that would permit them to "learn while helping." In terms of innovations in applying ethnography, the most notable characteristic of Tax's efforts was the extent to which the research team surrendered much of their control over the direction of their inquiries, which became increasingly dependent upon decisions made by the Fox in determining how they would respond to their own problems. The action anthropology proposed with the Fox Project (along with the work of sociologist Kurt Lewin) provided the impetus for much of the collaborative research to be discussed later in this chapter.

In the United States, much of the groundwork for an applied ethnography was established during and within the first decade after World War II. In addition to the contributions mentioned above, ethnographers of this era were involved in a wide variety of applications, including work in industrial relations and organizational behavior (e.g., Whyte, 1984); large-scale nutritional studies (Montgomery & Bennett, 1979); research with the War Relocation Authority related to the internment of the Japanese (Leighton, 1945; Spicer, 1979); ethnographic research in the Pacific Trust Territories, newly acquired by the United States (Barnett, 1956); and numerous projects in rural and international development (e.g., Foster, 1969; Holmberg, 1958; Spicer, 1952). At least some of the impetus for an increased interest in applied ethnography at this time can be attributed to the emergence of the United States as a global power and the recognition of a practical need for an improved understanding of cultural differences. The research clients of the time appear not to have been particularly interested in ethnography as a specific method; it just came along with the methodological preferences of most of the "cultural experts" of the time.

◆ From Stasis to Process

As noted above, the development of ethnographic methods and strategies has been closely associated with anthropology. Anthropologists continue to take the lead in insisting on linking their inquiries to the understanding of culturally based behaviors and values, thereby distinguishing ethnography from the broader category of qualitative research methods. By the same token, applied ethnography has never been defined solely as a property of anthropology. For example, the Society for Applied Anthropology was founded in 1941 as an organization devoted to encouraging interdisciplinary contributions to culturally based research and practice. Unlike the leaders of other professional organizations for anthropologists of the time, the founders of the Society for Applied Anthropology seemed less concerned with drawing disciplinary boundaries or maintaining methodological distinctions between disciplines than they were with establishing the status of culture as an important variable in matters of human change and adaptation.

Over the past few decades, a major shift in the way anthropologists, and some others, think about culture and its significance in human relations has led to a variety of innovations in ethnographic research. The kinds of inquiries discussed above were based on an assumption that the practical value of ethnography was to prepare cultural profiles of different human groups that could inform decision makers who were responsible for policies or programs that affected the lives of these people. Sol Tax's action anthropology was an exception to this trend, although it shared with the others a strong focus on viewing subjects in terms of the integrity of their "traditional," usually non-Western, cultural base.

Early applied ethnography was broadly influenced by anthropology's focus on peoples who had been marginalized, generally as a result of Western expansion, and by the discipline's prevailing interest in describing these peoples' traditional cultures before they disappeared altogether (another manifestation of early applied anthropology, sometimes called "salvage anthropology"). The consequence, if not the intent, of this research was to describe a people in terms of cultural ideals and behaviors that were presumed to be enduring and homogeneous. These "cultures" were often presumed to have changed little prior to Western contact, and their standards of behavior were generally described as being uniform within the prescribed statuses and roles of each culture. The usual ethnographic monograph of the time was written in what has been called the "ethnographic present," which was in reality an attempt to describe an idealized ethnographic past, largely out of time and with little or no reference to the present conditions of cultures that had been "adulterated" by Western influence (see, for example, Rosaldo, 1989). The impression was one of cultures that did not change in terms of any kind of internal dynamic, and that generally resisted change from the outside. Accordingly, much of the applied anthropology of the time was devoted to providing the kinds of cultural information that might help change agents respond to the resistance they almost invariably faced in the field.

So long as anthropologists focused their attention on small-scale societies and maintained the (generally erroneous) presumptions that

the cultures they studied had been homogeneous, isolated from other major cultural influences, and had experienced little change prior to Western intrusion, their methods of research were based principally on their commitment to *being there* and on their ability to observe behaviors systematically in the cultural settings in which they naturally occurred. Anthropology emphasized, and undoubtedly romanticized, the position of the lone field-worker immersed in another culture and confident in her or his ability to discover the salient patterns of that culture through sustained participant observation. As a rule, anthropology students received little training in methods prior to entering the field, and fieldwork instructions were directed as much to practical matters of how to survive in another society as they were to methods of inquiry. The methods were much like, and frequently likened to, those of the naturalist, who assumed little significant variation in the patterns of species behavior that he or she observed in the wild.

Early ethnographic research was also influenced by a secondary mission within anthropology. A major goal of anthropology has been to serve as an antidote to ethnocentric values, especially when those values lead to misunderstandings about other cultures. This mission has led many anthropologists to emphasize the uniqueness of a culture and to focus on rationalizing and defending differences rather than similarities between cultures. The role of the anthropologist as an investigator came to play an interesting part in this quest. Ethnographies were frequently written as narratives in which the anthropologist validated his or her discovery of the rationale of human difference by recounting her or his own naïveté, misunderstandings, and eventual enlightenment during the process of doing fieldwork. Again, the methods that seemed best suited to such a perspective were those that were the most informal, experiential, and reflexive.

Although early anthropologists did on occasion apply ethnographic methods to a variety of situations outside the preferences described above, it seems fair to assert that this model did predominate until the late 1960s. At that time, several events served as stimuli to a fairly rapid transformation in the development of ethnographic methods and in the use of those methods in applied settings. One of these events was the advent of more systematic approaches to ethnographic inquiry, including ethnoscientific, or cognitive, research methods, and increased attention to the quantification of field data (Poggie, DeWalt, & Dressler 1992). During the same period of time, anthropology experienced a rather profound shift in orientation from its focus on small-scale societies in relative isolation to an increased interest in seemingly more complex and heterogeneous social groupings. This was not an entirely new situation for anthropologists, but its increased legitimation within in the field helped transform the discipline in at least three major ways. First, as anthropologists attempted to deal with larger, more stratified, and more diverse populations, the need for a systematic and somewhat more formal approach to field research and ethnographic methods became apparent. These new research interests also put anthropologists in closer association with practitioners of other social science disciplines—sometimes in cooperation, and occasionally in direct competition. Closer association with specific applied research strategies, such as evaluation research and social impact assessment, encouraged some applied ethnographers to adapt their inquiries to these models. Finally, and importantly, the experience of doing research with populations in which heterogeneity was obvious led some anthropologists to challenge many of their earlier assumptions concerning the relative "simplicity" and seeming passivity of the smaller-scale societies in which they had been doing research.

These transformations were especially apparent in the development of applied ethnographic methods. Here, the greater and most apparent opportunity for anthropologists was still to try to assist change agents in interpreting the behaviors of marginal groups. It no longer seemed sufficient, however, to devote so much attention to traditional culture, at least not at the expense of understanding how these groups did indeed interact with, adapt to, and

participate in the larger political and economic systems of which they were clearly a part. In ethnography devoted to agricultural development, for example, the original questions had focused on understanding what it was in a people's traditional culture that prevented them from participating fully in a newly introduced development scheme. The new research questions were framed in a context in which research subjects could be seen as rational actors in a development process (e.g., Bartlett, 1980; Warren, Slikkerveer, & Brokensha, 1995).

All these factors led to a rather rapid shift of focus. For many applied ethnographers, the object of research changed from the study of particular cultures or social groups in place to the study of the cultural processes that occur in efforts to respond to particular human problems. Applied ethnographers have become increasingly interested in such matters as how social groups collide and mix in situations of change and in the cultural meanings that result from the interactions of interested groups or stakeholders. They have become less convinced of the value of viewing culture as a quality that people possess (or, in turn, a quality that possesses them) and more interested in discovering how cultural meanings might be exchanged and negotiated as a result of intracultural attempts to find solutions to problems. In this sense, the culture described by many applied ethnographers has shifted from being a durable repository of a people's traditions to an unstable and mutable process by which people actively strive to derive meaning from their continually changing relationships and circumstances.

◆ Varieties of Applied Ethnography

Much of the value of ethnography lies in its narrative—in the telling of a story that is based in cultural representations. Whereas traditional ethnography has focused almost exclusively on telling stories about "other" and generally distant peoples, many contemporary ethnographic approaches tend to focus on the ways in which people fashion culturally meaningful expressions from fields of experience in which meaning is routinely contested, and where culture is perennially under construction. This has been particularly true of applied ethnography, which is by its very nature interventionist and culturally intrusive. As noted above, the problem of the applied ethnographer has largely shifted from telling stories about others to describing what happens when cultural systems overlap as a result of some sort of deliberate, recent, or anticipated intervention.

Cognitive Approaches

Cognitive, semiotic, and semantic approaches have played a significant role in the development of applied ethnography. These approaches follow a variety of language or discourse models and ethnographic methodologies in order to provide, much as Malinowski espoused, "the native point of view" in relation to particular kinds of interventions. Classic ethnographies in this vein include James Spradley's *You Owe Yourself a Drunk: An Ethnography of Urban Nomads* (1975), Michael Agar's *Ripping and Running: A Formal Ethnography of Urban Heroin Addicts* (1973), and Peter Manning's *Police Work: The Social Organization of Policing* (1977). These and similar contributions differ from standard (i.e., nonapplied) ethnographies in that they are focused on a research population that is at least in part defined by some larger social "problem." Spradley's study is grounded in public perception of the problem of street alcoholics and in police approaches to solving the problem, largely through incarceration. Agar's study was conducted in a treatment facility for heroin addicts. Other ethnographies, such as Manning's study of police work and Michael Agar's more recent *Independents Declared: The Dilemmas of Independent Trucking* (1986a), focus on particular occupational groups that are subject to significant public interest or institutional intervention—Agar's study is concerned, for example, with the impacts of federal transportation regulation on independent truckers.

In an applied sense, the value of cognitive approaches to ethnography is that they often reveal patterns of cultural construction within a target group that vary considerably from the interpretations of that group that are made by outsiders, and most particularly by those who have some authority over the group under study. The ethnographies often reveal considerable disparities between policies, programs, or treatments directed to the group and the real-world exigencies that provide a cultural landscape and help determine behaviors within the group. To my mind, the most appealing of these ethnographies treat culture as a consequence of practical instances of intervention (including, interestingly enough, the interventions of research). As Agar (1994) notes in his discussion of the role of the intercultural practitioner (ICP), culture should not be thought of as an abstract set of principles that belong to a particular group, but rather as an orientation toward resolving differences:

> Culture is something the ICP creates, a story he or she tells that highlights and explains the differences that cause breakdowns. Culture is not something people *have*; it is something that fills the spaces *between* them. And culture is not an exhaustive description of anything; it focuses on differences, rich points, differences that can vary from task to task and group to group. (p. 236)

Cognitive approaches to applied ethnography derive much of their practical value from the fact that they tend to focus on failures of communication, or cultural "breakdowns" (see, e.g., Agar, 1986b; Briggs, 1986). Such failures are easily translated to applied situations, and cognitive ethnographic methods seem readily adaptable to the particular situations and communicative dilemmas that arise when one group attempts to intervene upon another. Although the approaches seem to hark back most closely to Malinowski's defense of applied ethnography in terms of eliciting a "native point of view," there are also parallels to Kluckhohn's attempt to describe a unique role for applied ethnographers in their ability to expose more tacit dimensions of culture. Cognitive and language-based ethnographies tend to be built on those communicative breakdowns that are directly experienced by the researcher and that are to be resolved by the researcher's attempts to understand what made the breakdowns occur. This is different from an applied approach that reports problems as expressed by change agents or by the groups they are attempting to change. There is also an assumption, seldom made entirely clear, that the ethnographer is better positioned to unravel communicative disorders between groups than are members of the groups themselves. This is not simply because researchers might have less at stake in anticipated actions, but also because they initially understand much less of the situation and are therefore more likely to experience firsthand the kinds of blunders and breakdowns that yield rich data and point toward communicative resolutions. Stakeholders, who are more closely associated with the problem at hand, are likely to have already developed cognitive defenses that insulate them from direct experience of the kinds of breakdowns that yield significant data or understanding. James Spradley (1979) has, for example, suggested that his own techniques of ethnosemantic elicitation seem to work best when the ethnographer comes to a cultural situation with little prior knowledge.

Approaches of Micro/Macro Analysis

Although ethnography has traditionally dwelled upon the local and relied heavily upon qualitative research techniques and methods, a variety of current approaches to applied ethnography have served to expand upon both the subjects and the methods of inquiry. Two factors have played major roles in this transition. One has been the recent tendency within the social sciences to resituate the local within the larger contexts of regional, national, and even global events. This focus seems particularly relevant to applied research and action, where deliberate efforts to intervene and bring about change invariably place the populations subject to such efforts in a relationship with a larger sphere of influence. Increasingly, applied ethnography is *about* these relationships, rather than about the experiences of particular groups or populations in isolation. The other factor has been the ten-

dency for applied ethnography to expand its methodological reach, not only with the use of increasingly sophisticated qualitative methods, but also by adopting or at least responding to more quantitative research methods. Some of this shift can be attributed to changes in the ways in which social scientists and practitioners have become involved in applied work. (Again, I am speaking here primarily on the basis of my experience with applied anthropology, although I suspect these comments apply to the social sciences more generally.) In the past, anthropologists normally became involved in applied research when they were called upon to provide expertise based on their knowledge of a particular people. They were most likely to become involved in a project after something had already gone wrong, and their involvement in the overall project or research activity was minimal. In other words, their ethnography was largely independent of the larger intervention, and their role was primarily that of expert witness or troubleshooter.

There have always been exceptions to this practice, and now the exception is often the rule. Applied ethnographers are more likely, for example, to be involved in a project or research effort from its inception, and to play a role in research design. They are also more likely to be a part of the analysis or interpretation stage of applied research efforts. This greater degree of integration of applied ethnography within larger research projects and interventions has meant that a considerable amount of the qualitative, field-based applied ethnography being done today has been developed in studied relation to other research approaches. One way in which this has occurred is when the applied ethnographer becomes a participant in a larger, more quantitative research activity, generally as a qualitative researcher. The other approach has been when applied ethnographers themselves adopt quantitative methods as a part of their own ethnographic research plan—this has occurred to the extent that some applied ethnography now relies predominantly upon quantitative rather than qualitative methods. (Here it is again important to keep in mind that ethnography is being defined in this chapter in relation to its subject matter, rather than as a particular kind of methodology.)

In terms of methodological innovativeness, the most interesting examples of ethnographic inquiry that include qualitative and quantitative approaches, as well as varied levels of analysis, are those in which the ethnographer plays an active if not leading role in research design and is thereby able to maintain a primary interest in cultural analysis. Within anthropology, the qualitative/quantitative approaches to ethnography, with a focus on application, are perhaps most thoroughly described in Pertti Pelto and Gretel Pelto's *Anthropological Research: The Structure of Inquiry* (1978), H. Russell Bernard's *Research Methods in Anthropology: Qualitative and Quantitative Approaches* (1994), and Bernard's *Handbook of Research Methods in Cultural Anthropology* (1998). The shift within anthropology from local or community levels of analysis to approaches that include "macro" analyses in several dimensions (space, causal, and time) is evidenced by the contributions to be found in Billie DeWalt and Pertti Pelto's *Micro and Macro Levels of Analysis in Anthropology: Issues in Theory and Research* (1985) and in Poggie et al.'s *Anthropological Research: Process and Application* (1992).

These kinds of research experiences have provided opportunities for applied ethnographers to articulate ways in which the qualitative aspects of their work can be integrated with larger research activities. Qualitative approaches have, for example, proven particularly useful at the beginning of a research effort, often to help define the parameters of survey research (e.g., Kempton, Boster, & Hartley, 1995). In other work, qualitative field research has proven to be particularly useful at the analysis stage of research, in helping to explain anomalies in the data, especially in research that relies heavily upon reported data from a number of sites, where there might be unaccounted-for variation in how the sites interpret reporting requirements (Trend, 1978).

Where research requires accurate portrayals of stakeholder values or opinions, qualitative ethnographic data have often proven superior to survey data, particularly in cases that involve long-term field exposure and in situations where informants might feel at risk or have other reasons to provide incorrect responses, or where their "truer" responses might develop over time. In some cases, as I will discuss later in this chapter, qualitative ethnographic data have also proven to be more credible to particular research clients and stakeholders.

It is rare to find reports that explicitly compare qualitative and quantitative data obtained in the same applied research project. Susan Scrimshaw (1985) offers one such instance, related to a study of practices and attitudes concerning induced abortion in Ecuador. She notes that the ethnographic (i.e., field-based) data were in most cases validated through the comparison of these results with those obtained as a result of the larger and more rigorously defined sampling procedures developed for the surveys. On the other hand, Scrimshaw cautiously suggests that the ethnographic data might have been more accurate in those few instances in which significant anomalies between the two data sets did exist. This appears to have been the case, for example, where research subjects were asked to report practices or attitudes that were particularly sensitive or potentially embarrassing. In these instances, the longer-term familiarity gained as a result of ethnographic experience enabled the researchers to gain a deeper and more accurate grounding from which to discern the subjects' attitudes.

Action and Clinical Approaches

A number of current approaches to applied ethnography follow the early action or advocacy models offered by Sol Tax (1958) and, in another context, discussed by psychologist Kurt Lewin (1948), who emphasized participatory research based on client-oriented attempts to resolve particular social problems. Some of the models derive directly from these earlier examples, whereas others have been encouraged by recent interest on the part of research funding agencies, particularly some federal agencies, in sponsoring applied research that is participatory and that involves the "subjects" of research or intervention in one or several stages of inquiry. The actual extent of participation required for these activities varies considerably from one research effort to another, and in some cases mandated "participatory" research has earned a reputation for superficiality that is not dissimilar from earlier mandates that called for "citizen participation" in public decision making.

There is nothing necessarily ethnographic about action or advocacy research, although some researchers have suggested that ethnographic research strategies may be more accessible than other strategies, and, at the stage of interpretation, might provide kinds of data that are more convincing to those participants and community members who have not been trained as social scientists. As in the other approaches to applied research discussed here, much of what has been identified as applied "ethnography" would not conform to the definition offered above—it may be good and informative qualitative research, but it lacks the association with understanding cultural processes that would make it ethnographic.

Notwithstanding these provisos, there remain plenty of instances in which applied ethnographic methods have been incorporated into action and advocacy research strategies. Jean Schensul (1985) has described action-oriented research within the context of a collaborative model in which researchers and community activists form "policy research clusters" that are focused on important community problems. She notes that, in these settings, the ethnography is shaped in part by "the constraints of field situations including the social and political realities of the dissemination/utilization context," as well as by considerations that the research not violate "cultural principles" within the community (p. 193). William Foote Whyte (1984) has offered a similar model, which he calls "participatory action research." Dianne Argyris (1990) has provided perhaps the most detailed accounting of applied ethnography within the action context, and she suggests that a major goal of action research is to encourage participants to test their own "theories-in-use" as they relate to particular social problems.

The major innovation to applied ethnography resulting from action models has been the tendency to include individuals who are not professional social scientists in various stages of the research, including project selection and design, fieldwork, and research analysis. Conversely, and probably more than any other approach, advocacy research has also resulted in the professionalism of any number of traditional research subjects as social scientists in their own right—a practice extending back again to Sol Tax, who devoted considerable time during the later years of his career to facilitating the education of Native American students in the social sciences and in other fields. Davydd Greenwood and Morten Levin (1998) have offered a survey of action research that focuses on its criteria of scientific evidence and commitment to "democratizing" the research process.

Allied in many respects with action and advocacy research is the clinical approach to applied ethnography, which in the simplest of terms seeks to train people to use ethnographic strategies to gain a better understanding of their own cultural situations, or to understand more fully those cultural processes that influence others with whom they are involved. The clinical model has referred most often to those activities in which professionals of various kinds are encouraged to think about their practice in ethnographic terms. It has most often been applied to settings in which the professional is likely to encounter considerable cultural diversity, as in medicine and health (e.g., Shimkin & Golde, 1983), education (e.g., Heath, 1982), and social work (e.g., Green, 1982). Howard Stein (1982) describes the clinical model as one of "ethnographic teaching," in which the professionals (in this case, medical school students) are encouraged to use an ethnographic perspective and at least some methods of ethnographic inquiry to first conduct "self-ethnography," and later to apply principles of ethnography to understanding cultural diversity within the clinical setting.

Edgar Schein (1987) has argued the clinical perspective somewhat differently. His *clinicians* are organizational researchers and advisers who rely on fieldwork approaches that Schein claims are distinct in several respects from those of ethnographers. It is difficult, however, to determine how Schein derives his model of ethnography—what he describes as the opposing clinical model seems in actuality to be quite similar to the approaches of *applied* ethnography described in this chapter.

It seems likely that attention to ethnography as a way of thinking and problem solving will increase as social scientists learn that applied work is not simply a matter of affixing existing research paradigms to human problems. In the examples cited above, an ethnographic perspective is offered to aid practitioners in a variety of fields, presumably to increase their sensitivity toward issues related to cultural differences and cultural process. It is equally important to recognize that practitioners do have their own models of change and intervention, and that these models might conflict with an ethnographic perspective and militate against the effective use of ethnography in clinical or applied settings. Peter Rigby and Peter Sevareid (1992) have, for example, contrasted the ways in which lawyers and ethnographers deal with "facts" and "evidence," and Drake (1988) has contrasted ethnographic thinking with that of the government bureaucrat.

◆ Major Issues in Applied Ethnography

The increased use of ethnographic methods and perspectives in applied research has led to a variety of emergent issues, some of which are unique to the ethnographic approach and others of which are more general and relate primarily to differences between applied and basic research.

Criticisms of Ethnography in Applied Work

Issues of reliability and internal validity remain significant concerns related to the use of ethnographic approaches in applied research.

These issues have become more prominent as ethnographers increase their involvement with research teams that include social scientists who approach their work from a more quantitative perspective. By the same token, such experiences have contributed to an increased sophistication on the part of many ethnographers, both in terms of expanding their methodological repertoires and in terms of their being better able to articulate measures of reliability and validity within the more qualitative aspects of their inquiries (e.g., Bernard, 1994; Kirk & Miller, 1986), although some ethnographers have argued that ethnographic research requires distinct criteria for judging the validity of its methods (e.g., Guba & Lincoln, 1989). As Hammersley (1992) notes, criteria of validity ultimately have their point of reference in concepts of "truth." This allows for the possibility that the "truths" derived from attempts to understand and interpret cultural processes are different from those of other phenomena (e.g., Geertz, 1983). It also allows for the certainty that the "truths" of applied research are generally more contingent and subject to varied criteria of utility (see below) than are those drawn from the framework of "pure" and discipline-bound research. If validity is not entirely in the eye of the beholder, it clearly does stand in relation to the needs and judgments of those who have in a stake in any particular applied research activity.

Another criticism of ethnography has related to the wealth and richness of the data that applied ethnographers typically retrieve, particularly when they are involved in large-scale research efforts that might involve collecting data over periods of several years, and that include a number of ethnographers or qualitative researchers producing data from several different research sites. Early efforts of this kind were often initiated without adequate attention to how the field data would later be analyzed or the extent to which data collected by different fieldworkers at different sites would be comparable. More recently, the adoption of computer-based ethnographic programs, such as NUD•IST and the Ethnograph, has proven useful, in terms of both managing ethnographic data and facilitating preliminary data analyses. The use of ethnography in applied research has also been criticized as taking too long to serve as an effective tool for decision making, and as being too broadly focused (ethnographers do not always stick to the "problem" specified by their clients). In regard to timeliness, ethnographers have made considerable progress in developing "rapid assessment" procedures, particularly in areas of development research and resource management. In defense of their usually broad or holistic focus, ethnographers have countered that their methods are often fundamental to exploring the extent to which the "problem" identified in applied research efforts might have been misconstrued or might fall off the mark—an argument that may have considerable merit but has not proved particularly comforting to some research clients.

The potential for perceptions of researcher bias in applied ethnographic research and practice extends beyond issues of reliability and validity. Whether their efforts are applied or not, ethnographers have often been regarded as advocates for the people they study, and at least some ethnographers would themselves not dispute such a claim. This seems particularly true of work in anthropology, where a claim to representing and protecting the "best" interests of those people typically studied by anthropologists has long been a part of the disciplinary standard. Although ethnographers certainly need to be attentive to the extent to which their traditions of advocacy contribute to biases, it is equally apparent that criticisms concerning possible bias can come about simply as a result of the kinds of conclusions for which ethnographers aim. In an applied setting, the strength of ethnography is its capacity to identify cultural patterns that provide reason and meaningfulness to human values and behaviors. Change agents and other potential clients for applied research are themselves usually close enough to the problem that they have their own interpretations of the values and behaviors that are being studied. Ethnography has the potential to provide alternative interpretations that might be greeted with enthusiasm by some research clients, or that might be so incompatible with client expectations as to be dismissed as biased and rejected outright.

Defenses of Ethnography in Applied Work

Many of the characteristics that have given rise to criticisms of the value of ethnography for applied research can also be offered as strengths particular to the method. The long-term and relatively intimate acquaintance with research subjects that is characteristic of much ethnography provides rich, contextual information that can increase the depth of our knowledge of particular subjects. Ethnographic and qualitative research approaches have been successfully applied to research situations in which subjects are not likely to be candid in response to such instruments as survey questionnaires, or where there are likely to be significant differences of interpretation regarding the appropriate responses to direct questions, cultural differences in the etiquette of inquiry, or even in the meaning of particular questions or responses. In terms of analysis and interpretation of research results, ethnography adds a cultural dimension that is likely to be absent in other approaches.

Recent approaches to applied ethnography have also served the useful purpose of simply helping people (clients, research subjects, and so on) think about the idea of culture, how culture "works," and culture's consequences. In some instances, this might require ethnographers to help others unlearn the popular, more static concepts of culture taught by earlier ethnographers, and most particularly by anthropologists (Chambers, 1986).

Research Clients and Applied Ethnographic Methods

Whereas basic research methods are generally developed within disciplinary boundaries and subject almost solely to peer review, applied research invariably entails convincing a client of the appropriateness and effectiveness of a research strategy. This may require the ethnographer to adapt his or her methods to the particular needs and constraints expressed by the client. Approaches to rapid ethnographic methods have, for example, derived specifically from the need of particular clients to receive data in a timely fashion (e.g., R. Chambers, 1985; Harris, Jerome, & Fawcett, 1997; van Willigan & Finan, 1991). Similarly, ethnographic methods have been adapted to the special needs of clients who feel the need to conduct assessments of the potential social or cultural impacts of their interventions (e.g., Cernea, 1985; Cochrane, 1979).

Rapid research might include a variety of techniques, but those that seem to be most commonly associated with ethnography are (a) the use of focus group interviews; (b) "stepwise" research, in which long-term field presence is replaced by brief ethnographic "visits" to solve particular research problems posed by an ongoing research project; and (c) participatory research strategies that involve those at the research site in data collection efforts. These approaches, as they relate to applied ethnographic research, are discussed in greater detail by the contributors to van Willigan and Finan's (1991) edited volume.

Applied ethnographers are not of a single mind as to the extent to which their research approaches should be adapted to the declared needs or expectations of research clients. For example, Wolcott (1994) has expressed concern about the influence of evaluation research models on ethnographic research in education. Wolcott argues for a more descriptive and nonevaluative approach. In contrast, others have built their approaches to applied ethnography directly upon evaluation research models (e.g., Fetterman 1984; Ryan, Greene, Lincoln, Mathison, & Mertens, 1998).

Criteria of Utility in Applied Ethnography

By and large, applied ethnographers have not been attentive to the task of proving the value of their inquiries. Although there has been considerable discussion of ways in which ethnographic research *might* be useful, there has been relatively little effort made to establish actual uses. Within anthropology, the usual genre for discussing the practical uses of ethnography has been the case study, which relies heavily upon establishing the reasonableness of an ethnographic interpretation, but seldom offers clues as to whether those interpretations were actually incorporated into client decision making, policy construction, or program intervention. A major exception is *Making Our Research Useful: Case Studies in the Utilization of Anthropological Knowledge* (van Willigan, Rylko-Bauer, & McElroy, 1989). Although the authors in this volume identify numerous factors that appear to contribute to effective utilization, many of them cluster around issues of collaboration and communication. The effective application of ethnography seems related to the extent to which the research client is actively involved in the research effort and the extent to which the ethnographers are willing to serve as advocates of their research and to communicate their findings in different ways to a variety of stakeholders.

In a similar vein, I have argued that criteria of utility are as vital for effective applied research as might be the more usual and variable criteria for establishing scientific reliability and validity (E. Chambers, 1985). I have identified five such criteria. The *accessibility* of research findings refers to the criterion that knowledge be available in an appropriate manner to those who have a stake in a program of change. Applied ethnography should also be *relevant* to the goals and prescribed activities of stakeholders and clients. It also needs to be responsive to different claims upon the *significance* of a course of action (understanding, for example, that the claims of the significance of maintaining historic structures might well be different among historic preservationists and among community members who more acutely feel the need for a modern shopping center). Fourth, applied ethnography should meet a criterion of *credibility* in terms of being responsive to those standards of evidence and proof that are favored by clients and stakeholders. Finally, applied research needs to address matters of *prospect* and judgment (or, in other words, to understand that stakeholders and clients are often more interested in what could be, or even in what should be, than they are in what currently is).

What Kind of Science?

As far as I can determine, there has never been agreement among applied ethnographers as to the kind of science they practice. I am certain this is true within anthropology. Early accounts range from the interpretive and even speculative sciences (e.g., Kluckhohn, 1947) to models that emulate the natural sciences in their attention to precision and predictability (e.g., Chapple, 1941). Most current applied ethnography follows one or the other of these models, with some researchers basing their work on a natural science paradigm that places emphasis on the search for testable and causal statements related to cultural processes (e.g., Bernard, 1994; Poggie et al., 1992) and others focusing on interpretive models that, to an extent at least, emphasize the uniqueness of particular cultural circumstances and events (e.g., Agar, 1996; Wolcott, 1994). In this regard, Wolcott has gone so far as to question whether a preoccupation with validity in applied ethnography might actually detract from an ethnographer's quest for understanding.

A major difference in the ways qualitative ethnography plays out in these two models is in the manner in which the method is integrated into a research project. For the natural science model, qualitative ethnography is often accompanied by, and sometimes dominated by, more quantitative methods. Interpretive researchers and practitioners tend to rely more fully on qualitative approaches as the basis for their inquiries.

In contrast to developments in general anthropology and elsewhere in the social sciences, postmodernism has played a relatively minor role in the further development of applied ethnography, and in some quarters there is open antagonism toward the approach (e.g., Young, 1998). Other have suggested that some aspects of the postmodern critique might contribute positively to a more critical understanding of

applied ethnographers' own positions in the processes of inquiry, as well as to an exploration of alternative approaches to textual representation (e.g., Johannsen, 1992).

Issues of Ethics and Morality

Applied research often has immediate consequences for those who become subject to its gaze. In many cases, where applied ethnography is employed as a part of a knowledge base from which to make decisions about the fate of communities and their environments, the ethical and moral considerations can be daunting. Not infrequently, applied ethnography is conducted under conditions of planned or unplanned change, in which communities are experiencing the pressures of disruption and manipulation of their lives. Ethnographers vary considerably in the extent to which they feel their primary role in such situations is to try to understand what is going on or to try to help alleviate human suffering.

Beyond those issues that affect social science researchers in general, applied ethnographers have encountered a number of ethical and moral dilemmas that arise as a result of the researchers' unique relationships to research clients. One of the more intriguing of these is the question of whether or not ethnographers should be engaged in research with clients whose policies or actions might not conform to professional or personal standards of morality. In putting forth the idea that anthropologists could serve useful purposes related to British colonial administration in Africa, Malinowski (1929) walked a thin line between complicity and arguing that the presence of anthropology would help humanize the colonial mission. Similarly, social scientists involved as community analysts in the relocation camps established for Japanese Americans during World War II have sought to distance themselves from the policy and have described themselves primarily as "cultural brokers" between the Japanese internees and the War Relocation Authority (Spicer, 1979). This idea that involvement is better than boycott pervades much of current applied research, although others have argued that association is the equivalent of complicity and have recommended that applied researchers excuse themselves from work with a wide variety of clients (e.g., Berreman, 1991; Escobar, 1991).

Three issues of professional ethics have proven particularly difficult for applied ethnographers. One of these is the principle of informed consent. Within anthropology, Fluehr-Lobban (1994) has suggested that the tendency of field-workers to resist informed consent may result in part from their assumption that they are in a better position than their research subjects to determine and to mitigate any potentially harmful consequences of their research. She decries this attitude as being inappropriately paternalistic. On the other hand, Murray Wax (1995) has argued that there are instances in which strict adherence to principles of informed consent would make field-work difficult if not impossible—especially in cases where ethnographers are investigating illegal activity or are investigating elites (i.e., "studying up") who are likely to resist their inquiries.

Applied ethnographers also face ethical dilemmas related to the protection of the confidentiality of research subjects. This problem can relate to research subjects in general, as it does in cases in which research clients have or request access to records that identify research subjects. It can also relate to particular research subjects whose identities cannot be concealed by virtue of their unique positions in an institution. The professional codes of both the American Anthropological Association and the Society for Applied Anthropology, which at one time specified that the confidentiality of research subjects should be maintained in all cases, have recently been revised to indicate that subjects should at least be informed of those cases in which confidentiality cannot be assured.

In general, the social science professions have encouraged open and public dissemination of the results of research. During the 1960s, the American Anthropological Association went so far as to proscribe "secret" research altogether. This prohibition seemed unreasonable to some applied ethnographers,

who found themselves engaged in research in which their clients appeared to have legitimate proprietary interests over the data. Such interests included, for example, research devoted to the test marketing of new products, evaluations of marketable techniques for counseling and consultation, and long-term social experiment research in which the early release of preliminary results might compromise the experiment. These claims have by and large been held to have merit, and most professional associations, including the American Anthropological Association in its 1998 revision of its principles of professional responsibility, have revised their codes to allow for the withholding of research results in cases in which there appear to be legitimate proprietary interests.

◆ Summary

Early attempts to apply ethnographic research to problem solving and social intervention introduced three major rationales that retain much of their influence. These point to the strengths of ethnography in eliciting the "native point of view," in uncovering the more tacit dimensions of culture, and in facilitating collaborative or "action" research strategies. On the other hand, a major change in the ethnographic perspective has been the gradual shift from viewing cultures as relatively closed and geographically bounded systems to focusing attention upon those cultural processes that emerge as a result of programs of intervention and change. In this respect, applied ethnographic research has kept pace with more general trends in tracing the interplay of local and global aspects of cultural expression.

The past two decades have seen changes and improvements in the development of applied ethnographic research methods and techniques. These changes have included the following:

- Increased sophistication in developing cultural (and cognitive) models in response to issues of intervention and problem solving;

- A greater diversification of research methodologies and techniques to include both qualitative and quantitative approaches, and the use of computer-assisted ethnographic research programs;
- More complete involvement of ethnographers in the various stages of applied research (project design, analysis, dissemination, and so on), resulting in greater understanding of specifically applied and policy-oriented research strategies;
- A greater tendency for ethnographers to work as members of research teams, either within their own disciplinary framework or as participants in interdisciplinary research;
- A tendency for ethnographers to pay greater attention to the importance of matching research strategies to specific client needs for information and insight, and to pay heed to "criteria of utility";
- Increased experience in applying ethnographic methods to participatory and "action" research strategies.

Within anthropology as a whole, this same period has seen increased acceptance of specifically applied research as a legitimate and important enterprise. Increased support and institutionalization of applied ethnography from within the discipline, as well as increased interest from outside the discipline, suggest that the progress made to date will continue well into the future.

Are there other areas in which applied ethnography has not progressed? I think there are. One of these is the failure of many ethnographers to follow up on the actual uses of their contributions. Except in occasional asides and anecdotes, no clear conceptualizations of utilization have emerged from the practice of applied ethnography. As in the past, ethnographers seem content to stress the supposed usefulness of their inquiries rather than to explore empirically what happens when their knowledge enters the fray of public recognition, intervention, and decision making. In this respect, much applied ethnography seems locked

in the "positivist" assumption that good knowledge will find good uses without much effort or commitment on the part of the investigator. More critical analyses of the actual uses (and misuses) of ethnographic knowledge are badly needed.

Related to this is the ethical and moral stance of applied ethnography. Although guided in a general way by a preference for advocating for those who often have the least voice in public affairs, applied ethnographers have not resolved for themselves the vexing issue of the proper role for their inquiries. Are they specialists in the production of knowledge whose services should be available without discrimination, much as physicians and lawyers endeavor to respond equally to the needs of all potential clients? Or do they limit their participation to those clients they feel are most deserving? Although it might be that this issue will never be resolved beyond the level of individual choices, a higher level of discussion of the issues would be helpful.

Another area in which we have made few advances is in the translation of the ethnographic perspective to clinical modes of practice other than research. Although there is precedence for such an interest, which I have discussed above, our efforts to understand how ethnographic inquiry can better inform the practices of individuals who enter careers related to the human services, planning, and decision making fall short of the situation in which we find ourselves. In anthropology, for example, the dominant role of academic practice has begun to yield to a much broader sense of the kinds of careers that are appropriate to the discipline. We need to pay more attention to the ways in which such a major and distinct mode of inquiry as ethnography might prepare individuals for these new career modes—increasing our appreciation for the possibility that the "method" has salience beyond its more formal applications.

If I can speculate as to where the field will be 10 years from now, I would certainly hope for improvements in the areas just mentioned. Beyond this, I would place my bets on (a) increased sophistication in research methods and techniques, and advances in integrating ethnographic inquiries with other approaches to problem solving; and (b) in terms of research directions, greater emphasis upon convincing decision makers and research clients of the importance of paying heed to "indigenous knowledge systems," not only as means to understanding more fully the needs of people and their communities, but also as a vital source of potential solutions to communities' problems. Too often, "top-down" responses in attempts to solve social problems have served to erode if not destroy those very social and cultural resources and survival strategies that have helped keep troubled communities alive.

■ *References*

Agar, M. H. (1973). *Ripping and running: A formal ethnography of urban heroin addicts.* New York: Seminar.

Agar, M. H. (1986a). *Independents declared: The dilemmas of independent trucking.* Washington, DC: Smithsonian Institution.

Agar, M. H. (1986b). *Speaking of ethnography.* Beverly Hills, CA: Sage.

Agar, M. H. (1994). The intercultural frame. *International Journal of Intercultural Relations, 18,* 221-237.

Agar, M. H. (1996). *The professional stranger: An informal introduction to ethnography.* San Diego, CA: Academic Press.

Argyris, D. (1990). The ethnographic approach to intervention and fundamental change. In C. Argyris, R. Putnam, & D. M. Smith (Eds.), *Action science* (pp. 158-189). San Francisco: Jossey-Bass.

Barnett, H. G. (1956). *Anthropology in administration.* Evanston, IL: Row, Peterson.

Bartlett, P. F. (Ed.). (1980). *Agricultural decision making: Anthropological contributions to rural development.* New York: Academic Press.

Bernard, H. R. (1994). *Research methods in anthropology: Qualitative and quantitative approaches* (2nd ed.). Walnut Creek, CA: AltaMira.

Bernard, H. R. (Ed.). (1998). *Handbook of research methods in cultural anthropology.* Walnut Creek, CA: AltaMira.

Berreman, G. D. (1991). Anthropological ethics in the 1980s: A positive approach. In C. Fluehr-Lobban (Ed.), *Ethics and the profession of anthropology: A dialogue for a new era* (pp. 36-71). Philadelphia: University of Pennsylvania Press.

Briggs, C. L. (1986). *Learning how to ask: A sociologuist appraisal of the role of the interview in social science research.* Cambridge: Cambridge University Press.

Cernea, M. M. (Ed.). (1985). *Putting people first: Sociological variables in rural development.* New York: Oxford University Press.

Chambers, E. (1985). *Applied anthropology: A practical guide.* Prospect Heights, IL: Waveland.

Chambers, E. (1986). The cultures of science and policy. In W. N. Dunn (Ed.), *Policy analysis: Perspectives, concepts, and methods* (pp. 93-110). Greenwich, CT: JAI.

Chambers, R. (1985). Shortcut and participatory methods for gaining social information for projects. In M. M. Cernea (Ed.), *Putting people first: Sociological variables in rural development* (pp. 515-537). New York: Oxford University Press.

Chapple, E. D. (1941). Anthropological engineering: Its use to administrators. *Applied Anthropology, 2*(2), 23-32.

Cochrane, G. (1979). *The cultural appraisal of development projects.* New York: Praeger.

DeWalt, B. R., & Pelto, P. J. (Eds.). (1985). *Micro and macro levels of analysis in anthropology: Issues in theory and research.* Boulder, CO: Westview.

Drake, H. M. (1988). *Mainstreaming anthropology: Experiences in government employment.* Washington, DC: American Anthropological Association.

Escobar, A. (1991). Anthropology and the development encounter: The making and marketing of development anthropology. *American Ethnologist, 18,* 658-682.

Fetterman, D. M. (Ed.). (1984). *Ethnography in educational evaluation.* Beverly Hills, CA: Sage.

Fluehr-Lobban, C. (1994). Informed consent in anthropological research: We are not exempt. *Human Organization, 53,* 1-10.

Geertz, C. (1983). *Local knowledge: Further essays in interpretive anthropology.* New York: Basic Books.

Green, J. W. (1982). *Cultural awareness in the human services.* Englewood Cliffs, NJ: Prentice Hall.

Greenwood, D. J., & Levin, M. (1998). *Introduction to action research: Social research for social change.* Thousand Oaks, CA: Sage.

Guba, E. G., & Lincoln, Y. S. (1989). *Fourth generation evaluation.* Newbury Park, CA: Sage.

Hammersley, M. (1992). *What's wrong with ethnography? Methodological explorations.* London: Routledge.

Harris, K. J., Jerome, N. W., & Fawcett, S. B. (1997). Rapid assessment procedures: A review and critique. *Human Organization, 56,* 375-378.

Heath, S. B. (1982). Questioning at home and at school: A comparative study. In G. Spindler (Ed.), *Doing the ethnography of schooling.* New York: Holt, Rinehart & Winston.

Holmberg, A. R. (1958). The research and development approach to the study of change. *Human Organization, 17,* 12-16.

Johannsen, A. M. (1992). Applied anthropology and post-modernist ethnography. *Human Organization, 51,* 71-81.

Kempton, W., Boster, J. S., & Hartley, J. A. (1995). *Environmental values in American culture.* Cambridge: MIT Press.

Kirk, J., & Miller, M. L. (1986). *Reliability and validity in qualitative research.* Beverly Hills, CA: Sage.

Kluckhohn, C. (1947). Covert culture and administrative problems. *American Anthropologist, 45,* 213-229.

Leighton, A. H. (1945). *The governing of men.* Princeton, NJ: Princeton University Press.

Lewin, K. (1948). *Resolving social conflicts.* New York: Harper & Row.

Malinowski, B. (1929). Practical anthropology. *Africa, 2,* 23-38.

Manning, P. K. (1977). *Police work: The social organization of policing.* Cambridge: MIT Press.

Montgomery, E., & Bennett, J. W. (1979). Anthropological studies of food and nutrition: The 1940s and the 1970s. In W. Goldschmidt (Ed.), *The uses of anthropology* (pp. 124-144). Washington, DC: American Anthropological Association.

Pelto, P. J., & Pelto, G. H. (1978). *Anthropological research: The structure of inquiry* (2nd ed.). New York: Cambridge University Press.

Poggie, J. J., Jr., DeWalt, B. R., & Dressler, W. W. (Eds.). (1992). *Anthropological research: Process and application.* Albany: State University of New York Press.

Rigby, P., & Sevareid, P. (1992). Lawyers, anthropologists, and the knowledge of facts. In R. F. Kandel (Ed.), *Double vision: Anthropologists at law* (pp. 5-21). Washington, DC: American Anthropological Association.

Rosaldo, R. (1989). *Culture and truth: The remaking of social analysis.* Boston: Beacon.

Ryan, K. E., Greene, J. C., Lincoln, Y. S., Mathison, S., & Mertens, D. (1998). Advantages and challenges of using inclusive evaluation approaches in evaluation practice. *American Journal of Evaluation, 19,* 101-122.

Schein, E. H. (1987). *The clinical perspective in fieldwork.* Newbury Park, CA: Sage.

Schensul, J. J. (1985). Systems consistency in field research, dissemination, and social change. *American Behavioral Scientist, 29,* 186-204.

Scrimshaw, S. C. M. (1985). Bringing the period down: Government and squatter settlement confront induced abortion in Ecuador. In B. R. DeWalt & P. J. Pelto (Eds.), *Micro and macro levels of analysis in anthropology: Issues in theory and research* (pp. 121-146). Boulder, CO: Westview.

Shimkin, D. B., & Golde, P. (Eds.). (1983). *Clinical anthropology: A new approach to American health.* Lanham, MD: University Press of America.

Spicer, E. H. (1952). *Human problems in technological change.* New York: John Wiley.

Spicer, E. H. (1979). Anthropologists and the War Relocation Authority. In W. Goldschmidt (Ed.), *The uses of anthropology* (pp. 217-237). Washington, DC: American Anthropological Association.

Spradley, J. P. (1975). *You owe yourself a drunk: An ethnography of urban nomads.* Boston: Little, Brown.

Spradley, J. P. (1979). *The ethnographic interview.* New York: Holt, Rinehart & Winston.

Stein, H. F. (1982). The ethnographic mode of teaching clinical behavioral science. In N. J. Chrisman & T. W. Maretzki (Eds.), *Clinically applied anthropology: Anthropologists*

Chrisman & T. W. Maretzki (Eds.), *Clinically applied anthropology: Anthropologists in health science settings* (pp. 61-82). Boston: D. Reidel.

van Willigan, J., & Finan, T. L. (Eds.). (1991). *Soundings: Rapid and reliable research methods for practicing anthropologists.* Washington, DC: American Anthropological Association.

van Willigan, J., Rylko-Bauer, B., & McElroy, A. (Eds.). (1989). *Making our research useful: Case studies in the utilization of anthropological knowledge.* Boulder, CO: Westview.

Tax, S. (1958). The Fox Project. *Human Organization, 17,* 17-19.

Trend, M. G. (1978). On the reconciliation of qualitative and quantitative analysis: A case study. *Human Organization, 37,* 345-354.

Warren, D. M., Slikkerveer, L. J., & Brokensha, D. (Eds.). (1995). *The cultural dimension of development: Indigenous knowledge systems.* London: Intermediate Technology.

Wax, M. L. (1995). Informed consent in applied research: A comment. *Human Organization, 54,* 330-331.

Whyte, W. F. (with Whyte, K. K.). (1984). *Learning from the field: A guide from experience.* Beverly Hills, CA: Sage.

Wolcott, H. F. (1994). *Transforming qualitative data: Description, analysis, and interpretation.* Thousand Oaks, CA: Sage.

Wolcott, H. F. (1995). Making a study "more ethnographic." In J. Van Maanen (Ed.), *Representation in ethnography* (pp. 44-72). Thousand Oaks, CA: Sage.

Young, J. (1998). SfAA president's letter. *Society for Anthropology Newsletter, 9*(4), 1-2.

THE ART AND PRACTICES OF INTERPRETATION, EVALUATION, AND REPRESENTATION

n conventional terms, Part V of this *Handbook* signals the terminal phase of qualitative inquiry. The researcher or evaluator now assesses, analyzes, and interprets the empirical materials that have been collected. This process, conventionally conceived, involves a set of analytic procedures that produce interpretations, which are then integrated into a theory or put forward as a set of policy recommendations. The resulting interpretations are assessed in terms of a set of criteria, from the positivist or postpositivist tradition, that include validity, reliability, and objectivity. Those interpretations that stand up to scrutiny are put forward as the findings of the research.

The contributors to Part V explore the art, practices, and politics of interpretation, evaluation, and representation. In so doing, they return to the themes raised by the authors in Part I—asking, that is, *How can we use the discourses of qualitative research to help create and imagine a free democratic society?* It is understood that the processes of analysis, evaluation, and interpretation are neither terminal nor mechanical. They are like a dance, to invoke the metaphor used by Valerie Janesick in Chapter 13 of this volume. This dance is informed at every step of the way by a commitment to this civic agenda. The processes that define the practices of interpretation and representation are always ongoing, emergent, unpredictable, and unfinished.

We begin by assessing a number of criteria that have been used traditionally (as well as recently) to judge the adequacy of qualitative research. These criteria flow from the major paradigms now operating in this field (in Chapter 34, John Smith and Deborah Deemer explore these criteria in detail).

◆ *Criteria for Evaluating Qualitative Research*

Smith and Deemer remind us that we live in an age of relativism. They note that in the social sciences today there is no longer a God's-eye view that guarantees absolute methodological certainty; to assert such is to court embarrassment. Indeed, as Lincoln and Guba discuss in detail in Chapter 6, there is considerable debate over what constitutes good interpretation in qualitative research. Nonetheless, there seems to be an emerging consensus that all inquiry reflects the standpoint of the inquirer, that all observation is theory laden, and that there is no possibility of theory-free knowledge. We can no longer think of ourselves as neutral spectators of the social world.

Consequently, as Smith and Deemer observe, in the current discourses of qualitative inquiry it is no longer possible to speak in terms of a foundational epistemology and a direct ontological realism. No method is a neutral tool of inquiry, and hence the notion of procedural objectivity cannot be sustained. The days of naïve realism and naïve positivism are over. In their place stand critical and historical realism and various versions of relativism. The criteria for evaluating research are now relative.

Extending Smith and Deemer's argument, there are three basic positions on the issue of evaluative criteria: foundational, quasi-foundational, and nonfoundational. There are still those who think in terms of a foundational epistemology. They would apply the same criteria to qualitative research as are employed in quantitative inquiry, contending that is there is nothing special about qualitative research that demands a special set of evaluative criteria. As we indicate in our introduction to Part II, the positivist and postpositivist paradigms apply four standard criteria to disciplined inquiry: internal validity, external validity, reliability, and objectivity. The use of these criteria, or their variants, is consistent with the *foundational* position.

In contrast, *quasi-foundationalists* approach the criteria issue from the standpoint of a nonnaïve neorealism or subtle realism. They contend that the discussion of criteria must take place within the context of an ontological neorealism and a constructivist epistemology. They believe in a real world that is independent of our fallible knowledge of it. Their constructivism commits them to the position that there can be no theory-free knowledge.

Proponents of the quasi-foundational position argue for the development of a set of criteria unique to qualitative research. Hammersley (1992, p. 64; also 1995, p. 18; see also Wolcott, 1999, p. 194) is a leading proponent of this position. He wants to maintain the correspondence theory of truth while suggesting that researchers assess a work in terms of its ability (a) to generate generic/formal theory; (b) to be empirically grounded and scientifically credible; (c) to produce findings that can be generalized, or transferred to other settings; and (d) to be internally reflexive in terms of taking account of the effects of the researcher and the research strategy on the findings that have been produced.

Hammersley reduces his criteria to three essential terms: plausibility (Is a claim plausible?), credibility (Is the claim based on credible evidence?), and relevance (What is the claim's relevance for knowledge about the world?). Of course, these criteria require social judgments. They cannot be assessed in terms of any set of external or foundational criteria. Their meanings are arrived at through consensus and discussion in the scientific community. Smith and Deemer note that within Hammersley's model there is no satisfactory method for resolving this issue of how to evaluate an empirical claim.

For the *nonfoundationalists,* relativism is not an issue. They accept the argument that there is no theory-free knowledge. As Smith and Deemer note, relativism, or uncertainty, is the inevitable consequence of the fact that as human beings we have finite knowledge of ourselves and the world we live in. Nonfoundationalists contend that the injunction to pursue knowledge cannot be given epistemologically; rather, the injunction is moral and political.

Accordingly, the criteria for evaluating qualitative work are also moral and fitted to the pragmatic, ethical, and political contingencies of concrete situations. Good or bad inquiry in any given context is assessed in terms of such criteria as those outlined by Greenwood and Levin (Chapter 3), Fine, Weis, Weseen, and Wong (Chapter 4), Christians (Chapter 5), Lincoln and Guba (Chapter 6), Schwandt (Chapter 7), Kemmis and McTaggart (Chapter 22), Angrosino and Pérez (Chapter 25), and Madriz (Chapter 32). These are the criteria that flow from a feminist, communitarian moral ethic of empowerment, community, and moral solidarity. Returning to Christians, this moral ethic calls for research rooted in the concepts of care, shared governance, neighborliness, love, and kindness. Further, this work should provide the foundations for social criticism and social action.

◆ The Practices and Politics of Interpretation

In Chapter 35, Norman Denzin proposes to reengage the methods and promises of qualitative inquiry as forms of radical democratic practice. He explores new and older writing forms, working back and forth among the new, civic, and intimate journalism, calls for performance-based ethnographies, and variations on a Chicano/a and African American aesthetic. He explores the relationships between these practices and critical race theory. Like Ladson-Billings (Chapter 9), Denzin seeks to align critical theory with the poststructural turn in ethnography.

◆ Writing as Inquiry

Writers interpret as they write, so writing is a form of inquiry, a way of making sense of the world. In Chapter 36, Laurel Richardson explores new writing and interpretive styles that follow from the narrative, literary turn in the social sciences. She calls these different forms of writing CAP (creative analytic practices) ethnography. These new forms include autoethnography, fiction stories, poetry, drama, performance texts, polyvocal texts, readers' theater, responsive readings, aphorisms, comedy and satire, visual presentations, conversation, layered accounts, writing-stories, and mixed genres. Richardson discusses in detail one class of experimental genre that she calls evocative representations. Work in this genre includes narratives of the self, microprocess writing-stories, ethnographic fictional representations, poetic representations, ethnographic dramas, and mixed genres.

The crystal is a central image in Richardson's text; she contrasts the crystal with the triangle. Traditional postpositivist research has relied upon triangulation, including the use of multiple methods, as a method of validation. This model implies a fixed point of reference that can be triangulated. Mixed-genre texts, in contrast, do not triangulate. The central image is the crystal, which "combines symmetry and substance with an infinite variety of shapes, substances, transmutations, . . . and angles of approach." Crystals are prisms that reflect and refract, creating ever-changing images and pictures of reality. Crystallization deconstructs the traditional idea of validity, for now there can be no single, or triangulated, truth.

Richardson offers five criteria for evaluating CAP ethnography: substantive contribution, aesthetic merit, reflexivity, impactfulness, and ability to evoke lived experience. She concludes with a list of writing practices, ways of using writing as a method of knowing.

◆ *Anthropological Poetics*

Anthropologists have been writing experimental, literary, and poetic ethnographic texts for at least 40 years. In Chapter 37, Ivan Brady analyzes three subcategories of this writing: ethnopoetics, literary anthropology, and anthropological poetry. Ethnopoetics focuses on the poetic productions, proverbs, riddles, laments, prayers, and oral performances of indigenous verbal artists. Literary anthropology includes the fiction in realistic ethnographies, ethnographic novels, and the many different CAP ethnographies discussed by Richardson. Anthropological poetry is just that, poetry written by anthropologists.

In the literary, poetic form, anthropologists enact a moral aesthetic, an aesthetic that allows them to say things they could not otherwise say. In so doing, they push the boundaries of artful ethnographic discourse. Thus are the boundaries between the humanities and the human sciences blurred. In this blurring, our moral sensibilities are enlivened. We are able to imagine new ways of being ourselves in this bewilderingly complex world called the postmodern.

◆ *The Practice and Promise of Qualitative Program Evaluation*

Program evaluation, of course, is a major site of qualitative research (the contributions to this *Handbook* by Greenwood & Levin, Stake, Kemmis & McTaggart, Miller & Crabtree, and Chambers help to establish this fact). Evaluators are interpreters. Their texts tell stories. These stories, Jennifer Greene argues in Chapter 38, are inherently moral and political. She examines four contemporary genres of evaluation work: postpositivism, utilitarian pragmatism, interpretivism/constructivism, and critical social science. She reviews the work of the major figures in this area, including Guba and Lincoln, Schwandt, Greenwood and Levin, and Stake. She presents evaluation as a narrative craft, asking, How good is this story? She calls for a morally engaged, constructivist, qualitative genre of evaluation practice.

◆ *Influencing Policy with Qualitative Research*

Qualitative researchers can influence social policy, and in Chapter 39, Ray Rist shows how they do this. He shows how qualitative research has pivotal relevance in each stage of the policy cycle, from the problem formulation to the implementation and accountability stages. Qualitative researchers can isolate target populations, show the immediate effects of certain programs on such groups, and isolate the constraints that operate against policy changes in such settings. Unlike other models that relegate qualitative research to a secondary position in this process, Rist's model gives this research a central part in the shaping of social policy.

Greene's and Rist's contributions here connect back to the applied research traditions identified by Greenwood and Levin, Stake, Chambers, and Kemmis and McTaggart. They show how the interpretive, qualitative text can morally empower citizens and shape government policies. At the same time, they chart new lines of action for evaluators who are themselves part of the ruling apparatuses of society (Ryan, 1995). Rist and Greene reclaim a new moral authority for the evaluator. This claim can also empower the qualitative researcher who does not engage in direct program evaluation.

◆ *Conclusion*

The readings in Part V affirm our position that qualitative research has come of age. Multiple discourses now surround topics that in earlier historical moments where contained within the broad grasp of the positivist and postpositivist epistemologies. There are now many ways to write, read, assess, evaluate, and apply qualitative research texts. This complex field invites reflexive appraisal, which is the topic of Part IV of this *Handbook*.

■ *References*

Hammersley, M. (1992). *What's wrong with ethnography? Methodological explorations.* London: Routledge.

Hammersley, M. (1995). *The politics of social research.* Thousand Oaks, CA: Sage.

Ryan, K. E. (1995). Evaluation ethics and issues of social justice: Contributions from female moral thinking. In N. K. Denzin (Ed.), *Studies in symbolic interaction: A research annual* (Vol. 19, pp. 143-151). Greenwich, CT: JAI.

Wolcott, H. F. (1999). *Ethnography: A way of seeing.* Walnut Creek, CA: AltaMira.

34

THE PROBLEM OF CRITERIA
IN THE AGE OF RELATIVISM

◆ John K. Smith and Deborah K. Deemer

In the introduction to the third volume in his series on the nature of inquiry, Hazelrigg (1995) talks about "issues of relativism and its contrary" (p. ix). He then goes on to say about the latter, "which is what, now that we no longer speak the name of absolutism without embarrassment?" (p. ix). His point, which has been noted by many others, such as Bernstein (1983), is that there no longer is a "contrary" to place in opposition to relativism. If this is the case, then it is clear that in this age when the God's-eye view is no longer a realizable hope, relativism, in some form or another, is a consequence that is inescapable (Hesse, 1980, p. xiv). Thus any discussion of criteria for judging social and educational inquiry must confront the issue of relativism—but, of course, as we shall see, how relativism is understood or conceptualized matters greatly.

We begin this chapter with a brief historical review of how we have arrived at this point where we must accept relativism, not only as the crucial feature in any discussion of criteria, but also as the central condition of our very being in the world. At the core of this journey stands the realization, which has been expressed in innumerable ways, that all observation is theory laden or that there is no possibility of theory-free observation or knowledge. Although this idea well predates the work of people such as Hanson (1958) and Kuhn (1962), one can argue it is their writings that have forced upon us the recognition that as knowing subjects we are intimately a part of any understanding we have of what counts as knowledge or of any claim we make to knowledge. With the end of the possibility that we could think of ourselves as neutral spectators at the game of knowledge, the central problem that has preoccupied the thoughts of numerous researchers for the past few decades is that of "Now what are we going to do with us?" This is a preoccupation that has been expressed with great frequency and in all manner of ways: Gallagher's (1995) revisiting of her role in her dissertation research, Sparkes's (1993) concerns over reciprocity, various aspects of Wolcott's (1995) discussion of the art of fieldwork, Punch's (1994) discussion of the politics and ethics of field inquiry, and on and on. The discussions that focus on the position or role of the inquirer seemingly have become endless.

Following this brief historical review, we examine some of the ways the issue of criteria has been addressed in this age of relativism. One of the most prominent of these is what we call the *quasi-foundationalist* response. At the center of the quasi-foundationalist project is the desire to deny the relativism that must accompany the realization that there can be no theory-free knowledge or observation. This group has drawn much of its intellectual sustenance from various neorealist philosophers (*neorealist* is a general term used to distinguish this group from what are often referred to, especially by the neorealists themselves, as naïve, direct, or unsophisticated realists). From at least the time of Popper's (1959) rejection of positivism in favor of a sophisticated or scientific realism, the neorealists have attempted to thread a line between their acceptance of a constructivist epistemology on the one side and, on the other, their adoption of a neorealist ontology. The latter commits them to the position that there is a reality out there that, because it can be known, at least in principle, as it really is, acts as a constraint on any claim to knowledge. The former announces their recognition that there can be no theory-free knowledge or theory-free observation.

In the second half of the chapter we address how our ideas about criteria must change when we realize that the epistemological project is over and relativism must be accepted. This examination begins with the very important point that relativism need not and must not be seen in terms of "anything goes." Rather, relativism is nothing more or less than our condition in the world—it announces that as human beings we are, and can be nothing but, finite. This understanding of relativism is then coupled with a concern that we must change our imageries and metaphors from those of discovery and finding to those of constructing and making. Based on this transition, the central issues become those of how do we as individuals make judgments, which we all must, and the extent to which we allow our judgments to move into a public space, which to a certain degree we also must, to engage the judgments of others.

As is always the case, before we begin at least two caveats are necessary. First, the issues we address are complex. Given the space available and, much more important, our limited capacities, there is no way we can do them full justice. Second, contrary to what is generally the case for others who have addressed this topic, we offer no particular criteria and instructions on how they might be applied. Our intent is to discuss the limits and possibilities of judgment—both individual and within social spaces—in this age of relativism.

◆ Historical Background

The long-standing problem empiricists constructed for themselves was how to reconnect that which they had separated—the knowing subject from the object of knowing. After having established a dualism of subject and object, empiricists of all varieties were compelled to spend considerable time and energy attempting to rework or get around this duality in a way that would allow them to claim the knowing subject could have access to reality in such a way that it could be depicted accurately. Put differently, empiricists had developed a situation in which the referent point for judging claims to knowledge was, and could only be, that which was outside, and independently so, of the knower. Knowledge was a matter of accurate representation, and thus was born the correspondence theory of truth. The solution of choice to make good on this correspondence theory was, as has long been announced in our research textbooks, a methodical one. The idea was quite straightforward: If the proper procedures or methods were properly applied, the subjectivities of the knowing subject would be contained and the knower would thereby gain an accurate, objective depiction of reality. This is what Kerlinger (1979) meant when he said that "the procedures of science are objective—not the scientists. Scientists, like all men and women are opinionated, dogmatic, ideological . . . that is the very reason for insisting on procedural objectivity; to get the whole business outside of ourselves" (p. 264).

Given this line of thought, a judgment about the quality of research, at least in the first instance, was a judgment about whether or not the proper procedures had been properly applied. The methods were seen as neutral and hence established that neutral arena within which judgments could be made about the goodness or badness of any individual research. Of course, there still remained a second level of interest—that of the significance of any particular study. It has long been recognized by the proceduralists that even the most appropriately conducted study could still be judged insignificant because it focused on a trivial problem. In any event, for empiricists the issue can be summarized as follows: Because method allowed for undistorted contact with reality, it was the basis for distinguishing good from bad inquiry but not important from unimportant research.

The attempts by empiricists over the past few hundred years to reconnect subject and object—from Locke's "blank slate" to the ostensive reference of the logical empiricists— need not be discussed. These moves are quite well-known and, more important, such a discussion would take us far afield from the main topic at hand (for a brief recounting of this history, see Smith, 1993). A few brief comments, however, must be made with regard to what has happened over the past 30 or 40 years as traditional empiricism has unraveled and we have witnessed the demise of the methodical solution to the problem of criteria. The problems associated with the dualism of subject and ob-

ject were apparent to many philosophers prior to the middle of the 20th century. However, within Anglo-American philosophical circles, a good case can be made that it was Hanson (1958) and then, most definitely, Kuhn (1962) who brought the problematic associated with the dualism of subject and object to the forefront.

At the core of Hanson's (1958) arguments was the now seemingly obvious point that "the theory, hypothesis, framework, or background knowledge held by an investigator can strongly influence what is observed" (p. 7). A few short years later Kuhn (1962) followed up on this line of reasoning with his talk of incommensurable paradigms, paradigm shifts, that all knowledge is framework dependent, and so on. By the mid-to-late 1980s, the work of numerous people made it apparent that any claim of or hope for "theory-free knowledge" was untenable on all counts. To cite just a few examples, there were Putnam's (1981) arguments about "no God's-eye point of view," Nagel's (1986) claim that there was no possibility of a "view from nowhere," Bernstein's (1983) discussion of no "Archimedean point," Taylor's (1971) undermining of the hope for access to "brute data," Gadamer's (1995) discussion of "effective history," and Goodman's (1978) elaboration of the ways we make the world.

All of these arguments, and others, combined with another series of arguments that focused directly on, and cast grave doubt upon, the claim that method itself was neutral and could thereby be the repository of procedural objectivity. This certainly was one of the main messages that could be taken from the work of Hesse (1980), Giddens (1976), MacKenzie (1981), Cherryholmes (1988), Smith (1985), and so on. In the end, the result of all of this intellectual ferment was the elaboration of a number of points of great consequence for any discussion of criteria: There is no possibility of theory-free observation and knowledge, the duality of subject and object is untenable, no special epistemic privilege can be attached to any particular method or set of methods, and we cannot have the kind of objective access to an external, extralinguistic referent that would allow us to adjudicate from among different knowledge claims.

The legacy of all of this, of course, is that we no longer can talk in terms of a foundational epistemology and a direct ontological realism. To the contrary, if the discussions of the past few decades have made anything clear to us, it is that we cannot adopt a God's-eye point of view; all we can have are "the various points of view of actual persons reflecting various interests and purposes that their descriptions and theories subserve" (Putnam, 1981, p. 50). Under these conditions, with the demise of empiricism and the methodical stance, any discussion of criteria must come to terms, in one form or another or in one way or another, with the issue of relativism.

◆ *The Quasi-Foundationalist Response*

The quasi-foundationalists, who have attempted to address the criteria issue from the perspective of some form of nonnaïve realism, have had to contend with a very interesting problem. Any elaboration of criteria must take place within the context of their commitment to ontological realism on the one side and, on the other, their realization that they are obligated to accept a constructivist epistemology. The former announces a commitment to the proposition that there is a real world out there independent of our interest in, or knowledge of, it. The latter announces a commitment to the proposition that we can never know if we have depicted this real world as it really is. In short, nonnaïve realists or neorealists "assert a belief in a real world independent of our knowledge while also making it clear that our knowledge of this metacognitive world is quite fallible" (Leary, 1984, p. 918).

In light of these dual commitments, many neorealist philosophers have felt compelled to express their positions with the use of the term *relativism*. Bhaskar (1983), for example, says that his transcendental realism presupposes "ontological realism and epistemological relativism" (p. 259). Similarly, House (1991) notes

that the world can be "known only under particular descriptions and is, in that limited sense, epistemologically relative" (p. 5). Even more directly, Manicas (1987) has written that "knowledge is a social product and the standards of inquiry are generated in the course of inquiry. This is a relativism. But it is not irrationalism, because it presupposes a realism" (p. 261).

There is no question, then, that neorealist acceptance of epistemological constructivism entails the realization that there can be no "God's-eye view" in that any claim to knowledge must take into account the perspective of the person making the claim. Maxwell (1992) notes quite clearly the key aspects of the neorealist response to the consequences of this realization. First, he recognizes that "as observers and interpreters . . . we cannot step outside of our own experience to obtain some observer-independent account of what we experience. Thus, it is always possible for there to be different, equally valid accounts from different perspectives" (p. 283). That said, however, it is also equally clear that he, like the other neorealists, does not accept a situation in which "all possible accounts . . . are equally useful, credible, or legitimate" (p. 283). Thus "understanding is relative," there is no account that can stand "independent of any particular perspective" (p. 284), but this does not mean that our only option is to descend into a relativism of all-accounts-are-equal or "anything goes." Finally, in that the neorealists acknowledge that the methodical stance of their empiricist predecessors is not possible, the way to avoid relativism is to call upon a "realist conception of validity that sees the validity of an account as inherent, not in the procedures used to produce and validate it, but in its relationship to those things that it is intended to be an account of" (p. 281).

To examine how well they have done with this quasi-foundationalist project, with its obvious truth-as-correspondence overtones, we turn to exemplars—beginning with a particular emphasis on the work of Hammersley, in that he has presented one of the clearest and most sophisticated attempts to develop criteria from a neorealist perspective. In one very well attended piece of work, Hammersley (1990) begins with the assertion that "we do not need to abandon the concept of truth as correspondence to an independent reality. We can retain this concept of truth by adopting a more subtle realism" (p. 61). Following this assertion that we can retain the empiricist concept of truth but must reject naïve interpretations of it, he then attempts to elaborate criteria in order to prevent a slide into what is, for him, the void of relativism. These are criteria that must be worked out in light of a constructivist epistemology and a realist, however subtle, ontology. Hammersley frames this task in terms of how researchers can validate their accounts and argues that the only basis for validation is to engage in judgments of the "likelihood of error" (p. 61). This is a position that has distinct Popperian overtones and, accordingly, shares in the problems attendant to Popper's account of falsification. We return to this point shortly.

Hammersley (1990) proposes that the two key elements of validity are plausibility and credibility. The former issue is one of whether or not a claim seems plausible; "that is, whether we judge it as likely to be true given our existing knowledge" (p. 61). He adds that some claims are so plausible we can immediately accept them at face value, whereas others require the presentation of evidence. In the latter instance, a judgment about the credibility of a claim must be taken "given the nature of the phenomena concerned, the circumstances of the research" (p. 61), and so on. In both instances, then, Hammersley recognizes that when a claim has neither face plausibility nor face credibility, evidence is required. However, he further recognizes that the particular evidence presented by a researcher in support of the plausibility and credibility of a study must itself be assessed as to its own plausibility and credibility. And, as he continues, "we may require further evidence to support that evidence, which we shall judge in terms of plausibility and credibility" (p. 62).

It is clear Hammersley fully acknowledges that plausibility and credibility are social judgments, and, not surprisingly, his attempt to establish criteria has become entangled in an infinite regress—if not a hermeneutic circle. At this point, it would seem prudent to call upon ontological realism and make it do some serious work—in particular, the work of making contact with reality in such a way as to blunt the infinite regress of social judgments or, to put it differently, to blunt the relativism that would seem to lie at the end of it all.

This is not the case, however, and the notion of correspondence and realism, no matter how subtle or sophisticated, plays no role of consequence for the balance of his discussion. Hammersley's (1990) movement away from neorealism begins when he says that "plausibility and credibility form a relatively weak basis for judging claims, compared to the idea that we can assess claims directly according to their correspondence with reality or by relying on some body of knowledge whose validity is certain" (p. 62). He continues this movement when he reinvokes a constructivist epistemology and thereby acknowledges that judgments will not "necessarily be consensual, since there may be different views about what is plausible and credible" (p. 62).

Ultimately, Hammersley's line of argument ends in a discussion of the norms that should govern discourse among members of a scientific community. He lists what he considers to be three key features of this scientific community. First, all findings should be subject to "communal assessment," with an effort to "resolve disagreements by seeking common grounds . . . and trying to work back to a resolution of the dispute relying only on what is accepted as valid by all disputants" (p. 63). Second, all involved should not only attempt to persuade, but be willing to be persuaded and to change their views. Finally, the community is open to those who are "willing to operate on the basis of the first two rules" (p. 63). In the end, then, judgments about plausibility and credibility are social judgments, and they should be made based upon as free and open a dialogue and discussion as possible. There is nothing in Hammersley's discussion that shows us how we can make contact with an external referent—a reality—that would give the criteria of plausibility and credibility a standing beyond the social process and the inevitable relativism that lurks behind this process.

A similar point can be made about the well-known work of Manicas and Secord (1983). They admit that "knowledge is a social and historical product" (p. 401), there is "no preinterpreted 'given' and the test of truth cannot be 'correspondence.' Epistemologically, there can be nothing known to which our ideas (sentences, theories) can correspond" (p. 401). But, if that is so, then, as Leary (1984) notes, "Exactly how Manicas and Secord propose to link experiences—which they admit to be culturally and historically mediated—with reality independent from experience is an issue I shall leave for them to clarify" (p. 918). They do not do well with this task, for as Leary further notes, their best response is the negative assertion that there is no theory-free observation, which "does not eliminate the possibility of objectivity, construed here as warranted assertibility" (p. 410). But, of course, the problem they face here is the same one Hammersley (1990) faces; the warrants one brings to judgments are themselves socially and historically conditioned—as are the warrants that warrant the warrants, and on and on. In both of these instances, and generally for neorealists, any attempt to elaborate on the issue of criteria in a way that gives criteria force beyond socially and historically conditioned judgments must involve an explanation of exactly how their ontological realism does some serious work and is not merely an assertion.

A further example of the same situation occurs in Maxwell's (1992) discussion of five aspects of validity: descriptive, interpretive, theoretical, generalizability, and evaluative. We focus only on his discussion of descriptive validity, as this is the one that seems to make the most use of the realist commitment. Maxwell argues that this is the first concern for qualitative inquirers in that it focuses on the factual accuracy of an account—that researchers are "not making up or distorting the things they saw and heard" (p. 285). On the face of it, this concern seems to be very unproblematic, especially if one confines description to the level of did the researcher actually speak with the person she said she did or did the researcher actually enter the classroom to observe the goings on. However, as soon as one moves that short distance to

the level of "description" on the order of did or did not the student "throw an eraser on a specific occasion" (p. 286) or did she raise her arm or did she thrust her arm in the air, the prospects for a viable concept of descriptive validity disappear. Put differently, as soon as we move past the most minimal level of the depiction of the movement of physical bodies in time and space, the coercive or constraining quality that is desired from the real or from reality itself has been left behind long ago in the name of the need for context.

Maxwell (1992) recognizes this issue in that he further notes even descriptive validity is "by no means independent of theory . . . even if this theory is implicit or common sense" (p. 287). This understanding then leads to the comment that although there can be disagreement about the descriptive validity of an account, this can be resolved "in principle" by the data. Further, however, he brings this line of argument to its inevitable outcome when he notes, "Of course, the theory could be made problematic by one of the participants in the discussion—for example, by challenging the applicability of 'throwing' to what the student did with the eraser" (p. 287). One might counter at this point that to challenge the applicability of "throwing" is not only to make theory problematic, it is to make the description problematic. For example, one might say that "throwing" cannot be applied here because the student "tossed" the eraser. If someone were to raise this point, then what would be at stake would not be just a matter of making the theory problematic; to the contrary, it would be a fundamental challenge to the very accuracy of depiction, with each accusing the other of an incorrect or inaccurate accounting of the facts.

Maxwell (1992) responds to this complication with a shift of validity categories and says that this then is no longer an issue of descriptive validity, but rather one of interpretive validity. But this will not do because the whole point of the idea that there can be no theory-free observation is that it is virtually impossible to disentangle the descriptive from the interpretive. How we describe the world is an interpretation—or, put differently, interpretation cuts very, very deep indeed. That much of the time we can agree on "throwing" versus "tossing" is not because reality stands over against us, but because we happen to share a theoretical or pretheoretical disposition and a language for depicting movement in time and space. In his next paragraph, Maxwell recognizes this point when he says, "Descriptive understanding pertains, by definition, to matters for which we have a framework for resolving such disagreement, a framework provided in large part by taken-for-granted ideas about time, space, physical objects, behavior, and our perception of these" (p. 286). In other words, if we start from the same perspective, sharing a language and so on, we will tend to describe/interpret things in basically the same ways. If we start from different theoretical or pretheoretical perspectives, our descriptions/interpretations of events and actions will differ. This is exactly the point made by Hanson (1958), Kuhn (1962), and many others, including the neorealists. Accordingly, just like Hammersley (1990) and Manicas and Secord (1983), Maxwell is unable to show us how to get reality to do some serious work—work that would give his discussion of validity, and by extension criteria, the kind of force that will allow it to stand over and against or beyond a process of socially and historically constrained judgments.

We close this section by noting that the problems faced by the neorealists are little different from the ones faced by one of their major intellectual precursors, Popper (1959, 1972), who, although he as much as anyone else contributed to the retreat from logical empiricism, still attempted to salvage something from the remains of that project. Popper freely accepted that there could be no theory-free observation. That point granted, he still wanted to preserve the capacity to test theories against observational statements. In order to do so, he appealed to a version of realism as the key element in our ability to falsify hypotheses. The problem with his appeal is that if falsification is a matter of a disjuncture between a theory, or a hypothesis derived from a theory, and the facts, the latter must be independent of the former. This is precisely what is not possible if all obser-

vation is theory laden. That is, it is impossible to think of the comparison of a hypothesis with theory-mediated facts as the same as testing a hypothesis against an independently existing reality. Hindess (1977) clearly notes the incoherence present in this line of thought: "If theory is inescapably implicated in observation then testing cannot be a rational procedure. If testing is a rational procedure then there must be an atheoretical mode of observation governed by a preestablished harmony between language and the real. To maintain . . . both the rationality of testing and the thesis that observation is an interpretation in light of theory is . . . [a] contradiction" (p. 186).

The problems with Popper's realism are further evident in his claims about inquiry and approximations to truth. This is a claim that Hammersley (1990) reiterates in slightly different terms when he mentions the possibility of research producing "cumulative knowledge" (p. 62). The basic idea sponsoring these claims is that over time our research gets us closer and closer to truth or reality. Unfortunately, this whole line of thought, as is well noted by Hazelrigg (1989), lacks cogency because the "notion of approximation requires an existent referent to which one can achieve proximity, yet how can we know that existent? According to Popper we cannot; but if we cannot, then how are we possibly to judge the question of proximity?" (p. 78). Again, the neorealist claim that it is reality itself that can serve as the bottom line for judgments cannot be made good.

In summary, then, it is clear the neorealists cannot grant us the kind of purchase on the criteria issue that they desire. This lack is evident in the work of Hammersley (1990), Maxwell (1992), and others. In the cases of the aforementioned, both begin with, in the first instance, the claim that we can retain the concept of "truth as correspondence to an independent reality" (p. 61) and, in the second, that a judgment about the validity of a study can be taken with regard to its "relationship to those things that it is intended to be an account of" (p. 281). However, in both cases this is as far as their neorealism goes, and both eventually turn to judgment as a social process. For Hammersley this move appears with full force when he fails to show us how to make contact with an external referent and, in response to this failure, he turns his full attention in the only direction possible—to the issue of the norms that should guide discourse among researchers. For Maxwell, the signal that he should abandon his neorealism comes when he notes that even a judgment about descriptive validity, which he says is about the "factual accuracy of [an] account" (p. 285), requires a shared framework for resolving disagreements (p. 287) and, accordingly, "validity is relative in this sense because understanding is relative" (p. 284).

◆ A Transition

With the failure of the neorealists to salvage the last remnants of the empiricist project, it is time to make a transition and begin to change the conversation. In other words, it is time to move beyond any lingering hopes for a foundational or quasi-foundational epistemology, to change our metaphors and imageries from those of discoverers/finders to those of constructors/makers, and to accept that relativism is our inescapable condition as finite beings. There is no question that we must, as both inquirers and laypersons, learn to live with uncertainty and contingency, and forgo the hope that something will come along that will enable us to transcend our human finitude. But, that said, the relativism that arrives with this perspective does not mean we must give ourselves over to the neorealist fear that all judgments are equally valid, or that "anything goes" in our assessments of the quality of inquiry. Schwandt (1996) summarizes the nonfoundationalist situation quite succinctly: "We must learn to live with uncertainty, with the absence of final vindications, without the hope of solutions in the form of epistemological guarantees. Contingency, fallibilism, dialogue, and deliberation mark our way of being in the world. But these ontological conditions are not the equivalent to eternal ambiguity, the lack of commitment, the inability to act in the face of uncertainty" (p. 59). In short, the

problematic for nonfoundationalists, which is profoundly unsettling for us as individuals and as a community of inquirers (if such a sense of an overall community is even possible), is that of how to make and defend judgments when there can be no appeal to foundations or to something outside of the social processes of knowledge construction.

Discussion of this problematic, and of what it means for the judgments we make about inquiry, must begin by clearing some ground and establishing some points. Most immediately, a response is required to the oft-expressed charge that relativism is self-refuting. The refrain here is quite well-known: To say that all things are relative is to make a nonrelative statement. As such, relativism is self-refuting and an untenable position to adopt. We must address two issues in order to demonstrate why this charge is of no consequence.

First, is it the case that relativism is self-refuting? Given the form of logic we normally bring to such questions, the answer, of course, must be yes. But this then leads to the second point: Does it matter, again given this form of logic, that relativism is self-refuting? In this instance, the answer is no. This second point obviously requires elaboration.

One could attempt to argue that this point about being self-refuting should be a crippling blow to nonfoundationalists and their approach to criteria, if only because other schools of philosophical thought have met their demise in similar circumstances. For example, logical empiricism certainly unraveled over the verification issue. As is well-known, logical empiricists said that any statement that cannot be empirically verified is meaningless. But, of course, that statement itself cannot be empirically verified and so, logically, it is meaningless. As Putnam (1981) so clearly points out, it was this problem as much as anything else that led to the end of logical empiricism. So, why should not the same strictures be applied to relativism?

The initial answers to this self-refuting situation came from Gadamer and Rorty. Gadamer's (1995) response is to agree that relativism is self-refuting, but then to shrug it off by saying that to make this point is to make a point of no interest, or one that does "not express any superior insight of value" (p. 344). Rorty's (1985) tactic is to argue that it is a mistake to think of relativism as another theory of knowledge. Quite to the contrary, he dispenses with the self-refuting problem by saying that because his type of pragmatist is not interested in advancing any "epistemology, *a fortiori* he does not have a relativistic one" (p. 6).

Although we agree with much of how both Gadamer (1995) and Rorty (1985) have approached this issue, we feel a further comment remains necessary. One reason the self-refuting claim is and should be devastating to logical empiricism, and, for that matter, to other schools of thought, but not to relativism, depends on the aspirations expressed by these philosophical dispositions. We would argue that empiricism in any form, for example, was based on the claim and the hope that we could deny our human finitude and adopt a God's-eye point of view. That is, the claim was that we could "bracket" ourselves in some way or another, predominantly through submission to method, such that it would become possible for us to seize upon some external referent (i.e., reality known as it really is) to adjudicate different knowledge claims and resolve our differences. Given this claim, it is quite appropriate to apply the logic of self-refuting—the strength of the claim and the aspirations advanced must be directly related to the strength of the argument brought forth in support of those claims and aspirations.

Relativism as understood here, quite to the contrary, is not a theory of knowledge and advances no pretense that we can escape our finite condition of being in the world. As such, the issue of self-refuting, even though it is a logically correct position given a standard form of logic, is unimportant. Taking a page from Godel's idea of incompleteness (see Hofstadter, 1979), this situation is only what one would expect from any human, social and historical, construction. Relativism is not something to be transcended, it is merely something with which we, as finite beings, must learn to live.

Does this understanding of relativism leave nonfoundationalists enmeshed in a situation of "anything goes"—a situation where all judgments about inquiry, and, for that matter, everything else, are equal? There are two intimately related reasons why relativism should not and need not be understood in these terms. First, the charge of relativism as anything goes does not make sense because this charge requires for its vitality a viable concept of the absolute. As previously noted with reference to Hazelrigg (1995), if we no longer can speak of the absolute without embarrassment, then we must realize we cannot speak of "anything goes" without embarrassment.

Second, and more tangibly, it is very clear we all already do make judgments, and as far as anyone can see, we will continue to do so for a long time to come. To say these judgments cannot be grounded extralinguistically does not mean we are exempt from engaging in as open and unconstrained dialogue as possible in order to attempt to justify our assessments. But to attempt to persuade another further requires that one is open to being persuaded. All relativism brings to the table with regard to the issue of criteria is that to be a finite human being who must live with and make judgments in concert with other finite human beings can be, with some frequency, very tough work indeed. This is, in effect, what Schwandt (1996) means when he says, as noted above, that learning to live with uncertainty and the impossibility of final vindication does not mean that we must abandon commitment and our ability to make judgments.

What, then, does this understanding of relativism as a recognition and acceptance of our human finitude mean for social and educational inquiry—especially for the issue of criteria for judging the quality of our studies? One very important way to frame this question is to introduce the difference between depictions of inquiry with the use of the metaphors and imagery of discovery or finding versus the metaphors and imagery of making or constructing. If one accepts a constructivist stance, this means that, as Rorty (1979) so well notes, the metaphors and imageries of discovery and finding no longer can be made good. However, Rorty also goes on to add that we might as well stay with the language of a found world. Part of his justification for this injunction is that "nothing deep turns on the choice between these two phrases—between the imagery of making and of finding" (p. 344).

However, Hazelrigg (1989) has been persuasive in helping us understand that a great deal of consequence turns on this distinction. This is so because, as he puts it, "the difference in consequence is not merely of imageries and stories but of practices—of who we are, of what we do, of what world we make" (p. 167). The problem is that to continue to employ the language of a "discovered world" is to continue a "passivity in regard to responsibility for the world" (p. 168). And, as Hazelrigg continues, to think in terms of finding is to place the world "outside the domain of human will. That is an enormously dangerous consequence of any retention of the 'found world' language of storytelling" (p. 168).

To illustrate this point, we note that in the histories, especially more recent, of both educational practice and research there has been a strong tendency to categorize children as this or that—as learning disabled (LD), for example. For those who operate with the image of researchers as "discoverers," LD is a natural category—there always were LD children, and the reason we have recently discovered them is that our inquiries have become increasingly sophisticated. For those who use the language of making or constructing, LD is a constructed category—a way we have chosen, for whatever social/historical reasons, to categorize children. The point is not that we dispense with categorization, which in any case is impossible for the finite human mind. To the contrary, the point is to examine and fully discuss why we construct the world as we do. This is a discussion that is practical and moral, framed by contingent social and historical circumstances, and certainly not epistemological in any theory-of-knowledge sense of the word. Put differently, for those possessed by the metaphors of discovery, issues of moral responsibility are at best contingent because "discovery" is only a matter of contact with reality and what reality is telling us. For those who accept the metaphors of constructing, moral responsibility is central because one must be morally responsible for what one constructs or makes (for a further example and discussion, see Smith, 1989, especially chap. 4).

It is in this sense that the relativism of the nonfoundationalists requires that inquiry be seen as an act of construction that is practical and moral and not epistemological. Likewise, as must follow from this requirement, any judgments about the goodness or badness of research must themselves be practical and moral judgments and not epistemological ones. For the nonfoundationalists, to move away from epistemology is to recognize inquiry as a social process in which we construct reality as we go along and as a social process in which we, at one and the same time, construct our criteria for judging inquiries as we go along.

◆ Changing the Conversation

Relativism is nothing more or less than the expression of our human finitude; we must see ourselves as practical and moral beings, and abandon hope for knowledge that is not embedded within our historical, cultural, and engendered ways of being. If this so, then to continue to talk in the vocabularies of theories of knowledge is to continue to talk in the shadows of the unrealizable desire that something will come along to allow us to get off of Montaigne's wheel or out of the hermeneutic circle. Chisholm's (1973) paraphrase of Montaigne clearly summarizes the unresolved and unresolvable epistemological problematic:

> To know whether things really are as they seem to be, we must have a *procedure* for distinguishing appearances that are true from appearances that are false. But to know whether our procedure is a good procedure, we have to know whether it really *succeeds* in distinguishing appearances that are true from appearances that are false. And we cannot know whether it does really succeed unless we already know which appearances are *true* and which ones are *false*. And so we are caught in a circle. (p. 3)

The neorealists have been unsuccessful in their attempt to cling to an organizing narrative of epistemology free of time and place. They have not been able to show us a way to get off of the wheel or out of the circle. We suspect it is time to move on; it is time to change the conversation by asking what making judgments is about when we can no longer be epistemological. Although we are certainly able to talk about knowledge, especially its social production, there is little point in talking about theories of knowledge and pursuing the ambition to solve the problematic.

That we can no longer play the game of philosophy as epistemology and find solace in a foundational narrative can be nothing but profoundly unsettling to us. This is a break, a rupture, that appears to leave social and educational inquiry "undone"—to use a word from the title of a recent book by Stronach and Maclure (1997). Put differently, all of this talk about judging can no longer take place within that seemingly abstracted, disembodied public space that was fostered by the desire to be epistemological and to thereby specify the context of judgment apart from the actual judgment process. In the age of relativism the issue of who is making judgments, about what inquiries, for what purposes, and with whom one shares these judgments is of critical importance. As individuals we must make judgments, and as members of social groups, however loosely organized, we must be witness to situations in which our individual judgments are played out with the judgments of other individuals.

But, we must immediately note, there is at least one very apparent and often practiced way to avoid the difficulty of judgment. Certainly one could turn to power, in one or another of its numerous guises, to render the social context and process of judgment very specifiable indeed. There is the use of power in a rather raw or open application—for example, the all-too-common situation where a reviewer rejects an article with little or no explanation. Or there is the power of the shrug of the shoulder that seems so popular today with various people when they are questioned. The questioner just does not get the point and the situation is so hopeless that there is no reason to attempt to engage any further. In these instances and many, many others of similar nature with

which we are all familiar, an individual has made a judgment, criteria have been applied, but engagement with the judgment and criteria has been denied. To engage this defensive stance, based on the claim of theoretical, standpoint, or whatever differences, works to narrow the public space or social group with whom one shares judgments—all others are read out of the exchange. In any event, although the possibilities for the application of power to solve the problem of criteria seem almost endless, they also seem very unsatisfying and undesirable.

This should not be taken to mean that we are so naïve as to hold that power should and can be eliminated from judgments as they are played out socially. We have no intention to embrace some sort of romanticized "intellectualist flight from power" (Hazelrigg, 1995, p. 202). Rather, the issue for us centers on the responsible use of power while avoiding its excesses. But we also are well aware that it is impossible to specify in some permanent way exactly when one has crossed the line from responsible to excessive. Likewise, it would seem there are often good reasons to narrow the social group. When marginalized groups seek to have their voices heard, solidarity can be very important. In fact, we would argue that this was the case for many qualitative inquirers a few years ago. But, again, the question arises as to how to honor this need while avoiding its excesses—fully realizing that we are unable to specify exactly when the line has been crossed. In short, then, we recognize that power is ever and always present, but we also hold that the temptation (also ever and always present?) to use power as a way to avoid critique and the risk of one's prejudices denies the value of and need for public discourse. So the issue remains: What can be said about judgment when relativism demands attention to context and forgoes the possibility of appeal to an abstract, disembodied (epistemological) public space?

One response to this question from some people is the claim that any discussion of criteria is pointless. Although we will not engage Rosenau's (1992) rendering of affirmative versus skeptical postmodern and poststructural perspectives, we must acknowledge that some of her comments successfully surface issues that have been troubling many within the academy. Those whom Rosenau calls skeptic postmodernists argue that we can only be "nonjudgmental" (p. 55) because "good/bad criteria are unavailable" (p. 175) and all interpretations are equally interesting or uninteresting. In the absence of established criteria for sorting the good from the less so, there is no choice but to simply throw up our hands and leave the field of judgment behind. Certainly this sentiment is not unknown, at least to us. There are times as we review articles for publication, grade papers, accept the dissertation even though it disappointed, that the thought arises: Who are we to judge? The field should be left open to the play of differences, and so on. A similar arena of self-doubt, given the fallibility of human judgment, seems to be the driving force behind the often agonized and agonizing discussions of voice, writing the other, the crisis of representation, and so on.

But to begin from this point or to pretend (even hope?) that we can lead a life free of judgment is to immediately go astray, and obviously so. Judgments must be made and must be argued and justified, unless, in the latter instance, one simply resorts to raw power. As Schwandt (1996) has noted for us, that we all must live with uncertainty and contingency does not mean that we can dismiss commitment and abandon judgment (p. 59). There is no question that we all think some things are better than others and that we make judgments accordingly, often even when we say we do not. This process of judgment making has been going on for quite some time now, and will continue to do so for as far as can be seen.

It is impossible to imagine a person leading a life without making judgments or without making discriminations. To attempt to do so evokes the image of Ebenezer in Barth's novel *The Sot-Weed Factor* (1960), who, because he found all things equally interesting, "threw up his hands at choice" and "sat immobile in the window seat in his nightshirt and stared at the activity in the street below" (p. 11). The same immobility must be the fate of all those who would claim to find everything equally uninteresting.

Taylor (1989) has expressed this situation and its consequences very clearly: "To know who you are is to be oriented in moral space, a space in which questions arise about what is good or bad, what is worth doing and what not, what has meaning and importance for you and what is trivial and secondary" (p. 28). To not make judgments is to lose sight of one's orientation in moral space, which is to lose one's grounding as a human being.

In our roles as inquirers, educators, evaluators, we are always making judgments about papers for publication, presentations, books, dissertations, student papers, and so on. As we approach judgment in any given case, we have in mind or bring to the task a list, for lack of a better term, of characteristics that we use to judge the quality of that production. The use of the term *list* should not be taken to mean that we are referring to something like an enclosed and precisely specified or specifiable shopping or laundry list. Put differently, to talk of a list in this sense is not at all to talk about, for example, an accumulation of 20 items, scaled 1 to 5, where everyone's presentation proposal is then numerically scored with a cutoff point for acceptance. Obviously, to think of a list in these terms is to miss the entire point, so much so that it makes a mockery of the idea of qualitative inquiry, of what relativism means, and of what it means to realize that we can no longer be epistemological.

To the contrary, for us a list of characteristics must be seen as always open-ended, in part unarticulated, and, even when a characteristic is more or less articulated, it is always and ever subject to constant reinterpretation. Moreover, the items on the list can never be the distillation of some abstracted epistemology, they must inevitably be rooted in one's standpoint or, to use Gadamer's (1995) term, they must inevitably evolve out of and reflect one's "effective history" (pp. 301-302). These points require brief comment.

The lists we bring to judgment are and can only be open-ended in that we have the permanent capacity to add items to and subtract items from the lists—although, as we shall soon note, doing so involves risk. Should we accept the risk, then the limits for recasting our lists derive not from theoretical labor, but from the use to which the lists are put. The limits on modification are a practical matter; they are worked and reworked within the context of actual practices/applications and cannot be set down in abstracted formulas.

Second, any lists we bring to judgment are only partly articulated. Some items can be more or less specified, whereas others seem to resist such specification. Polanyi's (1962) idea of tacit knowledge applies here very well indeed. When we make judgments we more or less can specify some of the reasons, but other things seem to be out there—there is surplus that seems to stand just beyond our grasp, just beyond our language. This does not mean that we should not and do not attempt to bring this surplus to fuller conscious articulation; it only means that it can never be done completely. That this is so should not be surprising, because as finite beings we can never be fully transparent, not only to others, but even to ourselves. Similarly, even those items on our lists that are more or less well articulated can be reinterpreted, even if subtly and gradually over time. And, finally, the importance we assign to items on our lists may easily change over time. A characteristic of research that we thought important at one time and in one place may take on diminished importance at another time and place (D. Gallagher, personal communication, 1998).

But what is most important to reiterate here is that our lists are challenged, changed, and modified not through abstracted discussions of the lists and items in and of themselves, but in application to actual inquiries. That is, very often something "new" comes along, such as Sparkes's (1996) self-reflective narrative of the fragile body-self, the developing genre of ethnographic fiction, or readers' theater. The new does not fit well with one's existing list of characteristics. To read these "new" things that come along or to attend the challenge seriously immediately opens up the possibility that one must reformulate one's list and possibly replace the exemplars one calls upon in the never-ending process of making judgments. However,

the key here is possibility, because inquirers may choose to preserve their lists, as many often seem to do, and judge the production as not even qualifying to be considered research. The latter is a comment, by the way, that was often heard about qualitative inquiry in years past.

The lists we hold are part of us—they are expressions of our own particular standpoints or effective histories. In other words, to refer again to Gadamer (1995), a list is an expression of our prejudices and, as he notes, it is the prejudices of an individual that "constitute the historical reality of his being" (p. 277). In any encounter with a production, especially something "new," as noted above, one must be willing to risk one's prejudices. Just as in the process of judgment one asks questions of a text or a person, the person or a text must be allowed to ask questions in return. As per the example of Sparkes's (1996) work mentioned above, to approach this inquiry requires that one be open, that one be willing to allow the text to challenge one's prejudices and possibly change one's list and one's idea about what is and is not good inquiry. But two important points must be made here. First, to reiterate, the word *possibly* is crucial here because to be open does not mean automatically to accept. One may still offer reasons for not accepting something new. Second, there is no method for engaging in the risking of prejudices. If anything, to risk one's prejudices is a matter of disposition—or, better said, moral obligation—that requires one to accept that if one wishes to persuade others, one must be equally open to being persuaded.

It is time to turn to an exemplar to illustrate these points. The work of Lather (1986a, 1986b, 1993, 1998a, 1998b) over the past 10 or 12 years, in various articles and presentations and in her book with Smithies (1997), stands as an almost paradigmatic example of the fact that we all approach a piece of work with something in mind. Lather's discussions both participate in and trouble our discourse about criteria for judging inquiry. In the process, Lather struggles with lists of characteristics that are open, evolving over time, and always in flux, and that resist full articulation. The items Lather has brought forth under the banner of validity have clearly evolved over the years. In 1986, Lather was talking about validity with reference to triangulation, face validity, catalytic validity, and so on. By 1993 this list had evolved to a discussion of transgressive validity, with her interest focused on such concepts as simulacra/ironic validity, paralogy/neopragmatic validity, rhizomatic validity, and voluptuous/situated validity.

There are two important points to be noted here. First, Lather is well aware that her lists are not composed of highly specified items that are enclosed, complete, can be numerically scored, and so on. In fact, when she develops a "checklist" it is only to mimic and thereby disrupt the very idea or possibility of a checklist. Second, she also is well aware that her theorizing is and can only be grounded in practice or in the actual process of applying the lists and making judgments. This is a point she noted in her work in 1986 and that she has reiterated, to one degree or another, in her more recent efforts (1998a, 1998b).

Lather sees the task of judgment not only as a practical engagement, but also as a moral one. Although we must acknowledge her resistance to the appropriation of poststructuralist perspectives within unproblematized concerns of critical theorists, we also must acknowledge that she clearly is and has been concerned deeply with such things as oppression, exploitation, and domination. There is no question that she holds a normative frame of reference in which some definitive preferences are expressed. Not surprisingly, then, Lather holds, as we assume do most other inquirers, that social and educational inquiry can, should, and must have an ameliorative purpose—that what we do as inquirers has the purpose of contributing to making people's lives and futures better (again, with full recognition that whatever *better* might mean in any given context cannot be precisely specified).

However, at this point a version of the problem of Ebenezer's paralysis (as noted above) seems to be lurking in the shadows. Lather (1993, pp. 684-685) poses a number of worrisome questions that arose as she participated in a project involving women with HIV/AIDS. These are problems that are, as she puts it,

"grounded in the crisis of representation" (p. 684). Her concerns range widely over issues about voice, the other, the methodological interest she advances, her goals as a researcher, and so on. These concerns seem to be echoed, even if expressed in a different sense and in different terminology, by Scheurich's (1997) fears about the "resourcefulness of the Same to reappear with new masks that only seem to be the Other" (p. 90) and about the "anonymous imperial violence that slips quietly and invisibly into our best intentions and practices" (p. 90). In both instances, we argue that at the core of the problem is these authors' concern that any judgment must close off other possibilities, that any writing discloses in its silences as much as it reveals in its articulations, that to write the other is to appropriate the other, that any judgment is quietly but immediately turned on itself, and so on.

We have no doubt that the questions are important and the concerns are genuine, and we agree that we must always question the judgments we make and guard against the reappearance of the Same. In this sense, both Lather and Scheurich have raised important issues that have moved us at least partly away from the epistemological project. But still we must ask: Can this questioning be taken too far? Is the quest framed by a desire for answers that can never be had and guarantees that can never be given? In a text that presents the voices of the women who live with the reality of being HIV-positive, Lather and Smithies (1997) demonstrate that they understand what might be called the imperialist position of the author and own their particular judgments to do one thing as opposed to another in telling the stories of these women. However, in later discussions about her judgments, Lather (1998a, 1998b) seemingly works to undo the responsibility she has enacted, reinvoking a concern that she is still seeking a way to alleviate human vulnerability and contingency in judgment.

These points also can be noted in the responses of Lather (1993) and Scheurich (1997) to the questions she asks and the concerns he expresses. We argue that because the answers sought remain unavailable, as they must, and the concerns resist relief, as they must, they have turned too far to the other side with the call for a "loud clamor of a polyphonous, open, tumultuous, subversive conversation on validity as the wild, unknowable play of differences" (Scheurich, 1997, p. 90) and "a disjunctive affirmation of incommensurates" (Lather, 1993, p. 687). But if these injunctions that everything should be an unknowable play of differences and that all contributions are incommensurable are taken seriously or taken to conclusion, have they arrived at the point of "everything goes" such that nothing is left for judgment? Their lingering concern with the epistemological project has left them in an untenable situation where, intellectually or conceptually, they have rendered judgment pointless if not impossible, whereas practically and morally they do and must make judgments. A hypothetical example is necessary to make our point as clear as possible. We are confident that if Lather and Scheurich were to review for publication an article with racist overtones, as a practical and moral affair they would reject that paper for just that reason. However, at another level, on what basis could this be done? Given their comments above, why should not this paper be seen as simply another element in the play of differences or as another affirmation of incommensurates?

For us, it is time to accept our vulnerability and contingency, drop the last traces of the epistemological project, and thus change the conversation. There is no way off of the wheel or out of the circle and, in what may seem an odd twist, in a strange way there is no epistemological crisis of representation, but only a practical and moral problem of representation. We are finite human beings who must learn to accept, for example, that anything we write must always and inevitably leave silences, that to speak at all must always and inevitably be to speak for the someone else, and that we cannot make judgments and at the same time have a "constantly moving speaking position that fixes neither subject or object" (Lather, 1993, p. 684). To lament this condition and to search for a solution to these "problems" is actually to lament and search for a so-

lution to our human finitude. But that we are finite is something we can do nothing about. Hazelrigg (1995) puts it very well: These are our "deficiencies" as human beings, if you will. But they are deficiencies "proper to the fields of human knowing and doing" because "what the human creature is not, no matter what the strength of will, is omniscient and omnipotent" (p. 102).

But a caution must be reiterated lest we be misinterpreted. There is no doubt that there is a problem of representation. Silences must be questioned, we must be careful of what we speak in that we speak for others, and we must be cautious in our judgments and be willing to risk our prejudices as we share and justify our judgments in a public space. But these are not epistemological issues; to the contrary, they are practical and moral issues. We inquire, we make judgments about inquiries, we must give reasons for our judgments, offer up these reasons to others and simply attempt to do the best we can. Knowledge is a human social production. As finite beings, all we can do is construct social and educational worlds, social and educational constructed realities for which we are morally responsible. To realize that we are finite human beings is to realize that there may be little more to say than this about judgment, criteria, and validity.

Be that as it may, our remaining comments must turn more directly toward the fact that judgment obviously is not a solitary engagement. As teachers and researchers, we are members of social groups and, as briefly indicated at various times above, our individual judgments inevitably must be moved into a public space where they are placed in concert with the judgments of others. To a certain extent the public space for sharing judgments, certainly the initial and immediate public space, has been predetermined because of institutional and organizational arrangements. For example, grading papers must at least involve a public space with a student; dissertation approval/disapproval must involve the student, the committee, and whoever comes to the defense; reviewing a paper for journal publication must necessarily involve the author and the editor. In a broader sense, however, there is room for choice as to the public space within which or with whom one's judgments will be allowed play and the extent to which one allows one's prejudices to be tested and challenged.

This is possible because, although the ideal of community is important, in practice there is no overarching social and/or educational research community. Educational researchers, for example, are dispersed along numerous lines from what are referred to as subfields, to theoretical and methodological differences, to differences based on characteristics like gender, race, and sexual orientation, and so on. That we are dispersed in this way is what allows for some degree of individual choice in terms of with whom one will share judgments and risk one's prejudices.

There is no question that over the past few years the rejection of metanarratives and appeals to final vindications have promoted the concern to open new spaces of inquiry and increase the number of possible groups, however loosely formed, with which one can choose to share or not share judgments. This is a recognition that has appeared in the work of numerous people, including, for example, Denzin (1997) and Lincoln (1995). For the latter, one of the key points is that all texts "are always partial and incomplete; socially, culturally, historically, racially, and sexually located; and can therefore never represent any truth except those truths that exhibit the same characteristics" (p. 280). This is further coupled with the recognition "that research takes place in, and is addressed to, a community; it is also accurately labeled because of the desire of those who discuss such research to have it serve the purposes of the community in which it was carried out" (p. 280). And, very important, Lincoln says that these ideas must be understood within the context of ethics and social amelioration. About the latter she says we must have a "vision of research that enables and promotes social justice, community, diversity, civic discourse, and caring" (pp. 277-278).

For Denzin (1997), we have entered the era of the new ethnography, one that has left science behind, that finds no "break between empirical activity . . . theorizing and social criticism" (p. 86), and where we will encounter the contin-uing development of "standpoint epistemologies of race, class, nation, gender, and sexuality" (p. 87). Denzin continues by noting three shared commitments that stand behind the advent of standpoint epistemologies. First, our research must be undertaken from the "point of view of the historically and culturally situated individual" (p. 87). Second, "ethnographers will continue to work outward from their own biographies to the worlds of experience that surround them" (p. 87). Third, the desire is to produce inquiry that will "speak clearly and powerfully about these worlds [of experience]" (p. 87). Thus, in the end, "the stories ethnographers tell to one another will change, and the criteria for reading stories will also change" (p. 87).

To the extent that this new ethnography brings with it an increasing pluralism, multiplicity, and the play of differences to open new spaces and new possible futures, we think the move must be applauded. However, as alluded to above, the issue of honoring pluralism and multiplicity while avoiding its excesses is ever and always present. Schrag (1992) frames the possibilities quite well. On the one side, he says that it is possible that a multiplicity of stories can be "assembled in such a manner that lines of similitude remain operative and a binding of multiple discourses and practices remain possible" (p. 33). If this can be accomplished, then we could offer up our judgments to others in the name of the "possibilities for rational critique, articulation, and disclosure as these are geared to an understanding of shared experience, evaluation, and emancipation" (p. 49). However, on the other side, he also notes that if this multiplicity and plurality engage nothing beyond an endless play of local and localized stories, vocabularies, and judgments, then we may be ensnared in a never-ending process of "dissensus, incommensurability, irretrievable conflicts of interpretation, and hermeneutical nihilism" (p. 33).

As a practical and moral matter, Schrag (1992) centers a number of important questions: How does one preserve diversity and multiplicity while avoiding its excesses? With whom and under what conditions am I obligated to risk my prejudices by offering up my work and my judgments for comment and criticism? Or, put differently, What is there that will allow us to put faith in Denzin's (1997) claim that in the era of the new ethnography inquirers will work out from their own standpoints? But two points arise immediately to madden any discussion of these questions. First, what does it even mean to say that we have reached an excess of diversity; when and how does one know when the line of excess has been crossed? Second, it is naïve to hold that one should constantly offer work and judgments to a total diversity of localized communities or social spaces. At times there may be very good reasons, physical and mental exhaustion aside, for not reaching out and engaging in extended dialogue with others. For example, there are times when dialogue has been engaged, progress has not been made, and there seems no reason to continue. As has been so throughout this change of conversation, the issues are illusive indeed and resist easy solution.

That said, we begin by noting that we value Schrag's (1992) hope that lines of similitude can remain open and effective across a range of discourses and practices. The reason for this is framed by the fact that our inquiries do not discover reality, but rather construct reality—a constructed social and educational reality for which we are morally responsible, as individuals and collectively. And this point must be coupled with the injunction from Marx that our task is not merely to study the world, but to help change it. We thereby have a moral obligation to maximize our collective influence on actual policies and practices. To do this requires that we engage across lines, that we move out from our individual standpoints and risk our individual prejudices to keep lines of connection open to others.

If these lines cannot be kept open, then there may well be a Balkanization of, or a deep heterogeneity among, inquirer-based standpoints, theoretical differences, or whatever, and we could well end up with deep dissensus and a permanent conflict of interpretations. The play of differences to open spaces could easily tip over into little more than the announcement of differences, and the affirmation of incommensurates easily could become exactly that. This would seem to lead to inquirers' talking past one another, or not talking to each other at all, as they construct their localized communities, realities, and criteria. Under these conditions, it is difficult to imagine how our work can have moral purpose and social influence. The point is straightforward: If we cannot talk and listen to each other, it is difficult to imagine why anyone else would want to talk with us, listen to us, or attend to our judgments.

But the main problem is that there is no method or process to which we can appeal to energize Denzin's claim (hope?) that in this era of the new ethnography inquirers will work outward from their own biographies to engage the biographies of others. If inquirers are to do this, then it can only be a matter of disposition, not method. This is a disposition—or, as noted above, a moral obligation—that enjoins one to risk one's prejudices and defend one's judgments in a social space with others, even with those whose standpoints may seem seriously different from one's own. At the core of this moral obligation is the requirement that we accept that just as we attempt to persuade others to accept our judgments of good versus bad inquiries, we must in turn be equally willing to be persuaded by the judgments of others. And, to reiterate, it is only with this obligation in mind that we can maximize the possibility that our inquiries will assist in the construction of more just social and educational worlds.

◆ Summary

The quasi-foundationalists have attempted to establish criteria within the context of an epistemological constructivism on the one side and, on the other, an ontological realism. The latter announces their claim that there is a reality independent of us that can be known as it is—at least in principle; the former assumption directs their attention to the idea that knowledge is socially constructed and always fallible. This has led them to talk about criteria with the use of terms on the order of *plausibility, credibility,* and *descriptive validity.* Moreover, because the neorealists claim they are able to have contact with reality, however subtle this contact may be, they further claim that these criteria have force beyond particular time and place.

Unfortunately, the neorealists have not been able to present a convincing case, or an adequate justification, for their position. Neither Hammersley (1990) nor Maxwell (1992), for example, is able to demonstrate how his realist commitment does any real work in terms of moving us beyond a continual process of social judgments. In fact, were the neorealists to drop their realist ontology and their attempt to salvage something from the remains of empiricism, they would look very much like relativists of a Gadamerian variety.

Nonfoundationalists have fully accepted the relativist implications of the fact that there can be no theory-free observation or knowledge. However, for them relativism is not a problem, it is just the inevitable result of the fact that we, as human beings, are finite—a finitude we should learn to live with and not lament. For nonfoundationalists, the issue of criteria for judging inquiry is a practical and moral affair, not an epistemological one. They take very seriously Rorty's (1985) injunction that our pursuit of knowledge, as is the case for all human social activities, "has only an ethical base, not an epistemological or metaphysical one" (p. 6). Accordingly, criteria should not be thought of in abstraction, but as a list of features that we think, or more or less agree at any given time and place, characterize good versus bad inquiry. This is a list that can be challenged, added to, subtracted from, modified, and so on, as it is applied in actual practice—in actual application to actual inquiries. Relativists also recognize the need for and value of plurality, multiplicity, the acceptance and celebration of differences, and so on. The essential problem, however, is to honor this need without giving over to excesses—to inquiry that is so fragmented that lines of connection have been lost and the social

amelioration possibilities of our work have been rendered moot.

So, we have come to the end with, as promised, no discussion of particular criteria and how to apply them. Rather, we have attempted to elaborate some of the conditions under which we must think about the possibility of criteria and the possibility of individual and collective judgment in this age of relativism.

■ *References*

Barth, J. (1960). *The sot-weed factor.* Garden City, NY: Doubleday.

Bernstein, R. (1983). *Beyond objectivism and relativism.* Philadelphia: University of Pennsylvania Press.

Bhaskar, R. (1983). [Review of the book *Scientific revolutions*]. *Isis, 74,* 259.

Cherryholmes, C. (1988). *Power and criticism.* New York: Teachers College Press.

Chisholm, R. (1973). *The problem of the criterion.* Milwaukee, WI: Marquette University Press.

Denzin, N. K. (1997). *Interpretive ethnography: Ethnographic practices for the 21st century.* Thousand Oaks, CA: Sage.

Gadamer, H.-G. (1995). *Truth and method* (2nd rev. ed.; J. Weinsheimer & D. G. Marshall, Trans.). New York: Crossroad.

Gallagher, D. (1995). In search of the rightful role of method: Reflections on conducting a qualitative dissertation. In T. Tiller, A. Sparkes, S. Karhus, & F. Dowling-Naess (Eds.), *The qualitative challenge* (pp. 17-35). Oslo, Norway: Casper.

Giddens, A. (1976). *New rules of sociological method: A positive critique of interpretative sociologies.* New York: Basic Books.

Goodman, N. (1978). *Ways of worldmaking.* Indianapolis: Hackett.

Hammersley, M. (1990). *Reading ethnographic research: A critical guide.* London: Longman.

Hanson, N. (1958). *Patterns of discovery.* Cambridge: Cambridge University Press.

Hazelrigg, L. (1989). *Claims of knowledge.* Tallahassee: Florida State University Press.

Hazelrigg, L. (1995). *Cultures of nature.* Tallahassee: Florida State University Press.

Hesse, M. (1980). *Revolutions and reconstructions in the philosophy of science.* Brighton: Harvester.

Hindess, B. (1977). *Philosophy and methodology in the social sciences.* Atlantic Highlands, NJ: Humanities Press.

Hofstadter, D. (1979). *Godel, Escher, Bach: An eternal golden braid.* New York: Basic Books.

House, E. (1991). Realism in research. *Educational Researcher, 20*(6), 2-9.

Kerlinger, F. (1979). *Behavioral research.* New York: Holt, Rinehart & Winston.

Kuhn, T. S. (1962). *The structure of scientific revolutions.* Chicago: University of Chicago Press.

Lather, P. (1986a). Issues of validity in openly ideological research: Between a rock and a soft place. *Interchange, 17*(4), 63-84.

Lather, P. (1986b). Research as praxis. *Harvard Educational Review, 56,* 257-277.

Lather, P. (1993). Fertile obsession: Validity after poststructuralism. *Sociological Quarterly, 34,* 673-693.

Lather, P. (1998a, April). *Against empathy, voice, and authenticity.* Paper presented at the annual meeting of the American Educational Research Association, San Diego, CA.

Lather, P. (1998b, April). *Troubling praxis: The work of mourning.* Paper presented at the annual meeting of the American Educational Research Association, San Diego, CA.

Lather, P., & Smithies, C. (1997). *Troubling the angels: Women living with HIV/AIDS.* Boulder, CO: Westview.

Leary, D. (1984). Philosophy, psychology, and reality. *American Psychologist, 39,* 917-919.

Lincoln, Y. S. (1995). Emerging criteria for quality in qualitative and interpretive inquiry. *Qualitative Inquiry, 1,* 275-289.

MacKenzie, D. (1981). *Statistics in Great Britain: 1885-1930.* Edinburgh: Edinburgh University Press.

Manicas, P. (1987). *A history and philosophy of the social sciences.* Oxford: Basil Blackwell.

Manicas, P., & Secord, P. (1983). Implications for psychology of the new philosophy of science. *American Psychologist, 38,* 399-413.

Maxwell, J. (1992). Understanding and validity in qualitative research. *Harvard Educational Review, 62,* 279-300.

Nagel, T. (1986). *The view from nowhere.* New York: Oxford University Press.

Polanyi, M. (1962). *Personal knowledge.* Chicago: University of Chicago Press.

Popper, K. (1959). *The logic of scientific discovery.* London: Hutchinson.

Popper, K. (1972). *Objective knowledge.* Oxford: Clarendon.

Punch, M. (1994). Politics and ethics in qualitative research. In N. K. Denzin & Y. S. Lincoln (Eds.), *Handbook of qualitative research* (pp. 83-97). Thousand Oaks, CA: Sage.

Putnam, H. (1981). *Reason, truth and history.* Cambridge: Cambridge University Press.

Rorty, R. (1979). *Philosophy and the mirror of nature.* Princeton, NJ: Princeton University Press.

Rorty, R. (1985). Solidarity or objectivity? In J. Rajchman & C. West (Eds.), *Post-analytic philosophy* (pp. 3-19). New York: Columbia University Press.

Rosenau, P. M. (1992). *Post-modernism and the social sciences: Insights, inroads, and intrusions.* Princeton, NJ: Princeton University Press.

Scheurich, J. J. (1997). *Research method in the postmodern.* London: Falmer.

Schrag, C. (1992). *The resources of rationality.* Bloomington: Indiana University Press.

Schwandt, T. A. (1996). Farewell to criteriology. *Qualitative Inquiry, 2,* 58-72.

Smith, J. (1985). Social reality as mind-dependent versus mind-independent and the interpretation of test validity. *Journal of Research and Development in Education, 1,* 1-9.

Smith, J. (1989). *The nature of social and educational inquiry: Empiricism versus interpretation.* Norwood, NJ: Ablex.

Smith, J. (1993). *After the demise of empiricism: The problem of judging social and educational inquiry.* Norwood, NJ: Ablex.

Sparkes, A. (1993). Reciprocity in critical research? Some unsettling thoughts. In G. Shacklock & J. Smyth (Eds.), *Being reflexive in critical educational and social research* (pp. 67-82). London: Falmer.

Sparkes, A. (1996). The fatal flaw: A narrative of the fragile body-self. *Qualitative Inquiry, 2,* 463-494.

Stronach, I., & Maclure, M. (1997). *Educational research undone.* Milton Keynes, England: Open University Press.

Taylor, C. (1971). Interpretation and the sciences of man. *Review of Metaphysics, 25,* 3-51.

Taylor, C. (1989). *Sources of the self.* Cambridge: Cambridge University Press.

Wolcott, H. F. (1995). *The art of fieldwork.* Walnut Creek, CA: AltaMira.

35

THE PRACTICES AND POLITICS OF INTERPRETATION

◆ Norman K. Denzin

A marginalized group needs to be wary of the seductive power of realism, of accepting all that a realistic representation implies.

> Wahneema Lubiano, "But, Compared to What? Reading Realism,Representation, and Essentialism in School Daze, Do the Right Thing, and the Spike Lee Discourse," 1997

> You've taken my blues and gone—
> You sing 'em on Broadway
> . . . And you fixed 'em
> So they don't sound like me.
> Yes, you done taken my blues and gone.
>
> You also took my spiritual and gone.
> . . . But someday somebody'll
> Stand up and write about me,
> And write about me—
> Black and Beautiful—
> And sing about me,
> And put on plays about me!
> I reckon it'll be
> Me myself!

> Langston Hughes, "Yes, It'll Be Me," 1940/1994*

AUTHOR'S NOTE: I would like to thank Meaghan Morris, Ivan Brady, Yvonna Lincoln, Jack Bratich, Laurel Richardson, and Katherine Ryan for their comments on earlier versions of this chapter. All asterisked material is used by permission.

I
have seen it
and like it: The blood
the way like Sand Creek
even its name brings fear,
because I am an American
Indian and have learned
words are another kind of violence.

Sherman Alexie, "Texas Chainsaw Massacre," 1993*

At the beginning of the end of the sixth moment it is necessary to reengage the promise of qualitative research and interpretive ethnography as forms of radical democratic practice.[1] The narrative turn in the social sciences has been taken, we have told our tales from the field, and we understand today that we write culture (Brady, 1998; Richardson, 1998). Writing is not an innocent practice, although in the social sciences and the humanities there is only interpretation (Rinehart, 1998). Nonetheless, Marx (1888/1983, p. 158) continues to remind us that we are in the business of not just interpreting but changing the world.

In this chapter I explore new (and old) forms of writing, forms that are intended to forward the project of interpreting and changing the world—and this is the global world, not just the world as it is known in North America. Specifically, I work back and forth among three interpretive practices: the new civic, intimate, and literary journalisms (Charity, 1995; Dash, 1997; Harrington, 1992, 1997a, 1997b; Kramer, 1995; Sims, 1995); calls for critical, performance-based ethnographies (Ceglowski, 1997; Cohen-Cruz, 1998; Degh, 1995; Denison, 1996; Denzin, 1997, 1999a, 1999b, 1999c; Diversi, 1998; Dunbar, 1999; Jackson, 1998; Jones, 1999; Jordan, 1998; Lincoln, 1997; Rinehart, 1998; Ronai, 1998; Smith, 1993, 1994); and variations on a Chicano/a (Gonzalez, 1998; Pizarro, 1998) and African American aesthetic (Davis, 1998; hooks, 1990, 1996) and the relationship between these practices and critical race theory (Ladson-Billings, 1998; Parker, 1998).

Although there have been efforts to bring critical race theory into qualitative research, few have merged this theory with the poststructural turn in ethnography (see hooks, 1990, pp. 123-134; also Ladson-Billings, Chapter 9, this volume). Nor have critical race theory and qualitative inquiry been connected to the radical performance texts stemming from the black arts movement of the 1960s and 1970s (Baker, 1997; Baraka, 1997; Harris, 1998). These interconnections are now being established in the various black cultural studies projects of the new black public intellectuals and cultural critics (Hall, Gilroy, hooks, Gates, West, Reed, Morrison, Wallace, Steele). A current generation of blues, rap, hip-hop, and popular singers, jazz performers, poets (Angelou, Dove, Jordan, Knight, Cortez), novelists (Walker, Morrison, Bambara), playwrights (Wilson, Shange, Smith), and filmmakers (Lee, Singleton, Burnett, Dash) are also making these links (see Christian, 1997, pp. 2019-2020; Harris, 1998, pp. 1344-1345).[2]

This chapter is a utopian project in which I attempt to bring these multiple discourses together into a unified framework. I present examples of writing from each these frameworks. In so doing, I assume that words and language have a material presence in the world—that words have effects on people. Amiri Baraka (1969/1998, p. 1502*) puts it this way:

we want poems that wrestle cops into alleys

and take their weapons . . .

We want a black poem. And a Black
World.

Let the world be a Black Poem.

And Let All Black People Speak This
Poem

Silently

Or LOUD.

Words matter.

I imagine a world where race, ethnicity,
class, gender, and sexual orientation intersect;
a world where language empowers and humans
are free to become who they can be, free of
prejudice, repression, and discrimination
(Jackson, 1998, p. 21; see also Parker, Deyhle,
Villenas, & Nebeker, 1998, p. 5). Those who
write culture must learn to use language in a
way that brings people together. The goal is to
create sacred, loving texts that "demonstrate a
strong fondness . . . for freedom and an affectionate concern for the lives of people" (Joyce,
1987, p. 344). This writing addresses and demonstrates the benevolence and kindness that
people should feel toward one another (Joyce,
1987, p. 344).

Thus I examine new ways of writing culture,
new ways of making qualitative research central to the workings of a free democratic society. I begin with the civic, public affairs, and intimate journalists.

◆ An Intimate, Civic Journalism

As qualitative researchers engage experimental
writing forms, a parallel movement is occurring in journalism, and there is much to be
learned from these developments. Building on
earlier calls for a new journalism (Wolfe,
1973), a current generation of journalists (Harrington, 1997a, 1997b; Kramer, 1995; Sims,
1995) is producing a new writing genre variously termed literary, intimate, or creative nonfiction journalism (Harrington, 1997a, p. xv).
This intimate journalism extends the project of

the new journalism of the 1970s. That project
was based on seven understandings. The new
writers of Wolfe's generation treated facts as social constructions. They blurred writing genres
and combined literary and investigative journalism with the realist novel, the confession, the
travel report, and the autobiography. They used
the scenic method to show rather than tell. They
wrote about real people and created composite
characters. They used multiple points of view, including third-person narration to establish
authorial presence, and deployed multiple narrative strategies (flashbacks, foreshadowing, interior monologues, parallel plots) to build dramatic tension. They positioned themselves as
moral witnesses to the radical changes going on
in U.S. society (Denzin, 1997, p. 131). These
writers understood that social life and the reports about it are social constructions. Journalists do not map, or report on, an objective reality.

I have no desire to reproduce arguments that
maintain some distinction between fictional (literary) and nonfictional (journalism, ethnography) texts. Nor do I distinguish literary, nonliterary, fictional, and nonfictional textual forms.
These are socially and politically constructed
categories. They are too often used to police certain transgressive writing forms, such as fictional
ethnographies. There is only narrative—that is,
only different genre-defined ways of representing and writing about experiences and their multiple realities. The discourses of the postmodern
world constantly intermingle literary, poetic,
journalistic, fictional, cinematic, documentary,
factual, and ethnographic writing and representation. No form is privileged over others. Each
simply performs a different function for a writer
and an interpretive community.

These practices and understandings shape the
work of the intimate journalists. Writers such as
Harrington (1992) use the methods of descriptive realism to produce in-depth, narrative accounts of everyday life, lived up close. They use
real-life dialogue, intimate first- and third-person voice, multiple points of view, interior
monologues, scene-by-scene narration, and a
plain, spare style (Harrington, 1997b, pp. xlii-
xlv; Kramer, 1995, p. 24). The writer may be in-

visible in the text or present as narrator and participant. Here is Harrington (1992) talking about himself; the story is "Family Portrait in Black and White":

> My journey begins in the dentist's chair. The nurse . . . and the doctor are [telling] funny stories about their kids, when in walks another dentist. . . . "I've got a good one," he says cheerfully, and then he tells a racist joke. I can't recall the joke, only that it ends with a black man who is stupid. Dead silence. It's just us white folks here in the room, but my dentist and his nurse know my wife, who is black, and they know my son and daughter, who are, as they describe themselves, tan and bright tan. How many racist jokes have I heard in my life? . . . for the first time . . . I am struck with a deep sharp pain. I look at this man, with his pasty face, pale hair and weak lips, and I think: This idiot is talking about my children! (p. 1)

Compare this telling, with its first-person narration, to Leon Dash's (1997) description of Rosa Lee:

> Rosa Lee Cunningham is thankful that she doesn't have to get up early this morning. She is dozing, floating back and forth between sleep and drowsiness. Occasionally she hears the muted conversations of the nurses and doctors puttering around the nurse's station. . . . She's tired and worn down. . . . A full night's sleep and daylong quiet are rare luxuries in her life. This is the closest she ever comes to having a vacation. . . . Rosa Lee . . . is fifty-two years old, a longtime heroin addict . . . a member of the urban underclass. . . . [She] has no intention of ending her heroin use. (p. 3)

Harrington speaks only for himself. He is fully present in his text. Dash is invisible. He is the all-knowing observer. He is the fly on the wall narrating an unfolding scene. Dash describes a world, whereas Harrington talks about how it feels to be present in a world. Each writer creates a scene. Each penetrates the images that surround a situation. Harrington and Dash both use sparse, clean prose. Each creates a vivid image of his subject, Harrington of himself, Dash of Rosa Lee. On the other hand, Dash presumes to know what Rosa Lee is feeling and thinking. Hers is a story waiting to be told, and he will tell

it. In contrast, Harrington's text suggests that stories are not waiting to be told; rather, they are constructed by the writer, who attempts to impose order on some set of experiences or perceived events.

Both writers ground their prose in facts and their meanings. Dash, however, works with so-called verifiable, factually accurate facts, whereas Harrington writes of impressions and truths that, although not necessarily factually accurate, are aesthetically and emotionally true. If something did not happen, it could have happened, and it will happen in Harrington's text.

Accounts like Harrington's and Dash's invoke the felt life. The goal of such writers is to understand "other people's worlds from the inside out, to understand and portray people as they understand themselves" (Harrington, 1997b, p. xxv). The intent is to build an emotional relationship joining the writer, the life told about, and the reader.

A year later, Harrington (1992) returns to his experience in the dentist's chair:

> What I discovered while waiting in the dentist's chair more than a year ago . . . still remains the greatest insight I have to share: *The idiot was talking about my kids!*
>
> I remember a time when my son was a baby. It was late at night . . . I sat in the dark of my son's room. . . . I watched his face grimace . . . in the shadows. And then, in time so short it passed only in the mind, my son was gone and I was the boy . . . and my father was me. . . . just as suddenly, I was gone again and the light was falling across the knees of my son, who was grown, who was a father, who was me. . . . this kind of understanding changes everything. Only when I *became* black by proxy—through my son, through my daughter—could I see the racism I had been willing to tolerate. Becoming black, even for a fraction of an instant, created an urgency for justice that I couldn't feel as only a white man, no matter how good-hearted. . . . no white man in his or her right mind would yet volunteer to trade places, become black, in America today. (p. 447)

Such writing connects readers to their newspapers by producing narratives about people in extreme and ordinary situations. These stories, or journalistic case studies, politicize the everyday world, illuminating the structures and processes that shape individuals' lives and their relations with others. In so doing, they "nurture civic transformation" (Harrington, 1997a, p. xiv; see also Harrington, 1997b, p. xviii).[3]

Civic Transformations

At the moment of civic transformation, intimate journalism joins with the call for public journalism, a critical ethnographic journalism that fuses persons and their troubles with public issues and the public arena. A pragmatic, civic journalism invites readers to become participants, not mere spectators, in the public dramas that define meaningful, engaged life in society today. Public journalism creates the space for local ethnographies of problematic community and personal experiences. This is a socially responsible civic journalism. It advocates participatory democracy. It gives a public voice to the biographically meaningful, epiphanic experiences that occur within the confines of the local moral community.[4] This form of journalistic ethnography speaks to the morally committed reader. This is a reader who is a coparticipant in a public project that demands democratic solutions to personal and public problems (Charity, 1995, p. 146).[5]

Taken to the next level, transformed into public-journalism-as-ethnography, this writing answers to the following goals. Critical, intimate, public ethnography does the following things:

- It presents the public with in-depth, intimate stories of problematic everyday life, lived up close. These stories create moral compassion and help citizens make intelligent decisions and take public action on private troubles that have become public issues, including helping to get these action proposals carried out (Charity, 1995, p. 2; Mills, 1959, p. 8).
- It promotes interpretive works that raise public and private consciousness. These works help persons collectively work through the decision-making process. They help isolate choices, core values, uti-

lize expert and local systems of knowledge, and facilitate deliberative, civic discourse (Charity, 1995, pp. 4-8).

- It rejects the classic model of investigative journalism, where the reporter exposes corruption, goes on crusades, roots "out the inside story, tells the brave truth, faces down the Joseph McCarthy's and Richard Nixon's . . . comforts the afflicted and afflicts the comfortable" (Charity, 1995, p. 9).
- It seeks the ethnographer and journalist who is an expert in the history and public life of the local community, who knows how to listen to and talk to citizens, and how to hear and present consensus when it emerges, and who is also a full-time citizen and committed to the belief that public life can be made to work (Charity, 1995, p. 10).
- It sees the writer as a watchdog for the local community, a person who writes stories that contribute to deliberative, participatory discourse, thereby maintaining the public's awareness of its own voice (Charity, 1995, pp. 104-105, 127).
- It values writing that moves a public to meaningful judgment and meaningful action (Charity, 1995, p. 50). A central goal is civic transformation (Christians, Ferre, & Fackler, 1993, p. 14).
- It exposes complacency, bigotry, and wishful thinking (Charity, 1995, p. 146) while "attempting to strengthen the political community's capacity to understand itself, converse well, and make choices" (Rosen, 1994, p. 381).
- It seeks dramatic stories, narratives that separate facts from stories, telling moving accounts that join private troubles with public issues (Charity, 1995, p. 72; Mills, 1959, p. 8).
- It promotes a form of textuality that turns citizens into readers and readers into persons who take democratic action in the world (Charity, 1995, pp. 19, 83-84).

These are goals, ideals, ways of merging critical ethnography with applied action research, with the new public journalism, and with qualitative research in the seventh moment. (They presume the feminist, communitarian ethical model discussed by Christians in Chapter 5 of this volume.)

These goals assume an ethnographer who functions and writes like a literary and intimate public journalist. This means that ethnography as a performer-centered form of storytelling will be given greater emphasis (Degh, 1995, p. 8). A shared public consciousness is sought, a common awareness of troubles that have become issues in the public arena. This consciousness is shaped by a form of writing that merges the personal, the biographical, with the public. Janet Cooke's (1980) fictional story "Jimmy's World" is an instance of such writing. Such stories expose complacency and bigotry in the public sphere.

Writing Norms

A feminist, communitarian ethical model produces a series of norms for the public ethnographic writing project.[6] These norms build on and elaborate the four nonnegotiable journalistic norms of accuracy, nonmaleficence, the right to know, and making one's moral position public.[7] The ethnographer's moral tales are not written to produce harm for those who have been oppressed by the culture's systems of domination and repression (the principle of nonmaleficence). The identities of those written about should always be protected. These tales are factually and fictionally correct.[8] When fiction, or imaginative narrative, is written, or when composite cases are molded into a single story, the writer is under an obligation to report this to the reader (see Christians et al., 1993, p. 55).

The reader has the right to read what the ethnographer has learned, but the right to know should be balanced against the principle of nonmaleficence. Accounts should exhibit "interpretive sufficiency" (Christians et al., 1993, p. 120), that is, they should possess depth, detail, emotionality, nuance, and coherence. These qualities assist the reader in forming a critical interpretive consciousness. Such texts should also exhibit representational adequacy,

including the absence of racial, class, and gender stereotyping.[9]

The writer must be honest with the reader.[10] The text must be realistic, concrete as to character, setting, atmosphere, and dialogue. The text should provide a forum for the search for moral truths about the self. This forum may explore the unpresentable in the culture; the discontents and violence of contemporary life are documented and placed in narrative form. This writer stirs up the world, and the writer's story ("mystory") becomes part of the tale that is told. The writer has a theory about how the world works, and this theory is never far from the surface of the text. Self-reflexive readers are presumed—readers who seek honest but reflexive works that draw them into the many experiences of daily life.

There remains the struggle to find a narrative voice that writes against a long tradition that favors autobiography and lived experience as the sites for reflexivity and self-hood (Clough, 1994, p. 157). This form of subjective reflexivity can be a trap. It too easily reproduces sad, celebratory, and melodramatic conceptions of self, agency, gender, desire, and sexuality. There is a pressing need to invent a reflexive form of writing that turns ethnography and experimental literary texts back "onto each other" (Clough, 1994, p. 162; 1998, p. 134).

Always a skeptic, this new writer is suspicious of conspiracies, alignments of power and desire that turn segments of the public into victims. So these works trouble traditional, realist notions of truth and verification, asking always who stands to benefit from a particular version of the truth. The intimate journalist as public ethnographer enacts an ethics of practice that privileges the client-public relationship. The ethnographer is a moral advocate for the public, although their own personal moral codes may lead individual researchers to work against the so-called best interests of their clients or particular segments of the public.

The ethnographer's tale is always allegorical, a symbolic tale, a parable that is not just a record of human experience. This tale is a means of experience, a method of empowerment for the reader. It is a vehicle through which readers may discover moral truths about themselves. More deeply, the tale is a utopian story of self and social redemption, a tale that brings a moral compass back into the reader's (and the writer's) life. The ethnographer discovers the multiple "truths" that operate in the social world, the stories people tell one another about the things that matter to them. The intimate journalist writes stories that stimulate critical public discourse. Thus these stories enable transformations in the public and private spheres of everyday life.

◆ *Performing Ethnography*

I turn next to the concept of the performance text (Conquergood, 1992; Turner, 1986), illustrating my arguments with materials drawn from an ongoing interpretive ethnography of a small Montana town (Denzin, 1999a, 1999b, 1999c).[11] I seek a set of writing practices that turn notes from the field into texts that are performed. A single, yet complex thesis organizes my argument.

We inhabit a performance-based, dramaturgical culture. The dividing line between performer and audience blurs, and culture itself becomes a dramatic performance. Performance ethnography enters a gendered culture with nearly invisible boundaries separating everyday theatrical performances from formal theater, dance, music, MTV, video, and film (Birringer, 1993, p. 182; Butler, 1990, p. 25; 1997, p. 159; 1999, p. 19). But the matter goes even deeper then blurred boundaries. The performance has become reality. Of this, speaking of gender and personal identity, Butler (1990) is certain. Gender is performative, gender is always doing, "though not a doing by a subject who might be said to preexist the deed. . . . there is no being behind doing. . . . the deed is everything. . . . there is no gender identity behind the expressions of gender. . . . identity is performatively constituted by the very 'expressions' that are said to be its results" (p. 25). Fur-

ther, the linguistic act is performative, and words can hurt (Butler, 1997, p. 4).

Performance texts are situated in complex systems of discourse, where traditional, everyday, and avant-garde meanings of theater, film, video, ethnography, cinema, performance, text, and audience all circulate and inform one another. As Collins (1990, p. 210) has suggested, the meanings of lived experience are inscribed and sometimes made visible in these performances (see also Brady, 1999, p. 245).

Anna Deavere Smith's *Fires in the Mirror* (1993) is an example. In this play, Smith offers a series of performance pieces based on interviews with people involved in a racial conflict in Crown Heights, Brooklyn, on August 19, 1991. The conflict was set in motion when a young black Guyanese boy, Gavin Cato, was accidentally killed by an auto in a police-escorted entourage carrying Lubavitcher Grand Rebbe Menachem Schneerson. Later that day, a group of black men fatally stabbed Yankel Rosenbaum, a 29-year-old Hasidic scholar from Australia. This killing was followed by a racial conflict that lasted 3 days and involved many members of the community. A jury acquitted Yankel Rosenbaum's accused murderer, causing considerable pain for his family as well as feelings of victimization for the Lubavitchers (Smith, 1993, p. xiv).[12] Smith's play has speaking parts for gang members, police officers, anonymous young girls and boys, mothers, fathers, rabbis, the Reverend Al Sharpton, playwright Ntozake Shange, and African American cultural critic Angela Davis.

Cornel West (1993) observes that *Fires in the Mirror* is a "grand example of how art can constitute a public space that is perceived by people as empowering rather than disempowering" (p. xix). Thus blacks, gang members, the police, and the Jewish community all come together and talk in this play. The drama crosses racial boundaries. Smith's text shows that "American character lives not on one place or the other, but in the gaps between places, and in our struggle to be together in our differences" (p. xii).

An Anonymous Young Man #1 Wa Wa Wa, a Caribbean American with dreadlocks, describes the auto accident:

What I saw was

she was pushin'

her brother on the bike like

this,

right?

She was pushin'

him

and he keep dippin' around

like he didn't know how

to ride the bike . . .

So she was already runnin'

when the car was comin' . . .

we was watchin' the car

weavin',

and we was goin'

"Oh, yo

it's a Jew man.

He broke the stop light, they never get

arrested." (Smith, 1993, pp. 79-80)*

And so in performing this young man's words, Smith contextualizes this drama, showing how it looked from the standpoint of a person who watched the accident unfold.

Performance ethnography simultaneously creates and enacts moral texts, texts that move from the personal to the political, the local to the historical and the cultural. Following Conquergood (1985), these dialogical works create spaces for give and take, doing more than turning the other into the object of a voyeuristic, fetishistic, custodial, or paternalistic gaze.

Texts turned into radical street performances act to question and "re-envision ingrained social arrangements of power" (Cohen-Cruz, 1998, p. 1). Such works, in the forms of rallies, puppet shows, marches, vigils, choruses, clown shows, and ritual performances, transport spectators and performers out of everyday reality into idealized spaces where the taken for granted is contested (Cohen-Cruz, 1998, p. 3). Street, or public place, performances offer members of the culture alternative scripts or ways of acting in and hence of changing the world (Cohen-Cruz, 1998, p. 1).

Cohen-Cruz (1998, p. 5) suggests that these performances can take several overlapping forms, including *agit-prop,* or attempts to mobilize people around a partisan view; *witnessing,* or making a spectacle out of an act that perhaps cannot be changed; *confrontation,* or inserting a performance into people's everyday life, thereby asking them to confront a scenario that is otherwise distant; *utopia,* or enacting an idealized version of reality; and *tradition,* that is, honoring a set of culturally shared beliefs, as in Fourth of July parades in small-town America.

In my performance project I seek minimalist social science, one that uses few concepts. This is a dramaturgical (Branaman, 1997, p. xlix; Goffman, 1959; Lemert, 1997, p. xxiv) or performative anthropology (Jackson, 1998; Turner, 1986) that attempts to stay close to how people represent everyday life experiences. A performative ethnography simultaneously writes and studies performances, showing how people enact cultural meanings in their daily lives.

Shaped by the sociological imagination (Mills, 1959), this version of qualitative inquiry attempts to show how terms such as *biography, gender, race, ethnicity, family,* and *history* interact and shape one another in concrete social situations. These works are usually written in the first-person voice, from the point of view of the sociologist doing the observing and the writing. A minimalist, performative social science is also about stories, performances, and storytelling. When performed well, these stories create a ritual space "where people gather to listen, to experience, to better understand the world and their place in it" (Jenkins, 1999, p. 19).

The Performance Turn

The performance turn in the human disciplines (Bochner & Ellis, 1996; Conquergood, 1992) poses three closely interrelated problems for a critical, interdisciplinary interpretive project—namely, how to construct, perform, and critically analyze performance texts (see Stern & Henderson, 1993). Glossing the issues involved in construction and critical analysis, I will privilege performance and coperformance (audience-performer) texts in contrast to single performer, text-centered approaches to interpretation (see Denzin, 1997, p. 96). Through the act of coparticipation, these works bring audiences back into the text, creating a field of shared emotional experience. The phenomenon being described is created through the act of representation. A resistance model of textual performance and interpretation is foregrounded. A good performance text must be more than cathartic, it must be political, moving people to action and reflection.

The attention to performance is interdisciplinary; sociologists (Bochner & Ellis, 1996; Clough, 1994; Denzin, 1997; Ellis, 1997; Ellis & Bochner, 1992, 1996; Ellis & Flaherty, 1992; Kotarba, 1998; Richardson, 1997), anthropologists (Behar, 1996; Brady, 1999; Bruner, 1986, 1989, 1996; Cruikshank, 1997; Jackson, 1998; Turner, 1986), communication scholars (Conquergood, 1992; Hill, 1997), and education theorists (Lather, 1993; Lather & Smithies, 1997; Lincoln, 1995a, 1995b, 1997; Tierney, 1997) are calling for texts that move beyond the purely representational and toward the presentational. At the same time, action (Stringer, 1996), communitarian (Christians et al., 1993), feminist (Lather, 1993), constructivist (Lincoln, 1995a, 1995b, 1997), cooperative inquiry (Reason, 1993, 1994), and participant researchers (Carspecken, 1996) are exploring nontraditional presentational performance formats. Such works allow community researchers and community members to co-construct meaning through action-based performance projects (Stringer, 1996; see also Conquergood, 1998; Schwandt, 1997, p. 307). This call merges a feminist, communitarian ethic with a moral ethnography that presumes a researcher who builds collaborative, reciprocal, trusting, friendly relations with those studied (Lincoln, 1995a).

Performed texts "have narrators, drama, action, shifting points of view . . . [and] make experience concrete, anchoring it in the here and now" (Paget, 1993 p. 27; see also Donmoyer & Yennie-Donmoyer, 1995; Mienczakowski, 1995). Centered in the audience-researcher nexus, these texts are the site for "mystories" (Ulmer, 1989); that is, reflexive, critical stories that feel the sting of memory, stories that enact

liminal experiences. These are storied retellings that seek the truth of life's fictions via evocation rather than explanation or analysis. In them ethnographers, audiences, and performers meet in a shared field of experience, emotion, and action.

Such performances return to memory, not lived experience, as the site of criticism, interpretation, and action. It is understood that experience exists only in its representation, it does not stand outside memory or perception. The meanings of facts are always reconstituted in the telling, as they are remembered and connected to other events. Hence the appeal of the performance text does not lie in its offer of the certainty of the factual. The appeal is more complicated than that. Working from the site of memory, the reflexive, performed text asks readers as viewers (or coperformers) to relive the experience through the writer's or performer's eyes. Readers thus move through the re-created experience with the performer. This allows them to relive the experience for themselves.

Thus we can share in Harrington's experiences when he tells us about remembering the night he held his young son in his arms. The writer acting in this manner re-creates in the mind's eye a series of emotional moments. Life is then retraced through that moment, interpreting the past from the point of view of the present. Here is Susan Krieger (1996):

> I have just come back from a trip to Florida to settle the affairs of my lover's aunt [Maxine], who died suddenly at the age of seventy. She was carrying her groceries up the stairs to her apartment when she dropped dead of a heart attack. . .
>   . . . It was an otherworldly experience: going to Florida . . . to clean out the house of a woman I did not know—sorting through her clothes and jewelry, finding snapshots she recently took, using her bathroom, meeting her friends. (pp. 65, 68).

On her last day in Florida, Krieger finds Aunt Maxine's silver flatware inside an old accordion case in the back corner of a greasy kitchen cabinet. Maxine's silver is cheap. It had been a replacement set. It is tarnished, not the real thing like the family silver her mother had gotten from her mother. Krieger asks, "What determines the value of a person's life, is value different if you are a woman, how do you separate a woman from the things she owns, leaves behind, her clothes, the cheap family silver?" (p. 70). This cheap set of silver flatware is not an adequate measure of Aunt Maxine.

Laurel Richardson's mother died of breast cancer in Miami Beach on June 8, 1968. Nearly 30 years later, Richardson (1997) wrote about her mother's death:

> On June 8, I awoke determined to drive to Key West for the day. I sponge-bathed Mother, greeted the nurse, kissed my parents good-bye, and drove off in Father's Dodge Dart. When I got to Long Key, I was overwhelmed with the need to phone my parents. Mother had just died—less than a minute ago—Father said. (p. 234)

Of this news she observes, "I was grateful to have not witnessed her passing-on. I was thirty years old" (p. 235).

Ten years after her mother's death, Richardson wrote a poem, "Last Conversation" (1997, p. 234):

> I want to hold your
>
> weightless body to my
>
> breasts, cradle you,
>
> rock you to sleep.

The truth of a person's and a culture's ways are given in texts like these. Such works, when performed or read, become symbolic representations of what the culture and the person values. In their performances, performers embody these values.

Now listen to Angela Davis. In her recent study of the female blues singers Ma Rainey, Bessie Smith, and Billie Holiday, Davis (1998) observes that within African American culture the "blues marked the advent of a popular culture of performance, with the borders of performer and audience becoming increasing differentiated. . . . this . . . mode of presenting popular music crystallized into a performance culture that has had an enduring influence on African-American music" (p. 5).

In their performances, Ma Rainey, Bessie Smith, and Billie Holiday presented a set of black feminist understandings concerning class, race, gender, violence, sexuality, marriage, men, and intimacy (Collins, 1990, p. 209). This blues legacy is deeply entrenched in an indigenous, class-conscious, black feminism. The female blues singers created performance spaces for black women, spaces to sing and live the blues, black female voices talking about and doing black culture on stage, a public, critical performance art (see Jones, 1999).

The blues are improvised songs sung from the heart about love and about women and men gone wrong (Collins, 1990, p. 210). Rainey, Smith, and Holiday sang in ways that went beyond the written text. They turned the blues into a living art form, a form that would with Holiday move into the spaces of jazz. And jazz, like the blues and culture, is an improvisational, not static, art form. Bill Evans, the great bebop pianist, put it this way, "Jazz is not a what . . . it is a how. If it were a what, it would be static, never growing. The how is that the music comes from the moment, it is spontaneous, it exists at the time it is created" (quoted in Lee, 1996, p. 426). The improvised coperformance text, the jazz solo, like Billie Holiday singing the blues, is a spontaneous production, it lives in the moment of creation. The how of culture as it connects people to one another in loving, conflictual, and disempowering ways is what performance ethnography seeks to capture (see Jackson, 1998, p. 21).

◆ Red Lodge, Montana: Experiences and Performances

William Kittredge (1996, p. 97) says that the West is an enormous empty and innocent stage waiting for a performance (see also Kittredge, 1987, 1994). He continues, "We see the history of our performances everywhere . . . inscribed on the landscape (fences, roads, canals, power lines, city plans, bomb ranges" (p. 97). Moreover, the West is contained in the stories people tell about it. Montana is both a performance and a place for performances. It is not possible to write an objective, authoritative, neutral account of performing Montana. Every account is personal and locally situated. Here are some of the ways Montana is performed.

In 1994, my wife and I bought a little piece of land outside Red Lodge, Montana, population 1,875.[13] We got an acre with a cabin on a river called Rock Creek and a big bluff of a rock outcropping behind the cabin. Our little valley is marked by lakes, snowcapped mountain ranges, alpine meadows, and sprawling ranches where people live in double-wide mobile homes. Early June brings fields of yellow sunflowers, Indian paintbrush, and lupine.

In the summer, horses and deer graze in the valley above the road to our cabin. Off the big boulder under the big cottonwood tree, I catch rainbow and brook trout for breakfast. I fish; my wife quilts, hikes, and collects wildflowers. Last Christmas my wife took up cross-country skiing. In the summer we go to auctions and yard sales, and drive into town for groceries.

Red Lodge is 4 miles from our cabin. It was primarily a mining town until the 1943 mine explosion that killed 74 miners. Hit hard by the Depression, even before the mines closed, looking for a way to stay alive, the town fathers pushed for a "high road" (the Hi-Road) that would connect Red Lodge to Cooke City and Silver Gate, the two little mining communities just outside the northeast entrance to Yellowstone National Park. It took a 1931 act of Congress and 5 years of hard work to build the road over the mountain; The Beartooth Highway officially opened in 1936. Ever since, Red Lodge has been marketed as the eastern gateway to Yellowstone. That's what got us there in 1990.[14]

After reading Kittredge and studying Turner (1986) and Bruner (1986, 1989, 1996), I have come to see our little part of Montana as a liminal place, a place for new performances, new stories. Caught up in the shadows of the new, mythologized culture of the West (Limerick, 1997, p. 151; Wilkinson, 1997, p. 114), we are learning how to perform Montana. We are learning to engage in the ritual performances

that people do when they are in and around Red Lodge, performances such as going to parades; shopping in the little craft and antique stores; buying things for the cabin; driving over the mountain; eating out; having an espresso on the sidewalk in front of the Coffee Factory Roasters; having a fancy dinner at the Pollard (which is on the National Registry of Hotels); picking up pictures from Flash's Image Factory; buying quilting materials at Granny Hugs; volunteering in the local library, which is computerizing its entire collection; and chatting with the owner of the Village Shoppe, who at one time dated the niece of the former University of Illinois basketball coach.

We watch other people do what we are doing, separating the experience of being in Montana from its performances and representations, constructing culture and meaning as they go along (Bruner, 1989, p. 113). Three years ago, I overheard a man talking to the owner of the tackle shop in Big Timber. His BMW was still running out front, the driver's door open. He had on an Orvis fishing vest. He had driven with his family from Connecticut. "The kids saw that movie *A River Runs Through It.* Where do we have to go to catch fish like they did in that movie? Can somebody around here give me fly-fishing lessons?" The owner said no on the lessons, but told the man to "go about 20 miles upriver, past Four-Mile Bridge. You can't miss it" (see also Dawson, 1996, p. 11).

Of course, the meanings of these Montana performance experiences are constantly changing. It is not appropriate to judge them in terms of their authenticity or originality. There is absolutely no original against which any given performance can be measured. There are only performances that seem to work and those that don't.

Creating Local History

Every year, we try to observe part of Red Lodge's Festival of Nations celebration. This is a 9-day ritual performance that reenacts the town's white European ethnic history. It involves white rituals such as colorful Old World costumes; Finnish, Irish, and Scottish dances and songs; bagpipes and the New Caledonia Drum and Bugle Corps; and cowboy poets—"whiteness as race, as privilege, as social construction" (Fine, Powell, Weis, & Wong, 1997, p. vii). This is whiteness as moral community. The souls of white folk are on public display (Du Bois, 1920, p. 29; Hughes, 1962).

Each day of the festival is given a name—7 days are devoted to specific nationalities (Irish-English-Welsh, German, Scandinavian, Finnish, Italian, Slavic, and Scottish), and the other days are Montana Day and All Nations Day. At the beginning of the 20th century, men from the European countries saluted in the festival came to Montana and became miners. Later they married, and their wives taught school, cooked, had children, helped run little shops, and carried on native crafts from their home countries. Red Lodge tries to keep this history alive.

According to local history, the festival started shortly after World War II. Local community leaders decided to build a civic center. They wanted a place for community activities, for an annual summer music festival, for art and craft exhibits and the display of flags and cultural items from each of the nations represented in the town. Thus was born the Festival of Nations, and Red Lodge was soon transformed into a "tourist town, a place that offered good scenery, fine fishing, the Hi-Road, the rodeo, cool summers" (Red Lodge Chamber of Commerce, 1982, p. 4). But the town had more to offer: "The inhabitants themselves were a resource" (p. 4). For 9 days every summer, Red Lodge puts its version of local ethnic culture on display, turning everyday people into performers of their respective ethnic heritages.

In these performances, residents only had their own histories to go on, so they made it up as they went along, one day for each ethnic group, but each group would do pretty much the same thing: a parade down Broadway with national flags from the country of origin, people in native costume, an afternoon performance of some sort (singing, storytelling, rug making), ethnic food in the Labor Temple (every day from 3:00 to 5:00 p.m.), an evening of music and dance in the civic center. This is improvised ethnicity connected to the performance of made-up rituals handed down from one generation to the next, white privilege, white cultural memory, Montana style (see also Hill, 1997, p. 245).

Montana Jazz

I like Montana Day, especially that part that involves ranch women reading their stories about being Montana wives. This is improvised theater, cowgirl women singing their version of the blues—Montana jazz. A tent is set up over the dance pavilion in Lions Park, just next to the Depot Gallery, which is housed in a converted red train caboose, across the street from the Carnegie Library. White plastic chairs are lined up in rows on the lawn. Loudspeakers are on each side of the stage. An old-fashioned Montana rancher meal is served afterward: barbecued beef, baked beans, coleslaw, baked potatoes, Jell-o salad, brownies for dessert, coffee and ice tea for beverages.

Tall and short middle-aged suntanned women take the stage. These are hardworking women, mothers, daughters, and grandmothers who live in the ranches in the Beartooth Valley, along the East Rosebud, Rock Creek, Willow Creek, and Stillwater River south of Columbus and Absarokee. Some have on cowboy boots, others wear Nike sneakers. They are dressed in blue jeans and decorated red, white, and blue cowboy shirts and skirts, and have red bandannas around their necks. They have short and long hair, ponytails and curls. They read cowboy poetry, tell short stories about hard winters and horses that freeze to death in snowbanks. Some sing songs. Country music plays quietly, and people come and go, some stopping and listening for a while. As these women perform, old ranchers in wide-brimmed cowboy hats close their eyes and tap their feet to the music. Young children run around through the crowd, and husbands proudly watch their wives read their poetry. Like Ma Rainey, Bessie Smith, and Billie Holiday, these women sing their version of the cowgirl blues. And there is a certain firm truth in the way they do this.

Dead Indians

Fiedler (1988) argues that Montana as a white territory became psychologically possible only after the Native Americans, the Nez Percé, Blackfeet, Sioux, Assinboine, Gros Ventre, Cheyenne, Chipewayan, Cree, and Crow were killed, driven away, or forced onto reservations. He asserts that the struggle to rid the West of the "noble savage" and the "redskin" was integral to the myth of the Montana frontier as a wild wilderness (p. 745). According to Fiedler, the Indian was Montana's Negro, an outcast living in an open-air ghetto (p. 752). With the passing of the redskin came trappers, mountain men, explorers, General Custer, Chief Joseph, and then ranchers and homesteaders. Indian sites were marked with names such as Dead Indian Pass.

Entering Red Lodge, you drive past a wooden statue of a Native American, a male Indian face sitting on a big stone. It was carved by a non-Native American. The history of Montana's relations with the Native American is folded into mountain man festivals and events like Montana Day in Red Lodge. It is a history that simultaneously honors the dead Indian while denying the violent past that is so central to white supremacy.

Two summers ago, we drove over Dead Indian Pass, taking the Chief Joseph Highway back from Yellowstone Park. Chief Joseph led the Nez Percé over this pass just months before Custer's last stand. At the top of the mountain there is a turnoff where you can stop and look back across the valley, 10,000 feet below. Although this place is called Dead Indian Pass, there is no mention of Chief Joseph on the little plaque at this viewing spot. Instead, there is a story about the ranch families who settled the valley while fighting off the Indians—hence the name Dead Indian Pass. The whites, and not the Indians, are honored in popular memory.

Performing Montana

There are many ways to perform Montana. Montana is a place where locals and tourists constantly commingle, where Orvis-outfitted fly fishermen from Connecticut connect with Huck Finn look-alike local kids who fish with worms and old bamboo poles. These Montana performances mix up many different things at the same time—different identities, different selves: cowboys, rodeos, classical music, antique hunters, skiers, mountain men, Finnish women who make rugs, ranchers' wives who write poetry, fishing for trout.

Being in nature is a major part of the Montana self. My wife and I enact nature; we bring it to ourselves through the very act of bending down and smelling a wildflower, of walking along the river. This contact with the "natural world is an experience that comes to us like a gift" (Kittredge, 1996, p. 108). And so our corner of Montana is a sacred place, a hole, or house of sky, to use phrases from Kittredge (1994) and Doig (1978), a place where wonderful things happen, and they happen when we perform them.

These are the kinds of things a minimalist, storytelling, performative form of qualitative inquiry makes visible. In these tellings the world comes alive. The qualitative researcher attempts to make these meanings available to the reader, hoping to show how this version of the sociological imagination engages some of the things that matter in everyday life. But sometimes words fail, for in its naturalness Montana is a place that is stunning in its beauty, a world of images beyond words.

I turn now to an aesthetic of color[15] and critical race theory. I explore how critical race theory can use experimental forms of narrative to criticize and resist racist cultural practices.

◆ An Aesthetic of Color and Critical Race Theory

A feminist, Chicano/a, and black performance-based aesthetic uses art, photography, music, dance, poetry, painting, theater, cinema, performance texts, autobiography, narrative, storytelling, and poetic, dramatic language to create a critical race consciousness, thereby extending the post-civil rights Chicano/a and black arts cultural movements into the next century (see Harrington, 1992, p. 208). These practices serve to implement critical race theory (Anzaldúa, 1987; Collins, 1990; Davis, 1998, p. 155; Gonzalez, 1998; hooks, 1990, p. 105; Joyce, 1987; Ladson-Billings, 1998; Parker, 1998; Parker et al., 1998; Scheurich, 1997, pp. 144-158; Smith, 1993, p. xxvi; Smith, 1994, p. xxii; Trinh, 1992). Critical race theory "seeks to decloak the seemingly race-neutral, and color-blind ways . . . of constructing and administering race-based appraisals . . . of the law, administrative policy, electoral politics . . . political discourse [and education] in the USA" (Parker et al., 1998, p. 5).

Thus Collins's (1990, 1998) Afrocentric feminist agenda for the 1990s is moved into the next century; that is, theorists and practitioners enact a standpoint epistemology that sees the world from the point of view of oppressed persons of color. Representative sociopoetic and interpretive works in this tradition include those of Baraka (1969/1998), Jones (1966), Shange (1977), Joyce (1987), Neal (1988), and Jordan (1998), as well as the more recent arguments of hooks (1990, 1996), Smith (1993, 1994), Davis (1998), Anzaldúa (1987), Noriega (1996), and others. This aesthetic is also informed by the successive waves of activism among Asian Americans and Native Americans, women, and gays, lesbians, and bisexuals who "use their art as a weapon for political activism" (Harris, 1998, p. 1384; also Nero, 1998, p. 1973).

Theorists critically engage and interrogate the anti-civil rights agendas of the New Right (see Jordan, 1998), but this is not a protest or integrationist initiative aimed solely at informing a white audience of racial injustice. It dismisses these narrow agendas. In so doing it rejects classical Eurocentric and postpositivist standards for evaluating literary, artistic, and research work.

The following understandings shape this complex project:

- Ethics, aesthetics, political praxis and epistemology are joined; every act of represen-

tation, artistic or research, is a political and ethical statement (see Neal, 1988/1998, p. 1451). There is not a separate aesthetic or epistemological realm regulated by transcendent ideals, although an ethics of care should always be paramount.

- Claims to truth and knowledge are assessed in terms of multiple criteria, including asking if a text (a) interrogates existing cultural, sexist, and racial stereotypes, especially those connected to family, femininity, masculinity, marriage, and intimacy (Neal, 1988/1998, p. 1457); (b) gives primacy to concrete lived experience; (c) uses dialogue and an ethics of personal responsibility, values beauty, spirituality, and love of others; (d) implements an emancipatory agenda committed to equality, freedom, social justice, and participatory democratic practices; and (e) emphasizes community, collective action, solidarity, and group empowerment (Denzin, 1997, p. 65; hooks, 1990, p. 111; Pizarro, 1998, pp. 63-65).

- No topic is taboo, including sexuality, sexual abuse, death, and violence.

- This project presumes an artist and social researcher who is part of, and a spokesperson for, a local moral community, a community with its own symbolism, mythology, and heroic figures.

- This project asks that the writer-artist draw upon vernacular, folk, and popular culture forms of representation, including proverbs, work songs, spirituals, sermons, prayers, poems, choreopoems (Shange, 1977), folktales, blues (Davis, 1998), jazz, rap, film, paintings, theater, movies, photographs, performance art, murals, and *corridos* (see Fregoso, 1993; Gates & McKay, 1997, p. xxvii; Hill, 1998; Noriega, 1996; Pizarro, 1998, p. 65).

- This project includes a search for texts that speak to women and children of color and to persons who suffer from violence, rape, and racist and sexist injustice.

- This project seeks artists-researchers-writers who produce works that speak to and represent the needs of the community (e.g., concerning drug addiction, teenage pregnancy, murder, gang warfare, AIDS, school dropout).

- It is understood, of course, that no single representation or work can speak to the collective needs of the community. Rather, local communities are often divided along racial, ethnic, gender, residential, age, and class lines.

Thus this project seeks emancipatory, utopian texts grounded in the distinctive styles, rhythms, idioms, and personal identities of local folk and vernacular culture. As historical documents, these texts record the histories of injustices experienced by the members of oppressed groups. They show how members of local groups have struggled to find places of dignity and respect in a violent, racist, and sexist civil society (see Gates & McKay, 1997, p. xxvii).

These texts are sites of resistance. They are places where meanings, politics, and identities are negotiated. They transform and challenge all forms of cultural representation: white, black, Chicano/a, Asian American, Native American, gay or straight.

In her poem "Power," black lesbian poet Audre Lorde (1978/1998b, p. 1627)* talks about taking action in the world:

The difference between poetry and rhetoric
is being
ready to kill
yourself
instead of your children.

In lines such as these, critical race theory is connected to a heightened reflexive and moral sense of race consciousness. Lorde (1973/1998a, pp. 1626-1627)* again, this time from "Coal":

I
is the total black, being spoken

from the earth's inside.
There are many kinds of open
how a diamond comes into a knot of
flame
how a sound comes into a word
coloured
by who pays what for speaking . . .

Love is a word, another kind of open.
As the diamond comes into a knot of
flame
I am black because I come from the
earth's inside
Now take my word for jewel in the open
light.

Lorde (1986/1998c, pp. 1630-1631)* once more, from her poem "Stations":

Some women love
to wait
for life for a ring
for a touch . . . for another
woman's voice to make them whole . . .
Some women wait for something
to change and nothing
does change
so they change
themselves.

In "Taking in Wash," Rita Dove (1993/1998, pp. 1966-1967)* speaks to drinking, drunkenness, and violence in the house:

Papa called her Pearl when he came home
drunk, swaying as if the wind touched
only him . . . Mama never changed:
when the dog crawled under the stove
and the back gate slammed, Mama hid
the laundry . . . Papa is making the hankies
sail. Her foot upon a silk
stitched rose, she waits

he turns, his smile sliding over.

Mama a tight dark fist.

Touch that child

And I'll cut you down

Just like the Cedar of Lebanon.

Ntozake Shange's (1977)* powerful, Obie Award-winning choreopoem *For Colored Girls Who Have Considered Suicide When the Rainbow Is Enuf* ends this way. Six of the seven women in the company, the ladies in red, purple, orange, blue, green, and yellow, have spoken. The lady in red summarizes (pp. 60, 63-64):

lady in red

i waz missin somethin . . .

i sat up one nite walkin a boardin house

screamin/cryin/the ghost of another woman

who was missin what I waz missin

i wanted to jump up outta my bones

& be done wit myself

leave me alone . . .

i fell into a numbness

til the only tree I cd see . . .

held me in the breeze

made me dawn dew

that chill at daybreak

the sun wrapped me up swingin rose light everywhere

the sky laid over me like a million men

i waz cold/I waz burnin up/a child

& endlessly weaving garments for the moon

wit me tears

i found god in myself

& i loved her/i loved her fiercely

> All of the ladies repeat to themselves softly the lines 'i found god in myself & I loved her.' It soon becomes a

song of joy, started by the lady in blue. The ladies sing first to each other, then gradually to the audience. After the song peaks the ladies enter a closed tight circle.

lady in brown

& this is for colored girls who have considered

suicide/but are movin to the ends of their own

rainbows

And so the world is taken back, and we dream of another day of lightness and being free, of making our own rainbow.

Aesthetics and Cinematic Practices

Within the contemporary black and Chicano/a film communities, there are specific sets of film practices associated with this aesthetic project.[16] These practices inform and shape the narrative and visual content of these experimental texts. They include the following:

- Experiments with narrative forms, folk ballads, and *corridos* that honor long-standing Chicano/a discourse traditions (Fregoso, 1993, pp. 70-76; Noriega, 1992, pp. 152-153);
- The use of improvisation, mise-en-scène, and montage to fill the screen with multiracial images and to manipulate bicultural visual and linguistic codes;
- The use of personal testimonials, life stories, voice-overs, and offscreen narration to provide overall narrative unity to texts (Noriega, 1992, pp. 156-159);
- Celebration of key elements in Chicano/a culture, especially the themes of resistance, maintenance, affirmation, and neo-indigenism, or *mestizaje* (Noriega, 1992, p. 150), thereby challenging assimilation and melting-pot narratives;
- Production of texts that deconstruct machismo, the masculine identity, and the celebration of works that give the Chicana

subject an active part in the text while criticizing such timeworn stereotypes as the virgin, whore, supportive wife, and homegirl (Fregoso, 1993, pp. 29, 93-94);

- Rejection of essentializing approaches to identity and emphasis on a processual, gendered, performance view of self and the location of identity within, not outside of, systems of cultural and media representation;

- Refusal to accept the official race-relations narrative of the culture, which privileges the ideology of assimilation while contending that black and Hispanic youth pose grave threats to white society (Fregoso, 1993, p. 29).

Return to Anna Deavere Smith's *Fires in the Mirror* (1993)*, and listen now to An Anonymous Young Man #2 Bad Boy. The time is evening; the season, spring. The setting is the same recreation room where the interview with Anonymous Young Man #1 took place. Young Man #2 has dreadlocks. On his head is a "very odd-shaped multicolored hat" (p. 100). He is wearing a black jacket over his clothes. He has a gold tooth. He is soft-spoken.

That youth,

that sixteen-year-old

didn't murder that Jew . . .

mostly the Black youth in Crown Heights have two things to do—

You either

DJ, be a MC, a rapper

or Jamaican rapper,

ragamuffin,

or you be a bad boy

you sell drugs or you rob people.

What do you do?

I sell drugs

What do you do?

I rap.

That's how it is in Crown Heights.
(pp. 100, 102)

In this speech Smith catches the language of youth, its rhythm, syntax, and semantics. She uses the personal testimonial as a way of bringing another voice into the text, as well as providing narrative unity to the play. Her young man rejects essentializing views of identity, but notes that in Crown Heights young people have few choices or options in life. Young Man #2 resists these interpretations.

Artistic representations such as those presented here from Lorde, Dove, and Smith (and Jordan—see below) are based on the notion of a radical and constantly changing set of aesthetic practices. As hooks (1990) observes: "There can never be one critical paradigm for the evaluation of artistic work. . . . a radical aesthetic acknowledges that we are constantly changing positions, locations, that our needs and concerns vary, that these diverse directions must correspond with shifts in critical thinking" (p. 111).

At this level, there is no preferred aesthetic. For example, realistic art is not necessarily better than abstract, expressionist, or impressionist art. In the worlds of jazz, ragtime, New Orleans, classic, and swing are not necessarily more or less politically correct or aesthetically better than bebop, cool, hard bop, Latin, avant-garde, and fusion. Nor is Charlie Parker less politically correct then Lester Young, or Ben Webster, Ella Fitzgerald, Nina Simone, Nancy Wilson, Billie Holiday, Bessie Smith, John Coltrane, or Miles Davis.

But then, June Jordan (1998)* might put it differently. In her jazz prose poem "A Good News Blues," she pays homage to Billie and Louis, Nina, and Bessie, to anyone who sings the blues. In the following lines she praises Billie Holiday (pp. 199-200):

Since the blues left my sky

I'm runnin out on Monday

To chase down all my Sundays

Now a man must be pushing and shoving

But a woman's born to strut and stretch

To go outside (for /catch some) lovin

Get over past regrets

I'm liftin' weights and wearin sweats . . .

And thrillin through the night . . .

And if I want to rewrite

all the sorry-ass/

victim/passive/feminine/

traditional

propaganda

spinnin out here

    ain' nobody's business

    if I do

I been lost

but

I been found

    I am bound

    for Billie's land

that place of longing

where the angels learn

to sing and play

    the syncopated music

    of my soul

And brilliant rainbows cut through the blue-and-white clouds, connecting distant hills and mountains to the places where I live.

Each text, each performance should be valued in terms of the collective and individual reflection and critical action it produces, including conversations that cross the boundaries of race, class, gender, and nation. We ask how each work of art and each instance of qualitative inquiry promotes the development of human agency, "resistance . . . and critical consciousness" (hooks, 1990, p. 111).

This aesthetic also seeks and values beauty, and looks to find beauty in the everyday, especially in "the lives of poor people" (hooks, 1990, p. 111). Here is an illustration from bell hooks, who recalls the houses of her childhood, especially the house of Baba, her grandmother. Looking back into her childhood, hooks observes that she now sees how this black woman was struggling to create, in spite of poverty and hardship, an oppositional world of beauty. Baba had a clean house crowded with many precious objects. Baba was also a quilt maker. She turned worn-out everyday clothing into beautiful works of art, and her quilts were present in every room of her small house.

Baba's house was like an art gallery. Late at night, hooks would sit alone in an upstairs room in the house, and light from the moon would send crisscrossing patterns and shadows across the floor and the wall. In the stillness of the night, in the reflections from the moon's light, hooks came to see darkness and beauty in different ways.

Now, in a different time, late at night, she and her sisters "think about our skin as a dark room, a place of shadows. We talk often about color politics, and the ways racism has created an aesthetic that wounds us, we talk about the need to see darkness differently. . . . in that space of shadows we long for an aesthetic of blackness—strange and oppositional" (hooks, 1990, p. 113). Baba, the quilt maker, shows her how to do this.

Aesthetics, art, performance, history, culture, and politics are thus intertwined, for in the artful, interpretive production, cultural heroes, heroines, mythic pasts, and senses of moral community are created. It remains to chart the future—to return to the beginning, to reimagine the ways in which qualitative inquiry and interpretive ethnography can advance the agendas of radical democratic practice, to ask where these practices will take us next.

◆ Into the Future

Of course, persons who do interpretations feel uncomfortable making predictions. But where the fields of interpretation, qualitative inquiry, and the practices and politics of telling stories will be in 10 years must be addressed. If the past predicts the future, and if the decade of the 1990s is to be taken seriously, then interpretation is moving more and more deeply into the regions of the postmodern, multicultural sensibility. A new postinterpretive, postfoundational paradigm is emerging. This framework is attaching itself to new and less foundational interpretive criteria. A more expansive framework shaped by an aesthetics of color and critical race theory principles informs these criteria.

Epistemologies and aesthetics of color will proliferate, building on Afrocentric, Chicano/a, Native American, Asian, and Third World perspectives. More elaborated epistemologies of gender (and class) will appear, including queer theory (see Gamson, Chapter 12, this volume) and feminisms of color (see Ladson-Billings, Chapter 9, this volume). These interpretive communities and their scholars will draw on their group experiences as the basis of the texts they write, and they will seek texts that speak to the logic and cultures of these communities. They will be committed to advancing the political, economic, cultural, and educational practices of critical race theory.

These race-, ethnic-, and gender-specific interpretive communities will fashion interpretive criteria out of their interactions with postpositivist, constructivist, critical theory, and poststructural sensibilities. These criteria will be local, aesthetic, emic, existential, political, and emotional. They will push the personal to the forefront of the political, where the social text becomes the vehicle for the expression of politics.

This projected proliferation of interpretive communities does not mean that the field of qualitative research will splinter into warring factions, or into groups that cannot speak to one another. Underneath the complexities and contradictions that define this field rest four common commitments. The first reflects the belief that the world of human experience must be studied from the point of view of the historically and culturally situated individual. Second, qualitative researchers will persist in working outward from their own biographies to the worlds of experience that surround them. Third, scholars will continue to value and seek to produce works that speak clearly and powerfully about these worlds. As Raymond Carver (1989, p. 24) observes, the real experimenters will always be those who make it new, who find things out for themselves, and who want to carry this news from their world to ours. Thus will qualitative researchers find new and different ways of joining their interpretive work with constantly changing forms of radical democratic practice.

Fourth, these texts will be committed not just to describing the world, but to changing it. These texts will be performance based and informed by the practices of civic, intimate, and public journalism. They will be committed to creating civic transformations and to using minimalist social theory. They will inscribe and perform utopian dreams, dreams shaped by critical race theory, dreams of a world where all are free to be who they choose to be, free of gender, class, race, religious, or ethnic prejudice or discrimination. The seventh moment will be one in which the practices of qualitative inquiry finally move, without hesitation or encumbrance, from the personal to the political. This move is a spiraling process. It builds on previous levels of expression. It does not abandon the personal, for example, in the name of the political.[17]

So the stories we tell one another will change, and the criteria for reading stories will also change. And this is how it should be. The good stories are always told by those who have learned well the stories of the past but are unable to tell them any longer. This is so because the stories from the past no longer speak to them or to us.

In the end, then, to summarize, I seek an existential, interpretive ethnography, an ethnography that offers a blueprint for cultural criticism. This criticism is grounded in the specific worlds made visible in the ethnography. It understands that all ethnography is theory and value laden. There can be no objective account of a culture and its ways (see Smith & Deemer, Chapter 34, this volume). Taking a lead from midcentury African American cultural critics (Du Bois, Hurston, Ellison, Wright, Baldwin, Hines), we now know that the ethnographic, the aesthetic, and the political can never be neatly separated. Ethnography, like art, is always political.

Accordingly, after Ford (1950/1998), a critical, civic, literary ethnography is one that must meet four criteria. It must evidence a mastery of literary craftsmanship, the art of good writing. It should present a well-plotted, compelling, but minimalist narrative. This narrative should be based on realistic, natural conversation, with a focus on memorable, recognizable characters. These characters should be located in well-described, "unforgettable scenes" (Ford, 1950/1998, p. 1112). Second, the work should present clearly identifiable cultural and political issues, including injustices based on the structures and meanings of race, class, gender, and sexual orientation. Third, the work should articulate a politics of hope. It should criticize how things are and imagine how they could be different. Finally, it should do these things through direct and indirect symbolic and rhetorical means. Writers who do these things are fully immersed in the oppressions and injustices of their time. They direct their ethnographic energies to higher, utopian, morally sacred goals.

Finally, this performative ethnography searches for new ways to locate and represent the gendered, sacred self in its ethical relationships to nature. An exploration of other forms of writing is sought, including personal diaries, nature writing, and performance texts anchored in the natural world (see Denzin, 1999a; see also Lincoln & Denzin, Chapter 41, this volume).

■ Notes

* I am indebted to Sage Publications and the Institute of Communications Research for supplying the funds to pay the permissions fees for quoted material used in this chapter.

1. To repeat, as Yvonna Lincoln and I assert in Chapter 1 of this volume, the seven moments of qualitative inquiry are traditional (1900-1950); modernist (1950-1970); blurred genres (1970-1986); crisis of representation (1986-1990); postmodern, a period of experimental and new ethnographies (1990-1995); postexperimental inquiry (1995-2000); and the future, which is now (2000-).

2. A parallel movement (see below) is occurring in the worlds of cinema, where Chicano/a and black filmmakers are using voice-overs, first-person and offscreen narration, mise-en-scène, and montage as ways of disturbing traditional gendered images of the racial subject (Fregoso, 1993, pp. 70-76; Noriega, 1992, pp. 152-153; see also Hall, 1989). This movement is a consequence, in part, of a 1968 U.S. Office of Economic Opportunity-funded program called the New Communicators, "designed to train minorities for employment in the film industry" (Noriega, 1996, p. 7).

3. The following section draws from Denzin (1997, pp. 280-281).

4. At the same time, it is understood that "participating in a citizen's initiative to clean up a polluted harbor is no less political than debating in cultural journals the pejorative presentation of certain groups in terms of stereotypical images" (Benhabib, 1992, p. 104).

5. Public journalism is not without its critics, including those who say it is news by focus group, that it is a marketing device to sell newspapers, that it is a conservative reform movement aimed at increasing the power of professional journalists, and that its advocates do not understand the real meanings of community, public life, and civic discourse. See the essays in Graber, McQuail, and Norris (1998) and Glasser (1999), but see also Carey (1995).

6. This ethic values community, solidarity, care, love, empowerment, morally involved observers, and caring relations with the community (see Denzin, 1997, p. 275).

7. These are extensions of the norms that Christians et al. (1993, pp. 55-57) see as operating for journalists.

8. Things are known only through their representations. Each representational form is regulated by a set of conventions. Factual tales should be objective and should conform to certain rules of verification. Fictional tales are regulated by understandings connected to emotional verisimilitude, emotional realism, and so on.

9. I thank Clifford Christians for this principle.

10. The rules in this paragraph plagiarize Raymond Chandler's "Twelve Notes on the Mystery Story" (1995).

11. This section draws from and reworks portions of Denzin (1999b).

12. As Meaghan Morris has indicated to me in conversation, the Australians involved in this case felt that justice was not served, that they had to deal with the loss of a loved one strictly within American political terms. Rosenbaum became a cipher in these accounts.

13. There are various stories about how the town got its name. "The generally accepted theory is that the Crow Indians who inhabited the

area colored their lodges with red clay" (Graetz, 1997, p. 23).

14. The town has a Web site. Using a search engine such as Yahoo, you can simply type "Red Lodge, Montana" and within seconds you can be looking at a map of downtown Red Lodge.

15. I borrow this phrase from bell hooks's (1990) essay "An Aesthetic of Blackness."

16. The implementation of the 1968 New Communicators program (see note 2, above) at the University of Southern California and the University of California at Los Angeles produced first- and second-generation minority filmmakers called by some the black and brown Los Angeles schools (see Diawara, 1993; Fregoso, 1993, pp. 31, 129; Masilela, 1993; Noriega, 1992, p. 142; Noriega, 1996, pp. 7-8). Among this group of filmmakers are such names as Burnett, Dash, Van Peebles, Rich, Duke, Trevino, Vasquez, Martinez, Valdez, Nair, Wang, hooks, and Nava. More recent names include Lee, Singleton, and Hughes. These post-civil rights filmmakers are implementing a cinematic version of critical race theory, and their works should be read alongside those of hooks, West, and others. Funding for this project was cut back under the Reagan administration in the 1980s.

17. Ivan Brady clarified this point for me.

■ *References*

Alexie, S. (1993). *Old shirts and new skins.* Los Angeles: University of California, American Indian Studies Center. (Used by permission.)

Anzaldúa, G. (1987). *Borderlands/la frontera: The new mestiza.* San Francisco: Aunt Lute.

Baker, H., Jr. (1997). The black arts movement. In H. L. Gates, Jr., & N. Y. McKay (Eds.), *The Norton anthology of African American literature* (pp. 1791-1806). New York: W. W. Norton.

Baraka, A. (1997). *The autobiography of Leroi Jones.* Chicago: Lawrence Hill.

Baraka, A. (1998). Black art. In P. L. Hill (Ed.), *Call and response: The Riverside anthology of the African American literary tradition* (pp. 1501-1502). Boston: Houghton Mifflin. (Original work published 1969. Reprinted by permission of Sterling Lord Literistic, Inc. Copyright by Amiri Baraka.)

Behar, R. (1996). *The vulnerable observer: Anthropology that breaks your heart.* Boston: Beacon.

Benhabib, S. (1992). *Situating the self: Gender, community and postmodernism in contemporary ethics.* New York: Routledge.

Birringer, J. (1993). *Theatre, history, postmodernism.* Bloomington: Indiana University Press.

Bochner, A. P., & Ellis, C. (1996). Taking ethnography into the twenty-first century. *Journal of Contemporary Ethnography, 25,* 3-5.

Brady, I. (1998). A gift of the journey. *Qualitative Inquiry, 4,* 463.

Brady, I. (1999). Review essay: Ritual as cognitive process, performance as history. *Current Anthropology, 40,* 243-248.

Branaman, A. (1997). Goffman's social theory. In C. Lemert & A. Branaman (Eds.), *The Goffman reader* (pp. xvi-lxxxii). Malden, MA: Blackwell.

Bruner, E. M. (1986). Experience and its expressions. In V. Turner & E. M. Bruner (Eds.), *The anthropology of experience* (pp. 3-30). Urbana: University of Illinois Press.

Bruner, E. M. (1989). Tourism, creativity, and authenticity. In N. K. Denzin (Ed.), *Studies in symbolic interaction: A research annual* (Vol. 10, pp. 109-114). Greenwich, CT: JAI.

Bruner, E. M. (1996). Abraham Lincoln as authentic reproduction: A critique of postmodernism. *American Anthropologist, 96,* 397-415.

Butler, J. (1990). *Gender trouble: Feminism and the subversion of identity.* New York: Routledge.

Butler, J. (1997). *Excitable speech: A politics of the performative.* New York: Routledge.

Butler, J. (1999). Revisiting bodies and pleasures. *Theory, Culture & Society, 16,* 11-20.

Carey, J. W. (1995). The press, public opinion, and public discourse. In T. L. Glasser & C. T. Salmon (Eds.), *Public opinion and the communication of consent* (pp. 380-402). New York: Guilford.

Carspecken, P. F. (1996). *Critical ethnography in educational research: A theoretical and practical guide.* New York: Routledge.

Carver, R. (1989). *Fires.* New York: Vantage.

Ceglowski, D. (1997). That's a good story, but is it really research? *Qualitative Inquiry, 3,* 188-201.

Chandler, R. (1995). Twelve notes on the mystery story. In R. Chandler, *Later novels and other writings* (pp. 1004-1011). New York: Penguin.

Charity, A. (1995). *Doing public journalism.* New York: Guilford.

Christian, B. T. (1997). Literature since 1970. In H. L. Gates, Jr., & N. Y. McKay (Eds.), *The Norton anthology of African American literature* (pp. 2011-2020). New York: W. W. Norton.

Christians, C. G., Ferre, J. P., & Fackler, P. M. (1993). *Good news: Social ethics and the press.* New York: Oxford University Press.

Clough, P. T. (1994). *Feminist thought: Desire, power and academic discourse.* Cambridge, MA: Blackwell.

Clough, P. T. (1998). *The end(s) of ethnography: From realism to social criticism* (2nd ed.). New York: Peter Lang.

Cohen-Cruz, J. (1998). General introduction. In J. Cohen-Cruz (Ed.), *Radical street performance: An international anthology* (pp. 1-6). New York: Routledge.

Collins, P. H. (1990). *Black feminist thought: Knowledge, consciousness, and the politics of empowerment.* New York: Routledge, Chapman & Hall.

Collins, P. H. (1998). *Fighting words: Black women and the search for justice.* Minneapolis: University of Minnesota Press.

Conquergood, D. (1985). Performing as a moral act: Ethical dimensions of the ethnography of performance. *Literature in Performance, 5,* 1-13.

Conquergood, D. (1992). Ethnography, rhetoric and performance. *Quarterly Journal of Speech, 78,* 80-97.

Conquergood, D. (1998). Health theatre in a Hmong refugee camp: Performance, communication and culture. In J. Cohen-Cruz (Ed.), *Radical street performance: An international anthology* (pp. 220-229). New York: Routledge.

Cooke, J. (1980, September 28). Jimmy's world. *Washington Post,* p. A1.

Cruikshank, J. (1997). Negotiating with narrative: Establishing cultural identity at the Yukon International Storytelling Festival. *American Anthropologist, 99,* 56-69.

Dash, L. (1997). *Rosa Lee: A mother and her family in urban America.* New York: Penguin.

Davis, A. Y. (1998). *Blues legacies and black feminism: Gertrude Ma Rainey, Bessie Smith, and Billie Holiday.* New York: Pantheon.

Dawson, P. (1996). Not another fish story from occupied Montana. In R. Newby & S. Hunger (Eds.), *Writing Montana: Literature under the big sky* (pp. 10-23). Helena: Montana Center for the Book.

Degh, L. (1995). *Narratives in society: A performer-centered study of narration.* Bloomington: Indiana University Press.

Denison, J. (1996). Sports narratives. *Qualitative Inquiry, 2,* 351-362.

Denzin, N. K. (1997). *Interpretive ethnography: Ethnographic practices for the 21st century.* Thousand Oaks, CA: Sage.

Denzin, N. K. (1999a). An interpretive ethnography for the next century. *Journal of Contemporary Ethnography, 28,* 510-519.

Denzin, N. K. (1999b). Performing Montana. In B. Glassner & R. Hertz (Eds.), *Qualitative sociology as everyday life* (pp. 147-158). Thousand Oaks, CA: Sage.

Denzin, N. K. (1999c). Performing Montana, part II. *Symbolic Interaction, 23,* 76-89.

Diawara, M. (1993). Black American cinema: The new realism. In M. Diawara (Ed.), *Black American cinema* (pp. 3-25). New York: Routledge.

Diversi, M. (1998). Glimpses of street life: Representing lived experience through short stories. *Qualitative Inquiry, 4,* 131-137.

Doig, I. (1978). *This house of sky.* New York: Harcourt Brace.

Donmoyer, R., & Yennie-Donmoyer, J. (1995). Data as drama: Reflections on the use of readers theater as a mode of qualitative data display. *Qualitative Inquiry, 1,* 402-428.

Dove, R. (1998). Taking in wash. In P. L. Hill (Ed.), *Call and response: The Riverside anthology of the African American literary tradition* (pp. 1966-1967). Boston: Houghton Mifflin. (Reprinted from R. Dove, *Selected poems,* 1993, New York: Vantage)

Du Bois, W. E. B. (1920). *Darkwater: Voices from within the veil.* New York: Schocken.

Dunbar, C., Jr. (1999). Three short stories. *Qualitative Inquiry, 5,* 130-140.

Ellis, C. (1997). Evocative autoethnography: Writing emotionally about our lives. In W. G. Tierney & Y. S. Lincoln (Eds.), *Representation and the text: Re-framing the narrative voice* (pp. 115-139). Albany: State University of New York Press.

Ellis, C., & Bochner, A. P. (1992). Telling and performing personal stories: The constraints of choice in abortion. In C. Ellis & M. G. Flaherty (Eds.), *Investigating subjectivity: Research on lived experience* (pp. 79-101). Newbury Park, CA: Sage.

Ellis, C., & Bochner, A. P. (Eds.). (1996). *Composing ethnography: Alternative forms of qualitative writing.* Walnut Creek, CA: AltaMira.

Ellis, C., & Flaherty, M. G. (Eds.). (1992). *Investigating subjectivity: Research on lived experience.* Newbury Park, CA: Sage.

Fiedler, L. (1988). The Montana face. In W. Kittredge & A. Smith (Eds.), *The last best place: A Montana anthology* (pp. 744-752). Seattle: University of Washington Press.

Fine, M., Powell, L. C., Weis, L., & Wong, L. M. (1997). Preface. In M. Fine, L. C. Powell, L. Weis, & L. M. Wong (Eds.), *Off white: Readings on race, power and society* (pp. vii-xii). New York: Routledge.

Ford, N. A. (1998). A blueprint for Negro authors. In P. L. Hill (Ed.), *Call and response: The Riverside anthology of the African American literary tradition* (pp. 1112-1114). Boston: Houghton Mifflin. (Original work published 1950)

Fregoso, R. L. (1993). *The bronze screen: Chicana and Chicano film culture.* Minneapolis: University of Minnesota Press.

Gates, H. L., Jr., & McKay, N. Y. (1997). Preface: Talking books. In H. L. Gates, Jr., & N. Y. McKay (Eds.), *The Norton anthology of African American literature* (pp. xxvii-xli). New York: W. W. Norton.

Glasser, T. L. (Ed.). (1999). *The idea of public journalism.* New York: Guilford.

Goffman, E. (1959). *The presentation of self in everyday life.* Garden City, NY: Doubleday.

Gonzalez, F. E. (1998). Formations of Mexicananess: Trenzas de identidades multiples/ Growing up Mexicana: Braids of multiple identities. *International Journal of Qualitative Studies in Education, 11,* 81-102.

Graber, D., McQuail, D., & Norris, P. (Eds.). (1998). *The politics of news: The news of politics.* Washington, DC: Congressional Quarterly Press.

Graetz, R. (1997, July-August). Sojourn to the sky: The Beartooth Highway. *Montana Magazine,* pp. 18-26.

Hall, S. (1989). Cultural identity and cinematic representation. *Framework, 36,* 68-81.

Harrington, W. (1992). *Crossings: A white man's journey into black America.* New York: HarperCollins.

Harrington, W. (1997a). Prologue: The job of remembering for the tribe. In W. Harrington (Ed.), *Intimate journalism: The art and craft of reporting everyday life* (pp. vii-xvi). Thousand Oaks, CA: Sage.

Harrington, W. (1997b). A writer's essay: Seeking the extraordinary in the ordinary. In W. Harrington (Ed.), *Intimate journalism: The art and craft of reporting everyday life* (pp. xvii-xlvi). Thousand Oaks, CA: Sage.

Harris, W. J. (1998). Cross roads blues: African American history and culture, 1960 to the present. In P. L. Hill (Ed.), *Call and response: The Riverside anthology of the African American literary tradition* (pp. 1343-1385). Boston: Houghton Mifflin.

Hill, P. L. (Ed.). (1998). *Call and response: The Riverside anthology of the African American literary tradition.* Boston: Houghton Mifflin.

Hill, R. T. G. (1997). Performance and the "political anatomy" of pioneer Colorado. *Text and Performance Quarterly, 17,* 236-255.

hooks, b. (1990). *Yearning: Race, gender, and cultural politics.* Boston: South End.

hooks, b. (1996). *Reel to real: Race, sex, and class at the movies.* New York: Routledge.

Hughes, L. (1962). *The ways of white folks.* New York: Vintage.

Hughes, L. (1994). *Collected poems by Langston Hughes.* New York: Alfred A. Knopf. (Permission granted by the Estate of Langston Hughes. Reprinted by permission of Alfred A. Knopf, a Division of Random House, Inc.)

Jackson, M. (1998). *Minima ethnographica: Intersubjectivity and the anthropological project.* Chicago: University of Chicago Press.

Jenkins, J. E. (1999, May 2). Narrating the action while taking part in it. *New York Times,* Arts and Leisure sec., pp. 9, 19.

Jones, L. (1966). *Home: Social essays.* Hopewell, NJ: Ecco.

Jones, S. H. (1999). Torch. *Qualitative Inquiry, 5,* 235-250.

Jordan, J. (1998). *Affirmative acts.* Garden City NY: Anchor. (Copyright © 1998 by June Jordan. Used by permission of Doubleday, a division of Random House, Inc.)

Joyce, J. A. (1987). The black canon: Reconstructing black American literary criticism. *New Literary History, 18,* 335-344.

Kittredge, W. (1987). *Owning it all.* San Francisco: Murray House.

Kittredge, W. (1994). *Hole in the sky: A memoir.* San Francisco: Murray House.

Kittredge, W. (1996). *Who owns the West?* San Francisco: Murray House.

Kotarba, J. A. (1998). Black men, black voices: The role of the producer in synthetic performance ethnography. *Qualitative Inquiry, 4,* 389-404.

Kramer, M. (1995). Breakable rules for literary journalists. In N. Sims & M. Kramer (Eds.), *Literary journalism: A new collection of the best American nonfiction* (pp. 21-34). New York: Ballantine.

Krieger, S. (1996). *The family silver: Essays on relationships among women.* Berkeley: University of California Press.

Ladson-Billings, G. (1998). Just what is critical race theory and what is it doing in a "nice" field like education? *International Journal of Qualitative Studies in Education, 11,* 7-24.

Lather, P. (1993). Fertile obsession: Validity after poststructuralism. *Sociological Quarterly, 34,* 673-693.

Lather, P., & Smithies, C. (1997). *Troubling the angels: Women living with HIV/AIDS.* Boulder, CO: Westview.

Lee, G. (1996). The poet: Bill Evans. In R. Gottlieb (Ed.), *Reading jazz: A gathering of autobiography, reportage, and criticism from 1919 to now* (pp. 419-444). New York: Pantheon.

Lemert, C. (1997). Goffman. In C. Lemert & A. Branaman (Eds.), *The Goffman reader* (pp. ix-xliii). Malden, MA: Blackwell.

Limerick, P. N. (1997). The shadows of heaven itself. In W. E. Reibsame (Ed.), *Atlas of the new West* (pp. 151-178). New York: W. W. Norton.

Lincoln, Y. S. (1995a). Emerging criteria for quality in qualitative and interpretive inquiry. *Qualitative Inquiry, 1,* 275-289.

Lincoln, Y. S. (1995b). The sixth moment: Emerging problems in qualitative research. In N. K. Denzin (Ed.), *Studies in symbolic interaction: A research annual* (Vol. 19, pp. 37-55). Greenwich, CT: JAI.

Lincoln, Y. S. (1997). Self, subject, audience, text: Living at the edge, writing in the margins. In W. G. Tierney & Y. S. Lincoln (Eds.), *Representation and the text: Re-framing the narrative voice* (pp. 37-56). Albany: State University of New York Press.

Lincoln, Y. S. (1998, November). *When research is not enough: Community, care, and love.* Presidential Address delivered at the annual meeting of the Association for the Study of Higher Education, Miami, FL.

Lorde, A. (1998a). Coal. In P. L. Hill (Ed.), *Call and response: The Riverside anthology of the African American literary tradition* (pp. 1626-1627). Boston: Houghton Mifflin. (Copyright © 1986 by Audre Lorde, from *Collected Poems* by Audre Lorde. Used by permission of W. W. Norton & Company, Inc.)

Lorde, A. (1998b). Power. In P. L. Hill (Ed.), *Call and response: The Riverside anthology of the African American literary tradition* (p. 1627). Boston: Houghton Mifflin. (Reprinted from A. Lorde, *The black unicorn: Poems,* 1978, New York: W. W. Norton)

Lorde, A. (1998c). Stations. In P. L. Hill (Ed.), *Call and response: The Riverside anthology of the African American literary tradition* (pp. 1630-1631). Boston: Houghton Mifflin. (Copyright © 1988 by Audre Lorde, from *Collected Poems* by Audre Lorde. Used by permission of W. W. Norton & Company, Inc.)

Lubiano, W. (1997). But, compared to what? Reading realism, representation, and essentialism in *School Daze, Do the Right Thing,* and the Spike Lee discourse. In V. Smith (Ed.), *Representing blackness: Issues in film and video* (pp. 1-12). New Brunswick, NJ: Rutgers University Press.

Marx, K. (1983). Theses on Feuerbach. In E. Kamenka (Ed.), *The portable Karl Marx* (pp. 155-158). New York: Penguin. (Original work published 1888)

Masilela, N. (1993). The Los Angeles school of black filmmakers. In M. Diawara (Ed.),

Black American cinema (pp. 107-117). New York: Routledge.

Mills, C. W. (1959). *The sociological imagination*. New York: Oxford University Press.

Mienczakowski, J. (1995). The reconstruction of ethnography into theater with emancipatory potential. *Qualitative Inquiry, 1,* 360-375.

Neal, L. (1988). *Visions of a liberated future.* New York: Thunder's Mouth.

Neal, L. (1998). The black arts movement. In P. L. Hill (Ed.), *Call and response: The Riverside anthology of the African American literary tradition* (pp. 1450-1458). Boston: Houghton Mifflin. (Reprinted from L. Neal, *Visions of a liberated future,* 1988, New York: Thunder's Mouth)

Nero, C. L. (1998). Toward a gay black aesthetic: Signifying in contemporary black gay literature. In P. L. Hill (Ed.), *Call and response: The Riverside anthology of the African American literary tradition* (pp. 1973-1987). Boston: Houghton Mifflin.

Noriega, C. A. (1992). Between a weapon and a formula: Chicano cinema and its contexts. In C. A. Noriega (Ed.), *Chicanos and film: Representation and resistance* (pp. 141-167). Minneapolis: University of Minnesota Press.

Noriega, C. A. (1996). Imagined borders: Locating Chicano cinema in America/America. In C. A. Noriega & A. M. López (Eds.), *The ethnic eye: Latino media arts* (pp. 3-21). Minneapolis: University of Minnesota Press.

Paget, M. A. (1993). *A complex sorrow* (M. L. DeVault, Ed.). Philadelphia: Temple University Press.

Parker, L. (1998). Race is . . . race ain't: An exploration of the utility of critical race theory in qualitative research in education. *International Journal of Qualitative Studies in Education, 11,* 43-55.

Parker, L., Deyhle, D., Villenas, S., & Nebeker, K. C. (1998). Guest editors' introduction: Critical race theory and qualitative studies in education. *International Journal of Qualitative Studies in Education, 11,* 5-6.

Pizarro, M. (1998). "Chicana/o power": Epistemology and methodology for social justice and empowerment in Chicana/o communities. *International Journal of Qualitative Studies in Education, 11,* 57-79.

Red Lodge Chamber of Commerce. (1982). *Festival of Nations, Red Lodge, Montana* [brochure]. Red Lodge, MT: Author.

Reason, P. (1993). Sacred experience and sacred science. *Journal of Management Inquiry, 2,* 10-27.

Reason, P. (Ed.). (1994). *Participation in human inquiry.* London: Sage.

Richardson, L. (1997). *Fields of play: Constructing an academic life.* New Brunswick, NJ: Rutgers University Press.

Richardson, M. (1998). Poetics in the field and on the page. *Qualitative Inquiry, 4,* 451-462.

Rinehart, R. (1998). Fictional methods in ethnography: Believability, specks of glass, and Chekhov. *Qualitative Inquiry, 4,* 200-224.

Ronai, C. R. (1998). Sketching with Derrida: An ethnography of a researcher/erotic dancer. *Qualitative Inquiry, 4,* 405-420.

Rorty, R. (1979). *Philosophy and the mirror of nature.* Princeton, NJ: Princeton University Press.

Rosen, J. (1994). Making things more public: On the political responsibility of the media intellectual. *Critical Studies in Mass Communication, 11,* 362-388.

Scheurich, J. J. (1997). *Research method in the postmodern.* London: Falmer.

Schwandt, T. A. (1997). Textual gymnastics, ethics and angst. In W. G. Tierney & Y. S. Lincoln (Eds.), *Representation and the text: Re-framing the narrative voice* (pp. 305-311). Albany: State University of New York Press.

Shange, N. (1977). *For colored girls who have considered suicide when the rainbow is enuf.* New York: Simon & Schuster. (Reprinted with the permission of Scribner, a Division of Simon & Schuster. Copyright © 1975, 1976, 1977 by Ntozake Shange.)

Sims, N. (1995). The art of literary journalism. In N. Sims & M. Kramer (Eds.), *Literary journalism: A new collection of the best American nonfiction* (pp. 3-19). New York: Ballantine.

Smith, A. D. (1993). *Fires in the mirror: Crown Heights, Brooklyn, and other identities.* Garden City, NY: Anchor. (Copyright © 1993 by Anna Deavere Smith. Used by permission of Doubleday, a division of Random House, Inc.)

Smith, A. D. (1994). *Twilight: Los Angeles, 1992.* Garden City, NY: Anchor.

Stern, C. S., & Henderson, B. (1993). *Performance texts and contexts*. New York: Longman.

Stringer, E. T. (1996). *Action research*. Thousand Oaks, CA: Sage.

Tierney, W. G. (1997). Lost in translation: Time and voice in qualitative research. In W. G. Tierney & Y. S. Lincoln (Eds.), *Representation and the text: Re-framing the narrative voice* (pp. 23-36). Albany: State University of New York Press.

Trinh T. M. (1992). *Framer framed*. New York: Routledge.

Turner, V. (1986). *The anthropology of performance*. New York: Performing Arts Journal Publications.

Ulmer, G. (1989). *Teletheory*. New York: Routledge.

West, C. (1993). Foreword. In A. D. Smith, *Fires in the mirror: Crown Heights, Brooklyn, and other identities* (pp. xvii-xxii). Garden City, NY: Anchor.

West, C. (1994). *Race matters*. New York: Vantage.

Wilkinson, C. (1997). Paradise revisited. In W. E. Reibsame (Ed.), *Atlas of the new West* (pp. 15-65). New York: W. W. Norton.

Wolfe, T. (1973). The new journalism. In T. Wolfe & E. W. Johnson (Eds.), *The new journalism: An anthology* (pp. 1-52). New York: Harper & Row.

36

WRITING

A Method of Inquiry

◆ Laurel Richardson

*The writer's object is—or should be—to hold the reader's attention. . . . I want the reader to turn
the page and keep on turning to the end.*

Barbara Tuchman, *New York Times,* February 2, 1989

In the spirit of affectionate irreverence toward qualitative research, I consider writing as a *method of inquiry,* a way of finding out about yourself and your topic. Although we usually think about writing as a mode of "telling" about the social world, writing is not just a mopping-up activity at the end of a research project. Writing is also a way of "knowing"—a method of discovery and analysis. By writing in different ways, we discover new aspects of our topic and our relationship to it. Form and content are inseparable.

Writing as a method of inquiry departs from standard social science practices. It offers an ad- ditional—or alternative—research practice. In standard social scientific discourse, methods for acquiring data are distinct from the writing of the research report, the latter presumed to be an unproblematic activity, a transparent report about the world studied. When we view writing as a *method,* however, we experience "language-in-use," how we "word the world" into existence (Rose, 1992). And then we "reword" the world, erase the computer screen, check the thesaurus, move a paragraph, again and again. This "worded world" never accurately, precisely, completely captures the studied world, yet we persist in trying. Writing as a method of

AUTHOR'S NOTE: I thank Ernest Lockridge for many discussions about this chapter, and his reading of it multiple times. I also thank Arthur Bochner, Norman Denzin, Carolyn Ellis, Michelle Fine, Patti Lather, Yvonna Lincoln, Meaghan Morris, and John Van Maanen for their generous and valuable critiques. And, finally, I am grateful to the many students who have told me they found the earlier version of this chapter useful; they have given me the energy and the will to revise it.

inquiry honors and encourages the trying, recognizing it as embryonic to the full-fledged attention to the significance of language.

Writing as a method of inquiry, then, provides a research practice through which we can investigate how we construct the world, ourselves, and others, and how standard objectifying practices of social science unnecessarily limit us and social science. Writing as method does not take writing for granted, but offers multiple ways to learn to do it, and to nurture the writer.

I have composed this chapter into two *equally* important, but differently formatted, sections. I emphasize the *equally* because the first section, an essay, has rhetorical advantages over its later-born sib. In the first section, "Writing in Contexts," I position myself as a reader/writer of qualitative research. Then, I discuss (a) the historical roots of social scientific writing, including its dependence upon metaphor and prescribed writing formats; (b) the postmodernist possibilities for qualitative writing, including creative analytic practices and their ethnographic products; and (c) the future of ethnography. In the second section, "Writing Practices," I offer a compendium of writing suggestions and exercises.

Necessarily, the chapter reflects my own process and preferences. I encourage researchers to explore their own processes and preferences through writing. Writing from our Selves should strengthen the community of qualitative researchers and the individual voices within it, because we will be more fully present in our work, more honest, more engaged.

◆ Writing in Contexts

I have a confession to make. For 30 years, I had yawned my way through numerous supposedly exemplary qualitative studies. Countless numbers of texts I abandoned half read, half scanned. I would order a new book with great anticipation—the topic was one I was interested in, the author was someone I wanted to read—

only to find the text boring. It was not that the writing was complex and difficult, but that it suffered from acute and chronic passivity: passive-voiced author, passive "subjects." "Coming out" to colleagues and students about my secret displeasure with much of qualitative writing, I found a community of like-minded discontents. Undergraduates, graduates, and colleagues alike say they have found much of qualitative writing—yes—boring.

We have a serious problem: Research topics are riveting and research valuable, but qualitative books are underread. Unlike quantitative work, which can be interpreted through its tables and summaries, qualitative work carries its meaning in its entire text. Just as a piece of literature is not equivalent to its "plot summary," qualitative research is not contained in its abstracts. Qualitative research has to be read, not scanned; its meaning is in the reading.

Qualitative work could be reaching wide and diverse audiences, not just devotees of individual topics or authors. It seems foolish at best, and narcissistic and wholly self-absorbed at worst, to spend months or years doing research that ends up not being read and not making a difference to anything but the author's career. Can something be done? That is the question that drives this chapter: How do we create texts that are vital? That are attended to? That make a difference? One way to create those texts is to turn our attention to writing as a method of inquiry.

I write because I want to find something out. I write in order to learn something that I did not know before I wrote it. I was taught, however, as perhaps you were, too, not to write until I knew what I wanted to say, until my points were organized and outlined. No surprise, this static writing model coheres with mechanistic scientism and quantitative research. But, I will argue, this static writing model is itself a sociohistorical invention that reifies the static social world imagined by our 19th-century foreparents. The model has serious problems: It ignores the role of writing as a dynamic, creative process; it undermines the confidence of beginning qualitative researchers because their experience of research is inconsistent with the writing model;

and it contributes to the flotilla of qualitative writing that is simply not interesting to read because adherence to the model requires writers to silence their own voices and to view themselves as contaminants.

Qualitative researchers commonly speak of the importance of the individual researcher's skills and aptitudes. The researcher—rather than the survey, the questionnaire, or the census tape—is the "instrument." The more honed the researcher, the better the possibility of excellent research. Students are taught to be open, to observe, listen, question, and participate. Yet they are taught to conceptualize writing as "writing-up" the research, rather than as an open place, a method of discovery. Promulgating "writing-up" validates a mechanistic model of writing, shutting down the creativity and sensibilities of the individual writer/researcher.

One reason, then, that some of our texts may be boring is that our sense of Self is diminished as we are homogenized through professional socialization, rewards, and punishments. Homogenization occurs through the suppression of individual voices and the acceptance of the omniscient voice of science as if it were our own. How do we put ourselves in our own texts, and with what consequences? How do we nurture our own individuality and at the same time lay claim to "knowing" something? These are both philosophically and practically difficult problems.

Historical Contexts: Writing Conventions

Language is a constitutive force, creating a particular view of reality and of the Self. Producing "things" always involves value—what to produce, what to name the productions, and what the relationship between the producers and the named things will be. Writing "things" is no exception. No textual staging is ever innocent (including this one). Styles of writing are neither fixed nor neutral but reflect the historically shifting domination of particular schools or paradigms. Social scientific writing, like all

other forms of writing, is a sociohistorical construction, and, therefore, mutable.

Since the 17th century, the world of writing has been divided into two separate kinds: literary and scientific. Literature, from the 17th century onward, was associated with fiction, rhetoric, and subjectivity, whereas science was associated with fact, "plain language," and objectivity (Clifford, 1986, p. 5). Fiction was "false" because it invented reality, unlike science, which was "true" because it purportedly "reported" "objective" reality in an unambiguous voice.

During the 18th century, assaults upon literature intensified. John Locke cautioned adults to forgo figurative language lest the "conduit" between "things" and "thought" be obstructed. David Hume depicted poets as professional liars. Jeremy Bentham proposed that the ideal language would be one without words, only unambiguous symbols. Samuel Johnson's dictionary sought to fix "univocal meanings in perpetuity, much like the univocal meanings of standard arithmetic terms" (Levine, 1985, p. 4).

Into this linguistic world the Marquis de Condorcet introduced the term *social science*. He contended that "knowledge of the truth" would be "easy and error almost impossible" if one adopted precise language about moral and social issues (quoted in Levine, 1985, p. 6). By the 19th century, literature and science stood as two separate domains. Literature was aligned with "art" and "culture"; it contained the values of "taste, aesthetics, ethics, humanity, and morality" (Clifford, 1986, p. 6) and the rights to metaphoric and ambiguous language. Given to science was the belief that its words were objective, precise, unambiguous, noncontextual, and nonmetaphoric.

But because literary writing was taking a second seat to science in importance, status, impact, and truth value, some literary writers attempted to make literature a part of science. By the late 19th century, "realism" dominated both science and fiction writing (Clough, 1992). Honoré de Balzac spearheaded the realism movement in literature. He viewed society as an "historical organism" with "social species" akin to "zoological species." Writers deserving of praise, he contended, must investigate "the reasons or causes" of "social effects"—the "first principles" upon which society is based (Balzac, 1842/1965, pp. 247-249). For Balzac, the novel was an "instrument of scientific inquiry" (Crawford, 1951, p. 7). Following Balzac's lead, Emile Zola argued for "naturalism" in literature. In his famous essay "The Novel as Social Science," he argued that the "return to nature, the naturalistic evolution which marks the century, drives little by little all the manifestation of human intelligence into the same scientific path." Literature is to be "governed by science" (Zola, 1880/1965, p. 271).

As the 20th century unfolded, the relationships between social scientific writing and literary writing grew in complexity. The presumed solid demarcations between "fact" and "fiction" and between "true" and "imagined" were blurred. The blurring was most hotly debated around writing for the public—or journalism. In what Tom Wolfe dubbed the "new journalism," writers consciously blurred the boundaries between "fact" and "fiction" and consciously made themselves the center of the story. (For an excellent extended discussion of the new journalism, see Denzin, 1997, chap. 5.)

New journalists also encroached upon ethnography's province, borrowing its methods and reporting social and cultural life not as "reporters," but as social analysts. Joining those trespassers were fiction writers such as Truman Capote, Joan Didion, and Norman Mailer. Professors of literature awakened and reawakened interest in novels by minority and postcolonial writers by positioning them as "ethnographic novels"—narratives that tell about cultures through characters (see Ba, 1987; Hurston, 1942/1991).

By the 1970s, "crossovers" between writing forms spawned the naming of oxymoronic genres: "creative nonfiction," "faction," "ethnographic fiction," the "nonfiction novel," and "true fiction." By 1980, the novelist E. L. Doctorow would assert, "There is no longer any such things as fiction or nonfiction, there is only narrative" (quoted in Fishkin, 1985, p. 7).

Despite the actual blurring of genres, and despite our contemporary understanding that all

writing is narrative writing, I would contend that there is still one major difference separating fiction from science writing. The difference is not whether the text *really* is fiction or nonfiction, but the claim the author makes for the text. Claiming to write "fiction" is different from claiming to write "science" in terms of the audience one seeks, the impact one might have on different publics, and how one expects "truth claims" to be evaluated. These differences should not be overlooked or minimized.

Whenever there are changes in writing styles and formats, we can expect intellectual interest in documenting and tracing those changes. Today, scholars in a host of disciplines are tracing the relationships between scientific and literary writing and are deconstructing the differences between them (see Agger, 1989; Brodkey, 1987; Brown, 1977; Clough, 1992; Edmondson, 1984; Mishler, 1989; Nelson, Megill, & McCloskey, 1987; Simons, 1990). Their deconstructive analyses concretely show how all disciplines have their own sets of literary devices—not necessarily *fiction writing* devices—and rhetorical appeals such as probability tables, archival records, and first-person accounts.

Each social science writing convention could be discussed at length, but I will address here only (a) metaphor and (b) writing format. I choose these conventions because they are omnipresent, and because I believe they are good sites for experimenting with writing as a method of inquiry (see the section headed "Writing Practices").

Metaphor

Metaphor, a literary device, is the backbone of social science writing. Like the spine, it bears weight, permits movement, is buried beneath the surface, and links parts together into a functional, coherent whole. As this metaphor about metaphor suggests, the essence of metaphor is experiencing and understanding one thing in terms of another. This is accomplished through comparison (e.g., "My love is like a green, green toad") or analogy (e.g. "the evening of life").

Social scientific writing uses metaphors at every "level." Social science depends upon a deep epistemic code regarding the way "that knowledge and understanding in general are figured" (Shapiro, 1985-1986, p. 198). Metaphors external to a particular piece of research prefigure the analysis with a "truth-value" code belonging to another domain (Jameson, 1981). For example, the use of *enlighten* for knowledge is a light-based metaphor, what Derrida (1982) refers to as the heliocentric view of knowledge, the passive receipt of rays. Immanent in such metaphors are philosophical and value commitments so entrenched and familiar that they can do their partisan work in the guise of neutrality, passing as literal.

Theoretical schemata are always situated in complex, systematic metaphors. Consider the following statements about theory (examples inspired by Lakoff & Johnson, 1980, p. 46):

- What is the *foundation* of your theory?
- Your theory needs *support*.
- Your position is *shaky*.
- Your argument is *falling apart*.
- Let's *construct* an argument.
- The *form* of your argument needs *buttressing*.
- Given your *framework,* no wonder your argument *fell apart*.

The italicized words express our customary, unconscious use of the metaphor "Theory is architecture." The metaphor, moreover, structures the actions we take in theorizing and what we believe constitutes theory. We try to *build* a theoretical *structure,* which we then experience as a *structure,* which has a *form* and a *foundation,* which we then experience as an *edifice,* sometimes quite *grand,* sometimes in need of *shoring up,* and sometimes in need of *dismantling,* or, more recently, *deconstructing.*

Historically, theory constructors have *deployed* combative metaphors. *Sport, game,* and *war* are common ones. These metaphoric schemes do not resonate with many women's interests, and, in addition, they have contributed to an academic intellectual culture of hos-

tility, argumentativeness, and confrontation. In the 1970s, feminist researchers introduced and acted upon a different metaphor: "Theory is story." Not only is the personal the political, the personal is the grounding for theory. With the new metaphor for their work, many feminists altered their research and writing practices; women talking about their experience, narrativizing their lives, telling individual and collective stories became understood as women *theorizing* their lives. The boundary between "narrative" and "analysis" dissolved.

Metaphors are everywhere. Consider *functionalism, role* theory, *game* theory, *dramaturgical* analogy, *organicism,* social *evolutionism,* the social *system, ecology, labeling* theory, *equilibrium, human capital, resource mobilization,* ethnic *insurgency, developing* countries, *stratification* and *significance* tests. Metaphors organize social scientific work and affect the interpretations of the "facts"; indeed, facts are interpretable ("make sense") only in terms of their place within a metaphoric structure. The "sense making" is always value constituting—making sense in a particular way, privileging one ordering of the "facts" over others.

Writing Format

In addition to the metaphoric basis of social scientific writing, there are prescribed writing formats: How we are expected to write affects what we can write about. The referencing system in social science, for example, discourages the use of footnotes, a place for secondary arguments, novel conjectures, and related ideas. Knowledge is constituted as "focused," "problem" (hypothesis) centered, "linear," straightforward. Other thoughts are extraneous. Inductively accomplished research is to be reported deductively; the argument is to be abstracted in 150 words or less; and researchers are to identify explicitly with a theoretical label. Each of these conventions favors—creates and sustains—a particular vision of what constitutes knowledge. The conventions hold tremendous material and symbolic power over social scientists. Using them increases the probability of one's work being accepted into "core" social science journals, but they are not prima facie evidence of greater—or lesser—truth value or significance than social science writing using other conventions.

Additional social science writing conventions have governed ethnographies. Needful of distinguishing their work from travelers' and missionaries' reports as well as from imaginative writing, ethnographers adopted an impersonal, third-person voice to explain "observed phenomena" and to trumpet the authenticity of their representations (see Tedlock, Chapter 17, this volume). John Van Maanen (1988) identifies four conventions used in traditional ethnographies, or "realist tales": (a) *experiential author(ity),* where the author exists only in the preface to establish "I was there" and "I am a researcher" credentials; (b) *documentary style,* or a plethora of concrete, particular details that presume to represent the typical activity, pattern, culture member; (c) *the culture member's point of view,* putatively presented through quotations, explanations, syntax, cultural clichés, and so on; and (d) *interpretive omnipotence* of the ethnographer. Many of the classic books in the social sciences are realist tales. These include Kai Erikson's *Everything in Its Path* (1976), William Foote Whyte's *Street Corner Society* (1943), Elliot Liebow's *Tally's Corner* (1967), and Carol Stack's *All Our Kin* (1974).

Other genres of qualitative writing—such as texts based on life histories or in-depth interviews—have their own sets of traditional conventions (see Mishler, 1989; Richardson, 1990). In these qualitative texts, researchers establish their credentials in the introductory or methods section; they write the body of the text as though the document and quotation snippets are naturally present, valid, reliable, and fully representative, rather than selected, pruned, and spruced up by the author for their textual appearance. As in cultural ethnographies, the assumption of *scientific authority* is rhetorically displayed in these other qualitative texts. Examples of conventional "life story" texts include Lillian Rubin's *Worlds of Pain* (1976), Sharon Kaufman's *The Ageless Self* (1986), and my own *The New Other Woman* (Richardson, 1985).

Postmodernist Context

We are fortunate, now, to be working in a postmodernist climate (see Agger, 1990; Clifford & Marcus, 1986; Denzin, 1986, 1991, 1995; Hutcheon, 1988; Lehman, 1991; Lyotard, 1984; Nicholson, 1990; Turner & Bruner, 1986), a time when a multitude of approaches to knowing and telling exist side by side. The core of postmodernism is the *doubt* that any method or theory, discourse or genre, tradition or novelty, has a universal and general claim as the "right" or the privileged form of authoritative knowledge. Postmodernism *suspects* all truth claims of masking and serving particular interests in local, cultural, and political struggles. But it does not automatically reject conventional methods of knowing and telling as false or archaic. Rather, it opens those standard methods to inquiry and introduces new methods, which are also, then, subject to critique.

The postmodernist context of *doubt,* then, distrusts all methods equally. No method has a privileged status. The superiority of "science" over "literature"—or, from another vantage point, "literature" over "science"—is challenged. But a postmodernist position does allow us to know "something" without claiming to know everything. Having a partial, local, historical knowledge is still knowing. In some ways, "knowing" is easier, however, because postmodernism recognizes the situational limitations of the knower. Qualitative writers are off the hook, so to speak. They don't have to try to play God, writing as disembodied omniscient narrators claiming universal, atemporal general knowledge; they can eschew the questionable metanarrative of scientific objectivity and still have plenty to say as situated speakers, subjectivities engaged in knowing/telling about the world as they perceive it.

A particular kind of postmodernist thinking that I have found especially helpful is *poststructuralism* (for an overview, see Weedon, 1987; for application of the perspective in a research setting, see Davies, 1994). Poststructuralism links language, subjectivity, social organization, and power. The centerpiece is language. Language does not "reflect" social reality, but produces meaning, creates social reality. Different languages and different discourses within a given language divide up the world and give it meaning in ways that are not reducible to one another. Language is how social organization and power are defined and contested and the place where our sense of selves, our *subjectivity,* is constructed. Understanding language as competing discourses, competing ways of giving meaning and of organizing the world, makes language a site of exploration and struggle.

Language is not the result of one's individuality; rather, language constructs the individual's subjectivity in ways that are historically and locally specific. What something means to individuals is dependent on the discourses available to them. For example, being hit by one's spouse is differently experienced if it is thought of within the discourse of "normal marriage," "husbands' rights," or "wife battering." If a woman sees male violence as "normal" or a "husband's right," then she is unlikely to see it as "wife battering," an illegitimate use of power that should not be tolerated. Similarly, when a man is exposed to the discourse of "childhood sexual abuse," he may recategorize and remember his own traumatic childhood experiences. Experience and memory are thus open to contradictory interpretations governed by social interests and prevailing discourses. The individual is both site and subject of these discursive struggles for identity and for remaking memory. Because individuals are subject to multiple and competing discourses in many realms, their subjectivity is shifting and contradictory, not stable, fixed, rigid.

Poststructuralism thus points to the *continual cocreation of Self and social science:* Each is known through the other. Knowing the self and knowing about the subject are intertwined, partial, historical, local knowledges. Poststructuralism, then, permits—nay, invites—no, incites—us to reflect upon our method and explore new ways of knowing.

Specifically, poststructuralism suggests two important things to qualitative writers: First, it directs us to understand ourselves reflexively as persons writing from particular positions at specific times; and second, it frees us from trying to write a single text in which we say everything at once to everyone. Nurturing our own voices releases the censorious hold of "science writing" on our consciousness, as well as the arrogance it fosters in our psyche: Writing is validated as a method of knowing.

Creative Analytic Practices: CAP Ethnography

In the wake of postmodernist—including poststructuralist, feminist, queer, and critical race theory—critiques of traditional qualitative writing practices, qualitative work now appears in multiple venues in different forms. Science-writing prose is not held sacrosanct. The ethnographic genre has been blurred, enlarged, altered to include poetry, drama, conversations, readers' theater, and so on. These ethnographies are like each other in that they are produced through *creative analytic practices.* I have settled upon calling this class of ethnographies *creative analytic practice ethnography,* or *CAP ethnography.* This label can include new work, future work, and older work, wherever the author has moved outside conventional social scientific writing.

I know that any concept or acronym is problematic, subject to critique. Yet the more I thought about what to name these genre-breaking ethnographies, the more I liked the complex metaphoric resonances of the acronym CAP. The English word *cap* comes from the Latin for head, *caput.* Using "head" to signal ethnographic breaching work can help break down the mind/body duality. The "head" is both mind and body and more, too. Producers of CAP ethnography are using their "heads." The products, although mediated throughout the body, cannot manifest without "headwork."

Cap—both noun (product) and verb (process)—has multiple common and idiomatic meanings and associations, some of which refract the playfulness of the genre: a rounded head covering; a special head covering indicating occupation or membership in a particular group; the top of a building, or fungus; a small explosive charge; any of several sizes of writing paper; putting the final touches on; lying on top of; surpassing, outdoing. And then there are the other associated words from the Latin root, such as *capillary* and *capital(ism)*, which humble and contextualize the labor.

The practices that produce CAP ethnography are *both* creative *and* analytic. Those holding the dinosaurian belief that "creative" and "analytic" are contradictory and incompatible modes are standing in the path of a meteor. They are doomed for extinction. Witness the evolution, proliferation, and diversity of new ethnographic "species" during the past two decades.

Here is but a sampling of the many "species" of CAP ethnography: *autoethnography* (Behar, 1993, 1996; Bruner, 1996; Church, 1995; Ellis, 1993, 1995a, 1995b, 1998; Frank, 1995; Geertz, 1988; Gerla, 1995; Goetting & Fenstermaker, 1995; Karp, 1996; Kondo, 1990; Krieger, 1991, 1996; Lawrence-Lightfoot, 1994; McMahon, 1996; Shostak, 1996; Slobin, 1995; Steedman, 1986; Yu, 1997; Zola, 1982), *fiction-stories* (Cherry, 1995; Diversi, 1998a, 1998b; Frohock, 1992; Richardson & Lockridge, 1998; Rinehart, 1998; Shelton, 1995; Sparkes, 1997; Stewart, 1989; Williams, 1991; Wilson, 1965; Wolf, 1992), *poetry* (Baff, 1997; Brady, 1991; Diamond, 1982; Glesne, 1997; Norum, in press; Patai, 1988; Prattis, 1985; Richardson, 1992a), *drama* (Ellis & Bochner, 1992; Paget, 1990; Richardson, 1993, 1996a; Richardson & Lockridge, 1991), *performance texts* (Denzin, 1997; McCall & Becker, 1990; Mienczakowski, 1996; Richardson, 1998, 1999a, 1999b), *polyvocal texts* (see Butler & Rosenblum, 1991; Daly & Dienhart, 1998; Krieger, 1983; Pandolfo, 1997; Schneider, 1991), *readers' theater* (see Donmoyer & Yennie-Donmoyer, 1995), *responsive readings* (see Richardson, 1992b), *aphorisms* (Rose, 1992, 1993), *comedy and satire* (see Barley, 1986, 1988), *visual presentations* (see Harper, 1987; Jacobs, 1984; McCall, Gammel, & Taylor, 1994), *allegory* (Lawton, 1997, pp. 193-214), *conversation* (see Ellis & Bochner, 1996b; Richardson & Lockridge, 1998), *layered accounts* (Jago, 1996; Ronai, 1992, 1995), *writing-stories* (see Lawton, 1997; Richardson, 1995, 1997; St. Pierre, 1997a, 1997b), and *mixed genres* (see Angrosino, 1998; Brown,

1991; Church, 1999: Davies, 1989; Dorst, 1989; Fine, 1992; hooks, 1990; Jipson & Paley, 1997; Jones, 1998; Lather, 1991; Lather & Smithies, 1997; Lee, 1996; Linden, 1992; Pfohl, 1992; Richardson, 1997; Rose, 1989; Stoller, 1989; Trinh, 1989; Ulmer, 1989; Visweswaran, 1994; Walkerdine, 1990; Williams, 1991; Wolf, 1992).

For more than a decade, what I am calling CAP ethnography has been labeled *experimental* or *alternative* (see Van Maanen, 1995). Unintentionally, however, those labels have reinscribed traditional ethnographic practices as the standard, the known, accepted, preferred, tried-and-true mode of doing and representing qualitative research. I believe that reinscription is now unnecessary, false, and deleterious. CAP ethnographies are not alternative or experimental; they are in and of themselves valid and desirable representations of the social. Into the foreseeable future, these ethnographies may indeed be the most valid and desirable representations, for they invite people in; they open spaces for thinking about the social that elude us now.

CAP ethnography displays the *writing process* and the *writing product* as deeply intertwined; both are privileged. The product cannot be separated from the producer or the mode of production or the method of knowing. Because all research—traditional and CAP ethnography—is now produced within the broader postmodernist climate of "doubt," readers (and reviewers) want and deserve to know how the researcher claims to know. How does the author position the Self as a knower and teller? These questions engage intertwined problems of subjectivity, authority, authorship, reflexivity, and process on the one hand and representational form on the other.

Postmodernism claims that writing is always partial, local, and situational, and that our Self is always present, no matter how much we try to suppress it—but only partially present, for in our writing we repress parts of ourselves, too. Working from that premise frees us to write material in a variety of ways: to tell and retell. There is no such thing as "getting it right"—

only "getting it" differently contoured and nuanced. When using creative analytic practices, ethnographers learn about their topics and about themselves that which was unknowable and unimaginable using conventional analytic procedures, metaphors, and writing formats. Even if one chooses to write an article in a conventional form, trying on different modes of writing is a practical and powerful way to expand one's interpretive skills, raise one's consciousness, and bring a fresh perspective to one's research.

It is beyond this chapter's scope for me to outline or comment here on the scores of new ethnographic practices and forms. And it is far beyond that scope for me to discuss practices that exceed the written page—performance pieces, readers' theater, museum displays, choreographed research findings, fine-art representations, hypertexts, and so on—although I welcome these additions to the qualitative repertoire. Instead, I will address a class of genres that deploy literary devices to re-create lived experience and evoke emotional responses. I call these *evocative representations*. I resist providing the reader with snippets from these forms, because snippets will not do them justice. I will describe some texts, but I have no - desire to valorize a new canon. Again, *process* rather than product is the purpose of this chapter.

Evocative forms display interpretive frameworks that demand analysis of themselves as cultural products and as methods for rendering the social. Evocative representations are a striking way of seeing through and beyond social scientific naturalisms. Casting social science into evocative forms reveals the rhetoric and the underlying labor of the production, as well as social science's potential as a human endeavor, because evocative writing touches us where we live, in our bodies. Through it we can experience the self-reflexive and transformational process of self-creation. Trying out evocative forms, we relate differently to our material; we know it differently. We find ourselves attending to feelings, ambiguities, temporal sequences, blurred experiences, and so on; we

struggle to find a textual place for ourselves and our doubts and uncertainties.

One form of evocative writing is *autoethnography*. (This topic is fully covered by Ellis & Bochner in Chapter 28 of this volume; see also Fine et al., Chapter 4.) Autoethnographies are highly personalized, revealing texts in which authors tell stories about their own lived experiences, relating the personal to the cultural. The power of these narratives depends upon their rhetorical staging as "true stories," stories about events that really happened to the writers. In telling these stories, the writers call upon such fiction-writing techniques as dramatic recall, strong imagery, fleshed-out characters, unusual phrasings, puns, subtexts, allusions, flashbacks and flashforwards, tone shifts, synecdoche, dialogue, and interior monologue. Through these techniques, the writers construct sequences of events, or "plots," holding back on interpretation, asking readers to "relive" the events emotionally, with the writers. These narratives seek to meet literary criteria of coherence, verisimilitude, and interest. Some narratives of the Self are staged as imaginative renderings; others are staged as personal essays, striving for honesty, revelation, the "larger picture." In either case, autoethnographers are somewhat relieved of the problem of speaking for the "Other," because they are the "Other" in their texts.

Related to autoethnography without necessarily invoking the writing strategies mentioned above are narratives about the writing process itself. I call these *writing-stories* (Richardson, 1997). These are narratives about contexts in which the writing is produced. They situate the author's writing in other parts of the author's life, such as disciplinary constraints, academic debates, departmental politics, social movements, community structures, research interests, familial ties, and personal history. They offer critical reflexivity about the writing-self in different contexts as a valuable creative analytic practice. They evoke new questions about the self and the subject; they remind us that our work is grounded, contextual, and rhizomatic. They can evoke deeper parts of the Self, heal wounds, enhance the sense of self—or even alter one's sense of identity.

In *Fields of Play: Constructing an Academic Life* (1997), I make extensive use of writing-stories to contextualize 10 years of my sociological work, creating a text more congruent with poststructural understandings of the situated nature of knowledge. Putting my papers and essays in the chronological order in which they were conceptualized, I sorted them into two piles—"keeper" and "reject." When I reread my first keeper—a presidential address to the North Central Sociological Association—memories of being patronized, marginalized, and punished by my department chair and dean reemerged. I stayed with those memories and wrote a writing-story about the disjunction between my departmental life and my disciplinary reputation. Writing the story was not emotionally easy; in the writing I was reliving horrific experiences, but writing it released the anger and pain. Many academics who read that story recognize it as congruent with their experiences, their untold stories.

I worked chronologically through the keeper pile, rereading and then writing the writing-story evoked by the rereading. Different facets, different contexts. Some stories required checking my journals and files, but most did not. Some stories were painful and took an interminable length of time to write, but writing them loosened their shadow hold on me. Other stories are joyful and remind me of the good fortunes I have in friends, colleagues, family.

Writing-stories sensitize us to the potential consequences of all of our writing by bringing home—inside our homes and workplaces—the ethics of representation. Writing-stories are not about people and cultures "out there"—ethnographic subjects (or objects)—they are about ourselves, our work spaces, disciplines, friends, and families. What can we say? With what consequences? Writing-stories bring the danger and poignancy of ethnographic representation up close and personal.

Each writing-story offers its writer an opportunity to make a situated and pragmatic ethical decision about whether and where to publish the story. For the most part, I have found no ethical problem in publishing stories that reflect the abuse of power by administrators; I consider the damage done by them far greater than any discomfort my stories might cause them. In contrast, I feel constraint when writing about my family members. Anything I have published about them, I have checked out with them; in the case of more distant family members, I have changed their names and identifying characteristics. Some of my recent writing I will not publish for a while because it would be too costly to me and my familial relations to do so.

Graduate students have found the idea of the writing-story useful for thinking through and writing about their research experiences. Some use the writing-story as an alternative or supplement to the traditional methods chapter and, as Judith Lawton (1997) has done, to link the narratives of those they have researched.

Yet to be developed as a subgenre of writing-stories are what we might call *microprocess writing-stories* (see also Meloy, 1993). Who has not looked at the computer screen, read a paragraph he or she has written, and then chosen to alter it? Who has not had their subsequent writing affected by what they have already written? How does the process of writing passages and reading them back to yourself "open new questions and issues that feed back and emanate from the earlier passages?" (A. P. Bochner, personal communication, May 10, 1998). How is a changed Self evoked through the hands-on/ eyes-on feedback process?

Related to this subgenre is computer technology and the textual page layout: typefaces, font sizes, split pages, boxed inserts, running bottom text, images, frames. How are choices made? With what impact on the producer and the reader? How does the ease of manipulating page formats and typographical style contribute to—or distract from—the evocativeness of the text? Authors' discoveries about their topics and themselves? These are questions looking for writing-stories.

Unlike the two forms discussed above, an evocative form about which there is an extensive literature is *ethnographic fiction* (see Banks & Banks, 1998). (For a more extended discussion of this and other narrative forms, see Tedlock, Chapter 17, this volume.) "Fiction writing," according to novelist Ernest Lockridge (personal communication, 1998), "is using the imagination to discover and embody truth." Social science writers who claim that their work is fiction privilege their imaginations, seeking to express their visions of social scientific "truth." Usually they encase their stories—whether about themselves or a group or culture—in settings they have studied ethnographically; they display cultural norms through their characters. In addition to the techniques used by self-narrators (see above), ethnographic fiction writers might draw upon devices such as alternative points of view, deep characterization, third-person voice, and the omniscient narrator. (I do not think any ethnographic fiction writers, yet, write from the point of view of the unreliable narrator; see Lockridge, 1987.)

There are some advantages and some disadvantages to claiming one's ethnographic writing is fiction. Staging qualitative research as fiction frees the author from some constraints, protects the author from criminal or other charges, and may protect the identities of those studied. But competing in the publishing world of "literary fiction" is very difficult. Few succeed. Moreover, if one's desire is to effect social change through one's research, fiction is a rhetorically poor writing strategy. Policy makers prefer materials that claim to be not "nonfiction" even, but "true research."

Another evocative form is *poetic representation*. A poem, as Robert Frost articulates it, is "the shortest emotional distance between two points"—the speaker and the reader. Writing sociological interviews as poetry, for example, displays the role of the *prose trope* in constituting knowledge. When we read or hear poetry, we are continually nudged into recognizing that the text has been constructed. But all texts are constructed—prose ones, too; therefore, poetry helps problematize reliability, validity, transparency, and "truth."

Writing "data" as poetic representations reveals the constraining belief that the purpose of a social science text is to convey information as facts or themes or notions existing independent of the contexts in which they were found or produced—as if the story we have recorded, transcribed, edited, and written up in prose snippets is the one and only true one: a "science" story. Standard prose writing conceals the handprint of the sociologist who produced the final written text.

When people talk, moreover, whether as conversants, storytellers, informants, or interviewees, their speech is closer to poetry than it is to sociological prose (Tedlock, 1983). Writing up interviews as poems, honoring the speaker's pauses, repetitions, alliterations, narrative strategies, rhythms, and so on, may actually better represent the speaker than the practice of quoting in prose snippets. Further, poetic devices—rhythms, silences, spaces, breath points, alliterations, meter, cadence, assonance, rhyme, and off-rhyme—engage the listener's body, even if the mind resists and denies. "Poetry is above all a concentration of the power of language which is the power of our ultimate relationship to everything in the universe. It is as if forces we can lay claim to in no other way become present to us in sensuous form" (DeShazer, 1986, p. 138). Settling words together in new configurations lets us hear, see, and *feel* the world in new dimensions. Poetry is thus a *practical* and *powerful* method for analyzing social worlds.

"Louisa May's Story of Her Life" is an example of poetic construction that challenges epistemological assumptions (Richardson, 1997). It is a 5-page narrative poem I created from a 36-page transcript of my in-depth interview with "Louisa May," an unwed mother. In writing Louisa May's story, I drew upon both scientific and literary criteria. This was a greater literary challenge than a sociological one because Louisa May used no images or sensory words and very few idioms. The poem, therefore, had to build upon other poetic devices, such as repetition, pauses, meter, rhyme, and off-rhyme. Without putting words in her mouth, which would violate my sociological sensibilities, I used her voice, diction, hill-southern rhythms, and tone. I wrote her life—as she told it to me—as a historically situated exemplar of sense making. Her life, as she speaks it, is a "normal one." The political subtext, as I wrote it, is "Mother Courage in America."

Ethnographic drama is another evocative way of shaping an experience without losing the experience. It can blend realist, fictional, and poetic techniques; it can reconstruct the "sense" of an event from multiple "as-lived" perspectives; it can allow all the conflicting "voices" to be heard, relieving the researcher of having to be judge and arbiter (Davies et al., 1997; Johnston, 1997); and it can give voice to what is unspoken but present, for example, "cancer" as portrayed in Paget's (1990) ethnographic drama or abortion as in Ellis and Bochner's (1992) drama. When the material to be displayed is intractable, unruly, multisited, and emotionally laden, drama is more likely to recapture the experience than is standard writing.

Constructing drama raises the postmodern debates about "oral" and "written" texts. Which comes first? Which one should be (is) privileged, and with what consequences? Why the bifurcation between "oral" and "written"? Originating in the lived experience, encoded as field notes, transformed into an ethnographic play, performed, taped-recorded, and then re-edited for publication, the printed script might well be fancied the definitive or "valid" version, particularly to those who privilege the published over the "original," the performance, or even the lived experience. What happens if we accept this validity claim? Dramatic construction provides multiple sites of invention and potential contestation for validity, the blurring of oral and written texts, rhetorical moves, ethical dilemmas, and authority/authorship. It doesn't just "talk about" these issues, *it is* these issues (see Davies et al., 1997; Johnston, 1997; Richardson, 1997).

A last evocative form to consider is *mixed genres*. The scholar draws freely in his or her productions from literary, artistic, and scientific genres, often breaking the boundaries of each of those as well. In these productions, the scholar might have different "takes" on the same topic, what I think of as a postmodernist deconstruction of triangulation.

In traditionally staged research, we valorize "triangulation." (For discussion of triangulation

as method, see Denzin, 1978; Flick, 1998. For an application, see Statham, Richardson, & Cook, 1991). In triangulation, a researcher deploys "different methods"—such as interviews, census data, and documents—to "validate" findings. These methods, however, carry the *same domain* assumptions, including the assumption that there is a "fixed point" or "object" that can be triangulated. But in postmodernist mixed-genre texts, we do not triangulate; we *crystallize*. We recognize that there are far more than "three sides" from which to approach the world.

I propose that the central imaginary for "validity" for postmodernist texts is not the triangle—a rigid, fixed, two-dimensional object. Rather, the central imaginary is the crystal, which combines symmetry and substance with an infinite variety of shapes, substances, transmutations, multidimensionalities, and angles of approach. Crystals grow, change, alter, but are not amorphous. Crystals are prisms that reflect externalities *and* refract within themselves, creating different colors, patterns, and arrays, casting off in different directions. What we see depends upon our angle of repose. Not triangulation, crystallization. In postmodernist mixed-genre texts, we have moved from plane geometry to light theory, where light can be *both* waves *and* particles.

Crystallization, without losing structure, deconstructs the traditional idea of "validity" (we feel how there is no single truth, we see how texts validate themselves), and crystallization provides us with a deepened, complex, thoroughly partial, understanding of the topic. Paradoxically, we know more and doubt what we know. Ingeniously, we know there is always more to know.

The construction and reception of the narrative poem mentioned above, "Louisa May's Story of Her Life" (Richardson, 1997), is emblematic of crystallization. That work generated alternate theories and perspectives for writing and for living, deconstructed traditional notions of validity, glancingly touching some projects, lighting others. My life has been deeply altered through the research and writing of the poem, and "Louisa May" has touched wide and diverse audiences, even inspiring some to change their research and writing practices.

In one section of *Fields of Play* (1997), I tell two interwoven stories of "writing illegitimacy": Louisa May's story and the research story—its production, dissemination, reception, and consequences for me. There are multiple illegitimacies in the stories: a child out of wedlock; poetic representation of research findings; a feminine voice in social sciences; ethnographic research on ethnographers and dramatic representation of that research; emotional presence of the writer; and work *jouissance*.

I had thought the research story was complete, not necessarily the only story that could be told, but one that reflected fairly, honestly, and sincerely what my research experiences have been. I still believe that. But missing from the research story, I came to realize, were the personal, biographical experiences that led me to author such a story.

The idea of "illegitimacy," I have come to acknowledge, has had a compelling hold on me. In my research journal I wrote, "My career in the social sciences might be viewed as one long adventure into illegitimacies." I asked myself, Why am I drawn to constructing "texts of illegitimacy," including the text of my academic life? What is this struggle I have with the academy—being in it and against it at the same time? How is my story like and unlike the stories of others struggling to make sense of themselves, to retrieve suppressed selves, to act ethically?

Refracting "illegitimacy" through allusions, glimpses, extended views, I came to write a personal essay, "Vespers," the final essay in *Fields of Play*. "Vespers" located my academic life in childhood experiences and memories; it deepened my knowledge of myself and has resonated with others' experiences in academia. In turn, the writing of "Vespers" has refracted, again, giving me desire, strength, and enough self-knowledge to narrativize other memories and experiences—to give myself agency, to construct myself anew, for better or for worse.

We also see this crystallization process in several recent mixed-genre books. Margery

Wolf, in *A Thrice-Told Tale* (1992), takes the same event and tells it as fictional story, field notes, and a social scientific paper. John Stewart, in *Drinkers, Drummers and Decent Folk* (1989), writes poetry, fiction, ethnographic accounts, and field notes about Village Trinidad. In *Schoolgirl Fictions* (1990), Valerie Walkerdine develops/displays the theme that "masculinity and femininity are fictions which take on the status of fact" (p. xiii) by incorporating into the book journal entries, poems, essays, photographs of herself, drawings, cartoons, and annotated transcripts. Ruth Linden's *Making Stories, Making Selves: Feminist Reflections on the Holocaust* (1992) intertwines autobiography, academic writing, and survivors' stories in a Helen Hooven Santmyer Prize in Women's Studies book, which was her dissertation. John Van Maanen's *Tales from the Field* (1988) presents his research on police as realist, confessional, and impressionist narratives. Patti Lather and Chris Smithies's *Troubling the Angels: Women Living With HIV/AIDS* (1997) displays high theory, researchers' stories, women's support group transcripts, and historical and medical information, using innovative text layouts. John Dorst's *The Written Suburb* (1989) presents a geographic site as site, image, idea, discourse, and an assemblage of texts. Stephen Pfohl's *Death at the Parasite Cafe* (1992) employs collage strategies and synchronic juxtapositions, blurring critical theory and militant art forms.

In some mixed-genre productions, the writer/artist roams freely around topics, breaking our sense of the externality of topics, developing our sense of how topic and self are twin constructed. Susan Krieger's *Social Science and the Self: Personal Essays on an Art Form* (1991) is a superb example. The book is "design oriented," reflecting Krieger's attachment to Pueblo potters and Georgia O'Keeffe, and, as she says, it "looks more like a pot or a painting than a hypothesis" (p. 120). Trinh T. Minh-ha's *Woman Native Other* (1989) breaks down writing conventions within each of the essays that constitute the book, mixing poetry, self-reflection, feminist criticism, photographs, and quotations to help readers experience postcoloniality. In *I've Known Rivers: Lives of Loss and Libera-*

tion (1994), Sara Lawrence-Lightfoot uses fiction-writing techniques and self-reflexivity to tell stories of being Afro-American and professional. Anthologies also reflect these mixed genres. My own book *Fields of Play: Constructing an Academic Life* (1997) in its entirety tells the story of my intellectual and political struggles in academia through personal essays, dramas, poems, writing-stories, e-mail messages, and sociology articles. Anthologies also present mixed genres. Some examples are Carolyn Ellis and Arthur Bochner's *Composing Ethnography: Alternative Forms of Qualitative Writing* (1996a), Ellis and Michael Flaherty's *Investigating Subjectivity: Research on Lived Experience* (1992), Ruth Behar and Deborah Gordon's *Women Writing Culture* (1995). The book series *Studies in Symbolic Interaction,* and the journal *Qualitative Inquiry* mix genres in their pages.

Whither and Whence?

The contemporary postmodernist context in which we work as qualitative researchers is a propitious one. It provides an opportunity for us to review, critique, and re-vision writing. Although we are freer to present our texts in a variety of forms to diverse audiences, we have different constraints arising from self-consciousness about claims to authorship, authority, truth, validity, reliability. Self-reflexivity brings to consciousness some of the complex political/ideological agendas hidden in our writing. Truth claims are less easily validated now; desires to speak "for" others are suspect. The greater freedom to experiment with textual form, however, does not guarantee a better product. The opportunities for writing worthy texts—books and articles that are "good reads"—are multiple, exciting, and demanding. But the work is harder. The guarantees are fewer. There is a lot more for us to think about.

One thing for us to think about is whether writing CAP ethnography for publication is a luxury open only to those who have academic sinecure. Are the tenured doing a disservice to students by introducing them to these different forms of writing? Will teaching students hereticisms "deskill" them? Alienate them from

their discipline? (Would we ask these questions about students' learning a second language?) A related issue is, if students are taught writing as inquiry, what criteria should be brought to bear upon their work? These are heady ethical, pedagogical, aesthetic, and practical questions. I struggle with them in my teaching, writing, and collegial discussions. I have no definitive answers, but I do have some thoughts on the issues.

Writing is a process of discovery. My purpose is not to turn us into poets, novelists, or dramatists—few of us will write well enough to succeed in those competitive fields. Most of us, like Poe, will be at best only almost poets. Rather, my intention is to encourage individuals to accept and nurture their own voices. The researcher's self-knowledge and knowledge of the topic develop through experimentation with point of view, tone, texture, sequencing, metaphor, and so on. Another skill, another language—the student's own—is added to the student's repertoire. The science-writing enterprise is demystified. The deepened understanding of a Self deepens the text. Even the analysis paralysis that afflicts some readers of postmodernism is attenuated when writers view their work as process rather than as definitive representation.

Students will not lose the language of science when they learn to write in other ways, any more than students who learn a second language lose their first (Y. S. Lincoln, personal communication, 1998). Rather, acquiring a second language enriches students in two ways: It gains them entry into a new culture and literature, and it leads them to a deepened understanding of their first language, not just grammatically, but as a language that constructs how they view the world.

Writing in traditional ways does not prevent us from writing in other ways for other audiences at other times (Denzin, 1994; Richardson, 1990). There is no single way—much less one "right" way—of staging a text. Like wet clay, the material can be shaped. Learning alternative ways of writing increases our repertoires, increases the numbers and kinds of audiences we might reach.

As I write this chapter, I imagine four friendly audiences: graduate students, curious quantitative researchers, traditionally inclined qualitative researchers, and creative analytic practitioners. I want to clarify and teach—and, yes, proselytize.

Who is your audience? What are your purposes? Understanding how to stage your writing *rhetorically* increases your chances of getting published and reaching your intended audiences. Deconstructing traditional writing practices makes writers more conscious of writing conventions and, therefore, more competently able to make choices.

The new ways of writing do, however, invoke conversation about criteria for judging an ethnographic work—new or traditional. Traditional ethnographers of goodwill have legitimate concerns about how their students' work will be evaluated if they choose to write CAP ethnography. I have no definitive answers to ease their concerns, but I do have some ideas and preferences.

I see the ethnographic project as humanly situated, always filtered through human eyes and human perceptions, bearing both the limitations and the strengths of human feelings. Scientific superstructure is always resting on the foundation of human activity, belief, understandings. I emphasize ethnography as constructed through *research practices*. Research practices are concerned with enlarged understanding. Science offers some research practices; literature, creative arts, memory work (Davies, 1994; Davies et al., 1997), and introspection (Ellis, 1991) offer still others. Researchers have many practices from which to choose, and ought not be constrained by habits of other people's minds.

I believe in holding CAP ethnography to high and difficult standards; mere novelty does not suffice. Here are five of the criteria I use when reviewing papers or monographs submitted for social scientific publication.

1. *Substantive contribution:* Does this piece contribute to our *understanding* of social life? Does the writer demonstrate a deeply grounded (if embedded) social scientific perspective? How has this perspective informed the construction of the text? (See "Writing Practices," below, for some suggestions on how to accomplish this.)

2. *Aesthetic merit:* Rather than reducing standards, CAP ethnography adds another standard. Does this piece succeed aesthetically? Does the use of creative analytic practices open up the text, invite interpretive responses? Is the text artistically shaped, satisfying, complex, and not boring? (Creative writing is a skill that can be developed through reading, courses, workshops, and practice; see the suggestions listed in the "Writing Practices" section.)

3. *Reflexivity:* Is the author cognizant of the epistemology of postmodernism? How did the author come to write this text? How was the information gathered? Are there ethical issues? How has the author's subjectivity been both a producer and a product of this text? Is there adequate self-awareness and self-exposure for the reader to make judgments about the point of view? Does the author hold him- or herself accountable to the standards of knowing and telling of the people he or she has studied?

4. *Impact:* Does this affect me? Emotionally? Intellectually? Does it generate new questions? Move me to write? Move me to try new research practices? Move me to action?

5. *Expression of a reality:* Does this text embody a fleshed out, embodied sense of lived experience? Does it seem "true"—a credible account of a cultural, social, individual, or communal sense of the "real"?

These are five of my criteria. Science is one lens; creative arts another. We see more deeply using two lenses. I want to look through both lenses, to see a "social science art form."

I strongly disagree, then, with those who claim ethnography should be a "science guild," a "craft" with "tacit rules," apprentices, trade "secrets," and "disciplined," "responsible" journeymen (i.e., professors) who enact rules that check "artistic pretensions and excesses" (see Schwalbe, 1995; see also Richardson, 1996b). This medieval vision limits ethnographic exploration, patrols the boundaries of intellectual thought, and aligns qualitative research ideologically with those who would discipline and punish postmodern ideas within social science. Policing, however, is always about bodies. It is always about real live people. Should the medieval vision triumph, what real live people are likely to be excluded?

What I have learned from my teaching and conversations with colleagues is this: Minorities within academia, including ethnic and racial, postcolonial, gay and lesbian, physically challenged, and returning students, find the turn to creative analytic practices as beckoning. These researchers desire the opportunity to be "responsible" to the "guild" while honoring their responsibilities to their traditions, their cultures, and their sense of the meaningful life.

Welcoming these researchers creates an enriched, diversified, socially engaged, nonhegemonic community of qualitative researchers. Everyone profits—the communities of origin and identification and the qualitative research community. The implications of race and gender would be stressed not because it would be "politically correct," but because race and gender *are axes* through which symbolic and actual worlds have been constructed. Members of nondominant worlds know that, and would insist that this knowledge be honored (see Margolis & Romero, 1998). The blurring of humanities and social sciences would be welcomed not because it is "trendy," but because the blurring coheres more truly with the life senses and learning styles of so many. This new qualitative community could, through its theory, analytic practices, and diverse membership, reach beyond academia, teaching all of us about social injustice and methods for alleviating it. What qualitative researcher interested in social life would not feel enriched by membership in such a culturally diverse and inviting community?

Furthermore, CAP ethnography is now firmly established within the social sciences. There are prestigious places for students and others to publish. *Sociological Quarterly, Symbolic Interaction, American Anthropologist, Journal of Contemporary Ethnography, Journal of Aging Studies, Qualitative Inquiry, International Journal of Qualitative Research in Education, Qualitative Studies in Psychology, Qualitative Sociology, Waikato Journal of Education,* and *Text and Performance Quarterly* routinely publish CAP ethnography. The annuals *Studies in Symbolic Interaction* and *Cultural Studies* showcase evocative writing. Publishers such as Routledge, University of Chicago Press, University of Michigan Press, Indiana University Press, University of Pennsylvania Press, Rutgers University Press, Temple University Press, and Sage Publications regularly publish new ethnography by both well-known and lesser-known authors. AltaMira Press (formerly a division of Sage) boasts the excellent Ethnographic Alternatives book series, which is dedicated to qualitative research that blurs the boundaries between the social sciences and humanities. New York University Press has launched the Qualitative Studies in Psychology series, which is receptive to creative-analytic texts. Trade and university presses are increasingly resistant to publishing old-style monographs, and traditional ethnographers are writing more reflexively and self-consciously (see Thorne, 1993). Even those opposed to postmodernism legitimate it through dialogue (Whyte, 1992). Throughout the social sciences, convention papers include transgressive presentations. Entire conferences are devoted to experimentation, such as the "Redesigning Ethnography" conference at the University of Colorado and the Year 2000 Couch-Stone Symbolic Interaction Symposium.

At least three well-respected interpretive programs—at the University of Illinois (under Norman Denzin), the University of South Florida (under Arthur Bochner and Carolyn Ellis), and the University of Nevada at Las Vegas (with Andrea Fontana and Kate Hausbreck)—teach creative analytic practices. The Ohio State University's Folklore Studies (under Amy Shuman) and its Cultural Studies in Education Ph.D. program (under Patti Lather) privilege postpositivism. Dissertations violating the traditional five-chapter, social science writing style format are accepted in the United States, Canada, England, New Zealand, and Australia. Elliot Eisner (1996), art educator and past president of the American Educational Research Association, has gone further. He proposes that novels should be accepted as Ph.D. dissertations in education. All of these changes in academic practices are signs of *paradigm changes.*

In the 1950s, the sociology of science was a new, reflexively critical area. Today, the sociology of science undergirds theory, methods, and interdisciplinary science studies. In the 1960s, "gender" emerged as a theoretical perspective. Today, gender studies is one of the largest (if not the largest) subfield in the social sciences. In part, science studies and gender studies thrived because they identified normative assumptions of social science that falsely limited knowledge. They spoke "truly" to the everyday experiences of social scientists. The new areas hit us where we lived—in our work and in our bodies. They offered alternative perspectives for understanding the experienced world.

Today, the postmodernist critique is having the same impact on the social sciences that science studies and gender have had, and for similar reasons. Postmodernism identifies unspecified assumptions that hinder us in our search for understanding "truly," and it offers different practices that work. We feel its "truth"—its moral, intellectual, aesthetic, emotional, intuitive, embodied pull. Each researcher is likely to respond to that pull differently, which should lead to writing that is more diverse, more author centered, less boring, and humbler. These are propitious times. Some even speak of their work as spiritual.

And Thence

The ethnographic life is not separable from the Self. Who we are and what we can be—what we can study, how we can write about that which we study—is tied to how a knowledge system disciplines itself and its members, its methods for claiming authority over both the subject matter and its members.

We have inherited some ethnographic rules that are arbitrary, narrow, exclusionary, distorting, and alienating. Our task is to find concrete practices through which we can construct ourselves as ethical subjects engaged in ethical ethnography—inspiring to read and to write. Some of these practices involve working within theoretical schemata (sociology of knowledge, feminism, critical race theory, constructionism, poststructuralism) that challenge grounds of authority; writing on topics that matter, personally and collectively; *jouissance*; experimenting with different writing formats and audiences simultaneously; locating ourselves in multiple discourses and communities; developing critical literacy; finding ways to write/present/teach that are less hierarchal and univocal; revealing institutional secrets; using positions of authority to increase diversity, both in academic appointments and in journal publications; self-reflexivity; giving in to synchronicity; asking for what we want, like cats; not flinching from where the writing takes us, emotionally or spiritually; and honoring the embodiedness and spatiality of our labors.

What creative analytic practices in ethnography will eventually produce, I do not know. But I do know that the ground has been staked, the foundation laid, the scaffolding erected, and diverse and adventurous settlers have moved on in.

. . . and Forever After

The *Handbook* editors really do want all the contributors to predict the future of qualitative research. I thought I had. Oh, how I resist! But here goes.

Forty years ago, I was an undergraduate who detested the yearlong course "History of Western Civilization"—2,500 years, five continents, 700 countries, six trillion names, dates, wars, and places. I thought the final would decimate me. But fortune smiled. In addition to the zillions of "objective" questions, we were given a take-home essay: "What is the future of history?" I said—in 10 pages or less—that the future of history was *both* toward unity *and* toward diversity. I got an A+ on that essay. I think I'll stick with it. That's the way I see the future of qualitative research, too. We will be clearer about its domain and more welcoming of diverse representations.

The domain's metaphor will be the "text"—or some other equally outrageously encompassing image—but the meaning and construction of text will far exceed the written page, the computer screen, and even the hypertext: two-dimensional, three-dimensions, refractive, layered texts. Discussions of the boundaries between literature and science will seem quaint, as "writing"—in the future understood as any textual construction—will be routinely understood as a "method of inquiry." And, therefore, it will have to be challenged!

Oh, dear!

◆ Writing Practices

Writing, the creative effort, should come first—at least for some part of every day of your life. It is a wonderful blessing if you will use it. You will become happier, more enlightened, alive, impassioned, light hearted and generous to everybody else. Even your health will improve. Colds will disappear and all the other ailments of discouragement and boredom.

Brenda Ueland, *If You Want to Write*, 1938/1987

In what follows, I suggest some ways of using writing as a method of knowing. I have chosen exercises that have been productive for students because they demystify writing, nurture the researcher's voice, and serve the process of discovery. I wish I could guarantee them to bring good health as well. The practices are organized around topics discussed in the text.

Metaphor

Using old, worn-out metaphors, although easy and comfortable, after a while invites stodginess and stiffness. The stiffer you get, the less flexible you are. Your ideas get ignored. If your writing is clichéd, you'll not "stretch your own imagination" (Ouch! Hear the cliché of pointing out the cliché!) and you'll bore people.

1. In traditional social scientific writing, the metaphor for theory is that it is a "building" (structure, foundation, construction, deconstruction, framework, grand, and so on). Consider a different metaphor, such as "theory as a tapestry" or "theory as an illness." Write a paragraph about "theory" using your metaphor. Do you "see" differently and "feel" differently about theorizing using an unusual metaphor?

2. Consider alternative sensory metaphors for "knowledge" other than the heliocentric one mentioned in the text. What happens when you rethink/resense "knowledge" as situated in voice? In touch?

3. Look at one of your papers and highlight your metaphors and images. What are you saying through metaphors that you did not realize you were saying? What are you reinscribing? Do you want to? Can you find different metaphors that change how you "see" ("feel") the material? your relationship to it? Are your mixed metaphors pointing to confusion in yourself or to social science's glossing over of ideas?

4. Take a look at George Lakoff and Mark Johnson's *Metaphors We Live By* (1980). It is a wonderful book, a compendium of examples of metaphors in everyday life and how they affect our ways of perceiving, thinking, and acting. What everyday metaphors are shaping your knowing/writing?

Writing Formats

1. Choose a journal article that exemplifies the mainstream writing conventions of your discipline. How is the argument staged? Who is the presumed audience? How does the paper inscribe ideology? How does the author claim authority over the material? Where is the author? Where are you in this paper? Who are the subjects and who are the objects of research?

2. Choose a journal article that exemplifies excellence in qualitative research. How has the article built upon normative social science writing? How is authority claimed? Where is the author? Where are you in the article? Who are the subjects and who are the objects of research?

3. Choose a paper you have written for a class or that you have published that you think is

pretty good. How did you follow the norms of your discipline? Were you conscious of doing so? How did you stage your paper? What parts did the professor/reviewer laud? How did you depend upon those norms to carry your argument? Did you elide some difficult areas through vagueness, jargon, calls to authorities, or other rhetorical devices? What voices did you exclude in your writing? Who is the audience? Where are the subjects in the paper? Where are you? How do you feel about the paper now? About your process of constructing it?

Creative Analytic Writing Practices

1. Join or start a writing group. This could be a writing support group, a creative writing group, a poetry group, a dissertation group, or another kind of group. (On dissertation and article writing, see Becker, 1986; Fox, 1985; Richardson, 1990; Wolcott, 1990.)

2. Work through a creative writing guidebook. Natalie Goldberg (1986, 1990), Rust Hills (1987), Brenda Ueland (1938/1987), and Deena Weinstein (1993) all provide excellent guides.

3. Enroll in a creative writing workshop or class. These experiences are valuable for both beginning and experienced researchers.

4. Use "writing up" your field notes as an opportunity to expand your writing vocabulary, habits of thought, and attentiveness to your senses, and as a bulwark against the censorious voice of science. Where better to develop your sense of self, your voice, than in the process of doing your research? Apply creative writing skills to your field notes. You may need to rethink what you've have been taught about objectivity, science, and the ethnographic project. What works for me is to give different labels to different content. Building on the work of Glaser and Strauss (1967), I use four categories, which you may find of value:

- *Observation notes* (ON): These are as concrete and detailed as I am able to make

them. I want to think of them as fairly accurate renditions of what I see, hear, feel, taste, and so on. I stay close to the scene as I experience it through my senses.

- *Methodological notes* (MN): These are messages to myself regarding how to collect "data"—who to talk to, what to wear, when to phone, and so on. I write a lot of these because I like methods, and I like to keep a process diary of my work.

- *Theoretical notes* (TN): These are hunches, hypotheses, poststructuralist connections, critiques of what I am doing/thinking/seeing. I like writing these because they open my field note texts to alternative interpretations and a critical epistemological stance. They provide a way of keeping me from being hooked on one view of reality.

- *Personal notes* (PN): These are uncensored feeling statements about the research, the people I am talking to, my doubts, my anxieties, my pleasures. I want all my feelings out on paper because I know they are affecting what/how I lay claim to know. I also know they are a great source for hypotheses; if I am feeling a certain way in a setting, it is likely that others might feel that way too. Finally, writing personal notes is a way for me to know myself better, a way of using writing as method of inquiry into the self.

5. Keep a journal. In it, write about your feelings about your work. This not only frees up your writing, it becomes the "historical record" for the writing of a narrative of the Self or a writing-story about the writing process.

6. Write a writing autobiography. This would be the story of how you learned to write: the dicta of English classes (topic sentences? outlines? the five-paragraph essay?), the dicta of social science professors, your experiences with teachers' comments on your papers, how and where you write now, your idiosyncratic "writing needs," your feelings about writing and about the writing process. (This is an exercise that Arthur Bochner uses.)

7. If you wish to experiment with evocative writing, a good place to begin is by transforming

your field notes into drama. See what ethnographic rules you are using (such as fidelity to the speech of the participants, fidelity in the order of the speakers and events) and what literary ones you are invoking (such as limits on how long a speaker speaks, keeping the "plot" moving along, developing character through actions). Writing dramatic presentations accentuates ethical considerations. If you doubt that, contrast writing up an ethnographic event as a "typical" event with writing it as a play, with you and your hosts cast in roles that will be performed before others. Who has ownership of spoken words? How is authorship attributed? What if people do not like how they are characterized? Are courtesy norms being violated? Experiment here with both oral and written versions of your drama.

8. Experiment with transforming an in-depth interview into a poetic representation. Try using only the words, rhythms, figures of speech, breath points, pauses, syntax, and diction of the speaker. Where are you in the poem? What do you know about the interviewee and about yourself that you did not know before you wrote the poem? What poetic devices have you sacrificed in the name of science?

9. Experiment with writing narratives of the self. Keep in mind Barbara Tuchman's warning: "The writer's object is—or should be—to hold the reader's attention. . . . I want the reader to turn the page and keep on turning to the end. This is accomplished only when the narrative moves steadily ahead, not when it comes to a weary standstill, overlaced with every item uncovered in the research" (in *New York Times,* February 2, 1989).

10. Try writing a text using different typefaces, font sizes, and textual placement. How have the traditional ways of using print affected what you know and how you know it?

11. Write a "layered text" (see Lather & Smithies, 1997; Ronai, 1992). The layered text is a strategy for putting yourself into your text and putting your text into the literatures and traditions of social science. Here is one possibility. First, write a short narrative of the Self about some event that is especially meaningful to you.

Then step back and look at the narrative from your disciplinary perspective and insert into the narrative—beginning, midsections, end, wherever—relevant analytic statements or references, using a different typescript, alternative page placement, split pages, or other ways to mark the text. The layering can be multiple, with different ways of marking different theoretical levels, theories, speakers, and so on. (This is an exercise that Carolyn Ellis uses.)

12. Try some other strategy for writing new ethnography for social scientific publications. Try the "seamless" text, in which previous literature, theory, and methods are placed in textually meaningful ways, rather than in disjunctive sections (for a excellent example, see Bochner, 1997); try the "sandwich" text, in which traditional social science themes are the "white bread" around the "filling" (C. Ellis, personal communication, April 27, 1998); or try an "epilogue" explicating the theoretical analytic work of the creative text (see Eisner, 1996).

13. Consider a fieldwork setting. Consider the various subject positions you have or have had within it. For example, in a store you might be a salesclerk, customer, manager, feminist, capitalist, parent, child, and so on. Write about the setting (or an event in the setting) from several different subject positions. What do you "know" from the different positions? Next, let the different points of view dialogue with each other. What do you discover through these dialogues?

14. Consider a paper you have written (or your field notes). What have you left out? Who is not present in this text? Who has been repressed or marginalized? Rewrite the text from that point of view.

15. Write your "data" in three different ways—for example, as a narrative account, as a poetic representation, and as readers' theater. What do you know in each rendition that you did not know in the other renditions? How do the different renditions enrich each other?

16. Write a narrative of the Self from your point of view (such as something that happened in your family or in a seminar). Then interview another participant (such as family or seminar

member) and have that person tell you his or her story of the event. See yourself as part of the other person's story in the same way he or she is part of your story. How do you rewrite your story from the other person's point of view? (This is an exercise Carolyn Ellis uses.)

17. Collaborative writing is a way to see beyond one's own naturalisms of style and attitude. This is an exercise that I have used in my teaching, but it would be appropriate for a writing group as well. Each member writes a story of his or her life. It could be a feminist story, a success story, quest story, cultural story, professional socialization story, realist tale, confessional tale, or another kind of story. All persons' stories are photocopied for the group. The group is then broken into subgroups (I prefer groups of three), and each subgroup collaborates on writing a new story, the collective story of its members. The collaboration can take any form: drama, poetry, fiction, narrative of the selves, realism, whatever the subgroup chooses. The collaboration is shared with the entire group. All members then write about their feelings about the collaboration and what happened to their stories, their lives, in the process.

18. Memory work (see Davies, 1994; Davies et al., 1997) is another collaborative research and writing strategy. Stories shared in the group are discussed and then rewritten, with attention paid to the discourses that are shaping the stories in each of their tellings. As more people tell their stories, individuals remember more details of their own stories, or develop new stories. Participants discover what their stories have in common, perhaps even writing what Bronwyn Davies (1994) calls a "collective biography."

19. Consider a part of your life outside of or before academia with which you have deeply resonated. Use that resonance as a "working metaphor" for understanding and reporting your research. Students have created excellent reports by using unexpected lenses, such as choreography, principles of flower arrangement, art composition, and sportscasting, to view their lives and the lives of others. Writing

from that which resonates with your life nurtures a more integrated life.

20. Different forms of writing are appropriate for different audiences and different occasions. Try writing the same piece of research for an academic audience, a trade audience, the popular press, policy makers, research hosts, and so on (see Richardson, 1990). This is an especially powerful exercise for dissertation students who may want to share their results in a "user-friendly" way with those they studied.

21. Write writing-stories (see Richardson, 1997), or reflexive accounts of how you happened to write pieces you have written. Your writing-stories can be about disciplinary politics, departmental events, friendship networks, collegial ties, family, and personal biographical experiences. Writing-stories situate your work in contexts, tying what can be a lonely and seemingly separative task to the ebbs and flows of your life, your self. Writing these stories reminds us of the continual cocreation of the self and social science.

Willing is doing something you know already—there is no new imaginative understanding in it. And presently your soul gets frightfully sterile and dry because you are so quick, snappy, and efficient about doing one thing after another that you have no time for your own ideas to come in and develop and gently shine.

Brenda Ueland, *If You Want to Write*, 1938/1987

■ *References*

Agger, B. (1989). *Reading science: A literary, political and sociological analysis.* Dix Hills, NY: General Hall.

Agger, B. (1990). *The decline of discourse: Reading, writing and resistance in postmodern capitalism.* Bristol, PA: Falmer.

Angrosino, M. V. (1998). *Opportunity House: Ethnographic stories of mental retardation.* Walnut Creek, CA: AltaMira.

Ba, M. (1987). *So long a letter* (M. Bode-Thomas, Trans.). Portsmouth, NH: Heinemann.

Baff, S. J. (1997). Realism and naturalism and dead dudes: Talking about literature in 11th grade English. *Qualitative Inquiry, 3,* 468-490.

Balzac, H. de (1965). Preface to *The human comedy,* from *At the Sign of the cat and racket* (C. Bell, Trans., 1897). In R. Ellman & C. Feidelson, Jr. (Eds.), *The modern tradition: Backgrounds of modern literature* (pp. 246-254). New York: Oxford University Press. (Original work published 1842)

Banks, A., & Banks, S. P. (Eds.). (1998). *Fiction and social research: By ice or fire.* Walnut Creek, CA: AltaMira.

Barley, N. (1986). *Ceremony: An anthropologist's misadventures in the African bush.* New York: Henry Holt.

Barley, N. (1988). *Not a pleasant sport.* New York: Henry Holt.

Becker, H. S. (1986). *Writing for social scientists: How to finish your thesis, book, or article.* Chicago: University of Chicago Press.

Behar, R. (1993). *Translated woman: Crossing the border with Esperanza's story.* Boston: Beacon.

Behar, R. (1996). *The vulnerable observer: Anthropology that breaks your heart.* Boston: Beacon.

Behar, R., & Gordon, D. A. (Eds.). (1995). *Women writing culture.* Berkeley: University of California Press.

Bochner, A. (1997). It's about time: Narrative and the divided self. *Qualitative Inquiry, 3,* 418-438.

Brady, I. (Ed.). (1991). *Anthropological poetics.* Savage, MD: Rowman & Littlefield.

Brodkey, L. (1987). *Academic writing as social practice.* Philadelphia: Temple University Press.

Brown, K. M. (1991). *Mama Lola: A Vodou priestess in Brooklyn.* Berkeley: University of California Press.

Brown, R. H. (1977). *A poetic for sociology.* Cambridge: Cambridge University Press.

Bruner, E. M. (1996). My life in an ashram. *Qualitative Inquiry, 2,* 300-319.

Butler, S., & Rosenblum, B. (1991). *Cancer in two voices.* San Francisco: Spinster.

Cherry, K. (1995). The best years of their lives: A portrait of a residential home for people with AIDS. *Symbolic Interaction, 18,* 463-486.

Church, K. (1995). *Forbidden narratives: Critical autobiography as social science.* Newark, NJ: Gordon & Breach.

Church, K. (1999). *Fabrications: Stitching ourselves together* [Online]. Ottawa: Canadian Museum of Civilization. Available Internet: http://www/grannyg.bc.ca/Fabrications/index.html

Clifford, J. (1986). Introduction: Partial truths. In J. Clifford & G. E. Marcus (Eds.), *Writing culture: The poetics and politics of ethnography* (pp. 1-26). Berkeley: University of California Press.

Clifford, J., & Marcus, G. E. (Eds.). (1986). *Writing culture: The poetics and politics of ethnography.* Berkeley: University of California Press.

Clough, P. T. (1992). *The end(s) of ethnography: From realism to social criticism.* Newbury Park, CA: Sage.

Crawford, M. A. (1951). *Introduction to* Old Goriot. New York: Penguin.

Daly, K., & Dienhart, A. (1998). Navigating the family domain: Qualitative field dilemmas. In S. Grills (Ed.), *Doing ethnographic research: Fieldwork settings* (pp. 97-120). Thousand Oaks, CA: Sage.

Davies, B. (1989). *Frogs and snails and feminist tales: Preschool children.* St. Leonards, Australia: Allen & Unwin.

Davies, B. (1994). *Poststructuralist theory and classroom practice.* Geelong, Victoria, Australia: Deakin University Press.

Davies, B., Dormer, S., Honan, E., McAllister, N., O'Reilly, R., Rocco, S., & Walker, A. (1997). Ruptures in the skin of silence: A collective biography. *Hecate: A Woman's Interdisciplinary Journal, 23*(1), 62-79.

Denzin, N. K. (1978). *The research act: A theoretical introduction to sociological methods* (2nd ed.). New York: McGraw-Hill.

Denzin, N. K. (1986). A postmodern social theory. *Sociological Theory, 4,* 194-204.

Denzin, N. K. (1991). *Images of postmodern society.* Newbury Park, CA: Sage.

Denzin, N. K. (1994). Evaluating qualitative research in the poststructural moment: The lessons James Joyce teaches us. *International Journal of Qualitative Studies in Education, 7,* 295-308.

Denzin, N. K. (1995). *The cinematic society: The voyeur's gaze*. Thousand Oaks, CA: Sage.

Denzin, N. K. (1997). *Interpretive ethnography: Ethnographic practices for the 21st century*. Thousand Oaks, CA: Sage.

Derrida, J. (1982). *Margins of philosophy* (A. Bass, Trans.). Chicago: University of Chicago Press.

DeShazer, M. K. (1986). *Inspiring women: Reimagining the muse*. New York: Pergamon.

Diamond, S. (1982). *Totems*. Barrytown, NY: Open Book/Station Hill.

Diversi, M. (1998a). Glimpses of street life: Representing lived experience through short stories. *Qualitative Inquiry, 4,* 131-147.

Diversi, M. (1998b). Late for school. *Waikato Journal of Education, 4,* 78-86.

Donmoyer, R., & Yennie-Donmoyer, J. (1995). Data as drama: Reflections on the use of readers theater as a mode of qualitative data display. *Qualitative Inquiry, 1,* 402-428.

Dorst, J. D. (1989). *The written suburb: An American site, an ethnographic dilemma*. Philadelphia: University of Pennsylvania Press.

Edmondson, R. (1984). *Rhetoric in sociology*. London: Macmillan.

Eisner, E. (1996). Should a novel count as a dissertation in education? *Research in the Teaching of English, 30,* 403-427.

Ellis, C. (1991). Sociological introspection and emotional experience. *Symbolic Interaction, 14,* 23-50.

Ellis, C. (1993). Telling the story of sudden death. *Sociological Quarterly, 34,* 711-730.

Ellis, C. (1995a). *Final negotiations: A story of love, loss, and chronic illness*. Philadelphia: Temple University Press.

Ellis, C. (1995b). The other side of the fence: Seeing black and white in a small southern town. *Qualitative Inquiry, 1,* 147-168.

Ellis, C. (1998). "I hate my voice": Coming to terms with minor bodily stigmas. *Sociological Quarterly, 39,* 517-537.

Ellis, C., & Bochner, A. P. (1992). Telling and performing personal stories: The constraints of choice in abortion. In C. Ellis & M. G. Flaherty (Eds.), *Investigating subjectivity: Research on lived experience* (pp. 79-101). Newbury Park, CA: Sage.

Ellis, C., & Bochner, A. P. (Eds.). (1996a). *Composing ethnography: Alternative forms of qualitative writing*. Walnut Creek, CA: AltaMira.

Ellis, C., & Bochner, A. P. (1996b). Introduction: Talking over ethnography. In C. Ellis & A. P. Bochner (Eds.), *Composing ethnography: Alternative forms of qualitative writing* (pp. 13-48). Walnut Creek, CA: AltaMira.

Ellis, C., & Flaherty, M. G. (Eds.). (1992). *Investigating subjectivity: Research on lived experience*. Newbury Park, CA: Sage.

Erikson, K. T. (1976). *Everything in its path: Destruction of the community in the Buffalo Creek flood*. New York: Simon & Schuster.

Fine, M. (1992). *Disruptive voices: The possibility of feminist research*. Ann Arbor: University of Michigan Press.

Fishkin, S. F. (1985). *From fact to fiction: Journalism and imaginative writing in America*. Baltimore: Johns Hopkins University Press.

Flick, U. (1998). *An introduction to qualitative research: Theory, method and applications*. London: Sage.

Fox, M. F. (Ed.). (1985). *Scholarly writing and publishing: Issues, problems, and solutions*. Boulder, CO: Westview.

Frank, A. (1995). *The wounded storyteller: Body, illness, and ethics*. Chicago: University of Chicago Press.

Frohock, F. (1992). *Healing powers*. Chicago: University of Chicago Press.

Geertz, C. (1988). *Works and lives: The anthropologist as author*. Stanford, CA: Stanford University Press.

Gerla, J. P. (1995). An uncommon friendship: Ethnographic fiction around finance equity in Texas. *Qualitative Inquiry, 1,* 168-188.

Glaser, B. G., & Strauss, A. L. (1967). *The discovery of grounded theory: Strategies for qualitative research*. Chicago: Aldine.

Glesne, C. E. (1997). That rare feeling: Re-presenting research through poetic transcription. *Qualitative Inquiry, 3,* 202-221.

Goetting, A., & Fenstermaker, S. (1995). *Individual voices, collective visions: Fifty years of women in sociology*. Philadelphia: Temple University Press.

Goldberg, N. (1986). *Writing down the bones: Freeing the writer within*. Boston: Shambala.

Goldberg, N. (1990). *Wild mind: Living the writer's life*. New York: Bantam.

Harper, D. (1987). *Working knowledge: Skill and community in a small shop.* Chicago: University of Chicago Press.

Hills, R. (1987). *Writing in general and the short story in particular.* Boston: Houghton Mifflin.

hooks, b. (1990). *Yearning: Race, gender, and cultural politics.* Boston: South End.

Hurston, Z. N. (1991). *Dust tracks on a road.* New York: HarperCollins. (Original work published 1942)

Hutcheon, L. (1988). *A poetics for postmodernism: History, theory, fiction.* New York: Routledge.

Jacobs, J. (1984). *The mall: An attempted escape from everyday life.* Prospect Heights, IL: Waveland.

Jago, B. J. (1996). Postcards, ghosts, and fathers: Revising family stories. *Qualitative Inquiry, 2,* 495-516.

Jameson, F. (1981). *The political unconscious: Narrative as a socially symbolic act.* Ithaca, NY: Cornell University Press.

Jipson, J., & Paley, N. (Eds.). (1997). *Daredevil research: Re-creating analytic practice.* New York: Peter Lang.

Johnston, M. (with Educators for Collaborative Change). (1997). *Contradictions in collaboration: New thinking on school/university partnerships.* New York: Teachers College Press.

Jones, S. H. (1998). *Kaleidoscope notes: Writing women's music and organizational culture.* Walnut Creek, CA: AltaMira.

Karp, D. (1996). *Speaking of sadness.* New York: Oxford University Press.

Kaufman, S. (1986). *The ageless self: Sources of meaning in later life.* Madison: University of Wisconsin Press.

Kondo, D. K. (1990). *Crafting selves: Power, gender, and discourses of identity in a Japanese workplace.* Chicago: University of Chicago Press.

Krieger, S. (1983). *The mirror dance: Identity in a women's community.* Philadelphia: Temple University Press.

Krieger, S. (1991). *Social science and the self: Personal essays on an art form.* New Brunswick, NJ: Rutgers University Press.

Krieger, S. (1996). *The family silver: Essays on relationships among women.* Berkeley: University of California Press.

Lakoff, G., & Johnson, M. (1980). *Metaphors we live by.* Chicago: University of Chicago Press.

Lather, P. (1991). *Getting smart: Feminist research and pedagogy with/in the postmodern.* New York: Routledge.

Lather, P., & Smithies, C. (1997). *Troubling the angels: Women living with HIV/AIDS.* Boulder, CO: Westview.

Lawrence-Lightfoot, S. (1994). *I've known rivers: Lives of loss and liberation.* Boston: Addison-Wesley.

Lawton, J. E. (1997). *Reconceptualizing a horizontal career line: A study of seven experienced urban English teachers approaching career end.* Unpublished doctoral dissertation, Ohio State University.

Lee, V. (1996). *Granny midwives and black women writers.* New York: Routledge.

Lehman, D. (1991). *Signs of the times: Deconstruction and the fall of Paul de Man.* New York: Poseidon.

Levine, D. N. (1985). *The flight from ambiguity: Essays in social and cultural theory.* Chicago: University of Chicago Press.

Liebow, E. (1967). *Tally's corner: A study of Negro street corner men.* Boston: Little, Brown.

Linden, R. R. (1992). *Making stories, making selves: Feminist reflections on the Holocaust.* Columbus: Ohio State University Press.

Lockridge, E. (1987). F. Scott Fitzgerald's *Trompe l'oeil* and *The great Gatsby*'s buried plot. *Journal of Narrative Technique, 17,* 163-183.

Lyotard, J.-F. (1984). *The postmodern condition: A report on knowledge* (G. Bennington & B. Massumi, Trans.). Minneapolis: University of Minnesota Press.

Margolis, E., & Romero, M. (1998). The department is very male, very white, very old, and very conservative: The functioning of the hidden curriculum in graduate sociology departments. *Harvard Educational Review, 68,* 1-32.

McCall, M. M., & Becker, H. S. (1990). Performance science. *Social Problems, 37,* 116-132.

McCall, M. M., Gammel, L., & Taylor, S. (1994). *The one about the farmer's daughter: Stereotypes and self portraits.* Minneapolis: Country Characters.

McMahon, M. (1996). Significant absences. *Qualitative Inquiry, 2,* 320-336.

Meloy, J. M. (1993). Problems of writing and representation in qualitative inquiry. *International Journal of Qualitative Studies in Education, 6,* 315-330.

Mienczakowski, J. (1996). An ethnographic act: The construction of consensual theater. In C. Ellis & A. P. Bochner (Eds.), *Composing ethnography: Alternative forms of qualitative writing* (pp. 244-266). Walnut Creek, CA: AltaMira.

Mishler, E. G. (1989). *Research interviewing: Context and narrative.* Cambridge, MA: Harvard University Press.

Nelson, J. S., Megill, A., & McCloskey, D. N. (Eds.). (1987). *The rhetoric of the human sciences: Language and argument in scholarship and human affairs.* Madison: University of Wisconsin Press.

Nicholson, L. J. (Ed.). (1990). *Feminism/postmodernism.* New York: Routledge.

Norum, K. E. (in press). School patterns: A sextet. *International Journal of Qualitative Studies in Education.*

Paget, M. (1990). Performing the text. *Journal of Contemporary Ethnography, 19,* 136-155.

Pandolfo, S. (1997). *Impasse of the angels: Scenes from a Moroccan space of memory.* Chicago: University of Chicago Press.

Patai, D. (1988). Constructing a self: A Brazilian life story. *Feminist Studies, 14,* 142-163.

Pfohl, S. J. (1992). *Death at the Parasite Cafe: Social science (fictions) and the postmodern.* New York: St. Martin's.

Prattis, I. (Ed.). (1985). *Reflections: The anthropological muse.* Washington, DC: American Anthropological Association.

Richardson, L. (1985). *The new other woman: Contemporary single women in affairs with married men.* New York: Free Press.

Richardson, L. (1990). *Writing strategies: Reaching diverse audiences.* Thousand Oaks, CA: Sage.

Richardson, L. (1992a). The consequences of poetic representation: Writing the other, rewriting the self. In C. Ellis & M. G. Flaherty (Eds.), *Investigating subjectivity: Research on lived experience.* Newbury Park, CA: Sage.

Richardson, L. (1992b). Resisting resistance narratives: A representation for communication. In N. K. Denzin (Ed.), *Studies in symbolic interaction: A research annual* (Vol. 13, pp. 77-83). Greenwich, CT: JAI.

Richardson, L. (1993). The case of the skipped line: Poetics, dramatics and transgressive validity. *Sociological Quarterly, 34,* 695-710.

Richardson, L. (1995). Writing-stories: Coauthoring "The sea monster," a writing-story. *Qualitative Inquiry, 1,* 189-203.

Richardson, L. (1996a). Educational birds. *Journal of Contemporary Ethnography, 25,* 6-15.

Richardson, L. (1996b). A sociology of responsibility. *Qualitative Research, 19,* 519-524.

Richardson, L. (1997). *Fields of play: Constructing an academic life.* New Brunswick, NJ: Rutgers University Press.

Richardson, L. (1998). The politics of location: Where am I now? *Qualitative Inquiry, 4,* 41-48.

Richardson, L. (1999a). Dead again in Berkeley. *Qualitative Inquiry, 5,* 141-144.

Richardson, L. (1999b). Paradigms lost [Distinguished Lecture]. *Symbolic Interaction, 22,* 79-91.

Richardson, L., & Lockridge, E. (1991). *The sea monster: An ethnographic drama. Symbolic Interaction, 14,* 335-340.

Richardson, L., & Lockridge, E. (1998). Fiction and ethnography: A conversation. *Qualitative Inquiry, 4,* 328-336.

Rinehart, R. (1998). Sk8ing. *Waikato Journal of Education, 4,* 87-100.

Ronai, C. R. (1992). The reflexive self through narrative: A night in the life of an erotic dancer/researcher. In C. Ellis & M. G. Flaherty (Eds.), *Investigating subjectivity: Research on lived experience* (pp. 102-124). Newbury Park, CA: Sage.

Ronai, C. R. (1995). Multiple reflections of child sexual abuse: An argument for a layered account. *Journal of Contemporary Ethnography, 23,* 395-426.

Rose, D. (1989). *Patterns of American culture: Ethnography and estrangement.* Philadelphia: University of Pennsylvania Press.

Rose, E. (1992). *The werald.* Boulder, CO: Waiting Room.

Rose, E. (1993). *The worulde.* Boulder, CO: Waiting Room.

Rubin, L. B. (1976). *Worlds of pain: Life in the working-class family.* New York: Basic Books.

Schneider, J. (1991). Troubles with textual authority in sociology. *Symbolic Interaction, 14,* 295-320.

Schwalbe, M. (1995). The responsibilities of sociological poets. *Qualitative Sociology, 18,* 393-412.

Shapiro, M. (1985-1986). Metaphor in the philosophy of the social sciences. *Cultural Critique, 2,* 191-214.

Shelton, A. (1995). The man at the end of the machine. *Symbolic Interaction, 18,* 505-518.

Shostak, A. (Ed.). (1996). *Private sociology: Unsparing reflections, uncommon gains.* Dix Hills, NY: General Hall.

Simons, H. W. (1990). *Rhetoric in the human sciences.* London: Sage.

Slobin, K. (1995). Fieldwork and subjectivity: On the ritualization of seeing a burned child. *Symbolic Interaction, 18,* 487-504.

Sparkes, A. C. (1997). Ethnographic fiction and representing the absent other. *Sport, Education, and Society, 2,* 25-40.

Stack, C. B. (1974). *All our kin: Strategies for survival in a black community.* New York: Harper & Row.

Statham, A., Richardson, L., & Cook, J. A. (1991). *Gender and university teaching: A negotiated difference.* Albany: State University of New York Press.

Steedman, K. (1986). *Landscape for a good woman: A story of two lives.* New Brunswick, NJ: Rutgers University Press.

Stewart, J. (1989). *Drinkers, drummers and decent folk: Ethnographic narratives of Village Trinidad.* Albany: State University of New York Press.

Stoller, P. (1989). *The taste of ethnographic things: The senses in anthropology.* Philadelphia: University of Pennsylvania Press.

St. Pierre, E. A. (1997a). Circling the text: Nomadic writing practices. *Qualitative Inquiry, 3,* 403-417.

St. Pierre, E. A. (1997b). Nomadic inquiry in the smooth spaces of the field: A preface. *International Journal of Qualitative Studies in Education, 10,* 175-189.

Tedlock, D. (1983). *The spoken word and the work of interpretation.* Philadelphia: University of Pennsylvania Press.

Thorne, B. (1993). *Gender play.* New Brunswick, NJ: Rutgers University Press.

Trinh T. M. (1989). *Woman, native, other: Writing postcoloniality and feminism.* Bloomington: Indiana University Press.

Turner, V., & Bruner, E. M. (Eds.). (1986). *The anthropology of experience.* Urbana: University of Illinois Press.

Ueland, B. (1987). *If you want to write: A book about art, independence and spirit.* Saint Paul, MN: Graywolf. (Original work published 1938)

Ulmer, G. (1989). *Teletheory: Grammatology in the age of video.* New York: Routledge.

Van Maanen, J. (1988). *Tales of the field: On writing ethnography.* Chicago: University of Chicago Press.

Van Maanen, J. (Ed.). (1995). *Representation in ethnography.* Thousand Oaks, CA: Sage.

Visweswaran, K. (1994). *Fictions of feminist ethnography.* Minneapolis: University of Minnesota Press.

Walkerdine, V. (1990). *Schoolgirl fictions.* London: Verso.

Weedon, C. (1987). *Feminist practice and poststructuralist theory.* New York: Basil Blackwell.

Weinstein, D. (1993). *Writing for your life: A guide and companion to the inner worlds.* New York: HarperCollins.

Whyte, W. F. (1943). *Street corner society: The social structure of an Italian slum.* Chicago: University of Chicago Press.

Whyte, W. F. (1992). In defense of *Street corner society. Journal of Contemporary Ethnography, 21,* 52-68.

Williams, P. J. (1991). *The alchemy of race and rights: Diary of a law professor.* Cambridge, MA: Harvard University Press.

Wilson, C. (1965). *Crazy February: Death and life in the Mayan highlands of Mexico.* Berkeley: University of California Press.

Wolcott, H. F. (1990). *Writing up qualitative research.* Newbury Park, CA: Sage.

Wolf, M. A. (1992). *A thrice-told tale: Feminism, postmodernism, and ethnographic responsibility.* Stanford, CA: Stanford University Press.

Yu, P.-L. (1997). *Hungry lightning: Notes of a woman anthropologist in Venezuela.* Albuquerque: University of New Mexico Press.

Zola, E. (1965). The novel as social science. In R. Ellman & C. Feidelson, Jr. (Eds.), *The modern tradition: Backgrounds of modern literature* (pp. 270-289). New York: Oxford University Press. (Original work published 1880)

Zola, I. K. (1982). *Missing pieces: A chronicle of living with a disability.* Philadelphia: Temple University Press.

37

ANTHROPOLOGICAL POETICS

◆ Ivan Brady

oetics is a topic usually associated with the systematic study of literature, but, especially in its modern concern with texts as "cultural artifacts," it extends to anthropology in several ways.[1] One obvious connection is that, like other academic disciplines, anthropology is "literary" in that it conveys its information primarily through writing. This textual base lets anthropology share with more conventional studies of poetics an interest in text construction, the authority of the text, semiotic behavior and the production of meaning in discourse, and, in general, all the philosophical and critical problems associated with mimesis—the representation and successful communication of experience in any form, especially as problematized in texts. It also brings to the fore

something that anthropology is predisposed to engage because of its own diverse history: debate over the place of art and science in the social sciences and the humanities. Anthropology has intellectual camps at both extremes, that is, strong science orientations that conscientiously attempt to exclude more artistic or humanistic methods and interpretations, and vice versa (see Fujimara, 1998). Overall there is a compromise of identity: Anthropology sees itself as an "artful science" (Brady, 1990a, 1993). That leaves room for engaging a variety of postmodern challenges from other disciplines, including much that has arisen under the labels *literary* and *poetic* (Brady, 1991b).

Cultural anthropology in particular encompasses both individualized studies and system-

AUTHOR'S NOTE: This chapter is a substantially revised and expanded version of Brady (1996). It has benefitted from generous readings by James A. Boon, Norman K. Denzin, Robert Borofsky, Dan Rose, Miles Richardson, Yvonna S. Lincoln, James W. Fernandez, and Barbara Tedlock, and I wish to thank them. Any remaining wrongheadedness is entirely my own. "Shaman's Song" is reprinted with permission of Station Hill Press (Barrytown, New York), from Stanley Diamond's *Totems* (1982, p. 94).

atic comparisons of cross-cultural experience, so its potential poetic sources are broadly based. That has allowed anthropologists to feed into and draw reciprocally on several disciplines while developing their own specialized studies of the forms and content of poetic production in their own societies, in other cultures, as well as in their communications *about* other cultures.[2] Playing in such fields begs a variety of critical issues, from cultural relativism to competing philosophies of representation that have long histories of contemplation in other disciplines and less attention in anthropology. Theorists from other disciplines have reached into anthropology on similar issues (see Clifford, 1988; Clifford & Marcus, 1986; Krupat, 1992). But the cross-poaching that underwrites anthropology's "literarization" and the "anthropologizing" of literary studies is hard to measure and subject to various interpretations.[3] It has also resulted in some confusion over the degree to which anthropology ought to rely on other disciplines instead of creating its own adaptive solutions to the challenges posed, for example, regarding "the effort to situate discourses sociologically, to show how discourses function, compete, and clash within sociopolitical arenas, and to trace how discourses are transformed historically" (Fischer, 1988, p. 8; compare Krupat, 1992, pp. 51-52; Taylor, 1996).

One famous connection between anthropology and other disciplines that study poetics is structuralism. Although now less popular (having been relegated mistakenly by some to the graveyard of things buried by "postmodern" growth—see Brady, 1993), the structuralism developed in this century by linguists Ferdinand de Saussure and Noam Chomsky, psychologist Jean Piaget, and especially anthropologist Claude Lévi-Strauss had a profound impact on literary studies in the 1960s and 1970s.[4] The concept of poetics and what might constitute a legitimate study of it has been permanently changed as a result, and the possibilities for demarcating something clearly as *anthropological* poetics have been complicated in the process.[5] That doesn't disappoint most of the modern critics who operate happily between the cracks

of conventional divisions. Poetics is now more than ever an interdisciplinary topic that rightfully resists such reductions. Nevertheless, anthropology's footprints tend to be distinctive, so marking its path through this terrain is not impossible. Even though anthropological inquiry into poetics lacks coherence as a specialized field, we can locate it pragmatically by inspecting what anthropologists have done with it and by marking the intersections of their work with like-minded activities from elsewhere.

Without departing entirely from the common literary grounds of writing as a form of expression and what constitutes *author*-ity in the first place, anthropological studies of poetics differ from those of most other disciplines by reaching into performance issues in discourse, including studies of ritual and worldview, from tribal societies to modern theater, and their relationships to language and culture.[6] Ethnopoets in particular—cultural anthropologists, linguists, and poets who study other cultures from a poetic perspective—never lose sight of the language that structures and facilitates discourse, in oral or written form.[7] These are some of the reasons the subject of anthropological poetics gravitates naturally to sociolinguistics and linguistics in general (which has its own gradations of science-minded versus more artful practitioners), residually to the empirically rigorous studies of semantics and culture popularized in anthropology in the 1960s and 1970s as "cognitive anthropology" (see Tyler, 1969), and directly to discourse-centered production in any form, including writing. They are tied together by the instrumental role language plays in each instance.

The emphasis on the centrality of language in culture was also one of the original attractions of structuralism and poetics to linguistics and at the same time a brace for some of the earliest discontents with logical positivism in ethnography, which historically has tried to keep its rhetorical bases and authorship "invisible" as a pretext of clinical distance. An increased understanding of the collaborative nature of fieldwork and the need for more "reflexive" perspectives on it relative to constructivist (e.g., the reader reception theories of scholars such as semiologist Umberto Eco and literary critic Roland Barthes) and multivocal interpretations of literature (following especially the seminal work of Russian critic Mikhail Bakhtin) have also spurred the development of a critical dialogics for linguistics and anthropology as a whole.[8] The challenge for a dialogic poetics is that it "must first of all be able to identify and arrange relations between points of view: It must be adequate to the complex architectonics that shape the viewpoint of the author toward his characters, the characters toward the author, and all of these toward each other" (Holquist, 1990, p. 162). Ethnographers have been attracted to this kind of argument precisely because it defines both the relationships and the constraints on self-conscious cross-cultural research and writing. But the subsequent turn to linguistics as science and model for cultural and textual studies and to language in some strict sense as the key to ethnographic investigation has proved to be inadequate—or at least incomplete—and is the source of many of the indeterminacies in philosophy and method that characterize current debate on ethnographic representation and interpretation.[9]

The interdisciplinary stretch of what can be marked as the anthropological version of poetics thus covers a lot of ground. It ranges from a self-conscious interest in *poetry,* conceived brightly by poet Rita Dove (1994) as "the art of making the interior life of one individual available to others" (p. 25; see also Prattis, 1986, 1997), on the one hand, to much more inclusive analytic interests that are perhaps best contained by French critic Paul Valéry's (1964) concept of poetics as "everything that bears on the creation or composition of works having language at once as their substance and their instrument" (p. 86; see also Brady, 1991a), on the other. Splicing into that fuzzy framework from many directions, anthropological poetics nevertheless settles mainly into three subcategories of inquiry, which are not mutually exclusive: (a) ethnopoetics, (b) literary anthropology, and (c) anthropological poetry.

◆ Ethnopoetics

Ethnopoetics may be the most conspicuously anthropological activity in a poetic domain. Dennis Tedlock (1992), a pioneer in the field, defines it as the "study of the verbal arts in a worldwide range of languages and cultures" (p. 81). It focuses primarily on "the vocal-auditory channel of communication in which speaking, chanting, or singing voices give shape to proverbs, riddles, curses, laments, praises, prayers, prophecies, public announcements, and narratives" (p. 81). The goal in such studies is "not only to analyze and interpret oral performances but also to make them directly accessible through transcriptions and translations that display their qualities as works of art" (p. 81). Much has been done to reach this goal since ethnopoetics was invented as a special genre of inquiry in the United States in the late 1960s.

Poet-ethnographer Jerome Rothenberg coined the term *ethnopoetics* in 1968 and is properly considered to be "the father of American ethnopoetics" (Tarn, 1991, p. 75). His most instructive thoughts on this topic are collected in edited volumes that also illustrate the diverse intellectual inspiration this movement owes to various social scientists, ethnographers, and poets (including especially Henry David Thoreau, Gertrude Stein, Ezra Pound, Arthur Rimbaud, and William Blake), and to other influential social thinkers (such as Giambattista Vico and surrealist Tristan Tzara—see Rothenberg & Rothenberg, 1983). Some of Rothenberg's other work (e.g., 1981, 1985) digs deeper into the roots of "oral poetry" (see Finnegan, 1992a, 1992b) and related traditions as old as the late Pleistocene (see Brady, 1990b; Tarn, 1991, p. 15) and as momentous as the birth of theater and poetry in shamanism (Rothenberg, 1981). A common theme throughout is an attempt to close the distance modern thinking tends to put between "us" and "them," both historically and as these artificial boundaries are used to separate us from the performative traditions of "ex-primitives" around the globe today (see Bauman, 1977, 1992; MacCannell, 1992; Schechner, 1995). The author of numerous books of poetry, Rothenberg was also a cofounder (with Dennis Tedlock) and coeditor of the radical magazine *Alcheringa/Ethnopoetics,* which featured "transcripts, translations, and tear-out disc recordings of performances by indigenous verbal artists from Africa, Asia, Oceania, and the Americas" (D. Tedlock, 1992, pp. 81-82). It was keenly focused on developing ethnopoetics, on freeing poetries of all kinds from the "monolithic great tradition" of Western literature, and on exploring new techniques of translating the poetry of tribal societies. Although *Alcheringa* is no longer in print, its experimentalism continues to characterize the field of ethnopoetics today (see especially Tedlock, 1983, 1990, 1992).

The innovative work of linguist-anthropologists Dell Hymes, Robert Duncan, and George Quasha, anthropologist-poet Stanley Diamond, and other poets who, like Rothenberg, have had some training in anthropology or linguistics, including David Antin and Gary Snyder, must also be considered in calculating the intellectual history of ethnopoetics. Their collective scholarship has influenced all the others who have contributed to the development and preservation of this genre since the early 1970s. One such person was anthropologist Victor Turner. Writing more than a decade and half ago about the connection of ethnopoetics to his own work on ritual, Turner (1983) suggested that ethnopoetics offers a way of renewing recognition of "the deep bonds between body and mentality, unconscious and conscious thinking, species and self" that "have been treated without respect, as though they were irrelevant for analytical purposes" in much of the intellectual discourse from anthropology's colonial period (p. 338). He also noted poignantly that the resurgence of ethnopoetics "comes at a time when knowledge is being increased of other cultures, other worldviews, other life styles, when Westerners, endeavoring to trap non-Western philosophies and poetries in the corrals of their own cognitive constructions, find that they have caught sublime monsters, eastern dragons, lords of fructile chaos, whose wisdom makes our knowledge look somehow shrunken and inadequate" (p. 338). Appropriate to bridging ethnopoetics

and anthropology's struggle for a postcolonial identity, such concerns also lead directly into the realm of humanistic anthropology.[10]

Anthropologist-linguist Keith Basso (1988) points to another major problem still on the ethnopoetic horizon that is centered in the larger issue of hegemonic discourse—a cultural bias or override in the linguistic and intellectual forms we use to appropriate and represent cross-cultural experience. There is, Basso says, "a growing conviction among linguistic anthropologists that the oral literatures of Native American people have been inaccurately characterized, wrongly represented, and improperly translated." For the better part of a century, "the spoken productions of Native American storytellers have been presented as pieces of prose whose formal divisions are marked by paragraphs and sentences." Recent research indicates that this is a fundamental distortion of the record. It appears that "Native American storytellers often spoke—and in some Indian communities continue to speak today—in forms of measured verse" (p. 809).[11] The ethnopoetic task is to decide on the kinds of evidence that "attest to the existence of these poetic forms" and to answer a variety of related questions: "Given a properly recorded text, together with a knowledge of the language in which it was made, how should analysis proceed? What kinds of theoretical constructs are called for along the way, and how should these constructs be modified and refined?" (Basso, 1988, p. 809).[12] Answering these questions sweeps through many of the postmodern challenges that have surfaced in ethnopoetics and anthropology in general in the past 20 years. The concerns cluster around cultural and historical "situatedness"—our inability to devise a culture-free or purely objective view of anything. It is hard to avoid the argument that scholarly work is culturally constructed, rhetorically conditioned, tropological, empowered with a point of view, and addled with imperfections, distortion, and incompleteness. Everything a scholar produces is, in effect, "textual" in every sense of the term (see also Rorty, 1979, 1981; White, 1973, p. xii). Just how "literary" anthropology wants to be in the face of these challenges has emerged as a serious question and a point of much debate.

◆ Literary Anthropology

While the study of relations between anthropology and literary theory is still unfolding,[13] the major points of entry into them were pioneered in anthropology by Clifford Geertz (1973, 1983, 1988). In much the same way that Hayden White's celebrated "contention of the inherent 'literariness' of history significantly prefigured the way a number of theorists and historians are now reading anthropology, that is, as text, as writing that is necessarily bound within the parameters of discourse," so it is that "Clifford Geertz's anthropological writings over the past two decades have similarly affirmed the ultimately discursive nature of anthropology by holding that cultural interplay is itself semiotic, a system of signs that can be interpreted by the culture-reader" (Manganaro, 1990b, p. 15). Pursuing this has had a dramatic effect on ideas about the craft and purpose of ethnography, but the linking up with literary interests has not been too much of a stretch for anthropology in some respects: "We know many reasons to emphasize what literature shares with other kinds of human expression. We know how readily we transform literary to non-literary knowledge, and vice versa. We also know how fuzzy matters may be at their intellectual margins" (Miner, 1990, p. 12)—and therein lies much of the problem: It is "fuzzy" on the boundaries. That notwithstanding for the moment, with both the same and a different subject by metaphoric extension—"texts" and "cultures as texts"—some anthropologists have pushed Geertz's premises to argue that their discipline can function as a form of cultural critique not unlike that promoted in more obviously literary circles.[14] Transcending the naïve conception of ethnography as easily apprehended cross-cultural description, influential anthropologist-critic George Marcus (1988) gives its poetic a simultaneous shot of

aesthetic value and authority: "When done artfully," he says, "description takes the form of authoritative narration of cultural processes" (p. 68). It has the character of allegory (Clifford, 1988) in any case and produces a kind of layered artifact loaded with variable cultural dispositions and competing political concerns that are situated in "terms of the social construction of literary realism" (Feld, 1987, p. 190). The much-discussed perspectives of "interpretive anthropology" were born of such concerns.[15]

By keeping questions of authorship at center focus and by exploring the evocative equation of cultures *as* texts that participant observers must learn how to "read" in culturally authentic ways,[16] Marcus and several other anthropologists have since the early 1980s devoted considerable effort to evaluating the utility of such metaphors and to understanding how the methods and theories of interpreting literature might transfer to the interpretation of their own writings, to the study of other cultures so conceived, as well as to the specific study of indigenous oral narratives.[17] The "rich contemporary production of fiction and literature from most parts of the third world" is another "object of analysis that combines ethnography and literary criticism" (Marcus & Fischer, 1986, p. 74).[18] It is "important not only as a guide for . . . inquiries in the field . . . [but also] for suggesting ways in which the form of the ethnography might be altered to reflect the kind of cultural experiences that find expression both in indigenous writing and in the ethnographer's fieldwork" (Marcus & Fischer, 1986, p. 74) and ultimately function "as a form of cultural critique of ourselves" (Marcus & Fischer, 1986, p. 1; see also Williams, 1998).

This work has been expanded critically[19] and extended creatively[20] in various ethnographic and historical contexts. But the growing literariness of the process has become increasingly problematic, including the issue of *how* to write as an anthropologist and questions about the place of fiction in "realistic" ethnographies (see Banks & Banks, 1998; Ellis & Bochner, 1996; Rapport, 1997). Geertz (1988) first raised the issue of anthropological writing's being inescapably fictional in the sense of being "something made, something constructed"—a strategic fabrication that is not necessarily untrue, but cannot escape its fictional character simply by adopting realism as a mode of exposition or by claiming clear authority on another form of life only on the basis of having "been there" (pp. 4-5). Ethnographic authority derives necessarily from a much more creative, self-interested, historically and culturally situated circumstance in which the author is inevitably a confabulator between his or her own experiences and those of Others in some mutually constructed communication. It is established most directly as a "writerly act" (Geertz, 1988); ethnographic knowledge is *really* created by conventions of writing" (Fabian, 1990, p. 762). By being dedicated generally to representing peoples without writing, ethnography differentiates itself from the writing of literature and history per se (Manganaro, 1990b). But, despite its needs for objectivity and the defiance of ethnocentrism, ethnographic writing can "no longer be seen as a natural or organic extension of content"; the anthropological writer "either plugs into preexisting plot structures or creates a new structure out of the amalgam of old forms" (Manganaro, 1990b, p. 15). By allowing no culturally or linguistically unconstructed access to reality—no story structures unconditioned by history—and by virtue of its roots in the "fuzzy" cross-cultural margins of anthropological fieldwork, ethnographic representation is thus conducive to developing the kinds of competing interpretations that go with the declaration of "fuzzy" boundaries on any topic. In that capacity it easily lends itself to further analogizing of the situation as ambiguous "text."[21]

The attempt to reconcile the role of the author, the place of fiction, and related literary enmeshments in ethnography's realist writing tradition leads to two underexamined developments in the field, one old and one new, and it begs a third. First, it shows the need for a critical reexamination of writing constructions and realist assumptions in anthropology's only established poetic genre, the ethnographic novel.[22] Second, there is an active search on in many quarters of anthropology to adopt more obviously literary forms that can be used to enhance

communication of the ethnographic experience in the realist tradition, including those with greater "writer consciousness" (e.g., where the author appears in first person as narrator and actor in the ethnographic account, contrary to the positivist tradition).[23] Although there are now many variations on this theme,[24] Lévi-Strauss's *Tristes Tropiques* (1961) is by far the best known of all such works and was foundational in "its resistance to the duty of directly rendering the anthropological subject."[25] It "represents the anthropological text that perhaps most influenced current speculation on the nature of anthropological representation" (Manganaro, 1990b, p. 17). One enduring consequence is that anthropologists are much more alert to their roles as writers and critics today in ethnographic and historical research,[26] and to the role of writing and criticism more generally in anthropological method and theory.[27]

Third, the new emphasis on creative construction and prolonged attention to anthropology's inevitable textual involvement has created a kind of epistemological havoc. It not only pits positivism against all of the great deconstructive "undoings" of late, it also means the loss of invisibility in writing as part of the realist tradition. That is a direct challenge to science's mythical perpetuation of the unobtrusive sign (compare Barthes, 1972). By accentuating the form of the message rather than the contents of its speech acts, the literary or poetic takes for its primary object what science does not. In the formalist sense, we can cull out a measure of literariness in any text and call it *poeticity:* the degree to which a work flags the linguistic nature of its own being; the degree to which it emphasizes materiality versus transparency through self-referencing linguistic forms (see Jakobson, 1987). A text high in poeticity, whether prose or verse, in this sense signals itself in place instead of disappearing; it celebrates the signifier over the signified without abandoning the basic communication function it shares as discourse with more scientific or historically authentic calculations, albeit through very different channels (compare Levine, 1987, 1994). Writing in a way that does not call attention to itself in order to allow the objective observer to focus directly on the "reality" of the subject is a delusion—a special kind of fiction and desire that helps to turn "culture" into "nature" in the common view. It hides precepts and politics alike behind the power of the sign and makes them look invisible (Brady, 1991a, p. 216). The narrative discourse of science, as in art, is created out of the interaction of such cultural conventions and situations, the way the author deploys them through particular language codes, and the reader's process of reception (creative construction) that releases meaning from the text. Clarity of meaning itself takes on new meaning in this context. It lacks absolutes. It becomes a manipulable cultural code, reckoned with familiarity and history—still "fuzzy" around the edges. It cannot be a culture-free peek at the universe enabled by a mythical objectivity (Brady, 1991b, p. 19; see also Bruner, 1986, 1990; compare Barthes, 1968).

Science, of course, needs language to function, but unlike literature, it neither asserts nor sees itself as situated *within* language. The conspicuously poetic author willingly appears in his or her text as an artisan whose constant display is the craft of language (the language and form of the poem is claimed by the poet and must be read through that claim—a proprietary function) or as a person who visibly leads the prose narrative from within. The scientific author tries to avoid both, aspiring to invisibility in every place except the opening credits of his or her cover page (compare Geertz, 1988, pp. 7-8; Manganaro, 1990b, pp. 15-16). The resulting gap between author and text is a pit for various detached composition strategies, including anthropology's great timeless fiction of writing in the ethnographic present. Authorial invisibility enhances the prospect for smuggling distancing time frames (we are "present" and full of time; Others are "past" and "timeless")[28] into the argument, not to mention excessively clinical assumptions of philosophy, including the possibility of "mirror of nature minds" in observation and communication and related forms of objectivity (Rorty, 1979). Calling "into question the very language by which modern science knows its language," thereby bringing its invisible signs back

into conscious orbit, Barthes (1986, p. 5) concludes, can thus only be done by writing, itself a condition of language.

Philosophical justification in the criticism of interpretive anthropology and its textual turn have waned since Dreyfus and Rabinow's (1983) challenging evaluation of Michel Foucault's thinking and its relevance to cultural anthropology.[29] Any serious reengagement of interpretive anthropology with modern science (and, to some degree, with archaeology and physical anthropology—compare Hodder, 1986; Tilley, 1990) will have to resurrect the historical points at which epistemological concerns began to recede in anthropology and then build from there. Literary anthropology, as part of the emerging critical tradition in textual studies, rests on a similar fate if it is ever to close the loop of its critical departure from modern science concerns with *explanation* per se and much that has been rejected arbitrarily in the zeal to construct powerful arguments about representation, historical situatedness, and *author*-ity in general. As Fabian (1990) suggests, "Dialogical and poetic conceptions of ethnographic knowledge touch the heart of questions about othering. But they have a chance to change the shape of ethnography only if they lead to literary processes that are hermeneutic-dialectical, or 'practical,' rather than representational" (p. 766). On the other hand, many of the participants in anthropology's literary turn have no interest whatsoever in closing that larger loop with any method, theory, or language that resembles the status quo ante in their field (Brady, 1991b, pp. 12-13). Theirs is a more creative turn to be considered critically before any larger inclusions are attempted.[30] Following ideas that have "already been claimed by various forms of radical anthropology," which see "the discipline as a handmaiden to an era of European and American imperialism," Nathaniel Tarn (1991) suggests that intellectual studies—perhaps properly conceived as Wittgensteinian language games—should keep their identities as such and not be promoted to some Archimedian level of essential Truth or "used for oppressive purposes or any pretence at superior knowledge" (p. 57).[31] Anthropological poetry has surfaced in a similar humanistically grounded context as a distinctly literary activity crossed over to social science.

◆ Anthropological Poetry

If ethnopoetics is the most conspicuous anthropological activity in a poetics domain, anthropological poetry is easily qualified in the converse as the most conspicuously poetic activity in an anthropological domain.[32] Such work tends to focus on cross-cultural themes, esoteric cultural information, the experiences of doing fieldwork in other cultures, and so on. Its distinctive characteristic is the presentation of that information in marked poetic form. Set in an anthropological mode, poetry is a conspicuously linguistic message loaded with critical commentary on the nature of the world and our place in it (Brady, 1991a, p. 216). Through poetic portrayal, although perhaps fictional at the level of precise time and sequence of events, anthropological poets often attempt to convey the cross-cultural circumstances and events of their fieldwork in an authentic and penetrating way (see Flores, 1982, 1999; Prattis, 1986). The aim in this poetry is not to exist only for its own sake or self, or merely to entertain, but to flag its language without losing its historical or ethnographic referentiality and authenticity—thereby constituting a paradox of the first order.[33] But it is the conspicuously linguistic forms (such as the self-halting process of poetic line phrasing) that give it poeticity, not its commentary—that is its anthropological part. This raises the issue of writer consciousness once again, the degree to which authors should or must appear as such in their discourse, and therefore crosses the boundary that traditionally has divided scientific writing (and observation) from other forms.

Poetics leads to the aesthetic, which, as part of a general concern for the making of meaning in what we do and study (see Brady, 1991b; Flores, 1985), can be engaged in radical forms, including but not limited to poetry, without completely abandoning seemingly contrary interests such as scientific observation. Although poetry is not science and does not aspire to be science (Diamond, 1986c, p. 132), some of the work of at least the kind of science produced by ethnographers is intruded upon by the anthropological poet. By varying their forms of expression to include poetry, anthropologists attempt to say things that might not be said as effectively or at all any other way. This is consistent with the need to discover and examine critically all of the ways a subject (including social and cultural relationships) can be represented. In that diversity the anthropological poet finds a measure of truth. But the Cartesian critic sees another version: By reporting fieldwork experiences through poetry, the author invokes a form of subjectivity to do the work of a form of objectivity, the conventional ethnography (see Tarn, 1991, p. 246). In the process, information may be conveyed more as what "might" or "could be" than "what is" or "what was" as concrete historical fact, and that is problematic (counterintuitive) to modern science and to ethnography that emulates its methods.

The pecking order of arguments in this instance has not always been the same. Poetry has occupied more respectable positions in some of the Truth camps of the past. It has not always been so marginalized as intellectual activity.[34] Aristotle recognized 2,400 years ago that because poetry exacts universal judgments from action, from history, it can be considered (with more than a little irony for the present argument) at one level *more* scientific (or philosophical) than history. It is a medium in which "the lessons of history do not become any more intelligible and they remain undemonstrated and therefore merely probable, but they become more compendious and therefore more useful" (Collingwood, 1956, p. 25). Nevertheless, rejected as method by the received wisdom of science since the Enlightenment, in part for its declaration of "ringing true" rather than "being true" in some particular empirical and historical accountability of "what actually happened," in part for working in a kind of "fifth dimension," independent of time and therefore "of a sort that scientists cannot recognize" (Graves, 1971, p. 35; see also Bruner, 1986, p. 52), poetry is reintroduced only with difficulty to any context of specific empirical accountability, such as concerns anthropology and the social sciences.[35]

The challenge of poetry for anthropology thus has several aspects. In addition to studying the uses to which poetry can be put, the contexts in which it appears as discourse, and the variability of its forms in specific cultures (its ethnopoetic dimensions), the challenge includes the development of a genre of writing and reporting that systematically tries to incorporate satisfying and edifying poetic quality (foregrounding for clarity as well as aesthetic functions and the practical use of metaphor as a tool of discovery) without sacrificing the essence of ethnographic accountability. In writing anthropological poetry, an author attempts to evoke a comparable experience or set of experiences through the reader's experience with the text on the twin assumptions that all humans are tied together through certain substantive universals of being and that the beings we encounter are sufficiently like ourselves to be open to empathic construction, discovery, and reporting (Quine's principal of charity—see Shweder, 1996).

Perhaps one can also "extend to all discourse what has been said of poetic discourse alone, because it manifests to the highest degree, when it is successful, the effect which consists in awakening experiences which vary from one individual to another. . . . The paradox of communication is that it presupposes a common medium, but one which works—as is clearly seen in the limiting case in which, as often in poetry, the aim is to transmit emotions—only by eliciting and reviving singular, and therefore socially marked, experiences" (Bourdieu, 1991, p. 39). In this way, whether through poetry, a great novel, or a play, the anthropological writer invites us to "live through" other experiences vicariously and, "through the power of metaphor, to come away with a deeper understanding of . . . the human condition" (Coward & Royce, 1981, p. 132). Anthropological humanists (some of whom are poets) look at this as the challenge of writing "from within" rather than "without"

and that of "good writing" in general, which, as mentioned earlier, is an important part of anthropology's emerging poetics.[36]

Clifford Geertz is well-known for the quality of his writing, as are a few other anthropologists.[37] But theirs is not typical writing in the discipline. In fact, as noted previously, and contrary to the kind of disciplinary protection history claims generally for the public accessibility of its writings against the obtuse jargonizing of the social sciences, not all anthropologists strive for more interesting and edifying ways of communicating anthropological experience. Appearing "too literary" (and certainly writing poetry begs the issue) is generally believed to undermine scientific authority.[38] It can put the writer in the "wrong" intellectual camp, and that can have severe career consequences for research funding, promotions, and other political concerns. Some of the resistance is simply against passion in discourse (see Fabian, 1994, p. 100; Taussig, 1987). For holistic anthropology (with its interest in preserving the four-field character of the discipline: cultural anthropology, archaeology, physical anthropology, and linguistics), the real danger in exaggerating the focus on "author-centrism" is slipping into a purely rhetorical or aesthetic legitimation of ethnography "by ontologizing representation, writing, and literary form" (Fabian, 1994, p. 91). That may elide or preempt altogether the question of objectivity, which—as one of the few gates of conversation open to reconciling conventional scientific concerns with advancing poetics and the need for epistemological study in ethnography—nevertheless is a neglected issue in postmodern anthropology (Fabian, 1994, p. 91; see also Megill, 1994; Tiles, 1984). In the middle of it all is an ongoing confusion between powerful explanation and good vocabulary (Rorty, 1981, p. 158; see also Abrahams, 1986; Brady, 1991b).

Lamenting the generally sad state of anthropological discourse today—that it is often "painful to read," enormously self-serving, corrupted with esoteric and bland jargon, incestuous in its preoccupations when it might be better served with a more outward vision of its purposes and communication strategies—Tarn (1991) suggests that "if the latest generation writes well it may be due to mass alienation from the academic side of the discipline (with all its dangers) and to such phenomena as 'ethnopoetics' " (p. 56)—with its emphasis on comparative expression. A properly modern anthropology would find a way to reintegrate its writing of science and its humanisms. "It would pay the greatest attention to the way in which . . . ethnography was written, striving to go beyond *belles lettres* toward a language with scientific and literary properties both, but governed primarily by literature, so that its results could be available to all culturally literate readers" (Tarn, 1991, p. 57). Addressing in particular what authors have attempted in what he calls "auto-anthropologies" ("personal ethnography," "reflexive ethnography," and so on; see Crapanzano, 1980; Dumont, 1978; Rabinow, 1977), Tarn (1991) says that such efforts run parallel to his "argument that the genre so long looked for which would assure a complete union of the poetic and anthropological enterprises [without reducing either completely to the other, without sacrificing the option of lopsided emphasis, of an anti-union, or of for all practical purposes complete independence in the conscious formulation of anthropological discourse] (should such be desirable) lies not in the keeping of the anthropologist who cannot, for all his/her efforts, get beyond *belles lettres,* but with the poet who, in theory, still can. This is the question of a language which, without turning away from scientific veracity, abdicates not one jot of its literary potential. Undoubtedly utopian, the search is at home in poetry, incurably utopian, and probably nowhere else" (p. 256; see also Richardson, 1994; Rose, 1991b).

As poets, anthropologists still have to get some purchase on their audiences. Will it be poetry addressed to the existing elite, to anthropologists as such, perhaps as a form of extending the ethnographic tradition, or addressed to "the people at large, or that section of it which has not been consumerized out of existence as a reading and listening public?" (Tarn, 1991, p. 64). Market matters, and some poetry published in the social sciences is of dubious quality by literary standards and therefore less marketable.[39] But what makes the distinction? What is

defensibly good or agreeably bad poetry? There is a whole industry of writing about this in general, of course, and there has been since the first critics forayed as experts into a world not of their own making. I will not attempt to sort that pile out here, especially at the level of craft (although such discussion is relevant), except to echo some early-in-the-century thinking by I. A. Richards (1929): "It is less important to like 'good' poetry and dislike 'bad,' than to be able to use them both as a means of ordering our minds"; and that what matters is the quality of the reading we give to poems, "not the correctness with which we classify them" as good or bad, right or wrong (p. 327). The ease with which a poem might slip into the mind to good effect is as much a function of the reader's susceptibility by topic and variable inclination to appropriate such things as it is a function of form. There may be wide agreement on the value of a particular poem or body of work, but there are no absolutes of poetic stimulation and effectiveness. Much depends on the situation at hand. As with any text, the same poem can travel with very different effects across personal and cultural boundaries.

Nonetheless, after all is said and done, perhaps we can agree that the most effective poetry stirs something up in you—an emotion or passion that reaches beyond the shallow, that gravitates to deeper experiences and the sublime. The best of it is powerfully orienting, inspirational, if not more directly mantic or prophetic.[40] In ethnographic or cross-cultural poetry, the effect is likely to be a significant realization of identity with what otherwise could not possibly be claimed as Own. Through words and their specialized forms, a kinship is evoked that is grounded in empathy and interpretation. It huddles with the universality of being human and sends a large message: Perhaps we are all Cheyenne, Arapaho, Tuvaluan, and Ik. Perhaps we are also all ethnographers now, as Rose (1991b, 1993) says. The best poets can make these things work as ideas and as platforms for social action (compare Rothenberg, 1994).

The late anthropologist-poet-social-activist Stanley Diamond (1987), reflecting on the ugly, the beautiful, and the sublime in poetry (and quarreling with Keats's famous line that "a thing of beauty is a joy for ever"), wrote:

> The mere deepening of gratification from the "joyful" experience of beauty as truth does not achieve the sublime. The experience of the sublime is both transcendental and quintessentially cultural at the same time. Language itself is the transcendence of the biological, it is the medium of culture, and culture is a rope-bridge thrown across a biological chasm. As the objective realizations of the human essence, that is, as the existentializing of our human possibilities, culture(s) is the arena for the construction of meanings: it represents a struggle that is constant and renewed in each generation, and evident in the lives of individuals as they strive to become cultured human beings. . . . There are no certainties here, only struggle and contingency, pain and realization. Gratification, satisfaction, or happiness are not at issue. But, we encounter *joy*. This is the joy that one finds in Lear, as he hurls his words into the terrible gulf that engulfs him. The joy is in the words, in his matured sensibility, in his challenge to nature and human defeat. The joy is in the challenge, and in the formulation of his meanings. Or observe the final shuffling off of guilt by Oedipus at Colonnus, as Sophocles etherealizes him in a beam of light. Or the conclusion of the Winnebago medicine rite, when the initiate finally achieves his emancipation from society, after bearing all the abuse that society may heap upon him. Or, for that matter, the ordinary rituals of maturing and variegated experience known in every primitive society, whereby growth is attended by pain, where a new name may be earned, and where the past is arduously incorporated into the present, preparing the individual for the next ritual round as he moves higher in the spiritual hierarchy of his society. That is where the joy is. And finally, it is this joy, not Keats's beauty or truth, which defines the sublime, beyond the confines of the merely aesthetic, breaking all the formal rules of aesthetics, beyond the range of the romantic imagination. For we are not talking of imagination here, but of experience and its meanings, whether in the culture of dreams, the culture of the hunt, or in the ceremonies of rebirth. And finally, I am talking of the sacred space, the sacred silence that lies beyond language, but remains grounded in language. (pp. 270-271; compare Burke, 1958)

All but the most serious and sensitive writers would be hard-pressed to capture these existential dimensions in generally accessible language. Ethnopoets strive for such experience and communication, even as they eschew as unrealistic any expectations of ever reducing the sacred or the sublime to strictly clinical or analytic forms. A battle is fit on this very quest: If the artist sees it, she believes she has some prospect of saying it poetically, of conveying with less prospect of empirical distortion the nature of the experience as panhuman emotion; if the scientist sees it or grips its "felt meaning," she can only hasten its transformation into something else (or some things else) by attempting to appropriate and express it through clinical forms. Either way, there is a problem. Coleridge's "The Rime of the Ancient Mariner" refuses reduction to the subject of sailors and seawater or to critical summaries of its formal properties and inspirations, just as the statistical expression of cross-cultural trait distributions in the ancient Middle East cannot yield its exactness and rhetorical integrity to interpretive statements high in poeticity or uncommon metaphor.[41] Poetizing such things may reveal new dimensions of the problem, to be sure, and that can be a profound contribution to humanistic concerns, but it is not necessarily a proper substitute for the original statement or form. While the upshot of such things can be shared widely in language, culture, and experience, the confining exactitudes of competing poetic and scientific linguistic forms restrict movements and thus hook again into that entangled truth of disciplinary and intellectual discourse: Not all subjects travel equally well.[42] The movement is not hopeless. Translation is possible. But it is by definition a changing frame.

Beyond that we need to ask who does the poet speak *for*? There is debate over this in anthropology, not only for its poets but for all of its writers, as there is in every discipline that has entered the crisis of representation. Sticking to anthropological poets for the moment, for they may have stretched the forms of representation in the social sciences the most, consider Diamond's (1982, p. 94) poem "Shaman's Song":

I talk to flowers

My fingertips withstand

The glance of roses

What do you know of the Bear

His body, my spirit

Rises everywhere

Seeing what the leaf sees

And the cloud

Ambiguous as a woman

Drifting through stones

I have lain with the otter

Under white water

On beds softer than birds

What do you know of the Fox

Bearing the message of death?

Diamond was not a shaman. He was not a Native American, although the spirit of indigenous cultures of the Americas resonates through this work and through the multiple (Native American, Anglo, and anthropomorphized animal) voices that structure his epic poem *Going West* (1986a).[43] In these works, as in all others he produced, especially in the waning years of his life, Diamond aimed for the sublime by drawing on the Everyman he met time and again through cross-cultural experience and by taking on that persona. Here was Aristotle's universal—and Diamond's mine. Penetrating and conspicuous experiences were laid out before him like so much crackable glass and Diamond felt it under his feet with every cross-cultural step. Tread lightly, he said, and his poetry was the gateway sign: "Things can break here." In that he spoke for everyone, as brother, as kin, as alienated Jew, as Everyman who has ever suffered the great smotherings of life and identity that flow from cross-cultural oppression. Translation and multivoice reporting of human commonalities in purpose, interests, pasts, and futures were not only possible, they were, to Diamond's eternal credit, imperative (see Rose, 1983/1991a). Everyman was for him simultaneously author, subject, and audience, a social unit whose variable parts were collapsed into reciprocal self-awareness through the rituals of poetry.

Two related themes found throughout Diamond's work, including his provocative "How to Die in America" (1986b), are that individuals and cultures transcend that which consumes them, no matter how painful the circumstances, or perhaps because of the pain, and that vast unintended consequences come from colonial cannibalizing, with its miles and miles of cross-cultural casualties on the beachheads of the world, in Biafra, India, New Mexico, the Dakotas, New York, and California—not to mention the great erasures of tribal peoples in Russia, Spain, Iraq, Australia, China, and the other Americas. Diamond's poetry seems to come from everywhere because his quest for internalizing and expressing the sublime had no firm cultural boundaries. Transcultural mysteries and truths were in his view everywhere subject to appropriation through the carefully opened eye and ear, once saturated with experience. Diamond believed that no culture could hide its fundamental life from the prying eyes of the mystic or the excavations of the traveling poet, especially when a mature social scientist carried them both on his shoulders. His discourse was full of crossovers and changing centers. He knew that anthropology struggled for such knowledge and he believed that none of it would come without intellectual passion in discovery and representation. By shucking preconceptions to the best of his ability and immersing himself in the lives of others, he devoted the last years of his life to saying these things through poetry, having been, as he said, "first a poet, then an anthropologist, then a poet again" (personal communication, March 1983; see also Diamond, 1982; Rose, 1991b). His writings make it obvious that he never really changed professions, only from time to time his manner of professing.

Is the truth of Diamond's poetic work mixed up with beauty and yet anchored empirically in valid ethnography (compare McAllister, 1998)? Is it best judged as poetry, as skill in form, plussed by the enJOYment or illuminating and edifying introspection it produces? Or is it best judged like all fiction, not exclusively or necessarily in terms of its historical accuracy, but on a sliding scale of erotics and believability in the realm of being human? Does it stir something valuable up in us, perhaps rare or otherwise unobtainable, even as it rings true on life as we know it, or argue it, or both? These are but a few problematic slices of Geertz's (1973) claim that all ethnography is in important ways fictional—something constructed, something fashioned, and never from whole cloth. The crisis of representation in anthropology followed most directly from that pioneering work. The poets have never held center stage in the ensuing melee, but we can assert here that the fundamental issues of ethnographic representation do not change for conspicuously poetic versus more clinical texts. They are textual through and through, no matter what the purported form of representation.[44]

By the same token, as convention would have it in society generally, and specifically in the curious mix of subtle inferences, methodological mandates, and editorial imperialism in the Western world concerning appropriate language for scientific reporting, the form of address often depends heavily on the nature of the problem to be addressed. As it happens, Miles Richardson (1998a) says, "social scientists have long turned to poetry" as a reportorial mode, but the content generally has diverged from the academic centers of their fieldwork and therefore from a collision course with more conventional forms of ethnographic reporting: "Their poems . . . rarely addressed the rich ethnographic record they compiled nor the anguish they felt about the free individual encountering coercive culture" (p. 461). Some of the most notable poetry written by anthropologists in previous generations—by Edward Sapir, Loren Eiseley, and Ruth Benedict, who make up most of a short list—was similarly decentered as ethnography per se but competitive enough to be published in nonanthropological media oriented toward such concerns. But no anthropology journals catered to such interests, and the mainstream sentiment was generally then what it is now: Poetry is an aside, an amusement, that belongs elsewhere. Other than what might be called a "poetic mentality" in the humanism of the

times, and for some an affinity with the enticingly poetic work of Sir James Frazer, there was no ideology afoot that might sponsor or enfranchise a more specifically poetic genre of anthropological writing, including poetry.

That climate has changed perceptibly with the growth of more explicitly interpretive works in the field, that is, with the advent of postmodernism, the growth of "textualism" because of its focus on text construction and consumption, and the linguistic emphases of influential structuralists such as Jakobson (1987) and Lévi-Strauss (1962). Iain Prattis's *Reflections: The Anthropological Muse* (1986), a collection of poetry and artwork specifically addressed to fieldwork experiences by cultural anthropologists and linguists, established a precedent. So did reviews of Stanley Diamond's and Paul Friedrich's poetry in anthropology's flagship journal, the *American Anthropologist,* in the early 1980s.[45] At a time when much of this was at least a source of heated debate in the field, then editor George Marcus published Diamond's "How to Die in America" (1986b) poem in the first volume of *Cultural Anthropology.* As the editor of *Anthropology and Humanism Quarterly,* Miles Richardson initiated a poetry and fiction competition that featured the winners in the journal. The competition has been continued by the present editor, Edith Turner, and by her poetry editor, Dell Hymes, and the topics continue to widen. Friedrich's *Bastard Moons* (1979a), Diamond's *Going West* (1986a), and Dennis Tedlock's Turner Prize-winning *Days From a Dream Almanac* (1990) "explore issues of language, ethnographic truth, and shamanic dreams" (Richardson, 1998a, p. 461). Recent poetry in the *American Anthropologist,* under the editorship of Barbara and Dennis Tedlock, includes contributions by Friedrich (1995), Hymes (1995), and Richardson (1998b) on a variety of themes central to ethnographic experience. A new journal devoted to poetry, poetics, ethnography, and cultural and ethnic studies, called appropriately *Cross-Cultural Poetics [Xcp]* and edited by Mark Nowak, published its first issue in 1997. Now the journal *Qualitative Inquiry,* under the editorship of Yvonna Lincoln and Norman Denzin, is following suit (see Brady, 1998a; Richardson, 1998a). It will carry poetry and fiction as regular features, not because it is trendy to do so, say the editors, but because "social scientists have for too long ignored these important forms of ethnographic representation and interpretation" (N. K. Denzin, personal communication, November 8, 1998).

Looking in another direction, if the anthropologist-poets have been few in number to date (albeit increasing in the postmodern afterglow), anthropology as a whole has inspired numerous poets from other disciplines. "Poets precisely because of their 'otherness' in their home societies are attuned to otherness wherever it may be found. Hence they find an affinity, and to their own delight a *social* affinity, with the fruits of other cultures, particularly those of the 'despised and rejected' " (Turner, 1983, p. 339). To which Tarn (1991) adds: "The inspiration that anthropology has afforded poets—to go no further back than Pound or Eliot, or St. John Perse and Segalen, or Neruda, Vallejo, and Paz, in the age of Frazer, Harrison, or the author of *From Ritual to Romance*—to say nothing of Marx and Engles, Freud or Jung, Mauss, Durkheim or Lévi-Strauss—can scarcely be said to have abated when we now have a virtual school of 'ethnopoetics' devoted both to the accessing of 'primitive and archaic poetries' into our culture through the best available techniques of *twentieth century* translation *and* to the mutual effect upon each other of such poetries and our own—granted that Native poets very much continue to produce poetry all over this world" (p. 63).

Anticipating mutual effects, it is reasonable to ask where one goes with a penchant to write poetry in anthropology. Just adopting poetry as a form of writing guarantees nothing. But poetry can be informative and useful, even exhilarating when it reaches the sublime. Properly cast, it can be both fire bellows for and bubbling lid on the pot of intellectual life, a source of transformation that is admirably unquiet in any position: It "turns everything into life. It is that form of life that turns everything into language" (Meschonnic, 1988, p. 90). It is in fact an art "far larger than any description of its powers"

(Vendler, 1988, p. 6). For these reasons and others already detailed, some competition between poetry and science as genres may in fact be "healthy and entertaining" (Fabian, 1990, p. 766), even functional (Brady, 1993). It follows that having a hall full of poets (as nightmarish as that may seem to some scientists) can give academies of arts and sciences a better overall pulse, if not a better future of discourse and discovery. Writing poetry has also "helped individual anthropologists to overcome alienation from experience" (Fabian, 1990, p. 766) and that, as much as anything, has serious implications for engaging postmodern concerns about authority in ethnography. The penchant of the anthropologist to wax poetic, if honed and pointed in these ways, can push into the heart of ethnographic contemplation, epistemology, and theory. Hanging out in that zone for a while (as nightmarish as that may seem to some poets) might give way to progress in the conversation over what divides us so readily in the academy today.

There are many other paths to that end, of course. Poetry is not necessarily the right tool for every job. As the old adage goes, if one has only a hammer to work with, after a while everything starts to look like a nail. In this instance, "To seek the solution for a problem regarding the production of knowledge in different or better representations of knowledge is to reaffirm, not to overcome, the representationist stance," with all of its compulsions to order in conceptions of language and culture and related problems (Fabian, 1990, p. 766; see also Friedrich, 1979b). Remaining attentive to "the transformative, creative aspects of ethnographic knowledge" (Fabian, 1990, p. 766) is not entailed automatically by writing poetry (or reproducing dialogues) as an alternative to strict representational ethnography. "To preserve the dialogue with our interlocutors, to assure the Other's presence against the distancing devices of anthropological discourse, is to continue conversing with the Other on all levels of writing, not just to reproduce dialogues" (Fabian, 1990, p. 766) or to slip unwittingly from being "natural historians into itinerant bards, clowns, or preachers" in a humanistic or poetic commitment to "being with others" (Fabian, 1990, pp. 766-767; see also Tarn, 1991, p. 75). We can do better—and more.

One more thing to do in this writer's arena is to counter sole reliance on the centrifugal or "distancing" devices of anthropological discourse—the "Others are never Us" ideas, substituting third-person writing for first-person experiences, writing in the ethnographic present, and so on. Developing alternatives depends on paying special attention to the processes through which ethnographic knowledge is produced in the first place (Fabian, 1994).[46] That does not require a lapse into the old static models of structuralism, although much of what a poetics yields as the sublime might be seen as the recognition of common deep structures (*langue*) in a variable field of surface particulars (*parole*). Certainly there is room for some edifying resuscitation here. But the movement to more centripetal or "closing" discourse in anthropology should at minimum include an ontological and ethnopoetic emphasis on the performative aspects of culture, those that can be "acted out," as opposed to focusing exclusively on the more limited category of "what members of a culture know [that] is 'informative' in the sense that it can be elicited and produced as discursive information" (Fabian, 1994, p. 97).[47]

Such concerns necessarily draw ethnographers and poets into the larger philosophical fields of process, structure, and agency—including the dynamics of knowledge and ritual, theater and history (see Brady, 1999; Richardson, 1994)—and thereby increase the prospects of producing larger-level understandings of the experiential fields we draw from as observers and contribute to as actors and writers. But it should also be remembered that the original point of creative mystery in every study is also where the Muses call on the writer, and that is precisely "where humanistic anthropology must both stall the process of knowing and open it up intellectually—where we must catch ourselves in the act of rushing headlong into conventional formats, of jumping to conclusions about where the experience must take us and how to communicate it to others, and be-

gin to build a successful poetics into the framework" (Brady, 1991b, p. 20). By attempting to reconcile the spread in this connection between analytic problems and the substance of fieldwork, anthropological poetics can do more than capture (or create) and convey the poetries and literatures of various cultures. It can require greater philosophical justification for its ethnographic endeavors and at the same time help to erase some unnecessary distortions of detachment from its objects of inquiry.

◆ Coda

Here, then, is the poetic turf more anthropologists than ever are traversing nowadays. It is neither defined nor covered exclusively by anthropologists or traditional anthropological interests. As observers of common problems (in and out of their own societies), anthropologists differ in research methods and strategies and sometimes produce incomparable results. Adding other disciplines from the wings only seems to complicate matters. But common ground for all is not beyond the pale. One source of that for anthropologists and other social scientists is that they all seek ways of "speaking in the name of the real" about the people and behaviors they study—of representing fairly and accurately what cannot easily be known or demonstrated in the foggy partialities of cross-cultural experience, the imperfections of culturally situated observations, and the many voices insinuated in mutually constructed truths (compare Brady, 1983, 1991c). Another, as poet Tarn (1991) says, lies in the knowledge that "nothing can hide from us for long the fact that we all face the same problems in the end; that the poetic fate, like the human, is universal" (p. 14).

Discovering and assessing the common denominators of human existence has always had some priority in anthropology,[48] and the need to bridge the inherently hermeneutic studies of ethnography and larger-level statements about the whole organism (universals of language, culture, cognition, and behavior) is getting renewed attention—in full view of past limitations, such as incommensurate theory construction, language biases, political and pragmatic relations between ethnographers and the groups they study, the impossibility of absolute objectivity, and the need for successful measures of validity in ethnographic assertions.[49] But the poets have traditionally approached human commonalities differently, hanging more on meaning than behavior—more on humanistic interpretations than clinically validatable truths. From the perspective of anthropological poetics, resurrecting a systematic scientific examination of what is universal in life and culture—"thinking big" again (see Simpson, 1994)—is more than a big task. It requires jumping the gap of irony and paradox from a great (Geertzian) descent into details of local knowledge, "thick descriptions," and related critical intellectual developments over the past 20 years, back into the whole package of logical positivist methods and assumptions that have been criticized so extensively by the great descenders. Besides, as Aristotle discovered, the poets' generality is exposed in the rich particulars of their work. The poets believe that the commonalities of life can be plucked from there by large-minded observers of whatever persuasion. Whether or not these apparent sharings can be defended as unassailable or universal truths by other standards is another matter. The paths for collecting them are different, so are the logbooks, and therefore the form of the arguments down the line. Scientists normally create conglomerates from heavily laundered particulars, drawn from wide fields of clinically cut cloth, to reach their generalities.

So which to choose? No matter which extreme is harnessed—soft art, hard science—let me reiterate what can be called by now (via my pressing redundancies) the maxim that some things can't be said exactly or as effectively any other way. Extremes are validated and perpetuated by that defensible fact, even as the proponents themselves exaggerate it in their bookend fights over turf and exclusivity. But what about the stretch in between? Rifts are made to be mended; the challenge in gulfs is to bridge them. The boldest of anthropology's new interpreters and poets have gone halfway around the horns of this problem by trying to raise the illumina-tion of our human commonalities to an art form without losing the ability to inform more traditional social science concerns at the same time, in part on the premise that the collective work of scientists and poets is in the broadest view complementary. In the pool of common knowledge, the pattern is ancient and very human: many in the one, one in the many. How you travel depends on where you start. The destination is in the longest of long runs the same: the audiovisual room, the bookshelf, the electronic library, and, perhaps above all else, the mirror in the center of the house of Who-Are-We?[50] Inquiring minds want to know. We have always wanted to know. Who has the key? Never mind. There seems to be more than one door and some of them aren't locked. See you inside.

[Refrain: *Is this just more anthropological borrowing from the multiple-reality world of physics? No. An argument for uncompromising relativism, or just for tolerance of diversity of argument and approach in the absence of an overarching paradigm for cultural anthropology? Neither. Do ethnographic methods have to be reduced to "deep hanging out" (Geertz, 1998)? No. Do we have to abandon the search for commensurate theories and universals of language, culture, and behavior? No. Should we force nostalgia-driven models of the past on present ethnographic research for the next millennium? No need to ask. Won't work.*]

■ Notes

1. But compare Bachelard (1964) on the "poetics of space," Bachelard (1971) on the "poetics of reverie," Brown (1977) on a "poetic for sociology," and Hallyn (1990) on the "poetic structure of the world."

2. For ethnographers, the poetic focus on communications about other cultures is as much a concern about how the story of fieldwork is told as anything else. See Bruner (1984), Prattis (1986), Van Maanen (1988), Manganaro (1990a), Brady (1991a), and O'Nell (1994).

3. See Beaujour (1987, p. 470) and Fischer (1988, p. 8); compare Burke (1989, p. 188), Krupat (1992, pp. 51-52), Robbins (1987), Tarn

(1991, p. 63), Tsing (1994), and James, Hockey, and Dawson (1997).

4. See Lévi-Strauss (1962, 1967, 1969), Riffaterre (1970), Scholes (1974), Culler (1975, 1977), Todorov (1977, 1981), and Harland (1987).

5. See Boon (1972), Todorov (1981), Eagleton (1983), Brady (1991a), and Brooks (1994). The burgeoning domain of "cultural studies" also begs the question of disciplinary division and proprietary interests in these subjects (compare Marcus, 1998). Although there is much more in book form and articles elsewhere using this label, a comparison of the range of interests covered in the literary journals *Cultural Critique* and *Poetics Today* relative to those of the *American Anthropologist, Cultural Anthropology,* and *Anthropology and Humanism* is instructive.

6. See Turner (1974, 1982a, 1982b), Bauman (1977, 1992), Schechner (1985, 1995), Graham (1995), Dening (1996), and Brady (1999).

7. Drawing on the oral behavior of the speech community, for example, ethnopoet David Antin (1983), paraphrasing Dell Hymes, writes: "All over the world in a great variety of languages people announce, greet, take leave, invoke, introduce, inquire, request, demand, command, coax, entreat, encourage, beg, answer, name, report, describe, narrate, interpret, analyze, instruct, advise, defer, refuse, apologize, reproach, joke, taunt, insult, praise, discuss, gossip. Among this grab-bag of human language activities are a number of more or less well-defined universal discourse genres, whose expectation structures are the source of all poetic activity. If there is any place that we should look for an ETHNOPOETICS it is here, among these universal genres, where all linguistic invention begins. . . . I take the 'poetics' part of ETHNOPOETICS to be . . . the structure of those linguistic acts of invention and discovery through which the mind explores the transformational power of language and discovers and invents the world itself" (p. 451). Albeit less dynamic in orientation and less concerned with cultural process than product, there is also connective tissue in that perception for structural studies of the ways what has been discovered and invented is put into place in particular societies, that is, the logical and symbolic arrangements that characterize the cognitive content and social relations of whole cultures (including

anthropology itself—see Boon, 1982, 1984, 1989; Brady, 1993).

8. For more on dialogics, see Tedlock (1983, 1987b), Hill (1986), Feld (1987), Holquist (1990), Weiss (1990), Brady (1991b), Bruner and Gorfain (1991), Duranti (1993), and Emerson (1997).

9. See Harland (1987), Clifford and Marcus (1986), Clifford (1988), Fabian (1994), Marcus (1998), and Geertz (1998).

10. See, for example, Tarn (1991), Wilk (1991), Scott (1992), and Brady and Turner (1994).

11. See also Rothenberg (1981, 1985), Swann (1983), Tedlock (1983), Tedlock and Tedlock (1985), Kroskrity (1985), and Sherzer and Woodbury (1987). On the anthropology of folk narratives, see Jackson (1982), Wilbert and Simoneau (1982), Swann (1983), Sherzer and Woodbury (1987), Narayan (1989), Abu-Lughod (1993), Basso (1995), Graham (1995), Candre and Echeverri (1996), and Reichel-Dolmatoff (1996).

12. Compare D. Tedlock (1972, 1985, 1987a, 1991, 1993), Culler (1977, p. 8), Riffaterre (1984), Sherzer (1987), and Graham (1995).

13. If not literature per se—see, for example, Spradley and McDonough (1973), Langness and Frank (1978), Dennis and Aycock (1989), Handler (1983, 1985, 1990), Handler and Segal (1987), Richardson (1990), and Benson (1993).

14. See also Marcus and Fischer (1986), Handler (1983, 1985, 1990), Handler and Segal (1987), Fischer (1991), and Marcus (1998).

15. Of course, the whole enterprise is "interpretive." Furthermore, interpretive anthropology—as part of the poststructuralist, deconstructionist movement in contemporary philosophy and social science—is not necessarily (a) antiempirical (How can any discipline operate without an empirical ground?), (b) antiobjective (see Brady, 1991b; Rorty, 1979, pp. 361-363; Spiegelberg, 1975, pp. 72-73), or (c) antiscience (compare Barrett, 1996; Holton, 1993; Jennings, 1983; Knauft, 1996; Lett, 1997; Maxwell, 1984; O'Meara, 1989; Sangren, 1991; Shankman, 1984). But responsible social science of this kind does reject (as necessarily incomplete, among other problems) dogmatic empiric-*ism* that forecloses on the study of meaning in favor of an exclusive focus on behavior (see Brady, 1993, p. 277, n. 28; Fernandez, 1974; Polanyi & Prosch, 1975; Rabinow & Sullivan, 1987).

16. Following especially Geertz's (1973) classic observations on a Balinese cockfight.

17. See Marcus and Fischer (1986, p. 72), Marcus (1980, 1998), Marcus and Cushman (1982), Boon (1972, 1982, 1989), Clifford and Marcus (1986), Fernandez (1974, 1985, 1986, 1988, 1989), and much that has been published in the journal *Cultural Anthropology,* the discussion of anthropology and Irish discourse in Taylor (1996), and note 11, above, on folk narratives. See also Fischer (1988, 1989, 1991), Fabian (1990, p. 767: "If writing is part of a system of intellectual and political oppression of the Other, how can we avoid contributing to that oppression if we go on writing?"), Manganaro (1990a), Tarn (1991), Karp and Levine (1991), Said (1991), Krupat (1992), Marcus's (1993) review of Krupat, and Mascia-Lees, Sharpe, and Cohen (1993) on some important aspects of the politicizing that follows from ethnographic encapsulations of other people's texts and customs.

18. See, for example, the best-selling novels by Silko (1977) and Momaday (1989), and Slater's (1982) ethnographic exegesis of Brazilian *literatura de cordel.*

19. See, for example, Dennis and Aycock (1989), Rosaldo (1989), Manganaro (1990a), B. Tedlock (1991), Brady (1991b), Benson (1993), James et al. (1997), and Marcus (1998).

20. See, for example, Feld (1982), Jackson (1986), Turner (1987), Dennis (1989), Fox (1989), Stewart (1989), Richardson (1990), B. Tedlock (1992), Gottlieb and Graham (1993), Limón (1994), Behar (1993, 1996), Stewart (1996), and Dening (1998a, 1998b).

21. For related readings on textual authority and ethnographic representation, see Geertz (1973, 1983, 1988, 1995, 1998), Lanser (1981), Bruner (1984), Fernandez (1985, 1986), Webster (1986), Fabian (1990), Weinstein (1990a, 1990b), Simms (1991), Tsing (1994), Dening (1996, 1998a, 1998b), Rapport (1997), and Banks and Banks (1998); compare Taussig (1993) and Motzafi-Haller (1998). For a recent debate on who speaks for whom in historical ethnography, see Obeyesekere (1992), Sahlins (1996), and Borofsky (1997); compare Brady (1985).

22. On that account, see the diverse works of LaFarge (1929), Bohannan (writing as Elenore Smith Bowen, 1954), Turnbull (1962), Stewart (1962), Matthiessen (1963, 1975), Kurten (1980), Thomas (1987), Handy (1973), Thompson (1983), Jackson (1986), and Knab (1995);

compare the narrative form in Turner's (1987) empathic memoir.

23. See Turnbull (1962, 1972), Rabinow (1977), Dumont (1978), Crapanzano (1980), Turner (1987), Dennis (1989), Dennis and Aycock (1989), and B. Tedlock (1992).

24. See especially the innovative combination of Gottlieb and Graham (1993), Fischer (1988) on Michel Leiris's effort "to combine sympathetic observation of the Other, the unavoidability of literary self-inscription, and the imperative of cultural critique" (p. 8); compare Beaujoir (1987), Tarn (1991), and Wolf (1992).

25. Tarn (1991) echoes a sentiment shared by many about Lévi-Strauss: He might have been a creative writer with equal success, "had he chosen that path of expression" (p. 56). Manganaro (1990b) adds, "The writerly sense of *Tristes Tropiques,* importantly, arises not only out of a literary style adopted by the anthropologist-author, but from the very perspective that the writer takes to his subject" (p. 16). It is also noteworthy that Lévi-Strauss has been roundly criticized for the formalism of his other works (see, e.g., Eagleton, 1983; Geertz, 1973, pp. 345-359; Harland, 1987; Prattis, 1986; compare Boon, 1972, 1982; Brady, 1993). The large-minded Lévi-Strauss seems to have touched all the bases at one time or another.

26. A theme plainly visible in Dening (1980, 1998a), Geertz (1998), and Borofsky (2000).

27. See Fox (1991), Poggie, DeWalt, and Dressler (1992), Borofsky (1994), Barrett (1996), Jessor, Colby, and Shweder (1996), Knauft (1996), Denzin (1997), Lett (1997), James et al. (1997), Layton (1997), Rapport (1997), and Marcus (1998); compare O'Meara (1997).

28. For important statements on this problem, see Wolf (1982), Fabian (1983), Borofsky (1987, 2000), Thomas (1989, 1991), and Dening (1995, 1996).

29. See Rabinow (1983, 1984, 1986), Jarvie (1983), Wuthnow, Hunter, Bergesen, and Kurzweil (1984), Ulin (1984), Rabinow and Sullivan (1987), Boon (1982), Swearingen (1986), Loriggio (1990), Brady (1991a, 1993), Duranti (1993), and Rapport (1997); compare Scholte (1966) for some earlier thinking, and, more recently, continuing the epistemological effort in anthropology with smart and practical arguments, Davies (1999).

30. See, for example, Reck's (1978) Mexican ethnography, Rose (1993) on the death of "Malinowski-style" ethnography and the birth of a more poetic and multigenre manifesto as its replacement, Boon (1982, pp. 9-12) on some of the confusions of this style and its supposed differentiation as "ethnography" from the "armchair" speculations of Sir James George Frazer, Burke (1989, pp. 188ff.) on the need for anthropologists to "recognize the factor of rhetoric in their own field" (Marcus, 1980), and Boon (1982) on "standards of 'convincingness' in various cross-cultural styles and genres, just as there are canons of verisimilitude in realist ethnography" (p. 21).

31. For more on the relativity and eligibility of such material as language games or similar focus frames, see Guetti (1984), de Zengotita (1989), Denzin (1997), and Gellner (1998).

32. This is less true on both counts in linguistics—see, for example, Napoli and Rando (1979) and Bright (1983, 1985).

33. Dilemma is the other side of paradox. As Paul de Man once observed: "It is in the essence of language to be capable of origination, but of never achieving the absolute identity with itself that exists in the natural object. Poetic language can do nothing but originate anew over and over again; it is always constitutive, able to posit regardless of presence but, by the same token, unable to give a foundation to what it posits except as an intent of consciousness" (quoted in Donoghue, 1989, p. 37).

34. See Vendler (1985, 1988) on the variable marginality of poetry. Not all cultures share America's questionable valuation of poetry. It has conspicuously more status as an activity elsewhere (Brazil, Spain, England—to name a few). See Bishop and Brasil (1972), Lorde (1984, p. 87) on poetry being something other than a luxury, Tarn (1991, p. 15) on poetry's "survival value" for humankind, Lavie (1990) and Behar's (1993) sensitive and rich texts on the tribulations of letting their poetry and poetic mentalities out in oppressive contexts, and Richardson (1994) on poetry being a *practical* and *powerful* method for analyzing social worlds" (p. 522).

35. Tarn (1991, p. 254) sees this as a kind of competition of "vocations" that can be most discouraging in its personal, political, and philosophical entanglements. But it should be remembered that these seemingly insurmountable

problems do not prevent great artists from also being great scientists (and vice versa—e.g., Goethe; see Gould, 1991), that "contempt for one is no qualification for citizenship in the other" (Brann, 1991, p. 775), and that the opposition that pits imagination against reason, when overdrawn on the battlegrounds of art and science, may be a kind "synecdochic fallacy" anyway—a category mistake in its opposition (see Brady, 1991a; Burke, 1989, p. 87).

36. For more on anthropological humanism and writing, see Wilk (1991) and Brady and Turner (1994); compare Harris (1997, p. 293) and Lett (1997).

37. See, for example, Lévi-Strauss (1961), Turnbull (1962, 1972), Van Lawick-Goodall (1971), Harris (1977, 1987), Dening (1980), Sahlins (1981, 1985, 1996), Jackson (1986), Thomas (1987), Rosaldo (1989), Narayan (1989), D. Tedlock (1990), Laderman (1991), B. Tedlock (1992), Rose (1993), and Behar (1993, 1996). Fabian (1990) notes wryly that "Geertz probably deserves credit for initiating the new literary awareness in anthropology not so much because he fraternized with literary critics but because he dared to write well and got away with it" (p. 761). Fernandez (personal communication, February 27, 1998), playing on some of his own influential work (e.g., 1974, 1986), says that Geertz is above all else a "master metaphorist."

38. However, separating these genres and doing both can generate a laudable effect. Scientists who also write novels, poetry, or very "literary" memoirs only seem to enhance their reputations (see, e.g., Levi, 1984; Lightman, 1993; Sagan, 1980, 1985). On a related matter, when asked if his exercises in poetry improved his science, Nobel Prize-winning chemist and estimable poet Roald Hoffmann said no, at least not directly. Writing poetry for Hoffmann makes him feel better about himself as a person, as a human being, and *that* helps his science considerably (personal communication, February 26, 1997; see also Chandrasekhar, 1987; Hoffmann, 1987, 1990a, 1990b, 1995). Even with separation in practice or redefinition in humanistic terms, the functional linkage of art-*in*-science cannot be denied. It may be less direct, less obvious, less explored, and less reported than it could be. But it is always present.

39. There are important exceptions. See, for example, Friedrich (1979a), Diamond (1982, 1986a, 1986b), some of Prattis (1986), various

contributions over the years to *Anthropology and Humanism (Quarterly)*, Fox (1989), Stewart (1989), Tedlock (1990), Richardson (1998a, 1998b), and Flores (1999); compare Hall (1988) on phases in becoming a poet.

40. Leavitt (1997) is pioneering work on poetry and prophecy, words and power, mantic prose and ecstatic experiences—"stirrings" that range from the aesthetic and emotional to fundamentally physical responses and their diverse cultural expressions in ritual, politics, healing, and messianic movements, to name a few. See also Abu-Lughod (1986), Trawick (1988, 1997), Dobin (1990), and Csordas (1997).

41. See Fernandez (1974) for an important argument (with discussion) on sensitivity to and the mastery of metaphors (tropes) in ethnographic narration and related highly organized expressive activities, Lakoff and Johnson (1980) and Lakoff and Turner (1989) for a clear enunciation of common versus uncommon metaphors in everyday life, Van Den Abbeele (1992) on travel as a common metaphor and much that is smuggled into its use, and Fernandez (1986) and Fernandez and Herzfeld (1998) on the place of social and cultural poetics in the study of meaning in performance.

42. Playing out these constraints is in part how logical positivism got to be known less as the backbone of universally applicable methods and more as a list of things that could not (or were not allowed to) be studied in depth, or at all (e.g., meaning versus behavior, aesthetics and emotions, and so on).

43. It is not the same thing as letting multiple authentic voices surface in a single text or performance (see Trawick, 1997), of course, but Diamond believed in—and displayed (by assuming the roles of other speakers) in some of his poetry—the prospect that some people could speak for others to advantage for all on some occasions; that certain knowledge boundaries could be crossed with insight and power, without imperialism or blind cultural exploitation, without a franchise of superiority or oppressive ethnocentrism. Early in his *Going West* (1986a), for example, the anthropomorphized Otter speaks for the Mohicans and Algonquins (as representatives of still other Native Americans) through esoteric knowledge of their impending collision with history: "Because we knew the future / And we understood their [Mohican, Algonquin] legends / Better than they did" (p. 11).

A larger point of this boundary crossing that is not always obvious, especially where ethnic pride is at stake, is that indigenous identity doesn't necessarily translate to expert on all that contextualizes it. Much depends on the form and cultural origins of the questions asked and the cultural and intellectual range of answers sought (see Brady, 1985).

44. There are no separate languages for science and poetry, only specialized vocabularies and variable contexts—cultural "pre-texts" and "subtexts" that reassure, inform, and might even misinform through manipulations designed to present the truth we *want* to find, as opposed to something that might be calculated through other measures as more accurate, analytically satisfying, or less prejudicial. Moreover, there is plenty of slippage in the division of labor between scientific and poetic texts. Asserting bias control, for example, including unmasking ethnocentrism, is seen as obligatory in scientific observation. Disclosing observational bias directly by emulating ("flagging") it in performance and text is a poetic option that may accomplish much the same thing, albeit through a radically different channel and probably for different ends. Here, as elsewhere, context is practically everything for determining meaning, and on occasion it can itself be all but slave to authorial intentions and sociolinguistic form.

45. As book review editor of the *American Anthropologist* at the time, I commissioned these reviews (see Rose, 1983/1991a; Tyler, 1984). One earlier and interesting example of poetry in the *AA* was published by then editor Sol Tax. Referred to as "Puzzled Ph.D. Candidate," and published anonymously (Anonymous, 1954), the poem was sent to Tax by Melville Herskovits, who took it off the bulletin board at the Department of Anthropology, Northwestern University. It was actually "Wasn't It a Thought Titanic" by then graduate student (and now anthropologist and poetics scholar at the University of Chicago) James W. Fernandez.

46. For special takes on the production of ethnographic knowledge, see Borofsky (1987, 2000), Geertz (1973, 1983, 1988, 1995, 1998), Dening (1980, 1996, 1998a, 1998b), Brady (1991b), and Behar (1993, 1996).

47. See also Tedlock (1983, 1990), Schechner (1985, 1995), Fernandez (1988), Graham (1995), Dening (1996), and Taylor (1996). Poetry, of course, fits into the performative tradi-

tions of its makers directly, and it can be an important source for understanding indigenous histories. As Charlot (1985) says of Hawaiian poetry, "The fact that poetry has been used frequently for important occasions and purposes suggests that it has a utility thus far overlooked by historians" (p. 29). See also Vendler (1995, p. 6) on the historical meaning of rhythms, stanza forms, personae, and genre; and Fernandez and Herzfeld (1998) for a strong argument that "poetic principles guide all *effective* and *affective* social interaction" (p. 94) and a discussion of how that articulates with the problem of performativity in human action generally.

48. See Brown (1991) and Lévi-Strauss's whole corpus of writings; see also Whitten (1988) and Kilbride (1993),

49. See, for example, Jessor et al. (1996), Shore (1996), Bloch (1998), and Brady (1998b); compare Wierzbicka (1996).

50. Some poets live there, along with a group of narcissists, clever historians, and a tinhorn totalitarian or two. They are visited regularly by social and natural scientists. The project is to see what makes the residents tick. The problem is that everyone in the room is ticking. Everyone is looking back at everyone who's looking at. Nobody knows for sure who's studying whom, or, for that matter, whose conversation should dominate. Somebody said there was order in the chaos. Two poets and the ghost of Aristotle said, "We told you so." Two scientists wanted to bottle it but couldn't get a grip on either its substance or its meaning. New schools of methods grew up in the exact spot of this discovery. A plaque marks it to this very day: THE FOUNTAIN OF MUSES STARTED HERE. LANGUAGE OF TRUTH SOLD NEAR HERE. PLEASE DO NOT LOITER.

■ References

Abrahams, R. D. (1986). Ordinary and extraordinary experience. In V. Turner & E. M. Bruner (Eds.), *The anthropology of experience* (pp. 45-72). Urbana: University of Illinois Press.

Abu-Lughod, L. (1986). *Veiled sentiments: Honor and poetry in a Bedouin society.* Berkeley: University of California Press.

Abu-Lughod, L. (1993). *Writing women's worlds: Bedouin stories.* Berkeley: University of California Press.

Anonymous (J. W. Fernandez). (1954). Puzzled Ph.D. candidate. In S. Tax, This issue and others. *American Anthropologist, 56,* 742.

Antin, D. (1983). Talking to discover. In J. Rothenberg & D. Rothenberg (Eds.), *Symposium of the whole: A range of discourse toward an ethnopoetics* (pp. 450-461). Berkeley: University of California Press.

Bachelard, G. (1964). *The poetics of space.* Boston: Beacon.

Bachelard, G. (1971). *On poetic imagination and reverie* (C. Gandin, Trans.). Indianapolis: Bobbs-Merrill.

Banks, A., & Banks, S. P. (Eds.). (1998). *Fiction and social research: By ice or fire.* Walnut Creek, CA: AltaMira.

Barrett, S. R. (1996). *Anthropology: A student's guide to theory and method.* Toronto: University of Toronto Press.

Barthes, R. (1968). *Writing degree zero* (A. Lavers & C. Smith, Trans.). New York: Noonday.

Barthes, R. (1972). *Mythologies* (A. Lavers, Trans.). New York: Hill & Wang.

Barthes, R. (1986). From science to literature. In R. Barthes, *The rustle of language* (R. Howard, Trans.; pp. 3-10). Berkeley: University of California Press.

Basso, K. (1988). A review of *Native American discourse: Poetics and rhetoric* (J. Sherzer & A. C. Woodbury, Eds.). *American Ethnologist, 15,* 805-810.

Basso, E. (1995). *The last cannibals: A South American oral history.* Austin: University of Texas Press.

Bauman, R. (1977). *Verbal art as performance.* Prospect Heights, IL: Waveland.

Bauman, R. (Ed.). (1992). *Folklore, cultural performances, and popular entertainments.* New York: Oxford University Press.

Beaujoir, M. (1987). Michel Leiris: Ethnography or self-portrayal? Review essay of Sulfur 15, featuring new translations of Michel Leiris's work. *Cultural Anthropology, 2,* 470-480.

Behar, R. (1993). *Translated woman: Crossing the border with Esperanza's story.* Boston: Beacon.

Behar, R. (1996). *The vulnerable observer: Anthropology that breaks your heart.* Boston: Beacon.

Benson, P. (Ed.). (1993). *Anthropology and literature*. Urbana: University of Illinois Press.

Bishop, E., & Brasil, E. (Eds.). (1972). *An anthology of twentieth-century Brazilian poetry*. Middletown, CT: Wesleyan University Press.

Bloch, M. E. F. (1998). *How we think they think: Anthropological approaches to cognition, memory, and literacy*. Boulder, CO: Westview.

Boon, J. A. (1972). *From symbolism to structuralism: Lévi-Strauss in a literary tradition*. New York: Harper & Row.

Boon, J. A. (1982). *Other tribes, other scribes: Symbolic anthropology in the comparative study of cultures, histories, religions, and texts*. Cambridge: Cambridge University Press.

Boon, J. A. (1984). Folly, Bali, and anthropology, or satire across cultures. In E. M. Bruner (Ed.), *Text, play, and story: The construction and reconstruction of self and society* (pp. 156-177). Washington, DC: American Ethnological Society.

Boon, J. A. (1989). *Affinities and extremes: Criss-crossing the bittersweet ethnology of East Indies history, Hindu-Balinese culture, and Indo-European allure*. Chicago: University of Chicago Press.

Borofsky, R. (1987). *Making history: Pukapukan and anthropological constructions of knowledge*. New York: Cambridge University Press.

Borofsky, R. (1994). *Assessing cultural anthropology*. New York: McGraw-Hill.

Borofsky, R. (1997). Cook, Lono, Obeyesekere, and Sahlins [with commentary]. *Current Anthropology, 38*, 255-282.

Borofsky, R. (Ed.). (2000). *Remembrance of Pacific pasts: An invitation to remake history*. Honolulu: University of Hawaii Press.

Bourdieu, P. (1991). *Language and symbolic power*. Cambridge, MA: Harvard University Press.

Bowen, E. S. (pseudonym of L. Bohannan). (1954). *Return to laughter: An anthropological novel*. New York: Harper & Row.

Brady, I. (Ed.). (1983). Speaking in the name of the real: Freeman and Mead on Samoa [Special section]. *American Anthropologist, 85*, 908-947.

Brady, I. (1985). Review of *Tuvalu: A history*, by S. Faniu, V. Ielemia, T. Isako, et al. In *Pacific History Bibliography and Comment, 1985* (pp. 52-54). Canberra: Journal of Pacific History.

Brady, I. (1990a). Comment on "Is anthropology art or science?" by M. Carrithers. *Current Anthropology, 31*, 273-274.

Brady, I. (1990b). Review of *The violent imagination*, by R. Fox. *American Anthropologist, 92*, 1078-1079.

Brady, I. (Ed.). (1991a). *Anthropological poetics*. Savage, MD: Rowman & Littlefield.

Brady, I. (1991b). Harmony and argument: Bringing forth the artful science. In I. Brady (Ed.), *Anthropological poetics* (pp. 3-30). Savage, MD: Rowman & Littlefield.

Brady, I. (1991c). The Samoa reader: Last word or lost horizon? *Current Anthropology, 32*, 497-500.

Brady, I. (1993). Tribal fire and scribal ice. In P. Benson (Ed.), *Anthropology and literature* (pp. 248-278). Urbana: University of Illinois Press.

Brady, I. (1996). Poetics. In D. Levinson & M. Ember (Eds.), *The encyclopedia of cultural anthropology* (Vol. 3, pp. 951-959). New York: Holt.

Brady, I. (1998a). A gift of the journey. *Qualitative Inquiry, 4*, 463.

Brady, I. (1998b). Two thousand and what? Anthropological moments and methods for the next century. *American Anthropologist, 100*, 510-516.

Brady, I. (1999). Ritual as cognitive process, performance as history. *Current Anthropology, 40*, 243-248.

Brady, I., & Turner, E. (1994, June). Introduction. In I. Brady & E. Turner (Eds.), Humanism in anthropology, 1994 [Special issue]. *Anthropology and Humanism, 19*, 3-11.

Brann, E. T. H. (1991). *The world of the imagination: Sum and substance*. Savage, MD: Rowman & Littlefield.

Bright, W. (Ed.). (1983). *Discovered tongues: Poems by linguists*. San Francisco: Corvine.

Bright, W. (1985). *Word formations: Poems by linguists*. San Francisco: Corvine.

Brooks, P. (1994). Aesthetics and ideology: What happened to poetics? *Critical Inquiry, 20*, 509-523.

Brown, D. E. (1991). *Human universals.* New York: McGraw-Hill.

Brown, R. H. (1977). *A poetic for sociology: Toward a logic of discovery for the human sciences.* Cambridge: Cambridge University Press.

Bruner, E. M. (Ed.). (1984). *Text, play, and story: The construction and reconstruction of self and society.* Washington, DC: American Ethnological Society.

Bruner, E. M., & Gorfain, P. (1991). Dialogic narration and the paradoxes of Masada. In I. Brady (Ed.), *Anthropological poetics* (pp. 177-203). Savage, MD: Rowman & Littlefield.

Bruner, J. (1986). *Actual minds, possible worlds.* Cambridge, MA: Harvard University Press.

Bruner, J. (1990). *Acts of meaning.* Cambridge, MA: Harvard University Press.

Burke, E. (1958). *A philosophical enquiry into the origin of ideas of the sublime and beautiful.* Notre Dame, IN: University of Notre Dame Press.

Burke, K. (1989). *On symbols and society* (J. R. Gusfield, Ed.). Chicago: University of Chicago Press.

Candre, H., & Echeverri, J. A. (1996). *Cool tobacco, sweet coca: Teachings of an Indian sage from the Colombian Amazon.* Devon: Themis.

Chandrasekhar, S. (1987). *Truth and beauty: Aesthetics and motivations In science.* Chicago: University of Chicago Press.

Charlot, J. (1985). *The Hawaiian poetry of religion and politics.* Honolulu: Institute for Polynesian Studies.

Clifford, J. (1988). *The predicament of culture: Twentieth-century ethnography, literature, and art.* Cambridge, MA: Harvard University Press.

Clifford, J., & Marcus, G. E. (Eds.). (1986). *Writing culture: The poetics and politics of ethnography.* Berkeley: University of California Press.

Collingwood, R. G. (1956). *The idea of history.* New York: Oxford University Press.

Coward, H. G., & Royce, J. R. (1981). Toward an epistemological basis for humanistic psychology. In J. R. Royce & L. P. Mos (Eds.), *Humanistic psychology: Concepts and criticisms* (pp. 109-134). New York: Plenum.

Crapanzano, V. (1980). *Tuhami: Portrait of a Moroccan.* Chicago: University of Chicago Press.

Csordas, T. J. (1997). Prophecy and the performance of metaphor. *American Anthropologist, 99,* 321-332.

Culler, J. (1975). *Structuralist poetics: Structuralism, linguistics, and the study of literature.* Ithaca, NY: Cornell University Press.

Culler, J. (1977). Foreword. In T. Torodov, *The poetics of prose* (pp. 7-13). Ithaca, NY: Cornell University Press.

Davies, C. A. (1999). *Reflexive ethnography: A guide to researching selves and others.* New York: Routledge.

Dening, G. (1980). *Islands and beaches: Discourse on a silent land: Marquesas 1774-1880.* Honolulu: University of Hawaii Press.

Dening, G. (1995). *The death of William Gooch: A history's anthropology.* Honolulu: University of Hawaii Press.

Dening, G. (1996). *Performances.* Chicago: University of Chicago Press.

Dening, G. (1998a). *Readings/writings.* Victoria: Melbourne University Press.

Dening, G. (1998b). Writing, rewriting the beach: An essay. *Rethinking History, 2*(2), 143-172.

Dennis, P. A. (1989). Oliver LaFarge, writer and anthropologist. In P. A. Dennis & W. Aycock (Eds.), *Literature and anthropology* (pp. 209-219). Lubbock: Texas Tech University Press.

Dennis, P. A., & Aycock, W. (Eds.). (1989). *Literature and anthropology.* Lubbock: Texas Tech University Press.

Denzin, N. K. (1997). *Interpretive ethnography: Ethnographic practices for the 21st century.* Thousand Oaks, CA: Sage.

de Zengotita, T. (1989). On Wittgenstein's remarks on Frazer's *Golden bough. Cultural Anthropology, 4,* 390-398.

Diamond, S. (1982). *Totems.* Barrytown, NY: Open Book/Station Hill.

Diamond, S. (1986a). *Going west.* Northhampton, MA: Hermes House.

Diamond, S. (1986b). How to die in America. *Cultural Anthropology, 1,* 447-448.

Diamond, S. (1986c). Preface. *Dialectical Anthropology, 11,* 131-132.

Diamond, S. (1987). The beautiful and the ugly are one thing, the sublime another: A reflection on culture. *Cultural Anthropology, 2,* 268-271.

Dobin, H. (1990). *Merlin's disciples: Prophecy, poetry, and power in Renaissance England.* Stanford, CA: Stanford University Press.

Donoghue, D. (1989, June 29). The strange case of Paul de Man. *New York Review of Books,* pp. 32, 37.

Dove, R. (1994, January-February). What does poetry do for us? *Virginia* (University of Virginia alumni newsletter), pp. 22-27.

Dreyfus, H. L., & Rabinow, P. (1983). *Michel Foucault: Beyond structuralism and hermeneutics* (2nd ed.). Chicago: University of Chicago Press.

Dumont, J.-P. (1978). *The headman and I: Ambiguity and ambivalence in the fieldworking experience.* Austin: University of Texas Press.

Duranti, A. (1993). Truth and intentionality: An ethnographic critique. *Cultural Anthropology, 8,* 214-245.

Eagleton, T. (1983). *Literary theory: An introduction.* Minneapolis: University of Minnesota Press.

Eco, U. (1979). *The role of the reader: Explorations in the semiotics of texts.* Bloomington: Indiana University Press.

Ellis, C., & Bochner, A. P. (Eds.). (1996). *Composing ethnography: Alternative forms of qualitative writing.* Walnut Creek, CA: AltaMira.

Emerson, C. (1997). *The first hundred years of Mikhail Bakhtin.* Princeton, NJ: Princeton University Press.

Fabian, J. (1983). *Time and the other: How anthropology makes its object.* New York: Columbia University Press.

Fabian, J. (1990). Presence and representation: The other and anthropological writing. *Critical Inquiry, 16,* 753-772.

Fabian, J. (1994). Ethnographic objectivity revisited: From rigor to vigor. In A. Megill (Ed.), *Rethinking objectivity* (pp. 81-108). Durham, NC: Duke University Press.

Feld, S. (1982). *Sound and sentiment: Birds, weeping, poetics, and song in Kaluli expression.* Philadelphia: University of Pennsylvania Press.

Feld, S. (1987). Dialogic editing: Interpreting how Kaluli read sound and sentiment. *Cultural Anthropology, 2,* 190-210.

Fernandez, J. W. (1974). The mission of metaphor in expressive culture [with commentary]. *Current Anthropology, 15,* 119-145.

Fernandez, J. W. (1985). Exploded worlds: Texts as a metaphor for ethnography (and vice-versa). In S. Diamond (Ed.), Anthropology after '84: State of the art, state of society, part II [Special issue]. *Dialectical Anthropology, 10*(1-2), 15-26.

Fernandez, J. W. (1986). *Persuasions and performances: The play of tropes in culture.* Bloomington: Indiana University Press.

Fernandez, J. W. (1988). Andalusia on our minds: Two contrasting places in Spain as seen in a vernacular poetic duel of the late 19th century. *Cultural Anthropology, 3,* 21-35.

Fernandez, J. W. (1989). Comment on Keesing's exotic readings of cultural texts. *Current Anthropology, 30,* 470-471.

Fernandez, J. W., & Herzfeld, M. (1998). In search of meaningful methods. In H. R. Bernard (Ed.), *A handbook of method in cultural anthropology* (pp. 89-129). Thousand Oaks, CA: Sage.

Finnegan, R. (1992a). Oral poetry. In R. Bauman (Ed.), *Folklore, cultural performances, and popular entertainments* (pp. 119-127). New York: Oxford University Press.

Finnegan, R. (1992b). *Oral poetry: Its nature, significance, and social context.* Bloomington: Indiana University Press.

Fischer, M. M. J. (1988). Scientific dialogue and critical hermeneutics. *Cultural Anthropology, 3,* 3-15.

Fischer, M. M. J. (1989). Museums and festivals: Poetics and politics of Representations Conference, the Smithsonian Institution, September 26-28, 1988, I. Karp and S. Levine, organizers. *Cultural Anthropology, 4,* 204-221.

Fischer, M. M.J. (1991). Anthropology as cultural critique: Inserts for the 1990s: Cultural studies of science, visual virtual-realities, and post-trauma politics. *Cultural Anthropology, 6,* 525-537.

Flores, T. (1982). Field poetry. *Anthropology and Humanism Quarterly, 7*(1), 16-22.

Flores, T. (1985). The anthropology of aesthetics. In S. Diamond (Ed.), Anthropology after '84: State of the art, state of society, part II

[Special issue]. *Dialectical Anthropology,* *10*(1-2), 27-41.

Flores, T. (1999). *In place: Poems by Toni Flores.* Geneva, NY: Hobart & William Smith Colleges Press.

Fox, R. (1989). *The violent imagination.* New Brunswick, NJ: Rutgers University Press.

Fox, R. G. (Ed.). (1991). *Recapturing anthropology: Working in the present.* Santa Fe, NM: School of American Research Press.

Friedrich, P. (1979a). *Bastard moons.* Chicago: Benjamin & Martha Waite.

Friedrich, P. (1979b). Linguistic relativity and the order-to-chaos continuum. In J. Maquet (Ed.), *On linguistic anthropology: Essays in honor of Harry Hoijer* (pp. 89-139). Malibu, CA: Undena.

Friedrich, P. (1995). The world-listener & Cities (two poems). *American Anthropologist, 97,* 658-659.

Fujimara, J. H. (1998). Authorizing knowledge in science and anthropology. *American Anthropologist, 100,* 347-360.

Geertz, C. (1973). *The interpretation of cultures: Selected essays.* New York: Basic Books.

Geertz, C. (1983). *Local knowledge: Further essays in interpretive anthropology.* New York: Basic Books.

Geertz, C. (1988). *Works and lives: The anthropologist as author.* Stanford, CA: Stanford University Press.

Geertz, C. (1995). Disciplines. *Raritan, 14*(3), 65-102.

Geertz, C. (1998, October 22). Deep hanging out. *New York Review of Books,* pp. 69-70.

Gellner, E. (1998). *Language and solitude: Wittgenstein, Malinowski, and the Habsburg dilemma.* New York: Cambridge University Press.

Gottlieb, A., & Graham, P. (1993). *Parallel worlds: An anthropologist and a writer encounter Africa.* New York: Crown.

Gould, S. J. (1991). More light on leaves: Can a great artist also be a great scientist? *Natural History, 2,* 16-23.

Graham, L. (1995). *Performing dreams: Discourse of immortality among the Xavante of central Brazil.* Austin: University of Texas Press.

Graves, R. (1971, December 2). Science, technology, and poetry. *New Scientist,* pp. 34-35.

Guetti, J. (1984). Wittgenstein and literary theory. *Raritan, 4*(2), 67-84.

Hall, D. (1988). *Poetry and ambition: Essays 1982-88.* Ann Arbor: University of Michigan Press.

Hallyn, F. (1990). *The poetic structure of the world: Copernicus and Kepler.* New York: Urzone.

Handler, R. (1983). The dainty and the hungry man: Literature and anthropology in the work of Edward Sapir. In G. W. Stocking, Jr. (Ed.), *Observers observed: Essays on ethnographic research* (pp. 208-231). Madison: University of Wisconsin Press.

Handler, R. (1985). On dialogue and destructive analysis: Problems in narrating nationalism and ethnicity. *Journal of Anthropological Research, 41,* 171-181.

Handler, R. (1990). Ruth Benedict and the modernist sensibility. In M. Manganaro (Ed.), *Modernist anthropology: From fieldwork to text* (pp. 163-180). Princeton, NJ: Princeton University Press.

Handler, R., & Segal, D. (1987). Narrating multiple realities: Some lessons from Jane Austen for ethnographers. *Anthropology and Humanism Quarterly, 12*(4), 15-21.

Handy, W. C. (1973). *Thunder from the sea.* Honolulu: University of Hawaii Press.

Harland, R. (1987). *Superstructuralism: The philosophy of structuralism and post-structuralism.* New York: Methuen.

Harris, J. (1997). Giotto's invisible sheep: Lacanian mirroring and modeling in Walcott's "Another life." *South Atlantic Quarterly, 96,* 293-309.

Harris, M. (1977). *Cannibals and kings.* New York: Random House.

Harris, M. (1987). *The sacred cow and the abominable pig: Riddles of food and culture.* New York: Simon & Schuster.

Hill, J. H. (1986). The refiguration of the anthropology of language. *Cultural Anthropology, 1,* 89-102.

Hodder, I. (1986). *Reading the past: Current approaches to interpretation in archaeology.* New York: Cambridge University Press.

Hoffmann, R. (1987). *The metamict state: Poems by Roald Hoffmann.* Gainesville: University Presses of Florida.

Hoffmann, R. (1990a). *Gaps and verges: Poems by Roald Hoffmann.* Gainesville: University Presses of Florida.

Hoffmann, R. (1990b). Molecular beauty. *Journal of Aesthetics and Art Criticism, 48,* 191-204.

Hoffmann, R. (1995). *The same and not the same.* New York: Columbia University Press.

Holquist, M. (1990). *Dialogism: Bakhtin and his world.* New York: Routledge.

Holton, G. (1993). *Science and anti-science.* Cambridge, MA: Harvard University Press.

Jackson, M. (1982). *Allegories of the wilderness: Ethics and ambiguity in Kuranko narratives.* Bloomington: Indiana University Press.

Jackson, M. (1986). *Barawa and the ways birds fly in the sky.* Washington, DC: Smithsonian Institution Press.

Jakobson, R. (1987). *Language in literature* (K. Pomorska & S. Rudy, Eds.). Cambridge, MA: Harvard University Press.

James, A., Hockey, J., & Dawson, A. (Eds.). (1997). *After writing culture: Epistemology and praxis in contemporary anthropology.* New York: Routledge.

Jarvie, I. C. (1983). The problem of the ethnographic real. *Current Anthropology, 24,* 313-325.

Jennings, B. (1983). Interpretive social science and policy analysis. In D. Callahan & B. Jennings (Eds.), *Ethics, the social sciences, and policy analysis* (pp. 3-35). New York: Plenum.

Jessor, R., Colby, A., & Shweder, R. A. (Eds.). (1996). *Ethnography and human development: Context and meaning in social inquiry.* Chicago: University of Chicago Press.

Karp, I., & Levine, S. D. (Eds.). (1991). *Exhibiting cultures: The poetics and politics of museum display.* Washington, DC: Smithsonian Institution Press.

Kilbride, P. L. (1993). Anti-anti-universalism: Rethinking cultural psychology and anti-anti-relativism. *Reviews in Anthropology, 22*(1), 1-11.

Knab, T. J. (1995). *A war of witches: A journey into the underworld of the contemporary Aztecs.* New York: HarperCollins.

Knauft, B. M. (1996). *Genealogies for the present in cultural anthropology.* New York: Routledge.

Kroskrity, P. V. (1985). Growing with stories: Line, verse, and genre in an Arizona Tewa text. *Journal of Anthropological Research, 41,* 183-199.

Krupat, A. (1992). *Ethno-criticism: Ethnography, history, literature.* Berkeley: University of California Press.

Kurten, B. (1980). *Dance of the tiger.* New York: Berkeley.

Laderman, C. (1991). *Taming the wind of desire: Psychology, medicine, and aesthetics in Malay shamanistic performance.* Berkeley: University of California Press.

LaFarge, O. (1929). *Laughing boy.* Boston: Houghton Mifflin.

Lakoff, G., & Johnson, M. (1980). *Metaphors we live by.* Chicago: University of Chicago Press.

Lakoff, G., & Turner, M. (1989). *More than cool reason: A field guide to poetic metaphor.* Chicago: University of Chicago Press.

Langness, L. L., & Frank, G. (1978). Fact, fiction, and the ethnographic novel. *Anthropology and Humanism Quarterly, 3*(1-2), 18-22.

Lanser, S. S. (1981). *The narrative act.* Princeton, NJ: Princeton University Press.

Lavie, S. (1990). *The poetics of military occupation: Mzeina allegories of Bedouin identity under Israeli and Egyptian rule.* Berkeley: University of California Press.

Layton, R. (1997). *An introduction to theory in anthropology.* Cambridge: Cambridge University Press.

Leavitt, J. (Ed.). (1997). *Poetry and prophecy: The anthropology of inspiration.* Ann Arbor: University of Michigan Press.

Lett, J. (1997). *Science, reason, and anthropology: The principles of rational inquiry.* Lanham, MD: Roman & Littlefield.

Levi, P. (1984). *The periodic table.* New York: Schocken.

Levine, G. (1987). Literary science—scientific literature. *Raritan, 6*(3), 24-41.

Levine, G. (1994). Why science isn't literature: The importance of differences. In A. Megill (Ed.), *Rethinking objectivity* (pp. 65-79). Durham, NC: Duke University Press.

Lévi-Strauss, C. (1961). *Tristes tropiques: An anthropological study of primitive societies in Brazil* (J. Russell, Trans.). New York: Atheneum.

Lévi-Strauss, C. (1962). "Les chats" de Charles Baudelaire. *L'Homme, 2*(1), 5-21.

Lévi-Strauss, C. (1967). *Structural anthropology* (C. Jacobson & B. G. Schoepf, Trans.). Garden City, NY: Doubleday.

Lévi-Strauss, C. (1969). *The raw and the cooked* (J. Weightman & D. Weightman, Trans.). New York: Harper & Row.

Lightman, A. (1993). *Einstein's dreams*. New York: Time Warner.

Limón, J. (1994). *Dancing with the devil: Society and cultural poetics in Mexican-American South Texas*. Madison: University of Wisconsin Press.

Lorde, A. (1984). *Sister outsider*. Trumansburg, NY: Crossing.

Loriggio, F. (1990). Anthropology, literary theory, and the traditions of modernism. In M. Manganaro (Ed.), *Modernist anthropology: From fieldwork to text* (pp. 215-242). Princeton, NJ: Princeton University Press.

MacCannell, D. (1992). *Empty meeting grounds: The tourist papers*. New York: Routledge.

Manganaro, M. (Ed.). (1990a). *Modernist anthropology: From fieldwork to text*. Princeton, NJ: Princeton University Press.

Manganaro, M. (1990b). Textual play, power, and cultural critique: An orientation to modernist anthropology. In M. Manganaro (Ed.), *Modernist anthropology: From fieldwork to text* (pp. 3-47). Princeton, NJ: Princeton University Press.

Marcus, G. E. (1980). Rhetoric and the ethnographic genre in anthropological research. *Current Anthropology, 21*, 507-510.

Marcus, G. (1988). Parody and the parodic in Polynesian cultural history. *Cultural Anthropology, 3*, 68-76.

Marcus, G. E. (1993). A review of *Ethno-criticism: Ethnography, history, literature*, by A. Krupat. *American Anthropologist, 395*, 766.

Marcus, G. E. (1998). *Ethnography through thick and thin: A new research imaginary for anthropology's changing professional culture*. Princeton, NJ: Princeton University Press.

Marcus, G. E., & Cushman, D. (1982). Ethnographies as texts. *Annual Review of Anthropology, 11*, 25-69.

Marcus, G. E., & Fischer, M. M. J. (1986). *Anthropology as cultural critique: An experimental moment in the human sciences*. Chicago: University of Chicago Press.

Mascia-Lees, F. E., Sharpe, P., & Cohen, C. B. (1993). The postmodernist turn in anthropology: Cautions from a feminist perspective. In P. Benson (Ed.), *Anthropology and literature* (pp. 225-248). Urbana: University of Illinois Press.

Matthiessen, P. (1963). *At play in the fields of the Lord*. New York: Vintage.

Matthiessen, P. (1975). *Far Tortuga*. New York: Vintage.

Maxwell, N. (1984). *From knowledge to wisdom: A revolution in the aims and methods of science*. New York: Blackwell.

McAllister, J. W. (1998). Is beauty a sign of truth in scientific theories? *American Scientist, 86*, 178-183.

Megill, A. (Ed.). (1994). *Rethinking objectivity*. Durham, NC: Duke University Press.

Meschonnic, H. (1988). Rhyme and life. *Critical Inquiry, 15*, 90-107.

Miner, E. (1990). *Comparative poetics: An intercultural essay on theories of literature*. Princeton, NJ: Princeton University Press.

Momaday, N. S. (1989). *The ancient child*. New York: HarperCollins.

Motzafi-Haller, P. (1998). Beyond textual analysis: Practice, interacting discourses, and the experience of distinction in Botswana. *Cultural Anthropology, 13*, 522-547.

Napoli, D. J., & Rando, E. N. (Eds.). (1979). *Linguistic muse*. Edmonton: Linguistic Research.

Narayan, K. (1989). *Storytellers, saints, and scoundrels: Folk narrative in Hindu religious teaching*. Philadelphia: University of Pennsylvania Press.

Obeyesekere, G. (1992). *The apotheosis of Captain Cook: European mythmaking in the Pacific*. Princeton, NJ: Princeton University Press.

O'Meara, J. T. (1989). Anthropology as empirical science. *American Anthropologist, 91*, 354-369.

O'Meara, J. T. (1997). Causation and the struggle for a science of culture [with commentary]. *Current Anthropology, 38*, 399-418.

O'Nell, T. D. (1994). Telling about whites, talking about Indians: Oppression, resistance, and contemporary Indian identity. *Cultural Anthropology, 9*, 94-126.

Poggie, J. J., Jr., DeWalt, B. R., & Dressler, W. W. (Eds.). (1992). *Anthropological research: Process and application*. Albany: State University of New York Press.

Polanyi, M., & Prosch, H. (1975). *Meaning*. Chicago: University of Chicago Press.

Prattis, J. I. (Ed.). (1986). *Reflections: The anthropological muse.* Washington, DC: American Anthropological Association.

Prattis, J. I. (1997). *Anthropology at the edge: Essays on culture, symbol, and consciousness.* Lanham, MD: University Press of America.

Rabinow, P. (1977). *Reflections on fieldwork in Morocco.* Berkeley: University of California Press.

Rabinow, P. (1983). Humanism as nihilism. In N. Haan, R. N. Bellah, P. Rabinow, & W. M. Sullivan (Eds.), *Social science as moral inquiry* (pp. 52-75). New York: Columbia University Press.

Rabinow, P. (Ed.). (1984). *The Foucault reader.* New York: Pantheon.

Rabinow, P. (1986). Representations are social facts: Modernity and post-modernity in anthropology. In J. Clifford & G. E. Marcus (Eds.), *Writing culture: The poetics and politics of ethnography* (pp. 234-261). Berkeley: University of California Press.

Rabinow, P., & Sullivan, W. M. (Eds.). (1987). *Interpretive social science: A second look.* Berkeley: University of California Press.

Rapport, N. (1997). *Transcendent individual: Towards a literary and liberal anthropology.* New York: Routledge.

Reck, G. G. (1978). *In the shadow of Tlaloc: Life in a Mexican village.* Prospect Heights, IL: Waveland.

Reichel-Dolmatoff, G. (1996). *Yuruparí: Studies of an Amazonian foundation myth.* Cambridge, MA: Harvard University Press.

Richards, I. A. (1929). *Practical criticism.* New York: Harcourt Brace Jovanovich.

Richardson, L. (1994). Writing: A method of inquiry. In N. K. Denzin & Y. S. Lincoln (Eds.), *Handbook of qualitative research* (pp. 516-529). Thousand Oaks, CA: Sage.

Richardson, M. (1990). *Cry lonesome and other accounts of the anthropologist's project.* Albany: State University of New York Press.

Richardson, M. (1998a). Poetics in the field and on the page. *Qualitative Inquiry, 4,* 451-462.

Richardson, M. (1998b). The poetics of a resurrection: Re-seeing 30 years of change in a Colombian community and in the anthropological enterprise. *American Anthropologist, 100,* 11-21.

Riffaterre, M. (1970). Describing poetic structures: Two approaches to Baudelaire's "Les chats." In J. Ehrmann (Ed.), *Structuralism* (pp. 189-230). Garden City, NY: Doubleday.

Riffaterre, M. (1984). *Semiotics of poetry.* Bloomington: Indiana University Press.

Robbins, B. (1987). Poaching off the disciplines. *Raritan, 6*(4), 81-96.

Rorty, R. (1979). *Philosophy and the mirror of nature.* Princeton, NJ: Princeton University Press.

Rorty, R. (1981). Nineteenth-century idealism and twentieth-century textualism. *Monist, 64,* 155-174.

Rosaldo, R. (1989). *Culture and truth: The remaking of social analysis.* Boston: Beacon.

Rose, D. (1991a). In search of experience: The anthropological poetics of Stanley Diamond. In I. Brady (Ed.), *Anthropological poetics* (pp. 219-233). Savage, MD: Rowman & Littlefield. (Reprinted from *American Anthropologist,* 1983, *85*)

Rose, D. (1991b). Reversal. In I. Brady (Ed.), *Anthropological poetics* (pp. 283-301). Savage, MD: Rowman & Littlefield.

Rose, D. (1993). Ethnography as a form of life. In P. Benson (Ed.), *Anthropology and literature* (pp. 192-224). Urbana: University of Illinois Press.

Rothenberg, J. (1981). *Pre-faces and other writings.* New York: New Directions.

Rothenberg, J. (Ed.). (1985). *Technicians of the sacred: A range of poetries from Africa, America, Asia, Europe, and Oceania.* Berkeley: University of California Press.

Rothenberg, J. (1994). "Je est un autre": Ethnopoetics and the poet as other. *American Anthropologist, 96,* 523-524.

Rothenberg, J., & Rothenberg, D. (Eds.). (1983). *Symposium of the whole: A range of discourse toward an ethnopoetics.* Berkeley: University of California Press.

Sagan, C. (1980). *Cosmos.* New York: Ballantine.

Sagan, C. (1985). *Contact.* New York: Pocket Books.

Sahlins, M. (1981). *Historical metaphors and mythical realities: Structure in the early history of the Sandwich Islands kingdom.* Ann Arbor: University of Michigan Press.

Sahlins, M. (1985). *Islands of history.* Chicago: University of Chicago Press.

Sahlins, M. (1996). *How "natives" think: About Captain Cook, for example.* Chicago: University of Chicago Press.

Said, E. (1991). The politics of knowledge. *Raritan, 11*(1), 17-31.

Sangren, P. S. (1991). Rhetoric and the authority of ethnography. In S. Silverman (Ed.), *Inquiry and debate in the human sciences* (pp. 277-307). Chicago: University of Chicago Press.

Schechner, R. (1985). *Between theater and anthropology.* Philadelphia: University of Pennsylvania Press.

Schechner, R. (1995). *The future of ritual: Writings on culture and performance.* New York: Routledge.

Scholes, R. (1974). *Structuralism in literature: An introduction.* New Haven, CT: Yale University Press.

Scholte, B. (1966). Epistemic paradigms: Some problems in cross-cultural research on social anthropological history and theory. *American Anthropologist, 68,* 1192-1201.

Scott, D. (1992). Anthropology and colonial discourse: Aspects of the demonological construction of Sinhala cultural practice. *Cultural Anthropology, 7,* 301-326.

Shankman, P. (1984). On semiotics and science: Reply to Renner and Scholte. *Current Anthropology, 25,* 691-692.

Sherzer, J. (1987). A discourse-centered approach to language and culture. *American Anthropologist, 89,* 295-309.

Sherzer, J., & Woodbury, A. C. (Eds.). (1987). *Native American discourse: Poetics and rhetoric.* New York: Cambridge University Press.

Shore, B. (1996). *Cognition, culture, and the problem of meaning.* New York: Oxford University Press.

Shweder, R. A. (1996). True ethnography: The lore, the law, and the lure. In R. Jessor, A. Colby, & R. A. Shweder (Eds.), *Ethnography and human development: Context and meaning in social inquiry* (pp. 4-52). Chicago: University of Chicago Press.

Silko, L. M. (1977). *Ceremony.* New York: Penguin.

Simms, N. T. (1991). *Points of contact: A study of the interplay and intersection of traditional and non-traditional literatures, cultures, and mentalities.* New York: Pace University Press.

Simpson, D. (1994). Literary criticism, localism, and local knowledge. *Raritan, 14*(1), 70-88.

Slater, C. (1982). *Stories on a string: The Brazilian literatura de cordel.* Berkeley: University of California Press.

Spiegelberg, H. (1975). *Doing phenomenology: Essays on and in phenomenology.* The Hague: Martinus Nijhoff.

Spradley, J. E., & McDonough, G. P. (Eds.). (1973). *Anthropology through literature.* Boston: Little, Brown.

Stewart, J. (1962). *Curving road: Stories by John Stewart.* Urbana: University of Illinois Press.

Stewart, J. (1989). *Drinkers, drummers, and decent folk.* Albany: State University of New York Press.

Stewart, K. (1996). *A space on the side of the road: Cultural poetics in an "other" America.* Princeton, NJ: Princeton University Press.

Swann, B. (Ed.). (1983). *Smoothing the ground: Essays in Native American oral literature.* Berkeley: University of California Press.

Swearingen, J. (1986). Oral hermeneutics during the transition to literacy: The contemporary debate. *Cultural Anthropology, 1,* 138-156.

Tarn, N. (1991). *Views from the weaving mountain: Selected essays in poetics and anthropology.* Albuquerque: University of New Mexico.

Taussig, M. (1987). *Shamanism, colonialism, and the wild man.* Chicago: University of Chicago Press.

Taussig, M. (1993). *Mimesis and alterity: A particular history of the senses.* New York: Routledge.

Taylor, L. J. (1996). "There are two things that people don't like to hear about themselves": The anthropology of Ireland and the Irish view of anthropology. *South Atlantic Quarterly, 95,* 213-226.

Tedlock, B. (1991). From participant observation to the observation of participation: The emergence of narrative ethnography. *Journal of Anthropological Research, 47,* 69-94.

Tedlock, B. (1992). *The beautiful and the dangerous: Dialogues with the Zuni Indians.* New York: Penguin.

Tedlock, B., & Tedlock, D. (1985). Text and textile: Language and technology in the arts of the Quich Maya. *Journal of Anthropological Research, 41,* 121-146.

Tedlock, D. (Trans.). (1972). *Finding the center: Narrative poetry of the Zuni Indians.* New York: Dial.

Tedlock, D. (1983). *The spoken word and the work of interpretation.* Philadelphia: University of Pennsylvania Press.

Tedlock, D. (Trans. & Commentator). (1985). *Popol Vuh: The Mayan book of the dawn of life.* New York: Simon & Schuster.

Tedlock, D. (1987a). Hearing a voice in an ancient text: Quich Maya poetics in performance. In J. Sherzer & A. C. Woodbury (Eds.), *Native American discourse: Poetics and rhetoric* (pp. 140-175). Cambridge: Cambridge University Press.

Tedlock, D. (1987b). Questions concerning dialogical anthropology (with a response from Stephen Tyler). *Journal of Anthropological Research, 43,* 325-344.

Tedlock, D. (1990). *Days from a dream almanac.* Urbana: University of Illinois Press.

Tedlock, D. (1991). The speaker of tales has more than one string to play on. In I. Brady (Ed.), *Anthropological poetics* (pp. 309-340). Savage, MD: Rowman & Littlefield.

Tedlock, D. (1992). Ethnopoetics. In R. Bauman (Ed.), *Folklore, cultural performances, and popular entertainments* (pp. 81-85). New York: Oxford University Press.

Tedlock, D. (1993). *Breath on the mirror: Mythic voices and visions of the living Maya.* Albuquerque: University of New Mexico Press.

Thomas, E. M. (1987). *Reindeer moon.* New York: Pocket Books.

Thomas, N. (1989). *Out of time: History and evolution in anthropological discourse.* New York: Cambridge University Press.

Thomas, N. (1991). Against ethnography. *Cultural Anthropology, 6,* 306-322.

Thompson, W. I. (1983). *Blue jade from the morning star: An essay and a cycle of poems on Quetzalcoatl.* West Stockbridge, MA: Lindisfarne.

Tiles, M. (1984). *Bachelard: Science and objectivity.* New York: Cambridge University Press.

Tilley, C. (Ed.). (1990). *Reading material culture.* Cambridge, MA: Blackwell.

Todorov, T. (1977). *The poetics of prose* (R. Howard, Trans.). Ithaca, NY: Cornell University Press.

Todorov, T. (1981). *Introduction to poetics* (R. Howard, Trans.). Minneapolis: University of Minnesota Press.

Trawick, M. (1988). Spirits and voices in Tamil song. *American Ethnologist, 15,* 193-215.

Trawick, M. (1997). Time and mother: Conversations with a possessing spirit. In J. Leavitt (Ed.), *Poetry and prophecy: The anthropology of inspiration* (pp. 61-75). Ann Arbor: University of Michigan Press.

Tsing, A. L. (1994). From the margins. *Cultural Anthropology, 9,* 279-297.

Turnbull, C. (1962). *The forest people.* Garden City, NY: Doubleday.

Turnbull, C. (1972). *The mountain people.* New York: Simon & Schuster.

Turner, E. (1987). *The spirit and the drum: A memoir of Africa.* Tucson: University of Arizona Press.

Turner, V. (1974). *Dramas, fields, and metaphors: Symbolic action in human society.* Ithaca, NY: Cornell University Press.

Turner, V. (Ed.). (1982a). *Celebration: Studies in festivity and ritual.* Washington, DC: Smithsonian Institution Press.

Turner, V. (1982b). *From ritual to theatre: The human seriousness of play.* New York: Performing Arts Journal Publications.

Turner, V. (1983). A review of "Ethnopoetics." In J. Rothenberg & D. Rothenberg (Eds.), *Symposium of the whole: A range of discourse toward an ethnopoetics* (pp. 337-342). Berkeley: University of California Press.

Tyler, S. A. (Ed.). (1969). *Cognitive anthropology.* New York: Holt, Rinehart & Winston.

Tyler, S. A. (1984). The poetic turn in postmodern anthropology: The poetry of Paul Friedrich. *American Anthropologist, 86,* 328-336.

Ulin, R. C. (1984). *Understanding cultures: Perspectives in anthropology and social theory.* Austin: University of Texas Press.

Valéry, P. (1964). *Aesthetics* (R. Mennheim, Trans.). New York: Bollingen Foundation.

Van Den Abbeele, G. (1992). *Travel as metaphor: From Montaigne to Rousseau.* Minneapolis: University of Minnesota Press.

Van Lawick-Goodall, J. (1971). *In the shadow of man.* New York: Delta.

Van Maanen, J. (1988). *Tales of the field: On writing ethnography*. Chicago: University of Chicago Press.

Vendler, H. (1985, November 7). Looking for poetry in America. *New York Review of Books*, pp. 53-60.

Vendler, H. (1988). *The music of what happens: Poems, poets, critics*. Cambridge, MA: Harvard University Press.

Vendler, H. (1995). *Soul says: On recent poetry*. Cambridge, MA: Harvard University Press.

Webster, S. (1986). Realism and reification in the ethnographic genre. *Critique of Anthropology, 6,* 39-62.

Weinstein, F. (1990a). *History and theory after the fall: An essay on interpretation*. Chicago: University of Chicago Press.

Weinstein, F. (1990b). Who should write history? *SUNY Research, 10*(3), 20-21.

Weiss, W. A. (1990). Challenge to authority: Bakhtin and ethnographic description. *Cultural Anthropology, 5,* 414-430.

White, H. (1973). *Metahistory: The historical imagination in nineteenth-century Europe*. Baltimore: Johns Hopkins University Press.

Whitten, N. E., Jr. (1988). Toward a critical anthropology. *American Ethnologist, 15,* 732-742.

Wierzbicka, A. (1996). *Semantics: Primes and universals*. Oxford: Oxford University Press.

Wilbert, J., & Simoneau, K. (Eds.). (1982). *Folk literature of the Mataco Indians*. Los Angeles: UCLA Latin America Center Publications.

Wilk, S. (1991). *Humanistic anthropology*. Knoxville: University of Tennessee Press.

Williams, B. (1998, November 19). The end of explanation? *New York Review of Books*, pp. 40-44.

Wolf, E. (1982). *Europe and the people without history*. Berkeley: University of California Press.

Wolf, M. A. (1992). *A thrice-told tale: Feminism, postmodernism, and ethnographic responsibility*. Stanford, CA: Stanford University Press.

Wuthnow, R., Hunter, J. D., Bergesen, A., & Kurzweil, E. (Eds.). (1984). *Cultural analysis: The work of Peter L. Berger, Mary Douglas, Michel Foucault, and Jürgen Habermas*. Boston: Routledge & Kegan Paul.

38

UNDERSTANDING SOCIAL PROGRAMS THROUGH EVALUATION

◆ Jennifer C. Greene

S̲ocial program evaluation is a field of applied social inquiry uniquely distinguished by the explicit value dimensions of its knowledge claims, by the overt political character of its contexts, and by the inevitable pluralism and polyvocality of its actors.[1] Social program evaluators use the methods and tools of the social sciences to address not abstract theoretical questions of interest to some scholarly colleagues, but rather the priority policy and practice questions of diverse social actors—decision makers, program administrators, direct service staff, program participants, and others. Social program evaluators aim to inform and improve the services, programs, policies, and public conversations at hand, in contexts like these:

> Annette Barlow directs a county United Way in rural Georgia. Like the boards of directors of United Ways elsewhere, Annette's board has in-

creasingly asked for information about the *outcomes* of the programs they fund. Are babies in the county being born any healthier as a result of the prenatal program? Are children who participate in the peer tutoring program reading any better? Are seniors in the volunteer grandparent program less isolated, and, if so, does this meaningfully affect their physical health, their quality of life, and their economic self-sufficiency?

Martin Seguro is a newly elected U.S. senator from Arizona who finds himself the junior minority member on the Senate Foreign Relations Committee. As he learns more about American relationships around the world, he wonders about the influence on these relationships of international monetary policies, such as structural adjustment, tariffs, and trade agreements.

Evelyn Reynolds has 20 years of service as a social worker in her county social service department, working primarily with public assistance programs and clients. As the programs have changed over the years—from a proliferation of categorical benefits to more-integrated benefit and service packages to a phasing out of welfare altogether—so has Evelyn's job. She finds herself with increasingly less authority yet more responsibility and with more and more desperate demands for fewer and fewer resources. "There must be some way to make this system work better!" she asserted at a recent staff meeting.

Thomas Greenbaum is the director of social services in Evelyn Reynolds's state. He is also experiencing tensions and contradictions in his job. However, the pressures Thomas experiences—and thus his priority information needs—revolve around minimizing program costs, meeting federal regulations, and responding to the conflicting demands of political action lobbyists.

Michael Grey Wolf has been active in the Native American sovereignty movement for more than a decade. His recent work has focused on comparing Native and non-Native public elementary and secondary schools, toward the goal of developing charter school legislation for Native schools in his home state.[2]

In this chapter, I endeavor to use these and other specific contexts to redirect attention to the sociopolitical role of evaluation. I do so by highlighting the sociopolitical dimensions of evaluation approaches that incorporate qualitative methods and the changing face of this genre as it responds to challenges from within and without. These highlights are embedded within the following organization for the chapter. The next two sections locate evaluation within the social policy arena and qualitative approaches within the overall landscape of social program evaluation, respectively. The subsequent two sections portray the philosophy and practice of evaluation approaches that rely on qualitative methods. *Philosophy* refers to the general epistemological logic of justification for these approaches, and *practice* describes key facets of application. The final section then locates approaches in this genre historically, connects them to significant theoretical developments in evaluation, and guides them through contemporary challenges toward a promising future identity and role.

◆ *The Contexts of Program Evaluation*

The scenarios just above, presented as characteristic contexts of social program evaluation, clearly evince its political inherence (Cronbach & Associates, 1980; Patton, 1987; Weiss, 1987). They directly engage the pluralistic values of contemporary American democracy. These are contexts about contested social policies and programs, about how and by whom resources are allocated, and about competing civic values, both in the global arena and in the local community. The core content of social program evaluation is thus intertwined with political power and decision making about societal priorities and directions. Evaluators working in these politicized contexts must negotiate identities for themselves that maximize their credibility and potential effectiveness. Different evaluators choose different grounds for negotiation, grounds that lead to different evaluation purposes and roles, yet all are concerned with power and all are value based (Greene, 1997).

Moreover, the work of social program evaluators is steered by the interests of selected members of the setting being evaluated. (Interests here are value-based claims on resources.) In all evaluation contexts there are multiple, often competing, potential audiences for evaluation—groups and individuals who have vested interests in the programs being evaluated, called *stakeholders* in evaluation jargon. These range from the powerful to the powerless, from policy makers and funders like Annette Barlow's United Way board and the U.S. Senate to program administrators like Thomas Greenbaum and program staff members like Evelyn Reynolds, to advocates like Michael Grey Wolf, and to the citizenry at large. Thus evaluators must also negotiate whose questions will be addressed and whose interests will be served by their work, negotiations that again are inherently value based.

Evaluation results then enter the political arena of social program and policy decision making not as decontextualized, abstract, or theoretical knowledge claims, but rather as interested knowledge claims, as empirically justified value judgments about the merit or worth of the programs evaluated. Evaluators do not just claim to know about something, they claim to know how good it is from selected vantage points. At root, evaluation is about valuing (Scriven, 1967) and judging (Stake, 1967). Values permeate the evaluation landscape, from values that are constitutive of the programs being evaluated to values as professional ethics, to values as the ethical aim of the practice of evaluation (Schwandt, 1997b). Hence, in addition to negotiating evaluation purpose and audience, evaluators must negotiate the criteria and standards upon which judgments of quality will be made. These criteria and the resulting judgments are inescapably power and value based and thereby matters of debate and conflict in all contemporary democracies.

◆ Locating Qualitative Program Evaluation

Because social program evaluation is inextricably intertwined with politics and values, and because evaluators must navigate carefully amid competing political and value agendas, it is essential that evaluators have a diverse set of approaches to help guide practice. Currently, the diverse approaches available to evaluators offer not only choices of methods, but also alternative epistemological assumptions (about knowledge, the social world, human nature) and distinct ideological stances (about the desired ends of social programs and of social inquiry). These alternative philosophies and methods (concerned with what and how we know) and alternative ideological stances (concerning the meaning of social and community life) are constitutive of their respective approaches.

Table 38.1 offers a *descriptive* categorization of four contemporary genres of evaluation approaches. Like all such categorizations, the boundaries of these genres are clear only in the

presentation of them. In historical evolution, conceptual argument, and actual practice, genre boundaries are considerably more fluid. The first genre, which represents the historically dominant tradition in program evaluation, is oriented around the interests of policy makers and funders—characteristically, it involves causal questions about the degree to which a program has attained desired outcomes while retaining cost-efficiency compared to its critical competitors. Recurrent demands for accountability in social expenditures are well addressed by this genre. These include Annette Barlow's United Way board's desire for information on program outcomes and state administrator Thomas Greenbaum's need for information on his social welfare program's costs versus benefits. Also in this genre, science, in the guise of program evaluation, is especially valued for its presumed objectivity and truth claims, still held as regulative ideals.

The second genre of evaluation approaches arose largely in response to the failure of classic experimental science to provide trustworthy, timely, and useful information for program decision making. As early trials clearly demonstrated (one classic is the Head Start evaluation; Cicirelli & Associates, 1969), the logic of experimentalism simply does not transfer well to real-world social contexts. This second genre then refocused attention on the needs of decision makers, especially the practical needs of on-site decision makers for program information useful for management decisions. Evelyn Reynolds's plea for information useful for program improvement is well answered by this genre. With its utilitarian value base, this genre of evaluation embraces eclectic methods choices in the service of practical problem solving. Michael Patton's (1997) utilization-oriented evaluation is a quintessential example of this genre. His approach to qualitative evaluation also falls within this genre, given its utilitarian value base (Patton, 1990).

But it is in the third cluster that qualitative approaches to evaluation that are rooted in longstanding philosophical and disciplinary traditions, such as interpretivism and ethnography, respectively, have found their home. In both theory and practice, qualitative approaches to eval-

TABLE 38.1 Major Contemporary Approaches to Formal Program Evaluation

Epistemology	Primary Values Promoted	Key Audiences	Preferred Methods	Typical Evaluation Questions
Postpositivism (Cook, 1985)	Efficiency, accountability, cost-effectiveness, policy enlightenment	High-level policy and decision makers, funders, the social science community	Quantitative: experiments and quasi-experiments, surveys, causal modeling, cost-benefit analysis	Are intended outcomes attained and attributable to the program? Is this program the most efficient alternative?
Utilitarian pragmatism (Patton, 1997)	Utility, practicality, managerial effectiveness	Midlevel program managers and on-site administrators	Eclectic, mixed: structured and unstructured surveys, interviews, observations, document analyses, panel reviews	Which program components work well and which need improvement? How effective is the program with respect to the organization's goals and mission? Who likes the program?
Interpretivism, constructivism (Stake, 1995)	Pluralism, understanding, contextualism, personal experience	Program directors, staff, and beneficiaries	Qualitative: case studies, open-ended interviews and observations, document reviews, dialectics	How is the program experienced by various stakeholders? In what ways is the program meaningful?
Critical social sciences (Fay, 1987)	Emancipation, empowerment, social change, egalitarianism, critical enlightenment	Program beneficiaries and their communities, activists	Participatory, action oriented: stakeholder participation in evaluation agenda setting, data collection, interpretation, and action	In what ways are the premises, goals, or activities of the program serving to maintain power and resource inequities in this context?

uation span multiple "moments" in qualitative inquiry (see Lincoln & Denzin, Chapter 41, this volume), from the blurred genres and representation/legitimation crises of the 1970s and 1980s to the experimental postmodernism of today. Yet most of these approaches *in evaluation* share a hermeneutic view of social scientific knowledge claims, a value orientation that promotes pluralism, and a preference for qualitative methods. Also influenced by the responsive tradition within program evaluation (Abma, 1997a; Stake, 1975), these approaches characteristically seek to address the interests and honor the experiences of stakeholders closest to the programs evaluated—namely, program staff and beneficiaries—by giving voice to their contextualized program understanding. In-depth, contextualized understanding may also be of interest to other stakeholders, for example, Arizona Senator Martin Seguro's interest in the connections between international monetary policies and U.S. relations abroad. The early work of Robert Stake (1975) and of Egon Guba and Yvonna Lincoln (1981) significantly shaped the contours of this genre. As discussed later in this chapter (and as illustrated throughout this volume), contemporary work in this genre is reshaping it in significant ways.

Finally, the fourth genre represents evaluation approaches that are "openly ideological," that *explicitly* advance a particular value agenda, for example, of Rawlsian social justice (House, 1990), empowerment (Fetterman, 1994), critical race consciousness (Ladson-Billings, 1998), or social change (Ryan, Greene, Lincoln, Mathison, & Mertens, 1998; Whitmore, 1994). Michael Grey Wolf's explicit desire to advocate for Native American sovereignty in his evaluative work well illustrates this genre. As noted, all evaluation approaches advance certain ideals and values. "They privilege the stakeholder audiences who share those ideals and they summon the methodologies that enable their realization" (Greene, 1997, p. 27). Distinctively in the fourth genre, the essential rationales for evaluation are, first, the advocacy of ideals and values and, second, the answering of certain program questions. For most other evaluators, answering program questions is the stated first priority. Within this fourth genre of contemporary evaluation approaches are a diverse array of philosophical arguments, including critical social science, feminisms, and neo-Marxism. Within evaluation, British and Australian democratic evaluation (MacDonald, 1976) and action-oriented evaluation (Carr & Kemmis, 1986) are early exemplars. Guba and Lincoln's (1989) fourth-generation evaluation also warrants examination as it advances an activist ideology with grounding in a constructivist philosophy.

Even as I endeavor in Table 38.1 to present the four genres of evaluation approaches as significantly differentiated by ideology, in addition to epistemology and technique, the methodological domination of evaluative thinking still reigns (Greene, 1992; Schwandt, 1998). This is nowhere more evident than in the naming of different approaches to evaluation by their primary methods, as in *qualitative evaluation*. This naming obscures important differences among evaluative approaches that rely on qualitative methods, such as those promoted by Stake, Guba and Lincoln, Patton, Eisner, Schwandt, and Mac-Donald (which I discuss in my contribution to the first edition of this *Handbook*; Greene, 1994). It also misdirects attention toward *how* an evaluation is done (qualitatively) instead of *why* (to be contextually responsive, to help improve the program, to promote democratizing conversations, to advocate for pluralism). Further, the methodological domination of evaluative theory and practice falsely simplifies the political complexities of the contexts in which evaluators work.

◆ The Logic of Justification for Evaluations Conducted Qualitatively

Although variations exist in the philosophical underpinnings of different qualitative approaches to evaluation, most share a core set of assumptions and stances that are aptly labeled *constructivist* or *interpretivist*. As Schwandt (1994) notes:

> Proponents of these persuasions share the goal of understanding the complex world of lived experience from the point of view of those who live it. This goal is variously spoken of as an abiding concern for the life world, for the emic point of view, for understanding meaning, for grasping the actor's definition of a situation, for *Verstehen*. The world of lived reality and situation-specific meanings that constitute the general object of investigation is thought to be constructed by social actors. That is, particular actors, in particular places, at particular times, fashion meaning out of events and phenomena through prolonged, complex processes of social interaction involving history, language, and action. (p. 118)

He goes on:

> Constructivists are deeply committed to the . . . view that what we take to be objective knowledge and truth is the result of perspective. Knowledge and truth are created, not discovered by mind. They emphasize the pluralistic and plastic character of reality—pluralistic in the sense that reality is expressible in a variety of symbol and language systems; plastic in the sense that reality is stretched and shaped to fit purposeful acts of intentional human agents. (p. 125)

Constructivism

Constructivist inquirers seek to *understand contextualized meaning,* to understand the meaningfulness of human actions and interactions—as experienced and construed by the actors—in a given context. This aim is based on the assumption that the social world, as distinct from the physical world, does not exist independently, "out there," waiting to be discovered by smart and technically expert social inquirers. Rather, the emotional, linguistic, symbolic, interactive, political dimensions of the social world—and their meaningfulness, or lack thereof—are all constructed by agentic human actors. These constructions are influenced by specific historical, geopolitical, and cultural practices and discourses, and by the intentions—noble and otherwise—of those doing the constructing. So these constructions are multiple and plural, contingent and contextual.

And so the basic task of social inquiry is not to discover lawful properties of the external world, to answer population representation questions, or to extract and connect observed effects with causes. Rather, the first task is to understand people's constructions of meanings in the context being studied, because it is these constructions that constitute social realities and underlie all human action. This task itself is an interpretive one, requiring the inquirer to "elucidate the process of meaning construction . . . to construct a reading of these meanings; it is to offer the inquirer's construction of the constructions of the actors one studies" (Schwandt, 1994, p. 118). That is, the interpretive inquirer cannot know the meanings of another's life experience, but only the inquirer's own inscriptions or representations of said meanings (Lather, 1991). In these ways, interpretivist, constructivist inquiry is unapologetically subjectivist—the inquirer's worldview becomes part of the construction and representation of meaning in any particular context. Inquirer bias, experience, expertise, and insight are all part of the meanings constructed and inscribed.

Values are therefore also intertwined with knowing, as knowing is intertwined with being and acting. In constructivist, interpretive work, there are "no facts without values, and different values can actually lead to different facts" (Smith, 1989, p. 111). That is, different knowers holding different ideals and values can construct different meanings, even in the same situation. So constructivist, interpretive inquiry honors the value dimensions of lived experience and human meaning, but does not prescribe or advance any particular set of values. Rather, the values of a particular constructivist inquiry become those held dear by the constructors of meaning in that inquiry—the members of the setting studied, the inquirer, and the larger society. Constructivism is thereby value pluralistic.

Methodologically, constructivism is most consonant with natural settings, with the human inquirer as the primary gatherer and interpreter of meaning, with qualitative methods, with emergent inquiry designs, and with contextual, holistic understanding, in contrast to interventionist prediction and control, as the overall goal of inquiry (Guba & Lincoln, 1989; Lincoln, 1990; Patton, 1990).

Perhaps more significant, constructivism supports the decentering of inquiry/evaluation discourse from questions of method to questions of purpose and role. The quality of technique becomes secondary to the quality and meaningfulness of understanding. Yet, unlike some of their more radical peers who disclaim the existence of any privileged procedures that will enhance the acceptability of an inquirer's interpretations (e.g., Barone, 1992; Smith, 1989, p. 160), most constructivist evaluators favor some procedural structure for their work. This is partly because the contexts of social program evaluation continue to demand assurances of methodological quality and data integrity. Evaluations conducted qualitatively can make little contribution to social policies and programs if they are not perceived as credible—defensible, enlightening, and useful—by at least some evaluation users.

In this respect, evaluators are particularly concerned about criteria and methods for warranting their evaluative knowledge claims as empirically based representations of program experiences and not as biased inquirer opinions. Philosophically, this poses a contradiction, that being "the attempt to provide a methodological foundation for knowledge based on nonfoundational assumptions" (Smith, 1989, p. 159). The practice section that follows outlines some of the ways evaluators do this, for example, using time-honored procedures of triangulation. These responses to the criteria problem generally follow Smith's (1989, 1990) lead in recasting the concerns from ones of foundational methods to ones of heuristic procedures, appealing, for example, to procedural criteria as grounds for judging the goodness of interpretations (Schwandt, 1994, p. 130). For many qualitative evaluators, nonetheless, the contradictory demands of philosophy and practice, especially around criteria and procedures for warranting quality, remain strong.

Beyond Constructivism

Constructivism characterizes the philosophical logic justifying many of the evaluations conducted qualitatively today. But constructivism itself is not unchallenged, and some evaluators have engaged these challenges. Two brief examples here will illustrate these developments at the level of philosophy.[3] I will return to the topic of contemporary challenges and future directions in the concluding section of the chapter.

First, for more than a decade, Thomas Schwandt (1989, 1996, 1997a, 1997c, 1998) has offered *practical philosophy* as an alternative way of conceptualizing the practice and discourse of social science, including evaluation. "Practical philosophy is concerned with the mode of activity called the practical (praxis). Its subject matter is how an individual conducts her or his life and affairs as a member of society" (Schwandt, 1998, p. 9). To practice evaluation practically means to shift radically from a methodological to a political-ethical frame, and to be less concerned about perfecting and warranting our knowledge claims (Schwandt, 1996) and more concerned about helping practitioners to deliberate well and to develop their own wise practice.

Second, postmodern challenges exist to all contemporary forms of evaluation practice (Mabry, 1997). In much postmodern thought, for example, claims to know are not just partial and contingent, but also fundamentally indeterminate. Further, not only is the author of a postmodern representation of knowing also a major constructor of what is claimed to be known, but so is the reader. One response to these challenges is to abandon modernist principles and preoccupations in favor of actually practicing evaluation postmodernly. Tineke Abma (1997a, 1997b, 1998) offers inspirational examples of postmodern evaluation practice that accept postmodern incredulity and doubt without giving way to nihilism and disengagement. For example, Abma (1997a) promotes in her work the idea and experience of *playfulness:* "A playful person is not too attached to his or her personal persuasions and appreciates the power of redescribing, the power of language to make new and different things possible and important" (p. 44). Abma also invokes the "self-reflexive, polyvocal, and multi-interpretable" (1998, p. 434) texts of postmodern writers in endeavoring to craft her evaluation reports as "open, ambiguous, and unpredictable . . . without summary, conclusions and recommendations" (1997b, p. 106) and thereby as invitations to dialogue (1998).

◆ The Practice of Evaluations Conducted Qualitatively

So far, I have described the unique contexts and character of social program evaluation, presented a typology of contemporary genres of evaluation theory and practice, and explicated the constructivist philosophy underlying most "qualitative" evaluation approaches. In turning now to practice, I need to acknowledge that in the field, evaluators rarely practice a "pure" form of their craft, either philosophically or methodologically. The complex, pluralistic demands of evaluation field contexts evoke instead multiple, diverse frames for guiding practice and invite dialogue among them. In fact, evaluation expertise today is marked by its *dialectical, dialogical temperament,* its openness to multiple forms and layers of understanding, and its responsiveness to contextual needs for understanding, rather than its adherence to any singular philosophy or approach.

I offer here an example of evaluation practiced qualitatively that illustrates common features of this genre. After highlighting these features, I will discuss the continuing challenges of this approach to evaluation.

An Example

Envision an evaluation of a state-level welfare reform initiative, a reform that aims to shift three-quarters of the people currently on the state's welfare rolls to sustainable jobs over the next 5 years. This reform is based on the premise that long-term economic self-sufficiency for

many of the people currently dependent on welfare requires an approach that first concentrates on "developing human capital" and then shifts to work placements. The development phase of this program includes intensive, individualized education, personal development, job training, and job search activities.

To address evaluative questions about the quality and effectiveness of this welfare reform for both policy and local program audiences, the qualitatively minded evaluator would seek primarily to *understand* how the program is experienced by individual participants—welfare clients, program staff, educational and economic development leaders—in particular contexts, for it is in these contextualized experiences that the meanings of program quality and effectiveness are shaped and molded. The qualitative evaluator of this welfare reform would likely purposefully sample for intensive data gathering a small number of program communities and participants to obtain heterogeneous samples on relevant characteristics (for example, demographics, economic and employment histories, cultural norms) in order to capture a broad range of diversity of experiences and meanings expected. For this sample, then, the evaluator would likely conduct extended on-site observations in order to develop a descriptive portrayal of what happens in the new welfare program and how this portrayal varies across contexts. How is the concept of "human capital" envisioned and implemented in these varied program sites? What is a typical program experience like for different types of welfare clients? How do community characteristics shape the definitions of *long-term employment* variously adopted by the program sites?

The evaluator would likely sample 10-15 welfare clients in each site for individual interviews and reviews of their program records in order to understand what program participants find meaningful, or not, in the program and how this meaning is reflected in their program journeys. The evaluator would also likely sample some program staff and managers, some economic development leaders, and some key community members in each site for individual or group interviews regarding their perceptions of and experiences with the new welfare program. What is the range of views regarding the human and the economic development emphases of the new program? What agreements and disagreements exist within the community about the kinds of economic self-sufficiency being fostered in the new program? Alternatively, these program staff and community perceptions might be more effectively and representatively gathered with structured, quantitative mail surveys.

The evaluator would then integrate these multiple individual stories about program engagement and experience into community narratives. These community narratives would convey the evaluator's representations of the contextualized, experiential meaning of the welfare reform initiative in each locality studied. One community narrative, for example, might highlight the disjuncture between the "professional advancement" rhetoric of the welfare reform program and the program's limited, mostly low-skilled set of educational offerings. Another might highlight the complementarity of the program's activity schedule with the daily rhythms and practices of a significant proportion, although not all, of the program participants in that setting. Yet another might centrally feature program participants' experiences of *their* program as oppressive and dehumanizing, and core program staff who are bitterly resentful about their recent transfer to this, "the worst of the neighborhood welfare offices." Community narratives, that is, would holistically describe and analyze or explain the meaningful connections and disjunctures of this welfare reform initiative within each of its multiple contexts. Beyond description and analysis, political policy and action interpretations of these narratives (Wolcott, 1994) would invoke the values and beliefs of individual evaluators and stakeholders.

Furthermore, these community narratives are shaped not just by micro-level events and interactions, but also by macro-level economic, political, and especially job market factors, forces, and trends. The narratives would gain more meaning if placed within their larger state and regional economic and political context. Further, a cost-benefit analysis of this reform initiative is, in all probability, an expected part of the evaluation. So, in addition to the intensive study of selected community cases, this evaluation would access and analyze macro-level information—most probably in quantitative form—on relevant welfare dependence, economic, and job market indicators and would assess program costs against outcomes.

These evaluative data would then be woven into an overall portrayal of program quality and effectiveness as grounded in insider experiences and meanings and as bounded by the opportunities and constraints of the broader marketplace. This portrayal would be offered as a holistic representation of those studied, with possible but not assured extensions and relevance to those not studied. This portrayal would be filled with snapshots of program activities and vignettes about accomplishment and disappointment, fulfillment and disengagement. This portrayal would thus offer a contextualized, complex, dynamic, value-laden, but necessarily partial statement about welfare reform. Although holistic, hermeneutic understanding is the goal of evaluation practice qualitatively, human phenomena in their sociopolitical contexts remain extraordinarily complex. All representations of interpretive understanding are thus necessarily partial.

Evaluation as the Telling of Stories

As highlighted by this example, evaluation practiced qualitatively is a narrative craft that involves the telling of *stories*—stories about individuals and groups of people in their own complex and dynamic communities, stories that enable understanding of what these communities share with others and what is unique to them, stories with an explicit authorial signature (Barone, 1992), and stories with the aim of understanding, and often action, as the improvement of practice or the reframing of the policy conversation, toward the appreciation of pluralism and complexity.

As a narrative craft, this approach to evaluation heavily favors *qualitative methods,* methods that require direct engagement with members of the settings being studied and that gather information about their experiences in their own words. Such methods uniquely enable understanding of insider experiences and perspectives. On-site observations and personal interviews are thus the mainstays of evaluation practiced qualitatively, supported by reviews of relevant documents and records. However, most evaluations also require information about a large, representative sample of program participants or information about macro social-political-economic factors and trends or cost-benefit information, as illustrated by the welfare reform example above. For these kinds of purposes, *quantitative methods* are clearly acceptable within qualitative evaluation. In fact, in all genres of evaluation practice, evaluators are likely to attain more comprehensive and in-depth program understanding by explicitly inviting dialogue around data from different methods and approaches (Greene & Caracelli, 1997).

Good storytellers carefully select and richly portray their settings and make the actions of their protagonists explicable within these settings. In like fashion, qualitative evaluations are framed by the careful selection of one or more *cases* to study and by the rich, multilayered descriptions of the *contexts* of those cases. The welfare reform example is framed by the selection of several communities as *instrumental cases* (Stake, 1995)—cases selected not for their intrinsic interest but for their potential to provide insight into the overall reform initiative. Understanding the interpersonal, civic, socioeconomic, cultural rhythms of these communities is essential, as constructivist meaning is greatly embedded in context. What community characteristics, for example, might influence a program participant's sense of hopefulness or despair, connectedness or isolation, and then how are these feelings related to her or his program experience? Locating these instrumental cases within the larger state economic context—through more quantitative methods and indicators—is also a critical part of meaning making and understanding the overall reform endeavor.

As a narrative craft, evaluation practiced qualitatively is highly dependent on the narrator-evaluator. Different evaluators will tell different stories, and more experienced, knowledgeable, sensitive, and insightful evaluators can usually tell more meaningful stories. An *evaluator's own position* in his or her work reflects both personal biography and political partisanship, both who the evaluator is, as an individual and an evaluator, and whose interests he or she chooses to advance in the study (Greene, 1996, p. 285). With a constructivist worldview, most evaluators in this genre are partial to the interests of those closest to the program being studied, namely, program staff and participants. These are the voices and perspectives most prominently featured in the welfare reform example above. But, with a constructivist worldview, most evaluators in this genre are also committed to pluralism and thus to representing the full array of perspectives and meanings in their stories—for a comprehensive story, all are also needed.

Finally, evaluators must define and position not just themselves in their work, but their work in the world (Greene, 1996, 1998b). Evaluators must be accountable for the differences their stories make. With their constructivist worldview, evaluators in this genre most comfortably *position their stories* as guides for the improvement of specific contextual practices (Patton, 1997), as opportunities for program learning and insight by diverse interested stakeholders (Stake, 1997), or as vehicles for reframing the larger policy conversation (Weiss, 1998). Perhaps less comfortably, constructivist and interpretivist evaluators can position their stories as insistent demands to attend to the vital complexities, the legitimate pluralism, and the politics of power that constitute the fabric of contemporary social life in the United States. To have a voice in the future direction of the social practices and policies they study, evaluators in this genre must offer not only convincing stories, but challenging ones, and they need not only to tell their stories but also actively and assertively to claim space on the social agenda for them.

The Challenges of Evaluation as Storytelling

But how do those who read and listen to the evaluator's story about the meaningfulness of this state-level welfare reform decide if it is a good story? How do they know the evaluator is not just advocating for her own viewpoint about welfare reform in the telling of this story? How does the evaluator know where the boundaries of her own advocacy lie? And how does she as a "qualitative" evaluator fairly and justly fulfill her responsibilities—to those who have commissioned the evaluation, to the members of the settings studied, and to the larger citizenry, the collective good? Whose interests are advanced, for example, when the evaluator judges this state's approach to welfare reform to be an effective one, but welfare reform itself to be a misguided policy direction?

These questions reveal the essential value dimensions of all social program evaluation, across all genres. They contest the criteria to be used in judging the quality of the inquiry (How good is this story?) and the quality of the program evaluated (How good is this program?). They challenge the presence of the evaluator in the story (Are you just advocating for your own viewpoint?) and they query the very purpose of evaluation (Whose interests are being advanced?). As noted, these questions are germane to all forms of evaluation. They are more visible in evaluations practiced qualitatively because this evaluation genre explicitly acknowledges the value strands of knowledge claims. And they are more problematic because this evaluation genre is philosophically nonfoundational and practically value pluralistic. The constructivist justification for this genre provides no ready answers to these challenges, which instead must be addressed by each evaluator in each context.

In the welfare reform evaluation example above, the evaluator may rely on recognizable inquiry criteria, for example, some of the trustworthiness criteria of Lincoln and Guba

(1985). These criteria (credibility, applicability, dependability, and confirmability) are constructed to parallel conventional inquiry criteria (internal validity, external validity, reliability, and neutrality, respectively) and thus can be recognized as familiar and understood as legitimate by critical evaluation audiences, site-level program staff, and state-level program decision makers alike.[4] Procedural guides for fulfilling these criteria are also familiar, as they rely heavily on methodological arguments and techniques—sampling for diversity, triangulating for agreement, and monitoring bias. Many important evaluation clients need familiar or recognizable evaluation constructs like these in order to accept unfamiliar ways of knowing and thinking. Although not as respectful of the nature of constructivist thought as some other proposed lists of inquiry criteria—for example, Harry Wolcott's (1990) *understanding,* Guba and Lincoln's (1989) *authenticity,* and action researchers' *warranted action* (Greenwood & Levin, 1998)—these trustworthiness constructs are pragmatic choices for evaluators concerned about the acceptability and usefulness of their stories, especially for "modernist clients" (Robert Stake, personal communication, May 6, 1999).

But still, usefulness for what purposes, for whose aims? Whereas qualitative inquirers in other domains can uninhibitedly experiment with various political and action agendas for their work, social program evaluators are more constrained, both by tradition and by context. Advocacy is a daunting specter in many evaluation circles, challenging as it does the traditional stance of the disinterested, distanced, neutral evaluator whose only job is to find out the "truth" about the effectiveness of the social program at hand (Greene, 1997). But advocacy as the promotion of some interests over others is unavoidable in contemporary social program evaluation. There are simply too many stakeholders with too many varied interests for any single evaluation to address all of their concerns fairly and justly. In this regard, evaluation practiced qualitatively—characteristically more than other genres—strives to reach pluralistic ideals while clearly acknowledging its partialities. Pluralistic ideals imply inclusiveness of perspective and voice. That is, the views of both the usually vocal and the usually silent stakeholders are sought, the latter often with an extra stretch of an outreached hand. But even such concerted efforts will fall short, and pluralistic inclusiveness is rarely fully attained.

Moreover, evaluators in this genre know that their claims to understand are constitutive of the perspectives that do get privileged and thereby unavoidably interested and partial. The welfare reform evaluator, with her constructivist worldview, is likely to emphasize contextual meaningfulness over cost-efficiency in her judgments of program quality. In like manner, Patton's (1990, 1997) utilization ideals privilege the interests of on-site decision makers, Guba and Lincoln's (1989) fourth-generation evaluation integrates a constructivist philosophy with an empowerment ideology to champion the interests of the least powerful, and Stake's (1997) constructivist beliefs and reformist principles engender sympathies for those who are also struggling mightily and meaningfully with reform. In short, while soundly disclaiming advocacy as bias, evaluators of this genre recognize the undeniable leanings of all evaluation and embrace those most comfortable with their own philosophy and biography. My own leanings underscore the importance of complexity and pluralism as critical markers of social meaning and action.

◆ The Journey of Evaluations Conducted Qualitatively

Beginnings

Constructivist, qualitative approaches to program evaluation emerged within the U.S. evaluation community in the 1970s (Stake, 1967, 1975), in tandem with two significant evolutions in intellectual thought and societal beliefs (Cook, 1985; Greene & McClintock, 1991).[5] The first (r)evolution was the dethroning of experimental science as the paradigm for social program evaluation (and other applied social sciences), a dethroning resulting from major fractures in the positivist philosophy of science that had guided most scientific practice since the Enlightenment era of the 18th century.[6] It was amid the debates and discussions that ensued regarding alternatives to experimentalism that interpretivist philosophies and qualitative approaches entered evaluative discourse. Initially contested on both methodological and practical grounds (as expressed in evaluation's *qualitative-quantitative debate*, e.g., Cook & Reichardt, 1979; Reichardt & Rallis, 1994), qualitative approaches to evaluation took strong root in the thinking of many evaluation theorists and methodologists. Largely through their sensible and appealing practice, such approaches have now become an accepted alternative throughout the evaluation community.

The second major set of changes that encouraged and enabled the emergence and growth of qualitative approaches to evaluation involved changes in the belief systems of the larger U.S. society during the 1960s and 1970s. Thomas Cook (1985) describes these changes as follows:

1. The decline in authority accorded standard social science theory following the perceived failures of the Great Society (see also House, 1993);
2. The decline in authority accorded political figures following the Vietnam War, the Watergate scandal, and other government debacles; and,
3. An increase in the cultural, value, and political pluralism of society, as manifest, for example, in the civil rights and women's movements.

There was considerable consonance between these shifts in societal thinking and the emergence of alternative paradigms, including interpretivism and constructivism, for understanding and doing social science.

Present-Day Connections to Important Evaluation Theories

In its contemporary form, social program evaluation is a young field, just beginning to develop and refine its own theories (Shadish, Cook, & Leviton, 1991). Among the important theoretical developments likely to continue to shape evaluative thinking and practice over the coming decade are two sets of ideas: (a) the reclamation of *theories of program action and change* as significant conceptual frameworks for evaluation, and (b) the redefinition of evaluation's primary role as an opportunity for *active, generative, and inclusive learning,* a redefinition that emphasizes the *process* of evaluation over its products. What these developments in evaluation theory share is a recentering of evaluation around its sociopolitical role, instead of its methods and techniques, and a valuing of the educative and action potential of evaluation. They also derive strength from evaluation practiced qualitatively, through significant but not exclusive reliance on interpretive methods, and through support for, if not complete allegiance to, a constructivist worldview. I describe each development briefly below.

Evaluating Program Theories

Early program evaluations in the Great Society era of the United States were styled after experimental tests of program theories, of the hypothesized causal links between program inputs and expected program outcomes. Evaluations of that era aspired to measure outcomes for program participants and to compare these to measured outcomes for similar people who did not participate in the programs. Little attention was given to gathering data on the actual programs, as implemented or experienced. So the processes by which observed program effects happened or did not happen were unknown—thus the label of "black box" evaluations for these early studies, signaling the disfavor into which they generally fell as stand-alone studies. As Lee Cronbach and Associates (1980) observed, "A good evaluative

question invites a differentiated answer instead of leaving the program plan, the delivery of the program, and the response of clients as unexamined elements within a closed black box" (p. 5).

Starting in the early 1980s, a number of evaluation theorists (notably Len Bickman, 1987; Huey Chen & Peter Rossi, 1983; and Carol Weiss, 1972) began to reargue for the importance of "theory-driven evaluation" and evaluation directed at understanding and assessing a program's "theory of change." From Carol Weiss (1998):

> The [program] theory gives guidance to the evaluator about where to look and what to find out. (p. 65)

> The mere construction of a [program] theory can expose naïve and simplistic expectations. . . . The . . . theory can be a learning tool long before the evaluation begins. (p. 66)

> Once the data are in hand, [the analysis assesses] how well the theory describes what actually happened. . . . This is important information for the directors and staff of the program under study, so that they can rethink the understandings and replan the activities that did not work out as anticipated. (p. 66)

> Theory-based evaluation [also] provides explanations, stories of means and ends, that communicate readily to policymakers and the public. (p. 68)

Another key argument for theory-based evaluation is its potential to contribute to generalizable knowledge about how social interventions work and the conditions and factors that enable and obstruct their success (Cronbach, 1982; Weiss, 1998). Evaluation practiced qualitatively has much to offer this goal of social problem solving. Holistic program portrayals can translate program constructs into contextualized lived experiences within diverse community values. Evaluators' program portrayals can complement regression coefficients, say, for net earnings increases of job training program participants, with stories of human pride and shame, accomplishment and failure. Program portrayals can also challenge the generation of effect sizes, which homogenize and centralize program participation, with the dissonance and complexity of human diversity. Indeed, this increasingly urgent dialogue about social problems and how best to solve them requires the dialectical participation of all evaluation perspectives, and a critical if not leadership role for the insistence on complexity, contextuality, and human agency offered by qualitative approaches to evaluation.

Evaluating With Stakeholder Engagement

Offering some counterpoint to the reclamation of program theory as an important evaluation agenda is the expanding development and application of participatory and collaborative approaches to evaluation (Ryan et al., 1998; Whitmore, 1998). These approaches emphasize the active engagement of stakeholders in the evaluation process for purposes of enhancing ownership and thus usefulness of the evaluation results (Cousins & Earl, 1995; Patton, 1997) *or* for purposes of promoting some form of democratizing social change, such as social justice (House, 1990) or empowerment (Fetterman, 1994).[7] In these (admittedly diverse) ways, participatory evaluators frame evaluation primarily as an opportunity for engagement, learning, and action in that context. And the *process* of conducting the evaluation—the ways in which stakeholders are involved, which particular stakeholders participate, how less-powerful voices can be fairly heard, who speaks for and with whom—becomes of central importance, not the issue of what methods are used or even what substantive results are obtained.

In ongoing developments, utilization-oriented participatory evaluators are advancing the significant role evaluation can play in *organizational learning,* forging connections to contemporary emphases on strategic planning and quality management within organizational development circles (Cousins & Earl, 1995; Patton, 1994; Preskill & Torres, 1998). And social action-oriented participatory evaluators are advancing the significance of evaluation's potential for broadening and deepening our deliberations and dialogues about important social issues (Greene, 1997; House & Howe, 1998; Ryan et al., 1998). In all dimensions of these ongoing advances in participatory evaluation, qualitative evaluation is playing and will continue to play a central, although again not exclusive, role. Inclusion, not exclusivity, is the defining character of contemporary dialectical, dialogical evaluation.

◆ Future Directions

As vividly illustrated throughout this volume, ways of thinking about and doing "qualitative research" continue to evolve and change. Social program evaluators, like other applied social scientists, are challenged by the ongoing evolutions in the philosophy and ideology of science. Here is a sampling.[8]

Challenges to the Very Nature of Our Qualitative Data

The [qualitative] interview is fundamentally indeterminate. The complex play of conscious and unconscious thoughts, feelings, fears, powers, desires, and needs on the part of both the interviewer and interviewee cannot be captured and categorized. . . . When we think we "interpret" what the meaning or meanings of an interview are, through various data reduction techniques, we are overlaying indeterminacy with the determinacies of our meaning-making, replacing ambiguities with [our] findings or constructions. When we proceed as if we have "found" or "constructed" the best, or the key, or the most important interpretation, we are misportraying what has occurred. . . . [Instead in the analysis] the researcher fills . . . [the interview's] indeterminate openness with her or his interpretive baggage; imposes names, categories, constructions, conceptual schemes, theories upon the unknowable; and believes that the indeterminate is now located, constructed, known. Order has been created. The restless, appropriative spirit of the researcher is (temporarily) at peace. (Scheurich, 1995, p. 249)

Challenges to Our Representations as Meanings

> Postmodernism opens space for new forms of representing social science inquiry by challenging the assumptions of what are seen as accepted forms of presenting the findings of inquiry. Paget . . . points out, "there is something odd about privileging an analysis of discourse in its least robust form, a written text, exploring it in great detail while ignoring the speakers' miens and intentions.". . .
>
> . . . In the creation of new representations of inquiry, we need to struggle to represent the complexities and indeterminacies of participants' experiences . . . [and] to acknowledge our role in the construction of the representation, our voice in the presentation. [Further] as, in postmodern terms, knowledge is partial, conditional and contextual, so are representations. (Goodyear, 1997, pp. 64-65, 69)

Challenges Regarding the Political Ethics of Our Work

> How do we handle "hot" information, especially in times when poor and working-class women and men are being demonized by the Right and by Congress? . . . For instance, what do we do with information about the ways in which women on welfare virtually have to become welfare cheats to survive? *("Sure he comes once a month and gives me some money. I may have to take a beating, but the kids need the money.")* A few [of those we study] use more drugs than we wish to know . . . some underattend to their children well beyond neglect. . . . To ignore these data is to deny the effects [of hard economic times]. To report the data is to risk their likely misinterpretation.
>
> In a moment in history when there are few audiences willing to reflect on the complex social roots of community and domestic violence and the impossibility of sole reliance on welfare, or even to appreciate the complexity, love, hope, and pain that fills the poor and working class, how do we display the voyeuristic dirty laundry that litters our database? At the same time, how can we risk romanticizing or denying the devastating impact of the current assault on poor and working-class families launched by the State, the economy, neighbors, and sometimes kin? (Fine & Weis, 1996, pp. 258-259)

These challenges to the very core of what it is we do when we practice the craft of social program evaluation with a constructivist, qualitative worldview are daunting but not defeating. They continue the erosion, partially initiated by constructivism, of evaluation's preoccupation with methodological rigor and technical expertise. They affirm the constructivist evaluator's emphasis on the meaningfulness of lived experience, even as they unravel our confidence in our ability to know, understand, and interpret such experience. They also substantiate constructivist evaluators' self-consciousness about values, about our own position in our work, and about the location of our work in the world.

As social program evaluators, we have responsibilities to multiple audiences, including the powerful policy makers, the all-but-powerless poor people who are often the intended beneficiaries of the programs we evaluate, and the citizenry at large. Our work, therefore, must respectfully balance social scientific theories of knowledge construction, interpretation, and representation with the political realities of social policy making. Such balance is attained not through partisanship, but through explicit commitment to inclusiveness, to pluralism, to ensuring that all stakeholder voices are part of the conversation (Datta, 1999; House & Howe, 1998). Inclusiveness respects both constructivist holism *and* democratic dialogue. We must acknowledge that making such a commitment explicit is often viewed as advocacy or partisanship, and so our challenge becomes one of creating impartial, nonconfrontational expressions of this commitment (Datta, 1999).

The need is not to find the *one correct way* to do program evaluation, but rather to conduct our craft so that it responds to multiple audiences, includes multiple perspectives, constructs multiple and diverse understandings and equally diverse representations of those understandings, and encourages dialogue and conversations. I believe that the constructivist, qualitative genre of evaluation—with its valuing of responsiveness and pluralism—is extremely well positioned to be an active player in this dialogical evaluation evolution. It is now up to us, each of us as constructivist evaluators, to claim a seat at the table.

■ Notes

1. Social program evaluators work at all levels of government and thus social programming, from positions both inside and external to government agencies. Their work is frequently mandated by program funders—namely, government and foundations—traditionally for knowledge, development, or accountability purposes (Chelimsky, 1997). Practicing evaluators have been trained in applied social science graduate programs or in policy analysis and evaluation graduate programs. In addition to social programs, evaluations are conducted on objects (product evaluation), on people (personnel evaluation), and on programs in the private sector such as executive development and human resource training. Although Scriven (1995) and others argue that the logic of evaluation is the same across these different objects of evaluation, I believe they constitute essentially different tasks, and so require qualitatively and politically different responses. In this chapter, I focus on qualitative evaluation of social programs and the policies they embody, predominantly in the U.S. public domain. My arguments here may not transfer well to other evaluation contexts; this is a judgment for the reader.

2. I am indebted to Alyce Spotted Bear for the idea of this evaluation context.

3. These two examples are drawn from Greene (1998a).

4. From Lincoln and Guba (1985): Evaluation findings will be (a) *credible* when consonant with contextualized lived experience, (b) *applicable* to other similar contexts when so judged by those doing the applying, (c) *dependable* when the methods decisions made are defensible and reasonable for that context, and (d) *confirmable* when inferences can be traced back through analyses to data actually collected.

5. See my chapter in the first edition of this *Handbook* for an elaborated discussion of the history of qualitative program evaluation (Greene, 1994).

6. Among the numerous accounts of this revolution in the philosophy of science, the works of philosopher Richard Bernstein (1983, 1992) are among the most accessible.

7. These two clusters of purposes for participatory evaluation reflect its dual origins in (a) utilization (Patton, 1997) and stakeholder-based (Gold, 1983) evaluation, and (b) from outside the evaluation field, liberatory traditions of participatory and participatory action research (Freire, 1972; Greenwood & Levin, 1998). See Whitmore (1998) for elaborated discussions of participatory evaluation's histories, theories, and practices.

8. These examples are drawn from Greene (1998a).

■ References

Abma, T. A. (1997a). Playing with/in plurality. *Evaluation, 3,* 25-48.

Abma, T. A. (1997b). Sharing power, facing ambiguity. In L. Mabry (Ed.), *Evaluation and the postmodern dilemma* (pp. 105-119). Greenwich, CT: JAI.

Abma, T. A. (1998). Text in an evaluative context: Writing for dialogue. *Evaluation, 4,* 434-454.

Barone, T. E. (1992). On the demise of subjectivity in educational inquiry. *Curriculum Inquiry, 22,* 25-38.

Bernstein, R. J. (1983). *Beyond objectivism and relativism.* Philadelphia: University of Pennsylvania Press.

Bernstein, R. J. (1992). *The new constellation: The ethical-political horizons of modernity/postmodernity.* Cambridge: MIT Press.

Bickman, L. (Ed.). (1987). *Using program theory in evaluation.* San Francisco: Jossey-Bass.

Carr, W. L., & Kemmis, S. (1986). *Becoming critical: Education, knowledge, and action research.* London: Falmer.

Chelimsky, E. (1997). The coming transformations in evaluation. In E. Chelimsky & W. R. Shadish (Eds.), *Evaluation for the 21st century* (pp. 1-26). Thousand Oaks, CA: Sage.

Chen, H.-T., & Rossi, P. H. (1983). Evaluating with sense: The theory-driven approach. *Evaluation Review, 7,* 283-302.

Cicirelli, V. G., & Associates. (1969). *The impact of Head Start: An evaluation of the effects of Head Start on children's cognitive and affective development* (Report to the Office of Economic Opportunity). Athens: Ohio University/Westinghouse Learning Corporation.

Cook, T. D. (1985). Postpositivist critical multiplism. In L. Shotland & M. M. Mark (Eds.), *Social science and social policy* (pp. 21-62). Beverly Hills, CA: Sage.

Cook, T. D., & Reichardt, C. S. (Eds.). (1979). *Qualitative and quantitative methods in evaluation research.* Beverly Hills, CA: Sage.

Cousins, J. B., & Earl, L. (1995). *Participatory evaluation in education: Studies in evaluation use and organizational learning.* New York: Falmer.

Cronbach, L. J. (1982). *Designing evaluations of educational and social programs.* San Francisco: Jossey-Bass.

Cronbach, L. J., & Associates. (1980). *Toward reform of program evaluation.* San Francisco: Jossey-Bass.

Datta, L.-E. (1999). The ethics of evaluation neutrality and advocacy. In J. L. Fitzpatrick & M. Morris (Eds.), *Current and emerging ethical challenges in evaluation* (pp. 77-88). San Francisco: Jossey-Bass.

Fay, B. (1987). *Critical social science.* Ithaca, NY: Cornell University Press.

Fetterman, D. M. (1994). Empowerment evaluation. *Evaluation Practice, 15,* 1-16.

Fine, M., & Weis, L. (1996). Writing the "wrongs" of fieldwork: Confronting our own research/writing dilemmas in urban ethnographies. *Qualitative Inquiry, 2,* 251-274.

Freire, P. (1972). *Pedagogy of the oppressed.* New York: Herder & Herder.

Gold, N. (1983). Stakeholders and program evaluation: Characterizations and reflections. In A. S. Bryk (Ed.), *Stakeholder-based evaluation* (pp. 63-72). San Francisco: Jossey-Bass.

Goodyear, L. K. (1997). *"A circle that it's time to open": Using performance as a representation of a participatory evaluation.* Unpublished master's thesis, Cornell University.

Greene, J. C. (1992). The practitioner's perspective. *Curriculum Inquiry, 22,* 39-45.

Greene, J. C. (1994). Qualitative program evaluation: Practice and promise. In N. K. Denzin & Y. S. Lincoln (Eds.), *Handbook of qualitative research* (pp. 530-544). Thousand Oaks, CA: Sage.

Greene, J. C. (1996). Qualitative evaluation and scientific citizenship: Reflections and refractions. *Evaluation, 2,* 277-289.

Greene, J. C. (1997). Evaluation as advocacy. *Evaluation Practice, 18,* 25-35.

Greene, J. C. (1998a). Balancing philosophy and practicality in qualitative evaluation. In R. Davis (Ed.), *Proceedings of the Stake Symposium on Educational Evaluation* (pp. 35-49). Champaign-Urbana: University of Illinois Press.

Greene, J. C. (1998b). Qualitative, interpretive evaluation. In A. J. Reynolds & H. J. Walberg (Eds.), *Evaluation research for educational productivity* (pp. 135-154). Greenwich, CT: JAI.

Greene, J. C., & Caracelli, V. J. (Eds.). (1997). *Advances in mixed-method evaluation: The challenges and benefits of integrating diverse paradigms.* San Francisco: Jossey-Bass.

Greene, J. C., & McClintock, C. (1991). The evolution of evaluation methodology. *Theory Into Practice, 30,* 13-21.

Greenwood, D. J., & Levin, M. (1998). *Introduction to action research.* Thousand Oaks, CA: Sage.

Guba, E. G., & Lincoln, Y. S. (1981). *Effective evaluation: Improving the usefulness of evaluation results through responsive and naturalistic approaches.* San Francisco: Jossey-Bass.

Guba, E. G., & Lincoln, Y. S. (1989). *Fourth generation evaluation.* Newbury Park, CA: Sage.

House, E. R. (1990). Methodology and justice. In K. A. Sirotnik (Ed.), *Evaluation and social justice* (pp. 23-36). San Francisco: Jossey-Bass.

House, E. R. (1993). *Professional evaluation: Social impact and political consequences.* Newbury Park, CA: Sage.

House, E. R., & Howe, K. (1998). *Deliberative evaluation.* Paper presented at the annual meeting of the American Evaluation Association, Chicago.

Ladson-Billings, G. (1998). Just what is critical race theory and what is it doing in a "nice" field like education? *International Journal of Qualitative Studies in Education, 11,* 7-24.

Lather, P. (1991). *Getting smart: Feminist research and pedagogy with/in the postmodern.* New York: Routledge.

Lincoln, Y. S. (1990). The making of a constructivist: A remembrance of transformations past. In E. G. Guba (Ed.), *The paradigm dialog* (pp. 67-87). Newbury Park, CA: Sage.

Lincoln, Y. S., & Guba, E. G. (1985). *Naturalistic inquiry.* Beverly Hills, CA: Sage.

Mabry, L. (1997). A postmodern test on postmodernism? In L. Mabry (Ed.), *Evaluation and the postmodern dilemma* (pp. 1-19). Greenwich, CT: JAI.

MacDonald, B. (1976). Evaluation and the control of education. In D. A. Tawney (Ed.), *Curriculum evaluation today: Trends and implications.* London: Falmer.

Patton, M. Q. (1987). Evaluation's political inherency: Practical implications for design and use. In D. J. Palumbo (Ed.), *The politics of program evaluation* (pp. 100-145). Newbury Park, CA: Sage.

Patton, M. Q. (1990). *Qualitative evaluation and research methods* (2nd ed.). Newbury Park, CA: Sage.

Patton, M. Q. (1994). Development evaluation. *Evaluation Practice, 15,* 311-320.

Patton, M. Q. (1997). *Utilization-focused evaluation: New century edition.* Thousand Oaks, CA: Sage.

Preskill, H. S., & Torres, R. (1998). *Evaluative learning in organizations.* Thousand Oaks, CA: Sage.

Reichardt, C. S., & Rallis, S. F. (Eds.). (1994). *The qualitative-quantitative debate: New perspectives.* San Francisco: Jossey-Bass.

Ryan, K. E., Greene, J. C., Lincoln, Y. S., Mathison, S., & Mertens, D. (1998). Advantages and challenges of using inclusive evaluation approaches in evaluation practice. *American Journal of Evaluation, 19,* 101-122.

Scheurich, J. J. (1995). A postmodern review of research interviewing. *International Journal of Qualitative Studies in Education, 8,* 239-252.

Schwandt, T. A. (1989). Recapturing moral discourse in evaluation. *Educational Researcher, 18*(8), 11-16, 34.

Schwandt, T. A. (1994). Constructivist, interpretivist approaches to human inquiry. In N. K. Denzin & Y. S. Lincoln (Eds.), *Handbook of qualitative research* (pp. 118-137). Thousand Oaks, CA: Sage.

Schwandt, T. A. (1996). Farewell to criteriology. *Qualitative Inquiry, 2,* 58-72.

Schwandt, T. A. (1997a). Evaluation as practical hermeneutics. *Evaluation, 3,* 69-83.

Schwandt, T. A. (1997b). Reading the "problem of evaluation" in social inquiry. *Qualitative Inquiry, 3,* 4-25.

Schwandt, T. A. (1997c). Whose interests are being served? Program evaluation as a conceptual practice of power. In L. Mabry (Ed.), *Evaluation and the postmodern dilemma* (pp. 89-104). Greenwich, CT: JAI.

Schwandt, T. A. (1998, April). *Recapturing moral discourse in evaluation—revisited.* Keynote address delivered at the annual Kelly Conference, Ottawa, ON.

Scriven, M. (1967). The methodology of evaluation. *AERA Monograph Series in Curriculum Evaluation, 1,* 39-83.

Scriven, M. (1995). The logic of evaluation and evaluation practice. In D. Fournier (ed.), *Reasoning in evaluation: Inferential links and leaps* (pp. 49-70). San Francisco: Jossey-Bass.

Shadish, W. R., Cook, T. D., & Leviton, L. C. (1991). *Foundations of program evaluation.* Newbury Park, CA: Sage.

Smith, J. K. (1989). *The nature of social and educational inquiry: Empiricism versus interpretation.* Norwood, NJ: Ablex.

Smith, J. K. (1990). Alternative research paradigms and the problem of criteria. In E. G. Guba (Ed.), *The paradigm dialog* (pp. 167-187). Newbury Park, CA: Sage.

Stake, R. E. (1967). The countenance of educational evaluation. *Teachers College Record, 68,* 523-540.

Stake, R. E. (1975). *Evaluating the arts in education: A responsive approach.* Columbus, OH: Merrill.

Stake, R. E. (1995). *The art of case study research.* Thousand Oaks, CA: Sage.

Stake, R. E. (1997). The fleeting discernment of quality. In L. Mabry (Ed.), *Evaluation and the postmodern dilemma* (pp. 41-59). Greenwich, CT: JAI.

Weiss, C. H. (1972). *Evaluation.* Englewood Cliffs, NJ: Prentice Hall.

Weiss, C. H. (1987). Where politics and evaluation research meet. In D. J. Palumbo (Ed.), *The politics of program evaluation* (pp. 47-70). Thousand Oaks, CA: Sage.

Weiss, C. H. (1998). *Evaluation* (2nd ed.). Upper Saddle River, NJ: Prentice Hall.

Whitmore, E. (1994). To tell the truth: Working with oppressed groups in participatory approaches to inquiry. In P. Reason (Ed.), *Participation in human inquiry* (pp. 82-98). Thousand Oaks, CA: Sage.

Whitmore, E. (Ed.). (1998). *Understanding and practicing participatory evaluation.* San Francisco: Jossey-Bass.

Wolcott, H. F. (1990). On seeking—and rejecting—validity in qualitative research. In E. W. Eisner & A. Peshkin (Eds.), *Qualitative inquiry in education: The continuing debate* (pp. 121-152). New York: Teachers College Press.

Wolcott, H. F. (1994). *Transforming qualitative data: Description, analysis, and interpretation.* Thousand Oaks, CA: Sage.

39

INFLUENCING THE POLICY PROCESS WITH QUALITATIVE RESEARCH

◆ Ray C. Rist

More than 20 years ago, James Coleman wrote, "There is no body of methods; no comprehensive methodology for the study of the impact of public policy as an aid to future policy." This now-famous quote still rings true. Indeed, one can argue that in the intervening decades, the tendency in policy research and analysis has become ever more centrifugal, spinning off more methodologies and variations on methodologies, more conceptual frameworks, and more disarray among those who call themselves policy analysts or see themselves working in the area of policy studies. A number of critics of the current scene of policy studies and the attendant applications of so many different methodologies have argued that any improvements in the techniques of policy research have not led to

greater clarity about what to think or what to do. More charitably, it could be said that the multiplicity of approaches to policy research should be welcomed, as they bring different skills and strengths to what are admittedly difficult and complex issues.

Regardless of whether one supports or challenges the contention that policy research has had a centrifugal impact on the knowledge base relevant to policy making, the bottom line remains much the same: What policy researchers tend to consider as improvements in their craft have not significantly enhanced the role of research in policy making. Instead, the proliferation of persons, institutes, and centers conducting policy-related work has led to more variation in the manner by which problems are defined, more divergence in the ways in which

AUTHOR'S NOTE: The views expressed here are those of the author, and no endorsement by the World Bank is intended or should be inferred.

studies are designed and conducted, and more disagreement and controversy over the ways in which data are analyzed and findings reported. The policy maker now confronts a veritable glut of differing (if not conflicting) research information.

A sobering but provocative counterintuitive logic is at work here: Increased personnel, greater allocation of resources, and growing sophistication of methods have not had the anticipated or demonstrated effect of greater clarity and understanding of the policy issues before the country. Rather, current efforts have led to a more complex, complicated, and partial view of the issues and their solutions. Further, as Smith (1991) would argue, this tendency to greater complexity has left both the policy makers and the citizens less able to understand the issues and to see how their actions might affect the present condition.

Whereas one may grant that early analyses, for example, in the areas of education or social welfare, were frequently simplistic and not especially sophisticated in either the design or application of policy methods, the inverse does not, in and of itself, work to the advantage of the policy maker. Stated differently, to receive a report resplendent with "state-of-the-art" methodologies and complex analyses that tease out every nuance and shade of meaning on an issue may provide just as little guidance for effective decision making as did the former circumstances. The present fixation on the technical adequacy of policy research without a commensurate concern for its utilization is to relegate that work to quick obscurity (Chelimsky, 1982).

If this admittedly brief description of the current state of policy research approximates the reality, then a fundamental question arises: Is the presumption correct that research cannot be conducted that is relevant to the policy process? It is my view that the presumption is not correct. Research can contribute to informed decision making, but the manner in which this is done needs to be reformulated. We are well past the time when it is possible to argue that good research will, because it is good, influence the policy process. That kind of linear relation of research to action simply is not a viable way in which to think about how knowledge can in-

form decision making. The relation is both more subtle and more tenuous. Still, there is a relation. It is my intent in this chapter to address how some of the linkages of knowledge and action are formed, particularly for the kinds of knowledge generated through qualitative research.[1]

◆ The Nature of Policy Decision Making

Policy making is multidimensional and multifaceted. Research is but one (and often minor at that) among the number of frequently contradictory and competing sources that seek to influence what is an ongoing and constantly evolving process. The emphasis here on policy making being a *process* is deliberate. It is a process that evolves through cycles, with each cycle more or less bounded, more or less constrained by time, funds, political support, and other events. It is also a process that circles back on itself, iterates the same decision issue time and again, and often does not come to closure. Choosing not to decide is a frequent outcome.

Such a description of the policy process suggests the need for a modification, if not a fundamental reframing, of the traditional understanding of policy making. In this latter, more traditional approach, decision making in the policy arena is understood as a discrete event, undertaken by a defined set of actors working in "real time" and moving to their decision on the basis of an analysis of their alternatives. Weiss (1982) has nicely summarized this notion of "decision making as an event":

> Both the popular and the academic literature picture decision making as an event; a group of authorized decision makers assemble at particular times and places, review a problem (or opportunity), consider a number of alternative courses of action with more or less explicit calculation of the advantages and disadvantages of each option, weigh the alternatives against their goals or preferences, and then select an alternative that seems well suited for achieving their purposes. The result is a decision. (p. 23)

She also nicely demolishes this view when she writes:

> Given the fragmentation of authority across multiple bureaus, departments, and legislative committees, and the disjointed stages by which actions coalesce into decisions, the traditional model of decision making is a highly stylized rendition of reality. Identification of any clear-cut group of decision makers can be difficult. (Sometimes a middle-level bureaucrat has taken the key action, although he or she may be unaware that his or her action was going to be—or was—decisive.) The goals of policy are often equally diffuse, except in terms of "taking care of" some undesirable situation. Which opinions are considered, and what set of advantages or disadvantages are assessed, may be impossible to tell in the interactive, multi-participant, diffuse process of formulating policy. The complexity of governmental decision making often defies neat compartmentalization. (p. 26)

Of particular relevance here is that the focus on decision making as an ongoing set of adjustments, or midcourse corrections, eliminates the bind of having to pinpoint the event—that is, the exact time, place, and manner—in which research has been influential on policy. Parenthetically, because the specifics can seldom be supplied, the notion that research *should* have an impact on decision making seems to have become more and more an article of faith. That researchers have so persistently misunderstood decision making, and yet have constantly sought to be of influence, is a situation deserving of considerably more analysis than it receives. So long as researchers presume that research findings must be brought to bear upon a single event, a discrete act of decision making, they will be missing those circumstances and processes where, in fact, research can be useful. However, the reorientation away from "event decision making" and to "process decision making" necessitates looking at research as serving an "enlightenment function" in contrast to an "engineering function" (see Janowitz, 1971; Patton, 1988; Weiss, 1988).

Viewing policy research as serving an enlightenment function suggests that policy researchers work with policy makers and their staffs over time to create a contextual understanding about an issue, build linkages that will exist over time, and strive constantly to educate about new developments and research findings in the area. This is in contrast to the engineering perspective, where it is presumed that sufficient data can be brought to bear to determine the direction and intensity of the intended policy initiative, much as one can develop the specifications for the building of a bridge. If the policy direction is sufficiently explicit, then the necessary information relevant to the development of the policy can be collected, so this view would contend, and the policy actions can be deliberate, directed, and successful.

These comments should not be taken as a diatribe against research or an argument that knowledge counts for naught. Quite the contrary. Systematic knowledge generated by research is an important and necessary component in the decision-making process. Further, it is fair to note that there is seldom enough research-based information available in the policy arena. William Ruckelshaus once noted that although he was the administrator of the Environmental Protection Agency, he made many decisions when there was less than 10% of the necessary research information available to him and his staff. The relevance and usefulness of policy research will not become apparent, however, unless there is a reconsideration of what is understood by decision making in the policy process. A redefinition is needed of the context in which to look for a linkage between knowledge and action. Unpacking the nature of the policy cycle is the strategy employed here to address this redefinition of policy decision making.

◆ The Policy Cycle and Qualitative Research

There are two levels of decision making in the policy arena. The first involves the establishment of the broad parameters of government action, such as providing national health insurance, establishing a national energy policy, restructuring the national immigration laws, or reexamining the criteria for determining the safety and soundness of the country's financial institutions. At this level and in these instances, policy research input is likely to be quite small, if not nil. The setting of these national priorities is a political event, a coming together of a critical mass of politicians, special interest groups, and persons in the media who are able among them to generate the attention and focus necessary for the items to reach the national agenda.

"Iron triangles" built by the informal linking of supporters in each of these three arenas are not created by the presence or absence of policy research. One or another research study might be quoted in support of the contention that the issue deserves national attention, but it is incidental to the more basic task of first working to place the issue on the national agenda. If one wishes to influence any of the players during this phase of the policy process, it is much more likely to be done through personal contact, by organizations taking positions, or through the creation of sufficient static in the policy system (for example, lining up special interest groups in opposition to a proposal, even as there are groups in favor). This works to the benefit of the opposition in that media coverage will have to be seen to be "balanced" and coverage of the opposition can create the impression that there is not the strong unified support for a position that otherwise would seem to be the case.

Once the issue is on the agenda of key actors or organizations within the policy establishment, there are possibilities for the introduction and utilization of policy research. It is here at this second level of policy making—the level where there are concerns about translating policy intentions into policy and programmatic realities—that I will focus in this chapter.

The framework in which the contributions of policy research in general and qualitative research in particular can best be understood is that of the policy cycle, a concept that has been addressed for more than a decade (see, e.g., Chelimsky, 1985; Guba, 1984; Nakamura & Smallwood, 1980; Rist, 1989, 1990, 1993). I will develop my discussion of the policy cycle here according to its three phases—policy for-

mulation, policy implementation, and policy accountability. Each of these three phases has its own order and logic, its own information requirements, and its own policy actors. Further, there is only some degree of overlap among the three phases, suggesting that they do merit individual analysis and understanding.

The opportunities for qualitative research within the policy cycle are thus defined and differentiated by the information requirements at each phase. The questions asked at each phase are distinct, and the information generated in response to these same questions is used to different ends. It is to a detailed examination of these three phases of the policy cycle and the manner in which qualitative research can inform each phase that I now turn.

◆ Policy Formulation

Nakamura and Smallwood (1980) define a policy as follows: "A policy can be thought of as a set of instructions from policy makers to policy implementers that spell out both goals and the means for achieving those goals" (p. 31). How is it that these instructions are crafted, by whom, and with what relevant policy information and analysis? The answers can provide important insights into the process of policy formulation. Nakamura and Smallwood offer a relevant departure point with their description of the actors involved in policy formulation:

In general, the principal actors in policy formulation are the "legitimate" or formal policy makers: people who occupy positions in the governmental arena that entitle them to authoritatively assign priorities and commit resources. These people include elected officials, legislators, and high-level administrative appointees, each of whom must follow prescribed paths to make policy. . . . Since these formal policy makers represent diverse constituencies—electoral, administrative, and bureaucratic—the policy making process offers many points of access through which interest groups and others from arenas outside government can exercise influence. Thus policy making usually involves a diverse set of authoritative, or formal, policy makers, who operate within the governmental arena, plus a diverse set of special interest and other constituency groups from outside arenas, who press their demands on these formal leaders. (pp. 31-32)

As the formulation process begins, there are a number of pressing questions. Answering each question necessitates the compiling of whatever information is currently available plus the development of additional information when the gaps are too great in what is currently known. The information needs can generally be clustered around three broad sets of questions. Each of these clusters is highly relevant to policy formulation; in each there are important opportunities for the presentation and utilization of qualitative research.

The first set of information needs revolves around an understanding of the policy issue at hand. What are the contours of this issue? Is the problem or condition one that is larger now than before, about the same, or smaller? Is anything known about whether the nature of the condition has changed? Do the same target populations, areas, or institutions experience this condition now as earlier? How well can the condition be defined? How well can the condition be measured? What are the different interpretations and understandings about the condition, its causes and its effects? The issue here, stated differently, is one of the ability of policy makers to define clearly and understand the problem or condition that they are facing and for which they are expected to develop a response.

Charles Lindblom (1968) has nicely captured some of the conceptual complexity facing policy makers as they try to cope with the definition of a policy problem or condition:

Policy makers are not faced with a given problem. Instead they have to identify and formulate their problem. Rioting breaks out in dozens of American cities. What is the problem? Maintaining law and order? Racial discrimination? Incipient revolution? Black power? Low income? Lawlessness at the fringe of an otherwise

relatively peaceful reform movement? Urban disorganization? Alienation? (p. 13)

The second cluster of questions focuses on what has taken place previously in response to this condition or problem. What programs or projects have previously been initiated? How long did they last? How successful were they? What level of funding was required? How many staff members were required? How receptive were the populations or institutions to these initiatives? Did they request help or did they resist the interventions? Did the previous efforts address the same condition or problem as currently exists, or was it different? If it was different, how so? If it was the same, why are yet additional efforts necessary? Are the same interest groups involved? What may explain any changes in the present interest group coalition?

The third cluster of questions relevant to the policy formulation stage of the cycle focuses on what is known of the previous efforts and their impacts that would help one choose among present-day options. Considering trade-offs among various levels of effort in comparison to different levels of cost is but one among several kinds of data relevant to considering the policy options. There may also be data on the time frames necessary before one could hope to see impacts. Trade-offs between the length of the developmental stage of the program and the eventual impacts are relevant, particularly if there are considerable pressures for short-term solutions. The tendency to go to "weak thrust, weak effect" strategies is well understood in these circumstances. Alternatively, if previous efforts did necessitate a considerable period of time for measurable outcomes to appear, how did the policy makers in those circumstances hold on to the public support and keep the coalitions intact long enough for the results to emerge?

Qualitative research is highly relevant to the information needs at this stage in the policy cycle. Studies on the social construction of problems, on the differing interpretations of social conditions, on the building and sustaining of coalitions for change, on previous program initiatives and their impacts, on community and organizational receptivity to programs, on organizational stability and cohesion during the formulation stage, and on the changing nature of social conditions are all germane to the questions posed here.

There is an additional contribution that qualitative work can make at this stage of the policy process, and it is that of studying the intended and unintended consequences of the various policy instruments or tools that might be selected as the means to implement the policy (Salamon, 1989). There is a present need within the policy community to ascertain what tools work best in which circumstances and for which target populations. Very little systematic work has been done in this area—which frequently leaves policy makers essentially to guess as to the trade-offs between the choice of one tool and another.

Information of the kind provided by qualitative research can be of significant help in making decisions, for example, about whether to provide direct services in health, housing, and education or provide vouchers to recipients, whether to provide direct cash subsidies or tax credits to employers who will hire unemployed youth, and whether to increase funding for information campaigns or to increase taxes as strategies to discourage smoking. These are but three examples where different policy tools are available and where choices will have to be made among them.

Key among the activities in the policy formulation stage is the selection of the most appropriate policy strategy to achieve the desired objective. Central to the design of this strategy is the selection of one or more tools available to the government as the means to carry out its intentions. Qualitative studies of how different tools are understood and responded to by target populations is of immense importance at this stage of the policy process.

Unfortunately, although the demand for analysis of this type is great, the supply is extremely limited. The qualitative study of policy tools is an area that is yet to be even modestly explored within the research community.

Although qualitative research can be relevant at this stage, it is also the case that its appli-

cations are problematic. The basic reason is that seldom is there enough time to both commission and complete new qualitative research within the existing window of opportunity during policy formulation. Thus the applications have to rely on existing qualitative research— and that may or may not exist. Here is one key means by which good, well-crafted qualitative work on topical social issues can find its way into the policy arena. As policy makers start on the formulation effort, their need to draw quickly on existing work puts a premium on those research studies that have worked through matters of problem definition, the social construction of problems, community studies, retrospective assessments of prior initiatives, and so on.

The problematic nature of the applications of qualitative research at this stage is further reinforced by the fact that seldom are research funds available for studies that address the kinds of questions noted above in the three clusters. If the problem or condition is not seen to be above the horizon and thus on the policy screen, there is little incentive for a policy maker or program manager to use scarce funds for what would appear to be nonpragmatic, "theoretical" studies. And by the time the condition has sufficiently changed or become highly visible as a social issue for the policy community, qualitative work is hard-pressed to be sufficiently time sensitive and responsive. The window for policy formulation is frequently very small and open only a short time. The information that can be passed through has to be ready and in a form that enhances quick understanding.

The above constraints on the use of qualitative research at this stage of the policy cycle should not be taken as negative judgments on either the utility or the relevance of such information. Rather, it is only realistic to acknowledge that having the relevant qualitative research available when it is needed for policy formulation is not always possible. As noted earlier, this is an area where there are potentially significant uses for qualitative studies. But the uses are likely to come because of scholars and researchers who have taken on an area of study for their own interest and to inform basic understandings in the research community, rather than presuming before they begin that they would influence the formulation process. It is only the infrequent instance where there is sufficient time during the formulation stage for new qualitative work to be conducted.

It should be stressed here that the restrictions on the use of qualitative work during the formulation phase of the policy cycle come much more from the nature of the policy process than from the nature of qualitative work. The realities of the legislative calendar, the short lives of most senior political appointees in any one position, the mad scramble among competing special interest groups for their proposals to be addressed and acted upon, and the lack of concentration by the media on any issue for very long all inhibit the development of research agendas that address the underlying issues. This is ironic because it is clear that the country will face well into the foreseeable future the issues of health care allocation and quality, immigration controls and border security, educational retraining of dislocated workers, and youth unemployment, to name but four areas that have heretofore persistently stayed near or at the top of the national policy agenda. Basic, in-depth qualitative work in these and other key areas could inform the policy formulation process for years to come. But the pressures and structural incentives in the policy system all go in the other direction. To wit: Develop short-term proposals with quick impacts to show responsiveness and accommodate all the vested interests in the iron triangle.

In sum, with respect to this first phase of the policy cycle, qualitative research can be highly influential. This is particularly so with respect to problem definition, understanding of prior initiatives, community and organizational receptivity to particular programmatic approaches, and the kinds of impacts (both anticipated and unanticipated) that might emerge from different intervention strategies. This information would be invaluable to policy makers. But, as noted, the use of the material can be hindered by such factors as whether or not the information exists, is known to the policy community, and is available in a form that makes it quickly accessible. Overcoming these obstacles does not guarantee the use of qualitative research in the formulation process, but one can be strongly assured that if these obstacles are present, the likelihood of the use of qualitative material drastically diminishes.

◆ Policy Implementation

The second phase of the policy cycle is that of policy implementation. It is in this stage that the policy initiatives and goals established during policy formulation are to be transformed into programs, procedures, and regulations. The knowledge base that policy makers need to be effective in this phase necessitates the collection and analysis of different information from that found in policy formulation. With the transformation of policies into programs, the concern moves to the operational activities of the policy tool and the allocation of resources. The concern becomes one of how to use the available resources in the most efficient and effective manner in order to have the most robust impact on the program or condition at hand. As Pressman and Wildavsky (1984) have written in this regard:

> Policies imply theories. Whether stated explicitly or not, policies point to a chain of causation between initial conditions and future consequences. If X, then Y. Policies become programs when, by authoritative action, the initial conditions are created. X now exists. Programs make the theories operational by forging the first link in the causal chain connecting actions to objectives. Given X, we act to obtain Y. Implementation, then, is the ability to forge subsequent links in the causal chain so as to obtain the desired results. (p. xxii)

The research literature on policy and program implementation indicates that that is a particularly difficult task to accomplish (see, e.g., Hargrove, 1985; Pressman & Wildavsky, 1984; Yin, 1985). Again, quoting Pressman and Wildavsky:

Our normal expectations should be that new programs will fail to get off the ground and that, at best, they will take considerable time to get started. The cards in this world are stacked against things happening, as so much effort is required to make them work. The remarkable thing is that new programs work at all. (p. 109)

It is in this context of struggling to find ways of making programs work that the data and analyses from qualitative research can come into play. The information needs from qualitative research at this stage of the policy cycle cluster into several areas. First, there is a pressing need for information on the implementation process per se. Qualitative researchers, through case studies, program monitoring, and process evaluations, can inform program managers responsible for the implementation of the policy initiative.

Qualitative work can focus on such questions as the degree to which the program is reaching the intended target audience, the similarities and contrasts in implementation strategies across sites, the aspects of the program that are or are not operational, whether the services slated to be delivered are in fact the ones delivered, and the operational burdens placed on the institution or organization responsible for implementation (i.e., Is there the institutional capacity to respond effectively to the new policy initiative?). The focus is on the day-to-day realities of bringing a new program or policy into existence. This "ground-level" view of implementation is best done through qualitative research. The study of the rollout of an implementation effort is an area where qualitative work is at a clear advantage over other data collection strategies.

A second cluster of research questions amenable to qualitative work in the implementation arena focuses on the problem or condition that prompted the policy or program response in the first place. No problem or condition stands still simply because the policy community has decided to take action on what was known at the time the decision was made. Problems and conditions change—both before and after a policy response is decided upon. Thus the challenge for qualitative researchers is to continue to track

the condition, even as the implementation effort swings into action. Qualitative work can provide ongoing monitoring of the situation—whether the condition has improved, worsened, remained static; whether the same target population is involved as earlier; whether the condition has spread or contracted; and whether the aims of the program still match the assumptions and previous understandings of the condition. Qualitative work can provide an important reality check for program managers as to whether the program is or is not appropriate to the current condition. Qualitative work that monitors the condition in real time can play a key role in the continuous efforts of program managers to match their services or interventions to the present circumstances.

The third cluster of necessary policy questions during this implementation phase of the policy cycle focuses on the efforts made by the organization or institution to respond to the initiative. Here, for example, qualitative data would be relevant for learning how the organizational response to the condition or problem has been conceptualized. Are the social constructions of the problem that were accepted at the policy formulation stage by federal policy makers accepted during implementation by the program managers and staff months later and perhaps thousands of miles away? What has been the transformation of the understandings that have taken place when the policy or program is actually being implemented? Do the policy makers and the program implementation folks accept the same understandings as to the intent of the policy—let alone the same understandings of the problem that the policy is suppose to address?

Another aspect of this need for qualitative data concerns the organizational response. Here questions would be asked that address the expertise and qualifications of those responsible for the implementation effort, the interest shown by management and staff, the controls in place regarding the allocation of resources, the organizational structure and whether it adequately reflects the demands on the organization to respond to this initiative, what means exist in the organization for deciding among competing demands, the strategies the organization uses to clarify misunderstandings or ambiguities in how it defines its role in implementation, and, finally, what kinds of interactive information or feedback loops are in place to assist managers in their ongoing efforts to move the program toward the stated objectives of the policy. It is information of precisely this type on the implementation process that Robert Behn (1988) notes is so critical to managers as they struggle to "grope along" and move toward organizational goals.

◆ Policy Accountability

The third stage in the policy cycle comes when the policy or program is sufficiently mature that one can address questions of accountability, impacts, or outcomes. Here again, the information needs are different from those in the two previous stages of the policy cycle. The contributions of qualitative research can be pivotal in assessing the consequences of the policy and program initiative. Just as the questions change from one part of the policy cycle to another, so too does the focus of the qualitative research necessary to answer these same questions.

First there is the matter of what the program or policy did or did not accomplish: Were the objectives for the program met? Qualitative research can specifically help in this regard by addressing, for example, whether the community and police were actively working together in a neighborhood "crime watch" program, whether the appropriate target audience of homeless persons in another program received the health services they were promised, and whether in a third program youth were given the type and quantity of on-the-job training that resulted in successful placements in permanent positions.

When a program reaches the stage that it is appropriate to discuss and assess impacts, qualitative research provides a window on the program that is simply not available in any other way. Qualitative research allows for the study of both anticipated and unanticipated outcomes, changes in understandings and perceptions as a result of the efforts of the program or policy, the direction and intensity of any social change that results from the program, and the strengths and weaknesses of the administrative/organizational structure that was used to operationalize the program. Policy makers have no equally grounded means of learning about program impacts and outcomes as they do with qualitative research findings.

These grounded means of knowing also carry over into what one might traditionally think of as quantitative assessments of policy. Qualitative work can provide to program managers and policy makers information on how confident they can or should be in the measures being used to determine program influence. Although the intent may be that of a highly reliable and replicable instrument that allows for sophisticated quantification, it is the qualitative work that can address the issue of validity.

The issues of reliability and validity are well known in the research literature and need not be reviewed here. Suffice it to say that policy makers and program managers have been misled more than once by investing a great deal of time and effort on their instrumentation without equal emphasis on answering the question of whether their measures were the appropriate ones to the problem or condition at hand. Studies of school desegregation and busing or health care in nursing homes are but two areas where a heavy emphasis on quantifying outcomes and processes have left key aspects of the condition undocumented and thus unattended to by those who should have been paying attention.

There is an additional aspect of this first cluster of information needs that merits special attention vis-à-vis qualitative research. This has to do with whether the original objectives and goals of the policy stayed in place through implementation. One message has come back to policy makers time and again: Do not take for granted that what was intended to be established or put in place through a policy initiative will be what one finds after the implementation process is complete. Programs and policies make countless midcourse corrections, tacking constantly, making changes in funding levels, staff stability, target population movements, political support, community acceptance, and the like.

It is through the longitudinal perspective of qualitative work that such issues can be directly addressed. Blitzkrieg assessments of programs are simply unable to pick up the backstage issues and conflicts that will inevitably be present and that may directly influence the direction and success of the program (Rist, 1980). To ignore staff turnover in a program that is highly staff-intensive in the provision of services, for instance, is to miss what may be the key ingredient in any study of implementation. But recognizing that it may be an issue in the first place is one of the ways in which qualitative work distinguishes itself from other research strategies.

The second cluster of information needs that emerge when a program is being assessed for impacts and outcomes is that of addressing whether and what changes may have occurred in the problem or condition. Central to any study of outcomes is the determination of whether in fact the condition itself has changed or not and what relevance the program or policy did or did not have to the present circumstances.

Although it is rudimentary to say so, it is worth stating explicitly that problems can change or not, totally independently of any policy or program initiative. Conceptually what we have is a situation in which impacts could or could not have occurred, and the consequence would be change or no change in a program or condition.

For example, a positive outcome of a policy could be no worsening of a condition, that is, no change in the original status that first prompted the policy response. Developing local intervention programs that stalled any growth in the number of child abuse cases could be considered a positive outcome. The key question is, of course, whether the evidence of no growth can be attributed to the intervention program or some other factor that was affecting the community independent of the intervention program itself, such as broad media coverage of a particularly savage beating of a child and, in the aftermath, considerable additional media coverage of how parents can cope with their urges to injure their children.

Qualitative work in this instance could focus on such impacts as the outreach efforts of the program to attract parents who had previously abused their children; efforts to reach parents who are seeking help to build better skills in working with their children; patterns and trends in child abuse as discussed by school teachers, day care providers, and others who have ongoing and consistent contact with children; and whether and how parents are now coping with the stresses that might cause them to abuse their children.

The above discussion also generates an additional area in which qualitative work can assist at this stage of the policy cycle. It is the close-in and intensive familiarity with the problem or condition that comes from conducting qualitative work that would allow the researcher to make judgments on whether the situation is of a magnitude and nature that further action is necessary. If the study indicates that the problem or condition is diminishing in severity and prevalence, then further funding of a programmatic response may not be necessary. As a contrary example, the data from qualitative work may suggest that the condition has changed directions—that is, moved to a new target population—and a refocusing of the program is necessary if it is to be responsive.

Social conditions do not remain static, and the realization that the characteristics of a condition can change necessitates periodic reexamination of the original policy intent (policy formulation). Qualitative researchers can position themselves so that they can closely monitor the ongoing characteristics of a condition. With this firsthand and close-in information, they are well suited to suggest any necessary changes to both the policy formulation and implementation strategies for subsequent intervention efforts.

The third information need at this stage of the policy cycle where qualitative work can be of direct use comes with the focus on accountability. Here qualitative work can address concerns of management supervision, leadership of the organization with clear goals in mind, the attention to processes and procedures that would strengthen the capacity of the organization to implement the policy initiative effectively, the use of data-based decision making, and the degree of alignment or congruence between the leadership and the staff. All of these issues speak directly to the capacity of an organization to mobilize itself to provide effective service to its customers. If the organization is not positioned to do so, then there are clear issues of accountability that rest with the leadership.

Qualitative researchers who come to know an organization thoroughly and from the inside will be in a unique position from which to address the treatment and training of staff, reasons for attrition and low morale, the service-oriented philosophy (or lack of it) among the staff and leadership, the beliefs of the staff in the viability and worthiness of the program to address the problem, the quality and quantity of information used within the program for decision making, and the like. These are true qualitative dimensions of organizational life. It is essential that these be studied if judgments are to be made on the efficiency and effectiveness of any particular programmatic strategy. These judgments become central to subsequent decisions on the potential selection of a policy tool that would require a similar program intervention.

There are clear concerns of management accountability that must be discussed and assessed whenever programs are to be funded anew or redirected. Some of these concerns deal directly with impacts on the problem or condition, whereas others focus on the internal order and logic of the organization itself. Stated differently, it is important during the accountability phase to determine the degree to which any changes in the condition or problem

can be directly attributed to the program and whether the program optimized or suboptimized the impact it had. Likewise, it is important to ascertain whether the presence (or absence) of any documented impacts is the result of the coherence of the policy formulation or the nature of program implementation. Finding that instance where coherent and robust policy initiatives are operationalized within a well-managed organization necessitates the complex assessment of what impacts can be attributed to the policy and what to its successful implementation. Qualitative research has a perspective on how to undertake this kind of assessment that other research approaches do not and for which the other approaches would have to rely heavily on proxy measures.

◆ Policy Tools

The analysis thus far has focused on the nature of the policy cycle and how each phase of the cycle has different information requirements for policy makers and program managers. The effort has been to document how qualitative research can play an active and positive role in answering the information needs at each of these phases and for both the policy makers and the program managers. In this section, the attention shifts to a focus on what are termed *policy tools*.

Such an emphasis is important because a deeper understanding of the tools available to government and how each can be more or less effectively used to achieve policy objectives can clearly inform all three stages of the policy cycle. Key to the efforts in policy formulation is the selection of an appropriate tool—be it a grant, a subsidy, a tax credit, a loan, a new regulation, the creation of a government-sponsored enterprise, or the provision of direct services, to name but 7 of the more than 30 tools currently used by government.

The selection of one tool rather than another is a policy choice for which few guiding data are available. Further, research to help policy makers in this regard is extremely sparse. Policy makers decide either based on past experience with a tool ("We used tax credits before, let's use tax credits again") or because they have a clear proclivity for or against a particular tool (conservatives would resist direct government services and seek instead a tool that locates the activity in the private sector, e.g., grants for the construction of public housing or the privatization of all concessions in national parks). It is safe to assert that neither qualitative nor quantitative researchers have shown much interest in this area. Beyond the works of Linder (1988), Linder and Peters (1984, 1989), May (1981), and Salamon (1981, 1989), there is not much research, either theoretical or empirical, to be cited.

What follows is an effort to identify four areas where qualitative work could be highly valuable to discussions regarding policy tools. For each of these areas, there is at present a nearly complete research void. It should be stressed that the short discussion to follow is not meant to be a definitive statement on how qualitative work can address the information needs of policy makers as they choose among tools, nor is it the definitive research agenda on the strengths and weaknesses of different tools.

It needs to be restated that few researchers of any persuasion have moved into this difficult but highly policy-relevant area. The reasons for this hesitancy are outside the bounds of this discussion, but it is clear that the policy analysis and research communities have, with few exceptions, steered wide of this port of inquiry. Building primarily on the works of Linder, Peters, and Salamon, what follows is offered as a modest agenda for those qualitative researchers who are interested in exploring new and untested ways of involving qualitative work within the policy arena. A more elaborate and detailed research agenda in this area is still well over the horizon.

As noted, four areas amenable to qualitative study will be briefly discussed. These are resource intensiveness, targeting, institutional constraints, and political risks. The tentative-

ness of this proposal has to be stressed yet again. There may well be multiple other ways in which to frame the qualitative study of policy tools. What follows here is predicated on the previous discussion regarding the policy cycle. The framework for the qualitative study of policy tools is essentially a matrix analysis, whereby each of these four areas can be studied in each of the three phases of the policy cycle. All 12 combinations will not be individually addressed here; rather, the focus will be on the four broad areas that can help to clarify the trade-offs among tools.

Resource intensiveness refers to the constellation of concerns involving the complexity of the operations, the relative costliness of different options, and the degree of administrative burden that different tools place on organizations. Tools vary widely in their complexity, their demands on organizations for technical expertise to administer and manage, their direct and indirect costs by sector, and the degree to which they are direct or indirect in their intent. And just to complicate matters more, the mix of these concerns for any given tool will shift as one moves from one phase of the policy cycle to another. Keeping the financial costs low and federal involvement to a minimum, for example, may be high priorities in Washington during the policy formulation stage, but these will also have the consequences during the policy implementation stage of serving few of the eligible target population, adding complexity through mandated state administration, and reducing direct impacts. Managing toxic waste cleanups is but one example that is somewhat parallel to this brief scenario.

For qualitative researchers, the challenges here are multiple, not the least because they would necessitate more direct attention to organizational analysis. But there is also the clear opportunity to ask questions within organizations and to assess organizational capacity in ways that have not traditionally been done. Administrative burden has not been a topic of much (if any) qualitative research, but it is a very real consideration in the policy arena. Learning more of how to conceptualize this concern, how it is understood at various levels of government and within the private sector, and how different tools vary in this regard would be of considerable interest to policy makers in departments as well as those responsible for regulator and administrative oversight in organizations such as the Office of Management and Budget in the White House.

At present, a concept such as administrative burden is ill defined and subject to widely varying interpretations. In the absence of any systematic research, one person's definition and experience with "administrative burden" is as good as any other person's—and maybe better if he or she has more institutional or organizational influence. Additional examples concerning such concepts as "operational complexity" and "institutional capacity" are readily apparent.

Targeting refers to the capacity of the policy tool to be aimed at particular populations, problems, or institutions for whom the tool is primarily intended. A tool that, for example, seeks to help homeless persons who are mentally ill and also veterans would be highly targeted. Such a tool would be differentiated from a tool that is either diffuse or low in target specificity, for example, a tax credit for the interest earned in individual retirement accounts.

There are several key aspects of the targeting issue for a policy tool that qualitative researchers could address. First, there is the matter of the precision of the targeting. Qualitative researchers, in reference to the example just given, could help policy makers work through the strategies and definitional problems inherent in determining who is or is not homeless, who has or has not been diagnosed as mentally ill, and how to screen homeless veterans for service when documentation, service records, and so on are all likely to be lost or when persons simply cannot remember their own names.

A second aspect of targeting in selecting a policy tool is that of the amenability of the tool to adjustment and fine tuning. If the character-

istics of the target population start to change, can the tool be adjusted to respond to this change? Flexibility in some instances would be highly desirable, whereas in others it may be irrelevant. For example, it would be beneficial to choose a policy instrument that responds to fluctuations and variations in the refugee populations coming into the United States, whereas it would be unnecessary in the instance of an entitlement program for which age is the only criterion for access to services.

Qualitative studies of different populations targeted by tools and the need (or lack thereof) of specificity in the targeting would be highly useful in policy formulation. There is also the opportunity in this area to explore whether those who have been targeted by a program believe this to be the case. Establishing community mental health centers could have some in the target population coming because of the "community health" emphasis, others coming for the "mental health" emphasis, and still others not showing up at all because they are not certain whose community is being referred or because they would never want anyone in their own neighborhood to know they have mental health problems. Linking services to target populations in the absence of such qualitative information suggests immediately the vulnerability and precariousness of presuming to establish service centers without the detailed knowledge of the populations for whom the effort is intended.

The example of community mental health centers leads to a third consideration in the targeting area—that of adaptability across uses. Can community mental health centers also serve other needs of the designated population, for example, nutrition and education, as well as serve as centers for entirely other target populations who are in the same residential vicinity? Can they serve as centers for the elderly, for latchkey children, for infant nutrition programs, and so on? The issue is one of flexibility and acceptance as well as neutrality in the perceptions of the other target groups. There may be groups who would not want to come to a mental health center, but who would be quite pleased to meet in a church or at a school. Gaining insight on these matters is clearly important as decisions are made on the location and mix of community services to be offered at any one location. Qualitative studies on these issues can inform policy makers and program managers in ways that will clearly affect the success or failure of different strategies.

Institutional capacity refers to the ability of the institution to deliver on the tasks that have been delegated to it. When a policy option clearly relies on a single institution to achieve certain objectives—for example, using the public schools as the vehicle to teach English to non-English-speaking children—there has to be some degree of certainty that the institution has the capacity to do so. Countless experiences with different policy initiatives have shown time and again that some institutions simply did not have, at the time, the capacity to do what was expected of them.

Further, there can be constraints placed on the institution that make it difficult if not impossible for the objective to be achieved. In addition to the more readily anticipated constraints of funding, staff availability, quality of facilities, and low political support, there are also constraints associated with the degree of intrusiveness the institution can exercise as well as the level of coerciveness allowed. The hesitancy of policy makers to allow intrusive efforts by the Internal Revenue Service to collect unpaid taxes has a clear impact on the ability of the organization to do so. The same can be said with respect to the IRS on the matter of coerciveness. Policy makers have simply decided to keep some organizations more constrained than others in carrying out their functions, for fear of abuse. Policy tools that have to rely on voluntary compliance or are framed to have an indirect effect face constraints different from those where these do not apply.

Qualitative research into the domain of institutional constraints and how it is that these constraints play out in the relation of the organization to the fulfillment of its mission is not, to my knowledge, now being done. It may be argued

that it is not necessary, as the constraint dimension for any policy tool is too removed from research influence. That is, any constraints on an organization are more philosophical and ideological than operational. Yet the issue of institutional capacity and what does or does not hinder the ability of the organization to achieve its stated objectives is important to understand explicitly. If policy makers establish the parameters around an organization to the degree that it can never clearly achieve its goal (e.g., the IRS and unpaid back taxes), then there is a built-in level of failure that ought not be ignored and for which the institution should not be held accountable.

Political risk is the fourth dimension of the study of policy tools where qualitative research can directly contribute. Here the issues cluster around concerns of unanticipated risk, chances of failure, and timing. The selection of a policy tool is made with some outcome in mind—either direct or indirect. Yet there is always the possibility of unanticipated outcomes—again either direct or indirect. The selection of a tool necessarily has to take into account the risk of unknown outcomes and how these might affect the success of the policy.

Qualitative research, by the nature of its being longitudinal, done in naturalistic settings, and focused on the constructions of meaning developed by participants, is in a unique position from which to assess the possibility of tools having the impacts intended by policy makers. Low risk of unknown outcomes—for example, in increasing the security at U.S. federal courthouses—eliminates some level of uncertainty from the decision that does not happen when the risk of unknown outcomes is quite high, such as moving to year-round school schedules or as was learned when the movement to deinstitutionalize the mentally ill resulted in tens of thousands of mentally ill persons being left on their own with no means of support or treatment.

One other aspect of the political risk factor that qualitative research can address is the sustainability of the policy initiative. Close-in studies of the operational life of a policy initiative can gain a perspective on the commitment of those involved, their belief in the worthiness of the effort, the amount of political support they are or are not engendering, and the receptivity of the target population to the effort. If all these indicators are decidedly negative, then the sustainability of the initiative is surely low.

It is difficult to achieve success in policy efforts in the best of circumstances; it is that much harder when all the indicators point in the opposite direction. Qualitative research should have a distinct window from which to judge matters of political risk. Understanding of the participants, willingness to assume the causal linkage posited in the policy itself, and the degree of risk of unknown outcomes all influence the likelihood that any policy tool will achieve its intended results.

◆ Concluding Observations

In reviewing this assessment of the contributions of qualitative work to the policy process, it is apparent that the contributions are more in the realm of the potential than the actual. There is no broad-based and sustained tradition within contemporary social science of focusing qualitative work specifically on policy issues, especially given the real time constraints that the policy process necessitates. Yet it is also clear that the opportunities are multiple for such contributions to be made. The issue is chiefly one of how to link those in the research and academic communities who are knowledgeable in conducting qualitative research studies to those in the policy arena who can commission such work and who will make use of the findings. The analysis of different strategies for building these linkages would require a separate chapter; suffice it to say here that much hard thinking and numerous exploratory efforts will be required for the potential to become the actual. The issues of institutional cul-

tures, academic reward systems, publication requirements, funding sources, and methodological limitations are but five among many that will have to be addressed if the linkages are to be built. And even beyond the resolution of (or at least the careful thinking about) these issues is the fundamental question of whether there is the will to bring qualitative work directly into the policy arena. Much of what has been written here will remain speculative unless and until there is some consensus among the practitioners of qualitative research that making this transition is worthwhile. The policy community is, I believe, ready for and would be receptive to anything those in the qualitative research community could offer, should they choose to make the effort to do so.

■ Note

1. I want to stress early on that in this chapter I will not seek to develop distinctions among various conventionally used terms for qualitative research. Thus, in the pages that follow, terms such as *qualitative work, qualitative research,* and *qualitative methods* will all be used to denote the same frame of reference. I most frequently use the term that appears in the title of this handbook, *qualitative research.* I leave it to other authors in this volume to develop those distinctions as appropriate. I would also note, in defense of not trying to specify in much detail just exactly what the meaning is behind the use of any one of these terms, that early reviewers of this chapter suggested at least four other terms I might use in lieu of those I have. These terms included *naturalistic, constructionist, interpretive,* and *ethnographies.* I am sure that the delineation of distinctions has an important place in this book; it is just not my intent to do so here.

I also want to note early on that I am not going to try to differentiate among various qualitative data collection strategies, or means of analysis, as to their particular spheres of potential influence. Thus in this chapter I will not try to indicate what policy relevance or influence one might expect from case studies (and there are multiple variations in this single area alone) in contrast, for example, to multimethod studies. My intent is to place qualitative work broadly within the policy arena, not to develop a prescriptive set of categories about which methods or modes of analysis are likely to lead to what types of influence.

■ *References*

Behn, R. D. (1988). Managing by groping along. *Journal of Policy Analysis and Management, 7*(4).

Chelimsky, E. (1982). Making evaluations relevant to congressional needs. *GAO Review, 17*(1).

Chelimsky, E. (1985). Old patterns and new directions in program evaluation. In E. Chelimsky (Ed.), *Program evaluation: Patterns and directions*. Washington, DC: American Society for Public Administration.

Guba, E. G. (1984). The effect of definitions of policy on the nature and outcomes of policy analysis. *Educational Leadership, 42*(2).

Hargrove, E. (1985). *The missing link: The study of the implementation of social policy.* Washington, DC: Urban Institute Press.

Janowitz, M. (1971). *Sociological methods and social policy.* New York: General Learning Press.

Lindblom, C. E. (1968). *The policy making process.* Englewood Cliffs, NJ: Prentice Hall.

Linder, S. H. (1988). Managing support for social research and development: Research goals, risk, and policy instruments. *Journal of Policy Analysis and Management, 7*(4).

Linder, S. H., & Peters, B. G. (1984). From social theory to policy design. *Journal of Public Policy, 4*(3).

Linder, S. H., & Peters, B. G. (1989). Instruments of government: Perceptions and contexts. *Journal of Public Policy, 9*(1).

May, P. J. (1981). Hints for crafting alternative policies. *Policy Analysis, 7*(2).

Nakamura, R. T., & Smallwood, F. (1980). *The politics of policy implementation.* New York: St. Martin's.

Patton, M. Q. (1988). *Qualitative evaluation and research methods* (2nd ed.). Newbury Park, CA: Sage.

Pressman, J. L., & Wildavsky, A. (1984). *Implementation* (3rd ed.). Berkeley: University of California Press.

Rist, R. C. (1980). Blitzkrieg ethnography: On the transformation of a method into a movement. *Educational Researcher, 9*(2).

Rist, R. C. (1989). Management accountability: The signals sent by auditing and evaluation. *Journal of Public Policy, 9*(3).

Rist, R. C. (Ed.). (1990). *Program evaluation and the management of government: Patterns and prospects across eight nations.* New Brunswick, NJ: Transaction Books.

Rist, R. C. (1993). Program evaluation in the United States General Accounting Office: Reflections on question formulation and utilization. In R. Conner et al. (Eds.), *Advancing public policy evaluation: Learning from international experiences.* Amsterdam: Elsevier.

Salamon, L. M. (1981). Rethinking public management: Third-party government and the changing forms of government action. *Public Policy, 29*(3).

Salamon, L. M. (1989). *Beyond privatization: The tools of government action.* Washington, DC: Urban Institute Press.

Smith, J. A. (1991). *The idea brokers: Think tanks and the rise of the new policy elite.* New York: Free Press.

Weiss, C. H. (1982). Policy research in the context of diffuse decision making. In R. C. Rist (Ed.), *Policy studies review annual.* Beverly Hills, CA: Sage.

Weiss, C. H. (1988). Evaluations for decisions: Is anybody there? Does anybody care? *Evaluation Practice, 9*(1).

Yin, R. K. (1985). Studying the implementation of public programs. In W. Williams (Ed.), *Studying implementation.* Chatham, NJ: Chatham House.

■ *Suggested Further Readings*

Bemelmans-Videc, M. L., Rist, R. C., & Vedung, E. (Eds.). (1998). *Carrots, sticks, and sermons: Policy instruments and their evaluation.* New Brunswick, NJ: Transaction Books.

Elmore, R. (1987). Instruments and strategy in public policy. *Policy Studies Review, 7*(1), 63-78.

Gray, A., Jenkins, B., & Segsworth, B. (Eds.). (1992). *Budgeting, auditing and evaluation:*

Functions and integration in seven governments. New Brunswick, NJ: Transaction.

Hood, C. C. (1986). *The tools of government.* Chatham, NJ: Chatham House.

Leeuw, F. L., Rist, R. C., & Sonnichsen, R. (Eds.). (1994). *Can governments learn? Comparative perspectives on evaluation and organizational learning.* New Brunswick, NJ: Transaction.

Mayne, J., & Zapico-Goni, E. (Eds.). (1997). *Monitoring performance in the public sector: Future directions from international ex-*perience. New Brunswick, NJ: Transaction Books.

Rist, R. C. (1990). Management accountability: The signals sent by auditing and evaluation. *Journal of Public Policy, 9,* 355-369.

Toulemonde, J., & Rieper, O. (Eds.). (1997). *Politics and practices of intergovernmental evaluation.* New Brunswick, NJ: Transaction Books.

Vedung, E. (1997). *Public policy and program evaluation.* New Brunswick, NJ: Transaction Books.

Part VI

THE FUTURE OF QUALITATIVE RESEARCH

A nd so we come to the end, which is only the starting point for a new beginning. Several observations have structured our arguments to this point. The field of qualitative research continues to transform itself. The changes that took shape in the early 1990s are gaining momentum. The gendered, narrative turn has been taken. Foundational epistemologies, what Schwandt (1997, p. 40) calls epistemologies with a big *E*, have been replaced by constructivist, hermeneutic, feminist, poststructural, pragmatist, critical race, and queer theory approaches to social inquiry. Epistemology with a small *e* has become normative, displaced by discourses on ethics and values, conversations on and about the good, and about the just and moral society.

The chapters in this volume collectively speak to the great need for a compassionate, critical, interpretive civic social science. This is an interpretive social science that blurs both boundaries and genres. Its participants are committed to politically informed action research, inquiry directed to praxis and social change. Hence as the reformist movement called qualitative research gains momentum, its places in the discourses of a free democratic society become ever more clear. With the action researchers, we seek a set of disciplined interpretive practices that will produce radical democratizing transformations in the public and private spheres of the global postcapitalist world. Qualitative research is the means to these ends. It is the bridge that joins multiple interpretive communities. It stretches across many different landscapes and horizons, moving back and forth between the public and the private, the sacred and the secular.

Paradigm shifts and dialogues have become a constant presence within and across the theoretical frameworks that organize both qualitative inquiry and the social and human sciences. The move to standpoint epistemologies has accelerated. No one any longer believes in the concept of a unified sexual subject or, indeed, any unified subject. Epistemology has come out of the closet. The desire for critical, multivoiced, postcolonial ethnographies increases as capitalism extends its global reach.

We now understand that the civic-minded qualitative researcher uses a set of material practices that bring the world into play. These practices are not neutral tools. This researcher thinks historically and interactionally, always mindful of the structural processes that make race, gender, and class potentially repressive presences in daily life. The material practices of qualitative inquiry turn the researcher into a methodological (and epistemological) *bricoleur.* This person is an artist, a quilt maker, a skilled craftsperson, a maker of montages and collages. The interpretive *bricoleur* can interview, observe, study material culture, think within and beyond visual methods; write poetry, fiction, and autoethnography; construct narratives that tell explanatory stories; use qualitative computer software; do text-based inquiries; construct *testimonios* using focus group interviews; even engage in applied ethnography and policy formulation.

It is apparent that the constantly changing field of qualitative research is defined by a series of tensions and contradictions as well as emergent understandings. These tensions and understandings have been felt in every chapter in this volume. Here, as in the first edition of the *Handbook,* we list many of them for purposes of summary only. They take the form of questions and assertions:

1. How will the emphasis on multiple standpoint epistemologies and moral philosophies crystallize around a set of shared understandings concerning the contributions of qualitative inquiry to civil society, civic discourse, and critical race theory?
2. How will studies of ourselves as research subjects lead to greater understandings of the other?
3. If the meanings of experience are given only in representations, then will the performance turn in ethnography produce a shift away from attempts to represent the stream of consciousness and the world of internal meanings of the conscious subject?
4. How will feminist, communitarian, and race-based ethical codes change institutional review boards?
5. Will a new interpretive paradigm, with new methods and strategies of inquiry, emerge out of the interactions that exist among the many paradigms and perspectives presented in this volume?
6. How will ethnic, queer, postcolonial, and feminist paradigms be fitted to this new synthesis, if it comes?
7. How will the next generation of cultural studies scholars, with their critical focus on textual (narrative) and contextual (ethnographic) models of analysis, shape qualitative inquiry?
8. How will the next generation of qualitative researchers react to computer-assisted models of analysis, especially as these models continue to redefine (and erode) issues surrounding privacy and personal, sacred space?
9. Will the postmodern, antifoundational sensibility begin to form its own foundational criteria for evaluating the written and performed text?
10. What place will postpositivism and its successors have in research endeavors that favor local interpretation, question the existence of a guiding "truth," and emphasize subjectivity in the research process?
11. What part can "sixth and seventh moments" qualitative research, including program evaluation and analysis, play in the understanding and improvement of programs and policy?
12. When all universals are gone, including the postmodern worldview, in favor of local interpretations, how can we continue to talk and learn from one another?

There are no definitive answers to any of these questions. Here we can only suggest, in the barest of detail, our responses to them. In our concluding chapter we elaborate these responses, grouping them around several basic themes, or issues: text and voice; the existential, sacred text; reflexivity and being in the text; working the hyphen; ethics and critical moral consciousness; and the textual subject, including our presence in the text. Examined from another angle, the questions listed above focus on the social text, history, politics, ethics, the other, and interpretive paradigms more broadly.

◆   *Into the Future*

Chapter 40, by Mary Gergen and Kenneth Gergen, reflexively moves qualitative inquiry into the next century. Gergen and Gergen validate our argument that this field is filled with creativity, enthusiasm, intellectual ferment, cross-fertilizations, catalytic dialogues, and a prevailing sense of participation in a living revolution. They analyze these fractious cross-currents, focusing explicitly on the crisis in validity, the rights of representation, and the place of the political in qualitative inquiry.

The collapse of foundational epistemologies has led to emerging innovations in methodology that have reframed what is meant by *validity*. They have shaped the call for increased textual reflexivity, greater textual self-exposure, multiple voicing, stylized forms of literary representation, and performance texts. These innovations shade into the next, issues surrounding representation.

Representational issues involve how the other will be presented in the text. Gergen and Gergen discuss several different types of representation: empowerment, conjoint, distributed, and multivoiced. These representational strategies converge with a concern over the place of politics in the text. We can no longer separate ideology and politics from methodology. Gergen and Gergen are quite forceful on this point. Methods always acquire their meaning within broader systems of meaning, from epistemology to ontology. These systems are themselves embedded in ethical and ideological frameworks as well as in particular interpretive communities. In a parallel vein, as Gergen and Gergen note, studies of individual consciousness support the ideology of individualism. Our methods are always grafted onto our politics.

To repeat: Scientific practice does not stand outside ideology. As we argued in the first edition of this *Handbook,* a poststructural social science project seeks its external grounding not in science, but rather in a commitment to post-Marxism and an emancipatory feminism. A good text is one that invokes these commitments. A good text exposes how race, class, and gender work their ways into the concrete lives of interacting individuals.

Gergen and Gergen foresee a future where research becomes more relational, where working the hyphen becomes easier, and more difficult, for researchers are always on both sides of the hyphen. They also see a massive spawning of populist technology. This technology will serve to undermine qualitative inquiry as we know it, including disrupting what we mean by a "stable" subject (where is the cyberself located?). The new information technologies also increase the possibilities of dialogue and communication across time and space. We may be, as Gergen and Gergen observe, participating in the reconstruction of the social sciences. If so, qualitative inquiry is taking the lead in this reconstruction.

Finally, we predict that there will be no dominant form of qualitative textuality in the sixth and seventh moments; rather, several different hybrid textual forms will circulate alongside one another. The first form will be the classic, realist ethnographic text, redefined in poststructural terms. We will hear more from first-person voices in these texts. The second hybrid textual form will blend and combine poetic, fictional, and performance texts into critical interventionist presentations. The third textual form will include *testimonios* and first-person (autoethnographic) texts. The fourth form will be narrative evaluation texts, which work back and forth between first-person voices and the *testimonio*. These forms will be evaluated in terms of an increasingly sophisticated set of local, antifoundational, moral, and ethical criteria.

Variations on these textual forms will rest on a critical rethinking of the notion of the reflexive, self-aware subject. Lived experience cannot be studied directly. We study representations of experience: stories, narratives, performances, dramas. We have no direct access to the inner psychology and inner world of meanings of the reflexive subject. The subject in performance ethnographies becomes a performer. We study performers and performances, persons making meaning together, the how of culture as it connects persons in moments of cocreation and coperformance.

◆ *History, Paradigms, Politics, Ethics, and the Other*

Many things are changing as we write our way out of writing culture and move into the seventh moment of qualitative research. Multiple histories and theoretical frameworks, where before there were just a few, now circulate in this field. Today foundationalism and postpositivism are challenged and supplemented by a host of competing paradigms and perspectives. Many different applied action and participatory research agendas inform program evaluation and analysis.

We now understand that we study the other to learn about ourselves, and many of the lessons we have learned have not been pleasant. We seek a new body of ethical directives fitted to postmodernism. The old ethical codes failed to examine research as a morally engaged project. They never seriously located the researcher within the ruling apparatuses of society. A feminist, communitarian ethical system will continue to evolve, informed at every step by critical race, postcolonial, and queer theory sensibilities. Blatant voyeurism in the name of science or the state will continue to be challenged.

Performance-based cultural studies and critical theory perspectives, with their emphases on moral criticism, will alter the traditional empiricist foundations of qualitative research. The dividing line between science and morality will continue to be erased. A postmodern, feminist, poststructural, communitarian science will move closer to a sacred science of the moral universe.

As we edge our way into the 21st century, looking back, and borrowing Max Weber's metaphor, we see more clearly how we were trapped by the 20th century and its iron cage of reason and rationality. Like a bird in a cage, for too long we were unable to see the pattern in which we were caught. Coparticipants in a secular science of the social world, we became part of the problem. Entangled in the ruling apparatuses we wished to undo, we perpetuated systems of knowledge and power that we found, underneath, to be all too oppressive. It's not too late for us to get out of that cage—today we leave the cage behind.

And so we enter, or leave, the sixth moment. In our concluding chapter we elaborate our thoughts about the next generation of qualitative research.

■ *Reference*

Schwandt, T. A. (1997). *Qualitative inquiry: A dictionary of terms.* Thousand Oaks, CA: Sage.

40

QUALITATIVE INQUIRY

Tensions and Transformations

◆ Mary M. Gergen and Kenneth J. Gergen

The domain of qualitative inquiry offers some of the richest and most rewarding explorations available in contemporary social science. This bounty is the outcome of a host of historical convergences. The area has welcomed scores of scholars who have found their disciplinary traditions narrow and constraining. Other denizens have found outlets for expressing particular commitments or skills; here there is space for societal critique and political activism, just as there are clearings for literary, artistic, and dramatic expressions. Further, scholars from diverse arenas—AIDS researchers, market analysts, ethnographers, and more—have entered in search of ways to bring vitality to their customary pursuits. Perhaps most significant, the tidal wave of theoretical and metatheoretical debates dashing across the intellectual world—variably indexed as postfoundational, poststructural, post-Enlightenment, and postmodern—has swept into the qualitative harbor. Here these turbulent interchanges have produced profound challenges to the ways in which the social sciences are understood and practiced.

As a result of these convergences, the field of qualitative inquiry is replete with enthusiasm, creativity, intellectual ferment, and action. As one researcher, Virginia Olesen, has described it, "I don't think there's ever been a more exciting moment in terms of careful thought about the epistemologies of the methods, relations with participants, new modes and the growing strength of qualitative methods in important substantive fields such as education and nursing" (e-mail, November 25, 1998). There are cross-fertilizations, catalytic dialogues, and a prevailing sense of participation in a living revolution. Contrasting beliefs, skeptical challenges, and resistance are also in evidence. In the present chapter we turn our attention to some of these fractious crosscurrents in order to highlight some of the more salient differences and to deliberate on possible futures. We do so, however, not with the aim of settling the disputes or of moving the field toward coherence or univocality. We do not view the doubts and disagreements as the birth pangs of a new methodological foundation, but rather as opportunities for new conversations and new evolutions in practice. Approaching the issues from a social constructionist standpoint, we treat these tumultuous dialogues as harboring the generative potential that will sustain the vitality of the qualitative domain in the new century. We also explore what we feel to be some of the more promising vistas of inquiry, emerging challenges that may significantly shape the future of the field.

We do not embark on this enterprise alone. To sharpen and expand our deliberations, we surveyed distinguished colleagues who are contributors to the present volume and members of the *Handbook*'s International Advisory Board. We asked them where they see themselves moving in the qualitative domain during the next 5 years, what kinds of projects they have under way, what particular turns of methodology seem especially inviting and exciting to them, and what modes of inquiry seem most appealing to their graduate students. The replies were most generous, enlightening, and provocative; we wish to thank all who gave of their views for the enrichment of this chapter.

In what follows we attend specifically to three sites of controversy in qualitative inquiry: the crisis of validity, the rights of representation, and the place of the political in qualitative investigations. In each case we review the principal lines of development, exploring the ways in which controversy has sparked development. And in each case we point to what we believe to be the most useful lines of emerging argument and practice. Following this discussion, we address specific agendas for the new century. As we see it, developments within the major sites of controversy position the field for new and significant transformations. We pay special attention to research as relational process, transformations through technology, and the reconstruction of the self.

◆ The Crisis of Validity

One of the most catalytic influences on the qualitative domain within the past 10 years has been the lively dialogue on the nature of language, and particularly the relationship of language to the world it purports to describe. Developments in poststructural semiotics, literary theory, and rhetorical theory all challenge the pivotal assumption that scientific accounts can accurately and objectively represent the world as it is. At a minimum, such work makes clear the impossibility of linguistic mimesis; there is no means of privileging any particular account on the grounds of its unique match to the world. The intelligibility of our accounts of the world derive not from the world itself, but from our immersion within a tradition of cultural practices we inherit from previous generations. It is only as our accounts approximate these conventions that we make sense at all. Thus it is from our relationships within interpretive communities that our constructions of the world derive.[1]

Deteriorating Foundations of Methodology

This view of language has led to substantial skepticism concerning the epistemological foundations of scientific practices. The pursuit of universal or general laws, the capacity of science to produce accurate portrayals of its subject matter, the possibility of scientific progression toward objective truth, and the right to claims of scientific expertise are all undermined. We confront, then, what Denzin and Lincoln (1994) have called a crisis of validity. If there is no means of correctly matching word to world, then the warrant for scientific validity is lost, and researchers are left to question the role of methodology and criteria of evaluation. As Denzin and Lincoln cogently ask, "How are qualitative studies to be evaluated in the poststructural moment?" (p. 11).

Within the qualitative arena these developments have simultaneously stimulated heated debate and bursts of creative energy. For many qualitative researchers, critiques of validity resonate with other long-standing misgivings about nomothetic methodologies for their inability to reflect the complexities of human experience and action. Indeed, such researchers turn to qualitative methods in the hope of generating richer and more finely nuanced accounts of human action. Within these circles, many argue that the empiricist emphasis on quantifiable behavior left out the crucial ingredient of human understanding, namely, the private experiences of the agent. Both of these views—that qualitative methods are more faithful to the social world than quantitative ones and that individual human experiences are important—remain robust in today's qualitative community, with diverse proponents of grounded theory research (Strauss & Corbin, 1990, 1994), phenomenology (Georgi, 1994; Moustakas, 1994), and feminist standpoint researchers (Belenky, Clinchy, Goldberger, & Tarule, 1986; Brown & Gilligan, 1992; Harding, 1986, 1991; Komesaroff, Rothfield, & Daly, 1997; Miller & Stiver, 1997) among them.

Yet, as the validity critiques have played out, they bite the hand of the qualitative enthusiasts who feed them. If the idea of language as a picture or map of the real is rejected, then there is no rationale by which qualitative researchers can claim that their methods are superior to quantitative ones in terms of accuracy or sensitivity to what exists. A thousand-word description is no more valid a "picture of the person" than a single score on a standardized test. By the same token, the validity critiques challenge the presumption that language can adequately map individual experience (Bohan, 1993; Butler, 1990). In what sense, it is asked, can words map or picture an inner world? Accounts of "experience" seem more adequately understood as the outcome of a particular textual/cultural history in which people learn to tell stories of their lives to themselves and others. Such narratives are embedded within the sense-making processes of historically and culturally situated communities (see Bruner, 1986, 1990; Gergen, 1992, in press; Morawski, 1994; Sarbin, 1986).

Emerging Innovations in Methodology

Although sometimes accused of no-exit nihilism, such skepticism has had enormous catalytic effects in the qualitative arena. An effulgent range of methodological innovation has resulted from efforts to replace the traditional effort to discover and record the truth. We consider here four of these innovations: reflexivity, multiple voicing, literary representation, and performance. Their particular importance derives in part from the way in which they challenge the traditional binary between research and representation, that is, between acts of observing or "gathering data" and subsequent reports on this process. There is increasing recognition that because observation is inevitably saturated with interpretation, and research reports are essentially exercises in interpretation, research and representation are inextricably entwined (Behar & Gordon, 1995; Gergen, Chrisler, & LoCicero, 1999; Visweswaran, 1994). Let us explore.

Reflexivity

Among the primary innovations have been those emphasizing reflexivity. Here investigators seek ways of demonstrating to their audiences their historical and geographic situatedness, their personal investments in the research, various biases they bring to the work, their surprises and "undoings" in the process of the research endeavor, the ways in which their choices of literary tropes lend rhetorical force to the research report, and/or the ways in which they have avoided or suppressed certain points of view (see Behar, 1996; Kiesinger, 1998). Rosanna Hertz elaborates on these implications for her work:

> After delving into issues of voice and reflexivity, I find myself freer to think about how to incorporate my own voice into a piece of work where I have no personal experience. I want a reader to understand that . . . I bring to the topic my own history and perspective. I still believe that my primary obligation as a social scientist is to tell the stories of the people I have studied. But I also find that the accounts they tell have been constructed through the dialogue that my respondents created in conjunction with me. (e-mail, April 9, 1998)

Such forms of self-exposure have more recently led to the flourishing of autoethnography (Ellis & Bochner, 1996). Here investigators explore in depth the ways in which their personal histories saturate the ethnographic inquiry. However, rather than giving the reader pause to consider the biases, here the juxtaposition of self and subject matter is used to enrich the ethnographic report. The reader finds the subject/object binary deteriorating and is informed of ways in which confronting the world from moment to moment is also confronting the self. In all these reflexive moves, the investigator relinquishes the "God's-eye view" and reveals his or her work as historically, culturally, and personally situated. In the case of autoethnography, the distinction between the research and the report or representation is also fully challenged. Personal investments in the observational act are not only recognized but become a subject of the research. Although a valuable addition to the vocabulary of inquiry, reflexive moves are not entirely successful in subverting the concept of validity. Ultimately, the act of reflexivity asks the reader to accept itself as authentic, that is, as a conscientious effort to "tell the truth" about the making of the account. We are thus poised at the threshold of an infinite regress of reflections on reflection.

Multiple Voicing

A second significant means of disclaiming validity is to remove the single voice of omniscience and to relativize it by including multiple voices within the research report. There are many variations on this theme. For example, research subjects or clients may be invited to speak on their own behalf—to describe, express, or interpret within the research report itself (Anderson, 1997; Lather & Smithies, 1997; Reinharz, 1992). In other cases researchers may seek out respondents with wide-ranging perspectives on a given matter and include the varying views without pressing them into coherence (Fox, 1996). Or researchers may reflexively locate a range of conflicting interpretations that they find plausible and thereby avoid reaching a single, integrative conclusion (Ellis, Kiesinger, &

Tillmann-Healy, 1997). Some researchers also work collectively with their subjects so that their conclusions do not eradicate minority views. Multiple voicing is especially promising in its capacity to recognize the problems of validity while simultaneously providing a potentially rich array of interpretations or perspectives (Hertz, 1997). Doubt gives way to the positive potentials of multiplicity.

Yet multiple voicing is not without its complexities. One of the most difficult questions is how the author/researcher should treat his or her own voice. Should it simply be one among many, or should it have special privileges by virtue of professional training? There is also the question of identifying who the author and the participants truly are; once we realize the possibility of multiple voicing, it also becomes evident that each individual participant is polyvocal (Franklin, 1997). Which of these voices is speaking in the research and why? What is, at the same time, suppressed? The way in which Shulamit Reinharz raises this question has significant implications for deliberating on this issue:

> Using detailed field notes from a project I completed quite a while ago, . . . I trace the way I referred to myself during the course of the year, and saw how different parts of my self became relevant over time. I discuss these "selves" as emergent through the process of immersion in the field. At first, the most obvious "difference" with the [other group] members is what defines myself there. After that, more layers are unpeeled. As these different layers are uncovered, people get to know me in different ways, which leads to their telling me different things. This in turn allows me to know them in different ways over time. . . . Different lengths of time in the field therefore yield different types of knowledge. At first glance this seems self-evident because clearly a one-day visit is different from a one-year stay (for example). But this difference has not been explained or demonstrated. I think my notes demonstrate the process. (e-mail, April 18, 1998)

Finally, moves toward multiplicity are not always successful in giving all sides their due. Typically, the investigator functions as the ultimate author of the work (or the coordinator of the voices) and thus serves as the ultimate arbiter of inclusion, emphasis, and integration. The author's arts of literary rendering are often invisible to the reader.

Literary Styling

A third important reaction to validity critiques is the deployment of stylized representation, and particularly the replacement of traditional realist discourse with forms of writing cast in opposition to "truth telling." For example, the investigator's descriptions may take the form of fiction, poetry, or autobiographical invention. The use of literary styling signals to the reader that the account does not function as a map of the world (and, indeed, that the mapping metaphor is flawed), but as an interpretive activity addressed to a community of interlocutors. For many qualitative researchers, such writing is especially appealing because it offers a greater expressive range and an opportunity to reach audiences outside the academy (Communication Studies 298, 1999; Diversi, 1998; S. H. Jones, 1998, 1999; Richardson, 1997, 1998; Rinehart, 1998) and to do significant political work (Behar & Gordon, 1995). While generating significant openings for creative expression, such writing is vulnerable to the criticism of singularity of voice. The lone author commands the discursive domain in full rhetorical regalia. Again, however, critique gives way to innovation: Literary styling may be combined with other methodologies to offset the criticism. For example, in her dissertation on relationships among African Americans after the Million Man March, Deborah Austin (1996) co-constructed a narrative poem with one of the participants. This is a small excerpt:

Africans are the same

wherever we are, she says to me

matter-of-factly

I look at her and smile

and ask

like a good researcher should

How so?

I can't explain, she says

with that voice that sounds

like the rush of many rivers.
(pp. 207-208)

Many of the issues brought forth about reflexivity and multiple voicings can also be directed at forms of nontraditional writing. Although certain pitfalls of traditional literary forms are avoided in these innovations, claims that they are not appropriate for scientific representations are prevalent. These critiques are even more pronounced with regard to performance.

Performance

Finally, to remove the thrall of objectivity while sustaining voice, an increasing number of scholars are moving toward *performance* as a mode of research/representation. This move is justified by the notion that if the distinction between fact and fiction is largely a matter of textual tradition, as the validity critiques suggest, then forms of scientific writing are not the only mode of expression that might be employed. Although visual aids such as film and photography have also been accepted as a means of "capturing reality," they have generally been viewed as auxiliary modes within written traditions. However, when we realize that the communicative medium itself has a formative effect on what we take to be the object of research, the distinction between film as recording device as opposed to performance (e.g. "a film for an audience") is blurred (Gergen & Gergen, 1991). And with this blurring, investigators are invited into considering the entire range of communicative expression in the arts and entertainment world—graphic arts, video, drama, dance, magic, multimedia, and so on—as forms of research and presentation. Again, in moving toward performance the investigator avoids the mystifying claims of truth and simultaneously expands the range of communities in which the work can stimulate dialogue.

Significant contributions to this developing form of research/representation include Carlson's *Performance: A Critical Introduction* (1996) and Case, Brett, and Foster's edited volume *Cruising* the *Performative* (1995), as well as work by Blumenfeld-Jones (1995), Case (1997), Clark (1996), Denzin (1997), Donmoyer and Yennie-Donmoyer (1995), Jipson and Paley (in press), Mienczakowski (1996), Morris (1995), and Van Maanen (1995). An example specifically relevant to the qualitative domain is a performance piece concerning the lives of Mexican American migrants by Jim Scheurich, Gerardo Lopez, and Miguel Lopez. The performance includes music, video, and a slide show—all operating simultaneously. In addition, there is a script that requires the participation of a cast along with members of the audience. Apropos the issue of validity, Scheurich notes, "The originators make no assumptions about the nature of these experiences or their relationship to Mexican American migrant life" (e-mail, April 19, 1998). In effect, the performance provides the audience with possibilities for a rich engagement with the issues, but leaves them free to interpret as they wish. In another format, Glenda Russell and Janis Bohan (1999) responded performatively to the passage of Amendment 2 to the Colorado State Constitution (which removed legal recourse from those who encounter discrimination based on sexual orientation). Using themes and statements taken from the transcripts of interviews with persons opposed to the legislation, the researchers helped to create two highly sophisticated and complex artistic projects: one a five-part oratorio, *Fire,* written by a professional composer and sung by a highly skilled choir at a national competition; and the other a professionally produced television documentary aired on PBS. In their work one senses the blurring of many boundaries, between professional and amateur, insider and outsider, researcher and researched, and performer and audience.

Enrichment or Erosion?

Judging from the reactions of our correspondents, investments in these groundbreaking explorations are likely to increase considerably. As John Frow put it, "Where do I go from here? I suspect into ever greater levels of suspicion of the protocols of intellectual discourse, and into

exploration of the limits of the genre of 'academic' knowledge. . . . the use of nonlinear and recursive textual structures, seems to me increasingly unavoidable as I try to work my way out of the constraints and certainties of routine academic argument" (e-mail, April 5, 1998). And as Kathy Charmaz wrote, "One top priority for me is finishing a handbook about writing research. My approach combines methods of qualitative analysis with writing techniques . . . that professional writers use" (e-mail, May 30, 1998). Similarly, Jim Scheurich commented, "I have turned to video in search of a . . . more multidimensional medium. I like adding visual and sound to written words. I also like the storying aspect though I don't want to tell conventional stories. I see this medium as supportive of more levels of meaning" (e-mail, April 19, 1998).

Yet, in spite of the bold and creative zest accompanying many of these ventures, there is also a growing unease among some qualitative researchers with the drift from conventional scientific standards. Epithets of excess—narcissistic, navel gazing, exhibitionistic—are familiar reframes. In this vein, George Marcus suggested that "new thinking . . . and to some degree discursive practice in the things we write about reflexivity, subjectivity, power in intersubjectivity has run its course, nearly so, and that conditions of research—especially of fieldwork—need attention now" (e-mail, April 4, 1998). Marcus argues that anthropologists must continue to engage in the long, hard work required to produce "thick descriptions," and not let other intellectual pursuits distract from that duty (Marcus, 1998). Patricia Clough (1997) takes emotionally charged autoethnographic writing to task for its symbiotic relationship with television drama and for "keeping theoretically motivated critical interventions at a distance" (p. 101). In a similar vein, William Tierney worries that too often "adventurous texts are little more than experiments with words. Those of us who are critics are increasingly skeptical of literary wordsmithing without any concern for change" (e-mail, April 10, 1998). The harshest words among those we surveyed came from David Silverman, who wrote: "The last two decades have been obsessed with fashions that will quickly be forgotten or integrated into other ways of working. The best of Post-Modernism (Foucault, Latour) will be incorporated into sober studies of institutional practices. The 'fun and games' (wordplays, experimental writing etc.) will be dismissed. [The] endless open-ended interviews will be understood as the Oprah Winfrey cop-out it really is" (e-mail, April 3, 1998).

Vistas of Validity

One might view such critiques as numbing in consequence, possibly functioning as an enervating backlash, a return to the conventional, and the end to methodological experiments. It could also fragment the field, as researchers may simply terminate dialogue and go their separate ways. However, such outcomes would be both unfortunate and unwarranted. At the outset, it would be intellectually irresponsible simply to return to business as usual—as if the validity critiques had never occurred. At the same time, those engaged in the new endeavors can scarcely declare that the validity critiques are fully justified. By their own account, there are no foundational rationalities from which such warrants could be derived. Further, few of any persuasion would welcome a unified field of inquiry—guided by a coherent, conceptually rigid framework—in which all methods are prescribed in advance. Thus, rather than a domain of noncommunicating, nomadic tribes, we may properly reinvoke the metaphor of generative tension. Placing these innovations and their critiques into an appreciative dialogue, which is where we think they should be, what new avenues are now encouraged? What futures could be opened? Drawing from disparate dialogues, the following would appear prominent.

Reframing Validity

In the conventional terms by which it has been formulated, the debate on validity has reached an impasse. On the one hand, those pursuing their work as if their descriptions and explanations were transparent reflections of

their subject matter lack any rationale for this posture. They are vulnerable to host of deconstructive logics. Yet those who find fault with this tradition are, in the end, without means of justifying their critique. In the very process of depriviledging they are relying on the selfsame assumptions of language as correspondent with its object. Thus, rather than either reinstantiating the modernist tradition of objective truth or opening the throttle on anything goes, discussion is invited into ways of reconceptualizing the issue. At a minimum, we might profitably revisit the issue of linguistic reference. If research or critique is "about" something, and this relationship is not one of mimesis, how can it be otherwise envisioned? Even those employing fictional genres or performance in their work do not treat their work as mere entertainment; the underlying presumption is that in some fashion it is a contribution to understanding. Frow's communiqué offers an attractive beginning to the task of rethinking reference:

> The concept of "text" or "discourse" refers to a matter which is ontologically heterogeneous: that is, which is not reducible either to *language* or to a reality which is external to the symbolic, but is rather a heterogeneous mix of language and other (e.g. iconic) symbolizations, of social relations, of built environments, of consolidated institutional structure, of roles and hierarchies of authority, of bodies, etc. It's only on this basis, I believe, that the metaphor of textuality or discursivity can work without being reductive either to language or to social relations. (e-mail, April 5, 1998)

Here we begin to consider the achievement of reference in far richer terms than heretofore. If reference is born of such heterogeneity, then we are positioned to reconsider the means by which validity is achieved, by whom, for whom, and under what conditions.

We might also abandon concern with validity, an option favored by not a few, including several reviewers of this chapter, who cautioned us to avoid the term, given its embattled history and predicted demise. However, a more promising direction for us seemed to be toward reconceptualizing the concept. Here Patti Lather's (1991, 1993) work on validity is particularly catalytic. Lather proposes a "transgressive-list" of ways in which validity might be reconceptualized: Ironic validity foregrounds the insufficiencies of language in picturing the world; paralogical validity is concerned with undecidables, limits, paradoxes, discontinuities, and complexities in language; rhizomatic validity, symbolized by the taproot metaphor, expresses how conventional research procedures are undermined and new locally determined norms of understanding are generated; and voluptuous validity—"excessive," "leaky," "risky," and "unbounded"—brings issues of ethics and epistemology together. Robin McTaggart (1997b) has also raised the interesting question of validity in relation to participatory action research. He suggests that the concept might be reconceptualized in terms of the efficacy of research in changing relevant social practices. "Our thinking about validity must engage much more than mere knowledge claims. . . . [It must be] comprehensive enough to reflect [what] the social action researchers . . . are committed to, by the trenchant and withering critiques of other more inert and detached forms of social enquiry" (pp. 17-18). Conversations around such viewpoints are rich in potential for reconfiguring the concept of validity.

Situated Knowledge

Closely related to the revisioning of validity, but raising questions of its own, are explorations into situated knowledge. As Donna Haraway (1988) as well as other theorists have suggested, the concept typically serves an ameliorating function, reconciling constructionist and realist positions. Because few traditionalists wish to argue that their interpretations are uniquely articulated with the subject matter they wish to portray, and few constructionists would maintain that there is "nothing outside of text," a space is opened for situated truth, that is, "truth" located within particular communities at particular times and used indexically to represent their condition (see Landrine, 1995). In this way we can commonly speak as if the term *sunset* maps the sinking sun in the evening sky and astronomers can simultaneously agree

that "the sun does not set." Descriptions and explanations can be valid so long as one does not mistake local conventions for universal truth. It is in this vein that Jim Holstein wrote positively of research that "tries to be mindful of the constructed, the ephemeral, the hyperreal, while not giving up on empirical analysis of lived experience in a world that still seems quite real and solid to its inhabitants (even if it doesn't seem as solid as it might once have felt)" (e-mail, April 23, 1998).

Yet, although a useful beginning, further dialogues on the conceptual possibilities of situated knowledge are needed. It borders on the banal to suggest that everything can be valid for someone, sometime, somewhere. Such a conclusion both closes off dialogue among diverse group and leads to the result that no one can speak about another. Such an outcome would spell the end of social science inquiry. Dialogue is invited, then, into how situated validity is achieved, maintained, and subverted. Further, how do various qualitative methods function in this regard, and for whom? By what means do they variously achieve a sense of validity?

One important option is for the qualitative community to develop methods by which situated knowledges can be brought into productive (as opposed to conflicting) relationships with each other. Frequently our methods of inquiry support (or "empower") particular groups. This outcome contributes to the situated knowledge of these groups, but also tends to diminish or erase alternative realities. The challenge, then, is to develop methods of inquiry that can generate productive exchanges at the border of competing or clashing "situations." Here we found the words of Yen Espiritu provocative:

> I am trying to think about how scholars of color can expand upon the premise of studying "our own" by studying other "others." For example, as a Vietnam-born woman who studies Filipino Americans, I come to the research project not as an "objective" outsider but as a fellow Asian immigrant who shares some of the life experiences of my respondents. I do not claim that these shared struggles grant me "insider status" into the Filipino American community. But I do claim that these shared experiences enable me to bring to the work a comparative perspective that is im-

plicit, intuitive, and informed by my own identities and positionalities. These implicitly comparative aspects are important because they permit us to highlight the different and differentiating functional forces of racialization. (e-mail, April 12, 1998)

More broadly, however, the need is for transversing conversations, dialogues that crisscross the moguled terrains of discourse and practice (see Cooperrider & Dutton, 1999). We return to this issue later in the chapter.

Rhetorical/Political Deliberation

Finally, our contemporary debates would be enriched by an extension of the process of rhetorical/political deliberation. That is, we might usefully bracket the question of validity in favor of a range of alternative queries into the ways various methods/representations function within the culture. Given the impact of social science pursuits on cultural life, how do we estimate the comparative value of various methodological/representational forms? There is already an extensive sociopolitical critique of the patriarchal, colonialist, individualist, and hegemonic aspects of realism/objectivism (Braidotti, 1995; hooks, 1990; Penley & Ross, 1985; Said, 1978; Smith, in press). Although such work represents an important opening, there has been little exploration of what many would consider to be the positive functions of the realist orientation—both politically and in terms of rhetorical potential. For example, the language of statistics is but one form of rhetoric; however, it is a rhetoric that, for certain audiences and in certain circumstances, can be more compelling and more functional than a case study, poem, or autoethnographic report. More significant is that we have yet to explore the various sociopolitical and rhetorical implications of the new developments discussed above. For example, do ventures into multivoicing or fictional styling diminish or enhance audience interest or engagement? As Jay Gubrium, after expressing reservations about the work, declared, "The stuff can be riveting and, to me, that's important enough in its own

right" (e-mail, April 2, 1998). Yet in a society where clear, no-nonsense answers to serious issues are often demanded, such offerings may seem too impractical, irrelevant, or playful. As Linda Smircich wrote: "I am located in a business school . . . and the dominant mode of thinking and researching is still positivist/quantitative/functionalist and directed toward managerial interests. . . . I rarely get a daring student" who will challenge these barriers of tradition (e-mail, April 23, 1998). Either way, we must continue the inquiry into societal functions and repercussions of diverse modes of communicating.

In a different dimension, we might ask whether self-reflexivity and autoethnographic reportage function in such a way that individual experience is privileged over social or communal renditions. Can these orientations be faulted for their contribution to an ideology of self-contained individualism? In sum, broadscale comparative analyses are needed of the various rhetorical/political assets and liabilities of the many emerging methodologies. Lincoln's (1995, 1998) analyses of the criteria for qualitative research furnish a significant background to this conversation (see also Garratt & Hodkinson, 1998). However, a closer analysis of the relational repercussions of alternative forms of discourse is much to be welcomed.

◆ Rights of Representation

Critical reflection on the empiricist program has provoked a second roiling of the qualitative waters, in this case over issues of representation, its control, responsibilities, and ramifications (Tierney & Lincoln, 1997). It is perhaps Foucault's (1979, 1980) disquisitions on power/knowledge that have figured most centrally in these critiques. For Foucault, knowledge-generating disciplines—including the social sciences—function as sources of authority, and as their descriptions, explanations, and diagnoses are disseminated through education and other practices they enlarge the potential realm of subjugation. For example, as the concept of mental disorders and the diagnostic categories of the psychiatric profession are recognized by all professionals and laypersons involved with such issues, so does the culture capitulate to the disciplining power of psychiatry. The implications of such arguments are sobering to the research community. Increasingly painful questions are confronted: To what extent does research convert the commonsense, unscrutinized realities of the culture to disciplinary discourse? In what ways does research empower the discipline as opposed to those under study? When is the researcher exploiting his or her subjects for purposes of personal or institutional prestige? Does research serve agencies of surveillance, increasing their capacities of control over the research subject?

Confrontation with such issues has been intensified by increasing resistance among those subjected to social science inquiry. Feminists were among the first to issue complaints, regarding both omissions and commissions in characterizations of women in the research literature (Bohan, 1992). Minority group members have become increasingly aware that the long-standing critiques of the public media's distortion or misrepresentation of their lives apply no less to human science research. The psychiatric establishment was among the first of the professional groups to be targeted when it was forced by 1960s gay activists to withdraw homosexuality from the nosology of mental illness. It has also been the message delivered by African Americans angered by a social science literature depicting them as unintelligent or criminal. Similarly, the elderly, AIDS victims, "psychiatric survivors," and many others now join to question the rights of scientists to represent (appropriate) their experience, actions, and/or traditions. Given the problems of validity discussed above, these various critiques have troubling implications for future research.

Yet such contentions are not without their limitations. When extended to their extreme, they are as problematic as what they challenge. In reply to Foucauldian critiques, human science research often functions in counter-hegemonic ways, bringing into critical focus the

institutions of governance, economic control, educational institutions, the media, and so on. In this sense, such research can function as a force of resistance and social justice. Further, to suspend all knowledge claims would be to terminate virtually all traditions—ethnic, religious, and otherwise—that depend on the capacity to "name the world." In addition, there are limits to the claims and critiques of interest groups as well. For one, claims to rights of self-representation exist alongside a host of competing claims made by human scientists—including rights to freedom of speech, to speak the truth from one's own perspective, to contribute to science, and to pursue one's own moral ends. Self-representation may be a good, but it is not the only good. Further, the concept of self-representation is not unproblematic. If it were pressed to its conclusion, no one would have the right to speak for or describe anyone else. One might even question the possibility of individuals' representing themselves, for to do so would require that they appropriate the language of other persons. The solitary individual would have no private voice, no language of private experience. Without depending on the language of others, we cannot achieve intelligibility.

Expanding the Methodological Arena

With these crosscurrents of opinion in motion, what is again required is a more tolerant and mutually reflective orientation to the research process. Consistent with the central theme of this chapter, we see these various tensions as generative in potential. They have already stimulated a range of significant developments and currently set agendas for a creative future. Let us consider three such developments garnered from the qualitative domain.

Empowerment Research

Perhaps the most obvious response to the critical concerns with representation, and one already well developed within the qualitative community, is empowerment research. Here the researcher offers his or her skills and resources in order to assist groups in developing projects of mutual interest. Participatory action research is the most well developed genre of this kind (Lykes, 1996; McTaggart, 1997a; Reason, 1994; Smyth, 1991). In one variation on the empowerment theme, Elijah Anderson (1978, 1990) has mounted research aimed at fostering connection among members of otherwise hostile communities. Anderson essentially "hung out" for many years in the public housing projects and on the streets of Philadelphia, creating focus groups and collecting extensive narratives from clusters of people frequenting street corners and other public places. His recent book, *Code of the Street* (1999), is designed to speak to sociologists but also to public policy planners, neighborhood groups, educators, and others involved with diverse client populations. While not abandoning an explanatory goal of making sense of the "code" of the street and its functions, Anderson develops an interpretive framework that has meaning for both marginalized and mainstream society and thus functions as a bridge between them. The attempt is to reduce the mutual disrespect and sense of alienated difference that otherwise prevail.

Conjoint Representations

The use of conjoint representations to deal with issues of validity, as mentioned above, also has ramifications for issues of representation. As researchers join participants in inquiry and writing, the line between researcher and subject is blurred, and control over representation is increasingly shared. In early attempts of this sort, research participants were given a broader space in which to "tell their own stories." Often, however, the researcher's hand subtly, but strongly, shaped the voice through editing and interpretation. To compensate, some researchers now ask participants to join in writing the research accounts themselves. One of the most innovative and far-reaching examples of the genre is Lather and Smithies's volume *Troubling the Angels* (1997). Here the investigators worked in a support group composed of women with the AIDS virus. The report in-

cludes the women's firsthand accounts of their lives and what they want to share with the world about their conditions. Rather than obscuring their own positions, the investigators devote special sections of the book to their own experiences and understandings. To compensate for the ways in which these various accounts are cut away from the discourses of medicine, economics, and media, Lather and Smithies supplement with more formal academic and scientific materials. Before publication, the entire volume was submitted to the participants for their comments.

Distributed Representation

Representational critiques are also countered with emerging explorations into distributed representation, that is, attempts by the investigator to set in motion an array of different voices in dialogical relationship. A fascinating example is provided by Karen Fox (1996), who combines her own views, as researcher, with the related experiences of a survivor of child sexual abuse, along with the rarely available views of the abuser himself. The account is based on extensive open-ended interviews and participant observation in which Fox attended a therapy session with the convicted sex offender. The piece is arranged in a three-column format, with the columns representing the three voices. The flow of the text encourages the reader to consider the three different perspectives—separately and in relationship. All of the words are those of the speakers. Although the selection and arrangement are Fox's, each of the participants had the opportunity to read and comment on all of the materials. Ultimately, the arrangement facilitates a full expression of emotion—ambivalence, sorrow, rage, and affection. Fox also includes her own abuse story within the frame, thus breaking with the tradition of author insularity.

Another variation of distributed representation is offered by a group of three researchers who are also the objects of their mutual study (Ellis et al., 1997). For 5 months, the trio met in various configurations in diverse settings to discuss the topic of bulimia. Two of the researchers have long histories of eating disorders. The culmination of their research is a jointly written and edited account in which they describe a dinner at an elegant restaurant. This setting is very provocative for their particular involvements with food and permits the authors to treat complex relations as they write of ordering and eating food among others who are aware of their "problems." The text of their combined efforts reveals the private reflections and active engagement of each within a single narrative. Unlike the presentation by Fox discussed above, in which quotations are separated by blank spaces and individual perspectives are clearly delineated, this presentation is seamless. One achieves a form of "God's-eye view" by discovering almost simultaneously the private reactions of each author. For example, the reader discovers how ordering dessert takes on momentous significance for each woman, and how each resolves her interpersonal dilemmas concerning this challenge. Such experiments in representation open new and exciting vistas.

◆ The Place of the Political

A third site of controversy is closely related to issues of validity and representation but raises issues of a distinct nature. The focal point in this case concerns the political or valuational investments of the researcher. Thirty years ago, it was commonly argued that rigorous methods of research are politically or valuationally neutral. Ideological interests might, or might not, determine the topic of research or the ways in which the results are used, but the methods should themselves be ideologically free. However, as the postmodern critiques of validity have become more sophisticated, it has become increasingly clear that there is no simple means of separating method from ideology. For one, methods acquire their meaning and significance within broader networks of meaning—metaphysical, epistemological, ontological—which are themselves wedded to ideological and ethical traditions. For example, to conduct psychological experiments on individuals is to presume the centrality of individual mental functioning in the production of human affairs. Much the same privilege is granted by qualitative methods attempting to tap individual experience. In this way, both methods implicitly support an ideology of individualism. In the same way, methods that presume a separation of the researcher from the object of study (a subject/object binary) favor an instrumentalist attitude toward the world and a fundamental condition of alienation between the researcher and the researched.

This expanding realization of the political has had a significant impact on the posture of research. If inquiry is inevitably ideological, the major challenge is to pursue the research that most deeply expresses one's political and valuational investments (Smith, 1999). To paraphrase: If science is politics by other means, then we should pursue the inquiry that most effectively achieves our ends. It is also within the qualitative domain, with its lack of a fixed metaphysics, ontology, or epistemology, that the politically invested are most at liberty to generate methods uniquely crafted to their political or valuational commitments (Crawford & Kimmel, 1999).

It is this realization of the political potentials of methodology that now leads to significant tension within the qualitative sphere. We confront a range of highly partisan but quite separate commitments—to feminism, Marxism, lesbian and gay activism, ethnic consciousness-raising, and anticolonialism, among others.[2] Each group champions a particular vision of the good, and, by implication, those not participating in the effort are less than good and possibly obstructionist. Many also wish to see qualitative research become fully identified with a particular political position. For example, as Lincoln and Denzin (1994) propose: "A poststructural social science project seeks its external grounding not in science . . . but rather in a commitment to a post-Marxism and a feminism. . . . A good text is one that invokes these commitments. A good text exposes how race, class, and gender work their ways in the concrete lives of interacting individuals" (p. 579). For others, however, such cementing of the political agenda threatens to remove them from the dialogue. There are many whose humane concerns turn toward other groups—the aged, abused, ill, handicapped, and so on—and still others who find much to value in the long-standing traditions and use of their research to enlighten policy makers, organizational leaders, and so on.

It is here, however, that the same logic inviting unabashed ideological commitment begins to turn reflexively and critically upon these very commitments. If the postmodern turn undermines validity claims, it simultaneously opens a space for political or valuational investments; however, all reality posits serving to ground ideologically based research are simultaneously thrown into question. If one cannot legitimately claim truth through observational method, then accounts of poverty, marginality, oppression, and the like are similarly rendered rhetorical. Remove the rational and evidential foundations from empirical science and you simultaneously remove them from the sphere of value critique. And, as this form of critique has become progressively articulated, so has it produced a new range of tensions. The politically partisan turn on the postmodern arguments once favoring their causes to condemn them variously as "relativist," "conservative," and "irrelevant" (see, e.g., Reason, 1994).

From Partisanship to Polyvocality

Given such conflicts over matters of political partisanship, we again find opportunity for expanding the potential of qualitative methodology. Perhaps the most promising development in this domain is in conceptual and methodological explorations of polyvocality. There is a pervasive tendency for scholars—at least in their public writings—to presume coherence of self. Informed by Enlightenment conceptions of the rational and morally informed mind, they place a premium on coherence, integration, and clarity of purpose. The ideal scholar should know where he or she stands and should be responsible to his or her conception of the good. It is in this same sense that one may lay claim, for example, to being "a Marxist," "a masculinist," or a "Gray Panther." Yet, as the

postmodern literatures on "the death of self," social construction, dialogism, and the like have made increasingly clear, the conception of the singular or unified self is both intellectually and politically problematic. There is much to be gained by suspending such an orientation in favor of polyvocality. Specifically, we are encouraged in this case to recognize both within ourselves as scholars and within those who join our research as participants the multiplicity of competing and often contradictory values, political impulses, conceptions of the good, notions of desire, and senses of our "selves" as persons (Banister, 1999). We may each carry impulses toward Marxism, liberalism, anarchism, and so on, along with potentials for those ideologies most antagonistic to them.

This view of polyvocal subjects offers a significant means of going beyond the animosities pervading the qualitative arena. Rosie Braidotti (1995), a feminist theorist, avails this end with her conception of "nomadic subjectivity." A nomadic consciousness "entails a total dissolution of the notion of a center and consequently of originary sites of authentic identities of any kind" (p. 5). Chantal Mouffe (1993), a political theorist, suggests that a liberal socialist conception of citizenship "allows for the multiplicity of identities that constitute an individual" (p. 84). As we see it, the presumption of polyvocality opens the door to new forms of research methodology. We have already touched on methods in which multiple voices are given entry into the interpretive arena—voices of the research participants, the scientific literature, the private views of the investigators, the media, and so on (Ribbens & Edwards, 1998). However, the challenge of polyvocality is more radical in that we are sensitized to the possibility that all parties to the research may "contain multitudes." The question is whether researchers enable participating parties (and themselves) to give expression to their multiplicity—to the full complexity and range of contradictions that are typical of life in postindustrial society. There is movement in this direction (see, e.g., Jacobs, Munor, & Adams, 1995; Richardson, 1998; Travisano, 1998), but we have scarcely crossed the threshold. Two pieces that work toward this end involve the practice of overwriting, in which the author allows each overlay of description to erase, revise, and change her identities and activities. Among those under reconstruction are all of the principal actors—herself as stripper, dancer, wrestler, researcher, and professor (Ronai, 1998, 1999). Performance pieces that cut between character expositions and reflexive commentary also serve to undermine univocal subject positions (Gergen, in press).

◆ *New-Century Agendas*

Thus far, our discussion has remained closely interwoven with debates currently circulating within the qualitative arena, along with a focus on propitious opportunities for further development. In this final section we wish to explore three domains of future exploration that are congenially related to the preceding but considerably expand the domain of possibility. In our view, to follow these paths could potentially transform the conception of methodology, along with our understanding of social science and its subject matter. More important, we glimpse the potential of the social sciences to enter more actively into cultural life, transforming both common conceptions and forms of action. These are bracing challenges, but in our view the dialogues on qualitative methodology now deposit us on the threshold of just such reformations. We outline, then, the potentials of research as relational process, the vistas of technology, and the refiguring of the Western conception of self.

Research as Relational Process

As we find, the qualitative field has become a major source of creative innovation in modes of representation. Experiments in reflexivity, literary form, and multiple voicing, for example, have injected new vitality into the research endeavor. Yet there is good reason to press farther in such pursuits. Earlier, we stressed the inextricable relationship between research and representation: Any form of recording or describing is simultaneously a form of representation. At the same time, however, representation is inevitably "for an audience." To write, for example, is to invite an audience into a particular form of relationship. At a minimum, the act of writing serves to position both self and reader, to give each an identity and a role within a relationship. In this sense every form of representation—like a move in a dance—favors certain forms of relationship while discouraging others. Thus the various genres of social science writing—ranging from the mystical and the democratic to the ludic—all favor differing forms of relationship (Gergen, 1997). More broadly, we may say that our forms of representation in social sciences are themselves invitations to particular forms of cultural life.

In this context, we are enjoined to pay critical attention to our existing forms of representation and to consider future developments in methodology in terms of the kinds of relationships they favor. For example, much traditional writing tends to sustain structures of privilege: We write from the position of "knowing" to an audience positioned as "not knowing." The form tends toward the monological, inasmuch as the audience has no opportunity to participate and the choice of vocabulary and sentence structure tends to insulate the writing from examination by the broader public. We have also seen how various literary experiments within the qualitative domain open new forms of relationship. New forms of writing enable the author to abdicate the position of authority, for example, and invite the reader into a more egalitarian relationship. The immediate challenge for the future is that of expanding forms of representation to achieve specific relational ends. How can we set in motion particular processes of relationship, and more specifically processes with positive potentials for the culture at large?

It is here that we might ask, with Michelle Fine, "What elements of qualitative research are productively engaging toward democratic/revolutionary practices; toward community organizing; toward progressive social policy; toward democratizing public engagement with social critique?" (personal communication, 1998). To illustrate, in her work attempting to enhance the understanding of medical practitioners working with aging populations, Arlene Katz and her colleagues have established a panel of the elderly who serve as dialogical resources for students at the Harvard Medical School (see Katz & Shotter, 1996). The traditional "subjects of research" are positioned here as "cultural insiders" in matters of living with illness or its threat. In the same vein, researchers who provide ghetto inhabitants with cameras or video cameras and enable them to generate visual materials of their own choosing re-create the "research subject" as both learner and teacher/informer/performer. Further, the Public Conversations Project has generated methods for bringing together bitter antagonists (for example, prolife and prochoice advocates) for productive conversation (Becker, Chasin, Chasin, Herzig, & Roth, 1995; Chasin et al., 1996); David Cooperrider and his colleagues have developed a method of exchange, called "appreciative inquiry," that wholly transforms relationships among otherwise hostile members of an organization or community (see Cooperrider, 1990; Hammond, 1996; Hammond & Royal, 1998). In all these cases, new forms of relationship are forged.

There is a latent potential in these moves that, if allowed full expression, would wholly reconstitute the conception and practice of research. If we first abandon the long-standing scopic metaphor of *re/search* and replace it with the relational metaphor of *re/present,* then those formerly serving as the subjects of research and the readers of research outcomes become relational participants. And if we abandon the traditional goal of research as the accumulation of *products*—static or frozen findings—and replace it with the generation of communicative *process,* then a chief aim of research becomes that of establishing productive forms of relationship. The researcher ceases to be a passive bystander who generates representational products communicating to a minuscule audience of researchers. Rather, he or she becomes an active participant in forging generative, communicative relationships, in building ongoing dialogues and expanding the domain of civic deliberation. For example, much has been said about the value of global forums of exchange, national dialogues on prejudice, and the revitalization of communities (the "civil society"). Yet efforts to achieve these ends have been scattered and have infrequently included social science researchers. At present, our skills in creating social forms are meager; with this challenging reconceptualization of research we can and should become progenitors of relational practices. We shall return to this issue shortly.

The Challenge of the Technorevolution

The massive spawning of populist technology—including the telephone, radio, television, the automobile, mass-transit systems, jet travel, television, mass publication, and computer communication—may well constitute the most significant cultural transformation of the 20th century. To be sure, there is a rapidly growing corpus of work treating the myriad dimensions of this transformation. However, as yet there has been little exploration of the implications of such changes for research methodology. As William G. Tierney wrote to us, "I keep getting this sense that the way we do qualitative research over the next generation will change incredibly because of technology" (e-mail, April 10, 1998). We wholly concur. It is not simply that new sites for research are opened (e.g., Internet communication, MUDs), nor is it that as researchers we can now reach many populations more effectively and efficiently than heretofore. Rather, the technological watershed invites new ways of conceptualizing research methods, along with a refiguring of the very idea of research, including the identities of the researcher, researched, and audience. Let us speak to the conceptual issues first, and then turn to methodological implications.

Of preeminent significance for the researcher is the challenge of a *vanishing subject matter.* Traditional research methodologies are wedded to a conception of a relatively fixed object of study. One may spend several years in studying a topic within a given population or subculture; several years later the work may be published, with the hope that it will remain informative for the foreseeable future. The underlying presumption is that the subject matter will remain relatively stable and the research will retain relevance. Yet, with the global proliferation of communication technologies in particular, processes of meaning making are also accelerated. Values, attitudes, and opinions are all subject to rapid fluctuation, and with them patterns of related action. In effect, the temporal relevance of a research study is increasingly circumscribed, and the half-life of cultural analysis increasingly shortened. The question, then, is whether our traditional methods of research/representation are rapidly becoming irrelevant to contemporary conditions. How are we to justify studying various cultures or subcultures, for example, when the very conception of culture as a group of people who share an enduring pattern of meaning and action is being eroded (Hermans & Kempen, 1993)? Cultures, like those who make them up, are everywhere in motion (S. G. Jones, 1998).

At the outset the condition of vanishing subject matter invites researchers to envision themselves more as journalists than as traditional scientists—commentators on the contemporary as opposed to stonemasons at the edifice of progressive knowledge. Our mission should be that of contributing to the cultural dialogues on the here and now as opposed to the there and then. However, there are limits to this conclusion as well. In particular, as communication linkages are extended in all directions, we move into a condition of broadscale *interdependency of meaning*. The traditional conception of research methods in the social sciences was developed under conditions of relatively low technological saturation. In this circumstance, research subjects could make themselves available to scrutiny with little concern for repercussions. Not only were their identities typically shielded, but accounts of their activities (invariably value laden) were subject to great temporal delay and shared with only a small community of scientists. As we move into conditions of sophisticated communication technology, the situation changes dramatically. Traces of an individual's identity as research participant accumulate (consider the challenge of Internet privacy), and

the information a person conveys to a researcher may be immediately transmitted to an extended population. Further, these very technologies have also enhanced consciousness of the political and moral uses to which research is put (Ceglowski, in press). Thus the very fact of being invited to participate in a research project may generate defensive caution or may be seen as an opportunity to proselytize. As telephone researchers are well aware, there is now broad sensitivity to such questions as, What group is sponsoring this research, and how will it use the results? In a metaphoric sense, we approach a condition not unlike that of contemporary physics. No longer are we studying independent individuals (social atoms); instead, we are entering a field of relationships in which we as researchers are integers. And, as with the Heisenberg effect, as we embark on our research we alter the composition of the field. To act as a researcher is inherently to perturb the system of relationships, and, much like the butterfly wing in China, the effects of research itself may give rise to multiple unanticipated events at a distance.

Further deliberation on these issues is essential, and we see three significant research vistas opening to the social scientist. The first grows from our preceding proposal for *establishing communities of dialogue*. If the subject matter of social research is in continuous motion, and our research inevitably alters the flow, then there is further reason to generate research sites of active dialogue. The Internet serves as a significant context for such inquiry. Consider, for example, the political configuration of the World Wide Web. Thousands of political, religious, ethnic, and value-centered groups now offer sites informing and inviting participation. One can join with neo-Nazis, the KKK, or Druids as easily as one can participate in the Democratic, Republican, or Reform Party. Yet, while each of these groups is essentially centripetal in form, inviting others into a relatively closed circle of reiterative meanings, there are virtually no efforts to generate dialogue across sites of meaning making. Particularly in the case of antagonistic groups, there is a vital need for productive dialogue. In our view, research undertakings that would foster on-line interchange across lines of difference would be salutary. Further, for many persons who cannot physically be in contact with others with whom they share vital interests, computer-mediated interchanges would be highly desirable. Again, the research community could actively generate such resources.

The development of *conduit methods*—that is, technological efforts bringing into public visibility the voices, opinions, needs, and aspirations of various marginalized or suppressed groups of the world—would also be favored. Such efforts are already evident in print media. Social researchers have been highly effective over the years in representing the voices and conditions of numerous subaltern groups in writing. Yet these contributions are typically written for a professional audience with circumscribed circulation. With the availability of the Internet, the potentials for rendering visibility and effective communication are exponentially increased. An ample illustration of these potentials is provided by the revolutionary grassroots movement in the Mexican state of Chiapas. This group could have been eradicated by the government militia, but their ability to take their case before a global audience through the Internet radically altered their political circumstances. Numerous groups throughout the world came to their aid, intense communication was directed toward Mexican government officials, and government policies were significantly restrained. It is precisely such efforts that current social sciences curricula should facilitate.

Finally, and most challengingly, the technological transformation currently taking place invites the creation of what may be viewed as *living laboratories*. That is, the technological conditions allow social experimentation on an unprecedented scale—the creation of new conditions of interchange that could provide a sense of possible futures or, indeed, achieve those futures in fact. Just as in the case of politics in Chiapas, the grassroots culture points the way. Internet technologies have now spawned the development of myriad cybercommunities (see, e.g., S. G. Jones, 1998; Markham, 1998; Porter, 1997) and sites where

individuals may experiment with multiple identities or participate in new and imaginary ones (Rochlin, 1997; Turkle, 1995). As a research community, then, we are confronted with the possibility of moving from theoretical and political abstractions into the construction of virtual worlds that could shape the future. These virtual worlds could enable us to experiment with relational processes—such as forms of dialogue for reducing conflict, depression, or anomie—or, indeed, provide participants with new and growth-inviting experiences. In one relevant line of inquiry, the Dutch public administration scholar Paul Frissen and his colleagues work with policy makers concerned with how and whether the government should develop and enforce laws regarding Internet communication. Recognizing the rapid transformation taking place in the Internet world, Frissen and his colleagues have established a virtual community existing beyond the law of any particular nation. Without any public mandate, this community generates its own "laws" of Internet communication. Government officials are then invited into this world to speak with participants, sample the powers of the network, and explore its potentials as they unfold. It is through this immersion in this world—virtual yet potentially palpable in consequence—that both participants and policy makers enrich their perspectives (Gergen, 2000). In our view, the possibilities for creating experimental worlds are enormous.

Qualitative Methods and the Reconstruction of Self

Most qualitative methodologies are deeply infused with individualist conceptions and ideologies. To focus research on the individual's experience, feelings, identity, suffering, or life story, for example, is to presume the primacy of the individual mind. To employ methodology that attempts to give voice to "the other" is already to favor a metaphysics of self/other difference. Similarly, forms of representation that favor hierarchy and monologue tend toward reifying the "knowing one." Even the recognition of authorship on the research report constructs a world of separate, self-contained individuals. By and large, qualitative methods sustain a posture of methodological and ideological individualism. At the same time, as we have outlined above, with the influx of postmodern, constructionist, and dialogical formulations, we have become increasingly aware of the limitations—both conceptual and ideological—of the individualist tradition. Further, as many of the qualitative innovations begin to suggest, there are alternatives to this tradition. In our view, the most important of these alternatives may be termed *relational*. As our methodologies become increasingly sensitive to the relationship of researchers to their subjects as dialogical and co-constructive, the relationship of researchers to their audiences as interdependent, and the negotiation of meaning within any relationship as potentially ramifying outward into the society, individual agency ceases to be our major concern. We effectively create the reality of relational process.

It is thus that innovations in co-constructed narratives, multivoiced methods, participatory performance, conjoint and distributed representation, and participatory action research, for example, do far more than expand the methodological arena. Rather, in subverting methodological individualism they begin to generate a new form of consciousness. It is not the private mind that is celebrated, but integral connectivity. Dialogical methodologies nicely illustrate the point. For example, Mary Gergen (in press) introduced the topic of menopause to a discussion group of eight women as a means of counteracting the medical model of menopause and opening new spaces of meaning making. Through extended dialogue, the group generated new and more positive visions of the aging process. In a similar vein, Frigga Haug and her students (1987; Crawford, Kippax, Onyx, Gault, & Benton, 1992) arranged situations in which women shared their stories of their emotional development. Through their mutual dialogues and interpretive sessions, they were able to reconstruct their past and to generate a sense of how the culture creates femininity. In these cases the dialogue was circumscribed to the researcher/participants. To extend the preceding

concern with research as relationship, one can see the potential for using research to generate dialogue that expands as it moves outward from the originary site. The goal of the research becomes one of inciting dialogue that may undergo continuous change as it moves through an extended network.

In our view, these are but beginning moves in what should become a new vocabulary of research methodology and ultimately a relational reconceptualization of self. Such methodologies will become more integral to emerging concepts of communal memory, distributed cognition, and relational emotion. Invited will be concepts specifically illuminating the relational process out of which the very concept of individual mind emerges. With both practices and theory set in motion, the qualitative community may come to play a vital role in cultural transformation.

◆ Conclusion

In their introduction to the 1994 edition of the *Handbook of Qualitative Research,* Denzin and Lincoln aver that "we are in a new age where messy, uncertain, multivoiced texts, cultural criticisms, and new experimental works will become more common" (p. 15). At the same time, they suggest that "the field of qualitative research is defined by a series of tensions, contradictions, and hesitations" (p. 15). This analysis lends strong support to their prognoses. Along with the critique and experimentation, the tensions, contradictions, and hesitations they mention are present, but in our view, they are scarcely signs of deterioration. Rather, it is from within this matrix of uncertainty, where we are unceasingly crossing the boundaries of established enclaves—appropriating, reflecting, creating—that the vitality of qualitative inquiry is drawn. It is here that we locate the innovative power that is transforming the face of the social sciences. If we can avoid impulses toward elimination, the rage to order, and the desire for unity and singularity, we can anticipate the continued flourishing of qualitative inquiry, full of serendipitous incidents and generative expansions. In particular, if we bear out the implications of the increasing centrality of relationship over individuals—and realize these implications practically within the emerging spheres of technology—we may effectively participate in the reconstruction of the social sciences and alteration of the trajectories of the cultures in which we participate.

■ Notes

1. For further discussion of these arguments and their implications for the social sciences, see Gergen (1994, 1999).

2. Michelle Fine (personal communication, 1998) questioned this line: "Are only feminism, Marxism, lesbian, gays . . . political? What happened to good old right-wing, mainstream, run-of-the-mill psychology—isn't that deeply political? Are the rules different with explicitly political (or left) work?"

■ References

Anderson, E. (1978). *A place on the corner.* Chicago: University of Chicago Press.

Anderson, E. (1990). *Streetwise: Race, class, and change in an urban community.* Chicago: University of Chicago Press.

Anderson, E. (1999). *Code of the street.* New York: W. W. Norton.

Anderson, H. (1997). *Conversation, language, and possibilities: A postmodern approach to therapy.* New York: HarperCollins.

Austin, D. (1996). Kaleidoscope: The same and different. In C. Ellis & A. P. Bochner (Eds.), *Composing ethnography: Alternative forms of qualitative writing* (pp. 206-230). Walnut Creek, CA: AltaMira.

Banister, E. M. (1999). Evolving reflexivity: Negotiating meaning of women's midlife experience. *Qualitative Inquiry, 5,* 3-23.

Becker, C., Chasin, L., Chasin, R., Herzig, M., & Roth, S. (1995). From stuck debate to new conversation on controversial issues: A report from the Public Conversations Pro-

ject. *Journal of Feminist Family Therapy, 7,* 143-163.

Behar, R. (1996). *The vulnerable observer: Anthropology that breaks your heart.* Boston: Beacon.

Behar, R., & Gordon, D. A. (Eds.). (1995). *Women writing culture.* Berkeley: University of California Press.

Belenky, M. F., Clinchy, B. M., Goldberger, N. R., & Tarule, J. M. (1986). *Women's ways of knowing: The development of self, voice, and mind.* New York: Basic Books.

Blumenfeld-Jones, D. S. (1995). Dance as a mode of research representation. *Qualitative Inquiry, 1,* 391-401.

Bohan, J. (Ed.). (1992). *Seldom seen, rarely heard: Women's place in psychology.* Boulder, CO: Westview.

Bohan, J. (1993). Regarding gender: Essentialism, constructionism, and feminist psychology. *Psychology of Women Quarterly, 17,* 5-21.

Braidotti, R. (1995). *Nomadic subjects: Embodiment and sexual difference in contemporary feminist theory.* New York: Columbia University Press.

Brown, L. M., & Gilligan, C. (1992). *Meeting at the crossroads: Women's psychology and girls' development.* Cambridge, MA: Harvard University Press.

Bruner, J. (1986). *Actual minds: Possible worlds.* Cambridge, MA: Harvard University Press.

Bruner, J. (1990). *Acts of meaning.* Cambridge, MA: Harvard University Press.

Butler, J. (1990). *Gender trouble: Feminism and the subversion of identity.* New York: Routledge.

Carlson, M. (1996). *Performance: A critical introduction.* New York: Routledge.

Case, S.-E. (1997). *The domain-matrix; Performing lesbian at the end of print culture.* Bloomington: Indiana University Press.

Case, S.-E., Brett, P., & Foster, S. L. (Eds.). (1995). *Cruising the performative: Interventions into the representation of ethnicity, nationality, and sexuality.* Bloomington: Indiana University Press.

Ceglowski, D. (in press). *Research as relationship.* New York: Teachers College Press.

Chasin, R., Herzig, M., Roth, S., Chasin, L., Becher, C., & Stains, R., Jr. (1996). From diatribe to dialogue on divisive public issues: Approaches drawn from family therapy. *Mediation Quarterly, 13,* 4.

Clark, C. D. (1996). Interviewing children in qualitative research: A show and tell. *Canadian Journal of Marketing Research, 15,* 74-78.

Clough, P. T. (1997). Autotelecommunication and autoethnography: A reading of Carolyn Ellis's *Final negotiations. Sociological Quarterly, 38,* 95-110.

Communication Studies 298. (1999). Shopping for family. *Qualitative Inquiry, 5,* 147-180.

Cooperrider, D. L. (1990). Positive image, positive action: The affirmative basis of organizing. In S. Srivastva & D. L. Cooperrider (Eds.), *Appreciative management and leadership: The power of positive thought and action in organizations.* San Francisco: Jossey-Bass.

Cooperrider, D. L., & Dutton, J. E. (Eds.). (1999). *Organizational dimensions of global change: No limits to cooperation.* Thousand Oaks, CA: Sage.

Crawford, J., Kippax, S., Onyx, J., Gault, U., & Benton, P. (1992). *Emotion and gender: Constructing meaning from memory.* London: Sage.

Crawford, M., & Kimmel, E. (Eds.). (1999). Innovative methods in feminist psychology [Special issue]. *Psychology of Women Quarterly, 23*(4).

Denzin, N. K. (1997). *Interpretive ethnography: Ethnographic practices for the 21st century.* Thousand Oaks, CA: Sage.

Denzin, N. K., & Lincoln, Y. S. (1994). Introduction: Entering the field of qualitative research. In N. K. Denzin & Y. S. Lincoln (Eds.), *Handbook of qualitative research* (pp. 1-17). Thousand Oaks, CA: Sage.

Diversi, M. (1998). Glimpses of street life: Representing lived experience through short stories. *Qualitative Inquiry, 4,* 131-147.

Donmoyer, R., & Yennie-Donmoyer, J. (1995). Data as drama: Reflections on the use of readers theater as a mode of qualitative data display. *Qualitative Inquiry, 1,* 402-428.

Ellis, C., & Bochner, A. P. (Eds.). (1996). *Composing ethnography: Alternative forms of qualitative writing.* Walnut Creek, CA: AltaMira.

Ellis, C., Kiesinger, C. E., & Tillmann-Healy, L. (1997). Interactive interviewing: Talking about emotional experience. In R. Hertz (Ed.), *Reflexivity and voice* (pp. 119-149). Thousand Oaks, CA: Sage.

Foucault, M. (1979). *Discipline and punish: The birth of the prison* (A. Sheridan, Trans.). New York: Vintage.

Foucault, M. (1980). *Power/knowledge: Selected interviews and other writings, 1972-1977* (C. Gordon, Ed.; L. Marshall, J. Mepham, & K. Soper, Trans.). New York: Pantheon.

Fox, K. V. (1996). Silent voices: A subversive reading of child sexual abuse. In C. Ellis & A. P. Bochner (Eds.), *Composing ethnography: Alternative forms of qualitative writing* (pp. 330-356). Walnut Creek, CA: AltaMira.

Franklin, M. B. (1997). Making sense: Interviewing and narrative representation. In M. Gergen & S. N. Davis (Eds.), *Toward a new psychology of gender* (pp. 99-116). New York: Routledge.

Garratt, D., & Hodkinson, P. (1998). Can there be criteria for selecting research criteria? A hermeneutical analysis of an inescapable dilemma. *Qualitative Inquiry, 4,* 515-539.

Georgi, A. (1994). *Phenomenology and psychological research.* Pittsburgh, PA: Duquesne University Press.

Gergen, K. J. (1994). *Realities and relationships: Soundings in social construction.* Cambridge, MA: Harvard University Press.

Gergen, K. J. (1997). Who speaks and who responds in the human sciences? *History of the Human Sciences, 10,* 151-173.

Gergen, K. J. (1999). *An invitation to social construction.* Thousand Oaks, CA: Sage.

Gergen, K. J. (2000). *The saturated self* (2nd ed.). New York: Perseus.

Gergen, K. J., & Gergen, M. M. (1991). From theory to reflexivity in research practice. In F. Steier (Ed.), *Method and reflexivity: Knowing as systemic social construction* (pp. 76-95). London: Sage.

Gergen, M. M. (1992). Life stories: Pieces of a dream. In G. Rosenwald & R. Ochberg (Eds.), *Storied lives* (pp. 127-144). New Haven, CT: Yale University Press.

Gergen, M. M. (in press). *Impious improvisations: Feminist reconstructions in psychology.* Thousand Oaks, CA: Sage.

Gergen, M. M., Chrisler, J. C., & LoCicero, A. (1999). Innovative methods: Resources for research, teaching and publishing. *Psychology of Women Quarterly, 23*(4).

Hammond, S. A. (1996). *The thin book of appreciative inquiry.* Plano, TX: CSS.

Hammond, S. A., & Royal, C. (Eds.). (1998). *Lessons from the field: Applying appreciative inquiry.* Plano, TX: Practical Press.

Haraway, D. J. (1988). Situated knowledges: The science question in feminism and the privilege of partial perspective. *Feminist Studies, 14,* 575-599.

Harding, S. (1986). *The science question in feminism.* Ithaca, NY: Cornell University Press.

Harding, S. (1991). *Whose science? Whose knowledge? Thinking from women's lives.* Ithaca, NY: Cornell University Press.

Haug, F., et al. (1987). *Female sexualization: A collective work of memory* (E. Carter, Trans.). New York: Verso.

Hermans, H. J. M., & Kempen, H. J. G. (1993). *The dialogical self: Meaning as movement.* New York: Academic Press.

Hertz, R. (Ed.). (1997). *Reflexivity and voice.* Thousand Oaks, CA: Sage.

hooks, b. (1990). *Yearning: Race, gender, and cultural politics.* Boston: South End.

Jacobs, M.-E., Munor, P., & Adams, N. (1995). Palimpsest: (Re)reading women's lives. *Qualitative Inquiry, 1,* 327-345.

Jipson, J., & Paley, N. (Eds.). (in press). *Daredevil research.* New York: Peter Lang.

Jones, S. G. (Ed.). (1998). *Cybersociety 2.0.* Thousand Oaks, CA: Sage.

Jones, S. H. (1998). Kaleidoscope notes: Writing women's music and organizational culture. *Qualitative Inquiry, 4,* 148-177.

Jones, S. H. (1999). Torch. *Qualitative Inquiry, 5,* 235-250.

Katz, A. M., & Shotter, J. (1996). Hearing the patient's "voice": Toward a social poetics in diagnostic interviews. *Social Science and Medicine, 43,* 919-931.

Kiesinger, C. E. (1998). From interview to story: Writing Abbie's life. *Qualitative Inquiry, 4,* 71-95.

Komesaroff, P., Rothfield, P., & Daly, J. (1997). *Reinterpreting menopause: Cultural and philosophical issues.* New York: Routledge.

Landrine, H. (Ed.). (1995). *Bringing cultural diversity to feminist psychology: Theory, research, and practice.* Washington, DC: American Psychological Association.

Lather, P. (1991). *Getting smart: Feminist research and pedagogy with/in the postmodern.* New York: Routledge.

Lather, P. (1993). Fertile obsession: Validity after poststructuralism. *Sociological Quarterly, 34,* 673-693.

Lather, P., & Smithies, C. (1997). *Troubling the angels: Women living with HIV/AIDS.* Boulder, CO: Westview.

Lincoln, Y. S. (1995). Emerging criteria for quality in qualitative and interpretive inquiry. *Qualitative Inquiry, 1,* 275-289.

Lincoln, Y. S. (1998). From understanding to action: New imperatives, new criteria, new methods for interpretive researchers. *Theory and Research in Social Education, 26,* 12-29.

Lincoln, Y. S., & Denzin, N. K. (1994). The fifth moment. In N. K. Denzin & Y. S. Lincoln (Eds.), *Handbook of qualitative research* (pp. 575-586). Thousand Oaks, CA: Sage.

Lykes, M. B. (1996). Meaning making in a context of genocide and silencing. In M. B. Lykes, A. Banuazizi, R. Liem, & M. Morris (Eds.), *Myths about the powerless: Contesting social inequalities* (pp. 159-178). Philadelphia: Temple University Press.

Marcus, G. E. (1998). *Ethnography through thick and thin: A new research imaginary for anthropology's changing professional culture.* Princeton, NJ: Princeton University Press.

Markham, A. (1998). *Life online: Researching real experience in virtual space.* Thousand Oaks, CA: Sage.

McTaggart, R. (Ed.). (1997a). *Participatory action research: International contexts and consequences.* Albany: State University of New York Press.

McTaggart, R. (1997b). Reading the collection. In R. McTaggart (Ed.), *Participatory action research: International contexts and consequences* (pp. 1-24). Albany: State University of New York Press.

Mienczakowski, J. (1996). An ethnographic act: The construction of consensual theater. In C. Ellis & A. P. Bochner (Eds.), *Composing ethnography: Alternative forms of qualitative writing* (pp. 244-266). Walnut Creek, CA: AltaMira.

Miller, J. B., & Stiver, I. P. (1997). *The healing connection: How women form relationships in therapy and in life.* Boston: Beacon.

Morawski, J. G. (1994). *Practicing feminisms, reconstructing psychology: Notes on a liminal science.* Ann Arbor: University of Michigan Press.

Morris, R. C. (1995). All made up: Performance theory and the new anthropology of sex and gender. *Annual Review of Anthropology, 24,* 567-592.

Mouffe, C. (1993). Liberal socialism and pluralism: Which citizenship? In J. Squires (Ed.), *Principled positions: Postmodernism and the rediscovery of value.* London: Lawrence & Wishart.

Moustakas, C. (1994). *Phenomenological research methods.* Thousand Oaks, CA: Sage.

Penley, C., & Ross, A. (1985). Interview with Trinh T. Minh-ha. *Camera Obscura, 13-14,* 87-103.

Porter, D. (Ed.). (1997). *Internet culture.* New York: Routledge.

Reason, P. (1994). Three approaches to participative inquiry. In N. K. Denzin & Y. S. Lincoln (Eds.), *Handbook of qualitative research* (pp. 324-339). Thousand Oaks, CA: Sage.

Reinharz, S. (1992). *Feminist methods in social research.* New York: Oxford University Press.

Ribbens, J., & Edwards, R. (Eds.). (1998). *Feminist dilemmas in qualitative research: Public knowledge and private lives.* Thousand Oaks, CA: Sage.

Richardson, L. (1997). *Fields of play: Constructing an academic life.* New Brunswick, NJ: Rutgers University Press.

Richardson, L. (1998). Meta-jeopardy. *Qualitative Inquiry, 4,* 464-468.

Rinehart, R. (1998). Fictional methods in ethnography: Believability, specks of glass, and Chekhov. *Qualitative Inquiry, 4,* 200-224.

Rochlin, G. I. (1997). *Trapped in the Net: The unanticipated consequences of computerization.* Princeton, NJ: Princeton University Press.

Ronai, C. R. (1998). Sketching with Derrida: An ethnography of a researcher/erotic dancer. Qualitative Inquiry, 4, 405-420.

Ronai, C. R. (1999). The next night *sou rature:* Wrestling with Derrida's mimesis. *Qualitative Inquiry, 5,* 114-129.

Russell, G. M., & Bohan, J. S. (1999). Hearing voices: The use of research and the politics of change. *Psychology of Women Quarterly,* 23(4).

Said, E. W. (1978). *Orientalism.* New York: Pantheon.

Sarbin, T. (Ed.). (1986). *Narrative psychology: The storied nature of human conduct.* New York: Praeger.

Smith, L. T. (in press). *De-colonizing methodology: Research and indigenous peoples.* London: Zed.

Smith, P. (1999). Food truck's party hat. *Qualitative Inquiry, 5,* 244-262.

Smyth, A. (1991). The floozie in the jacuzzi: The problematics of culture and identity for an Irish woman. *Feminist Studies, 17,* 7-28.

Strauss, A. L., & Corbin, J. (1990). *Basics of qualitative research: Grounded theory procedures and techniques.* Newbury Park, CA: Sage.

Strauss, A. L., & Corbin, J. (1994). Grounded theory methodology: An overview. In N. K. Denzin & Y. S. Lincoln (Eds.), *Handbook of qualitative research* (pp. 273-285). Thousand Oaks, CA: Sage.

Tierney, W. G., & Lincoln, Y. S. (Eds.). (1997). *Representation and the text: Re-framing the narrative voice.* Albany: State University of New York Press.

Travisano, R. V. (1998). On becoming Italian American: An autobiography of an ethnic identity. *Qualitative Inquiry, 4,* 540-563.

Turkle, S. (1995). *Life on the screen: Identity in the age of the Internet.* New York: Simon & Schuster.

Van Maanen, J. (Ed.). (1995). *Representation in ethnography.* Thousand Oaks, CA: Sage.

Visweswaran, K. (1994). *Fictions of feminist ethnography.* Minneapolis: University of Minnesota Press.

41

THE SEVENTH MOMENT

Out of the Past

◆ Yvonna S. Lincoln and Norman K. Denzin

A s we have argued in our conclusion to the first edition of the *Handbook of Qualitative Research,* writing the present is always dangerous, a biased project conditioned by distorted readings of the past and utopian hopes for the future. In what follows we once again sketch our hopeful vision of the future of qualitative research. This vision is based on our reading of the seventh moment. We begin by delineating the central characteristics of this moment and the problems that define it. We conclude with predictions about the seventh moment based on our readings of the present.[1]

Four theses organize our discussion. First, as we have repeatedly observed, the history of qualitative research is defined more by breaks and ruptures than by a clear, evolutionary, progressive movement from one stage to the next. These breaks and ruptures move in cycles and phases, so that what is passé today may be in

vogue a decade from now, and vice versa. Just as the postmodern, for example, reacts to the modern, someday there may well be a retro-postmodern phase that extols Boas, Mead, Benedict, Strauss, Becker, Goffman, and the Chicago school and finds the current postexperimental, "messy" moment flawed and unacceptable.

Our second assumption builds on the tensions that now define qualitative research. There is an elusive center emerging in this contradictory, tension-riddled enterprise. We seem to be moving farther and farther away from grand narratives and single, overarching ontological, epistemological, and methodological paradigms. The center lies in the humanistic commitment of the qualitative researcher to study the world always from the perspective of the gendered, historically situated, interacting individual. From this complex commitment flows the liberal and radical politics of qualitative research. Action, feminist, clinical, constructionist, cultural studies, queer, and critical race theory researchers are all united on this point. They all share the belief that a politics of liberation must always begin with the perspective, desires, and dreams of those individuals and groups who have been oppressed by the larger ideological, economic, and political forces of a society or a historical moment.

This commitment defines an ever-present, but shifting, center in the discourses of qualitative research. The center shifts as new, previously oppressed or silenced voices enter the discourse. Thus, for example, feminists and critical race researchers have articulated their own relationship to the postpositivist, poststructuralist, and critical paradigms. These new articulations then refocus and redefine previous ontologies, epistemologies, and methodologies, including empiricism, postpositivism, and postmodernism.

Third, we anticipate a continued performance turn in qualitative inquiry, with more and more writers performing their texts for others. As ethnographic stagings, performances are always "enmeshed in moral matters" (Conquergood, 1985, p. 2). Such performances ask audiences to take a stand on the performances and their meanings and, indeed, to join the performances and the creation of meaning. In these productions, performers and the audience members become cultural critics. If culture is an ongoing performance, then performers bring the spaces, meanings, ambiguities, and contradictions of culture critically alive in their performances (Conquergood, 1985). The performed text is one of qualitative research's last frontiers. It is a version of Victor Turner's (1986, p. 25) "liminal space," an old, but new, border to be crossed. When fully embraced, this crossing will forever transform qualitative research methodology. It will serve, at the same time, to redefine the meanings of this project in its other moments and formations.

Fourth, the future, the seventh moment, is concerned with moral discourse, and with the development of sacred textualities. The seventh moment asks that the social sciences and the humanities become sites for critical conversations about democracy, race, gender, class, nation, freedom, and community.

These four theses suggest that only the broad outlines of the future, the seventh moment, can be predicted. Returning to our opening metaphor of the bridge, we seek to outline a project that connects the past with the present and the future. In charting this future, we group our discussion around the following themes, or issues: text and voice; the existential, sacred performance text; the return to narrative as a political act; text, reflexivity, and being vulnerable in the text; and inquiry as a moral act, ethics, and critical moral consciousness. These are the hallmarks of the sixth and seventh moments.

◆ Defining the Present

Recall our definition of this sprawling field. Slightly rephrased, it reads:

> Qualitative research is an interdisciplinary, transdisciplinary, and sometimes counterdisciplinary field. It crosscuts the humanities, the social sciences, and the physical sciences. Qualitative research is many things at the same time. It is multiparadigmatic in focus. Its practitioners are sensitive to the value of the multimethod approach. They are committed to the naturalistic perspective and to the interpretive understanding of human experience. At the same time, the field is inherently political and shaped by multiple ethical and political allegiances.
>
> Qualitative research embraces two tensions at the same time. On the one hand, it is drawn to a broad, interpretive, postexperimental, postmodern, feminist, and critical sensibility. On the other hand, it is shaped to more narrowly defined positivist, postpositivist, humanistic, and naturalistic conceptions of human experience and its analysis.

In the seventh moment all of these tensions will continue to operate as the field confronts and continues to define itself in the face of six fundamental issues that are embedded in these tensions.

The first issue involves the collapse of foundationalism. The present moment is characterized, in part, by a continuing critique of postpositivism and by poststructuralism and postmodernism. This critique is coupled with ongoing self-criticism and self-appraisal. Every contributor to this volume has reflectively wrestled with the location of his or her topic in the present moment, discussing its relationship to postpositivist and antifoundational formulations.

On this, Smith and Deemer (Chapter 34) remind us that the "demise of empiricism" created a new space for human interpretation and, in turn, for new criteria for judging and honoring human knowledge in all its forms. As Smith and Deemer make clear, relativism is not about paradigm choice; it is about the way we are in the world, about living contingent lives, about having to find new rationales for the judgments we make, because absolutes and foundationalist principles are little more than smoke and mirrors.

The second and third issues are what we have called the crises of representation and legitimation. These two crises speak, respectively, to the Other and the representation of the Other in our texts and to the authority we claim for our texts. Although these crises have circulated widely for two decades, their critiques have only recently reached full flower. Fourth, there is the continued emergence of a cacophony of voices speaking with varying agendas from specific gender, race, class, ethnic, and Third World perspectives.

Fifth, throughout its history, qualitative research has been defined in terms of shifting scientific, moral, sacred, and religious discourses. Vidich and Lyman clearly establish this fact in the history of colonial ethnography that they present in Chapter 2 of this volume. Since the Enlightenment, science and religion have been separated, but only at the ideological level, for in practice, as Vidich and Lyman argue, religion has constantly informed science and the scientific project. The divisions between these two systems of meaning are becoming more and more blurred. Critics increasingly see science from within a magical, interpretive framework (Rosaldo, 1989, p. 219), whereas others imagine a sacred epistemology (Bateson,

1979). Others are moving science away from its empiricist foundations and closer to a critical, interpretivist project that stresses ethics and moral standards of evaluation (Clough, 1992, pp. 136-137; see also Clough, 1998). Sixth, conceptualizing inquiry as a moral act returns our dialogue to the topics of ethics, vulnerability, and truth.

To summarize: The tensions that surround these six issues and the strategies that are developed to address them will continue to define the center and the margins of qualitative research well into the first decade of the 21st century. We begin with a discussion of the present.

◆ Coping With the Present

Of the following, we continue to be certain:

- The qualitative researcher is not an objective, authoritative, politically neutral observer standing outside and above the text.
- The qualitative researcher is "historically positioned and locally situated [as] an all-too-human [observer] of the human condition" (Bruner, 1993, p. 1).
- Meaning is "radically plural, always open, and . . . there is politics in every account" (Bruner, 1993, p. 1).
- Qualitative inquiry is properly conceptualized as a civic, participatory, collaborative project. This joins the researcher and the researched in an ongoing moral dialogue.

These certainties shape the questions we have listed in our introduction to Part VI.

Correcting Excesses and Revisiting the Past

This moment addresses these certainties in three ways. First, it continues to sharpen the above critique while, second, it attempts to correct its excesses. Qualitative research, like other scholarly domains, displays a tendency to move from one intellectual fashion to another, from critical race theory to queer theory, from semiotics to poststructuralism, from postmodernism to posthumanism, and so on. In such moves there is often a tendency to reject wholesale entire theoretical perspectives, or paradigms, as if postpositivism were passé, for example. It should not work this way. There is a real need to return, as Bruner (1993) argues, to "the originals of out-of-fashion texts" (p. 24). Such a return is necessary for two reasons: First, we need to relearn these texts and see if standard criticisms of them still hold today; second, we need to study the best works from these traditions so as to understand how the masters in a given "passé" perspective in fact did their work.

It must be noted that revisiting works from earlier historical moments operates at different levels of abstraction. Although colonialist, positivist ethnography may be passé, the basic strategies and techniques of case studies, ethnographies, observation, interviewing, and textual analysis still form the basis for sixth- and seventh-moment research. In a parallel vein, although certain of the assumptions of the grounded theory approach may be criticized, the generic method of building interpretations up out of observations and interactions with the world will not change.

Third, as we have argued in the first edition of this *Handbook,* it is time to get on with the multidisciplinary project called qualitative research. Too much critique will stifle this project. This critique, it must be noted, assumes two forms, and both can be counterproductive. Endless self-referential criticisms by the poststructuralist can produce mountains of texts, with few referents to concrete human experience. Such are not needed. The same conclusion holds for positivist and postpositivist criticisms of poststructuralism (and the responses to these criticisms). These criticisms and exchanges can operate at a level of abstraction, with opposing sides preaching to the already converted. No dialogue occurs, and the discourse does little to help the people who seek to engage the world empirically.

The basic issue is simple: How best to describe and interpret the experiences of other peoples and cultures? The problems of representation and legitimation flow from this commitment.

The Crisis of Representation

As indicated above, this crisis asks the questions, Who is the Other? Can we ever hope to speak authentically of the experience of the Other, or an Other? And if not, how do we create a social science that includes the Other? The short answer to these questions is that we move to including the Other in the larger research processes that we have developed. For some, this means participatory, or collaborative, research and evaluation efforts (see in this volume Greenwood & Levin, Chapter 3; Ladson-Billings, Chapter 9; Kemmis & McTaggart, Chapter 22; Miller & Crabtree, Chapter 23; Greene, Chapter 38; Rist, Chapter 39). These activities can occur in a variety of institutional sites, including clinical, educational, corporate, and social welfare settings.

For others, it means a form of liberatory investigation wherein Others are trained to engage in their own social and historical interrogative efforts and then are assisted in devising answers to questions of historical and contemporary oppression that are rooted in the values and cultural artifacts that characterize their communities. In this volume, Kemmis and McTaggart (Chapter 22) and Greene (Chapter 38) discuss various strategies for undertaking such inquiries, including the major different forms of participatory action and evaluation research.

For yet other social scientists, including the Other means becoming coauthors in narrative adventures. And for still others, it means constructing what are called "experimental," or "messy," texts where multiple voices speak (see in this volume Ellis & Bochner, Chapter 28; Richardson, Chapter 36), often in conflict, and where readers are left to sort out which experiences speak to their personal lives. For still others, it means presenting to the inquiry and policy community a series of autohistories, personal narratives, lived experiences, poetic representations, and sometimes fictive and/or fictional texts (see in this volume Tierney, Chapter 20; Beverley, Chapter 21; Richardson, Chapter 36) that allow the Other to speak for her- or himself. The inquirer or evaluator becomes merely the connection joining the field text, the research text, and the consuming community in making certain that such voices are heard. Sometimes, increasingly, it is the Institutionalized Other who speaks, especially as the Other gains access to the knowledge-producing corridors of power and achieves *entrée* into the particular group of elites known as intellectuals and academics or faculty. In Chapter 9 of this volume, Gloria Ladson-Billings elaborates the issues that are involved when this happens.

The point is that both the Other and more mainstream social scientists recognize that there is no such thing as unadulterated truth; that speaking from a faculty, an institution of higher education, or a corporate perspective automatically means speaking from a privileged and powerful vantage point; and that this vantage point is one to which many do not have access, through either social station or education.

Virginia Olesen (Chapter 8) speaks of the difficulties involved in representing the experiences of the Other about whom texts are written. Writing from a critical feminist perspective, she argues that a major contradiction exists in this project, despite the qualitative researcher's desire to engage in egalitarian research characterized by authenticity, reciprocity, and trust. This is so because actual differences of power, knowledge, and structural mobility still exist in the researcher-subject relationship. The subject is always at grave risk of manipulation and betrayal by the ethnographer. In addition, there is the crucial fact that the final product is too often controlled by the researcher, no matter how much it has been modified or influenced by the subject. Thus even when research is written from the perspective of the Other—for example, women writing about women—the women doing the writing may perpetuate the very power relations they most oppose. A proper feminist solution requires a merger of politics with collaborative, participatory scholarship.

The Author's Place in the Text

The feminist solution clarifies the issue of the author's place in the interpretations that are written. This problem is directly connected to the problem of representation. It is often phrased in terms of a false dichotomy—that is, "the extent to which the personal self should have a place in the scientific scholarly text" (Bruner, 1993, p. 2). This false division between the personal and the ethnographic self rests on the assumption that it is possible for an author to write a text that does not bear the traces of its author. Of course, this is impossible. As Geertz (1988) has demonstrated, all texts are personal statements.

The correct phrasing of this issue turns on the amount of the personal, subjective, poetic self that is openly given in the text. As Ellis and Bochner (Chapter 28) and Richardson (Chapter 36) observe, there are many ways to return the author openly to the qualitative research text. Fictional narratives of the self may be written. Performance texts can be produced. Dramatic readings can be given. Field interviews can be transformed into poetic texts and poetry; short stories and plays can be written as well (McCall, Chapter 15). The author can engage in a dialogue with those studied. The author may write through a narrator, "directly as a character . . . or through multiple characters, or one character may speak in many voices, or the writer may come in and then go out of the [text]" (Bruner, 1993, p. 6).

The Crisis of Legitimation

It is clear that critical race theory, queer theory, and feminist arguments are moving farther and farther away from postpositivist models of validity and textual authority. This is the crisis of legitimation that follows the collapse of foundational epistemologies. This so-called crisis arose when anthropologists and other social scientists addressed the authority of the text. By *the authority of the text* we reference the claim any text makes to being accurate, true, and complete—a "God's-eye view." Is a text, that is, faithful to the context and the individuals it is supposed to represent? Does the text have the right to assert that it is a report to the larger world that addresses not only the researcher's interests, but also the interests of those studied?

This is not an illegitimate set of questions, and it affects all of us and the work that we do. Although social scientists might enter the question from many different angles, all of them confront these twin crises.

◆ A Bridge Into the Future: Toward a Sacred Discourse

We imagine a form of qualitative inquiry in the 21st century that is simultaneously minimal, existential, autoethnographic, vulnerable, performative, and critical. This form of inquiry erases traditional distinctions among epistemology, ethics, and aesthetics; nothing is value-free. It seeks to ground the self in a sense of the sacred, to connect the ethical, respectful self dialogically to nature and the worldly environment (Christians, 1995, p. 129). It seeks to embed this self in deeply storied histories of sacred spaces and local places, to illuminate the unity of the self in its relationship to the reconstructed, moral, and sacred natural world (see Abram, 1996, p. 269; Christians, 1998, p. 3; Kittredge, 1996, p. 4; Macnaghten & Urry, 1998, p. 7). This model of inquiry seeks a sacred epistemology that recognizes the essential ethical unity of mind and nature (Bateson, 1972, pp. 336-337; Bateson, 1979, p. 213; Bateson & Bateson, 1987, pp. 8-9, 11; Christians, 1998, p. 3). A sacred, existential epistemology places us in a noncompetitive, nonhierarchical relationship to the earth, to nature, and to the larger world (Bateson, 1972, p. 335; Reason, 1993). This sacred epistemology is political, presuming a feminist, communitarian moral ethic stressing the values of empowerment, shared governance, care, solidarity, love, community, covenant, morally involved observers, and civic transformation (Denzin, 1997, p. 275; Lincoln, 1995, p. 287).

This epistemology recovers the moral values that were excluded by the Enlightenment science project (Christians, 1997, p. 6). This sacred epistemology, as we have argued in our introduction to Part I, is based on a philosophical anthropology that declares, "All humans are worthy of dignity and sacred status without exception for class or ethnicity" (Christians, 1995, p. 129; see also Christians, 1997, p. 13; 1998, p. 6). A universal human ethic emphasizing the sacredness of life, human dignity, truth telling, and nonviolence (Christians, 1997, pp. 12-15) derives from this position. This sacred epistemology interrogates the ways in which race, class, and gender operate as important systems of oppression in the world today (Collins, 1990, p. 227; West, 1989).

After Behar (1996) and Jackson (1998), this project works outward from those moments of existential crisis in the culture, from those moments that affirm the truth that says humans must have "some say in the world into which they are thrown, that they must in some measure choose their own lives and feel that they have a right to be here, to be free to make a difference" (Jackson, 1998, p. 3). This is an ethnography that interrogates and illuminates those interactional moments when humans come together in their struggles over love, loss, pain, joy, shame, violence, betrayal, dignity; those instances "when self and other are constituted in mutuality and acceptance rather than violence and contempt" (Jackson, 1998, p. 208).

This is interpretive scholarship that refuses to retreat to abstractions and high theory. It is a way of being in the world that avoids jargon and incomprehensible discourse. It celebrates the local, the sacred, the act of constructing meaning. Viewing culture as a complex process of improvisation, it seeks to understand how people enact and construct meaning in their daily lives. It celebrates autoethnography, the personal account, "mystories," myth, and folklore.

This is a return to narrative as a political act (Jackson, 1998, p. 35), a minimal ethnography with political teeth. It asks how power is exercised in concrete human relationships, understanding that power means empowerment, the give-and-take of scarce material resources. The play of power in daily lives is best revealed in performance texts, in narrative accounts that tell stories about how humans experience moral community.

Here is an example from one of the stories ("An Island in the Stream") Michael Jackson (1998) tells in his recent book. It is about a man named Desmond, a "wiry, weather-beaten man in bare feet . . . part aboriginal" (p. 196), who lives on an island in the middle of a river. One Sunday, Jackson, his wife (Francine), and his two children (Heidi and Joshua) call on Desmond. As Jackson relates, they are sitting in the middle of the buffalo grass near Desmond's hut. Desmond is rolling a cigarette. Heidi asks him if he would prefer a tailor-made, and she tosses him her pack of Winfields and cigarette lighter. Desmond has to lean forward to pick up the cigarettes and lighter. As he does so, he snaps, "Don't throw things at me! Don't treat me like a dog! Don't make me take them. If you meant to give them to me you should have got up and put them in my hand. Then I would have received them gladly. . . . Do you know what I say to people at the mission? I say to them, 'Name me one white person who has ever done anything for you?' "

Jackson replies, "We're whites."

Desmond retorts, "Well, you might be okay. I don't know. You might have an ulterior motive here, I don't know" (pp. 198-199).

It can be argued that Desmond believed that Jackson and Heidi (as whites) were denying him some degree of control and dignity in his life. Clearly, he felt that whites routinely did this to Aboriginals.

With Jackson (1998, p. 204), West (1989, p. 233), Collins (1990, pp. 226-227), and Du Bois (1903/1989, p. 9), we seek a redemptive, pragmatically prophetic, existential ethnography, a vulnerable scholarship that shows us how to act morally, in solidarity, with passion, with dignity; to engage the world and its dispossessed in complementary, not competitive or destructive, ways. Such an ethnography moves from the researcher's biography to the biographies of others, to those rare moments when our lives connect, as when Jackson's daughter gives Desmond her cigarettes.

This project asks that we make ourselves visible in our texts. Each of us is a universal singular, universalizing in our singularity the crises and experiences of our historical epoch (Sartre, 1981, p. ix). In this way, this version of the social sciences attempts to inscribe and represent the human crises of a specific culture. It endeavors to connect those crises to the public sphere, to the media, and to the apparatuses of the culture that commodify the personal, turning it into political, public spectacle: a movie of the week about this or that personal trouble.

In so doing, this ethnography attempts to understand more fully the conditions of oppression and commodification that operate in the culture, seeking to make these ways of the world more visible to others. The moral ethnographer searches for those moments when humans resist these structures of oppression and representation and attempt, in the process, to take control over their lives and the stories about them. Consider Ralph Ellison's (1964, pp. 307-308) interrogations of the image of the American Negro as given in the work of Robert E. Park. Park (1918/1950) states:

> The Negro has always been interested rather in expression than in action; interested in life itself rather than in its reconstruction or reformation. The Negro is by natural disposition, neither an intellectual nor an idealist, like the Jew; nor a brooding introspective, like the East Indian; nor a pioneer and frontiersman, like the Anglo-Saxon. He is primarily an artist, loving life for its own sake. His metier is expression rather than action. He is, so to speak, the lady among the races. (p. 280)

Ellison (1964) responds:

> Park's metaphor is so pregnant with mixed motives as to birth a thousand compromises and indecisions. Imagine the effect such teachings have had upon Negro students alone! Thus what started as part of a democratic attitude, ends not only uncomfortably close to the preachings of Sumner, but to those of Dr. Goebbels as well. (p. 308)

An existential, interpretive form of qualitative inquiry offers a blueprint for cultural criticism. This criticism is grounded in the specific worlds made visible in the ethnography. It understands that all ethnography is theory and value laden. There can be no value-free ethnography, no objective, dispassionate, value-neutral account of a culture and its ways (see Smith & Deemer, Chapter 34). Taking a lead from midcentury African American cultural critics (Du Bois, Hurston, Ellison, Wright, Baldwin, Hines), it is presumed that the ethnographic, the aesthetic, and the political can never be neatly separated. Ethnography, like art, is always political. It speaks to and for its historical moment as a political reflection.

Accordingly, after Ford (1950/1998), a critical, literary ethnography is one that must meet four criteria. It must evidence a mastery of literary craft, the art of good writing. It should present a well-plotted, compelling, but minimalist narrative, based on realistic, natural conversation, with a focus on memorable, recognizable characters. These characters should be located in well-described, "unforgettable scenes" (Ford, 1950/1998, p. 1112). Second, the work should articulate clearly identifiable cultural and political issues, including injustices based on the structures and meanings of race, class, gender, and sexual orientation. Third, the work should articulate a politics of hope. It should criticize how things are and imagine how they could be different. Finally, it should do all this through direct and indirect symbolic and rhetorical means. Writers who do these things are fully immersed in the oppressions and injustices of their time. They direct their ethnographic energies to higher, utopian, morally sacred goals.

Such work is vulnerable precisely at that moment when it makes its values and criticisms public, when it risks taking sides, aligning itself with one political and moral position and not another. This is a political vulnerability that goes beyond Behar's (1996, p. 177) call for an anthropology that breaks your heart. It is more than writing that inserts the personal into the ethnographic. It is more than stories that move others to tears, more than first-person narratives that turn the self and its experiences into the site of inquiry (Behar, 1996, pp. 19, 167). It

is more than autoethnography born of regret, fear, self-loathing, and anger.

This is writing that angers and sorrows the reader, writing that challenges the reader to take action in the world, to reconsider the conditions under which the moral terms of the self and community are constituted. This critical vulnerability dares to use the particular and the personal as vehicles for criticizing the status quo. Thus Ellison moves from his own experiences to criticize Park's theory of race relations in America. In the same way, Jackson presents Desmond's refusal of Heidi's cigarettes as an instance of perceived cultural prejudice toward Aboriginals.

Behar's vulnerability, on the other hand, is a modernist emotion. It is a product of an age that insists on maintaining a division between private troubles and public issues. Behar's self becomes vulnerable when its private experiences, fears, and doubts are made public. Her vulnerability presumes a gendered, multilayered self hiding behind many masks; it is a self with much to lose if it displays too much emotion. But it is not clear what Behar's term, *vulnerability*, means in an age when little is hidden, or invisible, as in the postmodern moment. How does vulnerability operate when freedom means only that there is "nothing left to lose," as Kris Kristofferson argues in his famous road song "Me and Bobbie McGee"? The existentially vulnerable researcher no longer has anywhere left to hide. The insertion of personal tales into the ethnographic text becomes a moot issue. The writing self is now called to a higher purpose, to use its experiences for social criticism, for imagining new configurations of the morally sacred self.

A vulnerable, performative ethnography moves in three directions at the same time. On the one hand, it represents *a call to action and morally informed social criticism.* Second, in so doing, it *asks the ethnographer always to connect good and bad stories to the circumstances of the media (and media representations), to history, culture, and political economy.* This structural move introduces another layer into the account. In connecting the personal to the historical, the political, and the representational, the writer contextualizes the story being told. This pinpoints local conditions that require change, and thereby provides the grounds for moving from the particular (the singular) to the universal.

In this move, the writer produces "mystory" accounts—multimedia, personal texts grafted onto scholarly, scientific, media, and popular culture discourses (Denzin, 1997, p. 116; Ulmer, 1989; White, Mogilka, & Slack, 1998). These mystory texts function as personal mythologies, improvised (and rehearsed) public performance stories. These narratives begin with the sting of personal memory, epiphanies, and existential crises in the person's biography. The writer moves from these moments into critical readings of those personal, community, popular, and expert systems of discourse that offer interpretations of such experiences. From these critical rereadings, the author fashions a mystory. In these tellings the writer claims ownership over a story previously interpreted from within other systems of discourse. These interpretations are, accordingly, replaced by empowerment narratives suited to personal, political, and community purposes.

The truth of these new texts is determined pragmatically, by their truth effects; by the critical, moral discourse they produce; by the "empathy they generate, the exchange of experience they enable, and the social bonds they mediate" (Jackson, 1998, p. 180). The power of these texts is not a question of whether "they mirror the world as it 'really' is" (Jackson, 1998, p. 180). The world is always already constructed through narrative texts. Rorty (1979) is firm on this point. There is no mirror of nature. The world as it is known is constructed through acts of representation and interpretation.

Third, this performative ethnography *searches for new ways to locate and represent the gendered, sacred self in its ethical relationships to nature.* It seeks an exploration of other forms of writing, including personal diaries, nature writing, and performance texts anchored in the natural world (Berry, 1981; Hasselstrom, Collier, & Curtis, 1997, p. xv; Rawlins, 1994; Stegner, 1980; Turner, 1986). These texts, written in the first-person voice, from the point of view of the ethnographer, focus on performance and experience as the sites of meaning. (As the emphasis on performance implies, there is little attempt to enter the minds of other people, to argue about what a performance means for the other person.)

A sacred ethnography celebrates the small performance rituals that bring us together in the natural world. This project understands that in these moments we become something more than our everyday lives allow. Thus an interpretive ethnography for the next century endeavors to ennoble this all-too-human project called making culture together. These moments display the sacredness of the organization of the natural and cultural world (Bateson & Bateson, 1987, p. 9). They show us how to enact the sacred, existential epistemology discussed above.

And so we must learn how to enact an enabling, interpretive ethnography, an ethnography that aspires to higher, sacred goals. We can scarcely afford to do otherwise. We are at a critical crossroads in the histories of our disciplines and our nation (Lincoln, 1998). Cornel West (1994) reminds us that "we simply cannot enter the twenty-first century at each other's throats" (p. 159). But with West we must ask, "Do we have the intelligence, humor, imagination, courage, tolerance, love, respect, and will to meet the challenge?" (p. 159).

◆ The Crisis of Vocality: New and Old Voices Coping With the Present

A variety of new and old voices—those of critical theory, feminist, ethnic, and other scholars—have also entered the present situation, offering solutions to the crises and problems we have identified above. The move is toward pluralism, and many social scientists now recognize that no picture is ever complete—that we need to employ many perspectives, hear many voices, before we can achieve deep understandings of social phenomena and before we can assert that a narrative is complete.

The modernist dream of a grand or master narrative is now a dead project. The recognition

1056 ◆ THE FUTURE OF QUALITATIVE RESEARCH

of the futility and oppression of such a project is the postmodern condition. The postmodern project challenges the modernist belief in (and desire to develop) a progressive program for incorporating all the cultures of the world under a single umbrella. The postmodern era is defined, in part, by the belief that there has been no single umbrella in the history of the world that might incorporate and represent fairly the dreams, aspirations, and experiences of all peoples.

Critical Theorists

The critical theorists, from the Frankfurt to the Annales, world-system, and participatory action research schools, continue to be a major presence in qualitative research, as Kincheloe and McLaren observe in Chapter 10 of this volume. The critique and concern of the critical theorists has been an effort to design a pedagogy of resistance within communities of difference. The pedagogy of resistance, of taking back "voice," of reclaiming narrative for one's own rather than adapting to the narratives of a dominant majority, was most explicitly laid out by Paolo Freire in his work with adults in Brazil. His work is echoed most faithfully by a group of activist priests and scholars who are exploring "liberation theology"—the joining of the Catholic Church to egalitarian ends for the purposes of overturning oppression and achieving social justice through empowerment of the marginalized, the poor, the nameless, the voiceless. Their program is nothing less than the radical restructuring of society toward the ends of reclaiming historic cultural legacies, social justice, the redistribution of power, and the achievement of truly democratic societies.

Feminist Researchers

The feminists have argued that there is a missing voice, and a missing picture, in the history of the sciences, religion, and the arts. Three different groups—feminist philosophers, scientists, and theologians—are represented in this discourse. Each has had an unsettling—if not

unnerving—effect on arguments about how we "do" qualitative research.

The first two groups—the philosophers and the scientists—have mounted two separate, but related, arguments. The first argument is that traditional science has acted to maintain the Enlightenment dualism, with its major premise that there is a separate and distinct "social reality," "out there" somewhere, separated from those who experience it, and that it is the scientist's job to uncover this separate reality and report on it, for that is the essence of "Truth."

Poststructural feminists urge the abandonment of any distinction between empirical science and social criticism. That is, they seek a morally informed social criticism that is not committed to the traditional concerns or criteria of empirical science. This traditional science, they argue, rests a considerable amount of its authority on the ability to make public what has traditionally been understood to be private (Clough, 1992, p. 137). Feminists dispute this distinction. They urge a social criticism that takes back from science the traditional authority to inscribe and create subjects within the boundaries and frameworks of an objective social science. This social criticism "gives up on data collection and instead offers rereadings of representations in every form of information processing, empirical science, literature, film, television, and computer simulation" (Clough, 1992, p. 137).

A second set of feminist philosophers notes distinct problems with several of the scientific method's most basic premises: the idea that scientific objectivity is possible, the effect that the mandate for objectivity has on the subjects of research, and the possibility of conducting unbiased science at all. Olesen reviews these arguments, which explicate the disastrous consequences of objectifying the targets, subjects, and participants of our research, in Chapter 8 of this volume.

Liberation and feminist theologians are central to this new discourse. They ask hard questions, including, Where and what are the places of women, persons of color, the poor, the homeless, and the hungry, in the church, in science, in art, and literature?

Critical Race and Queer Theory Scholars

There is yet another group of concerned scholars determining the course of qualitative research; these are the critical race and queer theory scholars, who examine the question of whether history has deliberately silenced and/or misrepresented them and their cultures. The members of this new generation of scholars, many of them persons of color, challenge both historical and contemporary social scientists on the accuracy, veracity, and authenticity of the latter's work, contending that no picture can be considered final when the perspectives and narratives of so many are missing or distorted to serve dominant majority interests. The results of such challenges have been twofold: First has been the reconsideration of the Western canon, and second has been an increase in the number of historical and scientific works that recognize and reconstruct the perspectives of those whose perspectives and constructions have been for so long missing. Gloria Ladson-Billings outlines this literature and its major moments, figures, and arguments in Chapter 9 of this volume. She offers a scathing criticism of traditional science and its inability to speak to these questions.

Thus have we written the present, the sixth moment. It is a messy moment, full of multiple voices, experimental texts, breaks, ruptures, crises of legitimation and representation, self-critique, new moral discourses, and technologies. We venture now into the future, attempting to inscribe and describe the possibilities of the seventh moment. Several themes emerge, or will not go away: the voice and presence of the other, historically called "the native"; the social text; and the sacred, the humanistic, and the technological.

◆ Back to the Future

We cannot foretell the future, but we can speculate about it, because the future never repre-

sents a clean break with the past. Indeed, many moments overlap. It is up to the reader to choose from among the voices in the contest of moments and to choose the future.

The Other's Voice

Throughout its 20th-century history, up to a scant quarter century ago, qualitative research was still seriously concerned about the problem of researchers' "going native"—*native* being the word that then inscribed the Other in qualitative discourse. Who today can even use that term? In after-hours tales, over drinks, mostly white, male, middle-class North American ethnographic researchers whispered of those of their colleagues who had engaged that final perdition, overidentification with those they had studied. Today, no one takes seriously talk of "going native." In fact, its disappearance as a category of concern among sociologists and anthropologists is scarcely remarked, but, like the silences between lovers, it is all the more significant for its absence. In its place looms the "Other," whose voice researchers now struggle to hear.

The disappearance of the word *native* is significant. Its silence is deafening. In the postmodern world we are executing as our own heirs, in the legacy we have left ourselves and the students who come after us, "going native" is a category that speaks volumes to both our distorted sense of scientific objectivity and our colonial past. We struggle to find ways to make our texts meaningful beyond the artificial structures of conventional objectivity. We try to come to terms with our own "critical subjectivities." All the while, we have also admitted our guilt and complicity in the colonizing aspects of our work, pointedly subsumed by the term *native* itself. Even using the term is offensive.

But worse than politically incorrect, it stands as witness to our conceits as field-workers. How could we have considered ourselves civilized and objective alongside another class of individuals clearly not "civilized," or well below us on a presumed continuum of becoming civilized? Vidich and Lyman, in Chapter 2 of this volume, trace the history of those ideas that undergirded and supported the very concepts that gave rise to the professional tragedy of "going native." Key to this was the Enlightenment legacy that led us to believe we could, indeed, prepare texts that purported to be whole and truthful accounts, objective accounts, of those "native-Others."

So we are not likely to hear much about "going native" again. That world has passed, and few mourn its passing. Quite the opposite—today we are trying to live ever closer to the lives about which we write. Many examples are discussed in this volume, and others are forthcoming. We are today trying to show not that we can live those lives, but that we have lived close enough to them to begin to understand how the people who live those lives have constructed their worlds.

The Social Text: Telling Stories From the Field

This brings us to our second theme: We are become extremely conscious of how our "tales of the field" can be categorized. We now understand at least the flaws that accompany "realist" and "confessional" tales, if not other kinds (Van Maanen, 1988). And many researchers are trying to move toward extended understandings, extended vicariousness, in their texts. Many now are experimenting with form, format, voice, shape, and style. Laurel Richardson, in her excellent and moving chapter in this volume, shares with us some of the more powerful literary narrative styles contemporary ethnographers are using.

This experimentation with text grows from several sources: our concern with representation of the Other; our willingness to all but abandon, or at least drastically modify, the realist text; and our growing sophistication surrounding the problems of situatedness in texts. We know that our texts have specific locations. We know that they represent—whether in some hidden way or openly—our baggage as individual social scientists. We care less about our "objectivity" as scientists than we do about providing our readers with some powerful propositional, tacit, intuitive, emotional, historical,

poetic, and empathic experience of the Other via the texts we write.

The problem of representation will not go away. Indeed, at its heart lies an inner tension, an ongoing dialectic, a contradiction that will never be resolved. On the one hand, there is the concern for validity, or certainty in the text as a form of isomorphism and authenticity. On the other hand, there is the sure and certain knowledge that all texts are socially, historically, politically, and culturally located. We, like the texts we write, can never be transcendent.

So the experiments will continue, proliferate, grow both more "ironic" and simultaneously less self-mocking. There will also be an expansion of the genres of literature from which they borrow. The tension of this dialectic will continue to be felt throughout the ethnographic community, but it will be resolved publicly and privately in many more ways than we have yet seen.

Vulnerability and Truth, Vulnerability Versus Truth

Rigoberta Menchú (1984), the book and the woman, has created a firestorm. On the one hand are readers who are sympathetic to the message of the book, which captures some sense of the suffering of the Guatemalan indigenous peoples at the hands of the *ladinos*, the primarily European-descent, landowning class in Guatemala. The *ladinos*, as one might expect, also control the national army, a group comprising European-descent officers and regulars as well as *mestizo* and indigenous soldiers.

On the other side of the argument are both scholars (Gugelberger, 1996; Stoll, 1999) and assorted others who study thoughtfully, laud, reject, and sometimes revile *I, Rigoberta Menchú* because it is a chronicle proven patently false in some (or all) of its facts and therefore suspect. The radical right wing of the culture war militia has accused the "liberal left" of using the book to propagandize on behalf of some unspecified liberal agenda, primarily Latin American revolution. The evidence that Rigoberta

Menchú, the person, provided so-called facts that are not true, that have no basis in her experience or witness, is not complete, but it is strong and nearly overwhelming (Lincoln, 2000, in press).

What do we do with a text like *I, Rigoberta Menchú*? John Beverley provides some answers in his thoughtful chapter here on the *testimonio* form. Instead of treating such works as subject to Eurocentric validity criteria, we need to look at them through another lens. They are, in fact, a bridge into subalternity, an avenue for us to use in crossing into the world of the subaltern, the border dweller, the margin-definer previously without voice. They represent power turned on its head in several directions. They signal a capture of authority by colonized voices, a reestablishment of the authority of indigenous peoples to speak for themselves, in their own terms. They also portend a refusal of the colonized to have their stories told solely by outsiders, by those with little political stake, or by those whose major interests are not historically perceived to be with indigenous others.

They signify, too, that although Stoll (1999) and others may argue on epistemological grounds, their arguments are all too often political (Beverley, 1996; see also in this volume Beverley, Chapter 21; Tierney, Chapter 20). Just as researchers, particularly feminist theorists, recognize that the personal is the political, subaltern voices recognize that the epistemological is also the political. *How* we know is intimately bound up with *what* we know, where we learned it, and what we have experienced. Enlisting the storytelling tradition to make statements that are epistemologically political narratives leaves the traditions of Western ethnography unsettled, threatened, vulnerable, and adrift from their moorings. The firestorm surrounding *I, Rigoberta Menchú* is the precise consequence of the meeting of majority criteria with subaltern purposes. Thus we are left with a new form of truth: the "truth" as civic sociology shaped by the experiences of alterity.

Just as we argued earlier that we will need to revisit the old texts to see, criticism aside, just what they taught us and what their purposes and uses might be for a postmodern era, we will have to consider carefully the issues of the civic social science for which we as editors call in light of what a civic social science means for, and from, subaltern voices. Clearly, a subaltern social science, a call for action from alterity, is shaped differently from a civic social science envisioned by Eurocentric and mainstream voices. Taking *I, Rigoberta* and Menchú on their own terms radically remakes what constitutes an entire genre of ethnographic work. This refashioning might ultimately include life histories, autoethnographies, "mystories," autobiographies, critical journals, and other narrative forms in this genre. The debut of *testimonio* as a form of critical ethnography has literally sent life history spinning out of control into another lane on the bridge.

Getting on With It

We confront another problematic in the sixth moment. Arguments around paradigms previously have centered on whether "competitor" paradigms are worthwhile (Guba & Lincoln, 1981, 1989; Lincoln & Guba, 1985) and whether students and others entering the fray might usefully select to operate in nonconventional scientific modes. Smith and Deemer (Chapter 34) show that this was a foolish argument (although perhaps a useful place to start the conversation). Ensuring that students and new practitioners did have choices in the paradigms they applied to their work at least kept us from "closing down the conversation" prematurely. But as Smith and Deemer make clear, it is not really about paradigm choices now. Rather, it is about taking account of the world that we have inherited. Recent understandings in the social sciences now convince us that there *is* no "God's-eye view"; there is no "voice from nowhere," no "voice from everywhere." It is not that we might elect to engage in work that is postmodern. Rather, it is that we have inherited a postmodern world, and there is no going back.

We do not "choose" to be postmodern. The historical moment has chosen us.

The implications of this understanding, of this resituating of the argument, are enormous. We have come and gone in the "great paradigm wars." The wars are over. While we were fighting, the boundaries and borders over which we were fighting were redrawn until they were meaningless. We are not free to "choose" postmodernism. It is the historical moment when the modernist epoch ends: contingent, pluralistic, ambiguous, freed (or jettisoned) from the certainties of yesterday, decentered, noisy with previously unheard voices. We may still hear, for some years to come, echoes of modernism. Assuredly, our more conservative intellectual and political organizations (such as universities) will long cling to modernist forms and structures, even as the mind-set of a new era takes shape.

Whose Self? What/Which Self?

We confront, too, the issue of self: Whose self? What self? Which self? The decentering of the Eurocentric grand narrative, the centering of polyvocality, the ragged race between margin and center, the deconstruction of the "authentic self"—all signal that the time of the fiction of a single, true, authentic self has come and gone. It is hard to know whether, in fact, it will even be missed, except as a psychoanalytic figment of the imagination. Instead, we confront multiple identities: identities formed in and around our social locations, identities evoked in the field, identities created as a result of the interaction between our data and our selves, in and out of the field, experience-near and time-distant. Bridges to the self seem to be as many as bridges to our respondents, each of them eliciting new glimpses, new images of what our own possibilities might be, of how we might become, of how and in what ways we might come to know.

The flowering of multiple paradigms and methods has been accompanied, to some extent, by a flowering of possibilities for the human spirit. Just as the Enlightenment opened possibilities for lives of choice not dictated by theological doctrine, so this abandonment of a rigid Eurocentrism in our social sciences leaves open the potential for a new flowering of the human spirit, a new sense of the sacredness of the human spirit, human community, and human flourishing. Rather than viewing multiple identities as a mark of psychic disorder, we see in them possibilities and potential. The reflexive self is a self freed to choose, to enact, to perform new roles, new relationships. The multiple selves summoned by a more complex and committed social science possess richness beyond our ability to understand or tell at the moment.

Mary Gergen and Ken Gergen (Chapter 40) argue that we are already in the "post"-post period—post-poststructuralism, post-postmodernism—an age of reconstruction. What this means for interpretive, ethnographic practices is still not clear. But it is certain that things will never again be the same. We are in a new age where multivoiced texts, cultural criticism, and post-experimental works will become more common, as will more reflexive forms of fieldwork, analysis, and intertextual representation.

Another way, then, of describing this moment in time and space is to paraphrase Thomas Berry, who has commented that we are between stories. The Old Story will no longer do, and we know that it is inadequate. But the New Story is not yet in place. And so we look for the pieces of the Story, the ways of telling it, and the elements that will make it whole, but it hasn't come to us yet. So we are now the ultimate *bricoleurs,* trying to cobble together a story that we are beginning to suspect will never enjoy the unity, the smoothness, the wholeness that the Old Story had. As we assemble different pieces of the Story, our *bricolage* begins to take not one, but many shapes.

Slowly it dawns on us that there may not be one future, one "moment," but rather many; not one "voice," but polyvocality; not one story, but many tales, dramas, pieces of fiction, fables, memories, histories, autobiographies, poems, and other texts to inform our sense of lifeways, to extend our understandings of the Other, to provide us with the material for "cultural critique" (Marcus & Fischer, 1986). The modernist project has bent and is breaking under the weight of postmodern resistance to its narratives, to what Berry calls "the Old Story."

◆ Conclusion: The Seventh Moment

It is hard to know whether it is easier to live in a time of certainty or a time of great uncertainty. John Naisbitt (1982), author of *Megatrends,* has observed:

> We are living in the *time of the parenthesis,* the time between eras. Those who are willing to handle the ambiguity of this in-between period and to anticipate the new era will be a quantum leap ahead of those who hold on to the past. The time of the parenthesis is a time of change and questioning.
>
> Although the time between eras is uncertain, it is a great and yeasty time, filled with opportunity. If we can learn to make uncertainty our friend, we can achieve much more than in stable eras. In stable eras, everything has a name, and everything knows its place, and we can leverage very little.
>
> But in the time of the parenthesis, we have extraordinary leverage and influence—individually, professionally and institutionally—if we can only get a clear sense, a clear conception, a clear vision, of the road ahead. (pp. 249-252)

We believe that Naisbitt is suggesting that while we are letting go of the certainties and absolutes of the past, we also have enormous opportunity to make of the future what we wish it to be.

◆ Coda

The answer to the question, Where have we come to? is unclear, as is the answer to the question, What are the many futures that lie ahead for qualitative research? We are not wandering, for that implies that we have no direction. But likewise, as is plain from the several ontologies and many epistemologies that inform and contradict each other, we are not necessarily marching in a column toward a common future. Like the *bricoleurs* of Lévi-Strauss, we are creating solutions to our problems with makeshift equipment, spare parts, and assemblage.

But interpretive *bricoleurs* are more than simply jacks-of-all-trades; they are also inventors, in the best sense of the word. *Bricoleurs* know that they have few tools, and little by way of appropriate parts, and so becomes inventors. They invent ways of repairing; they recycle fabric and cloth into beautiful quilts; they, like Pirsig's hero in *Zen and the Art of Motorcycle Maintenance,* know that for a particular repair, nothing is better than a strip of Coors beer aluminum can; having no art lessons, they become Grandma Moses. In the interpretive *bricoleur's world, invention is not only the child of necessity, it is the demand of restless art.*

The methods of qualitative research thereby become the "invention," and the telling of the tales—the representation—becomes the art, even though, as *bricoleurs,* we all know we are not working with standard-issue parts, and we have come to suspect that there are no longer any "standard-issue parts" made (if ever there were). And so we cobble. We cobble together stories that we may tell each other, some to share our profoundest links with those whom we studied; some to help us see how we can right a wrong or relieve oppression; some to help us and others to understand how and why we did what we did, and how it all went very wrong; and some simply to sing of difference.

And perhaps it is the case that this *Handbook* itself is the sixth moment. Perhaps it is the particular time in our history to take stock of where we are, to think about where we are going, to try to imagine a new future. Perhaps what we have asked our authors to do is to define this sixth moment and to speculate about what the seventh moment might be like—whether it will be a time when the Story is once again in place, or whether it will continue to be a time when fields and disciplines appear to be in disarray. This book, this effort, might well become, to historians long after us, a moment unto itself, a chapter in an evolution that we ourselves are not able to bound, to frame, or to capture for its essence.

We believe we are poised to cross the bridge into the seventh moment. We cannot see that landscape clearly yet, but we can discern some of its contours. First, we are not the only scholars calling for a social science that is more responsive—not to the policy community, which has often used research for its own ends, but to the communities in which we do our work. The press for a civic sociology (see in this volume Christians, Chapter 5; Denzin, Chapter 35) is not without its dangers. We may find that as we work more often with communities to answer their questions, we have less funding available with which we can do such work. We may also find that this work takes us away from campuses far more than our home institutions would like. Certainly, such work is far more labor-intensive and time-devouring than our traditional ethnographies dictated (Lincoln, in press). The calls for a civic sociology—by which we mean fieldwork located not only in sociology, but in an extended, enriched, cultivated social science embracing all the disciplines—nevertheless characterize a whole new generation of qualitative researchers: educationists, sociologists, political scientists, clinical practitioners in psychology and medicine, nurses, communications and media specialists, cultural studies workers, and a score of other assorted disciplines.

The moral imperatives of such work cannot be ignored. There have been several generations of social science that not only has not solved serious human problems, but many times has only worsened the plight of the persons studied (see Fine, Weis, Weseen, & Wong, Chapter 4, this volume). Beyond morality is something equally important—the mandates for such work come from our own sense of the human community. A detached social science frequently serves only those with the means, the social designations, and the intellectual capital to keep themselves detached. We face a choice, in the seventh moment, of declaring ourselves committed to detachment or in solidarity with the human community. We come to know, and we come to exist meaningfully, only in community. We have the opportunity to rejoin that community as its resident intellectuals and change agents.

An interesting, and significant, concomitant to expressions of interest in a civic social science is the implied end of the commitment to the Enlightenment dualism of means and ends. We are emerging from many moments in social science where ends and means have been carefully, objectively, separated. The implications of a civic social science go far beyond human solidarity. Such a social science also signals the dying of means-ends dualism. In a civic social science, the ends of ethnography—strong, just, egalitarian communities—are reconciled with the means for achieving those ends. In the seventh moment, the means (methods) of social science are developed, refined, and cherished for their contributions to communities characterized by respectful and loving difference, social justices and equal access to material, social, educational, and cultural capital (the ends of ethnography). Methods vie among themselves not for experimental robustness, but for vitality and vigor in illuminating the ways to achieve profound understanding of how we can create human flourishing.

We are also seeing an emerging dialogue around what paradigms mean and how we learn to trust their results (Lincoln, in press). The vast array of methods, paradigms, and proposals for trustworthiness has the power to blind us to the fact that many individuals and paradigm adherents, working from very different embarkation points, have arrived at quite similar destinations. The feminists, for example, with their critical emphasis on women's ways of knowing, share many understandings with the race and ethnic theorists, who likewise argue that nondominant, subaltern ways of knowing, while different from majority, academic, or conventional scientific epistemologies, have much to offer to our understanding of the vast array and variety of human social life. Critical theorists and those who work with life history and *testimonio* forms intuitively understand that the epistemological is the political, and both have similar proposals for how we might view validity and therefore the "truth" of any account.

As a consequence, we have before us the possibility of entering into more meaningful dialogue with each other, not about how we can create a new metaparadigm, but about the similarities we are uncovering in our work. We see many affinities and parallels emerging from methodological reflections on fieldwork under way. If a seventh moment is yet to be charted, such dialogues among paradigm and methodological adherents might well be undertaken.

One final characteristic that marks this moment is the activity and ferment between margins and center. What was center is now decentered; what was margin and border is now taking center stage. The staggering array of new materials, new resources, new stories, new critiques, new methods, new epistemological proposals, new forms of validity, new textual improvisations, new performed interpretations—all demonstrate an undeniably new, if shifting, center to this work. What was marked formerly by the firm and rigid shapes of a Eurocentric geometry is now the fluid, shape-shifting image of chemical flux and transformation, as margins move to the center, the center moves to the margins, and the whole is reconstituted again in some new form. The whole concept of center and margins is being transfigured by methods, methodologies, research practices, and epistemologies scarcely dreamed of a generation ago—or even when the first edition of this *Handbook* was published.

For whatever the moment, we hope that this volume is a prompt for new tales, improvisations, experiments, interpolations, dialogues, and additional interpretations. The Story is by no means in place yet, although we await the visit of yet another blind Homer to piece together not only what we know of this fabulous land, but a new set of chapters for us. And as we wait, we remember that our most powerful effects as storytellers come when we expose the cultural plots and the cultural practices that guide our writing hands. These practices and plots lead us to see coherence where there is none, or to create meaning without an understanding of the broader structures that tell us to tell things in a particular way. Erasing the boundaries separating self, other, and history,

we seek to learn how to tell new stories, stories no longer contained within or confined to the tales of the past. And so we embark together on a new project, a project with its own as yet not fully understood cultural plots and cultural practices.

And what remains, throughout, will be the steady but always changing commitment of all qualitative researchers—the commitment, that is, to study human experience from the ground up, from the point of interacting individuals who, together and alone, make and live histories that have been handed down to them from the ghosts of the past.

■ Note

1. The moments once more: traditional (1900-1950); modernist (1950-1970); blurred genres (1970-1986); crisis of representation (1986-1990); postmodern, a period of experimental and new ethnographies (1990-1995); postexperimental inquiry (1995-2000); and the future, which is now (2000-).

■ References

Abram, D. (1996). *The spell of the sensuous.* New York: Vintage.

Bateson, G. (1972). *Steps to an ecology of mind.* New York: Ballantine.

Bateson, G. (1979). *Mind and nature: A necessary unity.* New York: E. P. Dutton.

Bateson, G. P., & Bateson, M. C. (1987). *Anger's fear: Towards an epistemology of the sacred.* New York: Macmillan.

Behar, R. (1996). *The vulnerable observer: Anthropology that breaks your heart.* Boston: Beacon.

Berry, W. (1981). *Recollected essays: 1965-1980.* New York: Farrar, Strauss & Giroux.

Beverley, J. (1996). The real thing. In G. M. Gugelberger (Ed.), *The real thing: Testimonial discourse and Latin America* (pp. 266-286). Durham, NC: Duke University Press.

Bruner, E. M. (1993). Introduction: The ethnographic self and the personal self. In P.

Benson (Ed.), *Anthropology and literature* (pp. 1-26). Urbana: University of Illinois Press.

Christians, C. G. (1995). The naturalistic fallacy in contemporary interactionist-interpretive research. In N. K. Denzin (Ed.), *Studies in symbolic interaction: A research annual* (Vol. 19, pp. 125-130). Greenwich, CT: JAI.

Christians, C. G. (1997). The ethics of being. In C. G. Christians & M. Traber (Eds.), *Communication ethics and universal values* (pp. 3-23). Thousand Oaks, CA: Sage.

Christians, C. G. (1998). The sacredness of life. *Media Development, 45*(2), 3-7.

Clough, P. T. (1992). *The end(s) of ethnography: From realism to social criticism.* Newbury Park, CA: Sage.

Clough, P. T. (1998). *The end(s) of ethnography: From realism to social criticism* (2nd ed.). New York: Peter Lang.

Collins, P. H. (1990). *Black feminist thought: Knowledge, consciousness, and the politics of empowerment.* New York: Routledge, Chapman & Hall.

Conquergood, D. (1985). Performing as a moral act: Ethical dimensions of the ethnography of performance. *Literature in Performance, 5,* 1-13.

Denzin, N. K. (1997). *Interpretive ethnography: Ethnographic practices for the 21st century.* Thousand Oaks, CA: Sage.

Du Bois, W. E. B. (1989). *The souls of black folk.* New York: Bantam. (Original work published 1903)

Ellison, R. (1964). *Shadow and act.* New York: Random House.

Ford, N. A. (1998). A blueprint for Negro authors. In P. L. Hill (Ed.), *Call and response: The Riverside anthology of the African American literary tradition* (pp. 1112-1114). Boston: Houghton Mifflin. (Original work published 1950)

Geertz, C. (1988). *Works and lives: The anthropologist as author.* Stanford, CA: Stanford University Press.

Guba, E. G., & Lincoln, Y. S. (1981). *Effective evaluation: Improving the usefulness of evaluation results through responsive and naturalistic approaches.* San Francisco: Jossey-Bass.

Guba, E. G., & Lincoln, Y. S. (1989). *Fourth generation evaluation.* Newbury Park, CA: Sage.

Gugelberger, G. M. (Ed.). (1996). *The real thing: Testimonial discourse and Latin America.* Durham, NC: Duke University Press.

Hasselstrom, L., Collier, G., & Curtis, N. (1997). Introduction: Grass widows and wrinklebelly women. In L. Hasselstrom, G. Collier, & N. Curtis (Eds.), *Leaning into the wind: Women write from the heart of the West* (pp. xiii-xxi). Boston: Houghton Mifflin.

Jackson, M. (1998). *Minima ethnographica: Intersubjectivity and the anthropological project.* Chicago: University of Chicago Press.

Kittredge, W. (1996). *Who owns the West?* San Francisco: Murray House.

Lincoln, Y. S. (1995). Emerging criteria for quality in qualitative and interpretive inquiry. *Qualitative Inquiry, 1,* 275-289.

Lincoln, Y. S. (1998, November). *When research is not enough: Community, care, and love.* Presidential Address delivered at the annual meeting of the Association for the Study of Higher Education, Miami, FL.

Lincoln, Y. S. (1999, June). *Courage, vulnerability and truth.* Keynote address delivered at the conference "Reclaiming Voice II: Ethnographic Inquiry and Qualitative Research in a Postmodern Age," University of California, Irvine.

Lincoln, Y. S. (in press). Varieties of validities. In J. S. Smart (Ed.), *Higher education: Handbook of theory and research* (Vol. 14). Lexington, MA: Agathon.

Lincoln, Y. S., & Guba, E. G. (1985). *Naturalistic inquiry.* Beverly Hills, CA: Sage.

Macnaghten, P., & Urry, J. (1998). *Contested natures.* London: Sage.

Marcus, G. E., & Fischer, M. M. J. (1986). *Anthropology as cultural critique: An experimental moment in the human sciences.* Chicago: University of Chicago Press.

Menchú, R. (1984). *I, Rigoberta Menchú: An Indian woman in Guatemala* (E. Burgos-Debray, Ed.; A. Wright, Trans.). London: Verso.

Naisbitt, J. (1982). *Megatrends: Ten new directions transforming our lives.* New York: Time Warner.

Park, R. E. (1950). Education in its relation to the conflict and fusion of cultures. In R. E. Park, *Race and culture* (pp. 261-283). Glencoe, IL: Free Press. (Reprinted from

Publications of the American Sociological Society, 13, 1918, 38-63)

Rawlins, C. L. (1994). The meadow at the corner of your eye. In D. Clow & D. Snow (Eds.), *Northern lights: A selection of new writing from the American West* (pp. 389-395). New York: Vantage.

Reason, P. (1993). Sacred experience and sacred science. *Journal of Management Inquiry, 2,* 10-27.

Rorty, R. (1979). *Philosophy and the mirror of nature.* Princeton, NJ: Princeton University Press.

Rosaldo, R. (1989). *Culture and truth: The remaking of social analysis.* Boston: Beacon.

Sartre, J.-P. (1981). *The family idiot: Gustave Flaubert, 1821-1857* (Vol. 1). Chicago: University of Chicago Press.

Stegner, W. (1980). *The sound of mountain water: The changing American West.* Garden City, NY: Doubleday.

Stoll, D. (1999). *Rigoberta Menchú and the story of all poor Guatemalans.* Boulder, CO: Westview.

Turner, V. (1986). *The anthropology of performance.* New York: Performing Arts Journal Publications.

Ulmer, G. (1989). *Teletheory.* New York: Routledge.

Van Maanen, J. (1988). *Tales of the field: On writing ethnography.* Chicago: University of Chicago Press.

West, C. (1989). *The American evasion of philosophy: A genealogy of pragmatism.* Madison: University of Wisconsin Press.

West, C. (1994). *Race matters.* New York: Vantage.

White, C. J., Mogilka, J., & Slack, P. J. F. (1998). Disturbing the colonial frames of ethnographic representation: Releasing feminist imagination on the academy. *Cultural Studies: A Research Annual, 3,* 3-27.

AUTHOR INDEX

SUBJECT INDEX

Aboriginal teachers, 581-582
Academia/academics, 60, 85-105
    career and, 86, 88
    changes influencing, 319
    feminist research and, 236
    income generation and, 415-416
    participatory research and, 568
    partisan research and, 290-292
    See also Universities
Academic science, goals of, 32
Accommodation, 158, 169-174
Acculturation, 53
Action:
    applied ethnography and, 641, 859-860
    authenticity criteria and, 180, 181
    call to, 174-175
    clinical research, 611
    communicative, 301
    critical reasoning and, 585
    critical research stimulating, 292
    ethnomethodology and, 490-491, 498
    feminist research and, 216
    grounded theory and, 518
    individual, 576-577
    interpretivist philosophies, 191-194
    knowledge and, 1002-1003
    material culture and, 710
    moral commitments, 146, 147
    participatory research, 568
    performance texts moving people to, 905, 910,
        914
    photos documenting, 717-731
    policy research and, 1001-1016
    political, 181
    praxis and, 158
    public journalism, 901
    racialized discourses and, 271-272
    reflexive practice and, 578

    sexual communities and, 352
    social, 181
    social program evaluation and, 989, 993
    testimonio and, 560
Action anthropology, 854
Action learning, 570, 584
Action research, 32, 85-105, 1019
    classroom, 569-570
    critical, 568-569
    ethics and, 234
    industrial, 571-572
    key features of, 595-601
    participatory. *See* Participatory action research
Action science, 570-571, 584
Action theory, 588-589
Activism, 17
    participatory action research, 376
    persons of color and, 910
    See also Action
Advocacy, clinical research and, 616
Advocacy research, applied ethnography and, 641,
    859-860
Aesthetic forms, 322, 325, 326
Aesthetic issues, 4
Affirmative action, 264
African American(s):
    cultural studies, 318, 320
    identity and, 260, 318, 320
    resistance to inquiry, 1034
    music of, 906
    as Other, 51
    See also Black culture
African American performance-based aesthetic, 909
African American women:
    collective stories, 843
    feminists, 219, 223
    oppression of, 842
    standpoint research, 223

text, 1051
Autobiographies, 556, 742, 899
    ethnography drawing on, 372
    testimonio and, 541
    women's, 468
Autoethnographies, 636, 733-761, 930
    context of, 232
    evocativeness of, 931
    feminists and, 466
    future and, 1052
    individualism and, 1033
    literary structures and, 540
    interpretation and, 1029
    overcoming abstractions using, 179
    validity and, 1028
    voice in, 1022
Autohistories, 1050
Autopoesis, participatory evaluation versus,
    102-103
Axiology, 158, 175
Axiomatic-modeling methods, 58

Basic research, 851
Behavior:
    material traces of, 703-714
    norms, 685, 686
Being, great chain of, 43
Belief systems, worldviews and, 6
Belongingness, need for, 321
Bias, 754, 1027
    applied ethnography, 862
    description of, 389
    feminist research, 229
    fieldwork, 682
    ideologically-driven research and, 385
    paternalistic, 659
    social program evaluation, 991
    sociohistorically inherited, 194
Bible, 40
Biographical description, interviews and, 647
Biographical memory, 656
Biographical method, 539
Biographies, 459-461
    autoethnographies as. *See* Autoethnographies
    case centered, 438
    clinical research and, 614
    collective, 943
Biomedical research, 376, 690, 691
Biomedicine, 609, 610-612, 614-615
Bisexuality, 355, 358
Black arts movement, 898
Black cultural studies, 318, 320
Black culture, 44. *See also* African American(s)
Body art, 423
Body language, 300-301
Boolean tests, 787
Boundaries:
    case, 436
    crossing cultural, 466
    ethnography and, 461

Bounded system, 436
Bracketing, 390-391
Bricoleur:
    interpretive *bricoleur*, researcher as, 3, 4, 6, 31,
        157, 367, 371, 1020, 1060, 1061
    methodological *bricoleur*, 6
    narrative *bricoleur*, 6
    political *bricoleur*, 6
    theoretical *bricoleur*, 6
British cultural studies, 331

Capitalism:
    contradictions, 48-49
    critical theory and, 280
    exploitation and, 298, 303
    feminist research and, 681
    global reach, 1019
    nation building and, 44
Care:
    clinical research and, 615
    ethic of, 142, 143, 204, 235, 741, 754
    reciprocal, 145
    sacred epistomology and, 1052
Cartesian rationalism, 594
Case(s):
    cases within, 447
    identification, 436, 446
    instrumental, 990
    negative, 370, 782, 784, 787
    single versus multiple, 812
    social program evaluation, 990
Case method, 57, 61
Case record, 436
Case studies, 15, 393, 435-450
    biography and, 438
    clinical research, 621
    collective, 437, 446, 447
    conceptual structures, 372
    instrumental, 437, 440, 444, 446
    intrinsic, 370, 437, 439, 440, 444, 446
    journalistic, 900-901
    long term, 396
Catalytic authenticity, 181
Catalytic validity, 297
Categories/categorization:
    coding, 783, 786, 825
    computer-assisted analysis, 638
    culture and, 770
    grounded theory, 515 516, 519-520, 524,
        525-526
    interviews, 653
    life stories, 544
    membership categorization analysis, 826-828
    participants', 826
    participatory action research, 598
    reasons for, 886
    sexual, 349, 352, 353, 354
    social, 489, 493
Causal generalizations, 57
Causal narratives, 14

ABOUT THE CONTRIBUTORS

Michael V. Angrosino is Professor of Anthropology at the University of South Florida, where he specializes in mental health policy analysis, the influence of organized religion on contemporary social policy, and the methodology of oral history. He has served as editor of *Human Organization,* the journal of the Society for Applied Anthropology, and is currently general editor of the Southern Anthropological Society's Proceedings Series for the University of Georgia Press. His most recent book, *Opportunity House: Ethnographic Stories of Mental Retardation* (1998), is an experiment in alternative ethnographic writing.

H. Russell Bernard (Ph.D., Illinois, 1968) is Professor of Anthropology at the University of Florida. He has taught at Washington State University, West Virginia University, and the University of Florida. He has also taught or done research at the University of Athens, the University of Cologne, the National Museum of Ethnology (Osaka), and Scripps Institution of Oceanography. He works with indigenous people to develop publishing outlets for works in previously nonwritten languages. He also does research in social network analysis, particularly on the problem of estimating the size of uncountable populations. His publications include *Native Ethnography: An Otomí Indian Describes His Culture* (with Jesús Salinas Pedraza, 1989), *Technology and Social Change* (edited with Pertti Pelto; second edition, 1983), and *Research Methods in Anthropology* (second edition, 1994). He has served as editor of *Human Organization* (1976-1981), the *American Anthropologist* (1981-1989), and *Cultural Anthropology Methods Journal* (1989-1998), and is currently editor of *Field Methods.*

John Beverley is Professor of Spanish and Latin American literature and cultural studies at the University of Pittsburgh. He has taught at the University of California at San Diego, Stanford University, University of Minnesota, University of Washington, and Universidad Andina in Quito, Ecuador. His 1989 essay "The Margin at the Center: On Testimonio" helped inaugurate the extensive critical discussion of testimonio in Latin American studies in the 1990s. His publications related to the theme of testimonio include *Literature and Politics in the Central American Revolutions* (with Marc Zimmerman; 1990), *Against Literature* (1993), *Una modernidad obsoleta: Estudios sobre el barroco* (1999), *Subalternity and Representation: Arguments in Cultural Theory* (in press), and two coedited collections: *La voz del otro: Testimonio, subalternidad y verdad narrativa* (1992) and *The*

Postmodernism Debate in Latin America (1995). He is one of the founding members of the Latin American Subaltern Studies Group.

Arthur P. Bochner is Professor of Communication and Codirector of the Institute for Interpretive Human Studies at the University of South Florida. He is the coauthor of *Understanding Family Communication* and coeditor of *Composing Ethnography: Alternative Forms of Qualitative Writing* (1996) as well as the AltaMira Press book series Ethnographic Alternatives. He has published more than 50 articles and monographs on close relationships, communication theory, and narrative inquiry. His current research focuses on geriatric care managers as ethnographers of aging.

Ivan Brady is Distinguished Teaching Professor of Anthropology at the State University of New York at Oswego and a SUNY Faculty Exchange Scholar. A former President of the Society for Humanistic Anthropology and book review editor of the *American Anthropologist,* his special interests include Pacific Islands ethnography, ethnopoetics, and the philosophy of science. He is the editor or co-editor of several books, dozens of chapters, articles, and reviews, and is currently developing a new version of his book on *Anthropological Poetics* (1991). His poetry has appeared in various books and journals, including *Reflections: The Anthropological Muse* (edited by I. Prattis, 1985), the *Neuroanthropology Network Newsletter, Anthropology and Humanism* (Quarterly), and *Qualitative Inquiry.*

Erve Chambers is Professor of Anthropology at the University of Maryland, College Park. He is founding editor of the publication *Practicing Anthropology* and a past President of the Society for Applied Anthropology. His current research interests include ethnographic approaches to decision making in the areas of tourism development, natural resources management, and urban and regional planning. He is the author of *Applied Anthropology: A Practical Guide* (1985) and *Native Tours: The Anthropology of Travel and Tourism* (2000). His edited volumes include *Housing, Culture, and Design: A Comparative Perspective* (1989) and *Tourism and Culture: An Applied Perspective* (1997).

Kathy Charmaz is Professor of Sociology and Faculty Writing Coordinator at Sonoma State University. Her recent works have concerned qualitative research methods, suffering chronic illness, and professional writing. She serves as the editor of *Symbolic Interaction* and is the 1999-2000 President of the Pacific Sociological Association.

Julianne Cheek is Professor of Health at the University of South Australia, Adelaide, South Australia. She is currently Dean: Research for the Division of Health Sciences and Director: Centre for Research into Nursing and Health Care at the University of South Australia, a university-funded, performance-based research center. She has attracted funding for many qualitative research projects, with some 16 projects funded in the past four years. She has also attracted large sums of funding for projects related to teaching that have qualitative principles embedded within them. She is the author of *Postmodern and Poststructural Approaches to Nursing Research* and coauthor of *Society and Health: Social Theory for Health Workers* and *Finding Out: Information Literacy for the 21st Century.*

Clifford G. Christians is a Research Professor of Communications at the University of Illinois, Urbana-Champaign, where he is Director of the Institute of Communications Research. He has been a visiting scholar in philosophical ethics at Princeton University, in social ethics at the University of Chicago, and a PEW Fellow in Ethics at Oxford University. He completed the third edition of Rivers and Schramm's *Responsibility in Mass Communication,* has coauthored *Jacques Ellul: Interpretive Essays* with Jay Van Hook, and has written *Teaching Ethics in Journalism Education* with Catherine Covert. He is also the coauthor, with John Ferre and Mark Fackler, of *Good News: Social Ethics and the Press* (1993). His *Media Ethics: Cases and Moral Reasoning,* with Kim Rotzoll and Mark Fackler, is now in its fifth edition (1983, 1987, 1991, 1995, 1998). *Communication Ethics and Universal Values,* which he coauthored with Michael Traber, was published in 1997. He has lectured or given academic papers on ethics in Norway, Russia, Finland, France, Belgium, Italy, Netherlands, Switzerland, England, Singapore, Korea, Scotland, Philippines, Slovenia, Canada, Brazil, Mexico, Puerto Rico, Spain, and Sweden.

Benjamin F. Crabtree, Ph.D., is Professor and Research Director, University of Medicine and Dentistry of New Jersey, Robert Wood Johnson Medical School. He has written and contributed to numerous articles and chapters on both qualitative and quantitative methods, covering topics ranging from time-series analysis and log-linear models to in-depth interviews, case study research, and qualitative analysis strategies. He is coeditor of *Exploring Collaborative Research in Primary Care* (1994) and *Doing Qualitative Research* (second edition, 1999).

Deborah K. Deemer is Assistant Professor of Education at the University of Northern Iowa. Her interest in criteria for qualitative inquiry began when she was working in program evaluation as a Research Associate at Alverno College's Office of Research and Evaluation. For more than a decade she has struggled to disentangle her subjectivity from realist pretensions. Her coauthored contribution to this volume reflects her movement into working fully within the qualitative paradigm. In her current writing she continues to grapple with the meaning of quality while striving to utilize qualitative inquiry in writing the self, in depicting the lives of women, and in reflecting on educational practice.

Norman K. Denzin is Distinguished Professor of Communications, College of Communications Scholar, and Research Professor of Communications, Sociology and Humanities at the University of Illinois, Urbana-Champaign. He is the author of numerous books, including *Interpretive Ethnography: Ethnographic Practices for the 21st Century, The Cinematic Society: The Voyeur's Gaze, Images of Postmodern Society, The Research Act: A Theoretical Introduction to Sociological Methods, Interpretive Interactionism, Hollywood Shot by Shot, The Recovering Alcoholic,* and *The Alcoholic Self,* which won the Charles Cooley Award from the Society for the Study of Symbolic Interaction in 1988. In 1997 he was awarded the George Herbert Award from the Study of Symbolic Interaction. He is the editor of the *Sociological Quarterly,* coeditor of *Qualitative Inquiry,* and editor of the annual journals *Cultural Studies: A Research Annual* and *Studies in Symbolic Interaction.*

Carolyn Ellis is Professor of Communication and Sociology and Codirector of the Institute for Interpretive Human Studies at the University of South Florida. She is the author of *Final Negotiations: A Story of Love, Loss, and Chronic Illness* (1995) and *Fisher Folk: Two Communities on Chesapeake Bay* (1986). She is coeditor of *Composing Ethnography: Alternative Forms of Qualitative Writing* (1996), *Investigating Subjectivity: Research on Lived Experience* (1992), *Social Perspectives on Emotion* (volume 3), and the AltaMira book series Ethnographic Alternatives. Her current research focuses on illness narratives, autoethnography, and emotional sociology.

Michelle Fine is Professor of Social/Personality Psychology at the Graduate School and University Center at the City University of New York. She has authored and coauthored numerous books, including, most recently, *The Unknown City: The Lives of Poor and Working-Class Young Adults* (with Lois Weis, 1998), *Becoming Gentlemen: Women, Law School and Institutional Change* (with Lani Guinier and Jane Balin, 1997), and *Off White: Readings on Race, Power and Society* (with Linda Powell, Lois Weis, and Loonmun Wong, 1997). An activist in urban school reform, she is now working closely with a prison-based college program in New York State.

Andrea Fontana is Professor of Sociology at the University of Nevada, Las Vegas. He received his Ph.D. from the University of California, San Diego, in 1976. He has published articles on aging, leisure, theory, and postmodernism. He is the author of *The Last Frontier: The Social Meaning of Getting Old,* co-author of *Social Problems* and *Sociologies of Everyday Life,* and coeditor of *The Existential Self in Society* and *Postmodernism and Social Inquiry.* He is former President of the Society for the Study of Symbolic Interaction and a former editor of the journal *Symbolic Interaction.* His two most recently published essays are, respectively, a deconstruction of the work of Hieronymus Bosch and a performance/play about Farinelli, the castrato.

James H. Frey is Dean of the College of Liberal Arts, Professor of Sociology, and founder and former Director of the Center for Survey Research at the University of Nevada, Las Vegas. He is author of *Survey Research by Telephone* and *Government and Sport: Public Policy Issues.* He has published papers on survey research, group interviewing, sport sociology, deviance, and work in the leisure industry. He recently edited an issue of the *Annals of the American Academy of Political and Social Science* on the social and economic impacts of gambling.

John Frow is Regius Professor of Rhetoric and English Literature at the University of Edinburgh. He is the author of *Marxism and Literary History* (1986), *Cultural Studies and Cultural Value* (1995), *Time and Commodity Culture* (1997), and, with Tony Bennett and Michael Emmison, *Accounting for Tastes: Australian Everyday Cultures* (1999). With Meaghan Morris he edited *Australian Cultural Studies: A Reader* (1993). He is currently working on a book on cultural memory and another on the moral economy of everyday life, and he and Meaghan Morris are editing a reader in cultural theory.

Joshua Gamson is Associate Professor of Sociology at Yale University. In addition to numerous academic and nonacademic articles, he is the author of *Freaks Talk Back: Tabloid Television and Sexual Nonconformity* (1998) and *Claims to Fame: Celebrity in Contemporary America* (1994), and a participating author of *Ethnography Unbound: Power and Resistance in the Modern Metropolis* (1991). His research, teaching, and writing focus on the sociology of culture, with an emphasis on contemporary Western commercial culture and mass media; social movements, especially on cultural aspects of contemporary movements; on participant observation methodology and techniques, particularly as applied in urban settings; and on the history, theory, and sociology of sexuality.

Kenneth J. Gergen is Mustin Professor of Psychology at Swarthmore College and founder of the Swarthmore College Program in Interpretation Theory. He is a joint editor of the Sage Ltd series Inquiry in Social Construction and associate editor of *Theory and Psychology* and the *American Psychologist.* He is a cofounder of the Taos Institute, a nonprofit organization dedicated to the cross-fertilization of social constructionist theory and societal practice. His edited works include *Historical Social Psychology* (with Mary Gergen) and *Psychological Discourse in Historical Perspective* (with Carl Graumann). His authored volumes include *The Saturated Self* (1991), *Toward Transformation in Social Knowledge* (1993), *Realities and Relationships* (1994), and *An Invitation to Social Construction* (1999).

Mary M. Gergen is Professor of Psychology and Women's Studies at Pennsylvania State University, Delaware County. She works at the crossroads of social constructionism and feminist psychology. She is coeditor, with Sara N. Davis, of *Toward a New Psychology of Gender* (1997). Her most recent work is *Impious Improvisations: Feminist Reconstructions in Psychology* (in press), a collection of innovative experiences in the quantitative realm. She recently published, with Joan C. Chrisler and Alice LoCicero, "Innovative Methods: Resources for Research, Teaching and Publishing" (in *Psychology of Women Quarterly*), which endeavors to expand the range of methods available to academic psychologists. She is a cofounder of the Taos Institute, a nonprofit organization dedicated to the cross-fertilization of social constructionist theory and societal practice. She also writes and acts in performative psychology pieces.

Jennifer C. Greene received her Ph.D. in educational psychology from Stanford University in 1976. Since then, she has been engaged in the field of social and educational program evaluation. Working first at the University of Rhode Island, then at Cornell University, and currently at the University of Illinois, she has concentrated on making her work useful and socially responsible, both in theory and in practice. Her work has emphasized the development and refinement of various approaches to evaluation, primarily using qualitative methodologies, participatory approaches, and "mixed-method" perspectives and value stances. She has evaluated a wide range of programs, including public policy education, natural resource leadership training, remedial education, and youth employment. Her work generally focuses on educational programs and programs for families and children. In her publications she endeavors to share the lessons she has learned about evaluation practice across multiple contexts.

Davydd J. Greenwood is Goldwin Smith Professor of Anthropology at Cornell University and a Corresponding Member of the Spanish Royal Academy of Moral and Political Sciences. His work centers on action research, political economy, and the Spanish Basque Country. His action research work includes work in the health care system, industrial cooperatives, community development, industrial work reorganization, and higher-education reform. He serves on the editorial boards of *Dialogues on Work and Innovation, Concepts and Transformation, Systemic Practice and Action Research, Action Research International,* and *Revista de Antropología Aplicada.* Four of his books deal with action research, including two collaborative volumes written with the members of the Mondragón industrial cooperatives and one book coauthored with Morten Levin, *Introduction to Action Research: Social Research for Social Change* (1998).

Egon G. Guba is Professor Emeritus of Education, Indiana University. He received his Ph.D. from the University of Chicago in quantitative inquiry (education) in 1952, and thereafter served on the faculties of the University of Chicago, the University of Kansas City, the Ohio State University, and Indiana University. For the past 20 years, he has studied paradigms alternative to the received view and has espoused a personal commitment to one of these: constructivism. He is the coauthor of *Effective Evaluation* (1981), *Naturalistic Inquiry* (1985), and *Fourth Generation Evaluation* (1989), all with Yvonna S. Lincoln, and he is editor of *The Paradigm Dialog* (1990), which explores the implications of alternative paradigms for social and educational inquiry. He is the author of more than 150 journal articles and more than 100 conference presentations, many of them concerned with elements of new-paradigm inquiry and methods.

Jaber F. Gubrium is Professor of Sociology at the University of Florida. He is the author of several research monographs, including *Living and Dying at Murray Manor* (1975), *Caretakers* (1979), *Describing Care* (1982), *Oldtimers and Alzheimer's* (1986), *Out of Control* (1992), and *Speaking of Life* (1993). He is the editor of the *Journal of Aging Studies* and has coedited a number of volumes dealing with time, experience, and method in old age. In collaboration with Jim Holstein, he continues to examine empirically the interpretive horizons of social forms, including the self, family, the life course, aging, normality, health, and illness. Their most recent project is *Institutional Selves: Troubled Identities in a Postmodern World.*

Douglas Harper is Professor and Chair of the Department of Sociology and Codirector of the Graduate Center for Social and Public Policy at Duquesne University. He has held faculty appointments at the University of Amsterdam, the University of Bologna, the State University of New York at Potsdam, and the University of South Florida. He is the founding editor of *Visual Sociology,* the journal of the International Visual Sociology Association. His books include *Good Company* (the sociology of the tramp), *Working Knowledge: Skill and Community in a Small Shop* (the microsociology of the shop), and *Changing Works* (on cows and their keepers). He has coedited books on visual sociology published by academic presses in Italy and Holland. His first book, *Good Company,* has been translated into Italian and French; his papers have appeared in translation in French, German, and Italian. He is also codirector of the film *Ernie's Sawmill.* His current sociological interests center on the sociology of jazz. His 1998 ASA panel on that topic featured the first musical sociology in ASA history, as performed by H. S. Becker and Robert Faulkner.

Ian Hodder obtained his B.A. degree in archaeology from the University of London in 1971 and his Ph.D. from Cambridge University in 1975. From 1974 to 1977 he taught in the Department of Archaeology at Leeds University, and since then he has taught at Cambridge, ending up as Professor of Archaeology. Since September 1999 he has been Professor in the Cultural and Social Anthropology Department at Stanford University. He is also a Fellow of the British Academy and has taught as a Visiting Professor at the University of Amsterdam, Paris 1/Sorbonne, the State University of New York at Binghamton, the University of California at Berkeley, and the University of Vienna. His books include *Spatial Analysis in Archaeology* (with Clive Orton, 1976), *Reading the Past* (1986), *The Domestication of Europe* (1990), and *The Archaeological Process* (1999).

James A. Holstein is Professor of Sociology at Marquette University. He has published numerous books, including *Court-Ordered Insanity* (1993), and, with Gale Miller, *Reconsidering Social Constructionism* (1993), *Dispute Domains and Welfare Claims* (1996), and *Social Problems in Everyday Life* (1997). He is coauthor with Jay Gubrium of *The New Language of Qualitative Method* (1997) and *The Active Interview* (1995). Their most recent book, *The Self We Live By,* is a qualitative examination of self-construction in a postmodern world.

Valerie J. Janesick, Ph.D., is Professor of Educational Leadership and Organizational Change at Roosevelt University. She teaches classes in qualitative research methods, participatory action research, narrative methods of research, curriculum planning and evaluation, curriculum theory and inquiry, and ethics in the professions. Her research interests include qualitative research methods, ethics in research and evaluation, and comparative curriculum issues. She incorporates the arts and humanities into her research and writing projects. Her text *Stretching Exercises for Qualitative Researchers* (1998) and other writings use dance as a metaphor for clarifying and expanding our notions of qualitative inquiry. Her next project is focused on ethics and qualitative research.

Stephen Kemmis is Director of Stephen Kemmis Research & Consulting Pty Ltd; Professor Emeritus, University of Ballarat; Honorary Associate, Faculty of Education, Monash University; and Adjunct Professor, School of Education and Professional Studies, Griffith University. He is coauthor, with Wilfred Carr, of *Becoming Critical: Education, Knowledge and Action Research* (1986); and, with Robin McTaggart, of *The Action Research Planner* (1986). His research and consultancy interests include the development of critical theory and critical social scientific approaches in educational research and evaluation, participatory action research, curriculum theory, university development (especially research development), and indigenous education.

Joe L. Kincheloe is Belle Zeller Chair of Public Policy and Administration at City University of New York, Brooklyn College, and Professor of Cultural Studies and Pedagogy at Pennsylvania State University. He has written articles and books in the area of research and interpretation as well as culture, politics, cognition, and teaching. His latest books include *The Sign of the Burger: McDonald's and the*

Culture of Control; How Do We Tell the Workers? The Socio-Economic Foundations of Work and Vocational Education; The Post-Formal Reader: Cognition and Education (with Shirley Steinberg and Patricia Hinchey); *The Stigma of Genius: Einstein, Consciousness, and Education* (with Shirley Steinberg and Deborah Tippins); *Rethinking Intelligence: Confronting Psychological Assumptions About Teaching and Learning* (with Shirley Steinberg and Leila Villaverde); and *What Is Indigenous Knowledge? Voices From the Academy* (with Ladislaus Semali).

Gloria Ladson-Billings is Professor in the Department of Curriculum and Instruction at the University of Wisconsin–Madison and a Senior Fellow in Urban Education at the Annenberg Institute for School Reform at Brown University. The focus of her work is on examining new notions of pedagogical expertise for African American students and critical race theory applications to education.

Morten Levin is Professor in the Department of Sociology and Political Science at the Norwegian University of Science and Technology in Trondheim. He holds graduate degrees in engineering and sociology. Throughout his professional life, he has worked as an action researcher, with a particular focus on processes and structures of social change in the relationships between technology and organization. This action research has taken place in industrial contexts, in local communities, and in university teaching, where he has developed and been in charge of Ph.D. programs in action research. The author of a number of books and articles, he serves on the editorial boards of *Systemic Practice and Action Research, Action Research International, The Handbook of Qualitative Inquiry,* and *The Handbook of Action Research.*

Yvonna S. Lincoln is Professor of Higher Education, Texas A&M University, and coeditor of this volume and the first edition of the *Handbook of Qualitative Research* (1994). She is also coeditor of the journal *Qualitative Inquiry,* with Norman K. Denzin. She is, with her husband Egon G. Guba, coauthor of *Effective Evaluation* (1981), *Naturalistic Inquiry* (1985), and *Fourth Generation Evaluation* (1989); she is also the editor of *Organizational Theory and Inquiry* (1985) and coeditor of *Representation and the Text* (1997). She has been the recipient of numerous awards for research, including the AERA-Division J Research Achievement Award, the AIR Sidney Suslow Award for Research Contributions to Institutional Research, and the American Evaluation Association's Paul Lazarsfeld Award for Contributions to Evaluation Theory. She is the author of numerous journal articles, chapters, and conference presentations on constructivist and interpretive inquiry, and also on higher education.

Stanford M. Lyman is Robert J. Morrow Eminent Scholar and Professor of Social Science, Florida Atlantic University. In addition to holding posts at major universities in the United States, he has served as Fulbright Lecturer in Japan (1981), Visiting Foreign Expert at Beijing Foreign Studies University, China (1986), and U.S. Information Agency Lecturer in Singapore, Taiwan, Hong Kong, Ghana, Liberia, Nigeria, former Yugoslavia, and post-apartheid South Africa. In 1976, he was elected to a lifetime honorary appointment as Senior Lecturer, Linacre College, Oxford. He is author or coauthor of 21 books, including *Civilization: Contents, Discontents, Malcontents, and Other Essays in Social Theory* (1990), *The Seven Deadly Sins: Society and Evil* (revised and expanded edition, 1989), *A Sociology of the Absurd* (with Marvin B. Scott; second edition, 1989), *Social Order and the Public Philosophy: An Analysis and Interpretation of the Work of Herbert Blumer* (with Arthur J. Vidich; 1988); *Color, Culture, Civilization: Race and Minority Issues in American Society* (1994); *Postmodernism and a Sociology of the Absurd and Other Essays on the 'Nouvelle Vague' in American Social Science* (1997).

Esther Madriz is Associate Professor of Sociology and Associate Director of the Center for Latino Studies in the Americas at the University of San Francisco. She has a master's degree in criminal justice administration from California State University in Sacramento and a Ph.D. in sociology from

Vanderbilt University. She previously taught at Hunter College in New York City. She teaches classes in criminology, violence against women, and juvenile delinquency. Her field of expertise is fear of crime. She is the author of many articles on the topic and has also published papers on the use of focus groups as a feminist methodology. Her recent book *Nothing Bad Happens to Good Girls: Fear of Crime in Women's Lives* (1997) was nominated for the C. Wright Mills Award in 1998. She is a member of the board of directors of the Instituto Familiar La Raza in San Francisco and sits on the editorial boards of *Social Justice* and *Peace Review*.

Kimberly A. Mays de Pérez is a nontraditional student holding a B.A. in anthropology from the University of South Florida. She is especially interested in the role of culture in the practice of medicine. She currently works as a medical translator at a Tampa, Florida, clinic that serves a variety of Hispanic populations. She plans to use her background in anthropology in her chosen career as a medical doctor.

Michal M. McCall is Professor of Sociology at Macalester College in St. Paul, Minnesota, where she teaches courses on consumer society, sustainable agriculture, and social theory. Whenever possible, she lives with her husband, Paul Meshejian, on their 4.6-acre farm in Birchrunville, Pennsylvania.

Peter McLaren is Professor in the Division of Urban Schooling, Graduate School of Education and Information Studies at the University of California, Los Angeles. He has authored or edited more than 30 books on topics that include the sociology of education, critical ethnography, ritual and resistance, critical social theory, critical literacy, critical pedagogy, Marxist theory, and the politics of multiculturalism. A social activist, he travels worldwide. His works have been published in 12 languages. His most recent books include *Critical Pedagogy and Predatory Culture* (1995), *Revolutionary Multiculturalism* (1997), *Schooling as a Ritual Performance* (third edition, 1999), and *Che Guevara and Paulo Freire: An Introduction to the Pedagogy of Revolution* (1999).

Robin McTaggart is Professor and Pro Vice-Chancellor Staff Development and Student Affairs at James Cook University, Townsville and Cairns, Queensland, Australia, and Adjunct Professor in the International Graduate School of Management of the University of South Australia. A former high school chemistry and biology teacher, he completed his Ph.D. at the Center for Instructional Research and Curriculum Evaluation at the University of Illinois. Formerly Head of the School of Administration and Curriculum Studies and Chair of the Education Studies Centre at Deakin University in Geelong, he has conducted evaluation and research studies of action research by educators, discipline-based arts education, arts programs for disadvantaged youth, instructional computing programs for intellectually disabled adults, coeducation and gender equity in private schooling, AIDS/HIV professional development for rural health workers, Aboriginal education in traditionally oriented remote communities, scientific literacy, and distance education provision in technical and further education. He has also conducted research training workshops for a variety of professions and community groups in the United States, Canada, Thailand, Indonesia, Hong Kong, Malaysia, Indonesia, New Zealand, and Singapore.

William L. Miller, M.D., M.A., is Chair and Program Director, Department of Family Medicine, Lehigh Valley Hospital, Allentown, Pennsylvania; he is also a family physician anthropologist. He is active in an effort to make qualitative research more accessible to health care researchers. He has written and contributed to book chapters and articles detailing step-by-step applications of qualitative methods. His research interests center on the role of the patient-physician relationship in health care, on physician and patient understanding of pain and pain management, and on hypertension. In his current work, he is using case study designs to model primary care practices as nonlinear complex adaptive systems.

Meaghan Morris is Chair Professor of Cultural Studies at Lingnan University, Hong Kong, and Adjunct Professor to the Faculty of Humanities and Social Sciences, University of Technology, Sydney. Her books include *Too Soon, Too Late: History in Popular Culture* (1998), *Australian Cultural Studies: A Reader* (coedited with John Frow, 1993), and *The Pirate's Fiancee: Feminism, Reading, Postmodernism* (1988).

Virginia L. Olesen, Professor Emerita of Sociology at the University of California, San Francisco, teaches seminars on feminisms and qualitative research and on the sociology of the body and emotions. She is coeditor, with Sheryl Ruzek and Adele Clarke, of *Women's Health: Complexities and Diversities* (1997) and, with Adele Clarke, of *Revisioning Women, Health and Healing: Feminist, Cultural and Technoscience Perspectives* (1999). She is currently working on issues of skepticism in qualitative research and the problems of "the third voice" constituted between and among participants and researchers.

Laurel Richardson is Professor Emerita of Sociology, Professor of Cultural Studies in the College of Education, and Graduate Professor of Women's Studies at the Ohio State University. She has written extensively on qualitative research methods, ethics, and issues of representation. She is the author of seven books, including *Fields of Play: Constructing an Academic Life* (1997), which was honored with the C. H. Cooley Award for the 1998 Best Book in Symbolic Interaction. Currently, she is interested in the relationships between conceptual and personal constructions of "timeplaces," narratives of the self, and knowledge practices.

Ray C. Rist is the Evaluation Adviser for the World Bank Institute (WBI). He is also the Head of the Evaluation and Scholarship Unit within the WBI. Prior to his coming to the World Bank in 1996, his career had included 15 years in the U.S. government, with appointments in both the executive and legislative branches. He also served for 12 years as a university professor, with positions at the Johns Hopkins University, Cornell University, and George Washington University. He was the Senior Fulbright Fellow at the Max Planck Institute in Berlin, Germany, in 1976 and 1977. He has authored or edited 23 books, written more than 125 articles, and lectured in more than 40 countries. For the past 15 years, he has chaired an international working group with representative from 17 countries who are collaborating on research related to evaluation and governance. He also has a 4-year-old granddaughter named Molly.

Gery W. Ryan is Assistant Professor of Anthropology at the University of Missouri–Columbia. He has served as coeditor of *Cultural Anthropology Methods Journal* (1993-1998) and has written and lectured on qualitative data collection and analysis techniques, ethnographic decision modeling, and response biases in the field. For 2 years, he was Associate Director of the Fieldwork and Qualitative Data Laboratory at the UCLA Medical School, where he consulted with and trained researchers in text analysis. His substantive interests in medical anthropology focus on how laypersons select among treatment alternatives across illnesses and cultures. He has conducted fieldwork in Mexico and Cameroon and has published in *Social Science and Medicine, Human Organization,* and *Archives of Medical Research.*

Thomas A. Schwandt is Professor of Educational Psychology at the University of Illinois, Urbana-Champaign. His research and teaching focus on interpretive methodologies, social science epistemology, and theory of evaluation. His most recent publications include *Qualitative Inquiry: A Dictionary of Terms* and, with Luise McCarty, "Seductive Illusions: Von Glasersfeld and Gergen on Epistemology and Education," to appear in *Constructivism and Education: Opinions and Second Opinions on Controversial Issues,* edited by D. C. Phillips. He is at work on a book of essays tentatively titled *Evaluation Practice Reconsidered.*

David Silverman's interests are in nonromantic qualitative methodologies, professional-client communication, and conversation analysis. He is the author of 14 books, the most recent of which are *Interpreting Qualitative Data* (1993), *Discourses of Counselling* (1997), *Harvey Sacks: Social Science and Conversation Analysis* (1998), and *Doing Qualitative Research: A Practical Handbook* (2000). Since 1999, he has been Professor Emeritus at Goldsmiths College, London University. He continues to argue for a rigorous, theoretically based social science that maintains a dialogue with the wider community.

John K. Smith is Professor of Education at the University of Northern Iowa. For the past 20 years, his interests have centered on the philosophy of social and educational inquiry, with a special emphasis on the issue of criteria. His work has appeared in such journals as the *Educational Researcher, Journal of Educational Administration,* and *Educational Evaluation and Policy Analysis.* He also has published two books: *The Nature of Social and Educational Inquiry* and *After the Demise of Empiricism.*

Robert E. Stake is Professor of Education and Director of the Center for Instructional Research and Curriculum Evaluation at the University of Illinois. Since 1963 he has been a specialist in the evaluation of educational programs. Among the evaluative studies directed were works in science and mathematics in elementary and secondary schools, model programs and conventional teaching of the arts in schools, development of teaching with sensitivity to gender equity, education of teachers for the deaf and for youth in transition from school to work settings, environmental education and special programs for gifted students, and the reform of urban education. He is the author of *Quieting Reform,* a book on Charles Murray's evaluation of Cities-in-Schools; two books on methodology, *Evaluating the Arts in Education* and *The Art of Case Study Research*; and, with Liora Bresler and Linda Mabry, *Custom and Cherishing,* a book on teaching the arts in ordinary elementary school classrooms in the United States. Recently, he led a multiyear evaluation study of the Chicago Teachers Academy for Mathematics and Science. For his evaluation work, in 1988 he received the Lazarsfeld Award from the American Evaluation Association, and in 1994 he received an honorary doctorate from the University of Uppsala.

Barbara Tedlock is Full Professor and Chair of the Anthropology Department, State University of New York at Buffalo. She has served as editor in chief of the *American Anthropologist* (1993-1998), the flagship journal of the American Anthropological Association. Her publications include four ethnographies and more than 60 articles and essays. She has done extensive ethnographic research with Mayan peoples in Guatemala and Belize, the Zuni of Arizona and New Mexico, and most recently with the Roycrofters-At-Large, an arts and crafts community (a capitalist utopia of sorts) in East Aurora, New York.

William G. Tierney (Ph.D., Stanford University) is Wilbur Kieffer Professor of Higher Education and Director of the Center for Higher Education Policy Analysis at the University of Southern California. His research interests pertain to issues of access, equity, and organizational effectiveness in higher education. He has recently edited a special issue on life histories for *Qualitative Inquiry,* and he is coeditor, with Yvonna S. Lincoln, of *Representation and the Text: Re-framing the Narrative Voice.* Some of his other works include *Academic Outlaws: Queer Theory and Cultural Studies in the Academy; Naming Silenced Lives: Personal Narratives and the Process of Educational Change* (with Daniel McLaughlin); and *Building Communities of Difference: Higher Education in the 21st Century.*

Arthur J. Vidich is Emeritus Professor of Sociology and Anthropology at the Graduate Faculty of the New School for Social Research. He has conducted research on the United States, the Western Caroline Island of Palau, Colombia, Puerto Rico, and Slovenia. His books include *The Political Impact of Colo-*

nial Administration, Small Town in Mass Society (coauthored), *American Society: The Welfare State and Beyond* (coauthored), *American Sociology: Wordly Rejections of Religion and Their Directions* (coauthored), *The New Middle Classes: Lifestyles, Status Claims and Political Orientations,* and *Collaboration, Reputation and Ethics in American Academic Life: Haus H. Gerth and C. Wright Mills* (with Guy Oakes). His sociological analyses of the United States are published in *Arthur J. Vidich: Cultura, Economia e classi sociali mella politica degli stati Uniti d'America.* He is coeditor, with Robert Jackall, of a 12-volume series titled *Main Trends in the Modern World.*

Lois Weis is Professor of Sociology of Education at the State University of New York at Buffalo. She is the author and/or editor of numerous books and articles on the subject of social class, race, gender, and schooling. Her most recent publications include *The Unknown City: The Lives of Poor and Working-Class Young Adults* (with Michelle Fine, 1998), *Working Class Without Work: High School Students in a De-Industrializing Economy* (1990), *Beyond Silenced Voices* (with Michelle Fine, 1994), *Beyond Black and White* (with Maxine Seller, 1997), and *Off White: Readings on Race, Power and Society* (with Michelle Fine, Linda Powell, and Loonmun Wong, 1997). She is the recipient of two Spencer Foundation grants and a Carnegie Foundation grant. She sits on numerous editorial boards and is a former editor of *Education Policy.*

Eben A. Weitzman received his Ph.D. in social and organizational psychology from Columbia University. He is currently Assistant Professor, Graduate Programs in Dispute Resolution, University of Massachusetts Boston, and Research Associate at the International Center for Cooperation and Conflict Resolution. He is also the book and software reviews editor for the journal *Field Methods.* During 1993-1995, he was a Visiting Professor of Psychology in the New York University Psychology Department's program in industrial/organizational psychology. His interests are in organizational development, cross-cultural conflict, conflict resolution, and intergroup relations. His current research focuses on intragroup conflict in mediation, cultural differences in attitudes toward conflict, organizational conflict, and the effects of cooperation and competition on small group processes. His recent publications on the use of software in qualitative research include articles such as "Analyzing Qualitative Data With Computer Software" and, with the late Matthew B. Miles, "The State of Qualitative Analysis Software: What Do We Need?" and "Choosing Software for Qualitative Data Analysis: An Overview," and the book *Computer Programs for Qualitative Data Analysis* (1995), which he is currently revising in collaboration with Nigel Fielding and Ray Lee.

Susan Weseen is an advanced doctoral student in social-personality psychology who has previously published on issues related to qualitative research. She is currently researching the ways in which first-time mothers negotiate cultural constructions of motherhood.

Loonmun Wong, Ph.D., is a social psychologist and works for a nongovernmental organization dealing with issues of aging in Singapore. His work focuses on care management and caregiving in relation to the elderly. In addition, he is collaborating with a local hospice on the psychosocial aspects of cancer. He is one of the editors of *Off White: Readings on Race, Power and Society* (1997).